COLLINS ITALIAN COLLEGE DICTIONARY

COLLINS ITALIAN COLLEGE DICTIONARY

ITALIAN ▶ ENGLISH ENGLISH ▶ ITALIAN

HarperCollins*Publishers*

second edition/seconda edizione 1995

© **HarperCollins Publishers 1995**
© **William Collins Sons & Co. Ltd. 1989**

HarperCollins Publishers
P.O. Box, Glasgow G4 0NB, Great Britain.
ISBN 0 00 470209 3 (Paperback)
ISBN 0 00 470728 1 (College)

Arnoldo Mondadori Editore,
ISBN 88-04-40172-9

Catherine E. Love • Michela Clari

contributors to second edition/hanno collaborato alla seconda edizione
Gabriella Bacchelli • Donatella Boi
Angela Jack • Daphne Day

editorial staff/segreteria di redazione
Megan Thomson
Elspeth Anderson • Anne Convery •Anne Marie Banks

series editor/collana a cura di
Lorna Sinclair Knight
editorial management/coordinamento redazionale
Vivian Marr

Typeset by Morton Word Processing Ltd, Scarborough

*Printed in Great Britain by
HarperCollins Manufacturing, Glasgow*

INDICE

CONTENTS

INTRODUZIONE

Se desiderate imparare l'inglese o approfondire le conoscenze già acquisite, se volete leggere o redigere dei testi in inglese, oppure conversare con interlocutori di madrelingua inglese, se siete studenti, turisti, uomini o donne d'affari avete scelto il compagno di viaggio ideale per esprimervi e comunicare in inglese sia a voce che per iscritto. Strumento pratico e moderno, il vostro dizionario dà largo spazio al linguaggio quotidiano in campi quali l'attualità, gli affari, la gestione d'ufficio, l'informatica e il turismo. Come in tutti i nostri dizionari, grande importanza è stata data alla lingua contemporanea e alle espressioni idiomatiche.

COME USARE IL DIZIONARIO

Troverete qui di seguito alcune spiegazioni sul modo in cui le informazioni sono state presentate nel testo. L'obiettivo del dizionario è quello di darvi il maggior numero possibile di informazioni senza tuttavia sacrificare la chiarezza all'interno delle voci.

Le voci

Qui di seguito verranno descritti i vari elementi di cui si compone una voce tipo del vostro dizionario.

La trascrizione fonetica

Come regola generale è stata data la pronuncia di tutte le parole inglesi e quella delle parole italiane che potevano presentare qualche difficoltà per il parlante inglese. Nella parte inglese-italiano, tuttavia, per la pronuncia di nomi composti formati da due parole non unite dal trattino si dovrà cercare la trascrizione di ciascuna di queste parole alla rispettiva posizione alfabetica. La pronuncia si trova tra parentesi quadra, subito dopo il lemma. Come nella maggior parte dei dizionari moderni è stato adottato il sistema noto come "alfabeto fonetico internazionale". Troverete qui di seguito, a pagina xiii e xiv, un elenco completo dei caratteri utilizzati in questo sistema.

La categorie grammaticali

Tutte le parole appartengono ad una categoria grammaticale, cioè possono essere sostantivi, verbi, aggettivi, avverbi, pronomi, articoli, congiunzioni o abbreviazioni. I sostantivi possono essere singolari o plurali, sia in italiano che in inglese, e maschili o femminili in italiano. I verbi possono essere transitivi o intransitivi in entrambe le lingue, ma anche riflessivi o impersonali in italiano. La categoria grammaticale è stata introdotta in *corsivo* subito dopo la pronuncia ed eventuali informazioni di tipo morfologico (plurali irregolari ecc.).

Numerose voci sono state suddivise in varie categorie grammaticali. Per esempio la parola italiana **bene** può essere sia un avverbio che un aggettivo o un sostantivo, e la parola inglese **sneeze** può essere sia un sostantivo (starnuto) che un verbo intransitivo (starnutire). Analogamente il verbo italiano **correre** può essere usato sia come verbo intransitivo ("correre alla stazione") che come transitivo ("correre un rischio"). Per presentare la voce con maggiore chiarezza e permettervi di trovare rapidamente la traduzione che cercate, è stato introdotto il simbolo ◆ per contrassegnare il passaggio da una categoria grammaticale ad un'altra.

Suddivisioni semantiche

La maggior parte delle parole ha più di un significato. Per esempio, la parola **fiocco** può essere sia un'annodatura di un nastro che una falda di neve. Molte parole si traducono in modo diverso a seconda del contesto in cui sono usate: per esempio **scala** si tradurrà in inglese con "staircase" o "stairs" se si tratta di una scala con gradini, con "ladder" se è una scala a pioli. Per permettervi di scegliere la traduzione giusta per ciascuno dei contesti in cui la parola si può trovare, le voci sono state suddivise in categorie di significato. Ciascuna suddivisione è introdotta da un "indicatore d'uso" tra parentesi in *corsivo*. Le voci **fiocco** e **scala** compariranno quindi nel testo nel modo seguente:

fiocco, chi *sm (di nastro)* bow; (*di stoffa, lana*) flock; (*di neve*) flake
scala *sf (a gradini etc)* staircase, stairs pl; (*a pioli, di corda*) ladder

Per segnalare la traduzione appropriata sono stati introdotti anche degli indicatori d'ambito d'uso in CORSIVO MAIUSCOLO tra parentesi, spesso in forma abbreviata, come per esempio nel caso della voce **tromba**:

tromba *sf (MUS)* trumpet; (*AUT*) horn

Troverete un elenco completo delle abbreviazioni adottate all'interno del dizionario alle pp x, xi, xii.

Le traduzioni

Per la maggior parte delle parole inglesi ed italiane ci sono traduzioni precise a seconda del significato o del contesto, come risulta dagli esempi riportati fin qui. A volte, tuttavia, le parole non hanno un preciso equivalente nella lingua d'arrivo: in questi casi è stato fornito un equivalente approssimativo, preceduto dal segno ≈, come ad esempio per l'abbreviazione **RAC**, per cui è stato dato l'equivalente italiano "A.C.I.", dato che le due associazioni svolgono nei due paesi funzioni analoghe:

RAC *n abbr (BRIT. = Royal Automobile Club)* ≈ **A.C.I.** *m (= Automobile Club d' Italia)*

A volte è persino impossibile trovare un equivalente approssimativo. Questo è il caso, per esempio, di piatti tipici di un certo paese, come ad esempio **pandoro**:

pandoro *sm type of sponge cake eaten at Christmas*

In questi casi, al posto della traduzione, che non esiste, comparirà una spiegazione: per maggiore chiarezza questa spiegazione o glossa è stata messa in *corsivo*.

Molto spesso la traduzione di una parola può non funzionare all'interno di una data locuzione. Ad esempio alla voce **dare**, verbo spesso tradotto con "to give" in inglese, troviamo varie locuzioni per alcune delle quali la traduzione fornita all'inizio della voce non si può utilizzare: **quanti anni mi dai?** "how old do you think I am?" **danno ancora quel film?** "is that film still showing?", **dare per certo qc** "to consider sth certain", e così via. Ed è proprio in questi casi che potrete verificare l'utilità e la completezza del dizionario, che contiene una ricca gamma di composti, locuzioni e frasi idiomatiche.

Il registro linguistico

In italiano sapete istintivamente scegliere l'espressione corretta da usare a seconda del contesto in cui vi esprimete. Per esempio saprete quando dire **Non me ne importa!** e quando invece potete dire **Chi se ne frega?** Più difficile sarà farlo in inglese, dove avete minore consapevolezza delle sfumature di registro linguistico. Per questo motivo nella parte inglese-italiano le parole ed espressioni inglesi di uso più familiare sono segnalate dall'abbreviazione (*col*), mentre (*col!*) segnala le parole ed espressioni volgari. Nella parte italiano-inglese (*!*) dopo una traduzione segnala che si tratta di una parola od espressione volgare.

Parole chiave

Come vedrete, ad alcune voci è stato riservato un trattamento particolare sia dal punto di vista grafico che da quello linguistico. Si tratta di voci come **essere** o **fare**, o dei loro equivalenti inglesi **be** e **do**, che per la loro importanza e complessità meritano una strutturazione più articolata ed un maggior numero di locuzioni illustrative. Queste voci sono strutturate in diverse categorie di significato contrassegnate da numeri, e le costruzioni sintattiche e locuzioni che illustrano quel particolare significato sono riportate all'interno della relativa categoria.

Informazioni culturali

Le voci che compaiono nel testo delimitate da due linee approfondiscono aspetti della cultura italiana o di quella dei paesi di lingua inglese in argomenti quali la politica, la scuola, i mass media e le festività nazionali.

INTRODUCTION

You may be starting to learn Italian, or you may wish to extend your knowledge of the language. Perhaps you want to read and study Italian books, newspapers and magazines, or perhaps simply have a conversation with Italian speakers. Whatever the reason, whether you're a student, a tourist or want to use Italian for business, this is the ideal book to help you understand and communicate. This modern, user-friendly dictionary gives priority to everyday vocabulary and the language of current affairs, business and tourism. As in all Collins dictionaries, the emphasis is firmly placed on contemporary language and expressions.

HOW TO USE THE DICTIONARY

Below you will find an outline of how information is presented in your dictionary. Our aim is to give you the maximum amount of detail in the clearest and most helpful way.

Entries

A typical entry in your dictionary will be made up of the following elements:

Phonetic transcription

Phonetics appear in square brackets immediately after the headword. They are shown using the International Phonetic Alphabet (IPA), and a complete list of the symbols used in this system can be found on pages xiii and xiv.

Grammatical information

All words belong to one of the following parts of speech: noun, verb, adjective, adverb, pronoun, article, conjunction, preposition, abbreviation. Nouns can be singular or plural and, in Italian, masculine or feminine. Verbs can be transitive, intransitive, reflexive or impersonal. Parts of speech appear in *italics* immediately after the phonetic spelling of the headword.

Often a word can have more than one part of speech. Just as the English word **chemical** can be an adjective or a noun, the Italian word **fondo** can be an adjective ("deep") or a masculine noun ("bottom"). In the same way the verb **to walk** is sometimes transitive, ie it takes an object ("to walk the dog") and sometimes intransitive, ie it doesn't take an object ("to walk to school"). To help you find the meaning you are looking for quickly and for clarity of presentation, the different part of speech categories are separated by a black lozenge ♦.

Meaning divisions

Most words have more than one meaning. Take, for example, **punch** which can be, amongst other things, a blow with the fist or an object used for making holes. Other words are translated differently depending on the context in which they are used. The transitive verb **to roll up**, for example, can be translated by "arrotolare" or "rimboccare" depending on *what* it is you are rolling up. To help you select the most appropriate translation in every context, entries are divided according to meaning. Each different meaning is introduced by an "indicator" in *italics* and in brackets. Thus, the examples given above will be shown as follows:

    punch n (*blow*) pugno; (*tool*) punzone m
    roll up vt (*carpet, cloth, map*) arrotolare; (*sleeves*) rimboccare

Likewise, some words can have a different meaning when used to talk about a specific subject area or field. For example, **bishop**, which is generally used to mean a high-ranking clergyman, is also the name of a chess piece. To show English speakers which translation to use, we have added "subject field labels" in capitals and in brackets, in this case (*CHESS*):

bishop *n* vescovo; (*CHESS*) alfiere *m*

Field labels are often shortened to save space. You will find a complete list of abbreviations used in the dictionary on pages x, xi, xii.

Translations

Most English words have a direct translation in Italian and vice versa, as shown in the examples given above. Sometimes, however, no exact equivalent exists in the target language. In such cases we have given an approximate equivalent, indicated by the sign ≈. Such is the case of **National Insurance**, the Italian equivalent of which is "Previdenza Sociale". This is not an exact translation since the systems of the two countries in question are quite different:

National Insurance *n* (*BRIT*) ≈ Previdenza Sociale

On occasion it is impossible to find even an approximate equivalent. This may be the case, for example, with the names of types of food:

cottage pie *n piatto a base di carne macinata in sugo e purè di patate*

Here the translation (which doesn't exist) is replaced by an explanation. For increased clarity the explanation, or "gloss", is shown in *italics*.

It is often the case that a word, or a particular meaning of a word, cannot be translated in isolation. The translation of **Dutch**, for example, is "olandese". However, the phrase **to go Dutch** is rendered by "fare alla romana". Even an expression as simple as **washing powder** needs a separate translation since it translates as "detersivo (in polvere)", not "polvere per lavare". This is where your dictionary will prove to be particularly informative and useful since it contains an abundance of compounds, phrases and idiomatic expressions.

Levels of formality and familiarity

In English you instinctively know when to say **I'm broke** *or* **I'm a bit short of cash** and when to say **I don't have any money**. When you are trying to understand someone who is speaking Italian, however, or when you yourself try to speak Italian, it is important to know what is polite and what is less so, and what you can say in a relaxed situation but not in a formal context. To help you with this, on the Italian-English side we have added the label (*fam*) to show that an Italian word or expression is colloquial, while those word or expressions which are vulgar are given an exclamation mark (*fam!*), warning you they can cause serious offence. Note also that on the English-Italian side, translations which are vulgar are followed by an exclamation mark in brackets.

Keywords

Words labelled in the text as *KEYWORDS*, such as **be** and **do** or their Italian equivalents **essere** and **fare**, have been given special treatment because they form the basic elements of the language. This extra help will ensure that you know how to use these complex words with confidence.

Cultural information

Entries which appear separated from the main text by a line above and below them explain aspects of culture in Italy and English-speaking countries. Subject areas covered include politics, education, media and national festivals.

ABBREVIAZIONI

ABBREVIATIONS

abbreviazione	**abbr**	abbreviation
aggettivo	**adj**	adjective
amministrazione	**ADMIN**	administration
avverbio	**adv**	adverb
aeronautica, viaggi aerei	**AER**	flying, air travel
aggettivo	**ag**	adjective
agricoltura	**AGR**	agriculture
amministrazione	**AMM**	administration
anatomia	**ANAT**	anatomy
architettura	**ARCHIT**	architecture
astronomia, astrologia	**ASTR**	astronomy, astrology
l'automobile	**AUT**	the motor car and motoring
verbo ausiliare	**aux vb**	auxiliary verb
avverbio	**av**	adverb
aeronautica, viaggi aerei	**AVIAT**	flying, air travel
biologia	**BIOL**	biology
botanica	**BOT**	botany
inglese della Gran Bretagna	**BRIT**	British English
consonante	**C**	consonant
chimica	**CHIM, CHEM**	chemistry
familiare (! da evitare)	**col(!)**	colloquial usage (! particularly offensive)
commercio, finanza, banca	**COMM**	commerce, finance, banking
informatica	**COMPUT**	computing
congiunzione	**cong**	conjunction
congiunzione	**conj**	conjunction
edilizia	**CONSTR**	building
sostantivo usato come aggettivo, non può essere usato né come attributo, né dopo il sostantivo qualificato	**cpd**	compound element: noun used as adjective and which cannot follow the noun it qualifies
cucina	**CUC, CULIN**	cookery
davanti a	**dav**	before
determinante: articolo, aggettivo dimostrativo o indefinito etc	**det**	determiner: article, demonstrative etc
diritto	**DIR**	law
economia	**ECON**	economics
edilizia	**EDIL**	building
elettricità, elettronica	**ELETTR, ELEC**	electricity, electronics
esclamazione, interiezione	**escl, excl**	exclamation, interjection
specialmente	**esp**	especially
femminile	**f**	feminine
familiare (! da evitare)	**fam(!)**	colloquial usage (! particularly offensive)
ferrovia	**FERR**	railways
figurato	**fig**	figurative use
fisiologia	**FISIOL**	physiology
fotografia	**FOT**	photography
(verbo inglese) la cui particella è inseparabile dal verbo	**fus**	(phrasal verb) where the particle cannot be separated from main verb
nella maggior parte dei sensi; generalmente	**gen**	in most or all senses; generally
geografia, geologia	**GEO**	geography, geology
geometria	**GEOM**	geometry
impersonale	**impers**	impersonal

informatica	*INFORM*	computing
insegnamento, sistema scolastico e universitario	*INS*	schooling, schools and universities
invariabile	*inv*	invariable
irregolare	*irreg*	irregular
grammatica, linguistica	*LING*	grammar, linguistics
maschile	*m*	masculine
matematica	*MAT(H)*	mathematics
termine medico, medicina	*MED*	medical term, medicine
il tempo, meteorologia	*METEOR*	the weather, meteorology
maschile o femminile	*m/f*	either masculine or feminine depending on sex
esercito, lingua militare	*MIL*	military matters
musica	*MUS*	music
sostantivo	*n*	noun
nautica	*NAUT*	sailing, navigation
sostantivo che non si usa al plurale	*no pl*	uncountable noun: not used in the plural
numerale (aggettivo, sostantivo)	*num*	numeral adjective or noun
	o.s.	oneself
peggiorativo	*peg, pej*	derogatory, pejorative
fotografia	*PHOT*	photography
fisiologia	*PHYSIOL*	physiology
plurale	*pl*	plural
politica	*POL*	politics
participio passato	*pp*	past participle
preposizione	*prep*	preposition
pronome	*pron*	pronoun
psicologia, psichiatria	*PSIC, PSYCH*	psychology, psychiatry
tempo passato	*pt*	past tense
qualcosa	*qc*	
qualcuno	*qn*	
religione, liturgia	*REL*	religions, church service
sostantivo	*s*	noun
	sb	somebody
insegnamento, sistema scolastico e universitario	*SCOL*	schooling, schools and universities
singolare	*sg*	singular
soggetto (grammaticale)	*sog*	(grammatical) subject
	sth	something
congiuntivo	*sub*	subjunctive
soggetto (grammaticale)	*subj*	(grammatical) subject
termine tecnico, tecnologia	*TECN, TECH*	technical term, technology
telecomunicazioni	*TEL*	telecommunications
tipografia	*TIP*	typography, printing
televisione	*TV*	television
tipografia	*TYP*	typography, printing
inglese degli Stati Uniti	*US*	American English
vocale	*V*	vowel
verbo (ausiliare)	*vb (aus)*	(auxiliary) verb
verbo o gruppo verbale con funzione intransitiva	*vi*	verb or phrasal verb used intransitively
verbo riflessivo	*vr*	reflexive verb
verbo o gruppo verbale con funzione transitiva	*vt*	verb or phrasal verb used transitively
zoologia	*ZOOL*	zoology
marchio registrato	®	registered trademark
introduce un'equivalenza culturale	≈	introduces a cultural equivalent

TRASCRIZIONE FONETICA

Consonanti

Consonants

NB. **p, b, t, d, k, g** sono seguite da un'aspirazione in inglese.

NB. **p, b, t, d, k, g** are not aspirated in Italian.

padre	p	puppy
bambino	b	baby
tutto	t	tent
dado	d	daddy
cane che	k	cork kiss chord
gola ghiro	g	gag guess
sano	s	so rice kiss
svago esame	z	cousin buzz
scena	ʃ	sheep sugar
	ʒ	pleasure beige
pece lanciare	tʃ	church
giro gioco	dʒ	judge general
afa faro	f	farm raffle
vero bravo	v	very rev
	θ	thin maths
	ð	that other
letto ala	l	little ball
gli	ʎ	
rete arco	r	rat brat
ramo madre	m	mummy comb
no fumante	n	no ran
gnomo	ɲ	
	ŋ	singing bank
	h	hat reheat
buio piacere	j	yet
uomo guaio	w	wall bewail
	x	loch

Varie

Miscellaneous

per l'inglese: la "r" finale viene pronunciata se seguita da una vocale	*	
precede la sillaba accentata	'	precedes the stressed syllable

Come regola generale, in tutte le voci la trascrizione fonetica in parentesi quadra segue il termine cui si riferisce. Tuttavia, dalla parte inglese-italiano del dizionario, per la pronuncia di composti che sono formati da più parole non unite da trattino che appaiono comunque nel dizionario, si veda la trascrizione fonetica di ciascuna di queste parole alla rispettiva posizione alfabetica.

PHONETIC TRANSCRIPTION

Vocali		Vowels

NB. La messa in equivalenza di certi suoni indica solo una rassomiglianza approssimativa.		NB. The pairing of some vowel sounds only indicates approximate equivalence.

vino idea	i iː	heel bead
	ɪ	hit pity
stella edera	e	
epoca eccetto	ɛ	set tent
mamma amore	a æ	apple bat
	ɑː	after car calm
	ʌ	fun cousin
	ə	over above
	əː	urn fern work
rosa occhio	ɔ	wash pot
	ɔː	born cork
ponte ognuno	o	
utile zucca	u	full soot
	uː	boon lewd

Dittonghi   Diphthongs

ɪə	beer tier
ɛə	tear fair there
eɪ	date plaice day
aɪ	life buy cry
au	owl foul now
əu	low no
ɔɪ	boil boy oily
uə	poor tour

In general, we give the pronunciation of each entry in square brackets after the word in question. However, on the English-Italian side, where the entry is composed of two or more unhyphenated words, each of which is given elsewhere in this dictionary, you will find the pronunciation of each word in its alphabetical position.

ITALIAN PRONUNCIATION

Vowels

Where the vowel **e** or the vowel **o** appears in a stressed syllable it can be either open [ɛ], [ɔ] or closed [e], [o]. As the open or closed pronunciation of these vowels is subject to regional variation, the distinction is of little importance to the user of this dictionary. Phonetic transcription for headwords containing these vowels will therefore only appear where other pronunciation difficulties are present.

Consonants

c before "e" or "i" is pronounced *tch*.

ch is pronounced like the "k" in "kit".

g before "e" or "i" is pronounced like the "j" in "jet".

gh is pronounced like the "g" in "get".

gl before "e" or "i" is normally pronounced like the "lli" in "million", and in a few cases only like the "gl" in "glove".

gn is pronounced like the "ny" in "canyon".

sc before "e" or "i" is pronounced *sh*.

z is pronounced like the "ts" in "stetson", or like the "d's" in "bird's-eye".

Headwords containing the above consonants and consonantal groups have been given full phonetic transcription in this dictionary.

NB. All double written consonants in Italian are fully sounded: e.g. the *tt* in "tutto" is pronounced as in "ha*t t*rick".

ITALIAN VERBS

1 Gerundio *2* Participio passato *3* Presente *4* Imperfetto *5* Passato remoto *6* Futuro *7* Condizionale *8* Congiuntivo presente *9* Congiuntivo passato *10* Imperativo

accadere *like* **cadere**
accedere *like* **concedere**
accendere *2* acceso *5* accesi, accendesti
accludere *like* **alludere**
accogliere *like* **cogliere**
accondiscendere *like* **scendere**
accorgersi *like* **scorgere**
accorrere *like* **correre**
accrescere *like* **crescere**
addirsi *like* **dire**
addurre *like* **ridurre**
affiggere *2* affisso *5* affissi, affiggesti
affliggere *2* afflitto *5* afflissi, affliggesti
aggiungere *like* **giungere**
alludere *2* alluso *5* allusi, alludesti
ammettere *like* **mettere**
andare *3* vado, vai, va, andiamo, andate, vanno *6* andrò *etc* *8* vada *10* va'!, vada!, andate!, vadano!
annettere *2* annesso *5* annessi *o* annettei, annettesti
apparire *2* apparso *3* appaio, appari *o* apparisci, appare *o* apparisce, appaiono *o* appariscono *5* apparvi *o* apparsi, appariesti, apparve *o* apparì *o* apparse, apparvero *o* apparirono *o* apparsero *8* appaia *o* apparisca
appartenere *like* **tenere**
appendere *2* appeso *5* appesi, appendesti
apporre *like* **porre**
apprendere *like* **prendere**
aprire *2* aperto *3* apro *5* aprii *o* apersi, apristi *8* apra
ardere *2* arso *5* arsi, ardesti
ascendere *like* **scendere**
aspergere *2* asperso *5* aspersi, aspergesti
assalire *like* **salire**
assistere *2* assistito
assolvere *2* assolto *5* assolsi *o* assolvei *o* assolvetti, assolvesti
assumere *2* assunto *5* assunsi, assumesti
astenersi *like* **tenere**
attendere *like* **tendere**
attingere *like* **tingere**
AVERE *3* ho, hai, ha, abbiamo, avete, hanno *5* ebbi, avesti, ebbe, avemmo, aveste, ebbero *6* avrò *etc* *8* abbia *etc* *10* abbi!, abbia!, abbiate!, abbiano!
avvedersi *like* **vedere**
avvenire *like* **venire**
avvincere *like* **vincere**
avvolgere *like* **volgere**
benedire *like* **dire**
bere *1* bevendo *2* bevuto *3* bevo *etc* *4* bevevo *etc* *5* bevvi *o* bevetti, bevesti *6* berrò

etc *8* beva *etc* *9* bevessi *etc*
cadere *5* caddi, cadesti *6* cadrò *etc*
chiedere *2* chiesto *5* chiesi, chiedesti
chiudere *2* chiuso *5* chiusi, chiudesti
cingere *2* cinto *5* cinsi, cingesti
cogliere *2* colto *3* colgo, colgono *5* colsi, cogliesti *8* colga
coincidere *2* coinciso *5* coincisi, coincidesti
coinvolgere *like* **volgere**
commettere *like* **mettere**
commuovere *like* **muovere**
comparire *like* **apparire**
compiacere *like* **piacere**
compiangere *like* **piangere**
comporre *like* **porre**
comprendere *like* **prendere**
comprimere *2* compresso *5* compressi, comprimesti
compromettere *like* **mettere**
concedere *2* concesso *o* conceduto *5* concessi *o* concedei *o* concedetti, concedesti
concludere *like* **alludere**
concorrere *like* **correre**
condurre *like* **ridurre**
confondere *like* **fondere**
congiungere *like* **giungere**
connettere *like* **annettere**
conoscere *2* conosciuto *5* conobbi, conoscesti
consistere *like* **assistere**
contendere *like* **tendere**
contenere *like* **tenere**
contorcere *like* **torcere**
contraddire *like* **dire**
contraffare *like* **fare**
contrarre *like* **trarre**
convenire *like* **venire**
convincere *like* **vincere**
coprire *like* **aprire**
correggere *like* **reggere**
correre *2* corso *5* corsi, corresti
corrispondere *like* **rispondere**
corrompere *like* **rompere**
costringere *like* **stringere**
costruire *5* costrussi, costruisti
crescere *2* cresciuto *5* crebbi, crescesti
cuocere *2* cotto *3* cuocio, cociamo, cuociono *5* cossi, cocesti
dare *3* do, dai, dà, diamo, date, danno *5* diedi *o* detti, desti *6* darò *etc* *8* dia *etc* *9* dessi *etc* *10* da'!, dai!, date!, diano!
decidere *2* deciso *5* decisi, decidesti
decrescere *like* **crescere**
dedurre *like* **ridurre**

deludere *like* **alludere**
deporre *like* **porre**
deprimere *like* **comprimere**
deridere *like* **ridere**
descrivere *like* **scrivere**
desumere *like* **assumere**
detergere *like* **tergere**
devolvere *2* devoluto
difendere *2* difeso *5* difesi, difendesti
diffondere *like* **fondere**
dipendere *like* **appendere**
dipingere *like* **tingere**
dire *1* dicendo *2* detto *3* dico, dici, dice, diciamo, dite, dicono *4* dicevo *etc* *5* dissi, dicesti *6* dirò *etc* *8* dica, diciamo, diciate, dicano *9* dicessi *etc* *10* di'!, dica!, dite!, dicano!
dirigere *2* diretto *5* diressi, dirigesti
discendere *like* **scendere**
dischiudere *like* **chiudere**
disciogliere *like* **sciogliere**
discorrere *like* **correre**
discutere *2* discusso *5* discussi, discutesti
disfare *like* **fare**
disilludere *like* **alludere**
disperdere *like* **perdere**
dispiacere *like* **piacere**
disporre *like* **porre**
dissolvere *2* dissolto *o* dissoluto *5* dissolsi *o* dissolvetti *o* dissolvei, dissolvesti
dissuadere *like* **persuadere**
distendere *like* **tendere**
distinguere *2* distinto *5* distinsi, distinguesti
distogliere *like* **togliere**
distrarre *like* **trarre**
distruggere *like* **struggere**
divenire *like* **venire**
dividere *2* diviso *5* divisi, dividesti
dolere *3* dolgo, duoli, duole, dolgono *5* dolsi, dolesti *6* dorrò *etc* *8* dolga
DORMIRE *1* GERUNDIO dormendo
    2 PARTICIPIO PASSATO dormito
    3 PRESENTE dormo, dormi, dorme, dormiamo, dormite, dormono
    4 IMPERFETTO dormivo, dormivi, dormiva, dormivamo, dormivate, dormivano
    5 PASSATO REMOTO dormii, dormisti, dormì, dormimmo, dormiste, dormirono
    6 FUTURO dormirò, dormirai, dormirà, dormiremo, dormirete, dormiranno
    7 CONDIZIONALE dormirei, dormiresti, dormirebbe, dormiremmo, dormireste, dormirebbero
    8 CONGIUNTIVO PRESENTE dorma, dorma, dorma, dormiamo, dormiate, dormano
    9 CONGIUNTIVO PASSATO dormissi, dormissi, dormisse, dormissimo, dormiste, dormissero
    10 IMPERATIVO dormi!, dorma!, dormite!, dormano!
dovere *3* devo *o* debbo, devi, deve, dobbiamo, dovete, devono *o* debbono *6* dovrò *etc*

8 debba, dobbiamo, dobbiate, devano *o* debbano
eccellere *2* eccelso *5* eccelsi, eccellesti
eludere *like* **alludere**
emergere *2* emerso *5* emersi, emergesti
emettere *like* **mettere**
erigere *like* **dirigere**
escludere *like* **alludere**
esigere *2* esatto
esistere *2* esistito
espellere *2* espulso *5* espulsi, espellesti
esplodere *2* esploso *5* esplosi, esplodesti
esporre *like* **porre**
esprimere *like* **comprimere**
ESSERE *2* stato *3* sono, sei, è, siamo, siete, sono *4* ero, eri, era, eravamo, eravate, erano *5* fui, fosti, fu, fummo, foste, furono *6* sarò *etc* *8* sia *etc* *9* fossi, fossi, fosse, fossimo, foste, fossero *10* sii!, sia!, siate!, siano!
estendere *like* **tendere**
estinguere *like* **distinguere**
estrarre *like* **trarre**
evadere *2* evaso *5* evasi, evadesti
evolvere *2* evoluto
fare *1* facendo *2* fatto *3* faccio, fai, fa, facciamo, fate, fanno *4* facevo *etc* *5* feci, facesti *6* farò *etc* *8* faccia *etc* *9* facessi *etc* *10* fa'!, faccia!, fate!, facciano!
fingere *like* **cingere**
FINIRE *1* GERUNDIO finendo
    2 PARTICIPIO PASSATO finito
    3 PRESENTE finisco, finisci, finisce, finiamo, finite, finiscono
    4 IMPERFETTO finivo, finivi, finiva, finivamo, finivate, finivano
    5 PASSATO REMOTO finii, finisti, finì, finimmo, finiste, finirono
    6 FUTURO finirò, finirai, finirà, finiremo, finirete, finiranno
    7 CONDIZIONALE finirei, finiresti, finirebbe, finiremmo, finireste, finirebbero
    8 CONGIUNTIVO PRESENTE finisca, finisca, finisca, finiamo, finiate, finiscano
    9 CONGIUNTIVO PASSATO finissi, finissi, finisse, finissimo, finiste, finissero
    10 IMPERATIVO finisci!, finisca!, finite!, finiscano!
flettere *2* flesso
fondere *2* fuso *5* fusi, fondesti
friggere *2* fritto *5* frissi, friggesti
fungere *2* funto *5* funsi, fungesti
giacere *3* giaccio, giaci, giace, giac(c)iamo, giacete, giacciono *5* giacqui, giacesti *8* giaccia *etc* *10* giaci!, giaccia!, giac(c)iamo!, giacete!, giacciano!
giungere *2* giunto *5* giunsi, giungesti
godere *6* godrò *etc*
illudere *like* **alludere**
immergere *like* **emergere**
immettere *like* **mettere**
imporre *like* **porre**
imprimere *like* **comprimere**

incidere *like* **decidere**
includere *like* **alludere**
incorrere *like* **correre**
incutere *like* **discutere**
indulgere *2* indulto *5* indulsi, indulgesti
indurre *like* **ridurre**
inferire[1] *2* inferto *5* infersi, inferisti
inferire[2] *2* inferito *5* inferii, inferisti
infliggere *like* **affliggere**
infrangere *2* infranto *5* infransi, infrangesti
infondere *like* **fondere**
insistere *like* **assistere**
intendere *like* **tendere**
interdire *like* **dire**
interporre *like* **porre**
interrompere *like* **rompere**
intervenire *like* **venire**
intraprendere *like* **prendere**
introdurre *like* **ridurre**
invadere *like* **evadere**
irrompere *like* **rompere**
iscrivere *like* **scrivere**
istruire *like* **costruire**
ledere *2* leso *5* lesi, ledesti
leggere *2* letto *5* lessi, leggesti
maledire *like* **dire**
mantenere *like* **tenere**
mettere *2* messo *5* misi, mettesti
mordere *2* morso *5* morsi, mordesti
morire *2* morto *3* muoio, muori, muore, moriamo, morite, muoiono *6* morirò *o* morrò *etc 8* muoia
mungere *2* munto *5* munsi, mungesti
muovere *2* mosso *5* mossi, movesti
nascere *2* nato *5* nacqui, nascesti
nascondere *2* nascosto *5* nascosi, nascondesti
nuocere *2* nuociuto *3* nuoccio, nuoci, nuoce, nociamo *o* nuociamo, nuocete, nuocciono *4* nuocevo *etc 5* nocqui, nuocesti *6* nuocerò *etc 7* nuoccia
occorrere *like* **correre**
offendere *like* **difendere**
offrire *2* offerto *3* offro *5* offersi *o* offrii, offristi *8* offra
omettere *like* **mettere**
opporre *like* **porre**
opprimere *like* **comprimere**
ottenere *like* **tenere**
parere *2* parso *3* paio, paiamo, paiono *5* parvi *o* parsi, paresti *6* parrò *etc 8* paia, paiamo, paiate, paiano
PARLARE *1 GERUNDIO* parlando
  2 PARTICIPIO PASSATO parlato
  3 PRESENTE parlo, parli, parla, parliamo, parlate, parlano
  4 IMPERFETTO parlavo, parlavi, parlava, parlavamo, parlavate, parlavano
  5 PASSATO REMOTO parlai, parlasti, parlò, parlammo, parlaste, parlarono
  6 FUTURO parlerò, parlerai, parlerà, parleremo, parlerete, parleranno

  7 CONDIZIONALE parlerei, parleresti, parlerebbe, parleremmo, parlereste, parlerebbero
  8 CONGIUNTIVO PRESENTE parli, parli, parli, parliamo, parliate, parlino
  9 CONGIUNTIVO PASSATO parlassi, parlassi, parlasse, parlassimo, parlaste, parlassero
  10 IMPERATIVO parla!, parli!, parlate!, parlino!
percorrere *like* **correre**
percuotere *2* percosso *5* percossi, percotesti
perdere *2* perso *o* perduto *5* persi *o* perdei *o* perdetti, perdesti
permettere *like* **mettere**
persuadere *2* persuaso *5* persuasi, persuadesti
pervenire *like* **venire**
piacere *2* piaciuto *3* piaccio, piacciamo, piacciono *5* piacqui, piacesti *8* piaccia *etc*
piangere *2* pianto *5* piansi, piangesti
piovere *5* piovve
porgere *2* porto *5* porsi, porgesti
porre *1* ponendo *2* posto *3* pongo, poni, pone, poniamo, ponete, pongono *4* ponevo *etc 5* posi, ponesti *6* porrò *etc 8* ponga, poniamo, poniate, pongano *9* ponessi *etc*
posporre *like* **porre**
possedere *like* **sedere**
potere *3* posso, puoi, può, possiamo, potete, possono *6* potrò *etc 8* possa, possiamo, possiate, possano
prediligere *2* prediletto *5* predilessi, prediligesti
predire *like* **dire**
prefiggersi *like* **affiggere**
preludere *like* **alludere**
prendere *2* preso *5* presi, prendesti
preporre *like* **porre**
prescrivere *like* **scrivere**
presiedere *like* **sedere**
presumere *like* **assumere**
pretendere *like* **tendere**
prevalere *like* **valere**
prevedere *like* **vedere**
prevenire *like* **venire**
produrre *like* **ridurre**
proferire *like* **inferire**[2]
profondere *like* **fondere**
promettere *like* **mettere**
promuovere *like* **muovere**
proporre *like* **porre**
prorompere *like* **rompere**
proscrivere *like* **scrivere**
proteggere *2* protetto *5* protesi, proteggesti
provenire *like* **venire**
provvedere *like* **vedere**
pungere *2* punto *5* punsi, pungesti
racchiudere *like* **chiudere**
raccogliere *like* **cogliere**
radere *2* raso *5* rasi, radesti

raggiungere *like* giungere
rapprendere *like* prendere
ravvedersi *like* vedere
recidere *like* decidere
redigere *2* redatto
redimere *2* redento *5* redensi, redimesti
reggere *2* retto *5* ressi, reggesti
rendere *2* reso *5* resi, rendesti
reprimere *like* comprimere
rescindere *like* scindere
respingere *like* spingere
restringere *like* stringere
ricadere *like* cadere
richiedere *like* chiedere
riconoscere *like* conoscere
ricoprire *like* coprire
ricorrere *like* correre
ridere *2* riso *5* risi, ridesti
ridire *like* dire
ridurre *1* riducendo *2* ridotto *3* riduco *etc 4* riducevo *etc 5* ridussi, riducesti *6* ridurrò *etc 8* riduca *etc 9* riducessi *etc*
riempire *1* riempiendo *3* riempio, riempi, riempie, riempiono
rifare *like* fare
riflettere *2* riflettuto *o* riflesso
rifrangere *like* infrangere
rimanere *2* rimasto *3* rimango, rimangono *5* rimasi, rimanesti *6* rimarrò *etc 8* rimanga
rimettere *like* mettere
rimpiangere *like* piangere
rinchiudere *like* chiudere
rincrescere *like* crescere
rinvenire *like* venire
ripercuotere *like* percuotere
riporre *like* porre
riprendere *like* prendere
riprodurre *like* ridurre
riscuotere *like* scuotere
risolvere *like* assolvere
risorgere *like* sorgere
rispondere *2* risposto *5* risposi, rispondesti
ritenere *like* tenere
ritrarre *like* trarre
riuscire *like* uscire
rivedere *like* vedere
rivivere *like* vivere
rivolgere *like* volgere
rodere *2* roso *5* rosi, rodesti
rompere *2* rotto *5* ruppi, rompesti
salire *3* salgo, sali, salgono *8* salga
sapere *3* so, sai, sa, sappiamo, sapete, sanno *5* seppi, sapesti *6* saprò *etc 8* sappia *etc 10* sappi!, sappia!, sappiate!, sappiano!
scadere *like* cadere
scegliere *2* scelto *3* scelgo, scegli, sceglie, scegliamo, scegliete, scelgono *5* scelsi, scegliesti *8* scelga, scegliamo, scegliate, scelgano *10* scegli!, scelga!, scegliamo!, scegliete!, scelgano!
scendere *2* sceso *5* scesi, scendesti

schiudere *like* chiudere
scindere *2* scisso *5* scissi, scindesti
sciogliere *2* sciolto *3* sciolgo, sciolgi, scioglie, sciogliamo, sciogliete, sciolgono *5* sciolsi, sciogliesti *8* sciolga, sciogliamo, sciogliate, sciolgano *10* sciogli!, sciolga!, sciogliamo!, sciogliete!, sciolgano!
scommettere *like* mettere
scomparire *like* apparire
scomporre *like* porre
sconfiggere *2* sconfitto *5* sconfissi, sconfiggesti
sconvolgere *like* volgere
scoprire *like* aprire
scorgere *2* scorto *5* scorsi, scorgesti
scorrere *like* correre
scrivere *2* scritto *5* scrissi, scrivesti
scuotere *2* scosso *3* scuoto, scuoti, scuote, scotiamo, scotete, scuotono *5* scossi, scotesti *6* scoterò *etc 8* scuota, scotiamo, scotiate, scuotano *10* scuoti!, scuota!, scotiamo!, scotete!, scuotano!
sedere *3* siedo, siedi, siede, siedono *8* sieda
seppellire *2* sepolto
smettere *like* mettere
smuovere *like* muovere
socchiudere *like* chiudere
soccorrere *like* correre
soddisfare *like* fare
soffriggere *like* friggere
soffrire *2* sofferto *5* soffersi *o* soffrii, soffristi
soggiungere *like* giungere
solere *2* solito *3* soglio, suoli, suole, sogliamo, solete, sogliono *8* soglia, sogliamo, sogliate, sogliano
sommergere *like* emergere
sopprimere *like* comprimere
sorgere *2* sorto *3* sorsi, sorgesti
sorprendere *like* prendere
sorreggere *like* reggere
sorridere *like* ridere
sospendere *like* appendere
sospingere *like* spingere
sostenere *like* tenere
sottintendere *like* tendere
spandere *2* spanto
spargere *2* sparso *5* sparsi, spargesti
sparire *5* sparii *o* sparvi, sparisti
spegnere *2* spento *3* spengo, spengono *5* spensi, spegnesti *8* spenga
spendere *2* speso *5* spesi, spendesti
spingere *2* spinto *5* spinsi, spingesti
sporgere *like* porgere
stare *2* stato *3* sto, stai, sta, stiamo, state, stanno *5* stetti, stesti *6* starò *etc 8* stia *etc 9* stessi *etc 10* sta'!, stia!, state!, stiano!
stendere *like* tendere
storcere *like* torcere
stringere *2* stretto *5* strinsi, stringesti
struggere *2* strutto *5* strussi, struggesti
succedere *like* concedere

supporre *like* **porre**
svenire *like* **venire**
svolgere *like* **volgere**
tacere *2* taciuto *3* taccio, tacciono *5* tacqui, tacesti *8* taccia
tendere *2* teso *5* tesi, tendesti *etc*
tenere *3* tengo, tieni, tiene, tengono *5* tenni, tenesti *6* terrò *etc* *8* tenga
tingere *2* tinto *5* tinsi, tingesti
togliere *2* tolto *3* tolgo, togli, toglie, togliamo, togliete, tolgono *5* tolsi, togliesti *8* tolga, togliamo, togliate, tolgano *10* togli!, tolga!, togliamo!, togliete!, tolgano!
torcere *2* torto *5* torsi, torcesti
tradurre *like* **ridurre**
trafiggere *like* **sconfiggere**
transigere *like* **esigere**
trarre *1* traendo *2* tratto *3* traggo, trai, trae, traiamo, traete, traggono *4* traevo *etc* *5* trassi, traesti *6* trarrò *etc* *8* tragga *9* traessi *etc*
trascorrere *like* **correre**
trascrivere *like* **scrivere**
trasmettere *like* **mettere**
trasparire *like* **apparire**
trattenere *like* **tenere**
uccidere *2* ucciso *5* uccisi, uccidesti
udire *3* odo, odi, ode, odono *8* oda
ungere *2* unto *5* unsi, ungesti
uscire *3* esco, esci, esce, escono *8* esca
valere *2* valso *3* valgo, valgono *5* valsi, valesti *6* varrò *etc* *8* valga

vedere *2* visto *o* veduto *5* vidi, vedesti *6* vedrò *etc*
VENDERE *1* GERUNDIO vendendo
   2 PARTICIPIO PASSATO venduto
   3 PRESENTE vendo, vendi, vende, vendiamo, vendete, vendono
   4 IMPERFETTO vendevo, vendevi, vendeva, vendevamo, vendevate, vendevano
   5 PASSATO REMOTO vendei *o* vendetti, vendesti, vendé *o* vendette, vendemmo, vendeste, venderono *o* vendettero
   6 FUTURO venderò, venderai, venderà, venderemo, venderete, venderanno
   7 CONDIZIONALE venderei, venderesti, venderebbe, venderemmo, vendereste, venderebbero
   8 CONGIUNTIVO PRESENTE venda, venda, venda, vendiamo, vendiate, vendano
   9 CONGIUNTIVO PASSATO vendessi, vendessi, vendesse, vendessimo, vendeste, vendessero
   10 IMPERATIVO vendi!, venda!, vendete!, vendano!
venire *2* venuto *3* vengo, vieni, viene, vengono *5* venni, venisti *6* verrò *etc* *8* venga
vincere *2* vinto *5* vinsi, vincesti
vivere *2* vissuto *5* vissi, vivesti
volere *3* voglio, vuoi, vuole, vogliamo, volete, vogliono *5* volli, volesti *6* vorrò *etc* *8* voglia *etc* *10* vogli!, voglia!, vogliate!, vogliano!
volgere *2* volto *5* volsi, volgesti

VERBI INGLESI

present	pt	pp	present	pt	pp
arise	arose	arisen	drive	drove	driven
awake	awoke	awoken	dwell	dwelt	dwelt
be (am, is,	was, were	been	eat	ate	eaten
are;			fall	fell	fallen
being)			feed	fed	fed
bear	bore	born(e)	feel	felt	felt
beat	beat	beaten	fight	fought	fought
become	became	become	find	found	found
befall	befell	befallen	flee	fled	fled
begin	began	begun	fling	flung	flung
behold	beheld	beheld	fly	flew	flown
bend	bent	bent	forbid	forbad(e)	forbidden
beset	beset	beset	forecast	forecast	forecast
bet	bet, betted	bet, betted	forget	forgot	forgotten
bid (at	bid	bid	forgive	forgave	forgiven
auction,			forsake	forsook	forsaken
cards)			freeze	froze	frozen
bid (say)	bade	bidden	get	got	got, (US)
bind	bound	bound			gotten
bite	bit	bitten	give	gave	given
bleed	bled	bled	go (goes)	went	gone
blow	blew	blown	grind	ground	ground
break	broke	broken	grow	grew	grown
breed	bred	bred	hang	hung	hung
bring	brought	brought	hang	hanged	hanged
build	built	built	(execute)		
burn	burnt,	burnt,	have	had	had
	burned	burned	hear	heard	heard
burst	burst	burst	hide	hid	hidden
buy	bought	bought	hit	hit	hit
can	could	(been able)	hold	held	held
cast	cast	cast	hurt	hurt	hurt
catch	caught	caught	keep	kept	kept
choose	chose	chosen	kneel	knelt,	knelt,
cling	clung	clung		kneeled	kneeled
come	came	come	know	knew	known
cost	cost	cost	lay	laid	laid
cost (work	costed	costed	lead	led	led
out price			lean	leant,	leant,
of)				leaned	leaned
creep	crept	crept	leap	leapt,	leapt,
cut	cut	cut		leaped	leaped
deal	dealt	dealt	learn	learnt,	learnt,
dig	dug	dug		learned	learned
do (3rd	did	done	leave	left	left
person:			lend	lent	lent
he/she/it			let	let	let
does)			lie (lying)	lay	lain
draw	drew	drawn	light	lit, lighted	lit, lighted
dream	dreamed,	dreamed,	lose	lost	lost
	dreamt	dreamt	make	made	made
drink	drank	drunk	may	might	—

xxi

present	pt	pp	present	pt	pp
mean	meant	meant	**speed**	sped,	sped,
meet	met	met		speeded	speeded
mistake	mistook	mistaken	**spell**	spelt,	spelt,
mow	mowed	mown,		spelled	spelled
		mowed	**spend**	spent	spent
must	(had to)	(had to)	**spill**	spilt,	spilt,
pay	paid	paid		spilled	spilled
put	put	put	**spin**	spun	spun
quit	quit,	quit,	**spit**	spat	spat
	quitted	quitted	**spoil**	spoiled,	spoiled,
read	read	read		spoilt	spoilt
rid	rid	rid	**spread**	spread	spread
ride	rode	ridden	**spring**	sprang	sprung
ring	rang	rung	**stand**	stood	stood
rise	rose	risen	**steal**	stole	stolen
run	ran	run	**stick**	stuck	stuck
saw	sawed	sawed,	**sting**	stung	stung
		sawn	**stink**	stank	stunk
say	said	said	**stride**	strode	stridden
see	saw	seen	**strike**	struck	struck
seek	sought	sought	**strive**	strove	striven
sell	sold	sold	**swear**	swore	sworn
send	sent	sent	**sweep**	swept	swept
set	set	set	**swell**	swelled	swollen,
sew	sewed	sewn			swelled
shake	shook	shaken	**swim**	swam	swum
shear	sheared	shorn,	**swing**	swung	swung
		sheared	**take**	took	taken
shed	shed	shed	**teach**	taught	taught
shine	shone	shone	**tear**	tore	torn
shoot	shot	shot	**tell**	told	told
show	showed	shown	**think**	thought	thought
shrink	shrank	shrunk	**throw**	threw	thrown
shut	shut	shut	**thrust**	thrust	thrust
sing	sang	sung	**tread**	trod	trodden
sink	sank	sunk	**wake**	woke,	woken,
sit	sat	sat		waked	waked
slay	slew	slain			
sleep	slept	slept	**wear**	wore	worn
slide	slid	slid	**weave**	wove	woven
sling	slung	slung	**weave**	weaved	weaved
slit	slit	slit	*(wind)*		
smell	smelt,	smelt,	**wed**	wedded,	wedded,
	smelled	smelled		wed	wed
sow	sowed	sown,	**weep**	wept	wept
		sowed	**win**	won	won
speak	spoke	spoken	**wind**	wound	wound
			wring	wrung	wrung
			write	wrote	written

I NUMERI

NUMBERS

Italiano	Numero	English
uno(a)	1	one
due	2	two
tre	3	three
quattro	4	four
cinque	5	five
sei	6	six
sette	7	seven
otto	8	eight
nove	9	nine
dieci	10	ten
undici	11	eleven
dodici	12	twelve
tredici	13	thirteen
quattordici	14	fourteen
quindici	15	fifteen
sedici	16	sixteen
diciassette	17	seventeen
diciotto	18	eighteen
diciannove	19	nineteen
venti	20	twenty
ventuno	21	twenty-one
ventidue	22	twenty-two
ventitré	23	twenty-three
ventotto	28	twenty-eight
trenta	30	thirty
quaranta	40	forty
cinquanta	50	fifty
sessanta	60	sixty
settanta	70	seventy
ottanta	80	eighty
novanta	90	ninety
cento	100	a hundred, one hundred
centouno	101	a hundred and one
duecento	200	two hundred
mille	1 000	a thousand, one thousand
milleduecentodue	1 202	one thousand two hundred and two
cinquemila	5 000	five thousand
un milione	1 000 000	a million, one million

I NUMERI

NUMBERS

primo(a), 1°	first, 1st
secondo(a), 2°	second, 2nd
terzo(a), 3°	third, 3rd
quarto(a)	fourth, 4th
quinto(a)	fifth, 5th
sesto(a)	sixth, 6th
settimo(a)	seventh
ottavo(a)	eighth
nono(a)	ninth
decimo(a)	tenth
undicesimo(a)	eleventh
dodicesimo(a)	twelfth
tredicesimo(a)	thirteenth
quattordicesimo(a)	fourteenth
quindicesimo(a)	fifteenth
sedicesimo(a)	sixteenth
diciassettesimo(a)	seventeenth
diciottesimo(a)	eighteenth
diciannovesimo(a)	nineteenth
ventesimo(a)	twentieth
ventunesimo(a)	twenty-first
ventiduesimo(a)	twenty-second
ventitreesimo(a)	twenty-third
ventottesimo(a)	twenty-eighth
trentesimo(a)	thirtieth
centesimo(a)	hundredth
centunesimo(a)	hundred-and-first
millesimo(a)	thousandth
milionesimo(a)	millionth

L'ORA

THE TIME

che ora è?, che ore sono?	*what time is it?*
è ..., sono ...	*it's ...*

mezzanotte	midnight
l'una (del mattino)	one o'clock (in the morning) , one (am)
l'una e cinque	five past one
l'una e dieci	ten past one
l'una e un quarto, l'una e quindici	a quarter past one, one fifteen
l'una e venticinque	twenty-five past one, one twenty-five
l'una e mezzo *o* mezza, l'una e trenta	half past one, one thirty
l'una e trentacinque	twenty-five to two, one thirty-five
le due meno venti, l'una e quaranta	twenty to two, one forty
le due meno un quarto, l'una e quarantacinque	a quarter to two, one forty-five
le due meno dieci, l'una e cinquanta	ten to two, one fifty
mezzogiorno	twelve o'clock, midday, noon
le tre, le quindici	three o'clock (in the afternoon), three (pm)
le sette (di sera), le diciannove	seven o'clock (in the evening), seven (pm)

a che ora?	*at what time?*

a mezzanotte	at midnight
alle sette	at seven o'clock
fra venti minuti	in twenty minutes
venti minuti fa	twenty minutes ago

LA DATA

THE DATE

oggi	today
domani	tomorrow
dopodomani	the day after tomorrow
ieri	yesterday
l'altro ieri	the day before yesterday
il giorno prima	the day before, the previous day
il giorno dopo	the next *or* following day

la mattina	morning
la sera	evening
stamattina	this morning
stasera	this evening
questo pomeriggio	this afternoon
ieri mattina	yesterday morning
ieri sera	yesterday evening
domani mattina	tomorrow morning
domani sera	tomorrow evening
nella notte tra sabato e domenica	during Saturday night, during the night of Saturday to Sunday
viene sabato	he's coming on Saturday
il sabato	on Saturdays
tutti i sabati	every Saturday
sabato scorso, lo scorso sabato	last Saturday
il prossimo sabato	next Saturday
fra due sabati	a week on Saturday
fra tre sabati	a fortnight *or* two weeks on Saturday
da lunedì a sabato	from Monday to Saturday
tutti i giorni	every day
una volta alla settimana	once a week
una volta al mese	once a month
due volte alla settimana	twice a week
una settimana fa	a week ago
quindici giorni fa	a fortnight *or* two weeks ago
l'anno scorso *or* passato	last year
fra due giorni	in two days
fra una settimana	in a week
fra quindici giorni	in a fortnight *or* two weeks
il mese prossimo	next month
l'anno prossimo	next year

che giorno è oggi?	*what day is it?*
il primo/24 ottobre 1996	the 1st/24th of October 1996, October 1st/24th 1996
nel 1996	in 1996
il millenovecentonovantacinque	nineteen ninety-five
44 a.C.	44 BC
14 d.C.	14 AD
nel diciannovesimo secolo, nel XIX secolo, nell'Ottocento	in the nineteenth century
negli anni trenta	in the thirties
c'era una volta ...	once upon a time ...

Italiano-Inglese
Italian-English

Aa

A, a [a] *sf o m inv* (*lettera*) A, a; **A come Ancona** ≈ A for Andrew (*BRIT*), A for Able (*US*); **dalla a alla z** from a to z.
A *abbr* (= *altezza*) h; (= *area*) A; (= *autostrada*) ≈ M (*BRIT*).

=========== *PAROLA CHIAVE*

a (*a* + *il* = **al**, *a* + *lo* = **allo**, *a* + *l'* = **all'**, *a* + *la* = **alla**, *a* + *i* = **ai**, *a* + *gli* = **agli**, *a* + *le* = **alle**) *prep* **1** (*stato in luogo*) at; (: *in*) in; **essere alla stazione** to be at the station; **essere ~ casa/~ scuola/~ Roma** to be at home/at school/in Rome; **è ~ 10 km da qui** it's 10 km from here, it's 10 km away; **restare ~ cena** to stay for dinner
2 (*moto a luogo*) to; **andare ~ casa/~ scuola/alla stazione** to go home/to school/to the station; **andare ~ Roma/al mare** to go to Rome/to the seaside
3 (*tempo*) at; (*epoca, stagione*) in; **alle cinque** at five (o'clock); **~ mezzanotte/Natale** at midnight/Christmas; **al mattino** in the morning; **~ maggio/primavera** in May/spring; **~ cinquant'anni** at fifty (years of age); **~ domani!** see you tomorrow!; **~ lunedì!** see you on Monday!; **~ giorni** within (a few) days
4 (*complemento di termine*) to; **dare qc ~ qn** to give sb sth, give sth to sb; **l'ho chiesto ~ lui** I asked him
5 (*mezzo, modo*) with, by; **~ piedi/cavallo** on foot/horseback; **viaggiare ~ 100 km all'ora** to travel at 100 km an *o* per hour; **alla televisione/radio** on television/the radio; **fatto ~ mano** made by hand, handmade; **una barca ~ motore** a motorboat; **una stufa ~ gas** a gas heater; **~ uno ~ uno** one by one; **~ fatica** with difficulty; **all'italiana** the Italian way, in the Italian fashion
6 (*rapporto*) a, per; (: *con prezzi*) at; **due volte al giorno/mese** twice a day/month; **prendo 500.000 lire al mese** I get 500,000 lire a *o* per month; **pagato ~ ore** paid by the hour; **vendere qc ~ 500 lire il chilo** to sell sth at 500 lire a *o* per kilo; **cinque ~ zero** (*punteggio*) five nil.

AA *sigla* = Alto Adige.
AAS *sigla f* = Azienda Autonoma di Soggiorno.
AA.VV. *abbr* = autori vari.
ab. *abbr* = abitante.
a'bate *sm* abbot.
abbacchi'ato, a [abbak'kjato] *ag* downhearted, in low spirits.
abbacin'are [abbatʃi'nare] *vt* to dazzle.
abbagli'ante [abbaʎ'ʎante] *ag* dazzling; **~i** *smpl* (*AUT*): **accendere gli ~i** to put one's headlights on full (*BRIT*) *o* high (*US*) beam.
abbagli'are [abbaʎ'ʎare] *vt* to dazzle; (*illudere*) to delude.
ab'baglio [ab'baʎʎo] *sm* blunder; **prendere un ~** to blunder, make a blunder.
abbai'are *vi* to bark.
abba'ino *sm* dormer window; (*soffitta*) attic room.
abbando'nare *vt* to leave, abandon, desert; (*trascurare*) to neglect; (*rinunciare a*) to abandon, give up; **~rsi** *vr* to let o.s. go; **~ il campo** (*MIL*) to retreat; **~ la presa** to let go; **~rsi a** (*ricordi, vizio*) to give o.s. up to.
abbando'nato, a *ag* (*casa*) deserted;

(*miniera*) disused; (*tràscurato: terreno, podere*) neglected; (*bambino*) abandoned.

abban'dono *sm* abandoning; neglecting; (*stato*) abandonment; neglect; (*SPORT*) withdrawal; (*fig*) abandon; **in** ~ (*edificio, giardino*) neglected.

abbarbi'carsi *vr*: ~ **(a)** (*anche fig*) to cling (to).

abbassa'mento *sm* lowering; (*di pressione, livello dell'acqua*) fall; (*di prezzi*) reduction; ~ **di temperatura** drop in temperature.

abbas'sare *vt* to lower; (*radio*) to turn down; ~**rsi** *vr* (*chinarsi*) to stoop; (*livello, sole*) to go down; (*fig: umiliarsi*) to demean o.s.; ~ **i fari** (*AUT*) to dip (*BRIT*) o dim (*US*) one's lights; ~ **le armi** (*MIL*) to lay down one's arms.

ab'basso *escl*: ~ **il re!** down with the king!

abbas'tanza [abbas'tantsa] *av* (*a sufficienza*) enough; (*alquanto*) quite, rather, fairly; **non è** ~ **furbo** he's not shrewd enough; **un vino** ~ **dolce** quite a sweet wine, a fairly sweet wine; **averne** ~ **di qn/qc** to have had enough of sb/sth.

ab'battere *vt* (*muro, casa, ostacolo*) to knock down; (*albero*) to fell; (: *sog: vento*) to bring down; (*bestie da macello*) to slaughter; (*cane, cavallo*) to destroy, put down; (*selvaggina, aereo*) to shoot down; (*fig: sog: malattia, disgrazia*) to lay low; ~**rsi** *vr* (*avvilirsi*) to lose heart; ~**rsi a terra** o **al suolo** to fall to the ground; ~**rsi su** (*sog: maltempo*) to beat down on; (: *disgrazia*) to hit, strike.

abbatti'mento *sm* knocking down; felling; (*di casa*) demolition; (*prostrazione: fisica*) exhaustion; (: *morale*) despondency.

abbat'tuto, a *ag* despondent, depressed.

abba'zia [abbat'tsia] *sf* abbey.

abbece'dario [abbetʃe'darjo] *sm* primer.

abbelli'mento *sm* embellishment.

abbel'lire *vt* to make beautiful; (*ornare*) to embellish.

abbeve'rare *vt* to water; ~**rsi** *vr* to drink.

abbevera'toio *sm* drinking trough.

'abbi, 'abbia, abbi'amo, 'abbiano, abbi'ate *vb vedi* **avere**.

abbicci [abbit'tʃi] *sm inv* alphabet; (*sillabario*) primer; (*fig*) rudiments *pl*.

abbi'ente *ag* well-to-do, well-off.

abbi'etto, a *ag* = **abietto**.

abbiezi'one [abbjet'tsjone] *sf* = **abiezione**.

abbiglia'mento [abbiʎʎa'mento] *sm* dress *no pl*; (*indumenti*) clothes *pl*; (*industria*) clothing industry.

abbigli'are [abbiʎʎ'ʎare] *vt* to dress up.

abbina'mento *sm* combination; linking; matching.

abbi'nare *vt*: ~ **(con** o **a)** (*gen*) to combine (with); (*nomi*) to link (with); ~ **qc a qc** (*colori etc*) to match sth with sth.

abbindo'lare *vt* (*fig*) to cheat, trick.

abbocca'mento *sm* (*colloquio*) talks *pl*, meeting; (*TECN: di tubi*) connection.

abboc'care *vt* (*tubi, canali*) to connect, join up ♦ *vi* (*pesce*) to bite; (*tubi*) to join; ~ **(all'amo)** (*fig*) to swallow the bait.

abboc'cato, a *ag* (*vino*) sweetish.

abbona'mento *sm* subscription; (*alle ferrovie etc*) season ticket; **in** ~ **for** subscribers only; for season ticket holders only; **fare l'**~ **(a)** to take out a subscription (to); to buy a season ticket (for).

abbo'nare *vt* (*cifra*) to deduct; (*fig: perdonare*) to forgive; ~**rsi** *vr*: ~**rsi a un giornale** to take out a subscription to a newspaper; ~**rsi al teatro/alle ferrovie** to take out a season ticket for the theatre/the train.

abbo'nato, a *smf* subscriber; season-ticket holder; **elenco degli** ~**i** telephone directory.

abbon'dante *ag* abundant, plentiful; (*giacca*) roomy.

abbon'danza [abbon'dantsa] *sf* abundance; plenty.

abbon'dare *vi* to abound, be plentiful; ~ **in** o **di** to be full of, abound in.

abbor'dabile *ag* (*persona*) approachable; (*prezzo*) reasonable.

abbor'dare *vt* (*nave*) to board; (*persona*) to approach; (*argomento*) to tackle; ~ **una curva** to take a bend.

abbotto'nare *vt* to button up, do up; ~**rsi** *vr* to button (up).

abbotto'nato, a *ag* (*camicia etc*) buttoned (up); (*fig*) reserved.

abbottona'tura *sf* buttons *pl*; **questo cappotto ha l'**~ **da uomo/da donna** this coat buttons on the man's/woman's side.

abboz'zare [abbot'tsare] *vt* to sketch, outline; (*SCULTURA*) to rough-hew; ~ **un sorriso** to give a hint of a smile.

ab'bozzo [ab'bottso] *sm* sketch, outline; (*DIR*) draft.

abbracci'are [abbrat'tʃare] *vt* to embrace; (*persona*) to hug, embrace; (*professione*) to take up; (*contenere*) to include; ~**rsi** *vr* to hug o embrace (one another).

ab'braccio [ab'brattʃo] *sm* hug, embrace.

abbrevi'are *vt* to shorten; (*parola*) to abbreviate, shorten.

abbreviazi'one [abbrevjat'tsjone] *sf* abbreviation.

abbron'zante [abbron'dzante] *ag* tanning,

sun *cpd*.

abbron'zare [abbron'dzare] *vt* (*pelle*) to tan; (*metalli*) to bronze; **~rsi** *vr* to tan, get a tan.

abbron'zato, a [abbron'dzato] *ag* (sun)tanned.

abbronza'tura [abbrondza'tura] *sf* tan, suntan.

abbrusto'lire *vt* (*pane*) to toast; (*caffè*) to roast.

abbruti'mento *sm* exhaustion; degradation.

abbru'tire *vt* (*snervare, stancare*) to exhaust; (*degradare*) to degrade; **essere abbrutito dall'alcool** to be ruined by drink.

abbuf'farsi *vr* (*fam*): **~ (di qc)** to stuff o.s. (with sth).

abbuf'fata *sf* (*fam*) nosh-up; (*fig*) binge; **farsi un'~** to stuff o.s.

abbuo'nare *vt* = **abbonare**.

abbu'ono *sm* (*COMM*) allowance, discount; (*SPORT*) handicap.

abdi'care *vi* to abdicate; **~ a** to give up, renounce.

abdicazi'one [abdikat'tsjone] *sf* abdication.

aberrazi'one [aberrat'tsjone] *sf* aberration.

abe'taia *sf* fir wood.

a'bete *sm* fir (tree); **~ bianco** silver fir; **~ rosso** spruce.

abi'etto, a *ag* despicable, abject.

abiezi'one [abjet'tsjone] *sf* abjection.

'abile *ag* (*idoneo*): **~ (a qc/a fare qc)** fit (for sth/to do sth); (*capace*) able; (*astuto*) clever; (*accorto*) skilful; **~ al servizio militare** fit for military service.

abilità *sf inv* ability; cleverness; skill.

abili'tante *ag* qualifying; **corsi ~i** (*INS*) ≈ teacher training *sg*.

abili'tare *vt*: **~ qn a qc/a fare qc** to qualify sb for sth/to do sth; **è stato abilitato all'insegnamento** he has qualified as a teacher.

abili'tato, a *ag* qualified; (*TEL*) which has an outside line.

abilitazi'one [abilitat'tsjone] *sf* qualification.

abis'sale *ag* abysmal; (*fig: senza limiti*) profound.

abis'sino, a *ag, sm/f* Abyssinian.

a'bisso *sm* abyss, gulf.

abitabilità *sf:* **licenza di ~** *document stating that a property is fit for habitation.*

abi'tacolo *sm* (*AER*) cockpit; (*AUT*) inside; (*di camion*) (driver's) cab.

abi'tante *sm/f* inhabitant.

abi'tare *vt* to live in, dwell in ♦ *vi*: **~ in** **campagna/a Roma** to live in the country/ in Rome.

abi'tato, a *ag* inhabited; lived in ♦ *sm* (*anche*: **centro ~**) built-up area.

abitazi'one [abitat'tsjone] *sf* residence; house.

'abito *sm* dress *no pl*; (*da uomo*) suit; (*da donna*) dress; (*abitudine, disposizione, REL*) habit; **~i** *smpl* (*vestiti*) clothes; **in ~ da cerimonia** in formal dress; **in ~ da sera** in evening dress; **"è gradito l'~ scuro"** "dress formal"; **~ mentale** way of thinking.

abitu'ale *ag* usual, habitual; (*cliente*) regular.

abitual'mente *av* usually, normally.

abitu'are *vt*: **~ qn a** to get sb used *o* accustomed to; **~rsi a** to get used to, accustom o.s. to.

abitudi'nario, a *ag* of fixed habits ♦ *sm/f* creature of habit.

abi'tudine *sf* habit; **aver l'~ di fare qc** to be in the habit of doing sth; **d'~** usually; **per ~** from *o* out of habit.

abiu'rare *vt* to renounce.

abla'tivo *sm* ablative.

abnegazi'one [abnegat'tsjone] *sf* (self-) abnegation, self-denial.

ab'norme *ag* (*enorme*) extraordinary; (*anormale*) abnormal.

abo'lire *vt* to abolish; (*DIR*) to repeal.

abolizi'one [abolit'tsjone] *sf* abolition; repeal.

abomi'nevole *ag* abominable.

abo'rigeno [abo'ridʒeno] *sm* aborigine.

abor'rire *vt* to abhor, detest.

abor'tire *vi* (*MED: accidentalmente*) to miscarry, have a miscarriage; (*: deliberatamente*) to have an abortion; (*fig*) to miscarry, fail.

abor'tista, i, e *ag* pro-choice, pro-abortion ♦ *sm/f* pro-choicer.

a'borto *sm* miscarriage; abortion; (*fig*) freak; **~ clandestino** backstreet abortion.

abrasi'one *sf* abrasion.

abra'sivo, a *ag, sm* abrasive.

abro'gare *vt* to repeal, abrogate.

abrogazi'one [abrogat'tsjone] *sf* repeal.

abruz'zese [abrut'tsese] *ag* of (*o* from) the Abruzzi.

A'bruzzo [a'bruttso] *sm:* **l'~, gli ~i** the Abruzzi.

'abside *sf* apse.

'Abu 'Dhabi *sf* Abu Dhabi.

a'bulico, a, ci, che *ag* lacking in willpower.

abu'sare *vi*: **~ di** to abuse, misuse; (*approfittare, violare*) to take advantage of;

~ **dell'alcool/dei cibi** to drink/eat to excess.

abusi'vismo *sm* (*anche:* ~ **edilizio**) unlawful building, building without planning permission (*BRIT*).

abu'sivo, a *ag* unauthorized, unlawful; (**occupante**) ~ (*di una casa*) squatter.

a'buso *sm* abuse, misuse; excessive use; **fare** ~ **di** (*stupefacenti, medicine*) to abuse.

a.C. *abbr av* (= *avanti Cristo*) BC.

a'cacia, cie [a'katʃa] *sf* acacia.

'acca *sf* letter H; **non capire un'**~ not to understand a thing.

ac'cadde *vb vedi* **accadere**.

acca'demia *sf* (*società*) learned society; (*scuola: d'arte, militare*) academy; ~ **di Belle Arti** art school.

acca'demico, a, ci, che *ag* academic ♦ *sm* academician.

acca'dere *vi* to happen, occur.

acca'duto *sm* event; **raccontare l'**~ to describe what has happened.

accalappia'cani *sm inv* dog-catcher.

accalappi'are *vt* to catch; (*fig*) to trick, dupe.

accal'care *vt*, ~**rsi** *vr* to crowd, throng.

accal'darsi *vr* to grow hot.

accalo'rarsi *vr* (*fig*) to get excited.

accampa'mento *sm* camp.

accam'pare *vt* to encamp; (*fig*) to put forward, advance; ~**rsi** *vr* to camp; ~ **scuse** to make excuses.

accani'mento *sm* fury; (*tenacia*) tenacity, perseverance.

acca'nirsi *vr* (*infierire*) to rage; (*ostinarsi*) to persist.

accanita'mente *av* fiercely; assiduously.

acca'nito, a *ag* (*odio, gelosia*) fierce, bitter; (*lavoratore*) assiduous; (*giocatore*) inveterate; (*tifoso, sostenitore*) keen; **fumatore** ~ chain smoker.

ac'canto *av* near, nearby; ~ **a** *prep* near, beside, close to; **la casa** ~ the house next door.

accanto'nare *vt* (*problema*) to shelve; (*somma*) to set aside.

accaparra'mento *sm* (*COMM*) cornering, buying up.

accapar'rare *vt* (*COMM*) to corner, buy up; (*versare una caparra*) to pay a deposit on; ~**rsi** *vr:* ~**rsi qc** (*fig: simpatia, voti*) to secure sth (for o.s.).

accapigli'arsi [akkapiʎ'ʎarsi] *vr* to come to blows; (*fig*) to quarrel.

accappa'toio *sm* bathrobe.

accappo'nare *vi:* **far** ~ **la pelle a qn** (*fig*) to bring sb out in goosepimples.

accarez'zare [akkaret'tsare] *vt* to caress, stroke, fondle; (*fig*) to toy with.

accartocci'are [akkartot'tʃare] *vt* (*carta*) to roll up, screw up; ~**rsi** *vr* (*foglie*) to curl up.

acca'sarsi *vr* to set up house; to get married.

accasci'arsi [akkaʃ'ʃarsi] *vr* to collapse; (*fig*) to lose heart.

accatas'tare *vt* to stack, pile.

accatto'naggio [akkatto'naddʒo] *sm* begging.

accat'tone, a *sm/f* beggar.

accaval'lare *vt* (*gambe*) to cross; ~**rsi** *vr* (*sovrapporsi*) to overlap; (*addensarsi*) to gather.

acce'care [attʃe'kare] *vt* to blind ♦ *vi* to go blind.

ac'cedere [at'tʃɛdere] *vi:* ~ **a** to enter; (*richiesta*) to grant, accede to; (*fonte*) to gain access to.

accele'rare [attʃele'rare] *vt* to speed up ♦ *vi* (*AUT*) to accelerate; ~ **il passo** to quicken one's pace.

accele'rato, a [attʃele'rato] *ag* quick, rapid ♦ *sm* (*FERR*) local train, stopping train.

accelera'tore [attʃelera'tore] *sm* (*AUT*) accelerator.

accelerazi'one [attʃelerat'tsjone] *sf* acceleration.

ac'cendere [at'tʃɛndere] *vt* (*fuoco, sigaretta*) to light; (*luce, televisione*) to put o switch o turn on; (*AUT: motore*) to switch on; (*COMM: conto*) to open; (: *debito*) to contract; (: *ipoteca*) to raise; (*fig: suscitare*) to inflame, stir up; ~**rsi** *vr* (*luce*) to come o go on; (*legna*) to catch fire, ignite; (*fig: lotta, conflitto*) to break out.

accen'dino [attʃen'dino], **accendi'sigaro** [attʃendi'sigaro] *sm* (*cigarette*) lighter.

accen'nare [attʃen'nare] *vt* to indicate, point out; (*MUS*) to pick out the notes of; to hum ♦ *vi:* ~ **a** (*fig: alludere a*) to hint at; (: *far atto di*) to make as if; ~ **un saluto** (*con la mano*) to make as if to wave; (*col capo*) to half nod; ~ **un sorriso** to half smile; **accenna a piovere** it looks as if it's going to rain.

ac'cenno [at'tʃenno] *sm* (*cenno*) sign; nod; (*allusione*) hint.

accensi'one [attʃen'sjone] *sf* (*vedi accendere*) lighting; switching on; opening; (*AUT*) ignition.

accen'tare [attʃen'tare] *vt* (*parlando*) to stress; (*scrivendo*) to accent.

accentazi'one [attʃentat'tsjone] *sf* accentuation; stressing.

ac'cento [at'tʃɛnto] *sm* accent; (*FONETICA,*

fig) stress; (*inflessione*) tone (of voice).
accentra'mento [attʃentra'mento] *sm* centralization.
accen'trare [attʃen'trare] *vt* to centralize.
accentra'tore, 'trice [attʃentra'tore] *ag* (*persona*) unwilling to delegate; **politica ~trice** policy of centralization.
accentu'are [attʃentu'are] *vt* to stress, emphasize; **~rsi** *vr* to become more noticeable.
accerchi'are [attʃer'kjare] *vt* to surround, encircle.
accerta'mento [attʃerta'mento] *sm* check; assessment.
accer'tare [attʃer'tare] *vt* to ascertain; (*verificare*) to check; (*reddito*) to assess; **~rsi** *vr*: **~rsi (di qc/che)** to make sure (of sth/that).
ac'ceso, a [at'tʃeso] *pp di* **accendere ♦** *ag* lit; on; open; (*colore*) bright; **~ di** (*ira, entusiasmo etc*) burning with.
acces'sibile [attʃes'sibile] *ag* (*luogo*) accessible; (*persona*) approachable; (*prezzo*) reasonable; (*idea*): **~ a qn** within the reach of sb.
ac'cesso [at'tʃɛsso] *sm* (*anche INFORM*) access; (*MED*) attack, fit; (*impulso violento*) fit, outburst; **programmi dell'~** (*TV*) educational programmes; **tempo di ~** (*INFORM*) access time; **~ casuale/seriale/ sequenziale** (*INFORM*) random/serial/ sequential access.
accessori'ato, a [attʃesso'rjato] *ag* with accessories.
acces'sorio, a [attʃes'sɔrjo] *ag* secondary, of secondary importance; **~i** *smpl* accessories.
ac'cetta [at'tʃetta] *sf* hatchet.
accet'tabile [attʃet'tabile] *ag* acceptable.
accet'tare [attʃet'tare] *vt* to accept; **~ di fare qc** to agree to do sth.
accettazi'one [attʃettat'tsjone] *sf* acceptance; (*locale di servizio pubblico*) reception; **~ bagagli** (*AER*) check-in (desk); **~ con riserva** qualified acceptance.
ac'cetto, a [at'tʃɛtto] *ag* (*persona*) welcome; **(ben) ~ a tutti** well-liked by everybody.
accezi'one [attʃet'tsjone] *sf* meaning.
acchiap'pare [akkjap'pare] *vt* to catch; (*afferrare*) to seize.
ac'chito [ak'kito] *sm*: **a primo ~** at first sight.
acciac'cato, a [attʃak'kato] *ag* (*persona*) full of aches and pains; (*abito*) crushed.
acci'acco, chi [at'tʃakko] *sm* ailment; **~chi** *smpl* aches and pains.

acciaie'ria [attʃaje'ria] *sf* steelworks *sg*.
acci'aio [at'tʃajo] *sm* steel; **~ inossidabile** stainless steel.
acciden'tale [attʃiden'tale] *ag* accidental.
accidental'mente [attʃidental'mente] *av* (*per caso*) by chance; (*non deliberatamente*) accidentally, by accident.
acciden'tato, a [attʃiden'tato] *ag* (*terreno etc*) uneven.
acci'dente [attʃi'dɛnte] *sm* (*caso imprevisto*) accident; (*disgrazia*) mishap; **~i!** (*fam: per rabbia*) damn (it)!; (*: per meraviglia*) good heavens!; **~i a lui!** damn him!; **non vale un ~** it's not worth a damn; **non capisco un ~** it's as clear as mud to me; **mandare un ~ a qn** to curse sb.
ac'cidia [at'tʃidja] *sf* (*REL*) sloth.
accigli'ato, a [attʃiʎ'ʎato] *ag* frowning.
ac'cingersi [at'tʃindʒersi] *vr*: **~ a fare** to be about to do.
acciotto'lato [attʃotto'lato] *sm* cobbles *pl*.
acciuf'fare [attʃuf'fare] *vt* to seize, catch.
acci'uga, ghe [at'tʃuga] *sf* anchovy; **magro come un'~** as thin as a rake.
accla'mare *vt* (*applaudire*) to applaud; (*eleggere*) to acclaim.
acclamazi'one [akklamat'tsjone] *sf* applause; acclamation.
acclima'tare *vt* to acclimatize; **~rsi** *vr* to become acclimatized.
acclimatazi'one [akklimatat'tsjone] *sf* acclimatization.
ac'cludere *vt* to enclose.
ac'cluso, a [at'tʃuso] *pp di* **accludere ♦** *ag* enclosed.
accocco'larsi *vr* to crouch.
acco'darsi *vr* to follow, tag on (behind).
accogli'ente [akkoʎ'ʎɛnte] *ag* welcoming, friendly.
accogli'enza [akkoʎ'ʎɛntsa] *sf* reception; welcome; **fare una buona ~ a qn** to welcome sb.
ac'cogliere [ak'kɔʎʎere] *vt* (*ricevere*) to receive; (*dare il benvenuto*) to welcome; (*approvare*) to agree to, accept; (*contenere*) to hold, accommodate.
ac'colgo *etc vb vedi* **accogliere.**
ac'coll'are *vt* (*fig*): **~ qc a qn** to force sth on sb; **~rsi** *vr*: **~rsi qc** to take sth upon o.s., shoulder sth.
accol'lato, a *ag* (*vestito*) high-necked.
ac'colsi *etc vb vedi* **accogliere.**
accoltel'lare *vt* to knife, stab.
ac'colto, a *pp di* **accogliere.**
accoman'dita *sf* (*DIR*) limited partnership.
accomia'tare *vt* to dismiss; **~rsi** *vr*: **~rsi (da)** to take one's leave (of).
accomoda'mento *sm* agreement,

settlement.

accomo'dante *ag* accommodating.

accomo'dare *vt* (*aggiustare*) to repair, mend; (*riordinare*) to tidy; (*sistemare: questione, lite*) to settle; ~**rsi** *vr* (*sedersi*) to sit down; (*fig: risolversi: situazione*) to work out; **si accomodi!** (*venga avanti*) come in!; (*si sieda*) take a seat!

accompagna'mento [akkompaɲɲa'mento] *sm* (*MUS*) accompaniment; (*COMM*): **lettera di** ~ accompanying letter.

accompa'gnare [akkompaɲ'ɲare] *vt* to accompany, come *o* go with; (*MUS*) to accompany; (*unire*) to couple; ~**rsi** *vr* (*armonizzarsi*) to go well together; ~ **qn a casa** to see sb home; ~ **qn alla porta** to show sb out; ~ **un regalo con un biglietto** to put in *o* send a card with a present; ~ **qn con lo sguardo** to follow sb with one's eyes; ~ **la porta** to close the door gently; ~**rsi a** (*frequentare*) to frequent; (*colori*) to go with, match; (*cibi*) to go with.

accompagna'tore, 'trice [akkompaɲɲa 'tore] *sm/f* companion, escort; (*guida turistica*) courier; (*MUS*) accompanist; (*SPORT*) team manager.

accomu'nare *vt* to pool, share; (*avvicinare*) to unite.

acconcia'tura [akkontʃa'tura] *sf* hairstyle.

accondiscen'dente [akkondiʃʃen'dɛnte] *ag* affable.

accondi'scendere [akkondiʃ'ʃendere] *vi*: ~ **a** to agree *o* consent to.

accondi'sceso, a [akkondiʃ'ʃeso] *pp di* **accondiscendere.**

acconsen'tire *vi*: ~ **(a)** to agree *o* consent (to); **chi tace acconsente** silence means consent.

acconten'tare *vt* to satisfy; ~**rsi** *vr*: ~**rsi di** to be satisfied with, content o.s. with; **chi si accontenta gode** there's no point in complaining.

ac'conto *sm* part payment; **pagare una somma in** ~ to pay a sum of money as a deposit; ~ **di dividendo** interim dividend.

accoppia'mento *sm* pairing off; mating; (*ELETTR, INFORM*) coupling.

accoppi'are *vt* to couple, pair off; (*BIOL*) to mate; ~**rsi** *vr* to pair off; to mate.

accoppia'tore *sm* (*TECN*) coupler; ~ **acustico** (*INFORM*) acoustic coupler.

acco'rato, a *ag* heartfelt.

accorci'are [akkor'tʃare] *vt* to shorten; ~**rsi** *vr* to become shorter; (*vestiti: nel lavaggio*) to shrink.

accor'dare *vt* to reconcile; (*colori*) to match; (*MUS*) to tune; (*LING*): ~ **qc con qc** to make sth agree with sth; (*DIR*) to

grant; ~**rsi** *vr* to agree, come to an agreement; (*colori*) to match.

ac'cordo *sm* agreement; (*armonia*) harmony; (*MUS*) chord; **essere d'**~ to agree; **andare d'**~ to get on well together; **d'**~! all right!, agreed!; **mettersi d'**~ **(con qn)** to agree *o* come to an agreement with sb; **prendere** ~**i con** to reach an agreement with; ~ **commerciale** trade agreement; **A**~ **generale sulle tariffe ed il commercio** General Agreement on Tariffs and Trade, GATT.

ac'corgersi [ak'kɔrdʒersi] *vr*: ~ **di** to notice; (*fig*) to realize.

accorgi'mento [akkordʒi'mento] *sm* shrewdness *no pl*; (*espediente*) trick, device.

ac'correre *vi* to run up.

ac'corsi *vb vedi* **accorgersi; accorrere.**

ac'corso, a *pp di* **accorrere.**

accor'tezza [akkor'tettsa] *sf* (*avvedutezza*) good sense; (*astuzia*) shrewdness.

ac'corto, a *pp di* **accorgersi ♦** *ag* shrewd; **stare** ~ to be on one's guard.

accosta'mento *sm* (*di colori etc*) combination.

accos'tare *vt* (*avvicinarsi a*) to approach; (*socchiudere: imposte*) to half-close; (: *porta*) to leave ajar ♦ *vi*: ~ **(a)** (*NAUT*) to come alongside; (*AUT*) to draw up (at); ~**rsi** *vr*: ~**rsi a** to draw near, approach; (*somigliare*) to be like, resemble; (*fede, religione*) to turn to; (*idee politiche*) to come to agree with; ~ **qc a** (*avvicinare*) to bring sth near to, put sth near to; (*colori, stili*) to match sth with; (*appoggiare: scala etc*) to lean sth against.

accovacci'arsi [akkovat'tʃarsi] *vr* to crouch.

accoz'zaglia [akkot'tsaʎʎa] *sf* (*peg: di idee, oggetti*) jumble, hotchpotch; (: *di persone*) odd assortment.

ac'crebbi *etc vb vedi* **accrescere.**

accredi'tare *vt* (*notizia*) to confirm the truth of; (*COMM*) to credit; (*diplomatico*) to accredit; ~**rsi** *vr* (*fig*) to gain credit.

ac'credito *sm* (*COMM: atto*) crediting; (: *effetto*) credit.

ac'crescere [ak'kreʃʃere] *vt* to increase; ~**rsi** *vr* to increase, grow.

accresci'mento [akkreʃʃi'mento] *sm* increase, growth.

accresci'tivo, a [akkreʃʃi'tivo] *ag, sm* (*LING*) augmentative.

accresci'uto, a [akkreʃ'ʃuto] *pp di* **accrescere.**

accucci'arsi [akkut'tʃarsi] *vr* (*cane*) to lie down; (*persona*) to crouch down.

accu'dire *vi*: ~ **a** *vt* to attend to; to look

after.

acculturazi'one [akkulturat'tsjone] *sf* (*SOCIOLOGIA*) integration.

accumu'lare *vt* to accumulate; **~rsi** *vr* to accumulate; (*FINANZA*) to accrue.

accumula'tore *sm* (*ELETTR*) accumulator.

accumulazi'one [akkumulat'tsjone] *sf* accumulation.

ac'cumulo *sm* accumulation.

accurata'mente *av* carefully.

accura'tezza [akkura'tettsa] *sf* care; accuracy.

accu'rato, a *ag* (*diligente*) careful; (*preciso*) accurate.

ac'cusa *sf* accusation; (*DIR*) charge; **l'~, la pubblica ~** (*DIR*) the prosecution; **mettere qn sotto ~** to indict sb; **in stato di ~** committed for trial.

accu'sare *vt* (*sentire: dolore*) to feel; **~ qn di qc** to accuse sb of sth; (*DIR*) to charge sb with sth; **~ ricevuta di** (*COMM*) to acknowledge receipt of; **~ la fatica** to show signs of exhaustion; **ha accusato il colpo** (*anche fig*) you could see that he had felt the blow.

accusa'tivo *sm* accusative.

accu'sato, a *sm/f* accused.

accusa'tore, 'trice *ag* accusing ♦ *sm/f* accuser ♦ *sm* (*DIR*) prosecutor.

a'cerbo, a [a't∫erbo] *ag* bitter; (*frutta*) sour, unripe; (*persona*) immature.

'acero ['at∫ero] *sm* maple.

a'cerrimo, a [a't∫errimo] *ag* very fierce.

ace'tato [at∫e'tato] *sm* acetate.

a'ceto [a't∫eto] *sm* vinegar; **mettere sotto ~** to pickle.

ace'tone [at∫e'tone] *sm* nail varnish remover.

'A.C.I. ['at∫i] *sigla m* (= *Automobile Club d'Italia*) ≈ AA (*BRIT*), AAA (*US*).

acidità [at∫idi'ta] *sf* acidity; sourness; **~ (di stomaco)** heartburn.

'acido, a ['at∫ido] *ag* (*sapore*) acid, sour; (*CHIM, colore*) acid ♦ *sm* (*CHIM*) acid.

a'cidulo, a [a't∫idulo] *ag* slightly sour, slightly acid.

'acino ['at∫ino] *sm* berry; **~ d'uva** grape.

'ACLI *sigla fpl* (= *Associazioni Cristiane dei Lavoratori Italiani*) *Christian Trade Union Association.*

'acme *sf* (*fig*) acme, peak; (*MED*) crisis.

'acne *sf* acne.

ACNUR *sigla m* (= *Alto Commissariato delle Nazioni Unite per i Rifugiati*) UNHCR.

'acqua *sf* water; (*pioggia*) rain; **~e** *sfpl* waters; **fare ~** (*NAUT*) to leak, take in water; **essere con** *o* **avere l'~ alla gola** to be in great difficulty; **tirare ~ al proprio**
mulino to feather one's own nest; **navigare in cattive ~e** (*fig*) to be in deep water; **~ in bocca!** mum's the word!; **~ corrente** running water; **~ dolce** fresh water; **~ di mare** sea water; **~ minerale** mineral water; **~ ossigenata** hydrogen peroxide; **~ piovana** rain water; **~ potabile** drinking water; **~ salata** *o* **salmastra** salt water; **~ tonica** tonic water.

acqua'forte, *pl* acque'forti *sf* etching.

a'cquaio *sm* sink.

acqua'ragia [akkwa'radʒa] *sf* turpentine.

a'cquario *sm* aquarium; (*dello zodiaco*): **A~** Aquarius; **essere dell'A~** to be Aquarius.

acquartie'rare *vt* (*MIL*) to quarter.

acqua'santa *sf* holy water.

a'cquatico, a, ci, che *ag* aquatic; (*sport, sci*) water *cpd*.

acquat'tarsi *vr* to crouch (down).

acqua'vite *sf* brandy.

acquaz'zone [akkwat'tsone] *sm* cloudburst, heavy shower.

acque'dotto *sm* aqueduct; waterworks *pl*, water system.

'acqueo, a *ag*: **vapore ~** water vapour (*BRIT*) *o* vapor (*US*); **umore ~** aqueous humour (*BRIT*) *o* humor (*US*).

acque'rello *sm* watercolour (*BRIT*), watercolor (*US*).

acque'rugiola [akkwe'rudʒola] *sf* drizzle.

acquie'tare *vt* to appease; (*dolore*) to ease; **~rsi** *vr* to calm down.

acqui'rente *sm/f* purchaser, buyer.

acqui'sire *vt* to acquire.

acquisizi'one [akkwizit'tsjone] *sf* acquisition.

acquis'tare *vt* to purchase, buy; (*fig*) to gain ♦ *vi* to improve; **~ in bellezza** to become more beautiful; **ha acquistato in salute** his health has improved.

a'cquisto *sm* purchase; **fare ~i** to go shopping; **ufficio ~i** (*COMM*) purchasing department; **~ rateale** instalment purchase, hire purchase (*BRIT*).

acqui'trino *sm* bog, marsh.

acquo'lina *sf*: **far venire l'~ in bocca a qn** to make sb's mouth water.

a'cquoso, a *ag* watery.

'acre *ag* acrid, pungent; (*fig*) harsh, biting.

a'credine *sf* (*fig*) bitterness.

a'crilico, a, ci, che *ag, sm* acrylic.

a'critico, a, ci, che *ag* uncritical.

a'crobata, i, e *sm/f* acrobat.

acro'batico, a, ci, che *ag* (*ginnastica*) acrobatic; (*AER*) aerobatic ♦ *sf* acrobatics *sg*.

acroba'zia [akrobat'tsia] *sf* acrobatic feat;

~**e aeree** aerobatics.

a'**cronimo** *sm* acronym.

a'**cropoli** *sf inv:* **l'A**~ the Acropolis.

acu'**ire** *vt* to sharpen; ~**rsi** *vr* (*gen*) to increase; (*crisi*) to worsen.

a'**culeo** *sm* (*ZOOL*) sting; (*BOT*) prickle.

a'**cume** *sm* acumen, perspicacity.

acumi'**nato, a** *ag* sharp.

a'**custico, a, ci, che** *ag* acoustic ♦ *sf* (*scienza*) acoustics *sg*; (*di una sala*) acoustics *pl*; **apparecchio** ~ hearing aid; **cornetto** ~ ear trumpet.

acu'**tezza** [aku'tettsa] *sf* sharpness; shrillness; acuteness; high pitch; intensity; keenness.

acutiz'**zare** [akutid'dzare] *vt* (*fig*) to intensify; ~**rsi** *vr* (*fig: crisi, malattia*) to become worse, worsen.

a'**cuto, a** *ag* (*appuntito*) sharp, pointed; (*suono, voce*) shrill, piercing; (*MAT, LING, MED*) acute; (*MUS*) high-pitched; (*fig: dolore, desiderio*) intense; (*: perspicace*) acute, keen ♦ *sm* (*MUS*) high note.

A.D. *sigla f* (*POL*) = **Alleanza Democratica**.

ad *prep* (*dav V*) = **a**.

adagi'**are** [ada'dʒare] *vt* to lay *o* set down carefully; ~**rsi** *vr* to lie down, stretch out.

a'**dagio** [a'dadʒo] *av* slowly ♦ *sm* (*MUS*) adagio; (*proverbio*) adage, saying.

ada'**mitico, a, ci, che** *ag:* **in costume** ~ in one's birthday suit.

adat'**tabile** *ag* adaptable.

adattabilità *sf* adaptability.

adatta'**mento** *sm* adaptation; **avere spirito di** ~ to be adaptable.

adat'**tare** *vt* to adapt; (*sistemare*) to fit; ~**rsi** *vr:* ~**rsi (a)** (*ambiente, tempi*) to adapt (to); (*essere adatto*) to be suitable (for); (*accontentarsi*): ~**rsi a qc/a fare qc** to make the best of sth/of doing sth.

adatta'**tore** *sm* (*ELETTR*) adapter, adaptor.

a'**datto, a** *ag:* ~ (**a**) suitable (for), right (for).

addebi'**tare** *vt:* ~ **qc a qn** to debit sb with sth; (*fig: incolpare*) to blame sb for sth.

ad'**debito** *sm* (*COMM*) debit.

addensa'**mento** *sm* thickening; gathering.

adden'**sare** *vt* to thicken; ~**rsi** *vr* to thicken; (*nuvole*) to gather.

adden'**tare** *vt* to bite into.

adden'**trarsi** *vr:* ~ **in** to penetrate, go into.

ad'**dentro** *av* (*fig*): **essere molto** ~ **in qc** to be well-versed in sth.

addestra'**mento** *sm* training; ~ **aziendale** company training.

addes'**trare** *vt*, ~**rsi** *vr* to train; ~**rsi in qc** to practise (*BRIT*) *o* practice (*US*) sth.

ad'**detto, a** *ag:* ~ **a** (*persona*) assigned to; (*oggetto*) intended for ♦ *sm* employee; (*funzionario*) attaché; ~ **commerciale/stampa** commercial/press attaché; ~ **al telex** telex operator; **gli** ~**i ai lavori** authorized personnel; (*fig*) those in the know; "**vietato l'ingresso ai non** ~**i ai lavori**" "authorized personnel only".

addì *av* (*AMM*): ~ **3 luglio 1989** on the 3rd of July 1989 (*BRIT*), on July 3rd 1989 (*US*).

addi'**accio** [ad'djattʃo] *sm* (*MIL*) bivouac; **dormire all'**~ to sleep in the open.

addi'**etro** *av* (*indietro*) behind; (*nel passato, prima*) before, ago.

ad'**dio** *sm*, *escl* goodbye, farewell.

addirit'**tura** *av* (*veramente*) really, absolutely; (*perfino*) even; (*direttamente*) directly, right away.

ad'**dirsi** *vr:* ~ **a** to suit, be suitable for.

'**Addis A'beba** *sf* Addis Ababa.

addi'**tare** *vt* to point out; (*fig*) to expose.

addi'**tivo** *sm* additive.

addizio'**nale** [addittsjo'nale] *ag* additional ♦ *sf* (*anche:* **imposta** ~) surtax.

addizio'**nare** [addittsjo'nare] *vt* (*MAT*) to add (up).

addizi'**one** [addit'tsjone] *sf* addition.

addob'**bare** *vt* to decorate.

ad'**dobbo** *sm* decoration.

addol'**cire** [addol'tʃire] *vt* (*caffè etc*) to sweeten; (*acqua, fig: carattere*) to soften; ~**rsi** *vr* (*fig*) to mellow, soften; ~ **la pillola** (*fig*) to sugar the pill.

addolo'**rare** *vt* to pain, grieve; ~**rsi** *vr:* ~**rsi (per)** to be distressed (by).

addolo'**rato, a** *ag* distressed, upset; **l'A**~**a** (*REL*) Our Lady of Sorrows.

ad'**dome** *sm* abdomen.

addomesti'**care** *vt* to tame.

addomi'**nale** *ag* abdominal; (**muscoli** *mpl*) ~**i** stomach muscles.

addormen'**tare** *vt* to put to sleep; ~**rsi** *vr* to fall asleep, go to sleep.

addormen'**tato, a** *ag* sleeping, asleep; (*fig: tardo*) stupid, dopey.

addos'**sare** *vt* (*appoggiare*): ~ **qc a qc** to lean sth against sth; (*fig*): ~ **la colpa a qn** to lay the blame on sb; ~**rsi** *vr:* ~**rsi qc** (*responsabilità etc*) to shoulder sth.

ad'**dosso** *av* (*sulla persona*) on; ~ **a** *prep* (*sopra*) on; (*molto vicino*) right next to; **mettersi** ~ **il cappotto** to put one's coat on; **andare** (*o* **venire**) ~ **a** (*AUT: altra macchina*) to run into; (*: pedone*) to run over; **non ho soldi** ~ I don't have any money on me; **stare** ~ **a qn** (*fig*) to breathe down sb's neck; **dare** ~ **a qn** (*fig*) to attack sb; **mettere gli occhi** ~ **a qn/qc** to take quite a fancy to sb/sth; **mettere le** mani ~ a qn (*picchiare*) to hit sb; (*catturare*) to seize sb; (*molestare*: *donna*) to touch sb up.

ad'dotto, a *pp di* addurre.

ad'duco *etc vb vedi* addurre.

ad'durre *vt* (*DIR*) to produce; (*citare*) to cite.

ad'dussi *etc vb vedi* addurre.

adegu'are *vt*: ~ qc a to adjust sth to; ~rsi *vr* to adapt.

adegua'tezza [adegwa'tettsa] *sf* adequacy; suitability; fairness.

adegu'ato, a *ag* adequate; (*conveniente*) suitable; (*equo*) fair.

a'dempiere *vt* to fulfil (*BRIT*), fulfill (*US*), carry out; (*comando*) to carry out.

adempi'mento *sm* fulfilment (*BRIT*), fulfillment (*US*); carrying out; nell'~ del proprio dovere in the performance of one's duty.

adem'pire *vt* = adempiere.

'Aden: il golfo di ~ *sm* the Gulf of Aden.

ade'noidi *sfpl* adenoids.

a'depto *sm* disciple, follower.

ade'rente *ag* adhesive; (*vestito*) close-fitting ♦ *sm/f* follower.

ade'renza [ade'rɛntsa] *sf* adhesion; ~e *sfpl* (*fig*) connections, contacts.

ade'rire *vi* (*stare attaccato*) to adhere, stick; ~ a to adhere to, stick to; (*fig*: *società, partito*) to join; (: *opinione*) to support; (*richiesta*) to agree to.

ades'care *vt* (*attirare*) to lure, entice; (*TECN*: *pompa*) to prime.

adesi'one *sf* adhesion; (*fig*: *assenso*) agreement, acceptance; (*appoggio*) support.

ade'sivo, a *ag, sm* adhesive.

a'desso *av* (*ora*) now; (*or ora, poco fa*) just now; (*tra poco*) any moment now; da ~ in poi from now on; per ~ for the moment, for now.

adia'cente [adja'tʃɛnte] *ag* adjacent.

adi'bire *vt* (*usare*): ~ qc a to turn sth into.

'Adige ['adidʒe] *sm*: l'~ the Adige.

'adipe *sm* fat.

adi'poso, a *ag* (*tessuto, zona*) adipose.

adi'rarsi *vr*: ~ (con o contro qn per qc) to get angry (with sb over sth).

adi'rato, a *ag* angry.

a'dire *vt* (*DIR*): ~ le vie legali to take legal proceedings; ~ un'eredità to take legal possession of an inheritance.

'adito *sm*: dare ~ a (*sospetti*) to give rise to.

ADN *sigla m* (= *acido deossiribonucleico*) DNA.

adocchi'are [adok'kjare] *vt* (*scorgere*) to catch sight of; (*occhieggiare*) to eye.

adole'scente [adoleʃ'ʃɛnte] *ag, sm/f* adolescent.

adole'scenza [adoleʃ'ʃɛntsa] *sf* adolescence.

adolescenzi'ale [adoleʃʃen'tsjale] *ag* adolescent.

adom'brarsi *vr* (*cavallo*) to shy; (*persona*) to grow suspicious; (: *aversene a male*) to be offended.

adope'rare *vt* to use; ~rsi *vr* to strive; ~rsi per qn/qc to do one's best for sb/sth.

ado'rabile *ag* adorable.

ado'rare *vt* to adore; (*REL*) to adore, worship.

adorazi'one [adorat'tsjone] *sf* adoration; worship.

ador'nare *vt* to adorn.

a'dorno, a *ag*: ~ (di) adorned (with).

adot'tare *vt* to adopt; (*decisione, provvedimenti*) to pass.

adot'tivo, a *ag* (*genitori*) adoptive; (*figlio, patria*) adopted.

adozi'one [adot'tsjone] *sf* adoption.

adrena'linico, a, ci, che *ag* (*fig*: *vivace, eccitato*) charged-up.

adri'atico, a, ci, che *ag* Adriatic ♦ *sm*: l'A~, il mare A~ the Adriatic, the Adriatic Sea.

adu'lare *vt* to flatter.

adula'tore, 'trice *sm/f* flatterer.

adula'torio, a *ag* flattering.

adulazi'one [adulat'tsjone] *sf* flattery.

adulte'rare *vt* to adulterate.

adul'terio *sm* adultery.

a'dultero, a *ag* adulterous ♦ *sm/f* adulterer/adulteress.

a'dulto, a *ag* adult; (*fig*) mature ♦ *sm* adult, grown-up.

adu'nanza [adu'nantsa] *sf* assembly, meeting.

adu'nare *vt*, ~rsi *vr* to assemble, gather.

adu'nata *sf* (*MIL*) parade, muster.

a'dunco, a, chi, che *ag* hooked.

AEDA *sigla mpl* (= *Autori Editori Associati*) *association of authors and publishers*.

aerazi'one [aerat'tsjone] *sf* ventilation; (*TECN*) aeration.

a'ereo, a *ag* air *cpd*; (*radice*) aerial ♦ *sm* aerial; (*aeroplano*) plane; ~ da caccia fighter (plane); ~ di linea airliner; ~ a reazione jet (plane).

ae'robica *sf* aerobics *sg*.

aerodi'namico, a, ci, che *ag* aerodynamic; (*affusolato*) streamlined ♦ *sf* aerodynamics *sg*.

aeromo'dello *sm* model aircraft.

aero'nautica *sf* (*scienza*) aeronautics *sg*; ~ militare air force.

aerona'vale *ag* (*forze, manovre*) air and sea

cpd.

aero'plano *sm* (aero)plane (*BRIT*), (air)plane (*US*).

aero'porto *sm* airport.

aeroportu'ale *ag* airport *cpd*.

aeros'calo *sm* airstrip.

aero'sol *sm inv* aerosol.

aerospazi'ale [aerospat'tsjale] *ag* aerospace.

aeros'tatico, a, ci, che *ag* aerostatic; **pallone** ~ air balloon.

ae'rostato *sm* aerostat.

A.F. *abbr* (= *alta frequenza*) HF; (*AMM*) = **assegni familiari**.

'afa *sf* sultriness.

af'fabile *ag* affable.

affabilità *sf* affability.

affaccen'darsi [affattʃen'darsi] *vr*: ~ **intorno a qc** to busy o.s. with sth.

affaccen'dato, a [affattʃen'dato] *ag* busy.

affacci'arsi [affat'tʃarsi] *vr*: ~ **(a)** to appear (at); ~ **alla vita** to come into the world.

affa'mato, a *ag* starving; (*fig*): ~ **(di)** eager (for).

affan'nare *vt* to leave breathless; (*fig*) to worry; ~**rsi** *vr*: ~**rsi per qn/qc** to worry about sb/sth.

af'fanno *sm* breathlessness; (*fig*) anxiety, worry.

affannosa'mente *av* with difficulty; anxiously.

affan'noso, a *ag* (*respiro*) difficult; (*fig*) troubled, anxious.

af'fare *sm* (*faccenda*) matter, affair; (*COMM*) piece of business, (business) deal; (*occasione*) bargain; (*DIR*) case; (*fam: cosa*) thing; ~**i** *smpl* (*COMM*) business *sg*; ~ **fatto!** done!, it's a deal!; **sono ~i miei** that's my business; **bada agli ~i tuoi!** mind your own business!; **uomo d'~i** businessman; **ministro degli A~i Esteri** Foreign Secretary (*BRIT*), Secretary of State (*US*).

affa'rista, i *sm* profiteer, unscrupulous businessman.

affasci'nante [affaʃʃi'nante] *ag* fascinating.

affasci'nare [affaʃʃi'nare] *vt* to bewitch; (*fig*) to charm, fascinate.

affatica'mento *sm* tiredness.

affati'care *vt* to tire; ~**rsi** *vr* (*durar fatica*) to tire o.s. out.

af'fatto *av* completely; **non ... ~** not ... at all; **niente ~** not at all.

affer'mare *vi* (*dire di sì*) to say yes ♦ *vt* (*dichiarare*) to maintain, affirm; ~**rsi** *vr* to assert o.s., make one's name known.

affermativa'mente *av* in the affirmative, affirmatively.

afferma'tivo, a *ag* affirmative.

affer'mato, a *ag* established, well-known.

affermazi'one [affermat'tsjone] *sf* affirmation, assertion; (*successo*) achievement.

affer'rare *vt* to seize, grasp; (*fig: idea*) to grasp; ~**rsi** *vr*: ~**rsi a** to cling to.

Aff. Est. *abbr* = *Affari Esteri*.

affet'tare *vt* (*tagliare a fette*) to slice; (*ostentare*) to affect.

affet'tato, a *ag* sliced; affected ♦ *sm* sliced cold meat.

affetta'trice [affetta'tritʃe] *sf* meat slicer.

affettazi'one [affettat'tsjone] *sf* affectation.

affet'tivo, a *ag* emotional, affective.

af'fetto, a *ag*: **essere** ~ **da** to suffer from ♦ *sm* affection; **gli ~i familiari** one's nearest and dearest.

affettuosa'mente *av* affectionately; (*nelle lettere*): **(ti saluto)** ~, **Maria** love, Maria.

affettuosità *sf inv* affection; ~ *sfpl* (*manifestazioni*) demonstrations of affection.

affettu'oso, a *ag* affectionate.

affezio'narsi [affettsjo'narsi] *vr*: ~ **a** to grow fond of.

affezio'nato, a [affettsjo'nato] *ag*: ~ **a qn/qc** fond of sb/sth; (*attaccato*) attached to sb/sth.

affezi'one [affet'tsjone] *sf* (*affetto*) affection; (*MED*) ailment, disorder.

affian'care *vt* to place side by side; (*MIL*) to flank; (*fig*) to support; ~ **qc a qc** to place sth next to *o* beside sth; ~**rsi** *vr*: ~**rsi a qn** to stand beside sb.

affiata'mento *sm* understanding.

affia'tato, a *ag*: **essere** ~**i** to work well together *o* get on; **formano una squadra** ~**a** they make a good team.

affibbi'are *vt* to buckle, do up; (*fig: dare*) to give.

affi'dabile *ag* reliable.

affidabilità *sf* reliability.

affida'mento *sm* (*DIR: di bambino*) custody; (*fiducia*): **fare** ~ **su qn** to rely on sb; **non dà nessun** ~ he's not to be trusted.

affi'dare *vt*: ~ **qc** *o* **qn a qn** to entrust sth *o* sb to sb; ~**rsi** *vr*: ~**rsi a** to place one's trust in.

affievo'lirsi *vr* to grow weak.

af'figgere [af'fiddʒere] *vt* to stick up, post up.

affi'lare *vt* to sharpen.

affi'lato, a *ag* (*gen*) sharp; (*volto, naso*) thin.

affili'are *vt* to affiliate; ~**rsi** *vr*: ~**rsi a** to become affiliated to.

affi'nare *vt* to sharpen.

affinché [affin'ke] *cong* in order that, so that.

af'fine *ag* similar.

affinità *sf inv* affinity.

affio'rare *vi* to emerge.

af'fissi *etc vb vedi* **affiggere**.

affissi'one *sf* billposting.

af'fisso, a *pp di* **affiggere** ♦ *sm* bill, poster; (*LING*) affix.

affitta'camere *smf inv* landlord/landlady.

affit'tare *vt* (*dare in affitto*) to let, rent (out); (*prendere in affitto*) to rent.

af'fitto *sm* rent; (*contratto*) lease; **dare in ~** to rent (out), let; **prendere in ~** to rent.

affittu'ario *sm* lessee.

af'fliggere [af'fliddʒere] *vt* to torment; **~rsi** *vr* to grieve.

af'flissi *etc vb vedi* **affliggere**.

af'flitto, a *pp di* **affliggere**.

afflizi'one [afflit'tsjone] *sf* distress, torment.

afflosci'arsi [affloʃ'ʃarsi] *vr* to go limp; (*frutta*) to go soft.

afflu'ente *sm* tributary.

afflu'enza [afflu'ɛntsa] *sf* flow; (*di persone*) crowd.

afflu'ire *vi* to flow; (*fig: merci, persone*) to pour in.

af'flusso *sm* influx.

affo'gare *vt, vi* to drown; **~rsi** *vr* to drown; (*deliberatamente*) to drown o.s.

affo'gato, a *ag* drowned; (*CUC: uova*) poached.

affolla'mento *sm* crowding; (*folla*) crowd.

affol'lare *vt*, **~rsi** *vr* to crowd.

affol'lato, a *ag* crowded.

affonda'mento *sm* (*di nave*) sinking.

affon'dare *vt* to sink.

affran'care *vt* to free, liberate; (*AMM*) to redeem; (*lettera*) to stamp; (: *meccanicamente*) to frank (*BRIT*), meter (*US*); **~rsi** *vr* to free o.s.

affranca'trice [affranka'tritʃe] *sf* franking machine (*BRIT*), postage meter (*US*).

affranca'tura *sf* (*di francobollo*) stamping; franking (*BRIT*), metering (*US*); (*tassa di spedizione*) postage; **~ a carico del destinatario** postage paid.

af'franto, a *ag* (*esausto*) worn out; (*abbattuto*) overcome.

af'fresco, schi *sm* fresco.

affret'tare *vt* to quicken, speed up; **~rsi** *vr* to hurry; **~rsi a fare qc** to hurry o hasten to do sth.

affret'tato, a *ag* (*veloce: passo, ritmo*) quick, fast; (*frettoloso: decisione*) hurried, hasty; (: *lavoro*) rushed.

affron'tare *vt* (*pericolo etc*) to face; (*assalire: nemico*) to confront; **~rsi** *vr* (*reciproco*) to confront each other.

af'fronto *sm* affront, insult; **fare un ~ a qn** to insult sb.

affumi'care *vt* to fill with smoke; to blacken with smoke; (*alimenti*) to smoke.

affuso'lato, a *ag* tapering.

af'gano, a *ag, smf* Afghan.

Af'ghanistan [af'ganistan] *sm*: **l'~** Afghanistan.

af'ghano, a *ag, smf* = **afgano**.

afo'risma, i *sm* aphorism.

a'foso, a *ag* sultry, close.

'Africa *sf*: **l'~** Africa.

afri'cano, a *ag, smf* African.

afroasi'atico, ci, che *ag* Afro-Asian.

afrodi'siaco, a, ci, che *ag, sm* aphrodisiac.

AG *sigla* = Agrigento.

a'genda [a'dʒɛnda] *sf* diary; **~ tascabile/da tavolo** pocket/desk diary.

a'gente [a'dʒɛnte] *sm* agent; **~ di cambio** stockbroker; **~ di custodia** prison officer; **~ marittimo** shipping agent; **~ di polizia** police officer; **~ provocatore** agent provocateur; **~ delle tasse** tax inspector; **~ di vendita** sales agent; **resistente agli ~i atmosferici** weather-resistant.

agen'zia [adʒen'tsia] *sf* agency; (*succursale*) branch; **~ di collocamento** employment agency; **~ immobiliare** estate agent's (office) (*BRIT*), real estate office (*US*); **A~ Internazionale per l'Energia Atomica (AIEA)** International Atomic Energy Agency (IAEA); **~ matrimoniale** marriage bureau; **~ pubblicitaria** advertising agency; **~ di stampa** press agency; **~ viaggi** travel agency.

agevo'lare [adʒevo'lare] *vt* to facilitate, make easy.

agevolazi'one [adʒevolat'tsjone] *sf* (*facilitazione economica*) facility; **~ di pagamento** payment on easy terms; **~i creditizie** credit facilities; **~i fiscali** tax concessions.

a'gevole [a'dʒevole] *ag* easy; (*strada*) smooth.

agganci'are [aggan'tʃare] *vt* to hook up; (*FERR*) to couple; **~rsi** *vr*: **~rsi a** to hook up to; (*fig: pretesto*) to seize on.

ag'gancio [ag'gantʃo] *sm* (*TECN*) coupling; (*fig: conoscenza*) contact.

ag'geggio [ad'dʒeddʒo] *sm* gadget, contraption.

agget'tivo [addʒet'tivo] *sm* adjective.

agghiacci'ante [aggjat'tʃante] *ag* (*fig*) chilling.

agghiacci'are [aggjat'tʃare] *vt* to freeze;

(fig) to make one's blood run cold; ~**rsi** *vr* to freeze.

agghin'darsi [aggin'darsi] *vr* to deck o.s. out.

aggiorna'mento [addʒorna'mento] *sm* updating; revision; postponement; **corso di** ~ refresher course.

aggior'nare [addʒor'nare] *vt (opera, manuale)* to bring up-to-date; (: *rivedere*) to revise; (*listino*) to maintain, up-date; (*seduta etc*) to postpone; ~**rsi** *vr* to bring (o keep) o.s. up-to-date.

aggior'nato, a [addʒor'nato] *ag* up-to-date.

aggio'taggio [addʒo'taddʒo] *sm (ECON)* rigging the market.

aggi'rare [addʒi'rare] *vt* to go round; (*fig: ingannare*) to trick; ~**rsi** *vr* to wander about; **il prezzo s'aggira sul milione** the price is around the million mark.

aggiudi'care [addʒudi'kare] *vt* to award; (*all'asta*) to knock down; ~**rsi qc** to win sth.

aggi'ungere [ad'dʒundʒere] *vt* to add.

aggi'unsi [ad'dʒunsi] *etc vb vedi* **aggiungere**.

aggi'unto, a [ad'dʒunto] *pp di* **aggiungere** ♦ *ag* assistant *cpd* ♦ *sm* assistant ♦ *sf* addition; **sindaco** ~ deputy mayor; **in** ~**a ...** what's more ....

aggius'tare [addʒus'tare] *vt (accomodare)* to mend, repair; (*riassettare*) to adjust; (*fig: lite*) to settle; ~**rsi** *vr (arrangiarsi)* to make do; (*con senso reciproco*) to come to an agreement; **ti aggiusto io!** I'll fix you!

agglome'rato *sm (di rocce)* conglomerate; (*di legno*) chipboard; ~ **urbano** built-up area.

aggrap'parsi *vr*: ~ **a** to cling to.

aggrava'mento *sm* worsening.

aggra'vante *ag (DIR)* aggravating ♦ *sf* aggravation.

aggra'vare *vt (aumentare)* to increase; (*appesantire: anche fig*) to weigh down, make heavy; (*fig: pena*) to make worse; ~**rsi** *vr (fig)* to worsen, become worse.

ag'gravio *sm*: ~ **di costi** increase in costs.

aggrazi'ato, a [aggrat'tsjato] *ag* graceful.

aggre'dire *vt* to attack, assault.

aggre'gare *vt*: ~ **qn a qc** to admit sb to sth; ~**rsi** *vr* to join; ~**rsi a** to join, become a member of.

aggre'gato, a *ag* associated ♦ *sm* aggregate; ~ **urbano** built-up area.

aggressi'one *sf* aggression; (*atto*) attack; ~ **a mano armata** armed assault.

aggressività *sf* aggressiveness.

aggres'sivo, a *ag* aggressive.

aggres'sore *sm* aggressor, attacker.

aggrot'tare *vt*: ~ **le sopracciglia** to frown.

aggrovigli'are [aggroviʎ'ʎare] *vt* to tangle; ~**rsi** *vr (fig)* to become complicated.

agguan'tare *vt* to catch, seize.

aggu'ato *sm* trap; (*imboscata*) ambush; **tendere un** ~ **a qn** to set a trap for sb.

agguer'rito, a *ag (sostenitore, nemico)* fierce.

agia'tezza [adʒa'tettsa] *sf* prosperity.

agi'ato, a [a'dʒato] *ag (vita)* easy; (*persona*) well-off, well-to-do.

'agile ['adʒile] *ag* agile, nimble.

agilità [adʒili'ta] *sf* agility, nimbleness.

'agio ['adʒo] *sm* ease, comfort; ~**i** *smpl* comforts; **mettersi a proprio** ~ to make o.s. at home *o* comfortable; **dare** ~ **a qn di fare qc** to give sb the chance of doing sth.

a'gire [a'dʒire] *vi* to act; (*esercitare un'azione*) to take effect; (*TECN*) to work, function; ~ **contro qn** (*DIR*) to take action against sb.

agi'tare [adʒi'tare] *vt (bottiglia)* to shake; (*mano, fazzoletto*) to wave; (*fig: turbare*) to disturb; (: *incitare*) to stir (up); ~**rsi** *vr (mare)* to be rough; (*malato, dormitore*) to toss and turn; (*bambino*) to fidget; (*emozionarsi*) to get upset; (*POL*) to agitate.

agi'tato, a [adʒi'tato] *ag* rough; restless; fidgety; upset, perturbed.

agita'tore, 'trice [adʒita'tore] *sm/f (POL)* agitator.

agitazi'one [adʒitat'tsjone] *sf* agitation; (*POL*) unrest, agitation; **mettere in** ~ **qn** to upset *o* distress sb.

'agli ['aʎʎi] *prep + det vedi* **a**.

'aglio ['aʎʎo] *sm* garlic.

a'gnello [aɲ'ɲello] *sm* lamb.

a'gnostico, a, ci, che [aɲ'ɲostiko] *ag, sm/f* agnostic.

'ago, *pl* **'aghi** *sm* needle; ~ **da calza** knitting needle.

ago. *abbr* (= *agosto*) Aug.

ago'nia *sf* agony.

ago'nistico, a, ci, che *ag* athletic; (*fig*) competitive.

agoniz'zante [agonid'dzante] *ag* dying.

agoniz'zare [agonid'dzare] *vi* to be dying.

agopun'tura *sf* acupuncture.

agorafo'bia *sf* agoraphobia.

a'gosto *sm* August; *per fraseologia vedi* **luglio**.

a'grario, a *ag* agrarian, agricultural; (*riforma*) land *cpd* ♦ *sm* landowner ♦ *sf* agriculture.

a'gricolo, a *ag* agricultural, farm *cpd*.

agricol'tore *sm* farmer.

agricol'tura *sf* agriculture, farming.

agri'foglio [agri'fɔʎʎo] *sm* holly.

agrimen'sore *sm* land surveyor.
agritu'rismo *sm* farm holidays *pl*.
agritu'ristico, a, ci, che *ag* farm holiday *cpd*.
'agro, a *ag* sour, sharp.
agro'dolce [agro'doltʃe] *ag* bittersweet; (*salsa*) sweet and sour.
agrono'mia *sf* agronomy.
a'gronomo *sm* agronomist.
a'grume *sm* (*spesso al pl: pianta*) citrus; (: *frutto*) citrus fruit.
agru'meto *sm* citrus grove.
aguz'zare [agut'tsare] *vt* to sharpen; ~ gli orecchi to prick up one's ears; ~ l'ingegno to use one's wits.
aguz'zino, a [agud'dzino] *sm/f* jailer; (*fig*) tyrant.
a'guzzo, a [a'guttso] *ag* sharp.
'ahi *escl* (*dolore*) ouch!
ahimè *escl* alas!
'ai *prep* + *det vedi* a.
'Aia *sf*: L'~ The Hague.
'aia *sf* threshing floor.
AIDDA *sigla f* (= *Associazione Imprenditrici Donne Dirigenti d'Azienda*) *association of women entrepreneurs and managers*.
AIDS ['aids] *abbr m o f* AIDS.
AIE *sigla f* (= *Associazione Italiana degli Editori*) *publishers' association*.
AIEA *sigla f vedi* Agenzia Internazionale per l'Energia Atomica.
AIED *sigla f* (= *Associazione Italiana Educazione Demografica*) ≈ FPA (= *Family Planning Association*).
AIG *sigla f* (= *Associazione Italiana Alberghi per la Gioventù*) ≈ YHA (*BRIT*).
ai'ola *sf* = aiuola.
AIPI *sigla f* = *Associazione Italiana Protezione Infanzia*.
airbag *sm inv* air bag.
AIRC *abbr f* = *associazione italiana per la ricerca sul cancro*.
ai'rone *sm* heron.
ai'tante *ag* robust.
aiu'ola *sf* flower bed.
aiu'tante *sm/f* assistant ♦ *sm* (*MIL*) adjutant; (*NAUT*) master-at-arms; ~ di campo aide-de-camp.
aiu'tare *vt* to help; ~ qn (a fare) to help sb (to do).
ai'uto *sm* help, assistance, aid; (*aiutante*) assistant; venire in ~ di qn to come to sb's aid; ~ chirurgo assistant surgeon.
aiz'zare [ait'tsare] *vt* to incite; ~ i cani contro qn to set the dogs on sb.
al *prep* + *det vedi* a.
a.l. *abbr* = anno luce.
'ala, *pl* 'ali *sf* wing; fare ~ to fall back,

make way; ~ destra/sinistra (*SPORT*) right/left wing.
ala'bastro *sm* alabaster.
'alacre *ag* quick, brisk.
alacrità *sf* promptness, speed.
alam'bicco, chi *sm* still (*CHIM*).
a'lano *sm* Great Dane.
a'lare *ag* wing *cpd*; ~i *smpl* firedogs.
A'laska *sf*: l'~ Alaska.
a'lato, a *ag* winged.
'alba *sf* dawn; all'~ at dawn.
alba'nese *ag, sm/f, sm* Albanian.
Alba'nia *sf*: l'~ Albania.
'albatro *sm* albatross.
albeggi'are [albed'dʒare] *vi, vb impers* to dawn.
albe'rato, a *ag* (*viale, piazza*) lined with trees, tree-lined.
albera'tura *sf* (*NAUT*) masts *pl*.
alber'gare *vt* (*dare albergo*) to accommodate ♦ *vi* (*poetico*) to dwell.
alberga'tore, 'trice *sm/f* hotelier, hotel owner.
alberghi'ero, a [alber'gjɛro] *ag* hotel *cpd*.
al'bergo, ghi *sm* hotel; ~ diurno *public toilets with washing and shaving facilities etc*; ~ della gioventù youth hostel.
'albero *sm* tree; (*NAUT*) mast; (*TECN*) shaft; ~ a camme camshaft; ~ genealogico family tree; ~ a gomiti crankshaft; ~ maestro mainmast; ~ di Natale Christmas tree; ~ di trasmissione transmission shaft.
albi'cocca, che *sf* apricot.
albi'cocco, chi *sm* apricot tree.
al'bino, a *ag, sm/f* albino.
'albo *sm* (*registro*) register, roll; (*AMM*) notice board.
'album *sm* album; ~ da disegno sketch book.
al'bume *sm* albumen; (*bianco d'uovo*) egg white.
albu'mina *sf* albumin.
'alce ['altʃe] *sm* elk.
al'chimia [al'kimja] *sf* alchemy.
alchi'mista, i [alki'mista] *sm* alchemist.
'alcol *sm inv* = alcool.
alcolicità [alkolitʃi'ta] *sf* alcohol(ic) content.
al'colico, a, ci, che *ag* alcoholic ♦ *sm* alcoholic drink.
alco'lismo *sm* alcoholism.
alco'lista, i, e *sm/f* alcoholic.
alcoliz'zato, a [alkolid'dzato] *sm/f* alcoholic.
'alcool *sm inv* alcohol; ~ denaturato methylated spirits *pl* (*BRIT*), wood alcohol (*US*); ~ etilico ethyl alcohol; ~ metilico

methyl alcohol.

alco'olico *etc vedi* **alcolico** *etc.*

alco'test *sm inv* Breathalyser ® (*BRIT*), Breathalyzer ® (*US*).

al'cova *sf* alcove.

al'cuno, a *det* (*dav sm:* **alcun** + *C, V,* **alcuno** + *s impura, gn, pn, ps, x, z; dav sf:* **alcuna** + *C,* **alcun'** + *V*) (*nessuno*): **non ... ~** no, not any; **~i(e)** *det pl, pron pl* some, a few; **non c'è ~a fretta** there's no hurry, there isn't any hurry; **senza alcun riguardo** without any consideration.

aldilà *sm inv:* **l'~** the next life, the after-life.

alea'torio, a *ag* (*incerto*) uncertain.

aleggi'are [aled'dʒare] *vi* (*fig: profumo, sospetto*) to be in the air.

Ales'sandria *sf* (*anche:* **~ d'Egitto**) Alexandria.

a'letta *sf* (*TECN*) fin; tab.

alet'tone *sm* (*AER*) aileron.

Aleu'tine *sfpl:* **le isole ~** the Aleutian Islands.

alfa'betico, a, ci, che *ag* alphabetical.

alfa'beto *sm* alphabet.

alfanu'merico, a, ci, che *ag* alphanumeric.

alfi'ere *sm* standard-bearer; (*SCACCHI*) bishop.

al'fine *av* finally, in the end.

'alga, ghe *sf* seaweed *no pl,* alga.

'algebra ['aldʒebra] *sf* algebra.

Al'geri [al'dʒeri] *sf* Algiers.

Alge'ria [aldʒe'ria] *sf:* **l'~** Algeria.

alge'rino, a [aldʒe'rino] *ag, sm/f* Algerian.

algo'ritmo *sm* algorithm.

ALI *sigla f* (= *Associazione Librai Italiani*) *booksellers' association.*

ali'ante *sm* (*AER*) glider.

'alibi *sm inv* alibi.

a'lice [a'litʃe] *sf* anchovy.

alie'nare *vt* (*DIR*) to transfer; (*rendere ostile*) to alienate; **~rsi qn** to alienate sb.

alie'nato, a *ag* alienated; transferred; (*fuor di senno*) insane ♦ *sm* lunatic, insane person.

alienazi'one [aljenat'tsjone] *sf* alienation; transfer; insanity.

ali'eno, a *ag* (*avverso*): **~ (da)** opposed (to), averse (to) ♦ *sm/f* alien.

alimen'tare *vt* to feed; (*TECN*) to feed, supply; (*fig*) to sustain ♦ *ag* food *cpd;* **~i** *smpl* foodstuffs; (*anche:* **negozio di ~i**) grocer's shop; **regime ~** diet.

alimenta'tore *sm* (*ELETTR*) feeder.

alimentazi'one [alimentat'tsjone] *sf* feeding; (*cibi*) diet; **~ di fogli** (*INFORM*) sheet feed.

ali'mento *sm* food; **~i** *smpl* food *sg;* (*DIR*)

alimony.

a'liquota *sf* share; **~ d'imposta** tax rate; **~ minima** (*FISCO*) basic rate.

alis'cafo *sm* hydrofoil.

'alito *sm* breath.

all. *abbr* (= *allegato*) enc., encl.

'alla *prep* + *det vedi* **a.**

allaccia'mento [allattʃa'mento] *sm* (*TECN*) connection.

allacci'are [allat'tʃare] *vt* (*scarpe*) to tie, lace (up); (*cintura*) to do up, fasten; (*due località*) to link; (*luce, gas*) to connect; (*amicizia*) to form; **~rsi** *vr* (*vestito*) to fasten; **~ o ~rsi la cintura** to fasten one's belt.

allaccia'tura [allattʃa'tura] *sf* fastening.

allaga'mento *sm* flooding *no pl;* flood.

alla'gare *vt,* **~rsi** *vr* to flood.

allampa'nato, a *ag* lanky.

allar'gare *vt* to widen; (*vestito*) to let out; (*aprire*) to open; (*fig: dilatare*) to extend; **~rsi** *vr* (*gen*) to widen; (*scarpe, pantaloni*) to stretch; (*fig: problema, fenomeno*) to spread.

allar'mare *vt* to alarm; **~rsi** *vr* to become alarmed.

al'larme *sm* alarm; **mettere qn in ~** to alarm sb; **~ aereo** air-raid warning.

allar'mismo *sm* scaremongering.

allar'mista, i, e *sm/f* scaremonger, alarmist.

allat'tare *vt* (*sog: donna*) to (breast-)feed; (*: animale*) to suckle; **~ artificialmente** to bottle-feed.

'alle *prep* + *det vedi* **a.**

alle'anza [alle'antsa] *sf* alliance; **A~ Democratica** (*POL*) *moderate centre-left party;* **A~ Nazionale** (*POL*) *party on the far right.*

alle'arsi *vr* to form an alliance.

alle'ato, a *ag* allied ♦ *sm/f* ally.

alleg. *abbr* = **all.**

alle'gare *vt* (*accludere*) to enclose; (*DIR: citare*) to cite, adduce; (*denti*) to set on edge.

alle'gato, a *ag* enclosed ♦ *sm* enclosure; **in ~** enclosed; **in ~ Vi inviamo ...** please find enclosed ....

allegge'rire [alleddʒe'rire] *vt* to lighten, make lighter; (*fig: sofferenza*) to alleviate, lessen; (*: lavoro, tasse*) to reduce.

allego'ria *sf* allegory.

alle'gorico, a, ci, che *ag* allegorical.

alle'gria *sf* gaiety, cheerfulness.

al'legro, a *ag* cheerful, merry; (*un po' brillo*) merry, tipsy; (*vivace: colore*) bright ♦ *sm* (*MUS*) allegro.

allena'mento *sm* training.

alle'nare *vt*, **~rsi** *vr* to train.
allena'tore *sm* (*SPORT*) trainer, coach.
allen'tare *vt* to slacken; (*disciplina*) to relax; **~rsi** *vr* to become slack; (*ingranaggio*) to work loose.
aller'gia, 'gie [aller'dʒia] *sf* allergy.
al'lergico, a, ci, che [al'lɛrdʒiko] *ag* allergic.
allesti'mento *sm* preparation, setting up; **in ~** in preparation.
alles'tire *vt* (*cena*) to prepare; (*esercito, nave*) to equip, fit out; (*spettacolo*) to stage.
allet'tante *ag* attractive, alluring.
allet'tare *vt* to lure, entice.
alleva'mento *sm* breeding, rearing; (*luogo*) stock farm; **pollo d'~** battery hen.
alle'vare *vt* (*animale*) to breed, rear; (*bambino*) to bring up.
alleva'tore *sm* breeder.
allevi'are *vt* to alleviate.
alli'bire *vi* to turn pale; (*essere turbato*) to be disconcerted.
alli'bito, a *ag* pale; disconcerted.
allibra'tore *sm* bookmaker.
allie'tare *vt* to cheer up, gladden.
alli'evo *sm* pupil; (*apprendista*) apprentice; **~ ufficiale** cadet.
alliga'tore *sm* alligator.
allinea'mento *sm* alignment.
alline'are *vt* (*persone, cose*) to line up; (*TIP*) to align; (*fig: economia, salari*) to adjust, align; **~rsi** *vr* to line up; (*fig: a idee*): **~rsi a** to come into line with.
alline'ato, a *ag* aligned, in line; **paesi non ~i** (*POL*) non-aligned countries.
'allo *prep + det vedi* **a**.
allo'care *vt* to allocate.
al'locco, a, chi, che *sm* tawny owl ♦ *sm/f* oaf.
allocuzi'one [allokut'tsjone] *sf* address, solemn speech.
al'lodola *sf* (sky)lark.
alloggi'are [allod'dʒare] *vt* to accommodate ♦ *vi* to live.
al'loggio [al'lɔddʒo] *sm* lodging, accommodation (*BRIT*), accommodations (*US*); (*appartamento*) flat (*BRIT*), apartment (*US*).
allontana'mento *sm* removal; dismissal; estrangement.
allonta'nare *vt* to send away, send off; (*impiegato*) to dismiss; (*pericolo*) to avert, remove; (*estraniare*) to alienate; **~rsi** *vr*: **~rsi (da)** to go away (from); (*estraniarsi*) to become estranged (from).
al'lora *av* (*in quel momento*) then ♦ *cong* (*in questo caso*) well then; (*dunque*) well

then, so; **la gente d'~** people then *o* in those days; **da ~ in poi** from then on; **e ~?** (*che fare?*) what now?; (*e con ciò?*) so what?
allor'ché [allor'ke] *cong* (*formale*) when, as soon as.
al'loro *sm* laurel; **riposare** *o* **dormire sugli ~i** to rest on one's laurels.
'alluce ['allutʃe] *sm* big toe.
alluci'nante [allutʃi'nante] *ag* (*scena, spettacolo*) awful, terrifying; (*fam: incredibile*) amazing.
alluci'nato, a [allutʃi'nato] *ag* terrified; (*fuori di sé*) bewildered, confused.
allucinazi'one [allutʃinat'tsjone] *sf* hallucination.
al'ludere *vi*: **~ a** to allude to, hint at.
allu'minio *sm* aluminium (*BRIT*), aluminum (*US*).
allu'naggio [allu'naddʒo] *sm* moon landing.
allu'nare *vi* to land on the moon.
allun'gare *vt* to lengthen; (*distendere*) to prolong, extend; (*diluire*) to water down; **~rsi** *vr* to lengthen; (*ragazzo*) to stretch, grow taller; (*sdraiarsi*) to lie down, stretch out; **~ le mani** (*rubare*) to pick pockets; **gli allungò uno schiaffo** he took a swipe at him.
al'lusi *etc vb vedi* **alludere**.
allusi'one *sf* hint, allusion.
al'luso, a *pp di* **alludere**.
alluvi'one *sf* flood.
alma'nacco, chi *sm* almanac.
al'meno *av* at least ♦ *cong*: (**se**) **~** if only; (**se**) **~ piovesse!** if only it would rain!
a'logeno, a [a'lɔdʒeno] *ag*: **lampada ~a** halogen lamp.
a'lone *sm* halo.
al'pestre *ag* (*delle alpi*) alpine; (*montuoso*) mountainous.
'Alpi *sfpl*: **le ~** the Alps.
alpi'nismo *sm* mountaineering, climbing.
alpi'nista, i, e *sm/f* mountaineer, climber.
al'pino, a *ag* Alpine; mountain *cpd*; **~i** *smpl* (*MIL*) Italian Alpine troops.
al'quanto *av* rather, a little; **~, a** *det* a certain amount of, some ♦ *pron* a certain amount, some; **~i(e)** *det pl, pron pl* several, quite a few.
Al'sazia [al'sattsja] *sf* Alsace.
alt *escl* halt!, stop! ♦ *sm*: **dare l'~** to call a halt.
alta'lena *sf* (*a funi*) swing; (*in bilico, anche fig*) seesaw.
alta'mente *av* extremely, highly.
al'tare *sm* altar.
alte'rare *vt* to alter, change; (*cibo*) to adulterate; (*registro*) to falsify; (*persona*)

to irritate; ~**rsi** *vr* to alter; (*cibo*) to go bad; (*persona*) to lose one's temper.

alterazi'one [alterat'tsjone] *sf* alteration, change; adulteration; falsification; annoyance.

al'terco, chi *sm* altercation, wrangle.

alter'nanza [alter'nantsa] *sf* alternation; (*AGR*) rotation.

alter'nare *vt*, ~**rsi** *vr* to alternate.

alterna'tivo, a *ag* alternative ♦ *sf* alternative; **non abbiamo** ~**e** we have no alternative.

alter'nato, a *ag* alternate; (*ELETTR*) alternating.

alterna'tore *sm* alternator.

al'terno, a *ag* alternate; **a giorni** ~**i** on alternate days, every other day; **circolazione a targhe** ~**e** (*AUT*) *system of restricting vehicle use to odd/even registrations on alternate days.*

al'tero, a *ag* proud.

al'tezza [al'tettsa] *sf* (*di edificio, persona*) height; (*di tessuto*) width, breadth; (*di acqua, pozzo*) depth; (*di suono*) pitch; (*GEO*) latitude; (*titolo*) highness; (*fig: nobiltà*) greatness; **essere all'**~ **di** to be on a level with; (*fig*) to be up to *o* equal to; **all'**~ **della farmacia** near the chemist's.

altez'zoso, a [altet'tsoso] *ag* haughty.

al'ticcio, a, ci, ce [al'tittʃo] *ag* tipsy.

altipi'ano *sm* = **altopiano.**

altiso'nante *ag* (*fig*) high-sounding, pompous.

alti'tudine *sf* altitude.

'alto, a *ag* high; (*persona*) tall; (*tessuto*) wide, broad; (*sonno, acque*) deep; (*suono*) high(-pitched); (*GEO*) upper; (*: settentrionale*) northern ♦ *sm* top (part) ♦ *av* high; (*parlare*) aloud, loudly; **il palazzo è** ~ **20 metri** the building is 20 metres high; **il tessuto è** ~ **70 cm** the material is 70 cm wide; **ad** ~**a voce** aloud; **a notte** ~**a** in the dead of night; **in** ~ up, upwards; **at the top; mani in** ~**!** hands up!; **dall'**~ **in** *o* **al basso** up and down; **degli** ~**i e bassi** (*fig*) ups and downs; **andare a testa** ~**a** (*fig*) to carry one's head high; **essere in** ~ **mare** (*fig*) to be far from a solution; ~**a fedeltà** high fidelity, hi-fi; ~**a moda** haute couture; **l'A~ Medioevo** the Early Middle Ages; **l'**~ **Po** the upper reaches of the Po.

altoate'sino, a *ag* of (*o* from) the Alto Adige.

alto'forno *sm* blast furnace.

altolo'cato, a *ag* of high rank, highly placed.

altopar'lante *sm* loudspeaker.

altopi'ano, *pl* **alti'piani** *sm* upland plain, plateau.

'Alto 'Volta *sm:* **l'**~ Upper Volta.

altret'tanto, a *ag, pron* as much; (*pl*) as many ♦ *av* equally; **tanti auguri! — grazie,** ~ all the best! — thank you, the same to you.

'altri *pron inv* (*qualcuno*) somebody; (: *in espressioni negative*) anybody; (*un'altra persona*) another (person).

altri'menti *av* otherwise.

=========================== *PAROLA CHIAVE*

'altro, a *det* **1** (*diverso*) other, different; **questa è un'**~**a cosa** that's another *o* a different thing; **passami l'**~**a penna** give me the other pen

2 (*supplementare*) other; **prendi un** ~ **cioccolatino** have another chocolate; **hai avuto** ~**e notizie?** have you had any more *o* any other news?; **hai** ~ **pane?** have you got any more bread?

3 (*nel tempo*): **l'**~ **giorno** the other day; **l'altr'anno** last year; **l'**~ **ieri** the day before yesterday; **domani l'**~ the day after tomorrow; **quest'**~ **mese** next month

4: **d'**~**a parte** on the other hand

♦ *pron* **1** (*persona, cosa diversa o supplementare*): **un** ~**, un'**~**a** another (one); **lo farà un** ~ someone else will do it; ~**i, e** others; **gli** ~**i** (*la gente*) others, other people; **l'uno e l'**~ both (of them); **aiutarsi l'un l'**~ to help one another; **prendine un** ~ have another (one); **da un giorno all'**~ from day to day; (*nel giro di 24 ore*) from one day to the next; (*da un momento all'altro*) any day now

2 (*sostantivato: solo maschile*) something else; (: *in espressioni interrogative*) anything else; **non ho** ~ **da dire** I have nothing else *o* I don't have anything else to say; **desidera** ~**?** do you want anything else?; **più che** ~ above all; **se non** ~ if nothing else, at least; **tra l'**~ among other things; **ci mancherebbe** ~**!** that's all we need!; **non faccio** ~ **che lavorare** I do nothing but work; **contento** — ~ **che!** are you pleased? — I certainly am!; *vedi anche* **senza; noialtri; voialtri; tutto.**

altroché [altro'ke] *escl* certainly!, and how!

al'tronde *av:* **d'**~ on the other hand.

al'trove *av* elsewhere, somewhere else.

al'trui *ag inv* other people's ♦ *sm:* **l'**~ other people's belongings *pl.*

altru'ismo *sm* altruism.

altru'ista, i, e *ag* altruistic ♦ *sm/f* altruist.

al'tura *sf* (*rialto*) height, high ground; (*alto mare*) open sea; **pesca d'~** deep-sea fishing.

a'lunno, a *sm/f* pupil.

alve'are *sm* hive.

'alveo *sm* riverbed.

alzabandi'era [altsaban'djera] *sm inv* (*MIL*): l'~ the raising of the flag.

al'zare [al'tsare] *vt* to raise, lift; (*issare*) to hoist; (*costruire*) to build, erect; **~rsi** *vr* to rise; (*dal letto*) to get up; (*crescere*) to grow tall (*o* taller); **~ le spalle** to shrug one's shoulders; **~ le carte** to cut the cards; **~ il gomito** to drink too much; **~ le mani su qn** to raise one's hand to sb; **~ i tacchi** to take to one's heels; **~rsi in piedi** to stand up, get to one's feet; **~rsi col piede sbagliato** to get out of bed on the wrong side.

al'zata [al'tsata] *sf* lifting, raising; **un'~ di spalle** a shrug.

A.M. *abbr* = **aeronautica militare**.

a'mabile *ag* lovable; (*vino*) sweet.

'AMAC *sigla f* = *Aeronautica Militare-Aviazione Civile*.

a'maca, che *sf* hammock.

amalga'mare *vt*, **~rsi** *vr* to amalgamate.

a'mante *ag*: **~ di** (*musica etc*) fond of ♦ *sm/f* lover/mistress.

amara'mente *av* bitterly.

ama'ranto *sm* (*BOT*) love-lies-bleeding ♦ *ag inv*: **color ~** reddish purple.

a'mare *vt* to love; (*amico, musica, sport*) to like.

amareggi'are [amared'dʒare] *vt* to sadden, upset; **~rsi** *vr* to get upset; **~rsi la vita** to make one's life a misery.

amareggi'ato, a [amared'dʒato] *ag* upset, saddened.

ama'rena *sf* sour black cherry.

ama'retto *sm* (*dolce*) macaroon; (*liquore*) *bitter liqueur made with almonds*.

ama'rezza [ama'rettsa] *sf* bitterness.

a'maro, a *ag* bitter ♦ *sm* bitterness; (*liquore*) bitters *pl*.

ama'rognolo, a [ama'roɲɲolo] *ag* slightly bitter.

a'mato, a *ag* beloved, loved, dear ♦ *sm/f* loved one.

ama'tore, 'trice *sm/f* (*amante*) lover; (*intenditore: di vini etc*) connoisseur; (*dilettante*) amateur.

a'mazzone [a'maddzone] *sf* (*MITOLOGIA*) Amazon; (*cavallerizza*) horsewoman; (*abito*) riding habit; **cavalcare all'~** to ride sidesaddle; **il Rio delle A~i** the (river) Amazon.

Amaz'zonia [amad'dzonja] *sf* Amazonia.

amaz'zonico, a, ci, che [amad'dzɔniko] *ag* Amazonian; Amazon *cpd*.

ambasce'ria [ambaʃʃe'ria] *sf* embassy.

ambasci'ata [ambaʃ'ʃata] *sf* embassy; (*messaggio*) message.

ambascia'tore, 'trice [ambaʃʃa'tore] *sm/f* ambassador/ambassadress.

ambe'due *ag inv*: **~ i ragazzi** both boys ♦ *pron inv* both.

ambi'destro, a *ag* ambidextrous.

ambien'tale *ag* (*temperatura*) ambient *cpd*; (*problemi, tutela*) environmental.

ambienta'lismo *sm* environmentalism.

ambienta'lista, i, e *ag* environmental ♦ *sm/f* environmentalist.

ambien'tare *vt* to acclimatize; (*romanzo, film*) to set; **~rsi** *vr* to get used to one's surroundings.

ambientazi'one [ambjentat'tsjone] *sf* setting.

ambi'ente *sm* environment; (*fig: insieme di persone*) milieu; (*stanza*) room.

ambiguità *sf inv* ambiguity.

am'biguo, a *ag* ambiguous; (*persona*) shady.

am'bire *vt* (*anche: vi*: **~ a**) to aspire to; **un premio molto ambito** a much sought-after prize.

'ambito *sm* sphere, field.

ambiva'lente *ag* ambivalent; **questo apparecchio è ~** this is a dual-purpose device.

ambizi'one [ambit'tsjone] *sf* ambition.

ambizi'oso, a [ambit'tsjoso] *ag* ambitious.

'ambo *ag inv* both.

'ambra *sf* amber; **~ grigia** ambergris.

ambu'lante *ag* travelling, itinerant.

ambu'lanza [ambu'lantsa] *sf* ambulance.

ambulatori'ale *ag* (*MED*) outpatients *cpd*; **operazione ~** operation as an outpatient; **visita ~** visit to the doctor's surgery (*BRIT*) *o* office (*US*).

ambula'torio *sm* (*studio medico*) surgery (*BRIT*), doctor's office (*US*).

'AMDI *sigla f* = *Associazione Medici Dentisti Italiani*.

'AME *sigla m* = *Accordo Monetario Europeo*.

a'meba *sf* amoeba (*BRIT*), ameba (*US*).

amenità *sf inv* pleasantness *no pl*; (*facezia*) pleasantry.

a'meno, a *ag* pleasant; (*strano*) funny, strange; (*spiritoso*) amusing.

A'merica *sf*: l'~ America; l'~ **latina** Latin America; l'~ **del sud** South America.

america'nata *sf* (*peg*): **le Olimpiadi sono state una vera ~** the Olympics were a typically vulgar American extravaganza.

america'nismo *sm* Americanism;

(*ammirazione*) love of America.
ameri'cano, a *ag, sm/f* American.
ame'tista *sf* amethyst.
ami'anto *sm* asbestos.
a'mica *sf vedi* **amico.**
ami'chevole [ami'kevole] *ag* friendly.
ami'cizia [ami'tʃittsja] *sf* friendship; **~e** *sfpl* (*amici*) friends; **fare ~ con qn** to make friends with sb.
a'mico, a, ci, che *sm/f* friend; (*amante*) boyfriend/girlfriend; **~ del cuore** *o* **intimo** bosom friend; **~ d'infanzia** childhood friend.
'amido *sm* starch.
ammac'care *vt* (*pentola*) to dent; (*persona*) to bruise; **~rsi** *vr* to bruise.
ammacca'tura *sf* dent; bruise.
ammaes'trare *vt* (*animale*) to train; (*persona*) to teach.
ammai'nare *vt* to lower, haul down.
amma'larsi *vr* to fall ill.
amma'lato, a *ag* ill, sick ♦ *sm/f* sick person; (*paziente*) patient.
ammali'are *vt* (*fig*) to enchant, charm.
ammalia'tore, 'trice *sm/f* enchanter/ enchantress.
am'manco, chi *sm* (*ECON*) deficit.
ammanet'tare *vt* to handcuff.
ammani'cato, a, ammanigli'ato, a [ammaniʎ'ʎato] *ag* (*fig*) with friends in high places.
amman'sire *vt* (*animale*) to tame; (*fig*: *persona*) to calm down, placate.
amman'tarsi *vr*: **~ di** (*persona*) to wrap o.s. in; (*fig*: *prato etc*) to be covered in.
amma'raggio [amma'raddʒo] *sm* (sea) landing; splashdown.
amma'rare *vi* (*AER*) to make a sea landing; (*astronave*) to splash down.
ammas'sare *vt* (*ammucchiare*) to amass; (*raccogliere*) to gather together; **~rsi** *vr* to pile up; to gather.
am'masso *sm* mass; (*mucchio*) pile, heap; (*ECON*) stockpile.
ammat'tire *vi* to go mad.
ammaz'zare [ammat'tsare] *vt* to kill; **~rsi** *vr* (*uccidersi*) to kill o.s.; (*rimanere ucciso*) to be killed; **~rsi di lavoro** to work o.s. to death.
am'menda *sf* amends *pl*; (*DIR, SPORT*) fine; **fare ~ di qc** to make amends for sth.
am'messo, a *pp di* **ammettere** ♦ *cong*: **~ che** supposing that.
am'mettere *vt* to admit; (*riconoscere: fatto*) to acknowledge, admit; (*permettere*) to allow, accept; (*supporre*) to suppose; **ammettiamo che ...** let us suppose that ....

(*ammirazione*) love of America.
ammez'zato [ammed'dzato] *sm* (*anche*: **piano ~**) entresol, mezzanine.
ammic'care *vi*: **~ (a)** to wink (at).
amminis'trare *vt* to run, manage; (*REL, DIR*) to administer.
amministra'tivo, a *ag* administrative.
amministra'tore *sm* administrator; (*COMM*) director; **~ aggiunto** associate director; **~ delegato** managing director; **~ fiduciario** trustee; **~ unico** sole director.
amministrazi'one [amministrat'tsjone] *sf* management; administration; **consiglio d'~** board of directors; **l'~ comunale** local government; **~ fiduciaria** trust.
ammi'raglia [ammi'raʎʎa] *sf* flagship.
ammiragli'ato [ammiraʎ'ʎato] *sm* admiralty.
ammi'raglio [ammi'raʎʎo] *sm* admiral.
ammi'rare *vt* to admire.
ammira'tore, 'trice *sm/f* admirer.
ammirazi'one [ammirat'tsjone] *sf* admiration.
am'misi *etc vb vedi* **ammettere.**
ammis'sibile *ag* admissible, acceptable.
ammissi'one *sf* admission; (*approvazione*) acknowledgment.
Amm.ne *abbr* = **amministrazione.**
ammobili'are *vt* to furnish.
ammobili'ato, a *ag* (*camera, appartamento*) furnished.
ammoder'nare *vt* to modernize.
am'modo, a 'modo *av* properly ♦ *ag inv* respectable, nice.
ammogli'are [ammoʎ'ʎare] *vt* to find a wife for; **~rsi** *vr* to marry, take a wife.
am'mollo *sm*: **lasciare in ~** to leave to soak.
ammo'niaca *sf* ammonia.
ammoni'mento *sm* warning; admonishment.
ammo'nire *vt* (*avvertire*) to warn; (*rimproverare*) to admonish; (*DIR*) to caution.
ammonizi'one [ammonit'tsjone] *sf* (*monito: anche SPORT*) warning; (*rimprovero*) reprimand; (*DIR*) caution.
ammon'tare *vi*: **~ a** to amount to ♦ *sm* (total) amount.
ammonticchi'are [ammontik'kjare] *vt* to pile up, heap up.
ammor'bare *vt* (*diffondere malattia*) to infect; (*sog: odore*) to taint, foul.
ammorbi'dente *sm* fabric softener.
ammorbi'dire *vt* to soften.
ammorta'mento *sm* redemption; amortization; **~ fiscale** capital allowance.
ammor'tare *vt* (*FINANZA: debito*) to pay off,

redeem; (: *spese d'impianto*) to write off.

ammortiz'zare [ammortid'dzare] *vt*
(*FINANZA*) to pay off, redeem; (: *spese d'impianto*) to write off; (*AUT, TECN*) to absorb, deaden.

ammortizza'tore [ammortiddza'tore] *sm*
(*AUT, TECN*) shock absorber.

Amm.re *abbr* = **amministratore.**

ammucchi'are [ammuk'kjare] *vt, ~rsi vr* to pile up, accumulate.

ammuf'fire *vi* to go mouldy (*BRIT*) *o* moldy (*US*).

ammutina'mento *sm* mutiny.

ammuti'narsi *vr* to mutiny.

ammuti'nato, a *ag* mutinous ♦ *sm* mutineer.

ammuto'lire *vi* to be struck dumb.

amne'sia *sf* amnesia.

amnis'tia *sf* amnesty.

'amo *sm* (*PESCA*) hook; (*fig*) bait.

amo'rale *ag* amoral.

a'more *sm* love; ~i *smpl* love affairs; **il tuo bambino è un ~** your baby's a darling; **fare l'~ o all'~** to make love; **andare d'~ e d'accordo con qn** to get on like a house on fire with sb; **per ~ o per forza** by hook or by crook; **amor proprio** self-esteem, pride.

amoreggi'are [amored'dʒare] *vi* to flirt.

amo'revole *ag* loving, affectionate.

a'morfo, a *ag* amorphous; (*fig: persona*) lifeless.

amo'rino *sm* cupid.

amo'roso, a *ag* (*affettuoso*) loving, affectionate; (*d'amore: sguardo*) amorous; (: *poesia, relazione*) love *cpd*.

am'pere [ã'pɛr] *sm inv* amp(ère).

ampi'ezza [am'pjettsa] *sf* width, breadth; spaciousness; (*fig: importanza*) scale, size; ~ **di vedute** broad-mindedness.

'ampio, a *ag* wide, broad; (*spazioso*) spacious; (*abbondante: vestito*) loose; (: *gonna*) full; (: *spiegazione*) ample, full.

am'plesso *sm* (*sessuale*) intercourse.

amplia'mento *sm* (*di strada*) widening; (*di aeroporto*) expansion; (*fig*) broadening.

ampli'are *vt* (*allargare*) to widen; (*fig: discorso*) to enlarge on; ~rsi *vr* to grow, increase; ~ **la propria cultura** to broaden one's mind.

amplifi'care *vt* to amplify; (*magnificare*) to extol.

amplifica'tore *sm* (*TECN, MUS*) amplifier.

amplificazi'one [amplifikat'tsjone] *sf* amplification.

am'polla *sf* (*vasetto*) cruet.

ampol'loso, a *ag* bombastic, pompous.

ampu'tare *vt* (*MED*) to amputate.

amputazi'one [amputat'tsjone] *sf* amputation.

'Amsterdam *sf* Amsterdam.

amu'leto *sm* lucky charm.

AN *sigla* = *Ancona.*

A.N. *sigla f* (*POL*) = **Alleanza Nazionale.**

'ANA *sigla f* (*MIL*) = *Associazione Nazionale Alpini.*

ANAAO *sigla f* (= *Associazione Nazionale Aiuti e Assistenti Ospedalieri*) *trade union for hospital workers.*

anabbagli'ante [anabbaʎ'ʎante] *ag* (*AUT*) dipped (*BRIT*), dimmed (*US*); ~i *smpl* dipped *o* dimmed headlights.

anacro'nismo *sm* anachronism.

a'nagrafe *sf* (*registro*) register of births, marriages and deaths; (*ufficio*) registry office (*BRIT*), office of vital statistics (*US*).

ana'grafico, a, ci, che *ag* (*AMM*): **dati ~ci** personal data; **comune di residenza ~a** district where resident.

ana'gramma, i *sm* anagram.

anal'colico, a, ci, che *ag* non-alcoholic ♦ *sm* soft drink; **bevanda ~a** soft drink.

a'nale *ag* anal.

analfa'beta, i, e *ag, smf* illiterate.

analfabe'tismo *sm* illiteracy.

anal'gesico, a, ci, che [anal'dʒɛziko] *ag, sm* analgesic.

a'nalisi *sf inv* analysis; (*MED: esame*) test; **in ultima ~** in conclusion, in the final analysis; ~ **grammaticale** parsing; ~ **del sangue** blood test; ~ **dei sistemi/costi** systems/cost analysis.

ana'lista, i, e *smf* analyst; (*PSIC*) (psycho)analyst; ~ **finanziario** financial analyst; ~ **di sistemi** systems analyst.

ana'litico, a, ci, che *ag* analytic(al).

analiz'zare [analid'dzare] *vt* to analyse (*BRIT*), analyze (*US*); (*MED*) to test.

analo'gia, 'gie [analo'dʒia] *sf* analogy.

ana'logico, a, ci, che [ana'lɔdʒiko] *ag* analogical; (*calcolatore, orologio*) analog(ue).

a'nalogo, a, ghi, ghe *ag* analogous.

'ananas *sm inv* pineapple.

anar'chia [anar'kia] *sf* anarchy.

a'narchico, a, ci, che [a'narkiko] *ag* anarchic(al) ♦ *smf* anarchist.

'A.N.A.S. *sigla f* (= *Azienda Nazionale Autonoma delle Strade*) *national roads department.*

ana'tema, i *sm* anathema.

anato'mia *sf* anatomy.

ana'tomico, a, ci, che *ag* anatomical; (*sedile*) contoured.

'anatra *sf* duck; ~ **selvatica** mallard.

ana'troccolo *sm* duckling.

'ANCA *sigla f* = *Associazione Nazionale Cooperative Agricole.*

'anca, che *sf* (*ANAT*) hip; (*ZOOL*) haunch.

'ANCAB *sigla f* (= *Associazione Nazionale delle Cooperative di Abitazione*) *national association of housing cooperatives.*

ANCC *sigla f* = *Associazione Nazionale Carabinieri.*

'ANCE ['antʃe] *sigla f* (= *Associazione Nazionale Costruttori Edili*) *national association of builders.*

'anche ['anke] *cong* also; (*perfino*) even; **vengo anch'io!** I'm coming too!; ~ **se** even if; ~ **volendo, non finiremmo in tempo** even if we wanted to, we wouldn't finish in time.

ancheggi'are [anked'dʒare] *vi* to wiggle (one's hips).

anchilo'sato, a [ankilo'zato] *ag* stiff.

'ANCI ['antʃi] *sigla f* (= *Associazione Nazionale dei Comuni Italiani*) *national confederation of local authorities.*

ancone'tano, a *ag* of (*o* from) Ancona.

an'cora *av* still; (*di nuovo*) again; (*di più*) some more; (*persino*) ~ **più forte** even stronger; **non** ~ not yet; ~ **una volta** once more, once again; ~ **un po'** a little more; (*di tempo*) a little longer.

'ancora *sf* anchor; **gettare/levare l'**~ to cast/weigh anchor; ~ **di salvezza** (*fig*) last hope.

anco'raggio [anko'raddʒo] *sm* anchorage.

anco'rare *vt*, ~**rsi** *vr* to anchor.

ANCR *sigla f* (= *Associazione Nazionale Combattenti e Reduci*) *servicemen's and ex-servicemen's association.*

Andalu'sia *sf*: **l'**~ Andalusia.

anda'luso, a *ag*, *sm/f* Andalusian.

anda'mento *sm* (*di strada, malattia*) course; (*del mercato*) state.

an'dante *ag* (*corrente*) current; (*di poco pregio*) cheap, second-rate ♦ *sm* (*MUS*) andante.

an'dare *sm*: **a lungo** ~ in the long run; **con l'andar del tempo** with the passing of time; **racconta storie a tutto** ~ she's forever talking rubbish ♦ *vi* (*gen*) to go; (*essere adatto*): ~ **a** to suit; (*piacere*): **il suo comportamento non mi va** I don't like the way he behaves; **ti va di** ~ **al cinema?** do you feel like going to the cinema?; ~ **a cavallo** to ride; ~ **in macchina/aereo** to go by car/plane; ~ **a fare qc** to go and do sth; ~ **a pescare/sciare** to go fishing/skiing; **andarsene** to go away; **vado e vengo** I'll be back in a minute; ~ **per i 50** (*età*) to be getting on for 50; ~ **a male** to go bad; ~ **fiero di qc/qn** to be proud of sth/sb; ~

perduto to be lost; **come va?** (*lavoro, progetto*) how are things?; **come va?** — **bene, grazie!** how are you? — fine, thanks!; **va fatto entro oggi** it's got to be done today; **ne va della nostra vita** our lives are at stake; **se non vado errato** if I'm not mistaken; **le mele vanno molto** apples are selling well; **va da sé** (*è naturale*) it goes without saying; **per questa volta vada** let's say no more about it this time.

an'data *sf* (*viaggio*) outward journey; **biglietto di sola** ~ single (*BRIT*) *o* one-way ticket; **biglietto di** ~ **e ritorno** return (*BRIT*) *o* round-trip (*US*) ticket.

anda'tura *sf* (*modo di andare*) walk, gait; (*SPORT*) pace; (*NAUT*) tack.

an'dazzo [an'dattso] *sm* (*peg*): **prendere un brutto** ~ to take a turn for the worse.

'Ande *sfpl*: **le** ~ the Andes.

an'dino, a *ag* Andean.

andirivi'eni *sm inv* coming and going.

'andito *sm* corridor, passage.

An'dorra *sf* Andorra.

andrò *etc vb vedi* **andare**.

an'drone *sm* entrance hall.

ANDS *sigla f* (= *Associazione Nazionale Docenti Subalterni*) *teachers' union.*

'ANDU *sigla f* (= *Associazione Nazionale Docenti Universitari*) *association of university teachers.*

a'neddoto *sm* anecdote.

ane'lare *vi*: ~ **a** (*fig*) to long for, yearn for.

a'nelito *sm* (*fig*): ~ **di** longing *o* yearning for.

a'nello *sm* ring; (*di catena*) link.

ane'mia *sf* anaemia (*BRIT*), anemia (*US*).

a'nemico, a, ci, che *ag* anaemic (*BRIT*), anemic (*US*).

a'nemone *sm* anemone.

aneste'sia *sf* anaesthesia (*BRIT*), anesthesia (*US*).

aneste'sista, i, e *sm/f* anaesthetist (*BRIT*), anesthetist (*US*).

anes'tetico, a, ci, che *ag*, *sm* anaesthetic (*BRIT*), anesthetic (*US*).

anestetiz'zare [anestetid'dzare] *vt* to anaesthetize (*BRIT*), anesthetize (*US*).

anfeta'mina *sf* amphetamine.

anfeta'minico, a, ci, che *ag* (*fig*) hyper.

an'fibio, a *ag* amphibious ♦ *sm* amphibian; (*AUT*) amphibious vehicle.

anfite'atro *sm* amphitheatre (*BRIT*), amphitheater (*US*).

anfitri'one *sm* host.

'anfora *sf* amphora.

an'fratto *sm* ravine.

an'gelico, a, ci, che [an'dʒɛliko] *ag*

angelic(al).

'**angelo** ['andʒelo] *sm* angel; ~ **custode** guardian angel; **l'~ del focolare** (*fig*) the perfect housewife.

anghe'ria [ange'ria] *sf* vexation.

an'gina [an'dʒina] *sf* tonsillitis; ~ **pectoris** angina.

angli'cano, a *ag* Anglican.

angli'cismo [angli'tʃizmo] *sm* anglicism.

an'glofilo, a *ag* anglophilic ♦ *sm/f* anglophile.

anglo'sassone *ag* Anglo-Saxon.

An'gola *sf*: **l'~** Angola.

ango'lano, a *ag, sm/f* Angolan.

ango'lare *ag* angular.

angola'tura *sf* angle.

angolazi'one [angolat'tsjone] *sf* (*di angolo*) angulation; (*FOT, CINE, TV, fig*) angle.

'**angolo** *sm* corner; (*MAT*) angle; ~ **cottura** (*di appartamento etc*) cooking area; **fare** ~ **con** (*strada*) to run into; **dietro l'~** (*anche fig*) round the corner.

ango'loso, a *ag* (*oggetto*) angular; (*volto, corpo*) angular, bony.

'**angora** *sf*: **lana d'~** angora.

an'goscia, sce [an'gɔʃʃa] *sf* deep anxiety, anguish *no pl*.

angosci'are [angoʃ'ʃare] *vt* to cause anguish to; ~**rsi** *vr*: ~**rsi (per)** (*preoccuparsi*) to become anxious (about); (*provare angoscia*) to get upset (about *o* over).

angosci'oso, a [angoʃ'ʃoso] *ag* (*d'angoscia*) anguished; (*che dà angoscia*) distressing, painful.

angu'illa *sf* eel.

an'guria *sf* watermelon.

an'gustia *sf* (*ansia*) anguish, distress; (*povertà*) poverty, want.

angusti'are *vt* to distress; ~**rsi** *vr*: ~**rsi (per)** to worry (about).

an'gusto, a *ag* (*stretto*) narrow; (*fig*) mean, petty.

'**anice** ['anitʃe] *sm* (*CUC*) aniseed; (*BOT*) anise; (*liquore*) anisette.

ani'dride *sf* (*CHIM*): ~ **carbonica/solforosa** carbon/sulphur dioxide.

'**anima** *sf* soul; (*abitante*) inhabitant; ~ **gemella** soul mate; **un'~ in pena** (*anche fig*) a tormented soul; **non c'era** ~ **viva** there wasn't a living soul; **volere un bene dell'~ a qn** to be extremely fond of sb; **rompere l'~ a qn** to drive sb mad; **il nonno buon'~** ... Grandfather, God rest his soul ....

ani'male *sm, ag* animal.

anima'lesco, a, schi, sche *ag* (*gesto, atteggiamento*) animal-like.

anima'lista, i, e *ag* animal rights *cpd* ♦ *sm/f* animal rights activist.

ani'mare *vt* to give life to, liven up; (*incoraggiare*) to encourage; ~**rsi** *vr* to become animated, come to life.

ani'mato, a *ag* animate; (*vivace*) lively, animated; (: *strada*) busy.

anima'tore, 'trice *sm/f* guiding spirit; (*CINE*) animator; (*di festa*) life and soul.

animazi'one [animat'tsjone] *sf* liveliness; (*di strada*) bustle; (*CINE*) animation; ~ **teatrale** amateur dramatics.

'**animo** *sm* (*mente*) mind; (*cuore*) heart; (*coraggio*) courage; (*disposizione*) character, disposition; **avere in** ~ **di fare qc** to intend *o* have a mind to do sth; **farsi** ~ to pluck up courage; **fare qc di buon/ mal** ~ to do sth willingly/unwillingly; **perdersi d'~** to lose heart.

animosità *sf* animosity.

A'NITA *sigla f = Associazione Nazionale dell'Industria dei Trasporti Automobilistici*; *Associazione Naturista Italiana.*

'**anitra** *sf* = **anatra.**

'**Ankara** *sf* Ankara.

ANM *sigla f* (= *Associazione Nazionale dei Magistrati*) *national association of magistrates.*

ANMI *sigla f* (= *Associazione Nazionale Marinai d'Italia*) *national association of seamen.*

ANMIG *sigla f* (= *Associazione Nazionale fra Mutilati e Invalidi di Guerra*) *national association for disabled ex-servicemen.*

anna'cquare *vt* to water down, dilute.

annaffi'are *vt* to water.

annaffia'toio *sm* watering can.

an'nali *smpl* annals.

annas'pare *vi* (*nell'acqua*) to flounder; (*fig*: *nel buio, nell'incertezza*) to grope.

an'nata *sf* year; (*importo annuo*) annual amount; **vino di** ~ vintage wine.

annebbi'are *vt* (*fig*) to cloud; ~**rsi** *vr* to become foggy; (*vista*) to become dim.

annega'mento *sm* drowning.

anne'gare *vt, vi* to drown; ~**rsi** *vr* (*accidentalmente*) to drown; (*deliberatamente*) to drown o.s.

anne'rire *vt* to blacken ♦ *vi* to become black.

annessi'one *sf* (*POL*) annexation.

an'nesso, a *pp di* **annettere** ♦ *ag* attached; (*POL*) annexed; ... **e tutti gli** ~**i e connessi** ... and so on and so forth.

an'nettere *vt* (*POL*) to annex; (*accludere*) to attach.

annichi'lire [anniki'lire] *vt* to annihilate.

anni'darsi *vr* to nest.

annienta'mento *sm* annihilation, destruction.

annien'tare *vt* to annihilate, destroy.

anniver'sario *sm* anniversary.

'anno *sm* year; **quanti ~i hai? — ho 40 ~i** how old are you? — I'm 40 (years old); **gli ~i 20** the 20s; **porta bene gli ~i** she doesn't look her age; **porta male gli ~i** she looks older than she is; **~ commerciale** business year; **~ giudiziario** legal year; **~ luce** light year; **gli ~i di piombo** *the Seventies in Italy, characterized by terrorist attacks and killings.*

anno'dare *vt* to knot, tie; (*fig: rapporto*) to form.

annoi'are *vt* to bore; (*seccare*) to annoy; **~rsi** *vr* to be bored; to be annoyed.

an'noso, a *ag* (*albero*) old; (*fig: problema etc*) age-old.

anno'tare *vt* (*registrare*) to note, note down (*BRIT*); (*commentare*) to annotate.

annotazi'one [annotat'tsjone] *sf* note; annotation.

annove'rare *vt* to number.

annu'ale *ag* annual.

annual'mente *av* annually, yearly.

annu'ario *sm* yearbook.

annu'ire *vi* to nod; (*acconsentire*) to agree.

annulla'mento *sm* annihilation, destruction; cancellation; annulment; quashing.

annul'lare *vt* to annihilate, destroy; (*contratto, francobollo*) to cancel; (*matrimonio*) to annul; (*sentenza*) to quash; (*risultati*) to declare void.

an'nullo *sm* (*AMM*) cancelling.

annunci'are [annun't∫are] *vt* to announce; (*dar segni rivelatori*) to herald.

annuncia'tore, 'trice [annunt∫a'tore] *smlf* (*RADIO, TV*) announcer.

Annunciazi'one [annunt∫at'tsjone] *sf* (*REL*): **l'~** the Annunciation.

an'nuncio [an'nunt∫o] *sm* announcement; (*fig*) sign; **~ pubblicitario** advertisement; **~i economici** classified advertisements, small ads; **piccoli ~i** small ads, classified ads; **~i mortuari** (*colonna*) obituary column.

'annuo, a *ag* annual, yearly.

annu'sare *vt* to sniff, smell; **~ tabacco** to take snuff.

annuvola'mento *sm* clouding (over).

annuvo'lare *vt* to cloud; **~rsi** *vr* to become cloudy, cloud over.

'ano *sm* anus.

'anodo *sm* anode.

anoma'lia *sf* anomaly.

a'nomalo, a *ag* anomalous.

anoni'mato *sm* anonymity; **conservare l'~** to remain anonymous.

a'nonimo, a *ag* anonymous ♦ *sm* (*autore*) anonymous writer (*o* painter *etc*); **un tipo ~** (*peg*) a colourless (*BRIT*) *o* colorless (*US*) character.

anores'sia *sf* anorexia; **~ nervosa** anorexia nervosa.

ano'ressico, a, ci, che *ag* anorexic.

anor'male *ag* abnormal ♦ *smlf* subnormal person; (*eufemismo*) homosexual.

anormalità *sf inv* abnormality.

'ANSA *sigla f* (= *Agenzia Nazionale Stampa Associata*) *national press agency.*

'ansa *sf* (*manico*) handle; (*di fiume*) bend, loop.

an'sante *ag* out of breath, panting.

'ANSEA *sigla f* (= *Associazione delle Nazioni del Sud-Est asiatico*) ASEAN.

'ansia *sf* anxiety; **stare in ~ (per qn/qc)** to be anxious (about sb/sth).

ansietà *sf* anxiety.

ansi'mare *vi* to pant.

ansi'oso, a *ag* anxious.

'anta *sf* (*di finestra*) shutter; (*di armadio*) door.

antago'nismo *sm* antagonism.

antago'nista, i, e *smlf* antagonist.

an'tartico, a, ci, che *ag* Antarctic ♦ *sm*: **l'A~** the Antarctic.

An'tartide *sf*: **l'~** Antarctica.

ante'bellico, a, ci, che *ag* prewar *cpd.*

antece'dente [antet∫e'dɛnte] *ag* preceding, previous.

ante'fatto *sm* previous events *pl*; previous history.

antegu'erra *sm* pre-war period.

ante'nato *sm* ancestor, forefather.

an'tenna *sf* (*RADIO, TV*) aerial; (*ZOOL*) antenna, feeler; **rizzare le ~e** (*fig*) to prick up one's ears; **~ parabolica** (*TV*) satellite dish.

ante'porre *vt*: **~ qc a qc** to place *o* put sth before sth.

ante'posto, a *pp di* **anteporre.**

ante'prima *sf* preview.

anteri'ore *ag* (*ruota, zampa*) front *cpd*; (*fatti*) previous, preceding.

antesi'gnano [antesiɲ'ɲano] *sm* (*STORIA*) standard-bearer; (*fig*) forerunner.

antia'ereo, a *ag* anti-aircraft *cpd.*

antial'lergico, a [antial'lɛrdʒiko] *ag, sm* hypoallergenic.

antia'tomico, a, ci, che *ag* anti-nuclear; **rifugio ~** fallout shelter.

antibi'otico, a, ci, che *ag, sm* antibiotic.

anti'caglia [anti'kaʎʎa] *sf* junk *no pl.*

anti'camera *sf* anteroom; **fare** ~ to be kept waiting; **non mi passerebbe neanche per l'**~ **del cervello** it wouldn't even cross my mind.

anti'carie *ag inv* which fights tooth decay.

antichità [antiki'ta] *sf inv* antiquity; (*oggetto*) antique.

antici'clone [antitʃi'klone] *sm* anticyclone.

antici'pare [antitʃi'pare] *vt* (*consegna, visita*) to bring forward, anticipate; (*somma di denaro*) to pay in advance; (*notizia*) to disclose ♦ *vi* to be ahead of time.

antici'pato, a [antitʃi'pato] *ag* (*prima del previsto*) early; **pagamento** ~ payment in advance.

anticipazi'one [antiʃipat'tsjone] *sf* anticipation; (*di notizia*) advance information; (*somma di denaro*) advance.

an'ticipo [an'titʃipo] *sm* anticipation; (*di denaro*) advance; **in** ~ early, in advance; **con un sensibile** ~ well in advance.

antic'lan *ag inv* (*magistrato, processo*) anti-Mafia.

an'tico, a, chi, che *ag* (*quadro, mobili*) antique; (*dell'antichità*) ancient; **all'**~**a** old-fashioned.

anticoncezio'nale [antikontʃettsjo'nale] *sm* contraceptive.

anticonfor'mista, i, e *ag, sm/f* nonconformist.

anticonge'lante [antikondʒe'lante] *ag, sm* antifreeze.

anticongiuntu'rale [antikondʒuntu'rale] *ag* (*ECON*): **misure** ~**i** measures to remedy the economic situation.

anti'corpo *sm* antibody.

anticostituzio'nale [antikostituttsjo'nale] *ag* unconstitutional.

antidiluvi'ano, a *ag* (*fig: antiquato*) ancient.

anti'doping *sm inv* (*SPORT*) dope test.

an'tidoto *sm* antidote.

anti'droga *ag inv* anti-drugs *cpd*.

antie'stetico, a, ci, che *ag* unsightly.

an'tifona *sf* (*MUS, REL*) antiphon; **capire l'**~ (*fig*) to take the hint.

anti'furto *sm* anti-theft device.

anti'gelo [anti'dʒɛlo] *ag inv* antifreeze *cpd* ♦ *sm* (*per motore*) antifreeze; (*per cristalli*) de-icer.

an'tigene [an'tidʒene] *sm* antigen.

antigi'enico, a, ci, che [anti'dʒɛniko] *ag* unhygienic.

An'tille *sfpl*: **le** ~ the West Indies.

an'tilope *sf* antelope.

anti'mafia *ag inv* anti-mafia *cpd*.

antin'cendio [antin'tʃɛndjo] *ag inv* fire *cpd*; **bombola** ~ fire extinguisher.

anti'nebbia *sm inv* (*anche:* **faro** ~): (*AUT*) fog lamp.

antine'vralgico, a, ci, che [antine'vraldʒiko] *ag* painkilling ♦ *sm* painkiller.

antio'rario *ag*: **in senso** ~ in an anticlockwise (*BRIT*) *o* counterclockwise (*US*) direction, anticlockwise, counterclockwise.

anti'pasto *sm* hors d'œuvre.

antipa'tia *sf* antipathy, dislike.

anti'patico, a, ci, che *ag* unpleasant, disagreeable.

an'tipodi *smpl*: **essere agli** ~ (*fig: di idee opposte*) to be poles apart.

antiquari'ato *sm* antique trade; **un pezzo d'**~ an antique.

anti'quario *sm* antique dealer.

anti'quato, a *ag* antiquated, old-fashioned.

antirici'claggio [antiritʃi'kladdʒo] *ag* (*attività, operazioni*) anti-laundering.

antiri'flesso *ag inv* (*schermo*) non-glare *cpd*.

anti'ruggine [anti'ruddʒine] *ag* anti-rust *cpd* ♦ *sm inv* rust-preventer.

antise'mita, i, e *ag* anti-semitic.

antisemi'tismo *sm* anti-semitism.

anti'settico, a, ci, che *ag, sm* antiseptic.

antista'minico, a, ci, che *ag, sm* antihistamine.

anti'stante *ag* opposite.

antiterro'rismo *sm* anti-terrorist measures *pl*.

an'titesi *sf* antithesis.

antolo'gia, 'gie [antolo'dʒia] *sf* anthology.

antono'masia *sf* antonomasia; **per** ~ par excellence.

antra'cite [antra'tʃite] *sf* anthracite.

'antro *sm* cavern.

antro'pofago, gi *sm* cannibal.

antropolo'gia [antropolo'dʒia] *sf* anthropology.

antropo'logico, a, ci, che [antropo'lɔdʒiko] *ag* anthropological.

antro'pologo, a, gi, ghe *sm/f* anthropologist.

anu'lare *ag* ring *cpd* ♦ *sm* ring finger.

An'versa *sf* Antwerp.

'anzi ['antsi] *av* (*invece*) on the contrary; (*o meglio*) or rather, or better still.

anzianità [antsjani'ta] *sf* old age; (*AMM*) seniority.

anzi'ano, a [an'tsjano] *ag* old; (*AMM*) senior ♦ *sm/f* old person; senior member.

anziché [antsi'ke] *cong* rather than.

anzi'tempo [antsi'tɛmpo] *av* (*in anticipo*) early.

anzi'tutto [antsi'tutto] *av* first of all.

AO *sigla* = *Aosta*.

a'orta *sf* aorta.

aos'tano, a *ag* of (*o* from) Aosta.
AP *sigla* = *Ascoli Piceno*.
a'partheid [a'partheit] *sm* apartheid.
apar'titico, a, ci, che *ag* (*POL*) non-party *cpd*.
apa'tia *sf* apathy, indifference.
a'patico, a, ci, che *ag* apathetic, indifferent.
a.p.c. *abbr* = **a pronta cassa**.
'ape *sf* bee.
aperi'tivo *sm* aperitif.
aperta'mente *av* openly.
a'perto, a *pp di* aprire ♦ *ag* open ♦ *sm*: **all'~** in the open (air); **rimanere a bocca ~a** (*fig*) to be taken aback.
aper'tura *sf* opening; (*ampiezza*) width, spread; (*POL*) approach; (*FOT*) aperture; **~ alare** wing span; **~ mentale** open-mindedness; **~ di credito** (*COMM*) granting of credit.
API *sigla f* = *Associazione Piccole e Medie Industrie*.
'apice ['apitʃe] *sm* apex; (*fig*) height.
apicol'tore *sm* beekeeper.
apicol'tura *sf* beekeeping.
ap'nea *sf*: **immergersi in ~** to dive without breathing apparatus.
apoca'lisse *sf* apocalypse.
apo'geo [apo'dʒɛo] *sm* (*ASTR*) apogee; (*fig*: *culmine*) zenith.
a'polide *ag* stateless.
apo'litico, a, ci, che *ag* (*neutrale*) nonpolitical; (*indifferente*) apolitical.
apolo'gia, gie [apolo'dʒia] *sf* (*difesa*) apologia; (*esaltazione*) praise; **~ di reato** attempt to defend criminal acts.
apoples'sia *sf* (*MED*) apoplexy.
apop'lettico, a, ci, che *ag* apoplectic; **colpo ~** apoplectic fit.
a'postolo *sm* apostle.
apostro'fare *vt* (*parola*) to write with an apostrophe; (*persona*) to address.
a'postrofo *sm* apostrophe.
app. *abbr* (= *appendice*) app.
appaga'mento *sm* satisfaction; fulfilment.
appa'gare *vt* to satisfy; (*desiderio*) to fulfil; **~rsi** *vr*: **~rsi di** to be satisfied with.
appa'gato, a *ag* satisfied.
appai'are *vt* to couple, pair.
ap'paio *etc vb vedi* apparire.
Appa'lachi [appa'laki] *smpl*: **i Monti ~** the Appalachian Mountains.
appallotto'lare *vt* (*carta, foglio*) to screw into a ball; **~rsi** *vr* (*gatto*) to roll up into a ball.
appalta'tore *sm* contractor.
ap'palto *sm* (*COMM*) contract; **dare/ prendere in ~ un lavoro** to let out/

undertake a job on contract.
appan'naggio [appan'naddʒo] *sm* (*compenso*) annuity; (*fig*) privilege, prerogative.
appan'nare *vt* (*vetro*) to mist; (*metallo*) to tarnish; (*vista*) to dim; **~rsi** *vr* to mist over; (*metallo*) to tarnish; to grow dim.
appa'rato *sm* equipment, machinery; (*ANAT*) apparatus; **~ scenico** (*TEAT*) props *pl*.
apparecchi'are [apparek'kjare] *vt* to prepare; (*tavola*) to set ♦ *vi* to set the table.
apparecchia'tura [apparekkja'tura] *sf* equipment; (*macchina*) machine, device.
appa'recchio [appa'rekkjo] *sm* piece of apparatus, device; (*aeroplano*) aircraft *inv*; **~i sanitari** bathroom *o* sanitary appliances; **~ televisivo/telefonico** television set/telephone.
appa'rente *ag* apparent.
apparente'mente *av* apparently.
appa'renza [appa'rɛntsa] *sf* appearance; **in *o* all'~** apparently, to all appearances.
appa'rire *vi* to appear; (*sembrare*) to seem, appear.
appari'scente [appariʃ'ʃɛnte] *ag* (*colore*) garish, gaudy; (*bellezza*) striking.
apparizi'one [apparit'tsjone] *sf* apparition.
ap'parso, a *pp di* apparire.
apparta'mento *sm* flat (*BRIT*), apartment (*US*).
appar'tarsi *vr* to withdraw.
appar'tato, a *ag* (*luogo*) secluded.
apparte'nenza [apparte'nɛntsa] *sf*: **~ (a)** (*gen*) belonging (to); (*a un partito, club*) membership (of).
apparte'nere *vi*: **~ a** to belong to.
ap'parvi *etc vb vedi* apparire.
appassio'nante *ag* thrilling, exciting.
appassio'nare *vt* to thrill; (*commuovere*) to move; **~rsi** *vr*: **~rsi a qc** to take a great interest in sth; to be deeply moved by sth.
appassio'nato, a *ag* passionate; (*entusiasta*): **~ (di)** keen (on).
appas'sire *vi* to wither.
appel'larsi *vr* (*ricorrere*): **~ a** to appeal to; (*DIR*): **~ contro** to appeal against.
ap'pello *sm* roll-call; (*implorazione, DIR*) appeal; (*sessione d'esame*) exam session; **fare ~ a** to appeal to; **fare l'~** (*INS*) to call the register *o* roll; (*MIL*) to call the roll.
ap'pena *av* (*a stento*) hardly, scarcely; (*solamente, da poco*) just ♦ *cong* as soon as; **(non) ~ furono arrivati ...** as soon as they had arrived ...; **~ ... che *o* quando** no sooner ... than.

ap'pendere *vt* to hang (up).
appendi'abiti *sm inv* hook, peg; (*mobile*) hall stand (*BRIT*), hall tree (*US*).
appen'dice [appen'ditʃe] *sf* appendix; **romanzo d'~** popular serial.
appendi'cite [appendi'tʃite] *sf* appendicitis.
appen'dino *sm* (coat) hook.
Appen'nini *smpl*: **gli ~** the Apennines.
appesan'tire *vt* to make heavy; **~rsi** *vr* to grow stout.
ap'peso, a *pp di* **appendere.**
appe'tito *sm* appetite.
appeti'toso, a *ag* appetising; (*fig*) attractive, desirable.
appezza'mento [appettsa'mento] *sm* (*anche*: **~ di terreno**) plot, piece of ground.
appia'nare *vt* to level; (*fig*) to smooth away, iron out; **~rsi** *vr* (*divergenze*) to be ironed out.
appiat'tire *vt* to flatten; **~rsi** *vr* to become flatter; (*farsi piatto*) to flatten o.s.; **~rsi al suolo** to lie flat on the ground.
appic'care *vt*: **~ il fuoco a** to set fire to, set on fire.
appicci'care [appittʃi'kare] *vt* to stick; (*fig*): **~ qc a qn** to palm sth off on sb; **~rsi** *vr* to stick; (*fig: persona*) to cling.
appiccica'ticcio, a, ci, ce [appittʃika'tittʃo] *ag*, **appicci'coso, a** [appittʃi'koso] *ag* sticky; (*fig: persona*): **essere ~** to cling like a leech.
appie'dato, a *ag*: **rimanere ~** to be left without means of transport.
appi'eno *av* fully.
appigli'arsi [appiʎ'ʎarsi] *vr*: **~ a** (*afferrarsi*) to take hold of; (*fig*) to cling to.
ap'piglio [ap'piʎʎo] *sm* hold; (*fig*) pretext.
appiop'pare *vt*: **~ qc a qn** (*nomignolo*) to pin sth on sb; (*compito difficile*) to saddle sb with sth; **gli ha appioppato un pugno sul muso** he punched him in the face.
appiso'larsi *vr* to doze off.
applau'dire *vt, vi* to applaud.
ap'plauso *sm* applause *no pl*.
appli'cabile *ag*: **~ (a)** applicable (to).
appli'care *vt* to apply; (*regolamento*) to enforce; **~rsi** *vr* to apply o.s.
appli'cato, a *ag* (*arte, scienze*) applied ♦ *sm* (*AMM*) clerk.
applica'tore *sm* applicator.
applicazi'one [applikat'tsjone] *sf* application; enforcement; **~i tecniche** (*INS*) practical subjects.
appoggi'are [appod'dʒare] *vt* (*mettere contro*): **~ qc a qc** to lean *o* rest sth against sth; (*fig: sostenere*) to support; **~rsi** *vr*: **~rsi a** to lean against; (*fig*) to rely

upon.
ap'poggio [ap'pɔddʒo] *sm* support.
appollai'arsi *vr* (*anche fig*) to perch.
ap'pongo, ap'poni *etc vb vedi* **apporre.**
ap'porre *vt* to affix.
appor'tare *vt* to bring.
ap'porto *sm* (*gen*, *FINANZA*) contribution.
ap'posi *etc vb vedi* **apporre.**
apposita'mente *av* (*apposta*) on purpose; (*specialmente*) specially.
ap'posito, a *ag* appropriate.
ap'posta *av* on purpose, deliberately; **neanche a farlo ~, ...** by sheer coincidence, ...
appos'tarsi *vr* to lie in wait.
ap'posto, a *pp di* **apporre.**
ap'prendere *vt* (*imparare*) to learn; (*comprendere*) to grasp.
apprendi'mento *sm* learning.
appren'dista, i, e *sm/f* apprentice.
apprendi'stato *sm* apprenticeship.
apprensi'one *sf* apprehension.
appren'sivo, a *ag* apprehensive.
ap'preso, a *pp di* **apprendere.**
ap'presso *av* (*accanto, vicino*) close by, near; (*dietro*) behind; (*dopo, più tardi*) after, later ♦ *ag inv* (*dopo*): **il giorno ~** the next day; **~ a** *prep* (*vicino a*) near, close to.
appres'tare *vt* to prepare, get ready; **~rsi** *vr*: **~rsi a fare qc** to prepare *o* get ready to do sth.
ap'pretto *sm* starch.
apprez'zabile [appret'tsabile] *ag* (*notevole*) noteworthy, significant; (*percepibile*) appreciable.
apprezza'mento [apprettsa'mento] *sm* appreciation; (*giudizio*) opinion; (*commento*) comment.
apprez'zare [appret'tsare] *vt* to appreciate.
ap'proccio [ap'prɔttʃo] *sm* approach.
appro'dare *vi* (*NAUT*) to land; (*fig*): **non ~ a nulla** to come to nothing.
ap'prodo *sm* landing; (*luogo*) landing place.
approfit'tare *vi*: **~ di** (*persona, situazione*) to take advantage of; (*occasione, opportunità*) to make the most of, profit by.
approfon'dire *vt* to deepen; (*fig*) to study in depth; **~rsi** *vr* (*gen, fig*) to deepen; (*peggiorare*) to get worse.
appron'tare *vt* to prepare, get ready.
appropri'arsi *vr*: **~ di qc** to appropriate sth, take possession of sth; **~ indebitamente di** to embezzle.
appropri'ato, a *ag* appropriate.
appropriazi'one [approprjat'tsjone] *sf* appropriation; **~ indebita** (*DIR*)

embezzlement.

approssi'mare *vt* (*cifra*): ~ **per eccesso/per difetto** to round up/down; **~rsi** *vr*: **~rsi a** to approach, draw near.

approssima'tivo, a *ag* approximate, rough; (*impreciso*) inexact, imprecise.

approssimazi'one [approssimat'tsjone] *sf* approximation; **per** ~ approximately, roughly.

appro'vare *vt* (*condotta, azione*) to approve of; (*candidato*) to pass; (*progetto di legge*) to approve.

approvazi'one [approvat'tsjone] *sf* approval.

approvvigiona'mento [approvvidʒona 'mento] *sm* supplying; stocking up; **~i** *smpl* (*MIL*) supplies.

approvvigio'nare [approvvidʒo'nare] *vt* to supply; **~rsi** *vr* to lay in provisions, stock up; ~ **qn di qc** to supply sb with sth.

appunta'mento *sm* appointment; (*amoroso*) date; **darsi** ~ to arrange to meet (one another).

appun'tare *vt* (*rendere aguzzo*) to sharpen; (*fissare*) to pin, fix; (*annotare*) to note down.

appun'tato *sm* (*CARABINIERI*) corporal.

appun'tino *av* perfectly.

appun'tire *vt* to sharpen.

ap'punto *sm* note; (*rimprovero*) reproach ♦ *av* (*proprio*) exactly, just; **per l'**~**!**, ~**!** exactly!

appu'rare *vt* to check, verify.

apr. *abbr* (= *aprile*) Apr.

apribot'tiglie [apribot'tiʎʎe] *sm inv* bottleopener.

a'prile *sm* April; **pesce d'**~**!** April Fool!; *per fraseologia vedi* **luglio**.

a'prire *vt* to open; (*via, cadavere*) to open up; (*gas, luce, acqua*) to turn on ♦ *vi* to open; **~rsi** *vr* to open; ~ **le ostilità** (*MIL*) to start up *o* begin hostilities; ~ **una sessione** (*INFORM*) to log on; **~rsi a qn** to confide in sb, open one's heart to sb; **mi si è aperto lo stomaco** I feel rather peckish; **apriti cielo!** heaven forbid!

apris'catole *sm inv* tin (*BRIT*) *o* can opener.

APT *sigla f* (= *Azienda di Promozione Turistica*) ≈ tourist board.

AQ *sigla* = *Aquila*.

a'quario *sm* = **acquario**.

'aquila *sf* (*ZOOL*) eagle; (*fig*) genius.

aqui'lino, a *ag* aquiline.

aqui'lone *sm* (*giocattolo*) kite; (*vento*) North wind.

AR *sigla* = *Arezzo*.

ara'besco *sm* (*decorazione*) arabesque.

A'rabia Sau'dita *sf*: **l'**~ Saudi Arabia.

a'rabico, a, ci, che *ag*: **il Deserto** ~ the Arabian Desert.

a'rabile *ag* arable.

'arabo, a *ag, sm/f* Arab ♦ *sm* (*LING*) Arabic; **parlare** ~ (*fig*) to speak double Dutch (*BRIT*).

a'rachide [a'rakide] *sf* peanut.

ara'gosta *sf* spiny lobster.

a'raldica *sf* heraldry.

a'raldo *sm* herald.

aran'ceto [aran'tʃeto] *sm* orange grove.

a'rancia, ce [a'rantʃa] *sf* orange.

aranci'ata [aran'tʃata] *sf* orangeade.

a'rancio [a'rantʃo] *sm* (*BOT*) orange tree; (*colore*) orange ♦ *ag inv* (*colore*) orange; **fiori di** ~ orange blossom *sg*.

aranci'one [aran'tʃone] *ag inv*: **(color)** ~ bright orange.

a'rare *vt* to plough (*BRIT*), plow (*US*).

ara'tore *sm* ploughman (*BRIT*), plowman (*US*).

a'ratro *sm* plough (*BRIT*), plow (*US*).

ara'tura *sf* ploughing (*BRIT*), plowing (*US*).

a'razzo [a'rattso] *sm* tapestry.

arbi'traggio [arbi'traddʒo] *sm* (*SPORT*) refereeing; umpiring; (*DIR*) arbitration; (*COMM*) arbitrage.

arbi'trare *vt* (*SPORT*) to referee; to umpire; (*DIR*) to arbitrate.

arbi'trario, a *ag* arbitrary.

arbi'trato *sm* arbitration.

ar'bitrio *sm* will; (*abuso, sopruso*) arbitrary act.

'arbitro *sm* arbiter, judge; (*DIR*) arbitrator; (*SPORT*) referee; (*: TENNIS, CRICKET*) umpire.

arbo'scello [arboʃ'ʃɛllo] *sm* sapling.

ar'busto *sm* shrub.

'arca, che *sf* (*sarcofago*) sarcophagus; **l'**~ **di Noè** Noah's ark.

ar'caico, a, ci, che *ag* archaic.

arca'ismo *sm* (*LING*) archaism.

ar'cangelo [ar'kandʒelo] *sm* archangel.

ar'cano, a *ag* arcane, mysterious ♦ *sm* mystery.

ar'cata *sf* (*ARCHIT, ANAT*) arch; (*ordine di archi*) arcade.

archeolo'gia [arkeolo'dʒia] *sf* arch(a)eology.

archeo'logico, a, ci, che [arkeo'lɔdʒiko] *ag* arch(a)eological.

arche'ologo, a, gi, ghe [arke'ɔlogo] *sm/f* arch(a)eologist.

ar'chetipo [ar'kɛtipo] *sm* archetype.

ar'chetto [ar'ketto] *sm* (*MUS*) bow.

architet'tare [arkitet'tare] *vt* (*fig: ideare*) to devise; (*: macchinare*) to plan, concoct.

archi'tetto [arki'tetto] *sm* architect.

architet'tonico, a, ci, che [arkitet'tɔniko] *ag* architectural.

architet'tura [arkitet'tura] *sf* architecture.

archivi'are [arki'vjare] *vt* (*documenti*) to file; (*DIR*) to dismiss.

archiviazi'one [arkivjat'tsjone] *sf* filing; dismissal.

ar'chivio [ar'kivjo] *sm* archives *pl*; (*INFORM*) file; ~ **principale** (*INFORM*) master file.

archi'vista, i, e [arki'vista] *sm/f* (*AMM*) archivist; (*in ufficio*) filing clerk.

'ARCI ['artʃi] *sigla f* (= *Associazione Ricreativa Culturale Italiana*) *cultural society.*

arci'duca, chi [artʃi'duka] *sm* archduke.

arci'ere [ar'tʃɛre] *sm* archer.

ar'cigno, a [ar'tʃiɲɲo] *ag* grim, severe.

arci'one [ar'tʃone] *sm* saddlebow.

arci'pelago, ghi [artʃi'pɛlago] *sm* archipelago.

arci'vescovo [artʃi'veskovo] *sm* archbishop.

'arco, chi *sm* (*arma, MUS*) bow; (*ARCHIT*) arch; (*MAT*) arc; **nell'~ di 3 settimane** within the space of 3 weeks; ~ **costituzionale** *political parties involved in formulating Italy's post-war constitution.*

arcoba'leno *sm* rainbow.

arcu'ato, a *ag* curved, bent; **dalle gambe** ~**e** bow-legged.

ar'dente *ag* burning; (*fig*) burning, ardent.

'ardere *vt, vi* to burn; **legna da** ~ firewood.

ar'desia *sf* slate.

ardi'mento *sm* daring.

ar'dire *vi* to dare ♦ *sm* daring.

ar'dito, a *ag* brave, daring, bold; (*sfacciato*) bold.

ar'dore *sm* blazing heat; (*fig*) ardour, fervour.

'arduo, a *ag* arduous, difficult.

'area *sf* area; (*EDIL*) land, ground; **nell'~ dei partiti di sinistra** among the parties of the left; ~ **fabbricabile** building land; ~ **di rigore** (*SPORT*) penalty area; ~ **di servizio** (*AUT*) service area.

a'rena *sf* arena; (*per corride*) bullring; (*sabbia*) sand.

are'naria *sf* sandstone.

are'narsi *vr* to run aground; (*fig: trattative*) to come to a standstill.

areo'plano *sm* = **aeroplano.**

are'tino, a *ag* of (*o* from) Arezzo.

'argano *sm* winch.

argen'tato, a [ardʒen'tato] *ag* silver-plated; (*colore*) silver, silvery; (*capelli*) silver(-grey).

ar'genteo, a [ar'dʒenteo] *ag* silver, silvery.

argente'ria [ardʒente'ria] *sf* silverware,

silver.

Argen'tina [ardʒen'tina] *sf*: **l'**~ Argentina.

argen'tino, a [ardʒen'tino] *ag, sm/f* (*dell'Argentina*) Argentinian ♦ *sf* crewneck sweater.

ar'gento [ar'dʒɛnto] *sm* silver; ~ **vivo** quicksilver; **avere l'**~ **(vivo) addosso** (*fig*) to be fidgety.

ar'gilla [ar'dʒilla] *sf* clay.

argil'loso, a [ardʒil'loso] *ag* (*contenente argilla*) clayey; (*simile ad argilla*) clay-like.

argi'nare [ardʒi'nare] *vt* (*fiume, acque*) to embank; (: *con diga*) to dyke up; (*fig: inflazione, corruzione*) to check; (: *spese*) to limit.

'argine ['ardʒine] *sm* embankment, bank; (*diga*) dyke, dike; **far** ~ **a, porre un** ~ **a** (*fig*) to check, hold back.

argomen'tare *vi* to argue.

argo'mento *sm* argument; (*materia, tema*) subject; **tornare sull'**~ to bring the matter up again.

argu'ire *vt* to deduce.

ar'guto, a *ag* sharp, quick-witted; (*spiritoso*) witty.

ar'guzia [ar'guttsja] *sf* wit; (*battuta*) witty remark.

'aria *sf* air; (*espressione, aspetto*) air, look; (*MUS: melodia*) tune; (: *di opera*) aria; **all'**~ **aperta** in the open (air); **manca l'**~ it's stuffy; **andare all'**~ (*piano, progetto*) to come to nothing; **mandare all'**~ **qc** to ruin *o* upset sth; **darsi delle** ~**e** to put on airs and graces; **ha la testa per** ~ his head is in the clouds; **che** ~ **tira?** (*fig: atmosfera*) what's the atmosphere like?

aridità *sf* aridity, dryness; (*fig*) lack of feeling.

'arido, a *ag* arid.

arieggi'are [arjed'dʒare] *vt* (*cambiare aria*) to air; (*imitare*) to imitate.

ari'ete *sm* ram; (*MIL*) battering ram; (*dello zodiaco*): **A**~ Aries; **essere dell'A**~ to be Aries.

a'ringa, ghe *sf* herring *inv*; ~ **affumicata** smoked herring, kipper; ~ **marinata** pickled herring.

ari'oso, a *ag* (*ambiente, stanza*) airy; (*MUS*) ariose.

'arista *sf* (*CUC*) chine of pork.

aristo'cratico, a, ci, che *ag* aristocratic.

aristocra'zia [aristokrat'tsia] *sf* aristocracy.

arit'metica *sf* arithmetic.

arit'metico, a, ci, che *ag* arithmetical.

arlec'chino [arlek'kino] *sm* harlequin.

'arma, i *sf* weapon, arm; (*parte dell'esercito*) arm; **alle** ~**i!** to arms!; **chiamare alle** ~**i** to call up (*BRIT*), draft (*US*); **sotto le** ~**i** in the army (*o* forces); **combattere ad ~i pari** (*anche fig*) to fight on equal terms; **essere alle prime ~i** (*fig*) to be a novice; **passare qn per le ~i** to execute sb; **battersi all'~ bianca** to fight with blades; **~ a doppio taglio** (*anche fig*) double-edged weapon; **~ da fuoco** firearm.

ar'**madio** *sm* cupboard; (*per abiti*) wardrobe; **~ a muro** built-in cupboard.

armamen'**tario** *sm* equipment, instruments *pl.*

arma'**mento** *sm* (*MIL*) armament; (: *materiale*) arms *pl*, weapons *pl*; (*NAUT*) fitting out; manning; **la corsa agli ~i** the arms race.

ar'**mare** *vt* to arm; (*arma da fuoco*) to cock; (*NAUT: nave*) to rig, fit out; to man; (*EDIL: volta, galleria*) to prop up, shore up; **~rsi** *vr* to arm o.s.; (*MIL*) to take up arms.

ar'**mato, a** *ag*: **~ (di)** (*anche fig*) armed (with) ♦ *sf* (*MIL*) army; (*NAUT*) fleet; **rapina a mano ~a** armed robbery.

arma'**tore** *sm* shipowner.

arma'**tura** *sf* (*struttura di sostegno*) framework; (*impalcatura*) scaffolding; (*STORIA*) armour *no pl* (*BRIT*), armor *no pl* (*US*), suit of armo(u)r.

armeggi'**are** [armed'dʒare] *vi* (*affaccendarsi*): **~ (intorno a qc)** to mess about (with sth).

Ar'**menia** *sf*: **l'~** Armenia.

ar'**meno, a** *ag, sm/f, sm* Armenian.

ar'**meria** *sf* (*deposito*) armoury (*BRIT*), armory (*US*); (*collezione*) collection of arms.

armis'**tizio** [armis'tittsjo] *sm* armistice.

armo'**nia** *sf* harmony.

ar'**monico, a, ci, che** *ag* harmonic; (*fig*) harmonious ♦ *sf* (*MUS*) harmonica; **~a a bocca** mouth organ.

armoni'**oso, a** *ag* harmonious.

armoniz'**zare** [armonid'dzare] *vt* to harmonize; (*colori, abiti*) to match ♦ *vi* to be in harmony; to match.

ar'**nese** *sm* tool, implement; (*oggetto indeterminato*) thing, contraption; **male in ~** (*malvestito*) badly dressed; (*di salute malferma*) in poor health; (*di condizioni economiche*) down-at-heel.

'**arnia** *sf* hive.

a'**roma, i** *sm* aroma; fragrance; **~i** *smpl* herbs and spices; **~i naturali/artificiali** natural/artificial flavouring *sg* (*BRIT*) *o* flavoring *sg* (*US*).

aromatera'**pia** *sf* aromatherapy.

aro'**matico, a, ci, che** *ag* aromatic; (*cibo*) spicy.

aromatiz'**zare** [aromatid'dzare] *vt* to

season, flavour (*BRIT*), flavor (*US*).

'**arpa** *sf* (*MUS*) harp.

ar'**peggio** [ar'peddʒo] *sm* (*MUS*) arpeggio.

ar'**pia** *sf* (*anche fig*) harpy.

arpi'**one** *sm* (*gancio*) hook; (*cardine*) hinge; (*PESCA*) harpoon.

arrabat'**tarsi** *vr* to do all one can, strive.

arrabbi'**are** *vi* (*cane*) to be affected with rabies; **~rsi** *vr* (*essere preso dall'ira*) to get angry, fly into a rage.

arrabbi'**ato, a** *ag* (*cane*) rabid, with rabies; (*persona*) furious, angry.

arrabbia'**tura** *sf*: **prendersi un'~ (per qc)** to become furious (over sth).

arraf'**fare** *vt* to snatch, seize; (*sottrarre*) to pinch.

arrampi'**carsi** *vr* to climb (up); **~ sui vetri** *o* **sugli specchi** (*fig*) to clutch at straws.

arrampi'**cata** *sf* climb.

arrampica'**tore, 'trice** *sm/f* (*gen, SPORT*) climber; **~ sociale** (*fig*) social climber.

arran'**care** *vi* to limp, hobble; (*fig*) to struggle along.

arrangia'**mento** [arrandʒa'mento] *sm* (*MUS*) arrangement.

arran'**giare** [arran'dʒare] *vt* to arrange; **~rsi** *vr* to manage, do the best one can.

arre'**care** *vt* to bring; (*causare*) to cause.

arreda'**mento** *sm* (*studio*) interior design; (*mobili etc*) furnishings *pl.*

arre'**dare** *vt* to furnish.

arreda'**tore, 'trice** *sm/f* interior designer.

ar'**redo** *sm* fittings *pl*, furnishings *pl*; **~ per uffici** office furnishings.

arrem'**baggio** [arrem'baddʒo] *sm* (*NAUT*) boarding.

ar'**rendersi** *vr* to surrender; **~ all'evidenza (dei fatti)** to face (the) facts.

arren'**devole** *ag* (*persona*) yielding, compliant.

arrendevo'**lezza** [arrendevo'lettsa] *sf* compliancy.

ar'**reso, a** *pp di* **arrendersi**.

arres'**tare** *vt* (*fermare*) to stop, halt; (*catturare*) to arrest; **~rsi** *vr* (*fermarsi*) to stop.

arres'**tato, a** *sm/f* person under arrest.

ar'**resto** *sm* (*cessazione*) stopping; (*fermata*) stop; (*cattura, MED*) arrest; (*COMM: in produzione*) stoppage; **subire un ~** to come to a stop *o* standstill; **mettere agli ~i** to place under arrest; **~i domiciliari** (*DIR*) house arrest.

arre'**trare** *vt, vi* to withdraw.

arre'**trato, a** *ag* (*lavoro*) behind schedule; (*paese, bambino*) backward; (*numero di giornale*) back *cpd*; **~i** *smpl* arrears; **gli ~i dello stipendio** back pay *sg.*

arricchi'mento [arrikki'mento] *sm* enrichment.

arric'chire [arrik'kire] *vt* to enrich; **~rsi** *vr* to become rich.

arric'chito, a [arrik'kito] *sm/f* nouveau riche.

arricci'are [arrit't∫are] *vt* to curl; **~ il naso** to turn up one's nose.

ar'ridere *vi*: **~ a qn** (*fortuna, successo*) to smile on sb.

ar'ringa, ghe *sf* harangue; (*DIR*) address by counsel.

arrischi'are [arris'kjare] *vt* to risk; **~rsi** *vr* to venture, dare.

arrischi'ato, a [arris'kjato] *ag* risky; (*temerario*) reckless, rash.

ar'riso, a *pp di* **arridere**.

arri'vare *vi* to arrive; (*avvicinarsi*) to come; (*accadere*) to happen, occur; **~ a** (*livello, grado etc*) to reach; **lui arriva a Roma alle 7** he gets to *o* arrives at Rome at 7; **~ a fare qc** to manage to do sth, succeed in doing sth; **non ci arrivo** I can't reach it; (*fig: non capisco*) I can't understand it.

arri'vato, a *ag* (*persona: di successo*) successful ♦ *sm/f*: **essere un ~** to have made it; **nuovo ~** newcomer; **ben ~!** welcome!; **non sono l'ultimo ~!** (*fig*) I'm no fool!

arrive'derci [arrive'dert∫i] *escl* goodbye!

arrive'derla *escl* (*forma di cortesia*) goodbye!

arri'vismo *sm* (*ambizione*) ambitiousness; (*sociale*) social climbing.

arri'vista, i, e *sm/f* go-getter.

ar'rivo *sm* arrival; (*SPORT*) finish, finishing line.

arro'gante *ag* arrogant.

arro'ganza [arro'gantsa] *sf* arrogance.

arro'gare *vt*: **~rsi il diritto di fare qc** to assume the right to do sth; **~rsi il merito di qc** to claim credit for sth.

arro'lare *vb* = **arruolare**.

arrossa'mento *sm* reddening.

arros'sare *vt* (*occhi, pelle*) to redden, make red; **~rsi** *vr* to go *o* become red.

arros'sire *vi* (*per vergogna, timidezza*) to blush; (*per gioia*) to flush, blush.

arros'tire *vt* to roast; (*pane*) to toast; (*ai ferri*) to grill.

ar'rosto *sm, ag inv* roast; **~ di manzo** roast beef.

arro'tare *vt* to sharpen; (*investire con un veicolo*) to run over.

arro'tino *sm* knife-grinder.

arroto'lare *vt* to roll up.

arroton'dare *vt* (*forma, oggetto*) to round; (*stipendio*) to add to; (*somma*) to round off.

arrovel'larsi *vr* (*anche*: **~ il cervello**) to rack one's brains.

arroven'tato, a *ag* red-hot.

arruf'fare *vt* to ruffle; (*fili*) to tangle; (*fig: questione*) to confuse.

arruggi'nire [arrudd3i'nire] *vt* to rust; **~rsi** *vr* to rust; (*fig*) to become rusty.

arruola'mento *sm* (*MIL*) enlistment.

arruo'lare *vt* (*MIL*) to enlist; **~rsi** *vr* to enlist, join up.

arse'nale *sm* (*MIL*) arsenal; (*cantiere navale*) dockyard.

ar'senico *sm* arsenic.

'arsi *vb vedi* **ardere**.

'arso, a *pp di* **ardere** ♦ *ag* (*bruciato*) burnt; (*arido*) dry.

ar'sura *sf* (*calore opprimente*) burning heat; (*siccità*) drought.

art. *abbr* (= *articolo*) art.

'arte *sf* art; (*abilità*) skill; **a regola d'~** (*fig*) perfectly; **senz'~ né parte** penniless and out of a job; **~i figurative** visual arts.

arte'fatto, a *ag* (*stile, modi*) affected; (*cibo*) adulterated.

ar'tefice [ar'tefit∫e] *sm/f* craftsman/woman; (*autore*) author.

ar'teria *sf* artery.

arterioscle'rosi *sf* arteriosclerosis, hardening of the arteries.

arteri'oso, a *ag* arterial.

'artico, a, ci, che *ag* Arctic ♦ *sm*: **l'A~** the Arctic; **il Circolo polare ~** the Arctic Circle; **l'Oceano ~** the Arctic Ocean.

artico'lare *ag* (*ANAT*) of the joints, articular ♦ *vt* to articulate; (*suddividere*) to divide, split up; **~rsi** *vr*: **~rsi in** (*discorso, progetto*) to be divided into.

artico'lato, a *ag* (*linguaggio*) articulate; (*AUT*) articulated.

articolazi'one [artikolat'tsjone] *sf* (*ANAT, TECN*) joint; (*di voce, concetto*) articulation.

ar'ticolo *sm* article; **~ di fondo** (*STAMPA*) leader, leading article; **~i di marca** branded goods; **un bell'~** (*fig*) a real character.

'Artide *sm*: **l'~** the Arctic.

artifici'ale [artifi't∫ale] *ag* artificial.

artifici'ere [artifi't∫ere] *sm* (*MIL*) artificer; (*: per disinnescare bombe*) bomb-disposal expert.

arti'ficio [arti'fit∫o] *sm* (*espediente*) trick, artifice; (*ricerca di effetto*) artificiality.

artifici'oso, a [artifi't∫oso] *ag* cunning; (*non spontaneo*) affected.

artigia'nale [artid3a'nale] *ag* craft *cpd*.

artigia'nato [artid3a'nato] *sm*

craftsmanship; craftsmen *pl.*

artigi'ano, a [arti'dʒano] *smlf* craftsman/ woman.

artigli'ere [artiʎ'ʎɛre] *sm* artilleryman.

artiglie'ria [artiʎʎe'ria] *sf* artillery.

ar'tiglio [ar'tiʎʎo] *sm* claw; (*di rapaci*) talon; **sfoderare gli ~i** (*fig*) to show one's claws.

ar'tista, i, e *smlf* artist; **un lavoro da ~** (*fig*) a professional piece of work.

ar'tistico, a, ci, che *ag* artistic.

'arto *sm* (*ANAT*) limb.

ar'trite *sf* (*MED*) arthritis.

ar'trosi *sf* osteoarthritis.

arzigogo'lato, a [ardzigogo'lato] *ag* tortuous.

arzi'gogolo [ardzi'gɔgolo] *sm* tortuous expression.

ar'zillo, a [ar'dzillo] *ag* lively, sprightly.

a'scella [aʃ'ʃɛlla] *sf* (*ANAT*) armpit.

ascen'dente [aʃʃen'dɛnte] *sm* ancestor; (*fig*) ascendancy; (*ASTR*) ascendant.

a'scendere [aʃ'ʃendere] *vi*: **~ al trono** to ascend the throne.

ascen'sione [aʃʃen'sjone] *sf* (*ALPINISMO*) ascent; (*REL*): **l'A~** the Ascension; **isola dell'A~** Ascension Island.

ascen'sore [aʃʃen'sore] *sm* lift.

a'scesa [aʃ'ʃesa] *sf* ascent; (*al trono*) accession; (*al potere*) rise.

a'scesi [aʃ'ʃezi] *sf* asceticism.

a'sceso, a [aʃ'ʃeso] *pp di* **ascendere**.

a'scesso [aʃ'ʃɛsso] *sm* (*MED*) abscess.

a'sceta, i [aʃ'ʃɛta] *sm* ascetic.

'ascia, *pl* **'asce** ['aʃʃa] *sf* axe.

asciugaca'pelli [aʃʃugaka'pelli] *sm* hair dryer.

asciuga'mano [aʃʃuga'mano] *sm* towel.

asciu'gare [aʃʃu'gare] *vt* to dry; **~rsi** *vr* to dry o.s.; (*diventare asciutto*) to dry.

asciuga'trice [aʃʃuga'tritʃe] *sf* spin-dryer.

asciut'tezza [aʃʃut'tettsa] *sf* dryness; leanness; curtness.

asci'utto, a [aʃ'ʃutto] *ag* dry; (*fig: magro*) lean; (: *burbero*) curt ♦ *sm*: **restare all'~** (*fig*) to be left penniless; **restare a bocca ~a** (*fig*) to be disappointed.

asco'lano, a *ag of* (*o* from) Ascoli.

ascol'tare *vt* to listen to; **~ il consiglio di qn** to listen to *o* heed sb's advice.

ascolta'tore, 'trice *smlf* listener.

as'colto *sm*: **essere** *o* **stare in ~** to be listening; **dare** *o* **prestare ~ (a)** to pay attention (to); **indice di ~** (*TV, RADIO*) audience rating.

AS. COM. *sigla f* = *Associazione Commercianti*.

as'critto, a *pp di* **ascrivere**.

as'crivere *vt* (*attribuire*): **~ qc a qn** to

attribute sth to sb; **~ qc a merito di qn** to give sb credit for sth.

a'settico, a, ci, che *ag* aseptic.

asfal'tare *vt* to asphalt.

as'falto *sm* asphalt.

asfis'sia *sf* asphyxia, asphyxiation.

asfissi'ante *ag* (*gas*) asphyxiating; (*fig: calore, ambiente*) stifling, suffocating; (: *persona*) tiresome.

asfissi'are *vt* to asphyxiate, suffocate; (*fig: opprimere*) to stifle; (: *infastidire*) to get on sb's nerves ♦ *vi* to suffocate, asphyxiate.

'Asia *sf*: **l'~** Asia.

asi'atico, a, ci, che *ag, smlf* Asiatic, Asian.

a'silo *sm* refuge, sanctuary; **~ (d'infanzia)** nursery(-school); **~ nido** day nursery, crèche (*for children aged 0 to 3*); **~ politico** political asylum.

asim'metrico, a, ci, che *ag* asymmetric(al).

'asino *sm* donkey, ass; **la bellezza dell'~** (*fig: di ragazza*) the beauty of youth; **qui casca l'~!** there's the rub!

'asma *sf* asthma.

as'matico, a, ci, che *ag, smlf* asthmatic.

asoci'ale [aso'tʃale] *ag* antisocial.

'asola *sf* buttonhole.

as'parago, gi *sm* asparagus *no pl.*

as'pergere [as'pɛrdʒere] *vt*: **~ (di** *o* **con)** to sprinkle (with).

asperità *sf inv* roughness *no pl*; (*fig*) harshness *no pl.*

as'persi *etc vb vedi* **aspergere**.

as'perso, a *pp di* **aspergere**.

aspet'tare *vt* to wait for; (*anche COMM*) to await; (*aspettarsi*) to expect; (*essere in serbo: notizia, evento etc*) to be in store for, lie ahead of ♦ *vi* to wait; **~rsi qc** to expect sth; **~ un bambino** to be expecting (a baby); **questo non me l'aspettavo** I wasn't expecting this; **me l'aspettavo!** I thought as much!

aspetta'tiva *sf* expectation; **inferiore all'~** worse than expected; **essere/mettersi in ~** (*AMM*) to be on/take leave of absence.

as'petto *sm* (*apparenza*) aspect, appearance, look; (*punto di vista*) point of view; **di bell'~** good-looking.

aspi'rante *ag* (*attore etc*) aspiring ♦ *smlf* candidate, applicant.

aspira'polvere *sm inv* vacuum cleaner.

aspi'rare *vt* (*respirare*) to breathe in, inhale; (*sog: apparecchi*) to suck (up) ♦ *vi*: **~ a** to aspire to.

aspira'tore *sm* extractor fan.

aspirazi'one [aspirat'tsjone] *sf* (*TECN*) suction; (*anelito*) aspiration.

aspi'rina *sf* aspirin.

aspor'tare *vt* (*anche MED*) to remove, take away.

as'prezza [as'prettsa] *sf* sourness, tartness; pungency; harshness; roughness; rugged nature.

'aspro, a *ag* (*sapore*) sour, tart; (*odore*) acrid, pungent; (*voce, clima, fig*) harsh; (*superficie*) rough; (*paesaggio*) rugged.

Ass. *abbr* = **assicurazione; assicurata; assegno.**

assaggi'are [assad'dʒare] *vt* to taste.

assag'gini [assad'dʒini] *smpl* (*CUC*) *selection of first courses.*

as'saggio [as'saddʒo] *sm* tasting; (*piccola quantità*) taste; (*campione*) sample.

as'sai *av* (*molto*) a lot, much; (: *con ag*) very; (*a sufficienza*) enough ♦ *ag inv* (*quantità*) a lot of, much; (*numero*) a lot of, many; ~ **contento** very pleased.

as'salgo *etc vb vedi* **assalire.**

assa'lire *vt* to attack, assail.

assali'tore, 'trice *sm/f* attacker, assailant.

assal'tare *vt* (*MIL*) to storm; (*banca*) to raid; (*treno, diligenza*) to hold up.

as'salto *sm* attack, assault; **prendere d'~** (*fig: negozio, treno*) to storm; (: *personalità*) to besiege; **d'~** (*editoria, giornalista etc*) aggressive.

assapo'rare *vt* to savour (*BRIT*), savor (*US*).

assassi'nare *vt* to murder; (*POL*) to assassinate; (*fig*) to ruin.

assas'sinio *sm* murder; assassination.

assas'sino, a *ag* murderous ♦ *sm/f* murderer; assassin.

'asse *sm* (*TECN*) axle; (*MAT*) axis ♦ *sf* board; ~ **da stiro** ironing board.

assecon'dare *vt*: ~ **qn** (**in qc**) to go along with sb (in sth); ~ **i desideri di qn** to go along with sb's wishes; ~ **i capricci di qn** to give in to sb's whims.

assedi'are *vt* to besiege.

as'sedio *sm* siege.

asse'gnare [assɲ'ɲare] *vt* to assign, allot; (*premio*) to award.

assegna'tario [asseɲɲa'tarjo] *sm* (*DIR*) assignee; (*COMM*) recipient; **l'~ del premio** the person awarded the prize.

assegnazi'one [asseɲɲat'tsjone] *sf* (*di casa, somma*) allocation; (*di carica*) assignment; (*di premio, borsa di studio*) awarding.

as'segno [as'seɲɲo] *sm* allowance; (*anche:* ~ **bancario**) cheque (*BRIT*), check (*US*); **contro** ~ cash on delivery; ~ **circolare** bank draft; ~ **di invalidità** *o* **di malattia** injury *o* sickness benefit; ~ **post-datato** post-dated cheque; ~ **sbarrato** crossed cheque; ~ **non sbarrato** uncrossed cheque; ~ **di studio** study grant; "~ **non**

trasferibile" "account payee only"; ~ **di viaggio** travel(l)er's cheque; ~ **a vuoto** dud cheque; ~**i alimentari** alimony *sg*; ~**i familiari** ≈ child benefit *sg*.

assem'blaggio [assem'bladdʒo] *sm* (*INDUSTRIA*) assembly.

assem'blare *vt* to assemble.

assem'blea *sf* assembly; (*raduno, adunanza*) meeting.

assembra'mento *sm* public gathering; **divieto di** ~ ban on public meetings.

assen'nato, a *ag* sensible.

as'senso *sm* assent, consent.

assen'tarsi *vr* to go out.

as'sente *ag* absent; (*fig*) faraway, vacant ♦ *sm/f* absentee.

assente'ismo *sm* absenteeism.

assente'ista, i, e *sm/f* (*dal lavoro*) absentee.

assen'tire *vi*: ~ **(a)** to agree (to), assent (to).

as'senza [as'sɛntsa] *sf* absence.

asse'rire *vt* to maintain, assert.

asserragli'arsi [asserraʎ'ʎarsi] *vr*: ~ **(in)** to barricade o.s. (in).

asser'vire *vt* to enslave; (*fig: animo, passioni*) to subdue; ~**rsi** *vr*: ~**rsi (a)** to submit (to).

asserzi'one [asser'tsjone] *sf* assertion.

assesso'rato *sm* councillorship.

asses'sore *sm* councillor.

assesta'mento *sm* (*sistemazione*) arrangement; (*EDIL, GEO*) settlement.

asses'tare *vt* (*mettere in ordine*) to put in order, arrange; ~**rsi** *vr* to settle in; (*GEO*) to settle; ~ **un colpo a qn** to deal sb a blow.

asse'tato, a *ag* thirsty, parched.

as'setto *sm* order, arrangement; (*NAUT, AER*) trim; **in** ~ **di guerra** on a war footing; ~ **territoriale** country planning.

assicu'rare *vt* (*accertare*) to ensure; (*infondere certezza*) to assure; (*fermare, legare*) to make fast, secure; (*fare un contratto di assicurazione*) to insure; ~**rsi** *vr* (*accertarsi*): ~**rsi (di)** to make sure (of); (*contro il furto etc*): ~**rsi (contro)** to insure o.s. (against).

assicu'rato, a *ag* insured ♦ *sf* (*anche:* **lettera** ~**a**) registered letter.

assicura'tore, 'trice *ag* insurance *cpd* ♦ *sm/f* insurance agent; **società** ~**trice** insurance company.

assicurazi'one [assikurat'tsjone] *sf* assurance; insurance; ~ **multi-rischio** comprehensive insurance.

assidera'mento *sm* exposure.

asside'rare *vt* to freeze; ~**rsi** *vr* to freeze; **morire assiderato** to die of exposure.

as'siduo, a *ag (costante)* assiduous; *(regolare)* regular.

assi'eme *av (insieme)* together ♦ *prep:* ~ **a** (together) with.

assil'lante *ag (dubbio, pensiero)* nagging; *(creditore)* pestering.

assil'lare *vt* to pester, torment.

as'sillo *sm (fig)* worrying thought.

assimi'lare *vt* to assimilate.

assimilazi'one [assimilat'tsjone] *sf* assimilation.

assi'oma, i *sm* axiom.

assio'matico, a, ci, che *ag* axiomatic.

as'sise *sfpl (DIR)* assizes *(BRIT)*; **corte** *f* **d'** ~ court of assizes, ≈ crown court *(BRIT)*; *vedi anche* **Corte d'Assise.**

assis'tente *sm/f* assistant; ~ **sociale** social worker; ~ **universitario** (assistant) lecturer; ~ **di volo** *(AER)* steward/stewardess.

assis'tenza [assis'tɛntsa] *sf* assistance; ~ **legale** legal aid; ~ **ospedaliera** free hospital treatment; ~ **sanitaria** health service; ~ **sociale** welfare services *pl.*

assistenzi'ale [assisten'tsjale] *ag (ente, organizzazione)* welfare *cpd;* *(opera)* charitable.

assistenzia'lismo [assistentsja'lizmo] *sm (peg)* excessive state aid.

as'sistere *vt (aiutare)* to assist, help; *(curare)* to treat ♦ *vi:* ~ **(a qc)** *(essere presente)* to be present (at sth), attend (sth).

assis'tito, a *pp di* **assistere.**

'asso *sm* ace; **piantare qn in** ~ to leave sb in the lurch.

associ'are [asso'tʃare] *vt* to associate; *(rendere partecipe):* ~ **qn a** *(affari)* to take sb into partnership in; *(partito)* to make sb a member of; ~**rsi** *vr* to enter into partnership; ~**rsi a** to become a member of, join; *(dolori, gioie)* to share in; ~ **qn alle carceri** to take sb to prison.

associazi'one [assot'tsjone] *sf* association; ~ **di categoria** trade association; ~ **a o per delinquere** *(DIR)* criminal association; **A**~ **Europea di Libero Scambio** European Free Trade Association, EFTA; ~ **in partecipazione** *(COMM)* joint venture.

asso'dare *vt (muro, posizione)* to strengthen; *(fatti, verità)* to ascertain.

asso'dato, a *ag* well-founded.

assogget'tare [assoddʒet'tare] *vt* to subject, subjugate; ~**rsi** *vr:* ~**rsi a** to submit to.

asso'lato, a *ag* sunny.

assol'dare *vt* to recruit.

as'solsi *etc vb vedi* **assolvere.**

as'solto, a *pp di* **assolvere.**

assoluta'mente *av* absolutely.

asso'luto, a *ag* absolute.

assoluzi'one [assolut'tsjone] *sf (DIR)* acquittal; *(REL)* absolution.

as'solvere *vt (DIR)* to acquit; *(REL)* to absolve; *(adempiere)* to carry out, perform.

assomigli'are [assomiʎ'ʎare] *vi:* ~ **a** to resemble, look like.

asson'nato, a *ag* sleepy.

asso'pirsi *vr* to doze off.

assor'bente *ag* absorbent ♦ *sm:* ~ **igienico** sanitary towel; ~ **interno** tampon.

assor'bire *vt* to absorb; *(fig: far proprio)* to assimilate.

assor'dante *ag (rumore, musica)* deafening.

assor'dare *vt* to deafen.

assorti'mento *sm* assortment.

assor'tire *vt (disporre)* to arrange.

assor'tito, a *ag* assorted; *(colori)* matched, matching.

as'sorto, a *ag* absorbed, engrossed.

assottigli'are [assottiʎ'ʎare] *vt* to make thin, thin; *(aguzzare)* to sharpen; *(ridurre)* to reduce; ~**rsi** *vr* to grow thin; *(fig: ridursi)* to be reduced.

A.S.S.T. *sigla f* (= *Azienda di Stato per i Servizi Telefonici*) *state-run telecommunications company.*

assue'fare *vt* to accustom; ~**rsi** *vr:* ~**rsi a** to get used to, accustom o.s. to.

assue'fatto, a *pp di* **assuefare.**

assuefazi'one [assuefat'tsjone] *sf (MED)* addiction.

as'sumere *vt (impiegato)* to take on, engage; *(responsabilità)* to assume, take upon o.s.; *(contegno, espressione)* to assume, put on; *(droga)* to consume.

as'sunsi *etc vb vedi* **assumere.**

as'sunto, a *pp di* **assumere** ♦ *sm (tesi)* proposition.

assunzi'one [assun'tsjone] *sf (di impiegati)* employment, engagement; *(REL):* **l'A**~ the Assumption.

assurdità *sf inv* absurdity; **dire delle** ~ to talk nonsense.

as'surdo, a *ag* absurd.

'asta *sf* pole; *(modo di vendita)* auction.

as'tante *sm* bystander.

astante'ria *sf* casualty department.

as'temio, a *ag* teetotal ♦ *sm/f* teetotaller.

aste'nersi *vr:* ~ **(da)** to abstain (from), refrain (from); *(POL)* to abstain (from).

astensi'one *sf* abstention.

astensio'nista, i, e *sm/f (POL)* abstentionist.

aste'risco, schi *sm* asterisk.

aste'roide *sm* asteroid.
'astice ['astitʃe] *sm* lobster.
astigi'ano, a [asti'dʒano] *ag* of (*o* from) Asti.
astig'matico, a, ci, che *ag* astigmatic.
asti'nenza [asti'nɛntsa] *sf* abstinence; **essere in crisi di** ~ to suffer from withdrawal symptoms.
'astio *sm* rancour, resentment.
asti'oso, a *ag* resentful.
astrat'tismo *sm* (*ARTE*) abstract art.
as'tratto, a *ag* abstract.
astrin'gente [astrin'dʒɛnte] *ag, sm* astringent.
'astro *sm* star.
astrolo'gia [astrolo'dʒia] *sf* astrology.
astro'logico, a, ci, che [astro'lɔdʒiko] *ag* astrological.
as'trologo, a, ghi, ghe *sm/f* astrologer.
astro'nauta, i, e *sm/f* astronaut.
astro'nautica *sf* astronautics *sg*.
astro'nave *sf* space ship.
astrono'mia *sf* astronomy.
astro'nomico, a, ci, che *ag* astronomic(al).
as'tronomo *sm* astronomer.
as'truso, a *ag* (*discorso, ragionamento*) abstruse.
as'tuccio [as'tuttʃo] *sm* case, box, holder.
as'tuto, a *ag* astute, cunning, shrewd.
as'tuzia [as'tuttsja] *sf* astuteness, shrewdness; (*azione*) trick.
AT *sigla* = *Asti*.
A.T. *abbr* (= *alta tensione*) HT.
ATA *sigla f* = *Associazione Turistica Albergatori*.
a'tavico, a, ci, che *ag* atavistic.
ate'ismo *sm* atheism.
atelier [atə'lje] *sm inv* (*laboratorio*) workshop; (*studio*) studio; (*sartoria*) fashion house.
A'tene *sf* Athens.
ate'neo *sm* university.
ateni'ese *ag, sm/f* Athenian.
'ateo, a *ag, sm/f* atheist.
a'tipico, a, ci, che *ag* atypical.
at'lante *sm* atlas; **i Monti dell'A**~ the Atlas Mountains.
at'lantico, a, ci, che *ag* Atlantic ♦ *sm*: **l'A**~, **l'Oceano A**~ the Atlantic, the Atlantic Ocean.
at'leta, i, e *sm/f* athlete.
at'letica *sf* athletics *sg*; ~ **leggera** track and field events *pl*; ~ **pesante** weightlifting and wrestling.
ATM *sigla f* = *Azienda Tranviaria Municipale*.
atmos'fera *sf* atmosphere.
atmos'ferico, a, ci, che *ag* atmospheric.

a'tollo *sm* atoll.
a'tomico, a, ci, che *ag* atomic; (*nucleare*) atomic, atom *cpd*, nuclear.
atomizza'tore [atomiddza'tore] *sm* (*di acqua, lacca*) spray; (*di profumo*) atomizer.
'atomo *sm* atom.
'atono, a *ag* (*FONETICA*) unstressed.
'atrio *sm* entrance hall, lobby.
a'troce [a'trotʃe] *ag* (*che provoca orrore*) dreadful; (*terribile*) atrocious.
atrocità [atrotʃi'ta] *sf inv* atrocity.
atro'fia *sf* atrophy.
attacca'brighe [attakka'brige] *sm/f inv* quarrelsome person.
attacca'mento *sm* (*fig*) attachment, affection.
attacca'panni *sm* hook, peg; (*mobile*) hall stand.
attac'care *vt* (*unire*) to attach; (*cucendo*) to sew on; (*far aderire*) to stick (on); (*appendere*) to hang (up); (*assalire: anche fig*) to attack; (*iniziare*) to begin, start; (*fig: contagiare*) to pass on ♦ *vi* to stick, adhere; ~**rsi** *vr* to stick, adhere; (*trasmettersi per contagio*) to be contagious; (*afferrarsi*): ~**rsi (a)** to cling (to); (*fig: affezionarsi*): ~**rsi (a)** to become attached (to); ~ **discorso** to start a conversation; **con me non attacca!** that won't work with me!
attacca'ticcio, a, ci, ce [attakka'tittʃo] *ag* sticky.
attacca'tura *sf* (*di manica*) join; ~ **(dei capelli)** hairline.
at'tacco, chi *sm* (*azione offensiva: anche fig*) attack; (*MED*) attack, fit; (*SCI*) binding; (*ELETTR*) socket.
attanagli'are [attanaʎ'ʎare] *vt* (*anche fig*) to grip.
attar'darsi *vr*: ~ **a fare qc** (*fermarsi*) to stop to do sth; (*stare più a lungo*) to stay behind to do sth.
attec'chire [attek'kire] *vi* (*pianta*) to take root; (*fig*) to catch on.
atteggia'mento [attedddʒa'mento] *sm* attitude.
atteggi'arsi [atted'dʒarsi] *vr*: ~ **a** to pose as.
attem'pato, a *ag* elderly.
atten'dente *sm* (*MIL*) orderly, batman.
at'tendere *vt* to wait for, await ♦ *vi*: ~ **a** to attend to.
atten'dibile *ag* (*scusa, storia*) credible; (*fonte, testimone, notizia*) reliable; (*persona*) trustworthy.
atte'nersi *vr*: ~ **a** to keep *o* stick to.
atten'tare *vi*: ~ **a** to make an attempt on.
atten'tato *sm* attack; ~ **alla vita di qn** attempt on sb's life.
at'tento, a *ag* attentive; (*accurato*) careful,

thorough ♦ *escl* be careful!; **stare ~ a qc** to pay attention to sth; **~i!** (*MIL*) attention!; **~i al cane** beware of the dog.

attenu'ante *sf* (*DIR*) extenuating circumstance.

attenu'are *vt* to alleviate, ease; (*diminuire*) to reduce; **~rsi** *vr* to ease, abate.

attenuazi'one [attenuat'tsjone] *sf* alleviation; easing; reduction.

attenzi'one [atten'tsjone] *sf* attention ♦ *escl* watch out!, be careful!; **coprire qn di ~i** to lavish attention on sb.

atter'raggio [atter'raddʒo] *sm* landing; **~ di fortuna** emergency landing.

atter'rare *vt* to bring down ♦ *vi* to land.

atter'rire *vt* to terrify.

at'tesa *sf vedi* **atteso**.

at'tesi *etc vb vedi* **attendere**.

at'teso, a *pp di* **attendere** ♦ *sf* waiting; (*tempo trascorso aspettando*) wait; **essere in ~a di qc** to be waiting for sth; **in ~a di una vostra risposta** (*COMM*) awaiting your reply; **restiamo in ~a di Vostre ulteriori notizie** (*COMM*) we look forward to hearing (further) from you.

attes'tare *vt*: **~ qc/che** to testify to sth/(to the fact) that.

attes'tato *sm* certificate.

attestazi'one [attestat'tsjone] *sf* (*certificato*) certificate; (*dichiarazione*) statement.

'attico, ci *sm* attic.

at'tiguo, a *ag* adjacent, adjoining.

attil'lato, a *ag* (*vestito*) close-fitting, tight; (*persona*) dressed up.

'attimo *sm* moment; **in un ~** in a moment.

atti'nente *ag*: **~ a** relating to, concerning.

atti'nenza [atti'nɛntsa] *sf* connection.

at'tingere [at'tindʒere] *vt*: **~ a o da** (*acqua*) to draw from; (*denaro, notizie*) to obtain from.

at'tinto, a *pp di* **attingere**.

atti'rare *vt* to attract; **~rsi delle critiche** to incur criticism.

atti'tudine *sf* (*disposizione*) aptitude; (*atteggiamento*) attitude.

atti'vare *vt* to activate; (*far funzionare*) to set going, start.

atti'vista, i, e *smf* activist.

attività *sf inv* activity; (*COMM*) assets *pl*; **~ liquide** (*COMM*) liquid assets.

at'tivo, a *ag* active; (*COMM*) profit-making ♦ *sm* (*COMM*) assets *pl*; **in ~** in credit; **chiudere in ~** to show a profit; **avere qc al proprio ~** (*fig*) to have sth to one's credit.

attiz'zare [attit'tsare] *vt* (*fuoco*) to poke; (*fig*) to stir up.

attizza'toio [attittsa'tojo] *sm* poker.

'atto, a *ag*: **~ a** fit for, capable of ♦ *sm* act;

(*azione, gesto*) action, act, deed; (*DIR: documento*) deed, document; **~i** *smpl* (*di congressi etc*) proceedings; **essere in ~** to be under way; **mettere in ~** to put into action; **fare ~ di fare qc** to make as if to do sth; **all'~** in practice; **dare ~ a qn di qc** to give sb credit for sth; **~ di nascita/morte** birth/death certificate; **~ di proprietà** title deed; **~ pubblico** official document; **~ di vendita** bill of sale; **~i osceni (in luogo pubblico)** (*DIR*) indecent exposure; **~i verbali** transactions.

at'tonito, a *ag* dumbfounded, astonished.

attorcigli'are [attortʃiʎ'ʎare] *vt*, **~rsi** *vr* to twist.

at'tore, 'trice *sm/f* actor/actress.

attorni'are *vt* (*circondare*) to surround; **~rsi** *vr*: **~rsi di** to surround o.s. with.

at'torno *av*, **~ a** *prep* round, around, about.

attrac'care *vt, vi* (*NAUT*) to dock, berth.

at'tracco, chi *sm* (*NAUT: manovra*) docking, berthing; (*luogo*) berth.

at'trae *etc vb vedi* **attrarre**.

attra'ente *ag* attractive.

at'traggo *etc vb vedi* **attrarre**.

at'trarre *vt* to attract.

at'trassi *etc vb vedi* **attrarre**.

attrat'tiva *sf* attraction, charm.

at'tratto, a *pp di* **attrarre**.

attraversa'mento *sm* crossing; **~ pedonale** pedestrian crossing.

attraver'sare *vt* to cross; (*città, bosco, fig: periodo*) to go through; (*sog: fiume*) to run through.

attra'verso *prep* through; (*da una parte all'altra*) across.

attrazi'one [attrat'tsjone] *sf* attraction.

attrez'zare [attret'tsare] *vt* to equip; (*NAUT*) to rig.

attrezza'tura [attrettsa'tura] *sf* equipment *no pl*; rigging; **~e per uffici** office equipment.

at'trezzo [at'trettso] *sm* tool, instrument; (*SPORT*) piece of equipment.

attribu'ire *vt*: **~ qc a qn** (*assegnare*) to give *o* award sth to sb; (*quadro etc*) to attribute sth to sb.

attri'buto *sm* attribute.

at'trice [at'tritʃe] *sf vedi* **attore**.

at'trito *sm* (*anche fig*) friction.

attu'abile *ag* feasible.

attuabilità *sf* feasibility.

attu'ale *ag* (*presente*) present; (*di attualità*) topical; (*che è in atto*) actual.

attualità *sf inv* topicality; (*avvenimento*) current event; **notizie d'~** (*TV*) the news *sg*.

attualiz'zare [attualid'dzare] *vt* to update,

bring up to date.
attual'mente *av* at the moment, at present.
attu'are *vt* to carry out; ~**rsi** *vr* to be realized.
attuazi'one [attuat'tsjone] *sf* carrying out.
attu'tire *vt* to deaden, reduce; ~**rsi** *vr* to die down.
A.U. *abbr* = **allievo ufficiale.**
au'dace [au'datʃe] *ag* audacious, daring; bold; (*provocante*) provocative; (*sfacciato*) impudent, bold.
au'dacia [au'datʃa] *sf* audacity, daring; boldness; provocativeness; impudence.
'audio *sm* (*TV, RADIO, CINE*) sound.
audiocas'setta *sf* (audio) cassette.
audio'leso, a *sm/f* person who is hard of hearing.
audiovi'sivo, a *ag* audiovisual.
audi'torio *sm*, **audi'torium** *sm inv* auditorium.
audizi'one [audit'tsjone] *sf* hearing; (*MUS*) audition.
'auge ['audʒe] *sf* (*della gloria, carriera*) height, peak; **essere in** ~ to be at the top.
augu'rale *ag*: **messaggio** ~ greeting; **biglietto** ~ greetings card.
augu'rare *vt* to wish; ~**rsi qc** to hope for sth.
au'gurio *sm* (*presagio*) omen; (*voto di benessere etc*) (good) wish; **essere di buon/cattivo** ~ to be of good omen/be ominous; **fare gli** ~**i a qn** to give sb one's best wishes; **tanti** ~**i!** all the best!
'aula *sf* (*scolastica*) classroom; (*universitaria*) lecture theatre; (*di edificio pubblico*) hall; ~ **magna** main hall; ~ **del tribunale** courtroom.
aumen'tare *vt, vi* to increase; ~ **di peso** (*persona*) to put on weight; **la produzione è aumentata del 50%** production has increased by 50%.
au'mento *sm* increase.
'aureo, a *ag* (*di oro*) gold *cpd*; (*fig: colore, periodo*) golden.
au'reola *sf* halo.
au'rora *sf* dawn.
ausili'are *ag, sm, sm/f* auxiliary.
au'silio *sm* aid.
auspi'cabile *ag* desirable.
auspi'care *vt* to call for, express a desire for.
aus'picio [aus'pitʃo] *sm* omen; (*protezione*) patronage; **sotto gli** ~**i di** under the auspices of; **è di buon** ~ it augurs well.
austerità *sf inv* austerity.
aus'tero, a *ag* austere.
aus'trale *ag* southern.

Aus'tralia *sf*: **l'**~ Australia.
australi'ano, a *ag, sm/f* Australian.
'Austria *sf*: **l'**~ Austria.
aus'triaco, a, ci, che *ag, sm/f* Austrian.
au'tarchico, a, ci, che [au'tarkiko] *ag* (*sistema*) self-sufficient, autarkic; (*prodotto*) home *cpd*, home-produced.
'aut 'aut *sm inv* ultimatum.
autenti'care *vt* to authenticate.
autenticità [autentitʃi'ta] *sf* authenticity.
au'tentico, a, ci, che *ag* (*quadro, firma*) authentic, genuine; (*fatto*) true, genuine.
au'tista, i *sm* driver; (*personale*) chauffeur.
'auto *sf inv* car; ~ **blu** official car.
autoade'sivo, a *ag* self-adhesive ♦ *sm* sticker.
autoartico'lato *sm* articulated lorry (*BRIT*), semi (trailer) (*US*).
autobiogra'fia *sf* autobiography.
autobio'grafico, a, ci, che *ag* autobiographic(al).
auto'blinda *sf* armoured (*BRIT*) o armored (*US*) car.
auto'bomba *sf inv* car carrying a bomb; **l'**~ **si trovava a pochi metri** the car bomb was a few metres away.
auto'botte *sf* tanker.
'autobus *sm inv* bus.
auto'carro *sm* lorry (*BRIT*), truck.
autocertificazi'one [autotʃertifikat'tsjone] *sf* self-declaration.
autocis'terna [autotʃis'tɛrna] *sf* tanker.
autoco'lonna *sf* convoy.
autocon'trollo *sm* self-control.
autocopia'tivo, a *ag*: **carta** ~**a** carbonless paper.
autocorri'era *sf* coach, bus.
auto'cratico, a, ci, che *ag* autocratic.
auto'critica, che *sf* self-criticism.
au'toctono, a *ag, sm/f* native.
autodemolizi'one [autodemolit'tsjone] *sf* breaker's yard (*BRIT*).
autodi'datta, i, e *sm/f* autodidact, self-taught person.
autodi'fesa *sf* self-defence.
autoferrotranvi'ario, a *ag* public transport *cpd*.
autogesti'one [autodʒes'tjone] *sf* worker management.
autoges'tito, a [autodʒes'tito] *ag* under worker management.
au'tografo, a *ag, sm* autograph.
auto'grill *sm inv* motorway café (*BRIT*), roadside restaurant (*US*).
autoim'mune *ag* autoimmune.
autolesio'nismo *sm* (*fig*) self-destruction.
auto'linea *sf* bus route.
au'toma, i *sm* automaton.

auto'matico, a, ci, che *ag* automatic ♦ *sm* (*bottone*) snap fastener; (*fucile*) automatic; **selezione** ~**a** (*TEL*) direct dialling.

automazi'one [automat'tsjone] *sf*: ~ **delle procedure d'ufficio** office automation.

automedicazi'one [automedikat'tsjone] *sf* (*medicine, farmaci*): **medicinale di** ~ self-medication.

auto'mezzo [auto'mɛddzo] *sm* motor vehicle.

auto'mobile *sf* (motor) car; ~ **da corsa** racing car (*BRIT*), race car (*US*).

automobi'lismo *sm* (*gen*) motoring; (*SPORT*) motor racing.

automobi'lista, i, e *sm/f* motorist.

automobi'listico, a, ci, che *ag* car *cpd* (*BRIT*), automobile *cpd* (*US*); (*sport*) motor *cpd*.

autono'leggio [autono'leddʒo] *sm* car hire (*BRIT*), car rental.

autono'mia *sf* autonomy; (*di volo*) range.

au'tonomo, a *ag* autonomous; (*sindacato, pensiero*) independent.

auto'parco, chi *sm* (*parcheggio*) car park (*BRIT*), parking lot (*US*); (*insieme di automezzi*) transport fleet.

auto'pompa *sf* fire engine.

autop'sia *sf* post-mortem (examination), autopsy.

auto'radio *sf inv* (*apparecchio*) car radio; (*autoveicolo*) radio car.

au'tore, 'trice *sm/f* author; **l'**~ **del furto** the person who committed the robbery; **diritti d'**~ copyright *sg*; (*compenso*) royalties.

autoregolamentazi'one [autoregolamentat'tsjone] *sf* self-regulation.

auto'revole *ag* authoritative; (*persona*) influential.

autori'messa *sf* garage.

autorità *sf inv* authority.

autori'tratto *sm* self-portrait.

autoriz'zare [autorid'dzare] *vt* to authorize, give permission for.

autorizzazi'one [autoriddzat'tsjone] *sf* authorization; ~ **a procedere** (*DIR*) authorization to proceed.

autos'catto *sm* (*FOT*) timer.

autos'contro *sm* dodgem car (*BRIT*), bumper car (*US*).

autoscu'ola *sf* driving school.

autosno'dato *sm* articulated vehicle.

autos'top *sm* hitchhiking.

autostop'pista, i, e *sm/f* hitchhiker.

autos'trada *sf* motorway (*BRIT*), highway (*US*).

autosuffici'ente [autosuffi'tʃɛnte] *ag* self-sufficient.

autosuffici'enza [autosuffi'tʃɛntsa] *sf* self-sufficiency.

autotassazi'one [autotassat'tsjone] *sf* system of taxation where individual himself assesses and pays tax due.

auto'treno *sm* articulated lorry (*BRIT*), semi (trailer) (*US*).

autove'icolo *sm* motor vehicle.

autovet'tura *sf* (motor) car.

autun'nale *ag* (*di autunno*) autumn *cpd*; (*da autunno*) autumnal.

au'tunno *sm* autumn.

AV *sigla* = *Avellino*.

a/v *abbr* = **a vista**.

aval'lare *vt* (*FINANZA*) to guarantee; (*fig: sostenere*) to back; (: *confermare*) to confirm.

a'vallo *sm* (*FINANZA*) guarantee.

avam'braccio, *pl(f)* -**cia** [avam'brattʃo] *sm* forearm.

avam'posto *sm* (*MIL*) outpost.

A'vana *sf*: **l'**~ Havana.

a'vana *sm inv* (*sigaro*) Havana (cigar); (*colore*) Havana brown.

avangu'ardia *sf* vanguard; (*ARTE*) avant-garde.

avansco'perta *sf* (*MIL*) reconnaissance; **andare in** ~ to reconnoitre.

a'vanti *av* (*stato in luogo*) in front; (*moto: andare, venire*) forward; (*tempo: prima*) before ♦ *prep* (*luogo*): ~ **a** before, in front of; (*tempo*): ~ **Cristo** before Christ ♦ *escl* (*entrate*) come (*o* go) in!; (*MIL*) forward!; (*coraggio*) come on! ♦ *sm inv* (*SPORT*) forward; **il giorno** ~ the day before; ~ **e indietro** backwards and forwards; **andare** ~ to go forward; (*continuare*) to go on; (*precedere*) to go (on) ahead; (*orologio*) to be fast; **essere** ~ **negli studi** to be well advanced with one's studies; **mandare** ~ **la famiglia** to provide for one's family; **mandare** ~ **un'azienda** to run a business; ~ **il prossimo!** next please!

avan'treno *sm* (*AUT*) front chassis.

avanza'mento [avantsa'mento] *sm* (*gen*) advance; (*fig*) progress; promotion.

avan'zare [avan'tsare] *vt* (*spostare in avanti*) to move forward, advance; (*domanda*) to put forward; (*promuovere*) to promote; (*essere creditore*): ~ **qc da qn** to be owed sth by sb ♦ *vi* (*andare avanti*) to move forward, advance; (*fig: progredire*) to make progress; (*essere d'avanzo*) to be left, remain; **basta e avanza** that's more than enough.

avan'zato, a [avan'tsato] *ag* (*teoria, tecnica*)

advanced ♦ sf (MIL) advance; **in età ~a** advanced in years, up in years.

a'**vanzo** [a'vantso] sm (residuo) remains pl, left-overs pl; (MAT) remainder; (COMM) surplus; (eccedenza di bilancio) profit carried forward; **averne d'~ di qc** to have more than enough of sth; **~ di cassa** cash in hand; **~ di galera** (fig) jailbird.

ava'**ria** sf (guasto) damage; (: meccanico) breakdown.

avari'**ato, a** ag (merce) damaged; (cibo) off.

ava'**rizia** [ava'rittsja] sf avarice; **crepi l'~!** to hang with the expense!

a'**varo, a** ag avaricious, miserly ♦ sm miser.

a'**vena** sf oats pl.

===================== PAROLA CHIAVE

a'**vere** sm (COMM) credit; **gli ~i** (ricchezze) wealth sg, possessions

♦ vt **1** (possedere) to have; **ha due bambini/una bella casa** she has (got) two children/a lovely house; **ha i capelli lunghi** he has (got) long hair; **non ho da mangiare/bere** I've (got) nothing to eat/drink, I don't have anything to eat/drink

2 (indossare) to wear, have on; **aveva una maglietta rossa** he was wearing o he had on a red T-shirt; **ha gli occhiali** he wears o has glasses

3 (ricevere) to get; **hai avuto l'assegno?** did you get o have you had the cheque?

4 (età, dimensione) to be; **ha 9 anni** he is 9 (years old); **la stanza ha 3 metri di lunghezza** the room is 3 metres in length; vedi **fame; paura; sonno** etc

5 (tempo): **quanti ne abbiamo oggi?** what's the date today?; **ne hai per molto?** will you be long?

6 (fraseologia): **avercela con qn** to be angry with sb; **cos'hai?** what's wrong o what's the matter (with you)?; **non ha niente a che vedere** o **fare con me** it's got nothing to do with me

♦ vb aus **1** to have; **aver bevuto/mangiato** to have drunk/eaten; **l'ho già visto** I have seen it already; **l'ho visto ieri** I saw it yesterday; **ci ha creduto?** did he believe it?

2 (+ da + infinito): **~ da fare qc** to have to do sth; **non ho niente da dire** I have nothing to say; **non hai che da chiederlo** you only have to ask him.

avia'**tore, 'trice** sm/f aviator, pilot.

aviazi'**one** [avjat'tsjone] sf aviation; (MIL) air force; **~ civile** civil aviation.

avicol'**tura** sf bird breeding; (di pollame) poultry farming.

avidi'**tà** sf eagerness; greed.

'**avido** a ag eager; (: peg) greedy.

avi'**ere** sm (MIL) airman.

avitami'**nosi** sf vitamin deficiency.

'**avo** sm (antenato) ancestor; **i nostri ~i** our ancestors.

avo'**cado** sm avocado.

a'**vorio** sm ivory.

a'**vulso, a** ag: **parole ~e dal contesto** words out of context; **~ dalla società** (fig) cut off from society.

Avv. abbr = **avvocato.**

avva'**lersi** vr: **~ di** to avail o.s. of.

avvalla'**mento** sm sinking no pl; (effetto) depression.

avvalo'**rare** vt to confirm.

avvantaggi'**are** [avvantad'dʒare] vt to favour (BRIT), favor (US); (trarre vantaggio): **~rsi di** to take advantage of; (prevalere): **~rsi negli affari/sui concorrenti** to get ahead in business/of one's competitors.

avve'**dersi** vr: **~ di qn/qc** to notice sb/sth.

avve'**duto, a** ag (accorto) prudent; (scaltro) astute.

avvelena'**mento** sm poisoning.

avvele'**nare** vt to poison.

avve'**nente** ag attractive, charming.

avve'**nenza** [avve'nɛntsa] sf good looks pl.

av'**vengo** etc vb vedi **avvenire.**

avveni'**mento** sm event.

avve'**nire** vi, vb impers to happen, occur ♦ sm future.

av'**venni** etc vb vedi **avvenire.**

avven'**tarsi** vr: **~ su** o **contro qn/qc** to hurl o.s. o rush at sb/sth.

avven'**tato, a** ag rash, reckless.

avven'**tizio, a** [avven'tittsjo] ag (impiegato) temporary; (guadagno) casual.

av'**vento** sm advent, coming; (REL): **l'A~** Advent.

avven'**tore** sm customer.

avven'**tura** sf adventure; (amorosa) affair; **avere spirito d'~** to be adventurous.

avventu'**rarsi** vr to venture.

avventuri'**ero, a** sm/f adventurer/ adventuress.

avventu'**roso, a** ag adventurous.

avve'**nuto, a** pp di **avvenire.**

avve'**rarsi** vr to come true.

av'**verbio** sm adverb.

av'**verrò** etc vb vedi **avvenire.**

avver'**sare** vt to oppose.

avver'**sario, a** ag opposing ♦ sm opponent, adversary.

avversi'**one** sf aversion.

avversi'**tà** sf inv adversity, misfortune.

av'verso, a *ag* (*contrario*) contrary; (*sfavorevole*) unfavourable (*BRIT*), unfavorable (*US*).

avver'tenza [avver'tɛntsa] *sf* (*ammonimento*) warning; (*cautela*) care; (*premessa*) foreword; ~**e** *sfpl* (*istruzioni per l'uso*) instructions.

avverti'mento *sm* warning.

avver'tire *vt* (*avvisare*) to warn; (*rendere consapevole*) to inform, notify; (*percepire*) to feel.

av'vezzo, a [av'vettso] *ag*: ~ **a** used to.

avvia'mento *sm* (*atto*) starting; (*effetto*) start; (*AUT*) starting; (*: dispositivo*) starter; (*COMM*) goodwill.

avvi'are *vt* (*mettere sul cammino*) to direct; (*impresa, trattative*) to begin, start; (*motore*) to start; ~**rsi** *vr* to set off, set out.

avvicenda'mento [avvitʃenda'mento] *sm* alternation; (*AGR*) rotation; **c'è molto ~ di personale** there is a high turnover of staff.

avvicen'dare [avvitʃen'dare] *vt*, ~**rsi** *vr* to alternate.

avvicina'mento [avvitʃina'mento] *sm* approach.

avvici'nare [avvitʃi'nare] *vt* to bring near; (*trattare con: persona*) to approach; ~**rsi** *vr*: ~**rsi (a qn/qc)** to approach (sb/sth), draw near (to sb/sth); (*somigliare*) to be similar (to sb/sth), be close (to sb/sth).

avvi'lente *ag* (*umiliante*) humiliating; (*scoraggiante*) discouraging, disheartening.

avvili'mento *sm* humiliation; disgrace; discouragement.

avvi'lire *vt* (*umiliare*) to humiliate; (*degradare*) to disgrace; (*scoraggiare*) to dishearten, discourage; ~**rsi** *vr* (*abbattersi*) to lose heart.

avvilup'pare *vt* (*avvolgere*) to wrap up; (*ingarbugliare*) to entangle.

avvinaz'zato, a [avvinat'tsato] *ag* drunk.

avvin'cente [avvin'tʃɛnte] *ag* (*film, racconto*) enthralling.

av'vincere [av'vintʃere] *vt* to charm, enthral.

avvinghi'are [avvin'gjare] *vt* to clasp; ~**rsi** *vr*: ~**rsi a** to cling to.

av'vinsi *etc vb vedi* **avvincere**.

av'vinto, a *pp di* **avvincere**.

av'vio *sm* start, beginning; **dare l'~ a qc** to start sth off; **prendere l'~** to get going, get under way.

avvi'saglia [avvi'zaʎʎa] *sf* (*sintomo: di temporale etc*) sign; (*di malattia*) manifestation, sign, symptom; (*scaramuccia*) skirmish.

avvi'sare *vt* (*far sapere*) to inform; (*mettere in guardia*) to warn.

avvisa'tore *sm* (*apparecchio d'allarme*) alarm; ~ **acustico** horn; ~ **d'incendio** fire alarm.

av'viso *sm* warning; (*annuncio*) announcement; (*affisso*) notice; (*inserzione pubblicitaria*) advertisement; **a mio ~** in my opinion; **mettere qn sull'~** to put sb on their guard; **fino a nuovo ~** until further notice; ~ **di consegna/spedizione** (*COMM*) delivery/consignment note; ~ **di garanzia** (*DIR*) notification (*of impending investigation and of the right to name a defence laywer*); ~ **di pagamento** (*COMM*) payment advice.

avvista'mento *sm* sighting.

avvis'tare *vt* to sight.

avvi'tare *vt* to screw down (*o* in).

avviz'zire [avvit'tsire] *vi* to wither.

avvo'cato, 'essa *sm/f* (*DIR*) barrister (*BRIT*), lawyer; (*fig*) defender, advocate; ~ **del diavolo: fare l'~ del diavolo** to play devil's advocate; ~ **difensore** counsel for the defence; ~ **di parte civile** counsel for the plaintiff.

av'volgere [av'vɔldʒere] *vt* to roll up; (*bobina*) to wind up; (*avviluppare*) to wrap up; ~**rsi** *vr* (*avvilupparsi*) to wrap o.s. up.

avvol'gibile [avvol'dʒibile] *sm* roller blind (*BRIT*), blind.

avvolgi'mento [avvoldʒi'mento] *sm* winding.

av'volsi *etc vb vedi* **avvolgere**.

av'volto, a *pp di* **avvolgere**.

avvol'toio *sm* vulture.

aza'lea [addza'lɛa] *sf* azalea.

Azerbaigi'an [addzɛrbai'dʒan] *sm* Azerbaijan.

azerbaig'iano, a [addzɛrbaı'dʒano] *ag* Azerbaijani ♦ *sm/f* (*abitante*) Azerbaijani ♦ *sm* (*LING*) Azerbaijani.

a'zero, a [ad'dzɛro] *sm/f* Azeri.

azi'enda [ad'dzjɛnda] *sf* business, firm, concern; ~ **agricola** farm; ~ (**autonoma**) **di soggiorno** tourist board; ~ **a partecipazione statale** *business in which the State has a financial interest*; ~**e pubbliche** public corporations.

azien'dale [addzjen'dale] *ag* company *cpd*; **organizzazione** ~ business administration.

azio'nare [attsjo'nare] *vt* to activate.

azio'nario, a [attsjo'narjo] *ag* share *cpd*; **capitale** ~ share capital; **mercato** ~ stock market.

azi'one [at'tsjone] *sf* action; (*COMM*) share;

~ **sindacale** industrial action; ~**i preferenziali** preference shares (*BRIT*), preferred stock *sg* (*US*).

azio'nista, i, e [attsjo'nista] *sm/f* (*COMM*) shareholder.

a'zoto [ad'dzɔto] *sm* nitrogen.

az'teco, a, ci, che [as'tɛko] *ag*, *sm/f* Aztec.

azzan'nare [attsan'nare] *vt* to sink one's teeth into.

azzar'dare [addzar'dare] *vt* (*soldi, vita*) to risk, hazard; (*domanda, ipotesi*) to hazard, venture; ~**rsi** *vr*: ~**rsi a fare** to dare (to) do.

azzar'dato, a [addzar'dato] *ag* (*impresa*) risky; (*risposta*) rash.

az'zardo [ad'dzardo] *sm* risk; **gioco d'**~ game of chance.

azzec'care [attsek'kare] *vt* (*bersaglio*) to hit, strike; (*risposta, pronostico*) to get right; (*fig: indovinare*) to guess.

azzera'mento [addzera'mento] *sm* (*INFORM*) reset.

azze'rare [addze'rare] *vt* (*MAT, FISICA*) to make equal to zero, reduce to zero; (*TECN: strumento*) to (re)set to zero.

'azzimo, a ['addzimo] *ag* unleavened ♦ *sm* unleavened bread.

azzop'pare [attsop'pare] *vt* to lame, make lame.

Az'zorre [ad'dzorre] *sfpl*: **le** ~ the Azores.

azzuf'farsi [attsuf'farsi] *vr* to come to blows.

az'zurro, a [ad'dzurro] *ag* blue ♦ *sm* (*colore*) blue; **gli** ~**i** (*SPORT*) the Italian national team.

azzur'rognolo, a [addzur'roɲɲolo] *ag* bluish.

Bb

B, b [bi] *sf o m inv* (*lettera*) B, b; ~ **come Bologna** ≈ B for Benjamin (*BRIT*), B for Baker (*US*).

BA *sigla* = *Bari*.

ba'bau *sm inv* ogre, bogey man.

bab'beo *sm* simpleton.

'babbo *sm* (*fam*) dad, daddy; **B**~ **Natale** Father Christmas.

bab'buccia, ce [bab'buttʃa] *sf* slipper; (*per neonati*) bootee.

babbu'ino *sm* baboon.

babilo'nese *ag*, *sm/f* Babylonian.

Babi'lonia *sf* Babylonia.

ba'bordo *sm* (*NAUT*) port side.

baby'sitter ['beɪbɪsɪtə*] *sm/f inv* baby-sitter.

ba'cato, a *ag* worm-eaten, rotten; (*fig: mente*) diseased; (*: persona*) corrupt.

'bacca, che *sf* berry.

baccalà *sm* dried salted cod; (*fig: peg*) dummy.

bac'cano *sm* din, clamour (*BRIT*), clamor (*US*).

bac'cello [bat'tʃɛllo] *sm* pod.

bac'chetta [bak'ketta] *sf* (*verga*) stick, rod; (*di direttore d'orchestra*) baton; (*di tamburo*) drumstick; **comandare a** ~ to rule with a rod of iron; ~ **magica** magic wand.

ba'checa, che [ba'kɛka] *sf* (*mobile*) showcase, display case; (*UNIVERSITÀ, in ufficio*) notice board (*BRIT*), bulletin board (*US*).

bacia'mano [batʃa'mano] *sm*: **fare il** ~ **a qn** to kiss sb's hand.

baci'are [ba'tʃare] *vt* to kiss; ~**rsi** *vr* to kiss (one another).

ba'cillo [ba'tʃillo] *sm* bacillus, germ.

baci'nella [batʃi'nɛlla] *sf* basin.

ba'cino [ba'tʃino] *sm* basin; (*MINERALOGIA*) field, bed; (*ANAT*) pelvis; (*NAUT*) dock; ~ **carbonifero** coalfield; ~ **di carenaggio** dry dock; ~ **petrolifero** oilfield.

'bacio ['batʃo] *sm* kiss.

'baco, chi *sm* worm; ~ **da seta** silkworm.

'bada *sf*: **tenere qn a** ~ (*tener d'occhio*) to keep an eye on sb; (*tenere a distanza*) to hold sb at bay.

ba'dare *vi* (*fare attenzione*) to take care, be careful; ~ **a** (*occuparsi di*) to look after, take care of; (*dar ascolto*) to pay attention to; **è un tipo che non bada a spese** money is no object to him; **bada ai fatti tuoi!** mind your own business!

ba'dia *sf* abbey.

ba'dile *sm* shovel.

'baffi *smpl* moustache *sg*, mustache *sg* (*US*); (*di animale*) whiskers; **leccarsi i** ~ to lick one's lips; **ridere sotto i** ~ to laugh up one's sleeve.

bagagli'aio [bagaʎ'ʎajo] *sm* luggage van (*BRIT*) *o* car (*US*); (*AUT*) boot (*BRIT*), trunk (*US*).

ba'gaglio [ba'gaʎʎo] *sm* luggage *no pl*, baggage *no pl*; **fare/disfare i** ~**i** to pack/unpack; ~ **a mano** hand luggage.

bagat'tella *sf* trifle, trifling matter.

Bag'dad *sf* Baghdad.

baggia'nata [baddʒa'nata] *sf* foolish action; **dire** ~**e** to talk nonsense.

bagli'ore [baʎ'ʎore] *sm* flash, dazzling light;

un ~ **di speranza** a sudden ray of hope.

ba'gnante [baɲ'ɲante] *sm/f* bather.

ba'gnare [baɲ'ɲare] *vt* to wet; (*inzuppare*) to soak; (*innaffiare*) to water; (*sog: fiume*) to flow through; (: *mare*) to wash, bathe; (*brindare*) to drink to, toast; ~**rsi** *vr* (*al mare*) to go swimming *o* bathing; (*in vasca*) to have a bath.

ba'gnato, a [baɲ'ɲato] *ag* wet; **era come un pulcino** ~ he looked like a drowned rat.

ba'gnino [baɲ'ɲino] *sm* lifeguard.

'bagno ['baɲɲo] *sm* bath; (*locale*) bathroom; ~**i** *smpl* (*stabilimento*) baths; **fare il** ~ to have a bath; (*nel mare*) to go swimming *o* bathing; **fare il** ~ **a qn** to give sb a bath; **mettere a** ~ to soak.

bagnoma'ria [baɲɲoma'ria] *sm*: **cuocere a** ~ to cook in a double saucepan (*BRIT*) *o* double boiler (*US*).

bagnoschi'uma [baɲɲoskj'uma] *sm inv* bubble bath.

Ba'hama [ba'ama] *sfpl*: **le** ~ the Bahamas.

Bah'rein [ba'rein] *sm*: **il** ~ Bahrain *o* Bahrein.

'baia *sf* bay.

baio'netta *sf* bayonet.

'baita *sf* mountain hut.

balaus'trata *sf* balustrade.

balbet'tare *vi* to stutter, stammer; (*bimbo*) to babble ♦ *vt* to stammer out.

bal'buzie [bal'buttsje] *sf* stammer.

balbuzi'ente [balbut'tsjɛnte] *ag* stuttering, stammering.

Bal'cani *smpl*: **i** ~ the Balkans.

bal'canico, a, ci, che *ag* Balkan.

bal'cone *sm* balcony.

baldac'chino [baldak'kino] *sm* canopy; **letto a** ~ four-poster (bed).

bal'danza [bal'dantsa] *sf* self-confidence; boldness.

'baldo, a *ag* bold, daring.

bal'doria *sf*: **fare** ~ to have a riotous time.

Bale'ari *sfpl*: **le isole** ~ the Balearic Islands.

ba'lena *sf* whale.

bale'nare *vb impers*: **balena** there's lightning ♦ *vi* to flash; **mi balenò un'idea** an idea flashed through my mind.

baleni'era *sf* (*per la caccia*) whaler, whaling ship.

ba'leno *sm* flash of lightning; **in un** ~ in a flash.

ba'lera *sf* (*locale*) dance hall; (*pista*) dance floor.

ba'lestra *sf* crossbow.

'balia *sf* wet-nurse; ~ **asciutta** nanny.

ba'lia *sf*: **in** ~ **di** at the mercy of; **essere lasciato in** ~ **di se stesso** to be left to

one's own devices.

ba'lilla *sm inv* (*STORIA*) member of Fascist youth group.

ba'listico, a, ci, che *ag* ballistic ♦ *sf* ballistics *sg*; **perito** ~ ballistics expert.

'balla *sf* (*di merci*) bale; (*fandonia*) (tall) story.

bal'labile *sm* dance number, dance tune.

bal'lare *vt, vi* to dance.

bal'lata *sf* ballad.

balla'toio *sm* (*terrazzina*) gallery.

balle'rina *sf* dancer; ballet dancer; (*scarpa*) pump; ~ **di rivista** chorus girl.

balle'rino *sm* dancer; ballet dancer.

bal'letto *sm* ballet.

'ballo *sm* dance; (*azione*) dancing *no pl*; ~ **in maschera** *o* **mascherato** fancy-dress ball; **essere in** ~ (*fig: persona*) to be involved; (: *cosa*) to be at stake; **tirare in** ~ **qc** to bring sth up, raise sth.

ballot'taggio [ballot'taddʒo] *sm* (*POL*) second ballot.

balne'are *ag* seaside *cpd*; (*stagione*) bathing.

ba'locco, chi *sm* toy.

ba'lordo, a *ag* stupid, senseless.

bal'samico, a, ci, che *ag* (*aria, brezza*) balmy; **pomata** ~**a** balsam.

'balsamo *sm* (*aroma*) balsam; (*lenimento, fig*) balm; (*per capelli*) (hair) conditioner.

'baltico, a, ci, che *ag* Baltic; **il (mar) B**~ the Baltic (Sea).

balu'ardo *sm* bulwark.

'balza ['baltsa] *sf* (*dirupo*) crag; (*di stoffa*) frill.

bal'zano, a [bal'tsano] *ag* (*persona, idea*) queer, odd.

bal'zare [bal'tsare] *vi* to bounce; (*lanciarsi*) to jump, leap; **la verità balza agli occhi** the truth of the matter is obvious.

'balzo ['baltso] *sm* bounce; jump, leap; (*del terreno*) crag; **prendere la palla al** ~ (*fig*) to seize one's opportunity.

bam'bagia [bam'badʒa] *sf* (*ovatta*) cotton wool (*BRIT*), absorbent cotton (*US*); (*cascame*) cotton waste; **tenere qn nella** ~ (*fig*) to mollycoddle sb.

bam'bina *sf vedi* **bambino**.

bambi'naia *sf* nanny, nurse(maid).

bam'bino, a *sm/f* child; **fare il** ~ to behave childishly.

bam'boccio [bam'bɔttʃo] *sm* plump child; (*pupazzo*) rag doll.

'bambola *sf* doll.

bambo'lotto *sm* male doll.

bambù *sm* bamboo.

ba'nale *ag* banal, commonplace.

banalità *sf inv* banality.

ba'nana *sf* banana.
ba'nano *sm* banana tree.
'banca, che *sf* bank; ~ **d'affari** merchant bank; ~ **(di) dati** data bank.
banca'rella *sf* stall.
ban'cario, a *ag* banking, bank *cpd* ♦ *sm* bank clerk.
banca'rotta *sf* bankruptcy; **fare** ~ to go bankrupt.
bancarotti'ere *sm* bankrupt.
ban'chetto [ban'ketto] *sm* banquet.
banchi'ere [ban'kjɛre] *sm* banker.
ban'china [ban'kina] *sf* (*di porto*) quay; (*per pedoni, ciclisti*) path; (*di stazione*) platform; ~ **cedevole** (*AUT*) soft verge (*BRIT*) o shoulder (*US*); ~ **spartitraffico** (*AUT*) central reservation (*BRIT*), median (strip) (*US*).
ban'chisa [ban'kiza] *sf* pack ice.
'banco, chi *sm* bench; (*di negozio*) counter; (*di mercato*) stall; (*di officina*) (work)bench; (*GEO, banca*) bank; **sotto** ~ (*fig*) under the counter; **tenere il** ~ (*nei giochi*) to be (the) banker; **tener** ~ (*fig*) to monopolize the conversation; **medicinali da** ~ over-the-counter medicines; ~ **di chiesa** pew; ~ **di corallo** coral reef; ~ **degli imputati** dock; ~ **del Lotto** lottery-ticket office; ~ **di prova** (*fig*) testing ground; ~ **dei testimoni** witness box (*BRIT*) o stand (*US*).
banco'giro [banko'dʒiro] *sm* credit transfer.
'Bancomat ® *sm inv* automated banking; (*tessera*) cash card.
banco'nota *sf* banknote.
'banda *sf* band; (*di stoffa*) band, stripe; (*lato, parte*) side; (*di calcolatore*) tape; ~ **perforata** punch tape.
banderu'ola *sf* (*METEOR*) weathercock, weathervane; **essere una** ~ (*fig*) to be fickle.
bandi'era *sf* flag, banner; **battere** ~ **italiana** (*nave etc*) to fly the Italian flag; **cambiare** ~ (*fig*) to change sides; ~ **di comodo** flag of convenience.
ban'dire *vt* to proclaim; (*esiliare*) to exile; (*fig*) to dispense with.
ban'dito *sm* outlaw, bandit.
bandi'tore *sm* (*di aste*) auctioneer.
'bando *sm* proclamation; (*esilio*) exile, banishment; **mettere al** ~ **qn** to exile sb; (*fig*) to freeze sb out; ~ **alle ciance!** that's enough talk!
'bandolo *sm* (*di matassa*) end; **trovare il** ~ **della matassa** (*fig*) to find the key to the problem.
Bang'kok [ban'kɔk] *sf* Bangkok.

Bangla'desh [bangla'dɛʃ] *sm*: **il** ~ Bangladesh.
bar *sm inv* bar.
'bara *sf* coffin.
ba'racca, che *sf* shed, hut; (*peg*) hovel; **mandare avanti la** ~ to keep things going; **piantare** ~ **e burattini** to throw everything up.
barac'cato, a *sm/f person living in temporary camp*.
barac'chino [barak'kino] *sm* (*chiosco*) stall; (*apparecchio*) CB radio.
barac'cone *sm* booth, stall; ~**i** *smpl* (*luna park*) funfair *sg* (*BRIT*), amusement park; **fenomeno da** ~ circus freak.
barac'copoli *sf inv* shanty town.
bara'onda *sf* hubbub, bustle.
ba'rare *vi* to cheat.
'baratro *sm* abyss.
barat'tare *vt*: ~ **qc con** to barter sth for, swap sth for.
ba'ratto *sm* barter.
ba'rattolo *sm* (*di latta*) tin; (*di vetro*) jar; (*di coccio*) pot.
'barba *sf* beard; **farsi la** ~ to shave; **farla in** ~ **a qn** (*fig*) to fool sb; **servire qn di** ~ **e capelli** (*fig*) to teach sb a lesson; **che** ~! what a bore!
barbabi'etola *sf* beetroot (*BRIT*), beet (*US*); ~ **da zucchero** sugar beet.
Bar'bados *sf sg* Barbados.
bar'barico, a, ci, che *ag* (*invasione*) barbarian; (*usanze, metodi*) barbaric.
bar'barie *sf* barbarity.
'barbaro, a *ag* barbarous ♦ *sm* barbarian; **i** B~ the Barbarians.
'barbecue ['baːbikjuː] *sm inv* barbecue.
barbi'ere *sm* barber.
barbi'turico, a, ci, che *ag* barbituric ♦ *sm* barbiturate.
bar'bone *sm* (*cane*) poodle; (*vagabondo*) tramp.
bar'buto, a *ag* bearded.
'barca, che *sf* boat; **una** ~ **di** (*fig*) heaps of, tons of; **mandare avanti la** ~ (*fig*) to keep things going; ~ **a remi** rowing boat (*BRIT*), rowboat (*US*); ~ **a vela** sailing boat (*BRIT*), sailboat (*US*).
barcai'olo *sm* boatman.
barcame'narsi *vr* (*nel lavoro*) to get by; (*a parole*) to beat about the bush.
Barcel'lona [bartʃel'lona] *sf* Barcelona.
barcol'lare *vi* to stagger.
bar'cone *sm* (*per ponti di barche*) pontoon.
ba'rella *sf* (*lettiga*) stretcher.
'Barents: il mar di ~ *sm* the Barents Sea.
ba'rese *ag* of (*o* from) Bari.
bari'centro [bari'tʃentro] *sm* centre (*BRIT*) *o*

center (*US*) of gravity.

ba'rile *sm* barrel, cask.

ba'rista, i, e *smlf* barman/barmaid; bar owner.

ba'ritono *sm* baritone.

bar'lume *sm* glimmer, gleam.

'baro *sm* (*CARTE*) cardsharp.

ba'rocco, a, chi, che *ag, sm* baroque.

ba'rometro *sm* barometer.

ba'rone *sm* baron; i ~i della medicina (*fig peg*) the top brass in the medical faculty.

baro'nessa *sf* baroness.

'barra *sf* bar; (*NAUT*) helm; (*segno grafico*) stroke.

bar'rare *vt* to bar.

barri'care *vt* to barricade.

barri'cata *sf* barricade; essere dall'altra parte della ~ (*fig*) to be on the other side of the fence.

barri'era *sf* barrier; (*GEO*) reef; la Grande B~ Corallina the Great Barrier Reef.

bar'roccio [bar'rɔttʃo] *sm* cart.

ba'ruffa *sf* scuffle; fare ~ to squabble.

barzel'letta [bardzel'letta] *sf* joke, funny story.

basa'mento *sm* (*parte inferiore, piedestallo*) base; (*TECN*) bed, base plate.

ba'sare *vt* to base, found; ~rsi *vr*: ~rsi su (*sog: fatti, prove*) to be based *o* founded on; (: *persona*) to base one's arguments on.

'basco, a, schi, sche *ag* Basque ♦ *smlf* Basque ♦ *sm* (*lingua*) Basque; (*copricapo*) beret.

bas'culla *sf* weighing machine, weighbridge.

'base *sf* base; (*fig: fondamento*) basis; (*POL*) rank and file; di ~ basic; in ~ a on the basis of, according to; in ~ a ciò ... on that basis ...; a ~ di caffè coffee-based; essere alla ~ di qc to be at the root of sth; gettare le ~i per qc to lay the basis *o* foundations for sth; avere buone ~i (*INS*) to have a sound educational background.

'baseball ['beisbɔːl] *sm* baseball.

ba'setta *sf* sideburn.

basi'lare *ag* basic, fundamental.

Basi'lea *sf* Basle.

ba'silica, che *sf* basilica.

ba'silico *sm* basil.

bas'sezza [bas'settsa] *sf* (*d'animo, di sentimenti*) baseness; (*azione*) base action.

'basso, a *ag* low; (*di statura*) short; (*meridionale*) southern ♦ *sm* bottom, lower part; (*MUS*) bass; a occhi ~i with eyes lowered; a ~ prezzo cheap; scendere da ~ to go downstairs; cadere in ~ (*fig*) to come down in the world; la ~a Italia

southern Italy; il ~ Medioevo the late Middle Ages.

basso'fondo, *pl* bassi'fondi *sm* (*GEO*) shallows *pl*; i bassifondi (della città) the seediest parts of the town.

bassorili'evo *sm* bas-relief.

bas'sotto, a *ag* squat ♦ *sm* (*cane*) dachshund.

bas'tardo, a *ag* (*animale, pianta*) hybrid, crossbreed; (*persona*) illegitimate, bastard (*peg*) ♦ *smlf* illegitimate child, bastard (*peg*); (*cane*) mongrel.

bas'tare *vi, vb impers* to be enough, be sufficient; ~ a qn to be enough for sb; ~ a se stesso to be self-sufficient; basta chiedere *o* che chieda a un vigile you have only to *o* need only ask a policeman; basti dire che ... suffice it to say that ...; basta! that's enough!, that will do!; basta così? (*al bar etc*) will that be all?; punto e basta! and that's that!

basti'an *sm*: ~ contrario awkward customer.

basti'mento *sm* ship, vessel.

basti'one *sm* bastion.

basto'nare *vt* to beat, thrash; avere l'aria di un cane bastonato to look crestfallen.

basto'nata *sf* blow (with a stick); prendere qn a ~e to give sb a good beating.

baston'cino [baston'tʃino] *sm* (*piccolo bastone*) small stick; (*TECN*) rod; (*SCI*) ski pole; ~i di pesce (*CUC*) fish fingers (*BRIT*), fish sticks (*US*).

bas'tone *sm* stick; ~i *smpl* (*CARTE*) *suit in Neapolitan pack of cards*; ~ da passeggio walking stick; mettere i ~i fra le ruote a qn to put a spoke in sb's wheel.

bat'tage [ba'taʒ] *sm inv*: ~ promozionale *o* pubblicitario publicity campaign.

bat'taglia [bat'taʎʎa] *sf* battle.

bat'taglio [bat'taʎʎo] *sm* (*di campana*) clapper; (*di porta*) knocker.

battagli'one [battaʎ'ʎone] *sm* battalion.

bat'tello *sm* boat.

bat'tente *sm* (*imposta: di porta*) wing, flap; (: *di finestra*) shutter; (*per bussare*) knocker; (*di orologio*) hammer; chiudere i ~i (*fig*) to shut up shop.

'battere *vt* to beat; (*grano*) to thresh; (*percorrere*) to scour; (*rintoccare: le ore*) to strike ♦ *vi* (*bussare*) to knock; (*urtare*): ~ contro to hit *o* strike against; (*pioggia, sole*) to beat down; (*cuore*) to beat; (*TENNIS*) to serve; ~rsi *vr* to fight; ~ le mani to clap; ~ i piedi to stamp one's feet; ~ su un argomento to hammer home an argument; ~ a macchina to type; ~ il marciapiede (*peg*) to walk the

streets, be on the game; ~ **un rigore**
(*CALCIO*) to take a penalty; ~ **in testa**
(*AUT*) to knock; **in un batter d'occhio** in
the twinkling of an eye; **senza ~ ciglio**
without batting an eyelid; **battersela** to
run off.

batte'ria *sf* battery; (*MUS*) drums *pl*; ~ **da
cucina** pots and pans *pl*.

bat'terio *sm* bacterium; ~**i** *smpl* bacteria.

batteriolo'gia [batterjolo'dʒia] *sf*
bacteriology.

bat'tesimo *sm* (*sacramento*) baptism; (*rito*)
baptism, christening; **tenere qn a ~** to be
godfather (*o* godmother) to sb.

battez'zare [batted'dzare] *vt* to baptize; to
christen.

battiba'leno *sm*: **in un ~** in a flash.

batti'becco, chi *sm* squabble.

batticu'ore *sm* palpitations *pl*; **avere il ~** to
be frightened to death.

bat'tigia [bat'tidʒa] *sf* water's edge.

batti'mano *sm* applause.

batti'panni *sm inv* carpet-beater.

battis'tero *sm* baptistry.

battis'trada *sm inv* (*di pneumatico*) tread;
(*di gara*) pacemaker.

battitap'peto *sm inv* upright vacuum
cleaner.

'battito *sm* beat, throb; ~ **cardiaco**
heartbeat; ~ **della pioggia/dell'orologio**
beating of the rain/ticking of the clock.

batti'tore *sm* (*CRICKET*) batsman;
(*BASEBALL*) batter; (*CACCIA*) beater.

batti'tura *sf* (*anche*: ~ **a macchina**) typing;
(*del grano*) threshing.

bat'tuta *sf* blow; (*di macchina da scrivere*)
stroke; (*MUS*) bar; beat; (*TEAT*) cue; (*di
caccia*) beating; (*POLIZIA*) combing,
scouring; (*TENNIS*) service; **fare una ~** to
crack a joke, make a witty remark; **aver
la ~ pronta** (*fig*) to have a ready answer;
è ancora alle prime ~e it's just started.

ba'tuffolo *sm* wad.

ba'ule *sm* trunk; (*AUT*) boot (*BRIT*), trunk
(*US*).

bau'xite [bauk'site] *sf* bauxite.

'bava *sf* (*di animale*) slaver, slobber; (*di
lumaca*) slime; (*di vento*) breath.

bava'glino [bavaʎ'ʎino] *sm* bib.

ba'vaglio [ba'vaʎʎo] *sm* gag.

bava'rese *ag*, *sm/f* Bavarian.

'bavero *sm* collar.

Bavi'era *sf* Bavaria.

ba'zar [bad'dzar] *sm inv* bazaar.

baz'zecola [bad'dzekola] *sf* trifle.

bazzi'care [battsi'kare] *vt* (*persona*) to hang
about with; (*posto*) to hang about ♦ *vi*: ~
in/con to hang about/hang about with.

be'arsi *vr*: ~ **di qc/a fare qc** to delight in
sth/in doing sth; ~ **alla vista di** to enjoy
looking at.

beati'tudine *sf* bliss.

be'ato, a *ag* blessed; (*fig*) happy; ~ **te!**
lucky you!

bebè *sm inv* baby.

bec'caccia, ce [bek'kattʃa] *sf* woodcock.

bec'care *vt* to peck; (*fig: raffreddore*) to pick
up, catch; ~**rsi** *vr* (*fig*) to squabble.

bec'cata *sf* peck.

beccheggi'are [bekked'dʒare] *vi* to
pitch.

beccherò *etc* [bekke'rɔ] *vb vedi* **beccare**.

bec'chime [bek'kime] *sm* birdseed.

bec'chino [bek'kino] *sm* gravedigger.

'becco, chi *sm* beak, bill; (*di caffettiera etc*)
spout; lip; (*fig fam*) cuckold; **mettere ~**
(*fam*) to butt in; **chiudi il ~!** (*fam*) shut
your mouth!, shut your trap!; **non ho il ~
di un quattrino** (*fam*) I'm broke.

Be'fana *sf* old woman who, according to
legend, brings children their presents at
the Epiphany; (*Epifania*) Epiphany; (*donna
brutta*): **b~** hag, witch.

---

*The **Befana** is a national holiday, falling on
the feast of the Epiphany (Jan. 6th), which
marks the end of the Christmas period. It
takes its name from an imaginary old
woman, **la Befana**, who comes down the
chimney during the night, bringing gifts to
children who have been good and leaving
coal for those who have not.*

'beffa *sf* practical joke; **farsi ~ o ~e di qn**
to make a fool of sb.

bef'fardo, a *ag* scornful, mocking.

bef'fare *vt* (*anche*: ~**rsi di**) to make a fool
of, mock.

'bega, ghe *sf* quarrel.

'begli ['beʎʎi], **'bei** *ag vedi* **bello**.

beige [bɛʒ] *ag inv* beige.

Bei'rut *sf* Beirut.

bel *ag vedi* **bello**.

be'lare *vi* to bleat.

be'lato *sm* bleating.

'belga, gi, ghe *ag*, *sm/f* Belgian.

'Belgio ['bɛldʒo] *sm*: **il ~** Belgium.

Bel'grado *sf* Belgrade.

'bella *sf vedi* **bello**.

bel'lezza [bel'lettsa] *sf* beauty; **chiudere** *o*
finire qc in ~ to finish sth with a flourish;
che ~! fantastic!; **ho pagato la ~ di
60.000 lire** I paid 60,000 lire, no less.

belli'coso, a *ag* warlike.

bellige'rante [bellidʒe'rante] *ag* belligerent.

bellim'busto *sm* dandy.

═══════════════ *PAROLA CHIAVE*

'**bello, a** (*ag: dav sm* **bel** + *C*, **bell'** + *V*, **bello** + *s impura, gn, pn, ps, x, z, pl* **bei** + *C*, **begli** + *s impura etc o V*) *ag* **1** (*oggetto, donna, paesaggio*) beautiful; (*uomo*) handsome; (*tempo*) beautiful, fine, lovely; **farsi ~ di qc** to show off about sth; **fare la ~a vita** to have an easy life; **le ~e arti** fine arts

2 (*quantità*): **una ~a cifra** a considerable sum of money; **un bel niente** absolutely nothing

3 (*rafforzativo*): **è una truffa ~a e buona!** it's a real fraud!; **oh ~a!, anche questa è ~a!** (*ironico*) that's nice!; **è bell'e finito** it's already finished

♦ *smf* (*innamorato*) sweetheart

♦ *sm* **1** (*bellezza*) beauty; (*tempo*) fine weather

2: **adesso viene il ~** now comes the best bit; **sul più ~** at the crucial point; **cosa fai di ~?** are you doing anything interesting?

♦ *sf* (*anche*: **~a copia**) fair copy; (*SPORT, CARTE*) decider

♦ *av*: **fa ~** the weather is fine, it's fine; **alla bell'e meglio** somehow or other.

bellu'nese *ag* of (*o* from) Belluno.

'**belva** *sf* wild animal.

belve'dere *sm inv* panoramic viewpoint.

benché [ben'ke] *cong* although.

'**benda** *sf* bandage; (*per gli occhi*) blindfold.

ben'dare *vt* to bandage; to blindfold.

bendis'posto, a *ag*: **~ a qn/qc** well disposed towards sb/sth.

'**bene** *av* well; (*completamente, affatto*): **è ben difficile** it's very difficult ♦ *ag inv*: **gente ~** well-to-do people ♦ *sm* good; (*COMM*) asset; **~i** *smpl* (*averi*) property *sg*, estate *sg*; **io sto ~/poco ~** I'm well/not very well; **va ~** all right; **ben più lungo/caro** much longer/more expensive; **lo spero ~** I certainly hope so; **volere un ~ dell'anima a qn** to love sb very much; **un uomo per ~** a respectable man; **fare ~ to** do the right thing; **fare ~ a** (*salute*) to be good for; **fare del ~ a qn** to do sb a good turn; **di ~ in meglio** better and better; **~i ambientali** environmental assets; **~i di consumo** consumer goods; **~i di consumo durevole** consumer durables; **~i culturali** cultural heritage; **~i immateriali** immaterial *o* intangible assets; **~i patrimoniali** fixed assets; **~i privati** private property *sg*; **~i pubblici** public property *sg*; **~i reali** tangible assets.

bene'detto, a *pp di* **benedire** ♦ *ag* blessed, holy.

bene'dire *vt* to bless; to consecrate; **l'ho mandato a farsi ~** (*fig*) I told him to go to hell.

benedizi'one [benedit'tsjone] *sf* blessing.

benedu'cato, a *ag* well-mannered.

benefat'tore, 'trice *smlf* benefactor/benefactress.

benefi'cenza [benefi'tʃɛntsa] *sf* charity.

benefici'are [benefi'tʃare] *vi*: **~ di** to benefit by, benefit from.

benefici'ario, a [benefi'tʃarjo] *ag, smlf* beneficiary.

bene'ficio [bene'fitʃo] *sm* benefit; **con ~ d'inventario** (*fig*) with reservations.

be'nefico, a, ci, che *ag* beneficial; charitable.

'**Benelux** *sm*: **il ~** Benelux, the Benelux countries.

beneme'renza [beneme'rɛntsa] *sf* merit.

bene'merito, a *ag* meritorious.

bene'placito [bene'platʃito] *sm* (*approvazione*) approval; (*permesso*) permission.

be'nessere *sm* well-being.

benes'tante *ag* well-to-do.

benes'tare *sm* consent, approval.

benevo'lenza [benevo'lɛntsa] *sf* benevolence.

be'nevolo, a *ag* benevolent.

ben'godi *sm* land of plenty.

benia'mino, a *smlf* favourite (*BRIT*), favorite (*US*).

be'nigno, a [be'ɲiɲo] *ag* kind, kindly; (*critica etc*) favourable (*BRIT*), favorable (*US*); (*MED*) benign.

benintenzio'nato, a [benintentsjo'nato] *ag* well-meaning.

benin'teso *av* of course; **~ che** *cong* provided that.

benpen'sante *smlf* conformist.

benser'vito *sm*: **dare il ~ a qn** (*sul lavoro*) to give sb the sack, fire sb; (*fig*) to send sb packing.

bensì *cong* but (rather).

benve'nuto, a *ag, sm* welcome; **dare il ~ a qn** to welcome sb.

ben'visto, a *ag*: **essere ~ (da)** to be well thought of (by).

benvo'lere *vt*: **farsi ~ da tutti** to win everybody's affection; **prendere a ~ qn/qc** to take a liking to sb/sth.

ben'zina [ben'dzina] *sf* petrol (*BRIT*), gas (*US*); **fare ~** to get petrol *o* gas; **rimanere senza ~** to run out of petrol *o* gas; **~ verde** unleaded petrol, lead-free petrol.

benzi'naio [bendzi'najo] *sm* petrol (*BRIT*) *o* gas (*US*) pump attendant.

be'one *sm* heavy drinker.

'bere *vt* to drink; (*assorbire*) to soak up; **questa volta non me la dai a** ~! I won't be taken in this time!

berga'masco, a, schi, sche *ag* of (*o* from) Bergamo.

'Bering ['beriŋ]: **il mar di** ~ *sm* the Bering Sea.

ber'lina *sf* (*AUT*) saloon (car) (*BRIT*), sedan (*US*); **mettere alla** ~ (*fig*) to hold up to ridicule.

Ber'lino *sf* Berlin; ~ **est/ovest** East/West Berlin.

ber'muda *sfpl*: **le** ~ Bermuda *sg*.

ber'muda *smpl* (*calzoncini*) Bermuda shorts.

'Berna *sf* Bern.

ber'noccolo *sm* bump; (*inclinazione*) flair.

ber'retto *sm* cap.

berrò *etc vb vedi* **bere**.

bersagli'are [bersaʎ'ʎare] *vt* to shoot at; (*colpire ripetutamente, fig*) to bombard; **bersagliato dalla sfortuna** dogged by ill fortune.

bersagli'ere [bersaʎ'ʎɛre] *sm member of rifle regiment in Italian army*.

ber'saglio [ber'saʎʎo] *sm* target.

bes'temmia *sf* curse; (*REL*) blasphemy.

bestemmi'are *vi* to curse, swear; to blaspheme ♦ *vt* to curse, swear at; to blaspheme; ~ **come un turco** to swear like a trooper.

'bestia *sf* animal; **lavorare come una** ~ to work like a dog; **andare in** ~ (*fig*) to fly into a rage; **una** ~ **rara** (*fig: persona*) an oddball; ~ **da soma** beast of burden.

besti'ale *ag* bestial, brutish; (*fam*): **fa un caldo** ~ it's terribly hot; **fa un freddo** ~ it's bitterly cold.

bestialità *sf inv* (*qualità*) bestiality; **dire/fare una** ~ **dopo l'altra** to say/do one idiotic thing after another.

besti'ame *sm* livestock; (*bovino*) cattle *pl*.

Bet'lemme *sf* Bethlehem.

betoni'era *sf* cement mixer.

'bettola *sf* (*peg*) dive.

be'tulla *sf* birch.

be'vanda *sf* drink, beverage.

bevi'tore, 'trice *sm/f* drinker.

'bevo *etc vb vedi* **bere**.

be'vuto, a *pp di* **bere** ♦ *sf* drink.

'bevvi *etc vb vedi* **bere**.

BG *sigla* = Bergamo.

BI *sigla f* = Banca d'Italia ♦ *sigla* = Biella.

bi'ada *sf* fodder.

bianche'ria [bjanke'ria] *sf* linen; ~ **intima** underwear; ~ **da donna** ladies' underwear, lingerie.

bi'anco, a, chi, che *ag* white; (*non scritto*) blank ♦ *sm* white; (*intonaco*) whitewash ♦ *sm/f* white, white man/woman; **in** ~ (*foglio, assegno*) blank; **in** ~ **e nero** (*TV, FOT*) black and white; **mangiare in** ~ to follow a bland diet; **pesce in** ~ boiled fish; **andare in** ~ (*non riuscire*) to fail; (*in amore*) to be rejected; **notte** ~**a** *o* **in** ~ sleepless night; **voce** ~**a** (*MUS*) treble (voice); **votare scheda** ~**a** to return a blank voting slip; ~ **dell'uovo** egg-white.

bianco'segno [bjanko'seɲɲo] *sm* signature to a blank document.

biancos'pino *sm* hawthorn.

biasci'care [bjaʃʃi'kare] *vt* to mumble.

biasi'mare *vt* to disapprove of, censure.

bi'asimo *sm* disapproval, censure.

'bibbia *sf* bible.

bibe'ron *sm inv* feeding bottle.

'bibita *sf* (soft) drink.

bibliogra'fia *sf* bibliography.

biblio'teca, che *sf* library; (*mobile*) bookcase.

bibliote'cario, a *sm/f* librarian.

bicame'rale *ag* (*POL*) two-chamber *cpd*.

bicarbo'nato *sm*: ~ (**di sodio**) bicarbonate (of soda).

bicchi'ere [bik'kjɛre] *sm* glass; **è (facile) come bere un bicchier d'acqua** it's as easy as pie.

bici'cletta [bitʃi'kletta] *sf* bicycle; **andare in** ~ to cycle.

bi'cipite [bi'tʃipite] *sm* bicep.

bidè *sm inv* bidet.

bi'dello, a *sm/f* (*INS*) janitor.

bi'det *sm inv* = **bidè**.

bidirezio'nale [bidirettsjo'nale] *ag* bidirectional.

bido'nare *vt* (*fam: piantare in asso*) to let down; (: *imbrogliare*) to cheat, swindle.

bido'nata *sf* (*fam*) swindle.

bi'done *sm* drum, can; (*anche*: ~ **dell'immondizia**) (dust)bin; (*fam: truffa*) swindle; **fare un** ~ **a qn** (*fam*) to let sb down; to cheat sb.

bidon'ville [bidɔ̃'vil] *sf inv* shanty town.

bi'eco, a, chi, che *ag* sinister.

bi'ella *sf* (*TECN*) connecting rod.

Bielo'russia *sf* Belarus, Belorussia.

bielo'russo, a *ag*, *sm/f* Belarussian, Belorussian.

bien'nale *ag* biennial ♦ *sf*: **la B**~ **di Venezia** the Venice Arts Festival.

---

*The **Biennale di Venezia** is an international contemporary art festival. It takes place every two years, at Giardini, and first began in 1895. In its current form it includes*

National Pavilions, with exhibits organized by the various countries taking part, an exhibition on a particular theme and a section for young artists.

bi'ennio *sm* period of two years.

bi'erre *sm/f member of the Red Brigades.*

bi'etola *sf* beet.

bifo'cale *ag* bifocal.

bi'folco, a, chi, che *sm/f* (*peg*) bumpkin, yokel.

'bifora *sf* (ARCHIT) mullioned window.

bifor'carsi *vr* to fork.

biforcazi'one [biforkat'tsjone] *sf* fork.

bifor'cuto, a *ag* (*anche fig*) forked.

biga'mia *sf* bigamy.

'bigamo, a *ag* bigamous ♦ *sm/f* bigamist.

bighello'nare [bigello'nare] *vi* to loaf (about).

bighel'lone, a [bigel'lone] *sm/f* loafer.

bigiotte'ria [bidʒotte'ria] *sf* costume jewellery (BRIT) o jewelry (US); (*negozio*) jeweller's (shop) (BRIT) o jewelry store (US) (*selling only costume jewellery*).

bigli'ardo [biʎ'ʎardo] *sm* = **biliardo**.

bigliet'taio, a [biʎʎet'tajo] *sm/f* (*nei treni*) ticket inspector; (*in autobus etc*) conductor/conductress; (CINE, TEAT) box-office attendant.

bigliette'ria [biʎʎette'ria] *sf* (*di stazione*) ticket office; booking office; (*di teatro*) box office.

bigli'etto [biʎ'ʎetto] *sm* (*per viaggi, spettacoli etc*) ticket; (*cartoncino*) card; (*anche: ~ di banca*) (bank)note; ~ **d'auguri/da visita** greetings/visiting card; ~ **d'andata e ritorno** return (BRIT) o round-trip (US) ticket; ~ **omaggio** complimentary ticket.

bignè [biɲ'ɲɛ] *sm inv* cream puff.

bigo'dino *sm* roller, curler.

bi'gotto, a *ag* over-pious ♦ *sm/f* church fiend.

bi'kini *sm inv* bikini.

bi'lancia, ce [bi'lantʃa] *sf* (*pesa*) scales *pl*; (: *di precisione*) balance; (*dello zodiaco*): **B~** Libra; **essere della B~** to be Libra; ~ **commerciale/dei pagamenti** balance of trade/payments.

bilanci'are [bilan'tʃare] *vt* (*pesare*) to weigh; (: *fig*) to weigh up; ~ **le uscite e le entrate** (COMM) to balance expenditure and revenue.

bi'lancio [bi'lantʃo] *sm* (COMM) balance (sheet); (*statale*) budget; **far quadrare il** ~ to balance the books; **chiudere il** ~ **in attivo/passivo** to make a profit/loss; **fare il** ~ **di** (*fig*) to assess; ~ **consolidato**

consolidated balance; ~ **consuntivo** (final) balance; ~ **preventivo** budget; ~ **pubblico** national budget; ~ **di verifica** trial balance.

bilate'rale *ag* bilateral.

'bile *sf* bile; (*fig*) rage, anger.

bili'ardo *sm* billiards *sg*; (*tavolo*) billiard table.

'bilico, chi *sm*: **essere in** ~ to be balanced; (*fig*) to be undecided; **tenere qn in** ~ to keep sb in suspense.

bi'lingue *ag* bilingual.

bili'one *sm* (*mille milioni*) thousand million, billion (US); (*milione di milioni*) billion (BRIT), trillion (US).

'bimbo, a *sm/f* little boy/girl.

bimen'sile *ag* fortnightly.

bimes'trale *ag* two-monthly, bimonthly.

bi'mestre *sm* two-month period; **ogni** ~ every two months.

bi'nario, a *ag* binary ♦ *sm* (railway) track *o* line; (*piattaforma*) platform; ~ **morto** dead-end track.

bi'nocolo *sm* binoculars *pl*.

bio... *prefisso* bio....

bio'chimica [bio'kimika] *sf* biochemistry.

biodegra'dabile *ag* biodegradable.

biodiversità *sf* biodiversity.

bio'etica *sf* bioethics *sg*.

bio'etico, a, ci, che *ag* bioethical.

bio'fabbrica *sf factory producing biological control agents.*

bio'fisica *sf* biophysics *sg*.

biogra'fia *sf* biography.

bio'grafico, a, ci, che *ag* biographical.

bi'ografo, a *sm/f* biographer.

biolo'gia [biolo'dʒia] *sf* biology.

bio'logico, a, ci, che [bio'lɔdʒiko] *ag* biological.

bi'ologo, a, ghi, ghe *sm/f* biologist.

bi'ondo, a *ag* blond, fair.

bi'onico, a, ci, che *ag* bionic.

biop'sia *sf* biopsy.

bio'ritmo *sm* biorhythm.

bios'fera *sf* biosphere.

bipar'tito, a *ag* (POL) two-party *cpd* ♦ *sm* (POL) two-party alliance.

'birba *sf* rascal, rogue.

bir'bante *sm* rascal, rogue.

birbo'nata *sf* naughty trick.

bir'bone, a *ag* (*bambino*) naughty ♦ *sm/f* little rascal.

biri'chino, a [biri'kino] *ag* mischievous ♦ *sm/f* scamp, little rascal.

bi'rillo *sm* skittle (BRIT), pin (US); **~i** *smpl* (*gioco*) skittles *sg* (BRIT), bowling *no pl* (US).

Bir'mania *sf*: **la** ~ Burma.

bir'mano, a *ag*, *sm/f* Burmese (*inv*).

'**biro** ® *sf inv* biro ®.

'**birra** *sf* beer; ~ **scura** stout; **a tutta** ~ (*fig*) at top speed.

birre'ria *sf* (*locale*) ≈ bierkeller; (*fabbrica*) brewery.

bis *escl, sm inv* encore ♦ *ag inv* (*treno, autobus*) relief *cpd* (*BRIT*), additional; (*numero*): **12** ~ **12a**.

bi'saccia, ce [bi'zattʃa] *sf* knapsack.

Bi'sanzio [bi'zantsjo] *sf* Byzantium.

bis'betico, a, ci, che *ag* ill-tempered, crabby.

bisbigli'are [bizbiʎ'ʎare] *vt, vi* to whisper.

bis'biglio [biz'biʎʎo] *sm* whisper; (*notizia*) rumour (*BRIT*), rumor (*US*).

bisbi'glio [bizbiʎ'ʎio] *sm* whispering.

bis'boccia, ce [biz'bɔttʃa] *sf* binge, spree; **fare** ~ to have a binge.

'**bisca, sche** *sf* gambling house.

Bis'caglia [bis'kaʎʎa] *sf*: **il golfo di** ~ the Bay of Biscay.

'**bischero** ['biskero] *sm* (*MUS*) peg; (*fam: toscano*) fool, idiot.

'**biscia, sce** ['biʃʃa] *sf* snake; ~ **d'acqua** water snake.

biscot'tato, a *ag* crisp; **fette** ~**e** rusks.

bis'cotto *sm* biscuit.

bisessu'ale *ag, sm/f* bisexual.

bises'tile *ag*: **anno** ~ leap year.

bisezi'one [biset'tsjone] *sf* dichotomy.

bis'lacco, a, chi, che *ag* odd, weird.

bis'lungo, a, ghi, ghe *ag* oblong.

biso'gnare [bizoɲ'ɲare] *vb impers*: **bisogna che tu parta/lo faccia** you'll have to go/do it; **bisogna parlargli** we'll (*o* I'll) have to talk to him ♦ *vi* (*esser utile*) to be necessary.

bi'sogno [bi'zoɲɲo] *sm* need; ~**i** *smpl* (*necessità corporali*): **fare i propri** ~**i** to relieve o.s.; **avere** ~ **di qc/di fare qc** to need sth/to do sth; **al** ~, **in caso di** ~ if need be.

biso'gnoso, a [bizoɲ'ɲoso] *ag* needy, poor; ~ **di** in need of, needing.

bi'sonte *sm* (*ZOOL*) bison.

bis'tecca, che *sf* steak, beefsteak; ~ **al sangue/ai ferri** rare/grilled steak.

bisticci'are [bistit'tʃare] *vi*, ~**rsi** *vr* to quarrel, bicker.

bis'ticcio [bis'tittʃo] *sm* quarrel, squabble; (*gioco di parole*) pun.

bistrat'tare *vt* to maltreat.

'**bisturi** *sm inv* scalpel.

bi'sunto, a *ag* very greasy.

bi'torzolo [bi'tortsolo] *sm* (*sulla testa*) bump; (*sul corpo*) lump.

'**bitter** *sm inv* bitters *pl*.

bi'tume *sm* bitumen.

bivac'care *vi* (*MIL*) to bivouac; (*fig*) to bed down.

bi'vacco, chi *sm* bivouac.

'**bivio** *sm* fork; (*fig*) dilemma.

bizan'tino, a [biddzan'tino] *ag* Byzantine.

'**bizza** ['biddza] *sf* tantrum; **fare le** ~**e** to throw a tantrum.

biz'zarro, a [bid'dzarro] *ag* bizarre, strange.

biz'zeffe [bid'dzeffe]: **a** ~ *av* in plenty, galore.

BL *sigla* = **Belluno**.

blan'dire *vt* to soothe; to flatter.

'**blando, a** *ag* mild, gentle.

blas'femo, a *ag* blasphemous ♦ *sm/f* blasphemer.

bla'sone *sm* coat of arms.

blate'rare *vi* to chatter.

'**blatta** *sf* cockroach.

blin'dare *vt* to armour (*BRIT*), armor (*US*).

blin'data *sf* (*macchina*) armoured car *o* limousine.

blin'dato, a *ag* armoured (*BRIT*), armored (*US*); **camera** ~**a** strongroom; **mezzo** ~ armoured vehicle; **porta** ~**a** reinforced door; **vita** ~**a** life amid maximum security; **vetro** ~ bulletproof glass.

bloc'care *vt* to block; (*isolare*) to isolate, cut off; (*porto*) to blockade; (*prezzi, beni*) to freeze; (*meccanismo*) to jam; ~**rsi** *vr* (*motore*) to stall; (*freni, porta*) to jam, stick; (*ascensore*) to get stuck, stop; **ha bloccato la macchina** (*AUT*) he jammed on the brakes.

bloccas'terzo [blokkas'tɛrtso] *sm* (*AUT*) steering lock.

blocche'rò *etc* [blokke'rɔ] *vb vedi* **bloccare**.

bloc'chetto [blok'ketto] *sm* notebook.

'**blocco, chi** *sm* block; (*MIL*) blockade; (*dei fitti*) restriction; (*quadernetto*) pad; (*fig: unione*) coalition; (*il bloccare*) blocking; isolating, cutting-off; blockading; freezing; jamming; **in** ~ (*nell'insieme*) as a whole; (*COMM*) in bulk; ~ **cardiaco** cardiac arrest.

bloc-'notes [blɔk'nɔt] *sm inv* notebook, notepad.

blu *ag inv, sm inv* dark blue.

bluff [blɛf] *sm inv* bluff.

bluf'fare *vi* (*anche fig*) to bluff.

'**blusa** *sf* (*camiciotto*) smock; (*camicetta*) blouse.

BMT *sigla m* = **bollettino meteorologico**.

BN *sigla* = **Benevento**.

BO *sigla* = **Bologna**.

'**boa** *sm inv* (*ZOOL*) boa constrictor; (*sciarpa*) feather boa ♦ *sf* buoy.

bo'ato *sm* rumble, roar.

bob [bɔb] *sm inv* bobsleigh.
bo'bina *sf* reel, spool; (*di pellicola*) spool; (*di film*) reel; (*ELETTR*) coil.
'bocca, che *sf* mouth; **essere di buona ~ to** be a hearty eater; (*fig*) to be easily satisfied; **essere sulla ~ di tutti** (*persona, notizia*) to be the talk of the town; **rimanere a ~ asciutta** to have nothing to eat; (*fig*) to be disappointed; **in ~ al lupo!** good luck!; **~ di leone** (*BOT*) snapdragon.
boc'caccia, ce [bok'kattʃa] *sf* (*malalingua*) gossip; (*smorfia*): **fare le ~ce** to pull faces.
boc'caglio [bok'kaʎʎo] *sm* (*TECN*) nozzle; (*di respiratore*) mouthpiece.
boc'cale *sm* jug; **~ da birra** tankard.
bocca'scena [bokkaʃ'ʃɛna] *sm inv* proscenium.
boc'cata *sf* mouthful; (*di fumo*) puff; **prendere una ~ d'aria** to go out for a breath of (fresh) air.
boc'cetta [bot'tʃetta] *sf* small bottle.
boccheggi'are [bokked'dʒare] *vi* to gasp.
boc'chino [bok'kino] *sm* (*di sigaretta, sigaro: cannella*) cigarette-holder; cigar-holder; (*di pipa, strumenti musicali*) mouthpiece.
'boccia, ce ['bottʃa] *sf* bottle; (*da vino*) decanter, carafe; (*palla di legno, metallo*) bowl; **gioco delle ~ce** bowls *sg*.
bocci'are [bot'tʃare] *vt* (*proposta, progetto*) to reject; (*INS*) to fail; (*BOCCE*) to hit.
boccia'tura [bottʃa'tura] *sf* failure.
bocci'olo [bot'tʃɔlo] *sm* bud.
'boccolo *sm* curl.
boccon'cino [bokkon'tʃino] *sm* (*pietanza deliziosa*) delicacy.
boc'cone *sm* mouthful, morsel; **mangiare un ~** to have a bite to eat.
boc'coni *av* face downwards.
Bo'emia *sf* Bohemia.
bo'emo, a *ag, sm/f* Bohemian.
bofonchi'are [bofon'kjare] *vi* to grumble.
Bogotá *sf* Bogotá.
'boia *sm inv* executioner; hangman; **fa un freddo ~** (*fam*) it's cold as hell; **mondo ~!, ~ d'un mondo ladro!** (*fam*) damn!, blast!
boi'ata *sf* botch.
boicot'taggio [boikot'taddʒo] *sm* boycott.
boicot'tare *vt* to boycott.
'bolgia, ge ['bɔldʒa] *sf* (*fig*): **c'era una tale ~ al cinema** the cinema was absolutely mobbed.
'bolide *sm* (*ASTR*) meteor; (*macchina: da corsa*) racing car (*BRIT*), race car (*US*); (: *elaborata*) performance car; **come un ~** like a flash, at top speed; **entrare/uscire come un ~** to charge in/out.
Bo'livia *sf*: **la ~** Bolivia.

bolivi'ano, a *ag, sm/f* Bolivian.
'bolla *sf* bubble; (*MED*) blister; (*COMM*) bill, receipt; **finire in una ~ di sapone** (*fig*) to come to nothing; **~ di accompagnamento** waybill; **~ di consegna** delivery note; **~ papale** papal bull.
bol'lare *vt* to stamp; (*fig*) to brand.
bol'lente *ag* boiling; boiling hot; **calmare i ~i spiriti** to sober up, calm down.
bol'letta *sf* bill; (*ricevuta*) receipt; **essere in ~** to be hard up; **~ di consegna** delivery note; **~ doganale** clearance certificate; **~ di trasporto aereo** air waybill.
bollet'tino *sm* bulletin; (*COMM*) note; **~ meteorologico** weather forecast; **~ di ordinazione** order form; **~ di spedizione** consignment note.
bol'lire *vt, vi* to boil; **qualcosa bolle in pentola** (*fig*) there's something brewing.
bol'lito *sm* (*CUC*) boiled meat.
bolli'tore *sm* (*TECN*) boiler; (*CUC: per acqua*) kettle; (: *per latte*) milk pan.
bolli'tura *sf* boiling.
'bollo *sm* stamp; **imposta di ~** stamp duty; **~ auto** road tax; **~ per patente** driving licence tax; **~ postale** postmark.
bol'lore *sm*: **dare un ~ a qc** to bring sth to the boil (*BRIT*) *o* a boil (*US*); **i ~i della gioventù** youthful enthusiasm *sg*.
Bo'logna [bo'loɲɲa] *sf* Bologna.
bolo'gnese [bolo'ɲɲese] *ag* Bolognese; **spaghetti alla ~** spaghetti bolognese.
'bomba *sf* bomb; **tornare a ~** (*fig*) to get back to the point; **sei stato una ~!** you were tremendous!; **~ atomica** atom bomb; **~ a mano** hand grenade; **~ ad orologeria** time bomb.
bombarda'mento *sm* bombardment; bombing.
bombar'dare *vt* to bombard; (*da aereo*) to bomb.
bombardi'ere *sm* bomber.
bom'betta *sf* bowler (hat) (*BRIT*), derby (*US*).
'bombola *sf* cylinder; **~ del gas** gas cylinder.
bomboni'era *sf* box of sweets (*as souvenir at weddings, first communions etc*).
bo'naccia, ce [bo'nattʃa] *sf* dead calm.
bonacci'one, a [bonat'tʃone] *ag* good-natured, easy-going ♦ *sm/f* good-natured sort.
bo'nario, a *ag* good-natured, kind.
bo'nifica, che *sf* reclamation; reclaimed land.
bo'nifico, ci *sm* (*riduzione, abbuono*) discount; (*versamento a terzi*) credit transfer.

Bonn *sf* Bonn.

bontà *sf* goodness; (*cortesia*) kindness; **aver la ~ di fare qc** to be good *o* kind enough to do sth.

'**bonus-'malus** *sm inv* ≈ no-claims bonus.

bor'bonico, a, ci, che *ag* Bourbon; (*fig*) backward, out of date.

borbot'tare *vi* to mumble; (*stomaco*) to rumble.

borbot'tio, ii *sm* mumbling; rumbling.

'**borchia** ['borkja] *sf* stud.

borda'tura *sf* (*SARTORIA*) border, trim.

bor'deaux [bor'dɔ] *sm* (*colore*) burgundy, maroon; (*vino*) Bordeaux.

bor'dello *sm* brothel.

'**bordo** *sm* (*NAUT*) ship's side; (*orlo*) edge; (*striscia di guarnizione*) border, trim; **a ~ di** (*nave, aereo*) aboard, on board; (*macchina*) in; **sul ~ della strada** at the roadside; **persona d'alto ~** (*fig*) VIP.

bor'dura *sf* border.

bor'gata *sf* hamlet; (*a Roma*) working-class suburb.

bor'ghese [bor'geze] *ag* (*spesso peg*) middle-class; bourgeois; **abito ~** civilian dress; **poliziotto in ~** plainclothes policeman.

borghe'sia [borge'zia] *sf* middle classes *pl*; bourgeoisie.

'**borgo, ghi** *sm* (*paesino*) village; (*quartiere*) district; (*sobborgo*) suburb.

'**boria** *sf* self-conceit, arrogance.

bori'oso, a *ag* arrogant.

bor'lotto *sm* kidney bean.

'**Borneo** *sm*: **il ~** Borneo.

boro'talco *sm* talcum powder.

bor'raccia, ce [bor'rattʃa] *sf* canteen, water-bottle.

'**borsa** *sf* bag; (*anche: ~ da signora*) handbag; (*ECON*): **la B~ (valori)** the Stock Exchange; **~ dell'acqua calda** hot-water bottle; **B~ merci** commodity exchange; **~ nera** black market; **~ della spesa** shopping bag; **~ di studio** grant.

borsai'olo *sm* pickpocket.

bor'seggio [bor'seddʒo] *sm* pickpocketing.

borsel'lino *sm* purse.

bor'sello *sm* gent's handbag.

bor'setta *sf* handbag.

bor'sista, i, e *smlf* (*ECON*) speculator; (*INS*) grant-holder.

bos'caglia [bos'kaʎʎa] *sf* woodlands *pl*.

boscai'olo, boscaiu'olo *sm* woodcutter; forester.

bos'chetto [bos'ketto] *sm* copse, grove.

'**bosco, schi** *sm* wood.

bos'coso, a *ag* wooded.

bos'niaco, a, ci, che *ag, smlf* Bosnian.

'**Bosnia-Erze'govina** ['bɔsnja erdze'govina] *sf*: **la ~** Bosnia-Herzegovina.

'**bossolo** *sm* cartridge case.

Bot, bot *sigla m inv vedi* **buono ordinario del Tesoro**.

bo'tanico, a, ci, che *ag* botanical ♦ *sm* botanist ♦ *sf* botany.

'**botola** *sf* trap door.

Bots'wana [bots'vana] *sm*: **il ~** Botswana.

'**botta** *sf* blow; (*rumore*) bang; **dare (un sacco di) ~e a qn** to give sb a good thrashing; **~ e risposta** (*fig*) cut and thrust.

'**botte** *sf* barrel, cask; **essere in una ~ di ferro** (*fig*) to be as safe as houses; **volere la ~ piena e la moglie ubriaca** to want to have one's cake and eat it.

bot'tega, ghe *sf* shop; (*officina*) workshop; **stare a ~ (da qn)** to serve one's apprenticeship (with sb); **le B~ghe Oscure** *headquarters of the P.D.S.*

botte'gaio, a *smlf* shopkeeper.

botte'ghino [botte'gino] *sm* ticket office; (*del lotto*) public lottery office.

bot'tiglia [bot'tiʎʎa] *sf* bottle.

bottiglie'ria [bottiʎʎe'ria] *sf* wine shop.

bot'tino *sm* (*di guerra*) booty; (*di rapina, furto*) loot; **fare ~ di qc** (*anche fig*) to make off with sth.

'**botto** *sm* bang; crash; **di ~** suddenly; **d'un ~** (*fam*) in a flash.

bot'tone *sm* button; (*BOT*) bud; **stanza dei ~i** control room; (*fig*) nerve centre; **attaccare (un) ~ a *o* con qn** to buttonhole sb; **botton d'oro** buttercup.

bo'vino, a *ag* bovine; **~i** *smpl* cattle.

box [bɔks] *sm inv* (*per cavalli*) horsebox; (*per macchina*) lock-up; (*per macchina da corsa*) pit; (*per bambini*) playpen.

boxe [bɔks] *sf* boxing.

'**boxer** ['bɔkser] *sm inv* (*cane*) boxer ♦ *smpl* (*mutande*): **un paio di ~** a pair of boxer shorts.

'**bozza** ['bɔttsa] *sf* draft; (*TIP*) proof; **~ di stampa/impaginata** galley/page proof.

boz'zetto [bot'tsetto] *sm* sketch.

'**bozzolo** ['bɔttsolo] *sm* cocoon.

BR *sigla fpl* = **Brigate Rosse** ♦ *sigla* = Brindisi.

'**braca, che** *sf* (*gamba di pantalone*) trouser leg; **~che** *sfpl* (*fam*) trousers, pants (*US*); (*mutandoni*) drawers; **calare le ~che** (*fig fam*) to chicken out.

brac'care *vt* to hunt.

brac'cetto [brat'tʃetto] *sm*: **a ~** arm in arm.

bracche'rò *etc* [brakke'rɔ] *vb vedi* **braccare**.

bracci'ale [brat'tʃale] *sm* bracelet; (*distintivo*) armband.

braccia'letto [brattʃa'letto] *sm* bracelet,

bangle.

bracci'ante [brat'tʃante] *sm* (*AGR*) day labourer.

bracci'ata [brat'tʃata] *sf* armful; (*nel nuoto*) stroke.

'braccio ['brattʃo] *sm* (*pl(f*) **braccia**: *ANAT*) arm; (*pl(m*) **bracci**: *di gru, fiume*) arm; (*: di edificio*) wing; **camminare sotto** ~ to walk arm in arm; **è il suo** ~ **destro** he's his right-hand man; ~ **di ferro** (*anche fig*) trial of strength; ~ **di mare** sound.

bracci'olo [brat'tʃɔlo] *sm* (*appoggio*) arm.

'bracco, chi *sm* hound.

bracconi'ere *sm* poacher.

'brace ['bratʃe] *sf* embers *pl*.

braci'ere [bra'tʃɛre] *sm* brazier.

braci'ola [bra'tʃɔla] *sf* (*CUC*) chop.

'bradipo *sm* (*ZOOL*) sloth.

'brado, a *ag*: **allo stato** ~ in the wild *o* natural state.

'brama *sf*: ~ (**di/di fare**) longing (for/to do), yearning (for/to do).

bra'mare *vt*: ~ (**qc/di fare qc**) to long (for sth/to do sth), yearn (for sth/to do sth).

bramo'sia *sf*: ~ (**di**) longing (for), yearning (for).

'branca, che *sf* branch.

'branchia ['brankja] *sf* (*ZOOL*) gill.

'branco, chi *sm* (*di cani, lupi*) pack; (*di uccelli, pecore*) flock; (*peg: di persone*) gang, pack.

branco'lare *vi* to grope, feel one's way.

'branda *sf* camp bed.

bran'dello *sm* scrap, shred; **a** ~**i** in tatters, in rags; **fare a** ~**i** to tear to shreds.

bran'dina *sf* camp bed (*BRIT*), cot (*US*).

bran'dire *vt* to brandish.

'brano *sm* piece; (*di libro*) passage.

bra'sare *vt* to braise.

bra'sato *sm* braised beef.

Bra'sile *sm*: **il** ~ Brazil.

Bra'silia *sf* Brasilia.

brasili'ano, a *ag, sm/f* Brazilian.

bra'vata *sf* (*azione spavalda*) act of bravado.

'bravo, a *ag* (*abile*) clever, capable, skilful; (*buono*) good, honest; (*: bambino*) good; (*coraggioso*) brave; ~! well done!; (*al teatro*) bravo!; **su da** ~! (*fam*) there's a good boy!; **mi sono fatto le mie** ~**e 8 ore di lavoro** I put in a full 8 hours' work.

bra'vura *sf* cleverness, skill.

'breccia, ce ['brettʃa] *sf* breach; **essere sulla** ~ (*fig*) to be going strong; **fare** ~ **nell'animo** *o* **nel cuore di qn** to find the way to sb's heart.

'Brema *sf* Bremen.

bre'saola *sf* kind of dried salted beef.

bresci'ano, a [breʃ'ʃano] *ag* of (*o* from) Brescia.

Bre'tagna [bre'tanɲa] *sf*: **la** ~ Brittany.

bre'tella *sf* (*AUT*) link; ~**e** *sfpl* braces.

'bret(t)one *ag, sm/f* Breton.

'breve *ag* brief, short; **in** ~ in short; **per farla** ~ to cut a long story short; **a** ~ (*COMM*) short-term.

brevet'tare *vt* to patent.

bre'vetto *sm* patent; ~ **di pilotaggio** pilot's licence (*BRIT*) *o* license (*US*).

brevità *sf* brevity.

'brezza ['breddza] *sf* breeze.

'bricco, chi *sm* jug; ~ **del caffè** coffeepot.

bricco'nata *sf* mischievous trick.

bric'cone, a *sm/f* rogue, rascal.

'briciola ['britʃola] *sf* crumb.

'briciolo ['britʃolo] *sm* (*specie fig*) bit.

bridge [bridʒ] *sm* bridge.

'briga, ghe *sf* (*fastidio*) trouble, bother; **attaccar** ~ to start a quarrel; **pigliarsi la** ~ **di fare qc** to take the trouble to do sth.

brigadi'ere *sm* (*dei carabinieri etc*) ≈ sergeant.

bri'gante *sm* bandit.

bri'gata *sf* (*MIL*) brigade; (*gruppo*) group, party; **le B**~**e Rosse** (*POL*) the Red Brigades.

briga'tismo *sm* phenomenon of the Red Brigades.

briga'tista, i, e *sm/f* (*POL*) member of the Red Brigades.

'briglia ['briʎʎa] *sf* rein; **a** ~ **sciolta** at full gallop; (*fig*) at full speed.

bril'lante *ag* bright; (*anche fig*) brilliant; (*che luccica*) shining ♦ *sm* diamond.

brillan'tina *sf* brilliantine.

bril'lare *vi* to shine; (*mina*) to blow up ♦ *vt* (*mina*) to set off.

'brillo, a *ag* merry, tipsy.

'brina *sf* hoarfrost.

brin'dare *vi*: ~ **a qn/qc** to drink to *o* toast sb/sth.

'brindisi *sm inv* toast.

'brio *sm* liveliness, go.

bri'oche [bri'ɔʃ] *sf inv* brioche (bun).

bri'oso, a *ag* lively.

'briscola *sf* type of card game; (*seme vincente*) trump(s); (*carta*) trump card.

bri'tannico, a, ci, che *ag* British ♦ *sm/f* Briton; **i B**~**ci** the British *pl*.

'brivido *sm* shiver; (*di ribrezzo*) shudder; (*fig*) thrill; **racconti del** ~ suspense stories.

brizzo'lato, a [brittso'lato] *ag* (*persona*) going grey; (*barba, capelli*) greying.

'brocca, che *sf* jug.

broc'cato *sm* brocade.

broccolo – buffone

'**broccolo** sm broccoli no pl.
bro'daglia [bro'daʎʎa] sf (peg) dishwater.
'**brodo** sm broth; (per cucinare) stock; ~
  ristretto consommé; **lasciare (cuocere) qn
  nel suo** ~ to let sb stew (in his own
  juice); **tutto fa** ~ every little bit helps.
'**broglio** ['brɔʎʎo] sm: ~ **elettorale**
  gerrymandering; **~i** smpl (DIR)
  malpractices.
'**bromo** sm (CHIM) bromine.
bron'chite [bron'kite] sf (MED) bronchitis.
'**broncio** ['brontʃo] sm sulky expression;
  tenere il ~ to sulk.
'**bronco, chi** sm bronchial tube.
bronto'lare vi to grumble; (tuono, stomaco)
  to rumble.
bronto'lio sm grumbling, mumbling.
bronto'lone, a ag grumbling ♦ sm/f
  grumbler.
bron'zina [bron'dzina] sf (TECN) bush.
'**bronzo** ['brondzo] sm bronze; **che faccia di
  ~!** what a brass neck!
bross. abbr = **in brossura**.
bros'sura sf: **in** ~ (libro) limpback.
bru'care vt to browse on, nibble at.
brucherà etc [bruke'ra] vb vedi **brucare**.
bruciacchi'are [brutʃak'kjare] vt to singe,
  scorch; **~rsi** vr to become singed o
  scorched.
brucia'pelo [brutʃa'pelo]: **a** ~ av point-
  blank.
bruci'are [bru'tʃare] vt to burn; (scottare) to
  scald ♦ vi to burn; ~ **gli avversari** (SPORT, fig)
  to leave the rest of the field behind; ~ **le
  tappe** o **i tempi** (SPORT, fig) to shoot ahead;
  ~rsi la carriera to put an end to one's career.
brucia'tore [brutʃa'tore] sm burner.
brucia'tura [brutʃa'tura] sf (atto) burning no
  pl; (segno) burn; (scottatura) scald.
bruci'ore [bru'tʃore] sm burning o smarting
  sensation.
'**bruco, chi** sm grub; (di farfalla) caterpillar.
'**brufolo** sm pimple, spot.
brughi'era [bru'gjɛra] sf heath, moor.
bruli'care vi to swarm.
bruli'chio, ii [bruli'kio] sm swarming.
'**brullo, a** ag bare, bleak.
'**bruma** sf mist.
'**bruno, a** ag brown, dark; (persona) dark(-
  haired).
brusca'mente av (frenare, fermarsi)
  suddenly; (rispondere, reagire) sharply.
'**brusco, schi, sche** ag (sapore) sharp;
  (modi, persona) brusque, abrupt;
  (movimento) abrupt, sudden.
bru'sio sm buzz, buzzing.
bru'tale ag brutal.
brutalità sf inv brutality.

'**bruto, a** ag (forza) brute cpd ♦ sm brute.
'**brutta** sf vedi **brutto**.
brut'tezza [brut'tettsa] sf ugliness.
'**brutto, a** ag ugly; (cattivo) bad; (malattia,
  strada, affare) nasty, bad ♦ sm: **guardare qn
  di** ~ to give sb a nasty look ♦ sf rough
  copy, first draft; ~ **tempo** bad weather;
  passare un ~ **quarto d'ora** to have a nasty
  time of it; **vedersela ~a** (per un attimo) to
  have a nasty moment; (per un periodo) to
  have a bad time of it.
brut'tura sf (cosa brutta) ugly thing;
  (sudiciume) filth; (azione meschina) mean
  action.
Bru'xelles [bry'sɛl] sf Brussels.
BS sigla = **Brescia**.
B.T. abbr (= bassa tensione) LT ♦ sigla m inv
  = **buono del Tesoro**.
btg abbr = **battaglione**.
Btp sigla m (= buono del Tesoro poliennale,
  vedi **buono**.
bub'bone sm swelling.
'**buca, che** sf hole; (avvallamento) hollow; ~
  delle lettere letterbox.
buca'neve sm inv snowdrop.
bu'care vt (forare) to make a hole (o holes)
  in; (pungere) to pierce; (biglietto) to
  punch; **~rsi** vr (con eroina) to mainline; ~
  una gomma to have a puncture; **avere le
  mani bucate** (fig) to be a spendthrift.
'**Bucarest** sf Bucharest.
bu'cato sm (operazione) washing; (panni)
  wash, washing.
'**buccia, ce** ['buttʃa] sf skin, peel; (corteccia)
  bark.
bucherel'lare [bukerel'lare] vt to riddle
  with holes.
bucherò etc [buke'rɔ] vb vedi **bucare**.
'**buco, chi** sm hole; **fare un** ~ **nell'acqua** to
  fail, draw a blank; **farsi un** ~ (fam:
  drogarsi) to have a fix; ~ **nero** (anche fig)
  black hole.
'**Budapest** sf Budapest.
'**Budda** sm inv Buddha.
bud'dismo sm Buddhism.
bu'dello sm intestine; (fig: tubo) tube;
  (vicolo) alley; **~a** sfpl bowels, guts.
bu'dino sm pudding.
'**bue**, pl **bu'oi** sm ox; (anche: **carne di** ~)
  beef; **uovo all'occhio di** ~ fried egg.
Bu'enos 'Aires sf Buenos Aires.
'**bufalo** sm buffalo.
bu'fera sf storm.
buf'fetto sm flick.
'**buffo, a** ag funny; (TEAT) comic.
buffo'nata sf (azione) prank, jest; (parola)
  jest.
buf'fone sm buffoon.

bugge'rare [buddʒe'rare] *vt* to swindle, cheat.

bu'gia, 'gie [bu'dʒia] *sf* lie; (*candeliere*) candleholder.

bugi'ardo, a [bu'dʒardo] *ag* lying, deceitful ♦ *smf* liar.

bugi'gattolo [budʒi'gattolo] *sm* poky little room.

'buio, a *ag* dark ♦ *sm* dark, darkness; **fa ~ pesto** it's pitch-dark.

'bulbo *sm* (*BOT*) bulb; **~ oculare** eyeball.

Bulga'ria *sf*: **la ~** Bulgaria.

'bulgaro, a *ag, smf, sm* Bulgarian.

buli'mia *sf* bulimia.

'bullo *sm* (*persona*) tough.

bul'lone *sm* bolt.

bu'oi *smpl di* **bue**.

buona'fede *sf* good faith.

buon'anima *sf* = **buon'anima**; *vedi* **anima**.

buona'notte *escl* good night! ♦ *sf*: **dare la ~ a** to say good night to.

buona'sera *escl* good evening!

buoncos'tume *sm* public morality; **la (squadra del) ~** (*POLIZIA*) the vice squad.

buondì *escl* hello!

buongi'orno [bwon'dʒorno] *escl* good morning (*o afternoon*)!

buon'grado *av*: **di ~** willingly.

buongus'taio, a *smf* gourmet.

buon'gusto *sm* good taste.

═══════════════════ *PAROLA CHIAVE*

bu'ono, a (*ag*: *dav sm* **buon** + *C o V*, **buono** + *s impura, gn, pn, ps, x, z*; *dav sf* **buon'** + *V*) *ag* **1** (*gen*) good; **un buon pranzo/ ristorante** a good lunch/restaurant; (**stai**) **~!** behave!; **che ~!** (*cibo*) this is nice!

2 (*benevolo*): **~ (con)** good (to), kind (to)

3 (*giusto, valido*) right; **al momento ~** at the right moment

4 (*adatto*): **~ a/da** fit for/to; **essere ~ a nulla** to be no good *o* use at anything

5 (*auguri*): **buon compleanno!** happy birthday!; **buon divertimento!** have a nice time!; **~a fortuna!** good luck!; **buon riposo!** sleep well!; **buon viaggio!** have a good trip!

6: **ad ogni buon conto** in any case; **tante ~e cose!** all the best!; **di buon cuore** (*persona*) goodhearted; **di buon grado** willingly; **le ~e maniere** good manners; **di buon mattino** early in the morning; **a buon mercato** cheap; **di buon'ora** early; **mettere una ~a parola** to put in a good word; **di buon passo** at a good pace; **buon pro ti faccia!** much good may it do you!; **buon senso** common sense; **la ~a società** the upper classes; **una ~a volta** once and

for all; **alla ~a** *ag* simple ♦ *av* in a simple way, without any fuss; **un tipo alla ~a** an easy-going sort ♦ *smf*: **essere un ~/una ~a** to be a good person; **~ a nulla** good for nothing; **i ~i e i cattivi** (*in storia, film*) the goodies and the baddies; **accetterà con le ~e o con le cattive** one way or another he's going to agree to it ♦ *sm* **1** (*bontà*) goodness, good

2 (*COMM*) voucher, coupon; **~ d'acquisto** credit note; **~ di cassa** cash voucher; **~ di consegna** delivery note; **~ fruttifero** interest-bearing bond; **~ ordinario del Tesoro** short-term Treasury bond; **~ postale fruttifero** interest-bearing bond (*issued by Italian Post Office*); **~ del Tesoro** Treasury bill.

buon'senso *sm* = **buon senso**.

buontem'pone, a *smf* jovial person.

buonu'scita [bwonuʃ'ʃita] *sf* (*INDUSTRIA*) golden handshake; (*di affitti*) sum paid for the relinquishing of tenancy rights.

buratti'naio *sm* puppeteer, puppet master.

burat'tino *sm* puppet.

'burbero, a *ag* surly, gruff.

'burla *sf* prank, trick.

bur'lare *vt*: **~ qc/qn, ~rsi di qc/qn** to make fun of sth/sb.

bu'rocrate *sm* bureaucrat.

buro'cratico, a, ci, che *ag* bureaucratic.

burocra'zia [burokrat'tsia] *sf* bureaucracy.

bur'rasca, sche *sf* storm.

burras'coso, a *ag* stormy.

'burro *sm* butter.

bur'rone *sm* ravine.

bus'care *vt* (*anche*: **~rsi**: *raffreddore*) to get, catch; **buscarle** (*fam*) to get a hiding.

buscherò *etc* [buske'rɔ] *vb vedi* **buscare**.

bus'sare *vi* to knock; **~ a quattrini** (*fig*) ask for money.

'bussola *sf* compass; **perdere la ~** (*fig*) to lose one's bearings.

'busta *sf* (*da lettera*) envelope; (*astuccio*) case; **in ~ aperta/chiusa** in an unsealed/ sealed envelope; **~ paga** pay packet.

busta'rella *sf* bribe, backhander.

bus'tina *sf* (*piccola busta*) envelope; (*di cibi, farmaci*) sachet; (*MIL*) forage cap; **~ di tè** tea bag.

'busto *sm* bust; (*indumento*) corset, girdle; **a mezzo ~** (*fotografia, ritratto*) half-length.

bu'tano *sm* butane.

but'tare *vt* to throw; (*anche*: **~ via**) to throw away; **~rsi** *vr* (*saltare*) to jump; **~ giù** (*scritto*) to scribble down, dash off;·

(*cibo*) to gulp down; (*edificio*) to pull down, demolish; (*pasta, verdura*) to put into boiling water; **ho buttato là una frase** I mentioned it in passing; **buttiamoci!** (*saltiamo*) let's jump!; (*rischiamo*) let's have a go!; **~rsi dalla finestra** to jump out of the window.

'**buzzo** ['buddzo] *sm* (*fam: pancia*) belly, paunch; **di ~ buono** (*con impegno*) with a will.

Cc

C, c [tʃi] *sf o m inv* (*lettera*) C, c ♦ *abbr* (*GEO*) = **capo**; (= *Celsius, centigrado*) C; (= *conto*) a/c; **~ come Como** ≈ C for Charlie.

CA *sigla* = *Cagliari*.

c.a. *abbr* (*ELETTR*) *vedi* **corrente alternata**; (*COMM*) = **corrente anno**.

cab. *abbr* = *cablogramma*.

caba'ret [kaba'rɛ] *sm inv* cabaret.

ca'bina *sf* (*di nave*) cabin; (*da spiaggia*) beach hut; (*di autocarro, treno*) cab; (*di aereo*) cockpit; (*di ascensore*) cage; **~ di proiezione** (*CINE*) projection booth; **~ di registrazione** recording booth; **~ telefonica** callbox, (tele)phone box *o* booth.

cabi'nato *sm* cabin cruiser.

ca'blaggio [ka'bladdʒo] *sm* wiring.

cablo'gramma *sm* cable(gram).

ca'cao *sm* cocoa.

'**cacca** *sf* (*fam: anche fig*) shit (*!*).

'**caccia** ['kattʃa] *sf* hunting; (*con fucile*) shooting; (*inseguimento*) chase; (*cacciagione*) game ♦ *sm inv* (*aereo*) fighter; (*nave*) destroyer; **andare a ~** to go hunting; **andare a ~ di guai** to be asking for trouble; **~ grossa** big-game hunting; **~ all'uomo** manhunt.

cacciabombardi'ere [kattʃabombar'djɛre] *sm* fighter-bomber.

cacciagi'one [kattʃa'dʒone] *sf* game.

cacci'are [kat'tʃare] *vt* to hunt; (*mandar via*) to chase away; (*ficcare*) to shove, stick ♦ *vi* to hunt; **~rsi** *vr* (*fam: mettersi*): **~rsi tra la folla** to plunge into the crowd; **dove s'è cacciata la mia borsa?** where has my bag got to?; **~rsi nei guai** to get into trouble; **~ fuori qc** to whip *o* pull sth out; **~ un**

urlo to let out a yell.

caccia'tora [kattʃa'tora] *sf* (*giacca*) hunting jacket; (*CUC*): **pollo** *etc* **alla ~** chicken *etc* chasseur.

caccia'tore [kattʃa'tore] *sm* hunter; **~ di frodo** poacher; **~ di dote** fortune-hunter.

cacciatorpedini'ere [kattʃatorpedi'njɛre] *sm* destroyer.

caccia'vite [kattʃa'vite] *sm inv* screwdriver.

cache'mire [kaʃ'mir] *sm inv* cashmere.

ca'chet [ka'ʃɛ] *sm* (*MED*) capsule; (*: compressa*) tablet; (*compenso*) fee; (*colorante per capelli*) rinse.

'**cachi** ['kaki] *sm inv* (*albero, frutto*) persimmon; (*colore*) khaki ♦ *ag inv* khaki.

'**cacio** ['katʃo] *sm* cheese; **essere come il ~ sui maccheroni** (*fig*) to turn up at the right moment.

'**cactus** *sm inv* cactus.

ca'davere *sm* (dead) body, corpse.

cada'verico, a, ci, che *ag* (*fig*) deathly pale.

'**caddi** *etc vb vedi* **cadere**.

ca'dente *ag* falling; (*casa*) tumbledown; (*persona*) decrepit.

ca'denza [ka'dɛntsa] *sf* cadence; (*andamento ritmico*) rhythm; (*MUS*) cadenza.

ca'dere *vi* to fall; (*denti, capelli*) to fall out; (*tetto*) to fall in; **questa gonna cade bene** this skirt hangs well; **lasciar ~** (*anche fig*) to drop; **~ dal sonno** to be falling asleep on one's feet; **~ ammalato** to fall ill; **~ dalle nuvole** (*fig*) to be taken aback.

ca'detto *sm* cadet.

cadrò *etc vb vedi* **cadere**.

ca'duto, a *ag* (*morto*) dead ♦ *sm* dead soldier ♦ *sf* fall; **monumento ai ~i** war memorial; **~a di temperatura** drop in temperature; **la ~a dei capelli** hair loss; **~a del sistema** (*INFORM*) system failure.

caffè *sm inv* coffee; (*locale*) café; **~ corretto** coffee with liqueur; **~ in grani** coffee beans; **~ macchiato** coffee with a dash of milk; **~ macinato** ground coffee.

caffe'ina *sf* caffeine.

caffel'latte *sm inv* white coffee.

caffette'ria *sf* coffee shop.

caffetti'era *sf* coffeepot.

ca'fone *sm* (*contadino*) peasant; (*peg*) boor.

cagio'nare [kadʒo'nare] *vt* to cause, be the cause of.

cagio'nevole [kadʒo'nevole] *ag* delicate, weak.

cagli'are [kaʎ'ʎare] *vi* to curdle.

cagliari'tano, a [kaʎʎari'tano] *ag* of (*o* from) Cagliari.

'**cagna** ['kaɲɲa] *sf* (*ZOOL, peg*) bitch.

ca'gnara [kaɲ'ɲara] *sf* (*fig*) uproar.

ca'gnesco, a, schi, sche [kaɲ'ɲesko] *ag* (*fig*): guardare qn in ~ to scowl at sb.

CAI *sigla m* = *Club Alpino Italiano.*

'Cairo *sm*: il ~ Cairo.

cala'brese *ag, smf* Calabrian.

cala'brone *sm* hornet.

Cala'hari [kala'ari]: il Deserto di ~ *sm* the Kalahari Desert.

cala'maio *sm* inkpot; inkwell.

cala'maro *sm* squid.

cala'mita *sf* magnet.

calamità *sf inv* calamity, disaster; ~ naturale natural disaster.

ca'lare *vt* (*far discendere*) to lower; (*MAGLIA*) to decrease ♦ *vi* (*discendere*) to go (*o* come) down; (*tramontare*) to set, go down; ~ di peso to lose weight.

ca'lata *sf* (*invasione*) invasion.

'calca *sf* throng, press.

cal'cagno [kal'kaɲɲo] *sm* heel.

cal'care *sm* limestone ♦ *vt* (*premere coi piedi*) to tread, press down; (*premere con forza*) to press down; (*mettere in rilievo*) to stress; ~ la mano to overdo it, exaggerate; ~ le scene (*fig*) to be on the stage; ~ le orme di qn (*fig*) to follow in sb's footsteps.

'calce ['kaltʃe] *sm*: in ~ at the foot of the page ♦ *sf* lime; ~ viva quicklime.

calces'truzzo [kaltʃes'truttso] *sm* concrete.

calcherò *etc* [kalke'rɔ] *vb vedi* calcare.

calci'are [kal'tʃare] *vt*, *vi* to kick.

calcia'tore [kaltʃa'tore] *sm* footballer (*BRIT*), (football) player.

cal'cina [kal'tʃina] *sf* (*lime*) mortar.

calci'naccio [kaltʃi'nattʃo] *sm* flake of plaster.

'calcio ['kaltʃo] *sm* (*pedata*) kick; (*sport*) football, soccer; (*di pistola, fucile*) butt; (*CHIM*) calcium; ~ d'angolo (*SPORT*) corner (kick); ~ di punizione (*SPORT*) free kick.

'calco, chi *sm* (*ARTE*) casting, moulding (*BRIT*), molding (*US*); cast, mo(u)ld.

calco'lare *vt* to calculate, work out, reckon; (*ponderare*) to weigh (up).

calcola'tore, 'trice *ag* calculating ♦ *sm* calculator; (*fig*) calculating person ♦ *sf* (*anche:* macchina calcolatrice) calculator; ~ digitale digital computer; ~ elettronico computer; ~ da tavolo desktop computer.

'calcolo *sm* (*anche MAT*) calculation; (*infinitesimale etc*) calculus; (*MED*) stone; fare il ~ di qc to work sth out; fare i propri ~i (*fig*) to weigh the pros and cons; per ~ out of self-interest.

cal'daia *sf* boiler.

caldar'rosta *sf* roast chestnut.

caldeggi'are [kalded'dʒare] *vt* to support.

'caldo, a *ag* warm; (*molto* ~) hot; (*fig: appassionato*) keen ♦ *sm* heat; ho ~ I'm warm; I'm hot; fa ~ it's warm; it's hot; non mi fa né ~ né freddo I couldn't care less; a ~ (*fig*) in the heat of the moment.

caleidos'copio *sm* kaleidoscope.

calen'dario *sm* calendar.

ca'lende *sfpl* calends; rimandare qc alle ~ greche to put sth off indefinitely.

ca'lesse *sm* gig.

'calibro *sm* (*di arma*) calibre, bore; (*TECN*) callipers *pl*; (*fig*) calibre; di grosso ~ (*fig*) prominent.

'calice ['kalitʃe] *sm* goblet; (*REL*) chalice.

Cali'fornia *sf* California.

californi'ano, a *ag* Californian.

ca'ligine [ka'lidʒine] *sf* fog; (*mista con fumo*) smog.

calligra'fia *sf* (*scrittura*) handwriting; (*arte*) calligraphy.

'callo *sm* callus; (*ai piedi*) corn; fare il ~ a qc to get used to sth.

'calma *sf* calm; faccia con ~ take your time.

cal'mante *sm* sedative, tranquillizer.

cal'mare *vt* to calm; (*lenire*) to soothe; ~rsi *vr* to grow calm, calm down; (*vento*) to abate; (*dolori*) to ease.

calmi'ere *sm* controlled price.

'calmo, a *ag* calm, quiet.

'calo *sm* (*COMM: di prezzi*) fall; (*: di volume*) shrinkage; (*: di peso*) loss.

ca'lore *sm* warmth; (*intenso, FISICA*) heat; essere in ~ (*ZOOL*) to be on heat.

calo'ria *sf* calorie.

calo'rifero *sm* radiator.

calo'roso, a *ag* warm; essere ~ not to feel the cold.

calpes'tare *vt* to tread on, trample on; "è vietato ~ l'erba" "keep off the grass".

ca'lunnia *sf* slander; (*scritta*) libel.

calunni'are *vt* to slander.

cal'vario *sm* (*fig*) affliction, cross.

cal'vizie [kal'vittsje] *sf* baldness.

'calvo, a *ag* bald.

'calza ['kaltsa] *sf* (*da donna*) stocking; (*da uomo*) sock; fare la ~ to knit; ~e di nailon nylons, (nylon) stockings.

calza'maglia [kaltsa'maʎʎa] *sf* tights *pl*; (*per danza, ginnastica*) leotard.

cal'zare [kal'tsare] *vt* (*scarpe, guanti: mettersi*) to put on; (*: portare*) to wear ♦ *vi* to fit; ~ a pennello to fit like a glove.

calza'tura [kaltsa'tura] *sf* footwear.

calzaturi'ficio [kaltsaturi'fitʃo] *sm* shoe *o* footwear factory.

cal'zetta [kal'tsetta] *sf* ankle sock; **una mezza ~** (*fig*) a nobody.

calzet'tone [kaltset'tone] *sm* heavy knee-length sock.

cal'zino [kal'tsino] *sm* sock.

calzo'laio [kaltso'lajo] *sm* shoemaker; (*che ripara scarpe*) cobbler.

calzole'ria [kaltsole'ria] *sf* (*negozio*) shoe shop; (*arte*) shoemaking.

calzon'cini [kaltson'tʃini] *smpl* shorts; **~ da bagno** (swimming) trunks.

cal'zone [kal'tsone] *sm* trouser leg; (*CUC*) savoury turnover made with pizza dough; **~i** *smpl* trousers (*BRIT*), pants (*US*).

camale'onte *sm* chameleon.

cambi'ale *sf* bill (of exchange); (*pagherò cambiario*) promissory note; **~ di comodo** *o* **di favore** accommodation bill.

cambia'mento *sm* change.

cambi'are *vt* to change; (*modificare*) to alter, change; (*barattare*): **~ (qc con qn/ qc)** to exchange (sth with sb/for sth) ♦ *vi* to change, alter; **~rsi** *vr* (*variare abito*) to change; **~ casa** to move (house); **~ idea** to change one's mind; **~ treno** to change trains; **~ le carte in tavola** (*fig*) to change one's tune; **~ (l')aria in una stanza** to air a room; **è ora di ~ aria** (*andarsene*) it's time to move on.

cambiava'lute *sm inv* exchange office.

'cambio *sm* change; (*modifica*) alteration, change; (*scambio, COMM*) exchange; (*corso dei cambi*) rate (of exchange); (*TECN, AUT*) gears *pl*; **in ~ di** in exchange for; **dare il ~ a qn** to take over from sb; **fare il** *o* **un ~** to change (over); **~ a termine** (*COMM*) forward exchange.

'Cambital *sigla m* = Ufficio Italiano dei Cambi.

Cam'bogia [kam'bɔdʒa] *sf*: **la ~** Cambodia.

cambogi'ano, a [kambo'dʒano] *ag, smlf* Cambodian.

cam'busa *sf* storeroom.

'camera *sf* room; (*anche*: **~ da letto**) bedroom; (*POL*) chamber, house; **~ ardente** mortuary chapel; **~ d'aria** inner tube; (*di pallone*) bladder; **~ blindata** strongroom; **C~ di Commercio** Chamber of Commerce; **C~ dei Deputati** Chamber of Deputies, ≈ House of Commons (*BRIT*), ≈ House of Representatives (*US*); **~ a gas** gas chamber; **~ del lavoro** trades union centre (*BRIT*), labor union center (*US*); **~ a un letto/a due letti/ matrimoniale** single/twin-bedded/double room; **~ oscura** (*FOT*) dark room; **~ da pranzo** dining room.

The **Camera dei deputati** *is the lower chamber of the Italian parliament. It has legislative power and is presided over by the* **Presidente della Camera** *who is elected by the* 630 **deputati***. Elections are normally held every 5 years. The electoral reform of 1993 has meant that candidates are now elected by a combination of a first-past-the-post system and proportional representation. See also* **Parlamento**.

---

came'rata, i, e *sm/f* companion, mate ♦ *sf* dormitory.

camera'tismo *sm* comradeship.

cameri'era *sf* (*domestica*) maid; (*che serve a tavola*) waitress; (*che fa le camere*) chambermaid.

cameri'ere *sm* (man)servant; (*di ristorante*) waiter.

came'rino *sm* (*TEAT*) dressing room.

'Camerun *sm*: **il ~** Cameroon.

'camice ['kamitʃe] *sm* (*REL*) alb; (*per medici etc*) white coat.

cami'cetta [kami'tʃetta] *sf* blouse.

ca'micia, cie [ka'mitʃa] *sf* (*da uomo*) shirt; (*da donna*) blouse; **nascere con la ~** (*fig*) to be born lucky; **sudare sette ~cie** (*fig*) to have a hell of a time; **~ di forza** straitjacket; **~ da notte** (*da donna*) nightdress; (*da uomo*) nightshirt; **C~ nera** (*fascista*) Blackshirt.

camici'aio, a [kami'tʃajo] *sm/f* (*sarto*) shirtmaker; (*che vende camicie*) shirtseller.

camici'ola [kami'tʃɔla] *sf* vest.

camici'otto [kami'tʃɔtto] *sm* casual shirt; (*per operai*) smock.

cami'netto *sm* hearth, fireplace.

ca'mino *sm* chimney; (*focolare*) fireplace, hearth.

'camion *sm inv* lorry (*BRIT*), truck (*US*).

camion'cino [kamjon'tʃino] *sm* van.

camio'netta *sf* jeep.

camio'nista, i *sm* lorry driver (*BRIT*), truck driver (*US*).

'camma *sf* cam; **albero a ~e** camshaft.

cam'mello *sm* (*ZOOL*) camel; (*tessuto*) camel hair.

cam'meo *sm* cameo.

cammi'nare *vi* to walk; (*funzionare*) to work, go; **~ a carponi** *o* **a quattro zampe** to go on all fours.

cammi'nata *sf* walk; **fare una ~** to go for a walk.

cam'mino *sm* walk; (*sentiero*) path; (*itinerario, direzione, tragitto*) way; **mettersi in ~** to set *o* start off; **cammin facendo** on the way; **riprendere il** ~ to continue on one's way.

camo'milla *sf* camomile; (*infuso*) camomile tea.

ca'morra *sf* Camorra; (*fig*) racket.

camor'rista, i, e *smlf* member of the Camorra; (*fig*) racketeer.

ca'moscio [ka'moʃʃo] *sm* chamois.

cam'pagna [kam'paɲɲa] *sf* country, countryside; (*POL, COMM, MIL*) campaign; **in** ~ in the country; **andare in** ~ to go to the country; **fare una** ~ to campaign; ~ **promozionale vendite** sales campaign.

campa'gnolo, a [kampaɲ'ɲɔlo] *ag* country *cpd* ♦ *sf* (*AUT*) cross-country vehicle.

cam'pale *ag* field *cpd*; (*fig*): **una giornata** ~ a hard day.

cam'pana *sf* bell; (*anche:* ~ **di vetro**) bell jar; **sordo come una** ~ as deaf as a doorpost; **sentire l'altra** ~ (*fig*) to hear the other side of the story.

campa'nella *sf* small bell; (*di tenda*) curtain ring.

campa'nello *sm* (*all'uscio, da tavola*) bell.

campa'nile *sm* bell tower, belfry.

campani'lismo *sm* parochialism.

cam'pano, a *ag* of (*o* from) Campania.

cam'pare *vi* to live; (*tirare avanti*) to get by, manage; ~ **alla giornata** to live from day to day.

cam'pato, a *ag*: ~ **in aria** unsound, unfounded.

campeggi'are [kamped'dʒare] *vi* to camp; (*risaltare*) to stand out.

campeggia'tore, 'trice [kampeddʒa'tore] *smlf* camper.

cam'peggio [kam'peddʒo] *sm* camping; (*terreno*) camp site; **fare (del)** ~ to go camping.

cam'pestre *ag* country *cpd*, rural; **corsa** ~ cross-country race.

Campi'doglio [kampi'dɔʎʎo] *sm*: **il** ~ the Capitol.

The **Campidoglio**, one of the Seven Hills of Rome, is the site of the Comune di Roma.

'camping ['kæmpiŋ] *sm inv* camp site.

campiona'mento *sm* sampling.

campio'nario, a *ag*: **fiera** ~**a** trade fair ♦ *sm* collection of samples.

campio'nato *sm* championship.

campiona'tura *sf* (*COMM*) production of samples; (*STATISTICA*) sampling.

campi'one, 'essa *smlf* (*SPORT*) champion ♦ *sm* (*COMM*) sample; ~ **gratuito** free sample; **prelievi di** ~ product samples.

'campo *sm* (*gen*) field; (*MIL*) field;

(*: accampamento*) camp; (*spazio delimitato: sportivo etc*) ground; field; (*di quadro*) background; **i** ~**i** (*campagna*) the countryside; **padrone del** ~ (*fig*) victor; ~ **da aviazione** airfield; ~ **di concentramento** concentration camp; ~ **di golf** golf course; ~ **lungo** (*CINE, TV, FOT*) long shot; ~ **da tennis** tennis court; ~ **visivo** field of vision.

campobas'sano, a *ag* of (*o* from) Campobasso.

campo'santo, *pl* **campi'santi** *sm* cemetery.

camuf'fare *vt* to disguise; ~**rsi** *vr*: ~**rsi (da)** to disguise o.s. (as); (*per ballo in maschera*) to dress up (as).

CAN *abbr* (= *Costo, Assicurazione e Nolo*) CIF.

Can. *abbr* (*GEO*) = **canale**.

'Canada *sm*: **il** ~ Canada.

cana'dese *ag, smlf* Canadian ♦ *sf* (*anche:* **tenda** ~) ridge tent.

ca'naglia [ka'naʎʎa] *sf* rabble, mob; (*persona*) scoundrel, rogue.

ca'nale *sm* (*anche fig*) channel; (*artificiale*) canal.

'canapa *sf* hemp; ~ **indiana** cannabis.

Ca'narie *sfpl*: **le (isole)** ~ the Canary Islands, the Canaries.

cana'rino *sm* canary.

Can'berra *sf* Canberra.

cancel'lare [kantʃel'lare] *vt* (*con la gomma*) to rub out, erase; (*con la penna*) to strike out; (*annullare*) to annul, cancel; (*disdire*) to cancel.

cancel'lata [kantʃel'lata] *sf* railing(s) (*pl*).

cancelle'ria [kantʃelle'ria] *sf* chancery; (*quanto necessario per scrivere*) stationery.

cancelli'ere [kantʃel'ljɛre] *sm* chancellor; (*di tribunale*) clerk of the court.

can'cello [kan'tʃɛllo] *sm* gate.

cance'rogeno, a [kantʃe'rɔdʒeno] *ag* carcinogenic ♦ *sm* carcinogen.

cance'rologo, a, gi, ghe [kantʃe'rɔlogo] *smlf* cancer specialist.

cance'roso, a [kantʃe'roso] *ag* cancerous ♦ *smlf* cancer patient.

can'crena *sf* gangrene.

'cancro *sm* (*MED*) cancer; (*dello zodiaco*): **C**~ Cancer; **essere del C**~ to be Cancer.

candeggi'are [kanded'dʒare] *vt* to bleach.

candeg'gina [kanded'ʒina] *sf* bleach.

can'deggio [kan'deddʒo] *sm* bleaching.

can'dela *sf* candle; ~ (**di accensione**) (*AUT*) spark(ing) plug; **una lampadina da 100** ~**e** (*ELETTR*) a 100 watt bulb; **a lume di** ~ by candlelight; **tenere la** ~ (*fig*) to play gooseberry (*BRIT*), act as chaperone.

cande'labro sm candelabra.

candeli'ere sm candlestick.

cande'lotto sm candle; ~ di dinamite stick of dynamite; ~ lacrimogeno tear gas grenade.

candi'dare vt to present as candidate; ~rsi vr to present o.s. as candidate.

candi'dato, a sm/f candidate; (aspirante a una carica) applicant.

candida'tura sf candidature; application.

'candido, a ag white as snow; (puro) pure; (sincero) sincere, candid.

can'dito, a ag candied.

can'dore sm brilliant white; purity; sincerity, candour (BRIT), candor (US).

'cane sm dog; (di pistola, fucile) cock; fa un freddo ~ it's bitterly cold; non c'era un ~ there wasn't a soul; quell'attore è un ~ he's a rotten actor; ~ da caccia hunting dog; ~ da guardia guard dog; ~ lupo alsatian; ~ da salotto lap dog; ~ da slitta husky.

ca'nestro sm basket; fare un ~ (SPORT) to shoot a basket.

'canfora sf camphor.

cangi'ante [kan'dʒante] ag iridescent; seta ~ shot silk.

can'guro sm kangaroo.

ca'nicola sf scorching heat.

ca'nile sm kennel; (di allevamento) kennels pl; ~ municipale dog pound.

ca'nino, a ag, sm canine.

'canna sf (pianta) reed; (: indica, da zucchero) cane; (bastone) stick, cane; (di fucile) barrel; (di organo) pipe; (DROGA: gergo) joint; ~ fumaria chimney flue; ~ da pesca (fishing) rod; ~ da zucchero sugar cane.

can'nella sf (CUC) cinnamon; (di conduttura, botte) tap.

cannel'loni smpl pasta tubes stuffed with sauce and baked.

can'neto sm bed of reeds.

can'nibale sm cannibal.

cannocchi'ale [kannok'kjale] sm telescope.

canno'nata sf: è una vera ~! (fig) it's (o he's etc) fantastic!

can'none sm (MIL) gun; (: STORIA) cannon; (tubo) pipe, tube; (piega) box pleat; (fig) ace; donna ~ fat woman.

cannoni'ere sm (NAUT) gunner; (CALCIO) goal scorer.

can'nuccia, ce [kan'nuttʃa] sf (drinking) straw.

'canone sm canon, criterion; (mensile, annuo) rent; fee; legge dell'equo ~ fair rent act.

ca'nonica, che sf presbytery.

ca'nonico, ci sm (REL) canon.

canoniz'zare [kanonid'dzare] vt to canonize.

ca'noro, a ag (uccello) singing, song cpd.

ca'notta sf vest.

canot'taggio [kanot'taddʒo] sm rowing.

canotti'era sf vest (BRIT), undershirt (US).

ca'notto sm small boat, dinghy; canoe.

cano'vaccio [kano'vattʃo] sm (tela) canvas; (strofinaccio) duster; (trama) plot.

can'tante sm/f singer.

can'tare vt, vi to sing; ~ vittoria to crow; fare ~ qn (fig) to make sb talk.

cantas'torie sm/f inv storyteller.

cantau'tore, 'trice sm/f singer-composer.

canterel'lare vt, vi to hum, sing to o.s.

canticchi'are [kantik'kjare] vt, vi to hum, sing to o.s.

canti'ere sm (EDIL) (building) site; (anche: ~ navale) shipyard.

canti'lena sf (filastrocca) lullaby; (fig) singsong voice.

can'tina sf (locale) cellar; (bottega) wine shop.

'canto sm song; (arte) singing; (REL) chant; chanting; (POESIA) poem, lyric; (parte di una poesia) canto; (parte, lato): da un ~ on the one hand; d'altro ~ on the other hand.

canto'nata sf (di edificio) corner; prendere una ~ (fig) to blunder.

can'tone sm (in Svizzera) canton.

cantoni'era ag: (casa) ~ road inspector's house.

can'tuccio [kan'tuttʃo] sm corner, nook.

ca'nuto, a ag white, whitehaired.

canzo'nare [kantso'nare] vt to tease.

canzona'tura [kantsona'tura] sf teasing; (beffa) joke.

can'zone [kan'tsone] sf song; (POESIA) canzone.

canzoni'ere [kantso'njɛre] sm (MUS) songbook; (LETTERATURA) collection of poems.

'caos sm inv chaos.

ca'otico, a, ci, che ag chaotic.

CAP sigla m vedi codice di avviamento postale.

cap. abbr (= capitolo) ch.

ca'pace [ka'patʃe] ag able, capable; (ampio, vasto) large, capacious; sei ~ di farlo? can you o are you able to do it?; ~ d'intendere e di volere (DIR) in full possession of one's faculties.

capacità [kapatʃi'ta] sf inv ability; (DIR, di recipiente) capacity; ~ produttiva production capacity.

capaci'tarsi [kapatʃi'tarsi] vr: ~ di to make out, understand.

ca'panna *sf* hut.

capan'nello *sm* knot (of people).

ca'panno *sm* (*di cacciatori*) hide; (*da spiaggia*) bathing hut.

capan'none *sm* (*AGR*) barn; (*fabbricato industriale*) (*factory*) shed.

caparbietà *sf* stubbornness.

ca'parbio, a *ag* stubborn.

ca'parra *sf* deposit, down payment.

capa'tina *sf*: **fare una ~ da qn/in centro** to pop in on sb/into town.

capeggi'are [kaped'dʒare] *vt* (*rivolta etc*) to head, lead.

ca'pello *sm* hair; ~**i** *smpl* (*capigliatura*) hair *sg*; **averne fin sopra i ~i di qc/qn** to be fed up to the (back) teeth with sth/sb; **mi ci hanno tirato per i ~i** (*fig*) they dragged me into it; **tirato per i ~i** (*spiegazione*) far-fetched.

capel'lone *a smlf* hippie.

capel'luto, a *ag*: **cuoio ~** scalp.

capez'zale [kapet'tsale] *sm* bolster; (*fig*) bedside.

ca'pezzolo [ka'pettsolo] *sm* nipple.

capi'ente *ag* capacious.

capi'enza [ka'pjɛntsa] *sf* capacity.

capiglia'tura [kapiʎʎa'tura] *sf* hair.

capil'lare *ag* (*fig*) detailed ♦ *sm* (*ANAT: anche: vaso ~*) capillary.

ca'pire *vt* to understand; ~ **al volo** to catch on straight away; **si capisce!** (*certamente!*) of course!, certainly!

capi'tale *ag* (*mortale*) capital; (*fondamentale*) main *cpd*, chief *cpd* ♦ *sf* (*città*) capital ♦ *sm* (*ECON*) capital; ~ **azionario** equity capital, share capital; ~ **d'esercizio** working capital; ~ **fisso** capital assets, fixed capital; ~ **immobile** real estate; ~ **liquido** cash assets *pl*; ~ **mobile** movables *pl*; ~ **di rischio** risk capital; ~ **sociale** (*di società*) authorized capital; (*di club*) funds *pl*; ~ **di ventura** venture capital, risk capital.

capita'lismo *sm* capitalism.

capita'lista, i, e *ag, smlf* capitalist.

capitaliz'zare [kapitalid'dzare] *vt* to capitalize.

capitalizzazi'one [kapitaliddzat'tsjone] *sf* capitalization.

capita'nare *vt* to lead; (*CALCIO*) to captain.

capitane'ria *sf*: ~ (**di porto**) port authorities *pl*.

capi'tano *sm* captain; ~ **di lungo corso** master mariner; ~ **di ventura** (*STORIA*) mercenary leader.

capi'tare *vi* (*giungere casualmente*) to happen to go, find o.s.; (*accadere*) to happen; (*presentarsi: cosa*) to turn up,

present itself ♦ *vb impers* to happen; ~ **a proposito/bene/male** to turn up at the right moment/at a good time/at a bad time; **mi è capitato un guaio** I've had a spot of trouble.

capi'tello *sm* (*ARCHIT*) capital.

capito'lare *vi* to capitulate.

capitolazi'one [kapitolat'tsjone] *sf* capitulation.

ca'pitolo *sm* chapter; ~**i** *smpl* (*COMM*) items; **non ho voce in** ~ (*fig*) I have no say in the matter.

capi'tombolo *sm* headlong fall, tumble.

'capo *sm* (*ANAT*) head; (*persona*) head, leader; (*: in ufficio*) head, boss; (*: in tribù*) chief; (*estremità: di tavolo, scale*) head, top; (*: di filo*) end; (*GEO*) cape; **andare a ~** to start a new paragraph; "**punto a ~**" "full stop — new paragraph"; **da ~** over again; **in ~ a** (*tempo*) within; **da un ~ all'altro** from one end to the other; **fra ~ e collo** (*all'improvviso*) out of the blue; **un discorso senza né ~ né coda** a senseless *o* meaningless speech; ~ **d'accusa** (*DIR*) charge; ~ **di bestiame** head *inv* of cattle; **C~ di Buona Speranza** Cape of Good Hope; ~ **di vestiario** item of clothing.

capo'banda, *pl* **capi'banda** *sm* (*MUS*) bandmaster; (*di malviventi, fig*) gang leader.

ca'poccia [ka'pɔttʃa] *sm inv* (*di lavoranti*) overseer; (*peg: capobanda*) boss.

capo'classe, *pl(m)* **capi'classe**, *pl(f) inv smlf* (*INS*) ≈ form captain (*BRIT*), class president (*US*).

capocu'oco, chi *sm* head cook.

Capo'danno *sm* New Year.

capofa'miglia, *pl(m)* **capifa'miglia**, *pl(f) inv* [kapofa'miʎʎa] *smlf* head of the family.

capo'fitto: a ~ *av* headfirst, headlong.

capo'giro [kapo'dʒiro] *sm* dizziness *no pl*; **da ~** (*fig*) astonishing, staggering.

capo'gruppo, *pl(m)* **capi'gruppo**, *pl(f) inv smlf* group leader.

capola'voro, i *sm* masterpiece.

capo'linea, *pl* **capi'linea** *sm* terminus; (*fig*) end of the line.

capo'lino *sm*: **far ~** to peep out (*o in etc*).

capo'lista, *pl(m)* **capi'lista**, *pl(f) inv smlf* (*POL*) top candidate on electoral list.

capolu'ogo, *pl* **ghi** *o* **capilu'oghi** *sm* chief town, administrative centre (*BRIT*) *o* center (*US*).

capo'mastro, *pl* **i** *o* **capi'mastri** *sm* master builder.

capo'rale *sm* (*MIL*) lance corporal (*BRIT*), private first class (*US*).

capore'parto, *pl(m)* **capire'parto**, *pl(f) inv*

smlf (*di operai*) foreman; (*di ufficio, negozio*) head of department.

capo'sala *sf inv* (*MED*) ward sister.

capo'saldo, pl capi'saldi *sm* stronghold; (*fig: fondamento*) basis, cornerstone.

capo'squadra, pl capi'squadra *sm* (*di operai*) foreman, ganger; (*MIL*) squad leader; (*SPORT*) team captain.

capostazi'one, pl capistazi'one [kapostat'tsjone] *sm* station master.

capos'tipite *sm* progenitor; (*fig*) earliest example.

capo'tavola, pl(m) capi'tavola, pl(f) inv *smlf* (*persona*) head of the table; **sedere a** ~ to sit at the head of the table.

ca'pote [ka'pɔt] *sf inv* (*AUT*) hood (*BRIT*), soft top.

capo'treno, pl capi'treno *o* **capo'treni** *sm* guard.

capouf'ficio, pl(m) capiuf'ficio, pl(f) inv [kapouf'fitʃo] *smlf* head clerk.

'Capo 'Verde *sm*: **il** ~ Cape Verde.

capo'verso *sm* (*di verso, periodo*) first line; (*TIP*) indent; (*paragrafo*) paragraph; (*DIR*: *comma*) section.

capo'volgere [kapo'voldʒere] *vt* to overturn; (*fig*) to reverse; ~**rsi** *vr* to overturn; (*barca*) to capsize; (*fig*) to be reversed.

capovolgi'mento [kapovoldʒi'mento] *sm* (*fig*) reversal, complete change.

capo'volto, a *pp di* **capovolgere** ♦ *ag* upside down; (*barca*) capsized.

'cappa *sf* (*mantello*) cape, cloak; (*del camino*) hood.

cap'pella *sf* (*REL*) chapel.

cappel'lano *sm* chaplain.

cap'pello *sm* hat; **ti faccio tanto di** ~! (*fig*) I take my hat off to you!; ~ **a bombetta** bowler (hat), derby (*US*); ~ **a cilindro** top hat.

'cappero *sm* caper.

cap'pone *sm* capon.

cappot'tare *vi* (*AUT*) to overturn.

cap'potto *sm* (over)coat.

cappuc'cino [kapput'tʃino] *sm* (*frate*) Capuchin monk; (*bevanda*) frothy white coffee.

cap'puccio [kap'puttʃo] *sm* (*copricapo*) hood; (*della biro*) cap.

'capra *sf* (she-)goat.

ca'prese *ag* from (*o* of) Capri.

ca'pretto *sm* kid.

ca'priccio [ka'prittʃo] *sm* caprice, whim; (*bizza*) tantrum; **fare i** ~**i** to be very naughty; ~ **della sorte** quirk of fate.

capricci'oso, a [kaprit'tʃoso] *ag* capricious, whimsical; naughty.

Capri'corno *sm* Capricorn; **essere del** ~ (*dello zodiaco*) to be Capricorn.

capri'foglio [kapri'fɔʎʎo] *sm* honeysuckle.

capri'ola *sf* somersault.

capri'olo *sm* roe deer.

'capro *sm* billy-goat; ~ **espiatorio** (*fig*) scapegoat.

ca'prone *sm* billy-goat.

'capsula *sf* capsule; (*di arma, per bottiglie*) cap.

cap'tare *vt* (*RADIO, TV*) to pick up; (*cattivarsi*) to gain, win.

CAR *sigla m* = *Centro Addestramento Reclute*.

cara'bina *sf* rifle.

carabini'ere *sm* *member of Italian military police force.*

Originally part of the armed forces, the **Carabinieri** *are police who now perform both military and civil duties such as maintaining public order. They consist of, among other things, paratroop units and mounted divisions and come under the control of either the Minister of the Interior or the Minister of Defence, depending on the function they are performing.*

Ca'racas *sf* Caracas.

ca'raffa *sf* carafe.

Ca'raibi *smpl*: **il mar dei** ~ the Caribbean (Sea).

cara'ibico, a, ci, che *ag* Caribbean.

cara'mella *sf* sweet.

cara'mello *sm* caramel.

ca'rato *sm* (*di oro, diamante etc*) carat.

ca'rattere *sm* character; (*caratteristica*) characteristic, trait; **avere un buon** ~ to be good-natured; **informazione di** ~ **tecnico/confidenziale** information of a technical/confidential nature; **essere in** ~ **con qc** (*intonarsi*) to be in harmony with sth.

caratte'rino *sm* difficult nature *o* character.

caratte'ristico, a, ci, che *ag* characteristic ♦ *sf* characteristic, feature; **segni** ~**ci** (*su passaporto etc*) distinguishing marks.

caratteriz'zare [karatterid'dzare] *vt* to characterize, distinguish.

carboi'drato *sm* carbohydrate.

carbo'naio *sm* (*chi fa carbone*) charcoal-burner; (*commerciante*) coalman, coal merchant.

car'bone *sm* coal; ~ **fossile** (pit) coal; **essere** *o* **stare sui** ~**i ardenti** to be like a cat on hot bricks.

car'bonio *sm* (*CHIM*) carbon.

carboniz'zare [karbonid'dzare] *vt* (*legna*) to carbonize; (: *parzialmente*) to char; **morire carbonizzato** to be burned to death.
carbu'rante *sm* (motor) fuel.
carbura'tore *sm* carburettor.
car'cassa *sf* carcass; (*fig: peg: macchina etc*) (old) wreck.
carce'rato, a [kartʃe'rato] *sm/f* prisoner.
'carcere ['kartʃere] *sm* prison; (*pena*) imprisonment; ~ **di massima sicurezza** top-security prison.
carceri'ere, a [kartʃe'rjɛre] *sm/f* (*anche fig*) jailer.
carci'ofo [kar'tʃɔfo] *sm* artichoke.
cardel'lino *sm* goldfinch.
car'diaco, a, ci, che *ag* cardiac, heart *cpd.*
cardi'nale *ag, sm* cardinal.
'cardine *sm* hinge.
cardiolo'gia [kardjolo'dʒia] *sf* cardiology.
cardi'ologo, gi *sm* heart specialist, cardiologist.
'cardo *sm* thistle.
ca'rente *ag*: ~ **di** lacking in.
ca'renza [ka'rɛntsa] *sf* lack, scarcity; (*vitaminica*) deficiency.
cares'tia *sf* famine; (*penuria*) scarcity, dearth.
ca'rezza [ka'rettsa] *sf* caress; **dare** *o* **fare una** ~ **a** (*persona*) to caress; (*animale*) to stroke, pat.
carez'zare [karet'tsare] *vt* to caress, stroke, fondle.
carez'zevole [karet'tsevole] *ag* sweet, endearing.
'cargo, ghi *sm* (*nave*) cargo boat, freighter; (*aereo*) freighter.
cari'are *vt*, ~**rsi** *vr* (*denti*) to decay.
'carica *sf vedi* **carico**.
caricabatte'rie *sm inv* (*ELETTR*) battery charger.
cari'care *vt* to load; (*aggravare: anche fig*) to weigh down; (*orologio*) to wind up; (*batteria, MIL*) to charge; (*INFORM*) to load; ~**rsi** *vr*: ~**rsi di** to burden *o* load o.s. with; (*fig: di responsabilità, impegni*) to burden o.s. with.
carica'tura *sf* caricature.
'carico, a, chi, che *ag* (*che porta un peso*): ~ **di** loaded *o* laden with; (*fucile*) loaded; (*orologio*) wound up; (*batteria*) charged; (*colore*) deep; (*caffè, tè*) strong ♦ *sm* (*il caricare*) loading; (*ciò che si carica*) load; (*COMM*) shipment; (*fig: peso*) burden, weight ♦ *sf* (*mansione ufficiale*) office, position; (*MIL, TECN, ELETTR*) charge; ~ **di debiti** up to one's ears in debt; **persona a** ~ dependent; **essere a** ~ **di qn** (*spese etc*) to be charged to sb; (*accusa, prova*) to be

against sb; **testimone a** ~ witness for the prosecution; **farsi** ~ **di** (*problema, responsabilità*) to take on; **a** ~ **del cliente** at the customer's expense; ~ **di lavoro** (*di ditta, reparto*) workload; ~ **utile** payload; **capacità di** ~ cargo capacity; **entrare/ essere in** ~a to come into/be in office; **ricoprire** *o* **rivestire una** ~a to hold a position; **uscire di** ~a to leave office; **dare la** ~a **a** (*orologio*) to wind up; (*fig: persona*) to back up; **tornare alla** ~a (*fig*) to insist, persist; **ha una forte** ~a **di simpatia** he's very likeable.
'carie *sf* (*dentaria*) decay.
ca'rino, a *ag* lovely, pretty, nice; (*simpatico*) nice.
ca'risma [ka'rizma] *sm* charisma.
caris'matico, a, ci, che *ag* charismatic.
carità *sf* charity; **per** ~! (*escl di rifiuto*) good heavens, no!
carita'tevole *ag* charitable.
carnagi'one [karna'dʒone] *sf* complexion.
car'nale *ag* (*amore*) carnal; (*fratello*) blood *cpd.*
'carne *sf* flesh; (*bovina, ovina etc*) meat; **in** ~ **e ossa** in the flesh, in person; **essere (bene) in** ~ to be well padded, be plump; **non essere né** ~ **né pesce** (*fig*) to be neither fish nor fowl; ~ **di manzo/ maiale/pecora** beef/pork/mutton; ~ **in scatola** tinned *o* canned meat; ~ **tritata** mince (*BRIT*), hamburger meat (*US*), minced (*BRIT*) *o* ground (*US*) meat.
car'nefice [kar'nefitʃe] *sm* executioner; hangman.
carnefi'cina [karnefi'tʃina] *sf* carnage; (*fig*) disaster.
carne'vale *sm* carnival.

Carnevale *is the period between Epiphany (Jan. 6th) and the beginning of Lent when many festivities take place. It is marked by parties, processions of floats, bonfires in the piazze and people dressing up and wearing masks. It reaches its peak in the period immediately before Lent, culminating in the festivities of* **Martedì grasso** *(Shrove Tuesday).*

---

car'nivoro, a *ag* carnivorous.
car'noso, a *ag* fleshy; (*pianta, frutto, radice*) pulpy; (*labbra*) full.
'caro, a *ag* (*amato*) dear; (*costoso*) dear, expensive; **se ti è** ~**a la vita** if you value your life.
ca'rogna [ka'roɲɲa] *sf* carrion; (*fig fam*) swine.
caro'sello *sm* merry-go-round.

ca'rota *sf* carrot.
caro'vana *sf* caravan.
caro'vita *sm* high cost of living.
'carpa *sf* carp.
Car'pazi [kar'patsi] *smpl*: **i** ~ the Carpathian Mountains.
carpente'ria *sf* carpentry.
carpenti'ere *sm* carpenter.
car'pire *vt*: ~ **qc a qn** (*segreto etc*) to get sth out of sb.
car'poni *av* on all fours.
car'rabile *ag* suitable for vehicles; **"passo ~"** "keep clear".
car'raio, a *ag*: **passo** ~ vehicle entrance.
carré *sm* (*acconciatura*) bob.
carreggi'ata [karred'dʒata] *sf* carriageway (*BRIT*), roadway; **rimettersi in** ~ (*fig: recuperare*) to catch up; **tenersi in** ~ (*fig*) to keep to the right path.
carrel'lata *sf* (*CINE, TV: tecnica*) tracking; (: *scena*) running shot; ~ **di successi** medley of hit tunes.
car'rello *sm* trolley; (*AER*) undercarriage; (*CINE*) dolly; (*di macchina da scrivere*) carriage.
car'retta *sf*: **tirare la** ~ (*fig*) to plod along.
car'retto *sm* handcart.
carri'era *sf* career; **fare** ~ to get on; **ufficiale di** ~ (*MIL*) regular officer; **a gran** ~ at full speed.
carri'ola *sf* wheelbarrow.
'carro *sm* cart, wagon; **il Gran/Piccolo C~** (*ASTR*) the Great/Little Bear; **mettere il** ~ **avanti ai buoi** (*fig*) to put the cart before the horse; ~ **armato** tank; ~ **attrezzi** (*AUT*) breakdown van (*BRIT*), tow truck (*US*); ~ **funebre** hearse; ~ **merci/bestiame** (*FERR*) goods/animal wagon.
car'roccio [kar'rotʃo] *sm* (*POL*): **il C~** *symbol of Lega Nord*.
car'rozza [kar'rɔttsa] *sf* carriage, coach; ~ **letto** (*FERR*) sleeper; ~ **ristorante** (*FERR*) dining car.
carroz'zella [karrot'tsɛlla] *sf* (*per bambini*) pram (*BRIT*), baby carriage (*US*); (*per invalidi*) wheelchair.
carrozze'ria [karrottse'ria] *sf* body, coachwork (*BRIT*); (*officina*) coachbuilder's workshop (*BRIT*), body shop.
carrozzi'ere [karrot'tsjɛre] *sm* (*AUT: progettista*) car designer; (: *meccanico*) coachbuilder.
carroz'zina [karrot'tsina] *sf* pram (*BRIT*), baby carriage (*US*).
carroz'zone [karrot'tsone] *sm* (*da circo, di zingari*) caravan.
car'rucola *sf* pulley.

'carta *sf* paper; (*al ristorante*) menu; (*GEO*) map; plan; (*documento, da gioco*) card; (*costituzione*) charter; ~**e** *sfpl* (*documenti*) papers, documents; **alla** ~ (*al ristorante*) à la carte; **cambiare le** ~**e in tavola** (*fig*) to shift one's ground; **fare** ~**e false** (*fig*) to go to great lengths; ~ **assegni** bank card; ~ **assorbente** blotting paper; ~ **bollata** *o* **da bollo** (*AMM*) official stamped paper; ~ **di credito** credit card; ~ **di debito** cash card; ~ **(geografica)** map; ~ **d'identità** identity card; ~ **igienica** toilet paper; ~ **d'imbarco** (*AER, NAUT*) boarding card, boarding pass; ~ **da lettere** writing paper; ~ **libera** (*AMM*) unstamped paper; ~ **millimetrata** graph paper; ~ **oleata** waxed paper; ~ **da pacchi,** ~ **da imballo** wrapping paper, brown paper; ~ **da parati** wallpaper; ~ **verde** (*AUT*) green card; ~ **vetrata** sandpaper; ~ **da visita** visiting card.
cartacar'bone, *pl* **cartecar'bone** *sf* carbon paper.
car'taccia, ce [kar'tattʃa] *sf* waste paper.
cartamo'dello *sm* (*CUCITO*) paper pattern.
cartamo'neta *sf* paper money.
carta'pecora *sf* parchment.
carta'pesta *sf* papier-mâché.
cartas'traccia [kartas'trattʃa] *sf* waste paper.
car'teggio [kar'teddʒo] *sm* correspondence.
car'tella *sf* (*scheda*) card; (*custodia: di cartone*) folder; (: *di uomo d'affari etc*) briefcase; (: *di scolaro*) schoolbag, satchel; ~ **clinica** (*MED*) case sheet.
cartel'lino *sm* (*etichetta*) label; (*su porta*) notice; (*scheda*) card; **timbrare il** ~ (*all'entrata*) to clock in; (*all'uscita*) to clock out; ~ **di presenza** clock card, timecard.
car'tello *sm* sign; (*pubblicitario*) poster; (*stradale*) sign, signpost; (*in dimostrazioni*) placard; (*ECON*) cartel.
cartel'lone *sm* (*pubblicitario*) advertising poster; (*della tombola*) scoring frame; (*TEAT*) playbill; **tenere il** ~ (*spettacolo*) to have a long run.
carti'era *sf* paper mill.
carti'lagine [karti'ladʒine] *sf* cartilage.
car'tina *sf* (*AUT, GEO*) map.
car'toccio [kar'tɔttʃo] *sm* paper bag; **cuocere al** ~ (*CUC*) to bake in tinfoil.
cartogra'fia *sf* cartography.
carto'laio, a *sm/f* stationer.
cartole'ria *sf* stationer's (shop (*BRIT*)).
carto'lina *sf* postcard; ~ **di auguri** greetings card; ~ **precetto** *o* **rosa** (*MIL*) call-up card.
carto'mante *sm/f* fortune-teller (*using*

cards).

carton'cino [karton'tʃino] *sm* (*materiale*) thin cardboard; (*biglietto*) card; ~ **della società** compliments slip.

car'tone *sm* cardboard; (*del latte, dell'aranciata*) carton; (*ARTE*) cartoon; ~**i animati** (*CINE*) cartoons.

car'tuccia, ce [kar'tuttʃa] *sf* cartridge; ~ **a salve** blank cartridge; **mezza** ~ (*fig: persona*) good-for-nothing.

'casa *sf* house; (*specialmente la propria* ~) home; (*COMM*) firm, house; **essere a** ~ **to** be at home; **vado a** ~ **mia/tua** I'm going home/to your house; ~ **di correzione** ≈ community home (*BRIT*), reformatory (*US*); ~ **di cura** nursing home; ~ **editrice** publishing house; ~ **dello studente** student hostel; ~ **di tolleranza,** ~ **d'appuntamenti** brothel; ~**e popolari** ≈ council houses (*o* flats) (*BRIT*), ≈ public housing units (*US*).

Casa'blanca *sf* Casablanca.

ca'sacca, che *sf* military coat; (*di fantino*) blouse.

ca'sale *sm* (*gruppo di case*) hamlet; (*casa di campagna*) farmhouse.

casa'lingo, a, ghi, ghe *ag* household, domestic; (*fatto a casa*) home-made; (*semplice*) homely; (*amante della casa*) home-loving ♦ *sf* housewife; ~**ghi** *smpl* (*oggetti*) household articles; **cucina** ~**a** plain home cooking.

ca'sata *sf* family lineage.

ca'sato *sm* family name.

Casc. *abbr* (*GEO*) = **cascata**.

casca'morto *sm* woman-chaser; **fare il** ~ **to** chase women.

cas'care *vi* to fall; ~ **bene/male** (*fig*) to land lucky/unlucky; ~ **dalle nuvole** (*fig*) to be taken aback; ~ **dal sonno** to be falling asleep on one's feet; **caschi il mondo** no matter what; **non cascherà il mondo se ...** it won't be the end of the world if ....

cas'cata *sf* fall; (*d'acqua*) cascade, waterfall.

cascherò *etc* [kaske'rɔ] *vb vedi* **cascare**.

ca'scina [kaʃ'ʃina] *sf* farmstead.

casci'nale [kaʃʃi'nale] *sm* (*casolare*) farmhouse; (*cascina*) farmstead.

'casco, schi *sm* helmet; (*del parrucchiere*) hair-dryer; (*di banane*) bunch; ~ **blu** (*MIL*) blue helmet (*UN soldier*).

caseggi'ato [kased'dʒato] *sm* (*edificio*) large block of flats (*BRIT*) *o* apartment building (*US*); (*gruppo di case*) group of houses.

casei'ficio [kazei'fitʃo] *sm* creamery.

ca'sella *sf* pigeonhole; ~ **postale (C.P.)** post

office box (*P.O. box*).

casel'lario *sm* (*mobile*) filing cabinet; (*raccolta di pratiche*) files *pl*; ~ **giudiziale** court records *pl*; ~ **penale** police files *pl*.

ca'sello *sm* (*di autostrada*) tollgate.

case'reccio, a, ci, ce [kase'rettʃo] *ag* home-made.

ca'serma *sf* barracks *pl*.

caser'tano, a *ag* of (*o* from) Caserta.

ca'sino *sm* (*confusione*) row, racket; (*casa di prostituzione*) brothel.

casinò *sm inv* casino.

ca'sistica *sf* (*MED*) record of cases; **secondo la** ~ **degli incidenti stradali** according to road accident data.

'caso *sm* chance; (*fatto, vicenda*) event, incident; (*possibilità*) possibility; (*MED, LING*) case; **a** ~ at random; **per** ~ by chance, by accident; **in ogni** ~, **in tutti i** ~**i** in any case, at any rate; **in** ~ **contrario** otherwise; **al** ~ should the opportunity arise; **nel** ~ **che** in case; ~ **mai** if by chance; **far** ~ **a qc/qn** to pay attention to sth/sb; **fare** *o* **porre** *o* **mettere il** ~ **che** to suppose that; **fa proprio al** ~ **nostro** it's just what we need; **guarda** ~ ... strangely enough ...; **è il** ~ **che ce ne andiamo** we'd better go; ~ **limite** borderline case.

caso'lare *sm* cottage.

'Caspio *sm*: **il mar** ~ the Caspian Sea.

'caspita *escl* (*di sorpresa*) good heavens!; (*di impazienza*) for goodness' sake!

'cassa *sf* case, crate, box; (*bara*) coffin; (*mobile*) chest; (*involucro: di orologio etc*) case; (*macchina*) cash register; (*luogo di pagamento*) cash desk, checkout (*counter*); (*fondo*) fund; (*istituto bancario*) bank; **battere** ~ (*fig*) to come looking for money; ~ **automatica prelievi** automatic telling machine, cash dispenser; ~ **continua** night safe; **mettere in** ~ **integrazione** ≈ to lay off; **C~ del Mezzogiorno** *development fund for the South of Italy*; ~ **mutua** *o* **malattia** health insurance scheme; ~ **di risonanza** (*MUS*) soundbox; (*fig*) platform; ~ **di risparmio** savings bank; ~ **rurale e artigiana** credit institution (*serving farmers and craftsmen*); ~ **toracica** (*ANAT*) chest.

cassa'forte, *pl* **casse'forti** *sf* safe.

cassa'panca, *pl* **cassa'panche** *o* **casse'panche** *sf* settle.

casseru'ola, casse'rola *sf* saucepan.

cas'setta *sf* box; (*per registratore*) cassette; (*CINE, TEAT*) box-office takings *pl*; **pane a** *o* **in** ~ toasting loaf; **film di** ~ (*commerciale*) box-office draw; **far** ~ to be a box-office success; ~ **delle lettere** letterbox; ~ **di**

sicurezza strongbox.

cas'setto sm drawer.

casset'tone sm chest of drawers.

cassi'ere, a smlf cashier; (di banca) teller.

cassinte'grato, a smlf person who has been laid off.

cas'sone sm (cassa) large case, large chest.

'casta sf caste.

cas'tagna [kas'tanɲa] sf chestnut; prendere qn in ~ (fig) to catch sb in the act.

cas'tagno [kas'tanɲo] sm chestnut (tree).

cas'tano, a ag chestnut (brown).

cas'tello sm castle; (TECN) scaffolding.

casti'gare vt to punish.

casti'gato, a ag (casto, modesto) pure, chaste; (emendato: prosa, versione) expurgated, amended.

cas'tigo, ghi sm punishment.

castità sf chastity.

'casto, a ag chaste, pure.

cas'toro sm beaver.

cas'trante ag frustrating.

cas'trare vt to castrate; to geld; to doctor (BRIT), fix (US); (fig: iniziativa) to frustrate.

castrone'ria sf (fam): dire ~e to talk rubbish.

casu'ale ag chance cpd.

ca'supola sf simple little cottage.

catac'lisma, i sm (fig) catastrophe.

cata'comba sf catacomb.

cata'fascio [kata'faʃʃo] sm: andare a ~ to collapse; mandare a ~ to wreck.

cata'litico, a, ci, che ag: marmitta ~a (AUT) catalytic converter.

cataliz'zare [katalid'dzare] vt (fig) to act as a catalyst (up)on.

cataliz'zato, a [katalid'dzato] ag (AUT) with catalytic converter.

catalizza'tore [kataliddza'tore] sm (anche fig) catalyst; (AUT) catalytic converter.

Cata'logna [kata'lonɲa] sf: la ~ Catalonia.

ca'talogo, ghi sm catalogue; ~ dei prezzi price list.

cata'nese ag of (o from) Catania.

catanza'rese [katandza'rese] ag of (o from) Catanzaro.

cata'pecchia [kata'pekkja] sf hovel.

cata'pulta sf catapult.

catarifran'gente [katarifran'dʒɛnte] sm (AUT) reflector.

ca'tarro sm catarrh.

ca'tarsi sf inv catharsis.

ca'tasta sf stack, pile.

ca'tasto sm land register; land registry office.

ca'tastrofe sf catastrophe, disaster.

catas'trofico, a, ci, che ag (evento) catastrophic; (persona, previsione) pessimistic.

cate'chismo [kate'kizmo] sm catechism.

catego'ria sf category; (di albergo) class.

cate'gorico, a, ci, che ag categorical.

ca'tena sf chain; reazione a ~ chain reaction; susseguirsi a ~ to happen in quick succession; ~ alimentare food chain; ~ di montaggio assembly line; ~ montuosa mountain range; ~e da neve (AUT) snow chains.

cate'naccio [kate'nattʃo] sm bolt.

cate'nella sf (ornamento) chain; (di orologio) watch chain; (di porta) door chain.

cate'ratta sf cataract; (chiusa) sluice gate.

ca'terva sf (di cose) loads pl, heaps pl; (di persone) horde.

cate'tere sm (MED) catheter.

cati'nella sf: piovere a ~e to pour, rain cats and dogs.

ca'tino sm basin.

ca'todico, a, ci, che ag: tubo a raggi ~ci cathode-ray tube.

ca'torcio [ka'tɔrtʃo] sm (peg) old wreck.

ca'trame sm tar.

'cattedra sf teacher's desk; (di università) chair; salire o montare in ~ (fig) to pontificate.

catte'drale sf cathedral.

catte'dratico, a, ci, che ag (insegnamento) university cpd; (ironico) pedantic ♦ smlf professor.

catti'veria sf (qualità) wickedness; (di bambino) naughtiness; (azione) wicked action; fare una ~ to do something wicked; to be naughty.

cattività sf captivity.

cat'tivo, a ag bad; (malvagio) bad, wicked; (turbolento: bambino) bad, naughty; (: mare) rough; (odore, sapore) nasty, bad ♦ smlf bad o wicked person; farsi ~ sangue to worry, get in a state; farsi un ~ nome to earn o.s. a bad reputation; i ~i (nei film) the baddies (BRIT), the bad guys (US).

cattocomu'nista, i, e ag combining Catholic and communist ideas.

cattoli'cesimo [kattoli'tʃezimo] sm Catholicism.

cat'tolico, a, ci, che ag, smlf (Roman) Catholic.

cat'tura sf capture.

cattu'rare vt to capture.

cau'casico, a, ci, che ag, smlf Caucasian.

'Caucaso sm: il ~ the Caucasus.

cauccSiù [kaut'tʃu] sm rubber.

'causa sf cause; (DIR) lawsuit, case, action;

a ~ **di** because of; **per ~ sua** because of him; **fare** *o* **muovere ~ a qn** to take legal action against sb; **parte in ~** litigant.

cau'sale *ag* (*LING*) causal ♦ *sf* cause, reason.

cau'sare *vt* to cause.

'caustico, a, ci, che *ag* caustic.

cau'tela *sf* caution, prudence.

caute'lare *vt* to protect; **~rsi** *vr*: **~rsi (da** *o* **contro)** to take precautions (against).

'cauto, a *ag* cautious, prudent.

cauzio'nare [kauttsjo'nare] *vt* to guarantee.

cauzi'one [kaut'tsjone] *sf* security; (*DIR*) bail; **rilasciare dietro ~** to release on bail.

cav. *abbr* = **cavaliere.**

'cava *sf* quarry.

caval'care *vt* (*cavallo*) to ride; (*muro*) to sit astride; (*sog: ponte*) to span.

caval'cata *sf* ride; (*gruppo di persone*) riding party.

cavalca'via *sm inv* flyover.

cavalci'oni [kaval'tʃoni]: **a ~ di** *prep* astride.

cavali'ere *sm* rider; (*feudale, titolo*) knight; (*soldato*) cavalryman; (*al ballo*) partner.

cavalleg'gero [kavalled'dʒɛro] *sm* (*MIL*) light cavalryman.

cavalle'resco, a, schi, sche *ag* chivalrous.

cavalle'ria *sf* chivalry; (*milizia a cavallo*) cavalry.

cavalle'rizzo, a [kavalle'rittso] *sm/f* riding instructor; circus rider.

caval'letta *sf* grasshopper; (*dannosa*) locust.

caval'letto *sm* (*FOT*) tripod; (*da pittore*) easel.

caval'lina *sf* (*GINNASTICA*) horse; (*gioco*) leap-frog; **correre la ~** (*fig*) to sow one's wild oats.

ca'vallo *sm* horse; (*SCACCHI*) knight; (*AUT: anche: ~* **vapore**) horsepower; (*dei pantaloni*) crotch; **a ~** on horseback; **a ~ di** astride, straddling; **siamo a ~** (*fig*) we've made it; **da ~** (*fig: dose*) drastic; (*: febbre*) raging; **vivere a ~ tra due periodi** to straddle two periods; **~ di battaglia** (*TEAT*) tour de force; (*fig*) hobbyhorse; **~ da corsa** racehorse; **~ a dondolo** rocking horse; **~ da sella** saddle horse; **~ da soma** packhorse.

ca'vare *vt* (*togliere*) to draw out, extract, take out; (*: giacca, scarpe*) to take off; (*: fame, sete, voglia*) to satisfy; **~rsi** *vr*: **~rsi da** (*guai, problemi*) to get out of; **cavarsela** to get away with it; to manage, get on all right; **non ci caverà un bel nulla** you'll get nothing out of it (*o* him *etc*).

cava'tappi *sm inv* corkscrew.

ca'verna *sf* cave.

caver'noso, a *ag* (*luogo*) cavernous; (*fig: voce*) deep; (*: tosse*) raucous.

ca'vezza [ka'vettsa] *sf* halter.

'cavia *sf* guinea pig.

cavi'ale *sm* caviar.

ca'viglia [ka'viʎʎa] *sf* ankle.

cavil'lare *vi* to quibble.

ca'villo *sm* quibble.

cavil'loso, a *ag* quibbling, hair-splitting.

cavità *sf inv* cavity.

'cavo, a *ag* hollow ♦ *sm* (*ANAT*) cavity; (*grossa corda*) rope, cable; (*ELETTR, TEL*) cable.

cavo'lata *sf* (*fam*) stupid thing, foolish thing.

cavolfi'ore *sm* cauliflower.

'cavolo *sm* cabbage; **non m'importa un ~** (*fam*) I don't give a hoot; **che ~ vuoi?** (*fam*) what the heck do you want?; **~ di Bruxelles** Brussels sprout.

caz'zata [kat'tsata] *sf* (*fam!: stupidaggine*) stupid thing, something stupid.

'cazzo ['kattso] *sm* (*fam!: pene*) prick (*!*); **non gliene importa un ~** (*fig fam!*) he doesn't give a damn about it; **fatti i ~i tuoi** (*fig fam!*) mind your own damn business.

caz'zotto [kat'tsɔtto] *sm* punch; **fare a ~i** to have a punch-up.

cazzu'ola [kat'tswɔla] *sf* trowel.

CB *sigla* = Campobasso.

CC *abbr* = Carabinieri.

cc *abbr* (= *centimetro cubico*) cc.

C.C. *abbr* = **codice civile.**

c.c. *abbr* (= *conto corrente*) c/a, a/c; (*ELETTR*) *vedi* **corrente continua.**

c/c *abbr* (= *conto corrente*) c/a, a/c.

C.C.D. *sigla m* (*POL* = *Centro Cristiano Democratico*) *party originating from Democrazia Cristiana.*

CCI *sigla f* (= *Camera di Commercio Internazionale*) ICC (= *International Chamber of Commerce*).

CCIAA *abbr* = *Camera di Commercio Industria, Agricoltura e Artigianato.*

CCT *sigla m vedi* **certificato di credito del Tesoro.**

C.D. *abbr* (= *Corpo Diplomatico*) CD ♦ *sm inv* (= *compact disc*) CD.

c.d. *abbr* = **cosiddetto.**

c.d.d. *abbr* (= *come dovevasi dimostrare*) QED (= *quod erat demonstrandum*).

C.d.M. *abbr* = **Cassa del Mezzogiorno.**

CD-Rom [tʃidi'rɔm] *sigla m inv* (= *Compact Disc Read Only Memory*) CD-Rom.

CE *sigla* = Caserta.

ce [tʃe] *pron, av vedi* **ci.**

C.E. *sigla* = **Consiglio d'Europa.**

CECA sigla f (= Comunità Europea del Carbone e dell'Acciaio) ECSC (= European Coal and Steel Community).

cec'chino [tʃek'kino] sm sniper; (POL) member of parliament who votes against his own party.

'cece ['tʃetʃe] sm chickpea, garbanzo (US).

cecità [tʃetʃi'ta] sf blindness.

'ceco, a, chi, che ['tʃɛko] ag, sm/f, sm Czech; **la Repubblica C~a** the Czech Republic.

Cecoslo'vacchia [tʃekozlo'vakkja] sf: **la ~** Czechoslovakia.

cecoslo'vacco, a, chi, che [tʃekozlo'vakko] ag, sm/f Czechoslovakian.

CED [tʃɛd] sigla m = **centro elaborazione dati**.

'cedere ['tʃɛdere] vt (concedere: posto) to give up; (DIR) to transfer, make over ♦ vi (cadere) to give way, subside; **~ (a)** to surrender (to), yield (to), give in (to); **~ il passo (a qn)** to let (sb) pass in front; **~ il passo a qc** (fig) to give way to sth; **~ la parola (a qn)** to hand over (to sb).

ce'devole [tʃe'devole] ag (terreno) soft; (fig) yielding.

'cedola ['tʃɛdola] sf (COMM) coupon; voucher.

ce'drata [tʃe'drata] sf citron juice.

'cedro ['tʃɛdro] sm cedar; (albero da frutto, frutto) citron.

'CEE ['tʃɛe] sigla f vedi **Comunità Economica Europea**.

'ceffo ['tʃeffo] sm (peg) ugly mug.

cef'fone [tʃef'fone] sm slap, smack.

'ceko, a ['tʃɛko] ag, sm/f, sm = **ceco**.

ce'lare [tʃe'lare] vt to conceal; **~rsi** vr to hide.

cele'brare [tʃele'brare] vt to celebrate; (cerimonia) to hold; **~ le lodi di qc/qn** to sing the praises of sth/sb.

celebrazi'one [tʃelebrat'tsjone] sf celebration.

'celebre ['tʃɛlebre] ag famous, celebrated.

celebrità [tʃelebri'ta] sf inv fame; (persona) celebrity.

'celere ['tʃɛlere] ag fast, swift; (corso) crash cpd ♦ sf (POLIZIA) riot police.

ce'leste [tʃe'lɛste] ag celestial; heavenly; (colore) sky-blue.

'celia [tʃɛlja] sf joke; **per ~** for a joke.

celi'bato [tʃeli'bato] sm celibacy.

'celibe ['tʃɛlibe] ag single, unmarried ♦ sm bachelor.

'cella ['tʃɛlla] sf cell; **~ di rigore** punishment cell.

cello'phane ® [sɛlo'fan] sm cellophane ®.

'cellula ['tʃɛllula] sf (BIOL, ELETTR, POL) cell.

cellu'lare [tʃellu'lare] ag cellular ♦ sm (furgone) police van; (telefono) cellphone; **segregazione ~** (DIR) solitary confinement.

cellu'lite [tʃellu'lite] sf cellulitis.

'celta ['tʃɛlta] sm/f Celt.

'celtico, a, ci, che ['tʃɛltiko] ag, sm Celtic.

'cembalo ['tʃembalo] sm (MUS) harpsichord.

cemen'tare [tʃemen'tare] vt (anche fig) to cement.

ce'mento [tʃe'mento] sm cement; **~ armato** reinforced concrete.

'cena ['tʃena] sf dinner; (leggera) supper.

ce'nacolo [tʃe'nakolo] sm (circolo) coterie, circle; (REL, dipinto) Last Supper.

ce'nare [tʃe'nare] vi to dine, have dinner.

'cencio ['tʃentʃo] sm piece of cloth, rag; (per spolverare) duster; **essere bianco come un ~** to be as white as a sheet.

'cenere ['tʃenere] sf ash.

Cene'rentola [tʃene'rɛntola] sf (anche fig) Cinderella.

'cenno ['tʃenno] sm (segno) sign, signal; (gesto) gesture; (col capo) nod; (con la mano) wave; (allusione) hint, mention; (breve esposizione) short account; **far ~ di sì/no** to nod (one's head)/shake one's head; **~ d'intesa** sign of agreement; **~i di storia dell'arte** an outline of the history of art.

censi'mento [tʃensi'mento] sm census.

cen'sire [tʃen'sire] vt to take a census of.

'CENSIS ['tʃensis] sigla m (= Centro Studi Investimenti Sociali) independent institute carrying out research on Italy's social and cultural welfare.

cen'sore [tʃen'sore] sm censor.

cen'sura [tʃen'sura] sf censorship; censor's office; (fig) censure.

censu'rare [tʃensu'rare] vt to censor; to censure.

cent. abbr = **centesimo**.

centelli'nare [tʃentelli'nare] vt to sip; (fig) to savour (BRIT), savor (US).

cente'nario, a [tʃente'narjo] ag (che ha cento anni) hundred-year-old; (che ricorre ogni cento anni) centennial, centenary cpd ♦ sm/f centenarian ♦ sm centenary.

cen'tesimo, a [tʃen'tezimo] ag, sm hundredth; **essere senza un ~** to be penniless.

cen'tigrado, a [tʃen'tigrado] ag centigrade; **20 gradi ~i** 20 degrees centigrade.

cen'tilitro [tʃen'tilitro] sm centilitre.

cen'timetro [tʃen'timetro] sm centimetre (BRIT), centimeter (US); (nastro) measuring tape (in centimetres).

centi'naio, a pl(f) **-aia** [tʃenti'najo] sm: **un ~**

(di) a hundred; about a hundred.
'**cento** ['tʃɛnto] *num* a hundred, one hundred; **per** ~ per cent; **al** ~ **per** ~ **a** hundred per cent; ~ **di questi giorni!** many happy returns (of the day)!
centodi'eci [tʃɛnto'djɛtʃi] *num* one hundred and ten; ~ **e lode** (*UNIVERSITÀ*) ≈ first-class honours.
cento'mila [tʃɛnto'mila] *num* a o one hundred thousand; **te l'ho detto** ~ **volte** (*fig*) I've told you a thousand times.
Cen'trafrica [tʃen'trafrika] *sm*: **il** ~ the Central African Republic.
cen'trale [tʃen'trale] *ag* central ♦ *sf*: ~ **elettrica** electric power station; ~ **del latte** dairy; ~ **di polizia** police headquarters *pl*; ~ **telefonica** (telephone) exchange; **sede** ~ head office.
centrali'nista [tʃentrali'nista] *sm/f* operator.
centra'lino [tʃentra'lino] *sm* (telephone) exchange; (*di albergo etc*) switchboard.
centraliz'zare [tʃentralid'dzare] *vt* to centralize.
cen'trare [tʃen'trare] *vt* to hit the centre (*BRIT*) o center (*US*) of; (*TECN*) to centre; ~ **una risposta** to get the right answer; **ha centrato il problema** you've hit the nail on the head.
centra'vanti [tʃentra'vanti] *sm inv* centre forward.
cen'trifuga [tʃen'trifuga] *sf* spin-dryer.
centrifu'gare [tʃentrifu'gare] *vt* (*TECN*) to centrifuge; (*biancheria*) to spin-dry.
'**centro** ['tʃɛntro] *sm* centre (*BRIT*), center (*US*); **fare** ~ to hit the bull's eye; (*CALCIO*) to score; (*fig*) to hit the nail on the head; ~ **balneare** seaside resort; ~ **commerciale** shopping centre; (*città*) commercial centre; ~ **di costo** cost centre; ~ **elaborazione dati** data-processing unit; ~ **ospedaliero** hospital complex; ~ **sociale** community centre; ~**i vitali** (*anche fig*) vital organs.
centromedi'ano [tʃentrome'djano] *sm* (*CALCIO*) centre half.
'**ceppo** ['tʃeppo] *sm* (*di albero*) stump; (*pezzo di legno*) log.
'**cera** ['tʃera] *sf* wax; (*aspetto*) appearance, look; ~ **per pavimenti** floor polish.
cera'lacca [tʃera'lakka] *sf* sealing wax.
ce'ramica, che [tʃe'ramika] *sf* ceramic; (*ARTE*) ceramics *sg*.
cerbi'atto [tʃer'bjatto] *sm* fawn.
'**cerca** ['tʃerka] *sf*: **in** o **alla** ~ **di** in search of.
cercaper'sone [tʃerkaper'sone] *sm inv* bleeper.
cer'care [tʃer'kare] *vt* to look for, search for ♦ *vi*: ~ **di fare qc** to try to do sth.

cercherò *etc* [tʃerke'rɔ] *vb vedi* **cercare.**
'**cerchia** ['tʃerkja] *sf* circle.
cerchi'ato, a [tʃer'kjato] *ag*: **occhiali** ~**i d'osso** horn-rimmed spectacles; **avere gli occhi** ~**i** to have dark rings under one's eyes.
'**cerchio** ['tʃerkjo] *sm* circle; (*giocattolo, di botte*) hoop; **dare un colpo al** ~ **e uno alla botte** (*fig*) to keep two things going at the same time.
cerchi'one [tʃer'kjone] *sm* (wheel)rim.
cere'ale [tʃere'ale] *sm* cereal.
cere'brale [tʃere'brale] *ag* cerebral.
ceri'monia [tʃeri'mɔnja] *sf* ceremony; **senza tante** ~**e** (*senza formalità*) informally; (*bruscamente*) unceremoniously, without so much as a by-your-leave.
cerimoni'ale [tʃerimo'njale] *sm* etiquette; ceremonial.
cerimoni'ere [tʃerimo'njɛre] *sm* master of ceremonies.
cerimoni'oso, a [tʃerimo'njoso] *ag* formal, ceremonious.
ce'rino [tʃe'rino] *sm* wax match.
CERN [tʃern] *sigla m* (= *Comitato Europeo di Ricerche Nucleari*) CERN.
'**cernia** ['tʃɛrnja] *sf* (*ZOOL*) stone bass.
cerni'era [tʃer'njɛra] *sf* hinge; ~ **lampo** zip (fastener) (*BRIT*), zipper (*US*).
'**cernita** ['tʃɛrnita] *sf* selection; **fare una** ~ **di** to select.
'**cero** ['tʃero] *sm* (church) candle.
ce'rone [tʃe'rone] *sm* (*trucco*) greasepaint.
ce'rotto [tʃe'rɔtto] *sm* sticking plaster.
certa'mente [tʃerta'mente] *av* certainly, surely.
cer'tezza [tʃer'tettsa] *sf* certainty.
certifi'care [tʃertifi'kare] *vt* to certify.
certifi'cato [tʃertifi'kato] *sm* certificate; ~ **medico/di nascita** medical/birth certificate; ~ **di credito del Tesoro (CCT)** treasury bill.
certificazi'one [tʃertifikat'tsjone] *sf* certification; ~ **di bilancio** (*COMM*) external audit.

════════════════════ *PAROLA CHIAVE*

'**certo, a** ['tʃɛrto] *ag* (*sicuro*): ~ **(di/che)** certain o sure (of/that)
♦ *det* **1** (*tale*) certain; **un** ~ **signor Smith** a (certain) Mr Smith
2 (*qualche; con valore intensivo*) some; **dopo un** ~ **tempo** after some time; **un fatto di una** ~**a importanza** a matter of some importance; **di una** ~**a età** past one's prime, not so young
♦ *pron*: ~**i, e** *pl* some

♦ *av* (*certamente*) certainly; (*senz'altro*) of course; **di** ~ certainly; **no** (**di**) ~!, ~ **che no!** certainly not!; **sì** ~ yes indeed, certainly.

certo'sino [tʃerto'zino] *sm* Carthusian monk; (*liquore*) chartreuse; **è un lavoro da** ~ it's a pernickety job.
cer'tuni [tʃer'tuni] *pron pl* some (people).
ce'rume [tʃe'rume] *sm* (ear) wax.
'cerva ['tʃerva] *sf* (female) deer, doe.
cer'vello, *pl* **i** (*anche:* *pl(f)* **a** *o* **e**) [tʃer'vɛllo] *sm* brain; ~ **elettronico** computer; **avere il** *o* **essere un** ~ **fino** to be sharp-witted; **è uscito di** ~, **gli è dato di volta il** ~ he's gone off his head.
cervi'cale [tʃervi'kale] *ag* cervical.
'cervo, a ['tʃɛrvo] *sm/f* stag/hind ♦ *sm* deer; ~ **volante** stag beetle.
cesel'lare [tʃezel'lare] *vt* to chisel; (*incidere*) to engrave.
ce'sello [tʃe'zɛllo] *sm* chisel.
'CESIS ['tʃesis] *sigla m* (= *Comitato Esecutivo per i Servizi di Informazione e di Sicurezza*) *committee on intelligence and security matters, reporting to the Prime Minister.*
ce'soie [tʃe'zoje] *sfpl* shears.
ces'puglio [tʃes'puʎʎo] *sm* bush.
ces'sare [tʃes'sare] *vi, vt* to stop, cease; ~ **di fare qc** to stop doing sth; "**cessato allarme**" "all clear".
ces'sate il fu'oco [tʃes'sate-] *sm* ceasefire.
cessazi'one [tʃessat'tsjone] *sf* cessation; (*interruzione*) suspension.
cessi'one [tʃes'sjone] *sf* transfer.
'cesso ['tʃɛsso] *sm* (*fam: gabinetto*) bog.
'cesta ['tʃesta] *sf* (large) basket.
ces'tello [tʃes'tɛllo] *sm* (*per bottiglie*) crate; (*di lavatrice*) drum.
cesti'nare [tʃesti'nare] *vt* to throw away; (*fig: proposta*) to turn down; (: *romanzo*) to reject.
ces'tino [tʃes'tino] *sm* basket; (*per la carta straccia*) wastepaper basket; ~ **da viaggio** (*FERR*) packed lunch (*o* dinner).
'cesto ['tʃesto] *sm* basket.
ce'sura [tʃe'zura] *sf* caesura.
ce'taceo [tʃe'tatʃeo] *sm* sea mammal.
'ceto ['tʃɛto] *sm* (social) class.
'cetra ['tʃetra] *sf* zither; (*fig: di poeta*) lyre.
cetrio'lino [tʃetrio'lino] *sm* gherkin.
cetri'olo [tʃetri'olo] *sm* cucumber.
Cf., Cfr. *abbr* (= *confronta*) cf.
CFC [tʃieffe'tʃi] *abbr mpl* (= *clorofluorocarburi*) CFC.
CFS *sigla m* (= *Corpo Forestale dello Stato*) *body responsible for the planting and management of forests.*

cg *abbr* (= *centigrammo*) cg.
C.G.I.L. [tʃidʒi'ɛlle] *sigla f* (= *Confederazione Generale Italiana del Lavoro*) *trades union organization.*
CH *sigla* = *Chieti.*
cha'let [ʃa'lɛ] *sm inv* chalet.
cham'pagne [ʃã'paɲ] *sm inv* champagne.
chance [ʃãs] *sf inv* chance.
charme [ʃarm] *sm* charm.
'charter ['tʃaːtər] *ag inv* (*volo*) charter *cpd*; (*aereo*) chartered ♦ *sm inv* chartered plane.

════════════════ PAROLA CHIAVE

che [ke] *pron* **1** (*relativo: persona: soggetto*) who; (: *oggetto*) whom, that; (: *cosa, animale*) which, that; **il ragazzo** ~ **è venuto** the boy who came; **l'uomo** ~ **io vedo** the man (whom) I see; **il libro** ~ **è sul tavolo** the book which *o* that is on the table; **il libro** ~ **vedi** the book (which *o* that) you see; **la sera** ~ **ti ho visto** the evening I saw you
2 (*interrogativo, esclamativo*) what; ~ (**cosa**) **fai?** what are you doing?; **a** ~ (**cosa**) **pensi?** what are you thinking about?; **non sa** ~ (**cosa**) **fare** he doesn't know what to do; **sai di** ~ **si tratta?** do you know what it's about?; ~ (**cosa**) **succede?** what's happening?; **ma** ~ **dici!** what are you saying!
3 (*indefinito*): **quell'uomo ha un** ~ **di losco** there's something suspicious about that man; **un certo non so** ~ an indefinable something; **non è un gran** ~ it's nothing much
♦ *det* **1** (*interrogativo: tra tanti*) what; (: *tra pochi*) which; ~ **tipo di film preferisci?** what sort of film do you prefer?; ~ **vestito ti vuoi mettere?** what (*o* which) dress do you want to put on?
2 (*esclamativo: seguito da aggettivo*) how; (: *seguito da sostantivo*) what; ~ **buono!** how delicious!; ~ **bel vestito!** what a lovely dress!; ~ **macchina!** what a car!
♦ *cong* **1** (*con proposizioni subordinate*) that; **credo** ~ **verrà** I think he'll come; **voglio** ~ **tu studi** I want you to study; **so** ~ **tu c'eri** I know (that) you were there; **non** ~ **sia sbagliato, ma** ... not that it's wrong, but ...
2 (*finale*) so that; **vieni qua,** ~ **ti veda** come here, so (that) I can see you; **stai attento** ~ **non cada** mind it doesn't fall
3 (*temporale*): **arrivai** ~ **eri già partito** you had already left when I arrived; **sono anni** ~ **non lo vedo** I haven't seen him for years
4 (*in frasi imperative, concessive*): ~ **venga**

pure! let him come by all means!; ~ **tu sia benedetto!** may God bless you!; ~ **tu venga o no partiamo lo stesso** we're going whether you come or not **5** (*comparativo: con più, meno*) than; **è più lungo ~ largo** it's longer than it's wide; **più bella ~ mai** more beautiful than ever; *vedi anche* **più; meno; così** *etc.*

'**checca, che** ['kekka] *sf* (*fam: omosessuale*) fairy.

chef [ʃɛf] *sm inv* chef.

chemiotera'pia [kemjotera'pia] *sf* chemotherapy.

chero'sene [kero'zɛne] *sm* kerosene.

cheru'bino [keru'bino] *sm* cherub.

che'tare [ke'tare] *vt* to hush, silence; ~**rsi** *vr* to quieten down, fall silent.

cheti'chella [keti'kella]: **alla ~** *av* stealthily, unobtrusively; **andarsene alla ~** to slip away.

'**cheto, a** ['keto] *ag* quiet, silent.

=============== *PAROLA CHIAVE*

chi [ki] *pron* **1** (*interrogativo: soggetto*) who; (*: oggetto*) who, whom; ~ **è?** who is it?; **di ~ è questo libro?** whose book is this?, whose is this book?; **con ~ parli?** who are you talking to?; **a ~ pensi?** who are you thinking about?; ~ **di voi?** which of you?; **non so a ~ rivolgermi** I don't know who to ask

2 (*relativo*) whoever, anyone who; **dillo a ~ vuoi** tell whoever you like; **portate ~ volete** bring anyone you like; **so io di ~ parlo** I know who I'm talking about; **lo riferirò a ~ di dovere** I'll pass it on to the relevant person

3 (*indefinito*): ~ **... ~ ...** some ... others ...; ~ **dice una cosa, ~ dice un'altra** some say one thing, others say another.

chiacchie'rare [kjakkje'rare] *vi* to chat; (*discorrere futilmente*) to chatter; (*far pettegolezzi*) to gossip.

chiacchie'rata [kjakkje'rata] *sf* chat; **farsi una ~** to have a chat.

chi'acchiere ['kjakkjere] *sfpl* chatter *no pl*; gossip *no pl*; **fare due** *o* **quattro ~** to have a chat; **perdersi in ~** to waste time talking.

chiacchie'rone, a [kjakkje'rone] *ag* talkative, chatty; gossipy ♦ *sm/f* chatterbox; gossip.

chia'mare [kja'mare] *vt* to call; (*rivolgersi a qn*) to call (in), send for; ~**rsi** *vr* (*aver nome*) to be called; **mi chiamo Paolo** my name is Paolo, I'm called Paolo; **mandare**

a ~ qn to send for sb, call sb in; ~ **alle armi** to call up; ~ **in giudizio** to summon; ~ **qn da parte** to take sb aside.

chia'mata [kja'mata] *sf* (*TEL*) call; (*MIL*) call-up; ~ **interurbana** long-distance call; ~ **con preavviso** person-to-person call; ~ **alle urne** (*POL*) election.

chi'appa ['kjappa] *sf* (*fam: natica*) cheek; ~**e** *sfpl* bottom *sg*.

chi'ara ['kjara] *sf* egg white.

chia'rezza [kja'rettsa] *sf* clearness; clarity.

chiarifi'care [kjarifi'kare] *vt* (*anche fig*) to clarify.

chiarificazi'one [kjarifikat'tsjone] *sf* clarification.

chiari'mento [kjari'mento] *sm* clarification *no pl*, explanation.

chia'rire [kja'rire] *vt* to make clear; (*fig: spiegare*) to clear up, explain; ~**rsi** *vr* to become clear; **si sono chiariti** they've sorted things out.

chi'aro, a ['kjaro] *ag* clear; (*luminoso*) clear, bright; (*colore*) pale, light ♦ *av* (*parlare, vedere*) clearly; **si sta facendo ~** the day is dawning; **sia ~a una cosa** let's get one thing straight; **mettere in ~** (*fig*) to clear sth up; **parliamoci ~** let's be frank; **trasmissione in ~** (*TV*) uncoded broadcast.

chia'rore [kja'rore] *sm* (*diffuse*) light.

chiaroveg'gente [kjaroved'dʒɛnte] *sm/f* clairvoyant.

chi'asso ['kjasso] *sm* uproar, row; **far ~** to make a din; (*fig*) to make a fuss; (*: scalpore*) to cause a stir.

chias'soso, a [kjas'soso] *ag* noisy, rowdy; (*vistoso*) showy, gaudy.

'**chiatta** ['kjatta] *sf* barge.

chi'ave ['kjave] *sf* key ♦ *ag inv* key *cpd*; **chiudere a ~** to lock; ~ **d'accensione** (*AUT*) ignition key; ~ **a forcella** fork spanner; ~ **inglese** monkey wrench; **in ~ politica** in political terms; ~ **di volta** (*anche fig*) keystone; ~**i in mano** (*contratto*) turn-key *cpd*; **prezzo ~i in mano** (*di macchina*) on-the-road price.

chiavis'tello [kjavis'tɛllo] *sm* bolt.

chi'azza ['kjattsa] *sf* stain, splash.

chiaz'zare [kjat'tsare] *vt* to stain, splash.

chic [ʃik] *ag inv* chic, elegant.

chicches'sia [kikkes'sia] *pron* anyone, anybody.

'**chicco, chi** ['kikko] *sm* (*di cereale, riso*) grain; (*di caffè*) bean; ~ **di grandine** hailstone; ~ **d'uva** grape.

chi'edere [kjɛdere] *vt* (*per sapere*) to ask; (*per avere*) to ask for ♦ *vi*: ~ **di qn** to ask after sb; (*al telefono*) to ask for *o* want sb;

~rsi *vr*: ~rsi (se) to wonder (whether); ~ qc a qn to ask sb sth; to ask sb for sth; ~ scusa a qn to apologize to sb; ~ l'elemosina to beg; non chiedo altro that's all I want.

chieri'chetto [kjeri'ketto] *sm* altar boy.

chi'erico, ci ['kjɛriko] *sm* cleric; altar boy.

chi'esa ['kjɛza] *sf* church.

chi'esi *etc* ['kjɛzi] *vb vedi* chiedere.

chi'esto, a ['kjɛsto] *pp di* chiedere.

'Chigi ['kidʒi]: palazzo ~ *sm* (*POL*) *offices of the Italian Prime Minister.*

'chiglia ['kiʎʎa] *sf* keel.

'chilo ['kilo] *sm* kilo.

chilo'grammo [kilo'grammo] *sm* kilogram(me).

chilome'traggio [kilome'traddʒo] *sm* (*AUT*) ≈ mileage.

chilo'metrico, a, ci, che [kilo'mɛtriko] *ag* kilometric; (*fig*) endless.

chi'lometro [ki'lɔmetro] *sm* kilometre (*BRIT*), kilometer (*US*).

'chimico, a, ci, che ['kimiko] *ag* chemical ♦ *sm/f* chemist ♦ *sf* chemistry.

chi'mono [ki'mɔno] *sm inv* kimono.

'china ['kina] *sf* (*pendio*) slope, descent; (*BOT*) cinchona; (inchiostro di) ~ Indian ink; risalire la ~ (*fig*) to be on the road to recovery.

chi'nare [ki'nare] *vt* to lower, bend; ~rsi *vr* to stoop, bend.

chincaglie'ria [kinkaʎʎe'ria] *sf* fancy-goods shop; ~e *sfpl* fancy goods, knick-knacks.

chi'nino [ki'nino] *sm* quinine.

'chino, a ['kino] *ag*: a capo ~, a testa ~a head bent *o* bowed.

chi'occia, ce ['kjɔttʃa] *sf* brooding hen.

chi'occio, a, ci, ce ['kjɔttʃo] *ag* (*voce*) clucking.

chi'occiola ['kjɔttʃola] *sf* snail; scala a ~ spiral staircase.

chi'odo ['kjɔdo] *sm* nail; (*fig*) obsession; ~ scaccia ~ (*proverbio*) one problem drives away another; roba da ~i! it's unbelievable!; ~ di garofano (*CUC*) clove.

chi'oma ['kjɔma] *sf* (*capelli*) head of hair; (*di albero*) foliage.

chi'osco, schi ['kjɔsko] *sm* kiosk, stall.

chi'ostro ['kjɔstro] *sm* cloister.

chiro'mante [kiro'mante] *sm/f* palmist; (*indovino*) fortune-teller.

chirur'gia [kirur'dʒia] *sf* surgery.

chi'rurgico, a, ci, che [ki'rurdʒiko] *ag* (*anche fig*) surgical.

chi'rurgo, ghi *o* gi [ki'rurgo] *sm* surgeon.

chissà [kis'sa] *av* who knows, I wonder.

chi'tarra [ki'tarra] *sf* guitar.

chitar'rista, i, e [kitar'rista] *sm/f* guitarist, guitar player.

chi'udere ['kjudere] *vt* to close, shut; (*luce, acqua*) to put off, turn off; (*definitivamente: fabbrica*) to close down, shut down; (*strada*) to close; (*recingere*) to enclose; (*porre termine*) to end ♦ *vi* to close, shut; to close down, shut down; to end; ~rsi *vr* to shut, close; (*ritirarsi: anche fig*) to shut o.s. away; (*ferita*) to close up; ~ un occhio su (*fig*) to turn a blind eye to; chiudi la bocca! *o* il becco! (*fam*) shut up!

chi'unque [ki'unkwe] *pron* (*relativo*) whoever; (*indefinito*) anyone, anybody; ~ sia whoever it is.

'chiusi *etc* ['kjusi] *vb vedi* chiudere.

chi'uso, a ['kjuso] *pp di* chiudere ♦ *ag* (*porta*) shut, closed; (: *a chiave*) locked; (*senza uscita: strada etc*) blocked off; (*rubinetto*) off; (*persona*) uncommunicative; (*ambiente, club*) exclusive ♦ *sm*: stare al ~ (*fig*) to be shut up ♦ *sf* (*di corso d'acqua*) sluice, lock; (*recinto*) enclosure; (*di discorso etc*) conclusion, ending; "~" (*negozio etc*) "closed"; "~ al pubblico" "no admittance to the public".

chiu'sura [kju'sura] *sf* closing; shutting; closing *o* shutting down; enclosing; putting *o* turning off; ending; (*dispositivo*) catch; fastening; fastener; orario di ~ closing time; ~ lampo ® zip (fastener) (*BRIT*), zipper (*US*).

═══════════ PAROLA CHIAVE

ci [tʃi] (*dav lo, la, li, le, ne diventa* ce) *pron* 1 (*personale: complemento oggetto*) us; (: *a noi: complemento di termine*) to us; (: *riflessivo*) ourselves; (: *reciproco*) each other, one another; (*impersonale*): ~ si veste we get dressed; ~ ha visti he's seen us; non ~ ha dato niente he gave us nothing; ~ vestiamo we get dressed; ~ amiamo we love one another *o* each other; ~ siamo divertiti we had a good time

2 (*dimostrativo: di ciò, su ciò, in ciò etc*) about (*o* on *o* of) it; non ~ capisco nulla I can't make head nor tail of it; non so cosa far~ I don't know what to do about it; che ~ posso fare? what can I do about it?; che c'entro io? what have I got to do with it?; ~ puoi giurare you can bet on it; ~ puoi contare you can depend on it; ~ sei? (*sei pronto?*) are you ready?; (*hai capito?*) are you with me?

♦ *av* (*qui*) here; (*lì*) there; (*moto attraverso*

luogo): ~ **passa sopra un ponte** a bridge passes over it; **non ~ passa più nessuno** nobody comes this way any more; **qui ~ abito da un anno** I've been living here for a year; **esser**~ *vedi* **essere**.

CIA ['tʃia] *sigla f* (= *Central Intelligence Agency*) CIA.

C.ia *abbr* (= *compagnia*) Co.

cia'batta [tʃa'batta] *sf* mule, slipper.

ciabat'tino [tʃabat'tino] *sm* cobbler.

ciac [tʃak] *sm* (*CINE*) clapper board; ~, **si gira!** action!

Ci'ad [tʃad] *sm*: **il ~** Chad.

ci'alda ['tʃalda] *sf* (*CUC*) wafer.

cial'trone [tʃal'trone] *sm* good-for-nothing.

ciam'bella [tʃam'bɛlla] *sf* (*CUC*) ring-shaped cake; (*salvagente*) rubber ring.

ci'ancia, ce ['tʃantʃa] *sf* gossip *no pl*, tittle-tattle *no pl*.

cianfru'saglie [tʃanfru'zaʎʎe] *sfpl* bits and pieces.

cia'nuro [tʃa'nuro] *sm* cyanide.

ci'ao ['tʃao] *escl* (*all'arrivo*) hello!; (*alla partenza*) cheerio! (*BRIT*), bye!

ciar'lare [tʃar'lare] *vi* to chatter; (*peg*) to gossip.

ciarla'tano [tʃarla'tano] *sm* charlatan.

cias'cuno, a [tʃas'kuno] (*dav sm*: **ciascun** + *C, V,* **ciascuno** + *s impura, gn, pn, ps, x, z*; *dav sf*: **ciascuna** + *C,* **ciascun'** + *V*) *det, pron* each.

ci'bare [tʃi'bare] *vt* to feed; ~**rsi** *vr*: ~**rsi di** to eat.

ci'barie [tʃi'barje] *sfpl* foodstuffs.

ciber'netica [tʃiber'nɛtika] *sf* cybernetics *sg*.

'cibo ['tʃibo] *sm* food.

ci'cala [tʃi'kala] *sf* cicada.

cica'trice [tʃika'tritʃe] *sf* scar.

cicatriz'zarsi [tʃikatrid'dzarsi] *vr* to form a scar, heal (up).

'cicca, che ['tʃikka] *sf* cigarette end; (*fam*: *sigaretta*) fag; **non vale una ~** (*fig*) it's worthless.

'ciccia ['tʃittʃa] *sf* (*fam*: *carne*) meat; (: *grasso umano*) fat, flesh.

cicci'one, a [tʃit'tʃone] *sm/f* (*fam*) fatty.

cice'rone [tʃitʃe'rone] *sm* guide.

cicla'mino [tʃikla'mino] *sm* cyclamen.

ci'clismo [tʃi'klizmo] *sm* cycling.

ci'clista, i, e [tʃi'klista] *sm/f* cyclist.

'ciclo ['tʃiklo] *sm* cycle; (*di malattia*) course.

ciclomo'tore [tʃiklomo'tore] *sm* moped.

ci'clone [tʃi'klone] *sm* cyclone.

ciclos'tile [tʃiklos'tile] *sm* cyclostyle (*BRIT*).

ci'cogna [tʃi'koɲɲa] *sf* stork.

ci'coria [tʃi'kɔrja] *sf* chicory.

'CIDA ['tʃida] *sigla f* = *Confederazione Italiana Dirigenti d'Azienda*.

ci'eco, a, chi, che ['tʃɛko] *ag* blind ♦ *sm/f* blind man/woman; **alla ~a** (*anche fig*) blindly.

ciel'lino, a [tʃiel'lino] *sm/f* (*POL*) member of *CL* movement.

ci'elo ['tʃɛlo] *sm* sky; (*REL*) heaven; **toccare il ~ con un dito** (*fig*) to walk on air; **per amor del ~**! for heavens' sake!

'cifra ['tʃifra] *sf* (*numero*) figure, numeral; (*somma di denaro*) sum, figure; (*monogramma*) monogram, initials *pl*; (*codice*) code, cipher.

ci'frare [tʃi'frare] *vt* (*messaggio*) to code; (*lenzuola etc*) to embroider with a monogram.

'ciglio ['tʃiʎʎo] *sm* (*margine*) edge, verge; (*pl(f)* **ciglia**: *delle palpebre*) (eye)lash; (*sopracciglio*) eyebrow; **non ha battuto ~** (*fig*) he didn't bat an eyelid.

'cigno ['tʃiɲɲo] *sm* swan.

cigo'lante [tʃigo'lante] *ag* squeaking, creaking.

cigo'lare [tʃigo'lare] *vi* to squeak, creak.

CIIS *sigla m* (= *Comitato Interparlamentare per l'Informazione e la Sicurezza*) all-party committee on intelligence and security.

'Cile ['tʃile] *sm*: **il ~** Chile.

ci'lecca [tʃi'lekka] *sf*: **far ~** to fail.

ci'leno, a [tʃi'lɛno] *ag*, *sm/f* Chilean.

cili'egia, gie *o* **ge** [tʃi'ljɛdʒa] *sf* cherry.

cilie'gina [tʃilje'dʒina] *sf* glacé cherry; **la ~ sulla torta** (*fig*) the icing *o* cherry on the cake.

cili'egio [tʃi'ljɛdʒo] *sm* cherry tree.

cilin'drata [tʃilin'drata] *sf* (*AUT*) (cubic) capacity; **una macchina di grossa ~** a big-engined car.

ci'lindro [tʃi'lindro] *sm* cylinder; (*cappello*) top hat.

CIM [tʃim] *sigla m* = *centro d'igiene mentale*.

'cima ['tʃima] *sf* (*sommità*) top; (*di monte*) top, summit; (*estremità*) end; (*fig*: *persona*) genius; **in ~ a** at the top of; **da ~ a fondo** from top to bottom; (*fig*) from beginning to end.

ci'melio [tʃi'mɛljo] *sm* relic.

cimen'tarsi [tʃimen'tarsi] *vr*: ~**rsi in** (*atleta, concorrente*) to try one's hand at.

'cimice ['tʃimitʃe] *sf* (*ZOOL*) bug; (*puntina*) drawing pin (*BRIT*), thumbtack (*US*).

cimini'era [tʃimi'njɛra] *sf* chimney; (*di nave*) funnel.

cimi'tero [tʃimi'tɛro] *sm* cemetery.

ci'murro [tʃi'murro] *sm* (*di cani*) distemper.

'Cina ['tʃina] *sf*: **la ~** China.

cin'cin, cin cin [tʃin'tʃin] *escl* cheers!
cincischi'are [tʃintʃis'kjare] *vi* to mess about, fiddle about.
'cine ['tʃine] *sm inv* (*fam*) cinema.
cine'asta, i, e [tʃine'asta] *sm/f* person in the film industry; film-maker.
cinegior'nale [tʃineʤor'nale] *sm* newsreel.
'cinema ['tʃinema] *sm inv* cinema; ~ muto silent films; ~ d'essai (*locale*) avant-garde cinema, experimental cinema.
cinemato'grafico, a, ci, che [tʃinemato'grafiko] *ag* (*attore, critica*) movie *cpd*, film *cpd*; (*festival*) film *cpd*; sala ~a cinema; successo ~ box-office success.
cinema'tografo [tʃinema'tɔgrafo] *sm* cinema.
cine'presa [tʃine'presa] *sf* cine-camera.
ci'nese [tʃi'nese] *ag*, *sm/f*, *sm* Chinese *inv*.
cine'teca, che [tʃine'tɛka] *sf* (*collezione*) film collection, film library; (*locale*) film library.
ci'netico, a, ci, che [tʃi'nɛtiko] *ag* kinetic.
'cingere ['tʃinʤere] *vt* (*attorniare*) to surround, encircle; ~ la vita con una cintura to put a belt round one's waist; ~ d'assedio to besiege, lay siege to.
'cinghia ['tʃingja] *sf* strap; (*cintura, TECN*) belt; tirare la ~ (*fig*) to tighten one's belt.
cinghi'ale [tʃin'gjale] *sm* wild boar.
cinguet'tare [tʃingwet'tare] *vi* to twitter.
'cinico, a, ci, che ['tʃiniko] *ag* cynical ♦ *sm/f* cynic.
ci'nismo [tʃi'nizmo] *sm* cynicism.
cin'quanta [tʃin'kwanta] *num* fifty.
cinquante'nario [tʃinkwante'narjo] *sm* fiftieth anniversary.
cinquan'tenne [tʃinkwan'tɛnne] *sm/f* fifty-year-old man/woman.
cinquan'tesimo, a [tʃinkwan'tɛzimo] *num* fiftieth.
cinquan'tina [tʃinkwan'tina] *sf* (*serie*): una ~ (di) about fifty; (*età*): essere sulla ~ to be about fifty.
'cinque ['tʃinkwe] *num* five; avere ~ anni to be five (years old); il ~ dicembre 1988 the fifth of December 1988; alle ~ (*ora*) at five (o'clock); siamo in ~ there are five of us.
cinquecen'tesco, a, schi, sche [tʃinkwetʃen'tesko] *ag* sixteenth-century.
cinque'cento [tʃinkwe'tʃɛnto] *num* five hundred ♦ *sm*: il C~ the sixteenth century.
cinque'mila [tʃinkwe'mila] *num* five thousand.
'cinsi *etc* ['tʃinsi] *vb vedi* cingere.
'cinta ['tʃinta] *sf* (*anche*: ~ muraria) city walls *pl*; muro di ~ (*di giardino etc*)

surrounding wall.
cin'tare [tʃin'tare] *vt* to enclose.
'cinto, a ['tʃinto] *pp di* cingere.
'cintola ['tʃintola] *sf* (*cintura*) belt; (*vita*) waist.
cin'tura [tʃin'tura] *sf* belt; ~ di salvataggio lifebelt (*BRIT*), life preserver (*US*); ~ di sicurezza (*AUT, AER*) safety o seat belt.
cintu'rino [tʃintu'rino] *sm* strap; ~ dell'orologio watch strap.
CIO *sigla m* (= Comitato Internazionale Olimpico) IOC (= International Olympic Committee).
ciò [tʃɔ] *pron* this; that; ~ che what; ~ nonostante o nondimeno nevertheless, in spite of that; con tutto ~ for all that, in spite of everything.
ci'occa, che ['tʃɔkka] *sf* (*di capelli*) lock.
ciocco'lata [tʃokko'lata] *sf* chocolate; (*bevanda*) (hot) chocolate; ~ al latte/ fondente milk/plain chocolate.
cioccola'tino [tʃokkola'tino] *sm* chocolate.
ciocco'lato [tʃokko'lato] *sm* chocolate.
cio'è [tʃo'ɛ] *av* that is (to say).
ciondo'lare [tʃondo'lare] *vt* (*far dondolare*) to dangle, swing ♦ *vi* to dangle; (*fig*) to loaf (about).
ci'ondolo ['tʃondolo] *sm* pendant; ~ portafortuna charm.
ciondo'loni [tʃondo'loni] *av*: con le braccia/ gambe ~ with arms/legs dangling.
ciononos'tante [tʃononos'tante] *av* nonetheless, nevertheless.
ci'otola ['tʃɔtola] *sf* bowl.
ci'ottolo ['tʃɔttolo] *sm* pebble; (*di strada*) cobble(stone).
C.I.P. [tʃip] *sigla m* (= comitato interministeriale prezzi) *vedi* comitato.
Cipe ['tʃipe] *sigla m* (= comitato interministeriale per la programmazione economica) *vedi* comitato.
'Cipi ['tʃipi] *sigla m* (= comitato interministeriale per lo sviluppo industriale) *vedi* comitato.
ci'piglio [tʃi'piʎʎo] *sm* frown.
ci'polla [tʃi'polla] *sf* onion; (*di tulipano etc*) bulb.
ci'presso [tʃi'presso] *sm* cypress (tree).
'cipria ['tʃiprja] *sf* (*face*) powder.
cipri'ota, i, e [tʃipri'ɔta] *ag*, *sm/f* Cypriot.
'Cipro ['tʃipro] *sm* Cyprus.
'circa ['tʃirka] *av* about, roughly ♦ *prep* about, concerning; a mezzogiorno ~ about midday.
'circo, chi ['tʃirko] *sm* circus.
circo'lare [tʃirko'lare] *vi* to circulate; (*AUT*) to drive (along), move (along) ♦ *ag* circular ♦ *sf* (*AMM*) circular; (*di autobus*) circle (line); circola voce che ... there is a

rumour going about that ...; **assegno** ~ banker's draft.

circolazi'one [tʃirkolat'tsjone] *sf* circulation; (*AUT*): **la** ~ (the) traffic; **libretto di** ~ log book, registration book; **tassa di** ~ road tax.

Circolazione a targhe alterne *is a practice introduced by some town councils to combat the increase in traffic and pollution in town centres. It stipulates that on days with an even date, only cars whose numberplate ends in an even number or a zero may be on the road, while on days with an odd date, only cars whose numberplate ends in an odd number may be on the road. Generally, public holidays are not affected by this bylaw, but may be included at the council's discretion.*

'circolo ['tʃirkolo] *sm* circle; **entrare in** ~ (*ANAT*) to enter the bloodstream.

circoncisi'one [tʃirkontʃi'zjone] *sf* circumcision.

circon'dare [tʃirkon'dare] *vt* to surround.

circondari'ale [tʃirkonda'rjale] *ag*: **casa di pena** ~ district prison.

circon'dario [tʃirkon'darjo] *sm* (*DIR*) administrative district; (*zona circostante*) neighbourhood (*BRIT*), neighborhood (*US*).

circonfe'renza [tʃirkonfe'rɛntsa] *sf* circumference.

circonvallazi'one [tʃirkonvallat'tsjone] *sf* ring road (*BRIT*), beltway (*US*); (*per evitare una città*) by-pass.

circos'critto, a [tʃirkos'kritto] *pp di* **circoscrivere**.

circos'crivere [tʃirkos'krivere] *vt* to circumscribe; (*fig*) to limit, restrict.

circoscrizi'one [tʃirkoskrit'tsjone] *sf* (*AMM*) district, area; ~ **elettorale** constituency.

circos'petto, a [tʃirkos'pɛtto] *ag* circumspect, cautious.

circos'tante [tʃirkos'tante] *ag* surrounding, neighbouring (*BRIT*), neighboring (*US*).

circos'tanza [tʃirkos'tantsa] *sf* circumstance; (*occasione*) occasion; **parole di** ~ words suited to the occasion.

circu'ire [tʃirku'ire] *vt* (*fig*) to fool, take in.

cir'cuito [tʃir'kuito] *sm* circuit; **andare in** *o* **fare corto** ~ to short-circuit; ~ **integrato** integrated circuit.

ci'rillico, a, ci, che [tʃi'rilliko] *ag* Cyrillic.

cir'rosi [tʃir'rɔzi] *sf*: ~ **epatica** cirrhosis (of the liver).

'C.I.S.A.L. ['tʃizal] *sigla f* (= *Confederazione Italiana Sindacati Autonomi dei Lavoratori*) *trades union organization.*

C.I.S.L. [tʃizl] *sigla f* (= *Confederazione Italiana Sindacati Lavoratori*) *trades union organization.*

'C.I.S.N.A.L. ['tʃiznal] *sigla f* (= *Confederazione Italiana Sindacati Nazionali dei Lavoratori*) *trades union organization.*

'ciste ['tʃiste] *sf* = **cisti**.

cis'terna [tʃis'tɛrna] *sf* tank, cistern.

'cisti ['tʃisti] *sf inv* cyst.

cis'tite [tʃis'tite] *sf* cystitis.

C.I.T. [tʃit] *sigla f* = *Compagnia Italiana Turismo.*

cit. *abbr* (= *citato, citata*) cit.

ci'tare [tʃi'tare] *vt* (*DIR*) to summon; (*autore*) to quote; (*a esempio, modello*) to cite; ~ **qn per danni** to sue sb.

citazi'one [tʃitat'tsjone] *sf* summons *sg*; quotation; (*di persona*) mention.

ci'tofono [tʃi'tɔfono] *sm* entry phone; (*in uffici*) intercom.

cito'logico, a, ci, che [tʃito'lɔdʒiko] *ag*: **esame** ~ test for detection of cancerous cells.

'citrico, a, ci, che ['tʃitriko] *ag* citric.

città [tʃit'ta] *sf inv* town; (*importante*) city; ~ **giardino** garden city; ~ **mercato** shopping centre, mall; ~ **universitaria** university campus; **C**~ **del Capo** Cape Town.

citta'della [tʃitta'dɛlla] *sf* citadel, stronghold.

cittadi'nanza [tʃittadi'nantsa] *sf* citizens *pl*, inhabitants *pl* of a town (*o* city); (*DIR*) citizenship.

citta'dino, a [tʃitta'dino] *ag* town *cpd*; city *cpd* ♦ *smlf* (*di uno Stato*) citizen; (*abitante di città*) town dweller, city dweller.

ci'uccio ['tʃuttʃo] *sm* (*fam*) comforter, dummy (*BRIT*), pacifier (*US*).

ci'uco, a, chi, che ['tʃuko] *smlf* ass.

ci'uffo ['tʃuffo] *sm* tuft.

ci'urma ['tʃurma] *sf* (*di nave*) crew.

ci'vetta [tʃi'vetta] *sf* (*ZOOL*) owl; (*fig: donna*) coquette, flirt ♦ *ag inv*: **auto/nave** ~ decoy car/ship; **fare la** ~ **con qn** to flirt with sb.

civet'tare [tʃivet'tare] *vt* to flirt.

civette'ria [tʃivette'ria] *sf* coquetry, coquettishness.

civettu'olo, a [tʃivet'twɔlo] *ag* flirtatious.

'civico, a, ci, che ['tʃiviko] *ag* civic; (*museo*) municipal, town *cpd*; **guardia** ~**a** town policeman; **senso** ~ public spirit.

ci'vile [tʃi'vile] *ag* civil; (*non militare*) civilian; (*nazione*) civilized ♦ *sm* civilian; **stato** ~ marital status; **abiti** ~**i** civvies.

civi'lista, i, e [tʃivi'lista] *smlf* (*avvocato*) civil lawyer; (*studioso*) expert in civil law.

civiliz'zare [tʃivilid'dzare] *vt* to civilize.
civilizzazi'one [tʃiviliddzat'tsjone] *sf* civilization.
civiltà [tʃivil'ta] *sf* civilization; (*cortesia*) civility.
ci'vismo [tʃi'vizmo] *sm* public spirit.
CL [tʃi'elle] *sigla f* (*POL*: = *Comunione e Liberazione*) *Catholic youth movement* ♦ *sigla* = *Caltanissetta*.
cl *abbr* (= *centilitro*) cl.
'clacson *sm inv* (*AUT*) horn.
cla'more *sm* (*frastuono*) din, uproar, clamour (*BRIT*), clamor (*US*); (*fig*) outcry.
clamo'roso, a *ag* noisy; (*fig*) sensational.
clan *sm inv* clan.
clandestinità *sf* (*di attività*) secret nature; **vivere nella** ~ to live in hiding; (*ricercato politico*) to live underground.
clandes'tino, a *ag* clandestine; (*POL*) underground, clandestine ♦ *sm/f* stowaway.
clari'netto *sm* clarinet.
'classe *sf* class; **di** ~ (*fig*) with class; of excellent quality; ~ **turistica** (*AER*) economy class.
classi'cismo [klassi'tʃizmo] *sm* classicism.
'classico, a, ci, che *ag* classical; (*tradizionale: moda*) classic(al) ♦ *sm* classic; classical author; (*anche: liceo* ~) *secondary school with emphasis on the humanities.*
clas'sifica, che *sf* classification; (*SPORT*) placings *pl*; (*di dischi*) charts *pl*, hit parade.
classifi'care *vt* to classify; (*candidato, compito*) to grade; ~**rsi** *vr* to be placed.
classifica'tore *sm* filing cabinet.
classificazi'one [klassifikat'tsjone] *sf* classification; grading.
clas'sista, i, e *ag* class-conscious ♦ *sm/f* class-conscious person.
claudi'cante *ag* (*zoppo*) lame; (*fig: prosa*) halting.
'clausola *sf* (*DIR*) clause.
claustro'fobico, a, ci, che *ag* claustrophobic.
clau'sura *sf* (*REL*): **monaca di** ~ nun belonging to an enclosed order; **fare una vita di** ~ (*fig*) to lead a cloistered life.
'clava *sf* club.
clavi'cembalo [klavi'tʃembalo] *sm* harpsichord.
cla'vicola *sf* (*ANAT*) collarbone.
cle'mente *ag* merciful; (*clima*) mild.
cle'menza [kle'mɛntsa] *sf* mercy, clemency; mildness.
clep'tomane *sm/f* kleptomaniac.
cleri'cale *ag* clerical.

'clero *sm* clergy.
cles'sidra *sf* (*a sabbia*) hourglass; (*ad acqua*) water clock.
cliché [kli'ʃe] *sm inv* (*TIP*) plate; (*fig*) cliché.
cli'ente *sm/f* customer, client.
clien'tela *sf* customers *pl*, clientèle.
cliente'lismo *sm*: ~ **politico** political nepotism.
'clima, i *sm* climate.
cli'matico, a, ci, che *ag* climatic; **stazione** ~**a** health resort.
climatizzazi'one [klimatiddzat'tsjone] *sf* air conditioning.
'clinico, a, ci, che *ag* clinical ♦ *sm* (*medico*) clinician ♦ *sf* (*scienza*) clinical medicine; (*casa di cura*) clinic, nursing home; (*settore d'ospedale*) clinic; **quadro** ~ anamnesis; **avere l'occhio** ~ (*fig*) to have an expert eye.
clis'tere *sm* (*MED*) enema; (: *apparecchio*) *device used to give an enema*.
clo'aca, che *sf* sewer.
cloche [klɔʃ] *sf inv* (*AER*) control stick, joystick; **cambio a** ~ (*AUT*) floor-mounted gear lever.
'cloro *sm* chlorine.
cloro'filla *sf* chlorophyll.
cloro'formio *sm* chloroform.
club *sm inv* club.
cm *abbr* (= *centimetro*) cm.
c.m. *abbr* (= *corrente mese*) inst.
CN *sigla* = *Cuneo.*
c/n *abbr* = *conto nuovo.*
CNEN *sigla m* (= *Comitato Nazionale per l'Energia Nucleare*) ≈ AEA (*BRIT*), AEC (*US*).
CNIOP *sigla m* = *Centro Nazionale per l'Istruzione e l'Orientamento Professionale.*
CNR *sigla m* (= *Consiglio Nazionale delle Ricerche*) *science research council.*
CNRN *sigla m* = *Comitato Nazionale Ricerche Nucleari.*
CO *sigla* = *Como.*
Co. *abbr* (= *compagnia*) Co.
c/o *abbr* (= *care of*) c/o.
coabi'tare *vi* to live together, live under the same roof.
coagu'lare *vt* to coagulate ♦ *vi*, ~**rsi** *vr* to coagulate; (*latte*) to curdle.
coalizi'one [koalit'tsjone] *sf* coalition.
co'atto, a *ag* (*DIR*) compulsory, forced; **condannare al domicilio** ~ to place under house arrest.
'COBAS *sigla mpl* (= *Comitati di base*) *independent trades unions.*
'cobra *sm inv* cobra.
'coca 'cola ® *sf* coca cola ®.
coca'ina *sf* cocaine.

coc'carda *sf* cockade.

cocchi'ere [kok'kjɛre] *sm* coachman.

'cocchio ['kɔkkjo] *sm* (*carrozza*) coach; (*biga*) chariot.

cocci'nella [kottʃi'nɛlla] *sf* ladybird (*BRIT*), ladybug (*US*).

'coccio ['kɔttʃo] *sm* earthenware; (*vaso*) earthenware pot; ~**i** *smpl* fragments (of pottery).

cocciu'taggine [kottʃu'taddʒine] *sf* stubbornness, pig-headedness.

cocci'uto, a [kot'tʃuto] *ag* stubborn, pigheaded.

'cocco, chi *sm* (*pianta*) coconut palm; (*frutto*): **noce di** ~ coconut ♦ *sm/f* (*fam*) darling; **è il** ~ **della mamma** he's mummy's darling.

cocco'drillo *sm* crocodile.

cocco'lare *vt* to cuddle, fondle.

co'cente [ko'tʃɛnte] *ag* (*anche fig*) burning.

cocerò *etc* [kotʃe'rɔ] *vb vedi* **cuocere.**

co'comero *sm* watermelon.

co'cuzzolo [ko'kuttsolo] *sm* top; (*di capo, cappello*) crown.

cod. *abbr* = **codice.**

'coda *sf* tail; (*fila di persone, auto*) queue (*BRIT*), line (*US*); (*di abiti*) train; **con la ~ dell'occhio** out of the corner of one's eye; **mettersi in** ~ to queue (up) (*BRIT*), line up (*US*); to join the queue *o* line; ~ **di cavallo** (*acconciatura*) ponytail; **avere la ~ di paglia** (*fig*) to have a guilty conscience; ~ **di rospo** (*CUC*) frogfish tail.

codar'dia *sf* cowardice.

co'dardo, a *ag* cowardly ♦ *sm/f* coward.

co'desto, a *ag, pron* (*poetico*) this; that.

'codice ['kɔditʃe] *sm* code; (*manoscritto antico*) codex; ~ **di avviamento postale** (**CAP**) postcode (*BRIT*), zip code (*US*); ~ **a barre** bar code; ~ **civile** civil code; ~ **fiscale** tax code; ~ **penale** penal code; ~ **segreto** (*di tessera magnetica*) PIN (number); ~ **della strada** highway code.

co'difica *sf* codification; (*INFORM: di programma*) coding.

codifi'care *vt* (*DIR*) to codify; (*cifrare*) to code.

codificazi'one [kodifikat'tsjone] *sf* coding.

coercizi'one [koertʃit'tsjone] *sf* coercion.

coe'rente *ag* coherent.

coe'renza [koe'rɛntsa] *sf* coherence.

coesi'one *sf* cohesion.

coe'sistere *vi* to coexist.

coe'taneo, a *ag, sm/f* contemporary; **essere ~ di qn** to be the same age as sb.

cofa'netto *sm* casket; ~ **dei gioielli** jewel case.

'cofano *sm* (*AUT*) bonnet (*BRIT*), hood (*US*); (*forziere*) chest.

'coffa *sf* (*NAUT*) top.

'cogli ['kɔʎʎi] *prep* + *det vedi* **con.**

'cogliere ['kɔʎʎere] *vt* (*fiore, frutto*) to pick, gather; (*sorprendere*) to catch, surprise; (*bersaglio*) to hit; (*fig: momento opportuno etc*) to grasp, seize, take; (: *capire*) to grasp; ~ **l'occasione (per fare)** to take the opportunity (to do); ~ **sul fatto** *o* **in flagrante/alla sprovvista** to catch redhanded/unprepared; ~ **nel segno** (*fig*) to hit the nail on the head.

cogli'one [koʎ'ʎone] *sm* (*fam!: testicolo*): ~**i** balls (*!*); (: *fig: persona sciocca*) jerk; **rompere i ~i a qn** to get on sb's tits (*!*).

co'gnac [kɔ'ɲak] *sm inv* cognac.

co'gnato, a [koɲ'ɲato] *sm/f* brother-/sister-in-law.

cognizi'one [koɲɲit'tsjone] *sf* knowledge; **con ~ di causa** with full knowledge of the facts.

co'gnome [koɲ'ɲome] *sm* surname.

'coi *prep* + *det vedi* **con.**

coi'bente *ag* insulating.

coinci'denza [kointʃi'dɛntsa] *sf* coincidence; (*FERR, AER, di autobus*) connection.

coin'cidere [koin'tʃidere] *vi* to coincide.

coin'ciso, a [koin'tʃizo] *pp di* **coincidere.**

coinqui'lino *sm* fellow tenant.

cointeres'senza [kointeres'sɛntsa] *sf* (*COMM*): **avere una ~ in qc** to own shares in sth; ~ **dei lavoratori** profit-sharing.

coin'volgere [koin'vɔldʒere] *vt*: ~ **in** to involve in.

coinvolgi'mento [koinvoldʒi'mento] *sm* involvement.

coin'volto, a *pp di* **coinvolgere.**

col *prep* + *det vedi* **con.**

Col. *abbr* (= *colonnello*) Col.

colà *av* there.

cola'brodo *sm inv* strainer.

cola'pasta *sm inv* colander.

co'lare *vt* (*liquido*) to strain; (*pasta*) to drain; (*oro fuso*) to pour ♦ *vi* (*sudore*) to drip; (*botte*) to leak; (*cera*) to melt; ~ **a picco** *vt, vi* (*nave*) to sink.

co'lata *sf* (*di lava*) flow; (*FONDERIA*) casting.

colazi'one [kolat'tsjone] *sf* (*anche*: **prima ~**) breakfast; (*anche*: **seconda ~**) lunch; **fare ~** to have breakfast (*o* lunch); ~ **di lavoro** working lunch.

Coldi'retti *abbr f* (= *Confederazione nazionale coltivatori diretti*) *federation of Italian farmers*.

co'lei *pron vedi* **colui.**

co'lera *sm* (*MED*) cholera.

coleste'rolo *sm* cholesterol.

colf *abbr f* = **collaboratrice familiare.**
'**colgo** *etc vb vedi* **cogliere.**
colibrì *sm* hummingbird.
'**colica** *sf* (*MED*) colic.
co'lino *sm* strainer.
'**colla** *prep* + *det vedi* **con** ♦ *sf* glue; (*di farina*)
  paste.
collabo'rare *vi* to collaborate; (*con la
  polizia*) to co-operate; ~ **a** to collaborate
  on; (*giornale*) to contribute to.
collabora'tore, 'trice *sm/f* collaborator; (*di
  giornale, rivista*) contributor; ~ **esterno**
  freelance; ~**trice familiare** home help; ~
  di giustizia = **pentito, a.**
collaborazi'one [kollaborat'tsjone] *sf*
  collaboration; contribution.
col'lana *sf* necklace; (*collezione*) collection,
  series.
col'lant [kɔ'lã] *sm inv* tights *pl.*
col'lare *sm* collar.
col'lasso *sm* (*MED*) collapse.
collate'rale *ag* collateral; **effetti** ~**i** side
  effects.
col'laudo *sm* testing *no pl*; test.
'**colle** *prep* + *det vedi* **con** ♦ *sm* hill.
col'lega, ghi, ghe *sm/f* colleague.
collega'mento *sm* connection; (*MIL*)
  liaison; (*RADIO*) link(-up); **ufficiale di** ~
  liaison officer.
colle'gare *vt* to connect, join, link; ~**rsi** *vr*
  (*RADIO, TV*) to link up; ~**rsi con** (*TEL*) to
  get through to.
collegi'ale [kolle'dʒale] *ag* (*riunione,
  decisione*) collective; (*INS*) boarding
  school *cpd* ♦ *sm/f* boarder; (*fig: persona
  timida e inesperta*) schoolboy/girl.
col'legio [kol'lɛdʒo] *sm* college; (*convitto*)
  boarding school; ~ **elettorale** (*POL*)
  constituency.
'**collera** *sf* anger; **andare in** ~ to get angry.
col'lerico, a, ci, che *ag* quick-tempered,
  irascible.
col'letta *sf* collection.
collettività *sf* community.
collet'tivo, a *ag* collective; (*interesse*)
  general, everybody's; (*biglietto, visita etc*)
  group *cpd* ♦ *sm* (*POL*) (political) group;
  società in nome ~ (*COMM*) partnership.
col'letto *sm* collar; ~**i bianchi** (*fig*) white-
  collar workers.
collezio'nare [kollettsjo'nare] *vt* to collect.
collezi'one [kollet'tsjone] *sf* collection.
collezio'nista [kollettsjo'nista] *sm/f*
  collector.
colli'mare *vi* to correspond, coincide.
col'lina *sf* hill.
colli'nare *ag* hill *cpd.*
col'lirio *sm* eyewash.

collisi'one *sf* collision.
'**collo** *prep* + *det vedi* **con** ♦ *sm* neck; (*di abito*)
  neck, collar; (*pacco*) parcel; ~ **del piede**
  instep.
colloca'mento *sm* (*impiego*) employment;
  (*disposizione*) placing, arrangement;
  ufficio di ~ ≈ Jobcentre (*BRIT*), state (*o
  federal*) employment agency (*US*); ~ **a
  riposo** retirement.
collo'care *vt* (*libri, mobili*) to place;
  (*persona: trovare un lavoro per*) to find a job
  for, place; (*COMM: merce*) to find a market
  for; ~ **qn a riposo** to retire sb.
collocazi'one [kollokat'tsjone] *sf* placing;
  (*di libro*) classification.
colloqui'ale *ag* (*termine etc*) colloquial;
  (*tono*) informal.
col'loquio *sm* conversation, talk; (*ufficiale,
  per un lavoro*) interview; (*INS*)
  preliminary oral exam; **avviare un** ~ **con
  qn** (*POL etc*) to start talks with sb.
col'loso, a *ag* sticky.
col'lottola *sf* nape *o* scruff of the neck;
  afferrare qn per la ~ to grab sb by the
  scruff of the neck.
collusi'one *sf* (*DIR*) collusion.
colluttazi'one [kolluttat'tsjone] *sf* scuffle.
col'mare *vt*: ~ **di** (*anche fig*) to fill with;
  (*dare in abbondanza*) to load *o* overwhelm
  with; ~ **un divario** (*fig*) to bridge a gap.
'**colmo, a** *ag*: ~ (**di**) full (of) ♦ *sm* summit,
  top; (*fig*) height; **al** ~ **della disperazione** in
  the depths of despair; **è il** ~! it's the last
  straw!; **e per** ~ **di sfortuna** ... and to cap it
  all ...
co'lomba *sf vedi* **colombo.**
Co'lombia *sf*: **la** ~ Colombia.
colombi'ano, a *ag, sm/f* Colombian.
co'lombo, a *sm/f* dove; pigeon; ~**i** (*fig fam*)
  lovebirds.
Co'lonia *sf* Cologne.
co'lonia *sf* colony; (*per bambini*) holiday
  camp; (*acqua di*) ~ (eau de) cologne.
coloni'ale *ag* colonial ♦ *sm/f* colonist,
  settler.
co'lonico, a, ci, che *ag*: **casa** ~**a**
  farmhouse.
coloniz'zare [kolonid'dzare] *vt* to colonize.
co'lonna *sf* column; ~ **sonora** (*CINE*) sound
  track; ~ **vertebrale** spine, spinal column.
colon'nello *sm* colonel.
co'lono *sm* (*coltivatore*) tenant farmer.
colo'rante *sm* colouring (*BRIT*), coloring
  (*US*).
colo'rare *vt* to colour (*BRIT*), color (*US*);
  (*disegno*) to colo(u)r in.
co'lore *sm* colour (*BRIT*), color (*US*); (*CARTE*)
  suit; **a** ~**i** in colo(u)r, colo(u)r *cpd*; **la**

gente di ~ colo(u)red people; **diventare di
tutti i** ~**i** to turn scarlet; **farne di tutti i** ~**i**
to get up to all sorts of mischief;
passarne di tutti i ~**i** to go through all
sorts of problems.

colo'rito, a *ag* coloured (*BRIT*), colored
(*US*); (*viso*) rosy, pink; (*linguaggio*)
colourful (*BRIT*), colorful (*US*) ♦ *sm* (*tinta*)
colour (*BRIT*), color (*US*); (*carnagione*)
complexion.

co'loro *pron pl vedi* **colui**.

colos'sale *ag* colossal, enormous.

co'losso *sm* colossus.

'colpa *sf* fault; (*biasimo*) blame;
(*colpevolezza*) guilt; (*azione colpevole*)
offence; (*peccato*) sin; **di chi è la** ~**?**
whose fault is it?; **è** ~ **sua** it's his fault;
per ~ **di** through, owing to; **senso di** ~
sense of guilt; **dare la** ~ **a qn di qc** to
blame sb for sth.

col'pevole *ag* guilty.

colpevoliz'zare [kolpevolid'dzare] *vt:* ~ **qn**
to make sb feel guilty.

col'pire *vt* to hit, strike; (*fig*) to strike;
rimanere colpito da qc to be amazed *o*
struck by sth; **è stato colpito da ordine di
cattura** there is a warrant out for his
arrest; ~ **nel segno** (*fig*) to hit the nail on
the head, be spot on (*BRIT*).

'colpo *sm* (*urto*) knock; (*fig: affettivo*) blow,
shock; (*: aggressivo*) blow; (*di pistola*) shot;
(*MED*) stroke; (*furto*) raid; **di** ~**, tutto d'un**
~ suddenly; **fare** ~ to make a strong
impression; **il motore perde** ~**i** (*AUT*) the
engine is misfiring; **è morto sul** ~ he died
instantly; **mi hai fatto venire un** ~**!** what a
fright you gave me!; **ti venisse un** ~**!**
(*fam*) drop dead!; ~ **d'aria** chill; ~ **in
banca** bank job *o* raid; ~ **basso**
(*PUGILATO, fig*) punch below the belt; ~ **di
fulmine** love at first sight; ~ **di grazia**
coup de grâce; (*fig*) finishing blow; **a** ~
d'occhio at a glance; ~ **di scena** (*TEAT*)
coup de théâtre; (*fig*) dramatic turn of
events; ~ **di sole** sunstroke; ~**i di sole**
(*nei capelli*) highlights; ~ **di Stato** coup
d'état; ~ **di telefono** phone call; ~ **di testa**
(sudden) impulse *o* whim; ~ **di vento**
gust (of wind).

col'poso, a *ag:* **omicidio** ~ manslaughter.

'colsi *etc vb vedi* **cogliere**.

coltel'lata *sf* stab.

col'tello *sm* knife; **avere il** ~ **dalla parte del
manico** (*fig*) to have the whip hand; ~ **a
serramanico** clasp knife.

colti'vare *vt* to cultivate; (*verdura*) to grow,
cultivate.

coltiva'tore *sm* farmer; ~ **diretto** small

independent farmer.

coltivazi'one [koltivat'tsjone] *sf*
cultivation; growing; ~ **intensiva**
intensive farming.

'colto, a *pp di* **cogliere** ♦ *ag* (*istruito*)
cultured, educated.

'coltre *sf* blanket.

col'tura *sf* cultivation; ~ **alternata** crop
rotation.

co'lui, co'lei, *pl* **co'loro** *pron* the one;
~ **che parla** the one *o* the man *o* the
person who is speaking; **colei che
amo** the one *o* the woman *o* the person
(whom) I love.

com. *abbr* = **comunale; commissione**.

'coma *sm inv* coma.

comanda'mento *sm* (*REL*) commandment.

coman'dante *sm* (*MIL*) commander,
commandant; (*di reggimento*)
commanding officer; (*NAUT, AER*) captain.

coman'dare *vi* to be in command ♦ *vt* to
command; (*imporre*) to order, command;
~ **a qn di fare** to order sb to do.

co'mando *sm* (*ingiunzione*) order,
command; (*autorità*) command; (*TECN*)
control; ~ **generale** general headquarters
pl; ~ **a distanza** remote control.

co'mare *sf* (*madrina*) godmother; (*donna
pettegola*) gossip.

co'masco, a, schi, sche *ag* of (*o* from)
Como.

combaci'are [komba'tʃare] *vi* to meet; (*fig:
coincidere*) to coincide, correspond.

combat'tente *ag* fighting ♦ *sm* combatant;
ex-~ ex-serviceman.

com'battere *vt* to fight; (*fig*) to combat,
fight against ♦ *vi* to fight.

combatti'mento *sm* fight; fighting *no pl*; (*di
pugilato*) match; **mettere fuori** ~ to knock
out.

combat'tivo, a *ag* pugnacious.

combat'tuto, a *ag* (*incerto: persona*)
uncertain, undecided; (*gara, partita*) hard
fought.

combi'nare *vt* to combine; (*organizzare*) to
arrange; (*fam: fare*) to make, cause ♦ *vi*
(*corrispondere*): ~ **(con)** to correspond
(with).

combinazi'one [kombinat'tsjone] *sf*
combination; (*caso fortuito*) coincidence;
per ~ by chance.

com'briccola *sf* (*gruppo*) party; (*banda*)
gang.

combus'tibile *ag* combustible ♦ *sm*
fuel.

combusti'one *sf* combustion.

com'butta *sf* (*peg*) gang; **in** ~ in
league.

============================= *PAROLA CHIAVE*

'come *av* **1** (*alla maniera di*) like; **ti comporti** ~ **lui** you behave like him *o* like he does; **bianco** ~ **la neve** (as) white as snow; ~ **se** as if, as though; **com'è vero Dio!** as God is my witness!

2 (*in qualità di*) as a; **lavora** ~ **autista** he works as a driver

3 (*interrogativo*) how; ~ **ti chiami?** what's your name?; ~ **sta?** how are you?; **com'è il tuo amico?** what is your friend like?; ~**?** (*prego?*) pardon?, sorry?; ~ **mai?** how come?; ~ **mai non ci hai avvertiti?** how come you didn't warn us?

4 (*esclamativo*): ~ **sei bravo!** how clever you are!; ~ **mi dispiace!** I'm terribly sorry!

♦ *cong* **1** (*in che modo*) how; **mi ha spiegato** ~ **l'ha conosciuto** he told me how he met him; **non so** ~ **sia successo** I don't know how it happened; **attento a** ~ **parli!** watch your mouth!

2 (*correlativo*) as; (*con comparativi di maggioranza*) than; **non è bravo** ~ **pensavo** he isn't as clever as I thought; **è meglio di** ~ **pensassi** it's better than I thought

3 (*quasi se*) as; **è** ~ **se fosse ancora qui** it's as if he was still here; ~ **se niente fosse** as if nothing had happened; ~ **non detto!** let's forget it!

4 (*appena che, quando*) as soon as; ~ **arrivò, iniziò a lavorare** as soon as he arrived, he set to work; *vedi anche* **così; oggi; ora.**

'COMECON *abbr m* (= *Consiglio di Mutua Assistenza Economica*) COMECON.

come'done *sm* blackhead.

co'meta *sf* comet.

'comico, a, ci, che *ag* (*TEAT*) comic; (*buffo*) comical ♦ *sm* (*attore*) comedian, comic actor; (*comicità*) comic spirit, comedy.

co'mignolo [ko'miɲɲolo] *sm* chimney top.

cominci'are [komin'tʃare] *vt, vi* to begin, start; ~ **a fare/col fare** to begin to do/by doing; **cominciamo bene!** (*ironico*) we're off to a fine start!

comi'tato *sm* committee; ~ **direttivo** steering committee; ~ **di gestione** works council; ~ **interministeriale prezzi** interdepartmental committee on prices; ~ **interministeriale per la programmazione economica** interdepartmental committee for economic planning; ~ **interministeriale per lo sviluppo industriale** interdepartmental committee for industrial development.

comi'tiva *sf* party, group.

co'mizio [ko'mittsjo] *sm* (*POL*) meeting, assembly; ~ **elettorale** election rally.

'comma, i *sm* (*DIR*) subsection.

com'mando *sm inv* commando (squad).

com'media *sf* comedy; (*opera teatrale*) play; (: *che fa ridere*) comedy; (*fig*) playacting *no pl*.

commedi'ante *sm/f* (*peg*) third-rate actor/ actress; (: *fig*) sham.

commedi'ografo, a *sm/f* (*autore*) comedy writer.

commemo'rare *vt* to commemorate.

commemorazi'one [kommemorat'tsjone] *sf* commemoration.

commenda'tore *sm official title awarded for services to one's country.*

commen'sale *sm/f* table companion.

commen'tare *vt* to comment on; (*testo*) to annotate; (*RADIO, TV*) to give a commentary on.

commenta'tore, 'trice *sm/f* commentator.

com'mento *sm* comment; (*a un testo, RADIO, TV*) commentary; ~ **musicale** (*CINE*) background music.

commerci'ale [kommer'tʃale] *ag* commercial, trading; (*peg*) commercial.

commercia'lista, i, e [kommertʃa'lista] *sm/f* (*laureato*) graduate in economics and commerce; (*consulente*) business consultant.

commercializ'zare [kommertʃalid'dzare] *vt* to market.

commercializzazi'one [kommertʃaliddzat 'tsjone] *sf* marketing.

commerci'ante [kommer'tʃante] *sm/f* trader, dealer; (*negoziante*) shopkeeper; ~ **all'ingrosso** wholesaler; ~ **in proprio** sole trader.

commerci'are [kommer'tʃare] *vi*: ~ **in** *vt* to deal *o* trade in.

com'mercio [kom'mertʃo] *sm* trade, commerce; **essere in** ~ (*prodotto*) to be on the market *o* on sale; **essere nel** ~ (*persona*) to be in business; ~ **all'ingrosso/al minuto** wholesale/retail trade.

com'messo, a *pp di* **commettere** ♦ *sm/f* shop assistant (*BRIT*), sales clerk (*US*) ♦ *sm* (*impiegato*) clerk ♦ *sf* (*COMM*) order; ~ **viaggiatore** commercial traveller.

commes'tibile *ag* edible; ~**i** *smpl* foodstuffs.

com'mettere *vt* to commit; (*ordinare*) to commission, order.

commi'ato *sm* leave-taking; **prendere** ~ **da**

qn to take one's leave of sb.

commi'nare *vt* (*DIR*) to make provision for.

commise'rare *vt* to sympathize with, commiserate with.

commiserazi'one [kommizerat'tsjone] *sf* commiseration.

com'misi *etc vb vedi* **commettere.**

commissaria'mento *sm* temporary receivership.

commissari'are *vt* to put under temporary receivership.

commissari'ato *sm* (*AMM*) commissionership; (*: sede*) commissioner's office; (*: di polizia*) police station.

commis'sario *sm* commissioner; (*di pubblica sicurezza*) ≈ (police) superintendent (*BRIT*), (police) captain (*US*); (*SPORT*) steward; (*membro di commissione*) member of a committee *o* board; **alto** ~ high commissioner; ~ **di bordo** (*NAUT*) purser; ~ **d'esame** member of an examining board; ~ **di gara** race official; ~ **tecnico** (*SPORT*) national coach.

commissio'nare *vt* to order, place an order for.

commissio'nario *sm* (*COMM*) agent, broker.

commissi'one *sf* (*incarico*) errand; (*comitato, percentuale*) commission; (*COMM: ordinazione*) order; ~**i** *sfpl* (*acquisti*) shopping *sg*; ~ **d'esame** examining board; ~ **d'inchiesta** committee of enquiry; ~ **permanente** standing committee; ~**i bancarie** bank charges.

commit'tente *smlf* (*COMM*) purchaser, customer.

com'mosso, a *pp di* **commuovere.**

commo'vente *ag* moving.

commozi'one [kommot'tsjone] *sf* emotion, deep feeling; ~ **cerebrale** (*MED*) concussion.

commu'overe *vt* to move, affect; ~**rsi** *vr* to be moved.

commu'tare *vt* (*pena*) to commute; (*ELETTR*) to change *o* switch over.

commutazi'one [kommutat'tsjone] *sf* (*DIR, ELETTR*) commutation.

comò *sm inv* chest of drawers.

como'dino *sm* bedside table.

comodità *sf inv* comfort; convenience.

'comodo, a *ag* comfortable; (*facile*) easy; (*conveniente*) convenient; (*utile*) useful, handy ♦ *sm* comfort; convenience; **con** ~ at one's convenience *o* leisure; **fare il proprio** ~ to do as one pleases; **far** ~ to be useful *o* handy; **stia** ~! don't bother to

get up!

'compact disc *sm inv* compact disc.

compae'sano, a *smlf* fellow-countryman/woman; person from the same town.

com'pagine [kom'padʒine] *sf* (*squadra*) team.

compa'gnia [kompaɲ'ɲia] *sf* company; (*gruppo*) gathering; **fare** ~ **a qn** to keep sb company; **essere di** ~ to be sociable.

com'pagno, a [kom'paɲɲo] *smlf* (*di classe, gioco*) companion; (*POL*) comrade; ~ **di lavoro** workmate; ~ **di scuola** schoolfriend; ~ **di viaggio** fellow traveller.

com'paio *etc vb vedi* **comparire.**

compa'rare *vt* to compare.

compara'tivo, a *ag, sm* comparative.

comparazi'one [komparat'tsjone] *sf* comparison.

com'pare *sm* (*padrino*) godfather; (*complice*) accomplice; (*fam: amico*) old pal, old mate.

compa'rire *vi* to appear; ~ **in giudizio** (*DIR*) to appear before the court.

comparizi'one [komparit'tsjone] *sf* (*DIR*) appearance; **mandato di** ~ summons *sg*.

com'parso, a *pp di* **comparire** ♦ *sf* appearance; (*TEAT*) walk-on; (*CINE*) extra.

comparteci'pare [kompartetʃi'pare] *vi* (*COMM*): ~ **a** to have a share in.

compartecipazi'one [kompartetʃipat 'tsjone] *sf* sharing; (*quota*) share; ~ **agli utili** profit- sharing; **in** ~ jointly.

comparti'mento *sm* compartment; (*AMM*) district.

com'parvi *etc vb vedi* **comparire.**

compas'sato, a *ag* (*persona*) composed; **freddo e** ~ cool and collected.

compassi'one *sf* compassion, pity; **avere** ~ **di qn** to feel sorry for sb, pity sb; **fare** ~ to arouse pity.

compassio'nevole *ag* compassionate.

com'passo *sm* (pair of) compasses *pl*; callipers *pl*.

compa'tibile *ag* (*scusabile*) excusable; (*conciliabile, INFORM*) compatible.

compati'mento *sm* compassion; indulgence; **con aria di** ~ with a condescending air.

compa'tire *vt* (*aver compassione di*) to sympathize with, feel sorry for; (*scusare*) to make allowances for.

compatri'ota, i, e *smlf* compatriot.

compat'tezza [kompat'tettsa] *sf* (*solidità*) compactness; (*fig: unità*) solidarity.

com'patto, a *ag* compact; (*roccia*) solid; (*folla*) dense; (*fig: gruppo, partito*) united, close-knit.

com'pendio *sm* summary; (*libro*) compendium.

compen'sare *vt* (*equilibrare*) to compensate for, make up for; ~**rsi** *vr* (*reciproco*) to balance each other out; ~ **qn di** (*rimunerare*) to pay *o* remunerate sb for; (*risarcire*) to pay compensation to sb for; (*fig: fatiche, dolori*) to reward sb for.

compen'sato *sm* (*anche:* **legno** ~) plywood.

com'penso *sm* compensation; payment, remuneration; reward; **in** ~ (*d'altra parte*) on the other hand.

'compera *sf* purchase; **fare le** ~**e** to do the shopping.

compe'rare *vt* = **comprare**.

compe'tente *ag* competent; (*mancia*) apt, suitable; (*capace*) qualified; **rivolgersi all'ufficio** ~ to apply to the office concerned.

compe'tenza [kompe'tɛntsa] *sf* competence; (*DIR: autorità*) jurisdiction; (*TECN, COMM*) expertise; ~**e** *sfpl* (*onorari*) fees; **definire le** ~**e** to establish responsibilities.

com'petere *vi* to compete, vie; (*DIR: spettare*): ~ **a** to lie within the competence of.

competitività *sf inv* competitiveness.

competi'tivo, a *ag* competitive.

competi'tore, 'trice *sm/f* competitor.

competizi'one [kompetit'tsjone] *sf* competition; **spirito di** ~ competitive spirit.

compia'cente [kompja'tʃɛnte] *ag* courteous, obliging.

compia'cenza [kompja'tʃɛntsa] *sf* courtesy.

compia'cere [kompja'tʃere] *vi:* ~ **a** to gratify, please ♦ *vt* to please; ~**rsi** *vr* (*provare soddisfazione*): ~**rsi di** *o* **per qc** to be delighted at sth; (*rallegrarsi*): ~**rsi con qn** to congratulate sb; (*degnarsi*): ~**rsi di fare** to be so good as to do.

compiaci'mento [kompjatʃi'mento] *sm* satisfaction.

compiaci'uto, a [kompja'tʃuto] *pp di* **compiacere**.

compi'angere [kom'pjandʒere] *vt* to sympathize with, feel sorry for.

compi'anto, a *pp di* **compiangere** ♦ *ag:* **il** ~ **presidente** the late lamented president ♦ *sm* mourning, grief.

'compiere *vt* (*concludere*) to finish, complete; (*adempiere*) to carry out, fulfil; ~**rsi** *vr* (*avverarsi*) to be fulfilled, come true; ~ **gli anni** to have one's birthday.

compi'lare *vt* to compile; (*modulo*) to

complete, fill in (*BRIT*), fill out (*US*).

compila'tore, 'trice *sm/f* compiler.

compilazi'one [kompilat'tsjone] *sf* compilation; completion.

compi'mento *sm* (*termine, conclusione*) completion, fulfilment; **portare a** ~ **qc** to conclude sth, bring sth to a conclusion.

com'pire *vb* = **compiere**.

'compito *sm* (*incarico*) task, duty; (*dovere*) duty; (*INS*) exercise; (*: a casa*) piece of homework; **fare i** ~**i** to do one's homework.

com'pito, a *ag* well-mannered, polite.

compiu'tezza [kompju'tettsa] *sf* (*completezza*) completeness; (*perfezione*) perfection.

compi'uto, a *pp di* **compiere** ♦ *ag:* **a 20 anni** ~**i** at 20 years of age, at age 20; **un fatto** ~ a fait accompli.

comple'anno *sm* birthday.

complemen'tare *ag* complementary; (*INS: materia*) subsidiary.

comple'mento *sm* complement; (*MIL*) reserve (troops); ~ **oggetto** (*LING*) direct object.

comples'sato, a *ag, sm/f:* **essere (un)** ~ to be full of complexes *o* hang-ups (*fam*).

complessità *sf* complexity.

complessiva'mente *av* (*nell'insieme*) on the whole; (*in tutto*) altogether.

comples'sivo, a *ag* (*globale*) comprehensive, overall; (*totale: cifra*) total; **visione** ~**a** overview.

com'plesso, a *ag* complex ♦ *sm* (*PSIC, EDIL*) complex; (*MUS: corale*) ensemble; (*: orchestrina*) band; (*: di musica pop*) group; **in** *o* **nel** ~ on the whole.

completa'mento *sm* completion.

comple'tare *vt* to complete.

com'pleto, a *ag* complete; (*teatro, autobus*) full ♦ *sm* suit; **al** ~ full; (*tutti presenti*) all present; **essere al** ~ (*teatro*) to be sold out; ~ **da sci** ski suit.

compli'care *vt* to complicate; ~**rsi** *vr* to become complicated.

complicazi'one [komplikat'tsjone] *sf* complication; **salvo** ~**i** unless any difficulties arise.

'complice ['kɔmplitʃe] *sm/f* accomplice.

complicità [komplitʃi'ta] *sf inv* complicity; **un sorriso/uno sguardo di** ~ a knowing smile/look.

complimen'tarsi *vr:* ~ **con** to congratulate.

compli'mento *sm* compliment; ~**i** *smpl* (*cortesia eccessiva*) ceremony *sg*; ~**i!** congratulations!; **senza** ~**i!** don't stand on ceremony!; make yourself at home!;

help yourself!

complot'tare *vi* to plot, conspire.

com'plotto *sm* plot, conspiracy.

com'pone *etc vb vedi* **comporre**.

compo'nente *smlf* member ♦ *sm* component.

com'pongo *etc vb vedi* **comporre**.

compo'nibile *ag* (*mobili, cucina*) fitted.

componi'mento *sm* (*DIR*) settlement; (*INS*) composition; (*poetico, teatrale*) work.

com'porre *vt* (*musica, testo*) to compose; (*mettere in ordine*) to arrange; (*DIR: lite*) to settle; (*TIP*) to set; (*TEL*) to dial; **comporsi** *vr*: **comporsi di** to consist of, be composed of.

comportamen'tale *ag* behavioural (*BRIT*), behavioral (*US*).

comporta'mento *sm* behaviour (*BRIT*), behavior (*US*); (*di prodotto*) performance.

compor'tare *vt* (*implicare*) to involve, entail; (*consentire*) to permit, allow (of); ~**rsi** *vr* (*condursi*) to behave.

com'posi *etc vb vedi* **comporre**.

composi'tore, 'trice *smlf* composer; (*TIP*) compositor, typesetter.

composizi'one [kompozit'tsjone] *sf* composition; (*DIR*) settlement.

com'posta *sf vedi* **composto**.

compos'tezza [kompos'tettsa] *sf* composure; decorum.

com'posto, a *pp di* **comporre** ♦ *ag* (*persona*) composed, self-possessed; (*: decoroso*) dignified; (*formato da più elementi*) compound *cpd* ♦ *sm* compound; (*CUC etc*) mixture ♦ *sf* (*CUC*) stewed fruit *no pl*; (*AGR*) compost.

com'prare *vt* to buy; (*corrompere*) to bribe.

compra'tore, 'trice *smlf* buyer, purchaser.

compra'vendita *sf* (*COMM*) (contract of) sale; **un atto di** ~ a deed of sale.

com'prendere *vt* (*contenere*) to comprise, consist of; (*capire*) to understand.

compren'donio *sm*: **essere duro di** ~ to be slow on the uptake.

compren'sibile *ag* understandable.

comprensi'one *sf* understanding.

compren'sivo, a *ag* (*prezzo*): ~ **di** inclusive of; (*indulgente*) understanding.

compren'sorio *sm* area, territory; (*AMM*) district.

com'preso, a *pp di* **comprendere** ♦ *ag* (*incluso*) included; **tutto** ~ all included, all-in (*BRIT*).

com'pressa *sf vedi* **compresso**.

compressi'one *sf* compression.

com'presso, a *pp di* **comprimere** ♦ *ag* (*vedi* **comprimere**) pressed; compressed; repressed ♦ *sf* (*MED: garza*) compress;

(*: pastiglia*) tablet.

compres'sore *sm* compressor; (*anche*: **rullo** ~) steamroller.

compri'mario, a *smlf* (*TEAT*) supporting actor/actress.

com'primere *vt* (*premere*) to press; (*FISICA*) to compress; (*fig*) to repress.

compro'messo, a *pp di* **compromettere** ♦ *sm* compromise.

compro'mettere *vt* to compromise; ~**rsi** *vr* to compromise o.s.

comproprietà *sf* (*DIR*) joint ownership.

compro'vare *vt* to confirm.

com'punto, a *ag* contrite; **con fare** ~ with a solemn air.

compunzi'one [kompun'tsjone] *sf* contrition; solemnity.

compu'tare *vt* to calculate; (*addebitare*): ~ **qc a qn** to debit sb with sth.

com'puter [kəm'pju:tər] *sm inv* computer.

computeriz'zato, a [komputerid'dzato] *ag* computerized.

computerizzazi'one [komputeriddzat 'tsjone] *sf* computerization.

computiste'ria *sf* accounting, book-keeping.

'computo *sm* calculation; **fare il** ~ **di** to count.

comu'nale *ag* municipal, town *cpd*; **consiglio/palazzo** ~ town council/hall; **è un impiegato** ~ he works for the local council.

Co'mune *sm* (*AMM*) town council; (*sede*) town hall.

The **Comune** *is the smallest autonomous political and administrative unit. Records of births, marriages and deaths are kept by the Comune, which has the power to impose taxes and approve plans for public works and town planning. It is run by a Giunta comunale which is elected by the* **Consiglio Comunale**. *Both groups are headed by the* **Sindaco** *(mayor). See also* **Provincia** *and* **Regione**.

---

co'mune *ag* common; (*consueto*) common, everyday; (*di livello medio*) average; (*ordinario*) ordinary ♦ *sf* (*di persone*) commune; **fuori del** ~ out of the ordinary; **avere in** ~ to have in common, share; **mettere in** ~ to share; **un nostro** ~ **amico** a mutual friend of ours; **fare cassa** ~ to pool one's money.

comuni'care *vt* (*notizia*) to pass on, convey; (*malattia*) to pass on; (*ansia etc*) to communicate; (*trasmettere: calore etc*) to transmit, communicate; (*REL*) to

administer communion to ♦ *vi* to
communicate; ~**rsi** *vr* (*propagarsi*): ~**rsi a**
to spread to; (*REL*) to receive communion.
comunica'tivo, a *ag* (*sentimento*)
infectious; (*persona*) communicative ♦ *sf*
communicativeness.
comuni'cato *sm* communiqué; ~ **stampa**
press release.
comunicazi'one [komunikat'tsjone] *sf*
communication; (*annuncio*)
announcement; (*TEL*): ~ **(telefonica)**
(telephone) call; **dare la** ~ **a qn** to put sb
through; **ottenere la** ~ to get through;
salvo ~**i contrarie da parte Vostra** unless
we hear from you to the contrary.
comuni'one *sf* communion; ~ **dei beni**
(*DIR*: *tra coniugi*) joint ownership of
property.
comu'nismo *sm* communism.
comu'nista, i, e *ag*, *sm/f* communist.
comunità *sf inv* community; **C**~ **Economica
Europea (CEE)** European Economic
Community (EEC); ~ **terapeutica**
*rehabilitation centre run by voluntary
organizations for people with drug,
alcohol etc dependency.*
comuni'tario, a *ag* community *cpd*.
co'munque *cong* however, no matter how
♦ *av* (*in ogni modo*) in any case; (*tuttavia*)
however, nevertheless.
con *prep* (*nei seguenti casi con può fondersi
con l'articolo definito: con + il* = **col**, *con +
la* = **colla**, *con + gli* = **cogli**, *con + i* = **coi**,
con + le = **colle**) with; **partire col treno** to
leave by train; ~ **mio grande stupore** to
my great astonishment; ~ **la forza** by
force; ~ **questo freddo** in this cold
weather; ~ **il 1° di ottobre** as of October
1st; ~ **tutto ciò** in spite of that, for all
that; ~ **tutto che era arrabbiato** even
though he was angry, in spite of the fact
that he was angry; **e** ~ **questo?** so what?
co'nato *sm*: ~ **di vomito** retching.
'**conca, che** *sf* (*GEO*) valley.
concate'nare *vt* to link up, connect; ~**rsi** *vr*
to be connected.
'**concavo, a** *ag* concave.
con'cedere [kon'tʃɛdere] *vt* (*accordare*) to
grant; (*ammettere*) to admit, concede;
~**rsi qc** to treat o.s. to sth, allow o.s.
sth.
concentra'mento [kontʃentra'mento] *sm*
concentration.
concen'trare [kontʃen'trare] *vt*, ~**rsi** *vr* to
concentrate.
concen'trato [kontʃen'trato] *sm*
concentrate; ~ **di pomodoro** tomato
purée.

concentrazi'one [kontʃentrat'tsjone] *sf*
concentration; ~ **orizzontale/verticale**
(*ECON*) horizontal/vertical integration.
con'centrico, a, ci, che [kon'tʃentriko] *ag*
concentric.
conce'pibile [kontʃe'pibile] *ag* conceivable.
concepi'mento [kontʃepi'mento] *sm*
conception.
conce'pire [kontʃe'pire] *vt* (*bambino*) to
conceive; (*progetto, idea*) to conceive (of);
(*metodo, piano*) to devise; (*situazione*) to
imagine, understand.
con'cernere [kon'tʃɛrnere] *vt* to concern;
per quanto mi concerne as far as I'm
concerned.
concer'tare [kontʃer'tare] *vt* (*MUS*) to
harmonize; (*ordire*) to devise, plan; ~**rsi** *vr*
to agree.
concer'tista, i, e [kontʃer'tista] *sm/f* (*MUS*)
concert performer.
con'certo [kon'tʃɛrto] *sm* (*MUS*) concert;
(*: componimento*) concerto.
con'cessi *etc* [kon'tʃɛssi] *vb vedi* **concedere**.
concessio'nario [kontʃessjo'narjo] *sm*
(*COMM*) agent, dealer; ~ **esclusivo (di)**
sole agent (for).
concessi'one [kontʃes'sjone] *sf* concession.
con'cesso, a [kon'tʃɛsso] *pp di* **concedere**.
con'cetto [kon'tʃɛtto] *sm* (*pensiero, idea*)
concept; (*opinione*) opinion; **è un
impiegato di** ~ ≈ he's a white-collar
worker.
concezi'one [kontʃet'tsjone] *sf* conception;
(*idea*) view, idea.
con'chiglia [kon'kiʎʎa] *sf* shell.
'**concia** ['kontʃa] *sf* (*di pelli*) tanning; (*di
tabacco*) curing; (*sostanza*) tannin.
conci'are [kon'tʃare] *vt* (*pelli*) to tan;
(*tabacco*) to cure; (*fig: ridurre in cattivo
stato*) to beat up; ~**rsi** *vr* (*sporcarsi*) to get
in a mess; (*vestirsi male*) to dress badly; **ti
hanno conciato male o per le feste!**
they've really beaten you up!
concili'abile [kontʃi'ljabile] *ag* compatible.
concili'abolo [kontʃi'ljabolo] *sm* secret
meeting.
concili'ante [kontʃi'ljante] *ag* conciliatory.
concili'are [kontʃi'ljare] *vt* to reconcile;
(*contravvenzione*) to pay on the spot;
(*favorire: sonno*) to be conducive to,
induce; (*procurare: simpatia*) to gain; ~**rsi
qc** to gain o win sth (for o.s.); ~**rsi qn** to
win sb over; ~**rsi con** to be reconciled
with.
conciliazi'one [kontʃiljat'tsjone] *sf*
reconciliation; (*DIR*) settlement; **la C**~
(*STORIA*) the Lateran Pact.
con'cilio [kon'tʃiljo] *sm* (*REL*) council.

conci'mare [kontʃi'mare] *vt* to fertilize; (*con letame*) to manure.

con'cime [kon'tʃime] *sm* manure; (*chimico*) fertilizer.

concisi'one [kontʃi'zjone] *sf* concision, conciseness.

con'ciso, a [kon'tʃizo] *ag* concise, succinct.

conci'tato, a [kontʃi'tato] *ag* excited, emotional.

concitta'dino, a [kontʃitta'dino] *sm/f* fellow citizen.

con'clave *sm* conclave.

con'cludere *vt* to conclude; (*portare a compimento*) to conclude, finish, bring to an end; (*operare positivamente*) to achieve ♦ *vi* (*essere convincente*) to be conclusive; ~**rsi** *vr* to come to an end, close.

conclusi'one *sf* conclusion; (*risultato*) result.

conclu'sivo, a *ag* conclusive; (*finale*) final.

con'cluso, a *pp di* **concludere.**

concomi'tanza [konkomi'tantsa] *sf* (*di circostanze, fatti*) combination.

concor'danza [konkor'dantsa] *sf* (*anche* LING) agreement.

concor'dare *vt* (*prezzo*) to agree on; (*LING*) to make agree ♦ *vi* to agree; ~ **una tregua** to agree to a truce.

concor'dato *sm* agreement; (*REL*) concordat.

con'corde *ag* (*d'accordo*) in agreement; (*simultaneo*) simultaneous.

con'cordia *sf* harmony, concord.

concor'rente *ag* competing; (*MAT*) concurrent ♦ *sm/f* (*SPORT, COMM*) competitor; (*a un concorso di bellezza*) contestant.

concor'renza [konkor'rɛntsa] *sf* competition; ~ **sleale** unfair competition; **a prezzi di** ~ at competitive prices.

concorrenzi'ale [konkorren'tsjale] *ag* competitive.

con'correre *vi:* ~ (**in**) (*MAT*) to converge o meet (in); ~ (**a**) (*competere*) to compete (for); (: *INS: a una cattedra*) to apply (for); (*partecipare: a un'impresa*) to take part (in), contribute (to).

con'corso, a *pp di* **concorrere** ♦ *sm* competition; (*esame*) competitive examination; ~ **di bellezza** beauty contest; ~ **di circostanze** combination of circumstances; ~ **di colpa** (*DIR*) contributory negligence; **un** ~ **ippico** a showjumping event; ~ **in reato** (*DIR*) complicity in a crime; ~ **per titoli** competitive examination for qualified candidates.

con'creto, a *ag* concrete ♦ *sm:* **in** ~ in reality.

concu'bina *sf* concubine ♦ *sm:* **sono** ~**i** they are living together.

concussi'one *sf* (*DIR*) extortion.

con'danna *sf* condemnation; sentence; conviction; ~ **a morte** death sentence.

condan'nare *vt* (*disapprovare*) to condemn; (*DIR*): ~ **a** to sentence to; ~ **per** to convict of.

condan'nato, a *sm/f* convict.

con'densa *sf* condensation.

conden'sare *vt*, ~**rsi** *vr* to condense.

condensa'tore *sm* capacitor.

condensazi'one [kondensat'tsjone] *sf* condensation.

condi'mento *sm* seasoning; dressing.

con'dire *vt* to season; (*insalata*) to dress.

condiscen'dente [kondiʃʃen'dɛnte] *ag* obliging; compliant.

condiscen'denza [kondiʃʃen'dɛntsa] *sf* (*disponibilità*) obligingness; (*arrendevolezza*) compliance.

condi'scendere [kondiʃ'ʃendere] *vi:* ~ **a** to agree to.

condi'sceso, a [kondiʃ'ʃeso] *pp di* **condiscendere.**

condi'videre *vt* to share.

condi'viso, a *pp di* **condividere.**

condizio'nale [kondittsjo'nale] *ag* conditional ♦ *sm* (LING) conditional ♦ *sf* (*DIR*) suspended sentence.

condiziona'mento [kondittsjona'mento] *sm* conditioning; ~ **d'aria** air conditioning.

condizio'nare [kondittsjo'nare] *vt* to condition; **ad aria condizionata** air-conditioned.

condiziona'tore [kondittsjona'tore] *sm* air conditioner.

condizi'one [kondit'tsjone] *sf* condition; ~**i** *sfpl* (*di pagamento etc*) terms, conditions; **a** ~ **che** on condition that, provided that; **a nessuna** ~ on no account; ~**i a convenirsi** terms to be arranged; ~**i di lavoro** working conditions; ~**i di vendita** sales terms.

condogli'anze [kondoʎ'ʎantse] *sfpl* condolences.

condomini'ale *ag:* **riunione** ~ residents' meeting; **spese** ~**i** common charges.

condo'minio *sm* joint ownership; (*edificio*) jointly-owned building.

con'domino *sm* joint owner.

condo'nare *vt* (*DIR*) to remit.

con'dono *sm* remission; ~ **fiscale** *conditional amnesty for people evading tax.*

con'dotta *sf vedi* **condotto.**

con'dotto, a *pp di* **condurre** ♦ *ag:* **medico** ~

local authority doctor (*in country district*)
♦ *sm* (*canale, tubo*) pipe, conduit; (*ANAT*)
duct ♦ *sf* (*modo di comportarsi*) conduct,
behaviour (*BRIT*), behavior (*US*); (*di un
affare etc*) handling; (*di acqua*) piping;
(*incarico sanitario*) *country medical
practice controlled by a local authority.*

condu'cente [kondu'tʃɛnte] *sm* driver.

con'duco *etc vb vedi* **condurre.**

con'durre *vt* to conduct; (*azienda*) to
manage; (*accompagnare: bambino*) to take;
(*automobile*) to drive; (*trasportare: acqua,
gas*) to convey, conduct; (*fig*) to lead ♦ *vi*
to lead; **condursi** *vr* to behave, conduct
o.s.; ~ **a termine** to conclude.

con'dussi *etc vb vedi* **condurre.**

condut'tore, 'trice *ag*: **filo** ~ (*fig*) thread;
motivo ~ leitmotiv ♦ *sm* (*di mezzi pubblici*)
driver; (*FISICA*) conductor.

condut'tura *sf* (*gen*) pipe; (*di acqua, gas*)
main.

conduzi'one [kondut'tsjone] *sf* (*di affari,
ditta*) management; (*DIR: locazione*) lease;
(*FISICA*) conduction.

confabu'lare *vi* to confab.

confa'cente [konfa'tʃɛnte] *ag*: ~ **a qn/qc**
suitable for sb/sth; **clima** ~ **alla salute**
healthy climate.

CONFAGRICOL'TURA *abbr f*
(= *Confederazione generale dell'Agricoltura
Italiana*) *confederation of Italian farmers.*

CON'FAPI *sigla f* = *Confederazione Nazionale
della Piccola Industria.*

con'farsi *vr*: ~ **a** to suit, agree with.

CONFARTIGIA'NATO [konfartidʒa'nato]
abbr f = *Confederazione Generale
dell'Artigianato Italiano.*

con'fatto, a *pp di* **confarsi.**

CONFCOM'MERCIO [konfkom'mertʃo]
abbr f = *Confederazione Generale del
Commercio.*

confederazi'one [konfederat'tsjone] *sf*
confederation; ~ **imprenditoriale**
employers' association.

confe'renza [konfe'rɛntsa] *sf* (*discorso*)
lecture; (*riunione*) conference; ~ **stampa**
press conference.

conferenzi'ere, a [konferen'tsjɛre] *sm/f*
lecturer.

conferi'mento *sm* conferring, awarding.

confe'rire *vt*: ~ **qc a qn** to give sth to sb,
confer sth on sb ♦ *vi* to confer.

con'ferma *sf* confirmation.

confer'mare *vt* to confirm.

confes'sare *vt*, ~**rsi** *vr* to confess; **andare a**
~**rsi** (*REL*) to go to confession.

confessio'nale *ag, sm* confessional.

confessi'one *sf* confession; (*setta religiosa*)

denomination.

con'fesso, a *ag*: **essere reo** ~ to have
pleaded guilty.

confes'sore *sm* confessor.

con'fetto *sm* sugared almond; (*MED*) pill.

confet'tura *sf* (*gen*) jam; (*di arance*)
marmalade.

confezio'nare [konfettsjo'nare] *vt* (*vestito*)
to make (up); (*merci, pacchi*) to package.

confezi'one [konfet'tsjone] *sf* (*di abiti: da
uomo*) tailoring; (: *da donna*)
dressmaking; (*imballaggio*) packaging; ~
regalo gift pack; ~ **risparmio** economy
size; ~ **da viaggio** travel pack; ~**i per
signora** ladies' wear *no pl*; ~**i da uomo**
menswear *no pl*.

confic'care *vt*: ~ **qc in** to hammer *o* drive
sth into; ~**rsi** *vr* to stick.

confi'dare *vi*: ~ **in** to confide in, rely on
♦ *vt* to confide; ~**rsi con qn** to confide in
sb.

confi'dente *sm/f* (*persona amica*) confidant/
confidante; (*informatore*) informer.

confi'denza [konfi'dɛntsa] *sf* (*familiarità*)
intimacy, familiarity; (*fiducia*) trust,
confidence; (*rivelazione*) confidence;
prendersi (troppe) ~**e** to take liberties;
fare una ~ **a qn** to confide something to
sb.

confidenzi'ale [konfiden'tsjale] *ag* familiar,
friendly; (*segreto*) confidential; **in via** ~
confidentially.

configu'rare *vt* (*INFORM*) to set; ~**rsi** *vr*: ~ **a**
to assume the shape *o* form of.

configurazi'one [konfigurat'tsjone] *sf*
configuration; (*INFORM*) setting.

confi'nante *ag* neighbouring (*BRIT*),
neighboring (*US*).

confi'nare *vi*: ~ **con** to border on ♦ *vt* (*POL*)
to intern; (*fig*) to confine; ~**rsi** *vr* (*isolarsi*):
~**rsi in** to shut o.s. up in.

confi'nato, a *ag* interned ♦ *sm/f* internee.

CONFIN'DUSTRIA *sigla f* (= *Confederazione
Generale dell'Industria Italiana*) *employers'
association*, ≈ CBI (*BRIT*).

con'fine *sm* boundary; (*di paese*) border,
frontier; **territorio di** ~ border zone.

con'fino *sm* internment.

con'fisca *sf* confiscation.

confis'care *vt* to confiscate.

conflagrazi'one [konflagrat'tsjone] *sf*
conflagration.

con'flitto *sm* conflict; **essere in** ~ **con qc** to
clash with sth; **essere in** ~ **con qn** to be at
loggerheads with sb.

conflittu'ale *ag*: **rapporto** ~ relationship
based on conflict.

conflittualità *sf* conflicts *pl*.

conflu'enza [konflu'ɛntsa] *sf* (*di fiumi*)
confluence; (*di strade*) junction.
conflu'ire *vi* (*fiumi*) to flow into each other,
meet; (*strade*) to meet.
con'fondere *vt* to mix up, confuse;
(*imbarazzare*) to embarrass; ~**rsi** *vr*
(*mescolarsi*) to mingle; (*turbarsi*) to be
confused; (*sbagliare*) to get mixed up; ~
le idee a qn to mix sb up, confuse sb.
confor'mare *vt* (*adeguare*): ~ **a** to adapt *o*
conform to; ~**rsi** *vr*: ~**rsi** (**a**) to conform
(to).
con'forme *ag*: ~ **a** (*simile*) similar to;
(*corrispondente*) in keeping with.
conforme'mente *av* accordingly; ~ **a** in
accordance with.
confor'mismo *sm* conformity.
confor'mista, i, e *sm/f* conformist.
conformità *sf* conformity; **in** ~ **a** in
conformity with.
confor'tare *vt* to comfort, console.
confor'tevole *ag* (*consolante*) comforting;
(*comodo*) comfortable.
con'forto *sm* (*consolazione, sollievo*)
comfort, consolation; (*conferma*) support;
a ~ **di qc** in support of sth; **i** ~**i** (**religiosi**)
the last sacraments.
confra'ternita *sf* brotherhood.
confron'tare *vt* to compare; ~**rsi** *vr*
(*scontrarsi*) to have a confrontation.
con'fronto *sm* comparison; (*DIR, MIL, POL*)
confrontation; **in** *o* **a** ~ **di** in comparison
with, compared to; **nei miei** (*o* **tuoi** *etc*) ~**i**
towards me (*o* you *etc*).
con'fusi *etc vb vedi* **confondere**.
confusi'one *sf* confusion; (*imbarazzo*)
embarrassment; **far** ~ (*disordine*) to make
a mess; (*chiasso*) to make a racket;
(*confondere*) to confuse things.
con'fuso, a *pp di* **confondere** ♦ *ag* (*vedi
confondere*) confused; embarrassed.
confu'tare *vt* to refute.
conge'dare [kondʒe'dare] *vt* to dismiss;
(*MIL*) to demobilize; ~**rsi** *vr* to take one's
leave.
con'gedo [kon'dʒedo] *sm* (*anche MIL*) leave;
prendere ~ **da qn** to take one's leave of
sb; ~ **assoluto** (*MIL*) discharge.
conge'gnare [kondʒeɲ'ɲare] *vt* to
construct, put together.
con'gegno [kon'dʒeɲɲo] *sm* device,
mechanism.
congela'mento [kondʒela'mento] *sm* (*gen*)
freezing; (*MED*) frostbite; ~ **salariale**
wage freeze.
conge'lare [kondʒe'lare] *vt*, ~**rsi** *vr* to
freeze.
congela'tore [kondʒela'tore] *sm* freezer.

con'genito, a [kon'dʒɛnito] *ag* congenital.
con'gerie [kon'dʒɛrje] *sf inv* (*di oggetti*)
heap; (*di idee*) muddle, jumble.
congestio'nare [kondʒestjo'nare] *vt* to
congest; **essere congestionato** (*persona,
viso*) to be flushed; (*zona: per traffico*) to be
congested.
congesti'one [kondʒes'tjone] *sf*
congestion.
conget'tura [kondʒet'tura] *sf* conjecture,
supposition.
con'giungere [kon'dʒundʒere] *vt*, ~**rsi** *vr* to
join (together).
congiunti'vite [kondʒunti'vite] *sf*
conjunctivitis.
congiun'tivo [kondʒun'tivo] *sm* (*LING*)
subjunctive.
congi'unto, a [kon'dʒunto] *pp di*
congiungere ♦ *ag* (*unito*) joined ♦ *sm/f*
(*parente*) relative.
congiun'tura [kondʒun'tura] *sf* (*giuntura*)
junction, join; (*ANAT*) joint; (*circostanza*)
juncture; (*ECON*) economic situation.
congiuntu'rale [kondʒuntu'rale] *ag* of the
economic situation; **crisi** ~ economic
crisis.
congiunzi'one [kondʒun'tsjone] *sf* (*LING*)
conjunction.
congi'ura [kon'dʒura] *sf* conspiracy.
congiu'rare [kondʒu'rare] *vi* to conspire.
conglome'rato *sm* (*GEO*) conglomerate;
(*fig*) conglomeration; (*EDIL*) concrete.
'Congo *sm*: **il** ~ the Congo.
congo'lese *ag, sm/f* Congolese *inv*.
congratu'larsi *vr*: ~ **con qn per qc** to
congratulate sb on sth.
congratulazi'oni [kongratulat'tsjoni] *sfpl*
congratulations.
con'grega, ghe *sf* band, bunch.
congregazi'one [kongregat'tsjone] *sf*
congregation.
congres'sista, i, e *sm/f* participant at a
congress.
con'gresso *sm* congress.
'congruo, a *ag* (*prezzo, compenso*)
adequate, fair; (*ragionamento*) coherent,
consistent.
conguagli'are [kongwaʎ'ʎare] *vt* to
balance; (*stipendio*) to adjust.
congu'aglio [kon'gwaʎʎo] *sm* balancing;
adjusting; (*somma di denaro*) balance; **fare
il** ~ **di** to balance; to adjust.
coni'are *vt* to mint, coin; (*fig*) to coin.
coniazi'one [konjat'tsjone] *sf* mintage.
'conico, a, ci, che *ag* conical.
co'nifere *sfpl* conifers.
conigli'era [koniʎ'ʎɛra] *sf* (*gabbia*) rabbit
hutch; (*più grande*) rabbit run.

conigli'etta [koniʎ'ʎetta] *sf* bunny girl.
conigli'etto [koniʎ'ʎetto] *sm* bunny.
co'niglio [ko'niʎʎo] *sm* rabbit; **sei un** ~!
 (*fig*) you're chicken!
coniu'gale *ag* (*amore, diritti*) conjugal; (*vita*)
 married, conjugal.
coniu'gare *vt* to combine; (*LING*) to
 conjugate; ~**rsi** *vr* to get married.
coniu'gato, a *ag* (*AMM*) married.
coniugazi'one [konjugat'tsjone] *sf* (*LING*)
 conjugation.
'coniuge ['kɔnjudʒe] *sm/f* spouse.
connatu'rato, a *ag* inborn.
connazio'nale [konnattsjo'nale] *sm/f*
 fellow-countryman/woman.
connessi'one *sf* connection.
con'nesso, a *pp di* **connettere**.
con'nettere *vt* to connect, join ♦ *vi* (*fig*) to
 think straight.
connet'tore *sm* (*ELETTR*) connector.
conni'vente *ag* conniving.
conno'tati *smpl* distinguishing marks;
 rispondere ai ~**i** to fit the description;
 cambiare i ~**i a qn** (*fam*) to beat sb up.
con'nubio *sm* (*matrimonio*) marriage; (*fig*)
 union.
'cono *sm* cone; ~ **gelato** ice-cream cone.
co'nobbi *etc vb vedi* **conoscere**.
cono'scente [konoʃ'ʃɛnte] *sm/f*
 acquaintance.
cono'scenza [konoʃ'ʃɛntsa] *sf* (*il sapere*)
 knowledge *no pl*; (*persona*) acquaintance;
 (*facoltà sensoriale*) consciousness *no pl*;
 essere a ~ **di qc** to know sth; **portare qn a**
 ~ **di qc** to inform sb of sth; **per vostra** ~
 for your information; **fare la** ~ **di qn** to
 make sb's acquaintance; **perdere** ~ to
 lose consciousness; ~ **tecnica** know-how.
co'noscere [ko'noʃʃere] *vt* to know; **ci
 siamo conosciuti a Firenze** we (first) met
 in Florence; ~ **qn di vista** to know sb by
 sight; **farsi** ~ (*fig*) to make a name for o.s.
conosci'tore, 'trice [konoʃʃi'tore] *sm/f*
 connoisseur.
conosci'uto, a [konoʃ'ʃuto] *pp di* **conoscere**
 ♦ *ag* well-known.
con'quista *sf* conquest.
conquis'tare *vt* to conquer; (*fig*) to gain,
 win.
conquista'tore, 'trice *sm/f* (*in guerra*)
 conqueror ♦ *sm* (*seduttore*) lady-killer.
cons. *abbr* = **consiglio**.
consa'crare *vt* (*REL*) to consecrate;
 (*: sacerdote*) to ordain; (*dedicare*) to
 dedicate; (*fig: uso etc*) to sanction; ~**rsi a**
 to dedicate o.s. to.
consangu'ineo, a *sm/f* blood relation.
consa'pevole *ag*: ~ **di** aware *o* conscious

of.
consapevo'lezza [konsapevo'lettsa] *sf*
 awareness, consciousness.
conscia'mente [konʃa'mente] *av*
 consciously.
'conscio, a, sci, sce ['kɔnʃo] *ag*: ~ **di**
 aware *o* conscious of.
consecu'tivo, a *ag* consecutive;
 (*successivo: giorno*) following, next.
con'segna [kon'seɲɲa] *sf* delivery; (*merce
 consegnata*) consignment; (*custodia*) care,
 custody; (*MIL: ordine*) orders *pl*;
 (*: punizione*) confinement to barracks; **alla**
 ~ on delivery; **dare qc in** ~ **a qn** to
 entrust sth to sb; **passare le** ~**e a qn** to
 hand over to sb; ~ **a domicilio** home
 delivery; ~ **in contrassegno, pagamento
 alla** ~ cash on delivery; ~ **sollecita**
 prompt delivery.
conse'gnare [konseɲ'ɲare] *vt* to deliver;
 (*affidare*) to entrust, hand over; (*MIL*) to
 confine to barracks.
consegna'tario [konseɲɲa'tarjo] *sm*
 consignee.
consegu'ente *ag* consequent.
conseguente'mente *av* consequently.
consegu'enza [konse'gwɛntsa] *sf*
 consequence; **per** *o* **di** ~ consequently.
consegui'mento *sm* (*di scopo, risultato etc*)
 achievement, attainment; **al** ~ **della
 laurea** on graduation.
consegu'ire *vt* to achieve ♦ *vi* to follow,
 result; ~ **la laurea** to graduate, obtain
 one's degree.
con'senso *sm* approval, consent.
consensu'ale *ag* (*DIR*) by mutual consent.
consen'tire *vi*: ~ **a** to consent *o* agree to
 ♦ *vt* to allow, permit; **mi si consenta di
 ringraziare ...** I would like to thank ....
consenzi'ente [konsen'tsjɛnte] *ag* (*gen, DIR*)
 consenting.
con'serto, a *ag*: **a braccia** ~**e** with one's
 arms folded.
con'serva *sf* (*CUC*) preserve; ~ **di frutta**
 jam; ~ **di pomodoro** tomato purée; ~**e
 alimentari** tinned (*o* canned *o* bottled)
 foods.
conser'vare *vt* (*CUC*) to preserve;
 (*custodire*) to keep; (*: dalla distruzione etc*)
 to preserve, conserve; ~**rsi** *vr* to keep.
conserva'tore, 'trice *ag, sm/f* (*POL*)
 conservative.
conserva'torio *sm* (*di musica*)
 conservatory.
conserva'torismo *sm* (*POL*) conservatism.
conservazi'one [konservat'tsjone] *sf*
 preservation; conservation; **istinto di** ~
 instinct for self-preservation; **a lunga** ~

(*latte, panna*) long-life *cpd.*
con'sesso *sm* (*assemblea*) assembly; (*riunione*) meeting.
conside'rabile *ag* worthy of consideration.
conside'rare *vt* to consider; (*reputare*) to consider, regard; ~ **molto qn** to think highly of sb.
conside'rato, a *ag* (*prudente*) cautious, careful; (*stimato*) highly thought of, esteemed.
considerazi'one [konsiderat'tsjone] *sf* (*esame, riflessione*) consideration; (*stima*) regard, esteem; (*pensiero, osservazione*) observation; **prendere in** ~ to take into consideration.
conside'revole *ag* considerable.
consigli'abile [konsiʎ'ʎabile] *ag* advisable.
consigli'are [konsiʎ'ʎare] *vt* (*persona*) to advise; (*metodo, azione*) to recommend, advise, suggest; ~**rsi** *vr*: ~**rsi con qn** to ask sb for advice.
consigli'ere, a [konsiʎ'ʎɛre] *sm/f* adviser ♦ *sm*: ~ **d'amministrazione** board member; ~ **comunale** town councillor; ~ **delegato** (*COMM*) managing director.
con'siglio [kon'siʎʎo] *sm* (*suggerimento*) advice *no pl*, piece of advice; (*assemblea*) council; ~ **d'amministrazione** board; **C~ d'Europa** Council of Europe; ~ **di fabbrica** works council; **il C~ dei Ministri** (*POL*) ≈ the Cabinet; **C~ di stato** *advisory body to the Italian government on administrative matters and their legal implications*; **C~ superiore della magistratura** *state body responsible for judicial appointments and regulations*; *vedi anche* **Comune; Provincia; Regione.**

The **Consiglio dei Ministri**, *the Italian Cabinet, is headed by the* **Presidente del Consiglio**, *the Italian prime minister, and is made up of government ministers. See also* **Presidente del Consiglio** *and* **Presidente della Repubblica**.
The **Consiglio superiore della Magistratura**, *the magistrates' governing body, ensures their continued autonomy and independence as enshrined in the constitution. It deals principally with appointments and transfers of magistrates, and disciplinary action against individual members where required. The Consiglio has a total of 32 members and is chaired by the Presidente della Repubblica. Of the 30 magistrates elected to the Consiglio for a period of 4 years, 20 are elected by their fellow magistrates and 10 by Parliament. The remaining two are the Presidente della Repubblica and the Vicepresidente who are ex officio members.*

con'simile *ag* similar.
consis'tente *ag* solid; (*fig*) sound, valid.
consis'tenza [konsis'tɛntsa] *sf* (*di impasto*) consistency; (*di stoffa*) texture; **senza** ~ (*sospetti, voci*) ill-founded, groundless; ~ **di cassa/di magazzino** cash/stock in hand; ~ **patrimoniale** financial solidity.
con'sistere *vi*: ~ **in** to consist of.
consis'tito, a *pp di* **consistere.**
'CONSOB *sigla f* (= *Commissione nazionale per le società e la borsa*) *regulatory body for the Italian Stock Exchange.*
consoci'arsi [konso'tʃarsi] *vr* to go into partnership.
consociati'vismo [konsotʃati'vizmo] *sm* (*POL*) pact-building.
consocia'tivo, a [konsotʃa'tivo] *ag* (*POL: democrazia*) based on pacts.
consoci'ato, a [konso'tʃato] *ag* associated ♦ *sm/f* associate.
conso'lante *ag* consoling, comforting.
conso'lare *ag* consular ♦ *vt* (*confortare*) to console, comfort; (*rallegrare*) to cheer up; ~**rsi** *vr* to be comforted; to cheer up.
conso'lato *sm* consulate.
consolazi'one [konsolat'tsjone] *sf* consolation, comfort.
'console *sm* consul ♦ *sf* [kɔ'sɔl] (*quadro di comando*) console.
consolida'mento *sm* strengthening; consolidation.
consoli'dare *vt* to strengthen, reinforce; (*MIL, terreno*) to consolidate; ~**rsi** *vr* to consolidate.
consolidazi'one [konsolidat'tsjone] *sf* strengthening; consolidation.
consommé [kɔsɔ'me] *sm inv* consommé.
conso'nante *sf* consonant.
conso'nanza [konso'nantsa] *sf* consonance.
'consono, a *ag*: ~ **a** consistent with, consonant with.
con'sorte *sm/f* consort.
con'sorzio [kon'sɔrtsjo] *sm* consortium; ~ **agrario** farmers' cooperative; ~ **di garanzia** (*COMM*) underwriting syndicate.
con'stare *vi*: ~ **di** to consist of ♦ *vb impers*: **mi consta che** it has come to my knowledge that, it appears that; **a quanto mi consta** as far as I know.
consta'tare *vt* to establish, verify; (*notare*) to notice, observe.
constatazi'one [konstatat'tsjone] *sf* observation; ~ **amichevole** (*in incidenti*) jointly-agreed statement for insurance purposes.

consu'eto, a *ag* habitual, usual ♦ *sm*: **come di ~** as usual.

consuetudi'nario, a *ag*: **diritto ~** (*DIR*) common law.

consue'tudine *sf* habit; (*usanza*) custom.

consu'lente *sm/f* consultant; **~ aziendale/ tecnico** management/technical consultant.

consu'lenza [konsu'lɛntsa] *sf* consultancy; **~ medica/legale** medical/legal advice; **ufficio di ~ fiscale** tax consultancy office; **~ tecnica** technical consultancy *o* advice.

consul'tare *vt* to consult; **~rsi** *vr*: **~rsi con qn** to seek the advice of sb.

consultazi'one [konsultat'tsjone] *sf* consultation; **~i** *sfpl* (*POL*) talks, consultations; **libro di ~** reference book.

consul'tivo, a *ag* consultative.

consul'torio *sm*: **~ familiare** *o* **matrimoniale** marriage guidance centre; **~ pediatrico** children's clinic.

consu'mare *vt* (*logorare: abiti, scarpe*) to wear out; (*usare*) to consume, use up; (*mangiare, bere*) to consume; (*DIR*) to consummate; **~rsi** *vr* to wear out; to be used up; (*anche fig*) to be consumed; (*combustibile*) to burn out.

consu'mato, a *ag* (*vestiti, scarpe, tappeto*) worn; (*persona: esperto*) accomplished.

consuma'tore *sm* consumer.

consumazi'one [konsumat'tsjone] *sf* (*bibita*) drink; (*spuntino*) snack; (*DIR*) consummation.

consu'mismo *sm* consumerism.

con'sumo *sm* consumption; wear; use; **generi** *o* **beni di ~** consumer goods; **beni di largo ~** basic commodities; **imposta sui ~i** tax on consumer goods.

consun'tivo *sm* (*ECON*) final balance.

con'sunto, a *ag* worn-out; (*viso*) wasted.

'conta *sf* (*nei giochi*): **fare la ~** to see who is going to be "it".

con'tabile *ag* accounts *cpd*, accounting ♦ *sm/f* accountant.

contabilità *sf* (*attività, tecnica*) accounting, accountancy; (*insieme dei libri etc*) books *pl*, accounts *pl*; (*ufficio*) **~** accounts department; **~ finanziaria** financial accounting; **~ di gestione** management accounting.

contachi'lometri [kontaki'lɔmetri] *sm inv* ≈ mileometer.

conta'dino, a *sm/f* countryman/woman; farm worker; (*peg*) peasant.

contagi'are [konta'dʒare] *vt* to infect.

con'tagio [kon'tadʒo] *sm* infection; (*per contatto diretto*) contagion; (*epidemia*) epidemic.

contagi'oso, a [konta'dʒoso] *ag* infectious; contagious.

conta'giri [konta'dʒiri] *sm inv* (*AUT*) rev counter.

conta'gocce [konta'gottʃe] *sm inv* dropper.

contami'nare *vt* to contaminate.

contaminazi'one [kontaminat'tsjone] *sf* contamination.

con'tante *sm* cash; **pagare in ~i** to pay cash.

con'tare *vt* to count; (*considerare*) to consider ♦ *vi* to count, be of importance; **~ su qn** to count *o* rely on sb; **~ di fare qc** to intend to do sth; **ha i giorni contati, ha le ore contate** his days are numbered; **la gente che conta** people who matter.

contas'catti *sm inv* telephone meter.

conta'tore *sm* meter.

contat'tare *vt* to contact.

con'tatto *sm* contact; **essere in ~ con qn** to be in touch with sb; **fare ~** (*ELETTR: fili*) to touch.

'conte *sm* count.

con'tea *sf* (*STORIA*) earldom; (*AMM*) county.

conteggi'are [konted'dʒare] *vt* to charge, put on the bill.

con'teggio [kon'teddʒo] *sm* calculation.

con'tegno [kon'teɲɲo] *sm* (*comportamento*) behaviour (*BRIT*), behavior (*US*); (*atteggiamento*) attitude; **darsi un ~** (*ostentare disinvoltura*) to act nonchalant; (*ricomporsi*) to pull o.s. together.

conte'gnoso, a [konteɲ'ɲoso] *ag* reserved, dignified.

contem'plare *vt* to contemplate, gaze at; (*DIR*) to make provision for.

contempla'tivo, a *ag* contemplative.

contemplazi'one [kontemplat'tsjone] *sf* contemplation.

con'tempo *sm*: **nel ~** meanwhile, in the meantime.

contemporanea'mente *av* simultaneously; at the same time.

contempo'raneo, a *ag*, *sm/f* contemporary.

conten'dente *sm/f* opponent, adversary.

con'tendere *vi* (*competere*) to compete; (*litigare*) to quarrel ♦ *vt*: **~ qc a qn** to contend with *o* be in competition with sb for sth.

conte'nere *vt* to contain; **~rsi** *vr* to contain o.s.

conteni'tore *sm* container.

conten'tabile *ag*: **difficilmente ~** difficult to please.

conten'tare *vt* to please, satisfy; **~rsi** *vr*: **~rsi di** to be satisfied with, content o.s. with; **si contenta di poco** he is easily satisfied.

conten'tezza [konten'tettsa] *sf* contentment.

conten'tino *sm* sop.

con'tento, a *ag* pleased, glad; ~ **di** pleased with.

conte'nuto *ag* (*ira, entusiasmo*) restrained, suppressed; (*forza*) contained ♦ *sm* contents *pl*; (*argomento*) content.

contenzi'oso, a [konten'tsjɔso] *ag* (*DIR*) contentious ♦ *sm* (*AMM: ufficio*) legal department.

con'teso, a *pp di* **contendere** ♦ *sf* dispute, argument.

con'tessa *sf* countess.

contes'tare *vt* (*DIR*) to notify; (*fig*) to dispute; ~ **il sistema** to protest against the system.

contesta'tore, 'trice *ag* anti-establishment ♦ *sm/f* protester.

contestazi'one [kontestat'tsjone] *sf* (*DIR: disputa*) dispute; (*: notifica*) notification; (*POL*) anti-establishment activity; **in caso di** ~ if there are any objections.

con'testo *sm* context.

con'tiguo *ag*: ~ **(a)** adjacent (to).

continen'tale *ag* continental.

conti'nente *ag* continent ♦ *sm* (*GEO*) continent; (*: terra ferma*) mainland.

conti'nenza [konti'nɛntsa] *sf* continence.

contin'gente [kontin'dʒɛnte] *ag* contingent ♦ *sm* (*COMM*) quota; (*MIL*) contingent.

contin'genza [kontin'dʒɛntsa] *sf* circumstance; (**indennità di**) ~ cost-of-living allowance.

continua'mente *av* (*senza interruzione*) continuously, nonstop; (*ripetutamente*) continually.

continu'are *vt* to continue (with), go on with ♦ *vi* to continue, go on; ~ **a fare qc** to go on *o* continue doing sth; **continua a nevicare/a fare freddo** it's still snowing/ cold.

continua'tivo, a *ag* (*occupazione*) permanent; (*periodo*) consecutive.

continuazi'one [kontinuat'tsjone] *sf* continuation.

continuità *sf* continuity.

con'tinuo, a *ag* (*numerazione*) continuous; (*pioggia*) continual, constant; (*ELETTR: corrente*) direct; **di** ~ continually.

'conto *sm* (*calcolo*) calculation; (*COMM, ECON*) account; (*di ristorante, albergo*) bill; (*fig: stima*) consideration, esteem; **avere un** ~ **in sospeso (con qn)** to have an outstanding account (with sb); (*fig*) to have a score to settle (with sb); **fare i** ~**i con qn** to settle one's account with sb;

fare ~ **su qn** to count *o* rely on sb; **fare** ~ **che** (*supporre*) to suppose that; **rendere** ~ **a qn di qc** to be accountable to sb for sth; **rendersi** ~ **di qc/che** to realize sth/that; **tener** ~ **di qn/qc** to take sb/sth into account; **tenere qc da** ~ to take great care of sth; **ad ogni buon** ~ in any case; **di poco/nessun** ~ of little/no importance; **per** ~ **di** on behalf of; **per** ~ **mio** as far as I'm concerned; (*da solo*) on my own; **a** ~**i fatti, in fin dei** ~**i** all things considered; **mi hanno detto strane cose sul suo** ~ I've heard some strange things about him; ~ **capitale** capital account; ~ **cifrato** numbered account; ~ **corrente** current account (*BRIT*), checking account (*US*); ~ **corrente postale** Post Office account; ~ **economico** profit and loss account; ~ **in partecipazione** joint account; ~ **passivo** account payable; ~ **profitti e perdite** profit and loss account; ~ **alla rovescia** countdown; ~ **valutario** foreign currency account.

con'torcere [kon'tɔrtʃere] *vt* to twist; (*panni*) to wring (out); ~**rsi** *vr* to twist, writhe.

contor'nare *vt* to surround; ~**rsi** *vr*: ~**rsi di** to surround o.s. with.

con'torno *sm* (*linea*) outline, contour; (*ornamento*) border; (*CUC*) vegetables *pl*; **fare da** ~ **a** to surround.

contorsi'one *sf* contortion.

con'torto, a *pp di* **contorcere.**

contrabban'dare *vt* to smuggle.

contrabbandi'ere *sm/f* smuggler.

contrab'bando *sm* smuggling, contraband; **merce di** ~ contraband, smuggled goods *pl*.

contrab'basso *sm* (*MUS*) (double) bass.

contraccambi'are *vt* (*favore etc*) to return; **vorrei** ~ I'd like to show my appreciation.

contraccet'tivo, a [kontrattʃet'tivo] *ag, sm* contraceptive.

contrac'colpo *sm* rebound; (*di arma da fuoco*) recoil; (*fig*) repercussion.

con'trada *sf* street; district; *vedi anche* **Palio.**

contrad'detto, a *pp di* **contraddire.**

contrad'dire *vt* to contradict; ~**rsi** *vr* to contradict o.s.; (*uso reciproco: persone*) to contradict each other *o* one another; (*: testimonianze etc*) to be contradictory.

contraddis'tinguere *vt* (*merce*) to mark; (*fig: atteggiamento, persona*) to distinguish.

contraddis'tinto, a *pp di* **contraddistinguere.**

contraddit'torio, a *ag* contradictory; (*sentimenti*) conflicting ♦ *sm* (*DIR*) cross-examination.

contraddizi'one [kontraddit'tsjone] *sf* contradiction; **cadere in** ~ to contradict o.s.; **essere in** ~ (*tesi, affermazioni*) to contradict one another; **spirito di** ~ argumentativeness.

con'trae *etc vb vedi* **contrarre.**

contra'ente *sm* contractor.

contra'erea *sf* (*MIL*) anti-aircraft artillery.

contra'ereo, a *ag* anti-aircraft.

contraf'fare *vt* (*persona*) to mimic; (*voce*) to disguise; (*firma*) to forge, counterfeit.

contraf'fatto, a *pp di* **contraffare ♦** *ag* counterfeit.

contraffazi'one [kontraffat'tsjone] *sf* mimicking *no pl*; disguising *no pl*; forging *no pl*; (*cosa contraffatta*) forgery.

contraf'forte *sm* (*ARCHIT*) buttress; (*GEO*) spur.

con'traggo *etc vb vedi* **contrarre.**

con'tralto *sm* (*MUS*) contralto.

contrap'pello *sm* (*MIL*) second roll call.

contrappe'sare *vt* to counterbalance; (*fig: decisione*) to weigh up.

contrap'peso *sm* counterbalance, counterweight.

contrap'porre *vt*: ~ **qc a qc** to counter sth with sth; (*paragonare*) to compare sth with sth; **contrapporsi** *vr*: **contrapporsi a qc** to contrast with sth, be opposed to sth.

contrap'posto, a *pp di* **contrapporre.**

contraria'mente *av*: ~ **a** contrary to.

contrari'are *vt* (*contrastare*) to thwart, oppose; (*irritare*) to annoy, bother; ~**rsi** *vr* to get annoyed.

contrari'ato, a *ag* annoyed.

contrarietà *sf* adversity; (*fig*) aversion.

con'trario, a *ag* opposite; (*sfavorevole*) unfavourable (*BRIT*), unfavorable (*US*) **♦** *sm* opposite; **essere** ~ **a qc** (*persona*) to be against sth; **al** ~ on the contrary; **in caso** ~ otherwise; **avere qualcosa in** ~ to have some objection; **non ho niente in** ~ I have no objection.

con'trarre *vt* (*malattia, debito*) to contract; (*muscoli*) to tense; (*abitudine, vizio*) to pick up; (*accordo, patto*) to enter into; **contrarsi** *vr* to contract; ~ **matrimonio** to marry.

contrasse'gnare [kontrassen'ɲare] *vt* to mark.

contras'segno [kontras'senɲo] *sm* (*distintivo*) distinguishing mark; **spedire in** ~ (*COMM*) to send COD.

con'trassi *etc vb vedi* **contrarre.**

contras'tante *ag* contrasting.

contras'tare *vt* (*avversare*) to oppose; (*impedire*) to bar; (*negare: diritto*) to

contest, dispute **♦** *vi*: ~ **(con)** (*essere in disaccordo*) to contrast (with); (*lottare*) to struggle (with).

con'trasto *sm* contrast; (*conflitto*) conflict; (*litigio*) dispute.

contrat'tacco *sm* counterattack; **passare al** ~ (*fig*) to fight back.

contrat'tare *vt, vi* to negotiate.

contrat'tempo *sm* hitch.

con'tratto, a *pp di* **contrarre ♦** *sm* contract; ~ **di acquisto** purchase agreement; ~ **di affitto,** ~ **di locazione** lease; ~ **collettivo di lavoro** collective agreement; ~ **di lavoro** contract of employment; ~ **a termine** forward contract.

contrattu'ale *ag* contractual; **forza** ~ (*di sindacato*) bargaining power.

contravve'nire *vi*: ~ **a** (*legge*) to contravene; (*obbligo*) to fail to meet.

contravven'tore, 'trice *sm/f* offender.

contravve'nuto, a *pp di* **contravvenire.**

contravvenzi'one [kontravven'tsjone] *sf* contravention; (*ammenda*) fine.

contrazi'one [kontrat'tsjone] *sf* contraction; (*di prezzi etc*) reduction.

contribu'ente *sm/f* taxpayer; ratepayer (*BRIT*), property tax payer (*US*).

contribu'ire *vi* to contribute.

contribu'tivo, a *ag* contributory.

contri'buto *sm* contribution; (*sovvenzione*) subsidy, contribution; (*tassa*) tax; ~**i previdenziali** ≈ national insurance (*BRIT*) *o* welfare (*US*) contributions; ~**i sindacali** trade union dues.

con'trito, a *ag* contrite, penitent.

'contro *prep* against; ~ **di me/lui** against me/him; **pastiglie** ~ **la tosse** throat lozenges; ~ **pagamento** (*COMM*) on payment; ~ **ogni mia aspettativa** contrary to my expectations; **per** ~ on the other hand.

contro'battere *vt* (*fig: a parole*) to answer back; (*: confutare*) to refute.

controbilanci'are [kontrobilan'tʃare] *vt* to counterbalance.

controcor'rente *av*: **andare** ~ (*anche fig*) to swim against the tide.

controcul'tura *sf* counterculture.

contro'esodo *sm* return from holiday.

contro'fax *sm inv* reply to a fax.

controffen'siva *sf* counteroffensive.

controfi'gura *sf* (*CINE*) double.

controfir'mare *vt* to countersign.

control'lare *vt* (*accertare*) to check; (*sorvegliare*) to watch, control; (*tenere nel proprio potere, fig: dominare*) to control; ~**rsi** *vr* to control o.s.

control'lato, a *ag* (*persona*) self-possessed;

(*reazioni*) controlled ♦ *sf* (*COMM: società*) associated company.

con'trollo *sm* check; watch; control; **base di** ~ (*AER*) ground control; **telefono sotto** ~ tapped telephone; **visita di** ~ (*MED*) checkup; ~ **doganale** customs inspection; ~ **di gestione** management control; ~ **delle nascite** birth control; ~ **di qualità** quality control.

control'lore *sm* (*FERR, AUTOBUS*) (ticket) inspector; ~ **di volo** *o* **del traffico aereo** air traffic controller.

contro'luce [kontro'lutʃe] *sf inv* (*FOT*) backlit shot ♦ *av*: (**in**) ~ against the light; (*fotografare*) into the light.

contro'mano *av*: **guidare** ~ to drive on the wrong side of the road; (*in un senso unico*) to drive the wrong way up a one-way street.

contropar'tita *sf* (*fig: compenso*): **come** ~ in return.

contropi'ede *sm* (*SPORT*): **azione di** ~ sudden counter-attack; **prendere qn in** ~ (*fig*) to catch sb off his (*o* her) guard.

controprodu'cente [kontroprodu'tʃɛnte] *ag* counterproductive.

con'trordine *sm* counter-order; **salvo** ~ unless I (*o* you *etc*) hear to the contrary.

contro'senso *sm* (*contraddizione*) contradiction in terms; (*assurdità*) nonsense.

controspio'naggio [kontrospio'naddʒo] *sm* counterespionage.

controva'lore *sm* equivalent (value).

contro'vento *av* against the wind; **navigare** ~ (*NAUT*) to sail to windward.

contro'versia *sf* controversy; (*DIR*) dispute; ~ **sindacale** industrial dispute.

contro'verso, a *ag* controversial.

contro'voglia [kontro'vɔʎʎa] *av* unwillingly.

contu'mace [kontu'matʃe] *ag* (*DIR*): **rendersi** ~ to default, fail to appear in court ♦ *smf* (*DIR*) defaulter.

contu'macia [kontu'matʃa] *sf* (*DIR*) default.

contun'dente *ag*: **corpo** ~ blunt instrument.

contur'bante *ag* (*sguardo, bellezza*) disturbing.

contur'bare *vt* to disturb, upset.

contusi'one *sf* (*MED*) bruise.

convale'scente [konvaleʃ'ʃɛnte] *ag, smf* convalescent.

convale'scenza [konvaleʃ'ʃɛntsa] *sf* convalescence.

con'valida *sf* (*DIR*) confirmation; (*di biglietto*) stamping.

convali'dare *vt* (*AMM*) to validate; (*fig:*

sospetto, dubbio) to confirm.

con'vegno [kon'veɲɲo] *sm* (*incontro*) meeting; (*congresso*) convention, congress; (*luogo*) meeting place.

conve'nevoli *smpl* civilities.

conveni'ente *ag* suitable; (*vantaggioso*) profitable; (: *prezzo*) cheap.

conveni'enza [konve'njɛntsa] *sf* suitability; advantage; cheapness; ~**e** *sfpl* social conventions.

conve'nire *vi* to agree upon ♦ *vi* (*riunirsi*) to gather, assemble; (*concordare*) to agree; (*tornare utile*) to be worthwhile ♦ *vb impers*: **conviene fare questo** it is advisable to do this; **conviene andarsene** we should go; **ne convengo** I agree; **come convenuto** as agreed; **in data da** ~ on a date to be agreed; **come (si) conviene ad una signorina** as befits a young lady.

conven'ticola *sf* (*cricca*) clique; (*riunione*) secret meeting.

con'vento *sm* (*di frati*) monastery; (*di suore*) convent.

conve'nuto, a *pp di* **convenire** ♦ *sm* (*cosa pattuita*) agreement ♦ *smf* (*DIR*) defendant; **i** ~**i** (*i presenti*) those present.

convenzio'nale [konventsjo'nale] *ag* conventional.

convenzio'nato, a [konventsjo'nato] *ag* (*ospedale, clinica*) providing free health care, ≈ National Health Service *cpd* (*BRIT*).

convenzi'one [konven'tsjone] *sf* (*DIR*) agreement; (*nella società*) convention; **le** ~**i** (*sociali*) social conventions.

conver'gente [konver'dʒɛnte] *ag* convergent.

conver'genza [konver'dʒɛntsa] *sf* convergence.

con'vergere [kon'vɛrdʒere] *vi* to converge.

con'versa *sf* (*REL*) lay sister.

conver'sare *vi* to have a conversation, converse.

conversazi'one [konversat'tsjone] *sf* conversation; **fare** ~ (*chiacchierare*) to chat, have a chat.

conversi'one *sf* conversion; ~ **ad U** (*AUT*) U-turn.

con'verso, a *pp di* **convergere**; **per** ~ *av* conversely.

conver'tire *vt* (*trasformare*) to change; (*INFORM, POL, REL*) to convert; ~**rsi** *vr*: ~**rsi (a)** to be converted (to).

conver'tito, a *smf* convert.

converti'tore *sm* (*ELETTR*) converter.

con'vesso, a *ag* convex.

convin'cente [konvin'tʃɛnte] *ag* convincing.

con'vincere [kon'vintʃere] *vt* to convince; ~ **qn di qc** to convince sb of sth; (*DIR*) to prove sb guilty of sth; ~ **qn a fare qc** to persuade sb to do sth.

con'vinto, a *pp di* **convincere** ♦ *ag*: **reo** ~ (*DIR*) convicted criminal.

convinzi'one [konvin'tsjone] *sf* conviction, firm belief.

convis'suto, a *pp di* **convivere**.

convi'tato, a *smf* guest.

con'vitto *sm* (*INS*) boarding school.

convi'venza [konvi'vɛntsa] *sf* living together; (*DIR*) cohabitation.

con'vivere *vi* to live together.

convivi'ale *ag* convivial.

convo'care *vt* to call, convene; (*DIR*) to summon.

convocazi'one [konvokat'tsjone] *sf* meeting; summons *sg*; **lettera di** ~ (letter of) notification to appear *o* attend.

convogli'are [konvoʎ'ʎare] *vt* to convey; (*dirigere*) to direct, send.

con'voglio [kon'vɔʎʎo] *sm* (*di veicoli*) convoy; (*FERR*) train; ~ **funebre** funeral procession.

convo'lare *vi*: ~ **a (giuste) nozze** (*scherzoso*) to tie the knot.

convulsi'one *sf* convulsion.

con'vulso, a *ag* (*pianto*) violent, convulsive; (*attività*) feverish.

COOP *abbr f* = **cooperativa**.

coope'rare *vi*: ~ **(a)** to cooperate (in).

coopera'tiva *sf* cooperative.

cooperazi'one [kooperat'tsjone] *sf* cooperation.

coordina'mento *sm* coordination.

coordi'nare *vt* to coordinate.

coordi'nato, a *ag* (*movimenti*) coordinated ♦ *sf* (*LING, GEO, MAT*) coordinate ♦ *smpl*: ~**i** (*MODA*) coordinates.

coordinazi'one [koordinat'tsjone] *sf* coordination.

co'perchio [ko'pɛrkjo] *sm* cover; (*di pentola*) lid.

co'perta *sf* cover; (*di lana*) blanket; (*da viaggio*) rug; (*NAUT*) deck.

coper'tina *sf* (*STAMPA*) cover, jacket.

co'perto, a *pp di* **coprire** ♦ *ag* covered; (*cielo*) overcast ♦ *sm* place setting; (*posto a tavola*) place; (*al ristorante*) cover charge; ~ **di** covered in *o* with.

coper'tone *sm* (*telo impermeabile*) tarpaulin; (*AUT*) rubber tyre.

coper'tura *sf* (*anche ECON, MIL*) cover; (*di edificio*) roofing; **fare un gioco di** ~ (*SPORT*) to play a defensive game; ~ **assicurativa** insurance cover.

'copia *sf* copy; (*FOT*) print; **brutta/bella** ~ rough/final copy; ~ **conforme** (*DIR*) certified copy; ~ **omaggio** presentation copy.

copi'are *vt* to copy.

copia'trice [kopja'tritʃe] *sf* copier, copying machine.

copi'one *sm* (*CINE, TEAT*) script.

'coppa *sf* (*bicchiere*) goblet; (*per frutta, gelato*) dish; (*trofeo*) cup, trophy; ~**e** *sfpl* (*CARTE*) suit in Neapolitan pack of cards; ~ **dell'olio** oil sump (*BRIT*) *o* pan (*US*).

'coppia *sf* (*di persone*) couple; (*di animali, SPORT*) pair.

cop'rente *ag* (*colore, cosmetico*) covering; (*calze*) opaque.

copri'capo *sm* headgear; (*cappello*) hat.

coprifu'oco, chi *sm* curfew.

copri'letto *sm* bedspread.

co'prire *vt* to cover; (*occupare: carica, posto*) to hold; ~**rsi** *vr* (*cielo*) to cloud over; (*vestirsi*) to wrap up, cover up; (*ECON*) to cover o.s.; ~**rsi di** (*macchie, muffa*) to become covered in; ~ **qn di baci** to smother sb with kisses; ~ **le spese** to break even; ~**rsi le spalle** (*fig*) to cover o.s.

coque [kɔk] *sf*: **uovo alla** ~ boiled egg.

co'raggio [ko'raddʒo] *sm* courage, bravery; ~! (*forza!*) come on!; (*animo!*) cheer up!; **farsi** ~ to pluck up courage; **hai un bel** ~! (*sfacciataggine*) you've got a nerve *o* a cheek!

coraggi'oso, a [korad'dʒoso] *ag* courageous, brave.

co'rale *ag* choral; (*approvazione*) unanimous.

co'rallo *sm* coral; **il mar dei C~i** the Coral Sea.

co'rano *sm* (*REL*) Koran.

co'razza [ko'rattsa] *sf* armour (*BRIT*), armor (*US*); (*di animali*) carapace, shell; (*MIL*) armo(u)r(-plating).

coraz'zato, a [korat'tsato] *ag* (*MIL*) armoured (*BRIT*), armored (*US*) ♦ *sf* battleship.

corazzi'ere [korat'tsjɛre] *sm* (*STORIA*) cuirassier; (*guardia presidenziale*) *carabiniere of the President's guard.*

corbelle'ria *sf* stupid remark; ~**e** *sfpl* (*sciocchezze*) nonsense *no pl*.

'corda *sf* cord; (*fune*) rope; (*spago, MUS*) string; **dare** ~ **a qn** (*fig*) to let sb have his (*o* her) way; **tenere sulla** ~ **qn** (*fig*) to keep sb on tenterhooks; **tagliare la** ~ (*fig*) to slip away, sneak off; **essere giù di** ~ to feel down; ~**e vocali** vocal cords.

cor'data *sf* (*ALPINISMO*) roped party; (*fig*) *alliance system in financial and business* *world.*

cordi'ale *ag* cordial, warm ♦ *sm* (*bevanda*) cordial.

cordialità *sf inv* warmth, cordiality; ~ *sfpl* (*saluti*) best wishes.

cor'doglio [kor'dɔʎʎo] *sm* grief; (*lutto*) mourning.

cor'done *sm* cord, string; (*linea: di polizia*) cordon; ~ **ombelicale** umbilical cord; ~ **sanitario** quarantine line.

Co'rea *sf*: **la** ~ Korea; **la** ~ **del Nord/Sud** North/South Korea.

core'ano, a *a, ag, sm/f* Korean.

coreogra'fia *sf* choreography.

core'ografo, a *sm/f* choreographer.

cori'aceo, a [ko'rjatʃeo] *ag* (*BOT, ZOOL*) coriaceous; (*fig*) tough.

cori'andolo *sm* (*BOT*) coriander; ~**i** *smpl* (*per carnevale etc*) confetti *no pl*.

cori'care *vt* to put to bed; ~**rsi** *vr* to go to bed.

coricherò *etc* [korike'rɔ] *vb vedi* **coricare**.

Co'rinto *sf* Corinth.

co'rista, i, e *sm/f* (*REL*) choir member, chorister; (*TEAT*) member of the chorus.

'corna *sfpl vedi* **corno**.

cor'nacchia [kor'nakkja] *sf* crow.

corna'musa *sf* bagpipes *pl*.

'cornea *sf* (*ANAT*) cornea.

'corner *sm inv* (*CALCIO*) corner (kick); **salvarsi in** ~ (*fig: in gara, esame etc*) to get through by the skin of one's teeth.

cor'netta *sf* (*MUS*) cornet; (*TEL*) receiver.

cor'netto *sm* (*CUC*) croissant; ~ **acustico** ear trumpet.

cor'nice [kor'nitʃe] *sf* frame; (*fig*) background, setting.

cornici'one [korni'tʃone] *sm* (*di edificio*) ledge; (*ARCHIT*) cornice.

'corno *sm* (*ZOOL: pl(f)* ~**a**, *MUS*) horn; (*fam*): **fare le** ~**a a qn** to be unfaithful to sb; **dire peste e** ~**a di qn** to call sb every name under the sun; **un** ~! not on your life!

Corno'vaglia [korno'vaʎʎa] *sf*: **la** ~ Cornwall.

cor'nuto, a *ag* (*con corna*) horned; (*fam!: marito*) cuckolded ♦ *sm* (*fam!*) cuckold; (*: insulto*) bastard (*!*).

'coro *sm* chorus; (*REL*) choir.

corol'lario *sm* corollary.

co'rona *sf* crown; (*di fiori*) wreath.

corona'mento *sm* (*di impresa*) completion; (*di carriera*) crowning achievement; **il** ~ **dei propri sogni** the fulfilment of one's dreams.

coro'nare *vt* to crown.

coro'naria *sf* coronary artery.

'corpo *sm* body; (*cadavere*) (dead) body;

(*militare, diplomatico*) corps *inv*; (*di opere*) corpus; **prendere** ~ to take shape; **darsi anima e** ~ **a** to give o.s. heart and soul to; **a** ~ **a** ~ hand-to-hand; ~ **d'armata** army corps; ~ **di ballo** corps de ballet; ~ **dei carabinieri** ≈ police force; ~ **celeste** heavenly body; ~ **di guardia** (*soldati*) guard; (*locale*) guardroom; ~ **insegnante** teaching staff; ~ **del reato** material evidence.

corpo'rale *ag* bodily; (*punizione*) corporal.

corpora'tura *sf* build, physique.

corporazi'one [korporat'tsjone] *sf* corporation.

cor'poreo, a *ag* bodily, physical.

cor'poso, a *ag* (*vino*) full-bodied.

corpu'lento, a *ag* stout, corpulent.

corpu'lenza [korpu'lɛntsa] *sf* stoutness, corpulence.

cor'puscolo *sm* corpuscle.

corre'dare *vt*: ~ **di** to provide *o* furnish with; **domanda corredata dai seguenti documenti** application accompanied by the following documents.

cor'redo *sm* equipment; (*di sposa*) trousseau.

cor'reggere [kor'rɛddʒere] *vt* to correct; (*compiti*) to correct, mark.

cor'rente *ag* (*fiume*) flowing; (*acqua del rubinetto*) running; (*moneta, prezzo*) current; (*comune*) everyday ♦ *sm*: **essere al** ~ (**di**) to be well-informed (about) ♦ *sf* (*movimento di liquido*) current, stream; (*spiffero*) draught; (*ELETTR, METEOR*) current; (*fig*) trend, tendency; **mettere al** ~ (**di**) to inform (of); **la vostra lettera del 5** ~ **mese** (*in lettere commerciali*) in your letter of the 5th inst.; **articoli di qualità** ~ average-quality products; ~ **alternata** (**c.a.**) alternating current (AC); ~ **continua** (**c.c.**) direct current (DC).

corrente'mente *av* (*comunemente*) commonly; **parlare una lingua** ~ to speak a language fluently.

corren'tista, i, e *sm/f* (current (*BRIT*) *o* checking (*US*)) account holder.

cor'reo, a *sm/f* (*DIR*) accomplice.

'correre *vi* to run; (*precipitarsi*) to rush; (*partecipare a una gara*) to race, run; (*fig: diffondersi*) to go round ♦ *vt* (*SPORT: gara*) to compete in; (*rischio*) to run; (*pericolo*) to face; ~ **dietro a qn** to run after sb; **corre voce che ...** it is rumoured that ....

corresponsabilità *sf* joint responsibility; (*DIR*) joint liability.

corresponsi'one *sf* payment.

cor'ressi *etc vb vedi* **correggere**.

corret'tezza [korret'tettsa] *sf* (*di*

comportamento) correctness; (*SPORT*) fair play.

cor'retto, , **a** *pp di* **correggere** ♦ *ag* (*comportamento*) correct, proper; **caffè** ~ **al cognac** coffee laced with brandy.

corret'tore, 'trice *sm/f*: ~ **di bozze** proofreader ♦ *sm*: (**liquido**) ~ correction fluid.

correzi'one [korret'tsjone] *sf* correction; marking; ~ **di bozze** proofreading.

cor'rida *sf* bullfight.

corri'doio *sm* corridor; **manovre di** ~ (*POL*) lobbying *sg*.

corri'dore *sm* (*SPORT*) runner; (: *su veicolo*) racer.

corri'era *sf* coach (*BRIT*), bus.

corri'ere *sm* (*diplomatico, di guerra*) courier; (*posta*) mail, post; (*spedizioniere*) carrier.

corri'mano *sm* handrail.

corrispet'tivo *sm* amount due; **versare a qn il** ~ **di una prestazione** to pay sb the amount due for his (*o her*) services.

corrispon'dente *ag* corresponding ♦ *sm/f* correspondent.

corrispon'denza [korrispon'dɛntsa] *sf* correspondence; ~ **in arrivo/partenza** incoming/outgoing mail.

corris'pondere *vi* (*equivalere*): ~ (**a**) to correspond (to); (*per lettera*): ~ **con** to correspond with ♦ *vt* (*stipendio*) to pay; (*fig: amore*) to return.

corris'posto, a *pp di* **corrispondere**.

corrobo'rare *vt* to strengthen, fortify; (*fig*) to corroborate, bear out.

cor'rodere *vt*, ~**rsi** *vr* to corrode.

cor'rompere *vt* to corrupt; (*comprare*) to bribe.

corrosi'one *sf* corrosion.

corro'sivo, a *ag* corrosive.

cor'roso, a *pp di* **corrodere**.

cor'rotto, a *pp di* **corrompere** ♦ *ag* corrupt.

corrucci'arsi [korrut'tʃarsi] *vr* to grow angry *o* vexed.

corru'gare *vt* to wrinkle; ~ **la fronte** to knit one's brows.

cor'ruppi *etc vb vedi* **corrompere**.

corrut'tela *sf* corruption, depravity.

corruzi'one [korrut'tsjone] *sf* corruption; bribery; ~ **di minorenne** (*DIR*) corruption of a minor.

'corsa *sf* running *no pl*; (*gara*) race; (*di autobus, taxi*) journey, trip; **fare una** ~ to run, dash; (*SPORT*) to run a race; **andare** *o* **essere di** ~ to be in a hurry; ~ **ad ostacoli** (*IPPICA*) steeplechase; (*ATLETICA*) hurdles race.

cor'saro, a *ag*: **nave** ~**a** privateer ♦ *sm* privateer.

'corsi *etc vb vedi* **correre**.

cor'sia *sf* (*AUT, SPORT*) lane; (*di ospedale*) ward; ~ **preferenziale** ≈ bus lane; (*fig*) fast track; ~ **di sorpasso** (*AUT*) overtaking lane.

'Corsica *sf*: **la** ~ Corsica.

cor'sivo *sm* cursive (writing); (*TIP*) italics *pl*.

'corso, a *pp di* **correre** ♦ *ag, sm/f* Corsican ♦ *sm* course; (*strada cittadina*) main street; (*di unità monetaria*) circulation; (*di titoli, valori*) rate, price; **dar libero** ~ **a** to give free expression to; **in** ~ in progress, under way; (*annata*) current; ~ **d'acqua** river; stream; (*artificiale*) waterway; ~ **serale** evening class; **aver** ~ **legale** to be legal tender.

'corte *sf* (court)yard; (*DIR, regale*) court; **fare la** ~ **a qn** to court sb; ~ **d'appello** court of appeal; ~ **di cassazione** final court of appeal; **C**~ **dei Conti** *State audit court*; **C**~ **Costituzionale** *special court dealing with constitutional and ministerial matters*; ~ **marziale** court-martial.

Various **Corti** *exist to deal with different types of offence. The* **Corte d'Appello** *hears appeals against sentences passed by courts dealing with civil and criminal prosecutions and is empowered to modify sentences where justification is shown. The* **Corte d'Assise** *tries serious crimes such as manslaughter and murder and its judges comprise both legal professionals and members of the public. The* **Corte d'Assise d'Appello** *is structured in a similar way to the* **Corte d'Assise** *and hears appeals against sentences imposed by this court and by the* **Corte d'Appello**. *The* **Corte di Cassazione** *is the highest judicial authority in the country, dealing solely with the legitimacy of judicial decisions. It ensures that the law is correctly applied by the other courts and may call for a re-trial where it deems a violation to have taken place. The* **Corte Costituzionale** *is a politically independent body which ensures that laws comply with the principles of the constitution. It has the power to impeach the Presidente della Repubblica. The* **Corte dei Conti** *ensures the government's compliance with the law and the constitution. Reporting directly to Parliament, it oversees the management of the state budget and the finances of nationalized industries.*

cor'teccia, , ce [kor'tettʃa] *sf* bark.
corteggia'mento [korteddʒa'mento] *sm* courtship.
corteggi'are [korted'dʒare] *vt* to court.
corteggia'tore [korteddʒa'tore] *sm* suitor.
cor'teo *sm* procession; ~ **funebre** funeral cortège.
cor'tese *ag* courteous.
corte'sia *sf* courtesy; **fare una** ~ **a qn** to do sb a favour; **per** ~, **dov'è …?** excuse me, please, where is …?
cortigi'ano, a [korti'dʒano] *sm/f* courtier
♦ *sf* courtesan.
cor'tile *sm* (court)yard.
cor'tina *sf* curtain; (*anche fig*) screen.
corti'sone *sm* cortisone.
'corto, a *ag* short ♦ *av*: **tagliare** ~ to come straight to the point; **essere a** ~ **di qc** to be short of sth; **essere a** ~ **di parole** to be at a loss for words; **la settimana** ~**a** the 5-day week; ~ **circuito** short-circuit.
cortocir'cuito [kortotʃir'kuito] *sm* = **corto circuito.**
cortome'traggio [kortome'traddʒo] *sm* short (feature film).
cor'vino, a *ag* (*capelli*) jet-black.
'corvo *sm* raven.
'cosa *sf* thing; (*faccenda*) affair, matter, business *no pl*; (**che**) ~? what?; (**che**) **cos'è?** what is it?; **a** ~ **pensi?** what are you thinking about?; **tante belle** ~**e!** all the best!; **ormai è** ~ **fatta!** (*positivo*) it's in the bag!; (*negativo*) it's done now!; **a** ~**e fatte** when it's all over.
'Cosa 'Nostra *sf* Cosa Nostra.
'cosca, sche *sf* (*di mafiosi*) clan.
'coscia, sce ['kɔʃʃa] *sf* thigh; ~ **di pollo** (*CUC*) chicken leg.
cosci'ente [koʃ'ʃɛnte] *ag* conscious; ~ **di** conscious *o* aware of.
cosci'enza [koʃ'ʃɛntsa] *sf* conscience; (*consapevolezza*) consciousness; ~ **politica** political awareness.
coscienzi'oso, a [koʃʃen'tsjoso] *ag* conscientious.
cosci'otto [koʃ'ʃɔtto] *sm* (*CUC*) leg.
cos'critto *sm* (*MIL*) conscript.
coscrizi'one [koskrit'tsjone] *sf* conscription.

======================= *PAROLA CHIAVE*

così *av* 1 (*in questo modo*) like this, (in) this way; (*in tal modo*) so; **le cose stanno** ~ this is the way things stand; **non ho detto** ~**!** I didn't say that!; **come stai? — (e)** ~ how are you? — so-so; **e** ~ **via** and so on; **per** ~ **dire** so to speak; ~ **sia** amen
2 (*tanto*) so; ~ **lontano** so far away; **un**

ragazzo ~ **intelligente** such an intelligent boy
♦ *ag inv* (*tale*): **non ho mai visto un film** ~ I've never seen such a film
♦ *cong* 1 (*perciò*) so, therefore; **e** ~ **ho deciso di lasciarlo** so I decided to leave him
2: ~ … **come** as … as; **non è** ~ **bravo come te** he's not as good as you; ~ … **che** so … that.

cosicché [kosik'ke] *cong* so (that).
cosid'detto, a *ag* so-called.
cos'mesi *sf* (*scienza*) cosmetics *sg*; (*prodotti*) cosmetics *pl*; (*trattamento*) beauty treatment.
cos'metico, a, ci, che *ag*, *sm* cosmetic.
'cosmico, a, ci, che *ag* cosmic.
'cosmo *sm* cosmos.
cosmo'nauta, i, e *sm/f* cosmonaut.
cosmopo'lita, i, e *ag* cosmopolitan.
'coso *sm* (*fam*: *oggetto*) thing, thingumajig; (: *aggeggio*) contraption; (: *persona*) what's his name, thingumajig.
cos'pargere [kos'pardʒere] *vt*: ~ **di** to sprinkle with.
cos'parso, a *pp di* cospargere.
cos'petto, a *sm*: **al** ~ **di** in front of; in the presence of.
cospicuità *sf* vast quantity.
cos'picuo, a *ag* considerable, large.
cospi'rare *vi* to conspire.
cospira'tore, 'trice *sm/f* conspirator.
cospirazi'one [kospirat'tsjone] *sf* conspiracy.
'cossi *etc vb vedi* cuocere.
Cost. *abbr* = **costituzione.**
'costa *sf* (*tra terra e mare*) coast(line); (*litorale*) shore; (*pendio*) slope; (*ANAT*) rib; **navigare sotto** ~ to hug the coast; **la C**~ **Azzurra** the French Riviera; **la C**~ **d'Avorio** the Ivory Coast; **velluto a** ~**e** corduroy.
costà *av* there.
cos'tante *ag* constant; (*persona*) steadfast
♦ *sf* constant.
cos'tanza [kos'tantsa] *sf* (*gen*) constancy; (*fermezza*) constancy, steadfastness; **il Lago di C**~ Lake Constance.
cos'tare *vi*, *vt* to cost; ~ **caro** to be expensive, cost a lot; ~ **un occhio della testa** to cost a fortune; **costi quel che costi** no matter what.
'Costa 'Rica *sf*: **la** ~ Costa Rica.
cos'tata *sf* (*CUC*: *di manzo*) large chop.
cos'tato *sm* (*ANAT*) ribs *pl*.
costeggi'are [kosted'dʒare] *vt* to be close to; to run alongside.

cos'tei *pron vedi* **costui.**

costellazi'one [kostellat'tsjone] *sf* constellation.

coster'nare *vt* to dismay.

coster'nato, a *ag* dismayed.

costernazi'one [kosternat'tsjone] *sf* dismay, consternation.

costi'ero, a *ag* coastal, coast *cpd* ♦ *sf* stretch of coast.

costi'pato, a *ag* (*stitico*) constipated.

costitu'ire *vt* (*comitato, gruppo*) to set up, form; (*collezione*) to put together, build up; (*sog: elementi, parti: comporre*) to make up, constitute; (*rappresentare*) to constitute; (*DIR*) to appoint; **~rsi** *vr*: **~rsi (alla polizia)** to give o.s. up (to the police); **~rsi parte civile** (*DIR*) *to associate in an action with the public prosecutor for damages*; **il fatto non costituisce reato** this is not a crime.

costitu'tivo, a *ag* constituent, component; **atto ~** (*DIR: di società*) memorandum of association.

costituzio'nale [kostituttsjo'nale] *ag* constitutional.

costituzi'one [kostitut'tsjone] *sf* setting up; building up; constitution.

'costo *sm* cost; **sotto ~** for less than cost price; **a ogni** *o* **qualunque ~, a tutti i ~i** at all costs; **~i di esercizio** running costs; **~i fissi** fixed costs; **~i di gestione** operating costs; **~i di produzione** production costs.

'costola *sf* (*ANAT*) rib; **ha la polizia alle ~e** the police are hard on his heels.

costo'letta *sf* (*CUC*) cutlet.

cos'toro *pron pl vedi* **costui.**

cos'toso, a *ag* expensive, costly.

cos'tretto, a *pp di* **costringere.**

cos'tringere [kos'trindʒere] *vt*: **~ qn a fare qc** to force sb to do sth.

costrit'tivo, a *ag* coercive.

costrizi'one [kostrit'tsjone] *sf* coercion.

costru'ire *vt* to construct, build.

costrut'tivo, a *ag* (*EDIL*) building *cpd*; (*fig*) constructive.

costruzi'one [kostrut'tsjone] *sf* construction, building; **di ~ inglese** British-made.

cos'tui, cos'tei, *pl* **cos'toro** *pron* (*soggetto*) he/she; *pl* they; (*complemento*) him/her; *pl* them; **si può sapere chi è ~?** (*peg*) just who is that fellow?

cos'tume *sm* (*uso*) custom; (*foggia di vestire, indumento*) costume; **il buon ~** public morality; **donna di facili ~i** woman of easy morals; **~ da bagno** bathing *o* swimming costume (*BRIT*), swimsuit; (*da uomo*) bathing *o* swimming trunks *pl.*

costu'mista, i, e *smlf* costume maker, costume designer.

co'tenna *sf* bacon rind.

co'togna [ko'toɲɲa] *sf* quince.

coto'letta *sf* (*di maiale, montone*) chop; (*di vitello, agnello*) cutlet.

coto'nare *vt* (*capelli*) to backcomb.

co'tone *sm* cotton; **~ idrofilo** cotton wool (*BRIT*), absorbent cotton (*US*).

cotoni'ficio [kotoni'fitʃo] *sm* cotton mill.

'cotta *sf* (*REL*) surplice; (*fam: innamoramento*) crush.

'cottimo *sm*: **lavorare a ~** to do piecework.

'cotto, a *pp di* **cuocere** ♦ *ag* cooked; (*fam: innamorato*) head-over-heels in love ♦ *sm* brickwork; **~ a puntino** cooked to perfection; **dirne di ~e e di crude a qn** to call sb every name under the sun; **farne di ~e e di crude** to get up to all kinds of mischief; **mattone di ~** fired brick; **pavimento in ~** tile floor.

cot'tura *sf* cooking; (*in forno*) baking; (*in umido*) stewing; **~ a fuoco lento** simmering; **angolo (di) ~** cooking area.

co'vare *vt* to hatch; (*fig: malattia*) to be sickening for; (*: odio, rancore*) to nurse ♦ *vi* (*fuoco, fig*) to smoulder (*BRIT*), smolder (*US*).

co'vata *sf* (*anche fig*) brood.

'covo *sm* den; **~ di terroristi** terrorist base.

co'vone *sm* sheaf.

'cozza ['kɔttsa] *sf* mussel.

coz'zare [kot'tsare] *vi*: **~ contro** to bang into, collide with.

'cozzo ['kɔttso] *sm* collision.

C.P. *abbr* (= *cartolina postale*) pc; (*POSTA*) *vedi* **casella postale**; (*NAUT*) = **capitaneria (di porto)**; (*DIR*) = **codice penale.**

crack *sm inv* (*droga*) crack.

Cra'covia *sf* Cracow.

'crampo *sm* cramp.

'cranio *sm* skull.

cra'tere *sm* crater.

cra'vatta *sf* tie; **~ a farfalla** bow tie.

cravat'tino *sm* bow tie.

cre'anza [kre'antsa] *sf* manners *pl*; **per buona ~** out of politeness.

cre'are *vt* to create.

creatività *sf* creativity.

cre'ato *sm* creation.

crea'tore, 'trice *ag* creative ♦ *smlf* creator; **un ~ di alta moda** fashion designer; **andare al C~** to go to meet one's maker.

crea'tura *sf* creature; (*bimbo*) baby, infant.

creazi'one [kreat'tsjone] *sf* creation; (*fondazione*) foundation, establishment.

'crebbi *etc vb vedi* **crescere.**

cre'dente *smlf* (*REL*) believer.

cre'denza [kre'dɛntsa] *sf* belief; (*armadio*) sideboard.
credenzi'ali [kreden'tsjali] *sfpl* credentials.
'credere *vt* to believe ♦ *vi*: ~ **in**, ~ **a** to believe in; ~ **qn onesto** to believe sb (to be) honest; ~ **che** to believe *o* think that; ~**rsi furbo** to think one is clever; **lo credo bene!** I can well believe it!; **fai quello che credi** *o* **come credi** do as you please.
cre'dibile *ag* credible, believable.
credibilità *sf* credibility.
credi'tizio, a [kredi'tittsjo] *ag* credit.
'credito *sm* (*anche COMM*) credit; (*reputazione*) esteem, repute; **comprare a** ~ to buy on credit; ~ **agevolato** easy credit terms; ~ **d'imposta** tax credit.
credi'tore, 'trice *sm/f* creditor.
'credo *sm inv* creed.
'credulo, a *ag* credulous.
credu'lone, a *sm/f* simpleton, sucker (*fam*).
'crema *sf* cream; (*con uova, zucchero etc*) custard; ~ **idratante** moisturizing cream; ~ **pasticciera** confectioner's custard; ~ **solare** sun cream.
cre'mare *vt* to cremate.
crema'torio *sm* crematorium.
cremazi'one [kremat'tsjone] *sf* cremation.
'cremisi *ag inv*, *sm inv* crimson.
Crem'lino *sm*: **il** ~ the Kremlin.
cremo'nese *ag* of (*o* from) Cremona.
cre'moso, a *ag* creamy.
'crepa *sf* crack.
cre'paccio [kre'pattʃo] *sm* large crack, fissure; (*di ghiacciaio*) crevasse.
crepacu'ore *sm* broken heart.
crepa'pelle *av*: **ridere a** ~ to split one's sides laughing.
cre'pare *vi* (*fam: morire*) to snuff it (*BRIT*), kick the bucket; ~ **dalle risa** to split one's sides laughing; ~ **dall'invidia** to be green with envy.
crepi'tare *vi* (*fuoco*) to crackle; (*pioggia*) to patter.
crepi'tio, ii *sm* crackling; pattering.
cre'puscolo *sm* twilight, dusk.
cre'scendo [kreʃ'ʃɛndo] *sm* (*MUS*) crescendo.
cre'scente [kreʃ'ʃɛnte] *ag* (*gen*) growing, increasing; (*luna*) waxing.
'crescere ['kreʃʃere] *vi* to grow ♦ *vt* (*figli*) to raise.
cre'scione [kreʃ'ʃone] *sm* watercress.
'crescita ['kreʃʃita] *sf* growth.
cresci'uto, a [kreʃ'ʃuto] *pp di* **crescere**.
'cresima *sf* (*REL*) confirmation.
cresi'mare *vt* to confirm.
'crespo, a *ag* (*capelli*) frizzy; (*tessuto*) puckered ♦ *sm* crêpe.

'cresta *sf* crest; (*di polli, uccelli*) crest, comb; **alzare la** ~ (*fig*) to become cocky; **abbassare la** ~ (*fig*) to climb down; **essere sulla** ~ **dell'onda** (*fig*) to be riding high.
'Creta *sf* Crete.
'creta *sf* (*gesso*) chalk; (*argilla*) clay.
cre'tese *ag*, *sm/f* Cretan.
creti'nata *sf* (*fam*): **dire/fare una** ~ to say/do a stupid thing.
cre'tino, a *ag* stupid ♦ *sm/f* idiot, fool.
CRI *sigla f* = *Croce Rossa Italiana*.
cric *sm inv* (*TECN*) jack.
'cricca, che *sf* clique.
'cricco, chi *sm* = **cric**.
cri'ceto [kri'tʃɛto] *sm* hamster.
crimi'nale *ag*, *sm/f* criminal.
criminalità *sf* crime; ~ **organizzata** organized crime.
'Criminalpol *abbr* = *polizia criminale*.
'crimine *sm* (*DIR*) crime.
criminolo'gia [kriminolo'dʒia] *sf* criminology.
crimi'noso, a *ag* criminal.
cri'nale *sm* ridge.
'crine *sm* horsehair.
crini'era *sf* mane.
'cripta *sf* crypt.
crip'tare *vt* (*TV: programma*) to encrypt.
crip'tato, a *ag* (*programma, messaggio*) encrypted.
crisan'temo *sm* chrysanthemum; *vedi anche* **Giorno dei Morti**.
'crisi *sf inv* crisis; (*MED*) attack, fit; **essere in** ~ (*partito, impresa etc*) to be in a state of crisis; ~ **energetica** energy crisis; ~ **di nervi** attack *o* fit of nerves.
cristalle'ria *sf* (*fabbrica*) crystal glassworks *sg*; (*oggetti*) crystalware.
cristal'lino, a *ag* (*MINERALOGIA*) crystalline; (*fig: suono, acque*) crystal clear ♦ *sm* (*ANAT*) crystalline lens.
cristalliz'zare [kristallid'dzare] *vi*, ~**rsi** *vr* to crystallize; (*fig*) to become fossilized.
cris'tallo *sm* crystal.
cristia'nesimo *sm* Christianity.
cristianità *sf* Christianity; (*i cristiani*) Christendom.
cristi'ano, a *ag*, *sm/f* Christian; **un povero** ~ (*fig*) a poor soul *o* beggar; **comportarsi da** ~ (*fig*) to behave in a civilized manner.
'cristo *sm*: **C**~ Christ; (**un**) **povero** ~ (a) poor beggar.
cri'terio *sm* criterion; (*buon senso*) (common) sense.
'critica, che *sf vedi* **critico**.
criti'care *vt* to criticize.
'critico, a, ci, che *ag* critical ♦ *sm* critic ♦ *sf*

criticism; **la ~a** (*attività*) criticism; (*persone*) the critics *pl*.
criti'cone, a *sm/f* faultfinder.
crivel'lare *vt*: **~ (di)** to riddle (with).
cri'vello *sm* riddle.
cro'ato, a *ag*, *sm/f* Croatian, Croat.
Cro'azia [kro'attsja] *sf*: **la ~** Croatia.
croc'cante *ag* crisp, crunchy ♦ *sm* (*CUC*) almond crunch.
'crocchia ['krɔkkja] *sf* chignon, bun.
'crocchio ['krɔkkjo] *sm* (*di persone*) small group, cluster.
'croce ['krotʃe] *sf* cross; **in ~** (*di traverso*) crosswise; (*fig*) on tenterhooks; **mettere in ~** (*anche fig*: *criticare*) to crucify; (: *tormentare*) to nag to death; **la C~ Rossa** the Red Cross; **~ uncinata** swastika.
croce'figgere *etc* [krotʃe'fiddʒere] **= crocifiggere** *etc*.
croceros'sina [krotʃeros'sina] *sf* Red Cross nurse.
croce'via [krotʃe'via] *sm inv* crossroads *sg*.
croci'ato, a [kro'tʃato] *ag* cross-shaped ♦ *sm* (*anche fig*) crusader ♦ *sf* crusade.
cro'cicchio [kro'tʃikkjo] *sm* crossroads *sg*.
croci'era [kro'tʃɛra] *sf* (*viaggio*) cruise; (*ARCHIT*) transept; **altezza di ~** (*AER*) cruising height; **velocità di ~** (*AER*, *NAUT*) cruising speed.
croci'figgere [krotʃi'fiddʒere] *vt* to crucify.
crocifissi'one [krotʃifis'sjone] *sf* crucifixion.
croci'fisso, a [krotʃi'fisso] *pp di* **crocifiggere** ♦ *sm* crucifix.
crogio'larsi [krodʒo'larsi] *vr*: **~ al sole** to bask in the sun.
crogi'olo [kro'dʒɔlo], **crogiu'olo** [kro'dʒwɔlo] *sm* crucible; (*fig*) melting pot.
crol'lare *vi* to collapse.
'crollo *sm* collapse; (*di prezzi*) slump, sudden fall.
'croma *sf* (*MUS*) quaver (*BRIT*), eighth note (*US*).
cro'mato, a *ag* chromium-plated.
'cromo *sm* chrome, chromium.
cromo'soma, i *sm* chromosome.
'cronaca, che *sf* chronicle; (*STAMPA*) news *sg*; (: *rubrica*) column; (*TV*, *RADIO*) commentary; **fatto** *o* **episodio di ~** news item; **~ nera** crime news *sg*; crime column.
'cronico, a, ci, che *ag* chronic.
cro'nista, i *sm* (*STAMPA*) reporter, columnist.
cronis'toria *sf* chronicle; (*fig*: *ironico*) blow-by-blow account.
cro'nografo *sm* (*strumento*) chronograph.
cronolo'gia [kronolo'dʒia] *sf* chronology.

cronome'trare *vt* to time.
cro'nometro *sm* chronometer; (*a scatto*) stopwatch.
'crosta *sf* crust; (*MED*) scab; (*ZOOL*) shell; (*di ghiaccio*) layer; (*fig peg*: *quadro*) daub.
cros'tacei [kros'tatʃei] *smpl* shellfish.
cros'tata *sf* (*CUC*) tart.
cros'tino *sm* (*CUC*) croûton; (: *da antipasto*) canapé.
crucci'are [krut'tʃare] *vt* to torment, worry; **~rsi** *vr*: **~rsi per** to torment o.s. over.
'cruccio ['kruttʃo] *sm* worry, torment.
cruci'ale [kru'tʃale] *ag* crucial.
cruci'verba [krutʃi'vɛrba] *sm inv* crossword (puzzle).
cru'dele *ag* cruel.
crudeltà *sf* cruelty.
'crudo, a *ag* (*non cotto*) raw; (*aspro*) harsh, severe.
cru'ento, a *ag* bloody.
cru'miro *sm* (*peg*) blackleg (*BRIT*), scab.
'cruna *sf* eye (of a needle).
'crusca *sf* bran.
crus'cotto *sm* (*AUT*) dashboard.
CS *sigla* = Cosenza.
C.S. *sigla* (*MIL*) = *comando supremo*; (*AUT*) = *codice della strada*.
c.s. *abbr* = *come sopra*.
Csce [tʃi'esse'tʃie] *sigla f* (= *Conferenza sulla sicurezza e la cooperazione in Europa*) CSCE.
CSI [tʃi'esse'i] *sigla f* (= *Comunità di Stati Indipendenti*) CIS.
CSM [tʃiesse'emme] *sigla m* (= *consiglio superiore della magistratura*) Magistrates' Board of Supervisors.
CT *sigla* = Catania.
c.t. *abbr* = **commissario tecnico**.
'Cuba *sf* Cuba.
cu'bano, a *ag*, *sm/f* Cuban.
cu'betto *sm* (small) cube; **~ di ghiaccio** ice cube.
'cubico, a, ci, che *ag* cubic.
'cubo, a *ag* cubic ♦ *sm* cube; **elevare al ~** (*MAT*) to cube.
cuc'cagna [kuk'kaɲɲa] *sf*: **paese della ~** land of plenty; **albero della ~** greasy pole (*fig*).
cuc'cetta [kut'tʃetta] *sf* (*FERR*) couchette; (*NAUT*) berth.
cucchiai'ata [kukkja'jata] *sf* spoonful; tablespoonful.
cucchia'ino [kukkja'ino] *sm* teaspoon; coffee spoon.
cucchi'aio [kuk'kjajo] *sm* spoon; (*da tavola*) tablespoon; (*cucchiaiata*) spoonful; tablespoonful.
'cuccia, ce ['kuttʃa] *sf* dog's bed; **a ~!** down!

cuccio'lata [kuttʃo'lata] *sf* litter.
'cucciolo ['kuttʃolo] *sm* cub; (*di cane*) puppy.
cu'cina [ku'tʃina] *sf* (*locale*) kitchen; (*arte culinaria*) cooking, cookery; (*le vivande*) food, cooking; (*apparecchio*) cooker; **di ~** (*libro, lezione*) cookery *cpd*; **~ componibile** fitted kitchen; **~ economica** kitchen range.
cuci'nare [kutʃi'nare] *vt* to cook.
cuci'nino [kutʃi'nino] *sm* kitchenette.
cu'cire [ku'tʃire] *vt* to sew, stitch; **~ la bocca a qn** (*fig*) to shut sb up.
cu'cito, a [ku'tʃito] *sm* sewing; (*INS*) sewing, needlework.
cuci'trice [kutʃi'tritʃe] *sf* (*TIP: per libri*) stitching machine; (*per fogli*) stapler.
cuci'tura [kutʃi'tura] *sf* sewing, stitching; (*costura*) seam.
cucù *sm inv*, **cu'culo** *sm* cuckoo.
'cuffia *sf* bonnet, cap; (*da infermiera*) cap; (*da bagno*) (bathing) cap; (*per ascoltare*) headphones *pl*, headset.
cu'gino, a [ku'dʒino] *sm/f* cousin.

========== *PAROLA CHIAVE* ==========

'cui *pron* **1** (*nei complementi indiretti: persona*) whom; (*: oggetto, animale*) which; **la persona/le persone a ~ accennavi** the person/people you were referring to *o* to whom you were referring; **la penna con ~ scrivo** the pen I'm writing with; **il paese da ~ viene** the country he comes from; **i libri di ~ parlavo** the books I was talking about *o* about which I was talking; **parla varie lingue, fra ~ l'inglese** he speaks several languages, including English; **il quartiere in ~ abito** the district where I live; **visto il modo in ~ ti ha trattato ...** considering how he treated you ...; **la ragione per ~** the reason why; **per ~ non so più che fare** that's why I don't know what to do
2 (*inserito tra articolo e sostantivo*) whose; **la donna i ~ figli sono scomparsi** the woman whose children have disappeared; **il signore, dal ~ figlio ho avuto il libro** the man from whose son I got the book.

culi'naria *sf* cookery.
culi'nario, a *ag* culinary.
'culla *sf* cradle.
cul'lare *vt* to rock; (*fig: idea, speranza*) to cherish; **~rsi** *vr* (*gen*) to sway; **~rsi in vane speranze** (*fig*) to cherish fond hopes; **~rsi nel dolce far niente** (*fig*) to sit back and relax.

culmi'nante *ag*: **posizione ~** (*ASTR*) highest point; **punto** *o* **momento ~** (*fig*) climax.
culmi'nare *vi*: **~ in** *o* **con** to culminate in.
'culmine *sm* top, summit.
'culo *sm* (*fam!*) arse (*BRIT!*), ass (*US!*); (: *fig: fortuna*): **aver ~** to have the luck of the devil; **prendere qn per il ~** to take the piss out of sb (*!*).
'culto *sm* (*religione*) religion; (*adorazione*) worship, adoration; (*venerazione: anche fig*) cult.
cul'tura *sf* (*gen*) culture; (*conoscenza*) education, learning; **di ~** (*persona*) cultured; (*istituto*) cultural, of culture; **~ generale** general knowledge; **~ di massa** mass culture.
cultu'rale *ag* cultural.
cultu'rismo *sm* body-building.
cumu'lare *vt* to accumulate, amass.
cumula'tivo, a *ag* cumulative; (*prezzo*) inclusive; (*biglietto*) group *cpd*.
'cumulo *sm* (*mucchio*) pile, heap; (*METEOR*) cumulus; **~ dei redditi** (*FISCO*) combined incomes; **~ delle pene** (*DIR*) consecutive sentences.
'cuneo *sm* wedge.
cu'netta *sf* (*di strada etc*) bump; (*scolo: nelle strade di città*) gutter; (: *di campagna*) ditch.
cu'nicolo *sm* (*galleria*) tunnel; (*di miniera*) pit, shaft; (*di talpa*) hole.
cu'oca *sf* vedi cuoco.
cu'ocere ['kwɔtʃere] *vt* (*alimenti*) to cook; (*mattoni etc*) to fire ♦ *vi* to cook; **~ in umido/a vapore/in padella** to stew/steam/fry; **~ al forno** (*pane*) to bake; (*arrosto*) to roast.
cu'oco, a, chi, che *sm/f* cook; (*di ristorante*) chef.
cuoi'ame *sm* leather goods *pl*.
cu'oio *sm* leather; **~ capelluto** scalp; **tirare le ~a** (*fam*) to kick the bucket.
cu'ore *sm* heart; **~i** *smpl* (*CARTE*) hearts; **avere buon ~** to be kind-hearted; **stare a ~ a qn** to be important to sb; **un grazie di ~** heartfelt thanks; **ringraziare di ~** to thank sincerely; **nel profondo del ~** in one's heart of hearts; **avere la morte nel ~** to be sick at heart; **club dei ~i solitari** lonely hearts club.
cupi'digia [kupi'didʒa] *sf* greed, covetousness.
'cupo, a *ag* dark; (*suono*) dull; (*fig*) gloomy, dismal.
'cupola *sf* dome; (*più piccola*) cupola; (*fig*) Mafia high command.
'cura *sf* care; (*MED: trattamento*) (course of)

treatment; **aver ~ di** (*occuparsi di*) to look after; **a ~ di** (*libro*) edited by; **fare una ~** to follow a course of treatment; **~ dimagrante** diet.

cu'rabile *ag* curable.

cu'rante *ag:* **medico ~** doctor (in charge of a patient).

cu'rare *vt* (*malato, malattia*) to treat; (: *guarire*) to cure; (*aver cura di*) to take care of; (*testo*) to edit; **~rsi** *vr* to take care of o.s.; (*MED*) to follow a course of treatment; **~rsi di** to pay attention to; (*occuparsi di*) to look after.

cu'rato *sm* parish priest; (*protestante*) vicar, minister.

cura'tore, 'trice *sm/f* (*DIR*) trustee; (*di antologia etc*) editor; **~ fallimentare** (official) receiver.

'curdo, a *ag* Kurdish ♦ *sm/f* Kurd.

'curia *sf* (*REL*): **la ~ romana** the Roman curia; **~ notarile** notaries' association *o* guild.

curio'saggine [kurjo'saddʒine] *sf* nosiness.

curio'sare *vi* to look round, wander round; (*tra libri*) to browse; **~ nei negozi** to look *o* wander round the shops; **~ nelle faccende altrui** to poke one's nose into other people's affairs.

curiosità *sf inv* curiosity; (*cosa rara*) curio, curiosity.

curi'oso, a *ag* (*che vuol sapere*) curious, inquiring; (*ficcanaso*) curious, inquisitive; (*bizzarro*) strange, curious ♦ *sm/f* busybody, nosy parker; **essere ~ di** to be curious about; **una folla di ~i** a crowd of onlookers.

cur'riculum *sm inv:* **~ (vitae)** curriculum vitae.

cur'sore *sm* (*INFORM*) cursor.

'curva *sf* curve; (*stradale*) bend, curve.

cur'vare *vt* to bend ♦ *vi* (*veicolo*) to take a bend; (*strada*) to bend, curve; **~rsi** *vr* to bend; (*legno*) to warp.

'curvo, a *ag* curved; (*piegato*) bent.

CUS *sigla m* = *Centro Universitario Sportivo.*

cusci'netto [kuʃʃi'netto] *sm* pad; (*TECN*) bearing ♦ *ag inv:* **stato ~** buffer state; **~ a sfere** ball bearing.

cu'scino [kuʃ'ʃino] *sm* cushion; (*guanciale*) pillow.

'cuspide *sf* (*ARCHIT*) spire.

cus'tode *sm/f* (*di museo*) keeper, custodian; (*di parco*) warden; (*di casa*) concierge; (*di fabbrica, carcere*) guard.

cus'todia *sf* care; (*DIR*) custody; (*astuccio*) case, holder; **avere qc in ~** to look after sth; **dare qc in ~ a qn** to entrust sth to sb's care; **agente di ~** prison warder; **~**

delle carceri prison security; **~ cautelare** (*DIR*) remand.

custo'dire *vt* (*conservare*) to keep; (*assistere*) to look after, take care of; (*fare la guardia*) to guard.

'cute *sf* (*ANAT*) skin.

cu'ticola *sf* cuticle.

C.V. *abbr* = *cavallo vapore.*

c.v.d. *abbr* (= *come volevasi dimostrare*) QED (= *quod erat demonstrandum*).

c.vo *abbr* = *corsivo.*

cy'clette ® [si'klɛt] *sf inv* exercise bike.

CZ *sigla* = *Catanzaro.*

D d

D, d [di] *sf o m inv* (*lettera*) D, d; **D come Domodossola** ≈ D for David (*BRIT*), D for Dog (*US*).

D *abbr* (= *destra*) R; (*FERR*) = *diretto.*

━━━━━ *PAROLA CHIAVE*

da (*da + il = dal, da + lo = dallo, da + l' = dall', da + la = dalla, da + i = dai, da + gli = dagli, da + le = dalle*) *prep* **1** (*agente*) by; **dipinto ~ un grande artista** painted by a great artist

2 (*causa*) with; **tremare dalla paura** to tremble with fear

3 (*stato in luogo*) at; **abito ~ lui** I'm living at his house *o* with him; **sono dal giornalaio** I'm at the newsagent's; **era ~ Francesco** she was at Francesco's (house)

4 (*moto a luogo*) to; (*moto per luogo*) through; **vado ~ Pietro/dal giornalaio** I'm going to Pietro's (house)/to the newsagent's; **sono passati dalla finestra** they came in through the window

5 (*provenienza, allontanamento*) from; **~ ... a** from ... to; **arrivare/partire ~ Milano** to arrive/depart from Milan; **scendere dal treno/dalla macchina** to get off the train/out of the car; **viene ~ una famiglia povera** he comes from a poor background; **viene dalla Scozia** he comes from Scotland; **ti chiamo ~ una cabina** I'm phoning from a call box; **si trova a 5 km ~ qui** it's 5 km from here

6 (*tempo: durata*) for; (: *a partire da: nel passato*) since; (: *nel futuro*) from; **vivo qui ~ un anno** I've been living here for a year; **è dalle 3 che ti aspetto** I've been waiting for you since 3 (o'clock); ~ **mattina a sera** from morning till night; ~ **oggi in poi** from today onwards; ~ **bambino** as a child, when I (*o he etc*) was a child

7 (*modo, maniera*) like; **comportarsi ~ uomo** to behave like a man; **l'ho fatto ~ me** I did it (by) myself; **non è ~ lui** it's not like him

8 (*descrittivo*): **una macchina ~ corsa** a racing car; **è una cosa ~ poco** it's nothing special; **una ragazza dai capelli biondi** a girl with blonde hair; **sordo ~ un orecchio** deaf in one ear; **abbigliamento ~ uomo** menswear; **un vestito ~ 100.000 lire** a 100,000 lire dress; **qualcosa ~ bere/mangiare** something to drink/eat.

dà *vb vedi* **dare**.

dab'bene *ag inv* honest, decent.

'Dacca *sf* Dacca.

dac'capo, da 'capo *av* (*di nuovo*) (once) again; (*dal principio*) all over again, from the beginning.

dacché [dak'ke] *cong* since.

'dado *sm* (*da gioco*) dice *o* die (*pl* dice); (*CUC*) stock cube (*BRIT*), bouillon cube (*US*); (*TECN*) (screw) nut; ~**i** *smpl* (game of) dice.

daf'fare, da 'fare *sm* work, toil; **avere un gran ~** to be very busy.

'dagli ['daʎʎi], **'dai** *prep + det vedi* **da**.

'daino *sm* (fallow) deer *inv*; (*pelle*) buckskin.

Da'kar *sf* Dakar.

dal *prep + det vedi* **da**.

dal. *abbr* (= decalitro) dal.

dall', 'dalla, 'dalle, 'dallo *prep + det vedi* **da**.

dal'tonico, a, ci, che *ag* colour-blind (*BRIT*), colorblind (*US*).

dam. *abbr* (= decametro) dam.

'dama *sf* lady; (*nei balli*) partner; (*gioco*) draughts *sg* (*BRIT*), checkers *sg* (*US*); **far ~** (*nel gioco*) to make a crown; ~ **di compagnia** lady's companion; ~ **di corte** lady-in-waiting.

Da'masco *sf* Damascus.

dami'gella [dami'dʒɛlla] *sf* (*STORIA*) damsel; (: *titolo*) mistress; ~ **d'onore** (*di sposa*) bridesmaid.

damigi'ana [dami'dʒana] *sf* demijohn.

dam'meno *ag inv*: **per non essere ~ di qn** so as not to be outdone by sb.

DAMS *sigla m* (= Disciplina delle Arti, della Musica, dello Spettacolo) study of the performing arts.

da'naro *sm* = **denaro**.

dana'roso, a *ag* wealthy.

da'nese *ag* Danish ♦ *sm/f* Dane ♦ *sm* (*LING*) Danish.

Dani'marca *sf*: **la ~** Denmark.

dan'nare *vt* (*REL*) to damn; ~**rsi** *vr*: ~**rsi** (**per**) (*fig: tormentarsi*) to be worried to death (by); **far ~ qn** to drive sb mad; ~**rsi l'anima per qc** (*affannarsi*) to work o.s. to death for sth; (*tormentarsi*) to worry o.s. to death over sth.

dan'nato, a *ag* damned.

dannazi'one [dannat'tsjone] *sf* damnation.

danneggi'are [danned'dʒare] *vt* to damage; (*rovinare*) to spoil; (*nuocere*) to harm; **la parte danneggiata** (*DIR*) the injured party.

'danno *vb vedi* **dare** ♦ *sm* damage; (*a persona*) harm, injury; ~**i** *smpl* (*DIR*) damages; **a ~ di qn** to sb's detriment; **chiedere/risarcire i ~i** to sue for/pay damages.

dan'noso, a *ag*: ~ (**a o per**) harmful (to), bad (for).

dan'tesco, a, schi, sche *ag* Dantesque; **l'opera ~a** Dante's work.

Da'nubio *sm*: **il ~** the Danube.

'danza ['dantsa] *sf*: **la ~** dancing; **una ~** a dance.

dan'zante [dan'tsante] *ag* dancing; **serata ~** dance.

dan'zare [dan'tsare] *vt, vi* to dance.

danza'tore, 'trice [dantsa'tore] *sm/f* dancer.

dapper'tutto *av* everywhere.

dap'poco *ag inv* inept; worthless.

dap'prima *av* at first.

Darda'nelli *smpl*: **i ~** the Dardanelles.

'dardo *sm* dart.

'dare *sm* (*COMM*) debit ♦ *vt* to give; (*produrre: frutti, suono*) to produce ♦ *vi* (*guardare*): ~ **su** to look (out) onto; ~**rsi** *vr*: ~**rsi a** to dedicate o.s. to; **quanti anni mi dai?** how old do you think I am?; **danno ancora quel film?** is that film still showing?; ~ **da mangiare a qn** to give sb something to eat; ~ **per certo qc** to consider sth certain; ~ **ad intendere a qn che ...** to lead sb to believe that ...; ~ **per morto qn** to give sb up for dead; ~ **qc per scontato** to take sth for granted; ~**rsi ammalato** to report sick; ~**rsi alla bella vita** to have a good time; ~**rsi al bere** to take to drink; ~**rsi al commercio** to go into business; ~**rsi da fare per fare qc** to go to a lot of bother to do sth; ~**rsi per vinto** to give in; **può ~rsi** maybe, perhaps; **si dà il caso che ...** it so happens that ...; **darsela a gambe** to take to one's heels; **il ~ e l'avere** (*ECON*) debits and credits *pl*.

Dar-es-Sa'laam *sf* Dar-es-Salaam.

'darsena *sf* dock.

'data *sf* date; **in ~ da destinarsi** on a date still to be announced; **in ~ odierna** as of today; **amicizia di lunga** *o* **vecchia ~** long-standing friendship; **~ di emissione** date of issue; **~ di nascita** date of birth; **~ di scadenza** expiry date.

da'tare *vt* to date ♦ *vi*: **~ da** to date from.

da'tato, a *ag* dated.

da'tivo *sm* dative.

'dato, a *ag* (*stabilito*) given ♦ *sm* datum; **~i** *smpl* data *pl*; **~ che** given that; **in ~i casi** in certain cases; **è un ~ di fatto** it's a fact.

da'tore, 'trice *sm/f*: **~ di lavoro** employer.

'dattero *sm* date (*BOT*).

dattilogra'fare *vt* to type.

dattilogra'fia *sf* typing.

datti'lografo, a *sm/f* typist.

dattilos'critto *sm* typescript.

da'vanti *av* in front; (*dirimpetto*) opposite ♦ *ag inv* front ♦ *sm* front; **~ a** *prep* in front of; (*dirimpetto a*) facing, opposite; (*in presenza di*) before, in front of.

davan'zale [davan'tsale] *sm* windowsill.

da'vanzo, d'a'vanzo [da'vantso] *av* more than enough.

dav'vero *av* really, indeed; **dico ~** I mean it.

dazi'ario, a [dat'tsjarjo] *ag* excise *cpd*.

'dazio ['dattsjo] *sm* (*somma*) duty; (*luogo*) customs *pl*; **~ d'importazione** import duty.

db *abbr* (= *decibel*) dB.

DC *sigla f* = **Democrazia Cristiana** (*former political party*).

d.C. *av abbr* (= *dopo Cristo*) A.D.

D.D.T. *abbr m* (= *dicloro-difenil-tricloroetano*) D.D.T.

'dea *sf* goddess.

'debbo *etc vb vedi* **dovere**.

debel'lare *vt* to overcome, conquer.

debili'tare *vt* to debilitate.

debita'mente *av* duly, properly.

'debito, a *ag* due, proper ♦ *sm* debt; (*COMM: dare*) debit; **a tempo ~** at the right time; **portare a ~ di qn** to debit sb with; **~ consolidato** consolidated debt; **~ d'imposta** tax liability; **~ pubblico** national debt.

debi'tore, 'trice *sm/f* debtor.

'debole *ag* weak, feeble; (*suono*) faint; (*luce*) dim ♦ *sm* weakness.

debo'lezza [debo'lettsa] *sf* weakness.

debut'tante *sm/f* (*gen*) beginner, novice; (*TEAT*) actor/actress at the beginning of his (*o* her) career.

debut'tare *vi* to make one's début.

de'butto *sm* début.

'decade *sf* period of ten days.

deca'dente *ag* decadent.

deca'denza [deka'dɛntsa] *sf* decline; (*DIR*) loss, forfeiture.

deca'dere *vi* to decline.

deca'duto, a *ag* (*persona*) impoverished; (*norma*) lapsed.

decaffei'nato, a *ag* decaffeinated.

de'calogo *sm* (*fig*) rulebook.

de'cano *sm* (*REL*) dean.

decan'tare *vt* (*virtù, bravura etc*) to praise; (*persona*) to sing the praises of.

decapi'tare *vt* to decapitate, behead.

decappot'tabile *ag, sf* convertible.

dece'duto, a [detʃe'duto] *ag* deceased.

decele'rare [detʃele'rare] *vt, vi* to decelerate, slow down.

decen'nale [detʃen'nale] *ag* (*che dura 10 anni*) ten-year *cpd*; (*che ricorre ogni 10 anni*) ten-yearly, every ten years ♦ *sm* (*ricorrenza*) tenth anniversary.

de'cenne [de'tʃɛnne] *ag*: **un bambino ~** a ten-year-old child, a child of ten.

de'cennio [de'tʃɛnnjo] *sm* decade.

de'cente [de'tʃɛnte] *ag* decent, respectable, proper; (*accettabile*) satisfactory, decent.

decentraliz'zare [detʃentralid'dzare] *vt* (*AMM*) to decentralize.

decentra'mento [detʃentra'mento] *sm* decentralization.

decen'trare [detʃen'trare] *vt* to decentralize, move out of *o* away from the centre.

de'cenza [de'tʃɛntsa] *sf* decency, propriety.

de'cesso [de'tʃɛsso] *sm* death; **atto di ~** death certificate.

de'cidere [de'tʃidere] *vi* to decide, make up one's mind ♦ *vt*: **~ qc** to decide on sth; (*questione, lite*) to settle sth; **~rsi** *vr*: **~rsi (a fare)** to decide (to do), make up one's mind (to do); **~ di fare/che** to decide to do/that; **~ di qc** (*sog: cosa*) to determine sth.

deci'frare [detʃi'frare] *vt* to decode; (*fig*) to decipher, make out.

de'cilitro [de'tʃilitro] *sm* decilitre (*BRIT*), deciliter (*US*).

deci'male [detʃi'male] *ag* decimal.

deci'mare [detʃi'mare] *vt* to decimate.

de'cimetro [de'tʃimetro] *sm* decimetre.

'decimo, a ['dɛtʃimo] *num* tenth.

de'cina [de'tʃina] *sf* ten; (*circa dieci*): **una ~ (di)** about ten.

de'cisi [de'tʃizi] *etc vb vedi* **decidere**.

decisio'nale [detʃizjo'nale] *ag* decision-making *cpd*.

decisi'one [detʃi'zjone] *sf* decision; **prendere una** ~ to make a decision; **con** ~ decisively, resolutely.

deci'sivo, a [detʃi'zivo] *ag* (*gen*) decisive; (*fattore*) deciding.

de'ciso, a [de'tʃizo] *pp di* **decidere ♦** *ag* (*persona, carattere*) determined; (*tono*) firm, resolute.

declas'sare *vt* to downgrade; to lower in status; **1ª declassata** (*FERR*) *first-class carriage which may be used by second-class passengers.*

decli'nare *vi* (*pendio*) to slope down; (*fig: diminuire*) to decline; (*tramontare*) to set, go down **♦** *vt* to decline; ~ **le proprie generalità** (*fig*) to give one's particulars; ~ **ogni responsabilità** to disclaim all responsibility.

declinazi'one [deklinat'tsjone] *sf* (*LING*) declension.

de'clino *sm* decline.

de'clivio *sm* (downward) slope.

decodifi'care *vt* to decode.

decodifica'tore *sm* decoder.

decol'lare *vi* (*AER*) to take off.

décolleté [dekol'te] *ag inv* (*abito*) low-necked, low-cut **♦** *sm* (*di abito*) low neckline; (*di donna*) cleavage.

de'collo *sm* take-off.

decolo'rare *vt* to bleach.

decom'porre *vt*, **decomporsi** *vr* to decompose.

decomposizi'one [dekompozit'tsjone] *sf* decomposition.

decom'posto, a *pp di* **decomporre**.

decompressi'one *sf* decompression.

deconge'lare [dekondʒe'lare] *vt* to defrost.

decongestio'nare [dekondʒestjo'nare] *vt* (*MED, traffico*) to relieve congestion in.

deco'rare *vt* to decorate.

decora'tivo, a *ag* decorative.

decora'tore, 'trice *sm/f* (interior) decorator.

decorazi'one [dekorat'tsjone] *sf* decoration.

de'coro *sm* decorum.

deco'roso, a *ag* decorous, dignified.

decor'renza [dekor'rɛntsa] *sf*: **con** ~ **da** (as) from.

de'correre *vi* to pass, elapse; (*avere effetto*) to run, have effect.

de'corso, a *pp di* **decorrere ♦** *sm* (*evoluzione: anche MED*) course.

de'crebbi *etc vb vedi* **decrescere**.

de'crepito, a *ag* decrepit.

de'crescere [de'krɛʃʃere] *vi* (*diminuire*) to

decrease, diminish; (*acque*) to subside, go down; (*prezzi*) to go down.

decresci'uto, a [dekreʃ'ʃuto] *pp di* **decrescere**.

decre'tare *vt* (*norma*) to decree; (*mobilitazione*) to order; ~ **lo stato d'emergenza** to declare a state of emergency; ~ **la nomina di qn** to decide on the appointment of sb.

de'creto *sm* decree; ~ **legge** *decree with the force of law*; ~ **di sfratto** eviction order.

decur'tare *vt* (*debito, somma*) to reduce.

decurtazi'one [dekurtat'tsjone] *sf* reduction.

'dedalo *sm* maze, labyrinth.

'dedica, che *sf* dedication.

dedi'care *vt* to dedicate; ~**rsi** *vr*: ~**rsi a** (*votarsi*) to devote o.s. to.

dedicherò *etc* [dedike'rɔ] *vb vedi* **dedicare**.

'dedito, a *ag*: ~ **a** (*studio etc*) dedicated *o* devoted to; (*vizio*) addicted to.

de'dotto, a *pp di* **dedurre**.

de'duco *etc vb vedi* **dedurre**.

de'durre *vt* (*concludere*) to deduce; (*defalcare*) to deduct.

de'dussi *etc vb vedi* **dedurre**.

deduzi'one [dedut'tsjone] *sf* deduction.

defal'care *vt* to deduct.

defenes'trare *vt* to throw out of the window; (*fig*) to remove from office.

defe'rente *ag* respectful, deferential.

defe'rire *vt* (*DIR*): ~ **a** to refer to.

defezi'one [defet'tsjone] *sf* defection, desertion.

defici'ente [defi'tʃɛnte] *ag* (*mancante*): ~ **di** deficient in; (*insufficiente*) insufficient **♦** *sm/f* mental defective; (*peg: cretino*) idiot.

defici'enza [defi'tʃɛntsa] *sf* deficiency; (*carenza*) shortage; (*fig: lacuna*) weakness.

'deficit ['dɛfitʃit] *sm inv* (*ECON*) deficit.

defi'nire *vt* to define; (*risolvere*) to settle; (*questione*) to finalize.

defini'tivo, a *ag* definitive, final **♦** *sf*: **in** ~**a** (*dopotutto*) when all is said and done; (*dunque*) well then.

defi'nito, a *ag* definite; **ben** ~ clear, clear cut.

definizi'one [definit'tsjone] *sf* (*gen*) definition; (*di disputa, vertenza*) settlement; (*di tempi, obiettivi*) establishment.

deflagrazi'one [deflagrat'tsjone] *sf* explosion.

deflazi'one [deflat'tsjone] *sf* (*ECON*) deflation.

deflet'tore *sm* (*AUT*) quarterlight (*BRIT*),

deflector (*US*).

deflu'ire *vi*: ~ **da** (*liquido*) to flow away from; (*fig*: *capitali*) to flow out of.

de'flusso *sm* (*della marea*) ebb.

defor'mare *vt* (*alterare*) to put out of shape; (*corpo*) to deform; (*pensiero, fatto*) to distort; ~**rsi** *vr* to lose its shape.

deformazi'one [deformat'tsjone] *sf* (*MED*) deformation; **questa è ~ professionale!** that's force of habit because of your (*o* his *etc*) job!

de'forme *ag* deformed; disfigured.

deformità *sf inv* deformity.

defrau'dare *vt*: ~ **qn di qc** to defraud sb of sth, cheat sb out of sth.

de'funto, a *ag* late *cpd* ♦ *sm/f* deceased.

degene'rare [dedʒene'rare] *vi* to degenerate.

degenerazi'one [dedʒenerat'tsjone] *sf* degeneration.

de'genere [de'dʒenere] *ag* degenerate.

de'gente [de'dʒɛnte] *sm/f* bedridden person; (*ricoverato in ospedale*) in-patient.

de'genza [de'dʒɛntsa] *sf* confinement to bed; ~ **ospedaliera** period in hospital.

'degli ['deʎʎi] *prep + det vedi* **di.**

deglu'tire *vt* to swallow.

de'gnare [deɲ'ɲare] *vt*: ~ **qn della propria presenza** to honour sb with one's presence; ~**rsi** *vr*: ~**rsi di fare qc** to deign *o* condescend to do sth; **non mi ha degnato di uno sguardo** he wouldn't even look at me.

'degno, a ['deɲɲo] *ag* dignified; ~ **di** worthy of; ~ **di lode** praiseworthy.

degra'dare *vt* (*MIL*) to demote; (*privare della dignità*) to degrade; ~**rsi** *vr* to demean o.s.

de'grado *sm*: ~ **urbano** urban decline.

degus'tare *vt* to sample, taste.

degustazi'one [degustat'tsjone] *sf* sampling, tasting; ~ **di vini** (*locale*) specialist wine bar; ~ **di caffè** (*locale*) specialist coffee shop.

'dei *smpl di* **dio** ♦ *prep + det vedi* **di.**

del *prep + det vedi* **di.**

dela'tore, 'trice *sm/f* police informer.

delazi'one [delat'tsjone] *sf* informing.

'delega, ghe *sf* (*procura*) proxy; **per ~ notarile** ≈ through a solicitor (*BRIT*) *o* lawyer.

dele'gare *vt* to delegate.

dele'gato *sm* delegate.

delegazi'one [delegat'tsjone] *sf* delegation.

delegherò *etc* [delege'rɔ] *vb vedi* **delegare.**

dele'terio, a *ag* deleterious, noxious.

del'fino *sm* (*ZOOL*) dolphin; (*STORIA*) dauphin; (*fig*) probable successor.

'Delhi ['dɛli] *sf* Delhi.

de'libera *sf* decision.

delibe'rare *vt* to come to a decision on ♦ *vi* (*DIR*): ~ **(su qc)** to rule (on sth).

delica'tezza [delika'tettsa] *sf* delicacy; frailty; thoughtfulness; tactfulness.

deli'cato, a *ag* delicate; (*salute*) delicate, frail; (*fig*: *gentile*) thoughtful, considerate; (: *che dimostra tatto*) tactful.

delimi'tare *vt* (*anche fig*) to delimit.

deline'are *vt* to outline; ~**rsi** *vr* to be outlined; (*fig*) to emerge.

delin'quente *sm/f* criminal, delinquent.

delin'quenza [delin'kwɛntsa] *sf* criminality, delinquency; ~ **minorile** juvenile delinquency.

de'liquio *sm* (*MED*) swoon; **cadere in ~** to swoon.

deli'rante *ag* (*MED*) delirious; (*fig*: *folla*) frenzied; (: *discorso, mente*) insane.

deli'rare *vi* to be delirious, rave; (*fig*) to rave.

de'lirio *sm* delirium; (*ragionamento insensato*) raving; (*fig*): **andare/mandare in ~** to go/send into a frenzy.

de'litto *sm* crime; ~ **d'onore** *crime committed to avenge one's honour.*

delittu'oso, a *ag* criminal.

de'lizia [de'littsja] *sf* delight.

delizi'are [delit'tsjare] *vt* to delight; ~**rsi** *vr*: ~**rsi di qc/a fare qc** to take delight in sth/ in doing sth.

delizi'oso, a [delit'tsjoso] *ag* delightful; (*cibi*) delicious.

dell', 'della, 'delle, 'dello *prep + det vedi* **di.**

'delta *sm inv* delta.

delta'plano *sm* hang-glider; **volo col ~** hang-gliding.

delucidazi'one [delutʃidat'tsjone] *sf* clarification *no pl.*

delu'dente *ag* disappointing.

de'ludere *vt* to disappoint.

delusi'one *sf* disappointment.

de'luso, a *pp di* **deludere** ♦ *ag* disappointed.

dema'gogico, a, ci, che [dema'gɔdʒiko] *ag* popularity-seeking, demagogic.

dema'gogo, ghi *sm* demagogue.

de'manio *sm* state property.

de'mente *ag* (*MED*) demented, mentally deranged; (*fig*) crazy, mad.

de'menza [de'mɛntsa] *sf* dementia; madness; ~ **senile** senile dementia.

demenzi'ale [demen'tsjale] *ag* (*fig*) off-the-wall.

'demmo *vb vedi* **dare.**

demo'cratico, a, ci, che *ag* democratic.

democra'zia [demokrat'tsia] *sf* democracy; **la D~ Cristiana** the Christian Democrat Party.

democristi'ano, a *ag, sm/f* Christian Democrat.

demogra'fia *sf* demography.

demo'grafico, a, ci, che *ag* demographic; **incremento** ~ increase in population.

demo'lire *vt* to demolish.

demolizi'one [demolit'tsjone] *sf* demolition.

'demone *sm* demon.

de'monio *sm* demon, devil; **il D~** the Devil.

demoniz'zare [demonid'dzare] *vt* to make a monster of.

demonizzazi'one [demoniddzat'tsjone] *sf* demonizing, demonization.

demoraliz'zare [demoralid'dzare] *vt* to demoralize; ~**rsi** *vr* to become demoralized.

de'mordere *vi*: **non** ~ **(da)** to refuse to give up.

demoti'vare *vt*: ~ **qn** to take away sb's motivation.

demoti'vato, a *ag* unmotivated, lacking motivation.

de'naro *sm* money; ~**i** *smpl* (*CARTE*) suit in Neapolitan pack of cards.

denatu'rato, a *ag vedi* **alcool.**

deni'grare *vt* to denigrate, run down.

denomi'nare *vt* to name; ~**rsi** *vr* to be named *o* called.

denomina'tore *sm* (*MAT*) denominator.

denominazi'one [denominat'tsjone] *sf* name; denomination; ~ **di origine controllata (D.O.C.)** *label guaranteeing the quality and origin of a wine.*

deno'tare *vt* to denote, indicate.

densità *sf inv* density; (*di nebbia*) thickness, denseness; **ad alta/bassa** ~ **di popolazione** densely/sparsely populated.

'denso, a *ag* thick, dense.

den'tale *ag* dental.

den'tario, a *ag* dental.

denta'tura *sf* set of teeth, teeth *pl*; (*TECN: di ruota*) serration.

'dente *sm* tooth; (*di forchetta*) prong; (*GEO: cima*) jagged peak; **al** ~ (*CUC: pasta*) cooked so as to be firm when eaten; **mettere i** ~**i** to teethe; **mettere qc sotto i** ~**i** to have a bite to eat; **avere il** ~ **avvelenato contro** *o* **con qn** to bear sb a grudge; ~ **di leone** (*BOT*) dandelion; ~**i del giudizio** wisdom teeth.

'dentice ['dɛntitʃe] *sm* (*ZOOL*) sea bream.

denti'era *sf* (set of) false teeth *pl*.

denti'fricio [denti'fritʃo] *sm* toothpaste.

den'tista, i, e *sm/f* dentist.

'dentro *av* inside; (*in casa*) indoors; (*fig: nell'intimo*) inwardly ♦ *prep*: ~ **(a)** in;

piegato in ~ folded over; **qui/là** ~ in here/there; ~ **di sé** (*pensare, brontolare*) to oneself; **tenere tutto** ~ to keep everything bottled up (inside o.s.); **darci** ~ (*fig fam*) to slog away, work hard.

denucleariz'zato, a [denuklearid'dzato] *ag* denuclearized, nuclear-free.

denu'dare *vt* (*persona*) to strip; (*parte del corpo*) to bare; ~**rsi** *vr* to strip.

de'nuncia, ce *o* **cie** [de'nuntʃa], **de'nunzia** [de'nuntsja] *sf* denunciation; declaration; **fare una** ~ *o* **sporgere** ~ **contro qn** (*DIR*) to report sb to the police; ~ **del reddito** (income) tax return.

denunci'are [denun'tʃare], **denunzi'are** [denun'tsjare] *vt* to denounce; (*dichiarare*) to declare; ~ **qn/qc (alla polizia)** to report sb/sth to the police.

denu'trito, a *ag* undernourished.

denutrizi'one [denutrit'tsjone] *sf* malnutrition.

deodo'rante *sm* deodorant.

deontolo'gia [deontolo'dʒia] *sf* (*professionale*) professional code of conduct.

depenalizzazi'one [depenaliddzat'tsjone] *sf* decriminalization.

dépen'dance [depã'dãs] *sf inv* outbuilding.

depe'ribile *ag* perishable; **merce** ~ perishables *pl*, perishable goods *pl*.

deperi'mento *sm* (*di persona*) wasting away; (*di merci*) deterioration.

depe'rire *vi* to waste away.

depi'lare *vt* to depilate.

depila'torio, a *ag* hair-removing, depilatory ♦ *sm* hair remover, depilatory.

depilazi'one [depilat'tsjone] *sf* hair removal, depilation.

depis'taggio [depis'taddʒo] *sm* diversion.

depis'tare *vt* to set on the wrong track.

dépli'ant [depli'ã] *sm inv* leaflet; (*opuscolo*) brochure.

deplo'rare *vt* to deplore; to lament.

deplo'revole *ag* deplorable.

de'pone, de'pongo *etc vb vedi* **deporre.**

de'porre *vt* (*depositare*) to put down; (*rimuovere: da una carica*) to remove; (*: re*) to depose; (*DIR*) to testify; ~ **le armi** (*MIL*) to lay down arms; ~ **le uova** to lay eggs.

depor'tare *vt* to deport.

depor'tato, a *sm/f* deportee.

deportazi'one [deportat'tsjone] *sf* deportation.

de'posi *etc vb vedi* **deporre.**

deposi'tante *sm* (*COMM*) depositor.

deposi'tare *vt* (*gen, GEO, ECON*) to deposit; (*lasciare*) to leave; (*merci*) to store; ~**rsi** *vr* (*sabbia, polvere*) to settle.

deposi'tario *sm* (*COMM*) depository.
de'posito *sm* deposit; (*luogo*) warehouse; depot; (: *MIL*) depot; ~ **bagagli** left-luggage office; ~ **di munizioni** ammunition dump.
deposizi'one [depozit'tsjone] *sf* deposition; (*da una carica*) removal; **rendere una falsa** ~ to perjure o.s.
de'posto, a *pp di* **deporre**.
depra'vare *vt* to corrupt, pervert.
depra'vato, a *ag* depraved ♦ *sm/f* degenerate.
depre'care *vt* to deprecate, deplore.
depre'dare *vt* to rob, plunder.
depressi'one *sf* depression; **area** *o* **zona di** ~ (*METEOR*) area of low pressure; (*ECON*) depressed area.
de'presso, a *pp di* **deprimere** ♦ *ag* depressed.
deprezza'mento [deprettsa'mento] *sm* depreciation.
deprez'zare [depret'tsare] *vt* (*ECON*) to depreciate.
depri'mente *ag* depressing.
de'primere *vt* to depress.
depu'rare *vt* to purify.
depura'tore *sm*: ~ **d'acqua** water purifier; ~ **di gas** scrubber.
depu'tato, a *sm/f* (*POL*) deputy, ≈ Member of Parliament (*BRIT*), ≈ Congressman/ woman (*US*); *vedi anche* **Camera dei Deputati**.
deputazi'one [deputat'tsjone] *sf* deputation; (*POL*) position of deputy, ≈ parliamentary seat (*BRIT*), ≈ seat in Congress (*US*).
deraglia'mento [deraʎʎa'mento] *sm* derailment.
deragli'are [deraʎ'ʎare] *vi* to be derailed; **far** ~ to derail.
dera'pare *vi* (*veicolo*) to skid; (*SCI*) to sideslip.
derattizzazi'one [derattiddzat'tsjone] *sf* rodent control.
deregolamen'tare *vt* to deregulate.
deregolamentazi'one [deregolamentat'tsjone] *sf* deregulation.
dere'litto, a *ag* derelict.
dere'tano *sm* (*fam*) bottom, buttocks *pl*.
de'ridere *vt* to mock, deride.
de'risi *etc vb vedi* **deridere**.
derisi'one *sf* derision, mockery.
de'riso, a *pp di* **deridere**.
deri'sorio, a *ag* (*gesto, tono*) mocking.
de'riva *sf* (*NAUT, AER*) drift; (*dispositivo: AER*) fin; (: *NAUT*) centre-board (*BRIT*), centerboard (*US*); **andare alla** ~ (*anche fig*) to drift.

deri'vare *vi*: ~ **da** to derive from ♦ *vt* to derive; (*corso d'acqua*) to divert.
deri'vato, a *ag* derived ♦ *sm* (*CHIM, LING*) derivative; (*prodotto*) by-product.
derivazi'one [derivat'tsjone] *sf* derivation; diversion.
derma'tite *sf* dermatitis.
dermatolo'gia [dermatolo'dʒia] *sf* dermatology.
derma'tologo, a, gi, ghe *sm/f* dermatologist.
dermoprotet'tivo, a *ag* (*crema, azione*) protecting the skin.
'deroga, ghe *sf* (special) dispensation; **in** ~ **a** as a (special) dispensation to.
dero'gare *vi*: ~ **a** (*DIR*) to repeal in part.
der'rate *sfpl* commodities; ~ **alimentari** foodstuffs.
deru'bare *vt* to rob.
des'critto, a *pp di* **descrivere**.
des'crivere *vt* to describe.
descrizi'one [deskrit'tsjone] *sf* description.
de'serto, a *ag* deserted ♦ *sm* (*GEO*) desert; **isola** ~**a** desert island.
deside'rabile *ag* desirable.
deside'rare *vt* to want, wish for; (*sessualmente*) to desire; ~ **fare/che qn faccia** to want *o* wish to do/sb to do; **desidera fare una passeggiata?** would you like to go for a walk?; **farsi** ~ (*fare il prezioso*) to play hard to get; (*farsi aspettare*) to take one's time; **lascia molto a** ~ it leaves a lot to be desired.
desi'derio *sm* wish; (*più intenso, carnale*) desire.
deside'roso, a *ag*: ~ **di** longing *o* eager for.
desi'gnare [desiɲ'ɲare] *vt* to designate, appoint; (*data*) to fix; **la vittima designata** the intended victim.
designazi'one [desiɲɲat'tsjone] *sf* designation, appointment.
desi'nare *vi* to dine, have dinner ♦ *sm* dinner.
desi'nenza [dezi'nentsa] *sf* (*LING*) ending, inflexion.
de'sistere *vi*: ~ **da** to give up, desist from.
desis'tito, a *pp di* **desistere**.
deso'lante *ag* distressing.
deso'lato, a *ag* (*paesaggio*) desolate; (*persona: spiacente*) sorry.
desolazi'one [dezolat'tsjone] *sf* desolation.
'despota, i *sm* despot.
'dessi *etc vb vedi* **dare**.
destabiliz'zare [destabilid'dzare] *vt* to destabilize.
des'tare *vt* to wake (up); (*fig*) to awaken, arouse; ~**rsi** *vr* to wake (up).

'**deste** *etc vb vedi* **dare**.

desti'nare *vt* to destine; (*assegnare*) to appoint, assign; (*indirizzare*) to address; ~ **qc a qn** to intend to give sth to sb, intend sb to have sth.

destina'tario, a *sm/f* (*di lettera*) addressee; (*di merce*) consignee; (*di mandato*) payee.

destinazi'one [destinat'tsjone] *sf* destination; (*uso*) purpose.

des'tino *sm* destiny, fate.

destitu'ire *vt* to dismiss, remove.

destituzi'one [destitut'tsjone] *sf* dismissal, removal.

'**desto, a** *ag* (wide) awake.

'**destra** *sf vedi* **destro**.

destreggi'arsi [destred'dʒarsi] *vr* to manoeuvre (*BRIT*), maneuver (*US*).

des'trezza [des'trettsa] *sf* skill, dexterity.

'**destro, a** *ag* right, right-hand; (*abile*) skilful (*BRIT*), skillful (*US*), adroit ♦ *sf* (*mano*) right hand; (*parte*) right (side); (*POL*): **la ~a** the right ♦ *sm* (*BOXE*) right; **a ~a** (*essere*) on the right; (*andare*) to the right; **tenere la ~a** to keep to the right.

de'sumere *vt* (*dedurre*) to infer, deduce; (*trarre: informazioni*) to obtain.

de'sunto, a *pp di* **desumere**.

detas'sare *vt* to remove the duty (*o* tax) from.

dete'nere *vt* (*incarico, primato*) to hold; (*proprietà*) to have, possess; (*in prigione*) to detain, hold.

de'tengo, de'tenni *etc vb vedi* **detenere**.

deten'tivo, a *ag*: **mandato ~** imprisonment order; **pena ~a** prison sentence.

deten'tore, 'trice *sm/f* (*di titolo, primato etc*) holder.

dete'nuto, a *sm/f* prisoner.

detenzi'one [deten'tsjone] *sf* holding; possession; detention.

deter'gente [deter'dʒɛnte] *ag* detergent; (*crema, latte*) cleansing ♦ *sm* detergent.

de'tergere [de'tɛrdʒere] *vt* (*gen*) to clean; (*pelle, viso*) to cleanse; (*sudore*) to wipe (away).

deteriora'mento *sm*: ~ (**di**) deterioration (in).

deterio'rare *vt* to damage; ~**rsi** *vr* to deteriorate.

deteri'ore *ag* (*merce*) second-rate; (*significato*) pejorative; (*tradizione letteraria*) lesser, minor.

determi'nante *ag* decisive, determining.

determi'nare *vt* to determine.

determina'tivo, a *ag* determining; **articolo ~** (*LING*) definite article.

determi'nato, a *ag* (*gen*) certain;

(*particolare*) specific; (*risoluto*) determined, resolute.

determinazi'one [determinat'tsjone] *sf* determination; (*decisione*) decision.

deter'rente *ag, sm* deterrent.

deter'rò *etc vb vedi* **detenere**.

deter'sivo *sm* detergent; (*per bucato: in polvere*) washing powder (*BRIT*), soap powder.

de'terso, a *pp di* **detergere**.

detes'tare *vt* to detest, hate.

deti'ene *etc vb vedi* **detenere**.

deto'nare *vi* to detonate.

detona'tore *sm* detonator.

detonazi'one [detonat'tsjone] *sf* (*di esplosivo*) detonation, explosion; (*di arma*) bang; (*di motore*) pinking (*BRIT*), knocking.

de'trae, de'traggo *etc vb vedi* **detrarre**.

de'trarre *vt*: ~ (**da**) to deduct (from), take away (from).

de'trassi *etc vb vedi* **detrarre**.

de'tratto, a *pp di* **detrarre**.

detrazi'one [detrat'tsjone] *sf* deduction; ~ **d'imposta** tax allowance.

detri'mento *sm* detriment, harm; **a ~ di** to the detriment of.

de'trito *sm* (*GEO*) detritus.

detroniz'zare [detronid'dzare] *vt* to dethrone.

'**detta** *sf*: **a ~ di** according to.

dettagli'ante [dettaʎ'ʎante] *sm/f* (*COMM*) retailer.

dettagli'are [dettaʎ'ʎare] *vt* to detail, give full details of.

dettagliata'mente [dettaʎʎata'mente] *av* in detail.

det'taglio [det'taʎʎo] *sm* detail; (*COMM*): **il ~** retail; **al ~** (*COMM*) retail; separately.

det'tame *sm* dictate, precept.

det'tare *vt* to dictate; ~ **legge** (*fig*) to lay down the law.

det'tato *sm* dictation.

detta'tura *sf* dictation.

'**detto, a** *pp di* **dire** ♦ *ag* (*soprannominato*) called, known as; (*già nominato*) above-mentioned ♦ *sm* saying; ~ **fatto** no sooner said than done; **presto ~!** it's easier said than done!

detur'pare *vt* to disfigure; (*moralmente*) to sully.

devas'tante *ag* (*anche fig*) devastating.

devas'tare *vt* to devastate; (*fig*) to ravage.

devastazi'one [devastat'tsjone] *sf* devastation, destruction.

devi'are *vi*: ~ (**da**) to turn off (from) ♦ *vt* to divert.

devi'ato, a *ag* (*fig: persona, organizzazione*)

corrupt, bent (*col*).

deviazi'one [devjat'tsjone] *sf* (*anche AUT*) diversion; **fare una** ~ to make a detour.

'**devo** *etc vb vedi* **dovere.**

devo'luto, a *pp di* **devolvere.**

devoluzi'one [devolut'tsjone] *sf* (*DIR*) devolution, transfer.

de'volvere *vt* (*DIR*) to transfer, devolve; ~ **qc in beneficenza** to give sth to charity.

de'voto, a *ag* (*REL*) devout, pious; (*affezionato*) devoted.

devozi'one [devot'tsjone] *sf* devoutness; (*anche REL*) devotion.

dg *abbr* (= *decigrammo*) dg.

<hr>
===== PAROLA CHIAVE

di (*di* + *il* = **del**, *di* + *lo* = **dello**, *di* + *l'* = **dell'**, *di* + *la* = **della**, *di* + *i* = **dei**, *di* + *gli* = **degli**, *di* + *le* = **delle**) *prep* **1** (*possesso, specificazione*) of; (*composto da, scritto da*) by; **la macchina** ~ **Paolo/**~ **mio fratello** Paolo's/my brother's car; **un amico** ~ **mio fratello** a friend of my brother's, one of my brother's friends; **la grandezza della casa** the size of the house; **le foto delle vacanze** the holiday photos; **la città** ~ **Firenze** the city of Florence; **il nome** ~ **Maria** the name Mary; **un quadro** ~ **Botticelli** a painting by Botticelli
2 (*caratterizzazione, misura*) of; **una casa** ~ **mattoni** a brick house, a house made of bricks; **un orologio d'oro** a gold watch; **un bimbo** ~ **3 anni** a child of 3, a 3-year-old child; **una trota** ~ **un chilo** a trout weighing a kilo; **una strada** ~ **10km** a road 10km long; **un quadro** ~ **valore** a valuable picture
3 (*causa, mezzo, modo*) with; **tremare** ~ **paura** to tremble with fear; **morire** ~ **cancro** to die of cancer; **spalmare** ~ **burro** to spread with butter
4 (*argomento*) about, of; **discutere** ~ **sport** to talk about sport; **parlare** ~ **politica/lavoro** to talk about politics/work
5 (*luogo: provenienza*) from; out of; **essere** ~ **Roma** to be from Rome; **uscire** ~ **casa** to come out of *o* leave the house
6 (*tempo*) in; **d'estate/d'inverno** in (the) summer/winter; ~ **notte** by night, at night; ~ **mattina/sera** in the morning/evening; ~ **lunedì** on Mondays; ~ **ora in ora** by the hour
7 (*partitivo*) of; **alcuni** ~ **voi/noi** some of you/us; **il più bravo** ~ **tutti** the best of all; **il migliore del mondo** the best in the world; **non c'è niente** ~ **peggio** there's nothing worse
8 (*paragone*) than; **più veloce** ~ **me** faster

than me; **guadagna meno** ~ **me** he earns less than me
♦ *det* (*una certa quantità di*) some; (: *negativo*) any; (: *interrogativo*) any, some; **del pane** (some) bread; **delle caramelle** (some) sweets; **degli amici miei** some friends of mine; **vuoi del vino?** do you want some *o* any wine?

dì *sm* day; **buon** ~! hallo!; **a** ~ = **addì.**

DIA *sigla f* = *Direzione investigativa antimafia.*

dia'bete *sm* diabetes *sg.*

dia'betico, a, ci, che *ag, sm/f* diabetic.

dia'bolico, a, ci, che *ag* diabolical.

di'acono *sm* (*REL*) deacon.

dia'dema, i *sm* diadem; (*di donna*) tiara.

di'afano, a *ag* (*trasparente*) diaphanous; (*pelle*) transparent.

dia'framma, i *sm* (*divisione*) screen; (*ANAT, FOT, contraccettivo*) diaphragm.

di'agnosi [di'aɲɲozi] *sf* diagnosis *sg.*

diagnosti'care [diaɲɲosti'kare] *vt* to diagnose.

dia'gnostico, a, ci, che [diaɲ'ɲɔstiko] *ag* diagnostic; **aiuti** ~**ci** (*INFORM*) debugging aids.

diago'nale *ag, sf* diagonal.

dia'gramma, i *sm* diagram; ~ **a barre** bar chart; ~ **di flusso** flow chart.

dialet'tale *ag* dialectal; **poesia** ~ poetry in dialect.

dia'letto *sm* dialect.

di'alisi *sf* dialysis.

dialo'gante *ag*: **unità** ~ (*INFORM*) interactive terminal.

dialo'gare *vi*: ~ (**con**) to have a dialogue (with); (*conversare*) to converse (with)
♦ *vt* (*scena*) to write the dialogue for.

di'alogo, ghi *sm* dialogue.

dia'mante *sm* diamond.

di'ametro *sm* diameter.

di'amine *escl*: **che** ~ ...? what on earth ...?

diaposi'tiva *sf* transparency, slide.

di'aria *sf* daily (expense) allowance.

di'ario *sm* diary; ~ **di bordo** (*NAUT*) log(book); ~ **di classe** (*INS*) class register; ~ **degli esami** (*INS*) exam timetable.

diar'rea *sf* diarrhoea.

dia'triba *sf* diatribe.

diavole'ria *sf* (*azione*) act of mischief; (*aggeggio*) weird contraption.

di'avolo *sm* devil; **è un buon** ~ he's a good sort; **avere un** ~ **per capello** to be in a foul temper; **avere una fame/un freddo del** ~ to be ravenously hungry/frozen stiff; **mandare qn al** ~ (*fam*) to tell sb to go to hell; **fare il** ~ **a quattro** to kick up a fuss.

di'battere *vt* to debate, discuss; ~**rsi** *vr* to struggle.

dibatti'mento *sm* (*dibattito*) debate, discussion; (*DIR*) hearing.

di'battito *sm* debate, discussion.

dic. *abbr* (= *dicembre*) Dec.

dicas'tero *sm* ministry.

'dice ['ditʃe] *vb vedi* **dire**.

di'cembre [di'tʃɛmbre] *sm* December; *per fraseologia vedi* **luglio**.

dice'ria [ditʃe'ria] *sf* rumour (*BRIT*), rumor (*US*), piece of gossip.

dichia'rare [dikja'rare] *vt* to declare; ~**rsi** *vr* to declare o.s.; (*innamorato*) to declare one's love; **si dichiara che** ... it is hereby declared that ...; ~**rsi vinto** to acknowledge defeat.

dichia'rato, a [dikja'rato] *ag* (*nemico, ateo*) avowed.

dichiarazi'one [dikjarat'tsjone] *sf* declaration; ~ **dei redditi** statement of income; (*modulo*) tax return.

dician'nove [ditʃan'nɔve] *num* nineteen.

dicianno'venne [ditʃanno'vɛnne] *ag, sm/f* nineteen-year-old.

dicias'sette [ditʃas'sɛtte] *num* seventeen.

diciasset'tenne [ditʃasset'tɛnne] *ag, sm/f* seventeen-year-old.

diciot'tenne [ditʃot'tɛnne] *ag, sm/f* eighteen-year-old.

dici'otto [di'tʃɔtto] *num* eighteen ♦ *sm inv* (*INS*) *minimum satisfactory mark awarded in Italian universities*.

dici'tura [ditʃi'tura] *sf* words *pl*, wording.

'dico *etc vb vedi* **dire**.

didasca'lia *sf* (*di illustrazione*) caption; (*CINE*) subtitle; (*TEAT*) stage directions *pl*.

di'dattico, a, ci, che *ag* didactic; (*metodo, programma*) teaching; (*libro*) educational ♦ *sf* didactics *sg*; teaching methodology.

di'dentro *av* inside, indoors.

didi'etro *av* behind ♦ *ag inv* (*ruota, giardino*) back, rear *cpd* ♦ *sm* (*di casa*) rear; (*fam: sedere*) backside.

di'eci ['djetʃi] *num* ten.

dieci'mila [djetʃi'mila] *num* ten thousand.

die'cina [dje'tʃina] *sf* = **decina**.

di'edi *etc vb vedi* **dare**.

di'eresi *sf* dieresis *sg*.

'diesel ['di:zəl] *sm inv* diesel engine.

di'eta *sf* diet; **essere a** ~ to be on a diet.

die'tetica *sf* dietetics *sg*.

die'tologo, a, gi, ghe *sm/f* dietician.

di'etro *av* behind; (*in fondo*) at the back ♦ *prep* behind; (*tempo: dopo*) after ♦ *sm* (*di foglio, giacca*) back; (*di casa*) back, rear ♦ *ag inv* back *cpd*; **le zampe di** ~ the hind

legs; ~ **ricevuta** against receipt; ~ **richiesta** on demand; (*scritta*) on application; **andare** ~ **a** (*anche fig*) to follow; **stare** ~ **a qn** (*sorvegliare*) to keep an eye on sb; (*corteggiare*) to hang around sb; **portarsi** ~ **qn/qc** to bring sb/sth with one, bring sb/sth along; **gli hanno riso/parlato** ~ they laughed at/talked about him behind his back.

di'etro 'front *escl* about turn! (*BRIT*), about face! (*US*) ♦ *sm* (*MIL*) about-turn, about-face; (*fig*) volte-face, about-turn, about-face; **fare** ~ (*MIL, fig*) to about-turn, about-face; (*tornare indietro*) to turn round.

di'fatti *cong* in fact, as a matter of fact.

di'fendere *vt* to defend; ~**rsi** *vr* (*cavarsela*) to get by; ~**rsi da/contro** to defend o.s. from/against; ~**rsi dal freddo** to protect o.s. from the cold; **sapersi** ~ to know how to look after o.s.

difen'sivo, a *ag* defensive ♦ *sf*: **stare sulla** ~**a** (*anche fig*) to be on the defensive.

difen'sore *sm/f* defender; **avvocato** ~ counsel for the defence (*BRIT*) *o* defense (*US*).

di'fesa *sf vedi* **difeso**.

di'fesi *etc vb vedi* **difendere**.

di'feso, a *pp di* **difendere** ♦ *sf* defence (*BRIT*), defense (*US*); **prendere le** ~**e di qn** to defend sb, take sb's part.

difet'tare *vi* to be defective; ~ **di** to be lacking in, lack.

difet'tivo, a *ag* defective.

di'fetto *sm* (*mancanza*): ~ **di** lack of; (*di fabbricazione*) fault, flaw, defect; (*morale*) fault, failing, defect; (*fisico*) defect; **far** ~ to be lacking; **in** ~ at fault; **in the wrong**.

difet'toso, a *ag* defective, faulty.

diffa'mare *vt* (*a parole*) to slander; (*per iscritto*) to libel.

diffama'torio, a *ag* slanderous; libellous.

diffamazi'one [diffamat'tsjone] *sf* slander; libel.

diffe'rente *ag* different.

diffe'renza [diffe'rɛntsa] *sf* difference; **a** ~ **di** unlike; **non fare** ~ (**tra**) to make no distinction (between).

differenzi'ale [differen'tsjale] *ag, sm* differential; **classi** ~**i** (*INS*) special classes (*for backward children*).

differenzi'are [differen'tsjare] *vt* to differentiate; ~**rsi da** to differentiate o.s. from; to differ from.

diffe'rire *vt* to postpone, defer ♦ *vi* to be different.

diffe'rita *sf*: **in** ~ (*trasmettere*) prerecorded.

dif'ficile [dif'fitʃile] *ag* difficult; (*persona*)

hard to please, difficult (to please); (*poco probabile*): **è ~ che sia libero** it is unlikely that he'll be free ♦ *sm/f*: **fare il(la) ~** to be difficult, be awkward ♦ *sm* difficult part; difficulty; **essere ~ nel mangiare** to be fussy about one's food.

difficil'mente [diffitʃil'mente] *av* (*con difficoltà*) with difficulty; **~ verrà** he's unlikely to come.

difficoltà *sf inv* difficulty.

difficol'toso, a *ag* (*compito*) difficult, hard; (*persona*) difficult, hard to please; **digestione ~a** poor digestion.

dif'fida *sf* (*DIR*) warning, notice.

diffi'dare *vi*: **~ di** to be suspicious *o* distrustful of ♦ *vt* (*DIR*) to warn; **~ qn dal fare qc** to warn sb not to do sth, caution sb against doing sth.

diffi'dente *ag* suspicious, distrustful.

diffi'denza [diffi'dɛntsa] *sf* suspicion, distrust.

dif'fondere *vt* (*luce, calore*) to diffuse; (*notizie*) to spread, circulate; **~rsi** *vr* to spread.

dif'fusi *etc vb vedi* **diffondere**.

diffusi'one *sf* diffusion; spread; (*anche di giornale*) circulation; (*FISICA*) scattering.

dif'fuso, a *pp di* **diffondere** ♦ *ag* (*FISICA*) diffuse; (*notizia, malattia etc*) widespread; **è opinione ~a che ...** it's widely held that ....

difi'lato *av* (*direttamente*) straight, directly; (*subito*) straight away.

difte'rite *sf* diphtheria.

'diga, ghe *sf* dam; (*portuale*) breakwater.

dige'rente [didʒe'rɛnte] *ag* (*apparato*) digestive.

dige'rire [didʒe'rire] *vt* to digest.

digesti'one [didʒes'tjone] *sf* digestion.

diges'tivo, a [didʒes'tivo] *ag* digestive ♦ *sm* (after-dinner) liqueur.

Digi'one [di'dʒone] *sf* Dijon.

digi'tale [didʒi'tale] *ag* digital; (*delle dita*) finger *cpd*, digital ♦ *sf* (*BOT*) foxglove.

digi'tare [didʒi'tare] *vt* (*dati*) to key (in); (*tasto*) to press.

digiu'nare [didʒu'nare] *vi* to starve o.s.; (*REL*) to fast.

digi'uno, a [di'dʒuno] *ag*: **essere ~** not to have eaten ♦ *sm* fast; **a ~** on an empty stomach.

dignità [diɲɲi'ta] *sf inv* dignity.

digni'tario [diɲɲi'tarjo] *sm* dignitary.

digni'toso, a [diɲɲi'toso] *ag* dignified.

'DIGOS *sigla f* (= *Divisione Investigazioni Generali e Operazioni Speciali*) *police department dealing with political security.*

digressi'one *sf* digression.

digri'gnare [digriɲ'ɲare] *vt*: **~ i denti** to grind one's teeth.

dila'gare *vi* to flood; (*fig*) to spread.

dilani'are *vt* to tear to pieces.

dilapi'dare *vt* to squander, waste.

dila'tare *vt* to dilate; (*gas*) to cause to expand; (*passaggio, cavità*) to open (up); **~rsi** *vr* to dilate; (*FISICA*) to expand.

dilatazi'one [dilatat'tsjone] *sf* (*ANAT*) dilation; (*di gas, metallo*) expansion.

dilazio'nare [dilattsjo'nare] *vt* to delay, defer.

dilazi'one [dilat'tsjone] *sf* deferment.

dileggi'are [diled'dʒare] *vt* to mock, deride.

dilegu'are *vi*, **~rsi** *vr* to vanish, disappear.

di'lemma, i *sm* dilemma.

dilet'tante *sm/f* dilettante; (*anche SPORT*) amateur.

dilet'tare *vt* to give pleasure to, delight; **~rsi** *vr*: **~rsi di** to take pleasure in, enjoy.

dilet'tevole *ag* delightful.

di'letto, a *ag* dear, beloved ♦ *sm* pleasure, delight.

dili'gente [dili'dʒɛnte] *ag* (*scrupoloso*) diligent; (*accurato*) careful, accurate.

dili'genza [dili'dʒɛntsa] *sf* diligence; care; (*carrozza*) stagecoach.

dilu'ire *vt* to dilute.

dilun'garsi *vr* (*fig*): **~ su** to talk at length on *o* about.

diluvi'are *vb impers* to pour (down).

di'luvio *sm* downpour; (*inondazione, fig*) flood; **il ~ universale** the Flood.

dima'grante *ag* slimming *cpd*.

dima'grire *vi* to get thinner, lose weight.

dime'nare *vt* to wave, shake; **~rsi** *vr* to toss and turn; (*fig*) to struggle; **~ la coda** (*sog: cane*) to wag its tail.

dimensi'one *sf* dimension; (*grandezza*) size; **considerare un discorso nella sua ~ politica** to look at a speech in terms of its political significance.

dimenti'canza [dimenti'kantsa] *sf* forgetfulness; (*errore*) oversight, slip; **per ~** inadvertently.

dimenti'care *vt* to forget; **~rsi** *vr*: **~rsi di qc** to forget sth.

dimentica'toio *sm* (*scherzoso*): **cadere/ mettere nel ~** to sink into/consign to oblivion.

di'mentico, a, chi, che *ag*: **~ di** (*che non ricorda*) forgetful of; (*incurante*) oblivious of, unmindful of.

di'messo, a *pp di* **dimettere** ♦ *ag* (*voce*) subdued; (*uomo, abito*) modest, humble.

dimesti'chezza [dimesti'kettsa] *sf* familiarity.

di'mettere *vt*: ~ **qn da** to dismiss sb from; (*dall'ospedale*) to discharge sb from; **~rsi** *vr*: **~rsi (da)** to resign (from).

dimez'zare [dimed'dzare] *vt* to halve.

diminu'ire *vt* to reduce, diminish; (*prezzi*) to bring down, reduce ♦ *vi* to decrease, diminish; (*rumore*) to die down, die away; (*prezzi*) to fall, go down.

diminu'tivo, a *ag, sm* diminutive.

diminuzi'one [diminut'tsjone] *sf* decreasing, diminishing; **in** ~ on the decrease; ~ **della produttività** fall in productivity.

di'misi *etc vb vedi* **dimettere**.

dimissio'nario, a *ag* outgoing, resigning.

dimissi'oni *sfpl* resignation *sg*; **dare** *o* **presentare le** ~ to resign, hand in one's resignation.

di'mora *sf* residence; **senza fissa** ~ of no fixed address *o* abode.

dimo'rare *vi* to reside.

dimos'trante *sm/f* (*POL*) demonstrator.

dimos'trare *vt* to demonstrate, show; (*provare*) to prove, demonstrate; **~rsi** *vr*: **~rsi molto abile** to show o.s. *o* prove to be very clever; **non dimostra la sua età** he doesn't look his age; **dimostra 30 anni** he looks about 30 (years old).

dimostra'tivo, a *ag* (*anche LING*) demonstrative.

dimostrazi'one [dimostrat'tsjone] *sf* demonstration; proof.

di'namico, a, ci, che *ag* dynamic ♦ *sf* dynamics *sg*.

dina'mismo *sm* dynamism.

dinami'tardo, a *ag*: **attentato** ~ dynamite attack ♦ *sm/f* dynamiter.

dina'mite *sf* dynamite.

'dinamo *sf inv* dynamo.

di'nanzi [di'nantsi]: ~ **a** *prep* in front of.

dinas'tia *sf* dynasty.

dini'ego, ghi *sm* (*rifiuto*) refusal; (*negazione*) denial.

dinocco'lato, a *ag* lanky; **camminare** ~ to walk with a slouch.

dino'sauro *sm* dinosaur.

din'torno *av* round, (round) about; **~i** *smpl* outskirts; **nei ~i di** in the vicinity *o* neighbourhood of.

'dio, *pl* **'dei** *sm* god; **D~** God; **gli dei** the gods; **si crede un** ~ he thinks he's wonderful; **D~ mio!** my God!; **D~ ce la mandi buona** let's hope for the best; **D~ ce ne scampi e liberi!** God forbid!

di'ocesi [di'ɔtʃezi] *sf inv* diocese.

dios'sina *sf* dioxin.

dipa'nare *vt* (*lana*) to wind into a ball; (*fig*) to disentangle, sort out.

diparti'mento *sm* department.

dipen'dente *ag* dependent ♦ *sm/f* employee.

dipen'denza [dipen'dɛntsa] *sf* dependence; **essere alle ~e di qn** to be employed by sb *o* in sb's employ.

di'pendere *vi*: ~ **da** to depend on; (*finanziariamente*) to be dependent on; (*derivare*) to come from, be due to.

di'pesi *etc vb vedi* **dipendere**.

di'peso, a *pp di* **dipendere**.

di'pingere [di'pindʒere] *vt* to paint.

di'pinsi *etc vb vedi* **dipingere**.

di'pinto, a *pp di* **dipingere** ♦ *sm* painting.

di'ploma, i *sm* diploma.

diplo'mare *vt* to award a diploma to, graduate (*US*) ♦ *vi* to obtain a diploma, graduate (*US*).

diplo'matico, a, ci, che *ag* diplomatic ♦ *sm* diplomat.

diplo'mato, a *ag* qualified ♦ *sm/f* qualified person, holder of a diploma.

diploma'zia [diplomat'tsia] *sf* diplomacy.

di'porto *sm*: **imbarcazione** *f* **da** ~ pleasure craft.

dira'dare *vt* to thin (out); (*visite*) to reduce, make less frequent; **~rsi** *vr* to disperse; (*nebbia*) to clear (up).

dira'mare *vt* to issue ♦ *vi*, **~rsi** *vr* (*strade*) to branch.

'dire *vt* to say; (*segreto, fatto*) to tell; ~ **qc a qn** to tell sb sth; ~ **a qn di fare qc** to tell sb to do sth; ~ **di sì/no** to say yes/no; **si dice che ...** they say that ...; **mi si dice che ...** I am told that ...; **si direbbe che ...** it looks (*o* sounds) as though ...; **dica, signora?** (*in un negozio*) yes, Madam, can I help you?; **sa quello che dice** he knows what he's talking about; **lascialo** ~ (*esprimersi*) let him have his say; (*ignoralo*) just ignore him; **come sarebbe a ~?** what do you mean?; **che ne diresti di andarcene?** how about leaving?; **chi l'avrebbe mai detto!** who would have thought it!; **si dicono esperti** they say they are experts; **per così** ~ so to speak; **a dir poco** to say the least; **non c'è che** ~ there's no doubt about it; **non dico di no** I can't deny it; **il che è tutto** ~ need I say more?

di'ressi *etc vb vedi* **dirigere**.

di'retta *sf vedi* **diretto**.

diretta'mente *av* (*immediatamente*) directly, straight; (*personalmente*) directly; (*senza intermediari*) direct, straight.

diret'tissima *sf* (*tragitto*) most direct route; (*DIR*): **processo per** ~ summary trial.

diret'tissimo *sm* (*FERR*) fast (through) train.

diret'tivo, a *ag* (*POL, AMM*) executive; (*COMM*) managerial, executive ♦ *sm* leadership, leaders *pl* ♦ *sf* directive, instruction.

di'retto, a *pp di* **dirigere** ♦ *ag* direct ♦ *sm* (*FERR*) through train ♦ *sf*: **in** (**linea**) **~a** (*RADIO, TV*) live; **il mio ~ superiore** my immediate superior.

diret'tore, 'trice *sm/f* (*di azienda*) director; manager/ess; (*di scuola elementare*) head (teacher) (*BRIT*), principal (*US*); **~ amministrativo** company secretary (*BRIT*), corporate executive secretary (*US*); **~ del carcere** prison governor (*BRIT*) *o* warden (*US*); **~ di filiale** branch manager; **~ d'orchestra** conductor; **~ di produzione** (*CINE*) producer; **~ sportivo** team manager; **~ tecnico** (*SPORT*) trainer, coach.

direzi'one [diret'tsjone] *sf* (*senso: anche fig*) direction; (*conduzione: gen*) running; (: *di partito*) leadership; (: *di società*) management; (: *di giornale*) editorship; (*direttori*) management; **in ~ di** in the direction of, towards.

diri'gente [diri'dʒɛnte] *ag* managerial ♦ *sm/f* executive; (*POL*) leader; **classe ~** ruling class.

diri'genza [diri'dʒɛntsa] *sf* management; (*POL*) leadership.

dirigenzi'ale [diridʒen'tsjale] *ag* managerial.

di'rigere [di'ridʒere] *vt* to direct; (*impresa*) to run, manage; (*MUS*) to conduct; **~rsi** *vr*: **~rsi verso** *o* **a** to make *o* head for; **~ i propri passi verso** to make one's way towards; **il treno era diretto a Pavia** the train was heading for Pavia.

diri'gibile [diri'dʒibile] *sm* airship.

dirim'petto *av* opposite; **~ a** *prep* opposite, facing.

di'ritto, a *ag* straight; (*onesto*) straight, upright ♦ *av* straight, directly ♦ *sm* right side; (*TENNIS*) forehand; (*MAGLIA*) plain stitch, knit stitch; (*prerogativa*) right; (*leggi, scienza*): **il ~** law; **stare ~** to stand up straight; **aver ~ a qc** to be entitled to sth; **punto ~** plain (stitch); **andare ~** to go straight on; **a buon ~** quite rightly; **~i** (**d'autore**) royalties; **~ di successione** right of succession.

dirit'tura *sf* (*SPORT*) straight; (*fig*) rectitude.

diroc'cato, a *ag* tumbledown, in ruins.

dirom'pente *ag* (*anche fig*) explosive.

dirotta'mento *sm*: **~** (**aereo**) hijack.

dirot'tare *vt* (*nave, aereo*) to change the course of; (*aereo: sotto minaccia*) to hijack; (*traffico*) to divert ♦ *vi* (*nave, aereo*) to change course.

dirotta'tore, 'trice *sm/f* hijacker.

di'rotto, a *ag* (*pioggia*) torrential; (*pianto*) unrestrained; **piovere a ~** to pour, rain cats and dogs; **piangere a ~** to cry one's heart out.

di'rupo *sm* crag, precipice.

disabi'tato, a *ag* uninhabited.

disabitu'arsi *vr*: **~ a** to get out of the habit of.

disac'cordo *sm* disagreement.

disadat'tato, a *ag* (*PSIC*) maladjusted.

disa'dorno, a *ag* plain, unadorned.

disaffezi'one [dizaffet'tsjone] *sf* disaffection.

disa'gevole [disa'dʒevole] *ag* (*scomodo*) uncomfortable; (*difficile*) difficult.

disagi'ato, a [diza'dʒato] *ag* poor, needy; (*vita*) hard.

di'sagio [di'zadʒo] *sm* discomfort; (*disturbo*) inconvenience; (*fig: imbarazzo*) embarrassment; **~i** *smpl* hardship *sg*, poverty *sg*; **essere a ~** to be ill at ease.

di'samina *sf* close examination.

disappro'vare *vt* to disapprove of.

disapprovazi'one [dizapprovat'tsjone] *sf* disapproval.

disap'punto *sm* disappointment.

disarcio'nare [dizartʃo'nare] *vt* to unhorse.

disar'mante *ag* (*fig*) disarming.

disar'mare *vt, vi* to disarm.

di'sarmo *sm* (*MIL*) disarmament.

di'sastro *sm* disaster.

disas'troso, a *ag* disastrous.

disat'tento, a *ag* inattentive.

disattenzi'one [dizatten'tsjone] *sf* carelessness, lack of attention.

disatti'vare *vt* (*bomba*) to de-activate, defuse.

disa'vanzo [diza'vantso] *sm* (*ECON*) deficit.

disavven'tura *sf* misadventure, mishap.

dis'brigo, ghi *sm* (*prompt*) clearing up *o* settlement.

dis'capito *sm*: **a ~ di** to the detriment of.

dis'carica, che *sf* (*di rifiuti*) rubbish tip *o* dump.

discen'dente [diʃʃen'dɛnte] *ag* descending ♦ *sm/f* descendant.

di'scendere [diʃ'ʃɛndere] *vt* to go (*o* come) down ♦ *vi* to go (*o* come) down; (*smontare*) to get off; **~ da** (*famiglia*) to be descended from; **~ dalla macchina/dal treno** to get out of the car/out of *o* off the train; **~ da cavallo** to dismount, get off one's horse.

di'scepolo, a [diʃ'ʃepolo] *sm/f* disciple.

di'scernere [diʃ'ʃernere] *vt* to discern.

discerni'mento [diʃʃerni'mento] *sm* discernment.

disce'sista [diʃʃe'sista] *sm/f* downhill skier.

di'sceso, a [diʃ'ʃeso] *pp di* **discendere** ♦ *sf* descent; (*pendio*) slope; **in ~a** (*strada*) downhill *cpd*, sloping; **~a libera** (*SCI*) downhill race.

dischi'udere [dis'kjudere] *vt* (*aprire*) to open; (*fig: rivelare*) to disclose, reveal.

dischi'usi *etc* [dis'kjusi] *vb vedi* **dischiudere**.

dischi'uso, a [dis'kjuso] *pp di* **dischiudere**.

di'scinto, a [diʃ'ʃinto] *ag* (*anche*: **in abiti ~i**) half-undressed.

disci'ogliere [diʃ'ʃɔʎʎere] *vt*, **~rsi** *vr* to dissolve; (*fondere*) to melt.

disci'plina [diʃʃi'plina] *sf* discipline.

discipli'nare [diʃʃipli'nare] *ag* disciplinary ♦ *vt* to discipline.

'disco, schi *sm* disc, disk; (*SPORT*) discus; (*fonografico*) record; (*INFORM*) disk; **~ magnetico** (*INFORM*) magnetic disk; **~ orario** (*AUT*) parking disc; **~ rigido** (*INFORM*) hard disk; **~ volante** flying saucer.

discogra'fia *sf* (*tecnica*) recording, record-making; (*industria*) record industry.

disco'grafico, a, ci, che *ag* record *cpd*, recording *cpd* ♦ *sm* record producer; **casa ~a** record(ing) company.

'discolo, a *ag* (*bambino*) undisciplined, unruly ♦ *sm/f* rascal.

discol'pare *vt* to clear of blame; **~rsi** *vr* to clear o.s., prove one's innocence; (*giustificarsi*) to excuse o.s.

disco'noscere [disko'noʃʃere] *vt* (*figlio*) to disown; (*meriti*) to ignore, disregard.

disconosci'uto, a [diskonoʃ'ʃuto] *pp di* **disconoscere**.

discon'tinuo, a *ag* (*linea*) broken; (*rendimento, stile*) irregular; (*interesse*) sporadic.

dis'corde *ag* conflicting, clashing.

dis'cordia *sf* discord; (*dissidio*) disagreement, clash.

dis'correre *vi*: **~ (di)** to talk (about).

dis'corso, a *pp di* **discorrere** ♦ *sm* speech; (*conversazione*) conversation, talk.

dis'costo, a *ag* faraway, distant ♦ *av* far away; **~ da** *prep* far from.

disco'teca, che *sf* (*raccolta*) record library; (*luogo di ballo*) disco(theque).

discre'panza [diskre'pantsa] *sf* discrepancy.

dis'creto, a *ag* discreet; (*abbastanza buono*) reasonable, fair.

discrezi'one [diskret'tsjone] *sf* discretion;

(*giudizio*) judgment, discernment; **a ~ di** at the discretion of.

discrimi'nante *ag* (*fattore, elemento*) decisive ♦ *sf* (*DIR*) extenuating circumstance.

discrimi'nare *vt* to discrimate.

discriminazi'one [diskriminat'tsjone] *sf* discrimination.

dis'cussi *etc vb vedi* **discutere**.

discussi'one *sf* discussion; (*litigio*) argument; **mettere in ~** to bring into question; **fuori ~** out of the question.

dis'cusso, a *pp di* **discutere**.

dis'cutere *vt* to discuss, debate; (*contestare*) to question, dispute ♦ *vi* (*conversare*): **~ (di)** to discuss; (*litigare*) to argue.

discu'tibile *ag* questionable.

disde'gnare [dizdeɲ'ɲare] *vt* to scorn.

dis'degno [diz'deɲɲo] *sm* scorn, disdain.

disde'gnoso, a [dizdeɲ'ɲoso] *ag* disdainful, scornful.

dis'detto, a *pp di* **disdire** ♦ *sf* cancellation; (*sfortuna*) bad luck.

disdi'cevole [dizdi'tʃevole] *ag* improper, unseemly.

dis'dire *vt* (*prenotazione*) to cancel; **~ un contratto d'affitto** (*DIR*) to give notice (to quit).

dise'gnare [diseɲ'ɲare] *vt* to draw; (*progettare*) to design; (*fig*) to outline.

disegna'tore, 'trice [diseɲɲa'tore] *sm/f* designer.

di'segno [di'zeɲɲo] *sm* drawing; (*su stoffa etc*) design; (*fig: schema*) outline; **~ industriale** industrial design; **~ di legge** (*DIR*) bill.

diser'bante *sm* weedkiller.

disere'dare *vt* to disinherit.

diser'tare *vt*, *vi* to desert.

diser'tore *sm* (*MIL*) deserter.

diserzi'one [dizer'tsjone] *sf* (*MIL*) desertion.

disfaci'mento [disfatʃi'mento] *sm* (*di cadavere*) decay; (*fig: di istituzione, impero, società*) decline, decay; **in ~** in decay.

dis'fare *vt* to undo; (*valigie*) to unpack; (*meccanismo*) to take to pieces; (*lavoro, paese*) to destroy; (*neve*) to melt; **~rsi** *vr* to come undone; (*neve*) to melt; **~ il letto** to strip the bed; **~rsi di qn** (*liberarsi*) to get rid of sb.

dis'fatta *sf vedi* **disfatto**.

disfat'tista, i, e *sm/f* defeatist.

dis'fatto, a *pp di* **disfare** ♦ *ag* (*gen*) undone, untied; (*letto*) unmade; (*persona: sfinito*) exhausted, worn-out; (: *addolorato*) grief-stricken ♦ *sf* (*sconfitta*) rout.

disfunzi'one [disfun'tsjone] *sf* (*MED*)

dysfunction; ~ **cardiaca** heart trouble.
disge'lare [dizdʒe'lare] vt, vi, ~**rsi** vr to
thaw.
dis'gelo [diz'dʒɛlo] sm thaw.
dis'grazia [diz'grattsja] sf (sventura)
misfortune; (incidente) accident, mishap.
disgrazi'ato, a [dizgrat'tsjato] ag
unfortunate ♦ sm/f wretch.
disgre'gare vt, ~**rsi** vr to break up.
disgu'ido sm hitch; ~ **postale** error in
postal delivery.
disgus'tare vt to disgust; ~**rsi** vr: ~**rsi di** to
be disgusted by.
dis'gusto sm disgust.
disgus'toso, a ag disgusting.
disidra'tare vt to dehydrate.
disidra'tato, a ag dehydrated.
disil'ludere vt to disillusion, disenchant.
disillusi'one sf disillusion,
disenchantment.
disimpa'rare vt to forget.
disimpe'gnare [dizimpeɲ'ɲare] vt (persona:
da obblighi): ~ **da** to release from;
(oggetto dato in pegno) to redeem, get out
of pawn; ~**rsi** vr: ~**rsi da** (obblighi) to
release o.s. from, free o.s. from.
disincagli'are [dizinkaʎ'ʎare] vt (barca) to
refloat; ~**rsi** vr to get afloat again.
disincan'tato, a ag disenchanted,
disillusioned.
disincenti'vare [dizintʃenti'vare] vt to
discourage.
disinfes'tare vt to disinfest.
disinfestazi'one [dizinfestat'tsjone] sf
disinfestation.
disinfet'tante ag, sm disinfectant.
disinfet'tare vt to disinfect.
disinfezi'one [dizinfet'tsjone] sf
disinfection.
disingan'nare vt to disillusion.
disin'ganno sm disillusion.
disini'bito, a ag uninhibited.
disinnes'care vt to defuse.
disinnes'tare vt (marcia) to disengage.
disinqui'nare vt to free from pollution.
disinte'grare vt, vi to disintegrate.
disinteres'sarsi vr: ~ **di** to take no interest
in.
disinte'resse sm indifference; (generosità)
unselfishness.
disintossi'care vt (alcolizzato, drogato) to
treat for alcoholism (o drug addiction);
~**rsi** vr to clear out one's system;
(alcolizzato, drogato) to be treated for
alcoholism (o drug addiction).
disintossicazi'one [dizintossikat'tsjone] sf
treatment for alcoholism (o drug
addiction).

disin'volto, a ag casual, free and easy.
disinvol'tura sf casualness, ease.
disles'sia sf dyslexia.
disli'vello sm difference in height; (fig)
gap.
dislo'care vt to station, position.
dismi'sura sf excess; **a** ~ to excess,
excessively.
disobbe'dire etc = **disubbidire** etc.
disoccu'pato, a ag unemployed ♦ sm/f
unemployed person.
disoccupazi'one [dizokkupat'tsjone] sf
unemployment.
disonestà sf dishonesty.
diso'nesto, a ag dishonest.
disono'rare vt to dishonour (BRIT),
dishonor (US), bring disgrace upon.
diso'nore sm dishonour (BRIT), dishonor
(US), disgrace.
di'sopra av (con contatto) on top; (senza
contatto) above; (al piano superiore)
upstairs ♦ ag inv (superiore) upper ♦ sm inv
top, upper part; **la gente** ~ the people
upstairs; **il piano** ~ the floor above.
disordi'nare vt to mess up, disarrange;
(MIL) to throw into disorder.
disordi'nato, a ag untidy; (privo di misura)
irregular, wild.
di'sordine sm (confusione) disorder,
confusion; (sregolatezza) debauchery; ~**i**
smpl (POL etc) disorder sg; (tumulti) riots.
disor'ganico, a, ci, che ag incoherent,
disorganized.
disorganiz'zato, a [dizorganid'dzato] ag
disorganized.
disorienta'mento sm (fig) confusion,
bewilderment.
disorien'tare vt to disorientate; ~**rsi** vr (fig)
to get confused, lose one's bearings.
disorien'tato, a ag disorientated.
disos'sare vt (CUC) to bone.
di'sotto av below, underneath; (in fondo) at
the bottom; (al piano inferiore) downstairs
♦ ag inv (inferiore) lower; bottom cpd ♦ sm
inv (parte inferiore) lower part; bottom; **la
gente** ~ the people downstairs; **il piano** ~
the floor below.
dis'paccio [dis'pattʃo] sm dispatch.
dispa'rato, a ag disparate.
'dispari ag inv odd, uneven.
disparità sf inv disparity.
dis'parte: in ~ av (da lato) aside, apart;
tenersi o **starsene in** ~ to keep to o.s.,
hold aloof.
dis'pendio sm (di denaro, energie)
expenditure; (: spreco) waste.
dispendi'oso, a ag expensive.
dis'pensa sf pantry, larder; (mobile)

sideboard; (*DIR*) exemption; (*REL*) dispensation; (*fascicolo*) number, issue.

dispen'sare *vt* (*elemosine, favori*) to distribute; (*esonerare*) to exempt.

dispe'rare *vi*: ~ (**di**) to despair (of); ~**rsi** *vr* to despair.

dispe'rato, a *ag* (*persona*) in despair; (*caso, tentativo*) desperate.

disperazi'one [disperat'tsjone] *sf* despair.

dis'perdere *vt* (*disseminare*) to disperse; (*MIL*) to scatter, rout; (*fig: consumare*) to waste, squander; ~**rsi** *vr* to disperse; to scatter.

dispersi'one *sf* dispersion, dispersal; (*FISICA, CHIM*) dispersion.

disper'sivo, a *ag* (*lavoro etc*) disorganized.

dis'perso, a *pp di* **disperdere** ♦ *sm/f* missing person; (*MIL*) missing soldier.

dis'petto *sm* spite *no pl*, spitefulness *no pl*; **fare un** ~ **a qn** to play a (nasty) trick on sb; **a** ~ **di** in spite of; **con suo grande** ~ much to his annoyance.

dispet'toso, a *ag* spiteful.

dispia'cere [dispja'tʃere] *sm* (*rammarico*) regret, sorrow; (*dolore*) grief ♦ *vi*: ~ **a** to displease ♦ *vb impers*: **mi dispiace (che)** I am sorry (that); ~**i** *smpl* (*preoccupazioni*) troubles, worries; **se non le dispiace, me ne vado adesso** if you don't mind, I'll go now.

dispiaci'uto, a [dispja'tʃuto] *pp di* **dispiacere** ♦ *ag* sorry.

dis'pone, dis'pongo *etc vb vedi* **disporre**.

dispo'nibile *ag* available; (*persona: solerte, gentile*) helpful.

disponibilità *sf inv* availability; (*solerzia, gentilezza*) helpfulness; **disponibilità** *sfpl* (*economiche*) resources.

dis'porre *vt* (*sistemare*) to arrange; (*preparare*) to prepare; (*DIR*) to order; (*persuadere*): ~ **qn a** to incline *o* dispose sb towards ♦ *vi* (*decidere*) to decide; (*usufruire*): ~ **di** to use, have at one's disposal; (*essere dotato*): ~ **di** to have; **disporsi** *vr* (*ordinarsi*) to place o.s., arrange o.s.; **disporsi a fare** to get ready to do; **disporsi all'attacco** to prepare for an attack; **disporsi in cerchio** to form a circle.

dis'posi *etc vb vedi* **disporre**.

disposi'tivo *sm* (*meccanismo*) device; (*DIR*) pronouncement; ~ **di controllo** *o* **di comando** control device; ~ **di sicurezza** (*gen*) safety device; (*di arma da fuoco*) safety catch.

disposizi'one [dispozit'tsjone] *sf* arrangement, layout; (*stato d'animo*) mood; (*tendenza*) bent, inclination; (*comando*) order; (*DIR*) provision, regulation; **a** ~ **di qn** at sb's disposal; **per** ~ **di legge** by law; ~ **testamentaria** provisions of a will.

dis'posto, a *pp di* **disporre** ♦ *ag* (*incline*): ~ **a fare** disposed *o* prepared to do.

dis'potico, a, ci, che *ag* despotic.

dispo'tismo *sm* despotism.

disprez'zare [dispret'tsare] *vt* to despise.

dis'prezzo [dis'prɛttso] *sm* contempt; **con** ~ **del pericolo** with a total disregard for the danger involved.

'disputa *sf* dispute, quarrel.

dispu'tare *vt* (*contendere*) to dispute, contest; (*SPORT: partita*) to play; (*: gara*) to take part in ♦ *vi* to quarrel; ~ **di** to discuss; ~**rsi qc** to fight for sth.

disqui'sire *vi* to discourse on.

disquisizi'one [diskwizit'tsjone] *sf* detailed analysis.

dissa'crare *vt* to desecrate.

dissangua'mento *sm* loss of blood.

dissangu'are *vt* (*fig: persona*) to bleed white; (*: patrimonio*) to suck dry; ~**rsi** *vr* (*MED*) to lose blood; (*fig*) to ruin o.s.; **morire dissanguato** to bleed to death.

dissa'pore *sm* slight disagreement.

'disse *vb vedi* **dire**.

disse'care *vt* to dissect.

dissec'care *vt*, ~**rsi** *vr* to dry up.

dissemi'nare *vt* to scatter; (*fig: notizie*) to spread.

dissenna'tezza [dissenna'tettsa] *sf* foolishness.

dis'senso *sm* dissent; (*disapprovazione*) disapproval.

dissente'ria *sf* dysentery.

dissen'tire *vi*: ~ (**da**) to disagree (with).

disseppel'lire *vt* (*esumare: cadavere*) to disinter, exhume; (*dissotterrare: anche fig*) to dig up, unearth; (*: rancori*) to resurrect.

dissertazi'one [dissertat'tsjone] *sf* dissertation.

disser'vizio [disser'vittsjo] *sm* inefficiency.

disses'tare *vt* (*ECON*) to ruin.

disses'tato, a *ag* (*fondo stradale*) uneven; (*economia, finanze*) shaky; **"strada ~a"** (*per lavori in corso*) "road up" (*BRIT*), "road out" (*US*).

dis'sesto *sm* (financial) ruin.

disse'tante *ag* refreshing.

disse'tare *vt* to quench the thirst of; ~**rsi** *vr* to quench one's thirst.

dissezi'one [disset'tsjone] *sf* dissection.

'dissi *vb vedi* **dire**.

dissi'dente *ag*, *sm/f* dissident.

dis'sidio *sm* disagreement.

dis'simile *ag* different, dissimilar.

dissimu'lare *vt* (*fingere*) to dissemble; (*nascondere*) to conceal.

dissimula'tore, 'trice *sm/f* dissembler.

dissimulazi'one [dissimulat'tsjone] *sf* dissembling; concealment.

dissi'pare *vt* to dissipate; (*scialacquare*) to squander, waste.

dissipa'tezza [dissipa'tettsa] *sf* dissipation.

dissi'pato, a *ag* dissolute, dissipated.

dissipazi'one [dissipat'tsjone] *sf* squandering.

dissoci'are [disso'tʃare] *vt* to dissociate.

dis'solto, a *pp di* **dissolvere**.

disso'lubile *ag* soluble.

dissolu'tezza [dissolu'tettsa] *sf* dissoluteness.

dissolu'tivo, a *ag* (*forza*) divisive; **processo ~** (*anche fig*) process of dissolution.

disso'luto, a *pp di* **dissolvere ♦** *ag* dissolute, licentious.

dissol'venza [dissol'vɛntsa] *sf* (*CINE*) fading.

dis'solvere *vt* to dissolve; (*neve*) to melt; (*fumo*) to disperse; **~rsi** *vr* to dissolve; to melt; to disperse.

disso'nante *ag* discordant.

disso'nanza [disso'nantsa] *sf* (*fig*: *di opinioni*) clash.

dissotter'rare *vt* (*cadavere*) to disinter, exhume; (*tesori, rovine*) to dig up, unearth; (*fig*: *sentimenti, odio*) to bring up again, resurrect.

dissu'adere *vt*: **~ qn da** to dissuade sb from.

dissuasi'one *sf* dissuasion.

dissu'aso, a *pp di* **dissuadere**.

distacca'mento *sm* (*MIL*) detachment.

distac'care *vt* to detach, separate; (*SPORT*) to leave behind; **~rsi** *vr* to be detached; (*fig*) to stand out; **~rsi da** (*fig*: *allontanarsi*) to grow away from.

dis'tacco, chi *sm* (*separazione*) separation; (*fig*: *indifferenza*) detachment; (*SPORT*): **vincere con un ~ di ...** to win by a distance of ....

dis'tante *av* far away ♦ *ag* distant, far away; **essere ~** (**da**) to be a long way (from); **è ~ da qui?** is it far from here?; **essere ~ nel tempo** to be in the distant past.

dis'tanza [dis'tantsa] *sf* distance; **comando a ~** remote control; **a ~ di 2 giorni** 2 days later; **tener qn a ~** to keep sb at arm's length; **prendere le ~e da qc/qn** to dissociate o.s. from sth/sb; **tenere o mantenere le ~e** to keep one's distance; **~ focale** focal length; **~ di sicurezza** safe distance; (*AUT*) braking distance; **~ di tiro** range; **~ di visibilità** visibility.

distanzi'are [distan'tsjare] *vt* to space out, place at intervals; (*SPORT*) to outdistance; (*fig*: *superare*) to outstrip, surpass.

dis'tare *vi*: **distiamo pochi chilometri da Roma** we are only a few kilometres (away) from Rome; **dista molto da qui?** is it far (away) from here?; **non dista molto** it's not far (away).

dis'tendere *vt* (*coperta*) to spread out; (*gambe*) to stretch (out); (*mettere a giacere*) to lay; (*rilassare: muscoli, nervi*) to relax; **~rsi** *vr* (*rilassarsi*) to relax; (*sdraiarsi*) to lie down.

distensi'one *sf* stretching; relaxation; (*POL*) détente.

disten'sivo, a *ag* (*gen*) relaxing, restful; (*farmaco*) tranquillizing; (*POL*) conciliatory.

dis'teso, a *pp di* **distendere ♦** *ag* (*allungato*: *persona, gamba*) stretched out; (*rilassato*: *persona, atmosfera*) relaxed ♦ *sf* expanse, stretch; **avere un volto ~** to look relaxed.

distil'lare *vt* to distil.

distil'lato *sm* distillate.

distillazi'one [distillat'tsjone] *sf* distillation.

distille'ria *sf* distillery.

dis'tinguere *vt* to distinguish; **~rsi** *vr* (*essere riconoscibile*) to be distinguished; (*emergere*) to stand out, be conspicuous, distinguish o.s.; **un vino che si distingue per il suo aroma** a wine with a distinctive bouquet.

dis'tinguo *sm inv* distinction.

dis'tinta *sf* (*nota*) note; (*elenco*) list; **~ di pagamento** receipt; **~ di versamento** pay-in slip.

distin'tivo, a *ag* distinctive; distinguishing ♦ *sm* badge.

dis'tinto, a *pp di* **distinguere ♦** *ag* (*dignitoso ed elegante*) distinguished; **~i saluti** (*in lettera*) yours faithfully.

distinzi'one [distin'tsjone] *sf* distinction; **non faccio ~i** (*tra persone*) I don't discriminate; (*tra cose*) it's all one to me; **senza ~ di razza/religione ...** no matter what one's race/creed ....

dis'togliere [dis'tɔʎʎere] *vt*: **~ da** to take away from; (*fig*) to dissuade from.

dis'tolto, a *pp di* **distogliere**.

dis'torcere [dis'tɔrtʃere] *vt* to twist; (*fig*) to twist, distort; **~rsi** *vr* (*contorcersi*) to twist.

distorsi'one *sf* (*MED*) sprain; (*FISICA, OTTICA*) distortion.

dis'torto, a *pp di* **distorcere**.

dis'trarre *vt* to distract; (*divertire*) to entertain, amuse; **distrarsi** *vr* (*non fare* *attenzione)* to be distracted, let one's mind wander; *(svagarsi)* to amuse *o* enjoy o.s.; ~ **lo sguardo** to look away; **non distrarti!** pay attention!

distratta'mente *av* absent-mindedly, without thinking.

dis'tratto, a *pp di* **distrarre** ♦ *ag* absent-minded; *(disattento)* inattentive.

distrazi'one [distrat'tsjone] *sf* absent-mindedness; inattention; *(svago)* distraction, entertainment; **errori di** ~ careless mistakes.

dis'tretto *sm* district.

distribu'ire *vt* to distribute; *(CARTE)* to deal (out); *(consegnare: posta)* to deliver; *(lavoro)* to allocate, assign; *(ripartire)* to share out.

distribu'tore *sm (di benzina)* petrol *(BRIT) o* gas *(US)* pump; *(AUT, ELETTR)* distributor; *(automatico)* vending machine.

distribuzi'one [distribut'tsjone] *sf* distribution; delivery; allocation, assignment; sharing out.

distri'care *vt* to disentangle, unravel; ~**rsi** *vr (tirarsi fuori):* ~**rsi da** to get out of, disentangle o.s. from; *(fig: cavarsela)* to manage, get by.

dis'truggere [dis'truddʒere] *vt* to destroy.

distrut'tivo, a *ag* destructive.

dis'trutto, a *pp di* **distruggere**.

distruzi'one [distrut'tsjone] *sf* destruction.

distur'bare *vt* to disturb, trouble; *(sonno, lezioni)* to disturb, interrupt; ~**rsi** *vr* to put o.s. out; **non si disturbi** please don't bother.

dis'turbo *sm* trouble, bother, inconvenience; *(indisposizione)* (slight) disorder, ailment; ~**i** *smpl (RADIO, TV)* static *sg;* ~ **della quiete pubblica** *(DIR)* disturbance of the peace; ~**i di stomaco** stomach trouble *sg.*

disubbidi'ente *ag* disobedient.

disubbidi'enza [dizubbi'djɛntsa] *sf* disobedience; ~ **civile** civil disobedience.

disubbi'dire *vi:* ~ **(a qn)** to disobey (sb).

disuguagli'anza [dizugwaʎ'ʎantsa] *sf* inequality.

disugu'ale *ag* unequal; *(diverso)* different; *(irregolare)* uneven.

disumanità *sf* inhumanity.

disu'mano, a *ag* inhuman; **un grido** ~ a terrible cry.

disuni'one *sf* disunity.

disu'nire *vt* to divide, disunite.

di'suso *sm:* **andare** *o* **cadere in** ~ to fall into disuse.

'dita *sfpl di* **dito**.

di'tale *sm* thimble.

di'tata *sf (colpo)* jab (with one's finger); *(segno)* fingermark.

'dito, *pl(f)* **'dita** *sm* finger; *(misura)* finger, finger's breadth; ~ **(del piede)** toe; **mettersi le** ~**a nel naso** to pick one's nose; **mettere il** ~ **sulla piaga** *(fig)* to touch a sore spot; **non ha mosso un** ~ **(per aiutarmi)** he didn't lift a finger (to help me); **ormai è segnato a** ~ everyone knows about him now.

'ditta *sf* firm, business; **macchina della** ~ company car.

dit'tafono *sm* Dictaphone ®.

ditta'tore *sm* dictator.

ditta'tura *sf* dictatorship.

dit'tongo, ghi *sm* diphthong.

di'urno, a *ag* day *cpd,* daytime *cpd;* **ore** ~**e** daytime *sg;* **spettacolo** ~ matinee; **turno** ~ day shift; *vedi anche* **albergo**.

'diva *sf vedi* **divo**.

diva'gare *vi* to digress.

divagazi'one [divagat'tsjone] *sf* digression; ~**i sul tema** variations on a theme.

divam'pare *vi* to flare up, blaze up.

di'vano *sm* sofa; *(senza schienale)* divan; ~ **letto** bed settee, sofa bed.

divari'care *vt* to open wide.

di'vario *sm* difference.

di'vengo *etc vb vedi* **divenire**.

dive'nire *vi =* **diventare**.

di'venni *etc vb vedi* **divenire**.

diven'tare *vi* to become; ~ **famoso/ professore** to become famous/a teacher; ~ **vecchio** to grow old; **c'è da** ~ **matti** it's enough to drive you mad.

dive'nuto, a *pp di* **divenire**.

di'verbio *sm* altercation.

diver'gente [diver'dʒɛnte] *ag* divergent.

diver'genza [diver'dʒɛntsa] *sf* divergence; ~ **d'opinioni** difference of opinion.

di'vergere [di'vɛrdʒere] *vi* to diverge.

diverrò *etc vb vedi* **divenire**.

diversa'mente *av (in modo differente)* differently; *(altrimenti)* otherwise; ~ **da quanto stabilito** contrary to what had been decided.

diversifi'care *vt* to diversify, vary; ~**rsi** *vr:* ~**rsi (per)** to differ (in).

diversificazi'one [diversifikat'tsjone] *sf* diversification; difference.

diversi'one *sf* diversion.

diversità *sf inv* difference, diversity; *(varietà)* variety.

diver'sivo, a *ag* diversionary ♦ *sm* diversion, distraction; **fare un'azione** ~**a** to create a diversion.

di'verso, a *ag (differente):* ~ **(da)** different (from) ♦ *sm (omosessuale)* homosexual;

~i, e *det pl* several, various; (*COMM*) sundry ♦ *pron pl* several (people), many (people).

diver'tente *ag* amusing.

diverti'mento *sm* amusement, pleasure; (*passatempo*) pastime, recreation; **buon ~!** enjoy yourself!, have a nice time!

diver'tire *vt* to amuse, entertain; **~rsi** *vr* to amuse *o* enjoy o.s.; **divertiti!** enjoy yourself, have a good time!; **~rsi alle spalle di qn** to have a laugh at sb's expense.

diver'tito, a *ag* amused.

divez'zare [divet'tsare] *vt* (*anche fig*): **~ (da)** to wean (from).

divi'dendo *sm* dividend.

di'videre *vt* (*anche MAT*) to divide; (*distribuire, ripartire*) to divide (up), split (up); **~rsi** *vr* (*persone*) to separate, part; (*coppia*) to separate; **~rsi (in)** (*scindersi*) to divide (into), split up (into); (*ramificarsi*) to fork; **è diviso dalla moglie** he's separated from his wife; **si divide tra casa e lavoro** he divides his time between home and work.

divi'eto *sm* prohibition; "**~ di accesso**" "no entry"; "**~ di caccia**" "no hunting"; "**~ di parcheggio**" "no parking"; "**~ di sosta**" (*AUT*) "no waiting".

divinco'larsi *vr* to wriggle, writhe.

divinità *sf inv* divinity.

di'vino, a *ag* divine.

di'visa *sf* (*MIL etc*) uniform; (*COMM*) foreign currency.

di'visi *etc vb vedi* **dividere**.

divisi'one *sf* division; **~ in sillabe** syllable division; (*a fine riga*) hyphenation.

di'vismo *sm* (*esibizionismo*) playing to the crowd.

di'viso, a *pp di* **dividere**.

divi'sorio, a *ag* (*siepe, muro esterno*) dividing; (*muro interno*) dividing, partition *cpd* ♦ *sm* (*in una stanza*) partition.

'divo, a *sm/f* star; **come una ~a** like a prima donna.

divo'rare *vt* to devour; **~ qc con gli occhi** to eye sth greedily.

divorzi'are [divor'tsjare] *vi*: **~ (da qn)** to divorce (sb).

divorzi'ato, a [divor'tsjato] *ag* divorced ♦ *sm/f* divorcee.

di'vorzio [di'vɔrtsjo] *sm* divorce.

divul'gare *vt* to divulge, disclose; (*rendere comprensibile*) to popularize; **~rsi** *vr* to spread.

divulgazi'one [divulgat'tsjone] *sf* (*vedi vb*) disclosure; popularization; spread.

dizio'nario [dittsjo'narjo] *sm* dictionary.

dizi'one [dit'tsjone] *sf* diction; pronunciation.

Dja'karta [dʒa'karta] *sf* Djakarta.

dl *abbr* (= *decilitro*) dl.

dm *abbr* (= *decimetro*) dm.

DNA [di'ennea] *sigla m* (*BIOL*: = *acido deossiribonucleico*) DNA ♦ *sigla f* = *direzione nazionale antimafia*.

do *sm* (*MUS*) C; (: *solfeggiando la scala*) do(h).

dobbi'amo *vb vedi* **dovere**.

D.O.C. [dɔk] *sigla vedi* **denominazione di origine controllata**.

doc. *abbr* = *documento*.

'doccia, ce ['dottʃa] *sf* (*bagno*) shower; (*condotto*) pipe; **fare la ~** to have a shower; **~ fredda** (*fig*) slap in the face.

do'cente [do'tʃɛnte] *ag* teaching ♦ *sm/f* teacher; (*di università*) lecturer; **personale non ~** non-teaching staff.

do'cenza [do'tʃɛntsa] *sf* university teaching *o* lecturing; **ottenere la libera ~** to become a lecturer.

D.O.C.G. *sigla* (= *denominazione di origine controllata e garantita*) *label guaranteeing the quality and origin of a wine*.

'docile ['dɔtʃile] *ag* docile.

docilità [dotʃili'ta] *sf* docility.

documen'tare *vt* to document; **~rsi** *vr*: **~rsi (su)** to gather information *o* material (about).

documen'tario, a *ag, sm* documentary.

documentazi'one [dokumentat'tsjone] *sf* documentation.

docu'mento *sm* document; **~i** *smpl* (*d'identità etc*) papers.

Dodecan'neso *sm*: **le Isole del ~** the Dodecanese Islands.

dodi'cenne [dodi'tʃɛnne] *ag, sm/f* twelve-year-old.

dodi'cesimo, a [dodi'tʃɛzimo] *num* twelfth.

'dodici ['doditʃi] *num* twelve.

do'gana *sf* (*ufficio*) customs *pl*; (*tassa*) (customs) duty; **passare la ~** to go through customs.

doga'nale *ag* customs *cpd*.

dogani'ere *sm* customs officer.

'doglie ['dɔʎʎe] *sfpl* (*MED*) labour *sg* (*BRIT*), labor *sg* (*US*), labo(u)r pains.

'dogma, i *sm* dogma.

dog'matico, a, ci, che *ag* dogmatic.

'dolce ['doltʃe] *ag* sweet; (*colore*) soft; (*carattere, persona*) gentle, mild; (*fig: mite: clima*) mild; (*non ripido: pendio*) gentle ♦ *sm* (*sapore ~*) sweetness, sweet taste; (*CUC: portata*) sweet, dessert; (: *torta*) cake; **il ~ far niente** sweet idleness.

dol'cezza [dol'tʃettsa] *sf* sweetness;

softness; mildness; gentleness.

dolci'ario, a [dol't∫arjo] *ag* confectionery *cpd*.

dolci'astro, a [dol't∫astro] *ag* (*sapore*) sweetish.

dolcifi'cante [dolt∫ifi'kante] *ag* sweetening ♦ *sm* sweetener.

dolci'umi [dol't∫umi] *smpl* sweets.

do'lente *ag* sorrowful, sad.

do'lere *vi* to be sore, hurt, ache; ~**rsi** *vr* to complain; (*essere spiacente*): ~**rsi di** to be sorry for; **mi duole la testa** my head aches, I've got a headache.

'dolgo *etc vb vedi* **dolere**.

'dollaro *sm* dollar.

'dolo *sm* (*DIR*) malice; (*frode*) fraud, deceit.

Dolo'miti *sfpl*: **le** ~ the Dolomites.

dolo'rante *ag* aching, sore.

do'lore *sm* (*fisico*) pain; (*morale*) sorrow, grief; **se lo scoprono sono** ~**i!** if they find out there'll be trouble!

dolo'roso, a *ag* painful; sorrowful, sad.

do'loso, a *ag* (*DIR*) malicious; **incendio** ~ arson.

'dolsi *etc vb vedi* **dolere**.

dom. *abbr* (= *domenica*) Sun.

do'manda *sf* (*interrogazione*) question; (*richiesta*) demand; (*: cortese*) request; (*DIR: richiesta scritta*) application; (*ECON*): **la** ~ demand; **fare una** ~ **a qn** to ask sb a question; **fare** ~ (**per un lavoro**) to apply (for a job); **far regolare** ~ (**di qc**) to apply through the proper channels (for sth); **fare** ~ **all'autorità giudiziaria** to apply to the courts; ~ **di divorzio** divorce petition; ~ **di matrimonio** proposal.

doman'dare *vt* (*per avere*) to ask for; (*per sapere*) to ask; (*esigere*) to demand; ~**rsi** *vr* to wonder, ask o.s.; ~ **qc a qn** to ask sb for sth; to ask sb sth.

do'mani *av* tomorrow ♦ *sm* (*l'indomani*) next day, following day; **il** ~ (*il futuro*) the future; (*il giorno successivo*) the next day; **un** ~ some day; ~ **l'altro** the day after tomorrow; ~ (**a**) **otto** tomorrow week, a week tomorrow; **a** ~**!** see you tomorrow!

do'mare *vt* to tame.

doma'tore, 'trice *sm/f* (*gen*) tamer; ~ **di cavalli** horsebreaker; ~ **di leoni** lion tamer.

domat'tina *av* tomorrow morning.

do'menica, che *sf* Sunday; *per fraseologia vedi* **martedì**.

domeni'cale *ag* Sunday *cpd*.

domeni'cano, a *ag, sm/f* Dominican.

do'mestica, che *sf vedi* **domestico**.

do'mestico, a, ci, che *ag* domestic ♦ *sm/f* servant, domestic; **le pareti** ~**che** one's

own four walls; **animale** *m* ~ pet; **una** ~**a a ore** a daily (woman).

domicili'are [domit∫i'ljare] *ag vedi* **arresto**.

domicili'arsi [domit∫i'ljarsi] *vr* to take up residence.

domi'cilio [domi't∫iljo] *sm* (*DIR*) domicile, place of residence; **visita a** ~ (*MED*) house call; **"recapito a** ~**"** "deliveries"; **violazione di** ~ (*DIR*) breaking and entering.

domi'nante *ag* (*colore, nota*) dominant; (*opinione*) prevailing; (*idea*) main *cpd*, chief *cpd*; (*posizione*) dominating *cpd*; (*classe, partito*) ruling *cpd*.

domi'nare *vt* to dominate; (*fig: sentimenti*) to control, master ♦ *vi* to be in the dominant position; ~**rsi** *vr* (*controllarsi*) to control o.s.; ~ **su** (*fig*) to surpass, outclass.

domina'tore, 'trice *ag* ruling *cpd* ♦ *sm/f* ruler.

dominazi'one [dominat'tsjone] *sf* domination.

domini'cano, a *ag*: **la Repubblica D**~**a** the Dominican Republic.

do'minio *sm* dominion; (*fig: campo*) field, domain; ~**i coloniali** colonies; **essere di** ~ **pubblico** (*notizia etc*) to be common knowledge.

don *sm* (*REL*) Father.

do'nare *vt* to give, present; (*per beneficenza etc*) to donate ♦ *vi* (*fig*): ~ **a** to suit, become; ~ **sangue** to give blood.

dona'tore, 'trice *sm/f* donor; ~ **di sangue/ di organi** blood/organ donor.

donazi'one [donat'tsjone] *sf* donation; **atto di** ~ (*DIR*) deed of gift.

'donde *av* (*poetico*) whence.

dondo'lare *vt* (*cullare*) to rock; ~**rsi** *vr* to swing, sway.

'dondolo *sm*: **sedia/cavallo a** ~ rocking chair/horse.

dongio'vanni [dondʒo'vanni] *sm* Don Juan, ladies' man.

'donna *sf* woman; (*titolo*) Donna; (*CARTE*) queen; **figlio di buona** ~**!** (*fam*) son of a bitch!; ~ **di casa** housewife; ~ **a ore** daily (help *o* woman); ~ **delle pulizie** cleaning lady, cleaner; ~ **di servizio** maid; ~ **di vita** *o* **di strada** prostitute, streetwalker.

donnai'olo *sm* ladykiller.

'donnola *sf* weasel.

'dono *sm* gift.

'dopo *av* (*tempo*) afterwards; (*: più tardi*) later; (*luogo*) after, next ♦ *prep* after ♦ *cong* (*temporale*): ~ **aver studiato** after having studied ♦ *ag inv*: **il giorno** ~ the following day; ~ **mangiato va a dormire**

after having eaten *o* after a meal he goes for a sleep; **un anno** ~ a year later; ~ **di me/lui** after me/him; ~ **che** = **dopoché**.

dopo'barba *sm inv* after-shave.

dopoché [dopo'ke] *cong* after, when.

dopodiché [dopodi'ke] *av* after which.

dopodo'mani *av* the day after tomorrow.

dopogu'erra *sm* postwar years *pl.*

dopola'voro *sm* recreational club.

dopo'pranzo [dopo'prandzo] *av* after lunch (*o* dinner).

doposcì [dopoʃ'ʃi] *sm inv* après-ski outfit.

doposcu'ola *sm inv* school club *offering extra tuition and recreational facilities.*

dopo'tutto *av* after all.

doppi'aggio [dop'pjaddʒo] *sm* (*CINE*) dubbing.

doppi'are *vt* (*NAUT*) to round; (*SPORT*) to lap; (*CINE*) to dub.

doppia'tore, 'trice *sm/f* dubber.

doppi'etta *sf* (*fucile*) double-barrelled (*BRIT*) *o* double-barreled (*US*) shotgun; (*sparo*) shot from both barrels; (*CALCIO*) double; (*PUGILATO*) one-two; (*AUT*) double-declutch (*BRIT*), double-clutch (*US*).

doppi'ezza [dop'pjettsa] *sf* (*fig: di persona*) duplicity, double-dealing.

'doppio, a *ag* double; (*fig: falso*) double-dealing, deceitful ♦ *sm* (*quantità*): **il** ~ **(di)** twice as much (*o* many), double the amount (*o* number) of; (*SPORT*) doubles *pl* ♦ *av* double; **battere una lettera in** ~**a copia** to type a letter with a carbon copy; **fare il** ~ **gioco** (*fig*) to play a double game; **chiudere a** ~**a mandata** to double-lock; ~ **senso** double entendre; **frase a** ~ **senso** sentence with a double meaning; **un utensile a** ~ **uso** a dual-purpose utensil.

doppio'fondo *sm* (*di valigia*) false bottom; (*NAUT*) double hull.

doppi'one *sm* duplicate (copy).

doppio'petto *sm* double-breasted jacket.

dop'pista *sm/f* (*TENNIS*) doubles player.

do'rare *vt* to gild; (*CUC*) to brown; ~ **la pillola** (*fig*) to sugar the pill.

do'rato, a *ag* golden; (*ricoperto d'oro*) gilt, gilded.

dora'tura *sf* gilding.

dormicchi'are [dormik'kjare] *vi* to doze.

dormi'ente *ag* sleeping ♦ *sm/f* sleeper.

dormigli'one, a [dormiʎ'ʎone] *sm/f* sleepyhead.

dor'mire *vi* to sleep; (*essere addormentato*) to be asleep, be sleeping; **il caffè non mi fa** ~ coffee keeps me awake; ~ **come un ghiro** to sleep like a log; ~ **della grossa** to sleep soundly, be dead to the world; ~ **in**

piedi (*essere stanco*) to be asleep on one's feet.

dor'mita *sf*: **farsi una** ~ to have a good sleep.

dormi'torio *sm* dormitory; ~ **pubblico** doss house (*BRIT*) *o* flophouse (*US*) (*run by local authority*).

dormi'veglia [dormi'veʎʎa] *sm* drowsiness.

dorrò *etc vb vedi* **dolere**.

dor'sale *ag*: **spina** ~ backbone, spine.

'dorso *sm* back; (*di montagna*) ridge, crest; (*di libro*) spine; (*NUOTO*) backstroke; **a** ~ **di cavallo** on horseback.

do'saggio [do'zaddʒo] *sm* (*atto*) measuring out; **sbagliare il** ~ to get the proportions wrong.

do'sare *vt* to measure out; (*MED*) to dose.

'dose *sf* quantity, amount; (*MED*) dose.

dossi'er [do'sje] *sm inv* dossier, file.

'dosso *sm* (*rilievo*) rise; (: *di strada*) bump; (*dorso*): **levarsi di** ~ **i vestiti** to take one's clothes off; **levarsi un peso di** ~ (*fig*) to take a weight off one's mind.

do'tare *vt*: ~ **di** to provide *o* supply with; (*fig*) to endow with.

do'tato, a *ag*: ~ **di** (*attrezzature*) equipped with; (*bellezza, intelligenza*) endowed with; **un uomo** ~ a gifted man.

dotazi'one [dotat'tsjone] *sf* (*insieme di beni*) endowment; (*di macchine etc*) equipment; **dare qc in** ~ **a qn** to issue sb with sth, issue sth to sb; **i macchinari in** ~ **alla fabbrica** the machinery in use in the factory.

'dote *sf* (*di sposa*) dowry; (*assegnata a un ente*) endowment; (*fig*) gift, talent.

Dott. *abbr* (= *dottore*) Dr.

'dotto, a *ag* (*colto*) learned ♦ *sm* (*sapiente*) scholar; (*ANAT*) duct.

dotto'rato *sm* degree; ~ **di ricerca** doctorate, doctor's degree.

dot'tore, 'essa *sm/f* doctor.

dot'trina *sf* doctrine.

Dott.ssa *abbr* (= *dottoressa*) Dr.

double-'face [dubl'fas] *ag inv* reversible.

'dove *av* where; (*in cui*) where, in which; (*dovunque*) wherever ♦ *sm*: **per ogni** ~ everywhere; **di, dov'è?** where are you from?; **da** ~ **abito vedo tutta la città** I can see the whole city from where I live; **per** ~ **si passa?** which way should we go?; **le dò una mano fin** ~ **posso** I'll help you as much as I can.

do'vere *sm* (*obbligo*) duty ♦ *vt* (*essere debitore*): ~ **qc (a qn)** to owe (sb) sth ♦ *vi* (*seguito dall'infinito: obbligo*) to have to; **lui deve farlo** he has to do it, he must do it; **è dovuto partire** he had to leave; **ha dovuto**

pagare he had to pay; (: *intenzione*): **devo partire domani** I'm (due) to leave tomorrow; (: *probabilità*) **dev'essere tardi** it must be late; **doveva accadere** it was bound to happen; **avere il senso del** ~ **to** have a sense of duty; **rivolgersi a chi di** ~ to apply to the appropriate authority *o* person; **a** ~ (*bene*) properly; (*debitamente*) as he (*o* she *etc*) deserves; **come si deve** (*bene*) properly; (*meritatamente*) properly, as he (*o* she *etc*) deserves; **una persona come si deve** a respectable person.

dove'roso, a *ag* (right and) proper.

do'vizia [do'vittsja] *sf* abundance.

dovrò *etc vb vedi* **dovere**.

do'vunque *av* (*in qualunque luogo*) wherever; (*dappertutto*) everywhere; ~ **io vada** wherever I go.

dovuta'mente *av* (*debitamente*: *redigere, compilare*) correctly; (: *rimproverare*) as he (*o* she *etc*) deserves.

do'vuto, a *ag* (*causato*): ~ **a** due to ♦ *sm* due; **nel modo** ~ in the proper way; **ho lavorato più del** ~ I worked more than was necessary.

doz'zina [dod'dzina] *sf* dozen; **una** ~ **di uova** a dozen eggs; **di** *o* **da** ~ (*scrittore, spettacolo*) second-rate.

dozzi'nale [doddzi'nale] *ag* cheap, second-rate.

DP *sigla f* (= *Democrazia Proletaria*) *political party.*

'draga, ghe *sf* dredger.

dra'gare *vt* to dredge.

dragherò *etc* [drage'rɔ] *vb vedi* **dragare**.

'drago, ghi *sm* dragon; (*fig fam*) genius.

'dramma, i *sm* drama; **fare un** ~ **di qc** to make a drama out of sth.

dram'matico, a, ci, che *ag* dramatic.

drammatiz'zare [drammatid'dzare] *vt* to dramatize.

dramma'turgo, ghi *sm* playwright, dramatist.

drappeggi'are [drapped'dʒare] *vt* to drape.

drap'peggio [drap'peddʒo] *sm* (*tessuto*) drapery; (*di abito*) folds.

drap'pello *sm* (*MIL*) squad; (*gruppo*) band, group.

'drappo *sm* cloth.

'drastico, a, ci, che *ag* drastic.

dre'naggio [dre'naddʒo] *sm* drainage.

dre'nare *vt* to drain.

'Dresda *sf* Dresden.

drib'blare *vi* (*CALCIO*) to dribble ♦ *vt* (*avversario*) to dodge, avoid.

'dritto, a *ag, av* = **diritto** ♦ *sm/f* (*fam*: *furbo*): **è un** ~ he's a crafty *o* sly one ♦ *sf* (*destra*)

right, right hand; (*NAUT*) starboard; **a** ~**a e a manca** (*fig*) on all sides, right, left and centre.

driz'zare [drit'tsare] *vt* (*far tornare diritto*) to straighten; (*volgere*: *sguardo, occhi*) to turn, direct; (*innalzare*: *antenna, muro*) to erect; ~**rsi** *vr* to stand up; ~ **le orecchie** to prick up one's ears; ~**rsi in piedi** to rise to one's feet; ~**rsi a sedere** to sit up.

'droga, ghe *sf* (*sostanza aromatica*) spice; (*stupefacente*) drug; ~**ghe pesanti/leggere** hard/soft drugs.

dro'gare *vt* to season, spice; to drug, dope; ~**rsi** *vr* to take drugs.

dro'gato, a *sm/f* drug addict.

droghe'ria [droge'ria] *sf* grocer's (shop) (*BRIT*), grocery (store) (*US*).

drogherò *etc* [droge'rɔ] *vb vedi* **drogare**.

droghi'ere, a [dro'gjɛre] *sm/f* grocer.

drome'dario *sm* dromedary.

D.T. *abbr* = **direttore tecnico**.

'dubbio, a *ag* (*incerto*) doubtful, dubious; (*ambiguo*) dubious ♦ *sm* (*incertezza*) doubt; **avere il** ~ **che** to be afraid that, suspect that; **essere in** ~ **fra** to hesitate between; **mettere in** ~ **qc** to question sth; **nutrire seri** ~**i su qc** to have grave doubts about sth; **senza** ~ doubtless, no doubt.

dubbi'oso, a *ag* doubtful, dubious.

dubi'tare *vi*: ~ **di** (*onestà*) to doubt; (*risultato*) to be doubtful of; ~ **di qn** to mistrust sb; ~ **di sé** to be unsure of o.s.

Du'blino *sf* Dublin.

'duca, chi *sm* duke.

'duce ['dutʃe] *sm* (*STORIA*) captain; (: *del fascismo*) duce.

du'chessa [du'kessa] *sf* duchess.

'due *num* two; **a** ~ **a** ~ two at a time, two by two; **dire** ~ **parole** to say a few words; **ci metto** ~ **minuti** I'll have it done in a tick (*BRIT*) *o* jiffy.

duecen'tesco, a, schi, sche [duetʃen'tesko] *ag* thirteenth-century.

due'cento [due'tʃɛnto] *num* two hundred ♦ *sm*: **il D**~ the thirteenth century.

duel'lare *vi* to fight a duel.

du'ello *sm* duel.

due'mila *num* two thousand ♦ *sm inv*: **il** ~ the year two thousand.

due'pezzi [due'pettsi] *sm* (*costume da bagno*) two-piece swimsuit; (*abito femminile*) two-piece suit.

du'etto *sm* duet.

'dulcis in 'fundo ['dultʃisin'fundo] *av* to cap it all.

'duna *sf* dune.

'dunque *cong* (*perciò*) so, therefore; (*riprendendo il discorso*) well (then) ♦ *sm*

inv: **venire al** ~ to come to the point.
'duo *sm inv* (*MUS*) duet; (*TEAT, CINE, fig*) duo.
du'ole *etc vb vedi* **dolere**.
du'omo *sm* cathedral.
'duplex *sm inv* (*TEL*) party line.
dupli'cato *sm* duplicate.
'duplice ['duplitʃe] *ag* double, twofold; **in** ~ **copia** in duplicate.
duplicità [duplitʃi'ta] *sf* (*fig*) duplicity.
du'rante *prep* during; **vita natural** ~ for life.
du'rare *vi* to last; **non può** ~! this can't go on any longer!; ~ **fatica a** to have difficulty in; ~ **in carica** to remain in office.
du'rata *sf* length (of time); duration; **per tutta la** ~ **di** throughout; ~ **media della vita** life expectancy.
dura'turo, a *ag*, **du'revole** *ag* (*ricordo*) lasting; (*materiale*) durable.
du'rezza [du'rettsa] *sf* hardness; stubbornness; harshness; toughness.
'duro, a *ag* (*pietra, lavoro, materasso, problema*) hard; (*persona: ostinato*) stubborn, obstinate; (: *severo*) harsh, hard; (*voce*) harsh; (*carne*) tough ♦ *sm/f* (*persona*) tough one ♦ *av*: **tener** ~ (*resistere*) to stand firm, hold out; **avere la pelle** ~**a** (*fig: persona*) to be tough; **fare il** ~ to act tough; ~ **di comprendonio** slow-witted; ~ **d'orecchi** hard of hearing.
du'rone *sm* hard skin.
'duttile *ag* (*sostanza*) malleable; (*fig: carattere*) docile, biddable; (: *stile*) adaptable.

E e

E, e [e] *sf o m inv* (*lettera*) E, e; **E come Empoli** ≈ E for Edward (*BRIT*), E for Easy (*US*).
E *abbr* (= *est*) E; (*AUT*) = *itinerario europeo*.
e, *dav V spesso* **ed** *cong* and; (*eppure*) and yet; ~ **lui?** what about him?; ~ **compralo!** well buy it then!
è *vb vedi* **essere**.
E.A. *abbr* = *ente autonomo*.
E.A.D. *sigla f vedi* **elaborazione automatica dei dati**.
ebaniste'ria *sf* cabinet-making; (*negozio*) cabinet-maker's shop.
'ebano *sm* ebony.

eb'bene *cong* well (then).
'ebbi *etc vb vedi* **avere**.
eb'brezza [eb'brettsa] *sf* intoxication.
'ebbro, a *ag* drunk; ~ **di** (*gioia etc*) beside o.s. *o* wild with.
'ebete *ag* stupid, idiotic.
ebe'tismo *sm* stupidity.
ebollizi'one [ebollit'tsjone] *sf* boiling; **punto di** ~ boiling point.
e'braico, a, ci, che *ag* Hebrew, Hebraic ♦ *sm* (*LING*) Hebrew.
e'breo, a *ag* Jewish ♦ *sm/f* Jew/Jewess.
'Ebridi *sfpl*: **le (isole)** ~ the Hebrides.
e'burneo, a *ag* ivory *cpd*.
E/C *abbr* = *estratto conto*.
eca'tombe *sf* (*strage*) slaughter, massacre.
ecc *abbr av* (= *eccetera*) etc.
ecce'dente [ettʃe'dɛnte] *sm* surplus.
ecce'denza [ettʃe'dɛntsa] *sf* excess, surplus; (*INFORM*) overflow.
ec'cedere [et'tʃɛdere] *vt* to exceed ♦ *vi* to go too far; ~ **nel bere/mangiare** to indulge in drink/food to excess.
eccel'lente [ettʃel'lɛnte] *ag* excellent; (*cadavere, arresto*) of a prominent person.
eccel'lenza [ettʃel'lɛntsa] *sf* excellence; (*titolo*): **Sua E**~ His Excellency.
ec'cellere [et'tʃɛllere] *vi*: ~ **(in)** to excel (at); ~ **su tutti** to surpass everyone.
ec'celso, a [et'tʃɛlso] *pp di* **eccellere** ♦ *ag* (*cima, montagna*) high; (*fig: ingegno*) great, exceptional.
ec'centrico, a, ci, che [et'tʃɛntriko] *ag* eccentric.
ecces'sivo, a [ettʃes'sivo] *ag* excessive.
ec'cesso [et'tʃɛsso] *sm* excess; **all'**~ (*gentile, generoso*) to excess, excessively; **dare in** ~**i** to fly into a rage; ~ **di velocità** (*AUT*) speeding; ~ **di zelo** overzealousness.
ec'cetera [et'tʃɛtera] *av* et cetera, and so on.
ec'cetto [et'tʃɛtto] *prep* except, with the exception of; ~ **che** *cong* except, other than; ~ **che (non)** unless.
eccettu'are [ettʃettu'are] *vt* to except; **eccettuati i presenti** present company excepted.
eccezio'nale [ettʃettsjo'nale] *ag* exceptional; **in via del tutto** ~ in this instance, exceptionally.
eccezi'one [ettʃet'tsjone] *sf* exception; (*DIR*) objection; **a** ~ **di** with the exception of, except for; **d'**~ exceptional; **fare un'**~ **alla regola** to make an exception to the rule.
ec'chimosi [ek'kimozi] *sf inv* bruise.
ec'cidio [et'tʃidjo] *sm* massacre.

ecci'tante [ettʃi'tante] *ag* (*gen*) exciting; (*sostanza*) stimulating ♦ *sm* stimulant.

ecci'tare [ettʃi'tare] *vt* to excite, arouse; (*folla*) to incite; **~rsi** *vr* to get excited; (*sessualmente*) to become aroused.

eccitazi'one [ettʃitat'tsjone] *sf* excitement.

ecclesi'astico, a, ci, che *ag* ecclesiastical, church *cpd*; clerical ♦ *sm* ecclesiastic.

'ecco *av* (*per dimostrare*): ~ **il treno!** here's *o* here comes the train!; (*dav pronome*): **~mi!** here I am!; **~ne uno!** here's one (of them)!; (*dav pp*): ~ **fatto!** there, that's it done!

ec'come *av* rather; **ti piace?** — **~!** do you like it? — I'll say! *o* and how! *o* rather! (*BRIT*).

ECG *sigla m* = **elettrocardiogramma**.

echeggi'are [eked'dʒare] *vi* to echo.

e'clettico, a, ci, che *ag, sm/f* eclectic.

eclet'tismo *sm* eclecticism.

eclis'sare *vt* to eclipse; (*fig*) to eclipse, overshadow; **~rsi** *vr* (*persona: scherzoso*) to slip away.

e'clissi *sf* eclipse.

'eco, *pl(m)* **'echi** *sm o f* echo; **suscitò** *o* **ebbe una profonda** ~ it caused quite a stir.

ecogra'fia *sf* (*MED*) ultrasound.

ecolo'gia [ekolo'dʒia] *sf* ecology.

eco'logico, a, ci, che [eko'lɔdʒiko] *ag* ecological.

ecolo'gista, i, e [ekolo'dʒista] *ag* ecological ♦ *sm/f* ecologist, environmentalist.

e'cologo, a, gi, ghe *sm/f* ecologist.

econo'mato *sm* (*INS*) bursar's office.

econo'mia *sf* economy; (*scienza*) economics *sg*; (*risparmio: azione*) saving; **fare** ~ to economize, make economies; **l'~ sommersa** the black (*BRIT*) *o* underground (*US*) economy; ~ **di mercato** market economy; ~ **pianificata** planned economy.

eco'nomico, a, ci, che *ag* economic; (*poco costoso*) economical; **edizione** ~**a** economy edition.

econo'mista, i *sm* economist.

economiz'zare [ekonomid'dzare] *vt, vi* to save.

e'conomo, a *ag* thrifty ♦ *sm/f* (*INS*) bursar.

ecosis'tema, i *sm* ecosystem.

'ECU, 'ecu *abbr m inv* (= *European Currency Unit*) ECU, ecu.

'Ecuador *sm*: **l'~** Ecuador.

ecu'menico, a, ci, che *ag* ecumenical.

ec'zema [ek'dzɛma] *sm* eczema.

ed *cong vedi* **e**.

Ed. *abbr* = **editore**.

ed. *abbr* = **edizione**.

'edera *sf* ivy.

e'dicola *sf* newspaper kiosk *o* stand (*US*).

edico'lante *sm/f* news vendor (*in kiosk*).

edifi'cante *ag* edifying.

edifi'care *vt* to build; (*fig: teoria, azienda*) to establish; (*indurre al bene*) to edify.

edi'ficio [edi'fitʃo] *sm* building; (*fig*) structure.

e'dile *ag* building *cpd*.

edi'lizio, a [edi'littsjo] *ag* building *cpd* ♦ *sf* building, building trade.

Edim'burgo *sf* Edinburgh.

'edito, a *ag* published.

edi'tore, 'trice *ag* publishing *cpd* ♦ *sm/f* publisher; (*curatore*) editor.

edito'ria *sf* publishing.

editori'ale *ag* publishing *cpd* ♦ *sm* (*articolo di fondo*) editorial, leader.

e'ditto *sm* edict.

edizi'one [edit'tsjone] *sf* edition; (*tiratura*) printing; ~ **a tiratura limitata** limited edition.

edo'nismo *sm* hedonism.

e'dotto, a *ag* informed; **rendere qn** ~ **su qc** to inform sb about sth.

edu'canda *sf* boarder.

edu'care *vt* to educate; (*gusto, mente*) to train; ~ **qn a fare** to train sb to do.

educa'tivo, a *ag* educational.

edu'cato, a *ag* polite, well-mannered.

educazi'one [edukat'tsjone] *sf* education; (*familiare*) upbringing; (*comportamento*) (good) manners *pl*; **per** ~ out of politeness; **questa è pura mancanza d'~!** this is sheer bad manners!; ~ **fisica** (*INS*) physical training *o* education.

educherò *etc* [eduke'rɔ] *vb vedi* **educare**.

E.E.D. *sigla f vedi* **elaborazione elettronica dei dati**.

EEG *sigla m* = **elettroencefalogramma**.

e'felide *sf* freckle.

effemi'nato, a *ag* effeminate.

effe'rato, a *ag* brutal, savage.

efferve'scente [efferveʃ'ʃɛnte] *ag* effervescent.

effettiva'mente *av* (*in effetti*) in fact; (*a dire il vero*) really, actually.

effet'tivo, a *ag* (*reale*) real, actual; (*impiegato, professore*) permanent; (*MIL*) regular ♦ *sm* (*MIL*) strength; (*di patrimonio etc*) sum total.

ef'fetto *sm* effect; (*COMM: cambiale*) bill; (*fig: impressione*) impression; **far** ~ (*medicina*) to take effect, (*start to*) work; **cercare l'~** to seek attention; **in ~i** in fact; **~i attivi** (*COMM*) bills receivable; **~i passivi** (*COMM*) bills payable; **~i personali** personal effects, personal belongings; ~

serra greenhouse effect; ~**i speciali** (*CINE*) special effects.
effettu'are *vt* to effect, carry out.
effi'cace [effi'katʃe] *ag* effective.
effi'cacia [effi'katʃa] *sf* effectiveness.
effici'ente [effi'tʃɛnte] *ag* efficient.
efficien'tismo [effitʃen'tizmo] *sm* maximum efficiency.
effici'enza [effi'tʃɛntsa] *sf* efficiency.
effigi'are [effi'dʒare] *vt* to represent, portray.
ef'figie [ef'fidʒe] *sf inv* effigy.
ef'fimero, a *ag* ephemeral.
ef'fluvio *sm* (*anche peg, ironico*) scent, perfume.
effusi'one *sf* effusion.
e.g. *abbr* (= *exempli gratia*) e.g.
egemo'nia [edʒemo'nia] *sf* hegemony.
E'geo [e'dʒɛo] *sm*: **l'~, il mare ~** the Aegean (Sea).
'egida ['ɛdʒida] *sf*: **sotto l'~ di** under the aegis of.
E'gitto [e'dʒitto] *sm*: **l'~** Egypt.
egizi'ano, a [edʒit'tsjano] *ag, sm/f* Egyptian.
e'gizio, a [e'dʒittsjo] *ag, sm/f* (ancient) Egyptian.
'egli ['eʎʎi] *pron* he; ~ **stesso** he himself.
'ego *sm inv* (*PSIC*) ego.
ego'centrico, a, ci, che [ego'tʃɛntriko] *ag* egocentric(al) ♦ *sm/f* self-centred (*BRIT*) o self-centered (*US*) person.
egocen'trismo [egotʃen'trizmo] *sm* egocentricity.
ego'ismo *sm* selfishness, egoism.
ego'ista, i, e *ag* selfish, egoistic ♦ *sm/f* egoist.
ego'istico, a, ci, che *ag* egoistic, selfish.
ego'tismo *sm* egotism.
ego'tista, i, e *ag* egotistic ♦ *sm/f* egotist.
Egr. *abbr* = **Egregio.**
e'gregio, a, gi, gie [e'grɛdʒo] *ag* distinguished; (*nelle lettere*): **E~ Signore** Dear Sir.
eguagli'anza *etc* [egwaʎ'ʎantsa] *vedi* **uguaglianza** *etc.*
eguali'tario, a *ag, sm/f* egalitarian.
E.I. *abbr* = *Esercito Italiano.*
eiaculazi'one [ejakulat'tsjone] *sf* ejaculation; ~ **precoce** premature ejaculation.
elabo'rare *vt* (*progetto*) to work out, elaborate; (*dati*) to process; (*digerire*) to digest.
elabora'tore *sm* (*INFORM*): ~ **elettronico** computer.
elaborazi'one [elaborat'tsjone] *sf* elaboration; processing; digestion; ~ **automatica dei dati (E.A.D.)** (*INFORM*)

automatic data processing (A.D.P.); ~ **elettronica dei dati (E.E.D.)** (*INFORM*) electronic data processing (E.D.P.); ~ **testi** (*INFORM*) text processing.
elar'gire [elar'dʒire] *vt* to hand out.
elargizi'one [elardʒit'tsjone] *sf* donation.
elasticiz'zato, a [elastitʃid'dzato] *ag* (*tessuto*) stretch *cpd*.
e'lastico, a, ci, che *ag* elastic; (*fig: andatura*) springy; (*: decisione, vedute*) flexible ♦ *sm* (*gommino*) rubber band; (*per il cucito*) elastic *no pl*.
ele'fante *sm* elephant.
ele'gante *ag* elegant.
ele'ganza [ele'gantsa] *sf* elegance.
e'leggere [e'lɛddʒere] *vt* to elect.
elemen'tare *ag* elementary; **le (scuole)** ~**i** *vedi* **scuola elementare**; **prima** ~ first year of primary school, ≈ infants' class (*BRIT*), ≈ 1st grade (*US*).
ele'mento *sm* element; (*parte componente*) element, component, part; ~**i** *smpl* (*della scienza etc*) elements, rudiments.
ele'mosina *sf* charity, alms *pl*; **chiedere l'~** to beg.
elemosi'nare *vt* to beg for, ask for ♦ *vi* to beg.
elen'care *vt* to list.
elencherò *etc* [elenke'rɔ] *vb vedi* **elencare.**
e'lenco, chi *sm* list; ~ **nominativo** list of names; ~ **telefonico** telephone directory.
e'lessi *etc vb vedi* **eleggere.**
elet'tivo, a *ag* (*carica etc*) elected.
e'letto, a *pp di* **eleggere** ♦ *sm/f* (*nominato*) elected member.
eletto'rale *ag* electoral, election *cpd*.
eletto'rato *sm* electorate.
elet'tore, 'trice *sm/f* voter, elector.
elet'trauto *sm inv* workshop for car electrical repairs; (*tecnico*) car electrician.
elettri'cista, i [elettri'tʃista] *sm* electrician.
elettricità [elettritʃi'ta] *sf* electricity.
e'lettrico, a, ci, che *ag* electric(al).
elettrifi'care *vt* to electrify.
elettriz'zante [elettrid'dzante] *ag* (*fig*) electrifying, thrilling.
elettriz'zare [elettrid'dzare] *vt* to electrify; ~**rsi** *vr* to become charged with electricity; (*fig: persona*) to be thrilled.
e'lettro... *prefisso* electro....
elettrocardio'gramma, i *sm* electrocardiogram.
e'lettrodo *sm* electrode.
elettrodo'mestico, a, ci, che *ag*: **apparecchi** ~**ci** domestic (electrical) appliances.
elettroencefalo'gramma, i

[elettroentʃefalo'gramma] _sm_ electroencephalogram.

elet'trogeno, a [elet'trɔdʒeno] _ag_: **gruppo** ~ generator.

elet'trolisi _sf_ electrolysis.

elettroma'gnetico, a, ci, che [elettromaɲ'ɲɛtiko] _ag_ electromagnetic.

elettromo'trice [elettromo'tritʃe] _sf_ electric train.

elet'trone _sm_ electron.

elet'tronico, a, ci, che _ag_ electronic ♦ _sf_ electronics _sg_.

elettro'shock [elettroʃ'ʃɔk] _sm inv_ (electro)shock treatment.

elettro'tecnico, a, ci, che _ag_ electrotechnical ♦ _sm_ electrical engineer.

ele'vare _vt_ to raise; (_edificio_) to erect; (_multa_) to impose; ~ **un numero al quadrato** to square a number.

eleva'tezza [eleva'tettsa] _sf_ (_altezza_) elevation; (_di animo, pensiero_) loftiness.

ele'vato, a _ag_ (_gen_) high; (_cime_) high, lofty; (_fig: stile, sentimenti_) lofty.

elevazi'one [elevat'tsjone] _sf_ elevation; (_l'elevare_) raising.

elezi'one [elet'tsjone] _sf_ election; ~**i** _sfpl_ (_POL_) election(s); **patria d'**~ chosen country.

'elica, che _sf_ propeller.

eli'cottero _sm_ helicopter.

e'lidere _vt_ (_FONETICA_) to elide; ~**rsi** _vr_ (_forze_) to cancel each other out, neutralize each other.

elimi'nare _vt_ to eliminate.

elimina'toria _sf_ eliminating round.

eliminazi'one [eliminat'tsjone] _sf_ elimination.

'elio _sm_ helium.

eli'porto _sm_ heliport.

elisabetti'ano, a _ag_ Elizabethan.

eli'sir _sm inv_ elixir.

e'liso, a _pp di_ **elidere**.

eli'tario, a _ag_ elitist.

é'lite [e'lit] _sf inv_ élite.

'ella _pron_ she; (_forma di cortesia_) you; ~ **stessa** she herself; you yourself.

el'lisse _sf_ ellipse.

el'littico, a, ci, che _ag_ elliptic(al).

el'metto _sm_ helmet.

'elmo _sm_ helmet.

elogi'are [elo'dʒare] _vt_ to praise.

elogia'tivo, a [elodʒa'tivo] _ag_ laudatory.

e'logio [e'lɔdʒo] _sm_ (_discorso, scritto_) eulogy; (_lode_) praise; ~ **funebre** funeral oration.

elo'quente _ag_ eloquent; **questi dati sono** ~**i** these facts speak for themselves.

elo'quenza [elo'kwɛntsa] _sf_ eloquence.

e'loquio _sm_ speech, language.

elucu'brare _vt_ (_piano_) to ponder about, ponder over.

elucubrazi'oni [elukubrat'tsjoni] _sfpl_ (_anche ironico_) cogitations, ponderings.

e'ludere _vt_ to evade.

e'lusi _etc vb vedi_ **eludere**.

elusi'one _sf_: ~ **d'imposta** tax evasion.

elu'sivo, a _ag_ evasive.

e'luso, a _pp di_ **eludere**.

el'vetico, a, ci, che _ag_ Swiss.

emaci'ato, a [ema'tʃato] _ag_ emaciated.

ema'nare _vt_ to send out, give off; (_fig: leggi_) to promulgate; (: _decreti_) to issue ♦ _vi_: ~ **da** to come from.

emanazi'one [emanat'tsjone] _sf_ (_di raggi, calore_) emanation; (_di odori_) exhalation; (_di legge_) promulgation; (_di ordine, circolare_) issuing.

emanci'pare [emantʃi'pare] _vt_ to emancipate; ~**rsi** _vr_ (_fig_) to become liberated _o_ emancipated.

emancipazi'one [emantʃipat'tsjone] _sf_ emancipation.

emargi'nare [emardʒi'nare] _vt_ (_fig: socialmente_) to cast out.

emargi'nato, a [emardʒi'nato] _sm/f_ outcast.

ematolo'gia [ematolo'dʒia] _sf_ haematology (_BRIT_), hematology (_US_).

ema'toma, i _sm_ haematoma (_BRIT_), hematoma (_US_).

em'blema, i _sm_ emblem.

emble'matico, a, ci, che _ag_ emblematic; (_fig: atteggiamento, parole_) symbolic.

embo'lia _sf_ embolism.

embrio'nale, i, e _ag_ embryonic, embryo _cpd_; **allo stadio** ~ at the embryo stage.

embri'one _sm_ embryo.

emenda'mento _sm_ amendment.

emen'dare _vt_ to amend.

emer'gente [emer'dʒɛnte] _ag_ emerging.

emer'genza [emer'dʒɛntsa] _sf_ emergency; **in caso di** ~ in an emergency.

e'mergere [e'mɛrdʒere] _vi_ to emerge; (_sommergibile_) to surface; (_fig: distinguersi_) to stand out.

e'merito, a _ag_ (_insigne_) distinguished; **è un** ~ **cretino!** he's a complete idiot!

e'mersi _etc vb vedi_ **emergere**.

e'merso, a _pp di_ **emergere** ♦ _ag_ (_GEO_): **terre** ~**e** lands above sea level.

e'messo, a _pp di_ **emettere**.

e'mettere _vt_ (_suono, luce_) to give out, emit; (_onde radio_) to send out; (_assegno, francobollo, ordine_) to issue; (_fig: giudizio_) to express, voice; ~ **la sentenza** (_DIR_) to pass sentence.

emi'crania _sf_ migraine.

emi'grante *ag, sm/f* emigrant.
emi'grare *vi* to emigrate.
emi'grato, a *ag* emigrant ♦ *sm/f* emigrant; (*STORIA*) émigré.
emigrazi'one [emigrat'tsjone] *sf* emigration.
emili'ano, a *ag* of (*o* from) Emilia.
emi'nente *ag* eminent, distinguished.
emi'nenza [emi'nɛntsa] *sf* eminence; ~ **grigia** (*fig*) éminence grise.
emi'rato *sm* emirate; **gli E~i Arabi Uniti** the United Arab Emirates.
e'miro *sm* emir.
emis'fero *sm* hemisphere; ~ **boreale/ australe** northern/southern hemisphere.
e'misi *etc vb vedi* **emettere**.
emis'sario *sm* (*GEO*) outlet, effluent; (*inviato*) emissary.
emissi'one *sf* (*vedi emettere*) emission; sending out; issue; (*RADIO*) broadcast.
emit'tente *ag* (*banca*) issuing; (*RADIO*) broadcasting, transmitting ♦ *sf* (*RADIO*) transmitter.
emofi'lia *sf* haemophilia (*BRIT*), hemophilia (*US*).
emofi'liaco, a, ci, che *ag, sm/f* haemophiliac (*BRIT*), hemophiliac (*US*).
emoglo'bina *sf* haemoglobin (*BRIT*), hemoglobin (*US*).
emolli'ente *ag* soothing.
emorra'gia, 'gie [emorra'dʒia] *sf* haemorrhage (*BRIT*), hemorrhage (*US*).
emor'roidi *sfpl* haemorrhoids (*BRIT*), hemorrhoids (*US*).
emos'tatico, a, ci, che *ag* haemostatic (*BRIT*), hemostatic (*US*); **laccio** ~ tourniquet; **matita** ~a styptic pencil.
emotività *sf* emotionalism.
emo'tivo, a *ag* emotional.
emozio'nante [emottsjo'nante] *ag* exciting, thrilling.
emozio'nare [emottsjo'nare] *vt* (*appassionare*) to thrill, excite; (*commuovere*) to move; (*innervosire*) to upset; ~**rsi** *vr* to be excited; to be moved; to be upset.
emozi'one [emot'tsjone] *sf* emotion; (*agitazione*) excitement.
'empio, a *ag* (*sacrilego*) impious; (*spietato*) cruel, pitiless; (*malvagio*) wicked, evil.
em'pirico, a, ci, che *ag* empirical.
em'porio *sm* general store.
emu'lare *vt* to emulate.
'emulo, a *sm/f* imitator.
emulsi'one *sf* emulsion.
EN *sigla = Enna*.
en'ciclica, che [en'tʃiklika] *sf* (*REL*) encyclical.
enciclope'dia [entʃiklope'dia] *sf* encyclop(a)edia.
encomi'abile *ag* commendable, praiseworthy.
encomi'are *vt* to commend, praise.
en'comio *sm* commendation; ~ **solenne** (*MIL*) mention in dispatches.
endove'noso, a *ag* (*MED*) intravenous ♦ *sf* intravenous injection.
E'NEA *sigla f = Comitato nazionale per la ricerca e lo sviluppo dell'Energia Nucleare e delle Energie Alternative*.
'E.N.E.L. *sigla m* (*= Ente Nazionale per l'Energia Elettrica*) *national electricity company*.
ener'getico, a, ci, che [ener'dʒɛtiko] *ag* (*risorse, crisi*) energy *cpd*; (*sostanza, alimento*) energy-giving.
ener'gia, 'gie [ener'dʒia] *sf* (*FISICA*) energy; (*fig*) energy, strength, vigour (*BRIT*), vigor (*US*).
e'nergico, a, ci, che [e'nɛrdʒiko] *ag* energetic, vigorous.
'enfasi *sf* emphasis; (*peg*) bombast, pomposity.
en'fatico, a, ci, che *ag* emphatic; pompous.
enfatiz'zare [enfatid'dzare] *vt* to emphasize, stress.
enfi'sema *sm* emphysema.
'ENI *sigla m = Ente Nazionale Idrocarburi*.
e'nigma, i *sm* enigma.
enig'matico, a, ci, che *ag* enigmatic.
'ENIT *sigla m* (*= Ente Nazionale Italiano per il Turismo*) *Italian tourist authority*.
en'nesimo, a *ag* (*MAT, fig*) nth; **per l'~a volta** for the umpteenth time.
enolo'gia [enolo'dʒia] *sf* oenology (*BRIT*), enology (*US*).
e'nologo, gi *sm* wine expert.
e'norme *ag* enormous, huge.
enormità *sf inv* enormity, huge size; (*assurdità*) absurdity; **non dire** ~! don't talk nonsense!
eno'teca, che *sf* (*negozio*) wine bar.
'E.N.P.A. *sigla m* (*= Ente Nazionale Protezione Animali*) ≈ RSPCA (*BRIT*), ≈ SPCA (*US*).
'E.N.P.A.S. *sigla m* (*= Ente Nazionale di Previdenza e Assistenza per i Dipendenti Statali*) *welfare organization for State employees*.
'ente *sm* (*istituzione*) body, board, corporation; (*FILOSOFIA*) being; ~ **locale** local authority (*BRIT*), local government (*US*); ~ **pubblico** public body; ~ **di ricerca** research organization.
ente'rite *sf* enteritis.

entità *sf* (*FILOSOFIA*) entity; (*di perdita, danni, investimenti*) extent; (*di popolazione*) size; **di molta/poca** ~ (*avvenimento, incidente*) of great/little importance.

en'trambi, e *pron pl* both (of them) ♦ *ag pl*: ~ **i ragazzi** both boys, both of the boys.

en'trante *ag* (*prossimo: mese, anno*) next, coming.

en'trare *vi* to enter, go (*o come*) in; ~ **in** (*luogo*) to enter, go (*o come*) into; (*trovar posto, poter stare*) to fit into; (*essere ammesso a: club etc*) to join, become a member of; ~ **in automobile** to get into the car; **far** ~ **qn** (*visitatore etc*) to show sb in; ~ **in società/in commercio con qn** to go into partnership/business with sb; **questo non c'entra** (*fig*) that's got nothing to do with it.

en'trata *sf* entrance, entry; ~**e** *sfpl* (*COMM*) receipts, takings; (*ECON*) income *sg*; "~ **libera**" "admission free"; **con l'**~ **in vigore dei nuovi provvedimenti** ... once the new measures come into effect ...; ~**e tributarie** tax revenue *sg*.

'entro *prep* (*temporale*) within; ~ **domani** by tomorrow; ~ **e non oltre il 25 aprile** no later than 25th April.

entro'terra *sm inv* hinterland.

entusias'mante *ag* exciting.

entusias'mare *vt* to excite, fill with enthusiasm; ~**rsi** *vr*: ~**rsi** (**per qc/qn**) to become enthusiastic (about sth/sb).

entusi'asmo *sm* enthusiasm.

entusi'asta, i, e *ag* enthusiastic ♦ *sm/f* enthusiast.

entusi'astico, a, ci, che *ag* enthusiastic.

enucle'are *vt* (*formale: chiarire*) to explain.

enume'rare *vt* to enumerate, list.

enunci'are [enun'tʃare] *vt* (*teoria*) to enunciate, set out.

en'zima, i *sm* enzyme.

e'patico, a, ci, che *ag* hepatic; **cirrosi** ~**a** cirrhosis of the liver.

epa'tite *sf* hepatitis.

'epico, a, ci, che *ag* epic.

epide'mia *sf* epidemic.

epi'dermico, a, ci, che *ag* (*ANAT*) skin *cpd*; (*fig: interesse, impressioni*) superficial.

epi'dermide *sf* skin, epidermis.

Epifa'nia *sf* Epiphany.

e'pigono *sm* imitator.

e'pigrafe *sf* epigraph; (*su libro*) dedication.

epiles'sia *sf* epilepsy.

epi'lettico, a, ci, che *ag*, *sm/f* epileptic.

e'pilogo, ghi *sm* conclusion.

epi'sodico, a, ci, che *ag* (*romanzo, narrazione*) episodic; (*fig: occasionale*) occasional.

epi'sodio *sm* episode; **sceneggiato a** ~**i** serial.

e'pistola *sf* epistle.

episto'lare *ag* epistolary; **essere in rapporto** *o* **relazione** ~ **con qn** to correspond *o* be in correspondence with sb.

e'piteto *sm* epithet.

'epoca, che *sf* (*periodo storico*) age, era; (*tempo*) time; (*GEO*) age; **mobili d'**~ period furniture; **fare** ~ (*scandalo*) to cause a stir; (*cantante, moda*) to mark a new era.

epo'pea *sf* (*anche fig*) epic.

ep'pure *cong* and yet, nevertheless.

EPT *sigla m* (= *Ente Provinciale per il Turismo*) district tourist bureau.

epu'rare *vt* (*POL*) to purge.

equ'anime *ag* (*imparziale*) fair, impartial.

equa'tore *sm* equator.

equazi'one [ekwat'tsjone] *sf* (*MAT*) equation.

e'questre *ag* equestrian.

equi'latero, a *ag* equilateral.

equili'brare *vt* to balance.

equili'brato, a *ag* (*carico, fig: giudizio*) balanced; (*vita*) well-regulated; (*persona*) stable, well-balanced.

equi'librio *sm* balance, equilibrium; **perdere l'**~ to lose one's balance; **stare in** ~ **su** (*persona*) to balance on; (*oggetto*) to be balanced on.

equili'brismo *sm* tightrope walking; (*fig*) juggling.

e'quino, a *ag* horse *cpd*, equine.

equi'nozio [ekwi'nɔttsjo] *sm* equinox.

equipaggia'mento [ekwipaddʒa'mento] *sm* (*operazione: di nave*) equipping, fitting out; (: *di spedizione, esercito*) equipping, kitting out; (*attrezzatura*) equipment.

equipaggi'are [ekwipad'dʒare] *vt* to equip; ~**rsi** *vr* to equip o.s.

equi'paggio [ekwi'paddʒo] *sm* crew.

equipa'rare *vt* to make equal.

é'quipe [e'kip] *sf* (*SPORT, gen*) team.

equità *sf* equity, fairness.

equitazi'one [ekwitat'tsjone] *sf* (horse-) riding.

equiva'lente *ag*, *sm* equivalent.

equiva'lenza [ekwiva'lɛntsa] *sf* equivalence.

equiva'lere *vi*: ~ **a** to be equivalent to; ~**rsi** *vr* (*forze etc*) to counterbalance each other; (*soluzioni*) to amount to the same thing; **equivale a dire che** ... that is the same as saying that ....

equi'valso, a *pp di* **equivalere**.

equivo'care *vi* to misunderstand.

e'**quivoco, a, ci, che** *ag* equivocal, ambiguous; (*sospetto*) dubious ♦ *sm* misunderstanding; **a scanso di** ~**ci** to avoid any misunderstanding; **giocare sull'**~ to equivocate.
'**equo, a** *ag* fair, just.
'**era** *sf* era.
'**era** *etc vb vedi* **essere**.
erari'ale *ag*: **ufficio** ~ ≈ tax office; **imposte** ~**i** revenue taxes; **spese** ~**i** public expenditure *sg.*
e'**rario** *sm*: **l'**~ ≈ the Treasury.
'**erba** *sf* grass; (*aromatica, medicinale*) herb; **in** ~ (*fig*) budding; **fare di ogni** ~ **un fascio** (*fig*) to lump everything (*o* everybody) together.
er'**baccia, ce** [er'battʃa] *sf* weed.
er'**bivoro, a** *ag* herbivorous ♦ *sm/f* herbivore.
erbo'**rista, i, e** *sm/f* herbalist.
erboriste'**ria** *sf* (*scienza*) study of medicinal herbs; (*negozio*) herbalist's (shop).
er'**boso, a** *ag* grassy.
e'**rede** *sm/f* heir; ~ **legittimo** heir-at-law.
eredi**tà** *sf* (*DIR*) inheritance; (*BIOL*) heredity; **lasciare qc in** ~ **a qn** to leave *o* bequeath sth to sb.
eredi'**tare** *vt* to inherit.
eredi'**tario, a** *ag* hereditary.
erediti'**era** *sf* heiress.
ere'**mita, i** *sm* hermit.
eremi'**taggio** [eremi'taddʒo] *sm* hermitage.
'**eremo** *sm* hermitage; (*fig*) retreat.
ere'**sia** *sf* heresy.
e'**ressi** *etc vb vedi* **erigere**.
e'**retico, a, ci, che** *ag* heretical ♦ *sm/f* heretic.
e'**retto, a** *pp di* **erigere** ♦ *ag* erect, upright.
erezi'**one** [eret'tsjone] *sf* (*FISIOL*) erection.
ergasto'**lano, a** *sm/f* prisoner serving a life sentence, lifer (*fam*).
er'**gastolo** *sm* (*DIR: pena*) life imprisonment; (*: luogo di pena*) prison (*for those serving life sentences*).
ergono'**mia** *sf* ergonomics *sg.*
ergo'**nomico, a, ci, che** *ag* ergonomic(al).
'**erica** *sf* heather.
e'**rigere** [e'ridʒere] *vt* to erect, raise; (*fig: fondare*) to found.
eri'**tema** *sm* (*MED*) inflammation, erythema; ~ **solare** sunburn.
Eri'**trea** *sf* Eritrea.
ermel'**lino** *sm* ermine.
er'**metico, a, ci, che** *ag* hermetic.
'**ernia** *sf* (*MED*) hernia; ~ **del disco** slipped disc.
'**ero** *vb vedi* **essere**.

e'**rodere** *vt* to erode.
e'**roe** *sm* hero.
ero'**gare** *vt* (*somme*) to distribute; (*gas, servizi*) to supply.
erogazi'**one** [erogat'tsjone] *sf* distribution; supply.
e'**roico, a, ci, che** *ag* heroic.
ero'**ina** *sf* heroine; (*droga*) heroin.
ero'**ismo** *sm* heroism.
'**eros** *sm* Eros.
erosi'**one** *sf* erosion.
e'**roso, a** *pp di* **erodere**.
e'**rotico, a, ci, che** *ag* erotic.
ero'**tismo** *sm* eroticism.
'**erpete** *sm* herpes *sg.*
'**erpice** ['erpitʃe] *sm* (*AGR*) harrow.
er'**rare** *vi* (*vagare*) to wander, roam; (*sbagliare*) to be mistaken.
er'**roneo, a** *ag* erroneous, wrong.
er'**rore** *sm* error, mistake; (*morale*) error; **per** ~ by mistake; ~ **giudiziario** miscarriage of justice.
'**erto, a** *ag* (very) steep ♦ *sf* steep slope; **stare all'**~**a** to be on the alert.
eru'**dire** *vt* to teach, educate.
eru'**dito, a** *ag* learned, erudite.
erut'**tare** *vt* (*sog: vulcano*) to throw out, belch.
eruzi'**one** [erut'tsjone] *sf* eruption; (*MED*) rash.
es. *abbr* (= *esempio*) e.g.
E.S. *sigla m* (= *elettroshock*) ECT.
E.S.A. ['eza] *sigla m* (= *European Space Agency*) ESA.
esacer'**bare** [ezatʃer'bare] *vt* to exacerbate.
esage'**rare** [ezadʒe'rare] *vt* to exaggerate ♦ *vi* to exaggerate; (*eccedere*) to go too far; **senza** ~ without exaggeration.
esage'**rato, a** [ezadʒe'rato] *ag* (*notizia, proporzioni*) exaggerated; (*curiosità, pignoleria*) excessive; (*prezzo*) exorbitant ♦ *sm/f*: **sei il solito** ~ you are exaggerating as usual.
esagerazi'**one** [ezadʒerat'tsjone] *sf* exaggeration.
esago'**nale** *ag* hexagonal.
e'**sagono** *sm* hexagon.
esa'**lare** *vt* (*odori*) to give off ♦ *vi*: ~ (**da**) to emanate (from); ~ **l'ultimo respiro** (*fig*) to breathe one's last.
esalazi'**one** [ezalat'tsjone] *sf* (*emissione*) exhalation; (*odore*) fumes *pl.*
esal'**tante** *ag* exciting.
esal'**tare** *vt* to exalt; (*entusiasmare*) to excite, stir; ~**rsi** *vr*: ~**rsi (per qc)** to grow excited (about sth).
esal'**tato, a** *sm/f* fanatic.
esaltazi'**one** [ezaltat'tsjone] *sf* (*elogio*)

extolling, exalting; (*nervosa*) intense excitement; (*mistica*) exaltation.

e'same *sm* examination; (*INS*) exam, examination; **fare** *o* **dare un** ~ to sit *o* take an exam; **fare un** ~ **di coscienza** to search one's conscience; ~ **di guida** driving test; ~ **del sangue** blood test.

esami'nare *vt* to examine.

e'sangue *ag* bloodless; (*fig: pallido*) pale, wan; (: *privo di vigore*) lifeless.

e'sanime *ag* lifeless.

esaspe'rare *vt* to exasperate; (*situazione*) to exacerbate; ~**rsi** *vr* to become annoyed *o* exasperated.

esasperazi'one [ezasperat'tsjone] *sf* exasperation.

esatta'mente *av* exactly; accurately, precisely.

esat'tezza [ezat'tettsa] *sf* exactitude, accuracy, precision; **per l'**~ to be precise.

e'satto, a *pp di* **esigere** ♦ *ag* (*calcolo, ora*) correct, right, exact; (*preciso*) accurate, precise; (*puntuale*) punctual.

esat'tore *sm* (*di imposte etc*) collector.

esatto'ria *sf*: ~ **comunale** district rates office (*BRIT*) *o* assessor's office (*US*).

esau'dire *vt* to grant, fulfil (*BRIT*), fulfill (*US*).

esauri'ente *ag* exhaustive.

esauri'mento *sm* exhaustion; ~ **nervoso** nervous breakdown; **svendita (fino) ad** ~ **della merce** clearance sale.

esau'rire *vt* (*stancare*) to exhaust, wear out; (*provviste, miniera*) to exhaust; ~**rsi** *vr* to exhaust o.s., wear o.s. out; (*provviste*) to run out.

esau'rito, a *ag* exhausted; (*merci*) sold out; (*libri*) out of print; **essere** ~ (*persona*) to be run down; **registrare il tutto** ~ (*TEAT*) to have a full house.

e'sausto, a *ag* exhausted.

esauto'rare *vt* (*dirigente, funzionario*) to deprive of authority.

esazi'one [ezat'tsjone] *sf* collection (of taxes).

'esca, *pl* **'esche** *sf* bait.

escamo'tage [ɛskamɔ'taʒ] *sm* subterfuge.

escande'scenza [eskandeʃ'ʃentsa] *sf*: **dare in** ~**e** to lose one's temper, fly into a rage.

'esce ['ɛʃʃe] *vb vedi* **uscire**.

eschi'mese [eski'mese] *ag, sm/f, sm* Eskimo.

'esci ['ɛʃʃi] *vb vedi* **uscire**.

escl. *abbr* (= *escluso*) excl.

escla'mare *vi* to exclaim, cry out.

esclama'tivo, a *ag*: **punto** ~ exclamation mark.

esclamazi'one [esklamat'tsjone] *sf* exclamation.

es'cludere *vt* to exclude.

es'clusi *etc vb vedi* **escludere**.

esclusi'one *sf* exclusion; **a** ~ **di, fatta** ~ **per** except (for), apart from; **senza** ~ (**alcuna**) without exception; **procedere per** ~ to follow a process of elimination; **senza** ~ **di colpi** (*fig*) with no holds barred.

esclu'siva *sf vedi* **esclusivo**.

esclusiva'mente *av* exclusively, solely.

esclu'sivo, a *ag* exclusive ♦ *sf* (*DIR, COMM*) exclusive *o* sole rights *pl*.

es'cluso, a *pp di* **escludere** ♦ *ag*: **nessuno** ~ without exception; **IVA** ~**a** excluding VAT, exclusive of VAT.

'esco *vb vedi* **uscire**.

escogi'tare [eskodʒi'tare] *vt* to devise, think up.

'escono *vb vedi* **uscire**.

escoriazi'one [eskorjat'tsjone] *sf* abrasion, graze.

escre'menti *smpl* excrement *sg*, faeces.

es'cudo *sm* (*pl* ~**s**) escudo.

escursi'one *sf* (*gita*) excursion, trip; (: *a piedi*) hike, walk; (*METEOR*): ~ **termica** temperature range.

escursio'nista, i, e *sm/f* (*gitante*) (day) tripper; (: *a piedi*) hiker, walker.

ese'crare *vt* to loathe, abhor.

esecu'tivo, a *ag, sm* executive.

esecu'tore, 'trice *sm/f* (*MUS*) performer; (*DIR*) executor.

esecuzi'one [ezekut'tsjone] *sf* execution, carrying out; (*MUS*) performance; ~ **capitale** execution.

ese'geta, i [eze'dʒɛta] *sm* commentator.

esegu'ire *vt* to carry out, execute; (*MUS*) to perform, execute.

e'sempio *sm* example; **per** ~ for example, for instance; **fare un** ~ to give an example.

esem'plare *ag* exemplary ♦ *sm* example; (*copia*) copy; (*BOT, ZOOL, GEO*) specimen.

esemplifi'care *vt* to exemplify.

esen'tare *vt*: ~ **qn/qc da** to exempt sb/sth from.

esen'tasse *ag inv* tax-free.

e'sente *ag*: ~ **da** (*dispensato da*) exempt from; (*privo di*) free from.

esenzi'one [ezen'tsjone] *sf* exemption.

e'sequie *sfpl* funeral rites; funeral service *sg*.

eser'cente [ezer'tʃɛnte] *sm/f* trader, dealer; shopkeeper.

eserci'tare [ezertʃi'tare] *vt* (*professione*) to practise (*BRIT*), practice (*US*); (*allenare:*

corpo, mente) to exercise, train; (*diritto*) to exercise; (*influenza, pressione*) to exert; ~**rsi** *vr* to practise; ~**rsi nella guida** to practise one's driving.

esercitazi'one [ezertʃitat'tsjone] *sf* (*scolastica, militare*) exercise; ~**i di tiro** target practice *sg*.

e'sercito [e'zertʃito] *sm* army.

eser'cizio [ezer'tʃittsjo] *sm* practice; (*compito, movimento*) exercise; (*azienda*) business, concern; (*ECON*): ~ **finanziario** financial year; **in** ~ (*medico etc*) practising (*BRIT*), practicing (*US*); **nell'**~ **delle proprie funzioni** in the execution of one's duties.

esfoli'ante *sm* exfoliator.

esi'bire *vt* to exhibit, display; (*documenti*) to produce, present; ~**rsi** *vr* (*attore*) to perform; (*fig*) to show off.

esibizi'one [ezibit'tsjone] *sf* exhibition; (*di documento*) presentation; (*spettacolo*) show, performance.

esibizio'nista, i, e [ezibittsjo'nista] *sm/f* exhibitionist.

esi'gente [ezi'dʒɛnte] *ag* demanding.

esi'genza [ezi'dʒɛntsa] *sf* demand, requirement.

e'sigere [e'zidʒere] *vt* (*pretendere*) to demand; (*richiedere*) to demand, require; (*imposte*) to collect.

esi'gibile [ezi'dʒibile] *ag* payable.

e'siguo, a *ag* small, slight.

esila'rante *ag* hilarious; **gas** ~ laughing gas.

'esile *ag* (*persona*) slender, slim; (*stelo*) thin; (*voce*) faint.

esili'are *vt* to exile.

esili'ato, a *ag* exiled ♦ *sm/f* exile.

e'silio *sm* exile.

e'simere *vt*: ~ **qn/qc da** to exempt sb/sth from; ~**rsi** *vr*: ~**rsi da** to get out of.

esis'tente *ag* existing; (*attuale*) present, current.

esis'tenza [ezis'tɛntsa] *sf* existence.

esistenzia'lismo [ezistentsja'lizmo] *sm* existentialism.

e'sistere *vi* to exist; **esiste più di una versione dell'opera** there is more than one version of the work; **non esiste!** (*fam*) no way!

esis'tito, a *pp di* **esistere**.

esi'tante *ag* hesitant; (*voce*) faltering.

esi'tare *vi* to hesitate.

esitazi'one [ezitat'tsjone] *sf* hesitation.

'esito *sm* result, outcome.

'eskimo *sm* (*giaccone*) parka.

'esodo *sm* exodus.

e'sofago, gi *sm* oesophagus (*BRIT*),

esophagus (*US*).

esone'rare *vt*: ~ **qn da** to exempt sb from.

esorbi'tante *ag* exorbitant, excessive.

esor'cismo [ezor'tʃizmo] *sm* exorcism.

esor'cista, i [ezor'tʃista] *sm* exorcist.

esorciz'zare [ezortʃid'dzare] *vt* to exorcize.

esordi'ente *sm/f* beginner.

e'sordio *sm* debut.

esor'dire *vi* (*nel teatro*) to make one's debut; (*fig*) to start out, begin (one's career); **esordì dicendo che ...** he began by saying (that) ....

esor'tare *vt*: ~ **qn a fare** to urge sb to do.

esortazi'one [ezortat'tsjone] *sf* exhortation.

e'soso, a *ag* (*prezzo*) exorbitant; (*persona: avido*) grasping.

eso'terico, a, ci, che *ag* esoteric.

e'sotico, a, ci, che *ag* exotic.

es'pandere *vt* to expand; (*confini*) to extend; (*influenza*) to extend, spread; ~**rsi** *vr* to expand.

espansi'one *sf* expansion.

espansività *sf* expansiveness.

espan'sivo, a *ag* expansive, communicative.

es'panso, a *pp di* **espandere**.

espatri'are *vi* to leave one's country.

es'patrio *sm* expatriation; **permesso di** ~ authorization to leave the country.

espedi'ente *sm* expedient; **vivere di** ~**i** to live by one's wits.

es'pellere *vt* to expel.

esperi'enza [espe'rjɛntsa] *sf* experience; (*SCIENZA: prova*) experiment; **parlare per** ~ to speak from experience.

esperi'mento *sm* experiment; **fare un** ~ to carry out *o* do an experiment.

es'perto, a *ag, sm/f* expert.

espi'anto *sm* (*MED*) removal.

espi'are *vt* to atone for.

espiazi'one [espiat'tsjone] *sf*: ~ (**di**) expiation (of), atonement (for).

espi'rare *vt, vi* to breathe out.

espleta'mento *sm* (*AMM*) carrying out.

esple'tare *vt* (*AMM*) to carry out.

espli'care *vt* (*attività*) to carry out, perform.

esplica'tivo, a *ag* explanatory.

es'plicito, a [es'plitʃito] *ag* explicit.

es'plodere *vi* (*anche fig*) to explode ♦ *vt* to fire.

esplo'rare *vt* to explore.

esplora'tore, 'trice *sm/f* explorer; (*anche: giovane* ~) (boy) scout/(girl) guide (*BRIT*) *o* scout (*US*) ♦ *sm* (*NAUT*) scout (ship).

esplorazi'one [esplorat'tsjone] *sf* exploration; **mandare qn in** ~ (*MIL*) to send sb to scout ahead.

esplosi'one *sf (anche fig)* explosion.

esplo'sivo, a *ag, sm* explosive.

es'ploso, a *pp di* **esplodere.**

es'pone *etc vb vedi* **esporre.**

espo'nente *smlf (rappresentante)* representative.

esponenzi'ale [esponen'tsjale] *ag (MAT)* exponential.

es'pongo, es'poni *etc vb vedi* **esporre.**

es'porre *vt (merci)* to display; *(quadro)* to exhibit, show; *(fatti, idee)* to explain, set out; *(porre in pericolo, FOT)* to expose; **esporsi** *vr:* **esporsi a** *(sole, pericolo)* to expose o.s. to; *(critiche)* to lay o.s. open to.

espor'tare *vt* to export.

esporta'tore, 'trice *ag* exporting ♦ *sm* exporter.

esportazi'one [esportat'tsjone] *sf (azione)* exportation, export; *(insieme di prodotti)* exports *pl.*

es'pose *etc vb vedi* **esporre.**

espo'simetro *sm* exposure meter.

esposizi'one [espozit'tsjone] *sf* displaying; exhibiting; setting out; *(anche FOT)* exposure; *(mostra)* exhibition; *(narrazione)* explanation, exposition.

es'posto, a *pp di* **esporre** ♦ *ag:* ~ **a nord** facing north, north-facing ♦ *sm (AMM)* statement, account; *(: petizione)* petition.

espressi'one *sf* expression.

espres'sivo, a *ag* expressive.

es'presso, a *pp di* **esprimere** ♦ *ag* express ♦ *sm (lettera)* express letter; *(anche:* **treno** ~*)* express train; *(anche:* **caffè** ~*)* espresso.

es'primere *vt* to express; ~**rsi** *vr* to express o.s.

espropri'are *vt (terreni, edifici)* to place a compulsory purchase order on; *(persona)* to dispossess.

espropriazi'one [esproprjat'tsjone] *sf,* **es'proprio** *sm* expropriation; ~ **per pubblica utilità** compulsory purchase.

espu'gnare [espuɲ'ɲare] *vt* to take by force, storm.

es'pulsi *etc vb vedi* **espellere.**

espulsi'one *sf* expulsion.

es'pulso, a *pp di* **espellere.**

'essa *pron f,* **'esse** *pron fpl vedi* **esso.**

es'senza [es'sɛntsa] *sf* essence.

essenzi'ale [essen'tsjale] *ag* essential; *(stile, linea)* simple ♦ *sm:* **l'**~ the main *o* most important thing.

═════════════════ *PAROLA CHIAVE*

'essere *sm* being; ~ **umano** human being

♦ *vb copulativo* **1** *(con attributo, sostantivo)* to be; **sei giovane/simpatico** you are *o* you're young/nice; **è medico** he is *o* he's a doctor

2 *(+ di: appartenere)* to be; **di chi è la penna?** whose pen is it?; **è di Carla** it is *o* it's Carla's, it belongs to Carla

3 *(+ di: provenire)* to be; **è di Venezia** he is *o* he's from Venice

4 *(data, ora):* **è il 15 agosto** it is *o* it's the 15th of August; **è lunedì** it is *o* it's Monday; **che ora è?, che ore sono?** what time is it?; **è l'una** it is *o* it's one o'clock; **sono le due** it is *o* it's two o'clock

5 *(costare):* **quant'è?** how much is it?; **sono 20.000 lire** it's 20,000 lire

♦ *vb aus* **1** *(attivo):* ~ **arrivato/venuto** to have arrived/come; **è già partita** she has already left

2 *(passivo)* to be; ~ **fatto da** to be made by; **è stata uccisa** she has been killed

3 *(riflessivo):* **si sono lavati** they washed, they got washed

4 *(+ da + infinito):* **è da farsi subito** it must be done *o* is to be done immediately

♦ *vi* **1** *(esistere, trovarsi)* to be; **sono a casa** I'm at home; ~ **in piedi/seduto** to be standing/sitting

2 *(succedere):* **sarà quel che sarà** what will be will be; **sia quel che sia, io me ne vado** come what may, I'm going now

3: esserci: c'è there is; **ci sono** there are; **che c'è?** what's the matter?, what is it?; **non c'è niente da fare** there's nothing we can do; **c'è da sperare che ...** one can only hope that ...; **ci sono!** *(sono pronto)* I'm ready!; *(ho capito)* I get it!; *vedi anche* **ci**

♦ *vb impers:* **è tardi/Pasqua** it's late/Easter; **è mezzanotte** it's midnight; **è bello/ caldo/freddo** it's nice/hot/cold; **è possibile che venga** he may come; **è così** that's the way it is.

'essi *pron mpl vedi* **esso.**

essic'care *vt (gen)* to dry; *(legname)* to season; *(cibi)* to desiccate; *(bacino, palude)* to drain; ~**rsi** *vr (fiume, pozzo)* to dry up; *(vernice)* to dry (out).

'esso, a *pron* it; *(riferito a persona: soggetto)* he/she; *(: complemento)* him/her; ~**i, e** *pron pl* they; *(complemento)* them.

est *sm* east; **i paesi dell'E**~ the Eastern bloc *sg.*

'estasi *sf* ecstasy.

estasi'are *vt* to send into raptures; ~**rsi** *vr*: ~**rsi (davanti a)** to go into ecstasies (over), go into raptures (over).

es'tate *sf* summer.

es'tatico, a, ci, che *ag* ecstatic.

estempo'raneo, a *ag* (*discorso*) extempore, impromptu; (*brano musicale*) impromptu.

es'tendere *vt* to extend; ~**rsi** *vr* (*diffondersi*) to spread; (*territorio, confini*) to extend.

estensi'one *sf* extension; (*di superficie*) expanse; (*di voce*) range.

estenu'ante *ag* wearing, tiring.

estenu'are *vt* (*stancare*) to wear out, tire out.

esteri'ore *ag* outward, external.

esteriorità *sf inv* outward appearance.

esterioriz'zare [esterjorid'dzare] *vt* (*gioia etc*) to show.

ester'nare *vt* to express; ~ **un sospetto** to voice a suspicion.

es'terno, a *ag* (*porta, muro*) outer, outside; (*scala*) outside; (*alunno, impressione*) external ♦ *sm* outside, exterior ♦ *smlf* (*allievo*) day pupil; "**per uso ~**" "for external use only"; **gli ~i sono stati girati a Glasgow** (*CINE*) the location shots were taken in Glasgow.

'**estero, a** *ag* foreign ♦ *sm*: **all'~** abroad; **Ministero degli E~i, gli E~i** Ministry for Foreign Affairs, ≈ Foreign Office (*BRIT*), ≈ State Department (*US*).

esterofi'lia *sf* excessive love of foreign things.

esterre'fatto, a *ag* (*costernato*) horrified; (*sbalordito*) astounded.

es'tesi *etc vb vedi* **estendere**.

es'teso, a *pp di* **estendere** ♦ *ag* extensive, large; **scrivere per ~** to write in full.

estetica'mente *av* aesthetically.

es'tetico, a, ci, che *ag* aesthetic ♦ *sf* (*disciplina*) aesthetics *sg*; (*bellezza*) attractiveness; **chirurgia ~a** cosmetic surgery; **cura ~a** beauty treatment.

este'tista, i, e *smlf* beautician.

'**estimo** *sm* valuation; (*disciplina*) surveying.

es'tinguere *vt* to extinguish, put out; (*debito*) to pay off; (*conto*) to close; ~**rsi** *vr* to go out; (*specie*) to become extinct.

es'tinsi *etc vb vedi* **estinguere**.

es'tinto, a *pp di* **estinguere**.

estin'tore *sm* (*fire*) extinguisher.

estinzi'one [estin'tsjone] *sf* putting out; (*di specie*) extinction; (*di debito*) payment; (*di conto*) closing.

estir'pare *vt* (*pianta*) to uproot, pull up; (*dente*) to extract; (*tumore*) to remove;

(*fig: vizio*) to eradicate.

es'tivo, a *ag* summer *cpd*.

'**estone** *ag, smlf, sm* Estonian.

Es'tonia *sf*: **l'~** Estonia.

es'torcere [es'tɔrtʃere] *vt*: ~ **qc (a qn)** to extort sth (from sb).

estorsi'one *sf* extortion.

es'torto, a *pp di* **estorcere**.

estra'dare *vt* to extradite.

estradizi'one [estradit'tsjone] *sf* extradition.

es'trae, es'traggo *etc vb vedi* **estrarre**.

es'traneo, a *ag* foreign; (*discorso*) extraneous, unrelated ♦ *smlf* stranger; **rimanere ~ a qc** to take no part in sth; **sentirsi ~ a** (*famiglia, società*) to feel alienated from; "**ingresso vietato agli ~i**" "no admittance to unauthorized personnel".

estrani'arsi *vr*: ~ **(da)** to cut o.s. off (from).

es'trarre *vt* to extract; (*minerali*) to mine; (*sorteggiare*) to draw; ~ **a sorte** to draw lots.

es'trassi *etc vb vedi* **estrarre**.

es'tratto, a *pp di* **estrarre** ♦ *sm* extract; (*di documento*) abstract; ~ **conto** (bank) statement; ~ **di nascita** birth certificate.

estrazi'one [estrat'tsjone] *sf* extraction; mining; drawing *no pl*; draw.

estrema'mente *av* extremely.

estre'mismo *sm* extremism.

estre'mista, i, e *smlf* extremist.

estremità *sf inv* extremity, end ♦ *sfpl* (*ANAT*) extremities.

es'tremo, a *ag* extreme; (*ultimo: ora, tentativo*) final, last ♦ *sm* extreme; (*di pazienza, forza*) limit, end; ~**i** *smpl* (*DIR*) essential elements; (*AMM: dati essenziali*) details, particulars; **l'E~ Oriente** the Far East.

estrinse'care *vt* to express, show.

'**estro** *sm* (*capriccio*) whim, fancy; (*ispirazione creativa*) inspiration.

estro'messo, a *pp di* **estromettere**.

estro'mettere *vt*: ~ **(da)** (*partito, club etc*) to expel (from); (*discussione*) to exclude (from).

estromissi'one *sf* expulsion.

es'troso, a *ag* whimsical, capricious; inspired.

estro'verso, a *ag, sm* extrovert.

estu'ario *sm* estuary.

esube'rante *ag* exuberant; (*COMM*) redundant (*BRIT*).

esube'ranza [ezube'rantsa] *sf* (*di persona*) exuberance; ~ **di personale** (*COMM*) overmanning (*BRIT*), over-staffing (*US*).

e'subero *sm*: ~ **di personale** surplus staff; **in** ~ redundant, due to be laid off.

esu'lare *vi*: ~ **da** (*competenza*) to be beyond; (*compiti*) not to be part of.

'esule *sm/f* exile.

esul'tanza [ezul'tantsa] *sf* exultation.

esul'tare *vi* to exult.

esu'mare *vt* (*salma*) to exhume, disinter; (*fig*) to unearth.

età *sf inv* age; **all'**~ **di 8 anni** at the age of 8, at 8 years of age; **ha la mia** ~ he (*o* she) is the same age as me *o* as I am; **di mezza** ~ middle-aged; **raggiungere la maggiore** ~ to come of age; **essere in** ~ **minore** to be under age; **in** ~ **avanzata** advanced in years.

eta'nolo *sm* ethanol.

etc. *abbr* etc.

'etere *sm* ether; **via** ~ on the airwaves.

e'tereo, a *ag* ethereal.

eternità *sf* eternity.

e'terno, a *ag* eternal; (*interminabile: lamenti, attesa*) never-ending; **in** ~ for ever, eternally.

etero'geneo, a [etero'dʒɛneo] *ag* heterogeneous.

eterosessu'ale *ag*, *sm/f* heterosexual.

'etica *sf vedi* **etico**.

eti'chetta [eti'ketta] *sf* label; (*cerimoniale*): **l'**~ etiquette.

'etico, a, ci, che *ag* ethical ♦ *sf* ethics *sg*.

eti'lometro *sm* Breathalyzer ⓡ.

etimolo'gia, 'gie [etimolo'dʒia] *sf* etymology.

etimo'logico, a, ci, che [etimo'lɔdʒiko] *ag* etymological.

e'tiope *ag*, *sm/f* Ethiopian.

Eti'opia *sf*: **l'**~ Ethiopia.

eti'opico, a, ci, che *ag*, *sm* (*LING*) Ethiopian.

'Etna *sm*: **l'**~ Etna.

'etnico, a, ci, che *ag* ethnic.

e'trusco, a, schi, sche *ag*, *sm/f* Etruscan.

'ettaro *sm* hectare (= *10,000 m²*).

'etto *sm abbr* = **ettogrammo**.

etto'grammo *sm* hectogram(me) (= *100 grams*).

et'tolitro *sm* hectolitre (*BRIT*), hectoliter (*US*).

et'tometro *sm* hectometre.

EU *abbr* = **Europa**.

euca'lipto *sm* eucalyptus.

Eucaris'tia *sf*: **l'**~ the Eucharist.

eufe'mismo *sm* euphemism.

eufe'mistico, a, ci, che *ag* euphemistic.

eufo'ria *sf* euphoria.

eu'forico, a, ci, che *ag* euphoric.

Eu'rasia *sf* Eurasia.

eurasi'atico, a, ci, che *ag*, *sm/f* Eurasian.

Eura'tom *sigla f* (= *Comunità Europea dell'Energia Atomica*) Euratom.

euro'corpo *sm* European force.

eurodepu'tato *sm* Euro MP.

eurodi'visa *sf* Eurocurrency.

euro'dollaro *sm* Eurodollar.

euromer'cato *sm* Euromarket.

euro'missile *sm* Euro-missile.

Eu'ropa *sf*: **l'**~ Europe.

euro'peo, a *ag*, *sm/f* European.

euro'scettico, a, ci, che [euroʃ'ʃettiko] *sm/f* Euro-sceptic.

eutana'sia *sf* euthanasia.

E.V. *abbr* = *Eccellenza Vostra*.

evacu'are *vt* to evacuate.

evacuazi'one [evakuat'tsjone] *sf* evacuation.

e'vadere *vi* (*fuggire*): ~ **da** to escape from ♦ *vt* (*sbrigare*) to deal with, dispatch; (*tasse*) to evade.

evan'gelico, a, ci, che [evan'dʒɛliko] *ag* evangelical.

evange'lista, i [evandʒe'lista] *sm* evangelist.

evapo'rare *vi* to evaporate.

evaporazi'one [evaporat'tsjone] *sf* evaporation.

e'vasi *etc vb vedi* **evadere**.

evasi'one *sf* (*vedi* **evadere**) escape; dispatch; **dare** ~ **ad un ordine** to carry out *o* execute an order; **letteratura d'**~ escapist literature; ~ **fiscale** tax evasion.

eva'sivo, a *ag* evasive.

e'vaso, a *pp di* **evadere** ♦ *sm* escapee.

eva'sore *sm*: ~ (**fiscale**) tax evader.

eveni'enza [eve'njɛntsa] *sf*: **nell'**~ **che ciò succeda** should that happen; **essere pronto ad ogni** ~ to be ready for anything *o* any eventuality.

e'vento *sm* event.

eventu'ale *ag* possible.

eventualità *sf inv* eventuality, possibility; **nell'**~ **di** in the event of.

eventual'mente *av* if need be, if necessary.

'Everest *sm*: **l'**~, **il Monte** ~ (Mount) Everest.

eversi'one *sf* subversion.

ever'sivo, a *ag* subversive.

evi'dente *ag* evident, obvious.

evidente'mente *av* evidently; (*palesemente*) obviously, evidently.

evi'denza [evi'dɛntsa] *sf* obviousness; **mettere in** ~ to point out, highlight; **tenere in** ~ **qc** to bear sth in mind.

evidenzi'are [eviden'tsjare] *vt* (*sottolineare*) to emphasize, highlight; (*con

evidenziatore) to highlight.
evidenzia'tore [evidentsja'tore] *sm* (*penna*) highlighter.
evi'rare *vt* to castrate.
evi'tabile *ag* avoidable.
evi'tare *vt* to avoid; ~ **di fare** to avoid doing; ~ **qc a qn** to spare sb sth.
'evo *sm* age, epoch.
evo'care *vt* to evoke.
evoca'tivo, a *ag* evocative.
evocherò *etc* [evoke'rɔ] *vb vedi* **evocare**.
evolu'tivo, a *ag* (*gen*, *BIOL*) evolutionary; (*MED*) progressive.
evo'luto, a *pp di* **evolversi** ♦ *ag* (*popolo*, *civiltà*) (highly) developed, advanced; (*persona: emancipato*) independent; (: *senza pregiudizi*) broad-minded.
evoluzi'one [evolut'tsjone] *sf* evolution.
e'volversi *vr* to evolve; **con l'~ della situazione** as the situation develops.
ev'viva *escl* hurrah!; ~ **il re!** long live the king!, hurrah for the king!
ex *prefisso* ex-, former ♦ *sm/f inv* ex-boyfriend/girlfriend.
ex 'aequo [ɛg'zɛkwo] *av*: **classificarsi primo** ~ to come joint first, come equal first.
'extra *ag inv*, *sm inv* extra.
extracomuni'tario, a *ag* non-EEC ♦ *sm/f* non-EEC national (*often referring to non-European immigrant*).
extraconiu'gale *ag* extramarital.
extraparlamen'tare *ag* extraparliamentary.
extrasensori'ale *ag*: **percezione** *f* ~ extrasensory perception.
extrater'restre *ag*, *sm/f* extraterrestrial.
extraur'bano, a *ag* suburban.

Ff

F, f ['effe] *sf o m inv* (*lettera*) F, f; **F come Firenze** ≈ F for Frederick (*BRIT*), F for Fox (*US*).
F *abbr* (= *Fahrenheit*) F.
F. *abbr* (= *fiume*) R.
fa *vb vedi* **fare** ♦ *sm inv* (*MUS*) F; (: *solfeggiando la scala*) fa ♦ *av*: **10 anni** ~ 10 years ago.
fabbi'sogno [fabbi'zoɲɲo] *sm* needs *pl*, requirements *pl*; **il** ~ **nazionale di petrolio** the country's oil requirements; ~ **del**

settore pubblico public sector borrowing requirement (*BRIT*), government debt borrowing (*US*).
'fabbrica *sf* factory.
fabbri'cante *sm* manufacturer, maker.
fabbri'care *vt* to build; (*produrre*) to manufacture, make; (*fig*) to fabricate, invent.
fabbri'cato *sm* building.
fabbricazi'one [fabbrikat'tsjone] *sf* building, fabrication; making, manufacture, manufacturing.
'fabbro *sm* (black)smith.
fac'cenda [fat'tʃenda] *sf* matter, affair; (*cosa da fare*) task, chore; **le** ~**e domestiche** the housework *sg*.
faccendi'ere [fattʃen'djɛre] *sm* wheeler-dealer, (shady) operator.
fac'cetta [fat'tʃetta] *sf* (*di pietra preziosa*) facet.
fac'chino [fak'kino] *sm* porter.
'faccia, ce ['fattʃa] *sf* face; (*di moneta*, *medaglia*) side; ~ **a** ~ face to face; **di** ~ **a** opposite, facing; **avere la** ~ **(tosta) di dire/fare qc** to have the cheek *o* nerve to say/do sth; **fare qc alla** ~ **di qn** to do sth to spite sb; **leggere qc in** ~ **a qn** to see sth written all over sb's face.
facci'ata [fat'tʃata] *sf* façade; (*di pagina*) side.
'faccio *etc* ['fattʃo] *vb vedi* **fare**.
fa'cente [fa'tʃente]: ~ **funzione** *sm* (*AMM*) deputy.
fa'cessi *etc* [fa'tʃessi] *vb vedi* **fare**.
fa'ceto, a [fa'tʃeto] *ag* witty, humorous.
fa'cevo *etc* [fa'tʃevo] *vb vedi* **fare**.
fa'cezia [fa'tʃɛttsja] *sf* witticism, witty remark.
fa'chiro [fa'kiro] *sm* fakir.
'facile ['fatʃile] *ag* easy; (*affabile*) easy-going; (*disposto*): ~ **a** inclined to, prone to; (*probabile*): **è** ~ **che piova** it's likely to rain; **donna di** ~**i costumi** woman of easy virtue, loose woman.
facilità [fatʃili'ta] *sf* easiness; (*disposizione*, *dono*) aptitude.
facili'tare [fatʃili'tare] *vt* to make easier.
facilitazi'one [fatʃilitat'tsjone] *sf* (*gen*) facilities *pl*; ~**i di pagamento** easy terms, credit facilities.
facil'mente [fatʃil'mente] *av* (*gen*) easily; (*probabilmente*) probably.
faci'lone, a [fatʃi'lone] *sm/f* (*peg*) happy-go-lucky person.
facino'roso, a [fatʃino'roso] *ag* violent.
facoltà *sf inv* faculty; (*CHIM*) property; (*autorità*) power.
facolta'tivo, a *ag* optional; (*fermata*

d'autobus) request *cpd*.

facol'toso, a *ag* wealthy, rich.

fac'simile *sm* facsimile.

'faggio ['faddʒo] *sm* beech.

fagi'ano [fa'dʒano] *sm* pheasant.

fagio'lino [fadʒo'lino] *sm* French (*BRIT*) *o* string bean.

fagi'olo [fa'dʒɔlo] *sm* bean; **capitare a** ~ to come at the right time.

fagoci'tare [fagotʃi'tare] *vt* (*fig: industria etc*) to absorb, swallow up; (*scherzoso: cibo*) to devour.

fa'gotto *sm* bundle; (*MUS*) bassoon; **far** ~ (*fig*) to pack up and go.

'fai *vb vedi* **fare**.

'faida *sf* feud.

'fai-da-'te *sm inv* DIY, do-it-yourself.

fa'ina *sf* (*ZOOL*) stone marten.

'Fahrenheit ['faːrənheit] *sm* Fahrenheit.

fa'lange [fa'landʒe] *sf* (*ANAT, MIL*) phalanx.

fal'cata *sf* stride.

'falce ['faltʃe] *sf* scythe; ~ **e martello** (*POL*) hammer and sickle.

fal'cetto [fal'tʃetto] *sm* sickle.

falci'are [fal'tʃare] *vt* to cut; (*fig*) to mow down.

falcia'trice [faltʃa'tritʃe] *sf* (*per fieno*) reaping machine; (*per erba*) mowing machine.

'falco, chi *sm* (*anche fig*) hawk.

fal'cone *sm* falcon.

'falda *sf* (*GEO*) layer, stratum; (*di cappello*) brim; (*di cappotto*) tails *pl*; (*di monte*) lower slope; (*di tetto*) pitch; (*di neve*) flake; **abito a** ~**e** tails *pl*.

fale'gname [falen'ɲame] *sm* joiner.

fa'lena *sf* (*ZOOL*) moth.

'Falkland ['fɔːlklənd] *sfpl*: **le isole** ~ the Falkland Islands.

fal'lace [fal'latʃe] *ag* misleading, deceptive.

'fallico, a, ci, che *ag* phallic.

fallimen'tare *ag* (*COMM*) bankruptcy *cpd*; **bilancio** ~ negative balance, deficit; **diritto** ~ bankruptcy law.

falli'mento *sm* failure; bankruptcy.

fal'lire *vi* (*non riuscire*): ~ (**in**) to fail (in); (*DIR*) to go bankrupt ♦ *vt* (*colpo, bersaglio*) to miss.

fal'lito, a *ag* unsuccessful; bankrupt ♦ *smf* bankrupt.

'fallo *sm* error, mistake; (*imperfezione*) defect, flaw; (*SPORT*) foul; fault; (*ANAT*) phallus; **senza** ~ without fail; **cogliere qn in** ~ to catch sb out; **mettere il piede in** ~ to slip.

fal'locrate *sm* male chauvinist.

falò *sm inv* bonfire.

fal'sare *vt* to distort, misrepresent.

falsa'riga, ghe *sf* lined page, ruled page; **sulla** ~ **di** ... (*fig*) along the lines of ....

fal'sario *sm* forger; counterfeiter.

falsifi'care *vt* to forge; (*monete*) to forge, counterfeit.

falsità *sf inv* (*di persona, notizia*) falseness; (*bugia*) falsehood, lie.

'falso, a *ag* false; (*errato*) wrong; (*falsificato*) forged; fake; (: *oro, gioielli*) imitation *cpd* ♦ *sm* forgery; **essere un** ~ **magro** to be heavier than one looks; **giurare il** ~ to commit perjury; ~ **in atto pubblico** forgery (of a legal document).

'fama *sf* fame; (*reputazione*) reputation, name.

'fame *sf* hunger; **aver** ~ to be hungry; **fare la** ~ (*fig*) to starve, exist at subsistence level.

fa'melico, a, ci, che *ag* ravenous.

famige'rato, a [famidʒe'rato] *ag* notorious, ill-famed.

fa'miglia [fa'miʎʎa] *sf* family.

famili'are *ag* (*della propria famiglia*) family *cpd*; (*ben noto*) familiar; (*rapporti, atmosfera*) friendly; (*LING*) informal, colloquial ♦ *smf* relative, relation; **una vettura** ~ a family car.

familiarità *sf* familiarity; friendliness; informality.

familiariz'zare [familjarid'dzare] *vi*: ~ **con qn** to get to know sb; **abbiamo familiarizzato subito** we got on well together from the start.

fa'moso, a *ag* famous, well-known.

fa'nale *sm* (*AUT*) light, lamp (*BRIT*); (*luce stradale, NAUT*) light; (*di faro*) beacon.

fa'natico, a, ci, che *ag* fanatical; (*del teatro, calcio etc*): ~ **di** *o* **per** mad *o* crazy about ♦ *smf* fanatic; (*tifoso*) fan.

fana'tismo *sm* fanaticism.

fanciul'lezza [fantʃul'lettsa] *sf* childhood.

fanci'ullo, a [fan'tʃullo] *smf* child.

fan'donia *sf* tall story; ~**e** *sfpl* nonsense *sg*.

fan'fara *sf* brass band; (*musica*) fanfare.

fanfa'rone *sm* braggart.

fan'ghiglia [fan'giʎʎa] *sf* mire, mud.

'fango, ghi *sm* mud; **fare i** ~**ghi** (*MED*) to take a course of mud baths.

fan'goso, a *ag* muddy.

'fanno *vb vedi* **fare**.

fannul'lone, a *smf* idler, loafer.

fantasci'enza [fantaʃ'ʃɛntsa] *sf* science fiction.

fanta'sia *sf* fantasy, imagination; (*capriccio*) whim, caprice ♦ *ag inv*: **vestito** ~ patterned dress.

fantasi'oso, a *ag* (*dotato di fantasia*) imaginative; (*bizzarro*) fanciful, strange.

fan'tasma, i *sm* ghost, phantom.
fantasti'care *vi* to daydream.
fantasti'che'ria [fantastike'ria] *sf* daydream.
fan'tastico, a, ci, che *ag* fantastic; (*potenza, ingegno*) imaginative.
'fante *sm* infantryman; (*CARTE*) jack, knave (*BRIT*).
fante'ria *sf* infantry.
fan'tino *sm* jockey.
fan'toccio [fan'tɔttʃo] *sm* puppet.
fanto'matico, a, ci, che *ag* (*nave, esercito*) phantom *cpd*; (*personaggio*) mysterious.
FAO *sigla f* FAO (= *Food and Agriculture Organization*).
fara'butto *sm* crook.
fara'ona *sf* guinea fowl.
fara'one *sm* (*STORIA*) Pharaoh.
fara'onico, a, ci, che *ag* of the Pharaohs; (*fig*) enormous, huge.
far'cire [far'tʃire] *vt* (*carni, peperoni etc*) to stuff; (*torte*) to fill.
fard [far] *sm inv* blusher.
far'dello *sm* bundle; (*fig*) burden.

========= *PAROLA CHIAVE* =========

'fare *sm* 1 (*modo di fare*): **con ~ distratto** absent-mindedly; **ha un ~ simpatico** he has a pleasant manner
2: **sul far del giorno/della notte** at daybreak/nightfall
♦ *vt* 1 (*fabbricare, creare*) to make; (: *casa*) to build; (: *assegno*) to make out; **~ una promessa/un film** to make a promise/a film; **~ rumore** to make a noise
2 (*effettuare: lavoro, attività, studi*) to do; (: *sport*) to play; **cosa fa?** (*adesso*) what are you doing?; (*di professione*) what do you do?; **~ psicologia/italiano** to do psychology/Italian; **~ tennis** to play tennis; **~ un viaggio** to go on a trip *o* journey; **~ una passeggiata** to go for a walk; **~ la spesa** to do the shopping
3 (*funzione*) to be; (*TEAT*) to play; **~ il medico** to be a doctor; **~ il malato** (*fingere*) to act the invalid
4 (*suscitare: sentimenti*): **~ paura a qn** to frighten sb; **mi fa rabbia** it makes me angry; **(non) fa niente** (*non importa*) it doesn't matter
5 (*ammontare*): **3 più 3 fa 6** 3 and 3 are *o* make 6; **fanno 6.000 lire** that's 6,000 lire; **Roma fa oltre 2.000.000 di abitanti** Rome has over 2,000,000 inhabitants; **che ora fai?** what time do you make it?
6 (+ *infinito*): **far ~ qc a qn** (*obbligare*) to make sb do sth; (*permettere*) to let sb do sth; **~ piangere/ridere qn** to make sb

cry/laugh; **~ venire qn** to send for sb; **fammi vedere** let me see; **far partire il motore** to start (up) the engine; **far riparare la macchina/costruire una casa** to get *o* have the car repaired/a house built
7: **~rsi**: **~rsi una gonna** to make o.s. a skirt; **~rsi un nome** to make a name for o.s.; **~rsi la permanente** to get a perm; **~rsi notare** to get o.s. noticed; **~rsi tagliare i capelli** to get one's hair cut; **~rsi operare** to have an operation
8 (*fraseologia*): **farcela** to succeed, manage; **non ce la faccio più** I can't go on; **ce la faremo** we'll make it; **me l'hanno fatta!** I've been done!; **lo facevo più giovane** I thought he was younger; **fare sì/no con la testa** to nod/shake one's head
♦ *vi* 1 (*agire*) to act, do; **fate come volete** do as you like; **~ presto** to be quick; **~ da** to act as; **non c'è niente da ~** it's no use; **saperci ~ con qn/qc** to know how to deal with sb/sth; **ci sa ~** she's very good at it; **faccia pure!** go ahead!
2 (*dire*) to say; **"davvero?" fece** "really?" he said
3: **~ per** (*essere adatto*) to be suitable for; **~ per ~ qc** to be about to do sth; **fece per andarsene** he made as if to leave
4: **~rsi: si fa così** you do it like this, this is the way it's done; **non si fa così!** (*rimprovero*) that's no way to behave!; **la festa non si fa** the party is off
5: **~ a gara con qn** to compete with sb; **~ a pugni** to come to blows; **~ in tempo a ~** to be in time to do
♦ *vb impers*: **fa bel tempo** the weather is fine; **fa caldo/freddo** it's hot/cold; **fa notte** it's getting dark
♦ *vr*: **~rsi** 1 (*diventare*) to become; **~rsi prete** to become a priest; **~rsi grande/vecchio** to grow tall/old
2 (*spostarsi*): **~rsi avanti/indietro** to move forward/back; **fatti più in là** move along a bit
3 (*fam: drogarsi*) to be a junkie.

fa'retra *sf* quiver.
far'falla *sf* butterfly.
farfugli'are [farfuʎ'ʎare] *vt, vi* to mumble, mutter.
fa'rina *sf* flour; **~ gialla** maize (*BRIT*) *o* corn (*US*) flour; **~ integrale** wholemeal (*BRIT*) *o* whole-wheat (*US*) flour; **questa non è ~ del tuo sacco** (*fig*) this isn't your own idea (*o* work).
fari'nacei [fari'natʃei] *smpl* starches.
fa'ringe [fa'rindʒe] *sf* (*ANAT*) pharynx.
farin'gite [farin'dʒite] *sf* pharyngitis.

fari'noso, a *ag* (*patate*) floury; (*neve, mela*) powdery.

farma'ceutico, a, ci, che [farma'tʃeutiko] *ag* pharmaceutical.

farma'cia, 'cie [farma'tʃia] *sf* pharmacy; (*negozio*) chemist's (shop) (*BRIT*), pharmacy.

farma'cista, i, e [farma'tʃista] *sm/f* chemist (*BRIT*), pharmacist.

'farmaco, ci *o* **chi** *sm* drug, medicine.

farneti'care *vi* to rave, be delirious.

'faro *sm* (*NAUT*) lighthouse; (*AER*) beacon; (*AUT*) headlight, headlamp (*BRIT*).

farragi'noso, a [farradʒi'noso] *ag* (*stile*) muddled, confused.

'farsa *sf* farce.

far'sesco, a, schi, sche *ag* farcical.

fasc. *abbr* = **fascicolo**.

'fascia, sce ['faʃʃa] *sf* band, strip; (*MED*) bandage; (*di sindaco, ufficiale*) sash; (*parte di territorio*) strip, belt; (*di contribuenti etc*) group, band; **essere in ~sce** (*anche fig*) to be in one's infancy; **~ oraria** time band.

fasci'are [faʃ'ʃare] *vt* to bind; (*MED*) to bandage; (*bambino*) to put a nappy (*BRIT*) *o* diaper (*US*) on.

fascia'tura [faʃʃa'tura] *sf* (*azione*) bandaging; (*fascia*) bandage.

fa'scicolo [faʃ'ʃikolo] *sm* (*di documenti*) file, dossier; (*di rivista*) issue, number; (*opuscolo*) booklet, pamphlet.

'fascino ['faʃʃino] *sm* charm, fascination.

'fascio ['faʃʃo] *sm* bundle, sheaf; (*di fiori*) bunch; (*di luce*) beam; (*POL*): **il F~** the Fascist Party.

fa'scismo [faʃ'ʃizmo] *sm* fascism.

fa'scista, i, e [faʃ'ʃista] *ag, sm/f* fascist.

'fase *sf* phase; (*TECN*) stroke; **in ~ di espansione** in a period of expansion; **essere fuori ~** (*motore*) to be rough (*BRIT*), run roughly; (*fig*) to feel rough (*BRIT*) *o* rotten.

fas'tidio *sm* bother, trouble; **dare ~ a qn** to bother *o* annoy sb; **sento ~ allo stomaco** my stomach's upset; **avere ~i con la polizia** to have trouble *o* bother with the police.

fastidi'oso, a *ag* annoying, tiresome; (*schifiltoso*) fastidious.

'fasto *sm* pomp, splendour (*BRIT*), splendor (*US*).

fas'toso, a *ag* sumptuous, lavish.

fa'sullo, a *ag* (*gen*) fake; (*dichiarazione, persona*) false; (*pretesto*) bogus.

'fata *sf* fairy.

fa'tale *ag* fatal; (*inevitabile*) inevitable; (*fig*) irresistible.

fata'lismo *sm* fatalism.

fatalità *sf inv* inevitability; (*avversità*) misfortune; (*fato*) fate, destiny.

fa'tato, a *ag* (*spada, chiave*) magic; (*castello*) enchanted.

fa'tica, che *sf* hard work, toil; (*sforzo*) effort; (*di metalli*) fatigue; **a ~** with difficulty; **respirare a ~** to have difficulty (in) breathing; **fare ~ a fare qc** to find it difficult to do sth; **animale da ~** beast of burden.

fati'caccia, ce [fati'kattʃa] *sf*: **fu una ~** it was hard work, it was a hell of a job (*fam*).

fati'care *vi* to toil; **~ a fare qc** to have difficulty doing sth.

fati'cata *sf* hard work.

fa'tichi *etc* [fa'tiki] *vb vedi* **faticare**.

fati'coso, a *ag* (*viaggio, camminata*) tiring, exhausting; (*lavoro*) laborious.

fa'tidico, a, ci, che *ag* fateful.

'fato *sm* fate, destiny.

Fatt. *abbr* (= **fattura**) inv.

fat'taccio [fat'tattʃo] *sm* foul deed.

fat'tezze [fat'tettse] *sfpl* features.

fat'tibile *ag* feasible, possible.

fattis'pecie [fattis'pɛtʃe] *sf*: **nella** *o* **in ~** in this case *o* instance.

'fatto, a *pp di* **fare** ♦ *ag*: **un uomo ~** a grown man ♦ *sm* fact; (*azione*) deed; (*avvenimento*) event, occurrence; (*di romanzo, film*) action, story; **~ a mano/in casa** hand-/home-made; **è ben ~a** she has a nice figure; **cogliere qn sul ~** to catch sb red-handed; **il ~ sta** *o* **è che** the fact remains *o* is that; **in ~ di** as for, as far as ... is concerned; **fare i ~i propri** to mind one's own business; **è uno che sa il ~ suo** he knows what he's about; **gli ho detto il ~ suo** I told him what I thought of him; **porre qn di fronte al ~ compiuto** to present sb with a fait accompli.

fat'tore *sm* (*AGR*) farm manager; (*MAT*: *elemento costitutivo*) factor.

fatto'ria *sf* farm; (*casa*) farmhouse.

fatto'rino *sm* errand boy; (*di ufficio*) office boy; (*d'albergo*) porter.

fattucchi'era [fattuk'kjɛra] *sf* witch.

fat'tura *sf* (*COMM*) invoice; (*di abito*) tailoring; (*malia*) spell; **pagamento contro presentazione ~** payment on invoice.

fattu'rare *vt* (*COMM*) to invoice; (*prodotto*) to produce; (*vino*) to adulterate.

fattu'rato *sm* (*COMM*) turnover.

fatturazi'one [fatturat'tsjone] *sf* billing, invoicing.

'fatuo, a *ag* vain, fatuous; **fuoco ~** (*anche fig*) will-o'-the-wisp.

'fauci ['fautʃi] *sfpl* (*di leone etc*) jaws; (*di vulcano*) mouth *sg*.

'fauna *sf* fauna.
'fausto, a *ag* (*formale*) happy; **un ~ presagio** a good omen.
fau'tore, 'trice *sm/f* advocate, supporter.
'fava *sf* broad bean.
fa'vella *sf* speech.
fa'villa *sf* spark.
'favo *sm* (*di api*) honeycomb.
'favola *sf* (*fiaba*) fairy tale; (*d'intento morale*) fable; (*fandonia*) yarn; **essere la ~ del paese** (*oggetto di critica*) to be the talk of the town; (*zimbello*) to be a laughing stock.
favo'loso, a *ag* fabulous; (*incredibile*) incredible.
fa'vore *sm* favour (*BRIT*), favor (*US*); **per ~** please; **prezzo/trattamento di ~** preferential price/treatment; **condizioni di ~** (*COMM*) favo(u)rable terms; **fare un ~ a qn** to do sb a favo(u)r; **col ~ delle tenebre** under cover of darkness.
favoreggia'mento [favoreddʒa'mento] *sm* (*DIR*) aiding and abetting.
favo'revole *ag* favourable (*BRIT*), favorable (*US*).
favo'rire *vt* to favour (*BRIT*), favor (*US*); (*il commercio, l'industria, le arti*) to promote, encourage; **vuole ~?** won't you help yourself?; **favorisca in salotto** please come into the sitting room; **mi favorisca i documenti** please may I see your papers?
favori'tismo *sm* favouritism (*BRIT*), favoritism (*US*).
favo'rito, a *ag, sm/f* favourite (*BRIT*), favorite (*US*).
fax *sm inv* fax; **mandare qc via ~** to fax sth.
fa'xare *vt* to fax.
fazi'one [fat'tsjone] *sf* faction.
faziosità [fattsjosi'ta] *sf* sectarianism.
fazzo'letto [fattso'letto] *sm* handkerchief; (*per la testa*) (head)scarf.
F.B.I. *sigla f* (= *Federal Bureau of Investigation*) FBI.
F.C. *abbr* = **fuoricorso.**
f.co *abbr* = **franco.**
FE *sigla* = **Ferrara.**
febb. *abbr* (= *febbraio*) Feb.
feb'braio *sm* February; *per fraseologia vedi* **luglio.**
'febbre *sf* fever; **aver la ~** to have a high temperature; **~ da fieno** hay fever.
feb'brile *ag* (*anche fig*) feverish.
'feccia, ce ['fettʃa] *sf* dregs *pl.*
'feci ['fɛtʃi] *sfpl* faeces, excrement *sg.*
'feci *etc* ['fɛtʃi] *vb vedi* **fare.**
'fecola *sf* potato flour.
fecon'dare *vt* to fertilize.

fecondazi'one [fekondat'tsjone] *sf* fertilization; **~ artificiale** artificial insemination.
fecondità *sf* fertility.
fe'condo, a *ag* fertile.
'Fedcom *sigla m* = *Fondo Europeo di Cooperazione Monetaria.*
'fede *sf* (*credenza*) belief, faith; (*REL*) faith; (*fiducia*) faith, trust; (*fedeltà*) loyalty; (*anello*) wedding ring; (*attestato*) certificate; **aver ~ in qn** to have faith in sb; **tener ~ a** (*ideale*) to remain loyal to; (*giuramento, promessa*) to keep; **in buona/ cattiva ~** in good/bad faith; "**in ~**" (*DIR*) "in witness whereof".
fe'dele *ag* (*leale*): **~ (a)** faithful (to); (*veritiero*) true, accurate ♦ *sm/f* follower; **i ~i** (*REL*) the faithful.
fedeltà *sf* faithfulness; (*coniugale*) fidelity; (*esattezza: di copia, traduzione*) accuracy; **alta ~** (*RADIO*) high fidelity.
'federa *sf* pillowslip, pillowcase.
fede'rale *ag* federal.
federa'lismo *sm* (*POL*) federalism.
federa'lista, i, e *ag, sm/f* (*POL*) federalist.
federazi'one [federat'tsjone] *sf* federation.
Feder'caccia [feder'kattʃa] *abbr f* (= *Federazione Italiana della Caccia*) hunting federation.
Feder'calcio [feder'kaltʃo] *abbr m* (= *Federazione Italiana Gioco Calcio*) Italian football association.
Federcon'sorzi [federkon'sɔrtsi] *abbr f* (= *Federazione Italiana dei Consorzi Agrari*) federation of farmers' cooperatives.
fe'difrago, a, ghi, ghe *ag* faithless, perfidious.
fe'dina *sf* (*DIR*): **~ (penale)** record; **avere la ~ penale sporca** to have a police record.
'fegato *sm* liver; (*fig*) guts *pl*, nerve; **mangiarsi o rodersi il ~** to be consumed with rage.
'felce ['feltʃe] *sf* fern.
fe'lice [fe'litʃe] *ag* happy; (*fortunato*) lucky.
felicità [felitʃi'ta] *sf* happiness.
felici'tarsi [felitʃi'tarsi] *vr* (*congratularsi*): **~ con qn per qc** to congratulate sb on sth.
felicitazi'oni [felitʃitat'tsjoni] *sfpl* congratulations.
fe'lino, a *ag, sm* feline.
'felpa *sf* sweatshirt.
fel'pato, a *ag* (*tessuto*) brushed; (*passo*) stealthy; **con passo ~** stealthily.
'feltro *sm* felt.
'femmina *sf* (*ZOOL, TECN*) female; (*figlia*) girl, daughter; (*spesso peg*) woman.
femmi'nile *ag* feminine; (*sesso*) female; (*lavoro, giornale*) woman's, women's;

(*moda*) women's ♦ *sm* (*LING*) feminine.
femmi'nilità *sf* femininity.
femmi'nismo *sm* feminism.
femmi'nista, i, e *ag, sm/f* feminist.
'femore *sm* thighbone, femur.
'fendere *vt* to cut through.
fendi'nebbia *sm inv* (*AUT*) fog lamp.
fendi'tura *sf* (*gen*) crack; (*di roccia*) cleft, crack.
fenome'nale *ag* phenomenal.
fe'nomeno *sm* phenomenon.
'feretro *sm* coffin.
feri'ale *ag*: **giorno** ~ weekday, working day.
'ferie *sfpl* holidays (*BRIT*), vacation *sg* (*US*); **andare in** ~ to go on holiday *o* vacation; **25 giorni di** ~ **pagate** 25 days' holiday *o* vacation with pay.
feri'mento *sm* wounding.
fe'rire *vt* to injure; (*deliberatamente: MIL etc*) to wound; (*colpire*) to hurt; ~**rsi** *vr* to hurt o.s., injure o.s.
fe'rito, a *sm/f* wounded *o* injured man/woman ♦ *sf* injury; wound.
feri'toia *sf* slit.
'ferma *sf* (*MIL*) (period of) service; (*CACCIA*): **cane da** ~ pointer.
ferma'carte *sm inv* paperweight.
fermacra'vatta *sm inv* tiepin (*BRIT*), tie tack (*US*).
fer'maglio [fer'maʎʎo] *sm* clasp; (*gioiello*) brooch; (*per documenti*) clip.
ferma'mente *av* firmly.
fer'mare *vt* to stop, halt; (*POLIZIA*) to detain, hold; (*bottone etc*) to fasten, fix ♦ *vi* to stop; ~**rsi** *vr* to stop, halt; ~**rsi a fare qc** to stop to do sth.
fer'mata *sf* stop; ~ **dell'autobus** bus stop.
fermen'tare *vi* to ferment; (*fig*) to be in a ferment.
fermentazi'one [fermentat'tsjone] *sf* fermentation.
fer'mento *sm* (*anche fig*) ferment; (*lievito*) yeast.
fer'mezza [fer'mettsa] *sf* (*fig*) firmness, steadfastness.
'fermo, a *ag* still, motionless; (*veicolo*) stationary; (*orologio*) not working; (*saldo: anche fig*) firm; (*voce, mano*) steady ♦ *escl* stop!; keep still! ♦ *sm* (*chiusura*) catch, lock; (*DIR*): ~ **di polizia** police detention; ~ **restando che** ... it being understood that ....
'fermo 'posta *av, sm inv* poste restante (*BRIT*), general delivery (*US*).
fe'roce [fe'rɔtʃe] *ag* (*animale*) wild, fierce, ferocious; (*persona*) cruel, fierce; (*fame, dolore*) raging.

fe'rocia, cie [fe'rɔtʃa] *sf* ferocity.
Ferr. *abbr* = **ferrovia.**
fer'raglia [fer'raʎʎa] *sf* scrap iron.
ferra'gosto *sm* (*festa*) feast of the Assumption; (*periodo*) August holidays *pl* (*BRIT*) *o* vacation (*US*).

> Ferragosto is a national holiday which falls on August 15th. Its origins are religious, marking the feast of the Assumption on that date. However, in recent years it has simply become the most important public holiday of the summer season. Most people now extend the holiday by taking the days around the 15th off too and head out of the towns and cities to the holiday resorts. Consequently, during this period, most of industry and commerce is at a standstill.

ferra'menta *sfpl* ironmongery *sg* (*BRIT*), hardware *sg*; **negozio di** ~ ironmonger's (*BRIT*), hardware shop *o* store (*US*).
fer'rare *vt* (*cavallo*) to shoe.
fer'rato, a *ag* (*FERR*): **strada** ~**a** a railway line (*BRIT*), railroad line (*US*); (*fig*): **essere** ~ **in** (*materia*) to be well up in.
ferra'vecchio [ferra'vɛkkjo] *sm* scrap merchant.
'ferreo, a *ag* iron *cpd*.
ferri'era *sf* ironworks *sg o pl*.
'ferro *sm* iron; **una bistecca ai** ~**i** a grilled steak; **mettere a** ~ **e fuoco** to put to the sword; **essere ai** ~**i corti** (*fig*) to be at daggers drawn; **tocca** ~! touch wood!; ~ **battuto** wrought iron; ~ **di cavallo** horseshoe; ~ **da stiro** iron; ~**i da calza** knitting needles; **i** ~**i del mestiere** the tools of the trade.
ferrotranvi'ario, a *ag* public transport *cpd*.
Ferrotranvi'eri *abbr f* (= *Federazione Nazionale Lavoratori Autoferrotranvieri e Internavigatori*) *transport workers' union*.
ferro'vecchio [ferro'vɛkkjo] *sm* = **ferravecchio.**
ferro'via *sf* railway (*BRIT*), railroad (*US*).
ferrovi'ario, a *ag* railway *cpd* (*BRIT*), railroad *cpd* (*US*).
ferrovi'ere *sm* railwayman (*BRIT*), railroad man (*US*).
'fertile *ag* fertile.
fertilità *sf* fertility.
fertiliz'zante [fertilid'dzante] *sm* fertilizer.
fertiliz'zare [fertilid'dzare] *vt* to fertilize.
fer'vente *ag* fervent, ardent.
'fervere *vi*: **fervono i preparativi per** ... they are making feverish preparations for ....
'fervido, a *ag* fervent, ardent.
fer'vore *sm* fervour (*BRIT*), fervor (*US*),

ardour (*BRIT*), ardor (*US*); (*punto culminante*) height.

'**fesa** *sf* (*CUC*) rump of veal.

fesse'ria *sf* stupidity; **dire ~e** to talk nonsense.

'**fesso, a** *pp di* **fendere** ♦ *ag* (*fam: sciocco*) crazy, cracked.

fes'sura *sf* crack, split; (*per gettone, moneta*) slot.

'**festa** *sf* (*religiosa*) feast; (*pubblica*) holiday; (*compleanno*) birthday; (*onomastico*) name day; (*ricevimento*) celebration, party; **far ~** to have a holiday; (*far baldoria*) to live it up; **far ~ a qn** to give sb a warm welcome; **essere vestito a ~** to be dressed up to the nines; **~ comandata** (*REL*) holiday of obligation; **la ~ della mamma/del papà** Mother's/Father's Day.

The **Festa della Repubblica**, *which takes place on June 2nd, celebrates the founding of the Italian Republic after the fall of the monarchy and the subsequent referendum in 1946. It is marked by military parades and political speeches.*

---

festeggia'menti [festeddʒa'menti] *smpl* celebrations.

festeggi'are [fested'dʒare] *vt* to celebrate; (*persona*) to have a celebration for.

fes'tino *sm* party; (*con balli*) ball.

fes'tivo, a *ag* (*atmosfera*) festive; **giorno ~** holiday.

fes'toso, a *ag* merry, joyful.

fe'tente *ag* (*puzzolente*) fetid; (*comportamento*) disgusting ♦ *sm/f* (*fam*) stinker, rotter (*BRIT*).

fe'ticcio [fe'tittʃo] *sm* fetish.

'**feto** *sm* foetus (*BRIT*), fetus (*US*).

fe'tore *sm* stench, stink.

'**fetta** *sf* slice.

fet'tuccia, ce [fet'tuttʃa] *sf* tape, ribbon.

fettuc'cine [fettut'tʃine] *sfpl* (*CUC*) ribbon-shaped pasta.

feu'dale *ag* feudal.

'**feudo** *sm* (*STORIA*) fief; (*fig*) stronghold.

ff *abbr* (*AMM*) = **facente funzione**; (= *fogli*) pp.

FF.AA. *abbr* = **forze armate**.

FF.SS. *abbr* (= *Ferrovie dello Stato*) Italian railways.

FG *sigla* = *Foggia*.

FI *sigla* = *Firenze*.

fi'aba *sf* fairy tale.

fia'besco, a, schi, sche *ag* fairy-tale *cpd*.

fi'acca *sf* weariness; (*svogliatezza*) listlessness; **battere la ~** to shirk.

fiac'care *vt* to weaken.

fiaccherò *etc* [fjakke'rɔ] *vb vedi* **fiaccare**.

fi'acco, a, chi, che *ag* (*stanco*) tired, weary; (*svogliato*) listless; (*debole*) weak; (*mercato*) slack.

fi'accola *sf* torch.

fiacco'lata *sf* torchlight procession.

fi'ala *sf* phial.

fi'amma *sf* flame; (*NAUT*) pennant.

fiam'mante *ag* (*colore*) flaming; **nuovo ~** brand new.

fiam'mata *sf* blaze.

fiammeggi'are [fjammed'dʒare] *vi* to blaze.

fiam'mifero *sm* match.

fiam'mingo, a, ghi, ghe *ag* Flemish ♦ *sm/f* Fleming ♦ *sm* (*LING*) Flemish; (*ZOOL*) flamingo; **i F~ghi** the Flemish.

fian'cata *sf* (*di nave etc*) side; (*NAUT*) broadside.

fiancheggi'are [fjanked'dʒare] *vt* to border; (*fig*) to support, back (up); (*MIL*) to flank.

fi'anco, chi *sm* side; (*di persona*) hip; (*MIL*) flank; **di ~** sideways, from the side; **a ~ a ~** side by side; **prestare il proprio ~ alle critiche** to leave o.s. open to criticism; **~ destr/sinistr!** (*MIL*) right/left turn!

Fi'andre *sfpl*: **le ~** Flanders *sg*.

fiaschette'ria [fjaskette'ria] *sf* wine shop.

fi'asco, schi *sm* flask; (*fig*) fiasco; **fare ~** to be a fiasco.

fia'tare *vi* (*fig: parlare*): **senza ~** without saying a word.

fi'ato *sm* breath; (*resistenza*) stamina; **~i** *smpl* (*MUS*) wind instruments; **avere il ~ grosso** to be out of breath; **prendere ~** to catch one's breath; **bere qc tutto d'un ~** to drink sth in one go *o* gulp.

'**fibbia** *sf* buckle.

'**fibra** *sf* fibre, fiber (*US*); (*fig*) constitution; **~ ottica** optical fibre; **~ di vetro** fibreglass (*BRIT*), fiberglass (*US*).

ficca'naso, *pl(m)* **~i**, *pl(f)* *inv sm/f* busybody, nos(e)y parker.

fic'care *vt* to push, thrust, drive; **~rsi** *vr* (*andare a finire*) to get to; **~ il naso negli affari altrui** (*fig*) to poke o stick one's nose into other people's business; **~rsi nei pasticci** *o* **nei guai** to get into hot water *o* a fix.

ficcherò *etc* [fikke'rɔ] *vb vedi* **ficcare**.

fiche [fiʃ] *sf inv* (*nei giochi d'azzardo*) chip.

'**fico, chi** *sm* (*pianta*) fig tree; (*frutto*) fig; **~ d'India** prickly pear; **~ secco** dried fig.

fidanza'mento [fidantsa'mento] *sm* engagement.

fidan'zarsi [fidan'tsarsi] *vr* to get engaged.

fidan'zato, a [fidan'tsato] *sm/f* fiancé/fiancée.

fi'darsi *vr*: **~ di** to trust; **~rsi è bene non**

~rsi è meglio (*proverbio*) better safe than sorry.

fi'dato, a *ag* reliable, trustworthy.

fide'ismo *sm* unquestioning belief.

fide'istico, a, ci, che *ag* (*atteggiamento, posizione*) totally uncritical.

fideius'sore *sm* (*DIR*) guarantor.

'fido, a *ag* faithful, loyal ♦ *sm* (*COMM*) credit.

fi'ducia [fi'dutʃa] *sf* confidence, trust; **incarico di** ~ position of trust, responsible position; **persona di** ~ reliable person; **è il mio uomo di** ~ he is my right-hand man; **porre la questione di** ~ (*POL*) to ask for a vote of confidence.

fiduci'oso, a [fidu'tʃoso] *ag* trusting.

fi'ele *sm* (*MED*) bile; (*fig*) bitterness.

fie'nile *sm* hayloft.

fi'eno *sm* hay.

fi'era *sf* fair; (*animale*) wild beast; ~ **di beneficenza** charity bazaar; ~ **campionaria** trade fair.

fie'rezza [fje'rettsa] *sf* pride.

fi'ero, a *ag* proud; (*crudele*) fierce, cruel; (*audace*) bold.

fi'evole *ag* (*luce*) dim; (*suono*) weak.

F.I.F.A. *sigla f* (= *Fédération Internationale de Football Association*) FIFA.

'fifa *sf* (*fam*): **aver** ~ to have the jitters.

fi'fone, a *sm/f* (*fam, scherzoso*) coward.

fig. *abbr* (= *figura*) fig.

FIGC *sigla f* (= *Federazione Italiana Gioco Calcio*) *Italian football association.*

'Figi ['fidʒi] *sfpl*: **le isole** ~ Fiji, the Fiji Islands.

'figlia ['fiʎʎa] *sf* daughter; (*COMM*) counterfoil (*BRIT*), stub.

figli'are [fiʎ'ʎare] *vi* to give birth.

figli'astro, a [fiʎ'ʎastro] *sm/f* stepson/daughter.

'figlio ['fiʎʎo] *sm* son; (*senza distinzione di sesso*) child; ~ **d'arte: essere** ~ **d'arte** to come from a theatrical (*o* musical *etc*) family; ~ **di puttana** (*fam!*) son of a bitch (!); ~ **unico** only child.

figli'occio, a, ci, ce [fiʎ'ʎɔttʃo] *sm/f* godchild, godson/daughter.

figli'ola [fiʎ'ʎɔla] *sf* daughter; (*fig: ragazza*) girl.

figli'olo [fiʎ'ʎɔlo] *sm* (*anche fig: ragazzo*) son.

fi'gura *sf* figure; (*forma, aspetto esterno*) form, shape; (*illustrazione*) picture, illustration; **far** ~ to look smart; **fare una brutta** ~ to make a bad impression; **che** ~! how embarrassing!

figu'raccia, ce [figu'rattʃa] *sf*: **fare una** ~ to create a bad impression.

figu'rare *vi* to appear ♦ *vt*: ~**rsi qc** to

imagine sth; ~**rsi** *vr*: **figurati!** imagine that!; **ti do noia?** — **ma figurati!** am I disturbing you? — not at all! ·

figura'tivo, a *ag* figurative.

figu'rina *sf* (*statuetta*) figurine; (*cartoncino*) picture card.

figuri'nista, i, e *sm/f* dress designer.

figu'rino *sm* fashion sketch.

fi'guro *sm*: **un losco** ~ a suspicious character.

figu'rone *sm*: **fare un** ~ (*persona, oggetto*) to look terrific; (*persona: con un discorso etc*) to make an excellent impression.

'fila *sf* row, line; (*coda*) queue; (*serie*) series, string; **di** ~ in succession; **fare la** ~ to queue; **in** ~ **indiana** in single file.

fila'mento *sm* filament.

fi'lanca ® *sf* stretch material.

fi'landa *sf* spinning mill.

fi'lante *ag*: **stella** ~ (*stella cadente*) shooting star; (*striscia di carta*) streamer.

filantro'pia *sf* philanthropy.

filan'tropico, a, ci, che *ag* philanthropic(al).

fi'lantropo *sm* philanthropist.

fi'lare *vt* to spin; (*NAUT*) to pay out ♦ *vi* (*baco, ragno*) to spin; (*formaggio fuso*) to go stringy; (*liquido*) to trickle; (*discorso*) to hang together; (*fam: amoreggiare*) to go steady; (*muoversi a forte velocità*) to go at full speed; (*andarsene lestamente*) to make o.s. scarce ♦ *sm* (*di alberi etc*) row, line; ~ **diritto** (*fig*) to toe the line.

filar'monico, a, ci, che *ag* philharmonic.

filas'trocca, che *sf* nursery rhyme.

filate'lia *sf* philately, stamp collecting.

fi'lato, a *ag* spun ♦ *sm* yarn ♦ *av*: **vai dritto** ~ **a casa** go straight home; **3 giorni** ~**i** 3 days running *o* on end.

fila'tura *sf* spinning; (*luogo*) spinning mill.

fi'letto *sm* (*ornamento*) braid, trimming; (*di vite*) thread; (*di carne*) fillet.

fili'ale *ag* filial ♦ *sf* (*di impresa*) branch.

filibusti'ere *sm* pirate; (*fig*) adventurer.

fili'grana *sf* (*in oreficeria*) filigree; (*su carta*) watermark.

fi'lippica *sf* invective.

Filip'pine *sfpl*: **le** ~ the Philippines.

filip'pino, a *ag, sm/f* Filipino.

film *sm inv* film.

fil'mare *vt* to film.

fil'mato *sm* short film.

fil'mina *sf* film strip.

'filo *sm* (*anche fig*) thread; (*filato*) yarn; (*metallico*) wire; (*di lama, rasoio*) edge; **con un** ~ **di voce** in a whisper; **un** ~ **d'aria** (*fig*) a breath of air; **dare del** ~ **da torcere a qn** to create difficulties for sb, make life difficult for sb; **fare il ~ a qn** (*corteggiare*) to be after sb, chase sb; **per ~ e per segno** in detail; **~ d'erba** blade of grass; **~ interdentale** dental floss; **~ di perle** string of pearls; **~ di Scozia** fine cotton yarn; **~ spinato** barbed wire.

filoameri'cano, a *ag* pro-American.

'**filobus** *sm inv* trolley bus.

filodiffusi'one *sf* rediffusion.

filodram'matico, a, ci, che *ag*: (**compagnia**) ~a amateur dramatic society ♦ *sm/f* amateur actor/actress.

filon'cino [filon'tʃino] *sm* ≈ French stick.

fi'lone *sm* (*di minerali*) seam, vein; (*pane*) ≈ Vienna loaf; (*fig*) trend.

filoso'fia *sf* philosophy.

filo'sofico, a, ci, che *ag* philosophical.

fi'losofo, a *sm/f* philosopher.

filosovi'etico, a, ci, che *ag* pro-Soviet.

filo'via *sf* (*linea*) trolley line; (*bus*) trolley bus.

fil'trare *vt, vi* to filter.

'**filtro** *sm* filter; (*pozione*) potion; **~ dell'olio** (*AUT*) oil filter.

'**filza** ['filtsa] *sf* (*anche fig*) string.

FIN *sigla f* = *Federazione Italiana Nuoto.*

fin *av, prep* = **fino.**

fi'nale *ag* final ♦ *sm* (*di libro, film*) end, ending; (*MUS*) finale ♦ *sf* (*SPORT*) final.

fina'lista, i, e *sm/f* finalist.

finalità *sf* (*scopo*) aim, purpose.

finaliz'zare [finalid'dzare] *vt*: **~ a** to direct towards.

final'mente *av* finally, at last.

fi'nanza [fi'nantsa] *sf* finance; **~e** *sfpl* (*di individuo, Stato*) finances; **(Guardia di) ~** (*di frontiera*) ≈ Customs and Excise (*BRIT*), ≈ Customs Service (*US*); **(Intendenza di) ~** ≈ Inland Revenue (*BRIT*), ≈ Internal Revenue Service (*US*); **Ministro delle ~e** Minister of Finance, ≈ Chancellor of the Exchequer (*BRIT*), ≈ Secretary of the Treasury (*US*).

finanzia'mento [finantsja'mento] *sm* (*azione*) financing; (*denaro fornito*) funds *pl.*

finanzi'are [finan'tsjare] *vt* to finance, fund.

finanzi'ario, a [finan'tsjarjo] *ag* financial ♦ *sf* (*anche*: **società ~a**) investment company; (*anche*: **legge ~a**) finance act, ≈ budget (*BRIT*).

finanzia'tore, 'trice *ag*: **ente ~, società ~trice** backer ♦ *sm/f* backer.

finanzi'ere [finan'tsjere] *sm* financier; (*guardia di finanza: doganale*) customs officer; (: *tributaria*) Inland Revenue official (*BRIT*), Internal Revenue official (*US*).

finché [fin'ke] *cong* (*per tutto il tempo che*) as long as; (*fino al momento in cui*) until; **~ vorrai** as long as you like; **aspetta ~ non esca** wait until he goes (*o* comes) out.

'**fine** *ag* (*lamina, carta*) thin; (*capelli, polvere*) fine; (*vista, udito*) keen, sharp; (*persona*: *raffinata*) refined, distinguished; (*osservazione*) subtle ♦ *sf* end ♦ *sm* aim, purpose; (*esito*) result, outcome; **in** *o* **alla ~** in the end, finally; **alla fin ~** at the end of the day, in the end; **che ~ ha fatto?** what became of him?; **buona ~ e buon principio!** (*augurio*) happy New Year!; **a fin di bene** with the best of intentions; **al ~ di fare qc** (in order) to do sth; **condurre qc a buon ~** to bring sth to a successful conclusion; **secondo ~** ulterior motive.

'**fine setti'mana** *sm o f inv* weekend.

fi'nestra *sf* window.

fines'trino *sm* (*di treno, auto*) window.

fi'nezza [fi'nettsa] *sf* thinness; fineness; keenness, sharpness; refinement; subtlety.

'**fingere** ['findʒere] *vt* to feign; (*supporre*) to imagine, suppose; **~rsi** *vr*: **~rsi ubriaco/pazzo** to pretend to be drunk/crazy; **~ di fare qc** (in order) to do sth; **condurre qc a buon ~** to bring sth to a successful conclusion; **secondo ~** ulterior motive.

fini'menti *smpl* (*di cavallo etc*) harness *sg*.

fini'mondo *sm* pandemonium.

fi'nire *vt* to finish ♦ *vi* to finish, end ♦ *sm*: **sul ~ della festa** towards the end of the party; **~ di fare** (*compiere*) to finish doing; (*smettere*) to stop doing; **~ in galera** to end up *o* finish up in prison; **farla finita** (*con la vita*) to put an end to one's life; **farla finita con qc** to have done with sth; **com'è andata a ~?** what happened in the end?; **finiscila!** stop it!

fini'tura *sf* finish.

finlan'dese *ag* Finnish ♦ *sm/f* Finn ♦ *sm* (*LING*) Finnish.

Fin'landia *sf*: **la ~** Finland.

'**fino, a** *ag* (*capelli, seta*) fine; (*oro*) pure; (*fig*: *acuto*) shrewd ♦ *av* (*spesso troncato in* **fin**: *pure, anche*) even ♦ *prep* (*spesso troncato in* **fin**: *tempo*): **fin quando?** till when?; (: *luogo*): **fin qui** as far as here; **~ a** (*tempo*) until, till; (*luogo*) as far as, (up) to; **fin da domani** from tomorrow onwards; **fin da ieri** since yesterday; **fin dalla nascita** from *o* since birth.

fi'nocchio [fi'nɔkkjo] *sm* fennel; (*fam peg*: *pederasta*) queer.

fi'nora *av* up till now.

'**finsi** *etc vb vedi* **fingere.**

'**finto, a** *pp di* **fingere** ♦ *ag* (*capelli, dente*) false; (*fiori*) artificial; (*cuoio, pelle*) imitation *cpd*; (*fig: simulato: pazzia etc*) feigned, sham ♦ *sf* pretence (*BRIT*), pretense (*US*), sham; (*SPORT*) feint; **far ~a (di fare)** to pretend (to do); **l'ho detto per ~a** I was only pretending; (*per scherzo*) I was only kidding.

finzi'one [fin'tsjone] *sf* pretence (*BRIT*), pretense (*US*), sham.

fioc'care *vi* (*neve*) to fall; (*fig: insulti etc*) to fall thick and fast.

fi'occo, chi *sm* (*di nastro*) bow; (*di stoffa, lana*) flock; (*di neve*) flake; (*NAUT*) jib; **coi ~chi** (*fig*) first-rate; **~chi di granoturco** cornflakes.

fi'ocina ['fjɔtʃina] *sf* harpoon.

fi'oco, a, chi, che *ag* faint, dim.

fi'onda *sf* catapult.

fio'raio, a *sm/f* florist.

fiorda'liso *sm* (*BOT*) cornflower.

fi'ordo *sm* fjord.

fi'ore *sm* flower; **~i** *smpl* (*CARTE*) clubs; **nel ~ degli anni** in one's prime; **a fior d'acqua** on the surface of the water; **a fior di labbra** in a whisper; **aver i nervi a fior di pelle** to be on edge; **fior di latte** cream; **è costato fior di soldi** it cost a pretty penny; **il fior ~ della società** the cream of society; **~ all'occhiello** feather in the cap; **~i di campo** wild flowers.

fio'rente *ag* (*industria, paese*) flourishing; (*salute*) blooming; (*petto*) ample.

fioren'tino, a *ag, sm/f* Florentine ♦ *sf* (*CUC*) T-bone steak.

fio'retto *sm* (*SCHERMA*) foil.

fio'rino *sm* florin.

fio'rire *vi* (*rosa*) to flower; (*albero*) to blossom; (*fig*) to flourish.

fio'rista, i, e *sm/f* florist.

fiori'tura *sf* (*di pianta*) flowering, blooming; (*di albero*) blossoming; (*fig: di commercio, arte*) flourishing; (*insieme dei fiori*) flowers *pl*; (*MUS*) fioritura.

fi'otto *sm* (*di lacrime*) flow, flood; (*di sangue*) gush, spurt.

'FIPE *sigla f* = Federazione Italiana Pubblici Esercizi.

Fi'renze [fi'rɛntse] *sf* Florence.

'firma *sf* signature; (*reputazione*) name.

firma'mento *sm* firmament.

fir'mare *vt* to sign.

firma'tario, a *sm/f* signatory.

fisar'monica, che *sf* accordion.

fis'cale *ag* fiscal, tax *cpd*; (*meticoloso*) punctilious; **medico ~** doctor employed by Social Security to verify cases of sick leave.

fisca'lista, i, e *sm/f* tax consultant.

fiscaliz'zare [fiskalid'dzare] *vt* to exempt from taxes.

fischi'are [fis'kjare] *vi* to whistle ♦ *vt* to whistle; (*attore*) to boo, hiss; **mi fischian le orecchie** my ears are singing; (*fig*) my ears are burning.

fischiet'tare [fiskjet'tare] *vi, vt* to whistle.

fischi'etto [fis'kjetto] *sm* (*strumento*) whistle.

'fischio ['fiskjo] *sm* whistle; **prendere ~i per fiaschi** to get hold of the wrong end of the stick.

'fisco *sm* tax authorities *pl*, ≈ Inland Revenue (*BRIT*), ≈ Internal Revenue Service (*US*).

'fisica *sf vedi* fisico.

fisica'mente *av* physically.

'fisico, a, ci, che *ag* physical ♦ *sm/f* physicist ♦ *sm* physique ♦ *sf* physics *sg*.

'fisima *sf* fixation.

fisiolo'gia [fizjolo'dʒia] *sf* physiology.

fisiono'mia *sf* face, physiognomy.

fisiotera'pia *sf* physiotherapy.

fisiotera'pista *sm/f* physiotherapist.

fis'saggio [fis'saddʒo] *sm* (*FOT*) fixing.

fis'sante *ag* (*spray, lozione*) holding.

fis'sare *vt* to fix, fasten; (*guardare intensamente*) to stare at; (*data, condizioni*) to fix, establish, set; (*prenotare*) to book; **~rsi** *vr*: **~rsi su** (*sog: sguardo, attenzione*) to focus on; (*fig: idea*) to become obsessed with.

fissazi'one [fissat'tsjone] *sf* (*PSIC*) fixation.

fissi'one *sf* fission.

'fisso, a *ag* fixed; (*stipendio, impiego*) regular ♦ *av*: **guardar ~ qn/qc** to stare at sb/sth; **avere un ragazzo ~** to have a steady boyfriend; **senza ~a dimora** of no fixed abode.

fitoterma'lismo *sm* herbal hydrotherapy.

'fitta *sf vedi* fitto.

fit'tavolo *sm* tenant.

fit'tizio, a [fit'tittsjo] *ag* fictitious, imaginary.

'fitto, a *ag* thick, dense; (*pioggia*) heavy ♦ *sm* (*affitto, pigione*) rent ♦ *sf* sharp pain; **una ~a al cuore** (*fig*) a pang of grief; **nel ~ del bosco** in the heart *o* depths of the wood.

fiu'mana *sf* torrent; (*fig*) stream, flood.

fi'ume *sm* river ♦ *ag inv*: **processo ~** long-running trial; **scorrere a ~i** (*acqua, sangue*) to flow in torrents.

fiu'tare *vt* to smell, sniff; (*sog: animale*) to scent; (*fig: inganno*) to get wind of, smell; **~ tabacco** to take snuff; **~ cocaina** to snort cocaine.

fi'uto *sm* (sense of) smell; (*fig*) nose.

'flaccido, a ['flattʃido] *ag* flabby.

fla'cone *sm* bottle.

flagel'lare [fladʒel'lare] *vt* to flog, scourge; (*sog: onde*) to beat against.

fla'gello [fla'dʒɛllo] *sm* scourge.

fla'grante *ag* flagrant; **cogliere qn in** ~ **to** catch sb red-handed.

fla'nella *sf* flannel.

flash [flaʃ] *sm inv* (*FOT*) flash; (*giornalistico*) newsflash.

flau'tista, i *sm/f* flautist.

'flauto *sm* flute.

'flebile *ag* faint, feeble.

fle'bite *sf* phlebitis.

'flemma *sf* (*calma*) coolness, phlegm; (*MED*) phlegm.

flem'matico, a, ci, che *ag* phlegmatic, cool.

fles'sibile *ag* pliable; (*fig: che si adatta*) flexible.

flessi'one *sf* (*gen*) bending; (*GINNASTICA: a terra*) sit-up; (: *in piedi*) forward bend; (: *sulle gambe*) knee-bend; (*diminuzione*) slight drop, slight fall; (*LING*) inflection; **fare una** ~ **to** bend; **una** ~ **economica** a downward trend in the economy.

'flesso, a *pp di* **flettere**.

flessu'oso, a *ag* supple, lithe; (*andatura*) flowing, graceful.

'flettere *vt* to bend.

'flipper ['flipper] *sm inv* pinball machine.

flirt [fləːt] *sm inv* brief romance, flirtation.

flir'tare *vi* to flirt.

F.lli *abbr* (= *fratelli*) Bros.

'flora *sf* flora.

'florido, a *ag* flourishing; (*fig*) glowing with health.

'floscio, a, sci, sce ['flɔʃʃo] *ag* (*cappello*) floppy, soft; (*muscoli*) flabby.

'flotta *sf* fleet.

flot'tante *sm* (*ECON*): **titoli a largo** ~ blue chips, stocks on the market.

'fluido, a *ag, sm* fluid.

flu'ire *vi* to flow.

fluore'scente [fluoreʃ'ʃɛnte] *ag* fluorescent.

flu'oro *sm* fluorine.

fluo'ruro *sm* fluoride.

'flusso *sm* flow; (*FISICA, MED*) flux; ~ **e riflusso** ebb and flow; ~ **di cassa** (*COMM*) cash flow.

'flutti *smpl* waves.

fluttu'are *vi* to rise and fall; (*ECON*) to fluctuate.

fluvi'ale *ag* river *cpd*, fluvial.

FM *abbr vedi* **modulazione di frequenza**.

FMI *sigla m vedi* **Fondo Monetario Internazionale**.

FO *sigla* = *Forlì*.

fo'bia *sf* phobia.

'foca, che *sf* (*ZOOL*) seal.

fo'caccia, ce [fo'kattʃa] *sf* kind of pizza; (*dolce*) bun; **rendere pan per** ~ **to** get one's own back, give tit for tat.

fo'cale *ag* focal.

focaliz'zare [fokalid'dzare] *vt* (*FOT: immagine*) to get into focus; (*fig: situazione*) to get into perspective; ~ **l'attenzione su** to focus one's attention on.

'foce ['fotʃe] *sf* (*GEO*) mouth.

fo'chista, i [fo'kista] *sm* (*FERR*) stoker, fireman.

foco'laio *sm* (*MED*) centre (*BRIT*) *o* center (*US*) of infection; (*fig*) hotbed.

foco'lare *sm* hearth, fireside; (*TECN*) furnace.

fo'coso, a *ag* fiery; (*cavallo*) mettlesome, fiery.

'fodera *sf* (*di vestito*) lining; (*di libro, poltrona*) cover.

fode'rare *vt* to line; to cover.

'fodero *sm* (*di spada*) scabbard; (*di pugnale*) sheath; (*di pistola*) holster.

'foga *sf* enthusiasm, ardour (*BRIT*), ardor (*US*).

'foggia, ge ['fɔddʒa] *sf* (*maniera*) style; (*aspetto*) form, shape; (*moda*) fashion, style.

foggi'are [fod'dʒare] *vt* to shape; to style.

'foglia ['fɔʎʎa] *sf* leaf; **ha mangiato la** ~ (*fig*) he's caught on; ~ **d'argento/d'oro** silver/gold leaf.

fogli'ame [foʎ'ʎame] *sm* foliage, leaves *pl*.

fogli'etto [foʎ'ʎetto] *sm* (*piccolo foglio*) slip of paper, piece of paper; (*manifestino*) leaflet, handout.

'foglio ['fɔʎʎo] *sm* (*di carta*) sheet (of paper); (*di metallo*) sheet; (*documento*) document; (*banconota*) (bank)note; ~ **rosa** (*AUT*) provisional licence; ~ **di via** (*DIR*) expulsion order; ~ **volante** pamphlet.

'fogna ['foɲɲa] *sf* drain, sewer.

fogna'tura [foɲɲa'tura] *sf* drainage, sewerage.

föhn [føːn] *sm inv* hair-dryer.

fo'lata *sf* gust.

fol'clore *sm* folklore.

folclo'ristico, a, ci, che *ag* folk *cpd*.

folgo'rare *vt* (*sog: fulmine*) to strike down; (: *alta tensione*) to electrocute.

folgorazi'one [folgorat'tsjone] *sf* electrocution; **ebbe una** ~ (*fig: idea*) he had a brainwave.

'folgore *sf* thunderbolt.

'folla *sf* crowd, throng.

'folle *ag* mad, insane; (*TECN*) idle; **in** ~ (*AUT*) in neutral.

folleggi'are [folled'dʒare] *vi* (*divertirsi*) to

paint the town red.
fol'letto *sm* elf.
fol'lia *sf* folly, foolishness; foolish act;
(*pazzia*) madness, lunacy; **amare qn alla ~**
to love sb to distraction; **costare una ~** to
cost the earth.
'folto, a *ag* thick.
fomen'tare *vt* to stir up, foment.
fon *sm inv* = **föhn.**
fon'dale *sm* (*del mare*) bottom; (*TEAT*)
backdrop; **il ~ marino** the sea bed.
fondamen'tale *ag* fundamental, basic.
fondamenta'lista, i, e *ag, sm/f* (*REL*)
fundamentalist.
fonda'mento *sm* foundation; **~a** *sfpl* (*EDIL*)
foundations.
fon'dare *vt* to found; (*fig: dar base*): **~ qc su**
to base sth on; **~rsi** *vr* (*teorie*): **~rsi (su)** to
be based (on).
fonda'tezza [fonda'tettsa] *sf* (*di ragioni*)
soundness; (*di dubbio, sospetto*) basis in
fact.
fon'dato, a *ag* (*ragioni*) sound; (*dubbio,
sospetto*) well-founded.
fondazi'one [fondat'tsjone] *sf* foundation.
'fondere *vt* (*neve*) to melt; (*metallo*) to fuse,
melt; (*fig: colori*) to merge, blend;
(*: imprese, gruppi*) to merge ♦ *vi* to melt;
~rsi *vr* to melt; (*fig: partiti, correnti*) to
unite, merge.
fonde'ria *sf* foundry.
fondi'ario, a *ag* land *cpd*.
fon'dina *sf* (*piatto fondo*) soup plate;
(*portapistola*) holster.
'fondo, a *ag* deep ♦ *sm* (*di recipiente, pozzo*)
bottom; (*di stanza*) back; (*quantità di
liquido che resta, deposito*) dregs *pl*;
(*sfondo*) background; (*unità immobiliare*)
property, estate; (*somma di denaro*) fund;
(*SPORT*) long-distance race; **~i** *smpl*
(*denaro*) funds; **a notte ~a** at dead of
night; **in ~ a** at the bottom of; at the back
of; (*strada*) at the end of; **laggiù in ~**
(*lontano*) over there; (*in profondità*) down
there; **in ~** (*fig*) after all, all things
considered; **andare fino in ~ a** (*fig*) to
examine thoroughly; **andare a ~** (*nave*) to
sink; **conoscere a ~** to know inside out;
dar ~ a (*fig: provvisti, soldi*) to use up;
toccare il ~ (*fig*) to plumb the depths; **a ~
perduto** (*COMM*) without security; **~
comune di investimento** investment
trust; **F~ Monetario Internazionale (FMI)**
International Monetary Fund (IMF); **~ di
previdenza** social insurance fund; **~ di
riserva** reserve fund; **~ urbano** town
property; **~i di caffè** coffee grounds; **~i
d'esercizio** working capital *sg*; **~i liquidi**

ready money *sg*, liquid assets; **~i di
magazzino** old *o* unsold stock *sg*; **~i neri**
slush fund *sg*.
fondo'tinta *sm inv* (*cosmetico*) foundation.
fo'nema *sm* phoneme.
fo'netica *sf* phonetics *sg*.
fo'netico, a, ci, che *ag* phonetic.
fon'tana *sf* fountain.
fonta'nella *sf* drinking fountain.
'fonte *sf* spring, source; (*fig*) source ♦ *sm*: **~
battesimale** (*REL*) font.
fon'tina *sm* full fat hard, sweet cheese
from Valle d'Aosta.
'footing ['futiŋ] *sm* jogging.
forag'giare [forad'dʒare] *vt* (*cavalli*) to
fodder; (*fig: partito etc*) to bankroll.
fo'raggio [fo'raddʒo] *sm* fodder, forage.
fo'rare *vt* to pierce, make a hole in;
(*pallone*) to burst; (*pneumatico*) to
puncture; (*biglietto*) to punch; **~rsi** *vr*
(*gen*) to develop a hole; (*AUT, pallone,
timpano*) to burst; **~ una gomma** to burst
a tyre (*BRIT*) *o* tire (*US*).
fora'tura *sf* piercing; bursting; puncturing;
punching.
'forbici ['fɔrbitʃi] *sfpl* scissors.
forbi'cina [forbi'tʃina] *sf* earwig.
for'bito, a *ag* (*stile, modi*) polished.
'forca, che *sf* (*AGR*) fork, pitchfork;
(*patibolo*) gallows *sg*.
for'cella [for'tʃella] *sf* (*TECN*) fork; (*di
monte*) pass.
for'chetta [for'ketta] *sf* fork; **essere una
buona ~** to enjoy one's food.
for'cina [for'tʃina] *sf* hairpin.
'forcipe ['fɔrtʃipe] *sm* forceps *pl*.
for'cone *sm* pitchfork.
fo'rense *ag* (*linguaggio*) legal; **avvocato ~**
barrister (*BRIT*), lawyer.
fo'resta *sf* forest; **la F~ Nera** the Black
Forest.
fores'tale *ag* forest *cpd*; **guardia ~** forester.
foreste'ria *sf* (*di convento, palazzo etc*) guest
rooms *pl*, guest quarters *pl*.
foresti'ero, a *ag* foreign ♦ *sm/f* foreigner.
for'fait [fɔr'fɛ] *sm inv*: (**prezzo a**) **~** fixed
price, set price; **dichiarare ~** (*SPORT*) to
withdraw; (*fig*) to give up.
forfe'tario, a *ag*: **prezzo ~** (*da pagare*) fixed
o set price; (*da ricevere*) lump sum.
'forfora *sf* dandruff.
'forgia, ge ['fɔrdʒa] *sf* forge.
forgi'are [for'dʒare] *vt* to forge.
'forma *sf* form; (*aspetto esteriore*) form,
shape; (*DIR: procedura*) procedure; (*per
calzature*) last; (*stampo da cucina*) mould
(*BRIT*), mold (*US*); **~e** *sfpl* (*del corpo*)
figure, shape; **le ~e** (*convenzioni*)

appearances; **errori di** ~ stylistic errors; **essere in** ~ to be in good shape; **tenersi in** ~ to keep fit; **in** ~ **ufficiale/privata** officially/privately; **una** ~ **di formaggio** a (whole) cheese.

formag'gino [formad'dʒino] *sm* processed cheese.

for'maggio [for'maddʒo] *sm* cheese.

for'male *ag* formal.

formalità *sf inv* formality.

formaliz'zare [formalid'dzare] *vt* to formalize.

for'mare *vt* to form, shape, make; (*numero di telefono*) to dial; (*fig: carattere*) to form, mould (*BRIT*), mold (*US*); ~**rsi** *vr* to form, take shape; **il treno si forma a Milano** the train starts from Milan.

for'mato *sm* format, size.

format'tare *vt* (*INFORM*) to format.

formattazi'one [formattat'tsjone] *sf* (*INFORM*) formatting.

formazi'one [format'tsjone] *sf* formation; (*fig: educazione*) training; ~ **professionale** vocational training.

for'mica, che *sf* ant.

formi'caio *sm* anthill.

formico'lare *vi* (*gamba, braccio*) to tingle; (*brulicare: anche fig*): ~ **di** to be swarming with; **mi formicola la gamba** I've got pins and needles in my leg, my leg's tingling.

formico'lio *sm* pins and needles *pl*; swarming.

formi'dabile *ag* powerful, formidable; (*straordinario*) remarkable.

for'moso, a *ag* shapely.

'formula *sf* formula; ~ **di cortesia** (*nelle lettere*) letter ending.

formu'lare *vt* to formulate.

for'nace [for'natʃe] *sf* (*per laterizi etc*) kiln; (*per metalli*) furnace.

for'naio *sm* baker.

for'nello *sm* (*elettrico, a gas*) ring; (*di pipa*) bowl.

for'nire *vt*: ~ **qn di qc,** ~ **qc a qn** to provide *o* supply sb with sth, supply sth to sb; ~**rsi** *vr*: ~**rsi di** (*procurarsi*) to provide o.s. with.

for'nito, a *ag*: **ben** ~ (*negozio*) well-stocked.

forni'tore, 'trice *ag*: **ditta** ~**trice di ...** company supplying ... ♦ *sm/f* supplier.

forni'tura *sf* supply.

'forno *sm* (*di cucina*) oven; (*panetteria*) bakery; (*TECN: per calce etc*) kiln; (: *per metalli*) furnace; **fare i** ~**i** (*MED*) to undergo heat treatment.

'foro *sm* (*buco*) hole; (*STORIA*) forum; (*tribunale*) (law) court.

'forse *av* perhaps, maybe; (*circa*) about; **essere in** ~ to be in doubt.

forsen'nato, a *ag* mad, crazy, insane.

'forte *ag* strong; (*suono*) loud; (*spesa*) considerable, great ♦ *av* strongly; (*velocemente*) fast; (*a voce alta*) loud(ly); (*violentemente*) hard ♦ *sm* (*edificio*) fort; (*specialità*) forte, strong point; **piatto** ~ (*CUC*) main dish; **avere un** ~ **mal di testa/raffreddore** to have a bad headache/cold; **essere** ~ **in qc** to be good at sth; **farsi** ~ **di qc** to make use of *o* avail o.s. of sth; **dare man** ~ **a qn** to back sb up, support sb; **usare le maniere** ~**i** to use strong-arm tactics.

for'tezza [for'tettsa] *sf* (*morale*) strength; (*luogo fortificato*) fortress.

fortifi'care *vt* to fortify, strengthen.

for'tuito, a *ag* fortuitous, chance *cpd*.

for'tuna *sf* (*destino*) fortune, luck; (*buona sorte*) success, fortune; (*eredità, averi*) fortune; **per** ~ luckily, fortunately; **di** ~ makeshift, improvised; **atterraggio di** ~ emergency landing.

fortu'nale *sm* storm.

fortunata'mente *av* luckily, fortunately.

fortu'nato, a *ag* lucky, fortunate; (*coronato da successo*) successful.

fortu'noso, a *ag* (*vita*) eventful; (*avvenimento*) unlucky.

fo'runcolo *sm* (*MED*) boil.

forvi'are *vt, vi* = **fuorviare.**

'forza ['fortsa] *sf* strength; (*potere*) power; (*FISICA*) force ♦ *escl* come on!; ~**e** *sfpl* (*fisiche*) strength *sg*; (*MIL*) forces; **per** ~ against one's will; (*naturalmente*) of course; **per** ~ **di cose** by force of circumstances; **a viva** ~ by force; **a** ~ **di** by dint of; **farsi** ~ (*coraggio*) to pluck up one's courage; **bella** ~! (*ironico*) how clever of you (*o* him *etc*)!; ~ **lavoro** work force, manpower; **per causa di** ~ **maggiore** (*DIR*) by reason of an act of God; (*per estensione*) due to circumstances beyond one's control; **la** ~ **pubblica** the police *pl*; ~ **di vendita** (*COMM*) sales force; ~ **di volontà** willpower; **le** ~**e armate** the armed forces; **F**~ **Italia** (*POL*) *moderate right-wing party.*

for'zare [for'tsare] *vt* to force; (*cassaforte, porta*) to force (open); (*voce*) to strain; ~ **qn a fare** to force sb to do.

for'zato, a [for'tsato] *ag* forced ♦ *sm* (*DIR*) prisoner sentenced to hard labour (*BRIT*) *o* labor (*US*).

forzi'ere [for'tsjɛre] *sm* strongbox; (*di pirati*) treasure chest.

for'zista, i, e [for'tsista] *ag* of Forza Italia ♦ *sm/f* member (*o* supporter) of Forza Italia.

for'zuto, a [for'tsuto] *ag* big and strong.

fos'chia [fos'kia] *sf* mist, haze.

'fosco, a, schi, sche *ag* dark, gloomy; dipingere qc a tinte ~sche (*fig*) to paint a gloomy picture of sth.

fos'fato *sm* phosphate.

fosfore'scente [fosforeʃ'ʃɛnte] *ag* phosphorescent; (*lancetta dell'orologio etc*) luminous.

'fosforo *sm* phosphorous.

'fossa *sf* pit; (*di cimitero*) grave; ~ biologica septic tank; ~ comune mass grave.

fos'sato *sm* ditch; (*di fortezza*) moat.

fos'setta *sf* dimple.

'fossi *etc vb vedi* essere.

'fossile *ag*, *sm* fossil (*cpd*).

'fosso *sm* ditch; (*MIL*) trench.

'foste *etc vb vedi* essere.

'foto *sf inv* photo; ~ ricordo souvenir photo; ~ tessera passport(-type) photo.

foto... *prefisso* photo....

fotocomposi'tore *sm* filmsetter.

fotocomposizi'one [fotokompozit'tsjone] *sf* film setting.

foto'copia *sf* photocopy.

fotocopi'are *vt* to photocopy.

foto'genico, a, ci, che [foto'dʒɛniko] *ag* photogenic.

fotogra'fare *vt* to photograph.

fotogra'fia *sf* (*procedimento*) photography; (*immagine*) photograph; fare una ~ to take a photograph; una ~ a colori/in bianco e nero a colour/black and white photograph.

foto'grafico, a, ci, che *ag* photographic; macchina ~a camera.

fo'tografo, a *smf* photographer.

foto'gramma, i *sm* (*CINE*) frame.

fotomo'dello, a *smf* fashion model.

fotomon'taggio [fotomon'taddʒo] *sm* photomontage.

fotore'porter *smf inv* newspaper (*o* magazine) photographer.

fotoro'manzo [fotoro'mandzo] *sm* romantic picture story.

foto'sintesi *sf* photosynthesis.

'fottere *vt* (*fam!*: *avere rapporti sessuali*) to fuck (*!*), screw (*!*); (: *rubare*) to pinch, swipe; (: *fregare*): mi hanno fottuto they played a dirty trick on me; vai a farti ~! fuck off! (*!*).

fot'tuto, a *ag* (*fam!*) bloody, fucking (*!*).

fou'lard [fu'lar] *sm inv* scarf.

FR *sigla* = Frosinone.

fr. *abbr* (*COMM*) = franco.

fra *prep* = tra.

fracas'sare *vt* to shatter, smash; ~rsi *vr* to shatter, smash; (*veicolo*) to crash.

fra'casso *sm* smash; crash; (*baccano*) din, racket.

'fradicio, a, ci, ce ['fraditʃo] *ag* (*guasto*) rotten; (*molto bagnato*) soaking (wet); ubriaco ~ blind drunk.

'fragile ['fradʒile] *ag* fragile; (*salute*) delicate; (*nervi, vetro*) brittle.

fragilità [fradʒili'ta] *sf* (*vedi ag*) fragility; delicacy; brittleness.

'fragola *sf* strawberry.

fra'gore *sm* (*di cascate, carro armato*) roar; (*di tuono*) rumble.

frago'roso, a *ag* deafening; ridere in modo ~ to roar with laughter.

fra'grante *ag* fragrant.

fraintendi'mento *sm* misunderstanding.

frain'tendere *vt* to misunderstand.

frain'teso, a *pp di* fraintendere.

fram'mento *sm* fragment.

fram'misto, a *ag*: ~ a interspersed with, mixed with.

'frana *sf* landslide; (*fig*: *persona*): essere una ~ to be useless, be a walking disaster area.

fra'nare *vi* to slip, slide down.

franca'mente *av* frankly.

fran'cese [fran'tʃeze] *ag* French ♦ *smf* Frenchman/woman ♦ *sm* (*LING*) French; i F~i the French.

fran'chezza [fran'kettsa] *sf* frankness, openness.

fran'chigia, gie [fran'kidʒa] *sf* (*AMM*) exemption; (*DIR*) franchise; (*NAUT*) shore leave; ~ doganale exemption from customs duty.

'Francia ['frantʃa] *sf*: la ~ France.

'franco, a, chi, che *ag* (*COMM*) free; (*sincero*) frank, open, sincere ♦ *sm* (*moneta*) franc; farla ~a (*fig*) to get off scot-free; ~ a bordo free on board; ~ di dogana duty-free; ~ a domicilio delivered free of charge; ~ fabbrica ex factory, ex works; prezzo ~ fabbrica ex-works price; ~ magazzino ex warehouse; ~ di porto carriage free; ~ vagone free on rail; ~ tiratore *sm* sniper; (*POL*) *member of parliament who votes against his own party*.

franco'bollo *sm* (postage) stamp.

franco-cana'dese *ag*, *smf* French Canadian.

Franco'forte *sf* Frankfurt.

fran'gente [fran'dʒɛnte] *sm* (*onda*) breaker; (*scoglio emergente*) reef; (*circostanza*) situation, circumstance.

'frangia, ge ['frandʒa] *sf* fringe.
frangi'flutti [frandʒi'flutti] *sm inv*
breakwater.
frangi'vento [frandʒi'vɛnto] *sm* windbreak.
fran'toio *sm* (*AGR*) olive press; (*TECN*)
crusher.
frantu'mare *vt*, **~rsi** *vr* to break into
pieces, shatter.
fran'tumi *smpl* pieces, bits; (*schegge*)
splinters; **andare in ~, mandare in ~** to
shatter, smash to pieces *o* smithereens.
frappé *sm* (*CUC*) milk shake.
fra'sario *sm* (*gergo*) vocabulary, language.
'frasca, sche *sf* (leafy) branch; **saltare di
palo in ~** to jump from one subject to
another.
'frase *sf* (*LING*) sentence; (*locuzione,
espressione, MUS*) phrase; **~ fatta** set
phrase.
fraseolo'gia [frazeolo'dʒia] *sf* phraseology.
'frassino *sm* ash (tree).
frastagli'ato, a [frasta'ʎʎato] *ag* (*costa*)
indented, jagged.
frastor'nare *vt* (*intontire*) to daze;
(*confondere*) to bewilder, befuddle.
frastor'nato, a *ag* dazed; bewildered.
frastu'ono *sm* hubbub, din.
'frate *sm* friar, monk.
fratel'lanza [fratel'lantsa] *sf* brotherhood;
(*associazione*) fraternity.
fratel'lastro *sm* stepbrother.
fra'tello *sm* brother; **~i** *smpl* brothers; (*nel
senso di fratelli e sorelle*) brothers and
sisters.
fra'terno, a *ag* fraternal, brotherly.
fratri'cida, i, e [fratri'tʃida] *ag* fratricidal
♦ *sm/f* fratricide; **guerra ~** civil war.
frat'taglie [frat'taʎʎe] *sfpl* (*CUC: gen*) offal
sg; (: *di pollo*) giblets.
frat'tanto *av* in the meantime, meanwhile.
frat'tempo *sm*: **nel ~** in the meantime,
meanwhile.
frat'tura *sf* fracture; (*fig*) split, break.
frattu'rare *vt* to fracture.
fraudo'lento, a *ag* fraudulent.
fraziona'mento [frattsjona'mento] *sm*
division, splitting up.
frazio'nare [frattsjo'nare] *vt* to divide, split
up.
frazi'one [frat'tsjone] *sf* fraction; (*borgata*):
~ di comune hamlet.
'freccia, ce ['frettʃa] *sf* arrow; **~ di
direzione** (*AUT*) indicator.
frec'ciata [fret'tʃata] *sf*: **lanciare una ~** to
make a cutting remark.
fred'dare *vt* to shoot dead.
fred'dezza [fred'dettsa] *sf* coldness.
'freddo, a *ag, sm* cold; **fa ~** it's cold; **aver ~**

to be cold; **soffrire il ~** to feel the cold; **a
~** (*fig*) deliberately.
freddo'loso, a *ag* sensitive to the cold.
fred'dura *sf* pun.
'freezer ['frizer] *sm inv* fridge-freezer.
fre'gare *vt* to rub; (*fam: truffare*) to take in,
cheat; (: *rubare*) to swipe, pinch;
fregarsene (*fam!*): **chi se ne frega?** who
gives a damn (about it)?
fre'gata *sf* rub; (*fam*) swindle; (*NAUT*)
frigate.
frega'tura *sf* (*fam: imbroglio*) rip-off;
(: *delusione*) let-down.
fregherò *etc* [frege'rɔ] *vb vedi* **fregare**.
'fregio ['fredʒo] *sm* (*ARCHIT*) frieze;
(*ornamento*) decoration.
'fremere *vi*: **~ di** to tremble *o* quiver with;
~ d'impazienza to be champing at the bit.
'fremito *sm* tremor, quiver.
fre'nare *vt* (*veicolo*) to slow down; (*cavallo*)
to rein in; (*lacrime*) to restrain, hold back
♦ *vi* to brake; **~rsi** *vr* (*fig*) to restrain o.s.,
control o.s.
fre'nata *sf*: **fare una ~** to brake.
frene'sia *sf* frenzy.
fre'netico, a, ci, che *ag* frenetic.
'freno *sm* brake; (*morso*) bit; **tenere a ~**
(*passioni etc*) to restrain; **tenere a ~ la
lingua** to hold one's tongue; **~ a disco**
disc brake; **~ a mano** handbrake.
'freon ® *sm inv* (*CHIM*) Freon ®.
frequen'tare *vt* (*scuola, corso*) to attend;
(*locale, bar*) to go to, frequent; (*persone*)
to see (often).
frequen'tato, a *ag* (*locale*) busy.
fre'quente *ag* frequent; **di ~** frequently.
fre'quenza [fre'kwɛntsa] *sf* frequency; (*INS*)
attendance.
fre'sare *vt* (*TECN*) to mill.
fres'chezza [fres'kettsa] *sf* freshness.
'fresco, a, schi, sche *ag* fresh;
(*temperatura*) cool; (*notizia*) recent, fresh
♦ *sm*: **godere il ~** to enjoy the cool air;
~ di bucato straight from the wash,
newly washed; **stare ~** (*fig*) to be in for it;
mettere al ~ to put in a cool place; (*fig: in
prigione*) to put inside *o* in the cooler.
fres'cura *sf* cool.
'fresia *sf* freesia.
'fretta *sf* hurry, haste; **in ~** in a hurry; **in ~
e furia** in a mad rush; **aver ~** to be in a
hurry; **far ~ a qn** to hurry sb.
frettolosa'mente *av* hurriedly, in a rush.
fretto'loso, a *ag* (*persona*) in a hurry;
(*lavoro etc*) hurried, rushed.
fri'abile *ag* (*terreno*) friable; (*pasta*)
crumbly.
'friggere ['friddʒere] *vt* to fry ♦ *vi* (*olio etc*)

to sizzle; **vai a farti** ~! (*fam*) get lost!
frigidità [fridʒidi'ta] *sf* frigidity.
'frigido, a ['fridʒido] *ag* (*MED*) frigid.
fri'gnare [friɲ'ɲare] *vi* to whine, snivel.
fri'gnone, a [friɲ'ɲone] *sm/f* whiner, sniveller.
'frigo, ghi *sm* fridge.
frigo'rifero, a *ag* refrigerating ♦ *sm* refrigerator; **cella** ~**a** cold store.
fringu'ello *sm* chaffinch.
'frissi *etc vb vedi* **friggere.**
frit'tata *sf* omelet(te); **fare una** ~ (*fig*) to make a mess of things.
frit'tella *sf* (*CUC*) pancake; (: *ripiena*) fritter.
'fritto, a *pp di* **friggere** ♦ *ag* fried ♦ *sm* fried food; **ormai siamo** ~**i**! (*fig fam*) now we've had it!; **è un argomento** ~ **e rifritto** that's old hat; ~ **misto** mixed fry.
frit'tura *sf* (*cibo*) fried food; ~ **di pesce** mixed fried fish.
friu'lano, a *ag* of (*o* from) Friuli.
frivo'lezza [frivo'lettsa] *sf* frivolity.
'frivolo, a *ag* frivolous.
frizi'one [frit'tsjone] *sf* friction; (*di pelle*) rub, rub-down; (*AUT*) clutch.
friz'zante [frid'dzante] *ag* (*anche fig*) sparkling.
'frizzo ['friddzo] *sm* witticism.
fro'dare *vt* to defraud, cheat.
'frode *sf* fraud; ~ **fiscale** tax evasion.
'frodo *sm*: **di** ~ illegal, contraband; **pescatore di** ~, **cacciatore di** ~ poacher.
'frogia, gie ['frɔdʒa] *sf* (*di cavallo etc*) nostril.
'frollo, a *ag* (*carne*) tender; (: *di selvaggina*) high; (*fig: persona*) soft; **pasta** ~**a** short(crust) pastry.
'fronda *sf* (leafy) branch; (*di partito politico*) internal opposition; ~**e** *sfpl* (*di albero*) foliage *sg.*
fron'tale *ag* frontal; (*scontro*) head-on.
'fronte *sf* (*ANAT*) forehead; (*di edificio*) front, façade ♦ *sm* (*MIL, POL, METEOR*) front; **a** ~, **di** ~ facing, opposite; **di** ~ **a** (*posizione*) opposite, facing, in front of; (*a paragone di*) compared with; **far** ~ **a** (*nemico, problema*) to confront; (*responsabilità*) to face up to; (*spese*) to cope with.
fronteggi'are [fronted'dʒare] *vt* (*avversari, difficoltà*) to face, stand up to; (*spese*) to cope with.
frontes'pizio [frontes'pittsjo] *sm* (*ARCHIT*) frontispiece; (*di libro*) title page.
fronti'era *sf* border, frontier.
fron'tone *sm* pediment.
'fronzolo ['frondzolo] *sm* frill.
'frotta *sf* crowd; **in** ~, **a** ~**e** in their

hundreds, in droves.
'frottola *sf* fib; **raccontare un sacco di** ~**e** to tell a pack of lies.
fru'gale *ag* frugal.
fru'gare *vi* to rummage ♦ *vt* to search.
frugherò *etc* [fruge'rɔ] *vb vedi* **frugare.**
frui'tore *sm* user.
fruizi'one [fruit'tsjone] *sf* use.
frul'lare *vt* (*CUC*) to whisk ♦ *vi* (*uccelli*) to flutter; **cosa ti frulla in mente?** what is going on in that mind of yours?
frul'lato *sm* (*CUC*) milk shake; (: *con solo frutta*) fruit drink.
frulla'tore *sm* electric mixer.
frul'lino *sm* whisk.
fru'mento *sm* wheat.
frusci'are [fruʃ'ʃare] *vi* to rustle.
fru'scio [fruʃ'ʃio] *sm* rustle; rustling.
'frusta *sf* whip; (*CUC*) whisk.
frus'tare *vt* to whip.
frus'tata *sf* lash.
frus'tino *sm* riding crop.
frus'trare *vt* to frustrate.
frus'trato, a *ag* frustrated.
frustrazi'one [frustrat'tsjone] *sf* frustration.
'frutta *sf* fruit; (*portata*) dessert; ~ **candita/secca** candied/dried fruit.
frut'tare *vi* (*investimenti, deposito*) to bear dividends, give a return; **il mio deposito in banca (mi) frutta il 10%** my bank deposits bring (me) in 10%; **quella gara gli fruttò la medaglia d'oro** he won the gold medal in that competition.
frut'teto *sm* orchard.
frutticol'tura *sf* fruit growing.
frut'tifero, a *ag* (*albero etc*) fruit-bearing; (*fig: che frutta*) fruitful, profitable; **deposito** ~ interest-bearing deposit.
frutti'vendolo, a *sm/f* greengrocer (*BRIT*), produce dealer (*US*).
'frutto *sm* fruit; (*fig: risultato*) result(s); (*ECON: interesse*) interest; (: *reddito*) income; **è** ~ **della tua immaginazione** it's a figment of your imagination; ~**i di mare** seafood *sg.*
fruttu'oso, a *ag* fruitful, profitable.
FS *abbr* (= *Ferrovie dello Stato*) *Italian railways.*
f.t. *abbr* = **fuori testo.**
f.to. *abbr* (= *firmato*) signed.
fu *vb vedi* **essere** ♦ *ag inv*: **il** ~ **Paolo Bianchi** the late Paolo Bianchi.
fuci'lare [futʃi'lare] *vt* to shoot.
fuci'lata [futʃi'lata] *sf* rifle shot.
fucilazi'one [futʃilat'tsjone] *sf* execution (by firing squad).
fu'cile [fu'tʃile] *sm* rifle, gun; (*da caccia*)

shotgun, gun; ~ **a canne mozze** sawn-off shotgun.

fu'cina [fu'tʃina] *sf* forge.

'fuco, chi *sm* drone.

'fucsia *sf* fuchsia.

'fuga, ghe *sf* escape, flight; (*di gas, liquidi*) leak; (*MUS*) fugue; **mettere qn in** ~ to put sb to flight; ~ **di cervelli** brain drain.

fu'gace [fu'gatʃe] *ag* fleeting, transient.

fu'gare *vt* (*dubbi, incertezze*) to dispel, drive out.

fug'gevole [fud'dʒevole] *ag* fleeting.

fuggi'asco, a, schi, sche [fud'dʒasko] *ag, sm/f* fugitive.

fuggi'fuggi [fuddʒi'fuddʒi] *sm* scramble, stampede.

fug'gire [fud'dʒire] *vi* to flee, run away; (*fig: passar veloce*) to fly ♦ *vt* to avoid.

fuggi'tivo, a [fuddʒi'tivo] *sm/f* fugitive, runaway.

'fui *vb vedi* **essere**.

'fulcro *sm* (*FISICA*) fulcrum; (*fig: di teoria, questione*) central *o* key point.

ful'gore *sm* brilliance, splendour (*BRIT*), splendor (*US*).

fu'liggine [fu'liddʒine] *sf* soot.

fulmi'nare *vt* (*sog: elettricità*) to electrocute; (*con arma da fuoco*) to shoot dead; ~**rsi** *vr* (*lampadina*) to go, blow; (*fig: con lo sguardo*): **mi fulminò (con uno sguardo)** he looked daggers at me.

'fulmine *sm* bolt of lightning; ~**i** *smpl* lightning *sg*; ~ **a ciel sereno** bolt from the blue.

ful'mineo, a *ag* (*fig: scatto*) rapid; (: *minaccioso*) threatening.

'fulvo, a *ag* tawny.

fumai'olo *sm* (*di nave*) funnel; (*di fabbrica*) chimney.

fu'mante *ag* (*piatto etc*) steaming.

fu'mare *vi* to smoke; (*emettere vapore*) to steam ♦ *vt* to smoke.

fu'mario, a *ag*: **canna ~a** flue.

fu'mata *sf* (*segnale*) smoke signal; **farsi una** ~ to have a smoke; ~ **bianca/nera** (*in Vaticano*) *signal that a new pope has/has not been elected*.

fuma'tore, 'trice *sm/f* smoker.

fu'metto *sm* comic strip; **giornale** *m* **a ~i** comic.

'fummo *vb vedi* **essere**.

'fumo *sm* smoke; (*vapore*) steam; (*il fumare tabacco*) smoking; ~**i** *smpl* (*industriali etc*) fumes; **vendere** ~ to deceive, cheat; **è tutto ~ e niente arrosto** it has no substance to it; **i ~i dell'alcool** (*fig*) the after-effects of drink; ~ **passivo** passive smoking.

fu'mogeno, a [fu'mɔdʒeno] *ag* (*candelotto*) smoke *cpd* ♦ *sm* smoke bomb; **cortina ~a** smoke screen.

fu'moso, a *ag* smoky; (*fig*) muddled.

fu'nambolo, a *sm/f* tightrope walker.

'fune *sf* rope, cord; (*più grossa*) cable.

'funebre *ag* (*rito*) funeral; (*aspetto*) gloomy, funereal.

fune'rale *sm* funeral.

fu'nesto, a *ag* (*incidente*) fatal; (*errore, decisione*) fatal, disastrous; (*atmosfera*) gloomy, dismal.

'fungere ['fundʒere] *vi*: ~ **da** to act as.

'fungo, ghi *sm* fungus; (*commestibile*) mushroom; ~ **velenoso** toadstool; **crescere come i ~ghi** (*fig*) to spring up overnight.

funico'lare *sf* funicular railway.

funi'via *sf* cable railway.

'funsi *etc vb vedi* **fungere**.

'funto, a *pp di* **fungere**.

funzio'nare [funtsjo'nare] *vi* to work, function; (*fungere*): ~ **da** to act as.

funzio'nario [funtsjo'narjo] *sm* official; ~ **statale** civil servant.

funzi'one [fun'tsjone] *sf* function; (*carica*) post, position; (*REL*) service; **in** ~ (*meccanismo*) in operation; **in** ~ **di** (*come*) as; **vive in** ~ **dei figli** he lives for his children; **far** ~ **di** to act as; **fare la** ~ **di qn** (*farne le veci*) to take sb's place.

fu'oco, chi *sm* fire; (*fornello*) ring; (*FOT, FISICA*) focus; **dare** ~ **a qc** to set fire to sth; **far** ~ (*sparare*) to fire; **prendere** ~ to catch fire; ~ **d'artificio** firework; ~ **di paglia** flash in the pan; ~ **sacro** *o* **di Sant'Antonio** (*MED fam*) shingles *sg*.

fuorché [fwor'ke] *cong, prep* except.

FU'ORI *sigla m* (= *Fronte Unitario Omosessuale Rivoluzionario Italiano*) *gay liberation movement*.

fu'ori *av* outside; (*all'aperto*) outdoors, outside; (~ *di casa, SPORT*) out; (*esclamativo*) get out! ♦ *prep*: ~ (**di**) out of, outside ♦ *sm* outside; **essere in** ~ (*sporgere*) to stick out; **lasciar** ~ **qc/qn** to leave sth/sb out; **far** ~ (*fam: soldi*) to spend; (: *cioccolatini*) to eat up; (: *rubare*) to nick; **far** ~ **qn** (*fam*) to kill sb, do sb in; **essere tagliato** ~ (*da un gruppo, ambiente*) to be excluded; **essere** ~ **di sé** to be beside oneself; ~ **luogo** (*inopportuno*) out of place, uncalled for; ~ **mano** out of the way, remote; ~ **pasto** between meals; ~ **pericolo** out of danger; ~ **dai piedi!** get out of the way!; ~ **servizio** out of order; ~ **stagione** out of season; **illustrazione** ~ **testo** (*STAMPA*) plate; ~ **uso** out of use.

fuori'bordo *sm inv* speedboat (with outboard motor); outboard motor.

fuori'busta *sm inv* unofficial payment.

fuori'classe *sm/f inv* (undisputed) champion.

fuori'corso *ag inv* (*moneta*) no longer in circulation; (*INS*): (**studente**) ~ *undergraduate who has not completed a course in due time.*

fuorigi'oco [fwori'dʒɔko] *sm* offside.

fuori'legge [fwori'leddʒe] *sm/f inv* outlaw.

fuoriprog'ramma *sm inv* (*TV*, *RADIO*) unscheduled programme; (*fig*) change of plan *o* programme.

fuori'serie *ag inv* (*auto etc*) custom-built ♦ *sf* custom-built car.

fuoris'trada *sm* (*AUT*) cross-country vehicle.

fuoru'scito, a, fuoriu'scito, a [fwor(i)uʃ'ʃito] *sm/f* exile ♦ *sf* (*di gas*) leakage, escape; (*di sangue, linfa*) seepage.

fuorvi'are *vt* to mislead; (*fig*) to lead astray ♦ *vi* to go astray.

furbacchi'one, a [furbak'kjone] *sm/f* cunning old devil.

fur'bizia [fur'bittsja] *sf* (*vedi ag*) cleverness; cunning; **una** ~ a cunning trick.

'furbo, a *ag* clever, smart; (*peg*) cunning ♦ *sm/f*: **fare il** ~ to (try to) be clever *o* smart; **fatti** ~! show a bit of sense!

fu'rente *ag*: ~ (**contro**) furious (with).

fure'ria *sf* (*MIL*) orderly room.

fu'retto *sm* ferret.

fur'fante *sm* rascal, scoundrel.

furgon'cino [furgon'tʃino] *sm* small van.

fur'gone *sm* van.

'furia *sf* (*ira*) fury, rage; (*fig: impeto*) fury, violence; (*fretta*) rush; **a** ~ **di** by dint of; **andare su tutte le** ~**e** to fly into a rage.

furi'bondo, a *ag* furious.

furi'ere *sm* quartermaster.

furi'oso, a *ag* furious; (*mare, vento*) raging.

'furono *vb vedi* **essere**.

fu'rore *sm* fury; (*esaltazione*) frenzy; **far** ~ to be all the rage.

furtiva'mente *av* furtively.

fur'tivo, a *ag* furtive.

'furto *sm* theft; ~ **con scasso** burglary.

'fusa *sfpl*: **fare le** ~ to purr.

fu'scello [fuʃ'ʃɛllo] *sm* twig.

fu'seaux *smpl inv* leggings.

'fusi *etc vb vedi* **fondere**.

fu'sibile *sm* (*ELETTR*) fuse.

fusi'one *sf* (*di metalli*) fusion, melting; (*colata*) casting; (*COMM*) merger; (*fig*) merging.

'fuso, a *pp di* **fondere** ♦ *sm* (*FILATURA*)

spindle; **diritto come un** ~ as stiff as a ramrod; ~ **orario** time zone.

fusoli'era *sf* (*AER*) fusillage.

fus'tagno [fus'taɲɲo] *sm* corduroy.

fus'tella *sf* (*su scatola di medicinali*) tear-off tab.

fusti'gare *vt* (*frustare*) to flog; (*fig: costumi*) to censure, denounce.

fus'tino *sm* (*di detersivo*) tub.

'fusto *sm* stem; (*ANAT, di albero*) trunk; (*recipiente*) drum, can; (*fam*) he-man.

'futile *ag* vain, futile.

futilità *sf inv* futility.

futu'rismo *sm* futurism.

Gg

G, g [dʒi] *sf o m inv* (*lettera*) G, g; **G come Genova** ≈ G for George.

g. *abbr* (= *grammo*) g.

G7 [dʒi'sɛtte] *smpl* G7 (*Group of Seven*).

gabar'dine [gabar'din] *sm* (*tessuto*) gabardine; (*soprabito*) gabardine raincoat.

gab'bare *vt* to take in, dupe; ~**rsi** *vr*: ~**rsi di qn** to make fun of sb.

'gabbia *sf* cage; (*DIR*) dock; (*da imballaggio*) crate; **la** ~ **degli accusati** (*DIR*) the dock; ~ **dell'ascensore** lift (*BRIT*) *o* elevator (*US*) shaft; ~ **toracica** (*ANAT*) rib cage.

gabbi'ano *sm* (sea)gull.

gabi'netto *sm* (*MED etc*) consulting room; (*POL*) ministry; (*di decenza*) toilet, lavatory; (*INS: di fisica etc*) laboratory.

Ga'bon *sm*: **il** ~ Gabon.

ga'elico, a, ci, che *ag, sm* Gaelic.

gaffe [gaf] *sf inv* blunder, boob (*fam*).

gagli'ardo, a [gaʎ'ʎardo] *ag* strong, vigorous.

gai'ezza [ga'jettsa] *sf* gaiety, cheerfulness.

'gaio, a *ag* cheerful.

'gala *sf* (*sfarzo*) pomp; (*festa*) gala.

ga'lante *ag* gallant, courteous; (*avventura, poesia*) amorous.

galante'ria *sf* gallantry.

galantu'omo, pl galantu'omini *sm* gentleman.

Ga'lapagos *sfpl*: **le (isole)** ~ the Galapagos Islands.

ga'lassia *sf* galaxy.

gala'teo *sm* (good) manners *pl*, etiquette.

gale'otto *sm* (*rematore*) galley slave; (*carcerato*) convict.

ga'lera *sf* (*NAUT*) galley; (*prigione*) prison.

'galla *sf*: **a** ~ afloat; **venire a** ~ to surface, come to the surface; (*fig: verità*) to come out.

galleggia'mento [galleddʒa'mento] *sm* floating; **linea di** ~ (*di nave*) waterline.

galleggi'ante [galled'dʒante] *ag* floating ♦ *sm* (*natante*) barge; (*di pescatore, lenza, TECN*) float.

galleggi'are [galled'dʒare] *vi* to float.

galle'ria *sf* (*traforo*) tunnel; (*ARCHIT, d'arte*) gallery; (*TEAT*) circle; (*strada coperta con negozi*) arcade; ~ **del vento** *o* **aerodinamica** (*AER*) wind tunnel.

'Galles *sm*: **il** ~ Wales.

gal'lese *ag* Welsh ♦ *smf* Welshman/woman ♦ *sm* (*LING*) Welsh; **i G~i** the Welsh.

gal'letta *sf* cracker; (*NAUT*) ship's biscuit.

gal'letto *sm* young cock, cockerel; (*fig*) cocky young man; **fare il** ~ to play the gallant.

'Gallia *sf*: **la** ~ Gaul.

gal'lina *sf* hen; **andare a letto con le** ~**e** to go to bed early.

gal'lismo *sm* machismo.

'gallo *sm* cock; **al canto del** ~ at daybreak, at cockcrow; **fare il** ~ to play the gallant.

gal'lone *sm* piece of braid; (*MIL*) stripe; (*unità di misura*) gallon.

galop'pare *vi* to gallop.

galop'pino *sm* errand boy; (*POL*) canvasser.

ga'loppo *sm* gallop; **al** *o* **di** ~ at a gallop.

galvaniz'zare [galvanid'dzare] *vt* to galvanize.

'gamba *sf* leg; (*asta: di lettera*) stem; **in** ~ (*in buona salute*) well; (*bravo, sveglio*) bright, smart; **prendere qc sotto** ~ (*fig*) to treat sth too lightly; **scappare a** ~**e levate** to take to one's heels; ~**e!** scatter!

gam'bale *sm* legging.

gambe'retto *sm* shrimp.

'gambero *sm* (*di acqua dolce*) crayfish; (*di mare*) prawn.

'Gambia *sf*: **la** ~ the Gambia.

gambiz'zare [gambid'dzare] *vt* to kneecap.

'gambo *sm* stem; (*di frutta*) stalk.

ga'mella *sf* mess tin.

'gamma *sf* (*MUS*) scale; (*di colori, fig*) range; ~ **di prodotti** product range.

ga'nascia, sce [ga'naʃʃa] *sf* jaw; ~**sce del freno** (*AUT*) brake shoes.

'gancio ['gantʃo] *sm* hook.

'Gange ['gandʒe] *sm*: **il** ~ the Ganges.

'gangheri ['gangeri] *smpl*: **uscire dai** ~ (*fig*) to fly into a temper.

gan'grena *sf* = **cancrena**.

'gara *sf* competition; (*SPORT*) competition; contest; match; (*: corsa*) race; **fare a** ~ to compete, vie; ~ **d'appalto** (*COMM*) tender.

ga'rage [ga'raʒ] *sm inv* garage.

ga'rante *smf* guarantor.

garan'tire *vt* to guarantee; (*debito*) to stand surety for; (*dare per certo*) to assure.

garan'tismo *sm* protection of civil liberties.

garan'tista, i, e *ag* concerned with civil liberties.

garan'zia [garan'tsia] *sf* guarantee; (*pegno*) security; **in** ~ under guarantee.

gar'bare *vi*: **non mi garba** I don't like it (*o* him *etc*).

garba'tezza [garba'tettsa] *sf* courtesy, politeness.

gar'bato, a *ag* courteous, polite.

'garbo *sm* (*buone maniere*) politeness, courtesy; (*di vestito etc*) grace, style.

gar'buglio [gar'buʎʎo] *sm* tangle; (*fig*) muddle, mess.

gareggi'are [gared'dʒare] *vi* to compete.

garga'nella *sf*: **a** ~ from the bottle.

garga'rismo *sm* gargle; **fare i** ~**i** to gargle.

ga'ritta *sf* (*di caserma*) sentry box.

ga'rofano *sm* carnation; **chiodo di** ~ clove.

gar'retto *sm* hock.

gar'rire *vi* to chirp.

'garrulo, a *ag* (*uccello*) chirping; (*persona: loquace*) garrulous, talkative.

'garza ['gardza] *sf* (*per bende*) gauze.

gar'zone [gar'dzone] *sm* (*di negozio*) boy.

gas *sm inv* gas; **a tutto** ~ at full speed; **dare** ~ (*AUT*) to accelerate; ~ **lacrimogeno** tear gas; ~ **naturale** natural gas.

ga'sare *etc* = **gassare** *etc*.

ga'sato, a *smf* (*fam: persona*) freak.

gas'dotto *sm* gas pipeline.

ga'solio *sm* diesel (oil).

ga's(s)are *vt* to aerate, carbonate; (*asfissiare*) to gas; ~**rsi** *vr* (*fam*) to get excited.

ga's(s)ato, a *ag* (*bibita*) aerated, fizzy.

gas'soso, a *ag* gaseous; gassy ♦ *sf* fizzy drink.

'gastrico, a, ci, che *ag* gastric.

gast'rite *sf* gastritis.

gastroente'rite *sf* gastroenteritis.

gastrono'mia *sf* gastronomy.

gas'tronomo, a *smf* gourmet, gastronome.

G.A.T.T. *sigla m* (= *General Agreement on Tariffs and Trade*) GATT.

'gatta *sf* cat, she-cat; **una** ~ **da pelare** (*fam*) a thankless task; **qui** ~ **ci cova!** I smell a rat!, there's something fishy going on

here!
gatta'buia *sf* (*fam scherzoso: prigione*)
clink.
gat'tino *sm* kitten.
'gatto *sm* cat, tomcat; ~ **delle nevi** (*AUT*,
SCI) snowcat; ~ **a nove code** cat-o'-nine-
tails; ~ **selvatico** wildcat.
gatto'pardo *sm*: ~ **africano** serval; ~
americano ocelot.
gat'tuccio [gat'tuttʃo] *sm* dogfish.
gau'dente *sm/f* pleasure-seeker.
'gaudio *sm* joy, happiness.
ga'vetta *sf* (*MIL*) mess tin; **venire dalla** ~
(*MIL*, *fig*) to rise from the ranks.
'gazza ['gaddza] *sf* magpie.
gaz'zarra [gad'dzarra] *sf* racket, din.
gaz'zella [gad'dzɛlla] *sf* gazelle; (*dei*
carabinieri) (high-speed) police car.
gaz'zetta [gad'dzetta] *sf* news sheet; **G~**
Ufficiale *official publication containing*
details of new laws.
gaz'zoso, a [gad'dzoso] *ag* = **gassoso**.
Gazz. Uff. *abbr* = **Gazzetta Ufficiale**.
GB *sigla* (= *Gran Bretagna*) GB.
G.C. *abbr* = **genio civile**.
G.d.F. *abbr* = **guardia di finanza**.
GE *sigla* = *Genova*.
gel [dʒɛl] *sm inv* gel.
ge'lare [dʒe'lare] *vt, vi, vb impers* to freeze;
mi ha gelato il sangue (*fig*) it made my
blood run cold.
ge'lata [dʒe'lata] *sf* frost.
gela'taio, a [dʒela'tajo] *sm/f* ice-cream
vendor.
gelate'ria [dʒelate'ria] *sf* ice-cream shop.
gela'tina [dʒela'tina] *sf* gelatine; ~
esplosiva gelignite; ~ **di frutta** fruit jelly.
gelati'noso, a [dʒelati'noso] *ag* gelatinous,
jelly-like.
ge'lato, a [dʒe'lato] *ag* frozen ♦ *sm* ice
cream.
'gelido, a ['dʒɛlido] *ag* icy, ice-cold.
'gelo ['dʒɛlo] *sm* (*temperatura*) intense cold;
(*brina*) frost; (*fig*) chill.
ge'lone [dʒe'lone] *sm* chilblain.
gelo'sia [dʒelo'sia] *sf* jealousy.
ge'loso, a [dʒe'loso] *ag* jealous.
'gelso ['dʒɛlso] *sm* mulberry (tree).
gelso'mino [dʒelso'mino] *sm* jasmine.
gemel'laggio [dʒemel'laddʒo] *sm* twinning.
gemel'lare [dʒemel'lare] *ag* twin *cpd* ♦ *vt*
(*città*) to twin.
ge'mello, a [dʒe'mɛllo] *ag, sm/f* twin; ~**i** *smpl*
(*di camicia*) cufflinks; (*dello zodiaco*): **G~i**
Gemini *sg*; **essere dei G~i** to be Gemini.
'gemere ['dʒɛmere] *vi* to moan, groan;
(*cigolare*) to creak; (*gocciolare*) to drip,
ooze.

'gemito ['dʒɛmito] *sm* moan, groan.
'gemma ['dʒɛmma] *sf* (*BOT*) bud; (*pietra*
preziosa) gem.
Gen *abbr* (*MIL*: = *generale*) Gen.
gen. *abbr* (= *generale, generalmente*) gen.
gen'darme [dʒen'darme] *sm* policeman;
(*fig*) martinet.
'gene ['dʒɛne] *sm* gene.
genealo'gia, 'gie [dʒenealo'dʒia] *sf*
genealogy.
genea'logico, a, ci, che [dʒenea'lɔdʒiko]
ag genealogical; **albero** ~ family tree.
gene'rale [dʒene'rale] *ag, sm* general; **in** ~
(*per sommi capi*) in general terms; (*di*
solito) usually, in general; **a** ~ **richiesta**
by popular request.
generalità [dʒenerali'ta] *sfpl* (*dati d'identità*)
particulars.
generaliz'zare [dʒeneralid'dzare] *vt, vi* to
generalize.
generalizzazi'one [dʒeneraliddzat'tsjone] *sf*
generalization.
general'mente [dʒeneral'mente] *av*
generally.
gene'rare [dʒene'rare] *vt* (*dar vita*) to give
birth to; (*produrre*) to produce; (*causare*)
to arouse; (*TECN*) to produce, generate.
genera'tore [dʒenera'tore] *sm* (*TECN*)
generator.
generazi'one [dʒenerat'tsjone] *sf*
generation.
'genere ['dʒɛnere] *sm* kind, type, sort;
(*BIOL*) genus; (*merce*) article, product;
(*LING*) gender; (*ARTE, LETTERATURA*) genre;
in ~ generally, as a rule; **cose del** *o* **di**
questo ~ such things; **il** ~ **umano**
mankind; ~**i alimentari** foodstuffs; ~**i di**
consumo consumer goods; ~**i di prima**
necessità basic essentials.
ge'nerico, a, ci, che [dʒe'nɛriko] *ag*
generic; (*vago*) vague, imprecise; **medico**
~ general practitioner.
'genero ['dʒɛnero] *sm* son-in-law.
generosità [dʒenerosi'ta] *sf* generosity.
gene'roso, a [dʒene'roso] *ag* generous.
'genesi ['dʒɛnezi] *sf* genesis.
ge'netico, a, ci, che [dʒe'nɛtiko] *ag*
genetic ♦ *sf* genetics *sg*.
gen'giva [dʒen'dʒiva] *sf* (*ANAT*) gum.
ge'nia [dʒe'nia] *sf* (*peg*) mob, gang.
geni'ale [dʒe'njale] *ag* (*persona*) of genius;
(*idea*) ingenious, brilliant.
'genio ['dʒɛnjo] *sm* genius; (*attitudine*,
talento) talent, flair, genius; **andare a** ~ **a**
qn to be to sb's liking, appeal to sb; ~
civile civil engineers *pl*; **il** ~ **(militare)** the
Engineers.
geni'tale [dʒeni'tale] *ag* genital; ~**i** *smpl*

genitals.

geni'tore [dʒeni'tore] *sm* parent, father *o* mother; **~i** *smpl* parents.

genn. *abbr* (= *gennaio*) Jan.

gen'naio [dʒen'najo] *sm* January; *per fraseologia vedi* **luglio.**

geno'cidio [dʒeno'tʃidjo] *sm* genocide.

'Genova ['dʒenova] *sf* Genoa.

geno'vese [dʒeno'vese] *ag*, *sm/f* Genoese (*pl inv*).

gen'taglia [dʒen'taʎʎa] *sf* (*peg*) rabble.

'gente ['dʒɛnte] *sf* people *pl*.

gentil'donna [dʒentil'dɔnna] *sf* lady.

gen'tile [dʒen'tile] *ag* (*persona, atto*) kind; (: *garbato*) courteous, polite; (*nelle lettere*): **G~ Signore** Dear Sir; (: *sulla busta*): **G~ Signor Fernando Villa** Mr Fernando Villa.

genti'lezza [dʒenti'lettsa] *sf* kindness; courtesy, politeness; **per ~** (*per favore*) please.

gentilu'omo, *pl* **gentilu'omini** [dʒenti'lwɔmo] *sm* gentleman.

genuflessi'one [dʒenufles'sjone] *sf* genuflection.

genu'ino, a [dʒenu'ino] *ag* (*prodotto*) natural; (*persona, sentimento*) genuine, sincere.

geogra'fia [dʒeogra'fia] *sf* geography.

geo'grafico, a, ci, che [dʒeo'grafiko] *ag* geographical.

ge'ografo, a [dʒe'ɔgrafo] *sm/f* geographer.

geolo'gia [dʒeolo'dʒia] *sf* geology.

geo'logico, a, ci, che [dʒeo'lɔdʒiko] *ag* geological.

ge'ometra, i, e [dʒe'ɔmetra] *sm/f* (*professionista*) surveyor.

geome'tria [dʒeome'tria] *sf* geometry.

geo'metrico, a, ci, che [dʒeo'mɛtriko] *ag* geometric(al).

geopo'litico, a, ci, che [dʒeopo'litiko] *ag* geopolitical.

Ge'orgia [dʒe'ɔrdʒa] *sf* Georgia.

geor'giano, a [dʒeor'dʒano] *ag*, *sm/f* Georgian.

ge'ranio [dʒe'ranjo] *sm* geranium.

ge'rarca, chi [dʒe'rarka] *sm* (*STORIA: nel fascismo*) party official.

gerar'chia [dʒerar'kia] *sf* hierarchy.

ge'rarchico, a, ci, che [dʒe'rarkiko] *ag* hierarchical.

ge'rente [dʒe'rɛnte] *sm/f* manager/ manageress.

ge'renza [dʒe'rɛntsa] *sf* management.

ger'gale [dʒer'gale] *ag* slang *cpd*.

'gergo, ghi ['dʒɛrgo] *sm* jargon; slang.

geria'tria [dʒerja'tria] *sf* geriatrics *sg*.

geri'atrico, a, ci, che [dʒe'rjatriko] *ag* geriatric.

'gerla ['dʒɛrla] *sf* conical wicker basket.

Ger'mania [dʒer'manja] *sf*: **la ~** Germany; **la ~ occidentale/orientale** West/East Germany.

'germe ['dʒɛrme] *sm* germ; (*fig*) seed.

germinazi'one [dʒerminat'tsjone] *sf* germination.

germogli'are [dʒermoʎ'ʎare] *vi* (*emettere germogli*) to sprout; (*germinare*) to germinate.

ger'moglio [dʒer'moʎʎo] *sm* shoot; (*gemma*) bud.

gero'glifico, ci [dʒero'glifiko] *sm* hieroglyphic.

geron'tologo, a, gi, ghe [dʒeron'tɔlogo] *sm/f* specialist in geriatrics.

ge'rundio [dʒe'rundjo] *sm* gerund.

Gerusa'lemme [dʒeruza'lɛmme] *sf* Jerusalem.

'gesso ['dʒɛsso] *sm* chalk; (*SCULTURA, MED, EDIL*) plaster; (*statua*) plaster figure; (*minerale*) gypsum.

'gesta ['dʒɛsta] *sfpl* (*letterario*) deeds, feats.

ges'tante [dʒes'tante] *sf* expectant mother.

gestazi'one [dʒestat'tsjone] *sf* gestation.

gestico'lare [dʒestiko'lare] *vi* to gesticulate.

gestio'nale [dʒestjo'nale] *ag* administrative, management *cpd*.

gesti'one [dʒes'tjone] *sf* management; **~ di magazzino** stock control; **~ patrimoniale** investment management.

ges'tire [dʒes'tire] *vt* to run, manage.

'gesto ['dʒɛsto] *sm* gesture.

ges'tore [dʒes'tore] *sm* manager.

Gesù [dʒe'zu] *sm* Jesus; **~ bambino** the Christ Child.

gesu'ita, i [dʒezu'ita] *sm* Jesuit.

get'tare [dʒet'tare] *vt* to throw; (*anche*: **~ via**) to throw away *o* out; (*SCULTURA*) to cast; (*EDIL*) to lay; (*acqua*) to spout; (*grido*) to utter; **~rsi** *vr*: **~rsi in** (*impresa*) to throw o.s. into; (*mischia*) to hurl o.s. into; (*sog*: *fiume*) to flow into; **~ uno sguardo su** to take a quick look at.

get'tata [dʒet'tata] *sf* (*di cemento, gesso, metalli*) cast; (*diga*) jetty.

'gettito ['dʒettito] *sm* revenue.

'getto ['dʒɛtto] *sm* (*di gas, liquido, AER*) jet; (*BOT*) shoot; **a ~ continuo** uninterruptedly; **di ~** (*fig*) straight off, in one go.

get'tone [dʒet'tone] *sm* token; (*per giochi*) counter; (: *roulette etc*) chip; **~ di presenza** attendance fee; **~ telefonico** telephone token.

gettoni'era [dʒetto'njɛra] *sf* telephone-token dispenser.

'geyser ['gaizə] *sm inv* geyser.
'Ghana ['gana] *sm*: **il** ~ Ghana.
'ghenga, ghe ['gɛnga] *sf (fam)* gang, crowd.
ghe'pardo [ge'pardo] *sm* cheetah.
gher'mire [ger'mire] *vt* to grasp, clasp, clutch.
'ghetta ['getta] *sf (gambale)* gaiter.
ghettiz'zare [gettid'dzare] *vt* to segregate.
'ghetto ['getto] *sm* ghetto.
ghiacci'aia [gjat'tʃaja] *sf (anche fig)* icebox.
ghiacci'aio [gjat'tʃajo] *sm* glacier.
ghiacci'are [gjat'tʃare] *vt* to freeze; *(fig)*: ~ **qn** to make sb's blood run cold ♦ *vi* to freeze, ice over.
ghiacci'ato, a [gjat'tʃato] *ag* frozen; *(bevanda)* ice-cold.
ghi'accio ['gjattʃo] *sm* ice.
ghiacci'olo [gjat'tʃɔlo] *sm* icicle; *(tipo di gelato)* ice lolly *(BRIT)*, popsicle *(US)*.
ghi'aia ['gjaja] *sf* gravel.
ghi'anda ['gjanda] *sf (BOT)* acorn.
ghi'andola ['gjandola] *sf* gland.
ghiando'lare [gjando'lare] *ag* glandular.
ghigliot'tina [giʎʎot'tina] *sf* guillotine.
ghi'gnare [giɲ'ɲare] *vi* to sneer.
'ghigno ['giɲɲo] *sm (espressione)* sneer; *(risata)* mocking laugh.
'ghingheri ['gingeri] *smpl*: **in** ~ all dolled up; **mettersi in** ~ to put on one's Sunday best.
ghi'otto, a ['gjotto] *ag* greedy; *(cibo)* delicious, appetizing.
ghiot'tone, a [gjot'tone] *sm/f* glutton.
ghiottone'ria [gjottone'ria] *sf* greed, gluttony; *(cibo)* delicacy, titbit *(BRIT)*, tidbit *(US)*.
ghiri'goro [giri'gɔro] *sm* scribble, squiggle.
ghir'landa [gir'landa] *sf* garland, wreath.
'ghiro ['giro] *sm* dormouse.
'ghisa ['giza] *sf* cast iron.
G.I. *abbr* = **giudice istruttore**.
già [dʒa] *av* already; *(ex, in precedenza)* formerly ♦ *escl* of course!, yes indeed!; ~ **che ci sei ...** while you are at it ....
gi'acca, che ['dʒakka] *sf* jacket; ~ **a vento** windcheater *(BRIT)*, windbreaker *(US)*.
giacché [dʒak'ke] *cong* since, as.
giac'chetta [dʒak'ketta] *sf* (light) jacket.
'giaccio *etc* ['dʒattʃo] *vb vedi* **giacere**.
giac'cone [dʒak'kone] *sm* heavy jacket.
gia'cenza [dʒa'tʃɛntsa] *sf*: **merce in** ~ goods in stock; **capitale in** ~ uninvested capital; ~**e di magazzino** unsold stock.
gia'cere [dʒa'tʃere] *vi* to lie.
giaci'mento [dʒatʃi'mento] *sm* deposit.
gia'cinto [dʒa'tʃinto] *sm* hyacinth.
giaci'uto, a [dʒa'tʃuto] *pp di* **giacere**.

gi'acqui *etc* ['dʒakkwi] *vb vedi* **giacere**.
gi'ada ['dʒada] *sf* jade.
giaggi'olo [dʒad'dʒɔlo] *sm* iris.
giagu'aro [dʒa'gwaro] *sm* jaguar.
gial'lastro, a [dʒal'lastro] *ag* yellowish; *(carnagione)* sallow.
gi'allo ['dʒallo] *ag* yellow; *(carnagione)* sallow ♦ *sm* yellow; *(anche:* **romanzo** ~*)* detective novel; *(anche:* **film** ~*)* detective film; ~ **dell'uovo** yolk; **il mar G**~ the Yellow Sea.
gial'lognolo, a [dʒal'loɲɲolo] *ag* yellowish, dirty yellow.
Gia'maica [dʒa'maika] *sf*: **la** ~ Jamaica.
giamai'cano, a [dʒamai'kano] *ag, sm/f* Jamaican.
giam'mai [dʒam'mai] *av* never.
Giap'pone [dʒap'pone] *sm*: **il** ~ Japan.
giappo'nese [dʒappo'nese] *ag, sm/f, sm* Japanese *inv*.
gi'ara ['dʒara] *sf* jar.
giardi'naggio [dʒardi'naddʒo] *sm* gardening.
giardi'netta [dʒardi'netta] *sf* estate car *(BRIT)*, station wagon *(US)*.
giardini'ere, a [dʒardi'njere] *sm/f* gardener ♦ *sf (misto di sottaceti)* mixed pickles *pl*; *(automobile)* = **giardinetta**.
giar'dino [dʒar'dino] *sm* garden; ~ **d'infanzia** nursery school; ~ **pubblico** public gardens *pl*, (public) park; ~ **zoologico** zoo.
giarretti'era [dʒarret'tjera] *sf* garter.
Gi'ava ['dʒava] *sf* Java.
giavel'lotto [dʒavel'lɔtto] *sm* javelin.
gib'boso, a [dʒib'boso] *ag (superficie)* bumpy; *(naso)* crooked.
Gibil'terra [dʒibil'tɛrra] *sf* Gibraltar.
gi'gante, 'essa [dʒi'gante] *sm/f* giant ♦ *ag* giant, gigantic; *(COMM)* giant-size.
gigan'tesco, a, schi, sche [dʒigan'tesko] *ag* gigantic.
gigantogra'fia [dʒigantogra'fia] *sf (FOT)* blow-up.
'giglio ['dʒiʎʎo] *sm* lily.
gilè [dʒi'lɛ] *sm inv* waistcoat.
gin [dʒin] *sm inv* gin.
gin'cana [dʒin'kana] *sf* gymkhana.
ginecolo'gia [dʒinekolo'dʒia] *sf* gynaecology *(BRIT)*, gynecology *(US)*.
gine'cologo, a, gi, ghe [dʒine'kɔlogo] *sm/f* gynaecologist *(BRIT)*, gynecologist *(US)*.
gi'nepro [dʒi'nepro] *sm* juniper.
gi'nestra [dʒi'nɛstra] *sf (BOT)* broom.
Gi'nevra [dʒi'nevra] *sf* Geneva; **il Lago di** ~ Lake Geneva.
gingil'larsi [dʒindʒil'larsi] *vr* to fritter away one's time; *(giocare)*: ~ **con** to fiddle with.

gin'gillo [dʒin'dʒillo] *sm* plaything.

gin'nasio [dʒin'nazjo] *sm* the 4th and 5th year of secondary school in Italy.

gin'nasta, i, e [dʒin'nasta] *smlf* gymnast.

gin'nastica [dʒin'nastika] *sf* gymnastics *sg*; (*esercizio fisico*) keep-fit exercises *pl*; (*INS*) physical education.

'ginnico, a, ci, che ['dʒinniko] *ag* gymnastic.

gi'nocchio [dʒi'nɔkkjo], *pl(m)* **gi'nocchi** *o* *pl(f)* **gi'nocchia** *sm* knee; **stare in** ~ to kneel, be on one's knees; **mettersi in** ~ to kneel (down).

ginocchi'oni [dʒinok'kjoni] *av* on one's knees.

gio'care [dʒo'kare] *vt* to play; (*scommettere*) to stake, wager, bet; (*ingannare*) to take in ♦ *vi* to play; (*a roulette etc*) to gamble; (*fig*) to play a part, be important; (*TECN: meccanismo*) to be loose; ~ **a** (*gioco, sport*) to play; (*cavalli*) to bet on; ~ **d'astuzia** to be crafty; ~**rsi la carriera** to put one's career at risk; ~**rsi tutto** to risk everything; **a che gioco giochiamo?** what are you playing at?

gioca'tore, 'trice [dʒoka'tore] *smlf* player; gambler.

gio'cattolo [dʒo'kattolo] *sm* toy.

giocherel'lare [dʒokerel'lare] *vi:* ~ **con** (*giocattolo*) to play with; (*distrattamente*) to fiddle with.

giocherò *etc* [dʒoke'rɔ] *vb vedi* **giocare**.

gio'chetto [dʒo'ketto] *sm* (*gioco*) game; (*tranello*) trick; (*fig*): **è un** ~ it's child's play.

gi'oco, chi ['dʒɔko] *sm* game; (*divertimento, TECN*) play; (*al casinò*) gambling; (*CARTE*) hand; (*insieme di pezzi etc necessari per un gioco*) set; **per** ~ for fun; **fare il doppio** ~ **con qn** to double-cross sb; **prendersi** ~ **di qn** to pull sb's leg; **stare al** ~ **di qn** to play along with sb; **è in** ~ **la mia reputazione** my reputation is at stake; ~ **d'azzardo** game of chance; ~ **della palla** ball game; ~ **degli scacchi** chess set; **i G**~**chi Olimpici** the Olympic Games.

gioco'forza [dʒoko'fɔrtsa] *sm*: **essere** ~ to be inevitable.

giocoli'ere [dʒoko'ljɛre] *sm* juggler.

gio'coso, a [dʒo'koso] *ag* playful, jesting.

gio'gaia [dʒo'gaja] *sf (GEO)* range of mountains.

gi'ogo, ghi ['dʒogo] *sm* yoke.

gi'oia ['dʒɔja] *sf* joy, delight; (*pietra preziosa*) jewel, precious stone.

gioielle'ria [dʒojelle'ria] *sf* jeweller's (*BRIT*) *o* jeweler's (*US*) craft; (*negozio*) jewel(l)er's (shop).

gioielli'ere, a [dʒojel'ljɛre] *smlf* jeweller (*BRIT*), jeweler (*US*).

gioi'ello [dʒo'jɛllo] *sm* jewel, piece of jewellery (*BRIT*) *o* jewelry (*US*); ~**i** *smpl* (*gioie*) jewel(l)ery *sg*.

gioi'oso, a [dʒo'joso] *ag* joyful.

Gior'dania [dʒor'danja] *sf*: **la** ~ Jordan.

Gior'dano [dʒor'dano] *sm*: **il** ~ the Jordan.

gior'dano, a [dʒor'dano] *ag, smlf* Jordanian.

giorna'laio, a [dʒorna'lajo] *smlf* newsagent (*BRIT*), newsdealer (*US*).

gior'nale [dʒor'nale] *sm* (news)paper; (*diario*) journal, diary; (*COMM*) journal; ~ **di bordo** (*NAUT*) ship's log; ~ **radio** radio news *sg*.

giorna'letto [dʒorna'letto] *sm* (children's) comic.

giornali'ero, a [dʒorna'ljɛro] *ag* daily; (*che varia: umore*) changeable ♦ *sm* day labourer (*BRIT*) *o* laborer (*US*).

giorna'lino [dʒorna'lino] *sm* children's comic.

giorna'lismo [dʒorna'lizmo] *sm* journalism.

giorna'lista, i, e [dʒorna'lista] *smlf* journalist.

giorna'listico, a, ci, che [dʒorna'listiko] *ag* journalistic; **stile** ~ journalese.

giornal'mente [dʒornal'mente] *av* daily.

gior'nata [dʒor'nata] *sf* day; (*paga*) day's wages, day's pay; **durante la** ~ **di ieri** yesterday; **fresco di** ~ (*uovo*) freshly laid; **vivere alla** ~ to live from day to day; ~ **lavorativa** working day.

gi'orno ['dʒorno] *sm* day; (*opposto alla notte*) day, daytime; (*luce del* ~) daylight; **al** ~ per day; **di** ~ by day; ~ **per** ~ day by day; **al** ~ **d'oggi** nowadays; **tutto il santo** ~ all day long.

Il Giorno dei Morti, *All Souls' Day, falls on November 2nd. On that day, relatives make a special visit to the graves of loved ones to lay flowers.*

---

gi'ostra ['dʒɔstra] *sf (per bimbi)* merry-go-round; (*torneo storico*) joust.

gios'trare [dʒos'trare] *vi (STORIA)* to joust, tilt; ~**rsi** *vr* to manage.

giov. *abbr* (= *giovedì*) Thur(s).

giova'mento [dʒova'mento] *sm* benefit, help.

gi'ovane ['dʒovane] *ag* young; (*aspetto*) youthful ♦ *smlf* youth/girl, young man/ woman; **i** ~**i** young people; **è** ~ **del mestiere** he's new to the job.

giova'netto, a [dʒova'netto] *smlf* young man/woman.

giova'nile [dʒova'nile] *ag* youthful; (*scritti*)

early; (*errore*) of youth.

giova'notto [dʒova'nɔtto] *sm* young man.

gio'vare [dʒo'vare] *vi*: ~ **a** (*essere utile*) to be useful to; (*far bene*) to be good for ♦ *vb impers* (*essere bene, utile*) to be useful; ~**rsi** *vr*: ~**rsi di qc** to make use of sth; **a che giova prendersela?** what's the point of getting upset?

Gi'ove ['dʒɔve] *sm* (*MITOLOGIA*) Jove; (*ASTR*) Jupiter.

giovedì [dʒove'di] *sm inv* Thursday; *per fraseologia vedi* **martedì.**

gio'venca, che [dʒo'vɛnka] *sf* heifer.

gioventù [dʒoven'tu] *sf* (*periodo*) youth; (*i giovani*) young people *pl*, youth.

giovi'ale [dʒo'vjale] *ag* jovial, jolly.

giovi'nastro [dʒovi'nastro] *sm* young thug.

giovin'cello [dʒovin'tʃello] *sm* young lad.

giovi'nezza [dʒovi'nettsa] *sf* youth.

gip [dʒip] *sigla m inv* (= *giudice per le indagini preliminari*) judge for preliminary enquiries.

gira'dischi [dʒira'diski] *sm inv* record player.

gi'raffa [dʒi'raffa] *sf* giraffe; (*TV, CINE, RADIO*) boom.

gira'mento [dʒira'mento] *sm*: ~ **di testa** fit of dizziness.

gira'mondo [dʒira'mondo] *sm/f inv* globetrotter.

gi'randola [dʒi'randola] *sf* (*fuoco d'artificio*) Catherine wheel; (*giocattolo*) toy windmill; (*banderuola*) weather vane, weathercock.

gi'rante [dʒi'rante] *sm/f* (*di assegno*) endorser.

gi'rare [dʒi'rare] *vt* (*far ruotare*) to turn; (*percorrere, visitare*) to go round; (*CINE*) to shoot; (: *film: come regista*) to make; (*COMM*) to endorse ♦ *vi* to turn; (*più veloce*) to spin; (*andare in giro*) to wander, go around; ~**rsi** *vr* to turn; ~ **attorno a** to go round; to revolve round; **si girava e rigirava nel letto** he tossed and turned in bed; **far** ~ **la testa a qn** to make sb dizzy; (*fig*) to turn sb's head; **gira al largo** keep your distance; **girala come ti pare** (*fig*) look at it whichever way you like; **gira e rigira** ... after a lot of driving (*o* walking) about ...; (*fig*) whichever way you look at it; **cosa ti gira?** (*fam*) what's got into you?; **mi ha fatto** ~ **le scatole** (*fam*) he drove me crazy.

girar'rosto [dʒirar'rɔsto] *sm* (*CUC*) spit.

gira'sole [dʒira'sole] *sm* sunflower.

gi'rata [dʒi'rata] *sf* (*passeggiata*) stroll; (*con veicolo*) drive; (*COMM*) endorsement.

gira'tario, a [dʒira'tarjo] *sm/f* endorsee.

gira'volta [dʒira'vɔlta] *sf* twirl, turn; (*curva*) sharp bend; (*fig*) about-turn.

gi'rello [dʒi'rɛllo] *sm* (*di bambino*) Babywalker ® (*BRIT*), go-cart (*US*); (*taglio di carne*) topside (*BRIT*), top round (*US*).

gi'retto [dʒi'retto] *sm* (*passeggiata*) walk, stroll; (: *in macchina*) drive, spin; (: *in bicicletta*) ride.

gi'revole [dʒi'revole] *ag* revolving, turning.

gi'rino [dʒi'rino] *sm* tadpole.

'giro ['dʒiro] *sm* (*circuito, cerchio*) circle; (*di chiave, manovella*) turn; (*viaggio*) tour, excursion; (*passeggiata*) stroll, walk; (*in macchina*) drive; (*in bicicletta*) ride; (*SPORT: della pista*) lap; (*di denaro*) circulation; (*CARTE*) hand; (*TECN*) revolution; **fare un** ~ to go for a walk (*o* a drive *o* a ride); **fare il** ~ **di** (*parco, città*) to go round; **andare in** ~ (*a piedi*) to go about, walk around; **guardarsi in** ~ to look around; **prendere in** ~ **qn** (*fig*) to take sb for a ride; **a stretto** ~ **di posta** by return of post; **nel** ~ **di un mese** in a month's time; **essere nel** ~ (*fig*) to belong to a circle (of friends); ~ **d'affari** (*viaggio*) business tour; (*COMM*) turnover; ~ **di parole** circumlocution; ~ **di prova** (*AUT*) test drive; ~ **turistico** sightseeing tour; ~ **vita** waist measurement.

giro'collo [dʒiro'kɔllo] *sm*: **a** ~ crewneck *cpd*.

giro'conto [dʒiro'konto] *sm* (*ECON*) credit transfer.

gi'rone [dʒi'rone] *sm* (*SPORT*) series of games; ~ **di andata/ritorno** (*CALCIO*) first/second half of the season.

gironzo'lare [dʒirondzo'lare] *vi* to stroll about.

giro'tondo [dʒiro'tondo] *sm* ring-a-ring-o'roses (*BRIT*), ring-around-the-rosey (*US*); **in** ~ in a circle.

girova'gare [dʒirova'gare] *vi* to wander about.

gi'rovago, a, ghi, ghe [dʒi'rɔvago] *sm/f* (*vagabondo*) tramp; (*venditore*) peddler; **una compagnia di** ~**ghi** (*attori*) a company of strolling actors.

'gita ['dʒita] *sf* excursion, trip; **fare una** ~ to go for a trip, go on an outing.

gi'tano, a [dʒi'tano] *sm/f* gipsy.

gi'tante [dʒi'tante] *sm/f* member of a tour.

giù [dʒu] *av* down; (*dabbasso*) downstairs; **in** ~ downwards, down; **la mia casa è un po' più in** ~ my house is a bit further on; ~ **di lì** (*pressappoco*) thereabouts; **bambini dai 6 anni in** ~ children aged 6 and under; **cadere** ~ **per le scale** to fall down the stairs; ~ **le mani!** hands off!; **essere**

~ (*fig*: *di salute*) to be run down;
(: *di spirito*) to be depressed; **quel tipo non mi va** ~ I can't stand that guy.
gi'ubba ['dʒubba] *sf* jacket.
giub'botto [dʒub'bɔtto] *sm* jerkin; ~ **antiproiettile** bulletproof vest.
giubi'lare [dʒubi'lare] *vi* to rejoice.
gi'ubilo ['dʒubilo] *sm* rejoicing.
giudi'care [dʒudi'kare] *vt* to judge; (*accusato*) to try; (*lite*) to arbitrate in; ~ **qn/qc bello** to consider sb/sth (to be) beautiful.
giudi'cato [dʒudi'kato] *sm* (*DIR*): **passare in** ~ to pass final judgment.
gi'udice ['dʒuditʃe] *sm* judge; ~ **collegiale** member of the court; ~ **conciliatore** justice of the peace; ~ **istruttore** examining (*BRIT*) *o* committing (*US*) magistrate; ~ **popolare** member of a jury.
giudizi'ale [dʒudit'tsjale] *ag* judicial.
giudizi'ario, a [dʒudit'tsjarjo] *ag* legal, judicial.
giu'dizio [dʒu'dittsjo] *sm* judgment; (*opinione*) opinion; (*DIR*) judgment, sentence; (: *processo*) trial; (: *verdetto*) verdict; **aver** ~ to be wise *o* prudent; **essere in attesa di** ~ to be awaiting trial; **citare in** ~ to summons; **l'imputato è stato rinviato a** ~ the accused has been committed for trial.
giudizi'oso, a [dʒudit'tsjoso] *ag* prudent, judicious.
gi'uggiola ['dʒuddʒola] *sf*: **andare in brodo di** ~**e** (*fam*) to be over the moon.
gi'ugno ['dʒuɲɲo] *sm* June; *per fraseologia vedi* **luglio.**
giu'livo, a [dʒu'livo] *ag* merry.
giul'lare [dʒul'lare] *sm* jester.
giu'menta [dʒu'menta] *sf* mare.
gi'unco, chi ['dʒunko] *sm* (*BOT*) rush.
gi'ungere ['dʒundʒere] *vi* to arrive ♦ *vt* (*mani etc*) to join; ~ **a** to arrive at, reach; ~ **nuovo a qn** to come as news to sb; ~ **in porto** to reach harbour; (*fig*) to be brought to a successful outcome.
gi'ungla ['dʒungla] *sf* jungle.
gi'unsi *etc* ['dʒunsi] *vb vedi* **giungere.**
gi'unto, a ['dʒunto] *pp di* **giungere** ♦ *sm* (*TECN*) coupling, joint ♦ *sf* addition; (*organo esecutivo, amministrativo*) council, board; **per** ~**a** into the bargain, in addition; ~**a militare** military junta; *vedi anche* **Comune; Provincia; Regione.**
giun'tura [dʒun'tura] *sf* joint.
giuo'care [dʒwo'kare] *vt, vi* = **giocare.**
giu'oco ['dʒwɔko] *sm* = **gioco.**
giura'mento [dʒura'mento] *sm* oath; ~ **falso**

perjury.
giu'rare [dʒu'rare] *vt* to swear ♦ *vi* to swear, take an oath; **gliel'ho giurata** I swore I would get even with him.
giu'rato, a [dʒu'rato] *ag*: **nemico** ~ sworn enemy ♦ *sm/f* juror, juryman/woman.
giu'ria [dʒu'ria] *sf* jury.
giu'ridico, a, ci, che [dʒu'ridiko] *ag* legal.
giurisdizi'one [dʒurizdit'tsjone] *sf* jurisdiction.
giurispru'denza [dʒurispru'dɛntsa] *sf* jurisprudence.
giu'rista, i, e [dʒu'rista] *sm/f* jurist.
giustap'porre [dʒustap'porre] *vt* to juxtapose.
giustapposizi'one [dʒustappozit'tsjone] *sf* juxtaposition.
giustap'posto, a [dʒustap'posto] *pp di* **giustapporre.**
giustifi'care [dʒustifi'kare] *vt* to justify; ~**rsi** *vr*: ~**rsi di** *o* **per qc** to justify *o* excuse o.s. for sth.
giustifica'tivo, a [dʒustifika'tivo] *ag* (*AMM*): **nota** *o* **pezza** ~**a** receipt.
giustificazi'one [dʒustifikat'tsjone] *sf* justification; (*INS*) (note of) excuse.
gius'tizia [dʒus'tittsja] *sf* justice; **farsi** ~ (**da sé**) (*vendicarsi*) to take the law into one's own hands.
giustizi'are [dʒustit'tsjare] *vt* to execute, put to death.
giustizi'ere [dʒustit'tsjɛre] *sm* executioner.
gi'usto, a ['dʒusto] *ag* (*equo*) fair, just; (*vero*) true, correct; (*adatto*) right, suitable; (*preciso*) exact, correct ♦ *av* (*esattamente*) exactly, precisely; (*per l'appunto, appena*) just; **arrivare** ~ to arrive just in time; **ho** ~ **bisogno di te** you're just the person I need.
'glabro, a *ag* hairless.
glaci'ale [gla'tʃale] *ag* glacial.
gla'diolo *sm* gladiolus.
'glandola *sf* = **ghiandola.**
'glassa *sf* (*CUC*) icing.
glau'coma *sm* glaucoma.
gli [ʎi] *det mpl* (*dav V, s impura, gn, pn, ps, x, z*) the ♦ *pron* (*a lui*) to him; (*a esso*) to it; (*in coppia con lo, la, li, le, ne: a lui, a lei, a loro etc*): **gliele do** I'm giving them to him (*o* her *o* them); **gliene ho parlato** I spoke to him (*o* her *o* them) about it; *vedi anche* **il.**
glice'mia [glitʃe'mia] *sf* glycaemia.
glice'rina [glitʃe'rina] *sf* glycerine.
'glicine ['glitʃine] *sm* wistaria.
gli'ela *etc* ['ʎela] *vedi* **gli.**
glo'bale *ag* overall; (*vista*) global.
'globo *sm* globe.
'globulo *sm* (*ANAT*): ~ **rosso/bianco** red/

white corpuscle.

'gloria *sf* glory; **farsi ~ di qc** to pride o.s. on sth, take pride in sth.

glori'arsi *vr:* **~ di qc** to pride o.s. on sth, glory *o* take pride in sth.

glorifi'care *vt* to glorify.

glori'oso, a *ag* glorious.

glos'sario *sm* glossary.

glu'cosio *sm* glucose.

'gluteo *sm* gluteus; **~i** *smpl* buttocks.

GM *abbr* = **genio militare.**

G.N. *abbr* = **gas naturale.**

'gnocchi ['ɲɔkki] *smpl* (*CUC*) small dumplings made of semolina pasta or potato.

'gnomo ['ɲɔmo] *sm* gnome.

'gnorri ['ɲɔrri] *sm/f inv:* **non fare lo ~!** stop acting as if you didn't know anything about it!

GO *sigla* = **Gorizia.**

'goal ['goul] *sm inv* (*SPORT*) goal.

'gobba *sf* (*ANAT*) hump; (*protuberanza*) bump.

'gobbo, a *ag* hunchbacked; (*ricurvo*) round-shouldered ♦ *sm/f* hunchback.

'Gobi *smpl:* **il Deserto dei ~** the Gobi Desert.

'goccia, ce ['gottʃa] *sf* drop; **~ di rugiada** dewdrop; **somigliarsi come due ~ce d'acqua** to be as like as two peas in a pod; **è la ~ che fa traboccare il vaso!** it's the last straw!

'goccio ['gottʃo] *sm* drop, spot.

goccio'lare [gottʃo'lare] *vi, vt* to drip.

goccio'lio [gottʃo'lio] *sm* dripping.

go'dere *vi* (*compiacersi*): **~ (di)** to be delighted (at), rejoice (at); (*trarre vantaggio*): **~ di** to enjoy, benefit from ♦ *vt* to enjoy; **~rsi la vita** to enjoy life; **godersela** to have a good time, enjoy o.s.

godi'mento *sm* enjoyment.

godrò *etc vb vedi* **godere.**

gof'faggine [gof'faddʒine] *sf* clumsiness.

'goffo, a *ag* clumsy, awkward.

'gogna ['goɲɲa] *sf* pillory.

gol *sm inv* = **goal.**

'gola *sf* (*ANAT*) throat; (*golosità*) gluttony, greed; (*di camino*) flue; (*di monte*) gorge; **fare ~** (*anche fig*) to tempt; **ricacciare il pianto** *o* **le lacrime in ~** to swallow one's tears.

go'letta *sf* (*NAUT*) schooner.

golf *sm inv* (*SPORT*) golf; (*maglia*) cardigan.

'golfo *sm* gulf.

goli'ardico, a, ci, che *ag* (*canto, vita*) student *cpd*.

go'loso, a *ag* greedy.

'golpe *sm inv* (*POL*) coup.

gomi'tata *sf:* **dare una ~ a qn** to elbow sb; **farsi avanti a (forza** *o* **furia di) ~e** to elbow one's way through; **fare a ~e per qc** to fight to get sth.

'gomito *sm* elbow; (*di strada etc*) sharp bend.

go'mitolo *sm* ball.

'gomma *sf* rubber; (*colla*) gum; (*per cancellare*) rubber, eraser; (*di veicolo*) tyre (*BRIT*), tire (*US*); **~ da masticare** chewing gum; **~ a terra** flat tyre.

gommapi'uma ® *sf* foam rubber.

gom'mino *sm* rubber tip; (*rondella*) rubber washer.

gom'mista, i, e *sm/f* tyre (*BRIT*) *o* tire (*US*) specialist; (*rivenditore*) tyre *o* tire merchant.

gom'mone *sm* rubber dinghy.

gom'moso, a *ag* rubbery.

'gondola *sf* gondola.

gondoli'ere *sm* gondolier.

gonfa'lone *sm* banner.

gonfi'are *vt* (*pallone*) to blow up, inflate; (*dilatare, ingrossare*) to swell; (*fig: notizia*) to exaggerate; **~rsi** *vr* to swell; (*fiume*) to rise.

'gonfio, a *ag* swollen; (*stomaco*) bloated; (*palloncino, gomme*) inflated, blown up; (*con pompa*) pumped up; (*vela*) full; **occhi ~i di pianto** eyes swollen with tears; **~ di orgoglio** (*persona*) puffed up (with pride); **avere il portafoglio ~** to have a bulging wallet.

gonfi'ore *sm* swelling.

gongo'lare *vi* to look pleased with o.s.; **~ di gioia** to be overjoyed.

'gonna *sf* skirt; **~ pantalone** culottes *pl*.

'gonzo ['gondzo] *sm* simpleton, fool.

gorgheggi'are [gorged'dʒare] *vi* to warble; to trill.

gor'gheggio [gor'geddʒo] *sm* (*MUS, di uccello*) trill.

'gorgo, ghi *sm* whirlpool.

gorgogli'are [gorgoʎ'ʎare] *vi* to gurgle.

gorgo'glio [gorgoʎ'ʎio] *sm* gurgling.

go'rilla *sm inv* gorilla; (*guardia del corpo*) bodyguard.

'Gotha *sm inv* (*del cinema, letteratura, industria*) leading lights *pl*.

'gotico, a, ci, che *ag, sm* Gothic.

'gotta *sf* gout.

gover'nante *sm/f* ruler ♦ *sf* (*di bambini*) governess; (*donna di servizio*) housekeeper.

gover'nare *vt* (*stato*) to govern, rule; (*pilotare, guidare*) to steer; (*bestiame*) to tend, look after.

governa'tivo, a *ag* (*politica, decreto*)

government *cpd*, governmental; (*stampa*) pro-government.
governa'tore *sm* governor.
go'verno *sm* government; ~ **ombra** shadow cabinet.
'gozzo ['gottso] *sm* (*ZOOL*) crop; (*MED*) goitre; (*fig fam*) throat.
gozzovigli'are [gottsoviʎ'ʎare] *vi* to make merry, carouse.
gpm *abbr* (= *giri per minuto*) rpm.
GR [dzi'erre] *sigla* = *Grosseto* ♦ *sigla m* (= **giornale radio**) radio news.
gracchi'are [grak'kjare] *vi* to caw.
graci'dare [gratʃi'dare] *vi* to croak.
graci'dio, ii [gratʃi'dio] *sm* croaking.
'gracile ['gratʃile] *ag* frail, delicate.
gra'dasso *sm* boaster.
gradata'mente *av* gradually, by degrees.
gradazi'one [gradat'tsjone] *sf* (*sfumatura*) gradation; ~ **alcolica** alcoholic content, strength.
gra'devole *ag* pleasant, agreeable.
gradi'mento *sm* pleasure, satisfaction; **essere di mio** (*o tuo etc*) ~ to be to my (*o* your *etc*) liking.
gradi'nata *sf* flight of steps; (*in teatro, stadio*) tiers *pl*.
gra'dino *sm* step; (*ALPINISMO*) foothold.
gra'dire *vt* (*accettare con piacere*) to accept; (*desiderare*) to wish, like; **gradisce una tazza di tè?** would you like a cup of tea?
gra'dito, a *ag* welcome.
'grado *sm* (*MAT, FISICA etc*) degree; (*stadio*) degree, level; (*MIL, sociale*) rank; **essere in** ~ **di fare** to be in a position to do; **di buon** ~ willingly; **per** ~i by degrees; **un cugino di primo/secondo** ~ a first/second cousin; **subire il terzo** ~ (*anche fig*) to be given the third degree.
gradu'ale *ag* gradual.
gradu'are *vt* to grade.
gradu'ato, a *ag* (*esercizi*) graded; (*scala, termometro*) graduated ♦ *sm* (*MIL*) non-commissioned officer.
gradua'toria *sf* (*di concorso*) list; (*per la promozione*) order of seniority.
'graffa *sf* (*gancio*) clip; (*segno grafico*) brace.
graf'fetta *sf* paper clip.
graffi'are *vt* to scratch.
graffia'tura *sf* scratch.
'graffio *sm* scratch.
graf'fiti *smpl* graffiti.
gra'fia *sf* spelling; (*scrittura*) handwriting.
'grafico, a, ci, che *ag* graphic ♦ *sm* graph; (*persona*) graphic designer ♦ *sf* graphic arts *pl*; ~ **a torta** pie chart.
gra'migna [gra'miɲɲa] *sf* weed; couch

grass.
gram'matica, che *sf* grammar.
grammati'cale *ag* grammatical.
'grammo *sm* gram(me).
gram'mofono *sm* gramophone.
'gramo, a *ag* (*vita*) wretched.
gran *ag vedi* **grande**.
'grana *sf* (*granello, di minerali, corpi spezzati*) grain; (*fam: seccatura*) trouble; (: *soldi*) cash ♦ *sm inv* cheese similar to Parmesan.
gra'naglie [gra'naʎʎe] *sfpl* corn *sg*, seed *sg*.
gra'naio *sm* granary, barn.
gra'nata *sf* (*frutto*) pomegranate; (*pietra preziosa*) garnet; (*proiettile*) grenade.
granati'ere *sm* (*MIL*) grenadier; (*fig*) fine figure of a man.
Gran Bre'tagna [granbre'taɲɲa] *sf*: **la** ~ Great Britain.
gran'cassa *sf* (*MUS*) bass drum.
'granchio ['grankjo] *sm* crab; (*fig*) blunder; **prendere un** ~ (*fig*) to blunder.
grandango'lare *sm* wide-angle lens *sg*.
gran'dangolo *sm* (*FOT*) wide-angle lens *sg*.
'grande *ag* (*qualche volta* **gran** +C, **grand'** +V) (*grosso, largo, vasto*) big, large; (*alto*) tall; (*lungo*) long; (*in sensi astratti*) great ♦ *sm/f* (*persona adulta*) adult, grown-up; (*chi ha ingegno e potenza*) great man/ woman; **mio fratello più** ~ my big *o* older brother; **il gran pubblico** the general public; **di gran classe** (*prodotto*) high-class; **cosa farai da** ~? what will you be *o* do when you grow up?; **fare le cose in** ~ to do things in style; **fare il** ~ (*strafare*) to act big; **una gran bella donna** a very beautiful woman; **non è una gran cosa** *o* **un gran che** it's nothing special; **non ne so gran che** I don't know very much about it.
grandeggi'are [granded'dʒare] *vi* (*emergere per grandezza*): ~ **su** to tower over; (*darsi arie*) to put on airs.
gran'dezza [gran'dettsa] *sf* (*dimensione*) size; (*fig*) greatness; **in** ~ **naturale** lifesize; **manie di** ~ delusions of grandeur.
grandi'nare *vb impers* to hail.
'grandine *sf* hail.
grandi'oso, a *ag* grand, grandiose.
gran'duca, chi *sm* grand duke.
grandu'cato *sm* grand duchy.
grandu'chessa [grandu'kessa] *sf* grand duchess.
gra'nello *sm* (*di cereali, uva*) seed; (*di frutta*) pip; (*di sabbia, sale etc*) grain.
gra'nita *sf* kind of water ice.
gra'nito *sm* granite.
'grano *sm* (*in quasi tutti i sensi*) grain;

(*frumento*) wheat; (*di rosario, collana*) bead; ~ **di pepe** peppercorn.

gran'turco *sm* maize.

'granulo *sm* granule; (*MED*) pellet.

'grappa *sf* rough, strong brandy.

'grappolo *sm* bunch, cluster.

'graspo *sm* bunch (of grapes).

gras'setto *sm* (*TIP*) bold (type) (*BRIT*), bold face.

'grasso, a *ag* fat; (*cibo*) fatty; (*pelle*) greasy; (*terreno*) rich; (*fig: guadagno, annata*) plentiful; (: *volgare*) coarse, lewd ♦ *sm* (*di persona, animale*) fat; (*sostanza che unge*) grease.

gras'soccio, a, ci, ce [gras'sɔttʃo] *ag* plump.

gras'sone, a *sm/f* (*fam: persona*) dumpling.

'grata *sf* grating.

gra'ticcio [gra'tittʃo] *sm* trellis; (*stuoia*) mat.

gra'ticola *sf* grill.

gra'tifica, che *sf* bonus; ~ **natalizia** Christmas bonus.

gratificazi'one [gratifikat'tsjone] *sf* (*soddisfazione*) satisfaction, reward.

grati'nare *vt* (*CUC*) to cook au gratin.

'gratis *av* free, for nothing.

grati'tudine *sf* gratitude.

'grato, a *ag* grateful.

gratta'capo *sm* worry, headache.

grattaci'elo [gratta'tʃɛlo] *sm* skyscraper.

grat'tare *vt* (*pelle*) to scratch; (*raschiare*) to scrape; (*pane, formaggio, carote*) to grate; (*fam: rubare*) to pinch ♦ *vi* (*stridere*) to grate; (*AUT*) to grind; ~**rsi** *vr* to scratch o.s.; ~**rsi la pancia** (*fig*) to twiddle one's thumbs.

grat'tata *sf* scratch; **fare una** ~ (*AUT: fam*) to grind the gears.

grat'tugia, gie [grat'tudʒa] *sf* grater.

grattugi'are [grattu'dʒare] *vt* to grate; **pane** *m* **grattugiato** breadcrumbs *pl*.

gratuità *sf* (*fig*) gratuitousness.

gra'tuito, a *ag* free; (*fig*) gratuitous.

gra'vame *sm* tax; (*fig*) burden, weight.

gra'vare *vt* to burden ♦ *vi*: ~ **su** to weigh on.

'grave *ag* (*danno, pericolo, peccato etc*) grave, serious; (*responsabilità*) heavy, grave; (*contegno*) grave, solemn; (*voce, suono*) deep, low-pitched; (*LING*): **accento** ~ grave accent ♦ *sm* (*FISICA*) (heavy) body; **un malato** ~ a person who is seriously ill.

grave'mente *av* (*ammalato, ferito*) seriously.

gravi'danza [gravi'dantsa] *sf* pregnancy.

'gravido, a *ag* pregnant.

gravità *sf* seriousness; (*anche FISICA*) gravity.

gravi'tare *vi* (*FISICA*): ~ **intorno a** to gravitate round.

gra'voso, a *ag* heavy, onerous.

'grazia ['grattsja] *sf* grace; (*favore*) favour (*BRIT*), favor (*US*); (*DIR*) pardon; **di** ~ (*ironico*) if you please; **troppa** ~! (*ironico*) you're too generous!; **quanta** ~ **di Dio!** what abundance!; **entrare nelle ~e di qn** to win sb's favour; **Ministero di G~ e Giustizia** Ministry of Justice, ≈ Lord Chancellor's Office (*BRIT*), ≈ Department of Justice (*US*).

grazi'are [grat'tsjare] *vt* (*DIR*) to pardon.

'grazie ['grattsje] *escl* thank you!; ~ **mille!** *o* **tante!** *o* **infinite!** thank you very much!; ~ **a** thanks to.

grazi'oso, a [grat'tsjoso] *ag* charming, delightful; (*gentile*) gracious.

'Grecia ['grɛtʃa] *sf*: **la** ~ Greece.

'greco, a, ci, che *ag, sm/f, sm* Greek.

gre'gario *sm* (*CICLISMO*) supporting rider.

'gregge, pl(*f*) **i** ['greddʒe] *sm* flock.

'greggio, a, gi, ge ['greddʒo] *ag* raw, unrefined; (*diamante*) rough, uncut; (*tessuto*) unbleached ♦ *sm* (*anche*: **petrolio** ~) crude (oil).

grembi'ule *sm* apron; (*sopravveste*) overall.

'grembo *sm* lap; (*ventre della madre*) womb.

gre'mito, a *ag*: ~ (**di**) packed *o* crowded (with).

'greto *sm* (exposed) gravel bed of a river.

'gretto, a *ag* mean, stingy; (*fig*) narrow-minded.

'greve *ag* heavy.

'grezzo, a ['greddzo] *ag* = **greggio**.

gri'dare *vi* (*per chiamare*) to shout, cry (out); (*strillare*) to scream, yell ♦ *vt* to shout (out), yell (out); ~ **aiuto** to cry *o* shout for help.

'grido, pl(*m*) **i** *o* **pl**(*f*) **a** *sm* shout, cry; scream, yell; (*di animale*) cry; **di** ~ famous; **all'ultimo** ~ in the latest style.

'grigio, a, gi, gie ['gridʒo] *ag, sm* grey (*BRIT*), gray (*US*).

'griglia ['griʎʎa] *sf* (*per arrostire*) grill; (*ELETTR*) grid; (*inferriata*) grating; **alla** ~ (*CUC*) grilled.

grigli'ata [griʎ'ʎata] *sf* (*CUC*) grill.

gril'letto *sm* trigger.

'grillo *sm* (*ZOOL*) cricket; (*fig*) whim; **ha dei** ~**i per la testa** his head is full of nonsense.

grimal'dello *sm* picklock.

'grinfia *sf*: **cadere nelle** ~**e di qn** (*fig*) to fall into sb's clutches.

'grinta *sf* grim expression; (*SPORT*) fighting

spirit; **avere molta** ~ to be very determined.

grintoso, a *ag* forceful.

'**grinza** ['grintsa] *sf* crease, wrinkle; (*ruga*) wrinkle; **il tuo ragionamento non fa una** ~ your argument is faultless.

grin'zoso, a [grin'tsoso] *ag* wrinkled; creased.

grip'pare *vi* (*TECN*) to seize.

gris'sino *sm* bread-stick.

groenlan'dese *ag* Greenland *cpd* ♦ *sm/f* Greenlander.

Groen'landia *sf*: **la** ~ Greenland.

'**gronda** *sf* eaves *pl*.

gron'daia *sf* gutter.

gron'dante *ag* dripping.

gron'dare *vi* to pour; (*essere bagnato*): ~ **di** to be dripping with ♦ *vt* to drip with.

'**groppa** *sf* (*di animale*) back, rump; (*fam*: *dell'uomo*) back, shoulders *pl*.

'**groppo** *sm* tangle; **avere un** ~ **alla gola** (*fig*) to have a lump in one's throat.

'**grossa** *sf* (*unità di misura*) gross.

gros'sezza [gros'settsa] *sf* size; thickness.

gros'sista, i, e *sm/f* (*COMM*) wholesaler.

'**grosso, a** *ag* big, large; (*di spessore*) thick; (*grossolano*: *anche fig*) coarse; (*grave, insopportabile*) serious, great; (*tempo, mare*) rough ♦ *sm*: **il** ~ **di** the bulk of; **un pezzo** ~ (*fig*) a VIP, a bigwig; **farla** ~**a** to do something very stupid; **dirle** ~**e** to tell tall stories (*BRIT*) *o* tales (*US*); **questa è** ~**a**! that's a good one!; **sbagliarsi di** ~ to be completely wrong; **dormire della** ~**a** to sleep like a log.

grossolanità *sf* coarseness.

grosso'lano, a *ag* rough, coarse; (*fig*) coarse, crude; (: *errore*) stupid.

grosso'modo *av* roughly.

'**grotta** *sf* cave; grotto.

grot'tesco, a, schi, sche *ag* grotesque.

grovi'era *sm o f* gruyère (cheese).

gro'viglio [gro'viʎʎo] *sm* tangle; (*fig*) muddle.

gru *sf inv* crane.

'**gruccia, ce** ['gruttʃa] *sf* (*per camminare*) crutch; (*per abiti*) coat-hanger.

gru'gnire [gruɲ'ɲire] *vi* to grunt.

gru'gnito [gruɲ'ɲito] *sm* grunt.

'**grugno** ['gruɲɲo] *sm* snout; (*fam*: *faccia*) mug.

'**grullo, a** *ag* silly, stupid.

'**grumo** *sm* (*di sangue*) clot; (*di farina etc*) lump.

gru'moso, a *ag* lumpy.

'**gruppo** *sm* group; ~ **sanguigno** blood group.

gruvi'era *sm o f* = **groviera**.

'**gruzzolo** ['gruttsolo] *sm* (*di denaro*) hoard.

GT *abbr* (*AUT*: = *gran turismo*) GT.

G.U. *abbr* = **Gazzetta Ufficiale**.

guada'gnare [gwada ɲ'ɲare] *vt* (*ottenere*) to gain; (*soldi, stipendio*) to earn; (*vincere*) to win; (*raggiungere*) to reach; **tanto di guadagnato!** so much the better!

gua'dagno [gwa'daɲɲo] *sm* earnings *pl*; (*COMM*) profit; (*vantaggio, utile*) advantage, gain; ~ **di capitale** capital gains *pl*; ~ **lordo/netto** gross/net earnings *pl*.

gu'ado *sm* ford; **passare a** ~ to ford.

gu'ai *escl*: ~ **a te** (*o lui etc*)! woe betide you (*o him etc*)!

gua'ina *sf* (*fodero*) sheath; (*indumento per donna*) girdle.

gu'aio *sm* trouble, mishap; (*inconveniente*) trouble, snag.

gua'ire *vi* to whine, yelp.

gua'ito *sm* (*di cane*) yelp, whine; (*il guaire*) yelping, whining.

gu'ancia, ce ['gwantʃa] *sf* cheek.

guanci'ale [gwan'tʃale] *sm* pillow; **dormire fra due** ~**i** (*fig*) to sleep easy, have no worries.

gu'anto *sm* glove; **trattare qn con i** ~**i** (*fig*) to handle sb with kid gloves; **gettare/raccogliere il** ~ (*fig*) to throw down/take up the gauntlet.

guan'tone *sm* boxing glove.

guarda'boschi [gwarda'bɔski] *sm inv* forester.

guarda'caccia [gwarda'kattʃa] *sm inv* gamekeeper.

guarda'coste *sm inv* coastguard; (*nave*) coastguard patrol vessel.

guarda'linee *sm inv* (*SPORT*) linesman.

guarda'macchine [gwarda'makkine] *sm/f inv* car-park (*BRIT*) *o* parking lot (*US*) attendant.

guar'dare *vt* (*con lo sguardo*: *osservare*) to look at; (*film, televisione*) to watch; (*custodire*) to look after, take care of ♦ *vi* to look; (*badare*): ~ **a** to pay attention to; (*luoghi*: *esser orientato*): ~ **a** to face; ~**rsi** *vr* to look at o.s.; ~ **di** to try to; ~**rsi da** (*astenersi*) to refrain from; (*stare in guardia*) to beware of; ~**rsi dal fare** to take care not to do; **ma guarda un po'!** good heavens!; **e guarda caso ...** as if by coincidence ...; ~ **qn dall'alto in basso** to look down on sb; **non** ~ **in faccia a nessuno** (*fig*) to have no regard for anybody; ~ **di traverso** to scowl *o* frown at; ~ **a vista qn** to keep a close watch on sb.

guarda'roba *sm inv* wardrobe; (*locale*)

cloakroom.

guardarobi'ere, a *sm/f* cloakroom attendant.

guardasi'gilli [gwardasi'dʒilli] *sm inv* ≈ Lord Chancellor (*BRIT*), ≈ Attorney General (*US*).

gu'ardia *sf* (*individuo, corpo*) guard; (*sorveglianza*) watch; **fare la ~ a qc/qn** to guard sth/sb; **stare in ~** (*fig*) to be on one's guard; **il medico di ~** the doctor on call; **il fiume ha raggiunto il livello di ~** the river has reached the high-water mark; **~ carceraria** (*prison*) warder (*BRIT*) *o* guard (*US*); **~ del corpo** bodyguard; **~ di finanza** (*corpo*) customs *pl*; (*persona*) customs officer; **~ forestale** forest ranger; **~ giurata** security guard; **~ medica** emergency doctor service; **~ municipale** town policeman; **~ notturna** night security guard; **~ di pubblica sicurezza** policeman.

> The **Guardia di Finanza** is *a military body which deals with infringements of the laws governing income tax and monopolies. In its various duties it reports to the Ministers of Finance, Justice or Agriculture.*

guardia'caccia [gwardja'kattʃa] *sm inv* = **guardacaccia.**

guardi'ano, a *sm/f* (*di carcere*) warder (*BRIT*), guard (*US*); (*di villa etc*) caretaker; (*di museo*) custodian; (*di zoo*) keeper; **~ notturno** night watchman.

guar'dina *sf* cell.

guar'dingo, a, ghi, ghe *ag* wary, cautious.

guardi'ola *sf* porter's lodge; (*MIL*) look-out tower.

guarigi'one [gwari'dʒone] *sf* recovery.

gua'rire *vt* (*persona, malattia*) to cure; (*ferita*) to heal ♦ *vi* to recover, be cured; to heal (up).

guarnigi'one [gwarni'dʒone] *sf* garrison.

guar'nire *vt* (*ornare: abiti*) to trim; (*CUC*) to garnish.

guarnizi'one [gwarnit'tsjone] *sf* trimming; garnish; (*TECN*) gasket.

guasta'feste *sm/f inv* spoilsport.

guas'tare *vt* to spoil, ruin; (*meccanismo*) to break; **~rsi** *vr* (*cibo*) to go bad; (*meccanismo*) to break down; (*tempo*) to change for the worse; (*amici*) to quarrel, fall out.

gu'asto, a *ag* (*non funzionante*) broken; (: *telefono etc*) out of order; (*andato a male*) bad, rotten; (: *dente*) decayed, bad; (*fig: corrotto*) depraved ♦ *sm* breakdown;

(*avaria*) failure; **~ al motore** engine failure.

Guate'mala *sm*: **il ~** Guatemala.

guatemal'teco, a, ci, che *ag, sm/f* Guatemalan.

guazza'buglio [gwattsa'buʎʎo] *sm* muddle.

gu'ercio, a, ci, ce ['gwertʃo] *ag* cross-eyed.

gu'erra *sf* war; (*tecnica: atomica, chimica etc*) warfare; **fare la ~ (a)** to wage war (against); **la ~ fredda** the Cold War; **~ mondiale** world war; **la prima/seconda ~ mondiale** the First/Second World War.

guerrafon'daio *sm* warmonger.

guerreggi'are [gwerred'dʒare] *vi* to wage war.

guer'resco, a, schi, sche *ag* (*di guerra*) war *cpd*; (*incline alla guerra*) warlike.

guerri'ero, a *ag* warlike ♦ *sm* warrior.

guer'riglia [gwer'riʎʎa] *sf* guerrilla warfare.

guerrigli'ero [gwerriʎ'ʎɛro] *sm* guerrilla.

'gufo *sm* owl.

'guglia ['guʎʎa] *sf* (*ARCHIT*) spire; (*di roccia*) needle.

Gui'ana *sf*: **la ~ francese** French Guiana.

gu'ida *sf* guide; (*comando, direzione*) guidance, direction; (*AUT*) driving; (: *sterzo*) steering; (*tappeto, di tenda, cassetto*) runner; **~ a destra/sinistra** (*AUT*) right-/left-hand drive; **essere alla ~ di** (*governo*) to head; (*spedizione, paese*) to lead; **far da ~ a qn** (*mostrare la strada*) to show sb the way; (*in una città*) to show sb (a)round; **~ telefonica** telephone directory.

gui'dare *vt* to guide; (*condurre a capo*) to lead; (*auto*) to drive; (*aereo, nave*) to pilot; **sa ~?** can you drive?

guida'tore, 'trice *sm/f* (*conducente*) driver.

Gui'nea *sf*: **la Repubblica di ~** the Republic of Guinea; **la ~ Equatoriale** Equatorial Guinea.

guin'zaglio [gwin'tsaʎʎo] *sm* leash, lead.

gu'isa *sf*: **a ~ di** like, in the manner of.

guiz'zare [gwit'tsare] *vi* to dart; to flicker; to leap; **~ via** (*fuggire*) to slip away.

gu'izzo ['gwittso] *sm* (*di animali*) dart; (*di fulmine*) flash.

'guru *sm inv* (*REL, anche fig*) guru.

'guscio ['guʃʃo] *sm* shell.

gus'tare *vt* (*cibi*) to taste; (: *assaporare con piacere*) to enjoy, savour (*BRIT*), savor (*US*); (*fig*) to enjoy, appreciate ♦ *vi*: **~ a** to please; **non mi gusta affatto** I don't like it at all.

gusta'tivo, a *ag*: **papille** *fpl* **~e** taste buds.

'gusto *sm* (*senso*) taste; (*sapore*) taste, flavour (*BRIT*), flavor (*US*); (*godimento*)

enjoyment; **al ~ di fragola** strawberry-flavo(u)red; **di ~ barocco** in the baroque style; **mangiare di ~** to eat heartily; **prenderci ~: ci ha preso ~** he's acquired a taste for it, he's got to like it.
gus'toso, a *ag* tasty; (*fig*) agreeable.
guttu'rale *ag* guttural.
Gu'yana [gu'jana] *sf:* **la ~** Guyana.

H h

H, h ['akka] *sf o m inv* (*lettera*) H, h ♦ *abbr* (= *ora*) hr; (= *etto, altezza*) h; **H come hotel** ≈ H for Harry (*BRIT*), H for How (*US*).
ha¹, 'hai [a, ai] *vb vedi* **avere**.
ha² *abbr* (= *ettaro*) ha.
Ha'iti [a'iti] *sf* Haiti.
haiti'ano, a [ai'tjano] *ag, sm/f* Haitian.
hall [hɔːl] *sf inv* hall, foyer.
'handicap ['handikap] *sm inv* handicap.
handicap'pato, a [andikap'pato] *ag* handicapped ♦ *sm/f* handicapped person, disabled person.
'hanno ['anno] *vb vedi* **avere**.
ha'scisc [aʃ'ʃiʃ] *sm* hashish.
hawai'ano, a [ava'jano] *ag, sm/f* Hawaiian.
Ha'waii [a'vai] *sfpl:* **le ~** Hawaii *sg*.
'Helsinki ['ɛlsinki] *sf* Helsinki.
'herpes ['ɛrpes] *sm* (*MED*) herpes *sg*; **~ zoster** shingles *sg*.
hg *abbr* (= *ettogrammo*) hg.
'hi-fi ['haifai] *sf inv, ag inv* hi-fi.
Hima'laia [ima'laja] *sm:* **l'~** the Himalayas *pl*.
hl *abbr* (= *ettolitro*) hl.
ho [ɔ] *vb vedi* **avere**.
'hobby ['hɔbi] *sm inv* hobby.
'hockey ['hɔki] *sm* hockey; **~ su ghiaccio** ice hockey.
'holding ['houldiŋ] *sf inv* holding company.
Hon'duras [on'duras] *sm* Honduras.
'Hong Kong ['ɔkɔg] *sf* Hong Kong.
Hono'lulu [ono'lulu] *sf* Honolulu.
'hostess ['houstis] *sf inv* air hostess (*BRIT*) *o* stewardess.
ho'tel [o'tɛl] *sm inv* hotel.
Hz *abbr* (= *hertz*) Hz.

I i

I, i [i] *sf o m inv* (*lettera*) I, i; **I come Imola** ≈ I for Isaac (*BRIT*), I for Item (*US*).
i *det mpl* the; *vedi anche* **il**.
IACP *sigla m* (= *Istituto Autonomo per le Case Popolari*) public housing association.
i'ato *sm* hiatus.
i'berico, a, ci, che *ag* Iberian; **la Penisola I~a** the Iberian Peninsula.
iber'nare *vi* to hibernate ♦ *vt* (*MED*) to induce hypothermia in.
ibernazi'one [ibernat'tsjone] *sf* hibernation.
ibid. *abbr* (= *ibidem*) ib(id).
'ibrido, a *ag, sm* hybrid.
'ICE ['itʃe] *sigla m* (= *Istituto nazionale per il Commercio Estero*) overseas trade board.
i'cona *sf* icon.
id *abbr* (= *idem*) do.
Id'dio *sm* God.
i'dea *sf* idea; (*opinione*) opinion, view; (*ideale*) ideal; **avere le ~e chiare** to know one's mind; **cambiare ~** to change one's mind; **dare l'~ di** to seem, look like; **neanche** *o* **neppure per ~!** certainly not!, no way!; **~ fissa** obsession.
ide'ale *ag, sm* ideal.
idea'lismo *sm* idealism.
idea'lista, i, e *sm/f* idealist.
idea'listico, a, ci, che *ag* idealistic.
idealiz'zare [idealid'dzare] *vt* to idealize.
ide'are *vt* (*immaginare*) to think up, conceive; (*progettare*) to plan.
idea'tore, 'trice *sm/f* author.
i'dentico, a, ci, che *ag* identical.
identifi'care *vt* to identify.
identificazi'one [identifikat'tsjone] *sf* identification.
identità *sf inv* identity.
ideolo'gia, 'gie [ideolo'dʒia] *sf* ideology.
ideo'logico, a, ci, che [ideo'lɔdʒiko] *ag* ideological.
idil'liaco, a, ci, che *ag* = **idillico**.
i'dillico, a, ci, che *ag* idyllic.
i'dillio *sm* idyll; **tra di loro è nato un ~** they have fallen in love.
idi'oma, i *sm* idiom, language.
idio'matico, a, ci, che *ag* idiomatic; **frase** *f* **~a** idiom.

idiosincra'sia *sf* idiosyncrasy.
idi'ota, i, e *ag* idiotic ♦ *smf* idiot.
idio'zia [idjot'tsia] *sf* idiocy; (*atto, discorso*) idiotic thing to do (*o* say).
ido'latra, i, e *ag* idolatrous ♦ *smf* idolater.
idola'trare *vt* to worship; (*fig*) to idolize.
idola'tria *sf* idolatry.
'idolo *sm* idol.
idoneità *sf* suitability; **esame** *m* **di** ~ qualifying examination.
i'doneo, a *ag*: ~ **a** suitable for, fit for; (*MIL*) fit for; (*qualificato*) qualified for.
i'drante *sm* hydrant.
idra'tante *ag* (*crema*) moisturizing ♦ *sm* moisturizer.
idra'tare *vt* (*pelle*) to moisturize.
idratazi'one [idratat'tsjone] *sf* moisturizing.
i'draulico, a, ci, che *ag* hydraulic ♦ *sm* plumber ♦ *sf* hydraulics *sg*.
'idrico, a, ci, che *ag* water *cpd*.
idrocar'buro *sm* hydrocarbon.
idroe'lettrico, a, ci, che *ag* hydroelectric.
i'drofilo, a *ag*: **cotone** *m* ~ cotton wool (*BRIT*), absorbent cotton (*US*).
idrofo'bia *sf* rabies *sg*.
i'drofobo, a *ag* rabid; (*fig*) furious.
i'drogeno [i'drɔdʒeno] *sm* hydrogen.
idroli'pidico, a, ci, che *ag* hydrolipid.
idro'porto *sm* (*AER*) seaplane base.
idrorepel'lente *ag* water-repellent.
idros'calo *sm* = **idroporto**.
idrovo'lante *sm* seaplane.
i'ella *sf* bad luck.
iel'lato, a *ag* plagued by bad luck.
i'ena *sf* hyena.
ie'ratico, a, ci, che *ag* (*REL: scrittura*) hieratic; (*fig: atteggiamento*) solemn.
i'eri *av, sm* yesterday; **il giornale di** ~ yesterday's paper; ~ **l'altro** the day before yesterday; ~ **sera** yesterday evening.
ietta'tore, 'trice *smf* jinx.
igi'ene [i'dʒɛne] *sf* hygiene; **norme d'**~ sanitary regulations; **ufficio d'**~ public health office; ~ **mentale** mental health; ~ **pubblica** public health.
igi'enico, a, ci, che [i'dʒɛniko] *ag* hygienic; (*salubre*) healthy.
IGM *sigla m* (= *Ispettorato Generale della Motorizzazione*) road traffic inspectorate.
i'gnaro, a [iɲ'ɲaro] *ag*: ~ **di** unaware of, ignorant of.
i'gnifugo, a, ghi, ghe [iɲ'ɲifugo] *ag* flame-resistant, fireproof.
i'gnobile [iɲ'ɲɔbile] *ag* despicable, vile.
igno'minia [iɲɲo'minja] *sf* ignominy.
igno'rante [iɲɲo'rante] *ag* ignorant.

igno'ranza [iɲɲo'rantsa] *sf* ignorance.
igno'rare [iɲɲo'rare] *vt* (*non sapere, conoscere*) to be ignorant *o* unaware of, not to know; (*fingere di non vedere, sentire*) to ignore.
i'gnoto, a [iɲ'ɲɔto] *ag* unknown ♦ *smf*: **figlio di** ~**i** child of unknown parentage; **il Milite I~** the Unknown Soldier.

================================ *PAROLA CHIAVE*

il (*pl* (*m*) **i**; *diventa* **lo** (*pl* **gli**) *davanti a s impura, gn, pn, ps, x, z, f* **la** (*pl* **le**)) *det m* **1** the; ~ **libro/lo studente/l'acqua** the book/the student/the water; **gli scolari** the pupils
2 (*astrazione*): ~ **coraggio/l'amore/la giovinezza** courage/love/youth
3 (*tempo*): ~ **mattino/la sera** in the morning/evening; ~ **venerdì** (*abitualmente*) on Fridays; (*quel giorno*) on (the) Friday; **la settimana prossima** next week
4 (*distributivo*) a, an; **2.500 lire** ~ **chilo/paio** 2,500 lire a *o* per kilo/pair
5 (*partitivo*) some, any; **hai messo lo zucchero?** have you added sugar?; **hai comprato** ~ **latte?** did you buy (some *o* any) milk?
6 (*possesso*): **aprire gli occhi** to open one's eyes; **rompersi la gamba** to break one's leg; **avere i capelli neri/**~ **naso rosso** to have dark hair/a red nose; **mettiti le scarpe** put your shoes on
7 (*con nomi propri*): ~ **Petrarca** Petrarch; ~ **Presidente Clinton** President Clinton; **dov'è la Francesca?** where's Francesca?
8 (*con nomi geografici*): ~ **Tevere** the Tiber; **l'Italia** Italy; ~ **Regno Unito** the United Kingdom; **l'Everest** Everest.

'ilare *ag* cheerful.
ilarità *sf* hilarity, mirth.
ill. *abbr* (= *illustrazione; illustrato*) ill.
illangui'dire *vi* to grow weak *o* feeble.
illazi'one [illat'tsjone] *sf* inference, deduction.
il'lecito, a [il'letʃito] *ag* illicit.
ille'gale *ag* illegal.
illegalità *sf* illegality.
illeg'gibile [illed'dʒibile] *ag* illegible.
illegittimità [illedʒittimi'ta] *sf* illegitimacy.
ille'gittimo, a [ille'dʒittimo] *ag* illegitimate.
il'leso, a *ag* unhurt, unharmed.
illette'rato, a *ag* illiterate.
illiba'tezza [illiba'tettsa] *sf* (*di donna*) virginity.
illi'bato, a *ag*: **donna** ~**a** virgin.
illimi'tato, a *ag* boundless; unlimited.

illivi'dire *vi* (*volto, mani*) to turn livid; (*cielo*) to grow leaden.

ill.mo *abbr* = **illustrissimo**.

il'logico, a, ci, che [il'lɔdʒiko] *ag* illogical.

il'ludere *vt* to deceive, delude; **~rsi** *vr* to deceive o.s., delude o.s.

illumi'nare *vt* to light up, illuminate; (*fig*) to enlighten; **~rsi** *vr* to light up; **~ a giorno** (*con riflettori*) to floodlight.

illumi'nato, a *ag* (*fig*: *sovrano, spirito*) enlightened.

illuminazi'one [illuminat'tsjone] *sf* lighting; illumination; floodlighting; (*fig*) flash of inspiration.

illumi'nismo *sm* (*STORIA*): **l'l~** the Enlightenment.

il'lusi *etc vb vedi* **illudere**.

illusi'one *sf* illusion; **farsi delle ~i** to delude o.s.

illusio'nismo *sm* conjuring.

illusio'nista, i, e *sm/f* conjurer.

il'luso, a *pp di* **illudere**.

illu'sorio, a *ag* illusory.

illus'trare *vt* to illustrate.

illustra'tivo, a *ag* illustrative.

illustrazi'one [illustrat'tsjone] *sf* illustration.

il'lustre *ag* eminent, renowned.

illus'trissimo, a *ag* (*negli indirizzi*) very revered.

'ILOR *sigla f vedi* **imposta locale sui redditi**.

IM *sigla* = *Imperia*.

imbacuc'care *vt*, **~rsi** *vr* to wrap up.

imbaldan'zire [imbaldan'tsire] *vt* to give confidence to; **~rsi** *vr* to grow bold.

imbal'laggio [imbal'laddʒo] *sm* packing *no pl*.

imbal'lare *vt* to pack; (*AUT*) to race; **~rsi** *vr* (*AUT*) to race.

imbalsa'mare *vt* to embalm.

imbalsa'mato, a *ag* embalmed.

imbambo'lato, a *ag* (*sguardo, espressione*) vacant, blank.

imban'dire *vt*: **~ un banchetto** to prepare a lavish feast.

imban'dito, a *ag*: **tavola ~a** lavishly *o* sumptuously decked table.

imbaraz'zante [imbarat'tsante] *ag* embarrassing, awkward.

imbaraz'zare [imbarat'tsare] *vt* (*mettere a disagio*) to embarrass; (*ostacolare*: *movimenti*) to hamper; (: *stomaco*) to lie heavily on; **~rsi** *vr* to become embarrassed.

imbaraz'zato, a [imbarat'tsato] *ag* embarrassed; **avere lo stomaco ~** to have an upset stomach.

imba'razzo [imba'rattso] *sm* (*disagio*)

embarrassment; (*perplessità*) puzzlement, bewilderment; **essere** *o* **trovarsi in ~** to be in an awkward situation *o* predicament; **mettere in ~** to embarrass; **~ di stomaco** indigestion.

imbarbari'mento *sm* (*di civiltà, costumi*) barbarization.

imbarca'dero *sm* landing stage.

imbar'care *vt* (*passeggeri*) to embark; (*merci*) to load; **~rsi** *vr*: **~rsi su** to board; **~rsi per l'America** to sail for America; **~rsi in** (*fig*: *affare*) to embark on.

imbarcazi'one [imbarkat'tsjone] *sf* (small) boat, (small) craft *inv*; **~ di salvataggio** lifeboat.

im'barco, chi *sm* embarkation; loading; boarding; (*banchina*) landing stage; **carta d'~** boarding pass (*BRIT*), boarding card.

imbastar'dire *vt* to bastardize, debase; **~rsi** *vr* to degenerate, become debased.

imbas'tire *vt* (*cucire*) to tack; (*fig*: *abbozzare*) to sketch, outline.

im'battersi *vr*: **~ in** (*incontrare*) to bump *o* run into.

imbat'tibile *ag* unbeatable, invincible.

imbavagli'are [imbavaʎ'ʎare] *vt* to gag.

imbec'care *vt* (*uccelli*) to feed; (*fig*) to prompt, put words into sb's mouth.

imbec'cata *sf* (*TEAT*) prompt; **dare l'~ a qn** to prompt sb; (*fig*) to give sb their cue.

imbe'cille [imbe'tʃille] *ag* idiotic ♦ *sm/f* idiot; (*MED*) imbecile.

imbecillità [imbetʃilli'ta] *sf inv* (*MED, fig*) imbecility, idiocy; **dire ~** to talk nonsense.

imbellet'tare *vt* (*viso*) to make up, put make-up on; **~rsi** *vr* to make o.s. up, put on one's make-up.

imbel'lire *vt* to adorn, embellish ♦ *vi* to grow more beautiful.

im'berbe *ag* beardless; **un giovanotto ~** a callow youth.

imbestia'lire *vt* to infuriate; **~rsi** *vr* to become infuriated, fly into a rage.

im'bevere *vt* to soak; **~rsi** *vr*: **~rsi di** to soak up, absorb.

imbe'vuto, a *ag*: **~ (di)** soaked (in).

imbian'care *vt* to whiten; (*muro*) to whitewash ♦ *vi* to become *o* turn white.

imbianca'tura *sf* (*di muro*: *con bianco di calce*) whitewashing; (: *con altre pitture*) painting.

imbian'chino [imbjan'kino] *sm* (house) painter, painter and decorator.

imbion'dire *vt* (*capelli*) to lighten; (*CUC*: *cipolla*) to brown; **~rsi** *vr* (*capelli*) to lighten, go blonde, go fair; (*messi*) to turn golden, ripen.

imbizzar'rirsi [imbiddzar'rirsi] *vr* (*cavallo*) to become frisky.

imboc'care *vt* (*bambino*) to feed; (*entrare*: *strada*) to enter, turn into ♦ *vi*: ~ **in** (*sog*: *strada*) to lead into; (: *fiume*) to flow into.

imbocca'tura *sf* mouth; (*di strada, porto*) entrance; (*MUS, del morso*) mouthpiece.

im'bocco, chi *sm* entrance.

imboni'tore *sm* (*di spettacolo, circo*) barker.

imborghe'sire [imborge'zire] *vi*, ~**rsi** *vr* to become bourgeois.

imbos'care *vt* to hide; ~**rsi** *vr* (*MIL*) to evade military service.

imbos'cata *sf* ambush.

imbos'cato *sm* draft dodger (*US*).

imboschi'mento [imboski'mento] *sm* afforestation.

imbottigli'are [imbotti'ʎ'ʎare] *vt* to bottle; (*NAUT*) to blockade; (*MIL*) to hem in; ~**rsi** *vr* to be stuck in a traffic jam.

imbot'tire *vt* to stuff; (*giacca*) to pad; ~**rsi** *vr*: ~**rsi di** (*rimpinzarsi*) to stuff o.s. with.

imbot'tito, a *ag* (*sedia*) upholstered; (*giacca*) padded ♦ *sf* quilt.

imbotti'tura *sf* stuffing; padding.

imbracci'are [imbrat'tʃare] *vt* (*fucile*) to shoulder; (*scudo*) to grasp.

imbra'nato, a *ag* clumsy, awkward ♦ *sm/f* clumsy person.

imbratta'carte *sm/f* (*peg*) scribbler.

imbrat'tare *vt* to dirty, smear, daub; ~**rsi** *vr*: ~**rsi (di)** to dirty o.s. (with).

imbratta'tele *sm/f* (*peg*) dauber.

imbrigli'are [imbri'ʎ'ʎare] *vt* to bridle.

imbroc'care *vt* (*fig*) to guess correctly.

imbrogli'are [imbro'ʎ'ʎare] *vt* to mix up; (*fig*: *raggirare*) to deceive, cheat; (: *confondere*) to confuse, mix up; ~**rsi** *vr* to get tangled; (*fig*) to become confused.

im'broglio [im'brɔʎʎo] *sm* (*groviglio*) tangle; (*situazione confusa*) mess; (*truffa*) swindle, trick.

imbrogli'one, a [imbroʎ'ʎone] *sm/f* cheat, swindler.

imbronci'ato, a [imbron'tʃato] *ag* (*persona*) sulky; (*cielo*) cloudy, threatening.

imbru'nire *vi*, *vb impers* to grow dark; **all'**~ at dusk.

imbrut'tire *vt* to make ugly ♦ *vi* to become ugly.

imbu'care *vt* to post.

imbur'rare *vt* to butter.

imbuti'forme *ag* funnel-shaped.

im'buto *sm* funnel.

I.M.C.T.C. *sigla* (= *Ispettorato Generale della Motorizzazione Civile e dei Trasporti in Concessione*) ≈ DVLA.

i'mene *sm* hymen.

imi'tare *vt* to imitate; (*riprodurre*) to copy; (*assomigliare*) to look like.

imita'tore, 'trice *sm/f* (*gen*) imitator; (*TEAT*) impersonator, impressionist.

imitazi'one [imitat'tsjone] *sf* imitation.

immaco'lato, a *ag* spotless; immaculate.

immagazzi'nare [immagaddzi'nare] *vt* to store.

immagi'nabile [immadʒi'nabile] *ag* imaginable.

immagi'nare [immadʒi'nare] *vt* to imagine; (*supporre*) to suppose; (*inventare*) to invent; **s'immagini!** don't mention it!, not at all!

immagi'nario, a [immadʒi'narjo] *ag* imaginary.

immagina'tiva [immadʒina'tiva] *sf* imagination.

immaginazi'one [immadʒinat'tsjone] *sf* imagination; (*cosa immaginata*) fancy.

im'magine [im'madʒine] *sf* image; (*rappresentazione grafica, mentale*) picture.

immagi'noso, a [immadʒi'noso] *ag* (*linguaggio, stile*) fantastic.

immalinco'nire *vt* to sadden, depress; ~**rsi** *vr* to become depressed, become melancholy.

imman'cabile *ag* unfailing.

immancabil'mente *av* without fail, unfailingly.

im'mane *ag* (*smisurato*) huge; (*spaventoso, inumano*) terrible.

imma'nente *ag* (*FILOSOFIA*) inherent, immanent.

immangi'abile [imman'dʒabile] *ag* inedible.

immatrico'lare *vt* to register; ~**rsi** *vr* (*INS*) to matriculate, enrol.

immatricolazi'one [immatrikolat'tsjone] *sf* registration; matriculation, enrolment.

immaturità *sf* immaturity.

imma'turo, a *ag* (*frutto*) unripe; (*persona*) immature; (*prematuro*) premature.

immedesi'marsi *vr*: ~ **in** to identify with.

immediata'mente *av* immediately, at once.

immedia'tezza [immedja'tettsa] *sf* immediacy.

immedi'ato, a *ag* immediate.

immemo'rabile *ag* immemorial; **da tempo** ~ from time immemorial.

im'memore *ag*: ~ **di** forgetful of.

immensità *sf* immensity.

im'menso, a *ag* immense.

im'mergere [im'mɛrdʒere] *vt* to immerse, plunge; ~**rsi** *vr* to plunge; (*sommergibile*) to dive, submerge; (*dedicarsi a*): ~**rsi in** to immerse o.s. in.

immeri'tato, a *ag* undeserved.

immeri'tevole *ag* undeserving, unworthy.

immersi'one *sf* immersion; (*di sommergibile*) submersion, dive; (*di palombaro*) dive; **linea di ~** (*NAUT*) water line.

im'merso, a *pp di* **immergere.**

im'messo, a *pp di* **immettere.**

im'mettere *vt*: **~ (in)** to introduce (into); **~ dati in un computer** to enter data on a computer.

immi'grante *ag, smf* immigrant.

immi'grare *vi* to immigrate.

immi'grato, a *smf* immigrant.

immigrazi'one [immigrat'tsjone] *sf* immigration.

immi'nente *ag* imminent.

immi'nenza [immi'nɛntsa] *sf* imminence.

immischi'are [immis'kjare] *vt*: **~ qn in** to involve sb in; **~rsi** *vr*: **~rsi in** to interfere *o* meddle in.

immiseri'mento *sm* impoverishment.

immise'rire *vt* to impoverish.

immis'sario *sm* (*GEO*) affluent, tributary.

immissi'one *sf* (*gen*) introduction; (*di aria, gas*) intake; **~ di dati** (*INFORM*) data entry.

im'mobile *ag* motionless, still; **(beni) ~i** *smpl* real estate *sg*.

immobili'are *ag* (*DIR*) property *cpd*; **patrimonio ~** real estate; **società ~** property company.

immobi'lismo *sm* inertia.

immobilità *sf* immobility.

immobiliz'zare [immobilid'dzare] *vt* to immobilize; (*ECON*) to lock up.

immobi'lizzo [immobi'liddzo] *sm*: **spese d'~** capital expenditure.

immo'destia *sf* immodesty.

immo'desto, a *ag* immodest.

immo'lare *vt* to sacrifice.

immondez'zaio [immondet'tsajo] *sm* rubbish dump.

immon'dizia [immon'dittsja] *sf* dirt, filth; (*spesso al pl: spazzatura, rifiuti*) rubbish *no pl*, refuse *no pl*.

immo'rale *ag* immoral.

immoralità *sf* immorality.

immorta'lare *vt* to immortalize.

immor'tale *ag* immortal.

immortalità *sf* immortality.

im'mune *ag* (*esente*) exempt; (*MED, DIR*) immune.

immunità *sf* immunity; **~ diplomatica** diplomatic immunity; **~ parlamentare** parliamentary privilege.

immuniz'zare [immunid'dzare] *vt* (*MED*) to immunize.

immunizzazi'one [immuniddzat'tsjone] *sf* immunization.

immunodefi'cienza [immunodefi'tʃɛntsa] *sf*: **~ acquisita** acquired immunodeficiency.

immuno'logico, a, ci, che [immuno'lɔdʒiko] *ag* immunological.

immu'tabile *ag* immutable; unchanging.

impac'care *vt* to pack.

impacchet'tare [impakket'tare] *vt* to pack up.

impacci'are [impat'tʃare] *vt* to hinder, hamper.

impacci'ato, a [impat'tʃato] *ag* awkward, clumsy; (*imbarazzato*) embarrassed.

im'paccio [im'pattʃo] *sm* obstacle; (*imbarazzo*) embarrassment; (*situazione imbarazzante*) awkward situation.

im'pacco, chi *sm* (*MED*) compress.

impadro'nirsi *vr*: **~ di** to seize, take possession of; (*fig: apprendere a fondo*) to master.

impa'gabile *ag* priceless.

impagi'nare [impadʒi'nare] *vt* (*TIP*) to paginate, page (up).

impaginazi'one [impadʒinat'tsjone] *sf* pagination.

impagli'are [impaʎ'ʎare] *vt* to stuff (with straw).

impa'lato, a *ag* (*fig*) stiff as a board.

impalca'tura *sf* scaffolding; (*anche fig*) framework.

impalli'dire *vi* to turn pale; (*fig*) to fade.

impalli'nare *vt* to riddle with shot.

impal'pabile *ag* impalpable.

impa'nare *vt* (*CUC*) to dip (*o* roll) in breadcrumbs, bread (*US*).

impanta'narsi *vr* to sink (in the mud); (*fig*) to get bogged down.

impape'rarsi *vr* to stumble over a word.

impappi'narsi *vr* to stammer, falter.

impa'rare *vt* to learn; **così impari!** that'll teach you!

impara'ticcio [impara'tittʃo] *sm* half-baked notions *pl*.

impareggi'abile [impared'dʒabile] *ag* incomparable.

imparen'tarsi *vr*: **~ con** (*famiglia*) to marry into.

'impari *ag inv* (*disuguale*) unequal; (*dispari*) odd.

impar'tire *vt* to bestow, give.

imparzi'ale [impar'tsjale] *ag* impartial, unbiased.

imparzialità [impartsjali'ta] *sf* impartiality.

impas'sibile *ag* impassive.

impas'tare *vt* (*pasta*) to knead; (*colori*) to mix.

impastic'carsi *vr* to pop pills.

im'pasto *sm* (*l'impastare: di pane*) kneading;

(: *di cemento*) mixing; (*pasta*) dough; (*anche fig*) mixture.

im'patto *sm* impact; ~ **ambientale** impact on the environment.

impau'rire *vt* to scare, frighten ♦ *vi* (*anche:* ~**rsi**) to become scared *o* frightened.

im'pavido, a *ag* intrepid, fearless.

impazi'ente [impat'tsjɛnte] *ag* impatient.

impazi'enza [impat'tsjɛntsa] *sf* impatience.

impaz'zata [impat'tsata] *sf*: **all'**~ (*precipitosamente*) at breakneck speed; (*colpire*) wildly.

impaz'zire [impat'tsire] *vi* to go mad; ~ **per qn/qc** to be crazy about sb/sth.

impec'cabile *ag* impeccable.

impedi'mento *sm* obstacle, hindrance.

impe'dire *vt* (*vietare*): ~ **a qn di fare** to prevent sb from doing; (*ostruire*) to obstruct; (*impacciare*) to hamper, hinder.

impe'gnare [impeɲ'ɲare] *vt* (*dare in pegno*) to pawn; (*onore etc*) to pledge; (*prenotare*) to book, reserve; (*obbligare*) to oblige; (*occupare*) to keep busy; (*MIL: nemico*) to engage; ~**rsi** *vr* (*vincolarsi*): ~**rsi a fare** to undertake to do; (*mettersi risolutamente*): ~**rsi in qc** to devote o.s. to sth; ~**rsi con qn** (*accordarsi*) to come to an agreement with sb.

impegna'tivo, a [impeɲɲa'tivo] *ag* binding; (*lavoro*) demanding, exacting.

impe'gnato, a [impeɲ'ɲato] *ag* (*occupato*) busy; (*fig: romanzo, autore*) committed, engagé.

im'pegno [im'peɲɲo] *sm* (*obbligo*) obligation; (*promessa*) promise, pledge; (*zelo*) diligence, zeal; (*compito, d'autore*) commitment; ~**i di lavoro** business commitments.

impego'larsi *vr* (*fig*): ~ **in** to get heavily involved in.

impela'garsi *vr* = **impegolarsi**.

impel'lente *ag* pressing, urgent.

impene'trabile *ag* impenetrable.

impen'narsi *vr* (*cavallo*) to rear up; (*AER*) to go into a climb; (*fig*) to bridle.

impen'nata *sf* (*di cavallo*) rearing up; (*di aereo*) climb, nose-up; (*fig: scatto d'ira*) burst of anger; (: *di prezzi etc*) sudden increase.

impen'sabile *ag* (*inaccettabile*) unthinkable; (*difficile da concepire*) inconceivable.

impen'sato, a *ag* unforeseen, unexpected.

impensie'rire *vt*, ~**rsi** *vr* to worry.

impe'rante *ag* prevailing.

impe'rare *vi* (*anche fig*) to reign, rule.

impera'tivo, a *ag*, *sm* imperative.

impera'tore, 'trice *sm/f* emperor/empress.

impercet'tibile [impertʃet'tibile] *ag* imperceptible.

imperdo'nabile *ag* unforgivable, unpardonable.

imper'fetto, a *ag* imperfect ♦ *sm* (*LING*) imperfect (tense).

imperfezi'one [imperfet'tsjone] *sf* imperfection.

imperi'ale *ag* imperial.

imperia'lismo *sm* imperialism.

imperia'lista, i, e *ag* imperialist.

imperi'oso, a *ag* (*persona*) imperious; (*motivo, esigenza*) urgent, pressing.

imperi'turo, a *ag* everlasting.

impe'rizia [impe'rittsja] *sf* lack of experience.

imperma'lirsi *vr* to take offence.

imperme'abile *ag* waterproof ♦ *sm* raincoat.

imperni'are *vt*: ~ **qc su** to hinge sth on; (*fig: discorso, relazione etc*) to base sth on; ~**rsi** *vr* (*fig*): ~**rsi su** to be based on.

im'pero *sm* empire; (*forza, autorità*) rule, control.

imperscru'tabile *ag* inscrutable.

imperso'nale *ag* impersonal.

imperso'nare *vt* to personify; (*TEAT*) to play, act (the part of); ~**rsi** *vr*: ~**rsi in un ruolo** to get into a part, live a part.

imper'territo, a *ag* unperturbed.

imperti'nente *ag* impertinent.

imperti'nenza [imperti'nɛntsa] *sf* impertinence.

impertur'babile *ag* imperturbable.

imperver'sare *vi* to rage.

im'pervio, a *ag* (*luogo*) inaccessible; (*strada*) impassable.

'impeto *sm* (*moto, forza*) force, impetus; (*assalto*) onslaught; (*fig: impulso*) impulse; (: *slancio*) transport; **con** ~ (*parlare*) forcefully, energetically.

impet'tito, a *ag* stiff, erect; **camminare** ~ to strut.

impetu'oso, a *ag* (*vento*) strong, raging; (*persona*) impetuous.

impian'tare *vt* (*motore*) to install; (*azienda, discussione*) to establish, start.

impian'tistica *sf* plant design and installation.

impi'anto *sm* (*installazione*) installation; (*apparecchiature*) plant; (*sistema*) system; ~ **elettrico** wiring; ~ **sportivo** sports complex; ~**i di risalita** (*SCI*) ski lifts.

impias'trare, impiastricci'are [impjastrit'tʃare] *vt* to smear, dirty.

impi'astro *sm* poultice; (*fig fam: persona*) nuisance.

impiccagi'one [impikka'dʒone] *sf* hanging.

impic'care *vt* to hang; ~**rsi** *vr* to hang o.s.

impicci'are [impit'tʃare] *vt* to hinder, hamper; ~**rsi** *vr* to meddle, interfere; **impicciati degli affari tuoi**! mind your own business!

im'piccio [im'pittʃo] *sm* (*ostacolo*) hindrance; (*seccatura*) trouble, bother; (*affare imbrogliato*) mess; **essere d'~** to be in the way; **cavare** *o* **togliere qn dagli** ~**i** to get sb out of trouble.

impicci'one, a [impit'tʃone] *sm/f* busybody.

impie'gare *vt* (*usare*) to use, employ; (*assumere*) to employ, take on; (*spendere: denaro, tempo*) to spend; (*investire*) to invest; ~**rsi** *vr* to get a job, obtain employment; **impiego un quarto d'ora per andare a casa** it takes me *o* I take a quarter of an hour to get home.

impiega'tizio, a [impjega'tittsjo] *ag* clerical, white-collar *cpd*; **lavoro/ceto** ~ clerical *o* white-collar work/workers *pl*.

impie'gato, a *sm/f* employee; ~ **statale** state employee.

impi'ego, ghi *sm* (*uso*) use; (*occupazione*) employment; (*posto di lavoro*) (regular) job, post; (*ECON*) investment; ~ **pubblico** job in the public sector.

impieto'sire *vt* to move to pity; ~**rsi** *vr* to be moved to pity.

impie'toso, a *ag* pitiless, cruel.

impie'trire *vt* (*anche fig*) to petrify.

impigli'are [impiʎ'ʎare] *vt* to catch, entangle; ~**rsi** *vr* to get caught up *o* entangled.

impi'grire *vt* to make lazy ♦ *vi* (*anche:* ~**rsi**) to grow lazy.

impingu'are *vt* (*maiale etc*) to fatten; (*fig: tasche, casse dello Stato*) to stuff with money.

impiom'bare *vt* (*pacco*) to seal (with lead); (*dente*) to fill.

impla'cabile *ag* implacable.

implemen'tare *vt* to implement.

impli'care *vt* to imply; (*coinvolgere*) to involve; ~**rsi** *vr*: ~**rsi (in)** to become involved (in).

implicazi'one [implikat'tsjone] *sf* implication.

im'plicito, a [im'plitʃito] *ag* implicit.

implo'rare *vt* to implore.

implorazi'one [implorat'tsjone] *sf* plea, entreaty.

impolli'nare *vt* to pollinate.

impollinazi'one [impollinat'tsjone] *sf* pollination.

impolve'rare *vt* to cover with dust; ~**rsi** *vr* to get dusty.

impoma'tare *vt* (*pelle*) to put ointment on;

(*capelli*) to pomade; (*baffi*) to wax; ~**rsi** *vr* (*fam*) to get spruced up.

imponde'rabile *ag* imponderable.

im'pone *etc vb vedi* **imporre**.

impo'nente *ag* imposing, impressive.

im'pongo *etc vb vedi* **imporre**.

impo'nibile *ag* taxable ♦ *sm* taxable income.

impopo'lare *ag* unpopular.

impopolarità *sf* unpopularity.

im'porre *vt* to impose; (*costringere*) to force, make; (*far valere*) to impose, enforce; **imporsi** *vr* (*persona*) to assert o.s.; (*cosa: rendersi necessario*) to become necessary; (*aver successo: moda, attore*) to become popular; ~ **a qn di fare** to force sb to do, make sb do.

impor'tante *ag* important.

impor'tanza [impor'tantsa] *sf* importance; **dare** ~ **a qc** to attach importance to sth; **darsi** ~ to give o.s. airs.

impor'tare *vt* (*introdurre dall'estero*) to import ♦ *vi* to matter, be important ♦ *vb impers* (*essere necessario*) to be necessary; (*interessare*) to matter; **non importa**! it doesn't matter!; **non me ne importa**! I don't care!

importa'tore, 'trice *ag* importing ♦ *sm/f* importer.

importazi'one [importat'tsjone] *sf* importation; (*merci importate*) imports *pl*.

im'porto *sm* (total) amount.

importu'nare *vt* to bother.

impor'tuno, a *ag* irksome, annoying.

im'posi *etc vb vedi* **imporre**.

imposizi'one [impozit'tsjone] *sf* imposition; (*ordine*) order, command; (*onere, imposta*) tax.

imposses'sarsi *vr*: ~ **di** to seize, take possession of.

impos'sibile *ag* impossible; **fare l'**~ to do one's utmost, do all one can.

impossibilità *sf* impossibility; **essere nell'**~ **di fare qc** to be unable to do sth.

impossibili'tato, a *ag*: **essere** ~ **a fare qc** to be unable to do sth.

im'posta *sf* (*di finestra*) shutter; (*tassa*) tax; ~ **indiretta sui consumi** excise duty *o* tax; ~ **locale sui redditi (ILOR)** tax on unearned income; ~ **patrimoniale** property tax; ~ **sul reddito** income tax; ~ **sul reddito delle persone fisiche (IRPEF)** personal income tax; ~ **di successione** capital transfer tax (*BRIT*), inheritance tax (*US*); ~ **sugli utili** tax on profits; ~ **sul valore aggiunto (I.V.A.)** value added tax (VAT) (*BRIT*), sales tax (*US*).

impos'tare *vt* (*imbucare*) to post; (*servizio,*

organizzazione) to set up; (*lavoro*) to organize, plan; (*resoconto, rapporto*) to plan; (*problema*) to set out, formulate; (*TIP: pagina*) to lay out; ~ **la voce** (*MUS*) to pitch one's voice.

impostazi'one [impostat'tsjone] *sf* (*di lettera*) posting (*BRIT*), mailing (*US*); (*di problema, questione*) formulation, statement; (*di lavoro*) organization, planning; (*di attività*) setting up; (*MUS: di voce*) pitch.

im'posto, a *pp di* **imporre.**

impos'tore, a *sm/f* impostor.

impo'tente *ag* weak, powerless; (*anche MED*) impotent.

impo'tenza [impo'tɛntsa] *sf* weakness, powerlessness; impotence.

impove'rire *vt* to impoverish ♦ *vi* (*anche*: ~**rsi**) to become poor.

imprati'cabile *ag* (*strada*) impassable; (*campo da gioco*) unplayable.

imprati'chire [imprati'kire] *vt* to train; ~**rsi** *vr*: ~**rsi in qc** to practise (*BRIT*) *o* practice (*US*) sth.

impre'care *vi* to curse, swear; ~ **contro** to hurl abuse at.

imprecazi'one [imprekat'tsjone] *sf* abuse, curse.

impreci'sato, a [impretʃi'zato] *ag* (*non preciso: quantità, numero*) indeterminate.

imprecisi'one [impretʃi'zjone] *sf* imprecision; inaccuracy.

impre'ciso, a [impre'tʃizo] *ag* imprecise, vague; (*calcolo*) inaccurate.

impre'gnare [impreɲ'ɲare] *vt*: ~ (**di**) (*imbevere*) to soak *o* impregnate (with); (*riempire: anche fig*) to fill (with).

imprendi'tore *sm* (*industriale*) entrepreneur; (*appaltatore*) contractor; **piccolo** ~ small businessman.

imprendito'ria *sf* enterprise; (*imprenditori*) entrepreneurs *pl*.

imprenditori'ale *ag* (*ceto, classe*) entrepreneurial.

imprepa'rato, a *ag*: ~ (**a**) (*gen*) unprepared (for); (*lavoratore*) untrained (for); **cogliere qn** ~ to catch sb unawares.

impreparazi'one [imprepparat'tsjone] *sf* lack of preparation.

im'presa *sf* (*iniziativa*) enterprise; (*azione*) exploit; (*azienda*) firm, concern; ~ **familiare** family firm; ~ **pubblica** state-owned enterprise.

impre'sario *sm* (*TEAT*) manager, impresario; ~ **di pompe funebri** funeral director.

imprescin'dibile [impreʃʃin'dibile] *ag* not to be ignored.

im'pressi *etc vb vedi* **imprimere.**

impressio'nante *ag* impressive; upsetting.

impressio'nare *vt* to impress; (*turbare*) to upset; (*FOT*) to expose; ~**rsi** *vr* to be easily upset.

impressi'one *sf* impression; (*fig: sensazione*) sensation, feeling; (*stampa*) printing; **fare** ~ (*colpire*) to impress; (*turbare*) to frighten, upset; **fare buona/ cattiva** ~ **a** to make a good/bad impression on.

im'presso, a *pp di* **imprimere.**

impres'tare *vt*: ~ **qc a qn** to lend sth to sb.

impreve'dibile *ag* unforeseeable; (*persona*) unpredictable.

imprevi'dente *ag* lacking in foresight.

imprevi'denza [imprevi'dɛntsa] *sf* lack of foresight.

impre'visto, a *ag* unexpected, unforeseen ♦ *sm* unforeseen event; **salvo** ~**i** unless anything unexpected happens.

imprezio'sire [imprettsjo'sire] *vt*: ~ **di** to embellish with.

imprigiona'mento [impridʒona'mento] *sm* imprisonment.

imprigio'nare [impridʒo'nare] *vt* to imprison.

im'primere *vt* (*anche fig*) to impress, stamp; (*comunicare: movimento*) to transmit, give.

impro'babile *ag* improbable, unlikely.

'improbo, a *ag* (*fatica, lavoro*) hard, laborious.

improdut'tivo, a *ag* (*investimento*) unprofitable; (*terreno*) unfruitful; (*fig: sforzo*) fruitless.

im'pronta *sf* imprint, impression, sign; (*di piede, mano*) print; (*fig*) mark, stamp; ~ **digitale** fingerprint; **rilevamento delle** ~**e genetiche** genetic fingerprinting.

impro'perio *sm* insult.

impropo'nibile *ag* which cannot be proposed *o* suggested.

im'proprio, a *ag* improper; **arma** ~**a** offensive weapon.

improro'gabile *ag* (*termine*) that cannot be extended.

improvvisa'mente *av* suddenly; unexpectedly.

improvvi'sare *vt* to improvise; ~**rsi** *vr*: ~**rsi cuoco** to (decide to) act as cook.

improvvi'sata *sf* (pleasant) surprise.

improvvisazi'one [improvvizat'tsjone] *sf* improvisation; **spirito d'**~ spirit of invention.

improv'viso, a *ag* (*imprevisto*) unexpected;

(*subitaneo*) sudden; **all'**~ unexpectedly; suddenly.

impru'dente *ag* foolish, imprudent; (*osservazione*) unwise.

impru'denza [impru'dɛntsa] *sf* foolishness, imprudence; **è stata un'**~ that was a foolish *o* an imprudent thing to do.

impu'dente *ag* impudent.

impu'denza [impu'dɛntsa] *sf* impudence.

impudi'cizia [impudi'tʃittsja] *sf* immodesty.

impu'dico, a, chi, che *ag* immodest.

impu'gnare [impuɲ'ɲare] *vt* to grasp, grip; (*DIR*) to contest.

impugna'tura [impuɲɲa'tura] *sf* grip, grasp; (*manico*) handle; (: *di spada*) hilt.

impulsività *sf* impulsiveness.

impul'sivo, a *ag* impulsive.

im'pulso *sm* impulse; **dare un** ~ **alle vendite** to boost sales.

impune'mente *av* with impunity.

impunità *sf* impunity.

impun'tarsi *vr* to stop dead, refuse to budge; (*fig*) to be obstinate.

impun'tura *sf* stitching.

impurità *sf inv* impurity.

im'puro, a *ag* impure.

impu'tare *vt* (*ascrivere*): ~ **qc a** to attribute sth to; (*DIR: accusare*): ~ **qn di** to charge sb with, accuse sb of.

impu'tato, a *sm/f* (*DIR*) accused, defendant.

imputazi'one [imputat'tsjone] *sf* (*DIR*) charge; (*di spese*) allocation.

imputri'dire *vi* to rot.

=========== *PAROLA CHIAVE*

in (*in* + *il* = **nel**, *in* + *lo* = **nello**, *in* + *l'* = **nell'**, *in* + *la* = **nella**, *in* + *i* = **nei**, *in* + *gli* = **negli**, *in* + *le* = **nelle**) *prep* **1** (*stato in luogo*) in; **vivere** ~ **Italia/città** to live in Italy/town; **essere** ~ **casa/ufficio** to be at home/the office; **è nel cassetto/**~ **salotto** it's in the drawer/in the sitting room; **se fossi** ~ **te** if I were you

2 (*moto a luogo*) to; (: *dentro*) into; **andare** ~ **Germania/città** to go to Germany/town; **andare** ~ **ufficio** to go to the office; **entrare** ~ **macchina/casa** to get into the car/go into the house

3 (*tempo*) in; **nel 1989** in 1989; ~ **giugno/estate** in June/summer; **l'ha fatto** ~ **sei mesi** he did it in six months; ~ **gioventù, io ...** when I was young, I ...

4 (*modo, maniera*) in; ~ **silenzio** in silence; **parlare** ~ **tedesco** to speak (in) German; ~ **abito da sera** in evening dress; ~ **guerra** at war; ~ **vacanza** on holiday; **Maria Bianchi** ~ **Rossi** Maria

Rossi née Bianchi

5 (*mezzo*) by; **viaggiare** ~ **autobus/treno** to travel by bus/train

6 (*materia*) made of; ~ **marmo** made of marble, marble *cpd*; **una collana** ~ **oro** a gold necklace

7 (*misura*) in; **siamo** ~ **quattro** there are four of us; ~ **tutto** in all

8 (*fine*): **dare** ~ **dono** to give as a gift; **spende tutto** ~ **alcool** he spends all his money on drink; ~ **onore di** in honour of.

i'nabile *ag*: ~ **a** incapable of; (*fisicamente, MIL*) unfit for.

inabilità *sf*: ~ **(a)** unfitness (for).

inabis'sare *vt* (*nave*) to sink; ~**rsi** *vr* to go down.

inabi'tabile *ag* uninhabitable.

inabi'tato, a *ag* uninhabited.

inacces'sibile [inattʃes'sibile] *ag* (*luogo*) inaccessible; (*persona*) unapproachable; (*mistero*) unfathomable.

inaccet'tabile [inattʃet'tabile] *ag* unacceptable.

inacer'bire [inatʃer'bire] *vt* to exacerbate; ~**rsi** *vr* (*persona*) to become embittered.

inaci'dire [inatʃi'dire] *vt* (*persona, carattere*) to embitter; ~**rsi** *vr* (*latte*) to go sour; (*fig: persona, carattere*) to become sour, become embittered.

ina'datto, a *ag*: ~ **(a)** unsuitable *o* unfit (for).

inadegu'ato, a *ag* inadequate.

inadempi'ente *ag* defaulting ♦ *sm/f* defaulter.

inadempi'enza [inadem'pjɛntsa] *sf*: ~ **a un contratto** non-fulfilment of a contract; **dovuto alle** ~**e dei funzionari** due to negligence on the part of the officials.

inadempi'mento *sm* non-fulfilment.

inaffer'rabile *ag* elusive; (*concetto, senso*) difficult to grasp.

'INAIL *sigla m* (= *Istituto Nazionale per l'Assicurazione contro gli Infortuni sul Lavoro*) state body providing sickness benefit in the event of accidents at work.

ina'lare *vt* to inhale.

inala'tore *sm* inhaler.

inalazi'one [inalat'tsjone] *sf* inhalation.

inalbe'rare *vt* (*NAUT*) to hoist, raise; ~**rsi** *vr* (*fig*) to flare up, fly off the handle.

inalte'rabile *ag* unchangeable; (*colore*) fast, permanent; (*affetto*) constant.

inalte'rato, a *ag* unchanged.

inami'dare *vt* to starch.

inami'dato, a *ag* starched.

inammis'sibile *ag* inadmissible.

inani'mato, a *ag* inanimate; (*senza vita*:

corpo) lifeless.

inappa'gabile *ag* insatiable.

inappel'labile *ag* (*decisione*) final, irrevocable; (*DIR*) final, not open to appeal.

inappe'tenza [inappe'tɛntsa] *sf* (*MED*) lack of appetite.

inappun'tabile *ag* irreproachable, flawless.

inar'care *vt* (*schiena*) to arch; (*sopracciglia*) to raise; ~**rsi** *vr* to arch.

inaridi'mento *sm* (*anche fig*) drying up.

inari'dire *vt* to make arid, dry up ♦ *vi* (*anche:* ~**rsi**) to dry up, become arid.

inarres'tabile *ag* (*processo*) irreversible; (*emorragia*) that cannot be stemmed; (*corsa del tempo*) relentless.

inascol'tato, a *ag* unheeded, unheard.

inaspettata'mente *av* unexpectedly.

inaspet'tato, a *ag* unexpected.

inas'prire *vt* (*disciplina*) to tighten up, make harsher; (*carattere*) to embitter; (*rapporti*) to make worse; ~**rsi** *vr* to become harsher; to become bitter; to become worse.

inattac'cabile *ag* (*anche fig*) unassailable; (*alibi*) cast-iron.

inatten'dibile *ag* unreliable.

inat'teso, a *ag* unexpected.

inat'tivo, a *ag* inactive, idle; (*CHIM*) inactive.

inattu'abile *ag* impracticable.

inau'dito, a *ag* unheard of.

inaugu'rale *ag* inaugural.

inaugu'rare *vt* to inaugurate, open; (*monumento*) to unveil.

inaugurazi'one [inaugurat'tsjone] *sf* inauguration; unveiling.

inavve'duto, a *ag* careless, inadvertent.

inavver'tenza [inavver'tɛntsa] *sf* carelessness, inadvertence.

inavvertita'mente *av* inadvertently, unintentionally.

inavvici'nabile [inavvitʃi'nabile] *ag* unapproachable.

'Inca *ag inv, sm/f inv* Inca.

incagli'are [inkaʎ'ʎare] *vi* (*NAUT: anche:* ~**rsi**) to run aground.

incalco'labile *ag* incalculable.

incal'lito, a *ag* calloused; (*fig*) hardened, inveterate; (: *insensibile*) hard.

incal'zante [inkal'tsante] *ag* urgent, insistent; (*crisi*) imminent.

incal'zare [inkal'tsare] *vt* to follow *o* pursue closely; (*fig*) to press ♦ *vi* (*urgere*) to be pressing; (*essere imminente*) to be imminent.

iname'rare *vt* (*DIR*) to expropriate.

incammi'nare *vt* (*fig: avviare*) to start up; ~**rsi** *vr* to set off.

incana'lare *vt* (*anche fig*) to channel; ~**rsi** *vr* (*folla*): ~**rsi verso** to converge on.

incancre'nire *vi*, **incancre'nirsi** *vi* to become gangrenous.

incande'scente [inkandeʃ'ʃɛnte] *ag* incandescent, white-hot.

incan'tare *vt* to enchant, bewitch; ~**rsi** *vr* (*rimanere intontito*) to be spellbound; to be in a daze; (*meccanismo: bloccarsi*) to jam.

incanta'tore, 'trice *ag* enchanting, bewitching ♦ *sm/f* enchanter/enchantress.

incan'tesimo *sm* spell, charm.

incan'tevole *ag* charming, enchanting.

in'canto *sm* spell, charm, enchantment; (*asta*) auction; **come per** ~ as if by magic; **ti sta d'**~! (*vestito etc*) it really suits you!; **mettere all'**~ to put up for auction.

incanu'tire *vi* to go white.

inca'pace [inka'patʃe] *ag* incapable.

incapacità [inkapatʃi'ta] *sf* inability; (*DIR*) incapacity; ~ **d'intendere e di volere** diminished responsibility.

incapo'nirsi *vr* to be stubborn, be determined.

incap'pare *vi*: ~ **in qc/qn** (*anche fig*) to run into sth/sb.

incappucci'are [inkapput'tʃare] *vt* to put a hood on; ~**rsi** *vr* (*persona*) to put on a hood.

incapricci'arsi [inkaprit'tʃarsi] *vr*: ~ **di** to take a fancy to *o* for.

incapsu'lare *vt* (*dente*) to crown.

incarce'rare [inkartʃe'rare] *vt* to imprison.

incari'care *vt*: ~ **qn di fare** to give sb the responsibility of doing; ~**rsi** *vr*: ~**rsi di** to take care *o* charge of.

incari'cato, a *ag*: ~ (**di**) in charge (of), responsible (for) ♦ *sm/f* delegate, representative; **docente** ~ (*di università*) lecturer without tenure; ~ **d'affari** (*POL*) chargé d'affaires.

in'carico, chi *sm* task, job; (*INS*) temporary post.

incar'nare *vt* to embody; ~**rsi** *vr* to be embodied; (*REL*) to become incarnate.

incarnazi'one [inkarnat'tsjone] *sf* incarnation; (*fig*) embodiment.

incarta'mento *sm* dossier, file.

incartapeco'rito, a *ag* (*pelle*) wizened, shrivelled (*BRIT*), shriveled (*US*).

incar'tare *vt* to wrap (in paper).

incasel'lare *vt* (*posta*) to sort; (*fig: nozioni*) to pigeonhole.

incas'sare *vt* (*merce*) to pack (in cases); (*gemma: incastonare*) to set; (*ECON: riscuotere*) to collect; (*PUGILATO: colpi*) to take, stand up to.

in'casso *sm* cashing, encashment; (*introito*) takings *pl*.

incasto'nare *vt* to set.

incastona'tura *sf* setting.

incas'trare *vt* to fit in, insert; (*fig: intrappolare*) to catch; ~**rsi** *vr* (*combaciare*) to fit together; (*restare bloccato*) to become stuck.

in'castro *sm* slot, groove; (*punto di unione*) joint; **gioco a** ~ interlocking puzzle.

incate'nare *vt* to chain up.

incatra'mare *vt* to tar.

incatti'vire *vt* to make wicked; ~**rsi** *vr* to turn nasty.

in'cauto, a *ag* imprudent, rash.

inca'vare *vt* to hollow out.

inca'vato, a *ag* hollow; (*occhi*) sunken.

in'cavo *sm* hollow; (*solco*) groove.

incavo'larsi *vr* (*fam*) to lose one's temper, get annoyed.

incaz'zarsi [inkat'tsarsi] *vr* (*fam!*) to get steamed up.

in'cedere [in'tʃɛdere] *vi* (*poetico*) to advance solemnly ♦ *sm* solemn gait.

incendi'are [intʃen'djare] *vt* to set fire to; ~**rsi** *vr* to catch fire, burst into flames.

incendi'ario, a [intʃen'djarjo] *ag* incendiary ♦ *sm/f* arsonist.

in'cendio [in'tʃendjo] *sm* fire.

incene'rire [intʃene'rire] *vt* to burn to ashes, incinerate; (*cadavere*) to cremate; ~**rsi** *vr* to be burnt to ashes.

inceneri'tore [intʃeneri'tore] *sm* incinerator.

in'censo [in'tʃɛnso] *sm* incense.

incensu'rato, a [intʃensu'rato] *ag* (*DIR*): **essere** ~ to have a clean record.

incenti'vare [intʃenti'vare] *vt* (*produzione, vendite*) to boost; (*persona*) to motivate.

incen'tivo [intʃen'tivo] *sm* incentive.

incen'trarsi [intʃen'trarsi] *vr*: ~ **su** (*fig*) to centre (*BRIT*) *o* center (*US*) on.

incep'pare [intʃep'pare] *vt* to obstruct, hamper; ~**rsi** *vr* to jam.

ince'rata [intʃe'rata] *sf* (*tela*) tarpaulin; (*impermeabile*) oilskins *pl*.

incer'tezza [intʃer'tettsa] *sf* uncertainty.

in'certo, a [in'tʃɛrto] *ag* uncertain; (*irresoluto*) undecided, hesitating ♦ *sm* uncertainty; **gli** ~**i del mestiere** the risks of the job.

incespi'care [intʃespi'kare] *vi*: ~ (**in qc**) to trip (over sth).

inces'sante [intʃes'sante] *ag* incessant.

in'cesto [in'tʃɛsto] *sm* incest.

incestu'oso, a [intʃestu'oso] *ag* incestuous.

in'cetta [in'tʃetta] *sf* buying up; **fare** ~ **di qc**

to buy up sth.

inchi'esta [in'kjɛsta] *sf* investigation, inquiry.

inchi'nare [inki'nare] *vt* to bow; ~**rsi** *vr* to bend down; (*per riverenza*) to bow; (: *donna*) to curtsy.

in'chino [in'kino] *sm* bow; curtsy.

inchio'dare [inkjo'dare] *vt* to nail (down); ~ **la macchina** (*AUT*) to jam on the brakes.

inchi'ostro [in'kjɔstro] *sm* ink; ~ **simpatico** invisible ink.

inciam'pare [intʃam'pare] *vi* to trip, stumble.

inci'ampo [in'tʃampo] *sm* obstacle; **essere d'**~ **a qn** (*fig*) to be in sb's way.

inciden'tale [intʃiden'tale] *ag* incidental.

incidental'mente [intʃidental'mente] *av* (*per caso*) by chance; (*per inciso*) incidentally, by the way.

inci'dente [intʃi'dɛnte] *sm* accident; (*episodio*) incident; **e con questo l'**~ **è chiuso** and that is the end of the matter; ~ **d'auto** car accident; ~ **diplomatico** diplomatic incident.

inci'denza [intʃi'dɛntsa] *sf* incidence; **avere una forte** ~ **su qc** to affect sth greatly.

in'cidere [in'tʃidere] *vi*: ~ **su** to bear upon, affect ♦ *vt* (*tagliare incavando*) to cut into; (*ARTE*) to engrave; to etch; (*canzone*) to record.

in'cinta [in'tʃinta] *ag f* pregnant.

incipi'ente [intʃi'pjɛnte] *ag* incipient.

incipri'are [intʃi'prjare] *vt* to powder.

in'circa [in'tʃirka] *av*: **all'**~ more or less, very nearly.

in'cisi *etc* [in'tʃizi] *vb vedi* **incidere**.

incisi'one [intʃi'zjone] *sf* cut; (*disegno*) engraving; etching; (*registrazione*) recording; (*MED*) incision.

inci'sivo, a [intʃi'zivo] *ag* incisive; (*ANAT*): (**dente**) ~ incisor.

in'ciso, a [in'tʃizo] *pp di* **incidere** ♦ *sm*: **per** ~ incidentally, by the way.

inci'sore [intʃi'zore] *sm* (*ARTE*) engraver.

incita'mento [intʃita'mento] *sm* incitement.

inci'tare [intʃi'tare] *vt* to incite.

inci'vile [intʃi'vile] *ag* uncivilized; (*villano*) impolite.

incivi'lire [intʃivi'lire] *vt* to civilize.

incivil'tà [intʃivil'ta] *sf* (*di popolazione*) barbarism; (*fig: di trattamento*) barbarity; (: *maleducazione*) incivility, rudeness.

incl. *abbr* (= *incluso*) encl.

incle'mente *ag* (*giudice, sentenza*) severe, harsh; (*fig: clima*) harsh; (: *tempo*) inclement.

incle'menza [inkle'mɛntsa] *sf* severity; harshness; inclemency.

incli'nabile *ag (schienale)* reclinable.
incli'nare *vt* to tilt ♦ *vi (fig):* ~ **a qc/a fare** to
incline towards sth/doing; to tend
towards sth/to do; ~**rsi** *vr (barca)* to list;
(aereo) to bank.
incli'nato, a *ag* sloping.
inclinazi'one [inklinat'tsjone] *sf* slope; *(fig)*
inclination, tendency.
in'cline *ag:* ~ **a** inclined to.
in'cludere *vt* to include; *(accludere)* to
enclose.
inclusi'one *sf* inclusion.
inclu'sivo, a *ag:* ~ **di** inclusive of.
in'cluso, a *pp di* **includere** ♦ *ag* included;
enclosed.
incoe'rente *ag* incoherent; *(contraddittorio)*
inconsistent.
incoe'renza [inkoe'rɛntsa] *sf* incoherence;
inconsistency.
in'cognito, a [in'kɔɲɲito] *ag* unknown ♦ *sm:*
in ~ incognito ♦ *sf (MAT, fig)* unknown
quantity.
incol'lare *vt* to glue, gum; *(unire con colla)*
to stick together; ~ **gli occhi addosso a**
qn *(fig)* to fix one's eyes on sb.
incolla'tura *sf (IPPICA):* **vincere/perdere di**
un'~ to win/lose by a head.
incolon'nare *vt* to draw up in columns.
inco'lore *ag* colourless *(BRIT),* colorless
(US).
incol'pare *vt:* ~ **qn di** to charge sb with.
in'colto, a *ag (terreno)* uncultivated;
(trascurato: capelli) neglected; *(persona)*
uneducated.
in'colume *ag* safe and sound, unhurt.
incolumità *sf* safety.
incom'bente *ag (pericolo)* imminent,
impending.
incom'benza [inkom'bɛntsa] *sf* duty, task.
in'combere *vi (sovrastare minacciando):* ~
su to threaten, hang over.
incominci'are [inkomin'tʃare] *vi, vt* to
begin, start.
incomo'dare *vt* to trouble, inconvenience;
~**rsi** *vr* to put o.s. out.
in'comodo, a *ag* uncomfortable;
(inopportuno) inconvenient ♦ *sm*
inconvenience, bother.
incompa'rabile *ag* incomparable.
incompa'tibile *ag* incompatible.
incompatibilità *sf* incompatibility; ~ **di**
carattere (mutual) incompatibility.
incompe'tente *ag* incompetent.
incompe'tenza [inkompe'tɛntsa] *sf*
incompetence.
incompi'uto, a *ag* unfinished, incomplete.
incom'pleto, a *ag* incomplete.
incompren'sibile *ag* incomprehensible.

incomprensi'one *sf* incomprehension.
incom'preso, a *ag* not understood;
misunderstood.
inconce'pibile [inkontʃe'pibile] *ag*
inconceivable.
inconcili'abile [inkontʃi'ljabile] *ag*
irreconcilable.
inconclu'dente *ag* inconclusive; *(persona)*
ineffectual.
incondizio'nato, a [inkondittsjo'nato] *ag*
unconditional.
inconfes'sabile *ag (pensiero, peccato)*
unmentionable.
inconfon'dibile *ag* unmistakable.
inconfu'tabile *ag* irrefutable.
incongru'ente *ag* inconsistent.
incongru'enza [inkongru'ɛntsa] *sf*
inconsistency.
in'congruo, a *ag* incongruous.
inconsa'pevole *ag:* ~ **di** unaware of,
ignorant of.
inconsapevo'lezza [inkonsapevo'lettsa] *sf*
ignorance, lack of awareness.
in'conscio, a, sci, sce [in'kɔnʃo] *ag*
unconscious ♦ *sm (PSIC):* **l'**~ the
unconscious.
inconsis'tente *ag (patrimonio)*
insubstantial; *(dubbio)* unfounded;
(ragionamento, prove) tenuous, flimsy.
inconsis'tenza [inkonsis'tɛntsa] *sf*
insubstantial nature; lack of foundation;
flimsiness.
inconso'labile *ag* inconsolable.
inconsu'eto, a *ag* unusual.
incon'sulto, a *ag* rash.
inconte'nibile *ag (rabbia)* uncontrollable;
(entusiasmo) irrepressible.
inconten'tabile *ag (desiderio, avidità)*
insatiable; *(persona: capriccioso)* hard to
please, very demanding.
incontes'tabile *ag* incontrovertible,
indisputable.
incontes'tato, a *ag* undisputed.
inconti'nenza [inkonti'nɛntsa] *sf*
incontinence.
incon'trare *vt* to meet; *(difficoltà)* to meet
with; ~**rsi** *vr* to meet.
incon'trario *av:* **all'**~ *(sottosopra)* upside
down; *(alla rovescia)* back to front;
(all'indietro) backwards; *(nel senso*
contrario) the other way round.
incontras'tabile *ag* incontrovertible,
indisputable.
incontras'tato, a *ag (successo, vittoria,*
verità) uncontested, undisputed.
in'contro *av:* ~ **a** *(verso)* towards ♦ *sm*
meeting; *(SPORT)* match; meeting;
(fortuito) encounter; **venire** ~ **a** *(richieste,*

esigenze) to comply with; ~ **di calcio** football match (*BRIT*), soccer game (*US*).
incontrol'labile *ag* uncontrollable.
inconveni'ente *sm* drawback, snag.
incoraggia'mento [inkoraddʒa'mento] *sm* encouragement; **premio d'~** consolation prize.
incoraggi'are [inkorad'dʒare] *vt* to encourage.
incor'nare *vt* to gore.
incornici'are [inkorni'tʃare] *vt* to frame.
incoro'nare *vt* to crown.
incoronazi'one [inkoronat'tsjone] *sf* coronation.
incorpo'rare *vt* to incorporate; (*fig: annettere*) to annex.
incorreg'gibile [inkorred'dʒibile] *ag* incorrigible.
in'correre *vi:* ~ **in** to meet with, run into.
incorrut'tibile *ag* incorruptible.
in'corso, a *pp di* **incorrere.**
incosci'ente [inkoʃ'ʃɛnte] *ag* (*inconscio*) unconscious; (*irresponsabile*) reckless, thoughtless.
incosci'enza [inkoʃ'ʃɛntsa] *sf* unconsciousness; recklessness, thoughtlessness.
incos'tante *ag* (*studente, impiegato*) inconsistent; (*carattere*) fickle, inconstant; (*rendimento*) sporadic.
incos'tanza [inkos'tantsa] *sf* inconstancy, fickleness.
incostituzio'nale [inkostituttsjo'nale] *ag* unconstitutional.
incre'dibile *ag* incredible, unbelievable.
incredulità *sf* incredulity.
in'credulo, a *ag* incredulous, disbelieving.
incremen'tare *vt* to increase; (*dar sviluppo a*) to promote.
incre'mento *sm* (*sviluppo*) development; (*aumento numerico*) increase, growth.
incresci'oso, a [inkreʃ'ʃoso] *ag* (*spiacevole*) unpleasant; regrettable.
incres'pare *vt* (*capelli*) to curl; (*acque*) to ripple; **~rsi** *vr* (*vedi vt*) to curl; to ripple.
incrimi'nare *vt* (*DIR*) to charge.
incriminazi'one [inkriminat'tsjone] *sf* (*atto d'accusa*) indictment, charge.
incri'nare *vt* to crack; (*fig: rapporti, amicizia*) to cause to deteriorate; **~rsi** *vr* to crack; to deteriorate.
incrina'tura *sf* crack; (*fig*) rift.
incroci'are [inkro'tʃare] *vt* to cross; (*incontrare*) to meet ♦ *vi* (*NAUT, AER*) to cruise; **~rsi** *vr* (*strade*) to cross, intersect; (*persone, veicoli*) to pass each other; ~ **le braccia/le gambe** to fold one's arms/cross one's legs.

incrocia'tore [inkrotʃa'tore] *sm* cruiser.
in'crocio [in'krotʃo] *sm* (*anche FERR*) crossing; (*di strade*) crossroads.
incrol'labile *ag* (*fede*) unshakeable, firm.
incros'tare *vt* to encrust; **~rsi** *vr:* **~rsi di** to become encrusted with.
incrostazi'one [inkrostat'tsjone] *sf* encrustation; (*di calcare*) scale; (*nelle tubature*) fur (*BRIT*), scale.
incru'ento, a *ag* (*battaglia*) without bloodshed, bloodless.
incuba'trice [inkuba'tritʃe] *sf* incubator.
incubazi'one [inkubat'tsjone] *sf* incubation.
'incubo *sm* nightmare.
in'cudine *sf* anvil; **trovarsi** *o* **essere tra l'~ e il martello** (*fig*) to be between the devil and the deep blue sea.
incul'care *vt:* ~ **qc in** to inculcate sth into, instill sth into.
incune'are *vt* to wedge.
incu'pire *vt* (*rendere scuro*) to darken; (*fig: intristire*) to fill with gloom ♦ *vi* (*vedi vt*) to darken; to become gloomy.
incu'rabile *ag* incurable.
incu'rante *ag:* ~ **(di)** heedless (of), careless (of).
in'curia *sf* negligence.
incurio'sire *vt* to make curious; **~rsi** *vr* to become curious.
incursi'one *sf* raid.
incur'vare *vt*, **~rsi** *vr* to bend, curve.
in'cusso, a *pp di* **incutere.**
incusto'dito, a *ag* unguarded, unattended; **passaggio a livello** ~ unmanned level crossing.
in'cutere *vt* to arouse; ~ **timore/rispetto a qn** to strike fear into sb/command sb's respect.
'indaco *sm* indigo.
indaffa'rato, a *ag* busy.
inda'gare *vt* to investigate.
indaga'tore, 'trice *ag* (*sguardo, domanda*) searching; (*mente*) inquiring.
in'dagine [in'dadʒine] *sf* investigation, inquiry; (*ricerca*) research, study; ~ **di mercato** market survey.
indebita'mente *av* (*immeritatamente*) undeservedly; (*erroneamente*) wrongfully.
indebi'tare *vt:* ~ **qn** to get sb into debt; **~rsi** *vr* to run *o* get into debt.
in'debito, a *ag* undeserved; wrongful.
indeboli'mento *sm* weakening; (*debolezza*) weakness.
indebo'lire *vt*, *vi* (*anche:* **~rsi**) to weaken.
inde'cente [inde'tʃɛnte] *ag* indecent.
inde'cenza [inde'tʃɛntsa] *sf* indecency; **è un'~!** (*vergogna*) it's scandalous!, it's a

disgrace!
indeci'frabile [indetʃi'frabile] *ag* indecipherable.
indecisi'one [indetʃi'zjone] *sf* indecisiveness; indecision.
inde'ciso, a [inde'tʃizo] *ag* indecisive; (*irresoluto*) undecided.
indeco'roso, a *ag* (*comportamento*) indecorous, unseemly.
inde'fesso, a *ag* untiring, indefatigable.
indefi'nibile *ag* indefinable.
indefi'nito, a *ag* (*anche LING*) indefinite; (*impreciso, non determinato*) undefined.
indefor'mabile *ag* crushproof.
in'degno, a [in'deɲɲo] *ag* (*atto*) shameful; (*persona*) unworthy.
inde'lebile *ag* indelible.
indelica'tezza [indelika'tettsa] *sf* tactlessness.
indeli'cato, a *ag* (*domanda*) indiscreet, tactless.
indemoni'ato, a *ag* possessed (by the devil).
in'denne *ag* unhurt, uninjured.
indennità *sf inv* (*rimborso: di spese*) allowance; (*: di perdita*) compensation, indemnity; ~ **di contingenza** cost-of-living allowance; ~ **di fine rapporto** severance payment (*on retirement, redundancy or when taking up other employment*); ~ **di trasferta** travel expenses *pl*.
indenniz'zare [indennid'dzare] *vt* to compensate.
inden'nizzo [inden'niddzo] *sm* (*somma*) compensation, indemnity.
indero'gabile *ag* binding.
indescri'vibile *ag* indescribable.
indeside'rabile *ag* undesirable.
indeside'rato, a *ag* unwanted.
indetermina'tezza [indetermina'tettsa] *sf* vagueness.
indetermina'tivo, a *ag* (*LING*) indefinite.
indetermi'nato, a *ag* indefinite, indeterminate.
in'detto, a *pp di* indire.
'India *sf*: l'~ India; **le** ~**e occidentali** the West Indies.
indi'ano, a *ag* Indian ♦ *smlf* (*d'India*) Indian; (*d'America*) Red Indian; **l'Oceano I**~ the Indian Ocean.
indiavo'lato, a *ag* possessed (by the devil); (*vivace, violento*) wild.
indi'care *vt* (*mostrare*) to show, indicate; (*: col dito*) to point to, point out; (*consigliare*) to suggest, recommend.
indica'tivo, a *ag* indicative ♦ *sm* (*LING*) indicative (mood).

indi'cato, a *ag* (*consigliato*) advisable; (*adatto*): ~ **per** suitable for, appropriate for.
indica'tore, 'trice *ag* indicating ♦ *sm* (*elenco*) guide; directory; (*TECN*) gauge; indicator; **cartello** ~ sign; ~ **della benzina** petrol (*BRIT*) *o* gas (*US*) gauge, fuel gauge; ~ **di velocità** (*AUT*) speedometer; (*AER*) airspeed indicator.
indicazi'one [indikat'tsjone] *sf* indication; (*informazione*) piece of information; ~**i per l'uso** instructions for use.
'indice ['inditʃe] *sm* (*ANAT: dito*) index finger, forefinger; (*lancetta*) pointer; (*fig: indizio*) sign; (*TECN, MAT, nei libri*) index; ~ **azionario** share index; ~ **di gradimento** (*RADIO, TV*) popularity rating; ~ **dei prezzi al consumo** ≈ retail price index.
indicherò *etc* [indike'rɔ] *vb vedi* **indicare**.
indi'cibile [indi'tʃibile] *ag* inexpressible.
indiciz'zare [inditʃid'dzare] *vt*: ~ **al costo della vita** to index-link (*BRIT*), index (*US*).
indiciz'zato, a [inditʃid'dzato] *ag* (*polizza, salario etc*) index-linked (*BRIT*), indexed (*US*).
indicizzazi'one [inditʃiddzat'tsjone] *sf* indexing.
indietreggi'are [indjetred'dʒare] *vi* to draw back, retreat.
indi'etro *av* back; (*guardare*) behind, back; (*andare, cadere: anche*: **all'**~) backwards; **rimanere** ~ to be left behind; **essere** ~ (*col lavoro*) to be behind; (*orologio*) to be slow; **rimandare qc** ~ to send sth back; **non vado né avanti né** ~ (*fig*) I'm not getting anywhere, I'm getting nowhere.
indi'feso, a *ag* (*città, confine*) undefended; (*persona*) defenceless (*BRIT*), defenseless (*US*), helpless.
indiffe'rente *ag* indifferent ♦ *sm*: **fare l'**~ to pretend to be indifferent, be *o* act casual; (*fingere di non vedere o sentire*) to pretend not to notice.
indiffe'renza [indiffe'rentsa] *sf* indifference.
in'digeno, a [in'didʒeno] *ag* indigenous, native ♦ *smlf* native.
indi'gente [indi'dʒente] *ag* poverty-stricken, destitute.
indi'genza [indi'dʒentsa] *sf* extreme poverty.
indigesti'one [indidʒes'tjone] *sf* indigestion.
indi'gesto, a [indi'dʒesto] *ag* indigestible.
indi'gnare [indiɲ'ɲare] *vt* to fill with indignation; ~**rsi** *vr* to be (*o get*) indignant.

indignazi'one [indiɲɲat'tsjone] *sf* indignation.

indimenti'cabile *ag* unforgettable.

'indio, a *ag, sm/f* (South American) Indian.

indipen'dente *ag* independent.

indipendente'mente *av* independently; ~ **dal fatto che gli piaccia o meno, verrà!** he's coming, whether he likes it or not!

indipen'denza [indipen'dɛntsa] *sf* independence.

in'dire *vt* (*concorso*) to announce; (*elezioni*) to call.

indi'retto, a *ag* indirect.

indiriz'zare [indirit'tsare] *vt* (*dirigere*) to direct; (*mandare*) to send; (*lettera*) to address; ~ **la parola a qn** to address sb.

indiriz'zario [indirit'tsarjo] *sm* mailing list.

indi'rizzo [indi'rittso] *sm* address; (*direzione*) direction; (*avvio*) trend, course; ~ **assoluto** (*INFORM*) absolute address.

indisci'plina [indiʃʃi'plina] *sf* indiscipline.

indiscipli'nato, a [indiʃʃipli'nato] *ag* undisciplined, unruly.

indis'creto, a *ag* indiscreet.

indiscrezi'one [indiskret'tsjone] *sf* indiscretion.

indiscrimi'nato, a *ag* indiscriminate.

indis'cusso, a *ag* unquestioned.

indiscu'tibile *ag* indisputable, unquestionable.

indispen'sabile *ag* indispensable, essential.

indispet'tire *vt* to irritate, annoy ♦ *vi* (*anche*: ~**rsi**) to get irritated *o* annoyed.

indispo'nente *ag* irritating, annoying.

indis'porre *vt* to antagonize.

indisposizi'one [indispozit'tsjone] *sf* (slight) indisposition.

indis'posto, a *pp di* **indisporre** ♦ *ag* indisposed, unwell.

indisso'lubile *ag* indissoluble.

indissolubil'mente *av* indissolubly.

indistinta'mente *av* (*senza distinzioni*) indiscriminately, without exception; (*in modo indefinito*: *vedere, sentire*) vaguely, faintly.

indis'tinto, a *ag* indistinct.

indistrut'tibile *ag* indestructible.

in'divia *sf* endive.

individu'ale *ag* individual.

individua'lismo *sm* individualism.

individua'lista, i, e *sm/f* individualist.

individualità *sf* individuality.

individual'mente *av* individually.

individu'are *vt* (*dar forma distinta a*) to characterize; (*determinare*) to locate; (*riconoscere*) to single out.

indi'viduo *sm* individual.

indivi'sibile *ag* indivisible; **quei due sono** ~**i** (*fig*) those two are inseparable.

indizi'are [indit'tsjare] *vt*: ~ **qn di qc** to cast suspicion on sb for sth.

indizi'ato, a [indit'tsjato] *ag* suspected ♦ *sm/f* suspect.

in'dizio [in'dittsjo] *sm* (*segno*) sign, indication; (*POLIZIA*) clue; (*DIR*) piece of evidence.

Indo'cina [indo'tʃina] *sf*: **l'**~ Indochina.

'indole *sf* nature, character.

indo'lente *ag* indolent.

indo'lenza [indo'lɛntsa] *sf* indolence.

indolen'zire [indolen'tsire] *vt* (*gambe, braccia etc*) to make stiff, cause to ache; (:*intorpidire*) to numb; ~**rsi** *vr* to become stiff; to go numb.

indolen'zito, a [indolen'tsito] *ag* stiff, aching; (*intorpidito*) numb.

indo'lore *ag* (*anche fig*) painless.

indo'mani *sm*: **l'**~ the next day, the following day.

Indo'nesia *sf*: **l'**~ Indonesia.

indonesi'ano, a *ag, sm/f, sm* Indonesian.

indo'rare *vt* (*rivestire in oro*) to gild; (*CUC*) to dip in egg yolk; ~ **la pillola** (*fig*) to sugar the pill.

indos'sare *vt* (*mettere indosso*) to put on; (*avere indosso*) to have on.

indossa'tore, 'trice *sm/f* model.

in'dotto, a *pp di* **indurre**.

indottri'nare *vt* to indoctrinate.

indovi'nare *vt* (*scoprire*) to guess; (*immaginare*) to imagine, guess; (*il futuro*) to foretell; **tirare a** ~ to make a shot in the dark.

indovi'nato, a *ag* successful; (*scelta*) inspired.

indovi'nello *sm* riddle.

indo'vino, a *sm/f* fortuneteller.

indù *ag, sm/f* Hindu.

indubbia'mente *av* undoubtedly.

in'dubbio, a *ag* certain, undoubted.

in'duco *etc vb vedi* **indurre**.

indugi'are [indu'dʒare] *vi* to take one's time, delay.

in'dugio [in'dudʒo] *sm* (*ritardo*) delay; **senza** ~ without delay.

indul'gente [indul'dʒɛnte] *ag* indulgent; (*giudice*) lenient.

indul'genza [indul'dʒɛntsa] *sf* indulgence; leniency.

in'dulgere [in'duldʒere] *vi*: ~ **a** (*accondiscendere*) to comply with; (*abbandonarsi*) to indulge in.

in'dulto, a *pp di* **indulgere** ♦ *sm* (*DIR*) pardon.

indu'mento *sm* article of clothing, garment; ~i *smpl* (*vestiti*) clothes; ~i intimi underwear *sg*.
induri'mento *sm* hardening.
indu'rire *vt* to harden ♦ *vi* (*anche:* ~rsi) to harden, become hard.
in'durre *vt*: ~ qn a fare qc to induce *o* persuade sb to do sth; ~ qn in errore to mislead sb; ~ in tentazione to lead into temptation.
in'dussi *etc vb vedi* **indurre**.
in'dustria *sf* industry; la piccola/grande ~ small/big business.
industri'ale *ag* industrial ♦ *sm* industrialist.
industrializ'zare [industrjalid'dzare] *vt* to industrialize.
industrializzazi'one [industrjaliddzat'tsjone] *sf* industrialization.
industri'arsi *vr* to do one's best, try hard.
industri'oso, a *ag* industrious, hard-working.
induzi'one [indut'tsjone] *sf* induction.
inebe'tito, a *ag* dazed, stunned.
inebri'are *vt* (*anche fig*) to intoxicate; ~rsi *vr* to become intoxicated.
inecce'pibile [inettʃe'pibile] *ag* unexceptionable.
i'nedia *sf* starvation.
i'nedito, a *ag* unpublished.
inef'fabile *ag* ineffable.
ineffi'cace [ineffi'katʃe] *ag* ineffective.
ineffi'cacia [ineffi'katʃa] *sf* inefficacy, ineffectiveness.
ineffici'ente [ineffi'tʃɛnte] *ag* inefficient.
ineffici'enza [ineffi'tʃɛntsa] *sf* inefficiency.
ineguagli'abile [inegwaʎ'ʎabile] *ag* incomparable, matchless.
ineguagli'anza [inegwaʎ'ʎantsa] *sf* (*sociale*) inequality; (*di superficie, livello*) unevenness.
inegu'ale *ag* unequal; (*irregolare*) uneven.
inelut'tabile *ag* inescapable.
ineluttabilità *sf* inescapability.
inenar'rabile *ag* unutterable.
inequivo'cabile *ag* unequivocal.
ine'rente *ag*: ~ a concerning, regarding.
i'nerme *ag* unarmed, defenceless (*BRIT*), defenseless (*US*).
inerpi'carsi *vr*: ~ (su) to clamber (up).
i'nerte *ag* inert; (*inattivo*) indolent, sluggish.
i'nerzia [i'nɛrtsja] *sf* inertia; indolence, sluggishness.
inesat'tezza [inezat'tettsa] *sf* inaccuracy.
ine'satto, a *ag* (*impreciso*) inaccurate, inexact; (*erroneo*) incorrect; (*AMM: non*

riscosso) uncollected.
inesau'ribile *ag* inexhaustible.
inesis'tente *ag* non-existent.
ineso'rabile *ag* inexorable, relentless.
inesorabil'mente *av* inexorably.
inesperi'enza [inespe'rjɛntsa] *sf* inexperience.
ines'perto, a *ag* inexperienced.
inespli'cabile *ag* inexplicable.
inesplo'rato, a *ag* unexplored.
ines'ploso, a *ag* unexploded.
inespres'sivo, a *ag* (*viso*) expressionless, inexpressive.
ines'presso, a *ag* unexpressed.
inespri'mibile *ag* inexpressible.
inespu'gnabile [inespuɲ'ɲabile] *ag* (*fortezza, torre etc*) impregnable.
ineste'tismo *sm* beauty problem.
inesti'mabile *ag* inestimable; (*valore*) incalculable.
inestir'pabile *ag* ineradicable.
inestri'cabile *ag* (*anche fig*) impenetrable.
inetti'tudine *sf* ineptitude.
i'netto, a *ag* (*incapace*) inept; (*che non ha attitudine*): ~ (a) unsuited (to).
ine'vaso, a *ag* (*ordine, corrispondenza*) outstanding.
inevi'tabile *ag* inevitable.
inevitabil'mente *av* inevitably.
i'nezia [i'nɛttsja] *sf* trifle, thing of no importance.
infagot'tare *vt* to bundle up, wrap up; ~rsi *vr* to wrap up.
infal'libile *ag* infallible.
infallibilità *sf* infallibility.
infa'mante *ag* (*accusa*) defamatory, slanderous.
infa'mare *vt* to defame.
in'fame *ag* infamous; (*fig: cosa, compito*) awful, dreadful.
in'famia *sf* infamy.
infan'gare *vt* (*sporcare*) to cover with mud; (*nome, reputazione*) to sully; ~rsi *vr* to get covered in mud; to be sullied.
infan'tile *ag* child *cpd*; childlike; (*adulto, azione*) childish; **letteratura** ~ children's books *pl*.
in'fanzia [in'fantsja] *sf* childhood; (*bambini*) children *pl*; **prima** ~ babyhood, infancy.
infari'nare *vt* to cover with (*o* sprinkle with *o* dip in) flour; ~ di zucchero to sprinkle with sugar.
infarina'tura *sf* (*fig*) smattering.
in'farto *sm* (*MED*): ~ (cardiaco) coronary.
infasti'dire *vt* to annoy, irritate; ~rsi *vr* to get annoyed *o* irritated.
infati'cabile *ag* tireless, untiring.
in'fatti *cong* as a matter of fact, in fact,

actually.

infatu'arsi *vr:* ~ **di** *o* **per** to become infatuated with, fall for.

infatuazi'one [infatuat'tsjone] *sf* infatuation.

in'fausto, a *ag* unpropitious, unfavourable (*BRIT*), unfavorable (*US*).

infecondità *sf* infertility.

infe'condo, a *ag* infertile.

infe'dele *ag* unfaithful.

infedeltà *sf* infidelity.

infe'lice [infe'litʃe] *ag* unhappy; (*sfortunato*) unlucky, unfortunate; (*inopportuno*) inopportune, ill-timed; (*mal riuscito: lavoro*) bad, poor.

infelicità [infelitʃi'ta] *sf* unhappiness.

infel'trire *vi*, ~**rsi** *vr* (*lana*) to become matted.

infe'renza [infe'rɛntsa] *sf* inference.

inferi'ore *ag* lower; (*per intelligenza, qualità*) inferior ♦ *sm/f* inferior; ~ **a** (*numero, quantità*) less *o* smaller than; (*meno buono*) inferior to; ~ **alla media** below average.

inferiorità *sf* inferiority.

infe'rire *vt* (*dedurre*) to infer, deduce.

inferme'ria *sf* infirmary; (*di scuola, nave*) sick bay.

infermi'ere, a *sm/f* nurse.

infermità *sf inv* illness; infirmity; ~ **di mente** mental illness.

in'fermo, a *ag* (*ammalato*) ill; (*debole*) infirm; ~ **di mente** mentally ill.

infer'nale *ag* infernal; (*proposito, complotto*) diabolical; **un tempo** ~ (*fam*) hellish weather.

in'ferno *sm* hell; **soffrire le pene dell'**~ (*fig*) to go through hell.

infero'cire [infero'tʃire] *vt* to make fierce ♦ *vi*, ~**rsi** *vr* to become fierce.

inferri'ata *sf* grating.

infervo'rare *vt* to arouse enthusiasm in; ~**rsi** *vr* to get excited, get carried away.

infes'tare *vt* to infest.

infet'tare *vt* to infect; ~**rsi** *vr* to become infected.

infet'tivo, a *ag* infectious.

in'fetto, a *ag* infected; (*acque*) polluted, contaminated.

infezi'one [infet'tsjone] *sf* infection.

infiac'chire [infjak'kire] *vt* to weaken ♦ *vi* (*anche:* ~**rsi**) to grow weak.

infiam'mabile *ag* inflammable.

infiam'mare *vt* to set alight; (*fig, MED*) to inflame; ~**rsi** *vr* to catch fire; (*MED*) to become inflamed; (*fig*): ~**rsi di** to be fired with.

infiammazi'one [infjammat'tsjone] *sf*

(*MED*) inflammation.

infias'care *vt* to bottle.

infici'are [infi'tʃare] *vt* (*DIR*: *atto, dichiarazione*) to challenge.

in'fido, a *ag* unreliable, treacherous.

infie'rire *vi*: ~ **su** (*fisicamente*) to attack furiously; (*verbalmente*) to rage at; (*epidemia*) to rage over.

in'figgere [in'fiddʒere] *vt*: ~ **qc in** to thrust *o* drive sth into.

infi'lare *vt* (*ago*) to thread; (*mettere: chiave*) to insert; (: *vestito*) to slip *o* put on; (*strada*) to turn into, take; ~**rsi** *vr*: ~**rsi in** to slip into; (*indossare*) to slip on; ~ **un anello al dito** to slip a ring on one's finger; ~ **l'uscio** to slip in; to slip out; ~**rsi la giacca** to put on one's jacket.

infil'trarsi *vr* to penetrate, seep through; (*MIL*) to infiltrate.

infil'trato, a *sm/f* infiltrator.

infiltrazi'one [infiltrat'tsjone] *sf* infiltration.

infil'zare [infil'tsare] *vt* (*infilare*) to string together; (*trafiggere*) to pierce.

'infimo, a *ag* lowest; **un albergo di** ~ **ordine** a third-rate hotel.

in'fine *av* finally; (*insomma*) in short.

infin'gardo, a *ag* lazy ♦ *sm/f* slacker.

infinità *sf* infinity; (*in quantità*): **un'**~ **di** an infinite number of.

infinitesi'male *ag* infinitesimal.

infi'nito, a *ag* infinite; (*LING*) infinitive ♦ *sm* infinity; (*LING*) infinitive; **all'**~ (*senza fine*) endlessly; (*LING*) in the infinitive.

infinocchi'are [infinok'kjare] *vt* (*fam*) to hoodwink.

infiore'scenza [infjoreʃ'ʃɛntsa] *sf* inflorescence.

infir'mare *vt* (*DIR*) to invalidate.

infischi'arsi [infis'kjarsi] *vr*: ~ **di** not to care about.

in'fisso, a *pp di* **infiggere** ♦ *sm* fixture; (*di porta, finestra*) frame.

infit'tire *vt, vi* (*anche:* ~**rsi**) to thicken.

inflazio'nare [inflattsjo'nare] *vt* to inflate.

inflazi'one [inflat'tsjone] *sf* inflation.

inflazio'nistico, a, ci, che [inflattsjo'nistiko] *ag* inflationary.

infles'sibile *ag* inflexible; (*ferreo*) unyielding.

inflessi'one *sf* inflexion.

in'fliggere [in'fliddʒere] *vt* to inflict.

in'flissi *etc vb vedi* **infliggere**.

in'flitto, a *pp di* **infliggere**.

influ'ente *ag* influential.

influ'enza [influ'ɛntsa] *sf* influence; (*MED*) influenza, flu.

influen'zare [influen'tsare] *vt* to influence, have an influence on.

influ'ire *vi*: ~ **su** to influence.
in'flusso *sm* influence.
INFN *sigla m* = *Istituto Nazionale di Fisica Nucleare.*
info'cato, a *ag* = **infuocato**.
info'gnarsi [infoɲ'ɲarsi] *vr* (*fam*) to get into a mess; ~ **in un mare di debiti** to be up to one's *o* the eyes in debt.
infol'tire *vt, vi* to thicken.
infon'dato, a *ag* unfounded, groundless.
in'fondere *vt*: ~ **qc in qn** to instill sth in sb; ~ **fiducia in qn** to inspire sb with confidence.
infor'care *vt* to fork (up); (*bicicletta, cavallo*) to get on; (*occhiali*) to put on.
infor'male *ag* informal.
infor'mare *vt* to inform, tell; ~rsi *vr*: ~rsi (**di** *o* **su**) to inquire (about); **tenere informato qn** to keep sb informed.
infor'matico, a, ci, che *ag* (*settore*) computer *cpd* ♦ *sf* computer science.
informa'tivo, a *ag* informative; **a titolo** ~ for information only.
informatiz'zare [informatid'dzare] *vt* to computerize.
infor'mato, a *ag* informed; **tenersi** ~ to keep o.s. (well-)informed.
informa'tore *sm* informer.
informazi'one [informat'tsjone] *sf* piece of information; ~**i** *sfpl* information *sg*; **chiedere un'**~ to ask for (some) information; ~ **di garanzia** (*DIR*) = **avviso di garanzia**.
in'forme *ag* shapeless.
informico'larsi *vr*, **informico'lirsi** *vr*: **mi si è informicolata una gamba** I've got pins and needles in my leg.
infor'nare *vt* to put in the oven.
infor'nata *sf* (*anche fig*) batch.
infortu'narsi *vr* to injure o.s., have an accident.
infortu'nato, a *ag* injured, hurt ♦ *sm/f* injured person.
infor'tunio *sm* accident; ~ **sul lavoro** industrial accident, accident at work.
infortu'nistica *sf* study of (industrial) accidents.
infos'sarsi *vr* (*terreno*) to sink; (*guance*) to become hollow.
infos'sato, a *ag* hollow; (*occhi*) deep-set; (*: per malattia*) sunken.
infradici'are [infradi'tʃare] *vt* (*inzuppare*) to soak, drench; (*marcire*) to rot; ~rsi *vr* to get soaked, get drenched; to rot.
in'frangere [in'frandʒere] *vt* to smash; (*fig: legge, patti*) to break; ~rsi *vr* to smash, break.
infran'gibile [infran'dʒibile] *ag*

unbreakable.
in'franto, a *pp di* **infrangere** ♦ *ag* broken.
infra'rosso, a *ag, sm* infrared.
infrasettima'nale *ag* midweek *cpd*.
infrastrut'tura *sf* infrastructure.
infrazi'one [infrat'tsjone] *sf*: ~ **a** breaking of, violation of.
infredda'tura *sf* slight cold.
infreddo'lito, a *ag* cold, chilled.
infre'quente *ag* infrequent, rare.
infrol'lire *vi*, ~rsi *vr* (*selvaggina*) to become high.
infruttu'oso, a *ag* fruitless.
infuo'cato, a *ag* (*metallo*) red-hot; (*sabbia*) burning; (*fig: discorso*) heated, passionate.
infu'ori *av* out; **all'**~ outwards; **all'**~ **di** (*eccetto*) except, with the exception of.
infuri'are *vi* to rage; ~rsi *vr* to fly into a rage.
infusi'one *sf* infusion.
in'fuso, a *pp di* **infondere** ♦ *ag*: **scienza** ~**a** (*anche ironico*) innate knowledge ♦ *sm* infusion; ~ **di camomilla** camomile tea.
Ing. *abbr* = **ingegnere**.
ingabbi'are *vt* to (put in a) cage.
ingaggi'are [ingad'dʒare] *vt* (*assumere con compenso*) to take on, hire; (*SPORT*) to sign on; (*MIL*) to engage.
in'gaggio [in'gaddʒo] *sm* hiring; signing on.
ingagliar'dire [ingaʎʎar'dire] *vt* to strengthen, invigorate ♦ *vi* (*anche*: ~rsi) to grow stronger.
ingan'nare *vt* to deceive; (*coniuge*) to be unfaithful to; (*fisco*) to cheat; (*eludere*) to dodge, elude; (*fig: tempo*) to while away ♦ *vi* (*apparenza*) to be deceptive; ~rsi *vr* to be mistaken, be wrong.
inganna'tore, 'trice *ag* deceptive; (*persona*) deceitful.
ingan'nevole *ag* deceptive.
in'ganno *sm* deceit, deception; (*azione*) trick; (*menzogna, frode*) cheat, swindle; (*illusione*) illusion.
ingarbugli'are [ingarbuʎ'ʎare] *vt* to tangle; (*fig*) to confuse, muddle; ~rsi *vr* to become confused *o* muddled.
ingarbu'gliato, a [ingarbuʎ'ʎato] *ag* tangled; confused, muddled.
inge'gnarsi [indʒeɲ'ɲarsi] *vr* to do one's best, try hard; ~ **per vivere** to live by one's wits; **basta** ~ **un po'** you just need a bit of ingenuity.
inge'gnere [indʒeɲ'ɲɛre] *sm* engineer; ~ **civile/navale** civil/naval engineer.
ingegne'ria [indʒeɲɲe'ria] *sf* engineering.
in'gegno [in'dʒeɲɲo] *sm* (*intelligenza*) intelligence, brains *pl*; (*capacità creativa*)

ingenuity; (*disposizione*) talent.

ingegnosità [indʒeɲɲosi'ta] *sf* ingenuity.

inge'gnoso, a [indʒeɲ'ɲoso] *ag* ingenious, clever.

ingelo'sire [indʒelo'sire] *vt* to make jealous ♦ *vi* (*anche:* ~**rsi**) to become jealous.

in'gente [in'dʒɛnte] *ag* huge, enormous.

ingenti'lire [indʒenti'lire] *vt* to refine, civilize; ~**rsi** *vr* to become more refined, become more civilized.

ingenuità [indʒenui'ta] *sf* ingenuousness.

in'genuo, a [in'dʒɛnuo] *ag* ingenuous, naïve.

inge'renza [indʒe'rɛntsa] *sf* interference.

inge'rire [indʒe'rire] *vt* to ingest.

inges'sare [indʒes'sare] *vt* (*MED*) to put in plaster.

ingessa'tura [indʒessa'tura] *sf* plaster.

Inghil'terra [ingil'tɛrra] *sf*: ~ England.

inghiot'tire [ingjot'tire] *vt* to swallow.

in'ghippo [in'gippo] *sm* trick.

ingial'lire [indʒal'lire] *vi* to go yellow.

ingigan'tire [indʒigan'tire] *vt* to enlarge, magnify ♦ *vi* to become gigantic *o* enormous.

inginocchi'arsi [indʒinok'kjarsi] *vr* to kneel (down).

inginocchia'toio [indʒinokkja'tojo] *sm* prie-dieu.

ingioiel'lare [indʒojel'lare] *vt* to bejewel, adorn with jewels.

ingiù [in'dʒu] *av* down, downwards.

ingi'ungere [in'dʒundʒere] *vt*: ~ **a qn di fare qc** to enjoin *o* order sb to do sth.

ingi'unto, a [in'dʒunto] *pp di* **ingiungere**.

ingiunzi'one [indʒun'tsjone] *sf* injunction, command; ~ **di pagamento** final demand.

ingi'uria [in'dʒurja] *sf* insult; (*fig: danno*) damage.

ingiuri'are [indʒu'rjare] *vt* to insult, abuse.

ingiuri'oso, a [indʒu'rjoso] *ag* insulting, abusive.

ingiusta'mente [indʒusta'mente] *av* unjustly.

ingiustifi'cabile [indʒustifi'kabile] *ag* unjustifiable.

ingiustifi'cato, a [indʒustifi'kato] *ag* unjustified.

ingius'tizia [indʒus'tittsja] *sf* injustice.

ingi'usto, a [in'dʒusto] *ag* unjust, unfair.

in'glese *ag* English ♦ *sm/f* Englishman/ woman ♦ *sm* (*LING*) English; **gli I~i** the English; **andarsene** *o* **filare all'**~ to take French leave.

inglori'oso, a *ag* inglorious.

ingob'bire *vi*, ~**rsi** *vr* to become stooped.

ingoi'are *vt* to gulp (down); (*fig*) to swallow (up); **ha dovuto** ~ **il rospo** (*fig*) he had to

accept the situation.

ingol'fare *vt*, ~**rsi** *vr* (*motore*) to flood.

ingolo'sire *vt*: ~ **qn** to make sb's mouth water; (*fig*) to attract sb ♦ *vi* (*anche:* ~**rsi**): ~ (**di**) (*anche fig*) to become greedy (for).

ingom'brante *ag* cumbersome.

ingom'brare *vt* (*strada*) to block; (*stanza*) to clutter up.

in'gombro, a *ag*: ~ **di** (*strada*) blocked by; (*stanza*) cluttered up with ♦ *sm* obstacle; **essere d'**~ to be in the way; **per ragioni di** ~ for reasons of space.

ingor'digia [ingor'didʒa] *sf*: ~ (**di**) greed (for); avidity (for).

in'gordo, a *ag*: ~ **di** greedy for; (*fig*) greedy *o* avid for ♦ *sm/f* glutton.

ingor'gare *vt* to block; ~**rsi** *vr* to be blocked up, be choked up.

in'gorgo, ghi *sm* blockage, obstruction; (*anche:* ~ **stradale**) traffic jam.

ingoz'zare [ingot'tsare] *vt* (*animali*) to fatten; (*fig: persona*) to stuff; ~**rsi** *vr*: ~**rsi** (**di**) to stuff o.s. (with).

ingra'naggio [ingra'naddʒo] *sm* (*TECN*) gear; (*di orologio*) mechanism; **gli** ~**i della burocrazia** the bureaucratic machinery.

ingra'nare *vi* to mesh, engage ♦ *vt* to engage; ~ **la marcia** to get into gear.

ingrandi'mento *sm* enlargement; extension; magnification; growth; expansion.

ingran'dire *vt* (*anche FOT*) to enlarge; (*estendere*) to extend; (*OTTICA, fig*) to magnify ♦ *vi* (*anche:* ~**rsi**) to become larger *o* bigger; (*aumentare*) to grow, increase; (*espandersi*) to expand.

ingrandi'tore *sm* (*FOT*) enlarger.

ingras'saggio [ingras'saddʒo] *sm* greasing.

ingras'sare *vt* to make fat; (*animali*) to fatten; (*AGR: terreno*) to manure; (*lubrificare*) to grease ♦ *vi* (*anche:* ~**rsi**) to get fat, put on weight.

ingrati'tudine *sf* ingratitude.

in'grato, a *ag* ungrateful; (*lavoro*) thankless, unrewarding.

ingrazi'are [ingrat'tsjare] *vt*: ~**rsi qn** to ingratiate o.s. with sb.

ingredi'ente *sm* ingredient.

in'gresso *sm* (*porta*) entrance; (*atrio*) hall; (*l'entrare*) entrance, entry; (*facoltà di entrare*) admission; "~ **libero**" "admission free"; ~ **principale** main entrance; ~ **di servizio** tradesmen's entrance.

ingros'sare *vt* to increase; (*folla, livello*) to swell ♦ *vi* (*anche:* ~**rsi**) to increase; to swell.

in'grosso *av*: **all'**~ (*COMM*) wholesale; (*all'incirca*) roughly, about.

ingru'gnato, a [ingruɲ'ɲato] *ag* grumpy.
inguai'arsi *vr* to get into trouble.
inguai'nare *vt* to sheathe.
ingual'cibile [ingwal'tʃibile] *ag* crease-resistant.
ingua'ribile *ag* incurable.
'inguine *sm* (ANAT) groin.
ingurgi'tare [ingurdʒi'tare] *vt* to gulp down.
ini'bire *vt* to forbid, prohibit; (PSIC) to inhibit.
ini'bito, a *ag* inhibited ♦ *smf* inhibited person.
inibi'torio, a *ag* (PSIC) inhibitory, inhibitive; (provvedimento, misure) restrictive.
inibizi'one [inibit'tsjone] *sf* prohibition; inhibition.
iniet'tare *vt* to inject; ~rsi *vr*: ~rsi di sangue (occhi) to become bloodshot.
iniet'tore *sm* injector.
iniezi'one [injet'tsjone] *sf* injection.
inimi'care *vt* to alienate, make hostile; ~rsi con qn to fall out with sb; si è inimicato gli amici di un tempo he has alienated his old friends.
inimi'cizia [inimi'tʃittsja] *sf* animosity.
inimi'tabile *ag* inimitable.
inimmagi'nabile [inimmadʒi'nabile] *ag* unimaginable.
ininfiam'mabile *ag* non-flammable.
inintelli'gibile [inintelli'dʒibile] *ag* unintelligible.
ininterrotta'mente *av* non-stop, continuously.
ininter'rotto, a *ag* (fila) unbroken; (rumore) uninterrupted.
iniquità *sf inv* iniquity; (atto) wicked action.
i'niquo, a *ag* iniquitous.
inizi'ale [init'tsjale] *ag*, *sf* initial.
inizializ'zare [inittsjalid'dzare] *vt* (INFORM) to boot.
inizial'mente [inittsjal'mente] *av* initially, at first.
inizi'are [init'tsjare] *vi*, *vt* to begin, start; ~ qn a to initiate sb into; (pittura etc) to introduce sb to; ~ a fare qc to start doing sth.
inizia'tiva [inittsja'tiva] *sf* initiative; ~ privata private enterprise.
inizia'tore, 'trice [inittsja'tore] *smf* initiator.
i'nizio [i'nittsjo] *sm* beginning; all'~ at the beginning, at the start; dare ~ a qc to start sth, get sth going; essere agli ~i (progetto, lavoro etc) to be in the initial stages.
innaffi'are *etc* = **annaffiare** *etc*.
innal'zare [innal'tsare] *vt* (sollevare, alzare)

to raise; (rizzare) to erect; ~rsi *vr* to rise.
innamora'mento *sm* falling in love.
innamo'rare *vt* to enchant, charm; ~rsi *vr*: ~rsi (di qn) to fall in love (with sb).
innamo'rato, a *ag* (che nutre amore): ~ (di) in love (with); (appassionato): ~ di very fond of ♦ *smf* lover; (anche scherzoso) sweetheart.
in'nanzi [in'nantsi] *av* (stato in luogo) in front, ahead; (moto a luogo) forward, on; (tempo: prima) before ♦ *prep* (prima) before; ~ a in front of; d'ora ~ from now on; farsi ~ to step forward; ~ tempo ahead of time.
innanzi'tutto [innantsi'tutto] *av* above all; (per prima cosa) first of all.
in'nato, a *ag* innate.
innatu'rale *ag* unnatural.
inne'gabile *ag* undeniable.
inneggi'are [inned'dʒare] *vi*: ~ a to sing hymns to; (fig) to sing the praises of.
innervo'sire *vt*: ~ qn to get on sb's nerves; ~rsi *vr* to get irritated o upset.
innes'care *vt* to prime.
in'nesco, schi *sm* primer.
innes'tare *vt* (BOT, MED) to graft; (TECN) to engage; (inserire: presa) to insert.
in'nesto *sm* graft; grafting no pl; (TECN) clutch; (ELETTR) connection.
'inno *sm* hymn; ~ nazionale national anthem.
inno'cente [inno'tʃɛnte] *ag* innocent.
inno'cenza [inno'tʃɛntsa] *sf* innocence.
in'nocuo, a *ag* innocuous, harmless.
innomi'nato, a *ag* unnamed.
inno'vare *vt* to change, make innovations in.
innova'tivo, a *ag* innovative.
innovazi'one [innovat'tsjone] *sf* innovation.
innume'revole *ag* innumerable.
inocu'lare *vt* (MED) to inoculate.
ino'doro, a *ag* odourless (BRIT), odorless (US).
inoffen'sivo, a *ag* harmless.
inol'trare *vt* (AMM) to pass on, forward; ~rsi *vr* (addentrarsi) to advance, go forward.
inol'trato, a *ag*: a notte ~a late at night; a primavera ~a late in the spring.
i'noltre *av* besides, moreover.
i'noltro *sm* (AMM) forwarding.
inon'dare *vt* to flood.
inondazi'one [inondat'tsjone] *sf* flooding no pl; flood.
inope'roso, a *ag* inactive, idle.
inopi'nato, a *ag* unexpected.
inoppor'tuno, a *ag* untimely, ill-timed; (poco adatto) inappropriate; (momento)

inopportune.

inoppu'gnabile [inoppuɲ'ɲabile] *ag* incontrovertible.

inor'ganico, a, ci, che *ag* inorganic.

inorgo'glire [inorgoʎ'ʎire] *vt* to make proud ♦ *vi* (*anche*: ~**rsi**) to become proud; ~**rsi di qc** to pride o.s. on sth.

inorri'dire *vt* to horrify ♦ *vi* to be horrified.

inospi'tale *ag* inhospitable.

inosser'vante *ag*: **essere** ~ **di** to fail to comply with.

inosser'vato, a *ag* (*non notato*) unobserved; (*non rispettato*) not observed, not kept; **passare** ~ to go unobserved, escape notice.

inossi'dabile *ag* stainless.

INPS *sigla m* (= *Istituto Nazionale Previdenza Sociale*) social security service.

inqua'drare *vt* (*foto, immagine*) to frame; (*fig*) to situate, set.

inquadra'tura *sf* (*CINE, FOT: atto*) framing; (: *immagine*) shot; (: *sequenza*) sequence.

inqualifi'cabile *ag* unspeakable.

inquie'tante *ag* disturbing, worrying.

inquie'tare *vt* (*turbare*) to disturb, worry; ~**rsi** *vr* to worry, become anxious; (*impazientirsi*) to get upset.

inqui'eto, a *ag* restless; (*preoccupato*) worried, anxious.

inquie'tudine *sf* anxiety, worry.

inqui'lino, a *sm/f* tenant.

inquina'mento *sm* pollution.

inqui'nare *vt* to pollute.

inqui'rente *ag* (*DIR*): **magistrato** ~ examining (*BRIT*) *o* committing (*US*) magistrate; **commissione** ~ commission of inquiry.

inqui'sire *vt, vi* to investigate.

inqui'sito, a *ag* (*persona*) under investigation.

inquisi'tore, 'trice *ag* (*sguardo*) inquiring.

inquisizi'one [inkwizit'tsjone] *sf* inquisition.

insabbia'mento *sm* (*fig*) shelving.

insabbi'are *vt* (*fig: pratica*) to shelve; ~**rsi** *vr* (*barca*) to run aground; (*fig: pratica*) to be shelved.

insac'care *vt* (*grano, farina etc*) to bag, put into sacks; (*carne*) to put into sausage skins.

insac'cati *smpl* (*CUC*) sausages.

insa'lata *sf* salad; (*pianta*) lettuce; ~ **mista** mixed salad.

insalati'era *sf* salad bowl.

insa'lubre *ag* unhealthy.

insa'nabile *ag* (*piaga*) which cannot be healed; (*situazione*) irremediable; (*odio*) implacable.

insangui'nare *vt* to stain with blood.

in'sania *sf* insanity.

in'sano, a *ag* (*pazzo, folle*) insane.

insapo'nare *vt* to soap; ~**rsi le mani** to soap one's hands.

insapo'nata *sf*: **dare un'**~ **a qc** to give sth a (quick) soaping.

insapo'rire *vt* to flavour (*BRIT*), flavor (*US*); (*con spezie*) to season; ~**rsi** *vr* to acquire flavo(u)r.

insa'poro, a *ag* tasteless, insipid.

insa'puta *sf*: **all'**~ **di qn** without sb knowing.

insazi'abile [insat'tsjabile] *ag* insatiable.

inscato'lare *vt* (*frutta, carne*) to can.

insce'nare [inʃe'nare] *vt* (*TEAT*) to stage, put on; (*fig*) to stage.

inscin'dibile [inʃin'dibile] *ag* (*fattori*) inseparable; (*legame*) indissoluble.

insec'chire [insek'kire] *vt* (*seccare*) to dry up; (: *piante*) to wither ♦ *vi* to dry up, become dry; to wither.

insedia'mento *sm* (*AMM: in carica, ufficio*) installation; (*villaggio, colonia*) settlement.

insedi'are *vt* (*AMM*) to install; ~**rsi** *vr* (*AMM*) to take up office; (*colonia, profughi etc*) to settle; (*MIL*) to take up positions.

in'segna [in'seɲɲa] *sf* sign; (*emblema*) sign, emblem; (*bandiera*) flag, banner; ~**e** *sfpl* (*decorazioni*) insignia *pl*.

insegna'mento [inseɲɲa'mento] *sm* teaching; **trarre** ~ **da un'esperienza** to learn from an experience, draw a lesson from an experience; **che ti serva da** ~ let this be a lesson to you.

inse'gnante [inseɲ'ɲante] *ag* teaching ♦ *sm/f* teacher.

inse'gnare [inseɲ'ɲare] *vt, vi* to teach; ~ **a qn qc** to teach sb sth; ~ **a qn a fare qc** to teach sb (how) to do sth; **come lei ben m'insegna** ... (*ironico*) as you will doubtless be aware ....

insegui'mento *sm* pursuit, chase; **darsi all'**~ **di qn** to give chase to sb.

insegu'ire *vt* to pursue, chase.

insegui'tore, 'trice *sm/f* pursuer.

insel'lare *vt* to saddle.

inselvati'chire [inselvati'kire] *vt* (*persona*) to make unsociable ♦ *vi* (*anche*: ~**rsi**) to grow wild; (*persona*) to become unsociable.

inseminazi'one [inseminat'tsjone] *sf* insemination.

insena'tura *sf* inlet, creek.

insen'sato, a *ag* senseless, stupid.

insen'sibile *ag* (*anche fig*) insensitive.

insensibilità *sf* insensitivity, insensibility.

insepa'rabile *ag* inseparable.

inse'polto, a *ag* unburied.

inseri'mento *sm* (*gen*) insertion; **problemi di** ~ (*di persona*) adjustment problems.

inse'rire *vt* to insert; (*ELETTR*) to connect; (*allegare*) to enclose; ~**rsi** *vr* (*fig*): ~**rsi in** to become part of; ~ **un annuncio sul giornale** to put *o* place an advertisement in the newspaper.

in'serto *sm* (*pubblicazione*) insert; ~ **filmato** (film) clip.

inser'vibile *ag* useless.

inservi'ente *sm/f* attendant.

inserzi'one [inser'tsjone] *sf* insertion; (*avviso*) advertisement; **fare un'**~ **sul giornale** to put an advertisement in the newspaper.

inserzio'nista, i, e [insertsjo'nista] *sm/f* advertiser.

insetti'cida, i [insetti'tʃida] *sm* insecticide.

in'setto *sm* insect.

insicu'rezza [insiku'rettsa] *sf* insecurity.

insi'curo, a *ag* insecure.

in'sidia *sf* snare, trap; (*pericolo*) hidden danger; **tendere un'**~ **a qn** to lay *o* set a trap for sb.

insidi'are *vt* (*MIL*) to harass; ~ **la vita di qn** to make an attempt on sb's life.

insidi'oso, a *ag* insidious.

insi'eme *av* together; (*contemporaneamente*) at the same time ♦ *prep:* ~ **a** *o* **con** together with ♦ *sm* whole; (*MAT, servizio, assortimento*) set; (*MODA*) ensemble, outfit; **tutti** ~ all together; **tutto** ~ all together; (*in una volta*) at one go; **nell'**~ on the whole; **d'**~ (*veduta etc*) overall.

in'signe [in'siɲɲe] *ag* (*persona*) famous, distinguished, eminent; (*città, monumento*) notable.

insignifi'cante [insiɲɲifi'kante] *ag* insignificant.

insi'gnire [insiɲ'ɲire] *vt:* ~ **qn di** to honour (*BRIT*) *o* honor (*US*) sb with, decorate sb with.

insin'cero, a [insin'tʃero] *ag* insincere.

insinda'cabile *ag* unquestionable.

insinu'ante *ag* (*osservazione, sguardo*) insinuating; (*maniere*) ingratiating.

insinu'are *vt* (*introdurre*): ~ **qc in** to slip *o* slide sth into; (*fig*) to insinuate, imply; ~**rsi** *vr:* ~**rsi in** to seep into; (*fig*) to creep into; to worm one's way into.

insinuazi'one [insinuat'tsjone] *sf* (*fig*) insinuation.

in'sipido, a *ag* insipid.

insis'tente *ag* insistent; (*pioggia, dolore*) persistent.

insistente'mente *av* repeatedly.

insis'tenza [insis'tɛntsa] *sf* insistence; persistence.

in'sistere *vi:* ~ **su qc** to insist on sth; ~ **in qc/a fare** (*perseverare*) to persist in sth/in doing.

insis'tito, a *pp di* **insistere**.

'insito, a *ag:* ~ **(in)** inherent (in).

insoddis'fatto, a *ag* dissatisfied.

insoddisfazi'one [insoddisfat'tsjone] *sf* dissatisfaction.

insoffe'rente *ag* intolerant.

insoffe'renza [insoffe'rɛntsa] *sf* impatience.

insolazi'one [insolat'tsjone] *sf* (*MED*) sunstroke.

inso'lente *ag* insolent.

insolen'tire *vi* to grow insolent ♦ *vt* to insult, be rude to.

inso'lenza [inso'lɛntsa] *sf* insolence.

in'solito, a *ag* unusual, out of the ordinary.

inso'lubile *ag* insoluble.

inso'luto, a *ag* (*non risolto*) unsolved; (*non pagato*) unpaid, outstanding.

insol'vente *ag* (*DIR*) insolvent.

insol'venza [insol'vɛntsa] *sf* (*DIR*) insolvency.

insol'vibile *ag* insolvent.

in'somma *av* (*in breve, in conclusione*) in short; (*dunque*) well ♦ *escl* for heaven's sake!

inson'dabile *ag* unfathomable.

in'sonne *ag* sleepless.

in'sonnia *sf* insomnia, sleeplessness.

insonno'lito, a *ag* sleepy, drowsy.

insonorizzazi'one [insonoriddzat'tsjone] *sf* soundproofing.

insoppor'tabile *ag* unbearable.

insoppri'mibile *ag* insuppressible.

insor'genza [insor'dʒentsa] *sf* (*di malattia*) onset.

in'sorgere [in'sordʒere] *vi* (*ribellarsi*) to rise up, rebel; (*apparire*) to come up, arise.

insormon'tabile *ag* (*ostacolo*) insurmountable, insuperable.

in'sorsi *etc vb vedi* **insorgere**.

in'sorto, a *pp di* **insorgere** ♦ *sm/f* rebel, insurgent.

insospet'tabile *ag* (*al di sopra di ogni sospetto*) above suspicion; (*inatteso*) unsuspected.

insospet'tire *vt* to make suspicious ♦ *vi* (*anche:* ~**rsi**) to become suspicious.

insoste'nibile *ag* (*posizione, teoria*) untenable; (*dolore, situazione*) intolerable, unbearable; **le spese di manutenzione sono** ~**i** the maintenance costs are excessive.

insostitu'ibile *ag* (*persona*) irreplaceable; (*aiuto, presenza*) invaluable.

insoz'zare [insot'tsare] *vt* (*pavimento*) to make dirty; (*fig: reputazione, memoria*) to tarnish, sully; ~**rsi** *vr* to get dirty.

inspe'rabile *ag:* **la guarigione/salvezza era** ~ there was no hope of a cure/of rescue; **abbiamo ottenuto risultati** ~**i** the results we achieved were far better than we had hoped.

inspe'rato, a *ag* unhoped-for.

inspie'gabile *ag* inexplicable.

inspi'rare *vt* to breathe in, inhale.

in'stabile *ag* (*carico, indole*) unstable; (*tempo*) unsettled; (*equilibrio*) unsteady.

instabilità *sf* instability; (*di tempo*) changeability.

instal'lare *vt* to install; ~**rsi** *vr* (*sistemarsi*): ~**rsi in** to settle in.

installazi'one [installat'tsjone] *sf* installation.

instan'cabile *ag* untiring, indefatigable.

instau'rare *vt* to establish.

instaurazi'one [instaurat'tsjone] *sf* establishment.

instil'lare *vt* to instil.

instra'dare *vt* = **istradare**.

insù *av* up, upwards; **guardare all'**~ to look up *o* upwards; **naso all'**~ turned-up nose.

insubordinazi'one [insubordinat'tsjone] *sf* insubordination.

insuc'cesso [insut'tʃɛsso] *sm* failure, flop.

insudici'are [insudi'tʃare] *vt* to dirty; ~**rsi** *vr* to get dirty.

insuffici'ente [insuffi'tʃɛnte] *ag* insufficient; (*compito, allievo*) inadequate.

insuffici'enza [insuffi'tʃɛntsa] *sf* insufficiency; inadequacy; (*INS*) fail; ~ **di prove** (*DIR*) lack of evidence.

insu'lare *ag* insular.

insu'lina *sf* insulin.

in'sulso, a *ag* (*sciocco*) inane, silly; (*persona*) dull, insipid.

insul'tare *vt* to insult, affront.

in'sulto *sm* insult, affront.

insupe'rabile *ag* (*ostacolo, difficoltà*) insuperable, insurmountable; (*eccellente: qualità, prodotto*) unbeatable; (*: persona, interpretazione*) unequalled.

insuper'bire *vt* to make proud, make arrogant; ~**rsi** *vr* to become arrogant.

insurrezi'one [insurret'tsjone] *sf* revolt, insurrection.

insussis'tente *ag* non-existent.

intac'care *vt* (*fare tacche*) to cut into; (*corrodere*) to corrode; (*fig: cominciare ad usare: risparmi*) to break into; (*: ledere*) to damage.

intagli'are [intaʎ'ʎare] *vt* to carve.

intaglia'tore, 'trice [intaʎʎa'tore] *sm/f*

engraver.

in'taglio [in'taʎʎo] *sm* carving.

intan'gibile [intan'dʒibile] *ag* (*bene, patrimonio*) untouchable; (*fig: diritto*) inviolable.

in'tanto *av* (*nel frattempo*) meanwhile, in the meantime; (*per cominciare*) just to begin with; ~ **che** *cong* while.

intarsi'are *vt* to inlay.

in'tarsio *sm* inlaying *no pl*, marquetry *no pl*; inlay.

intasa'mento *sm* (*ostruzione*) blockage, obstruction; (*AUT: ingorgo*) traffic jam.

inta'sare *vt* to choke (up), block (up); (*AUT*) to obstruct, block; ~**rsi** *vr* to become choked *o* blocked.

intas'care *vt* to pocket.

in'tatto, a *ag* intact; (*puro*) unsullied.

intavo'lare *vt* to start, enter into.

inte'gerrimo, a [inte'dʒɛrrimo] *ag* honest, upright.

inte'grale *ag* complete; (*pane, farina*) wholemeal (*BRIT*), wholewheat (*US*); **film in versione** ~ uncut version of a film; **calcolo** ~ (*MAT*) integral calculus; **edizione** ~ unabridged edition.

inte'grante *ag:* **parte** *f* ~ integral part.

inte'grare *vt* to complete; (*MAT*) to integrate; ~**rsi** *vr* (*persona*) to become integrated.

integra'tivo, a *ag* (*assegno*) supplementary; (*INS*): **esame** ~ *assessment test sat when changing schools.*

integra'tore *sm:* ~**i alimentari** nutritional supplements.

integrazi'one [integrat'tsjone] *sf* integration.

integrità *sf* integrity.

'integro, a *ag* (*intatto, intero*) complete, whole; (*retto*) upright.

intelaia'tura *sf* frame; (*fig*) structure, framework.

intel'letto *sm* intellect.

intellettu'ale *ag, sm/f* intellectual.

intellettua'loide (*peg*) *ag* pseudo-intellectual ♦ *sm/f* pseudo-intellectual, would-be intellectual.

intelli'gente [intelli'dʒɛnte] *ag* intelligent.

intelli'genza [intelli'dʒɛntsa] *sf* intelligence.

intelli'ghenzia [intelli'gɛntsja] *sf* intelligentsia.

intelli'gibile [intelli'dʒibile] *ag* intelligible.

inteme'rato, a *ag* (*persona, vita*) blameless, irreproachable; (*coscienza*) clear; (*fama*) unblemished.

intempe'rante *ag* intemperate,

immoderate.

intempe'ranza [intempe'rantsa] *sf* intemperance; ~**e** *sfpl* (*eccessi*) excesses.

intem'perie *sfpl* bad weather *sg*.

intempes'tivo, a *ag* untimely.

inten'dente *sm*: ~ **di Finanza** inland (*BRIT*) *o* internal (*US*) revenue officer.

inten'denza [inten'dɛntsa] *sf*: ~ **di Finanza** inland (*BRIT*) *o* internal (*US*) revenue office.

in'tendere *vt* (*avere intenzione*): ~ **fare qc** to intend *o* mean to do sth; (*comprendere*) to understand; (*udire*) to hear; (*significare*) to mean; ~**rsi** *vr* (*conoscere*): ~**rsi di** to know a lot about, be a connoisseur of; (*accordarsi*) to get on (well); ~**rsi con qn su qc** to come to an agreement with sb about sth; **intendersela con qn** (*avere una relazione amorosa*) to have an affair with sb; **mi ha dato a** ~ **che ...** he led me to believe that ...; **non vuole** ~ **ragione** he won't listen to reason; **s'intende!** naturally!, of course!; **intendiamoci** let's get it quite clear; **ci siamo intesi?** is that clear?, is that understood?

intendi'mento *sm* (*intelligenza*) understanding; (*proposito*) intention.

intendi'tore, 'trice *sm/f* connoisseur, expert; **a buon intenditor poche parole** (*proverbio*) a word is enough to the wise.

intene'rire *vt* (*fig*) to move (to pity); ~**rsi** *vr* (*fig*) to be moved.

intensifi'care *vt*, ~**rsi** *vr* to intensify.

intensità *sf* intensity; (*del vento*) force, strength.

inten'sivo, a *ag* intensive.

in'tenso, a *ag* (*luce, profumo*) strong; (*colore*) intense, deep.

inten'tare *vt* (*DIR*): ~ **causa contro qn** to start *o* institute proceedings against sb.

inten'tato, a *ag*: **non lasciare nulla d'**~ to leave no stone unturned, try everything.

in'tento, a *ag* (*teso, assorto*): ~ (**a**) intent (on), absorbed (in) ♦ *sm* aim, purpose; **fare qc con l'**~ **di** to do sth with the intention of; **riuscire nell'**~ to achieve one's aim.

intenzio'nale [intentsjo'nale] *ag* intentional; (*DIR: omicidio*) premeditated; **fallo** ~ (*SPORT*) deliberate foul.

intenzio'nato, a [intentsjo'nato] *ag*: **essere** ~ **a fare qc** to intend to do sth, have the intention of doing sth; **ben** ~ well-meaning, well-intentioned; **mal** ~ ill-intentioned.

intenzi'one [inten'tsjone] *sf* intention; (*DIR*) intent; **avere** ~ **di fare qc** to intend to do sth, have the intention of doing sth.

intera'gire [intera'dʒire] *vi* to interact.

intera'mente *av* entirely, completely.

interat'tivo, a *ag* interactive.

interazi'one [interat'tsjone] *sf* interaction.

interca'lare *sm* pet phrase, stock phrase ♦ *vt* to insert.

interca'pedine *sf* gap, cavity.

inter'cedere [inter'tʃedere] *vi* to intercede.

intercessi'one [intertʃes'sjone] *sf* intercession.

intercetta'mento [intertʃetta'mento] *sm* = **intercettazione**.

intercet'tare [intertʃet'tare] *vt* to intercept.

intercettazi'one [intertʃettat'tsjone] *sf*: ~ **telefonica** telephone tapping.

intercity [inter'siti] *sm inv* (*FERR*) ≈ intercity (train).

intercon'nettere *vt* to interconnect.

inter'correre *vi* (*esserci*) to exist; (*passare: tempo*) to elapse.

inter'corso, a *pp di* **intercorrere**.

inter'detto, a *pp di* **interdire** ♦ *ag* forbidden, prohibited; (*sconcertato*) dumbfounded ♦ *sm* (*REL*) interdict; **rimanere** ~ to be taken aback.

inter'dire *vt* to forbid, prohibit, ban; (*REL*) to interdict; (*DIR*) to deprive of civil rights.

interdizi'one [interdit'tsjone] *sf* prohibition, ban.

interessa'mento *sm* interest; (*intervento*) intervention, good offices *pl*.

interes'sante *ag* interesting; **essere in stato** ~ to be expecting (a baby).

interes'sare *vt* to interest; (*concernere*) to concern, be of interest to; (*far intervenire*): ~ **qn a** to draw sb's attention to ♦ *vi*: ~ **a** to interest, matter to; ~**rsi** *vr* (*mostrare interesse*): ~**rsi a** to take an interest in, be interested in; (*occuparsi*): ~**rsi di** to take care of; **precipitazioni che interessano le regioni settentrionali** rainfall affecting the north; **si è interessato di farmi avere quei biglietti** he took the trouble to get me those tickets.

interes'sato, a *ag* (*coinvolto*) interested, involved; (*peg*) **essere** ~ to act out of pure self-interest ♦ *sm/f* (*coinvolto*) person concerned; **a tutti gli** ~**i** to all those concerned, to all interested parties.

inte'resse *sm* (*anche COMM*) interest; (*tornaconto*): **fare qc per** ~ to do sth out of self-interest; ~ **maturato** (*ECON*) accrued interest; ~ **privato in atti di ufficio** (*AMM*) abuse of public office.

interes'senza [interes'sɛntsa] *sf* (*ECON*) profit-sharing.

inter'faccia, ce [inter'fattʃa] *sf* (*INFORM*)

interface; ~ **utente** user interface.
interfacci'are [interfat't∫are] *vt* (*INFORM*) to interface.
interfe'renza [interfe'rɛntsa] *sf* interference.
interfe'rire *vi* to interfere.
inter'fono *sm* intercom; (*apparecchio*) internal phone.
interiezi'one [interjet'tsjone] *sf* exclamation, interjection.
'interim *sm inv* (*periodo*) interim, interval; **ministro ad** ~ acting *o* interim minister; (*incarico*) temporary appointment.
interi'ora *sfpl* entrails.
interi'ore *ag* inner *cpd*; **parte** *f* ~ inside.
interiorità *sf* inner being.
interioriz'zare [interjorid'dzare] *vt* to internalize.
inter'linea *sf* (*DATTILOGRAFIA*) spacing; (*TIP*) leading; **doppia** ~ double spacing.
interlocu'tore, 'trice *sm/f* speaker.
interlocu'torio, a *ag* interlocutory.
inter'ludio *sm* (*MUS*) interlude.
intermedi'ario, a *ag, sm/f* intermediary.
intermediazi'one [intermedjat'tsjone] *sf* mediation.
inter'medio, a *ag* intermediate.
inter'mezzo [inter'mɛddzo] *sm* (*intervallo*) interval; (*breve spettacolo*) intermezzo.
intermi'nabile *ag* interminable, endless.
intermit'tente *ag* intermittent.
intermit'tenza [intermit'tɛntsa] *sf*: **ad** ~ intermittent.
interna'mento *sm* internment; confinement (to a mental hospital).
inter'nare *vt* (*arrestare*) to intern; (*MED*) to confine to a mental hospital.
inter'nato, a *ag* interned; confined (to a mental hospital) ♦ *sm/f* internee; (*of a mental hospital*) inmate ♦ *sm* (*collegio*) boarding school; (*MED*) period as a houseman (*BRIT*) *o* an intern (*US*).
internazio'nale [internattsjo'nale] *ag* international.
inter'nista, i, e *sm/f* specialist in internal medicine.
in'terno, a *ag* (*di dentro*) internal, interior, inner; (: *mare*) inland; (*nazionale*) domestic; (*allievo*) boarding ♦ *sm* inside, interior; (*di paese*) interior; (*fodera*) lining; (*di appartamento*) flat (*BRIT*) *o* apartment (*US*) (number); (*TEL*) extension ♦ *sm/f* (*INS*) boarder; ~**i** *smpl* (*CINE*) interior shots; **commissione** ~**a** (*INS*) internal examination board; **"per uso** ~**"** (*MED*) "to be taken internally"; **all'**~ inside; **Ministero degli I**~**i** Ministry of the Interior, ≈ Home Office (*BRIT*), ≈

Department of the Interior (*US*); **notizie dall'**~ (*STAMPA*) home news.
in'tero, a *ag* (*integro, intatto*) whole, entire; (*completo, totale*) complete; (*numero*) whole; (*non ridotto: biglietto*) full.
interpel'lanza [interpel'lantsa] *sf*: **presentare un'**~ (*POL*) to ask a (parliamentary) question; ~ **parlamentare** interpellation.
interpel'lare *vt* to consult; (*POL*) to question.
INTER'POL *sigla f* (= *International Criminal Police Organization*) INTERPOL.
inter'porre *vt* (*ostacolo*): ~ **qc a qc** to put sth in the way of sth; (*influenza*) to use; **interporsi** *vr* to intervene; ~ **appello** (*DIR*) to appeal; **interporsi fra** (*mettersi in mezzo*) to come between.
inter'posto, a *pp di* **interporre**.
interpre'tare *vt* (*spiegare, tradurre*) to interpret; (*MUS, TEAT*) to perform; (*personaggio, sonata*) to play; (*canzone*) to sing.
interpretari'ato *sm* interpreting.
interpretazi'one [interpretat'tsjone] *sf* interpretation.
in'terprete *sm/f* interpreter; (*TEAT*) actor/actress, performer; (*MUS*) performer; **farsi** ~ **di** to act as a spokesman for.
interpunzi'one [interpun'tsjone] *sf* punctuation; **segni di** ~ punctuation marks.
inter'rare *vt* (*seme, pianta*) to plant; (*tubature etc*) to lay underground; (*MIL: pezzo d'artiglieria*) to dig in; (*riempire di terra: canale*) to fill in.
interro'gare *vt* to question; (*INS*) to test.
interroga'tivo, a *ag* (*occhi, sguardo*) questioning, inquiring; (*LING*) interrogative ♦ *sm* question; (*fig*) mystery.
interroga'torio, a *ag* interrogatory, questioning ♦ *sm* (*DIR*) questioning *no pl*.
interrogazi'one [interrogat'tsjone] *sf* questioning *no pl*; (*INS*) oral test; (*POL*): ~ **(parlamentare)** question.
inter'rompere *vt* to interrupt; (*studi, trattative*) to break off, interrupt; ~**rsi** *vr* to break off, stop.
inter'rotto, a *pp di* **interrompere**.
interrut'tore *sm* switch.
interruzi'one [interrut'tsjone] *sf* (*vedi interrompere*) interruption; break; ~ **di gravidanza** termination of pregnancy.
interse'care *vt*, ~**rsi** *vr* to intersect.
inter'stizio [inter'stittsjo] *sm* interstice, crack.
interur'bano, a *ag* inter-city; (*TEL:*

chiamata) trunk *cpd* (*BRIT*), long-distance; (: *telefono*) long-distance ♦ *sf* trunk call (*BRIT*), long-distance call.

inter'vallo *sm* interval; (*spazio*) space, gap; ~ **pubblicitario** (*TV*) commercial break.

interve'nire *vi* (*partecipare*): ~ **a** to take part in; (*intromettersi: anche POL*) to intervene; (*MED: operare*) to operate.

interven'tista, i, e *ag, sm/f* interventionist.

inter'vento *sm* participation; (*intromissione*) intervention; (*MED*) operation; (*breve discorso*) speech; **fare un** ~ **nel corso di** (*dibattito, programma*) to take part in.

interve'nuto, a *pp di* **intervenire** ♦ *sm*: **gli** ~**i** those present.

inter'vista *sf* interview.

intervis'tare *vt* to interview.

intervista'tore, 'trice *sm/f* interviewer.

in'teso, a *pp di* **intendere** ♦ *ag* agreed ♦ *sf* understanding; (*accordo*) agreement, understanding; **resta** ~ **che** ... it is understood that ...; **non darsi per** ~ **di qc** to take no notice of sth; **uno sguardo d'**~**a** a knowing look.

in'tessere *vt* to weave together; (*fig: trama, storia*) to weave.

intes'tare *vt* (*lettera*) to address; (*proprietà*): ~ **a** to register in the name of; ~ **un assegno a qn** to make out a cheque to sb.

intesta'tario, a *sm/f* holder.

intestato, a *ag* (*proprietà, casa, conto*) in the name of; (*assegno*) made out to; **carta** ~**a** headed paper.

intestazi'one [intestat'tsjone] *sf* heading; (*su carta da lettere*) letterhead; (*registrazione*) registration.

intesti'nale *ag* intestinal.

intes'tino, a *ag* (*lotte*) internal, civil ♦ *sm* (*ANAT*) intestine.

intiepi'dire *vt* (*riscaldare*) to warm (up); (*raffreddare*) to cool (down); (*fig: amicizia etc*) to cool; ~**rsi** *vr* to warm (up); to cool (down); to cool.

Inti'fada *sf* Intifada.

intima'mente *av* intimately; **sono** ~ **convinto che** ... I'm firmly *o* deeply convinced that ...; **i due fatti sono** ~ **connessi** the two events are closely connected.

inti'mare *vt* to order, command; ~ **la resa a qn** (*MIL*) to call upon sb to surrender.

intimazi'one [intimat'tsjone] *sf* order, command.

intimida'torio, a *ag* threatening.

intimidazi'one [intimidat'tsjone] *sf* intimidation.

intimi'dire *vt* to intimidate ♦ *vi* (*anche:*

~**rsi**) to grow shy.

intimità *sf* intimacy; privacy; (*familiarità*) familiarity.

'intimo, a *ag* intimate; (*affetti, vita*) private; (*fig: profondo*) inmost ♦ *sm* (*persona*) intimate *o* close friend; (*dell'animo*) bottom, depths *pl*; **parti** ~**e** (*ANAT*) private parts; **rapporti** ~**i** (*sessuali*) intimate relations.

intimo'rire *vt* to frighten; ~**rsi** *vr* to become frightened.

in'tingere [in'tindʒere] *vt* to dip.

in'tingolo *sm* sauce; (*pietanza*) stew.

in'tinto, a *pp di* **intingere**.

intiriz'zire [intirid'dzire] *vt* to numb ♦ *vi* (*anche:* ~**rsi**) to go numb.

intiriz'zito, a [intirid'dzito] *ag* numb (with cold).

intito'lare *vt* to give a title to; (*dedicare*) to dedicate; ~**rsi** *vr* (*libro, film*) to be called.

intolle'rabile *ag* intolerable.

intolle'rante *ag* intolerant.

intolle'ranza [intolle'rantsa] *sf* intolerance.

intona'care *vt* to plaster.

in'tonaco, ci *o* **chi** *sm* plaster.

into'nare *vt* (*canto*) to start to sing; (*armonizzare*) to match; ~**rsi** *vr* (*colori*) to go together; ~**rsi a** (*carnagione*) to suit; (*abito*) to go with, match.

intonazi'one [intonat'tsjone] *sf* intonation.

inton'tire *vt* to stun, daze ♦ *vi*, ~**rsi** *vr* to be stunned *o* dazed.

inton'tito, a *ag* stunned, dazed; ~ **dal sonno** stupid with sleep.

in'toppo *sm* stumbling block, obstacle.

intorbi'dire *vt* (*liquido*) to make turbid; (*mente*) to cloud; ~ **le acque** (*fig*) to muddy the waters.

in'torno *av* around; ~ **a** *prep* (*attorno a*) around; (*riguardo, circa*) about.

intorpi'dire *vt* to numb; (*fig*) to make sluggish ♦ *vi* (*anche:* ~**rsi**) to grow numb; (*fig*) to become sluggish.

intossi'care *vt* to poison.

intossicazi'one [intossikat'tsjone] *sf* poisoning.

intradu'cibile [intradu'tʃibile] *ag* untranslatable.

intralci'are [intral'tʃare] *vt* to hamper, hold up.

in'tralcio [in'traltʃo] *sm* hitch.

intrallaz'zare [intrallat'tsare] *vi* to intrigue, scheme.

intral'lazzo [intral'lattso] *sm* (*POL*) intrigue, manoeuvre (*BRIT*), maneuver (*US*); (*traffico losco*) racket.

intramon'tabile *ag* timeless.

intramusco'lare *ag* intramuscular.

intransi'gente [intransi'dʒɛnte] *ag* intransigent, uncompromising.

intransi'genza [intransi'dʒɛntsa] *sf* intransigence.

intransi'tivo, a *ag, sm* intransitive.

intrappo'lare *vt* to trap; **rimanere intrappolato** to be trapped; **farsi** ~ to get caught.

intrapren'dente *ag* enterprising, go-ahead; *(con le donne)* forward, bold.

intrapren'denza [intrapren'dɛntsa] *sf* audacity, initiative; *(con le donne)* boldness.

intra'prendere *vt* to undertake; *(carriera)* to embark (up)on.

intra'preso, a *pp di* **intraprendere**.

intrat'tabile *ag* intractable.

intratte'nere *vt (divertire)* to entertain; *(chiacchierando)* to engage in conversation; *(rapporti)* to have, maintain; ~**rsi** *vr* to linger; ~**rsi su qc** to dwell on sth.

intratteni'mento *sm* entertainment.

intrave'dere *vt* to catch a glimpse of; *(fig)* to foresee.

intrecci'are [intret'tʃare] *vt (capelli)* to plait, braid; *(intessere: anche fig)* to weave, interweave, intertwine; ~**rsi** *vr* to intertwine, become interwoven; ~ **le mani** to clasp one's hands; ~ **una relazione amorosa** *(fig)* to begin an affair.

in'treccio [in'trettʃo] *sm (fig: trama)* plot, story.

in'trepido, a *ag* fearless, intrepid.

intri'care *vt (fili)* to tangle; *(fig: faccenda)* to complicate; ~**rsi** *vr* to become tangled; to become complicated.

in'trico, chi *sm (anche fig)* tangle.

intri'gante *ag* scheming ♦ *sm/f* schemer, intriguer.

intri'gare *vi* to manoeuvre *(BRIT)*, maneuver *(US)*, scheme.

in'trigo, ghi *sm* plot, intrigue.

in'trinseco, a, ci, che *ag* intrinsic.

in'triso, a *ag:* ~ **(di)** soaked (in).

intris'tire *vi (persona: diventare triste)* to grow sad; *(pianta)* to wilt.

intro'dotto, a *pp di* **introdurre**.

intro'durre *vt* to introduce; *(chiave etc):* ~ **qc in** to insert sth into; *(persona: far entrare)* to show in; **introdursi** *vr (moda, tecniche)* to be introduced; **introdursi in** *(persona: penetrare)* to enter; *(: entrare furtivamente)* to steal *o* slip into.

in'troito *sm* income, revenue.

intro'messo, a *pp di* **intromettersi**.

intro'mettersi *vr* to interfere, meddle; *(interporsi)* to intervene.

intromissi'one *sf* interference, meddling; intervention.

introspezi'one [introspet'tsjone] *sf* introspection.

intro'vabile *ag (persona, oggetto)* who *(o* which) cannot be found; *(libro etc)* unobtainable.

intro'verso, a *ag* introverted ♦ *sm/f* introvert.

intrufo'larsi *vr:* ~ **(in)** *(stanza)* to sneak in(to), slip in(to); *(conversazione)* to butt in (on).

in'truglio [in'truʎʎo] *sm* concoction.

intrusi'one *sf* intrusion; interference.

in'truso, a *sm/f* intruder.

intu'ire *vt* to perceive by intuition; *(rendersi conto)* to realize.

in'tuito *sm* intuition; *(perspicacia)* perspicacity.

intuizi'one [intuit'tsjone] *sf* intuition.

inturgi'dire [inturdʒi'dire] *vi,* ~**rsi** *vr* to swell.

inumanità *sf inv* inhumanity.

inu'mano, a *ag* inhuman.

inu'mare *vt (seppellire)* to bury, inter.

inumazi'one [inumat'tsjone] *sf* burial, interment.

inumi'dire *vt* to dampen, moisten; ~**rsi** *vr* to become damp *o* wet.

inurba'mento *sm* urbanization.

inusi'tato, a *ag* unusual.

i'nutile *ag* useless; *(superfluo)* pointless, unnecessary; **è stato tutto** ~**!** it was all in vain!

inutilità *sf* uselessness; pointlessness.

inutiliz'zabile [inutilid'dzabile] *ag* unusable.

inutil'mente *av (senza risultato)* fruitlessly; *(senza utilità, scopo)* unnecessarily, needlessly; **l'ho cercato** ~ I looked for him in vain; **ti preoccupi** ~ there's nothing for you to worry about, there's no need for you to worry.

inva'dente *ag (fig)* intrusive.

inva'denza [inva'dɛntsa] *sf* intrusiveness.

in'vadere *vt* to invade; *(affollare)* to swarm into, overrun; *(sog: acque)* to flood.

invadi'trice [invadi'tritʃe] *ag f vedi* **invasore**.

inva'ghirsi [inva'girsi] *vr:* ~ **di** to take a fancy to.

invali'cabile *ag (montagna)* impassable.

invali'dare *vt* to invalidate.

invalidità *sf* infirmity; disability; *(DIR)* invalidity.

in'valido, a *ag (infermo)* infirm; *(al lavoro)* disabled; *(DIR: nullo)* invalid ♦ *sm/f* invalid; disabled person; ~ **di guerra** disabled ex-serviceman; ~ **del lavoro** industrially disabled person.

in'valso, a *ag* (*diffuso*) established.
in'vano *av* in vain.
invari'abile *ag* invariable.
invari'ato, a *ag* unchanged.
inva'sare *vt* (*pianta*) to pot.
inva'sato, a *ag* possessed (by the devil)
♦ *sm/f* person possessed by the devil;
urlare come un ~ to shout like a
madman.
invasi'one *sf* invasion.
in'vaso, a *pp di* **invadere**.
inva'sore, invadi'trice [invadi'tritʃe] *ag*
invading ♦ *sm* invader.
invecchia'mento [invekkja'mento] *sm*
growing old; ageing; **questo whisky ha un**
~ **di 12 anni** this whisky has been
matured for 12 years.
invecchi'are [invek'kjare] *vi* (*persona*) to
grow old; (*vino, popolazione*) to age;
(*moda*) to become dated ♦ *vt* to age; (*far
apparire più vecchio*) to make look older; **lo
trovo invecchiato** I find he has aged.
in'vece [in'vetʃe] *av* instead; (*al contrario*)
on the contrary; ~ **di** *prep* instead of.
inve'ire *vi*: ~ **contro** to rail against.
invele'nire *vt* to embitter; ~**rsi** *vr* to
become bitter.
inven'duto, a *ag* unsold.
inven'tare *vt* to invent; (*pericoli,
pettegolezzi*) to make up, invent.
inventari'are *vt* to make an inventory of,
inventory.
inven'tario *sm* inventory; (*COMM*)
stocktaking *no pl*.
inven'tivo, a *ag* inventive ♦ *sf*
inventiveness.
inven'tore, 'trice *sm/f* inventor.
invenzi'one [inven'tsjone] *sf* invention;
(*bugia*) lie, story.
invere'condia *sf* shamelessness,
immodesty.
inver'nale *ag* winter *cpd*; (*simile all'inverno*)
wintry.
in'verno *sm* winter; **d'**~ in (the) winter.
invero'simile *ag* unlikely ♦ *sm*: **ha dell'**~
it's hard to believe, it's incredible.
inversi'one *sf* inversion; "**divieto d'**~"
(*AUT*) "no U-turns".
in'verso, a *ag* opposite; (*MAT*) inverse ♦ *sm*
contrary, opposite; **in senso** ~ in the
opposite direction; **in ordine** ~ in reverse
order.
inverte'brato, a *ag, sm* invertebrate.
inver'tire *vt* to invert; (*disposizione, posti*)
to change; (*ruoli*) to exchange; ~ **la
marcia** (*AUT*) to do a U-turn; ~ **la rotta**
(*NAUT*) to go about; (*fig*) to do a U-turn.
inver'tito, a *sm/f* homosexual.

investi'gare *vt, vi* to investigate.
investiga'tivo, a *ag*: **squadra** ~**a** detective
squad.
investiga'tore, 'trice *sm/f* investigator,
detective.
investigazi'one [investigat'tsjone] *sf*
investigation, inquiry.
investi'mento *sm* (*ECON*) investment; (*di
veicolo*) crash, collision; (*di pedone*)
knocking down.
inves'tire *vt* (*denaro*) to invest; (*sog:
veicolo: pedone*) to knock down; (: *altro
veicolo*) to crash into; (*apostrofare*) to
assail; (*incaricare*): ~ **qn di** to invest sb
with; ~**rsi** *vr* (*fig*): ~**rsi di una parte** to
enter thoroughly into a role.
investi'tore, 'trice *sm/f* driver responsible
for an accident.
investi'tura *sf* investiture.
invete'rato, a *ag* inveterate.
invet'tiva *sf* invective.
invi'are *vt* to send.
invi'ato, a *sm/f* envoy; (*STAMPA*)
correspondent.
in'vidia *sf* envy; **fare** ~ **a qn** to make sb
envious.
invidi'abile *ag* enviable.
invidi'are *vt*: ~ **qn (per qc)** to envy sb (for
sth); ~ **qc a qn** to envy sb sth; **non aver
nulla da** ~ **a nessuno** to be as good as the
next one.
invidi'oso, a *ag* envious.
invin'cibile [invin'tʃibile] *ag* invincible.
in'vio, 'vii *sm* sending; (*insieme di merci*)
consignment.
invio'labile *ag* inviolable.
invio'lato, a *ag* (*diritto, segreto*) inviolate;
(*foresta*) virgin *cpd*; (*montagna, vetta*)
unscaled.
invipe'rire *vi*, ~**rsi** *vr* to become furious,
fly into a temper.
invipe'rito, a *ag* furious.
invis'chiare [invis'kjare] *vt* (*fig*): ~ **qn in qc**
to involve sb in sth, mix sb up in sth; ~**rsi**
vr: ~**rsi (con qn/in qc)** to get mixed up *o*
involved (with sb/in sth).
invi'sibile *ag* invisible.
in'viso, a *ag*: ~ **a** unpopular with.
invi'tante *ag* (*proposta, odorino*) inviting;
(*sorriso*) appealing, attractive.
invi'tare *vt* to invite; ~ **qn a fare** to invite
sb to do.
invi'tato, a *sm/f* guest.
in'vito *sm* invitation; **dietro** ~ **del sig. Rossi**
at Mr Rossi's invitation.
invo'care *vt* (*chiedere: aiuto, pace*) to cry
out for; (*appellarsi: la legge, Dio*) to appeal
to, invoke.

invogli'are [invoʎ'ʎare] *vt*: ~ **qn a fare** to tempt sb to do, induce sb to do.

involon'tario, a *ag* (*errore*) unintentional; (*gesto*) involuntary.

invol'tino *sm* (*CUC*) roulade.

in'volto *sm* (*pacco*) parcel; (*fagotto*) bundle.

in'volucro *sm* cover, wrapping.

involu'tivo, a *ag*: **subire un processo** ~ to regress.

invo'luto, a *ag* involved, intricate.

involuzi'one [involut'tsjone] *sf* (*di stile*) convolutedness; (*regresso*): **subire un'**~ to regress.

invulne'rabile *ag* invulnerable.

inzacche'rare [intsakke'rare] *vt* to spatter with mud; ~**rsi** *vr* to get muddy.

inzup'pare [intsup'pare] *vt* to soak; ~**rsi** *vr* to get soaked; **inzuppò i biscotti nel latte** he dipped the biscuits in the milk.

'io *pron* I ♦ *sm inv*: **l'**~ the ego, the self; ~ **stesso(a)** I myself; **sono** ~ it's me.

i'odio *sm* iodine.

i'ogurt *sm inv* = **yoghurt**.

i'one *sm* ion.

I'onio *sm*: **lo** ~, **il mar** ~ the Ionian (Sea).

ionizza'tore [joniddza'tore] *sm* ioniser.

'iosa: a ~ *av* in abundance, in great quantity.

'IPAB *sigla fpl* (= *Istituzioni pubbliche di Assistenza e Beneficenza*) *charitable institutions.*

i'perbole *sf* (*LETTERATURA*) hyperbole; (*MAT*) hyperbola.

iper'bolico, a, ci, che *ag* (*LETTERATURA, MAT*) hyperbolic(al); (*fig: esagerato*) exaggerated.

ipermer'cato *sm* hypermarket.

ipersen'sibile *ag* (*persona*) hypersensitive; (*FOT: lastra, pellicola*) hypersensitized.

ipertecno'logico, a, ci, che [ipertekno'lɔdʒiko] *ag* hi-tech.

ipertensi'one *sf* high blood pressure, hypertension.

ip'nosi *sf* hypnosis.

ip'notico, a, ci, che *ag* hypnotic.

ipno'tismo *sm* hypnotism.

ipnotiz'zare [ipnotid'dzare] *vt* to hypnotize.

ipoaller'genico, a, ci, che [ipoaller'dʒɛniko] *ag* hypoallergenic.

ipocon'dria *sf* hypochondria.

ipocon'driaco, a, ci, che *ag, sm/f* hypochondriac.

ipocri'sia *sf* hypocrisy.

i'pocrita, i, e *ag* hypocritical ♦ *sm/f* hypocrite.

ipo'sodico, a, ci, che *ag* low sodium *cpd*.

ipo'teca, che *sf* mortgage.

ipote'care *vt* to mortgage.

ipote'nusa *sf* hypotenuse.

i'potesi *sf inv* hypothesis; **facciamo l'**~ **che ..., ammettiamo per** ~ **che ...** let's suppose *o* assume that ...; **nella peggiore/migliore delle** ~**i** at worst/best; **nell'**~ **che venga** should he come, if he comes; **se per** ~ **io partissi ...** just supposing I were to leave ....

ipo'tetico, a, ci, che *ag* hypothetical.

ipotiz'zare [ipotid'dzare] *vt*: ~ **che** to form the hypothesis that.

'ippico, a, ci, che *ag* horse *cpd* ♦ *sf* horse-racing.

ippocas'tano *sm* horse chestnut.

ip'podromo *sm* racecourse.

ippo'potamo *sm* hippopotamus.

'ipsilon *sf o m inv* (*lettera*) Y, y; (: *dell'alfabeto greco*) epsilon.

IP'SOA *sigla m* (= *Istituto Post-Universitario per lo Studio dell'Organizzazione Aziendale*) *postgraduate institute of business administration.*

IRA *sigla f* (= *Irish Republican Army*) IRA.

'ira *sf* anger, wrath.

ira'cheno, a [ira'kɛno] *ag, sm/f* Iraqi.

l'ran *sm*: **l'**~ Iran.

irani'ano, a *ag, sm/f* Iranian.

l'raq *sm*: **l'**~ Iraq.

iras'cibile [iraʃ'ʃibile] *ag* irascible, quick-tempered.

'IRCE ['irtʃe] *sigla m* = *Istituto per le relazioni culturali con l'Estero.*

'IRI *sigla m* (= *Istituto per la Ricostruzione Industriale*) *state-controlled industrial investment office.*

'iride *sf* (*arcobaleno*) rainbow; (*ANAT, BOT*) iris.

Ir'landa *sf*: **l'**~ Ireland; **l'**~ **del Nord** Northern Ireland, Ulster; **la Repubblica d'**~ Eire, the Republic of Ireland; **il mar d'**~ the Irish Sea.

irlan'dese *ag* Irish ♦ *sm/f* Irishman/woman; **gli l**~**i** the Irish.

iro'nia *sf* irony.

i'ronico, a, ci, che *ag* ironic(al).

ironiz'zare [ironid'dzare] *vt, vi*: ~ **su** to be ironical about.

i'roso, a *ag* (*sguardo, tono*) angry, wrathful; (*persona*) irascible.

'IRPEF *sigla f vedi* **imposta sul reddito delle persone fisiche.**

ir'pino, a *ag* of (*o* from) Irpinia.

irradi'are *vt* to radiate; (*sog: raggi di luce: illuminare*) to shine on ♦ *vi* (*diffondersi: anche:* ~**rsi**) to radiate.

irradiazi'one [irradjat'tsjone] *sf* radiation.

irraggiun'gibile [irraddʒun'dʒibile] *ag* unreachable; (*fig: meta*) unattainable.

irragio'nevole [irrad3o'nevole] *ag* (*privo di ragione*) irrational; (*fig: persona, pretese, prezzo*) unreasonable.

irrazio'nale [irrattsjo'nale] *ag* irrational.

irre'ale *ag* unreal.

irrealiz'zabile [irrealid'dzabile] *ag* (*sogno, desiderio*) unattainable, unrealizable; (*progetto*) unworkable, impracticable.

irrealtà *sf* unreality.

irrecupe'rabile *ag* (*gen*) irretrievable; (*fig: persona*) irredeemable.

irrecu'sabile *ag* (*offerta*) not to be refused; (*prova*) irrefutable.

irreden'tista, i, e *ag, sm/f* (*STORIA*) Irredentist.

irrefre'nabile *ag* uncontrollable.

irrefu'tabile *ag* irrefutable.

irrego'lare *ag* irregular; (*terreno*) uneven.

irregolarità *sf inv* irregularity; unevenness *no pl.*

irremo'vibile *ag* (*fig*) unshakeable, unyielding.

irrepa'rabile *ag* irreparable; (*fig*) inevitable.

irrepe'ribile *ag* nowhere to be found.

irrepren'sibile *ag* irreproachable.

irrequi'eto, a *ag* restless.

irresis'tibile *ag* irresistible.

irreso'luto, a *ag* irresolute.

irrespi'rabile *ag* (*aria*) unbreathable; (*fig: opprimente*) stifling, oppressive; (: *malsano*) unhealthy.

irrespon'sabile *ag* irresponsible.

irrestrin'gibile [irrestrin'dʒibile] *ag* unshrinkable, non-shrink (*BRIT*).

irre'tire *vt* to seduce.

irrever'sibile *ag* irreversible.

irrevo'cabile *ag* irrevocable.

irricono'scibile [irrikonoʃ'ʃibile] *ag* unrecognizable.

irridu'cibile [irridu'tʃibile] *ag* irreducible; (*fig*) unshakeable.

irrifles'sivo, a *ag* thoughtless.

irri'gare *vt* (*annaffiare*) to irrigate; (*sog: fiume etc*) to flow through.

irrigazi'one [irrigat'tsjone] *sf* irrigation.

irrigidi'mento [irridʒidi'mento] *sm* stiffening; hardening; tightening.

irrigi'dire [irridʒi'dire] *vt* to stiffen; (*disciplina*) to tighten; ~**rsi** *vr* to stiffen; (*posizione, atteggiamento*) to harden.

irriguar'doso, a *ag* disrespectful.

irrile'vante *ag* (*trascurabile*) insignificant.

irrimedi'abile *ag*: **un errore** ~ a mistake which cannot be rectified; **non è** ~! we can do something about it!

irrinunci'abile [irrinun'tʃabile] *ag* vital; which cannot be abandoned.

irripe'tibile *ag* unrepeatable.

irri'solto, a *ag* (*problema*) unresolved.

irri'sorio, a *ag* derisory.

irrispet'toso, a *ag* disrespectful.

irri'tabile *ag* irritable.

irri'tante *ag* (*atteggiamento*) irritating, annoying; (*MED*) irritant.

irri'tare *vt* (*mettere di malumore*) to irritate, annoy; (*MED*) to irritate; ~**rsi** *vr* (*stizzirsi*) to become irritated *o* annoyed; (*MED*) to become irritated.

irritazi'one [irritat'tsjone] *sf* irritation; annoyance.

irrive'rente *ag* irreverent.

irrobus'tire *vt* (*persona*) to make stronger, make more robust; (*muscoli*) to strengthen; ~**rsi** *vr* to become stronger.

ir'rompere *vi*: ~ **in** to burst into.

irro'rare *vt* to sprinkle; (*AGR*) to spray.

ir'rotto, a *pp di* **irrompere**.

irru'ente *ag* (*fig*) impetuous, violent.

irru'enza [irru'ɛntsa] *sf* impetuousness; **con** ~ impetuously.

ir'ruppi *etc vb vedi* **irrompere**.

irruvi'dire *vt* to roughen ♦ *vi* (*anche*: ~**rsi**) to become rough.

irruzi'one [irrut'tsjone] *sf*: **fare** ~ **in** to burst into; (*sog: polizia*) to raid.

ir'suto, a *ag* (*petto*) hairy; (*barba*) bristly.

'irto, a *ag* bristly; ~ **di** bristling with.

Is. *abbr* (= *isola*) I.

ISBN *abbr* (= *International Standard Book Number*) ISBN.

is'crissi *etc vb vedi* **iscrivere**.

is'critto, a *pp di* **iscrivere** ♦ *sm/f* member; **gli** ~**i alla gara** the competitors; **per** *o* **in** ~ in writing.

is'crivere *vt* to register, enter; (*persona*): ~ **(a)** to register (in), enrol (in); ~**rsi** *vr*: ~**rsi (a)** (*club, partito*) to join; (*università*) to register *o* enrol (at); (*esame, concorso*) to register *o* enter (for).

iscrizi'one [iskrit'tsjone] *sf* (*epigrafe etc*) inscription; (*a scuola, società etc*) enrolment; registration.

'ISEF *sigla m* = *Istituto Superiore di Educazione Fisica.*

Is'lam *sm*: **l'**~ Islam.

is'lamico, a, ci, che *ag* Islamic.

Is'landa *sf*: **l'**~ Iceland.

islan'dese *ag* Icelandic ♦ *sm/f* Icelander ♦ *sm* (*LING*) Icelandic.

'isola *sf* island; ~ **pedonale** (*AUT*) pedestrian precinct.

isola'mento *sm* isolation; (*TECN*) insulation; **essere in cella di** ~ to be in solitary confinement; ~ **acustico** soundproofing; ~ **termico** thermal

insulation.
iso'lano, a *ag* island *cpd* ♦ *sm/f* islander.
iso'lante *ag* insulating ♦ *sm* insulator.
iso'lare *vt* to isolate; (*TECN*) to insulate;
(*: acusticamente*) to soundproof.
iso'lato, a *ag* isolated; insulated ♦ *sm*
(*edificio*) block.
isolazio'nismo [isolattsjo'nismo] *sm*
isolationism.
i'sotopo *sm* isotope.
ispessi'mento *sm* thickening.
ispes'sire *vt* to thicken; ~**rsi** *vr* to get
thicker, thicken.
ispetto'rato *sm* inspectorate.
ispet'tore, 'trice *sm/f* inspector; (*COMM*)
supervisor; ~ **di zona** (*COMM*) area
supervisor *o* manager; ~ **di reparto** shop
walker (*BRIT*), floor walker (*US*).
ispezio'nare [ispettsjo'nare] *vt* to inspect.
ispezi'one [ispet'tsjone] *sf* inspection.
'ispido, a *ag* bristly, shaggy.
ispi'rare *vt* to inspire; ~**rsi** *vr*: ~**rsi a** to
draw one's inspiration from;
(*conformarsi*) to be based on; **l'idea
m'ispira** the idea appeals to me.
ispira'tore, 'trice *ag* inspiring ♦ *sm/f*
inspirer; (*di ribellione*) instigator.
ispirazi'one [ispirat'tsjone] *sf* inspiration;
secondo l'~ del momento according to
the mood of the moment.
israeli'ano, a *ag*, *sm/f* Israeli.
israe'lita, i, e *sm/f* Jew/Jewess; (*STORIA*)
Israelite.
israe'litico, a, ci, che *ag* Jewish.
is'sare *vt* to hoist; ~ **l'ancora** to weigh
anchor.
'Istanbul *sf* Istanbul.
istan'taneo, a *ag* instantaneous ♦ *sf* (*FOT*)
snapshot.
is'tante *sm* instant, moment; **all'~, sull'~**
instantly, immediately.
is'tanza [is'tantsa] *sf* petition, request;
giudice di prima ~ (*DIR*) judge of the
court of first instance; **giudizio di
seconda** ~ judgment on appeal; **in ultima**
~ (*fig*) finally; ~ **di divorzio** petition for
divorce.
'ISTAT *sigla m* = *Istituto Centrale di Statistica*.
'ISTEL *sigla f* = *Indagine sull'ascolto delle
televisioni in Italia*.
is'terico, a, ci, che *ag* hysterical.
isteri'lire *vt* (*terreno*) to render infertile;
(*fig: fantasia*) to dry up; ~**rsi** *vr* to become
infertile; to dry up.
iste'rismo *sm* hysteria.
isti'gare *vt* to incite.
istigazi'one [istigat'tsjone] *sf* instigation; ~
a delinquere (*DIR*) incitement to crime.

istin'tivo, a *ag* instinctive.
is'tinto *sm* instinct.
istitu'ire *vt* (*fondare*) to institute, found;
(*porre: confronto*) to establish;
(*intraprendere: inchiesta*) to set up.
isti'tuto *sm* institute; (*di università*)
department; (*ente, DIR*) institution; ~ **di
bellezza** beauty salon; ~ **di credito** bank,
banking institution; ~ **tecnico
commerciale** ≈ commercial college; ~
tecnico industriale statale ≈ technical
college.
istitu'tore, 'trice *sm/f* (*fondatore*) founder;
(*precettore*) tutor/governess.
istituzi'one [istitut'tsjone] *sf* institution; ~**i**
sfpl (*DIR*) institutes; **lotta alle** ~**i** struggle
against the Establishment.
'istmo *sm* (*GEO*) isthmus.
isto'gramma, i *sm* histogram.
istra'dare *vt* (*fig: persona*): ~ (**a/verso**) to
direct (to/towards).
istri'ano, a *ag*, *sm/f* Istrian.
'istrice ['istritʃe] *sm* porcupine.
istri'one *sm* (*peg*) ham (actor).
istru'ire *vt* (*insegnare*) to teach;
(*ammaestrare*) to train; (*informare*) to
instruct, inform; (*DIR*) to prepare.
istru'ito, a *ag* educated.
istrut'tivo, a *ag* instructive.
istrut'tore, 'trice *sm/f* instructor ♦ *ag*:
giudice ~ examining (*BRIT*) *o* committing
(*US*) magistrate.
istrut'toria *sf* (*DIR*) (preliminary)
investigation and hearing; **formalizzare
un'~** to proceed to a formal hearing.
istruzi'one [istrut'tsjone] *sf* (*gen*) training;
(*INS, cultura*) education; (*direttiva*)
instruction; (*DIR*) = **istruttoria; Ministero
della Pubblica I~** Ministry of Education;
~**i di spedizione** forwarding instructions;
~**i per l'uso** instructions (for use).
istupi'dire *vt* (*sog: colpo*) to stun, daze;
(*: droga, stanchezza*) to stupefy; ~**rsi** *vr* to
become stupid.
'ISVE *sigla m* (= *Istituto di Studi per lo
Sviluppo Economico*) *institute for research
into economic development*.
l'talia *sf*: **l'~** Italy.
itali'ano, a *ag* Italian ♦ *sm/f* Italian ♦ *sm*
(*LING*) Italian; **gli I~i** the Italians.
ITC *sigla m* = **istituto tecnico commerciale**.
'iter *sm* passage, course; **l'~ burocratico**
the bureaucratic process.
itine'rante *ag* wandering, itinerant;
mostra ~ touring exhibition; **spettacolo**
~ travelling (*BRIT*) *o* traveling (*US*) show,
touring show.
itine'rario *sm* itinerary.

'ITIS *sigla m* = **istituto tecnico industriale statale**.

itte'rizia [itte'rittsja] *sf* (*MED*) jaundice.

'ittico, a, ci, che *ag* fish *cpd*; fishing *cpd*.

IUD *sigla m inv* (= *intra-uterine device*) IUD.

Iugos'lavia *sf* = **Jugoslavia**.

iugos'lavo, a *ag*, *sm/f* = **jugoslavo, a**.

i'uta *sf* jute.

'I.V.A. *sigla f vedi* **imposta sul valore aggiunto**.

'ivi *av* (*formale, poetico*) therein; (*nelle citazioni*) ibid.

$$J\,j$$

J, j [i'lunga] *sm o f inv* (*lettera*) J, j; ~ **come Jersey** ≈ J for Jack (*BRIT*), J for Jig (*US*).

jazz [dʒaz] *sm* jazz.

jaz'zista, i [dʒad'dzista] *sm* jazz player.

jeans [dʒinz] *smpl* jeans.

jeep [dʒip] *sm inv* jeep.

'jersey ['dʒɛrzi] *sm inv* jersey (cloth).

'jockey ['dʒɔki] *sm inv* (*CARTE*) jack; (*fantino*) jockey.

'jogging ['dʒɔgiŋ] *sm* jogging; **fare** ~ to go jogging.

'jolly ['dʒɔli] *sm inv* joker.

jr. *abbr* (= *junior*) Jr., jr.

ju'do [dʒu'dɔ] *sm* judo.

Jugos'lavia [jugoz'lavja] *sf*: **la** ~ Yugoslavia.

jugos'lavo, a *ag*, *sm/f* Yugoslav(ian).

'juke 'box ['dʒuk'bɔks] *sm inv* jukebox.

$$K\,k$$

K, k ['kappa] *sf o m inv* (*lettera*) K, k ♦ *abbr* (= *kilo-, chilo-*) k; (*INFORM*) K; **K come Kursaal** ≈ K for King.

Kam'pala *sf* Kampala.

kara'kiri *sm* harakiri.

karatè [kara'tɛ] *sm* karate.

'Kashmir ['kaʃmir] *sm*: **il** ~ Kashmir.

ka'yak [ka'jak] *sm inv* kayak.

'Kenia ['kenja] *sm*: **il** ~ Kenya.

keni'ano, a, keni'ota, i, e *ag*, *sm/f* Kenyan.

'Kenya ['kenja] *sm*: **il** ~ Kenya.

kero'sene [kero'zɛne] *sm* = **cherosene**.

kg *abbr* (= *chilogrammo*) kg.

kib'butz [kib'buts] *sm inv* kibbutz.

Kilimangi'aro [kiliman'dʒaro] *sm*: **il** ~ Kilimanjaro.

'killer ['killer] *sm inv* gunman, hired gun.

'kilo *etc* = **chilo** *etc*.

kilt [kilt] *sm inv* kilt.

ki'mono [ki'mɔno] *sm* = **chimono**.

kitsch [kitʃ] *sm* kitsch.

'kiwi ['kiwi] *sm inv* kiwi (fruit).

km *abbr* (= *chilometro*) km.

kmq *abbr* (= *chilometro quadrato*) km².

ko'ala [ko'ala] *sm inv* koala (bear).

KR *sigla* = Crotone.

'krapfen ['krapfən] *sm inv* doughnut.

Ku'ala Lum'par *sf* Kuala Lumpur.

Ku'wait [ku'vait] *sm*: **il** ~ Kuwait.

kW *abbr* (= *kilowatt, chilowatt*) kW.

kWh *abbr* (= *kilowattora*) kW/h.

$$L\,l$$

L, l ['ɛlle] *sf o m inv* (*lettera*) L, l ♦ *abbr* (= *lira*) L; **L come Livorno** ≈ L for Lucy (*BRIT*), L for Love (*US*).

l *abbr* (= *litro*) l.

l' *det vedi* **la, lo**.

la *det f* (*dav V l'*) the ♦ *pron* (*dav V l'*) (*oggetto: persona*) her; (*: cosa*) it; (*: forma di cortesia*) you ♦ *sm inv* (*MUS*) A; (*: solfeggiando la scala*) la; *vedi anche* **il**.

là *av* there; **di** ~ (*da quel luogo*) from there; (*in quel luogo*) in there; (*dall'altra parte*) over there; **di** ~ **di** beyond; **per di** ~ that way; **più in** ~ further on; (*tempo*) later on; ~ **dentro/sopra/sotto** in/up (*o* on)/under there; ~ **per** ~ (*sul momento*) there and then; **essere in** ~ **con gli anni** to be getting on (in years); **essere più di** ~ **che di qua** to be more dead than alive; **va'** ~! come off it!; **stavolta è andato troppo in** ~ this time he's gone too far; *vedi anche* **quello**.

'labbro *sm* (*pl(f)*: **labbra**: *solo nel senso ANAT*) lip.

'labile *ag* fleeting, ephemeral.

labi'rinto *sm* labyrinth, maze.

labora'torio *sm* (*di ricerca*) laboratory; (*di arti, mestieri*) workshop; ~ **linguistico** language laboratory.

labori'oso, a *ag* (*faticoso*) laborious; (*attivo*) hard-working.

labu'rista, i, e *ag* Labour *cpd* (*BRIT*) ♦ *smf* Labour Party member (*BRIT*).

'lacca, che *sf* lacquer; (*per unghie*) nail varnish (*BRIT*), nail polish.

lac'care *vt* (*mobili*) to varnish, lacquer.

'laccio ['lattʃo] *sm* noose; (*legaccio, tirante*) lasso; (*di scarpa*) lace; ~ **emostatico** (*MED*) tourniquet.

lace'rante [latʃe'rante] *ag* (*suono*) piercing, shrill.

lace'rare [latʃe'rare] *vt* to tear to shreds, lacerate; **~rsi** *vr* to tear.

lacerazi'one [latʃerat'tsjone] *sf* (*anche MED*) tear.

'lacero, a ['latʃero] *ag* (*logoro*) torn, tattered; (*MED*) lacerated; **ferita ~- contusa** injury with lacerations and bruising.

la'conico, a, ci, che *ag* laconic, brief.

'lacrima *sf* tear; (*goccia*) drop; **in ~e** in tears.

lacri'mare *vi* to water.

lacri'mevole *ag* heartrending, pitiful.

lacri'mogeno, a [lakri'mɔdʒeno] *ag*: **gas ~** tear gas.

lacri'moso, a *ag* tearful.

la'cuna *sf* (*fig*) gap.

la'custre *ag* lake *cpd*.

lad'dove *cong* whereas.

'ladro *sm* thief; **al ~!** stop thief!

ladro'cinio [ladro'tʃinjo] *sm* theft, robbery.

la'druncolo, a *smf* petty thief.

laggiù [lad'dʒu] *av* down there; (*di là*) over there.

'lagna ['laɲɲa] *sf* (*fam: persona, cosa*) drag, bore; **fare la ~** to whine, moan.

la'gnanza [laɲ'ɲantsa] *sf* complaint.

la'gnarsi [laɲ'ɲarsi] *vr*: ~ (**di**) to complain (about).

'lago, ghi *sm* lake.

'Lagos ['lagos] *sf* Lagos.

'lagrima *etc* = **lacrima** *etc*.

la'guna *sf* lagoon.

lagu'nare *ag* lagoon *cpd*.

'laico, a, ci, che *ag* (*apostolato*) lay; (*vita*) secular; (*scuola*) non-denominational ♦ *smf* layman/woman ♦ *sm* lay brother.

'laido, a *ag* filthy, foul; (*fig: osceno*) obscene, filthy.

'lama *sf* blade ♦ *sm inv* (*ZOOL*) llama; (*REL*) lama.

lambic'care *vt* to distil; **~rsi il cervello** to rack one's brains.

lam'bire *vt* (*fig: sog: fiamme*) to lick; (: *acqua*) to lap.

lam'bretta ® *sf* scooter.

la'mella *sf* (*di metallo etc*) thin sheet, thin strip; (*di fungo*) gill.

lamen'tare *vt* to lament; **~rsi** *vr* (*emettere lamenti*) to moan, groan; (*rammaricarsi*): **~rsi** (**di**) to complain (about).

lamen'tela *sf* complaining *no pl*.

lamen'tevole *ag* (*voce*) complaining, plaintive; (*stato*) lamentable, pitiful.

la'mento *sm* moan, groan; (*per la morte di qn*) lament.

lamen'toso, a *ag* plaintive.

la'metta *sf* razor blade.

lami'era *sf* sheet metal.

'lamina *sf* (*lastra sottile*) thin sheet (*o* layer *o* plate); ~ **d'oro** gold leaf; gold foil.

lami'nare *vt* to laminate.

lami'nato, a *ag* laminated; (*tessuto*) lamé ♦ *sm* laminate.

'lampada *sf* lamp; ~ **a petrolio/a gas** oil/gas lamp; ~ **a spirito** blowlamp (*BRIT*), blowtorch; ~ **a stelo** standard lamp (*BRIT*), floor lamp; ~ **da tavolo** table lamp.

lampa'dario *sm* chandelier.

lampa'dina *sf* light bulb; ~ **tascabile** pocket torch (*BRIT*), flashlight (*US*).

lam'pante *ag* (*fig: evidente*) crystal clear, evident.

lam'para *sf* fishing lamp; (*barca*) boat for fishing by lamplight (*in Mediterranean*).

lampeggi'are [lamped'dʒare] *vi* (*luce, fari*) to flash ♦ *vb impers*: **lampeggia** there's lightning.

lampeggia'tore [lampeddʒa'tore] *sm* (*AUT*) indicator.

lampi'one *sm* street light *o* lamp (*BRIT*).

'lampo *sm* (*METEOR*) flash of lightning; (*di luce, fig*) flash ♦ *ag inv*: **cerniera ~** zip (*fastener*) (*BRIT*), zipper (*US*); **guerra ~** blitzkrieg; **~i** *smpl* (*METEOR*) lightning *no pl*; **passare come un ~** to flash past *o* by.

lam'pone *sm* raspberry.

'lana *sf* wool; ~ **d'acciaio** steel wool; **pura ~ vergine** pure new wool; ~ **di vetro** glass wool.

lan'cetta [lan'tʃetta] *sf* (*indice*) pointer, needle; (*di orologio*) hand.

'lancia, ce ['lantʃa] *sf* (*arma*) lance; (: *picca*) spear; (*di pompa antincendio*) nozzle; (*imbarcazione*) launch; **partire ~ in resta** (*fig*) to set off ready for battle; **spezzare una ~ in favore di qn** (*fig*) to come to sb's defence; ~ **di salvataggio** lifeboat.

lancia'bombe [lantʃa'bombe] *sm inv* (*MIL*) mortar.

lanciafi'amme [lantʃa'fjamme] *sm inv*

flamethrower.

lancia'missili [lantʃa'missili] *ag inv* missile-launching ♦ *sm inv* missile launcher.

lancia'razzi [lantʃa'raddzi] *ag inv* rocket-launching ♦ *sm inv* rocket launcher.

lanci'are [lan'tʃare] *vt* to throw, hurl, fling; (*SPORT*) to throw; (*far partire: automobile*) to get up to full speed; (*bombe*) to drop; (*razzo, prodotto, moda*) to launch; (*emettere: grido*) to give out; ~**rsi** *vr*: ~**rsi contro/su** to throw *o* hurl *o* fling o.s. against/on; ~**rsi in** (*fig*) to embark on; ~ **un cavallo** to give a horse his head; ~ **il disco** (*SPORT*) to throw the discus; ~ **il peso** (*SPORT*) to put the shot; ~**rsi all'inseguimento di qn** to set off in pursuit of sb; ~**rsi col paracadute** to parachute.

lanciasi'luri [lantʃasi'luri] *sm inv* torpedo tube.

lanci'ato, a [lan'tʃato] *ag* (*affermato: attore, prodotto*) well-known, famous; (*veicolo*) speeding along, racing along.

lanci'nante [lantʃi'nante] *ag* (*dolore*) shooting, throbbing; (*grido*) piercing.

'lancio ['lantʃo] *sm* throwing *no pl*; throw; dropping *no pl*; drop; launching *no pl*; launch; ~ **del disco** (*SPORT*) throwing the discus; ~ **del peso** (*SPORT*) putting the shot.

'landa *sf* (*GEO*) moor.

'languido, a *ag* (*fiacco*) languid, weak; (*tenero, malinconico*) languishing.

langu'ire *vi* to languish; (*conversazione*) to flag.

langu'ore *sm* weakness, languor.

lani'ero, a *ag* wool *cpd*, woollen (*BRIT*), woolen (*US*).

lani'ficio [lani'fitʃo] *sm* woollen (*BRIT*) *o* woolen (*US*) mill.

lano'lina *sf* lanolin(e).

la'noso, a *ag* woolly.

lan'terna *sf* lantern; (*faro*) lighthouse.

lanter'nino *sm*: **cercarsele col** ~ to be asking for trouble.

la'nugine [la'nudʒine] *sf* down.

'Laos *sm* Laos.

lapalissi'ano, a *ag* self-evident.

La 'Paz [la'pas] *sf* La Paz.

lapi'dare *vt* to stone.

lapi'dario, a *ag* (*fig*) terse.

'lapide *sf* (*di sepolcro*) tombstone; (*commemorativa*) plaque.

la'pin [la'pɛ̃] *sm inv* coney.

'lapis *sm inv* pencil.

'lappone *ag, sm/f, sm* Lapp.

Lap'ponia *sf*: **la** ~ Lapland.

'lapsus *sm inv* slip.

laptop ['læp tɔp] *sm inv* laptop (computer).

'lardo *sm* bacon fat, lard.

lar'ghezza [lar'gettsa] *sf* width; breadth; looseness; generosity; ~ **di vedute** broad-mindedness.

lar'gire [lar'dʒire] *vt* to give generously.

'largo, a, ghi, ghe *ag* wide, broad; (*maniche*) wide; (*abito: troppo ampio*) loose; (*fig*) generous ♦ *sm* width; breadth: (*mare aperto*): **il** ~ the open sea ♦ *sf*: **stare** *o* **tenersi alla** ~**a (da qn/qc)** to keep one's distance (from sb/sth), keep away (from sb/sth); ~ **due metri** two metres wide; ~ **di spalle** broad-shouldered; **di** ~**ghe vedute** broad-minded; **in** ~**a misura** to a great *o* large extent; **su** ~**a scala** on a large scale; **di manica** ~**a** generous, open-handed; **al** ~ **di Genova** off (the coast of) Genoa; **farsi** ~ **tra la folla** to push one's way through the crowd.

'larice ['laritʃe] *sm* (*BOT*) larch.

la'ringe [la'rindʒe] *sf* larynx.

larin'gite [larin'dʒite] *sf* laryngitis.

laringoi'atra, i, e *sm/f* (*medico*) throat specialist.

'larva *sf* larva; (*fig*) shadow.

la'sagne [la'zaɲɲe] *sfpl* lasagna *sg*.

lasciapas'sare [laʃʃapas'sare] *sm inv* pass, permit.

lasci'are [laʃ'ʃare] *vt* to leave; (*abbandonare*) to leave, abandon, give up; (*cessare di tenere*) to let go of ♦ *vb aux*: ~ **qn fare qc** to let sb do sth ♦ *vi*: ~ **di fare** (*smettere*) to stop doing; ~**rsi andare/truffare** to let o.s. go/be cheated; ~ **andare** *o* **correre** *o* **perdere** to let things go their own way; ~ **stare qc/qn** to leave sth/sb alone; ~ **qn erede** to make sb one's heir; ~ **la presa** to lose one's grip; ~ **il segno (su qc)** to leave a mark (on sth); (*fig*) to leave one's mark (on sth); ~ **(molto) a desiderare** to leave much to be desired; **ci ha lasciato la vita** it cost him his life.

'lascito ['laʃʃito] *sm* (*DIR*) legacy.

la'scivia [laʃ'ʃivja] *sf* lust, lasciviousness.

la'scivo, a [laʃ'ʃivo] *ag* lascivious.

'laser ['lazer] *ag, sm inv*: **(raggio)** ~ laser (beam).

lassa'tivo, a *ag, sm* laxative.

las'sismo *sm* laxity.

'lasso *sm*: ~ **di tempo** interval, lapse of time.

lassù *av* up there.

'lastra *sf* (*di pietra*) slab; (*di metallo, FOT*) plate; (*di ghiaccio, vetro*) sheet; (*radiografica*) X-ray (plate).

lastri'care *vt* to pave.

lastri'cato *sm* paving.

'**lastrico, ci** *o* **chi** *sm* paving; **essere sul** ~ (*fig*) to be penniless; **gettare qn sul** ~ (*fig*) to leave sb destitute.

las'trone *sm* (*ALPINISMO*) sheer rock face.

la'tente *ag* latent.

late'rale *ag* lateral, side *cpd*; (*uscita, ingresso etc*) side *cpd* ♦ *sm* (*CALCIO*) half-back.

lateral'mente *av* sideways.

late'rizio [late'rittsjo] *sm* (perforated) brick.

latifon'dista, i, e *sm/f* large agricultural landowner.

lati'fondo *sm* large estate.

la'tino, a *ag, sm* Latin.

la'tinoameri'cano, a *ag, sm/f* Latin-American.

lati'tante *ag*: **essere** ~ to be on the run ♦ *sm/f* fugitive (from justice).

lati'tanza [lati'tantsa] *sf*: **darsi alla** ~ to go into hiding.

lati'tudine *sf* latitude.

'**lato, a** *ag*: **in senso** ~ broadly speaking ♦ *sm* side; (*fig*) aspect, point of view; **d'altro** ~ (*d'altra parte*) on the other hand.

la'trare *vi* to bark.

lat'rato *sm* howling.

la'trina *sf* public lavatory.

latro'cinio [latro'tʃinjo] *sm* = **ladrocinio**.

'**latta** *sf* tin (plate); (*recipiente*) tin, can.

lat'taio, a *sm/f* (*distributore*) milkman/ woman; (*commerciante*) dairyman/ woman.

lat'tante *ag* unweaned ♦ *sm/f* breast-fed baby.

'**latte** *sm* milk; **fratello di** ~ foster brother; **avere ancora il** ~ **alla bocca** (*fig*) to be still wet behind the ears; **tutto** ~ **e miele** (*fig*) all smiles; ~ **detergente** cleansing milk *o* lotion; ~ **intero** full-cream milk; ~ **magro** *o* **scremato** skimmed milk; ~ **secco** *o* **in polvere** dried *o* powdered milk.

'**latteo, a** *ag* milky; (*dieta, prodotto*) milk *cpd*.

latte'ria *sf* dairy.

latti'cini [latti'tʃini] *smpl* dairy products.

lat'tina *sf* (*di birra etc*) can.

lat'tuga, ghe *sf* lettuce.

'**laurea** *sf* ≈ degree; ~ **breve** *university degree awarded at the end of a three-year course;* **avere una** ~ **in chimica** to have a degree in chemistry *o* a chemistry degree.

> *The* **Laurea** *is awarded to students upon successful completion of their degree courses. Courses take from 4 to 6 years and a major part of the final examinations is the presentation and discussion of a dissertation. A shorter, more vocational course of study, taking from 2 to 3 years, has been introduced at the end of which the* **Laurea breve**, *a diploma, is awarded.*

laure'ando, a *sm/f* final-year student.

laure'are *vt* to confer a degree on; ~**rsi** *vr* to graduate.

laure'ato, a *ag, sm/f* graduate.

'**lauro** *sm* laurel.

'**lauto, a** *ag* (*pranzo, mancia*) lavish; ~**i guadagni** handsome profits.

'**lava** *sf* lava.

lavabianche'ria [lavabjanke'ria] *sf inv* washing machine.

la'vabo *sm* washbasin.

la'vaggio [la'vaddʒo] *sm* washing *no pl*; ~ **del cervello** brainwashing *no pl*.

la'vagna [la'vaɲɲa] *sf* (*GEO*) slate; (*di scuola*) blackboard; ~ **luminosa** overhead projector.

la'vanda *sf* (*anche MED*) wash; (*BOT*) lavender; **fare una** ~ **gastrica a qn** to pump sb's stomach.

lavan'daia *sf* washerwoman.

lavande'ria *sf* (*di ospedale, caserma etc*) laundry; ~ **automatica** launderette; ~ **a secco** dry-cleaner's.

lavan'dino *sm* sink; (*del bagno*) washbasin.

lavapi'atti *sm/f* dishwasher.

la'vare *vt* to wash; ~**rsi** *vr* to wash, have a wash; ~ **a secco** to dry-clean; ~ **i panni sporchi in pubblico** (*fig*) to wash one's dirty linen in public; ~**rsi le mani/i denti** to wash one's hands/clean one's teeth.

lava'secco *sm o f inv* dry-cleaner's.

lavasto'viglie [lavasto'viʎʎe] *sm o f inv* (*macchina*) dishwasher.

la'vata *sf* wash; (*fig*): **dare una** ~ **di capo a qn** to give sb a good telling-off.

lava'tivo *sm* (*clistere*) enema; (*buono a nulla*) good-for-nothing, idler.

lava'toio *sm* (public) washhouse.

lava'trice [lava'tritʃe] *sf* washing machine.

lava'tura *sf* washing *no pl*; ~ **di piatti** dishwater.

la'vello *sm* (kitchen) sink.

la'vina *sf* snowslide.

lavo'rante *sm/f* worker.

lavo'rare *vi* to work; (*fig: bar, studio etc*) to do good business ♦ *vt* to work; ~ **a** to work on; ~ **a maglia** to knit; ~ **di fantasia** (*suggestionarsi*) to imagine things; (*fantasticare*) to let one's imagination run free; ~**rsi qn** (*fig: convincere*) to work on sb.

lavora'tivo, a *ag* working.

lavora'tore, 'trice *sm/f* worker ♦ *ag* working.

lavorazi'one [lavorat'tsjone] *sf* (*gen*) working; (*di legno, pietra*) carving; (*di film*) making; (*di prodotto*) manufacture; (*modo di esecuzione*) workmanship.

lavo'rio *sm* intense activity.

la'voro *sm* work; (*occupazione*) job, work *no pl*; (*opera*) piece of work, job; (*ECON*) labour (*BRIT*), labor (*US*); **Ministero del L~** Department of Employment (*BRIT*), Department of Labor (*US*); **(fare) i ~i di casa** (to do) the housework *sg*; **~i forzati** hard labour *sg*; **i ~i del parlamento** the parliamentary session *sg*; **~i pubblici** public works.

lazi'ale [lat'tsjale] *ag* of (*o* from) Lazio.

lazza'retto [laddza'retto] *sm* leper hospital.

lazza'rone [laddza'rone] *sm* scoundrel.

'lazzo ['laddzo] *sm* jest.

LC *sigla* = Lecco.

LE *sigla* = Lecce.

le *det fpl* the ♦ *pron* (*oggetto*) them; (: *a lei, a essa*) (to) her; (: *forma di cortesia*) (to) you; *vedi anche* **il**.

le'ale *ag* loyal; (*sincero*) sincere; (*onesto*) fair.

lea'lista, i, e *sm/f* loyalist.

lealtà *sf* loyalty; sincerity; fairness.

'leasing ['li:ziŋ] *sm* leasing; lease.

'lebbra *sf* leprosy.

'lecca 'lecca *sm inv* lollipop.

leccapi'edi *sm/f inv* (*peg*) toady, bootlicker.

lec'care *vt* to lick; (*sog: gatto: latte etc*) to lick *o* lap up; (*fig*) to flatter; **~rsi** *vr* (*fig*) to preen o.s.; **~rsi i baffi** to lick one's lips.

lec'cato, a *ag* affected ♦ *sf* lick.

leccherò *etc* [lekke'rɔ] *vb vedi* **leccare**.

'leccio ['lettʃo] *sm* holm oak, ilex.

leccor'nia *sf* titbit, delicacy.

'lecito, a ['letʃito] *ag* permitted, allowed; **se mi è ~** if I may; **mi sia ~ far presente che** ... may I point out that ....

'ledere *vt* to damage, injure; **~ gli interessi di qn** to be prejudicial to sb's interests.

'lega, ghe *sf* (*anche POL*) league; (*di metalli*) alloy; **metallo di bassa ~** base metal; **gente di bassa ~** common *o* vulgar people; **L~ Nord** (*POL*) *federalist party*.

le'gaccio [le'gattʃo] *sm* string, lace.

le'gale *ag* legal ♦ *sm* lawyer; **corso ~ delle monete** official exchange rate; **medicina ~** forensic medicine; **studio ~** lawyer's office.

legalità *sf* legality, lawfulness.

legaliz'zare [legalid'dzare] *vt* to legalize; (*documento*) to authenticate.

legalizzazi'one [legaliddzat'tsjone] *sf* (*vedi*

vt) legalization; authentication.

le'game *sm* (*corda, fig: affettivo*) tie, bond; (*nesso logico*) link, connection; **~ di sangue** *o* **di parentela** family tie.

lega'mento *sm* (*ANAT*) ligament.

le'gare *vt* (*prigioniero, capelli, cane*) to tie (up); (*libro*) to bind; (*CHIM*) to alloy; (*fig: collegare*) to bind, join ♦ *vi* (*far lega*) to unite; (*fig*) to get on well; **è pazzo da ~** (*fam*) he should be locked up.

lega'tario, a *sm/f* (*DIR*) legatee.

le'gato *sm* (*REL*) legate; (*DIR*) legacy, bequest.

legato'ria *sf* (*attività*) bookbinding; (*negozio*) bookbinder's.

lega'tura *sf* (*di libro*) binding; (*MUS*) ligature.

legazi'one [legat'tsjone] *sf* legation.

le'genda [le'dʒɛnda] *sf* (*di carta geografica etc*) = **leggenda**.

'legge ['leddʒe] *sf* law; **~ procedurale** procedural law.

leg'genda [led'dʒɛnda] *sf* (*narrazione*) legend; (*di carta geografica etc*) key, legend.

leggen'dario, a [leddʒen'darjo] *ag* legendary.

'leggere ['lɛddʒere] *vt, vi* to read; **~ il pensiero di qn** to read sb's mind *o* thoughts.

legge'rezza [leddʒe'rettsa] *sf* lightness; thoughtlessness; fickleness.

leg'gero, a [led'dʒɛro] *ag* light; (*agile, snello*) nimble, agile, light; (*tè, caffè*) weak; (*fig: non grave, piccolo*) slight; (: *spensierato*) thoughtless; (: *incostante*) fickle; free and easy; **una ragazza ~a** (*fig*) a flighty girl; **alla ~a** thoughtlessly.

leggi'adro, a [led'dʒadro] *ag* pretty, lovely; (*movimenti*) graceful.

leg'gibile [led'dʒibile] *ag* legible; (*libro*) readable, worth reading.

leg'gio, 'gii [led'dʒio] *sm* lectern; (*MUS*) music stand.

legherò *etc* [lege'rɔ] *vb vedi* **legare**.

le'ghismo [le'gismo] *sm political movement with federalist tendencies.*

le'ghista, i, e [le'gista] (*POL*) *ag* of a "lega" (*especially Lega Nord*) ♦ *sm/f* member (*o* supporter) of a "lega" (*especially Lega Nord*).

legife'rare [ledʒife'rare] *vi* to legislate.

legio'nario [ledʒo'narjo] *sm* (*romano*) legionary; (*volontario*) legionnaire.

legi'one [le'dʒone] *sf* legion; **~ straniera** foreign legion.

legisla'tivo, a [ledʒizla'tivo] *ag* legislative.

legisla'tore [ledʒizla'tore] *sm* legislator.

legisla'tura [ledʒizla'tura] *sf* legislature.
legislazi'one [ledʒizlat'tsjone] *sf*
legislation.
legitti'mare [ledʒitti'mare] *vt* (*figlio*) to
legitimize; (*comportamento etc*) to justify.
legittimità [ledʒittimi'ta] *sf* legitimacy.
le'gittimo, a [le'dʒittimo] *ag* legitimate;
(*fig: giustificato, lecito*) justified,
legitimate; **~a difesa** (*DIR*) self-defence
(*BRIT*), self-defense (*US*).
'legna ['leɲɲa] *sf* firewood.
le'gnaia [leɲ'ɲaja] *sf* woodshed.
legnai'olo [leɲɲa'jɔlo] *sm* woodcutter.
le'gname [leɲ'ɲame] *sm* wood, timber.
le'gnata [leɲ'ɲata] *sf* blow with a stick;
dare a qn un sacco di ~e to give sb a
good hiding.
'legno ['leɲɲo] *sm* wood; (*pezzo di ~*) piece
of wood; **di ~** wooden; **~ compensato**
plywood.
le'gnoso, a [leɲ'ɲoso] *ag* (*di legno*) wooden;
(*come il legno*) woody; (*carne*) tough.
le'gume *sm* (*BOT*) pulse; **~i** *smpl* (*fagioli,
piselli etc*) pulses.
'lei *pron* (*soggetto*) she; (*oggetto: per dare
rilievo, con preposizione*) her; (*forma di
cortesia: anche:* **L~**) you ♦ *sf inv:* **la mia ~**
my beloved ♦ *sm:* **dare del ~ a qn** to
address sb as "lei"; **~ stessa** she herself;
you yourself; **è ~** it's her.
'lembo *sm* (*di abito, strada*) edge; (*striscia
sottile: di terra*) strip.
'lemma, i *sm* headword.
'lemme 'lemme *av* (*very*) very slowly.
'lena *sf* (*fig*) energy, stamina; **di buona ~**
(*lavorare, camminare*) at a good pace.
Lenin'grado *sf* Leningrad.
le'nire *vt* to soothe.
'lente *sf* (*OTTICA*) lens *sg*; **~
d'ingrandimento** magnifying glass; **~i a
contatto, ~i corneali** contact lenses; **~i (a
contatto) morbide** soft lenses; **~i (a
contatto) rigide** hard lenses.
len'tezza [len'tettsa] *sf* slowness.
len'ticchia [len'tikkja] *sf* (*BOT*) lentil.
len'tiggine [len'tiddʒine] *sf* freckle.
'lento, a *ag* slow; (*molle: fune*) slack; (*non
stretto: vite, abito*) loose ♦ *sm* (*ballo*) slow
dance.
'lenza ['lɛntsa] *sf* fishing line.
lenzu'olo [len'tswɔlo] *sm* sheet; **~a** *sfpl* pair
of sheets; **~ funebre** shroud.
leon'cino [leon'tʃino] *sm* lion cub.
le'one *sm* lion; (*dello zodiaco*): **L~** Leo;
essere del L~ to be Leo.
leo'pardo *sm* leopard.
lepo'rino, a *ag:* **labbro ~** harelip.
'lepre *sf* hare.

'lercio, a, ci, ce ['lɛrtʃo] *ag* filthy.
lerci'ume [ler'tʃume] *sm* filth.
'lesbico, a, ci, che *ag, sf* lesbian.
'lesi *etc vb vedi* **ledere**.
lesi'nare *vt* to be stingy with ♦ *vi:* **~ (su)** to
skimp (on), be stingy (with).
lesi'one *sf* (*MED*) lesion; (*DIR*) injury,
damage; (*EDIL*) crack.
le'sivo, a *ag:* **~ (di)** damaging (to),
detrimental (to).
'leso, a *pp di* **ledere** ♦ *ag* (*offeso*) injured;
parte ~a (*DIR*) injured party; **~a maestà**
lese-majesty.
Le'sotho [le'soto] *sm* Lesotho.
les'sare *vt* (*CUC*) to boil.
'lessi *etc vb vedi* **leggere**.
lessi'cale *ag* lexical.
'lessico, ci *sm* vocabulary; (*dizionario*)
lexicon.
lessicogra'fia *sf* lexicography.
lessi'cografo, a *sm/f* lexicographer.
'lesso, a *ag* boiled ♦ *sm* boiled meat.
'lesto, a *ag* quick; (*agile*) nimble; **~ di
mano** (*per rubare*) light-fingered; (*per
picchiare*) free with one's fists.
lesto'fante *sm* swindler, con man.
le'tale *ag* lethal, deadly.
leta'maio *sm* dunghill.
le'tame *sm* manure, dung.
le'targo, ghi *sm* lethargy; (*ZOOL*)
hibernation.
le'tizia [le'tittsja] *sf* joy, happiness.
'letta *sf:* **dare una ~ a qc** to glance *o* look
through sth.
'lettera *sf* letter; **~e** *sfpl* (*letteratura*)
literature *sg*; (*studi umanistici*) arts
(subjects); **alla ~** literally; **in ~e** in
words, in full; **diventar ~ morta** (*legge*) to
become a dead letter; **restar ~ morta**
(*consiglio, invito*) to go unheeded; **~ di
accompagnamento** accompanying letter;
~ assicurata registered letter; **~ di
cambio** (*COMM*) bill of exchange; **~ di
credito** (*COMM*) letter of credit; **~ di
intenti** letter of intent; **~ di presentazione**
o **raccomandazione** letter of introduction;
~ raccomandata recorded delivery (*BRIT*)
o certified (*US*) letter; **~ di trasporto
aereo** (*COMM*) air waybill.
lette'rale *ag* literal.
letteral'mente *av* literally.
lette'rario, a *ag* literary.
lette'rato, a *ag* well-read, scholarly.
lettera'tura *sf* literature.
let'tiga, ghe *sf* (*portantina*) litter; (*barella*)
stretcher.
let'tino *sm* cot (*BRIT*), crib (*US*).
'letto, a *pp di* **leggere** ♦ *sm* bed; **andare a ~**

to go to bed; ~ **a castello** bunk beds *pl;* ~ **a una piazza/a due piazze** *o* **matrimoniale** single/double bed.

'lettone *ag, smf* Latvian ♦ *sm (LING)* Latvian, Lettish.

Let'tonia *sf:* **la** ~ Latvia.

lettorato *sm (INS)* lectorship, assistantship; *(REL)* lectorate.

let'tore, 'trice *smf* reader; *(INS)* (foreign language) assistant *(BRIT)*, (foreign) teaching assistant *(US)* ♦ *sm:* ~ **ottico (di caratteri)** optical character reader; ~ **CD** CD player.

let'tura *sf* reading.

leuce'mia [leutʃe'mia] *sf* leukaemia.

'leva *sf* lever; *(MIL)* conscription; **far** ~ **su qn** to work on sb; **essere di** ~ to be due for call-up; ~ **del cambio** *(AUT)* gear lever.

le'vante *sm* east; *(vento)* East wind; **il L**~ the Levant.

le'vare *vt (occhi, braccio)* to raise; *(sollevare, togliere: tassa, divieto)* to lift; *(: indumenti)* to take off, remove; *(rimuovere)* to take away; *(: dal di sopra)* to take off; *(: dal di dentro)* to take out; ~**rsi** *vr* to get up; *(sole)* to rise; ~ **le tende** *(fig)* to pack up and leave; ~**rsi il pensiero** to put one's mind at rest; **levati di mezzo** *o* **di lì** *o* **di torno!** get out of my way!

le'vata *sf (di posta)* collection.

leva'taccia, ce [leva'tattʃa] *sf* early rise.

leva'toio, a *ag:* **ponte** ~ drawbridge.

leva'trice [leva'tritʃe] *sf* midwife.

leva'tura *sf* intelligence, mental capacity.

levi'gare *vt* to smooth; *(con carta vetrata)* to sand.

levi'gato, a *ag (superficie)* smooth; *(fig: stile)* polished; *(: viso)* flawless.

levità *sf* lightness.

levri'ere *sm* greyhound.

lezi'one [let'tsjone] *sf* lesson; *(all'università, sgridata)* lecture; **fare** ~ to teach; to lecture.

lezi'oso, a [let'tsjoso] *ag* affected; simpering.

'lezzo ['leddzo] *sm* stench, stink.

lg *abbr (= lira sterlina)* £.

LI *sigla = Livorno.*

li *pron pl (oggetto)* them.

lì *av* there; **di** *o* **da** ~ from there; **per di** ~ that way; **di** ~ **a pochi giorni** a few days later; ~ **per** ~ there and then; at first; **essere** ~ **(~) per fare** to be on the point of doing, be about to do; ~ **dentro** in there; ~ **sotto** under there; ~ **sopra** on there; up there; **tutto** ~ that's all; *vedi anche* **quello**.

libagi'one [liba'dʒone] *sf* libation.

liba'nese *ag, smf* Lebanese *inv.*

Li'bano *sm:* **il** ~ the Lebanon.

'libbra *sf (peso)* pound.

li'beccio [li'bettʃo] *sm* south-west wind.

li'bello *sm* libel.

li'bellula *sf* dragonfly.

libe'rale *ag, smf* liberal.

liberaliz'zare [liberalid'dzare] *vt* to liberalize.

libe'rare *vt (rendere libero: prigioniero)* to release; *(: popolo)* to free, liberate; *(sgombrare: passaggio)* to clear; *(: stanza)* to vacate; *(produrre: energia)* to release; ~**rsi** *vr:* ~**rsi di qc/qn** to get rid of sth/sb.

libera'tore, 'trice *ag* liberating ♦ *smf* liberator.

liberazi'one [liberat'tsjone] *sf (di prigioniero)* release; *(di popolo)* liberation; **che** ~! what a relief!

The **Liberazione** *is a national holiday which falls on April 25th. It commemorates the liberation of Italy in 1945 from German forces and Mussolini's government and marks the end of the war on Italian soil.*

---

li'bercolo *sm (peg)* worthless book.

Li'beria *sf:* **la** ~ Liberia.

liberi'ano, a *ag, smf* Liberian.

libe'rismo *sm (ECON)* laissez-faire.

'libero, a *ag* free; *(strada)* clear; *(non occupato: posto etc)* vacant, free; *(TEL)* not engaged; ~ **di fare qc** free to do sth; ~ **da** free from; **una donna dai** ~**i costumi** a woman of loose morals; **avere via** ~**a** to have a free hand; **dare via** ~**a a qn** to give sb the go-ahead; **via** ~**a!** all clear!; ~ **arbitrio** free will; ~ **professionista** self-employed professional person; ~ **scambio** free trade; ~**a uscita** *(MIL)* leave.

liberoscam'bismo *sm (ECON)* free trade.

libertà *sf inv* freedom; *(tempo disponibile)* free time ♦ *sfpl (licenza)* liberties; **essere in** ~ **provvisoria/vigilata** to be released without bail/be on probation; ~ **di riunione** right to hold meetings.

liber'tario, a *ag* libertarian.

liber'tino, a *ag, smf* libertine.

'liberty ['liberti] *ag inv, sm* art nouveau.

'Libia *sf:* **la** ~ Libya.

'libico, a, ci, che *ag, smf* Libyan.

li'bidine *sf* lust.

libidi'noso, a *ag* lustful, libidinous.

li'bido *sf* libido.

li'braio *sm* bookseller.

li'brario, a *ag* book *cpd.*

li'brarsi *vr* to hover.

libre'ria *sf (bottega)* bookshop; *(stanza)*

library; (*mobile*) bookcase.

li'bretto *sm* booklet; (*taccuino*) notebook; (*MUS*) libretto; ~ **degli assegni** chequebook (*BRIT*), checkbook (*US*); ~ **di circolazione** (*AUT*) logbook; ~ **di deposito** (bank) deposit book; ~ **di risparmio** (savings) bankbook, passbook; ~ **universitario** student's report book.

'**libro** *sm* book; ~ **bianco** (*POL*) white paper; ~ **di cassa** cash book; ~ **di consultazione** reference book; ~ **mastro** ledger; ~ **paga** payroll; ~ **tascabile** paperback; ~ **di testo** textbook; ~**i contabili** (account) books; ~**i sociali** company records.

li'cantropo *sm* werewolf.

lice'ale [litʃe'ale] *ag* secondary school *cpd* (*BRIT*), high school *cpd* (*US*) ♦ *smf* secondary school *o* high school pupil.

li'cenza [li'tʃɛntsa] *sf* (*permesso*) permission, leave; (*di pesca, caccia, circolazione*) permit, licence (*BRIT*), license (*US*); (*MIL*) leave; (*INS*) school-leaving certificate; (*libertà*) liberty; (*sfrenatezza*) licentiousness; **andare in** ~ (*MIL*) to go on leave; **su** ~ **di ...** (*COMM*) under licence from ...; ~ **di esportazione** export licence; ~ **di fabbricazione** manufacturer's licence; ~ **poetica** poetic licence.

licenzia'mento [litʃentsja'mento] *sm* dismissal.

licenzi'are [litʃen'tsjare] *vt* (*impiegato*) to dismiss; (*INS*) to award a certificate to; ~**rsi** *vr* (*impiegato*) to resign, hand in one's notice; (*INS*) to obtain one's school-leaving certificate.

licenziosità [litʃentsjosi'ta] *sf* licentiousness.

licenzi'oso, a [litʃen'tsjoso] *ag* licentious.

li'ceo [li'tʃɛo] *sm* (*INS*) secondary (*BRIT*) *o* high (*US*) school (*for 14 to 19-year-olds*); ~ **classico/scientifico** secondary or high school specializing in classics/scientific subjects.

li'chene [li'kɛne] *sm* (*BOT*) lichen.

'**lido** *sm* beach, shore.

'**Liechtenstein** ['liktənstain] *sm*: **il** ~ Liechtenstein.

li'eto, a *ag* happy, glad; "**molto** ~" (*nelle presentazioni*) "pleased to meet you"; **a** ~ **fine** with a happy ending.

li'eve *ag* light; (*di poco conto*) slight; (*sommesso: voce*) faint, soft.

lievi'tare *vi* (*anche fig*) to rise ♦ *vt* to leaven.

li'evito *sm* yeast; ~ **di birra** brewer's yeast.

'**ligio, a, gi, gie** ['lidʒo] *ag* faithful, loyal.

li'gnaggio [liɲ'naddʒo] *sm* descent, lineage.

'**ligure** *ag* Ligurian; **la Riviera L**~ the Italian Riviera.

Li'kud [li'kud] *sm* Likud.

'**lilla, lillà** *sm inv* lilac.

'**Lima** *sf* Lima.

'**lima** *sf* file; ~ **da unghie** nail file.

limacci'oso, a [limat'tʃoso] *ag* muddy.

li'mare *vt* to file (down); (*fig*) to polish.

'**limbo** *sm* (*REL*) limbo.

li'metta *sf* nail file.

limi'tare *vt* to limit, restrict; (*circoscrivere*) to bound, surround.

limitata'mente *av* to a limited extent; ~ **alle mie possibilità** in so far as I am able.

limi'tato, a *ag* limited, restricted.

limitazi'one [limitat'tsjone] *sf* limitation, restriction.

'**limite** *sm* limit; (*confine*) border, boundary ♦ *ag inv*: **caso** ~ extreme case; **al** ~ if the worst comes to the worst (*BRIT*), if worst comes to worst (*US*); ~ **di velocità** speed limit.

li'mitrofo, a *ag* neighbouring (*BRIT*), neighboring (*US*).

'**limo** *sm* mud, slime; (*GEO*) silt.

limo'nata *sf* lemonade (*BRIT*), (lemon) soda (*US*); (*spremuta*) lemon squash (*BRIT*), lemonade (*US*).

li'mone *sm* (*pianta*) lemon tree; (*frutto*) lemon.

limpi'dezza [limpi'dettsa] *sf* clearness; (*di discorso*) clarity.

'**limpido, a** *ag* (*acqua*) limpid, clear; (*cielo*) clear; (*fig: discorso*) clear, lucid.

'**lince** ['lintʃe] *sf* lynx.

linci'aggio [lin'tʃaddʒo] *sm* lynching.

linci'are [lin'tʃare] *vt* to lynch.

'**lindo, a** *ag* tidy, spick and span; (*biancheria*) clean.

'**linea** *sf* (*gen*) line; (*di mezzi pubblici di trasporto: itinerario*) route; (: *servizio*) service; (*di prodotto: collezione*) collection; (: *stile*) style; **a grandi** ~**e** in outline; **mantenere la** ~ to look after one's figure; **è caduta la** ~ (*TEL*) I (*o* you *etc*) have been cut off; **di** ~: **aereo di** ~ airliner; **nave di** ~ liner; **volo di** ~ scheduled flight; **in** ~ **diretta da** (*TV, RADIO*) coming to you direct from; ~ **aerea** airline; ~ **continua** solid line; ~ **di partenza/d'arrivo** (*SPORT*) starting/finishing line; ~ **punteggiata** dotted line; ~ **di tiro** line of fire.

linea'menti *smpl* features; (*fig*) outlines.

line'are *ag* linear; (*fig*) coherent, logical.

line'etta *sf* (*trattino*) dash; (*d'unione*) hyphen.

'**linfa** *sf* (*BOT*) sap; (*ANAT*) lymph; ~ **vitale**

(*fig*) lifeblood.

lin'gotto *sm* ingot, bar.

'lingua *sf* (*ANAT, CUC*) tongue; (*idioma*) language; **mostrare la** ~ to stick out one's tongue; **di** ~ **italiana** Italian-speaking; ~ **madre** mother tongue; **una** ~ **di terra** a spit of land.

lingu'accia [lin'gwattʃa] *sf* (*fig*) spiteful gossip.

linguacci'uto, a [lingwat'tʃuto] *ag* gossipy.

lingu'aggio [lin'gwaddʒo] *sm* language; ~ **giuridico** legal language; ~ **macchina** (*INFORM*) machine language; ~ **di programmazione** (*INFORM*) programming language.

lingu'etta *sf* (*di strumento*) reed; (*di scarpa, TECN*) tongue; (*di busta*) flap.

lingu'ista, i, e *sm/f* linguist.

lingu'istico, a, ci, che *ag* linguistic ♦ *sf* linguistics *sg*.

lini'mento *sm* liniment.

'lino *sm* (*pianta*) flax; (*tessuto*) linen.

li'noleum *sm inv* linoleum, lino.

liofiliz'zare [liofilid'dzare] *vt* to freeze-dry.

liofiliz'zati [liofilid'dzati] *smpl* freeze-dried foods.

Li'one *sf* Lyons.

liposuzi'one [liposut'tsjone] *sf* liposuction.

'LIPU *sigla f* (= *Lega Italiana Protezione Uccelli*) *society for the protection of birds*.

liqu'ame *sm* liquid sewage.

lique'fare *vt* (*render liquido*) to liquefy; (*fondere*) to melt; ~**rsi** *vr* to liquefy; to melt.

lique'fatto, a *pp di* **liquefare**.

liqui'dare *vt* (*società, beni, persona: uccidere*) to liquidate; (*persona: sbarazzarsene*) to get rid of; (*conto, problema*) to settle; (*COMM: merce*) to sell off, clear.

liquidazi'one [likwidat'tsjone] *sf* (*di società, persona*) liquidation; (*di conto*) settlement; (*di problema*) settling; (*COMM: di merce*) clearance sale; (*AMM*) severance pay (*on retirement, redundancy, or when taking up other employment*).

liquidità *sf* liquidity.

'liquido, a *ag, sm* liquid; **denaro** ~ cash, ready money; ~ **per freni** brake fluid.

liqui'gas ® *sm inv* Calor gas ® (*BRIT*), butane.

liqui'rizia [likwi'rittsja] *sf* liquorice.

li'quore *sm* liqueur.

liquo'roso, a *ag*: **vino** ~ dessert wine.

'lira *sf* (*unità monetaria*) lira; (*MUS*) lyre; ~ **sterlina** pound sterling.

'lirico, a, ci, che *ag* lyric(al); (*MUS*) lyric ♦ *sf* (*poesia*) lyric poetry; (*componimento*

poetico) lyric; (*MUS*) opera; **cantante/teatro** ~ opera singer/house.

li'rismo *sm* lyricism.

Lis'bona *sf* Lisbon.

'lisca, sche *sf* (*di pesce*) fishbone.

lisci'are [liʃ'ʃare] *vt* to smooth; (*fig*) to flatter; ~**rsi i capelli** to straighten one's hair.

'liscio, a, sci, sce ['liʃʃo] *ag* smooth; (*capelli*) straight; (*mobile*) plain; (*bevanda alcolica*) neat; (*fig*) straightforward, simple ♦ *av*: **andare** ~ to go smoothly; **passarla** ~**a** to get away with it.

'liso, a *ag* worn out, threadbare.

'lista *sf* (*striscia*) strip; (*elenco*) list; ~ **elettorale** electoral roll; ~ **delle vivande** menu.

lis'tare *vt*: ~ (**di**) to edge (with), border (with).

lis'tato *sm* (*INFORM*) list, listing.

lis'tino *sm* list; ~ **di borsa** the Stock Exchange list; ~ **dei cambi** (foreign) exchange rate; ~ **dei prezzi** price list.

lita'nia *sf* litany.

'lite *sf* quarrel, argument; (*DIR*) lawsuit.

liti'gare *vi* to quarrel; (*DIR*) to litigate.

li'tigio [li'tidʒo] *sm* quarrel.

litigi'oso, a [liti'dʒoso] *ag* quarrelsome; (*DIR*) litigious.

litogra'fia *sf* (*sistema*) lithography; (*stampa*) lithograph.

lito'grafico, a, ci, che *ag* lithographic.

lito'rale *ag* coastal, coast *cpd* ♦ *sm* coast.

lito'raneo, a *ag* coastal.

'litro *sm* litre (*BRIT*), liter (*US*).

lit'torio, a *ag* (*STORIA*) lictorial; **fascio** ~ fasces *pl*.

Litu'ania *sf*: **la** ~ Lithuania.

litu'ano, a *ag, sm/f, sm* Lithuanian.

litur'gia, 'gie [litur'dʒia] *sf* liturgy.

li'uto *sm* lute.

li'vella *sf* level; ~ **a bolla d'aria** spirit level.

livel'lare *vt* to level, make level; ~**rsi** *vr* to become level; (*fig*) to level out, balance out.

livella'trice [livella'tritʃe] *sf* steamroller.

li'vello *sm* level; (*fig*) level, standard; **ad alto** ~ (*fig*) high-level; **a** ~ **mondiale** world-wide; **a** ~ **di confidenza** confidentially; ~ **di magazzino** stock level; ~ **del mare** sea level; **sul** ~ **del mare** above sea level; ~ **occupazionale** level of employment; ~ **retributivo** salary level.

'livido, a *ag* livid; (*per percosse*) bruised, black and blue; (*cielo*) leaden ♦ *sm* bruise.

li'vore *sm* malice, spite.

Li'vorno *sf* Livorno, Leghorn.

li'vrea *sf* livery.

'lizza ['littsa] *sf* lists *pl*; **essere in ~ per** (*fig*) to compete for; **scendere in ~** (*anche fig*) to enter the lists.

LO *sigla* = Lodi.

lo *det m* (*dav s impura, gn, pn, ps, x, z; dav V l'*) the ♦ *pron* (*dav V l'*) (*oggetto: persona*) him; (: *cosa*) it; **~ sapevo** I knew it; **~ so** I know; **sii buono, anche se lui non ~ è** be good, even if he isn't; *vedi anche* **il**.

lob'bista, i, e *sm/f* lobbyist.

'lobby *sf inv* lobby.

'lobo *sm* lobe; **~ dell'orecchio** ear lobe.

lo'cale *ag* local ♦ *sm* room; (*luogo pubblico*) premises *pl*; **~ notturno** nightclub.

località *sf inv* locality.

localiz'zare [lokalid'dzare] *vt* (*circoscrivere*) to confine, localize; (*accertare*) to locate, place.

lo'canda *sf* inn.

locandi'ere, a *sm/f* innkeeper.

locan'dina *sf* (*TEAT*) poster.

lo'care *vt* (*casa*) to rent out, let; (*macchina*) to hire out (*BRIT*), rent (out).

loca'tario, a *sm/f* tenant.

loca'tivo, a *ag* (*DIR*) rentable.

loca'tore, 'trice *sm/f* landlord/lady.

locazi'one [lokat'tsjone] *sf* (*da parte del locatario*) renting *no pl*; (*da parte del locatore*) renting *no pl*, letting *no pl*; (**contratto di**) **~** lease; (**canone di**) **~** rent; **dare in ~** to rent out, let.

locomo'tiva *sf* locomotive.

locomo'tore *sm* electric locomotive.

locomot'rice [lokomo'tritʃe] *sf* = **locomotore**.

locomozi'one [lokomot'tsjone] *sf* locomotion; **mezzi di ~** vehicles, means of transport.

'loculo *sm* burial recess.

lo'custa *sf* locust.

locuzi'one [lokut'tsjone] *sf* phrase, expression.

lo'dare *vt* to praise.

'lode *sf* praise; (*INS*): **laurearsi con 110 e ~** ≈ to graduate with first-class honours (*BRIT*), ≈ to graduate summa cum laude (*US*).

'loden *sm inv* (*stoffa*) loden; (*cappotto*) loden overcoat.

lo'devole *ag* praiseworthy.

loga'ritmo *sm* logarithm.

'loggia, ge ['lɔddʒa] *sf* (*ARCHIT*) loggia; (*circolo massonico*) lodge.

loggi'one [lod'dʒone] *sm* (*di teatro*): **il ~** the Gods *sg*.

logica'mente [lodʒika'mente] *av* naturally, obviously.

logicità [lodʒitʃi'ta] *sf* logicality.

'logico, a, ci, che ['lɔdʒiko] *ag* logical ♦ *sf* logic.

lo'gistica [lo'dʒistika] *sf* logistics *sg*.

'logo *sm inv* logo.

logora'mento *sm* (*di vestiti etc*) wear.

logo'rante *ag* exhausting.

logo'rare *vt* to wear out; (*sciupare*) to waste; **~rsi** *vr* to wear out; (*fig*) to wear o.s. out.

logo'rio *sm* wear and tear; (*fig*) strain.

'logoro, a *ag* (*stoffa*) worn out, threadbare; (*persona*) worn out.

'Loira *sf*: **la ~** the Loire.

lom'baggine [lom'baddʒine] *sf* lumbago.

Lombar'dia *sf*: **la ~** Lombardy.

lom'bardo, a *ag, sm/f* Lombard.

lom'bare *ag* (*ANAT, MED*) lumbar.

lom'bata *sf* (*taglio di carne*) loin.

'lombo *sm* (*ANAT*) loin.

lom'brico, chi *sm* earthworm.

londi'nese *ag* London *cpd* ♦ *sm/f* Londoner.

'Londra *sf* London.

lon'ganime *ag* forbearing.

longevità [londʒevi'ta] *sf* longevity.

lon'gevo, a [lon'dʒevo] *ag* long-lived.

longi'lineo, a [londʒi'lineo] *ag* long-limbed.

longi'tudine [londʒi'tudine] *sf* longitude.

lontana'mente *av* remotely; **non ci pensavo neppure ~** it didn't even occur to me.

lonta'nanza [lonta'nantsa] *sf* distance; absence.

lon'tano, a *ag* (*distante*) distant, faraway; (*assente*) absent; (*vago: sospetto*) slight, remote; (*tempo: remoto*) far-off, distant; (*parente*) distant, remote ♦ *av* far; **è ~a la casa?** is it far to the house?, is the house far from here?; **è ~ un chilometro** it's a kilometre away *o* a kilometre from here; **più ~** farther; **da** *o* **di ~** from a distance; **~ da** a long way from; **alla ~a** slightly, vaguely.

'lontra *sf* otter.

lo'quace [lo'kwatʃe] *ag* talkative, loquacious; (*fig: gesto etc*) eloquent.

loquacità [lokwatʃi'ta] *sf* talkativeness, loquacity.

'lordo, a *ag* dirty, filthy; (*peso, stipendio*) gross; **~ d'imposta** pre-tax.

Lo'rena *sf* (*GEO*) Lorraine.

'loro *pron pl* (*oggetto, con preposizione*) them; (*complemento di termine*) to them; (*soggetto*) they; (*forma di cortesia: anche:* **L~**) you; to you; **il(la) ~, i(le) ~** *det* their; (*forma di cortesia: anche:* **L~**) your ♦ *pron* theirs; (*forma di cortesia: anche:* **L~**) yours ♦ *sm inv*: **il ~** their (*o* your) money ♦ *sf inv*:

la ~ (*opinione*) their (*o* your) view; i ~
(*famiglia*) their (*o* your) family; (*amici etc*)
their (*o* your) own people; un ~ amico a
friend of theirs; è dalla ~ he's on their
(*o* your) side; ne hanno fatto un'altra
delle ~ they've (*o* you've) done it again;
~ stessi(e) they themselves; you
yourselves.

lo'sanga, ghe *sf* diamond, lozenge.

Lo'sanna *sf* Lausanne.

'losco, a, schi, sche *ag* (*fig*) shady,
suspicious.

'lotta *sf* struggle, fight; (*SPORT*) wrestling;
essere in ~ (con) to be in conflict (with);
fare la ~ (con) to wrestle (with); ~
armata armed struggle; ~ di classe (*POL*)
class struggle; ~ libera (*SPORT*) all-in
wrestling (*BRIT*), freestyle.

lot'tare *vi* to fight, struggle; to wrestle.

lotta'tore, 'trice *sm/f* wrestler.

lotte'ria *sf* lottery; (*di gara ippica*)
sweepstake.

lottiz'zare [lottid'dzare] *vt* to divide into
plots; (*fig*) to share out.

lottizzazi'one [lottiddzat'tsjone] *sf* division
into plots; (*fig*) share-out.

'lotto *sm* (*gioco*) (state) lottery; (*parte*) lot;
(*EDIL*) site; vincere un terno al ~ (*anche
fig*) to hit the jackpot.

lozi'one [lot'tsjone] *sf* lotion.

L.st. *abbr* (= *lire sterline*) £.

LT *sigla* = Latina.

LU *sigla* = Lucca.

lubrifi'cante *sm* lubricant.

lubrifi'care *vt* to lubricate.

lu'cano, a *ag* of (*o* from) Lucania.

luc'chetto [luk'ketto] *sm* padlock.

lucci'care [luttʃi'kare] *vi* (*o* sparkle; (*oro*) to
glitter; (*stella*) to twinkle; (*occhi*) to
glisten.

lucci'chio [luttʃi'kio] *sm* sparkling;
glittering; twinkling; glistening.

lucci'cone [luttʃi'kone] *sm*: avere i ~i agli
occhi to have tears in one's eyes.

'luccio ['luttʃo] *sm* (*ZOOL*) pike.

'lucciola ['luttʃola] *sf* (*ZOOL*) firefly; glow-
worm; (*fam, fig: prostituta*) girl (*o* woman)
on the game.

'luce ['lutʃe] *sf* light; (*finestra*) window; alla
~ di by the light of; fare qc alla ~ del sole
(*fig*) to do sth in the open; dare alla ~
(*bambino*) to give birth to; fare ~ su qc
(*fig*) to shed *o* throw light on sth; ~ del
sole/della luna sun/moonlight.

lu'cente [lu'tʃente] *ag* shining.

lucen'tezza [lutʃen'tettsa] *sf* shine.

lu'cerna [lu'tʃerna] *sf* oil lamp.

lucer'nario [lutʃer'narjo] *sm* skylight.

lu'certola [lu'tʃertola] *sf* lizard.

luci'dare [lutʃi'dare] *vt* to polish; (*ricalcare*)
to trace.

lucida'trice [lutʃida'tritʃe] *sf* floor polisher.

lucidità [lutʃidi'ta] *sf* lucidity.

'lucido, a ['lutʃido] *ag* shining, bright;
(*lucidato*) polished; (*fig*) lucid ♦ *sm* shine,
lustre (*BRIT*), luster (*US*); (*per scarpe etc*)
polish; (*disegno*) tracing.

lu'cignolo [lu'tʃiɲɲolo] *sm* wick.

luc'rare *vt* to make money out of.

lucra'tivo, a *ag* lucrative; a scopo ~ for
gain.

'lucro *sm* profit, gain; a scopo di ~ for gain;
organizzazione senza scopo di ~ non-
profit-making (*BRIT*) *o* non-profit (*US*)
organization.

lu'croso, a *ag* lucrative, profitable.

luculli'ano, a *ag* (*pasto*) sumptuous.

lu'dibrio *sm* mockery *no pl*; (*oggetto di
scherno*) laughing stock.

'lue *sf* syphilis.

'luglio ['luʎʎo] *sm* July; nel mese di ~ in
July, in the month of July; il primo ~ the
first of July; arrivare il 2 ~ to arrive on
the 2nd of July; all'inizio/alla fine di ~ at
the beginning/at the end of July; durante
il mese di ~ during July; a ~ del
prossimo anno in July of next year; ogni
anno a ~ every July; che fai a ~? what
are you doing in July?; ha piovuto molto
a ~ quest'anno July was very wet this
year.

'lugubre *ag* gloomy.

'lui *pron* (*soggetto*) he; (*oggetto: per dare
rilievo, con preposizione*) him ♦ *sm inv*: il mio
~ my beloved; ~ stesso he himself; è ~
it's him.

lu'maca, che *sf* slug; (*chiocciola*) snail.

luma'cone *sm* (*large*) slug; (*fig*) slowcoach
(*BRIT*), slowpoke (*US*).

'lume *sm* light; (*lampada*) lamp; ~ a olio oil
lamp; chiedere ~i a qn (*fig*) to ask sb for
advice; a ~ di naso (*fig*) by rule of thumb.

lumi'cino [lumi'tʃino] *sm* small *o* faint
light; essere (ridotto) al ~ (*fig*) to be at
death's door.

lumi'era *sf* chandelier.

lumi'nare *sm* luminary.

lumi'naria *sf* (*per feste*) illuminations *pl*.

lumine'scente [luminef'ʃente] *ag*
luminescent.

lu'mino *sm* small light; ~ da notte night-
light; ~ per i morti candle for the dead.

luminosità *sf* brightness; (*fig: di sorriso,
volto*) radiance.

lumi'noso, a *ag* (*che emette luce*) luminous;
(*cielo, colore, stanza*) bright; (*sorgente*) of

light, light *cpd*; (*fig: sorriso*) bright, radiant; **insegna** ~**a** neon sign.

lun. *abbr* (= *lunedì*) Mon.

'luna *sf* moon; ~ **nuova/piena** new/full moon; **avere la** ~ to be in a bad mood; ~ **di miele** honeymoon.

'luna park *sm inv* amusement park, funfair.

lu'nare *ag* lunar, moon *cpd*.

lu'nario *sm* almanac; **sbarcare il** ~ to make ends meet.

lu'natico, a, ci, che *ag* whimsical, temperamental.

lunedì *sm inv* Monday; *per fraseologia vedi* **martedì**.

lun'gaggine [lun'gaddʒine] *sf* slowness; ~**i della burocrazia** red tape.

lunga'mente *av* (*a lungo*) for a long time; (*estesamente*) at length.

lun'garno *sm* embankment along the Arno.

lun'ghezza [lun'gettsa] *sf* length; ~ **d'onda** (*FISICA*) wavelength.

'lungi ['lundʒi] *av*: ~ **da** *prep* far from.

lungimi'rante [lundʒimi'rante] *ag* far-sighted.

'lungo, a, ghi, ghe *ag* long; (*lento: persona*) slow; (*diluito: caffè, brodo*) weak, watery, thin ♦ *sm* length ♦ *prep* along; ~ **3 metri** 3 metres long; **avere la barba** ~**a** to be unshaven; **a** ~ for a long time; **a** ~ **andare** in the long run; **di gran** ~**a** (*molto*) by far; **andare in** ~ *o* **per le lunghe** to drag on; **saperla** ~**a** to know what's what; **in** ~ **e in largo** far and wide, all over; ~ **il corso dei secoli** throughout the centuries; **navigazione di** ~ **corso** ocean-going navigation.

lungofi'ume *sm* embankment.

lungo'lago *sm* road round a lake.

lungo'mare *sm* promenade.

lungome'traggio [lungome'traddʒo] *sm* (*CINE*) feature film.

lungo'tevere *sm* embankment along the Tiber.

lu'notto *sm* (*AUT*) rear *o* back window; ~ **termico** heated rear window.

lu'ogo, ghi *sm* place; (*posto: di incidente etc*) scene, site; (*punto, passo di libro*) passage; **in** ~ **di** instead of; **in primo** ~ in the first place; **aver** ~ to take place; **dar** ~ **a** to give rise to; ~ **comune** commonplace; ~ **del delitto** scene of the crime; ~ **geometrico** locus; ~ **di nascita** birthplace; (*AMM*) place of birth; ~ **di pena** prison, penitentiary; ~ **di provenienza** place of origin.

luogote'nente *sm* (*MIL*) lieutenant.

lupacchi'otto [lupak'kjɔtto] *sm* (*ZOOL*) (wolf) cub.

lu'para *sf* sawn-off shotgun.

lu'petto *sm* (*ZOOL*) (wolf) cub; (*negli scouts*) cub scout.

'lupo, a *sm/f* wolf/she-wolf; **cane** ~ alsatian (dog) (*BRIT*), German shepherd (dog); **tempo da** ~**i** filthy weather.

'luppolo *sm* (*BOT*) hop.

'lurido, a *ag* filthy.

luri'dume *sm* filth.

lu'singa, ghe *sf* (*spesso al pl*) flattery *no pl*.

lusin'gare *vt* to flatter.

lusinghi'ero, a [luzin'gjɛro] *ag* flattering, gratifying.

lus'sare *vt* (*MED*) to dislocate.

lussazi'one [lussat'tsjone] *sf* (*MED*) dislocation.

lussembur'ghese [lussembur'gese] *ag* of (*o* from) Luxembourg ♦ *sm/f* native (*o* inhabitant) of Luxembourg.

Lussem'burgo *sm* (*stato*): **il** ~ Luxembourg ♦ *sf* (*città*) Luxembourg.

'lusso *sm* luxury; **di** ~ luxury *cpd*.

lussu'oso, a *ag* luxurious.

lussureggi'are [lussured'dʒare] *vi* to be luxuriant.

lus'suria *sf* lust.

lussuri'oso, a *ag* lascivious, lustful.

lus'trare *vt* to polish, shine.

lustras'carpe *sm/f inv* shoeshine.

lus'trino *sm* sequin.

'lustro, a *ag* shiny; (*pelliccia*) glossy ♦ *sm* shine, gloss; (*fig*) prestige, glory; (*quinquennio*) five-year period.

lute'rano, a *ag*, *sm/f*, Lutheran.

'lutto *sm* mourning; **essere in/portare il** ~ to be in/wear mourning.

M m

M, m ['ɛmme] *sf o m inv* (*lettera*) M, m; **M come Milano** ≈ M for Mary (*BRIT*), M for Mike (*US*).

m. *abbr* = **mese; metro; miglia; monte.**

ma *cong* but; ~ **insomma!** for goodness sake!; ~ **no!** of course not!

'macabro, a *ag* gruesome, macabre.

ma'caco, chi *sm* (*ZOOL*) macaque.

macché [mak'ke] *escl* not at all!, certainly not!

macche'roni [makke'roni] *smpl* macaroni *sg.*

'macchia ['makkja] *sf* stain, spot; (*chiazza di diverso colore*) spot; splash, patch; (*tipo di boscaglia*) scrub; ~ **d'inchiostro** ink stain; **estendersi a** ~ **d'olio** (*fig*) to spread rapidly; **darsi/vivere alla** ~ (*fig*) to go into/live in hiding.

macchi'are [mak'kjare] *vt* (*sporcare*) to stain, mark; ~**rsi** *vr* (*persona*) to get o.s. dirty; (*stoffa*) to stain; to get stained *o* marked; ~**rsi di un delitto** to be guilty of a crime.

macchi'ato, a [mak'kjato] *ag* (*pelle, pelo*) spotted; ~ **di** stained with; **caffè** ~ coffee with a dash of milk.

macchi'etta [mak'kjetta] *sf* (*disegno*) sketch, caricature; (*TEAT*) caricature; (*fig: persona*) character.

'macchina ['makkina] *sf* machine; (*motore, locomotiva*) engine; (*automobile*) car; (*fig: meccanismo*) machinery; **andare in** ~ (*AUT*) to go by car; (*STAMPA*) to go to press; **salire in** ~ to get into the car; **venire in** ~ to come by car; **sala** ~**e** (*NAUT*) engine room; ~ **da cucire** sewing machine; ~ **fotografica** camera; ~ **da presa** cine *o* movie camera; ~ **da scrivere** typewriter; ~ **utensile** machine tool; ~ **a vapore** steam engine.

macchinal'mente [makkinal'mente] *av* mechanically.

macchi'nare [makki'nare] *vt* to plot.

macchi'nario [makki'narjo] *sm* machinery.

macchinazi'one [makkinat'tsjone] *sf* plot, machination.

macchi'netta [makki'netta] *sf* (*fam: caffettiera*) percolator; (*: accendino*) lighter.

macchi'nista, i [makki'nista] *sm* (*di treno*) engine-driver; (*di nave*) engineer; (*TEAT, TV*) stagehand.

macchi'noso, a [makki'noso] *ag* complex, complicated.

mace'donia [matʃe'dɔnja] *sf* fruit salad.

macel'laio [matʃel'lajo] *sm* butcher.

macel'lare [matʃel'lare] *vt* to slaughter, butcher.

macellazi'one [matʃellat'tsjone] *sf* slaughtering, butchering.

macelle'ria [matʃelle'ria] *sf* butcher's (shop).

ma'cello [ma'tʃɛllo] *sm* (*mattatoio*) slaughterhouse, abattoir (*BRIT*); (*fig*) slaughter, massacre; (*: disastro*) shambles *sg.*

mace'rare [matʃe'rare] *vt* to macerate; (*CUC*) to marinate; ~**rsi** *vr* to waste away; (*fig*): ~**rsi in** to be consumed with.

macerazi'one [matʃerat'tsjone] *sf* maceration.

ma'cerie [ma'tʃɛrje] *sfpl* rubble *sg*, debris *sg.*

'macero ['matʃero] *sm* (*operazione*) pulping; (*stabilimento*) pulping mill; **carta da** ~ paper for pulping.

machia'vellico, a, ci, che [makja'vɛlliko] *ag* (*anche fig*) Machiavellian.

ma'cigno [ma'tʃiɲɲo] *sm* (*masso*) rock, boulder.

maci'lento, a [matʃi'lɛnto] *ag* emaciated.

'macina ['matʃina] *sf* (*pietra*) millstone; (*macchina*) grinder.

macinacaffè [matʃinakaf'fɛ] *sm inv* coffee grinder.

macina'pepe [matʃina'pepe] *sm inv* peppermill.

maci'nare [matʃi'nare] *vt* to grind; (*carne*) to mince (*BRIT*), grind (*US*).

maci'nato [matʃi'nato] *sm* meal, flour; (*carne*) minced (*BRIT*) *o* ground (*US*) meat.

maci'nino [matʃi'nino] *sm* (*per caffè*) coffee grinder; (*per pepe*) peppermill; (*scherzoso: macchina*) old banger (*BRIT*), clunker (*US*).

maciul'lare [matʃul'lare] *vt* (*canapa, lino*) to brake; (*fig: braccio etc*) to crush.

'macro ... *prefisso* macro....

macrobi'otico, a *ag* macrobiotic ♦ *sf* macrobiotics *sg.*

macu'lato, a *ag* (*pelo*) spotted.

Ma'dama: palazzo ~ *sm* (*POL*) seat of the Italian Chamber of Senators.

made in Italy [meɪdɪ'nɪtəlɪ] *sm*: **il** ~ Italian exports *pl* (*especially fashion goods*).

Ma'dera *sf* (*GEO*) Madeira ♦ *sm inv* (*vino*) Madeira.

'madido, a *ag*: ~ (**di**) wet *o* moist (with).

Ma'donna *sf* (*REL*) Our Lady.

mador'nale *ag* enormous, huge.

'madre *sf* mother; (*matrice di bolletta*) counterfoil ♦ *ag inv* mother *cpd*; **ragazza** ~ unmarried mother; **scena** ~ (*TEAT*) principal scene; (*fig*) terrible scene.

madre'lingua *sf* mother tongue, native language.

madre'patria *sf* mother country, native land.

madre'perla *sf* mother-of-pearl.

Ma'drid *sf* Madrid.

madri'gale *sm* madrigal.

madri'leno, a *ag* of (*o* from) Madrid ♦ *sm/f* person from Madrid.

ma'drina *sf* godmother.

maestà *sf inv* majesty; **Sua M**~ **la Regina** Her Majesty the Queen.

maestosità *sf* majesty.

maes'toso, a *ag* majestic.

ma'estra *sf vedi* **maestro.**

maes'trale *sm* north-west wind.

maes'tranze [maes'trantse] *sfpl* workforce *sg.*

maes'tria *sf* mastery, skill.

ma'estro, a *sm/f* (*INS: anche*: ~ **di scuola** *o* **elementare**) primary (*BRIT*) *o* grade school (*US*) teacher; (*esperto*) expert ♦ *sm* (*artigiano, fig: guida*) master; (*MUS*) maestro ♦ *ag* (*principale*) main; (*di grande abilità*) masterly, skilful (*BRIT*), skillful (*US*); **un colpo da** ~ (*fig*) a masterly move; **muro** ~ main wall; **strada** ~**a** main road; ~**a d'asilo** nursery teacher; ~ **di ballo** dancing master; ~ **di cerimonie** master of ceremonies; ~ **d'orchestra** conductor, director (*US*); ~ **di scherma** fencing master; ~ **di sci** ski instructor.

'mafia *sf* Mafia.

mafi'oso *sm* member of the Mafia.

'maga, ghe *sf* sorceress.

ma'gagna [ma'gaɲɲa] *sf* defect, flaw, blemish; (*noia, guaio*) problem.

ma'gari *escl* (*esprime desiderio*): ~ **fosse vero!** if only it were true!; **ti piacerebbe andare in Scozia?** — ~! would you like to go to Scotland? — I certainly would! ♦ *av* (*anche*) even; (*forse*) perhaps.

magazzi'naggio [magaddzi'naddʒo] *sm*: (**spese di**) ~ storage charges *pl*, warehousing charges *pl*.

magazzini'ere [magaddzi'njɛre] *sm* warehouseman.

magaz'zino [magad'dzino] *sm* warehouse; **grande** ~ department store; ~ **doganale** bonded warehouse.

'maggio ['maddʒo] *sm* May; *per fraseologia vedi* **luglio.**

maggio'rana [maddʒo'rana] *sf* (*BOT*) (sweet) marjoram.

maggio'ranza [maddʒo'rantsa] *sf* majority; **nella** ~ **dei casi** in most cases.

maggio'rare [maddʒo'rare] *vt* to increase, raise.

maggiorazi'one [maddʒorat'tsjone] *sf* (*COMM*) rise, increase.

maggior'domo [maddʒor'dɔmo] *sm* butler.

maggi'ore [mad'dʒore] *ag* (*comparativo: più grande*) bigger, larger; taller; greater; (*: più vecchio: sorella, fratello*) older, elder; (*: di grado superiore*) senior; (*: più importante, MIL, MUS*) major; (*superlativo*) biggest, largest; tallest; greatest; oldest, eldest ♦ *sm/f* (*di grado*) superior; (*di età*) elder; (*MIL*) major; (*: AER*) squadron leader; **la maggior parte** the majority; **andare per la** ~ (*cantante, attore etc*) to be very popular, be "in".

maggio'renne [maddʒo'rɛnne] *ag* of age ♦ *sm/f* person who has come of age.

maggiori'tario, a [maddʒori'tarjo] *ag* majority *cpd* ♦ (*POL: anche*: **sistema** ~) first-past-the-post system.

maggior'mente [maddʒor'mente] *av* much more; (*con senso superlativo*) most.

ma'gia [ma'dʒia] *sf* magic.

'magico, a, ci, che ['madʒiko] *ag* magic; (*fig*) fascinating, charming, magical.

'magio ['madʒo] *sm* (*REL*): **i re Magi** the Magi, the Three Wise Men.

magis'tero [madʒis'tɛro] *sm* teaching; (*fig: maestria*) skill; (*INS*): **Facoltà di M~** ≈ teachers' training college.

magis'trale [madʒis'trale] *ag* primary (*BRIT*) *o* grade school (*US*) teachers', primary *o* grade school teaching *cpd*; (*abile*) skilful (*BRIT*), skillful (*US*); **istituto** ~ *secondary school for the training of primary teachers*.

magis'trato [madʒis'trato] *sm* magistrate.

magistra'tura [madʒistra'tura] *sf* magistrature; (*magistrati*): **la** ~ the Bench.

'maglia ['maʎʎa] *sf* stitch; (*lavoro ai ferri*) knitting *no pl*; (*tessuto, SPORT*) jersey; (*maglione*) jersey, sweater; (*di catena*) link; (*di rete*) mesh; **avviare/diminuire le** ~**e** to cast on/cast off; **lavorare a** ~, **fare la** ~ to knit; ~ **diritta/rovescia** plain/purl.

magli'aia [maʎ'ʎaja] *sf* knitter.

maglie'ria [maʎʎe'ria] *sf* knitwear; (*negozio*) knitwear shop; **macchina per** ~ knitting machine.

magli'etta [maʎ'ʎetta] *sf* (*canottiera*) vest; (*tipo camicia*) T-shirt.

magli'ficio [maʎʎi'fitʃo] *sm* knitwear factory.

ma'glina [maʎ'ʎina] *sf* (*tessuto*) jersey.

'maglio ['maʎʎo] *sm* mallet; (*macchina*) power hammer.

magli'one [maʎ'ʎone] *sm* jersey, sweater.

'magma *sm* magma; (*fig*) mass.

ma'gnaccia [maɲ'ɲattʃa] *sm inv* (*peg*) pimp.

magnanimità [maɲɲanimi'ta] *sf* magnanimity.

ma'gnanimo, a [maɲ'ɲanimo] *ag* magnanimous.

ma'gnate [maɲ'ɲate] *sm* tycoon, magnate.

ma'gnesia [maɲ'ɲɛzja] *sf* (*CHIM*) magnesia.

ma'gnesio [maɲ'ɲɛzjo] *sm* (*CHIM*) magnesium; **al** ~ (*lampada, flash*) magnesium *cpd*.

ma'gnete [maɲ'ɲɛte] *sm* magnet.

ma'gnetico, a, ci, che [maɲ'ɲɛtiko] *ag* magnetic.

magne'tismo [maɲɲe'tizmo] *sm* magnetism.

magnetiz'zare [maɲɲetid'dzare] *vt* (*FISICA*) to magnetize; (*fig*) to mesmerize.

magne'tofono [maɲɲe'tɔfono] *sm* tape recorder.

magnifica'mente [maɲɲifika'mente] *av* magnificently, extremely well.

magnifi'cenza [maɲɲifi'tʃɛntsa] *sf* magnificence, splendour (*BRIT*), splendor (*US*).

ma'gnifico, a, ci, che [maɲ'ɲifiko] *ag* magnificent, splendid; (*ospite*) generous.

'magno, a ['maɲɲo] *ag*: **aula ~a** main hall.

ma'gnolia [maɲ'ɲɔlja] *sf* magnolia.

'mago, ghi *sm* (*stregone*) magician, wizard; (*illusionista*) magician.

ma'grezza [ma'grettsa] *sf* thinness.

'magro, a *ag* (very) thin, skinny; (*carne*) lean; (*formaggio*) low-fat; (*fig: scarso, misero*) meagre (*BRIT*), meager (*US*), poor; (*: meschino: scusa*) poor, lame; **mangiare di ~** not to eat meat.

'mai *av* (*nessuna volta*) never; (*talvolta*) ever; **non ... ~** never; **~ più** never again; **come ~?** why (*o* how) on earth?; **chi/ dove/quando ~?** whoever/wherever/ whenever?

mai'ale *sm* (*ZOOL*) pig; (*carne*) pork.

mai'olica *sf* majolica.

maio'nese *sf* mayonnaise.

Mai'orca *sf* Majorca.

'mais *sm* maize (*BRIT*), corn (*US*).

mai'uscolo, a *ag* (*lettera*) capital ♦ *sf* capital letter ♦ *sm* capital letters *pl*; (*TIP*) upper case; **scrivere tutto (in) ~** to write everything in capitals *o* in capital letters.

mal *av, sm vedi* **male**.

'mala *sf* (*gergo*) underworld.

malac'corto, a *ag* rash, careless.

mala'fede *sf* bad faith.

malaf'fare: di ~ *ag* (*gente*) shady, dishonest; **donna di ~** prostitute.

mala'gevole [mala'dʒevole] *ag* difficult, hard.

mala'grazia [mala'grattsja] *sf*: **con ~** with bad grace, impolitely.

mala'lingua, *pl* **male'lingue** *sf* gossip (*person*).

mala'mente *av* badly; (*sgarbatamente*) rudely.

malan'dato, a *ag* (*persona: di salute*) in poor health; (*: di condizioni finanziarie*) badly off; (*trascurato*) shabby.

ma'lanimo *sm* ill will, malevolence; **di ~** unwillingly.

ma'lanno *sm* (*disgrazia*) misfortune;

(*malattia*) ailment.

mala'pena *sf*: **a ~** hardly, scarcely.

ma'laria *sf* malaria.

ma'larico, a, ci, che *ag* malarial.

mala'sorte *sf* bad luck.

mala'ticcio, a [mala'tittʃo] *ag* sickly.

ma'lato, a *ag* ill, sick; (*gamba*) bad; (*pianta*) diseased ♦ *sm/f* sick person; (*in ospedale*) patient; **darsi ~** (*sul lavoro etc*) to go sick.

malat'tia *sf* (*infettiva etc*) illness, disease; (*cattiva salute*) illness, sickness; (*di pianta*) disease; **mettersi in ~** to go on sick leave; **fare una ~ di qc** (*fig: disperarsi*) to get in a state about sth.

malaugu'rato, a *ag* ill-fated, unlucky.

malau'gurio *sm* bad *o* ill omen; **uccello del ~** bird of ill omen.

mala'vita *sf* underworld.

malavi'toso, a *sm/f* gangster.

mala'voglia [mala'vɔʎʎa]: **di ~** *av* unwillingly, reluctantly.

Ma'lawi [ma'lavi] *sm*: **il ~** Malawi.

Mala'ysia *sf* Malaysia.

malaysi'ano, a *ag*, *sm/f* Malaysian.

malcapi'tato, a *ag* unlucky, unfortunate ♦ *sm/f* unfortunate person.

mal'concio, a, ci, ce [mal'kontʃo] *ag* in a sorry state.

malcon'tento *sm* discontent.

malcos'tume *sm* immorality.

mal'destro, a *ag* (*inabile*) inexpert, inexperienced; (*goffo*) awkward.

maldi'cente [maldi'tʃɛnte] *ag* slanderous.

maldi'cenza [maldi'tʃɛntsa] *sf* malicious gossip.

maldis'posto, a *ag*: **~ (verso)** ill-disposed (towards).

Mal'dive *sfpl*: **le ~** the Maldives.

'male *av* badly ♦ *sm* (*ciò che è ingiusto, disonesto*) evil; (*danno, svantaggio*) harm; (*sventura*) misfortune; (*dolore fisico, morale*) pain, ache; **sentirsi ~** to feel ill; **aver mal di cuore/fegato** to have a heart/ liver complaint; **aver mal di denti/ d'orecchi/di testa** to have toothache/ earache/a headache; **aver mal di gola** to have a sore throat; **aver ~ ai piedi** to have sore feet; **far ~** (*dolere*) to hurt; **far ~ alla salute** to be bad for one's health; **far del ~ a qn** to hurt *o* harm sb; **parlar ~ di qn** to speak ill of sb; **restare** *o* **rimanere ~** to be sorry; to be disappointed; to be hurt; **trattar ~ qn** to ill-treat sb; **andare a ~** to go off *o* bad; **come va?** — **non c'è ~** how are you? — not bad; **di ~ in peggio** from bad to worse; **per ~ che vada** however badly things go; **non avertene a ~**, **non prendertela a ~** don't take it to heart; **mal**

comune mezzo gaudio (*proverbio*) a trouble shared is a trouble halved; **mal d'auto** carsickness; **mal di mare** seasickness.

male'detto, a *pp di* **maledire** ♦ *ag* cursed, damned; (*fig fam*) damned, blasted.

male'dire *vt* to curse.

maledizi'one [maledit'tsjone] *sf* curse; ~! damn it!

maledu'cato, a *ag* rude, ill-mannered.

maleducazi'one [maledukat'tsjone] *sf* rudeness.

male'fatta *sf* misdeed.

male'ficio [male'fitʃo] *sm* witchcraft.

ma'lefico, a, ci, che *ag* (*aria, cibo*) harmful, bad; (*influsso, azione*) evil.

ma'lese *ag, sm/f* Malay(an) ♦ *sm* (*LING*) Malay.

Ma'lesia *sf* Malaya.

ma'lessere *sm* indisposition, slight illness; (*fig*) uneasiness.

malevo'lenza [malevo'lɛntsa] *sf* malevolence.

ma'levolo, a *ag* malevolent.

malfa'mato, a *ag* notorious.

mal'fatto, a *ag* (*persona*) deformed; (*oggetto*) badly made; (*lavoro*) badly done.

malfat'tore, 'trice *sm/f* wrongdoer.

mal'fermo, a *ag* unsteady, shaky; (*salute*) poor, delicate.

malformazi'one [malformat'tsjone] *sf* malformation.

'malga, ghe *sf* Alpine hut.

malgo'verno *sm* maladministration.

mal'grado *prep* in spite of, despite ♦ *cong* although; **mio** (*o* **tuo** *etc*) ~ against my (*o* your *etc*) will.

ma'lia *sf* spell; (*fig: fascino*) charm.

mali'ardo, a *ag* (*occhi, sorriso*) bewitching ♦ *sf* enchantress.

maligna'mente [maliɲɲa'mente] *av* maliciously.

mali'gnare [maliɲ'ɲare] *vi:* ~ **su** to malign, speak ill of.

malignità [maliɲɲi'ta] *sf inv* (*qualità*) malice, spite; (*osservazione*) spiteful remark; **con** ~ spitefully, maliciously.

ma'ligno, a [ma'liɲɲo] *ag* (*malvagio*) malicious, malignant; (*MED*) malignant.

malinco'nia *sf* melancholy, gloom.

malin'conico, a, ci, che *ag* melancholy.

malincu'ore : a ~ *av* reluctantly, unwillingly.

malinfor'mato, a *ag* misinformed.

malintenzio'nato, a [malintentsjo'nato] *ag* ill-intentioned.

malin'teso, a *ag* misunderstood; (*riguardo, senso del dovere*) mistaken, wrong ♦ *sm* misunderstanding.

ma'lizia [ma'littsja] *sf* (*malignità*) malice; (*furbizia*) cunning; (*espediente*) trick.

malizi'oso, a [malit'tsjoso] *ag* malicious; cunning; (*vivace, birichino*) mischievous.

malle'abile *ag* malleable.

mal'loppo *sm* (*fam: refurtiva*) loot.

malme'nare, in to beat up; (*fig*) to ill-treat.

mal'messo, a *ag* shabby.

malnu'trito, a *ag* undernourished.

malnutrizi'one [malnutrit'tsjone] *sf* malnutrition.

'malo, a *ag:* **in** ~ **modo** badly.

ma'locchio [ma'lɔkkjo] *sm* evil eye.

ma'lora *sf* (*fam*): **andare in** ~ to go to the dogs; **va in** ~! go to hell!

ma'lore *sm* (sudden) illness.

malri'dotto, a *ag* (*abiti, scarpe, persona*) in a sorry state; (*casa, macchina*) dilapidated, in a poor state of repair.

mal'sano, a *ag* unhealthy.

malsi'curo, a *ag* unsafe.

'Malta *sf* Malta.

'malta *sf* (*EDIL*) mortar.

mal'tempo *sm* bad weather.

'malto *sm* malt.

mal'tolto *sm* ill-gotten gains *pl*.

maltratta'mento *sm* ill treatment.

maltrat'tare *vt* to ill-treat.

malu'more *sm* bad mood; (*irritabilità*) bad temper; (*discordia*) ill feeling; **di** ~ in a bad mood.

'malva *sf* (*BOT*) mallow ♦ *ag, sm inv* mauve.

mal'vagio, a, gi, gie [mal'vadʒo] *ag* wicked, evil.

malvagità [malvadʒi'ta] *sf inv* (*qualità*) wickedness; (*azione*) wicked deed.

malva'sia *sf* Italian dessert wine.

malversazi'one [malversat'tsjone] *sf* (*DIR*) embezzlement.

malves'tito, a *ag* badly dressed, ill-clad.

mal'visto, a *ag:* ~ (**da**) disliked (by), unpopular (with).

malvi'vente *sm* criminal.

malvolenti'eri *av* unwillingly, reluctantly.

malvo'lere *vt:* **farsi** ~ **da qn** to make o.s. unpopular with sb ♦ *sm:* **prendere qn a** ~ to take a dislike to sb.

'mamma *sf* mum(my) (*BRIT*), mom (*US*); ~ **mia!** my goodness!

mam'mario, a *ag* (*ANAT*) mammary.

mam'mella *sf* (*ANAT*) breast; (*di vacca, capra etc*) udder.

mam'mifero *sm* mammal.

mam'mismo *sm excessive attachment to one's mother.*

'mammola *sf* (*BOT*) violet.

'manager ['mænidʒə] *sm inv* manager.

manageri'ale [manadʒe'rjale] *ag*
managerial.
ma'nata *sf* (*colpo*) slap; (*quantità*) handful.
'manca *sf* left (hand); **a destra e a** ~ left,
right and centre, on all sides.
manca'mento *sm* (*di forze*) (feeling of)
faintness, weakness.
man'canza [man'kantsa] *sf* lack; (*carenza*)
shortage, scarcity; (*fallo*) fault;
(*imperfezione*) failing, shortcoming; **per** ~
di tempo through lack of time; **in** ~ **di**
meglio for lack of anything better;
sentire la ~ **di qc/qn** to miss sth/sb.
man'care *vi* (*essere insufficiente*) to be
lacking; (*venir meno*) to fail; (*sbagliare*) to
be wrong, make a mistake; (*non esserci*)
to be missing, not to be there; (*essere
lontano*): ~ (**da**) to be away (from) ♦ *vt* to
miss; ~ **di** to lack; ~ **a** (*promessa*) to fail
to keep; **tu mi manchi** I miss you; **mancò
poco che morisse** he very nearly died;
mancano ancora 10 sterline we're still
£10 short; **manca un quarto alle 6** it's a
quarter to 6; **non mancherò** I won't
forget, I'll make sure I do; **ci
mancherebbe altro!** of course I (*o* you
etc) will!; ~ **da casa** to be away from
home; ~ **di rispetto a** *o* **verso qn** to be
lacking in respect towards sb, be
disrespectful towards sb; ~ **di parola** not
to keep one's word, go back on one's
word; **sentirsi** ~ to feel faint.
man'cato, a *ag* (*tentativo*) unsuccessful;
(*artista*) failed.
manche [mãʃ] *sf inv* (*SPORT*) heat.
mancherò *etc* [manke'rɔ] *vb vedi* **mancare**.
man'chevole [man'kevole] *ag* (*insufficiente*)
inadequate, insufficient.
manchevo'lezza [mankevo'lettsa] *sf*
(*scorrettezza*) fault, shortcoming.
'mancia, ce ['mantʃa] *sf* tip; ~ **competente**
reward.
manci'ata [man'tʃata] *sf* handful.
man'cino, a [man'tʃino] *ag* (*braccio*) left;
(*persona*) left-handed; (*fig*) underhand.
'manco *av* (*nemmeno*): ~ **per sogno** *o* **per
idea!** not on your life!
man'dante *sm/f* (*DIR*) principal; (*istigatore*)
instigator.
manda'rancio [manda'rantʃo] *sm*
clementine.
man'dare *vt* to send; (*far funzionare:
macchina*) to drive; (*emettere*) to send out;
(*: grido*) to give, utter, let out; ~ **avanti**
(*persona*) to send ahead; (*fig: famiglia*) to
provide for; (*: ditta*) to look after, run;
(*: pratica*) to attend to; ~ **a chiamare qn** to
send for sb; ~ **giù** to send down; (*anche

fig) to swallow; ~ **in onda** (*RADIO, TV*) to
broadcast; ~ **in rovina** to ruin; ~ **via** to
send away; (*licenziare*) to fire.
manda'rino *sm* mandarin (orange);
(*cinese*) mandarin.
man'data *sf* (*quantità*) lot, batch; (*di chiave*)
turn; **chiudere a doppia** ~ to double-lock.
manda'tario *sm* (*DIR*) representative,
agent.
man'dato *sm* (*incarico*) commission; (*DIR:
provvedimento*) warrant; (*di deputato etc*)
mandate; (*ordine di pagamento*) postal *o*
money order; ~ **d'arresto,** ~ **di cattura**
warrant for arrest; ~ **di comparizione**
summons *sg*; ~ **di perquisizione** search
warrant.
man'dibola *sf* mandible, jaw.
mando'lino *sm* mandolin(e).
'mandorla *sf* almond.
mandor'lato *sm* nut brittle.
'mandorlo *sm* almond tree.
'mandria *sf* herd.
mandri'ano *sm* cowherd, herdsman.
man'drino *sm* (*TECN*) mandrel.
maneg'gevole [maned'dʒevole] *ag* easy to
handle.
maneggi'are [maned'dʒare] *vt* (*creta, cera*)
to mould (*BRIT*), mold (*US*), work, fashion;
(*arnesi, utensili*) to handle; (*: adoperare*) to
use; (*fig: persone, denaro*) to handle, deal
with.
ma'neggio [ma'neddʒo] *sm* moulding
(*BRIT*), molding (*US*); handling; use;
(*intrigo*) plot, scheme; (*per cavalli*) riding
school.
ma'nesco, a, schi, sche *ag* free with
one's fists.
ma'nette *sfpl* handcuffs.
manga'nello *sm* club.
manga'nese *sm* manganese.
mange'reccio, a, ci, ce [mandʒe'rettʃo] *ag*
edible.
mangi'abile [man'dʒabile] *ag* edible,
eatable.
mangia'dischi [mandʒa'diski] *sm inv* record
player.
mangia'nastri [mandʒa'nastri] *sm inv*
cassette-recorder.
mangi'are [man'dʒare] *vt* to eat; (*intaccare*)
to eat into *o* away; (*CARTE, SCACCHI etc*) to
take ♦ *vi* to eat ♦ *sm* eating; (*cibo*) food;
(*cucina*) cooking; **fare da** ~ to do the
cooking; ~**rsi le parole** to mumble; ~**rsi le
unghie** to bite one's nails.
mangia'soldi [mandʒa'sɔldi] *ag inv* (*fam*):
macchinetta ~ one-armed bandit.
mangia'toia [mandʒa'toja] *sf* feeding-
trough.

man'gime |man'dʒime| *sm* fodder.
mangiucchi'are |mandʒuk'kjare| *vt* to nibble.
'mango, ghi *sm* mango.
ma'nia *sf* (*PSIC*) mania; (*fig*) obsession, craze; **avere la ~ di fare qc** to have a habit of doing sth; **~ di persecuzione** persecution complex *o* mania.
mania'cale *ag* (*PSIC*) maniacal; (*fanatico*) fanatical.
ma'niaco, a, ci, che *ag* suffering from a mania; **~ (di)** obsessed (by), crazy (about).
'manica, che *sf* sleeve; (*fig: gruppo*) gang, bunch; (*GEO*): **la M~, il Canale della M~** the (English) Channel; **senza ~che** sleeveless; **essere in ~che di camicia** to be in one's shirt sleeves; **essere di ~ larga/stretta** to be easy-going/strict; **~ a vento** (*AER*) wind sock.
manica'retto *sm* titbit (*BRIT*), tidbit (*US*).
mani'chetta |mani'ketta| *sf* (*TECN*) hose.
mani'chino |mani'kino| *sm* (*di sarto, vetrina*) dummy.
'manico, ci *sm* handle; (*MUS*) neck; **~ di scopa** broomstick.
mani'comio *sm* mental hospital; (*fig*) madhouse.
mani'cotto *sm* muff; (*TECN*) coupling; sleeve.
mani'cure *sm o f inv* manicure ♦ *sf inv* manicurist.
mani'era *sf* way, manner; (*stile*) style, manner; **~e** *sfpl* manners; **in ~ che** so that; **in ~ da** so as to; **alla ~ di** in *o* after the style of; **in una ~ o nell'altra** one way or another; **in tutte le ~e** at all costs; **usare buone ~e con qn** to be polite to sb; **usare le ~e forti** to use strong-arm tactics.
manie'rato, a *ag* affected.
mani'ero *sm* manor.
manifat'tura *sf* (*lavorazione*) manufacture; (*stabilimento*) factory.
manifatturi'ero, a *ag* manufacturing.
manifes'tante *sm/f* demonstrator.
manifes'tare *vt* to show, display; (*esprimere*) to express; (*rivelare*) to reveal, disclose ♦ *vi* to demonstrate; **~rsi** *vr* to show o.s.; **~rsi amico** to prove o.s. (to be) a friend.
manifestazi'one |manifestat'tsjone| *sf* show, display; expression; (*sintomo*) sign, symptom; (*dimostrazione pubblica*) demonstration; (*cerimonia*) event.
manifes'tino *sm* leaflet.
mani'festo, a *ag* obvious, evident ♦ *sm* poster, bill; (*scritto ideologico*) manifesto.

ma'niglia |ma'niʎʎa| *sf* handle; (*sostegno: negli autobus etc*) strap.
Ma'nila *sf* Manila.
manipo'lare *vt* to manipulate; (*alterare: vino*) to adulterate.
manipolazi'one |manipolat'tsjone| *sf* manipulation; adulteration.
ma'nipolo *sm* (*drappello*) handful.

Mani pulite *is a term used to describe the judicial operation which identified, gathered evidence against, and brought to trial a number of politicians and industrialists implicated in bribery and corruption scandals. See also* **Tangentopoli**.

---

manis'calco, chi *sm* blacksmith, farrier (*BRIT*).
'manna *sf* (*REL*) manna.
man'naia *sf* (*del boia*) (executioner's) axe *o* ax (*US*); (*per carni*) cleaver.
man'naro, a *ag*: **lupo ~** werewolf.
'mano, i *sf* hand; (*strato: di vernice etc*) coat; **a ~** by hand; **cucito a ~** hand-sewn; **fatto a ~** handmade; **alla ~** (*persona*) easy-going; **fuori ~** out of the way; **di prima ~** (*notizia*) first-hand; **di seconda ~** second-hand; **man ~** little by little, gradually; **man ~ che** as; **a piene ~i** (*fig*) generously; **avere le ~i bucate** to spend money like water; **aver le ~i in pasta** to be in the know; **avere qc per le ~i** (*progetto, lavoro*) to have sth in hand; **dare una ~ a qn** to lend sb a hand; **dare una ~ di vernice a qc** to give sth a coat of paint; **darsi** *o* **stringersi la ~** to shake hands; **forzare la ~** to go too far; **mettere ~ a qc** to have a hand in sth; **mettere le ~i avanti** (*fig*) to safeguard o.s.; **restare a ~i vuote** to be left empty-handed; **venire alle ~i** to come to blows; **~i in aito! hands up!**
mano'dopera *sf* labour (*BRIT*), labor (*US*).
mano'messo, a *pp di* **manomettere**.
ma'nometro *sm* gauge, manometer.
mano'mettere *vt* (*alterare*) to tamper with; (*aprire indebitamente*) to break open illegally.
manomissi'one *sf* (*di prove etc*) tampering; (*di lettera*) opening.
ma'nopola *sf* (*dell'armatura*) gauntlet; (*guanto*) mitt; (*di impugnatura*) hand-grip; (*pomello*) knob.
manos'critto, a *ag* handwritten ♦ *sm* manuscript.
manova'lanza |manova'lantsa| *sf* unskilled workers *pl*.
mano'vale *sm* labourer (*BRIT*), laborer (*US*).

mano'vella *sf* handle; (*TECN*) crank.
ma'novra *sf* manoeuvre (*BRIT*), maneuver (*US*); (*FERR*) shunting; ~**e di corridoio** palace intrigues.
mano'vrare *vt* (*veicolo*) to manoeuvre (*BRIT*), maneuver (*US*); (*macchina, congegno*) to operate; (*fig: persona*) to manipulate ♦ *vi* to manoeuvre.
manro'vescio [manro'vɛʃʃo] *sm* slap (*with back of hand*).
man'sarda *sf* attic.
mansi'one *sf* task, duty, job.
mansu'eto, a *ag* (*animale*) tame; (*persona*) gentle, docile.
mansue'tudine *sf* tameness; gentleness, docility.
man'tello *sm* cloak; (*fig: di neve etc*) blanket, mantle; (*TECN: involucro*) casing, shell; (*ZOOL*) coat.
mante'nere *vt* to maintain; (*adempiere: promesse*) to keep, abide by; (*provvedere a*) to support, maintain; ~**rsi** *vr*: ~**rsi calmo/giovane** to stay calm/young; ~ **i contatti con qn** to keep in touch with sb.
manteni'mento *sm* maintenance.
mante'nuto, a *sm/f* gigolo/kept woman.
'mantice ['mantitʃe] *sm* bellows *pl*; (*di carrozza, automobile*) hood.
'manto *sm* cloak; ~ **stradale** road surface.
'Mantova *sf* Mantua.
manto'vano, a *ag* of (*o from*) Mantua.
manu'ale *ag* manual ♦ *sm* (*testo*) manual, handbook.
manua'listico, a, ci, che *ag* textbook *cpd*.
manual'mente *av* manually, by hand.
ma'nubrio *sm* handle; (*di bicicletta etc*) handlebars *pl*; (*SPORT*) dumbbell.
manu'fatto *sm* manufactured article; ~**i** *smpl* manufactured goods.
manutenzi'one [manuten'tsjone] *sf* maintenance, upkeep; (*d'impianti*) maintenance, servicing.
'manzo ['mandzo] *sm* (*ZOOL*) steer; (*carne*) beef.
Mao'metto *sm* Mohammed.
'mappa *sf* (*GEO*) map.
mappa'mondo *sm* map of the world; (*globo girevole*) globe.
ma'rasma, i *sm* (*fig*) decay, decline.
mara'tona *sf* marathon.
'marca, che *sf* mark; (*bollo*) stamp; (*COMM: di prodotti*) brand; (*contrassegno, scontrino*) ticket, check; **prodotti di (gran)** ~ high-class products; ~ **da bollo** official stamp.
mar'care *vt* (*munire di contrassegno*) to mark; (*a fuoco*) to brand; (*SPORT: gol*) to score; (*: avversario*) to mark; (*accentuare*) to stress; ~ **visita** (*MIL*) to report sick.

mar'cato, a *ag* (*lineamenti, accento etc*) pronounced.
'Marche ['marke] *sfpl*: **le** ~ the Marches (*region of central Italy*).
marcherò *etc* [marke'rɔ] *vb vedi* **marcare**.
mar'chese, a [mar'keze] *sm/f* marquis *o* marquess/marchioness.
marchi'ano, a [mar'kjano] *ag* (*errore*) glaring, gross.
marchi'are [mar'kjare] *vt* to brand.
marchigi'ano, a [marki'dʒano] *ag* of (*o from*) the Marches.
'marchio ['markjo] *sm* (*di bestiame, COMM, fig*) brand; ~ **depositato** registered trademark; ~ **di fabbrica** trademark.
'marcia, ce ['martʃa] *sf* (*anche MUS, MIL*) march; (*funzionamento*) running; (*il camminare*) walking; (*AUT*) gear; **mettere in** ~ to start; **mettersi in** ~ to get moving; **far** ~ **indietro** (*AUT*) to reverse; (*fig*) to back-pedal; ~ **forzata** forced march; ~ **funebre** funeral march.
marciapi'ede [martʃa'pjɛde] *sm* (*di strada*) pavement (*BRIT*), sidewalk (*US*); (*FERR*) platform.
marci'are [mar'tʃare] *vi* to march; (*andare: treno, macchina*) to go; (*funzionare*) to run, work.
'marcio, a, ci, ce ['martʃo] *ag* (*frutta, legno*) rotten, bad; (*MED*) festering; (*fig*) corrupt, rotten ♦ *sm*: **c'è del** ~ **in questa storia** (*fig*) there's something fishy about this business; **avere torto** ~ to be utterly wrong.
mar'cire [mar'tʃire] *vi* (*andare a male*) to go bad, rot; (*suppurare*) to fester; (*fig*) to rot.
marci'ume [mar'tʃume] *sm* (*parte guasta: di cibi etc*) rotten part, bad part; (*di radice, pianta*) rot; (*fig: corruzione*) rottenness, corruption.
'marco, chi *sm* (*unità monetaria*) mark.
'mare *sm* sea; **di** ~ (*brezza, acqua, uccelli, pesce*) sea *cpd*; **in** ~ at sea; **per** ~ by sea; **sul** ~ (*barca*) on the sea; (*villaggio, località*) by *o* beside the sea; **andare al** ~ (*in vacanza etc*) to go to the seaside; **il mar Caspio** the Caspian Sea; **il mar Morto** the Dead Sea; **il mar Nero** the Black Sea; **il** ~ **del Nord** the North Sea; **il mar Rosso** the Red Sea; **il mar dei Sargassi** the Sargasso Sea; **i** ~**i del Sud** the South Seas.
ma'rea *sf* tide; **alta/bassa** ~ high/low tide.
mareggi'ata [mared'dʒata] *sf* heavy sea.
ma'remma *sf* (*GEO*) maremma, swampy coastal area.
marem'mano, a *ag* (*zona, macchia*) swampy; (*della Maremma*) of (*o from*) the Maremma.

mare'moto *sm* seaquake.
maresci'allo [mareʃ'ʃallo] *sm* (*MIL*) marshal; (: *sottufficiale*) warrant officer.
marez'zato, a [mared'dzato] *ag* (*seta etc*) watered, moiré; (*legno*) veined; (*carta*) marbled.
marga'rina *sf* margarine.
marghe'rita [marge'rita] *sf* (ox-eye) daisy, marguerite; (*di stampante*) daisy wheel.
margheri'tina [margeri'tina] *sf* daisy.
margi'nale [mardʒi'nale] *ag* marginal.
'margine ['mardʒine] *sm* margin; (*di bosco, via*) edge, border; **avere un buon ~ di tempo/denaro** to have plenty of time/money; **~ di guadagno** *o* **di utile** profit margin; **~ di sicurezza** safety margin.
mariju'ana [mæri'wa:nə] *sf* marijuana.
ma'rina *sf* navy; (*costa*) coast; (*quadro*) seascape; **~ mercantile** merchant navy (*BRIT*) *o* marine (*US*); **~ militare (M.M.)** ≈ Royal Navy (RN) (*BRIT*), Navy (*US*).
mari'naio *sm* sailor.
mari'nare *vt* (*CUC*) to marinate; **~ la scuola** to play truant.
mari'naro, a *ag* (*tradizione, popolo*) seafaring; (*CUC*) with seafood; **alla ~a** (*vestito, cappello*) sailor *cpd*; **borgo ~** district where fishing folk live.
mari'nata *sf* marinade.
ma'rino, a *ag* sea *cpd*, marine.
mario'netta *sf* puppet.
mari'tare *vt* to marry; **~rsi** *vr*: **~rsi a** *o* **con qn** to marry sb, get married to sb.
mari'tato, a *ag* married.
ma'rito *sm* husband; **prendere ~** to get married; **ragazza (in età) da ~** girl of marriageable age.
ma'rittimo, a *ag* maritime, sea *cpd*.
mar'maglia [mar'maʎʎa] *sf* mob, riff-raff.
marmel'lata *sf* jam; (*di agrumi*) marmalade.
mar'mitta *sf* (*recipiente*) pot; (*AUT*) silencer; **~ catalitica** catalytic converter.
'marmo *sm* marble.
mar'mocchio [mar'mɔkkjo] *sm* (*fam*) (little) kid.
mar'motta *sf* (*ZOOL*) marmot.
maroc'chino, a [marok'kino] *ag, sm/f* Moroccan.
Ma'rocco *sm*: **il ~** Morocco.
ma'roso *sm* breaker.
'marra *sf* hoe.
Marra'kesh [marra'keʃ] *sf* Marrakesh.
mar'rone *ag inv* brown ♦ *sm* (*BOT*) chestnut.
mar'sala *sm inv* (*vino*) Marsala (wine).
Mar'siglia [mar'siʎʎa] *sf* Marseilles.
mar'sina *sf* tails *pl*, tail coat.
mar'supio *sm* (*ZOOL*) pouch, marsupium.

mart. *abbr* (= *martedì*) Tue(s).
'Marte *sm* (*ASTR, MITOLOGIA*) Mars.
martedì *sm inv* Tuesday; **di** *o* **il ~ on** Tuesdays; **oggi è ~ 3 aprile** (the date) today is Tuesday 3rd April; **~ stavo male** I wasn't well on Tuesday; **il giornale di ~** Tuesday's newspaper; **~ grasso** Shrove Tuesday.
martel'lante *ag* (*fig: dolore*) throbbing.
martel'lare *vt* to hammer ♦ *vi* (*pulsare*) to throb; (: *cuore*) to thump.
martel'letto *sm* (*di pianoforte*) hammer; (*di macchina da scrivere*) typebar; (*di giudice, nelle vendite all'asta*) gavel; (*MED*) percussion hammer.
mar'tello *sm* hammer; (*di uscio*) knocker; **suonare a ~** (*fig: campane*) to sound the tocsin; **~ pneumatico** pneumatic drill.
marti'netto *sm* (*TECN*) jack.
martin'gala *sf* (*di giacca*) half-belt; (*di cavallo*) martingale.
'martire *sm/f* martyr.
mar'tirio *sm* martyrdom; (*fig*) agony, torture.
martori'are *vt* to torment, torture.
mar'xismo *sm* Marxism.
mar'xista, i, e *ag, sm/f* Marxist.
marza'pane [martsa'pane] *sm* marzipan.
marzi'ale [mar'tsjale] *ag* martial.
'marzo ['martso] *sm* March; *per fraseologia vedi* **luglio**.
marzo'lino, a [martso'lino] *ag* March *cpd*.
mascalzo'nata [maskaltso'nata] *sf* dirty trick.
mascal'zone [maskal'tsone] *sm* rascal, scoundrel.
mas'cara *sm inv* mascara.
mascar'pone *sm* soft cream cheese often used in desserts.
ma'scella [maʃ'ʃɛlla] *sf* (*ANAT*) jaw.
'maschera ['maskera] *sf* mask; (*travestimento*) disguise; (: *per un ballo etc*) fancy dress; (*TEAT, CINE*) usher/usherette; (*personaggio del teatro*) stock character; **in ~** (*mascherato*) masked; **ballo in ~** fancy-dress ball; **gettare la ~** (*fig*) to reveal o.s.; **~ antigas/subacquea** gas/diving mask; **~ di bellezza** face pack.
masche'rare [maske'rare] *vt* to mask; (*travestire*) to disguise; to dress up; (*fig: celare*) to hide, conceal; (*MIL*) to camouflage; **~rsi** *vr*: **~rsi da** to disguise o.s. as; to dress up as; (*fig*) to masquerade as.
masche'rina [maske'rina] *sf* (*piccola maschera*) mask; (*di animale*) patch; (*di scarpe*) toe-cap; (*AUT*) radiator grill.
mas'chile [mas'kile] *ag* masculine; (*sesso,*

popolazione) male; *(abiti)* men's; *(per ragazzi: scuola)* boys'.

'maschio, a ['maskjo] *ag* (BIOL) male; *(virile)* manly ♦ *sm* (*anche* ZOOL, TECN) male; *(uomo)* man; *(ragazzo)* boy; *(figlio)* son.

masco'lino, a *ag* masculine.

mas'cotte [mas'kɔt] *sf inv* mascot.

maso'chismo [mazo'kizmo] *sm* masochism.

maso'chista, i, e [mazo'kista] *ag* masochistic ♦ *sm/f* masochist.

'massa *sf* mass; *(di errori etc)*: **una ~ di** heaps, masses of; *(di gente)* mass, multitude; *(ELETTR)* earth; **in ~** *(COMM)* in bulk; *(tutti insieme)* en masse; **adunata in ~** mass meeting; **manifestazione/cultura di ~** mass demonstration/culture; **produrre in ~** to mass-produce; **la ~ (del popolo)** the masses *pl*.

massa'crante *ag* exhausting, gruelling.

massa'crare *vt* to massacre, slaughter.

mas'sacro *sm* massacre, slaughter; *(fig)* mess, disaster.

massaggi'are [massad'dʒare] *vt* to massage.

massaggia'tore, 'trice [massaddʒa'tore] *sm/f* masseur/masseuse.

mas'saggio [mas'saddʒo] *sm* massage.

mas'saia *sf* housewife.

masse'ria *sf* large farm.

masse'rizie [masse'rittsje] *sfpl* (household) furnishings.

massicci'ata [massit'tʃata] *sf* (*di strada, ferrovia*) ballast.

mas'siccio, a, ci, ce [mas'sittʃo] *ag* (*oro, legno*) solid; *(palazzo)* massive; *(corporatura)* stout ♦ *sm* (GEO) massif.

'massima *sf vedi* **massimo**.

massi'male *sm* maximum; *(COMM)* ceiling, limit.

'massimo, a *ag*, *sm* maximum ♦ *sf* (*sentenza, regola*) maxim; (METEOR) maximum temperature; **in linea di ~a** generally speaking; **arrivare entro il tempo ~** to arrive within the time limit; **al ~** at (the) most; **sfruttare qc al ~** to make full use of sth; **arriverò al ~ alle 5** I'll arrive at 5 at the latest; **erano presenti le ~e autorità** all the most important dignitaries were there; **il ~ della pena** (DIR) the maximum penalty.

mas'sivo, a *ag* (*intervento*) en masse; *(emigrazione)* mass; *(emorragia)* massive.

'masso *sm* rock, boulder.

mas'sone *sm* freemason.

massone'ria *sf* freemasonry.

mas'sonico, a, ci, che *ag* masonic.

mas'tello *sm* tub.

masti'care *vt* to chew.

'mastice ['mastitʃe] *sm* mastic; *(per vetri)* putty.

mas'tino *sm* mastiff.

masto'dontico, a, ci, che *ag* gigantic, colossal.

mastur'barsi *vr* to masturbate.

masturbazi'one [masturbat'tsjone] *sf* masturbation.

ma'tassa *sf* skein.

mate'matico, a, ci, che *ag* mathematical ♦ *sm/f* mathematician ♦ *sf* mathematics *sg*.

materas'sino *sm* mat; **~ gonfiabile** air bed.

mate'rasso *sm* mattress; **~ a molle** spring *o* interior-sprung mattress.

ma'teria *sf* (FISICA) matter; *(TECN, COMM)* material, matter *no pl*; *(disciplina)* subject; *(argomento)* subject matter, material; **prima di entrare in ~ ...** before discussing the matter in hand ...; **un esperto in ~ (di musica** *etc)* an expert on the subject (of music *etc*); **sono ignorante in ~** I know nothing about it; **~ cerebrale** cerebral matter; **~ grassa** fat; **~ grigia** (*anche fig*) grey matter; **~e plastiche** plastics; **~e prime** raw materials.

materi'ale *ag* material; *(fig: grossolano)* rough, rude ♦ *sm* material; *(insieme di strumenti etc)* equipment *no pl*, materials *pl*; **~ da costruzione** building materials *pl*.

materia'lista, i, e *ag* materialistic ♦ *sm/f* materialist.

materializ'zarsi [materjalid'dzarsi] *vr* to materialize.

material'mente *av* (*fisicamente*) materially; *(economicamente)* financially.

mater'nità *sf* motherhood, maternity; *(clinica)* maternity hospital; **in (congedo di) ~** on maternity leave.

ma'terno, a *ag* (*amore, cura etc*) maternal, motherly; *(nonno)* maternal; *(lingua, terra)* mother *cpd; vedi anche* **scuola**.

ma'tita *sf* pencil; **~e colorate** crayons; **~ per gli occhi** eyeliner (pencil).

ma'trice [ma'tritʃe] *sf* matrix; *(COMM)* counterfoil; *(fig: origine)* background.

ma'tricola *sf* (*registro*) register; *(numero)* registration number; *(nell'università)* freshman, fresher *(BRIT fam)*.

ma'trigna [ma'triɲɲa] *sf* stepmother.

matrimoni'ale *ag* matrimonial, marriage *cpd*; **camera/letto ~** double room/bed.

matri'monio *sm* marriage, matrimony; *(durata)* marriage, married life; *(cerimonia)* wedding.

ma'trona *sf* (*fig*) matronly woman.

matta'toio *sm* abattoir *(BRIT)*, slaughterhouse.

mat'tina *sf* morning; **la** *o* **alla** *o* **di** ~ in the morning; **di prima** ~, **la** ~ **presto** early in the morning; **dalla** ~ **alla sera** (*continuamente*) from morning to night; (*improvvisamente: cambiare*) overnight.

matti'nata *sf* morning; (*spettacolo*) matinée, afternoon performance; **in** ~ in the course of the morning; **nella** ~ in the morning; **nella tarda** ~ at the end of the morning; **nella tarda** ~ **di sabato** late on Saturday morning.

mattini'ero, a *ag*: **essere** ~ to be an early riser.

mat'tino *sm* morning; **di buon** ~ early in the morning.

'matto, a *ag* mad, crazy; (*fig: falso*) false, imitation; (: *opaco*) matt, dull ♦ *sm/f* madman/woman; **avere una voglia** ~**a di qc** to be dying for sth; **far diventare** ~ **qn** to drive sb mad *o* crazy; **una gabbia di** ~**i** (*fig*) a madhouse.

mat'tone *sm* brick; (*fig*): **questo libro/film è un** ~ this book/film is heavy going.

matto'nella *sf* tile.

mattu'tino, a *ag* morning *cpd*.

matu'rare *vi* (*anche:* ~**rsi**) (*frutta, grano*) to ripen; (*ascesso*) to come to a head; (*fig: persona, idea, ECON*) to mature ♦ *vt* to ripen; to (make) mature; ~ **una decisione** to come to a decision.

maturità *sf* maturity; (*di frutta*) ripeness, maturity; (*INS*) school-leaving examination, ≈ GCE A-levels (*BRIT*).

ma'turo, a *ag* mature; (*frutto*) ripe, mature.

ma'tusa *sm/f inv* (*scherzoso*) old fogey.

Mauri'tania *sf*: **la** ~ Mauritania.

Mau'rizio [mau'rittsjo] *sf*: (**l'isola di**) ~ Mauritius.

mauso'leo *sm* mausoleum.

max. *abbr* (= *massimo*) max.

'maxi... *prefisso* maxi....

---

maxiprocesso *is a criminal trial characterized by the large number of co-accused involved. These are usually members of terrorist or criminal organizations. The trials are often lengthy and many witnesses may be called to give evidence.*

'mazza ['mattsa] *sf* (*bastone*) club; (*martello*) sledge-hammer; (*SPORT: da golf*) club; (: *da baseball, cricket*) bat.

maz'zata [mat'tsata] *sf* (*anche fig*) heavy blow.

maz'zetta [mat'tsetta] *sf* (*di banconote etc*) bundle; (*fig*) rake-off.

'mazzo ['mattso] *sm* (*di fiori, chiavi etc*) bunch; (*di carte da gioco*) pack.

MC *sigla* = Macerata.

m.c.d. *abbr* (= *minimo comune denominatore*) lcd.

m.c.m. *abbr* (= *minimo comune multiplo*) lcm.

ME *sigla* = Messina.

me *pron* me; **sei bravo quanto** ~ you are as clever as I (am) *o* as me.

me'andro *sm* meander.

M.E.C. [mɛk] *abbr m* = **Mercato Comune Europeo.**

'Mecca *sf* (*anche fig*): **La** ~ Mecca.

meccanica'mente *av* mechanically.

mec'canico, a, ci, che *ag* mechanical ♦ *sm* mechanic ♦ *sf* mechanics *sg*; (*attività tecnologica*) mechanical engineering; (*meccanismo*) mechanism; **officina** ~**a** garage.

mecca'nismo *sm* mechanism.

meccaniz'zare [mekkanid'dzare] *vt* to mechanize.

meccanizzazi'one [mekkaniddzat'tsjone] *sf* mechanization.

meccanogra'fia *sf* (*mechanical*) data processing.

meccano'grafico, a, ci, che *ag*: **centro** ~ data processing department.

mece'nate [metʃe'nate] *sm* patron.

mèche [mɛʃ] *sf inv* streak; **farsi le** ~ to have one's hair streaked.

me'daglia [me'daʎʎa] *sf* medal; ~ **d'oro** (*oggetto*) gold medal; (*persona*) gold medallist (*BRIT*) *o* medalist (*US*).

medagli'one [medaʎ'ʎone] *sm* (*ARCHIT*) medallion; (*gioiello*) locket.

me'desimo, a *ag* same; (*in persona*): **io** ~ I myself.

'media *sf vedi* **medio.**

media'mente *av* on average.

medi'ano, a *ag* median; (*valore*) mean ♦ *sm* (*CALCIO*) half-back.

medi'ante *prep* by means of.

medi'are *vt* (*fare da mediatore*) to act as mediator in; (*MAT*) to average.

medi'ato, a *ag* indirect.

media'tore, 'trice *sm/f* mediator; (*COMM*) middle man, agent; **fare da** ~ **fra** to mediate between.

mediazi'one [medjat'tsjone] *sf* mediation; (*COMM: azione, compenso*) brokerage.

medica'mento *sm* medicine, drug.

medi'care *vt* to treat; (*ferita*) to dress.

medi'cato, a *ag* (*garza, shampoo*) medicated.

medicazi'one [medikat'tsjone] *sf* treatment, medication; dressing; **fare una**

~ **a qn** to dress sb's wounds.
medi'cina [medi't∫ina] *sf* medicine; ~
legale forensic medicine.
medici'nale [medit∫i'nale] *ag* medicinal
♦ *sm* drug, medicine.
'**medico, a, ci, che** *ag* medical ♦ *sm* doctor;
~ **di bordo** ship's doctor; ~ **di famiglia**
family doctor; ~ **fiscale** *doctor who*
examines patients signed off sick for a
lengthy period by their private doctor; ~
generico general practitioner, GP.
medie'vale *ag* medieval.
'**medio, a** *ag* average; (*punto, ceto*) middle;
(*altezza, statura*) medium ♦ *sm* (*dito*)
middle finger ♦ *sf* average; (*MAT*) mean;
(*INS: voto*) end-of-term average; ~**e** *sfpl*
vedi **scuola media inferiore**; **licenza** ~**a**
leaving certificate awarded at the end of
3 years of secondary education; **in** ~**a** on
average; **al di sopra/sotto della** ~**a**
above/below average; **viaggiare ad una**
~**a di …** to travel at an average speed of
…; **il M**~ **Oriente** the Middle East.
medi'ocre *ag* (*gen*) mediocre; (*qualità,*
stipendio) poor.
mediocrità *sf* mediocrity; poorness.
medioe'vale *ag* = **medievale**.
Medio'evo *sm* Middle Ages *pl.*
medita'bondo, a *ag* thoughtful.
medi'tare *vt* to ponder over, meditate on;
(*progettare*) to plan, think out ♦ *vi* to
meditate.
medi'tato, a *ag* (*gen*) meditated; (*parole*)
carefully-weighed; (*vendetta*)
premeditated; **ben** ~ (*piano*) well
worked-out, neat.
meditazi'one [meditat'tsjone] *sf*
meditation.
mediter'raneo, a *ag* Mediterranean; **il**
(**mare**) **M**~ the Mediterranean (Sea).
'**medium** *sm/f inv* medium.
me'dusa *sf* (*ZOOL*) jellyfish.
me'gafono *sm* megaphone.
mega'lomane *ag, sm/f* megalomaniac.
me'gera [me'dʒɛra] *sf* (*peg: donna*) shrew.
'**meglio** ['mɛʎʎo] *av, ag inv* better; (*con senso*
superlativo) best ♦ *sm* (*la cosa migliore*): **il** ~
the best (thing); **faresti** ~ **ad andartene**
you had better leave; **alla** ~ as best one
can; **andar di bene in** ~ to get better and
better; **fare del proprio** ~ to do one's best;
per il ~ for the best; **aver la** ~ **su qn** to
get the better of sb.
'**mela** *sf* apple; ~ **cotogna** quince.
mela'grana *sf* pomegranate.
melan'zana [melan'dzana] *sf* aubergine
(*BRIT*), eggplant (*US*).
me'lassa *sf* molasses *sg*, treacle.

me'lenso, a *ag* dull, stupid.
me'lissa *sf* (*BOT*) balm.
mel'lifluo, a *ag* (*peg*) sugary, honeyed.
'**melma** *sf* mud, mire.
'**melo** *sm* apple tree.
melo'dia *sf* melody.
me'lodico, a, ci, che *ag* melodic.
melodi'oso, a *ag* melodious.
melo'dramma, i *sm* melodrama.
me'lone *sm* (musk) melon.
'**membra** *sfpl vedi* **membro**.
mem'brana *sf* membrane.
'**membro** *sm* member; (*pl(f)* ~**a**: *arto*) limb.
memo'rabile *ag* memorable.
memo'randum *sm inv* memorandum.
'**memore** *ag*: ~ **di** (*ricordando*) mindful of;
(*riconoscente*) grateful for.
me'moria *sf* (*anche INFORM*) memory; ~**e**
sfpl (*opera autobiografica*) memoirs; **a** ~
(*imparare, sapere*) by heart; **a** ~ **d'uomo**
within living memory; ~ **di sola lettura**
(*INFORM*) read-only memory; ~ **tampone**
(*INFORM*) buffer.
memori'ale *sm* (*raccolta di memorie*)
memoirs *pl*; (*DIR*) memorial.
memoriz'zare [memorid'dzare] *vt* (*gen*) to
memorize; (*INFORM*) to store.
memorizzazi'one [memoriddzat'tsjone] *sf*
memorization; storage.
'**mena** *sf* scheme.
mena'dito: a ~ *av* perfectly, thoroughly;
sapere qc a ~ to have sth at one's
fingertips.
mena'gramo *sm/f inv* jinx, Jonah.
me'nare *vt* to lead; (*picchiare*) to hit, beat;
(*dare: colpi*) to deal; ~ **la coda** (*cane*) to
wag its tail; ~ **qc per le lunghe** to drag
sth out; ~ **il can per l'aia** (*fig*) to beat
about (*BRIT*) o around (*US*) the bush.
mendi'cante *sm/f* beggar.
mendi'care *vt* to beg for ♦ *vi* to beg.
menefre'ghismo [menefre'gizmo] *sm* (*fam*)
couldn't-care-less attitude.
me'ninge [me'nindʒe] *sf* (*MED*) meninx;
spremersi le ~**i** to rack one's brains.
menin'gite [menin'dʒite] *sf* meningitis.
me'nisco *sm* (*ANAT, MAT, FISICA*) meniscus.

=============== *PAROLA CHIAVE*

'**meno** *av* **1** (*in minore misura*) less; **dovresti**
mangiare ~ you should eat less, you
shouldn't eat so much; **è sempre** ~ **facile**
it's getting less and less easy; **ne voglio**
di ~ I don't want so much
2 (*comparativo*): ~ … **di** not as … as, less
… than; **sono** ~ **alto di te** I'm not as tall as
you (are), I'm less tall than you (are); ~
… **che** not as … as, less … than; ~ **che mai**

less than ever; **è ~ intelligente che ricco** he's more rich than intelligent; **~ fumo più mangio** the less I smoke the more I eat; **~ di quanto pensassi** less than I thought
3 (*superlativo*) least; **il ~ dotato degli studenti** the least gifted of the students; **è quello che compro ~ spesso** it's the one I buy least often
4 (*MAT*) minus; **8 ~ 5** 8 minus 5, 8 take away 5; **sono le 8 ~ un quarto** it's a quarter to 8; **~ 5 gradi** 5 degrees below zero, minus 5 degrees; **mille lire in ~** a thousand lire less; **ha preso 6 ~** (*a scuola*) he scraped a pass; **centomila lire ~ le spese** a hundred thousand lire minus *o* less expenses
5 (*fraseologia*): **quanto ~ poteva telefonare** he could at least have phoned; **non so se accettare o ~** I don't know whether to accept or not; **non essere da ~ di** not to be outdone by; **fare a ~ di qc/ qn** to do without sth/sb; **non potevo fare a ~ di ridere** I couldn't help laughing; **~ male!** thank goodness!; **~ male che sei arrivato** it's a good job that you've come ♦ *ag inv* (*tempo, denaro*) less; (*errori, persone*) fewer; **ha fatto ~ errori di tutti** he made fewer mistakes than anyone, he made the fewest mistakes of all ♦ *sm inv* **1**: **il ~** (*il minimo*) the least; **parlare del più e del ~** to talk about this and that; **era il ~ che ti potesse succedere** it was the least you could have expected **2** (*MAT*) minus ♦ *prep* (*eccetto*) except (for), apart from; **tutti ~ lui** everybody except *o* apart from him; **a ~ che, a ~ di** unless; **a ~ che non piova** unless it rains; **non posso, a ~ di prendere ferie** I can't, unless I take some leave; *vedi anche* **più**.

meno'mare *vt* (*danneggiare*) to maim, disable.
meno'mato, a *ag* (*persona*) disabled ♦ *sm/f* disabled person.
menomazi'one [menomat'tsjone] *sf* disablement.
meno'pausa *sf* menopause.
'mensa *sf* (*locale*) canteen; (: *MIL*) mess; (: *nelle università*) refectory.
men'sile *ag* monthly ♦ *sm* (*periodico*) monthly (magazine); (*stipendio*) monthly salary.
mensil'mente *av* (*ogni mese*) every month; (*una volta al mese*) monthly.
'mensola *sf* bracket; (*ripiano*) shelf; (*ARCHIT*) corbel.

'menta *sf* mint; (*anche*: **~ piperita**) peppermint; (*bibita*) peppermint cordial; (*caramella*) mint, peppermint.
men'tale *ag* mental.
mentalità *sf inv* mentality.
mental'mente *av* mentally.
'mente *sf* mind; **imparare/sapere qc a ~** to learn/know sth by heart; **avere in ~ qc** to have sth in mind; **avere in ~ di fare qc** to intend to do sth; **fare venire in ~ qc a qn** to remind sb of sth; **mettersi in ~ di fare qc** to make up one's mind to do sth; **passare di ~ a qn** to slip sb's mind; **tenere a ~ qc** to bear sth in mind; **a ~ fredda** objectively; **lasciami fare ~ locale** let me think.
mente'catto, a *ag* half-witted ♦ *sm/f* halfwit, imbecile.
men'tire *vi* to lie.
men'tito, a *ag*: **sotto ~e spoglie** under false pretences (*BRIT*) *o* pretenses (*US*).
'mento *sm* chin; **doppio ~** double chin.
men'tolo *sm* menthol.
'mentre *cong* (*temporale*) while; (*avversativo*) whereas ♦ *sm*: **in quel ~** at that very moment.
menù *sm inv* (set) menu; **~ turistico** standard *o* tourists' menu.
menzio'nare [mentsjo'nare] *vt* to mention.
menzi'one [men'tsjone] *sf* mention; **fare ~ di** to mention.
men'zogna [men'tsɔɲɲa] *sf* lie.
menzo'gnero, a [mentsoɲ'ɲɛro] *ag* false, untrue.
mera'viglia [mera'viʎʎa] *sf* amazement, wonder; (*persona, cosa*) marvel, wonder; **a ~** perfectly, wonderfully.
meravigli'are [meraviʎ'ʎare] *vt* to amaze, astonish; **~rsi** *vr*: **~rsi (di)** to marvel (at); (*stupirsi*) to be amazed (at), be astonished (at); **mi meraviglio di te!** I'm surprised at you!; **non c'è da ~rsi** it's not surprising.
meravigli'oso, a [meraviʎ'ʎoso] *ag* wonderful, marvellous (*BRIT*), marvelous (*US*).
merc. *abbr* (= *mercoledì*) Wed.
mer'cante *sm* merchant; **~ d'arte** art dealer; **~ di cavalli** horse dealer.
mercanteggi'are [merkanted'dʒare] *vt* (*onore, voto*) to sell ♦ *vi* to bargain, haggle.
mercan'tile *ag* commercial, mercantile; (*nave, marina*) merchant *cpd* ♦ *sm* (*nave*) merchantman.
mercan'zia [merkan'tsia] *sf* merchandise, goods *pl*.
merca'tino *sm* (*rionale*) local street market; (*ECON*) unofficial stock market.

mer'cato *sm* market; **di** ~ (*economia, prezzo, ricerche*) market *cpd*; **mettere** *o* **lanciare qc sul** ~ to launch sth on the market; **a buon** ~ *ag, av* cheap; ~ **dei cambi** exchange market; **M~ Comune (Europeo)** (European) Common Market; ~ **del lavoro** labour market, job market; ~ **nero** black market; ~ **al rialzo/al ribasso** (*BORSA*) sellers'/buyers' market; ~ **a termine** forward market, futures market.

'merce ['mertʃe] *sf* goods *pl*, merchandise; ~ **deperibile** perishable goods *pl.*

mercé [mer'tʃe] *sf* mercy; **essere alla** ~ **di qn** to be at sb's mercy.

merce'nario, a [mertʃe'narjo] *ag, sm* mercenary.

merce'ria [mertʃe'ria] *sf* (*articoli*) haberdashery (*BRIT*), notions *pl* (*US*); (*bottega*) haberdasher's shop (*BRIT*), notions store (*US*).

mercoledì *sm inv* Wednesday; ~ **delle Ceneri** Ash Wednesday; *per fraseologia vedi* **martedì**.

Mercoledì delle Ceneri, *in the Catholic church, marks the beginning of Lent. On that day, people go to church and are marked on the forehead with ash from the burning of the blessed olive branch. Ash Wednesday is a day of fasting, abstinence and penitence.*

---

mer'curio *sm* mercury.

'merda *sf* (*fam!*) shit (*!*).

me'renda *sf* afternoon snack.

meridi'ano, a *ag* (*di mezzogiorno*) midday *cpd*, noonday ♦ *sm* meridian ♦ *sf* (*orologio*) sundial.

meridio'nale *ag* southern ♦ *smf* southerner.

meridi'one *sm* south.

me'ringa, ghe *sf* (*CUC*) meringue.

meri'tare *vt* to deserve, merit ♦ *vb impers* (*valere la pena*): **merita andare** it is worth going; **non merita neanche parlarne** it's not worth talking about; **per quel che merita** for what it's worth.

meri'tevole *ag* worthy.

'merito *sm* merit; (*valore*) worth; **dare** ~ **a qn di** to give sb credit for; **finire a pari** ~ to finish joint first (*o* second *etc*); to tie; **in** ~ **a** as regards, with regard to; **entrare nel** ~ **di una questione** to go into a matter; **non so niente in** ~ I don't know anything about it.

meritocra'zia [meritokrat'tsia] *sf* meritocracy.

meri'torio, a *ag* praiseworthy.

mer'letto *sm* lace.

'merlo *sm* (*ZOOL*) blackbird; (*ARCHIT*) battlement.

mer'luzzo [mer'luttso] *sm* (*ZOOL*) cod.

'mescere ['meʃʃere] *vt* to pour (out).

meschinità [meskini'ta] *sf* wretchedness; meagreness; meanness; narrow-mindedness.

mes'chino, a [mes'kino] *ag* wretched; (*scarso*) meagre (*BRIT*), meager (*US*); (*persona: gretta*) mean; (: *limitata*) narrow-minded, petty; **fare una figura** ~**a** to cut a poor figure.

'mescita ['meʃʃita] *sf* wine shop.

mesci'uto, a [meʃ'ʃuto] *pp di* **mescere.**

mesco'lanza [mesko'lantsa] *sf* mixture.

mesco'lare *vt* to mix; (*vini, colori*) to blend; (*mettere in disordine*) to mix up, muddle up; (*carte*) to shuffle; ~**rsi** *vr* to mix; to blend; to get mixed up; (*fig*): ~**rsi in** to get mixed up in, meddle in.

'mese *sm* month; **il** ~ **scorso** last month; **il corrente** ~ this month.

'messa *sf* (*REL*) mass; (*il mettere*): ~ **a fuoco** focusing; ~ **in moto** starting; ~ **in piega** (*acconciatura*) set; ~ **a punto** (*TECN*) adjustment; (*AUT*) tuning; (*fig*) clarification; ~ **in scena** = **messinscena.**

messagge'rie [messaddʒe'rie] *sfpl* (*ditta: di distribuzione*) distributors; (: *di trasporto*) freight company.

messag'gero [messad'dʒero] *sm* messenger.

mes'saggio [mes'saddʒo] *sm* message.

mes'sale *sm* (*REL*) missal.

'messe *sf* harvest.

Mes'sia *sm inv* (*REL*): **il** ~ the Messiah.

messi'cano, a *ag, smf* Mexican.

'Messico *sm*: **il** ~ Mexico; **Città del** ~ Mexico City.

messin'scena [messin'ʃena] *sf* (*TEAT*) production.

'messo, a *pp di* **mettere** ♦ *sm* messenger.

mestie'rante *smf* (*peg*) money-grubber; (: *scrittore*) hack.

mesti'ere *sm* (*professione*) job; (: *manuale*) trade; (: *artigianale*) craft; (*fig: abilità nel lavoro*) skill, technique; **di** ~ by *o* to trade; **essere del** ~ to know the tricks of the trade.

mes'tizia [mes'tittsja] *sf* sadness, melancholy.

'mesto, a *ag* sad, melancholy.

'mestola *sf* (*CUC*) ladle; (*EDIL*) trowel.

'mestolo *sm* (*CUC*) ladle.

mestru'ale *ag* menstrual.

mestruazi'one [mestruat'tsjone] *sf*

menstruation; **avere le ~i** to have one's period.

'meta *sf* destination; *(fig)* aim, goal.

metà *sf inv* half; *(punto di mezzo)* middle; **dividere qc a** *o* **per ~** to divide sth in half, halve sth; **fare a ~ (di qc con qn)** to go halves (with sb in sth); **a ~ prezzo** at half price; **a ~ settimana** midweek; **a ~ strada** halfway; **verso la ~ del mese** halfway through the month, towards the middle of the month; **dire le cose a ~** to leave some things unsaid; **fare le cose a ~** to leave things half-done; **la mia dolce ~** *(fam scherzoso)* my better half.

metabo'lismo *sm* metabolism.

meta'done *sm* methadone.

meta'fisica *sf* metaphysics *sg*.

me'tafora *sf* metaphor.

meta'forico, a, ci, che *ag* metaphorical.

me'tallico, a, ci, che *ag* (*di metallo*) metal *cpd*; (*splendore, rumore etc*) metallic.

metalliz'zato, a [metallid'dzato] *ag* (*verniciatura*) metallic.

me'tallo *sm* metal; **di ~** metal *cpd*.

metallur'gia [metallur'dʒia] *sf* metallurgy.

metalmec'canico, a, ci, che *ag* engineering *cpd* ♦ *sm* engineering worker.

meta'morfosi *sf* metamorphosis.

me'tano *sm* methane.

me'teora *sf* meteor.

meteo'rite *sm* meteorite.

meteorolo'gia [meteorolo'dʒia] *sf* meteorology.

meteoro'logico, a, ci, che [meteoro'lɔdʒiko] *ag* meteorological, weather *cpd*.

meteo'rologo, a, ghi, ghe *sm/f* meteorologist.

me'ticcio, a, ci, ce [me'tittʃo] *sm/f* half-caste, half-breed.

meticolosità *sf* meticulousness.

metico'loso, a *ag* meticulous.

me'todico, a, ci, che *ag* methodical.

'metodo *sm* method; (*manuale*) tutor (*BRIT*), manual; **far qc con/senza ~** to do sth methodically/unmethodically.

me'traggio [me'traddʒo] *sm* (*SARTORIA*) length; (*CINE*) footage; **film a lungo ~** feature film; **film a corto ~** short film.

metra'tura *sf* length.

'metrico, a, ci, che *ag* metric; (*POESIA*) metrical ♦ *sf* metrics *sg*.

'metro *sm* metre (*BRIT*), meter (*US*); (*nastro*) tape measure; (*asta*) (metre) rule.

metrò *sm inv* underground (*BRIT*), subway (*US*).

metro'notte *sm inv* night security guard.

me'tropoli *sf* metropolis.

metropoli'tano, a *ag* metropolitan ♦ *sf* underground (*BRIT*), subway (*US*); **~a leggera** metro (*mainly on the surface*).

'mettere *vt* to put; (*abito*) to put on; (: *portare*) to wear; (*installare: telefono*) to put in; (*fig: provocare*): **~ fame/allegria a qn** to make sb hungry/happy; (*supporre*): **mettiamo che ...** let's suppose *o* say that ...; **~rsi** *vr* (*persona*) to put o.s.; (*oggetto*) to go; (*disporsi: faccenda*) to turn out; **~rsi a piangere/ridere** to start crying/laughing, start *o* begin to cry/laugh; **~rsi a sedere** to sit down; **~rsi al lavoro** to set to work; **~rsi a letto** to get into bed; (*per malattia*) to take to one's bed; **~rsi il cappello** to put on one's hat; **~rsi sotto** to get down to things; **~rsi in società** to set up in business; **si sono messi insieme** (*coppia*) they've started going out together (*BRIT*) *o* dating (*US*); **~rci:** **~rci molta cura/molto tempo** to take a lot of care/a lot of time; **mettercela tutta** to do one's best; **ci ho messo 3 ore per venire** it's taken me 3 hours to get here; **~ un annuncio sul giornale** to place an advertisement in the paper; **~ a confronto** to compare; **~ in conto** (*somma etc*) to put on account; **~ in luce** (*problemi, errori*) to stress, highlight; **~ a tacere qn/qc** to keep sb/sth quiet; **~ su casa** to set up house; **~ su un negozio** to start a shop; **~ su peso** to put on weight; **~ via** to put away.

mez'zadro [med'dzadro] *sm* (*AGR*) sharecropper.

mezza'luna [meddza'luna], *pl* **mezze'lune** *sf* half-moon; (*dell'islamismo*) crescent; (*coltello*) (semicircular) chopping knife.

mezza'nino [meddza'nino] *sm* mezzanine (floor).

mez'zano, a [med'dzano] *ag* (*medio*) average, medium; (*figlio*) middle *cpd* ♦ *sm/f* (*intermediario*) go-between; (*ruffiano*) pimp.

mezza'notte [meddza'nɔtte] *sf* midnight.

'mezzo, a ['mɛddzo] *ag* half; **un ~ litro/panino** half a litre/roll ♦ *av* half-; **~ morto** half-dead ♦ *sm* (*metà*) half; (*parte centrale: di strada etc*) middle; (*per raggiungere un fine*) means *sg*; (*veicolo*) vehicle; (*nell'indicare l'ora*): **le nove e ~** half past nine; **mezzogiorno e ~** half past twelve ♦ *sf*: **la ~a** half-past twelve (in the afternoon); **~i** *smpl* (*possibilità economiche*) means; **di ~a età** middle-aged; **aver una ~a idea di fare qc** to have half a mind to do sth; **è stato un ~ scandalo** it almost caused a scandal; **un soprabito di ~a stagione** a spring (*o* autumn) coat; **a ~a**

voce in an undertone; **una volta e ~ più grande** one and a half times bigger; **di ~** middle, in the middle; **andarci di ~** (*patir danno*) to suffer; **esserci di ~** (*ostacolo*) to be in the way; **levarsi** *o* **togliersi di ~** to get out of the way; **mettersi di ~** to interfere; **togliere di ~** (*persona, cosa*) to get rid of; (*fam: uccidere*) to bump off; **non c'è una via di ~** there's no middle course; **in ~ a** in the middle of; **nel bel ~ (di)** right in the middle (of); **per** *o* **a ~ di** by means of; **a ~ corriere** by carrier; **~i di comunicazione di massa** mass media *pl*; **~i pubblici** public transport *sg*; **~i di trasporto** means of transport.

mezzogi'orno [meddzo'dʒorno] *sm* midday, noon; (*GEO*) south; **a ~ at** 12 (o'clock) *o* midday *o* noon; **il ~ d'Italia** southern Italy.

mez'z'ora, mez'zora [med'dzora] *sf* half-hour, half an hour.

MI *sigla* = Milano.

mi *pron* (*dav lo, la, li, le, ne diventa* **me**) (*oggetto*) me; (*complemento di termine*) (to) me; (*riflessivo*) myself ♦ *sm* (*MUS*) E; (*: solfeggiando la scala*) mi; **~ aiuti?** will you help me?; **me ne ha parlato** he spoke to me about it, he told me about it; **~ servo da solo** I'll help myself.

'mia *vedi* **mio**.

miago'lare *vi* to miaow, mew.

Mib *sigla m, ag* (= *indice borsa Milano*) Milan Stock Exchange Index.

'mica *sf* (*CHIM*) mica ♦ *av* (*fam*): **non ... ~** not ... at all; **non sono ~ stanco** I'm not a bit tired; **non sarà ~ partito?** he wouldn't have left, would he?; **~ male** not bad.

'miccia, ce ['mittʃa] *sf* fuse.

micidi'ale [mitʃi'djale] *ag* fatal; (*dannosissimo*) deadly.

'micio, a, ci, cie ['mitʃo] *sm/f* pussy (cat).

microbiolo'gia [mikrobiolo'dʒia] *sf* microbiology.

'microbo *sm* microbe.

microcir'cuito [mikrotʃir'kuito] *sm* microcircuit.

micro'film *sm inv* microfilm.

mi'crofono *sm* microphone.

microinfor'matica *sf* microcomputing.

micro'onda *sf* microwave.

microproces'sore [mikroprotʃes'sore] *sm* microprocessor.

micros'copico, a, ci, che *ag* microscopic.

micros'copio *sm* microscope.

micro'solco, chi *sm* (*solco*) microgroove; (*disco: a 33 giri*) long-playing record, LP; (*: a 45 giri*) extended-play record, EP.

micros'pia *sf* hidden microphone, bug

(*fam*).

mi'dollo, *pl(f)* **~a** *sm* (*ANAT*) marrow; **~ spinale** spinal cord.

'mie, mi'ei *vedi* **mio**.

mi'ele *sm* honey.

mi'etere *vt* (*AGR*) to reap, harvest; (*fig: vite*) to take, claim.

mietitrebbia'trice [mjetitrebbja'tritʃe] *sf* combine harvester.

mieti'trice [mjeti'tritʃe] *sf* (*macchina*) harvester.

mieti'tura *sf* (*raccolto*) harvest; (*lavoro*) harvesting; (*tempo*) harvest-time.

'miglia ['miʎʎa] *sfpl di* **miglio**.

migli'aio [miʎ'ʎajo], *pl(f)* **~a** *sm* thousand; **un ~ (di)** about a thousand; **a ~a** by the thousand, in thousands.

'miglio ['miʎʎo] *sm* (*BOT*) millet; (*pl(f)* **~a**: *unità di misura*) mile; **~ marino** *o* **nautico** nautical mile.

migliora'mento [miʎʎora'mento] *sm* improvement.

miglio'rare [miʎʎo'rare] *vt, vi* to improve.

migli'ore [miʎ'ʎore] *ag* (*comparativo*) better; (*superlativo*) best ♦ *sm*: **il ~** the best (thing) ♦ *sm/f*: **il(la) ~** the best (person); **il miglior vino di questa regione** the best wine in this area; **i ~i auguri** best wishes.

miglio'ria [miʎʎo'ria] *sf* improvement.

'mignolo ['miɲnolo] *sm* (*ANAT*) little finger, pinkie; (*: dito del piede*) little toe.

mi'grare *vi* to migrate.

migrazi'one [migrat'tsjone] *sf* migration.

'mila *pl di* **mille**.

mila'nese *ag* Milanese ♦ *sm/f* person from Milan; **i ~i** the Milanese; **cotoletta alla ~** (*CUC*) Wiener schnitzel; **risotto alla ~** (*CUC*) risotto with saffron.

Mi'lano *sf* Milan.

miliar'dario, a *ag, sm/f* millionaire.

mili'ardo *sm* thousand million (*BRIT*), billion (*US*).

mili'are *ag*: **pietra ~** milestone.

milio'nario, a *ag, sm/f* millionaire.

mili'one *sm* million; **un ~ di lire** a million lire.

mili'tante *ag, sm/f* militant.

mili'tanza [mili'tantsa] *sf* militancy.

mili'tare *vi* (*MIL*) to be a soldier, serve; (*fig: in un partito*) to be a militant ♦ *ag* military ♦ *sm* serviceman; **fare il ~** to do one's military service; **~ di carriera** regular (soldier).

milita'resco, a, schi, sche *ag* (*portamento*) military *cpd*.

'milite *sm* soldier.

mi'lizia [mi'littsja] *sf* (*corpo armato*) militia.

milizi'ano [milit'tsjano] *sm* militiaman.
millanta'tore, 'trice *sm/f* boaster.
millante'ria *sf (qualità)* boastfulness.
'mille *num (pl* **mila)** a *o* one thousand;
diecimila ten thousand.
mille'foglie [mille'fɔʎʎe] *sm inv (CUC)* cream
o vanilla slice.
mil'lennio *sm* millennium.
millepi'edi *sm inv* centipede.
mil'lesimo, a *ag, sm* thousandth.
milli'grammo *sm* milligram(me).
mil'lilitro *sm* millilitre *(BRIT)*, milliliter
(US).
mil'limetro *sm* millimetre *(BRIT)*,
millimeter *(US)*.
'milza ['miltsa] *sf (ANAT)* spleen.
mi'metico, a, ci, che *ag (arte)* mimetic;
tuta ~a *(MIL)* camouflage.
mime'tismo *sm* camouflage.
mimetiz'zare [mimetid'dzare] *vt* to
camouflage; **~rsi** *vr* to camouflage o.s.
'mimica *sf (arte)* mime.
'mimo *sm (attore, componimento)* mime.
mi'mosa *sf* mimosa.
min. *abbr (= minuto, minimo)* min.
'mina *sf (esplosiva)* mine; *(di matita)* lead.
mi'naccia, ce [mi'nattʃa] *sf* threat; **sotto la
~ di** under threat of.
minacci'are [minat'tʃare] *vt* to threaten; **~
qn di morte** to threaten to kill sb; **~ di
fare qc** to threaten to do sth; **minaccia di
piovere** it looks like rain.
minacci'oso, a [minat'tʃoso] *ag*
threatening.
mi'nare *vt (MIL)* to mine; *(fig)* to
undermine.
mina'tore *sm* miner.
mina'torio, a *ag* threatening.
minchi'one, a [min'kjone] *(fam) ag* idiotic
♦ *sm/f* idiot.
mine'rale *ag, sm* mineral.
mineralo'gia [mineralo'dʒia] *sf* mineralogy.
mine'rario, a *ag (delle miniere)* mining; *(dei
minerali)* ore *cpd*.
mi'nestra *sf* soup; **~ in brodo** noodle soup;
~ di verdura vegetable soup.
mines'trone *sm* thick vegetable and pasta
soup.
mingher'lino, a [minger'lino] *ag* thin,
slender.
'mini *ag inv* mini ♦ *sf inv* miniskirt.
minia'tura *sf* miniature.
minielabora'tore *sm* minicomputer.
mini'era *sf* mine; **~ di carbone** coalmine;
(impresa) colliery *(BRIT)*, coalmine.
mini'gonna *sf* miniskirt.
minima'lista, i, e *ag, sm/f* minimalist.
minimiz'zare [minimid'dzare] *vt* to

minimize.
'minimo, a *ag* minimum, least, slightest;
(piccolissimo) very small, slight; *(il più
basso)* lowest, minimum ♦ *sm* minimum;
al ~ at least; **girare al ~** *(AUT)* to idle; **il ~
indispensabile** the bare minimum; **il ~
della pena** the minimum sentence.
minis'tero *sm (POL, REL)* ministry;
(governo) government; *(DIR)*: **Pubblico M~**
State Prosecutor; **~ delle Finanze**
Ministry of Finance, ≈ Treasury.
mi'nistro *sm (POL, REL)* minister; **~ delle
Finanze** Minister of Finance, ≈
Chancellor of the Exchequer *(BRIT)*.
mino'ranza [mino'rantsa] *sf* minority;
essere in ~ to be in the minority.
mino'rato, a *ag* handicapped ♦ *sm/f*
physically *(o* mentally*)* handicapped
person.
minorazi'one [minorat'tsjone] *sf* handicap.
Mi'norca *sf* Minorca.
mi'nore *ag (comparativo)* less; *(: più piccolo)*
smaller; *(: numero)* lower; *(: inferiore)*
lower, inferior; *(: meno importante)*
minor; *(: più giovane)* younger;
(superlativo) least; smallest; lowest; least
important; youngest ♦ *sm/f (minorenne)*
minor, person under age; **in misura ~** to
a lesser extent; **questo è il male ~** this is
the lesser evil.
mino'renne *ag* under age ♦ *sm/f* minor,
person under age.
mino'rile *ag* juvenile; **carcere ~** young
offenders' institution; **delinquenza ~**
juvenile delinquency.
minori'tario, a *ag* minority *cpd*.
mi'nuscolo, a *ag (scrittura, carattere)* small;
(piccolissimo) tiny ♦ *sf* small letter ♦ *sm*
small letters *pl*; *(TIP)* lower case; **scrivere
tutto (in) ~** to write everything in small
letters.
mi'nuta *sf* rough copy, draft.
mi'nuto, a *ag* tiny, minute; *(pioggia)* fine;
(corporatura) delicate, fine; *(lavoro)*
detailed ♦ *sm (unità di misura)* minute; **al ~**
(COMM) retail; **avere i ~i contati** to have
very little time.
mi'nuzia [mi'nuttsja] *sf (cura)*
meticulousness; *(particolare)* detail.
minuziosa'mente [minuttsjosa'mente] *av*
meticulously; in minute detail.
minuzi'oso, a [minut'tsjoso] *ag (persona,
descrizione)* meticulous; *(esame)* minute.
'mio, 'mia, mi'ei, 'mie *det*: **il ~, la mia** *etc*
my ♦ *pronome*: **il ~, la mia** *etc* mine ♦ *sm*:
ho speso del ~ I spent my own money
♦ *sf*: **la mia** *(opinione)* my view; **i miei** my
family; **un ~ amico** a friend of mine; **per**

amor ~ for my sake; **è dalla mia** he is on my side; **anch'io ho avuto le mie** (*disavventure*) I've had my problems too; **ne ho fatta una delle mie!** (*sciocchezze*) I've done it again!; **cerco di stare sulle mie** I try to keep myself to myself.

'miope *ag* short-sighted.

mio'pia *sf* short-sightedness, myopia; (*fig*) short-sightedness.

'mira *sf* (*anche fig*) aim; **avere una buona/cattiva ~** to be a good/bad shot; **prendere la ~** to take aim; **prendere di ~ qn** (*fig*) to pick on sb.

mi'rabile *ag* admirable, wonderful.

mi'racolo *sm* miracle.

miraco'loso, a *ag* miraculous.

mi'raggio [mi'raddʒo] *sm* mirage.

mi'rare *vi*: **~ a** to aim at.

mi'riade *sf* myriad.

mi'rino *sm* (*TECN*) sight; (*FOT*) viewer, viewfinder.

mir'tillo *sm* bilberry (*BRIT*), blueberry (*US*), whortleberry.

'mirto *sm* myrtle.

mi'santropo, a *smf* misanthropist.

mi'scela [miʃ'ʃɛla] *sf* mixture; (*di caffè*) blend.

miscel'lanea [miʃʃel'lanea] *sf* miscellany.

'mischia ['miskja] *sf* scuffle; (*RUGBY*) scrum, scrummage.

mischi'are [mis'kjare] *vt*, **~rsi** *vr* to mix, blend.

misco'noscere [misko'noʃʃere] *vt* (*qualità, coraggio etc*) to fail to appreciate.

miscre'dente *ag* (*REL*) misbelieving; (: *incredulo*) unbelieving ♦ *smf* misbeliever; unbeliever.

mis'cuglio [mis'kuʎʎo] *sm* mixture, hotchpotch, jumble.

'mise *vb vedi* **mettere**.

mise'rabile *ag* (*infelice*) miserable, wretched; (*povero*) poverty-stricken; (*di scarso valore*) miserable.

mi'seria *sf* extreme poverty; (*infelicità*) misery; **~e** *sfpl* (*del mondo etc*) misfortunes, troubles; **costare una ~** to cost next to nothing; **piangere ~** to plead poverty; **ridursi in ~** to be reduced to poverty; **porca ~!** (*fam*) (bloody) hell!

miseri'cordia *sf* mercy, pity.

misericordi'oso, a *ag* merciful.

'misero, a *ag* miserable, wretched; (*povero*) poverty-stricken; (*insufficiente*) miserable.

mis'fatto *sm* misdeed, crime.

'misi *vb vedi* **mettere**.

mi'sogino [mi'zɔdʒino] *sm* misogynist.

'missile *sm* missile; **~ cruise** *o* **di crociera** cruise missile; **~ terra-aria** surface-to-air missile.

missio'nario, a *ag*, *smf* missionary.

missi'one *sf* mission.

misteri'oso, a *ag* mysterious.

mis'tero *sm* mystery; **fare ~ di qc** to make a mystery out of sth; **quanti ~i!** why all the mystery?

'mistico, a, ci, che *ag* mystic(al) ♦ *sm* mystic.

mistifi'care *vt* to fool, bamboozle.

'misto, a *ag* mixed; (*scuola*) mixed, coeducational ♦ *sm* mixture; **un tessuto in ~ lino** a linen mix.

mis'tura *sf* mixture.

mi'sura *sf* measure; (*misurazione, dimensione*) measurement; (*taglia*) size; (*provvedimento*) measure, step; (*moderazione*) moderation; (*MUS*) time; (: *divisione*) bar; (*fig: limite*) bounds *pl*, limit; **in ~ di** in accordance with, according to; **nella ~ in cui** inasmuch as, insofar as; **in giusta ~** moderately; **oltre ~** beyond measure; **su ~** made to measure; **in ugual ~** equally, in the same way; **a ~ d'uomo** on a human scale; **passare la ~** to overstep the mark, go too far; **prendere le ~e a qn** to take sb's measurements, measure sb; **prendere le ~e di qc** to measure sth; **ho preso le mie ~e** I've taken the necessary steps; **non ha il senso della ~** he doesn't know when to stop; **~ di lunghezza/capacità** measure of length/capacity; **~e di sicurezza/prevenzione** safety/precautionary measures.

misu'rare *vt* (*ambiente, stoffa*) to measure; (*terreno*) to survey; (*abito*) to try on; (*pesare*) to weigh; (*fig: parole etc*) to weigh up; (: *spese, cibo*) to limit ♦ *vi* to measure; **~rsi** *vr*: **~rsi con qn** to have a confrontation with sb; (*competere*) to compete with sb.

misu'rato, a *ag* (*ponderato*) measured; (*prudente*) cautious; (*moderato*) moderate.

misurazi'one [mizurat'tsjone] *sf* measuring; (*di terreni*) surveying.

'mite *ag* mild; (*prezzo*) moderate, reasonable.

'mitico, a, ci, che *ag* mythical.

miti'gare *vt* to mitigate, lessen; (*lenire*) to soothe, relieve; **~rsi** *vr* (*odio*) to subside; (*tempo*) to become milder.

'mitilo *sm* mussel.

'mito *sm* myth.

mitolo'gia, 'gie [mitolo'dʒia] *sf* mythology.

mito'logico, a, ci, che [mito'lɔdʒiko] *ag* mythological.

'**mitra** *sf(REL)* mitre (*BRIT*), miter (*US*) ♦ *sm inv* (*arma*) sub-machine gun.

mitragli'are [mitraʎˈʎare] *vt* to machine-gun.

mitraglia'tore, 'trice [mitraʎʎaˈtore] *ag:* **fucile** *m* ~ sub-machine gun ♦ *sf* machine gun.

mitteleuro'peo, a *ag* Central European.

mit'tente *sm/f* sender.

ml *abbr* (= *millilitro*) ml.

MLD *sigla m vedi* **Movimento per la Liberazione della Donna.**

MM *abbr* = *Metropolitana Milanese.*

mm *abbr* (= *millimetro*) mm.

M.M. *abbr vedi* **marina militare.**

MN *sigla* = *Mantova.*

M/N, m/n *abbr* (= *motonave*) MV.

MO *sigla* = *Modena.*

M.O. *abbr* = **Medio Oriente.**

mo' *sm*: **a** ~ **di** *prep* like; **a** ~ **di esempio** by way of example.

'**mobile** *ag* mobile; (*parte di macchina*) moving; (*DIR: bene*) movable, personal ♦ *sm* (*arredamento*) piece of furniture; ~**i** *smpl* furniture *sg.*

mo'bilia *sf* furniture.

mobili'are *ag* (*DIR*) personal, movable.

mo'bilio *sm* = **mobilia.**

mobilità *sf* mobility.

mobili'tare *vt* to mobilize; ~ **l'opinione pubblica** to rouse public opinion.

mobilitazi'one [mobilitatˈtsjone] *sf* mobilization.

mocas'sino *sm* moccasin.

mocci'oso, a [motˈtʃoso] *sm/f* (*bambino piccolo*) little kid; (*peg*) snotty-nosed kid.

'**moccolo** *sm* (*di candela*) candle end; (*fam: bestemmia*) oath; (: *moccio*) snot; **reggere il** ~ to play gooseberry (*BRIT*), act as chaperon(e).

'**moda** *sf* fashion; **alla** ~, **di** ~ fashionable, in fashion.

modalità *sf inv* formality; **seguire attentamente le** ~ **d'uso** to follow the instructions carefully; ~ **giuridiche** legal procedures; ~ **di pagamento** method of payment.

mo'della *sf* model.

model'lare *vt* (*creta*) to model, shape; ~**rsi** *vr*: ~**rsi su** to model o.s. on.

mo'dello *sm* model; (*stampo*) mould (*BRIT*), mold (*US*) ♦ *ag inv* model *cpd.*

'**modem** *sm inv* modem.

mode'nese *ag* of (*o* from) Modena.

mode'rare *vt* to moderate; ~**rsi** *vr* to restrain o.s.; ~ **la velocità** to reduce speed; ~ **i termini** to weigh one's words.

mode'rato, a *ag* moderate.

modera'tore, 'trice *sm/f* moderator.

moderazi'one [moderatˈtsjone] *sf* moderation.

moderniz'zare [modernidˈdzare] *vt* to bring up to date, modernize; ~**rsi** *vr* to get up to date.

mo'derno, a *ag* modern.

mo'destia *sf* modesty; ~ **a parte** ... in all modesty ..., though I say it myself ....

mo'desto, a *ag* modest.

'**modico, a, ci, che** *ag* reasonable, moderate.

mo'difica, che *sf* modification; **subire delle** ~**che** to undergo some modifications.

modifi'cabile *ag* modifiable.

modifi'care *vt* to modify, alter; ~**rsi** *vr* to alter, change.

mo'dista *sf* milliner.

'**modo** *sm* way, manner; (*mezzo*) means, way; (*occasione*) opportunity; (*LING*) mood; (*MUS*) mode; ~**i** *smpl* (*maniere*) manners; **a suo** ~, **a** ~ **suo** in his own way; **ad** *o* **in ogni** ~ anyway; **di** *o* **in** ~ **che** so that; **in** ~ **da** so as to; **in tutti i** ~**i** at all costs; (*comunque sia*) anyway; (*in ogni caso*) in any case; **in un certo qual** ~ in a way, in some ways; **in qualche** ~ somehow or other; **oltre** ~ extremely; ~ **di dire** turn of phrase; **per** ~ **di dire** so to speak; **fare a** ~ **proprio** to do as one likes; **fare le cose a** ~ to do things properly; **una persona a** ~ a well-mannered person; **c'è** ~ **e** ~ **di farlo** there's a right way and a wrong way of doing it.

modu'lare *vt* to modulate ♦ *ag* modular.

modulazi'one [modulatˈtsjone] *sf* modulation; ~ **di frequenza** (**FM**) frequency modulation (FM).

'**modulo** *sm* (*modello*) form; (*ARCHIT, lunare, di comando*) module; ~ **di domanda** application form; ~ **d'iscrizione** enrolment form; ~ **di versamento** deposit slip.

Moga'discio [mogaˈdiʃʃo] *sm* Mogadishu.

'**mogano** *sm* mahogany.

'**mogio, a, gi, gie** [ˈmɔdʒo] *ag* down in the dumps, dejected.

'**moglie** [ˈmoʎʎe] *sf* wife.

mo'hair [mɔˈɛr] *sm* mohair.

mo'ine *sfpl* cajolery *sg*; (*leziosità*) affectation *sg*; **fare le** ~ **a qn** to cajole sb.

'**mola** *sf* millstone; (*utensile abrasivo*) grindstone.

mo'lare *vt* to grind ♦ *ag* (*pietra*) mill *cpd* ♦ *sm* (*dente*) molar.

'**mole** *sf* mass; (*dimensioni*) size; (*edificio grandioso*) massive structure; **una** ~ **di lavoro** masses (*BRIT*) *o* loads of work.

mo'lecola *sf* molecule.
moles'tare *vt* to bother, annoy.
mo'lestia *sf* annoyance, bother; **recar ~ a qn** to bother sb; **~e sessuali** sexual harassment *sg.*
mo'lesto, a *ag* annoying.
moli'sano, a *ag* of (*o* from) Molise.
'molla *sf* spring; **~e** *sfpl* (*per camino*) tongs; **prendere qn con le ~e** to treat sb with kid gloves.
mol'lare *vt* to release, let go; (*NAUT*) to ease; (*fig: ceffone*) to give ♦ *vi* (*cedere*) to give in; **~ gli ormeggi** (*NAUT*) to cast off; **~ la presa** to let go.
'molle *ag* soft; (*muscoli*) flabby; (*fig: debole*) weak, feeble.
molleggi'ato, a [molled'dʒato] *ag* (*letto*) sprung; (*auto*) with good suspension.
mol'leggio [mol'leddʒo] *sm* (*per veicoli*) suspension; (*elasticità*) springiness; (*GINNASTICA*) knee-bends *pl.*
mol'letta *sf* (*per capelli*) hairgrip; (*per panni stesi*) clothes peg (*BRIT*) *o* pin (*US*); **~e** *sfpl* (*per zucchero*) tongs.
mol'lezza [mol'lettsa] *sf* softness; flabbiness; weakness, feebleness; **~e** *sfpl:* **vivere nelle ~e** to live in the lap of luxury.
mol'lica, che *sf* crumb, soft part.
mol'liccio, a, ci, ce [mol'littʃo] *ag* (*terreno, impasto*) soggy; (*frutta*) soft; (*floscio: mano*) limp; (: *muscolo*) flabby.
mol'lusco, schi *sm* mollusc.
'molo *sm* jetty, pier.
mol'teplice [mol'teplitʃe] *ag* (*formato di più elementi*) complex; **~i** *pl* (*svariati: interessi, attività*) numerous, various.
molteplicità [molteplitʃi'ta] *sf* multiplicity.
moltipli'care *vt* to multiply; **~rsi** *vr* to multiply; (*richieste*) to increase in number.
moltiplicazi'one [moltiplikat'tsjone] *sf* multiplication.
molti'tudine *sf* multitude; **una ~ di** a vast number *o* a multitude of.

═══════════════ *PAROLA CHIAVE*

'molto, a *det* (*quantità*) a lot of, much; (*numero*) a lot of, many; **~ pane/carbone** a lot of bread/coal; **~a gente** a lot of people, many people; **~i libri** a lot of books, many books; **non ho ~ tempo** I haven't got much time; **per ~ (tempo)** for a long time; **ci vuole ~ (tempo)?** will it take long?; **arriverà fra non ~** he'll arrive soon; **ne hai per ~?** will you be long?
♦ *av* **1** a lot, (very) much; **viaggia ~** he travels a lot; **non viaggia ~** he doesn't

travel much *o* a lot
2 (*intensivo: con aggettivi, avverbi*) very; (: *con participio passato*) (very) much; **~ buono** very good; **~ migliore, ~ meglio** much *o* a lot better
♦ *pron* much, a lot; **~i, e** *pron pl* many, a lot; **~i pensano che ...** many (people) think that ...; **~e sono rimaste a casa** a lot of them stayed at home; **c'era gente, ma non ~a** there were people there, but not many.

momentanea'mente *av* at the moment, at present.
momen'taneo, a *ag* momentary, fleeting.
mo'mento *sm* moment; **da un ~ all'altro** at any moment; (*all'improvviso*) suddenly; **al ~ di fare** just as I was (*o* you were *o* he was *etc*) doing; **a ~i** (*da un ~ all'altro*) any time *o* moment now; (*quasi*) nearly; **per il ~** for the time being; **dal ~ che** ever since; (*dato che*) since; **~ culminante** climax.
'monaca, che *sf* nun.
'Monaco *sf* Monaco; **~ (di Baviera)** Munich.
'monaco, ci *sm* monk.
mo'narca, chi *sm* monarch.
monar'chia [monar'kia] *sf* monarchy.
mo'narchico, a, ci, che [mo'narkiko] *ag* (*stato, autorità*) monarchic; (*partito, fede*) monarchist ♦ *sm/f* monarchist.
monas'tero *sm* (*di monaci*) monastery; (*di monache*) convent.
mo'nastico, a, ci, che *ag* monastic.
'monco, a, chi, che *ag* maimed; (*fig*) incomplete; **~ d'un braccio** one-armed.
mon'cone *sm* stump.
mon'dana *sf* prostitute.
mondanità *sf* (*frivolezza*) worldliness; **le ~** (*piaceri*) the pleasures of the world.
mon'dano, a *ag* (*anche fig*) worldly; (*dell'alta società*) society *cpd*; fashionable.
mon'dare *vt* (*frutta, patate*) to peel; (*piselli*) to shell; (*pulire*) to clean.
mondez'zaio [mondet'tsajo] *sm* rubbish (*BRIT*) *o* garbage (*US*) dump.
mondi'ale *ag* (*campionato, popolazione*) world *cpd*; (*influenza*) world-wide; **di fama ~** world famous.
'mondo *sm* world; (*grande quantità*): **un ~ di** lots of, a host of; **il gran** *o* **bel ~** high society; **per niente al ~, per nessuna cosa al ~** not for all the world; **da che ~ è** since time *o* the world began; **mandare qn all'altro ~** to kill sb; **mettere/venire al ~** to bring/come into the world; **vivere fuori dal ~** to be out of touch with the

real world; **(sono) cose dell'altro** ~! it's incredible!; **com'è piccolo il** ~! it's a small world!

mone'gasco, a, schi, sche *ag, sm/f* Monegasque.

monelle'ria *sf* prank, naughty trick.

mo'nello, a *sm/f* street urchin; (*ragazzo vivace*) scamp, imp.

mo'neta *sf* coin; (*ECON: valuta*) currency; (*denaro spicciolo*) (small) change; ~ **estera** foreign currency; ~ **legale** legal tender.

mone'tario, a *ag* monetary.

Mon'golia *sf:* **la** ~ Mongolia.

mon'golico, a, ci, che *ag* Mongolian.

mongo'lismo *sm* mongolism, Down's syndrome.

'mongolo, a *ag* Mongolian ♦ *sm/f, sm* Mongol, Mongolian.

mongo'loide *ag, sm/f* (*MED*) mongol.

'monito *sm* warning.

'monitor *sm inv* (*TECN, TV*) monitor.

monito'raggio [monito'raddʒo] *sm* monitoring.

monito'rare *vt* to monitor.

mo'nocolo *sm* (*lente*) monocle, eyeglass.

monoco'lore *ag* (*POL*): **governo** ~ one-party government.

monoga'mia *sf* monogamy.

mo'nogamo, a *ag* monogamous ♦ *sm* monogamist.

monogra'fia *sf* monograph.

mono'gramma, i *sm* monogram.

mono'lingue *ag* monolingual.

monolo'cale *sm* ≈ studio flat.

mo'nologo, ghi *sm* monologue.

mono'pattino *sm* scooter.

mono'polio *sm* monopoly; ~ **di stato** government monopoly.

monopoliz'zare [monopolid'dzare] *vt* to monopolize.

mono'sillabo, a *ag* monosyllabic ♦ *sm* monosyllable.

monoto'nia *sf* monotony.

mo'notono, a *ag* monotonous.

mono'uso *ag inv* disposable.

Mons. *abbr* (= *Monsignore*) Mgr.

monsi'gnore [monsiɲ'ɲore] *sm* (*REL: titolo*) Your (*o* His) Grace.

mon'sone *sm* monsoon.

monta'carichi [monta'kariki] *sm inv* hoist, goods lift.

mon'taggio [mon'taddʒo] *sm* (*TECN*) assembly; (*CINE*) editing.

mon'tagna [mon'taɲɲa] *sf* mountain; (*zona montuosa*): **la** ~ the mountains *pl*; **andare in** ~ to go to the mountains; **aria/strada di** ~ mountain air/road; **casa di** ~ house in the mountains; ~**e russe** roller coaster *sg*,

big dipper *sg* (*BRIT*).

monta'gnoso, a [montaɲ'ɲoso] *ag* mountainous.

monta'naro, a *ag* mountain *cpd* ♦ *sm/f* mountain dweller.

mon'tano, a *ag* mountain *cpd*.

mon'tante *sm* (*di porta*) jamb; (*di finestra*) upright; (*CALCIO: palo*) post; (*PUGILATO*) upper cut; (*COMM*) total amount.

mon'tare *vt* to go (*o* come) up; (*cavallo*) to ride; (*apparecchiatura*) to set up, assemble; (*CUC*) to whip; (*ZOOL*) to cover; (*incastonare*) to mount, set; (*CINE*) to edit; (*FOT*) to mount ♦ *vi* to go (*o* come) up; (*a cavallo*): ~ **bene/male** to ride well/badly; (*aumentare di livello, volume*) to rise; ~**rsi** *vr* to become big-headed; ~ **qc** to exaggerate sth; ~ **qn** *o* **la testa a qn** to turn sb's head; ~**rsi la testa** to become big-headed; ~ **in bicicletta/macchina/treno** to get on a bicycle/ into a car/on a train; ~ **a cavallo** to get on *o* mount a horse; ~ **la guardia** (*MIL*) to mount guard.

monta'tura *sf* assembling *no pl*; (*di occhiali*) frames *pl*; (*di gioiello*) mounting, setting; (*fig*): ~ **pubblicitaria** publicity stunt.

montavi'vande *sm inv* dumbwaiter.

'monte *sm* mountain; **a** ~ upstream; **andare a** ~ (*fig*) to come to nothing; **mandare a** ~ **qc** (*fig*) to upset sth, cause sth to fail; **il M**~ **Bianco** Mont Blanc; **il M**~ **Everest** Mount Everest; ~ **di pietà** pawnshop; ~ **premi** prize.

Monteci'torio [montetʃi'torjo] *sm:* **palazzo** ~ (*POL*) seat of the Italian Chamber of Deputies.

mont'gomery [mənt'gʌməri] *sm inv* duffel coat.

mon'tone *sm* (*ZOOL*) ram; (*anche:* **giacca di** ~) sheepskin (jacket); **carne di** ~ mutton.

montuosità *sf* mountainous nature.

montu'oso, a *ag* mountainous.

monu'mento *sm* monument.

mo'quette [mɔ'kɛt] *sf* fitted carpet.

'mora *sf* (*del rovo*) blackberry; (*del gelso*) mulberry; (*DIR*) delay; (: *somma*) arrears *pl*.

mo'rale *ag* moral ♦ *sf* (*scienza*) ethics *sg*, moral philosophy; (*complesso di norme*) moral standards *pl*, morality; (*condotta*) morals *pl*; (*insegnamento morale*) moral ♦ *sm* morale; **la** ~ **della favola** the moral of the tale; **essere giù di** ~ to be feeling down; **aver il** ~ **alto/a terra** to be in good/low spirits.

mora'lista, i, e *ag* moralistic ♦ *sm/f* moralist.

moralità *sf* morality; (*condotta*) morals *pl*.

moraliz'zare [moralid'dzare] *vt* (*costumi, vita pubblica*) to set moral standards for.

moralizzazi'one [moraliddzat'tsjone] *sf* setting of moral standards.

mora'toria *sf* (*DIR*) moratorium.

morbi'dezza [morbi'dettsa] *sf* softness; smoothness; tenderness.

'morbido, a *ag* soft; (*pelle*) soft, smooth; (*carne*) tender.

mor'billo *sm* (*MED*) measles *sg*.

'morbo *sm* disease.

mor'boso, a *ag* (*fig*) morbid.

'morchia ['mɔrkja] *sf* (*residuo grasso*) dregs *pl*; oily deposit.

mor'dente *sm* (*fig: di satira, critica*) bite; (: *di persona*) drive.

'mordere *vt* to bite; (*addentare*) to bite into; (*corrodere*) to eat into.

mordicchi'are [mordik'kjare] *vt* (*gen*) to chew at.

mo'rente *ag* dying ♦ *smf* dying man/woman.

mor'fina *sf* morphine.

mo'ria *sf* high mortality.

mori'bondo, a *ag* dying, moribund.

morige'rato, a [moridʒe'rato] *ag* of good morals.

mo'rire *vi* to die; (*abitudine, civiltà*) to die out; ~ **di dolore** to die of a broken heart; ~ **di fame** to die of hunger; (*fig*) to be starving; ~ **di freddo** to freeze to death; (*fig*) to be frozen; ~ **d'invidia** to be green with envy; ~ **di noia/paura** to be bored/scared to death; ~ **dalla voglia di fare qc** to be dying to do sth; **fa un caldo da** ~ it's terribly hot.

mormo'rare *vi* to murmur; (*brontolare*) to grumble; **si mormora che ...** it's rumoured (*BRIT*) *o* rumored (*US*) that ...; **la gente mormora** people are talking.

mormo'rio *sm* murmuring; grumbling.

'moro, a *ag* dark(-haired); dark(-complexioned); **i M~i** *smpl* (*STORIA*) the Moors.

mo'roso, a *ag* in arrears ♦ *smf* (*fam: innamorato*) sweetheart.

'morsa *sf* (*TECN*) vice (*BRIT*), vise (*US*); (*fig: stretta*) grip.

mor'setto *sm* (*TECN*) clamp; (*ELETTR*) terminal.

morsi'care *vt* to nibble (at), gnaw (at); (*sog: insetto*) to bite.

'morso, a *pp di* **mordere** ♦ *sm* bite; (*di insetto*) sting; (*parte della briglia*) bit; **dare un** ~ **a qc/qn** to bite sth/sb; **i ~i della fame** pangs of hunger.

morta'della *sf* (*CUC*) mortadella (*type of salted pork meat*).

mor'taio *sm* mortar.

mor'tale *ag, sm* mortal.

mortalità *sf* mortality; (*STATISTICA*) mortality, death rate.

'morte *sf* death; **in punto di** ~ at death's door; **ferito a** ~ (*soldato*) mortally wounded; (*in incidente*) fatally injured; **essere annoiato a** ~ to be bored to death *o* to tears; **avercela a** ~ **con qn** to be bitterly resentful of sb; **avere la** ~ **nel cuore** to have a heavy heart.

mortifi'care *vt* to mortify.

'morto, a *pp di* **morire** ♦ *ag* dead ♦ *smf* dead man/woman; **i** ~**i** the dead; **fare il** ~ (*nell'acqua*) to float on one's back; **un** ~ **di fame** (*fig peg*) a down-and-out; **le campane suonavano a** ~ the funeral bells were tolling; *vedi anche* **Giorno dei Morti**.

mor'torio *sm* (*anche fig*) funeral.

mo'saico, ci *sm* mosaic; **l'ultimo tassello del** ~ (*fig*) the last piece of the puzzle.

'Mosca *sf* Moscow.

'mosca, sche *sf* fly; **rimanere** *o* **restare con un pugno di** ~**sche** (*fig*) to be left empty-handed; **non si sentiva una** ~ (*fig*) you could have heard a pin drop; ~ **cieca** blind-man's buff.

mos'cato *sm* muscatel (wine).

mosce'rino [moʃʃe'rino] *sm* midge, gnat.

mos'chea [mos'kɛa] *sf* mosque.

mos'chetto [mos'ketto] *sm* musket.

moschet'tone [mosket'tone] *sm* (*gancia*) spring clip; (*ALPINISMO*) karabiner, snaplink.

moschi'cida, i, e [moski'tʃida] *ag* fly *cpd*; **carta** ~ flypaper.

'moscio, a, sci, sce ['moʃʃo] *ag* (*fig*) lifeless; **ha la "r"** ~**a** he can't roll his "r"s.

mos'cone *sm* (*ZOOL*) bluebottle; (*barca*) pedalo; (: *a remi*) *kind of pedalo with oars*.

mosco'vita, i, e *ag, smf* Muscovite.

'mossa *sf* movement; (*nel gioco*) move; **darsi una** ~ (*fig*) to give o.s. a shake; **prendere le** ~**e da qc** to come about as the result of sth.

'mossi *etc vb vedi* **muovere**.

'mosso, a *pp di* **muovere** ♦ *ag* (*mare*) rough; (*capelli*) wavy; (*FOT*) blurred; (*ritmo, prosa*) animated.

mos'tarda *sf* mustard.

'mosto *sm* must.

'mostra *sf* exhibition, show; (*ostentazione*) show; **in** ~ on show; **far** ~ **di** (*fingere*) to pretend; **far** ~ **di sé** to show off; **mettersi in** ~ to draw attention to o.s.

mos'trare *vt* to show ♦ *vi*: ~ **di fare** to pretend to do; ~**rsi** *vr* to appear; ~ **la**

lingua to stick out one's tongue.

'**mostro** *sm* monster.

mostru'oso, a *ag* monstrous.

mo'tel *sm inv* motel.

moti'vare *vt* (*causare*) to cause; (*giustificare*) to justify, account for.

motivazi'one [motivat'tsjone] *sf* justification; (*PSIC*) motivation.

mo'tivo *sm* (*causa*) reason, cause; (*movente*) motive; (*letterario*) (central) theme; (*disegno*) motif, design, pattern; (*MUS*) motif; **per quale** ~? why?, for what reason?; **per** ~**i di salute** for health reasons, on health grounds; ~**i personali** personal reasons.

'**moto** *sm* (*anche FISICA*) motion; (*movimento, gesto*) movement; (*esercizio fisico*) exercise; (*sommossa*) rising, revolt; (*commozione*) feeling, impulse ♦ *sf inv* (*motocicletta*) motorbike; **fare del** ~ to take some exercise; **un** ~ **d'impazienza** an impatient gesture; **mettere in** ~ to set in motion; (*AUT*) to start up.

moto'carro *sm* three-wheeler van.

motoci'cletta [motot∫i'kletta] *sf* motorcycle.

motoci'clismo [motot∫i'klizmo] *sm* motorcycling, motorcycle racing.

motoci'clista, i, e [motot∫i'klista] *sm/f* motorcyclist.

moto'nave *sf* motor vessel.

motopesche'reccio [motopeske'rett∫o] *sm* motor fishing vessel.

mo'tore, 'trice *ag* motor; (*TECN*) driving ♦ *sm* engine, motor ♦ *sf* (*TECN*) engine, motor; **albero** ~ drive shaft; **forza** ~**trice** driving force; **a** ~ motor *cpd*, power-driven; ~ **a combustione interna/a reazione** internal combustion/jet engine.

moto'rino *sm* moped; ~ **di avviamento** (*AUT*) starter.

motoriz'zato, a [motorid'dzato] *ag* (*truppe*) motorized; (*persona*) having a car *o* transport.

motorizzazi'one [motoriddzat'tsjone] *sf* (*ufficio tecnico e organizzativo*): (**ufficio della**) ~ road traffic office.

motos'cafo *sm* motorboat.

motove'detta *sf* motor patrol vessel.

mo'trice [mo'trit∫e] *sf vedi* **motore**.

mot'teggio [mot'tedd3o] *sm* banter.

'**motto** *sm* (*battuta scherzosa*) witty remark; (*frase emblematica*) motto, maxim.

mountain bike *sf inv* mountain bike.

mo'vente *sm* motive.

mo'venza [mo'ventsa] *sf* movement.

movimen'tare *vt* to liven up.

movimen'tato, a *ag* (*festa, partita*) lively; (*riunione*) animated; (*strada, vita*) busy; (*soggiorno*) eventful.

movi'mento *sm* movement; (*fig*) activity, hustle and bustle; (*MUS*) tempo, movement; **essere sempre in** ~ to be always on the go; **fare un po' di** ~ (*esercizio fisico*) to take some exercise; **c'è molto** ~ **in città** the town is very busy; ~ **di capitali** movement of capital; **M~ per la Liberazione della Donna (MLD)** Women's Movement.

movi'ola *sf* moviola; **rivedere qc alla** ~ to see an action (*BRIT*) *o* instant (*US*) replay of sth.

Mozam'bico [moddzam'biko] *sm*: **il** ~ Mozambique.

mozi'one [mot'tsjone] *sf* (*POL*) motion; ~ **d'ordine** (*POL*) point of order.

mozzafi'ato [mottsa'fjato] *ag inv* breathtaking.

moz'zare [mot'tsare] *vt* to cut off; (*coda*) to dock; ~ **il fiato** *o* **il respiro a qn** (*fig*) to take sb's breath away.

mozza'rella [mottsa'rella] *sf* mozzarella (*a moist Neapolitan curd cheese*).

mozzi'cone [mottsi'kone] *sm* stub, butt, end; (*anche*: ~ **di sigaretta**) cigarette end.

'**mozzo** *sm* ['mɔddzo] (*MECCANICA*) hub; ['mottso] (*NAUT*) ship's boy; ~ **di stalla** stable boy.

mq *abbr* (= *metro quadro*) sq.m.

MS *sigla* = *Massa Carrara*.

ms. *abbr* (= *manoscritto*) ms.

M.S.I. *sigla m* (= *Movimento Sociale Italiano*) former right-wing political party.

Mti *abbr* = *monti*.

'**mucca, che** *sf* cow.

'**mucchio** ['mukkjo] *sm* pile, heap; (*fig*): **un** ~ **di** lots of, heaps of.

mucil'lagine [mut∫il'ladʒine] *sf* (*BOT*) mucilage (*green slime produced by plants growing in water*).

'**muco, chi** *sm* mucus.

mu'cosa *sf* mucous membrane.

'**muffa** *sf* mould (*BRIT*), mold (*US*), mildew; **fare la** ~ to go mouldy (*BRIT*) *o* moldy (*US*).

mugghi'are [mug'gjare] *vi* (*fig: mare, tuono*) to roar; (*: vento*) to howl.

mug'gire [mud'dʒire] *vi* (*vacca*) to low, moo; (*toro*) to bellow; (*fig*) to roar.

mug'gito [mud'dʒito] *sm* low, moo; bellow; roar.

mu'ghetto [mu'getto] *sm* lily of the valley.

mu'gnaio, a [muɲ'najo] *sm/f* miller.

mugo'lare *vi* (*cane*) to whimper, whine; (*fig: persona*) to moan.

mugu'gnare [muguɲ'ɲare] *vi* (*fam*) to

mutter, mumble.

mulatti'era *sf* mule track.

mu'latto, a *ag, sm/f* mulatto.

muli'nare *vi* to whirl, spin (round and round).

muli'nello *sm (moto vorticoso)* eddy, whirl; *(di canna da pesca)* reel; *(NAUT)* windlass.

mu'lino *sm* mill; ~ **a vento** windmill.

'mulo *sm* mule.

'multa *sf* fine.

mul'tare *vt* to fine.

multico'lore *ag* multicoloured *(BRIT)*, multicolored *(US)*.

multi'forme *ag (paesaggio, attività, interessi)* varied; *(ingegno)* versatile.

multimedi'ale *ag* multimedia *cpd*.

multinazio'nale [multinattsjo'nale] *ag, sf* multinational; **forza ~ di pace** multinational peace-keeping force.

'multiplo, a *ag, sm* multiple.

multiu'tenza [multiu'tɛntsa] *sf (INFORM)* time sharing.

'mummia *sf* mummy.

'mungere ['mundʒere] *vt (anche fig)* to milk.

mungi'tura [mundʒi'tura] *sf* milking.

munici'pale [munitʃi'pale] *ag (gen)* municipal; **palazzo ~** town hall; **autorità ~i** local authorities *(BRIT)*, local government *sg*.

muni'cipio [muni'tʃipjo] *sm* town council; *(edificio)* town hall; **sposarsi in ~** ≈ to get married in a registry office *(BRIT)*, have a civil marriage.

munifi'cenza [munifi'tʃɛntsa] *sf* munificence.

mu'nifico, a, ci, che *ag* munificent, generous.

mu'nire *vt*: ~ **qc/qn di** to equip sth/sb with; ~ **di firma** *(documento)* to sign.

munizi'oni [munit'tsjoni] *sfpl (MIL)* ammunition *sg*.

'munsi *etc vb vedi* **mungere**.

'munto, a *pp di* **mungere**.

mu'oio *etc vb vedi* **morire**.

mu'overe *vt* to move; *(ruota, macchina)* to drive; *(sollevare: questione, obiezione)* to raise, bring up; *(: accusa)* to make, bring forward;* ~**rsi** *vr* to move; ~ **causa a qn** *(DIR)* to take legal action against sb; ~ **compassione** to move to pity; ~ **guerra a** *o* **contro qn** to wage war against sb; ~ **mari e monti** to move heaven and earth; ~ **al pianto** to move to tears; ~ **i primi passi** to take one's first steps; *(fig)* to be starting out; **muoviti!** hurry up!, get a move on!

'mura *sfpl vedi* **muro**.

mu'raglia [mu'raʎʎa] *sf* (high) wall.

mu'rale *ag* wall *cpd*; mural.

mu'rare *vt (persona, porta)* to wall up.

mu'rario, a *ag* building *cpd*; **arte ~a** masonry.

mura'tore *sm (con pietre)* mason; *(con mattoni)* bricklayer.

mura'tura *sf (lavoro murario)* masonry; **casa in ~** *(di pietra)* stonebuilt house; *(di mattoni)* brick house.

'muro *sm* wall; ~**a** *sfpl (cinta cittadina)* walls; **a ~** *cpd; (armadio etc)* built-in; **mettere al ~** *(fucilare)* to shoot *o* execute (by firing squad); ~ **di cinta** surrounding wall; ~ **divisorio** dividing wall; ~ **del suono** sound barrier.

'musa *sf* muse.

'muschio ['muskjo] *sm (ZOOL)* musk; *(BOT)* moss.

musco'lare *ag* muscular, muscle *cpd*.

muscola'tura *sf* muscle structure.

'muscolo *sm (ANAT)* muscle.

musco'loso, a *ag* muscular.

mu'seo *sm* museum.

museru'ola *sf* muzzle.

'musica *sf* music; ~ **da ballo/camera** dance/chamber music.

musi'cale *ag* musical.

musicas'setta *sf* (pre-recorded) cassette.

musi'cista, i, e [muzi'tʃista] *sm/f* musician.

musi'comane *sm/f* music lover.

'muso *sm* muzzle; *(di auto, aereo)* nose; **tenere il ~** to sulk.

mu'sone, a *sm/f* sulky person.

'mussola *sf* muslin.

mus(s)ul'mano, a *ag, sm/f* Muslim, Moslem.

'muta *sf (di animali)* moulting *(BRIT)*, molting *(US)*; *(di serpenti)* sloughing; *(per immersioni subacquee)* diving suit; *(gruppo di cani)* pack.

mu'tabile *ag* changeable.

muta'mento *sm* change.

mu'tande *sfpl (da uomo)* (under)pants.

mutan'dine *sfpl (da donna, bambino)* pants *(BRIT)*, briefs; ~ **di plastica** plastic pants.

mu'tare *vt, vi* to change, alter.

mutazi'one [mutat'tsjone] *sf* change, alteration; *(BIOL)* mutation.

mu'tevole *ag* changeable.

muti'lare *vt* to mutilate, maim; *(fig)* to mutilate, deface.

muti'lato, a *sm/f* disabled person *(through loss of limbs)*; ~ **di guerra** disabled ex-serviceman *(BRIT)* o war veteran *(US)*.

mutilazi'one [mutilat'tsjone] *sf* mutilation.

mu'tismo *sm (MED)* mutism; *(atteggiamento)* (stubborn) silence.

'muto, a *ag (MED)* dumb; *(emozione, dolore,*

CINE) silent; (LING) silent, mute; (carta geografica) blank; ~ **per lo stupore** etc speechless with amazement etc; **ha fatto scena** ~**a** he didn't utter a word.

'**mutua** sf (anche: **cassa** ~) health insurance scheme; **medico della** ~ ≈ National Health Service doctor (BRIT).

mutu'are vt (fig) to borrow.

mutu'ato, a sm/f member of a health insurance scheme.

'**mutuo, a** ag (reciproco) mutual ♦ sm (ECON) (long-term) loan; ~ **ipotecario** mortgage.

N n

N, n ['ɛnne] sf o m (lettera) N, n; **N come Napoli** ≈ N for Nellie (BRIT), N for Nan (US).

N abbr (= nord) N.

n abbr (= numero) no.

NA sigla = Napoli.

na'babbo sm (anche fig) nabob.

'**nacchere** ['nakkere] sfpl castanets.

NAD sigla m = nucleo anti-droga.

na'dir sm (ASTR) nadir.

'**nafta** sf naphtha; (per motori diesel) diesel oil.

nafta'lina sf (CHIM) naphthalene; (tarmicida) mothballs pl.

'**naia** sf (ZOOL) cobra; (MIL) slang term for national service.

na'if [na'if] ag inv naïve.

'**nailon** sm = nylon.

Nai'robi sf Nairobi.

'**nanna** sf (linguaggio infantile): **andare a** ~ to go to beddy-byes.

'**nano, a** ag, sm/f dwarf.

napole'tano, a ag, sm/f Neapolitan ♦ sf (macchinetta da caffè) Neapolitan coffee pot.

'**Napoli** sf Naples.

'**nappa** sf tassel.

nar'ciso [nar'tʃizo] sm narcissus.

'**narcos** sm inv (colombiano) Colombian drug trafficker.

narco'dollari smpl drug money sg.

nar'cosi sf general anaesthesia, narcosis.

nar'cotico, ci sm narcotic.

narcotraffi'cante sm/f drug trafficker.

narco'traffico sm drug trade.

na'rice [na'ritʃe] sf nostril.

nar'rare vt to tell the story of, recount.

narra'tivo, a ag narrative ♦ sf (branca letteraria) fiction.

narra'tore, 'trice sm/f narrator.

narrazi'one [narrat'tsjone] sf narration; (racconto) story, tale.

N.A.S.A. ['naza] sigla f (= National Aeronautics and Space Administration) NASA.

na'sale ag nasal.

na'scente [naʃ'ʃɛnte] ag (sole, luna) rising.

'**nascere** ['naʃʃere] vi (bambino) to be born; (pianta) to come o spring up; (fiume) to rise, have its source; (sole) to rise; (dente) to come through; (fig: derivare, conseguire): ~ **da** to arise from, be born out of; **è nata nel 1952** she was born in 1952; **da cosa nasce cosa** one thing leads to another.

'**nascita** ['naʃʃita] sf birth.

nasci'turo, a [naʃʃi'turo] sm/f future child; **come si chiamerà il** ~? what's the baby going to be called?

nas'condere vt to hide, conceal; ~**rsi** vr to hide.

nascon'diglio [naskon'diʎʎo] sm hiding place.

nascon'dino sm (gioco) hide-and-seek.

nas'cosi etc vb vedi **nascondere**.

nas'costo, a pp di **nascondere** ♦ ag hidden; **di** ~ secretly.

na'sello sm (ZOOL) hake.

'**naso** sm nose.

Nas'sau sf Nassau.

'**nastro** sm ribbon; (magnetico, isolante, SPORT) tape; ~ **adesivo** adhesive tape; ~ **trasportatore** conveyor belt.

nas'turzio [nas'turtsjo] sm nasturtium.

na'tale ag of one's birth ♦ sm (REL): **N**~ Christmas; (giorno della nascita) birthday; ~**i** smpl: **di illustri/umili** ~**i** of noble/humble birth.

natalità sf birth rate.

nata'lizio, a [nata'littsjo] ag (del Natale) Christmas cpd.

na'tante sm craft inv, boat.

'**natica, che** sf (ANAT) buttock.

na'tio, a, 'tii, 'tie ag native.

Natività sf (REL) Nativity.

na'tivo, a ag, sm/f native.

'**nato, a** pp di **nascere** ♦ ag: **un attore** ~ a born actor; ~**a Pieri** née Pieri.

'**N.A.T.O.** sigla f NATO (= North Atlantic Treaty Organization).

na'tura sf nature; **pagare in** ~ to pay in kind; ~ **morta** still life.

natu'rale ag natural ♦ sm: **al** ~ (alimenti) served plain; (ritratto) life-size; **(ma) è** ~!

(*in risposte*) of course!; **a grandezza** ~
life-size; **acqua** ~ spring water.
natura'lezza [natura'lettsa] *sf* naturalness.
natura'lista, i, e *smf* naturalist.
naturaliz'zare [naturalid'dzare] *vt* to
naturalize.
natural'mente *av* naturally; (*certamente,
si*) of course.
natu'rismo *sm* naturism, nudism.
natu'rista, i, e *ag, smf* naturist, nudist.
naufra'gare *vi* (*nave*) to be wrecked;
(*persona*) to be shipwrecked; (*fig*) to fall
through.
nau'fragio [nau'fradʒo] *sm* shipwreck; (*fig*)
ruin, failure.
'naufrago, ghi *sm* castaway, shipwreck
victim.
'nausea *sf* nausea; **avere la** ~ to feel sick
(*BRIT*) *o* ill (*US*); **fino alla** ~ ad nauseam.
nausea'bondo, a *ag*, nause'ante *ag*
nauseating, sickening.
nause'are *vt* to nauseate, make (feel) sick
(*BRIT*) *o* ill (*US*).
'nautico, a, ci, che *ag* nautical ♦ *sf* (art of)
navigation; **salone** ~ (*mostra*) boat show.
na'vale *ag* naval; **battaglia** ~ naval battle;
(*gioco*) battleships *pl*.
na'vata *sf* (*anche:* ~ **centrale**) nave; (*anche:*
~ **laterale**) aisle.
'nave *sf* ship, vessel; ~ **da carico** cargo
ship, freighter; ~ **cisterna** tanker; ~ **da
guerra** warship; ~ **di linea** liner; ~
passeggeri passenger ship; ~ **portaerei**
aircraft carrier; ~ **spaziale** spaceship.
na'vetta *sf* shuttle; (*servizio di
collegamento*) shuttle (service).
navi'cella [navi'tʃɛlla] *sf* (*di aerostato*)
gondola; ~ **spaziale** spaceship.
navi'gabile *ag* navigable.
navi'gante *sm* sailor, seaman.
navi'gare *vi* to sail; ~ **in cattive acque** (*fig*)
to be in deep water.
navi'gato, a *ag* (*fig: esperto*) experienced.
naviga'tore, 'trice *smf* (*gen*) navigator; ~
solitario single-handed sailor.
navigazi'one [navigat'tsjone] *sf* navigation;
dopo una settimana di ~ after a week at
sea.
na'viglio [na'viʎʎo] *sm* fleet, ships *pl*;
(*canale artificiale*) canal; ~ **da pesca**
fishing fleet.
'Nazaret(h) ['naddzaret] *sf* Nazareth.
nazio'nale [nattsjo'nale] *ag* national ♦ *sf*
(*SPORT*) national team.
naziona'lismo [nattsjona'lizmo] *sm*
nationalism.
naziona'lista, i, e [nattsjona'lista] *ag, smf*
nationalist.

nazionalità [nattsjonali'ta] *sf inv*
nationality.
nazionaliz'zare [nattsjonalid'dzare] *vt* to
nationalize.
nazionalizzazi'one [nattsjonalid-
dzat'tsjone] *sf* nationalization.
nazi'one [nat'tsjone] *sf* nation.
naziskin ['nɑːtsiskin] *sm inv* Nazi skinhead.
na'zismo [nat'tsizmo] *sm* Nazism.
na'zista, i, e [nat'tsista] *ag, smf* Nazi.
NB *abbr* (= *nota bene*) NB.
N.d.A. *abbr* (= *nota dell'autore*) author's
note.
N.d.D. *abbr* = *nota della direzione*.
N.d.E. *abbr* (= *nota dell'editore*) publisher's
note.
N.d.R. *abbr* (= *nota della redazione*) editor's
note.
'nd'rangheta [nd'rangeta] *sf* Calabrian
Mafia.
N.d.T. *abbr* (= *nota del traduttore*)
translator's note.

══════════════════ *PAROLA CHIAVE*

ne *pron* **1** (*di lui, lei, loro*) of him/her/them;
about him/her/them; ~ **riconosco la voce**
I recognize his (*o* her) voice
2 (*di questa, quella cosa*) of it; about it; ~
voglio ancora I want some more (of it *o*
them); **non parliamone più!** let's not talk
about it any more!
3 (*da ciò*) from this; ~ **deduco che l'avete
trovato** I gather you've found it; ~
consegue che ... it follows therefore
that ...
4 (*con valore partitivo*): **hai dei libri? — sì,
~ ho** have you any books? — yes, I have
(some); **hai del pane? — no, non ~ ho**
have you any bread? — no, I haven't any;
quanti anni hai? — ~ ho 17 how old are
you? — I'm 17
♦ *av* (*moto da luogo: da lì*) from there; ~
vengo ora I've just come from there.

né *cong:* ~ ... ~ neither ... nor; ~ **l'uno ~
l'altro lo vuole** neither of them wants it;
~ **più ~ meno** no more no less; **non parla
~ l'italiano ~ il tedesco** he speaks neither
Italian nor German, he doesn't speak
either Italian or German; **non piove ~
nevica** it isn't raining or snowing.
N.E. *abbr* (= *nordest*) NE.
ne'anche [ne'anke] *av, cong* not even; **non ...
~** not even; ~ **se volesse potrebbe venire**
he couldn't come even if he wanted to;
non l'ho visto — neanch'io I didn't see
him — neither did I *o* I didn't either; ~
per idea *o* **sogno!** not on your life!; **non ci**

penso ~! I wouldn't dream of it!; ~ **a pagarlo lo farebbe** he wouldn't do it even if you paid him.
'nebbia *sf* fog; (*foschia*) mist.
nebbi'oso, a *ag* foggy; misty.
nebulizza'tore [nebuliddza'tore] *sm* atomizer.
nebu'losa *sf* nebula.
nebulosità *sf* haziness.
nebu'loso, a *ag* (*atmosfera, cielo*) hazy; (*fig*) hazy, vague.
néces'saire [nesɛ'sɛr] *sm inv*: ~ **da viaggio** overnight case *o* bag.
necessaria'mente [netʃessarja'mente] *av* necessarily.
neces'sario, a [netʃes'sarjo] *ag* necessary ♦ *sm*: **fare il** ~ to do what is necessary; **lo stretto** ~ the bare essentials *pl*.
necessità [netʃessi'ta] *sf inv* necessity; (*povertà*) need, poverty; **trovarsi nella** ~ **di fare qc** to be forced *o* obliged to do sth, have to do sth.
necessi'tare [netʃessi'tare] *vt* to require ♦ *vi* (*aver bisogno*): ~ **di** to need.
necro'logio [nekro'lɔdʒo] *sm* obituary notice; (*registro*) register of deaths.
ne'fando, a *ag* infamous, wicked.
ne'fasto, a *ag* inauspicious, ill-omened.
ne'gare *vt* to deny; (*rifiutare*) to deny, refuse; ~ **di aver fatto/che** to deny having done/that.
negativa'mente *av* negatively; **rispondere** ~ to give a negative response.
nega'tivo, a *ag, sf, sm* negative.
negazi'one [negat'tsjone] *sf* negation.
negherò *etc* [nege'rɔ] *vb vedi* **negare**.
ne'gletto, a [ne'gletto] *ag* (*trascurato*) neglected.
'negli ['neʎʎi] *prep + det vedi* **in**.
négli'gé [negli'ʒe] *sm inv* negligee.
negli'gente [negli'dʒɛnte] *ag* negligent, careless.
negli'genza [negli'dʒɛntsa] *sf* negligence, carelessness.
negozi'abile [negot'tsjabile] *ag* negotiable.
negozi'ante [negot'tsjante] *sm/f* trader, dealer; (*bottegaio*) shopkeeper (*BRIT*), storekeeper (*US*).
negozi'are [negot'tsjare] *vt* to negotiate ♦ *vi*: ~ **in** to trade *o* deal in.
negozi'ato [negot'tsjato] *sm* negotiation.
negozia'tore, 'trice [negottsja'tore] *sm/f* negotiator.
ne'gozio [ne'gɔttsjo] *sm* (*locale*) shop (*BRIT*), store (*US*); (*affare*) (piece of) business *no pl*; (*DIR*): ~ **giuridico** legal

transaction.
negri'ere, a, negri'ero, a *sm* slave trader ♦ *sm/f* (*fig*) slave driver.
'negro, a *ag, sm/f* Negro.
negro'mante *sm/f* necromancer.
negroman'zia [negroman'tsia] *sf* necromancy.
'nei, nel, nell', 'nella, 'nelle, 'nello *prep + det vedi* **in**.
'nembo *sm* (*METEOR*) nimbus.
ne'mico, a, ci, che *ag* hostile; (*MIL*) enemy *cpd* ♦ *sm/f* enemy; **essere** ~ **di** to be strongly averse *o* opposed to.
nem'meno *av, cong* = **neanche**.
'nenia *sf* dirge; (*motivo monotono*) monotonous tune.
'neo *sm* mole; (*fig*) (slight) flaw.
'neo... *prefisso* neo....
neofa'scista, i, e [neofaʃ'ʃista] *sm/f* neofascist.
neolo'gismo [neolo'dʒizmo] *sm* neologism.
'neon *sm* (*CHIM*) neon.
neo'nato, a *ag* newborn ♦ *sm/f* newborn baby.
neozelan'dese [neoddzelan'dese] *ag* New Zealand *cpd* ♦ *sm/f* New Zealander.
Ne'pal *sm*: **il** ~ Nepal.
nepo'tismo *sm* nepotism.
nep'pure *av, cong* = **neanche**.
ner'bata *sf* (*colpo*) blow; (*sferzata*) whiplash.
'nerbo *sm* lash; (*fig*) strength, backbone.
nerbo'ruto, a *ag* muscular; robust.
ne'retto *sm* (*TIP*) bold type.
'nero, a *ag* black; (*scuro*) dark ♦ *sm* black; **nella miseria più** ~**a** in utter *o* abject poverty; **essere di umore** ~, **essere** ~ to be in a filthy mood; **mettere qc** ~ **su bianco** to put sth down in black and white; **vedere tutto** ~ to look on the black side (of things).
nero'fumo *sm* lampblack.
nerva'tura *sf* (*ANAT*) nervous system; (*BOT*) veining; (*ARCHIT, TECN*) rib.
'nervo *sm* (*ANAT*) nerve; (*BOT*) vein; **avere i** ~**i** to be on edge; **dare sui** ~**i a qn** to get on sb's nerves; **tenere/avere i** ~**i saldi** to keep/be calm; **che** ~**i!** damn (it)!
nervo'sismo *sm* (*PSIC*) nervousness; (*irritazione*) irritability.
ner'voso, a *ag* nervous; (*irritabile*) irritable ♦ *sm* (*fam*): **far venire il** ~ **a qn** to get on sb's nerves; **farsi prendere dal** ~ to let o.s. get irritated.
'nespola *sf* (*BOT*) medlar; (*fig*) blow, punch.
'nespolo *sm* medlar tree.
'nesso *sm* connection, link.

===================== *PAROLA CHIAVE*

nes'suno, a (*det: dav sm* **nessun** + *C, V,*
nessuno + *s impura, gn, pn, ps, x, z; dav sf*
nessuna + *C,* **nessun'** + *V*) *det* **1** (*non uno*)
no, *espressione negativa* + any; **non c'è**
nessun libro there isn't any book, there is
no book; **nessun altro** no one else, nobody
else; **nessun'altra cosa** nothing else; **in**
nessun luogo nowhere
2 (*qualche*) any; **hai ~a obiezione?** do you
have any objections?
♦ *pron* **1** (*non uno*) no one, nobody,
espressione negativa + any(one); (: *cosa*)
none, *espressione negativa* + any; **~ è venuto,**
non è venuto ~ nobody came
2 (*qualcuno*) anyone, anybody; **ha**
telefonato ~? did anyone phone?

netta'mente *av* clearly.
net'tare *vt* to clean ♦ *sm* ['nɛttare] nectar.
net'tezza [net'tettsa] *sf* cleanness,
cleanliness; **~ urbana** cleansing
department (*BRIT*), department of
sanitation (*US*).
'netto, a *ag* (*pulito*) clean; (*chiaro*) clear,
clear-cut; (*deciso*) definite; (*ECON*) net;
tagliare qc di ~ to cut sth clean off; **taglio**
~ col passato (*fig*) clean break with the
past.
nettur'bino *sm* dustman (*BRIT*), garbage
collector (*US*).
'neuro... *prefisso* neuro....
neurochirur'gia [neurokirur'dʒia] *sf*
neurosurgery.
neurolo'gia [neurolo'dʒia] *sf* neurology.
neuro'logico, a, ci, che [neuro'lɔdʒiko] *ag*
neurological.
neu'rologo a, gi, ghe *sm/f* neurologist.
neu'rosi *sf inv* = **nevrosi**.
neu'trale *ag* neutral.
neutralità *sf* neutrality.
neutraliz'zare [neutralid'dzare] *vt* to
neutralize.
'neutro, a *ag* neutral; (*LING*) neuter ♦ *sm*
(*LING*) neuter.
neu'trone *sm* neutron.
ne'vaio *sm* snowfield.
'neve *sf* snow; **montare a ~** (*CUC*) to whip
up; **~ carbonica** dry ice.
nevi'care *vb impers* to snow.
nevi'cata *sf* snowfall.
ne'vischio [ne'viskjo] *sm* sleet.
ne'voso, a *ag* snowy; snow-covered.
nevral'gia [nevral'dʒia] *sf* neuralgia.
ne'vralgico, a, ci, che [ne'vraldʒiko] *ag*:
punto ~ (*MED*) nerve centre; (*fig*) crucial
point.

nevras'tenico, a, ci, che *ag* (*MED*)
neurasthenic; (*fig*) hot-tempered ♦ *sm/f*
neurasthenic; hot-tempered person.
ne'vrosi *sf inv* neurosis.
ne'vrotico, a, ci, che *ag, sm/f* (*anche fig*)
neurotic.
Nia'gara *sm*: **le cascate del ~** the Niagara
Falls.
'nibbio *sm* (*ZOOL*) kite.
Nica'ragua *sm*: **il ~** Nicaragua.
nicaragu'ense *ag, sm/f* Nicaraguan.
'nicchia ['nikkja] *sf* niche; (*naturale*) cavity,
hollow; **~ di mercato** (*COMM*) niche
market.
nicchi'are [nik'kjare] *vi* to shilly-shally,
hesitate.
'nichel ['nikel] *sm* nickel.
nichi'lismo [niki'lizmo] *sm* nihilism.
Nico'sia *sf* Nicosia.
nico'tina *sf* nicotine.
nidi'ata *sf* (*di uccelli, fig: di bambini*) brood;
(*di altri animali*) litter.
nidifi'care *vi* to nest.
'nido *sm* nest ♦ *ag inv*: **asilo ~** day nursery,
crèche (*for children aged 0 to 3*); **a ~ d'ape**
(*tessuto etc*) honeycomb *cpd*.

===================== *PAROLA CHIAVE*

ni'ente *pron* **1** (*nessuna cosa*) nothing; **~**
può fermarlo nothing can stop him; **~ di**
~ absolutely nothing; **grazie! — di ~!**
thank you! — not at all!; **nient'altro**
nothing else; **nient'altro che** nothing but;
~ affatto not at all, not in the least; **come**
se ~ fosse as if nothing had happened;
cose da ~ trivial matters; **per ~** (*gratis,*
invano) for nothing; **non per ~, ma** ... not
for any particular reason, but ...; **poco o**
~ next to nothing; **un uomo da ~** a man
of no consequence
2 (*qualcosa*): **hai bisogno di ~?** do you
need anything?
3: **non** ... **~** nothing, *espressione negativa* +
anything; **non ho visto ~** I saw nothing, I
didn't see anything; **non può farci ~** he
can't do anything about it; **(non) fa ~** (*non*
importa) it doesn't matter; **non ho ~ da**
dire I have nothing *o* haven't anything to
say
♦ *ag inv*: **~ paura!** never fear!; **e ~ scuse!**
and I don't want to hear excuses!
♦ *sm* nothing; **un bel ~** absolutely
nothing; **basta un ~ per farla piangere** the
slightest thing is enough to make her
cry; **finire in ~** to come to nothing
♦ *av* (*in nessuna misura*): **non** ... **~** not ... at
all; **non è (per) ~ buono** it isn't good at
all; **non ci penso per ~** (*non ne ho nessuna*

intenzione) I wouldn't think of it; ~ **male!** not bad at all!

nientedi'meno, niente'meno *av* actually, even ♦ *escl* really!, I say!

'Niger ['nidʒer] *sm*: il ~ Niger; (*fiume*) the Niger.

Ni'geria [ni'dʒɛrja] *sf* Nigeria.

nigeri'ano, a [nidʒe'rjano] *ag*, *sm/f* Nigerian.

'Nilo *sm*: il ~ the Nile.

'nimbo *sm* halo.

'ninfa *sf* nymph.

nin'fea *sf* water lily.

nin'fomane *sf* nymphomaniac.

ninna'nanna *sf* lullaby.

'ninnolo *sm* (*balocco*) plaything; (*gingillo*) knick-knack.

ni'pote *sm/f* (*di zii*) nephew/niece; (*di nonni*) grandson/daughter, grandchild.

nip'ponico, a, ci, che *ag* Japanese.

niti'dezza [niti'dettsa] *sf* (*gen*) clearness; (*di stile*) clarity; (*FOT, TV*) sharpness.

'nitido, a *ag* clear; (*immagine*) sharp, well-defined.

ni'trato *sm* nitrate.

'nitrico, a, ci, che *ag* nitric.

ni'trire *vi* to neigh.

ni'trito *sm* (*di cavallo*) neighing *no pl*; neigh; (*CHIM*) nitrite.

nitroglice'rina [nitroglitʃe'rina] *sf* nitroglycerine.

'niveo, a *ag* snow-white.

'Nizza ['nittsa] *sf* Nice.

nn *abbr* (= *numeri*) nos.

NO *sigla* = Novara.

no *av* (*risposta*) no; **vieni o** ~? are you coming or not?; **come** ~! of course!, certainly!; **perché** ~? why not?

N.O. *abbr* (= *nordovest*) NW.

nobil'donna *sf* noblewoman.

'nobile *ag* noble ♦ *sm/f* noble, nobleman/woman.

nobili'are *ag* noble.

nobili'tare *vt* (*anche fig*) to ennoble; ~**rsi** *vr* (*rendersi insigne*) to distinguish o.s.

nobiltà *sf* nobility; (*di azione etc*) nobleness.

nobilu'omo *sm*, *pl* -**u'omini** nobleman.

'nocca, che *sf* (*ANAT*) knuckle.

'noccio *etc* ['nɔttʃo] *vb vedi* **nuocere**.

nocci'ola [not'tʃɔla] *sf* hazelnut ♦ *ag inv* (*anche: color* ~) hazel, light brown.

noccio'lina [nottʃo'lina] *sf* (*anche:* ~ **americana**) peanut.

'nocciolo ['nɔttʃolo] *sm* (*di frutto*) stone; (*fig*) heart, core; [not'tʃɔlo] (*albero*) hazel.

'noce ['notʃe] *sm* (*albero*) walnut tree ♦ *sf* (*frutto*) walnut; **una** ~ **di burro** (*CUC*) a knob of butter (*BRIT*), a dab of butter

(*US*); ~ **di cocco** coconut; ~ **moscata** nutmeg.

noce'pesca, sche [notʃe'pɛska] *sf* nectarine.

no'cevo *etc* [no'tʃevo] *vb vedi* **nuocere**.

noci'uto [no'tʃuto] *pp di* **nuocere**.

no'civo, a [no'tʃivo] *ag* harmful, noxious.

'nocqui *etc* *vb vedi* **nuocere**.

'nodo *sm* (*di cravatta, legname, NAUT*) knot; (*AUT, FERR*) junction; (*MED, ASTR, BOT*) node; (*fig: legame*) bond, tie; (: *punto centrale*) heart, crux; **avere un** ~ **alla gola** to have a lump in one's throat; **tutti i** ~**i vengono al pettine** (*proverbio*) your sins will find you out.

no'doso, a *ag* (*tronco*) gnarled.

'nodulo *sm* (*ANAT, BOT*) nodule.

'noi *pron* (*soggetto*) we; (*oggetto: per dare rilievo, con preposizione*) us; ~ **stessi(e)** we ourselves; (*oggetto*) ourselves; **da** ~ (*nel nostro paese*) in our country, where we come from; (*a casa nostra*) at our house.

'noia *sf* boredom; (*disturbo, impaccio*) bother *no pl*, trouble *no pl*; **avere qn/qc a** ~ not to like sb/sth; **mi è venuto a** ~ I'm tired of it; **dare** ~ **a** to annoy; **avere delle** ~**e con qn** to have trouble with sb.

noi'altri *pron* we.

noi'oso, a *ag* boring; (*fastidioso*) annoying, troublesome.

noleggi'are [noled'dʒare] *vt* (*prendere a noleggio*) to hire (*BRIT*), rent; (*dare a noleggio*) to hire out (*BRIT*), rent out; (*aereo, nave*) to charter.

noleggia'tore, 'trice [noleddʒa'tore] *sm/f* hirer (*BRIT*), renter; charterer.

no'leggio [no'leddʒo] *sm* hire (*BRIT*), rental; charter.

no'lente *ag*: **volente o** ~ whether one likes it or not, willy-nilly.

'nolo *sm* hire (*BRIT*), rental; charter; (*per trasporto merci*) freight; **prendere/dare a** ~ **qc** to hire/hire out sth (*BRIT*), rent/rent out sth.

'nomade *ag* nomadic ♦ *sm/f* nomad.

noma'dismo *sm* nomadism.

'nome *sm* name; (*LING*) noun; **in o a** ~ **di** in the name of; **di o per** ~ (*chiamato*) called, named; **conoscere qn di** ~ to know sb by name; **fare il** ~ **di qn** to name sb; **faccia pure il mio** ~ feel free to mention my name; ~ **d'arte** stage name; ~ **di battesimo** Christian name; ~ **depositato** trade name; ~ **di famiglia** surname; ~ **da ragazza** maiden name; ~ **da sposata** married name.

no'mea *sf* notoriety.

nomencla'tura *sf* nomenclature.

nomenkla'tura *sf (di partito, stato)* nomenklatura.

no'mignolo [no'miɲɲolo] *sm* nickname.

'nomina *sf* appointment.

nomi'nale *ag* nominal; *(LING)* noun *cpd.*

nomi'nare *vt* to name; *(eleggere)* to appoint; *(citare)* to mention; **non l'ho mai sentito** ~ I've never heard of it *(o* him).

nomina'tivo, a *ag (intestato: titolo)* registered; *(: libretto)* personal; *(LING)* nominative ♦ *sm (nome)* name; *(LING)* nominative; **elenco** ~ list of names.

non *av* not ♦ *prefisso* non-; **grazie — ~ c'è di che** thank you — don't mention it; **i ~ credenti** the unbelievers; *vedi* **affatto, appena** *etc.*

nonché [non'ke] *cong (tanto più, tanto meno)* let alone; *(e inoltre)* as well as.

nonconfor'mista, i, e *ag, sm/f* nonconformist.

noncu'rante *ag:* ~ **(di)** careless (of), indifferent (to); **con fare** ~ with a nonchalant air.

noncu'ranza [nonku'rantsa] *sf* carelessness, indifference; **un'aria di** ~ a nonchalant air.

nondi'meno *cong (tuttavia)* however; *(nonostante)* nevertheless.

'nonno, a *sm/f* grandfather/mother; *(in senso più familiare)* grandma/grandpa; ~**i** *smpl* grandparents.

non'nulla *sm inv:* **un** ~ nothing, a trifle.

'nono, a *num* ninth.

nonos'tante *prep* in spite of, notwithstanding ♦ *cong* although, even though.

non plus 'ultra *sm inv:* **il** ~ **(di)** the last word (in).

nontiscordardimé *sm inv (BOT)* forget-me-not.

nord *sm* north ♦ *ag inv* north; *(regione)* northern; **verso** ~ north, northwards; **l'America del N**~ North America.

nor'dest *sm* north-east.

'nordico, a, ci, che *ag* nordic, northern European.

nor'dista, i, e *ag, sm/f* Yankee.

nor'dovest *sm* north-west.

Norim'berga *sf* Nuremberg.

'norma *sf (principio)* norm; *(regola)* regulation, rule; *(consuetudine)* custom, rule; **di** ~ normally; **a** ~ **di legge** according to law, as laid down by law; **al di sopra della** ~ above average, above the norm; **per sua** ~ **e regola** for your information; **proporsi una** ~ **di vita** to set o.s. rules to live by; ~**e di sicurezza** safety regulations; ~**e per l'uso** instructions for use.

nor'male *ag* normal.

normalità *sf* normality.

normaliz'zare [normalid'dzare] *vt* to normalize, bring back to normal.

normal'mente *av* normally.

Norman'dia *sf:* **la** ~ Normandy.

nor'manno, a *ag, sm/f* Norman.

norma'tivo, a *ag* normative ♦ *sf* regulations *pl.*

norve'gese [norve'dʒese] *ag, sm/f, sm* Norwegian.

Nor'vegia [nor'vɛdʒa] *sf:* **la** ~ Norway.

noso'comio *sm* hospital.

nostal'gia [nostal'dʒia] *sf (di casa, paese)* homesickness; *(del passato)* nostalgia.

nos'talgico, a, ci, che [nos'taldʒiko] *ag* homesick; nostalgic ♦ *sm/f (POL)* person *who hopes for the return of Fascism.*

nos'trano, a *ag* local; *(pianta, frutta)* home-produced.

'nostro, a *det:* **il(la)** ~**(a)** *etc* our ♦ *pron:* **il(la)** ~**(a)** *etc* ours ♦ *sm:* **abbiamo speso del** ~ we spent our own money ♦ *sf:* **la** ~**a** *(opinione)* our view; **i** ~**i** our family; our own people; **è dei** ~**i** he's one of us; **è dalla** ~**a** *(parte)* he's on our side; **anche noi abbiamo avuto le** ~**e** *(disavventure)* we've had our problems too; **alla** ~**a!** *(brindisi)* to us!

nos'tromo *sm* boatswain.

'nota *sf (segno)* mark; *(comunicazione scritta, MUS)* note; *(fattura)* bill; *(elenco)* list; **prendere** ~ **di qc** to note sth, make a note of sth, write sth down; *(fig: fare attenzione)* to note sth, take note of sth; **degno di** ~ noteworthy, worthy of note; ~**e caratteristiche** distinguishing marks *o* features; ~**e a piè di pagina** footnotes.

no'tabile *ag* notable; *(persona)* important ♦ *sm* prominent citizen.

no'taio *sm* notary.

no'tare *vt (segnare: errori)* to mark; *(registrare)* to note (down), write down; *(rilevare, osservare)* to note, notice; **farsi** ~ to get o.s. noticed.

nota'rile *ag:* **atto** ~ legal document *(authorized by a notary)*; **studio** ~ notary's office.

notazi'one [notat'tsjone] *sf (MUS)* notation.

no'tevole *ag (talento)* notable, remarkable; *(peso)* considerable.

no'tifica, che *sf* notification.

notifi'care *vt (DIR):* ~ **qc a qn** to notify sb of sth, give sb notice of sth.

notificazi'one [notifikat'tsjone] *sf* notification.

no'tizia [no'tittsja] *sf* (piece of) news *sg*;

(*informazione*) piece of information; ~**e** *sfpl* news *sg*; information *sg*.

notizi'ario [notit'tsjarjo] *sm* (*RADIO, TV, STAMPA*) news *sg*.

'**noto, a** *ag* (well-)known.

notorietà *sf* fame; notoriety.

no'torio, a *ag* well-known; (*peg*) notorious.

not'tambulo, a *smf* night-bird (*fig*).

not'tata *sf* night.

'**notte** *sf* night; **di** ~ at night; (*durante la* ~) in the night, during the night; **questa** ~ (*passata*) last night; (*che viene*) tonight; **nella** ~ **dei tempi** in the mists of time; **come va?** — **peggio che andar di** ~ how are things? — worse than ever; ~ **bianca** sleepless night.

notte'tempo *av* at night; during the night.

'**nottola** *sf* (*ZOOL*) noctule.

not'turno, a *ag* nocturnal; (*servizio, guardiano*) night *cpd* ♦ *sf* (*SPORT*) evening fixture (*BRIT*) *o* match.

nov. *abbr* (= *novembre*) Nov.

no'vanta *num* ninety.

novan'tenne *ag, smf* ninety-year-old.

novan'tesimo, a *num* ninetieth.

novan'tina *sf*: **una** ~ **(di)** about ninety.

'**nove** *num* nine.

novecen'tesco, a, schi, sche [novetʃen'tesko] *ag* twentieth-century.

nove'cento [nove'tʃento] *num* nine hundred ♦ *sm*: **il N**~ the twentieth century.

no'vella *sf* (*LETTERATURA*) short story.

novel'lino, a *ag* (*pivello*) green, inexperienced.

novel'lista, i, e *smf* short-story writer.

novel'listica *sf* (*arte*) short-story writing; (*insieme di racconti*) short stories *pl*.

no'vello, a *ag* (*piante, patate*) new; (*insalata, verdura*) early; (*sposo*) newly-married.

no'vembre *sm* November; *per fraseologia vedi* **luglio.**

novem'brino, a *ag* November *cpd*.

nove'mila *num* nine thousand.

noven'nale *ag* (*che dura 9 anni*) nine-year *cpd*; (*ogni 9 anni*) nine-yearly.

novi'lunio *sm* (*ASTR*) new moon.

novità *sf inv* novelty; (*innovazione*) innovation; (*cosa originale, insolita*) something new; (*notizia*) (piece of) news *sg*; **le** ~ **della moda** the latest fashions.

novizi'ato [novit'tsjato] *sm* (*REL*) novitiate; (*tirocinio*) apprenticeship.

no'vizio, a [no'vittsjo] *smf* (*REL*) novice; (*tirocinante*) beginner, apprentice.

nozi'one [not'tsjone] *sf* notion, idea; ~**i** *sfpl* (*rudimenti*) basic knowledge *sg*, rudiments.

nozio'nismo [nottsjo'nizmo] *sm* superficial

knowledge.

nozio'nistico, a, ci, che [nottsjo'nistiko] *ag* superficial.

'**nozze** ['nɔttse] *sfpl* wedding *sg*, marriage *sg*; ~ **d'argento/d'oro** silver/golden wedding *sg*.

N.P.A. *abbr* = **nave portaerei.**

ns. *abbr* (*COMM*) = **nostro.**

NU *sigla* = *Nuoro*.

N.U. *sigla* (= *Nazioni Unite*) UN.

'**nube** *sf* cloud.

nubi'fragio [nubi'fradʒo] *sm* cloudburst.

'**nubile** *ag* (*donna*) unmarried, single.

'**nuca, che** *sf* nape of the neck.

nucle'are *ag* nuclear ♦ *sm*: **il** ~ nuclear energy.

'**nucleo** *sm* nucleus; (*gruppo*) team, unit, group; (*MIL, POLIZIA*) squad; ~ **antidroga** anti-drugs squad; **il** ~ **familiare** the family unit.

nu'dismo *sm* nudism.

nu'dista, i, e *smf* nudist.

nudità *sf inv* nudity, nakedness; (*di paesaggio*) bareness ♦ *sfpl* (*parti nude del corpo*) nakedness *sg*.

'**nudo, a** *ag* (*persona*) bare, naked, nude; (*membra*) bare, naked; (*montagna*) bare ♦ *sm* (*ARTE*) nude; **a occhio** ~ to the naked eye; **a piedi** ~**i** barefoot; **mettere a** ~ (*cuore, verità*) to lay bare; **gli ha detto** ~ **e crudo che** ... he told him bluntly that ....

'**nugolo** *sm*: **un** ~ **di** a whole host of.

'**nulla** *pron, av* = **niente** ♦ *sm*: **il** ~ nothing; **svanire nel** ~ to vanish into thin air; **basta un** ~ **per farlo arrabbiare** he gets annoyed over the slightest thing.

nulla'osta *sm inv* authorization.

nullate'nente *ag*: **essere** ~ to own nothing ♦ *smf* person with no property.

nullità *sf inv* nullity; (*persona*) nonentity.

'**nullo, a** *ag* useless, worthless; (*DIR*) null (and void); (*SPORT*): **incontro** ~ draw.

nume'rale *ag, sm* numeral.

nume'rare *vt* to number.

numera'tore *sm* (*MAT*) numerator; (*macchina*) numbering device.

numerazi'one [numerat'tsjone] *sf* numbering; (*araba, decimale*) notation.

nu'merico, a, ci, che *ag* numerical.

'**numero** *sm* number; (*romano, arabo*) numeral; (*di spettacolo*) act, turn; **dare i** ~**i** (*farneticare*) not to be all there; **tanto per fare** ~ **invitiamo anche lui** why don't we invite him to make up the numbers?; **ha tutti i** ~**i per riuscire** he's got what it takes to succeed; **che** ~ **tuo fratello!** your brother is a real character!; ~ **civico** house number; ~ **chiuso** (*UNIVERSITÀ*) selective entry system; ~ **doppio** (*di rivista*) issue with supplement; ~ **di scarpe** size of shoe; ~ **verde** (*TEL*) ≈ Freephone ®.

nume'roso, a *ag* numerous, many; (*folla, famiglia*) large.

numis'matica *sf* numismatics *sg*, coin collecting.

'nunzio ['nuntsjo] *sm* (*REL*) nuncio.

nu'occio *etc* **vb** *vedi* **nuocere**.

nu'ocere ['nwɔttʃere] *vi*: ~ **a** to harm, damage; **il tentar non nuoce** (*proverbio*) there's no harm in trying.

nuoci'uto, a [nwo'tʃuto] *pp di* **nuocere**.

nu'ora *sf* daughter-in-law.

nuo'tare *vi* to swim; (*galleggiare: oggetti*) to float; ~ **a rana/sul dorso** to do the breast stroke/backstroke.

nuo'tata *sf* swim.

nuota'tore, 'trice *sm/f* swimmer.

nu'oto *sm* swimming.

nu'ova *sf vedi* **nuovo**.

nuova'mente *av* again.

Nu'ova York *sf* New York.

Nu'ova Ze'landa [-dze'landa] *sf*: **la** ~ New Zealand.

nu'ovo, a *ag* new ♦ *sf* (*notizia*) (piece of) news *sg*; **come** ~ as good as new; **di** ~ again; **fino a** ~ **ordine** until further notice; **il suo volto non mi è** ~ I know his face; **rimettere a** ~ (*cosa, macchina*) to do up like new; **anno** ~, **vita** ~**a!** it's time to turn over a new leaf!; ~ **fiammante** *o* **di zecca** brand-new; **la N~a Guinea** New Guinea; **la N~a Inghilterra** New England; **la N~a Scozia** Nova Scotia.

nu'trice [nu'tritʃe] *sf* wet nurse.

nutri'ente *ag* nutritious, nourishing; (*crema, balsamo*) nourishing.

nutri'mento *sm* food, nourishment.

nu'trire *vt* to feed; (*fig: sentimenti*) to harbour (*BRIT*), harbor (*US*), nurse.

nutri'tivo, a *ag* nutritional; (*alimento*) nutritious.

nu'trito, a *ag* (*numeroso*) large; (*fitto*) heavy; **ben/mal** ~ well/poorly fed.

nutrizi'one [nutrit'tsjone] *sf* nutrition.

'nuvolo, a *ag* cloudy ♦ *sf* cloud.

nuvolosità *sf* cloudiness.

nuvo'loso, a *ag* cloudy.

nuzi'ale [nut'tsjale] *ag* nuptial; wedding *cpd*.

'nylon ['nailɔn] *sm* nylon.

O o

O, o [ɔ] *sf o m inv* (*lettera*) O, o; ~ **come Otranto** ≈ O for Oliver (*BRIT*), O for Oboe (*US*).

o *cong* (*dav V spesso* **od**) or; ~ ... ~ either ... or; ~ **l'uno** ~ **l'altro** either (of them); ~ **meglio** or rather.

O. *abbr* (= *ovest*) W.

'oasi *sf inv* oasis.

obbedi'ente *etc vedi* **ubbidiente** *etc*.

obbiet'tare *etc vedi* **obiettare** *etc*.

obbli'gare *vt* (*costringere*): ~ **qn a fare** to force *o* oblige sb to do; (*DIR*) to bind; ~**rsi** *vr*: ~**rsi a fare** to undertake to do; ~**rsi per qn** (*DIR*) to stand surety for sb, act as guarantor for sb.

obbliga'tissimo, a *ag* (*ringraziamento*): ~**!** much obliged!

obbli'gato, a *ag* (*costretto, grato*) obliged; (*percorso, tappa*) set, fixed; **passaggio** ~ (*fig*) essential requirement.

obbliga'torio, a *ag* compulsory, obligatory.

obbligazi'one [obbligat'tsjone] *sf* obligation; (*COMM*) bond, debenture; ~ **dello Stato** government bond; ~**i convertibili** convertible loan stock, convertible debentures.

obbligazio'nista, i, e [obbligattsjo'nista] *sm/f* bond-holder.

'obbligo, ghi *sm* obligation; (*dovere*) duty; **avere l'**~ **di fare, essere nell'**~ **di fare** to be obliged to do; **essere d'**~ (*discorso, applauso*) to be called for; **avere degli** ~**ghi con** *o* **verso qn** to be under an obligation to sb, be indebted to sb; **le formalità d'**~ the necessary formalities.

obb.mo *abbr* = **obbligatissimo**.

ob'brobrio *sm* disgrace; (*fig*) mess, eyesore.

obe'lisco, schi *sm* obelisk.

obe'rato, a *ag*: ~ **di** (*lavoro*) overloaded *o* overburdened with; (*debiti*) crippled with.

obesità *sf* obesity.

o'beso, a *ag* obese.

obiet'tare *vt*: ~ **che** to object that; ~ **su qc** to object to sth, raise objections concerning sth.

obiettiva'mente *av* objectively.
obiettività *sf* objectivity.
obiet'tivo, a *ag* objective ♦ *sm* (*OTTICA, FOT*) lens *sg*, objective; (*MIL, fig*) objective.
obiet'tore *sm* objector; ~ **di coscienza** conscientious objector.
obiezi'one [objet'tsjone] *sf* objection.
obi'torio *sm* morgue.
o'bliquo, a *ag* oblique; (*inclinato*) slanting; (*fig*) devious, underhand; **sguardo** ~ sidelong glance.
oblite'rare *vt* (*francobollo*) to cancel; (*biglietto*) to stamp.
oblitera'trice [oblitera'tritʃe] *sf* (*anche:* **macchina** ~) cancelling machine; stamping machine.
oblò *sm inv* porthole.
o'blungo, a, ghi, ghe *ag* oblong.
'oboe *sm* oboe.
'obolo *sm* (*elemosina*) (small) offering, mite.
obsole'scenza [obsoleʃ'ʃɛntsa] *sf* (*ECON*) obsolescence.
obso'leto, a *ag* obsolete.
OC *abbr* (= *onde corte*) SW.
'oca, *pl* **'oche** *sf* goose.
o'caggine [o'kaddʒine] *sf* silliness, stupidity.
occasio'nale *ag* (*incontro*) chance; (*cliente, guadagni*) casual, occasional.
occasi'one *sf* (*caso favorevole*) opportunity; (*causa, motivo, circostanza*) occasion; (*COMM*) bargain; **all'**~ should the need arise; **alla prima** ~ at the first opportunity; **d'**~ (*a buon prezzo*) bargain *cpd*; (*usato*) secondhand.
occhi'aia [ok'kjaja] *sf* eye socket; ~**e** *sfpl* (*sotto gli occhi*) shadows (under the eyes).
occhi'ali [ok'kjali] *smpl* glasses, spectacles; ~ **da sole** sunglasses.
occhi'ata [ok'kjata] *sf* look, glance; **dare un'**~ **a** to have a look at.
occhieggi'are [okkjed'dʒare] *vi* (*apparire qua e là*) to peep (out).
occhi'ello [ok'kjɛllo] *sm* buttonhole; (*asola*) eyelet.
'occhio ['ɔkkjo] *sm* eye; ~! careful!, watch out!; **a** ~ **nudo** with the naked eye; **a quattr'**~**i** privately, in private; **avere** ~ to have a good eye; **chiudere un** ~ (**su**) (*fig*) to turn a blind eye (to), shut one's eyes (to); **costare un** ~ **della testa** to cost a fortune; **dare all'**~ *o* **nell'**~ **a qn** to catch sb's eye; **fare l'**~ **a qc** to get used to sth; **tenere d'**~ **qn** to keep an eye on sb; **vedere di buon/mal** ~ **qc** to look favourably/unfavourably on sth.

occhio'lino [okkjo'lino] *sm*: **fare l'**~ **a qn** to wink at sb.
occiden'tale [ottʃiden'tale] *ag* western ♦ *sm/f* Westerner.
occi'dente [ottʃi'dɛnte] *sm* west; (*POL*): **l'O**~ the West; **a** ~ in the west.
oc'cipite [ot'tʃipite] *sm* back of the head, occiput (*ANAT*).
oc'cludere *vt* to block.
occlusi'one *sf* blockage, obstruction.
oc'cluso, a *pp di* **occludere**.
occor'rente *ag* necessary ♦ *sm* all that is necessary.
occor'renza [okkor'rɛntsa] *sf* necessity, need; **all'**~ in case of need.
oc'correre *vi* to be needed, be required ♦ *vb impers*: **occorre farlo** it must be done; **occorre che tu parta** you must leave, you'll have to leave; **mi occorrono i soldi** I need the money.
oc'corso, a *pp di* **occorrere**.
occulta'mento *sm* concealment.
occul'tare *vt* to hide, conceal.
oc'culto, a *ag* hidden, concealed; (*scienze, forze*) occult.
occu'pante *sm/f* (*di casa*) occupier, occupant; ~ **abusivo** squatter.
occu'pare *vt* to occupy; (*manodopera*) to employ; (*ingombrare*) to occupy, take up; ~**rsi** *vr* to occupy o.s., keep o.s. busy; (*impiegarsi*) to get a job; ~**rsi di** (*interessarsi*) to take an interest in; (*prendersi cura di*) to look after, take care of.
occu'pato, a *ag* (*MIL, POL*) occupied; (*persona: affaccendato*) busy; (*posto, sedia*) taken; (*toilette, TEL*) engaged.
occupazio'nale [okkupattsjo'nale] *ag* employment *cpd*, of employment.
occupazi'one [okkupat'tsjone] *sf* occupation; (*impiego, lavoro*) job; (*ECON*) employment.
Oce'ania [otʃe'anja] *sf*: **l'**~ Oceania.
o'ceano [o'tʃɛano] *sm* ocean.
'ocra *sf* ochre.
'OCSE *sigla f* (= *Organizzazione per la Cooperazione e lo Sviluppo Economico*) OECD (= *Organization for Economic Cooperation and Development*).
ocu'lare *ag* ocular, eye *cpd*; **testimone** ~ eye witness.
ocula'tezza [okula'tettsa] *sf* caution; shrewdness.
ocu'lato, a *ag* (*attento*) cautious, prudent; (*accorto*) shrewd.
ocu'lista, i, e *sm/f* eye specialist, oculist.
od *cong vedi* **o**.
'ode *sf* ode.

'**ode** *etc vb vedi* **udire.**

odi'are *vt* to hate, detest.

odi'erno, a *ag* today's, of today; (*attuale*) present; **in data** ~**a** (*formale*) today.

'**odio** *sm* hatred; **avere in** ~ **qc/qn** to hate *o* detest sth/sb.

odi'oso, a *ag* hateful, odious; **rendersi** ~ **(a)** to make o.s. unpopular (with).

'**odo** *etc vb vedi* **udire.**

odontoi'atra, i, e *sm/f* dentist, dental surgeon.

odontoia'tria *sf* dentistry.

odonto'tecnico, ci *sm* dental technician.

odo'rare *vt* (*annusare*) to smell; (*profumare*) to perfume, scent ♦ *vi*: ~ **(di)** to smell (of).

odo'rato *sm* sense of smell.

o'dore *sm* smell; **gli** ~**i** *smpl* (*CUC*) (aromatic) herbs; **sentire** ~ **di qc** to smell sth; **morire in** ~ **di santità** (*REL*) to die in the odour (*BRIT*) *o* odor (*US*) of sanctity.

odo'roso, a *ag* sweet-smelling.

of'fendere *vt* to offend; (*violare*) to break, violate; (*insultare*) to insult; (*ferire*) to hurt; ~**rsi** *vr* (*con senso reciproco*) to insult one another; (*risentirsi*): ~**rsi (di)** to take offence (at), be offended (by).

offen'sivo, a *ag, sf* offensive.

offen'sore *sm* offender; (*MIL*) aggressor.

offe'rente *sm* (*in aste*): **al migliore** ~ to the highest bidder.

of'ferto, a *pp di* **offrire** ♦ *sf* offer; (*donazione, anche REL*) offering; (*in gara d'appalto*) tender; (*in aste*) bid; (*ECON*) supply; **fare un'**~**a** to make an offer; (*per appalto*) to tender; (*ad un'asta*) to bid; ~**a pubblica d'acquisto (OPA)** takeover bid; ~**a pubblica di vendita (OPV)** public offer for sale; ~**a reale** tender; "~**e d'impiego**" (*STAMPA*) "situations vacant" (*BRIT*), "help wanted" (*US*).

of'feso, a *pp di* **offendere** ♦ *ag* offended; (*fisicamente*) hurt, injured ♦ *sm/f* offended party ♦ *sf* insult, affront; (*MIL*) attack; (*DIR*) offence (*BRIT*), offense (*US*); **essere** ~ **con qn** to be annoyed with sb; **parte** ~**a** (*DIR*) plaintiff.

offi'ciare [offi't∫are] *vi* (*REL*) to officiate.

offi'cina [offi't∫ina] *sf* workshop.

of'frire *vt* to offer; ~**rsi** *vr* (*proporsi*) to offer (o.s.), volunteer; (*occasione*) to present itself; (*esporsi*): ~**rsi a** to expose o.s. to; **ti offro da bere** I'll buy you a drink; "**offresi posto di segretaria**" "secretarial vacancy", "vacancy for secretary"; "**segretaria offresi**" "secretary seeks post".

offus'care *vt* to obscure, darken; (*fig: intelletto*) to dim, cloud; (: *fama*) to

obscure, overshadow; ~**rsi** *vr* to grow dark; to cloud, grow dim; to be obscured.

of'talmico, a, ci, che *ag* ophthalmic.

oggettività [oddʒettivi'ta] *sf* objectivity.

ogget'tivo, a [oddʒet'tivo] *ag* objective.

og'getto [od'dʒɛtto] *sm* object; (*materia, argomento*) subject (matter); (*in lettere commerciali*): ~ ... **re ...; essere** ~ **di** (*critiche, controversia*) to be the subject of; (*odio, pietà etc*) to be the object of; **essere** ~ **di scherno** to be a laughing stock; **in** ~ **a quanto detto** (*in lettere*) as regards the matter mentioned above; ~**i preziosi** valuables, articles of value; ~**i smarriti** lost property *sg* (*BRIT*), lost and found *sg* (*US*).

'**oggi** ['ɔddʒi] *av, sm* today; ~ **stesso** today, this very day; ~ **come** ~ at present, as things stand; **dall'** ~ **al domani** from one day to the next; **a tutt'**~ up till now, till today; **le spese a tutt'**~ **sono ...** expenses to date are ...; ~ **a otto** a week today.

oggigi'orno [oddʒi'dʒorno] *av* nowadays.

o'giva [o'dʒiva] *sf* ogive, pointed arch.

'**ogni** ['oɲɲi] *det* every, each; (*tutti*) all; (*con valore distributivo*) every; ~ **uomo è mortale** all men are mortal; **viene** ~ **due giorni** he comes every two days; ~ **cosa** everything; **ad** ~ **costo** at all costs, at any price; **in** ~ **luogo** everywhere; ~ **tanto** every so often; ~ **volta che** every time that.

Ognis'santi [oɲɲis'santi] *sm* All Saints' Day.

o'gnuno [oɲ'ɲuno] *pron* everyone, everybody.

'**ohi** *escl* oh!; (*esprimere dolore*) ow!

ohimè *escl* oh dear!

'**OIL** *sigla f* (= *Organizzazione Internazionale del Lavoro*) ILO.

OL *abbr* (= *onde lunghe*) LW.

O'landa *sf*: **l'**~ Holland.

olan'dese *ag* Dutch ♦ *sm* (*LING*) Dutch ♦ *sm/f* Dutchman/woman; **gli O**~**i** the Dutch.

ole'andro *sm* oleander.

ole'ato, a *ag*: **carta** ~**a** greaseproof paper (*BRIT*), wax paper (*US*).

oleo'dotto *sm* oil pipeline.

ole'oso, a *ag* oily; (*che contiene olio*) oil *cpd*.

o'lezzo [o'leddzo] *sm* fragrance.

ol'fatto *sm* sense of smell.

oli'are *vt* to oil.

olia'tore *sm* oil can, oiler.

oli'era *sf* oil cruet.

oligar'chia [oligar'kia] *sf* oligarchy.

olim'piadi *sfpl* Olympic Games.

o'limpico, a, ci, che *ag* Olympic.

'**olio** *sm* oil; (*PITTURA*): **un (quadro a)** ~ an oil painting; **sott'**~ (*CUC*) in oil; ~ **di fegato di merluzzo** cod liver oil; ~ **d'oliva** olive oil; ~ **santo** holy oil; ~ **di semi** vegetable oil; ~ **solare** suntan oil.

o'**liva** *sf* olive.

oli'**vastro, a** *ag* olive(-coloured) (*BRIT*), olive(-colored) (*US*); (*carnagione*) sallow.

oli'**veto** *sm* olive grove.

o'**livo** *sm* olive tree.

'**olmo** *sm* elm.

olo'**causto** *sm* holocaust.

OLP *sigla f* (= *Organizzazione per la Liberazione della Palestina*) PLO.

oltraggi'**are** [oltrad'dʒare] *vt* to offend, insult.

ol'**traggio** [ol'traddʒo] *sm* offence (*BRIT*), offense (*US*), insult; (*DIR*): ~ **al pudore** indecent behaviour (*BRIT*) *o* behavior (*US*); ~ **alla corte** contempt of court.

oltraggi'**oso, a** [oltrad'dʒoso] *ag* offensive.

ol'**tralpe** *av* beyond the Alps.

ol'**tranza** [ol'trantsa] *sf*: **a** ~ to the last, to the bitter end; **sciopero ad** ~ all-out strike.

oltran'**zismo** [oltran'tsizmo] *sm* (*POL*) extremism.

oltran'**zista, i, e** [oltran'tsista] *sm/f* (*POL*) extremist.

'**oltre** *av* (*più in là*) further; (*di più: aspettare*) longer, more ♦ *prep* (*di là da*) beyond, over, on the other side of; (*più di*) more than, over; (*in aggiunta a*) besides; (*eccetto*): ~ **a** except, apart from; ~ **a tutto** on top of all that.

oltrecor'**tina** *av* behind the Iron Curtain; **paesi d'**~ Iron Curtain countries.

oltre'**manica** *av* across the Channel.

oltre'**mare** *av* overseas.

oltre'**modo** *av* extremely, greatly.

oltreo'**ceano** [oltreo'tʃeano] *av* overseas ♦ *sm*: **paesi d'**~ overseas countries.

oltrepas'**sare** *vt* to go beyond, exceed.

oltre'**tomba** *sm inv*: **l'**~ the hereafter.

OM *abbr* (= *onde medie*) MW; (*MIL*) = *ospedale militare*.

o'**maggio** [o'maddʒo] *sm* (*dono*) gift; (*segno di rispetto*) homage, tribute; ~**i** *smpl* (*complimenti*) respects; **in** ~ (*copia, biglietto*) complimentary; **rendere** ~ **a** to pay homage *o* tribute to; **presentare i propri** ~**i a qn** (*formale*) to pay one's respects to sb.

'**Oman** *sm*: **l'**~ Oman.

ombeli'**cale** *ag* umbilical.

ombe'**lico, chi** *sm* navel.

'**ombra** *sf* (*zona non assolata, fantasma*) shade; (*sagoma scura*) shadow ♦ *ag inv*:

bandiera ~ flag of convenience; **governo** ~ (*POL*) shadow cabinet; **sedere all'**~ to sit in the shade; **nell'**~ (*tramare, agire*) secretly; **restare nell'**~ (*fig: persona*) to remain in obscurity; **senza** ~ **di dubbio** without the shadow of a doubt.

ombreggi'**are** [ombred'dʒare] *vt* to shade.

om'**brello** *sm* umbrella; ~ **da sole** parasol, sunshade.

ombrel'**lone** *sm* beach umbrella.

om'**bretto** *sm* eyeshadow.

om'**broso, a** *ag* shady, shaded; (*cavallo*) nervous, skittish; (*persona*) touchy, easily offended.

ome'**lette** [omə'lɛt] *sf inv* omelet(te).

ome'**lia** *sf* (*REL*) homily, sermon.

ome'**opata** *sm/f* hom(o)eopath.

omeopa'**tia** *sf* hom(o)eopathy.

omeo'**patico, a, ci, che** *ag* hom(o)eopathic ♦ *sm* hom(o)eopath.

omertà *sf* conspiracy of silence.

o'**messo, a** *pp di* **omettere**.

o'**mettere** *vt* to omit, leave out; ~ **di fare** to omit *o* fail to do.

omi'**cida, i, e** [omi'tʃida] *ag* homicidal, murderous ♦ *sm/f* murderer/murderess.

omi'**cidio** [omi'tʃidjo] *sm* murder; ~ **colposo** (*DIR*) culpable homicide; ~ **premeditato** (*DIR*) murder.

o'**misi** *etc vb vedi* **omettere**.

omissi'**one** *sf* omission; **reato d'**~ criminal negligence; ~ **di atti d'ufficio** negligence (*by a public employee*); ~ **di denuncia** failure to report a crime; ~ **di soccorso** (*DIR*) failure to stop and give assistance.

omogeneiz'**zato** [omodʒeneid'dzato] *sm* baby food.

omo'**geneo, a** [omo'dʒɛneo] *ag* homogeneous.

omolo'**gare** *vt* (*DIR*) to approve, recognize; (*ratificare*) to ratify.

omologazi'**one** [omologat'tsjone] *sf* approval; ratification.

o'**mologo, a, ghi, ghe** *ag* homologous, corresponding ♦ *sm/f* opposite number.

o'**monimo, a** *sm/f* namesake ♦ *sm* (*LING*) homonym.

omosessu'**ale** *ag, sm/f* homosexual.

O.M.S. *sigla f vedi* **Organizzazione Mondiale della Sanità**.

On. *abbr* (*POL*) = **onorevole**.

'**oncia, ce** ['ontʃa] *sf* ounce.

'**onda** *sf* wave; **mettere** *o* **mandare in** ~ (*RADIO, TV*) to broadcast; **andare in** ~ (*RADIO, TV*) to go on the air; ~**e corte/ medie/lunghe** short/medium/long wave *sg*; **l'**~ **verde** (*AUT*) synchronized traffic lights *pl*.

on'data *sf* wave, billow; (*fig*) wave, surge; **a ~e** in waves; **~ di caldo** heatwave; **~ di freddo** cold spell *o* snap.

'onde *cong* (*affinché: con il congiuntivo*) so that, in order that; (: *con l'infinito*) so as to, in order to.

ondeggi'are [onded'dʒare] *vi* (*acqua*) to ripple; (*muoversi sulle onde: barca*) to rock, roll; (*fig: muoversi come le onde, barcollare*) to sway; (: *essere incerto*) to waver.

on'doso, a *ag* (*moto*) of the waves.

ondu'lato, a *ag* (*capelli*) wavy; (*terreno*) undulating; **cartone ~** corrugated paper; **lamiera ~a** sheet of corrugated iron.

ondula'torio, a *ag* undulating; (*FISICA*) undulatory, wave *cpd.*

ondulazi'one [ondulat'tsjone] *sf* undulation; (*acconciatura*) wave.

one'rato, a *ag*: **~ di** burdened with, loaded with.

'onere *sm* burden; **~ finanziario** financial charge; **~i fiscali** taxes.

one'roso, a *ag* (*fig*) heavy, onerous.

onestà *sf* honesty.

onesta'mente *av* honestly; fairly; virtuously; (*in verità*) honestly, frankly.

o'nesto, a *ag* (*probo, retto*) honest; (*giusto*) fair; (*casto*) chaste, virtuous.

'onice ['ɔnitʃe] *sf* onyx.

o'nirico, a, ci, che *ag* dreamlike, dream *cpd.*

onnipo'tente *ag* omnipotent.

onnipre'sente *ag* omnipresent; (*scherzoso*) ubiquitous.

onnisci'ente [onniʃ'ʃɛnte] *ag* omniscient.

onniveg'gente [onnived'dʒɛnte] *ag* all-seeing.

ono'mastico, ci *sm* name day.

onomato'pea *sf* onomatopoeia.

onomato'peico, a, ci, che *ag* onomatopoeic.

ono'ranze [ono'rantse] *sfpl* honours (*BRIT*), honors (*US*).

ono'rare *vt* to honour (*BRIT*), honor (*US*); (*far onore a*) to do credit to; **~rsi** *vr*: **~rsi di qc/di fare** to feel hono(u)red by sth/to do.

ono'rario, a *ag* honorary ♦ *sm* fee.

onora'tissimo, a *ag* (*in presentazioni*): **~!** delighted to meet you!

ono'rato, a *ag* (*reputazione, famiglia, carriera*) distinguished; **essere ~ di fare qc** to have the honour to do sth *o* of doing sth; **~ di conoscerla!** (it is) a pleasure to meet you!

o'nore *sm* honour (*BRIT*), honor (*US*); **in ~ di** in hono(u)r of; **fare gli ~i di casa** to play host (*o* hostess); **fare ~ a** to hono(u)r; (*pranzo*) to do justice to; (*famiglia*) to be a credit to; **farsi ~** to distinguish o.s.; **posto d'~** place of hono(u)r; **a onor del vero ...** to tell the truth ....

ono'revole *ag* honourable (*BRIT*), honorable (*US*) ♦ *sm/f* (*POL*) ≈ Member of Parliament (*BRIT*), ≈ Congressman/woman (*US*).

onorifi'cenza [onorifi'tʃɛntsa] *sf* honour (*BRIT*), honor (*US*); decoration.

ono'rifico, a, ci, che *ag* honorary.

'onta *sf* shame, disgrace; **ad ~ di** despite, notwithstanding.

on'tano *sm* alder.

'O.N.U. *sigla f* (= *Organizzazione delle Nazioni Unite*) UN, UNO ....

OO.PP. *abbr vedi* opere pubbliche.

'OPA *sigla f vedi* offerta pubblica d'acquisto.

o'paco, a, chi, che *ag* (*vetro*) opaque; (*metallo*) dull, matt.

o'pale *sm o f* opal.

'O.P.E.C. *sigla f* (= *Organization of Petroleum Exporting Countries*) OPEC.

'opera *sf* (*gen*) work; (*azione rilevante*) action, deed, work; (*MUS*) work; opus; (: *melodramma*) opera; (: *teatro*) opera house; (*ente*) institution, organization; **per ~ sua** thanks to him; **fare ~ di persuasione presso qn** to try to convince sb; **mettersi/essere all'~** to get down to/be at work; **~ d'arte** work of art; **~ buffa** comic opera; **~ lirica** (grand) opera; **~ pia** religious charity; **~e pubbliche (OO.PP.)** public works; **~e di restauro/di scavo** restoration/excavation work *sg.*

ope'raio, a *ag* working-class; workers'; (*ZOOL: ape, formica*) worker *cpd* ♦ *sm/f* worker; **classe ~a** working class; **~ di fabbrica** factory worker; **~ a giornata** day labourer (*BRIT*) *o* laborer (*US*); **~ specializzato** *o* **qualificato** skilled worker; **~ non specializzato** semi-skilled worker.

ope'rare *vt* to carry out, make; (*MED*) to operate on ♦ *vi* to operate, work; (*rimedio*) to act, work; (*MED*) to operate; **~rsi** *vr* to occur, take place; (*MED*) to have an operation; **~rsi d'appendicite** to have one's appendix out; **~ qn d'urgenza** to perform an emergency operation on sb.

opera'tivo, a *ag* operative, operating; **piano ~** (*MIL*) plan of operations.

ope'rato *sm* (*comportamento*) actions *pl.*

opera'tore, 'trice *sm/f* operator; (*TV, CINE*) cameraman; (*COMM*) **aperto solo agli ~i** open to the trade only; **~ di borsa** dealer on the stock exchange; **~ ecologico** refuse collector; **~ economico** agent, broker; **~ del suono** sound recordist; **~ turistico** tour operator.

opera'torio, a *ag* (*MED*) operating.
operazi'one [operat'tsjone] *sf* operation.
ope'retta *sf* (*MUS*) operetta, light opera.
operosità *sf* industry.
ope'roso, a *ag* industrious, hard-working.
opi'ficio [opi'fitʃo] *sm* factory, works *pl*.
opi'nabile *ag* (*discutibile*) debatable,
  questionable; **è ~** it is a matter of
  opinion.
opini'one *sf* opinion; **avere il coraggio delle
  proprie ~i** to have the courage of one's
  convictions; **l'~ pubblica** public opinion.
opinio'nista, i, e *sm/f* (political) columnist.
op là *escl* (*per far saltare*) hup!; (*a bimbo che
  è caduto*) upsy-daisy!
'oppio *sm* opium.
oppi'omane *sm/f* opium addict.
oppo'nente *ag* opposing ♦ *sm/f* opponent.
op'pongo *etc vb vedi* **opporre**.
op'porre *vt* to oppose; **opporsi** *vr*: **opporsi
  (a qc)** to oppose (sth); to object (to sth); **~
  resistenza/un rifiuto** to offer resistance/
  to refuse.
opportu'nista, i, e *sm/f* opportunist.
opportunità *sf inv* opportunity;
  (*convenienza*) opportuneness, timeliness.
oppor'tuno, a *ag* timely, opportune;
  (*giusto*) right, appropriate; **a tempo ~** at
  the right o the appropriate time.
op'posi *etc vb vedi* **opporre**.
opposi'tore, 'trice *sm/f* opposer, opponent.
opposizi'one [oppozit'tsjone] *sf* opposition;
  (*DIR*) objection; **essere in netta ~** (*idee,
  opinioni*) to clash, be in complete
  opposition; **fare ~ a qn/qc** to oppose sb/
  sth.
op'posto, a *pp di* **opporre** ♦ *ag* opposite;
  (*opinioni*) conflicting ♦ *sm* opposite,
  contrary; **all'~** on the contrary.
oppressi'one *sf* oppression.
oppres'sivo, a *ag* oppressive.
op'presso, a *pp di* **opprimere**.
oppres'sore *sm* oppressor.
oppri'mente *ag* (*caldo, noia*) oppressive;
  (*persona*) tiresome; (: *deprimente*)
  depressing.
op'primere *vt* (*premere, gravare*) to weigh
  down; (*estenuare: sog: caldo*) to suffocate,
  oppress; (*tiranneggiare: popolo*) to
  oppress.
oppu'gnare [oppuɲ'ɲare] *vt* (*fig*) to refute.
op'pure *cong* or (else).
op'tare *vi*: **~ per** (*scegliere*) to opt for,
  decide upon; (*BORSA*) to take (out) an
  option on.
'optimum *sm inv* optimum.
opu'lento, a *ag* (*ricco*) rich, wealthy,
  affluent; (: *arredamento etc*) opulent.

opu'lenza [opu'lɛntsa] *sf* (*vedi ag*) richness,
  wealth, affluence; opulence.
o'puscolo *sm* booklet, pamphlet.
OPV *sigla f vedi* **offerta pubblica di vendita**.
opzio'nale [optsjo'nale] *ag* optional.
opzi'one [op'tsjone] *sf* option.
OR *sigla = Oristano*.
'ora *sf* (*60 minuti*) hour; (*momento*) time
  ♦ *av* (*adesso*) now; (*poco fa*): **è uscito
  proprio ~** he's just gone out; (*tra poco*)
  presently, in a minute; (*correlativo*):
  ~ ... ~ now ... now; **che ~ è?, che ~e
  sono?** what time is it?; **domani a quest'~**
  this time tomorrow; **non veder l'~ di fare**
  to long to do, look forward to doing; **fare
  le ~e piccole** to stay up till the early
  hours (of the morning) o the small hours;
  è ~ di partire it's time to go; **di buon' ~**
  early; **alla buon'~!** at last!; **~ legale** o
  estiva summer time (*BRIT*), daylight
  saving time (*US*); **~ locale** local time; **~ di
  pranzo** lunchtime; **~ di punta** (*AUT*) rush
  hour; **d'~ in avanti** o **poi** from now on; **or
  ~** just now, a moment ago; **~ come ~**
  right now, at present; **10 anni or sono** 10
  years ago.
o'racolo *sm* oracle.
'orafo *sm* goldsmith.
o'rale *ag, sm* oral.
oral'mente *av* orally.
ora'mai *av* = **ormai**.
o'rario, a *ag* hourly; (*fuso, segnale*) time
  cpd; (*velocità*) per hour ♦ *sm* timetable,
  schedule; (*di visite etc*) hours *pl*, time(s *pl*);
  ~ di apertura/chiusura opening/closing
  time; **~ di apertura degli sportelli** bank
  opening hours; **~ elastico** o **flessibile**
  (*INDUSTRIA*) flexitime; **~ ferroviario**
  railway timetable; **~ di lavoro/d'ufficio**
  working/office hours.
o'rata *sf* sea bream.
ora'tore, 'trice *sm/f* speaker; orator.
ora'torio, a *ag* oratorical ♦ *sm* (*REL*)
  oratory; (*MUS*) oratorio ♦ *sf* (*arte*) oratory.
orazi'one [orat'tsjone] *sf* (*REL*) prayer;
  (*discorso*) speech, oration.
or'bene *cong* so, well (then).
'orbita *sf* (*ASTR, FISICA*) orbit; (*ANAT*) (eye-)
  socket.
orbi'tare *vi* to orbit.
'orbo, a *ag* blind.
'Orcadi *sfpl*: **le (isole) ~** the Orkney
  Islands, the Orkneys.
or'chestra [or'kɛstra] *sf* orchestra.
orches'trale [orkes'trale] *ag* orchestral
  ♦ *sm/f* orchestra player.
orches'trare [orkes'trare] *vt* to orchestrate;
  (*fig*) to stage-manage.

orchi'dea [orki'dɛa] sf orchid.

'orcio ['ortʃo] sm jar.

'orco, chi sm ogre.

'orda sf horde.

or'digno [or'diɲɲo] sm: ~ **esplosivo** explosive device.

ordi'nale ag, sm ordinal.

ordina'mento sm order, arrangement; (regolamento) regulations pl, rules pl; ~ **scolastico/giuridico** education/legal system.

ordi'nanza [ordi'nantsa] sf (DIR, MIL) order; (AMM: decreto) decree; (persona: MIL) orderly, batman; **d'**~ (MIL) regulation cpd; **ufficiale d'**~ orderly; ~ **municipale** by(e)-law.

ordi'nare vt (mettere in ordine) to arrange, organize; (COMM) to order; (prescrivere: medicina) to prescribe; (comandare): ~ **a qn di fare qc** to order o command sb to do sth; (REL) to ordain.

ordi'nario, a ag (comune) ordinary; (grossolano) coarse, common ♦ sm ordinary; (di università) full professor.

ordina'tivo, a ag regulating, governing ♦ sm (COMM) order.

ordi'nato, a ag tidy, orderly.

ordinazi'one [ordinat'tsjone] sf (COMM) order; (REL) ordination; **fare un'**~ **di qc** to put in an order for sth, order sth; **eseguire qc su** ~ to make sth to order.

'ordine sm order; (carattere): **d'**~ **pratico** of a practical nature; **all'**~ (COMM: assegno) to order; **di prim'**~ first-class; **fino a nuovo** ~ until further notice; **essere in** ~ (documenti) to be in order; (persona, stanza) to be tidy; **mettere in** ~ to put in order, tidy (up); **richiamare all'**~ to call to order; **le forze dell'**~ the forces of law and order; ~ **d'acquisto** purchase order; **l'**~ **degli avvocati** ≈ the Bar; ~ **del giorno** (di seduta) agenda; (MIL) order of the day; **l'**~ **dei medici** ≈ the Medical Association; ~ **di pagamento** standing order (BRIT), automatic payment (US); **l'**~ **pubblico** law and order; ~**i (sacri)** (REL) holy orders.

or'dire vt (fig) to plot, scheme.

or'dito sm (di tessuto) warp.

orecchi'abile [orek'kjabile] ag (canzone) catchy.

orec'chino [orek'kino] sm earring.

o'recchio [o'rekkjo], pl(f) **o'recchie** sm (ANAT) ear; **avere** ~ to have a good ear (for music); **venire all'**~ **di qn** to come to sb's attention; **fare** ~**e da mercante (a)** to turn a deaf ear (to).

orecchi'oni [orek'kjoni] smpl (MED) mumps sg.

o'refice [o'refitʃe] sm goldsmith; jeweller (BRIT), jeweler (US).

orefice'ria [orefitʃe'ria] sf (arte) goldsmith's art; (negozio) jeweller's (shop) (BRIT), jewelry store (US).

'orfano, a ag orphan(ed) ♦ sm/f orphan; ~ **di padre/madre** fatherless/motherless.

orfano'trofio sm orphanage.

orga'netto sm barrel organ; (fam: armonica a bocca) mouth organ; (: fisarmonica) accordion.

or'ganico, a, ci, che ag organic ♦ sm personnel, staff.

organi'gramma, i sm organization chart; (INFORM) computer flow chart.

orga'nismo sm (BIOL) organism; (ANAT, AMM) body, organism.

orga'nista, i, e sm/f organist.

organiz'zare [organid'dzare] vt to organize; ~**rsi** vr to get organized.

organizza'tivo, a [organiddza'tivo] ag organizational.

organizza'tore, 'trice [organiddza'tore] ag organizing ♦ sm/f organizer.

organizzazi'one [organiddzat'tsjone] sf (azione) organizing, arranging; (risultato) organization; **O**~ **Mondiale della Sanità (O.M.S.)** World Health Organization (WHO).

'organo sm organ; (di congegno) part; (portavoce) spokesman/woman, mouthpiece; ~**i di trasmissione** (TECN) transmission (unit) sg.

or'gasmo sm (FISIOL) orgasm; (fig) agitation, anxiety.

'orgia, ge ['ɔrdʒa] sf orgy.

or'goglio [or'gɔʎʎo] sm pride.

orgogli'oso, a [orgoʎ'ʎoso] ag proud.

orien'tabile ag adjustable.

orien'tale ag (paese, regione) eastern; (tappeti, lingua, civiltà) oriental.

orienta'mento sm positioning; orientation; direction; **senso di** ~ sense of direction; **perdere l'**~ to lose one's bearings; ~ **professionale** careers guidance.

orien'tare vt (situare) to position; (carta, bussola) to orientate; (fig) to direct; ~**rsi** vr to find one's bearings; (fig: tendere) to tend, lean; (: indirizzarsi): ~**rsi verso** to take up, go in for.

orienta'tivo, a ag indicative, for guidance; **a scopo** ~ for guidance.

ori'ente sm east; **l'O**~ the East, the Orient; **il Medio/l'Estremo O**~ the Middle/Far East; **a** ~ in the east.

ori'ficio [ori'fitʃo], **ori'fizio** [ori'fittsjo] sm (apertura) opening; (: di tubo) mouth;

(*ANAT*) orifice.

o'rigano *sm* oregano.

origi'nale [oridʒi'nale] *ag* original; (*bizzarro*) eccentric ♦ *sm* original.

originalità [oridʒinali'ta] *sf* originality; eccentricity.

origi'nare [oridʒi'nare] *vt* to bring about, produce ♦ *vi*: ~ **da** to arise *o* spring from.

origi'nario, a [oridʒi'narjo] *ag* original; **essere ~ di** to be a native of; (*animale, pianta*) to be indigenous to, be native to.

o'rigine [o'ridʒine] *sf* origin; **all'~** originally; **d'~ inglese** of English origin; **avere ~ da** to originate from; **dare ~ a** to give rise to.

origli'are [oriʎ'ʎare] *vi*: ~ **(a)** to eavesdrop (on).

o'rina *sf* urine.

ori'nale *sm* chamberpot.

ori'nare *vi* to urinate ♦ *vt* to pass.

orina'toio *sm* (public) urinal.

ori'undo, a *ag*: **essere ~ di Milano** *etc* to be of Milanese *etc* extraction *o* origin ♦ *sm/f* person of foreign extraction *o* origin.

orizzon'tale [oriddzon'tale] *ag* horizontal.

oriz'zonte [orid'dzonte] *sm* horizon.

ORL *sigla f* (*MED*: = *otorinolaringoiatria*) ENT.

or'lare *vt* to hem.

orla'tura *sf* (*azione*) hemming *no pl*; (*orlo*) hem.

'orlo *sm* edge, border; (*di recipiente*) rim, brim; (*di vestito etc*) hem; **pieno fino all'~** full to the brim, brimful; **sull'~ della pazzia/della rovina** on the brink *o* verge of madness/ruin; ~ **a giorno** hemstitch.

'orma *sf* (*di persona*) footprint; (*di animale*) track; (*impronta, traccia*) mark, trace; **seguire** *o* **calcare le ~e di qn** to follow in sb's footsteps.

or'mai *av* by now, by this time; (*adesso*) now; (*quasi*) almost, nearly.

ormeggi'are [ormed'dʒare] *vt*, **~rsi** *vr* (*NAUT*) to moor.

or'meggio [or'meddʒo] *sm* (*atto*) mooring *no pl*; (*luogo*) moorings *pl*; **posto d'~** berth.

ormo'nale *ag* hormonal; (*disfunzione, cura*) hormone *cpd*; **terapia ~** hormone therapy.

or'mone *sm* hormone.

ornamen'tale *ag* ornamental, decorative.

orna'mento *sm* ornament, decoration.

or'nare *vt* to adorn, decorate; **~rsi** *vr*: **~rsi (di)** to deck o.s. (out) (with).

or'nato, a *ag* ornate.

ornitolo'gia [ornitolo'dʒia] *sf* ornithology.

orni'tologo, a, gi, ghe *sm/f* ornithologist.

'oro *sm* gold; **d'~, in ~** gold *cpd*; **d'~** (*colore, occasione*) golden; (*persona*) marvellous (*BRIT*), marvelous (*US*); **un affare d'~** a

real bargain; **prendere qc per ~ colato** to take sth as gospel (truth); ~ **nero** black gold; ~ **zecchino** pure gold.

orologe'ria [orolodʒe'ria] *sf* watchmaking *no pl*; watchmaker's (shop); clockmaker's (shop); **bomba a ~** time bomb.

orologi'aio [orolo'dʒajo] *sm* watchmaker; clockmaker.

oro'logio [oro'lɔdʒo] *sm* clock; (*da tasca, da polso*) watch; ~ **biologico** biological clock; ~ **da polso** wristwatch; ~ **al quarzo** quartz watch; ~ **a sveglia** alarm clock.

o'roscopo *sm* horoscope.

or'rendo, a *ag* (*spaventoso*) horrible, awful; (*bruttissimo*) hideous.

or'ribile *ag* horrible.

'orrido, a *ag* fearful, horrid.

orripi'lante *ag* hair-raising, horrifying.

or'rore *sm* horror; **avere in ~ qn/qc** to loathe *o* detest sb/sth; **mi fanno ~** I loathe *o* detest them.

orsacchi'otto [orsak'kjɔtto] *sm* teddy bear.

'orso *sm* bear; ~ **bruno/bianco** brown/polar bear.

orsù *escl* come now!

or'taggio [or'taddʒo] *sm* vegetable.

or'tensia *sf* hydrangea.

or'tica, che *sf* (stinging) nettle.

orti'caria *sf* nettle rash.

orticol'tura *sf* horticulture.

'orto *sm* vegetable garden, kitchen garden; (*AGR*) market garden (*BRIT*), truck farm (*US*); ~ **botanico** botanical garden(s *pl*).

orto'dosso, a *ag* orthodox.

ortofrut'ticolo, a *ag* fruit and vegetable *cpd*.

ortogo'nale *ag* perpendicular.

ortogra'fia *sf* spelling.

orto'lano, a *sm/f* (*venditore*) greengrocer (*BRIT*), produce dealer (*US*).

ortope'dia *sf* orthopaedics *sg* (*BRIT*), orthopedics *sg* (*US*).

orto'pedico, a, ci, che *ag* orthopaedic (*BRIT*), orthopedic (*US*) ♦ *sm* orthopaedic specialist (*BRIT*), orthopedist (*US*).

orzai'olo [ordza'jɔlo], **orzaiu'olo** [ordza'jwɔlo] *sm* (*MED*) stye.

or'zata [or'dzata] *sf* barley water.

'orzo ['ɔrdzo] *sm* barley.

'OSA *sigla f* (= *Organizzazione degli Stati Americani*) OAS (= *Organization of American States*).

o'sare *vt*, *vi* to dare; ~ **fare** to dare (to) do; **come osi?** how dare you?

oscenità [oʃʃeni'ta] *sf inv* obscenity.

o'sceno, a [oʃ'ʃɛno] *ag* obscene; (*ripugnante*) ghastly.

oscil'lare [oʃʃil'lare] *vi* (*pendolo*) to swing; (*dondolare: al vento etc*) to rock; (*variare*) to fluctuate; (*TECN*) to oscillate; (*fig*): ~ **fra** to waver between.

oscillazi'one [oʃʃillat'tsjone] *sf* oscillation; (*di prezzi, temperatura*) fluctuation.

oscura'mento *sm* darkening; obscuring; (*in tempo di guerra*) blackout.

oscu'rare *vt* to darken, obscure; (*fig*) to obscure; ~**rsi** *vr* (*cielo*) to darken, cloud over; (*persona*): **si oscurò in volto** his face clouded over.

oscurità *sf* (*vedi ag*) darkness; obscurity; gloominess.

os'curo, a *ag* dark; (*fig: incomprensibile*) obscure; (: *umile: vita, natali*) humble, obscure; (: *triste: pensiero*) gloomy, sombre ♦ *sm*: **all'**~ in the dark; **tenere qn all'**~ **di qc** to keep sb in the dark about sth.

'Oslo *sf* Oslo.

ospe'dale *sm* hospital.

ospedali'ero, a *ag* hospital *cpd*.

ospi'tale *ag* hospitable.

ospitalità *sf* hospitality.

ospi'tare *vt* to give hospitality to; (*sog: albergo*) to accommodate.

'ospite *smf* (*persona che ospita*) host/ hostess; (*persona ospitata*) guest.

os'pizio [os'pittsjo] *sm* (*per vecchi etc*) home.

'ossa *sfpl vedi* **osso**.

os'sario *sm* (*MIL*) war memorial (*with burial place*).

ossa'tura *sf* (*ANAT*) skeletal structure, frame; (*TECN, fig*) framework.

'osseo, a *ag* bony; (*tessuto etc*) bone *cpd*.

osse'quente *ag*: ~ **alla legge** law-abiding.

os'sequio *sm* deference, respect; ~**i** *smpl* (*saluto*) respects, regards; **porgere i propri** ~**i a qn** (*formale*) to pay one's respects to sb; ~**i alla signora!** (give my) regards to your wife!

ossequi'oso, a *ag* obsequious.

osser'vanza [osser'vantsa] *sf* observance.

osser'vare *vt* to observe, watch; (*esaminare*) to examine; (*notare, rilevare*) to notice, observe; (*DIR: la legge*) to observe, respect; (*mantenere: silenzio*) to keep, observe; **far** ~ **qc a qn** to point sth out to sb.

osserva'tore, 'trice *ag* observant, perceptive ♦ *smf* observer.

osserva'torio *sm* (*ASTR*) observatory; (*MIL*) observation post.

osservazi'one [osservat'tsjone] *sf* observation; (*di legge etc*) observance; (*considerazione critica*) observation,

remark; (*rimprovero*) reproof; **in** ~ under observation; **fare un'**~ to make a remark; to raise an objection; **fare un'**~ **a qn** to criticize sb.

ossessio'nare *vt* to obsess, haunt; (*tormentare*) to torment, harass.

ossessi'one *sf* obsession; (*seccatura*) nuisance.

osses'sivo, a *ag* obsessive, haunting; troublesome.

os'sesso, a *ag* (*spiritato*) possessed.

os'sia *cong* that is, to be precise.

ossi'buchi [ossi'buki] *smpl di* **ossobuco**.

ossi'dare *vt*, ~**rsi** *vr* to oxidize.

ossidazi'one [ossidat'tsjone] *sf* oxidization, oxidation.

'ossido *sm* oxide; ~ **di carbonio** carbon monoxide.

ossige'nare [ossidʒe'nare] *vt* to oxygenate; (*decolorare*) to bleach; **acqua ossigenata** hydrogen peroxide.

os'sigeno [os'sidʒeno] *sm* oxygen.

'osso *sm* (*pl*(*f*) **ossa** *nel senso ANAT*) bone; **d'**~ (*bottone etc*) of bone, bone *cpd*; **avere le** ~**a rotte** to be dead *o* dog tired; **bagnato fino all'**~ soaked to the skin; **essere ridotto all'**~ (*fig: magro*) to be just skin and bone; (: *senza soldi*) to be in dire straits; **rompersi l'**~ **del collo** to break one's neck; **rimetterci l'**~ **del collo** (*fig*) to ruin o.s., lose everything; **un** ~ **duro** (*persona, impresa*) a tough number; ~ **di seppia** cuttlebone.

osso'buco, *pl* **ossi'buchi** *sm* (*CUC*) marrowbone; (: *piatto*) *stew made with knuckle of veal in tomato sauce.*

os'suto, a *ag* bony.

ostaco'lare *vt* to block, obstruct.

os'tacolo *sm* obstacle; (*EQUITAZIONE*) hurdle, jump; **essere di** ~ **a qn/qc** (*fig*) to stand in the way of sb/sth.

os'taggio [os'taddʒo] *sm* hostage.

'oste, os'tessa *smf* innkeeper.

osteggi'are [osted'dʒare] *vt* to oppose, be opposed to.

os'tello *sm* hostel; ~ **della gioventù** youth hostel.

osten'sorio *sm* (*REL*) monstrance.

osten'tare *vt* to make a show of, flaunt.

ostentazi'one [ostentat'tsjone] *sf* ostentation, show.

oste'ria *sf* inn.

os'tessa *sf vedi* **oste**.

os'tetrico, a, ci, che *ag* obstetric ♦ *sm* obstetrician ♦ *sf* midwife.

'ostia *sf* (*REL*) host; (*per medicinali*) wafer.

'ostico, a, ci, che *ag* difficult, tough.

os'tile *ag* hostile.

ostilità *sf* hostility ♦ *sfpl* (*MIL*) hostilities.
osti'narsi *vr* to insist, dig one's heels in; ~ **a fare** to persist (obstinately) in doing.
osti'nato, a *ag* (*caparbio*) obstinate; (*tenace*) persistent, determined.
ostinazi'one [ostinat'tsjone] *sf* obstinacy; persistence.
ostra'cismo [ostra'tʃizmo] *sm* ostracism.
'ostrica, che *sf* oyster.
ostru'ire *vt* to obstruct, block.
ostruzi'one [ostrut'tsjone] *sf* obstruction, blockage.
ostruzio'nismo [ostruttsjo'nizmo] *sm* (*POL*) obstructionism; (*SPORT*) obstruction; **fare dell'**~ **a** (*progetto, legge*) to obstruct; ~ **sindacale** work-to-rule (*BRIT*), slowdown (*US*).
o'tite *sf* ear infection.
oto'rino(laringoi'atra), i, e *sm/f* ear, nose and throat specialist.
'otre *sm* (*recipiente*) goatskin.
ott. *abbr* (= *ottobre*) Oct.
ottago'nale *ag* octagonal.
ot'tagono *sm* octagon.
ot'tano *sm* octane; **numero di** ~**i** octane rating.
ot'tanta *num* eighty.
ottan'tenne *ag* eighty-year-old ♦ *sm/f* octogenarian.
ottan'tesimo, a *num* eightieth.
ottan'tina *sf*: **una** ~ (**di**) about eighty.
ot'tavo, a *num* eighth ♦ *sf* octave.
ottempe'ranza [ottempe'rantsa] *sf*: **in** ~ **a** (*AMM*) in accordance with, in compliance with.
ottempe'rare *vi*: ~ **a** to comply with, obey.
ottene'brare *vt* to darken; (*fig*) to cloud.
otte'nere *vt* to obtain, get; (*risultato*) to achieve, obtain.
'ottico, a, ci, che *ag* (*della vista: nervo*) optic; (*dell'ottica*) optical ♦ *sm* optician ♦ *sf* (*scienza*) optics *sg*; (*FOT: lenti, prismi etc*) optics *pl*.
otti'male *ag* optimal, optimum.
ottima'mente *av* excellently, very well.
otti'mismo *sm* optimism.
otti'mista, i, e *sm/f* optimist.
ottimiz'zare [ottimid'dzare] *vt* to optimize.
ottimizzazi'one [ottimiddzat'tsjone] *sf* optimization.
'ottimo, a *ag* excellent, very good.
'otto *num* eight.
ot'tobre *sm* October; *per fraseologia vedi* **luglio**.
otto'brino, a *ag* October *cpd*.
ottocen'tesco, a, schi, sche [ottotʃen'tesko] *ag* nineteenth-century.

otto'cento [otto'tʃɛnto] *num* eight hundred ♦ *sm*: **l'O**~ the nineteenth century.
otto'mila *num* eight thousand.
ot'tone *sm* brass; **gli** ~**i** (*MUS*) the brass.
ottuage'nario, a [ottuadʒe'narjo] *ag, sm/f* octogenarian.
ot'tundere *vt* (*fig*) to dull.
ottu'rare *vt* to close (up); (*dente*) to fill.
ottura'tore *sm* (*FOT*) shutter; (*nelle armi*) breechblock.
otturazi'one [otturat'tsjone] *sf* closing (up); (*dentaria*) filling.
ottusità *sf* (*vedi ag*) obtuseness; dullness.
ot'tuso, a *pp di* **ottundere** ♦ *ag* (*MAT, fig*) obtuse; (*suono*) dull.
o'vaia *sf*, **o'vaio** *sm* (*ANAT*) ovary.
o'vale *ag, sm* oval.
o'varico, a *ag* ovarian.
o'vatta *sf* cotton wool; (*per imbottire*) padding, wadding.
ovat'tare *vt* (*imbottire*) to pad; (*fig: smorzare*) to muffle.
ovazi'one [ovat'tsjone] *sf* ovation.
'ovest *sm* west; **a** ~ (**di**) west (of); **verso** ~ westward(s).
o'vile *sm* pen, enclosure; **tornare all'**~ (*fig*) to return to the fold.
o'vino, a *ag* sheep *cpd*, ovine.
'O.V.N.I. *sigla m* (= *oggetto volante non identificato*) UFO.
ovulazi'one [ovulat'tsjone] *sf* ovulation.
'ovulo *sm* (*FISIOL*) ovum.
o'vunque *av* = **dovunque**.
ov'vero *cong* (*ossia*) that is, to be precise; (*oppure*) or (else).
ovvi'are *vi*: ~ **a** to obviate.
'ovvio, a *ag* obvious.
ozi'are [ot'tsjare] *vi* to laze around.
'ozio ['ɔttsjo] *sm* idleness; (*tempo libero*) leisure; **ore d'**~ leisure time; **stare in** ~ to be idle.
ozi'oso, a [ot'tsjoso] *ag* idle.
o'zono [od'dzɔno] *sm* ozone; **lo strato d'**~ the ozone layer.
ozonos'fera [oddzonos'fɛra] *sf* ozone layer.

Pp

P, p [pi] *sf o m inv* (*lettera*) P, p; **P come Padova** ≈ P for Peter.
P *abbr* (= *peso*) wt; (= *posteggio*) P.
p *abbr* (= *pagina*) p.
P2 *abbr f*: **la (loggia)** ~ the P2 masonic lodge.
PA *sigla* = Palermo.
P.A. *abbr* = **pubblica amministrazione**.
pa'care *vt* to calm; ~**rsi** *vr* (*tempesta, disordini*) to subside.
paca'tezza [paka'tettsa] *sf* quietness, calmness.
pa'cato, a *ag* quiet, calm.
'pacca, che *sf* slap.
pac'chetto [pak'ketto] *sm* packet; ~ **applicativo** (*INFORM*) applications package; ~ **azionario** (*FINANZA*) shareholding; ~ **software** (*INFORM*) software package; ~ **turistico** package holiday (*BRIT*) *o* tour.
pacchi'ano, a [pak'kjano] *ag* (*colori*) garish; (*abiti, arredamento*) vulgar, garish.
'pacco, chi *sm* parcel; (*involto*) bundle; ~ **postale** parcel.
paccot'tiglia [pakkot'tiʎʎa] *sf* trash, junk.
'pace ['patʃe] *sf* peace; **darsi** ~ to resign o.s.; **fare (la)** ~ **con qn** to make it up with sb.
pachis'tano, a [pakis'tano] *ag, sm/f* Pakistani.
pacifi'care [patʃifi'kare] *vt* (*riconciliare*) to reconcile, make peace between; (*mettere in pace*) to pacify.
pacificazi'one [patʃifikat'tsjone] *sf* (*vedi vt*) reconciliation; pacification.
pa'cifico, a, ci, che [pa'tʃifiko] *ag* (*persona*) peaceable; (*vita*) peaceful; (*fig: indiscusso*) indisputable; (: *ovvio*) obvious, clear ♦ *sm*: **il P~, l'Oceano P~** the Pacific (Ocean).
paci'fismo [patʃi'fizmo] *sm* pacifism.
paci'fista, i, e [patʃi'fista] *sm/f* pacifist.
pa'dano, a *ag* of the Po; **la pianura ~a** the Lombardy plain.
pa'della *sf* frying pan; (*per infermi*) bedpan.
padigli'one [padiʎ'ʎone] *sm* pavilion.
'Padova *sf* Padua.
pado'vano, a *ag* of (*o* from) Padua.
'padre *sm* father; ~**i** *smpl* (*antenati*)

forefathers.
Padre'terno *sm*: **il** ~ God the Father.
pa'drino *sm* godfather.
padro'nale *ag* (*scala, entrata*) main, principal; **casa** ~ country house.
padro'nanza [padro'nantsa] *sf* command, mastery.
padro'nato *sm*: **il** ~ the ruling class.
pa'drone, a *sm/f* master/mistress; (*proprietario*) owner; (*datore di lavoro*) employer; **essere** ~ **di sé** to be in control of o.s.; ~**/a di casa** master/mistress of the house; (*per gli inquilini*) landlord/lady.
padroneggi'are [padroned'dʒare] *vt* (*fig: sentimenti*) to master, control; (: *materia*) to master, know thoroughly; ~**rsi** *vr* to control o.s.
pae'saggio [pae'zaddʒo] *sm* landscape.
paesag'gista, i, e [paezad'dʒista] *sm/f* (*pittore*) landscape painter.
pae'sano, a *ag* country *cpd* ♦ *sm/f* villager; countryman/woman.
pa'ese *sm* (*nazione*) country, nation; (*terra*) country, land; (*villaggio*) village; ~ **di provenienza** country of origin; **i P~i Bassi** the Netherlands.
paf'futo, a *ag* chubby, plump.
'paga, ghe *sf* pay, wages *pl*; **giorno di** ~ pay day.
pa'gabile *ag* payable; ~ **alla consegna/a vista** payable on delivery/on demand.
pa'gaia *sf* paddle.
paga'mento *sm* payment; ~ **anticipato** payment in advance; ~ **alla consegna** payment on delivery; ~ **all'ordine** cash with order; **la TV a** ~ pay TV.
pa'gano, a *ag, sm/f* pagan.
pa'gare *vt* to pay; (*acquisto, fig: colpa*) to pay for; (*contraccambiare*) to repay, pay back ♦ *vi* to pay; **quanto l'ha pagato?** how much did you pay for it?; ~ **con carta di credito** to pay by credit card; ~ **in contanti** to pay cash; ~ **di persona** (*fig*) to suffer the consequences; **l'ho pagata cara** (*fig*) I paid dearly for it.
pa'gella [pa'dʒɛlla] *sf* (*INS*) school report (*BRIT*), report card (*US*).
'paggio ['paddʒo] *sm* page(boy).
paghe'rò [page'rɔ] *vb vedi* **pagare** ♦ *sm inv* IOU; ~ **cambiario** promissory note.
'pagina ['padʒina] *sf* page.
'paglia ['paʎʎa] *sf* straw; **avere la coda di** ~ (*fig*) to have a guilty conscience; **fuoco di** ~ (*fig*) flash in the pan.
pagliac'cetto [paʎʎat'tʃetto] *sm* (*per bambini*) rompers *pl*.
pagliac'ciata [paʎʎat'tʃata] *sf* farce.
pagli'accio [paʎ'ʎattʃo] *sm* clown.

pagli'aio [paʎˈʎajo] *sm* haystack.
paglie'riccio [paʎʎeˈrittʃo] *sm* straw mattress.
paglie'rino, a [paʎʎeˈrino] *ag:* **giallo ~** pale yellow.
pagli'etta [paʎˈʎetta] *sf (cappello per uomo)* (straw) boater; *(per tegami etc)* steel wool.
pagli'uzza [paʎˈʎuttsa] *sf* (blade of) straw; *(d'oro etc)* tiny particle, speck.
pa'gnotta [paɲˈɲɔtta] *sf* round loaf.
'pago, a, ghi, ghe *ag:* **~ (di)** satisfied (with).
pa'goda *sf* pagoda.
pail'lette [paˈjɛt] *sf inv* sequin.
'paio, *pl(f)* **'paia** *sm* pair; **un ~ di occhiali** a pair of glasses; **un ~ di** *(alcuni)* a couple of; **è un altro ~ di maniche** *(fig)* that's another kettle of fish.
'paio *etc vb vedi* **parere.**
pai'olo, paiu'olo *sm* (copper) pot.
'Pakistan *sm:* **il ~** Pakistan.
pakis'tano, a *ag, sm/f* = **pachistano.**
pal. *abbr* = **palude.**
'pala *sf* shovel; *(di remo, ventilatore, elica)* blade; *(di ruota)* paddle.
palan'drana *sf (scherzoso: abito lungo e largo)* tent.
pa'lata *sf* shovelful; **fare soldi a ~e** to make a mint.
pala'tale *ag (ANAT, LING)* palatal.
pa'lato *sm* palate.
pa'lazzo [paˈlattso] *sm (reggia)* palace; *(edificio)* building; **~ di giustizia** courthouse; **~ dello sport** sports stadium.

Rome contains a number of **Palazzi,** *which are now associated with various government departments and political figures or groups.* **Palazzo Chigi,** *in Piazza Colonna, was built in the 16th century and acquired by the state in 1919, as the seat of the Foreign Ministry. Since 1961 it has been the Prime Minister's office and the place where the cabinet meets.* **Palazzo Madama,** *also constructed in the 16th century for the Medici family, has been the seat of the Senate since 1871.* **Palazzo di Montecitorio,** *which was completed in 1694, has housed the* **Camera dei deputati** *since 1870.* **Palazzo Viminale,** *which takes its name from one of the seven hills of Rome, on which it stands, is the home of the Ministry of the Interior.*

---

pal'chetto [palˈketto] *sm* shelf.
'palco, chi *sm (TEAT)* box; *(tavolato)* platform, stand; *(ripiano)* layer.
palco'scenico, ci [palkoʃˈʃɛniko] *sm (TEAT)* stage.

palermi'tano, a *ag* of *(o* from*)* Palermo
♦ *sm/f* person from Palermo.
Pa'lermo *sf* Palermo.
pale'sare *vt* to reveal, disclose; **~rsi** *vr* to reveal *o* show o.s.
pa'lese *ag* clear, evident.
Pales'tina *sf:* **la ~** Palestine.
palesti'nese *ag, sm/f* Palestinian.
pa'lestra *sf* gymnasium; *(esercizio atletico)* exercise, training; *(fig)* training ground, school.
paletot [palˈto] *sm inv* overcoat.
pa'letta *sf* spade; *(per il focolare)* shovel; *(del capostazione)* signalling disc.
pa'letto *sm* stake, peg; *(spranga)* bolt.
palin'sesto *sm (STORIA)* palimpsest; *(TV, RADIO)* programme *(BRIT) o* program *(US)* schedule.
'palio *sm (gara):* **il P~** horserace run at Siena; **mettere qc in ~** to offer sth as a prize.

The **Palio** *is a horse race which takes place in a number of Italian towns, the most famous being the race in* **Siena.** *It has its origins in the 13th century and nowadays is usually held twice a year, on July 2nd and August 16th in the Piazza del Campo, Siena. 10 of the 17* **contrade** *or districts take part. Each contrada is represented by a horse and rider, and the winner is the first horse to complete the course regardless of whether it still has its rider. The race is preceded by a procession of contrada members in historical dress.*

---

palis'sandro *sm* rosewood.
paliz'zata [palitˈtsata] *sf* palisade.
'palla *sf* ball; *(pallottola)* bullet; **prendere la ~ al balzo** *(fig)* to seize one's opportunity.
pallaca'nestro *sf* basketball.
pallanu'oto *sf* water polo.
palla'volo *sf* volleyball.
palleggi'are [palledˈdʒare] *vi (CALCIO)* to practise *(BRIT) o* practice *(US)* with the ball; *(TENNIS)* to knock up.
pallia'tivo *sm* palliative; *(fig)* stopgap measure.
'pallido, a *ag* pale.
pal'lina *sf (bilia)* marble.
pal'lino *sm (BILIARDO)* cue ball; *(BOCCE)* jack; *(proiettile)* pellet; *(pois)* dot; **bianco a ~i blu** white with blue dots; **avere il ~ di** *(fig)* to be crazy about.
pallon'cino [pallonˈtʃino] *sm* balloon; *(lampioncino)* Chinese lantern.
pal'lone *sm (palla)* ball; *(CALCIO)* football;

(*aerostato*) balloon; **gioco del** ~ ball game.

pal'lore *sm* pallor, paleness.

pal'lottola *sf* pellet; (*proiettile*) bullet.

'palma *sf* (*ANAT*) = **palmo**; (*BOT*) palm; ~ **da datteri** date palm.

pal'mato, a *ag* (*ZOOL: piede*) webbed; (*BOT*) palmate.

pal'mipede *ag* web-footed.

pal'mizio [pal'mittsjo] *sm* (*palma*) palm tree; (*ramo*) palm.

'palmo *sm* (*ANAT*) palm; **essere alto un** ~ (*fig*) to be tiny; **restare con un** ~ **di naso** (*fig*) to be badly disappointed.

'palo *sm* (*legno appuntito*) stake; (*sostegno*) pole; **fare da** *o* **il** ~ (*fig*) to act as look-out; **saltare di** ~ **in frasca** (*fig*) to jump from one topic to another.

palom'baro *sm* diver.

pa'lombo *sm* (*pesce*) dogfish.

pal'pare *vt* to feel, finger.

'palpebra *sf* eyelid.

palpi'tare *vi* (*cuore, polso*) to beat; (: *più forte*) to pound, throb; (*fremere*) to quiver.

palpitazi'one [palpitat'tsjone] *sf* palpitation.

'palpito *sm* (*del cuore*) beat; (*fig: d'amore etc*) throb.

paltò *sm inv* overcoat.

pa'lude *sf* marsh, swamp.

palu'doso, a *ag* marshy, swampy.

pa'lustre *ag* marsh *cpd*, swamp *cpd*.

'pampino *sm* vine leaf.

pana'cea [pana't ʃea] *sf* panacea.

'Panama *sf* Panama; **il canale di** ~ the Panama Canal.

pana'mense *ag, sm/f* Panamanian.

'panca, che *sf* bench.

pancarrè *sm* sliced bread.

pan'cetta [pan't ʃetta] *sf* (*CUC*) bacon.

pan'chetto [pan'ketto] *sm* stool; footstool.

pan'china [pan'kina] *sf* garden seat; (*di giardino pubblico*) (park) bench.

'pancia, ce ['pant ʃa] *sf* belly, stomach; **mettere** *o* **fare** ~ to be getting a paunch; **avere mal di** ~ to have stomach ache *o* a sore stomach.

panci'era [pan't ʃɛra] *sf* corset.

panci'olle [pan't ʃɔlle] *av*: **stare in** ~ to lounge about (*BRIT*) *o* around.

panci'otto [pan't ʃɔtto] *sm* waistcoat.

pan'ciuto, a [pan't ʃuto] *ag* (*persona*) potbellied; (*vaso, bottiglia*) rounded.

'pancreas *sm inv* pancreas.

'panda *sm inv* panda.

pande'monio *sm* pandemonium.

pan'doro *sm type of sponge cake eaten at Christmas.*

'pane *sm* bread; (*pagnotta*) loaf (of bread);

(*forma*): **un** ~ **di burro/cera** *etc* a pat of butter/bar of wax *etc*; **guadagnarsi il** ~ to earn one's living; **dire** ~ **al** ~, **vino al vino** (*fig*) to call a spade a spade; **rendere pan per focaccia** (*fig*) to give tit for tat; ~ **casereccio** homemade bread; ~ **a cassetta** sliced bread; ~ **integrale** wholemeal bread; ~ **di segale** rye bread; **pan di Spagna** sponge cake; ~ **tostato** toast.

pane'girico [pane'dʒiriko] *sm* (*fig*) panegyric.

panette'ria *sf* (*forno*) bakery; (*negozio*) baker's (shop), bakery.

panetti'ere, a *sm/f* baker.

panet'tone *sm a kind of spiced brioche with sultanas, eaten at Christmas.*

'panfilo *sm* yacht.

pan'forte *sm Sienese nougat-type delicacy.*

pangrat'tato *sm* breadcrumbs *pl*.

'panico, a, ci, che *ag, sm* panic; **essere in preda al** ~ to be panic-stricken; **lasciarsi prendere dal** ~ to panic.

pani'ere *sm* basket.

panifica'tore, trice *sm/f* bread-maker, baker.

pani'ficio [pani'fit ʃo] *sm* (*forno*) bakery; (*negozio*) baker's (shop), bakery.

pa'nino *sm* roll; ~ **imbottito** filled roll; sandwich.

panino'teca, che *sf* sandwich bar.

'panna *sf* (*CUC*) cream; (*AUT*) = **panne**; ~ **di cucina** cooking cream; ~ **montata** whipped cream.

'panne [pan] *sf inv* (*AUT*) breakdown; **essere in** ~ to have broken down.

pan'nello *sm* panel; ~ **di controllo** control panel; ~ **solare** solar panel.

'panno *sm* cloth; ~**i** *smpl* (*abiti*) clothes; **mettiti nei miei** ~**i** (*fig*) put yourself in my shoes.

pan'nocchia [pan'nɔkkja] *sf* (*di mais etc*) ear.

panno'lino *sm* (*per bambini*) nappy (*BRIT*), diaper (*US*).

pano'rama, i *sm* panorama.

pano'ramico, a, ci, che *ag* panoramic; **strada** ~**a** scenic route.

pantacol'lant *smpl* leggings.

panta'loni *smpl* trousers (*BRIT*), pants (*US*), pair *sg* of trousers *o* pants.

pan'tano *sm* bog.

pan'tera *sf* panther.

'pantheon ['panteon] *sm inv* pantheon.

pan'tofola *sf* slipper.

panto'mima *sf* pantomime.

pan'zana [pan'tsana] *sf* fib, tall story.

pao'nazzo, a [pao'nattso] *ag* purple.

'papa, i *sm* pope.

papà *sm inv* dad(dy); figlio di ~ spoilt young man.

pa'pale *ag* papal.

pa'pato *sm* papacy.

pa'pavero *sm* poppy.

'papero, a *sm/f* (*ZOOL*) gosling ♦ *sf* (*fig*) slip of the tongue, blunder.

papi'llon [papi'jɔ] *sm inv* bow tie.

pa'piro *sm* papyrus.

'pappa *sf* baby cereal.

pappa'gallo *sm* parrot; (*fig: uomo*) Romeo, wolf.

pappa'gorgia, ge [pappa'gɔrdʒa] *sf* double chin.

pappar'della *sf* (*fig*) rigmarole.

pap'pare *vt* (*fam: anche:* ~rsi) to gobble up.

par. *abbr* (= *paragrafo*) par.

'para *sf*: suole di ~ crepe soles.

parà *abbr m inv* (= *paracadutista*) para.

pa'rabola *sf* (*MAT*) parabola; (*REL*) parable.

para'bolico, a, ci, che *ag* (*MAT*) parabolic; *vedi anche* antenna.

para'brezza [para'breddza] *sm inv* (*AUT*) windscreen (*BRIT*), windshield (*US*).

paracadu'tare *vt*, ~rsi *vr* to parachute.

paraca'dute *sm inv* parachute.

paracadu'tismo *sm* parachuting.

paracadu'tista, i, e *sm/f* parachutist; (*MIL*) paratrooper.

para'carro *sm* kerbstone (*BRIT*), curbstone (*US*).

paradi'siaco, a, ci, che *ag* heavenly.

para'diso *sm* paradise; ~ fiscale tax haven.

parados'sale *ag* paradoxical.

para'dosso *sm* paradox.

para'fango, ghi *sm* mudguard.

paraf'fina *sf* paraffin, paraffin wax.

parafra'sare *vt* to paraphrase.

pa'rafrasi *sf inv* paraphrase.

para'fulmine *sm* lightning conductor.

pa'raggi [pa'raddʒi] *smpl*: nei ~ in the vicinity, in the neighbourhood (*BRIT*) o neighborhood (*US*).

parago'nare *vt*: ~ con/a to compare with/ to.

para'gone *sm* comparison; (*esempio analogo*) analogy, parallel; reggere al ~ to stand comparison.

pa'ragrafo *sm* paragraph.

paraguai'ano, a *ag*, *sm/f* Paraguayan.

Paragu'ay [para'gwai] *sm*: il ~ Paraguay.

pa'ralisi *sf inv* paralysis.

para'litico, a, ci, che *ag*, *sm/f* paralytic.

paraliz'zare [paralid'dzare] *vt* to paralyze.

parallela'mente *av* in parallel.

parallele'pipedo *sm* parallelepiped.

paralle'lismo *sm* (*MAT*) parallelism; (*fig:* *corrispondenza*) similarities *pl*.

paral'lelo, a *ag* parallel ♦ *sm* (*GEO*) parallel; (*comparazione*): fare un ~ tra to draw a parallel between ♦ *sf* parallel (line); ~e *sfpl* (*attrezzo ginnico*) parallel bars.

para'lume *sm* lampshade.

para'medico, a, ci, che *ag* paramedical.

para'menti *smpl* (*REL*) vestments.

pa'rametro *sm* parameter.

paramili'tare *ag* paramilitary.

pa'ranco, chi *sm* hoist.

para'noia *sf* paranoia; andare/mandare in ~ (*fam*) to freak/be freaked out.

para'noico, a, ci, che *ag*, *sm/f* paranoid; (*fam: angosciato*) freaked (out).

paranor'male *ag* paranormal.

para'occhi [para'ɔkki] *smpl* blinkers (*BRIT*), blinders (*US*).

para'petto *sm* parapet.

para'piglia [para'piʎʎa] *sm* commotion, uproar.

parapsicolo'gia [parapsikolo'dʒia] *sf* parapsychology.

pa'rare *vt* (*addobbare*) to adorn, deck; (*proteggere*) to shield, protect; (*scansare: colpo*) to parry; (*CALCIO*) to save ♦ *vi*: dove vuole andare a ~? what are you driving at?; ~rsi *vr* (*presentarsi*) to appear, present o.s.

parasco'lastico, a, ci, che *ag* (*attività*) extracurricular.

para'sole *sm inv* parasol, sunshade.

paras'sita, i *sm* parasite.

parassi'tario, a *ag* parasitic.

parasta'tale *ag* state-controlled.

paras'tato *sm* employees in the state-controlled sector.

pa'rata *sf* (*SPORT*) save; (*MIL*) review, parade.

pa'rati *smpl* hangings *pl*; carta da ~ wallpaper.

para'tia *sf* (*di nave*) bulkhead.

para'urti *sm inv* (*AUT*) bumper.

para'vento *sm* folding screen; fare da ~ a qn (*fig*) to shield sb.

par'cella [par'tʃɛlla] *sf* fee.

parcheggi'are [parked'dʒare] *vt* to park.

par'cheggio [par'keddʒo] *sm* parking *no pl*; (*luogo*) car park (*BRIT*), parking lot (*US*); (*singolo posto*) parking space.

par'chimetro [par'kimetro] *sm* parking meter.

'parco, chi *sm* park; (*spazio per deposito*) depot; (*complesso di veicoli*) fleet.

'parco, a, chi, che *ag*: ~ (in) (*sobrio*) moderate (in); (*avaro*) sparing (with).

pa'recchio, a [pa'rekkjo] *det* quite a lot of; (*tempo*) quite a lot of, a long ♦ *pron* quite a lot, quite a bit; (*tempo*) quite a while, a long time ♦ *av* (*con ag*) quite, rather; (*con vb*) quite a lot, quite a bit; ~**i(e)** *det pl* quite a lot of, several ♦ *pron pl* quite a lot, several.

pareggi'are [pared'dʒare] *vt* to make equal; (*terreno*) to level, make level; (*bilancio, conti*) to balance ♦ *vi* (*SPORT*) to draw.

pa'reggio [pa'reddʒo] *sm* (*ECON*) balance; (*SPORT*) draw.

paren'tado *sm* relatives *pl*, relations *pl*.

pa'rente *smf* relative, relation.

paren'tela *sf* (*vincolo di sangue, fig*) relationship; (*insieme dei parenti*) relations *pl*, relatives *pl*.

pa'rentesi *sf* (*segno grafico*) bracket, parenthesis; (*frase incisa*) parenthesis; (*digressione*) parenthesis, digression; **tra** ~ in brackets; (*fig*) incidentally.

pa'rere *sm* (*opinione*) opinion; (*consiglio*) advice, opinion; **a mio** ~ in my opinion ♦ *vi* to seem, appear ♦ *vb impers*: **pare che** it seems *o* appears that, they say that; **mi pare che** it seems to me that; **mi pare di sì/no** I think so/don't think so; **fai come ti pare** do as you like; **che ti pare del mio libro?** what do you think of my book?

pa'rete *sf* wall.

'pargolo, a *smf* child.

'pari *ag inv* (*uguale*) equal, same; (*in giochi*) equal; drawn, tied; (*MAT*) even ♦ *sm inv* (*POL: di Gran Bretagna*) peer ♦ *smf inv* (*POL*) peer, equal; **copiato** ~ ~ copied word for word; **siamo** ~ (*fig*) we are quits *o* even; **alla** ~ on the same level; (*BORSA*) at par; **ragazza alla** ~ au pair (girl); **mettersi alla** ~ **con** to place o.s. on the same level as; **mettersi in** ~ **con** to catch up with; **andare di** ~ **passo con qn** to keep pace with sb.

parifi'care *vt* (*scuola*) to recognize officially.

parifi'cato, a *ag*: **scuola** ~**a** *officially recognized private school.*

Pa'rigi [pa'ridʒi] *sf* Paris.

pari'gino, a [pari'dʒino] *ag, smf* Parisian.

pa'riglia [pa'riʎʎa] *sf* pair; **rendere la** ~ to give tit for tat.

parità *sf* parity, equality; (*SPORT*) draw, tie.

pari'tetico, a, ci, che *ag*: **commissione** ~**a** joint committee; **rapporto** ~ equal relationship.

parlamen'tare *ag* parliamentary ♦ *smf* ≈ Member of Parliament (*BRIT*), ≈ Congressman/woman (*US*) ♦ *vi* to negotiate, parley.

parla'mento *sm* parliament.

The **Parlamento** *has legislative power as laid down in the Italian constitution which came into force on January 1st 1948. It is made up of two chambers: the* **Camera dei deputati** *and the* **Senato**. *Parliamentary elections are held every 5 years.*

---

parlan'tina *sf* (*fam*) talkativeness; **avere una buona** ~ to have the gift of the gab.

par'lare *vi* to speak, talk; (*confidare cose segrete*) to talk ♦ *vt* to speak; ~ **(a qn) di** to speak *o* talk (to sb) about; ~ **chiaro** to speak one's mind; ~ **male di qn/qc** to speak ill of sb/sth; ~ **del più e del meno** to talk of this and that; **ne ho sentito** ~ I have heard it mentioned; **non parliamone più** let's just forget about it; **i dati parlano** (*fig*) the facts speak for themselves.

par'lata *sf* (*dialetto*) dialect.

parla'tore, 'trice *smf* speaker.

parla'torio *sm* (*di carcere etc*) visiting room; (*REL*) parlour (*BRIT*), parlor (*US*).

parlot'tare *vi* to mutter.

parmigi'ano, a [parmi'dʒano] *ag* Parma *cpd*, of (*o* from) Parma ♦ *sm* (*grana*) Parmesan (cheese); **alla** ~**a** (*CUC*) with Parmesan cheese.

paro'dia *sf* parody.

parodi'are *vt* to parody.

pa'rola *sf* word; (*facoltà*) speech; ~**e** *sfpl* (*chiacchiere*) talk *sg*; **chiedere la** ~ to ask permission to speak; **dare la** ~ **a qn** to call on sb to speak; **dare la propria** ~ **a qn** to give sb one's word; **mantenere la** ~ to keep one's word; **mettere una buona** ~ **per qn** to put in a good word for sb; **passare dalle** ~**e ai fatti** to get down to business; **prendere la** ~ to take the floor; **rimanere senza** ~ to be speechless; **rimangiarsi la** ~ to go back on one's word; **non ho** ~**e per ringraziarla** I don't know how to thank you; **rivolgere la** ~ **a qn** to speak to sb; **non è detta l'ultima** ~ that's not the end of the matter; **è una persona di** ~ he is a man of his word; **in** ~**e povere** in plain English; ~ **d'onore** word of honour; ~ **d'ordine** (*MIL*) password; ~**e incrociate** crossword (puzzle) *sg*.

paro'laccia, ce [paro'lattʃa] *sf* bad word, swearword.

paros'sismo *sm* paroxysm.

par'quet [par'kɛ] *sm* parquet (flooring).

parrò *etc vb vedi* **parere**.

par'rocchia [par'rɔkkja] *sf* parish; (*chiesa*) parish church.

parrocchi'ano, a [parrok'kjano] *sm/f* parishioner.

'**parroco, ci** *sm* parish priest.

par'rucca, che *sf* wig.

parrucchi'ere, a [parruk'kjɛre] *sm/f* hairdresser ♦ *sm* barber.

parruc'cone *sm* (*peg*) old fogey.

parsi'monia *sf* frugality, thrift.

parsimoni'oso, a *ag* frugal, thrifty.

'**parso, a** *pp di* **parere.**

'**parte** *sf* part; (*lato*) side; (*quota spettante a ciascuno*) share; (*direzione*) direction; (*POL*) party; faction; (*DIR*) party; **a ~** *ag* separate ♦ *av* separately; **scherzi a ~** joking aside; **a ~ ciò** apart from that; **inviare a ~** (*campioni etc*) to send under separate cover; **da ~** (*in disparte*) to one side, aside; **mettere/prendere da ~** to put/take aside; **d'altra ~** on the other hand; **da ~ di** (*per conto di*) on behalf of; **da ~ mia** as far as I'm concerned, as for me; **da ~ di madre** on his (*o* her *etc*) mother's side; **essere dalla ~ della ragione** to be in the right; **da ~ a ~** right through; **da qualche ~** somewhere; **da nessuna ~** nowhere; **da questa ~** (*in questa direzione*) this way; **da ogni ~** on all sides, everywhere; (*moto da luogo*) from all sides; **fare ~ di qc** to belong to sth; **prendere ~ a qc** to take part in sth; **prendere le ~i di qn** to take sb's side; **mettere qn a ~ di qc** to inform sb of sth; **costituirsi ~ civile contro qn** (*DIR*) to associate in an action with the public prosecutor against sb; **la ~ lesa** (*DIR*) the injured party; **le ~i in causa** the parties concerned.

parteci'pante [partetʃi'pante] *sm/f*: ~ **(a)** (*a riunione, dibattito*) participant (in); (*a gara sportiva*) competitor (in); (*a concorso*) entrant (to).

parteci'pare [partetʃi'pare] *vi*: ~ **a** to take part in, participate in; (*utili etc*) to share in; (*spese etc*) to contribute to; (*dolore, successo di qn*) to share (in) ♦ *vt*: ~ **le nozze (a)** to announce one's wedding (to).

partecipazi'one [partetʃipat'tsjone] *sf* participation; sharing; (*ECON*) interest; ~ **a banda armata** (*DIR*) belonging to an armed gang; ~ **di maggioranza/minoranza** controlling/minority interest; ~ **agli utili** profit-sharing; ~i **di nozze** *wedding announcement card*; **ministro delle P~i statali** *minister responsible for companies in which the state has a financial interest.*

par'tecipe [par'tetʃipe] *ag* participating; **essere ~ di** to take part in, participate in;

(*gioia, dolore*) to share (in); (*consapevole*) to be aware of.

parteggi'are [parted'dʒare] *vi*: ~ **per** to side with, be on the side of.

par'tenza [par'tɛntsa] *sf* departure; (*SPORT*) start; **essere in ~** to be about to leave, be leaving; **passeggeri in ~ per** passengers travelling (*BRIT*) *o* traveling (*US*) to; **siamo tornati al punto di ~** (*fig*) we are back where we started; **falsa ~** (*anche fig*) false start.

parti'cella [parti'tʃella] *sf* particle.

parti'cipio [parti'tʃipjo] *sm* participle.

partico'lare *ag* (*specifico*) particular; (*proprio*) personal, private; (*speciale*) special, particular; (*caratteristico*) distinctive; (*fuori dal comune*) peculiar ♦ *sm* detail, particular; **in ~** in particular, particularly; **entrare nei ~i** to go into details.

particolareggi'ato, a [partikolared'dʒato] *ag* (extremely) detailed.

particolarità *sf inv* (*carattere eccezionale*) peculiarity; (*dettaglio*) particularity, detail; (*caratteristica*) characteristic, feature.

partigi'ano, a [parti'dʒano] *ag* partisan ♦ *sm* (*fautore*) supporter, champion; (*MIL*) partisan.

par'tire *vi* to go, leave; (*allontanarsi*) to go (*o* drive *etc*) away *o* off; (*petardo, colpo*) to go off; (*fig*: *avere inizio, SPORT*) to start; **sono partita da Roma alle 7** I left Rome at 7; **il volo parte da Ciampino** the flight leaves from Ciampino; **a ~ da** from; **la seconda a ~ da destra** the second from the right; ~ **in quarta** to drive off at top speed; (*fig*) to be very enthusiastic.

par'tita *sf* (*COMM*) lot, consignment; (*ECON*: *registrazione*) entry, item; (*CARTE, SPORT*: *gioco*) game; (: *competizione*) match, game; ~ **di caccia** hunting party; ~ **IVA** VAT account; ~ **semplice/doppia** (*COMM*) single-/double-entry book-keeping.

par'tito *sm* (*POL*) party; (*decisione*) decision, resolution; (*persona da maritare*) match; **per ~ preso** on principle; **mettere la testa a ~** to settle down.

partitocra'zia [partitokrat'tsia] *sf* hijacking *of institutions by the party system.*

parti'tura *sf* (*MUS*) score.

'**parto** *sm* (*MED*) labour (*BRIT*), labor (*US*); **sala ~** labo(u)r room; **morire di ~** to die in childbirth.

partori'ente *sf* woman in labour (*BRIT*) *o* labor (*US*).

parto'rire *vt* to give birth to; (*fig*) to produce.

par'venza [par'vɛntsa] *sf* semblance.
'parvi *etc vb vedi* **parere**.
parzi'ale [par'tsjale] *ag* (*limitato*) partial;
(*non obiettivo*) biased, partial.
parzialità [partsjali'ta] *sf*: ~ **(a favore di)**
partiality (for), bias (towards); ~
(contro) bias (against).
'pascere ['paʃʃere] *vi* to graze ♦ *vt* (*brucare*)
to graze on; (*far pascolare*) to graze,
pasture.
pasci'uto, a [paʃ'ʃuto] *pp di* **pascere** ♦ *ag*:
ben ~ plump.
pasco'lare *vt, vi* to graze.
'pascolo *sm* pasture.
'Pasqua *sf* Easter; **isola di** ~ Easter Island.
pas'quale *ag* Easter *cpd*.
pasqu'etta *sf* Easter Monday.
pas'sabile *ag* fairly good, passable.
pas'saggio [pas'saddʒo] *sm* passing *no pl*,
passage; (*traversata*) crossing *no pl*,
passage; (*luogo, prezzo della traversata,
brano di libro etc*) passage; (*su veicolo
altrui*) lift (*BRIT*), ride; (*SPORT*) pass; **di** ~
(*persona*) passing through; ~ **pedonale/a
livello** pedestrian/level (*BRIT*) *o* grade
(*US*) crossing; ~ **di proprietà** transfer of
ownership.
passamane'ria *sf* braid, trimming.
passamon'tagna [passamon'taɲɲa] *sm inv*
balaclava.
pas'sante *sm/f* passer-by ♦ *sm* loop.
passa'porto *sm* passport.
pas'sare *vi* (*andare*) to go; (*veicolo, pedone*)
to pass (by), go by; (*fare una breve sosta:
postino etc*) to come, call; (: *amico: per fare
una visita*) to call *o* drop in; (*sole, aria,
luce*) to get through; (*trascorrere: giorni,
tempo*) to pass, go by; (*fig: proposta di
legge*) to be passed; (: *dolore*) to pass, go
away; (*CARTE*) to pass ♦ *vt* (*attraversare*) to
cross; (*trasmettere: messaggio*): ~ **qc a qn**
to pass sth on to sb; (*dare*): ~ **qc a qn**
to pass sth to sb, give sb sth; (*trascorrere:
tempo*) to spend; (*superare: esame*) to
pass; (*triturare: verdura*) to strain;
(*approvare*) to pass, approve; (*oltrepassare,
sorpassare: anche fig*) to go beyond, pass;
(*fig: subire*) to go through; ~ **da ... a** to
pass from ... to; ~ **di padre in figlio** to be
handed down *o* to pass from father to
son; ~ **per** (*anche fig*) to go through; ~ **per
stupido/un genio** to be taken for a fool/a
genius; ~ **sopra** (*anche fig*) to pass over;
~ **attraverso** (*anche fig*) to go through; ~
ad altro to change the subject; (*in una
riunione*) to discuss the next item; ~ **in
banca/ufficio** to call (in) at the bank/
office; ~ **alla storia** to pass into history; ~

a un esame to go up (to the next class)
after an exam; ~ **di moda** to go out of
fashion; ~ **a prendere qc/qn** to call and
pick sth/sb up; **le passo il Signor X** (*al
telefono*) here is Mr X, I'm putting you
through to Mr X; **farsi** ~ **per** to pass o.s.
off as, pretend to be; **lasciar** ~ **qn/qc** to
let sb/sth through; **col** ~ **degli anni**
(*riferito al presente*) as time goes by;
(*riferito al passato*) as time passed *o* went
by; **il peggio è passato** the worst is over;
30 anni e passa well over 30 years ago; ~
una mano di vernice su qc to give sth a
coat of paint; **passarsela: come te la
passi?** how are you getting on *o* along?
pas'sata *sf*: **dare una** ~ **di vernice a qc** to
give sth a coat of paint; **dare una** ~ **al
giornale** to have a look at the paper, skim
through the paper.
passa'tempo *sm* pastime, hobby.
pas'sato, a *ag* (*scorso*) last; (*finito: gloria,
generazioni*) past; (*usanze*) out of date;
(*sfiorito*) faded ♦ *sm* past; (*LING*) past
(tense); **l'anno** ~ last year; **nel corso degli
anni** ~**i** over the past years; **nei tempi** ~**i**
in the past; **sono le 8** ~**e** it's past *o* after 8
o'clock; **è acqua** ~**a** (*fig*) it's over and
done with; ~ **prossimo** (*LING*) present
perfect; ~ **remoto** (*LING*) past historic; ~
di verdura (*CUC*) vegetable purée.
passa'tutto *sm inv*, **passaver'dura** *sm inv*
vegetable mill.
passeg'gero, a [passed'dʒero] *ag* passing
♦ *sm/f* passenger.
passeggi'are [passed'dʒare] *vi* to go for a
walk; (*in veicolo*) to go for a drive.
passeggi'ata [passed'dʒata] *sf* walk; drive;
(*luogo*) promenade; **fare una** ~ to go for a
walk (*o* drive).
passeg'gino [passed'dʒino] *sm* pushchair
(*BRIT*), stroller (*US*).
pas'seggio [pas'seddʒo] *sm* walk, stroll;
(*luogo*) promenade; **andare a** ~ to go for a
walk *o* a stroll.
passe'rella *sf* footbridge; (*di nave, aereo*)
gangway; (*pedana*) catwalk.
'passero *sm* sparrow.
pas'sibile *ag*: ~ **di** liable to.
passio'nale *ag* (*temperamento*) passionate;
delitto ~ crime of passion.
passi'one *sf* passion.
passività *sf* (*qualità*) passivity,
passiveness; (*COMM*) liability.
pas'sivo, a *ag* passive ♦ *sm* (*LING*) passive;
(*ECON*) debit; (: *complesso dei debiti*)
liabilities *pl*.
'passo *sm* step; (*andatura*) pace; (*rumore*)
(foot)step; (*orma*) footprint; (*passaggio,*

fig: brano) passage; (*valico*) pass; **a ~ d'uomo** at walking pace; (*AUT*) dead slow; **~ (a) ~ step** by step; **fare due** *o* **quattro ~i** to go for a walk *o* a stroll; **andare al ~ coi tempi** to keep up with the times; **di questo ~** (*fig*) at this rate; **fare i primi ~i** (*anche fig*) to take one's first steps; **fare il gran ~** (*fig*) to take the plunge; **fare un ~ falso** (*fig*) to make the wrong move; **tornare sui propri ~i** to retrace one's steps; "*~* **carraio**" "vehicle entrance — keep clear".

'**pasta** *sf* (*CUC*) dough; (*: impasto per dolce*) pastry; (*: anche: ~* **alimentare**) pasta; (*massa molle di materia*) paste; (*fig: indole*) nature; *~***e** *sfpl* (*pasticcini*) pastries; *~* **in brodo** noodle soup; *~* **sfoglia** puff pastry *o* paste (*US*).

pastasci'utta [pastaʃ'ʃutta] *sf* pasta.

pasteggi'are [pasted'dʒare] *vi*: *~* **a vino/champagne** to have wine/champagne with one's meal.

pas'tella *sf* batter.

pas'tello *sm* pastel.

pas'tetta *sf* (*CUC*) = **pastella**.

pas'ticca, che *sf* = **pastiglia**.

pasticce'ria [pastittʃe'ria] *sf* (*pasticcini*) pastries *pl*, cakes *pl*; (*negozio*) cake shop; (*arte*) confectionery.

pasticci'are [pastit'tʃare] *vt* to mess up, make a mess of ♦ *vi* to make a mess.

pasticci'ere, a [pastit'tʃere] *sm/f* pastrycook; confectioner.

pastic'cino [pastit'tʃino] *sm* petit four.

pas'ticcio [pas'tittʃo] *sm* (*CUC*) pie; (*lavoro disordinato, imbroglio*) mess; **trovarsi nei ~i** to get into trouble.

pasti'ficio [pasti'fitʃo] *sm* pasta factory.

pas'tiglia [pas'tiʎʎa] *sf* pastille, lozenge.

pas'tina *sf* small pasta shapes used in soup.

pasti'naca, che *sf* parsnip.

'**pasto** *sm* meal; **vino da ~** table wine.

pas'toia *sf* (*fig*): *~* **burocratica** red tape.

pas'tone *sm* (*per animali*) mash; (*peg*) overcooked stodge.

pasto'rale *ag* pastoral.

pas'tore *sm* shepherd; (*REL*) pastor, minister; (*anche*: **cane ~**) sheepdog; *~* **scozzese** (*ZOOL*) collie; *~* **tedesco** (*ZOOL*) Alsatian (dog) (*BRIT*), German shepherd (dog).

pasto'rizia [pasto'rittsja] *sf* sheep-rearing, sheep farming.

pastoriz'zare [pastorid'dzare] *vt* to pasteurize.

pas'toso, a *ag* doughy; pasty; (*fig: voce, colore*) mellow, soft.

pas'trano *sm* greatcoat.

pas'tura *sf* pasture.

pa'tacca, che *sf* (*distintivo*) medal, decoration; (*fig: macchia*) grease spot, grease mark; (*: articolo scadente*) bit of rubbish.

pa'tata *sf* potato; *~***e fritte** chips (*BRIT*), French fries.

pata'tine *sfpl* (potato) crisps (*BRIT*) *o* chips (*US*).

pata'trac *sm* (*crollo: anche fig*) crash.

pâté [pa'te] *sm inv* pâté; *~* **di fegato d'oca** pâté de foie gras.

pa'tella *sf* (*ZOOL*) limpet.

pa'tema, i *sm* anxiety, worry.

paten'tato, a *ag* (*munito di patente*) licensed, certified; (*fig scherzoso: qualificato*) utter, thorough.

pa'tente *sf* licence (*BRIT*), license (*US*); (*anche*: *~* **di guida**) driving licence (*BRIT*), driver's license (*US*).

paten'tino *sm* temporary licence (*BRIT*) *o* license (*US*).

paterna'lismo *sm* paternalism.

paterna'lista *sm* paternalist.

paterna'listico, a, ci, che *ag* paternalistic.

paternità *sf* paternity, fatherhood.

pa'terno, a *ag* (*affetto, consigli*) fatherly; (*casa, autorità*) paternal.

pa'tetico, a, ci, che *ag* pathetic; (*commovente*) moving, touching.

'**pathos** ['patos] *sm* pathos.

pa'tibolo *sm* gallows *sg*, scaffold.

pati'mento *sm* suffering.

'**patina** *sf* (*su rame etc*) patina; (*sulla lingua*) fur, coating.

pa'tire *vt, vi* to suffer.

pa'tito, a *sm/f* enthusiast, fan, lover.

patolo'gia [patolo'dʒia] *sf* pathology.

pato'logico, a, ci, che [pato'lɔdʒiko] *ag* pathological.

pa'tologo, a, gi, ghe *sm/f* pathologist.

'**patria** *sf* homeland; **amor di ~** patriotism.

patri'arca, chi *sm* patriarch.

pa'trigno [pa'triɲɲo] *sm* stepfather.

patrimoni'ale *ag* (*rendita*) from property ♦ *sf* (*anche*: **imposta ~**) property tax.

patri'monio *sm* estate, property; (*fig*) heritage; **mi è costato un ~** (*fig*) it cost me a fortune, I paid a fortune for it; *~* **spirituale/culturale** spiritual/cultural heritage; *~* **ereditario** (*fig*) hereditary characteristics *pl*; *~* **pubblico** public property.

'**patrio, a, ii, ie** *ag* (*di patria*) native *cpd*, of one's country; (*DIR*): *~***a potestà** parental authority; **amor ~** love of one's country.

patri'ota, i, e *sm/f* patriot.
patri'ottico, a, ci, che *ag* patriotic.
patriot'tismo *sm* patriotism.
patroci'nare [patrotʃi'nare] *vt* (*DIR: difendere*) to defend; (*sostenere*) to sponsor, support.
patro'cinio [patro'tʃinjo] *sm* defence (*BRIT*), defense (*US*); support, sponsorship.
patro'nato *sm* patronage; (*istituzione benefica*) charitable institution *o* society.
pa'trono *sm* (*REL*) patron saint; (*socio di patronato*) patron; (*DIR*) counsel.
'patta *sf* flap; (*dei pantaloni*) fly.
patteggia'mento [patteddʒa'mento] *sm* (*DIR*) plea bargaining.
patteggi'are [patted'dʒare] *vt, vi* to negotiate.
patti'naggio [patti'naddʒo] *sm* skating.
patti'nare *vi* to skate; ~ **sul ghiaccio** to ice-skate.
pattina'tore, 'trice *sm/f* skater.
'pattino *sm* skate; (*di slitta*) runner; (*AER*) skid; (*TECN*) sliding block; **~i (da ghiaccio)** (ice) skates; **~i a rotelle** roller skates.
pat'tino *sm* (*barca*) kind *of pedalo with oars.*
pat'tista, i, e *ag* (*POL*) of Patto per l'Italia ♦ *sm/f* (*POL*) member (*o* supporter) of Patto per l'Italia.
'patto *sm* (*accordo*) pact, agreement; (*condizione*) term, condition; **a ~ che** on condition that; **a nessun ~** under no circumstances; **venire *o* scendere a ~i (con)** to come to an agreement (with); **P~ per l'Italia** (*POL*) centrist party.
pat'tuglia [pat'tuʎʎa] *sf* (*MIL*) patrol.
pattugli'are [pattuʎ'ʎare] *vt* to patrol.
pattu'ire *vt* to reach an agreement on.
pattumi'era *sf* (dust)bin (*BRIT*), ashcan (*US*).
pa'ura *sf* fear; **aver ~ di/di fare/che** to be frightened *o* afraid of/of doing/that; **far ~ a** to frighten; **per ~ di/che** for fear of/that; **ho ~ di sì/no** I am afraid so/not.
pau'roso, a *ag* (*che fa paura*) frightening; (*che ha paura*) fearful, timorous.
'pausa *sf* (*sosta*) break; (*nel parlare, MUS*) pause.
paven'tato, a *ag* much-feared.
pa'vese *ag* of (*o* from) Pavia.
'pavido, a *ag* (*letterario*) fearful.
pavimen'tare *vt* (*stanza*) to floor; (*strada*) to pave.
pavimentazi'one [pavimentat'tsjone] *sf* flooring; paving.
pavi'mento *sm* floor.
pa'vone *sm* peacock.

pavoneggi'arsi [pavoned'dʒarsi] *vr* to strut about, show off.
pazien'tare [pattsjen'tare] *vi* to be patient.
pazi'ente [pat'tsjɛnte] *ag, sm/f* patient.
pazi'enza [pat'tsjɛntsa] *sf* patience; **perdere la ~** to lose (one's) patience.
pazza'mente [pattsa'mente] *av* madly; **essere ~ innamorato** to be madly in love.
paz'zesco, a, schi, sche [pat'tsesko] *ag* mad, crazy.
paz'zia [pat'tsia] *sf* (*MED*) madness, insanity; (*di azione, decisione*) madness, folly; **è stata una ~!** it was sheer madness!
'pazzo, a [pat'tso] *ag* (*MED*) mad, insane; (*strano*) wild, mad ♦ *sm/f* madman/woman; ~ **di** (*gioia, amore etc*) mad *o* crazy with; ~ **per qc/qn** mad *o* crazy about sth/sb; **essere ~ da legare** to be raving mad *o* a raving lunatic.
PC *sigla* = Piacenza.
P.C. *abbr* = **polizza di carico.**
p.c. *abbr* = *per condoglianze; per conoscenza.*
p.c.c. *abbr* (= *per copia conforme*) cc.
P.C.I. *sigla m* (= *Partito Comunista Italiano*) *former political party.*
PCUS *sigla m* = *Partito Comunista dell'Unione Sovietica.*
PD *sigla* = Padova.
P.D. *abbr* = **partita doppia.**
P.D.S. *sigla m* (= *Partito Democratico della Sinistra*) *party originating from the P.C.I.*
PE *sigla* = Pescara.
'pecca, che *sf* defect, flaw, fault.
peccami'noso, a *ag* sinful.
pec'care *vi* to sin; (*fig*) to err.
pec'cato *sm* sin; **è un ~ che** it's a pity that; **che ~!** what a shame *o* pity!; **un ~ di gioventù** (*fig*) a youthful error *o* indiscretion.
pecca'tore, 'trice *sm/f* sinner.
pecche'rò *etc* [pekke'rɔ] *vb vedi* **peccare.**
'pece ['petʃe] *sf* pitch.
pechi'nese [peki'nese] *ag, sm/f* Pekin(g)ese (*inv*) ♦ *sm* (*anche:* **cane ~**) Pekin(g)ese *inv*, Peke.
Pe'chino [pe'kino] *sf* Beijing, Peking.
'pecora *sf* sheep; ~ **nera** (*fig*) black sheep.
peco'raio *sm* shepherd.
peco'rella *sf* lamb; **la ~ smarrita** the lost sheep; **cielo a ~e** (*fig: nuvole*) mackerel sky.
peco'rino *sm* sheep's milk cheese.
pecu'lato *sm* (*DIR*) embezzlement.
peculi'are *ag:* ~ **di** peculiar to.
peculiarità *sf* peculiarity.
pecuni'ario, a *ag* financial, money *cpd*.
pe'daggio [pe'daddʒo] *sm* toll.

pedago'gia [pedago'dʒia] *sf* pedagogy, educational methods *pl.*

peda'gogico, a, ci, che [peda'gɔdʒiko] *ag* pedagogic(al).

peda'gogo, a, ghi, ghe *sm/f* pedagogue.

peda'lare *vi* to pedal; (*andare in bicicletta*) to cycle.

pe'dale *sm* pedal.

pe'dana *sf* footboard; (*SPORT: nel salto*) springboard; (: *nella scherma*) piste.

pe'dante *ag* pedantic ♦ *sm/f* pedant.

pedante'ria *sf* pedantry.

pe'data *sf* (*impronta*) footprint; (*colpo*) kick; **prendere a ~e qn/qc** to kick sb/sth.

pede'rasta, i *sm* pederast.

pe'destre *ag* prosaic, pedestrian.

pedi'atra, i, e *sm/f* paediatrician (*BRIT*), pediatrician (*US*).

pedia'tria *sf* paediatrics *sg* (*BRIT*), pediatrics *sg* (*US*).

pedi'atrico, a, ci, che *ag* pediatric.

pedi'cure *sm/f inv* chiropodist (*BRIT*), podiatrist (*US*).

pedigree *sm inv* pedigree.

pedi'luvio *sm* footbath.

pe'dina *sf* (*della dama*) draughtsman (*BRIT*), draftsman (*US*); (*fig*) pawn.

pedi'nare *vt* to shadow, tail.

pe'dofilo, a *ag, sm/f* paedophile.

pedo'nale *ag* pedestrian.

pe'done, a *sm/f* pedestrian ♦ *sm* (*SCACCHI*) pawn.

peeling ['piling] *sm inv* (*COSMESI*) facial scrub.

'peggio ['pɛddʒo] *av, ag inv* worse ♦ *sm o f*: **il o la ~** the worst; **cambiare in ~** to get o become worse; **alla ~** at worst, if the worst comes to the worst; **tirare avanti alla meno ~** to get along as best one can; **avere la ~** to come off worse, get the worst of it.

peggiora'mento [peddʒora'mento] *sm* worsening.

peggio'rare [peddʒo'rare] *vt* to make worse, worsen ♦ *vi* to grow worse, worsen.

peggiora'tivo, a [peddʒora'tivo] *ag* pejorative.

peggi'ore [ped'dʒore] *ag* (*comparativo*) worse; (*superlativo*) worst ♦ *sm/f*: **il(la) ~** the worst (person); **nel ~ dei casi** if the worst comes to the worst.

'pegno ['peɲɲo] *sm* (*DIR*) security, pledge; (*nei giochi di società*) forfeit; (*fig*) pledge, token; **dare in ~ qc** to pawn sth; **in ~ d'amicizia** as a token of friendship; **banco dei ~i** pawnshop.

pelapa'tate *sm inv* potato peeler.

pe'lare *vt* (*spennare*) to pluck; (*spellare*) to skin; (*sbucciare*) to peel; (*fig*) to make pay through the nose; **~rsi** *vr* to go bald.

pe'lato, a *ag* (*sbucciato*) peeled; (*calvo*) bald; (**pomodori**) **~i** peeled tomatoes.

pel'lame *sm* skins *pl*, hides *pl.*

'pelle *sf* skin; (*di animale*) skin, hide; (*cuoio*) leather; **essere ~ ed ossa** to be skin and bone; **avere la ~ d'oca** to have goose pimples o goose flesh; **avere i nervi a fior di ~** to be edgy; **non stare più nella ~ dalla gioia** to be beside o.s. with delight; **lasciarci la ~** to lose one's life; **amici per la ~** firm o close friends.

pellegri'naggio [pellegri'naddʒo] *sm* pilgrimage.

pelle'grino, a *sm/f* pilgrim.

pelle'rossa, pelli'rossa, *pl* **pelli'rosse** *sm/f* Red Indian.

pellette'ria *sf* (*articoli*) leather goods *pl*; (*negozio*) leather goods shop.

pelli'cano *sm* pelican.

pellicce'ria [pellittʃe'ria] *sf* (*negozio*) furrier's (shop); (*quantità di pellicce*) furs *pl.*

pel'liccia, ce [pel'littʃa] *sf* (*mantello di animale*) coat, fur; (*indumento*) fur coat; **~ ecologica** fake fur.

pellicci'aio [pellit'tʃajo] *sm* furrier.

pel'licola *sf* (*membrana sottile*) film, layer; (*FOT, CINE*) film.

pelli'rossa *sm/f* = **pellerossa.**

'pelo *sm* hair; (*pelame*) coat, hair; (*pelliccia*) fur; (*di tappeto*) pile; (*di liquido*) surface; **per un ~:** **per un ~ non ho perduto il treno** I very nearly missed the train; **c'è mancato un ~ che affogasse** he narrowly escaped drowning; **cercare il ~ nell'uovo** (*fig*) to pick holes, split hairs; **non aver ~i sulla lingua** (*fig*) to speak one's mind.

pe'loso, a *ag* hairy.

'peltro *sm* pewter.

pe'luche [pə'lyʃ] *sm* plush; **giocattoli di ~** soft toys.

pe'luria *sf* down.

'pelvi *sf inv* pelvis.

'pelvico, a, ci, che *ag* pelvic.

'pena *sf* (*DIR*) sentence; (*punizione*) punishment; (*sofferenza*) sadness *no pl*, sorrow; (*fatica*) trouble *no pl*, effort; (*difficoltà*) difficulty; **far ~** to be pitiful; **mi fai ~** I feel sorry for you; **essere o stare in ~ (per qc/qn)** to worry o be anxious (about sth/sb); **prendersi o darsi la ~ di fare** to go to the trouble of doing; **vale la ~ farlo** it's worth doing, it's worth it; **non ne vale la ~** it's not worth the effort, it's not worth it; **~ di morte** death sentence;

~ **pecuniaria** fine.

pe'nale *ag* penal ♦ *sf* (*anche:* **clausola** ~) penalty clause; **causa** ~ criminal trial; **diritto** ~ criminal law; **pagare la** ~ to pay the penalty.

pena'lista, i, e *sm/f* (*avvocato*) criminal lawyer.

penalità *sf inv* penalty.

penaliz'zare [penalid'dzare] *vt* (*SPORT*) to penalize.

penalizzazi'one [penaliddzat'tsjone] *sf* (*SPORT*) penalty.

pe'nare *vi* (*patire*) to suffer; (*faticare*) to struggle.

pen'dente *ag* hanging; leaning ♦ *sm* (*ciondolo*) pendant; (*orecchino*) drop earring.

pen'denza [pen'dɛntsa] *sf* slope, slant; (*grado d'inclinazione*) gradient; (*ECON*) outstanding account.

'pendere *vi* (*essere appeso*): ~ **da** to hang from; (*essere inclinato*) to lean; (*fig: incombere*): ~ **su** to hang over.

pen'dice [pen'ditʃe] *sf* (*di monte*) slope.

pen'dio, ii *sm* slope, slant; (*luogo in pendenza*) slope.

'pendola *sf* pendulum clock.

pendo'lare *ag* pendulum *cpd*, pendular ♦ *sm/f* commuter.

pendola'rismo *sm* commuting.

'pendolo *sm* (*peso*) pendulum; (*anche:* **orologio a** ~) pendulum clock.

'pene *sm* penis.

pene'trante *ag* piercing, penetrating.

pene'trare *vi* to come *o* get in ♦ *vt* to penetrate; ~ **in** to enter; (*sog: proiettile*) to penetrate; (*: acqua, aria*) to go *o* come into.

penetrazi'one [penetrat'tsjone] *sf* penetration.

penicil'lina [penitʃil'lina] *sf* penicillin.

peninsu'lare *ag* peninsular; **l'Italia** ~ mainland Italy.

pe'nisola *sf* peninsula.

peni'tente *sm/f* penitent.

peni'tenza [peni'tɛntsa] *sf* penitence; (*punizione*) penance.

penitenzi'ario [peniten'tsjarjo] *sm* prison.

'penna *sf* (*di uccello*) feather; (*per scrivere*) pen; ~**e** *sfpl* (*CUC*) quills (*type of pasta*); ~ **a feltro/stilografica/a sfera** felt-tip/ fountain/ballpoint pen.

pen'nacchio [pen'nakkjo] *sm* (*ornamento*) plume; **un** ~ **di fumo** (*fig*) a plume *o* spiral of smoke.

penna'rello *sm* felt(-tip) pen.

pennel'lare *vi* to paint.

pennel'lata *sf* brushstroke.

pen'nello *sm* brush; (*per dipingere*) (paint)brush; **a** ~ (*perfettamente*) to perfection, perfectly; ~ **per la barba** shaving brush.

Pen'nini *smpl:* **i** ~ the Pennines.

pen'nino *sm* nib.

pen'none *sm* (*NAUT*) yard; (*stendardo*) banner, standard.

pen'nuto *sm* bird.

pe'nombra *sf* half-light, dim light.

pe'noso, a *ag* painful, distressing; (*faticoso*) tiring, laborious.

pen'sare *vi* to think ♦ *vt* to think; (*inventare, escogitare*) to think out; ~ **a** to think of; (*amico, vacanze*) to think of *o* about; (*problema*) to think about; ~ **di fare qc** to think of doing sth; ~ **bene/male di qn** to think well/badly of sb, have a good/bad opinion of sb; **penso di sì** I think so; **penso di no** I don't think so; **a pensarci bene ...** on second thoughts (*BRIT*) *o* thought (*US*) ...; **non voglio nemmeno pensarci** I don't even want to think about it; **ci farò io** I'll see to *o* take care of it.

pen'sata *sf* (*trovata*) idea, thought.

pensa'tore, 'trice *sm/f* thinker.

pensie'rino *sm* (*dono*) little gift; (*pensiero*): **ci farò un** ~ I'll think about it.

pensi'ero *sm* thought; (*modo di pensare, dottrina*) thinking *no pl*; (*preoccupazione*) worry, care, trouble; **darsi** ~ **per qc** to worry about sth; **stare in** ~ **per qn** to be worried about sb; **un** ~ **gentile** (*anche fig: dono etc*) a kind thought.

pensie'roso, a *ag* thoughtful.

'pensile *ag* hanging.

pensi'lina *sf* (*in stazione*) platform roof.

pensiona'mento *sm* retirement; ~ **anticipato** early retirement.

pensio'nante *sm/f* (*presso una famiglia*) lodger; (*di albergo*) guest.

pensio'nato, a *sm/f* pensioner ♦ *sm* (*istituto*) hostel.

pensi'one *sf* (*al prestatore di lavoro*) pension; (*vitto e alloggio*) board and lodging; (*albergo*) boarding house; **andare in** ~ to retire; **mezza** ~ half board; ~ **completa** full board; ~ **d'invalidità** disablement pension; ~ **per la vecchiaia** old-age pension.

pensio'nistico, a, ci, che *ag* pension *cpd*.

pen'soso, a *ag* thoughtful, pensive, lost in thought.

pen'tagono *sm* pentagon; **il P**~ the Pentagon.

pentag'ramma, i *sm* (*MUS*) staff, stave.

pentapar'tito *sm* (*POL*) five-party coalition government.

'pentathlon ['pɛntatlon] *sm* (*SPORT*) pentathlon.

Pente'coste *sf* Pentecost, Whit Sunday (*BRIT*).

penti'mento *sm* repentance, contrition.

pen'tirsi *vr*: ~ **di** to repent of; (*rammaricarsi*) to regret, be sorry for.

penti'tismo *sm confessions from terrorists and members of organized crime rackets.*

The practice of **pentitismo** *emerged in Italy during the period of major terrorist activity in the 1970s. Members of terrorist groups, who had been arrested, would collaborate with the authorities by providing information in return for a reduced sentence, or for their own ideological reasons. In recent years it has become common practice for members of Mafia organizations to become* **pentiti** *and special legislation has been passed to provide for their sentencing and personal protection.*

---

pen'tito, a *sm/f* ≈ supergrass (*BRIT*), *terrorist/criminal who turns police informer.*

'pentola *sf* pot; ~ **a pressione** pressure cooker.

pe'nultimo, a *ag* last but one (*BRIT*), next to last, penultimate.

pe'nuria *sf* shortage.

penzo'lare [pendzo'lare] *vi* to dangle, hang loosely.

penzo'loni [pendzo'loni] *av* dangling, hanging down; **stare** ~ to dangle, hang down.

pe'pato, a *ag* (*condito con pepe*) peppery, hot; (*fig: pungente*) sharp.

'pepe *sm* pepper; ~ **macinato/in grani/nero** ground/whole/black pepper.

pepero'nata *sf stewed peppers, tomatoes and onions.*

peperon'cino [peperon'tʃino] *sm* chilli pepper.

pepe'rone *sm*: ~ **(rosso)** red pepper, capsicum; ~ **(verde)** green pepper, capsicum; **rosso come un** ~ as red as a beetroot (*BRIT*), fire-engine red (*US*); ~**i ripieni** stuffed peppers.

pe'pita *sf* nugget.

═══════════ *PAROLA CHIAVE*

per *prep* **1** (*moto attraverso luogo*) through; **i ladri sono passati** ~ **la finestra** the thieves got in (*o* out) through the window; **l'ho cercato** ~ **tutta la casa** I've searched the whole house *o* all over the

house for it

2 (*moto a luogo*) for, to; **partire** ~ **la Germania/il mare** to leave for Germany/ the sea; **il treno** ~ **Roma** the Rome train, the train for *o* to Rome; **proseguire** ~ **Londra** to go on to London

3 (*stato in luogo*): **seduto/sdraiato** ~ **terra** sitting/lying on the ground

4 (*tempo*) for; ~ **anni/tanto tempo** for years/a long time; ~ **tutta l'estate** throughout the summer, all summer long; **lo rividi** ~ **Natale** I saw him again at Christmas; **lo faccio** ~ **lunedì** I'll do it for Monday

5 (*mezzo, maniera*) by; ~ **lettera/ferrovia/ via aerea** by letter/rail/airmail; **prendere qn** ~ **un braccio** to take sb by the arm

6 (*causa, scopo*) for; **assente** ~ **malattia** absent because of *o* through *o* owing to illness; **ottimo** ~ **il mal di gola** excellent for sore throats; ~ **abitudine** out of habit, from habit

7 (*limitazione*) for; **è troppo difficile** ~ **lui** it's too difficult for him; ~ **quel che mi riguarda** as far as I'm concerned; ~ **poco che sia** however little it may be; ~ **questa volta ti perdono** I'll forgive you this time

8 (*prezzo, misura*) for; (*distributivo*) a, per; **venduto** ~ **3 milioni** sold for 3 million; **la strada continua** ~ **3 km** the street goes on for 3 km; **1000 lire** ~ **persona** 1000 lire a *o* per person; **uno** ~ **volta** one at a time; **uno** ~ **uno** one by one; **giorno** ~ **giorno** day by day; **due** ~ **parte** two either side; **5** ~ **cento** 5 per cent; **3** ~ **4 fa 12** 3 times 4 equals 12; **dividere/moltiplicare 12** ~ **4** to divide/multiply 12 by 4

9 (*in qualità di*) as; (*al posto di*) for; **avere qn** ~ **professore** to have sb as a teacher; **ti ho preso** ~ **Mario** I mistook you for Mario, I thought you were Mario; **dare** ~ **morto qn** to give sb up for dead; **lo prenderanno** ~ **pazzo** they'll think he's crazy

10 (*seguito da vb: finale*): ~ **fare qc** (so as) to do sth, in order to do sth; (*: causale*): ~ **aver fatto qc** for having done sth; **studia** ~ **passare l'esame** he's studying in order to *o* (so as) to pass his exam; **l'hanno punito** ~ **aver rubato i soldi** he was punished for having stolen the money; **è abbastanza grande** ~ **andarci da solo** he's big enough to go on his own.

'pera *sf* pear.

pe'raltro *av* moreover, what's more.

per'bacco *escl* by Jove!

per'bene *ag inv* respectable, decent ♦ *av*

(*con cura*) properly, well.

perbe'nismo *sm* (so-called) respectability.

percentu'ale [pertʃentu'ale] *sf* percentage; (*commissione*) commission.

perce'pire [pertʃe'pire] *vt* (*sentire*) to perceive; (*ricevere*) to receive.

percet'tibile [pertʃet'tibile] *ag* perceptible.

percezi'one [pertʃet'tsjone] *sf* perception.

══════════════ *PAROLA CHIAVE*

perché [per'ke] *av* why; ~ **no?** why not?; ~ **non vuoi andarci?** why don't you want to go?; **spiegami** ~ **l'hai fatto** tell me why you did it

♦ *cong* **1** (*causale*) because; **non posso uscire** ~ **ho da fare** I can't go out because *o* as I've a lot to do

2 (*finale*) in order that, so that; **te lo do** ~ **tu lo legga** I'm giving it to you so (that) you can read it

3 (*consecutivo*): **è troppo forte** ~ **si possa batterlo** he's too strong to be beaten

♦ *sm inv* reason; **il** ~ **di** the reason for; **non c'è un vero** ~ there's no real reason for it.

perciò [per'tʃɔ] *cong* so, for this (*o* that) reason.

per'correre *vt* (*luogo*) to go all over; (: *paese*) to travel up and down, go all over; (*distanza*) to cover.

percor'ribile *ag* (*strada*) which can be followed.

per'corso, a *pp di* **percorrere** ♦ *sm* (*tragitto*) journey; (*tratto*) route.

per'cosso, a *pp di* **percuotere** ♦ *sf* blow.

percu'otere *vt* to hit, strike.

percussi'one *sf* percussion; **strumenti a** ~ (*MUS*) percussion instruments.

per'dente *ag* losing ♦ *smf* loser.

'perdere *vt* to lose; (*lasciarsi sfuggire*) to miss; (*sprecare: tempo, denaro*) to waste; (*mandare in rovina: persona*) to ruin ♦ *vi* to lose; (*serbatoio etc*) to leak; ~**rsi** *vr* (*smarrirsi*) to get lost; (*svanire*) to disappear, vanish; **saper** ~ to be a good loser; **lascia** ~**!** forget it!, never mind!; **non ho niente da** ~ (*fig*) I've got nothing to lose; **è un'occasione da non** ~ it's a marvellous opportunity; (*affare*) it's a great bargain; **è fatica persa** it's a waste of effort; ~ **al gioco** to lose money gambling; ~ **di vista qn** (*anche fig*) to lose sight of sb; ~**rsi di vista** to lose sight of each other; (*fig*) to lose touch; ~**rsi alla vista** to disappear from sight; ~**rsi in chiacchiere** to waste time talking.

perdifi'ato : **a** ~ *av* (*correre*) at breathtaking speed; (*gridare*) at the top of one's voice.

perdigi'orno [perdi'dʒorno] *smf inv* idler, waster.

'perdita *sf* loss; (*spreco*) waste; (*fuoriuscita*) leak; **siamo in** ~ (*COMM*) we are running at a loss; **a** ~ **d'occhio** as far as the eye can see.

perdi'tempo *smf inv* waster, idler.

perdizi'one [perdit'tsjone] *sf* (*REL*) perdition, damnation; **luogo di** ~ place of ill repute.

perdo'nare *vt* to pardon, forgive; (*scusare*) to excuse, pardon; **per farsi** ~ in order to be forgiven; **perdona la domanda** ... if you don't mind my asking ...; **vogliate** ~ **il (mio) ritardo** my apologies for being late; **un male che non perdona** an incurable disease.

per'dono *sm* forgiveness; (*DIR*) pardon; **chiedere** ~ **a qn (per)** to ask for sb's forgiveness (for); (*scusarsi*) to apologize to sb (for).

perdu'rare *vi* to go on, last; (*perseverare*) to persist.

perduta'mente *av* desperately, passionately.

per'duto, a *pp di* **perdere** ♦ *ag* (*gen*) lost; **sentirsi** *o* **vedersi** ~ (*fig*) to realize the hopelessness of one's position; **una donna** ~**a** (*fig*) a fallen woman.

peregri'nare *vi* to wander, roam.

pe'renne *ag* eternal, perpetual, perennial; (*BOT*) perennial.

peren'torio, a *ag* peremptory; (*definitivo*) final.

perfetta'mente *av* perfectly; **sai** ~ **che** ... you know perfectly well that ....

per'fetto, a *ag* perfect ♦ *sm* (*LING*) perfect (tense).

perfeziona'mento [perfettsjona'mento] *sm*: ~ (**di**) improvement (in), perfection (of); **corso di** ~ proficiency course.

perfezio'nare [perfettsjo'nare] *vt* to improve, perfect; ~**rsi** *vr* to improve.

perfezi'one [perfet'tsjone] *sf* perfection.

perfezio'nismo [perfettsjo'nizmo] *sm* perfectionism.

perfezio'nista, i, e [perfettsjo'nista] *smf* perfectionist.

per'fidia *sf* perfidy.

'perfido, a *ag* perfidious, treacherous.

per'fino *av* even.

perfo'rare *vt* to pierce; (*MED*) to perforate; (*banda, schede*) to punch; (*trivellare*) to drill.

perfora'tore, 'trice *smf* punch-card operator ♦ *sm* (*utensile*) punch; (*INFORM*):

~ **di schede** card punch ♦ *sf* (*TECN*) boring
o drilling machine; (*INFORM*) card punch.
perforazi'one [perforat'tsjone] *sf* piercing;
perforation; punching; drilling.
perga'mena *sf* parchment.
'pergola *sf* pergola.
pergo'lato *sm* pergola.
perico'lante *ag* precarious.
pe'ricolo *sm* danger; **essere fuori** ~ to be
out of danger; (*MED*) to be off the danger
list; **mettere in** ~ to endanger, put in
danger.
perico'loso, a *ag* dangerous.
perife'ria *sf* (*anche fig*) periphery; (*di città*)
outskirts *pl.*
peri'ferico, a, ci, che *ag* (*ANAT, INFORM*)
peripheral; (*zona*) outlying.
pe'rifrasi *sf inv* circumlocution.
pe'rimetro *sm* perimeter.
peri'odico, a, ci, che *ag* periodic(al);
(*MAT*) recurring ♦ *sm* periodical.
pe'riodo *sm* period; ~ **contabile**
accounting period; ~ **di prova** trial
period.
peripe'zie [peripet'tsie] *sfpl* ups and downs,
vicissitudes.
'periplo *sm* circumnavigation.
pe'rire *vi* to perish, die.
peris'copio *sm* periscope.
pe'rito, a *ag* expert, skilled ♦ *sm/f* expert;
(*agronomo, navale*) surveyor; **un** ~
chimico a qualified chemist.
perito'nite *sf* peritonitis.
pe'rizia [pe'rittsja] *sf* (*abilità*) ability;
(*giudizio tecnico*) expert opinion; expert's
report; ~ **psichiatrica** psychiatrist's
report.
'perla *sf* pearl.
per'lina *sf* bead.
perli'nato *sm* matchboarding.
perlo'meno *av* (*almeno*) at least.
perlopiù *av* (*quasi sempre*) in most cases,
usually.
perlus'trare *vt* to patrol.
perlustrazi'one [perlustrat'tsjone] *sf* patrol,
reconnaissance; **andare in** ~ to go on
patrol.
perma'loso, a *ag* touchy.
perma'nente *ag* permanent ♦ *sf*
permanent wave, perm.
perma'nenza [perma'nentsa] *sf*
permanence; (*soggiorno*) stay; **buona** ~!
enjoy your stay!
perma'nere *vi* to remain.
per'mango, per'masi *etc vb vedi*
permanere.
perme'abile *ag* permeable.
perme'are *vt* to permeate.

per'messo, a *pp di* **permettere** ♦ *sm*
(*autorizzazione*) permission, leave; (*dato a
militare, impiegato*) leave; (*licenza*) licence
(*BRIT*), license (*US*), permit; (*MIL: foglio*)
pass; ~?, **è** ~? (*posso entrare?*) may I
come in?; (*posso passare?*) excuse me; ~
di lavoro/pesca work/fishing permit.
per'mettere *vt* to allow, permit; ~ **a qn**
qc/di fare qc to allow sb sth/to do sth;
~**rsi** *vr:* ~**rsi qc/di fare qc** (*concedersi*) to
allow o.s. sth/to do sth; (*avere la
possibilità*) to afford sth/to do sth;
permettete che mi presenti let me
introduce myself, may I introduce
myself?; **mi sia permesso di sottolineare**
che ... may I take the liberty of pointing
out that ....
per'misi *etc vb vedi* **permettere.**
permis'sivo, a *ag* permissive.
'permuta *sf* (*DIR*) transfer; (*COMM*) trade-
in; **accettare qc in** ~ to take sth as a
trade-in; **valore di** ~ (*di macchina etc*)
trade-in value.
permu'tare *vt* to exchange; (*MAT*) to
permute.
per'nacchia [per'nakkja] *sf* (*fam*): **fare una**
~ to blow a raspberry.
per'nice [per'nitʃe] *sf* partridge.
pernici'oso, a [perni'tʃoso] *ag* pernicious.
'perno *sm* pivot.
pernotta'mento *sm* overnight stay.
pernot'tare *vi* to spend the night, stay
overnight.
'pero *sm* pear tree.
però *cong* (*ma*) but; (*tuttavia*) however,
nevertheless.
pero'rare *vt* (*DIR, fig*): ~ **la causa di qn** to
plead sb's case.
perpendico'lare *ag, sf* perpendicular.
perpen'dicolo *sm:* **a** ~ perpendicularly.
perpe'trare *vt* to perpetrate.
perpetu'are *vt* to perpetuate.
per'petuo, a *ag* perpetual.
perplessità *sf inv* perplexity.
per'plesso, a *ag* perplexed, puzzled.
perqui'sire *vt* to search.
perquisizi'one [perkwizit'tsjone] *sf* (*police*)
search; **mandato di** ~ search warrant.
'perse *etc vb vedi* **perdere.**
persecu'tore *sm* persecutor.
persecuzi'one [persekut'tsjone] *sf*
persecution.
persegu'ibile *ag* (*DIR*): **essere** ~ **per legge**
to be liable to prosecution.
persegu'ire *vt* to pursue; (*DIR*) to
prosecute.
persegui'tare *vt* to persecute.
perseve'rante *ag* persevering.

perseve'ranza [perseve'rantsa] *sf* perseverance.

perseve'rare *vi* to persevere.

'persi *etc vb vedi* **perdere**.

'Persia *sf*: **la** ~ Persia.

persi'ano, a *ag, smf* Persian ♦ *sf* shutter; **~a avvolgibile** roller blind.

'persico, a, ci, che *ag*: **il golfo P**~ the Persian Gulf; **pesce** ~ perch.

per'sino *av* = **perfino**.

persis'tente *ag* persistent.

persis'tenza [persis'tɛntsa] *sf* persistence.

per'sistere *vi* to persist; ~ **a fare** to persist in doing.

persis'tito, a *pp di* **persistere**.

'perso, a *pp di* **perdere** ♦ *ag* (*smarrito*: *anche fig*) lost; (*sprecato*) wasted; **fare qc a tempo** ~ to do sth in one's spare time; ~ **per** ~ I've (*o* we've *etc*) got nothing further to lose.

per'sona *sf* person; (*qualcuno*): **una** ~ someone, somebody, *espressione interrogativa* + anyone *o* anybody; **~e** *sfpl* people *pl*; **non c'è** ~ **che** ... there's nobody who ..., there isn't anybody who ...; **in** ~, **di** ~ in person; **per interposta** ~ through an intermediary *o* a third party; ~ **giuridica** (*DIR*) legal person.

perso'naggio [perso'naddʒo] *sm* (*persona ragguardevole*) personality, figure; (*tipo*) character, individual; (*LETTERATURA*) character.

perso'nale *ag* personal ♦ *sm* staff, personnel; (*figura fisica*) build ♦ *sf* (*mostra*) one-man (*o* one-woman) exhibition.

personalità *sf inv* personality.

personaliz'zare [personalid'dzare] *vt* (*arredamento, stile*) to personalize; (*adattare*) to customize.

personaliz'zato, a [personalid'dzato] *ag* personalized.

personal'mente *av* personally.

personifi'care *vt* to personify; (*simboleggiare*) to embody.

personificazi'one [personifikat'tsjone] *sf* (*vedi vb*) personification; embodiment.

perspi'cace [perspi'katʃe] *ag* shrewd, discerning.

perspi'cacia [perspi'katʃa] *sf* perspicacity, shrewdness.

persu'adere *vt*: ~ **qn** (**di qc/a fare**) to persuade sb (of sth/to do).

persuasi'one *sf* persuasion.

persua'sivo, a *ag* persuasive.

persu'aso, a *pp di* **persuadere**.

per'tanto *cong* (*quindi*) so, therefore.

'pertica, che *sf* pole.

perti'nace [perti'natʃe] *ag* determined; persistent.

perti'nente *ag*: ~ (**a**) relevant (to), pertinent (to).

perti'nenza [perti'nɛntsa] *sf* (*attinenza*) pertinence, relevance; (*competenza*): **essere di** ~ **di qn** to be sb's business.

per'tosse *sf* whooping cough.

per'tugio [per'tudʒo] *sm* hole, opening.

pertur'bare *vt* to disrupt; (*persona*) to disturb, perturb.

perturbazi'one [perturbat'tsjone] *sf* disruption; disturbance.

Perù *sm*: **il** ~ Peru.

peru'gino, a [peru'dʒino] *ag* of (*o* from) Perugia.

peruvi'ano, a *ag, smf* Peruvian.

per'vadere *vt* to pervade.

per'vaso, a *pp di* **pervadere**.

perve'nire *vi*: ~ **a** to reach, arrive at, come to; (*venire in possesso*): **gli pervenne una fortuna** he inherited a fortune; **far** ~ **qc a** to have sth sent to.

perve'nuto, a *pp di* **pervenire**.

perversi'one *sf* perversion.

perversità *sf* perversity.

per'verso, a *ag* perverted.

perver'tire *vt* to pervert.

perver'tito, a *smf* pervert.

pervi'cace [pervi'katʃe] *ag* stubborn, obstinate.

pervi'cacia [pervi'katʃa] *sf* stubbornness, obstinacy.

per'vinca, che *sf* periwinkle ♦ *sm inv* (*colore*) periwinkle (blue).

p.es. *abbr* (= *per esempio*) e.g.

'pesa *sf* weighing *no pl*; weighbridge.

pe'sante *ag* heavy; (*fig: noioso*) dull, boring.

pesan'tezza [pesan'tettsa] *sf* (*anche fig*) heaviness; **avere** ~ **di stomaco** to feel bloated.

pesaper'sone *ag inv*: (**bilancia**) ~ (weighing) scales *pl*; (*automatica*) weighing machine.

pe'sare *vt* to weigh ♦ *vi* (*avere un peso*) to weigh; (*essere pesante*) to be heavy; (*fig*) to carry weight; ~ **su** (*fig*) to lie heavy on; to influence; to hang over; **mi pesa sgridarlo** I find it hard to scold him; **tutta la responsabilità pesa su di lui** all the responsibility rests on his shoulders; **è una situazione che mi pesa** it's a difficult situation for me; **il suo parere pesa molto** his opinion counts for a lot; ~ **le parole** to weigh one's words.

'pesca *sf* (*pl* **pesche**: *frutto*) peach; (*il pescare*) fishing; **andare a** ~ to go fishing; ~ **di beneficenza** (*lotteria*) lucky dip; ~

con la lenza angling; ~ **subacquea** underwater fishing.

pes'caggio [pes'kaddʒo] *sm* (*NAUT*) draught (*BRIT*), draft (*US*).

pes'care *vt* (*pesce*) to fish for; to catch; (*qc nell'acqua*) to fish out; (*fig: trovare*) to get hold of, find.

pesca'tore *sm* fisherman; (*con lenza*) angler.

'pesce ['peʃʃe] *sm* fish *gen inv*; **P~i** (*dello zodiaco*) Pisces; **essere dei P~i** to be Pisces; **non saper che ~i prendere** (*fig*) not to know which way to turn; ~ **d'aprile!** April Fool!; ~ **martello** hammerhead; ~ **rosso** goldfish; ~ **spada** swordfish.

Il pesce d'aprile *is a sort of April Fool, played on April 1st each year. It took its name from the paper fish which was stuck to the back of the person who was the object of the joke. Nowadays all sorts of practical jokes are played on that day.*

---

pesce'cane [peʃʃe'kane] *sm* shark.

pesche'reccio [peske'rettʃo] *sm* fishing boat.

pesche'ria [peske'ria] *sf* fishmonger's (shop) (*BRIT*), fish store (*US*).

pescherò *etc* [peske'rɔ] *vb vedi* **pescare**.

peschi'era [pes'kjɛra] *sf* fishpond.

pesci'vendolo, a [peʃʃi'vendolo] *sm/f* fishmonger (*BRIT*), fish merchant (*US*).

'pesco, schi *sm* peach tree.

pes'coso, a *ag* teeming with fish.

pe'seta *sf* peseta.

'peso *sm* weight; (*SPORT*) shot; **dar ~ a qc** to attach importance to sth; **essere di ~ a qn** (*fig*) to be a burden to sb; **rubare sul ~** to give short weight; **lo portarono via di ~** they carried him away bodily; **avere due ~i e due misure** (*fig*) to have double standards; ~ **lordo/netto** gross/net weight; ~ **piuma/mosca/gallo/medio/ massimo** (*PUGILATO*) feather/fly/bantam/ middle/heavyweight.

pessi'mismo *sm* pessimism.

pessi'mista, i, e *ag* pessimistic ♦ *sm/f* pessimist.

'pessimo, a *ag* very bad, awful; **di ~a qualità** of very poor quality.

pes'tare *vt* to tread on, trample on; (*sale, pepe*) to grind; (*uva, aglio*) to crush; (*fig: picchiare*): ~ **qn** to beat sb up; ~ **i piedi** to stamp one's feet; ~ **i piedi a qn** (*anche fig*) to tread on sb's toes.

'peste *sf* plague; (*persona*) nuisance, pest.

pes'tello *sm* pestle.

pesti'cida, i [pesti'tʃida] *sm* pesticide.

pes'tifero, a *ag* (*anche fig*) pestilential, pestiferous; (*odore*) noxious.

pesti'lenza [pesti'lɛntsa] *sf* pestilence; (*fetore*) stench.

'pesto, a *ag*: **c'è buio ~** it's pitch dark ♦ *sm* (*CUC*) sauce made with basil, garlic, cheese and oil; **occhio ~** black eye.

'petalo *sm* (*BOT*) petal.

pe'tardo *sm* firecracker, banger (*BRIT*).

petizi'one [petit'tsjone] *sf* petition; **fare una ~ a** to petition.

'peto *sm* (*fam!*) fart (*!*).

petro'dollaro *sm* petrodollar.

petrol'chimica [petrol'kimika] *sf* petrochemical industry.

petroli'era *sf* (*nave*) oil tanker.

petroli'ere *sm* (*industriale*) oilman; (*tecnico*) worker in the oil industry.

petroli'ero, a *ag* oil *cpd*.

petro'lifero, a *ag* oil *cpd*.

pe'trolio *sm* oil, petroleum; (*per lampada, fornello*) paraffin (*BRIT*), kerosene (*US*); **lume a ~** oil *o* paraffin *o* kerosene lamp; ~ **grezzo** crude oil.

pettego'lare *vi* to gossip.

pettego'lezzo [pettego'leddzo] *sm* gossip *no pl*; **fare ~i** to gossip.

pet'tegolo, a *ag* gossipy ♦ *sm/f* gossip.

petti'nare *vt* to comb (the hair of); ~**rsi** *vr* to comb one's hair.

pettina'tura *sf* (*acconciatura*) hairstyle.

'pettine *sm* comb; (*ZOOL*) scallop.

petti'rosso *sm* robin.

'petto *sm* chest; (*seno*) breast, bust; (*CUC: di carne bovina*) brisket; (: *di pollo etc*) breast; **prendere qn/qc di ~** to face up to sb/sth; **a doppio ~** (*abito*) double-breasted.

petto'rale *ag* pectoral.

petto'rina *sf* (*di grembiule*) bib.

petto'ruto, a *ag* broad-chested; full-breasted.

petu'lante *ag* insolent.

pe'tunia *sf* petunia.

'pezza ['pettsa] *sf* piece of cloth; (*toppa*) patch; (*cencio*) rag, cloth; (*AMM*): ~ **d'appoggio** *o* **giustificativa** voucher; **trattare qn come una ~ da piedi** to treat sb like a doormat.

pez'zato, a [pet'tsato] *ag* piebald.

pez'zente [pet'tsɛnte] *sm/f* beggar.

'pezzo ['pettso] *sm* (*gen*) piece; (*brandello, frammento*) piece, bit; (*di macchina, arnese etc*) part; (*STAMPA*) article; (*di tempo*): **aspettare un ~** to wait quite a while *o* some time; **andare a ~i** to break into pieces; **essere a ~i** (*oggetto*) to be in pieces o bits; (*fig: persona*) to be shattered; **un bel ~ d'uomo** a fine figure of a man; **abito a due ~i** two-piece suit; **essere tutto d'un ~** (*fig*) to be a man (o woman) of integrity; **~ di cronaca** (*STAMPA*) report; **~ grosso** (*fig*) bigwig; **~ di ricambio** spare part.

P.F. *abbr* = **per favore; prossimo futuro.**

PG *sigla* = **Perugia.**

P.G. *abbr* = **procuratore generale.**

pH [pi'akka] *sm inv* (*CHIM*) pH.

PI *sigla* = *Pisa.*

P.I. *abbr* = **Pubblica Istruzione.**

pi'accio *etc* ['pjatt∫o] *vb vedi* **piacere.**

pia'cente [pja't∫ɛnte] *ag* attractive, pleasant.

pia'cere [pja't∫ere] *vi* to please; ♦ *sm* pleasure; (*favore*) favour (*BRIT*), favor (*US*); **una ragazza che piace** (*piacevole*) a likeable girl; (*attraente*) an attractive girl; **~ a: mi piace** I like it; **quei ragazzi non mi piacciono** I don't like those boys; **gli piacerebbe andare al cinema** he would like to go to the cinema; **il suo discorso è piaciuto molto** his speech was well received; **"~!"** (*nelle presentazioni*) "pleased to meet you!"; **con ~** certainly, with pleasure; **per ~** please; **fare un ~ a qn** to do sb a favour; **mi fa ~ per lui** I am pleased for him; **mi farebbe ~ rivederlo** I would like to see him again.

pia'cevole [pja't∫evole] *ag* pleasant, agreeable.

piaci'mento [pjat∫i'mento] *sm*: **a ~** (*a volontà*) as much as one likes, at will; **lo farà a suo ~** he'll do it when it suits him.

piaci'uto, a [pja't∫uto] *pp di* **piacere.**

pi'acqui *etc vb vedi* **piacere.**

pi'aga, ghe *sf* (*lesione*) sore; (*ferita: anche fig*) wound; (*fig: flagello*) scourge, curse; (: *persona*) pest, nuisance.

piagnis'teo [pjaɲɲis'tɛo] *sm* whining, whimpering.

piagnuco'lare [pjaɲɲuko'lare] *vi* to whimper.

piagnuco'lio, ii [pjaɲɲuko'lio] *sm* whimpering.

piagnuco'loso, a [pjaɲɲuko'loso] *ag* whiny, whimpering, moaning.

pi'alla *sf* (*arnese*) plane.

pial'lare *vt* to plane.

pialla'trice [pjalla'trit∫e] *sf* planing machine.

pi'ana *sf* stretch of level ground; (*più esteso*) plain.

pianeggi'ante [pjaned'dʒante] *ag* flat, level.

piane'rottolo *sm* landing.

pia'neta *sm* (*ASTR*) planet.

pi'angere ['pjandʒere] *vi* to cry, weep; (*occhi*) to water ♦ *vt* to cry, weep; (*lamentare*) to bewail, lament; **~ la morte di qn** to mourn sb's death.

pianifi'care *vt* to plan.

pianificazi'one [pjanifikat'tsjone] *sf* (*ECON*) planning; **~ aziendale** corporate planning.

pia'nista, i, e *sm/f* pianist.

pi'ano, a *ag* (*piatto*) flat, level; (*MAT*) plane; (*facile*) straightforward, simple; (*chiaro*) clear, plain ♦ *av* (*adagio*) slowly; (*a bassa voce*) softly; (*con cautela*) slowly, carefully ♦ *sm* (*MAT*) plane; (*GEO*) plain; (*livello*) level, plane; (*di edificio*) floor; (*programma*) plan; (*MUS*) piano; **pian ~** very slowly; (*poco a poco*) little by little; **una casa di 3 ~i** a 3-storey (*BRIT*) o 3-storied (*US*) house; **al ~ di sopra/di sotto** on the floor above/below; **all'ultimo ~** on the top floor; **al ~ terra** on the ground floor; **in primo/secondo ~** (*FOT, CINE etc*) in the foreground/background; **fare un primo ~** (*FOT, CINE*) to take a close-up; **di primo ~** (*fig*) prominent, high-ranking; **un fattore di secondo ~** a secondary o minor factor; **passare in secondo ~** to become less important; **mettere tutto sullo stesso ~** to lump everything together, give equal importance to everything; **tutto secondo i ~i** all according to plan; **~ di lavoro** (*superficie*) worktop; (*programma*) work plan; **~ regolatore** (*URBANISTICA*) town-planning scheme; **~ stradale** road surface.

piano'forte *sm* piano, pianoforte.

piano'terra *sm inv* = **piano terra.**

pi'ansi *etc vb vedi* **piangere.**

pi'anta *sf* (*BOT*) plant; (*ANAT: anche: ~ del piede*) sole (of the foot); (*grafico*) plan; (*cartina topografica*) map; **ufficio a ~ aperta** open-plan office; **in ~ stabile** on the permanent staff; **~ stradale** street map, street plan.

piantagi'one [pjanta'dʒone] *sf* plantation.

pianta'grane *sm/f inv* troublemaker.

pian'tare *vt* to plant; (*conficcare*) to drive o hammer in; (*tenda*) to put up, pitch; (*fig: lasciare*) to leave, desert; **~rsi** *vr*: **~rsi davanti a qn** to plant o.s. in front of sb; **~ qn in asso** to leave sb in the lurch; **~ grane** (*fig*) to cause trouble; **piantala!** (*fam*) cut it out!

pian'tato, a *ag*: **ben ~** (*persona*) well-built.

pianta'tore *sm* planter.

pianter'reno *sm* ground floor.

pi'anto, a *pp di* **piangere** ♦ *sm* tears *pl*, crying.

pianto'nare *vt* to guard, watch over.
pian'tone *sm* (*vigilante*) sentry, guard; (*soldato*) orderly; (*AUT*) steering column.
pia'nura *sf* plain.
pi'astra *sf* plate; (*di pietra*) slab; (*di fornello*) hotplate; **panino alla ~** ≈ toasted sandwich; **~ di registrazione** tape deck.
pias'trella *sf* tile.
piastrel'lare *vt* to tile.
pias'trina *sf* (*ANAT*) platelet; (*MIL*) identity disc (*BRIT*) o tag (*US*).
piatta'forma *sf* (*anche fig*) platform; **~ continentale** (*GEO*) continental shelf; **~ girevole** (*TECN*) turntable; **~ di lancio** (*MIL*) launching pad o platform; **~ rivendicativa** *document prepared by the unions in an industry, setting out their claims*.
piat'tello *sm* clay pigeon; **tiro al ~** clay-pigeon shooting (*BRIT*), trapshooting.
piat'tino *sm* (*di tazza*) saucer.
pi'atto, a *ag* flat; (*fig: scialbo*) dull ♦ *sm* (*recipiente, vivanda*) dish; (*portata*) course; (*parte piana*) flat (part); **~i** *smpl* (*MUS*) cymbals; **un ~ di minestra** a plate of soup; **~ fondo** soup dish; **~ forte** main course; **~ del giorno** dish of the day, plat du jour; **~ del giradischi** turntable; **~i già pronti** (*CUC*) ready-cooked dishes.
pi'azza ['pjattsa] *sf* square; (*COMM*) market; (*letto, lenzuolo*): **a una ~** single; **a due ~e** double; **far ~ pulita** to make a clean sweep; **mettere in ~** (*fig: rendere pubblico*) to make public; **scendere in ~** (*fig*) to take to the streets, demonstrate; **~ d'armi** (*MIL*) parade ground.
piazza'forte [pjattsa'forte], *pl* **piazze'forti** *sf* (*MIL*) stronghold.
piaz'zale [pjat'tsale] *sm* (large) square.
piazza'mento [pjattsa'mento] *sm* (*SPORT*) place, placing.
piaz'zare [pjat'tsare] *vt* to place; (*COMM*) to market, sell; **~rsi** *vr* (*SPORT*) to be placed; **~rsi bene** to finish with the leaders o in a good position.
piaz'zista, i [pjat'tsista] *sm* (*COMM*) commercial traveller.
piaz'zola [pjat'tsɔla] *sf* (*AUT*) lay-by (*BRIT*), (roadside) stopping place.
'picca, che *sf* pike; **~che** *sfpl* (*CARTE*) spades; **rispondere ~che a qn** (*fig*) to give sb a flat refusal.
pic'cante *ag* hot, pungent; (*fig*) racy.
pic'carsi *vr*: **~ di fare** to pride o.s. on one's ability to do; **~ per qc** to take offence (*BRIT*) o offense (*US*) at sth.
picchet'taggio [pikket'taddʒo] *sm* picketing.

picchet'tare [pikket'tare] *vt* to picket.
pic'chetto [pik'ketto] *sm* (*MIL, di scioperanti*) picket.
picchi'are [pik'kjare] *vt* (*persona: colpire*) to hit, strike; (*: prendere a botte*) to beat (up); (*battere*) to beat; (*sbattere*) to bang ♦ *vi* (*bussare*) to knock; (*: con forza*) to bang; (*colpire*) to hit, strike; (*sole*) to beat down.
picchi'ata [pik'kjata] *sf* knock; bang; blow; (*percosse*) beating, thrashing; (*AER*) dive; **scendere in ~** to (nose-)dive.
picchiet'tare [pikkjet'tare] *vt* (*punteggiare*) to spot, dot; (*colpire*) to tap.
'picchio ['pikkjo] *sm* woodpecker.
pic'cino, a [pit'tʃino] *ag* tiny, very small.
picci'olo [pit'tʃɔlo] *sm* (*BOT*) stalk.
piccio'naia [pittʃo'naja] *sf* pigeon-loft; (*TEAT*): **la ~** the gods *sg* (*BRIT*), the gallery.
picci'one [pit'tʃone] *sm* pigeon; **pigliare due ~i con una fava** (*fig*) to kill two birds with one stone.
'picco, chi *sm* peak; **a ~** vertically; **colare a ~** (*NAUT, fig*) to sink.
picco'lezza [pikko'lettsa] *sf* (*dimensione*) smallness; (*fig: grettezza*) meanness, pettiness; (*: inezia*) trifle.
'piccolo, a *ag* small; (*oggetto, mano, di età: bambino*) small, little (*dav sostantivo*); (*di breve durata: viaggio*) short; (*fig*) mean, petty ♦ *smlf* child, little one ♦ *sm*: **nel mio ~** in my own small way; **~i** *smpl* (*di animale*) young *pl*; **in ~** in miniature; **la ~a borghesia** the lower middle classes; (*peg*) the petty bourgeoisie.
pic'cone *sm* pick(-axe).
pic'cozza [pik'kɔttsa] *sf* ice-axe.
pic'nic *sm inv* picnic; **fare un ~** to have a picnic.
pidies'sino, a [pidjes'sino] *ag* (*POL*) of P.D.S. ♦ *smlf* member (*o* supporter) of P.D.S.
pi'docchio [pi'dɔkkjo] *sm* louse.
pidoc'chi'oso, a [pidok'kjoso] *ag* (*infestato*) lousy; (*fig: taccagno*) mean, stingy, tight.
pidu'ista, i, e *ag* P2 *cpd* (*masonic lodge*) ♦ *sm* member of the P2 masonic lodge.
piè *sm inv*: **a ogni ~ sospinto** (*fig*) at every step; **saltare a ~ pari** (*omettere*) to skip; **a ~ di pagina** at the foot of the page; **note a ~ di pagina** footnotes.
pi'ede *sm* foot; (*di mobile*) leg; **in ~i** standing; **a ~i** on foot; **a ~i nudi** barefoot; **su due ~i** (*fig*) at once; **mettere qc in ~i** (*azienda etc*) to set sth up; **prendere ~** (*fig*) to gain ground, catch on; **puntare i ~i** (*fig*) to dig one's heels in; **sentirsi mancare la terra sotto i ~i** to feel lost; **non sta in ~i** (*persona*) he can't stand; (*fig: scusa etc*) it doesn't hold water; **tenere in**

~i (*persona*) to keep on his (*o* her) feet; (*fig: ditta etc*) to keep going; a ~ **libero** (*DIR*) on bail; **sul ~ di guerra** (*MIL*) ready for action; ~ **di porco** crowbar.

piedipi'atti *sm inv* (*peg: poliziotto*) cop.

piedis'tallo, piedes'tallo *sm* pedestal.

pi'ega, ghe *sf* (*piegatura, GEO*) fold; (*di gonna*) pleat; (*di pantaloni*) crease; (*grinza*) wrinkle, crease; **prendere una brutta** *o* **cattiva ~** (*fig: persona*) to get into bad ways; (: *situazione*) to take a turn for the worse; **non fa una ~** (*fig: ragionamento*) it's faultless; **non ha fatto una ~** (*fig: persona*) he didn't bat an eye(lid) (*BRIT*) *o* an eye(lash) (*US*).

piega'mento *sm* folding; bending; ~ **sulle gambe** (*GINNASTICA*) kneebend.

pie'gare *vt* to fold; (*braccia, gambe, testa*) to bend ♦ *vi* to bend; ~**rsi** *vr* to bend; (*fig*): ~**rsi (a)** to yield (to), submit (to).

piega'tura *sf* folding *no pl*; bending *no pl*; fold; bend.

piegherò *etc* [pjege'rɔ] *vb vedi* **piegare**.

pieghet'tare [pjeget'tare] *vt* to pleat.

pie'ghevole [pje'gevole] *ag* pliable, flexible; (*porta*) folding; (*fig*) yielding, docile.

Pie'monte *sm*: **il ~** Piedmont.

piemon'tese *ag, sm/f* Piedmontese.

pi'ena *sf vedi* **pieno**.

pie'nezza [pje'nettsa] *sf* fullness.

pi'eno, a *ag* full; (*muro, mattone*) solid ♦ *sm* (*colmo*) height, peak; (*carico*) full load ♦ *sf* (*di fiume*) flood, spate; (*gran folla*) crowd, throng; ~ **di** full of; **a ~e mani** abundantly; **a tempo ~** full-time; **a ~i voti** (*eleggere*) unanimously; **laurearsi a ~i voti** to graduate with full marks; **in ~ giorno** in broad daylight; **in ~ inverno** in the depths of winter; **in ~a notte** in the middle of the night; **in ~a stagione** at the height of the season; **in ~** (*completamente: sbagliare*) completely; (*colpire, centrare*) bang *o* right in the middle; **avere ~i poteri** to have full powers; **nel ~ possesso delle sue facoltà** in full possession of his faculties; **fare il ~ (di benzina)** to fill up (with petrol).

pie'none *sm*: **c'era il ~ al cinema/al teatro** the cinema/the theatre was packed.

pietà *sf* pity; (*REL*) piety; **senza ~** (*agire*) ruthlessly; (*persona*) pitiless, ruthless; **avere ~ di** (*compassione*) to pity, feel sorry for; (*misericordia*) to have pity *o* mercy on; **far ~** to arouse pity; (*peg*) to be terrible.

pie'tanza [pje'tantsa] *sf* dish, course.

pie'toso, a *ag* (*compassionevole*) pitying,

compassionate; (*che desta pietà*) pitiful.

pi'etra *sf* stone; **mettiamoci una ~ sopra** (*fig*) let bygones be bygones; ~ **preziosa** precious stone, gem; ~ **dello scandalo** (*fig*) cause of scandal.

pie'traia *sf* (*terreno*) stony ground.

pietrifi'care *vt* to petrify; (*fig*) to transfix, paralyze.

piet'rina *sf* (*per accendino*) flint.

pie'trisco, schi *sm* crushed stone, road metal.

pi'eve *sf* parish church.

'piffero *sm* (*MUS*) pipe.

pigi'ama [pi'dʒama] *sm* pyjamas *pl.*

'pigia 'pigia ['pidʒa'pidʒa] *sm* crowd, press.

pigi'are [pi'dʒare] *vt* to press.

pigia'trice [pidʒa'tritʃe] *sf* (*macchina*) wine press.

pigi'one [pi'dʒone] *sf* rent.

pigli'are [piʎ'ʎare] *vt* to take, grab; (*afferrare*) to catch.

'piglio ['piʎʎo] *sm* look, expression.

pig'mento *sm* pigment.

pig'meo, a *sm/f* pygmy.

'pigna ['piɲɲa] *sf* pine cone.

pignole'ria [piɲɲole'ria] *sf* fastidiousness, fussiness.

pi'gnolo, a [piɲ'ɲɔlo] *ag* pernickety.

pigno'rare [piɲɲo'rare] *vt* (*DIR*) to distrain.

pigo'lare *vi* to cheep, chirp.

pigo'lio *sm* cheeping, chirping.

pigra'mente *av* lazily.

pi'grizia [pi'grittsja] *sf* laziness.

'pigro, a *ag* lazy; (*fig: ottuso*) slow, dull.

PIL *sigla m vedi* **prodotto interno lordo**.

'pila *sf* (*catasta, di ponte*) pile; (*ELETTR*) battery; (*fam: torcia*) torch (*BRIT*), flashlight; **a ~, ~e** battery-operated.

pi'lastro *sm* pillar.

'pillola *sf* pill; **prendere la ~** (*contraccettivo*) to be on the pill; ~ **del giorno dopo** morning-after pill.

pi'lone *sm* (*di ponte*) pier; (*di linea elettrica*) pylon.

pi'lota, i, e *sm/f* pilot; (*AUT*) driver ♦ *ag inv* pilot *cpd*; ~ **automatico** automatic pilot.

pilo'taggio [pilo'taddʒo] *sm*: **cabina di ~** flight deck.

pilo'tare *vt* to pilot; to drive.

piluc'care *vt* to nibble at.

pi'mento *sm* pimento, allspice.

pim'pante *ag* lively, full of beans.

pinaco'teca, che *sf* art gallery.

pi'neta *sf* pinewood.

ping-'pong [pɪŋ'pɔŋ] *sm* table tennis.

'pingue *ag* fat, corpulent.

pingu'edine *sf* corpulence.

pingu'ino *sm* (*ZOOL*) penguin.

'pinna sf fin; (di pinguino, spatola di gomma) flipper.

pin'nacolo sm pinnacle.

'pino sm pine (tree).

pi'nolo sm pine kernel.

'pinta sf pint.

'pinza ['pintsa] sf pliers pl; (MED) forceps pl; (ZOOL) pincer.

pinzette [pin'tsette] sfpl tweezers.

'pio, a, 'pii, 'pie ag pious; (opere, istituzione) charitable, charity cpd.

piogge'rella [pjoddʒe'rɛlla] sf drizzle.

pi'oggia, ge ['pjɔddʒa] sf rain; (fig: di regali, fiori) shower; (di insulti) hail; **sotto la ~** in the rain; **~ acida** acid rain.

pi'olo sm peg; (di scala) rung.

piom'bare vi to fall heavily; (gettarsi con impeto): **~ su** to fall upon, assail ♦ vt (dente) to fill.

piomba'tura sf (di dente) filling.

piom'bino sm (sigillo) (lead) seal; (del filo a piombo) plummet; (PESCA) sinker.

pi'ombo sm (CHIM) lead; (sigillo) (lead) seal; (proiettile) (lead) shot; **a ~** (cadere) straight down; (muro etc) plumb; **andare con i piedi di ~** (fig) to tread carefully; **senza ~** (benzina) unleaded, lead-free; **anni di ~** (fig) era of terrorist outrages.

pioni'ere, a sm/f pioneer.

pi'oppo sm poplar.

pio'vano, a ag: **acqua ~a** rainwater.

pi'overe vb impers to rain ♦ vi (fig: scendere dall'alto) to rain down; (: affluire in gran numero): **~ in** to pour into; **non ci piove sopra** (fig) there's no doubt about it.

pioviggi'nare [pjoviddʒi'nare] vb impers to drizzle.

piovosità sf rainfall.

pio'voso, a ag rainy.

pi'ovra sf octopus.

pi'ovve etc vb vedi **piovere**.

'pipa sf pipe.

pipì sf (fam): **fare ~** to have a wee (wee).

pipis'trello sm (ZOOL) bat.

pi'ramide sf pyramid.

pi'ranha sm inv piranha.

pi'rata, i sm pirate; **~ della strada** hit-and-run driver.

Pire'nei smpl: **i ~** the Pyrenees.

pi'retro sm pyrethrum.

'pirico, a, ci, che ag: **polvere ~a** gunpowder.

pi'rite sf pyrite.

piro'etta sf pirouette.

pi'rofilo, a ag heat-resistant ♦ sf heat-resistant glass; (tegame) heat-resistant dish.

pi'roga, ghe sf dug-out canoe.

pi'romane sm/f arsonist.

pi'roscafo sm steamer, steamship.

'Pisa sf Pisa.

pi'sano, a ag Pisan.

pisci'are [piʃ'ʃare] vi (fam!) to piss (!), pee (!).

pi'scina [piʃ'ʃina] sf (swimming) pool.

pi'sello sm pea.

piso'lino sm nap; **fare un ~** to have a nap.

'pista sf (traccia) track, trail; (di stadio) track; (di pattinaggio) rink; (da sci) run; (AER) runway; (di circo) ring; **~ da ballo** dance floor; **~ ciclabile** cycle track; **~ di lancio** launch(ing) pad; **~ di rullaggio** (AER) taxiway; **~ di volo** (AER) runway.

pis'tacchio [pis'takkjo] sm pistachio (tree); pistachio (nut).

pis'tillo sm (BOT) pistil.

pis'tola sf pistol, gun; **~ a spruzzo** spray gun; **~ a tamburo** revolver.

pis'tone sm piston.

pi'tocco, chi sm skinflint, miser.

pi'tone sm python.

'pittima sf (fig) bore.

pit'tore, 'trice sm/f painter.

pitto'resco, a, schi, sche ag picturesque.

pit'torico, a, ci, che ag of painting, pictorial.

pit'tura sf painting; **~ fresca** wet paint.

pittu'rare vt to paint.

═══════════ PAROLA CHIAVE

più av **1** (in maggiore quantità) more; **~ del solito** more than usual; **in ~, di ~** more; **ne voglio di ~** I want some more; **ci sono 3 persone in** o **di ~** there are 3 more o extra people; **costa di ~** it's more expensive; **una volta di ~** once more; **~ o meno** more or less; **né ~ né meno** no more, no less; **per di ~** (inoltre) what's more, moreover; **è sempre ~ difficile** it is getting more and more difficult; **chi ~ chi meno hanno tutti contribuito** everybody made a contribution of some sort; **~ dormo e ~ dormirei** the more I sleep the more I want to sleep

2 (comparativo) more; (se monosillabo, spesso): **+ ...er**; **~ ... di/che** more ... than; **~ intelligente di lui** more intelligent than him; **~ furbo di te** smarter than you; **~ tardi di ...** later than ...; **lavoro ~ di te/di Paola** I work harder than you/than Paola; **è ~ fortunato che bravo** he is lucky rather than skilled; **~ di quanto pensassi** more than I thought; **~ che altro** mainly; **~ che mai** more than ever

3 (superlativo) most; (se monosillabico, spesso): **+ ...est**; **il ~ grande/intelligente**

the biggest/most intelligent; **è quello che compro ~ spesso** that's the one I buy most often; **al ~ presto** as soon as possible; **al ~ tardi** at the latest
4 (*negazione*): **non ... ~** no more, no longer; **non ho ~ soldi** I've got no more money, I don't have any more money; **non lavoro ~** I'm no longer working, I don't work any more; **non ce n'è ~** there isn't any left; **non c'è ~ nessuno** there's no one left; **non c'è ~ niente da fare** there's nothing more to be done; **a ~ non posso** (*gridare*) at the top of one's voice; (*correre*) as fast as one can
5 (*MAT*) plus; **4 ~ 5 fa 9** 4 plus 5 equals 9; **~ 5 gradi** 5 degrees above freezing, plus 5; **6 ~** (*a scuola*) just above a pass
♦ *prep* plus; **500.000 ~ le spese** 500,000 plus expenses; **siamo in quattro ~ il nonno** there are four of us, plus grandpa
♦ *ag inv* **1**: **~ ... (di)** more ... (than); **~ denaro/tempo** more money/time; **~ persone di quante ci aspettassimo** more people than we expected
2 (*numerosi, diversi*) several; **l'aspettai per ~ giorni** I waited for it for several days
♦ *sm* **1** (*la maggior parte*): **il ~ è fatto** most of it is done; **il ~ delle volte** more often than not, generally; **parlare del ~ e del meno** to talk about this and that
2 (*MAT*) plus (sign)
3: **i ~** the majority.

piuccheper'fetto [pjukkeper'fɛtto] *sm* (*LING*) pluperfect, past perfect.
pi'uma *sf* feather; **~e** *sfpl* down *sg*; (*piumaggio*) plumage *sg*, feathers.
piu'maggio [pju'maddʒo] *sm* plumage, feathers *pl*.
piu'mino *sm* (eider)down; (*per letto*) eiderdown; (: *tipo danese*) duvet, continental quilt; (*giacca*) quilted jacket (*with goose-feather padding*); (*per cipria*) powder puff; (*per spolverare*) feather duster.
piut'tosto *av* rather; **~ che** (*anziché*) rather than.
'piva *sf*: **con le ~e nel sacco** (*fig*) empty-handed.
pi'vello, a *sm/f* greenhorn.
'pizza ['pittsa] *sf* (*CUC*) pizza; (*CINE*) reel.
pizze'ria [pittse'ria] *sf* place where pizzas are made, sold or eaten.
pizzi'cagnolo, a [pittsi'kaɲɲolo] *sm/f* specialist grocer.
pizzi'care [pittsi'kare] *vt* (*stringere*) to nip, pinch; (*pungere*) to sting; to bite; (*MUS*) to

pluck ♦ *vi* (*prudere*) to itch, be itchy; (*cibo*) to be hot *o* spicy.
pizziche'ria [pittsike'ria] *sf* delicatessen (shop).
'pizzico, chi ['pittsiko] *sm* (*pizzicotto*) pinch, nip; (*piccola quantità*) pinch, dash; (*d'insetto*) sting; bite.
pizzi'cotto [pittsi'kɔtto] *sm* pinch, nip.
'pizzo ['pittso] *sm* (*merletto*) lace; (*barbetta*) goatee beard; (*tangente*) protection money.
pla'care *vt* to placate, soothe; **~rsi** *vr* to calm down.
'placca, che *sf* plate; (*con iscrizione*) plaque; (*anche*: **~ dentaria**) (dental) plaque.
plac'care *vt* to plate; **placcato in oro/ argento** gold-/silver-plated.
pla'centa [pla'tʃɛnta] *sf* placenta.
placidità [platʃidi'ta] *sf* calm, peacefulness.
'placido, a ['platʃido] *ag* placid, calm.
plafoni'era *sf* ceiling light.
plagi'are [pla'dʒare] *vt* (*copiare*) to plagiarize; (*DIR*: *influenzare*) to coerce.
'plagio ['pladʒo] *sm* plagiarism; (*DIR*) duress.
plaid [plɛd] *sm inv* (travelling) rug (*BRIT*), lap robe (*US*).
pla'nare *vi* (*AER*) to glide.
'plancia, ce ['plantʃa] *sf* (*NAUT*) bridge; (*AUT*: *cruscotto*) dashboard.
'plancton *sm inv* plankton.
plane'tario, a *ag* planetary ♦ *sm* (*locale*) planetarium.
planis'fero *sm* planisphere.
plan'tare *sm* arch support.
'plasma *sm* plasma.
plas'mare *vt* to mould (*BRIT*), mold (*US*), shape.
'plastico, a, ci, che *ag* plastic ♦ *sm* (*rappresentazione*) relief model; (*esplosivo*): **bomba al ~** plastic bomb ♦ *sf* (*arte*) plastic arts *pl*; (*MED*) plastic surgery; (*sostanza*) plastic; **in materiale ~** plastic.
plasti'lina ® *sf* plasticine ®.
'platano *sm* plane tree.
pla'tea *sf* (*TEAT*) stalls *pl* (*BRIT*), orchestra (*US*).
plate'ale *ag* (*gesto, atteggiamento*) theatrical.
plateal'mente *av* theatrically.
'platino *sm* platinum.
pla'tonico, a, ci, che *ag* platonic.
plau'dire *vi*: **~ a** to applaud.
plau'sibile *ag* plausible.
'plauso *sm* (*fig*) approval.
'playback ['plei bæk] *sm*: **cantare in ~** to

mime.

'**playboy** ['pleibɔi] sm inv playboy.

'**playmaker** ['pleimeikə*] sm/f inv (SPORT) playmaker.

'**play-off** ['pleiɔf] sm inv (SPORT) play-off.

ple'**baglia** [ple'baʎʎa] sf (peg) rabble, mob.

'**plebe** sf common people.

ple'**beo, a** ag plebeian; (volgare) coarse, common.

plebi'**scito** [plebiʃ'ʃito] sm plebiscite.

ple'**nario, a** ag plenary.

pleni'**lunio** sm full moon.

plenipotenzi'**ario, a** [plenipoten'tsjarjo] ag plenipotentiary.

'**plenum** sm inv plenum.

'**plettro** sm plectrum.

'**pleura** sf (ANAT) pleura.

pleu'**rite** sf pleurisy.

P.L.I. sigla m (= Partito Liberale Italiano) former political party.

'**plico, chi** sm (pacco) parcel; **in ~ a parte** (COMM) under separate cover.

plissé [pli'se] ag inv plissé cpd ♦ sm inv (anche: **tessuto ~**) plissé.

plisset'**tato, a** ag plissé cpd.

plo'**tone** sm (MIL) platoon; **~ d'esecuzione** firing squad.

'**plumbeo, a** ag leaden.

plu'**rale** ag, sm plural.

plura'**lismo** sm pluralism.

pluralità sf plurality; (maggioranza) majority.

plusva'**lenza** [pluzva'lɛntsa] sf capital gain.

plusva'**lore** sm (ECON) surplus.

plu'**tonio** sm plutonium.

pluvi'**ale** ag rain cpd.

pluvi'**ometro** sm rain gauge.

P.M. abbr (POL) = **Pubblico Ministero**; (= Polizia Militare) MP (= Military Police).

pm abbr = peso molecolare.

PN sigla = Pordenone.

pneu'**matico, a, ci, che** ag inflatable; (TECN) pneumatic ♦ sm (AUT) tyre (BRIT), tire (US).

PNL sigla m vedi prodotto nazionale lordo.

PO sigla = Prato.

Po sm: **il ~** the Po.

po' av, sm vedi poco.

P.O. abbr = posta ordinaria.

po'**chezza** [po'kettsa] sf insufficiency, shortage; (fig: meschinità) meanness, smallness.

======= PAROLA CHIAVE

'**poco, a, chi, che** ag (quantità) little, not much; (numero) few, not many; **~ pane/ denaro/spazio** little o not much bread/ money/space; **con ~a spesa** without

spending much; **a ~ prezzo** at a low price, cheap; **~ (tempo) fa** a short time ago; **~che persone/idee** few o not many people/ideas; **è un tipo di ~che parole** he's a man of few words

♦ av **1** (in piccola quantità) little, not much; (numero limitato) few, not many; **guadagna ~** he doesn't earn much, he earns little

2 (con ag, av) (a) little, not very; **è ~ più vecchia di lui** she's a little o slightly older than him; **è ~ socievole** he's not very sociable; **sta ~ bene** he isn't very well

3 (tempo): **~ dopo/prima** shortly afterwards/before; **il film dura ~** the film doesn't last very long; **ci vediamo molto ~** we don't see each other very often, we hardly ever see each other

4: **un po'** a little, a bit; **è un po' corto** it's a little o a bit short; **arriverà fra un po'** he'll arrive shortly o in a little while

5: **a dir ~** to say the least; **a ~ a ~** little by little; **per ~ non cadevo** I nearly fell; **è una cosa da ~** it's nothing, it's of no importance; **una persona da ~** a worthless person

♦ pron (a) little; **~chi, ~che** pron pl (persone) few (people); (cose) few; **ci vediamo tra ~** see you soon; **~chi lo sanno** not many people know it; **ci vuole tempo ed io ne ho ~** it takes time, and I haven't got much to spare

♦ sm **1** little; **vive del ~ che ha** he lives on the little he has

2: **un po'** a little; **un po' di zucchero** a little sugar; **un bel po' di denaro** quite a lot of money; **un po' per ciascuno** a bit each.

po'**dere** sm (AGR) farm.

pode'**roso, a** ag powerful.

podestà sm inv (nel fascismo) podestà, mayor.

'**podio** sm dais, platform; (MUS) podium.

po'**dismo** sm (SPORT: marcia) walking; (: corsa) running.

po'**dista, i, e** sm/f walker; runner.

po'**ema, i** sm poem.

poe'**sia** sf (arte) poetry; (componimento) poem.

po'**eta, 'essa** sm/f poet/poetess.

poe'**tare** vi to write poetry.

po'**etico, a, ci, che** ag poetic(al).

poggi'**are** [pod'dʒare] vt to lean, rest; (posare) to lay, place.

poggia'**testa** [poddʒa'tɛsta] sm inv (AUT) headrest.

'**poggio** ['pɔddʒo] sm hillock, knoll.

poggi'olo [pod'dʒɔlo] *sm* balcony.

'poi *av* then; (*alla fine*) finally, at last ♦ *sm*: **pensare al** ~ to think of the future; **e** ~ (*inoltre*) and besides; **questa** ~ (**è bella**) (*ironico*) that's a good one!; **d'ora in** ~ from now on; **da domani in** ~ from tomorrow onwards.

poi'ana *sf* buzzard.

poiché [poi'ke] *cong* since, as.

pois [pwa] *sm inv* spot, (polka) dot; **a** ~ spotted, polka-dot *cpd*.

'poker *sm* poker.

po'lacco, a, chi, che *ag* Polish ♦ *sm/f* Pole.

po'lare *ag* polar.

polariz'zare [polarid'dzare] *vt* (*anche fig*) to polarize.

'polca, che *sf* polka.

po'lemico, a, ci, che *ag* polemic(al), controversial ♦ *sf* controversy; **fare** ~**che** to be contentious.

polemiz'zare [polemid'dzare] *vi*: ~ (**su qc**) to argue (about sth).

po'lenta *sf* (*CUC*) sort of thick porridge made with maize flour.

polen'tone, a *sm/f* slowcoach (*BRIT*), slowpoke (*US*).

pole'sano, a *ag* of (*o* from) Polesine (*area between the Po and the Adige*).

POL'FER *abbr f* = Polizia Ferroviaria.

'poli... *prefisso* poly....

poliambula'torio *sm* (*MED*) health clinic.

poli'clinico, ci *sm* general hospital, polyclinic.

poli'edro *sm* polyhedron.

poli'estere *sm* polyester.

poliga'mia *sf* polygamy.

polig'lotta, i, e *ag, sm/f* polyglot.

po'ligono *sm* polygon; ~ **di tiro** rifle range.

Poli'nesia *sf*: **la** ~ Polynesia.

polinesi'ano, a *ag, sm/f* Polynesian.

'polio(mie'lite) *sf* polio(myelitis).

'polipo *sm* polyp.

polisti'rolo *sm* polystyrene.

poli'tecnico, ci *sm* postgraduate technical college.

po'litica, che *sf vedi* politico.

politi'cante *sm/f* (*peg*) petty politician.

politiciz'zare [politit∫id'dzare] *vt* to politicize.

po'litico, a, ci, che *ag* political ♦ *sm/f* politician ♦ *sf* politics *sg*; (*linea di condotta*) policy; **elezioni** ~**che** parliamentary (*BRIT*) *o* congressional (*US*) election(s); **uomo** ~ politician; **darsi alla** ~**a** to go into politics; **fare** ~**a** (*militante*) to be a political activist; (*come professione*) to be in politics; **la** ~**a del governo** the government's policies; ~**a aziendale** company policy; ~**a estera** foreign policy; ~**a dei prezzi** prices policy; ~**a dei redditi** incomes policy.

poliva'lente *ag* multi-purpose.

poli'zia [polit'tsia] *sf* police; ~ **giudiziaria** ≈ Criminal Investigation Department (CID) (*BRIT*), Federal Bureau of Investigation (FBI) (*US*); ~ **sanitaria/ tributaria** health/tax inspectorate; ~ **stradale** traffic police.

> *The function of the* **polizia di stato** *is to maintain public order, to uphold law and prevent and investigate crime. They are a civil body and employ both male and female officers who perform similar duties. They report to the Minister of the Interior through a national committee on public order and security.*

polizi'esco, a, schi, sche [polit'tsjesko] *ag* police *cpd*; (*film, romanzo*) detective *cpd*.

polizi'otto [polit'tsjɔtto] *sm* policeman; **cane** ~ police dog; **donna** ~ policewoman.

'polizza ['pɔlittsa] *sf* (*COMM*) bill; ~ **di assicurazione** insurance policy; ~ **di carico** bill of lading.

pol'laio *sm* henhouse.

pollai'olo, a *sm/f* poulterer (*BRIT*), poultryman.

pol'lame *sm* poultry.

pol'lastra *sf* pullet; (*fig: ragazza*) chick, wench.

pol'lastro *sm* (*ZOOL*) cockerel.

'pollice ['pɔllit∫e] *sm* thumb; (*unità di misura*) inch.

'polline *sm* pollen.

polli'vendolo, a *sm/f* poulterer (*BRIT*), poultryman.

'pollo *sm* chicken; **far ridere i** ~**i** (*situazione, persona*) to be utterly ridiculous.

polmo'nare *ag* lung *cpd*, pulmonary.

pol'mone *sm* lung.

polmo'nite *sf* pneumonia.

'polo *sm* (*GEO, FISICA*) pole; (*gioco*) polo ♦ *sf inv* (*maglia*) polo shirt; **il P**~ **sud/nord** the South/North Pole.

Po'lonia *sf*: **la** ~ Poland.

'polpa *sf* flesh, pulp; (*carne*) lean meat.

pol'paccio [pol'patt∫o] *sm* (*ANAT*) calf.

polpas'trello *sm* fingertip.

pol'petta *sf* (*CUC*) meatball.

polpet'tone *sm* (*CUC*) meatloaf.

'polpo *sm* octopus.

pol'poso, a *ag* fleshy.

pol'sino *sm* cuff.

'polso *sm* (*ANAT*) wrist; (*pulsazione*) pulse;

(*fig: forza*) drive, vigour (*BRIT*), vigor (*US*); **avere** ~ (*fig*) to be strong; **un uomo di** ~ a man of nerve.

pol'tiglia [pol'tiʎʎa] *sf* (*composto*) mash, mush; (*di fango e neve*) slush.

pol'trire *vi* to laze about.

pol'trona *sf* armchair; (*TEAT: posto*) seat in the front stalls (*BRIT*) *o* the orchestra (*US*).

poltron'cina [poltron'tʃina] *sf* (*TEAT*) seat in the back stalls (*BRIT*) *o* the orchestra (*US*).

pol'trone *ag* lazy, slothful.

'polvere *sf* dust; (*anche*: ~ **da sparo**) (gun)powder; (*sostanza ridotta minutissima*) powder, dust; **caffè in** ~ instant coffee; **latte in** ~ dried *o* powdered milk; **sapone in** ~ soap powder; ~ **di ferro** iron filings *pl*; ~ **d'oro** gold dust; ~ **pirica** *o* **da sparo** gunpowder.

polveri'era *sf* powder magazine.

polve'rina *sf* (*gen*, *MED*) powder; (*gergo*: *cocaina*) snow.

polveriz'zare [polverid'dzare] *vt* to pulverize; (*nebulizzare*) to atomize; (*fig*) to crush, pulverize; (: *record*) to smash.

polve'rone *sm* thick cloud of dust.

polve'roso, a *ag* dusty.

po'mata *sf* ointment, cream.

po'mello *sm* knob.

pomeridi'ano, a *ag* afternoon *cpd*; **nelle ore** ~**e** in the afternoon.

pome'riggio [pome'riddʒo] *sm* afternoon; **nel primo/tardo** ~ in the early/late afternoon.

'pomice ['pomitʃe] *sf* pumice.

pomici'are [pomi'tʃare] *vi* (*fam: sbaciucchiarsi*) to neck.

'pomo *sm* (*mela*) apple; (*ornamentale*) knob; (*di sella*) pommel; ~ **d'Adamo** (*ANAT*) Adam's apple.

pomo'doro *sm* tomato.

'pompa *sf* pump; (*sfarzo*) pomp (and ceremony); ~ **antincendio** fire hose; ~ **di benzina** petrol (*BRIT*) *o* gas (*US*) pump; (*distributore*) filling *o* gas (*US*) station; (**impresa di**) ~**e funebri** funeral parlour *sg* (*BRIT*), undertaker's *sg*, mortician's (*US*).

pom'pare *vt* to pump; (*trarre*) to pump out; (*gonfiare d'aria*) to pump up.

pompei'ano, a *ag* of (*o* from) Pompei.

pom'pelmo *sm* grapefruit.

pompi'ere *sm* fireman.

pom'pon [pom'pɔn] *sm inv* pompom, pompon.

pom'poso, a *ag* pompous.

ponde'rare *vt* to ponder over, consider carefully.

ponde'roso, a *ag* (*anche fig*) weighty.

po'nente *sm* west.

'pongo, 'poni *etc vb vedi* **porre**.

'ponte *sm* bridge; (*di nave*) deck; (: *anche*: ~ **di comando**) bridge; (*impalcatura*) scaffold; **vivere sotto i** ~**i** to be a tramp; **fare il** ~ (*fig*) to take the extra day off (*between 2 public holidays*); **governo** ~ interim government; ~ **aereo** airlift; ~ **di barche** (*MIL*) pontoon bridge; ~ **di coperta** (*NAUT*) upper deck; ~ **levatoio** drawbridge; ~ **radio** radio link; ~ **sospeso** suspension bridge.

pon'tefice [pon'tefitʃe] *sm* (*REL*) pontiff.

ponti'cello [ponti'tʃello] *sm* (*di occhiali, MUS*) bridge.

pontifi'care *vi* (*anche fig*) to pontificate.

pontifi'cato *sm* pontificate.

ponti'ficio, a, ci, cie [ponti'fitʃo] *ag* papal; **Stato P**~ Papal State.

pon'tile *sm* jetty.

'pony ['pɔni] *sm inv* pony.

pool [puːl] *sm inv* (*consorzio*) consortium; (*organismo internazionale*) pool; (*di esperti, ricercatori*) team; (*antimafia, antidroga*) working party.

pop [pɔp] *ag inv* pop *cpd*.

'popcorn ['pɔpkɔːn] *sm inv* popcorn.

'popeline ['pɔpelin] *sm* poplin.

popò *sm inv* (*sedere*) botty.

popo'lano, a *ag* popular, of the people ♦ *sm/f* man/woman of the people.

popo'lare *ag* popular; (*quartiere, clientela*) working-class; (*POL*) of P.P.I. ♦ *sm/f* (*POL*) member (*o* supporter) of P.P.I. ♦ *vt* (*rendere abitato*) to populate; ~**rsi** *vr* to fill with people, get crowded; **manifestazione** ~ mass demonstration; **repubblica** ~ people's republic.

popolarità *sf* popularity.

popolazi'one [popolat'tsjone] *sf* population.

'popolo *sm* people.

popo'loso, a *ag* densely populated.

po'pone *sm* melon.

'poppa *sf* (*di nave*) stern; (*mammella*) breast; **a** ~ aft, astern.

pop'pante *sm/f* unweaned infant; (*fig: inesperto*) whippersnapper.

pop'pare *vt* to suck.

pop'pata *sf* (*allattamento*) feed.

poppa'toio *sm* (feeding) bottle.

popu'lista, i, e *ag* populist.

por'caio *sm* (*anche fig*) pigsty.

por'cata *sf* (*libro, film etc*) load of rubbish; **fare una** ~ **a qn** to play a dirty trick on sb.

porcel'lana [portʃel'lana] *sf* porcelain,

china; (*oggetto*) piece of porcelain.

porcel'lino, a [portʃel'lino] *sm/f* piglet; ~
d'India guinea pig.

porche'ria [porke'ria] *sf* filth, muck; (*fig:
oscenità*) obscenity; (: *azione disonesta*)
dirty trick; (: *cosa mal fatta*) rubbish.

por'chetta [por'ketta] *sf* roast sucking pig.

por'cile [por'tʃile] *sm* pigsty.

por'cino, a [por'tʃino] *ag* of pigs, pork *cpd*
♦ *sm* (*fungo*) *type of edible mushroom.*

'porco, ci *sm* pig; (*carne*) pork.

porcos'pino *sm* porcupine.

'porfido *sm* porphyry.

'porgere ['pɔrdʒere] *vt* to hand, give;
(*tendere*) to hold out.

'porno *ag inv* porn, porno.

pornogra'fia *sf* pornography.

porno'grafico, a, ci, che *ag* pornographic.

'poro *sm* pore.

po'roso, a *ag* porous.

'porpora *sf* purple.

'porre *vt* (*mettere*) to put; (*collocare*) to
place; (*posare*) to lay (down), put (down);
(*fig: supporre*): **poniamo (il caso) che ...**
let's suppose that ...; **porsi** *vr* (*mettersi*):
porsi a sedere/in cammino to sit down/
set off; ~ **le basi di** (*fig*) to lay the
foundations of, establish; ~ **una
domanda a qn** to ask sb a question, put
a question to sb; ~ **la propria fiducia in
qn** to place one's trust in sb; ~ **fine** *o*
termine a qc to put an end *o* a stop to sth;
posto che ... supposing that ..., on the
assumption that ...; **porsi in salvo** to save
o.s.

'porro *sm* (*BOT*) leek; (*MED*) wart.

'porsi *etc vb vedi* **porgere.**

'porta *sf* door; (*SPORT*) goal; (*INFORM*) port;
~**e** *sfpl* (*di città*) gates; **mettere qn alla** ~ to
throw sb out; **sbattere** *o* **chiudere la** ~ **in
faccia a qn** (*anche fig*) to slam the door in
sb's face; **trovare tutte le** ~**e chiuse** (*fig*)
to find the way barred; **a** ~**e chiuse** (*DIR*)
in camera; **l'inverno è alle** ~**e** (*fig*) winter
is upon us; **vendita** ~ **a** ~ door-to-door
selling; ~ **di servizio** tradesmen's
entrance; ~ **di sicurezza** emergency exit;
~ **stagna** watertight door.

portaba'gagli [portaba'gaʎʎi] *sm inv*
(*facchino*) porter; (*AUT, FERR*) luggage
rack.

portabandi'era *sm inv* standard bearer.

porta'borse *sm inv* (*peg*) lackey.

portabot'tiglie [portabot'tiʎʎe] *sm inv*
bottle rack.

porta'cenere [porta'tʃenere] *sm inv* ashtray.

portachi'avi [porta'kjavi] *sm inv* keyring.

porta'cipria [porta'tʃiprja] *sm inv* powder

compact.

porta'erei *sf inv* (*nave*) aircraft carrier ♦ *sm
inv* (*aereo*) aircraft transporter.

portafi'nestra, *pl* **portefi'nestre** *sf*
French window.

porta'foglio [porta'fɔʎʎo] *sm* (*busta*) wallet;
(*cartella*) briefcase; (*POL, BORSA*)
portfolio; ~ **titoli** investment portfolio.

portagi'oie [porta'dʒɔje] *sm inv*,
portagioi'elli [portadʒo'jɛlli] *sm inv*
jewellery (*BRIT*) *o* jewelry (*US*) box.

por'tale *sm* portal.

porta'lettere *sm/f inv* postman/woman
(*BRIT*), mailman/woman (*US*).

porta'mento *sm* carriage, bearing.

portamo'nete *sm inv* purse.

por'tante *ag* (*muro etc*) supporting, load-
bearing.

portan'tina *sf* sedan chair; (*per ammalati*)
stretcher.

portaog'getti [portaod'dʒetti] *ag inv:* **vano**
~ (*in macchina*) glove compartment.

portaom'brelli *sm inv* umbrella stand.

porta'pacchi [porta'pakki] *sm inv* (*di moto,
bicicletta*) luggage rack.

por'tare *vt* (*sostenere, sorreggere: peso,
bambino, pacco*) to carry; (*indossare: abito,
occhiali*) to wear; (: *capelli lunghi*) to have;
(*avere: nome, titolo*) to have, bear; (*recare*):
~ **qc a qn** to take (*o* bring) sth to sb; (*fig:
sentimenti*) to bear; ~**rsi** *vr* (*recarsi*) to go;
~ **avanti** (*discorso, idea*) to pursue; ~ **via**
to take away; (*rubare*) to take; ~ **i bambini
a spasso** to take the children for a walk;
~ **fortuna** to bring good luck; ~ **qc alla
bocca** to lift *o* put sth to one's lips; **porta
bene i suoi anni** he's wearing well; **dove
porta questa strada?** where does this
road lead?, where does this road take
you?; **il documento porta la tua firma** the
document has *o* bears your signature;
non gli porto rancore I don't bear him a
grudge; **la polizia si è portata sul luogo
del disastro** the police went to the scene
of the disaster.

portarit'ratti *sm inv* photo(graph) frame.

portari'viste *sm inv* magazine rack.

portasa'pone *sm inv* soap dish.

portasiga'rette *sm inv* cigarette case.

portas'pilli *sm inv* pincushion.

por'tata *sf* (*vivanda*) course; (*AUT*) carrying
(*o* loading) capacity; (*di arma*) range;
(*volume d'acqua*) (rate of) flow; (*fig: limite*)
scope, capability; (: *importanza*) impact,
import; **alla** ~ **di tutti** (*conoscenza*) within
everybody's capabilities; (*prezzo*) within
everybody's means; **a/fuori** ~ **(di)**
within/out of reach (of); **a** ~ **di mano**

within (arm's) reach; **di grande** ~ of great importance.

por'tatile *ag* portable.

por'tato, a *ag* (*incline*): ~ **a** inclined *o* apt to.

porta'tore, 'trice *sm/f* (*anche COMM*) bearer; (*MED*) carrier; **pagabile al** ~ payable to the bearer; ~ **di handicap** disabled person.

portatovagli'olo [portatovaʎˈʎɔlo] *sm* napkin ring.

portau'ovo *sm inv* eggcup.

porta'voce [portaˈvotʃe] *sm/f inv* spokesman/woman.

por'tello *sm* (*di portone*) door; (*NAUT*) hatch.

portel'lone *sm* (*NAUT, AER*) hold door.

por'tento *sm* wonder, marvel.

porten'toso, a *ag* wonderful, marvellous (*BRIT*), marvelous (*US*).

porti'cato *sm* portico.

'portico, ci *sm* portico; (*riparo*) lean-to.

porti'era *sf* (*AUT*) door.

porti'ere *sm* (*portinaio*) concierge, caretaker; (*di hotel*) porter; (*nel calcio*) goalkeeper.

porti'naio, a *sm/f* concierge, caretaker.

portine'ria *sf* caretaker's lodge.

'porto, a *pp di* **porgere** ♦ *sm* (*NAUT*) harbour (*BRIT*), harbor (*US*), port; (*spesa di trasporto*) carriage ♦ *sm inv* port (wine); **andare** *o* **giungere in** ~ (*fig*) to come to a successful conclusion; **condurre qc in** ~ to bring sth to a successful conclusion; ~ **d'armi** gun licence (*BRIT*) *o* license (*US*); ~ **fluviale** river port; ~ **franco** free port; ~ **marittimo** seaport; ~ **militare** naval base; ~ **pagato** carriage paid, post free *o* paid; ~ **di scalo** port of call.

Porto'gallo *sm*: **il** ~ Portugal.

porto'ghese [portoˈgese] *ag, sm/f, sm* Portuguese *inv*.

por'tone *sm* main entrance, main door.

portori'cano, a *ag, sm/f* Puerto Rican.

Porto'rico *sf* Puerto Rico.

portu'ale *ag* harbour *cpd* (*BRIT*), harbor *cpd* (*US*), port *cpd* ♦ *sm* dock worker.

porzi'one [porˈtsjone] *sf* portion, share; (*di cibo*) portion, helping.

'posa *sf* (*FOT*) exposure; (*atteggiamento, di modello*) pose; (*riposo*): **lavorare senza** ~ to work without a break; **mettersi in** ~ to pose; **teatro di** ~ photographic studio.

posa'cenere [posaˈtʃenere] *sm inv* ashtray.

po'sare *vt* to put (down), lay (down) ♦ *vi* (*ponte, edificio, teoria*): ~ **su** to rest on; (*FOT, atteggiarsi*) to pose; ~**rsi** *vr* (*ape, aereo*) to land; (*uccello*) to alight;

(*sguardo*) to settle.

po'sata *sf* piece of cutlery; ~**e** *sfpl* cutlery *sg*.

posa'tezza [posaˈtettsa] *sf* (*di persona*) composure; (*di discorso*) balanced nature.

po'sato, a *ag* steady; (*discorso*) balanced.

pos'critto *sm* postscript.

'posi *etc vb vedi* **porre**.

positiva'mente *av* positively; (*rispondere*) in the affirmative, affirmatively.

posi'tivo, a *ag* positive.

posizi'one [poziˈtsjone] *sf* position; **farsi una** ~ to make one's way in the world; **prendere** ~ (*fig*) to take a stand; **luci di** ~ (*AUT*) sidelights.

posolo'gia, 'gie [pozoloˈdʒia] *sf* dosage, directions *pl* for use.

pos'porre *vt* to place after; (*differire*) to postpone, defer.

pos'posto, a *pp di* **posporre**.

posse'dere *vt* to own, possess; (*qualità, virtù*) to have, possess; (*conoscere a fondo*: *lingua etc*) to have a thorough knowledge of; (*sog: ira etc*) to possess.

possedi'mento *sm* possession.

pos'sente *ag* strong, powerful.

posses'sivo, a *ag* possessive.

pos'sesso *sm* possession; **essere in** ~ **di qc** to be in possession of sth; **prendere** ~ **di qc** to take possession of sth; **entrare in** ~ **dell'eredità** to come into one's inheritance.

posses'sore *sm* owner.

pos'sibile *ag* possible ♦ *sm*: **fare tutto il** ~ to do everything possible; **nei limiti del** ~ as far as possible; **al più tardi** ~ as late as possible; **vieni prima** ~ come as soon as possible.

possibi'lista, i, e *ag*: **essere** ~ to keep an open mind.

possibilità *sf inv* possibility ♦ *sfpl* (*mezzi*) means; **aver la** ~ **di fare** to be in a position to do; to have the opportunity to do; **nei limiti delle nostre** ~ in so far as we can.

possibil'mente *av* if possible.

possi'dente *sm/f* landowner.

possi'edo *etc vb vedi* **possedere**.

'posso *etc vb vedi* **potere**.

post... *prefisso* post....

'posta *sf* (*servizio*) post, postal service; (*corrispondenza*) post, mail; (*ufficio postale*) post office; (*nei giochi d'azzardo*) stake; (*CACCIA*) hide (*BRIT*), blind (*US*); ~**e** *sfpl* (*amministrazione*) post office; **fare la** ~ **a qn** (*fig*) to lie in wait for sb; **la** ~ **in gioco è troppo alta** (*fig*) there's too much at stake; **a bella** ~ (*apposta*) on purpose;

piccola ~ (*su giornale*) letters to the editor, letters page; ~ **aerea** airmail; ~ **elettronica** electronic mail; ~ **ordinaria** ≈ second-class mail; **P~e e Telecomunicazioni (PP.TT.)** *postal and telecommunications service;* **ministro delle P~e e Telecomunicazioni** Postmaster General.

posta'giro [posta'dʒiro] *sm* post office cheque (*BRIT*) *o* check (*US*), postal giro (*BRIT*).

pos'tale *ag* postal, post office *cpd* ♦ *sm* (*treno*) mail train; (*nave*) mail boat; (*furgone*) mail van; **timbro** ~ postmark.

postazi'one [postat'tsjone] *sf* (*MIL*) emplacement.

post'bellico, a, ci, che *ag* postwar.

postda'tare *vt* to postdate.

posteggi'are [posted'dʒare] *vt, vi* to park.

posteggia'tore, 'trice [postedʒa'tore] *smf* car-park attendant (*BRIT*), parking-lot attendant (*US*).

pos'teggio [pos'teddʒo] *sm* car park (*BRIT*), parking lot (*US*); (*di taxi*) rank (*BRIT*), stand (*US*).

postelegra'fonico, a, ci, che *ag* postal and telecommunications *cpd*.

'posteri *smpl* posterity *sg;* **i nostri** ~ our descendants.

posteri'ore *ag* (*dietro*) back; (*dopo*) later ♦ *sm* (*fam*: *sedere*) behind.

posteri'ori: a ~ *ag inv* after the event (*dopo sostantivo*) ♦ *av* looking back.

posterità *sf* posterity.

pos'ticcio, a, ci, ce [pos'tittʃo] *ag* false ♦ *sm* hairpiece.

postici'pare [postitʃi'pare] *vt* to defer, postpone.

pos'tilla *sf* marginal note.

pos'tino *sm* postman (*BRIT*), mailman (*US*).

'posto, a *pp di* **porre** ♦ *sm* (*sito, posizione*) place; (*impiego*) job; (*spazio libero*) room, space; (*di parcheggio*) space; (*sedile: al teatro, in treno etc*) seat; (*MIL*) post; **a** ~ (*in ordine*) in place, tidy; (*fig*) settled; (: *persona*) reliable; **mettere a** ~ (*riordinare*) to tidy (up), put in order; (*faccende: sistemare*) to straighten out; **prender** ~ to take a seat; **al** ~ **di** in place of; **sul** ~ on the spot; ~ **di blocco** roadblock; ~ **di lavoro** job; ~ **di polizia** police station; ~ **telefonico pubblico (P.T.P.)** public telephone; ~ **di villeggiatura** holiday (*BRIT*) *o* tourist spot; ~**i in piedi** (*TEAT, in autobus*) standing room.

postopera'torio, a *ag* (*MED*) postoperative.

pos'tribolo *sm* brothel.

post'scriptum *sm inv* postscript.

'postumo, a *ag* posthumous; (*tardivo*) belated; ~**i** *smpl* (*conseguenze*) after-effects, consequences.

po'tabile *ag* drinkable; **acqua** ~ drinking water.

po'tare *vt* to prune.

po'tassio *sm* potassium.

pota'tura *sf* pruning.

po'tente *ag* (*nazione*) strong, powerful; (*veleno, farmaco*) potent, strong.

poten'tino, a *ag* of (*o* from) Potenza.

Po'tenza [po'tɛntsa] *sf* Potenza.

po'tenza [po'tɛntsa] *sf* power; (*forza*) strength; **all'ennesima** ~ to the nth degree; **le Grandi P~e** the Great Powers; ~ **militare** military might *o* strength.

potenzi'ale [poten'tsjale] *ag, sm* potential.

potenzia'mento [potentsja'mento] *sm* development.

potenzi'are [poten'tsjare] *vt* to develop.

═══════════ *PAROLA CHIAVE*

po'tere *sm* power; **al** ~ (*partito etc*) in power; ~ **d'acquisto** purchasing power; ~ **esecutivo** executive power; ~ **giudiziario** legal power; ~ **legislativo** legislative power

♦ *vb aus* **1** (*essere in grado di*) can, be able to; **non ha potuto ripararlo** he wasn't able to repair it; **non è potuto venire** he couldn't *o* he wasn't able to come; **spiacente di non poter aiutare** sorry not to be able to help

2 (*avere il permesso*) can, may, be allowed to; **posso entrare?** can *o* may I come in?; **posso chiederti dove sei stato?** where, may I ask, have you been?

3 (*eventualità*) may, might, could; **potrebbe essere vero** it might *o* could be true; **può aver avuto un incidente** he may *o* might *o* could have had an accident; **può darsi** perhaps; **può darsi** *o* **può essere che non venga** he may *o* might not come

4 (*augurio*): **potessi almeno parlargli!** if only I could speak to him!

5 (*suggerimento*): **potresti almeno scusarti!** you could at least apologize!

♦ *vt* can, be able to; **può molto per noi** he can do a lot for us; **non ne posso più** (*per stanchezza*) I'm exhausted; (*per rabbia*) I can't take any more.

potestà *sf* (*potere*) power; (*DIR*) authority.

potrò *etc vb vedi* **potere**.

pove'raccio, a, ci, ce [pove'rattʃo] *smf* poor devil.

'**povero, a** *ag* poor; (*disadorno*) plain, bare ♦ *sm/f* poor man/woman; **i ~i** the poor; **~ di** lacking in, having little; **minerale ~ di ferro** ore with a low iron content; **paese ~ di risorse** country short of *o* lacking in resources.

povertà *sf* poverty.

pozi'one [pot'tsjone] *sf* potion.

'**pozza** ['pottsa] *sf* pool.

poz'zanghera [pot'tsangera] *sf* puddle.

'**pozzo** ['pottso] *sm* well; (*cava: di carbone*) pit; (*di miniera*) shaft; **~ nero** cesspit; **~ petrolifero** oil well.

pp. *abbr* (= *pagine*) pp.

p.p. *abbr* (= *per procura*) pp.

P.P.I. *sigla m* (*POL*) (= *Partito Popolare Italiano*) *party originating from D.C.*

PP.SS. *abbr* = **partecipazioni statali.**

PP.TT. *abbr* = **Poste e Telecomunicazioni;** *vedi* **posta.**

PR *sigla* = *Parma* ♦ *sigla m* (*POL*) = *Partito Radicale.*

P.R. *abbr* = **piano regolatore; procuratore della Repubblica.**

'**Praga** *sf* Prague.

prag'matico, a, ci, che *ag* pragmatic.

pram'matica *sf* custom; **essere di ~** to be customary.

pran'zare [pran'dzare] *vi* to dine, have dinner; to lunch, have lunch.

'**pranzo** ['prandzo] *sm* dinner; (*a mezzogiorno*) lunch.

'**prassi** *sf* usual procedure.

'**pratica, che** *sf* practice; (*esperienza*) experience; (*conoscenza*) knowledge, familiarity; (*tirocinio*) training, practice; (*AMM: affare*) matter, case; (: *incartamento*) file, dossier; **in ~** (*praticamente*) in practice; **mettere in ~** to put into practice; **fare le ~che per** (*AMM*) to do the paperwork for; **~ restrittiva** restrictive practice; **~che illecite** dishonest practices.

prati'cabile *ag* (*progetto*) practicable, feasible; (*luogo*) passable, practicable.

pratica'mente *av* (*in modo pratico*) in a practical way, practically; (*quasi*) practically, almost.

prati'cante *sm/f* apprentice, trainee; (*REL*) (regular) churchgoer.

prati'care *vt* to practise (*BRIT*), practice (*US*); (*SPORT: tennis etc*) to play; (: *nuoto, scherma etc*) to go in for; (*eseguire: apertura, buco*) to make; **~ uno sconto** to give a discount.

praticità [pratit∫i'ta] *sf* practicality, practicalness; **per ~** for practicality's sake.

'**pratico, a, ci, che** *ag* practical; **~ di** (*esperto*) experienced *o* skilled in; (*familiare*) familiar with; **all'atto ~** in practice; **è ~ del mestiere** he knows his trade; **mi è più ~ venire di pomeriggio** it's more convenient for me to come in the afternoon.

'**prato** *sm* meadow; (*di giardino*) lawn.

preal'larme *sm* warning (signal).

Pre'alpi *sfpl*: **le ~** (the) Pre-Alps.

preal'pino, a *ag* of the Pre-Alps.

pre'ambolo *sm* preamble; **senza tanti ~i** without beating about (*BRIT*) *o* around (*US*) the bush.

preannunci'are [preannun't∫are], **preannunzi'are** [preannun'tsjare] *vt* to give advance notice of.

preavvi'sare *vt* to give advance notice of.

preav'viso *sm* notice; **telefonata con ~** personal *o* person to person call.

pre'bellico, a, ci, che *ag* prewar *cpd.*

precari'ato *sm* temporary employment.

precarietà *sf* precariousness.

pre'cario, a *ag* precarious; (*INS*) temporary, without tenure.

precauzio'nale [prekauttsjo'nale] *ag* precautionary.

precauzi'one [prekaut'tsjone] *sf* caution, care; (*misura*) precaution; **prendere ~i** to take precautions.

prece'dente [pret∫e'dente] *ag* previous ♦ *sm* precedent; **il discorso/film ~** the previous *o* preceding speech/film; **senza ~i** unprecedented; **~i penali** (*DIR*) criminal record *sg.*

precedente'mente [pret∫edente'mente] *av* previously.

prece'denza [pret∫e'dentsa] *sf* priority, precedence; (*AUT*) right of way; **dare ~ assoluta a qc** to give sth top priority.

pre'cedere [pre't∫edere] *vt* to precede, go (*o come*) before.

precet'tare [pret∫et'tare] *vt* (*lavoratori*) to order back to work (*via an injunction*).

precettazi'one [pret∫ettat'tsjone] *sf* (*di lavoratori*) order to resume work.

pre'cetto [pre't∫etto] *sm* precept; (*MIL*) call-up notice.

precet'tore [pret∫et'tore] *sm* (private) tutor.

precipi'tare [pret∫ipi'tare] *vi* (*cadere*) to fall headlong; (*fig: situazione*) to get out of control ♦ *vt* (*gettare dall'alto in basso*) to hurl, fling; (*fig: affrettare*) to rush; **~rsi** *vr* (*gettarsi*) to hurl *o* fling o.s.; (*affrettarsi*) to rush.

precipi'tato, a [pret∫ipi'tato] *ag* hasty ♦ *sm* (*CHIM*) precipitate.

precipitazi'one [pretʃipitat'tsjone] _sf_ (_METEOR_) precipitation; (_fig_) haste.

precipi'toso, a [pretʃipi'toso] _ag_ (_caduta, fuga_) headlong; (_fig: avventato_) rash, reckless; (: _affrettato_) hasty, rushed.

preci'pizio [pretʃi'pittsjo] _sm_ precipice; **a ~** (_fig: correre_) headlong.

pre'cipuo, a [pre'tʃipuo] _ag_ principal, main.

precisa'mente [pretʃiza'mente] _av_ (_gen_) precisely; (_con esattezza_) exactly.

preci'sare [pretʃi'zare] _vt_ to state, specify; (_spiegare_) to explain (in detail); **vi preciseremo la data in seguito** we'll let you know the exact date later; **tengo a ~ che ...** I must point out that ....

precisazi'one [pretʃizat'tsjone] _sf_ clarification.

precisi'one [pretʃi'zjone] _sf_ precision; accuracy; **strumenti di ~** precision instruments.

pre'ciso, a [pre'tʃizo] _ag_ (_esatto_) precise; (_accurato_) accurate, precise; (_deciso: idea_) precise, definite; (_uguale_): **2 vestiti ~i 2** dresses exactly the same; **sono le 9 ~e** it's exactly 9 o'clock.

pre'cludere _vt_ to block, obstruct.

pre'cluso, a _pp di_ **precludere**.

pre'coce [pre'kɔtʃe] _ag_ early; (_bambino_) precocious; (_vecchiaia_) premature.

precocità [prekotʃi'ta] _sf_ (_di morte_) untimeliness; (_di bambino_) precociousness.

precon'cetto, a [prekon'tʃetto] _ag_ preconceived ♦ _sm_ preconceived idea, prejudice.

pre'correre _vt_ to anticipate; **~ i tempi** to be ahead of one's time.

precorri'tore, 'trice _sm/f_ precursor, forerunner.

pre'corso, a _pp di_ **precorrere**.

precur'sore _sm_ forerunner, precursor.

'preda _sf_ (_bottino_) booty; (_animale, fig_) prey; **essere ~ di** to fall prey to; **essere in ~ a** to be prey to.

pre'dare _vt_ to plunder.

preda'tore _sm_ predator.

predeces'sore, a [predetʃes'sore] _sm/f_ predecessor.

pre'della _sf_ platform, dais; altar-step.

predesti'nare _vt_ to predestine.

predestinazi'one [predestinat'tsjone] _sf_ predestination.

pre'detto, a _pp di_ **predire** ♦ _ag_ aforesaid, aforementioned.

'predica, che _sf_ sermon; (_fig_) lecture, talking-to.

predi'care _vt, vi_ to preach.

predica'tivo, a _ag_ predicative.

predi'cato _sm_ (_LING_) predicate.

predi'letto, a _pp di_ **prediligere** ♦ _ag, sm/f_ favourite (_BRIT_), favorite (_US_).

predilezi'one [predilet'tsjone] _sf_ fondness, partiality; **avere una ~ per qc/qn** to be partial to sth/fond of sb.

predi'ligere [predi'lidʒere] _vt_ to prefer, have a preference for.

pre'dire _vt_ to foretell, predict.

predis'porre _vt_ to get ready, prepare; **~ qn a qc** to predispose sb to sth.

predisposizi'one [predispozit'tsjone] _sf_ (_MED_) predisposition; (_attitudine_) bent, aptitude; **avere ~ alla musica** to have a bent for music.

predis'posto, a _pp di_ **predisporre**.

predizi'one [predit'tsjone] _sf_ prediction.

predomi'nante _ag_ predominant.

predomi'nare _vi_ (_prevalere_) to predominate; (_eccellere_) to excel.

predo'minio _sm_ predominance; supremacy.

preesis'tente _ag_ pre-existent.

pree'sistere _vi_ to pre-exist.

preesis'tito, a _pp di_ **preesistere**.

prefabbri'cato, a _ag_ (_EDIL_) prefabricated.

prefazi'one [prefat'tsjone] _sf_ preface, foreword.

prefe'renza [prefe'rɛntsa] _sf_ preference; **a ~ di** rather than; **di ~** preferably, by preference; **non ho ~e** I have no preferences either way, I don't mind.

preferenzi'ale [preferen'tsjale] _ag_ preferential; **corsia ~** (_AUT_) bus and taxi lane.

prefe'ribile _ag_: **~ (a)** preferable (to), better (than); **sarebbe ~ andarsene** it would be better to go.

preferibil'mente _av_ preferably.

prefe'rire _vt_ to prefer, like better; **~ il caffè al tè** to prefer coffee to tea, like coffee better than tea.

pre'fetto _sm_ prefect.

prefet'tura _sf_ prefecture.

pre'figgersi [pre'fiddʒersi] _vr_: **~rsi uno scopo** to set o.s. a goal.

prefigu'rare _vt_ (_simboleggiare_) to foreshadow; (_prevedere_) to foresee.

pre'fisso, a _pp di_ **prefiggersi** ♦ _sm_ (_LING_) prefix; (_TEL_) dialling (_BRIT_) o dial (_US_) code.

Preg. _abbr_ = **pregiatissimo**.

pre'gare _vi_ to pray ♦ _vt_ (_REL_) to pray to; (_implorare_) to beg; (_chiedere_): **~ qn di fare** to ask sb to do; **farsi ~** to need coaxing o persuading.

pre'gevole [pre'dʒevole] _ag_ valuable.

pregherò _etc_ [prege'rɔ] _vb vedi_ **pregare**.

preghi'era [pre'gjɛra] *sf* (REL) prayer; (*domanda*) request.

pregi'arsi [pre'dʒarsi] *vr*: **mi pregio di farle sapere che ...** I am pleased to inform you that ....

pregia'tissimo, a [predʒa'tissimo] *ag* (*in lettere*): **~ Signor G. Agnelli** G. Agnelli Esquire.

pregi'ato, a [pre'dʒato] *ag* (*opera*) valuable; (*tessuto*) fine; (*valuta*) strong; **vino ~** vintage wine.

'pregio ['predʒo] *sm* (*stima*) esteem, regard; (*qualità*) (good) quality, merit; (*valore*) value, worth; **il ~ di questo sistema è ...** the merit of this system is ...; **oggetto di ~** valuable object.

pregiudi'care [predʒudi'kare] *vt* to prejudice, harm, be detrimental to.

pregiudi'cato, a [predʒudi'kato] *sm/f* (DIR) previous offender.

pregiu'dizio [predʒu'dittsjo] *sm* (*idea errata*) prejudice; (*danno*) harm *no pl*.

preg'nante [preɲ'ɲante] *ag* (*fig*) pregnant, meaningful.

'pregno, a ['preɲɲo] *ag* (*saturo*): **~ di** full of, saturated with.

'prego *escl* (*a chi ringrazia*) don't mention it!; (*invitando qn ad accomodarsi*) please sit down!; (*invitando qn ad andare prima*) after you!

pregus'tare *vt* to look forward to.

preis'toria *sf* prehistory.

preis'torico, a, ci, che *ag* prehistoric.

pre'lato *sm* prelate.

prela'vaggio [prela'vaddʒo] *sm* pre-wash.

prelazi'one [prelat'tsjone] *sf* (DIR) pre-emption; **avere il diritto di ~ su qc** to have the first option on sth.

preleva'mento *sm* (BANCA) withdrawal; (*di merce*) picking up, collection.

prele'vare *vt* (*denaro*) to withdraw; (*campione*) to take; (*merce*) to pick up, collect; (*sog: polizia*) to take, capture.

preli'evo *sm* (BANCA) withdrawal; (MED): **fare un ~ (di)** to take a sample (of).

prelimi'nare *ag* preliminary; **~i** *smpl* preliminary talks; preliminaries.

pre'ludere *vi*: **~ a** (*preannunciare: crisi, guerra, temporale*) to herald, be a sign of; (*introdurre: dibattito etc*) to introduce, be a prelude to.

pre'ludio *sm* prelude.

pre'luso, a *pp di* **preludere**.

pre-ma'man [prema'mã] *sm inv* maternity dress.

prematrimoni'ale *ag* premarital.

prema'turo, a *ag* premature.

premedi'tare *vt* to premeditate, plan.

premeditazi'one [premeditat'tsjone] *sf* (DIR) premeditation; **con ~** *ag* premeditated ♦ *av* with intent.

'premere *vt* to press ♦ *vi*: **~ su** to press down on; (*fig*) to put pressure on; **~ a** (*fig: importare*) to matter to; **~ il grilletto** to pull the trigger.

pre'messo, a *pp di* **premettere** ♦ *sf* introductory statement, introduction; **mancano le ~e per una buona riuscita** we lack the basis for a successful outcome.

pre'mettere *vt* to put before; (*dire prima*) to start by saying, state first; **premetto che ...** I must say first of all that ...; **premesso che ...** given that ...; **ciò premesso ...** that having been said ....

premi'are *vt* to give a prize to; (*fig: merito, onestà*) to reward.

premiazi'one [premjat'tsjone] *sf* prize giving.

'premier ['prɛmjer] *sm inv* premier.

premi'nente *ag* pre-eminent.

'premio *sm* prize; (*ricompensa*) reward; (COMM) premium; (AMM: *indennità*) bonus; **in ~ per** as a prize (*o* reward) for; **~ d'ingaggio** (SPORT) signing-on fee; **~ di produzione** productivity bonus.

pre'misi *etc vb vedi* **premettere**.

premoni'tore, 'trice *ag* premonitory.

premonizi'one [premonit'tsjone] *sf* premonition.

premu'nirsi *vr*: **~ di** to provide o.s. with; **~ contro** to protect o.s. from, guard o.s. against.

pre'mura *sf* (*fretta*) haste, hurry; (*riguardo*) attention, care; **aver ~** to be in a hurry; **far ~ a qn** to hurry sb; **usare ogni ~ nei riguardi di qn, circondare qn di ~e** to be very attentive to sb.

premu'roso, a *ag* thoughtful, considerate.

prena'tale *ag* antenatal.

'prendere *vt* to take; (*andare a prendere*) to get, fetch; (*ottenere*) to get; (*guadagnare*) to get, earn; (*catturare: ladro, pesce*) to catch; (*collaboratore, dipendente*) to take on; (*passeggero*) to pick up; (*chiedere: somma, prezzo*) to charge, ask; (*trattare: persona*) to handle ♦ *vi* (*colla, cemento*) to set; (*pianta*) to take; (*fuoco: nel camino*) to catch; (*voltare*): **~ a destra** to turn (to the) right; **~rsi** *vr* (*azzuffarsi*): **~rsi a pugni** to come to blows; **prende qualcosa?** (*da bere, da mangiare*) would you like something to eat (*o* drink)?; **prendo un caffè** I'll have a coffee; **~ a fare qc** to start doing sth; **~ qn/qc per** (*scambiare*) to take sb/sth for; **~ l'abitudine di** to get into the habit of; **~ fuoco** to catch fire; **~ le generalità di qn**

to take down sb's particulars; ~ **nota di** to take note of; ~ **parte a** to take part in; ~**rsi cura di qn/qc** to look after sb/sth; ~**rsi un impegno** to take on a commitment; **prendersela** (*adirarsi*) to get annoyed; (*preoccuparsi*) to get upset, worry.

prendi'sole *sm inv* sundress.

preno'tare *vt* to book, reserve.

prenotazi'one [prenotat'tsjone] *sf* booking, reservation.

'prensile *ag* prehensile.

preoccu'pante *ag* worrying.

preoccu'pare *vt* to worry; ~**rsi** *vr*: ~**rsi di qn/qc** to worry about sb/sth; ~**rsi per qn** to be anxious for sb.

preoccupazi'one [preokkupat'tsjone] *sf* worry, anxiety.

preordi'nato, a *ag* preordained.

prepa'rare *vt* to prepare; (*esame, concorso*) to prepare for; ~**rsi** *vr* (*vestirsi*) to get ready; ~**rsi a qc/a fare** to get ready *o* prepare (o.s.) for sth/to do; ~ **da mangiare** to prepare a meal.

prepara'tivi *smpl* preparations.

prepa'rato, a *ag* (*gen*) prepared; (*pronto*) ready ♦ *sm* (*prodotto*) preparation.

prepara'torio, a *ag* preparatory.

preparazi'one [preparat'tsjone] *sf* preparation; **non ha la necessaria ~ per svolgere questo lavoro** he lacks the qualifications necessary for the job.

prepensiona'mento *sm* early retirement.

preponde'rante *ag* predominant.

pre'porre *vt* to place before; (*fig*) to prefer.

preposizi'one [prepozit'tsjone] *sf* (*LING*) preposition.

pre'posto, a *pp di* **preporre**.

prepo'tente *ag* (*persona*) domineering, arrogant; (*bisogno, desiderio*) overwhelming, pressing ♦ *sm/f* bully.

prepo'tenza [prepo'tɛntsa] *sf* arrogance; (*comportamento*) arrogant behaviour (*BRIT*) *o* behavior (*US*).

pre'puzio [pre'puttsjo] *sm* (*ANAT*) foreskin.

preroga'tiva *sf* prerogative.

'presa *sf* taking *no pl*; catching *no pl*; (*di città*) capture; (*indurimento: di cemento*) setting; (*appiglio, SPORT*) hold; (*di acqua, gas*) (supply) point; (*ELETTR*): ~ **(di corrente)** socket; (: *al muro*) point; (*piccola quantità: di sale etc*) pinch; (*CARTE*) trick; **far ~** (*colla*) to set; **ha fatto ~ sul pubblico** (*fig*) it caught the public's imagination; **a ~ rapida** (*cemento*) quick-setting; **di forte ~** (*fig*) with wide appeal; **essere alle ~e con qc** (*fig*) to be struggling with sth;

macchina da ~ (*CINE*) cine camera (*BRIT*), movie camera (*US*); ~ **d'aria** air inlet; ~ **diretta** (*AUT*) direct drive; ~ **in giro** leg-pull (*BRIT*), joke; ~ **di posizione** stand.

pre'sagio [pre'zadʒo] *sm* omen.

presa'gire [preza'dʒire] *vt* to foresee.

presa'lario *sm* (*INS*) grant.

'presbite *ag* long-sighted.

presbiteri'ano, a *ag, sm/f* Presbyterian.

presbi'terio *sm* presbytery.

pre'scindere [preʃ'ʃindere] *vi*: ~ **da** to leave out of consideration; **a ~ da** apart from.

pre'scisso, a [preʃ'ʃisso] *pp di* **prescindere**.

presco'lastico, a, ci, che *ag* pre-school *cpd*.

pres'critto, a *pp di* **prescrivere**.

pres'crivere *vt* to prescribe.

prescrizi'one [preskrit'tsjone] *sf* (*MED, DIR*) prescription; (*norma*) rule, regulation; **cadere in ~** (*DIR*) to become statute-barred.

'prese *etc vb vedi* **prendere**.

presen'tare *vt* to present; (*far conoscere*): ~ **qn (a)** to introduce sb (to); (*AMM: inoltrare*) to submit; ~**rsi** *vr* (*recarsi, farsi vedere*) to present o.s., appear; (*farsi conoscere*) to introduce o.s.; (*occasione*) to arise; ~ **qc in un'esposizione** to show *o* display sth at an exhibition; ~ **qn in società** to introduce sb into society; ~**rsi come candidato** (*POL*) to stand (*BRIT*) *o* run (*US*) as a candidate; ~**rsi bene/male** to have a good/poor appearance; **la situazione si presenta difficile** things aren't looking too good, things look a bit tricky.

presentazi'one [prezentat'tsjone] *sf* presentation; introduction.

pre'sente *ag* present; (*questo*) this ♦ *sm* present ♦ *sf* (*lettera*): **con la ~ vi comunico ...** this is to inform you that ... ♦ *sm/f* person present; **i ~i** those present; **aver ~ qc/qn** to remember sth/sb; **essere ~ a una riunione** to be present at *o* attend a meeting; **tener ~ qn/qc** to keep sb/sth in mind; **esclusi i ~i** present company excepted.

presenti'mento *sm* premonition.

pre'senza [pre'zɛntsa] *sf* presence; (*aspetto esteriore*) appearance; **in ~ di** in (the) presence of; **di bella ~** of good appearance; ~ **di spirito** presence of mind.

presenzi'are [prezen'tsjare] *vi*: ~ **a** to be present at, attend.

pre'sepio, pre'sepe *sm* crib.

preser'vare *vt* to protect.

preserva'tivo *sm* sheath, condom.

'**presi** *etc vb vedi* **prendere.**

'**preside** *smf* (*INS*) head (teacher) (*BRIT*), principal (*US*); (*di facoltà universitaria*) dean.

presi'dente *sm* (*POL*) president; (*di assemblea*, *COMM*) chairman; **il P~ della Camera** (*POL*) ≈ the Speaker; **P~ del Consiglio (dei Ministri)** ≈ Prime Minister; **P~ della Repubblica** President of the Republic.

The **Presidente del Consiglio**, *the Italian prime minister, is the head of the government. He/She submits nominations for ministerial posts to the Presidente della Repubblica and is responsible for those ministers appointed. He/She is nominated by the Presidente della Repubblica, in consultation with the leaders of the parliamentary parties, former heads of state, the* **Presidente della Camera** *and the Presidente del Senato. See also* **Parlamento** *and* **Consiglio dei Ministri***. The* **Presidente della Repubblica** *is the head of state. He/She must be an Italian citizen of at least 50 years of age and is elected by Parliament and by 3 delegates from each region. He/She remains in office for 7 years. He/She has the power to call an election, dissolve one or both chambers of Parliament or call a referendum. He/She nominates the* **Presidente del Consiglio** *and in consultation with the latter appoints government Ministers. He/She also presides over the* **Consiglio Superiore della Magistratura***.*

presiden'tessa *sf* president; (*moglie*) president's wife; (*di assemblea*, *COMM*) chairwoman.

presi'denza [presi'dɛntsa] *sf* presidency; office of president; chairmanship; **assumere la ~** to become president; to take the chair; **essere alla ~** to be president (*o* chairman); **candidato alla ~** presidential candidate; candidate for the chairmanship.

presidenzi'ale [presidɛn'tsjale] *ag* presidential.

presidi'are *vt* to garrison.

pre'sidio *sm* garrison.

presi'edere *vt* to preside over ♦ *vi*: **~ a** to direct, be in charge of.

'**preso, a** *pp di* **prendere.**

'**pressa** *sf* (*TECN*) press.

pres'sante *ag* (*bisogno*, *richiesta*) urgent, pressing.

pressap'poco *av* about, roughly, approximately.

pres'sare *vt* (*anche fig*) to press; **~ qn con richieste** to pursue sb with demands.

pressi'one *sf* pressure; **far ~ su qn** to put pressure on sb; **subire forti ~i** to be under strong pressure; **~ sanguigna** blood pressure.

'**presso** *av* (*vicino*) nearby, close at hand ♦ *prep* (*vicino a*) near; (*accanto a*) beside, next to; (*in casa di*): **~ qn** at sb's home; (*nelle lettere*) care of (*abbr* c/o); (*alle dipendenze di*): **lavora ~ di noi** he works for *o* with us ♦ *smpl*: **nei ~i di** near, in the vicinity of; **ha avuto grande successo ~ i giovani** it has been a hit with young people.

pressoché [presso'ke] *av* nearly, almost.

pressuriz'zare [pressurid'dzare] *vt* to pressurize.

prestabi'lire *vt* to arrange beforehand, arrange in advance.

presta'nome *smf inv* (*peg*) figurehead.

pres'tante *ag* good-looking.

pres'tanza [pres'tantsa] *sf* (*robust*) good looks *pl*.

pres'tare *vt*: **~ (qc a qn)** to lend (sb sth *o* sth to sb); **~rsi** *vr* (*offrirsi*): **~rsi a fare** to offer to do; (*essere adatto*): **~rsi a** to lend itself to, be suitable for; **~ aiuto** to lend a hand; **~ ascolto** *o* **orecchio** to listen; **~ attenzione** to pay attention; **~ fede a qc/ qn** to give credence to sth/sb; **~ giuramento** to take an oath; **la frase si presta a molteplici interpretazioni** the phrase lends itself to numerous interpretations.

prestazi'one [prestat'tsjone] *sf* (*TECN*, *SPORT*) performance, **~i** *sfpl* (*di persona*: *servizi*) services.

prestigia'tore, 'trice [prestidʒa'tore] *smf* conjurer.

pres'tigio [pres'tidʒo] *sm* (*potere*) prestige; (*illusione*): **gioco di ~** conjuring trick.

prestigi'oso, a [presti'dʒoso] *ag* prestigious.

'**prestito** *sm* lending *no pl*; loan; **dar in ~** to lend; **prendere in ~** to borrow; **~ bancario** bank loan; **~ pubblico** public borrowing.

'**presto** *av* (*tra poco*) soon; (*in fretta*) quickly; (*di buon'ora*) early; **a ~** see you soon; **~ o tardi** sooner or later; **fare ~ a fare qc** to hurry up and do sth; (*non costare fatica*) to have no trouble doing sth; **si fa ~ a criticare** it's easy to criticize; **è ancora ~ per decidere** it's still too early *o* too soon to decide.

pre'sumere *vt* to presume, assume.

presu'mibile *ag* (*dati*, *risultati*) likely.

pre'sunsi *etc vb vedi* **presumere.**

pre'sunto, a *pp di* **presumere ♦** *ag*: **il ~ colpevole** the alleged culprit.

presuntu'oso, a *ag* presumptuous.

presunzi'one [prezun'tsjone] *sf* presumption.

presup'porre *vt* to suppose; to presuppose.

presup'posto, a *pp di* **presupporre ♦** *sm* (*premessa*) supposition, premise; **partendo dal ~ che** ... assuming that ...; **mancano i ~i necessari** the necessary conditions are lacking.

'prete *sm* priest.

preten'dente *sm/f* pretender **♦** *sm* (*corteggiatore*) suitor.

pre'tendere *vt* (*esigere*) to demand, require; (*sostenere*): **~ che** to claim that; **pretende di aver sempre ragione** he thinks he's always right.

pretenzi'oso, a [preten'tsjoso] *ag* pretentious.

preterintenzio'nale [preterintentsjo'nale] *ag* (*DIR*): **omicidio ~** manslaughter.

pre'teso, a *pp di* **pretendere ♦** *sf* (*esigenza*) claim, demand; (*presunzione, sfarzo*) pretentiousness; **avanzare una ~a** to put forward a claim *o* demand; **senza ~e** *ag* unpretentious **♦** *av* unpretentiously.

pre'testo *sm* pretext, excuse; **con il ~ di** on the pretext of.

pretestu'oso, a *ag* (*data, motivo*) used as an excuse.

pre'tore *sm* magistrate.

pre'tura *sf* (*DIR: sede*) magistrate's court (*BRIT*), circuit *o* superior court (*US*); (: *magistratura*) magistracy.

preva'lente *ag* prevailing.

prevalente'mente *av* mainly, for the most part.

preva'lenza [preva'lɛntsa] *sf* predominance.

preva'lere *vi* to prevail.

pre'valso, a *pp di* **prevalere.**

prevari'care *vi* (*abusare del potere*) to abuse one's power.

prevaricazi'one [prevarikat'tsjone] *sf* (*abuso di potere*) abuse of power.

preve'dere *vt* (*indovinare*) to foresee; (*presagire*) to foretell; (*considerare*) to make provision for; **nulla lasciava ~ che** ... there was nothing to suggest *o* to make one think that ...; **come previsto** as expected; **spese previste** anticipated expenditure; **previsto per martedì** scheduled for Tuesday.

prev'edibile *ag* predictable; **non era assolutamente ~ che** ... no one could have foreseen that ....

prevedibil'mente *av* as one would expect.

preve'nire *vt* (*anticipare: obiezione*) to forestall; (: *domanda*) to anticipate; (*evitare*) to avoid, prevent; (*avvertire*): **~ qn (di)** to warn sb (of); to inform sb (of).

preventi'vare *vt* (*COMM*) to estimate.

preven'tivo, a *ag* preventive **♦** *sm* (*COMM*) estimate; **fare un ~** to give an estimate; **bilancio ~** budget; **carcere ~** custody (*pending trial*).

preve'nuto, a *ag* (*mal disposto*): **~ (contro qc/qn)** prejudiced (against sth/sb).

prevenzi'one [preven'tsjone] *sf* prevention; (*preconcetto*) prejudice.

previ'dente *ag* showing foresight; prudent.

previ'denza [previ'dɛntsa] *sf* foresight; **istituto di ~** provident institution; **~ sociale** social security (*BRIT*), welfare (*US*).

pre'vidi *etc vb vedi* **prevedere.**

'previo, a *ag* (*COMM*): **~ avviso** upon notice; **~ pagamento** upon payment.

previsi'one *sf* forecast, prediction; **~i meteorologiche** *o* **del tempo** weather forecast *sg*.

pre'visto, a *pp di* **prevedere ♦** *sm*: **più/meno del ~** more/less than expected; **prima del ~** earlier than expected.

prezi'oso, a [pret'tsjoso] *ag* precious; (*aiuto, consiglio*) invaluable **♦** *sm* jewel; valuable.

prez'zemolo [pret'tsemolo] *sm* parsley.

'prezzo ['prɛttso] *sm* price; **a ~ di costo** at cost, at cost price (*BRIT*); **tirare sul ~** to bargain, haggle; **il ~ pattuito è 1.000.000 di lire** the agreed price is 1,000,000 lire; **~ d'acquisto/di vendita** buying/selling price; **~ di fabbrica** factory price; **~ di mercato** market price; **~ scontato** reduced price; **~ unitario** unit price.

P.R.I. *sigla m* (= *Partito Repubblicano Italiano*) *former political party.*

prigi'one [pri'dʒone] *sf* prison.

prigio'nia [pridʒo'nia] *sf* imprisonment.

prigioni'ero, a [pridʒo'njɛro] *ag* captive **♦** *sm/f* prisoner.

'prima *sf vedi* **primo ♦** *av* before; (*in anticipo*) in advance, beforehand; (*per l'addietro*) at one time, formerly; (*più presto*) sooner, earlier; (*in primo luogo*) first **♦** *cong*: **~ di fare/che parta** before doing/he leaves; **~ di** *prep* before; **~ o poi** sooner or later; **due giorni ~** two days before *o* earlier; **~ d'ora** before now.

pri'mario, a *ag* primary; (*principale*) chief, leading, primary **♦** *sm/f* (*medico*) head physician, chief physician.

pri'mate *sm* (*REL, ZOOL*) primate.
prima'tista, i, e *sm/f* (*SPORT*) record holder.
pri'mato *sm* supremacy; (*SPORT*) record.
prima'vera *sf* spring.
primave'rile *ag* spring *cpd.*
primeggi'are [primed'dʒare] *vi* to excel, be one of the best.
primi'tivo, a *ag* (*gen*) primitive; (*significato*) original.
pri'mizie [pri'mittsje] *sfpl* early produce *sg.*
'primo, a *ag* first; (*fig*) initial; basic; prime ♦ *sm/f* first (one) ♦ *sm* (*CUC*) first course; (*in date*): **il ~ luglio** the first of July ♦ *sf* (*TEAT*) first night; (*CINE*) première; (*AUT*) first (gear); **le ~e ore del mattino** the early hours of the morning; **di ~a mattina** early in the morning; **in ~a pagina** (*STAMPA*) on the front page; **ai ~i freddi** at the first sign of cold weather; **ai ~i di maggio** at the beginning of May; **i ~i del Novecento** the early twentieth century; **viaggiare in ~a** to travel first-class; **per ~a cosa** firstly; **in ~ luogo** first of all, in the first place; **di prim'ordine** *o* **~a qualità** first-class, first-rate; **in un ~ tempo** *o* **momento** at first; **~a donna** leading lady; (*di opera lirica*) prima donna.
primo'genito, a [primo'dʒɛnito] *ag, sm/f* firstborn.
pri'mordi *smpl* beginnings.
primordi'ale *ag* primordial.
'primula *sf* primrose.
princi'pale [printʃi'pale] *ag* main, principal ♦ *sm* manager, boss; **sede ~** head office.
principal'mente [printʃipal'mente] *av* mainly, principally.
princi'pato [printʃi'pato] *sm* principality.
'principe ['printʃipe] *sm* prince; **~ ereditario** crown prince.
princi'pesco, a, schi, sche [printʃi'pesko] *ag* (*anche fig*) princely.
princi'pessa [printʃi'pessa] *sf* princess.
principi'ante [printʃi'pjante] *sm/f* beginner.
principi'are [printʃi'pjare] *vt, vi* to start, begin.
prin'cipio [prin'tʃipjo] *sm* (*inizio*) beginning, start; (*origine*) origin, cause; (*concetto, norma*) principle; **al** *o* **in ~** at first; **fin dal ~** right from the start; **per ~** on principle; **una questione di ~** a matter of principle; **una persona di sani ~i morali** a person of sound moral principles; **~ attivo** active ingredient.
pri'ore *sm* (*REL*) prior.
pri'ori: a ~ *ag inv* prior; **a priori** ♦ *av* at first glance; initially; a priori.
priorità *sf* priority; **avere la ~ (su)** to have

priority (over).
priori'tario, a *ag* having priority, of utmost importance.
'prisma, i *sm* prism.
pri'vare *vt*: **~ qn di** to deprive sb of; **~rsi** *vr*: **~rsi di** to go *o* do without.
priva'tiva *sf* (*ECON*) monopoly.
privatiz'zare [privatid'dzare] *vt* to privatize.
privatizzazi'one [privatiddzat'tsjone] *sf* privatization.
pri'vato, a *ag* private ♦ *sm/f* (*anche*: **~ cittadino**) private citizen; **in ~** in private; **diritto ~** (*DIR*) civil law; **ritirarsi a vita ~a** to withdraw from public life; **"non vendiamo a ~i"** "wholesale only".
privazi'one [privat'tsjone] *sf* privation, hardship.
privilegi'are [privile'dʒare] *vt* to favour (*BRIT*), favor (*US*).
privilegi'ato, a [privile'dʒato] *ag* (*individuo, classe*) privileged; (*trattamento, COMM*: *credito*) preferential; **azioni ~e** preference shares (*BRIT*), preferred stock (*US*).
privi'legio [privi'lɛdʒo] *sm* privilege; **avere il ~ di fare** to have the privilege of doing, be privileged to do.
'privo, a *ag*: **~ di** without, lacking.
pro *prep* for, on behalf of ♦ *sm inv* (*utilità*) advantage, benefit; **a che ~?** what's the use?; **il ~ e il contro** the pros and cons.
pro'babile *ag* probable, likely.
probabilità *sf inv* probability; **con molta ~** very probably, in all probability.
probabil'mente *av* probably.
pro'bante *ag* convincing.
pro'blema, i *sm* problem.
proble'matico, a, ci, che *ag* problematic; (*incerto*) doubtful ♦ *sf* problems *pl.*
pro'boscide [pro'bɔʃʃide] *sf* (*di elefante*) trunk.
procacci'are [prokat'tʃare] *vt* to get, obtain.
procaccia'tore [prokattʃa'tore] *sm*: **~ d'affari** sales executive.
pro'cace [pro'katʃe] *ag* (*donna, aspetto*) provocative.
pro'cedere [pro'tʃɛdere] *vi* to proceed; (*comportarsi*) to behave; (*iniziare*): **~ a** to start; **~ contro** (*DIR*) to start legal proceedings against; **~ oltre** to go on ahead; **prima di ~ oltre** before going any further; **gli affari procedono bene** business is going well; **bisogna ~ con cautela** we have to proceed cautiously; **non luogo a ~** (*DIR*) nonsuit.
procedi'mento [protʃedi'mento] *sm* (*modo di condurre*) procedure; (*di avvenimenti*) course; (*TECN*) process; **~ penale** (*DIR*)

criminal proceedings *pl.*

proce'dura [protʃe'dura] *sf* (*DIR*) procedure.

proces'sare [protʃes'sare] *vt* (*DIR*) to try.

processi'one [protʃes'sjone] *sf* procession.

pro'cesso [pro'tʃɛsso] *sm* (*DIR*) trial; proceedings *pl*; (*metodo*) process; **essere sotto ~** to be on trial; **mettere sotto ~** (*anche fig*) to put on trial; **~ di fabbricazione** manufacturing process; **~ di pace** peace process.

processu'ale [protʃessu'ale] *ag* (*DIR*): **atti ~i** records of a trial; **spese ~i** legal costs.

Proc. Gen. *abbr* = **procuratore generale**.

pro'cinto [pro'tʃinto] *sm*: **in ~ di fare** about to do, on the point of doing.

pro'clama, i *sm* proclamation.

procla'mare *vt* to proclaim.

proclamazi'one [proklamat'tsjone] *sf* proclamation, declaration.

procrasti'nare *vt* (*data*) to postpone; (*pagamento*) to defer.

procre'are *vt* to procreate.

pro'cura *sf* (*DIR*) proxy, power of attorney; (*ufficio*) attorney's office; **per ~** by proxy; **la P~ della Repubblica** the Public Prosecutor's Office.

procu'rare *vt*: **~ qc a qn** (*fornire*) to get *o* obtain sth for sb; (*causare: noie etc*) to bring *o* give sb sth.

procura'tore, 'trice *smlf* (*DIR*) ≈ solicitor; (*: chi ha la procura*) holder of power of attorney; **~ generale** (*in corte d'appello*) public prosecutor; (*in corte di cassazione*) Attorney General; **~ legale** ≈ solicitor (*BRIT*), lawyer; **~ della Repubblica** (*in corte d'assise, tribunale*) public prosecutor.

prodi'gare *vt* to be lavish with; **~rsi** *vr*: **~rsi per qn** to do all one can for sb.

pro'digio [pro'didʒo] *sm* marvel, wonder; (*persona*) prodigy.

prodigi'oso, a [prodi'dʒoso] *ag* prodigious; phenomenal.

'prodigo, a, ghi, ghe *ag* lavish, extravagant.

pro'dotto, a *pp di* **produrre** ♦ *sm* product; **~ di base** primary product; **~ finale** end product; **~ interno lordo (PIL)** gross domestic product (GDP); **~ nazionale lordo (PNL)** gross national product (GNP); **~i agricoli** farm produce *sg*; **~i di bellezza** cosmetics; **~i chimici** chemicals.

pro'duco *etc vb vedi* **produrre**.

pro'durre *vt* to produce.

pro'dussi *etc vb vedi* **produrre**.

produttività *sf* productivity.

produt'tivo, a *ag* productive.

produt'tore, 'trice *ag* producing *cpd* ♦ *smlf* producer; **paese ~ di petrolio** oil-

producing country.

produzi'one [produt'tsjone] *sf* production; (*rendimento*) output; **~ in serie** mass production.

pro'emio *sm* introduction, preface.

Prof. *abbr* (= *professore*) Prof.

profa'nare *vt* to desecrate.

pro'fano, a *ag* (*mondano*) secular, profane; (*sacrilego*) profane.

profe'rire *vt* to utter.

profes'sare *vt* to profess; (*medicina etc*) to practise (*BRIT*), practice (*US*).

professio'nale *ag* professional; **scuola ~** training college.

professi'one *sf* profession; **di ~** professional, by profession; **libera ~** profession.

professio'nista, i, e *smlf* professional.

profes'sore, 'essa *smlf* (*INS*) teacher; (*: di università*) lecturer; (*: titolare di cattedra*) professor; **~ d'orchestra** member of an orchestra.

pro'feta, i *sm* prophet.

pro'fetico, a, ci, che *ag* prophetic.

profetiz'zare [profetid'dzare] *vt* to prophesy.

profe'zia [profet'tsia] *sf* prophecy.

pro'ficuo, a *ag* useful, profitable.

profi'lare *vt* to outline; (*ornare: vestito*) to edge; **~rsi** *vr* to stand out, be silhouetted; to loom up.

profi'lassi *sf* (*MED*) preventive treatment, prophylaxis.

profi'lattico, a, ci, che *ag* prophylactic ♦ *sm* (*anticoncezionale*) sheath, condom.

pro'filo *sm* profile; (*breve descrizione*) sketch, outline; **di ~** in profile.

profit'tare *vi*: **~ di** (*trarre profitto*) to profit by; (*approfittare*) to take advantage of.

pro'fitto *sm* advantage, profit, benefit; (*fig: progresso*) progress; (*COMM*) profit; **ricavare un ~ da** to make a profit from *o* out of; **vendere con ~** to sell at a profit; **conto ~i e perdite** profit and loss account.

pro'fondere *vt* (*lodi*) to lavish; (*denaro*) to squander; **~rsi** *vr*: **~rsi in** to be profuse in.

profondità *sf inv* depth.

pro'fondo, a *ag* deep; (*rancore, meditazione*) profound ♦ *sm* depth(s *pl*), bottom; **~ 8 metri** 8 metres deep.

pro'forma *ag* routine *cpd* ♦ *sm inv* formality ♦ *av*: **fare qc ~** to do sth as a formality.

'profugo, a, ghi, ghe *smlf* refugee.

profu'mare *vt* to perfume ♦ *vi* to be fragrant; **~rsi** *vr* to put on perfume *o* scent.

profumata'mente *av*: **pagare qc ~** to pay

through the nose for sth.

profu'mato, a *ag* (*fiore, aria*) fragrant; (*fazzoletto, saponetta*) scented; (*pelle*) sweet-smelling; (*persona*) with perfume on.

profume'ria *sf* perfumery; (*negozio*) perfume shop.

pro'fumo *sm* (*prodotto*) perfume, scent; (*fragranza*) fragrance.

profusi'one *sf* profusion; **a ~** in plenty.

pro'fuso, a *pp di* **profondere**.

progeni'tore, 'trice [prodʒeni'tore] *smf* ancestor.

proget'tare [prodʒet'tare] *vt* to plan; (*TECN*: *edificio*) to plan, design; **~ di fare qc** to plan to do sth.

progettazi'one [prodʒettat'tsjone] *sf* planning; **in corso di ~** at the planning stage.

proget'tista, i, e [prodʒet'tista] *smf* designer.

pro'getto [pro'dʒɛtto] *sm* plan; (*idea*) plan, project; **avere in ~ di fare qc** to be planning to do sth; **~ di legge** (*POL*) bill.

'prognosi ['proɲɲozi] *sf* (*MED*) prognosis; **essere in ~ riservata** to be on the danger list.

pro'gramma, i *sm* programme (*BRIT*), program (*US*); (*TV, RADIO*) program(me)s *pl*; (*INS*) syllabus, curriculum; (*INFORM*) program; **avere in ~ di fare qc** to be planning to do sth; **~ applicativo** (*INFORM*) application program.

program'mare *vt* (*TV, RADIO*) to put on; (*INFORM*) to program; (*ECON*) to plan.

programma'tore, 'trice *smf* (*INFORM*) computer programmer (*BRIT*) *o* programer (*US*).

programmazi'one [programmat'tsjone] *sf* programming (*BRIT*), programing (*US*); planning.

progre'dire *vi* to progress, make progress.

progressi'one *sf* progression.

progres'sista, i, e *ag, smf* progressive.

progressiva'mente *av* progressively.

progres'sivo, a *ag* progressive.

pro'gresso *sm* progress *no pl*; **fare ~i** to make progress.

proi'bire *vt* to forbid, prohibit; **~ a qn di fare qc** (*vietare*) to forbid sb to do sth; (*impedire*) to prevent sb from doing sth.

proibi'tivo, a *ag* prohibitive.

proi'bito, a *ag* forbidden; **"è ~ l'accesso"** "no admittance"; **"è ~ fumare"** "no smoking".

proibizi'one [proibit'tsjone] *sf* prohibition.

proibizio'nismo [proibittsjo'nizmo] *sm* prohibition.

proiet'tare *vt* (*gen, GEOM, CINE*) to project; (: *presentare*) to show, screen; (*luce, ombra*) to throw, cast, project.

proi'ettile *sm* projectile, bullet (*o shell etc*).

proiet'tore *sm* (*CINE*) projector; (*AUT*) headlamp; (*MIL*) searchlight.

proiezi'one [projet'tsjone] *sf* (*CINE*) projection; showing.

'prole *sf* children *pl*, offspring.

proletari'ato *sm* proletariat.

prole'tario, a *ag, smf* proletarian.

prolife'rare *vi* (*fig*) to proliferate.

pro'lifico, a, ci, che *ag* prolific.

pro'lisso, a *ag* verbose.

'prologo, ghi *sm* prologue.

pro'lunga, ghe *sf* (*di cavo elettrico etc*) extension.

prolunga'mento *sm* (*gen*) extension; (*di strada*) continuation.

prolun'gare *vt* (*discorso, attesa*) to prolong; (*linea, termine*) to extend.

prome'moria *sm inv* memorandum.

pro'messa *sf* promise; **fare/mantenere una ~** to make/keep a promise.

pro'messo, a *pp di* **promettere**.

promet'tente *ag* promising.

pro'mettere *vt* to promise ♦ *vi* to be *o* look promising; **~ a qn di fare** to promise sb that one will do.

promi'nente *ag* prominent.

promi'nenza [promi'nɛntsa] *sf* prominence.

promiscuità *sf* promiscuousness.

pro'miscuo, a *ag*: **matrimonio ~** mixed marriage; **nome ~** (*LING*) common-gender noun.

pro'misi *etc vb vedi* **promettere**.

promon'torio *sm* promontory, headland.

pro'mosso, a *pp di* **promuovere**.

promo'tore, 'trice *smf* promoter, organizer.

promozio'nale [promottsjo'nale] *ag* promotional; **"vendita ~"** "special offer".

promozi'one [promot'tsjone] *sf* promotion; **~ delle vendite** sales promotion.

promul'gare *vt* to promulgate.

promulgazi'one [promulgat'tsjone] *sf* promulgation.

promu'overe *vt* to promote.

proni'pote *smf* (*di nonni*) great-grandchild, great-grandson/granddaughter; (*di zii*) great-nephew/niece; **~i** *smpl* (*discendenti*) descendants.

pro'nome *sm* (*LING*) pronoun.

pronomi'nale *ag* pronominal.

pronosti'care *vt* to foretell, predict.

pro'nostico, ci *sm* forecast.

pron'tezza [pron'tettsa] *sf* readiness; quickness, promptness; ~ **di riflessi** quick reflexes; ~ **di spirito/mente** readiness of wit/mind.

'pronto, a *ag* ready; (*rapido*) fast, quick, prompt; ~! (*TEL*) hello!; **essere ~ a fare qc** to be ready to do sth; ~ **all'ira** quick-tempered; **a ~a cassa** (*COMM*) cash (*BRIT*) *o* collect (*US*) on delivery; ~**a consegna** (*COMM*) prompt delivery; ~ **soccorso** first aid.

prontu'ario *sm* manual, handbook.

pro'nuncia [pro'nuntʃa] *sf* pronunciation.

pronunci'are [pronun'tʃare] *vt* (*parola, sentenza*) to pronounce; (*dire*) to utter; (*discorso*) to deliver; ~**rsi** *vr* to declare one's opinion; ~**rsi a favore di/contro** to pronounce o.s. in favour of/against; **non mi pronuncio** I'm not prepared to comment.

pronunci'ato, a [pronun'tʃato] *ag* (*spiccato*) pronounced, marked; (*sporgente*) prominent.

pro'nunzia *etc* [pro'nuntsja] = **pronuncia** *etc*.

propa'ganda *sf* propaganda.

propagan'dare *vt* (*idea*) to propagandize; (*prodotto, invenzione*) to push, plug (*fam*).

propa'gare *vt* (*FISICA, BIOL*) to propagate; (*notizia, idea, malattia*) to spread; ~**rsi** *vr* to propagate; to spread.

propagaz'ione [propagat'tsjone] *sf* (*vedi vb*) propagation; spreading.

prope'deutico, a, ci, che *ag* (*corso, trattato*) introductory.

pro'pendere *vi*: ~ **per** to favour (*BRIT*), favor (*US*), lean towards.

propensi'one *sf* inclination, propensity; **avere ~ a credere che** ... to be inclined to think that ....

pro'penso, a *pp di* **propendere ♦** *ag*: **essere ~ a qc** to be in favour (*BRIT*) *o* favor (*US*) of sth; **essere ~ a fare qc** to be inclined to do sth.

propi'nare *vt* to administer.

pro'pizio, a [pro'pittsjo] *ag* favourable (*BRIT*), favorable (*US*).

pro'porre *vt* (*suggerire*): ~ **qc (a qn)** to suggest sth (to sb); (*candidato*) to put forward; (*legge, brindisi*) to propose; ~ **di fare** to suggest *o* propose doing; **proporsi di fare** to propose *o* intend to do; **proporsi una meta** to set o.s. a goal.

proporzio'nale [proportsjo'nale] *ag* proportional; (**sistema**) ~ (*POL*) proportional representation system.

proporzio'nato, a [proportsjo'nato] *ag*: ~ **a** proportionate to, proportional to; **ben ~** well-proportioned.

proporzi'one [propor'tsjone] *sf* proportion; **in ~ a** in proportion to.

pro'posito *sm* (*intenzione*) intention, aim; (*argomento*) subject, matter; **a ~ di** regarding, with regard to; **a questo ~** on this subject; **di ~** (*apposta*) deliberately, on purpose; **a ~** by the way; **capitare a ~** (*cosa, persona*) to turn up at the right time.

proposizi'one [propozit'tsjone] *sf* (*LING*) clause; (: *periodo*) sentence.

pro'posto, a *pp di* **proporre ♦** *sf* proposal; (*suggerimento*) suggestion; **fare una ~a** to put forward a proposal; to make a suggestion; ~**a di legge** (*POL*) bill.

propria'mente *av* (*correttamente*) properly, correctly; (*in modo specifico*) specifically; ~ **detto** in the strict sense of the word.

proprietà *sf inv* (*ciò che si possiede*) property *gen no pl*, estate; (*caratteristica*) property; (*correttezza*) correctness; **essere di ~ di qn** to belong to sb; ~ **edilizia** (developed) property; ~ **privata** private property.

proprie'tario, a *sm/f* owner; (*di albergo etc*) proprietor, owner; (*per l'inquilino*) landlord/lady; ~ **terriero** landowner.

'proprio, a *ag* (*possessivo*) own; (: *impersonale*) one's; (*esatto*) exact, correct, proper; (*senso, significato*) literal; (*LING: nome*) proper; (*particolare*): ~ **di** characteristic of, peculiar to **♦** *av* (*precisamente*) just, exactly; (*davvero*) really; (*affatto*): **non** ... ~ **not** ... at all **♦** *sm* (*COMM*): **mettersi in ~** to set up on one's own; **l'ha visto con i (suoi) ~i occhi** he saw it with his own eyes.

propu'gnare [propuɲ'ɲare] *vt* to support.

propulsi'one *sf* propulsion; **a ~ atomica** atomic-powered.

propul'sore *sm* (*TECN*) propeller.

'prora *sf* (*NAUT*) bow(s *pl*), prow.

'proroga, ghe *sf* extension; postponement.

proro'gare *vt* to extend; (*differire*) to postpone, defer.

pro'rompere *vi* to burst out.

pro'rotto, a *pp di* **prorompere**.

pro'ruppi *etc vb vedi* **prorompere**.

'prosa *sf* prose; (*TEAT*): **la stagione della ~** the theatre season; **attore di ~** theatre actor; **compagnia di ~** theatrical company.

pro'saico, a, ci, che *ag* (*fig*) prosaic, mundane.

pro'sciogliere [proʃ'ʃɔʎʎere] *vt* to release; (*DIR*) to acquit.

prosciogli'mento [proʃʃoʎʎi'mento] *sm*

acquittal.
prosci'olto, a [proʃ'ʃɔlto] *pp di*
prosciogliere.
prosciu'gare [proʃʃu'gare] *vt (terreni)* to
drain, reclaim; **~rsi** *vr* to dry up.
prosci'utto [proʃ'ʃutto] *sm* ham.
pros'critto, a *pp di* **proscrivere** ♦ *sm/f* exile;
outlaw.
pros'crivere *vt* to exile, banish.
proscrizi'one [proskrit'tsjone] *sf (esilio)*
banishment, exile.
prosecuzi'one [prosekut'tsjone] *sf*
continuation.
prosegui'mento *sm* continuation; **buon ~!**
all the best!; *(a chi viaggia)* enjoy the rest
of your journey!
prosegu'ire *vt* to carry on with, continue
♦ *vi* to carry on, go on.
pro'selito *sm (REL, POL)* convert.
prospe'rare *vi* to thrive.
prosperità *sf* prosperity.
'prospero, a *ag (fiorente)* flourishing,
thriving, prosperous.
prospe'roso, a *ag (robusto)* hale and
hearty; (: *ragazza*) buxom.
prospet'tare *vt (esporre)* to point out,
show; *(ipotesi)* to advance; *(affare)* to
outline; **~rsi** *vr* to look, appear.
prospet'tiva *sf (ARTE)* perspective;
(veduta) view; *(fig: previsione, possibilità)*
prospect.
pros'petto *sm (DISEGNO)* elevation;
(veduta) view, prospect; *(facciata)* façade,
front; *(tabella)* table; *(sommario)*
summary.
prospici'ente [prospi'tʃɛnte] *ag:* **~ qc**
facing *o* overlooking sth.
prossima'mente *av* soon.
prossimità *sf* nearness, proximity; **in ~ di**
near (to), close to; **in ~ delle feste
natalizie** as Christmas approaches.
'prossimo, a *ag (vicino):* **~ a** near (to),
close to; *(che viene subito dopo)* next;
(parente) close ♦ *sm* neighbour *(BRIT)*,
neighbor *(US)*, fellow man; **nei ~i giorni**
in the next few days; **in un ~ futuro** in
the near future; **~ venturo (pv)** *(AMM):*
venerdì ~ venturo next Friday.
'prostata *sf* prostate (gland).
prostitu'irsi *vr* to prostitute o.s.
prosti'tuta *sf* prostitute.
prostituzi'one [prostitut'tsjone] *sf*
prostitution.
pros'trare *vt (fig)* to exhaust, wear out;
~rsi *vr (fig)* to humble o.s.; **prostrato dal
dolore** overcome *o* prostrate with grief.
prostrazi'one [prostrat'tsjone] *sf*
prostration.

protago'nista, i, e *sm/f* protagonist.
pro'teggere [pro'tɛddʒere] *vt* to protect.
pro'teico, a, ci, che *ag* protein *cpd;*
altamente ~ high in protein.
prote'ina *sf* protein.
pro'tendere *vt* to stretch out.
'protesi *sf inv (MED)* prosthesis.
pro'teso, a *pp di* **protendere**.
pro'testa *sf* protest.
protes'tante *ag*, *sm/f* Protestant.
protes'tare *vt, vi* to protest; **~rsi** *vr:* **~rsi
innocente** *etc* to protest one's innocence
o that one is innocent *etc*.
pro'testo *sm (DIR)* protest; **mandare una
cambiale in ~** to dishonour *(BRIT) o*
dishonor *(US)* a bill.
protet'tivo, a *ag* protective.
pro'tetto, a *pp di* **proteggere**.
protet'torato *sm* protectorate.
protet'tore, 'trice *sm/f* protector;
(sostenitore) patron ♦ *ag (REL):* **santo ~**
patron saint; **società ~trice dei
consumatori** consumer protection
society.
protezi'one [protet'tsjone] *sf* protection;
(patrocinio) patronage; **misure di ~**
protective measures; **~ civile** civil
defence *(BRIT) o* defense *(US)*.
protezio'nismo [protettsjo'nizmo] *sm*
protectionism.
protocol'lare *vt* to register ♦ *ag* formal; of
protocol.
proto'collo *sm* protocol; *(registro)* register
of documents ♦ *ag inv:* **foglio ~** foolscap;
numero di ~ reference number.
pro'tone *sm* proton.
pro'totipo *sm* prototype.
pro'trarre *vt (prolungare)* to prolong;
protrarsi *vr* to go on, continue.
pro'tratto, a *pp di* **protrarre**.
protube'ranza [protube'rantsa] *sf*
protuberance, bulge.
Prov. *abbr (= provincia)* Prov.
'prova *sf (esperimento, cimento)* test,
trial; *(tentativo)* attempt, try; *(MAT,
testimonianza etc)* proof *no pl;* *(DIR)*
evidence *no pl,* proof *no pl;* *(INS)* exam,
test; *(TEAT)* rehearsal; *(di abito)* fitting; **a
~ di** *(in testimonianza di)* as proof of; **a ~
di fuoco** fireproof; **assumere in ~** *(per
lavoro)* to employ on a trial basis; **essere
in ~** *(persona: per lavoro)* to be on trial;
mettere alla ~ to put to the test; **giro di ~**
test *o* trial run; **fino a ~ contraria** until
(it's) proved otherwise; **~ a carico/a
discarico** *(DIR)* evidence for the
prosecution/for the defence; **~
documentale** *(DIR)* documentary

evidence; ~ **generale** (*TEAT*) dress rehearsal; ~ **testimoniale** (*DIR*) testimonial evidence.

pro'vare *vt* (*sperimentare*) to test; (*tentare*) to try, attempt; (*assaggiare*) to try, taste; (*sperimentare in sé*) to experience; (*sentire*) to feel; (*cimentare*) to put to the test; (*dimostrare*) to prove; (*abito*) to try on; ~**rsi** *vr*: ~**rsi (a fare)** to try *o* attempt (to do); ~ **a fare** to try *o* attempt to do.

proveni'enza [prove'njɛntsa] *sf* origin, source.

prove'nire *vi*: ~ **da** to come from.

pro'venti *smpl* revenue *sg*.

prove'nuto, a *pp di* **provenire**.

Pro'venza [pro'ventsa] *sf*: **la** ~ Provence.

proven'zale [proven'tsale] *ag* Provençal.

pro'verbio *sm* proverb.

pro'vetta *sf* test tube; **bambino in** ~ test-tube baby.

pro'vetto, a *ag* skilled, experienced.

pro'vincia, ce *o* **cie** [pro'vintʃa] *sf* province.

> The **Provincia** is the autonomous political and administrative unit intermediate between the *Comune* and the *Regione*. A **Provincia** includes several **Comuni**. It has responsiblity for public sanitation and health, maintenance of major roads and public buildings, such as schools, and for agriculture and fisheries. Each **Provincia** has a *capoluogo*, its chief town, and is run by a *Giunta Provinciale* which is elected by the *Consiglio Provinciale*. Each of these two bodies is presided over by a *Presidente*. There are 103 *province* in Italy. See also **Comune** and **Regione**.

provinci'ale [provin'tʃale] *ag* provincial; (**strada**) ~ main road (*BRIT*), highway (*US*).

pro'vino *sm* (*CINE*) screen test; (*campione*) specimen.

provo'cante *ag* (*attraente*) provocative.

provo'care *vt* (*causare*) to cause, bring about; (*eccitare: riso, pietà*) to arouse; (*irritare, sfidare*) to provoke.

provoca'tore, 'trice *smf* agitator ♦ *ag*: **agente** ~ agent provocateur.

provoca'torio, a *ag* provocative.

provocazi'one [provokat'tsjone] *sf* provocation.

provve'dere *vi* (*disporre*): ~ **(a)** to provide (for); (*prendere un provvedimento*) to take steps, act ♦ *vt*: ~ **qc a qn** to supply sth to sb; ~**rsi** *vr*: ~**rsi di** to provide o.s. with.

provvedi'mento *sm* measure; (*di*

previdenza) precaution; ~ **disciplinare** disciplinary measure.

provvedito'rato *sm* (*AMM*): ~ **agli studi** divisional education offices *pl*.

provvedi'tore *sm* (*AMM*): ~ **agli studi** divisional director of education.

provvi'denza [provvi'dɛntsa] *sf*: **la** ~ providence.

provvidenzi'ale [provviden'tsjale] *ag* providential.

provvigi'one [provvi'dʒone] *sf* (*COMM*) commission; **lavoro/stipendio a** ~ job/salary on a commission basis.

provvi'sorio, a *ag* temporary; (*governo*) temporary, provisional.

prov'vista *sf* (*riserva*) supply, stock; **fare** ~ **di** to stock up with.

prov'visto, a *pp di* **provvedere** ♦ *sf* provision, supply.

pro'zia [prot'tsia] *sf* great-aunt.

pro'zio, zii [prot'tsio] *sm* great-uncle.

'prua *sf* (*NAUT*) = **prora**.

pru'dente *ag* cautious, prudent; (*assennato*) sensible, wise.

pru'denza [pru'dɛntsa] *sf* prudence, caution; wisdom; **per** ~ as a precaution, to be on the safe side.

'prudere *vi* to itch, be itchy.

'prugna ['pruɲɲa] *sf* plum; ~ **secca** prune.

prurigi'noso, a [pruridʒi'noso] *ag* itchy.

pru'rito *sm* itchiness *no pl*; itch.

PS *sigla* = **Pesaro**.

P.S. *abbr* (= *postscriptum*) P.S.; (*COMM*) = **partita semplice** ♦ *sigla f vedi* **Pubblica Sicurezza**.

P.S.D.I. *sigla m* (= *Partito Socialista Democratico Italiano*) former political party.

pseu'donimo *sm* pseudonym.

PSI *sigla m* (*POL*) = *Partito Socialista Italiano*.

psica'nalisi *sf* psychoanalysis.

psicana'lista, i, e *smf* psychoanalyst.

psicanaliz'zare [psikanalid'dzare] *vt* to psychoanalyse.

'psiche ['psike] *sf* psyche.

psiche'delico, a, ci, che [psike'dɛliko] *ag* psychedelic.

psichi'atra, i, e [psi'kjatra] *smf* psychiatrist.

psichia'tria [psikja'tria] *sf* psychiatry.

psichi'atrico, a, ci, che [psi'kjatriko] *ag* (*caso*) psychiatric; (*reparto, ospedale*) psychiatric, mental.

'psichico, a, ci, che ['psikiko] *ag* psychological.

psico'farmaco, ci *sm* (*MED*) drug used in treatment of mental conditions.

psicolo'gia [psikolo'dʒia] *sf* psychology.

psico'logico, a, ci, che [psiko'lɔdʒiko] *ag* psychological.

psi'cologo, a, gi, ghe *sm/f* psychologist.

psico'patico, a, ci, che *ag* psychopathic ♦ *sm/f* psychopath.

psi'cosi *sf inv* (MED) psychosis; (*fig*) obsessive fear.

psicoso'matico, a, ci, che *ag* psychosomatic.

PT *sigla* = Pistoia.

Pt. *abbr* (GEO: = punta) Pt.

P.T. *abbr* (= Posta e Telegrafi) ≈ PO (= Post Office); (FISCO) = **polizia tributaria.**

P.ta *abbr* = **porta.**

P.T.P. *abbr vedi* **posto telefonico pubblico.**

pubbli'care *vt* to publish.

pubblicazi'one [pubblikat'tsjone] *sf* publication; ~ **periodica** periodical; ~**i** (**matrimoniali**) *sfpl* (marriage) banns.

pubbli'cista, i, e [pubbli'tʃista] *sm/f* (STAMPA) freelance journalist.

pubblicità [pubblitʃi'ta] *sf* (*diffusione*) publicity; (*attività*) advertising; (*annunci nei giornali*) advertisements *pl*; **fare** ~ **a qc** to advertise sth.

pubblici'tario, a [pubblitʃi'tarjo] *ag* advertising *cpd*; (*trovata, film*) publicity *cpd* ♦ *sm* advertising agent; **annuncio** *o* **avviso** ~ advertisement.

'pubblico, a, ci, che *ag* public; (*statale*: *scuola etc*) state *cpd* ♦ *sm* public; (*spettatori*) audience; **in** ~ in public; **la** ~**a amministrazione** public administration; **un** ~ **esercizio** a catering (*o* hotel *o* entertainment) business; ~ **funzionario** civil servant; **Ministero della P~a Istruzione** ≈ Department of Education and Science (BRIT), ≈ Department of Health, Education and Welfare (US); **P~ Ministero** Public Prosecutor's Office; **la P~a Sicurezza (P.S.)** the police.

'pube *sm* (ANAT) pubis.

pubertà *sf* puberty.

'pudico, a, ci, che *ag* modest.

pu'dore *sm* modesty.

puericul'tura *sf* infant care.

pue'rile *ag* childish.

pu'erpera *sf* woman who has just given birth.

pugi'lato [pudʒi'lato] *sm* boxing.

'pugile ['pudʒile] *sm* boxer.

pugli'ese [puʎ'ʎese] *ag* of (*o* from) Puglia.

pugna'lare [puɲɲa'lare] *vt* to stab.

pu'gnale [puɲ'ɲale] *sm* dagger.

'pugno ['puɲɲo] *sm* fist; (*colpo*) punch; (*quantità*) fistful; **avere qn in** ~ to have sb in the palm of one's hand; **tenere la situazione in** ~ to have control of the

situation; **scrivere qc di proprio** ~ to write sth in one's own hand.

'pulce ['pultʃe] *sf* flea.

pul'cino [pul'tʃino] *sm* chick.

pu'ledro, a *sm/f* colt/filly.

pu'leggia, ge [pu'leddʒa] *sf* pulley.

pu'lire *vt* to clean; (*lucidare*) to polish; **far** ~ **qc** to have sth cleaned; ~ **a secco** to dry-clean.

pu'lito, a *ag* (*anche fig*) clean; (*ordinato*) neat, tidy ♦ *sf* quick clean; **avere la coscienza** ~**a** to have a clear conscience.

puli'tura *sf* cleaning; ~ **a secco** dry-cleaning.

puli'zia [pulit'tsia] *sf* (*atto*) cleaning; (*condizione*) cleanness; **fare le** ~**e** to do the cleaning, do the housework; ~ **etnica** ethnic cleansing.

'pullman *sm inv* coach (BRIT), bus.

pul'lover *sm inv* pullover, jumper.

pullu'lare *vi* to swarm, teem.

pul'mino *sm* minibus.

'pulpito *sm* pulpit.

pul'sante *sm* (push-)button.

pul'sare *vi* to pulsate, beat.

pulsazi'one [pulsat'tsjone] *sf* beat.

pul'viscolo *sm* fine dust.

'puma *sm inv* puma.

pun'gente [pun'dʒɛnte] *ag* prickly; stinging; (*anche fig*) biting.

'pungere ['pundʒere] *vt* to prick; (*sog*: *insetto, ortica*) to sting; (: *freddo*) to bite; ~ **qn sul vivo** (*fig*) to cut sb to the quick.

pungigli'one [pundʒiʎ'ʎone] *sm* sting.

pungo'lare *vt* to goad.

pu'nire *vt* to punish.

puni'tivo, a *ag* punitive.

punizi'one [punit'tsjone] *sf* punishment; (SPORT) penalty.

'punsi *etc vb vedi* **pungere.**

'punta *sf* point; (*parte terminale*) tip, end; (*di monte*) peak; (*di costa*) promontory; (*minima parte*) touch, trace; **in** ~ **di piedi** on tiptoe; **ore di** ~ peak hours; **uomo di** ~ (SPORT, POL) front-rank *o* leading man; **doppie** ~**e** split ends.

pun'tare *vt* (*piedi a terra, gomiti sul tavolo*) to plant; (*dirigere*: *pistola*) to point; (*scommettere*): ~ **su** to bet on ♦ *vi* (*mirare*): ~ **a** to aim at; (*avviarsi*): ~ **su** to head *o* make for; (*fig*: *contare*): ~ **su** to count *o* rely on.

puntas'pilli *sm inv* = **portaspilli.**

pun'tata *sf* (*gita*) short trip; (*scommessa*) bet; (*parte di opera*) instalment (BRIT), installment (US); **farò una** ~ **a Parigi** I'll pay a flying visit to Paris; **romanzo a** ~**e** serial.

punteggi'are [punted'dʒare] *vt* to punctuate.
punteggia'tura [punteddʒa'tura] *sf* punctuation.
pun'teggio [pun'teddʒo] *sm* score.
puntel'lare *vt* to support.
pun'tello *sm* prop, support.
punteru'olo *sm* (*TECN*) punch; (: *per stoffa*) bodkin.
pun'tiglio [pun'tiʎʎo] *sm* obstinacy, stubbornness.
puntigli'oso, a [puntiʎ'ʎoso] *ag* punctilious.
pun'tina *sf*: ~ **da disegno** drawing pin (*BRIT*), thumb tack (*US*); ~**e** *sfpl* (*AUT*) points.
pun'tino *sm* dot; **fare qc a** ~ to do sth properly; **arrivare a** ~ to arrive just at the right moment; **cotto a** ~ cooked to perfection; **mettere i** ~**i sulle "i"** (*fig*) to dot the i's and cross the t's.
'punto, a *pp di* **pungere** ♦ *sm* (*segno, macchiolina*) dot; (*LING*) full stop; (*MAT, momento, di punteggio, fig: argomento*) point; (*posto*) spot; (*a scuola*) mark; (*nel cucire, nella maglia, MED*) stitch ♦ *av*: **non ...** ~ not ... at all; **due** ~**i** *sm inv* (*LING*) colon; **ad un certo** ~ at a certain point; **fino ad un certo** ~ (*fig*) to a certain extent; **sul** ~ **di fare** (just) about to do; **fare il** ~ (*NAUT*) to take a bearing; **fare il** ~ **della situazione** (*analisi*) to take stock of the situation; (*riassunto*) to sum up the situation; **alle 6 in** ~ at 6 o'clock sharp *o* on the dot; **essere a buon** ~ to have reached a satisfactory stage; **mettere a** ~ to adjust; (*motore*) to tune; (*cannocchiale*) to focus; (*fig*) to settle; **venire al** ~ to come to the point; **vestito di tutto** ~ all dressed up; **di** ~ **in bianco** point-blank; ~ **d'arrivo** arrival point; ~ **cardinale** point of the compass, cardinal point; ~ **debole** weak point; ~ **esclamativo/interrogativo** exclamation/question mark; ~ **d'incontro** meeting place, meeting point; ~ **morto** standstill; ~ **nero** (*comedone*) blackhead; ~ **nevralgico** (*anche fig*) nerve centre (*BRIT*) *o* center (*US*); ~ **di partenza** (*anche fig*) starting point; ~ **di riferimento** landmark; (*fig*) point of reference; ~ **di vendita** retail outlet; ~ **e virgola** semicolon; ~ **di vista** (*fig*) point of view; ~**i di sospensione** suspension points.
puntu'ale *ag* punctual.
puntualità *sf* punctuality.
puntualiz'zare [puntualid'dzare] *vt* to make clear.
puntual'mente *av* (*gen*) on time; (*ironico*:

al solito) as usual.
pun'tura *sf* (*di ago*) prick; (*di insetto*) sting, bite; (*MED*) puncture; (: *iniezione*) injection; (*dolore*) sharp pain.
punzecchi'are [puntsek'kjare] *vt* to prick; (*fig*) to tease.
punzo'nare [puntso'nare] *vt* (*TECN*) to stamp.
pun'zone [pun'tsone] *sm* (*per metalli*) stamp, die.
può, pu'oi *vb vedi* **potere.**
'pupa *sf* doll.
pu'pazzo [pu'pattso] *sm* puppet.
pu'pillo, a *smf* (*DIR*) ward; (*prediletto*) favourite (*BRIT*), favorite (*US*), pet ♦ *sf* (*ANAT*) pupil.
purché [pur'ke] *cong* provided that, on condition that.
'pure *cong* (*tuttavia*) and yet, nevertheless; (*anche se*) even if ♦ *av* (*anche*) too, also; **pur di** (*al fine di*) just to; **faccia** ~! go ahead!, please do!
purè *sm*, **pu'rea** *sf* (*CUC*) purée; (: *di patate*) mashed potatoes.
pu'rezza [pu'rettsa] *sf* purity.
'purga, ghe *sf* (*MED*) purging *no pl*; purge; (*POL*) purge.
pur'gante *sm* (*MED*) purgative, purge.
pur'gare *vt* (*MED, POL*) to purge; (*pulire*) to clean.
purga'torio *sm* purgatory.
purifi'care *vt* to purify; (*metallo*) to refine.
purificazi'one [purifikat'tsjone] *sf* purification; refinement.
puri'tano, a *ag, smf* puritan.
'puro, a *ag* pure; (*acqua*) clear, limpid; (*vino*) undiluted; **di razza** ~**a** thoroughbred; **per** ~ **caso** by sheer chance, purely by chance.
puro'sangue *smf inv* thoroughbred.
pur'troppo *av* unfortunately.
pus *sm* pus.
pusil'lanime *ag* cowardly.
'pustola *sf* pimple.
puta'caso *av* just supposing, suppose.
puti'ferio *sm* rumpus, row.
putre'fare *vi* to putrefy, rot.
putre'fatto, a *pp di* **putrefare.**
putrefazi'one [putrefat'tsjone] *sf* putrefaction.
'putrido, a *ag* putrid, rotten.
put'tana *sf* (*fam!*) whore (*!*).
'putto *sm* cupid.
'puzza ['puttsa] *sf* = **puzzo.**
puz'zare [put'tsare] *vi* to stink; **la faccenda puzza (d'imbroglio)** the whole business stinks.
'puzzo ['puttso] *sm* stink, foul smell.

'puzzola ['puttsola] *sf* polecat.
puzzo'lente [puttso'lente] *ag* stinking.
PV *sigla* = Pavia.
pv *abbr vedi* **prossimo venturo.**
P.V.C. [pivi't∫i] *sigla m* (= *polyvinyl chloride*)
PVC.
PZ *sigla* = Potenza.
p. zza *abbr* = **piazza.**

Q q

Q, q [ku] *sf o m inv* (*lettera*) Q, q; **Q come
Quarto** ≈ Q for Queen.
q *abbr* (= *quintale*) q.
Qa'tar [ka'tar] *sm*: **il ~** Qatar.
q.b. *abbr* (= *quanto basta*) as needed;
zucchero ~ sugar to taste.
Q.G. *abbr* = **quartier generale.**
Q.I. *abbr vedi* **quoziente d'intelligenza.**
qua *av* here; **in ~** (*verso questa parte*) this
way; **~ dentro/sotto** *etc* in/under here
etc; **da un anno in ~** for a year now; **da
quando in ~?** since when?; **per di ~**
(*passare*) this way; **al di ~ di** (*fiume,
strada*) on this side of; *vedi* **questo.**
'quacchero, a ['kwakkero] *sm/f* Quaker.
qua'derno *sm* notebook; (*per scuola*)
exercise book.
qua'drangolo *sm* quadrangle.
qua'drante *sm* quadrant; (*di orologio*) face.
qua'drare *vi* (*bilancio*) to balance, tally;
(*fig: corrispondere*): **~ (con)** to correspond
(with) ♦ *vt* (*MAT*) to square; **far ~ il
bilancio** to balance the books; **non mi
quadra** I don't like it.
qua'drato, a *ag* square; (*fig: equilibrato*)
level-headed, sensible; (: *peg*) square
♦ *sm* (*MAT*) square; (*PUGILATO*) ring; **5 al ~**
5 squared.
quadret'tato, a *ag* (*foglio*) squared;
(*tessuto*) checked.
qua'dretto *sm*: **a ~i** (*tessuto*) checked;
(*foglio*) squared.
quadrien'nale *ag* (*che dura 4 anni*) four-
year *cpd*; (*che avviene ogni 4 anni*) four-
yearly.
quadri'foglio [kwadri'fɔʎʎo] *sm* four-leaf
clover.
quadri'mestre *sm* (*periodo*) four-month
period; (*INS*) term.
'quadro *sm* (*pittura*) painting, picture;

(*quadrato*) square; (*tabella*) table, chart;
(*TECN*) board, panel; (*TEAT*) scene; (*fig:
scena, spettacolo*) sight; (: *descrizione*)
outline, description; **~i** *smpl* (*POL*) party
organizers; (*COMM*) managerial staff;
(*MIL*) cadres; (*CARTE*) diamonds; **a ~i**
(*disegno*) checked; **fare un ~ della
situazione** to outline the situation; **~
clinico** (*MED*) case history; **~ di comando**
control panel; **~i intermedi** middle
management *sg*.
qua'drupede *sm* quadruped.
quadrupli'care *vt* to quadruple.
'quadruplo, a *ag, sm* quadruple.
quaggiù [kwad'dʒu] *av* down here.
'quaglia ['kwaʎʎa] *sf* quail.

══════════════ *PAROLA CHIAVE*

'qualche ['kwalke] *det* **1** some, a few; (*in
interrogative*) any; **ho comprato ~ libro**
I've bought some *o* a few books; **~ volta**
sometimes; **hai ~ sigaretta?** have you any
cigarettes?
2 (*uno*): **c'è ~ medico?** is there a doctor?;
in ~ modo somehow
3 (*un certo, parecchio*) some; **un
personaggio di ~ rilievo** a figure of some
importance
4: **~ cosa** = **qualcosa.**

qualche'duno [kwalke'duno] *pron*
= **qualcuno.**
qual'cosa *pron* something; (*in espressioni
interrogative*) anything; **qualcos'altro**
something else; anything else; **~ di
nuovo** something new; anything new; **~
da mangiare** something to eat; anything
to eat; **c'è ~ che non va?** is there
something *o* anything wrong?
qual'cuno *pron* (*persona*) someone,
somebody; (: *in espressioni interrogative*)
anyone, anybody; (*alcuni*) some; **~ è
favorevole a noi** some are on our side;
qualcun altro someone *o* somebody else;
anyone *o* anybody else.

══════════════ *PAROLA CHIAVE*

'quale (*spesso troncato in* **qual**) *det* **1**
(*interrogativo*) what; (: *scegliendo tra due o
più cose o persone*) which; **~ uomo/
denaro?** what man/money?; which man/
money?; **~i sono i tuoi programmi?** what
are your plans?; **~ stanza preferisci?**
which room do you prefer?
2 (*relativo: come*): **il risultato fu ~ ci si
aspettava** the result was as expected
3 (*in elenchi*) such as, like; **piante ~i
l'edera** plants such as *o* like ivy

4 (*esclamativo*) what; ~ **disgrazia!** what bad luck!
5: in un certo qual modo in a way, in some ways; **per la qual cosa** for which reason
♦ *pron* **1** (*interrogativo*) which; ~ **dei due scegli?** which of the two do you want?
2 (*relativo*): **il(la)** ~ (*persona: soggetto*) who; (: *oggetto, con preposizione*) whom; (*cosa*) which; (*possessivo*) whose; **suo padre, il** ~ **è avvocato,** ... his father, who is a lawyer, ...; **a tutti coloro i** ~**i fossero interessati** ... to whom it may concern ...; **il signore con il** ~ **parlavo** the gentleman to whom I was speaking; **l'albergo al** ~ **ci siamo fermati** the hotel where we stayed *o* which we stayed at; **la signora della** ~ **ammiriamo la bellezza** the lady whose beauty we admire
♦ *av* (*in qualità di, come*) as; ~ **sindaco di questa città** as mayor of this town.

qua'lifica, che *sf* qualification; (*titolo*) title.
qualifi'care *vt* to qualify; (*definire*): ~ **qn/ qc come** to describe sb/sth as; ~**rsi** *vr* (*anche SPORT*) to qualify; ~**rsi a un concorso** to pass a competitive exam.
qualifica'tivo, a *ag* qualifying.
qualifi'cato, a *ag* (*dotato di qualifica*) qualified; (*esperto, abile*) skilled; **non mi ritengo** ~ **per questo lavoro** I don't think I'm qualified for this job; **è un medico molto** ~ he is a very distinguished doctor.
qualificazi'one [kwalifikat'tsjone] *sf* qualification; **gara di** ~ (*SPORT*) qualifying event.
qualità *sf inv* quality; **di ottima** *o* **prima** ~ top quality; **in** ~ **di** in one's capacity as; **in** ~ **di amica** as a friend; **articoli di ogni** ~ all sorts of goods; **controllo (di)** ~ quality control; **prodotto di** ~ quality product.
qualita'tivo, a *ag* qualitative.
qua'lora *cong* in case, if.
qual'siasi, qua'lunque *det inv* any; (*quale che sia*) whatever; (*discriminativo*) whichever; (*posposto: mediocre*) poor, indifferent; ordinary; **mettiti un vestito** ~ put on any old dress; ~ **cosa** anything; ~ **cosa accada** whatever happens; **a** ~ **costo** at any cost, whatever the cost; **l'uomo** ~ the man in the street; ~ **persona** anyone, anybody.
qualunqu'ista, i, e *smf* person indifferent to politics.
'quando *cong, av* when; ~ **sarò ricco** when I'm rich; **da** ~ (*dacché*) since;

(*interrogativo*): **da** ~ **sei qui?** how long have you been here?; **di** ~ **in** ~ from time to time; **quand'anche** even if.
quantifi'care *vt* to quantify.
quantità *sf inv* quantity; (*gran numero*): **una** ~ **di** a great deal of; a lot of; **in grande** ~ in large quantities.
quantita'tivo, a *ag* quantitative ♦ *sm* (*COMM: di merce*) amount, quantity.

══════════ *PAROLA CHIAVE*

'quanto, a *det* **1** (*interrogativo: quantità*) how much; (: *numero*) how many; ~ **pane/ denaro?** how much bread/money?; ~**i libri/ragazzi?** how many books/boys?; ~ **tempo?** how long?; ~**i anni hai?** how old are you?
2 (*esclamativo*): ~**e storie!** what a lot of nonsense!; ~ **tempo sprecato!** what a waste of time!
3 (*relativo: quantità*) as much ... as; (: *numero*) as many ... as; **ho** ~ **denaro mi occorre** I have as much money as I need; **prendi** ~**i libri vuoi** take as many books as you like
♦ *pron* **1** (*interrogativo: quantità*) how much; (: *numero*) how many; (: *tempo*) how long; ~ **mi dai?** how much will you give me?; ~**i me ne hai portati?** how many did you bring me?; ~ **starai via?** how long will you be away (for)?; **da** ~ **sei qui?** how long have you been here?; ~**i ne abbiamo oggi?** what's the date today?
2 (*relativo: quantità*) as much as; (: *numero*) as many as; **farò** ~ **posso** I'll do as much as I can; **a** ~ **dice lui** according to him; **in risposta a** ~ **esposto nella sua lettera** ... in answer to the points raised in your letter; **possono venire** ~**i sono stati invitati** all those who have been invited can come
♦ *av* **1** (*interrogativo: con ag, av*) how; (: *con vb*) how much; ~ **stanco ti sembrava?** how tired did he seem to you?; ~ **corre la tua moto?** how fast can your motorbike go?; ~ **costa?** how much does it cost?; **quant'è?** how much is it?
2 (*esclamativo: con ag, av*) how; (: *con vb*) how much; ~ **sono felice!** how happy I am!; **sapessi** ~ **abbiamo camminato!** if you knew how far we've walked!; **studierò** ~ **posso** I'll study as much as *o* all I can; ~ **prima** as soon as possible; ~ **più ... tanto meno** the more ... the less; ~ **più ... tanto più** the more ... the more
3: in ~ (*in qualità di*) as; (*perché, per il fatto che*) as, since; **in** ~ **legale della signora** as the lady's lawyer; **non è possibile in** ~

non possiamo permettercelo it isn't possible, since we can't afford it; **(in)** ~ **a** (*per ciò che riguarda*) as for, as regards; **(in)** ~ **a lui** as far as he's concerned **4**: **per** ~ (*nonostante, anche se*) however; **per** ~ **si sforzi, non ce la farà** try as he may, he won't manage it; **per** ~ **sia brava, fa degli errori** however good she may be, she makes mistakes; **per** ~ **io sappia** as far as I know.

quan'tunque *cong* although, though.
qua'ranta *num* forty.
quaran'tena *sf* quarantine.
quaran'tenne *ag, smf* forty-year-old.
quaran'tennio *sm* (period of) forty years.
quaran'tesimo, a *num* fortieth.
quaran'tina *sf*: **una** ~ **(di)** about forty.
quaran'totto *sm inv* forty-eight; **fare un** ~ (*fam*) to raise hell.
Qua'resima *sf*: **la** ~ Lent.
'quarta *sf vedi* quarto.
quar'tetto *sm* quartet(te).
quarti'ere *sm* district, area; (*MIL*) quarters *pl*; ~ **generale (Q.G.)** headquarters *pl* (HQ); ~ **residenziale** residential area *o* district; **i** ~**i alti** the smart districts.
'quarto, a *ag* fourth ♦ *sm* fourth; (*quarta parte*) quarter ♦ *sf* (*AUT*) fourth (gear); (*INS: elementare*) *fourth year of primary school*; (: *superiore*) *seventh year of secondary school*; **un** ~ **di vino** a quarter-litre (*BRIT*) *o* quarter-liter (*US*) bottle of wine; **le 6 e un** ~ a quarter past (*BRIT*) *o* after (*US*) 6; ~ **d'ora** quarter of an hour; **tre** ~**i d'ora** three quarters of an hour; **le otto e tre** ~**i, le nove meno un** ~ (a) quarter to (*BRIT*) *o* of (*US*) nine; **passare un brutto** ~ **d'ora** (*fig*) to have a bad *o* nasty time of it; ~**i di finale** (*SPORT*) quarter finals.
'quarzo ['kwartso] *sm* quartz.
'quasi *av* almost, nearly ♦ *cong* (*anche*: ~ **che**) as if; **(non)** ... ~ **mai** hardly ever; ~ ~ **me ne andrei** I've half a mind to leave.
quas'sù *av* up here.
'quatto, a *ag* crouched, squatting; (*silenzioso*) silent; ~ ~ very quietly; stealthily.
quattordi'cenne [kwattordi'tʃɛnne] *ag, smf* fourteen-year-old.
quat'tordici [kwat'torditʃi] *num* fourteen.
quat'trini *smpl* money *sg*, cash *sg*.
'quattro *num* four; **in** ~ **e quattr'otto** in less than no time; **dirne** ~ **a qn** to give sb a piece of one's mind; **fare il diavolo a** ~ to kick up a rumpus; **fare** ~ **chiacchiere** to have a chat; **farsi in** ~ **per qn** to go out of one's way for sb, put o.s. out for sb.

quat'trocchi [kwat'trɔkki] *sm inv* (*fig fam*: *persona con occhiali*) four-eyes; **a** ~ *av* (*tra 2 persone*) face to face; (*privatamente*) in private.
quattrocen'tesco, a, schi, sche [kwattrotʃen'tesko] *ag* fifteenth-century.
quattro'cento [kwattro'tʃento] *num* four hundred ♦ *sm*: **il Q**~ the fifteenth century.
quattro'mila *num* four thousand.

========= *PAROLA CHIAVE*

'quello, a (*dav sm* **quel** + *C*, **quell'** + *V*, **quello** + *s impura, gn, pn, ps, x, z; pl* **quei** + *C*, **quegli** + *V o s impura, gn, pn, ps, x, z; dav sf* **quella** + *C*, **quell'** + *V; pl* **quelle**) *det* that; those *pl*; ~**a casa** that house; **quegli uomini** those men; **voglio** ~**a camicia (lì o là)** I want that shirt; ~ **è mio fratello** that's my brother
♦ *pron* **1** (*dimostrativo*) that (one); those (ones) *pl*; (*ciò*) that; **conosci** ~**a?** do you know her?; **prendo** ~ **bianco** I'll take the white one; **chi è** ~**?** who's that?; **prendiamo** ~ **(lì o là)** let's take that one (there); **in quel di Milano** in the Milan area *o* region
2 (*relativo*): ~**(a) che** (*persona*) the one (who); (*cosa*) the one (which), the one (that); ~**i(e) che** (*persone*) those who; (*cose*) those which; **è lui** ~ **che non voleva venire** he's the one who didn't want to come; **ho fatto** ~ **che potevo** I did what I could; **è** ~**a che ti ho prestato** that's the one I lent you; **è proprio** ~ **che gli ho detto** that's exactly what I told him; **da** ~ **che ho sentito** from what I've heard.

'quercia, ce ['kwɛrtʃa] *sf* oak (tree); (*legno*) oak; **la Q**~(*POL*) *symbol of P.D.S.*
que'rela *sf* (*DIR*) (legal) action.
quere'lare *vt* to bring an action against.
que'sito *sm* question, query; problem.
'questi *pron* (*poetico*) this person.
questio'nario *sm* questionnaire.
questi'one *sf* problem, question; (*controversia*) issue; (*litigio*) quarrel; **in** ~ in question; **il caso in** ~ the matter at hand; **la persona in** ~ the person involved; **non voglio essere chiamato in** ~ I don't want to be dragged into the argument; **fuor di** ~ out of the question; **è** ~ **di tempo** it's a matter *o* question of time.

═══════════════ *PAROLA CHIAVE*

'questo, a *det* **1** (*dimostrativo*) this; these *pl*;
~ **libro (qui** *o* **qua)** this book; **io prendo ~
cappotto, tu quello** I'll take this coat, you
take that one; **quest'oggi** today; **~a sera**
this evening
2 (*enfatico*): **non fatemi più prendere di
~e paure** don't frighten me like that
again

♦ *pron* (*dimostrativo*) this (one); these
(ones) *pl*; (*ciò*) this; **prendo ~ (qui** *o* **qua)**
I'll take this one; **preferisci ~i** *o* **quelli?** do
you prefer these (ones) or those (ones)?;
~ **intendevo io** this is what I meant; ~
non dovevi dirlo you shouldn't have said
that; **e con ~?** so what?; **e con ~ se n'è
andato** and with that he left; **con tutto ~**
in spite of this, despite all this; ~ **è
quanto** that's all.

ques'tore *sm public official in charge of
the police in the provincial capital,
reporting to the prefetto*; ≈ chief
constable (*BRIT*), ≈ police commissioner
(*US*).

'questua *sf* collection (of alms).

ques'tura *sf* police headquarters *pl*.

questu'rino *sm* (*fam: poliziotto*) cop.

qui *av* here; **da** *o* **di ~** from here; **di ~ in
avanti** from now on; **di ~ a poco/una
settimana** in a little while/a week's time;
~ **dentro/sopra/vicino** in/up/near here;
vedi **questo.**

quie'scenza [kwjeʃˈʃɛntsa] *sf* (*AMM*): **porre
qn in ~** to retire sb.

quie'tanza [kwjeˈtantsa] *sf* receipt.

quie'tare *vt* to calm, soothe.

qui'ete *sf* quiet, quietness; calmness;
stillness; peace; **turbare la ~ pubblica**
(*DIR*) to disturb the peace.

qui'eto, a *ag* quiet; (*notte*) calm, still;
(*mare*) calm; **l'ho fatto per il ~ vivere** I did
it for a quiet life.

'quindi *av* then ♦ *cong* therefore, so.

quindi'cenne [kwindiˈtʃɛnne] *ag, sm/f*
fifteen-year-old.

'quindici [ˈkwinditʃi] *num* fifteen; ~ **giorni** a
fortnight (*BRIT*), two weeks.

quindi'cina [kwindiˈtʃina] *sf* (*serie*): **una ~
(di)** about fifteen; **fra una ~ di giorni** in a
fortnight (*BRIT*) *o* two weeks.

quindici'nale [kwinditʃiˈnale] *ag* fortnightly
(*BRIT*), semimonthly (*US*) ♦ *sm* (*rivista*)
fortnightly magazine (*BRIT*),
semimonthly (*US*).

quinquen'nale *ag* (*che dura 5 anni*) five-
year *cpd*; (*che avviene ogni 5 anni*) five-

yearly.

quin'quennio *sm* period of five years.

quinta *sf vedi* **quinto.**

quin'tale *sm* quintal (*100 kg*).

quin'tetto *sm* quintet(te).

'quinto, a *num* fifth ♦ *sf* (*AUT*) fifth (gear);
(*INS: elementare*) *fifth year of primary
school*; (*: superiore*) *final year of
secondary school*; (*TEAT*) wing; **un ~ della
popolazione** a fifth of the population; **tre
~i** three fifths; **in ~a pagina** on the fifth
page, on page five.

qui pro quo *sm inv* misunderstanding.

┌───┐
│ *The* **Quirinale**, *which takes its name from*
│ *one of the famous Seven Hills of Rome, on*
│ *which it stands, is the official residence of*
│ *the Presidente della Repubblica.*
└───┘

'Quito *sf* Quito.

quiz [kwidz] *sm inv* (*domanda*) question;
(*anche: gioco a ~*) quiz game.

'quorum *sm* quorum.

'quota *sf* (*parte*) quota, share; (*AER*) height,
altitude; (*IPPICA*) odds *pl*; **prendere/
perdere ~** (*AER*) to gain/lose height *o*
altitude; ~ **imponibile** taxable income; ~
d'iscrizione (*INS*) enrolment fee; (*ad una
gara*) entry fee; (*ad un club*) membership
fee; ~ **di mercato** market share.

quo'tare *vt* (*BORSA*) to quote; (*valutare:
anche fig*) to value; **è un pittore molto
quotato** he is rated highly as a painter.

quotazi'one [kwotatˈtsjone] *sf* quotation.

quotidiana'mente *av* daily, every day.

quotidi'ano, a *ag* daily; (*banale*) everyday
♦ *sm* (*giornale*) daily (paper).

quozi'ente [kwotˈtsjɛnte] *sm* (*MAT*)
quotient; ~ **di crescita zero** zero growth
rate; ~ **d'intelligenza (Q.I.)** intelligence
quotient (IQ).

R r

R, r [ˈɛrre] *sf* o *m* (*lettera*) R, r; **R come Roma**
≈ R for Robert (*BRIT*), R for Roger (*US*).

R *abbr* (*POSTA*) = **raccomandata**; (*FERR*)
= **rapido.**

RA *sigla* = Ravenna.

ra'barbaro *sm* rhubarb.

Ra'bat *sf* Rabat.

rabberci'are [rabber'tʃare] vt (anche fig) to patch up.

'rabbia sf (ira) anger, rage; (accanimento, furia) fury; (MED: idrofobia) rabies sg.

rab'bino sm rabbi.

rabbi'oso, a ag angry, furious; (facile all'ira) quick-tempered; (forze, acqua etc) furious, raging; (MED) rabid, mad.

rabbo'nire vt, ~**rsi** vr to calm down.

rabbrivi'dire vi to shudder, shiver.

rabbui'arsi vr to grow dark.

rabdo'mante sm water diviner.

racc. abbr (POSTA) = **raccomandata**.

raccapez'zarsi [rakkapet'tsarsi] vr: **non** ~ to be at a loss.

raccapricci'ante [rakkaprit'tʃante] ag horrifying.

racca'priccio [rakka'prittʃo] sm horror.

raccatta'palle sm inv (SPORT) ballboy.

raccat'tare vt to pick up.

rac'chetta [rak'ketta] sf (per tennis) racket; (per ping-pong) bat; ~ **da neve** snowshoe; ~ **da sci** ski stick.

'racchio, a ['rakkjo] ag (fam) ugly.

racchi'udere [rak'kjudere] vt to contain.

racchi'uso, a [rak'kjuso] pp di **racchiudere**.

rac'cogliere [rak'kɔʎʎere] vt to collect; (raccattare) to pick up; (frutti, fiori) to pick, pluck; (AGR) to harvest; (approvazione, voti) to win; (profughi) to take in; (vele) to furl; (capelli) to put up; ~**rsi** vr to gather; (fig) to gather one's thoughts; to meditate; **non ha raccolto** (allusione) he didn't take the hint; (frecciata) he took no notice of it; ~ **i frutti del proprio lavoro** (fig) to reap the benefits of one's work; ~ **le idee** (fig) to gather one's thoughts.

raccogli'mento [rakkoʎʎi'mento] sm meditation.

raccogli'tore [rakkoʎʎi'tore] sm (cartella) folder, binder; ~ **a fogli mobili** loose-leaf binder.

rac'colto, a pp di **raccogliere** ♦ ag (persona: pensoso) thoughtful; (luogo: appartato) secluded, quiet ♦ sm (AGR) crop, harvest ♦ sf collecting no pl; collection; (AGR) harvesting no pl, gathering no pl; harvest, crop; **fare la** ~**a di qc** to collect sth; **chiamare a** ~**a** to gather together.

raccoman'dabile ag (highly) commendable; **è un tipo poco** ~ he is not to be trusted.

raccoman'dare vt to recommend; (affidare) to entrust; ~**rsi** vr: ~**rsi a qn** to commend o.s. to sb; ~ **a qn di fare qc** to recommend that sb does sth; ~ **a qn di non fare qc** to tell o warn sb not to do sth; ~ **qn a qn/alle cure di qn** to entrust sb to

sb/to sb's care; **mi raccomando!** don't forget!

raccoman'dato, a ag (lettera, pacco) recorded-delivery (BRIT), certified (US); (candidato) recommended ♦ sm/f: **essere un(a)** ~**(a) di ferro** to have friends in high places ♦ sf (anche: **lettera** ~**a**) recorded-delivery letter; ~**a con ricevuta di ritorno** (Rrr) recorded-delivery letter with advice of receipt.

raccomandazi'one [rakkomandat'tsjone] sf recommendation; **lettera di** ~ letter of introduction.

raccomo'dare vt (riparare) to repair, mend.

raccon'tare vt: ~ **(a qn)** (dire) to tell (sb); (narrare) to relate (to sb), tell (sb) about; **a me non la racconti** don't try and kid me; **cosa mi racconti di nuovo?** what's new?

rac'conto sm telling no pl, relating no pl; (fatto raccontato) story, tale; (genere letterario) short story; ~**i per bambini** children's stories.

raccorci'are [rakkor'tʃare] vt to shorten.

raccor'dare vt to link up, join.

rac'cordo sm (TECN: giunzione) connection, joint; (AUT: di autostrada) slip road (BRIT), entrance (o exit) ramp (US); ~ **anulare** (AUT) ring road (BRIT), beltway (US).

ra'chitico, a, ci, che [ra'kitiko] ag suffering from rickets; (fig) scraggy, scrawny.

rachi'tismo [raki'tizmo] sm (MED) rickets sg.

racimo'lare [ratʃimo'lare] vt (fig) to scrape together, glean.

'rada sf (natural) harbour (BRIT) o harbor (US).

'radar sm inv radar.

raddol'cire [raddol'tʃire] vt (persona, carattere) to soften; ~**rsi** vr (tempo) to grow milder; (persona) to soften, mellow.

raddoppia'mento sm doubling.

raddoppi'are vt, vi to double.

rad'doppio sm (gen) doubling; (BILIARDO) double; (EQUITAZIONE) gallop.

raddriz'zare [raddrit'tsare] vt to straighten; (fig: correggere) to put straight, correct.

'radere vt (barba) to shave off; (mento) to shave; (fig: rasentare) to graze; to skim; ~**rsi** vr to shave (o.s.); ~ **al suolo** to raze to the ground.

radi'ale ag radial.

radi'ante ag (calore, energia) radiant.

radi'are vt to strike off.

radia'tore sm radiator.

radiazi'one [radjat'tsjone] sf (FISICA) radiation; (cancellazione) striking off.

'**radica** *sf* (*BOT*): ~ **di noce** walnut (wood).
radi'cale *ag* radical ♦ *sm* (*LING*) root; (*MAT, POL*) radical.
radi'cato, a *ag* (*pregiudizio, credenza*) deep-seated, deeply-rooted.
ra'dicchio [ra'dikkjo] *sm variety of chicory.*
ra'dice [ra'ditʃe] *sf* root; **segno di** ~ (*MAT*) radical sign; **colpire alla** ~ (*fig*) to strike at the root; **mettere** ~**i** (*idee, odio etc*) to take root; (*persona*) to put down roots; ~ **quadrata** (*MAT*) square root.
'**radio** *sf inv* radio ♦ *sm* (*CHIM*) radium; **trasmettere per** ~ to broadcast; **stazione/ponte** ~ radio station/link; ~ **ricevente/trasmittente** receiver/transmitter.
radioabbo'nato, a *sm/f* radio subscriber.
radioama'tore, 'trice *sm/f* amateur radio operator, ham (*fam*).
radioascolta'tore, 'trice *sm/f* (radio) listener.
radioattività *sf* radioactivity.
radioat'tivo, a *ag* radioactive.
radiocoman'dare *vt* to operate by remote control.
radiocoman'dato, a *ag* remote-controlled.
radioco'mando *sm* remote control.
radiocomunicazi'one [radjokomunikat'tsjone] *sf* radio message.
radio'cronaca, che *sf* radio commentary.
radiocro'nista, i, e *sm/f* radio commentator.
radiodiffusi'one *sf* (radio) broadcasting.
radio'fonico, a, ci, che *ag* radio *cpd.*
radiogra'fare *vt* to X-ray.
radiogra'fia *sf* radiography; (*foto*) X-ray photograph.
radio'lina *sf* portable radio, transistor (radio).
radiolo'gia [radjolo'dʒia] *sf* radiology.
radi'ologo, a, gi, ghe *sm/f* radiologist.
radiorice'vente [radjoritʃe'vɛnte] *sf* (*anche:* **apparecchio** ~) receiver.
radi'oso, a *ag* radiant.
radiostazi'one [radjostat'tsjone] *sf* radio station.
radios'veglia [radjoz'veʎʎa] *sf* radio alarm.
radio'taxi *sm inv* radio taxi.
radio'tecnico, a, ci, che *ag* radio engineering *cpd* ♦ *sm* radio engineer.
radiotelegra'fista, i, e *sm/f* radiotelegrapher.
radiotera'pia *sf* radiotherapy.
radiotrasmit'tente *ag* (radio) broadcasting *cpd* ♦ *sf* (radio) broadcasting station.
'**rado, a** *ag* (*capelli*) sparse, thin; (*visite*) infrequent; **di** ~ rarely; **non di** ~ not uncommonly.
radu'nare *vt,* ~**rsi** *vr* to gather, assemble.
radu'nata *sf* (*MIL*) muster.
ra'duno *sm* gathering, meeting.
ra'dura *sf* clearing.
'**rafano** *sm* horseradish.
raffazzo'nare [raffattso'nare] *vt* to patch up.
raf'fermo, a *ag* stale.
'**raffica, che** *sf* (*METEOR*) gust (of wind); ~ **di colpi** (*di fucile*) burst of gunfire.
raffigu'rare *vt* to represent.
raffigurazi'one [raffigurat'tsjone] *sf* representation, depiction.
raffi'nare *vt* to refine.
raffina'tezza [raffina'tettsa] *sf* refinement.
raffi'nato, a *ag* refined.
raffinazi'one [raffinat'tsjone] *sf* (*di sostanza*) refining; ~ **del petrolio** oil refining.
raffine'ria *sf* refinery.
raffor'zare [raffor'tsare] *vt* to reinforce.
rafforza'tivo, a [raffortsa'tivo] *ag* (*LING*) intensifying ♦ *sm* (*LING*) intensifier.
raffredda'mento *sm* cooling.
raffred'dare *vt* to cool; (*fig*) to dampen, have a cooling effect on; ~**rsi** *vr* to grow cool *o* cold; (*prendere un raffreddore*) to catch a cold; (*fig*) to cool (off).
raffred'dato, a *ag* (*MED*): **essere** ~ to have a cold.
raffred'dore *sm* (*MED*) cold.
raffron'tare *vt* to compare.
raf'fronto *sm* comparison.
'**rafia** *sf* (*fibra*) raffia.
raga'nella *sf* (*ZOOL*) tree frog.
ra'gazzo, a [ra'gattso] *sm/f* boy/girl; (*fam: fidanzato*) boyfriend/girlfriend; **nome da** ~**a** maiden name; ~**a madre** unmarried mother; ~**a squillo** call girl.
ragge'lare [raddʒe'lare] *vt, vi,* ~**rsi** *vr* to freeze.
raggi'ante [rad'dʒante] *ag* radiant, shining; ~ **di gioia** beaming *o* radiant with joy.
raggi'era [rad'dʒɛra] *sf* (*di ruota*) spokes *pl*; **a** ~ with a sunburst pattern.
'**raggio** ['raddʒo] *sm* (*di sole etc*) ray; (*MAT, distanza*) radius; (*di ruota etc*) spoke; **nel** ~ **di 20 km** within a radius of 20 km *o* a 20-km radius; **a largo** ~ (*esplorazione, incursione*) wide-ranging; ~ **d'azione** range; ~ **laser** laser beam; ~**i X** X-rays.
raggi'rare [raddʒi'rare] *vt* to take in, trick.
rag'giro [rad'dʒiro] *sm* trick.
raggi'ungere [rad'dʒundʒere] *vt* to reach; (*persona: riprendere*) to catch up (with); (*bersaglio*) to hit; (*fig: meta*) to achieve; ~

il proprio scopo to reach one's goal, achieve one's aim; **~ un accordo** to come to *o* reach an agreement.

raggi'unto, a [rad'dʒunto] *pp di* **raggiungere**.

raggomito'larsi *vr* to curl up.

raggranel'lare *vt* to scrape together.

raggrin'zare [raggrin'tsare] *vt, vi* (*anche:* ~**rsi**) to wrinkle.

raggrin'zire [raggrin'tsire] *vt* = **raggrinzare**.

raggru'mare *vt,* ~**rsi** *vr* (*sangue, latte*) to clot.

raggruppa'mento *sm* (*azione*) grouping; (*gruppo*) group; (: *MIL*) unit.

raggrup'pare *vt* to group (together).

ragguagli'are [raggwaʎ'ʎare] *vt* (*paragonare*) to compare; (*informare*) to inform.

raggu'aglio [rag'gwaʎʎo] *sm* comparison; (*informazione, relazione*) piece of information.

ragguar'devole *ag* (*degno di riguardo*) distinguished, notable; (*notevole: somma*) considerable.

'ragia ['radʒa] *sf*: **acqua ~** turpentine.

ragiona'mento [radʒona'mento] *sm* reasoning *no pl*; argument.

ragio'nare [radʒo'nare] *vi* (*usare la ragione*) to reason; (*discorrere*): **~ (di)** to argue (about); **cerca di ~** try and be reasonable.

ragi'one [ra'dʒone] *sf* reason; (*dimostrazione, prova*) argument, reason; (*diritto*) right; **aver ~** to be right; **aver ~ di qn** to get the better of sb; **dare ~ a qn** (*sog: persona*) to side with sb; (: *fatto*) to prove sb right; **farsi una ~ di qc** to accept sth, come to terms with sth; **in ~ di** at the rate of; **a *o* con ~** rightly, justly; **perdere la ~** to become insane; (*fig*) to take leave of one's senses; **a ragion veduta** after due consideration; **per ~i di famiglia** for family reasons; **~ di scambio** terms of trade; **~ sociale** (*COMM*) corporate name; **ragion di stato** reason of State.

ragione'ria [radʒone'ria] *sf* accountancy; (*ufficio*) accounts department.

ragio'nevole [radʒo'nevole] *ag* reasonable.

ragioni'ere, a [radʒo'njɛre] *sm/f* accountant.

ragli'are [raʎ'ʎare] *vi* to bray.

ragna'tela [raɲɲa'tela] *sf* cobweb, spider's web.

'ragno ['raɲɲo] *sm* spider; **non cavare un ~ dal buco** (*fig*) to draw a blank.

ragù *sm inv* (*CUC*) meat sauce (*for pasta*).

RAI-TV [raiti'vu] *sigla f* (= *Radio televisione italiana*) Italian Broadcasting Company.

rallegra'menti *smpl* congratulations.

ralle'grare *vt* to cheer up; ~**rsi** *vr* to cheer up; (*provare allegrezza*) to rejoice; ~**rsi con qn** to congratulate sb.

rallenta'mento *sm* slowing down; slackening.

rallen'tare *vt, vi* to slow down; **~ il passo** to slacken one's pace.

rallenta'tore *sm* (*CINE*) slow-motion camera; **al ~** (*anche fig*) in slow motion.

raman'zina [raman'dzina] *sf* lecture, telling-off.

ra'mare *vt* (*superficie*) to copper, coat with copper; (*AGR: vite*) to spray with copper sulphate.

ra'marro *sm* green lizard.

ra'mato, a *ag* (*oggetto: rivestito di rame*) copper-coated, coppered; (*capelli, barba*) coppery, copper-coloured (*BRIT*), copper-colored (*US*).

'rame *sm* (*CHIM*) copper; **di ~** copper *cpd*; **incisione su ~** copperplate.

ramifi'care *vi* (*BOT*) to put out branches; ~**rsi** *vr* (*diramarsi*) to branch out; (*MED: tumore, vene*) to ramify; ~**rsi in** (*biforcarsi*) to branch into.

ramificazi'one [ramifikat'tsjone] *sf* ramification.

ra'mingo, a, ghi, ghe *ag* (*poetico*): **andare ~** to go wandering, wander.

ra'mino *sm* (*CARTE*) rummy.

rammari'carsi *vr*: **~ (di)** (*rincrescersi*) to be sorry (about), regret; (*lamentarsi*) to complain (about).

ram'marico, chi *sm* regret.

rammen'dare *vt* to mend; (*calza*) to darn.

ram'mendo *sm* mending *no pl*; darning *no pl*; mend; darn.

rammen'tare *vt* to remember, recall; ~**rsi** *vr*: ~**rsi (di qc)** to remember (sth); **~ qc a qn** to remind sb of sth.

rammol'lire *vt* to soften ♦ *vi* (*anche:* ~**rsi**) to go soft.

rammol'lito, a *ag* weak ♦ *sm/f* weakling.

'ramo *sm* branch; (*di commercio*) field; **non è il mio ~** it's not my field *o* line.

ramo'scello [ramoʃ'ʃello] *sm* twig.

'rampa *sf* flight (of stairs); **~ di lancio** launching pad.

rampi'cante *ag* (*BOT*) climbing.

ram'pino *sm* (*gancio*) hook; (*NAUT*) grapnel.

ram'pollo *sm* (*di acqua*) spring; (*BOT: germoglio*) shoot; (*fig: discendente*) descendant.

ram'pone *sm* harpoon; (*ALPINISMO*) crampon.

'rana *sf* frog; **~ pescatrice** angler fish.

'rancido, a ['rantʃido] *ag* rancid.

'rancio ['rantʃo] _sm_ (MIL) mess; **ora del** ~ mess time.

ran'core _sm_ rancour (BRIT), rancor (US), resentment; **portare** ~ **a qn, provare** ~ **per** _o_ **verso qn** to bear sb a grudge.

ran'dagio, a, gi, gie _o_ **ge** [ran'dadʒo] _ag_ (_gatto, cane_) stray.

ran'dello _sm_ club, cudgel.

'rango, ghi _sm_ (_grado_) rank; (_condizione sociale_) station, social standing; **persone di** ~ **inferiore** people of lower standing; **uscire dai** ~**ghi** to fall out; (_fig_) to step out of line.

Ran'gun _sf_ Rangoon.

rannicchi'arsi [rannik'kjarsi] _vr_ to crouch, huddle.

rannuvo'larsi _vr_ to cloud over, become overcast.

ra'nocchio [ra'nɔkkjo] _sm_ (edible) frog.

ranto'lare _vi_ to wheeze.

ranto'lio _sm_ (_il respirare affannoso_) wheezing; (: _di agonizzante_) death rattle.

'rantolo _sm_ wheeze; death rattle.

ra'nuncolo _sm_ (BOT) buttercup.

'rapa _sf_ (BOT) turnip.

ra'pace [ra'patʃe] _ag_ (_animale_) predatory; (_fig_) rapacious, grasping ♦ _sm_ bird of prey.

ra'pare _vt_ (_capelli_) to crop, cut very short.

'rapida _sf vedi_ **rapido**.

rapida'mente _av_ quickly, rapidly.

rapidità _sf_ speed.

'rapido, a _ag_ fast; (_esame, occhiata_) quick, rapid ♦ _sm_ (FERR) express (train) ♦ _sf_ (_di fiume_) rapid.

rapi'mento _sm_ kidnapping; (_fig_) rapture.

ra'pina _sf_ robbery; ~ **in banca** bank robbery; ~ **a mano armata** armed robbery.

rapi'nare _vt_ to rob.

rapina'tore, 'trice _sm/f_ robber.

ra'pire _vt_ (_cose_) to steal; (_persone_) to kidnap; (_fig_) to enrapture, delight.

ra'pito, a _ag_ (_persona_) kidnapped; (_fig: in estasi_): **ascoltare** ~ **qn** to be captivated by sb's words ♦ _sm/f_ kidnapped person.

rapi'tore, 'trice _sm/f_ kidnapper.

rappacifi'care [rappatʃifi'kare] _vt_ (_riconciliare_) to reconcile; ~**rsi** _vr_ (_uso reciproco_) to be reconciled, make it up (_fam_).

rappacificazi'one [rappatʃifikat'tsjone] _sf_ reconciliation.

rappez'zare [rappet'tsare] _vt_ to patch.

rappor'tare _vt_ (_confrontare_) to compare; (_riprodurre_) to reproduce.

rap'porto _sm_ (_resoconto_) report; (_legame_) relationship; (MAT, TECN) ratio; ~**i** _smpl_

(_fra persone, paesi_) relations; **in** ~ **a quanto è successo** with regard to _o_ in relation to what happened; **fare** ~ **a qn su qc** to report sth to sb; **andare a** ~ **da qn** to report to sb; **chiamare qn a** ~ (MIL) to summon sb; **essere in buoni/cattivi** ~**i con qn** to be on good/bad terms with sb; ~ **d'affari,** ~ **di lavoro** business relations; ~ **di compressione** (TECN) pressure ratio; ~ **coniugale** marital relationship; ~ **di trasmissione** (TECN) gear; ~**i sessuali** sexual intercourse _sg_.

rap'prendersi _vr_ to coagulate, clot; (_latte_) to curdle.

rappre'saglia [rappre'saʎʎa] _sf_ reprisal, retaliation.

rappresen'tante _sm/f_ representative; ~ **di commercio** sales representative, sales rep (_fam_); ~ **sindacale** union delegate _o_ representative.

rappresen'tanza [rapprezen'tantsa] _sf_ delegation, deputation; (COMM: _ufficio, sede_) agency; **in** ~ **di qn** on behalf of sb; **spese di** ~ entertainment expenses; **macchina di** ~ official car; **avere la** ~ **di** to be the agent for; ~ **esclusiva** sole agency; **avere la** ~ **esclusiva** to be sole agent.

rappresen'tare _vt_ to represent; (TEAT) to perform; **farsi** ~ **dal proprio legale** to be represented by one's lawyer.

rappresenta'tivo, a _ag_ representative ♦ _sf_ (_di partito, sindacale_) representative group; (SPORT: _squadra_) representative (team).

rappresentazi'one [rapprezentat'tsjone] _sf_ representation; performing _no pl_; (_spettacolo_) performance; **prima** ~ **assoluta** world première.

rap'preso, a _pp di_ **rapprendere**.

rapso'dia _sf_ rhapsody.

'raptus _sm inv_: ~ **di follia** fit of madness.

rara'mente _av_ seldom, rarely.

rare'fare _vt,_ ~**rsi** _vr_ to rarefy.

rare'fatto, a _pp di_ **rarefare** ♦ _ag_ rarefied.

rarefazi'one [rarefat'tsjone] _sf_ rarefaction.

rarità _sf inv_ rarity.

'raro, a _ag_ rare.

ra'sare _vt_ (_barba etc_) to shave off; (_siepi, erba_) to trim, cut; ~**rsi** _vr_ to shave (o.s.).

ra'sato, a _ag_ (_erba_) trimmed, cut; (_tessuto_) smooth; **avere la barba** ~**a** to be clean-shaven.

rasa'tura _sf_ shave.

raschia'mento [raskja'mento] _sm_ (MED) curettage; ~ **uterino** D and C.

raschi'are [ras'kjare] _vt_ to scrape; (_macchia, fango_) to scrape off ♦ _vi_ to clear one's throat.

rasen'tare *vt* (*andar rasente*) to keep close to; (*sfiorare*) to skim along (*o* over); (*fig*) to border on.

ra'sente *prep*: ~ (**a**) close to, very near.

'raso, a *pp di* **radere** ♦ *ag* (*barba*) shaved; (*capelli*) cropped; (*con misure di capacità*) level; (*pieno*: *bicchiere*) full to the brim ♦ *sm* (*tessuto*) satin; ~ **terra** close to the ground; **volare** ~ **terra** to hedgehop; **un cucchiaio** ~ a level spoonful.

ra'soio *sm* razor; ~ **elettrico** electric shaver *o* razor.

ras'pare *vt* (*levigare*) to rasp; (*grattare*) to scratch.

'raspo *sm* (*di uva*) grape stalk.

ras'segna [ras'seɲɲa] *sf* (*MIL*) inspection, review; (*esame*) inspection; (*resoconto*) review, survey; (*pubblicazione letteraria etc*) review; (*mostra*) exhibition, show; **passare in** ~ (*MIL*, *fig*) to review.

rasse'gnare [rasseɲ'ɲare] *vt*: ~ **le dimissioni** to resign, hand in one's resignation; ~**rsi** *vr* (*accettare*): ~**rsi (a qc/ a fare)** to resign o.s. (to sth/to doing).

rassegnazi'one [rasseɲɲat'tsjone] *sf* resignation.

rassere'nare *vt* (*persona*) to cheer up; ~**rsi** *vr* (*tempo*) to clear up.

rasset'tare *vt* to tidy, put in order; (*aggiustare*) to repair, mend.

rassicu'rante *ag* reassuring.

rassicu'rare *vt* to reassure; ~**rsi** *vr* to take heart, recover one's confidence.

rassicurazi'one [rassikurat'tsjone] *sf* reassurance.

rasso'dare *vt* to harden, stiffen; (*fig*) to strengthen, consolidate.

rassomigli'anza [rassomiʎ'ʎantsa] *sf* resemblance.

rassomigli'are [rassomiʎ'ʎare] *vi*: ~ **a** to resemble, look like.

rastrella'mento *sm* (*MIL*, *di polizia*) (thorough) search.

rastrel'lare *vt* to rake; (*fig*: *perlustrare*) to comb.

rastrelli'era *sf* rack; (*per piatti*) dish rack.

ras'trello *sm* rake.

'rata *sf* (*quota*) instalment, installment (*US*); **pagare a** ~**e** to pay by instal(l)ments *o* on hire purchase (*BRIT*); **comprare/vendere a** ~**e** to buy/sell on hire purchase (*BRIT*) *o* on the installment plan (*US*).

rate'ale *ag*: **pagamento** ~ payment by instal(l)ments; **vendita** ~ hire purchase (*BRIT*), installment plan (*US*).

rate'are, rateiz'zare [rateid'dzare] *vt* to divide into instal(l)ments.

rateazi'one [rateat'tsjone] *sf* division into instal(l)ments.

'rateo *sm* (*COMM*) accrual.

ra'tifica, che *sf* ratification.

ratifi'care *vt* (*DIR*) to ratify.

'ratto *sm* (*DIR*) abduction; (*ZOOL*) rat.

rattop'pare *vt* to patch.

rat'toppo *sm* patching *no pl*; patch.

rattrap'pire *vt* to make stiff; ~**rsi** *vr* to be stiff.

rattris'tare *vt* to sadden; ~**rsi** *vr* to become sad.

rau'cedine [rau'tʃɛdine] *sf* hoarseness.

'rauco, a, chi, che *ag* hoarse.

rava'nello *sm* radish.

raven'nate *ag* of (*o* from) Ravenna.

ravi'oli *smpl* ravioli *sg*.

ravve'dersi *vr* to mend one's ways.

ravvi'are *vt* (*capelli*) to tidy; ~**rsi i capelli** to tidy one's hair.

ravvicina'mento [ravvitʃina'mento] *sm* (*tra persone*) reconciliation; (*POL*: *tra paesi etc*) rapprochement.

ravvici'nare [ravvitʃi'nare] *vt* (*avvicinare*): ~ **qc a** to bring sth nearer to; (*oggetti*) to bring closer together; (*fig*: *persone*) to reconcile, bring together; ~**rsi** *vr* to be reconciled.

ravvi'sare *vt* to recognize.

ravvi'vare *vt* to revive; (*fig*) to brighten up, enliven; ~**rsi** *vr* to revive; to brighten up.

Rawal'pindi [raval'pindi] *sf* Rawalpindi.

razio'cinio [rattsjo'tʃinjo] *sm* reasoning *no pl*; reason; (*buon senso*) common sense.

razio'nale [rattsjo'nale] *ag* rational.

razionalità [rattsjonali'ta] *sf* rationality; (*buon senso*) common sense.

razionaliz'zare [rattsjonalid'dzare] *vt* (*metodo, lavoro, programma*) to rationalize; (*problema, situazione*) to approach rationally.

raziona'mento [rattsjona'mento] *sm* rationing.

razio'nare [rattsjo'nare] *vt* to ration.

razi'one [rat'tsjone] *sf* ration; (*porzione*) portion, share.

'razza ['rattsa] *sf* race; (*ZOOL*) breed; (*discendenza, stirpe*) stock, race; (*sorta*) sort, kind.

raz'zia [rat'tsia] *sf* raid, foray.

razzi'ale [rat'tsjale] *ag* racial.

raz'zismo [rat'tsizmo] *sm* racism, racialism.

raz'zista, i, e [rat'tsista] *ag*, *sm/f* racist, racialist.

'razzo ['raddzo] *sm* rocket; ~ **di segnalazione** flare; ~ **vettore** vector rocket.

razzo'lare [rattso'lare] *vi* (*galline*) to scratch about.

RC *sigla* = *Reggio Calabria*.

RDT *sigla f vedi* **Repubblica Democratica Tedesca**.

RE *sigla* = *Reggio Emilia*.

re *sm inv* (*sovrano*) king; (*MUS*) D; (: *solfeggiando la scala*) re.

rea'gente [rea'dʒɛnte] *sm* reagent.

rea'gire [rea'dʒire] *vi* to react.

re'ale *ag* real; (*di, da re*) royal ♦ *sm*: **il ~** reality; **i R~i** the Royal family.

rea'lismo *sm* realism.

rea'lista, i, e *sm/f* realist; (*POL*) royalist.

rea'listico, a, ci, che *ag* realistic.

realiz'zare [realid'dzare] *vt* (*progetto etc*) to realize, carry out; (*sogno, desiderio*) to realize, fulfil; (*scopo*) to achieve; (*COMM: titoli etc*) to realize; (*CALCIO etc*) to score; **~rsi** *vr* to be realized.

realizzazi'one [realiddzat'tsjone] *sf* realization; fulfilment; achievement; **~ scenica** stage production.

rea'lizzo [rea'liddzo] *sm* (*conversione in denaro*) conversion into cash; (*vendita forzata*) clearance sale.

real'mente *av* really, actually.

realtà *sf inv* reality; **in ~** (*in effetti*) in fact; (*a dire il vero*) really.

re'ame *sm* kingdom, realm; (*fig*) realm.

re'ato *sm* offence (*BRIT*), offense (*US*).

reat'tore *sm* (*FISICA*) reactor; (*AER: aereo*) jet; (: *motore*) jet engine.

reazio'nario, a [reattsjo'narjo] *ag, sm/f* (*POL*) reactionary.

reazi'one [reat'tsjone] *sf* reaction; **motore/ aereo a ~** jet engine/plane; **forze della ~** reactionary forces; **~ a catena** (*anche fig*) chain reaction.

'rebbio *sm* prong.

'rebus *sm inv* rebus; (*fig*) puzzle; enigma.

recapi'tare *vt* to deliver.

re'capito *sm* (*indirizzo*) address; (*consegna*) delivery; **ha un ~ telefonico?** do you have a telephone number where you can be reached?; **~ a domicilio** home delivery (service).

re'care *vt* (*portare*) to bring; (*avere su di sé*) to carry, bear; (*cagionare*) to cause, bring; **~rsi** *vr* to go; **~ danno a qn** to harm sb, cause harm to sb.

re'cedere [re't∫ɛdere] *vi* to withdraw.

recensi'one [ret∫en'sjone] *sf* review.

recen'sire [ret∫en'sire] *vt* to review.

recen'sore, a [ret∫en'sore] *sm/f* reviewer.

re'cente [re't∫ɛnte] *ag* recent; **di ~** recently; **più ~** latest, most recent.

recente'mente [ret∫ente'mente] *av* recently.

rece'pire [ret∫e'pire] *vt* to understand, take in.

recessi'one [ret∫es'sjone] *sf* (*ECON*) recession.

re'cesso [re't∫ɛsso] *sm* (*azione*) recession, receding; (*DIR*) withdrawal; (*luogo*) recess.

recherò *etc* [reke'rɔ] *vb vedi* **recare**.

re'cidere [re't∫idere] *vt* to cut off, chop off.

reci'divo, a [ret∫i'divo] *sm/f* (*DIR*) second (*o* habitual) offender, recidivist ♦ *sf* recidivism.

recin'tare [ret∫in'tare] *vt* to enclose, fence off.

re'cinto [re't∫into] *sm* enclosure; (*ciò che recinge*) fence; surrounding wall.

recinzi'one [ret∫in'tsjone] *sf* (*azione*) enclosure, fencing-off; (*recinto: di legno*) fence; (: *di mattoni*) wall; (: *reticolato*) wire fencing; (: *a sbarre*) railings *pl*.

recipi'ente [ret∫i'pjɛnte] *sm* container.

re'ciproco, a, ci, che [re't∫iproko] *ag* reciprocal.

re'ciso, a [re't∫izo] *pp di* **recidere**.

'recita ['rɛt∫ita] *sf* performance.

'recital ['rɛt∫ital] *sm inv* recital.

reci'tare [ret∫i'tare] *vt* (*poesia, lezione*) to recite; (*dramma*) to perform; (*ruolo*) to play *o* act (the part of).

recitazi'one [ret∫itat'tsjone] *sf* recitation; (*di attore*) acting; **scuola di ~** drama school.

recla'mare *vi* to complain ♦ *vt* (*richiedere*) to demand.

ré'clame [re'klam] *sf inv* advertising *no pl*; advertisement, advert (*BRIT*), ad (*fam*).

reclamiz'zare [reklamid'dzare] *vt* to advertise.

re'clamo *sm* complaint; **sporgere ~ a** to complain to, make a complaint to.

recli'nabile *ag* (*sedile*) reclining.

recli'nare *vt* (*capo*) to bow, lower; (*sedile*) to tilt.

reclusi'one [ret∫lu'zjone] *sf* (*DIR*) imprisonment.

re'cluso, a *sm/f* prisoner.

'recluta *sf* recruit.

recluta'mento *sm* recruitment.

reclu'tare *vt* to recruit.

re'condito, a *ag* secluded; (*fig*) secret, hidden.

'record *ag inv* record *cpd* ♦ *sm inv* record; **in tempo ~, a tempo di ~** in record time; **detenere il ~ di** to hold the record for; **~ mondiale** world record.

recrimi'nare *vi*: **~ (su qc)** to complain (about sth).

recriminazi'one [rekriminat'tsjone] *sf* recrimination.

recrude'scenza [rekrudeʃ'ʃɛntsa] *sf* fresh outbreak.

recupe'rare *etc* = **ricuperare** *etc*.

redargu'ire *vt* to rebuke.

re'dassi *etc vb vedi* **redigere**.

re'datto, a *pp di* **redigere**.

redat'tore, 'trice *sm/f* (*STAMPA*) editor; (*: di articolo*) writer; (*di dizionario etc*) compiler; ~ **capo** chief editor.

redazi'one [redat'tsjone] *sf* editing; writing; (*sede*) editorial office(s); (*personale*) editorial staff; (*versione*) version.

reddi'tizio, a [reddi'tittsjo] *ag* profitable.

'reddito *sm* income; (*dello Stato*) revenue; (*di un capitale*) yield; ~ **complessivo** gross income; ~ **disponibile** disposable income; ~ **fisso** fixed income; ~ **imponibile/non imponibile** taxable/non-taxable income; ~ **da lavoro** earned income; ~ **nazionale** national income; ~ **pubblico** public revenue.

re'densi *etc vb vedi* **redimere**.

re'dento, a *pp di* **redimere**.

reden'tore *sm*: **il R**~ the Redeemer.

redenzi'one [reden'tsjone] *sf* redemption.

re'digere [re'didʒere] *vt* to write; (*contratto*) to draw up.

re'dimere *vt* to deliver; (*REL*) to redeem.

'redini *sfpl* reins.

redi'vivo, a *ag* returned to life, reborn.

'reduce ['rɛdutʃe] *ag* (*gen*): ~ **da** returning from, back from ♦ *sm/f* survivor; (*veterano*) veteran; **essere** ~ **da** (*esame, colloquio*) to have been through; (*malattia*) to be just over.

'refe *sm* thread.

refe'rendum *sm inv* referendum.

refe'renza [refe'rɛntsa] *sf* reference.

re'ferto *sm* medical report.

refet'torio *sm* refectory.

refezi'one [refet'tsjone] *sf* (*INS*) school meal.

refrat'tario, a *ag* refractory; (*fig*): **essere** ~ **alla matematica** to have no aptitude for mathematics.

refrige'rante [refridʒe'rante] *ag* (*TECN*) cooling, refrigerating; (*bevanda*) refreshing ♦ *sm* (*CHIM: fluido*) coolant; (*TECN: apparecchio*) refrigerator.

refrige'rare [refridʒe'rare] *vt* to refrigerate; (*rinfrescare*) to cool, refresh.

refrigerazi'one [refridʒerat'tsjone] *sf* refrigeration; (*TECN*) cooling; ~ **ad acqua** (*AUT*) water-cooling.

refri'gerio [refri'dʒɛrjo] *sm*: **trovare** ~ to find somewhere cool.

refur'tiva *sf* stolen goods *pl*.

Reg. *abbr* (= **reggimento**) Regt; (*AMM*) = **regolamento**.

rega'lare *vt* to give (as a present), make a present of.

re'gale *ag* regal.

re'galo *sm* gift, present ♦ *ag inv*: **confezione** ~ gift pack; **fare un** ~ **a qn** to give sb a present; **"articoli da** ~**"** "gifts".

re'gata *sf* regatta.

reg'gente [red'dʒɛnte] *ag* (*proposizione*) main; (*sovrano*) reigning ♦ *sm/f* regent; **principe** ~ prince regent.

reg'genza [red'dʒɛntsa] *sf* regency.

'reggere ['rɛddʒere] *vt* (*tenere*) to hold; (*sostenere*) to support, bear, hold up; (*portare*) to carry, bear; (*resistere*) to withstand; (*dirigere: impresa*) to manage, run; (*governare*) to rule, govern; (*LING*) to take, be followed by ♦ *vi* (*resistere*): ~ **a** to stand up to, hold out against; (*sopportare*): ~ **a** to stand; (*durare*) to last; (*fig: teoria etc*) to hold water; ~**rsi** *vr* (*stare ritto*) to stand; (*fig: dominarsi*) to control o.s.; ~**rsi sulle gambe** *o* **in piedi** to stand up.

'reggia, ge ['rɛddʒa] *sf* royal palace.

reggi'calze [reddʒi'kaltse] *sm inv* suspender belt.

reggi'mento [reddʒi'mento] *sm* (*MIL*) regiment.

reggi'petto [reddʒi'pɛtto] *sm*, **reggi'seno** [reddʒi'seno] *sm* bra.

re'gia, 'gie [re'dʒia] *sf* (*TV, CINE etc*) direction.

re'gime [re'dʒime] *sm* (*POL*) regime; (*DIR: aureo, patrimoniale etc*) system; (*MED*) diet; (*TECN*) (engine) speed; ~ **di giri** (*di motore*) revs *pl* per minute; ~ **vegetariano** vegetarian diet.

re'gina [re'dʒina] *sf* queen.

'regio, a, gi, gie ['rɛdʒo] *ag* royal.

regio'nale [redʒo'nale] *ag* regional.

regi'one [re'dʒone] *sf* (*gen*) region; (*territorio*) region, area.

The **Regione** is the main administrative unit in Italy. There are 20 of these, each being subdivided into **Province**, which in turn are divided into **Comuni**. Each **Regione** has a **capoluogo**, which is its chief **provincia**. For example, in the Regione of Tuscany, Florence is the chief **Provincia** and therefore the **capoluogo di regione**. The number of **province** in a **regione** varies. Five **regioni** have special status: Val d'Aosta, Friuli-Venezia Giulia, Trentino-Alto Adige, Sicily and Sardinia and these enjoy wider powers.

*The **Regione** is run by the Giunta regionale which is elected by the Consiglio regionale. Each of these two bodies is presided over by a Presidente. The Giunta regionale has legislative powers within the region over the police, public health, schools, town planning and agriculture. See also **Comune** and* **Provincia**.

re'gista, i, e [re'dʒista] *sm/f* (*TV, CINE etc*) director.

regis'trare [redʒis'trare] *vt* (*AMM*) to register; (*COMM*) to enter; (*notare*) to report, note; (*canzone, conversazione, sog: strumento di misura*) to record; (*mettere a punto*) to adjust, regulate; ~ **i bagagli** (*AER*) to check in one's luggage; ~ **i freni** (*TECN*) to adjust the brakes.

registra'tore [redʒistra'tore] *sm* (*strumento*) recorder, register; (*magnetofono*) tape recorder; ~ **di cassa** cash register; ~ **a cassette** cassette recorder; ~ **di volo** (*AER*) flight recorder, black box (*fam*).

registrazi'one [redʒistrat'tsjone] *sf* registration; entry; reporting; recording; adjustment; ~ **bagagli** (*AER*) check-in.

re'gistro [re'dʒistro] *sm* (*libro*) register; (*DIR*) registry; (*MUS, TECN*) register; (*COMM*): ~ (**di cassa**) ledger; **ufficio del** ~ registrar's office; ~ **di bordo** logbook; ~**i contabili** (account) books.

re'gnante [reɲ'ɲante] *ag* reigning, ruling ♦ *sm/f* ruler.

re'gnare [reɲ'ɲare] *vi* to reign, rule; (*fig*) to reign.

'regno ['reɲɲo] *sm* kingdom; (*periodo*) reign; (*fig*) realm; **il** ~ **animale/vegetale** the animal/vegetable kingdom; **il R~ Unito** the United Kingdom.

'regola *sf* rule; **a** ~ **d'arte** duly; perfectly; **essere in** ~ (*dipendente*) to be a registered employee; (*fig: essere pulito*) to be clean; **fare le cose in** ~ to do things properly; **avere le carte in** ~ (*gen*) to have one's papers in order; (*fig: essere adatto*) to be the right person; **per tua (norma e)** ~ for your information; **un'eccezione alla** ~ an exception to the rule.

rego'labile *ag* adjustable.

regolamen'tare *ag* (*distanza, velocità*) regulation *cpd*, proper; (*disposizione*) statutory ♦ *vt* (*gen*) to control; **entro il tempo** ~ within the time allowed, within the prescribed time.

regola'mento *sm* (*complesso di norme*) regulations *pl*; (*di debito*) settlement; ~ **di conti** (*fig*) settling of scores.

rego'lare *ag* regular; (*velocità*) steady;

(*superficie*) even; (*passo*) steady, even; (*in regola: documento*) in order ♦ *vt* to regulate, control; (*apparecchio*) to adjust, regulate; (*questione, conto, debito*) to settle; ~**rsi** *vr* (*moderarsi*): ~**rsi nel bere/ nello spendere** to control one's drinking/ spending; (*comportarsi*) to behave, act; **presentare** ~ **domanda** to apply through the proper channels; ~ **i conti** (*fig*) to settle old scores.

regolarità *sf inv* regularity; steadiness; evenness; (*nel pagare*) punctuality.

regolariz'zare [regolarid'dzare] *vt* (*posizione*) to regularize; (*debito*) to settle.

rego'lata *sf*: **darsi una** ~ to pull o.s. together.

regola'tezza [regola'tettsa] *sf* (*ordine*) orderliness; (*moderazione*) moderation.

rego'lato, a *ag* (*ordinato*) orderly; (*moderato*) moderate.

regola'tore *sm* (*TECN*) regulator; ~ **di frequenza/di volume** frequency/volume control.

'regolo *sm* ruler; ~ **calcolatore** slide rule.

regre'dire *vi* to regress.

regressi'one *sf* regression.

re'gresso *sm* (*fig: declino*) decline.

rei'etto, a *sm/f* outcast.

reincarnazi'one [reinkarnat'tsjone] *sf* reincarnation.

reinte'grare *vt* (*produzione*) to restore; (*energie*) to recover; (*dipendente*) to reinstate.

reintegrazi'one [reintegrat'tsjone] *sf* (*di produzione*) restoration; (*di dipendente*) reinstatement.

relativa'mente *av* relatively.

relatività *sf* relativity.

rela'tivo, a *ag* relative; (*attinente*) relevant; (*rispettivo*) respective; ~ **a** (*che concerne*) relating to, concerning; (*proporzionato*) in proportion to.

rela'tore, 'trice *sm/f* (*gen*) spokesman/ woman; (*INS: di tesi*) supervisor.

re'lax [re'laks] *sm* relaxation.

relazi'one [relat'tsjone] *sf* (*fra cose, persone*) relation(ship); (*resoconto*) report, account; ~**i** *sfpl* (*conoscenze*) connections; **essere in** ~ to be connected; **mettere in** ~ (*fatti, elementi*) to make the connection between; **in** ~ **a quanto detto prima** with regard to what has already been said; **essere in buone** ~**i con qn** to be on good terms with sb; **fare una** ~ to make a report, give an account; ~**i pubbliche (RP)** public relations (PR).

rele'gare *vt* to banish; (*fig*) to relegate.

religi'one [reli'dʒone] *sf* religion.

religi'oso, a [reli'dʒoso] *ag* religious ♦ *sm/f* monk/nun.

re'liquia *sf* relic.

re'litto *sm* wreck; (*fig*) down-and-out.

re'mainder [ri'meində*] *sm inv* (*libro*) remainder.

're'make ['riː'meik] *sm inv* (*CINE*) remake.

re'mare *vi* to row.

remini'scenze [reminiʃ'ʃɛntse] *sfpl* reminiscences.

remissi'one *sf* remission; (*deferenza*) submissiveness, compliance; ~ **del debito** remission of debt; ~ **di querela** (*DIR*) withdrawal of an action.

remissività *sf* submissiveness.

remis'sivo, a *ag* submissive, compliant.

'remo *sm* oar.

'remora *sf* (*poetico: indugio*) hesitation.

re'moto, a *ag* remote.

remune'rare *etc* = **rimunerare** *etc*.

'rena *sf* sand.

re'nale *ag* kidney *cpd*.

'rendere *vt* (*ridare*) to return, give back; (: *saluto etc*) to return; (*produrre*) to yield, bring in; (*esprimere, tradurre*) to render; (*far diventare*): ~ **qc possibile** to make sth possible ♦ *vi* (*fruttare: ditta*) to be profitable; (: *investimento, campo*) to yield, be productive; ~ **grazie a qn** to thank sb; ~ **omaggio a qn** to honour sb; ~ **un servizio a qn** to do sb a service; ~ **una testimonianza** to give evidence; ~ **la visita** to pay a return visit; **non so se rendo l'idea** I don't know whether I'm making myself clear; ~**rsi utile** to make o.s. useful; ~**rsi conto di qc** to realize sth.

rendi'conto *sm* (*rapporto*) report, account; (*AMM, COMM*) statement of account.

rendi'mento *sm* (*reddito*) yield; (*di manodopera, TECN*) efficiency; (*capacità di produrre*) output; (*di studenti*) performance.

'rendita *sf* (*di individuo*) private *o* unearned income; (*COMM*) revenue; ~ **annua** annuity; ~ **vitalizia** life annuity.

'rene *sm* kidney.

'reni *sfpl* back *sg*.

reni'tente *ag* reluctant, unwilling; ~ **ai consigli di qn** unwilling to follow sb's advice; **essere** ~ **alla leva** (*MIL*) to fail to report for military service.

'renna *sf* reindeer *inv*.

'Reno *sm*: **il** ~ the Rhine.

'reo, a *sm/f* (*DIR*) offender.

re'parto *sm* department, section; (*MIL*) detachment; ~ **acquisti** purchasing office.

repel'lente *ag* repulsive; (*CHIM: insettifugo*): **liquido** ~ (liquid) repellant.

repen'taglio [repen'taʎʎo] *sm*: **mettere a** ~ to jeopardize, risk.

repen'tino, a *ag* sudden, unexpected.

repe'ribile *ag* available.

repe'rire *vt* to find, trace.

re'perto *sm* (*ARCHEOLOGIA*) find; (*MED*) report; (*anche*: ~ **giudiziario**) exhibit.

reper'torio *sm* (*TEAT*) repertory; (*elenco*) index, (alphabetical) list.

'replica, che *sf* repetition; reply, answer; (*obiezione*) objection; (*TEAT, CINE*) repeat performance; (*copia*) replica.

repli'care *vt* (*ripetere*) to repeat; (*rispondere*) to answer, reply.

repor'tage [rəpɔr'taʒ] *sm inv* (*STAMPA*) report.

repressi'one *sf* repression.

repres'sivo, a *ag* repressive.

re'presso, a *pp di* **reprimere**.

re'primere *vt* to suppress, repress.

re'pubblica, che *sf* republic; **la R~ Democratica Tedesca (RDT)** the German Democratic Republic (GDR); **la R~ Federale Tedesca (RFT)** the Federal Republic of Germany (FRG); **la Prima/la Seconda R~** *terms used to refer to Italy before and after the political changes resulting from the 1994 elections; vedi anche* **Festa della Repubblica; Seconda Repubblica**.

repubbli'cano, a *ag, sm/f* republican.

repu'tare *vt* to consider, judge.

reputazi'one [reputat'tsjone] *sf* reputation; **farsi una cattiva** ~ to get o.s. a bad name.

'requie *sf* rest; **dare** ~ **a qn** to give sb some peace; **senza** ~ unceasingly.

'requiem *sm inv* (*preghiera*) requiem, prayer for the dead; (*fig: ufficio funebre*) requiem.

requi'sire *vt* to requisition.

requi'sito *sm* requirement; **avere i** ~**i necessari per un lavoro** to have the necessary qualifications for a job.

requisi'toria *sf* (*DIR*) closing speech (for the prosecution).

requisizi'one [rekwizit'tsjone] *sf* requisition.

'resa *sf* (*l'arrendersi*) surrender; (*restituzione, rendimento*) return; ~ **dei conti** rendering of accounts; (*fig*) day of reckoning.

re'scindere [reʃ'ʃindere] *vt* (*DIR*) to rescind, annul.

re'scisso, a [reʃ'ʃisso] *pp di* **rescindere**.

reset'tare *vt* (*INFORM*) to reset.

'resi *etc vb vedi* **rendere**.

resi'dente *ag* resident.
resi'denza [resi'dɛntsa] *sf* residence.
residenzi'ale [residen'tsjale] *ag* residential.
residu'ale *ag* residual.
re'siduo, a *ag* residual, remaining ♦ *sm* remainder; (*CHIM*) residue; **~i industriali** industrial waste *sg*.
'resina *sf* resin.
resis'tente *ag* (*che resiste*): **~ a** resistant to; (*forte*) strong; (*duraturo*) long-lasting, durable; **~ all'acqua** waterproof; **~ al caldo** heat-resistant; **~ al fuoco** fireproof; **~ al gelo** frost-resistant.
resis'tenza [resis'tɛntsa] *sf* (*gen*, *ELETTR*) resistance; (*di persona*: *fisica*) stamina, endurance; (*: mentale*) endurance, resistance; **opporre ~ (a)** to offer *o* put up resistance (to); (*decisione, scelta*) to show opposition (to).

*The **Resistenza** in Italy fought against both the Nazis and Fascists during the Second World War. It was particularly active after the fall of the Fascist government on July 25th 1943, during the German occupation and the period of Mussolini's Republic of Salò in Northern Italy. Members of the Resistance spanned the whole political spectrum and played a vital role in the Liberation and in the formation of the new democratic government.*

re'sistere *vi* to resist; **~ a** (*assalto, tentazioni*) to resist; (*dolore, sog*: *pianta*) to withstand; (*non patir danno*) to be resistant to.
resis'tito, a *pp di* **resistere**.
'reso, a *pp di* **rendere**.
reso'conto *sm* report, account.
respin'gente [respin'dʒɛnte] *sm* (*FERR*) buffer.
res'pingere [res'pindʒere] *vt* to drive back, repel; (*rifiutare*: *pacco, lettera*) to return; (*: invito*) to refuse; (*: proposta*) to reject, turn down; (*INS*: *bocciare*) to fail.
res'pinto, a *pp di* **respingere**.
respi'rare *vi* to breathe; (*fig*) to get one's breath; to breathe again ♦ *vt* to breathe (in), inhale.
respira'tore *sm* respirator.
respira'torio, a *ag* respiratory.
respirazi'one [respirat'tsjone] *sf* breathing; **~ artificiale** artificial respiration; **~ bocca a bocca** mouth-to-mouth resuscitation, kiss of life (*fam*).
res'piro *sm* breathing *no pl*; (*singolo atto*) breath; (*fig*) respite, rest; **mandare un ~ di sollievo** to give a sigh of relief;

trattenere il ~ to hold one's breath; **lavorare senza ~** to work non-stop; **di ampio ~** (*opera, lavoro*) far-reaching.
respon'sabile *ag* responsible ♦ *sm/f* person responsible; (*capo*) person in charge; **~ di** responsible for; (*DIR*) liable for.
responsabilità *sf inv* responsibility; (*legale*) liability; **assumere la ~ di** to take on the responsibility for; **affidare a qn la ~ di qc** to make sb responsible for sth; **~ patrimoniale** debt liability; **~ penale** criminal liability.
responsabiliz'zare [responsabilid'dzare] *vt*: **~ qn** to make sb feel responsible.
res'ponso *sm* answer; (*DIR*) verdict.
'ressa *sf* crowd, throng.
'ressi *etc vb vedi* **reggere**.
res'tare *vi* (*rimanere*) to remain, stay; (*diventare*): **~ orfano/cieco** to become *o* be left an orphan/become blind; (*trovarsi*): **~ sorpreso** to be surprised; (*avanzare*) to be left, remain; **~ d'accordo** to agree; **non resta più niente** there's nothing left; **restano pochi giorni** there are only a few days left; **che resti tra di noi** this is just between ourselves; **~ in buoni rapporti** to remain on good terms; **~ senza parole** to be left speechless.
restau'rare *vt* to restore.
restaura'tore, 'trice *sm/f* restorer.
restaurazi'one [restaurat'tsjone] *sf* (*POL*) restoration.
res'tauro *sm* (*di edifici etc*) restoration; **in ~** under repair; **sotto ~** (*dipinto*) being restored; **chiuso per ~i** closed for repairs.
res'tio, a, 'tii, 'tie *ag* restive; (*persona*): **~ a** reluctant to.
restitu'ire *vt* to return, give back; (*energie, forze*) to restore.
restituzi'one [restitut'tsjone] *sf* return; (*di soldi*) repayment.
'resto *sm* remainder, rest; (*denaro*) change; (*MAT*) remainder; **~i** *smpl* leftovers; (*di città*) remains; **del ~** moreover, besides; **~i mortali** (mortal) remains.
res'tringere [res'trindʒere] *vt* to reduce; (*vestito*) to take in; (*stoffa*) to shrink; (*fig*) to restrict, limit; **~rsi** *vr* (*strada*) to narrow; (*stoffa*) to shrink.
restrit'tivo, a *ag* restrictive.
restrizi'one [restrit'tsjone] *sf* restriction.
resurrezi'one [resurret'tsjone] *sf* = **risurrezione**.
resusci'tare [resuʃʃi'tare] *vt, vi* = **risuscitare**.
re'tata *sf* (*PESCA*) haul, catch; **fare una ~ di** (*fig*: *persone*) to round up.
'rete *sf* net; (*di recinzione*) wire netting;

(*AUT, FERR, di spionaggio etc*) network; (*fig*) trap, snare; **segnare una** ~ (*CALCIO*) to score a goal; ~ **ferroviaria/stradale/di distribuzione** railway/road/distribution network; ~ **del letto** (sprung) bed base; ~ **da pesca** fishing net; ~ **(televisiva)** (*sistema*) network; (*canale*) channel.

reti'cente [reti'tʃɛnte] *ag* reticent.

reti'cenza [reti'tʃɛntsa] *sf* reticence.

retico'lato *sm* grid; (*rete metallica*) wire netting; (*di filo spinato*) barbed wire fence.

'**retina** *sf* (*ANAT*) retina.

re'torico, a, ci, che *ag* rhetorical ♦ *sf* rhetoric.

retribu'ire *vt* to pay; (*premiare*) to reward; **un lavoro mal retribuito** a poorly-paid job.

retribu'tivo, a *ag* pay *cpd*.

retribuzi'one [retribut'tsjone] *sf* payment; reward.

re'trivo, a *ag* (*fig*) reactionary.

'**retro** *sm inv* back ♦ *av* (*dietro*): **vedi** ~ see over(leaf).

retroattività *sf* retroactivity.

retroat'tivo, a *ag* (*DIR: legge*) retroactive; (*AMM: salario*) backdated.

retrobot'tega, ghe *sf* back shop.

retro'cedere [retro'tʃɛdere] *vi* to withdraw ♦ *vt* (*CALCIO*) to relegate; (*MIL*) to degrade; (*AMM*) to demote.

retrocessi'one [retrotʃes'sjone] *sf* (*di impiegato*) demotion.

retro'cesso, a [retro'tʃɛsso] *pp di* **retrocedere**.

retroda'tare *vt* (*AMM*) to backdate.

re'trogrado, a *ag* (*fig*) reactionary, backward-looking.

retrogu'ardia *sf* (*anche fig*) rearguard.

retro'marcia [retro'martʃa] *sf* (*AUT*) reverse; (: *dispositivo*) reverse gear.

retro'scena [retroʃ'ʃɛna] *sf inv* (*TEAT*) backstage ♦ *sm inv* (*fig*) behind-the-scenes activity.

retrospet'tivo, a *ag* retrospective ♦ *sf* (*ARTE*) retrospective (exhibition).

retros'tante *ag*: ~ **(a)** at the back (of).

retro'terra *sm* hinterland.

retro'via *sf* (*MIL*) zone behind the front; **mandare nelle** ~**e** to send to the rear.

retrovi'sore *sm* (*AUT*) (rear-view) mirror.

'**retta** *sf* (*MAT*) straight line; (*di convitto*) charge for bed and board; (*fig: ascolto*): **dar** ~ **a** to listen to, pay attention to.

rettango'lare *ag* rectangular.

ret'tangolo, a *ag* right-angled ♦ *sm* rectangle.

ret'tifica, che *sf* rectification, correction.

rettifi'care *vt* (*curva*) to straighten; (*fig*) to rectify, correct.

'**rettile** *sm* reptile.

retti'lineo *ag* rectilinear.

retti'tudine *sf* rectitude, uprightness.

'**retto, a** *pp di* **reggere** ♦ *ag* straight; (*MAT*): **angolo** ~ right angle; (*onesto*) honest, upright; (*giusto, esatto*) correct, proper, right.

ret'tore *sm* (*REL*) rector; (*di università*) ≈ chancellor.

reuma'tismo *sm* rheumatism.

Rev. *abbr* (= *Reverendo*) Rev(d).

reve'rendo, a *ag*: **il** ~ **padre Belli** the Reverend Father Belli.

reve'rente *ag* = **riverente**.

reve'renza [reve'rɛntsa] *sf* = **riverenza**.

rever'sibile *ag* reversible.

revisio'nare *vt* (*conti*) to audit; (*TECN*) to overhaul, service; (*DIR: processo*) to review; (*componimento*) to revise.

revisi'one *sf* auditing *no pl*; audit; servicing *no pl*; overhaul; review; revision; ~ **di bilancio** audit; ~ **di bozze** proofreading; ~ **contabile interna** internal audit.

revi'sore *sm*: ~ **di conti/bozze** auditor/ proofreader.

'**revoca** *sf* revocation.

revo'care *vt* to revoke.

re'volver *sm inv* revolver.

revolve'rata *sf* revolver shot.

'**Reykjavik** ['reikjavik] *sf* Reykjavik.

RFT *sigla f vedi* **Repubblica Federale Tedesca**.

ri'abbia *etc vb vedi* **riavere**.

riabili'tare *vt* to rehabilitate; (*fig*) to restore to favour (*BRIT*) *o* favor (*US*).

riabilitazi'one [riabilitat'tsjone] *sf* rehabilitation.

riac'cendere [riat'tʃɛndere] *vt* (*sigaretta, fuoco, gas*) to light again; (*luce, radio, TV*) to switch on again; (*fig: sentimenti, interesse*) to rekindle, revive; ~**rsi** *vr* (*fuoco*) to catch again; (*luce, radio, TV*) to come back on again; (*fig: sentimenti*) to revive, be rekindled.

riac'ceso, a [riat'tʃeso] *pp di* **riaccendere**.

riacqui'stare *vt* (*gen*) to buy again; (*ciò che si era venduto*) to buy back; (*fig: buonumore, sangue freddo, libertà*) to regain; ~ **la salute** to recover (one's health); ~ **le forze** to regain one's strength.

Ri'ad *sf* Riyadh.

riaddormen'tare *vt* to put to sleep again; ~**rsi** *vr* to fall asleep again.

riallac'ciare [riallat'tʃare] *vt* (*cintura, cavo etc*) to refasten, tie up *o* fasten again; (*fig: rapporti, amicizia*) to resume, renew; ~**rsi**

vr: ~**rsi a** (*fig: a discorso, tema*) to resume, take up again.

rial'zare [rial'tsare] *vt* to raise, lift; (*alzare di più*) to heighten, raise; (*aumentare: prezzi*) to increase, raise ♦ *vi* (*prezzi*) to rise, increase.

rial'zato, a [rial'tsato] *ag:* **piano** ~ mezzanine, entresol.

rial'zista, i [rial'tsista] *sm* (*BORSA*) bull.

ri'alzo [ri'altso] *sm* (*di prezzi*) increase, rise; (*sporgenza*) rise; **giocare al** ~ (*BORSA*) to bull.

rian'dare *vi:* ~ **(in)**, ~ **(a)** to go back (to), return (to).

riani'mare *vt* (*MED*) to resuscitate; (*fig: rallegrare*) to cheer up; (: *dar coraggio*) to give heart to; ~**rsi** *vr* to recover consciousness; to cheer up; to take heart.

rianimazi'one [rianimat'tsjone] *sf* (*MED*) resuscitation; **centro di** ~ intensive care unit.

ria'perto, a *pp di* **riaprire.**

riaper'tura *sf* reopening.

riappa'rire *vi* to reappear.

riap'parso, a *pp di* **riapparire.**

riap'pendere *vt* to rehang; (*TEL*) to hang up.

ria'prire *vt*, ~**rsi** *vr* to reopen, open again.

ri'armo *sm* (*MIL*) rearmament.

ri'arso, a *ag* (*terreno*) arid; (*gola*) parched; (*labbra*) dry.

riasset'tare *vt* (*vedi sm*) to rearrange; to reorganize.

rias'setto *sm* (*di stanza etc*) rearrangement; (*ordinamento*) reorganization.

rias'sumere *vt* (*riprendere*) to resume; (*impiegare di nuovo*) to re-employ; (*sintetizzare*) to summarize.

rias'sunto, a *pp di* **riassumere** ♦ *sm* summary.

riattac'care *vt* (*attaccare di nuovo*): ~ **(a)** (*manifesto, francobollo*) to stick back (on); (*bottone*) to sew back (on); (*quadro, chiavi*) to hang back up (on); ~ **(il telefono o il ricevitore)** to hang up (the receiver).

riatti'vare *vt* to reactivate.

ria'vere *vt* to have again; (*avere indietro*) to get back; (*riacquistare*) to recover; ~**rsi** *vr* to recover; (*da svenimento, stordimento*) to come round.

riba'dire *vt* (*fig*) to confirm.

ri'balta *sf* (*sportello*) flap; (*TEAT: proscenio*) front of the stage; (: *apparecchio d'illuminazione*) footlights *pl*; (*fig*) limelight; **tornare alla** ~ (*personaggio*) to make a comeback; (*problema*) to come up again.

ribal'tabile *ag* (*sedile*) tip-up.

ribal'tare *vt*, *vi* (*anche:* ~**rsi**) to turn over, tip over.

ribas'sare *vt* to lower, bring down ♦ *vi* to come down, fall.

ribas'sista, i *sm* (*BORSA*) bear.

ri'basso *sm* reduction, fall; **essere in** ~ (*azioni, prezzi*) to be down; (*fig: popolarità*) to be on the decline; **giocare al** ~ (*BORSA*) to bear.

ri'battere *vt* (*battere di nuovo*) to beat again; (*con macchina da scrivere*) to type again; (*palla*) to return; (*confutare*) to refute; ~ **che** to retort that.

ribattez'zare [ribatted'dzare] *vt* to rename.

ribel'larsi *vr:* ~ **(a)** to rebel (against).

ri'belle *ag* (*soldati*) rebel; (*ragazzo*) rebellious ♦ *smf* rebel.

ribelli'one *sf* rebellion.

'ribes *sm inv* currant; ~ **nero** blackcurrant; ~ **rosso** redcurrant.

ribol'lire *vi* (*fermentare*) to ferment; (*fare bolle*) to bubble, boil; (*fig*) to seethe.

ri'brezzo [ri'breddzo] *sm* disgust, loathing; **far** ~ **a** to disgust.

ribut'tante *ag* disgusting, revolting.

ricacci'are [rikat'tʃare] *vt* (*respingere*) to drive back; ~ **qn fuori** to throw sb out.

rica'dere *vi* to fall again; (*scendere a terra, fig: nel peccato etc*) to fall back; (*vestiti, capelli etc*) to hang (down); (*riversarsi: fatiche, colpe*): ~ **su** to fall on.

rica'duta *sf* (*MED*) relapse.

rical'care *vt* (*disegni*) to trace; (*fig*) to follow faithfully.

ricalci'trare [rikaltʃi'trare] *vi* (*cavalli, asini, muli*) to kick.

rica'mare *vt* to embroider.

ricambi'are *vt* to change again; (*contraccambiare*) to return.

ri'cambio *sm* exchange, return; (*FISIOL*) metabolism; ~**i** *smpl*, **pezzi di** ~ spare parts; ~ **della manodopera** labour turnover.

ri'camo *sm* embroidery; **senza** ~**i** (*fig*) without frills.

ricapito'lare *vt* to recapitulate, sum up.

ricapitolazi'one [rikapitolat'tsjone] *sf* recapitulation, summary.

ricari'care *vt* (*arma, macchina fotografica*) to reload; (*penna*) to refill; (*orologio, giocattolo*) to rewind; (*ELETTR*) to recharge.

ricat'tare *vt* to blackmail.

ricatta'tore, 'trice *smf* blackmailer.

ri'catto *sm* blackmail; **fare un** ~ **a qn** to blackmail sb; **subire un** ~ to be blackmailed.

rica'vare *vt* (*estrarre*) to draw out, extract;

(*ottenere*) to obtain, gain.

rica'vato *sm* (*di vendite*) proceeds *pl*.

ri'cavo *sm* proceeds *pl*; (*CONTABILITÀ*) revenue.

ric'chezza [rik'kettsa] *sf* wealth; (*fig*) richness; **~e** *sfpl* (*beni*) wealth *sg*, riches; **~e naturali** natural resources.

'**riccio, a, ci, ce** ['rittʃo] *ag* curly ◆ *sm* (*ZOOL*) hedgehog; (: *anche*: ~ **di mare**) sea urchin.

'**ricciolo** ['rittʃolo] *sm* curl.

ricci'uto, a [rit'tʃuto] *ag* curly.

'**ricco, a, chi, che** *ag* rich; (*persona, paese*) rich, wealthy ◆ *sm/f* rich man/woman; **i ~chi** the rich; ~ **di** (*idee, illustrazioni etc*) full of; (*risorse, fauna etc*) rich in.

ri'cerca, che [ri'tʃerka] *sf* search; (*indagine*) investigation, inquiry; (*studio*): **la ~** research; **una ~** piece of research; **mettersi alla ~ di** to go in search of, look *o* search *o* hunt for; **essere alla ~ di** to be searching for, be looking for; ~ **di mercato** market research; ~ **operativa** operational research.

ricer'care [ritʃer'kare] *vt* (*motivi, cause*) to look for, try to determine; (*successo, piacere*) to pursue; (*onore, gloria*) to seek.

ricerca'tezza [ritʃerka'tettsa] *sf* (*raffinatezza*) refinement; (: *peg*) affectation.

ricer'cato, a [ritʃer'kato] *ag* (*apprezzato*) much sought-after; (*affettato*) studied, affected ◆ *sm/f* (*POLIZIA*) wanted man/woman.

ricerca'tore, 'trice [ritʃerka'tore] *sm/f* (*INS*) researcher.

ricetrasmit'tente [ritʃetrazmit'tɛnte] *sf* two-way radio, transceiver.

ri'cetta [ri'tʃetta] *sf* (*MED*) prescription; (*CUC*) recipe; (*fig*: *antidoto*): ~ **contro** remedy for.

ricet'tacolo [ritʃet'takolo] *sm* (*peg*: *luogo malfamato*) den.

ricet'tario [ritʃet'tarjo] *sm* (*MED*) prescription pad; (*CULIN*) recipe book.

ricetta'tore, 'trice [ritʃetta'tore] *sm/f* (*DIR*) receiver (of stolen goods).

ricettazi'one [ritʃettat'tsjone] *sf* (*DIR*) receiving (stolen goods).

ricet'tivo, a [ritʃet'tivo] *ag* receptive.

rice'vente [ritʃe'vɛnte] *ag* (*RADIO, TV*) receiving ◆ *sm/f* (*COMM*) receiver.

ri'cevere [ri'tʃevere] *vt* to receive; (*stipendio, lettera*) to get, receive; (*accogliere*: *ospite*) to welcome; (*vedere*: *cliente, rappresentante etc*) to see; "**confermiamo di aver ricevuto tale merce**" (*COMM*) "we acknowledge receipt

of these goods".

ricevi'mento [ritʃevi'mento] *sm* receiving *no pl*; (*trattenimento*) reception; **al ~ della merce** on receipt of the goods.

ricevi'tore [ritʃevi'tore] *sm* (*TECN*) receiver; ~ **delle imposte** tax collector.

ricevito'ria [ritʃevito'ria] *sf* (*FISCO*): ~ (**delle imposte**) Inland Revenue (*BRIT*) *o* Internal Revenue (*US*) Office; ~ **del lotto** lottery office.

rice'vuta [ritʃe'vuta] *sf* receipt; **accusare ~ di qc** (*COMM*) to acknowledge receipt of sth; ~ **fiscale** official receipt (for tax purposes); ~ **di ritorno** (*POSTA*) advice of receipt; ~ **di versamento** receipt of payment.

ricezi'one [ritʃet'tsjone] *sf* (*RADIO, TV*) reception.

richia'mare [rikja'mare] *vt* (*chiamare indietro, ritelefonare*) to call back; (*ambasciatore, truppe*) to recall; (*rimproverare*) to reprimand; (*attirare*) to attract, draw; **~rsi** *vr*: **~rsi a** (*riferirsi a*) to refer to; ~ **qn all'ordine** to call sb to order; **desidero ~ la vostra attenzione su** ... I would like to draw your attention to ....

richi'amo [ri'kjamo] *sm* call; recall; reprimand; attraction.

richie'dente [rikje'dɛnte] *sm/f* applicant.

richi'edere [ri'kjɛdere] *vt* to ask again for; (*chiedere indietro*): ~ **qc** to ask for sth back; (*chiedere*: *per sapere*) to ask; (: *per avere*) to ask for; (*AMM*: *documenti*) to apply for; (*esigere*) to need, require; **essere molto richiesto** to be in great demand.

richi'esto, a [ri'kjɛsto] *pp di* **richiedere** ◆ *sf* (*domanda*) request; (*AMM*) application, request; (*esigenza*) demand, request; **a ~a** on request.

rici'claggio [ritʃi'kladdʒo] *sm* (*fig*) laundering; ~ **di materiale** recycling; ~ **di denaro sporco** money laundering.

rici'clare [ritʃi'klare] *vt* (*vetro, carta, bottiglie*) to recycle; (*fig*: *personale*) to retrain.

'**ricino** ['ritʃino] *sm*: **olio di ~** castor oil.

ricogni'tore [rikoɲɲi'tore] *sm* (*AER*) reconnaissance aircraft.

ricognizi'one [rikoɲɲit'tsjone] *sf* (*MIL*) reconnaissance; (*DIR*) recognition, acknowledgement.

ricolle'gare *vt* (*collegare nuovamente*: *gen*) to join again, link again; (*connettere*: *fatti*): ~ (**a, con**) to connect (with); **~rsi** *vr*: **~rsi a** (*sog*: *fatti*: *connettersi*) to be connected to; (: *persona*: *riferirsi*) to refer to.

ri'colmo, a *ag*: ~ (**di**) (*bicchiere*) full to the

brim (with); (*stanza*) full (of).

ricominci'are [rikomin'tʃare] *vt, vi* to start again, begin again; ~ **a fare qc** to begin doing *o* to do sth again, start doing *o* to do sth again.

ricom'pensa *sf* reward.

ricompen'sare *vt* to reward.

ricom'porsi *vr* to compose o.s., regain one's composure.

ricom'posto, a *pp di* **ricomporsi.**

riconcili'are [rikontʃi'ljare] *vt* to reconcile; ~**rsi** *vr* to be reconciled.

riconciliazi'one [rikontʃiliat'tsjone] *sf* reconciliation.

ricon'dotto, a *pp di* **ricondurre.**

ricon'durre *vt* to bring (*o* take) back.

ricon'ferma *sf* reconfirmation.

riconfer'mare *vt* to reconfirm.

ricono'scente [rikonoʃ'ʃɛnte] *ag* grateful.

ricono'scenza [rikonoʃ'ʃɛntsa] *sf* gratitude.

rico'noscere [riko'noʃʃere] *vt* to recognize; (*DIR: figlio, debito*) to acknowledge; (*ammettere: errore*) to admit, acknowledge; ~ **qn colpevole** to find sb guilty.

riconosci'mento [rikonoʃʃi'mento] *sm* recognition; acknowledgment; (*identificazione*) identification; **come ~ dei servizi resi** in recognition of services rendered; **documento di ~** means of identification; **segno di ~** distinguishing mark.

riconosci'uto, a [rikonoʃ'ʃuto] *pp di* **riconoscere.**

riconquis'tare *vt* (*MIL*) to reconquer; (*libertà, stima*) to win back.

rico'perto, a *pp di* **ricoprire.**

ricopi'are *vt* to copy.

rico'prire *vt* to re-cover; (*coprire*) to cover; (*occupare: carica*) to hold.

ricor'dare *vt* to remember, recall; (*richiamare alla memoria*): ~ **qc a qn** to remind sb of sth; ~**rsi** *vr*: ~**rsi (di)** to remember; ~**rsi di qc/di aver fatto** to remember sth/having done.

ri'cordo *sm* memory; (*regalo*) keepsake, souvenir; (*di viaggio*) souvenir; ~**i** *smpl* (*memorie*) memoirs.

ricor'rente *ag* recurrent, recurring.

ricor'renza [rikor'rɛntsa] *sf* recurrence; (*festività*) anniversary.

ri'correre *vi* (*ripetersi*) to recur; ~ **a** (*rivolgersi*) to turn to; (: *DIR*) to appeal to; (*servirsi di*) to have recourse to; ~ **in appello** to lodge an appeal.

ri'corso, a *pp di* **ricorrere** ♦ *sm* recurrence; (*DIR*) appeal; **far ~ a = ricorrere a.**

ricostitu'ente *ag* (*MED*): **cura ~** tonic treatment ♦ *sm* (*MED*) tonic.

ricostitu'ire *vt* (*società*) to build up again; (*governo, partito*) to re-form; ~**rsi** *vr* (*gruppo etc*) to re-form.

ricostru'ire *vt* (*casa*) to rebuild; (*fatti*) to reconstruct.

ricostruzi'one [rikostrut'tsjone] *sf* rebuilding *no pl*; reconstruction.

ri'cotta *sf soft white unsalted cheese made from sheep's milk.*

ricove'rare *vt* to give shelter to; ~ **qn in ospedale** to admit sb to hospital.

ricove'rato, a *sm/f* patient.

ri'covero *sm* shelter, refuge; (*MIL*) shelter; (*MED*) admission (to hospital); ~ **antiaereo** air-raid shelter.

ricre'are *vt* to recreate; (*rinvigorire*) to restore; (*fig: distrarre*) to amuse.

ricrea'tivo, a *ag* recreational.

ricreazi'one [rikreat'tsjone] *sf* recreation, entertainment; (*INS*) break.

ri'credersi *vr* to change one's mind.

ricupe'rare *vt* (*rientrare in possesso di*) to recover, get back; (*tempo perduto*) to make up for; (*NAUT*) to salvage; (: *naufraghi*) to rescue; (*delinquente*) to rehabilitate; ~ **lo svantaggio** (*SPORT*) to close the gap.

ri'cupero *sm* (*gen*) recovery; (*di relitto etc*) salvaging; **capacità di ~** resilience.

ricu'sare *vt* to refuse.

ridacchi'are [ridak'kjare] *vi* to snigger.

ri'dare *vt* to return, give back.

'ridda *sf* (*di ammiratori etc*) swarm; (*di pensieri*) jumble.

ri'dente *ag* (*occhi, volto*) smiling; (*paesaggio*) delightful.

'ridere *vi* to laugh; (*deridere, beffare*): ~ **di** to laugh at, make fun of; **non c'è niente da ~, c'è poco da ~** it's not a laughing matter.

rides'tare *vt* (*fig: ricordi, passioni*) to reawaken.

ri'detto, a *pp di* **ridire.**

ridico'laggine [ridiko'laddʒine] *sf* (*di situazione*) absurdity; (*cosa detta o fatta*) nonsense *no pl*.

ridicoliz'zare [ridikolid'dzare] *vt* to ridicule.

ri'dicolo, a *ag* ridiculous, absurd ♦ *sm*: **cadere nel ~** to become ridiculous; **rendersi ~** to make a fool of o.s.

ridimensiona'mento *sm* reorganization; (*di fatto storico*) reappraisal.

ridimensio'nare *vt* to reorganize; (*fig*) to see in the right perspective.

ri'dire *vt* to repeat; (*criticare*) to find fault with; to object to; **trova sempre qualcosa da ~** he always manages to find fault.

ridon'dante *ag* redundant.

ri'dosso *sm*: a ~ di (*dietro*) behind; (*contro*) against.

ri'dotto, a *pp di* ridurre.

ri'duco *etc vb vedi* ridurre.

ri'durre *vt* (*anche CHIM, MAT*) to reduce; (*prezzo, spese*) to cut, reduce; (*accorciare: opera letteraria*) to abridge; (: *RADIO, TV*) to adapt; ridursi *vr* (*diminuirsi*) to be reduced, shrink; ridursi a to be reduced to; ridursi a pelle e ossa to be reduced to skin and bone.

ri'dussi *etc vb vedi* ridurre.

ridut'tore *sm* (*TECN, CHIM, ELETTR*) reducer.

riduzi'one [ridut'tsjone] *sf* reduction; abridgement; adaptation.

ri'ebbi *etc vb vedi* riavere.

riecheg'giare [rieked'dʒare] *vi* to re-echo.

riedu'care *vt* (*persona, arto*) to re-educate; (*malato*) to rehabilitate.

rieducazi'one [riedukat'tsjone] *sf* re-education; rehabilitation; centro di ~ rehabilitation centre.

rie'leggere [rie'lɛddʒere] *vt* to re-elect.

rie'letto, a *pp di* rieleggere.

riempi'mento *sm* filling (up).

riem'pire *vt* to fill (up); (*modulo*) to fill in *o* out; ~rsi *vr* to fill (up); (*mangiare troppo*) to stuff o.s.; ~ qc di to fill sth (up) with.

riempi'tivo, a *ag* filling ♦ *sm* (*anche fig*) filler.

rien'tranza [rien'trantsa] *sf* recess; indentation.

rien'trare *vi* (*entrare di nuovo*) to go (*o* come) back in; (*tornare*) to return; (*fare una rientranza*) to go in, curve inwards; to be indented; (*riguardare*): ~ in to be included among, form part of; ~ (a casa) to get back home; non rientriamo nelle spese we are not within our budget.

ri'entro *sm* (*ritorno*) return; (*di astronave*) re-entry; è iniziato il grande ~ (*estivo*) people are coming back from their (summer) holidays.

riepilo'gare *vt* to summarize ♦ *vi* to recapitulate.

rie'pilogo, ghi *sm* recapitulation; fare un ~ di qc to summarize sth.

rie'same *sm* re-examination.

riesami'nare *vt* to re-examine.

ri'esco *etc vb vedi* riuscire.

ri'essere *vi*: ci risiamo! (*fam*) we're back to this again!

rievo'care *vt* (*passato*) to recall; (*commemorare: figura, meriti*) to commemorate.

rievocazi'one [rievokat'tsjone] *sf* (*vedi vt*) recalling; commemoration.

rifaci'mento [rifatʃi'mento] *sm* (*di film*) remake; (*di opera letteraria*) rehashing.

ri'fare *vt* to do again; (*ricostruire*) to make again; (*nodo*) to tie again, do up again; (*imitare*) to imitate, copy; ~rsi *vr* (*risarcirsi*): ~rsi di to make up for; (*vendicarsi*): ~rsi di qc su qn to get one's own back on sb for sth; (*riferirsi*): ~rsi a (*periodo, fenomeno storico*) to go back to; ~ il letto to make the bed; ~rsi una vita to make a new life for o.s.

ri'fatto, a *pp di* rifare.

riferi'mento *sm* reference; in *o* con ~ a with reference to; far ~ a to refer to.

rife'rire *vt* (*riportare*) to report; (*ascrivere*): ~ qc a to attribute sth to ♦ *vi* to do a report; ~rsi *vr*: ~rsi a to refer to; riferirò I'll pass on the message.

rifi'lare *vt* (*tagliare a filo*) to trim; (*fam: affibbiare*): ~ qc a qn to palm sth off on sb.

rifi'nire *vt* to finish off, put the finishing touches to.

rifini'tura *sf* finishing touch; ~e *sfpl* (*di mobile, auto*) finish *sg*.

rifiu'tare *vt* to refuse; ~ di fare to refuse to do.

rifi'uto *sm* refusal; ~i *smpl* (*spazzatura*) rubbish *sg*, refuse *sg*; ~i solidi urbani solid urban waste *sg*.

riflessi'one *sf* (*FISICA*) reflection; (*il pensare*) thought, reflection; (*osservazione*) remark.

rifles'sivo, a *ag* (*persona*) thoughtful, reflective; (*LING*) reflexive.

ri'flesso, a *pp di* riflettere ♦ *sm* (*di luce, su specchio*) reflection; (*FISIOL*) reflex; (*su capelli*) light; (*fig*) effect; di *o* per ~ indirectly; avere i ~i pronti to have quick reflexes.

ri'flettere *vt* to reflect ♦ *vi* to think; ~rsi *vr* to be reflected; (*ripercuotersi*): ~rsi su to have repercussions on; ~ su to think over.

riflet'tore *sm* reflector; (*proiettore*) floodlight; (: *MIL*) searchlight.

ri'flusso *sm* flowing back; (*della marea*) ebb; un'epoca di ~ an era of nostalgia.

rifocil'larsi [rifotʃil'larsi] *vr* (*poetico*) to take refreshment.

rifondazi'one [rifondat'tsjone] *sf* (*POL*): R~ Comunista *hard left party, originating from former P.C.I.*

ri'fondere *vt* (*rimborsare*) to refund, repay; ~ le spese a qn to refund sb's expenses; ~ i danni a qn to compensate sb for damages.

ri'forma *sf* reform; (*MIL*) declaration of unfitness for service; discharge (*on*

health grounds); **la R~** (REL) the
Reformation.
rifor'mare vt to re-form; (cambiare,
innovare) to reform; (MIL: recluta) to
declare unfit for service; (: soldato) to
invalid out, discharge.
riforma'tore, 'trice ag reforming ♦ sm/f
reformer.
riforma'torio sm (DIR) community home
(BRIT), reformatory (US).
rifor'mista, i, e ag, sm/f reformist.
riforni'mento sm supplying; providing;
restocking; (di carburante) refuelling; **~i**
smpl supplies, provisions; **fare ~ di** (viveri)
to stock up with; (benzina) to fill up with;
posto di ~ filling o gas (US) station.
rifor'nire vt (provvedere): **~ di** to supply o
provide with; (fornire di nuovo: casa etc) to
restock.
ri'frangere [ri'frandʒere] vt to refract.
ri'fratto, a pp di **rifrangere.**
rifrazi'one [rifrat'tsjone] sf refraction.
rifug'gire [rifud'dʒire] vi to escape again;
(fig): **~ da** to shun.
rifugi'arsi [rifu'dʒarsi] vr to take refuge.
rifugi'ato, a [rifu'dʒato] sm/f refugee.
ri'fugio [ri'fudʒo] sm refuge, shelter; (in
montagna) shelter; **~ antiaereo** air-raid
shelter.
ri'fuso, a pp di **rifondere.**
'riga, ghe sf line; (striscia) stripe; (di
persone, cose) line, row; (regolo) ruler;
(scriminatura) parting; **mettersi in ~** to
line up; **a ~ghe** (foglio) lined; (vestito)
striped; **buttare giù due ~ghe** (note) to jot
down a few notes; **mandami due ~ghe**
appena arrivi drop me a line as soon as
you arrive.
ri'gagnolo [ri'ɡaɲɲolo] sm rivulet.
ri'gare vt (foglio) to rule ♦ vi: **~ diritto** (fig)
to toe the line.
riga'toni smpl (CUC) short, ridged pasta
shapes.
rigatti'ere sm junk dealer.
riga'tura sf (di pagina, quaderno) lining,
ruling; (di fucile) rifling.
rigene'rare [ridʒene'rare] vt (gen, TECN) to
regenerate; (forze) to restore; (gomma) to
retread; **~rsi** vr (gen) to regenerate;
(ramo, tumore) to regenerate, grow again;
gomma rigenerata retread.
rigenerazi'one [ridʒenerat'tsjone] sf
regeneration.
riget'tare [ridʒet'tare] vt (gettare indietro) to
throw back; (fig: respingere) to reject;
(vomitare) to bring o throw up.
ri'getto [ri'dʒetto] sm (anche MED)
rejection.

ri'ghello [ri'ɡɛllo] sm ruler.
righerò etc [rige'rɔ] vb vedi **rigare.**
rigi'dezza [ridʒi'dettsa], **rigidità** [ridʒidi'ta]
sf rigidity; stiffness; severity, rigours pl
(BRIT), rigors pl (US); strictness.
'rigido, a ['ridʒido] ag rigid, stiff; (membra
etc: indurite) stiff; (METEOR) harsh, severe;
(fig) strict.
rigi'rare [ridʒi'rare] vt to turn; **~rsi** vr to
turn round; (nel letto) to turn over; **~ qc
tra le mani** to turn sth over in one's
hands; **~ il discorso** to change the
subject.
'rigo, ghi sm line; (MUS) staff, stave.
rigogli'oso, a [riɡoʎ'ʎoso] ag (pianta)
luxuriant; (fig: commercio, sviluppo)
thriving.
rigonfia'mento sm (ANAT) swelling; (su
legno, intonaco etc) bulge.
ri'gonfio, a ag swollen; (grembiule, sporta):
~ di bulging with.
ri'gore sm (METEOR) harshness, rigours pl
(BRIT), rigors pl (US); (fig) severity,
strictness; (anche: calcio di ~) penalty; **di
~ compulsory; "è di ~ l'abito da sera"**
"evening dress"; **area di ~** (CALCIO)
penalty box (BRIT); **a rigor di termini**
strictly speaking.
rigorosità sf strictness; rigour (BRIT), rigor
(US).
rigo'roso, a ag (severo: persona, ordine)
strict; (preciso) rigorous.
rigover'nare vt to wash (up).
riguar'dare vt to look at again;
(considerare) to regard, consider;
(concernere) to regard, concern; **~rsi** vr
(aver cura di sé) to look after o.s.; **per quel
che mi riguarda** as far as I'm concerned;
sono affari che non ti riguardano it's none
of your business.
rigu'ardo sm (attenzione) care;
(considerazione) regard, respect; **~ a**
concerning, with regard to; **per ~ a** out
of respect for; **ospite/persona di ~** very
important guest/person; **non aver ~i**
nell'agire/nel parlare to act/speak freely.
riguar'doso, a ag (rispettoso) respectful;
(premuroso) considerate, thoughtful.
rigurgi'tare [rigurdʒi'tare] vi (liquido): **~ da**
to gush out from; (recipiente: traboccare):
~ di to overflow with.
ri'gurgito [ri'gurdʒito] sm (MED)
regurgitation; (fig: ritorno, risveglio)
revival.
rilanci'are [rilan'tʃare] vt (lanciare di nuovo:
gen) to throw again; (: moda) to bring
back; (: prodotto) to re-launch; **~
un'offerta** (asta) to make a higher bid.

ri'lancio [ri'lantʃo] *sm* (*CARTE, di offerta*) raising.

rilasci'are [rilaʃ'ʃare] *vt* (*rimettere in libertà*) to release; (*AMM: documenti*) to issue; (*intervista*) to give; ~ **delle dichiarazioni** to make a statement.

ri'lascio [ri'laʃʃo] *sm* release; issue.

rilassa'mento *sm* (*gen, MED*) relaxation.

rilas'sare *vt* to relax; ~**rsi** *vr* to relax; (*fig: disciplina*) to become slack.

rilassa'tezza [rilassa'tettsa] *sf* (*fig: di costumi, disciplina*) laxity.

rilas'sato, a *ag* (*persona, muscoli*) relaxed; (*disciplina, costumi*) lax.

rile'gare *vt* (*libro*) to bind.

rilega'tura *sf* binding.

ri'leggere [ri'lɛddʒere] *vt* to reread, read again; (*rivedere*) to read over.

ri'lento: a ~ *av* slowly.

ri'letto, a *pp di* **rileggere**.

rilet'tura *sf* (*vedi vt*) rereading; reading over.

rileva'mento *sm* (*topografico, statistico*) survey; (*NAUT*) bearing.

rile'vante *ag* considerable; important.

rile'vanza [rile'vantsa] *sf* importance.

rile'vare *vt* (*ricavare*) to find; (*notare*) to notice; (*mettere in evidenza*) to point out; (*venire a conoscere: notizia*) to learn; (*raccogliere: dati*) to gather, collect; (*TOPOGRAFIA*) to survey; (*MIL*) to relieve; (*COMM*) to take over.

rilevazi'one [rilevat'tsjone] *sf* survey.

rili'evo *sm* (*ARTE, GEO*) relief; (*fig: rilevanza*) importance; (*osservazione*) point, remark; (*TOPOGRAFIA*) survey; **dar** ~ **a** *o* **mettere in** ~ **qc** (*fig*) to bring sth out, highlight sth; **di poco/nessun** ~ (*fig*) of little/no importance; **un personaggio di** ~ an important person.

rilut'tante *ag* reluctant.

rilut'tanza [rilut'tantsa] *sf* reluctance.

'rima *sf* rhyme; (*verso*) verse; **far** ~ **con** to rhyme with; **rispondere a qn per le** ~**e** to give sb tit for tat.

riman'dare *vt* to send again; (*restituire, rinviare*) to send back, return; (*differire*): ~ **qc (a)** to postpone sth *o* put sth off (till); (*fare riferimento*): ~ **qn a** to refer sb to; **essere rimandato** (*INS*) to have to resit one's exams.

ri'mando *sm* (*rinvio*) return; (*dilazione*) postponement; (*riferimento*) cross-reference.

rimaneggi'are [rimaned'dʒare] *vt* (*testo*) to reshape, recast; (*POL*) to reshuffle.

rima'nente *ag* remaining ♦ *sm* rest, remainder; **i** ~**i** (*persone*) the rest of them, the others.

rima'nenza [rima'nɛntsa] *sf* rest, remainder; ~**e** *sfpl* (*COMM*) unsold stock *sg*.

rima'nere *vi* (*restare*) to remain, stay; (*avanzare*) to be left, remain; (*restare stupito*) to be amazed; (*restare, mancare*): **rimangono poche settimane a Pasqua** there are only a few weeks left till Easter; (*diventare*): ~ **vedovo** to be left a widower; (*trovarsi*): ~ **confuso/sorpreso** to be confused/surprised; **rimane da vedere se** it remains to be seen whether.

rimangi'are [riman'dʒare] *vt* to eat again; ~**rsi la parola/una promessa** (*fig*) to go back on one's word/one's promise.

ri'mango *etc vb vedi* **rimanere**.

ri'mare *vt, vi* to rhyme.

rimargi'nare [rimardʒi'nare] *vt, vi* (*anche*: ~**rsi**) to heal.

ri'masto, a *pp di* **rimanere**.

rima'sugli [rima'suʎʎi] *smpl* leftovers.

rimbal'zare [rimbal'tsare] *vi* to bounce back, rebound; (*proiettile*) to ricochet.

rim'balzo [rim'baltso] *sm* rebound; ricochet.

rimbam'bire *vi* to be in one's dotage; (*rincretinire*) to grow foolish.

rimbam'bito, a *ag* senile, gaga (*fam*); **un vecchio** ~ a doddering old man.

rimbec'care *vt* (*persona*) to answer back; (*offesa*) to return.

rimbecil'lire [rimbetʃil'lire] *vi,* ~**rsi** *vr* to become stupid.

rimboc'care *vt* (*orlo*) to turn up; (*coperta*) to tuck in; (*maniche, pantaloni*) to turn *o* roll up.

rimbom'bare *vi* to resound; (*artiglieria*) to boom; (*tuono*) to rumble.

rim'bombo *sm* (*vedi vi*) boom; rumble.

rimbor'sare *vt* to pay back, repay; ~ **qc a qn** to reimburse sb for sth.

rim'borso *sm* repayment; (*di spese, biglietto*) refund; ~ **d'imposta** tax rebate.

rimboschi'mento [rimboski'mento] *sm* reafforestation.

rimbos'chire [rimbos'kire] *vt* to reafforest.

rimbrot'tare *vt* to reproach.

rim'brotto *sm* reproach.

rimedi'are *vi*: ~ **a** to remedy ♦ *vt* (*fam: procurarsi*) to get *o* scrape together; ~ **da vivere** to scrape a living.

ri'medio *sm* (*medicina*) medicine; (*cura, fig*) remedy, cure; **porre** ~ **a qc** to remedy sth; **non c'è** ~ there's no way out, there's nothing to be done about it.

rimesco'lare *vt* to mix well, stir well; (*carte*) to shuffle; **sentirsi** ~ **il sangue** (*per* *rabbia*) to feel one's blood boil.

ri'**messa** *sf* (*locale: per veicoli*) garage; (: *per aerei*) hangar; (*COMM: di merce*) consignment; (: *di denaro*) remittance; (*TENNIS*) return; (*CALCIO: anche*: ~ **in gioco**) throw-in.

ri'**messo, a** *pp di* **rimettere**.

rimes'**tare** *vt* (*mescolare*) to mix well, stir well; (*fig: passato*) to drag up again.

ri'**mettere** *vt* (*mettere di nuovo*) to put back; (*indossare di nuovo*): ~ **qc** to put sth back on, put sth on again; (*restituire*) to return, give back; (*affidare*) to entrust; (: *decisione*) to refer; (*condonare*) to remit; (*COMM: merci*) to deliver; (: *denaro*) to remit; (*vomitare*) to bring up; (*perdere: anche*: **rimetterci**) to lose; ~**rsi** *vr*: ~**rsi a** (*affidarsi*) to trust; ~ **a nuovo** (*casa etc*) to do up (*BRIT*) o over (*US*); **rimetterci di tasca propria** to be out of pocket; ~**rsi al bello** (*tempo*) to clear up; ~**rsi in cammino** to set off again; ~**rsi al lavoro** to start working again; ~**rsi in salute** to get better, recover one's health.

rimi'**nese** *ag* (*of* (*o* from) Rimini.

ri'**misi** *etc vb vedi* **rimettere**.

'**rimmel** ® *sm inv* mascara.

rimoderna'**mento** *sm* modernization.

rimoder'**nare** *vt* to modernize.

ri'**monta** *sf* (*SPORT, gen*) recovery.

rimon'**tare** *vt* (*meccanismo*) to reassemble; (*tenda*) to put up again ♦ *vi* (*salire di nuovo*): ~ **in** (*macchina, treno*) to get back into; (*SPORT*) to close the gap.

rimorchi'**are** [rimor'kjare] *vt* to tow; (*fig: ragazza*) to pick up.

rimorchia'**tore** [rimorkja'tore] *sm* (*NAUT*) tug(boat).

ri'**morchio** [ri'mɔrkjo] *sm* tow; (*veicolo*) trailer; **andare a** ~ to be towed; **prendere a** ~ to tow; **cavo da** ~ towrope; **autocarro con** ~ articulated lorry (*BRIT*), semi(trailer) (*US*).

ri'**morso** *sm* remorse; **avere il** ~ **di aver fatto qc** to deeply regret having done sth.

ri'**mosso, a** *pp di* **rimuovere**.

rimos'**tranza** [rimos'trantsa] *sf* protest, complaint; **fare le proprie** ~**e a qn** to remonstrate with sb.

rimozi'**one** [rimot'tsjone] *sf* removal; (*da un impiego*) dismissal; (*PSIC*) repression; "~ **forzata**" "illegally parked vehicles will be removed at owner's expense".

rimpas'**tare** *vt* (*POL: ministero*) to reshuffle.

rim'**pasto** *sm* (*POL*) reshuffle; ~ **ministeriale** cabinet reshuffle.

rimpatri'**are** *vi* to return home ♦ *vt* to repatriate.

rim'**patrio** *sm* repatriation.

rimpi'**angere** [rim'pjandʒere] *vt* to regret; (*persona*) to miss; ~ **di (non) aver fatto qc** to regret (not) having done sth.

rimpi'**anto, a** *pp di* **rimpiangere** ♦ *sm* regret.

rimpiat'**tino** *sm* hide-and-seek.

rimpiaz'**zare** [rimpjat'tsare] *vt* to replace.

rimpiccio'**lire** [rimpittʃo'lire] *vt* to make smaller ♦ *vi* (*anche*: ~**rsi**) to become smaller.

rimpin'**zare** [rimpin'tsare] *vt*: ~ **di** to cram o stuff with.

rimprove'**rare** *vt* to rebuke, reprimand.

rim'**provero** *sm* rebuke, reprimand; **di** ~ (*tono, occhiata*) reproachful; (*parole*) of reproach.

rimugi'**nare** [rimudʒi'nare] *vt* (*fig*) to turn over in one's mind.

rimune'**rare** *vt* (*retribuire*) to remunerate; (*ricompensare: sacrificio etc*) to reward; **un lavoro ben rimunerato** a well-paid job.

rimunera'**tivo, a** *ag* (*lavoro, attività*) remunerative, profitable.

rimunerazi'**one** [rimunerat'tsjone] *sf* remuneration; (*premio*) reward.

rimu'**overe** *vt* to remove; (*destituire*) to dismiss; (*fig: distogliere*) to dissuade.

rinascimen'**tale** [rinaʃʃimen'tale] *ag* Renaissance *cpd*, of the Renaissance.

Rinasci'**mento** [rinaʃʃi'mento] *sm*: **il** ~ the Renaissance.

ri'**nascita** [ri'naʃʃita] *sf* rebirth, revival.

rincal'**zare** [rinkal'tsare] *vt* (*palo, albero*) to support, prop up; (*lenzuola*) to tuck in.

rin'**calzo** [rin'kaltso] *sm* support, prop; (*rinforzo*) reinforcement; (*SPORT*) reserve (player); ~**i** *smpl* (*MIL*) reserves.

rinca'**rare** *vt* to increase the price of ♦ *vi* to go up, become more expensive; ~ **la dose** (*fig*) to pile it on.

rin'**caro** *sm*: ~ (**di**) (*prezzi, costo della vita*) increase (in); (*prodotto*) increase in the price (of).

rinca'**sare** *vi* to go home.

rinchi'**udere** [rin'kjudere] *vt* to shut (*o* lock) up; ~**rsi** *vr*: ~**rsi in** to shut o.s. up in; ~**rsi in se stesso** to withdraw into o.s.

rinchi'**uso, a** [rin'kjuso] *pp di* **rinchiudere**.

rincitrul'**lirsi** [rintʃitrul'lirsi] *vr* to grow foolish.

rin'**correre** *vt* to chase, run after.

rin'**corso, a** *pp di* **rincorrere** ♦ *sf* short run.

rin'**crescere** [rin'kreʃʃere] *vb impers*: **mi rincresce che/di non poter fare** I'm sorry that/I can't do, I regret that/being unable to do.

rincresci'**mento** [rinkreʃʃi'mento] *sm*

regret.

rincresci'uto, a [rinkreʃ'ʃuto] *pp di* **rincrescere**.

rincu'lare *vi* to draw back; (*arma*) to recoil.

rinfacci'are [rinfat'tʃare] *vt* (*fig*): ~ qc a qn to throw sth in sb's face.

rinfoco'lare *vt* (*fig: odio, passioni*) to rekindle; (: *risentimento, rabbia*) to stir up.

rinfor'zare [rinfor'tsare] *vt* to reinforce, strengthen ♦ *vi* (*anche:* ~rsi) to grow stronger.

rin'forzo [rin'fortso] *sm*: **mettere un ~ a** to strengthen; ~i *smpl* (*MIL*) reinforcements; **di ~** (*asse, sbarra*) strengthening; (*esercito*) supporting; (*personale*) extra, additional.

rinfran'care *vt* to encourage, reassure.

rinfres'cante *ag* (*bibita*) refreshing.

rinfres'care *vt* (*atmosfera, temperatura*) to cool (down); (*abito, pareti*) to freshen up ♦ *vi* (*tempo*) to grow cooler; ~rsi *vr* (*ristorarsi*) to refresh o.s.; (*lavarsi*) to freshen up; ~ **la memoria a qn** to refresh sb's memory.

rin'fresco, schi *sm* (*festa*) party; ~schi *smpl* (*cibi e bevande*) refreshments.

rin'fusa *sf*: **alla ~** in confusion, higgledy-piggledy.

ringhi'are [rin'gjare] *vi* to growl, snarl.

ringhi'era [rin'gjɛra] *sf* railing; (*delle scale*) banister(s *pl*).

'ringhio ['ringjo] *sm* growl, snarl.

ringhi'oso, a [rin'gjoso] *ag* growling, snarling.

ringiova'nire [rindʒova'nire] *vt* (*sog: vestito, acconciatura etc*): ~ **qn** to make sb look younger; (: *vacanze etc*) to rejuvenate ♦ *vi* (*anche:* ~rsi) to become (*o* look) younger.

ringrazia'mento [ringrattsja'mento] *sm* thanks *pl*; **lettera/biglietto di ~** thank you letter/card.

ringrazi'are [ringrat'tsjare] *vt* to thank; ~ **qn di qc** to thank sb for sth; ~ **qn per aver fatto qc** to thank sb for doing sth.

rinne'gare *vt* (*fede*) to renounce; (*figlio*) to disown, repudiate.

rinne'gato, a *sm/f* renegade.

rinnova'mento *sm* renewal; (*economico*) revival.

rinno'vare *vt* to renew; (*ripetere*) to repeat, renew; ~rsi *vr* (*fenomeno*) to be repeated, recur.

rin'novo *sm* (*di contratto*) renewal; "chiuso per ~ **(dei) locali**" (*negozio*) "closed for alterations".

rinoce'ronte [rinotʃe'ronte] *sm* rhinoceros.

rino'mato, a *ag* renowned, celebrated.

rinsal'dare *vt* to strengthen.

rinsa'vire *vi* to come to one's senses.

rinsec'chito, a [rinsek'kito] *ag* (*vecchio, albero*) thin, gaunt.

rinta'narsi *vr* (*animale*) to go into its den; (*persona: nascondersi*) to hide.

rintoc'care *vi* (*campana*) to toll; (*orologio*) to strike.

rin'tocco, chi *sm* toll.

rintracci'are [rintrat'tʃare] *vt* to track down; (*persona scomparsa, documento*) to trace.

rintro'nare *vi* to boom, roar ♦ *vt* (*assordare*) to deafen; (*stordire*) to stun.

rintuz'zare [rintut'tsare] *vt* (*fig: sentimento*) to check, repress; (: *accusa*) to refute.

ri'nuncia [ri'nuntʃa] *sf* renunciation; ~ **a** (*carica*) resignation from; (*eredità*) relinquishment of; ~ **agli atti del giudizio** (*DIR*) abandonment of a claim.

rinunci'are [rinun'tʃare] *vi*: ~ **a** to give up, renounce; ~ **a fare qc** to give up doing sth.

rinuncia'tario, a [rinuntʃa'tarjo] *ag* defeatist.

ri'nunzia *etc* [ri'nuntsja] = **rinuncia** *etc*.

rinveni'mento *sm* (*ritrovamento*) recovery; (*scoperta*) discovery; (*METALLURGIA*) tempering.

rinve'nire *vt* to find, recover; (*scoprire*) to discover, find out ♦ *vi* (*riprendere i sensi*) to come round; (*riprendere l'aspetto naturale*) to revive.

rinve'nuto, a *pp di* **rinvenire**.

rinver'dire *vi* (*bosco, ramo*) to become green again.

rinvi'are *vt* (*rimandare indietro*) to send back, return; (*differire*): ~ **qc (a)** to postpone sth *o* put sth off (till); (: *seduta*) to adjourn sth (till); (*fare un rimando*): ~ **qn a** to refer sb to; ~ **a giudizio** (*DIR*) to commit for trial.

rinvigo'rire *vt* to strengthen.

rin'vio, 'vii *sm* (*rimando*) return; (*differimento*) postponement; (: *di seduta*) adjournment; (*in un testo*) cross-reference; ~ **a giudizio** (*DIR*) indictment.

riò *etc vb vedi* **riavere**.

'Rio de Ja'neiro ['riodedʒa'neiro] *sf* Rio de Janeiro.

rio'nale *ag* (*mercato, cinema*) local, district *cpd*.

ri'one *sm* district, quarter.

riordina'mento *sm* (*di ente, azienda*) reorganization.

riordi'nare *vt* (*rimettere in ordine*) to tidy; (*riorganizzare*) to reorganize.

riorganiz'zare [riorganid'dzare] *vt* to reorganize.

riorganizzazi'one [riorganiddzat'tsjone] *sf* reorganization.

ripa'gare *vt* to repay.

ripa'rare *vt* (*proteggere*) to protect, defend; (*correggere: male, torto*) to make up for; (: *errore*) to put right; (*aggiustare*) to repair ♦ *vi* (*mettere rimedio*): ~ **a** to make up for; ~**rsi** *vr* (*rifugiarsi*) to take refuge *o* shelter.

ripa'rato, a *ag* (*posto*) sheltered.

riparazi'one [riparat'tsjone] *sf* (*di un torto*) reparation; (*di guasto, scarpe*) repairing *no pl*; repair; (*risarcimento*) compensation; (*INS*): **esame di** ~ resit (*BRIT*), test retake (*US*).

ri'paro *sm* (*protezione*) shelter, protection; (*rimedio*) remedy; **al** ~ **da** (*sole, vento*) sheltered from; **mettersi al** ~ to take shelter; **correre ai** ~**i** (*fig*) to take remedial action.

ripar'tire *vt* (*dividere*) to divide up; (*distribuire*) to share out, distribute ♦ *vi* to leave again; (*motore*) to start again.

ripartizi'one [ripartit'tsjone] *sf* division; sharing out, distribution; (*AMM: dipartimento*) department.

ripas'sare *vi* to come (*o* go) back ♦ *vt* (*scritto, lezione*) to go over (again).

ri'passo *sm* (*di lezione*) revision (*BRIT*), review (*US*).

ripensa'mento *sm* second thoughts *pl* (*BRIT*), change of mind; **avere un** ~ to have second thoughts, change one's mind.

ripen'sare *vi* to think; (*cambiare idea*) to change one's mind; (*tornare col pensiero*): ~ **a** to recall; **a ripensarci** ... on thinking it over ....

riper'correre *vt* (*itinerario*) to travel over again; (*strada*) to go along again; (*fig: ricordi, passato*) to go back over.

riper'corso, a *pp di* **ripercorrere**.

riper'cosso, a *pp di* **ripercuotersi**.

ripercu'otersi *vr*: ~ **su** (*fig*) to have repercussions on.

ripercussi'one *sf* (*fig*): **avere una** ~ *o* **delle** ~**i su** to have repercussions on.

ripes'care *vt* (*pesce*) to catch again; (*persona, cosa*) to fish out; (*fig: ritrovare*) to dig out.

ripe'tente *sm/f* student repeating the year, repeater (*US*).

ri'petere *vt* to repeat; (*ripassare*) to go over.

ripeti'tore *sm* (*RADIO, TV*) relay.

ripetizi'one [ripetit'tsjone] *sf* repetition; (*di lezione*) revision; ~**i** *sfpl* (*INS*) private tutoring *o* coaching *sg*; **fucile a** ~

repeating rifle.

ripetuta'mente *av* repeatedly, again and again.

ripi'ano *sm* (*GEO*) terrace; (*di mobile*) shelf.

ri'picca *sf*: **per** ~ out of spite.

'ripido, a *ag* steep.

ripiega'mento *sm* (*MIL*) retreat.

ripie'gare *vt* to refold; (*piegare più volte*) to fold (up) ♦ *vi* (*MIL*) to retreat, fall back; (*fig: accontentarsi*): ~ **su** to make do with; ~**rsi** *vr* to bend.

ripi'ego, ghi *sm* expedient; **una soluzione di** ~ a makeshift solution.

ripi'eno, a *ag* full; (*CUC*) stuffed; (: *panino*) filled ♦ *sm* (*CUC*) stuffing.

ri'pone, ri'pongo *etc vb vedi* **riporre**.

ri'porre *vt* (*porre al suo posto*) to put back, replace; (*mettere via*) to put away; (*fiducia, speranza*): ~ **qc in qn** to place *o* put sth in sb.

ripor'tare *vt* (*portare indietro*) to bring (*o* take) back; (*riferire*) to report; (*citare*) to quote; (*ricevere*) to receive, get; (*vittoria*) to gain; (*successo*) to have; (*MAT*) to carry; (*COMM*) to carry forward; ~**rsi** *vr*: ~**rsi a** (*anche fig*) to go back to; (*riferirsi a*) to refer to; ~ **danni** to suffer damage; **ha riportato gravi ferite** he was seriously injured.

ri'porto *sm* amount carried over; amount carried forward.

ripo'sante *ag* (*gen*) restful; (*musica, colore*) soothing.

ripo'sare *vt* (*bicchiere, valigia*) to put down; (*dare sollievo*) to rest ♦ *vi* to rest; ~**rsi** *vr* to rest; **qui riposa** ... (*su tomba*) here lies ....

ripo'sato, a *ag* (*viso, aspetto*) rested; (*mente*) fresh.

ri'posi *etc vb vedi* **riporre**.

ri'poso *sm* rest; (*MIL*): ~**!** at ease!; **a** ~ (*in pensione*) retired; **giorno di** ~ day off; "**oggi** ~" (*CINE, TEAT*) "no performance today"; (*ristorante*) "closed today".

ripos'tiglio [ripos'tiʎʎo] *sm* lumber room (*BRIT*), storage room (*US*).

ri'posto, a *pp di* **riporre** ♦ *ag* (*fig: senso, significato*) hidden.

ri'prendere *vt* (*prigioniero, fortezza*) to recapture; (*prendere indietro*) to take back; (*ricominciare: lavoro*) to resume; (*andare a prendere*) to fetch, come back for; (*assumere di nuovo: impiegati*) to take on again, re-employ; (*rimproverare*) to tell off; (*restringere: abito*) to take in; (*CINE*) to shoot; ~**rsi** *vr* to recover; (*correggersi*) to correct o.s.; ~ **a fare qc** to start doing sth again; ~ **il cammino** to set off again; ~ **i sensi** to recover consciousness; ~ **sonno**

to go back to sleep.

ripresen'tare *vt* (*certificato*) to submit again; (*domanda*) to put forward again; (*persona*) to introduce again; ~**rsi** *vr* (*ritornare: persona*) to come back; (*: occasione*) to arise again; ~**rsi a** (*esame*) to sit (*BRIT*) *o* take (*US*) again; (*concorso*) to enter again; ~**rsi come candidato** (*POL*) to stand (*BRIT*) *o* run (*US*) again (as a candidate).

ri'preso, a *pp di* **riprendere** ♦ *sf* recapture; resumption; (*economica, da malattia, emozione*) recovery; (*AUT*) acceleration *no pl*; (*TEAT, CINE*) rerun; (*CINE: presa*) shooting *no pl*; shot; (*SPORT*) second half; (*: PUGILATO*) round; **a più ~e** on several occasions, several times.

ripristi'nare *vt* to restore.

ri'pristino *sm* (*gen*) restoration; (*di tradizioni*) revival.

ripro'dotto, a *pp di* **riprodurre**.

ripro'durre *vt* to reproduce; **riprodursi** *vr* (*BIOL*) to reproduce; (*riformarsi*) to form again.

riprodut'tivo, a *ag* reproductive.

riprodut'tore, 'trice *ag* (*organo*) reproductive ♦ *sm*: ~ **acustico** pick-up; ~ **a cassetta** cassette player.

riproduzi'one [riprodut'tsjone] *sf* reproduction; ~ **vietata** all rights reserved.

ripro'messo, a *pp di* **ripromettersi**.

ripro'mettersi *vt* (*aspettarsi*): ~ **qc da** to expect sth from; (*intendere*): ~ **di fare qc** to intend to do sth.

ripro'porre *vt*: **riproporsi di fare qc** to intend to do sth.

ripro'posto, a *pp di* **riproporre**.

ri'prova *sf* confirmation; **a ~ di** as confirmation of.

ripro'vare *vt* (*provare di nuovo: gen*) to try again; (*: vestito*) to try on again; (*: sensazione*) to experience again ♦ *vi* (*tentare*): ~ **(a fare qc)** to try (to do sth) again; **riproverò più tardi** I'll try again later.

ripro'vevole *ag* reprehensible.

ripudi'are *vt* to repudiate, disown.

ri'pudio *sm* repudiation, disowning.

ripu'gnante [ripuɲ'ɲante] *ag* disgusting, repulsive.

ripu'gnanza [ripuɲ'ɲantsa] *sf* repugnance, disgust.

ripu'gnare [ripuɲ'ɲare] *vi*: ~ **a qn** to repel *o* disgust sb.

ripu'lire *vt* to clean up; (*sog: ladri*) to clean out; (*perfezionare*) to polish, refine.

ripulsi'one *sf* (*FISICA, fig*) repulsion.

ri'quadro *sm* square; (*ARCHIT*) panel.

ri'sacca, che *sf* backwash.

ri'saia *sf* paddy field.

risa'lire *vi* (*ritornare in su*) to go back up; ~ **a** (*ritornare con la mente*) to go back to; (*datare da*) to date back to, go back to.

risa'lita *sf*: **mezzi di ~** (*SCI*) ski lifts.

risal'tare *vi* (*fig: distinguersi*) to stand out; (*ARCHIT*) to project, jut out.

ri'salto *sm* prominence; (*sporgenza*) projection; **mettere** *o* **porre in ~ qc** to make sth stand out.

risana'mento *sm* (*economico*) improvement; (*bonifica*) reclamation; ~ **del bilancio** reorganization of the budget; ~ **edilizio** building improvement.

risa'nare *vt* (*guarire*) to heal, cure; (*palude*) to reclaim; (*economia*) to improve; (*bilancio*) to reorganize.

risa'pere *vt*: ~ **qc** to come to know of sth.

risa'puto, a *ag*: **è** ~ **che ...** everyone knows that ..., it's common knowledge that ....

risarci'mento [risartʃi'mento] *sm*: ~ **(di)** compensation (for); **aver diritto al ~ dei danni** to be entitled to damages.

risar'cire [risar'tʃire] *vt* (*cose*) to pay compensation for; (*persona*): ~ **qn di qc** to compensate sb for sth; ~ **i danni a qn** to pay sb damages.

ri'sata *sf* laugh.

riscalda'mento *sm* heating; ~ **centrale** central heating.

riscal'dare *vt* (*scaldare*) to heat; (*: mani, persona*) to warm; (*minestra*) to reheat; ~**rsi** *vr* to warm up.

ris'caldo *sm* (*fam*) (slight) inflammation.

riscat'tare *vt* (*prigioniero*) to ransom, pay a ransom for; (*DIR*) to redeem; ~**rsi** *vr* (*da disonore*) to redeem o.s.

ris'catto *sm* ransom; redemption.

rischia'rare [riskja'rare] *vt* (*illuminare*) to light up; (*colore*) to make lighter; ~**rsi** *vr* (*tempo*) to clear up; (*cielo*) to clear; (*fig: volto*) to brighten up; ~**rsi la voce** to clear one's throat.

rischi'are [ris'kjare] *vt* to risk ♦ *vi*: ~ **di fare qc** to risk *o* run the risk of doing sth.

'rischio ['riskjo] *sm* risk; **a ~** (*zona, situazione*) at risk, vulnerable; **a proprio ~ e pericolo** at one's own risk; **correre il ~ di fare qc** to run the risk of doing sth; ~ **del mestiere** occupational hazard.

rischi'oso, a [ris'kjoso] *ag* risky, dangerous.

risciac'quare [riʃʃak'kware] *vt* to rinse.

risci'acquo [riʃ'ʃakkwo] *sm* rinse.

riscon'trare *vt* (*confrontare: due cose*) to compare; (*esaminare*) to check, verify;

(*rilevare*) to find.
ris'contro *sm* comparison; check, verification; (*AMM: lettera di risposta*) reply; **mettere a ~** to compare; **in attesa di un vostro cortese ~** we look forward to your reply.
risco'perto, a *pp di* **riscoprire**.
risco'prire *vt* to rediscover.
riscossi'one *sf* collection.
ris'cosso, a *pp di* **riscuotere** ♦ *sf* (*riconquista*) recovery, reconquest.
riscu'otere *vt* (*ritirare una somma dovuta*) to collect; (: *stipendio*) to draw, collect; (*fig: successo etc*) to win, earn; **~rsi** *vr:* **~rsi (da)** to shake o.s. (out of), rouse o.s. (from); **~ un assegno** to cash a cheque.
'rise *etc vb vedi* **ridere**.
risenti'mento *sm* resentment.
risen'tire *vt* to hear again; (*provare*) to feel ♦ *vi:* **~ di** to feel (*o* show) the effects of; **~rsi** *vr:* **~rsi di** *o* **per** to take offence (*BRIT*) *o* offense (*US*) at, resent.
risen'tito, a *ag* resentful.
ri'serbo *sm* reserve.
ri'serva *sf* reserve; (*di caccia, pesca*) preserve; (*restrizione, di indigeni*) reservation; **fare ~ di** (*cibo*) to get in a supply of; **tenere di ~** to keep in reserve; **con le dovute ~e** with certain reservations; **ha accettato con la ~ di potersi ritirare** he accepted with the proviso that he could pull out.
riser'vare *vt* (*tenere in serbo*) to keep, put aside; (*prenotare*) to book, reserve; **~rsi** *vr:* **~rsi di fare qc** to intend to do sth; **~rsi il diritto di fare qc** to reserve the right to do sth.
riserva'tezza [riserva'tettsa] *sf* reserve.
riser'vato, a *ag* (*prenotato, fig: persona*) reserved; (*confidenziale*) confidential; (*lettera, informazione*) confidential.
'risi *etc vb vedi* **ridere**.
ri'sibile *ag* laughable.
risi'cato, a *ag* (*vittoria etc*) very narrow.
risi'edere *vi:* **~ a** *o* **in** to reside in.
'risma *sf* (*di carta*) ream; (*fig*) kind, sort.
'riso, a *pp di* **ridere** ♦ *sm* (*pianta*) rice; (*pl(f)* **~a**: *il ridere*): **un ~** a laugh; **il ~** laughter; **uno scoppio di ~a** a burst of laughter.
riso'lino *sm* snigger.
risolle'vare *vt* (*sollevare di nuovo: testa*) to raise again, lift up again; (*fig: questione*) to raise again, bring up again; (: *morale*) to raise; **~rsi** *vr* (*da terra*) to rise again; (*fig: da malattia*) to recover; **~ le sorti di qc** to improve the chances of sth.
ri'solsi *etc vb vedi* **risolvere**.
ri'solto, a *pp di* **risolvere**.

risolu'tezza [risolu'tettsa] *sf* determination.
risolu'tivo, a *ag* (*determinante*) decisive; (*che risolve*): **arrivare ad una formula ~a** to come up with a formula to resolve a situation.
riso'luto, a *ag* determined, resolute.
risoluzi'one [risolut'tsjone] *sf* solving *no pl*; (*MAT*) solution; (*decisione, di immagine*) resolution; (*DIR: di contratto*) annulment, cancellation.
ri'solvere *vt* (*difficoltà, controversia*) to resolve; (*problema*) to solve; (*decidere*): **~ di fare** to resolve to do; **~rsi** *vr* (*decidersi*): **~rsi a fare** to make up one's mind to do; (*andare a finire*): **~rsi in** to end up, turn out; **~rsi in nulla** to come to nothing.
risol'vibile *ag* solvable.
riso'nanza [riso'nantsa] *sf* resonance; **aver vasta ~** (*fig: fatto etc*) to be known far and wide.
riso'nare *vt, vi* = **risuonare**.
ri'sorgere [ri'sordʒere] *vi* to rise again.
risorgimen'tale [risordʒimen'tale] *ag* of the Risorgimento.
risorgi'mento [risordʒi'mento] *sm* revival; **il R~** (*STORIA*) the Risorgimento.

> *The* **Risorgimento**, *which began in the early nineteenth century and ended in 1861, with the proclamation of the Kingdom of Italy, was a period of great upheaval and change. Political and personal freedom took on a new importance under the influence of the events of the French Revolution. It eventually led to the unification of Italy in 1871.*

ri'sorsa *sf* expedient, resort; **~e** *sfpl* (*naturali, finanziarie etc*) resources; **persona piena di ~e** resourceful person.
ri'sorsi *etc vb vedi* **risorgere**.
ri'sorto, a *pp di* **risorgere**.
ri'sotto *sm* (*CUC*) risotto.
rispar'miare *vt* to save; (*non uccidere*) to spare ♦ *vi* to save; **~ qc a qn** to spare sb sth; **~ fatica/fiato** to save one's energy/breath; **risparmiati il disturbo** *o* **la fatica** (*anche ironico*) save yourself the trouble.
risparmia'tore, 'trice *sm/f* saver.
ris'parmio *sm* saving *no pl*; (*denaro*) savings *pl*.
rispecchi'are [rispek'kjare] *vt* to reflect; **~rsi** *vr* to be reflected.
rispe'dire *vt* to send back; **~ qc a qn** to send sth back to sb.
rispet'tabile *ag* respectable; (*considerevole: somma*) sizeable, considerable.

rispet'tare *vt* to respect; (*legge*) to obey, comply with, abide by; (*promessa*) to keep; **farsi** ~ to command respect; ~ **le distanze** to keep one's distance; ~ **i tempi** to keep to schedule; **ogni medico che si rispetti** every self-respecting doctor.

rispettiva'mente *av* respectively.

rispet'tivo, a *ag* respective.

ris'petto *sm* respect; ~**i** *smpl* (*saluti*) respects, regards; ~ **a** (*in paragone a*) compared to; (*in relazione a*) as regards, as for; ~ **(di o per)** (*norme, leggi*) observance (of), compliance (with); **portare** ~ **a qn/qc** to have o feel respect for sb/sth; **mancare di** ~ **a qn** to be disrespectful to sb; **con** ~ **parlando** with respect, if you will excuse my saying so; **(porga) i miei** ~**i alla signora** (give) my regards to your wife.

rispet'toso, a *ag* respectful.

risplen'dente *ag* (*giornata, sole*) bright, shining; (*occhi*) sparkling.

ris'plendere *vi* to shine.

rispon'dente *ag:* ~ **a** in keeping o conformity with.

rispon'denza [rispon'dɛntsa] *sf* correspondence.

ris'pondere *vi* to answer, reply; (*freni*) to respond; ~ **a** (*domanda*) to answer, reply to; (*persona*) to answer; (*invito*) to reply to; (*provocazione, sog: veicolo, apparecchio*) to respond to; (*corrispondere a*) to correspond to; (*: speranze, bisogno*) to answer; ~ **a qn di qc** (*essere responsabile*) to be answerable to sb for sth.

rispo'sarsi *vr* to get married again, remarry.

ris'posto, a *pp di* **rispondere** ♦ *sf* answer, reply; **in** ~**a a** in reply to; **dare una** ~**a a** to give an answer; **diamo** ~**a alla vostra lettera del** ... in reply to your letter of ....

'rissa *sf* brawl.

ris'soso, a *ag* quarrelsome.

rist. *abbr* = **ristampa**.

ristabi'lire *vt* to re-establish, restore; (*persona: sog: riposo etc*) to restore to health; ~**rsi** *vr* to recover.

rista'gnare [ristaɲ'ɲare] *vi* (*acqua*) to become stagnant; (*sangue*) to cease flowing; (*fig: industria*) to stagnate.

ris'tagno [ris'taɲɲo] *sm* stagnation; **c'è un** ~ **delle vendite** business is slack.

ris'tampa *sf* reprinting *no pl*; reprint.

ristam'pare *vt* to reprint.

risto'rante *sm* restaurant.

risto'rare *vt* (*persona, forze*) to revive, refresh; ~**rsi** *vr* (*rifocillarsi*) to have

something to eat and drink; (*riposarsi*) to rest, have a rest.

ristora'tore, 'trice *ag* refreshing, reviving ♦ *sm* (*gestore di ristorante*) restaurateur.

ris'toro *sm* (*bevanda, cibo*) refreshment; **posto di** ~ (*FERR*) buffet, snack bar; **servizio di** ~ (*FERR*) refreshments *pl*.

ristret'tezza [ristret'tettsa] *sf* (*strettezza*) narrowness; (*fig: scarsezza*) scarcity, lack; (*: meschinità*) meanness; ~**e** *sfpl* (*povertà*) poverty *sg*.

ris'tretto, a *pp di* **restringere** ♦ *ag* (*racchiuso*) enclosed, hemmed in; (*angusto*) narrow; (*limitato*): ~ **(a)** restricted o limited (to); (*CUC: brodo*) thick; (*: caffè*) extra strong.

ristruttu'rare *vt* (*azienda*) to reorganize; (*edificio*) to restore; (*appartamento*) to alter; (*sog: crema, balsamo*) to repair.

ristrutturazi'one [ristrutturat'tsjone] *sf* reorganization; restoration; alteration.

risucchi'are [risuk'kjare] *vt* to suck in.

ri'succhio [ri'sukkjo] *sm* (*di acqua*) undertow, pull; (*di aria*) suction.

risul'tare *vi* (*dimostrarsi*) to prove (to be), turn out (to be); (*riuscire*): ~ **vincitore** to emerge as the winner; ~ **da** (*provenire*) to result from, be the result of; **mi risulta che** ... I understand that ..., as far as I know ...; **(ne) risulta che** ... it follows that ...; **non mi risulta** not as far as I know.

risul'tato *sm* result.

risuo'nare *vi* (*rimbombare*) to resound.

risurrezi'one [risurret'tsjone] *sf* (*REL*) resurrection.

risusci'tare [risuʃʃi'tare] *vt* to resuscitate, restore to life; (*fig*) to revive, bring back ♦ *vi* to rise (from the dead).

risvegli'are [rizveʎ'ʎare] *vt* (*gen*) to wake up, waken; (*fig: interesse*) to stir up, arouse; (*: curiosità*) to arouse; (*fig: dall'inerzia etc*): ~ **qn (da)** to rouse sb (from); ~**rsi** *vr* to wake up, awaken; (*fig: interesse, curiosità*) to be aroused.

ris'veglio [riz've λλo] *sm* waking up; (*fig*) revival.

ris'volto *sm* (*di giacca*) lapel; (*di pantaloni*) turn-up (*BRIT*), cuff (*US*); (*di manica*) cuff; (*di tasca*) flap; (*di libro*) inside flap; (*fig*) implication.

ritagli'are [ritaλ'λare] *vt* (*tagliar via*) to cut out.

ri'taglio [ri'taλλo] *sm* (*di giornale*) cutting, clipping; (*di stoffa etc*) scrap; **nei** ~**i di tempo** in one's spare time.

ritar'dare *vi* (*persona, treno*) to be late; (*orologio*) to be slow ♦ *vt* (*rallentare*) to slow down; (*impedire*) to delay, hold up;

(*differire*) to postpone, delay; ~ **il pagamento** to defer payment.

ritarda'tario, a *smlf* latecomer.

ritar'dato, a *ag* (*PSIC*) retarded.

ri'tardo *sm* delay; (*di persona aspettata*) lateness *no pl*; (*fig: mentale*) backwardness; **in** ~ late.

ri'tegno [ri'teɲɲo] *sm* restraint.

ritem'prare *vt* (*forze, spirito*) to restore.

rite'nere *vt* (*trattenere*) to hold back; (: *somma*) to deduct; (*giudicare*) to consider, believe.

ri'tengo, ri'tenni *etc vb vedi* **ritenere**.

riten'tare *vt* to try again, make another attempt at.

rite'nuta *sf* (*sul salario*) deduction; ~ **d'acconto** advance deduction of tax; ~ **alla fonte** (*FISCO*) taxation at source.

riterrò, riti'ene *etc vb vedi* **ritenere**.

riti'rare *vt* to withdraw; (*POL: richiamare*) to recall; (*andare a prendere: pacco etc*) to collect, pick up; ~**rsi** *vr* to withdraw; (*da un'attività*) to retire; (*stoffa*) to shrink; (*marea*) to recede; **gli hanno ritirato la patente** they disqualified him from driving (*BRIT*), they took away his licence (*BRIT*) *o* license (*US*); ~**rsi a vita privata** to withdraw from public life.

riti'rata *sf* (*MIL*) retreat; (*latrina*) lavatory.

riti'rato, a *ag* secluded; **fare vita ~a** to live in seclusion.

ri'tiro *sm* (*di truppe, candidati, soldi*) withdrawal; (*di pacchi*) collection; (*di passaporto*) confiscation; (*da attività*) retirement; (*luogo appartato*) retreat.

rit'mato, a *ag* rhythmic(al).

'ritmico, a, ci, che *ag* rhythmic(al).

'ritmo *sm* rhythm; (*fig*) rate; (: *della vita*) pace, tempo; **al ~ di** at a speed *o* rate of; **ballare al ~ di valzer** to waltz.

'rito *sm* rite; **di ~** usual, customary.

ritoc'care *vt* (*disegno, fotografia*) to touch up; (*testo*) to alter.

ri'tocco, chi *sm* touching up *no pl*; alteration.

ri'torcere [ri'tɔrtʃere] *vt* (*filato*) to twist; (*fig: accusa, insulto*) to throw back; ~**rsi** *vr* (*tornare a danno di*): ~**rsi contro** to turn against.

ritor'nare *vi* to return, go (*o* come) back; (*ripresentarsi*) to recur; (*ridiventare*): ~ **ricco** to become rich again ♦ *vt* (*restituire*) to return, give back.

ritor'nello *sm* refrain.

ri'torno *sm* return; **durante il (viaggio di) ~** on the return trip, on the way back; **al ~** (*tornando*) on the way back; **essere di ~** to be back; **far ~** to return; **avere un ~ di**

fiamma (*AUT*) to backfire; (*fig: persona*) to be back in love again.

ritorsi'one *sf* (*rappresaglia*) retaliation.

ri'torto, a *pp di* **ritorcere** ♦ *ag* (*cotone, corda*) twisted.

ri'trarre *vt* (*trarre indietro, via*) to withdraw; (*distogliere: sguardo*) to turn away; (*rappresentare*) to portray, depict; (*ricavare*) to get, obtain; **ritrarsi** *vr* to move back.

ritrat'tare *vt* (*disdire*) to retract, take back; (*trattare nuovamente*) to deal with again.

ritrattazi'one [ritrattat'tsjone] *sf* withdrawal.

ritrat'tista, i, e *smlf* portrait painter.

ri'tratto, a *pp di* **ritrarre** ♦ *sm* portrait.

ritro'sia *sf* (*riluttanza*) reluctance, unwillingness; (*timidezza*) shyness.

ri'troso, a *ag* (*restio*): ~ (**a**) reluctant (to); (*schivo*) shy; **andare a ~** to go backwards.

ritrova'mento *sm* (*di cadavere, oggetto smarrito etc*) finding; (*oggetto ritrovato*) find.

ritro'vare *vt* to find; (*salute*) to regain; (*persona*) to find; to meet again; ~**rsi** *vr* (*essere, capitare*) to find o.s.; (*raccapezzarsi*) to find one's way; (*con senso reciproco*) to meet (again).

ritro'vato *sm* discovery.

ri'trovo *sm* meeting place; ~ **notturno** night club.

'ritto, a *ag* (*in piedi*) standing, on one's feet; (*levato in alto*) erect, raised; (: *capelli*) standing on end; (*posto verticalmente*) upright.

ritu'ale *ag, sm* ritual.

riuni'one *sf* (*adunanza*) meeting; (*riconciliazione*) reunion; **essere in ~** to be at a meeting.

riu'nire *vt* (*ricongiungere*) to join (together); (*riconciliare*) to reunite, bring together (again); ~**rsi** *vr* (*adunarsi*) to meet; (*tornare a stare insieme*) to be reunited; **siamo qui riuniti per festeggiare il vostro anniversario** we are gathered here to celebrate your anniversary.

riu'scire [riuʃ'ʃire] *vi* (*uscire di nuovo*) to go out again, go back out; (*aver esito: fatti, azioni*) to go, turn out; (*aver successo*) to succeed, be successful; (*essere, apparire*) to be, prove; (*raggiungere il fine*) to manage, succeed; ~ **a fare qc** to manage *o* be able to do sth; **questo mi riesce nuovo** this is new to me.

riu'scita [riuʃ'ʃita] *sf* (*esito*) result, outcome; (*buon esito*) success.

riutiliz'zare [riutilid'dzare] *vt* to use again, re-use.

'riva *sf (di fiume)* bank; *(di lago, mare)* shore; **in ~ al mare** on the (sea) shore.

ri'vale *ag* rival *cpd* ♦ *smf* rival; **non avere ~i** *(anche fig)* to be unrivalled.

rivaleggi'are [rivaled'dʒare] *vi* to compete, vie.

rivalità *sf* rivalry.

ri'valsa *sf (rivincita)* revenge; *(risarcimento)* compensation; **prendersi una ~ su qn** to take revenge on sb.

rivalu'tare *vt (ECON)* to revalue.

rivalutazi'one [rivalutat'tsjone] *sf (ECON)* revaluation; *(fig)* re-evaluation.

rivan'gare *vt (ricordi etc)* to dig up (again).

rive'dere *vt* to see again; *(ripassare)* to revise; *(verificare)* to check.

rivedrò *etc vb vedi* **rivedere**.

rive'lare *vt* to reveal; *(divulgare)* to reveal, disclose; *(dare indizio)* to reveal, show; **~rsi** *vr (manifestarsi)* to be revealed; **~rsi onesto** *etc* to prove to be honest *etc*.

rivela'tore, 'trice *ag* revealing ♦ *sm (TECN)* detector; *(FOT)* developer.

rivelazi'one [rivelat'tsjone] *sf* revelation.

ri'vendere *vt (vendere: di nuovo)* to resell, sell again; *(: al dettaglio)* to retail, sell retail.

rivendi'care *vt* to claim, demand.

rivendicazi'one [rivendikat'tsjone] *sf* claim; **~i salariali** wage claims.

ri'vendita *sf (bottega)* retailer's (shop); **~ di tabacchi** tobacconist's (shop).

rivendi'tore, 'trice *smf* retailer; **~ autorizzato** authorized dealer.

riverbe'rare *vt* to reflect.

ri'verbero *sm (di luce, calore)* reflection; *(di suono)* reverberation.

rive'rente *ag* reverent, respectful.

rive'renza [rive'rɛntsa] *sf* reverence; *(inchino)* bow; curtsey.

rive'rire *vt (rispettare)* to revere; *(salutare)* to pay one's respects to.

river'sare *vt (anche fig)* to pour; **~rsi** *vr (fig: persone)* to pour out.

rivesti'mento *sm* covering; coating.

rives'tire *vt* to dress again; *(ricoprire)* to cover; *(: con vernice)* to coat; *(fig: carica)* to hold; **~rsi** *vr* to get dressed again; to change (one's clothes); **~ di piastrelle** to tile.

ri'vidi *etc vb vedi* **rivedere**.

rivi'era *sf* coast; **la ~ italiana** the Italian Riviera.

ri'vincita [ri'vintʃita] *sf (SPORT)* return match; *(fig)* revenge; **prendersi la ~ (su qn)** to take *o* get one's revenge (on sb).

rivis'suto, a *pp di* **rivivere**.

ri'vista *sf* review; *(periodico)* magazine,

review; *(TEAT)* revue; variety show.

ri'visto, a *pp di* **rivedere**.

rivitaliz'zante [rivitalid'dzante] *ag* revitalizing.

rivitaliz'zare [rivitalid'dzare] *vt* to revitalize.

ri'vivere *vi (riacquistare forza)* to come alive again; *(tornare in uso)* to be revived ♦ *vt* to relive.

'rivo *sm* stream.

ri'volgere [ri'vɔldʒere] *vt (attenzione, sguardo)* to turn, direct; *(parole)* to address; **~rsi** *vr* to turn round; *(fig: dirigersi per informazioni)*: **~rsi a** to go and see, go and speak to; **~ un'accusa/una critica a qn** to accuse/criticize sb; **~rsi all'ufficio competente** to apply to the office concerned.

rivolgi'mento [rivoldʒi'mento] *sm* upheaval.

ri'volsi *etc vb vedi* **rivolgere**.

ri'volta *sf* revolt, rebellion.

rivol'tante *ag* revolting, disgusting.

rivol'tare *vt* to turn over; *(con l'interno all'esterno)* to turn inside out; *(disgustare: stomaco)* to upset, turn; *(: fig)* to revolt, disgust; **~rsi** *vr (ribellarsi)*: **~rsi (a)** to rebel (against).

rivol'tella *sf* revolver.

ri'volto, a *pp di* **rivolgere**.

rivol'toso, a *ag* rebellious ♦ *smf* rebel.

rivoluzio'nare [rivoluttsjo'nare] *vt* to revolutionize.

rivoluzio'nario, a [rivoluttsjo'narjo] *ag, smf* revolutionary.

rivoluzi'one [rivolut'tsjone] *sf* revolution.

riz'zare [rit'tsare] *vt* to raise, erect; **~rsi** *vr* to stand up; *(capelli)* to stand on end; **~rsi in piedi** to stand up, get to one's feet.

RN *sigla = Rimini.*

RNA *sigla m* RNA *(= ribonucleic acid)*.

RO *sigla = Rovigo.*

'roba *sf* stuff, things *pl*; *(possessi, beni)* belongings *pl*, things *pl*, possessions *pl*; **~ da mangiare** things to eat, food; **~ da matti!** it's sheer madness *o* lunacy!

robi'vecchi [robi'vɛkki] *smf inv* junk dealer.

'robot *sm inv* robot.

ro'botica *sf* robotics *sg*.

robus'tezza [robus'tettsa] *sf (di persona, pianta)* robustness, sturdiness; *(di edificio, ponte)* soundness.

ro'busto, a *ag* robust, sturdy; *(solido: catena)* strong; *(: edificio, ponte)* sound, solid; *(vino)* full-bodied.

'rocca, che *sf* fortress.

rocca'forte *sf* stronghold.

roc'chetto [rok'ketto] *sm* reel, spool.

'**roccia, ce** ['rɔttʃa] *sf* rock; **fare** ~ (*SPORT*) to go rock climbing.

roccia'tore, 'trice [rottʃa'tore] *sm/f* rock climber.

rocci'oso, a [rot't'ʃoso] *ag* rocky; **le Montagne R~e** the Rocky Mountains.

'**roco, a, chi, che** *ag* hoarse.

ro'daggio [ro'daddʒo] *sm* running (*BRIT*) *o* breaking (*US*) in; **in** ~ running *o* breaking in; **periodo di** ~ (*fig*) period of adjustment.

'**Rodano** *sm*: **il** ~ the Rhone.

ro'dare *vt* (*AUT, TECN*) to run (*BRIT*) *o* break (*US*) in.

ro'deo *sm* rodeo.

'**rodere** *vt* to gnaw (at); (*distruggere poco a poco*) to eat into.

'**Rodi** *sf* Rhodes.

rodi'tore *sm* (*ZOOL*) rodent.

rodo'dendro *sm* rhododendron.

'**rogito** ['rɔdʒito] *sm* (*DIR*) (notary's) deed.

'**rogna** ['rɔɲɲa] *sf* (*MED*) scabies *sg*; (*di animale*) mange; (*fig*) bother, nuisance.

ro'gnone [roɲ'ɲone] *sm* (*CUC*) kidney.

ro'gnoso, a [roɲ'ɲoso] *ag* (*persona*) scabby; (*animale*) mangy; (*fig*) troublesome.

'**rogo, ghi** *sm* (*per cadaveri*) (funeral) pyre; (*supplizio*): **il** ~ the stake.

rol'lare *vi* (*NAUT, AER*) to roll.

rol'lino *sm* = **rullino**.

rol'lio *sm* roll(ing).

'**Roma** *sf* Rome.

roma'gnolo, a [romaɲ'ɲɔlo] *ag* of (*o* from) Romagna.

roma'nesco, a, schi, sche *ag* Roman ♦ *sm* Roman dialect.

Roma'nia *sf*: **la** ~ Romania.

ro'manico, a, ci, che *ag* Romanesque.

ro'mano, a *ag, sm/f* Roman; **fare alla** ~**a** to go Dutch.

romantiche'ria [romantike'ria] *sf* sentimentality.

romanti'cismo [romanti'tʃizmo] *sm* romanticism.

ro'mantico, a, ci, che *ag* romantic.

ro'manza [ro'mandza] *sf* (*MUS, LETTERATURA*) romance.

roman'zare [roman'dzare] *vt* to romanticize.

roman'zesco, a, schi, sche [roman'dzesko] *ag* (*stile, personaggi*) fictional; (*fig*) storybook *cpd*.

romanzi'ere [roman'dzjere] *sm* novelist.

ro'manzo, a [ro'mandzo] *ag* (*LING*) romance *cpd* ♦ *sm* (*medievale*) romance; (*moderno*) novel; ~ **d'amore** love story; ~ **d'appendice** serial (story); ~ **cavalleresco** tale of chivalry; ~ **poliziesco**, ~ **giallo**

detective story; ~ **rosa** romantic novel.

rom'bare *vi* to rumble, thunder, roar.

'**rombo** *sm* rumble, thunder, roar; (*MAT*) rhombus; (*ZOOL*) turbot.

ro'meno, a *ag, sm/f, sm* = **rumeno**.

'**rompere** *vt* to break; (*conversazione, fidanzamento*) to break off ♦ *vi* to break; ~**rsi** *vr* to break; **mi rompe le scatole** (*fam*) he (*o* she) is a pain in the neck; ~**rsi un braccio** to break an arm.

rompi'capo *sm* worry, headache; (*indovinello*) puzzle; (*in enigmistica*) brain-teaser.

rompi'collo *sm* daredevil.

rompighi'accio [rompi'gjattʃo] *sm* (*NAUT*) icebreaker.

rompis'catole *sm/f inv* (*fam*) pest, pain in the neck.

'**ronda** *sf* (*MIL*) rounds *pl*, patrol.

ron'della *sf* (*TECN*) washer.

'**rondine** *sf* (*ZOOL*) swallow.

ron'done *sm* (*ZOOL*) swift.

ron'fare *vi* (*russare*) to snore.

ron'zare [ron'dzare] *vi* to buzz, hum.

ron'zino [ron'dzino] *sm* (*peg: cavallo*) nag.

ron'zio, ii [ron'dzio] *sm* buzzing, humming; ~ **auricolare** (*MED*) tinnitus *sg*.

'**rosa** *sf* rose; (*fig: gruppo*): ~ **dei candidati** list of candidates ♦ *ag inv, sm* pink.

ro'saio *sm* (*pianta*) rosebush, rose tree; (*giardino*) rose garden.

ro'sario *sm* (*REL*) rosary.

ro'sato, a *ag* pink, rosy ♦ *sm* (*vino*) rosé (wine).

ro'seo, a *ag* (*anche fig*) rosy.

ro'seto *sm* rose garden.

ro'setta *sf* (*diamante*) rose-cut diamond; (*rondella*) washer.

'**rosi** *vb vedi* **rodere**.

rosicchi'are [rosik'kjare] *vt* to gnaw (at); (*mangiucchiare*) to nibble (at).

rosma'rino *sm* rosemary.

'**roso, a** *pp di* **rodere**.

roso'lare *vt* (*CUC*) to brown.

roso'lia *sf* (*MED*) German measles *sg*, rubella.

'**rospo** *sm* (*ZOOL*) toad; **mandar giù** *o* **ingoiare un** *o* **il** ~ (*fig*) to swallow a bitter pill; **sputa il** ~! out with it!

ros'setto *sm* (*per labbra*) lipstick; (*per guance*) rouge.

ros'siccio, a, ci, ce [ros'sittʃo] *ag* reddish.

'**rosso, a** *ag, sm, sm/f* red; **diventare** ~ (**per la vergogna**) to blush *o* go red (with *o* for shame); **il mar R**~ the Red Sea; ~ **d'uovo** egg yolk.

ros'sore *sm* flush, blush.

rosticce'ria [rostittʃe'ria] *sf* shop selling

roast meat and other cooked food.

'ro'stro *sm* rostrum; (*becco*) beak.

ro'tabile *ag* (*percorribile*): strada ~ roadway; (*FERR*): materiale ~ rolling stock.

ro'taia *sf* rut, track; (*FERR*) rail.

ro'tare *vt, vi* to rotate.

rota'tivo, a *ag* rotating, rotation *cpd*.

rotazi'one [rotat'tsjone] *sf* rotation.

rote'are *vt, vi* to whirl; ~ gli occhi to roll one's eyes.

ro'tella *sf* small wheel; (*di mobile*) castor.

roto'calco, chi *sm* (*TIP*) rotogravure; (*rivista*) illustrated magazine.

roto'lare *vt, vi* to roll; ~rsi *vr* to roll (about).

roto'lio *sm* rolling.

'rotolo *sm* (*di carta, stoffa*) roll; (*di corda*) coil; andare a ~i (*fig*) to go to rack and ruin; mandare a ~i (*fig*) to ruin.

ro'tondo, a *ag* round ♦ *sf* rotunda.

ro'tore *sm* rotor.

'rotta *sf* (*AER, NAUT*) course, route; (*MIL*) rout; a ~ di collo at breakneck speed; essere in ~ con qn to be on bad terms with sb; fare ~ su *o* per *o* verso to head for *o* towards; cambiare ~ (*anche fig*) to change course; in ~ di collisione on a collision course; ufficiale di ~ navigator, navigating officer.

rot'tame *sm* fragment, scrap, broken bit; ~i *smpl* (*di nave, aereo etc*) wreckage *sg*; ~i di ferro scrap iron *sg*.

'rotto, a *pp di* rompere ♦ *ag* broken; (*calzoni*) torn, split; (*persona: pratico, resistente*): ~ a accustomed *o* inured to ♦ *sm*: per il ~ della cuffia by the skin of one's teeth; ~i *smpl*: 20.000 lire e ~i 20,000-odd lire.

rot'tura *sf* (*azione*) breaking *no pl*; (*di rapporti*) breaking off; (*MED*) fracture, break.

rou'lotte [ru'lɔt] *sf inv* caravan.

ro'vente *ag* red-hot.

'rovere *sm* oak.

ro'vescia [ro'vɛʃʃa] *sf*: alla ~ upside-down; inside-out; oggi mi va tutto alla ~ everything is going wrong (for me) today.

rovesci'are [roveʃ'ʃare] *vt* (*versare in giù*) to pour; (*: accidentalmente*) to spill; (*capovolgere*) to turn upside down; (*gettare a terra*) to knock down; (*: fig: governo*) to overthrow; (*piegare all'indietro: testa*) to throw back; ~rsi *vr* (*sedia, macchina*) to overturn; (*barca*) to capsize; (*liquido*) to spill; (*fig: situazione*) to be reversed.

ro'vescio, sci [ro'vɛʃʃo] *sm* other side, wrong side; (*della mano*) back; (*di moneta*) reverse; (*pioggia*) sudden downpour; (*fig*) setback; (*MAGLIA: anche: punto* ~) purl (stitch); (*TENNIS*) backhand (stroke); a ~ (*sottosopra*) upside-down; (*con l'esterno all'interno*) inside-out; capire qc a ~ to misunderstand sth; ~ di fortuna setback.

ro'vina *sf* ruin; ~e *sfpl* ruins; andare in ~ (*andare a pezzi*) to collapse; (*fig*) to go to rack and ruin; mandare qc/qn in ~ to ruin sth/sb.

rovi'nare *vi* to collapse, fall down ♦ *vt* (*far cadere giù: casa*) to demolish; (*danneggiare, fig*) to ruin.

rovi'nato, a *ag* ruined, damaged; (*fig: persona*) ruined.

rovi'noso, a *ag* ruinous.

rovis'tare *vt* (*casa*) to ransack; (*tasche*) to rummage in (*o* through).

'rovo *sm* (*BOT*) blackberry bush, bramble bush.

roz'zezza [rod'dzettsa] *sf* roughness, coarseness.

'rozzo, a ['roddzo] *ag* rough, coarse.

RP *sigla fpl vedi* relazioni pubbliche.

R.R. *abbr* (*POSTA*) = ricevuta di ritorno.

Rrr *abbr* (*POSTA*) = raccomandata con ricevuta di ritorno.

RSVP *abbr* (= *répondez s'il vous plaît*) RSVP.

'ruba *sf*: andare a ~ to sell like hot cakes.

rubacu'ori *sm inv* ladykiller.

ru'bare *vt* to steal; ~ qc a qn to steal sth from sb.

rubi'condo, a *ag* ruddy.

rubi'netto *sm* tap, faucet (*US*).

ru'bino *sm* ruby.

ru'bizzo, a [ru'bittso] *ag* lively, sprightly.

'rublo *sm* rouble.

ru'brica, che *sf* (*di giornale: colonna*) column; (*: pagina*) page; (*quadernetto*) index book; (*: per indirizzi*) address book.

'rude *ag* tough, rough.

'rudere *sm* (*rovina*) ruins *pl*.

rudimen'tale *ag* rudimentary, basic.

rudi'menti *smpl* rudiments; basic principles.

ruffi'ano *sm* pimp.

'ruga, ghe *sf* wrinkle.

'ruggine ['ruddʒine] *sf* rust.

rug'gire [rud'dʒire] *vi* to roar.

rug'gito [rud'dʒito] *sm* roar.

rugi'ada [ru'dʒada] *sf* dew.

ru'goso, a *ag* wrinkled; (*scabro: superficie etc*) rough.

rul'lare *vi* (*tamburo, nave*) to roll; (*aereo*) to taxi.

rul'lino *sm* (*FOT*) roll of film, spool.

rul'lio, ii *sm* (*di tamburi*) roll.

'rullo *sm* (*di tamburi*) roll; (*arnese cilindrico,*

TIP) roller; ~ **compressore** steam roller; ~ **di pellicola** roll of film.

rum *sm* rum.

ru'meno, a *ag, sm/f, sm* Romanian.

rumi'nante *sm* (*ZOOL*) ruminant.

rumi'nare *vt* (*ZOOL*) to ruminate; (*fig*) to ruminate on *o* over, chew over.

ru'more *sm*: **un** ~ a noise, a sound; **il** ~ noise; **fare** ~ to make a noise; **un** ~ **di passi** the sound of footsteps; **la notizia ha fatto molto** ~ (*fig*) the news aroused great interest.

rumoreggi'are [rumored'dʒare] *vi* (*tuono etc*) to rumble; (*fig: folla*) to clamour (*BRIT*), clamor (*US*).

rumo'roso, a *ag* noisy.

ru'olo *sm* (*TEAT, fig*) role, part; (*elenco*) roll, register, list; **di** ~ permanent, on the permanent staff; **professore di** ~ (*INS*) ≈ lecturer with tenure; **fuori** ~ (*personale, insegnante*) temporary.

ru'ota *sf* wheel; **a** ~ (*forma*) circular; ~ **anteriore/posteriore** front/back wheel; **andare a** ~ **libera** to freewheel; **parlare a** ~ **libera** (*fig*) to speak freely; ~ **di scorta** spare wheel.

ruo'tare *vt, vi* = rotare.

'rupe *sf* cliff, rock.

ru'pestre *ag* rocky.

ru'pia *sf* rupee.

'ruppi *etc vb vedi* rompere.

ru'rale *ag* rural, country *cpd*.

ru'scello [ruʃ'ʃɛllo] *sm* stream.

'ruspa *sf* excavator.

rus'pante *ag* (*pollo*) free-range.

rus'sare *vi* to snore.

'Russia *sf*: **la** ~ Russia.

'russo, a *ag, sm/f, sm* Russian.

'rustico, a, ci, che *ag* country *cpd*, rural; (*arredamento*) rustic; (*fig*) rough, unrefined ♦ *sm* (*fabbricato: per attrezzi*) shed; (*per abitazione*) farm labourer's (*BRIT*) *o* farmhand's cottage.

'ruta *sf* (*BOT*) rue.

rut'tare *vi* to belch.

'rutto *sm* belch.

'ruvido, a *ag* rough, coarse.

ruzzo'lare [ruttso'lare] *vi* to tumble down.

ruzzo'lone [ruttso'lone] *sm* tumble, fall.

ruzzo'loni [ruttso'loni] *av*: **cadere** ~ to tumble down; **fare le scale** ~ to tumble down the stairs.

S s

S, s ['ɛsse] *sf o m* (*lettera*) S, s; **S come Savona** ≈ S for Sugar.

s *abbr* (= *secondo*) sec.

S. *abbr* (= *sud*) S; (= *santo*) St.

SA *sigla* = Salerno ♦ *abbr vedi* **società anonima.**

sa *vb vedi* **sapere.**

sab. *abbr* (= *sabato*) Sat.

'sabato *sm* Saturday; *per fraseologia vedi* **martedì.**

'sabbia *sf* sand; ~**e mobili** quicksand(s *pl*).

sabbia'tura *sf* (*MED*) sand bath; (*TECN*) sand-blasting; **fare le** ~**e** to take sand baths.

sabbi'oso, a *ag* sandy.

sabo'taggio [sabo'taddʒo] *sm* sabotage.

sabo'tare *vt* to sabotage.

sabota'tore, 'trice *sm/f* saboteur.

'sacca, che *sf* bag; (*bisaccia*) haversack; (*insenatura*) inlet; ~ **d'aria** air pocket; ~ **da viaggio** travelling bag.

sacca'rina *sf* saccharin(e).

sac'cente [sat'tʃɛnte] *sm/f* know-all (*BRIT*), know-it-all (*US*).

saccheggi'are [sakked'dʒare] *vt* to sack, plunder.

sac'cheggio [sak'keddʒo] *sm* sack(ing).

sac'chetto [sak'ketto] *sm* (small) bag; (small) sack; ~ **di carta/di plastica** paper/plastic bag.

'sacco, chi *sm* bag; (*per carbone etc*) sack; (*ANAT, BIOL*) sac; (*tela*) sacking; (*saccheggio*) sack(ing); (*fig: grande quantità*): **un** ~ **di** lots of, heaps of; **cogliere** *o* **prendere qn con le mani nel** ~ to catch sb red-handed; **vuotare il** ~ to confess, spill the beans; **mettere qn nel** ~ to cheat sb; **colazione** *f* **al** ~ packed lunch; ~ **a pelo** sleeping bag; ~ **per i rifiuti** bin bag (*BRIT*), garbage bag (*US*).

sacer'dote [satʃer'dote] *sm* priest.

sacer'dozio [satʃer'dɔttsjo] *sm* priesthood.

'Sacra Co'rona U'nita *sf* the mafia in Puglia.

sacra'mento *sm* sacrament.

sa'crario *sm* memorial chapel.

sacres'tano *sm* = sagrestano.

sacres'tia *sf* = sagrestia.

sacrifi'care *vt* to sacrifice; **~rsi** *vr* to sacrifice o.s.; (*privarsi di qc*) to make sacrifices.

sacrifi'cato, a *ag* sacrificed; (*non valorizzato*) wasted; **una vita ~a** a life of sacrifice.

sacri'ficio [sakri'fitʃo] *sm* sacrifice.

sacri'legio [sacri'lɛdʒo] *sm* sacrilege.

sa'crilego, a, ghi, ghe *ag* (*REL*) sacrilegious.

'sacro, a *ag* sacred.

sacro'santo, a *ag* sacrosanct.

'sadico, a, ci, che *ag* sadistic ♦ *sm/f* sadist.

sa'dismo *sm* sadism.

sadomaso'chismo [sadomazo'kismo] *sm* sadomasochism.

sa'etta *sf* arrow; (*fulmine: anche fig*) thunderbolt.

sa'fari *sm inv* safari.

sa'gace [sa'gatʃe] *ag* shrewd, sagacious.

sa'gacia [sa'gatʃa] *sf* sagacity, shrewdness.

sag'gezza [sad'dʒettsa] *sf* wisdom.

saggi'are [sad'dʒare] *vt* (*metalli*) to assay; (*fig*) to test.

'saggio, a, gi, ge ['saddʒo] *ag* wise ♦ *sm* (*persona*) sage; (*operazione sperimentale*) test; (: *dell'oro*) assay; (*fig: prova*) proof; (*campione indicativo*) sample; (*scritto: letterario*) essay; (: *INS*) written test; **dare ~ di** to give proof of; **in ~** as a sample.

sag'gistica [sad'dʒistika] *sf* ≈ non-fiction.

Sagit'tario [sadʒit'tarjo] *sm* Sagittarius; **essere del ~** to be Sagittarius.

'sagoma *sf* (*profilo*) outline, profile; (*forma*) form, shape; (*TECN*) template; (*bersaglio*) target; (*fig: persona*) character.

'sagra *sf* festival.

sa'grato *sm* churchyard.

sagres'tano *sm* sacristan; sexton.

sagres'tia *sf* sacristy; (*culto protestante*) vestry.

Sa'hara [sa'ara] *sm*: **il (Deserto del) ~** the Sahara (Desert).

sahari'ana [saa'rjana] *sf* bush jacket.

'sai *vb vedi* **sapere**.

Sai'gon *sf* Saigon.

'saio *sm* (*REL*) habit.

'sala *sf* hall; (*stanza*) room; **~ d'aspetto** waiting room; **~ da ballo** ballroom; **~ (dei) comandi** control room; **~ per concerti** concert hall; **~ per conferenze** (*INS*) lecture hall; (*in aziende*) conference room; **~ da gioco** gaming room; **~ macchine** (*NAUT*) engine room; **~ operatoria** (*MED*) operating theatre (*BRIT*) *o* room (*US*); **~ da pranzo** dining room; **~ per ricevimenti** banqueting hall; **~ delle udienze** (*DIR*) courtroom.

sa'lace [sa'latʃe] *ag* (*spinto, piccante*) salacious, saucy; (*mordace*) cutting, biting.

sala'mandra *sf* salamander.

sa'lame *sm* salami *no pl*, salami sausage.

sala'moia *sf* (*CUC*) brine.

sa'lare *vt* to salt.

salari'ale *ag* wage *cpd*, pay *cpd*; **aumento ~** wage *o* pay increase (*BRIT*) *o* raise (*US*).

salari'ato, a *sm/f* wage-earner.

sa'lario *sm* pay, wages *pl*; **~ base** basic wage; **~ minimo garantito** guaranteed minimum wage.

salas'sare *vt* (*MED*) to bleed.

sa'lasso *sm* (*MED*) bleeding, bloodletting; (*fig: forte spesa*) drain.

sala'tino *sm* cracker, salted biscuit.

sa'lato, a *ag* (*sapore*) salty; (*CUC*) salted, salt *cpd*; (*fig: discorso etc*) biting, sharp; (: *prezzi*) steep, stiff.

sal'dare *vt* (*congiungere*) to join, bind; (*parti metalliche*) to solder; (: *con saldatura autogena*) to weld; (*conto*) to settle, pay.

salda'tore *sm* (*operaio*) solderer; welder; (*utensile*) soldering iron.

salda'trice [salda'tritʃe] *sf* (*macchina*) welder, welding machine; **~ ad arco** arc welder.

salda'tura *sf* soldering; welding; (*punto saldato*) soldered joint; weld; **~ autogena** welding; **~ dolce** soft soldering.

sal'dezza [sal'dettsa] *sf* firmness, strength.

'saldo, a *ag* (*resistente, forte*) strong, firm; (*fermo*) firm, steady, stable; (*fig*) firm, steadfast ♦ *sm* (*svendita*) sale; (*di conto*) settlement; (*ECON*) balance; **pagare a ~** to pay in full; **~ attivo** credit; **~ passivo** deficit; **~ da riportare** balance carried forward.

'sale *sm* salt; (*fig*) wit; **~i** *smpl* (*MED: da annusare*) smelling salts; **sotto ~** salted; **restare di ~** (*fig*) to be dumbfounded; **ha poco ~ in zucca** he doesn't have much sense; **~ da cucina, ~ grosso** cooking salt; **~ da tavola, ~ fino** table salt; **~i da bagno** bath salts; **~i minerali** mineral salts; **~i e tabacchi** tobacconist's (shop).

sal'gemma [sal'dʒemma] *sm* rock salt.

'salgo *etc vb vedi* **salire**.

'salice ['salitʃe] *sm* willow; **~ piangente** weeping willow.

sali'ente *ag* (*fig*) salient, main.

sali'era *sf* salt cellar.

sa'lino, a *ag* saline ♦ *sf* saltworks *sg*.

sa'lire *vi* to go (*o* come) up; (*aereo etc*) to climb, go up; (*passeggero*) to get on; (*sentiero, prezzi, livello*) to go up, rise ♦ *vt* (*scale, gradini*) to go (*o* come) up; **~ su** to climb (up); ~ **sul treno/sull'autobus** to board the train/the bus; ~ **in macchina** to get into the car; ~ **a cavallo** to mount; ~ **al potere** to rise to power; ~ **al trono** to ascend the throne; ~ **alle stelle** (*prezzi*) to rocket.

sali'scendi [saliʃˈʃendi] *sm inv* latch.

sa'lita *sf* climb, ascent; (*erta*) hill, slope; **in ~** *ag, av* uphill.

sa'liva *sf* saliva.

'salma *sf* corpse.

sal'mastro, a *ag* (*acqua*) salt *cpd*; (*sapore*) salty ♦ *sm* (*sapore*) salty taste; (*odore*) salty smell.

salmi *sm* (*CUC*) salmi; **lepre in ~** salmi of hare.

'salmo *sm* psalm.

sal'mone *sm* salmon.

salmo'nella *sf* salmonella.

Salo'mone: le isole ~ *sfpl* the Solomon Islands.

sa'lone *sm* (*stanza*) sitting room, lounge; (*in albergo*) lounge; (*di ricevimento*) reception room; (*su nave*) lounge, saloon; (*mostra*) show, exhibition; (*negozio: di parrucchiere*) hairdresser's (salon); ~ **dell'automobile** motor show; ~ **di bellezza** beauty salon.

salo'pette [salɔˈpɛt] *sf inv* dungarees *pl*.

salotti'ero, a *ag* mundane.

sa'lotto *sm* lounge, sitting room; (*mobilio*) lounge suite.

sal'pare *vi* (*NAUT*) to set sail; (*anche:* ~ **l'ancora**) to weigh anchor.

'salsa *sf* (*CUC*) sauce; **in tutte le ~e** (*fig*) in all kinds of ways; ~ **di pomodoro** tomato sauce.

sal'sedine *sf* (*del mare, vento*) saltiness; (*incrostazione*) (dried) salt.

sal'siccia, ce [salˈsittʃa] *sf* pork sausage.

salsi'era *sf* sauceboat (*BRIT*), gravy boat.

'salso *sm* saltiness.

sal'tare *vi* to jump, leap; (*esplodere*) to blow up, explode; (*: valvola*) to blow; (*venir via*) to pop off; (*non aver luogo: corso etc*) to be cancelled ♦ *vt* to jump (over), leap (over); (*fig: pranzo, capitolo*) to skip, miss (out); (*CUC*) to sauté; **far ~** to blow up; (*serratura: forzare*) to break; **far ~ il banco** (*GIOCO*) to break the bank; **farsi ~ le cervella** to blow one's brains out; **ma che ti salta in mente?** what are you thinking of?; ~ **da un argomento all'altro** to jump from one subject to another; ~ **addosso a qn** (*aggredire*) to attack sb; ~ **fuori** to jump out, leap out; (*venire trovato*) to turn up; ~ **fuori con** (*frase, commento*) to come out with; ~ **giù da qc** to jump off sth, jump down from sth.

saltel'lare *vi* to skip; to hop.

sal'tello *sm* hop, little jump.

saltim'banco, chi *sm* acrobat.

'salto *sm* jump; (*SPORT*) jumping; (*dislivello*) drop; **fare un ~** to jump, leap; **fare un ~ da qn** to pop over to sb's (place); ~ **in alto/lungo** high/long jump; ~ **con l'asta** pole vaulting; ~ **mortale** somersault; **un ~ di qualità** (*miglioramento*) significant improvement.

saltu'ario, a *ag* occasional, irregular.

sa'lubre *ag* healthy, salubrious.

sa'lume *sm* (*CUC*) cured pork; ~**i** *smpl* (*insaccati*) cured pork meats.

salume'ria *sf* delicatessen.

salumi'ere, a *sm/f* ≈ delicatessen owner.

salumi'ficio [salumiˈfitʃo] *sm* cured pork meat factory.

salu'tare *ag* healthy; (*fig*) salutary, beneficial ♦ *vt* (*per dire buon giorno, fig*) to greet; (*per dire addio*) to say goodbye to; (*MIL*) to salute; **mi saluti sua moglie** my regards to your wife.

sa'lute *sf* health; ~! (*a chi starnutisce*) bless you!; (*nei brindisi*) cheers!; **bere alla ~ di qn** to drink (to) sb's health; **la ~ pubblica** public welfare; **godere di buona ~** to be healthy, enjoy good health.

sa'luto *sm* (*gesto*) wave; (*parola*) greeting; (*MIL*) salute; **gli ha tolto il ~** he no longer says hello to him; **cari ~i, tanti ~i** best regards; **vogliate gradire i nostri più distinti ~i** yours faithfully; **i miei ~i alla sua signora** my regards to your wife.

'salva *sf* salvo.

salvacon'dotto *sm* (*MIL*) safe-conduct.

salvada'naio *sm* moneybox, piggy bank.

salvado'regno, a [salvadoˈreɲɲo] *ag, sm/f* Salvadorean.

salva'gente [salvaˈdʒɛnte] *sm* (*NAUT*) lifebuoy; (*pl inv: stradale*) traffic island; ~ **a ciambella** lifebelt; ~ **a giubbotto** lifejacket (*BRIT*), life preserver (*US*).

salvaguar'dare *vt* to safeguard.

salvagu'ardia *sf* safeguard; **a ~ di** for the safeguard of.

sal'vare *vt* to save; (*trarre da un pericolo*) to rescue; (*proteggere*) to protect; ~**rsi** *vr* to save o.s.; to escape; ~ **la vita a qn** to save sb's life; ~ **le apparenze** to keep up appearances; **si salvi chi può!** every man for himself!

salva'taggio [salvaˈtaddʒo] *sm* rescue.

salva'tore, 'trice *sm/f* saviour (*BRIT*), savior (*US*).

salvazi'one [salvatˈtsjone] *sf* (*REL*) salvation.

'salve *escl* (*fam*) hi!

sal'vezza [sal'vettsa] *sf* salvation; (*sicurezza*) safety.

'salvia *sf* (*BOT*) sage.

salvi'etta *sf* napkin, serviette.

'salvo, a *ag* safe, unhurt, unharmed; (*fuori pericolo*) safe, out of danger ♦ *sm*: **in ~ safe** ♦ *prep* (*eccetto*) except; **~ che** *cong* (*a meno che*) unless; (*eccetto che*) except (that); **mettere qc in ~** to put sth in a safe place; **mettersi in ~** to reach safety; **portare qn in ~** to lead sb to safety; **~ contrordini** barring instructions to the contrary; **~ errori e omissioni** errors and omissions excepted; **~ imprevisti** barring accidents.

sam'buca *sf* (*liquore*) sambuca (*type of anisette*).

sam'buco *sm* elder (tree).

sa'nare *vt* to heal, cure; (*economia*) to put right.

sana'toria *sf* (*DIR*) act of indemnity.

sana'torio *sm* sanatorium (*BRIT*), sanitarium (*US*).

san'cire [san'tʃire] *vt* to sanction.

'sandalo *sm* (*BOT*) sandalwood; (*calzatura*) sandal.

sang'ria [san'gria] *sf* (*bibita*) sangria.

'sangue *sm* blood; **farsi cattivo ~** to fret, get worked up; **all'ultimo ~** (*duello, lotta*) to the death; **non corre buon ~ tra di loro** there's bad blood between them; **buon ~ non mente!** blood will out!; **~ freddo** (*fig*) sang-froid, calm; **a ~ freddo** in cold blood.

sangu'igno, a [san'gwiɲɲo] *ag* blood *cpd*; (*colore*) blood-red.

sangui'nante *ag* bleeding.

sangui'nare *vi* to bleed.

sangui'nario, a *ag* bloodthirsty.

sangui'noso, a *ag* bloody.

sangui'suga, ghe *sf* leech.

sanità *sf* health; (*salubrità*) healthiness; **Ministero della S~** Department of Health; **~ mentale** sanity; **~ pubblica** public health.

sani'tario, a *ag* health *cpd*; (*condizioni*) sanitary ♦ *sm* (*AMM*) doctor; **Ufficiale S~** Health Officer; (*impianti*) **~i** *smpl* bathroom *o* sanitary fittings.

San Ma'rino *sf*: **la Repubblica di ~** the Republic of San Marino.

'sanno *vb vedi* **sapere**.

'sano, a *ag* healthy; (*denti, costituzione*) healthy, sound; (*integro*) whole, unbroken; (*fig: politica, consigli*) sound; **~ di mente** sane; **di ~a pianta** completely, entirely; **~ e salvo** safe and sound.

Santi'ago *sf*: **~ (del Cile)** Santiago (de Chile).

santifi'care *vt* to sanctify; (*feste*) to observe.

san'tino *sm* holy picture.

san'tissimo, a *ag*: **il S~ Sacramento** the Holy Sacrament; **il Padre S~** (*papa*) the Holy Father.

santità *sf* sanctity; holiness; **Sua/Vostra ~** (*titolo di papa*) His/Your Holiness.

'santo, a *ag* holy; (*fig*) saintly; (*seguito da nome proprio: dav sm* **san** + *C*, **sant'** + *V*, **santo** + *s impura, gn, pn, ps, x, z; dav sf* **santa** + *C*, **sant'** + *V*) saint ♦ *sm/f* saint; **parole ~e!** very true!; **tutto il ~ giorno** the whole blessed day, all day long; **non c'è ~ che tenga!** that's no excuse!; **la S~a Sede** the Holy See.

san'tone *sm* holy man.

santu'ario *sm* sanctuary.

sanzio'nare [santsjo'nare] *vt* to sanction.

sanzi'one [san'tsjone] *sf* sanction; (*penale, civile*) sanction, penalty; **~i economiche** economic sanctions.

sa'pere *vt* to know; (*essere capace di*): **so nuotare** I know how to swim, I can swim ♦ *vi*: **~ di** (*aver sapore*) to taste of; (*aver odore*) to smell of ♦ *sm* knowledge; **far ~ qc a qn** to inform sb about sth, let sb know sth; **venire a ~ qc (da qn)** to find out *o* hear about sth (from sb); **non ne vuole più ~ di lei** he doesn't want to have anything more to do with her; **mi sa che non sia vero** I don't think that's true.

sapi'ente *ag* (*dotto*) learned; (*che rivela abilità*) masterly ♦ *sm/f* scholar.

sapien'tone, a *sm/f* (*peg*) know-all (*BRIT*), know-it-all (*US*).

sapi'enza [sa'pjɛntsa] *sf* wisdom.

sa'pone *sm* soap; **~ da barba** shaving soap; **~ da bucato** washing soap; **~ liquido** liquid soap; **~ in scaglie** soapflakes *pl*.

sapo'netta *sf* cake *o* bar *o* tablet of soap.

sa'pore *sm* taste, flavour (*BRIT*), flavor (*US*).

sapo'rito, a *ag* tasty; (*fig: arguto*) witty; (*: piccante*) racy.

sappi'amo *vb vedi* **sapere**.

saprò *etc vb vedi* **sapere**.

sapu'tello, a *sm/f* know-all (*BRIT*), know-it-all (*US*).

sarà *etc vb vedi* **essere**.

sara'banda *sf* (*fig*) uproar.

saraci'nesca, sche [saratʃi'neska] *sf* (*serranda*) rolling shutter.

sar'casmo *sm* sarcasm *no pl*; sarcastic remark.

sar'castico, a, ci, che *ag* sarcastic.

sarchi'are [sar'kjare] *vt* (*AGR*) to hoe.

sar'cofago, gi *o* **ghi** *sm* sarcophagus.

Sar'degna [sar'deɲɲa] *sf*: **la** ~ Sardinia.
sar'dina *sf* sardine.
'sardo, a *ag, sm/f* Sardinian.
sar'donico, a, ci, che *ag* sardonic.
sa'rei *etc vb vedi* **essere**.
'sarta *sf vedi* **sarto**.
'sartia *sf* (*NAUT*) stay.
sarti'ame *sm* (*NAUT*) stays *pl*.
'sarto, a *sm/f* tailor/dressmaker; ~ **d'alta moda** couturier.
sarto'ria *sf* tailor's (shop); dressmaker's (shop); (*casa di moda*) fashion house; (*arte*) couture.
sassai'ola *sf* hail of stones.
sas'sata *sf* blow with a stone; **tirare una** ~ **contro** *o* **a qc/qn** to throw a stone at sth/sb.
'sasso *sm* stone; (*ciottolo*) pebble; (*masso*) rock; **restare** *o* **rimanere di** ~ to be dumbfounded.
sassofo'nista, i, e *sm/f* saxophonist.
sas'sofono *sm* saxophone.
sas'sone *ag, sm/f, sm* Saxon.
sas'soso, a *ag* stony; pebbly.
'Satana *sm* Satan.
sa'tanico, a, ci, che *ag* satanic, fiendish.
sa'tellite *sm, ag* satellite.
'satira *sf* satire.
satireggi'are [satired'dʒare] *vt* to satirize ♦ *vi* (*fare della satira*) to be satirical; (*scrivere satire*) to write satires.
sa'tirico, a, ci, che *ag* satiric(al).
sa'tollo, a *ag* full, replete.
satu'rare *vt* to saturate.
saturazi'one [saturat'tsjone] *sf* saturation.
'saturo, a *ag* saturated; (*fig*): ~ **di** full of; ~ **d'acqua** (*terreno*) waterlogged.
'SAUB *sigla f* (= *Struttura Amministrativa Unificata di Base*) state welfare system.
'sauna *sf* sauna; **fare la** ~ to have *o* take a sauna.
sa'vana *sf* savannah.
'savio, a *ag* wise, sensible ♦ *sm* wise man.
Sa'voia *sf*: **la** ~ Savoy.
savoi'ardo, a *ag* of Savoy, Savoyard ♦ *sm* (*biscotto*) sponge finger.
sazi'are [sat'tsjare] *vt* to satisfy, satiate; ~**rsi** *vr* (*riempirsi di cibo*): ~**rsi (di)** to eat one's fill (of); (*fig*): ~**rsi di** to grow tired *o* weary of.
sazietà [sattsje'ta] *sf* satiety, satiation.
'sazio, a ['sattsjo] *ag*: ~ **(di)** sated (with), full (of); (*fig*: *stufo*) fed up (with), sick (of).
sbada'taggine [zbada'taddʒine] *sf* (*sventatezza*) carelessness; (*azione*) oversight.
sba'dato, a *ag* careless, inattentive.

sbadigli'are [zbadiʎ'ʎare] *vi* to yawn.
sba'diglio [zba'diʎʎo] *sm* yawn; **fare uno** ~ to yawn.
'sbafo *sm*: **a** ~ at somebody else's expense.
sbagli'are [zbaʎ'ʎare] *vt* to make a mistake in, get wrong ♦ *vi* (*fare errori*) to make a mistake (*o* mistakes), be mistaken; (*ingannarsi*) to be wrong; (*operare in modo non giusto*) to err; ~**rsi** *vr* to make a mistake, be mistaken, be wrong; ~ **la mira/strada** to miss one's aim/take the wrong road; **scusi, ho sbagliato numero** (*TEL*) sorry, I've got the wrong number; **non c'è da** ~**rsi** there can be no mistake.
sbagli'ato, a [zbaʎ'ʎato] *ag* (*gen*) wrong; (*compito*) full of mistakes; (*conclusione*) erroneous.
'sbaglio ['zbaʎʎo] *sm* mistake, error; (*morale*) error; **fare uno** ~ to make a mistake.
sbales'trato, a *ag* (*persona*: *scombussolato*) unsettled.
sbal'lare *vt* (*merce*) to unpack ♦ *vi* (*nel fare un conto*) to overestimate; (*DROGA*: *gergo*) to get high.
sbal'lato, a *ag* (*calcolo*) wrong; (*fam*: *ragionamento, persona*) screwy.
'sballo *sm* (*DROGA*: *gergo*) trip.
sballot'tare *vt* to toss (about).
sbalor'dire *vt* to stun, amaze ♦ *vi* to be stunned, be amazed.
sbalordi'tivo, a *ag* amazing; (*prezzo*) incredible, absurd.
sbal'zare [zbal'tsare] *vt* to throw, hurl; (*fig*: *da una carica*) to remove, dismiss ♦ *vi* (*balzare*) to bounce; (*saltare*) to leap, bound.
'sbalzo ['zbaltso] *sm* (*spostamento improvviso*) jolt, jerk; **a** ~**i** jerkily; (*fig*) in fits and starts; **uno** ~ **di temperatura** a sudden change in temperature.
sban'care *vt* (*nei giochi*) to break the bank at (*o* of); (*fig*) to ruin, bankrupt.
sbanda'mento *sm* (*NAUT*) list; (*AUT*) skid; (*fig*: *di persona*) confusion; **ha avuto un periodo di** ~ he went off the rails for a bit.
sban'dare *vi* (*NAUT*) to list; (*AUT*) to skid; ~**rsi** *vr* (*folla*) to disperse; (*truppe*) to scatter; (*fig*: *famiglia*) to break up.
sban'data *sf* (*AUT*) skid; (*NAUT*) list; **prendere una** ~ **per qn** (*fig*) to fall for sb.
sban'dato, a *sm/f* mixed-up person.
sbandie'rare *vt* (*bandiera*) to wave; (*fig*) to parade, show off.
'sbando *sm*: **essere allo** ~ to drift.
sbarac'care *vt* (*libri, piatti etc*) to clear (up).
sbaragli'are [zbaraʎ'ʎare] *vt* (*MIL*) to rout;

(*in gare sportive etc*) to beat, defeat.

sba'raglio [zba'raλλo] *sm*: **gettarsi allo ~** (*soldato*) to throw o.s. into the fray; (*fig*) to risk everything.

sbaraz'zarsi [zbarat'tsarsi] *vr*: **~ di** to get rid of, free o.s. of.

sbaraz'zino, a [zbarat'tsino] *ag* impish, cheeky.

sbar'bare *vt*, **~rsi** *vr* to shave.

sbarba'tello *sm* novice, greenhorn.

sbar'care *vt* (*passeggeri*) to disembark; (*merci*) to unload ♦ *vi* to disembark.

'sbarco *sm* disembarkation; unloading; (*MIL*) landing.

'sbarra *sf* bar; (*di passaggio a livello*) barrier; (*DIR*): **mettere/presentarsi alla ~** to bring/appear before the court.

sbarra'mento *sm* (*stradale*) barrier; (*diga*) dam, barrage; (*MIL*) barrage; (*POL*) cut-off point (*level of support below which a political party is excluded from representation in Parliament*).

sbar'rare *vt* (*bloccare*) to block, bar; (*cancellare*: *assegno*) to cross (*BRIT*); **~ il passo** to bar the way; **~ gli occhi** to open one's eyes wide.

sbar'rato, a *ag* (*porta*) barred; (*passaggio*) blocked, barred; (*strada*) blocked, obstructed; (*occhi*) staring; (*assegno*) crossed (*BRIT*).

'sbattere *vt* (*porta*) to bang; (*tappeti, ali, CUC*) to beat; (*urtare*) to knock, hit ♦ *vi* (*porta, finestra*) to bang; (*agitarsi*: *ali, vele etc*) to flap; **~ qn fuori/in galera** to throw sb out/into prison; **me ne sbatto!** (*fam*) I don't give a damn!

sbat'tuto, a *ag* (*viso, aria*) dejected, worn out; (*uovo*) beaten.

sba'vare *vi* to dribble; (*colore*) to smear, smudge.

sbava'tura *sf* (*di persone*) dribbling; (*di lumache*) slime; (*di rossetto, vernice*) smear.

sbelli'carsi *vr*: **~ dalle risa** to split one's sides laughing.

'sberla *sf* slap.

sber'leffo *sm*: **fare uno ~ a qn** to make a face at sb.

sbia'dire *vi* (*anche*: **~rsi**), *vt* to fade.

sbia'dito, a *ag* faded; (*fig*) colourless (*BRIT*), colorless (*US*), dull.

sbian'care *vt* to whiten; (*tessuto*) to bleach ♦ *vi* (*impallidire*) to grow pale *o* white.

sbi'eco, a, chi, che *ag* (*storto*) squint, askew; **di ~**: **guardare qn di ~** (*fig*) to look askance at sb; **tagliare una stoffa di ~** to cut material on the bias.

sbigot'tire *vt* to dismay, stun ♦ *vi* (*anche*:

~rsi) to be dismayed.

sbilanci'are [zbilan'tʃare] *vt* to throw off balance; **~rsi** *vr* (*perdere l'equilibrio*) to overbalance, lose one's balance; (*fig*: *compromettersi*) to compromise o.s.

sbi'lenco, a, chi, che *ag* (*persona*) crooked, misshapen; (*fig*: *idea, ragionamento*) twisted.

sbirci'are [zbir'tʃare] *vt* to cast sidelong glances at, eye.

sbirci'ata [zbir'tʃata] *sf*: **dare una ~ a qc** to glance at sth, have a look at sth.

'sbirro *sm* (*peg*) cop.

sbizzar'rirsi [zbiddzar'rirsi] *vr* to indulge one's whims.

sbloc'care *vt* to unblock, free; (*freno*) to release; (*prezzi, affitti*) to free from controls; **~rsi** *vr* (*gen*) to become unblocked; (*passaggio, strada*) to clear, become unblocked; **la situazione si è sbloccata** things are moving again.

'sblocco, chi *sm* (*vedi vt*) unblocking, freeing; release.

sboc'care *vi*: **~ in** (*fiume*) to flow into; (*strada*) to lead into; (*persona*) to come (out) into; (*fig*: *concludersi*) to end (up) in.

sboc'cato, a *ag* (*persona*) foul-mouthed; (*linguaggio*) foul.

sbocci'are [zbot'tʃare] *vi* (*fiore*) to bloom, open (out).

'sbocco, chi *sm* (*di fiume*) mouth; (*di strada*) end; (*di tubazione, COMM*) outlet; (*uscita*: *anche fig*) way out; **una strada senza ~** a dead end; **siamo in una situazione senza ~chi** there's no way out of this for us.

sbocconcel'lare [zbokkontʃel'lare] *vt*: **~ (qc)** to nibble (at sth).

sbollen'tare *vt* (*CUC*) to parboil.

sbol'lire *vi* (*fig*) to cool down, calm down.

'sbornia *sf* (*fam*): **prendersi una ~** to get plastered.

sbor'sare *vt* (*denaro*) to pay out.

sbot'tare *vi*: **~ in una risata/per la collera** to burst out laughing/explode with anger.

sbotto'nare *vt* to unbutton, undo.

sbra'cato, a *ag* slovenly.

sbracci'arsi [zbrat'tʃarsi] *vr* to wave (one's arms about).

sbracci'ato, a [zbrat'tʃato] *ag* (*camicia*) sleeveless; (*persona*) bare-armed.

sbrai'tare *vi* to yell, bawl.

sbra'nare *vt* to tear to pieces.

sbricio'lare [zbritʃo'lare] *vt*, **~rsi** *vr* to crumble.

sbri'gare *vt* to deal with, get through; (*cliente*) to attend to, deal with; **~rsi** *vr* to hurry (up).

sbriga'tivo, a *ag* (*persona, modo*) quick, expeditious; (*giudizio*) hasty.
sbrina'mento *sm* defrosting.
sbri'nare *vt* to defrost.
sbrindel'lato, a *ag* tattered, in tatters.
sbrodo'lare *vt* to stain, dirty.
sbron'zarsi [zbron'tsarsi] *vr* (*fam*) to get sozzled.
'sbronzo, a ['zbrontso] (*fam*) *ag* sozzled
♦ *sf*: **prendersi una ~a** to get sozzled.
sbruf'fone, a *sm/f* boaster, braggart.
sbu'care *vi* (*apparire*) to pop out (o up).
sbucci'are [zbut'tʃare] *vt* (*arancia, patata*) to peel; (*piselli*) to shell; **~rsi un ginocchio** to graze one's knee.
sbucherò *etc* [zbuke'rɔ] *vb vedi* **sbucare**.
sbudel'larsi *vr*: **~ dalle risa** to split one's sides laughing.
sbuf'fare *vi* (*persona, cavallo*) to snort; (: *ansimare*) to puff, pant; (*treno*) to puff.
'sbuffo *sm* (*di aria, fumo, vapore*) puff; **maniche a ~** puff(ed) sleeves.
sc. *abbr* (*TEAT:* = *scena*) sc.
S.C. *abbr* = **stato civile; Suprema Corte (di Cassazione)**.
'scabbia *sf* (*MED*) scabies *sg*.
'scabro, a *ag* rough, harsh; (*fig*) concise, terse.
sca'broso, a *ag* (*fig: difficile*) difficult, thorny; (: *imbarazzante*) embarrassing; (: *sconcio*) indecent.
scacchi'era [skak'kjɛra] *sf* chessboard.
scacchiere [skak'kjɛre] *sm* (*MIL*) sector; **S~** (*in Gran Bretagna*) Exchequer.
scaccia'cani [skattʃa'kani] *sm o f inv* pistol with blanks.
scacciapensi'eri [skattʃapen'sjɛri] *sm inv* (*MUS*) jew's-harp.
scacci'are [skat'tʃare] *vt* to chase away o out, drive away o out; **~ qn di casa** to turn sb out of the house.
'scacco, chi *sm* (*pezzo del gioco*) chessman; (*quadretto di scacchiera*) square; (*fig*) setback, reverse; **~chi** *smpl* (*gioco*) chess *sg*; **a ~chi** (*tessuto*) check(ed); **subire uno ~** (*fig: sconfitta*) to suffer a setback.
scacco'matto *sm* checkmate; **dare ~ a qn** (*anche fig*) to checkmate sb.
'scaddi *etc vb vedi* **scadere**.
sca'dente *ag* shoddy, of poor quality.
sca'denza [ska'dɛntsa] *sf* (*di cambiale, contratto*) maturity; (*di passaporto*) expiry date; **a breve/lunga ~** short-/long-term; **data di ~** expiry date; **~ a termine** fixed deadline.
sca'dere *vi* (*contratto etc*) to expire; (*debito*) to fall due; (*valore, forze, peso*) to decline, go down.

sca'fandro *sm* (*di palombaro*) diving suit; (*di astronauta*) spacesuit.
scaffala'tura *sf* shelving, shelves *pl*.
scaf'fale *sm* shelf; (*mobile*) set of shelves.
'scafo *sm* (*NAUT, AER*) hull.
scagio'nare [skadʒo'nare] *vt* to exonerate, free from blame.
'scaglia ['skaʎʎa] *sf* (*ZOOL*) scale; (*scheggia*) chip, flake.
scagli'are [skaʎ'ʎare] *vt* (*lanciare: anche fig*) to hurl, fling; **~rsi** *vr*: **~rsi su** *o* **contro** to hurl *o* fling o.s. at; (*fig*) to rail at.
scagliona'mento [skaʎʎona'mento] *sm* (*MIL*) arrangement in echelons.
scaglio'nare [skaʎʎo'nare] *vt* (*pagamenti*) to space out, spread out; (*MIL*) to echelon.
scagli'one [skaʎ'ʎone] *sm* (*MIL*) echelon; (*GEO*) terrace; **a ~i** in groups.
sca'gnozzo [skaɲ'ɲottso] *sm* (*peg*) lackey.
'scala *sf* (*a gradini etc*) staircase, stairs *pl*; (*a pioli, di corda*) ladder; (*MUS, GEO, di colori, valori, fig*) scale; **~e** *sfpl* (*scalinata*) stairs; **su larga** *o* **vasta ~** on a large scale; **su piccola ~**, **su ~ ridotta** on a small scale; **su ~ nazionale/mondiale** on a national/worldwide scale; **in ~ di 1 a 100.000** on a scale of 1 cm to 1 km; **riproduzione in ~** reproduction to scale; **~ a chiocciola** spiral staircase; **~ a libretto** stepladder; **~ di misure** system of weights and measures; **~ mobile** escalator; (*ECON*) sliding scale; **~ mobile (dei salari)** index-linked pay scale; **~ di sicurezza** (*antincendio*) fire escape.

Milan's **la Scala** *theatre first opened its doors in 1778 with a performance of Salieri's opera, "L'Europa riconosciuta". Built on the site of the former church of Santa Maria della Scala, it suffered serious damage in the bombing of Milan in 1943. It re-opened in 1946 with a concert conducted by Toscanini. Enjoying world-wide renown for its opera performances, it also has a famous classical dance school.*

---

sca'lare *vt* (*ALPINISMO, muro*) to climb, scale; (*debito*) to scale down, reduce; **questa somma vi viene scalata dal prezzo originale** this sum is deducted from the original price.
sca'lata *sf* scaling *no pl*, climbing *no pl*; (*arrampicata, fig*) climb; **dare la ~ a** (*fig*) to make a bid for.
scala'tore, 'trice *sm/f* climber.
scalca'gnato, a [skalkaɲ'ɲato] *ag* (*logoro*) worn; (*persona*) shabby.
scalci'are [skal'tʃare] *vi* to kick.

scalci'nato, a [skaltʃi'nato] *ag (fig peg)* shabby.

scalda'bagno [skalda'baɲɲo] *sm* water heater.

scal'dare *vt* to heat; ~**rsi** *vr* to warm up, heat up; (*al fuoco, al sole*) to warm o.s.; (*fig*) to get excited; ~ **la sedia** (*fig*) to twiddle one's thumbs.

scaldavi'vande *sm inv* dish warmer.

scal'dino *sm* (*per mani*) hand-warmer; (*per piedi*) foot-warmer; (*per letto*) bedwarmer.

scal'fire *vt* to scratch.

scalfit'tura *sf* scratch.

scali'nata *sf* staircase.

sca'lino *sm* (*anche fig*) step; (*di scala a pioli*) rung.

scal'mana *sf* (hot) flush.

scalma'narsi *vr* (*affaticarsi*) to rush about, rush around; (*agitarsi, darsi da fare*) to get all hot and bothered; (*arrabbiarsi*) to get excited, get steamed up.

scalma'nato, a *sm/f* hothead.

'scalo *sm* (*NAUT*) slipway; (: *porto d'approdo*) port of call; (*AER*) stopover; **fare** ~ **(a)** (*NAUT*) to call (at), put in (at); (*AER*) to land (at), make a stop (at); **volo senza** ~ non-stop flight; ~ **merci** (*FERR*) goods (*BRIT*) o freight yard.

sca'logna [ska'loɲɲa] *sf* (*fam*) bad luck.

scalo'gnato, a [skaloɲ'ɲato] *ag* (*fam*) unlucky.

scalop'pina *sf* (*CUC*) escalope.

scal'pello *sm* chisel.

scalpi'tare *vi* (*cavallo*) to paw the ground; (*persona*) to stamp one's feet.

scal'pore *sm* noise, row; **far** ~ (*notizia*) to cause a sensation o a stir.

'scaltro, a *ag* cunning, shrewd.

scal'zare [skal'tsare] *vt* (*albero*) to bare the roots of; (*muro, fig: autorità*) to undermine.

'scalzo, a ['skaltso] *ag* barefoot.

scambi'are *vt* to exchange; (*confondere*): ~ **qn/qc per** to take o mistake sb/sth for; **mi hanno scambiato il cappello** they've given me the wrong hat.

scambi'evole *ag* mutual, reciprocal.

'scambio *sm* exchange; (*COMM*) trade; (*FERR*) points *pl*; **fare (uno)** ~ to make a swap; **libero** ~ free trade; ~**i con l'estero** foreign trade.

scamosci'ato, a [skamoʃ'ʃato] *ag* suede.

scampa'gnata [skampaɲ'ɲata] *sf* trip to the country.

scampa'nare *vi* to peal.

scam'pare *vt* (*salvare*) to rescue, save; (*evitare: morte, prigione*) to escape ♦ *vi*: ~ (**a qc**) to survive (sth), escape (sth); **scamparla bella** to have a narrow escape.

'scampo *sm* (*salvezza*) escape; (*ZOOL*) prawn; **cercare** ~ **nella fuga** to seek safety in flight; **non c'è (via di)** ~ there's no way out.

'scampolo *sm* remnant.

scanala'tura *sf* (*incavo*) channel, groove.

scandagli'are [skandaʎ'ʎare] *vt* (*NAUT*) to sound; (*fig*) to sound out; to probe.

scanda'listico, a, ci, che *ag* (*settimanale etc*) sensational.

scandaliz'zare [skandalid'dzare] *vt* to shock, scandalize; ~**rsi** *vr* to be shocked.

'scandalo *sm* scandal; **dare** ~ to cause a scandal.

scanda'loso, a *ag* scandalous, shocking.

Scandi'navia *sf*: **la** ~ Scandinavia.

scandi'navo, a *ag, sm/f* Scandinavian.

scan'dire *vt* (*versi*) to scan; (*parole*) to articulate, pronounce distinctly; ~ **il tempo** (*MUS*) to beat time.

scan'nare *vt* (*animale*) to butcher, slaughter; (*persona*) to cut o slit the throat of.

'scanno *sm* seat, bench.

scansafa'tiche [skansafa'tike] *sm/f inv* idler, loafer.

scan'sare *vt* (*rimuovere*) to move (aside), shift; (*schivare: schiaffo*) to dodge; (*sfuggire*) to avoid; ~**rsi** *vr* to move aside.

scan'sia *sf* shelves *pl*; (*per libri*) bookcase.

'scanso *sm*: **a** ~ **di** in order to avoid, as a precaution against; **a** ~ **di equivoci** to avoid (any) misunderstanding.

scanti'nato *sm* basement.

scanto'nare *vi* to turn the corner; (*svignarsela*) to sneak off.

scanzo'nato, a [skantso'nato] *ag* easygoing.

scapacci'one [skapat'tʃone] *sm* clout, slap.

scapes'trato, a *ag* dissolute.

'scapito *sm* (*perdita*) loss; (*danno*) damage, detriment; **a** ~ **di** to the detriment of.

'scapola *sf* shoulder blade.

'scapolo *sm* bachelor.

scappa'mento *sm* (*AUT*) exhaust.

scap'pare *vi* (*fuggire*) to escape; (*andare via in fretta*) to rush off; ~ **di prigione** to escape from prison; ~ **di mano** (*oggetto*) to slip out of one's hands; ~ **di mente a qn** to slip sb's mind; **lasciarsi** ~ (*occasione, affare*) to miss, let go by; (*dettaglio*) to overlook; (*parola*) to let slip; (*prigioniero*) to let escape; **mi scappò detto** I let it slip.

scap'pata *sf* quick visit o call.

scappa'tella *sf* escapade.

scappa'toia *sf* way out.

scara'beo *sm* beetle.

scarabocchi'are [skarabok'kjare] *vt* to scribble, scrawl.

scara'bocchio [skara'bɔkkjo] *sm* scribble, scrawl.

scara'faggio [skara'faddʒo] *sm* cockroach.

scaraman'zia [skaraman'tsia] *sf*: **per ~ for** luck.

scara'muccia, ce [skara'muttʃa] *sf* skirmish.

scaraven'tare *vt* to fling, hurl.

scarce'rare [skartʃe'rare] *vt* to release (from prison).

scarcerazi'one [skartʃerat'tsjone] *sf* release (from prison).

scardi'nare *vt* to take off its hinges.

'scarica, che *sf* (*di più armi*) volley of shots; (*di sassi, pugni*) hail, shower; (*ELETTR*) discharge; **~ di mitra** burst of machine-gun fire.

scari'care *vt* (*merci, camion etc*) to unload; (*passeggeri*) to set down; (*arma*) to unload; (: *sparare, ELETTR*) to discharge; (*sog: corso d'acqua*) to empty, pour; (*fig: liberare da un peso*) to unburden, relieve; **~rsi** *vr* (*orologio*) to run o wind down; (*batteria, accumulatore*) to go flat (*BRIT*) o dead; (*fig: rilassarsi*) to unwind; (: *sfogarsi*) to let off steam; **~ le proprie responsabilità su qn** to off-load one's responsibilities onto sb; **~ la colpa addosso a qn** to blame sb; **il fulmine si scaricò su un albero** the lightning struck a tree.

scarica'tore *sm* loader; (*di porto*) docker.

'scarico, a, chi, che *ag* unloaded; (*orologio*) run down; (*batteria, accumulatore*) dead, flat (*BRIT*) ♦ *sm* (*di merci, materiali*) unloading; (*di immondizie*) dumping, tipping (*BRIT*); (: *luogo*) rubbish dump; (*TECN: deflusso*) draining; (: *dispositivo*) drain; (*AUT*) exhaust; **~ del lavandino** waste outlet.

scarlat'tina *sf* scarlet fever.

scar'latto, a *ag* scarlet.

'scarno, a *ag* thin, bony.

'scarpa *sf* shoe; **fare le ~e a qn** (*fig*) to double-cross sb; **~e da ginnastica** gym shoes; **~e coi tacchi (alti)** high-heeled shoes; **~e col tacco basso** low-heeled shoes; **~e senza tacco** flat shoes; **~e da tennis** tennis shoes.

scar'pata *sf* escarpment.

scarpi'era *sf* shoe rack.

scar'pone *sm* boot; **~i da montagna** climbing boots; **~i da sci** ski-boots.

scarroz'zare [skarrot'tsare] *vt* to drive around.

scarseggi'are [skarsed'dʒare] *vi* to be scarce; **~ di** to be short of, lack.

scar'sezza [skar'settsa] *sf* scarcity, lack.

'scarso, a *ag* (*insufficiente*) insufficient, meagre (*BRIT*), meager (*US*); (*povero: annata*) poor, lean; (*INS: voto*) poor; **~ di** lacking in; **3 chili ~i** just under 3 kilos, barely 3 kilos.

scartabel'lare *vt* to skim through, glance through.

scarta'faccio [skarta'fattʃo] *sm* notebook.

scarta'mento *sm* (*FERR*) gauge; **~ normale/ridotto** standard/narrow gauge.

scar'tare *vt* (*pacco*) to unwrap; (*idea*) to reject; (*MIL*) to declare unfit for military service; (*carte da gioco*) to discard; (*CALCIO*) to dodge (past) ♦ *vi* to swerve.

'scarto *sm* (*cosa scartata, anche COMM*) reject; (*di veicolo*) swerve; (*differenza*) gap, difference; **~ salariale** wage differential.

scar'toffie *sfpl* (*peg*) papers *pl.*

scas'sare *vt* (*fam: rompere*) to wreck.

scassi'nare *vt* to break, force.

'scasso *sm vedi* **furto.**

scate'nare *vt* (*fig*) to incite, stir up; **~rsi** *vr* (*temporale*) to break; (*rivolta*) to break out; (*persona: infuriarsi*) to rage.

scate'nato, a *ag* wild.

'scatola *sf* box; (*di latta*) tin (*BRIT*), can; **cibi in ~** tinned (*BRIT*) o canned foods; **una ~ di cioccolatini** a box of chocolates; **comprare qc a ~ chiusa** to buy sth sight unseen; **~ cranica** cranium.

scat'tante *ag* quick off the mark; (*agile*) agile.

scat'tare *vt* (*fotografia*) to take ♦ *vi* (*congegno, molla etc*) to be released; (*balzare*) to spring up; (*SPORT*) to put on a spurt; (*fig: dare per l'ira*) to fly into a rage; (*legge, provvedimento*) to come into effect; **~ in piedi** to spring to one's feet; **far ~** to release.

'scatto *sm* (*dispositivo*) release; (: *di arma da fuoco*) trigger mechanism; (*rumore*) click; (*balzo*) jump, start; (*SPORT*) spurt; (*fig: di ira etc*) fit; (: *di stipendio*) increment; **di ~** suddenly; **serratura a ~** spring lock.

scatu'rire *vi* to gush, spring.

scaval'care *vt* (*ostacolo*) to pass (o climb) over; (*fig*) to get ahead of, overtake.

sca'vare *vt* (*terreno*) to dig; (*legno*) to hollow out; (*pozzo, galleria*) to bore; (*città sepolta etc*) to excavate.

scava'trice [skava'tritʃe] *sf* (*macchina*) excavator.

scavezza'collo [skavettsa'kɔllo] *sm* daredevil.

'**scavo** *sm* excavating *no pl*; excavation.
scazzot'tare [skattsot'tare] *vt* (*fam*) to beat up, give a thrashing to.
'**scegliere** ['ʃeʎʎere] *vt* (*gen*) to choose; (*candidato, prodotto*) to choose, select; ~ **di fare** to choose to do.
sce'icco, chi [ʃe'ikko] *sm* sheik.
'**scelgo** *etc* ['ʃelgo] *vb vedi* **scegliere**.
scelle'rato, a [ʃelle'rato] *ag* wicked, evil.
scel'lino [ʃel'lino] *sm* shilling.
'**scelto, a** ['ʃelto] *pp di* **scegliere** ♦ *ag* (*gruppo*) carefully selected; (*frutta, verdura*) choice, top quality; (*MIL: specializzato*) crack *cpd*, highly skilled ♦ *sf* choice; (*selezione*) selection, choice; **frutta o formaggi a** ~**a** choice of fruit or cheese; **fare una** ~**a** to make a choice, choose; **non avere** ~**a** to have no choice *o* option; **di prima** ~**a** top grade *o* quality.
sce'mare [ʃe'mare] *vt, vi* to diminish.
sce'menza [ʃe'mɛntsa] *sf* stupidity *no pl*; stupid thing (to do *o* say).
'**scemo, a** ['ʃemo] *ag* stupid, silly.
'**scempio** ['ʃempjo] *sm* slaughter, massacre; (*fig*) ruin; **far** ~ **di** (*fig*) to play havoc with, ruin.
'**scena** ['ʃɛna] *sf* (*gen*) scene; (*palcoscenico*) stage; **le** ~**e** (*fig: teatro*) the stage; **andare in** ~ to be staged *o* put on *o* performed; **mettere in** ~ to stage; **uscire di** ~ to leave the stage; (*fig*) to leave the scene; **fare una** ~ (*fig*) to make a scene; **ha fatto** ~ **muta** (*fig*) he didn't open his mouth.
sce'nario [ʃe'narjo] *sm* scenery; (*di film*) scenario.
sce'nata [ʃe'nata] *sf* row, scene.
'**scendere** ['ʃendere] *vi* to go (*o* come) down; (*strada, sole*) to go down; (*notte*) to fall; (*passeggero: fermarsi*) to get out, alight; (*fig: temperatura, prezzi*) to fall, drop ♦ *vt* (*scale, pendio*) to go (*o* come) down; ~ **dalle scale** to go (*o* come) down the stairs; ~ **dal treno** to get off *o* out of the train; ~ **dalla macchina** to get out of the car; ~ **da cavallo** to dismount, get off one's horse; ~ **ad un albergo** to put up *o* stay at a hotel.
sceneggi'ato [ʃened'dʒato] *sm* television drama.
sceneggia'tore, 'trice [ʃeneddʒa'tore] *sm/f* script-writer.
sceneggia'tura [ʃeneddʒa'tura] *sf* (*TEAT*) scenario; (*CINE*) screenplay, scenario.
'**scenico, a, ci, che** ['ʃeniko] *ag* stage *cpd*.
scenogra'fia [ʃenogra'fia] *sf* (*TEAT*) stage design; (*CINE*) set design; (*elementi scenici*) scenery.
sce'nografo, a [ʃe'nɔgrafo] *sm/f* set designer.

sce'riffo [ʃe'riffo] *sm* sheriff.
scervel'larsi [ʃervel'larsi] *vr:* ~ (**su qc**) to rack one's brains (over sth).
scervel'lato, a [ʃervel'lato] *ag* featherbrained, scatterbrained.
'**sceso, a** ['ʃeso] *pp di* **scendere**.
scetti'cismo [ʃetti'tʃizmo] *sm* scepticism (*BRIT*), skepticism (*US*).
'**scettico, a, ci, che** ['ʃettiko] *ag* sceptical (*BRIT*), skeptical (*US*).
'**scettro** ['ʃettro] *sm* sceptre (*BRIT*), scepter (*US*).
'**scheda** ['skɛda] *sf* (*index*) card; (*TV, RADIO*) (*brief*) report; ~ **a circuito stampato** printed-circuit board; ~ **elettorale** ballot paper; ~ **perforata** punch card; ~ **telefonica** phone card.
sche'dare [ske'dare] *vt* (*dati*) to file; (*libri*) to catalogue; (*registrare: anche POLIZIA*) to put on one's files.
sche'dario [ske'darjo] *sm* file; (*mobile*) filing cabinet.
sche'dato, a [ske'dato] *ag* with a (police) record ♦ *sm/f* person with a (police) record.
sche'dina [ske'dina] *sf* ≈ pools coupon (*BRIT*).
'**scheggia, ge** ['skeddʒa] *sf* splinter, sliver; ~ **impazzita** (*fig*) maverick.
sche'letrico, a, ci, che [ske'lɛtriko] *ag* (*anche ANAT*) skeletal; (*fig: essenziale*) skeleton *cpd*.
'**scheletro** ['skɛletro] *sm* skeleton; **avere uno** ~ **nell'armadio** (*fig*) to have a skeleton in the cupboard.
'**schema, i** ['skɛma] *sm* (*diagramma*) diagram, sketch; (*progetto, abbozzo*) outline, plan; **ribellarsi agli** ~**i** to rebel against traditional values; **secondo gli** ~**i tradizionali** in accordance with traditional values.
sche'matico, a, ci, che [ske'matiko] *ag* schematic.
schematiz'zare [skematid'dzare] *vt* to schematize.
'**scherma** ['skerma] *sf* fencing.
scher'maglia [sker'maʎʎa] *sf* (*fig*) skirmish.
scher'mirsi [sker'mirsi] *vr* to defend o.s., protect o.s.
'**schermo** ['skermo] *sm* shield, screen; (*CINE, TV*) screen.
schermogra'fia [skermogra'fia] *sf* X-rays *pl*.
scher'nire [sker'nire] *vt* to mock, sneer at.
'**scherno** ['skerno] *sm* mockery, derision; **farsi** ~ **di** to sneer at; **essere oggetto di** ~ to be a laughing stock.

scher'zare [sker'tsare] *vi* to joke.

'scherzo ['skertso] *sm* joke; (*tiro*) trick; (*MUS*) scherzo; **è uno ~!** (*una cosa facile*) it's child's play!, it's easy!; **per ~** for a joke *o* a laugh; **fare un brutto ~ a qn** to play a nasty trick on sb; **~i a parte** seriously, joking apart.

scher'zoso, a [sker'tsoso] *ag* (*tono, gesto*) playful; (*osservazione*) facetious; **è un tipo ~** he likes a joke.

schiaccia'noci [skjattʃa'notʃi] *sm inv* nutcracker.

schiacci'ante [skjat'tʃante] *ag* overwhelming.

schiacci'are [skjat'tʃare] *vt* (*dito*) to crush; (*noci*) to crack; **~ un pisolino** to have a nap.

schiaffeggi'are [skjaffed'dʒare] *vt* to slap.

schi'affo ['skjaffo] *sm* slap; **prendere qn a ~i** to slap sb's face; **uno ~ morale** a slap in the face, a rebuff.

schiamaz'zare [skjamat'tsare] *vi* to squawk, cackle.

schia'mazzo [skja'mattso] *sm* (*fig: chiasso*) din, racket.

schian'tare [skjan'tare] *vt* to break, tear apart; **~rsi** to break (up), shatter; **~rsi al suolo** (*aereo*) to crash (to the ground).

schi'anto ['skjanto] *sm* (*rumore*) crash; tearing sound; **è uno ~!** (*fam*) it's (*o* he's *o* she's) terrific!; **di ~** all of a sudden.

schia'rire [skja'rire] *vt* to lighten, make lighter ♦ *vi* (*anche*: **~rsi**) to grow lighter; (*tornar sereno*) to clear, brighten up; **~rsi la voce** to clear one's throat.

schia'rita [skja'rita] *sf* (*METEOR*) bright spell; (*fig*) improvement, turn for the better.

schiat'tare [skjat'tare] *vi* to burst; **~ d'invidia** to be green with envy; **~ di rabbia** to be beside o.s. with rage.

schiavitù [skjavi'tu] *sf* slavery.

schiaviz'zare [skjavid'dzare] *vt* to enslave.

schi'avo, a [ˈskjavo] *sm/f* slave.

schi'ena [ˈskjɛna] *sf* (*ANAT*) back.

schie'nale [skjeˈnale] *sm* (*di sedia*) back.

schi'era [ˈskjɛra] *sf* (*MIL*) rank; (*gruppo*) group, band; **villette a ~** ≈ terraced houses.

schiera'mento [skjeraˈmento] *sm* (*MIL, SPORT*) formation; (*fig*) alliance.

schie'rare [skjeˈrare] *vt* (*esercito*) to line up, draw up, marshal; **~rsi** *vr* to line up; (*fig*): **~rsi con** *o* **dalla parte di/contro qn** to side with/oppose sb.

schi'etto, a [ˈskjɛtto] *ag* (*puro*) pure; (*fig*) frank, straightforward.

schi'fare [skiˈfare] *vt* to disgust.

schi'fezza [skiˈfettsa] *sf*: **essere una ~** (*cibo, bibita etc*) to be disgusting; (*film, libro*) to be dreadful.

schifil'toso, a [skifilˈtoso] *ag* fussy, difficult.

'schifo [ˈskifo] *sm* disgust; **fare ~** (*essere fatto male, dare pessimi risultati*) to be awful; **mi fa ~** it makes me sick, it's disgusting; **quel libro è uno ~** that book's rotten.

schi'foso, a [skiˈfoso] *ag* disgusting, revolting; (*molto scadente*) rotten, lousy.

schioc'care [skjokˈkare] *vt* (*frusta*) to crack; (*dita*) to snap; (*lingua*) to click; **~ le labbra** to smack one's lips.

schioppet'tata [skjoppetˈtata] *sf* gunshot.

schi'oppo [ˈskjɔppo] *sm* rifle, gun.

schi'udere [ˈskjudere] *vt*, **~rsi** *vr* to open.

schi'uma [ˈskjuma] *sf* foam; (*di sapone*) lather; (*di latte*) froth.

schiu'mare [skjuˈmare] *vt* to skim ♦ *vi* to foam.

schi'uso, a [ˈskjuso] *pp di* **schiudere**.

schi'vare [skiˈvare] *vt* to dodge, avoid.

'schivo, a [ˈskivo] *ag* (*ritroso*) stand-offish, reserved; (*timido*) shy.

schizofre'nia [skiddzofreˈnia] *sf* schizophrenia.

schizo'frenico, a, ci, che [skiddzoˈfrɛniko] *ag* schizophrenic.

schiz'zare [skitˈtsare] *vt* (*spruzzare*) to spurt, squirt; (*sporcare*) to splash, spatter; (*fig: abbozzare*) to sketch ♦ *vi* to spurt, squirt; (*saltar fuori*) to dart up (*o* off *etc*); **~ via** (*animale, persona*) to dart away; (*macchina, moto*) to accelerate away.

schizzi'noso, a [skittsiˈnoso] *ag* fussy, finicky.

'schizzo [ˈskittso] *sm* (*di liquido*) spurt; splash, spatter; (*abbozzo*) sketch.

sci [ʃi] *sm inv* (*attrezzo*) ski; (*attività*) skiing; **~ di fondo** cross-country skiing, ski touring (*US*); **~ nautico** water-skiing.

'scia, *pl* **'scie** [ˈʃia] *sf* (*di imbarcazione*) wake; (*di profumo*) trail.

scià [ʃa] *sm inv* shah.

sci'abola [ˈʃabola] *sf* sabre (*BRIT*), saber (*US*).

scia'callo [ʃaˈkallo] *sm* jackal; (*fig peg: profittatore*) shark, profiteer; (*: ladro*) looter.

sciac'quare [ʃakˈkware] *vt* to rinse.

scia'gura [ʃaˈgura] *sf* disaster, calamity.

sciagu'rato, a [ʃaguˈrato] *ag* unfortunate; (*malvagio*) wicked.

scialac'quare [ʃalakˈkware] *vt* to squander.

scia'lare [ʃaˈlare] *vi* to throw one's money

around.

sci'albo, a ['ʃalbo] *ag* pale, dull; (*fig*) dull, colourless (*BRIT*), colorless (*US*).

sci'alle ['ʃalle] *sm* shawl.

sci'alo ['ʃalo] *sm* squandering, waste.

scia'luppa [ʃa'luppa] *sf* (*NAUT*) sloop; (*anche*: ~ **di salvataggio**) lifeboat.

scia'mare [ʃa'mare] *vi* to swarm.

sci'ame ['ʃame] *sm* swarm.

scian'cato, a [ʃan'kato] *ag* lame; (*mobile*) rickety.

sci'are [ʃi'are] *vi* to ski; **andare a** ~ to go skiing.

sci'arpa ['ʃarpa] *sf* scarf; (*fascia*) sash.

scia'tore, 'trice [ʃia'tore] *sm/f* skier.

sciat'tezza [ʃat'tettsa] *sf* slovenliness.

sci'atto, a ['ʃatto] *ag* (*persona: nell'aspetto*) slovenly, unkempt; (: *nel lavoro*) sloppy, careless.

'scibile ['ʃibile] *sm* knowledge.

scien'tifico, a, ci, che [ʃen'tifiko] *ag* scientific; **la (polizia)** ~**a** the forensic department.

sci'enza ['ʃɛntsa] *sf* science; (*sapere*) knowledge; ~**e** *sfpl* (*INS*) science *sg*; ~**e naturali** natural sciences; ~**e politiche** political science *sg*.

scienzi'ato, a [ʃen'tsjato] *sm/f* scientist.

'Scilly ['ʃilli]: **le isole** ~ *sfpl* the Scilly Isles.

'scimmia ['ʃimmja] *sf* monkey.

scimmiot'tare [ʃimmjot'tare] *vt* to ape, mimic.

scimpanzé [ʃimpan'tse] *sm inv* chimpanzee.

scimu'nito, a [ʃimu'nito] *ag* silly, idiotic.

'scindere ['ʃindere] *vt*, ~**rsi** *vr* to split (up).

scin'tilla [ʃin'tilla] *sf* spark.

scintil'lare [ʃintil'lare] *vi* to spark; (*acqua, occhi*) to sparkle.

scintil'lio [ʃintil'lio] *sm* sparkling.

scioc'care [ʃok'kare] *vt* to shock.

scioc'chezza [ʃok'kettsa] *sf* stupidity *no pl*; stupid *o* foolish thing; **dire** ~**e** to talk nonsense.

sci'occo, a, chi, che ['ʃɔkko] *ag* stupid, foolish.

sci'ogliere ['ʃɔʎʎere] *vt* (*nodo*) to untie; (*capelli*) to loosen; (*persona, animale*) to untie, release; (*fig: persona*): ~ **da** to release from; (*neve*) to melt; (*nell'acqua: zucchero etc*) to dissolve; (*fig: mistero*) to solve; (*porre fine a: contratto*) to cancel; (: *società, matrimonio*) to dissolve; (: *riunione*) to bring to an end; ~**rsi** *vr* to loosen, come untied; to melt; to dissolve; (*assemblea, corteo, duo*) to break up; ~ **i muscoli** to limber up; ~ **il ghiaccio** (*fig*) to break the ice; ~ **le vele** (*NAUT*) to set sail; ~**rsi dai legami** (*fig*) to free o.s. from all

ties.

sci'olgo *etc* ['ʃɔlgo] *vb vedi* **sciogliere**.

sciol'tezza [ʃol'tettsa] *sf* agility; suppleness; ease.

sci'olto, a ['ʃɔlto] *pp di* **sciogliere** ♦ *ag* loose; (*agile*) agile, nimble; (*disinvolto*) free and easy; **essere** ~ **nei movimenti** to be supple; **versi** ~**i** (*POESIA*) blank verse.

sciope'rante [ʃope'rante] *sm/f* striker.

sciope'rare [ʃope'rare] *vi* to strike, go on strike.

sci'opero ['ʃopero] *sm* strike; **fare** ~ to strike; **entrare in** ~ to go on *o* come out on strike; ~ **bianco** work-to-rule (*BRIT*), slowdown (*US*); ~ **della fame** hunger strike; ~ **selvaggio** wildcat strike; ~ **a singhiozzo** on-off strike; ~ **di solidarietà** sympathy strike.

sciori'nare [ʃori'nare] *vt* (*ostentare*) to show off, display.

scio'via [ʃio'via] *sf* ski lift.

sciovi'nismo [ʃovi'nizmo] *sm* chauvinism.

sciovi'nista, i, e [ʃovi'nista] *sm/f* chauvinist.

sci'pito, a [ʃi'pito] *ag* insipid.

scip'pare [ʃip'pare] *vt*: ~ **qn** to snatch sb's bag.

scippa'tore [ʃippa'tore] *sm* bag-snatcher.

'scippo ['ʃippo] *sm* bag-snatching.

sci'rocco [ʃi'rokko] *sm* sirocco.

sci'roppo [ʃi'rɔppo] *sm* syrup; ~ **per la tosse** cough syrup, cough mixture.

'scisma, i ['ʃizma] *sm* (*REL*) schism.

scissi'one [ʃis'sjone] *sf* (*anche fig*) split, division; (*FISICA*) fission.

'scisso, a ['ʃisso] *pp di* **scindere**.

sciu'pare [ʃu'pare] *vt* (*abito, libro, appetito*) to spoil, ruin; (*tempo, denaro*) to waste; ~**rsi** *vr* to get spoilt *o* ruined; (*rovinarsi la salute*) to ruin one's health.

scivo'lare [ʃivo'lare] *vi* to slide *o* glide along; (*involontariamente*) to slip, slide.

'scivolo ['ʃivolo] *sm* slide; (*TECN*) chute.

scivo'loso, a [ʃivo'loso] *ag* slippery.

scle'rosi *sf* sclerosis.

scoc'care *vt* (*freccia*) to shoot ♦ *vi* (*guizzare*) to shoot up; (*battere: ora*) to strike.

scoccherò *etc* [skokke'rɔ] *vb vedi* **scoccare**.

scocci'are [skot'tʃare] *vt* to bother, annoy; ~**rsi** *vr* to be bothered *o* annoyed.

scoccia'tore, 'trice [skottʃa'tore] *sm/f* nuisance, pest (*fam*).

scoccia'tura [skottʃa'tura] *sf* nuisance, bore.

sco'della *sf* bowl.

scodinzo'lare [skodintso'lare] *vi* to wag its tail.

scogli'era [skoʎ'ʎɛra] *sf* reef; (*rupe*) cliff.

'scoglio ['skɔʎʎo] *sm* (*al mare*) rock; (*fig: ostacolo*) difficulty, stumbling block.

scogli'oso, a [skoʎ'ʎoso] *ag* rocky.

scoi'attolo *sm* squirrel.

scola'pasta *sm inv* colander.

sco'lare *ag*: **età ~** school age ♦ *vt* to drain ♦ *vi* to drip.

scola'resca *sf* schoolchildren *pl*, pupils *pl*.

sco'laro, a *sm/f* pupil, schoolboy/girl.

sco'lastico, a, ci, che *ag* (*gen*) scholastic; (*libro, anno, divisa*) school *cpd*.

scol'lare *vt* (*staccare*) to unstick; **~rsi** *vr* to come unstuck.

scol'lato, a *ag* (*vestito*) low-cut, low-necked; (*donna*) wearing a low-cut dress (*o blouse etc*).

scolla'tura *sf* neckline.

'scolo *sm* drainage; (*sbocco*) drain; (*acqua*) waste water; **canale di ~** drain; **tubo di ~** drainpipe.

scolo'rire *vt* to fade; to discolour (*BRIT*), discolor (*US*) ♦ *vi* (*anche:* **~rsi**) to fade; to become discolo(u)red; (*impallidire*) to turn pale.

scol'pire *vt* to carve, sculpt.

scombi'nare *vt* to mess up, upset.

scombi'nato, a *ag* confused, muddled.

scombusso'lare *vt* to upset.

scom'messo, a *pp di* **scommettere** ♦ *sf* bet, wager; **fare una ~a** to bet.

scom'mettere *vt, vi* to bet.

scomo'dare *vt* to trouble, bother, disturb; (*fig: nome famoso*) to involve, drag in; **~rsi** *vr* to put o.s. out; **~rsi a fare** to go to the bother *o* trouble of doing.

scomodità *sf inv* (*di sedia, letto etc*) discomfort; (*di orario, sistemazione etc*) inconvenience.

'scomodo, a *ag* uncomfortable; (*sistemazione, posto*) awkward, inconvenient.

scompagi'nare [skompadʒi'nare] *vt* to upset, throw into disorder.

scompag'nato, a [skompaɲ'ɲato] *ag* (*calzini, guanti*) odd.

scompa'rire *vi* (*sparire*) to disappear, vanish; (*fig*) to be insignificant.

scom'parso, a *pp di* **scomparire** ♦ *sf* disappearance; (*fig: morte*) passing away, death.

scomparti'mento *sm* (*FERR*) compartment; (*sezione*) division.

scom'parto *sm* compartment, division.

scom'penso *sm* imbalance, lack of balance.

scompigli'are [skompiʎ'ʎare] *vt* (*cassetto, capelli*) to mess up, disarrange; (*fig: piani*) to upset.

scom'piglio [skom'piʎʎo] *sm* mess, confusion.

scom'porre *vt* (*parola, numero*) to break up; (*CHIM*) to decompose; **scomporsi** *vr* (*CHIM*) to decompose; (*fig*) to get upset, lose one's composure; **senza scomporsi** unperturbed.

scom'posto, a *pp di* **scomporre** ♦ *ag* (*gesto*) unseemly; (*capelli*) ruffled, dishevelled.

sco'munica, che *sf* excommunication.

scomuni'care *vt* to excommunicate.

sconcer'tante [skontʃer'tante] *ag* disconcerting.

sconcer'tare [skontʃer'tare] *vt* to disconcert, bewilder.

'sconcio, a, ci, ce ['skontʃo] *ag* (*osceno*) indecent, obscene ♦ *sm* (*cosa riprovevole, mal fatta*) disgrace.

sconclusio'nato, a *ag* incoherent, illogical.

sconfes'sare *vt* to renounce, disavow; to repudiate.

scon'figgere [skon'fiddʒere] *vt* to defeat, overcome.

sconfi'nare *vi* to cross the border; (*in proprietà privata*) to trespass; (*fig*): **~ da** to stray *o* digress from.

sconfi'nato, a *ag* boundless, unlimited.

scon'fitto, a *pp di* **sconfiggere** ♦ *sf* defeat.

sconfor'tante, a *ag* discouraging, disheartening.

sconfor'tare *vt* to discourage, dishearten; **~rsi** *vr* to become discouraged, become disheartened, lose heart.

scon'forto *sm* despondency.

sconge'lare [skondʒe'lare] *vt* to defrost.

scongiu'rare [skondʒu'rare] *vt* (*implorare*) to beseech, implore; (*eludere: pericolo*) to ward off, avert.

scongi'uro [skon'dʒuro] *sm* (*esorcismo*) exorcism; **fare gli ~i** to touch wood (*BRIT*), knock on wood (*US*).

scon'nesso, a *ag* (*fig: discorso*) incoherent, rambling.

sconosci'uto, a [skonoʃ'ʃuto] *ag* unknown; new, strange ♦ *sm/f* stranger, unknown person.

sconquas'sare *vt* to shatter, smash.

scon'quasso *sm* (*danno*) damage; (*fig*) confusion.

sconside'rato, a *ag* thoughtless, rash.

sconsigli'are [skonsiʎ'ʎare] *vt*: **~ qc a qn** to advise sb against sth; **~ qn dal fare qc** to advise sb not to do *o* against doing sth.

sconso'lato, a *ag* disconsolate.

scon'tare *vt* (*COMM: detrarre*) to deduct; (*: debito*) to pay off; (*: cambiale*) to discount; (*pena*) to serve; (*colpa, errori*) to pay for, suffer for.

scon'tato, a *ag* (*previsto*) foreseen, taken for granted; (*prezzo, merce*) discounted, at a discount; **dare per ~ che** to take it for granted that.

sconten'tare *vt* to displease, dissatisfy.

sconten'tezza [skonten'tettsa] *sf* displeasure, dissatisfaction.

scon'tento, a *ag:* **~ (di)** discontented *o* dissatisfied (with) ♦ *sm* discontent, dissatisfaction.

'sconto *sm* discount; **fare** *o* **concedere uno ~** to give a discount; **uno ~ del 10%** a 10% discount.

scon'trarsi *vr* (*treni etc*) to crash, collide; (*venire ad uno scontro, fig*) to clash; **~ con** to crash into, collide with.

scon'trino *sm* ticket.

'scontro *sm* (*MIL, fig*) clash; (*di veicoli*) crash, collision; **~ a fuoco** shoot-out.

scon'troso, a *ag* sullen, surly; (*permaloso*) touchy.

sconveni'ente *ag* unseemly, improper.

sconvol'gente [skonvol'dʒɛnte] *ag* (*notizia, brutta esperienza*) upsetting, disturbing; (*bellezza*) amazing; (*passione*) overwhelming.

scon'volgere [skon'vɔldʒere] *vt* to throw into confusion, upset; (*turbare*) to shake, disturb, upset.

scon'volto, a *pp di* **sconvolgere** ♦ *ag* (*persona*) distraught, very upset.

'scopa *sf* broom; (*CARTE*) Italian card game.

sco'pare *vt* to sweep; (*fam!*) to bonk (!).

sco'pata *sf* (*fam!*) bonk (!).

scoperchi'are [skoper'kjare] *vt* (*pentola, vaso*) to take the lid off, uncover; (*casa*) to take the roof off.

sco'perto, a *pp di* **scoprire** ♦ *ag* uncovered; (*capo*) uncovered, bare; (*macchina*) open; (*MIL*) exposed, without cover; (*conto*) overdrawn ♦ *sf* discovery ♦ *sm*: **allo ~** (*dormire etc*) out in the open; **assegno ~** uncovered cheque; **avere un conto ~** to be overdrawn.

'scopo *sm* aim, purpose; **a che ~?** what for?; **adatto allo ~** fit for its purpose; **allo ~ di fare qc** in order to do sth; **a ~ di lucro** for gain *o* money; **senza ~** (*fare, cercare*) pointlessly.

scoppi'are *vi* (*spaccarsi*) to burst; (*esplodere*) to explode; (*fig*) to break out; **~ in pianto** *o* **a piangere** to burst out crying; **~ dalle risa** *o* **dal ridere** to split one's sides laughing; **~ dal caldo** to be boiling; **~ di salute** to be the picture of health.

scoppiet'tare *vi* to crackle.

'scoppio *sm* explosion; (*di tuono, arma etc*) crash, bang; (*di pneumatico*) bang; (*fig: di guerra*) outbreak; **a ~ ritardato** delayed-action; **reazione a ~ ritardato** delayed *o* slow reaction; **uno ~ di risa** a burst of laughter; **uno ~ di collera** an explosion of anger.

sco'prire *vt* to discover; (*liberare da ciò che copre*) to uncover; (: *monumento*) to unveil; **~rsi** *vr* to put on lighter clothes; (*fig*) to give o.s. away.

scopri'tore, 'trice *sm/f* discoverer.

scoraggi'are [skorad'dʒare] *vt* to discourage; **~rsi** *vr* to become discouraged, lose heart.

scor'butico, a, ci, che *ag* (*fig*) cantankerous.

scorcia'toia [skortʃa'toja] *sf* short cut.

'scorcio ['skortʃo] *sm* (*ARTE*) foreshortening; (*di secolo, periodo*) end, close; **~ panoramico** vista.

scor'dare *vt* to forget; **~rsi** *vr*: **~rsi di qc/di fare** to forget sth/to do.

sco'reggia [sko'reddʒa] (*fam!*) *sf* fart (!).

scoreggi'are [skored'dʒare] (*fam!*) *vi* to fart (!).

'scorgere ['skɔrdʒere] *vt* to make out, distinguish, see.

sco'ria *sf* (*di metalli*) slag; (*vulcanica*) scoria; **~e radioattive** (*FISICA*) radioactive waste *sg*.

'scorno *sm* ignominy, disgrace.

scorpacci'ata [skorpat'tʃata] *sf*: **fare una ~ (di)** to stuff o.s. (with), eat one's fill (of).

scorpi'one *sm* scorpion; (*dello zodiaco*): **S~** Scorpio; **essere dello S~** to be Scorpio.

'scorporo *sm* (*POL*) *transfer of votes aimed at increasing the chances of representation for minority parties*.

scorraz'zare [skorrat'tsare] *vi* to run about.

'scorrere *vt* (*giornale, lettera*) to run *o* skim through ♦ *vi* (*liquido, fiume*) to run, flow; (*fune*) to run; (*cassetto, porta*) to slide easily; (*tempo*) to pass (by).

scorre'ria *sf* raid, incursion.

scorret'tezza [skorret'tettsa] *sf* incorrectness; lack of politeness, rudeness; unfairness; **commettere una ~** (*essere sleale*) to be unfair.

scor'retto, a *ag* (*sbagliato*) incorrect; (*sgarbato*) impolite; (*sconveniente*) improper; (*sleale*) unfair; (*gioco*) foul.

scor'revole *ag* (*porta*) sliding; (*fig: stile*) fluent, flowing.

scorri'banda *sf* (*MIL*) raid; (*escursione*) trip, excursion.

'scorsi *etc vb vedi* **scorgere**.

'scorso, a *pp di* **scorrere** ♦ *ag* last ♦ *sf* quick look, glance; **lo ~ mese** last month.

scor'soio, a *ag*: **nodo ~** noose.

'scorta *sf* (*di personalità, convoglio*) escort; (*provvista*) supply, stock; **sotto la ~ di due agenti** escorted by two policemen; **fare ~ di** to stock up with, get in a supply of; **di ~** (*materiali*) spare; **ruota di ~** spare wheel.

scor'tare *vt* to escort.

scor'tese *ag* discourteous, rude.

scorte'sia *sf* discourtesy, rudeness; (*azione*) discourtesy.

scorti'care *vt* to skin.

'scorto, a *pp di* **scorgere**.

'scorza ['skɔrdza] *sf* (*di albero*) bark; (*di agrumi*) peel, skin.

sco'sceso, a [skoʃ'ʃeso] *ag* steep.

'scosso, a *pp di* **scuotere** ♦ *ag* (*turbato*) shaken, upset ♦ *sf* jerk, jolt, shake; (*ELETTR, fig*) shock; **prendere la ~a** to get an electric shock; **~a di terremoto** earth tremor.

scos'sone *sm*: **dare uno ~ a qn** to give sb a shake; **procedere a ~i** to jolt *o* jerk along.

scos'tante *ag* (*fig*) off-putting (*BRIT*), unpleasant.

scos'tare *vt* to move (away), shift; **~rsi** *vr* to move away.

scostu'mato, a *ag* immoral, dissolute.

scotch [skɔtʃ] *sm inv* (*whisky*) Scotch; ® (*nastro adesivo*) Scotch tape ®, Sellotape ®.

scot'tante *ag* (*fig*: *urgente*) pressing; (: *delicato*) delicate.

scot'tare *vt* (*ustionare*) to burn; (: *con liquido bollente*) to scald ♦ *vi* to burn; (*caffè*) to be too hot.

scotta'tura *sf* burn; scald.

'scotto, a *ag* overcooked ♦ *sm* (*fig*): **pagare lo ~ (di)** to pay the penalty (for).

sco'vare *vt* to drive out, flush out; (*fig*) to discover.

'Scozia ['skɔttsja] *sf*: **la ~** Scotland.

scoz'zese [skot'tsese] *ag* Scottish ♦ *smf* Scot.

screan'zato, a [skrean'tsato] *ag* ill-mannered ♦ *smf* boor.

scredi'tare *vt* to discredit.

scre'mare *vt* to skim.

scre'mato, a *ag* skimmed; **parzialmente ~** semi-skimmed.

screpo'lare *vt*, **~rsi** *vr* to crack.

screpola'tura *sf* cracking *no pl*; crack.

screzi'ato, a [skret'tsjato] *ag* streaked.

'screzio ['skrɛttsjo] *sm* disagreement.

scribac'chino [skribak'kino] *sm* (*peg*: *impiegato*) penpusher; (: *scrittore*) hack.

scricchio'lare [skrikkjo'lare] *vi* to creak, squeak.

scricchio'lio [skrikkjo'lio] *sm* creaking.

'scricciolo ['skrittʃolo] *sm* wren.

'scrigno ['skriɲɲo] *sm* casket.

scrimina'tura *sf* parting.

'scrissi *etc vb vedi* **scrivere**.

'scritto, a *pp di* **scrivere** ♦ *ag* written ♦ *sm* writing; (*lettera*) letter, note ♦ *sf* inscription; **~i** *smpl* (*letterari etc*) work(s), writings; **per** *o* **in ~** in writing.

scrit'toio *sm* writing desk.

scrit'tore, 'trice *sm/f* writer.

scrit'tura *sf* writing; (*COMM*) entry; (*contratto*) contract; (*REL*): **la Sacra S~** the Scriptures *pl*; **~e** *sfpl* (*COMM*) accounts, books.

scrittu'rare *vt* (*TEAT, CINE*) to sign up, engage; (*COMM*) to enter.

scriva'nia *sf* desk.

scri'vano *sm* (*amanuense*) scribe; (*impiegato*) clerk.

scri'vente *sm/f* writer.

'scrivere *vt* to write; **come si scrive?** how is it spelt?, how do you write it?; **~ qc a qn** to write sth to sb; **~ qc a macchina** to type sth; **~ a penna/matita** to write in pen/pencil; **~ qc maiuscolo/minuscolo** to write sth in capital/small letters.

scroc'care *vt* (*fam*) to scrounge, cadge.

scroc'cone, a *sm/f* scrounger.

'scrofa *sf* (*ZOOL*) sow.

scrol'lare *vt* to shake; **~rsi** *vr* (*anche fig*) to give o.s. a shake; **~ le spalle/il capo** to shrug one's shoulders/shake one's head; **~rsi qc di dosso** (*ache fig*) to shake sth off.

scrol'lata *sf* shake; **~ di spalle** shrug (of one's shoulders).

scrosci'ante [skroʃ'ʃante] *ag* (*pioggia*) pouring; (*fig*: *applausi*) thunderous.

scrosci'are [skroʃ'ʃare] *vi* (*pioggia*) to pour down, pelt down; (*torrente, fig*: *applausi*) to thunder, roar.

'scroscio ['skrɔʃʃo] *sm* pelting; thunder, roar; (*di applausi*) burst.

scros'tare *vt* (*intonaco*) to scrape off, strip; **~rsi** *vr* to peel off, flake off.

'scrupolo *sm* scruple; (*meticolosità*) care, conscientiousness; **essere senza ~i** to be unscrupulous.

scrupo'loso, a *ag* scrupulous; conscientious.

scru'tare *vt* to scrutinize; (*intenzioni, causa*) to examine, scrutinize.

scruta'tore, trice *sm/f* (*POL*) scrutineer.

scruti'nare *vt* (*voti*) to count.

scru'tinio *sm* (*votazione*) ballot; (*insieme*

delle operazioni) poll; (*INS*) (*meeting for*) assignment of marks at end of a term or year.

scu'cire [sku'tʃire] *vt* (*orlo etc*) to unpick, undo; ~**rsi** *vr* to come unstitched.

scude'ria *sf* stable.

scu'detto *sm* (*SPORT*) (championship) shield; (*distintivo*) badge.

scu'discio [sku'diʃʃo] *sm* (riding) crop, (riding) whip.

'**scudo** *sm* shield; **farsi** ~ **di** *o* **con qc** to shield o.s. with sth; ~ **aereo/missilistico** air/missile defence (*BRIT*) *o* defense (*US*); ~ **termico** heat shield.

sculacci'are [skulat'tʃare] *vt* to spank.

sculacci'one [skulat'tʃone] *sm* spanking.

scul'tore, 'trice *sm/f* sculptor.

scul'tura *sf* sculpture.

scu'ola *sf* school; ~ **elementare** primary (*BRIT*) *o* grade (*US*) school (*for children from 6 to 11 years of age*); ~ **guida** driving school; ~ **materna** nursery school (*for children aged 3 to 5*); ~ **media inferiore** *first 3 years of secondary school, for children from 11 to 14 years of age*; ~ **dell'obbligo** compulsory education; ~ **privata/pubblica** private/state school; ~**e serali** evening classes, night school *sg*; ~ **tecnica** technical college.

> *Italian children first attend* **la scuola** *from the age of 3. They remain at* **la scuola materna** *until the age of 6 when they move on to the* **scuola elementare** *for a period of 5 years. After this there is the* **scuola media inferiore**, *which lasts another 3 years. Its completion marks the end of compulsory education. Students who want to continue their education then go to the* **scuola media superiore**, *which consists of a number of different establishments offering different specialisations: these are the* **liceo classico**, *the* **liceo scientifico** *and the liceo artistico, which take a further 5 years, the* **istituto magistrale**, *which takes 4 years, and the istituto tecnico e professionale, which takes between 3 and 5 years.*

scu'otere *vt* to shake; ~**rsi** *vr* to jump, be startled; (*fig: muoversi*) to rouse o.s., stir o.s.; (: *turbarsi*) to be shaken.

'**scure** *sf* axe, ax (*US*).

scu'rire *vt* to darken, make darker.

'**scuro, a** *ag* dark; (*fig: espressione*) grim ♦ *sm* darkness; dark colour (*BRIT*) *o* color (*US*); (*imposta*) (window) shutter; **verde/rosso** *etc* ~ dark green/red *etc*.

scur'rile *ag* scurrilous.

'**scusa** *sf* excuse; ~**e** *sfpl* apology *sg*, apologies; **chiedere** ~ **a qn (per)** to apologize to sb (for); **chiedo** ~ I'm sorry; (*disturbando etc*) excuse me; **vi prego di accettare le mie** ~**e** please accept my apologies.

scu'sare *vt* to excuse; ~**rsi** *vr*: ~**rsi (di)** to apologize (for); **(mi) scusi** I'm sorry; (*per richiamare l'attenzione*) excuse me.

S.C.V. *sigla* = *Stato della Città del Vaticano.*

sdebi'tarsi *vt*: ~**rsi (con qn di o per qc)** (*anche fig*) to repay (sb for sth).

sde'gnare [zdeɲ'ɲare] *vt* to scorn, despise; ~**rsi** *vr* (*adirarsi*) to get angry.

sde'gnato, a [zdeɲ'ɲato] *ag* indignant, angry.

'**sdegno** ['zdeɲɲo] *sm* scorn, disdain.

sde'gnoso, a [zdeɲ'ɲoso] *ag* scornful, disdainful.

sdilin'quirsi *vr* (*illanguidirsi*) to become sentimental.

sdoga'nare *vt* (*COMM*) to clear through customs.

sdolci'nato, a [zdoltʃi'nato] *ag* mawkish, oversentimental.

sdoppia'mento *sm* (*CHIM: di composto*) splitting; (*PSIC*): ~ **della personalità** split personality.

sdoppi'are *vt* (*dividere*) to divide *o* split in two.

sdrai'arsi *vr* to stretch out, lie down.

'**sdraio** *sm*: **sedia a** ~ deck chair.

sdrammatiz'zare [zdrammatid'dzare] *vt* to play down, minimize.

sdruccio'lare [zdruttʃo'lare] *vi* to slip, slide.

sdrucci'olevole [zdruttʃo'levole] *ag* slippery.

sdru'cito, a [zdru'tʃito] *ag* (*strappato*) torn; (*logoro*) threadbare.

═══════════════ *PAROLA CHIAVE*

se *pron vedi* **si**

♦ *cong* **1** (*condizionale, ipotetica*) if; ~ **nevica non vengo** I won't come if it snows; ~ **fossi in te** if I were you; **sarei rimasto** ~ **me l'avessero chiesto** I would have stayed if they'd asked me; **non puoi fare altro** ~ **non telefonare** all you can do is phone; ~ **mai** if, if ever; **siamo noi** ~ **mai che le siamo grati** it is we who should be grateful to you; ~ **no** (*altrimenti*) or (else), otherwise; ~ **non** (*anzi*) if not; (*tranne*) except; ~ **non altro** if nothing else, at least; ~ **solo** *o* **solamente** if only

2 (*in frasi dubitative, interrogative indirette*) if, whether; **non so** ~ **scrivere o telefonare** I don't know whether *o* if I should write or phone.

S.E. *abbr* (= *sud-est*) SE; (= *Sua Eccellenza*) HE.

sé *pron* (*gen*) oneself; (*esso, essa, lui, lei, loro*) itself; himself; herself; themselves; ~ **stesso(a)** *pron* oneself; itself; himself; herself; ~ **stessi(e)** *pron pl* themselves; **di per ~ non è un problema** it's no problem in itself; **parlare tra ~ e ~** to talk to oneself; **va da ~ che** ... it goes without saying that ..., it's obvious that ..., it stands to reason that ...; **è un caso a ~ o a ~ stante** it's a special case.

S.E.A.T.O. *sigla f* (= *Southeast Asia Treaty Organization*) SEATO.

seb'bene *cong* although, though.

'sebo *sm* sebum.

sec. *abbr* (= *secolo*) c.

'SECAM *sigla m* (= *séquentiel couleur à mémoire*) SECAM.

'secca *sf vedi* **secco.**

sec'care *vt* to dry; (*prosciugare*) to dry up; (*fig: importunare*) to annoy, bother ♦ *vi* to dry; to dry up; ~**rsi** *vr* to dry; to dry up; (*fig*) to grow annoyed; **si è seccato molto** he was very annoyed.

sec'cato, a (*fig: infastidito*) bothered, annoyed; (: *stufo*) fed up.

secca'tore, 'trice *sm/f* nuisance, bother.

secca'tura *sf* (*fig*) bother *no pl*, trouble *no pl*.

seccherò *etc* [sekke'rɔ] *vb vedi* **seccare.**

'secchia ['sekkja] *sf* bucket, pail.

secchi'ello [sek'kjɛllo] *sm* (*per bambini*) pail, bucket.

'secchio ['sekkjo] *sm* bucket, pail; ~ **della spazzatura** *o* **delle immondizie** dustbin (*BRIT*), garbage can (*US*).

'secco, a, chi, che *ag* dry; (*fichi, pesce*) dried; (*foglie, ramo*) withered; (*magro: persona*) thin, skinny; (*fig: risposta, modo di fare*) curt, abrupt; (: *colpo*) clean, sharp ♦ *sm* (*siccità*) drought ♦ *sf* (*del mare*) shallows *pl*; ~**rsi** (*fig: morire sul colpo*) to drop dead; **avere la gola ~a** to feel dry, be parched; **lavare a ~** to dry-clean; **tirare a ~** (*barca*) to beach.

secen'tesco, a, schi, sche [setʃen'tesko] *ag* = **seicentesco.**

se'cernere [se'tʃɛrnere] *vt* to secrete.

seco'lare *ag* age-old, centuries-old; (*laico, mondano*) secular.

'secolo *sm* century; (*epoca*) age.

se'conda *sf vedi* **secondo.**

The **Seconda Repubblica** *is the name used especially by the media to refer to the government and country in general since the elections of 1994 when the old party*

system collapsed and a new system was adopted. The collapse followed the Tangentopoli scandals (see **Tangentopoli**) *which provoked a general wish for radical change. The political parties representing this new system were formed only recently and 1994 saw the first elections to be decided by the first-past-the-post method rather than by proportional representation.*

secondaria'mente *av* secondly.

secon'dario, a *ag* secondary; **scuola/istruzione** ~**a** secondary school/education.

secon'dino *sm* prison officer, warder (*BRIT*).

se'condo, a *ag* second ♦ *sm* second; (*di pranzo*) main course ♦ *sf* (*AUT*) second (gear); (*FERR*) second class ♦ *prep* according to; (*nel modo prescritto*) in accordance with; ~ **me** in my opinion, to my mind; ~ **la legge/quanto si era deciso** in accordance with the law/the decision taken; **di** ~**a classe** second-class; **di** ~**a mano** second-hand; **viaggiare in** ~**a** to travel second-class; **comandante** *m* **in** ~**a** second-in-command; **a** ~**a di** *prep* according to; in accordance with.

secondo'genito, a [sekondo'dʒɛnito] *sm/f* second-born.

secrezi'one [sekret'tsjone] *sf* secretion.

'sedano *sm* celery.

se'dare *vt* (*dolore*) to soothe; (*rivolta*) to put down, suppress.

seda'tivo, a *ag, sm* sedative.

'sede *sf* (*luogo di residenza*) (place of) residence; (*di ditta: principale*) head office; (: *secondaria*) branch (office); (*di organizzazione*) headquarters *pl*; (*di governo, parlamento*) seat; (*REL*) see; **in** ~ **di** (*in occasione di*) during; **in altra** ~ on another occasion; **in** ~ **legislativa** in legislative sitting; **prendere** ~ to take up' residence; **un'azienda con diverse** ~**i in città** a firm with several branches in the city; ~ **centrale** head office; ~ **sociale** registered office.

seden'tario, a *ag* sedentary.

se'dere *vi* to sit, be seated; ~**rsi** *vr* to sit down ♦ *sm* (*deretano*) bottom; **posto a** ~ seat.

'sedia *sf* chair; ~ **elettrica** electric chair; ~ **a rotelle** wheelchair.

sedi'cenne [sedi'tʃɛnne] *ag, sm/f* sixteen-year-old.

sedi'cente [sedi'tʃɛnte] *ag* self-styled.

sedi'cesimo, a [sedi'tʃɛzimo] *num* sixteenth.

'**sedici** ['seditʃi] *num* sixteen.

se'**dile** *sm* seat; (*panchina*) bench.

sedimen'**tare** *vi* to leave a sediment.

sedi'**mento** *sm* sediment.

sedizi'**one** [sedit'tsjone] *sf* revolt, rebellion.

sedizi'**oso, a** [sedit'tsjoso] *ag* seditious.

se'**dotto, a** *pp di* **sedurre.**

sedu'**cente** [sedu'tʃɛnte] *ag* seductive; (*proposta*) very attractive.

se'**durre** *vt* to seduce.

se'**duta** *sf* session, sitting; (*riunione*) meeting; **essere in ~** to be in session, be sitting; **~ stante** (*fig*) immediately; **~ spiritica** seance.

sedut'**tore, 'trice** *sm/f* seducer/seductress.

seduzi'**one** [sedut'tsjone] *sf* seduction; (*fascino*) charm, appeal.

SEeO *abbr* (= *salvo errori e omissioni*) E and OE.

'**sega, ghe** *sf* saw; **~ circolare** circular saw; **~ a mano** handsaw.

'**segale** *sf* rye.

se'**gare** *vt* to saw; (*recidere*) to saw off.

sega'**tura** *sf* (*residuo*) sawdust.

'**seggio** ['sɛddʒo] *sm* seat; **~ elettorale** polling station.

'**seggiola** ['sɛddʒola] *sf* chair.

seggio'**lino** [seddʒo'lino] *sm* seat; (*per bambini*) child's chair; **~ di sicurezza** (*AUT*) child safety seat.

seggio'**lone** [seddʒo'lone] *sm* (*per bambini*) highchair.

seggio'**via** [seddʒo'via] *sf* chairlift.

seghe'**ria** [sege'ria] *sf* sawmill.

seghe'**rò** *etc* [sege'rɔ] *vb vedi* **segare.**

seghet'**tato, a** [seget'tato] *ag* serrated.

se'**ghetto** [se'getto] *sm* hacksaw.

seg'**mento** *sm* segment.

segna'**lare** [seɲɲa'lare] *vt* (*essere segno di*) to indicate, be a sign of; (*avvertire*) to signal; (*menzionare*) to indicate; (: *fatto, risultato, aumento*) to report; (: *errore, dettaglio*) to point out; (*AUT*) to signal, indicate; **~rsi** *vr* (*distinguersi*) to distinguish o.s.; **~ qn a qn** (*per lavoro etc*) to bring sb to sb's attention.

segnalazi'**one** [seɲɲalat'tsjone] *sf* (*azione*) signalling; (*segnale*) signal; (*annuncio*) report; (*raccomandazione*) recommendation.

se'**gnale** [seɲ'ɲale] *sm* signal; (*cartello*): **~ stradale** road sign; **~ acustico** acoustic *o* sound signal; **~ d'allarme** alarm; (*FERR*) communication cord; **~ di linea libera** (*TEL*) dialling (*BRIT*) *o* dial (*US*) tone; **~ luminoso** light signal; **~ di occupato** (*TEL*) engaged tone (*BRIT*), busy signal (*US*); **~ orario** (*RADIO*) time signal.

segna'**letica** [seɲɲa'lɛtika] *sf* signalling, signposting; **~ stradale** road signs *pl*.

segna'**libro** [seɲɲa'libro] *sm* bookmark(er).

segna'**punti** [seɲɲa'punti] *sm/f inv* scorer, scorekeeper.

se'**gnare** [seɲ'ɲare] *vt* to mark; (*prendere nota*) to note; (*indicare*) to indicate, mark; (*SPORT: goal*) to score; **~rsi** *vr* (*REL*) to make the sign of the cross, cross o.s.

'**segno** ['seɲɲo] *sm* sign; (*impronta, contrassegno*) mark; (*bersaglio*) target; **fare ~ di si/no** to nod (one's head)/shake one's head; **fare ~ a qn di fermarsi** to motion (to) sb to stop; **cogliere o colpire nel ~** (*fig*) to hit the mark; **in o come ~ d'amicizia** as a mark *o* token of friendship; "**~i particolari**" (*su documento etc*) "distinguishing marks".

segre'**gare** *vt* to segregate, isolate.

segregazi'**one** [segregat'tsjone] *sf* segregation.

se'**greta** *sf vedi* **segreto.**

segre'**tario, a** *sm/f* secretary; **~ comunale** town clerk; **~ del partito** party leader; **~ di Stato** Secretary of State.

segrete'**ria** *sf* (*di ditta, scuola*) (secretary's) office; (*d'organizzazione internazionale*) secretariat; (*POL etc: carica*) office of Secretary; **~ telefonica** answering service.

segre'**tezza** [segre'tettsa] *sf* secrecy; **notizie della massima ~** confidential information; **in tutta ~** in secret; (*confidenzialmente*) in confidence.

se'**greto, a** *ag* secret ♦ *sm* secret ♦ *sf* dungeon; **in ~** in secret, secretly; **il ~ professionale** professional secrecy; **un ~ professionale** a professional secret.

segu'**ace** [se'gwatʃe] *sm/f* follower, disciple.

segu'**ente** *ag* following, next; **nel modo ~** as follows, in the following way.

se'**gugio** [se'gudʒo] *sm* hound, hunting dog; (*fig*) private eye, sleuth.

segu'**ire** *vt* to follow; (*frequentare: corso*) to attend ♦ *vi* to follow; (*continuare: testo*) to continue; **~ i consigli di qn** to follow *o* to take sb's advice; **~ gli avvenimenti di attualità** to follow *o* keep up with current events; **come segue** as follows; "**segue**" "to be continued".

segui'**tare** *vt* to continue, carry on with ♦ *vi* to continue, carry on.

'**seguito** *sm* (*scorta*) suite, retinue; (*discepoli*) followers *pl*; (*serie*) sequence, series *sg*; (*continuazione*) continuation; (*conseguenza*) result; **di ~** at a stretch, on

end; **in** ~ later on; **in** ~ **a, a** ~ **di**
following; (*a causa di*) as a result of,
owing to; **essere al** ~ **di qn** to be among
sb's suite, be one of sb's retinue; **non
aver** ~ (*conseguenze*) to have no
repercussions; **facciamo** ~ **alla lettera del**
... further in *o* in answer to your letter
of ....

'**sei** *vb vedi* **essere** ♦ *num* six.
Sei'celle [sei'tʃɛlle] *sfpl*: **le** ~ the
Seychelles.
seicen'tesco, a, schi, sche [seitʃen'tesko]
ag seventeenth-century.
sei'cento [sei'tʃɛnto] *num* six hundred ♦ *sm*:
il S~ the seventeenth century.
sei'mila *num* six thousand.
'**selce** ['seltʃe] *sf* flint, flintstone.
selci'ato [sel'tʃato] *sm* cobbled surface.
selet'tivo, a *ag* selective.
selet'tore *sm* (*TECN*) selector.
selezio'nare [selettsjo'nare] *vt* to select.
selezi'one [selet'tsjone] *sf* selection; **fare
una** ~ to make a selection *o* choice.
'**sella** *sf* saddle.
sel'lare *vt* to saddle.
sel'lino *sm* saddle.
seltz *sm inv* soda (water).
'**selva** *sf* (*bosco*) wood; (*foresta*) forest.
selvag'gina [selvad'dʒina] *sf* (*animali*)
game.
sel'vaggio, a, gi, ge [sel'vaddʒo] *ag* wild;
(*tribù*) savage, uncivilized; (*fig: brutale*)
savage, brutal; (: *incontrollato: fenomeno,
aumento etc*) uncontrolled ♦ *sm/f* savage;
inflazione ~ a runaway inflation.
sel'vatico, a, ci, che *ag* wild.
S.Em. *abbr* (= *Sua Eminenza*) HE.
se'maforo *sm* (*AUT*) traffic lights *pl*.
se'mantico, a *ag* semantic ♦ *sf* semantics
sg.
sembi'anza [sem'bjantsa] *sf* (*poetico:
aspetto*) appearance; ~ **e** *sfpl* (*lineamenti*)
features; (*fig: falsa apparenza*) semblance
sg.
sem'brare *vi* to seem ♦ *vb impers*: **sembra
che** it seems that; **mi sembra che** it seems
to me that; (*penso che*) I think (that); ~ **di
essere** to seem to be; **non mi sembra
vero!** I can't believe it!
'**seme** *sm* seed; (*sperma*) semen; (*CARTE*)
suit.
se'mente *sf* seed.
semes'trale *ag* (*che dura 6 mesi*) six-month
cpd; (*che avviene ogni 6 mesi*) six-monthly.
se'mestre *sm* half-year, six-month period.
'**semi** ... *prefisso* **semi** ....
semi'cerchio [semi'tʃerkjo] *sm* semicircle.
semicondut'tore *sm* semiconductor.

semidetenzi'one [semideten'tsjone] *sf*
custodial sentence whereby individual
must spend a minimum of 10 hours per
day in prison.
semifi'nale *sf* semifinal.
semi'freddo, a *ag* (*CUC*) chilled ♦ *sm* ice-
cream cake.
semilibertà *sf* custodial sentence which
allows prisoner to study or work outside
prison for part of the day.
'**semina** *sf* (*AGR*) sowing.
semi'nare *vt* to sow.
semi'nario *sm* seminar; (*REL*) seminary.
semi'nato *sm*: **uscire dal** ~ (*fig*) to wander
off the point.
seminter'rato *sm* basement;
(*appartamento*) basement flat (*BRIT*) *o*
apartment (*US*).
semi'ologo, a, gi, ghe *sm/f* semiologist.
semi'otica *sf* semiotics *sg*.
se'mitico, a, ci, che *ag* semitic.
sem'mai = **se mai**.
'**semola** *sf* bran; ~ **di grano duro** durum
wheat.
semo'lato *ag*: **zucchero** ~ caster sugar.
semo'lino *sm* semolina.
'**semplice** ['semplitʃe] *ag* simple; (*di un solo
elemento*) single; **è una** ~ **formalità** it's a
mere formality.
semplice'mente [semplitʃe'mente] *av*
simply.
sempli'cistico, a, ci, che [sempli'tʃistiko]
ag simplistic.
semplicità [semplitʃi'ta] *sf* simplicity.
semplifi'care *vt* to simplify.
semplificazi'one [semplifikat'tsjone] *sf*
simplification; **fare una** ~ **di** to simplify.
'**sempre** *av* always; (*ancora*) still; **posso** ~
tentare I can always *o* still try; **da** ~
always; **per** ~ forever; **una volta per** ~
once and for all; ~ **che** *cong* provided
(that); ~ **più** more and more; ~ **meno**
less and less; **va** ~ **meglio** things are
getting better and better; **è** ~ **meglio che
niente** it's better than nothing; **è (pur)** ~
tuo fratello he is still your brother
(however); **c'è** ~ **la possibilità che** ...
there's still a chance that ..., there's
always the possibility that ....
sempre'verde *ag, sm o f* (*BOT*) evergreen.
Sen. *abbr* (= *senatore*) Sen.
'**senape** *sf* (*CUC*) mustard.
se'nato *sm* senate.

The **Senato** *is the upper chamber of the
Italian parliament, with similar functions to
the* **Camera dei deputati**. *To stand for the*
Senato, *one must be at least 40 years of age*

and to vote a candidate into the **Senato,** *one must be 25 years of age or over. Elections for the 315 senators are held every 5 years. Former heads of state are elected life senators as are 5 distinguished members of the public nominated by the head of state for their achievements in the scientific, social, artistic or literary fields. It is presided over by the Presidente del Senato who is elected by the senators.* See also **Parlamento.**

sena'tore, 'trice *sm/f* senator.

'Senegal *sm:* **il** ~ Senegal.

senega'lese *ag, sm/f* Senegalese *inv.*

se'nese *ag* of (*o* from) Siena.

se'nile *ag* senile.

'Senna *sf:* **la** ~ the Seine.

'senno *sm* judgment, (common) sense; **col** ~ **di poi** with hindsight.

sennò *av* = **se no.**

'seno *sm* (*ANAT: petto, mammella*) breast; (: *grembo, fig*) womb; (: *cavità*) sinus; (*GEO*) inlet, creek; (*MAT*) sine; **in** ~ **al partito/all'organizzazione** within the party/the organization.

sen'sale *sm* (*COMM*) agent.

sensa'tezza [sensa'tettsa] *sf* good sense, good judgment.

sen'sato, a *ag* sensible.

sensazio'nale [sensattsjo'nale] *ag* sensational.

sensazi'one [sensat'tsjone] *sf* feeling, sensation; **fare** ~ to cause a sensation, create a stir; **avere la** ~ **che** to have a feeling that.

sen'sibile *ag* sensitive; (*ai sensi*) perceptible; (*rilevante, notevole*) appreciable, noticeable; ~ **a** sensitive to.

sensibilità *sf* sensitivity.

sensibiliz'zare [sensibilid'dzare] *vt* (*fig*) to make aware, awaken.

'senso *sm* (*FISIOL, istinto*) sense; (*impressione, sensazione*) feeling, sensation; (*significato*) meaning, sense; (*direzione*) direction; ~**i** *smpl* (*coscienza*) consciousness *sg*; (*sensualità*) senses; **perdere/riprendere i** ~**i** to lose/regain consciousness; **avere** ~ **pratico** to be practical; **avere un sesto** ~ to have a sixth sense; **fare** ~ **a** (*ripugnare*) to disgust, repel; **ciò non ha** ~ that doesn't make sense; **senza** *o* **privo di** ~ meaningless; **nel** ~ **che** in the sense that; **nel vero** ~ **della parola** in the true sense of the word; **nel** ~ **della lunghezza** lengthwise, lengthways; **nel** ~ **della larghezza** widthwise; **ho dato disposizioni**

in quel ~ I've given instructions to that end *o* effect; ~ **comune** common sense; ~ **del dovere** sense of duty; **in** ~ **opposto** in the opposite direction; **in** ~ **orario/ antiorario** clockwise/anticlockwise; ~ **dell'umorismo** sense of humour; **a** ~ **unico** one-way; **"**~ **vietato"** (*AUT*) "no entry".

sensu'ale *ag* sensual; sensuous.

sensualità *sf* sensuality; sensuousness.

sen'tenza [sen'tentsa] *sf* (*DIR*) sentence; (*massima*) maxim.

sentenzi'are [senten'tsjare] *vi* (*DIR*) to pass judgment.

senti'ero *sm* path.

sentimen'tale *ag* sentimental; (*vita, avventura*) love *cpd.*

senti'mento *sm* feeling.

senti'nella *sf* sentry.

sen'tire *vt* (*percepire al tatto, fig*) to feel; (*udire*) to hear; (*ascoltare*) to listen to; (*odore*) to smell; (*avvertire con il gusto, assaggiare*) to taste ♦ *vi:* ~ **di** (*avere sapore*) to taste of; (*avere odore*) to smell of; ~**rsi** *vr* (*uso reciproco*) to be in touch; ~**rsi bene/male** to feel well/unwell *o* ill; ~**rsi di fare qc** (*essere disposto*) to feel like doing sth; ~ **la mancanza di qn** to miss sb; **ho sentito dire che ...** I have heard that ...; **a** ~ **lui ...** to hear him talk ...; **fatti** ~ keep in touch; **intendo** ~ **il mio legale/il parere di un medico** I'm going to consult my lawyer/a doctor.

sentita'mente *av* sincerely; **ringraziare** ~ to thank sincerely.

sen'tito, a *ag* (*sincero*) sincere, warm; **per** ~ **dire** by hearsay.

sen'tore *sm* rumour (*BRIT*), rumor (*US*), talk; **aver** ~ **di qc** to hear about sth.

'senza ['sentsa] *prep, cong* without; ~ **dir nulla** without saying a word; ~ **dire che ...** not to mention the fact that ...; ~ **contare che ...** without considering that ...; **fare** ~ **qc** to do without sth; ~ **di me** without me; ~ **che io lo sapessi** without me *o* my knowing; ~ **amici** friendless; **senz'altro** of course, certainly; ~ **dubbio** no doubt; ~ **scrupoli** unscrupulous; **i** ~ **lavoro** the jobless, the unemployed; **i** ~ **tetto** the homeless.

senza'tetto [sentsa'tetto] *sm/f inv* homeless person; **i** ~ the homeless.

sepa'rare *vt* to separate; (*dividere*) to divide; (*tenere distinto*) to distinguish; ~**rsi** *vr* (*coniugi*) to separate, part; (*amici*) to part; ~**rsi da** (*coniuge*) to separate *o* part from; (*amico, socio*) to part company with; (*oggetto*) to part with.

separata'mente *av* separately.
sepa'rato, a *ag* (*letti, conto etc*) separate;
(*coniugi*) separated.
separazi'one [separat'tsjone] *sf* separation;
~ **dei beni** division of property.
séparé [sepa're] *sm inv* screen.
se'polcro *sm* sepulchre (*BRIT*), sepulcher
(*US*).
se'polto, a *pp di* **seppellire**.
sepol'tura *sf* burial; **dare** ~ **a qn** to bury
sb.
seppel'lire *vt* to bury.
'seppi *etc vb vedi* **sapere**.
'seppia *sf* cuttlefish ♦ *ag inv* sepia.
sep'pure *cong* even if.
se'quela *sf* (*di avvenimenti*) series,
sequence; (*di offese, ingiurie*) string.
se'quenza [se'kwentsa] *sf* sequence.
sequenzi'ale [sekwen'tsjale] *ag* sequential.
seques'trare *vt* (*DIR*) to impound; (*rapire*)
to kidnap; (*costringere in un luogo*) to
keep, confine.
se'questro *sm* (*DIR*) impoundment; ~ **di**
persona kidnapping.
se'quoia *sf* sequoia.
'sera *sf* evening; **di** ~ in the evening;
domani ~ tomorrow evening, tomorrow
night; **questa** ~ this evening, tonight.
se'rale *ag* evening *cpd*; **scuola** ~ evening
classes *pl*, night school.
se'rata *sf* evening; (*ricevimento*) party.
ser'bare *vt* to keep; (*mettere da parte*) to put
aside; ~ **rancore/odio verso qn** to bear sb
a grudge/hate sb.
serba'toio *sm* tank; (*cisterna*) cistern.
'serbo *ag* Serbian ♦ *sm/f* Serbian, Serb ♦ *sm*
(*LING*) Serbian; (*il serbare*): **mettere/tenere**
o **avere in** ~ **qc** to put/keep sth aside.
serbocro'ato, a *ag, sm* Serbo-Croat.
serena'mente *av* serenely, calmly.
sere'nata *sf* (*MUS*) serenade.
serenità *sf* serenity.
se'reno, a *ag* (*tempo, cielo*) clear; (*fig*)
serene, calm ♦ *sm* (*tempo*) good weather;
un fulmine a ciel ~ (*fig*) a bolt from the
blue.
serg. *abbr* (= *sergente*) Sgt.
ser'gente [ser'dʒɛnte] *sm* (*MIL*) sergeant.
seri'ale *ag* (*INFORM*) serial.
seria'mente *av* (*con serietà, in modo grave*)
seriously; **lavorare** ~ to take one's job
seriously.
'serie *sf inv* (*successione*) series *inv*; (*gruppo,
collezione: di chiavi etc*) set; (*SPORT*)
division; league; (*COMM*): **modello di** ~ /
fuori ~ standard/custom-built model; **in**
~ in quick succession; (*COMM*) mass *cpd*;
tutta una ~ **di problemi** a whole string *o*

series of problems.
serietà *sf* seriousness; reliability.
'serio, a *ag* serious; (*impiegato*)
responsible, reliable; (*ditta, cliente*)
reliable, dependable; **sul** ~ (*davvero*)
really, truly; (*seriamente*) seriously, in
earnest; **dico sul** ~ I'm serious; **faccio sul**
~ I mean it; **prendere qc/qn sul** ~ to take
sth/sb seriously.
seri'oso, a *ag* (*persona, modi*): **un po'** ~ a
bit too serious.
ser'mone *sm* sermon.
'serpe *sf* snake; (*fig peg*) viper.
serpeggi'are [serped'dʒare] *vi* to wind; (*fig*)
to spread.
ser'pente *sm* snake; ~ **a sonagli**
rattlesnake.
'serra *sf* greenhouse; hothouse; (*GEO*)
sierra.
serra'manico *sm*: **coltello a** ~ jack-knife.
ser'randa *sf* roller shutter.
ser'rare *vt* to close, shut; (*a chiave*) to lock;
(*stringere*) to tighten; (*premere: nemico*) to
close in on; ~ **i pugni/i denti** to clench
one's fists/teeth; ~ **le file** to close ranks.
ser'rata *sf* (*INDUSTRIA*) lockout.
ser'rato, a *ag* (*veloce*): **a ritmo** ~ quickly,
fast.
serra'tura *sf* lock.
'serva *sf vedi* **servo**.
ser'vigio [ser'vidʒo] *sm* favour (*BRIT*), favor
(*US*), service.
ser'vire *vt* to serve; (*clienti: al ristorante*) to
wait on; (: *al negozio*) to serve, attend to;
(*fig: giovare*) to aid, help; (*CARTE*) to deal
♦ *vi* (*TENNIS*) to serve; (*essere utile*): ~ **a qn**
to be of use to sb; ~ **a qc/a fare** (*utensile
etc*) to be used for sth/for doing; ~ (**a qn**)
da to serve as (for sb); ~**rsi** *vr* (*usare*):
~**rsi di** to use; (*prendere: cibo*): ~**rsi (di)** to
help o.s. (to); (*essere cliente abituale*): ~**rsi**
da to be a regular customer at, go to; **non**
mi serve più I don't need it any more;
non serve che lei vada you don't need to
go.
servitù *sf* servitude; slavery; (*personale di
servizio*) servants *pl*, domestic staff.
servizi'evole [servit'tsjevole] *ag* obliging,
willing to help.
ser'vizio [ser'vittsjo] *sm* service; (*al
ristorante: sul conto*) service (charge);
(*STAMPA, TV, RADIO*) report; (*da tè, caffè
etc*) set, service; ~**i** *smpl* (*di casa*) kitchen
and bathroom; (*ECON*) services; **essere di**
~ to be on duty; **fuori** ~ (*telefono etc*) out
of order; ~ **compreso/escluso** service
included/not included; **entrata di** ~
service *o* tradesman's (*BRIT*) entrance;

casa con doppi ~i house with two bathrooms; ~ **assistenza clienti** after-sales service; ~ **civile** ≈ community service; ~ **in diretta** (*TV, RADIO*) live coverage; ~ **fotografico** (*STAMPA*) photo feature; ~ **militare** military service; ~ **d'ordine** (*POLIZIA*) police patrol; (*di manifestanti*) team of stewards (*responsible for crowd control*); ~**i segreti** secret service *sg*; ~**i di sicurezza** security forces.

'**servo, a** *sm/f* servant.

servo'**freno** *sm* (*AUT*) servo brake.

servos'**terzo** [servos'tɛrtso] *sm* (*AUT*) power steering.

'**sesamo** *sm* (*BOT*) sesame.

ses'**santa** *num* sixty.

sessan'**tenne** *ag, sm/f* sixty-year-old.

sessan'**tesimo, a** *num* sixtieth.

sessan'**tina** *sf*: una ~ (di) about sixty.

sessantot'**tino, a** *sm/f a person who took part in the events of 1968.*

Sessantotto, '68, *refers to the year 1968 when the student protest movement really took on major significance. Originating in France, it then spread to other industrialized countries including Italy. What began as a purely student movement gradually spread to other parts of society and led to major political and social change. Left-wing groups flourished, schools and universities became more democratic and the referendum on divorce was held.*

sessi'**one** *sf* session.

'**sesso** *sm* sex; il ~ **debole/forte** the weaker/stronger sex.

sessu'**ale** *ag* sexual, sex *cpd*.

sessualità *sf* sexuality.

sessu'**ologo, a, gi, ghe** *sm/f* sexologist, sex specialist.

ses'**tante** *sm* sextant.

'**sesto, a** *num* sixth ♦ *sm*: **rimettere in ~** (*aggiustare*) to put back in order; (*fig: persona*) to put back on his (*o* her) feet; **rimettersi in ~** (*riprendersi*) to recover, get well; (*riassettarsi*) to tidy o.s. up.

'**seta** *sf* silk.

setacci'**are** [setat't͡ʃare] *vt* (*farina etc*) to sift, sieve; (*fig: zona*) to search, comb.

se'**taccio** [se'tatt͡ʃo] *sm* sieve; **passare al ~** (*fig*) to search, comb.

'**sete** *sf* thirst; **avere ~** to be thirsty; ~ **di potere** thirst for power.

seti'**ficio** [seti'fit͡ʃo] *sm* silk factory.

'**setola** *sf* bristle.

sett. *abbr* (= *settembre*) Sept.

'**setta** *sf* sect.

set'**tanta** *num* seventy.

settan'**tenne** *ag, sm/f* seventy-year-old.

settan'**tesimo, a** *num* seventieth.

settan'**tina** *sf*: una ~ (di) about seventy.

'**sette** *num* seven.

settecen'**tesco, a, schi, sche** [settet͡ʃen'tesko] *ag* eighteenth-century.

sette'**cento** [sette't͡ʃɛnto] *num* seven hundred ♦ *sm*: **il S~** the eighteenth century.

set'**tembre** *sm* September; *per fraseologia vedi* **luglio.**

sette'**mila** *num* seven thousand.

settentrio'**nale** *ag* northern ♦ *sm/f* northerner.

settentri'**one** *sm* north.

'**settico, a, ci, che** *ag* (*MED*) septic.

setti'**mana** *sf* week; **la ~ scorsa/prossima** last/next week; **a metà ~** in the middle of the week.

The **settimana bianca** *is a winter-sports holiday taken by many Italians.*

settima'**nale** *ag, sm* weekly.

'**settimo, a** *num* seventh.

set'**tore** *sm* sector; ~ **privato/pubblico** private/public sector; ~ **terziario** service industries *pl*.

Se'**ul** *sf* Seoul.

severità *sf* severity.

se'**vero, a** *ag* severe.

sevizi'**are** [sevit't͡sjare] *vt* to torture.

se'**vizie** [se'vittsje] *sfpl* torture *sg*.

'**sexy** ['seksi] *ag inv* sexy.

sez. *abbr* = **sezione.**

sezio'**nare** [settsjo'nare] *vt* to divide into sections; (*MED*) to dissect.

sezi'**one** [set'tsjone] *sf* section; (*MED*) dissection.

sfaccen'**dato, a** [sfatt͡ʃen'dato] *ag* idle.

sfaccetta'**tura** [sfatt͡ʃetta'tura] *sf* (*azione*) faceting; (*parte sfaccettata, fig*) facet.

sfacchi'**nare** [sfakki'nare] *vi* (*fam*) to toil, drudge.

sfacchi'**nata** [sfakki'nata] *sf* (*fam*) chore, drudgery *no pl*.

sfaccia'**taggine** [sfatt͡ʃa'tadd͡ʒine] *sf* insolence, cheek.

sfacci'**ato, a** [sfat't͡ʃato] *ag* (*maleducato*) cheeky, impudent; (*vistoso*) gaudy.

sfa'**celo** [sfa't͡ʃɛlo] *sm* (*fig*) ruin, collapse.

sfal'**darsi** *vr* to flake (off).

sfal'**sare** *vt* to offset.

sfa'**mare** *vt* (*nutrire*) to feed; (*soddisfare la fame*): ~ **qn** to satisfy sb's hunger; ~**rsi** *vr* to satisfy one's hunger, fill o.s. up.

sfarfal'lio *sm* (*CINE, TV*) flickering.

'sfarzo ['sfartso] *sm* pomp, splendour (*BRIT*), splendor (*US*).

sfar'zoso, a [sfar'tsoso] *ag* splendid, magnificent.

sfasa'mento *sm* (*ELETTR*) phase displacement; (*fig*) confusion, bewilderment.

sfa'sato, a *ag* (*ELETTR, motore*) out of phase; (*fig: persona*) confused, bewildered.

sfasci'are [sfaʃ'ʃare] *vt* (*ferita*) to unbandage; (*distruggere: porta*) to smash, shatter; **~rsi** *vr* (*rompersi*) to smash, shatter.

sfa'tare *vt* (*leggenda*) to explode.

sfati'cato, a *sm/f* idler, loafer.

'sfatto, a *ag* (*letto*) unmade; (*orlo etc*) undone; (*gelato, neve*) melted; (*frutta*) overripe; (*riso, pasta etc*) overdone, overcooked; (*fam: persona, corpo*) flabby.

sfavil'lare *vi* to spark, send out sparks; (*risplendere*) to sparkle.

sfa'vore *sm* disfavour (*BRIT*), disfavor (*US*), disapproval.

sfavo'revole *ag* unfavourable (*BRIT*), unfavorable (*US*).

sfega'tato, a *ag* fanatical.

'sfera *sf* sphere.

'sferico, a, ci, che *ag* spherical.

sfer'rare *vt* (*fig: colpo*) to land, deal; (: *attacco*) to launch.

sfer'zante [sfer'tsante] *ag* (*critiche, parole*) stinging.

sfer'zare [sfer'tsare] *vt* to whip; (*fig*) to lash out at.

sfian'care *vt* to wear out, exhaust; **~rsi** *vr* to exhaust o.s., wear o.s. out.

sfia'tare *vi* to allow air (*o gas etc*) to escape.

sfiata'toio *sm* blowhole; (*TECN*) vent.

sfi'brante *ag* exhausting, energy-sapping.

sfi'brare *vt* (*indebolire*) to exhaust, enervate.

sfi'brato, a *ag* exhausted, worn out.

'sfida *sf* challenge.

sfi'dante *ag* challenging ♦ *sm/f* challenger.

sfi'dare *vt* to challenge; (*fig*) to defy, brave; **~ qn a fare qc** to challenge sb to do sth; **~ un pericolo** to brave a danger; **sfido che ...** I dare say (that) ....

sfi'ducia [sfi'dutʃa] *sf* distrust, mistrust; **avere ~ in qn/qc** to distrust sb/sth.

sfiduci'ato, a [sfidu'tʃato] *ag* lacking confidence.

sfigu'rare *vt* (*persona*) to disfigure; (*quadro, statua*) to deface ♦ *vi* (*far cattiva figura*) to make a bad impression.

sfilacci'are [sfilat'tʃare] *vt, vi*, **~rsi** *vr* to fray.

sfi'lare *vt* (*ago*) to unthread; (*abito, scarpe*) to slip off ♦ *vi* (*truppe*) to march past, parade; (*manifestanti*) to march; **~rsi** *vr* (*perle etc*) to come unstrung; (*orlo, tessuto*) to fray; (*calza*) to run, ladder.

sfi'lata *sf* (*MIL*) parade; (*di manifestanti*) march; **~ di moda** fashion show.

'sfilza ['sfiltsa] *sf* (*di case*) row; (*di errori*) series *inv*.

'sfinge ['sfindʒe] *sf* sphinx.

sfini'mento *sm* exhaustion.

sfi'nito, a *ag* exhausted.

sfio'rare *vt* to brush (against); (*argomento*) to touch upon; **~ la velocità di 150 km/h** to touch 150 km/h.

sfio'rire *vi* to wither, fade.

'sfitto, a *ag* vacant, empty.

sfo'cato, a *ag* (*FOT*) out of focus.

sfoci'are [sfo'tʃare] *vi*: **~ in** to flow into; (*fig: malcontento*) to develop into.

sfode'rato, a *ag* (*vestito*) unlined.

sfo'gare *vt* to vent, pour out; **~rsi** *vr* (*sfogare la propria rabbia*) to give vent to one's anger; (*confidarsi*): **~rsi (con)** to pour out one's feelings (to); **non sfogarti su di me!** don't take your bad temper out on me!

sfoggi'are [sfod'dʒare] *vt, vi* to show off.

'sfoggio ['sfoddʒo] *sm* show, display; **fare ~ di** to show off, display.

sfogherò *etc* [sfoge'rɔ] *vb vedi* **sfogare**.

'sfoglia ['sfoʎʎa] *sf* sheet of pasta dough; **pasta ~** (*CUC*) puff pastry.

sfogli'are [sfoʎ'ʎare] *vt* (*libro*) to leaf through.

'sfogo, ghi *sm* outlet; (*eruzione cutanea*) rash; (*fig*) outburst; **dare ~ a** (*fig*) to give vent to.

sfolgo'rante *ag* (*luce*) blazing; (*fig: vittoria*) brilliant.

sfolgo'rare *vi* to blaze.

sfolla'gente [sfolla'dʒɛnte] *sm inv* truncheon (*BRIT*), billy (*US*).

sfol'lare *vt* to empty, clear ♦ *vi* to disperse; **~ da** (*città*) to evacuate.

sfol'lato, a *ag* evacuated ♦ *sm/f* evacuee.

sfol'tire *vt*, **~rsi** *vr* to thin (out).

sfon'dare *vt* (*porta*) to break down; (*scarpe*) to wear a hole in; (*cesto, scatola*) to burst, knock the bottom out of; (*MIL*) to break through ♦ *vi* (*riuscire*) to make a name for o.s.

sfon'dato, a *ag* (*scarpe*) worn out; (*scatola*) burst; (*sedia*) broken, damaged; **essere ricco ~** to be rolling in it.

'sfondo *sm* background.

sfo'rare *vi* to overrun.
sfor'mare *vt* to put out of shape, knock out of shape; ~**rsi** *vr* to lose shape, get out of shape.
sfor'mato, a *ag* (*che ha perso forma*) shapeless ♦ *sm* (*CUC*) type of soufflé.
sfor'nare *vt* (*pane*) to take out of the oven; (*fig*) to churn out.
sfor'nito, a *ag*: ~ **di** lacking in, without; (*negozio*) out of.
sfor'tuna *sf* misfortune, ill luck *no pl*; **avere** ~ to be unlucky; **che** ~! how unfortunate!
sfortu'nato, a *ag* unlucky; (*impresa, film*) unsuccessful.
sfor'zare [sfor'tsare] *vt* to force; (*voce, occhi*) to strain; ~**rsi** *vr*: ~**rsi di** *o* **a** *o* **per fare** to try hard to do.
'sforzo ['sfɔrtso] *sm* effort; (*tensione eccessiva, TECN*) strain; **fare uno** ~ to make an effort; **essere sotto** ~ (*motore, macchina, fig: persona*) to be under stress.
'sfottere *vt* (*fam*) to tease.
sfracel'lare [sfratʃel'lare] *vt*, ~**rsi** *vr* to smash.
sfrat'tare *vt* to evict.
'sfratto *sm* eviction; **dare lo** ~ **a qn** to give sb notice to quit.
sfrecci'are [sfret'tʃare] *vi* to shoot *o* flash past.
sfre'gare *vt* (*strofinare*) to rub; (*graffiare*) to scratch; ~**rsi le mani** to rub one's hands; ~ **un fiammifero** to strike a match.
sfregi'are [sfre'dʒare] *vt* to slash, gash; (*persona*) to disfigure; (*quadro*) to deface.
'sfregio ['sfredʒo] *sm* gash; scar; (*fig*) insult.
sfre'nato, a *ag* (*fig*) unrestrained, unbridled.
sfron'dare *vt* (*albero*) to prune, thin out; (*fig: discorso, scritto*) to prune (down).
sfronta'tezza [sfronta'tettsa] *sf* impudence, cheek.
sfron'tato, a *ag* impudent, cheeky.
sfrutta'mento *sm* exploitation.
sfrut'tare *vt* (*terreno*) to overwork, exhaust; (*miniera*) to exploit, work; (*fig: operai, occasione, potere*) to exploit.
sfrutta'tore, 'trice *sm/f* exploiter.
sfug'gente [sfud'dʒɛnte] *ag* (*fig: sguardo*) elusive; (*mento*) receding.
sfug'gire [sfud'dʒire] *vi* to escape; ~ **a** (*custode*) to escape (from); (*morte*) to escape; ~ **a qn** (*dettaglio, nome*) to escape sb; ~ **di mano a qn** to slip out of sb's hand (*o* hands); **lasciarsi** ~ **un'occasione** to let an opportunity go by; ~ **al controllo** (*macchina*) to go out of control;

(*situazione*) to be no longer under control.
sfug'gita [sfud'dʒita] *sf*: **di** ~ (*rapidamente, in fretta*) in passing.
sfu'mare *vt* (*colori, contorni*) to soften, shade off ♦ *vi* to shade (off), fade; (*fig: svanire*) to vanish, disappear; (*: speranze*) to come to nothing.
sfuma'tura *sf* shading off *no pl*; (*tonalità*) shade, tone; (*fig*) touch, hint.
sfuo'cato, a *ag* = **sfocato**.
sfuri'ata *sf* (*scatto di collera*) fit of anger; (*rimprovero*) sharp rebuke.
'sfuso, a *ag* (*caramelle etc*) loose, unpacked; (*vino*) unbottled; (*birra*) draught (*BRIT*), draft (*US*).
sg. *abbr* = **seguente**.
S.G. *abbr* = **Sua Grazia**.
sga'bello *sm* stool.
sgabuz'zino [zgabud'dzino] *sm* lumber room.
sgambet'tare *vi* to kick one's legs about.
sgam'betto *sm*: **far lo** ~ **a qn** to trip sb up; (*fig*) to oust sb.
sganasci'arsi [zganaʃ'ʃarsi] *vr*: ~ **dalle risa** to roar with laughter.
sganci'are [zgan'tʃare] *vt* to unhook; (*chiusura*) to unfasten, undo; (*FERR*) to uncouple; (*bombe: da aereo*) to release, drop; (*fig: fam: soldi*) to fork out; ~**rsi** *vr* to come unhooked; to come unfastened, come undone; to uncouple; (*fig*): ~**rsi (da)** to get away (from).
sganghe'rato, a [zgange'rato] *ag* (*porta*) off its hinges; (*auto*) ramshackle; (*riso*) wild, boisterous.
sgar'bato, a *ag* rude, impolite.
'sgarbo *sm*: **fare uno** ~ **a qn** to be rude to sb.
sgargi'ante [zgar'dʒante] *ag* gaudy, showy.
sgar'rare *vi* (*persona*) to step out of line; (*orologio: essere avanti*) to gain; (*: essere indietro*) to lose.
'sgarro *sm* inaccuracy.
sgattaio'lare *vi* to sneak away *o* off.
sge'lare [zdʒe'lare] *vi*, *vt* to thaw.
'sghembo, a ['zgembo] *ag* (*obliquo*) slanting; (*storto*) crooked.
sghignaz'zare [zgiɲɲat'tsare] *vi* to laugh scornfully.
sghignaz'zata [zgiɲɲat'tsata] *sf* scornful laugh.
sgob'bare *vi* (*fam: scolaro*) to swot; (*: operaio*) to slog.
sgoccio'lare [zgottʃo'lare] *vt* (*vuotare*) to drain (to the last drop) ♦ *vi* (*acqua*) to drip; (*recipiente*) to drain.
'sgoccioli ['zgottʃoli] *smpl*: **essere agli** ~ (*lavoro, provviste etc*) to be nearly

finished; (*periodo*) to be nearly over; **siamo agli ~** we've nearly finished, the end is in sight.

sgo'larsi *vr* to talk (*o* shout *o* sing) o.s. hoarse.

sgomb(e)'rare *vt* to clear; (*andarsene da: stanza*) to vacate; (*evacuare*) to evacuate.

'sgombero *sm vedi* **sgombro**.

'sgombro, a *ag*: ~ **(di)** clear (of), free (from) ♦ *sm* (*ZOOL*) mackerel; (*anche*: **sgombero**) clearing; vacating; evacuation; (: *trasloco*) removal.

sgomen'tare *vt* to dismay; **~rsi** *vr* to be dismayed.

sgo'mento, a *ag* dismayed ♦ *sm* dismay, consternation.

sgomi'nare *vt* (*nemico*) to rout; (*avversario*) to defeat; (*fig*: *epidemia*) to overcome.

sgonfi'are *vt* to let down, deflate; **~rsi** *vr* to go down.

'sgonfio, a *ag* (*pneumatico, pallone*) flat.

'sgorbio *sm* blot; scribble.

sgor'gare *vi* to gush (out).

sgoz'zare [zgot'tsare] *vt* to cut the throat of.

sgra'devole *ag* unpleasant, disagreeable.

sgra'dito, a *ag* unpleasant, unwelcome.

sgraffi'gnare [zgraffiɲ'ɲare] *vt* (*fam*) to pinch, swipe.

sgrammati'cato, a *ag* ungrammatical.

sgra'nare *vt* (*piselli*) to shell; ~ **gli occhi** to open one's eyes wide.

sgran'chirsi [zgran'kirsi] *vr* to stretch; ~ **le gambe** to stretch one's legs.

sgranocchi'are [zgranok'kjare] *vt* to munch.

sgras'sare *vt* to remove the grease from.

'sgravio *sm*: ~ **fiscale** *o* **contributivo** tax relief.

sgrazi'ato, a [zgrat'tsjato] *ag* clumsy, ungainly.

sgreto'lare *vt* to cause to crumble; **~rsi** *vr* to crumble.

sgri'dare *vt* to scold.

sgri'data *sf* scolding.

sguai'ato, a *ag* coarse, vulgar.

sguai'nare *vt* to draw, unsheathe.

sgual'cire [zgwal'tʃire] *vt* to crumple (up), crease.

sgual'drina *sf* (*peg*) slut.

sgu'ardo *sm* (*occhiata*) look, glance; (*espressione*) look (in one's eye); **dare uno ~ a qc** to glance at sth, cast a glance *o* an eye over sth; **alzare** *o* **sollevare lo ~** to raise one's eyes, look up; **cercare qc/qn con lo ~** to look (a)round for sth/sb.

'sguattero, a *sm/f* scullery boy/maid.

sguaz'zare [zgwat'tsare] *vi* (*nell'acqua*) to splash about; (*nella melma*) to wallow; ~ **nell'oro** to be rolling in money.

sguinzagli'are [zgwintsaʎ'ʎare] *vt* to let off the leash; (*fig*: *persona*): ~ **qn dietro a qn** to set sb on sb.

sgusci'are [zguʃ'ʃare] *vt* to shell ♦ *vi* (*sfuggire di mano*) to slip; ~ **via** to slip *o* slink away.

'shaker ['ʃeikə*] *sm inv* (*cocktail*) shaker.

'shampoo ['ʃampo] *sm inv* shampoo.

shoc'care [ʃok'kare] *vt* = **shockare**.

shock [ʃɔk] *sm inv* shock.

shoc'kare [ʃok'kare] *vt* to shock.

SI *sigla* = Siena.

════════════════════ PAROLA CHIAVE

si (*dav lo, la, li, le, ne diventa* **se**) *pron* **1** (*riflessivo: maschile*) himself; (: *femminile*) herself; (: *neutro*) itself; (: *impersonale*) oneself; (: *pl*) themselves; **lavarsi** to wash (oneself); ~ **è tagliato** he has cut himself; ~ **credono importanti** they think a lot of themselves

2 (*con complemento oggetto*): **lavarsi le mani** to wash one's hands; **sporcarsi i pantaloni** to get one's trousers dirty; ~ **sta lavando i capelli** he (*o* she) is washing his (*o* her) hair

3 (*reciproco*) one another, each other; **si amano** they love one another *o* each other

4 (*passivo*): ~ **ripara facilmente** it is easily repaired; **affittasi camera** room to let

5 (*impersonale*): ~ **dice che ...** they *o* people say that ...; ~ **vede che è vecchio** one *o* you can see that it's old; **non ~ fa credito** we do not give credit; **ci ~ sbaglia facilmente** it's easy to make a mistake

6 (*noi*) we; **tra poco ~ parte** we're leaving soon.

─────────────────────────

sì *av* yes ♦ *sm*: **non mi aspettavo un ~** I didn't expect him (*o* her *etc*) to say yes; **per me è ~** I should think so, I expect so; **saranno stati ~ e no in 20** there must have been about 20 of them; **uno ~ e uno no** every other one; **un giorno ~ e uno no** every other day; **dire di ~** to say yes; **spero/penso di ~** I hope/think so; **fece di ~ col capo** he nodded (his head); **e ~ che ...** and to think that ....

'sia *cong*: ~ ... ~ (*o* ... *o*): ~ **che lavori, ~ che non lavori** whether he works or not; (*tanto ... quanto*): **verranno ~ Luigi ~ suo fratello** both Luigi and his brother will be coming.

'sia *etc vb vedi* **essere**.

SIAE *sigla f* = *Società Italiana Autori ed Editori.*
Si'am *sm*: **il** ~ Siam.
sia'mese *ag, sm/f* siamese *inv*.
si'amo *vb vedi* **essere**.
Si'beria *sf*: **la** ~ Siberia.
siberi'ano, a *ag, sm/f* Siberian.
sibi'lare *vi* to hiss; (*fischiare*) to whistle.
'sibilo *sm* hiss; whistle.
si'cario *sm* hired killer.
sicché [sik'ke] *cong* (*perciò*) so (that), therefore; (*e quindi*) (and) so.
siccità [sittʃi'ta] *sf* drought.
sic'come *cong* since, as.
Si'cilia [si'tʃilja] *sf*: **la** ~ Sicily.
sicili'ano, a [sitʃi'ljano] *ag, sm/f* Sicilian.
sico'moro *sm* sycamore.
'siculo, a *ag, sm/f* Sicilian.
si'cura *sf* (*di arma, spilla*) safety catch; (*di portiera*) safety lock.
sicura'mente *av* certainly.
sicu'rezza [siku'rettsa] *sf* safety; security; confidence; certainty; **di** ~ safety *cpd*; **la** ~ **stradale** road safety; **avere la** ~ **di qc** to be sure *o* certain of sth; **lo so con** ~ I am quite certain; **ha risposto con molta** ~ he answered very confidently.
si'curo, a *ag* safe; (*ben difeso*) secure; (*fiducioso*) confident; (*certo*) sure, certain; (*notizia, amico*) reliable; (*esperto*) skilled ♦ *av* (*anche*: **di** ~) certainly ♦ *sm*: **andare sul** ~ to play safe; **essere/mettere al** ~ to be safe/put in a safe place; ~ **di sé** self-confident, sure of o.s.; **sentirsi** ~ to feel safe *o* secure; **essere** ~ **di/che** to be sure of/that; **da fonte** ~**a** from reliable sources.
siderur'gia [siderur'dʒia] *sf* iron and steel industry.
side'rurgico, a, ci, che [side'rurdʒiko] *ag* iron and steel *cpd*.
'sidro *sm* cider.
si'edo *etc vb vedi* **sedere**.
si'epe *sf* hedge.
si'ero *sm* (*MED*) serum; ~ **antivipera** snake bite serum; ~ **del latte** whey.
sieronegatività *sf inv* HIV-negative status.
sieronega'tivo, a *ag* HIV-negative ♦ *sm/f* HIV-negative person.
sieropositività *sf inv* HIV-positive status.
sieroposi'tivo, a *ag* HIV-positive ♦ *sm/f* HIV-positive person.
si'erra *sf* (*GEO*) sierra.
Si'erra Le'one *sf*: **la** ~ Sierra Leone.
si'esta *sf* siesta, (afternoon) nap.
si'ete *vb vedi* **essere**.
si'filide *sf* syphilis.
si'fone *sm* siphon.

Sig. *abbr* (= *signore*) Mr.
siga'retta *sf* cigarette.
'sigaro *sm* cigar.
Sigg. *abbr* (= *signori*) Messrs.
sigil'lare [sidʒil'lare] *vt* to seal.
si'gillo [si'dʒillo] *sm* seal.
'sigla *sf* (*iniziali*) initials *pl*; (*abbreviazione*) acronym, abbreviation; ~ **automobilistica** *abbreviation of province on vehicle number plate*; ~ **musicale** signature tune.
si'glare *vt* to initial.
Sig.na *abbr* (= *signorina*) Miss.
signifi'care [siɲɲifi'kare] *vt* to mean; **cosa significa?** what does this mean?
significa'tivo, a [siɲɲifika'tivo] *ag* significant.
signifi'cato [siɲɲifi'kato] *sm* meaning.
si'gnora [siɲ'ɲora] *sf* lady; **la** ~ **X** Mrs ['mɪsɪz] X; **buon giorno S**~**/Signore/ Signorina** good morning; (*deferente*) good morning Madam/Sir/Madam; (*quando si conosce il nome*) good morning Mrs/Mr/ Miss X; **Gentile S**~**/Signore/Signorina** (*in una lettera*) Dear Madam/Sir/Madam; **Gentile** (*o* **Cara**) **S**~ **Rossi** Dear Mrs Rossi; **Gentile S**~ **Anna Rossi** (*sulle buste*) Mrs Anna Rossi; **il signor Rossi e** ~ Mr Rossi and his wife; ~**e e signori** ladies and gentlemen; **le presento la mia** ~ may I introduce my wife?
si'gnore [siɲ'ɲore] *sm* gentleman; (*padrone*) lord, master; (*REL*): **il S**~ the Lord; **il signor X** Mr ['mɪstə*] X; **signor Presidente** Mr Chairman; **Gentile** (*o* **Caro**) **Signor Rossi** (*in lettere*) Dear Mr Rossi; **Gentile Signor Paolo Rossi** (*sulle buste*) Mr Paolo Rossi; **i** ~**i Bianchi** (*coniugi*) Mr and Mrs Bianchi; *vedi anche* **signora**.
signo'ria [siɲɲo'ria] *sf* (*STORIA*) seignory, signoria; **S**~ **Vostra** (*S.V.*) (*AMM*) you.
signo'rile [siɲɲo'rile] *ag* refined.
signorilità [siɲɲorili'ta] *sf* (*raffinatezza*) refinement; (*eleganza*) elegance.
signo'rina [siɲɲo'rina] *sf* young lady; **la** ~ **X** Miss X; **Gentile** (*o* **Cara**) **S**~ **Rossi** (*in lettere*) Dear Miss Rossi; **Gentile S**~ **Anna Rossi** (*sulle buste*) Miss Anna Rossi; *vedi anche* **signora**.
signo'rino [siɲɲo'rino] *sm* young master.
Sig.ra *abbr* (= *signora*) Mrs.
silenzia'tore [silentsja'tore] *sm* silencer.
si'lenzio [si'lentsjo] *sm* silence; **fare** ~ to be quiet, stop talking; **far passare qc sotto** ~ to keep quiet about sth, hush sth up.
silenzi'oso, a [silen'tsjoso] *ag* silent, quiet.
'silice ['silitʃe] *sf* silica.
si'licio [si'litʃo] *sm* silicon; **piastrina di** ~

silicon chip.
sili'cone *sm* silicone.
'sillaba *sf* syllable.
silu'rare *vt* to torpedo; (*fig: privare del comando*) to oust.
si'luro *sm* torpedo.
simbi'osi *sf* (*BIOL, fig*) symbiosis.
simboleggi'are [simboled'dʒare] *vt* to symbolize.
sim'bolico, a, ci, che *ag* symbolic(al).
simbo'lismo *sm* symbolism.
'simbolo *sm* symbol.
simi'lare *ag* similar.
'simile *ag* (*analogo*) similar; (*di questo tipo*): **un uomo** ~ such a man, a man like this ♦ *sm* (*persona*) fellow man; **libri** ~**i** such books; ~ **a** similar to; **non ho mai visto niente di** ~ I've never seen anything like that; **è insegnante o qualcosa di** ~ he's a teacher or something like that; **vendono vasi e** ~**i** they sell vases and things like that; **i suoi** ~**i** one's fellow men; one's peers.
simili'tudine *sf* (*LING*) simile.
simme'tria *sf* symmetry.
sim'metrico, a, ci, che *ag* symmetric(al).
simpa'tia *sf* (*qualità*) pleasantness; (*inclinazione*) liking; **avere** ~ **per qn** to like sb, have a liking for sb; **con** ~ (*su lettera etc*) with much affection.
sim'patico, a, ci, che *ag* (*persona*) nice, pleasant, likeable; (*casa, albergo etc*) nice, pleasant.
simpatiz'zante [simpatid'dzante] *smf* sympathizer.
simpatiz'zare [simpatid'dzare] *vi:* ~ **con** to take a liking to.
sim'posio *sm* symposium.
simu'lacro *sm* (*monumento, statua*) image; (*fig*) semblance.
simu'lare *vt* to sham, simulate; (*TECN*) to simulate.
simulazi'one [simulat'tsjone] *sf* shamming; simulation.
simul'taneo, a *ag* simultaneous.
sin. *abbr* (= *sinistra*) L.
sina'goga, ghe *sf* synagogue.
sincera'mente [sintʃera'mente] *av* (*gen*) sincerely; (*francamente*) honestly, sincerely.
since'rarsi [sintʃe'rarsi] *vr:* ~ (**di qc**) to make sure (of sth).
sincerità [sintʃeri'ta] *sf* sincerity.
sin'cero, a [sin'tʃero] *ag* (*genuino*) sincere; (*onesto*) genuine.
'sincope *sf* syncopation; (*MED*) blackout.
sincro'nia *sf* (*di movimento*) synchronism.
sin'cronico, a, ci, che *ag* synchronic.

sincroniz'zare [sinkronid'dzare] *vt* to synchronize.
sinda'cale *ag* (trade-)union *cpd*.
sindaca'lista, i, e *smf* trade unionist.
sinda'care *vt* (*controllare*) to inspect; (*fig: criticare*) to criticize.
sinda'cato *sm* (*di lavoratori*) (trade) union; ~ **dei datori di lavoro** employers' association.
'sindaco, ci *sm* mayor.
'sindrome *sf* (*MED*) syndrome.
siner'gia, gie [siner'dʒia] *sf* (*anche fig*) synergy.
sinfo'nia *sf* (*MUS*) symphony.
sin'fonico, a, ci, che *ag* symphonic; (*orchestra*) symphony *cpd*.
singa'lese *ag, smf, sm* Sin(g)halese *inv*.
Singa'pore *sf* Singapore.
singhioz'zare [singjot'tsare] *vi* to sob; to hiccup.
singhi'ozzo [sin'gjottso] *sm* (*di pianto*) sob; (*MED*) hiccup; **avere il** ~ to have the hiccups; **a** ~ (*fig*) by fits and starts.
singo'lare *ag* (*insolito*) remarkable, singular; (*LING*) singular ♦ *sm* (*LING*) singular; (*TENNIS*): ~ **maschile/femminile** men's/women's singles.
singolar'mente *av* (*separatamente*) individually, one at a time; (*in modo strano*) strangely, peculiarly, oddly.
'singolo, a *ag* single, individual ♦ *sm* (*persona*) individual; (*TENNIS*) = **singolare**; **ogni** ~ **individuo** each individual; **camera** ~**a** a single room.
sinis'trato, a *ag* damaged ♦ *smf* disaster victim; **zona** ~**a** a disaster area.
si'nistro, a *ag* left, left-hand; (*fig*) sinister ♦ *sm* (*incidente*) accident ♦ *sf* (*POL*) left (wing); **a** ~**a** on the left; (*direzione*) to the left; **a** ~**a di** to the left of; **di** ~**a** left-wing; **tenere la** ~**a** to keep to the left; **guida a** ~**a** left-hand drive.
'sino *prep* = **fino**.
si'nonimo, a *ag* synonymous ♦ *sm* synonym; ~ **di** synonymous with.
sin'tassi *sf* syntax.
sin'tattico, a, ci, che *ag* syntactic.
'sintesi *sf* synthesis; (*riassunto*) summary, résumé; **in** ~ in brief, in short.
sin'tetico, a, ci, che *ag* synthetic; (*conciso*) brief, concise.
sintetiz'zare [sintetid'dzare] *vt* to synthesize; (*riassumere*) to summarize.
sintetizza'tore [sintetiddza'tore] *sm* (*MUS*) synthesizer; ~ **di voce** voice synthesizer.
sinto'matico, a, ci, che *ag* symptomatic.
'sintomo *sm* symptom.
sinto'nia *sf* (*RADIO*) tuning; **essere in** ~ **con**

qn (*fig*) to be on the same wavelength as
sb.

sintoniz'zare [sintonid'dzare] *vt* to tune
(in); **~rsi** *vr*: **~rsi su** to tune in to.

sintonizza'tore [sintoniddza'tore] *sm* tuner.

sinu'oso, a *ag* (*strada*) winding.

sinu'site *sf* sinusitis.

SIP *sigla f* (= *Società Italiana per l'esercizio
telefonico*) *Italian telephone company.*

si'pario *sm* (*TEAT*) curtain.

si'rena *sf* (*apparecchio*) siren; (*nella
mitologia, fig*) siren, mermaid; **~ d'allarme**
(*per incendio*) fire alarm; (*per furto*)
burglar alarm.

'Siria *sf*: **la ~** Syria.

siri'ano, a *ag, smf* Syrian.

si'ringa, ghe *sf* syringe.

'sisma, i *sm* earthquake.

'SISMI *sigla m* (= *Servizio per l'Informazione e
la Sicurezza Militari*) *military security
service.*

'sismico, a, ci, che *ag* seismic; (*zona*)
earthquake *cpd*.

sis'mografo *sm* seismograph.

sissi'gnore [sissiɲ'ɲore] *av* (*a un superiore*)
yes, sir; (*enfatico*) yes indeed, of course.

sis'tema, i *sm* system; (*metodo*) method,
way; **trovare il ~ per fare qc** to find a way
to do sth; **~ decimale/metrico** decimal/
metric system; **~ operativo** (*INFORM*)
operating system; **~ solare** solar system;
~ di vita way of life.

siste'mare *vt* (*mettere a posto*) to tidy, put
in order; (*risolvere: questione*) to sort out,
settle; (*procurare un lavoro a*) to find a job
for; (*dare un alloggio a*) to settle, find
accommodation (*BRIT*) o accommodations
(*US*) for; **~rsi** *vr* (*problema*) to be settled;
(*persona: trovare alloggio*) to find
accommodation(s); (: *trovarsi un lavoro*) to
get fixed up with a job; **ti sistemo io!** I'll
soon sort you out!; **~ qn in un albergo** to
fix sb up with a hotel.

sistematica'mente *av* sistematically.

siste'matico, a, ci, che *ag* systematic.

sistemazi'one [sistemat'tsjone] *sf*
arrangement, order; settlement;
employment; accommodation (*BRIT*),
accommodations (*US*).

'sito, a *ag* (*AMM*) situated ♦ *sm* (*letterario*)
place.

situ'are *vt* to site, situate.

situ'ato, a *ag*: **~ a/su** situated at/on.

situazi'one [situat'tsjone] *sf* situation; **vista
la sua ~ familiare** given your family
situation o circumstances; **nella sua ~** in
your position o situation; **mi trovo in una
~ critica** I'm in a very difficult situation o

position.

'skai ® *sm* Leatherette ®.

ski-lift [ski'lift] *sm inv* ski lift.

slacci'are [zlat'tʃare] *vt* to undo, unfasten.

slanci'arsi [zlan'tʃarsi] *vr* to dash, fling o.s.

slanci'ato, a [zlan'tʃato] *ag* slender.

'slancio ['zlantʃo] *sm* dash, leap; (*fig*) surge;
in uno ~ d'affetto in a burst o rush of
affection; **di ~** impetuously.

sla'vato, a *ag* faded, washed out; (*fig: viso,
occhi*) pale, colourless (*BRIT*), colorless
(*US*).

sla'vina *sf* snowslide.

'slavo, a *ag* Slav(onic), Slavic.

sle'ale *ag* disloyal; (*concorrenza etc*) unfair.

slealtà *sf* disloyalty; unfairness.

sle'gare *vt* to untie.

slip *sm inv* (*mutandine*) briefs *pl*; (*da bagno:
per uomo*) (swimming) trunks *pl*; (: *per
donna*) bikini bottoms *pl*.

'slitta *sf* sledge; (*trainata*) sleigh.

slitta'mento *sm* slipping; skidding;
postponement; **~ salariale** wage drift.

slit'tare *vi* to slip, slide; (*AUT*) to skid;
(*incontro, conferenza*) to be put off, be
postponed.

s.l.m. *abbr* (= *sul livello del mare*) a.s.l.

slo'gare *vt* (*MED*) to dislocate; (: *caviglia,
polso*) to sprain.

sloga'tura *sf* dislocation; sprain.

sloggi'are [zlod'dʒare] *vt* (*inquilino*) to turn
out; (*nemico*) to drive out, dislodge ♦ *vi* to
move out.

Slo'vacchia [zlo'vakkja] *sf* Slovakia.

slo'vacco, a, ci, che *ag, smf* Slovak,
Slovakian; **la Repubblica S~a** the Slovak
Republic.

Slo'venia *sf* Slovenia.

slo'veno, a *ag, smf* Slovene, Slovenian
♦ *sm* (*LING*) Slovene.

S.M. *abbr* (*MIL*) = **Stato Maggiore**; (= *Sua
Maestà*) HM.

smac'cato, a *ag* (*fig*) excessive.

smacchi'are [zmak'kjare] *vt* to remove
stains from.

smacchia'tore [zmakkja'tore] *sm* stain
remover.

'smacco, chi *sm* humiliating defeat.

smagli'ante [zmaʎ'ʎante] *ag* brilliant,
dazzling.

smagli'are [zmaʎ'ʎare] *vt*, **~rsi** *vr* (*calza*) to
ladder.

smaglia'tura [zmaʎʎa'tura] *sf* (*su maglia,
calza*) ladder (*BRIT*), run; (*MED: sulla pelle*)
stretch mark.

sma'grire *vt* to make thin ♦ *vi* to get o grow
thin, lose weight.

sma'grito, a *ag*: **essere ~** to have lost a lot

of weight.

smalizi'ato, a [smalit'tsjato] *ag* shrewd, cunning.

smal'tare *vt* to enamel; (*ceramica*) to glaze; (*unghie*) to varnish.

smalti'mento *sm* (*di rifiuti*) disposal.

smal'tire *vt* (*merce*) to sell off; (*rifiuti*) to dispose of; (*cibo*) to digest; (*peso*) to lose; (*rabbia*) to get over; ~ **la sbornia** to sober up.

'smalto *sm* (*anche di denti*) enamel; (*per ceramica*) glaze; ~ **per unghie** nail varnish.

smance'rie [zmantʃe'rie] *sfpl* mawkishness *sg*.

'smania *sf* agitation, restlessness; (*fig*): ~ **di** thirst for, craving for; **avere la** ~ **addosso** to have the fidgets; **avere la** ~ **di fare** to long *o* yearn to do.

smani'are *vi* (*agitarsi*) to be restless *o* agitated; (*fig*): ~ **di fare** to long *o* yearn to do.

smantella'mento *sm* dismantling.

smantel'lare *vt* to dismantle.

smar'carsi *vr* (*SPORT*) to get free of marking.

smargi'asso [zmar'dʒasso] *sm* show-off.

smarri'mento *sm* loss; (*fig*) bewilderment; dismay.

smar'rire *vt* to lose; (*non riuscire a trovare*) to mislay; ~**rsi** *vr* (*perdersi*) to lose one's way, get lost; (: *oggetto*) to go astray.

smar'rito, a *ag* (*oggetto*) lost; (*fig: confuso: persona*) bewildered, nonplussed; (: *sguardo*) bewildered; **ufficio oggetti** ~**i** lost property office (*BRIT*), lost and found (*US*).

smasche'rare [zmaske'rare] *vt* to unmask.

SME *abbr* = Stato Maggiore Esercito ♦ *sigla m* (= *Sistema Monetario Europeo*) EMS (= *European Monetary System*).

smem'brare *vt* (*gruppo, partito etc*) to split; ~**rsi** *vr* to split up.

smemo'rato, a *ag* forgetful.

smen'tire *vt* (*negare*) to deny; (*testimonianza*) to refute; (*reputazione*) to give the lie to; ~**rsi** *vr* to be inconsistent.

smen'tita *sf* denial; refutation.

sme'raldo *sm*, *ag inv* emerald.

smerci'are [zmer'tʃare] *vt* (*COMM*) to sell; (: *svendere*) to sell off.

'smercio ['zmertʃo] *sm* sale; **avere poco/ molto** ~ to have poor/good sales.

smerigli'ato, a [zmeriʎ'ʎato] *ag*: **carta** ~**a** emery paper; **vetro** ~ frosted glass.

sme'riglio [zme'riʎʎo] *sm* emery.

'smesso, a *pp di* **smettere** ♦ *ag*: **abiti** *mpl* ~**i** cast-offs.

'smettere *vt* to stop; (*vestiti*) to stop wearing ♦ *vi* to stop, cease; ~ **di fare** to stop doing.

smidol'lato, a *ag* spineless ♦ *sm/f* spineless person.

smilitarizzazi'one [zmilitariddzat'tsjone] *sf* demilitarization.

'smilzo, a ['zmiltso] *ag* thin, lean.

sminu'ire *vt* to diminish, lessen; (*fig*) to belittle; ~ **l'importanza di qc** to play sth down.

sminuz'zare [zminut'tsare] *vt* to break into small pieces; to crumble.

'smisi *etc vb vedi* **smettere**.

smista'mento *sm* (*di posta*) sorting; (*FERR*) shunting.

smis'tare *vt* (*pacchi etc*) to sort; (*FERR*) to shunt.

smisu'rato, a *ag* boundless, immeasurable; (*grandissimo*) immense, enormous.

smitiz'zare [zmitid'dzare] *vt* to debunk.

smobili'tare *vt* to demobilize.

smobilitazi'one [zmobilitat'tsjone] *sf* demobilization.

smobi'lizzo [zmobi'liddzo] *sm* (*COMM*) disinvestment.

smo'dato, a *ag* excessive, unrestrained.

smode'rato, a *ag* immoderate.

smog [zmɔg] *sm inv* smog.

'smoking ['smoukiŋ] *sm inv* dinner jacket (*BRIT*), tuxedo (*US*).

smon'tare *vt* (*mobile, macchina etc*) to take to pieces, dismantle; (*fig: scoraggiare*) to dishearten ♦ *vi* (*scendere: da cavallo*) to dismount; (: *da treno*) to get off; (*terminare il lavoro*) to stop (work); ~**rsi** *vr* to lose heart; to lose one's enthusiasm.

'smorfia *sf* grimace; (*atteggiamento lezioso*) simpering; **fare** ~**e** to make faces; to simper.

smorfi'oso, a *ag* simpering.

'smorto, a *ag* (*viso*) pale, wan; (*colore*) dull.

smor'zare [zmor'tsare] *vt* (*suoni*) to deaden; (*colori*) to tone down; (*luce*) to dim; (*sete*) to quench; (*entusiasmo*) to dampen; ~**rsi** *vr* (*suono, luce*) to fade; (*entusiasmo*) to dampen.

'smosso, a *pp di* **smuovere**.

smotta'mento *sm* landslide.

'smunto, a *ag* haggard, pinched.

smu'overe *vt* to move, shift; (*fig: commuovere*) to move; (: *dall'inerzia*) to rouse, stir; ~**rsi** *vr* to move, shift.

smus'sare *vt* (*angolo*) to round off, smooth; (*lama etc*) to blunt; ~**rsi** *vr* to become blunt.

s.n. *abbr* = senza numero.

snaturato – soffiata

snatu'rato, a *ag* inhuman, heartless.
snazionaliz'zare [znattsjonalid'dzare] *vt* to denationalize.
snelli'mento *sm* (*di traffico*) speeding up; (*di procedura*) streamlining.
snel'lire *vt* (*persona*) to make slim; (*traffico*) to speed up; (*procedura*) to streamline; ~**rsi** *vr* (*persona*) to (get) slim; (*traffico*) to speed up.
'snello, a *ag* (*agile*) agile; (*svelto*) slender, slim.
sner'vante *ag* (*attesa, lavoro*) exasperating.
sner'vare *vt* to enervate, wear out; ~**rsi** *vr* to become enervated.
sni'dare *vt* to drive out, flush out.
snob'bare *vt* to snub.
sno'bismo *sm* snobbery.
snoccio'lare [znottʃo'lare] *vt* (*frutta*) to stone; (*fig: orazioni*) to rattle off; (: *verità*) to blab; (: *fam: soldi*) to shell out.
sno'dabile *ag* (*lampada*) adjustable; (*tubo, braccio*) hinged; **rasoio con testina** ~ swivel-head razor.
sno'dare *vt* to untie, undo; (*rendere agile, mobile*) to loosen; ~**rsi** *vr* to come loose; (*articolarsi*) to bend; (*strada, fiume*) to wind.
SO *sigla* = Sondrio.
so *vb vedi* **sapere**.
S.O. *abbr* (= *sudovest*) SW.
so'ave *ag* (*voce, maniera*) gentle; (*volto*) delicate, sweet; (*musica*) soft, sweet; (*profumo*) delicate.
soavità *sf* gentleness; delicacy; sweetness; softness.
sobbal'zare [sobbal'tsare] *vi* to jolt, jerk; (*trasalire*) to jump, start.
sob'balzo [sob'baltso] *sm* jerk, jolt; jump, start.
sobbar'carsi *vr*: ~ **a** to take on, undertake.
sob'borgo, ghi *sm* suburb.
sobil'lare *vt* to stir up, incite.
'sobrio, a *ag* sober.
Soc. *abbr* (= *società*) Soc.
socchi'udere [sok'kjudere] *vt* (*porta*) to leave ajar; (*occhi*) to half-close.
socchi'uso, a [sok'kjuso] *pp di* **socchiudere** ♦ *ag* (*porta, finestra*) ajar; (*occhi*) half-closed.
soc'combere *vi* to succumb, give way.
soc'correre *vt* to help, assist.
soccorri'tore, 'trice *sm/f* rescuer.
soc'corso *pp di* **soccorrere** ♦ *sm* help, aid, assistance; ~**i** *smpl* relief *sg*, aid *sg*; **prestare** ~ **a qn** to help *o* assist sb; **venire in** ~ **di qn** to help sb, come to sb's aid; **operazioni di** ~ rescue operations; ~ **stradale** breakdown service.

socialdemo'cratico, a, ci, che [sotʃaldemo'kratiko] *sm/f* Social Democrat.
soci'ale [so'tʃale] *ag* social; (*di associazione*) club *cpd*, association *cpd*.
socia'lismo [sotʃa'lizmo] *sm* socialism.
socia'lista, i, e [sotʃa'lista] *ag, sm/f* socialist.
socializ'zare [sotʃalid'dzare] *vi* to socialize.
società [sotʃe'ta] *sf inv* society; (*sportiva*) club; (*COMM*) company; **in** ~ **con qn** in partnership with sb; **mettersi in** ~ **con qn** to go into business with sb; **l'alta** ~ high society; ~ **anonima (SA)** ≈ limited (*BRIT*) *o* incorporated (*US*) company; ~ **per azioni (S.p.A.)** joint-stock company; ~ **di comodo** shell company; ~ **fiduciaria** trust company; ~ **di mutuo soccorso** friendly society (*BRIT*), benefit society (*US*); ~ **a responsabilità limitata (S.r.l.)** *type of limited liability company.*
soci'evole [so'tʃevole] *ag* sociable.
socievo'lezza [sotʃevo'lettsa] *sf* sociableness.
'socio ['sɔtʃo] *sm* (*DIR, COMM*) partner; (*membro di associazione*) member.
sociolo'gia [sotʃolo'dʒia] *sf* sociology.
soci'ologo, a, gi, ghe [so'tʃɔlogo] *sm/f* sociologist.
'soda *sf* (*CHIM*) soda; (*acqua gassata*) soda (water).
soda'lizio [soda'littsjo] *sm* association, society.
soddisfa'cente [soddisfa'tʃɛnte] *ag* satisfactory.
soddis'fare *vt, vi*: ~ **a** to satisfy; (*impegno*) to fulfil; (*debito*) to pay off; (*richiesta*) to meet, comply with; (*offesa*) to make amends for.
soddis'fatto, a *pp di* **soddisfare** ♦ *ag* satisfied, pleased; **essere** ~ **di** to be satisfied *o* pleased with.
soddisfazi'one [soddisfat'tsjone] *sf* satisfaction.
'sodio *sm* (*CHIM*) sodium.
'sodo, a *ag* firm, hard ♦ *sm*: **venire al** ~ to come to the point ♦ *av* (*picchiare, lavorare*) hard; **dormire** ~ to sleep soundly.
sofà *sm inv* sofa.
soffe'renza [soffe'rɛntsa] *sf* suffering; (*COMM*): **in** ~ unpaid.
sof'ferto, a *pp di* **soffrire** ♦ *ag* (*vittoria*) hard-fought; (*distacco, decisione*) painful.
soffi'are *vt* to blow; (*notizia, segreto*) to whisper ♦ *vi* to blow; (*sbuffare*) to puff (and blow); ~**rsi il naso** to blow one's nose; ~ **qc/qn a qn** (*fig*) to pinch *o* steal sth/sb from sb; ~ **via qc** to blow sth away.
soffi'ata *sf* (*fam*) tip-off; **fare una** ~ **alla**

polizia to tip off the police.
'soffice ['sɔffitʃe] *ag* soft.
soffi'etto *sm* (*MUS, per fuoco*) bellows *pl*;
porta a ~ folding door.
'soffio *sm* (*di vento*) breath; (*di fumo*) puff;
(*MED*) murmur.
soffi'one *sm* (*BOT*) dandelion.
sof'fitta *sf* attic.
sof'fitto *sm* ceiling.
soffo'cante *ag* suffocating, stifling.
soffo'care *vi* (*anche:* ~**rsi**) to suffocate,
choke ♦ *vt* to suffocate, choke; (*fig*) to
stifle, suppress.
soffocazi'one [soffokat'tsjone] *sf*
suffocation.
sof'friggere [sof'friddʒere] *vt* to fry lightly.
sof'frire *vt* to suffer, endure; (*sopportare*)
to bear, stand ♦ *vi* to suffer; to be in pain;
~ (**di**) **qc** (*MED*) to suffer from sth.
sof'fritto, a *pp di* **soffriggere** ♦ *sm* (*CUC*)
fried mixture of herbs, bacon and onions.
sof'fuso, a *ag* (*di luce*) suffused.
So'fia *sf* (*GEO*) Sofia.
sofisti'care *vt* (*vino, cibo*) to adulterate.
sofisti'cato, a *ag* sophisticated; (*vino*)
adulterated.
sofisticazi'one [sofistikat'tsjone] *sf*
adulteration.
'software ['sɔftwɛə] *sm:* ~ **applicativo**
applications package.
sogget'tivo, a [soddʒet'tivo] *ag* subjective.
sog'getto [sod'dʒetto] *ag:* ~ **a**
(*sottomesso*) subject to; (*esposto: a
variazioni, danni etc*) subject *o* liable to
♦ *sm* subject; ~ **a tassa** taxable; **recitare
a** ~ (*TEAT*) to improvise.
soggezi'one [soddʒet'tsjone] *sf* subjection;
(*timidezza*) awe; **avere** ~ **di qn** to be ill at
ease in sb's presence.
sogghi'gnare [soggiɲ'ɲare] *vi* to sneer.
sog'ghigno [sog'giɲɲo] *sm* sneer.
soggia'cere [soddʒa'tʃere] *vi:* ~ **a** to be
subjected to.
soggio'gare [soddʒo'gare] *vt* to subdue,
subjugate.
soggior'nare [soddʒor'nare] *vi* to stay.
soggi'orno [sod'dʒorno] *sm* (*invernale,
marino*) stay; (*stanza*) living room.
soggi'ungere [sod'dʒundʒere] *vt* to add.
soggi'unto, a [sod'dʒunto] *pp di*
soggiungere.
'soglia ['sɔʎʎa] *sf* doorstep; (*anche fig*)
threshold.
'sogliola ['sɔʎʎola] *sf* (*ZOOL*) sole.
so'gnante [soɲ'ɲante] *ag* dreamy.
so'gnare [soɲ'ɲare] *vt, vi* to dream; ~ **a
occhi aperti** to daydream.
sogna'tore, 'trice [soɲɲa'tore] *sm/f*

dreamer.
'sogno ['soɲɲo] *sm* dream.
'soia *sf* (*BOT*) soya.
sol *sm* (*MUS*) G; (*: solfeggiando la scala*)
so(h).
so'laio *sm* (*soffitta*) attic.
sola'mente *av* only, just.
so'lare *ag* solar, sun *cpd.*
sol'care *vt* (*terreno, fig: mari*) to plough
(*BRIT*), plow (*US*).
'solco, chi *sm* (*scavo, fig: ruga*) furrow;
(*incavo*) rut, track; (*di disco*) groove; (*scia*)
wake.
sol'dato *sm* soldier; ~ **di leva** conscript; ~
semplice private.
'soldo *sm* (*fig*): **non avere un** ~ to be
penniless; **non vale un** ~ it's not worth a
penny; ~**i** *smpl* (*denaro*) money *sg.*
'sole *sm* sun; (*luce*) sun(light); (*tempo
assolato*) sun(shine); **prendere il** ~ to
sunbathe; **il S**~ **che ride** (*POL*) *symbol of
the Italian Green party.*
soleggi'ato, a [soled'dʒato] *ag* sunny.
so'lenne *ag* solemn.
solennità *sf* solemnity; (*festività*) holiday,
feast day.
so'lere *vt:* ~ **fare qc** to be in the habit of
doing sth ♦ *vb impers:* **come suole accadere**
as is usually the case, as usually
happens; **come si suol dire** as they say.
so'lerte *ag* diligent.
so'lerzia [so'lɛrtsja] *sf* diligence.
so'letta *sf* (*per scarpe*) insole.
sol'fato *sm* sulphate (*BRIT*), sulfate (*US*).
sol'forico, a, ci, che *ag* sulphuric (*BRIT*),
sulfuric (*US*); **acido** ~ sulphuric *o*
sulfuric acid.
sol'furo *sm* sulphur (*BRIT*), sulfur (*US*).
soli'dale *ag* in agreement; **essere** ~ **con qn**
(*essere d'accordo*) to be in agreement with
sb; (*appoggiare*) to be behind sb.
solidarietà *sf* solidarity.
solidifi'care *vt, vi* (*anche:* ~**rsi**) to solidify.
solidità *sf* solidity.
'solido, a *ag* solid; (*forte, robusto*) sturdy,
solid; (*fig: ditta*) sound, solid ♦ *sm* (*MAT*)
solid.
soli'loquio *sm* soliloquy.
so'lista, i, e *ag* solo ♦ *sm/f* soloist.
solita'mente *av* usually, as a rule.
soli'tario, a *ag* (*senza compagnia*) solitary,
lonely; (*solo, isolato*) solitary, lone;
(*deserto*) lonely ♦ *sm* (*gioiello, gioco*)
solitaire.
'solito, a *ag* usual; **essere** ~ **fare** to be in
the habit of doing; **di** ~ usually; **più tardi
del** ~ later than usual; **come al** ~ as
usual; **siamo alle** ~**e!** (*fam*) here we go

again!

soli'tudine *sf* solitude.

sollaz'zare [sollat'tsare] *vt* to entertain; ~**rsi** *vr* to amuse o.s.

sol'lazzo [sol'lattso] *sm* amusement.

solleci'tare [solletʃi'tare] *vt* (*lavoro*) to speed up; (*persona*) to urge on; (*chiedere con insistenza*) to press for, request urgently; (*stimolare*): ~ **qn a fare** to urge sb to do; (*TECN*) to stress.

sollecitazi'one [solletʃitat'tsjone] *sf* entreaty, request; (*fig*) incentive; (*TECN*) stress; **lettera di** ~ (*COMM*) reminder.

sol'lecito, a [sol'letʃito] *ag* prompt, quick ♦ *sm* (*COMM*) reminder; ~ **di pagamento** payment reminder.

solleci'tudine [solletʃi'tudine] *sf* promptness, speed.

solleti'care *vt* to tickle.

sol'letico *sm* tickling; **soffrire il** ~ to be ticklish.

solleva'mento *sm* raising; lifting; (*ribellione*) revolt; ~ **pesi** (*sport*) weight-lifting.

solle'vare *vt* to lift, raise; (*fig: persona: alleggerire*): ~ (**da**) to relieve (of); (: *dar conforto*) to comfort, relieve; (: *questione*) to raise; (: *far insorgere*) to stir (to revolt); ~**rsi** *vr* to rise; (*fig: riprendersi*) to recover; (: *ribellarsi*) to rise up; ~**rsi da terra** (*persona*) to get up from the ground; (*aereo*) to take off; **sentirsi sollevato** to feel relieved.

solli'evo *sm* relief; (*conforto*) comfort; **con mio grande** ~ to my great relief.

'solo, a *ag* alone; (*in senso spirituale: isolato*) lonely; (*unico*): **un** ~ **libro** only one book, a single book; (*con ag numerale*): **veniamo noi tre** ~**i** just *o* only the three of us are coming ♦ *av* (*soltanto*) only, just; ~ **che** *cong* but; **è il** ~ **proprietario** he's the sole proprietor; **l'incontrò due** ~**e volte** he only met him twice; **non** ~ ... **ma anche** not only ... but also; **fare qc da** ~ to do sth (all) by oneself; **vive (da)** ~ he lives on his own; **possiamo vederci da** ~**i?** can I see you in private?

sol'stizio [sol'stittsjo] *sm* solstice.

sol'tanto *av* only.

so'lubile *ag* (*sostanza*) soluble; **caffè** ~ instant coffee.

soluzi'one [solut'tsjone] *sf* solution; **senza** ~ **di continuità** uninterruptedly.

sol'vente *ag, sm* solvent; ~ **per unghie** nail polish remover; ~ **per vernici** paint remover.

sol'venza [sol'vɛntsa] *sf* (*COMM*) solvency.

'soma *sf* load, burden; **bestia da** ~ beast of burden.

So'malia *sf*: **la** ~ Somalia.

'somalo, a *ag, sm/f, sm* Somali.

so'maro *sm* ass, donkey.

so'matico, a, ci, che *ag* somatic.

somigli'anza [somiʎ'ʎantsa] *sf* resemblance.

somigli'are [somiʎ'ʎare] *vi*: ~ **a** to be like, resemble; (*nell'aspetto fisico*) to look like; ~**rsi** *vr* to be (*o* look) alike.

'somma *sf* (*MAT*) sum; (*di denaro*) sum (of money); (*complesso di varie cose*) whole amount, sum total; **tirare le** ~**e** (*fig*) to sum up; **tirate le** ~**e** (*fig*) all things considered.

som'mare *vt* to add up; (*aggiungere*) to add; **tutto sommato** all things considered.

som'mario, a *ag* (*racconto, indagine*) brief; (*giustizia*) summary ♦ *sm* summary.

som'mergere [som'mɛrdʒere] *vt* to submerge.

sommer'gibile [sommer'dʒibile] *sm* submarine.

som'merso, a *pp di* **sommergere**.

som'messo, a *ag* (*voce*) soft, subdued.

somminis'trare *vt* to give, administer.

sommità *sf inv* summit, top; (*fig*) height.

'sommo, a *ag* highest; (*rispetto*) highest, greatest; (*poeta, artista*) great, outstanding ♦ *sm* (*fig*) height; **per** ~**i capi** in short, in brief.

som'mossa *sf* uprising.

sommozza'tore [sommottsa'tore] *sm* (deep-sea) diver; (*MIL*) frogman.

so'naglio [so'naʎʎo] *sm* (*di mucche etc*) bell; (*per bambini*) rattle.

so'nante *ag*: **denaro** *o* **moneta** ~ (ready) cash.

so'nare *etc* = **suonare** *etc*.

'sonda *sf* (*MED, METEOR, AER*) probe; (*MINERALOGIA*) drill ♦ *ag inv*: **pallone** *m* ~ weather balloon.

son'daggio [son'daddʒo] *sm* sounding; probe; boring, drilling; (*indagine*) survey; ~ **d'opinioni** opinion poll.

son'dare *vt* (*NAUT*) to sound; (*atmosfera, piaga*) to probe; (*MINERALOGIA*) to bore, drill; (*fig: opinione etc*) to survey, poll.

so'netto *sm* sonnet.

son'nambulo, a *sm/f* sleepwalker.

sonnecchi'are [sonnek'kjare] *vi* to doze, nod.

sonnel'lino *sm* nap.

son'nifero *sm* sleeping drug (*o* pill).

'sonno *sm* sleep; **aver** ~ to be sleepy; **prendere** ~ to fall asleep.

sonno'lento, a *ag* sleepy, drowsy;

(*movimenti*) sluggish.

sonno'lenza [sonno'lɛntsa] *sf* sleepiness, drowsiness.

'sono *vb vedi* **essere.**

sonoriz'zare [sonorid'dzare] *vt* (*LING*) to voice; (*CINE*) to add a sound-track to.

so'noro, a *ag* (*ambiente*) resonant; (*voce*) sonorous, ringing; (*onde, film*) sound *cpd* ♦ *sm:* **il ~** (*CINE*) the talkies *pl.*

sontu'oso, a *ag* sumptuous.

so'pire *vt* (*fig: dolore, tensione*) to soothe.

so'pore *sm* drowsiness.

sopo'rifero, a *ag* soporific.

soppe'rire *vi:* **~ a** to provide for; **~ alla mancanza di qc** to make up for the lack of sth.

soppe'sare *vt* to weigh in one's hand(s), feel the weight of; (*fig*) to weigh up.

soppian'tare *vt* to supplant.

soppi'atto *av:* **di ~** secretly; furtively.

soppor'tabile *ag* tolerable, bearable.

soppor'tare *vt* (*reggere*) to support; (*subire: perdita, spese*) to bear, sustain; (*soffrire: dolore*) to bear, endure; (*sog: cosa: freddo*) to withstand; (*: persona: freddo, vino*) to take; (*tollerare*) to put up with, tolerate.

sopportazi'one [sopportat'tsjone] *sf* patience; **avere spirito di ~, avere capacità di ~** to be long-suffering.

soppressi'one *sf* abolition; withdrawal; suppression; deletion; elimination; liquidation.

sop'presso, a *pp di* **sopprimere.**

sop'primere *vt* (*carica, privilegi etc*) to abolish, do away with; (*servizio*) to withdraw; (*pubblicazione*) to suppress; (*parola, frase*) to delete; (*uccidere*) to eliminate, liquidate.

'sopra *prep* (*gen*) on; (*al di sopra di, più in alto di*) above; over; (*riguardo a*) on, about ♦ *av* on top; (*attaccato, scritto*) on it; (*al di sopra*) above; (*al piano superiore*) upstairs; **donne ~ i 30 anni** women over 30 (years of age); **100 metri ~ il livello del mare** 100 metres above sea level; **5 gradi ~ lo zero** 5 degrees above zero; **abito di ~** I live upstairs; **essere al di ~ di ogni sospetto** to be above suspicion; **per i motivi ~ illustrati** for the above-mentioned reasons, for the reasons shown above; **dormirci ~** (*fig*) to sleep on it; **passar ~ a qc** (*anche fig*) to pass over sth.

so'prabito *sm* overcoat.

sopraccen'nato, a [soprattʃen'nato] *ag* above-mentioned.

soprac'ciglio [soprat'tʃiλλo], *pl(f)* **soprac'ciglia** *sm* eyebrow.

sopracco'perta *sf* (*di letto*) bedspread; (*di*

libro) jacket.

soprad'detto, a *ag* aforesaid.

sopraf'fare *vt* to overcome, overwhelm.

sopraf'fatto, a *pp di* **sopraffare.**

sopraffazi'one [sopraffat'tsjone] *sf* overwhelming, overpowering.

sopraf'fino, a *ag* (*pranzo, vino*) excellent; (*fig*) masterly.

sopraggi'ungere [soprad'dʒundʒere] *vi* (*giungere all'improvviso*) to arrive (unexpectedly); (*accadere*) to occur (unexpectedly).

sopraggi'unto, a [soprad'dʒunto] *pp di* **sopraggiungere.**

soprallu'ogo, ghi *sm* (*di esperti*) inspection; (*di polizia*) on-the-spot investigation.

sopram'mobile *sm* ornament.

soprannatu'rale *ag* supernatural.

sopran'nome *sm* nickname.

soprannomi'nare *vt* to nickname.

sopran'numero *av:* **in ~** in excess.

so'prano, a *sm/f* (*persona*) soprano ♦ *sm* (*voce*) soprano.

soprappensi'ero *av* lost in thought.

soprappiù *sm* surplus, extra; **in ~** extra, surplus; (*per giunta*) besides, in addition.

sopras'salto *sm:* **di ~** with a start, with a jump.

soprasse'dere *vi:* **~ a** to delay, put off.

soprat'tassa *sf* surtax.

soprat'tutto *av* (*anzitutto*) above all; (*specialmente*) especially.

sopravvalu'tare *vt* (*persona, capacità*) to overestimate.

sopravve'nire *vi* to arrive, appear; (*fatto*) to occur.

soprav'vento *sm:* **avere/prendere il ~ su qn** to have/get the upper hand over sb.

sopravvis'suto, a *pp di* **sopravvivere** ♦ *sm/f* survivor.

sopravvi'venza [sopravvi'vɛntsa] *sf* survival.

soprav'vivere *vi* to survive; (*continuare a vivere*): **~ (in)** to live on (in); **~ a** (*incidente etc*) to survive; (*persona*) to outlive.

soprele'vata *sf* (*di strada, ferrovia*) elevated section.

soprinten'dente *sm/f* supervisor; (*statale: di belle arti etc*) keeper.

soprinten'denza [soprinten'dɛntsa] *sf* supervision; (*ente*): **~ alle Belle Arti** *government department responsible for monuments and artistic treasures.*

soprin'tendere *vi:* **~ a** to superintend, supervise.

soprin'teso, a *pp di* **soprintendere.**

so'pruso *sm* abuse of power; **subire un ~**

to be abused.

soq'quadro *sm*: **mettere a** ~ to turn upside-down.

sor'betto *sm* sorbet, water ice (*BRIT*).

sor'bire *vt* to sip; (*fig*) to put up with.

'sorcio ['sortʃo] *sm* mouse.

'sordido, a *ag* sordid; (*fig: gretto*) stingy.

sor'dina *sf*: **in** ~ softly; (*fig*) on the sly.

sordità *sf* deafness.

'sordo, a *ag* deaf; (*rumore*) muffled; (*dolore*) dull; (*lotta*) silent, hidden; (*odio, rancore*) veiled ♦ *sm/f* deaf person.

sordo'muto, a *ag* deaf-and-dumb ♦ *sm/f* deaf-mute.

so'rella *sf* sister.

sorel'lastra *sf* stepsister.

sor'gente [sor'dʒɛnte] *sf* (*acqua che sgorga*) spring; (*di fiume, FISICA, fig*) source; **acqua di** ~ spring water; ~ **di calore** source of heat; ~ **termale** thermal spring.

'sorgere ['sordʒere] *vi* to rise; (*scaturire*) to spring, rise; (*fig: difficoltà*) to arise ♦ *sm*: **al** ~ **del sole** at sunrise.

sori'ano, a *ag, sm/f* tabby.

sormon'tare *vt* (*fig*) to overcome, surmount.

sorni'one, a *ag* sly.

sorpas'sare *vt* (*AUT*) to overtake; (*fig*) to surpass; (: *eccedere*) to exceed, go beyond; ~ **in altezza** to be higher than; (*persona*) to be taller than.

sorpas'sato, a *ag* (*metodo, moda*) outmoded, old-fashioned; (*macchina*) obsolete.

sor'passo *sm* (*AUT*) overtaking.

sorpren'dente *ag* surprising; (*eccezionale, inaspettato*) astonishing, amazing.

sor'prendere *vt* (*cogliere: in flagrante etc*) to catch; (*stupire*) to surprise; ~**rsi** *vr*: ~**rsi (di)** to be surprised (at).

sor'preso, a *pp di* **sorprendere** ♦ *sf* surprise; **fare una** ~**a a qn** to give sb a surprise; **prendere qn di** ~**a** to take sb by surprise *o* unawares.

sor'reggere [sor'rɛddʒere] *vt* to support, hold up; (*fig*) to sustain.

sor'retto, a *pp di* **sorreggere**.

sor'ridere *vi* to smile.

sor'riso, a *pp di* **sorridere** ♦ *sm* smile.

sor'sata *sf* gulp; **bere a** ~**e** to gulp.

sorseggi'are [sorsed'dʒare] *vt* to sip.

'sorsi *etc vb vedi* **sorgere**.

'sorso *sm* sip; **d'un** ~, **in un** ~ **solo** at one gulp.

'sorta *sf* sort, kind; **di** ~ whatever, of any kind at all; **ogni** ~ **di** all sorts of; **di ogni** ~ of every kind.

'sorte *sf* (*fato*) fate, destiny; (*evento fortuito*) chance; **tirare a** ~ to draw lots; **tentare la** ~ to try one's luck.

sorteggi'are [sorted'dʒare] *vt* to draw for.

sor'teggio [sor'teddʒo] *sm* draw.

sorti'legio [sorti'lɛdʒo] *sm* witchcraft *no pl*; (*incantesimo*) spell; **fare un** ~ **a qn** to cast a spell on sb.

sor'tire *vt* (*ottenere*) to produce.

sor'tita *sf* (*MIL*) sortie.

'sorto, a *pp di* **sorgere**.

sorvegli'ante [sorveʎ'ʎante] *sm/f* (*di carcere*) guard, warder (*BRIT*); (*di fabbrica etc*) supervisor.

sorvegli'anza [sorveʎ'ʎantsa] *sf* watch; supervision; (*POLIZIA, MIL*) surveillance.

sorvegli'are [sorveʎ'ʎare] *vt* (*bambino, bagagli, prigioniero*) to watch, keep an eye on; (*malato*) to watch over; (*territorio, casa*) to watch *o* keep watch over; (*lavori*) to supervise.

sorvo'lare *vt* (*territorio*) to fly over ♦ *vi*: ~ **su** (*fig*) to skim over.

S.O.S. *sigla m* mayday, SOS.

'sosia *sm inv* double.

sos'pendere *vt* (*appendere*) to hang (up); (*interrompere, privare di una carica*) to suspend; (*rimandare*) to defer; ~ **un quadro al muro/un lampadario al soffitto** to hang a picture on the wall/a chandelier from the ceiling; ~ **qn dal suo incarico** to suspend sb from office.

sospensi'one *sf* (*anche CHIM, AUT*) suspension; deferment; ~ **condizionale della pena** (*DIR*) suspended sentence.

sos'peso, a *pp di* **sospendere** ♦ *ag* (*appeso*): ~ **a** hanging on (*o* from); (*treno, autobus*) cancelled; **in** ~ in abeyance; (*conto*) outstanding; **tenere in** ~ (*fig*) to keep in suspense; **col fiato** ~ with bated breath.

sospet'tare *vt* to suspect ♦ *vi*: ~ **di** to suspect; (*diffidare*) to be suspicious of.

sos'petto, a *ag* suspicious ♦ *sm* suspicion; **destare** ~**i** to arouse suspicion.

sospet'toso, a *ag* suspicious.

sos'pingere [sos'pindʒere] *vt* to drive, push.

sos'pinto, a *pp di* **sospingere**.

sospi'rare *vi* to sigh ♦ *vt* to long for, yearn for.

sos'piro *sm* sigh; ~ **di sollievo** sigh of relief.

'sosta *sf* (*fermata*) stop, halt; (*pausa*) pause, break; **senza** ~ non-stop, without a break.

sostanti'vato, a *ag* (*LING*): **aggettivo** ~ adjective used as a noun.

sostan'tivo *sm* noun, substantive.

sos'tanza [sos'tantsa] *sf* substance; ~**e** *sfpl*

(*ricchezze*) wealth *sg*, possessions; **in ~** in short, to sum up; **la ~ del discorso** the essence of the speech.

sostanzi'ale [sostan'tsjale] *ag* substantial.

sostanzi'oso, a [sostan'tsjoso] *ag* (*cibo*) nourishing, substantial.

sos'tare *vi* (*fermarsi*) to stop (for a while), stay; (*fare una pausa*) to take a break.

sos'tegno [sos'teɲɲo] *sm* support; **a ~ di** in support of; **muro di ~** supporting wall.

soste'nere *vt* to support; (*prendere su di sé*) to take on, bear; (*resistere*) to withstand, stand up to; (*affermare*): **~ che** to maintain that; **~rsi** *vr* to hold o.s. up, support o.s.; (*fig*) to keep up one's strength; **~ qn** (*moralmente*) to be a support to sb; (*difendere*) to stand up for sb, take sb's part; **~ gli esami** to sit exams; **~ il confronto** to bear *o* stand comparison.

soste'nibile *ag* (*tesi*) tenable; (*spese*) bearable; (*sviluppo*) sustainable.

sosteni'tore, 'trice *sm/f* supporter.

sostenta'mento *sm* maintenance, support; **mezzi di ~** means of support.

soste'nuto, a *ag* (*stile*) elevated; (*velocità, ritmo*) sustained; (*prezzo*) high ♦ *sm/f*: **fare il(la) ~(a)** to be standoffish, keep one's distance.

sostitu'ire *vt* (*mettere al posto di*): **~ qn/qc a** to substitute sb/sth for; (*prendere il posto di*) to replace, take the place of.

sostitu'tivo, a *ag* (*AMM: documento, certificato*) equivalent.

sosti'tuto, a *sm/f* substitute; **~ procuratore della Repubblica** (*DIR*) deputy public prosecutor.

sostituzi'one [sostitut'tsjone] *sf* substitution; **in ~ di** as a substitute for, in place of.

sosta'ceti [sotta'tʃeti] *smpl* pickles.

sot'tana *sf* (*sottoveste*) underskirt; (*gonna*) skirt; (*REL*) soutane, cassock.

sot'tecchi [sot'tekki] *av*: **guardare di ~** to steal a glance at.

sotter'fugio [sotter'fudʒo] *sm* subterfuge.

sotter'raneo, a *ag* underground ♦ *sm* cellar.

sotter'rare *vt* to bury.

sottigli'ezza [sottiʎ'ʎettsa] *sf* thinness; slimness; (*fig: acutezza*) subtlety; shrewdness; **~e** *sfpl* (*pedanteria*) quibbles.

sot'tile *ag* thin; (*figura, caviglia*) thin, slim, slender; (*fine: polvere, capelli*) fine; (*fig: leggero*) light; (*: vista*) sharp, keen; (*: olfatto*) fine, discriminating; (*: mente*) subtle; shrewd ♦ *sm*: **non andare per il ~** not to mince matters.

sottiliz'zare [sottilid'dzare] *vi* to split hairs.

sottin'tendere *vt* (*intendere qc non espresso*) to understand; (*implicare*) to imply; **lasciare ~ che** to let it be understood that.

sottin'teso, a *pp di* **sottintendere** ♦ *sm* allusion; **parlare senza ~i** to speak plainly.

'sotto *prep* (*gen*) under; (*più in basso di*) below ♦ *av* underneath, beneath; below; (*al piano inferiore*): **(al piano) di ~** downstairs; **~ il monte** at the foot of the mountain; **~ la pioggia/il sole** in the rain/ sun(shine); **tutti quelli ~ i 18 anni** all those under 18 (years of age) (*BRIT*) *o* under age 18 (*US*); **~ il livello del mare** below sea level; **~ il chilo** under *o* less than a kilo; **ha 5 impiegati ~ di sé** he has 5 clerks under him; **siamo ~ Natale/ Pasqua** it's nearly Christmas/Easter; **~ un certo punto di vista** in a sense; **~ forma di** in the form of; **~ falso nome** under a false name; **~ terra** underground; **~ voce** in a low voice; **chiuso ~ vuoto** vacuum packed.

sotto'banco *av* (*di nascosto: vendere, comprare*) under the counter; (*agire*) in an underhand way.

sottobicchi'ere [sottobik'kjɛre] *sm* mat, coaster.

sotto'bosco, schi *sm* undergrowth *no pl*.

sotto'braccio [sotto'brattʃo] *av* by the arm; **prendere qn ~** to take sb by the arm; **camminare ~ a qn** to walk arm in arm with sb.

sottochi'ave [sotto'kjave] *av* under lock and key.

sottoco'perta *av* (*NAUT*) below deck.

sotto'costo *av* below cost (price).

sottocu'taneo, a *ag* subcutaneous.

sottoes'posto, a *ag* (*fotografia, pellicola*) underexposed.

sotto'fondo *sm* background; **~ musicale** background music.

sotto'gamba *av*: **prendere qc ~** not to take sth seriously.

sotto'gonna *sf* underskirt.

sottogo'verno *sm* political patronage.

sotto'gruppo *sm* subgroup; (*di partito*) faction.

sottoline'are *vt* to underline; (*fig*) to emphasize, stress.

sot't'olio *av, ag inv* in oil.

sotto'mano *av* (*a portata di mano*) within reach, to hand; (*di nascosto*) secretly.

sottoma'rino, a *ag* (*flora*) submarine; (*cavo, navigazione*) underwater ♦ *sm* (*NAUT*) submarine.

sotto'messo, a *pp di* **sottomettere** ♦ *ag* submissive.

sotto'mettere *vt* to subdue, subjugate; **~rsi** *vr* to submit.

sottomissi'one *sf* submission.

sottopas'saggio [sottopas'saddʒo] *sm* (*AUT*) underpass; (*pedonale*) subway, underpass.

sotto'porre *vt* (*costringere*) to subject; (*fig: presentare*) to submit; **sottoporsi** *vr* to submit; **sottoporsi a** (*subire*) to undergo.

sotto'posto, a *pp di* **sottoporre**.

sottopro'dotto *sm* by-product.

sottoproduzi'one [sottoprodut'tsjone] *sf* underproduction.

sottoproletari'ato *sm*: **il ~** the underprivileged class.

sot'tordine *av*: **passare in ~** to become of minor importance.

sottos'cala *sm inv* (*ripostiglio*) cupboard (*BRIT*) *o* closet (*US*) under the stairs; (*stanza*) room under the stairs.

sottos'critto, a *pp di* **sottoscrivere** ♦ *sm/f*: **io ~, il ~** the undersigned.

sottos'crivere *vt* to sign ♦ *vi*: **~ a** to subscribe to.

sottoscrizi'one [sottoskrit'tsjone] *sf* signing; subscription.

sottosegre'tario *sm*: **S~ di Stato** undersecretary of state (*BRIT*), assistant secretary of state (*US*).

sotto'sopra *av* upside-down.

sottos'tante *ag* (*piani*) lower; **nella valle ~** in the valley below.

sottos'tare *vi*: **~ a** (*assoggettarsi a*) to submit to; (: *richieste*) to give in to; (*subire: prova*) to undergo.

sottosu'olo *sm* subsoil.

sottosvilup'pato, a *ag* underdeveloped.

sottosvi'luppo *sm* underdevelopment.

sottote'nente *sm* (*MIL*) second lieutenant.

sotto'terra *av* underground.

sotto'tetto *sm* attic.

sotto'titolo *sm* subtitle.

sottovalu'tare *vt* (*persona, prova*) to underestimate, underrate.

sotto'vento *av* (*NAUT*) leeward(s) ♦ *ag inv* (*lato*) leeward, lee.

sotto'veste *sf* underskirt.

sotto'voce [sotto'votʃe] *av* in a low voice.

sottovu'oto *av*: **confezionare ~** to vacuum-pack ♦ *ag*: **confezione** *f* **~** vacuum pack.

sot'trarre *vt* (*MAT*) to subtract, take away; **sottrarsi** *vr*: **sottrarsi a** (*sfuggire*) to escape; (*evitare*) to avoid; **~ qn/qc a** (*togliere*) to remove sb/sth from; (*salvare*) to save *o* rescue sb/sth from; **~ qc a qn**

(*rubare*) to steal sth from sb; **sottratte le spese** once expenses have been deducted.

sot'tratto, a *pp di* **sottrarre**.

sottrazi'one [sottrat'tsjone] *sf* (*MAT*) subtraction; (*furto*) removal.

sottuffici'ale [sottuffi'tʃale] *sm* (*MIL*) non-commissioned officer; (*NAUT*) petty officer.

soufflé [su'fle] *sm inv* (*CUC*) soufflé.

souve'nir [suv(ə)'nir] *sm inv* souvenir.

so'vente *av* often.

soverchi'are [sover'kjare] *vt* to overpower, overwhelm.

soverchie'ria [soverkje'ria] *sf* (*prepotenza*) abuse (of power).

sovi'etico, a, ci, che *ag* Soviet ♦ *sm/f* Soviet citizen.

sovrabbon'dante *ag* overabundant.

sovrabbon'danza [sovrabbon'dantsa] *sf* overabundance; **in ~** in excess.

sovraccari'care *vt* to overload.

sovrac'carico, a, chi, che *ag*: **~ (di)** overloaded (with) ♦ *sm* excess load; **~ di lavoro** extra work.

sovraesposizi'one [sovraespozit'tsjone] *sf* (*FOT*) overexposure.

sovraffol'lato, a *ag* overcrowded.

sovraimmagazzi'nare [sovraimmagaddzi-'nare] *vt* to overstock.

sovranità *sf* sovereignty; (*fig: superiorità*) supremacy.

sovrannatu'rale *ag* = **soprannaturale**.

so'vrano, a *ag* sovereign; (*fig: sommo*) supreme ♦ *sm/f* sovereign, monarch.

sovrappopolazi'one [sovrappopolat'tsjone] *sf* overpopulation.

sovrap'porre *vt* to place on top of, put on top of; (*FOT, GEOM*) to superimpose; **sovrapporsi** *vr* (*fig: aggiungersi*) to be added; (*FOT*) to be superimposed.

sovrapposizi'one [sovrapposit'tsjone] *sf* superimposition.

sovrap'posto, a *pp di* **sovrapporre**.

sovrapproduzi'one [sovrapprodut'tsjone] *sf* overproduction.

sovras'tante *ag* overhanging; (*fig*) imminent.

sovras'tare *vi*: **~ a** *vt* (*vallata, fiume*) to overhang; (*fig*) to hang over, threaten.

sovrastrut'tura *sf* superstructure.

sovrecci'tare [sovrettʃi'tare] *vt* to overexcite.

sovrimpressi'one *sf* (*FOT, CINE*) double exposure; **immagini in ~** superimposed images.

sovrinten'dente *etc* = **soprintendente** *etc*.

sovru'mano, a *ag* superhuman.

sovve'nire *vi* (*venire in mente*): ~ **a** to occur to.

sovvenzio'nare [sovventsjo'nare] *vt* to subsidize.

sovvenzi'one [sovven'tsjone] *sf* subsidy, grant.

sovver'sivo, a *ag* subversive.

sovverti'mento *sm* subversion, undermining.

sovver'tire *vt* (*POL: ordine, stato*) to subvert, undermine.

'sozzo, a ['sottso] *ag* filthy, dirty.

SP *sigla* = La Spezia.

S.P. *abbr* = **strada provinciale**; *vedi* **provinciale.**

S.p.A. *abbr vedi* **società per azioni.**

spac'care *vt* to split, break; (*legna*) to chop; (*fig*) to divide; **~rsi** *vr* to split, break.

spacca'tura *sf* split.

spaccherò [spakke'rɔ] *etc vb vedi* **spaccare.**

spacci'are [spat'tʃare] *vt* (*vendere*) to sell (off); (*mettere in circolazione*) to circulate; (*droga*) to peddle, push; **~rsi** *vr*: **~rsi per** (*farsi credere*) to pass o.s. off as, pretend to be.

spacci'ato, a [spat'tʃato] *ag* (*fam: malato, fuggiasco*): **essere** ~ to be done for.

spaccia'tore, 'trice [spattʃa'tore] *sm/f* (*di droga*) pusher; (*di denaro falso*) dealer.

'spaccio ['spattʃo] *sm* (*di merce rubata, droga*): ~ **(di)** trafficking (in); (*di denaro falso*): ~ **(di)** passing (of); (*vendita*) sale; (*bottega*) shop.

'spacco, chi *sm* (*fenditura*) split, crack; (*strappo*) tear; (*di gonna*) slit.

spac'cone *sm/f* boaster, braggart.

'spada *sf* sword.

spadroneggi'are [spadroned'dʒare] *vi* to swagger.

spae'sato, a *ag* disorientated, lost.

spaghet'tata [spaget'tata] *sf* spaghetti meal.

spa'ghetti [spa'getti] *smpl* (*CUC*) spaghetti *sg*.

'Spagna ['spaɲɲa] *sf*: **la** ~ Spain.

spa'gnolo, a [spaɲ'ɲɔlo] *ag* Spanish ♦ *sm/f* Spaniard ♦ *sm* (*LING*) Spanish; **gli S~i** the Spanish.

'spago, ghi *sm* string, twine; **dare** ~ **a qn** (*fig*) to let sb have his (*o* her) way.

spai'ato, a *ag* (*calza, guanto*) odd.

spalan'care *vt*, **~rsi** *vr* to open wide.

spa'lare *vt* to shovel.

'spalla *sf* shoulder; (*fig: TEAT*) stooge; **~e** *sfpl* (*dorso*) back; **di ~e** from behind; **seduto alle mie ~e** sitting behind me; **prendere/colpire qn alle ~e** to take/hit sb from behind; **mettere qn con le ~e al muro** (*fig*) to put sb with his (*o* her) back to the wall; **vivere alle ~e di qn** (*fig*) to live off sb.

spal'lata *sf* (*urto*) shove *o* push with the shoulder; **dare una** ~ **a qc** to give sth a push *o* shove with one's shoulder.

spalleggi'are [spalled'dʒare] *vt* to back up, support.

spal'letta *sf* (*parapetto*) parapet.

spalli'era *sf* (*di sedia etc*) back; (*di letto: da capo*) head(board); (: *da piedi*) foot(board); (*GINNASTICA*) wall bars *pl*.

spal'lina *sf* (*MIL*) epaulette; (*di sottoveste, maglietta*) strap; **senza ~e** strapless.

spal'mare *vt* to spread.

'spalti *smpl* (*di stadio*) terraces (*BRIT*), ≈ bleachers (*US*).

'spandere *vt* to spread; (*versare*) to pour (out); **~rsi** *vr* to spread; ~ **lacrime** to shed tears.

'spanto, a *pp di* **spandere.**

spa'rare *vt* to fire ♦ *vi* (*far fuoco*) to fire; (*tirare*) to shoot; ~ **a qn/qc** to shoot sb/sth, fire at sb/sth.

spa'rato *sm* (*di camicia*) dicky.

spara'tore *sm* gunman.

spara'toria *sf* exchange of shots.

sparecchi'are [sparek'kjare] *vt*: ~ **(la tavola)** to clear the table.

spa'reggio [spa'redd3o] *sm* (*SPORT*) play-off.

'spargere ['spardʒere] *vt* (*sparpagliare*) to scatter; (*versare: vino*) to spill; (: *lacrime, sangue*) to shed; (*diffondere*) to spread; (*emanare*) to give off (*o* out); **~rsi** *vr* (*voce, notizia*) to spread; (*persone*) to scatter; **si è sparsa una voce sul suo conto** there is a rumour going round about him.

spargi'mento [spardʒi'mento] *sm* scattering; spilling; shedding; ~ **di sangue** bloodshed.

spa'rire *vi* to disappear, vanish; ~ **dalla circolazione** (*fig fam*) to lie low, keep a low profile.

sparizi'one [sparit'tsjone] *sf* disappearance.

spar'lare *vi*: ~ **di** to run down, speak ill of.

'sparo *sm* shot.

sparpagli'are [sparpaʎ'ʎare] *vt*, **~rsi** *vr* to scatter.

'sparso, a *pp di* **spargere** ♦ *ag* scattered; (*sciolto*) loose; **in ordine** ~ (*MIL*) in open order.

sparti'acque *sm* (*GEO*) watershed.

sparti'neve *sm inv* snowplough (*BRIT*), snowplow (*US*).

spar'tire *vt* (*eredità, bottino*) to share out;

(*avversari*) to separate.
spar'tito *sm* (*MUS*) score.
sparti'traffico *sm inv* (*AUT*) central reservation (*BRIT*), median (strip) (*US*).
spartizi'one [spartit'tsjone] *sf* division.
spa'ruto, a *ag* (*viso etc*) haggard.
sparvi'ero *sm* (*ZOOL*) sparrowhawk.
spasi'mante *sm* suitor.
spasi'mare *vi* to be in agony; ~ **di fare** (*fig*) to yearn to do; ~ **per qn** to be madly in love with sb.
'spasimo *sm* pang.
'spasmo *sm* (*MED*) spasm.
spas'modico, a, ci, che *ag* (*angoscioso*) agonizing; (*MED*) spasmodic.
spas'sarsela *vi* to enjoy o.s., have a good time.
spassio'nato, a *ag* dispassionate, impartial.
'spasso *sm* (*divertimento*) amusement, enjoyment; **andare a** ~ to go out for a walk; **essere a** ~ (*fig*) to be out of work; **mandare qn a** ~ (*fig*) to give sb the sack.
spas'soso, a *ag* amusing, entertaining.
'spastico, a, ci, che *ag*, *sm/f* spastic.
'spatola *sf* spatula.
spau'racchio [spau'rakkjo] *sm* scarecrow.
spau'rire *vt* to frighten, terrify.
spavalde'ria *sf* boldness, arrogance.
spa'valdo, a *ag* arrogant, bold.
spaventa'passeri *sm inv* scarecrow.
spaven'tare *vt* to frighten, scare; ~**rsi** *vr* to become frightened, become scared.
spa'vento *sm* fear, fright; **far** ~ **a qn** to give sb a fright.
spaven'toso, a *ag* frightening, terrible; (*fig fam*) tremendous, fantastic.
spazi'ale [spat'tsjale] *ag* (*volo, nave, tuta*) space *cpd*; (*ARCHIT, GEOM*) spatial.
spazia'tura [spattsja'tura] *sf* (*TIP*) spacing.
spazien'tire [spattsjen'tire] *vi* (*anche*: ~**rsi**) to lose one's patience.
'spazio ['spattsjo] *sm* space; (*posto*) room, space; **fare** ~ **per qc/qn** to make room for sth/sb; **nello** ~ **di un'ora** within an hour, in the space of an hour; **dare** ~ **a** (*fig*) to make room for; ~ **aereo** airspace.
spazi'oso, a [spat'tsjoso] *ag* spacious.
spazzaca'mino [spattsaka'mino] *sm* chimney sweep.
spazza'neve [spattsa'neve] *sm inv* (*spartineve, SCI*) snowplough (*BRIT*), snowplow (*US*).
spaz'zare [spat'tsare] *vt* to sweep; (*foglie etc*) to sweep up; (*cacciare*) to sweep away.
spazza'tura [spattsa'tura] *sf* sweepings *pl*; (*immondizia*) rubbish.

spaz'zino [spat'tsino] *sm* street sweeper.
'spazzola ['spattsola] *sf* brush; **capelli a** ~ crew cut *sg*; ~ **per abiti** clothesbrush; ~ **da capelli** hairbrush.
spazzo'lare [spattso'lare] *vt* to brush.
spazzo'lino [spattso'lino] *sm* (*small*) brush; ~ **da denti** toothbrush.
specchi'arsi [spek'kjarsi] *vr* to look at o.s. in a mirror; (*riflettersi*) to be mirrored, be reflected.
specchi'era [spek'kjɛra] *sf* large mirror; (*mobile*) dressing table.
specchi'etto [spek'kjetto] *sm* (*tabella*) table, chart; ~ **da borsetta** pocket mirror; ~ **retrovisore** (*AUT*) rear-view mirror.
'specchio ['spɛkkjo] *sm* mirror; (*tabella*) table, chart; **uno** ~ **d'acqua** a sheet of water.
speci'ale [spe't∫ale] *ag* special; **in special modo** especially; **inviato** ~ (*RADIO, TV, STAMPA*) special correspondent; **offerta** ~ special offer; **poteri/leggi** ~**i** (*POL*) emegency powers/legislation.
specia'lista, i, e [spet∫a'lista] *sm/f* specialist.
specia'listico, a, ci, che [spet∫a'listiko] *ag* (*conoscenza, preparazione*) specialized.
specialità [spet∫ali'ta] *sf inv* speciality; (*branca di studio*) special field, speciality.
specializ'zare [spet∫alid'dzare] *vt* (*industria*) to make more specialized; ~**rsi** *vr*: ~**rsi (in)** to specialize (in).
specializ'zato, a [spet∫alid'dzato] *ag* (*manodopera*) skilled; **operaio non** ~ semiskilled worker; **essere** ~ **in** to be a specialist in.
specializzazi'one [spet∫aliddzat'tsjone] *sf* specialization; **prendere la** ~ **in** to specialize in.
special'mente [spet∫al'mente] *av* especially, particularly.
'specie ['spet∫e] *sf inv* (*BIOL, BOT, ZOOL*) species *inv*; (*tipo*) kind, sort ♦ *av* especially, particularly; **una** ~ **di** a kind of; **fare** ~ **a qn** to surprise sb; **la** ~ **umana** mankind.
spe'cifica, che [spe't∫ifika] *sf* specification.
specifi'care [spet∫ifi'kare] *vt* to specify, state.
specificata'mente [spet∫ifikata'mente] *av* in detail.
spe'cifico, a, ci, che [spe't∫ifiko] *ag* specific.
speck [∫pɛk] *sm inv* kind of smoked ham.
specu'lare *vi*: ~ **su** (*COMM*) to speculate in; (*sfruttare*) to exploit; (*meditare*) to speculate on.

specula'tore, 'trice *sm/f* (*COMM*) speculator.

speculazi'one [spekulat'tsjone] *sf* speculation.

spe'dire *vt* to send; (*COMM*) to dispatch, forward; ~ **per posta** to post (*BRIT*), mail (*US*); ~ **per mare** to ship.

spedita'mente *av* quickly; **camminare** ~ to walk at a brisk pace.

spe'dito, a *ag* (*gen*) quick; **con passo** ~ at a brisk pace.

spedizi'one [spedit'tsjone] *sf* sending; (*collo*) consignment; (*scientifica etc*) expedition; (*COMM*) forwarding; shipping; **fare una** ~ to send a consignment; **agenzia di** ~ forwarding agency; **spese di** ~ postal charges; (*COMM*) forwarding charges.

spedizioni'ere [spedittsjo'njɛre] *sm* forwarding agent, shipping agent.

'spegnere ['spɛɲɲere] *vt* (*fuoco, sigaretta*) to put out, extinguish; (*apparecchio elettrico*) to turn *o* switch off; (*gas*) to turn off; (*fig: suoni, passioni*) to stifle; (*debito*) to extinguish; ~**rsi** *vr* to go out; to go off; (*morire*) to pass away.

speleolo'gia [speleolo'dʒia] *sf* (*studio*) speleology; (*pratica*) potholing (*BRIT*), speleology.

spele'ologo, a, gi, ghe *sm/f* speleologist; potholer.

spel'lare *vt* (*scuoiare*) to skin; (*scorticare*) to graze; ~**rsi** *vr* to peel.

spendacci'one, a [spendat'tʃone] *sm/f* spendthrift.

'spendere *vt* to spend; ~ **una buona parola per qn** (*fig*) to put in a good word for sb.

'spengo *etc vb vedi* **spegnere**.

spen'nare *vt* to pluck.

'spensi *etc vb vedi* **spegnere**.

spensiera'tezza [spensjera'tettsa] *sf* carefreeness, lightheartedness.

spensie'rato, a *ag* carefree.

'spento, a *pp di* **spegnere** ♦ *ag* (*suono*) muffled; (*colore*) dull; (*sigaretta*) out; (*civiltà, vulcano*) extinct.

spe'ranza [spe'rantsa] *sf* hope; **nella** ~ **di rivederti** hoping to see *o* in the hope of seeing you again; **pieno di** ~**e** hopeful; **senza** ~ (*situazione*) hopeless; (*amare*) without hope.

speran'zoso, a [speran'tsoso] *ag* hopeful.

spe'rare *vt* to hope for ♦ *vi*: ~ **in** to trust in; ~ **che/di fare** to hope that/to do; **lo spero, spero di sì** I hope so; **tutto fa** ~ **per il meglio** everything leads one to hope for the best.

sper'duto, a *ag* (*isolato*) out-of-the-way; (*persona: smarrita, a disagio*) lost.

spergi'uro, a [sper'dʒuro] *sm/f* perjurer ♦ *sm* perjury.

sperico'lato, a *ag* fearless, daring; (*guidatore*) reckless.

sperimen'tale *ag* experimental; **fare qc in via** ~ to try sth out.

sperimen'tare *vt* to experiment with, test; (*fig*) to test, put to the test.

sperimentazi'one [sperimentat'tsjone] *sf* experimentation.

'sperma, i *sm* (*BIOL*) sperm.

spermato'zoo, i [spermatod'dzɔo] *sm* spermatozoon.

spe'rone *sm* spur.

sperpe'rare *vt* to squander.

'sperpero *sm* (*di denaro*) squandering, waste; (*di cibo, materiali*) waste.

'spesa *sf* (*soldi spesi*) expense; (*costo*) cost; (*acquisto*) purchase; (*fam: acquisto del cibo quotidiano*) shopping; ~**e** *sfpl* expenses; (*COMM*) costs; charges; **ridurre le** ~**e** (*gen*) to cut down; (*COMM*) to reduce expenditure; **fare la** ~ to do the shopping; **fare le** ~**e di qc** (*fig*) to pay the price for sth; **a** ~**e di** (*a carico di*) at the expense of; **con la modica** ~ **di un milione di lire** for the modest sum *o* outlay of one million lire; ~ **pubblica** public expenditure; ~**e accessorie** incidental expenses; ~**e generali** overheads; ~**e di gestione** operating expenses; ~**e d'impianto** initial outlay; ~**e legali** legal costs; ~**e di manutenzione**, ~**e di mantenimento** maintenance costs; ~**e postali** postage *sg*; ~**e di sbarco e sdoganamento** landing charges; ~**e di trasporto** handling charge; ~**e di viaggio** travelling (*BRIT*) *o* traveling (*US*) expenses.

spe'sare *vt*: **viaggio tutto spesato** all-expenses-paid trip.

'speso, a *pp da* **spendere**.

'spesso, a *ag* (*fitto*) thick; (*frequente*) frequent ♦ *av* often; ~**e volte** frequently, often.

spes'sore *sm* thickness; **ha uno** ~ **di 20 cm** it is 20 cm thick.

Spett. *abbr vedi* **spettabile**.

spet'tabile *ag* (*abbr:* **Spett.**: *in lettere*): ~ **ditta X** Messrs X and Co; **avvertiamo la** ~ **clientela ...** we inform our customers ....

spettaco'lare *ag* spectacular.

spet'tacolo *sm* (*rappresentazione*) performance, show; (*vista, scena*) sight; **dare** ~ **di sé** to make an exhibition *o* a spectacle of o.s.

spettaco'loso, a *ag* spectacular.

spet'tanza [spet'tantsa] *sf* (*competenza*)

concern; **non è di mia** ~ it's no concern of mine.

spet'tare *vi:* ~ **a** (*decisione*) to be up to; (*stipendio*) to be due to; **spetta a lei decidere** it's up to you to decide.

spetta'tore, 'trice *smlf* (*CINE, TEAT*) member of the audience; (*di avvenimento*) onlooker, witness.

spettego'lare *vi* to gossip.

spetti'nare *vt:* ~ **qn** to ruffle sb's hair; **~rsi** *vr* to get one's hair in a mess.

spet'trale *ag* spectral, ghostly.

'spettro *sm* (*fantasma*) spectre (*BRIT*), specter (*US*); (*FISICA*) spectrum.

'spezie ['spɛttsje] *sfpl* (*CUC*) spices.

spez'zare [spet'tsare] *vt* (*rompere*) to break; (*fig: interrompere*) to break up; **~rsi** *vr* to break.

spezza'tino [spettsa'tino] *sm* (*CUC*) stew.

spez'zato, a [spet'tsato] *ag* (*unghia, ramo, braccio*) broken ♦ *sm* (*abito maschile*) coordinated jacket and trousers (*BRIT*) *o* pants (*US*); **fare orario** ~ to work a split shift.

spezzet'tare [spettset'tare] *vt* to break up (*o chop*) into small pieces.

spez'zino, a [spet'tsino] *ag* of (*o from*) La Spezia.

spez'zone [spet'tsone] *sm* (*CINE*) clip.

'spia *sf* spy; (*confidente della polizia*) informer; (*ELETTR*) indicating light; warning light; (*fessura*) peephole; (*fig: sintomo*) sign, indication; ~ **dell'olio** (*AUT*) oil warning light.

spiacci'care [spjattʃi'kare] *vt* to squash, crush.

spia'cente [spja'tʃɛnte] *ag* sorry; **essere** ~ **di qc/di fare qc** to be sorry about sth/for doing sth; **siamo ~i di dovervi annunciare che** ... we regret to announce that ....

spia'cevole [spja'tʃevole] *ag* unpleasant, disagreeable.

spi'aggia, ge ['spjaddʒa] *sf* beach.

spia'nare *vt* (*terreno*) to level, make level; (*edificio*) to raze to the ground; (*pasta*) to roll out; (*rendere liscio*) to smooth (out).

spi'ano *sm:* **a tutto** ~ (*lavorare*) non-stop, without a break; (*spendere*) lavishly.

spian'tato, a *ag* penniless, ruined.

spi'are *vt* to spy on; (*occasione etc*) to watch *o* wait for.

spi'ata *sf* tip-off.

spiattel'lare *vt* (*fam: verità, segreto*) to blurt out.

spi'azzo ['spjattso] *sm* open space; (*radura*) clearing.

spic'care *vt* (*assegno, mandato di cattura*) to issue ♦ *vi* (*risaltare*) to stand out; ~ **il volo**

to fly off; (*fig*) to spread one's wings; ~ **un balzo** to jump, leap.

spic'cato, a *ag* (*marcato*) marked, strong; (*notevole*) remarkable.

spiccherò *etc* [spikke'rɔ] *vb vedi* **spiccare**.

'spicchio ['spikkjo] *sm* (*di agrumi*) segment; (*di aglio*) clove; (*parte*) piece, slice.

spicci'are [spit'tʃare] *vt* (*faccenda, impegno*) to finish off; **~rsi** *vr* (*fare in fretta*) to hurry up, get a move on.

'spiccio, a, ci, ce ['spittʃo] *ag* (*modi, mezzi*) quick; **andare per le ~ce** to be quick off the mark, waste no time.

spiccio'lata [spittʃo'lata] *av:* **alla** ~ in dribs and drabs, a few at a time.

'spicciolo, a [spittʃolo] *ag:* **moneta ~a, ~i** *smpl* (small) change.

'spicco, chi *sm:* **fare** ~ to stand out; **di** ~ outstanding, prominent; (*tema*) main, principal.

spie'dino *sm* (*utensile*) skewer; (*cibo*) kebab.

spi'edo *sm* (*CUC*) spit; **pollo allo** ~ spit-roasted chicken.

spiega'mento *sm* (*MIL*): ~ **di forze** deployment of forces.

spie'gare *vt* (*far capire*) to explain; (*tovaglia*) to unfold; (*vele*) to unfurl; **~rsi** *vr* to explain o.s., make o.s. clear; ~ **qc a qn** to explain sth to sb; **il problema si spiega** one can understand the problem; **non mi spiego come** ... I can't understand how ....

spiegazi'one [spjegat'tsjone] *sf* explanation; **avere una** ~ **con qn** to have it out with sb.

spiegaz'zare [spjegat'tsare] *vt* to crease, crumple.

spiegherò *etc* [spjege'rɔ] *vb vedi* **spiegare**.

spie'tato, a *ag* ruthless, pitiless.

spiffe'rare *vt* (*fam*) to blurt out, blab.

'spiffero *sm* draught (*BRIT*), draft (*US*).

'spiga, ghe *sf* (*BOT*) ear.

spigli'ato, a [spiʎ'ʎato] *ag* self-possessed, self-confident.

spigo'lare *vt* (*anche fig*) to glean.

'spigolo *sm* corner; (*GEOM*) edge.

spigo'loso, a *ag* (*mobile*) angular; (*persona, carattere*) difficult.

'spilla *sf* brooch; (*da cravatta, cappello*) pin.

spil'lare *vt* (*vino, fig*) to tap; ~ **denaro/ notizie a qn** to tap sb for money/ information.

'spillo *sm* pin; (*spilla*) brooch; **tacco a** ~ stiletto heel (*BRIT*), spike heel (*US*); ~ **di sicurezza** *o* **da balia** safety pin; ~ **di sicurezza** (*MIL*) (safety) pin.

spilorce'ria [spilortʃe'ria] *sf* meanness,

stinginess.

spi'lorcio, a, ci, ce [spi'lortʃo] *ag* mean, stingy.

spilun'gone *sm/f* beanpole.

'spina *sf* (*BOT*) thorn; (*ZOOL*) spine, prickle; (*di pesce*) bone; (*ELETTR*) plug; (*di botte*) bunghole; **birra alla ~** draught beer; **stare sulle ~e** (*fig*) to be on tenterhooks; **~ dorsale** (*ANAT*) backbone.

spi'nacio [spi'natʃo] *sm* spinach *no pl*; (*CUC*): **~i** spinach *sg*.

spi'nale *ag* (*ANAT*) spinal.

spi'nato, a *ag* (*fornito di spine*): **filo ~** barbed wire; (*tessuto*) herringbone *cpd*.

spi'nello *sm* (*DROGA: gergo*) joint.

'spingere ['spindʒere] *vt* to push; (*condurre: anche fig*) to drive; (*stimolare*): **~ qn a fare** to urge *o* press sb to do; **~rsi** *vr* (*inoltrarsi*) to push on, carry on; **~rsi troppo lontano** (*anche fig*) to go too far.

'spino *sm* (*BOT*) thorn bush.

spi'noso, a *ag* thorny, prickly.

'spinsi *etc vb vedi* **spingere**.

spinte'rogeno [spinte'rɔdʒeno] *sm* (*AUT*) coil ignition.

'spinto, a *pp di* **spingere** ♦ *sf* (*urto*) push; (*FISICA*) thrust; (*fig: stimolo*) incentive, spur; (*: appoggio*) string-pulling *no pl*; **dare una ~a a qn** (*fig*) to pull strings for sb.

spinto'nare *vt* to shove, push.

spin'tone *sm* push, shove.

spio'naggio [spio'naddʒo] *sm* espionage, spying.

spion'cino [spion'tʃino] *sm* peephole.

spi'one, a *sm/f* (*spia*) informer; (*ragazzino, collega*) telltale, sneak.

spio'nistico, a, ci, che *ag* (*organizzazione*) spy *cpd*; **rete ~a** spy ring.

spi'overe *vi* (*scorrere*) to flow down; (*ricadere*) to hang down, fall.

'spira *sf* coil.

spi'raglio [spi'raʎʎo] *sm* (*fessura*) chink, narrow opening; (*raggio di luce, fig*) glimmer, gleam.

spi'rale *sf* spiral; (*contraccettivo*) coil; **a ~** spiral(-shaped); **~ inflazionistica** inflationary spiral.

spi'rare *vi* (*vento*) to blow; (*morire*) to expire, pass away.

spiri'tato, a *ag* possessed; (*fig: persona, espressione*) wild.

spiri'tismo *sm* spiritualism.

'spirito *sm* (*REL, CHIM, disposizione d'animo, di legge etc, fantasma*) spirit; (*pensieri, intelletto*) mind; (*arguzia*) wit; (*umorismo*) humour, wit; **in buone condizioni di ~** in the right frame of mind; **è una persona di ~** he has a sense of humour (*BRIT*) *o*

humor (*US*); **battuta di ~** joke; **~ di classe** class consciousness; **non ha ~ di parte** he never takes sides; **lo S~ Santo** the Holy Spirit *o* Ghost.

spirito'saggine [spirito'saddʒine] *sf* witticism; (*peg*) wisecrack.

spiri'toso, a *ag* witty.

spiritu'ale *ag* spiritual.

splen'dente *ag* (*giornata*) bright, sunny; (*occhi*) shining; (*pavimento*) shining, gleaming.

'splendere *vi* to shine.

'splendido, a *ag* splendid; (*splendente*) shining; (*sfarzoso*) magnificent, splendid.

splen'dore *sm* splendour (*BRIT*), splendor (*US*); (*luce intensa*) brilliance, brightness.

spodes'tare *vt* to deprive of power; (*sovrano*) to depose.

'spoglia ['spɔʎʎa] *sf vedi* **spoglio**.

spogli'are [spoʎ'ʎare] *vt* (*svestire*) to undress; (*privare, fig: depredare*): **~ qn di qc** to deprive sb of sth; (*togliere ornamenti: anche fig*): **~ qn/qc di** to strip sb/sth of; **~rsi** *vr* to undress, strip; **~rsi di** (*ricchezze etc*) to deprive o.s. of, give up; (*pregiudizi*) to rid o.s. of.

spoglia'rello [spoʎʎa'rɛllo] *sm* striptease.

spoglia'toio [spoʎʎa'tojo] *sm* dressing room; (*di scuola etc*) cloakroom; (*SPORT*) changing room.

'spoglio, a ['spɔʎʎo] *ag* (*pianta, terreno*) bare; (*privo*): **~ di** stripped of; lacking in, without ♦ *sm* (*di voti*) counting ♦ *sf* (*ZOOL*) skin, hide; (*: di rettile*) slough; **~e** *sfpl* (*salma*) remains; (*preda*) spoils, booty *sg*.

'spola *sf* shuttle; (*bobina*) spool; **fare la ~** (*fra*) to go to and fro *o* shuttle (between).

spo'letta *sf* (*CUCITO: bobina*) spool; (*di bomba*) fuse.

spol'pare *vt* to strip the flesh off.

spolve'rare *vt* (*anche CUC*) to dust; (*con spazzola*) to brush; (*con battipanni*) to beat; (*fig: mangiare*) to polish off ♦ *vi* to dust.

spolve'rino *sm* (*soprabito*) dust coat.

'sponda *sf* (*di fiume*) bank; (*di mare, lago*) shore; (*bordo*) edge.

sponsoriz'zare [sponsorid'dzare] *vt* to sponsor.

sponsorizzazi'one [sponsoriddzat'tsjone] *sf* sponsorship.

spontanea'mente *av* (*comportarsi*) naturally; (*agire*) spontaneously; (*reagire*) instinctively, spontaneously.

spon'taneo, a *ag* spontaneous; (*persona*) unaffected, natural; **di sua ~a volontà** of his own free will.

spopo'lare *vt* to depopulate ♦ *vi* (*attirare folla*) to draw the crowds; **~rsi** *vr* to become depopulated.

spo'radico, a, ci, che *ag* sporadic.

sporcacci'one, a [sporkat't∫one] *sm/f (peg)* pig, filthy person.

spor'care *vt* to dirty, make dirty; *(fig)* to sully, soil; **~rsi** *vr* to get dirty.

spor'cizia [spor't∫ittsja] *sf (stato)* dirtiness; *(sudiciume)* dirt, filth; *(fig: cosa oscena)* obscenity.

'sporco, a, chi, che *ag* dirty, filthy; **avere la coscienza ~a** to have a guilty conscience.

spor'genza [spor'dʒɛntsa] *sf* projection.

'sporgere ['spɔrdʒere] *vt* to put out, stretch out ♦ *vi (venire in fuori)* to stick out; **~rsi** *vr* to lean out; **~ querela contro qn** *(DIR)* to take legal action against sb.

'sporsi *etc vb vedi* **sporgere**.

sport *sm inv* sport.

'sporta *sf* shopping bag.

spor'tello *sm (di treno, auto etc)* door; *(di banca, ufficio)* window, counter; **~ automatico** *(BANCA)* cash dispenser, automated telling machine.

spor'tivo, a *ag (gara, giornale)* sports *cpd*; *(persona)* sporty; *(abito)* casual; *(spirito, atteggiamento)* sporting ♦ *sm/f* sportsman/ woman; **campo ~** playing field; **giacca ~a** sports *(BRIT) o* sport *(US)* jacket.

'sporto, a *pp di* **sporgere**.

'sposa *sf* bride; *(moglie)* wife; **abito *o* vestito da ~** wedding dress.

sposa'lizio [spoza'littsjo] *sm* wedding.

spo'sare *vt* to marry; *(fig: idea, fede)* to espouse; **~rsi** *vr* to get married, marry; **~rsi con qn** to marry sb, get married to sb.

spo'sato, a *ag* married.

'sposo *sm* (bride)groom; *(marito)* husband; **gli ~i** the newlyweds.

spos'sante *ag* exhausting.

spossa'tezza [spossa'tettsa] *sf* exhaustion.

spos'sato, a *ag* exhausted, weary.

sposta'mento *sm* movement, change of position.

spos'tare *vt* to move, shift; *(cambiare: orario)* to change; **~rsi** *vr* to move; **hanno spostato la partenza di qualche giorno** they postponed *o* put off their departure by a few days.

spot [spɔt] *sm inv (faretto)* spotlight, spot; *(TV)* advert, commercial, ad.

'spranga, ghe *sf (sbarra)* bar; *(catenaccio)* bolt.

spran'gare *vt* to bar; to bolt.

spray ['sprai] *sm inv (dispositivo, sostanza)* spray ♦ *ag inv (bombola, confezione)* spray *cpd*.

'sprazzo ['sprattso] *sm (di sole etc)* flash; *(fig: di gioia etc)* burst.

spre'care *vt* to waste; **~rsi** *vr (persona)* to waste one's energy.

'spreco, chi *sm* waste.

spre'gevole [spre'dʒevole] *ag* contemptible, despicable.

'spregio ['spredʒo] *sm* scorn, disdain.

spregiudi'cato, a [spredʒudi'kato] *ag* unprejudiced, unbiased; *(peg)* unscrupulous.

'spremere *vt* to squeeze; **~rsi le meningi** *(fig)* to rack one's brains.

spre'muta *sf* fresh fruit juice; **~ d'arancia** fresh orange juice.

sprez'zante [spret'tsante] *ag* scornful, contemptuous.

'sprezzo ['sprɛttso] *sm* contempt, scorn, disdain.

sprigio'nare [spridʒo'nare] *vt* to give off, emit; **~rsi** *vr* to emanate; *(uscire con impeto)* to burst out.

spriz'zare [sprit'tsare] *vt, vi* to spurt; **~ gioia/salute** to be bursting with joy/ health.

sprofon'dare *vi* to sink; *(casa)* to collapse; *(suolo)* to give way, subside; **~rsi** *vr:* **~rsi in** *(poltrona)* to sink into; *(fig)* to become immersed *o* absorbed in.

sproloqui'are *vi* to ramble on.

spro'loquio *sm* rambling speech.

spro'nare *vt* to spur (on).

'sprone *sm (sperone, fig)* spur.

sproporzio'nato, a [sproportsjo'nato] *ag* disproportionate, out of all proportion.

sproporzi'one [spropor'tsjone] *sf* disproportion.

spropositato, a *ag (lettera, discorso)* full of mistakes; *(fig: costo)* excessive, enormous.

spro'posito *sm* blunder; **a ~** at the wrong time; *(rispondere, parlare)* irrelevantly.

sprovve'duto, a *ag* inexperienced, naïve.

sprov'visto, a *ag (mancante):* **~ di** lacking in, without; **ne siamo ~** *(negozio)* we are out of it *(o* them); **alla ~a** unawares.

spruz'zare [sprut'tsare] *vt (a nebulizzazione)* to spray; *(aspergere)* to sprinkle; *(inzaccherare)* to splash.

spruzza'tore [spruttsa'tore] *sm (per profumi)* spray, atomizer; *(per biancheria)* sprinkler, spray.

'spruzzo ['spruttso] *sm* spray; splash; **verniciatura a ~** spray painting.

spudora'tezza [spudora'tettsa] *sf* shamelessness.

spudo'rato, a *ag* shameless.

'spugna ['spuɲɲa] *sf (ZOOL)* sponge;

(*tessuto*) towelling.

spu'gnoso, a [spuɲ'ɲoso] *ag* spongy.

spulci'are [spul'tʃare] *vt* (*animali*) to rid of fleas; (*fig*: *testo, compito*) to examine thoroughly.

'spuma *sf* (*schiuma*) foam; (*bibita*) fizzy drink.

spu'mante *sm* sparkling wine.

spumeggi'ante [spumed'dʒante] *ag* (*vino, fig*) sparkling; (*birra, mare*) foaming.

spu'mone *sm* (*CUC*) mousse.

spun'tare *sm*: **allo ~ del sole** at sunrise; **allo ~ del giorno** at daybreak ♦ *vt* (*coltello*) to break the point of; (*capelli*) to trim; (*elenco*) to tick off (*BRIT*), check off (*US*) ♦ *vi* (*uscire: germogli*) to sprout; (: *capelli*) to begin to grow; (: *denti*) to come through; (*apparire*) to appear (suddenly); **~rsi** *vr* to become blunt, lose its point; **spuntarla** (*fig*) to make it, win through.

spun'tino *sm* snack.

'spunto *sm* (*TEAT, MUS*) cue; (*fig*) starting point; **dare lo ~ a** to give rise to; **prendere ~ da qc** to take sth as one's starting point.

spur'gare *vt* (*fogna*) to clean, clear; **~rsi** *vr* (*MED*) to expectorate.

spu'tare *vt* to spit out; (*fig*) to belch (out) ♦ *vi* to spit.

'sputo *sm* spittle *no pl*, spit *no pl*.

sputta'nare *vt* (*fam*) to bad-mouth.

'squadra *sf* (*strumento*) (set) square; (*gruppo*) team, squad; (*di operai*) gang, squad; (*MIL*) squad; (: *AER, NAUT*) squadron; (*SPORT*) team; **lavoro a ~e** teamwork; **~ mobile/del buon costume** (*POLIZIA*) flying/vice squad.

squa'drare *vt* to square, make square; (*osservare*) to look at closely.

squa'driglia [skwa'driʎʎa] *sf* (*AER*) flight; (*NAUT*) squadron.

squa'drone *sm* squadron.

squagli'arsi [skwaʎ'ʎarsi] *vr* to melt; (*fig*) to sneak off.

squa'lifica, che *sf* disqualification.

squalifi'care *vt* to disqualify.

'squallido, a *ag* wretched, bleak.

squal'lore *sm* wretchedness, bleakness.

'squalo *sm* shark.

'squama *sf* scale.

squa'mare *vt* to scale; **~rsi** *vr* to flake *o* peel (off).

squarcia'gola [skwartʃa'gola]: **a ~** *av* at the top of one's voice.

squarci'are [skwar'tʃare] *vt* (*muro, corpo*) to rip open; (*tessuto*) to rip; (*fig*: *tenebre, silenzio*) to split; (: *nuvole*) to pierce.

'squarcio ['skwartʃo] *sm* (*ferita*) gash; (*in lenzuolo, abito*) rip; (*in un muro*) breach; (*in una nave*) hole; (*brano*) passage, excerpt; **uno ~ di sole** a burst of sunlight.

squar'tare *vt* to quarter, cut up; (*cadavere*) to dismember.

squattri'nato, a *ag* penniless ♦ *sm/f* pauper.

squili'brare *vt* to unbalance.

squili'brato, a *ag* (*PSIC*) unbalanced ♦ *sm/f* deranged person.

squi'librio *sm* (*differenza, sbilancio*) imbalance; (*PSIC*) derangement.

squil'lante *ag* (*suono*) shrill, sharp; (*voce*) shrill.

squil'lare *vi* (*campanello, telefono*) to ring (out); (*tromba*) to blare.

'squillo *sm* ring, ringing *no pl*; blare ♦ *sf inv* (*anche*: **ragazza ~**) call girl.

squi'sito, a *ag* exquisite; (*cibo*) delicious; (*persona*) delightful.

squit'tire *vi* (*uccello*) to squawk; (*topo*) to squeak.

SR *sigla* = Siracusa.

sradi'care *vt* to uproot; (*fig*) to eradicate.

sragio'nare [zradʒo'nare] *vi* to talk nonsense, rave.

sregola'tezza [zregola'tettsa] *sf* (*nel mangiare, bere*) lack of moderation; (*di vita*) dissoluteness, dissipation.

srego'lato, a *ag* (*senza ordine: vita*) disorderly; (*smodato*) immoderate; (*dissoluto*) dissolute.

Sri 'Lanka [sri'lanka] *sm*: **il ~** Sri Lanka.

S.r.l. *abbr vedi* **società a responsabilità limitata.**

sroto'lare *vt*, **~rsi** *vr* to unroll.

SS *sigla* = Sassari.

S.S. *abbr* (*REL*) = Sua Santità; Santa Sede; santi, santissimo; (*AUT*) = **strada statale**; *vedi* **statale.**

S.S.N. *abbr* (= Servizio Sanitario Nazionale) ≈ NHS.

sta *etc vb vedi* **stare.**

'stabbio *sm* (*recinto*) pen, fold; (*di maiali*) pigsty; (*letame*) manure.

'stabile *ag* stable, steady; (*tempo: non variabile*) settled; (*TEAT: compagnia*) resident ♦ *sm* (*edificio*) building; **teatro ~** civic theatre.

stabili'mento *sm* (*edificio*) establishment; (*fabbrica*) plant, factory; **~ balneare** bathing establishment; **~ tessile** textile mill.

stabi'lire *vt* to establish; (*fissare: prezzi, data*) to fix; (*decidere*) to decide; **~rsi** *vr* (*prendere dimora*) to settle; **resta stabilito**

che ... it is agreed that ....
stabilità *sf* stability.
stabiliz'zare [stabilid'dzare] *vt* to stabilize.
stabilizza'tore [stabiliddza'tore] *sm* stabilizer; (*fig*) stabilizing force.
stabilizzazi'one [stabiliddzat'tsjone] *sf* stabilization.
stacano'vista, i, e *sm/f* (*ironico*) eager beaver.
stac'care *vt* (*levare*) to detach, remove; (*separare: anche fig*) to separate, divide; (*strappare*) to tear off (*o* out); (*scandire: parole*) to pronounce clearly; (*SPORT*) to leave behind; ~**rsi** *vr* (*bottone etc*) to come off; (*scostarsi*): ~**rsi** (**da**) to move away (from); (*fig: separarsi*): ~**rsi da** to leave; **non** ~ **gli occhi da qn** not to take one's eyes off sb; ~ **la televisione/il telefono** to disconnect the television/the phone; ~ **un assegno** to write a cheque.
staccio'nata [stattʃo'nata] *sf* (*gen*) fence; (*IPPICA*) hurdle.
'stacco, chi *sm* (*intervallo*) gap; (: *tra due scene*) break; (*differenza*) difference; (*SPORT: nel salto*) takeoff.
sta'dera *sf* lever scales *pl*.
'stadio *sm* (*SPORT*) stadium; (*periodo, fase*) phase, stage.
'staffa *sf* (*di sella, TECN*) stirrup; **perdere le** ~**e** (*fig*) to fly off the handle.
staf'fetta *sf* (*messo*) dispatch rider; (*SPORT*) relay race.
stagflazi'one [stagflat'tsjone] *sf* (*ECON*) stagflation.
stagio'nale [stadʒo'nale] *ag* seasonal ♦ *sm/f* seasonal worker.
stagio'nare [stadʒo'nare] *vt* (*legno*) to season; (*formaggi, vino*) to mature.
stagio'nato, a [stadʒo'nato] *ag* (*vedi vb*) seasoned; matured; (*scherzoso: attempato*) getting on in years.
stagi'one [sta'dʒone] *sf* season; **alta/bassa** ~ high/low season.
stagli'arsi [staʎ'ʎarsi] *vr* to stand out, be silhouetted.
sta'gnante [staɲ'ɲante] *ag* stagnant.
sta'gnare [staɲ'ɲare] *vt* (*vaso, tegame*) to tin-plate; (*barca, botte*) to make watertight; (*sangue*) to stop ♦ *vi* to stagnate.
sta'gnino [staɲ'ɲino] *sm* tinsmith.
'stagno, a ['staɲɲo] *ag* (*a tenuta d'acqua*) watertight; (*a tenuta d'aria*) airtight ♦ *sm* (*acquitrino*) pond; (*CHIM*) tin.
sta'gnola [staɲ'ɲɔla] *sf* tinfoil.
stalag'mite *sf* stalagmite.
stalat'tite *sf* stalactite.
stali'nismo *sm* (*POL*) Stalinism.

'stalla *sf* (*per bovini*) cowshed; (*per cavalli*) stable.
stalli'ere *sm* groom, stableboy.
'stallo *sm* stall, seat; (*SCACCHI*) stalemate; (*AER*) stall; **situazione di** ~ (*fig*) stalemate.
stal'lone *sm* stallion.
sta'mani, stamat'tina *av* this morning.
stam'becco, chi *sm* ibex.
stam'berga, ghe *sf* hovel.
'stampa *sf* (*TIP, FOT: tecnica*) printing; (*impressione, copia fotografica*) print; (*insieme di quotidiani, giornalisti etc*): **la** ~ the press; **andare in** ~ to go to press; **mandare in** ~ to pass for press; **errore di** ~ printing error; **prova di** ~ print sample; **libertà di** ~ freedom of the press; **"**~**e"** "printed matter".
stam'pante *sf* (*INFORM*) printer; ~ **seriale/termica** serial/thermal printer.
stam'pare *vt* to print; (*pubblicare*) to publish; (*coniare*) to strike, coin; (*imprimere: anche fig*) to impress.
stampa'tello *sm* block letters *pl*.
stam'pato, a *ag* printed ♦ *sm* (*opuscolo*) leaflet; (*modulo*) form; ~**i** *smpl* printed matter *sg*.
stam'pella *sf* crutch.
stampigli'are [stampiʎ'ʎare] *vt* to stamp.
stampiglia'tura [stampiʎʎa'tura] *sf* (*atto*) stamping; (*marchio*) stamp.
'stampo *sm* mould; (*fig: indole*) type, kind, sort.
sta'nare *vt* to drive out.
stan'care *vt* to tire, make tired; (*annoiare*) to bore; (*infastidire*) to annoy; ~**rsi** *vr* to get tired, tire o.s. out; ~**rsi (di)** (*stufarsi*) to grow weary (of), grow tired (of).
stan'chezza [stan'kettsa] *sf* tiredness, fatigue.
'stanco, a, chi, che *ag* tired; ~ **di** tired of, fed up with.
stand [stand] *sm inv* (*in fiera*) stand.
'standard ['standərd] *sm inv* (*livello*) standard.
standardiz'zare [standardid'dzare] *vt* to standardize.
stan'dista, i, e *sm/f* (*in una fiera etc*) person responsible for a stand.
'stanga, ghe *sf* bar; (*di carro*) shaft.
stan'gare *vt* (*fig: cliente*) to overcharge; (: *studente*) to fail.
stan'gata *sf* (*colpo: anche fig*) blow; (*cattivo risultato*) poor result; (*CALCIO*) shot.
stan'ghetta [stan'getta] *sf* (*di occhiali*) leg; (*MUS, di scrittura*) bar.
'stanno *vb vedi* **stare**.
sta'notte *av* tonight; (*notte passata*) last night.

'**stante** *prep* owing to, because of; **a sé** ~ (*appartamento, casa*) independent, separate.

stan'tio, a, 'tii, 'tie *ag* stale; (*burro*) rancid; (*fig*) old.

stan'tuffo *sm* piston.

'**stanza** ['stantsa] *sf* room; (*POESIA*) stanza; **essere di** ~ **a** (*MIL*) to be stationed in; ~ **da bagno** bathroom; ~ **da letto** bedroom.

stanzia'mento [stantsja'mento] *sm* allocation.

stanzi'are [stan'tsjare] *vt* to allocate.

stan'zino [stan'tsino] *sm* (*ripostiglio*) storeroom; (*spogliatoio*) changing room (*BRIT*), locker room (*US*).

stap'pare *vt* to uncork; (*tappo a corona*) to uncap.

star [star] *sf* (*attore, attrice etc*) star.

'**stare** *vi* (*restare in un luogo*) to stay, remain; (*abitare*) to stay, live; (*essere situato*) to be, be situated; (*anche*: ~ **in piedi**) to stand; (*essere, trovarsi*) to be; (*dipendere*): **se stesse in me** if it were up to me; **il depended on me**; (*seguito da gerundio*): **sta studiando** he's studying; ~ **per fare qc** to be about to do sth; **starci** (*esserci spazio*): **nel baule non ci sta più niente** there's no more room in the boot; (*accettare*): **ci stai?** is that okay with you?; ~ **a** (*attenersi a*) to follow, stick to; (*seguito dall'infinito*): ~ **a sentire** to listen; **staremo a vedere** let's wait and see; **stiamo a discutere** we're talking; (*toccare a*): **sta a te giocare** it's your turn to play; **sta a te decidere** it's up to you to decide; ~ **a qn** (*abiti etc*) to fit sb; **queste scarpe mi stanno strette** these shoes are tight for me; **il rosso ti sta bene** red suits you; **come sta?** how are you?; **io sto bene/male** I'm very well/not very well; ~ **fermo** to keep *o* stay still; ~ **seduto** to sit, be sitting; ~ **zitto** to keep quiet; **stando così le cose** given the situation; **stando a ciò che dice lui** according to him *o* to his version.

starnaz'zare [starnat'tsare] *vi* to squawk.

starnu'tire *vi* to sneeze.

star'nuto *sm* sneeze.

sta'sera *av* this evening, tonight.

'**stasi** *sf* (*MED, fig*) stasis.

sta'tale *ag* state *cpd*, government *cpd* ♦ *sm/f* state employee; (*nell'amministrazione*) ≈ civil servant; **bilancio** ~ national budget; **strada** ~ ≈ trunk (*BRIT*) *o* main road.

stataliz'zare [statalid'dzare] *vt* to nationalize, put under state control.

'**statico, a, ci, che** *ag* (*ELETTR, fig*) static.

sta'tista, i *sm* statesman.

sta'tistico, a, ci, che *ag* statistical ♦ *sf* statistic; (*scienza*) statistics *sg*; **fare una** ~**a** to carry out a statistical examination.

'**stato, a** *pp di* **essere, stare** ♦ *sm* (*condizione*) state, condition; (*POL*) state; (*DIR*) status; **essere in** ~ **d'accusa** (*DIR*) to be committed for trial; **essere in** ~ **d'arresto** (*DIR*) to be under arrest; **essere in** ~ **interessante** to be pregnant; ~ **d'assedio/d'emergenza** state of siege/emergency; ~ **civile** (*AMM*) marital status; ~ **di famiglia** (*AMM*) *certificate giving details of a household and its dependents*; ~ **maggiore** (*MIL*) general staff; ~ **patrimoniale** (*COMM*) statement of assets and liabilities; **gli S~i Uniti (d'America)** the United States (of America).

'**statua** *sf* statue.

statuni'tense *ag* United States *cpd*, of the United States.

sta'tura *sf* (*ANAT*) height; (*fig*) stature; **essere alto/basso di** ~ to be tall/short *o* small.

sta'tuto *sm* (*DIR*) statute; **regione a** ~ **speciale** *Italian region with political autonomy in certain matters*; ~ **della società** (*COMM*) articles *pl* of association.

sta'volta *av* this time.

staziona'mento [stattsjona'mento] *sm* (*AUT*) parking; (: *sosta*) waiting; **freno di** ~ handbrake.

stazio'nare [stattsjo'nare] *vi* (*veicoli*) to be parked.

stazio'nario, a [stattsjo'narjo] *ag* stationary; (*fig*) unchanged.

stazi'one [stat'tsjone] *sf* station; (*balneare, invernale etc*) resort; ~ **degli autobus** bus station; ~ **balneare** seaside resort; ~ **climatica** health resort; ~ **ferroviaria** railway (*BRIT*) *o* railroad (*US*) station; ~ **invernale** winter sports resort; ~ **di lavoro** work station; ~ **di polizia** police station (*in small town*); ~ **di servizio** service *o* petrol (*BRIT*) *o* filling station; ~ **termale** spa.

'**stazza** ['stattsa] *sf* tonnage.

st. civ. *abbr* = **stato civile**.

'**stecca, che** *sf* stick; (*di ombrello*) rib; (*di sigarette*) carton; (*MED*) splint; (*stonatura*): **fare una** ~ to sing (*o* play) a wrong note.

stec'cato *sm* fence.

stec'chito, a [stek'kito] *ag* dried up; (*persona*) skinny; **lasciar** ~ **qn** (*fig*) to leave sb flabbergasted; **morto** ~ stone dead.

'**stella** *sf* star; ~ **alpina** (*BOT*) edelweiss; ~ **cadente** *o* **filante** shooting star; ~ **di mare**

(*ZOOL*) starfish.

stel'lato, a *ag* (*cielo, notte*) starry.

'stelo *sm* stem; (*asta*) rod; **lampada a** ~ standard lamp (*BRIT*), floor lamp.

'stemma, i *sm* coat of arms.

'stemmo *vb vedi* **stare**.

stempe'rare *vt* (*calce, colore*) to dissolve.

stempi'ato, a *ag* with a receding hairline.

stempia'tura *sf* receding hairline.

sten'dardo *sm* standard.

'stendere *vt* (*braccia, gambe*) to stretch (out); (*tovaglia*) to spread (out); (*bucato*) to hang out; (*mettere a giacere*) to lay (down); (*spalmare: colore*) to spread; (*mettere per iscritto*) to draw up; ~**rsi** *vr* (*coricarsi*) to stretch out, lie down; (*estendersi*) to extend, stretch.

stendibianche'ria [stendibjanke'ria] *sm inv* clotheshorse.

stendi'toio *sm* (*locale*) drying room; (*stendibiancheria*) clotheshorse.

stenodattilogra'fia *sf* shorthand typing (*BRIT*), stenography (*US*).

stenodatti'lografo, a *sm/f* shorthand typist (*BRIT*), stenographer (*US*).

stenogra'fare *vt* to take down in shorthand.

stenogra'fia *sf* shorthand.

ste'nografo, a *sm/f* stenographer.

sten'tare *vi*: ~ **a fare** to find it hard to do, have difficulty doing.

sten'tato, a *ag* (*compito, stile*) laboured (*BRIT*), labored (*US*); (*sorriso*) forced.

'stento *sm* (*fatica*) difficulty; ~**i** *smpl* (*privazioni*) hardship *sg*, privation *sg*; **a** ~ *av* with difficulty, barely.

'steppa *sf* steppe.

'sterco *sm* dung.

stereofo'nia *sf* stereophony.

'stereo('fonico, a, ci, che) *ag* stereo(phonic).

stereoti'pato, a *ag* stereotyped.

stere'otipo *sm* stereotype; **pensare per** ~**i** to think in clichés.

'sterile *ag* sterile; (*terra*) barren; (*fig*) futile, fruitless.

sterilità *sf* sterility.

steriliz'zare [sterilid'dzare] *vt* to sterilize.

sterilizzazi'one [steriliddzat'tsjone] *sf* sterilization.

ster'lina *sf* pound (sterling).

stermi'nare *vt* to exterminate, wipe out.

stermi'nato, a *ag* immense, endless.

ster'minio *sm* extermination, destruction; **campo di** ~ death camp.

'sterno *sm* (*ANAT*) breastbone.

ster'paglia [ster'paʎʎa] *sf* brushwood.

'sterpo *sm* dry twig.

ster'rare *vt* to excavate.

ster'zare [ster'tsare] *vt, vi* (*AUT*) to steer.

'sterzo ['stertso] *sm* steering; (*volante*) steering wheel.

'steso, a *pp di* **stendere**.

'stessi *etc vb vedi* **stare**.

'stesso, a *ag* same; (*rafforzativo: in persona, proprio*): **il re** ~ the king himself *o* in person ♦ *pron*: **lo(la)** ~**(a)** the same (one); **quello** ~ **giorno** that very day; **i suoi** ~**i avversari lo ammirano** even his enemies admire him; **fa lo** ~ it doesn't matter; **parto lo** ~ I'm going all the same; **per me è lo** ~ it's all the same to me, it doesn't matter to me; *vedi* **io, tu** *etc*.

ste'sura *sf* (*azione*) drafting *no pl*, drawing up *no pl*; (*documento*) draft.

stetos'copio *sm* stethoscope.

'stetti *etc vb vedi* **stare**.

'stia *sf* hutch.

'stia *etc vb vedi* **stare**.

'stigma, i *sm* stigma.

'stigmate *sfpl* (*REL*) stigmata.

sti'lare *vt* to draw up, draft.

'stile *sm* style; (*classe*) style, class; (*SPORT*): ~ **libero** freestyle; **mobili in** ~ period furniture; **in grande** ~ in great style; **è proprio nel suo** ~ (*fig*) it's just like him.

sti'lismo *sm* concern for style.

sti'lista, i, e *sm/f* designer.

sti'listico, a, ci, che *ag* stylistic.

stiliz'zato, a [stilid'dzato] *ag* stylized.

stil'lare *vi* (*trasudare*) to ooze; (*gocciolare*) to drip.

stilli'cidio [stilli'tʃidjo] *sm* (*fig*) continual pestering (*o* moaning *etc*).

stilo'grafica, che *sf* (*anche:* **penna** ~) fountain pen.

Stim. *abbr* = **stimata**.

'stima *sf* esteem; valuation; assessment, estimate; **avere** ~ **di qn** to have respect for sb; **godere della** ~ **di qn** to enjoy sb's respect; **fare la** ~ **di qc** to estimate the value of sth.

sti'mare *vt* (*persona*) to esteem, hold in high regard; (*terreno, casa etc*) to value; (*stabilire in misura approssimativa*) to estimate, assess; (*ritenere*): ~ **che** to consider that; ~**rsi fortunato** to consider o.s. (to be) lucky.

Stim.ma *abbr* = **stimatissima**.

stimo'lante *ag* stimulating ♦ *sm* (*MED*) stimulant.

stimo'lare *vt* to stimulate; (*incitare*): ~ **qn (a fare)** to spur sb on (to do).

stimolazi'one [stimolat'tsjone] *sf* stimulation.

'stimolo *sm* (*anche fig*) stimulus.

'stinco, chi *sm* shin; shinbone.

'stingere ['stindʒere] *vt, vi* (*anche*: ~**rsi**) to fade.

'stinto, a *pp di* **stingere**.

sti'pare *vt* to cram, pack; ~**rsi** *vr* (*accalcarsi*) to crowd, throng.

stipendi'are *vt* (*pagare*) to pay (a salary to).

stipendi'ato, a *ag* salaried ♦ *sm/f* salaried worker.

sti'pendio *sm* salary.

'stipite *sm* (*di porta, finestra*) jamb.

stipu'lare *vt* (*redigere*) to draw up.

stipulazi'one [stipulat'tsjone] *sf* (*di contratto: stesura*) drafting; (: *firma*) signing.

stiracchi'are [stirak'kjare] *vt* (*fig: significato di una parola*) to stretch, force; ~**rsi** *vr* (*persona*) to stretch.

stira'mento *sm* (*MED*) sprain.

sti'rare *vt* (*abito*) to iron; (*distendere*) to stretch; (*strappare: muscolo*) to strain; ~**rsi** *vr* (*fam*) to stretch (o.s.).

stira'tura *sf* ironing.

'stirpe *sf* birth, stock; descendants *pl*.

stiti'chezza [stiti'kettsa] *sf* constipation.

'stitico, a, ci, che *ag* constipated.

'stiva *sf* (*di nave*) hold.

sti'vale *sm* boot.

stiva'letto *sm* ankle boot.

sti'vare *vt* to stow, load.

'stizza ['stittsa] *sf* anger, vexation.

stiz'zire [stit'tsire] *vt* to irritate ♦ *vi*, ~**rsi** *vr* to become irritated, become vexed.

stiz'zoso, a [stit'tsoso] *ag* (*persona*) quick-tempered, irascible; (*risposta*) angry.

stocca'fisso *sm* stockfish, dried cod.

Stoc'carda *sf* Stuttgart.

stoc'cata *sf* (*colpo*) stab, thrust; (*fig*) gibe, cutting remark.

Stoc'colma *sf* Stockholm.

stock [stɔk] *sm inv* (*COMM*) stock.

'stoffa *sf* material, fabric; (*fig*): **aver la ~ di** to have the makings of; **avere della ~** to have what it takes.

stoi'cismo [stoi'tʃizmo] *sm* stoicism.

'stoico, a, ci, che *ag* stoic(al).

sto'ino *sm* doormat.

'stola *sf* stole.

stol'tezza [stol'tettsa] *sf* stupidity; (*azione*) foolish action.

'stolto, a *ag* stupid, foolish.

'stomaco, chi *sm* stomach; **dare di ~** to vomit, be sick.

sto'nare *vt* to sing (*o* play) out of tune ♦ *vi* to be out of tune, sing (*o* play) out of tune; (*fig*) to be out of place, jar; (: *colori*) to clash.

sto'nato, a *ag* (*persona*) off-key; (*strumento*) off-key, out of tune.

stona'tura *sf* (*suono*) false note.

stop *sm inv* (*TELEGRAFIA*) stop; (*AUT: cartello*) stop sign; (: *fanalino d'arresto*) brake-light (*BRIT*), stoplight.

'stoppa *sf* tow.

'stoppia *sf* (*AGR*) stubble.

stop'pino *sm* (*di candela*) wick; (*miccia*) fuse.

'storcere ['stɔrtʃere] *vt* to twist; ~**rsi** *vr* to writhe, twist; ~ **il naso** (*fig*) to turn up one's nose; ~**rsi la caviglia** to twist one's ankle.

stordi'mento *sm* (*gen*) dizziness; (*da droga*) stupefaction.

stor'dire *vt* (*intontire*) to stun, daze; ~**rsi** *vr*: ~**rsi col bere** to dull one's senses with drink.

stor'dito, a *ag* stunned; (*sventato*) scatterbrained, heedless.

'storia *sf* (*scienza, avvenimenti*) history; (*racconto, bugia*) story; (*faccenda, questione*) business *no pl*; (*pretesto*) excuse, pretext; ~**e** *sfpl* (*smancerie*) fuss *sg*; **passare alla ~** to go down in history; **non ha fatto ~e** he didn't make a fuss.

storicità [storitʃi'ta] *sf* historical authenticity.

'storico, a, ci, che *ag* historic(al) ♦ *sm/f* historian.

storiogra'fia *sf* historiography.

stori'one *sm* (*ZOOL*) sturgeon.

stor'mire *vi* to rustle.

'stormo *sm* (*di uccelli*) flock.

stor'nare *vt* (*COMM*) to transfer.

stor'nello *sm* kind of folk song.

'storno *sm* starling.

storpi'are *vt* to cripple, maim; (*fig: parole*) to mangle; (: *significato*) to twist.

storpia'tura *sf* (*fig: di parola*) twisting, distortion.

'storpio, a *ag* crippled, maimed.

'storsi *etc vb vedi* **storcere**.

'storto, a *pp di* **storcere** ♦ *ag* (*chiodo*) twisted, bent; (*gamba, quadro*) crooked; (*fig: ragionamento*) false, wrong ♦ *sf* (*distorsione*) sprain, twist; (*recipiente*) retort ♦ *av*: **guardare ~ qn** (*fig*) to look askance at sb; **andar ~** to go wrong.

sto'viglie [sto'viʎʎe] *sfpl* dishes *pl*, crockery.

str. *abbr* (*GEO*) = **stretto**.

'strabico, a, ci, che *ag* squint-eyed; (*occhi*) squint.

strabili'ante *ag* astonishing, amazing.

strabili'are *vi* to astonish, amaze.

stra'bismo *sm* squinting.

strabuz'zare [strabud'dzare] *vt*: ~ **gli occhi** to open one's eyes wide.

stra'carico, a, chi, che *ag* overloaded.

strac'chino [strak'kino] *sm type of soft cheese*.

stracci'are [strat'tʃare] *vt* to tear.

'straccio, a, ci, ce ['strattʃo] *ag*: **carta** ~**a** waste paper ♦ *sm* rag; (*per pulire*) cloth, duster.

stracci'one, a [strat'tʃone] *sm/f* ragamuffin.

stracci'vendolo [strattʃi'vendolo] *sm* ragman.

'stracco, a, chi, che *ag*: ~ **(morto)** exhausted, dead tired.

stra'cotto, a *ag* overcooked ♦ *sm* (*CUC*) beef stew.

'strada *sf* road; (*di città*) street; (*cammino, via, fig*) way; ~ **facendo** on the way; **tre ore di** ~ **(a piedi)/(in macchina)** three hours' walk/drive; **essere sulla buona** ~ (*nella vita*) to be on the right road *o* path; (*con indagine etc*) to be on the right track; **essere fuori** ~ (*fig*) to be on the wrong track; **fare** ~ **a qn** to show sb the way; **fare** *o* **farsi** ~ (*fig: persona*) to get on in life; **portare qn sulla cattiva** ~ to lead sb astray; **donna di** ~ (*fig peg*) streetwalker; **ragazzo di** ~ (*fig peg*) street urchin; ~ **ferrata** railway (*BRIT*), railroad (*US*); ~ **principale** main road; ~ **senza uscita** dead end, cul-de-sac.

stra'dale *ag* road *cpd*; (*polizia, regolamento*) traffic *cpd*.

stra'dario *sm* street guide.

stra'dino *sm* road worker.

strafalci'one [strafal'tʃone] *sm* blunder, howler.

stra'fare *vi* to overdo it.

stra'fatto, a *pp di* **strafare**.

stra'foro: **di** ~ *av* (*di nascosto*) on the sly.

strafot'tente *ag*: **è** ~ he doesn't give a damn, he couldn't care less.

strafot'tenza [strafot'tɛntsa] *sf* arrogance.

'strage ['stradʒe] *sf* massacre, slaughter.

stra'grande *ag*: **la** ~ **maggioranza** the overwhelming majority.

stralci'are [stral'tʃare] *vt* to remove.

'stralcio ['straltʃo] *sm* (*COMM*): **vendere in** ~ to sell off (at bargain prices) ♦ *ag inv*: **legge** ~ abridged version of an act.

stralu'nato, a *ag* (*occhi*) rolling; (*persona*) beside o.s., very upset.

stramaz'zare [stramat'tsare] *vi* to fall heavily.

strambe'ria *sf* eccentricity.

'strambo, a *ag* strange, queer.

strampa'lato, a *ag* odd, eccentric.

strana'mente *av* oddly, strangely; **e lui, ~,**

ha accettato and, surprisingly, he agreed.

stra'nezza [stra'nettsa] *sf* strangeness.

strango'lare *vt* to strangle; **~rsi** *vr* to choke.

strani'ero, a *ag* foreign ♦ *sm/f* foreigner.

stra'nito, a *ag* dazed.

'strano, a *ag* strange, odd.

straordi'nario, a *ag* extraordinary; (*treno etc*) special ♦ *sm* (*lavoro*) overtime.

strapaz'zare [strapat'tsare] *vt* to ill-treat; **~rsi** *vr* to tire o.s. out, overdo things.

strapaz'zato, a [strapat'tsato] *ag*: **uova ~e** scrambled eggs.

stra'pazzo [stra'pattso] *sm* strain, fatigue; **da** ~ (*fig*) third-rate.

strapi'eno, a *ag* full to overflowing.

strapi'ombo *sm* overhanging rock; **a** ~ overhanging.

strapo'tere *sm* excessive power.

strappa'lacrime *ag inv* (*fam*): **romanzo** (*o* **film** *etc*) ~ tear-jerker.

strap'pare *vt* (*gen*) to tear, rip; (*pagina etc*) to tear off, tear out; (*sradicare*) to pull up; (*togliere*): ~ **qc a qn** to snatch sth from sb; (*fig*) to wrest sth from sb; **~rsi** *vr* (*lacerarsi*) to rip, tear; (*rompersi*) to break; **~rsi un muscolo** to tear a muscle.

strap'pato, a *ag* torn, ripped.

'strappo *sm* (*strattone*) pull, tug; (*lacerazione*) tear, rip; (*fig fam: passaggio*) lift (*BRIT*), ride (*US*); **fare uno** ~ **alla regola** to make an exception to the rule; ~ **muscolare** torn muscle.

strapun'tino *sm* jump *o* foldaway seat.

strari'pare *vi* to overflow.

Stras'burgo *sf* Strasbourg.

strasci'care [straʃʃi'kare] *vt* to trail; (*piedi*) to drag; ~ **le parole** to drawl.

'strascico, chi ['straʃʃiko] *sm* (*di abito*) train; (*conseguenza*) after-effect.

strata'gemma, i [strata'dʒɛmma] *sm* stratagem.

stra'tega, ghi *sm* strategist.

strate'gia, 'gie [strate'dʒia] *sf* strategy.

stra'tegico, a, ci, che [stra'tɛdʒiko] *ag* strategic.

'strato *sm* layer; (*rivestimento*) coat, coating; (*GEO, fig*) stratum; (*METEOR*) stratus.

stratos'fera *sf* stratosphere.

strat'tone *sm* tug, jerk; **dare uno** ~ **a qc** to tug *o* jerk sth, give sth a tug *o* jerk.

stravac'cato, a *ag* sprawling.

strava'gante *ag* odd, eccentric.

strava'ganza [strava'gantsa] *sf* eccentricity.

stra'vecchio, a [stra'vɛkkjo] *ag* very old.

strave'dere *vi*: ~ **per qn** to dote on sb.

stra'visto, a *pp di* **stravedere**.

stra'vizio [stra'vittsjo] *sm* excess.

stra'volgere [stra'vɔldʒere] *vt* (*volto*) to contort; (*fig: animo*) to trouble deeply; (: *verità*) to twist, distort.

stra'volto, a *pp di* **stravolgere** ♦ *ag* (*persona: per stanchezza etc*) in a terrible state; (: *per sofferenza*) distraught.

strazi'ante [strat'tsjante] *ag* (*scena*) harrowing; (*urlo*) bloodcurdling; (*dolore*) excruciating.

strazi'are [strat'tsjare] *vt* to torture, torment.

'strazio ['strattsjo] *sm* torture; (*fig: cosa fatta male*): **essere uno** ~ to be appalling; **fare** ~ **di** (*corpo, vittima*) to mutilate.

'strega, ghe *sf* witch.

stre'gare *vt* to bewitch.

stre'gone *sm* (*mago*) wizard; (*di tribù*) witch doctor.

stregone'ria *sf* (*pratica*) witchcraft; **fare una** ~ to cast a spell.

'stregua *sf*: **alla** ~ **di** by the same standard as.

stre'mare *vt* to exhaust.

'stremo *sm*: **essere allo** ~ to be at the end of one's tether.

'strenna *sf*: ~ **natalizia** (*regalo*) Christmas present; (*libro*) book published for the Christmas market.

'strenuo, a *ag* brave, courageous.

strepi'tare *vi* to yell and shout.

'strepito *sm* (*di voci, folla*) clamour (*BRIT*), clamor (*US*); (*di catene*) clanking, rattling.

strepi'toso, a *ag* clamorous, deafening; (*fig: successo*) resounding.

stres'sante *ag* stressful.

stres'sare *vt* to put under stress.

stres'sato, a *ag* under stress.

'stretta *sf vedi* **stretto**.

stretta'mente *av* tightly; (*rigorosamente*) strictly.

stret'tezza [stret'tettsa] *sf* narrowness; ~**e** *sfpl* (*povertà*) poverty *sg*, straitened circumstances.

'stretto, a *pp di* **stringere** ♦ *ag* (*corridoio, limiti*) narrow; (*gonna, scarpe, nodo, curva*) tight; (*intimo: parente, amico*) close; (*rigoroso: osservanza*) strict; (*preciso: significato*) precise, exact ♦ *sm* (*braccio di mare*) strait ♦ *sf* (*di mano*) grasp; (*finanziaria*) squeeze; (*fig: dolore, turbamento*) pang; **a denti** ~**i** with clenched teeth; **lo** ~ **necessario** the bare minimum; **una** ~**a di mano** a handshake; **una** ~**a al cuore** a sudden sadness; **essere alle** ~**e** to have one's back to the wall.

stret'toia *sf* bottleneck; (*fig*) tricky situation.

stri'ato, a *ag* streaked.

stria'tura *sf* (*atto*) streaking; (*effetto*) streaks *pl*.

stric'nina *sf* strychnine.

'strida *sfpl* screaming *sg*.

stri'dente *ag* strident.

'stridere *vi* (*porta*) to squeak; (*animale*) to screech, shriek; (*colori*) to clash.

'strido, *pl*(*f*) **strida** *sm* screech, shriek.

stri'dore *sm* screeching, shrieking.

'stridulo, a *ag* shrill.

'striglia ['striʎʎa] *sf* currycomb.

strigli'are [striʎ'ʎare] *vt* (*cavallo*) to curry.

strigli'ata [striʎ'ʎata] *sf* (*di cavallo*) currying; (*fig*): **dare una** ~ **a qn** to give sb a scolding.

stril'lare *vt, vi* to scream, shriek.

'strillo *sm* scream, shriek.

stril'lone *sm* newspaper seller.

strimin'zito, a [strimin'tsito] *ag* (*misero*) shabby; (*molto magro*) skinny.

strimpel'lare *vt* (*MUS*) to strum.

'stringa, ghe *sf* lace; (*INFORM*) string.

strin'gare *vt* (*fig: discorso*) to condense.

strin'gato, a *ag* (*fig*) concise.

'stringere ['strindʒere] *vt* (*avvicinare due cose*) to press (together), squeeze (together); (*tenere stretto*) to hold tight, clasp, clutch; (*pugno, mascella, denti*) to clench; (*labbra*) to compress; (*avvitare*) to tighten; (*abito*) to take in; (*sog: scarpe*) to pinch, be tight for; (*fig: concludere: patto*) to make; (: *accelerare: passo*) to quicken ♦ *vi* (*incalzare*) to be pressing; ~**rsi** *vr* (*accostarsi*): ~**rsi a** to press o.s. up against; ~ **la mano a qn** to shake sb's hand; ~ **gli occhi** to screw up one's eyes; ~ **amicizia con qn** to make friends with sb; **stringi stringi** in conclusion; **il tempo stringe** time is short.

'strinsi *etc vb vedi* **stringere**.

'striscia, sce ['striʃʃa] *sf* (*di carta, tessuto etc*) strip; (*riga*) stripe; ~**sce (pedonali)** zebra crossing *sg*; **a** ~**sce** striped.

strisci'ante [striʃ'ʃante] *ag* (*fig peg*) unctuous; (*ECON: inflazione*) creeping.

strisci'are [striʃ'ʃare] *vt* (*piedi*) to drag; (*muro, macchina*) to graze ♦ *vi* to crawl, creep.

'striscio ['striʃʃo] *sm* graze; (*MED*) smear; **colpire di** ~ to graze.

strisci'one [striʃ'ʃone] *sm* banner.

strito'lare *vt* to grind.

striz'zare [strit'tsare] *vt* (*arancia*) to squeeze; (*panni*) to wring (out); ~ **l'occhio** to wink.

striz'zata [strit'tsata] *sf*: **dare una ~ a qc** to give sth a wring; **una ~ d'occhio** a wink.

'strofa *sf*, **'strofe** *sf inv* strophe.

strofi'naccio [strofi'nattʃo] *sm* duster, cloth; (*per piatti*) dishcloth; (*per pavimenti*) floorcloth.

strofi'nare *vt* to rub.

stron'care *vt* to break off; (*fig: ribellione*) to suppress, put down; (*: film, libro*) to tear to pieces.

'stronzo ['strontso] *sm* (*sterco*) turd; (*fig fam!: persona*) shit (*!*).

stropicci'are [stropit'tʃare] *vt* to rub.

stroz'zare [strot'tsare] *vt* (*soffocare*) to choke, strangle; **~rsi** *vr* to choke.

strozza'tura [strottsa'tura] *sf* (*restringimento*) narrowing; (*di strada etc*) bottleneck.

stroz'zino, a [strot'tsino] *sm/f* (*usuraio*) usurer; (*fig*) shark.

struc'care *vt* to remove make-up from; **~rsi** *vr* to remove one's make-up.

'struggere ['struddʒere] *vt* (*fig*) to consume; **~rsi** *vr* (*fig*): **~rsi di** to be consumed with.

struggi'mento [struddʒi'mento] *sm* (*desiderio*) yearning.

strumen'tale *ag* (*MUS*) instrumental.

strumentaliz'zare [strumentalid'dzare] *vt* to exploit, use to one's own ends.

strumentalizzazi'one [strumentaliddzat'tsjone] *sf* exploitation.

strumentazi'one [strumentat'tsjone] *sf* (*MUS*) orchestration; (*TECN*) instrumentation.

stru'mento *sm* (*arnese, fig*) instrument, tool; (*MUS*) instrument; **~ a corda** *o* **ad arco/a fiato** string(ed)/wind instrument.

'strussi *etc vb vedi* **struggere**.

'strutto *sm* lard.

strut'tura *sf* structure.

struttu'rare *vt* to structure.

'struzzo ['struttso] *sm* ostrich; **fare lo ~, fare la politica dello ~** to bury one's head in the sand.

stuc'care *vt* (*muro*) to plaster; (*vetro*) to putty; (*decorare con stucchi*) to stucco.

stucca'tore, 'trice *sm/f* plasterer; (*artista*) stucco worker.

stuc'chevole [stuk'kevole] *ag* nauseating; (*fig*) tedious, boring.

'stucco, chi *sm* plaster; (*da vetri*) putty; (*ornamentale*) stucco; **rimanere di ~** (*fig*) to be dumbfounded.

stu'dente, 'essa *sm/f* student; (*scolaro*) pupil, schoolboy/girl.

studen'tesco, a, schi, sche *ag* student *cpd*.

studi'are *vt* to study; **~rsi** *vr* (*sforzarsi*): **~rsi**

di fare to try *o* endeavour (*BRIT*) *o* endeavor (*US*) to do.

studi'ato, a *ag* (*modi, sorriso*) affected.

'studio *sm* studying; (*ricerca, saggio, stanza*) study; (*di professionista*) office; (*di artista, CINE, TV, RADIO*) studio; (*di medico*) surgery (*BRIT*), office (*US*); **~i** *smpl* (*INS*) studies; **alla fine degli ~i** at the end of one's course (of studies); **secondo recenti ~i, appare che** ... recent research indicates that ...; **la proposta è allo ~** the proposal is under consideration; **~ legale** lawyer's office.

studi'oso, a *ag* studious, hardworking ♦ *sm/f* scholar.

'stufa *sf* stove; **~ elettrica** electric fire *o* heater; **~ a legna/carbone** wood-burning/coal stove.

stu'fare *vt* (*CUC*) to stew; (*fig fam*) to bore.

stu'fato *sm* (*CUC*) stew.

'stufo, a *ag* (*fam*): **essere ~ di** to be fed up with, be sick and tired of.

stu'oia *sf* mat.

stu'olo *sm* crowd, host.

stupefa'cente [stupefa'tʃente] *ag* stunning, astounding ♦ *sm* drug, narcotic.

stupe'fare *vt* to stun, astound.

stupe'fatto, a *pp di* **stupefare**.

stupefazi'one [stupefat'tsjone] *sf* astonishment.

stu'pendo, a *ag* marvellous, wonderful.

stupi'daggine [stupi'daddʒine] *sf* stupid thing (to do *o* say).

stupidità *sf* stupidity.

'stupido, a *ag* stupid.

stu'pire *vt* to amaze, stun ♦ *vi* (*anche:* **~rsi**): **~ (di)** to be amazed (at), be stunned (by); **non c'è da ~rsi** that's not surprising.

stu'pore *sm* amazement, astonishment.

stu'prare *vt* to rape.

stupra'tore *sm* rapist.

'stupro *sm* rape.

stu'rare *vt* (*lavandino*) to clear.

stuzzica'denti [stuttsika'dɛnti] *sm* toothpick.

stuzzi'cante [stuttsi'kante] *ag* (*gen*) stimulating; (*appetitoso*) appetizing.

stuzzi'care [stuttsi'kare] *vt* (*ferita etc*) to poke (at), prod (at); (*fig*) to tease; (*: appetito*) to whet; (*: curiosità*) to stimulate; **~ i denti** to pick one's teeth.

=============================== *PAROLA CHIAVE*

su (*su + il* = **sul**, *su + lo* = **sullo**, *su + l'* = **sull'**, *su + la* = **sulla**, *su + i* = **sui**, *su + gli** = **sugli**, *su + le* = **sulle**) *prep* **1** (*gen*) on; (*moto*) on(to); (*in cima a*) on (top of); **mettilo sul tavolo** put it on the table;

salire sul treno to get on the train; **un paesino sul mare** a village by the sea; **è sulla destra** it's on the right; **cento metri sul livello del mare** a hundred metres above sea level; **fecero rotta ~ Palermo** they set out for Palermo; **sul vestito portava un golf rosso** she was wearing a red sweater over her dress

2 (*argomento*) about, on; **un libro ~ Cesare** a book on *o* about Caesar

3 (*circa*) about; **costerà sui 3 milioni** it will cost about 3 million; **una ragazza sui 17 anni** a girl of about 17 (years of age)

4: ~ **misura** made to measure; ~ **ordinazione** to order; ~ **richiesta** on request; **3 casi ~ dieci** 3 cases out of 10

♦ *av* **1** (*in alto, verso l'alto*) up; **vieni ~ come** on up; **guarda ~** look up; **andare ~ e giù** to go up and down; ~ **le mani!** hands up!; **in ~** (*verso l'alto*) up(wards); (*in poi*) onwards; **vieni ~ da me?** are you going to come up?; **dai 20 anni in ~** from the age of 20 onwards

2 (*addosso*) on; **cos'hai ~?** what have you got on?

♦ *escl* come on!; ~ **avanti, muoviti!** come on, hurry up!; ~ **coraggio!** come on, cheer up!

'sua *vedi* **suo.**

sua'dente *ag* persuasive.

sub *sm/f inv* skin-diver.

su'bacqueo, a *ag* underwater ♦ *sm* skin-diver.

subaffit'tare *vt* to sublet.

subaf'fitto *sm* (*contratto*) sublet.

subal'terno, a *ag, sm* subordinate; (*MIL*) subaltern.

subappal'tare *vt* to subcontract.

subap'palto *sm* subcontract.

sub'buglio [sub'buʎʎo] *sm* confusion, turmoil; **essere/mettere in ~** to be in/throw into a turmoil.

sub'conscio, a [sub'kɔnʃo], **subcosci'ente** [subkoʃ'ʃɛnte] *ag, sm* subconscious.

'subdolo, a *ag* underhand, sneaky.

suben'trare *vi*: ~ **a qn in qc** to take over sth from sb; **sono subentrati altri problemi** other problems arose.

su'bire *vt* to suffer, endure.

subis'sare *vt* (*fig*): ~ **di** to overwhelm with, load with.

subi'taneo, a *ag* sudden.

'subito *av* immediately, at once, straight away.

subli'mare *vt* (*PSIC*) to sublimate; (*CHIM*) to sublime.

su'blime *ag* sublime.

sublo'care *vt* to sublease.

sublocazi'one [sublokat'tsjone] *sf* sublease.

subnor'male *ag* subnormal ♦ *sm/f* mentally handicapped person.

subodo'rare *vt* (*insidia etc*) to smell, suspect.

subordi'nare *vt* to subordinate.

subordi'nato, a *ag* subordinate; (*dipendente*): ~ **a** dependent on, subject to.

subordinazi'one [subordinat'tsjone] *sf* subordination.

su'bordine *sm*: **in ~** secondarily.

subur'bano, a *ag* suburban.

succe'daneo [suttʃe'daneo] *sm* substitute.

suc'cedere [sut'tʃɛdere] *vi* (*prendere il posto di qn*): ~ **a** to succeed; (*venire dopo*): ~ **a** to follow; (*accadere*) to happen; ~**rsi** *vr* to follow each other; ~ **al trono** to succeed to the throne; **sono cose che succedono** these things happen.

successi'one [suttʃes'sjone] *sf* succession; **tassa di ~** death duty (*BRIT*), inheritance tax (*US*).

successiva'mente [suttʃessiva'mente] *av* subsequently.

succes'sivo, a [suttʃes'sivo] *ag* successive; **il giorno ~** the following day; **in un momento ~** subsequently.

suc'cesso, a [sut'tʃɛsso] *pp di* **succedere** ♦ *sm* (*esito*) outcome; (*buona riuscita*) success; **di ~** (*libro, personaggio*) successful; **avere ~** (*persona*) to be successful; (*idea*) to be well received.

succes'sore [suttʃes'sore] *sm* successor.

succhi'are [suk'kjare] *vt* to suck (up).

succhi'otto [suk'kjɔtto] *sm* dummy (*BRIT*), pacifier (*US*), comforter (*US*).

suc'cinto, a [sut'tʃinto] *ag* (*discorso*) succinct; (*abito*) brief.

'succo, chi *sm* juice; (*fig*) essence, gist; ~ **di frutta/pomodoro** fruit/tomato juice.

suc'coso, a *ag* juicy; (*fig*) pithy.

'succube *sm/f* victim; **essere ~ di qn** to be dominated by sb.

succur'sale *sf* branch (office).

sud *sm* south ♦ *ag inv* south; (*regione*) southern; **verso ~** south, southwards; **l'Italia del S~** Southern Italy; **l'America del S~** South America.

Su'dafrica *sm*: **il ~** South Africa.

sudafri'cano, a *ag, sm/f* South African.

Suda'merica *sm*: **il ~** South America.

sudameri'cano, a *ag, sm/f* South American.

Su'dan *sm*: **il ~** (the) Sudan.

suda'nese *ag, sm/f* Sudanese *inv*.

su'dare *vi* to perspire, sweat; ~ **freddo** to

come out in a cold sweat.

su'dato, a *ag (persona, mani)* sweaty; *(fig: denaro)* hard-earned ♦ *sf (anche fig)* sweat; **una vittoria ~a** a hard-won victory; **ho fatto una bella ~a per finirlo in tempo** it was a real sweat to get it finished in time.

sud'detto, a *ag* above-mentioned.

suddi'tanza [suddi'tantsa] *sf* subjection; *(cittadinanza)* citizenship.

sud'dito, a *sm/f* subject.

suddi'videre *vt* to subdivide.

suddivisi'one *sf* subdivision.

suddi'viso, a *pp di* **suddividere**.

su'dest *sm* south-east; **vento di ~** south-easterly wind; **il ~ asiatico** South-East Asia.

sudice'ria [suditʃe'ria] *sf (qualità)* filthiness, dirtiness; *(cosa sporca)* dirty thing.

'sudicio, a, ci, ce ['suditʃo] *ag* dirty, filthy.

sudici'ume [sudi'tʃume] *sm* dirt, filth.

su'dore *sm* perspiration, sweat.

su'dovest *sm* south-west; **vento di ~** south-westerly wind.

'sue *vedi* **suo**.

'Suez ['suez] *sm*: **il Canale di ~** the Suez Canal.

suffici'ente [suffi'tʃɛnte] *ag* enough, sufficient; *(borioso)* self-important; *(INS)* satisfactory.

sufficiente'mente [suffitʃɛnte'mente] *av* sufficiently, enough; *(guadagnare, darsi da fare)* enough.

suffici'enza [suffi'tʃɛntsa] *sf (INS)* pass mark; **con un'aria di ~** *(fig)* with a condescending air; **a ~** enough; **ne ho avuto a ~!** I've had enough of this!

suf'fisso *sm (LING)* suffix.

suffra'gare *vt* to support.

suf'fragio [suf'fradʒo] *sm (voto)* vote; **~ universale** universal suffrage.

suggel'lare [suddʒel'lare] *vt (fig)* to seal.

suggeri'mento [suddʒeri'mento] *sm* suggestion; *(consiglio)* piece of advice, advice *no pl*; **dietro suo ~** on his advice.

sugge'rire [suddʒe'rire] *vt (risposta)* to tell; *(consigliare)* to advise; *(proporre)* to suggest; *(TEAT)* to prompt; **~ a qn di fare qc** to suggest to sb that he *(o she)* do sth.

suggeri'tore, 'trice [suddʒeri'tore] *sm/f (TEAT)* prompter.

suggestio'nare [suddʒestjo'nare] *vt* to influence.

suggesti'one [suddʒes'tjone] *sf (PSIC)* suggestion; *(istigazione)* instigation.

sugges'tivo, a [suddʒes'tivo] *ag (paesaggio)* evocative; *(teoria)* interesting, attractive.

'sughero ['sugero] *sm* cork.

'sugli ['suʎʎi] *prep +det vedi* **su**.

'sugo, ghi *sm (succo)* juice; *(di carne)* gravy; *(condimento)* sauce; *(fig)* gist, essence.

su'goso, a *ag (frutto)* juicy; *(fig: articolo etc)* pithy.

'sui *prep +det vedi* **su**.

sui'cida, i, e [sui'tʃida] *ag* suicidal ♦ *sm/f* suicide.

suici'darsi [suitʃi'darsi] *vr* to commit suicide.

sui'cidio [sui'tʃidjo] *sm* suicide.

su'ino, a *ag*: **carne ~a** pork ♦ *sm* pig; **~i** *smpl* swine *pl*.

sul, sull', 'sulla, 'sulle, 'sullo *prep + det vedi* **su**.

sulfa'midico, a, ci, che *ag, sm (MED)* sulphonamide.

sulta'nina *sf*: **(uva) ~** sultana.

sul'tano, a *sm/f* sultan/sultana.

Su'matra *sf* Sumatra.

'summit ['summit] *sm inv* summit.

S.U.N.I.A. *sigla m (= sindacato unitario nazionale inquilini e assegnatari) national association of tenants*.

sunnomi'nato, a *ag* aforesaid *cpd*.

'sunto *sm* summary.

'suo, 'sua, 'sue, su'oi *det*: **il ~, la sua** *etc (di lui)* his; *(di lei)* her; *(di esso)* its; *(con valore indefinito)* one's, his/her; *(forma di cortesia: anche:* **S~**) your ♦ *pron*: **il ~, la sua** *etc* his; hers; yours ♦ *sm*: **ha speso del ~** he *(o she etc)* spent his *(o her etc)* own money ♦ *sf*: **la ~a** *(opinione)* his *(o her etc)* view; **i suoi** *(parenti)* his *(o her etc)* family; **un ~ amico** a friend of his *(o hers etc)*; **è dalla ~a** he's on his *(o her etc)* side; **anche lui ha avuto le ~e** *(disavventure)* he's had his problems too; **sta sulle ~e** he keeps himself to himself.

su'ocero, a ['swɔtʃero] *sm/f* father/mother-in-law; **i ~i** *smpl* father- and mother-in-law.

su'oi *vedi* **suo**.

su'ola *sf (di scarpa)* sole.

su'olo *sm (terreno)* ground; *(terra)* soil.

suo'nare *vt (MUS)* to play; *(campana)* to ring; *(ore)* to strike; *(clacson, allarme)* to sound ♦ *vi* to play; *(telefono, campana)* to ring; *(ore)* to strike; *(clacson, fig: parole)* to sound.

suo'nato, a *ag (compiuto)*: **ha cinquant'anni ~i** he is well over fifty.

suona'tore, 'trice *sm/f* player; **~ ambulante** street musician.

suone'ria *sf* alarm.

su'ono *sm* sound.

su'ora *sf (REL)* nun; **Suor Maria** Sister

Maria.

'super *ag inv:* **(benzina)** ~ ≈ four-star (petrol) (*BRIT*), premium (*US*).

supera'mento *sm* (*di ostacolo*) overcoming; (*di montagna*) crossing.

supe'rare *vt* (*oltrepassare: limite*) to exceed, surpass; (*attraversare: fiume*) to cross; (*sorpassare: veicolo*) to overtake; (*fig: essere più bravo di*) to surpass, outdo; (*: difficoltà*) to overcome; (*: esame*) to get through; ~ **qn in altezza/peso** to be taller/heavier than sb; **ha superato la cinquantina** he's over fifty (years of age); ~ **i limiti di velocità** to exceed the speed limit; **stavolta ha superato se stesso** this time he has surpassed himself.

supe'rato, a *ag* outmoded.

supe'rattico, a *sm* penthouse.

su'perbia *sf* pride.

su'perbo, a *ag* proud; (*fig*) magnificent, superb.

supercondut'tore *sm* superconductor.

superfici'ale [superfi'tʃale] *ag* superficial.

superficialità [superfitʃali'ta] *sf* superficiality.

super'ficie, ci [super'fitʃe] *sf* surface; **tornare in** ~ (*a galla*) to return to the surface; (*fig: problemi etc*) to resurface; ~ **alare** (*AER*) wing area; ~ **velica** (*NAUT*) sail area.

su'perfluo, a *ag* superfluous.

superi'ora *sf* (*REL: anche:* **madre** ~) mother superior.

superi'ore *ag* (*piano, arto, classi*) upper; (*più elevato: temperatura, livello*): ~ **(a)** higher (than); (*migliore*): ~ **(a)** superior (to) ♦ *sf/pl:* **le** ~**i** (*INS*) *vedi* **scuola media superiore**; **il corso** ~ **di un fiume** the upper reaches of a river; **scuola media** ~ ≈ senior comprehensive school (*BRIT*); ≈ senior high (school) (*US*).

superiorità *sf* superiority.

superla'tivo, a *ag, sm* superlative.

superla'voro *sm* overwork.

super'market [super'market] *sm inv* = **supermercato**.

supermer'cato *sm* supermarket.

super'nova *sf* supernova.

superpo'tenza [superpo'tentsa] *sf* (*POL*) superpower.

super'sonico, a, ci, che *ag* supersonic.

su'perstite *ag* surviving ♦ *sm/f* survivor.

superstizi'one [superstit'tsjone] *sf* superstition.

superstizi'oso, a [superstit'tsjoso] *ag* superstitious.

super'strada *sf* ≈ expressway.

supervisi'one *sf* supervision.

supervi'sore *sm* supervisor.

su'pino, a *ag* supine; **accettazione** ~**a** (*fig*) blind acceptance.

suppel'lettile *sf* furnishings *pl.*

suppergiù [supper'dʒu] *av* more or less, roughly.

suppl. *abbr* (= *supplemento*) supp(l).

supplemen'tare *ag* extra; (*treno*) relief *cpd*; (*entrate*) additional.

supple'mento *sm* supplement.

sup'plente *ag* temporary; (*insegnante*) supply *cpd* (*BRIT*), substitute *cpd* (*US*) ♦ *sm/f* temporary member of staff; supply (*o* substitute) teacher.

sup'lenza [sup'plɛntsa] *sf:* **fare** ~ to do supply (*BRIT*) *o* substitute (*US*) teaching.

supple'tivo, a *ag* (*gen*) supplementary; (*sessione d'esami*) extra.

'supplica, che *sf* (*preghiera*) plea; (*domanda scritta*) petition, request.

suppli'care *vt* to implore, beseech.

suppli'chevole [suppli'kevole] *ag* imploring.

sup'plire *vi:* ~ **a** to make up for, compensate for.

sup'plizio [sup'plittsjo] *sm* torture.

sup'pongo, sup'poni *etc vb vedi* **supporre**.

sup'porre *vt* to suppose; **supponiamo che ...** let's *o* just suppose that ....

sup'porto *sm* (*sostegno*) support.

supposizi'one [suppozit'tsjone] *sf* supposition.

sup'posta *sf* (*MED*) suppository.

sup'posto, a *pp di* **supporre**.

suppu'rare *vi* to suppurate.

suprema'zia [supremat'tsia] *sf* supremacy.

su'premo, a *ag* supreme; **S~a Corte (di Cassazione)** Supreme Court.

surclas'sare *vt* to outclass.

surge'lare [surdʒe'lare] *vt* to (deep-)freeze.

surge'lato, a [surdʒe'lato] *ag* (deep-)frozen ♦ *smpl:* **i** ~**i** frozen food *sg.*

surme'nage [syrmə'naʒ] *sm* (*fisico*) overwork; (*mentale*) mental strain; (*SPORT*) overtraining.

sur'plus *sm inv* (*ECON*) surplus; ~ **di manodopera** overmanning.

surre'ale *ag* surrealistic.

surriscalda'mento *sm* (*gen, TECN*) overheating.

surriscal'dare *vt* to overheat.

surro'gato *sm* substitute.

suscet'tibile [suʃʃet'tibile] *ag* (*sensibile*) touchy, sensitive; (*soggetto*): ~ **di miglioramento** that can be improved, open to improvement.

suscettibilità [suʃʃettibili'ta] *sf* touchiness; **urtare la** ~ **di qn** to hurt sb's feelings.

susci'tare [suʃʃi'tare] vt to provoke, arouse.
su'sina sf plum.
su'sino sm plum (tree).
sussegu'ire vt to follow; **~rsi** vr to follow one another.
sussidi'ario, a ag subsidiary; (treno) relief cpd; (fermata) extra.
sus'sidio sm subsidy; (aiuto) aid; **~i didattici/audiovisivi** teaching/audiovisual aids; **~ di disoccupazione** unemployment benefit (BRIT) o benefits (US); **~ per malattia** sickness benefit.
sussi'ego sm haughtiness; **con aria di ~** haughtily.
sussis'tenza [sussis'tɛntsa] sf subsistence.
sus'sistere vi to exist; (essere fondato) to be valid o sound.
sussul'tare vi to shudder.
sus'sulto sm start.
sussur'rare vt, vi to whisper, murmur; **si sussurra che ...** it's rumoured (BRIT) o rumored (US) that ....
sus'surro sm whisper, murmur.
su'tura sf (MED) suture.
sutu'rare vt to stitch up, suture.
suv'via escl come on!
SV sigla = Savona.
S.V. abbr vedi **Signoria Vostra**.
sva'gare vt (divertire) to amuse; (distrarre): **~ qn** to take sb's mind off things; **~rsi** vr to amuse o.s.; to take one's mind off things.
sva'gato, a ag (persona) absent-minded; (scolaro) inattentive.
'svago, ghi sm (riposo) relaxation; (ricreazione) amusement; (passatempo) pastime.
svaligi'are [zvali'dʒare] vt to rob, burgle (BRIT), burglarize (US).
svaligia'tore, 'trice [zvalidʒa'tore] sm/f (di banca) robber; (di casa) burglar.
svalu'tare vt (ECON) to devalue; (fig) to belittle; **~rsi** vr (ECON) to be devalued.
svalutazi'one [zvalutat'tsjone] sf devaluation.
svam'pito, a ag absent-minded ♦ sm/f absent-minded person.
sva'nire vi to disappear, vanish.
sva'nito, a ag (fig: persona) absent-minded.
svantaggi'ato, a [zvantad'dʒato] ag at a disadvantage.
svan'taggio [zvan'taddʒo] sm disadvantage; (inconveniente) drawback, disadvantage; **tornerà a suo ~** it will work against you.
svantaggi'oso, a [zvantad'dʒoso] ag disadvantageous; **è un'offerta ~a per me** it's not in my interest to accept this

offer; **è un prezzo ~** it is not an attractive price.
svapo'rare vi to evaporate.
svapo'rato, a ag (bibita) flat.
svari'ato, a ag (vario, diverso) varied; (numeroso) various.
'svastica, che sf swastika.
sve'dese ag Swedish ♦ sm/f Swede ♦ sm (LING) Swedish.
'sveglia ['zveʎʎa] sf waking up; (orologio) alarm (clock); **suonare la ~** (MIL) to sound the reveille; **~ telefonica** alarm call.
svegli'are [zveʎ'ʎare] vt to wake up; (fig) to awaken, arouse; **~rsi** vr to wake up; (fig) to be revived, reawaken.
'sveglio, a ['zveʎʎo] ag awake; (fig) alert, quick-witted.
sve'lare vt to reveal.
svel'tezza [zvel'tettsa] sf (gen) speed; (mentale) quick-wittedness.
svel'tire vt (gen) to speed up; (procedura) to streamline.
'svelto, a ag (passo) quick; (mente) quick, alert; (linea) slim, slender; **alla ~a** quickly.
'svendere vt to sell off, clear.
'svendita sf (COMM) (clearance) sale.
sve'nevole ag mawkish.
'svengo etc vb vedi **svenire**.
sveni'mento sm fainting fit, faint.
sve'nire vi to faint.
sven'tare vt to foil, thwart.
sventa'tezza [zventa'tettsa] sf (distrazione) absent-mindedness; (mancanza di prudenza) rashness.
sven'tato, a ag (distratto) scatterbrained; (imprudente) rash.
'sventola sf (colpo) slap; **orecchie a ~** sticking-out ears.
svento'lare vt, vi to wave, flutter.
sven'trare vt to disembowel.
sven'tura sf misfortune.
sventu'rato, a ag unlucky, unfortunate.
sve'nuto, a pp di **svenire**.
svergo'gnare [zvergoɲ'ɲare] vt to shame.
svergo'gnato, a [zvergoɲ'ɲato] ag shameless ♦ sm/f shameless person.
sver'nare vi to spend the winter.
sverrò etc vb vedi **svenire**.
sves'tire vt to undress; **~rsi** vr to get undressed.
'Svezia ['zvettsja] sf: **la ~** Sweden.
svez'zare [zvet'tsare] vt to wean.
svi'are vt to divert; (fig) to lead astray; **~rsi** vr to go astray.
svico'lare vi to slip down an alley; (fig) to sneak off.
svi'gnarsela [zviɲ'ɲarsela] vr to slip away,

sneak off.

svili'mento *sm* debasement.

svi'lire *vt* to debase.

svilup'pare *vt*, **~rsi** *vr* to develop.

svi'luppo *sm* development; (*di industria*) expansion; **in via di ~** in the process of development; **paesi in via di ~** developing countries.

svinco'lare *vt* to free, release; (*merce*) to clear.

'svincolo *sm* (*COMM*) clearance; (*stradale*) motorway (*BRIT*) *o* expressway (*US*) intersection.

svisce'rare [zviʃʃe'rare] *vt* (*fig: argomento*) to examine in depth.

svisce'rato, a [zviʃʃe'rato] *ag* (*amore, odio*) passionate.

'svista *sf* oversight.

svi'tare *vt* to unscrew.

'Svizzera ['zvittsera] *sf*: **la ~** Switzerland.

'svizzero, a ['zvittsero] *ag, sm/f* Swiss.

svoglia'tezza [zvoʎʎa'tettsa] *sf* listlessness; indolence.

svogli'ato, a [zvoʎ'ʎato] *ag* listless; (*pigro*) lazy, indolent.

svolaz'zare [zvolat'tsare] *vi* to flutter.

'svolgere ['zvɔldʒere] *vt* to unwind; (*srotolare*) to unroll; (*fig: argomento*) to develop; (: *piano, programma*) to carry out; **~rsi** *vr* to unwind; to unroll; (*fig: aver luogo*) to take place; (: *procedere*) to go on; **tutto si è svolto secondo i piani** everything went according to plan.

svolgi'mento [zvɔldʒi'mento] *sm* development; carrying out; (*andamento*) course.

'svolsi *etc vb vedi* **svolgere**.

'svolta *sf* (*atto*) turning *no pl*; (*curva*) turn, bend; (*fig*) turning-point; **essere ad una ~ nella propria vita** to be at a crossroads in one's life.

svol'tare *vi* to turn.

'svolto, a *pp di* **svolgere**.

svuo'tare *vt* to empty (out).

'Swaziland ['swadziland] *sm*: **lo ~** Swaziland.

T t

T, t [ti] *sf o m inv* (*lettera*) T, t; **T come Taranto** ≈ T for Tommy.

T *abbr* = **tabaccheria**.

t *abbr* = **tara**; **tonnellata**.

TA *sigla* = **Taranto**.

tabac'caio, a *sm/f* tobacconist.

tabacche'ria [tabakke'ria] *sf* tobacconist's (shop).

tabacchi'era [tabak'kjɛra] *sf* snuffbox.

ta'bacco, chi *sm* tobacco.

ta'bella *sf* (*tavola*) table; (*elenco*) list; **~ di marcia** schedule; **~ dei prezzi** price list.

tabel'lone *sm* (*per pubblicità*) billboard; (*per informazioni*) notice board (*BRIT*), bulletin board (*US*); (: *in stazione*) timetable board.

taber'nacolo *sm* tabernacle.

tabù *ag, sm inv* taboo.

'tabula 'rasa *sf* tabula rasa; **fare ~** (*fig*) to make a clean sweep.

tabu'lare *vt* to tabulate.

tabu'lato *sm* (*INFORM*) printout.

tabula'tore *sm* tabulator.

TAC *sigla f* (*MED*: = *Tomografia Assiale Computerizzata*) CAT.

'tacca, che *sf* notch, nick; **di mezza ~** (*fig*) mediocre.

taccagne'ria [takkaɲɲe'ria] *sf* meanness, stinginess.

tac'cagno, a [tak'kaɲɲo] *ag* mean, stingy.

tac'cheggio [tak'keddʒo] *sm* shoplifting.

tac'chino [tak'kino] *sm* turkey.

'taccia, ce ['tattʃa] *sf* bad reputation.

tacci'are [tat'tʃare] *vt*: **~ qn di** (*vigliaccheria etc*) to accuse sb of.

'taccio *etc* ['tattʃo] *vb vedi* **tacere**.

'tacco, chi *sm* heel.

taccu'ino *sm* notebook.

ta'cere [ta'tʃere] *vi* to be silent *o* quiet; (*smettere di parlare*) to fall silent ♦ *vt* to keep to oneself, say nothing about; **far ~ qn** to make sb be quiet; (*fig*) to silence sb; **mettere a ~ qc** to hush sth up.

tachicar'dia [takikar'dia] *sf* (*MED*) tachycardia.

ta'chimetro [ta'kimetro] *sm* speedometer.

'tacito, a ['tatʃito] *ag* silent; (*sottinteso*) tacit, unspoken.

taci'turno, a [tatʃi'turno] *ag* taciturn.

taci'uto, a [ta'tʃuto] *pp di* **tacere**.
'tacqui *etc vb vedi* **tacere**.
ta'fano *sm* horsefly.
taffe'ruglio [taffe'ruʎʎo] *sm* brawl, scuffle.
taffettà *sm* taffeta.
'taglia ['taʎʎa] *sf (statura)* height; *(misura)* size; *(riscatto)* ransom; *(ricompensa)* reward; **~e forti** *(ABBIGLIAMENTO)* outsize.
taglia'boschi [taʎʎa'bɔski] *sm inv* woodcutter.
taglia'carte [taʎʎa'karte] *sm inv* paperknife.
taglia'legna [taʎʎa'leɲɲa] *sm inv* woodcutter.
tagli'ando [taʎ'ʎando] *sm* coupon.
tagli'are [taʎ'ʎare] *vt* to cut; *(recidere, interrompere)* to cut off; *(intersecare)* to cut across, intersect; *(carne)* to carve; *(vini)* to blend ♦ *vi* to cut; *(prendere una scorciatoia)* to take a short-cut; **~ la strada a qn** to cut across in front of sb; **~ corto** *(fig)* to cut short.
taglia'telle [taʎʎa'tɛlle] *sfpl* tagliatelle *pl.*
tagli'ato, a [taʎ'ʎato] *ag:* **essere ~ per qc** *(fig)* to be cut out for sth.
taglia'trice [taʎʎa'tritʃe] *sf (TECN)* cutter.
taglia'unghie [taʎʎa'ungje] *sm inv* nail clippers *pl.*
taglieggi'are [taʎʎed'dʒare] *vt* to exact a tribute from.
tagli'ente [taʎ'ʎɛnte] *ag* sharp.
tagli'ere [taʎ'ʎere] *sm* chopping board; *(per il pane)* bread board.
'taglio ['taʎʎo] *sm (anche fig)* cut; *(azione)* cutting *no pl; (di carne)* piece; *(di stoffa)* length; *(di vini)* blending; **di ~** on edge, edgeways; **banconote di piccolo/grosso ~** notes of small/large denomination; **un bel ~ di capelli** a nice haircut *o* hairstyle; **pizza al ~** pizza by the slice.
tagli'ola [taʎ'ʎɔla] *sf* trap, snare.
tagli'one [taʎ'ʎone] *sm:* **la legge del ~** the concept of an eye for an eye and a tooth for a tooth.
tagliuz'zare [taʎʎut'tsare] *vt* to cut into small pieces.
Ta'hiti [ta'iti] *sf* Tahiti.
tailan'dese *ag, sm/f, sm* Thai.
Tai'landia *sf:* **la ~** Thailand.
tai'lleur [ta'jœr] *sm inv* lady's suit.
Tai'wan [tai'wan] *sm:* **il ~** Taiwan.
'talamo *sm (poetico)* marriage bed.
'talco *sm* talcum powder.

================ *PAROLA CHIAVE*

'tale *det* **1** *(simile, così grande)* such; **un(a) ~ ... such (a) ...; non accetto ~i discorsi** I won't allow such talk; **è di una ~ arroganza** he is so arrogant; **fa una ~**

confusione! he makes such a mess!
2 *(persona o cosa indeterminata)* such-and-such; **il giorno ~ all'ora ~** on such-and-such a day at such-and-such a time; **la tal persona** that person; **ha telefonato una ~ Giovanna** somebody called Giovanna phoned
3 *(nelle similitudini):* **~ ... ~** like ... like; **~ padre ~ figlio** like father, like son; **hai il vestito ~ quale il mio** your dress is just *o* exactly like mine
♦ *pron (indefinito: persona):* **un(a) ~** someone; **quel** *(o* **quella)** **~** that person, that man *(o* woman); **il tal dei ~i** what's-his-name.

ta'lento *sm* talent.
talis'mano *sm* talisman.
talk-'show [tɔlk'ʃo] *sm inv* talk *o* chat show.
tallo'nare *vt* to pursue; **~ il pallone** *(CALCIO, RUGBY)* to heel the ball.
tallon'cino [tallon'tʃino] *sm* counterfoil *(BRIT)*, stub; **~ del prezzo** *(di medicinali)* tear-off tag.
tal'lone *sm* heel.
tal'mente *av* so.
ta'lora *av* = **talvolta**.
'talpa *sf (anche fig)* mole.
tal'volta *av* sometimes, at times.
tambu'rello *sm* tambourine.
tambu'rino *sm* drummer boy.
tam'buro *sm* drum; **freni a ~** drum brakes; **pistola a ~** revolver; **a ~ battente** *(fig)* immediately, at once.
Ta'migi [ta'midʒi] *sm:* **il ~** the Thames.
tampona'mento *sm (AUT)* collision; **~ a catena** pile-up.
tampo'nare *vt (otturare)* to plug; *(urtare: macchina)* to crash *o* ram into.
tam'pone *sm (MED)* wad, pad; *(per timbri)* ink-pad; *(respingente)* buffer; **~ assorbente** tampon.
'tamtam *sm inv (fig)* grapevine.
'tana *sf* lair, den; *(fig)* den, hideout.
'tanfo *sm (di muffa)* musty smell; *(puzza)* stench.
tan'gente [tan'dʒɛnte] *ag (MAT):* **~ a** tangential to ♦ *sf* tangent; *(quota)* share; *(denaro estorto)* rake-off *(fam)*, cut.
tangen'topoli [tandʒɛn'topoli] *sf (POL, MEDIA)* Bribesville.

Tangentopoli *is the term used to describe the corruption scandal involving a large number of politicians, from all political parties, including government ministers, leading industrialists and businessmen. Investigations exposed a complex system of* *illegal payments and bribes using both public and private money to benefit certain private individuals and political parties. The scandal began in Milan which was consequently called Tangentopoli or "Bribesville".*

tangenzi'ale [tandʒen'tsjale] *sf* (*strada*) bypass.
'Tangeri ['tandʒeri] *sf* Tangiers.
tan'gibile [tan'dʒibile] *ag* tangible.
'tango, ghi *sm* tango.
'tanica, che *sf* jerry can.
tan'nino *sm* tannin.
tan'tino: un ~ *av* a little, a bit.

================== *PAROLA CHIAVE*

'tanto, a *det* **1** (*molto: quantità*) a lot of, much; (: *numero*) a lot of, many; ~ **pane/latte** a lot of bread/milk; ~ **tempo** a lot of time, a long time; ~**i auguri!** all the best!; ~**e grazie** many thanks; ~ **persone** a lot of people, many people; ~**e volte** many times, often; **ogni** ~**i chilometri** every so many kilometres
2: (*così* ~: *quantità*) so much, such a lot of; (: *numero*) so many, such a lot of; ~**a fatica per niente!** a lot of trouble for nothing!; **ha** ~ **coraggio che** ... he's got so much courage that ..., he's so brave that ...; **ho aspettato per** ~ **tempo** I waited so long *o* for such a long time
3: ~ ... **quanto** (*quantità*) as much ... as; (*numero*) as many ... as; **ho** ~**a pazienza quanta ne hai tu** I have as much patience as you have *o* as you; **ha** ~**i amici quanti nemici** he has as many friends as he has enemies
♦ *pron* **1** (*molto*) much, a lot; (*così* ~) so much, such a lot; ~**i, e** many, a lot; so many, such a lot; **credevo ce ne fosse** ~ I thought there was (such) a lot, I thought there was plenty; **una persona come** ~**e** a person just like any other; **è passato** ~ (*tempo*) it's been so long; **è** ~ **che aspetto** I've been waiting for a long time; ~ **di guadagnato!** so much the better!
2: ~ **quanto** (*denaro*) as much as; (*cioccolatini*) as many as; **ne ho** ~ **quanto basta** I have as much as I need; **due volte** ~ twice as much
3 (*indeterminato*) so much; ~ **per l'affitto,** ~ **per il gas** so much for the rent, so much for the gas; **costa un** ~ **al metro** it costs so much per metre; **di** ~ **in** ~, **ogni** ~ every so often; ~ **vale che** ... I (*o* we *etc*) may as well ...; ~ **meglio!** so much the better!; ~ **peggio per lui!** so much the worse for him!; **se** ~ **mi dà** ~ if that's how things are; **guardare qc con** ~ **d'occhi** to gaze wide-eyed at sth
♦ *av* **1** (*molto*) very; **vengo** ~ **volentieri** I'd be very glad to come; **non ci vuole** ~ **a capirlo** it doesn't take much to understand it
2 (*così* ~: *con ag, av*) so; (: *con vb*) so much, such a lot; **è** ~ **bella!** she's so beautiful!; **non urlare** ~ (**forte**) don't shout so much; **sto** ~ **meglio adesso** I'm so much better now; **era** ~ **bella da non credere** she was incredibly beautiful; ~ ... **che** so ... (that); ~ ... **da** so ... as
3: ~ ... **quanto** as ... as; **conosco** ~ **Carlo quanto suo padre** I know both Carlo and his father; **non è poi** ~ **complicato quanto sembra** it's not as difficult as it seems; **è** ~ **bella quanto buona** she is as good as she is beautiful; ~ **più insisti,** ~ **più non mollerà** the more you insist, the more stubborn he'll be; **quanto più** ... ~ **meno** the more ... the less; **quanto più lo conosco** ~ **meno mi piace** the better I know him the less I like him
4 (*solamente*) just; ~ **per cambiare/scherzare** just for a change/a joke; **una volta** ~ for once
5 (*a lungo*) (for) long
♦ *cong* after all; **non insistere,** ~ **è inutile** don't keep on, it's no use; **lascia stare,** ~ **è troppo tardi** forget it, it's too late.

Tanza'nia [tandza'nia] *sf*: **la** ~ Tanzania.
tapi'oca *sf* tapioca.
ta'piro *sm* (*ZOOL*) tapir.
'tappa *sf* (*luogo di sosta, fermata*) stop, halt; (*parte di un percorso*) stage, leg; (*SPORT*) lap; **a** ~**e** in stages; **bruciare le** ~**e** (*fig*) to be a whizz kid.
tappa'buchi [tappa'buki] *sm inv* stopgap; **fare da** ~ to act as a stopgap.
tap'pare *vt* to plug, stop up; (*bottiglia*) to cork.
tappa'rella *sf* rolling shutter.
tap'peto *sm* carpet; (*anche:* **tappetino**) rug; (*di tavolo*) cloth; (*SPORT*): **andare al** ~ to go down for the count; **mettere sul** ~ (*fig*) to bring up for discussion.
tappez'zare [tappet'tsare] *vt* (*con carta*) to paper; (*rivestire*): ~ **qc (di)** to cover sth (with).
tappezze'ria [tappettse'ria] *sf* (*arredamento*) soft furnishings *pl*; (*carta da parati*) wall covering; (*di automobile*) upholstery; **far da** ~ (*fig*) to be a wallflower.
tappezzi'ere [tappet'tsjere] *sm* upholsterer.
'tappo *sm* stopper; (*in sughero*) cork; ~ **a**

corona bottle top; ~ **a vite** screw top.

TAR *sigla m* = *Tribunale Amministrativo Regionale.*

'tara *sf (peso)* tare; *(MED)* hereditary defect; *(difetto)* flaw.

taran'tella *sf* tarantella.

ta'rantola *sf* tarantula.

ta'rare *vt (COMM)* to tare; *(TECN)* to calibrate.

ta'rato, a *ag (COMM)* tared; *(MED)* with a hereditary defect.

tara'tura *sf (COMM)* taring; *(TECN)* calibration.

tarchi'ato, a [tar'kjato] *ag* stocky, thickset.

tar'dare *vi* to be late ♦ *vt* to delay; ~ **a fare** to delay doing.

'tardi *av* late; **più** ~ later (on); **al più** ~ at the latest; **sul** ~ *(verso sera)* late in the day; **far** ~ to be late; *(restare alzato)* to stay up late.

tar'divo, a *ag (primavera)* late; *(rimedio)* belated, tardy; *(fig: bambino)* retarded.

'tardo, a *ag (lento, fig: ottuso)* slow; *(tempo: avanzato)* late.

tar'dona *sf (peg)*: **essere una** ~ to be mutton dressed as lamb.

'targa, ghe *sf* plate; *(AUT)* number *(BRIT)* o license *(US)* plate; *vedi anche* **circolazione**.

tar'gare *vt (AUT)* to register.

targ'hetta [tar'getta] *sf (con nome: su porta)* nameplate; (: *su bagaglio)* name tag.

ta'riffa *sf (gen)* rate, tariff; *(di trasporti)* fare; *(elenco)* price list; tariff; **la** ~ **in vigore** the going rate; ~ **normale/ridotta** standard/reduced rate; *(su mezzi di trasporto)* full/concessionary fare; ~ **salariale** wage rate; ~ **unica** flat rate; ~**e doganali** customs rates o tariff; ~**e postali/telefoniche** postal/telephone charges.

tarif'fario, ii *ag*: **aumento** ~ increase in charges o rates ♦ *sm* tariff, table of charges.

'tarlo *sm* woodworm.

'tarma *sf* moth.

tarmi'cida, i [tarmi't∫ida] *ag, sm* mothkiller.

ta'rocco, chi *sm* tarot card; ~**chi** *smpl (gioco)* tarot *sg*.

tar'pare *vt (fig)*: ~ **le ali a qn** to clip sb's wings.

tartagli'are [tartaʎ'ʎare] *vi* to stutter, stammer.

'tartaro, a *ag, sm (in tutti i sensi)* tartar.

tarta'ruga, ghe *sf* tortoise; *(di mare)* turtle; *(materiale)* tortoiseshell.

tartas'sare *vt (fam)*: ~ **qn** to give sb the

works; ~ **qn a un esame** to give sb a grilling at an exam.

tar'tina *sf* canapé.

tar'tufo *sm (BOT)* truffle.

'tasca, sche *sf* pocket; **da** ~ pocket *cpd*; **fare i conti in** ~ **a qn** *(fig)* to meddle in sb's affairs.

tas'cabile *ag (libro)* pocket *cpd*.

tasca'pane *sm* haversack.

tas'chino [tas'kino] *sm* breast pocket.

Tas'mania *sf*: **la** ~ Tasmania.

'tassa *sf (imposta)* tax; *(doganale)* duty; *(per iscrizione: a scuola etc)* fee; ~ **di circolazione/di soggiorno** road/tourist tax.

tas'sametro *sm* taximeter.

tas'sare *vt* to tax; to levy a duty on.

tassa'tivo, a [tas'kino] *sm* peremptory.

tassazi'one [tassat'tsjone] *sf* taxation; **soggetto a** ~ taxable.

tas'sello *sm (di legno, pietra)* plug; *(assaggio)* wedge.

tassì *sm inv* = **taxi**.

tas'sista, i, e *sm/f* taxi driver.

'tasso *sm (di natalità, d'interesse etc)* rate; *(BOT)* yew; *(ZOOL)* badger; ~ **di cambio/ d'interesse** rate of exchange/interest; ~ **di crescita** growth rate.

tas'tare *vt* to feel; ~ **il terreno** *(fig)* to see how the land lies.

tasti'era *sf* keyboard.

tastie'rino *sm*: ~ **numerico** numeric keypad.

'tasto *sm* key; *(tatto)* touch, feel; **toccare un** ~ **delicato** *(fig)* to touch on a delicate subject; **toccare il** ~ **giusto** *(fig)* to strike the right note; ~ **funzione** *(INFORM)* function key; ~ **delle maiuscole** *(su macchina da scrivere etc)* shift key.

tas'toni *av*: **procedere (a)** ~ to grope one's way forward.

'tata *sf (linguaggio infantile)* nanny.

'tattico, a, ci, che *ag* tactical ♦ *sf* tactics *pl*.

'tatto *sm (senso)* touch; *(fig)* tact; **duro al** ~ hard to the touch; **aver** ~ to be tactful, have tact.

tatu'aggio [tatu'addʒo] *sm* tattooing; *(disegno)* tattoo.

tatu'are *vt* to tattoo.

tauma'turgico, a, ci, che [tauma'turdʒiko] *ag (fig)* miraculous.

ta'verna *sf (osteria)* tavern.

'tavola *sf* table; *(asse)* plank, board; *(lastra)* tablet; *(quadro)* panel (painting); *(illustrazione)* plate; ~ **calda** snack bar; ~ **pieghevole** folding table.

tavo'lata *sf* company at table.

tavo'lato *sm* boarding; *(pavimento)* wooden

floor.

tavo'letta *sf* tablet, bar; ~ (*AUT*) flat out.

tavo'lino *sm* small table; (*scrivania*) desk;
~ **da tè/gioco** coffee/card table; **mettersi
a** ~ to get down to work; **decidere qc a** ~
(*fig*) to decide sth on a theoretical level.

'tavolo *sm* table; ~ **da disegno** drawing
board; ~ **da lavoro** desk; (*TECN*)
workbench; ~ **operatorio** (*MED*) operating
table.

tavo'lozza [tavo'lɔttsa] *sf* (*ARTE*) palette.

'taxi *sm inv* taxi.

'tazza ['tattsa] *sf* cup; ~ **da caffè/tè**
coffee/tea cup; **una** ~ **di caffè/tè** a cup of
coffee/tea.

taz'zina [tat'tsina] *sf* coffee cup.

TBC *abbr f* (= *tubercolosi*) TB.

TCI *sigla m* = *Touring Club Italiano.*

TE *sigla* = *Teramo.*

te *pron* (*soggetto: in forme comparative,
oggetto*) you.

tè *sm inv* tea; (*trattenimento*) tea party.

tea'trale *ag* theatrical.

te'atro *sm* theatre; ~ **comico** comedy; ~ **di
posa** film studio.

'tecnico, a, ci, che *ag* technical ♦ *sm/f*
technician ♦ *sf* technique; (*tecnologia*)
technology.

tecnolo'gia [teknolo'dʒia] *sf* technology;
alta ~ high technology, hi-tech.

tecno'logico, a, ci, che [tekno'lɔdʒiko] *ag*
technological.

te'desco, a, schi, sche *ag, sm/f, sm*
German; ~ **orientale/occidentale** East/
West German.

tedi'are *vt* (*infastidire*) to bother, annoy;
(*annoiare*) to bore.

'tedio *sm* tedium, boredom.

tedi'oso, a *ag* tedious, boring.

te'game *sm* (*CUC*) pan; **al** ~ fried.

'teglia ['teʎʎa] *sf* (*CUC: per dolci*) (baking)
tin (*BRIT*), cake pan (*US*); (: *per arrosti*)
(roasting) tin.

'tegola *sf* tile.

Teh'ran *sf* Tehran.

tei'era *sf* teapot.

te'ina *sf* (*CHIM*) theine.

tel. *abbr* (= *telefono*) tel.

'tela *sf* (*tessuto*) cloth; (*per vele, quadri*)
canvas; (*dipinto*) canvas, painting; **di** ~
(*calzoni*) (heavy) cotton *cpd*; (*scarpe, borsa*)
canvas *cpd*; ~ **cerata** oilcloth; ~ **di ragno**
spider's web.

te'laio *sm* (*apparecchio*) loom; (*struttura*)
frame.

Tel A'viv *sf* Tel Aviv.

tele... *prefisso* tele....

teleabbo'nato *sm* television licence

holder.

tele'camera *sf* television camera.

telecoman'dare *vt* to operate by remote
control.

teleco'mando *sm* remote control;
(*dispositivo*) remote-control device.

telecomunicazi'oni [telekomunikat'tsjoni]
sfpl telecommunications.

tele'cronaca, che *sf* television report.

telecro'nista, i, e *sm/f* (television)
commentator.

tele'ferica, che *sf* cableway.

tele'film *sm inv* television film.

telefo'nare *vi* to telephone, ring; (*fare una
chiamata*) to make a phone call ♦ *vt* to
telephone; ~ **a qn** to telephone sb, phone
o ring o call sb (up).

telefo'nata *sf* (telephone) call; ~ **urbana/
interurbana** local/long-distance call; ~ **a
carico del destinatario** reverse charge
(*BRIT*) o collect (*US*) call; ~ **con preavviso**
person-to-person call.

telefonica'mente *av* by (tele)phone.

tele'fonico, a, ci, che *ag* (tele)phone *cpd.*

telefo'nino *sm* (*cellulare*) mobile phone.

telefo'nista, i, e *sm/f* telephonist;
(*d'impresa*) switchboard operator.

te'lefono *sm* telephone; **avere il** ~ to be on
the (tele)phone; ~ **a gettoni** ≈ pay phone;
~ **azzurro** ≈ Childline; ~ **interno** internal
phone; ~ **pubblico** public phone, call box
(*BRIT*); ~ **rosa** ≈ rape crisis.

telegior'nale [teledʒor'nale] *sm* television
news (programme).

telegra'fare *vt, vi* to telegraph, cable.

telegra'fia *sf* telegraphy.

tele'grafico, a, ci, che *ag* telegraph *cpd*,
telegraphic.

telegra'fista, i, e *sm/f* telegraphist,
telegraph operator.

te'legrafo *sm* telegraph; (*ufficio*) telegraph
office.

tele'gramma, i *sm* telegram.

tele'matica *sf* data transmission;
telematics *sg.*

teleno'vela *sf* soap opera.

teleobiet'tivo *sm* telephoto lens *sg.*

telepa'tia *sf* telepathy.

tele'quiz [tele'kwits] *sm inv* (*TV*) game show.

teles'chermo [teles'kermo] *sm* television
screen.

teles'copio *sm* telescope.

telescri'vente *sf* teleprinter (*BRIT*),
teletypewriter (*US*).

teleselet'tivo, a *ag*: **prefisso** ~ dialling
code (*BRIT*), dial code (*US*).

teleselezi'one [teleselet'tsjone] *sf* direct
dialling.

telespetta'tore, 'trice smlf (television) viewer.
tele'text sm inv teletext.
tele'video sm videotext service.
televisi'one sf television.

Televisione in Italy comprises public and private-sector channels. There are 3 state-owned channels, **RAI** 1, 2 and 3, and a large number of private channels. Some of these exist at local level only, while others are regional. Some form part of a network, others are independent. Being state-owned, RAI is responsible to the Ministero delle Poste e Telecomunicazioni. Both the state-owned RAI and the privately run channels compete for advertising to finance themselves.

---

televi'sore sm television set.
'telex sm inv telex.
'telo sm length of cloth.
te'lone sm (per merci etc) tarpaulin; (sipario) drop curtain.
'tema, i sm theme; (INS) essay, composition.
te'matica sf basic themes pl.
teme'rario, a ag rash, reckless.
te'mere vt to fear, be afraid of; (essere sensibile a: freddo, calore) to be sensitive to ♦ vi to be afraid; (essere preoccupato): ~ **per** to worry about, fear for; ~ **di/che** to be afraid of/that.
'tempera sf (pittura) tempera; (dipinto) painting in tempera.
temperama'tite sm inv pencil sharpener.
tempera'mento sm temperament.
tempe'rante ag moderate.
tempe'rare vt (aguzzare) to sharpen; (fig) to moderate, control, temper.
tempe'rato, a ag moderate, temperate; (clima) temperate.
tempera'tura sf temperature; ~ **ambiente** room temperature.
tempe'rino sm penknife.
tem'pesta sf storm; ~ **di sabbia/neve** sand/snowstorm.
tempes'tare vt (percuotere): ~ **qn di colpi** to rain blows on sb; (bombardare): ~ **qn di domande** to bombard sb with questions; (ornare) to stud.
tempestività sf timeliness.
tempes'tivo, a ag timely.
tempes'toso, a ag stormy.
'tempia sf (ANAT) temple.
'tempio sm (edificio) temple.
tem'pismo sm sense of timing.
tem'pistiche [tem'pistike] sfpl (COMM) time

and motion.
'tempo sm (METEOR) weather; (cronologico) time; (epoca) time, times pl; (di film, gioco: parte) part; (MUS) time; (: battuta) beat; (LING) tense; **un** ~ once; **da** ~ for a long time now; ~ **fa** some time ago; **poco** ~ **dopo** not long after; **a** ~ **e luogo** at the right time and place; **ogni cosa a suo** ~ we'll (o you'll etc) deal with it in due course; **al** ~ **stesso** o **a un** ~ at the same time; **per** ~ early; **per qualche** ~ for a while; **trovare il** ~ **di fare qc** to find the time to do sth; **aver fatto il proprio** ~ to have had its (o his etc) day; **primo/ secondo** ~ (TEAT) first/second part; (SPORT) first/second half; **rispettare i** ~**i** to keep to the timetable; **stringere i** ~**i** to speed things up; **con i** ~**i che corrono** these days; **in questi ultimi** ~**i** of late; **ai miei** ~**i** in my day; ~ **di cottura** cooking time; **in** ~ **utile** in due time o course; ~**i di esecuzione** (COMM) time scale sg; ~**i di lavorazione** (COMM) throughput time sg; ~**i morti** (COMM) downtime sg, idle time sg.
tempo'rale ag temporal ♦ sm (METEOR) (thunder)storm.
tempora'lesco, a, schi, sche ag stormy.
tempo'raneo, a ag temporary.
temporeggi'are [tempored'dʒare] vi to play for time, temporize.
'tempra sf (TECN: atto) tempering, hardening; (: effetto) temper; (fig: costituzione fisica) constitution; (: intellettuale) temperament.
tem'prare vt to temper.
te'nace [te'natʃe] ag strong, tough; (fig) tenacious.
te'nacia [te'natʃa] sf tenacity.
te'naglie [te'naʎʎe] sfpl pincers pl.
'tenda sf (riparo) awning; (di finestra) curtain; (per campeggio etc) tent.
ten'daggio [ten'daddʒo] sm curtaining, curtains pl, drapes pl (US).
ten'denza [ten'dɛntsa] sf tendency; (orientamento) trend; **avere** ~ **a** o **per qc** to have a bent for sth; ~ **al rialzo/ribasso** (BORSA) upward/downward trend.
tendenziosità [tendentsjosi'ta] sf tendentiousness.
tendenzi'oso, a [tenden'tsjoso] ag tendentious, bias(s)ed.
'tendere vt (allungare al massimo) to stretch, draw tight; (porgere: mano) to hold out; (fig: trappola) to lay, set ♦ vi: ~ **a qc/a fare** to tend towards sth/to do; **tutti i nostri sforzi sono tesi a** ... all our efforts are geared towards ...; ~ **l'orecchio** to

prick up one's ears; **il tempo tende al caldo** the weather is getting hot; **un blu che tende al verde** a greenish blue.

ten'dina *sf* curtain.

'tendine *sm* tendon, sinew.

ten'done *sm* (*da circo*) big top.

ten'dopoli *sf inv* (large) camp.

'tenebre *sfpl* darkness *sg*.

tene'broso, a *ag* dark, gloomy.

te'nente *sm* lieutenant.

te'nere *vt* to hold; (*conservare, mantenere*) to keep; (*ritenere, considerare*) to consider; (*spazio: occupare*) to take up, occupy; (*seguire: strada*) to keep to; (*dare: lezione, conferenza*) to give ♦ *vi* to hold; (*colori*) to be fast; (*dare importanza*): ~ **a** to care about; ~ **a fare** to want to do, be keen to do; ~**rsi** *vr* (*stare in una determinata posizione*) to stand; (*stimarsi*) to consider o.s.; (*aggrapparsi*): ~**rsi a** to hold on to; (*attenersi*): ~**rsi a** to stick to; ~ **in gran conto** *o* **considerazione qn** to have a high regard for sb, think highly of sb; ~ **conto di qc** to take sth into consideration; ~ **presente qc** to bear sth in mind; **non ci sono scuse che tengano** I'll take no excuses; ~**rsi per la mano** (*uso reciproco*) to hold hands; ~**rsi in piedi** to stay on one's feet.

tene'rezza [tene'rettsa] *sf* tenderness.

'tenero, a *ag* tender; (*pietra, cera, colore*) soft; (*fig*) tender, loving ♦ *sm*: **tra quei due c'è del** ~ there's a romance budding between those two.

'tengo *etc vb vedi* **tenere**.

'tenia *sf* tapeworm.

'tenni *etc vb vedi* **tenere**.

'tennis *sm* tennis; ~ **da tavolo** table tennis.

ten'nista, i, e *sm/f* tennis player.

te'nore *sm* (*tono*) tone; (*MUS*) tenor; ~ **di vita** way of life; (*livello*) standard of living.

tensi'one *sf* tension; **ad alta** ~ (*ELETTR*) high-voltage *cpd*, high-tension *cpd*.

tentaco'lare *ag* tentacular; (*fig: città*) magnet-like.

ten'tacolo *sm* tentacle.

ten'tare *vt* (*indurre*) to tempt; (*provare*): ~ **qc/di fare** to attempt *o* try sth/to do; ~ **la sorte** to try one's luck.

tenta'tivo *sm* attempt.

tentazi'one [tentat'tsjone] *sf* temptation; **aver la** ~ **di fare** to be tempted to do.

tentenna'mento *sm* (*fig*) hesitation, wavering; **dopo molti** ~**i** after much hesitation.

tenten'nare *vi* to shake, be unsteady; (*fig*) to hesitate, waver ♦ *vt*: ~ **il capo** to shake

one's head.

ten'toni *av*: **andare a** ~ (*anche fig*) to grope one's way.

'tenue *ag* (*sottile*) fine; (*colore*) soft; (*fig*) slender, slight.

te'nuta *sf* (*capacità*) capacity; (*divisa*) uniform; (*abito*) dress; (*AGR*) estate; **a** ~ **d'aria** airtight; ~ **di strada** roadholding power; **in** ~ **da lavoro** in one's working clothes; **in** ~ **da sci** in a skiing outfit.

teolo'gia [teolo'dʒia] *sf* theology.

teo'logico, a, ci, che [teo'lɔdʒiko] *ag* theological.

te'ologo, gi *sm* theologian.

teo'rema, i *sm* theorem.

teo'ria *sf* theory; **in** ~ in theory, theoretically.

te'orico, a, ci, che *ag* theoretic(al) ♦ *sm* theorist, theoretician; **a livello** ~, **in linea** ~**a** theoretically.

teoriz'zare [teorid'dzare] *vt* to theorize.

'tepido, a *ag* = **tiepido**.

te'pore *sm* warmth.

'teppa *sf* mob, hooligans *pl*.

tep'paglia [tep'paʎʎa] *sf* hooligans *pl*.

tep'pismo *sm* hooliganism.

tep'pista, i *sm* hooligan.

tera'peutico, a, ci, che *ag* therapeutic.

tera'pia *sf* therapy; ~ **di gruppo** group therapy.

tera'pista, i, e *sm/f* therapist.

tergicris'tallo [terdʒikris'tallo] *sm* windscreen (*BRIT*) *o* windshield (*US*) wiper.

tergiver'sare [terdʒiver'sare] *vi* to shilly-shally.

'tergo *sm*: **a** ~ behind; **vedi a** ~ please turn over.

'terital ® *sm inv* Terylene ®.

ter'male *ag* thermal.

'terme *sfpl* thermal baths.

'termico, a, ci, che *ag* thermal; **centrale** ~**a** thermal power station.

termi'nale *ag* (*fase, parte*) final; (*MED*) terminal ♦ *sm* terminal; **tratto** ~ (*di fiume*) lower reaches *pl*.

termi'nare *vt* to end; (*lavoro*) to finish ♦ *vi* to end.

terminazi'one [terminat'tsjone] *sf* (*fine*) end; (*LING*) ending; ~**i nervose** (*ANAT*) nerve endings.

'termine *sm* term; (*fine, estremità*) end; (*di territorio*) boundary, limit; **fissare un** ~ to set a deadline; **portare a** ~ **qc** to bring sth to a conclusion; **contratto a** ~ (*COMM*) forward contract; **a breve/lungo** ~ short-/long-term; **ai** ~**i di legge** by law; **in altri** ~**i** in other words; **parlare senza**

mezzi ~**i** to talk frankly, not to mince one's words.
terminolo'gia [terminolo'dʒia] *sf* terminology.
'**termite** *sf* termite.
termoco'perta *sf* electric blanket.
ter'mometro *sm* thermometer.
termonucle'are *ag* thermonuclear.
'**termos** *sm inv* = **thermos**.
termosi'fone *sm* radiator; (**riscaldamento a**) ~ central heating.
ter'mostato *sm* thermostat.
'**terna** *sf* set of three; (*lista di tre nomi*) list of three candidates.
'**terno** *sm* (*al lotto etc*) (set of) three winning numbers; **vincere un** ~ **al lotto** (*fig*) to hit the jackpot.
'**terra** *sf* (*gen, ELETTR*) earth; (*sostanza*) soil, earth; (*opposto al mare*) land; (*regione, paese*) land; (*argilla*) clay; ~**e** *sfpl* (*possedimento*) lands, land *sg*; **a o per** ~ (*stato*) on the ground (*o floor*); (*moto*) to the ground, down; **mettere a** ~ (*ELETTR*) to earth; **essere a** ~ (*fig: depresso*) to be at rock bottom; **via** ~ (*viaggiare*) by land, overland; **strada in** ~ **battuta** dirt track; ~ **di nessuno** no man's land; **la T**~ **Santa** the Holy Land; ~ **di Siena** sienna; ~ ~ (*fig: persona, argomento*) prosaic, pedestrian.
terra-'aria *ag inv* (*MIL*) ground-to-air.
terra'cotta *sf* terracotta; **vasellame di** ~ earthenware.
terra'ferma *sf* dry land, terra firma; (*continente*) mainland.
ter'raglia [ter'raʎʎa] *sf* pottery; ~**e** *pl* (*oggetti*) crockery *sg*, earthenware *sg*.
Terra'nova *sf*: **la** ~ Newfoundland.
terrapi'eno *sm* embankment, bank.
'**terra-'terra** *ag inv* (*MIL*) surface-to-surface.
ter'razza [ter'rattsa] *sf*, **ter'razzo** [ter'rattso] *sm* terrace.
terremo'tato, a *ag* (*zona*) devastated by an earthquake ♦ *sm/f* earthquake victim.
terre'moto *sm* earthquake.
ter'reno, a *ag* (*vita, beni*) earthly ♦ *sm* (*suolo, fig*) ground; (*COMM*) land *no pl*, plot (of land); site; (*SPORT, MIL*) field; **perdere** ~ (*anche fig*) to lose ground; **un** ~ **montuoso** a mountainous terrain; ~ **alluvionale** (*GEO*) alluvial soil.
'**terreo, a** *ag* (*viso, colorito*) wan.
ter'restre *ag* (*superficie*) of the earth, earth's; (*di terra: battaglia, animale*) land *cpd*; (*REL*) earthly, worldly.
ter'ribile *ag* terrible, dreadful.
ter'riccio [ter'rittʃo] *sm* soil.
terri'ero, a *ag*: **proprietà** ~**a** landed

property; **proprietario** ~ landowner.
terrifi'cante *ag* terrifying.
ter'rina *sf* (*zuppiera*) tureen.
territori'ale *ag* territorial.
terri'torio *sm* territory.
ter'rone, a *sm/f* derogatory term used by Northern Italians to describe Southern Italians.
ter'rore *sm* terror; **avere il** ~ **di qc** to be terrified of sth.
terro'rismo *sm* terrorism.
terro'rista, i, e *sm/f* terrorist.
terroriz'zare [terrorid'dzare] *vt* to terrorize.
'**terso, a** *ag* clear.
ter'zetto [ter'tsetto] *sm* (*MUS*) trio, terzetto; (*di persone*) trio.
terzi'ario, a [ter'tsjarjo] *ag* (*GEO, ECON*) tertiary.
ter'zino [ter'tsino] *sm* (*CALCIO*) fullback, back.
'**terzo, a** ['tɛrtso] *ag* third ♦ *sm* (*frazione*) third; (*DIR*) third party ♦ *sf* (*gen*) third; (*AUT*) third (gear); (*di trasporti*) third class; (*SCOL: elementare*) third year at primary school; (: *media*) third year at secondary school; (: *superiore*) sixth year at secondary school; ~**i** *smpl* (*altri*) others, other people; **agire per conto di** ~**i** to act on behalf of a third party; **assicurazione contro** ~**i** third-party insurance (*BRIT*), liability insurance (*US*); **la** ~**a età** old age; **il** ~ **mondo** the Third World; **di terz'ordine** third rate; **la** ~**a pagina** (*STAMPA*) the Arts page.
'**tesa** *sf* brim; **a larghe** ~**e** wide-brimmed.
'**teschio** ['tɛskjo] *sm* skull.
'**tesi** *sf inv* thesis; ~ **di laurea** degree thesis.
'**tesi** *etc vb vedi* **tendere**.
'**teso, a** *pp di* **tendere** ♦ *ag* (*tirato*) taut, tight; (*fig*) tense.
tesore'ria *sf* treasury.
tesori'ere *sm* treasurer.
te'soro *sm* treasure; **il Ministero del T**~ the Treasury; **far** ~ **dei consigli di qn** to take sb's advice to heart.
'**tessera** *sf* (*documento*) card; (*di abbonato*) season ticket; (*di giornalista*) pass; **ha la** ~ **del partito** he's a party member.
tesse'rare *vt* (*iscrivere*) to give a membership card to.
tesse'rato, a *sm/f* (*di società sportiva etc*) (fully paid-up) member; (*POL*) (card-carrying) member.
'**tessere** *vt* to weave; ~ **le lodi di qn** (*fig*) to sing sb's praises.
'**tessile** *ag, sm* textile.
tessi'tore, 'trice *sm/f* weaver.
tessi'tura *sf* weaving.

tes'suto *sm* fabric, material; (*BIOL*) tissue; (*fig*) web.

'testa *sf* head; (*di cose: estremità, parte anteriore*) head, front; **5.000 lire a** ~ 5,000 lire apiece *o* a head *o* per person; **a** ~ **alta** with one's head held high; **a** ~ **bassa** (*correre*) headlong; (*con aria dimessa*) with head bowed; **di** ~ *ag* (*vettura etc*) front; **dare alla** ~ to go to one's head; **fare di** ~ **propria** to go one's own way; **in** ~ (*SPORT*) in the lead; **essere in** ~ **alla classifica** (*corridore*) to be number one; (*squadra*) to be at the top of the league table; (*disco*) to be top of the charts, be number one; **essere alla** ~ **di qc** (*società*) to be the head of; (*esercito*) to be at the head of; **tenere** ~ **a qn** (*nemico etc*) to stand up to sb; **una** ~ **d'aglio** a bulb of garlic; ~ **o croce?** heads or tails?; **avere la** ~ **dura** to be stubborn; ~ **di serie** (*TENNIS*) seed, seeded player.

'testa-'coda *sm inv* (*AUT*) spin.

testamen'tario, a *ag* (*DIR*) testamentary; **le sue disposizioni** ~**e** the provisions of his will.

testa'mento *sm* (*atto*) will, testament; **l'Antico/il Nuovo T**~ (*REL*) the Old/New Testament.

testar'daggine [testar'daddʒine] *sf* stubbornness, obstinacy.

tes'tardo, a *ag* stubborn, pig-headed.

tes'tare *vt* to test.

tes'tata *sf* (*parte anteriore*) head; (*intestazione*) heading; **missile a** ~ **nucleare** missile with a nuclear warhead.

'teste *sm/f* witness.

tes'ticolo *sm* testicle.

testi'era *sf* (*del letto*) headboard; (*di cavallo*) headpiece.

testi'mone *sm/f* (*DIR*) witness; **fare da** ~ **alle nozze di qn** to be a witness at sb's wedding; ~ **oculare** eye witness.

testimoni'anza [testimo'njantsa] *sf* (*atto*) deposition; (*effetto*) evidence; (*fig: prova*) proof; **accusare qn di falsa** ~ to accuse sb of perjury; **rilasciare una** ~ to give evidence.

testimoni'are *vt* to testify; (*fig*) to bear witness to, testify to ◊ *vi* to give evidence, testify; ~ **il vero** to tell the truth; ~ **il falso** to perjure o.s.

tes'tina *sf* (*di giradischi, registratore*) head.

'testo *sm* text; **fare** ~ (*opera, autore*) to be authoritative; (*fig: dichiarazione*) to carry weight.

testoste'rone *sm* testosterone.

testu'ale *ag* textual; **le sue parole** ~**i** his (*o* her) actual words.

tes'tuggine [tes'tuddʒine] *sf* tortoise; (*di mare*) turtle.

'tetano *sm* (*MED*) tetanus.

'tetro, a *ag* gloomy.

'tetta *sf* (*fam*) boob, tit.

tetta'rella *sf* teat.

'tetto *sm* roof; **abbandonare il** ~ **coniugale** to desert one's family; ~ **a cupola** dome.

tet'toia *sf* roofing; canopy.

'Tevere *sm*: **il** ~ the Tiber.

TG [tid'dʒi] *abbr m* (= *telegiornale*) TV news *sg*.

'thermos ® ['tɛrmos] *sm inv* vacuum *o* Thermos ® flask.

'thriller ['θrilə], **'thrilling** ['θriliŋ] *sm inv* thriller.

ti *pron* (*dav lo, la, li, le, ne diventa* **te**) (*oggetto*) you; (*complemento di termine*) (to) you; (*riflessivo*) yourself; ~ **aiuto?** can I give you a hand?; **te lo ha dato?** did he give it to you?; ~ **sei lavato?** have you washed?

ti'ara *sf* (*REL*) tiara.

'Tibet *sm*: **il** ~ Tibet.

tibe'tano, a *ag, sm/f* Tibetan.

'tibia *sf* tibia, shinbone.

tic *sm inv* tic, (nervous) twitch; (*fig*) mannerism.

ticchet'tio [tikket'tio] *sm* (*di macchina da scrivere*) clatter; (*di orologio*) ticking; (*della pioggia*) patter.

'ticchio ['tikkjo] *sm* (*ghiribizzo*) whim; (*tic*) tic, (nervous) twitch.

'ticket *sm inv* (*MED*) prescription charge (*BRIT*).

ti'ene *etc vb vedi* **tenere**.

ti'epido, a *ag* lukewarm, tepid.

ti'fare *vi*: ~ **per** to be a fan of; (*parteggiare*) to side with.

'tifo *sm* (*MED*) typhus; (*fig*): **fare il** ~ **per** to be a fan of.

tifoi'dea *sf* typhoid.

ti'fone *sm* typhoon.

ti'foso, a *sm/f* (*SPORT etc*) fan.

tight ['tait] *sm inv* morning suit.

'tiglio ['tiʎʎo] *sm* lime (tree), linden (tree).

'tigna ['tiɲɲa] *sf* (*MED*) ringworm.

ti'grato, a *ag* striped.

'tigre *sf* tiger.

tilt *sm*: **andare in** ~ (*fig*) to go haywire.

tim'ballo *sm* (*strumento*) kettledrum; (*CUC*) timbale.

tim'brare *vt* to stamp; (*annullare: francobolli*) to postmark; ~ **il cartellino** to clock in.

'timbro *sm* stamp; (*MUS*) timbre, tone.

timi'dezza [timi'dettsa] *sf* shyness, timidity.

'timido, a *ag* shy, timid.

'timo *sm* thyme.

ti'mone *sm* (*NAUT*) rudder.

timoni'ere *sm* helmsman.

timo'rato, a *ag* conscientious; ~ **di Dio** God-fearing.

ti'more *sm* (*paura*) fear; (*rispetto*) awe; **avere** ~ **di qc/qn** (*paura*) to be afraid of sth/sb.

timo'roso, a *ag* timid, timorous.

'timpano *sm* (*ANAT*) eardrum; (*MUS*): ~**i** kettledrums, timpani.

'tinca, che *sf* (*ZOOL*) tench.

ti'nello *sm* small dining room.

'tingere ['tindʒere] *vt* to dye.

'tino *sm* vat.

ti'nozza [ti'nɔttsa] *sf* tub.

'tinsi *etc vb vedi* **tingere**.

'tinta *sf* (*materia colorante*) dye; (*colore*) colour (*BRIT*), color (*US*), shade.

tinta'rella *sf* (*fam*) (sun)tan.

tintin'nare *vi* to tinkle.

tintin'nio *sm* tinkling.

'tinto, a *pp di* **tingere**.

tinto'ria *sf* (*officina*) dyeworks *sg*; (*lavasecco*) dry cleaner's (shop).

tin'tura *sf* (*operazione*) dyeing; (*colorante*) dye; ~ **di iodio** tincture of iodine.

'tipico, a, ci, che *ag* typical.

'tipo *sm* type; (*genere*) kind, type; (*fam*) chap, fellow; **vestiti di tutti i ~i** all kinds of clothes; **sul** ~ **di questo** of this sort; **sei un bel ~!** you're a fine one!

tipogra'fia *sf* typography.

tipo'grafico, a, ci, che *ag* typographic(al).

ti'pografo *sm* typographer.

tip 'tap [tip'tap] *sm* (*ballo*) tap dancing.

T.I.R. *sigla m* (= *Transports Internationaux Routiers*) *International Heavy Goods Vehicle*.

'tira e 'molla *sm inv* tug-of-war.

ti'raggio [ti'raddʒo] *sm* (*di camino etc*) draught (*BRIT*), draft (*US*).

Ti'rana *sf* Tirana.

tiranneggi'are [tiranned'dʒare] *vt* to tyrannize.

tiran'nia *sf* tyranny.

ti'ranno, a *ag* tyrannical ♦ *sm* tyrant.

ti'rante *sm* (*NAUT, di tenda etc*) guy; (*EDIL*) brace.

tirapi'edi *smf inv* hanger-on.

tira'pugni [tira'puɲɲi] *sm inv* knuckle-duster.

ti'rare *vt* (*gen*) to pull; (*estrarre*): ~ **qc da** to take *o* pull sth out of; to get sth out of; to extract sth from; (*chiudere: tenda etc*) to draw, pull; (*tracciare, disegnare*) to draw, trace; (*lanciare: sasso, palla*) to throw; (*stampare*) to print; (*pistola, freccia*) to fire ♦ *vi* (*pipa, camino*) to draw; (*vento*) to

blow; (*abito*) to be tight; (*fare fuoco*) to fire; (*fare del tiro, CALCIO*) to shoot; ~ **qn da parte** to take *o* draw sb aside; ~ **un sospiro (di sollievo)** to heave a sigh (of relief); ~ **a indovinare** to take a guess; ~ **sul prezzo** to bargain; ~ **avanti** *vi* to struggle on ♦ *vt* (*famiglia*) to provide for; (*ditta*) to look after; ~ **fuori** to take out, pull out; ~ **giù** to pull down; ~ **su** to pull up; (*capelli*) to put up; (*fig: bambino*) to bring up; ~**rsi indietro** to move back; (*fig*) to back out; ~**rsi su** to pull o.s. up; (*fig*) to cheer o.s. up.

ti'rato, a *ag* (*teso*) taut; (*fig: teso, stanco*) drawn.

tira'tore *sm* gunman; **un buon** ~ a good shot; ~ **scelto** marksman.

tira'tura *sf* (*azione*) printing; (*di libro*) (print) run; (*di giornale*) circulation.

tirchie'ria [tirkje'ria] *sf* meanness, stinginess.

'tirchio, a ['tirkjo] *ag* mean, stingy.

tiri'tera *sf* drivel, hot air.

'tiro *sm* shooting *no pl*, firing *no pl*; (*colpo, sparo*) shot; (*di palla: lancio*) throwing *no pl*; throw; (*fig*) trick; **essere a** ~ to be in range; **giocare un brutto** ~ *o* **un** ~ **mancino a qn** to play a dirty trick on s.b.; **cavallo da** ~ draught (*BRIT*) *o* draft (*US*) horse; ~ **a segno** target shooting; (*luogo*) shooting range.

tiroci'nante [tirotʃi'nante] *ag, smf* apprentice (*cpd*); trainee (*cpd*).

tiro'cinio [tiro'tʃinjo] *sm* apprenticeship; (*professionale*) training.

ti'roide *sf* thyroid (gland).

ti'rolese *ag, smf* Tyrolean, Tyrolese *inv*.

Ti'rolo *sm*: **il** ~ the Tyrol.

tir'rennico, a, ci, che *ag* Tyrrhenian.

Tir'reno *sm*: **il** (*mar*) ~ the Tyrrhenian Sea.

ti'sana *sf* herb tea.

'tisi *sf* (*MED*) consumption.

'tisico, a, ci, che *ag* (*MED*) consumptive; (*fig: gracile*) frail ♦ *smf* consumptive (person).

ti'tanico, a, ci, che *ag* gigantic, enormous.

ti'tano *sm* (*MITOLOGIA, fig*) titan.

tito'lare *ag* appointed; (*sovrano*) titular ♦ *smf* incumbent; (*proprietario*) owner; (*CALCIO*) regular player.

tito'lato, a *ag* (*persona*) titled.

'titolo *sm* title; (*di giornale*) headline; (*diploma*) qualification; (*COMM*) security; (: *azione*) share; **a che** ~? for what reason?; **a** ~ **di amicizia** out of friendship; **a** ~ **di cronaca** for your information; **a** ~ **di premio** as a prize; ~ **di credito** share; ~ **obbligazionario** bond; ~ **al portatore**

bearer bond; ~ **di proprietà** title deed; ~**i di stato** government securities; ~**i di testa** (*CINE*) credits.

titu'bante *ag* hesitant, irresolute.

tivù *sf inv* (*fam*) telly (*BRIT*), TV.

'tizio, a ['tittsjo] *sm/f* fellow, chap.

tiz'zone [tit'tsone] *sm* brand.

T.M.G. *abbr* (= *tempo medio di Greenwich*) GMT.

TN *sigla* = *Trento*.

TNT *sigla m* (= *trinitrotoluolo*) TNT.

TO *sigla* = *Torino*.

toast [toust] *sm inv* toasted sandwich.

toc'cante *ag* touching.

toc'care *vt* to touch; (*tastare*) to feel; (*fig: riguardare*) to concern; (: *commuovere*) to touch, move; (: *pungere*) to hurt, wound; (: *far cenno a: argomento*) to touch on, mention ♦ *vi*: ~ **a** (*accadere*) to happen to; (*spettare*) to be up to; **tocca a te difenderci** it's up to you to defend us; **a chi tocca?** whose turn is it?; **mi toccò pagare** I had to pay; ~ **il fondo** (*in acqua*) to touch the bottom; (*fig*) to touch rock bottom; ~ **con mano** (*fig*) to find out for o.s.; ~ **qn sul vivo** to cut sb to the quick.

tocca'sana *sm inv* cure-all, panacea.

toccherò *etc* [tokke'rɔ] *vb vedi* toccare.

'tocco, chi *sm* touch; (*ARTE*) stroke, touch.

toe'letta *sf* = toilette.

'toga, ghe *sf* toga; (*di magistrato, professore*) gown.

'togliere ['tɔʎʎere] *vt* (*rimuovere*) to take away (*o* off), remove; (*riprendere, non concedere più*) to take away, remove; (*MAT*) to take away, subtract; (*liberare*) to free; ~ **qc a qn** to take sth (away) from sb; **ciò non toglie che ...** nevertheless ..., be that as it may ...; ~**rsi il cappello** to take off one's hat.

'Togo *sm*: il ~ Togo.

toilette [twa'lɛt] *sf inv* (*gabinetto*) toilet; (*cosmesi*) make-up; (*abbigliamento*) gown, dress; (*mobile*) dressing table; **fare** ~ to get made up, make o.s. beautiful.

'Tokyo *sf* Tokyo.

to'letta *sf* = toilette.

'tolgo *etc vb vedi* togliere.

tolle'rante *ag* tolerant.

tolle'ranza [tolle'rantsa] *sf* tolerance; **casa di** ~ brothel.

tolle'rare *vt* to tolerate; **non tollero repliche** I won't stand for objections; **non sono tollerati i ritardi** lateness will not be tolerated.

To'losa *sf* Toulouse.

'tolsi *etc vb vedi* togliere.

'tolto, a *pp di* togliere.

to'maia *sf* (*di scarpa*) upper.

'tomba *sf* tomb.

tom'bale *ag*: **pietra** ~ tombstone, gravestone.

tom'bino *sm* manhole cover.

'tombola *sf* (*gioco*) tombola; (*ruzzolone*) tumble.

'tomo *sm* volume.

tomogra'fia *sf* (*MED*) tomography; ~ **assiale computerizzata** computerized axial tomography.

'tonaca, che *sf* (*REL*) habit.

to'nare *vi* = tuonare.

'tondo, a *ag* round.

'tonfo *sm* splash; (*rumore sordo*) thud; (*caduta*): **fare un** ~ to take a tumble.

'tonico, a, ci, che *ag* tonic ♦ *sm* tonic; (*cosmetico*) toner.

tonifi'cante *ag* invigorating, bracing.

tonifi'care *vt* (*muscoli, pelle*) to tone up; (*irrobustire*) to invigorate, brace.

ton'nara *sf* tuna-fishing nets *pl*.

ton'nato, a *ag* (*CUC*): **salsa** ~**a** tuna fish sauce; **vitello** ~ veal with tuna fish sauce.

tonnel'laggio [tonnel'laddʒo] *sm* (*NAUT*) tonnage.

tonnel'lata *sf* ton.

'tonno *sm* tuna (fish).

'tono *sm* (*gen, MUS*) tone; (*di colore*) shade, tone; **rispondere a** ~ (*a proposito*) to answer to the point; (*nello stesso modo*) to answer in kind; (*per le rime*) to answer back.

ton'silla *sf* tonsil.

tonsil'lite *sf* tonsillitis.

ton'sura *sf* tonsure.

'tonto, a *ag* dull, stupid ♦ *sm/f* blockhead, dunce; **fare il finto** ~ to play dumb.

top [tɔp] *sm inv* (*vertice, camicetta*) top.

to'paia *sf* (*di topo*) mousehole; (*di ratto*) rat's nest; (*fig: casa etc*) hovel, dump.

to'pazio [to'pattsjo] *sm* topaz.

topi'cida, i [topi'tʃida] *sm* rat poison.

'topless ['tɔplis] *sm inv* topless bathing costume.

'topo *sm* mouse; ~ **d'albergo** (*fig*) hotel thief; ~ **di biblioteca** (*fig*) bookworm.

topogra'fia *sf* topography.

topog'rafico, a, ci, che *ag* topographic, topographical.

to'ponimo *sm* place name.

'toppa *sf* (*serratura*) keyhole; (*pezza*) patch.

to'race [to'ratʃe] *sm* chest.

'torba *sf* peat.

'torbido, a *ag* (*liquido*) cloudy; (: *fiume*) muddy; (*fig*) dark; troubled ♦ *sm*: **pescare nel** ~ (*fig*) to fish in troubled waters.

'torcere ['tɔrtʃere] *vt* to twist; (*biancheria*) to

wring (out); ~**rsi** *vr* to twist, writhe; **dare del filo da ~ a qn** to make life *o* things difficult for sb.

torchi'are [tor'kjare] *vt* to press.

'**torchio** ['tɔrkjo] *sm* press; **mettere qn sotto il ~** (*fig fam*: *interrogare*) to grill sb; **~ tipografico** printing press.

'**torcia, ce** ['tɔrtʃa] *sf* torch; **~ elettrica** torch (*BRIT*), flashlight (*US*).

torci'collo [tortʃi'kɔllo] *sm* stiff neck.

'**tordo** *sm* thrush.

to'rero *sm* bullfighter, toreador.

tori'nese *ag* of (*o* from) Turin ♦ *sm/f* person from Turin.

To'rino *sf* Turin.

tor'menta *sf* snowstorm.

tormen'tare *vt* to torment; ~**rsi** *vr* to fret, worry o.s.

tor'mento *sm* torment.

torna'conto *sm* advantage, benefit.

tor'nado *sm* tornado.

tor'nante *sm* hairpin bend (*BRIT*) *o* curve (*US*).

tor'nare *vi* to return, go (*o* come) back; (*ridiventare: anche fig*) to become (again); (*riuscire giusto, esatto: conto*) to work out; (*risultare*) to turn out (to be), prove (to be); **~ al punto di partenza** to start again; **~ a casa** to go (*o* come) home; **i conti tornano** the accounts balance; **~ utile** to prove *o* turn out (to be) useful.

torna'sole *sm inv* litmus.

tor'neo *sm* tournament.

'**tornio** *sm* lathe.

tor'nire *vt* (*TECN*) to turn (on a lathe); (*fig*) to shape, polish.

tor'nito, a *ag* (*gambe, caviglie*) well-shaped.

'**toro** *sm* bull; (*dello zodiaco*): **T~** Taurus; **essere del T~** to be Taurus.

tor'pedine *sf* torpedo.

torpedini'era *sf* torpedo boat.

tor'pore *sm* torpor.

'**torre** *sf* tower; (*SCACCHI*) rook, castle; **~ di controllo** (*AER*) control tower.

torrefazi'one [torrefat'tsjone] *sf* roasting.

torreggi'are [torred'dʒare] *vi*: **~ (su)** to tower (over).

tor'rente *sm* torrent.

torren'tizio, a [torren'tittsjo] *ag* torrential.

torrenzi'ale [torren'tsjale] *ag* torrential.

tor'retta *sf* turret.

'**torrido, a** *ag* torrid.

torri'one *sm* keep.

tor'rone *sm* nougat.

'**torsi** *etc vb vedi* **torcere**.

torsi'one *sf* twisting; (*TECN*) torsion.

'**torso** *sm* torso, trunk; (*ARTE*) torso; **a ~ nudo** bare-chested.

'**torsolo** *sm* (*di cavolo etc*) stump; (*di frutta*) core.

'**torta** *sf* cake.

tortel'lini *smpl* (*CUC*) tortellini.

torti'era *sf* cake tin (*BRIT*), cake pan (*US*).

'**torto, a** *pp di* **torcere** ♦ *ag* (*ritorto*) twisted; (*storto*) twisted, crooked ♦ *sm* (*ingiustizia*) wrong; (*colpa*) fault; **a ~** wrongly; **a ~ o a ragione** rightly or wrongly; **aver ~** to be wrong; **fare un ~ a qn** to wrong sb; **essere/passare dalla parte del ~** to be/put o.s. in the wrong; **lui non ha tutti i ~i** there's something in what he says.

'**tortora** *sf* turtle dove.

tortu'oso, a *ag* (*strada*) twisting; (*fig*) tortuous.

tor'tura *sf* torture.

tortu'rare *vt* to torture.

'**torvo, a** *ag* menacing, grim.

tosa'erba *sm o f inv* (lawn)mower.

to'sare *vt* (*pecora*) to shear; (*cane*) to clip; (*siepe*) to clip, trim.

tosa'tura *sf* (*di pecore*) shearing; (*di cani*) clipping; (*di siepi*) trimming, clipping.

Tos'cana *sf*: **la ~** Tuscany.

tos'cano, a *ag*, *sm/f* Tuscan ♦ *sm* (*anche*: **sigaro ~**) strong Italian cigar.

'**tosse** *sf* cough.

tossicità [tossitʃi'ta] *sf* toxicity.

'**tossico, a, ci, che** *ag* toxic.

tossicodipen'dente *sm/f* drug addict.

tossicodipen'denza [tossikodipen'dɛntsa] *sf* drug addiction.

tossi'comane *sm/f* drug addict.

tossicoma'nia *sf* drug addiction.

tos'sina *sf* toxin.

tos'sire *vi* to cough.

tosta'pane *sm inv* toaster.

tos'tare *vt* to toast; (*caffè*) to roast.

tosta'tura *sf* (*di pane*) toasting; (*di caffè*) roasting.

'**tosto, a** *ag*: **faccia ~a** cheek ♦ *av* at once, immediately; **~ che** as soon as.

to'tale *ag*, *sm* total.

totalità *sf*: **la ~ di** all of, the total amount (*o* number) of; **the whole + sg.**

totali'tario, a *ag* totalitarian; (*totale*) complete, total; **adesione ~a** complete support.

totalita'rismo *sm* (*POL*) totalitarianism.

totaliz'zare [totalid'dzare] *vt* to total; (*SPORT: punti*) to score.

totalizza'tore [totaliddza'tore] *sm* (*TECN*) totalizator; (*IPPICA*) totalizator, tote (*fam*).

to'tip *sm* gambling pool betting on horse racing.

toto'calcio [toto'kaltʃo] *sm* gambling pool betting on football results, ≈ (football) pools *pl* (*BRIT*).

tou'pet [tu'pɛ] *sm inv* toupee.

tour [tur] *sm inv* (*giro*) tour; (*CICLISMO*) tour de France.

tour de 'force ['tur də 'fɔrs] *sm inv* (*SPORT: anche fig*) tour de force.

tour'née [tur'ne] *sf* tour; **essere in** ~ to be on tour.

to'vaglia [to'vaʎʎa] *sf* tablecloth.

tovagli'olo [tovaʎ'ʎɔlo] *sm* napkin.

'tozzo, a ['tɔttso] *ag* squat ♦ *sm:* ~ **di pane** crust of bread.

TP *sigla* = Trapani.

TR *sigla* = Terni.

Tr *abbr* (*COMM*) = **tratta**.

tra *prep* (*di due persone, cose*) between; (*di più persone, cose*) among(st); (*tempo: entro*) within, in; **prendere qn ~ le braccia** to take sb in one's arms; **litigano ~ (di) loro** they're fighting amongst themselves; ~ **5 giorni** in 5 days' time; ~ **breve** *o* **poco** soon; ~ **sé e sé** (*parlare etc*) to oneself; **sia detto ~ noi ...** between you and me ...; ~ **una cosa e l'altra** what with one thing and another.

trabal'lante *ag* shaky.

trabal'lare *vi* to stagger, totter.

tra'biccolo *sm* (*peg: auto*) old banger (*BRIT*), jalopy.

traboc'care *vi* to overflow.

traboc'chetto [trabok'ketto] *sm* (*fig*) trap ♦ *ag inv* trap *cpd;* **domanda** ~ trick question.

traca'gnotto, a [trakaɲ'ɲɔtto] *ag* dumpy ♦ *sm/f* dumpy person.

tracan'nare *vt* to gulp down.

'traccia, ce ['trattʃa] *sf* (*segno, striscia*) trail, track; (*orma*) tracks *pl*; (*residuo, testimonianza*) trace, sign; (*abbozzo*) outline; **essere sulle ~ce di qn** to be on sb's trail.

tracci'are [trat'tʃare] *vt* to trace, mark (out); (*disegnare*) to draw; (*fig: abbozzare*) to outline; ~ **un quadro della situazione** to outline the situation.

tracci'ato [trat'tʃato] *sm* (*grafico*) layout, plan; ~ **di gara** (*SPORT*) race route.

tra'chea [tra'kɛa] *sf* windpipe, trachea.

tra'colla *sf* shoulder strap; **portare qc a** ~ to carry sth over one's shoulder; **borsa a** ~ shoulder bag.

tra'collo *sm* (*fig*) collapse, ruin; ~ **finanziario** crash; **avere un** ~ (*MED*) to have a setback; (*COMM*) to collapse.

traco'tante *ag* overbearing, arrogant.

traco'tanza [trako'tantsa] *sf* arrogance.

trad. *abbr* = **traduzione**.

tradi'mento *sm* betrayal; (*DIR, MIL*) treason; **a** ~ by surprise; **alto** ~ high treason.

tra'dire *vt* to betray; (*coniuge*) to be unfaithful to; (*doveri: mancare*) to fail in; (*rivelare*) to give away, reveal; **ha tradito le attese di tutti** he let everyone down.

tradi'tore, 'trice *sm/f* traitor.

tradizio'nale [tradittsjo'nale] *ag* traditional.

tradizi'one [tradit'tsjone] *sf* tradition.

tra'dotto, a *pp di* **tradurre** ♦ *sf* (*MIL*) troop train.

tra'durre *vt* to translate; (*spiegare*) to render, convey; (*DIR*): ~ **qn in carcere/tribunale** to take sb to prison/court; ~ **in cifre** to put into figures; ~ **in atto** (*fig*) to put into effect.

tradut'tore, 'trice *sm/f* translator.

traduzi'one [tradut'tsjone] *sf* translation; (*DIR*) transfer.

'trae *vb vedi* **trarre**.

tra'ente *sm/f* (*ECON*) drawer.

trafe'lato *ag* out of breath.

traffi'cante *sm/f* dealer; (*peg*) trafficker.

traffi'care *vi* (*commerciare*): ~ (**in**) to trade (in), deal (in); (*affaccendarsi*) to busy o.s. ♦ *vt* (*peg*) to traffic in.

traffi'cato, a *ag* (*strada, zona*) busy.

'traffico, ci *sm* traffic; (*commercio*) trade, traffic; ~ **aereo/ferroviario** air/rail traffic; ~ **di droga** drug trafficking; ~ **stradale** traffic.

tra'figgere [tra'fiddʒere] *vt* to run through, stab; (*fig*) to pierce.

tra'fila *sf* procedure.

trafi'letto *sm* (*di giornale*) short article.

tra'fitto, a *pp di* **trafiggere**.

trafo'rare *vt* to bore, drill.

trafo'ro *sm* (*azione*) boring, drilling; (*galleria*) tunnel.

trafu'gare *vt* to purloin.

tra'gedia [tra'dʒɛdja] *sf* tragedy.

'traggo *etc vb vedi* **trarre**.

traghet'tare [traget'tare] *vt* to ferry.

tra'ghetto [tra'getto] *sm* crossing; (*barca*) ferry(boat).

tragicità [tradʒitʃi'ta] *sf* tragedy.

'tragico, a, ci, che ['tradʒiko] *ag* tragic ♦ *sm* (*autore*) tragedian; **prendere tutto sul** ~ (*fig*) to take everything far too seriously.

tragi'comico, a, ci, che [tradʒi'kɔmiko] *ag* tragicomic.

tra'gitto [tra'dʒitto] *sm* (*passaggio*) crossing; (*viaggio*) journey.

tragu'ardo *sm* (*SPORT*) finishing line; (*fig*) goal, aim.

'trai *etc vb vedi* **trarre**.

traiet'toria *sf* trajectory.

trai'nante *ag (cavo, fune)* towing; *(fig: persona, settore)* driving.

trai'nare *vt* to drag, haul; *(rimorchiare)* to tow.

'training ['trɛinin(g)] *sm inv* training.

'traino *sm (carro)* wagon; *(slitta)* sledge; *(carico)* load.

tralasci'are [tralaʃ'ʃare] *vt (studi)* to neglect; *(dettagli)* to leave out, omit.

'tralcio ['traltʃo] *sm (BOT)* shoot.

tra'liccio [tra'littʃo] *sm (tela)* ticking; *(struttura)* trellis; *(ELETTR)* pylon.

tram *sm inv* tram *(BRIT)*, streetcar *(US)*.

'trama *sf (filo)* weft, woof; *(fig: argomento, maneggio)* plot.

traman'dare *vt* to pass on, hand down.

tra'mare *vt (fig)* to scheme, plot.

tram'busto *sm* turmoil.

trames'tio *sm* bustle.

tramez'zino [tramed'dzino] *sm* sandwich.

tra'mezzo [tra'mɛddzo] *sm* partition.

'tramite *prep* through ♦ *sm* means *pl*; **agire/ fare da** ~ to act as/be a go-between.

tramon'tana *sf (METEOR)* north wind.

tramon'tare *vi* to set, go down.

tra'monto *sm* setting; *(del sole)* sunset.

tramor'tire *vi* to faint ♦ *vt* to stun.

trampo'lino *sm (per tuffi)* springboard, diving board; *(per lo sci)* ski-jump.

'trampolo *sm* stilt.

tramu'tare *vt:* ~ **in** to change into, turn into.

trance [traːns] *sf inv (di medium)* trance; **cadere in** ~ to fall into a trance.

'trancia, ce ['trantʃa] *sf* slice; *(cesoia)* shearing machine.

tranci'are [tran'tʃare] *vt (TECN)* to shear.

'trancio ['trantʃo] *sm* slice.

tra'nello *sm* trap; **tendere un** ~ **a qn** to set a trap for sb; **cadere in un** ~ to fall into a trap.

trangugi'are [trangu'dʒare] *vt* to gulp down.

'tranne *prep* except (for), but (for); ~ **che** *cong* unless; **tutti i giorni** ~ **il venerdì** every day except *o* with the exception of Friday.

tranquil'lante *sm (MED)* tranquillizer.

tranquillità *sf* calm, stillness; quietness; peace of mind.

tranquilliz'zare [trankwillid'dzare] *vt* to reassure.

tran'quillo, a *ag* calm, quiet; *(bambino, scolaro)* quiet; *(sereno)* with one's mind at rest; **sta'** ~ don't worry.

transat'lantico, a, ci, che *ag* transatlantic ♦ *sm* transatlantic liner; *(POL)* corridor used as a meeting place by members of the lower chamber of the Italian Parliament.

The **transatlantico** is a room in the **Palazzo di Montecitorio** used by the **deputati**, between parliamentary sessions, for relaxing and conversing with other members and also for giving interviews and press conferences to the media.

tran'satto, a *pp di* **transigere**.

transazi'one [transat'tsjone] *sf (DIR)* settlement; *(COMM)* transaction, deal.

tran'senna *sf* barrier.

tran'setto *sm* transept.

transiberi'ano, a *ag* trans-Siberian.

tran'sigere [tran'sidʒere] *vi (DIR)* to reach a settlement; *(venire a patti)* to compromise, come to an agreement.

tran'sistor *sm inv*, **transis'tore** *sm* transistor.

transi'tabile *ag* passable.

transi'tare *vi* to pass.

transi'tivo, a *ag* transitive.

'transito *sm* transit; **di** ~ *(merci)* in transit; *(stazione)* transit *cpd*; **"divieto di** ~" "no entry"; **"**~ **interrotto"** "road closed".

transi'torio, a *ag* transitory, transient; *(provvisorio)* provisional.

transizi'one [transit'tsjone] *sf* transition.

tran 'tran *sm* routine; **il solito** ~ the same old routine.

tran'via *sf* tramway *(BRIT)*, streetcar line *(US)*.

tranvi'ario, a *ag* tram *cpd (BRIT)*, streetcar *cpd (US)*; **linea** ~ **a** tramline, streetcar line.

tranvi'ere *sm (conducente)* tram driver *(BRIT)*, streetcar driver *(US)*; *(bigliettaio)* tram *o* streetcar conductor.

trapa'nare *vt (TECN)* to drill.

'trapano *sm (utensile)* drill; *(: MED)* trepan.

trapas'sare *vt* to pierce.

trapas'sato *sm (LING)* past perfect.

tra'passo *sm* passage; ~ **di proprietà** *(di case)* conveyancing; *(di auto etc)* legal transfer.

trape'lare *vi* to leak, drip; *(fig)* to leak out.

tra'pezio [tra'pɛttsjo] *sm (MAT)* trapezium; *(attrezzo ginnico)* trapeze.

trape'zista, i, e [trapet'tsista] *sm/f* trapeze artist.

trapian'tare *vt* to transplant.

trapi'anto *sm* transplanting; *(MED)* transplant.

'trappola *sf* trap.

tra'punta *sf* quilt.

'trarre *vt* to draw, pull; *(prendere, tirare fuori)* to take (out), draw; *(derivare)* to obtain; ~ **beneficio** *o* **profitto da qc** to benefit from sth; ~ **le conclusioni** to draw one's own conclusions; ~ **esempio da qn** to follow sb's example; ~ **guadagno** to make a profit; ~ **qn d'impaccio** to get sb out of an awkward situation; ~ **origine da qc** to have its origins *o* originate in sth; ~ **in salvo** to rescue.

trasa'lire *vi* to start, jump.

trasan'dato, a *ag* shabby.

trasbor'dare *vt* to transfer; (*NAUT*) to tran(s)ship ♦ *vi* (*NAUT*) to change ship; (*AER*) to change plane; (*FERR*) to change (trains).

trascenden'tale [traʃʃenden'tale] *ag* transcendental.

tra'scendere [traʃ'ʃendere] *vt* (*FILOSOFIA*, *REL*) to transcend; (*fig: superare*) to surpass, go beyond.

tra'sceso, a [traʃ'ʃeso] *pp di* **trascendere**.

trasci'nare [traʃʃi'nare] *vt* to drag; ~**rsi** *vr* to drag o.s. along; (*fig*) to drag on.

tras'correre *vt* (*tempo*) to spend, pass ♦ *vi* to pass.

tras'corso, a *pp di* **trascorrere** ♦ *ag* past ♦ *sm* mistake.

tras'critto, a *pp di* **trascrivere**.

tras'crivere *vt* to transcribe.

trascrizi'one [traskrit'tsjone] *sf* transcription.

trascu'rare *vt* to neglect; (*non considerare*) to disregard.

trascura'tezza [traskura'tettsa] *sf* carelessness, negligence.

trascu'rato, a *ag* (*casa*) neglected; (*persona*) careless, negligent.

traseco'lato, a *ag* astounded, amazed.

trasferi'mento *sm* transfer; (*trasloco*) removal, move.

trasfe'rire *vt* to transfer; ~**rsi** *vr* to move.

tras'ferta *sf* transfer; (*indennità*) travelling expenses *pl*; (*SPORT*) away game.

trasfigu'rare *vt* to transfigure.

trasfor'mare *vt* to transform, change.

trasforma'tore *sm* transformer.

trasformazi'one [trasformat'tsjone] *sf* transformation.

trasfusi'one *sf* (*MED*) transfusion.

trasgre'dire *vt* to break, infringe; (*ordini*) to disobey.

trasgressi'one *sf* breaking, infringement; disobeying.

trasgres'sivo, a *ag* (*personaggio*, *atteggiamento*) rule-breaking.

trasgres'sore, trasgredi'trice [trazgredi'tritʃe] *sm/f* (*DIR*) transgressor.

tras'lato, a *ag* metaphorical, figurative.

traslo'care *vt* to move, transfer; ~**rsi** *vr* to move.

tras'loco, chi *sm* removal.

tras'messo, a *pp di* **trasmettere**.

tras'mettere *vt* (*passare*): ~ **qc a qn** to pass sth on to sb; (*mandare*) to send; (*TECN, TEL, MED*) to transmit; (*TV, RADIO*) to broadcast.

trasmetti'tore *sm* transmitter.

trasmissi'one *sf* (*gen, FISICA, TECN*) transmission; (*passaggio*) transmission, passing on; (*TV, RADIO*) broadcast.

trasmit'tente *sf* transmitting *o* broadcasting station.

traso'gnato, a [trasoɲ'ɲato] *ag* dreamy.

traspa'rente *ag* transparent.

traspa'renza [traspa'rentsa] *sf* transparency; **guardare qc in** ~ to look at sth against the light.

traspa'rire *vi* to show (through).

tras'parso, a *pp di* **trasparire**.

traspi'rare *vi* to perspire; (*fig*) to come to light, leak out.

traspirazi'one [traspirat'tsjone] *sf* perspiration.

tras'porre *vt* to transpose.

traspor'tare *vt* to carry, move; (*merce*) to transport, convey; **lasciarsi** ~ (**da qc**) (*fig*) to let o.s. be carried away (by sth).

tras'porto *sm* transport; (*fig*) rapture, passion; **con** ~ passionately; **compagnia di** ~ carriers *pl*; (*per strada*) hauliers *pl* (*BRIT*), haulers *pl* (*US*); **mezzi di** ~ means of transport; **nave/aereo da** ~ transport ship/aircraft *inv*; ~ (**funebre**) funeral procession; ~ **marittimo/aereo** sea/air transport; ~ **stradale** (road) haulage; **i** ~**i pubblici** public transport.

tras'posto, a *pp di* **trasporre**.

'trassi *etc vb vedi* **trarre**.

trastul'lare *vt* to amuse; ~**rsi** *vr* to amuse o.s.

tras'tullo *sm* game.

trasu'dare *vi* (*filtrare*) to ooze; (*sudare*) to sweat ♦ *vt* to ooze with.

trasver'sale *ag* (*taglio, sbarra*) cross(-); (*retta*) transverse; **via** ~ side street.

trasvo'lare *vt* to fly over.

'tratta *sf* (*ECON*) draft; (*di persone*): **la** ~ **delle bianche** the white slave trade; ~ **documentaria** documentary bill of exchange.

tratta'mento *sm* treatment; (*servizio*) service; **ricevere un buon** ~ (*cliente*) to get good service; ~ **di bellezza** beauty treatment; ~ **di fine rapporto** (*COMM*) severance pay.

trat'tare *vt* (*gen*) to treat; (*commerciare*) to

deal in; (*svolgere: argomento*) to discuss, deal with; (*negoziare*) to negotiate ♦ *vi*: ~ **di** to deal with; ~ **con** (*persona*) to deal with; **si tratta di ...** it's about ...; **si tratterebbe solo di poche ore** it would just be a matter of a few hours.

tratta'tiva *sf* negotiation; ~**e** *sfpl* (*tra governi, stati*) talks; **essere in** ~ **con** to be in negotiation with.

trat'tato *sm* (*testo*) treatise; (*accordo*) treaty; ~ **commerciale** trade agreement; ~ **di pace** peace treaty.

trattazi'one [trattat'tsjone] *sf* treatment.

tratteggi'are [tratted'dʒare] *vt* (*disegnare: a tratti*) to sketch, outline; (*: col tratteggio*) to hatch.

trat'teggio [trat'teddʒo] *sm* hatching.

tratte'nere *vt* (*far rimanere: persona*) to detain; (*tenere, frenare, reprimere*) to hold back, keep back; (*astenersi dal consegnare*) to hold, keep; (*detrarre: somma*) to deduct; ~**rsi** *vr* (*astenersi*) to restrain o.s., stop o.s.; (*soffermarsi*) to stay, remain; **sono stato trattenuto in ufficio** I was delayed at the office.

tratteni'mento *sm* entertainment; (*festa*) party.

tratte'nuta *sf* deduction.

trat'tino *sm* dash; (*in parole composte*) hyphen.

'tratto, a *pp di* **trarre** ♦ *sm* (*di penna, matita*) stroke; (*parte*) part, piece; (*di strada*) stretch; (*di mare, cielo*) expanse; (*di tempo*) period (of time); ~**i** *smpl* (*caratteristiche*) features; (*modo di fare*) ways, manners; **a un** ~, **d'un** ~ suddenly.

trat'tore *sm* tractor.

tratto'ria *sf* (small) restaurant.

'trauma, i *sm* trauma; ~ **cranico** concussion.

trau'matico, a, ci, che *ag* traumatic.

traumatiz'zare [traumatid'dzare] *vt* (*MED*) to traumatize; (*fig: impressionare*) to shock.

tra'vaglio [tra'vaʎʎo] *sm* (*angoscia*) pain, suffering; (*MED*) pains *pl*; ~ **di parto** labour pains.

trava'sare *vt* to pour; (*vino*) to decant.

tra'vaso *sm* pouring; decanting.

trava'tura *sf* beams *pl*.

'trave *sf* beam.

tra'veggole *sfpl*: **avere le** ~ to be seeing things.

tra'versa *sf* (*trave*) crosspiece; (*via*) sidestreet; (*FERR*) sleeper (*BRIT*), (railroad) tie (*US*); (*CALCIO*) crossbar.

traver'sare *vt* to cross.

traver'sata *sf* crossing; (*AER*) flight, trip.

traver'sie *sfpl* mishaps, misfortunes.

traver'sina *sf* (*FERR*) sleeper (*BRIT*), (railroad) tie (*US*).

tra'verso, a *ag* oblique; **di** ~ *ag* askew ♦ *av* sideways; **andare di** ~ (*cibo*) to go down the wrong way; **messo di** ~ sideways on; **guardare di** ~ to look askance at; **via** ~**a** side road; **ottenere qc per vie** ~**e** (*fig*) to obtain sth in an underhand way.

travesti'mento *sm* disguise.

traves'tire *vt* to disguise; ~**rsi** *vr* to disguise o.s.

traves'tito *sm* transvestite.

travi'are *vt* (*fig*) to lead astray.

travi'sare *vt* (*fig*) to distort, misrepresent.

travol'gente [travol'dʒɛnte] *ag* overwhelming.

tra'volgere [tra'vɔldʒere] *vt* to sweep away, carry away; (*fig*) to overwhelm.

tra'volto, a *pp di* **travolgere**.

trazi'one [trat'tsjone] *sf* traction; ~ **anteriore/posteriore** (*AUT*) front-wheel/rear-wheel drive.

tre *num* three.

tre'alberi *sm inv* (*NAUT*) three-master.

'trebbia *sf* (*AGR: operazione*) threshing; (*: stagione*) threshing season.

trebbi'are *vt* to thresh.

trebbia'trice [trebbja'tritʃe] *sf* threshing machine.

trebbia'tura *sf* threshing.

'treccia, ce ['trettʃa] *sf* plait, braid; **lavorato a** ~**ce** (*pullover etc*) cable-knit.

trecen'tesco, a, schi, sche [tretʃen'tesko] *ag* fourteenth-century.

tre'cento [tre'tʃento] *num* three hundred ♦ *sm*: **il T**~ the fourteenth century.

tredi'cenne [tredi'tʃɛnne] *ag, sm/f* thirteen-year-old.

tredi'cesimo, a [tredi'tʃɛzimo] *num* thirteenth ♦ *sf* Christmas bonus of a month's pay.

'tredici ['treditʃi] *num* thirteen ♦ *sm inv*: **fare** ~ (*TOTOCALCIO*) to win the pools (*BRIT*).

'tregua *sf* truce; (*fig*) respite; **senza** ~ non-stop, without stopping, uninterruptedly.

tre'mante *ag* trembling, shaking.

tre'mare *vi* to tremble, shake; ~ **di** (*freddo etc*) to shiver o tremble with; (*paura, rabbia*) to shake o tremble with.

trema'rella *sf* shivers *pl*.

tremen'tina *sf* turpentine.

tre'mila *num* three thousand.

'tremito *sm* trembling *no pl*; shaking *no pl*; shivering *no pl*.

tremo'lare *vi* to tremble; (*luce*) to flicker; (*foglie*) to quiver.

tremo'lio *sm* (*vedi vi*) tremble; flicker; quiver.

tre'more *sm* tremor.

'treno *sm* train; (*AUT*): ~ **di gomme** set of tyres; ~ **locale/diretto/espresso** local/fast/express train; ~ **merci** goods (*BRIT*) *o* freight train; ~ **rapido** express (train) (*for which supplement must be paid*); ~ **straordinario** special train; ~ **viaggiatori** passenger train.

> **Treni** *in Italy are of numerous different types: the regionali and interregionali are local trains which stop at every small town and village; the former operate within regional boundaries, while the latter may cross these. The* **diretti** *are ordinary trains for which no supplement need be paid and differ from the* **espressi** *principally in that the latter are long-distance trains which travel mainly during the night. The intercity and eurocity are faster trains for which a supplement must be paid when one buys one's ticket. The* **rapidi** *operate a first-class service only, and the high-speed pendolino, which offers both first and second-class travel, runs between Milan and Rome.*

'trenta *num* thirty ♦ *sm inv* (*INS*): ~ **e lode** full marks plus distinction *o* cum laude.

tren'tenne *ag*, *sm/f* thirty-year-old.

tren'tennio *sm* period of thirty years.

tren'tesimo, a *num* thirtieth.

tren'tina *sf*: **una** ~ (**di**) thirty or so, about thirty.

tren'tino, a *ag* of (*o* from) Trento.

trepi'dante *ag* anxious.

trepi'dare *vi* to be anxious; ~ **per qn** to be anxious about sb.

'trepido, a *ag* anxious.

treppi'ede *sm* tripod; (*CUC*) trivet.

tre'quarti *sm inv* three-quarter-length coat.

'tresca, sche *sf* (*fig*) intrigue; (*: relazione amorosa*) affair.

'trespolo *sm* trestle.

trevigi'ano, a [trevi'dʒano] *ag* of (*o* from) Treviso.

triango'lare *ag* triangular.

tri'angolo *sm* triangle.

tribo'lare *vi* (*patire*) to suffer; (*fare fatica*) to have a lot of trouble.

tribolazi'one [tribolat'tsjone] *sf* suffering, tribulation.

tri'bordo *sm* (*NAUT*) starboard.

tribù *sf inv* tribe.

tri'buna *sf* (*podio*) platform; (*in aule etc*) gallery; (*di stadio*) stand; ~ **della stampa/riservata al pubblico** press/public gallery.

tribu'nale *sm* court; **presentarsi** *o* **comparire in** ~ to appear in court; ~ **militare** military tribunal; ~ **supremo** supreme court.

tribu'tare *vt* to bestow; ~ **gli onori dovuti a qn** to pay tribute to sb.

tribu'tario, a *ag* (*imposta*) fiscal, tax *cpd*; (*GEO*): **essere** ~ **di** to be a tributary of.

tri'buto *sm* tax; (*fig*) tribute.

tri'checo, chi [tri'kɛko] *sm* (*ZOOL*) walrus.

tri'ciclo [tri'tʃiklo] *sm* tricycle.

trico'lore *ag* three-coloured (*BRIT*), three-colored (*US*) ♦ *sm* tricolo(u)r; (*bandiera italiana*) Italian flag.

tri'dente *sm* trident.

trien'nale *ag* (*che dura 3 anni*) three-year *cpd*; (*che avviene ogni 3 anni*) three-yearly.

tri'ennio *sm* period of three years.

tries'tino, a *ag* of (*o* from) Trieste.

tri'fase *ag* (*ELETTR*) three-phase.

tri'foglio [tri'fɔʎʎo] *sm* clover.

trifo'lato, a *ag* (*CUC*) cooked in oil, garlic and parsley.

'triglia ['triʎʎa] *sf* red mullet.

trigonome'tria *sf* trigonometry.

tril'lare *vi* (*MUS*) to trill.

'trillo *sm* trill.

tri'mestre *sm* period of three months; (*INS*) term, quarter (*US*); (*COMM*) quarter.

trimo'tore *sm* (*AER*) three-engined plane.

'trina *sf* lace.

trin'cea [trin'tʃea] *sf* trench.

trince'rare [trintʃe'rare] *vt* to entrench.

trinci'are [trin'tʃare] *vt* to cut up.

'Trinidad *sm*: ~ **e Tobago** Trinidad and Tobago.

Trinità *sf* (*REL*) Trinity.

'trio, *pl* **'trii** *sm* trio.

trion'fale *ag* triumphal, triumphant.

trion'fante *ag* triumphant.

trion'fare *vi* to triumph, win; ~ **su** to triumph over, overcome.

tri'onfo *sm* triumph.

tripli'care *vt* to triple.

'triplice ['triplitʃe] *ag* triple; **in** ~ **copia** in triplicate.

'triplo, a *ag* triple, treble ♦ *sm*: **il** ~ (**di**) three times as much (as); **la spesa è** ~**a** it costs three times as much.

'tripode *sm* tripod.

'Tripoli *sf* Tripoli.

'trippa *sf* (*CUC*) tripe.

tri'pudio *sm* triumph, jubilation; (*fig: di colori*) galaxy.

tris *sm inv* (*CARTE*): ~ **d'assi/di re** *etc* three aces/kings *etc*.

'triste *ag* sad; (*luogo*) dreary, gloomy.

tris'tezza [tris'tettsa] *sf* sadness;

gloominess.

'tristo, a *ag* (*cattivo*) wicked, evil; (*meschino*) sorry, poor.

trita'carne *sm inv* mincer, grinder (*US*).

trita'ghiaccio [trita'gjattʃo] *sm inv* ice crusher.

tri'tare *vt* to mince, grind (*US*).

trita'tutto *sm inv* mincer, grinder (*US*).

'trito, a *ag* (*tritato*) minced, ground (*US*); ~ e ritrito (*idee, argomenti, frasi*) trite, hackneyed.

tri'tolo *sm* trinitrotoluene.

tri'tone *sm* (*ZOOL*) newt.

'trittico, ci *sm* (*ARTE*) triptych.

tritu'rare *vt* to grind.

tri'vella *sf* drill.

trivel'lare *vt* to drill.

trivellazi'one [trivellat'tsjone] *sf* drilling; torre di ~ derrick.

trivi'ale *ag* vulgar, low.

trivialità *sf inv* (*volgarità*) coarseness, crudeness; (: *osservazione*) coarse *o* crude remark.

tro'feo *sm* trophy.

'trogolo *sm* (*per maiali*) trough.

'troia *sf* (*ZOOL*) sow; (*fig peg*) whore.

'tromba *sf* (*MUS*) trumpet; (*AUT*) horn; ~ d'aria whirlwind; ~ delle scale stairwell.

trombet'tista, i, e *sm/f* trumpeter, trumpet (player).

trom'bone *sm* trombone.

trom'bosi *sf* thrombosis.

tron'care *vt* to cut off; (*spezzare*) to break off.

'tronco, a, chi, che *ag* cut off; broken off; (*LING*) truncated ♦ *sm* (*BOT, ANAT*) trunk; (*fig: tratto*) section; (: *pezzo: di lancia*) stump; licenziare qn in ~ (*fig*) to fire sb on the spot.

troneggi'are [troned'dʒare] *vi:* ~ (su) to tower (over).

'tronfio, a *ag* conceited.

'trono *sm* throne.

tropi'cale *ag* tropical.

'tropico, ci *sm* tropic; ~ del Cancro/Capricorno Tropic of Cancer/Capricorn; i ~ci the tropics.

════════ *PAROLA CHIAVE*

'troppo, a *det* (*in eccesso: quantità*) too much; (: *numero*) too many; ho messo ~ zucchero I put too much sugar in; c'era ~a gente there were too many people ♦ *pron* (*in eccesso: quantità*) too much; (: *numero*) too many; ne hai messo ~ you've put in too much; meglio ~i che pochi better too many than too few ♦ *av* (*eccessivamente: con ag, av*) too; (: *con*

vb*) too much; ~ amaro/tardi too bitter/late; lavora ~ he works too much; ~ buono da parte tua! (*anche ironico*) you're too kind!; di ~ too much; too many; qualche tazza di ~ a few cups too many; 3000 lire di ~ 3000 lire too much; essere di ~ to be in the way.

'trota *sf* trout.

trot'tare *vi* to trot.

trotterel'lare *vi* to trot along; (*bambino*) to toddle.

'trotto *sm* trot.

'trottola *sf* spinning top.

tro'vare *vt* to find; (*giudicare*): trovo che I find *o* think that; ~rsi *vr* (*reciproco: incontrarsi*) to meet; (*essere, stare*) to be; (*arrivare, capitare*) to find o.s.; andare a ~ qn to go and see sb; ~ qn colpevole to find sb guilty; trovo giusto/sbagliato che ... I think/don't think it's right that ...; ~rsi bene/male (*in un luogo, con qn*) to get on well/badly; ~rsi d'accordo con qn to be in agreement with sb.

tro'vata *sf* good idea; ~ pubblicitaria advertising gimmick.

trova'tello, a *sm/f* foundling.

truc'care *vt* (*falsare*) to fake; (*attore etc*) to make up; (*travestire*) to disguise; (*SPORT*) to fix; (*AUT*) to soup up; ~rsi *vr* to make up (one's face).

trucca'tore, 'trice *sm/f* (*CINE, TEAT*) make-up artist.

'trucco, chi *sm* trick; (*cosmesi*) make-up; i ~chi del mestiere the tricks of the trade.

'truce ['trutʃe] *ag* fierce.

truci'dare [trutʃi'dare] *vt* to slaughter.

'truciolo ['trutʃolo] *sm* shaving.

'truffa *sf* fraud, swindle.

truf'fare *vt* to swindle, cheat.

truffa'tore, 'trice *sm/f* swindler, cheat.

'truppa *sf* troop.

TS *sigla* = Trieste.

tu *pron* you; ~ stesso(a) you yourself; dare del ~ a qn to address sb as "tu"; trovarsi a ~ per ~ con qn to find o.s. face to face with sb.

'tua *vedi* tuo.

'tuba *sf* (*MUS*) tuba; (*cappello*) top hat.

tu'bare *vi* to coo.

tuba'tura *sf*, tubazi'one [tubat'tsjone] *sf* piping *no pl*, pipes *pl*.

tuberco'losi *sf* tuberculosis.

'tubero *sm* (*BOT*) tuber.

tu'betto *sm* tube.

tu'bino *sm* (*cappello*) bowler (*BRIT*), derby (*US*); (*abito da donna*) sheath dress.

'tubo *sm* tube; (*per conduttore*) pipe; ~

digerente (*ANAT*) alimentary canal, digestive tract; ~ **di scappamento** (*AUT*) exhaust pipe.

tubo'lare *ag* tubular ♦ *sm* tubeless tyre (*BRIT*) *o* tire (*US*).

'tue *vedi* **tuo.**

tuf'fare *vt* to plunge; (*intingere*) to dip; ~**rsi** *vr* to plunge, dive.

tuffa'tore, 'trice *sm/f* (*SPORT*) diver.

'tuffo *sm* dive; (*breve bagno*) dip.

tu'gurio *sm* hovel.

tuli'pano *sm* tulip.

'tulle *sm* (*tessuto*) tulle.

tume'fare *vt* to cause to swell; ~**rsi** *vr* to swell.

'tumido, a *ag* swollen.

tu'more *sm* (*MED*) tumour (*BRIT*), tumor (*US*).

tumulazi'one [tumulat'tsjone] *sf* burial.

tu'multo *sm* uproar, commotion; (*sommossa*) riot; (*fig*) turmoil.

tumultu'oso, a *ag* rowdy, unruly; (*fig*) turbulent, stormy.

tungs'teno *sm* tungsten.

'tunica, che *sf* tunic.

'Tunisi *sf* Tunis.

Tuni'sia *sf*: **la** ~ Tunisia.

tuni'sino, a *ag, sm/f* Tunisian.

'tunnel *sm inv* tunnel.

'tuo, 'tua, tu'oi, 'tue *det*: **il** ~, **la tua** *etc* your ♦ *pron*: **il** ~, **la tua** *etc* yours ♦ *sm*: **hai speso del** ~? did you spend your own money? ♦ *sf*: **la** ~**a** (*opinione*) your view; **i tuoi** (*genitori, famiglia*) your family; **una** ~**a amica** a friend of yours; **è dalla** ~**a** he is on your side; **alla** ~**a!** (*brindisi*) your health!; **ne hai fatta una delle** ~**e!** (*sciocchezze*) you've done it again!

tuo'nare *vi* to thunder; **tuona** it is thundering, there's some thunder.

tu'ono *sm* thunder.

tu'orlo *sm* yolk.

tu'racciolo [tu'rattʃolo] *sm* cap, top; (*di sughero*) cork.

tu'rare *vt* to stop, plug; (*con sughero*) to cork; ~**rsi il naso** to hold one's nose.

'turba *sf* (*folla*) crowd, throng; (: *peg*) mob; ~**e** *sfpl* disorder(s); **soffrire di** ~**e psichiche** to suffer from a mental disorder.

turba'mento *sm* disturbance; (*di animo*) anxiety, agitation.

tur'bante *sm* turban.

tur'bare *vt* to disturb, trouble; ~ **la quiete pubblica** (*DIR*) to disturb the peace.

tur'bina *sf* turbine.

turbi'nare *vi* to whirl.

'turbine *sm* whirlwind; ~ **di neve** swirl of snow; ~ **di polvere/sabbia** dust/ sandstorm.

turbi'noso, a *ag* (*vento, danza etc*) whirling.

turbo'lento, a *ag* turbulent; (*ragazzo*) boisterous, unruly.

turbo'lenza [turbo'lɛntsa] *sf* turbulence.

turboreat'tore *sm* turbojet engine.

tur'chese [tur'kese] *ag, sm, sf* turquoise.

Tur'chia [tur'kia] *sf*: **la** ~ Turkey.

tur'chino, a [tur'kino] *ag* deep blue.

'turco, a, chi, che *ag* Turkish ♦ *sm/f* Turk/ Turkish woman ♦ *sm* (*LING*) Turkish; **parlare** ~ (*fig*) to talk double Dutch.

'turgido, a ['turdʒido] *ag* swollen.

tu'rismo *sm* tourism.

tu'rista, i, e *sm/f* tourist.

tu'ristico, a, ci, che *ag* tourist *cpd*.

tur'nista, i, e *sm/f* shift worker.

'turno *sm* turn; (*di lavoro*) shift; **di** ~ (*soldato, medico, custode*) on duty; **a** ~ (*rispondere*) in turn; (*lavorare*) in shifts; **fare a** ~ **a fare qc** to take turns to do sth; **è il suo** ~ it's your (*o* his *etc*) turn.

'turpe *ag* filthy, vile.

turpi'loquio *sm* obscene language.

'tuta *sf* overalls *pl*; (*SPORT*) tracksuit; ~ **mimetica** (*MIL*) camouflage clothing; ~ **spaziale** spacesuit; ~ **subacquea** wetsuit.

tu'tela *sf* (*DIR*: *di minore*) guardianship; (: *protezione*) protection; (*difesa*) defence (*BRIT*), defense (*US*); ~ **dell'ambiente** environmental protection; ~ **del consumatore** consumer protection.

tute'lare *vt* to protect, defend ♦ *ag* (*DIR*): **giudice** ~ *judge with responsibility for guardianship cases.*

tu'tore, 'trice *sm/f* (*DIR*) guardian.

tutta'via *cong* nevertheless, yet.

════════════════ *PAROLA CHIAVE*

'tutto, a *det* **1** (*intero*) all; ~ **il latte** all the milk; ~**a la notte** all night, the whole night; ~ **il libro** the whole book; ~**a una bottiglia** a whole bottle; **in** ~ **il mondo** all over the world

2 (*pl, collettivo*) all; every; ~**i i libri** all the books; ~**e le notti** every night; ~**i i venerdì** every Friday; ~**i gli uomini** all the men; (*collettivo*) all men; ~**e le volte che** every time (that); ~**i e due** both *o* each of us (*o* them *o* you); ~**i e cinque** all five of us (*o* them *o* you)

3 (*completamente*): **era** ~**a sporca** she was all dirty; **tremava** ~ he was trembling all over; **è** ~**a sua madre** she's just *o* exactly like her mother

4: **a tutt'oggi** so far, up till now; **a** ~**a velocità** at full *o* top speed

◆ *pron* **1** (*ogni cosa*) everything, all; (*qualsiasi cosa*) anything; **ha mangiato ~** he's eaten everything; **~ tell me** all about it; **~ compreso** all included, all-in (*BRIT*); **~ considerato** all things considered; **con ~ che** (*malgrado*) although; **del ~** completely; **10.000 lire in ~** 10,000 lire in all; **in ~ eravamo 50** there were 50 of us in all; **in ~ e per ~** completely; **il che è ~ dire** and that's saying a lot **2**: **~i, e** (*ognuno*) all, everybody; **vengono ~i** they are all coming, everybody's coming; **~i sanno che** everybody knows that; **~i quanti** all and sundry ◆ *av* (*completamente*) entirely, quite; **è ~ il contrario** it's quite *o* exactly the opposite; **tutt'al più: saranno stati tutt'al più una cinquantina** there were about fifty of them at (the very) most; **tutt'al più possiamo prendere un treno** if the worst comes to the worst we can take a train; **tutt'altro** on the contrary; **è tutt'altro che felice** he's anything but happy; **tutt'intorno** all around; **tutt'a un tratto** suddenly ◆ *sm*: **il ~** the whole lot, all of it; **il ~ si è svolto senza incidenti** it all went off without incident; **il ~ le costerà due milioni** the whole thing will cost you two million.

tutto'fare *ag inv*: **domestica ~** general maid; **ragazzo ~** office boy ◆ *sm/f inv* handyman/woman.
tut'tora *av* still.
tutù *sm inv* tutu, ballet skirt.
TV [ti'vu] *sf inv* (= *televisione*) TV ◆ *sigla* = *Treviso*.

U u

U, u [u] *sf o m inv* (*lettera*) U, u; **U come Udine** ≈ U for Uncle; **inversione ad U** U-turn.
ub'bia *sf* (*letterario*) irrational fear.
ubbidi'ente *ag* obedient.
ubbidi'enza [ubbi'djɛntsa] *sf* obedience.
ubbi'dire *vi* to obey; **~ a** to obey; (*sog: veicolo, macchina*) to respond to.
ubicazi'one [ubikat'tsjone] *sf* site, location.

ubiquità *sf*: **non ho il dono dell'~** I can't be everywhere at once.
ubria'care *vt*: **~ qn** to get sb drunk; (*sog: alcool*) to make sb drunk; (*fig*) to make sb's head spin *o* reel; **~rsi** *vr* to get drunk; **~rsi di** (*fig*) to become intoxicated with.
ubria'chezza [ubria'kettsa] *sf* drunkenness.
ubri'aco, a, chi, che *ag, sm/f* drunk.
ubria'cone *sm* drunkard.
uccellagi'one [uttʃella'dʒone] *sf* bird catching.
uccelli'era [uttʃel'ljɛra] *sf* aviary.
uccel'lino [uttʃel'lino] *sm* baby bird, chick.
uc'cello [ut'tʃello] *sm* bird.
uc'cidere [ut'tʃidere] *vt* to kill; **~rsi** *vr* (*suicidarsi*) to kill o.s.; (*perdere la vita*) to be killed.
uccisi'one [uttʃi'zjone] *sf* killing.
uc'ciso, a [ut'tʃizo] *pp di* **uccidere**.
ucci'sore [uttʃi'zore] *sm* killer.
U'craina *sf* Ukraine.
u'craino, a *ag, sm/f* Ukrainian.
UD *sigla* = *Udine*.
U.D.C. *sigla f* (*POL*: = *Unione di Centro*) centre party.
u'dente *sm/f*: **i non udenti** the hard of hearing.
u'dibile *ag* audible.
udi'enza [u'djɛntsa] *sf* audience; (*DIR*) hearing; **dare ~ (a)** to grant an audience (to); **~ a porte chiuse** hearing in camera.
u'dire *vt* to hear.
udi'tivo, a *ag* auditory.
u'dito *sm* (sense of) hearing.
udi'tore, 'trice *sm/f* listener; (*INS*) unregistered student (*attending lectures*).
udi'torio *sm* (*persone*) audience.
U.E. *abbr* = *uso esterno*.
UEFA *sigla f* UEFA (= *Union of European Football Associations*).
'uffa *escl* tut!
uffici'ale [uffi'tʃale] *ag* official ◆ *sm* (*AMM*) official, officer; (*MIL*) officer; **pubblico ~** public official; **~ giudiziario** clerk of the court; **~ di marina** naval officer; **~ sanitario** health inspector; **~ di stato civile** registrar.
ufficializ'zare [uffitʃalid'dzare] *vt* to make official.
uf'ficio [uf'fitʃo] *sm* (*gen*) office; (*dovere*) duty; (*mansione*) task, function, job; (*agenzia*) agency, bureau; (*REL*) service; **d'~** *ag* office *cpd*; official ◆ *av* officially; **provvedere d'~** to act officially; **convocare d'~** (*DIR*) to summons; **difensore *o* avvocato d'~** (*DIR*) court-appointed counsel for the defence; **~ brevetti** patent office; **~ di collocamento**

employment office; ~ **informazioni**
information bureau; ~ **oggetti smarriti**
lost property office (*BRIT*), lost and found
(*US*); ~ **postale** post office; ~ **vendite/del**
personale sales/personnel department.
uffici'oso, a [uffi't∫oso] *ag* unofficial.
'UFO *sm inv* (= *unidentified flying object*)
UFO.
'ufo: a ~ *av* free, for nothing.
U'ganda *sf:* **l'~** Uganda.
'uggia ['uddʒa] *sf* (*noia*) boredom; (*fastidio*)
bore; **avere/prendere qn in** ~ to dislike/
take a dislike to sb.
uggi'oso, a [ud'dʒoso] *ag* tiresome; (*tempo*)
dull.
'ugola *sf* uvula.
uguagli'anza [ugwaʎ'ʎantsa] *sf* equality.
uguagli'are [ugwaʎ'ʎare] *vt* to make equal;
(*essere uguale*) to equal, be equal to;
(*livellare*) to level; **~rsi** *vr*: **~rsi a** *o* **con qn**
(*paragonarsi*) to compare o.s. to sb.
ugu'ale *ag* equal; (*identico*) identical, the
same; (*uniforme*) level, even ♦ *av*: **costano**
~ they cost the same; **sono bravi** ~
they're equally good.
ugual'mente *av* equally; (*lo stesso*) all the
same.
U.I. *abbr* = *uso interno*.
UIL *sigla f* (= *Unione Italiana del Lavoro*)
trade union federation.
'ulcera ['ult∫era] *sf* ulcer.
ulcerazi'one [ult∫erat'tsjone] *sf* ulceration.
u'liva *etc* = *oliva etc.*
ulteri'ore *ag* further.
ultima'mente *av* lately, of late.
ulti'mare *vt* to finish, complete.
ulti'matum *sm inv* ultimatum.
ulti'missime *sfpl* latest news *sg*.
'ultimo, a *ag* (*finale*) last; (*estremo*)
farthest, utmost; (*recente: notizia, moda*)
latest; (*fig: sommo, fondamentale*) ultimate
♦ *sm/f* last (one); **fino all'~** to the last, until
the end; **da** ~, **in** ~ in the end; **per** ~
(*entrare, arrivare*) last; **abitare all'~ piano**
to live on the top floor; **in** ~**a pagina** (*di*
giornale) on the back page; **negli** ~**i tempi**
recently; **all'~ momento** at the last
minute; ... **la vostra lettera del 7 aprile** ~
scorso ... your letter of April 7th last; **in**
~**a analisi** in the final *o* last analysis; **in** ~
luogo finally.
ultrà *sm/f* ultra.
ultrasi'nistra *sf* (*POL*) extreme left.
ultrasu'ono *sm* ultrasound.
ultravio'letto, a *ag* ultraviolet.
ulu'lare *vi* to howl.
ulu'lato *sm* howling *no pl*; howl.
umana'mente *av* (*con umanità*) humanely;

(*nei limiti delle capacità umane*) humanly.
uma'nesimo *sm* humanism.
umanità *sf* humanity.
umani'tario, a *ag* humanitarian.
umaniz'zare [umanid'dzare] *vt* to
humanize.
u'mano, a *ag* human; (*comprensivo*)
humane.
umbi'lico *sm* = *ombelico*.
'umbro, a *ag* of (*o* from) Umbria.
umet'tare *vt* to dampen, moisten.
umi'diccio, a, ci, ce [umi'dittʃo] *ag*
(*terreno*) damp; (*mano*) moist, clammy.
umidifi'care *vt* to humidify.
umidifica'tore *sm* humidifier.
umidità *sf* dampness; moistness; humidity.
'umido, a *ag* damp; (*mano, occhi*) moist;
(*clima*) humid ♦ *sm* dampness, damp;
carne in ~ stew.
u'mile *ag* humble.
umili'ante *ag* humiliating.
umili'are *vt* to humiliate; **~rsi** *vr* to humble
o.s.
umiliazi'one [umiljat'tsjone] *sf* humiliation.
umiltà *sf* humility, humbleness.
u'more *sm* (*disposizione d'animo*) mood;
(*carattere*) temper; **di buon/cattivo** ~ in a
good/bad mood.
umo'rismo *sm* humour (*BRIT*), humor (*US*);
avere il senso dell'~ to have a sense of
humo(u)r.
umo'rista, i, e *sm/f* humorist.
umo'ristico, a, ci, che *ag* humorous,
funny.
un, un', una *vedi* **uno**.
u'nanime *ag* unanimous.
unanimità *sf* unanimity; **all'**~
unanimously.
'una 'tantum *ag* one-off *cpd* ♦ *sf* (*imposta*)
one-off tax.
unci'nato, a [unt∫i'nato] *ag* (*amo*) barbed;
(*ferro*) hooked; **croce** ~**a** swastika.
unci'netto [unt∫i'netto] *sm* crochet hook.
un'cino [un't∫ino] *sm* hook.
undi'cenne [undi't∫enne] *ag, sm/f* eleven-
year-old.
undi'cesimo, a [undi't∫ezimo] *ag* eleventh.
'undici ['undit∫i] *num* eleven.
U'NESCO *sigla f* (= *United Nations*
Educational, Scientific and Cultural
Organization) UNESCO.
'ungere ['undʒere] *vt* to grease, oil; (*REL*) to
anoint; (*fig*) to flatter, butter up; **~rsi** *vr*
(*sporcarsi*) to get covered in grease; **~rsi**
con la crema to put on cream.
unghe'rese [unge'rese] *ag, sm/f, sm*
Hungarian.
Unghe'ria [unge'ria] *sf:* **l'**~ Hungary.

'unghia ['ungja] *sf* (*ANAT*) nail; (*di animale*) claw; (*di rapace*) talon; (*di cavallo*) hoof; **pagare sull'~** (*fig*) to pay on the nail

unghi'ata [un'gjata] *sf* (*graffio*) scratch.

ungu'ento *sm* ointment.

unica'mente *av* only.

'UNICEF ['unitʃef] *sigla m* (= United Nations International Children's Emergency Fund) UNICEF.

'unico, a, ci, che *ag* (*solo*) only; (*ineguagliabile*) unique; (*singolo: binario*) single; **è figlio ~** he's an only child; **atto ~** (*TEAT*) one-act play; **agente ~** (*COMM*) sole agent.

uni'corno *sm* unicorn.

unifi'care *vt* to unite, unify; (*sistemi*) to standardize.

unificazi'one [unifikat'tsjone] *sf* unification; standardization.

unifor'mare *vt* (*terreno, superficie*) to level; **~rsi** *vr*: **~rsi a** to conform to; **~ qc a** to adjust *o* relate sth to.

uni'forme *ag* uniform; (*superficie*) even ♦ *sf* (*divisa*) uniform; **alta ~** dress uniform.

uniformità *sf* uniformity; evenness.

unilate'rale *ag* one-sided; (*DIR, POL*) unilateral.

uninomi'nale *ag* (*POL: collegio, sistema*) single-candidate *cpd*.

uni'one *sf* union; (*fig: concordia*) unity, harmony; **l'U~ Sovietica** the Soviet Union.

u'nire *vt* to unite; (*congiungere*) to join, connect; (*: ingredienti, colori*) to combine; (*in matrimonio*) to unite, join together; **~rsi** *vr* to unite; (*in matrimonio*) to be joined together; **~ qc a** to unite sth with; to join *o* connect sth with; to combine sth with; **~rsi a** (*gruppo, società*) to join.

u'nisono *sm*: **all'~** in unison.

unità *sf inv* (*unione, concordia*) unity; (*MAT, MIL, COMM, di misura*) unit; **~ centrale (di elaborazione)** (*INFORM*) central processing unit; **~ disco** (*INFORM*) disk drive; **~ monetaria** monetary unit.

uni'tario, a *ag* unitary; **prezzo ~** price per unit.

u'nito, a *ag* (*paese*) united; (*amici, famiglia*) close; **in tinta ~a** plain, self-coloured (*BRIT*), self-colored (*US*).

univer'sale *ag* universal; general.

universalità *sf* universality.

universal'mente *av* universally.

università *sf inv* university.

universi'tario, a *ag* university *cpd* ♦ *sm/f* (*studente*) university student; (*insegnante*) academic, university lecturer.

uni'verso *sm* universe.

u'nivoco, a, ci, che *ag* unambiguous.

━━━━━━━━━━━ *PAROLA CHIAVE*

'uno, a (*dav sm* **un** + *C, V,* **uno** + *s impura, gn, pn, ps, x, z; dav sf* **un'** + *V,* **una** + *C*) *det*
1 a; (*dav vocale*) an; **un bambino** a child; **~a strada** a street; **~ zingaro** a gypsy
2 (*intensivo*): **ho avuto ~a paura!** I got such a fright!
♦ *pron* **1** one; **ce n'è ~ qui** there's one here; **prendine ~** take one (of them); **l'~ o l'altro** either (of them); **l'~ e l'altro** both (of them); **aiutarsi l'un l'altro** to help one another *o* each other; **sono entrati l'~ dopo l'altro** they came in one after the other; **a ~ a ~** one by one; **metà per ~** half each
2 (*un tale*) someone, somebody; **ho incontrato ~ che ti conosce** I met somebody who knows you
3 (*con valore impersonale*) one, you; **se ~ vuole** if one wants, if you want; **cosa fa ~ in quella situazione?** what does one do in that situation?
♦ *num* one; **~a mela e due pere** one apple and two pears; **~ più ~ fa due** one plus one equals two, one and one are two
♦ *sf*: **è l'~a** it's one (o'clock).

━━━━━━━━━━━━━━━━━━━━━━━━━━

'unsi *etc vb vedi* **ungere**.

'unto, a *pp di* **ungere** ♦ *ag* greasy, oily ♦ *sm* grease.

untu'oso, a *ag* greasy, oily.

unzi'one [un'tsjone] *sf*: **l'Estrema U~** (*REL*) Extreme Unction.

u'omo, *pl* **u'omini** *sm* man; **da ~** (*abito, scarpe*) men's, for men; **a memoria d'~** since the world began; **a passo d'~** at walking pace; **~ d'affari** businessman; **~ d'azione** man of action; **~ di fiducia** right-hand man; **~ di mondo** man of the world; **~ di paglia** stooge; **~ rana** frogman; **l'~ della strada** the man in the street.

u'opo *sm*: **all'~** if necessary.

u'ovo, *pl(f)* **u'ova** *sm* egg; **cercare il pelo nell'~** (*fig*) to split hairs; **~ affogato** *o* **in camicia** poached egg; **~ bazzotto/sodo** soft-/hard-boiled egg; **~ alla coque** boiled egg; **~ di Pasqua** Easter egg; **~ al tegame** *o* **all'occhio di bue** fried egg; **uova strapazzate** scrambled eggs.

ura'gano *sm* hurricane.

U'rali *smpl*: **gli ~, i Monti ~** the Urals, the Ural Mountains.

u'ranio *sm* uranium.

urba'nesimo *sm* urbanization.

urba'nista, i, e *sm/f* town planner.

urba'nistica *sf* town planning.
urbanità *sf* urbanity.
ur'bano, a *ag* urban, city *cpd*, town *cpd*; (*TEL: chiamata*) local; (*fig*) urbane.
ur'gente [ur'dʒɛnte] *ag* urgent.
ur'genza [ur'dʒɛntsa] *sf* urgency; **in caso d'~** in (case of) an emergency; **d'~** *ag* emergency ♦ *av* urgently, as a matter of urgency; **non c'è** ~ there's no hurry; **questo lavoro va fatto con** ~ this work is urgent.
'urgere ['urdʒere] *vi* to be needed urgently.
u'rina *etc* = **orina** *etc*.
ur'lare *vi* (*persona*) to scream, yell; (*animale, vento*) to howl ♦ *vt* to scream, yell.
'urlo, *pl(m)* **'urli,** *pl(f)* **'urla** *sm* scream, yell; howl.
'urna *sf* urn; (*elettorale*) ballot box; **andare alle** ~**e** to go to the polls.
urrà *escl* hurrah!
U.R.S.S. *sigla f* (= *Unione delle Repubbliche Socialiste Sovietiche*): **l'~** the USSR.
ur'tare *vt* to bump into, knock against; (*fig: irritare*) to annoy ♦ *vi*: ~ **contro** *o* **in** to bump into, knock against; (*fig: imbattersi*) to come up against; ~**rsi** *vr* (*reciproco: scontrarsi*) to collide; (*: fig*) to clash; (*irritarsi*) to get annoyed.
'urto *sm* (*colpo*) knock, bump; (*scontro*) crash, collision; (*fig*) clash; **terapia d'~** (*MED*) shock treatment.
uruguai'ano, a *ag*, *sm/f* Uruguayan.
Urugu'ay *sm*: **l'~** Uruguay.
u.s. *abbr* = **ultimo scorso**.
'USA *smpl*: **gli** ~ the USA.
u'sanza [u'zantsa] *sf* custom; (*moda*) fashion.
u'sare *vt* to use, employ ♦ *vi* (*essere di moda*) to be fashionable; (*servirsi*): ~ **di** to use; (*: diritto*) to exercise; (*essere solito*): ~ **fare** to be in the habit of doing, be accustomed to doing ♦ *vb impers*: **qui usa così** it's the custom round here; ~ **la massima cura nel fare qc** to exercise great care when doing sth.
u'sato, a *ag* used; (*consumato*) worn; (*di seconda mano*) used, second-hand ♦ *sm* second-hand goods *pl*.
u'scente [uʃ'ʃɛnte] *ag* (*AMM*) outgoing.
usci'ere [uʃ'ʃɛre] *sm* usher.
'uscio ['uʃʃo] *sm* door.
u'scire [uʃ'ʃire] *vi* (*gen*) to come out; (*partire, andare a passeggio, a uno spettacolo etc*) to go out; (*essere sorteggiato: numero*) to come up; ~ **da** (*gen*) to leave; (*posto*) to go (*o* come) out of, leave; (*solco, vasca etc*) to come out of; (*muro*) to stick out of;

(*competenza etc*) to be outside; (*infanzia, adolescenza*) to leave behind; (*famiglia nobile etc*) to come from; ~ **da** *o* **di casa** to go out; (*fig*) to leave home; ~ **in automobile** to go out in the car, go for a drive; ~ **di strada** (*AUT*) to go off *o* leave the road.
u'scita [uʃ'ʃita] *sf* (*passaggio, varco*) exit, way out; (*per divertimento*) outing; (*ECON: somma*) expenditure; (*fig: battuta*) witty remark; **"vietata l'~"** "no exit"; ~ **di sicurezza** emergency exit.
usi'gnolo [uziɲ'ɲɔlo] *sm* nightingale.
U.S.L. [uzl] *sigla f* (= *unità sanitaria locale*) local health centre.
'uso *sm* (*utilizzazione*) use; (*esercizio*) practice (*BRIT*), practise (*US*); (*abitudine*) custom; **fare** ~ **di qc** to use sth; **con l'~** with practice; **a** ~ **di** for (the use of); **d'~** (*corrente*) in use; **fuori** ~ out of use; **essere in** ~ to be in common *o* current use.
ustio'nare *vt* to burn; ~**rsi** *vr* to burn o.s.
usti'one *sf* burn.
usu'ale *ag* common, everyday.
usufru'ire *vi*: ~ **di** (*giovarsi di*) to take advantage of, make use of.
usu'frutto *sm* (*DIR*) usufruct.
u'sura *sf* usury; (*logoramento*) wear (and tear).
usu'raio *sm* usurer.
usur'pare *vt* to usurp.
usurpa'tore, 'trice *sm/f* usurper.
uten'sile *sm* tool, implement ♦ *ag*: **macchina** ~ machine tool; ~**i da cucina** kitchen utensils.
utensile'ria *sf* (*utensili*) tools *pl*; (*reparto*) tool room.
u'tente *sm/f* user; (*di gas etc*) consumer; (*del telefono*) subscriber; ~ **finale** end user.
'utero *sm* uterus, womb; ~ **in affitto** host womb.
'utile *ag* useful ♦ *sm* (*vantaggio*) advantage, benefit; (*ECON: profitto*) profit; **rendersi** ~ to be helpful; **in tempo** ~ **per** in time for; **unire l'~ al dilettevole** to combine business with pleasure; **partecipare agli** ~**i** (*ECON*) to share in the profits.
utilità *sf* usefulness *no pl*; use; (*vantaggio*) benefit; **essere di grande** ~ to be very useful.
utili'tario, a *ag* utilitarian ♦ *sf* (*AUT*) economy car.
utiliz'zare [utilid'dzare] *vt* to use, make use of, utilize.
utilizzazi'one [utiliddzat'tsjone] *sf* utilization, use.

uti'lizzo [uti'liddzo] sm (AMM) utilization;
(BANCA: di credito) availment.
util'mente av usefully, profitably.
uto'pia sf utopia; è pura ~ that's sheer
utopianism.
uto'pistico, a, ci, che ag utopian.
UVA abbr = ultravioletto prossimo.
'uva sf grapes pl; ~ passa raisins pl; ~
spina gooseberry.

V v

V, v [vi, vu] sf o m inv (lettera) V, v; V come
Venezia ≈ V for Victor.
V abbr (= volt) V.
v. abbr (= vedi, verso, versetto) v.
VA sigla = Varese.
va, va' vb vedi andare.
va'cante ag vacant.
va'canza [va'kantsa] sf (l'essere vacante)
vacancy; (riposo, ferie) holiday(s pl) (BRIT),
vacation (US); (giorno di permesso) day
off, holiday; ~e sfpl (periodo di ferie)
holidays, vacation sg; essere/andare in ~
to be/go on holiday o vacation; far ~ to
have a holiday; ~e estive summer
holiday(s) o vacation.
'vacca, che sf cow.
vacci'nare [vattʃi'nare] vt to vaccinate;
farsi ~ to have a vaccination, get
vaccinated.
vaccinazi'one [vattʃinat'tsjone] sf
vaccination.
vac'cino [vat'tʃino] sm (MED) vaccine.
vacil'lante [vatʃil'lante] ag (edificio, vecchio)
shaky, unsteady; (fiamma) flickering;
(salute, memoria) shaky, failing.
vacil'lare [vatʃil'lare] vi to sway; (fiamma)
to flicker; (fig: memoria, coraggio) to be
failing, falter.
'vacuo, a ag (fig) empty, vacuous ♦ sm
vacuum.
'vado etc vb vedi andare.
vagabon'daggio [vagabon'daddʒo] sm
wandering, roaming; (DIR) vagrancy.
vagabon'dare vi to roam, wander.
vaga'bondo, a sm/f tramp, vagrant;
(fannullone) idler, loafer.
va'gare vi to wander.
vagheggi'are [vaged'dʒare] vt to long for,
dream of.

vagherò etc [vage'rɔ] vb vedi vagare.
va'ghezza [va'gettsa] sf vagueness.
va'gina [va'dʒina] sf vagina.
va'gire [va'dʒire] vi to whimper.
va'gito [va'dʒito] sm cry, wailing.
'vaglia ['vaʎʎa] sm inv money order; ~
cambiario promissory note; ~ postale
postal order.
vagli'are [vaʎ'ʎare] vt to sift; (fig) to weigh
up.
'vaglio ['vaʎʎo] sm sieve; passare al ~ (fig)
to examine closely.
'vago, a, ghi, ghe ag vague.
va'gone sm (FERR: per passeggeri) carriage
(BRIT), car (US); (: per merci) truck,
wagon; ~ letto sleeper, sleeping car; ~
ristorante dining o restaurant car.
'vai vb vedi andare.
vai'olo sm smallpox.
val. abbr = valuta.
va'langa, ghe sf avalanche.
va'lente ag able, talented.
va'lenza [va'lɛntsa] sf (fig: significato)
content; (CHIM) valency.
va'lere vi (avere forza, potenza) to have
influence; (essere valido) to be valid;
(avere vigore, autorità) to hold, apply;
(essere capace: poeta, studente) to be good,
be able ♦ vt (prezzo, sforzo) to be worth;
(corrispondere) to correspond to;
(procurare): ~ qc a qn to earn sb sth; ~rsi
vr: ~rsi di to make use of, take advantage
of; far ~ (autorità etc) to assert; far ~ le
proprie ragioni to make o.s. heard; farsi ~
to make o.s. appreciated o respected;
vale a dire that is to say; ~ la pena to be
worth the effort o worth it; l'uno vale
l'altro the one is as good as the other,
they amount to the same thing; non vale
niente it's worthless; ~rsi dei consigli di
qn to take sb's advice, act upon sb's
advice.
valeri'ana sf (BOT, MED) valerian.
va'levole ag valid.
'valgo etc vb vedi valere.
vali'care vt to cross.
'valico, chi sm (passo) pass.
validità sf validity.
'valido, a ag valid; (rimedio) effective;
(persona) worthwhile; essere di ~ aiuto a
qn to be a great help to sb.
valige'ria [validʒe'ria] sf (assortimento)
leather goods pl; (fabbrica) leather goods
factory; (negozio) leather goods shop.
va'ligia, gie o ge [va'lidʒa] sf (suit)case;
fare le ~gie to pack (up); ~ diplomatica
diplomatic bag.
val'lata sf valley.

'valle *sf* valley; **a ~** (*di fiume*) downstream; **scendere a ~** to go downhill.

val'letto *sm* valet.

valligi'ano, a [valli'dʒano] *sm/f* inhabitant of a valley.

va'lore *sm* (*gen, COMM*) value; (*merito*) merit, worth; (*coraggio*) valour (*BRIT*), valor (*US*), courage; (*FINANZA: titolo*) security; **~i** *smpl* (*oggetti preziosi*) valuables; **crescere/diminuire di ~** to go up/down in value, gain/lose in value; **è di gran ~** it's worth a lot, it's very valuable; **privo di ~** worthless; **~ contabile** book value; **~ effettivo** real value; **~ nominale** *o* **facciale** nominal value; **~ di realizzo** break-up value; **~ di riscatto** surrender value; **~i bollati** (revenue) stamps.

valoriz'zare [valorid'dzare] *vt* (*terreno*) to develop; (*fig*) to make the most of.

valo'roso, a *ag* courageous.

'valso, a *pp di* **valere**.

va'luta *sf* currency, money; (*BANCA*): **~ 15 gennaio** interest to run from January 15th; **~ estera** foreign currency.

valu'tare *vt* (*casa, gioiello, fig*) to value; (*stabilire: peso, entrate, fig*) to estimate.

valu'tario, a *ag* (*FINANZA: norme*) currency *cpd*.

valutazi'one [valutat'tsjone] *sf* valuation; estimate.

'valva *sf* (*ZOOL, BOT*) valve.

'valvola *sf* (*TECN, ANAT*) valve; (*ELETTR*) fuse; **~ a farfalla del carburatore** (*AUT*) throttle; **~ di sicurezza** safety valve.

'valzer ['valtser] *sm inv* waltz.

vam'pata *sf* (*di fiamma*) blaze; (*di calore*) blast; (: *al viso*) flush.

vam'piro *sm* vampire.

vana'gloria *sf* boastfulness.

van'dalico, a, ci, che *ag* vandal *cpd*; **atto ~** act of vandalism.

vanda'lismo *sm* vandalism.

'vandalo *sm* vandal.

vaneggia'mento [vaneddʒa'mento] *sm* raving, delirium.

vaneggi'are [vaned'dʒare] *vi* to rave.

va'nesio, a *ag* vain, conceited.

'vanga, ghe *sf* spade.

van'gare *vt* to dig.

van'gelo [van'dʒelo] *sm* gospel.

vanifi'care *vt* to nullify.

va'niglia [va'niʎʎa] *sf* vanilla.

vanigli'ato, a [vaniʎ'ʎato] *ag*: **zucchero ~** (*CUC*) vanilla sugar.

vanità *sf* vanity; (*di promessa*) emptiness; (*di sforzo*) futility.

vani'toso, a *ag* vain, conceited.

'vanno *vb vedi* **andare**.

'vano, a *ag* vain ♦ *sm* (*spazio*) space; (*apertura*) opening; (*stanza*) room; **il ~ della porta** the doorway; **il ~ portabagagli** (*AUT*) the boot (*BRIT*), the trunk (*US*).

van'taggio [van'taddʒo] *sm* advantage; **trarre ~ da qc** to benefit from sth; **essere/portarsi in ~** (*SPORT*) to be in/take the lead.

vantaggi'oso, a [vantad'dʒoso] *ag* advantageous, favourable (*BRIT*), favorable (*US*).

van'tare *vt* to praise, speak highly of; **~rsi** *vr*: **~rsi (di/di aver fatto)** to boast *o* brag (about/about having done).

vante'ria *sf* boasting.

'vanto *sm* boasting; (*merito*) virtue, merit; (*gloria*) pride.

'vanvera *sf*: **a ~** haphazardly; **parlare a ~** to talk nonsense.

va'pore *sm* vapour (*BRIT*), vapor (*US*); (*anche:* **~ acqueo**) steam; (*nave*) steamer; **a ~** (*turbina etc*) steam *cpd*; **al ~** (*CUC*) steamed.

vapo'retto *sm* steamer.

vapori'era *sf* (*FERR*) steam engine.

vaporiz'zare [vaporid'dzare] *vt* to vaporize.

vaporizza'tore [vaporiddza'tore] *sm* spray.

vaporizzazi'one [vaporiddzat'tsjone] *sf* vaporization.

vapo'roso, a *ag* (*tessuto*) filmy; (*capelli*) soft and full.

va'rare *vt* (*NAUT, fig*) to launch; (*DIR*) to pass.

var'care *vt* to cross.

'varco, chi *sm* passage; **aprirsi un ~ tra la folla** to push one's way through the crowd.

vare'china [vare'kina] *sf* bleach.

vari'abile *ag* variable; (*tempo, umore*) changeable, variable ♦ *sf* (*MAT*) variable.

vari'ante *sf* (*gen*) variation, change; (*di piano*) modification; (*LING*) variant; (*SPORT*) alternative route.

vari'are *vt, vi* to vary; **~ di opinione** to change one's mind.

variazi'one [varjat'tsjone] *sf* variation, change; (*MUS*) variation; **una ~ di programma** a change of plan.

va'rice [va'ritʃe] *sf* varicose vein.

vari'cella [vari'tʃɛlla] *sf* chickenpox.

vari'coso, a *ag* varicose.

varie'gato, a *ag* variegated.

varietà *sf inv* variety ♦ *sm inv* variety show.

'vario, a *ag* varied; (*parecchi: col sostantivo al pl*) various; (*mutevole: umore*) changeable; **~e** *sfpl*: **~e ed eventuali** (*nell'ordine del giorno*) any other business.

vario'pinto, a *ag* multicoloured (*BRIT*),

multicolored (US).

'**varo** sm (NAUT, fig) launch; (di leggi) passing.

varrò etc vb vedi **valere**.

Var'savia sf Warsaw.

va'saio sm potter.

'**vasca, sche** sf basin; (anche: ~ **da bagno**) bathtub, bath.

va'scello [vaʃ'ʃɛllo] sm (NAUT) vessel, ship.

vas'chetta [vas'ketta] sf (per gelato) tub; (per sviluppare fotografie) dish.

vase'lina sf vaseline.

vasel'lame sm (stoviglie) crockery; (: di porcellana) china; ~ **d'oro/d'argento** gold/silver plate.

'**vaso** sm (recipiente) pot; (: barattolo) jar; (: decorativo) vase; (ANAT) vessel; ~ **da fiori** vase; (per piante) flowerpot.

vas'sallo sm vassal.

vas'soio sm tray.

vastità sf vastness.

'**vasto, a** ag vast, immense; **di ~e proporzioni** (incendio) huge; (fenomeno, rivolta) widespread; **su ~a scala** on a vast o huge scale.

Vati'cano sm: **il ~** the Vatican; **la Città del ~** the Vatican City.

VB sigla = Vibo Valenza.

VC sigla = Vercelli.

VE sigla = Venezia ♦ abbr = Vostra Eccellenza.

ve pron, av vedi **vi**.

vecchi'aia [vek'kjaja] sf old age.

'**vecchio, a** ['vɛkkjo] ag old ♦ smf old man/woman; **i ~i** the old; **è un mio ~ amico** he's an old friend of mine; **è un uomo ~ stile** o **stampo** he's an old-fashioned man; **è ~ del mestiere** he's an old hand at the job.

'**vece** ['vetʃe] sf: **in ~ di** in the place of, for; **fare le ~i di qn** to take sb's place; **firma del padre o di chi ne fa le ~i** signature of the father or guardian.

ve'dere vt, vi to see; **~rsi** vr to meet, see one another; **~ di fare qc** to see (to it) that sth is done, make sure that sth is done; **avere a che ~ con** to have to do with; **far ~ qc a qn** to show sb sth; **farsi ~** to show o.s.; (farsi vivo) to show one's face; **farsi ~ da un medico** to go and see a doctor; **modo di ~** outlook, view of things; **vedi pagina 8** (rimando) see page 8; **è da ~ se ...** it remains to be seen whether ...; **non vedo la ragione di farlo** I can't see any reason to do it; **si era visto costretto a ...** he found himself forced to ...; **non (ci) si vede** (è buio etc) you can't see a thing; **ci vediamo domani!** see you tomorrow!; **non lo posso ~** (fig) I can't stand him.

ve'detta sf (sentinella, posto) look-out; (NAUT) patrol boat.

ve'dette [və'dɛt] sf inv (attrice) star.

'**vedovo, a** smf widower/widow; **rimaner ~** to be widowed.

vedrò etc vb vedi **vedere**.

ve'duta sf view; **di larghe** o **ampie ~e** broad-minded; **di ~e limitate** narrow-minded.

vee'mente ag (discorso, azione) vehement; (assalto) vigorous; (passione) overwhelming.

vee'menza [vee'mɛntsa] sf vehemence; **con ~** vehemently.

vege'tale [vedʒe'tale] ag, sm vegetable.

vege'tare [vedʒe'tare] vi (fig) to vegetate.

vegetari'ano, a [vedʒeta'rjano] ag, smf vegetarian.

vegeta'tivo, a ag vegetative.

vegetazi'one [vedʒetat'tsjone] sf vegetation.

'**vegeto, a** ['vɛdʒeto] ag (pianta) thriving; (persona) strong, vigorous.

veg'gente [ved'dʒɛnte] smf (indovino) clairvoyant.

'**veglia** ['veʎʎa] sf (sorveglianza) watch; (trattenimento) evening gathering; **tra la ~ e il sonno** half awake; **fare la ~ a un malato** to watch over a sick person; **~ funebre** wake.

vegli'ardo, a [veʎ'ʎardo] smf venerable old man/woman.

vegli'are [veʎ'ʎare] vi to stay o sit up; (stare vigile) to watch; to keep watch ♦ vt (malato, morto) to watch over, sit up with.

vegli'one [veʎ'ʎone] sm ball, dance.

ve'icolo sm vehicle; ~ **spaziale** spacecraft inv.

'**vela** sf (NAUT: tela) sail; (sport) sailing; **tutto va a gonfie ~e** (fig) everything is going perfectly.

ve'lare vt to veil; **~rsi** vr (occhi, luna) to mist over; (voce) to become husky; **~rsi il viso** to cover one's face (with a veil).

ve'lato, a ag veiled.

vela'tura sf (NAUT) sails pl.

veleggi'are [veled'dʒare] vi to sail; (AER) to glide.

ve'leno sm poison.

vele'noso, a ag poisonous.

ve'letta sf (di cappello) veil.

veli'ero sm sailing ship.

ve'lina sf (anche: **carta ~**: per imballare) tissue paper; (: per copie) flimsy paper; (copia) carbon copy.

ve'lista, i, e smf yachtsman/woman.

ve'livolo sm aircraft.

velleità sf inv vain ambition, vain desire.

vellei'tario, a *ag* unrealistic.

'vello *sm* fleece.

vellu'tato, a *ag* (*stoffa, pesca, colore*) velvety; (*voce*) mellow.

vel'luto *sm* velvet; ~ **a coste** cord.

'velo *sm* veil; (*tessuto*) voile.

ve'loce [ve'lotʃe] *ag* fast, quick ♦ *av* fast, quickly.

velo'cista, i, e [velo'tʃista] *sm/f* (*SPORT*) sprinter.

velocità [velotʃi'ta] *sf* speed; **a forte** ~ at high speed; ~ **di crociera** cruising speed.

ve'lodromo *sm* velodrome.

ven. *abbr* (*REL*) = **venerabile**; (= *venerdì*) Fri.

'vena *sf* (*gen*) vein; (*filone*) vein, seam; (*fig: ispirazione*) inspiration; (: *umore*) mood; **essere in** ~ **di qc** to be in the mood for sth.

ve'nale *ag* (*prezzo, valore*) market *cpd*; (*fig*) venal; mercenary.

venalità *sf* venality.

ve'nato, a *ag* (*marmo*) veined, streaked; (*legno*) grained.

vena'torio, a *ag* hunting; **la stagione** ~**a** the hunting season.

vena'tura *sf* (*di marmo*) vein, streak; (*di legno*) grain.

ven'demmia *sf* (*raccolta*) grape harvest; (*quantità d'uva*) grape crop, grapes *pl*; (*vino ottenuto*) vintage.

vendemmi'are *vt* to harvest ♦ *vi* to harvest the grapes.

'vendere *vt* to sell; ~ **all'ingrosso/al dettaglio** *o* **minuto** to sell wholesale/retail; ~ **all'asta** to auction, sell by auction; **"vendesi"** "for sale".

ven'detta *sf* revenge.

vendi'care *vt* to avenge; ~**rsi** *vr*: ~**rsi (di)** to avenge o.s. (for); (*per rancore*) to take one's revenge (for); ~**rsi su qn** to revenge o.s. on sb.

vendica'tivo, a *ag* vindictive.

'vendita *sf* sale; **la** ~ (*attività*) selling; (*smercio*) sales *pl*; **in** ~ on sale; **mettere in** ~ to put on sale; **in** ~ **presso** on sale at; **contratto di** ~ sales agreement; **reparto** ~**e** sales department; ~ **all'asta** sale by auction; ~ **al dettaglio** *o* **minuto** retail; ~ **all'ingrosso** wholesale.

vendi'tore, 'trice *sm/f* seller, vendor; (*gestore di negozio*) trader, dealer.

ven'duto, a *ag* (*merce*) sold; (*fig: corrotto*) corrupt.

ve'nefico, a, ci, che *ag* poisonous.

vene'rabile *ag*, **vene'rando, a** *ag* venerable.

vene'rare *vt* to venerate.

venerazi'one [venerat'tsjone] *sf* veneration.

venerdì *sm inv* Friday; **V**~ **Santo** Good Friday; *per fraseologia vedi* **martedì**.

'Venere *sm, sf* Venus.

ve'nereo, a *ag* venereal.

'veneto, a *ag* (*o* from) the Veneto.

'veneto-giuli'ano, a ['vɛnetodʒu'ljano] *ag* of (*o* from) Venezia-Giulia.

Ve'nezia [ve'nɛttsja] *sf* Venice.

venezi'ano, a [venet'tsjano] *ag, sm/f* Venetian.

Venezu'ela [venettsu'ela] *sm*: **il** ~ Venezuela.

venezue'lano, a [venettsue'lano] *ag, sm/f* Venezuelan.

'vengo *etc vb vedi* **venire**.

veni'ale *ag* venial.

ve'nire *vi* to come; (*riuscire: dolce, fotografia*) to turn out; (*come ausiliare: essere*): **viene ammirato da tutti** he is admired by everyone; ~ **da** to come from; **quanto viene?** how much does it cost?; **far** ~ (*mandare a chiamare*) to send for; (*medico*) to call, send for; ~ **a capo di qc** to unravel sth, sort sth out; ~ **al dunque** *o* **nocciolo** *o* **fatto** to come to the point; ~ **fuori** to come out; ~ **giù** to come down; ~ **meno** (*svenire*) to faint; ~ **meno a qc** not to fulfil sth; ~ **su** to come up; ~ **via** to come away; ~ **a sapere qc** to learn sth; ~ **a trovare qn** to come and see sb; **negli anni a** ~ in the years to come, in future; **è venuto il momento di ...** the time has come to ....

'venni *etc vb vedi* **venire**.

ven'taglio [ven'taʎʎo] *sm* fan.

ven'tata *sf* gust (of wind).

venten'nale *ag* (*che dura 20 anni*) twenty-year *cpd*; (*che ricorre ogni 20 anni*) which takes place every twenty years.

ven'tenne *ag, sm/f* twenty-year-old.

ven'tennio *sm* period of twenty years; **il** ~ **fascista** the Fascist period.

ven'tesimo, a *num* twentieth.

'venti *num* twenty.

venti'lare *vt* (*stanza*) to air, ventilate; (*fig: idea, proposta*) to air.

venti'lato, a *ag* (*camera, zona*) airy; **poco** ~ airless.

ventila'tore *sm* fan; (*su parete, finestra*) ventilator, fan.

ventilazi'one [ventilat'tsjone] *sf* ventilation.

ven'tina *sf*: **una** ~ **(di)** around twenty, twenty or so.

ventiquat'tr'ore *sfpl* (*periodo*) twenty-four hours ♦ *sf inv* (*SPORT*) twenty-four-hour race; (*valigetta*) overnight case.

venti'sette *num* twenty-seven; **il** ~ (*giorno di paga*) (monthly) pay day.

ventitré *num* twenty-three ♦ *sfpl*: **portava il cappello sulle** ~ he wore his hat at a jaunty angle.

'**vento** *sm* wind; **c'è** ~ it's windy; **un colpo di** ~ a gust of wind; **contro** ~ against the wind; ~ **contrario** (*NAUT*) headwind.

'**ventola** *sf* (*AUT, TECN*) fan.

ven'tosa *sf* (*ZOOL*) sucker; (*di gomma*) suction pad.

ven'toso, a *ag* windy.

ven'totto *num* twenty-eight.

'**ventre** *sm* stomach.

ven'triloquo *sm* ventriloquist.

ven'tuno *num* twenty-one.

ven'tura *sf*: **andare alla** ~ to trust to luck; **soldato di** ~ mercenary.

ven'turo, a *ag* next, coming.

ve'nuto, a *pp di* venire ♦ *sm/f*: **il(la) primo(a)** ~**(a)** the first person who comes along ♦ *sf* coming, arrival.

ver. *abbr* = **versamento**.

'**vera** *sf* wedding ring.

ve'race [ve'ratʃe] *ag* (*testimone*) truthful; (*testimonianza*) accurate; (*cibi*) real, genuine.

vera'mente *av* really.

ve'randa *sf* veranda(h).

ver'bale *ag* verbal ♦ *sm* (*di riunione*) minutes *pl*; **accordo** ~ verbal agreement; **mettere a** ~ to place in the minutes *o* on record.

'**verbo** *sm* (*LING*) verb; (*parola*) word; (*REL*): **il V**~ the Word.

ver'boso, a *ag* verbose, wordy.

ver'dastro, a *ag* greenish.

'**verde** *ag, sm* green; ~ **bottiglia/oliva** *ag inv* bottle/olive green; **benzina** ~ lead-free *o* unleaded petrol; **i V**~**i** (*POL*) the Greens; **essere al** ~ (*fig*) to be broke.

verdeggi'ante [verded'dʒante] *ag* green, verdant.

verde'rame *sm* verdigris.

ver'detto *sm* verdict.

ver'dura *sf* vegetables *pl*.

vere'condia *sf* modesty.

vere'condo, a *ag* modest.

'**verga, ghe** *sf* rod.

ver'gato a *ag* (*foglio*) ruled.

vergi'nale [verdʒi'nale] *ag* virginal.

'**vergine** ['verdʒine] *sf* virgin; (*dello zodiaco*): **V**~ Virgo ♦ *ag* virgin; (*ragazza*): **essere** ~ to be a virgin; **essere della V**~ (*dello zodiaco*) to be Virgo; **pura lana** ~ pure new wool; **olio** ~ **d'oliva** unrefined olive oil.

verginità [verdʒini'ta] *sf* virginity.

ver'gogna [ver'goɲɲa] *sf* shame; (*timidezza*) shyness, embarrassment.

vergo'gnarsi [vergoɲ'ɲarsi] *vr*: ~ (**di**) to be *o* feel ashamed (of); to be shy (about), be embarrassed (about).

vergo'gnoso, a [vergoɲ'ɲoso] *ag* ashamed; (*timido*) shy, embarrassed; (*causa di vergogna: azione*) shameful.

veridicità [veriditʃi'ta] *sf* truthfulness.

ve'ridico, a, ci, che *ag* truthful.

ve'rifica, che *sf* checking; check; **fare una** ~ **di** (*freni, testimonianza, firma*) to check; ~ **contabile** (*FINANZA*) audit.

verifi'care *vt* (*controllare*) to check; (*confermare*) to confirm, bear out; (*FINANZA*) to audit.

verità *sf inv* truth; **a dire la** ~, **per la** ~ truth to tell, actually.

veriti'ero, a *ag* (*che dice la verità*) truthful; (*conforme a verità*) true.

'**verme** *sm* worm.

vermi'celli [vermi'tʃɛlli] *smpl* vermicelli *sg*.

ver'miglio [ver'miʎʎo] *sm* vermilion, scarlet.

'**vermut** *sm inv* vermouth.

ver'nacolo *sm* vernacular.

ver'nice [ver'nitʃe] *sf* (*colorazione*) paint; (*trasparente*) varnish; (*pelle*) patent leather; "~ **fresca**" "wet paint".

vernici'are [verni'tʃare] *vt* to paint; to varnish.

vernicia'tura [vernitʃa'tura] *sf* painting; varnishing.

'**vero, a** *ag* (*veridico: fatti, testimonianza*) true; (*autentico*) real ♦ *sm* (*verità*) truth; (*realtà*) (real) life; **un** ~ **e proprio delinquente** a real criminal, an out and out criminal; **tant'è** ~ **che ...** so much so that ...; **a onor del** ~, **a dire il** ~ to tell the truth.

Ve'rona *sf* Verona.

vero'nese *ag* of (*o* from) Verona.

vero'simile *ag* likely, probable.

verrò *etc vb vedi* venire.

ver'ruca, che *sf* wart.

versa'mento *sm* (*pagamento*) payment; (*deposito di denaro*) deposit.

ver'sante *sm* slopes *pl*, side.

ver'sare *vt* (*fare uscire: vino, farina*) to pour (out); (*spargere: lacrime, sangue*) to shed; (*rovesciare*) to spill; (*ECON*) to pay; (: *depositare*) to deposit, pay in ♦ *vi*: ~ **in gravi difficoltà** to find o.s. with serious problems; ~**rsi** *vr* (*rovesciarsi*) to spill; (*fiume, folla*): ~**rsi (in)** to pour (into).

versa'tile *ag* versatile.

versatilità *sf* versatility.

ver'sato, a *ag:* ~ **in** to be (well-)versed in.
ver'setto *sm* (*REL*) verse.
versi'one *sf* version; (*traduzione*) translation.
'verso *sm* (*di poesia*) verse, line; (*di animale, uccello, venditore ambulante*) cry; (*direzione*) direction; (*modo*) way; (*di foglio di carta*) verse; (*di moneta*) reverse; ~**i** *smpl* (*poesia*) verse *sg*; **per un** ~ **o per l'altro** one way or another; **prendere qn/ qc per il** ~ **giusto** to approach sb/sth the right way; **rifare il** ~ **a qn** (*imitare*) to mimic sb; **non c'è** ~ **di persuaderlo** there's no way of persuading him, he can't be persuaded ♦ *prep* (*in direzione di*) toward(s); (*nei pressi di*) near, around (about); (*in senso temporale*) about, around; (*nei confronti di*) for; ~ **di me** towards me; ~ **l'alto** upwards; ~ **il basso** downwards; ~ **sera** towards evening.
'vertebra *sf* vertebra.
verte'brale *ag* vertebral; **colonna** ~ spinal column, spine.
verte'brato, a *ag, sm* vertebrate.
ver'tenza [ver'tɛntsa] *sf* (*lite*) lawsuit, case; (*sindacale*) dispute.
'vertere *vi:* ~ **su** to deal with, be about.
verti'cale *ag, sf* vertical.
'vertice ['vɛrtitʃe] *sm* summit, top; (*MAT*) vertex; **conferenza al** ~ (*POL*) summit conference.
ver'tigine [ver'tidʒine] *sf* dizziness *no pl*; dizzy spell; (*MED*) vertigo; **avere le** ~**i** to feel dizzy.
vertigi'noso, a [vertidʒi'noso] *ag* (*altezza*) dizzy; (*fig*) breathtakingly high (*o deep etc*).
'verza ['vɛrdza] *sf* Savoy cabbage.
ve'scica, che [veʃ'ʃika] *sf* (*ANAT*) bladder; (*MED*) blister.
vesco'vile *ag* episcopal.
'vescovo *sm* bishop.
'vespa *sf* wasp; (®: *veicolo*) (motor) scooter.
ves'paio *sm* wasps' nest; **suscitare un** ~ (*fig*) to stir up a hornets' nest.
vespasi'ano *sm* urinal.
'vespro *sm* (*REL*) vespers *pl*.
ves'sare *vt* to oppress.
vessazi'one [vessat'tsjone] *sf* oppression.
ves'sillo *sm* standard; (*bandiera*) flag.
ves'taglia [ves'taʎʎa] *sf* dressing gown, robe (*US*).
'veste *sf* garment; (*rivestimento*) covering; (*qualità, facoltà*) capacity; ~**i** *sfpl* clothes, clothing *sg*; **in** ~ **ufficiale** (*fig*) in an official capacity; **in** ~ **di** in the guise of, as; ~ **da camera** dressing gown, robe

(*US*); ~ **editoriale** layout.
vesti'ario *sm* wardrobe, clothes *pl*; **capo di** ~ article of clothing, garment.
ves'tibolo *sm* (entrance) hall.
ves'tigia [ves'tidʒa] *sfpl* (*tracce*) vestiges, traces; (*rovine*) ruins, remains.
ves'tire *vt* (*bambino, malato*) to dress; (*avere indosso*) to have on, wear; ~**rsi** *vr* to dress, get dressed; ~**rsi da** (*negozio, sarto*) to buy *o* get one's clothes at.
ves'tito, a *ag* dressed ♦ *sm* garment; (*da donna*) dress; (*da uomo*) suit; ~**i** *smpl* (*indumenti*) clothes; ~ **di bianco** dressed in white.
Ve'suvio *sm:* **il** ~ Vesuvius.
vete'rano, a *ag, sm/f* veteran.
veteri'nario, a *ag* veterinary ♦ *sm* veterinary surgeon (*BRIT*), veterinarian (*US*), vet ♦ *sf* veterinary medicine.
'veto *sm inv* veto; **porre il** ~ **a qc** to veto sth.
ve'traio *sm* glassmaker; (*per finestre*) glazier.
ve'trato, a *ag* (*porta, finestra*) glazed; (*che contiene vetro*) glass *cpd* ♦ *sf* glass door (*o window*); (*di chiesa*) stained glass window; **carta** ~**a** sandpaper.
vetre'ria *sf* (*stabilimento*) glassworks *sg*; (*oggetti di vetro*) glassware.
ve'trina *sf* (*di negozio*) (shop) window; (*armadio*) display cabinet.
vetri'nista, i, e *sm/f* window dresser.
ve'trino *sm* slide.
vetri'olo *sm* vitriol.
'vetro *sm* glass; (*per finestra, porta*) pane (of glass); ~ **blindato** bulletproof glass; ~ **infrangibile** shatterproof glass; ~ **di sicurezza** safety glass; **i** ~**i di Murano** Murano glassware *sg*.
ve'troso, a *ag* vitreous.
'vetta *sf* peak, summit, top.
vet'tore *sm* (*MAT, FISICA*) vector; (*chi trasporta*) carrier.
vetto'vaglie [vetto'vaʎʎe] *sfpl* supplies.
vet'tura *sf* (*carrozza*) carriage; (*FERR*) carriage (*BRIT*), car (*US*); (*auto*) car (*BRIT*), automobile (*US*); ~ **di piazza** hackney carriage.
vettu'rino *sm* coach driver, coachman.
vezzeggi'are [vettsedd'dʒare] *vt* to fondle, caress.
vezzeggia'tivo [vettseddʒa'tivo] *sm* (*LING*) term of endearment.
'vezzo ['vettso] *sm* habit; ~**i** *smpl* (*smancerie*) affected ways; (*leggiadria*) charms.
vez'zoso, a [vet'tsoso] *ag* (*grazioso*) charming, pretty; (*lezioso*) affected.
V.F. *abbr* = **vigili del fuoco**.

V.G. *abbr* = *Vostra Grazia*.

VI *sigla* = *Vicenza*.

vi (*dav lo, la, li, le, ne diventa* **ve**) *pron* (*oggetto*) you; (*complemento di termine*) (to) you; (*riflessivo*) yourselves; (*reciproco*) each other ♦ *av* (*lì*) there; (*qui*) here; (*per questo/quel luogo*) through here/there; ~ **è/sono** there is/are.

'via *sf* (*gen*) way; (*strada*) street; (*sentiero, pista*) path, track; (*AMM: procedimento*) channels *pl* ♦ *prep* (*passando per*) via, by way of ♦ *av* away ♦ *escl* go away!; (*suvvia*) come on!; (*SPORT*) go! ♦ *sm* (*SPORT*) starting signal; **per** ~ **di** (*a causa di*) because of, on account of; **in** *o* **per** ~ on the way; **in** ~ **di guarigione** (*fig*) on the road to recovery; **per** ~ **aerea** by air; (*lettere*) by airmail; ~ **satellite** by satellite; **andare/essere** ~ to go/be away; ~ ~ (*pian piano*) gradually; ~ ~ **che** (*a mano a mano*) as; **e** ~ **dicendo**, **e** ~ **di questo passo** and so on (and so forth); **dare il** ~ (*SPORT*) to give the starting signal; **dare il** ~ **a un progetto** to give the green light to a project; **hanno dato il** ~ **ai lavori** they've begun *o* started work; **in** ~ **amichevole** in a friendly manner; **comporre una disputa in** ~ **amichevole** (*DIR*) to settle a dispute out of court; **in** ~ **eccezionale** as an exception; **in** ~ **privata** *o* **confidenziale** (*dire etc*) in confidence; **in** ~ **provvisoria** provisionally; **V~ lattea** (*ASTR*) Milky Way; ~ **di mezzo** middle course; **non c'è** ~ **di scampo** *o* **d'uscita** there's no way out; ~**e di comunicazione** communication routes.

viabilità *sf* (*di strada*) practicability; (*rete stradale*) roads *pl*, road network.

via'dotto *sm* viaduct.

viaggi'are [viad'dʒare] *vi* to travel; **le merci viaggiano via mare** the goods go *o* are sent by sea.

viaggia'tore, 'trice [viadd'ʒa'tore] *ag* travelling (*BRIT*), traveling (*US*) ♦ *sm* traveller (*BRIT*), traveler (*US*); (*passeggero*) passenger.

vi'aggio [vi'addʒo] *sm* travel(ling); (*tragitto*) journey, trip; **buon** ~! have a good trip!; ~ **d'affari** business trip; ~ **di nozze** honeymoon; ~ **organizzato** package tour *o* holiday.

vi'ale *sm* avenue.

vian'dante *sm/f* vagrant.

vi'atico, ci *sm* (*REL*) viaticum; (*fig*) encouragement.

via'vai *sm* coming and going, bustle.

vi'brare *vi* to vibrate; (*agitarsi*): ~ (**di**) to quiver (with).

vibra'tore *sm* vibrator.

vibrazi'one [vibrat'tsjone] *sf* vibration.

vi'cario *sm* (*apostolico etc*) vicar.

'vice ['vitʃe] *sm/f* deputy ♦ *prefisso* vice.

vice'console [vitʃe'kɔnsole] *sm* vice-consul.

vicediret'tore, 'trice [vitʃediret'tore] *sm/f* assistant manager/manageress; (*di giornale etc*) deputy editor.

vi'cenda [vi'tʃɛnda] *sf* event; ~**e** *sfpl* (*sorte*) fortunes; **a** ~ in turn; **con alterne** ~**e** with mixed fortunes.

vicen'devole [vitʃen'devole] *ag* mutual, reciprocal.

vicen'tino, a [vitʃen'tino] *ag* of (*o* from) Vicenza.

vicepresi'dente [vitʃepresi'dɛnte] *sm* vice-president, vice-chairman.

vice'versa [vitʃe'vɛrsa] *av* vice versa; **da Roma a Pisa e** ~ from Rome to Pisa and back.

vi'chingo, a, ghi, ghe [vi'kingo] *ag, sm/f* Viking.

vici'nanza [vitʃi'nantsa] *sf* nearness, closeness; ~**e** *sfpl* (*paraggi*) neighbourhood (*BRIT*), neighborhood (*US*), vicinity.

vici'nato [vitʃi'nato] *sm* neighbourhood (*BRIT*), neighborhood (*US*); (*vicini*) neighbo(u)rs *pl*.

vi'cino, a [vi'tʃino] *ag* (*gen*) near; (*nello spazio*) near, nearby; (*accanto*) next; (*nel tempo*) near, close at hand ♦ *sm/f* neighbour (*BRIT*), neighbor (*US*) ♦ *av* near, close; **da** ~ (*guardare*) close up; (*esaminare, seguire*) closely; (*conoscere*) well, intimately; ~ **a** *prep* near (to), close to; (*accanto a*) beside; **mi sono stati molto** ~**i** (*fig*) they were very supportive towards me; ~ **di casa** neighbo(u)r.

vicissi'tudini [vitʃissi'tudini] *sfpl* trials and tribulations.

'vicolo *sm* alley; ~ **cieco** blind alley.

'video *sm inv* (*TV: schermo*) screen.

video'camera *sf* camcorder.

videocas'setta *sf* videocassette.

videogi'oco, chi [video'dʒɔko] *sm* video game.

videoregistra'tore [videoredʒistra'tore] *sm* (*apparecchio*) video (recorder).

video'teca, che *sf* video shop.

videotermi'nale *sm* visual display unit.

'vidi *etc vb vedi* **vedere**.

vidi'mare *vt* (*AMM*) to authenticate.

vidimazi'one [vidimat'tsjone] *sf* (*AMM*) authentication.

Vi'enna *sf* Vienna.

vien'nese *ag, sm/f* Viennese *inv*.

vie'tare *vt* to forbid; (*AMM*) to prohibit;

(*libro*) to ban; ~ **a qn di fare** to forbid sb
to do; to prohibit sb from doing.
vie'tato, a *ag* (*vedi vb*) forbidden;
prohibited; banned; "~ **fumare/**
l'ingresso" "no smoking/admittance"; ~
ai minori di 14/18 anni prohibited to
children under 14/18; "**senso** ~" (*AUT*)
"no entry"; "**sosta** ~**a**" (*AUT*) "no
parking".
Viet'nam *sm:* **il** ~ Vietnam.
vietna'mita, i, e *ag, sm/f, sm* Vietnamese
inv.
vi'eto, a *ag* worthless.
vi'gente [vi'dʒɛnte] *ag* in force.
'vigere ['vidʒere] *vi* (*difettivo: si usa solo alla*
terza persona) to be in force; **in casa mia**
vige l'abitudine di ... at home we are in
the habit of ....
vigi'lante [vidʒi'lante] *ag* vigilant,
watchful.
vigi'lanza [vidʒi'lantsa] *sf* vigilance;
(*sorveglianza: di operai, alunni*)
supervision; (: *di sospetti, criminali*)
surveillance; ~ **notturna** night-watchman
service.
vigi'lare [vidʒi'lare] *vt* to watch over, keep
an eye on; ~ **che** to make sure that, see
to it that.
vigi'lato, a [vidʒi'lato] *sm/f* (*DIR*) person
under police surveillance.
vigila'trice [vidʒila'tritʃe] *sf:* ~ **d'infanzia**
nursery-school teacher; ~ **scolastica**
school health officer.
'vigile ['vidʒile] *ag* watchful ♦ *sm* (*anche:* ~
urbano) policeman (*in towns*); ~ **del fuoco**
fireman.

> The **vigili urbani** *are a municipal police force*
> *whose sphere of activity is the* **Comune** *and*
> *daily life within it. Their duties involve the*
> *enforcing of laws relating to traffic, public*
> *works and services and commerce.*

vigi'lessa [vidʒi'lessa] *sf* (traffic)
policewoman.
vi'gilia [vi'dʒilja] *sf* (*giorno antecedente*) eve;
la ~ **di Natale** Christmas Eve.
vigliacche'ria [viʎʎakke'ria] *sf* cowardice.
vigli'acco, a, chi, che [viʎ'ʎakko] *ag*
cowardly ♦ *sm/f* coward.
'vigna ['viɲɲa] *sf,* **vi'gneto** [viɲ'ɲeto] *sm*
vineyard.
vi'gnetta [viɲ'ɲetta] *sf* cartoon.
vi'gogna [vi'goɲɲa] *sf* vicuña.
vi'gore *sm* vigour (*BRIT*), vigor (*US*); (*DIR*):
essere/entrare in ~ to be in/come into
force; **non è più in** ~ it is no longer in
force, it no longer applies.

vigo'roso, a *ag* vigorous.
'vile *ag* (*spregevole*) low, mean, base;
(*codardo*) cowardly.
vili'pendere *vt* to despise, scorn.
vili'pendio *sm* contempt, scorn.
vili'peso, a *pp di* **vilipendere**.
'villa *sf* villa.
vil'laggio [vil'laddʒo] *sm* village; ~ **turistico**
holiday village.
villa'nia *sf* rudeness, lack of manners; **fare**
(*o* **dire**) **una** ~ **a qn** to be rude to sb.
vil'lano, a *ag* rude, ill-mannered ♦ *sm/f*
boor.
villeggi'ante [villed'dʒante] *sm/f* holiday-
maker (*BRIT*), vacationer (*US*).
villeggi'are [villed'dʒare] *vi* to holiday,
spend one's holidays, vacation (*US*).
villeggia'tura [villeddʒa'tura] *sf* holiday(s
pl) (*BRIT*), vacation (*US*); **luogo di** ~
(holiday) resort.
vil'letta *sf,* **vil'lino** *sm* small house (with a
garden), cottage.
vil'loso, a *ag* hairy.
viltà *sf* cowardice *no pl*; (*gesto*) cowardly
act.

> The **Viminale**, *which takes its name from*
> *one of the famous Seven Hills of Rome, on*
> *which it stands, is the home of the Ministry*
> *of the Interior.*

'vimine *sm* wicker; **mobili di** ~**i** wicker
furniture *sg.*
vi'naio *sm* wine merchant.
'vincere ['vintʃere] *vt* (*in guerra, al gioco, a*
una gara) to defeat, beat; (*premio, guerra,*
partita) to win; (*fig*) to overcome, conquer
♦ *vi* to win; ~ **qn in** (*abilità, bellezza*) to
surpass sb in.
'vincita ['vintʃita] *sf* win; (*denaro vinto*)
winnings *pl.*
vinci'tore, 'trice [vintʃi'tore] *sm/f* winner;
(*MIL*) victor.
vinco'lante *ag* binding.
vinco'lare *vt* to bind; (*COMM: denaro*) to tie
up.
vinco'lato, a *ag:* **deposito** ~ (*COMM*) fixed
deposit.
'vincolo *sm* (*fig*) bond, tie; (*DIR*) obligation.
vi'nicolo, a *ag* wine *cpd*; **regione** ~**a** wine-
producing area.
vinificazi'one [vinifikat'tsjone] *sf* wine-
making.
'vino *sm* wine; ~ **bianco/rosso** white/red
wine.
'vinsi *etc vb vedi* **vincere**.
'vinto, a *pp di* **vincere** ♦ *ag:* **darla** ~**a a qn** to
let sb have his (*o* her) way; **darsi per** ~ to

give up, give in.

vi'ola *sf* (*BOT*) violet; (*MUS*) viola ♦ *ag, sm inv* (*colore*) purple.

vio'lare *vt* (*chiesa*) to desecrate, violate; (*giuramento, legge*) to violate.

violazi'one [violat'tsjone] *sf* desecration; violation; ~ **di domicilio** (*DIR*) breaking and entering.

violen'tare *vt* to use violence on; (*donna*) to rape.

vio'lento, a *ag* violent.

vio'lenza [vio'lɛntsa] *sf* violence; ~ **carnale** rape.

vio'letto, a *ag, sm* (*colore*) violet ♦ *sf* (*BOT*) violet.

violi'nista, i, e *smf* violinist.

vio'lino *sm* violin.

violoncel'lista, i, e [violontʃel'lista] *smf* cellist, cello player.

violon'cello [violon'tʃɛllo] *sm* cello.

vi'ottolo *sm* path, track.

VIP *smf inv* (= *Very Important Person*) VIP.

'vipera *sf* viper, adder.

vi'raggio [vi'raddʒo] *sm* (*NAUT, AER*) turn; (*FOT*) toning.

vi'rale *ag* viral.

vi'rare *vi* (*NAUT*) to come about; (*AER*) to turn; (*FOT*) to tone; ~ **di bordo** to change course.

vi'rata *sf* coming about; turning; change of course.

'virgola *sf* (*LING*) comma; (*MAT*) point.

virgo'lette *sfpl* inverted commas, quotation marks.

vi'rile *ag* (*proprio dell'uomo*) masculine; (*non puerile, da uomo*) manly, virile.

virilità *sf* masculinity; manliness; (*sessuale*) virility.

virtù *sf inv* virtue; **in** *o* **per** ~ **di** by virtue of, by.

virtu'ale *ag* virtual.

virtu'oso, a *ag* virtuous ♦ *smf* (*MUS etc*) virtuoso.

viru'lento, a *ag* virulent.

'virus *sm inv* virus.

visa'gista, i, e [viza'dʒista] *smf* beautician.

visce'rale [viʃʃe'rale] *ag* (*MED*) visceral; (*fig*) profound, deep-rooted.

'viscere ['viʃʃere] *sm* (*ANAT*) internal organ ♦ *sfpl* (*di animale*) entrails *pl*; (*fig*) depths *pl*, bowels *pl*.

'vischio ['viskjo] *sm* (*BOT*) mistletoe; (*pania*) birdlime.

vischi'oso, a [vis'kjoso] *ag* sticky.

visci'dità [viʃʃidi'ta] *sf* sliminess.

'viscido, a ['viʃʃido] *ag* slimy.

vis'conte, 'essa *smf* viscount/viscountess.

viscosità *sf* viscosity.

vis'coso, a *ag* viscous.

vi'sibile *ag* visible.

visi'bilio *sm*: **andare in** ~ to go into raptures.

visibilità *sf* visibility.

visi'era *sf* (*di elmo*) visor; (*di berretto*) peak.

visio'nare *vt* (*gen*) to look at, examine; (*CINE*) to screen.

visio'nario, a *ag, smf* visionary.

visi'one *sf* vision; **prendere** ~ **di qc** to examine sth, look sth over; **prima/seconda** ~ (*CINE*) first/second showing.

'visita *sf* visit; (*MED*) visit, call; (: *esame*) examination; **far** ~ **a qn, andare in** ~ **da qn** to visit sb, pay sb a visit; **in** ~ **ufficiale in Italia** on an official visit to Italy; **orario di** ~**e** (*ospedale*) visiting hours; ~ **di controllo** (*MED*) checkup; ~ **a domicilio** house call; ~ **guidata** guided tour; ~ **sanitaria** sanitary inspection.

visi'tare *vt* to visit; (*MED*) to visit, call on; (: *esaminare*) to examine.

visita'tore, 'trice *smf* visitor.

vi'sivo, a *ag* visual.

'viso *sm* face; **fare buon** ~ **a cattivo gioco** to make the best of things.

vi'sone *sm* mink.

vi'sore *sm* (*FOT*) viewer.

'vispo, a *ag* quick, lively.

'vissi *etc vb vedi* **vivere**.

vis'suto, a *pp di* **vivere** ♦ *ag* (*aria, modo di fare*) experienced.

'vista *sf* (*facoltà*) (eye)sight; (*fatto di vedere*): **la** ~ **di** the sight of; (*veduta*) view; **con** ~ **sul lago** with a view over the lake; **sparare a** ~ to shoot on sight; **pagabile a** ~ payable on demand; **in** ~ in sight; **avere in** ~ **qc** to have sth in view; **mettersi in** ~ to draw attention to o.s.; (*peg*) to show off; **perdere qn di** ~ to lose sight of sb; (*fig*) to lose touch with sb; **far** ~ **di fare** to pretend to do; **a** ~ **d'occhio** as far as the eye can see; (*fig*) before one's very eyes.

vis'tare *vt* to approve; (*AMM: passaporto*) to visa.

'visto, a *pp di* **vedere** ♦ *sm* visa; ~ **che** *cong* seeing (that); ~ **d'ingresso/di transito** entry/transit visa; ~ **permanente/di soggiorno** permanent/tourist visa.

vis'toso, a *ag* gaudy, garish; (*ingente*) considerable.

visu'ale *ag* visual.

visualiz'zare [vizualid'dzare] *vt* to visualize.

visualizza'tore [vizualiddza'tore] *sm* (*INFORM*) visual display unit, VDU.

visualizzazi'one [vizualiddzat'tsjone] *sf* (*INFORM*) display.

'vita *sf* life; (*ANAT*) waist; **essere in** ~ to be alive; **pieno di** ~ full of life; **a** ~ for life; **membro a** ~ life member.

vi'tale *ag* vital.

vitalità *sf* vitality.

vita'lizio, a [vita'littsjo] *ag* life *cpd* ♦ *sm* life annuity.

vita'mina *sf* vitamin.

'vite *sf* (*BOT*) vine; (*TECN*) screw; **giro di** ~ (*anche fig*) turn of the screw.

vi'tello *sm* (*ZOOL*) calf; (*carne*) veal; (*pelle*) calfskin.

vi'ticcio [vi'tittʃo] *sm* (*BOT*) tendril.

viticol'tore *sm* wine grower.

viticol'tura *sf* wine growing.

'vitreo, a *ag* vitreous; (*occhio, sguardo*) glassy.

'vittima *sf* victim.

vitti'mismo *sm* self-pity.

'vitto *sm* food; (*in un albergo etc*) board; ~ **e alloggio** board and lodging.

vit'toria *sf* victory.

vittori'ano, a *ag* Victorian.

vittori'oso, a *ag* victorious.

vitupe'rare *vt* to rail at *o* against.

vi'uzza [vi'uttsa] *sf* (*in città*) alley.

'viva *escl:* ~ **il re!** long live the king!

vivacchi'are [vivak'kjare] *vi* to scrape a living.

vi'vace [vi'vatʃe] *ag* (*vivo, animato*) lively; (*: mente*) lively, sharp; (*colore*) bright.

vivacità [vivatʃi'ta] *sf* liveliness; brightness.

vivaciz'zare [vivatʃid'dzare] *vt* to liven up.

vi'vaio *sm* (*di pesci*) hatchery; (*AGR*) nursery.

viva'mente *av* (*commuoversi*) deeply, profoundly; (*ringraziare etc*) sincerely, warmly.

vi'vanda *sf* food; (*piatto*) dish.

vi'vente *ag* living, alive; **i** ~**i** the living.

'vivere *vi* to live ♦ *vt* to live; (*passare: brutto momento*) to live through, go through; (*sentire: gioie, pene di qn*) to share ♦ *sm* life; (*anche:* **modo di** ~) way of life; ~**i** *smpl* food *sg*, provisions; ~ **di** to live on.

vi'veur [vi'vœr] *sm inv* pleasure-seeker.

'vivido, a *ag* (*colore*) vivid, bright.

vivifi'care *vt* to enliven, give life to; (*piante etc*) to revive.

vivisezi'one [viviset'tsjone] *sf* vivisection.

'vivo, a *ag* (*vivente*) alive, living; (*fig*) lively; (*: colore*) bright, brilliant ♦ *sm:* **entrare nel** ~ **di una questione** to get to the heart of a matter; **i** ~**i** the living; **esperimenti su animali** ~**i** experiments on live *o* living animals; ~ **e vegeto** hale and hearty; **farsi** ~ (*fig*) to show one's face; to keep in touch; **con** ~ **rammarico** with deep regret; **congratulazioni vivissime** heartiest congratulations; **con i più** ~**i ringraziamenti** with deepest *o* warmest thanks; **ritrarre dal** ~ to paint from life; **pungere qn nel** ~ (*fig*) to cut sb to the quick.

vivrò *etc vb vedi* **vivere**.

vizi'are [vit'tsjare] *vt* (*bambino*) to spoil; (*corrompere moralmente*) to corrupt; (*DIR*) to invalidate.

vizi'ato, a [vit'tsjato] *ag* spoilt; (*aria, acqua*) polluted; (*DIR*) invalid, invalidated.

'vizio ['vittsjo] *sm* (*morale*) vice; (*cattiva abitudine*) bad habit; (*imperfezione*) flaw, defect; (*errore*) fault, mistake; ~ **di forma** legal flaw *o* irregularity; ~ **procedurale** procedural error.

vizi'oso, a [vit'tsjoso] *ag* depraved; (*inesatto*) incorrect, wrong; **circolo** ~ vicious circle.

V.le *abbr* = **viale**.

vocabo'lario *sm* (*dizionario*) dictionary; (*lessico*) vocabulary.

vo'cabolo *sm* word.

vo'cale *ag* vocal ♦ *sf* vowel.

vocazi'one [vokat'tsjone] *sf* vocation; (*fig*) natural bent.

'voce ['votʃe] *sf* voice; (*diceria*) rumour (*BRIT*), rumor (*US*); (*di un elenco, in bilancio*) item; (*di dizionario*) entry; **parlare a alta/bassa** ~ to speak in a loud/low *o* soft voice; **fare la** ~ **grossa** to raise one's voice; **dar** ~ **a qc** to voice sth, give voice to sth; **a gran** ~ in a loud voice, loudly; **te lo dico a** ~ I'll tell you when I see you; **a una** ~ unanimously; **aver** ~ **in capitolo** (*fig*) to have a say in the matter; ~**i di corridoio** rumours.

voci'are [vo'tʃare] *vi* to shout, yell.

vocife'rante [votʃife'rante] *ag* noisy.

vo'cio [vo'tʃio] *sm* shouting.

'vodka *sf inv* vodka.

'voga *sf* (*NAUT*) rowing; (*usanza*): **essere in** ~ to be in fashion *o* in vogue.

vo'gare *vi* to row.

voga'tore, 'trice *sm/f* oarsman/woman ♦ *sm* rowing machine.

vogherò *etc* [voge'rɔ] *vb vedi* **vogare**.

'voglia ['vɔʎʎa] *sf* desire, wish; (*macchia*) birthmark; **aver** ~ **di qc/di fare** to feel like sth/like doing; (*più forte*) to want sth/ to do; **di buona** ~ willingly.

'voglio *etc* ['vɔʎʎo] *vb vedi* **volere**.

vogli'oso, a [voʎ'ʎoso] *ag* (*sguardo etc*) longing; (*più forte*) full of desire.

'voi *pron* you; ~ **stessi(e)** you yourselves.

voi'altri *pron* you.

vol. *abbr* (= *volume*) vol.
vo'lano *sm* (*SPORT*) shuttlecock; (*TECN*) flywheel.
vo'lant [vɔ'lã] *sm inv* frill.
vo'lante *ag* flying ♦ *sm* (steering) wheel ♦ *sf* (*POLIZIA: anche*: **squadra** ~) flying squad.
volanti'naggio [volanti'naddʒo] *sm* leafleting.
volanti'nare *vt* (*distribuire volantini*) to leaflet, hand out leaflets.
volan'tino *sm* leaflet.
vo'lare *vi* (*uccello, aereo, fig*) to fly; (*cappello*) to blow away *o* off, fly away *o* off; ~ **via** to fly away *o* off.
vo'lata *sf* flight; (*d'uccelli*) flock, flight; (*corsa*) rush; (*SPORT*) final sprint; **passare di ~ da qn** to drop in on sb briefly.
vo'latile *ag* (*CHIM*) volatile ♦ *sm* (*ZOOL*) bird.
volatiliz'zarsi [volatilid'dzarsi] *vr* (*CHIM*) to volatilize; (*fig*) to vanish, disappear.
vo'lente *ag*: **verrai ~ o nolente** you'll come whether you like it or not.
volente'roso, a *ag* willing, keen.
volenti'eri *av* willingly; "~" "with pleasure", "I'd be glad to".

========= *PAROLA CHIAVE*

vo'lere *sm* will, wish(es); **contro il ~ di** against the wishes of; **per ~ di qn** in obedience to sb's will *o* wishes
♦ *vt* **1** (*esigere, desiderare*) to want; ~ **fare qc** to want to do sth; ~ **che qn faccia qc** to want sb to do sth; **vorrei andarmene** I'd like to go; **vorrei che se ne andasse** I'd like him to go; **vorrei quello lì!** I'd like that one; **volevo parlartene** I meant to talk to you about it; **come vuoi** as you like; **la vogliono al telefono** there's a call for you; **che tu lo voglia o no** whether you like it or not; **vuoi un caffè?** would you like a coffee?; **senza ~** (*inavvertitamente*) without meaning to, unintentionally; **te la sei voluta** you asked for it; **la tradizione vuole che ...** custom requires that ...; **la leggenda vuole che ...** legend has it that ...
2 (*consentire*): **vogliate attendere, per piacere** please wait; **vogliamo andare?** shall we go?; **vuole essere così gentile da ...?** would you be so kind as to ...?; **non ha voluto ricevermi** he wouldn't see me
3: **volerci** (*essere necessario: materiale, attenzione*) to be needed; (: *tempo*) to take; **quanta farina ci vuole per questa torta?** how much flour do you need for this cake?; **ci vuole un'ora per arrivare a Venezia** it takes an hour to get to Venice; **è quel che ci vuole** it's just what is

needed
4: **voler bene a qn** (*amore*) to love sb; (*affetto*) to be fond of sb, like sb very much; **voler male a qn** to dislike sb; **volerne a qn** to bear sb a grudge; **voler dire** to mean; **voglio dire ...** I mean ...; **volevo ben dire!** I thought as much!

vol'gare *ag* vulgar.
volgarità *sf* vulgarity.
volgariz'zare [volgarid'dzare] *vt* to popularize.
volgar'mente *av* (*in modo volgare*) vulgarly, coarsely; (*del popolo*) commonly, popularly.
'volgere ['vɔldʒere] *vt* to turn ♦ *vi* to turn; (*tendere*): ~ **a**: **il tempo volge al brutto/al bello** the weather is breaking/is setting fair; **un rosso che volge al viola** a red verging on purple; ~**rsi** *vr* to turn; ~ **al peggio** to take a turn for the worse; ~ **al termine** to draw to an end.
'volgo *sm* common people.
voli'era *sf* aviary.
voli'tivo, a *ag* strong-willed.
'volli *etc vb vedi* **volere**.
'volo *sm* flight; **ci sono due ore di ~ da Londra a Milano** it's a two-hour flight between London and Milan; **al ~: colpire qc al ~** to hit sth as it flies past; **prendere al ~** (*autobus, treno*) to catch at the last possible moment; (*palla*) to catch as it flies past; (*occasione*) to seize; **capire al ~** to understand straight away; **veduta a ~ d'uccello** bird's-eye view; ~ **di linea** scheduled flight.
volontà *sf inv* will; **a ~** (*mangiare, bere*) as much as one likes; **buona/cattiva ~** goodwill/lack of goodwill; **le sue ultime ~** (*testamento*) his last will and testament *sg*.
volontaria'mente *av* voluntarily.
volontari'ato *sm* (*MIL*) voluntary service; (*lavoro*) voluntary work.
volon'tario, a *ag* voluntary ♦ *sm* (*MIL*) volunteer.
'volpe *sf* fox.
vol'pino, a *ag* (*pelo, coda*) fox's; (*aspetto, astuzia*) fox-like ♦ *sm* (*cane*) Pomeranian.
vol'pone, a *sm/f* (*fig*) old fox.
'volsi *etc vb vedi* **volgere**.
volt *sm inv* (*ELETTR*) volt.
'volta *sf* (*momento, circostanza*) time; (*turno, giro*) turn; (*curva*) turn, bend; (*ARCHIT*) vault; (*direzione*): **partire alla ~ di** to set off for; **a mia** (*o tua etc*) ~ in turn; **una ~** once; **una ~ sola** only once; **c'era una ~** once upon a time there was; **le cose di**

una ~ the things of the past; **due** ~**e** twice; **tre** ~**e** three times; **una cosa per** ~ one thing at a time; **una** ~ **o l'altra** one of these days; **una** ~ **per tutte** once and for all; **una** ~ **tanto** just for once; **lo facciamo un'altra** ~ we'll do it another time *o* some other time; **a** ~**e** at times, sometimes; **di** ~ **in** ~ from time to time; **una** ~ **che** (*temporale*) once; (*causale*) since; **3** ~**e 4** 3 times 4; **ti ha dato di** ~ **il cervello?** have you gone out of your mind?
volta'faccia [volta'fattʃa] *sm inv* (*fig*) volteface.
vol'taggio [vol'taddʒo] *sm* (*ELETTR*) voltage.
vol'tare *vt* to turn; (*girare: moneta*) to turn over; (*rigirare*) to turn round ♦ *vi* to turn; ~**rsi** *vr* to turn; to turn over; to turn round.
voltas'tomaco *sm* nausea; (*fig*) disgust.
volteggi'are [volted'dʒare] *vi* (*volare*) to circle; (*in equitazione*) to do trick riding; (*in ginnastica*) to vault.
'volto, a *pp di* **volgere** ♦ *ag* (*inteso a*): **il mio discorso è** ~ **a spiegare** ... in my speech I intend to explain ... ♦ *sm* face.
vo'lubile *ag* changeable, fickle.
vo'lume *sm* volume.
volumi'noso, a *ag* voluminous, bulky.
vo'luta *sf* (*gen*) spiral; (*ARCHIT*) volute.
voluttà *sf* sensual pleasure *o* delight.
voluttu'oso, a *ag* voluptuous.
vomi'tare *vt, vi* to vomit.
'vomito *sm* vomit; **ho il** ~ I feel sick.
'vongola *sf* clam.
vo'race [vo'ratʃe] *ag* voracious, greedy.
voracità [voratʃi'ta] *sf* voracity, voraciousness.
vo'ragine [vo'radʒine] *sf* abyss, chasm.
vorrò *etc vb vedi* **volere**.
'vortice ['vɔrtitʃe] *sm* whirl, vortex; (*fig*) whirl.
vorti'coso, a *ag* whirling.
'vostro, a *det*: **il(la)** ~**(a)** *etc* your ♦ *pron*: **il(la)** ~**(a)** *etc* yours ♦ *sm*: **avete speso dei** ~? did you spend your own money? ♦ *sf*: **la** ~**a** (*opinione*) your view; **i** ~**i** (*famiglia*) your family; **un** ~ **amico** a friend of yours; **è dei** ~**i, è dalla** ~**a** he's on your side; **l'ultima** ~**a** (*COMM: lettera*) your most recent letter; **alla** ~**a!** (*brindisi*) here's to you!, your health!
vo'tante *sm/f* voter.
vo'tare *vi* to vote ♦ *vt* (*sottoporre a votazione*) to take a vote on; (*approvare*) to vote for; (*REL*): ~ **qc a** to dedicate sth to; ~**rsi** *vr* to devote o.s. to.
votazi'one [votat'tsjone] *sf* vote, voting; ~**i** *sfpl* (*POL*) votes; (*INS*) marks.

'voto *sm* (*POL*) vote; (*INS*) mark (*BRIT*), grade (*US*); (*REL*) vow; (: *offerta*) votive offering; **aver** ~**i belli/brutti** (*INS*) to get good/bad marks *o* grades; **prendere i** ~**i** to take one's vows; ~ **di fiducia** vote of confidence.
V.P. *abbr* (= *vicepresidente*) VP.
VR *sigla* = *Verona*.
v.r. *abbr* (= *vedi retro*) PTO.
V.S. *abbr* = *Vostra Santità, Vostra Signoria*.
vs. *abbr* (= *vostro*) yr.
v.s. *abbr* = *vedi sopra*.
VT *sigla* = *Viterbo*.
V.U. *abbr* = **vigile urbano**.
vul'canico, a, ci, che *ag* volcanic.
vulcanizzazi'one [vulkaniddzat'tsjone] *sf* vulcanization.
vul'cano *sm* volcano.
vulne'rabile *ag* vulnerable.
vulnerabilità *sf* vulnerability.
vu'oi, vu'ole *vb vedi* **volere**.
vuo'tare *vt*, ~**rsi** *vr* to empty.
vu'oto, a *ag* empty; (*fig: privo*): ~ **di** (*senso etc*) devoid of ♦ *sm* empty space, gap; (*spazio in bianco*) blank; (*FISICA*) vacuum; (*fig: mancanza*) gap, void; **a mani** ~**e** empty-handed; **assegno a** ~ dud cheque (*BRIT*), bad check (*US*); ~ **d'aria** air pocket; "~ **a perdere**" "no deposit"; "~ **a rendere**" "returnable bottle".
v.v. *abbr* (= *vostro*) yr.

W w

W, w ['dɔppjovu] *sf o m inv* (*lettera*) W, w; **W come Washington** ≈ W for William.
W *abbr* = **viva, evviva**.
'wafer ['vafer] *sm inv* (*CUC, ELETTR*) wafer.
wagon-'lit [vagɔ'li] *sm inv* (*FERR*) sleeping car.
'walkman ® ['wɔːkmən] *sm inv* Walkman ®.
'water 'closet ['wɔːtə'klɔzit] *sm inv* toilet, lavatory.
watt [vat] *sm inv* (*ELETTR*) watt.
wat'tora [vat'tora] *sm inv* (*ELETTR*) watt-hour.
WC *sm inv* WC.
'weekend ['wiːkend] *sm inv* weekend.
'western ['wɛstern] *ag* (*CINE*) cowboy *cpd* ♦ *sm inv* western, cowboy film; ~ **all'italiana** spaghetti western.

'whisky ['wiski] *sm inv* whisky.
'windsurf ['windsə:f] *sm inv* (*tavola*)
windsurfer, sailboard; (*sport*)
windsurfing.
'würstel ['vyrstəl] *sm inv* frankfurter.

X x

X, x [iks] *sf o m inv* (*lettera*) X, x; **X come**
Xeres ≈ X for Xmas.
xenofo'bia [ksenofo'bia] *sf* xenophobia.
xe'nofobo, a [kse'nɔfobo] *ag* xenophobic
♦ *sm/f* xenophobe.
'xeres ['ksɛres] *sm inv* sherry.
xero'copia [ksero'kɔpja] *sf* xerox ®,
photocopy.
xerocopi'are [kseroko'pjare] *vt* to
photocopy.
xi'lofono [ksi'lɔfono] *sm* xylophone.

Y y

Y, y ['ipsilon] *sf o m inv* (*lettera*) Y, y; **Y come**
Yacht ≈ Y for Yellow (*BRIT*), Y for Yoke
(*US*).
yacht [jɔt] *sm inv* yacht.
'yankee ['jæŋki] *sm/f inv* Yank, Yankee.
Y.C.I. *abbr* = *Yacht Club d'Italia*.
'Yemen ['jemen] *sm*: **lo ~** Yemen.
yen [jen] *sm inv* (*moneta*) yen.
'yiddish ['jidiʃ] *ag inv, sm inv* Yiddish.
'yoga ['jɔga] *ag inv, sm* yoga (*cpd*).
yogurt ['jɔgurt] *sm inv* yog(h)urt.

Z z

Z, z ['dzɛta] *sf o m inv* (*lettera*) Z, z; **Z come**
Zara ≈ Z for Zebra.
zabai'one [dzaba'jone] *sm dessert made of
egg yolks, sugar and marsala.*
zaf'fata [tsaf'fata] *sf* (*tanfo*) stench.
zaffe'rano [dzaffe'rano] *sm* saffron.
zaf'firo [dzaf'firo] *sm* sapphire.
'zagara ['dzagara] *sf* orange blossom.
'zaino ['dzaino] *sm* rucksack.
Za'ire [dza'ire] *sm*: **lo ~** Zaire.
'Zambia ['dzambja] *sm*: **lo ~** Zambia.
'zampa ['tsampa] *sf* (*di animale: gamba*) leg;
(*: piede*) paw; **a quattro ~e** on all fours;
~e di gallina (*calligrafia*) scrawl; (*rughe*)
crow's feet.
zam'pata [tsam'pata] *sf* (*di cane, gatto*) blow
with a paw.
zampet'tare [tsampet'tare] *vi* to scamper.
zampil'lare [tsampil'lare] *vi* to gush, spurt.
zam'pillo [tsam'pillo] *sm* gush, spurt.
zam'pino [tsam'pino] *sm* paw; **qui c'è sotto**
il suo ~ (*fig*) he's had a hand in this.
zam'pogna [tsam'poɲɲa] *sf instrument
similar to bagpipes.*
'zanna ['tsanna] *sf* (*di elefante*) tusk; (*di
carnivori*) fang.
zan'zara [dzan'dzara] *sf* mosquito.
zanzari'era [dzandza'rjɛra] *sf* mosquito net.
'zappa ['tsappa] *sf* hoe.
zap'pare [tsap'pare] *vt* to hoe.
zappa'tore [tsappa'tore] *sm* (*AGR*) hoer.
zappa'tura [tsappa'tura] *sf* (*AGR*) hoeing.
zar, za'rina [tsar, tsa'rina] *sm/f* tsar/tsarina.
'zattera ['dzattera] *sf* raft.
za'vorra [dza'vɔrra] *sf* ballast.
'zazzera ['tsattsera] *sf* shock of hair.
'zebra ['dzɛbra] *sf* zebra; **~e** *sfpl* (*AUT*) zebra
crossing *sg* (*BRIT*), crosswalk *sg* (*US*).
ze'brato, a [dze'brato] *ag* with black and
white stripes; **strisce ~e,**
attraversamento ~ (*AUT*) zebra crossing
(*BRIT*), crosswalk (*US*).
'zecca, che ['tsekka] *sf* (*ZOOL*) tick; (*officina
di monete*) mint.
zec'chino [tsek'kino] *sm* gold coin; **oro ~**
pure gold.
ze'lante [dze'lante] *ag* zealous.
'zelo ['dzɛlo] *sm* zeal.

'**zenit** ['dzɛnit] *sm* zenith.
'**zenzero** ['dzendzero] *sm* ginger.
'**zeppa** ['tseppa] *sf* wedge.
'**zeppo, a** ['tseppo] *ag*: ~ **di** crammed *o* packed with.
zer'bino [dzer'bino] *sm* doormat.
'**zero** ['dzɛro] *sm* zero, nought; **vincere per tre a** ~ (*SPORT*) to win three-nil.
'**zeta** ['dzɛta] *sm o f* zed, (the letter) z.
'**zia** ['tsia] *sf* aunt.
zibel'lino [dzibel'lino] *sm* sable.
zi'gano, a [tsi'gano] *ag, sm/f* gypsy.
'**zigomo** ['dzigomo] *sm* cheekbone.
zigri'nare [dzigri'nare] *vt* (*gen*) to knurl; (*pellame*) to grain; (*monete*) to mill.
zig'zag [dzig'dzag] *sm inv* zigzag; **andare a** ~ to zigzag.
Zim'babwe [tsim'babwe] *sm*: **lo** ~ Zimbabwe.
zim'bello [dzim'bɛllo] *sm* (*oggetto di burle*) laughing-stock.
'**zinco** ['dzinko] *sm* zinc.
zinga'resco, a, schi, sche [dzinga'resko] *ag* gypsy *cpd*.
'**zingaro, a** ['dzingaro] *sm/f* gipsy.
'**zio** ['tsio], *pl* '**zii** *sm* uncle; **zii** *smpl* (*zio e zia*) uncle and aunt.
zi'tella [dzi'tɛlla] *sf* spinster; (*peg*) old maid.
zit'tire [tsit'tire] *vt* to silence, hush *o* shut up ♦ *vi* to hiss.
'**zitto, a** ['tsitto] *ag* quiet, silent; **sta'** ~! be quiet!
ziz'zania [dzid'dzanja] *sf* (*BOT*) darnel; (*fig*) discord; **gettare** *o* **seminare** ~ to sow discord.
'**zoccolo** ['tsɔkkolo] *sm* (*calzatura*) clog; (*di cavallo etc*) hoof; (*ARCHIT*) plinth; (*di parete*) skirting (board); (*di armadio*) base.
zodia'cale [dzodia'kale] *ag* zodiac *cpd*; **segno** ~ sign of the zodiac.
zo'diaco [dzo'diako] *sm* zodiac.
zolfa'nello [tsolfa'nɛllo] *sm* (sulphur) match.
'**zolfo** ['tsolfo] *sm* sulphur (*BRIT*), sulfur (*US*).
'**zolla** ['dzolla] *sf* clod (of earth).
zol'letta [dzol'letta] *sf* sugar lump.
'**zona** ['dzɔna] *sf* zone, area; ~ **di depressione** (*METEOR*) trough of low pressure; ~ **erogena** erogenous zone; ~ **pedonale** pedestrian precinct; ~ **verde** (*di abitato*) green area.

'**zonzo** ['dzondzo]: **a** ~ *av*: **andare a** ~ to wander about, stroll about.
'**zoo** ['dzɔo] *sm inv* zoo.
zoolo'gia [dzoolo'dʒia] *sf* zoology.
zoo'logico, a, ci, che [dzoo'lɔdʒiko] *ag* zoological.
zo'ologo, a, gi, ghe [dzo'ɔlogo] *sm/f* zoologist.
zoosa'fari [dzoosa'fari] *sm inv* safari park.
zoo'tecnico, a, ci, che [dzoo'tɛkniko] *ag* zootechnical; **il patrimonio** ~ **di un paese** a country's livestock resources.
zoppi'care [tsoppi'kare] *vi* to limp; (*fig: mobile*) to be shaky, rickety.
'**zoppo, a** ['tsɔppo] *ag* lame; (*fig: mobile*) shaky, rickety.
zoti'cone [dzoti'kone] *sm* lout.
zu'ava [dzu'ava] *sf*: **pantaloni** *mpl* **alla** ~ knickerbockers.
'**zucca, che** ['tsukka] *sf* (*BOT*) marrow (*BRIT*), vegetable marrow (*US*); pumpkin; (*scherzoso*) head.
zucche'rare [tsukke'rare] *vt* to put sugar in.
zucche'rato, a [tsukke'rato] *ag* sweet, sweetened.
zuccheri'era [tsukke'rjɛra] *sf* sugar bowl.
zuccheri'ficio [tsukkeri'fitʃo] *sm* sugar refinery.
zucche'rino, a [tsukke'rino] *ag* sugary, sweet.
'**zucchero** ['tsukkero] *sm* sugar; ~ **di canna** cane sugar; ~ **caramellato** caramel; ~ **filato** candy floss, cotton candy (*US*); ~ **a velo** icing sugar (*BRIT*), confectioner's sugar (*US*).
zucche'roso, a [tsukke'roso] *ag* sugary.
zuc'china, a [tsuk'kina] *sf*, **zuc'chino** [tsuk'kino] *sm* courgette (*BRIT*), zucchini (*US*).
zuc'cotto [tsuk'kɔtto] *sm* ice-cream sponge.
'**zuffa** ['tsuffa] *sf* brawl.
zufo'lare [tsufo'lare] *vt, vi* to whistle.
'**zufolo** ['tsufolo] *sm* (*MUS*) flageolet.
'**zuppa** ['tsuppa] *sf* soup; (*fig*) mixture, muddle; ~ **inglese** (*CUC*) dessert made with sponge cake, custard and chocolate, ≈ trifle (*BRIT*).
zuppi'era [tsup'pjɛra] *sf* soup tureen.
'**zuppo, a** ['tsuppo] *ag*: ~ **(di)** drenched (with), soaked (with).
Zu'rigo [dzu'rigo] *sf* Zurich.

English-Italian
Inglese-Italiano

Aa

A, a [eɪ] *n* (*letter*) A, a *for m inv*; (*SCOL*: *mark*)
≈ 10 (*ottimo*); (*MUS*): **A** la *m*; **A for Andrew**,
(*US*) **A for Able** ≈ A come Ancona;
from A to Z dall'A alla Z; **A road** *n* (*BRIT
AUT*) ≈ strada statale; **A shares** *npl* (*BRIT
STOCK EXCHANGE*) azioni *fpl* senza diritto
di voto; **A to Z** ® *n* stradario.

a [ə] (*before vowel or silent h*: **an**) *indef art* **1**
un (uno +*s impure, gn, pn, ps, x, z*), *f* una
(un' +*vowel*); ~ **book** un libro; ~ **mirror**
uno specchio; **an apple** una mela; **she's** ~
doctor è medico
2 (*instead of the number "one"*) un(o), *f*
una; ~ **year ago** un anno fa; ~ **hundred/
thousand pounds** cento/mille sterline
3 (*in expressing ratios, prices etc*) a, per; **3**
~ **day/week** 3 al giorno/alla settimana; **10
km an hour** 10 km all'ora; **£5** ~ **person** 5
sterline a persona *or* per persona.

a. *abbr* = **acre**.
AA *n abbr* (*BRIT*: = *Automobile Association*)
≈ A.C.I. *m* (= *Automobile Club d'Italia*);
(*US*: = *Associate in/of Arts*) titolo di studio;
(= *Alcoholics Anonymous*) A.A. *f*
(= *Anonima Alcolisti*); (*MIL*) = **anti-aircraft**.
AAA *n abbr* (= *American Automobile
Association*) ≈ A.C.I. *m* (= *Automobile
Club d'Italia*); (*BRIT*) = *Amateur Athletics
Association*.
A & R *n abbr* (*MUS*) = *artists and repertoire*; ~
man talent scout *m inv*.
AAUP *n abbr* (= *American Association of
University Professors*) *associazione dei
professori universitari*.
AB *abbr* (*BRIT*) *see* **able-bodied seaman**;

(*Canada*) = *Alberta*.
aback [ə'bæk] *adv*: **to be taken** ~ essere
sbalordito(a).
abacus, *pl* **abaci** ['æbəkəs, -saɪ] *n*
pallottoliere *m*, abaco.
abandon [ə'bændən] *vt* abbandonare ♦ *n*
abbandono; **to** ~ **ship** abbandonare la
nave.
abandoned [ə'bændənd] *adj* (*child, house
etc*) abbandonato(a); (*unrestrained*:
manner) disinvolto(a).
abase [ə'beɪs] *vt*: **to** ~ **o.s. (so far as to do)**
umiliarsi *or* abbassarsi (al punto di fare).
abashed [ə'bæʃt] *adj* imbarazzato(a).
abate [ə'beɪt] *vi* calmarsi.
abatement [ə'beɪtmənt] *n* (*of pollution,
noise*) soppressione *f*, eliminazione *f*;
noise ~ **society** associazione *f* per la lotta
contro i rumori.
abattoir ['æbətwɑ:*] *n* (*BRIT*) mattatoio.
abbey ['æbɪ] *n* abbazia, badia.
abbot ['æbət] *n* abate *m*.
abbreviate [ə'bri:vɪeɪt] *vt* abbreviare.
abbreviation [əbri:vɪ'eɪʃən] *n*
abbreviazione *f*.
ABC *n abbr* (= *American Broadcasting
Company*) *rete televisiva americana*.
abdicate ['æbdɪkeɪt] *vt* abdicare a ♦ *vi*
abdicare.
abdication [æbdɪ'keɪʃən] *n* abdicazione *f*.
abdomen ['æbdəmən] *n* addome *m*.
abdominal [æb'dɔmɪnl] *adj* addominale.
abduct [æb'dʌkt] *vt* rapire.
abduction [æb'dʌkʃən] *n* rapimento.
Aberdonian [æbə'dəunɪən] *adj* di Aberdeen
♦ *n* abitante *m/f* di Aberdeen; originario/a
di Aberdeen.
aberration [æbə'reɪʃən] *n* aberrazione *f*.

abet [ə'bɛt] *vt see* **aid.**

abeyance [ə'beɪəns] *n*: **in ~** in sospeso.

abhor [əb'hɔ:*] *vt* aborrire.

abhorrent [əb'hɔrənt] *adj* odioso(a).

abide [ə'baɪd] *vt* sopportare.

▶**abide by** *vt fus* conformarsi a.

abiding [ə'baɪdɪŋ] *adj* (*memory etc*) persistente, duraturo(a).

ability [ə'bɪlɪtɪ] *n* abilità *f inv*; **to the best of my ~** con il massimo impegno.

abject ['æbdʒɛkt] *adj* (*poverty*) abietto(a); (*apology*) umiliante; (*coward*) indegno(a), vile.

ablaze [ə'bleɪz] *adj* in fiamme; **~ with light** risplendente di luce.

able ['eɪbl] *adj* capace; **to be ~ to do sth** essere capace di fare qc, poter fare qc.

able-bodied ['eɪbl'bɔdɪd] *adj* robusto(a).

able-bodied seaman (AB) *n* (*BRIT*) marinaio scelto.

ably ['eɪblɪ] *adv* abilmente.

ABM *n abbr* (= *anti-ballistic missile*) ABM *m*.

abnormal [æb'nɔ:məl] *adj* anormale.

abnormality [æbnɔ:'mælɪtɪ] *n* (*condition*) anormalità; (*instance*) anomalia.

aboard [ə'bɔ:d] *adv* a bordo ♦ *prep* a bordo di; **~ the train** in *or* sul treno.

abode [ə'bəud] *n* (*old*) dimora; (*LAW*) domicilio, dimora; **of no fixed ~** senza fissa dimora.

abolish [ə'bɔlɪʃ] *vt* abolire.

abolition [æbəu'lɪʃən] *n* abolizione *f*.

abominable [ə'bɔmɪnəbl] *adj* abominevole.

aborigine [æbə'rɪdʒɪnɪ] *n* aborigeno/a.

abort [ə'bɔ:t] *vt* (*MED, fig*) abortire; (*COMPUT*) interrompere l'esecuzione di.

abortion [ə'bɔ:ʃən] *n* aborto; **to have an ~** avere un aborto, abortire.

abortionist [ə'bɔ:ʃənɪst] *n* abortista *m/f*.

abortive [ə'bɔ:tɪv] *adj* abortivo(a).

abound [ə'baund] *vi* abbondare; **to ~ in** abbondare di.

════════════ *KEYWORD*

about [ə'baut] *adv* **1** (*approximately*) circa, quasi; **~ a hundred/thousand** un centinaio/migliaio, circa cento/mille; **it takes ~ 10 hours** ci vogliono circa 10 ore; **at ~ 2 o'clock** verso le 2; **I've just ~ finished** ho quasi finito; **it's ~ here** è qui intorno, è qui vicino

2 (*referring to place*) qua e là, in giro; **to leave things lying ~** lasciare delle cose in giro; **to run ~** correre qua e là; **to walk ~** camminare; **is Paul ~?** (*BRIT*) hai visto Paul in giro?; **it's the other way ~** (*BRIT*) è il contrario

3: **to be ~ to do sth** stare per fare qc; **I'm**

not ~ to do all that for nothing non ho intenzione di fare tutto questo per niente

♦ *prep* **1** (*relating to*) su, di; **a book ~ London** un libro su Londra; **what is it ~?** di che si tratta?; (*book, film etc*) di cosa tratta?; **we talked ~ it** ne abbiamo parlato; **do something ~ it!** fai qualcosa!; **what** *or* **how ~ doing this?** che ne dici di fare questo?

2 (*referring to place*): **to walk ~ the town** camminare per la città; **her clothes were scattered ~ the room** i suoi vestiti erano sparsi *or* in giro per tutta la stanza.

about-face [ə'baut'feɪs] *n*, **about-turn** [ə'baut'tɔ:n] *n* (*MIL*) dietro front *m inv*.

above [ə'bʌv] *adv, prep* sopra; **mentioned ~** suddetto; **costing ~ £10** più caro di 10 sterline; **he's not ~ a bit of blackmail** non rifuggirebbe dal ricatto; **~ all** soprattutto.

aboveboard [ə'bʌv'bɔ:d] *adj* aperto(a); onesto(a).

abrasion [ə'breɪʒən] *n* abrasione *f*.

abrasive [ə'breɪzɪv] *adj* abrasivo(a).

abreast [ə'brɛst] *adv* di fianco; **3 ~** per 3 di fronte; **to keep ~ of** tenersi aggiornato su.

abridge [ə'brɪdʒ] *vt* ridurre.

abroad [ə'brɔ:d] *adv* all'estero; **there is a rumour ~ that ...** (*fig*) si sente dire in giro che ..., circola la voce che ....

abrupt [ə'brʌpt] *adj* (*steep*) erto(a); (*sudden*) improvviso(a); (*gruff, blunt*) brusco(a).

abscess ['æbsɪs] *n* ascesso.

abscond [əb'skɔnd] *vi* scappare.

absence ['æbsəns] *n* assenza; **in the ~ of** (*person*) in assenza di; (*thing*) in mancanza di.

absent ['æbsənt] *adj* assente; **to be ~ without leave (AWOL)** (*MIL etc*) essere assente ingiustificato.

absentee [æbsən'ti:] *n* assente *m/f*.

absenteeism [æbsən'ti:ɪzəm] *n* assenteismo.

absent-minded ['æbsənt'maɪndɪd] *adj* distratto(a).

absent-mindedness ['æbsənt'maɪndɪdnɪs] *n* distrazione *f*.

absolute ['æbsəlu:t] *adj* assoluto(a).

absolutely [æbsə'lu:tlɪ] *adv* assolutamente.

absolve [əb'zɔlv] *vt*: **to ~ sb (from)** (*sin etc*) assolvere qn (da); **to ~ sb from** (*oath*) sciogliere qn da.

absorb [əb'sɔ:b] *vt* assorbire; **to be ~ed in a book** essere immerso(a) in un libro.

absorbent [əb'sɔ:bənt] *adj* assorbente.

absorbent cotton *n* (*US*) cotone *m* idrofilo.

absorbing [əb'sɔ:bɪŋ] *adj* avvincente, molto

interessante.

absorption [əb'sɔːpʃən] *n* assorbimento.

abstain [əb'steɪn] *vi*: **to ~ (from)** astenersi (da).

abstemious [əb'stiːmɪəs] *adj* astemio(a).

abstention [əb'stɛnʃən] *n* astensione *f*.

abstinence ['æbstɪnəns] *n* astinenza.

abstract ['æbstrækt] *adj* astratto(a) ♦ *n* (*summary*) riassunto ♦ *vt* [æb'strækt] estrarre.

absurd [əb'sɔːd] *adj* assurdo(a).

absurdity [əb'sɔːdɪtɪ] *n* assurdità *f inv*.

ABTA ['æbtə] *n abbr* = Association of British Travel Agents.

Abu Dhabi ['æbuː'dɑːbɪ] *n* Abu Dhabi *f*.

abundance [ə'bʌndəns] *n* abbondanza.

abundant [ə'bʌndənt] *adj* abbondante.

abuse *n* [ə'bjuːs] abuso; (*insults*) ingiurie *fpl* ♦ *vt* [ə'bjuːz] abusare di; **open to ~** che si presta ad abusi.

abusive [ə'bjuːsɪv] *adj* ingiurioso(a).

abysmal [ə'bɪzməl] *adj* spaventoso(a).

abyss [ə'bɪs] *n* abisso.

AC *n abbr* (*US*) = athletic club.

a/c *abbr* (*BANKING etc*: = *account, account current*) c.

academic [ækə'dɛmɪk] *adj* accademico(a); (*pej: issue*) puramente formale ♦ *n* universitario/a.

academic year *n* anno accademico.

academy [ə'kædəmɪ] *n* (*learned body*) accademia; (*school*) scuola privata; **military/naval ~** scuola militare/navale; **~ of music** conservatorio.

ACAS ['eɪkæs] *n abbr* (*BRIT*: = Advisory, Conciliation and Arbitration Service) comitato governativo per il miglioramento della contrattazione collettiva.

accede [æk'siːd] *vi*: **to ~ to** (*request*) accedere a; (*throne*) ascendere a.

accelerate [æk'sɛləreɪt] *vt, vi* accelerare.

acceleration [æksɛlə'reɪʃən] *n* accelerazione *f*.

accelerator [æk'sɛləreɪtə*] *n* acceleratore *m*.

accent ['æksɛnt] *n* accento.

accentuate [æk'sɛntjueɪt] *vt* (*syllable*) accentuare; (*need, difference etc*) accentuare, mettere in risalto *or* in evidenza.

accept [ək'sɛpt] *vt* accettare.

acceptable [ək'sɛptəbl] *adj* accettabile.

acceptance [ək'sɛptəns] *n* accettazione *f*; **to meet with general ~** incontrare il favore *or* il consenso generale.

access ['æksɛs] *n* accesso ♦ *vt* (*COMPUT*) accedere a; **to have ~ to** avere accesso a;

the burglars gained ~ through a window i ladri sono riusciti a penetrare da *or* attraverso una finestra.

accessible [æk'sɛsəbl] *adj* accessibile.

accession [æk'sɛʃən] *n* (*addition*) aggiunta; (*to library*) accessione *f*, acquisto; (*of king*) ascesa *or* salita al trono.

accessory [æk'sɛsərɪ] *n* accessorio; **toilet accessories** *npl* (*BRIT*) articoli *mpl* da toilette.

access road *n* strada d'accesso; (*to motorway*) raccordo di entrata.

access time *n* (*COMPUT*) tempo di accesso.

accident ['æksɪdənt] *n* incidente *m*; (*chance*) caso; **to meet with** *or* **to have an ~** avere un incidente; **~s at work** infortuni *mpl* sul lavoro; **by ~** per caso.

accidental [æksɪ'dɛntl] *adj* accidentale.

accidentally [æksɪ'dɛntəlɪ] *adv* per caso.

accident insurance *n* assicurazione *f* contro gli infortuni.

accident-prone ['æksɪdənt'prəun] *adj*: **he's very ~** è un vero passaguai.

acclaim [ə'kleɪm] *vt* acclamare ♦ *n* acclamazione *f*.

acclamation [æklə'meɪʃən] *n* (*approval*) acclamazione *f*; (*applause*) applauso.

acclimatize [ə'klaɪmətaɪz], (*US*) **acclimate** [ə'klaɪmeɪt] *vt*: **to become ~d** acclimatarsi.

accolade ['ækəleɪd] *n* encomio.

accommodate [ə'kɒmədeɪt] *vt* alloggiare; (*oblige, help*) favorire; **this car ~s 4 people comfortably** quest'auto può trasportare comodamente 4 persone.

accommodating [ə'kɒmədeɪtɪŋ] *adj* compiacente.

accommodation, (*US*) **accommodations** [əkɒmə'deɪʃən(z)] *n(pl)* alloggio; **seating ~** (*BRIT*) posti a sedere; **"~ to let"** (*BRIT*) "camere in affitto"; **have you any ~?** avete posto?

accompaniment [ə'kʌmpənɪmənt] *n* accompagnamento.

accompanist [ə'kʌmpənɪst] *n* (*MUS*) accompagnatore/trice.

accompany [ə'kʌmpənɪ] *vt* accompagnare.

accomplice [ə'kʌmplɪs] *n* complice *m/f*.

accomplish [ə'kʌmplɪʃ] *vt* compiere; (*achieve*) ottenere.

accomplished [ə'kʌmplɪʃt] *adj* (*person*) esperto(a).

accomplishment [ə'kʌmplɪʃmənt] *n* compimento; (*thing achieved*) risultato; **~s** *npl* (*skills*) doti *fpl*.

accord [ə'kɔːd] *n* accordo ♦ *vt* accordare; **of his own ~** di propria iniziativa; **with one ~** all'unanimità, di comune accordo.

accordance [ə'kɔːdəns] *n*: **in ~ with** in

conformità con.

according [ə'kɔːdɪŋ]: ~ **to** prep secondo; **it went ~ to plan** è andata secondo il previsto.

accordingly [ə'kɔːdɪŋlɪ] adv in conformità.

accordion [ə'kɔːdɪən] n fisarmonica.

accost [ə'kɔst] vt avvicinare.

account [ə'kaunt] n (COMM) conto; (report) descrizione f; ~**s** npl (COMM) conti; "~ payee only" (BRIT) "assegno non trasferibile"; **to keep an ~ of** tenere nota di; **to bring sb to ~ for sth/for having done sth** chiedere a qn di render conto di qc/per aver fatto qc; **by all ~s** a quanto si dice; **of little ~** di poca importanza; **on ~** in acconto; **to buy sth on ~** comprare qc a credito; **on no ~** per nessun motivo; **on ~ of** a causa di; **to take into ~, take ~ of** tener conto di.

▸**account for** vt fus (explain) spiegare; giustificare; **all the children were ~ed for** nessun bambino mancava all'appello.

accountability [ə'kauntə'bɪlɪtɪ] n responsabilità.

accountable [ə'kauntəbl] adj responsabile; **to be held ~ for sth** dover rispondere di qc.

accountancy [ə'kauntənsɪ] n ragioneria.

accountant [ə'kauntənt] n ragioniere/a.

accounting [ə'kauntɪŋ] n contabilità.

accounting period n esercizio finanziario, periodo contabile.

account number n numero di conto.

account payable n conto passivo.

account receivable n conto da esigere.

accredited [ə'kredɪtɪd] adj accreditato(a).

accretion [ə'kriːʃən] n accrescimento.

accrue [ə'kruː] vi (mount up) aumentare; **to ~ to** derivare a; ~**d charges** ratei mpl passivi; ~**d interest** interesse m maturato.

accumulate [ə'kjuːmjuleɪt] vt accumulare ♦ vi accumularsi.

accumulation [əkjuːmju'leɪʃən] n accumulazione f.

accuracy ['ækjurəsɪ] n precisione f.

accurate ['ækjurɪt] adj preciso(a).

accurately ['ækjurɪtlɪ] adv precisamente.

accusation [ækju'zeɪʃən] n accusa.

accusative [ə'kjuːzətɪv] n (LING) accusativo.

accuse [ə'kjuːz] vt accusare.

accused [ə'kjuːzd] n accusato/a.

accuser [ə'kjuːzə*] n accusatore/trice.

accustom [ə'kʌstəm] vt abituare; **to ~ o.s. to sth** abituarsi a qc.

accustomed [ə'kʌstəmd] adj (usual) abituale; ~ **to** abituato(a) a.

AC/DC abbr (= alternating current/direct current) c.a./c.c.

ACE [eɪs] n abbr = American Council on Education.

ace [eɪs] n asso; **within an ~ of** (BRIT) a un pelo da.

acerbic [ə'sɜːbɪk] adj (also fig) acido(a).

acetate ['æsɪteɪt] n acetato.

ache [eɪk] n male m, dolore m ♦ vi (be sore) far male, dolere; (yearn): **to ~ to do sth** morire dalla voglia di fare qc; **I've got stomach ~** or (US) **a stomach ~** ho mal di stomaco; **my head ~s** mi fa male la testa; **I'm aching all over** mi duole dappertutto.

achieve [ə'tʃiːv] vt (aim) raggiungere; (victory, success) ottenere; (task) compiere.

achievement [ə'tʃiːvmənt] n compimento; successo.

Achilles heel [ə'kɪliːz-] n tallone m d'Achille.

acid ['æsɪd] adj acido(a) ♦ n acido.

acidity [ə'sɪdɪtɪ] n acidità.

acid rain n pioggia acida.

acid test n (fig) prova del fuoco.

acknowledge [ək'nɔlɪdʒ] vt riconoscere; (letter. also: ~ **receipt of**) accusare ricevuta di.

acknowledgement [ək'nɔlɪdʒmənt] n riconoscimento; (of letter) conferma; ~**s** (in book) ringraziamenti mpl.

ACLU n abbr (= American Civil Liberties Union) unione americana per le libertà civili.

acme ['ækmɪ] n culmine m, acme m.

acne ['æknɪ] n acne f.

acorn ['eɪkɔːn] n ghianda.

acoustic [ə'kuːstɪk] adj acustico(a); see also **acoustics**.

acoustic coupler [-'kʌplə*] n (COMPUT) accoppiatore m acustico.

acoustics [ə'kuːstɪks] n, npl acustica.

acquaint [ə'kweɪnt] vt: **to ~ sb with sth** far sapere qc a qn; **to be ~ed with** (person) conoscere.

acquaintance [ə'kweɪntəns] n conoscenza; (person) conoscente m/f; **to make sb's ~** fare la conoscenza di qn.

acquiesce [ækwɪ'ɛs] vi (agree): **to ~ (in)** acconsentire (a).

acquire [ə'kwaɪə*] vt acquistare.

acquired [ə'kwaɪəd] adj acquisito(a); **it's an ~ taste** è una cosa che si impara ad apprezzare.

acquisition [ækwɪ'zɪʃən] n acquisto.

acquisitive [ə'kwɪzɪtɪv] adj a cui piace accumulare le cose.

acquit [ə'kwɪt] vt assolvere; **to ~ o.s. well**

comportarsi bene.

acquittal [ə'kwɪtl] n assoluzione f.

acre ['eɪkə*] n acro (= 4047 m²).

acreage ['eɪkərɪdʒ] n superficie f in acri.

acrid ['ækrɪd] adj (smell) acre, pungente; (fig) pungente.

acrimonious [ækrɪ'məʊnɪəs] adj astioso(a).

acrobat ['ækrəbæt] n acrobata m/f.

acrobatic [ækrə'bætɪk] adj acrobatico(a).

acrobatics [ækrə'bætɪks] n acrobatica ♦ npl acrobazie fpl.

Acropolis [ə'krɔpəlɪs] n: the ~ l'Acropoli f.

across [ə'krɔs] prep (on the other side) dall'altra parte di; (crosswise) attraverso ♦ adv dall'altra parte; in larghezza; **to walk ~ (the road)** attraversare (la strada); **to take sb ~ the road** far attraversare la strada a qn; **~ from** di fronte a; **the lake is 12 km ~** il lago ha una larghezza di 12 km or è largo 12 km; **to get sth ~ to sb** (fig) far capire qc a qn.

acrylic [ə'krɪlɪk] adj acrilico(a) ♦ n acrilico.

ACT n abbr (= American College Test) esame di ammissione a college.

act [ækt] n atto; (in music-hall etc) numero; (LAW) decreto ♦ vi agire; (THEAT) recitare; (pretend) fingere ♦ vt (part) recitare; **to catch sb in the ~** cogliere qn in flagrante or sul fatto; **it's only an ~** è tutta scena, è solo una messinscena; **~ of God** (LAW) calamità f inv naturale; **to ~ Hamlet** (BRIT) recitare la parte di Amleto; **to ~ the fool** (BRIT) fare lo stupido; **to ~ as** agire da; **it ~s as a deterrent** serve da deterrente; **~ing in my capacity as chairman, I ...** in qualità di presidente, io ....

►**act on** vt: **to ~ on sth** agire in base a qc.

►**act out** vt (event) ricostruire; (fantasies) dare forma concreta a.

acting ['æktɪŋ] adj che fa le funzioni di ♦ n (of actor) recitazione f; (activity): **to do some ~** fare del teatro (or del cinema); **he is the ~ manager** fa le veci del direttore.

action ['ækʃən] n azione f; (MIL) combattimento; (LAW) processo; **to take ~** agire; **to put a plan into ~** realizzare un piano; **out of ~** fuori combattimento; (machine etc) fuori servizio; **killed in ~** (MIL) ucciso in combattimento; **to bring an ~ against sb** (LAW) intentare causa contro qn.

action replay n (BRIT TV) replay m inv.

activate ['æktɪveɪt] vt (mechanism) fare funzionare; (CHEM, PHYSICS) rendere attivo(a).

active ['æktɪv] adj attivo(a); **to play an ~ part in** partecipare attivamente a.

active duty (AD) n (US MIL) = **active service**.

actively ['æktɪvlɪ] adv attivamente.

active partner n (COMM) socio effettivo.

active service n (BRIT MIL): **to be on ~** prestar servizio in zona di operazioni.

activist ['æktɪvɪst] n attivista m/f.

activity [æk'tɪvɪtɪ] n attività f inv.

actor ['æktə*] n attore m.

actress ['æktrɪs] n attrice f.

actual ['æktjuəl] adj reale, vero(a).

actually ['æktjuəlɪ] adv veramente; (even) addirittura.

actuary ['æktjuərɪ] n attuario/a.

actuate ['æktjueɪt] vt attivare.

acuity [ə'kjuːɪtɪ] n acutezza.

acumen ['ækjumən] n acume m; **business ~** fiuto negli affari.

acupuncture ['ækjupʌŋktʃə*] n agopuntura.

AD adv abbr (= Anno Domini) d. C. ♦ n abbr (US MIL) see **active duty**.

ad [æd] n abbr = **advertisement**.

adamant ['ædəmənt] adj irremovibile.

Adam's apple ['ædəmz-] n pomo di Adamo.

adapt [ə'dæpt] vt adattare ♦ vi: **to ~ (to)** adattarsi (a).

adaptability [ədæptə'bɪlɪtɪ] n adattabilità.

adaptable [ə'dæptəbl] adj (device) adattabile; (person) che sa adattarsi.

adaptation [ædæp'teɪʃən] n adattamento.

adapter, adaptor [ə'dæptə*] n (ELEC) adattatore m.

ADC n abbr (MIL) = **aide-de-camp**; (US: = Aid to Dependent Children) sussidio per figli a carico.

add [æd] vt aggiungere; (figures) addizionare ♦ vi: **to ~ to** (increase) aumentare.

►**add on** vt aggiungere.

►**add up** vt (figures) addizionare ♦ vi (fig): **it doesn't ~ up** non ha senso; **it doesn't ~ up to much** non è un granché.

adder ['ædə*] n vipera.

addict ['ædɪkt] n tossicomane m/f; (fig) fanatico/a; **heroin ~** eroinomane m/f; **drug ~** tossicodipendente m/f, tossicomane m/f.

addicted [ə'dɪktɪd] adj: **to be ~ to** (drink etc) essere dedito(a) a; (fig: football etc) essere tifoso(a) di.

addiction [ə'dɪkʃən] n (MED) tossicomania.

adding machine ['ædɪŋ-] n addizionatrice f.

Addis Ababa ['ædɪs'æbəbə] n Addis Abeba f.

addition [ə'dɪʃən] n addizione f; **in ~** inoltre; **in ~ to** oltre.

additional [ə'dɪʃənl] adj supplementare.

additive ['ædɪtɪv] n additivo.

address [ə'drɛs] n (*gen*, *COMPUT*) indirizzo; (*talk*) discorso ♦ vt indirizzare; (*speak to*) fare un discorso a; **form of** ~ (*gen*) formula di cortesia; (*in letters*) formula d'indirizzo *or* di intestazione; **to** ~ **o.s. to sth** indirizzare le proprie energie verso qc; **absolute/relative** ~ (*COMPUT*) indirizzo assoluto/relativo.

address book n rubrica.

addressee [ædrɛ'si:] n destinatario/a.

Aden ['eɪdən] n: **the Gulf of** ~ il golfo di Aden.

adenoids ['ædɪnɔɪdz] npl adenoidi fpl.

adept ['ædɛpt] adj: ~ **at** esperto(a) in.

adequate ['ædɪkwɪt] adj (*description*, *reward*) adeguato(a); (*amount*) sufficiente; **to feel** ~ **to a task** sentirsi all'altezza di un compito.

adequately ['ædɪkwɪtlɪ] adv adeguatamente; sufficientemente.

adhere [əd'hɪə*] vi: **to** ~ **to** aderire a; (*fig*: *rule*, *decision*) seguire.

adhesion [əd'hi:ʒən] n adesione f.

adhesive [əd'hi:zɪv] adj adesivo(a) ♦ n adesivo; ~ **tape** (*BRIT*: *for parcels etc*) nastro adesivo; (*US*: *MED*) cerotto adesivo.

ad hoc [æd'hɔk] adj (*decision*) ad hoc inv; (*committee*) apposito(a).

ad infinitum ['ædɪnfɪ'naɪtəm] adv all'infinito.

adjacent [ə'dʒeɪsənt] adj adiacente; ~ **to** accanto a.

adjective ['ædʒɛktɪv] n aggettivo.

adjoin [ə'dʒɔɪn] vt essere contiguo(a) *or* attiguo(a) a.

adjoining [ə'dʒɔɪnɪŋ] adj accanto inv, adiacente ♦ prep accanto a.

adjourn [ə'dʒə:n] vt rimandare, aggiornare; (*US*: *end*) sospendere ♦ vi sospendere la seduta; (*PARLIAMENT*) sospendere i lavori; (*go*) spostarsi; **to** ~ **a meeting till the following week** aggiornare *or* rinviare un incontro alla settimana seguente; **they** ~**ed to the pub** (*col*) si sono trasferiti al pub.

adjournment [ə'dʒə:nmənt] n rinvio, aggiornamento; sospensione f.

Adjt abbr (*MIL*) = **adjutant**.

adjudicate [ə'dʒu:dɪkeɪt] vt (*contest*) giudicare; (*claim*) decidere su.

adjudication [ədʒu:dɪ'keɪʃən] n decisione f.

adjust [ə'dʒʌst] vt aggiustare; (*COMM*) rettificare ♦ vi: **to** ~ (**to**) adattarsi (a).

adjustable [ə'dʒʌstəbl] adj regolabile.

adjuster [ə'dʒʌstə*] n see **loss adjuster**.

adjustment [ə'dʒʌstmənt] n adattamento; (*of prices*, *wages*) aggiustamento.

adjutant ['ædʒətənt] n aiutante m.

ad-lib [æd'lɪb] vt, vi improvvisare ♦ n improvvisazione f ♦ adv: **ad lib** a piacere, a volontà.

adman ['ædmæn] n (*col*) pubblicitario/a.

admin [æd'mɪn] n abbr (*col*) = **administration**.

administer [əd'mɪnɪstə*] vt amministrare; (*justice*) somministrare.

administration [ədmɪnɪs'treɪʃən] n amministrazione f; **the A**~ (*US*) il Governo.

administrative [əd'mɪnɪstrətɪv] adj amministrativo(a).

administrator [əd'mɪnɪstreɪtə*] n amministratore/trice.

admirable ['ædmərəbl] adj ammirevole.

admiral ['ædmərəl] n ammiraglio.

Admiralty ['ædmərəltɪ] n (*BRIT*: *also*: ~ **Board**) Ministero della Marina.

admiration [ædmə'reɪʃən] n ammirazione f.

admirer [əd'maɪərə*] n ammiratore/trice.

admiring [əd'maɪərɪŋ] adj (*glance etc*) di ammirazione.

admissible [əd'mɪsəbl] adj ammissibile.

admission [əd'mɪʃən] n ammissione f; (*to exhibition*, *night club etc*) ingresso; (*confession*) confessione f; **by his own** ~ per sua ammissione; "~ **free**", "**free** ~" "ingresso gratuito".

admit [əd'mɪt] vt ammettere; far entrare; (*agree*) riconoscere; "**children not** ~**ted**" "vietato l'ingresso ai bambini"; **this ticket** ~**s two** questo biglietto è valido per due persone; **I must** ~ **that** ... devo ammettere *or* confessare che ....

► **admit of** vt fus lasciare adito a.

► **admit to** vt fus riconoscere.

admittance [əd'mɪtəns] n ingresso; "**no** ~" "vietato l'ingresso".

admittedly [əd'mɪtɪdlɪ] adv bisogna pur riconoscere (che).

admonish [əd'mɔnɪʃ] vt ammonire.

ad nauseam [æd'nɔ:zɪæm] adv fino alla nausea, a non finire.

ado [ə'du:] n: **without (any) more** ~ senza più indugi.

adolescence [ædəu'lɛsns] n adolescenza.

adolescent [ædəu'lɛsnt] adj, n adolescente (m/f).

adopt [ə'dɔpt] vt adottare.

adopted [ə'dɔptɪd] adj adottivo(a).

adoption [ə'dɔpʃən] n adozione f.

adore [ə'dɔ:*] vt adorare.

adoring [ə'dɔ:rɪŋ] adj adorante; **his** ~ **wife** sua moglie che lo adora.

adoringly [ə'dɔ:rɪŋlɪ] adv con adorazione.

adorn [ə'dɔ:n] vt ornare.

adornment [ə'dɔːnmənt] *n* ornamento.
ADP *n abbr see* **automatic data processing.**
adrenalin [ə'drɛnəlɪn] *n* adrenalina; **it gets the ~ going** ti dà una carica.
Adriatic (Sea) [eɪdrɪ'ætɪk-] *n* Adriatico.
adrift [ə'drɪft] *adv* alla deriva; **to come ~** (*boat*) andare alla deriva; (*wire, rope etc*) esersi staccato(a) *or* sciolto(a).
adroit [ə'drɔɪt] *adj* abile, destro(a).
ADT *abbr* (*US*: = *Atlantic Daylight Time*) ora legale di New York.
adult ['ædʌlt] *n* adulto/a.
adult education *n* scuola per adulti.
adulterate [ə'dʌltəreɪt] *vt* adulterare.
adulterer [ə'dʌltərə*] *n* adultero.
adulteress [ə'dʌltərɪs] *n* adultera.
adultery [ə'dʌltərɪ] *n* adulterio.
adulthood ['ædʌlthud] *n* età adulta.
advance [əd'vɑːns] *n* avanzamento; (*money*) anticipo ♦ *vt* avanzare; (*date, money*) anticipare ♦ *vi* avanzare; **in ~** in anticipo; **to make ~s to sb** (*gen*) fare degli approcci a qn; (*amorously*) fare delle avances a qn.
advanced [əd'vɑːnst] *adj* avanzato(a); (*SCOL: studies*) superiore; **~ in years** avanti negli anni.
advancement [əd'vɑːnsmənt] *n* avanzamento.
advance notice *n* preavviso.
advantage [əd'vɑːntɪdʒ] *n* (*also TENNIS*) vantaggio; **to take ~ of** approfittarsi di; **it's to our ~** è nel nostro interesse, torna a nostro vantaggio.
advantageous [ædvən'teɪdʒəs] *adj* vantaggioso(a).
advent ['ædvənt] *n* avvento; **A~** (*REL*) Avvento.
Advent calendar *n* calendario dell'Avvento.
adventure [əd'vɛntʃə*] *n* avventura.
adventure playground *n area attrezzata di giochi per bambini con funi, strutture in legno etc.*
adventurous [əd'vɛntʃərəs] *adj* avventuroso(a).
adverb ['ædvəːb] *n* avverbio.
adversary ['ædvəsərɪ] *n* avversario/a.
adverse ['ædvəːs] *adj* avverso(a); **in ~ circumstances** nelle avversità; **~ to** contrario(a) a.
adversity [əd'vəːsɪtɪ] *n* avversità.
advert ['ædvəːt] *n abbr* (*BRIT*) = **advertisement.**
advertise ['ædvətaɪz] *vi* (*vt*) fare pubblicità *or* réclame (a); fare un'inserzione (per vendere); **to ~ for** (*staff*) cercare tramite annuncio.

advertisement [əd'vəːtɪsmənt] *n* (*COMM*) réclame *f inv*, pubblicità *f inv*; (*in classified ads*) inserzione *f.*
advertiser ['ædvətaɪzə*] *n* azienda che reclamizza un prodotto; (*in newspaper*) inserzionista *m/f.*
advertising ['ædvətaɪzɪŋ] *n* pubblicità.
advertising agency *n* agenzia pubblicitaria *or* di pubblicità.
advertising campaign *n* campagna pubblicitaria.
advice [əd'vaɪs] *n* consigli *mpl*; (*notification*) avviso; **piece of ~** consiglio; **to ask (sb) for ~** chiedere il consiglio (di qn), chiedere un consiglio (a qn); **legal ~** consulenza legale.
advice note *n* (*BRIT*) avviso di spedizione.
advisable [əd'vaɪzəbl] *adj* consigliabile.
advise [əd'vaɪz] *vt* consigliare; **to ~ sb of sth** informare qn di qc; **to ~ sb against sth/against doing sth** sconsigliare qc a qn/a qn di fare qc; **you will be well/ill ~d to go** fareste bene/male ad andare.
advisedly [əd'vaɪzɪdlɪ] *adv* (*deliberately*) deliberatamente.
adviser [əd'vaɪzə*] *n* consigliere/a; (*in business*) consulente *m/f*, consigliere/a.
advisory [əd'vaɪzərɪ] *adj* consultivo(a); **in an ~ capacity** in veste di consulente.
advocate *n* ['ædvəkɪt] (*upholder*) sostenitore/trice ♦ *vt* ['ædvəkeɪt] propugnare; **to be an ~ of** essere a favore di.
advt. *abbr* = **advertisement.**
AEA *n abbr* (*BRIT*: = *Atomic Energy Authority*) ente di controllo sulla ricerca e lo sviluppo dell'energia atomica.
AEC *n abbr* (*US*: = *Atomic Energy Commission*) ente di controllo sulla ricerca e lo sviluppo dell'energia atomica.
Aegean (Sea) [iː'dʒiːən-] *n* (mare *m*) Egeo.
aegis ['iːdʒɪs] *n*: **under the ~ of** sotto gli auspici di.
aeon ['iːən] *n* eternità *f inv.*
aerial ['ɛərɪəl] *n* antenna ♦ *adj* aereo(a).
aerobatics ['ɛərəu'bætɪks] *npl* acrobazia aerea *sg*; (*stunts*) acrobazie *fpl* aeree.
aerobics [ɛə'rəubɪks] *n* aerobica.
aerodrome ['ɛərədrəum] *n* (*BRIT*) aerodromo.
aerodynamic ['ɛərəudaɪ'næmɪk] *adj* aerodinamico(a).
aeronautics [ɛərə'nɔːtɪks] *n* aeronautica.
aeroplane ['ɛərəpleɪn] *n* aeroplano.
aerosol ['ɛərəsɔl] *n* aerosol *m inv.*
aerospace industry ['ɛərəuspeɪs-] *n* industria aerospaziale.

aesthetic [ɪs'θɛtɪk] *adj* estetico(a).

afar [ə'fɑː*] *adv* lontano; **from** ~ da lontano.

AFB *n abbr* (*US*) = *Air Force Base*.

AFDC *n abbr* (*US:* = *Aid to Families with Dependent Children*) ≈ A.F. (= *assegni familiari*).

affable ['æfəbl] *adj* affabile.

affair [ə'fɛə*] *n* affare *m*; (*also:* **love** ~) relazione *f* amorosa; ~**s** (*business*) affari; **the Watergate** ~ il caso Watergate.

affect [ə'fɛkt] *vt* toccare; (*feign*) fingere.

affectation [æfɛk'teɪʃən] *n* affettazione *f*.

affected [ə'fɛktɪd] *adj* affettato(a).

affection [ə'fɛkʃən] *n* affezione *f*.

affectionate [ə'fɛkʃənɪt] *adj* affettuoso(a).

affectionately [ə'fɛkʃənɪtlɪ] *adv* affettuosamente.

affidavit [æfɪ'deɪvɪt] *n* (*LAW*) affidavit *m inv.*

affiliated [ə'fɪlɪeɪtɪd] *adj* affiliato(a); ~ **company** filiale *f.*

affinity [ə'fɪnɪtɪ] *n* affinità *f inv.*

affirm [ə'fəːm] *vt* affermare, asserire.

affirmation [æfə'meɪʃən] *n* affermazione *f.*

affirmative [ə'fəːmətɪv] *adj* affermativo(a) ♦ *n:* **in the** ~ affermativamente.

affix [ə'fɪks] *vt* apporre; attaccare.

afflict [ə'flɪkt] *vt* affliggere.

affliction [ə'flɪkʃən] *n* afflizione *f.*

affluence ['æfluəns] *n* ricchezza.

affluent ['æfluənt] *adj* ricco(a); **the** ~ **society** la società del benessere.

afford [ə'fɔːd] *vt* permettersi; (*provide*) fornire; **I can't** ~ **the time** non ho veramente il tempo; **can we** ~ **a car?** possiamo permetterci un'automobile?

affordable [ə'fɔːdəbl] *adj* (che ha un prezzo) abbordabile.

affray [ə'freɪ] *n* (*BRIT LAW*) rissa.

affront [ə'frʌnt] *n* affronto.

affronted [ə'frʌntɪd] *adj* insultato(a).

Afghan ['æfgæn] *adj, n* afgano(a).

Afghanistan [æf'gænɪstɑːn] *n* Afganistan *m.*

afield [ə'fiːld] *adv:* **far** ~ lontano.

AFL-CIO *n abbr* (= *American Federation of Labor and Congress of Industrial Organizations*) confederazione sindacale.

afloat [ə'fləut] *adj, adv* a galla.

afoot [ə'fut] *adv:* **there is something** ~ si sta preparando qualcosa.

aforementioned [ə'fɔːmɛnʃənd] *adj* suddetto(a).

aforesaid [ə'fɔːsɛd] *adj* suddetto(a), predetto(a).

afraid [ə'freɪd] *adj* impaurito(a); **to be** ~ **of** aver paura di; **to be** ~ **of doing** *or* **to do** aver paura di fare; **I am** ~ **that I'll be late** mi dispiace, ma farò tardi; **I'm** ~ **so!** ho

paura di sì!, temo proprio di sì!; **I'm** ~ **not** no, mi dispiace, purtroppo no.

afresh [ə'frɛʃ] *adv* di nuovo.

Africa ['æfrɪkə] *n* Africa.

African ['æfrɪkən] *adj, n* africano(a).

Afrikaans [æfrɪ'kɑːns] *n* afrikaans *m.*

Afrikaner [æfrɪ'kɑːnə*] *n* africander *m inv.*

Afro-American ['æfrəuə'mɛrɪkən] *adj* afroamericano(a).

AFT *n abbr* (= *American Federation of Teachers*) sindacato degli insegnanti.

aft [ɑːft] *adv* a poppa, verso poppa.

after ['ɑːftə*] *prep, adv* dopo; ~ **dinner** dopo cena; **the day** ~ **tomorrow** dopodomani; **what/who are you** ~? che/chi cerca?; **the police are** ~ **him** è ricercato dalla polizia; ~ **you!** prima lei!, dopo di lei!; ~ **all** dopo tutto.

afterbirth ['ɑːftəbəːθ] *n* placenta.

aftercare ['ɑːftəkɛə*] *n* (*BRIT MED*) assistenza medica post-degenza.

after-effects ['ɑːftərɪfɛkts] *npl* conseguenze *fpl*; (*of illness*) postumi *mpl.*

afterlife ['ɑːftəlaɪf] *n* vita dell'al di là.

aftermath ['ɑːftəmæθ] *n* conseguenze *fpl*; **in the** ~ **of** nel periodo dopo.

afternoon ['ɑːftə'nuːn] *n* pomeriggio; **good** ~! buon giorno!

afters ['ɑːftəz] *n* (*BRIT col: dessert*) dessert *m inv.*

after-sales service [ɑːftə'seɪlz-] *n* servizio assistenza clienti.

after-shave (lotion) ['ɑːftəʃeɪv-] *n* dopobarba *m inv.*

aftershock ['ɑːftəʃɔk] *n* scossa di assestamento.

aftertaste ['ɑːftəteɪst] *n* retrogusto.

afterthought ['ɑːftəθɔːt] *n:* **as an** ~ come aggiunta.

afterwards ['ɑːftəwədz] *adv* dopo.

again [ə'gɛn] *adv* di nuovo; **to begin/see** ~ ricominciare/rivedere; **he opened it** ~ l'ha aperto di nuovo, l'ha riaperto; **not ...** ~ non ... più; ~ **and** ~ ripetutamente; **now and** ~ di tanto in tanto, a volte.

against [ə'gɛnst] *prep* contro; ~ **a blue background** su uno sfondo azzurro; **leaning** ~ **the desk** appoggiato alla scrivania; **(as)** ~ (*BRIT*) in confronto a, contro.

age [eɪdʒ] *n* età *f inv* ♦ *vt, vi* invecchiare; **what** ~ **is he?** quanti anni ha?; **he is 20 years of** ~ ha 20 anni; **under** ~ minorenne; **to come of** ~ diventare maggiorenne; **it's been** ~**s since ...** sono secoli che ....

aged ['eɪdʒd] *adj:* ~ **10** di 10 anni; **the** ~ ['eɪdʒɪd] *npl* (*elderly*) gli anziani.

age group n generazione f; **the 40 to 50** ~ le persone fra i 40 e i 50 anni.

ageing ['eɪdʒɪŋ] adj che diventa vecchio(a); **an ~ filmstar** una diva stagionata.

ageless ['eɪdʒlɪs] adj senza età.

age limit n limite m d'età.

agency ['eɪdʒənsɪ] n agenzia; **through** or **by the ~ of** grazie a.

agenda [ə'dʒɛndə] n ordine m del giorno; **on the ~** all'ordine del giorno.

agent ['eɪdʒənt] n agente m.

aggravate ['æɡrəveɪt] vt aggravare, peggiorare; (annoy) esasperare.

aggravation [æɡrə'veɪʃən] n peggioramento; esasperazione f.

aggregate ['æɡrɪɡeɪt] n aggregato; **on ~** (SPORT) con punteggio complessivo.

aggression [ə'ɡrɛʃən] n aggressione f.

aggressive [ə'ɡrɛsɪv] adj aggressivo(a).

aggressiveness [ə'ɡrɛsɪvnɪs] n aggressività.

aggressor [ə'ɡrɛsə*] n aggressore m.

aggrieved [ə'ɡriːvd] adj addolorato(a).

aggro ['æɡrəʊ] n (col: behaviour) aggressività f inv; (: hassle) rottura.

aghast [ə'ɡɑːst] adj sbigottito(a).

agile ['ædʒaɪl] adj agile.

agility [ə'dʒɪlɪtɪ] n agilità f inv.

agitate ['ædʒɪteɪt] vt turbare; agitare ♦ vi: **to ~ for** agitarsi per.

agitator ['ædʒɪteɪtə*] n agitatore/trice.

AGM n abbr see **annual general meeting**.

agnostic [æɡ'nɔstɪk] adj, n agnostico(a).

ago [ə'ɡəʊ] adv: **2 days ~** 2 giorni fa; **not long ~** poco tempo fa; **as long ~ as 1960** già nel 1960; **how long ~?** quanto tempo fa?

agog [ə'ɡɔɡ] adj: **(all) ~ (for)** ansioso(a) (di), impaziente (di).

agonize ['æɡənaɪz] vi: **to ~ (over)** angosciarsi (per).

agonizing ['æɡənaɪzɪŋ] adj straziante.

agony ['æɡənɪ] n agonia; **I was in ~** avevo dei dolori atroci.

agony aunt n (BRIT col) chi tiene la rubrica della posta del cuore.

agony column n posta del cuore.

agree [ə'ɡriː] vt (price) pattuire ♦ vi: **to ~ (with)** essere d'accordo (con); (LING) concordare (con); **to ~ to sth/to do sth** accettare qc/di fare qc; **to ~ that** (admit) ammettere che; **to ~ on sth** accordarsi su qc; **it was ~d that ...** è stato deciso (di comune accordo) che ...; **garlic doesn't ~ with me** l'aglio non mi va.

agreeable [ə'ɡriːəbl] adj gradevole; (willing) disposto(a); **are you ~ to this?** è d'accordo con questo?

agreed [ə'ɡriːd] adj (time, place) stabilito(a); **to be ~** essere d'accordo.

agreement [ə'ɡriːmənt] n accordo; **in ~** d'accordo; **by mutual ~** di comune accordo.

agricultural [æɡrɪ'kʌltʃərəl] adj agricolo(a).

agriculture ['æɡrɪkʌltʃə*] n agricoltura.

aground [ə'ɡraʊnd] adv: **to run ~** arenarsi.

ahead [ə'hɛd] adv avanti; davanti; **~ of** davanti a; (fig: schedule etc) in anticipo su; **~ of time** in anticipo; **go ~!** avanti!; **go right** or **straight ~** tiri diritto; **they were (right) ~ of us** erano (proprio) davanti a noi.

AI n abbr = Amnesty International; (COMPUT) see **artificial intelligence**.

AIB n abbr (BRIT: = Accident Investigation Bureau) ufficio d'inchiesta per incidenti aerei e simili.

AID n abbr = artificial insemination by donor; (US: = Agency for International Development) A.I.D. f.

aid [eɪd] n aiuto ♦ vt aiutare; **with the ~ of** con l'aiuto di; **in ~ of** a favore di; **to ~ and abet** (LAW) essere complice di.

aide [eɪd] n (person) aiutante m.

aide-de-camp (ADC) ['eɪddə'kɔŋ] n (MIL) aiutante m di campo.

AIDS [eɪdz] n abbr (= acquired immune or immuno-deficiency syndrome) A.I.D.S. f.

AIH n abbr = artificial insemination by husband.

ailing ['eɪlɪŋ] adj sofferente; (fig: economy, industry etc) in difficoltà.

ailment ['eɪlmənt] n indisposizione f.

aim [eɪm] vt: **to ~ sth at** (gun) mirare qc a, puntare qc a; (camera, remark) rivolgere qc a; (missile) lanciare qc contro; (blow etc) tirare qc a ♦ vi (also: **to take ~**) prendere la mira ♦ n mira; **to ~ at** mirare; **to ~ to do** aver l'intenzione di fare.

aimless ['eɪmlɪs] adj, **aimlessly** ['eɪmlɪslɪ] adv senza scopo.

ain't [eɪnt] (col) = am not; aren't; isn't.

air [ɛə*] n aria ♦ vt (room, bed) arieggiare; (clothes) far prendere aria a; (idea, grievance) esprimere pubblicamente, manifestare; (views) far conoscere ♦ cpd (currents) d'aria; (attack) aereo(a); **by ~** (travel) in aereo; **to be on the ~** (RADIO, TV: station) trasmettere; (: programme) essere in onda.

air bag n airbag m inv.

air base n base f aerea.

airbed ['ɛəbɛd] n (BRIT) materassino.

airborne ['ɛəbɔːn] adj (plane) in volo; (troops) aerotrasportato(a); **as soon as**

the plane was ~ appena l'aereo ebbe decollato.

air cargo n carico trasportato per via aerea.

air-conditioned ['ɛəkən'dɪʃənd] adj con or ad aria condizionata.

air conditioning n condizionamento d'aria.

air-cooled ['ɛəku:ld] adj raffreddato(a) ad aria.

aircraft ['ɛəkrɑːft] n (pl inv) apparecchio.

aircraft carrier n portaerei f inv.

air cushion n cuscino gonfiabile; (TECH) cuscino d'aria.

airfield ['ɛəfiːld] n campo d'aviazione.

Air Force n aviazione f militare.

air freight n spedizione f di merci per via aerea; (goods) carico spedito per via aerea.

airgun ['ɛəgʌn] n fucile m ad aria compressa.

air hostess n hostess f inv.

airily ['ɛərɪlɪ] adv con disinvoltura.

airing ['ɛərɪŋ] n: **to give an** ~ **to** (linen) far prendere aria a; (room) arieggiare; (fig: ideas etc) ventilare.

air letter n (BRIT) aerogramma m.

airlift ['ɛəlɪft] n ponte m aereo.

airline ['ɛəlaɪn] n linea aerea.

airliner ['ɛəlaɪnə*] n aereo di linea.

airlock ['ɛəlɔk] n cassa d'aria.

air mail n posta aerea; **by** ~ per via or posta aerea.

air mattress n materassino gonfiabile.

airplane ['ɛəpleɪn] n (US) aeroplano.

air pocket n vuoto d'aria.

airport ['ɛəpɔːt] n aeroporto.

air raid n incursione f aerea.

air rifle n fucile m ad aria compressa.

airsick ['ɛəsɪk] adj: **to be** ~ soffrire di mal d'aereo.

airspace ['ɛəspeɪs] n spazio aereo.

airspeed ['ɛəspiːd] n velocità f inv di crociera (AER).

airstrip ['ɛəstrɪp] n pista d'atterraggio.

air terminal n air-terminal m inv.

airtight ['ɛətaɪt] adj ermetico(a).

air time n (RADIO) spazio radiofonico; (TV) spazio televisivo.

air traffic control n controllo del traffico aereo.

air traffic controller n controllore m del traffico aereo.

airway ['ɛəweɪ] n (AVIAT) rotte fpl aeree; (ANAT) vie fpl respiratorie.

airy ['ɛərɪ] adj arioso(a); (manners) noncurante.

aisle [aɪl] n (of church) navata laterale;

navata centrale; (of plane) corridoio.

ajar [ə'dʒɑː*] adj socchiuso(a).

AK abbr (US) = Alaska.

aka abbr (= also known as) alias.

akin [ə'kɪn] prep simile a.

AL abbr (US) = Alabama.

ALA n abbr = American Library Association.

Ala. abbr (US) = Alabama.

à la carte [ɑːlɑː'kɑːt] adv alla carta.

alacrity [ə'lækrɪtɪ] n: **with** ~ con prontezza.

alarm [ə'lɑːm] n allarme m ♦ vt allarmare.

alarm clock n sveglia.

alarmed [ə'lɑːmd] adj (person) allarmato(a); (house, car etc) dotato(a) di allarme.

alarming [ə'lɑːmɪŋ] adj allarmante, preoccupante.

alarmingly [ə'lɑːmɪŋlɪ] adv in modo allarmante; ~ **close** pericolosamente vicino.

alarmist [ə'lɑːmɪst] n allarmista m/f.

alas [ə'læs] excl ohimè!, ahimè!

Alas. abbr (US) = Alaska.

Alaska [ə'læskə] n Alasca.

Albania [æl'beɪnɪə] n Albania.

Albanian [æl'beɪnɪən] adj albanese ♦ n albanese m/f; (LING) albanese m.

albatross ['ælbətrɔs] n albatro, albatros m inv.

albeit [ɔːl'biːɪt] conj sebbene + sub, benché + sub.

album ['ælbəm] n album m inv; (L.P.) 33 giri m inv, L.P. m inv.

albumen ['ælbjumɪn] n albume m.

alchemy ['ælkɪmɪ] n alchimia.

alcohol ['ælkəhɔl] n alcool m.

alcohol-free ['ælkəhɔl'friː] adj analcolico(a).

alcoholic [ælkə'hɔlɪk] adj alcolico(a) ♦ n alcolizzato/a.

alcoholism ['ælkəhɔlɪzəm] n alcolismo.

alcove ['ælkəuv] n alcova.

Ald. abbr = alderman.

alderman ['ɔːldəmən] n consigliere m comunale.

ale [eɪl] n birra.

alert [ə'lɔːt] adj vivo(a); (watchful) vigile ♦ n allarme m ♦ vt: **to** ~ **sb (to sth)** avvisare qn (di qc), avvertire qn (di qc); **to** ~ **sb to the dangers of sth** mettere qn in guardia contro qc; **on the** ~ all'erta.

Aleutian Islands [ə'luːʃən-] npl isole fpl Aleutine.

A level n (BRIT) diploma di studi superiori.

Alexandria [ælɪg'zændrɪə] n Alessandria (d'Egitto).

alfresco [æl'frɛskəu] adj, adv all'aperto.

algebra ['ældʒɪbrə] n algebra.

Algeria [æl'dʒɪərɪə] n Algeria.

Algerian [æl'dʒɪərɪən] adj, n algerino(a).

Algiers [æl'dʒɪəz] n Algeri f.

algorithm ['ælgərɪðəm] n algoritmo.

alias ['eɪlɪəs] adv alias ♦ n pseudonimo, falso nome m.

alibi ['ælɪbaɪ] n alibi m inv.

alien ['eɪlɪən] n straniero/a ♦ adj: ~ **(to)** estraneo(a) (a).

alienate ['eɪlɪəneɪt] vt alienare.

alienation [eɪlɪə'neɪʃən] n alienazione f.

alight [ə'laɪt] adj acceso(a) ♦ vi scendere; (bird) posarsi.

align [ə'laɪn] vt allineare.

alignment [ə'laɪnmənt] n allineamento; **out of** ~ **(with)** non allineato (con).

alike [ə'laɪk] adj simile ♦ adv allo stesso modo; **to look** ~ assomigliarsi; **winter and summer** ~ sia d'estate che d'inverno.

alimony ['ælɪmənɪ] n (payment) alimenti mpl.

alive [ə'laɪv] adj vivo(a); (active) attivo(a); ~ **with** pieno(a) di; ~ **to** conscio(a) di.

alkali ['ælkəlaɪ] n alcali m inv.

================= KEYWORD

all [ɔːl] adj tutto(a); ~ **day** tutto il giorno; ~ **night** tutta la notte; ~ **men** tutti gli uomini; ~ **five girls** tutt'e cinque le ragazze; ~ **five came** sono venuti tutti e cinque; ~ **the books** tutti i libri; ~ **the food** tutto il cibo; ~ **the time** tutto il tempo; (always) sempre; ~ **his life** tutta la vita; **for** ~ **their efforts** nonostante tutti i loro sforzi

♦ pron 1 tutto(a); **is that** ~? non c'è altro?; (in shop) basta così?; ~ **of them** tutti(e); ~ **of it** tutto(a); **I ate it** ~, **I ate** ~ **of it** l'ho mangiato tutto; ~ **of us went** tutti noi siamo andati; ~ **of the boys went** tutti i ragazzi sono andati

2 (in phrases): **above** ~ soprattutto; **after** ~ dopotutto; **at** ~: **not at** ~ (in answer to question) niente affatto; (in answer to thanks) prego!, di niente!, s'immagini!; **I'm not at** ~ **tired** non sono affatto stanco; **anything at** ~ **will do** andrà bene qualsiasi cosa; ~ **in** ~ tutto sommato

♦ adv: ~ **alone** tutto(a) solo(a); **to be/feel** ~ **in** (BRIT col) essere/sentirsi sfinito(a) or distrutto(a); ~ **out** adv: **to go** ~ **out** mettercela tutta; **it's not as hard as** ~ **that** non è poi così difficile; ~ **the more/ the better** tanto più/meglio; ~ **but** quasi; **the score is two** ~ il punteggio è di due a due or è due pari.

allay [ə'leɪ] vt (fears) dissipare.

all clear n (MIL) cessato allarme m inv; (fig) okay m.

allegation [ælɪ'geɪʃən] n asserzione f.

allege [ə'lɛdʒ] vt asserire; **he is** ~**d to have said** ... avrebbe detto che ....

alleged [ə'lɛdʒd] adj presunto(a).

allegedly [ə'lɛdʒɪdlɪ] adv secondo quanto si asserisce.

allegiance [ə'liːdʒəns] n fedeltà.

allegory ['ælɪgərɪ] n allegoria.

all-embracing ['ɔːlɪm'breɪsɪŋ] adj universale.

allergic [ə'lɜːdʒɪk] adj: ~ **to** allergico(a) a.

allergy ['ælədʒɪ] n allergia.

alleviate [ə'liːvɪeɪt] vt alleviare.

alley ['ælɪ] n vicolo; (in garden) vialetto.

alleyway ['ælɪweɪ] n vicolo.

alliance [ə'laɪəns] n alleanza.

allied ['ælaɪd] adj alleato(a).

alligator ['ælɪgeɪtə*] n alligatore m.

all-important ['ɔːlɪm'pɔːtənt] adj importantissimo(a).

all-in ['ɔːlɪn] adj (BRIT: also adv: charge) tutto compreso.

all-in wrestling n (BRIT) lotta americana.

alliteration [əlɪtə'reɪʃən] n allitterazione f.

all-night ['ɔːl'naɪt] adj aperto(a) (or che dura) tutta la notte.

allocate ['æləkeɪt] vt (share out) distribuire; (duties, sum, time): **to** ~ **sth to** assegnare qc a; **to** ~ **sth for** stanziare qc per.

allocation [æləu'keɪʃən] n: ~ **(of money)** stanziamento.

allot [ə'lɔt] vt (share out) spartire; **to** ~ **sth to** (time) dare qc a; (duties) assegnare qc a; **in the** ~**ted time** nel tempo fissato or prestabilito.

allotment [ə'lɔtmənt] n (share) spartizione f; (garden) lotto di terra.

all-out ['ɔːlaut] adj (effort etc) totale ♦ adv: **to go all out for** mettercela tutta per.

allow [ə'lau] vt (practice, behaviour) permettere; (sum to spend etc) accordare; (sum, time estimated) dare; (concede): **to** ~ **that** ammettere che; **to** ~ **sb to do** permettere a qn di fare; **he is** ~**ed to (do it)** lo può fare; **smoking is not** ~**ed** è vietato fumare, non è permesso fumare; **we must** ~ **3 days for the journey** dobbiamo calcolare 3 giorni per il viaggio.

▶**allow for** vt fus tener conto di.

allowance [ə'lauəns] n (money received) assegno; (for travelling, accommodation) indennità f inv; (TAX) detrazione f di imposta; **to make** ~**(s) for** tener conto di; (person) scusare.

alloy ['ælɔɪ] n lega.

all right adv (feel, work) bene; (as answer) va bene.

all-round ['ɔ:l'raund] *adj* completo(a).
all-rounder [ɔ:l'raundə*] *n* (*BRIT*): **to be a good ~** essere bravo(a) in tutto.
allspice ['ɔ:lspaɪs] *n* pepe *m* della Giamaica.
all-time ['ɔ:l'taɪm] *adj* (*record*) assoluto(a).
allude [ə'lu:d] *vi*: **to ~ to** alludere a.
alluring [ə'ljuərɪŋ] *adj* seducente.
allusion [ə'lu:ʒən] *n* allusione *f*.
alluvium [ə'lu:vɪəm] *n* materiale *m* alluvionale.
ally *n* ['ælaɪ] alleato ♦ *vt* [ə'laɪ]: **to ~ o.s. with** allearsi con.
almighty [ɔ:l'maɪtɪ] *adj* onnipotente.
almond ['ɑ:mənd] *n* mandorla.
almost ['ɔ:lməust] *adv* quasi; **he ~ fell** per poco non è caduto.
alms [ɑ:mz] *n* elemosina.
aloft [ə'lɔft] *adv* in alto; (*NAUT*) sull'alberatura.
alone [ə'ləun] *adj, adv* solo(a); **to leave sb ~** lasciare qn in pace; **to leave sth ~** lasciare stare qc; **let ~ ...** figuriamoci poi ..., tanto meno ....
along [ə'lɔŋ] *prep* lungo ♦ *adv*: **is he coming ~?** viene con noi?; **he was hopping/limping ~** veniva saltellando/zoppicando; **~ with** insieme con.
alongside [ə'lɔŋ'saɪd] *prep* accanto a; lungo ♦ *adv* accanto; (*NAUT*) sottobordo; **we brought our boat ~** (*of a pier/shore etc*) abbiamo accostato la barca (al molo/alla riva *etc*).
aloof [ə'lu:f] *adj* distaccato(a) ♦ *adv* a distanza, in disparte; **to stand ~** tenersi a distanza *or* in disparte.
aloofness [ə'lu:fnɪs] *n* distacco, riserbo.
aloud [ə'laud] *adv* ad alta voce.
alphabet ['ælfəbɛt] *n* alfabeto.
alphabetical [ælfə'bɛtɪkəl] *adj* alfabetico(a); **in ~ order** in ordine alfabetico.
alphanumeric [ælfənju:'mɛrɪk] *adj* alfanumerico(a).
alpine ['ælpaɪn] *adj* alpino(a); **~ hut** rifugio alpino; **~ pasture** pascolo alpestre; **~ skiing** sci alpino.
Alps [ælps] *npl*: **the ~** le Alpi.
already [ɔ:l'rɛdɪ] *adv* già.
alright ['ɔ:l'raɪt] *adv* (*BRIT*) = **all right**.
Alsatian [æl'seɪʃən] *n* (*BRIT*: *dog*) pastore *m* tedesco, (cane *m*) lupo.
also ['ɔ:lsəu] *adv* anche.
Alta. *abbr* (*Canada*) = Alberta.
altar ['ɔltə*] *n* altare *m*.
alter ['ɔltə*] *vt, vi* alterare.
alteration [ɔltə'reɪʃən] *n* modificazione *f*, alterazione *f*; **~s** (*SEWING, ARCHIT*) modifiche *fpl*; **timetable subject to ~**

orario soggetto a variazioni.
altercation [ɔ:ltə'keɪʃən] *n* alterco, litigio.
alternate *adj* [ɔl'tə:nɪt] alterno(a) ♦ *vi* ['ɔltə:neɪt] alternare; **on ~ days** ogni due giorni.
alternately [ɔl'tə:nɪtlɪ] *adv* alternatamente.
alternating current ['ɔltəneɪtɪŋ-] *n* corrente *f* alternata.
alternative [ɔl'tə:nətɪv] *adj* (*solutions*) alternativo(a); (*solution*) altro(a) ♦ *n* (*choice*) alternativa; (*other possibility*) altra possibilità.
alternatively [ɔl'tə:nətɪvlɪ] *adv* altrimenti, come alternativa.
alternative medicine *n* medicina alternativa.
alternator ['ɔltə:neɪtə*] *n* (*AUT*) alternatore *m*.
although [ɔ:l'ðəu] *conj* benché + *sub*, sebbene + *sub*.
altitude ['æltɪtju:d] *n* altitudine *f*.
alto ['æltəu] *n* contralto.
altogether [ɔ:ltə'gɛðə*] *adv* del tutto, completamente; (*on the whole*) tutto considerato; (*in all*) in tutto; **how much is that ~?** quant'è in tutto?
altruism ['æltruɪzəm] *n* altruismo.
altruistic [æltru'ɪstɪk] *adj* altruistico(a).
aluminium [ælju'mɪnɪəm], (*US*) **aluminum** [ə'lu:mɪnəm] *n* alluminio.
always ['ɔ:lweɪz] *adv* sempre.
Alzheimer's ['æltshaɪməz] *n* (*also*: ~ **disease**) morbo di Alzheimer.
AM *abbr* (= *amplitude modulation*) AM.
am [æm] *vb see* **be**.
a.m. *adv abbr* (= *ante meridiem*) della mattina.
AMA *n abbr* = *American Medical Association*.
amalgam [ə'mælgəm] *n* amalgama *m*.
amalgamate [ə'mælgəmeɪt] *vt* amalgamare ♦ *vi* amalgamarsi.
amalgamation [əmælgə'meɪʃən] *n* amalgamazione *f*; (*COMM*) fusione *f*.
amass [ə'mæs] *vt* ammassare.
amateur ['æmətə*] *n* dilettante *m/f* ♦ *adj* (*SPORT*) dilettante; **~ dramatics** *n* filodrammatica.
amateurish ['æmətərɪʃ] *adj* (*pej*) da dilettante.
amaze [ə'meɪz] *vt* stupire; **to be ~d (at)** essere sbalordito(a) (da).
amazement [ə'meɪzmənt] *n* stupore *m*.
amazing [ə'meɪzɪŋ] *adj* sorprendente, sbalorditivo(a); (*bargain, offer*) sensazionale.
amazingly [ə'meɪzɪŋlɪ] *adv* incredibilmente, sbalorditivamente.
Amazon ['æməzən] *n* (*MYTHOLOGY*)

Amazzone *f*; (*river*): **the** ~ il Rio delle Amazzoni ♦ *cpd* (*basin, jungle*) amazzonico(a).

Amazonian [æmə'zəʊnɪən] *adj* amazzonico(a).

ambassador [æm'bæsədə*] *n* ambasciatore/trice.

amber ['æmbə*] *n* ambra; **at** ~ (*BRIT AUT*) giallo.

ambidextrous [æmbɪ'dɛkstrəs] *adj* ambidestro(a).

ambience ['æmbɪəns] *n* ambiente *m*.

ambiguity [æmbɪ'gjuɪtɪ] *n* ambiguità *f inv*.

ambiguous [æm'bɪgjuəs] *adj* ambiguo(a).

ambition [æm'bɪʃən] *n* ambizione *f*; **to achieve one's** ~ realizzare le proprie aspirazioni *or* ambizioni.

ambitious [æm'bɪʃəs] *adj* ambizioso(a).

ambivalent [æm'bɪvələnt] *adj* ambivalente.

amble ['æmbl] *vi* (*gen*: **to** ~ **along**) camminare tranquillamente.

ambulance ['æmbjuləns] *n* ambulanza.

ambush ['æmbuʃ] *n* imboscata ♦ *vt* fare un'imboscata a.

ameba [ə'miːbə] *n* (*US*) = **amoeba**.

ameliorate [ə'miːlɪəreɪt] *vt* migliorare.

amen ['ɑː'mɛn] *excl* così sia, amen.

amenable [ə'miːnəbl] *adj*: ~ **to** (*advice etc*) ben disposto(a) a.

amend [ə'mɛnd] *vt* (*law*) emendare; (*text*) correggere ♦ *vi* emendarsi; **to make** ~**s** fare ammenda.

amendment [ə'mɛndmənt] *n* emendamento; correzione *f*.

amenities [ə'miːnɪtɪz] *npl* attrezzature *fpl* ricreative e culturali.

amenity [ə'miːnɪtɪ] *n* amenità *f inv*.

America [ə'mɛrɪkə] *n* America.

American [ə'mɛrɪkən] *adj, n* americano(a).

americanize [ə'mɛrɪkənaɪz] *vt* americanizzare.

amethyst ['æmɪθɪst] *n* ametista.

Amex ['æmɛks] *n abbr* = *American Stock Exchange*.

amiable ['eɪmɪəbl] *adj* amabile, gentile.

amicable ['æmɪkəbl] *adj* amichevole.

amicably ['æmɪkəblɪ] *adv*: **to part** ~ lasciarsi senza rancori.

amid(st) [ə'mɪd(st)] *prep* fra, tra, in mezzo a.

amiss [ə'mɪs] *adj, adv*: **there's something** ~ c'è qualcosa che non va bene; **don't take it** ~ non avertene a male.

ammo ['æməʊ] *n abbr* (*col*) = **ammunition**.

ammonia [ə'məʊnɪə] *n* ammoniaca.

ammunition [æmju'nɪʃən] *n* munizioni *fpl*; (*fig*) arma.

ammunition dump *n* deposito di

munizioni.

amnesia [æm'niːzɪə] *n* amnesia.

amnesty ['æmnɪstɪ] *n* amnistia; **to grant an** ~ **to** concedere l'amnistia a, amnistiare.

Amnesty International *n* Amnesty International *f*.

amoeba, (*US*) **ameba** [ə'miːbə] *n* ameba.

amok [ə'mɔk] *adv*: **to run** ~ diventare pazzo(a) furioso(a).

among(st) [ə'mʌŋ(st)] *prep* fra, tra, in mezzo a.

amoral [eɪ'mɔrəl] *adj* amorale.

amorous ['æmərəs] *adj* amoroso(a).

amorphous [ə'mɔːfəs] *adj* amorfo(a).

amortization [əmɔːtaɪ'zeɪʃən] *n* (*COMM*) ammortamento.

amount [ə'maʊnt] *n* (*sum of money*) somma; (*of bill etc*) importo; (*quantity*) quantità *f inv* ♦ *vi*: **to** ~ **to** (*total*) ammontare a; (*be same as*) essere come; **this** ~**s to a refusal** questo equivale a un rifiuto.

amp(ère) ['æmp(ɛə*)] *n* ampere *m inv*; **a 13** ~ **plug** una spina con fusibile da 13 ampere.

ampersand ['æmpəsænd] *n* e *f* commerciale.

amphetamine [æm'fɛtəmiːn] *n* anfetamina.

amphibian [æm'fɪbɪən] *n* anfibio.

amphibious [æm'fɪbɪəs] *adj* anfibio(a).

amphitheatre, (*US*) **amphitheater** ['æmfɪθɪətə*] *n* anfiteatro.

ample ['æmpl] *adj* ampio(a); spazioso(a); (*enough*): **this is** ~ questo è più che sufficiente; **to have** ~ **time/room** avere assai tempo/posto.

amplifier ['æmplɪfaɪə*] *n* amplificatore *m*.

amplify ['æmplɪfaɪ] *vt* amplificare.

amply ['æmplɪ] *adv* ampiamente.

ampoule, (*US*) **ampule** ['æmpuːl] *n* (*MED*) fiala.

amputate ['æmpjuteɪt] *vt* amputare.

amputee [æmpju'tiː] *n* mutilato/a, chi ha subito un'amputazione.

Amsterdam [æmstə'dæm] *n* Amsterdam *f*.

amt *abbr* = **amount**.

amuck [ə'mʌk] *adv* = **amok**.

amuse [ə'mjuːz] *vt* divertire; **to** ~ **o.s. with sth/by doing sth** divertirsi con qc/a fare qc; **to be** ~**d at** essere divertito da; **he was not** ~**d** non l'ha trovato divertente.

amusement [ə'mjuːzmənt] *n* divertimento; **much to my** ~ con mio grande spasso.

amusement arcade *n* sala giochi (*solo con macchinette a gettoni*).

amusement park *n* luna park *m inv*.

amusing [ə'mjuːzɪŋ] *adj* divertente.

an [æn, ən, n] *indef art see* **a**.

ANA *n abbr* = *American Newspaper*

Association; _American Nurses Association._
anachronism [ə'nækrənızəm] _n_ anacronismo.
anaemia [ə'niːmɪə] _n_ anemia.
anaemic [ə'niːmɪk] _adj_ anemico(a).
anaesthetic [ænɪs'θεtɪk] _adj_ anestetico(a) ♦ _n_ anestetico; **local/general** ~ anestesia locale/totale; **under the** ~ sotto anestesia.
anaesthetist [æ'niːsθɪtɪst] _n_ anestesista _m/f._
anagram ['ænəɡræm] _n_ anagramma _m._
anal ['eɪnl] _adj_ anale.
analgesic [ænæl'dʒiːsɪk] _adj_ analgesico(a) ♦ _n_ analgesico.
analogous [ə'næləɡəs] _adj_: ~ **to** _or_ **with** analogo(a) a.
analog(ue) ['ænəlɔɡ] _adj_ (_watch_, _computer_) analogico(a).
analogy [ə'nælədʒɪ] _n_ analogia; **to draw an** ~ **between** fare un'analogia tra.
analyse ['ænəlaɪz] _vt_ (_BRIT_) analizzare.
analysis, _pl_ **analyses** [ə'næləsɪs, -siːz] _n_ analisi _f inv_; **in the last** ~ in ultima analisi.
analyst ['ænəlɪst] _n_ (_political_ ~ _etc_) analista _m/f_; (_US_) (psic)analista _m/f._
analytic(al) [ænə'lɪtɪk(l)] _adj_ analitico(a).
analyze ['ænəlaɪz] _vt_ (_US_) = **analyse.**
anarchic [æ'nɑːkɪk] _adj_ anarchico(a).
anarchist ['ænəkɪst] _adj_, _n_ anarchico(a).
anarchy ['ænəkɪ] _n_ anarchia.
anathema [ə'næθɪmə] _n_: **it is** ~ **to him** non ne vuol neanche sentir parlare.
anatomical [ænə'tɔmɪkl] _adj_ anatomico(a).
anatomy [ə'nætəmɪ] _n_ anatomia.
ANC _n abbr_ = _African National Congress._
ancestor ['ænsɪstə*] _n_ antenato/a.
ancestral [æn'sεstrəl] _adj_ avito(a).
ancestry ['ænsɪstrɪ] _n_ antenati _mpl_; ascendenza.
anchor ['æŋkə*] _n_ ancora ♦ _vi_ (_also_: **to drop** ~) gettare l'ancora ♦ _vt_ ancorare; **to weigh** ~ salpare _or_ levare l'ancora.
anchorage ['æŋkərɪdʒ] _n_ ancoraggio.
anchor man _n_ (_TV, RADIO_) anchorman _m inv._
anchor woman _n_ (_TV, RADIO_) anchorwoman _f inv._
anchovy ['æntʃəvɪ] _n_ acciuga.
ancient ['eɪnʃənt] _adj_ antico(a); (_fig_) anziano(a); ~ **monument** monumento storico.
ancillary [æn'sɪlərɪ] _adj_ ausiliario(a).
and [ænd] _conj_ e (_often ed before vowel_); ~ **so on** e così via; **try** ~ **do it** prova a farlo; **come** ~ **sit here** vieni a sedere qui; **better** ~ **better** sempre meglio; **more** ~ **more** sempre di più.
Andes ['ændiːz] _npl_: **the** ~ le Ande.
Andorra [æn'dɔːrə] _n_ Andorra.

anecdote ['ænɪkdəut] _n_ aneddoto.
anemia [ə'niːmɪə] _etc_ = **anaemia** _etc._
anemone [ə'nεmənɪ] _n_ (_BOT_) anemone _m_; (_sea_ ~) anemone _m_ di mare, attinia.
anesthetic [ænɪs'θεtɪk] _etc_ = **anaesthetic** _etc._
anew [ə'njuː] _adv_ di nuovo.
angel ['eɪndʒəl] _n_ angelo.
angel dust _n_ sedativo usato a scopo allucinogeno.
anger ['æŋɡə*] _n_ rabbia ♦ _vt_ arrabbiare.
angina [æn'dʒaɪnə] _n_ angina pectoris.
angle ['æŋɡl] _n_ angolo ♦ _vi_: **to** ~ **for** (_fig_) cercare di avere; **from their** ~ dal loro punto di vista.
angler ['æŋɡlə*] _n_ pescatore _m_ con la lenza.
Anglican ['æŋɡlɪkən] _adj_, _n_ anglicano(a).
anglicize ['æŋɡlɪsaɪz] _vt_ anglicizzare.
angling ['æŋɡlɪŋ] _n_ pesca con la lenza.
Anglo- ['æŋɡləu] _prefix_ anglo...; ~**Italian** _adj_, _n_ italobritannico(a).
Anglo-Saxon ['æŋɡləu'sæksən] _adj_, _n_ anglosassone (_m/f_).
Angola [æŋ'ɡəulə] _n_ Angola.
Angolan [æŋ'ɡəulən] _adj_, _n_ angolano(a).
angrily ['æŋɡrɪlɪ] _adv_ con rabbia.
angry ['æŋɡrɪ] _adj_ arrabbiato(a), furioso(a); **to be** ~ **with sb/at sth** essere in collera con qn/per qc; **to get** ~ arrabbiarsi; **to make sb** ~ fare arrabbiare qn.
anguish ['æŋɡwɪʃ] _n_ angoscia.
anguished ['æŋɡwɪʃt] _adj_ angosciato(a), pieno(a) d'angoscia.
angular ['æŋɡjulə*] _adj_ angolare.
animal ['ænɪməl] _adj_, _n_ animale (_m_).
animal rights _npl_ diritti _mpl_ degli animali.
animate _vt_ ['ænɪmeɪt] animare ♦ _adj_ ['ænɪmɪt] animato(a).
animated ['ænɪmeɪtɪd] _adj_ animato(a).
animation [ænɪ'meɪʃən] _n_ animazione _f._
animosity [ænɪ'mɔsɪtɪ] _n_ animosità.
aniseed ['ænɪsiːd] _n_ semi _mpl_ di anice.
Ankara ['æŋkərə] _n_ Ankara.
ankle ['æŋkl] _n_ caviglia.
ankle socks _npl_ calzini _mpl._
annex _n_ ['ænεks] (_also_: _BRIT_: **annexe**) edificio annesso ♦ _vt_ [ə'nεks] annettere.
annexation [ænεk'seɪʃən] _n_ annessione _f._
annihilate [ə'naɪəleɪt] _vt_ annientare.
annihilation [ənaɪə'leɪʃən] _n_ annientamento.
anniversary [ænɪ'vəːsərɪ] _n_ anniversario.
anniversary dinner _n_ cena commemorativa.
annotate ['ænəuteɪt] _vt_ annotare.
announce [ə'nauns] _vt_ annunciare; **he** ~**d that he wasn't going** ha dichiarato che

non (ci) sarebbe andato.

announcement [ə'naunsmənt] n annuncio; (*letter, card*) partecipazione f; **I'd like to make an ~** ho una comunicazione da fare.

announcer [ə'naunsə*] n (*RADIO, TV*: *between programmes*) annunciatore/trice; (*: in a programme*) presentatore/trice.

annoy [ə'nɔɪ] vt dare fastidio a; **to be ~ed (at sth/with sb)** essere seccato or irritato (per qc/con qn); **don't get ~ed!** non irritarti!

annoyance [ə'nɔɪəns] n fastidio; (*cause of ~*) noia.

annoying [ə'nɔɪɪŋ] adj irritante, seccante.

annual ['ænjuəl] adj annuale ♦ n (*BOT*) pianta annua; (*book*) annuario.

annual general meeting (AGM) n (*BRIT*) assemblea generale.

annually ['ænjuəlɪ] adv annualmente.

annual report n relazione f annuale.

annuity [ə'njuːɪtɪ] n annualità f inv; **life ~** vitalizio.

annul [ə'nʌl] vt annullare; (*law*) rescindere.

annulment [ə'nʌlmənt] n annullamento; rescissione f.

annum ['ænəm] n see **per annum.**

Annunciation [ənʌnsɪ'eɪʃən] n Annunciazione f.

anode ['ænəud] n anodo.

anoint [ə'nɔɪnt] vt ungere.

anomalous [ə'nɔmələs] adj anomalo(a).

anomaly [ə'nɔməlɪ] n anomalia.

anon. [ə'nɔn] abbr = **anonymous.**

anonymity [ænə'nɪmɪtɪ] n anonimato.

anonymous [ə'nɔnɪməs] adj anonimo(a); **to remain ~** mantenere l'anonimato.

anorak ['ænəræk] n giacca a vento.

anorexia [ænə'rɛksɪə] n (*also: ~ nervosa*) anoressia.

anorexic [ænə'rɛksɪk] adj, n anoressico(a).

another [ə'nʌðə*] adj: **~ book** (*one more*) un altro libro, ancora un libro; (*a different one*) un altro libro ♦ pron un altro(un'altra), ancora uno(a); **~ drink?** ancora qualcosa da bere?; **in ~ 5 years** fra altri 5 anni; see also **one.**

ANSI n abbr (= *American National Standards Institution*) Istituto americano di standardizzazione.

answer ['ɑːnsə*] n risposta; soluzione f ♦ vi rispondere ♦ vt (*reply to*) rispondere a; (*problem*) risolvere; (*prayer*) esaudire; **in ~ to your letter** in risposta alla sua lettera; **to ~ the phone** rispondere (al telefono); **to ~ the bell** rispondere al campanello; **to ~ the door** aprire la porta.

▶**answer back** vi ribattere.

▶**answer for** vt fus essere responsabile di.

▶**answer to** vt fus (*description*) corrispondere a.

answerable ['ɑːnsərəbl] adj: **~ (to sb/for sth)** responsabile (verso qn/di qc); **I am ~ to no one** non devo rispondere a nessuno.

answering machine ['ɑːnsərɪŋ-] n segreteria (telefonica) automatica.

ant [ænt] n formica.

ANTA n abbr = *American National Theater and Academy.*

antagonism [æn'tægənɪzəm] n antagonismo.

antagonist [æn'tægənɪst] n antagonista m/f.

antagonistic [æntægə'nɪstɪk] adj antagonistico(a).

antagonize [æn'tægənaɪz] vt provocare l'ostilità di.

Antarctic [ænt'ɑːktɪk] n: **the ~** l'Antartide f ♦ adj antartico(a).

Antarctica [ænt'ɑːktɪkə] n Antartide f.

Antarctic Circle n Circolo polare antartico.

Antarctic Ocean n Oceano antartico.

ante ['æntɪ] n (*CARDS, fig*): **to up the ~** alzare la posta in palio.

ante... ['æntɪ] prefix anti..., ante..., pre....

anteater ['æntiːtə*] n formichiere m.

antecedent [æntɪ'siːdənt] n antecedente m, precedente m.

antechamber ['æntɪtʃeɪmbə*] n anticamera.

antelope ['æntɪləup] n antilope f.

antenatal ['æntɪ'neɪtl] adj prenatale.

antenatal clinic n assistenza medica preparto.

antenna, pl **antennae** [æn'tɛnə, -niː] n antenna.

anthem ['ænθəm] n antifona; **national ~** inno nazionale.

ant-hill ['ænthɪl] n formicaio.

anthology [æn'θɔlədʒɪ] n antologia.

anthropologist [ænθrə'pɔlədʒɪst] n antropologo/a.

anthropology [ænθrə'pɔlədʒɪ] n antropologia.

anti- ['æntɪ] prefix anti....

anti-aircraft ['æntɪ'ɛəkrɑːft] adj antiaereo(a).

anti-aircraft defence n difesa antiaerea.

antiballistic ['æntɪbə'lɪstɪk] adj antibalistico(a).

antibiotic ['æntɪbaɪ'ɔtɪk] adj antibiotico(a) ♦ n antibiotico.

antibody ['æntɪbɔdɪ] n anticorpo.

anticipate [æn'tɪsɪpeɪt] vt prevedere;

pregustare; (*wishes, request*) prevenire;
as ~d come previsto; **this is worse than I**
~d è peggio di quel che immaginavo *or*
pensavo.
anticipation [æntɪsɪ'peɪʃən] *n* anticipazione
f; (*expectation*) aspettative *fpl*; **thanking
you in** ~ vi ringrazio in anticipo.
anticlimax ['æntɪ'klaɪmæks] *n*: **it was an** ~
fu una completa delusione.
anticlockwise ['æntɪ'klɔkwaɪz] *adj* in senso
antiorario.
antics ['æntɪks] *npl* buffonerie *fpl*.
anticyclone ['æntɪ'saɪkləun] *n* anticiclone
m.
antidote ['æntɪdəut] *n* antidoto.
antifreeze ['æntɪfriːz] *n* anticongelante *m*.
antihistamine [æntɪ'hɪstəmɪn] *n*
antistaminico.
Antilles [æn'tɪliːz] *npl*: **the** ~ le Antille.
antipathy [æn'tɪpəθɪ] *n* antipatia.
antiperspirant ['æntɪ'pəːspərənt] *adj*
antitraspirante.
Antipodean [æntɪpə'diːən] *adj* degli
Antipodi.
Antipodes [æn'tɪpədiːz] *npl*: **the** ~ gli
Antipodi.
antiquarian [æntɪ'kwɛərɪən] *adj*: ~
bookshop libreria antiquaria ♦ *n*
antiquario/a.
antiquated ['æntɪkweɪtɪd] *adj* antiquato(a).
antique [æn'tiːk] *n* antichità *f inv* ♦ *adj*
antico(a).
antique dealer *n* antiquario/a.
antique shop *n* negozio d'antichità.
antiquity [æn'tɪkwɪtɪ] *n* antichità *f inv*.
anti-semitic ['æntɪsɪ'mɪtɪk] *adj*
antisemitico(a), antisemita.
anti-semitism ['æntɪ'sɛmɪtɪzəm] *n*
antisemitismo.
antiseptic [æntɪ'sɛptɪk] *adj* antisettico(a)
♦ *n* antisettico.
antisocial ['æntɪ'səuʃəl] *adj* asociale;
(*against society*) antisociale.
antitank [æntɪ'tæŋk] *adj* anticarro *inv*.
antithesis, *pl* **antitheses** [æn'tɪθɪsɪs, -siːz]
n antitesi *f inv*; (*contrast*) carattere *m*
antitetico.
anti-trust [æntɪ'trʌst] *adj* (*COMM*): ~
legislation legislazione *f* antitrust *inv*.
antlers ['æntləz] *npl* palchi *mpl*.
Antwerp ['æntwəːp] *n* Anversa.
anus ['eɪnəs] *n* ano.
anvil ['ænvɪl] *n* incudine *f*.
anxiety [æŋ'zaɪətɪ] *n* ansia; (*keenness*): ~ **to
do** smania di fare.
anxious ['æŋkʃəs] *adj* ansioso(a),
inquieto(a); (*keen*): ~ **to do/that**
impaziente di fare/che + *sub*; **I'm very** ~

about you sono molto preoccupato *or* in
pensiero per te.
anxiously ['æŋkʃəslɪ] *adv* ansiosamente,
con ansia.

========================= KEYWORD

any ['ɛnɪ] *adj* **1** (*in questions etc*): **have you** ~
butter? hai del burro?, hai un po' di
burro?; **have you** ~ **children?** hai
bambini?; **if there are** ~ **tickets left** se ci
sono ancora (dei) biglietti, se c'è ancora
qualche biglietto
2 (*with negative*): **I haven't** ~ **money/
books** non ho soldi/libri; **without** ~
difficulty senza nessuna *or* alcuna
difficoltà
3 (*no matter which*) qualsiasi, qualunque;
choose ~ **book you like** scegli un libro
qualsiasi
4 (*in phrases*): **in** ~ **case** in ogni caso; ~
day now da un giorno all'altro; **at** ~
moment in qualsiasi momento, da un
momento all'altro; **at** ~ **rate** ad ogni
modo
♦ *pron* **1** (*in questions, with negative*): **have
you got** ~**?** ne hai?; **can** ~ **of you sing?**
qualcuno di voi sa cantare?; **I haven't** ~
(**of them**) non ne ho
2 (*no matter which one(s)*): **take** ~ **of those
books (you like)** prendi uno qualsiasi di
quei libri
♦ *adv* **1** (*in questions etc*): **do you want** ~
more soup/sandwiches? vuoi ancora un
po' di minestra/degli altri panini?; **are
you feeling** ~ **better?** ti senti meglio?
2 (*with negative*): **I can't hear him** ~ **more**
non lo sento più; **don't wait** ~ **longer** non
aspettare più.

anybody ['ɛnɪbɔdɪ] *pron* qualsiasi persona;
(*in interrogative sentences*) qualcuno; (*in
negative sentences*): **I don't see** ~ non vedo
nessuno.
anyhow ['ɛnɪhau] *adv* in qualsiasi modo;
(*haphazard*) come capita; **I shall go** ~ ci
andrò lo stesso *or* comunque.
anyone ['ɛnɪwʌn] *pron* = **anybody**.
anyplace ['ɛnɪpleɪs] *pron* (*US col*)
= **anywhere**.
anything ['ɛnɪθɪŋ] *pron* qualsiasi cosa; (*in
interrogative sentences*) qualcosa; (*in
negative sentences*) non ... niente, non ...
nulla; ~ **else?** (*in shop*) basta (così)?; **it
can cost** ~ **between £15 and £20** può
costare qualcosa come 15 o 20 sterline.
anytime ['ɛnɪtaɪm] *adv* in qualunque
momento; quando vuole.
anyway ['ɛnɪweɪ] *adv* in *or* ad ogni modo.

anywhere ['ɛnɪwɛə*] adv da qualsiasi parte; (in interrogative sentences) da qualche parte; **I don't see him** ~ non lo vedo da nessuna parte; ~ **in the world** dovunque nel mondo.

Anzac ['ænzæk] n abbr (= Australia-New Zealand Army Corps) A.N.Z.A.C. m; (soldier) soldato dell'A.N.Z.A.C.

L'**Anzac Day** è una festa nazionale australiana e neozelandese che cade il 25 aprile e commemora il famoso sbarco delle forze armate congiunte dei due paesi a Gallipoli nel 1915, durante la prima guerra mondiale.

apart [ə'pɑːt] adv (to one side) a parte; (separately) separatamente; **with one's legs** ~ con le gambe divaricate; **10 miles/a long way** ~ a 10 miglia di distanza/molto lontani l'uno dall'altro; **they are living** ~ sono separati; ~ **from** prep a parte, eccetto.

apartheid [ə'pɑːteɪt] n apartheid f.

apartment [ə'pɑːtmənt] n (US) appartamento; ~**s** npl appartamento ammobiliato.

apartment building n (US) stabile m, caseggiato.

apathetic [æpə'θɛtɪk] adj apatico(a).

apathy ['æpəθɪ] n apatia.

APB n abbr (US: = all points bulletin: police expression) espressione della polizia che significa "trovate e arrestate il sospetto".

ape [eɪp] n scimmia ♦ vt scimmiottare.

Apennines ['æpənaɪnz] npl: **the** ~ gli Apennini.

aperitif [ə'pɛrɪtiːf] n aperitivo.

aperture ['æpətʃjuə*] n apertura.

APEX ['eɪpɛks] n abbr (AVIAT: = advance purchase excursion) APEX m inv.

apex ['eɪpɛks] n apice m.

aphid ['æfɪd] n afide f.

aphrodisiac [æfrəu'dɪzɪæk] adj afrodisiaco(a) ♦ n afrodisiaco.

API n abbr = American Press Institute.

apiece [ə'piːs] adv ciascuno(a).

aplomb [ə'plɔm] n disinvoltura.

APO n abbr (US: = Army Post Office) ufficio postale dell'esercito.

apocalypse [ə'pɔkəlɪps] n apocalisse f.

apolitical [eɪpə'lɪtɪkl] adj apolitico(a).

apologetic [əpɔlə'dʒɛtɪk] adj (tone, letter) di scusa; **to be very** ~ **about** scusarsi moltissimo di.

apologetically [əpɔlə'dʒɛtɪkəlɪ] adv per scusarsi.

apologize [ə'pɔlədʒaɪz] vi: **to** ~ **(for sth to sb)** scusarsi (di qc a qn), chiedere scusa (a qn per qc).

apology [ə'pɔlədʒɪ] n scuse fpl; **please accept my apologies** la prego di accettare le mie scuse.

apoplectic [æpə'plɛktɪk] adj (MED) apoplettico(a); ~ **with rage** (col) livido(a) per la rabbia.

apoplexy ['æpəplɛksɪ] n apoplessia.

apostle [ə'pɔsl] n apostolo.

apostrophe [ə'pɔstrəfɪ] n (sign) apostrofo.

appal [ə'pɔːl] vt atterrire; sgomentare.

Appalachian Mountains [æpə'leɪʃən-] npl: **the** ~ i Monti Appalachi.

appalling [ə'pɔːlɪŋ] adj spaventoso(a); **she's an** ~ **cook** è un disastro come cuoca.

apparatus [æpə'reɪtəs] n apparato.

apparel [ə'pærl] n (US) abbigliamento, confezioni fpl.

apparent [ə'pærənt] adj evidente.

apparently [ə'pærəntlɪ] adv evidentemente, a quanto pare.

apparition [æpə'rɪʃən] n apparizione f.

appeal [ə'piːl] vi (LAW) appellarsi alla legge ♦ n (LAW) appello; (request) richiesta; (charm) attrattiva; **to** ~ **for** chiedere (con insistenza); **to** ~ **to** (subj: person) appellarsi a; (: thing) piacere a; **to** ~ **to sb for mercy** chiedere pietà a qn; **it doesn't** ~ **to me** mi dice poco; **right of** ~ diritto d'appello.

appealing [ə'piːlɪŋ] adj (moving) commovente; (attractive) attraente.

appear [ə'pɪə*] vi apparire; (LAW) comparire; (publication) essere pubblicato(a); (seem) sembrare; **it would** ~ **that** sembra che; **to** ~ **in Hamlet** recitare nell'Amleto; **to** ~ **on TV** presentarsi in televisione.

appearance [ə'pɪərəns] n apparizione f; (look, aspect) aspetto; **to put in** or **make an** ~ fare atto di presenza; **by order of** ~ (THEAT) in ordine di apparizione; **to keep up** ~**s** salvare le apparenze; **to all** ~**s** giudicar dalle apparenze.

appease [ə'piːz] vt calmare, appagare.

appeasement [ə'piːzmənt] n (POL) appeasement m inv.

append [ə'pɛnd] vt (COMPUT) aggiungere in coda.

appendage [ə'pɛndɪdʒ] n aggiunta.

appendicitis [əpɛndɪ'saɪtɪs] n appendicite f.

appendix, pl **appendices** [ə'pɛndɪks, -siːz] n appendice f; **to have one's** ~ **out** operarsi or farsi operare di appendicite.

appetite ['æpɪtaɪt] n appetito; **that walk has given me an** ~ la passeggiata mi ha

messo appetito.
appetizer ['æpɪtaɪzə*] n (food) stuzzichino; (drink) aperitivo.
appetizing ['æpɪtaɪzɪŋ] adj appetitoso(a).
applaud [ə'plɔːd] vt, vi applaudire.
applause [ə'plɔːz] n applauso.
apple ['æpl] n mela; (also: ~ tree) melo; **the ~ of one's eye** la pupilla dei propri occhi.
apple turnover n sfogliatella alle mele.
appliance [ə'plaɪəns] n apparecchio; **electrical ~s** elettrodomestici mpl.
applicable [ə'plɪkəbl] adj applicabile; **to be ~ to** essere valido per; **the law is ~ from January** la legge entrerà in vigore in gennaio.
applicant ['æplɪkənt] n candidato/a; (ADMIN: for benefit etc) chi ha fatto domanda or richiesta.
application [æplɪ'keɪʃən] n applicazione f; (for a job, a grant etc) domanda; **on ~** su richiesta.
application form n modulo di domanda.
application program n (COMPUT) programma applicativo.
applications package n (COMPUT) software m inv applicativo.
applied [ə'plaɪd] adj applicato(a); ~ **arts** arti fpl applicate.
apply [ə'plaɪ] vt: **to ~ (to)** (paint, ointment) dare (a); (theory, technique) applicare (a) ♦ vi: **to ~ to** (ask) rivolgersi a; (be suitable for, relevant to) riguardare, riferirsi a; **to ~ (for)** (permit, grant, job) fare domanda (per); **to ~ the brakes** frenare; **to ~ o.s. to** dedicarsi a.
appoint [ə'pɔɪnt] vt nominare.
appointee [əpɔɪn'tiː] n incaricato/a.
appointment [ə'pɔɪntmənt] n nomina; (arrangement to meet) appuntamento; **by ~** su or per appuntamento; **to make an ~ with sb** prendere un appuntamento con qn; (PRESS): "~**s (vacant)**" "offerte fpl di impiego".
apportion [ə'pɔːʃən] vt attribuire.
appraisal [ə'preɪzl] n valutazione f.
appraise [ə'preɪz] vt (value) valutare, fare una stima di; (situation etc) fare il bilancio di.
appreciable [ə'priːʃəbl] adj apprezzabile.
appreciably [ə'priːʃəblɪ] adv notevolmente, sensibilmente.
appreciate [ə'priːʃɪeɪt] vt (like) apprezzare; (be grateful for) essere riconoscente di; (be aware of) rendersi conto di ♦ vi (COMM) aumentare; **I ~d your help** ti sono grato per l'aiuto.
appreciation [əpriːʃɪ'eɪʃən] n apprezzamento; (FINANCE) aumento del

valore.
appreciative [ə'priːʃɪətɪv] adj (person) sensibile; (comment) elogiativo(a).
apprehend [æprɪ'hɛnd] vt (arrest) arrestare; (understand) comprendere.
apprehension [æprɪ'hɛnʃən] n (fear) inquietudine f.
apprehensive [æprɪ'hɛnsɪv] adj apprensivo(a).
apprentice [ə'prɛntɪs] n apprendista m/f ♦ vt: **to be ~d to** lavorare come apprendista presso.
apprenticeship [ə'prɛntɪsʃɪp] n apprendistato; **to serve one's ~** fare il proprio apprendistato or tirocinio.
appro. ['æprəu] abbr (BRIT COMM: col) = **approval**.
approach [ə'prəutʃ] vi avvicinarsi ♦ vt (come near) avvicinarsi a; (ask, apply to) rivolgersi a; (subject, passer-by) avvicinare ♦ n approccio; accesso; (to problem) modo di affrontare; **to ~ sb about sth** rivolgersi a qn per qc.
approachable [ə'prəutʃəbl] adj accessibile.
approach road n strada d'accesso.
approbation [æprə'beɪʃən] n approvazione f, benestare m.
appropriate vt [ə'prəuprɪeɪt] (take) appropriarsi di ♦ adj [ə'prəuprɪit] appropriato(a); adatto(a); **it would not be ~ for me to comment** non sta a me fare dei commenti.
appropriately [ə'prəuprɪitlɪ] adv in modo appropriato.
appropriation [əprəuprɪ'eɪʃən] n stanziamento.
approval [ə'pruːvəl] n approvazione f; **on ~** (COMM) in prova, in esame; **to meet with sb's ~** soddisfare qn, essere di gradimento di qn.
approve [ə'pruːv] vt, vi approvare.
▶**approve of** vt fus approvare.
approved school n (BRIT: old) riformatorio.
approvingly [ə'pruːvɪŋlɪ] adv in approvazione.
approx. abbr = **approximately**.
approximate adj [ə'prɔksɪmɪt] approssimativo(a) ♦ vt [ə'prɔksɪmeɪt] essere un'approssimazione di, avvicinarsi a.
approximately [ə'prɔksɪmətlɪ] adv circa.
approximation [ə'prɔksɪ'meɪʃən] n approssimazione f.
apr n abbr (= annual percentage rate) tasso di percentuale annuo.
Apr. abbr (= April) apr.
apricot ['eɪprɪkɔt] n albicocca.

April ['eɪprəl] *n* aprile *m*; ~ **fool!** pesce d'aprile!; *for phrases see also* **July.**

April Fool's Day *è il primo aprile, il giorno degli scherzi e delle burle. Il nome deriva dal fatto che, se una persona cade nella trappola che gli è stata tesa, fa la figura del* **fool**, *cioè dello sciocco. Di recente gli scherzi stanno diventando sempre più elaborati, e persino i giornalisti a volte inventano vicende incredibili per burlarsi dei lettori.*

---

apron ['eɪprən] *n* grembiule *m*; (*AVIAT*) area di stazionamento.
apse [æps] *n* (*ARCHIT*) abside *f.*
APT *n abbr* (*BRIT.* = *advanced passenger train*) *treno ad altissima velocità.*
apt [æpt] *adj* (*suitable*) adatto(a); (*able*) capace; (*likely*): **to be ~ to do** avere tendenza a fare.
Apt. *abbr* = **apartment.**
aptitude ['æptɪtjuːd] *n* abilità *f inv.*
aptitude test *n* test *m inv* attitudinale.
aptly ['æptlɪ] *adv* appropriatamente, in modo adatto.
aqualung ['ækwəlʌŋ] *n* autorespiratore *m.*
aquarium [ə'kwɛərɪəm] *n* acquario.
Aquarius [ə'kwɛərɪəs] *n* Acquario; **to be ~** essere dell'Acquario.
aquatic [ə'kwætɪk] *adj* acquatico(a).
aqueduct ['ækwɪdʌkt] *n* acquedotto.
AR *abbr* (*US*) = *Arkansas.*
ARA *n abbr* (*BRIT*) = *Associate of the Royal Academy.*
Arab ['ærəb] *adj*, *n* arabo(a).
Arabia [ə'reɪbɪə] *n* Arabia.
Arabian [ə'reɪbɪən] *adj* arabo(a).
Arabian Desert *n* Deserto arabico.
Arabian Sea *n* mare *m* Arabico.
Arabic ['ærəbɪk] *adj* arabico(a) ♦ *n* arabo.
Arabic numerals *npl* numeri arabi *mpl*, numerazione *f* araba.
arable ['ærəbl] *adj* arabile.
ARAM *n abbr* (*BRIT*) = *Associate of the Royal Academy of Music.*
arbiter ['aːbɪtə*] *n* arbitro.
arbitrary ['aːbɪtrərɪ] *adj* arbitrario(a).
arbitrate ['aːbɪtreɪt] *vi* arbitrare.
arbitration [aːbɪ'treɪʃən] *n* (*LAW*) arbitrato; (*INDUSTRY*) arbitraggio.
arbitrator ['aːbɪtreɪtə*] *n* arbitro.
ARC *n abbr* (= *American Red Cross*) C.R.I. *f* (= *Croce Rossa Italiana*).
arc [aːk] *n* arco.
arcade [aː'keɪd] *n* portico; (*passage with shops*) galleria.
arch [aːtʃ] *n* arco; (*of foot*) arco plantare

♦ *vt* inarcare ♦ *prefix*: ~(-) grande (*before n*); per eccellenza.
archaeological [aːkɪə'lɔdʒɪkəl] *adj* archeologico(a).
archaeologist [aːkɪ'ɔlədʒɪst] *n* archeologo/a.
archaeology [aːkɪ'ɔlədʒɪ] *n* archeologia.
archaic [aː'keɪɪk] *adj* arcaico(a).
archangel ['aːkeɪndʒəl] *n* arcangelo.
archbishop [aːtʃ'bɪʃəp] *n* arcivescovo.
arched [aːtʃt] *adj* arcuato(a), ad arco.
arch-enemy ['aːtʃ'ɛnɪmɪ] *n* arcinemico/a.
archeology [aːkɪ'ɔlədʒɪ] *etc* = **archaeology** *etc.*
archer ['aːtʃə*] *n* arciere *m.*
archery ['aːtʃərɪ] *n* tiro all'arco.
archetypal ['aːkɪtaɪpəl] *adj* tipico(a).
archetype ['aːkɪtaɪp] *n* archetipo.
archipelago [aːkɪ'pɛlɪɡəu] *n* arcipelago.
architect ['aːkɪtɛkt] *n* architetto.
architectural [aːkɪ'tɛktʃərəl] *adj* architettonico(a).
architecture ['aːkɪtɛktʃə*] *n* architettura.
archive file *n* (*COMPUT*) file *m inv* di archivio.
archives ['aːkaɪvz] *npl* archivi *mpl.*
archivist ['aːkɪvɪst] *n* archivista *m/f.*
archway ['aːtʃweɪ] *n* arco.
ARCM *n abbr* (*BRIT*) = *Associate of the Royal College of Music.*
Arctic ['aːktɪk] *adj* artico(a) ♦ *n*: **the ~** l'Artico.
Arctic Circle *n* Circolo polare artico.
Arctic Ocean *n* Oceano artico.
ARD *n abbr* (*US MED*) = *acute respiratory disease.*
ardent ['aːdənt] *adj* ardente.
ardour, (*US*) **ardor** ['aːdə*] *n* ardore *m.*
arduous ['aːdjuəs] *adj* arduo(a).
are [aː*] *vb see* **be.**
area ['ɛərɪə] *n* (*GEOM*) area; (*zone*) zona; (: *smaller*) settore *m*; **dining ~** zona pranzo; **the London ~** la zona di Londra.
area code *n* (*US TEL*) prefisso.
arena [ə'riːnə] *n* arena.
aren't [aːnt] = **are not.**
Argentina [aːdʒən'tiːnə] *n* Argentina.
Argentinian [aːdʒən'tɪnɪən] *adj*, *n* argentino(a).
arguable ['aːgjuəbl] *adj* discutibile; **it is ~ whether ...** è una cosa discutibile se ... + *sub.*
arguably ['aːgjuəblɪ] *adv*: **it is ~ ...** si può sostenere che sia ....
argue ['aːgjuː] *vi* (*quarrel*) litigare; (*reason*) ragionare ♦ *vt* (*debate: case, matter*) dibattere; **to ~ that** sostenere che; **to ~ about sth (with sb)** litigare per *or* a

proposito di qc (con qn).
argument ['ɑːgjumənt] *n* (*reasons*)
argomento; (*quarrel*) lite *f*; (*debate*)
discussione *f*; ~ **for/against** argomento a
or in favore di/contro.
argumentative [ɑːgju'mentətɪv] *adj*
litigioso(a).
aria ['ɑːrɪə] *n* aria.
ARIBA *n abbr* (*BRIT*) = *Associate of the Royal
Institute of British Architects.*
arid ['ærɪd] *adj* arido(a).
aridity [ə'rɪdɪtɪ] *n* aridità.
Aries ['ɛərɪz] *n* Ariete *m*; **to be** ~ essere
dell'Ariete.
arise, *pt* **arose**, *pp* **arisen** [ə'raɪz, ə'rəuz,
ə'rɪzn] *vi* alzarsi; (*opportunity, problem*)
presentarsi; **to** ~ **from** risultare da;
should the need ~ dovesse presentarsi la
necessità, in caso di necessità.
aristocracy [ærɪs'tɔkrəsɪ] *n* aristocrazia.
aristocrat ['ærɪstəkræt] *n* aristocratico/a.
aristocratic [ærɪstə'krætɪk] *adj*
aristocratico(a).
arithmetic [ə'rɪθmətɪk] *n* aritmetica.
arithmetical [ærɪθ'metɪkəl] *adj*
aritmetico(a).
Ariz. *abbr* (*US*) = *Arizona.*
ark [ɑːk] *n*: **Noah's A**~ l'arca di Noè.
Ark. *abbr* (*US*) = *Arkansas.*
arm [ɑːm] *n* braccio; (*MIL*: *branch*) arma ♦ *vt*
armare; ~ **in** ~ a braccetto; *see also* **arms**.
armaments ['ɑːməmənts] *npl* (*weapons*)
armamenti *mpl*.
armband ['ɑːmbænd] *n* bracciale *m*.
armchair ['ɑːmtʃɛə*] *n* poltrona.
armed [ɑːmd] *adj* armato(a).
armed forces *npl* forze *fpl* armate.
armed robbery *n* rapina a mano armata.
Armenia [ɑː'miːnɪə] *n* Armenia.
Armenian [ɑː'miːnɪən] *adj* armeno(a) ♦ *n*
armeno/a; (*LING*) armeno.
armful ['ɑːmful] *n* bracciata.
armistice ['ɑːmɪstɪs] *n* armistizio.
armour, (*US*) **armor** ['ɑːmə*] *n* armatura;
(*also*: ~**-plating**) corazza, blindatura; (*MIL*:
tanks) mezzi *mpl* blindati.
armo(u)red car *n* autoblinda *f inv*.
armo(u)ry ['ɑːmərɪ] *n* arsenale *m*.
armpit ['ɑːmpɪt] *n* ascella.
armrest ['ɑːmrest] *n* bracciolo.
arms [ɑːmz] *npl* (*weapons*) armi *fpl*;
(*HERALDRY*) stemma *m*.
arms control *n* controllo degli armamenti.
arms race *n* corsa agli armamenti.
army ['ɑːmɪ] *n* esercito.
aroma [ə'rəumə] *n* aroma.
aromatherapy [ərəumə'θɛrəpɪ] *n*
aromaterapia.

aromatic [ærə'mætɪk] *adj* aromatico(a).
arose [ə'rəuz] *pt of* **arise**.
around [ə'raund] *adv* attorno, intorno ♦ *prep*
intorno a; (*fig*: *about*): ~ **£5/3 o'clock** circa
5 sterline/le 3; **is he** ~? è in giro?
arousal [ə'rauzəl] *n* (*sexual etc*) eccitazione
f; (*awakening*) risveglio.
arouse [ə'rauz] *vt* (*sleeper*) svegliare;
(*curiosity, passions*) suscitare.
arrange [ə'reɪndʒ] *vt* sistemare;
(*programme*) preparare ♦ *vi*: **we have** ~**d**
for a taxi to pick you up la faremo venire
a prendere da un taxi; **it was** ~**d that** ... è
stato deciso *or* stabilito che ...; **to** ~ **to do**
sth mettersi d'accordo per fare qc.
arrangement [ə'reɪndʒmənt] *n*
sistemazione *f*; (*plans etc*): ~**s** progetti
mpl, piani *mpl*; **by** ~ su richiesta; **to come**
to an ~ (**with sb**) venire ad un accordo
(con qn), mettersi d'accordo *or*
accordarsi (con qn); **I'll make** ~**s for you**
to be met darò disposizioni *or* istruzioni
perché ci sia qualcuno ad incontrarla.
arrant ['ærənt] *adj*: ~ **nonsense** colossali
sciocchezze *fpl*.
array [ə'reɪ] *n* fila; (*COMPUT*) array *m inv*,
insiemi *mpl*.
arrears [ə'rɪəz] *npl* arretrati *mpl*; **to be in** ~
with one's rent essere in arretrato con
l'affitto.
arrest [ə'rest] *vt* arrestare; (*sb's attention*)
attirare ♦ *n* arresto; **under** ~ in arresto.
arresting [ə'restɪŋ] *adj* (*fig*) che colpisce.
arrival [ə'raɪvəl] *n* arrivo; (*person*)
arrivato/a; **new** ~ nuovo venuto.
arrive [ə'raɪv] *vi* arrivare.
▶**arrive at** *vt fus* arrivare a.
arrogance ['ærəgəns] *n* arroganza.
arrogant ['ærəgənt] *adj* arrogante.
arrow ['ærəu] *n* freccia.
arse [ɑːs] *n* (*BRIT col!*) culo(*!*).
arsenal ['ɑːsɪnl] *n* arsenale *m*.
arsenic ['ɑːsnɪk] *n* arsenico.
arson ['ɑːsn] *n* incendio doloso.
art [ɑːt] *n* arte *f*; (*craft*) mestiere *m*; **work of**
~ opera d'arte; *see also* **arts**.
artefact, (*US*) **artifact** ['ɑːtɪfækt] *n*
manufatto.
arterial [ɑː'tɪərɪəl] *adj* (*ANAT*) arterioso(a);
(*road etc*) di grande comunicazione; ~
roads le (grandi *or* principali) arterie.
artery ['ɑːtərɪ] *n* arteria.
artful ['ɑːtful] *adj* furbo(a).
art gallery *n* galleria d'arte.
arthritis [ɑː'θraɪtɪs] *n* artrite *f*.
artichoke ['ɑːtɪtʃəuk] *n* carciofo; **Jerusalem**
~ topinambur *m inv*.
article ['ɑːtɪkl] *n* articolo; ~**s** *npl* (*BRIT LAW*:

training) contratto di tirocinio; **~s of clothing** indumenti *mpl*.

articles of association *npl* (*COMM*) statuto sociale.

articulate *adj* [ɑː'tɪkjulɪt] (*person*) che si esprime forbitamente; (*speech*) articolato(a) ♦ *vi* [ɑː'tɪkjuleɪt] articolare.

articulated lorry *n* (*BRIT*) autotreno.

artifact ['ɑːtɪfækt] *n* (*US*) = **artefact**.

artifice ['ɑːtɪfɪs] *n* (*cunning*) abilità, destrezza; (*trick*) artificio.

artificial [ɑːtɪ'fɪʃəl] *adj* artificiale.

artificial insemination [-ɪnsɛmɪ'neɪʃən] *n* fecondazione *f* artificiale.

artificial intelligence (AI) *n* intelligenza artificiale (IA).

artificial respiration *n* respirazione *f* artificiale.

artillery [ɑː'tɪlərɪ] *n* artiglieria.

artisan ['ɑːtɪzæn] *n* artigiano/a.

artist ['ɑːtɪst] *n* artista *m/f*.

artistic [ɑː'tɪstɪk] *adj* artistico(a).

artistry ['ɑːtɪstrɪ] *n* arte *f*.

artless ['ɑːtlɪs] *adj* semplice, ingenuo(a).

arts [ɑːts] *npl* (*SCOL*) lettere *fpl*.

art school *n* scuola d'arte.

artwork ['ɑːtwəːk] *n* materiale *m* illustrativo.

ARV *n abbr* (= *American Revised Version*) *traduzione della Bibbia*.

AS *n abbr* (*US SCOL*: = *Associate in/of Sciences*) *titolo di studio* ♦ *abbr* (*US*) = *American Samoa*.

━━━━━━━━━━━━━━━ *KEYWORD*

as [æz] *conj* **1** (*referring to time*) mentre; ~ **the years went by** col passare degli anni; **he came in** ~ **I was leaving** arrivò mentre stavo uscendo; ~ **from tomorrow** da domani

2 (*in comparisons*): ~ **big** ~ grande come; **twice** ~ **big** ~ due volte più grande di; ~ **much/many** ~ tanto quanto/tanti quanti; ~ **soon** ~ **possible** prima possibile

3 (*since, because*) dal momento che, siccome

4 (*referring to manner, way*) come; **big** ~ **it is** grande com'è; **much** ~ **I like them, ...** per quanto mi siano simpatici, ...; **do** ~ **you wish** fa' come vuoi; ~ **she said** come ha detto lei

5 (*concerning*): ~ **for** *or* **to that** per quanto riguarda *or* quanto a quello

6: ~ **if** *or* **though** come se; **he looked** ~ **if he was ill** sembrava stare male; *see also* **long; such; well**

♦ *prep*: **he works** ~ **a driver** fa l'autista; ~ **chairman of the company, he ...** come

presidente della compagnia, lui ...; **he gave me it** ~ **a present** me lo ha regalato.

ASA *n abbr* (= *American Standards Association*) *associazione per la normalizzazione*.

a.s.a.p. *abbr* (= *as soon as possible*) prima possibile.

asbestos [æz'bɛstəs] *n* asbesto, amianto.

ascend [ə'sɛnd] *vt* salire.

ascendancy [ə'sɛndənsɪ] *n* ascendente *m*.

ascendant [ə'sɛndənt] *n*: **to be in the** ~ essere in auge.

ascension [ə'sɛnʃən] *n*: **the A~** (*REL*) l'Ascensione *f*.

Ascension Island *n* isola dell'Ascensione.

ascent [ə'sɛnt] *n* salita.

ascertain [æsə'teɪn] *vt* accertare.

ascetic [ə'sɛtɪk] *adj* ascetico(a).

asceticism [ə'sɛtɪsɪzəm] *n* ascetismo.

ASCII ['æskiː] *n abbr* (= *American Standard Code for Information Interchange*) ASCII *m*.

ascribe [ə'skraɪb] *vt*: **to** ~ **sth to** attribuire qc a.

ASCU *n abbr* (*US*) = *Association of State Colleges and Universities*.

ASE *n abbr* = *American Stock Exchange*.

ASH [æʃ] *n abbr* (*BRIT*: = *Action on Smoking and Health*) *iniziativa contro il fumo*.

ash [æʃ] *n* (*dust*) cenere *f*; ~ (*tree*) frassino.

ashamed [ə'ʃeɪmd] *adj* vergognoso(a); **to be** ~ **of** vergognarsi di; **to be** ~ (**of o.s.**) **for having done** vergognarsi di aver fatto.

ashen ['æʃən] *adj* (*pale*) livido(a).

ashore [ə'ʃɔː*] *adv* a terra; **to go** ~ sbarcare.

ashtray ['æʃtreɪ] *n* portacenere *m*.

Ash Wednesday *n* Mercoledì *m inv* delle Ceneri.

Asia Minor *n* Asia minore.

Asian ['eɪʃən] *adj*, *n* asiatico(a).

Asiatic [eɪsɪ'ætɪk] *adj* asiatico(a).

aside [ə'saɪd] *adv* da parte ♦ *n* a parte *m*; **to take sb** ~ prendere qn da parte; ~ **from** (*as well as*) oltre a; (*except for*) a parte.

ask [ɑːsk] *vt* (*request*) chiedere; (*question*) domandare; (*invite*) invitare; **to** ~ **sb sth/sb to do sth** chiedere qc a qn/a qn di fare qc; **to** ~ **sb about sth** chiedere a qn di qc; **to** ~ (**sb**) **a question** fare una domanda (a qn); **to** ~ **sb the time** chiedere l'ora a qn; **to** ~ **sb out to dinner** invitare qn a mangiare fuori; **you should** ~ **at the information desk** dovreste rivolgervi all'ufficio informazioni.

▶**ask after** *vt fus* chiedere di.

▶**ask for** vt fus chiedere; **it's just ~ing for trouble** or **for it** è proprio (come) andarsele a cercare.

askance [ə'skɑ:ns] adv: **to look ~ at sb** guardare qn di traverso.

askew [ə'skju:] adv di traverso, storto.

asking price ['ɑ:skɪŋ-] n prezzo di partenza.

asleep [ə'sli:p] adj addormentato(a); **to be ~** dormire; **to fall ~** addormentarsi.

ASLEF ['æzlɛf] n abbr (BRIT: = Associated Society of Locomotive Engineers and Firemen) sindacato dei conducenti dei treni e dei macchinisti.

asp [æsp] n cobra m inv egiziano.

asparagus [əs'pærəgəs] n asparagi mpl.

asparagus tips npl punte fpl d'asparagi.

ASPCA n abbr (= American Society for the Prevention of Cruelty to Animals) ≈ E.N.P.A. m (Ente Nazionale per la Protezione degli Animali).

aspect ['æspɛkt] n aspetto.

aspersions [əs'pə:ʃənz] npl: **to cast ~ on** diffamare.

asphalt ['æsfælt] n asfalto.

asphyxiate [æs'fɪksɪeɪt] vt asfissiare.

asphyxiation [æsfɪksɪ'eɪʃən] n asfissia.

aspiration [æspə'reɪʃən] n aspirazione f.

aspire [əs'paɪə*] vi: **to ~ to** aspirare a.

aspirin ['æsprɪn] n aspirina.

aspiring [əs'paɪərɪŋ] adj aspirante.

ass [æs] n asino; (US col!) culo(!).

assail [ə'seɪl] vt assalire.

assailant [ə'seɪlənt] n assalitore m.

assassin [ə'sæsɪn] n assassino.

assassinate [ə'sæsɪneɪt] vt assassinare.

assassination [əsæsɪ'neɪʃən] n assassinio.

assault [ə'sɔ:lt] n (MIL) assalto; (gen: attack) aggressione f, (LAW): **~ (and battery)** minacce e vie di fatto fpl ♦ vt assaltare; aggredire; (sexually) violentare.

assemble [ə'sɛmbl] vt riunire; (TECH) montare ♦ vi riunirsi.

assembly [ə'sɛmblɪ] n (meeting) assemblea; (construction) montaggio.

assembly language n (COMPUT) linguaggio assemblativo.

assembly line n catena di montaggio.

assent [ə'sɛnt] n assenso, consenso ♦ vi assentire; **to ~ (to sth)** approvare (qc).

assert [ə'sə:t] vt asserire; (insist on) far valere; **to ~ o.s.** farsi valere.

assertion [ə'sə:ʃən] n asserzione f.

assertive [ə'sə:tɪv] adj che sa imporsi.

assess [ə'sɛs] vt valutare.

assessment [ə'sɛsmənt] n valutazione f; (judgment): **~ (of)** giudizio (su).

assessor [ə'sɛsə*] n perito; funzionario del fisco.

asset ['æsɛt] n vantaggio; (person) elemento prezioso; **~s** npl (COMM) beni mpl; disponibilità fpl; attivo.

asset-stripping ['æsɛt'strɪpɪŋ] n (COMM) acquisto di una società in fallimento con lo scopo di rivenderne le attività.

assiduous [ə'sɪdjuəs] adj assiduo(a).

assign [ə'saɪn] vt: **to ~ (to)** (task) assegnare (a); (resources) riservare (a); (cause, meaning) attribuire (a); **to ~ a date to sth** fissare la data di qc.

assignment [ə'saɪnmənt] n compito.

assimilate [ə'sɪmɪleɪt] vt assimilare.

assimilation [əsɪmɪ'leɪʃən] n assimilazione f.

assist [ə'sɪst] vt assistere, aiutare.

assistance [ə'sɪstəns] n assistenza, aiuto.

assistant [ə'sɪstənt] n assistente m/f; (BRIT: also: **shop ~**) commesso/a.

assistant manager n vicedirettore m.

assizes [ə'saɪzɪz] npl assise fpl.

associate [ə'səuʃɪɪt] adj associato(a); (member) aggiunto(a) ♦ n collega m/f; (in business) socio/a ♦ vb [ə'səuʃɪeɪt] vt associare ♦ vi: **to ~ with sb** frequentare qn.

associated company [ə'səusɪ'eɪtɪd-] n società collegata.

associate director n amministratore m aggiunto.

association [əsəusɪ'eɪʃən] n associazione f; **in ~ with** in collaborazione con.

association football n (BRIT) (gioco del) calcio.

assorted [ə'sɔ:tɪd] adj assortito(a); **in ~ sizes** in diverse taglie.

assortment [ə'sɔ:tmənt] n assortimento.

Asst. abbr = **assistant**.

assuage [ə'sweɪdʒ] vt alleviare.

assume [ə'sju:m] vt supporre; (responsibilities etc) assumere; (attitude, name) prendere.

assumed name n nome m falso.

assumption [ə'sʌmpʃən] n supposizione f, ipotesi f inv; **on the ~ that ...** partendo dal presupposto che ....

assurance [ə'ʃuərəns] n assicurazione f; (self-confidence) fiducia in se stesso; **I can give you no ~s** non posso assicurarle or garantirle niente.

assure [ə'ʃuə*] vt assicurare.

assured [ə'ʃuəd] adj (confident) sicuro(a); (certain: promotion etc) assicurato(a).

AST abbr (US: = Atlantic Standard Time) ora invernale di New York.

asterisk ['æstərɪsk] n asterisco.

astern [ə'stə:n] adv a poppa.

asteroid ['æstərɔɪd] n asteroide m.
asthma ['æsmə] n asma.
asthmatic [æs'mætɪk] adj, n asmatico(a).
astigmatism [ə'stɪgmətɪzəm] n astigmatismo.
astir [ə'stəː*] adv in piedi; (excited) in fermento.
astonish [ə'stɔnɪʃ] vt stupire.
astonishing [ə'stɔnɪʃɪŋ] adj sorprendente, stupefacente; **I find it ~ that ...** mi stupisce che ....
astonishingly [ə'stɔnɪʃɪŋlɪ] adv straordinariamente, incredibilmente.
astonishment [ə'stɔnɪʃmənt] n stupore m; **to my ~** con mia gran meraviglia, con mio grande stupore.
astound [ə'staund] vt sbalordire.
astray [ə'streɪ] adv: **to go ~** smarrirsi; (fig) traviarsi; **to go ~ in one's calculations** sbagliare i calcoli.
astride [ə'straɪd] adv a cavalcioni ♦ prep a cavalcioni di.
astringent [əs'trɪndʒənt] adj, n astringente (m).
astrologer [əs'trɔlədʒə*] n astrologo/a.
astrology [əs'trɔlədʒɪ] n astrologia.
astronaut ['æstrənɔːt] n astronauta m/f.
astronomer [əs'trɔnəmə*] n astronomo/a.
astronomical [æstrə'nɔmɪkl] adj astronomico(a).
astronomy [əs'trɔnəmɪ] n astronomia.
astrophysics ['æstrəu'fɪzɪks] n astrofisica.
astute [əs'tjuːt] adj astuto(a).
asunder [ə'sʌndə*] adv: **to tear ~** strappare.
ASV n abbr (= American Standard Version) traduzione della Bibbia.
asylum [ə'saɪləm] n asilo; (lunatic ~) manicomio; **to seek political ~** chiedere asilo politico.
asymmetric(al) [eɪsɪ'mɛtrɪk(əl)] adj asimmetrico(a).

======================= KEYWORD

at [æt] prep **1** (referring to position, direction) a; **~ the top** in cima; **~ the desk** al banco, alla scrivania; **~ home/school** a casa/scuola; **~ Paolo's** da Paolo; **~ the baker's** dal panettiere; **to look ~ sth** guardare qc; **to throw sth ~ sb** lanciare qc a qn
2 (referring to time) a; **~ 4 o'clock** alle 4; **~ night** di notte; **~ Christmas** a Natale; **~ times** a volte
3 (referring to rates, speed etc) a; **~ £1 a kilo** a 1 sterlina al chilo; **two ~ a time** due alla volta, due per volta; **~ 50 km/h** a 50 km/h; **~ full speed** a tutta velocità
4 (referring to manner): **~ a stroke** d'un

solo colpo; **~ peace** in pace
5 (referring to activity): **to be ~ work** essere al lavoro; **to play ~ cowboys** giocare ai cowboy; **to be good ~ sth/doing sth** essere bravo in qc/a fare qc
6 (referring to cause): **shocked/surprised/annoyed ~ sth** colpito da/sorpreso da/arrabbiato per qc; **I went ~ his suggestion** ci sono andato dietro suo consiglio.

ate [eɪt] pt of **eat**.
atheism ['eɪθɪɪzəm] n ateismo.
atheist ['eɪθɪɪst] n ateo/a.
Athenian [ə'θiːnɪən] adj, n ateniese (m/f).
Athens ['æθɪnz] n Atene f.
athlete ['æθliːt] n atleta m/f.
athletic [æθ'lɛtɪk] adj atletico(a).
athletics [æθ'lɛtɪks] n atletica.
Atlantic [ət'læntɪk] adj atlantico(a) ♦ n: **the ~ (Ocean)** l'Atlantico, l'Oceano Atlantico.
atlas ['ætləs] n atlante m.
Atlas Mountains npl: **the ~** i Monti dell'Atlante.
A.T.M. abbr (= automated telling machine) cassa automatica prelievi, sportello automatico.
atmosphere ['ætməsfɪə*] n atmosfera; (air) aria.
atmospheric [ætməs'fɛrɪk] adj atmosferico(a).
atmospherics [ætməs'fɛrɪks] npl (RADIO) scariche fpl.
atoll ['ætɔl] n atollo.
atom ['ætəm] n atomo.
atomic [ə'tɔmɪk] adj atomico(a).
atom(ic) bomb n bomba atomica.
atomizer ['ætəmaɪzə*] n atomizzatore m.
atone [ə'təun] vi: **to ~ for** espiare.
atonement [ə'təunmənt] n espiazione f.
ATP n abbr = Association of Tennis Professionals.
atrocious [ə'trəuʃəs] adj atroce, pessimo(a).
atrocity [ə'trɔsɪtɪ] n atrocità f inv.
atrophy ['ætrəfɪ] n atrofia ♦ vi atrofizzarsi.
attach [ə'tætʃ] vt attaccare; (document, letter) allegare; (MIL: troops) assegnare; **to be ~ed to sb/sth** (to like) essere affezionato(a) a qn/qc; **the ~ed letter** la lettera acclusa or allegata.
attaché [ə'tæʃeɪ] n addetto.
attaché case n valigetta per documenti.
attachment [ə'tætʃmənt] n (tool) accessorio; (love): **~ (to)** affetto (per).
attack [ə'tæk] vt attaccare; (task etc) iniziare; (problem) affrontare ♦ n attacco; (also: heart ~) infarto.

attacker [ə'tækə*] n aggressore m, assalitore/trice.

attain [ə'teɪn] vt (also: to ~ to) arrivare a, raggiungere.

attainments [ə'teɪnmənts] npl cognizioni fpl.

attempt [ə'tɛmpt] n tentativo ♦ vt tentare; ~ed murder (LAW) tentato omicidio; to make an ~ on sb's life attentare alla vita di qn; he made no ~ to help non ha (neanche) tentato or cercato di aiutare.

attend [ə'tɛnd] vt frequentare; (meeting, talk) andare a; (patient) assistere.
►**attend to** vt fus (needs, affairs etc) prendersi cura di; (customer) occuparsi di.

attendance [ə'tɛndəns] n (being present) presenza; (people present) gente f presente.

attendant [ə'tɛndənt] n custode m/f; persona di servizio ♦ adj concomitante.

attention [ə'tɛnʃən] n attenzione f; ~s premure fpl, attenzioni fpl; ~! (MIL) attenti!; at ~ (MIL) sull'attenti; for the ~ of (ADMIN) per l'attenzione di; it has come to my ~ that ... sono venuto a conoscenza (del fatto) che ....

attentive [ə'tɛntɪv] adj attento(a); (kind) premuroso(a).

attentively [ə'tɛntɪvlɪ] adv attentamente.

attenuate [ə'tɛnjueɪt] vt attenuare ♦ vi attenuarsi.

attest [ə'tɛst] vi: to ~ to attestare.

attic ['ætɪk] n soffitta.

attire [ə'taɪə*] n abbigliamento.

attitude ['ætɪtjuːd] n (behaviour) atteggiamento; (posture) posa; (view): ~ (to) punto di vista (nei confronti di).

attorney [ə'təːnɪ] n (US: lawyer) avvocato; (having proxy) mandatario; power of ~ procura.

Attorney General n (BRIT) Procuratore m Generale; (US) Ministro della Giustizia.

attract [ə'trækt] vt attirare.

attraction [ə'trækʃən] n (gen pl: pleasant things) attrattiva; (PHYSICS, fig: towards sth) attrazione f.

attractive [ə'træktɪv] adj attraente; (idea, offer, price) allettante, interessante.

attribute n ['ætrɪbjuːt] attributo ♦ vt [ə'trɪbjuːt]: to ~ sth to attribuire qc a.

attrition [ə'trɪʃən] n: war of ~ guerra di logoramento.

Atty. Gen. abbr = Attorney General.

atypical [eɪ'tɪpɪkl] adj atipico(a).

aubergine ['əubəʒiːn] n melanzana.

auburn ['ɔːbən] adj tizianesco(a).

auction ['ɔːkʃən] n (also: sale by ~) asta ♦ vt (also: to sell by ~) vendere all'asta; (also: to put up for ~) mettere all'asta.

auctioneer [ɔːkʃə'nɪə*] n banditore m.

auction room n sala dell'asta.

audacious [ɔː'deɪʃəs] adj (bold) audace; (impudent) sfrontato(a).

audacity [ɔː'dæsɪtɪ] n audacia.

audible ['ɔːdɪbl] adj udibile.

audience ['ɔːdɪəns] n (people) pubblico; spettatori mpl; ascoltatori mpl; (interview) udienza.

audio-typist ['ɔːdɪəu'taɪpɪst] n dattilografo/a che trascrive da nastro.

audiovisual [ɔːdɪəu'vɪzjuəl] adj audiovisivo(a); ~ aids sussidi mpl audiovisivi.

audit ['ɔːdɪt] n revisione f, verifica ♦ vt rivedere, verificare.

audition [ɔː'dɪʃən] n (THEAT) audizione f; (CINE) provino ♦ vi fare un'audizione (or un provino).

auditor ['ɔːdɪtə*] n revisore m.

auditorium [ɔːdɪ'tɔːrɪəm] n sala, auditorio.

Aug. abbr (= August) ago., ag.

augment [ɔːg'mɛnt] vt, vi aumentare.

augur ['ɔːgə*] vt (be a sign of) predire ♦ vi: it ~s well promette bene.

August ['ɔːgəst] n agosto; for phrases see also July.

august [ɔː'gʌst] adj augusto(a).

aunt [ɑːnt] n zia.

auntie, aunty ['ɑːntɪ] n zietta.

au pair ['əu'pɛə*] n (also: ~ girl) (ragazza f) alla pari inv.

aura ['ɔːrə] n aura.

auspices ['ɔːspɪsɪz] npl: under the ~ of sotto gli auspici di.

auspicious [ɔːs'pɪʃəs] adj propizio(a).

austere [ɔs'tɪə*] adj austero(a).

austerity [ɔs'tɛrɪtɪ] n austerità f inv.

Australasia [ɔstrə'leɪzɪə] n Australasia.

Australia [ɔs'treɪlɪə] n Australia.

Australian [ɔs'treɪlɪən] adj, n australiano(a).

Austria ['ɔstrɪə] n Austria.

Austrian ['ɔstrɪən] adj, n austriaco(a).

AUT n abbr (BRIT: = Association of University Teachers) associazione dei docenti universitari.

authentic [ɔː'θɛntɪk] adj autentico(a).

authenticate [ɔː'θɛntɪkeɪt] vt autenticare.

authenticity [ɔːθɛn'tɪsɪtɪ] n autenticità.

author ['ɔːθə*] n autore/trice.

authoritarian [ɔːθɔrɪ'tɛərɪən] adj autoritario(a).

authoritative [ɔː'θɔrɪtətɪv] adj (account etc) autorevole; (manner) autoritario(a).

authority [ɔː'θɔrɪtɪ] n autorità f inv; (permission) autorizzazione f; the

authorities *npl* le autorità; **to have ~ to do sth** avere l'autorizzazione a fare *or* il diritto di fare qc.
authorization [ɔːθəraɪˈzeɪʃən] *n* autorizzazione *f*.
authorize [ˈɔːθəraɪz] *vt* autorizzare.
authorized capital *n* capitale *m* nominale.
authorship [ˈɔːθəʃɪp] *n* paternità (*letteraria etc*).
autistic [ɔːˈtɪstɪk] *adj* autistico(a).
auto [ˈɔːtəu] *n* (*US*) auto *f inv*.
autobiography [ɔːtəbaɪˈɔgrəfɪ] *n* autobiografia.
autocratic [ɔːtəˈkrætɪk] *adj* autocratico(a).
Autocue ® [ˈɔːtəukjuː] *n* (*BRIT*) gobbo (*TV*).
autograph [ˈɔːtəgrɑːf] *n* autografo ♦ *vt* firmare.
autoimmune [ɔːtəuɪˈmjuːn] *adj* autoimmune.
automat [ˈɔːtəmæt] *n* (*US*) tavola calda fornita esclusivamente di distributori automatici.
automated [ˈɔːtəmeɪtɪd] *adj* automatizzato(a).
automatic [ɔːtəˈmætɪk] *adj* automatico(a) ♦ *n* (*gun*) arma automatica; (*car*) automobile *f* con cambio automatico; (*washing machine*) lavatrice *f* automatica.
automatically [ɔːtəˈmætɪklɪ] *adv* automaticamente.
automatic data processing (ADP) *n* elaborazione *f* automatica dei dati (EAD).
automation [ɔːtəˈmeɪʃən] *n* automazione *f*.
automaton, *pl* **automata** [ɔːˈtɔmətən, -tə] *n* automa *m*.
automobile [ˈɔːtəməbiːl] *n* (*US*) automobile *f*.
autonomous [ɔːˈtɔnəməs] *adj* autonomo(a).
autopsy [ˈɔːtɔpsɪ] *n* autopsia.
autumn [ˈɔːtəm] *n* autunno.
auxiliary [ɔːgˈzɪlɪərɪ] *adj* ausiliario(a) ♦ *n* ausiliare *m/f*.
AV *n abbr* (= *Authorized Version*) traduzione inglese della Bibbia ♦ *abbr* = **audiovisual**.
Av. *abbr* = **avenue**.
avail [əˈveɪl] *vt*: **to ~ o.s. of** servirsi di; approfittarsi di ♦ *n*: **to no ~** inutilmente.
availability [əveɪləˈbɪlɪtɪ] *n* disponibilità.
available [əˈveɪləbl] *adj* disponibile; **every ~ means** tutti i mezzi disponibili; **to make sth ~ to sb** mettere qc a disposizione di qn; **is the manager ~?** è libero il direttore?
avalanche [ˈævəlɑːnʃ] *n* valanga.
avant-garde [ˈævãŋˈgɑːd] *adj* d'avanguardia.
avarice [ˈævərɪs] *n* avarizia.
avaricious [ævəˈrɪʃəs] *adj* avaro(a).

avdp. *abbr* (= *avoirdupois*) sistema ponderale anglosassone basato su libbra, oncia e multipli.
Ave. *abbr* = **avenue**.
avenge [əˈvɛndʒ] *vt* vendicare.
avenue [ˈævənjuː] *n* viale *m*.
average [ˈævərɪdʒ] *n* media ♦ *adj* medio(a) ♦ *vt* (*also*: ~ **out at**) aggirarsi in media su, essere in media di; **on ~** in media; **above/below (the)** ~ sopra/sotto la media.
averse [əˈvɔːs] *adj*: **to be ~ to sth/doing** essere contrario(a) a qc/a fare; **I wouldn't be ~ to a drink** non avrei nulla in contrario a bere qualcosa.
aversion [əˈvɔːʃən] *n* avversione *f*.
avert [əˈvɔːt] *vt* evitare, prevenire; (*one's eyes*) distogliere.
aviary [ˈeɪvɪərɪ] *n* voliera, uccelliera.
aviation [eɪvɪˈeɪʃən] *n* aviazione *f*.
avid [ˈævɪd] *adj* avido(a).
avidly [ˈævɪdlɪ] *adv* avidamente.
avocado [ævəˈkɑːdəu] *n* (*also*: *BRIT*: ~ **pear**) avocado *m inv*.
avoid [əˈvɔɪd] *vt* evitare.
avoidable [əˈvɔɪdəbl] *adj* evitabile.
avoidance [əˈvɔɪdəns] *n* l'evitare *m*.
avowed [əˈvaud] *adj* dichiarato(a).
AVP *n abbr* (*US*) = *assistant vice-president*.
AWACS [ˈeɪwæks] *n abbr* (= *airborne warning and control system*) sistema di allarme e controllo in volo.
await [əˈweɪt] *vt* aspettare; ~**ing attention** (*COMM: letter*) in attesa di risposta; (*: order*) in attesa di essere evaso; **long** ~**ed** tanto atteso(a).
awake [əˈweɪk] *adj* sveglio(a) ♦ *vb* (*pt* **awoke** [əˈwəuk], *pp* **awoken** [əˈwəukən] *or* **awaked**) *vt* svegliare ♦ *vi* svegliarsi; ~ **to** consapevole di.
awakening [əˈweɪknɪŋ] *n* risveglio.
award [əˈwɔːd] *n* premio; (*LAW*) decreto ♦ *vt* assegnare; (*LAW: damages*) decretare.
aware [əˈwɛə*] *adj*: ~ **of** (*conscious*) conscio(a) di; (*informed*) informato(a) di; **to become ~ of** accorgersi di; **politically/socially** ~ politicamente/socialmente preparato; **I am fully ~ that ...** mi rendo perfettamente conto che ....
awareness [əˈwɛənɪs] *n* consapevolezza; coscienza; **to develop people's ~ (of)** sensibilizzare la gente (a).
awash [əˈwɔʃ] *adj*: ~ **(with)** inondato(a) (da).
away [əˈweɪ] *adj, adv* via; lontano(a); **two kilometres** ~ a due chilometri di distanza; **two hours ~ by car** a due ore di

distanza in macchina; **the holiday was two weeks** ~ mancavano due settimane alle vacanze; ~ **from** lontano da; **he's** ~ **for a week** è andato via per una settimana; **he's** ~ **in Milan** è (andato) a Milano; **to take** ~ *vt* portare via; **he was working/pedalling** *etc* ~ *la particella indica la continuità e l'energia dell'azione:* lavorava/pedalava *etc* più che poteva; **to fade/wither** *etc* ~ *la particella rinforza l'idea della diminuzione.*

away game *n* (*SPORT*) partita fuori casa.

awe [ɔː] *n* timore *m*.

awe-inspiring ['ɔːɪnspaɪərɪŋ], **awesome** ['ɔːsəm] *adj* imponente.

awestruck ['ɔːstrʌk] *adj* sgomento(a).

awful ['ɔːfəl] *adj* terribile; **an** ~ **lot of** (*people, cars, dogs*) un numero incredibile di; (*jam, flowers*) una quantità incredibile di.

awfully ['ɔːflɪ] *adv* (*very*) terribilmente.

awhile [ə'waɪl] *adv* (per) un po'.

awkward ['ɔːkwəd] *adj* (*clumsy*) goffo(a); (*inconvenient*) scomodo(a); (*embarrassing*) imbarazzante; (*difficult*) delicato(a), difficile.

awkwardness ['ɔːkwədnɪs] *n* goffaggine *f*; scomodità; imbarazzo; delicatezza, difficoltà.

awl ['ɔːl] *n* punteruolo.

awning ['ɔːnɪŋ] *n* (*of tent*) veranda; (*of shop, hotel etc*) tenda.

awoke [ə'wəuk] *pt of* **awake.**

awoken [ə'wəukən] *pp of* **awake.**

AWOL ['eɪwɔl] *abbr* (*MIL etc*) *see* **absent without leave.**

awry [ə'raɪ] *adv* di traverso ♦ *adj* storto(a); **to go** ~ andare a monte.

axe, (*US*) **ax** [æks] *n* scure *f* ♦ *vt* (*project etc*) abolire; (*jobs*) sopprimere; **to have an** ~ **to grind** (*fig*) fare i propri interessi *or* ~ proprio tornaconto.

axiom ['æksɪəm] *n* assioma *m*.

axiomatic [æksɪəu'mætɪk] *adj* assiomatico(a).

axis, *pl* **axes** ['æksɪs, -siːz] *n* asse *m*.

axle ['æksl] *n* (*also:* ~**-tree**) asse *m*.

ay(e) [aɪ] *excl* (*yes*) sì.

AYH *n abbr* = *American Youth Hostels.*

AZ *abbr* (*US*) = *Arizona.*

azalea [ə'zeɪlɪə] *n* azalea.

Azerbaijan [æzəbaɪ'dʒɑːn] *n* Azerbaigian *m*.

Azerbaijani [æzəbaɪ'dʒɑːnɪ], **Azeri** [ə'zɛərɪ] *adj, n* azerbaigiano(a), azero(a).

Azores [ə'zɔːz] *npl:* **the** ~ le Azzorre.

AZT *n abbr* (= *azidothymidine*) AZT *m*.

Aztec ['æztɛk] *adj, n* azteco(a).

azure ['eɪʒə*] *adj* azzurro(a).

B b

B, b [biː] *n* (*letter*) B, b *f or m inv*; (*SCOL: mark*) ≈ 8 (*buono*); (*MUS*): **B** si *m*; **B for Benjamin,** (*US*) **B for Baker** ≈ B come Bologna; **B road** *n* (*BRIT AUT*) ≈ strada secondaria.

b. *abbr* = **born.**

BA *n abbr* = *British Academy*; (*SCOL*) *see* **Bachelor of Arts.**

babble ['bæbl] *vi* cianciare; mormorare ♦ *n* ciance *fpl*; mormorio.

babe [beɪb] *n* (*col*): **she's a real** ~ è uno schianto di ragazza.

baboon [bə'buːn] *n* babbuino.

baby ['beɪbɪ] *n* bambino/a.

baby carriage *n* (*US*) carrozzina.

baby grand *n* (*also:* ~ **piano**) pianoforte *m* a mezza coda.

babyhood ['beɪbɪhud] *n* prima infanzia.

babyish ['beɪbɪʃ] *adj* infantile.

baby-minder ['beɪbɪ'maɪndə*] *n* (*BRIT*) bambinaia (*che tiene i bambini mentre la madre lavora*).

baby-sit ['beɪbɪsɪt] *vi* fare il (*or* la) babysitter.

baby-sitter ['beɪbɪsɪtə*] *n* baby-sitter *m/f inv*.

bachelor ['bætʃələ*] *n* scapolo; **B**~ **of Arts/Science (BA/BSc)** ≈ laureato/a in lettere/scienze; **B**~ **of Arts/Science degree (BA/BSc)** *n* ≈ laurea in lettere/scienze.

Il **Bachelor's Degree** *è il riconoscimento che viene conferito a chi ha completato un corso di laurea di tre o quattro anni all'università. I Bachelor's degree più importanti sono il BA (Bachelor of Arts), il BSc (Bachelor of Science), il BEd (Bachelor of Education), e il LLB (Bachelor of Laws); vedi anche* **Master's degree, doctorate.**

bachelorhood ['bætʃələhud] *n* celibato.

bachelor party *n* (*US*) festa di addio al celibato.

back [bæk] *n* (*of person, horse*) dorso, schiena; (*of hand*) dorso; (*of house, car*) didietro; (*of train*) coda; (*of chair*) schienale *m*; (*of page*) rovescio; (*FOOTBALL*) difensore *m*; ~ **to front**

all'incontrario; **to break the** ~ **of a job**
(*BRIT*) fare il grosso *or* il peggio di un
lavoro; **to have one's** ~ **to the wall** (*fig*)
essere *or* trovarsi con le spalle al muro
♦ *vt* (*financially*) finanziare; (*candidate*: *also*:
~ **up**) appoggiare; (*horse*: *at races*)
puntare su; (*car*) guidare a marcia
indietro ♦ *vi* indietreggiare; (*car etc*) fare
marcia indietro ♦ *adj* (*in compounds*)
posteriore, di dietro; arretrato(a); ~
seats/wheels (*AUT*) sedili *mpl*/ruote *fpl*
posteriori; ~ **payments/rent** arretrati
mpl; ~ **garden/room** giardino/stanza sul
retro (della casa); **to take a** ~ **seat** (*fig*)
restare in secondo piano ♦ *adv* (*not
forward*) indietro; (*returned*): **he's** ~ **è**
tornato; **when will you be** ~**?** quando
torni?; **he ran** ~ tornò indietro di corsa;
(*restitution*): **throw the ball** ~ ritira la
palla; **can I have it** ~**?** posso riaverlo?;
(*again*): **he called** ~ ha richiamato.
▶**back down** *vi* (*fig*) fare marcia indietro.
▶**back on to** *vt fus*: **the house** ~**s on to the
golf course** il retro della casa dà sul
campo da golf.
▶**back out** *vi* (*of promise*) tirarsi indietro.
▶**back up** *vt* (*support*) appoggiare,
sostenere; (*COMPUT*) fare una copia di
riserva di.
backache ['bækeɪk] *n* mal *m* di schiena.
back benches *npl* posti in Parlamento
occupati dai backbencher.

Nella **House of Commons**, una delle camere
del Parlamento britannico, sono chiamati
back benches gli scanni dove siedono i
backbencher, parlamentari che non hanno
incarichi né al governo né all'opposizione.
Nelle file davanti ad essi siedono i
frontbencher; *vedi anche* **front bench**.

backbencher ['bæk'bɛntʃə*] *n* (*BRIT*)
parlamentare che non ha incarichi né al
governo né all'opposizione.
backbiting ['bækbaɪtɪŋ] *n* maldicenza.
backbone ['bækbəun] *n* spina dorsale; **the**
~ **of the organization** l'anima
dell'organizzazione.
backchat ['bæktʃæt] *n* (*BRIT col*)
impertinenza.
backcloth ['bækklɔθ] *n* (*BRIT*) scena di
sfondo.
backcomb ['bækkəum] *vt* (*BRIT*) cotonare.
backdate [bæk'deɪt] *vt* (*letter*) retrodatare;
~**d pay rise** aumento retroattivo.
backdrop ['bækdrɔp] *n* = **backcloth**.
backer ['bækə*] *n* sostenitore/trice; (*COMM*)
fautore *m*.

backfire ['bæk'faɪə*] *vi* (*AUT*) dar ritorni di
fiamma; (*plans*) fallire.
backgammon ['bækgæmən] *n* tavola reale.
background ['bækgraund] *n* sfondo; (*of
events*, *COMPUT*) background *m inv*; (*basic
knowledge*) base *f*; (*experience*) esperienza
♦ *cpd* (*noise*, *music*) di fondo; ~ **reading**
letture *fpl* sull'argomento; **family** ~
ambiente *m* familiare.
backhand ['bækhænd] *n* (*TENNIS*: *also*: ~
stroke) rovescio.
backhanded [bæk'hændɪd] *adj* (*fig*)
ambiguo(a).
backhander ['bækhændə*] *n* (*BRIT*: *bribe*)
bustarella.
backing [bækɪŋ] *n* (*COMM*) finanziamento;
(*MUS*) accompagnamento; (*fig*) appoggio.
backlash ['bæklæʃ] *n* contraccolpo,
ripercussione *f*.
backlog ['bæklɔg] *n*: ~ **of work** lavoro
arretrato.
back number *n* (*of magazine etc*) numero
arretrato.
backpack ['bækpæk] *n* zaino.
backpacker ['bækpækə*] *n* chi viaggia con
zaino e sacco a pelo.
back pay *n* arretrato di paga.
backpedal ['bækpɛdl] *vi* pedalare
all'indietro; (*fig*) far marcia indietro.
backseat driver ['bæksiːt-] *n* passeggero
che dà consigli non richiesti al guidatore.
backside [bæk'saɪd] *n* (*col*) sedere *m*.
backslash ['bækslæʃ] *n* backslash *m inv*,
barra obliqua inversa.
backslide ['bækslaɪd] *vi* ricadere.
backspace ['bækspeɪs] *vi* (*in typing*) battere
il tasto di ritorno.
backstage [bæk'steɪdʒ] *adv* nel retroscena.
back street *n* vicolo.
back-street ['bækstriːt] *adj*: ~ **abortionist**
praticante *m/f* di aborti clandestini.
backstroke ['bækstrəuk] *n* nuoto sul dorso.
backtrack ['bæktræk] *vi* = **backpedal**.
backup ['bækʌp] *adj* (*train*, *plane*)
supplementare; (*COMPUT*) di riserva ♦ *n*
(*support*) appoggio, sostegno; (*COMPUT*:
also: ~ **file**) file *m inv* di riserva.
backward ['bækwəd] *adj* (*movement*)
indietro *inv*; (*person*) tardivo(a); (*country*)
arretrato(a); ~ **and forward movement**
movimento avanti e indietro.
backwards ['bækwədz] *adv* indietro; (*fall*,
walk) all'indietro; **to know sth** ~ (*or* (*US*) ~
and forwards) (*col*) sapere qc a menadito.
backwater ['bækwɔːtə*] *n* (*fig*) posto
morto.
back yard *n* cortile *m* sul retro.
bacon ['beɪkən] *n* pancetta.

bacteria [bæk'tɪərɪə] *npl* batteri *mpl.*
bacteriology [bæktɪərɪ'ɔlədʒɪ] *n*
batteriologia.
bad [bæd] *adj* cattivo(a); (*child*)
cattivello(a); (*meat, food*) andato(a) a
male; **his ~ leg** la sua gamba malata; **to
go ~** (*meat, food*) andare a male; **to have
a ~ time of it** passarsela male; **I feel ~
about it** (*guilty*) mi sento un po' in colpa;
~ debt credito difficile da recuperare; **~
faith** malafede *f.*
baddie, baddy ['bædɪ] *n* (*col: CINE etc*)
cattivo/a.
bade [bæd] *pt of* **bid.**
badge [bædʒ] *n* insegna; (*of policeman*)
stemma *m*; (*stick-on*) adesivo.
badger ['bædʒə*] *n* tasso ♦ *vt* tormentare.
badly ['bædlɪ] *adv* (*work, dress etc*) male;
things are going ~ le cose vanno male; **~
wounded** gravemente ferito; **he needs it
~** ne ha gran bisogno; **~ off** *adj* povero(a).
bad-mannered [bæd'mænəd] *adj*
maleducato(a), sgarbato(a).
badminton ['bædmɪntən] *n* badminton *m.*
bad-tempered [bæd'tɛmpəd] *adj* irritabile;
(*in bad mood*) di malumore.
baffle ['bæfl] *vt* (*puzzle*) confondere.
baffling ['bæflɪŋ] *adj* sconcertante.
bag [bæg] *n* sacco; (*handbag etc*) borsa; (*of
hunter*) carniere *m*; bottino ♦ *vt* (*col: take*)
mettersi in tasca; prendersi; **~s of** (*col:
lots of*) un sacco di; **to pack one's ~s** fare
le valigie; **~s under the eyes** borse sotto
gli occhi.
bagful ['bægful] *n* sacco (pieno).
baggage ['bægɪdʒ] *n* bagagli *mpl.*
baggage car *n* (*US*) bagagliaio.
baggage claim *n* ritiro bagagli.
baggy ['bægɪ] *adj* largo(a), sformato(a).
Baghdad [bæg'dæd] *n* Bagdad *f.*
bag lady *n* (*col*) stracciona, barbona.
bagpipes ['bægpaɪps] *npl* cornamusa.
bag-snatcher ['bægsnætʃə*] *n* (*BRIT*)
scippatore/trice.
bag-snatching ['bægsnætʃɪŋ] *n* (*BRIT*)
scippo.
Bahamas [bə'hɑːməz] *npl*: **the ~** le isole
Bahama.
Bahrain [bɑː'reɪn] *n* Bahrein *m.*
bail [beɪl] *n* cauzione *f* ♦ *vt* (*prisoner: gen: to
grant ~ to*) concedere la libertà
provvisoria su cauzione a; (*NAUT: also: ~
out*) *see* **bale out**; **to be released on ~**
essere rilasciato(a) su cauzione.
▶**bail out** *vt* (*prisoner*) ottenere la libertà
provvisoria su cauzione di; (*fig*) tirare
fuori dai guai ♦ *vi see* **bale out.**
bailiff ['beɪlɪf] *n* usciere *m*; fattore *m.*

bait [beɪt] *n* esca ♦ *vt* (*hook*) innescare;
(*trap*) munire di esca; (*fig*) tormentare.
bake [beɪk] *vt* cuocere al forno ♦ *vi*
cuocersi al forno.
baked beans *npl* fagioli *mpl* all'uccelletto.
baker ['beɪkə*] *n* fornaio/a, panettiere/a.
bakery ['beɪkərɪ] *n* panetteria.
baking ['beɪkɪŋ] *n* cottura (al forno).
baking powder *n* lievito in polvere.
baking tin *n* stampo, tortiera.
baking tray *n* teglia.
balaclava [bælə'klɑːvə] *n* (*also: ~ helmet*)
passamontagna *m inv.*
balance ['bæləns] *n* equilibrio; (*COMM: sum*)
bilancio; (*scales*) bilancia ♦ *vt* tenere in
equilibrio; (*pros and cons*) soppesare;
(*budget*) far quadrare; (*account*)
pareggiare; (*compensate*) contrappesare;
~ of trade/payments bilancia
commerciale/dei pagamenti; **~ brought
forward** saldo riportato; **~ carried
forward** saldo da riportare; **to ~ the
books** fare il bilancio.
balanced ['bælənst] *adj* (*personality, diet*)
equilibrato(a).
balance sheet *n* bilancio.
balcony ['bælkənɪ] *n* balcone *m.*
bald [bɔːld] *adj* calvo(a).
baldness ['bɔːldnɪs] *n* calvizie *f.*
bale [beɪl] *n* balla.
▶**bale out** *vt* (*NAUT: water*) vuotare; (: *boat*)
aggottare ♦ *vi* (*of a plane*) gettarsi col
paracadute.
Balearic [bælɪ'ærɪk] *adj*: **the ~ Islands** le
(isole) Baleari.
baleful ['beɪlful] *adj* funesto(a).
balk [bɔːlk] *vi*: **to ~ (at)** tirarsi indietro
(davanti a); (*horse*) recalcitrare (davanti
a).
Balkan ['bɔːlkən] *adj* balcanico(a) ♦ *n*: **the
~s** i Balcani.
ball [bɔːl] *n* palla; (*football*) pallone *m*; (*for
golf*) pallina; (*dance*) ballo; **to play ~ (with
sb)** giocare a palla (con qn); (*fig*) stare al
gioco (di qn); **to be on the ~** (*fig:
competent*) essere in gamba; (: *alert*) stare
all'erta; **to start the ~ rolling** (*fig*) fare la
prima mossa; **the ~ is in your court** (*fig*) a
lei la prossima mossa; *see also* **balls.**
ballad ['bæləd] *n* ballata.
ballast ['bæləst] *n* zavorra.
ball bearing *n* cuscinetto a sfere.
ball cock *n* galleggiante *m.*
ballerina [bælə'riːnə] *n* ballerina.
ballet ['bæleɪ] *n* balletto.
ballet dancer *n* ballerino/a.
ballistic [bə'lɪstɪk] *adj* balistico(a).
ballistics [bə'lɪstɪks] *n* balistica.

balloon [bə'luːn] n pallone m; (in comic strip) fumetto ◆ vi gonfiarsi.
balloonist [bə'luːnɪst] n aeronauta m/f.
ballot ['bælət] n scrutinio.
ballot box n urna (per le schede).
ballot paper n scheda.
ballpark ['bɔːlpɑːk] n (US) stadio di baseball.
ballpark figure n (col) cifra approssimativa.
ball-point pen ['bɔːlpɔɪnt-] n penna a sfera.
ballroom ['bɔːlrum] n sala da ballo.
balls [bɔːlz] npl (col!) coglioni mpl (!).
balm [bɑːm] n balsamo.
balmy ['bɑːmɪ] adj (breeze, air) balsamico(a); (BRIT col) = **barmy**.
BALPA ['bælpə] n abbr (= British Airline Pilots' Association) sindacato dei piloti.
balsam ['bɔːlsəm] n balsamo.
balsa (wood) ['bɔːlsə-] n (legno di) balsa.
Baltic ['bɔːltɪk] adj, n: **the ~ (Sea)** il (mar) Baltico.
balustrade [bæləs'treɪd] n balaustrata.
bamboo [bæm'buː] n bambù m.
bamboozle [bæm'buːzl] vt (col) infinocchiare.
ban [bæn] n interdizione f ◆ vt interdire; **he was ~ned from driving** (BRIT) gli hanno ritirato la patente.
banal [bə'nɑːl] adj banale.
banana [bə'nɑːnə] n banana.
band [bænd] n banda; (at a dance) orchestra; (MIL) fanfara.
▶**band together** vi collegarsi.
bandage ['bændɪdʒ] n benda.
Band-Aid ® ['bændeɪd] n (US) cerotto.
bandit ['bændɪt] n bandito.
bandstand ['bændstænd] n palco dell'orchestra.
bandwagon ['bændwægən] n: **to jump on the ~** (fig) seguire la corrente.
bandy ['bændɪ] vt (jokes, insults) scambiare.
▶**bandy about** vt far circolare.
bandy-legged ['bændɪ'legɪd] adj dalle gambe storte.
bane [beɪn] n: **it (or he etc) is the ~ of my life** è la mia rovina.
bang [bæŋ] n botta; (of door) lo sbattere; (blow) colpo ◆ vt battere (violentemente); (door) sbattere ◆ vi scoppiare; sbattere; **to ~ at the door** picchiare alla porta; **to ~ into sth** sbattere contro qc ◆ adv: **to be ~ on time** (BRIT col) spaccare il secondo; see also **bangs**.
banger ['bæŋə*] n (BRIT: car: also: **old ~**) macinino; (BRIT col: sausage) salsiccia; (firework) mortaretto.

Bangkok ['bæŋkɔk] n Bangkok f.
Bangladesh [bɑːŋglə'dɛʃ] n Bangladesh m.
bangle ['bæŋgl] n braccialetto.
bangs [bæŋz] npl (US: fringe) frangia, frangetta.
banish ['bænɪʃ] vt bandire.
banister(s) ['bænɪstə(z)] n(pl) ringhiera.
banjo, **~es** or **~s** ['bændʒəu] n banjo m inv.
bank [bæŋk] n (for money) banca, banco; (of river, lake) riva, sponda; (of earth) banco ◆ vi (AVIAT) inclinarsi in virata; (COMM): **they ~ with Pitt's** sono clienti di Pitt's.
▶**bank on** vt fus contare su.
bank account n conto in banca.
bank balance n saldo; **a healthy ~** un solido conto in banca.
bank card n = **banker's card**.
bank charges npl (BRIT) spese fpl bancarie.
bank draft n assegno circolare or bancario.
banker ['bæŋkə*] n banchiere m; **~'s card** (BRIT) carta assegni; **~'s order** (BRIT) ordine m di banca.
bank giro n bancogiro.
bank holiday n (BRIT) giorno di festa.

Una **bank holiday**, in Gran Bretagna, è una giornata in cui le banche e i negozi sono chiusi. Generalmente le bank holiday cadono di lunedì e molti ne approfittano per fare una breve vacanza fuori città. Di conseguenza, durante questi fine settimana lunghi (**bank holiday weekend**) si verifica un notevole aumento del traffico sulle strade, negli aeroporti e nelle stazioni e molte località turistiche registrano il tutto esaurito.

---

banking ['bæŋkɪŋ] n attività bancaria; professione f di banchiere.
banking hours npl orario di sportello.
bank loan n prestito bancario.
bank manager n direttore m di banca.
banknote ['bæŋknəut] n banconota.
bank rate n tasso bancario.
bankrupt ['bæŋkrʌpt] adj, n fallito(a); **to go ~** fallire.
bankruptcy ['bæŋkrʌptsɪ] n fallimento.
bank statement n estratto conto.
banner ['bænə*] n bandiera.
bannister(s) ['bænɪstə(z)] n(pl) = **banister(s)**.
banns [bænz] npl pubblicazioni fpl di matrimonio.
banquet ['bæŋkwɪt] n banchetto.
bantam-weight ['bæntəmweɪt] n peso gallo.
banter ['bæntə*] n scherzi mpl bonari.

baptism ['bæptɪzəm] *n* battesimo.
Baptist ['bæptɪst] *adj, n* battista (*m/f*).
baptize [bæp'taɪz] *vt* battezzare.
bar [bɑ:*] *n* barra; (*of window etc*) sbarra;
(*of chocolate*) tavoletta; (*fig*) ostacolo;
restrizione *f*; (*pub*) bar *m inv*; (*counter: in
pub*) banco; (*MUS*) battuta ♦ *vt* (*road,
window*) sbarrare; (*person*) escludere;
(*activity*) interdire; ~ **of soap** saponetta;
the B~ (*LAW*) l'Ordine *m* degli avvocati;
behind ~s (*prisoner*) dietro le sbarre; ~
none senza eccezione.
Barbados [bɑ:'beɪdɔs] *n* Barbados *fsg*.
barbaric [bɑ:'bærɪk], **barbarous** ['bɑ:bərəs]
adj barbaro(a); barbarico(a).
barbecue ['bɑ:bɪkju:] *n* barbecue *m inv*.
barbed wire ['bɑ:bd-] *n* filo spinato.
barber ['bɑ:bə*] *n* barbiere *m*.
barbiturate [bɑ:'bɪtjurɪt] *n* barbiturico.
Barcelona [bɑ:sɪ'ləunə] *n* Barcellona.
bar chart *n* diagramma *m* di frequenza.
bar code *n* codice *m* a barre.
bare [bɛə*] *adj* nudo(a) ♦ *vt* scoprire,
denudare; (*teeth*) mostrare; **the ~
essentials** lo stretto necessario.
bareback ['bɛəbæk] *adv* senza sella.
barefaced ['bɛəfeɪst] *adj* sfacciato(a).
barefoot ['bɛəfut] *adj, adv* scalzo(a).
bareheaded [bɛə'hɛdɪd] *adj, adv* a capo
scoperto.
barely ['bɛəlɪ] *adv* appena.
Barents Sea ['bærənts-] *n*: **the ~** il mar di
Barents.
bargain ['bɑ:gɪn] *n* (*transaction*) contratto;
(*good buy*) affare *m* ♦ *vi* (*haggle*) tirare sul
prezzo; (*trade*) contrattare; **into the ~** per
giunta.
►**bargain for** *vt fus* (*col*): **to ~ for sth**
aspettarsi qc; **he got more than he ~ed
for** gli è andata peggio di quel che si
aspettasse.
bargaining ['bɑ:gənɪŋ] *n* contrattazione *f*.
bargaining position *n*: **to be in a weak/
strong ~** non avere/avere potere
contrattuale.
barge [bɑ:dʒ] *n* chiatta.
►**barge in** *vi* (*walk in*) piombare dentro;
(*interrupt talk*) intromettersi a sproposito.
►**barge into** *vt fus* urtare contro.
baritone ['bærɪtəun] *n* baritono.
barium meal ['bɛərɪəm-] *n* (pasto di) bario.
bark [bɑ:k] *n* (*of tree*) corteccia; (*of dog*)
abbaio ♦ *vi* abbaiare.
barley ['bɑ:lɪ] *n* orzo.
barley sugar *n* zucchero d'orzo.
barmaid ['bɑ:meɪd] *n* cameriera al banco.
barman ['bɑ:mən] *n* barista *m*.
barmy ['bɑ:mɪ] *adj* (*BRIT col*) tocco(a).

barn [bɑ:n] *n* granaio; (*for animals*) stalla.
barnacle ['bɑ:nəkl] *n* cirripede *m*.
barn owl *n* barbagianni *m inv*.
barometer [bə'rɔmɪtə*] *n* barometro.
baron ['bærən] *n* barone *m*; (*fig*) magnate *m*;
the oil ~s i magnati del petrolio; **the
press ~s** i baroni della stampa.
baroness ['bærənɪs] *n* baronessa.
baronet ['bærənɪt] *n* baronetto.
barrack ['bærək] *vt* (*BRIT*): **to ~ sb** subissare
qn di grida e fischi.
barracking ['bærəkɪŋ] *n* (*BRIT*): **to give sb a
~** subissare qn di grida e fischi.
barracks ['bærəks] *npl* caserma.
barrage ['bærɑ:ʒ] *n* (*MIL*) sbarramento; **a ~
of questions** una raffica di *or* un fuoco di
fila di domande.
barrel ['bærəl] *n* barile *m*; (*of gun*) canna.
barrel organ *n* organetto a cilindro.
barren ['bærən] *adj* sterile; (*soil*) arido(a).
barricade [bærɪ'keɪd] *n* barricata ♦ *vt*
barricare.
barrier ['bærɪə*] *n* barriera; (*BRIT: also:
crash ~*) guardrail *m inv*.
barrier cream *n* (*BRIT*) crema protettiva.
barring ['bɑ:rɪŋ] *prep* salvo.
barrister ['bærɪstə*] *n* (*BRIT*) avvocato.

Il **barrister** *è un membro della più
prestigiosa delle due branche della
professione legale (l'altra è quella dei*
solicitor*); la sua funzione è quella di
rappresentare i propri clienti in tutte le
corti (***magistrates' court***,* **crown court** *e*
Court of Appeal*), generalmente seguendo le
istruzioni del caso preparate dai solicitor.*

barrow ['bærəu] *n* (*cart*) carriola.
barstool ['bɑ:stu:l] *n* sgabello.
Bart. *abbr* (*BRIT*) = **baronet**.
bartender ['bɑ:tɛndə*] *n* (*US*) barista *m*.
barter ['bɑ:tə*] *n* baratto ♦ *vt*: **to ~ sth for**
barattare qc con.
base [beɪs] *n* base *f* ♦ *adj* vile ♦ *vt*: **to ~ sth
on** basare qc su; **to ~ at** (*troops*) mettere
di stanza a; **coffee-~d** a base di caffè; **a
Paris-~d firm** una ditta con sede centrale
a Parigi; **I'm ~d in London** sono di base
or ho base a Londra.
baseball ['beɪsbɔ:l] *n* baseball *m*.
baseboard ['beɪsbɔ:d] *n* (*US*) zoccolo,
battiscopa *m inv*.
base camp *n* campo *m* base *inv*.
Basel [bɑ:l] *n* = **Basle**.
baseline ['beɪslaɪn] *n* (*TENNIS*) linea di
fondo.
basement ['beɪsmənt] *n* seminterrato; (*of
shop*) sotterraneo.

base rate n tasso di base.
bases ['beɪsiːz] npl of **basis**; ['beɪsɪz] npl of **base**.
bash [bæʃ] vt (col) picchiare ♦ n: **I'll have a ~ (at it)** (BRIT col) ci proverò; **~ed in** adj sfondato(a).
▶**bash up** vt (col: car) sfasciare; (: BRIT: person) riempire di or prendere a botte.
bashful ['bæʃful] adj timido(a).
bashing ['bæʃɪŋ] n: **Paki-/queer-~** atti mpl di violenza contro i pachistani/gli omosessuali.
BASIC ['beɪsɪk] n (COMPUT) BASIC m.
basic ['beɪsɪk] adj (principles, precautions, rules) elementare; (salary) base inv (after n).
basically ['beɪsɪklɪ] adv fondamentalmente, sostanzialmente.
basic rate n (of tax) aliquota minima.
basil ['bæzl] n basilico.
basin ['beɪsn] n (vessel, also GEO) bacino; (also: **wash~**) lavabo; (BRIT: for food) terrina.
basis, pl **bases** ['beɪsis, -siːz] n base f; **on the ~ of what you've said** in base alle sue asserzioni.
bask [bɑːsk] vi: **to ~ in the sun** crogiolarsi al sole.
basket ['bɑːskɪt] n cesta; (smaller) cestino; (with handle) paniere m.
basketball ['bɑːskɪtbɔːl] n pallacanestro f.
basketball player n cestista m/f.
Basle [bɑːl] n Basilea.
basmati rice [bəz'mætɪ-] n riso basmati.
Basque [bæsk] adj, n basco(a).
bass [beɪs] n (MUS) basso.
bass clef n chiave f di basso.
bassoon [bə'suːn] n fagotto.
bastard ['bɑːstəd] n bastardo/a; (col!) stronzo (!).
baste [beɪst] vt (CULIN) ungere con grasso; (SEWING) imbastire.
bastion ['bæstɪən] n bastione m; (fig) baluardo.
bat [bæt] n pipistrello; (for baseball etc) mazza; (BRIT: for table tennis) racchetta; **off one's own ~** di propria iniziativa ♦ vt: **he didn't ~ an eyelid** non battè ciglio.
batch [bætʃ] n (of bread) infornata; (of papers) cumulo; (of applicants, letters) gruppo; (of work) sezione f; (of goods) partita, lotto.
batch processing n (COMPUT) elaborazione f a blocchi.
bated ['beɪtɪd] adj: **with ~ breath** col fiato sospeso.
bath [bɑːθ, pl bɑːðz] n bagno; (bathtub) vasca da bagno ♦ vt far fare il bagno a; **to**

have a ~ fare un bagno; see also **baths**.
bathchair ['bɑːθtʃɛə*] n (BRIT) poltrona a rotelle.
bathe [beɪð] vi fare il bagno ♦ vt bagnare; (wound etc) lavare.
bather ['beɪðə*] n bagnante m/f.
bathing ['beɪðɪŋ] n bagni mpl.
bathing cap n cuffia da bagno.
bathing costume, (US) **bathing suit** n costume m da bagno.
bathmat ['bɑːθmæt] n tappetino da bagno.
bathrobe ['bɑːθrəub] n accappatoio.
bathroom ['bɑːθrum] n stanza da bagno.
baths [bɑːðz] npl bagni mpl pubblici.
bath towel n asciugamano da bagno.
bathtub ['bɑːθtʌb] n (vasca da) bagno.
batman ['bætmən] n (BRIT MIL) attendente m.
baton ['bætən] n bastone m; (MUS) bacchetta.
battalion [bə'tælɪən] n battaglione m.
batten ['bætən] n (CARPENTRY) assicella, correntino; (for flooring) tavola per pavimenti; (NAUT) serretta; (: on sail) stecca.
▶**batten down** vt (NAUT): **to ~ down the hatches** chiudere i boccaporti.
batter ['bætə*] vt battere ♦ n pastetta.
battered ['bætəd] adj (hat) sformato(a); (pan) ammaccato(a); **~ wife/baby** consorte f/bambino(a) maltrattato(a).
battering ram ['bætərɪŋ-] n ariete m.
battery ['bætərɪ] n batteria; (of torch) pila.
battery charger n caricabatterie m inv.
battle ['bætl] n battaglia ♦ vi battagliare, lottare; **to fight a losing ~** (fig) battersi per una causa persa; **that's half the ~** (col) è già una mezza vittoria.
battle dress n uniforme f da combattimento.
battlefield ['bætlfiːld] n campo di battaglia.
battlements ['bætlmənts] npl bastioni mpl.
battleship ['bætlʃɪp] n nave f da guerra.
batty ['bætɪ] adj (col: person) svitato(a), strambo(a); (: behaviour, idea) strampalato(a).
bauble ['bɔːbl] n ninnolo.
baud [bɔːd] n (COMPUT) baud m inv.
baulk [bɔːlk] vi = **balk**.
bauxite ['bɔːksaɪt] n bauxite f.
Bavaria [bə'vɛərɪə] n Bavaria.
Bavarian [bə'vɛərɪən] adj, n bavarese (m/f).
bawdy ['bɔːdɪ] adj piccante.
bawl [bɔːl] vi urlare.
bay [beɪ] n (of sea) baia; (BRIT: for parking) piazzola di sosta; (loading) piazzale m di (sosta e) carico; **to hold sb at ~** tenere qn a bada.

bay leaf n foglia d'alloro.
bayonet ['beɪənɪt] n baionetta.
bay tree n alloro.
bay window n bovindo.
bazaar [bə'zɑː*] n bazar m inv; vendita di beneficenza.
bazooka [bə'zuːkə] n bazooka m inv.
BB n abbr (BRIT: = Boys' Brigade) organizzazione giovanile a fine educativo.
B & B n abbr see bed and breakfast.
BBB n abbr (US: = Better Business Bureau) organismo per la difesa dei consumatori.
BBC n abbr = British Broadcasting Corporation.

La **BBC** è l'azienda statale che fornisce il servizio radiofonico e televisivo in Gran Bretagna. Pur dovendo rispondere al Parlamento del proprio operato, la BBC non è soggetta al controllo dello stato per scelte e programmi, anche perché si autofinanzia con il ricavato dei canoni d'abbonamento. La BBC ha due reti televisive (BBC1 e BBC2), cinque stazioni radiofoniche nazionali e 37 emittenti locali; fornisce un servizio di informazione internazionale, il **BBC World Service**, trasmesso in tutto il mondo.

BBE n abbr (US: = Benevolent and Protective Order of Elks) organizzazione filantropica.
BC adv abbr (= before Christ) a.C. ♦ abbr (Canada) = British Columbia.
BCG n abbr (= Bacillus Calmette-Guérin) vaccino antitubercolare.
BD n abbr (= Bachelor of Divinity) titolo di studio.
B/D abbr = bank draft.
BDS n abbr (= Bachelor of Dental Surgery) titolo di studio.

═══════════════════ KEYWORD

be [biː] (pt was, were, pp been) aux vb 1 (with present participle: forming continuous tenses): **what are you doing?** che fai?, che stai facendo?; **they're coming tomorrow** vengono domani; **I've been waiting for her for hours** sono ore che l'aspetto
2 (with pp: forming passives) essere; **to ~ killed** essere or venire ucciso(a); **the box had been opened** la scatola era stata aperta; **the thief was nowhere to ~ seen** il ladro non si trovava da nessuna parte
3 (in tag questions): **it was fun, wasn't it?** è stato divertente, no?; **he's good-looking, isn't he?** è un bell'uomo, vero?; **she's back, is she?** così è tornata, eh?

4 (+ to + infinitive): **the house is to ~ sold** abbiamo (or hanno etc) intenzione di vendere casa; **you're to ~ congratulated for all your work** dovremo farvi i complimenti per tutto il vostro lavoro; **am I to understand that ...?** devo dedurre che ...?; **he's not to open it** non deve aprirlo; **he was to have come yesterday** sarebbe dovuto venire ieri
♦ vb + complement 1 (gen) essere; **I'm English** sono inglese; **I'm tired** sono stanco(a); **I'm hot/cold** ho caldo/freddo; **he's a doctor** è medico; **2 and 2 are 4** 2 più 2 fa 4; **~ careful!** sta attento!; **~ good** sii buono; **if I were you ...** se fossi in te ...
2 (of health) stare; **how are you?** come sta?; **he's very ill** sta molto male
3 (of age): **how old are you?** quanti anni hai?; **I'm sixteen (years old)** ho sedici anni
4 (cost) costare; **how much was the meal?** quant'era or quanto costava il pranzo?; **that'll ~ £5, please** (sono) 5 sterline, per favore
♦ vi 1 (exist, occur etc) essere, esistere; **the best singer that ever was** il migliore cantante mai esistito or di tutti tempi; **~ that as it may** comunque sia, sia come sia; **so ~ it** sia pure, e sia
2 (referring to place) essere, trovarsi; **I won't ~ here tomorrow** non ci sarò domani; **Edinburgh is in Scotland** Edimburgo si trova in Scozia
3 (referring to movement): **where have you been?** dove sei stato?; **I've been to China** sono stato in Cina
♦ impers vb 1 (referring to time, distance) essere; **it's 5 o'clock** sono le 5; **it's the 28th of April** è il 28 aprile; **it's 10 km to the village** di qui al paese sono 10 km
2 (referring to the weather) fare; **it's too hot/cold** fa troppo caldo/freddo; **it's windy** c'è vento
3 (emphatic): **it's me** sono io; **it's only me** sono solo io; **it was Maria who paid the bill** è stata Maria che ha pagato il conto.

B/E abbr = bill of exchange.
beach [biːtʃ] n spiaggia ♦ vt tirare in secco.
beach buggy n dune buggy f inv.
beachcomber ['biːtʃkəumə*] n vagabondo (che s'aggira sulla spiaggia).
beachwear ['biːtʃwɛə*] n articoli mpl da spiaggia.
beacon ['biːkən] n (lighthouse) faro; (marker) segnale m; (radio ~) radiofaro.
bead [biːd] n perlina; (of dew, sweat) goccia; ~**s** (necklace) collana.
beady ['biːdɪ] adj: ~ **eyes** occhi mpl piccoli e

penetranti.

beagle ['biːgl] *n* cane *m* da lepre.

beak [biːk] *n* becco.

beaker ['biːkəˀ] *n* coppa.

beam [biːm] *n* trave *f*; (*of light*) raggio; (*RADIO*) fascio (d'onde) ♦ *vi* brillare; (*smile*): **to ~ at sb** rivolgere un radioso sorriso a qn; **to drive on full** *or* **main ~** *or* (*US*) **high ~** guidare con gli abbaglianti accesi.

beaming ['biːmɪŋ] *adj* (*sun, smile*) raggiante.

bean [biːn] *n* fagiolo; (*of coffee*) chicco.

beanpole ['biːnpəul] *n* (*col*) spilungone/a.

beansprouts ['biːnsprauts] *npl* germogli *mpl* di soia.

bear [bɛəˀ] *n* orso; (*STOCK EXCHANGE*) ribassista *m/f* ♦ *vb* (*pt* **bore**, *pp* **borne** [bɔːˀ, bɔːn]) *vt* (*gen*) portare; (*produce: fruit*) produrre, dare; (: *traces, signs*) mostrare; (*COMM: interest*) fruttare; (*endure*) sopportare ♦ *vi*: **to ~ right/left** piegare a destra/sinistra; **to ~ the responsibility of** assumersi la responsabilità di; **to ~ comparison with** reggere al paragone con; **I can't ~ him** non lo posso soffrire *or* sopportare; **to bring pressure to ~ on sb** fare pressione su qn.

▶**bear out** *vt* (*theory, suspicion*) confermare, convalidare.

▶**bear up** *vi* farsi coraggio; **he bore up well under the strain** ha sopportato bene lo stress.

▶**bear with** *vt fus* (*sb's moods, temper*) sopportare (con pazienza); **~ with me a minute** solo un attimo, prego.

bearable ['bɛərəbl] *adj* sopportabile.

beard [bɪəd] *n* barba.

bearded ['bɪədɪd] *adj* barbuto(a).

bearer ['bɛərəˀ] *n* portatore *m*; (*of passport*) titolare *m/f*.

bearing ['bɛərɪŋ] *n* portamento; (*connection*) rapporto; (**ball**) **~s** *npl* cuscinetti *mpl* a sfere; **to take a ~** fare un rilevamento; **to find one's ~s** orientarsi.

beast [biːst] *n* bestia.

beastly ['biːstlɪ] *adj* meschino(a); (*weather*) da cani.

beat [biːt] *n* colpo; (*of heart*) battito; (*MUS*) tempo; battuta; (*of policeman*) giro ♦ *vt* (*pt* **beat**, *pp* **beaten**) battere; **off the ~en track** fuori mano; **to ~ about the bush** menare il cane per l'aia; **to ~ time** battere il tempo; **that ~s everything!** (*col*) questo è il colmo!

▶**beat down** *vt* (*door*) abbattere, buttare giù; (*price*) far abbassare; (*seller*) far scendere ♦ *vi* (*rain*) scrosciare; (*sun*) picchiare.

▶**beat off** *vt* respingere.

▶**beat up** *vt* (*col: person*) picchiare; (*eggs*) sbattere.

beater ['biːtəˀ] *n* (*for eggs, cream*) frullino.

beating ['biːtɪŋ] *n* botte *fpl*; (*defeat*) batosta; **to take a ~** prendere una (bella) batosta.

beat-up [biːt'ʌp] *adj* (*col*) scassato(a).

beautician [bjuː'tɪʃən] *n* estetista *m/f*.

beautiful ['bjuːtɪful] *adj* bello(a).

beautify ['bjuːtɪfaɪ] *vt* abbellire.

beauty ['bjuːtɪ] *n* bellezza; (*concept*) bello; **the ~ of it is that ...** il bello è che ....

beauty contest *n* concorso di bellezza.

beauty queen *n* miss *f inv*, reginetta di bellezza.

beauty salon *n* istituto di bellezza.

beauty sleep *n*: **to get one's ~** farsi un sonno ristoratore.

beauty spot *n* neo; (*BRIT: TOURISM*) luogo pittoresco.

beaver ['biːvəˀ] *n* castoro.

becalmed [bɪ'kɑːmd] *adj* in bonaccia.

became [bɪ'keɪm] *pt of* **become**.

because [bɪ'kɔz] *conj* perché; **~ of** *prep* a causa di.

beck [bɛk] *n*: **to be at sb's ~ and call** essere a completa disposizione di qn.

beckon ['bɛkən] *vt* (*also:* **~ to**) chiamare con un cenno.

become [bɪ'kʌm] *vt* (*irreg: like* **come**) diventare; **to ~ fat/thin** ingrassarsi/ dimagrire; **to ~ angry** arrabbiarsi; **it became known that ...** si è venuto a sapere che ...; **what has ~ of him?** che gli è successo?

becoming [bɪ'kʌmɪŋ] *adj* (*behaviour*) che si conviene; (*clothes*) grazioso(a).

BECTU ['bɛktuː] *n abbr* (*BRIT*) = *Broadcasting Entertainment Cinematographic and Theatre Union*.

BEd *n abbr* (= *Bachelor of Education*) *laurea con abilitazione all'insegnamento.*

bed [bɛd] *n* letto; (*of flowers*) aiuola; (*of coal, clay*) strato; (*of sea, lake*) fondo; **to go to ~** andare a letto.

▶**bed down** *vi* sistemarsi (per dormire).

bed and breakfast (B & B) *n* (*terms*) camera con colazione; (*place*) ≈ pensione *f* familiare.

I **bed and breakfast**, *anche* **B & B**, *sono piccole pensioni a conduzione familiare, in case private o fattorie, dove si affittano camere e viene servita al mattino la tradizionale colazione all'inglese. Segnalate da un cartello posto in giardino o alla finestra, queste graziose pensioni offrono un* servizio di camera con prima colazione, appunto bed and breakfast, a prezzi più contenuti rispetto agli alberghi.

bedbug ['bɛdbʌg] *n* cimice *f.*
bedclothes ['bɛdkləuðz] *npl* coperte e lenzuola *fpl.*
bedcover ['bɛdkʌvə*] *n* copriletto.
bedding ['bɛdɪŋ] *n* coperte e lenzuola *fpl.*
bedevil [bɪ'dɛvl] *vt* (*person*) tormentare; (*plans*) ostacolare continuamente.
bedfellow ['bɛdfɛləu] *n*: **they are strange ~s** (*fig*) fanno una coppia ben strana.
bedlam ['bɛdləm] *n* baraonda.
bedpan ['bɛdpæn] *n* padella.
bedpost ['bɛdpəust] *n* colonnina del letto.
bedraggled [bɪ'drægld] *adj* fradicio(a).
bedridden ['bɛdrɪdən] *adj* costretto(a) a letto.
bedrock ['bɛdrɔk] *n* (*GEO*) basamento; (*fig*) fatti *mpl* di base.
bedroom ['bɛdrum] *n* camera da letto.
Beds *abbr* (*BRIT*) = *Bedfordshire*.
bed settee *n* divano *m* letto *inv.*
bedside ['bɛdsaɪd] *n*: **at sb's ~** al capezzale di qn.
bedside lamp *n* lampada da comodino.
bedsit(ter) ['bɛdsɪt(ə*)] *n* (*BRIT*) monolocale *m.*
bedspread ['bɛdsprɛd] *n* copriletto.
bedtime ['bɛdtaɪm] *n*: **it's ~** è ora di andare a letto.
bee [bi:] *n* ape *f;* **to have a ~ in one's bonnet (about sth)** avere la fissazione (di qc).
beech [bi:tʃ] *n* faggio.
beef [bi:f] *n* manzo.
▶**beef up** *vt* (*col*) rinforzare.
beefburger ['bi:fbə:gə*] *n* hamburger *m inv.*
beefeater ['bi:fi:tə*] *n guardia della Torre di Londra.*
beehive ['bi:haɪv] *n* alveare *m.*
bee-keeping ['bi:ki:pɪŋ] *n* apicoltura.
beeline ['bi:laɪn] *n*: **to make a ~ for** buttarsi a capo fitto verso.
been [bi:n] *pp of* **be.**
beep [bi:p] *n* (*of horn*) colpo di clacson; (*of phone etc*) segnale *m* (acustico), bip *m inv* ♦ *vi* suonare.
beeper ['bi:pə*] *n* (*of doctor etc*) cercapersone *m inv.*
beer [bɪə*] *n* birra.
beer belly *n* (*col*) stomaco da bevitore.
beer can *n* lattina di birra.
beetle ['bi:tl] *n* scarafaggio; coleottero.
beetroot ['bi:tru:t] *n* (*BRIT*) barbabietola.
befall [bɪ'fɔ:l] *vi(vt)* (*irreg: like* **fall**) accadere (a).
befit [bɪ'fɪt] *vt* addirsi a.

before [bɪ'fɔ:*] *prep* (*in time*) prima di; (*in space*) davanti a ♦ *conj* prima che + *sub;* prima di ♦ *adv* prima; ~ **going** prima di andare; ~ **she goes** prima che vada; **the week** ~ la settimana prima; **I've seen it** ~ l'ho già visto; **I've never seen it** ~ è la prima volta che lo vedo.
beforehand [bɪ'fɔ:hænd] *adv* in anticipo.
befriend [bɪ'frɛnd] *vt* assistere; mostrarsi amico a.
befuddled [bɪ'fʌdld] *adj* confuso(a).
beg [bɛg] *vi* chiedere l'elemosina ♦ *vt* chiedere in elemosina; (*favour*) chiedere; (*entreat*) pregare; **I ~ your pardon** (*apologising*) mi scusi; (*not hearing*) scusi?; **this ~s the question of** ... questo presuppone che sia già risolto il problema di ....
began [bɪ'gæn] *pt of* **begin.**
beggar ['bɛgə*] *n* (*also:* ~**man,** ~**woman**) mendicante *m/f.*
begin, *pt* **began,** *pp* **begun** [bɪ'gɪn, bɪ'gæn, bɪ'gʌn] *vt, vi* cominciare; **to ~ doing** *or* **to do sth** incominciare *or* iniziare a fare qc; **I can't ~ to thank you** non so proprio come ringraziarla; **to ~ with, I'd like to know** ... tanto per cominciare vorrei sapere ...; ~**ning from Monday** a partire da lunedì.
beginner [bɪ'gɪnə*] *n* principiante *m/f.*
beginning [bɪ'gɪnɪŋ] *n* inizio, principio; **right from the** ~ fin dall'inizio.
begrudge [bɪ'grʌdʒ] *vt*: **to ~ sb sth** dare qc a qn a malincuore; invidiare qn per qc.
beguile [bɪ'gaɪl] *vt* (*enchant*) incantare.
beguiling [bɪ'gaɪlɪŋ] *adj* (*charming*) allettante; (*deluding*) ingannevole.
begun [bɪ'gʌn] *pp of* **begin.**
behalf [bɪ'hɑ:f] *n*: **on ~ of,** (*US*) **in ~ of** per conto di; a nome di.
behave [bɪ'heɪv] *vi* comportarsi; (*well: also:* ~ **o.s.**) comportarsi bene.
behaviour, (*US*) **behavior** [bɪ'heɪvjə*] *n* comportamento, condotta.
behead [bɪ'hɛd] *vt* decapitare.
beheld [bɪ'hɛld] *pt, pp of* **behold.**
behind [bɪ'haɪnd] *prep* dietro; (*followed by pronoun*) dietro di; (*time*) in ritardo con ♦ *adv* dietro, in ritardo ♦ *n* didietro; **we're ~ them in technology** siamo più indietro *or* più arretrati di loro nella tecnica; ~ **the scenes** dietro le quinte; **to be ~ (schedule) with sth** essere indietro con qc; (*payments*) essere in arretrato con qc; **to leave sth ~** dimenticare di prendere qc.
behold [bɪ'həuld] *vt* (*irreg: like* **hold**) vedere, scorgere.

beige [beɪʒ] *adj* beige *inv.*
Beijing ['beɪ'dʒɪŋ] *n* Pechino *f.*
being ['biːɪŋ] *n* essere *m;* **to come into** ~
cominciare ad esistere.
Beirut [beɪ'ruːt] *n* Beirut *f.*
Belarus ['bɛlærus] *n* Bielorussia.
Belarussian [bɛlə'rʌʃən] *adj* bielorusso(a)
♦ *n* bielorusso/a; (*LING*) bielorusso.
belated [bɪ'leɪtɪd] *adj* tardo(a).
belch [bɛltʃ] *vi* ruttare ♦ *vt* (*gen:* ~ **out:**
smoke etc) eruttare.
beleaguered [bɪ'liːɡəd] *adj* (*city*)
assediato(a); (*army*) accerchiato(a); (*fig*)
assillato(a).
Belfast ['bɛlfɑːst] *n* Belfast *f.*
belfry ['bɛlfrɪ] *n* campanile *m.*
Belgian ['bɛldʒən] *adj, n* belga (*m/f*).
Belgium ['bɛldʒəm] *n* Belgio.
Belgrade [bɛl'ɡreɪd] *n* Belgrado *f.*
belie [bɪ'laɪ] *vt* smentire; (*give false
impression of*) nascondere.
belief [bɪ'liːf] *n* (*opinion*) opinione *f,*
convinzione *f;* (*trust, faith*) fede *f;*
(*acceptance as true*) credenza; **in the** ~
that nella convinzione che; **it's beyond** ~
è incredibile.
believe [bɪ'liːv] *vt, vi* credere; **to** ~ **in** (*God*)
credere in; (*ghosts*) credere a; (*method*)
avere fiducia in; **I don't** ~ **in corporal
punishment** sono contrario alle punizioni
corporali; **he is** ~**d to be abroad** si pensa
(che) sia all'estero.
believer [bɪ'liːvə*] *n* (*REL*) credente *m/f;* (*in
idea, activity*): **to be a** ~ **in** credere in.
belittle [bɪ'lɪtl] *vt* sminuire.
Belize [bɛ'liːz] *n* Belize *m.*
bell [bɛl] *n* campana; (*small, on door, electric*)
campanello; **that rings a** ~ (*fig*) mi
ricorda qualcosa.
bell-bottoms ['bɛlbɔtəmz] *npl* calzoni *mpl* a
zampa d'elefante.
bellboy ['bɛlbɔɪ], (*US*) **bellhop** ['bɛlhɔp] *n*
ragazzo d'albergo, fattorino d'albergo.
belligerent [bɪ'lɪdʒərənt] *adj* (*at war*)
belligerante; (*fig*) bellicoso(a).
bellow ['bɛləu] *vi* muggire; (*cry*) urlare (a
squarciagola) ♦ *vt* (*orders*) urlare (a
squarciagola).
bellows ['bɛləuz] *npl* soffietto.
bell push *n* (*BRIT*) pulsante *m* del
campanello.
belly ['bɛlɪ] *n* pancia.
bellyache ['bɛlɪeɪk] *n* mal *m* di pancia ♦ *vi*
(*col*) mugugnare.
bellybutton ['bɛlɪbʌtn] *n* ombelico.
bellyful ['bɛlɪful] *n* (*col*): **to have had a** ~ **of**
(*fig*) averne piene le tasche (di).
belong [bɪ'lɔŋ] *vi:* **to** ~ **to** appartenere a;

(*club etc*) essere socio di; **this book** ~**s
here** questo libro va qui.
belongings [bɪ'lɔŋɪŋz] *npl* cose *fpl,* roba;
personal ~ effetti *mpl* personali.
Belorussia [bɛləu'rʌʃə] *n* Bielorussia.
Belorussian [bɛləu'rʌʃən] *adj, n*
= **Belarussian**.
beloved [bɪ'lʌvɪd] *adj* adorato(a).
below [bɪ'ləu] *prep* sotto, al di sotto di ♦ *adv*
sotto, di sotto; giù; **see** ~ vedi sotto *or*
oltre; **temperatures** ~ **normal**
temperature al di sotto del normale.
belt [bɛlt] *n* cintura; (*TECH*) cinghia ♦ *vt*
(*thrash*) picchiare ♦ *vi* (*BRIT col*) filarsela;
industrial ~ zona industriale.
▶**belt out** *vt* (*song*) cantare a squarciagola.
▶**belt up** *vi* (*BRIT col*) chiudere la
boccaccia.
beltway ['bɛltweɪ] *n* (*US AUT*)
circonvallazione *f;* (: *motorway*)
autostrada.
bemoan [bɪ'məun] *vt* lamentare.
bemused [bɪ'mjuːzd] *adj* perplesso(a),
stupito(a).
bench [bɛntʃ] *n* panca; (*in workshop*) banco;
the B~ (*LAW*) la Corte.
bench mark *n* banco di prova.
bend [bɛnd] *vb* (*pt, pp* **bent** [bɛnt]) *vt*
curvare; (*leg, arm*) piegare ♦ *vi* curvarsi;
piegarsi ♦ *n* (*BRIT: in road*) curva; (*in pipe,
river*) gomito.
▶**bend down** *vi* chinarsi.
▶**bend over** *vi* piegarsi.
bends [bɛndz] *npl* (*MED*) embolia.
beneath [bɪ'niːθ] *prep* sotto, al di sotto di;
(*unworthy of*) indegno(a) di ♦ *adv* sotto, di
sotto.
benefactor ['bɛnɪfæktə*] *n* benefattore *m.*
benefactress ['bɛnɪfæktrɪs] *n* benefattrice *f.*
beneficial [bɛnɪ'fɪʃəl] *adj* che fa bene;
vantaggioso(a); ~ **to** che giova a.
beneficiary [bɛnɪ'fɪʃərɪ] *n* (*LAW*)
beneficiario/a.
benefit ['bɛnɪfɪt] *n* beneficio, vantaggio;
(*allowance of money*) indennità *f inv* ♦ *vt* far
bene a ♦ *vi:* **he'll** ~ **from it** ne trarrà
beneficio *or* profitto.
benefit performance *n* spettacolo di
beneficenza.
Benelux ['bɛnɪlʌks] *n* Benelux *m.*
benevolent [bɪ'nɛvələnt] *adj* benevolo(a).
BEng *n abbr* (= *Bachelor of Engineering*)
laurea in ingegneria.
benign [bɪ'naɪn] *adj* benevolo(a); (*MED*)
benigno(a).
bent [bɛnt] *pt, pp of* **bend** ♦ *n* inclinazione *f*
♦ *adj* (*wire, pipe*) piegato(a), storto(a); (*col:
dishonest*) losco(a); **to be** ~ **on** essere

deciso(a) a.

bequeath [bɪ'kwiːð] *vt* lasciare in eredità.

bequest [bɪ'kwɛst] *n* lascito.

bereaved [bɪ'riːvd] *adj* in lutto ♦ *npl*: **the ~ i** familiari in lutto.

bereavement [bɪ'riːvmənt] *n* lutto.

beret ['bɛreɪ] *n* berretto.

Bering Sea ['bɛrɪŋ-] *n*: **the ~** il mar di Bering.

berk [bəːk] *n* (*BRIT col!*) coglione/a (*!*).

Berks *abbr* (*BRIT*) = *Berkshire.*

Berlin [bəː'lɪn] *n* Berlino *f*; **East/West ~** Berlino est/ovest.

berm [bəːm] *n* (*US AUT*) corsia d'emergenza.

Bermuda [bəː'mjuːdə] *n* le Bermude.

Bermuda shorts *npl* bermuda *mpl*.

Bern [bəːn] *n* Berna *f*.

berry ['bɛrɪ] *n* bacca.

berserk [bə'səːk] *adj*: **to go ~** montare su tutte le furie.

berth [bəːθ] *n* (*bed*) cuccetta; (*for ship*) ormeggio ♦ *vi* (*in harbour*) entrare in porto; (*at anchor*) gettare l'ancora; **to give sb a wide ~** (*fig*) tenersi alla larga da qn.

beseech, pt, pp besought [bɪ'siːtʃ, bɪ'sɔːt] *vt* implorare.

beset, pt, pp beset [bɪ'sɛt] *vt* assalire ♦ *adj*: **a policy ~ with dangers** una politica irta *or* piena di pericoli.

besetting [bɪ'sɛtɪŋ] *adj*: **his ~ sin** il suo più grande difetto.

beside [bɪ'saɪd] *prep* accanto a; (*compared with*) rispetto a, in confronto a; **to be ~ o.s. (with anger)** essere fuori di sé; **that's ~ the point** non c'entra.

besides [bɪ'saɪdz] *adv* inoltre, per di più ♦ *prep* oltre a; (*except*) a parte.

besiege [bɪ'siːdʒ] *vt* (*town*) assediare; (*fig*) tempestare.

besotted [bɪ'sɔtɪd] *adj* (*BRIT*): **~ with** infatuato(a) di.

besought [bɪ'sɔːt] *pt, pp of* **beseech**.

bespectacled [bɪ'spɛktɪkld] *adj* occhialuto(a).

bespoke [bɪ'spəuk] *adj* (*BRIT*: *garment*) su misura; **~ tailor** sarto.

best [bɛst] *adj* migliore ♦ *adv* meglio; **the ~ thing to do is ...** la cosa migliore da fare *or* farsi è ...; **the ~ part of** (*quantity*) la maggior parte di; **at ~** tutt'al più; **to make the ~ of sth** cavare il meglio possibile da qc; **to do one's ~** fare del proprio meglio; **to the ~ of my knowledge** per quel che ne so; **to the ~ of my ability** al massimo delle mie capacità; **he's not exactly patient at the ~ of times** non è mai molto paziente.

best man *n* testimone *m* dello sposo.

bestow [bɪ'stəu] *vt*: **to ~ sth on sb** conferire qc a qn.

bestseller ['bɛst'sɛlə*] *n* bestseller *m inv*.

bet [bɛt] *n* scommessa ♦ *vt, vi* (*pt, pp* **bet** *or* **betted**) scommettere; **it's a safe ~** (*fig*) è molto probabile.

Bethlehem ['bɛθlɪhɛm] *n* Betlemme *f*.

betray [bɪ'treɪ] *vt* tradire.

betrayal [bɪ'treɪəl] *n* tradimento.

better ['bɛtə*] *adj* migliore ♦ *adv* meglio ♦ *vt* migliorare ♦ *n*: **to get the ~ of** avere la meglio su; **you had ~ do it** è meglio che lo faccia; **he thought ~ of it** cambiò idea; **to get ~** migliorare; **a change for the ~** un cambiamento in meglio; **that's ~!** così va meglio!; **I had ~ go** dovrei andare; **~ off** *adj* più ricco(a); (*fig*): **you'd be ~ off this way** starebbe meglio così.

betting ['bɛtɪŋ] *n* scommesse *fpl*.

betting shop *n* (*BRIT*) ufficio dell'allibratore.

between [bɪ'twiːn] *prep* tra ♦ *adv* in mezzo, nel mezzo; **the road ~ here and London** la strada da qui a Londra; **we only had £5 ~ us** fra tutti e due avevamo solo 5 sterline.

bevel ['bɛvl] *n* (*also*: **~(led) edge**) profilo smussato.

beverage ['bɛvərɪdʒ] *n* bevanda.

bevy ['bɛvɪ] *n*: **a ~ of** una banda di.

bewail [bɪ'weɪl] *vt* lamentare.

beware [bɪ'wɛə*] *vt, vi*: **to ~ (of)** stare attento(a) (a).

bewildered [bɪ'wɪldəd] *adj* sconcertato(a), confuso(a).

bewildering [bɪ'wɪldərɪŋ] *adj* sconcertante, sbalorditivo(a).

bewitching [bɪ'wɪtʃɪŋ] *adj* affascinante.

beyond [bɪ'jɔnd] *prep* (*in space*) oltre; (*exceeding*) al di sopra di ♦ *adv* di là; **~ doubt** senza dubbio; **~ repair** irreparabile.

b/f *abbr see* **brought forward**.

BFPO *n abbr* (= *British Forces Post Office*) *recapito delle truppe britanniche all'estero.*

bhp *n abbr* (*AUT*: = *brake horsepower*) c.v. (= *cavallo vapore*).

bi... [baɪ] *prefix* bi....

biannual [baɪ'ænjuəl] *adj* semestrale.

bias ['baɪəs] *n* (*prejudice*) pregiudizio; (*preference*) preferenza.

bias(s)ed ['baɪəst] *adj* parziale; **to be ~ against** essere prevenuto(a) contro.

biathlon [baɪ'æθlən] *n* biathlon *m*.

bib [bɪb] *n* bavaglino.

Bible ['baɪbl] *n* Bibbia.

bibliography [bɪblɪˈɔgrəfɪ] *n* bibliografia.
bicarbonate of soda [baɪˈkɑːbənɪt-] *n* bicarbonato (di sodio).
bicentenary [baɪsɛnˈtiːnərɪ], **bicentennial** [baɪsɛnˈtɛnɪəl] *n* bicentenario.
biceps [ˈbaɪsɛps] *n* bicipite *m*.
bicker [ˈbɪkə*] *vi* bisticciare.
bicycle [ˈbaɪsɪkl] *n* bicicletta.
bicycle path *n*, **bicycle track** *n* sentiero ciclabile.
bicycle pump *n* pompa della bicicletta.
bid [bɪd] *n* offerta; (*attempt*) tentativo ♦ *vb* (*pt* **bade** [bæd] *or* **bid**, *pp* **bidden** [ˈbɪdn] *or* **bid**) *vi* fare un'offerta ♦ *vt* fare un'offerta di; **to ~ sb good day** dire buon giorno a qn.
bidder [ˈbɪdə*] *n*: **the highest ~** il maggior offerente.
bidding [ˈbɪdɪŋ] *n* offerte *fpl*.
bide [baɪd] *vt*: **to ~ one's time** aspettare il momento giusto.
bidet [ˈbiːdeɪ] *n* bidè *m inv*.
bidirectional [ˈbaɪdɪˈrɛkʃənl] *adj* bidirezionale.
biennial [baɪˈɛnɪəl] *adj* biennale ♦ *n* (pianta) biennale *f*.
bier [bɪə*] *n* bara.
bifocals [baɪˈfəuklz] *npl* occhiali *mpl* bifocali.
big [bɪg] *adj* grande; grosso(a); **my ~ brother** mio fratello maggiore; **to do things in a ~ way** fare le cose in grande.
bigamy [ˈbɪgəmɪ] *n* bigamia.
big dipper [-ˈdɪpə*] *n* montagne *fpl* russe, otto *m inv* volante.
big end *n* (*AUT*) testa di biella.
biggish [ˈbɪgɪʃ] *adj* (*see* **big**) piuttosto grande; piuttosto grosso(a); **a ~ rent** un affitto piuttosto alto.
bigheaded [ˈbɪgˈhɛdɪd] *adj* presuntuoso(a).
big-hearted [ˈbɪgˈhɑːtɪd] *adj* generoso(a).
bigot [ˈbɪgət] *n* persona gretta.
bigoted [ˈbɪgətɪd] *adj* gretto(a).
bigotry [ˈbɪgətrɪ] *n* grettezza.
big toe *n* alluce *m*.
big top *n* tendone *m* del circo.
big wheel *n* (*at fair*) ruota (panoramica).
bigwig [ˈbɪgwɪg] *n* (*col*) pezzo grosso.
bike [baɪk] *n* bici *f inv*.
bikini [bɪˈkiːnɪ] *n* bikini *m inv*.
bilateral [baɪˈlætərl] *adj* bilaterale.
bile [baɪl] *n* bile *f*.
bilingual [baɪˈlɪŋgwəl] *adj* bilingue.
bilious [ˈbɪlɪəs] *adj* biliare; (*fig*) bilioso(a).
bill [bɪl] *n* (*in hotel, restaurant*) conto; (*COMM*) fattura; (*for gas, electricity*) bolletta, conto; (*POL*) atto; (*US: banknote*) banconota; (*notice*) avviso; (*THEAT*): **on the ~** in cartellone; (*of bird*) becco ♦ *vt* mandare il conto a; **may I have the ~ please?** posso avere il conto per piacere?; **"stick *or* post no ~s"** "divieto di affissione"; **to fit *or* fill the ~** (*fig*) fare al caso; **~ of exchange** cambiale *f*, tratta; **~ of lading** polizza di carico; **~ of sale** atto di vendita.
billboard [ˈbɪlbɔːd] *n* tabellone *m*.
billet [ˈbɪlɪt] *n* alloggio ♦ *vt* (*troops etc*) alloggiare.
billfold [ˈbɪlfəuld] *n* (*US*) portafoglio.
billiards [ˈbɪljədz] *n* biliardo.
billion [ˈbɪljən] *n* (*BRIT*) bilione *m*; (*US*) miliardo.
billow [ˈbɪləu] *n* (*of smoke*) nuvola; (*of sail*) rigonfiamento ♦ *vi* (*smoke*) alzarsi in volute; (*sail*) gonfiarsi.
bills payable (B/P, b.p.) *npl* effetti *mpl* passivi.
bills receivable (B/R, b.r.) *npl* effetti *mpl* attivi.
billy goat [ˈbɪlɪgəut] *n* caprone *m*, becco.
bimbo [ˈbɪmbəu] *n* (*col*) pollastrella, svampitela.
bin [bɪn] *n* bidone *m*; (*BRIT*: *also*: **dust~**) pattumiera; (: *also*: **litter ~**) cestino.
binary [ˈbaɪnərɪ] *adj* binario(a).
bind, *pt*, *pp* **bound** [baɪnd, baund] *vt* legare; (*oblige*) obbligare.
▶**bind over** *vt* (*LAW*) dare la condizionale a.
▶**bind up** *vt* (*wound*) fasciare, bendare; **to be bound up in** (*work, research etc*) essere completamente assorbito da; **to be bound up with** (*person*) dedicarsi completamente a.
binder [ˈbaɪndə*] *n* (*file*) classificatore *m*.
binding [ˈbaɪndɪŋ] *n* (*of book*) legatura ♦ *adj* (*contract*) vincolante.
binge [bɪndʒ] *n* (*col*): **to go on a ~** fare baldoria.
bingo [ˈbɪŋgəu] *n* gioco simile alla tombola.
bin liner *n* sacchetto per l'immondizia.
binoculars [bɪˈnɔkjuləz] *npl* binocolo.
biochemistry [baɪəuˈkɛmɪstrɪ] *n* biochimica.
biodegradable [ˈbaɪəudɪˈgreɪdəbl] *adj* biodegradabile.
biodiversity [ˈbaɪəudaɪˈvəːsɪtɪ] *n* biodiversità *f inv*.
biofuel [ˈbaɪəufjuəl] *n* carburante *m* biologico.
biographer [baɪˈɔgrəfə*] *n* biografo/a.
biographic(al) [baɪəˈgræfɪk(l)] *adj* biografico(a).
biography [baɪˈɔgrəfɪ] *n* biografia.
biological [baɪəˈlɔdʒɪkl] *adj* biologico(a).
biological clock *n* orologio biologico.

biologist [baɪˈɔlədʒɪst] n biologo/a.
biology [baɪˈɔlədʒɪ] n biologia.
biophysics [baɪəuˈfɪzɪks] n biofisica.
biopic [ˈbaɪəupɪk] n film m inv biografia inv.
biosphere [ˈbaɪəusfɪə*] n biosfera.
biopsy [ˈbaɪɔpsɪ] n biopsia.
biotechnology [baɪəutɛkˈnɔlədʒɪ] n biotecnologia.
birch [bə:tʃ] n betulla.
bird [bə:d] n uccello; (*BRIT col*: *girl*) bambola.
bird of prey n (uccello) rapace m.
bird's-eye view [ˈbə:dzaɪ-] n vista panoramica.
bird watcher n ornitologo/a dilettante.
Biro ® [ˈbaɪrəu] n biro ® f inv.
birth [bə:θ] n nascita; **to give ~ to** dare alla luce; (*fig*) dare inizio a.
birth certificate n certificato di nascita.
birth control n controllo delle nascite; contraccezione f.
birthday [ˈbə:θdeɪ] n compleanno.
birthmark [ˈbə:θmɑ:k] n voglia.
birthplace [ˈbə:θpleɪs] n luogo di nascita.
birth rate n indice m di natalità.
Biscay [ˈbɪskeɪ] n: **the Bay of ~** il golfo di Biscaglia.
biscuit [ˈbɪskɪt] n (*BRIT*) biscotto; (*US*) panino al latte.
bisect [baɪˈsɛkt] vt tagliare in due (parti); (*MATH*) bisecare.
bisexual [baɪˈsɛksjuəl] adj, n bisessuale (m/f).
bishop [ˈbɪʃəp] n vescovo; (*CHESS*) alfiere m.
bistro [ˈbi:strəu] n bistrò m inv.
bit [bɪt] pt of **bite** ♦ n pezzo; (of tool) punta; (of horse) morso; (*COMPUT*) bit m inv; (*US*: coin) ottavo di dollaro; **a ~ of** un po' di; **a ~ mad/dangerous** un po' matto/pericoloso; **~ by** a poco a poco; **to do one's ~** fare la propria parte; **to come to ~s** (break) andare a pezzi; **bring all your ~s and pieces** porta tutte le tue cose.
bitch [bɪtʃ] n (dog) cagna; (col!) puttana (!).
bite [baɪt] vt, vi (pt **bit** [bɪt], pp **bitten** [ˈbɪtn]) mordere ♦ n morso; (insect ~) puntura; (mouthful) boccone m; **let's have a ~** (to eat) mangiamo un boccone; **to ~ one's nails** mangiarsi le unghie.
biting [ˈbaɪtɪŋ] adj pungente.
bit part n (*THEAT*) particina.
bitten [ˈbɪtn] pp of **bite**.
bitter [ˈbɪtə*] adj amaro(a); (wind, criticism) pungente; (icy: weather) gelido(a) ♦ n (*BRIT*: beer) birra amara; **to the ~ end** a oltranza.
bitterly [ˈbɪtəlɪ] adv (disappoint, complain,

weep) amaramente; (oppose, criticise) aspramente; (jealous) profondamente; **it's ~ cold** fa un freddo gelido.
bitterness [ˈbɪtənɪs] n amarezza; gusto amaro.
bittersweet [ˈbɪtəswi:t] adj agrodolce.
bitty [ˈbɪtɪ] adj (*BRIT col*) frammentario(a).
bitumen [ˈbɪtjumɪn] n bitume m.
bivouac [ˈbɪvuæk] n bivacco.
bizarre [bɪˈza:*] adj bizzarro(a).
bk abbr = **bank; book**.
BL n abbr (= Bachelor of Law(s), Bachelor of Letters) titolo di studio; (*US*: = Bachelor of Literature) titolo di studio.
bl abbr = **bill of lading**.
blab [blæb] vi parlare troppo ♦ vt (also: ~ out) spifferare.
black [blæk] adj nero(a) ♦ n nero; (person): **B~** negro/a ♦ vt (*BRIT INDUSTRY*) boicottare; **~ coffee** caffè m inv nero; **to give sb a ~ eye** fare un occhio nero a qn; **in the ~** (in credit) in attivo; **there it is in ~ and white** (fig) eccolo nero su bianco; **~ and blue** adj tutto(a) pesto(a).
▶**black out** vi (faint) svenire.
black belt n (*SPORT*) cintura nera; (*US*: area): **the ~** zona abitata principalmente da negri.
blackberry [ˈblækbərɪ] n mora.
blackbird [ˈblækbə:d] n merlo.
blackboard [ˈblækbɔ:d] n lavagna.
black box n (*AVIAT*) scatola nera.
Black Country n (*BRIT*): **the ~** zona carbonifera del centro dell'Inghilterra.
blackcurrant [blækˈkʌrənt] n ribes m inv.
black economy n (*BRIT*) economia sommersa.
blacken [ˈblækn] vt annerire.
Black Forest n: **the ~** la Foresta Nera.
blackhead [ˈblækhɛd] n punto nero, comedone m.
black hole n (*ASTRON*) buco nero.
black ice n strato trasparente di ghiaccio.
blackjack [ˈblækdʒæk] n (*CARDS*) ventuno; (*US*: truncheon) manganello.
blackleg [ˈblæklɛg] n (*BRIT*) crumiro.
blacklist [ˈblæklɪst] n lista nera ♦ vt mettere sulla lista nera.
blackmail [ˈblækmeɪl] n ricatto ♦ vt ricattare.
blackmailer [ˈblækmeɪlə*] n ricattatore/trice.
black market n mercato nero.
blackout [ˈblækaut] n oscuramento; (fainting) svenimento; (*TV*) interruzione f delle trasmissioni.
black pepper n pepe m nero.
Black Sea n: **the ~** il mar Nero.

black sheep n pecora nera.
blacksmith ['blæksmıθ] n fabbro ferraio.
black spot n (AUT) luogo famigerato per gli incidenti.
bladder ['blædə*] n vescica.
blade [bleıd] n lama; (of oar) pala; ~ **of grass** filo d'erba.
blame [bleım] n colpa ♦ vt: **to ~ sb/sth for sth** dare la colpa di qc a qn/qc; **who's to ~?** chi è colpevole?; **I'm not to ~** non è colpa mia.
blameless ['bleımlıs] adj irreprensibile.
blanch [blɑːntʃ] vi (person) sbiancare in viso ♦ vt (CULIN) scottare.
bland [blænd] adj mite; (taste) blando(a).
blank [blæŋk] adj bianco(a); (look) distratto(a) ♦ n spazio vuoto; (cartridge) cartuccia a salve; **to draw a ~** (fig) non aver nessun risultato.
blank cheque, (US) **blank check** n assegno in bianco; **to give sb a ~ to do** (fig) dare carta bianca a qn per fare.
blanket ['blæŋkıt] n coperta ♦ adj (statement, agreement) globale.
blanket cover n: **to give ~** (subj: insurance policy) coprire tutti i rischi.
blare [blɛə*] vi strombettare; (radio) suonare a tutto volume.
blasé ['blɑːzeı] adj blasé inv.
blasphemous ['blæsfıməs] adj blasfemo(a).
blasphemy ['blæsfımı] n bestemmia.
blast [blɑːst] n (of wind) raffica; (of air, steam) getto; (bomb ~) esplosione f ♦ vt far saltare ♦ excl (BRIT col) mannaggia!; **(at) full ~** a tutta forza.
▶**blast off** vi (SPACE) essere lanciato(a).
blast-off ['blɑːstɔf] n (SPACE) lancio.
blatant ['bleıtənt] adj flagrante.
blatantly ['bleıtəntlı] adv: **it's ~ obvious** è lampante.
blaze [bleız] n (fire) incendio; (glow: of fire, sun etc) bagliore m; (fig) vampata ♦ vi (fire) ardere, fiammeggiare; (fig) infiammarsi ♦ vt: **to ~ a trail** (fig) tracciare una via nuova; **in a ~ of publicity** circondato da grande pubblicità.
blazer ['bleızə*] n blazer m inv.
bleach [bliːtʃ] n (also: **household ~**) varechina ♦ vt (material) candeggiare.
bleached ['bliːtʃt] adj (hair) decolorato(a).
bleachers ['bliːtʃəz] npl (US) posti mpl di gradinata.
bleak [bliːk] adj (prospect, future) tetro(a); (landscape) desolato(a); (weather) gelido(a); (smile) pallido(a).
bleary-eyed ['blıərı'aıd] adj dagli occhi offuscati.
bleat [bliːt] vi belare.

bleed, pt, pp **bled** [bliːd, blɛd] vt dissanguare; (brakes, radiator) spurgare ♦ vi sanguinare; **my nose is ~ing** mi viene fuori sangue dal naso.
bleep [bliːp] n breve segnale m acustico, bip m inv ♦ vi suonare ♦ vt (doctor) chiamare con il cercapersone.
bleeper ['bliːpə*] n (of doctor etc) cercapersone m inv.
blemish ['blɛmıʃ] n macchia.
blend [blɛnd] n miscela ♦ vt mescolare ♦ vi (colours etc) armonizzare.
blender ['blɛndə*] n (CULIN) frullatore m.
bless, pt, pp **blessed** or **blest** [blɛs, blɛst] vt benedire; **~ you!** (sneezing) salute!; **to be ~ed with** godere di.
blessed ['blɛsıd] adj (REL: holy) benedetto(a); (happy) beato(a); **every ~ day** tutti i santi giorni.
blessing ['blɛsıŋ] n benedizione f; fortuna; **to count one's ~s** ringraziare Iddio, ritenersi fortunato; **it was a ~ in disguise** in fondo è stato un bene.
blest [blɛst] pt, pp of **bless.**
blew [bluː] pt of **blow.**
blight [blaıt] n (of plants) golpe f ♦ vt (hopes etc) deludere; (life) rovinare.
blimey ['blaımı] excl (BRIT col) accidenti!
blind [blaınd] adj cieco(a) ♦ n (for window) avvolgibile m; (Venetian ~) veneziana ♦ vt accecare; **to turn a ~ eye (on or to)** chiudere un occhio (su).
blind alley n vicolo cieco.
blind corner n (BRIT) svolta cieca.
blind date n appuntamento combinato (tra due persone che non si conoscono).
blinders ['blaındəz] npl (US) = **blinkers.**
blindfold ['blaındfəuld] n benda ♦ adj, adv bendato(a) ♦ vt bendare gli occhi a.
blinding ['blaındıŋ] adj (flash, light) accecante; (pain) atroce.
blindly ['blaındlı] adv ciecamente.
blindness ['blaındnıs] n cecità.
blind spot n (AUT etc) punto cieco; (fig) punto debole.
blink [blıŋk] vi battere gli occhi; (light) lampeggiare ♦ n: **to be on the ~** (col) essere scassato(a).
blinkers ['blıŋkəz] npl (BRIT) paraocchi mpl.
blinking ['blıŋkıŋ] adj (BRIT col): **this ~ ...** questo(a) maledetto(a) ....
blip [blıp] n (on radar etc) segnale m intermittente; (on graph) piccola variazione f; (fig) momentanea battuta d'arresto.
bliss [blıs] n estasi f.
blissful ['blısfəl] adj (event, day) stupendo(a), meraviglioso(a); (smile)

beato(a); **in ~ ignorance** nella (più) beata ignoranza.

blissfully ['blɪsfəlɪ] *adj (sigh, smile)* beatamente; **~ happy** magnificamente felice.

blister ['blɪstə*] *n (on skin)* vescica; *(on paintwork)* bolla ♦ *vi (paint)* coprirsi di bolle.

blithe [blaɪð] *adj* gioioso(a), allegro(a).

blithely ['blaɪðlɪ] *adv* allegramente.

blithering ['blɪðərɪŋ] *adj (col)*: **this ~ idiot** questa razza d'idiota.

BLit(t) *n abbr (= Bachelor of Literature)* titolo di studio.

blitz [blɪts] *n* blitz *m*; **to have a ~ on sth** *(fig)* prendere d'assalto qc.

blizzard ['blɪzəd] *n* bufera di neve.

BLM *n abbr (US: = Bureau of Land Management)* ≈ il demanio.

bloated ['bləutɪd] *adj* gonfio(a).

blob [blɔb] *n (drop)* goccia; *(stain, spot)* macchia.

bloc [blɔk] *n (POL)* blocco.

block [blɔk] *n (gen, COMPUT)* blocco; *(in pipes)* ingombro; *(toy)* cubo; *(of buildings)* isolato ♦ *vt (gen, COMPUT)* bloccare; **~ of flats** caseggiato; **3 ~s from here** a 3 isolati di distanza da qui; **mental ~** blocco mentale.

►**block up** *vt* bloccare; *(pipe)* ingorgare, intasare.

blockade [blɔ'keɪd] *n* blocco ♦ *vt* assediare.

blockage ['blɔkɪdʒ] *n* ostacolo.

block and tackle *n (TECH)* paranco.

block booking *n* prenotazione *f* in blocco.

blockbuster ['blɔkbʌstə*] *n* libro *or* film *etc* sensazionale.

block capitals *npl* stampatello.

blockhead ['blɔkhɛd] *n* testa di legno.

block letters *npl* stampatello.

block release *n (BRIT)* periodo pagato concesso al tirocinante per effettuare studi superiori.

block vote *n (BRIT)* voto per delega.

bloke [bləuk] *n (BRIT col)* tizio.

blond [blɔnd] *n (man)* biondo ♦ *adj* biondo(a).

blonde [blɔnd] *n (woman)* bionda ♦ *adj* biondo(a).

blood [blʌd] *n* sangue *m*; **new ~** *(fig)* nuova linfa.

blood bank *n* banca del sangue.

blood count *n* conteggio di globuli rossi e bianchi.

bloodcurdling ['blʌdkə:dlɪŋ] *adj* raccapricciante, da far gelare il sangue.

blood donor *n* donatore/trice di sangue.

blood group *n* gruppo sanguigno.

bloodhound ['blʌdhaund] *n* segugio.

bloodless ['blʌdlɪs] *adj (pale)* smorto(a), esangue; *(coup)* senza spargimento di sangue.

bloodletting ['blʌdlɛtɪŋ] *n (MED)* salasso; *(fig)* spargimento di sangue.

blood poisoning *n* setticemia.

blood pressure *n* pressione *f* sanguigna; **to have high/low ~** avere la pressione alta/bassa.

bloodshed ['blʌdʃɛd] *n* spargimento di sangue.

bloodshot ['blʌdʃɔt] *adj*: **~ eyes** occhi iniettati di sangue.

bloodstained ['blʌdsteɪnd] *adj* macchiato(a) di sangue.

bloodstream ['blʌdstri:m] *n* flusso del sangue.

blood test *n* analisi *f inv* del sangue.

bloodthirsty ['blʌdθə:stɪ] *adj* assetato(a) di sangue.

blood transfusion *n* trasfusione *f* di sangue.

blood type *n* gruppo sanguigno.

blood vessel *n* vaso sanguigno.

bloody ['blʌdɪ] *adj* sanguinoso(a); *(BRIT col!)*: **this ~ ...** questo maledetto ...; **a ~ awful day** *(col!)* una giornata di merda *(!)*; **~ good** *(col!)* maledettamente buono.

bloody-minded ['blʌdɪ'maɪndɪd] *adj (BRIT col)* indisponente.

bloom [blu:m] *n* fiore *m* ♦ *vi* essere in fiore.

blooming ['blu:mɪŋ] *adj (col)*: **this ~ ...** questo(a) dannato(a) ....

blossom ['blɔsəm] *n* fiore *m*; *(with pl sense)* fiori *mpl* ♦ *vi* essere in fiore; **to ~ into** *(fig)* diventare.

blot [blɔt] *n* macchia ♦ *vt* macchiare; **to be a ~ on the landscape** rovinare il paesaggio; **to ~ one's copy book** *(fig)* farla grossa.

►**blot out** *vt (memories)* cancellare; *(view)* nascondere; *(nation, city)* annientare.

blotchy ['blɔtʃɪ] *adj (complexion)* coperto(a) di macchie.

blotter ['blɔtə*] *n* tampone *m* (di carta assorbente).

blotting paper ['blɔtɪŋ-] *n* carta assorbente.

blotto ['blɔtəu] *adj (col)* sbronzo(a).

blouse [blauz] *n* camicetta.

blow [bləu] *n* colpo ♦ *vb (pt* **blew** [blu:]*, pp* **blown** [bləun])* *vi* soffiare ♦ *vt (fuse)* far saltare; **to come to ~s** venire alle mani; **to ~ one's nose** soffiarsi il naso; **to ~ a whistle** fischiare.

►**blow away** *vi* volare via ♦ *vt* portare via.

►**blow down** *vt* abbattere.

►**blow off** *vt* far volare via; **to ~ off course**

far uscire di rotta.

►**blow out** vi scoppiare.

►**blow over** vi calmarsi.

►**blow up** vi saltare in aria ♦ vt far saltare in aria; (tyre) gonfiare; (PHOT) ingrandire.

blow-dry ['bləudraɪ] n (hairstyle) messa in piega a föhn ♦ vt asciugare con il föhn.

blowlamp ['bləulæmp] n (BRIT) lampada a benzina per saldare.

blown [bləun] pp of **blow**.

blowout ['bləuaut] n (of tyre) scoppio; (col: big meal) abbuffata.

blowtorch ['bləutɔːtʃ] n lampada a benzina per saldare.

blowzy ['blauzɪ] adj trasandato(a).

BLS n abbr (US) = Bureau of Labor Statistics.

blubber ['blʌbə*] n grasso di balena ♦ vi (pej) piangere forte.

bludgeon ['blʌdʒən] vt prendere a randellate.

blue [bluː] adj azzurro(a), celeste; (darker) blu inv; ~ film/joke film/barzelletta pornografico(a); (only) once in a ~ moon a ogni morte di papa; out of the ~ (fig) all'improvviso; see also **blues**.

blue baby n neonato cianotico.

bluebell ['bluːbel] n giacinto di bosco.

bluebottle ['bluːbɒtl] n moscone m.

blue cheese n formaggio tipo gorgonzola.

blue-chip ['bluːtʃɪp] adj: ~ **investment** investimento sicuro.

blue-collar worker ['bluːkɒlə*-] n operaio/a.

blue jeans npl blue-jeans mpl.

blueprint ['bluːprɪnt] n cianografia; (fig): ~ (for) formula (di).

blues [bluːz] npl: **the** ~ (MUS) il blues; **to have the** ~ (col: feeling) essere a terra.

bluff [blʌf] vi bluffare ♦ n bluff m inv; (promontory) promontorio scosceso ♦ adj (person) brusco(a); **to call sb's** ~ mettere alla prova il bluff di qn.

blunder ['blʌndə*] n abbaglio ♦ vi prendere un abbaglio; **to** ~ **into sb/sth** andare a sbattere contro qn/qc.

blunt [blʌnt] adj (edge) smussato(a); (point) spuntato(a); (knife) che non taglia; (person) brusco(a) ♦ vt smussare; spuntare; **this pencil is** ~ questa matita non ha più la punta; ~ **instrument** (LAW) corpo contundente.

bluntly ['blʌntlɪ] adv (speak) senza mezzi termini.

bluntness ['blʌntnɪs] n (of person) brutale franchezza.

blur [blɔː*] n cosa offuscata ♦ vt offuscare.

blurb [blɔːb] n trafiletto pubblicitario.

blurred [blɔːd] adj (photo) mosso(a); (TV)

sfuocato(a).

blurt out [blɔːt-] vt lasciarsi sfuggire.

blush [blʌʃ] vi arrossire ♦ n rossore m.

blusher ['blʌʃə*] n fard m inv.

bluster ['blʌstə*] n spacconate fpl; (threats) vuote minacce fpl ♦ vi fare lo spaccone; minacciare a vuoto.

blustering ['blʌstərɪŋ] adj (tone etc) da spaccone.

blustery ['blʌstərɪ] adj (weather) burrascoso(a).

Blvd abbr = boulevard.

BM n abbr = British Museum; (SCOL: = Bachelor of Medicine) titolo di studio.

BMA n abbr = British Medical Association.

BMJ n abbr = British Medical Journal.

BMus n abbr (= Bachelor of Music) titolo di studio.

BMX n abbr (= bicycle motorcross) BMX f inv; ~ **bike** mountain bike f inv per cross.

BO n abbr (col: = body odour) odori mpl sgradevoli (del corpo); (US) = box office.

boar [bɔː*] n cinghiale m.

board [bɔːd] n tavola; (on wall) tabellone m; (for chess etc) scacchiera; (committee) consiglio, comitato; (in firm) consiglio d'amministrazione; (NAUT, AVIAT): **on** ~ a bordo ♦ vt (ship) salire a bordo di; (train) salire su; **full** ~ (BRIT) pensione f completa; **half** ~ (BRIT) mezza pensione; ~ **and lodging** vitto e alloggio; **above** ~ (fig) regolare; **across the** ~ (fig) adv per tutte le categorie ♦ adj generale; **to go by the** ~ venir messo(a) da parte.

►**board up** vt (door) chiudere con assi.

boarder ['bɔːdə*] n pensionante m/f; (SCOL) convittore/trice.

board game n gioco da tavolo.

boarding card ['bɔːdɪŋ-] n (AVIAT, NAUT) carta d'imbarco.

boarding house n pensione f.

boarding party n squadra di ispezione (del carico di una nave).

boarding pass n (BRIT) = boarding card.

boarding school n collegio.

board meeting n riunione f di consiglio.

board room n sala del consiglio.

boardwalk ['bɔːdwɔːk] n (US) passeggiata a mare.

boast [bəust] vi: **to** ~ (about or of) vantarsi (di) ♦ vt vantare ♦ n vanteria; vanto.

boastful ['bəustful] adj vanaglorioso(a).

boastfulness ['bəustfulnɪs] n vanagloria.

boat [bəut] n nave f; (small) barca; **to go by** ~ andare in barca or in nave; **we're all in the same** ~ (fig) siamo tutti nella stessa barca.

boater ['bəutə*] n (hat) paglietta.

boating ['bəutɪŋ] n canottaggio.
boat people n boat people mpl.
boatswain ['bəusn] n nostromo.
bob [bɔb] vi (boat, cork on water: also: ~ **up and down**) andare su e giù ♦ n (BRIT col) = **shilling**.
▶**bob up** vi saltare fuori.
bobbin ['bɔbɪn] n bobina; (of sewing machine) rocchetto.
bobby ['bɔbɪ] n (BRIT col) ≈ poliziotto.
bobsleigh ['bɔbsleɪ] n bob m inv.
bode [bəud] vi: **to ~ well/ill (for)** essere di buon/cattivo auspicio (per).
bodice ['bɔdɪs] n corsetto.
bodily ['bɔdɪlɪ] adj (comfort, needs) materiale; (pain) fisico(a) ♦ adv (carry) in braccio; (lift) di peso.
body ['bɔdɪ] n corpo; (of car) carrozzeria; (of plane) fusoliera; (organization) associazione f, organizzazione f; (quantity) quantità f inv; (of speech, document) parte f principale; (also: ~ **stocking**) body m inv; **in a ~** in massa; **ruling ~** direttivo; **a wine with ~** un vino corposo.
body blow n (fig) duro colpo.
body-building ['bɔdɪ'bɪldɪŋ] n culturismo.
bodyguard ['bɔdɪgɑːd] n guardia del corpo.
body language n linguaggio del corpo.
body repairs npl (AUT) lavori mpl di carrozzeria.
body search n perquisizione f personale; **to submit to** or **undergo a ~** essere sottoposto(a) a perquisizione personale.
bodywork ['bɔdɪwɜːk] n carrozzeria.
boffin ['bɔfɪn] n scienziato.
bog [bɔg] n palude f ♦ vt: **to get ~ged down** (fig) impantanarsi.
bogey ['bəugɪ] n (worry) spauracchio; (also: ~ **man**) babau m inv.
boggle ['bɔgl] vi: **the mind ~s** è incredibile.
Bogotá [bəugə'tɑː] n Bogotà f.
bogus ['bəugəs] adj falso(a); finto(a).
Bohemia [bəu'hiːmɪə] n Boemia.
Bohemian [bəu'hiːmɪən] adj, n boemo(a).
boil [bɔɪl] vt, vi bollire ♦ n (MED) foruncolo; **to come to the** or (US) **a ~** raggiungere l'ebollizione; **to bring to the** or (US) **a ~** portare a ebollizione; ~**ed egg** uovo alla coque; ~**ed potatoes** patate fpl bollite or lesse.
▶**boil down** vi (fig): **to ~ down to** ridursi a.
▶**boil over** vi traboccare (bollendo).
boiler ['bɔɪlə*] n caldaia.
boiler suit n (BRIT) tuta.
boiling ['bɔɪlɪŋ] adj bollente; **I'm ~** (hot) (col) sto morendo di caldo.

boiling point n punto di ebollizione.
boil-in-the-bag [bɔɪlɪnðə'bæg] adj (rice etc) da bollire nel sacchetto.
boisterous ['bɔɪstərəs] adj chiassoso(a).
bold [bəuld] adj audace; (child) impudente; (outline) chiaro(a); (colour) deciso(a).
boldness ['bəuldnɪs] n audacia; impudenza.
bold type n (TYP) neretto, grassetto.
Bolivia [bə'lɪvɪə] n Bolivia.
Bolivian [bə'lɪvɪən] adj, n boliviano(a).
bollard ['bɔləd] n (NAUT) bitta; (BRIT AUT) colonnina luminosa.
bolshy ['bɔlʃɪ] adj (BRIT col) piantagrane, ribelle; **to be in a ~ mood** essere in vena di piantar grane.
bolster ['bəulstə*] n capezzale m.
▶**bolster up** vt sostenere.
bolt [bəult] n chiavistello; (with nut) bullone m ♦ adv: ~ **upright** diritto(a) come un fuso ♦ vt serrare; (food) mangiare in fretta ♦ vi scappare via; **a ~ from the blue** (fig) un fulmine a ciel sereno.
bomb [bɔm] n bomba ♦ vt bombardare.
bombard [bɔm'bɑːd] vt bombardare.
bombardment [bɔm'bɑːdmənt] n bombardamento.
bombastic [bɔm'bæstɪk] adj ampolloso(a).
bomb disposal n: ~ **expert** artificiere m; ~ **unit** corpo degli artificieri.
bomber ['bɔmə*] n bombardiere m; (terrorist) dinamitardo/a.
bombing ['bɔmɪŋ] n bombardamento.
bomb scare n stato di allarme (per sospetta presenza di una bomba).
bombshell ['bɔmʃɛl] n (fig) notizia bomba.
bomb site n luogo bombardato.
bona fide ['bəunə'faɪdɪ] adj sincero(a); (offer) onesto(a).
bonanza [bə'nænzə] n cuccagna.
bond [bɔnd] n legame m; (binding promise, FINANCE) obbligazione f; **in ~** (of goods) in attesa di sdoganamento.
bondage ['bɔndɪdʒ] n schiavitù f.
bonded warehouse ['bɔndɪd-] n magazzino doganale.
bone [bəun] n osso; (of fish) spina, lisca ♦ vt disossare; togliere le spine a.
bone china n porcellana fine.
bone-dry ['bəun'draɪ] adj asciuttissimo(a).
bone idle adj: **to be ~** essere un(a) fannullone(a).
bone marrow n midollo osseo.
boner ['bəunə*] n (US) gaffe f inv.
bonfire ['bɔnfaɪə*] n falò m inv.
bonk [bɔŋk] vt, vi (hum, col) scopare (!).
bonkers ['bɔŋkəz] adj (BRIT col) suonato(a).
Bonn [bɔn] n Bonn f.
bonnet ['bɔnɪt] n cuffia; (BRIT: of car)

cofano.

bonny ['bɒnɪ] adj (esp Scottish) bello(a), carino(a).

bonus ['bəʊnəs] n premio; (on wages) gratifica.

bony ['bəʊnɪ] adj (thin: person) ossuto(a), angoloso(a); (arm, face, MED: tissue) osseo(a); (meat) pieno(a) di ossi; (fish) pieno(a) di spine.

boo [buː] excl ba! ♦ vt fischiare ♦ n fischio.

boob [buːb] n (col: breast) tetta; (: BRIT: mistake) gaffe f inv.

booby prize ['buːbɪ-] n premio per il peggior contendente.

booby trap ['buːbɪ-] n trabocchetto; (bomb) congegno che esplode al contatto.

booby-trapped ['buːbɪtræpt] adj: **a ~ car** una macchina con dell'esplosivo a bordo.

book [buk] n libro; (of stamps etc) blocchetto ♦ vt (ticket, seat, room) prenotare; (driver) multare; (football player) ammonire; **~s** npl (COMM) conti mpl; **to keep the ~s** (COMM) tenere la contabilità; **by the ~** secondo le regole; **to throw the ~ at sb** incriminare qn seriamente or con tutte le aggravanti.

►**book in** vi (BRIT: at hotel) prendere una camera.

►**book up** vt riservare, prenotare; **the hotel is ~ed up** l'albergo è al completo; **all seats are ~ed up** è tutto esaurito.

bookable ['bukəbl] adj: **seats are ~** si possono prenotare i posti.

bookcase ['bukkeɪs] n scaffale m.

book ends npl reggilibri mpl.

booking ['bukɪŋ] n (BRIT) prenotazione f.

booking office n (BRIT) biglietteria.

book-keeping ['buk'kiːpɪŋ] n contabilità.

booklet ['buklɪt] n opuscolo, libretto.

bookmaker ['bukmeɪkə*] n allibratore m.

bookseller ['bukselə*] n libraio.

bookshelf ['bukʃelf] n mensola (per libri); **bookshelves** npl (bookcase) libreria.

bookshop ['bukʃɒp] n libreria.

bookstall ['bukstɔːl] n bancarella di libri.

bookstore ['bukstɔː*] n = **bookshop**.

book token n buono m libri inv.

book value n valore m contabile.

bookworm ['bukwɜːm] n (fig) topo di biblioteca.

boom [buːm] n (noise) rimbombo; (busy period) boom m inv ♦ vi rimbombare; andare a gonfie vele.

boomerang ['buːməræŋ] n boomerang m inv ♦ vi (fig) avere effetto contrario; **to ~ on sb** (fig) ritorcersi contro qn.

boom town n città f inv in rapidissima espansione.

boon [buːn] n vantaggio.

boorish ['buərɪʃ] adj maleducato(a).

boost [buːst] n spinta ♦ vt spingere; (increase: sales, production) incentivare; **to give a ~ to** (morale) tirar su; **it gave a ~ to his confidence** è stata per lui un'iniezione di fiducia.

booster ['buːstə*] n (ELEC) amplificatore m; (TV) amplificatore m di segnale; (also: ~ rocket) razzo vettore; (MED) richiamo.

booster seat n (AUT: for children) seggiolino di sicurezza.

boot [buːt] n stivale m; (ankle ~) stivaletto; (for hiking) scarpone m da montagna; (for football etc) scarpa; (BRIT: of car) portabagagli m inv ♦ vt (COMPUT) inizializzare; **to ~** (in addition) per giunta, in più; **to give sb the ~** (col) mettere qn alla porta.

booth [buːð] n (at fair) baraccone m; (of cinema, telephone etc) cabina; (also: **voting ~**) cabina (elettorale).

bootleg ['buːtleg] adj di contrabbando; **~ record** registrazione f pirata inv.

booty ['buːtɪ] n bottino.

booze [buːz] (col) n alcool m ♦ vi trincare.

boozer ['buːzə*] n (col: person) beone m; (BRIT col: pub) osteria.

border ['bɔːdə*] n orlo; margine m; (of a country) frontiera; **the B~** la frontiera tra l'Inghilterra e la Scozia; **the B~s** la zona di confine tra l'Inghilterra e la Scozia.

►**border on** vt fus confinare con.

borderline ['bɔːdəlaɪn] n (fig) linea di demarcazione ♦ adj: **~ case** caso limite.

bore [bɔː*] pt of **bear** ♦ vt (hole) perforare; (person) annoiare ♦ n (person) seccatore/trice; (of gun) calibro; **he's ~d to tears** or **~d to death** or **~d stiff** è annoiato a morte, si annoia da morire.

boredom ['bɔːdəm] n noia.

boring ['bɔːrɪŋ] adj noioso(a).

born [bɔːn] adj: **to be ~** nascere; **I was ~ in 1960** sono nato nel 1960; **~ blind** cieco dalla nascita; **a ~ comedian** un comico nato.

born-again [bɔːnə'gen] adj: **~ Christian** convertito(a) alla chiesa evangelica.

borne [bɔːn] pp of **bear**.

Borneo ['bɔːnɪəʊ] n Borneo.

borough ['bʌrə] n comune m.

borrow ['bɒrəʊ] vt: **to ~ sth (from sb)** prendere in prestito qc (da qn); **may I ~ your car?** può prestarmi la macchina?

borrower ['bɒrəʊə*] n (gen) chi prende a prestito; (ECON) mutuatario/a.

borrowing ['bɒrəʊɪŋ] n prestito.

borstal ['bɔːstl] n (BRIT) riformatorio.

Bosnia ['bɒznɪə] *n* Bosnia.
Bosnia-Herzegovina
['bɒznɪəhɛrzə'gəuviːnə] *n* (*also:* **Bosnia-Hercegovina**) Bosnia-Erzegovina.
Bosnian ['bɒznɪən] *adj, n* bosniaco(a).
bosom ['buzəm] *n* petto; (*fig*) seno.
bosom friend *n* amico/a del cuore.
boss [bɒs] *n* capo ♦ *vt* (*also:* ~ **about** *or* **around**) comandare a bacchetta; **stop** ~**ing everyone about!** smettila di dare ordini a tutti!
bossy ['bɒsɪ] *adj* prepotente.
bosun ['bəusn] *n* nostromo.
botanical [bə'tænɪkl] *adj* botanico(a).
botanist ['bɒtənɪst] *n* botanico/a.
botany ['bɒtənɪ] *n* botanica.
botch [bɒtʃ] *vt* fare un pasticcio di.
both [bəuθ] *adj* entrambi(e), tutt'e due
♦ *pron:* ~ (**of them**) entrambi(e) ♦ *adv:* **they sell** ~ **meat and poultry** vendono insieme la carne ed il pollame; ~ **of us went, we** ~ **went** ci siamo andati tutt'e due.
bother ['bɒðə*] *vt* (*worry*) preoccupare; (*annoy*) infastidire ♦ *vi* (*gen:* ~ **o.s.**) preoccuparsi ♦ *n:* **it is a** ~ **to have to do** è una seccatura dover fare ♦ *excl* uffa!, accidenti!; **to** ~ **doing sth** darsi la pena di fare qc; **I'm sorry to** ~ **you** mi dispiace disturbarla; **please don't** ~ non si scomodi; **it's no** ~ non c'è problema.
Botswana [bɒt'swɑːnə] *n* Botswana *m*.
bottle ['bɒtl] *n* bottiglia; (*of perfume, shampoo etc*) flacone *m*; (*baby's*) biberon *m inv* ♦ *vt* imbottigliare; ~ **of wine/milk** bottiglia di vino/latte; **wine/milk** ~ bottiglia da vino/del latte.
▶**bottle up** *vt* contenere.
bottle bank *n* contenitore *m* per la raccolta del vetro.
bottle-fed ['bɒtlfɛd] *adj* allattato(a) artificialmente.
bottleneck ['bɒtlnɛk] *n* ingorgo.
bottle-opener ['bɒtləupnə*] *n* apribottiglie *m inv*.
bottom ['bɒtəm] *n* fondo; (*of mountain, tree, hill*) piedi *mpl*; (*buttocks*) sedere *m* ♦ *adj* più basso(a); ultimo(a); **at the** ~ **of** in fondo a; **to get to the** ~ **of sth** (*fig*) andare al fondo di *or* in fondo a qc.
bottomless ['bɒtəmlɪs] *adj* senza fondo.
bottom line *n:* **the** ~ **is ...** in ultima analisi ....
botulism ['bɒtjulɪzəm] *n* botulismo.
bough [bau] *n* ramo.
bought [bɔːt] *pt, pp of* buy.
boulder ['bəuldə*] *n* masso (tondeggiante).
boulevard ['buːlvɑːd] *n* viale *m*.
bounce [bauns] *vi* (*ball*) rimbalzare;

(*cheque*) essere restituito(a) ♦ *vt* far rimbalzare ♦ *n* (*rebound*) rimbalzo; **to** ~ **in** entrare di slancio *or* con foga; **he's got plenty of** ~ (*fig*) è molto esuberante.
bouncer ['baunsə*] *n* buttafuori *m inv*.
bouncy castle ® ['baunsɪ-] *n grande castello gonfiabile per giocare.*
bound [baund] *pt, pp of* bind ♦ *n* (*gen pl*) limite *m*; (*leap*) salto ♦ *vt* (*leap*) saltare; (*limit*) delimitare ♦ *adj:* **to be** ~ **to do sth** (*obliged*) essere costretto(a) a fare qc; **he's** ~ **to fail** (*likely*) è certo di fallire; ~ **for** diretto(a) a; **out of** ~**s** il cui accesso è vietato.
boundary ['baundrɪ] *n* confine *m*.
boundless ['baundlɪs] *adj* illimitato(a).
bountiful ['bauntɪful] *adj* (*person*) munifico(a); (*God*) misericordioso(a); (*supply*) abbondante.
bounty ['bauntɪ] *n* (*generosity*) liberalità, munificenza; (*reward*) taglia.
bounty hunter *n* cacciatore *m* di taglie.
bouquet ['bukeɪ] *n* bouquet *m inv*.
bourbon ['buəbən] *n* (*US: also:* ~ **whiskey**) bourbon *m inv*.
bourgeois ['buəʒwɑː] *adj, n* borghese (*m/f*).
bout [baut] *n* periodo; (*of malaria etc*) attacco; (*BOXING etc*) incontro.
boutique [buː'tiːk] *n* boutique *f inv*.
bow[1] *n* [bəu] nodo; (*weapon*) arco; (*MUS*) archetto; (*NAUT: also:* ~**s**) prua.
bow[2] [bau] *n* (*with body*) inchino ♦ *vi* inchinarsi; (*yield*): **to** ~ **to** *or* **before** sottomettersi a; **to** ~ **to the inevitable** rassegnarsi all'inevitabile.
bowels [bauəlz] *npl* intestini *mpl*; (*fig*) viscere *fpl*.
bowl [bəul] *n* (*for eating*) scodella; (*for washing*) bacino; (*ball*) boccia; (*of pipe*) fornello; (*US: stadium*) stadio ♦ *vi* (*CRICKET*) servire (la palla); *see also* **bowls**.
▶**bowl over** *vt* (*fig*) sconcertare.
bow-legged ['bəu'lɛgɪd] *adj* dalle gambe storte.
bowler ['bəulə*] *n* giocatore *m* di bocce; (*CRICKET*) giocatore che serve la palla; (*BRIT: also:* ~ **hat**) bombetta.
bowling ['bəulɪŋ] *n* (*game*) gioco delle bocce; bowling *m*.
bowling alley *n* pista da bowling.
bowling green *n* campo di bocce.
bowls [bəulz] *n* gioco delle bocce.
bow tie *n* cravatta a farfalla.
box [bɒks] *n* scatola; (*also:* **cardboard** ~) (scatola di) cartone *m*; (*crate; also for money*) cassetta; (*THEAT*) palco; (*BRIT AUT*) area d'incrocio ♦ *vi* fare pugilato ♦ *vt* mettere in (una) scatola; (*SPORT*)

combattere contro.

boxer ['bɔksə*] n (*person*) pugile m; (*dog*) boxer m inv.

boxing ['bɔksɪŋ] n (*SPORT*) pugilato.

Boxing Day n (*BRIT*) ≈ Santo Stefano.

---

*Il **Boxing Day** è il primo giorno infrasettimanale dopo Natale e cade generalmente il 26 di dicembre. Prende il nome dall'usanza di donare pacchi regalo natalizi, un tempo chiamati "Christmas boxes", a fornitori, dipendenti e così via.*

---

boxing gloves npl guantoni mpl da pugile.

boxing ring n ring m inv.

box number n (*for advertisements*) casella.

box office n biglietteria.

box room n ripostiglio.

boy [bɔɪ] n ragazzo m; (*small*) bambino; (*son*) figlio; (*servant*) servo.

boycott ['bɔɪkɔt] n boicottaggio ♦ vt boicottare.

boyfriend ['bɔɪfrɛnd] n ragazzo.

boyish ['bɔɪɪʃ] adj di or da ragazzo.

Bp abbr = bishop.

BR abbr see **British Rail**.

bra [brɑː] n reggipetto, reggiseno.

brace [breɪs] n sostegno; (*on teeth*) apparecchio correttore; (*tool*) trapano; (*TYP: also:* ~ **bracket**) graffa ♦ vt rinforzare, sostenere; **to** ~ **o.s.** (*fig*) farsi coraggio; see also **braces**.

bracelet ['breɪslɪt] n braccialetto.

braces ['breɪsɪz] npl (*BRIT*) bretelle fpl.

bracing ['breɪsɪŋ] adj invigorante.

bracken ['brækən] n felce f.

bracket ['brækɪt] n (*TECH*) mensola; (*group*) gruppo; (*TYP*) parentesi f inv ♦ vt mettere fra parentesi; (*fig: also:* ~ **together**) mettere insieme; (*in* ~s tra parentesi; **round/square** ~s parentesi tonde/quadre; **income** ~ fascia di reddito.

brackish ['brækɪʃ] adj (*water*) salmastro(a).

brag [bræg] vi vantarsi.

braid [breɪd] n (*trimming*) passamano; (*of hair*) treccia.

Braille [breɪl] n braille m.

brain [breɪn] n cervello; ~s npl cervella fpl; **he's got** ~s è intelligente.

brainchild ['breɪntʃaɪld] n creatura, creazione f.

braindead ['breɪndɛd] adj (*MED*) che ha subito morte cerebrale; (*col*) cerebroleso(a), deficiente.

brainless ['breɪnlɪs] adj deficiente, stupido(a).

brainstorm ['breɪnstɔːm] n (*fig*) attacco di pazzia; (*US*) = brainwave.

brainwash ['breɪnwɔʃ] vt fare un lavaggio di cervello a.

brainwave ['breɪnweɪv] n lampo di genio.

brainy ['breɪnɪ] adj intelligente.

braise [breɪz] vt brasare.

brake [breɪk] n (*on vehicle*) freno ♦ vt, vi frenare.

brake light n (fanalino dello) stop m inv.

brake pedal n pedale m del freno.

bramble ['bræmbl] n rovo; (*fruit*) mora.

bran [bræn] n crusca.

branch [brɑːntʃ] n ramo; (*COMM*) succursale f, filiale f ♦ vi diramarsi.

▶**branch out** vi: **to** ~ **out into** intraprendere una nuova attività nel ramo di.

branch line n (*RAIL*) linea secondaria.

branch manager n direttore m di filiale.

brand [brænd] n marca ♦ vt (*cattle*) marcare (a ferro rovente); (*fig: pej*): **to** ~ **sb a communist** etc definire qn come comunista etc.

brandish ['brændɪʃ] vt brandire.

brand name n marca.

brand-new ['brænd'njuː] adj nuovo(a) di zecca.

brandy ['brændɪ] n brandy m inv.

brash [bræʃ] adj sfacciato(a).

Brasilia [brə'zɪljə] n Brasilia.

brass [brɑːs] n ottone m; **the** ~ (*MUS*) gli ottoni.

brass band n fanfara.

brassière ['bræsɪə*] n reggipetto, reggiseno.

brass tacks npl: **to get down to** ~ (*col*) venire al sodo.

brat [bræt] n (*pej*) marmocchio, monello/a.

bravado [brə'vɑːdəu] n spavalderia.

brave [breɪv] adj coraggioso(a) ♦ n guerriero m pellerossa inv ♦ vt affrontare.

bravery ['breɪvərɪ] n coraggio.

bravo [brɑː'vəu] excl bravo!, bene!

brawl [brɔːl] n rissa ♦ vi azzuffarsi.

brawn [brɔːn] n muscolo; (*meat*) carne f di testa di maiale.

brawny ['brɔːnɪ] adj muscoloso(a).

bray [breɪ] n raglio ♦ vi ragliare.

brazen ['breɪzn] adj svergognato(a) ♦ vt: **to** ~ **it out** fare lo sfacciato.

brazier ['breɪzɪə*] n braciere m.

Brazil [brə'zɪl] n Brasile m.

Brazilian [brə'zɪljən] adj, n brasiliano(a).

Brazil nut n noce f del Brasile.

breach [briːtʃ] vt aprire una breccia in ♦ n (*gap*) breccia, varco; (*estrangement*) rottura; (*of duty*) abuso; (*breaking*): ~ **of contract** rottura di contratto; ~ **of the peace** violazione f dell'ordine pubblico; ~

of trust abuso di fiducia.

bread [brɛd] n pane m; (col: money) grana; **to earn one's daily** ~ guadagnarsi il pane; **to know which side one's** ~ **is buttered on** saper fare i propri interessi; ~ **and butter** n pane e burro; (fig) mezzi mpl di sussistenza.

breadbin ['brɛdbɪn] n (BRIT) cassetta f portapane inv.

breadboard ['brɛdbɔːd] n tagliere m (per il pane); (COMPUT) pannello per esperimenti.

breadbox ['brɛdbɔks] n (US) cassetta f portapane inv.

breadcrumbs ['brɛdkrʌmz] npl briciole fpl; (CULIN) pangrattato.

breadline ['brɛdlaɪn] n: **to be on the** ~ avere appena denaro per vivere.

breadth [brɛtθ] n larghezza.

breadwinner ['brɛdwɪnə*] n chi guadagna il pane per tutta la famiglia.

break [breɪk] vb (pt broke [brəuk], pp broken ['brəukən]) vt rompere; (law) violare; (promise) mancare a ♦ vi rompersi; (weather) cambiare ♦ n (gap) breccia; (fracture) rottura; (rest, also SCOL) intervallo; (: short) pausa; (chance) possibilità f inv; (holiday) vacanza; **to** ~ **one's leg** etc rompersi la gamba etc; **to** ~ **a record** battere un primato; **to** ~ **the news to sb** comunicare per primo la notizia a qn; **to** ~ **with sb** (fig) rompere con qn; **to** ~ **even** vi coprire le spese; **to** ~ **free** or **loose** liberarsi; **without a** ~ senza una pausa; **to have** or **take a** ~ (few minutes) fare una pausa; (holiday) prendere un po' di riposo; **a lucky** ~ un colpo di fortuna.

►**break down** vt (figures, data) analizzare; (door etc) buttare giù, abbattere; (resistance) stroncare ♦ vi crollare; (MED) avere un esaurimento (nervoso); (AUT) guastarsi.

►**break in** vt (horse etc) domare ♦ vi (burglar) fare irruzione.

►**break into** vt fus (house) fare irruzione in.

►**break off** vi (speaker) interrompersi; (branch) troncarsi ♦ vt (talks, engagement) rompere.

►**break open** vt (door etc) sfondare.

►**break out** vi evadere; **to** ~ **out in spots** coprirsi di macchie.

►**break through** vi: **the sun broke through** il sole ha fatto capolino tra le nuvole ♦ vt (defences, barrier) sfondare, penetrare in; (crowd) aprirsi un varco in or tra, aprirsi un passaggio in or tra.

►**break up** vi (partnership) sciogliersi; (friends) separarsi ♦ vt fare in pezzi, spaccare; (fight etc) interrompere, far cessare; (marriage) finire.

breakable ['breɪkəbl] adj fragile; ~**s** npl oggetti mpl fragili.

breakage ['breɪkɪdʒ] n rottura; **to pay for** ~**s** pagare i danni.

breakaway ['breɪkəweɪ] adj (group etc) scissionista, dissidente.

break-dancing ['breɪkdɑːnsɪŋ] n breakdance f.

breakdown ['breɪkdaun] n (AUT) guasto; (in communications) interruzione f; (MED: also: **nervous** ~) esaurimento nervoso; (of payments etc) resoconto.

breakdown service n (BRIT) servizio riparazioni.

breakdown van n carro m attrezzi inv.

breaker ['breɪkə*] n frangente m.

breakeven ['breɪk'iːvn] cpd: ~ **chart** diagramma m del punto di rottura or pareggio; ~ **point** punto di rottura or pareggio.

breakfast ['brɛkfəst] n colazione f.

breakfast cereal n fiocchi mpl d'avena or di mais etc.

break-in ['breɪkɪn] n irruzione f.

breaking point ['breɪkɪŋ-] n punto di rottura.

breakthrough ['breɪkθruː] n (MIL) breccia; (fig) passo avanti.

break-up ['breɪkʌp] n (of partnership, marriage) rottura.

break-up value n (COMM) valore m di realizzo.

breakwater ['breɪkwɔːtə*] n frangiflutti m inv.

breast [brɛst] n (of woman) seno; (chest) petto.

breast-feed ['brɛstfiːd] vt, vi (irreg: like feed) allattare (al seno).

breast pocket n taschino.

breast-stroke ['brɛststrəuk] n nuoto a rana.

breath [brɛθ] n fiato; **out of** ~ senza fiato; **to go out for a** ~ **of air** andare a prendere una boccata d'aria.

Breathalyser ® ['brɛθəlaɪzə*] n alcoltest m inv.

breathe [briːð] vt, vi respirare; **I won't** ~ **a word about it** non fiaterò.

►**breathe in** vi inspirare ♦ vt respirare.

►**breathe out** vt, vi espirare.

breather ['briːðə*] n attimo di respiro.

breathing ['briːðɪŋ] n respiro, respirazione f.

breathing space n (fig) attimo di respiro.

breathless ['brɛθlɪs] adj senza fiato; (with

excitement) con il fiato sospeso.
breath-taking ['brɛθteɪkɪŋ] *adj*
sbalorditivo(a).
breath test *n* ≈ prova del palloncino.
-bred [brɛd] *suffix*: **to be well/ill~** essere ben
educato(a)/maleducato(a).
breed [briːd] *vb* (*pt, pp* **bred** [brɛd]) *vt*
allevare; (*fig: hate, suspicion*) generare,
provocare ♦ *vi* riprodursi ♦ *n* razza,
varietà *f inv*.
breeder ['briːdə*] *n* (*PHYSICS: also:* ~
reactor) reattore *m* autofertilizzante.
breeding ['briːdɪŋ] *n* riproduzione *f*;
allevamento.
breeze [briːz] *n* brezza.
breeze block *n* (*BRIT*) *mattone composto
di scorie di coke*.
breezy ['briːzɪ] *adj* arioso(a); allegro(a).
Breton ['brɛtən] *adj*, *n* brettone (*m/f*).
brevity ['brɛvɪtɪ] *n* brevità.
brew [bruː] *vt* (*tea*) fare un infuso di; (*beer*)
fare; (*plot*) tramare ♦ *vi* (*tea*) essere in
infusione; (*beer*) essere in
fermentazione; (*fig*) bollire in pentola.
brewer ['bruːə*] *n* birraio.
brewery ['bruːərɪ] *n* fabbrica di birra.
briar ['braɪə*] *n* (*thorny bush*) rovo; (*wild
rose*) rosa selvatica.
bribe [braɪb] *n* bustarella ♦ *vt* comprare; **to
~ sb to do sth** pagare qn sottobanco
perché faccia qc.
bribery ['braɪbərɪ] *n* corruzione *f*.
bric-a-brac ['brɪkəbræk] *n* bric-a-brac *m*.
brick [brɪk] *n* mattone *m*.
bricklayer ['brɪkleɪə*] *n* muratore *m*.
brickwork ['brɪkwəːk] *n* muratura in
mattoni.
brickworks ['brɪkwəːks] *n* fabbrica di
mattoni.
bridal ['braɪdl] *adj* nuziale; ~ **party** corteo
nuziale.
bride [braɪd] *n* sposa.
bridegroom ['braɪdgruːm] *n* sposo.
bridesmaid ['braɪdzmeɪd] *n* damigella
d'onore.
bridge [brɪdʒ] *n* ponte *m*; (*NAUT*) ponte di
comando; (*of nose*) dorso; (*CARDS,
DENTISTRY*) bridge *m inv* ♦ *vt* (*river*) fare un
ponte sopra; (*gap*) colmare.
bridging loan ['brɪdʒɪŋ-] *n* (*BRIT*)
anticipazione *f* sul mutuo.
bridle ['braɪdl] *n* briglia ♦ *vt* tenere a freno;
(*horse*) mettere la briglia a ♦ *vi* (*in anger
etc*) adombrarsi, adontarsi.
bridle path *n* sentiero (per cavalli).
brief [briːf] *adj* breve ♦ *n* (*LAW*) comparsa
♦ *vt* (*MIL etc*) dare istruzioni a; **in ~** ... in
breve ..., a farla breve ...; **to ~ sb** (*about*

sth) mettere qn al corrente (di qc); *see
also* **briefs**.
briefcase ['briːfkeɪs] *n* cartella.
briefing ['briːfɪŋ] *n* istruzioni *fpl*.
briefly ['briːflɪ] *adv* (*speak, visit*)
brevemente; (*glimpse*) di sfuggita.
briefness ['briːfnɪs] *n* brevità.
briefs [briːfs] *npl* mutande *fpl*.
Brig. *abbr* = **brigadier**.
brigade [brɪ'geɪd] *n* (*MIL*) brigata.
brigadier [brɪgə'dɪə*] *n* generale *m* di
brigata.
bright [braɪt] *adj* luminoso(a); (*person*)
sveglio(a); (*colour*) vivace; **to look on the
~ side** vedere il lato positivo delle cose.
brighten ['braɪtn] (*also:* ~ **up**) *vt* (*room*)
rendere luminoso(a); rallegrare ♦ *vi*
schiarirsi; (*person*) rallegrarsi.
brightly ['braɪtlɪ] *adv* (*shine*) vivamente,
intensamente; (*smile*) radiosamente; (*talk*)
con animazione.
brill [brɪl] *excl* (*BRIT col*) stupendo!,
fantastico!
brilliance ['brɪljəns] *n* splendore *m*; (*fig: of
person*) genialità, talento.
brilliant ['brɪljənt] *adj* brillante; (*sunshine*)
sfolgorante.
brim [brɪm] *n* orlo.
brimful ['brɪm'ful] *adj* pieno(a) *or* colmo(a)
fino all'orlo; (*fig*) pieno(a).
brine [braɪn] *n* acqua salmastra; (*CULIN*)
salamoia.
bring, *pt*, *pp* **brought** [brɪŋ, brɔːt] *vt* portare;
to ~ sth to an end mettere fine a qc; **I
can't ~ myself to sack him** non so
risolvermi a licenziarlo.
▶**bring about** *vt* causare.
▶**bring back** *vt* riportare.
▶**bring down** *vt* (*lower*) far scendere;
(*shoot down*) abbattere; (*government*) far
cadere.
▶**bring forward** *vt* portare avanti; (*in time*)
anticipare; (*BOOK-KEEPING*) riportare.
▶**bring in** *vt* (*person*) far entrare; (*object*)
portare; (*POL: bill*) presentare;
(: *legislation*) introdurre; (*LAW: verdict*)
emettere; (*produce: income*) rendere.
▶**bring off** *vt* (*task, plan*) portare a
compimento; (*deal*) concludere.
▶**bring out** *vt* (*meaning*) mettere in
evidenza; (*new product*) lanciare; (*book*)
pubblicare, fare uscire.
▶**bring round** *or* **to** *vt* (*unconscious person*)
far rinvenire.
▶**bring up** *vt* allevare; (*question*)
introdurre.
brink [brɪŋk] *n* orlo; **on the ~ of doing sth**
sul punto di fare qc; **she was on the ~ of**

tears era lì lì per piangere.

brisk [brɪsk] *adj (person, tone)* spiccio(a), sbrigativo(a); (: *abrupt*) brusco(a); (*wind*) fresco(a); (*trade etc*) vivace, attivo(a); **to go for a ~ walk** fare una camminata di buon passo; **business is ~** gli affari vanno bene.

bristle ['brɪsl] *n* setola ♦ *vi* rizzarsi; **bristling with** irto(a) di.

bristly ['brɪslɪ] *adj (chin)* ispido(a); (*beard, hair*) irsuto(a), setoloso(a).

Brit [brɪt] *n abbr (col:* = *British person)* britannico/a.

Britain ['brɪtən] *n* Gran Bretagna.

British ['brɪtɪʃ] *adj* britannico(a); **the ~** *npl* i Britannici; **the ~ Isles** *npl* le Isole Britanniche.

British Rail (BR) *n compagnia ferroviaria britannica,* ≈ Ferrovie *fpl* dello Stato (F.S.).

British Summer Time *n* ora legale (*in Gran Bretagna*).

Briton ['brɪtən] *n* britannico/a.

Brittany ['brɪtənɪ] *n* Bretagna.

brittle ['brɪtl] *adj* fragile.

Br(o) *abbr (REL)* = **brother.**

broach [brəʊtʃ] *vt (subject)* affrontare.

broad [brɔːd] *adj* largo(a); (*distinction*) generale; (*accent*) spiccato(a) ♦ *n (US col)* bellona; **~ hint** allusione *f* esplicita; **in ~ daylight** in pieno giorno; **the ~ outlines** le grandi linee.

broad bean *n* fava.

broadcast ['brɔːdkɑːst] *n* trasmissione *f* ♦ *vb (pt, pp* **broadcast**) *vt* trasmettere per radio (*or* per televisione) ♦ *vi* fare una trasmissione.

broadcaster ['brɔːdkɑːstə*] *n* annunciatore/trice radiotelevisivo(a) (*or* radiofonico(a)).

broadcasting ['brɔːdkɑːstɪŋ] *n* radiodiffusione *f*; televisione *f*.

broadcasting station *n* stazione *f* trasmittente.

broaden ['brɔːdn] *vt* allargare ♦ *vi* allargarsi.

broadly ['brɔːdlɪ] *adv (fig)* in generale.

broad-minded ['brɔːd'maɪndɪd] *adj* di mente aperta.

broadsheet ['brɔːdʃiːt] *n (BRIT)* giornale *m* (*si contrappone al tabloid che è di formato più piccolo*).

broccoli ['brɒkəlɪ] *n (BOT)* broccolo; (*CULIN*) broccoli *mpl*.

brochure ['brəʊʃjʊə*] *n* dépliant *m inv.*

brogue [brəʊg] *n (shoe)* scarpa rozza in cuoio; (*accent*) accento irlandese.

broil [brɔɪl] *vt* cuocere a fuoco vivo.

broke [brəʊk] *pt of* **break** ♦ *adj (col)* squattrinato(a); **to go ~** fare fallimento.

broken ['brəʊkən] *pp of* **break** ♦ *adj (gen)* rotto(a); (*stick, promise, vow*) spezzato(a); (*marriage*) fallito(a); **he comes from a ~ home** i suoi sono divisi; **in ~ French/ English** in un francese/inglese stentato.

broken-down ['brəʊkən'daʊn] *adj (car)* in panne, rotto(a); (*machine*) guasto(a), fuori uso; (*house*) abbandonato(a), in rovina.

broken-hearted ['brəʊkən'hɑːtɪd] *adj:* **to be ~** avere il cuore spezzato.

broker ['brəʊkə*] *n* agente *m.*

brokerage ['brəʊkərɪdʒ] *n (COMM)* commissione *f* di intermediazione.

brolly ['brɒlɪ] *n (BRIT col)* ombrello.

bronchitis [brɒŋ'kaɪtɪs] *n* bronchite *f.*

bronze [brɒnz] *n* bronzo.

bronzed [brɒnzd] *adj* abbronzato(a).

brooch [brəʊtʃ] *n* spilla.

brood [bruːd] *n* covata ♦ *vi (hen)* covare; (*person*) rimuginare.

broody ['bruːdɪ] *adj (fig)* cupo(a) e taciturno(a).

brook [brʊk] *n* ruscello.

broom [brʊm] *n* scopa.

broomstick ['brʊmstɪk] *n* manico di scopa.

Bros. *abbr (COMM:* = *brothers)* F.lli (= *Fratelli*).

broth [brɒθ] *n* brodo.

brothel ['brɒθl] *n* bordello.

brother ['brʌðə*] *n* fratello.

brotherhood ['brʌðəhud] *n* fratellanza; confraternità *f inv.*

brother-in-law ['brʌðərɪnlɔː] *n* cognato.

brotherly ['brʌðəlɪ] *adj* fraterno(a).

brought [brɔːt] *pt, pp of* **bring.**

brought forward (b/f) *adj (COMM)* riportato(a).

brow [braʊ] *n* fronte *f*; (*rare, gen:* **eye~**) sopracciglio; (*of hill*) cima.

browbeat ['braʊbiːt] *vt* intimidire.

brown [braʊn] *adj* bruno(a), marrone; (*hair*) castano(a) ♦ *n (colour)* color *m* bruno *or* marrone ♦ *vt (CULIN)* rosolare; **to go ~** (*person*) abbronzarsi; (*leaves*) ingiallire.

brown bread *n* pane *m* integrale, pane nero.

brownie ['braʊnɪ] *n* giovane esploratrice *f.*

brown paper *n* carta da pacchi *or* da imballaggio.

brown rice *n* riso greggio.

brown sugar *n* zucchero greggio.

browse [braʊz] *vi (animal)* brucare; (*in bookshop etc*) curiosare ♦ *n:* **to have a ~ (around)** dare un'occhiata (in giro); **to ~ through a book** sfogliare un libro.

bruise [bru:z] *n* ammaccatura; (*on person*) livido ◆ *vt* ammaccare; (*leg etc*) farsi un livido a; (*fig: feelings*) urtare ◆ *vi* (*fruit*) ammaccarsi.

Brum [brʌm] *n abbr*, **Brummagem** ['brʌmədʒəm] *n* (*col*) = Birmingham.

Brummie ['brʌmɪ] *n* (*col*) abitante *m/f* di Birmingham; originario/a di Birmingham.

brunch [brʌntʃ] *n* ricca colazione consumata in tarda mattinata.

brunette [bru:'nɛt] *n* bruna.

brunt [brʌnt] *n*: **the ~ of** (*attack, criticism etc*) il peso maggiore di.

brush [brʌʃ] *n* spazzola; (*quarrel*) schermaglia ◆ *vt* spazzolare; (*gen*: ~ **past**, ~ **against**) sfiorare; **to have a ~ with sb** (*verbally*) avere uno scontro con qn; (*physically*) venire a diverbio *or* alle mani con qn; **to have a ~ with the police** avere delle noie con la polizia.

►**brush aside** *vt* scostare.

►**brush up** *vt* (*knowledge*) rinfrescare.

brushed [brʌʃt] *adj* (*TECH*: *steel, chrome etc*) sabbiato(a); (*nylon, denim etc*) pettinato(a).

brush-off ['brʌʃɔf] *n*: **to give sb the ~** dare il ben servito a qn.

brushwood ['brʌʃwud] *n* macchia.

brusque [bru:sk] *adj* (*person, manner*) brusco(a); (*tone*) secco(a).

Brussels ['brʌslz] *n* Bruxelles *f*.

Brussels sprout *n* cavolo di Bruxelles.

brutal ['bru:tl] *adj* brutale.

brutality [bru:'tælɪtɪ] *n* brutalità.

brutalize ['bru:tǝlaɪz] *vt* (*harden*) abbrutire; (*ill-treat*) brutalizzare.

brute [bru:t] *n* bestia; **by ~ force** con la forza, a viva forza.

brutish ['bru:tɪʃ] *adj* da bruto.

BS *n abbr* (*US*: = *Bachelor of Science*) titolo di studio.

bs *abbr* = **bill of sale**.

BSA *n abbr* (*US*) = *Boy Scouts of America*.

BSc *n abbr see* **Bachelor of Science**.

BSE *n abbr* (= *bovine spongiform encephalopathy*) encefalite *f* bovina spongiforme.

BSI *n abbr* (= *British Standards Institution*) associazione per la normalizzazione.

BST *abbr* (= *British Summer Time*) *ora legale.*

Bt. *abbr* (*BRIT*) = **baronet**.

btu *n abbr* (= *British thermal unit*) Btu *m* (= *1054.2 joules*).

bubble ['bʌbl] *n* bolla ◆ *vi* ribollire; (*sparkle, fig*) essere effervescente.

bubble bath *n* bagno *m* schiuma *inv*.

bubblejet printer ['bʌbldʒɛt-] *n* stampante *f* a getto d'inchiostro.

bubbly ['bʌblɪ] *adj* (*also fig*) frizzante ◆ *n* (*col*) (*champagne*) spumante *m*.

Bucharest [bu:kǝ'rɛst] *n* Bucarest *f*.

buck [bʌk] *n* maschio (*di camoscio, caprone, coniglio etc*); (*US col*) dollaro ◆ *vi* sgroppare; **to pass the ~ (to sb)** scaricare (su di qn) la propria responsabilità.

►**buck up** *vi* (*cheer up*) rianimarsi ◆ *vt*: **to ~ one's ideas up** mettere la testa a partito.

bucket ['bʌkɪt] *n* secchio ◆ *vi* (*BRIT col*): **the rain is ~ing (down)** piove a catinelle.

> **Buckingham Palace** *è la residenza ufficiale a Londra del sovrano britannico. Costruita nel 1703 per il duca di Buckingham, fu acquistata nel 1762 dal re Giorgio III e ricostruita tra il 1821 e il 1838 sotto la guida dell'architetto John Nash. All'inizio del Novecento alcune sue parti sono state ulteriormente modificate.*

buckle ['bʌkl] *n* fibbia ◆ *vt* affibbiare; (*warp*) deformare.

►**buckle down** *vi* mettersi sotto.

Bucks [bʌks] *abbr* (*BRIT*) = *Buckinghamshire*.

bud [bʌd] *n* gemma; (*of flower*) boccio ◆ *vi* germogliare; (*flower*) sbocciare.

Budapest [bju:dǝ'pɛst] *n* Budapest *f*.

Buddha ['budǝ] *n* Budda *m*.

Buddhism ['budɪzǝm] *n* buddismo.

Buddhist ['budɪst] *adj*, *n* buddista (*m/f*).

budding ['bʌdɪŋ] *adj* (*flower*) in boccio; (*poet etc*) in erba.

buddy ['bʌdɪ] *n* (*US*) compagno.

budge [bʌdʒ] *vt* scostare ◆ *vi* spostarsi.

budgerigar ['bʌdʒǝrɪgɑ:*] *n* pappagallino.

budget ['bʌdʒɪt] *n* bilancio preventivo ◆ *vi*: **to ~ for sth** fare il bilancio per qc; **I'm on a tight ~** devo contare la lira; **she works out her ~ every month** fa il preventivo delle spese ogni mese.

budgie ['bʌdʒɪ] *n* = **budgerigar**.

Buenos Aires ['bweɪnɔs'aɪrɪz] *n* Buenos Aires *f*.

buff [bʌf] *adj* color camoscio *inv* ◆ *n* (*enthusiast*) appassionato/a.

buffalo, *pl* ~ *or* ~**es** ['bʌfǝlǝu] *n* bufalo; (*US*) bisonte *m*.

buffer ['bʌfǝ*] *n* respingente *m*; (*COMPUT*) memoria tampone, buffer *m inv*.

buffering ['bʌfǝrɪŋ] *n* (*COMPUT*) bufferizzazione *f*, memorizzazione *f* transitoria.

buffer state *n* stato cuscinetto.

buffer zone *n* zona *f* cuscinetto *inv*.

buffet *n* ['bufeɪ] (*food, BRIT: bar*) buffet *m inv* ♦ *vt* ['bʌfɪt] schiaffeggiare; scuotere; urtare.
buffet car *n* (*BRIT RAIL*) ≈ servizio ristoro.
buffet lunch *n* pranzo in piedi.
buffoon [bə'fuːn] *n* buffone *m*.
bug [bʌg] *n* (*insect*) cimice *f*; (: *gen*) insetto; (*fig: germ*) virus *m inv*; (*spy device*) microfono spia; (*COMPUT*) bug *m inv*, errore *m* nel programma ♦ *vt* mettere sotto controllo; (*room*) installare microfoni spia in; (*annoy*) scocciare; **I've got the travel ~** (*fig*) mi è presa la mania dei viaggi.
bugbear ['bʌgbɛə*] *n* spauracchio.
bugger ['bʌgə*] (*col!*) *n* bastardo (*!*) ♦ *vb*: ~ **off!** vaffanculo! (*!*); ~ (**it**)! merda! (*!*).
bugle ['bjuːgl] *n* tromba.
build [bɪld] *n* (*of person*) corporatura ♦ *vt* (*pt, pp* **built** [bɪlt]) costruire.
▶**build on** *vt fus* (*fig*) prendere il via da.
▶**build up** *vt* (*establish: business*) costruire; (: *reputation*) fare, consolidare; (*increase: production*) allargare, incrementare; **don't ~ your hopes up too soon** non sperarci troppo.
builder ['bɪldə*] *n* costruttore *m*.
building ['bɪldɪŋ] *n* costruzione *f*; edificio; (*also*: ~ **trade**) edilizia.
building contractor *n* costruttore *m*, imprenditore *m* (edile).
building industry *n* industria edilizia.
building site *n* cantiere *m* di costruzione.
building society *n* società immobiliare e finanziaria.

Le **building society** *sono società immobiliari e finanziarie che forniscono anche numerosi servizi bancari ai clienti che vi investono i risparmi. Chi ha bisogno di un prestito per l'acquisto di una casa si rivolge in genere ad una building society.*

---

building trade *n* = **building industry**.
build-up ['bɪldʌp] *n* (*of gas etc*) accumulo; (*publicity*): **to give sb/sth a good ~** fare buona pubblicità a qn/qc.
built [bɪlt] *pt, pp of* **build**; **well-~** robusto(a).
built-in ['bɪlt'ɪn] *adj* (*cupboard*) a muro; (*device*) incorporato(a).
built-up area ['bɪltʌp-] *n* abitato.
bulb [bʌlb] *n* (*BOT*) bulbo; (*ELEC*) lampadina.
bulbous ['bʌlbəs] *adj* bulboso(a).
Bulgaria [bʌl'gɛərɪə] *n* Bulgaria.
Bulgarian [bʌl'gɛərɪən] *adj* bulgaro(a) ♦ *n* bulgaro/a; (*LING*) bulgaro.
bulge [bʌldʒ] *n* rigonfiamento; (*in birth rate, sales*) punta ♦ *vi* essere protuberante *or*

rigonfio(a); **to be bulging with** essere pieno(a) *or* zeppo(a) di.
bulimia [bə'lɪmɪə] *n* bulimia.
bulk [bʌlk] *n* massa, volume *m*; **the ~ of** il grosso di; (**to buy**) **in ~** (comprare) in grande quantità.
bulk buying *n* acquisto di merce in grande quantità.
bulk carrier *n* grossa nave *f* da carico.
bulkhead ['bʌlkhɛd] *n* paratia.
bulky ['bʌlkɪ] *adj* grosso(a); voluminoso(a).
bull [bul] *n* toro; (*STOCK EXCHANGE*) rialzista *m/f*; (*REL*) bolla (papale).
bulldog ['buldɔg] *n* bulldog *m inv*.
bulldoze ['buldəuz] *vt* aprire *or* spianare col bulldozer; **I was ~d into doing it** (*fig col*) mi ci hanno costretto con la prepotenza.
bulldozer ['buldəuzə*] *n* bulldozer *m inv*.
bullet ['bulɪt] *n* pallottola.
bulletin ['bulɪtɪn] *n* bollettino.
bulletin board *n* (*COMPUT*) bulletin board *m inv*.
bullet-proof ['bulɪtpruːf] *adj* a prova di proiettile; ~ **vest** giubbotto antiproiettile.
bullfight ['bulfaɪt] *n* corrida.
bullfighter ['bulfaɪtə*] *n* torero.
bullfighting ['bulfaɪtɪŋ] *n* tauromachia.
bullion ['buljən] *n* oro *or* argento in lingotti.
bullock ['bulək] *n* giovenco.
bullring ['bulrɪŋ] *n* arena (per corride).
bull's-eye ['bulzaɪ] *n* centro del bersaglio.
bullshit ['bulʃɪt] (*col!*) *excl, n* stronzate *fpl* (*!*) ♦ *vi* raccontare stronzate (*!*) ♦ *vt* raccontare stronzate a (*!*).
bully ['bulɪ] *n* prepotente *m* ♦ *vt* angariare; (*frighten*) intimidire.
bullying ['bulɪɪŋ] *n* prepotenze *fpl*.
bum [bʌm] *n* (*col: backside*) culo; (*tramp*) vagabondo/a; (*US: idler*) fannullone/a.
▶**bum around** *vi* (*col*) fare il vagabondo.
bumblebee ['bʌmblbiː] *n* (*ZOOL*) bombo.
bumf [bʌmf] *n* (*col: forms etc*) scartoffie *fpl*.
bump [bʌmp] *n* (*blow*) colpo; (*jolt*) scossa; (*noise*) botto; (*on road etc*) protuberanza; (*on head*) bernoccolo ♦ *vt* battere; (*car*) urtare, sbattere.
▶**bump along** *vi* procedere sobbalzando.
▶**bump into** *vt fus* scontrarsi con; (*col: meet*) imbattersi in, incontrare per caso.
bumper ['bʌmpə*] *n* (*BRIT*) paraurti *m inv* ♦ *adj*: ~ **harvest** raccolto eccezionale.
bumper cars *npl* (*US*) autoscontri *mpl*.
bumph [bʌmf] *n* = **bumf**.
bumptious ['bʌmpʃəs] *adj* presuntuoso(a).
bumpy ['bʌmpɪ] *adj* (*road*) dissestato(a);

(*journey, flight*) movimentato(a).
bun [bʌn] *n* focaccia; (*of hair*) crocchia.
bunch [bʌntʃ] *n* (*of flowers, keys*) mazzo; (*of bananas*) ciuffo; (*of people*) gruppo; ~ **of grapes** grappolo d'uva.
bundle ['bʌndl] *n* fascio ♦ *vt* (*also*: ~ **up**) legare in un fascio; (*put*): **to** ~ **sth/sb into** spingere qc/qn in.
▶**bundle off** *vt* (*person*) mandare via in gran fretta.
▶**bundle out** *vt* far uscire (senza tante cerimonie).
bun fight *n* (*BRIT: col*) tè *m inv* (*ricevimento*).
bung [bʌŋ] *n* tappo ♦ *vt* (*BRIT: throw: also*: ~ **into**) buttare; (*also*: ~ **up**: *pipe, hole*) tappare, otturare; **my nose is** ~**ed up** (*col*) ho il naso otturato.
bungalow ['bʌŋgələu] *n* bungalow *m inv*.
bungee jumping ['bʌndʒiː'dʒʌmpɪŋ] *n* salto nel vuoto da ponti, grattacieli etc con un cavo fissato alla caviglia.
bungle ['bʌŋgl] *vt* abborracciare.
bunion ['bʌnjən] *n* callo (al piede).
bunk [bʌŋk] *n* cuccetta.
▶**bunk off** *vi* (*BRIT col*): **to** ~ **off school** marinare la scuola; **I'll** ~ **off at 3 this afternoon** oggi me la filo dal lavoro alle 3.
bunk beds *npl* letti *mpl* a castello.
bunker ['bʌŋkə*] *n* (*coal store*) ripostiglio per il carbone; (*MIL, GOLF*) bunker *m inv*.
bunny ['bʌnɪ] *n* (*also*: ~ **rabbit**) coniglietto.
bunny girl *n* coniglietta.
bunny hill *n* (*US SKI*) pista per principianti.
bunting ['bʌntɪŋ] *n* pavesi *mpl*, bandierine *fpl*.
buoy [bɔɪ] *n* boa.
▶**buoy up** *vt* tenere a galla; (*fig*) sostenere.
buoyancy ['bɔɪənsɪ] *n* (*of ship*) galleggiabilità.
buoyant ['bɔɪənt] *adj* galleggiante; (*fig*) vivace; (*COMM: market*) sostenuto(a); (*prices, currency*) stabile.
burden ['bəːdn] *n* carico, fardello ♦ *vt* caricare; (*oppress*) opprimere; **to be a** ~ **to sb** essere di peso a qn.
bureau, *pl* ~**x** ['bjuərəu, -z] *n* (*BRIT: writing desk*) scrivania; (*US: chest of drawers*) cassettone *m*; (*office*) ufficio, agenzia.
bureaucracy [bjuə'rɔkrəsɪ] *n* burocrazia.
bureaucrat ['bjuərəkræt] *n* burocrate *m/f*.
bureaucratic [bjuərə'krætɪk] *adj* burocratico(a).
burgeon ['bəːdʒən] *vi* svilupparsi rapidamente.
burger ['bəːgə*] *n* hamburger *m inv*.
burglar ['bəːglə*] *n* scassinatore *m*.
burglar alarm *n* antifurto *m inv*.
burglarize ['bəːgləraɪz] *vt* (*US*) svaligiare.

burglary ['bəːglərɪ] *n* furto con scasso.
burgle ['bəːgl] *vt* svaligiare.
Burgundy ['bəːgəndɪ] *n* Borgogna.
burial ['bɛrɪəl] *n* sepoltura.
burial ground *n* cimitero.
burly ['bəːlɪ] *adj* robusto(a).
Burma ['bəːmə] *n* Birmania; *see* **Myanmar**.
Burmese [bəː'miːz] *adj* birmano(a) ♦ *n* (*pl inv*) birmano/a; (*LING*) birmano.
burn [bəːn] *vt, vi* (*pt, pp* **burned** *or* **burnt** [bəːnt]) bruciare ♦ *n* bruciatura, scottatura; (*MED*) ustione *f*; **I've** ~**t myself!** mi sono bruciato!; **the cigarette** ~**t a hole in her dress** si è fatta un buco nel vestito con la sigaretta.
▶**burn down** *vt* distruggere col fuoco.
▶**burn out** *vt* (*subj: writer etc*): **to** ~ **o.s. out** esaurirsi.
burner ['bəːnə*] *n* fornello.
burning ['bəːnɪŋ] *adj* (*building, forest*) in fiamme; (*issue, question*) scottante.
burnish ['bəːnɪʃ] *vt* brunire.

Burns night *è la festa celebrata il 25 gennaio per commemorare il poeta scozzese Robert Burns (1759-1796). Gli scozzesi festeggiano questa data con una cena a base di* haggis *e* whisky, *spesso al suono di una cornamusa; durante la cena vengono recitate le poesie di Robert Burns e vengono letti discorsi alla sua memoria.*

---

burnt [bəːnt] *pt, pp of* **burn**.
burnt sugar *n* (*BRIT*) caramello.
burp [bəːp] (*col*) *n* rutto ♦ *vi* ruttare.
burrow ['bʌrəu] *n* tana ♦ *vt* scavare.
bursar ['bəːsə*] *n* economo/a; (*BRIT: student*) borsista *m/f*.
bursary ['bəːsərɪ] *n* (*BRIT*) borsa di studio.
burst [bəːst] *vb* (*pt, pp* **burst**) *vt* far scoppiare *or* esplodere ♦ *vi* esplodere; (*tyre*) scoppiare ♦ *n* scoppio; (*also*: ~ **pipe**) rottura nel tubo, perdita; ~ **of energy/laughter** scoppio d'energia/di risa; **a** ~ **of applause** uno scroscio d'applausi; **a** ~ **of speed** uno scatto (di velocità); ~ **blood vessel** rottura di un vaso sanguigno; **the river has** ~ **its banks** il fiume ha rotto gli argini *or* ha straripato; **to** ~ **into flames/tears** scoppiare in fiamme/lacrime; **to be** ~**ing with** essere pronto a scoppiare di; **to** ~ **out laughing** scoppiare a ridere; **to** ~ **open** *vi* aprirsi improvvisamente; (*door*) spalancarsi.
▶**burst into** *vt fus* (*room etc*) irrompere in.
▶**burst out of** *vt fus* precipitarsi fuori da.
bury ['bɛrɪ] *vt* seppellire; **to** ~ **one's face in one's hands** nascondere la faccia tra le

mani; **to ~ one's head in the sand** (*fig*)
fare (la politica del)lo struzzo; **to ~ the
hatchet** (*fig*) seppellire l'ascia di guerra.
bus, **~es** [bʌs, 'bʌsɪz] *n* autobus *m inv.*
bus boy *n* (*US*) aiuto *inv* cameriere/a.
bush [buʃ] *n* cespuglio; (*scrub land*)
macchia.
bushed [buʃt] *adj* (*col*) distrutto(a).
bushel ['buʃl] *n* staio.
bushfire ['buʃfaɪə*] *n grande incendio in
aperta campagna.*
bushy ['buʃɪ] *adj* (*plant, tail, beard*) folto(a);
(*eyebrows*) irsuto(a).
busily ['bɪzɪlɪ] *adv* con impegno,
alacremente.
business ['bɪznɪs] *n* (*matter*) affare *m*;
(*trading*) affari *mpl*; (*firm*) azienda; (*job,
duty*) lavoro; **to be away on ~** essere
andato via per affari; **I'm here on ~** sono
qui per affari; **to do ~ with sb** fare affari
con qn; **he's in the insurance ~** lavora nel
campo delle assicurazioni; **it's none of
my ~** questo non mi riguarda; **he means
~** non scherza.
business address *n* indirizzo di lavoro *or*
d'ufficio.
business card *n* biglietto da visita della
ditta.
businesslike ['bɪznɪslaɪk] *adj* serio(a);
efficiente.
businessman ['bɪznɪsmən] *n* uomo d'affari.
business trip *n* viaggio d'affari.
businesswoman ['bɪznɪswumən] *n* donna
d'affari.
busker ['bʌskə*] *n* (*BRIT*) suonatore/trice
ambulante.
bus lane *n* (*BRIT*) corsia riservata agli
autobus.
bus shelter *n* pensilina (*alla fermata
dell'autobus*).
bus station *n* stazione *f* delle autolinee,
autostazione *f.*
bus stop *n* fermata d'autobus.
bust [bʌst] *n* (*ART*) busto; (*bosom*) seno ♦ *adj*
(*broken*) rotto(a) ♦ *vt* (*col: POLICE: arrest*)
pizzicare, beccare; **to go ~** fallire.
bustle ['bʌsl] *n* movimento, attività ♦ *vi*
darsi da fare.
bustling ['bʌslɪŋ] *adj* (*person*)
indaffarato(a); (*town*) animato(a).
bust-up ['bʌstʌp] *n* (*BRIT col*) lite *f.*
busty ['bʌstɪ] *adj* (*col*) tettone(a).
busy ['bɪzɪ] *adj* occupato(a); (*shop, street*)
molto frequentato(a) ♦ *vt*: **to ~ o.s.** darsi
da fare; **he's a ~ man** (*normally*) è un
uomo molto occupato; (*temporarily*) ha
molto da fare, è molto occupato.
busybody ['bɪzɪbɔdɪ] *n* ficcanaso *m/f inv.*

busy signal *n* (*US*) segnale *m* di occupato.

═══════════════════════════ KEYWORD

but [bʌt] *conj* ma; **I'd love to come, ~ I'm
busy** vorrei tanto venire, ma ho da fare
♦ *prep* (*apart from, except*) eccetto, tranne,
meno; **nothing ~** nient'altro che; **he was
nothing ~ trouble** non dava altro che
guai; **no-one ~ him** solo lui; **no-one ~ him
can do it** nessuno può farlo tranne lui;
the last ~ one (*BRIT*) il(la) penultimo(a);
~ for you/your help se non fosse per te/
per il tuo aiuto; **anything ~ that** tutto ma
non questo; **anything ~ finished** tutt'altro
che finito
♦ *adv* (*just, only*) solo, soltanto; **she's ~ a
child** è solo una bambina; **had I ~ known**
se solo avessi saputo; **I can ~ try** tentar
non nuoce; **all ~ finished** quasi finito.

butane ['bjuːteɪn] *n* (*also*: **~ gas**) butano.
butch [butʃ] *adj* (*woman: pej*) mascolino(a);
(*man*) macho *inv.*
butcher ['butʃə*] *n* macellaio ♦ *vt*
macellare; **~'s (shop)** macelleria.
butler ['bʌtlə*] *n* maggiordomo.
butt [bʌt] *n* (*cask*) grossa botte *f*; (*thick end*)
estremità *f inv* più grossa; (*of gun*) calcio;
(*of cigarette*) mozzicone *m*; (*BRIT fig: target*)
oggetto ♦ *vt* cozzare.
►**butt in** *vi* (*interrupt*) interrompere.
butter ['bʌtə*] *n* burro ♦ *vt* imburrare.
buttercup ['bʌtəkʌp] *n* ranuncolo.
butter dish *n* burriera.
butterfingers ['bʌtəfɪŋgəz] *n* (*col*) mani *fpl*
di ricotta.
butterfly ['bʌtəflaɪ] *n* farfalla; (*SWIMMING:
also*: **~ stroke**) (nuoto a) farfalla.
buttocks ['bʌtəks] *npl* natiche *fpl.*
button ['bʌtn] *n* bottone *m* ♦ *vt* (*also*: **~ up**)
abbottonare ♦ *vi* abbottonarsi.
buttonhole ['bʌtnhəul] *n* asola, occhiello
♦ *vt* (*person*) attaccar bottone a.
buttress ['bʌtrɪs] *n* contrafforte *m.*
buxom ['bʌksəm] *adj* formoso(a).
buy [baɪ] *vt* (*pt, pp* **bought** [bɔːt]) comprare,
acquistare ♦ *n*: **a good/bad ~** un buon/
cattivo acquisto *or* affare; **to ~ sb sth/
sth from sb** comprare qc per qn/qc da qn;
to ~ sb a drink offrire da bere a qn.
►**buy back** *vt* riprendersi, prendersi
indietro.
►**buy in** *vt* (*BRIT: goods*) far provvista di.
►**buy into** *vt fus* (*BRIT COMM*) acquistare
delle azioni di.
►**buy off** *vt* (*col: bribe*) comprare.
►**buy out** *vt* (*business*) rilevare.
►**buy up** *vt* accaparrare.

buyer ['baɪə*] n compratore/trice; ~'s **market** mercato favorevole ai compratori.

buy-out ['baɪaut] n (COMM) acquisto di una società da parte dei suoi dipendenti.

buzz [bʌz] n ronzio; (col: phone call) colpo di telefono ♦ vi ronzare ♦ vt (call on intercom) chiamare al citofono; (: with buzzer) chiamare col cicalino; (AVIAT: plane, building) passare rasente; **my head is** ~**ing** mi gira la testa.

▶**buzz off** vi (BRIT col) filare, levarsi di torno.

buzzard ['bʌzəd] n poiana.

buzzer ['bʌzə*] n cicalino.

buzz word n (col) termine m in voga.

===================== KEYWORD

by [baɪ] prep 1 (referring to cause, agent) da; **killed** ~ **lightning** ucciso da un fulmine; **surrounded** ~ **a fence** circondato da uno steccato; **a painting** ~ **Picasso** un quadro di Picasso

2 (referring to method, manner, means): ~ **bus/car/train** in autobus/macchina/treno, con l'autobus/la macchina/il treno; **to pay** ~ **cheque** pagare con (un) assegno; ~ **moonlight** al chiaro di luna; ~ **saving hard, he** ... risparmiando molto, lui ...

3 (via, through) per; **we came** ~ **Dover** siamo venuti via Dover

4 (close to, past) accanto a; **the house** ~ **the river** la casa sul fiume; **a holiday** ~ **the sea** una vacanza al mare; **she sat** ~ **his bed** si sedette accanto al suo letto; **she rushed** ~ **me** mi è passata accanto correndo; **I go** ~ **the post office every day** passo davanti all'ufficio postale ogni giorno

5 (not later than) per, entro; ~ **4 o'clock** per or entro le 4; ~ **this time tomorrow** domani a quest'ora; ~ **the time I got here it was too late** quando sono arrivato era ormai troppo tardi

6 (during): ~ **day/night** di giorno/notte

7 (amount) a; ~ **the kilo** a chili; **paid** ~ **the hour** pagato all'ora; **to increase** ~ **the hour** aumentare di ora in ora; **one** ~ **one** uno per uno; **little** ~ **little** a poco a poco

8 (MATH, measure): **to divide/multiply** ~ **3** dividere/moltiplicare per 3; **a room 3 metres** ~ **4** una stanza di 3 metri per 4; **it's broader** ~ **a metre** è un metro più largo, è più largo di un metro

9 (according to) per; **to play** ~ **the rules** attenersi alle regole; **it's all right** ~ **me** per me va bene

10: (all) ~ **oneself** (tutto(a)) solo(a); **he did**

it (all) ~ **himself** lo ha fatto (tutto) da solo

11: ~ **the way** a proposito; **this wasn't my idea** ~ **the way** tra l'altro l'idea non è stata mia

♦ adv 1 see **go**; **pass** etc

2: ~ **and** ~ (in past) poco dopo; (in future) fra breve; ~ **and large** nel complesso.

bye(-bye) ['baɪ'baɪ)] excl ciao!, arrivederci!

by(e)-law ['baɪlɔː] n legge f locale.

by-election ['baɪɪlɛkʃən] n (BRIT) elezione f straordinaria.

Una **by-election** in Gran Bretagna e in alcuni paesi del Commonwealth è un'elezione che si tiene per coprire un posto in Parlamento resosi vacante, a governo ancora in carica. È importante in quanto serve a misurare il consenso degli elettori in vista delle successive elezioni politiche.

Byelorussia [bjɛləu'rʌʃə] n Bielorussia, Belorussia.

Byelorussian [bjɛləu'rʌʃən] adj, n = **Belarussian**.

bygone ['baɪgɔn] adj passato(a) ♦ n: let ~**s** be ~**s** mettiamoci una pietra sopra.

bypass ['baɪpɑːs] n circonvallazione f; (MED) by-pass m inv ♦ vt fare una deviazione intorno a.

by-product ['baɪprɔdʌkt] n sottoprodotto; (fig) conseguenza secondaria.

byre ['baɪə*] n (BRIT) stalla.

bystander ['baɪstændə*] n spettatore/trice.

byte [baɪt] n (COMPUT) byte m inv.

byway ['baɪweɪ] n strada secondaria.

byword ['baɪwəːd] n: to be a ~ for essere sinonimo di.

by-your-leave ['baɪjɔː'liːv] n: without so much as a ~ senza nemmeno chiedere il permesso.

Cc

C, c [siː] *n* (*letter*) C, c *f or m inv*; (*SCOL: mark*) ≈ 6 (*sufficiente*); (*MUS*): **C** do; ~ **for Charlie** ≈ C come Como.

C *abbr* (= *Celsius, centigrade*) C.

c. *abbr* (= *century*) sec.; (= *circa*) c; (*US etc*) = **cent(s)**.

CA *abbr* = **Central America**; (*US*) = **California** ♦ *n abbr* (*BRIT*) *see* **chartered accountant**.

ca. *abbr* (= *circa*) ca.

c/a *abbr* = **capital account; credit account; current account**.

CAA *n abbr* (*BRIT*: = *Civil Aviation Authority*, *US*: = *Civil Aeronautics Authority*) organismo di controllo e di sviluppo dell'aviazione civile.

CAB *n abbr* (*BRIT*: = *Citizens' Advice Bureau*) organizzazione per la tutela del consumatore.

cab [kæb] *n* taxi *m inv*; (*of train, truck*) cabina; (*horsedrawn*) carrozza.

cabaret ['kæbəreɪ] *n* cabaret *m inv*.

cabbage ['kæbɪdʒ] *n* cavolo.

cabbie, cabby ['kæbɪ] *n* (*col*), **cab driver** *n* tassista *m/f*.

cabin ['kæbɪn] *n* capanna; (*on ship*) cabina.

cabin cruiser *n* cabinato.

cabinet ['kæbɪnɪt] *n* (*POL*) consiglio dei ministri; (*furniture*) armadietto; (*also*: **display ~**) vetrinetta; **cocktail ~** mobile *m* bar *inv*.

cabinet-maker ['kæbɪnɪt'meɪkə*] *n* stipettaio.

cabinet minister *n* ministro (*membro del Consiglio*).

cable ['keɪbl] *n* cavo; fune *f*; (*TEL*) cablogramma *m* ♦ *vt* telegrafare.

cable-car ['keɪblkɑː*] *n* funivia.

cablegram ['keɪblgræm] *n* cablogramma *m*.

cable railway *n* funicolare *f*.

cable television *n* televisione *f* via cavo.

cache [kæʃ] *n* nascondiglio; **a ~ of food** *etc* un deposito segreto di viveri *etc*.

cackle ['kækl] *vi* schiamazzare.

cactus, *pl* **cacti** ['kæktəs, -taɪ] *n* cactus *m inv*.

CAD *n abbr* (= *computer-aided design*) progettazione *f* con l'ausilio dell'elaboratore.

caddie ['kædɪ] *n* caddie *m inv*.

cadet [kə'dɛt] *n* (*MIL*) cadetto; **police ~** allievo poliziotto.

cadge [kædʒ] *vt* (*col*) scroccare; **to ~ a meal (off sb)** scroccare un pranzo (a qn).

cadre ['kædrɪ] *n* quadro.

Caesarean, (*US*) **Cesarean** [siː'zɛərɪən] *adj*: ~ **(section)** (taglio) cesareo.

CAF *abbr* (*BRIT*: = *cost and freight*) Caf *m*.

café ['kæfeɪ] *n* caffè *m inv*.

cafeteria [kæfɪ'tɪərɪə] *n* self-service *m inv*.

caffein(e) ['kæfiːn] *n* caffeina.

cage [keɪdʒ] *n* gabbia ♦ *vt* mettere in gabbia.

cagey ['keɪdʒɪ] *adj* (*col*) chiuso(a); guardingo(a).

cagoule [kə'guːl] *n* K-way ® *m inv*.

cahoots [kə'huːts] *n*: **to be in ~ (with sb)** essere in combutta (con qn).

CAI *n abbr* (= *computer-aided instruction*) istruzione *f* assistita dall'elaboratore.

Cairo ['kaɪərəu] *n* il Cairo.

cajole [kə'dʒəul] *vt* allettare.

cake [keɪk] *n* torta; ~ **of soap** saponetta; **it's a piece of ~** (*col*) è una cosa da nulla; **he wants to have his ~ and eat it (too)** (*fig*) vuole la botte piena e la moglie ubriaca.

caked [keɪkt] *adj*: ~ **with** incrostato(a) di.

cake shop *n* pasticceria.

Cal. *abbr* (*US*) = *California*.

calamitous [kə'læmɪtəs] *adj* disastroso(a).

calamity [kə'læmɪtɪ] *n* calamità *f inv*.

calcium ['kælsɪəm] *n* calcio.

calculate ['kælkjuleɪt] *vt* calcolare; (*estimate: chances, effect*) valutare.

▶**calculate on** *vt fus*: **to ~ on sth/on doing sth** contare su qc/di fare qc.

calculated ['kælkjuleɪtɪd] *adj* calcolato(a), intenzionale; **a ~ risk** un rischio calcolato.

calculating ['kælkjuleɪtɪŋ] *adj* calcolatore(trice).

calculation [kælkju'leɪʃən] *n* calcolo.

calculator ['kælkjuleɪtə*] *n* calcolatrice *f*.

calculus ['kælkjuləs] *n* calcolo; **integral/differential ~** calcolo integrale/differenziale.

calendar ['kæləndə*] *n* calendario.

calendar year *n* anno civile.

calf, *pl* **calves** [kɑːf, kɑːvz] *n* (*of cow*) vitello; (*of other animals*) piccolo; (*also*: ~**skin**) (pelle *f* di) vitello; (*ANAT*) polpaccio.

caliber ['kælɪbə*] *n* (*US*) = **calibre**.

calibrate ['kælɪbreɪt] *vt* (*gun etc*) calibrare; (*scale of measuring instrument*) tarare.

calibre, (*US*) **caliber** ['kælɪbə*] *n* calibro.

calico ['kælɪkəu] *n* tela grezza, cotone *m* grezzo; (*US*) cotonina stampata.

Calif. *abbr* (*US*) = *California*.
California [kælɪ'fɔːnɪə] *n* California.
calipers ['kælɪpəz] *npl* (*US*) = **callipers**.
call [kɔːl] *vt* (*gen, also TEL*) chiamare; (*announce: flight*) annunciare; (*meeting, strike*) indire, proclamare ♦ *vi* chiamare; (*visit: also:* ~ **in**, ~ **round**) passare ♦ *n* (*shout*) grido, urlo; (*summons: for flight etc*) chiamata; (*fig: lure*) richiamo; (*also:* **telephone** ~) telefonata; **to be on** ~ essere a disposizione; **to make a** ~ telefonare, fare una telefonata; **please give me a** ~ **at 7** per piacere mi chiami alle 7; **to pay a** ~ **on sb** fare (una) visita a qn; **there's not much** ~ **for these items** non c'è molta richiesta di questi articoli; **she's** ~**ed Jane** si chiama Jane; **who is** ~**ing?** (*TEL*) chi parla?; **London** ~**ing** (*RADIO*) qui Londra.
►**call at** *vt fus* (*subj: ship*) fare scalo a; (*: train*) fermarsi a.
►**call back** *vi* (*return*) ritornare; (*TEL*) ritelefonare, richiamare ♦ *vt* (*TEL*) ritelefonare a, richiamare.
►**call for** *vt fus* (*demand: action etc*) richiedere; (*collect: person*) passare a prendere; (*: goods*) ritirare.
►**call in** *vt* (*doctor, expert, police*) chiamare, far venire.
►**call off** *vt* (*meeting, race*) disdire; (*deal*) cancellare; (*dog*) richiamare; **the strike was** ~**ed off** lo sciopero è stato revocato.
►**call on** *vt fus* (*visit*) passare da; (*request*): **to** ~ **on sb to do** chiedere a qn di fare.
►**call out** *vi* urlare ♦ *vt* (*doctor, police, troops*) chiamare.
►**call up** *vt* (*MIL*) richiamare.
Callanetics ® [kælə'netɪks] *nsg* tipo di ginnastica basata sulla ripetizione di piccoli movimenti.
callbox ['kɔːlbɒks] *n* (*BRIT*) cabina telefonica.
caller ['kɔːlə*] *n* persona che chiama; visitatore/trice; **hold the line,** ~! (*TEL*) rimanga in linea, signore (*or* signora)!
call girl *n* ragazza *f* squillo *inv*.
call-in ['kɔːlɪn] *n* (*US*) = **phone-in**.
calling ['kɔːlɪŋ] *n* vocazione *f*.
calling card *n* (*US*) biglietto da visita.
callipers, (*US*) **calipers** ['kælɪpəz] *npl* (*MED*) gambale *m*; (*MATH*) calibro.
callous ['kæləs] *adj* indurito(a), insensibile.
callousness ['kæləsnɪs] *n* insensibilità.
callow ['kæləu] *adj* immaturo(a).
calm [kɑːm] *adj* calmo(a) ♦ *n* calma ♦ *vt* calmare.
►**calm down** *vi* calmarsi ♦ *vt* calmare.
calmly ['kɑːmlɪ] *adv* con calma.

calmness ['kɑːmnɪs] *n* calma.
Calor gas ® ['kælə*-] *n* (*BRIT*) butano.
calorie ['kælərɪ] *n* caloria; **low-**~ **product** prodotto a basso contenuto di calorie.
calve [kɑːv] *vi* figliare.
calves [kɑːvz] *npl of* **calf**.
CAM *n abbr* (= *computer-aided manufacturing*) fabbricazione *f* con l'ausilio dell'elaboratore.
camber ['kæmbə*] *n* (*of road*) bombatura.
Cambodia [kæm'bəudjə] *n* Cambogia.
Cambodian [kæm'bəudɪən] *adj, n* cambogiano(a).
Cambs *abbr* (*BRIT*) = *Cambridgeshire*.
camcorder ['kæmkɔːdə*] *n* videocamera.
came [keɪm] *pt of* **come**.
camel ['kæməl] *n* cammello.
cameo ['kæmɪəu] *n* cammeo.
camera ['kæmərə] *n* macchina fotografica; (*CINE, TV*) telecamera; (*also:* **cine**~, **movie** ~) cinepresa; **in** ~ a porte chiuse.
cameraman ['kæmərəmæn] *n* cameraman *m inv*.
Cameroon, Cameroun ['kæməruːn] *n* Camerun *m*.
camouflage ['kæməflɑːʒ] *n* camuffamento; (*MIL*) mimetizzazione *f* ♦ *vt* camuffare; mimetizzare.
camp [kæmp] *n* campeggio; (*MIL*) campo ♦ *vi* campeggiare; accamparsi; **to go** ~**ing** andare in campeggio.
campaign [kæm'peɪn] *n* (*MIL, POL etc*) campagna ♦ *vi:* **to** ~ (**for/against**) (*also fig*) fare una campagna (per/contro).
campaigner [kæm'peɪnə*] *n:* ~ **for** fautore/trice di; ~ **against** oppositore/trice di.
campbed ['kæmp'bed] *n* (*BRIT*) brandina.
camper ['kæmpə*] *n* campeggiatore/trice.
camping ['kæmpɪŋ] *n* campeggio.
camp(ing) site *n* campeggio.
campus ['kæmpəs] *n* campus *m inv*.
camshaft ['kæmʃɑːft] *n* albero a camme.
can [kæn] *aux vb see next headword* ♦ *n* (*of milk*) scatola; (*of oil*) bidone *m*; (*of water*) tanica; (*tin*) scatola ♦ *vt* mettere in scatola; **a** ~ **of beer** una lattina di birra; **to carry the** ~ (*BRIT col*) prendere la colpa.

━━━━━━━━━━━━━━━━━━━━ KEYWORD

can [kæn] (*negative* **cannot, can't**; *conditional and pt* **could**) *aux vb* **1** (*be able to*) potere; **I** ~**'t go any further** non posso andare oltre; **you** ~ **do it if you try** sei in grado di farlo — basta provarci; **I'll help you all I** ~ ti aiuterò come potrò; **I** ~**'t see you** non ti vedo; ~ **you hear me?** mi senti?, riesci a sentirmi?
2 (*know how to*) sapere, essere capace di;

I ~ **swim** so nuotare; ~ **you speak French?** parla francese?
3 (may) potere; **could I have a word with you?** posso parlarle un momento?
4 (expressing disbelief, puzzlement etc): **it ~'t be true!** non può essere vero!; **what CAN he want?** cosa può mai volere?
5 (expressing possibility, suggestion etc): **he could be in the library** può darsi che sia in biblioteca; **they could have forgotten** potrebbero essersene dimenticati; **she could have been delayed** può aver avuto un contrattempo.

Canada [ˈkænədə] n Canada m.
Canadian [kəˈneɪdɪən] adj, n canadese (m/f).
canal [kəˈnæl] n canale m.
canary [kəˈnɛərɪ] n canarino.
Canary Islands, Canaries [kəˈnɛərɪz] npl: **the ~** le (isole) Canarie.
Canberra [ˈkænbərə] n Camberra.
cancel [ˈkænsəl] vt annullare; (train) sopprimere; (cross out) cancellare.
▶**cancel out** vt (MATH) semplificare; (fig) annullare; **they ~ each other out** (also fig) si annullano a vicenda.
cancellation [kænsəˈleɪʃən] n annullamento; soppressione f; cancellazione f; (TOURISM) prenotazione f annullata.
cancer [ˈkænsə*] n cancro; **C~** (sign) Cancro; **to be C~** essere del Cancro.
cancerous [ˈkænsərəs] adj canceroso(a).
cancer patient n malato/a di cancro.
cancer research n ricerca sul cancro.
C and F abbr (BRIT: = cost and freight) Caf m.
candid [ˈkændɪd] adj onesto(a).
candidacy [ˈkændɪdəsɪ] n candidatura.
candidate [ˈkændɪdeɪt] n candidato/a.
candidature [ˈkændɪdətʃə*] n (BRIT) = **candidacy.**
candied [ˈkændɪd] adj candito(a); **~ apple** (US) mela caramellata.
candle [ˈkændl] n candela.
candlelight [ˈkændlˈlaɪt] n: **by ~** a lume di candela.
candlestick [ˈkændlstɪk] n (also: **candle holder**) bugia; (bigger, ornate) candeliere m.
candour, (US) **candor** [ˈkændə*] n sincerità.
candy [ˈkændɪ] n zucchero candito; (US) caramella; caramelle fpl.
candy-floss [ˈkændɪflɔs] n (BRIT) zucchero filato.
candy store n (US) ≈ pasticceria.
cane [keɪn] n canna; (for baskets, chairs etc) bambù m; (SCOL) verga; (for walking)

bastone m (da passeggio) ♦ vt (BRIT SCOL) punire a colpi di verga.
canine [ˈkænaɪn] adj canino(a).
canister [ˈkænɪstə*] n scatola metallica.
cannabis [ˈkænəbɪs] n canapa indiana.
canned [ˈkænd] adj (food) in scatola; (col: recorded: music) registrato(a); (BRIT col: drunk) sbronzo(a); (US col: worker) licenziato(a).
cannibal [ˈkænɪbəl] n cannibale m/f.
cannibalism [ˈkænɪbəlɪzəm] n cannibalismo.
cannon, pl ~ or ~**s** [ˈkænən] n (gun) cannone m.
cannonball [ˈkænənbɔːl] n palla di cannone.
cannon fodder n carne f da macello.
cannot [ˈkænɔt] = **can not.**
canny [ˈkænɪ] adj furbo(a).
canoe [kəˈnuː] n canoa; (SPORT) canotto.
canoeing [kəˈnuːɪŋ] n (sport) canottaggio.
canoeist [kəˈnuːɪst] n canottiere m.
canon [ˈkænən] n (clergyman) canonico; (standard) canone m.
canonize [ˈkænənaɪz] vt canonizzare.
can opener [-ˈəupnə*] n apriscatole m inv.
canopy [ˈkænəpɪ] n baldacchino.
cant [kænt] n gergo ♦ vt inclinare ♦ vi inclinarsi.
can't [kænt] = **can not.**
Cantab. abbr (BRIT: = cantabrigiensis) of Cambridge.
cantankerous [kænˈtæŋkərəs] adj stizzoso(a).
canteen [kænˈtiːn] n mensa; (BRIT: of cutlery) portaposate m inv.
canter [ˈkæntə*] n piccolo galoppo ♦ vi andare al piccolo galoppo.
cantilever [ˈkæntɪliːvə*] n trave f a sbalzo.
canvas [ˈkænvəs] n tela; **under ~** (camping) sotto la tenda; (NAUT) sotto la vela.
canvass [ˈkænvəs] vt (COMM: district) fare un'indagine di mercato in; (: citizens, opinions) fare un sondaggio di; (POL: district) fare un giro elettorale di; (: person) fare propaganda elettorale a.
canvasser [ˈkænvəsə*] n (COMM) agente m viaggiatore, piazzista m; (POL) propagandista m/f (elettorale).
canvassing [ˈkænvəsɪŋ] n sollecitazione f.
canyon [ˈkænjən] n canyon m inv.
CAP n abbr (= Common Agricultural Policy) PAC f.
cap [kæp] n (also FOOTBALL) berretto; (of pen) coperchio; (of bottle) tappo; (for swimming) cuffia; (BRIT: contraceptive: also: **Dutch ~**) diaframma m ♦ vt tappare; (outdo) superare; **~ped with** ricoperto(a) di; **and to ~ it all, he ...** (BRIT) e per

completare l'opera, lui ....

capability [keɪpə'bɪlɪtɪ] n capacità f inv, abilità f inv.

capable ['keɪpəbl] adj capace; ~ **of** capace di; suscettibile di.

capacious [kə'peɪʃəs] adj capace.

capacity [kə'pæsɪtɪ] n capacità f inv; (of lift etc) capienza; **in his** ~ **as** nella sua qualità di; **to work at full** ~ lavorare al massimo delle proprie capacità; **this work is beyond my** ~ questo lavoro supera le mie possibilità; **filled to** ~ pieno zeppo; **in an advisory** ~ a titolo consultativo.

cape [keɪp] n (garment) cappa; (GEO) capo.

Cape of Good Hope n Capo di Buona Speranza.

caper ['keɪpə*] n (CULIN: also: ~s) cappero; (leap) saltello; (escapade) birichinata.

Cape Town n Città del Capo.

capita ['kæpɪtə] see **per capita**.

capital ['kæpɪtl] n (also: ~ **city**) capitale f; (money) capitale m; (also: ~ **letter**) (lettera) maiuscola.

capital account n conto capitale.

capital allowance n ammortamento fiscale.

capital assets npl capitale m fisso.

capital expenditure n spese fpl in capitale.

capital gains tax n imposta sulla plusvalenza.

capital goods n beni mpl d'investimento, beni mpl capitali.

capital-intensive ['kæpɪtlɪn'tɛnsɪv] adj ad alta intensità di capitale.

capitalism ['kæpɪtəlɪzəm] n capitalismo.

capitalist ['kæpɪtəlɪst] adj, n capitalista (m/f).

capitalize ['kæpɪtəlaɪz] vt (provide with capital) capitalizzare.

►**capitalize on** vt fus (fig) trarre vantaggio da.

capital punishment n pena capitale.

capital transfer tax n (BRIT) imposta sui trasferimenti di capitali.

Capitol ['kæpɪtl] n: **the** ~ il Campidoglio.

Il **Capitol** è l'edificio che ospita le riunioni del Congresso degli Stati Uniti. È situato sull'omonimo colle, Capitol Hill, a Washington DC. In molti stati americani il termine Capitol viene usato per indicare l'edificio dove si riuniscono i rappresentanti dello stato.

---

capitulate [kə'pɪtjuleɪt] vi capitolare.

capitulation [kəpɪtju'leɪʃən] n capitolazione f.

capricious [kə'prɪʃəs] adj capriccioso(a).

Capricorn ['kæprɪkɔːn] n Capricorno; **to be** ~ essere del Capricorno.

caps [kæps] abbr = **capital letters**.

capsize [kæp'saɪz] vt capovolgere ♦ vi capovolgersi.

capstan ['kæpstən] n argano.

capsule ['kæpsjuːl] n capsula.

Capt. abbr (= captain) Cap.

captain ['kæptɪn] n capitano ♦ vt capitanare.

caption ['kæpʃən] n leggenda.

captivate ['kæptɪveɪt] vt avvincere.

captive ['kæptɪv] adj, n prigioniero(a).

captivity [kæp'tɪvɪtɪ] n prigionia; **in** ~ (animal) in cattività.

captor ['kæptə*] n (lawful) chi ha catturato; (unlawful) rapitore m.

capture ['kæptʃə*] vt catturare, prendere; (attention) attirare ♦ n cattura; (data ~) registrazione f or rilevazione f di dati.

car [kɑː*] n macchina, automobile f; (US RAIL) carrozza; **by** ~ in macchina.

Caracas [kə'rækəs] n Caracas f.

carafe [kə'ræf] n caraffa.

carafe wine n (in restaurant) ≈ vino sfuso.

caramel ['kærəməl] n caramello.

carat ['kærət] n carato; **18** ~ **gold** oro a 18 carati.

caravan ['kærəvæn] n roulotte f inv.

caravan site n (BRIT) campeggio per roulotte.

caraway ['kærəweɪ] n: ~ **seed** seme m di cumino.

carbohydrates [kɑːbəʊ'haɪdreɪts] npl (foods) carboidrati mpl.

carbolic acid [kɑː'bɒlɪk-] n acido fenico, fenolo.

car bomb n ordigno esplosivo collocato in una macchina; **a** ~ **went off yesterday** ieri è esplosa un'autobomba.

carbon ['kɑːbən] n carbonio.

carbonated ['kɑːbəneɪtəd] adj (drink) gassato(a).

carbon copy n copia f carbone inv.

carbon dioxide [-daɪ'ɒksaɪd] n diossido di carbonio.

carbon paper n carta carbone.

carbon ribbon n nastro carbonato.

car boot sale n mercatino dell'usato dove la merce viene esposta nel bagagliaio delle macchine.

carburettor, (US) **carburetor** [kɑːbjuˈrɛtə*] n carburatore m.

carcass ['kɑːkəs] n carcassa.

carcinogenic [kɑːsɪnə'dʒɛnɪk] adj cancerogeno(a).

card [kɑːd] n carta; (thin cardboard)

cartoncino; (*visiting* ~ *etc*) biglietto;
(*membership* ~) tessera; (*Christmas* ~ *etc*)
cartolina; **to play** ~**s** giocare a carte.
cardamom ['kɑːdəməm] *n* cardamomo.
cardboard ['kɑːdbɔːd] *n* cartone *m*.
cardboard box *n* (scatola di) cartone *m*.
cardboard city *n luogo dove dormono in
scatole di cartone emarginati senzatetto.*
card-carrying member ['kɑːd'kærɪɪŋ-] *n*
tesserato/a.
card game *n* gioco di carte.
cardiac ['kɑːdɪæk] *adj* cardiaco(a).
cardigan ['kɑːdɪɡən] *n* cardigan *m inv*.
cardinal ['kɑːdɪnl] *adj, n* cardinale (*m*).
card index *n* schedario.
cardphone ['kɑːdfəʊn] *n* telefono a scheda
(magnetica).
cardsharp ['kɑːdʃɑːp] *n* baro.
card vote *n* (*BRIT*) voto (palese) per
delega.
CARE [kɛə*] *n abbr* = *Cooperative for
American Relief Everywhere.*
care [kɛə*] *n* cura, attenzione *f*; (*worry*)
preoccupazione *f* ♦ *vi:* **to** ~ **about**
interessarsi di; **would you** ~ **to/for ...?** le
piacerebbe ...?; **I wouldn't** ~ **to do it** non
lo vorrei fare; **in sb's** ~ alle cure di qn; **to
take** ~ fare attenzione; **to take** ~ **of**
curarsi di; (*details, arrangements*)
occuparsi di; **I don't** ~ non me ne
importa; **I couldn't** ~ **less** non me ne
importa un bel niente; ~ **of (c/o)** (*on
letter*) presso; "**with** ~" "fragile"; **the
child has been taken into** ~ il bambino è
stato preso in custodia.
▶**care for** *vt fus* aver cura di; (*like*) voler
bene a.
careen [kə'riːn] *vi* (*ship*) sbandare ♦ *vt*
carenare.
career [kə'rɪə*] *n* carriera; (*occupation*)
professione *f* ♦ *vi* (*also:* ~ **along**) andare di
(gran) carriera.
career girl *n* donna dedita alla carriera.
careers officer *n* consulente *m/f*
d'orientamento professionale.
carefree ['kɛəfriː] *adj* sgombro(a) di
preoccupazioni.
careful ['kɛəful] *adj* attento(a); (*cautious*)
cauto(a); **(be)** ~! attenzione!; **he's very** ~
with his money bada molto alle spese.
carefully ['kɛəfəlɪ] *adv* con cura;
cautamente.
careless ['kɛəlɪs] *adj* negligente; (*remark*)
privo(a) di tatto.
carelessly ['kɛəlɪslɪ] *adv* negligentemente;
senza tatto; (*without thinking*)
distrattamente.
carelessness ['kɛəlɪsnɪs] *n* negligenza;

mancanza di tatto.
carer ['kɛərə*] *n chi si occupa di un
familiare anziano o invalido.*
caress [kə'rɛs] *n* carezza ♦ *vt* accarezzare.
caretaker ['kɛəteɪkə*] *n* custode *m*.
caretaker government *n* (*BRIT*) governo
m ponte *inv*.
car-ferry ['kɑːfɛrɪ] *n* traghetto.
cargo, ~**es** ['kɑːɡəʊ] *n* carico.
cargo boat *n* cargo.
cargo plane *n* aereo di linea da carico.
car hire *n* (*BRIT*) autonoleggio.
Caribbean [kærɪ'biːən] *adj* caraibico(a); **the**
~ **(Sea)** il Mar dei Caraibi.
caricature ['kærɪkətjuə*] *n* caricatura.
caring ['kɛərɪŋ] *adj* (*person*) premuroso(a);
(*society, organization*) umanitario(a).
carnage ['kɑːnɪdʒ] *n* carneficina.
carnal ['kɑːnl] *adj* carnale.
carnation [kɑː'neɪʃən] *n* garofano.
carnival ['kɑːnɪvəl] *n* (*public celebration*)
carnevale *m*; (*US: funfair*) luna park *m inv*.
carnivorous [kɑː'nɪvərəs] *adj* carnivoro(a).
carol ['kærəl] *n:* **(Christmas)** ~ canto di
Natale.
carouse [kə'raʊz] *vi* far baldoria.
carousel [kærə'sɛl] *n* (*US*) giostra.
carp [kɑːp] *n* (*fish*) carpa.
▶**carp at** *vt fus* trovare a ridire su.
car park *n* parcheggio.
carpenter ['kɑːpɪntə*] *n* carpentiere *m*.
carpentry ['kɑːpɪntrɪ] *n* carpenteria.
carpet ['kɑːpɪt] *n* tappeto; (*BRIT: fitted* ~)
moquette *f inv* ♦ *vt* coprire con tappeto.
carpet bombing *n* bombardamento a
tappeto.
carpet slippers *npl* pantofole *fpl*.
carpet sweeper *n* scopatappeti *m inv*.
car phone *n* telefonino per auto.
car rental *n* (*US*) autonoleggio.
carriage ['kærɪdʒ] *n* vettura; (*of goods*)
trasporto; (*of typewriter*) carrello;
(*bearing*) portamento; ~ **forward** porto
assegnato; ~ **free** franco di porto; ~ **paid**
porto pagato.
carriage return *n* (*on typewriter etc*) leva
(*or* tasto) del ritorno a capo.
carriageway ['kærɪdʒweɪ] *n* (*BRIT: part of
road*) carreggiata.
carrier ['kærɪə*] *n* (*of disease*) portatore/
trice; (*COMM*) impresa di trasporti;
(*NAUT*) portaerei *f inv*.
carrier bag *n* (*BRIT*) sacchetto.
carrier pigeon *n* colombo viaggiatore.
carrion ['kærɪən] *n* carogna.
carrot ['kærət] *n* carota.
carry ['kærɪ] *vt* (*subj: person*) portare;
(: *vehicle*) trasportare; (*a motion, bill*) far

passare; (*involve: responsibilities etc*) comportare; (*COMM: goods*) tenere; (*: interest*) avere; (*MATH: figure*) riportare ♦ *vi* (*sound*) farsi sentire; **this loan carries 10% interest** questo prestito è sulla base di un interesse del 10%; **to be carried away** (*fig*) farsi trascinare.

►**carry forward** *vt* (*MATH, COMM*) riportare.

►**carry on** *vi*: **to ~ on with sth/doing** continuare qc/a fare ♦ *vt* mandare avanti.

►**carry out** *vt* (*orders*) eseguire; (*investigation*) svolgere; (*accomplish etc: plan*) realizzare; (*perform, implement: idea, threat*) mettere in pratica.

carrycot ['kærɪkɔt] *n* (*BRIT*) culla portabile.

carry-on [kærɪ'ɔn] *n* (*col: fuss*) casino, confusione *f*; (*: annoying behaviour*): **I've had enough of your ~!** mi hai proprio scocciato!

cart [kɑːt] *n* carro ♦ *vt* (*col*) trascinare, scarrozzare.

carte blanche ['kɑːt'blɒnʃ] *n*: **to give sb ~** dare carta bianca a qn.

cartel [kɑː'tɛl] *n* (*COMM*) cartello.

cartilage ['kɑːtɪlɪdʒ] *n* cartilagine *f*.

cartographer [kɑː'tɔgrəfə*] *n* cartografo/a.

cartography [kɑː'tɔgrəfɪ] *n* cartografia.

carton ['kɑːtən] *n* (*box*) scatola di cartone; (*of yogurt*) cartone *m*; (*of cigarettes*) stecca.

cartoon [kɑː'tuːn] *n* (*in newspaper etc*) vignetta; (*CINE, TV*) cartone *m* animato; (*ART*) cartone.

cartoonist [kɑː'tuːnɪst] *n* vignettista *m/f*; cartonista *m/f*.

cartridge ['kɑːtrɪdʒ] *n* (*for gun, pen*) cartuccia; (*for camera*) caricatore *m*; (*music tape*) cassetta; (*of record player*) testina.

cartwheel ['kɑːtwiːl] *n*: **to turn a ~** (*SPORT etc*) fare la ruota.

carve [kɑːv] *vt* (*meat*) trinciare; (*wood, stone*) intagliare.

►**carve up** *vt* (*meat*) tagliare; (*fig: country*) suddividere.

carving ['kɑːvɪŋ] *n* (*in wood etc*) scultura.

carving knife *n* trinciante *m*.

car wash *n* lavaggio auto.

Casablanca [kæsə'blæŋkə] *n* Casablanca.

cascade [kæs'keɪd] *n* cascata ♦ *vi* scendere a cascata.

case [keɪs] *n* caso *m*; (*LAW*) causa, processo; (*box*) scatola; (*also*: **suit~**) valigia; (*TYP*): **lower/upper ~** (carattere *m*) minuscolo/maiuscolo; **to have a good ~** avere pretese legittime; **there's a strong ~ for reform** ci sono validi argomenti a favore della riforma; **in ~ of** in caso di; **in ~ he** caso mai lui; **just in ~** in caso di bisogno.

case history *n* (*MED*) cartella clinica.

case study *n* studio di un caso.

cash [kæʃ] *n* (*coins, notes*) soldi *mpl*, denaro; (*col: money*) quattrini *mpl* ♦ *vt* incassare; **to pay (in) ~** pagare in contanti; **to be short of ~** essere a corto di soldi; **~ with order/on delivery (COD)** (*COMM*) pagamento all'ordinazione/alla consegna.

►**cash in** *vt* (*insurance policy etc*) riscuotere, riconvertire.

►**cash in on** *vt fus*: **to ~ in on sth** sfruttare qc.

cash account *n* conto *m* cassa *inv*.

cash-and-carry ['kæʃənd'kærɪ] *n* cash and carry *m inv*.

cashbook ['kæʃbuk] *n* giornale *m* di cassa.

cash box *n* cassetta per il denaro spicciolo.

cash card *n* carta per prelievi automatici.

cash desk *n* (*BRIT*) cassa.

cash discount *n* sconto per contanti.

cash dispenser *n* sportello automatico.

cashew [kæ'ʃuː] *n* (*also*: **~ nut**) anacardio.

cash flow *n* cash-flow *m inv*, liquidità *f inv*.

cashier [kæ'ʃɪə*] *n* cassiere/a ♦ *vt* (*esp MIL*) destituire.

cashmere ['kæʃmɪə*] *n* cachemire *m*.

cash payment *n* pagamento in contanti.

cash price *n* prezzo per contanti.

cash register *n* registratore *m* di cassa.

cash sale *n* vendita per contanti.

casing ['keɪsɪŋ] *n* rivestimento.

casino [kə'siːnəu] *n* casinò *m inv*.

cask [kɑːsk] *n* botte *f*.

casket ['kɑːskɪt] *n* cofanetto; (*US: coffin*) bara.

Caspian Sea ['kæspɪən-] *n*: **the ~** il mar Caspio.

casserole ['kæsərəul] *n* casseruola; (*food*): **chicken ~** pollo in casseruola.

cassette [kæ'sɛt] *n* cassetta.

cassette deck *n* piastra di registrazione.

cassette player *n* riproduttore *m* a cassette.

cassette recorder *n* registratore *m* a cassette.

cast [kɑːst] *vt* (*pt, pp* **cast**) (*throw*) gettare; (*shed*) perdere; spogliarsi di; (*metal*) gettare, fondere ♦ *n* (*THEAT*) complesso di attori; (*mould*) forma; (*also*: **plaster ~**) ingessatura; (*THEAT*): **to ~ sb as Hamlet** scegliere qn per la parte di Amleto; **to ~ one's vote** votare, dare il voto.

►**cast aside** *vt* (*reject*) mettere da parte.

►**cast off** *vi* (*NAUT*) salpare; (*KNITTING*) diminuire, calare ♦ *vt* (*NAUT*)

disormeggiare; (*KNITTING*) diminuire, calare.
►**cast on** *vt* (*KNITTING*) avviare ♦ *vi* avviare (le maglie).
castanets [kæstə'nɛts] *npl* castagnette *fpl*.
castaway ['kɑːstəwəɪ] *n* naufrago/a.
caste [kɑːst] *n* casta.
caster sugar ['kɑːstə-] *n* zucchero semolato.
casting vote ['kɑːstɪŋ-] *n* (*BRIT*) voto decisivo.
cast iron *n* ghisa ♦ *adj*: **cast-iron** (*fig: will, alibi*) di ferro, d'acciaio.
castle ['kɑːsl] *n* castello; (*fortified*) rocca.
castor ['kɑːstə*] *n* (*wheel*) rotella.
castor oil *n* olio di ricino.
castrate [kæs'treɪt] *vt* castrare.
casual ['kæʒjul] *adj* (*by chance*) casuale, fortuito(a); (*irregular: work etc*) avventizio(a); (*unconcerned*) noncurante, indifferente; ~ **wear** casual *m*.
casual labour *n* manodopera avventizia.
casually ['kæʒjulɪ] *adv* con disinvoltura; (*by chance*) casualmente.
casualty ['kæʒjultɪ] *n* ferito/a; (*dead*) morto/a, vittima; **heavy casualties** *npl* grosse perdite *fpl*.
casualty ward *n* (*BRIT*) pronto soccorso.
cat [kæt] *n* gatto.
catacombs ['kætəkuːmz] *npl* catacombe *fpl*.
catalogue, (*US*) **catalog** ['kætəlɔg] *n* catalogo ♦ *vt* catalogare.
catalyst ['kætəlɪst] *n* catalizzatore *m*.
catalytic converter [kætə'lɪtɪkkən'vɜːtə*] *n* marmitta catalitica, catalizzatore *m*.
catapult ['kætəpʌlt] *n* catapulta; fionda.
cataract ['kætərækt] *n* (*also MED*) cateratta.
catarrh [kə'tɑː*] *n* catarro.
catastrophe [kə'tæstrəfɪ] *n* catastrofe *f*.
catastrophic [kætə'strɔfɪk] *adj* catastrofico(a).
catcall ['kætkɔːl] *n* (*at meeting etc*) fischio.
catch [kætʃ] *vb* (*pt, pp* **caught** [kɔːt]) *vt* (*train, thief, cold*) acchiappare; (*ball*) afferrare; (*person: by surprise*) sorprendere; (*understand*) comprendere; (*get entangled*) impigliare ♦ *vi* (*fire*) prendere ♦ *n* (*fish etc caught*) retata, presa; (*trick*) inganno; (*TECH*) gancio; **to** ~ **sb's attention** *or* **eye** attirare l'attenzione di qn; **to** ~ **fire** prendere fuoco; **to** ~ **sight of** scorgere.
►**catch on** *vi* (*become popular*) affermarsi, far presa; (*understand*): **to** ~ **on (to sth)** capire (qc).
►**catch out** *vt* (*BRIT fig: with trick question*) cogliere in fallo.
►**catch up** *vi* mettersi in pari ♦ *vt* (*also:* ~ **up with**) raggiungere.

catching ['kætʃɪŋ] *adj* (*MED*) contagioso(a).
catchment area ['kætʃmənt-] *n* (*BRIT SCOL*) circoscrizione *f* scolare; (*GEO*) bacino pluviale.
catch phrase *n* slogan *m inv*; frase *f* fatta.
catch-22 ['kætʃtwɛntɪ'tuː] *n*: **it's a** ~ **situation** non c'è via d'uscita.
catchy ['kætʃɪ] *adj* orecchiabile.
catechism ['kætɪkɪzəm] *n* catechismo.
categoric(al) [kætɪ'gɔrɪk(l)] *adj* categorico(a).
categorize ['kætɪgəraɪz] *vt* categorizzare.
category ['kætɪgərɪ] *n* categoria.
cater ['keɪtə*] *vi* (*gen*: ~ **for**) provvedere da mangiare (per).
►**cater for** *vt fus* (*BRIT: needs*) provvedere a; (*: readers, consumers*) incontrare i gusti di.
caterer ['keɪtərə*] *n* fornitore *m*.
catering ['keɪtərɪŋ] *n* approvvigionamento.
catering trade *n* settore *m* ristoranti.
caterpillar ['kætəpɪlə*] *n* (*ZOOL*) bruco ♦ *cpd* (*vehicle*) cingolato(a); ~ **track** cingolo.
cat flap *n* gattaiola.
cathedral [kə'θiːdrəl] *n* cattedrale *f*, duomo.
cathode ['kæθəud] *n* catodo.
cathode ray tube *n* tubo a raggi catodici.
catholic ['kæθəlɪk] *adj* universale; aperto(a); eclettico(a); **C**~ *adj, n* (*REL*) cattolico(a).
CAT scanner [kæt-] *n* (*MED*: = *computerized axial tomography scanner*) (rilevatore *m* per la) TAC *f inv*.
cat's-eye ['kætsaɪ] *n* (*BRIT AUT*) catarifrangente *m*.
catsup ['kætsəp] *n* (*US*) ketchup *m inv*.
cattle ['kætl] *npl* bestiame *m*, bestie *fpl*.
catty ['kætɪ] *adj* maligno(a), dispettoso(a).
catwalk ['kætwɔːk] *n* passerella.
Caucasian [kɔː'keɪzɪən] *adj, n* caucasico(a).
Caucasus ['kɔːkəsəs] *n* Caucaso.
caucus ['kɔːkəs] *n* (*US POL*) (riunione *f* del) comitato elettorale; (*BRIT POL: group*) comitato di dirigenti.

Caucus è il termine usato, specialmente negli Stati Uniti, per indicare una riunione informale dei rappresentanti di spicco di un partito politico che precede una riunione ufficiale. Con uso estensivo, la parola indica il nucleo direttivo di un partito politico.

---

caught [kɔːt] *pt, pp of* **catch**.
cauliflower ['kɔlɪflauə*] *n* cavolfiore *m*.
cause [kɔːz] *n* causa ♦ *vt* causare; **there is no** ~ **for concern** non c'è ragione di preoccuparsi; **to** ~ **sb to do sth** far fare qc a qn; **to** ~ **sth to be done** far fare qc.

causeway ['kɔːzweɪ] n strada rialzata.
caustic ['kɔːstɪk] adj caustico(a).
caution ['kɔːʃən] n prudenza; (warning) avvertimento ♦ vt ammonire.
cautious ['kɔːʃəs] adj cauto(a), prudente.
cautiously ['kɔːʃəslɪ] adv prudentemente.
cautiousness ['kɔːʃəsnɪs] n cautela.
cavalier [kævə'lɪə*] n (knight) cavaliere m ♦ adj (pej: offhand) brusco(a).
cavalry ['kævəlrɪ] n cavalleria.
cave [keɪv] n caverna, grotta ♦ vi: **to go caving** fare speleologia.
▶**cave in** vi (roof etc) crollare.
caveman ['keɪvmæn] n uomo delle caverne.
cavern ['kævən] n caverna.
caviar(e) ['kævɪɑː*] n caviale m.
cavity ['kævɪtɪ] n cavità f inv.
cavity wall insulation n isolamento per pareti a intercapedine.
cavort [kə'vɔːt] vi far capriole.
cayenne (pepper) [keɪ'ɛn-] n pepe m di Caienna.
CB n abbr (BRIT: = Companion (of the Order) of the Bath) titolo; (= Citizens' Band (Radio)) C.B. m; ~ **radio (set)** baracchino.
CBC n abbr = Canadian Broadcasting Corporation.
CBE n abbr (BRIT: = Companion (of the Order) of the British Empire) titolo.
CBI n abbr (= Confederation of British Industry) ≈ CONFINDUSTRIA (= Confederazione Generale dell'Industria Italiana).
CBS n abbr (US) = Columbia Broadcasting System.
CC abbr (BRIT) = county council.
cc abbr (= cubic centimetre) cc; (on letter etc) = carbon copy.
CCA n abbr (US: = Circuit Court of Appeals) corte f d'appello itinerante.
CCU n abbr (US: = coronary care unit) unità coronarica.
CD n abbr (= compact disk) compact disc m inv; ~ **player** lettore m CD; (MIL) = Civil Defence (Corps) (BRIT), Civil Defense (US) ♦ abbr (BRIT: = Corps Diplomatique) C.D.
CDC n abbr (US) = center for disease control.
CD-I ® n CD-I m inv, compact disc m inv interattivo.
Cdr. abbr (= commander) Com.
CD-ROM ['siː'diː'rɔm] n abbr (= compact disc read-only memory) CD-ROM m inv.
CDT abbr (US: = Central Daylight Time) ora legale del centro.
CDW n abbr see **collision damage waiver**.
cease [siːs] vt, vi cessare.
ceasefire ['siːsfaɪə*] n cessate il fuoco m inv.

ceaseless ['siːslɪs] adj incessante, continuo(a).
CED n abbr (US) = Committee for Economic Development.
cedar ['siːdə*] n cedro.
cede [siːd] vt cedere.
CEEB n abbr (US: = College Entrance Examination Board) commissione f per l'esame di ammissione al college.
ceilidh ['keɪlɪ] n festa con musiche e danze popolari scozzesi o irlandesi.
ceiling ['siːlɪŋ] n soffitto; (fig: upper limit) tetto, limite m massimo.
celebrate ['sɛlɪbreɪt] vt, vi celebrare.
celebrated ['sɛlɪbreɪtɪd] adj celebre.
celebration [sɛlɪ'breɪʃən] n celebrazione f.
celebrity [sɪ'lɛbrɪtɪ] n celebrità f inv.
celeriac [sə'lɛrɪæk] n sedano m rapa inv.
celery ['sɛlərɪ] n sedano.
celestial [sɪ'lɛstɪəl] adj celeste.
celibacy ['sɛlɪbəsɪ] n celibato.
cell [sɛl] n cella; (BIOL) cellula; (ELEC) elemento (di batteria).
cellar ['sɛlə*] n sottosuolo, cantina.
cellist ['tʃɛlɪst] n violoncellista m/f.
cello ['tʃɛləʊ] n violoncello.
cellophane ® ['sɛləfeɪn] n cellophane ® m.
cellphone ['sɛlfəʊn] n cellulare m.
cellular ['sɛljʊlə*] adj cellulare.
celluloid ['sɛljʊlɔɪd] n celluloide f.
cellulose ['sɛljʊləʊs] n cellulosa.
Celsius ['sɛlsɪəs] adj Celsius inv.
Celt [kɛlt, sɛlt] n celta m/f.
Celtic ['kɛltɪk, 'sɛltɪk] adj celtico(a) ♦ n (LING) celtico.
cement [sə'mɛnt] n cemento ♦ vt cementare.
cement mixer n betoniera.
cemetery ['sɛmɪtrɪ] n cimitero.
cenotaph ['sɛnətɑːf] n cenotafio.
censor ['sɛnsə*] n censore m ♦ vt censurare.
censorship ['sɛnsəʃɪp] n censura.
censure ['sɛnʃə*] vt censurare.
census ['sɛnsəs] n censimento.
cent [sɛnt] n (US: coin) centesimo (= 1:100 di un dollaro); see also **per cent**.
centenary [sɛn'tiːnərɪ], **centennial** [sɛn'tɛnɪəl] n centenario.
center ['sɛntə*] n, vt (US) = **centre**.
centigrade ['sɛntɪgreɪd] adj centigrado(a).
centilitre, (US) **centiliter** ['sɛntɪliːtə*] n centilitro.
centimetre, (US) **centimeter** ['sɛntɪmiːtə*] n centimetro.
centipede ['sɛntɪpiːd] n centopiedi m inv.
central ['sɛntrəl] adj centrale.
Central African Republic n Repubblica

centrafricana.
Central America n America centrale.
central heating n riscaldamento centrale.
centralize ['sɛntrəlaɪz] vt accentrare.
central processing unit (CPU) n
(*COMPUT*) unità f inv centrale di
elaborazione.
central reservation n (*BRIT AUT*) banchina
f spartitraffico inv.
centre, (*US*) **center** ['sɛntə*] n centro ♦ vt
(*concentrate*): **to ~ (on)** concentrare (su).
centrefold, (*US*) **centerfold** ['sɛntəfəuld] n
(*PRESS*) poster m (all'interno di rivista).
centre-forward ['sɛntə'fɔ:wəd] n (*SPORT*)
centroavanti m inv.
centre-half ['sɛntə'hɑ:f] n (*SPORT*)
centromediano.
centrepiece, (*US*) **centerpiece** ['sɛntəpi:s]
n centrotavola m; (*fig*) punto centrale.
centre spread n (*BRIT*) pubblicità a doppia
pagina.
centre-stage [sɛntə'steɪdʒ] n: **to take ~**
porsi al centro dell'attenzione.
centrifugal [sɛn'trɪfjugəl] adj centrifugo(a).
centrifuge ['sɛntrɪfju:ʒ] n centrifuga.
century ['sɛntjuri] n secolo; **in the
twentieth ~** nel ventesimo secolo.
CEO n abbr (*US*) see **chief executive officer**.
ceramic [sɪ'ræmɪk] adj ceramico(a).
cereal ['si:rɪəl] n cereale m.
cerebral ['sɛrɪbrəl] adj cerebrale.
ceremonial [sɛrɪ'məunɪəl] n cerimoniale m;
(*rite*) rito.
ceremony ['sɛrɪmənɪ] n cerimonia; **to stand
on ~** fare complimenti.
cert [sə:t] n (*BRIT col*): **it's a dead ~** non c'è
alcun dubbio.
certain ['sə:tən] adj certo(a); **to make ~ of**
assicurarsi di; **for ~** per certo, di sicuro.
certainly ['sə:tənlɪ] adv certamente, certo.
certainty ['sə:təntɪ] n certezza.
certificate [sə'tɪfɪkɪt] n certificato; diploma
m.
certified letter ['sə:tɪfaɪd-] n (*US*) lettera
raccomandata.
certified public accountant (CPA)
['sə:tɪfaɪd-] n (*US*) ≈ commercialista m/f.
certify ['sə:tɪfaɪ] vt certificare ♦ vi: **to ~ to**
attestare a.
cervical ['sə:vɪkl] adj: **~ cancer** cancro della
cervice, tumore m al collo dell'utero; **~
smear** Pap-test m inv.
cervix ['sə:vɪks] n cervice f.
Cesarean [si:'zɛərɪən] adj, n (*US*) =
Caesarean.
cessation [sə'seɪʃən] n cessazione f;
arresto.
cesspit ['sɛspɪt] n pozzo nero.

CET abbr (= *Central European Time*) fuso
orario.
Ceylon [sɪ'lɔn] n Ceylon f.
cf. abbr (= *compare*) cfr.
c/f abbr (*COMM*) = *carried forward*.
CFC n abbr (= *chlorofluorocarbon*) CFC m inv.
CG n abbr (*US*) = **coastguard**.
cg abbr (= *centigram*) cg.
CH n abbr (*BRIT*: = *Companion of Honour*)
titolo.
ch abbr (*BRIT*) = **central heating**.
ch. abbr (= *chapter*) cap.
Chad [tʃæd] n Chad m.
chafe [tʃeɪf] vt fregare, irritare ♦ vi (*fig*): **to
~ against** scontrarsi con.
chaffinch ['tʃæfɪntʃ] n fringuello.
chagrin ['ʃægrɪn] n disappunto, dispiacere
m.
chain [tʃeɪn] n catena ♦ vt (*also*: **~ up**)
incatenare.
chain reaction n reazione f a catena.
chain-smoke ['tʃeɪnsməuk] vi fumare una
sigaretta dopo l'altra.
chain store n negozio a catena.
chair [tʃɛə*] n sedia; (*armchair*) poltrona; (*of
university*) cattedra ♦ vt (*meeting*)
presiedere; **the ~** (*US*: *electric ~*) la sedia
elettrica.
chairlift ['tʃɛəlɪft] n seggiovia.
chairman ['tʃɛəmən] n presidente m.
chairperson ['tʃɛəpə:sn] n presidente/essa.
chairwoman ['tʃɛəwumən] n
presidentessa.
chalet ['ʃæleɪ] n chalet m inv.
chalice ['tʃælɪs] n calice m.
chalk [tʃɔ:k] n gesso.
▶**chalk up** vt scrivere col gesso; (*fig*:
success) ottenere; (: *victory*) riportare.
challenge ['tʃælɪndʒ] n sfida ♦ vt sfidare;
(*statement, right*) mettere in dubbio; **to ~
sb to a fight/game** sfidare qn a battersi/
ad una partita; **to ~ sb to do** sfidare qn a
fare.
challenger ['tʃælɪndʒə*] n (*SPORT*) sfidante
m/f.
challenging ['tʃælɪndʒɪŋ] adj sfidante;
(*remark, look*) provocatorio(a).
chamber ['tʃeɪmbə*] n camera; **~ of
commerce** camera di commercio.
chambermaid ['tʃeɪmbəmeɪd] n cameriera.
chamber music n musica da camera.
chamberpot ['tʃeɪmbəpɔt] n vaso da notte.
chameleon [kə'mi:lɪən] n camaleonte m.
chamois ['ʃæmwɑ:] n camoscio.
chamois leather ['ʃæmɪ-] n pelle f di
camoscio.
champagne [ʃæm'peɪn] n champagne m inv.
champers ['ʃæmpəz] nsg (*col*) sciampagna.

champion ['tʃæmpɪən] n campione/essa; (of cause) difensore m ♦ vt difendere, lottare per.

championship ['tʃæmpɪənʃɪp] n campionato.

chance [tʃɑːns] n caso; (opportunity) occasione f; (likelihood) possibilità f inv ♦ vt: **to ~ it** rischiare, provarci ♦ adj fortuito(a); **there is little ~ of his coming** è molto improbabile che venga; **to take a ~** rischiare; **by ~** per caso; **it's the ~ of a lifetime** è un'occasione unica; **the ~s are that** ... probabilmente ..., è probabile che ... + sub; **to ~ to do sth** (formal: happen) fare per caso qc.

►**chance (up)on** vt fus (person) incontrare per caso, imbattersi in; (thing) trovare per caso.

chancel ['tʃɑːnsəl] n coro.

chancellor ['tʃɑːnsələ*] n cancelliere m; (of university) rettore m (onorario); **C~ of the Exchequer** (BRIT) Cancelliere m dello Scacchiere.

chandelier [ʃændə'lɪə*] n lampadario.

change [tʃeɪndʒ] vt cambiare; (transform): **to ~ sb into** trasformare qn in ♦ vi cambiarsi; (be transformed): **to ~ into** trasformarsi in ♦ n cambiamento; (money) resto; **to ~ one's mind** cambiare idea; **to ~ gear** (AUT) cambiare (marcia); **she ~d into an old skirt** si è cambiata e ha messo una vecchia gonna; **a ~ of clothes** un cambio (di vestiti); **for a ~** tanto per cambiare; **small ~** spiccioli mpl, moneta; **keep the ~** tenga il resto; **can you give me ~ for £1?** mi può cambiare una sterlina?

changeable ['tʃeɪndʒəbl] adj (weather) variabile; (person) mutevole.

change machine n distributore m automatico di monete.

changeover ['tʃeɪndʒəuvə*] n cambiamento, passaggio.

changing ['tʃeɪndʒɪŋ] adj che cambia; (colours) cangiante.

changing room n (BRIT: in shop) camerino; (: SPORT) spogliatoio.

channel ['tʃænl] n canale m; (of river, sea) alveo ♦ vt canalizzare; (fig: interest, energies): **to ~ into** concentrare su, indirizzare verso; **through the usual ~s** per le solite vie; **the (English) C~** la Manica; **green/red ~** (CUSTOMS) uscita "niente da dichiarare"/"merci da dichiarare".

Channel Islands npl: **the ~** le Isole Normanne.

Channel Tunnel n: **the ~** il tunnel della Manica.

chant [tʃɑːnt] n canto; salmodia; (of crowd) slogan m inv ♦ vt cantare; salmodiare; **the demonstrators ~ed their disapproval** i dimostranti lanciavano slogan di protesta.

chaos ['keɪɔs] n caos m.

chaos theory n teoria del caos.

chaotic [keɪ'ɔtɪk] adj caotico(a).

chap [tʃæp] n (BRIT col: man) tipo ♦ vt (skin) screpolare; **old ~** vecchio mio.

chapel ['tʃæpl] n cappella.

chaperone ['ʃæpərəun] n accompagnatore/trice ♦ vt accompagnare.

chaplain ['tʃæplɪn] n cappellano.

chapped [tʃæpt] adj (skin, lips) screpolato(a).

chapter ['tʃæptə*] n capitolo.

char [tʃɑː*] vt (burn) carbonizzare ♦ vi (BRIT: cleaner) lavorare come domestica (a ore) ♦ n (BRIT) = **charlady**.

character ['kærɪktə*] n (gen, COMPUT) carattere m; (in novel, film) personaggio; (eccentric) originale m; **a person of good ~** una persona a modo.

character code n (COMPUT) codice m di carattere.

characteristic ['kærɪktə'rɪstɪk] adj caratteristico(a) ♦ n caratteristica; **~ of** tipico(a) di.

characterize ['kærɪktəraɪz] vt caratterizzare; (describe): **to ~ (as)** descrivere (come).

charade [ʃə'rɑːd] n sciarada.

charcoal ['tʃɑːkəul] n carbone m di legna.

charge [tʃɑːdʒ] n accusa; (cost) prezzo; (of gun, battery, MIL: attack) carica ♦ vt (gun, battery, MIL: enemy) caricare; (customer) fare pagare a; (sum) fare pagare; (LAW): **to ~ sb (with)** accusare qn (di) ♦ vi (gen with: up, along etc) lanciarsi; **~s** npl: **bank ~s** commissioni fpl bancarie; **labour ~s** costi mpl del lavoro; **to ~ in/out** precipitarsi dentro/fuori; **to ~ up/down** lanciarsi su/giù per; **is there a ~?** c'è da pagare?; **there's no ~** non c'è niente da pagare; **extra ~** supplemento; **to take ~ of** incaricarsi di; **to be in ~ of** essere responsabile per; **to have ~ of sb** aver cura di qn; **how much do you ~ for this repair?** quanto chiede per la riparazione?; **to ~ an expense (up) to sb** addebitare una spesa a qn; **~ it to my account** lo metta or addebiti sul mio conto.

charge account n conto.

charge card n carta di credito commerciale.

chargé d'affaires ['ʃɑːʒeɪdæ'feə*] n incaricato d'affari.

chargehand ['tʃɑːdʒhænd] n (BRIT) caposquadra m/f.

charger ['tʃɑːdʒə*] n (also: **battery** ~) caricabatterie m inv; (old: warhorse) destriero.

chariot ['tʃærɪət] n carro.

charitable ['tʃærɪtəbl] adj caritatevole.

charity ['tʃærɪtɪ] n carità; (organization) opera pia.

charlady ['tʃɑːleɪdɪ] n (BRIT) domestica a ore.

charlatan ['ʃɑːlətən] n ciarlatano.

charm [tʃɑːm] n fascino; (on bracelet) ciondolo ♦ vt affascinare, incantare.

charm bracelet n braccialetto con ciondoli.

charming ['tʃɑːmɪŋ] adj affascinante.

chart [tʃɑːt] n tabella; grafico; (map) carta nautica; (weather ~) carta del tempo ♦ vt fare una carta nautica di; (sales, progress) tracciare il grafico di; **to be in the ~s** (record, pop group) essere in classifica.

charter ['tʃɑːtə*] vt (plane) noleggiare ♦ n (document) carta; **on** ~ a nolo.

chartered accountant (CA) ['tʃɑːtəd-] n (BRIT) ragioniere/a professionista.

charter flight n volo m charter inv.

charwoman ['tʃɑːwumən] n = **charlady**.

chase [tʃeɪs] vt inseguire; (also: ~ **away**) cacciare ♦ n caccia.

▶**chase down** vt (US) = **chase up**.

▶**chase up** vt (BRIT: person) scovare; (: information) scoprire, raccogliere.

chasm ['kæzəm] n abisso.

chassis ['ʃæsɪ] n telaio.

chastened ['tʃeɪsnd] adj abbattuto(a), provato(a).

chastening ['tʃeɪsnɪŋ] adj che fa riflettere.

chastise [tʃæs'taɪz] vt punire, castigare.

chastity ['tʃæstɪtɪ] n castità.

chat [tʃæt] vi (also: **have a** ~) chiacchierare ♦ n chiacchierata.

▶**chat up** vt (BRIT col: girl) abbordare.

chatline ['tʃætlaɪn] n chatline f.

chat show n (BRIT) talk show m inv, conversazione f televisiva.

chattel ['tʃætl] n see **goods**.

chatter ['tʃætə*] vi (person) ciarlare ♦ n ciarle fpl; **her teeth were** ~**ing** batteva i denti.

chatterbox ['tʃætəbɔks] n chiacchierone/a.

chattering classes ['tʃætərɪŋ-] npl: **the** ~ (col, pej) ≈ gli intellettuali da salotto.

chatty ['tʃætɪ] adj (style) familiare; (person) chiacchierino(a).

chauffeur ['ʃəufə*] n autista m.

chauvinism ['ʃəuvɪnɪzəm] n (also: **male** ~) maschilismo; (nationalism) sciovinismo.

chauvinist ['ʃəuvɪnɪst] n (also: **male** ~) maschilista m; (nationalist) sciovinista m/f.

chauvinistic [ʃəuvɪ'nɪstɪk] adj sciovinistico(a).

ChE abbr = **chemical engineer**.

cheap [tʃiːp] adj a buon mercato; (reduced: fare, ticket) ridotto(a); (joke) grossolano(a); (poor quality) di cattiva qualità ♦ adv a buon mercato; ~**er** meno caro; ~ **money** denaro a basso tasso di interesse.

cheapen ['tʃiːpn] vt ribassare; (fig) avvilire.

cheaply ['tʃiːplɪ] adv a buon prezzo, a buon mercato.

cheat [tʃiːt] vi imbrogliare; (at school) copiare ♦ vt ingannare; (rob) defraudare ♦ n imbroglione m; copione m; (trick) inganno; **he's been** ~**ing on his wife** ha tradito sua moglie.

cheating ['tʃiːtɪŋ] n imbrogliare m; copiare m.

check [tʃɛk] vt verificare; (passport, ticket) controllare; (halt) fermare; (restrain) contenere ♦ vi (official etc) informarsi ♦ n verifica; controllo; (curb) freno; (bill) conto; (pattern: gen pl) quadretti mpl; (US) = **cheque** ♦ adj (also: ~**ed**: pattern, cloth) a scacchi, a quadretti; **to** ~ **with sb** chiedere a qn; **to keep a** ~ **on sb/sth** controllare qn/qc, fare attenzione a qn/qc.

▶**check in** vi (in hotel) registrare; (at airport) presentarsi all'accettazione ♦ vt (luggage) depositare.

▶**check off** vt segnare.

▶**check out** vi (from hotel) saldare il conto ♦ vt (luggage) ritirare; (investigate: story) controllare, verificare; (: person) prendere informazioni su.

▶**check up** vi: **to** ~ **up (on sth)** investigare (qc); **to** ~ **up on sb** informarsi sul conto di qn.

checkbook ['tʃɛkbuk] n (US) = **chequebook**.

checkered ['tʃɛkəd] adj (US) = **chequered**.

checkers ['tʃɛkəz] n (US) dama.

check guarantee card n (US) carta f assegni inv.

check-in ['tʃɛkɪn] n (also: ~ **desk**: at airport) check-in m inv, accettazione f (bagagli inv).

checking account ['tʃɛkɪŋ-] n (US) conto corrente.

checklist ['tʃɛklɪst] n lista di controllo.

checkmate ['tʃɛkmeɪt] n scaccomatto.

checkout ['tʃɛkaut] n (in supermarket)

cassa.

checkpoint ['tʃɛkpɔɪnt] *n* posto di blocco.

checkroom ['tʃɛkrum] *n* (*US*) deposito *m* bagagli *inv*.

checkup ['tʃɛkʌp] *n* (*MED*) controllo medico.

cheek [tʃiːk] *n* guancia; (*impudence*) faccia tosta.

cheekbone ['tʃiːkbəun] *n* zigomo.

cheeky ['tʃiːkɪ] *adj* sfacciato(a).

cheep [tʃiːp] *n* (*of bird*) pigolio ♦ *vi* pigolare.

cheer [tʃɪə*] *vt* applaudire; (*gladden*) rallegrare ♦ *vi* applaudire ♦ *n* (*gen pl*) applausi *mpl*; evviva *mpl*; ~s! salute!
►**cheer on** *vt* (*person etc*) incitare.
►**cheer up** *vi* rallegrarsi, farsi animo ♦ *vt* rallegrare.

cheerful ['tʃɪəful] *adj* allegro(a).

cheerfulness ['tʃɪəfulnɪs] *n* allegria.

cheerio ['tʃɪərɪ'əu] *excl* (*BRIT*) ciao!

cheerleader ['tʃɪəliːdə*] *n* cheerleader *f inv*.

cheerless ['tʃɪəlɪs] *adj* triste.

cheese [tʃiːz] *n* formaggio.

cheeseboard ['tʃiːzbɔːd] *n* piatto del (*or* per il) formaggio.

cheeseburger ['tʃiːzbɔːgə*] *n* cheeseburger *m inv*.

cheesecake ['tʃiːzkeɪk] *n* specie di torta di ricotta, a volte con frutta.

cheetah ['tʃiːtə] *n* ghepardo.

chef [ʃɛf] *n* capocuoco.

chemical ['kɛmɪkl] *adj* chimico(a) ♦ *n* prodotto chimico.

chemical engineering *n* ingegneria chimica.

chemist ['kɛmɪst] *n* (*BRIT: pharmacist*) farmacista *m/f*; (*scientist*) chimico/a; ~'s **shop** *n* (*BRIT*) farmacia.

chemistry ['kɛmɪstrɪ] *n* chimica.

chemotherapy [kiːməu'θɛrəpɪ] *n* chemioterapia.

cheque, (*US*) **check** [tʃɛk] *n* assegno; **to pay by** ~ pagare per assegno *or* con un assegno.

chequebook, (*US*) **checkbook** ['tʃɛkbuk] *n* libretto degli assegni.

cheque card *n* (*BRIT*) carta *f* assegni *inv*.

chequered, (*US*) **checkered** ['tʃɛkəd] *adj* (*fig*) movimentato(a).

cherish ['tʃɛrɪʃ] *vt* aver caro; (*hope etc*) nutrire.

cheroot [ʃə'ruːt] *n* sigaro spuntato.

cherry ['tʃɛrɪ] *n* ciliegia.

Ches *abbr* (*BRIT*) = Cheshire.

chess [tʃɛs] *n* scacchi *mpl*.

chessboard ['tʃɛsbɔːd] *n* scacchiera.

chessman ['tʃɛsmæn] *n* pezzo degli scacchi.

chessplayer ['tʃɛspleɪə*] *n* scacchista *m/f*.

chest [tʃɛst] *n* petto; (*box*) cassa; **to get sth off one's** ~ (*col*) sputare il rospo; ~ **of drawers** cassettone *m*.

chest measurement *n* giro *m* torace *inv*.

chestnut ['tʃɛsnʌt] *n* castagna; (*also:* ~ *tree*) castagno ♦ *adj* castano(a).

chesty ['tʃɛstɪ] *adj:* ~ **cough** tosse *f* bronchiale.

chew [tʃuː] *vt* masticare.

chewing gum ['tʃuːɪŋ-] *n* chewing gum *m*.

chic [ʃiːk] *adj* elegante.

chick [tʃɪk] *n* pulcino; (*US col*) pollastrella.

chicken ['tʃɪkɪn] *n* pollo; (*col: coward*) coniglio.
►**chicken out** *vi* (*col*) avere fifa; **to** ~ **out of sth** tirarsi indietro da qc per fifa *or* paura.

chicken feed *n* (*fig*) miseria.

chickenpox ['tʃɪkɪnpɔks] *n* varicella.

chickpea ['tʃɪkpiː] *n* cece *m*.

chicory ['tʃɪkərɪ] *n* cicoria.

chide [tʃaɪd] *vt* rimproverare.

chief [tʃiːf] *n* capo ♦ *adj* principale; **C~ of Staff** (*MIL*) Capo di Stato Maggiore.

chief constable *n* (*BRIT*) ≈ questore *m*.

chief executive, (*US*) **chief executive officer (CEO)** *n* direttore *m* generale.

chiefly ['tʃiːflɪ] *adv* per lo più, soprattutto.

chiffon ['ʃɪfɔn] *n* chiffon *m inv*.

chilblain ['tʃɪlbleɪn] *n* gelone *m*.

child, *pl* ~**ren** [tʃaɪld, 'tʃɪldrən] *n* bambino/a.

child abuse *n* molestie *fpl* a minori.

child abuser [-ə'bjuːzə*] *n* molestatore/trice di bambini.

child benefit *n* (*BRIT*) ≈ assegni *mpl* familiari.

childbirth ['tʃaɪldbɔːθ] *n* parto.

childhood ['tʃaɪldhud] *n* infanzia.

childish ['tʃaɪldɪʃ] *adj* puerile.

childless ['tʃaɪldlɪs] *adj* senza figli.

childlike ['tʃaɪldlaɪk] *adj* fanciullesco(a).

child minder *n* (*BRIT*) bambinaia.

child prodigy *n* bambino *m* prodigio *inv*.

children ['tʃɪldrən] *npl of* **child**.

children's home *n* istituto per l'infanzia.

Chile ['tʃɪlɪ] *n* Cile *m*.

Chilean ['tʃɪlɪən] *adj, n* cileno(a).

chill [tʃɪl] *n* freddo; (*MED*) infreddatura ♦ *adj* freddo(a), gelido(a) ♦ *vt* raffreddare; (*CULIN*) mettere in fresco; **"serve ~ed"** "servire fresco".
►**chill out** *vi* (*esp US: col*) darsi una calmata.

chilli, (*US*) **chili** ['tʃɪlɪ] *n* peperoncino.

chilling ['tʃɪlɪŋ] *adj* agghiacciante; (*wind*) gelido(a).

chilly ['tʃɪlɪ] *adj* freddo(a), fresco(a); (*sensitive to cold*) freddoloso(a); **to feel** ~ sentirsi infreddolito(a).

chime [tʃaɪm] *n* carillon *m inv* ♦ *vi* suonare, scampanare.

chimney ['tʃɪmnɪ] *n* camino.

chimney sweep *n* spazzacamino.

chimpanzee [tʃɪmpæn'ziː] *n* scimpanzé *m inv*.

chin [tʃɪn] *n* mento.

China ['tʃaɪnə] *n* Cina.

china ['tʃaɪnə] *n* porcellana.

Chinese [tʃaɪ'niːz] *adj* cinese ♦ *n* (*pl inv*) cinese *m/f*; (*LING*) cinese *m*.

chink [tʃɪŋk] *n* (*opening*) fessura; (*noise*) tintinnio.

chinwag ['tʃɪnwæg] *n* (*col*): **to have a** ~ fare una chiacchierata.

chip [tʃɪp] *n* (*gen pl: CULIN*) patatina fritta; (*: US: also*: **potato** ~) patatina; (*of wood, glass, stone*) scheggia; (*in gambling*) fiche *f inv*; (*COMPUT: micro*~) chip *m inv* ♦ *vt* (*cup, plate*) scheggiare; **when the** ~**s are down** (*fig*) al momento critico.

▶**chip in** *vi* (*col: contribute*) contribuire; (*: interrupt*) intromettersi.

chipboard ['tʃɪpbɔːd] *n* agglomerato.

chipmunk ['tʃɪpmʌŋk] *n* tamia *m* striato.

chippings ['tʃɪpɪŋz] *npl*: **loose** ~ brecciame *m*.

I **chip shop**, *anche chiamati* **fish-and-chip shop**, *sono friggitorie che vendono principalmente filetti di pesce impanati e patatine fritte che un tempo venivano serviti ai clienti avvolti in carta di giornale.*

---

chiropodist [kɪ'rɒpədɪst] *n* (*BRIT*) pedicure *m/f inv*.

chiropody [kɪ'rɒpədɪ] *n* (*BRIT*) mestiere *m* di callista.

chirp [tʃəːp] *n* cinguettio; (*of crickets*) cri cri *m* ♦ *vi* cinguettare.

chirpy ['tʃəːpɪ] *adj* (*col*) frizzante.

chisel ['tʃɪzl] *n* cesello.

chit [tʃɪt] *n* biglietto.

chitchat ['tʃɪttʃæt] *n* (*col*) chiacchiere *fpl*.

chivalrous ['ʃɪvəlrəs] *adj* cavalleresco(a).

chivalry ['ʃɪvəlrɪ] *n* cavalleria; cortesia.

chives [tʃaɪvz] *npl* erba cipollina.

chloride ['klɔːraɪd] *n* cloruro.

chlorinate ['klɔrɪneɪt] *vt* clorare.

chlorine ['klɔːriːn] *n* cloro.

chock [tʃɒk] *n* zeppa.

chock-a-block ['tʃɒkə'blɒk], **chockfull** ['tʃɒk'ful] *adj* pieno(a) zeppo(a).

chocolate ['tʃɒklɪt] *n* (*substance*) cioccolato, cioccolata; (*drink*) cioccolata; (*a sweet*) cioccolatino.

choice [tʃɔɪs] *n* scelta ♦ *adj* scelto(a); **a wide** ~ un'ampia scelta; **I did it by** *or* **from** ~ l'ho fatto di mia volontà *or* per mia scelta.

choir ['kwaɪə*] *n* coro.

choirboy ['kwaɪəbɔɪ] *n* corista *m* fanciullo.

choke [tʃəuk] *vi* soffocare ♦ *vt* soffocare; (*block*) ingombrare ♦ *n* (*AUT*) valvola dell'aria.

cholera ['kɒlərə] *n* colera *m*.

cholesterol [kə'lɛstərɔl] *n* colesterolo.

choose, *pt* **chose**, *pp* **chosen** [tʃuːz, tʃəuz, 'tʃəuzn] *vt* scegliere; **to** ~ **to do** decidere di fare; preferire fare; **to** ~ **between** scegliere tra; **to** ~ **from** scegliere da *or* tra.

choosy ['tʃuːzɪ] *adj*: (**to be**) ~ (fare lo(la)) schizzinoso(a).

chop [tʃɒp] *vt* (*wood*) spaccare; (*CULIN: also*: ~ **up**) tritare ♦ *n* colpo netto; (*CULIN*) costoletta; **to get the** ~ (*BRIT col: project*) essere bocciato(a); (*: person: be sacked*) essere licenziato(a); *see also* **chops**.

▶**chop down** *vt* (*tree*) abbattere.

choppy ['tʃɒpɪ] *adj* (*sea*) mosso(a).

chops [tʃɒps] *npl* (*jaws*) mascelle *fpl*.

chopsticks ['tʃɒpstɪks] *npl* bastoncini *mpl* cinesi.

choral ['kɔːrəl] *adj* corale.

chord [kɔːd] *n* (*MUS*) accordo.

chore [tʃɔː*] *n* faccenda; **household** ~**s** faccende *fpl* domestiche.

choreographer [kɒrɪ'ɒgrəfə*] *n* coreografo/a.

choreography [kɒrɪ'ɒgrəfɪ] *n* coreografia.

chorister ['kɒrɪstə*] *n* corista *m/f*.

chortle ['tʃɔːtl] *vi* ridacchiare.

chorus ['kɔːrəs] *n* coro; (*repeated part of song, also fig*) ritornello.

chose [tʃəuz] *pt of* **choose**.

chosen ['tʃəuzn] *pp of* **choose**.

chowder ['tʃaudə*] *n* zuppa di pesce.

Christ [kraɪst] *n* Cristo.

christen ['krɪsn] *vt* battezzare.

christening ['krɪsnɪŋ] *n* battesimo.

Christian ['krɪstɪən] *adj, n* cristiano(a).

Christianity [krɪstɪ'ænɪtɪ] *n* cristianesimo.

Christian name *n* nome *m* di battesimo.

Christmas ['krɪsməs] *n* Natale *m*; **happy** *or* **merry** ~! Buon Natale!

Christmas card *n* cartolina di Natale.

Christmas Day *n* il giorno di Natale.

Christmas Eve *n* la vigilia di Natale.

Christmas Island *n* isola di Christmas.

Christmas tree *n* albero di Natale.

chrome [krəum] *n* = **chromium**.

chromium ['krəumɪəm] *n* cromo; (*also*: ~

plating) cromatura.
chromosome ['krəuməsəum] n cromosoma m.
chronic ['krɔnɪk] adj cronico(a); (fig: liar, smoker) incallito(a).
chronicle ['krɔnɪkl] n cronaca.
chronological [krɔnə'lɔdʒɪkl] adj cronologico(a).
chrysanthemum [krɪ'sænθəməm] n crisantemo.
chubby ['tʃʌbɪ] adj paffuto(a).
chuck [tʃʌk] vt buttare, gettare; **to ~ (up** or **in)** (BRIT: job, person) piantare.
►**chuck out** vt buttar fuori.
chuckle ['tʃʌkl] vi ridere sommessamente.
chuffed [tʃʌft] adj (col): **to be ~ about sth** essere arcicontento(a) di qc.
chug [tʃʌg] vi (also: ~ **along**: train) muoversi sbuffando.
chum [tʃʌm] n compagno/a.
chump [tʃʌmp] n (col) idiota m/f.
chunk [tʃʌŋk] n pezzo; (of bread) tocco.
chunky [tʃʌŋkɪ] adj (furniture etc) basso(a) e largo(a); (person) ben piantato(a); (knitwear) di lana grossa.
Chunnel ['tʃʌnəl] n = **Channel Tunnel.**
church [tʃəːtʃ] n chiesa; **the C~ of England** la Chiesa anglicana.
churchyard ['tʃəːtʃjɑːd] n sagrato.
churlish ['tʃəːlɪʃ] adj rozzo(a), sgarbato(a).
churn [tʃəːn] n (for butter) zangola; (also: milk ~) bidone m.
►**churn out** vt sfornare.
chute [ʃuːt] n cascata; (also: **rubbish** ~) canale m di scarico; (BRIT: children's slide) scivolo.
chutney ['tʃʌtnɪ] n salsa piccante (di frutta, zucchero e spezie).
CIA n abbr (US: = Central Intelligence Agency) C.I.A. f.
CID n abbr (BRIT) see **Criminal Investigation Department.**
cider ['saɪdə*] n sidro.
CIF abbr (= cost, insurance and freight) C.I.F. m.
cigar [sɪ'gɑː*] n sigaro.
cigarette [sɪgə'rɛt] n sigaretta.
cigarette case n portasigarette m inv.
cigarette end n mozzicone m.
cigarette holder n bocchino.
C-in-C abbr see **commander-in-chief.**
cinch [sɪntʃ] n (col): **it's a ~** è presto fatto; (sure thing) è una cosa sicura.
cinder ['sɪndə*] n cenere f.
Cinderella [sɪndə'rɛlə] n Cenerentola.
cine-camera ['sɪnɪ'kæmərə] n (BRIT) cinepresa.
cine-film ['sɪnɪfɪlm] n (BRIT) pellicola.

cinema ['sɪnəmə] n cinema m inv.
cine-projector ['sɪnɪprə'dʒɛktə*] n (BRIT) proiettore m.
cinnamon ['sɪnəmən] n cannella.
cipher ['saɪfə*] n cifra; (fig: faceless employee etc) persona di nessun conto; **in ~** in codice.
circa ['səːkə] prep circa.
circle ['səːkl] n cerchio; (of friends etc) circolo; (in cinema) galleria ♦ vi girare in circolo ♦ vt (surround) circondare; (move round) girare intorno a.
circuit ['səːkɪt] n circuito.
circuit board n (COMPUT) tavola dei circuiti.
circuitous [səː'kjuɪtəs] adj indiretto(a).
circular ['səːkjulə*] adj circolare ♦ n (letter) circolare f; (as advertisement) volantino pubblicitario.
circulate ['səːkjuleɪt] vi circolare; (person: socially) girare e andare un po' da tutti ♦ vt far circolare.
circulating capital ['səːkjuleɪtɪŋ-] n (COMM) capitale m d'esercizio.
circulation [səːkju'leɪʃən] n circolazione f; (of newspaper) tiratura.
circumcise ['səːkəmsaɪz] vt circoncidere.
circumference [sə'kʌmfərəns] n circonferenza.
circumflex ['səːkəmflɛks] n (also: ~ **accent**) accento circonflesso.
circumscribe ['səːkəmskraɪb] vt circoscrivere; (fig: limit) limitare.
circumspect ['səːkəmspɛkt] adj circospetto(a).
circumstances ['səːkəmstənsɪz] npl circostanze fpl; (financial condition) condizioni fpl finanziarie; **in the ~s** date le circostanze; **under no ~s** per nessun motivo.
circumstantial ['səːkəm'stænʃəl] adj (report, statement) circostanziato(a), dettagliato(a); ~ **evidence** prova indiretta.
circumvent [səːkəm'vɛnt] vt (rule etc) aggirare.
circus ['səːkəs] n circo; (also: **C~**: in place names) piazza (di forma circolare).
cirrhosis [sɪ'rəusɪs] n (also: ~ **of the liver**) cirrosi f inv (epatica).
CIS n abbr (= Commonwealth of Independent States) CSI f.
cissy ['sɪsɪ] n = **sissy.**
cistern ['sɪstən] n cisterna; (in toilet) serbatoio d'acqua.
citation [saɪ'teɪʃən] n citazione f.
cite [saɪt] vt citare.
citizen ['sɪtɪzn] n (POL) cittadino/a;

(*resident*): **the ~s of this town** gli abitanti di questa città.

Citizens' Advice Bureau n (*BRIT*) organizzazione di volontari che offre gratuitamente assistenza legale e finanziaria.

citizenship ['sɪtɪznʃɪp] n cittadinanza.

citric ['sɪtrɪk] adj: ~ **acid** acido citrico.

citrus fruit ['sɪtrəs-] n agrume m.

city ['sɪtɪ] n città f inv; **the C~** la Città di Londra (*centro commerciale*).

city centre n centro della città.

City Hall n (*US*) ≈ Comune m.

City Technology College n (*BRIT*) istituto tecnico superiore (*finanziato dall'industria*).

civic ['sɪvɪk] adj civico(a).

civic centre n (*BRIT*) centro civico.

civil ['sɪvɪl] adj civile; (*polite*) educato(a), gentile.

civil disobedience n disubbidienza civile.

civil engineer n ingegnere m civile.

civil engineering n ingegneria civile.

civilian [sɪ'vɪlɪən] adj, n borghese (*m/f*).

civilization [sɪvɪlaɪ'zeɪʃən] n civiltà f inv.

civilized ['sɪvɪlaɪzd] adj civilizzato(a); (*fig*) cortese.

civil law n codice m civile; (*study*) diritto civile.

civil liberties npl libertà fpl civili.

civil rights npl diritti mpl civili.

civil servant n impiegato/a statale.

Civil Service n amministrazione f statale.

civil war n guerra civile.

civvies ['sɪvɪz] npl (*col*): **in ~** in borghese.

cl abbr (= centilitre) cl.

clad [klæd] adj: ~ **(in)** vestito(a) (di).

claim [kleɪm] vt (*rights etc*) rivendicare; (*damages*) richiedere; (*assert*) sostenere, pretendere ♦ vi (*for insurance*) fare una domanda d'indennizzo ♦ n rivendicazione f; pretesa; (*right*) diritto; **to ~ that/to be** sostenere che/di essere; (*insurance*) ~ domanda d'indennizzo; **to put in a ~ for sth** fare una richiesta di qc.

claimant ['kleɪmənt] n (*ADMIN, LAW*) richiedente m/f.

claim form n (*gen*) modulo di richiesta; (*for expenses*) modulo di rimborso spese.

clairvoyant [klɛə'vɔɪənt] n chiaroveggente m/f.

clam [klæm] n vongola.

►**clam up** vi (*col*) azzittirsi.

clamber ['klæmbə*] vi arrampicarsi.

clammy ['klæmɪ] adj (*weather*) caldo(a) umido(a); (*hands*) viscido(a).

clamour, (*US*) **clamor** ['klæmə*] n (*noise*) clamore m; (*protest*) protesta ♦ vi: **to ~ for**

sth chiedere a gran voce qc.

clamp [klæmp] n pinza; morsa ♦ vt ammorsare.

►**clamp down** vt fus (*fig*): **to ~ down (on)** dare un giro di vite (a).

clampdown ['klæmpdaun] n stretta, giro di vite; **a ~ on sth/sb** un giro di vite a qc/ qn.

clan [klæn] n clan m inv.

clandestine [klæn'dɛstɪn] adj clandestino(a).

clang [klæŋ] n fragore m, suono metallico.

clanger ['klæŋə*] n: **to drop a ~** (*BRIT col*) fare una gaffe.

clansman ['klænzmən] n membro di un clan.

clap [klæp] vi applaudire ♦ vt: **to ~ one's hands** battere le mani ♦ n: **a ~ of thunder** un tuono.

clapping ['klæpɪŋ] n applausi mpl.

claptrap ['klæptræp] n (*col*) stupidaggini fpl.

claret ['klærət] n vino di Bordeaux.

clarification [klærɪfɪ'keɪʃən] n (*fig*) chiarificazione f, chiarimento.

clarify ['klærɪfaɪ] vt chiarificare, chiarire.

clarinet [klærɪ'nɛt] n clarinetto.

clarity ['klærɪtɪ] n chiarezza.

clash [klæʃ] n frastuono; (*fig*) scontro ♦ vi (*MIL, fig: have an argument*) scontrarsi; (*colours*) stridere; (*dates, events*) coincidere.

clasp [klɑːsp] n fermaglio, fibbia ♦ vt stringere.

class [klɑːs] n classe f; (*group, category*) tipo, categoria ♦ vt classificare.

class-conscious ['klɑːskɔnʃəs] adj che ha coscienza di classe.

class consciousness n coscienza di classe.

classic ['klæsɪk] adj classico(a) ♦ n classico.

classical ['klæsɪkəl] adj classico(a).

classics ['klæsɪks] npl (*SCOL*) studi mpl umanistici.

classification [klæsɪfɪ'keɪʃən] n classificazione f.

classified ['klæsɪfaɪd] adj (*information*) segreto(a), riservato(a); ~ **ads** annunci economici.

classify ['klæsɪfaɪ] vt classificare.

classless society ['klɑːslɪs-] n società f inv senza distinzioni di classe.

classmate ['klɑːsmeɪt] n compagno/a di classe.

classroom ['klɑːsrum] n aula.

clatter ['klætə*] n acciottolio; scalpitio ♦ vi acciottolare; scalpitare.

clause [klɔːz] n clausola; (*LING*) proposizione f.

claustrophobia [klɔːstrə'fəubɪə] n claustrofobia.

claustrophobic [klɔːstrə'fəubɪk] adj claustrofobico(a).

claw [klɔː] n tenaglia; (of bird of prey) artiglio; (of lobster) pinza ♦ vt graffiare; afferrare.

clay [kleɪ] n argilla.

clean [kliːn] adj pulito(a); (clear, smooth) netto(a) ♦ vt pulire ♦ adv: **he ~ forgot** si è completamente dimenticato; **to come ~** (col: admit guilt) confessare; **to have a ~ driving licence** or (US) **record** non aver mai preso contravvenzioni; **to ~ one's teeth** (BRIT) lavarsi i denti.

▶**clean off** vt togliere.

▶**clean out** vt ripulire.

▶**clean up** vi far pulizia ♦ vt (also fig) ripulire; (fig: make profit): **to ~ up on** fare una barca di soldi con.

clean-cut ['kliːn'kʌt] adj (man) curato(a); (situation etc) ben definito(a).

cleaner ['kliːnə*] n (person) uomo/donna delle pulizie; (also: **dry ~**) tintore/a; (product) smacchiatore m.

cleaning ['kliːnɪŋ] n pulizia.

cleaning lady n donna delle pulizie.

cleanliness ['klɛnlɪnɪs] n pulizia.

cleanly ['kliːnlɪ] adv in modo netto.

cleanse [klɛnz] vt pulire; purificare.

cleanser ['klɛnzə*] n detergente m; (cosmetic) latte m detergente.

clean-shaven ['kliːn'ʃeɪvn] adj sbarbato(a).

cleansing department ['klɛnzɪŋ-] n (BRIT) nettezza urbana.

clean sweep n: **to make a ~ (of)** fare piazza pulita (di).

clean-up ['kliːnʌp] n pulizia.

clear [klɪə*] adj chiaro(a); (road, way) libero(a); (profit, majority) netto(a) ♦ vt sgombrare; liberare; (site, woodland) spianare; (COMM: goods) liquidare; (LAW: suspect) discolpare; (obstacle) superare; (cheque) fare la compensazione di ♦ vi (weather) rasserenarsi; (fog) andarsene ♦ adv: **~ of** distante da ♦ n: **to be in the ~** (out of debt) essere in attivo; (out of suspicion) essere a posto; (out of danger) essere fuori pericolo; **to ~ the table** sparecchiare (la tavola); **to ~ one's throat** schiarirsi la gola; **to ~ a profit** avere un profitto netto; **to make o.s. ~** spiegarsi bene; **to make it ~ to sb that ...** far capire a qn che ...; **I have a ~ day tomorrow** (BRIT) non ho impegni domani; **to keep ~ of sb/sth** tenersi lontano da qn/qc, stare alla larga da qn/qc.

▶**clear off** vi (col: leave) svignarsela.

▶**clear up** vi schiarirsi ♦ vt mettere in ordine; (mystery) risolvere.

clearance ['klɪərəns] n (removal) sgombro; (free space) spazio; (permission) autorizzazione f, permesso.

clearance sale n vendita di liquidazione.

clear-cut ['klɪə'kʌt] adj ben delineato(a), distinto(a).

clearing ['klɪərɪŋ] n radura; (BRIT BANKING) clearing m.

clearing bank n (BRIT) banca che fa uso della camera di compensazione.

clearing house n (COMM) camera di compensazione.

clearly ['klɪəlɪ] adv chiaramente.

clearway ['klɪəweɪ] n (BRIT) strada con divieto di sosta.

cleavage ['kliːvɪdʒ] n (of woman) scollatura.

cleaver ['kliːvə*] n mannaia.

clef [klɛf] n (MUS) chiave f.

cleft [klɛft] n (in rock) crepa, fenditura.

clemency ['klɛmənsɪ] n clemenza.

clement ['klɛmənt] adj (weather) mite, clemente.

clench [klɛntʃ] vt stringere.

clergy ['klɜːdʒɪ] n clero.

clergyman ['klɜːdʒɪmən] n ecclesiastico.

clerical ['klɛrɪkl] adj d'impiegato; (REL) clericale.

clerk [klɑːk, (US) klɜːrk] n impiegato/a; (US: salesman/woman) commesso/a; **C~ of the Court** (LAW) cancelliere m.

clever ['klɛvə*] adj (mentally) intelligente; (deft, skilful) abile; (device, arrangement) ingegnoso(a).

cleverly ['klɛvəlɪ] adv abilmente.

clew [kluː] n (US) = **clue**.

cliché ['kliːʃeɪ] n cliché m inv.

click [klɪk] vi scattare ♦ vt: **to ~ one's tongue** schioccare la lingua; **to ~ one's heels** battere i tacchi.

client ['klaɪənt] n cliente m/f.

clientele [kliːɑːn'tɛl] n clientela.

cliff [klɪf] n scogliera scoscesa, rupe f.

cliffhanger ['klɪfhæŋə*] n (TV, fig) episodio (or situazione etc) ricco(a) di suspense.

climactic [klaɪ'mæktɪk] adj culminante.

climate ['klaɪmɪt] n clima m.

climax ['klaɪmæks] n culmine m; (of play etc) momento più emozionante; (sexual ~) orgasmo.

climb [klaɪm] vi salire; (clamber) arrampicarsi; (plane) prendere quota ♦ vt salire; (CLIMBING) scalare ♦ n salita; arrampicata; scalata; **to ~ over a wall** scavalcare un muro.

▶**climb down** vi scendere; (BRIT fig) far

marcia indietro.

climbdown ['klaimdaun] n (BRIT) ritirata.

climber ['klaimə*] n (also: **rock** ~)
rocciatore/trice; alpinista m/f.

climbing ['klaimiŋ] n (also: **rock** ~)
alpinismo.

clinch [klintʃ] vt (deal) concludere.

clincher ['klintʃə*] n (col): **that was the** ~
quello è stato il fattore decisivo.

cling, pt, pp **clung** [kliŋ, klʌŋ] vi: **to** ~ **(to)**
tenersi stretto(a) (a); (of clothes) aderire
strettamente (a).

clingfilm ['kliŋfilm] n pellicola trasparente
(per alimenti).

clinic ['klinik] n clinica; (session) seduta;
serie f di sedute.

clinical ['klinikəl] adj clinico(a); (fig)
freddo(a), distaccato(a).

clink [kliŋk] vi tintinnare.

clip [klip] n (for hair) forcina; (also: **paper** ~)
graffetta; (BRIT: also: **bulldog** ~)
fermafogli m inv; (holding hose etc) anello
d'attacco ♦ vt (also: ~ **together**: papers)
attaccare insieme; (hair, nails) tagliare;
(hedge) tosare.

clippers ['klipəz] npl macchinetta per
capelli; (also: **nail** ~) forbicine fpl per le
unghie.

clipping ['klipiŋ] n (from newspaper)
ritaglio.

clique [kliːk] n cricca.

cloak [kləuk] n mantello ♦ vt avvolgere.

cloakroom ['kləukrum] n (for coats etc)
guardaroba m inv; (BRIT: W.C.) gabinetti
mpl.

clock [klɔk] n orologio; (of taxi) tassametro;
around the ~ ventiquattr'ore su
ventiquattro; **to sleep round the** ~ or **the**
~ **round** dormire un giorno intero; **to
work against the** ~ lavorare in gara col
tempo; **30,000 on the** ~ (BRIT AUT) 30.000
sul contachilometri.

►**clock in, clock on** vi (BRIT) timbrare il
cartellino (all'entrata).

►**clock off, clock out** vi (BRIT) timbrare il
cartellino (all'uscita).

►**clock up** vt (miles, hours etc) fare.

clockwise ['klɔkwaiz] adv in senso orario.

clockwork ['klɔkwəːk] n movimento or
meccanismo a orologeria ♦ adj (toy, train)
a molla.

clog [klɔg] n zoccolo ♦ vt intasare ♦ vi
intasarsi, bloccarsi.

cloister ['klɔistə*] n chiostro.

clone [kləun] n clone m.

close adj, adv and derivatives [kləus] adj
vicino(a); (writing, texture) fitto(a); (watch)
stretto(a); (examination) attento(a);

(weather) afoso(a) ♦ adv vicino,
dappresso; ~ **to** prep vicino a; ~ **by**, ~ **at
hand** qui (or lì) vicino; **how** ~ **is
Edinburgh to Glasgow?** quanto dista
Edimburgo da Glasgow?; **a** ~ **friend** un
amico intimo; **to have a** ~ **shave** (fig)
scamparla bella; **at** ~ **quarters** da vicino
♦ vb, n and derivatives [kləuz] vt chiudere;
(bargain, deal) concludere ♦ vi (shop etc)
chiudere; (lid, door etc) chiudersi; (end)
finire ♦ n (end) fine f; **to bring sth to a** ~
terminare qc.

►**close down** vt chiudere
(definitivamente) ♦ vi cessare
(definitivamente).

►**close in** vi (hunters) stringersi attorno;
(evening, night, fog) calare; **to** ~ **in on sb**
accerchiare qn; **the days are closing in** le
giornate si accorciano.

►**close off** vt (area) chiudere.

closed [kləuzd] adj chiuso(a).

closed-circuit ['kləuzd'səːkit] adj: ~
television televisione f a circuito chiuso.

closed shop n azienda o fabbrica che
impiega solo aderenti ai sindacati.

close-knit ['kləus'nit] adj (family,
community) molto unito(a).

closely ['kləusli] adv (examine, watch) da
vicino; **we are** ~ **related** siamo parenti
stretti; **a** ~ **guarded secret** un assoluto
segreto.

close season ['kləuz-] n (FOOTBALL)
periodo di vacanza del campionato;
(HUNTING) stagione f di chiusura (di
caccia, pesca etc).

closet ['klɔzit] n (cupboard) armadio.

close-up ['kləusʌp] n primo piano.

closing ['kləuziŋ] adj (stages, remarks)
conclusivo(a), finale; ~ **price** (STOCK
EXCHANGE) prezzo di chiusura.

closing time n orario di chiusura.

closure ['kləuʒə*] n chiusura.

clot [klɔt] n (also: **blood** ~) coagulo; (col:
idiot) scemo/a ♦ vi coagularsi.

cloth [klɔθ] n (material) tessuto, stoffa;
(BRIT: also: **tea**~) strofinaccio; (also:
table~) tovaglia.

clothe [kləuð] vt vestire.

clothes [kləuðz] npl abiti mpl, vestiti mpl; **to
put one's** ~ **on** vestirsi; **to take one's** ~
off togliersi i vestiti, svestirsi.

clothes brush n spazzola per abiti.

clothes line n corda (per stendere il
bucato).

clothes peg, (US) **clothes pin** n molletta.

clothing ['kləuðiŋ] n = **clothes**.

clotted cream ['klɔtid-] n (BRIT) panna
rappresa.

cloud [klaud] *n* nuvola; (*of dust, smoke, gas*) nube *f* ♦ *vt* (*liquid*) intorbidire; **to ~ the issue** distogliere dal problema; **every ~ has a silver lining** (*proverb*) non tutto il male vien per nuocere.

▶**cloud over** *vi* rannuvolarsi; (*fig*) offuscarsi.

cloudburst ['klaudbəːst] *n* acquazzone *m*.

cloud-cuckoo-land ['klaud'kuku:'lænd] *n* (*BRIT*) mondo dei sogni.

cloudy ['klaudɪ] *adj* nuvoloso(a); (*liquid*) torbido(a).

clout [klaut] *n* (*blow*) colpo; (*fig*) influenza ♦ *vt* dare un colpo a.

clove [kləuv] *n* chiodo di garofano; **~ of garlic** spicchio d'aglio.

clover ['kləuvə*] *n* trifoglio.

cloverleaf ['kləuvəliːf] *n* foglia di trifoglio; (*AUT*) raccordo (a quadrifoglio).

clown [klaun] *n* pagliaccio ♦ *vi* (*also:* ~ **about,** ~ **around**) fare il pagliaccio.

cloying ['klɔɪɪŋ] *adj* (*taste, smell*) nauseabondo(a).

club [klʌb] *n* (*society*) club *m inv*, circolo; (*weapon, GOLF*) mazza ♦ *vt* bastonare ♦ *vi*: **to ~ together** associarsi; **~s** *npl* (*CARDS*) fiori *mpl*.

club car *n* (*US RAIL*) carrozza *or* vagone *m* ristorante.

club class *n* (*AVIAT*) classe *f* club.

clubhouse ['klʌbhaus] *n* sede *f* del circolo.

club soda *n* (*US*) = **soda.**

cluck [klʌk] *vi* chiocciare.

clue [kluː] *n* indizio; (*in crosswords*) definizione *f*; **I haven't a ~** non ho la minima idea.

clued up, (*US*) **clued in** [kluːd-] *adj* (*col*) (ben) informato(a).

clump [klʌmp] *n*: **~ of trees** folto d'alberi.

clumsy ['klʌmzɪ] *adj* (*person*) goffo(a), maldestro(a); (*object*) malfatto(a), mal costruito(a).

clung [klʌŋ] *pt, pp of* **cling.**

cluster ['klʌstə*] *n* gruppo ♦ *vi* raggrupparsi.

clutch [klʌtʃ] *n* (*grip, grasp*) presa, stretta; (*AUT*) frizione *f* ♦ *vt* afferrare, stringere forte; **to ~ at** aggrapparsi a.

clutter ['klʌtə*] *vt* (*also:* ~ **up**) ingombrare ♦ *n* confusione *f*, disordine *m*.

CM *abbr* (*US POST*) = North Marianna Islands.

cm *abbr* (= *centimetre*) cm.

CNAA *n abbr* (*BRIT*: = *Council for National Academic Awards*) *organizzazione che conferisce premi accademici.*

CND *n abbr* = *Campaign for Nuclear Disarmament.*

CO *n abbr* (= *commanding officer*) Com.;

(*BRIT*) = *Commonwealth Office* ♦ *abbr* (*US*) = Colorado.

Co. *abbr* = *county*; (= *company*) C., C.ia.

c/o *abbr* (= *care of*) c/o.

coach [kəutʃ] *n* (*bus*) pullman *m inv*; (*horse-drawn, of train*) carrozza; (*SPORT*) allenatore/trice ♦ *vt* allenare.

coach trip *n* viaggio in pullman.

coagulate [kəu'ægjuleɪt] *vt* coagulare ♦ *vi* coagularsi.

coal [kəul] *n* carbone *m*.

coalface ['kəulfeɪs] *n* fronte *f*.

coalfield ['kəulfiːld] *n* bacino carbonifero.

coalition [kəuə'lɪʃən] *n* coalizione *f*.

coalman ['kəulmən] *n* negoziante *m* di carbone.

coalmine ['kəulmaɪn] *n* miniera di carbone.

coalminer ['kəulmaɪnə*] *n* minatore *m*.

coalmining ['kəulmaɪnɪŋ] *n* estrazione *f* del carbone.

coarse [kɔːs] *adj* (*salt, sand etc*) grosso(a); (*cloth, person*) rozzo(a); (*vulgar: character, laugh*) volgare.

coast [kəust] *n* costa ♦ *vi* (*with cycle etc*) scendere a ruota libera.

coastal ['kəustəl] *adj* costiero(a).

coaster ['kəustə*] *n* (*NAUT*) nave *f* da cabotaggio; (*for glass*) sottobicchiere *m*.

coastguard ['kəustgɑːd] *n* guardia costiera.

coastline ['kəustlaɪn] *n* linea costiera.

coat [kəut] *n* cappotto; (*of animal*) pelo; (*of paint*) mano *f* ♦ *vt* coprire; **~ of arms** *n* stemma *m*.

coat hanger *n* attaccapanni *m inv*.

coating ['kəutɪŋ] *n* rivestimento.

co-author ['kəu'ɔːθə*] *n* coautore/trice.

coax [kəuks] *vt* indurre (con moine).

cob [kɔb] *n see* **corn.**

cobbler ['kɔblə*] *n* calzolaio.

cobbles ['kɔblz], **cobblestones** ['kɔblstəunz] *npl* ciottoli *mpl*.

COBOL ['kəubɔl] *n* COBOL *m*.

cobra ['kəubrə] *n* cobra *m inv*.

cobweb ['kɔbwɛb] *n* ragnatela.

cocaine [kə'keɪn] *n* cocaina.

cock [kɔk] *n* (*rooster*) gallo; (*male bird*) maschio ♦ *vt* (*gun*) armare; **to ~ one's ears** (*fig*) drizzare le orecchie.

cock-a-hoop [kɔkə'huːp] *adj* euforico(a).

cockerel ['kɔkərəl] *n* galletto.

cock-eyed ['kɔkaɪd] *adj* (*fig*) storto(a); strampalato(a).

cockle ['kɔkl] *n* cardio.

cockney ['kɔknɪ] *n* cockney *m/f inv* (*abitante dei quartieri popolari dell'East End di Londra*).

cockpit ['kɔkpɪt] *n* abitacolo.

cockroach ['kɔkrəutʃ] n blatta.
cocktail ['kɔkteɪl] n cocktail m inv; **prawn ~**, (US) **shrimp ~** cocktail m inv di gamberetti.
cocktail cabinet n mobile m bar inv.
cocktail party n cocktail m inv.
cocktail shaker n shaker m inv.
cocky ['kɔkɪ] adj spavaldo(a), arrogante.
cocoa ['kəukəu] n cacao.
coconut ['kəukənʌt] n noce f di cocco.
cocoon [kə'ku:n] n bozzolo.
COD abbr see **cash on delivery, collect on delivery**.
cod [kɔd] n merluzzo.
code [kəud] n codice m; **~ of behaviour** regole fpl di condotta; **~ of practice** codice professionale.
codeine ['kəudi:n] n codeina.
codger ['kɔdʒə*] n (BRIT col): **an old ~** un simpatico nonnetto.
codicil ['kɔdɪsɪl] n codicillo.
codify ['kəudɪfaɪ] vt codificare.
cod-liver oil ['kɔdlɪvə*-] n olio di fegato di merluzzo.
co-driver ['kəu'draɪvə*] n (in race) copilota m; (of lorry) secondo autista m.
co-ed ['kəu'ɛd] adj abbr = **coeducational ♦** n abbr (US: female student) studentessa presso un'università mista; (BRIT: school) scuola mista.
coeducational ['kəuɛdju'keɪʃənl] adj misto(a).
coerce [kəu'ə:s] vt costringere.
coercion [kəu'ə:ʃən] n coercizione f.
coexistence ['kəuɪg'zɪstəns] n coesistenza.
C. of C. n abbr = **chamber of commerce**.
C of E abbr = **Church of England**.
coffee ['kɔfɪ] n caffè m inv; **white ~**, (US) **~ with cream** caffellatte m.
coffee bar n (BRIT) caffè m inv.
coffee bean n grano o chicco di caffè.
coffee break n pausa per il caffè.
coffeecake ['kɔfɪkeɪk] n (US) panino dolce all'uva.
coffee cup n tazzina da caffè.
coffeepot ['kɔfɪpɔt] n caffettiera.
coffee table n tavolino da tè.
coffin ['kɔfɪn] n bara.
C of I abbr = **Church of Ireland**.
C of S abbr = **Church of Scotland**.
cog [kɔg] n dente m.
cogent ['kəudʒənt] adj convincente.
cognac ['kɔnjæk] n cognac m inv.
cogwheel ['kɔgwi:l] n ruota dentata.
cohabit [kəu'hæbɪt] vi (formal): **to ~ (with sb)** coabitare (con qn).
coherent [kəu'hɪərənt] adj coerente.
cohesion [kəu'hi:ʒən] n coesione f.

cohesive [kəu'hi:sɪv] adj (fig) unificante, coesivo(a).
COI n abbr (BRIT) = Central Office of Information.
coil [kɔɪl] n rotolo; (one loop) anello; (AUT, ELEC) bobina; (contraceptive) spirale f; (of smoke) filo ♦ vt avvolgere.
coin [kɔɪn] n moneta ♦ vt (word) coniare.
coinage ['kɔɪnɪdʒ] n sistema m monetario.
coin-box ['kɔɪnbɔks] n (BRIT) cabina telefonica.
coincide [kəuɪn'saɪd] vi coincidere.
coincidence [kəu'ɪnsɪdəns] n combinazione f.
coin-operated ['kɔɪn'ɔpəreɪtɪd] adj (machine) (che funziona) a monete.
Coke ® [kəuk] n (Coca-Cola) coca f inv.
coke [kəuk] n coke m.
Col. abbr = **colonel**; (US) = Colorado.
COLA n abbr (US: = cost-of-living adjustment) ≈ scala mobile.
colander ['kɔləndə*] n colino.
cold [kəuld] adj freddo(a) ♦ n freddo; (MED) raffreddore m; **it's ~** fa freddo; **to be ~** aver freddo; **to catch ~** prendere freddo; **to catch a ~** prendere un raffreddore; **in ~ blood** a sangue freddo; **to have ~ feet** avere i piedi freddi; (fig) aver la fifa; **to give sb the ~ shoulder** ignorare qn.
cold-blooded [kəuld'blʌdɪd] adj (ZOOL) a sangue freddo.
cold cream n crema emolliente.
coldly ['kəuldlɪ] adv freddamente.
cold sore n erpete m.
cold sweat n: **to be in a ~ (about sth)** sudare freddo (per qc).
cold turkey n (col): **to go ~** avere la scimmia (drogato).
Cold War n: **the ~** la guerra fredda.
coleslaw ['kəulslɔ:] n insalata di cavolo bianco.
colic ['kɔlɪk] n colica.
colicky ['kɔlɪkɪ] adj che soffre di coliche.
collaborate [kə'læbəreɪt] vi collaborare.
collaboration [kəlæbə'reɪʃən] n collaborazione f.
collaborator [kə'læbəreɪtə*] n collaboratore/trice.
collage [kɔ'lɑ:ʒ] n (ART) collage m inv.
collagen ['kɔlədʒən] n collageno.
collapse [kə'læps] vi (gen) crollare; (government) cadere; (MED) avere un collasso; (plans) fallire ♦ n crollo; caduta; collasso; fallimento.
collapsible [kə'læpsəbl] adj pieghevole.
collar ['kɔlə*] n (of coat, shirt) colletto; (for dog) collare m; (TECH) anello, fascetta ♦ vt (col: person, object) beccare.

collarbone ['kɔləbəun] n clavicola.
collate [kɔ'leɪt] vt collazionare.
collateral [kɔ'lætərəl] n garanzia.
collation [kɔ'leɪʃən] n collazione f.
colleague ['kɔliːg] n collega m/f.
collect [kɔ'lɛkt] vt (gen) raccogliere; (as a hobby) fare collezione di; (BRIT: call for) prendere; (money owed, pension) riscuotere; (donations, subscriptions) fare una colletta di ♦ vi (people) adunarsi, riunirsi; (rubbish etc) ammucchiarsi ♦ adv (US TEL): **to call** ~ fare una chiamata a carico del destinatario; **to** ~ **one's thoughts** raccogliere le idee; ~ **on delivery (COD)** (US COMM) pagamento alla consegna.
collected [kɔ'lɛktɪd] adj: ~ **works** opere fpl raccolte.
collection [kɔ'lɛkʃən] n collezione f; raccolta; (for money) colletta; (POST) levata.
collective [kɔ'lɛktɪv] adj collettivo(a) ♦ n collettivo.
collective bargaining n trattative fpl (sindacali) collettive.
collector [kɔ'lɛktə*] n collezionista m/f; (of taxes) esattore m; ~'s **item** or **piece** pezzo da collezionista.
college ['kɔlɪdʒ] n (BRIT, US SCOL) college m inv; (of technology, agriculture etc) istituto superiore; (body) collegio; ~ **of education** ≈ facoltà f inv di Magistero.
collide [kɔ'laɪd] vi: **to** ~ **(with)** scontrarsi (con).
collie ['kɔlɪ] n (dog) collie m inv.
colliery ['kɔlɪərɪ] n (BRIT) miniera di carbone.
collision [kɔ'lɪʒən] n collisione f, scontro; **to be on a** ~ **course** (also fig) essere in rotta di collisione.
collision damage waiver (CDW) n (INSURANCE) copertura per i danni alla vettura.
colloquial [kɔ'ləukwɪəl] adj familiare.
collusion [kɔ'luːʒən] n collusione f; **in** ~ **with** in accordo segreto con.
Colo. abbr (US) = Colorado.
Cologne [kɔ'ləun] n Colonia.
cologne [kɔ'ləun] n (also: **eau de** ~) acqua di colonia.
Colombia [kɔ'lɔmbɪə] n Colombia.
Colombian [kɔ'lɔmbɪən] adj, n colombiano(a).
colon ['kəulən] n (sign) due punti mpl; (MED) colon m inv.
colonel ['kɔːnl] n colonnello.
colonial [kɔ'ləunɪəl] adj coloniale.
colonize ['kɔlənaɪz] vt colonizzare.

colony ['kɔlənɪ] n colonia.
color etc ['kʌlə*] (US) = **colour** etc.
Colorado beetle [kɔlə'rɑːdəu-] n dorifora.
colossal [kɔ'lɔsl] adj colossale.
colour, (US) **color** ['kʌlə*] n colore m ♦ vt colorare; (tint, dye) tingere; (fig: affect) influenzare ♦ vi arrossire ♦ cpd (film, photograph, television) a colori; ~**s** npl (of party, club) emblemi mpl.
colo(u)r bar n discriminazione f razziale (in locali etc).
colo(u)r-blind ['kʌləblaɪnd] adj daltonico(a).
colo(u)red ['kʌləd] adj colorato(a); (photo) a colori ♦ n: ~**s** gente f di colore.
colo(u)r film n (for camera) pellicola a colori.
colo(u)rful ['kʌləful] adj pieno(a) di colore, a vivaci colori; (personality) colorato(a).
colo(u)ring ['kʌlərɪŋ] n colorazione f; (complexion) colorito.
colo(u)r scheme combinazione f di colori.
colour supplement n (BRIT PRESS) supplemento a colori.
colo(u)r television n televisione f a colori.
colt [kəult] n puledro.
column ['kɔləm] n colonna; (fashion ~, sports ~ etc) rubrica; **the editorial** ~ l'articolo di fondo.
columnist ['kɔləmnɪst] n articolista m/f.
coma ['kəumə] n coma m inv.
comb [kəum] n pettine m ♦ vt (hair) pettinare; (area) battere a tappeto.
combat ['kɔmbæt] n combattimento ♦ vt combattere, lottare contro.
combination [kɔmbɪ'neɪʃən] n combinazione f.
combination lock n serratura a combinazione.
combine vb [kəm'baɪn] vt combinare; (one quality with another): **to** ~ **sth with sth** unire qc a qc ♦ vi unirsi; (CHEM) combinarsi ♦ n ['kɔmbaɪn] lega; (ECON) associazione f; **a** ~**d effort** uno sforzo collettivo.
combine (harvester) n mietitrebbia.
combo ['kɔmbəu] n (JAZZ etc) gruppo.
combustible [kəm'bʌstɪbl] adj combustibile.
combustion [kəm'bʌstʃən] n combustione f.
come, pt **came,** pp **come** [kʌm, keɪm] vi venire; (arrive) venire, arrivare; ~ **with me** vieni con me; **we've just** ~ **from Paris** siamo appena arrivati da Parigi; **nothing came of it** non è saltato fuori niente; **to** ~ **into sight** or **view** apparire; **to** ~ **to** (decision etc) raggiungere; **to** ~ **undone/**

loose slacciarsi/allentarsi; **coming!** vengo!; **if it ~s to it** nella peggiore delle ipotesi.

▶**come about** *vi* succedere.

▶**come across** *vt fus* trovare per caso; **to ~ across well/badly** fare una buona/cattiva impressione.

▶**come along** *vi* (*pupil, work*) fare progressi; **~ along!** avanti!, andiamo!, forza!

▶**come apart** *vi* andare in pezzi; (*become detached*) staccarsi.

▶**come away** *vi* venire via; (*become detached*) staccarsi.

▶**come back** *vi* ritornare; (*reply: col*): **can I ~ back to you on that one?** possiamo riparlarne più tardi?

▶**come by** *vt fus* (*acquire*) ottenere; procurarsi.

▶**come down** *vi* scendere; (*prices*) calare; (*buildings*) essere demolito(a).

▶**come forward** *vi* farsi avanti; presentarsi.

▶**come from** *vt fus* venire da; provenire da.

▶**come in** *vi* entrare.

▶**come in for** *vt fus* (*criticism etc*) ricevere.

▶**come into** *vt fus* (*money*) ereditare.

▶**come off** *vi* (*button*) staccarsi; (*stain*) andar via; (*attempt*) riuscire.

▶**come on** *vi* (*lights, electricity*) accendersi; (*pupil, undertaking*) fare progressi; **~ on!** avanti!, andiamo!, forza!

▶**come out** *vi* uscire; (*strike*) entrare in sciopero.

▶**come over** *vt fus*: **I don't know what's ~ over him!** non so cosa gli sia successo!

▶**come round** *vi* (*after faint, operation*) riprendere conoscenza, rinvenire.

▶**come through** *vi* (*survive*) sopravvivere, farcela; **the call came through** ci hanno passato la telefonata.

▶**come to** *vi* rinvenire ♦ *vt* (*add up to: amount*): **how much does it ~ to?** quanto costa?, quanto viene?

▶**come under** *vt fus* (*heading*) trovarsi sotto; (*influence*) cadere sotto, subire.

▶**come up** *vi* venire su.

▶**come up against** *vt fus* (*resistance, difficulties*) urtare contro.

▶**come up to** *vt fus* arrivare (fino) a; **the film didn't ~ up to our expectations** il film ci ha delusi.

▶**come up with** *vt fus*: **he came up with an idea** venne fuori con un'idea.

▶**come upon** *vt fus* trovare per caso.

comeback ['kʌmbæk] *n* (*THEAT etc*) ritorno; (*reaction*) reazione *f*; (*response*) risultato,

risposta.

COMECON ['kɒmɪkɒn] *n abbr* (= *Council for Mutual Economic Aid*) COMECON *m*.

comedian [kə'miːdɪən] *n* comico.

comedienne [kəmiːdɪ'ɛn] *n* attrice *f* comica.

comedown ['kʌmdaun] *n* rovescio.

comedy ['kɒmɪdɪ] *n* commedia.

comet ['kɒmɪt] *n* cometa.

comeuppance [kʌm'ʌpəns] *n*: **to get one's ~** ricevere ciò che si merita.

comfort ['kʌmfət] *n* comodità *f inv*, benessere *m*; (*solace*) consolazione *f*, conforto ♦ *vt* consolare, confortare; *see also* **comforts**.

comfortable ['kʌmfətəbl] *adj* comodo(a); (*income, majority*) più che sufficiente; **I don't feel very ~ about it** non mi sento molto tranquillo.

comfortably ['kʌmfətəblɪ] *adv* (*sit*) comodamente; (*live*) bene.

comforter ['kʌmfətə*] *n* (*US*) trapunta.

comforts ['kʌmfəts] *npl* comforts *mpl*, comodità *fpl*.

comfort station *n* (*US*) gabinetti *mpl*.

comic ['kɒmɪk] *adj* comico(a) ♦ *n* comico; (*magazine*) giornaletto.

comical ['kɒmɪkl] *adj* divertente, buffo(a).

comic strip *n* fumetto.

coming ['kʌmɪŋ] *n* arrivo ♦ *adj* (*next*) prossimo(a); (*future*) futuro(a); **in the ~ weeks** nelle prossime settimane.

coming(s) and going(s) *n(pl)* andirivieni *m inv*.

Comintern ['kɒmɪntəːn] *n* KOMINTERN *m*.

comma ['kɒmə] *n* virgola.

command [kə'mɑːnd] *n* ordine *m*, comando; (*MIL: authority*) comando; (*mastery*) padronanza; (*COMPUT*) command *m inv*, comando ♦ *vt* comandare; **to ~ sb to do** ordinare a qn di fare; **to have/take ~ of** avere/prendere il comando di; **to have at one's ~** (*money, resources etc*) avere a propria disposizione.

command economy *n* = **planned economy**.

commandeer [kɒmən'dɪə*] *vt* requisire.

commander [kə'mɑːndə*] *n* capo; (*MIL*) comandante *m*.

commander-in-chief (C-in-C) [kə'mɑːndər-ɪn'tʃiːf] *n* (*MIL*) comandante *m* in capo.

commanding [kə'mɑːndɪŋ] *adj* (*appearance*) imponente; (*voice, tone*) autorevole; (*lead, position*) dominante.

commanding officer *n* comandante *m*.

commandment [kə'mɑːndmənt] *n* (*REL*) comandamento.

command module n (*SPACE*) modulo di comando.

commando [kə'mɑːndəu] n commando m inv; membro di un commando.

commemorate [kə'mɛməreɪt] vt commemorare.

commemoration [kəmɛmə'reɪʃən] n commemorazione f.

commemorative [kə'mɛmərətɪv] adj commemorativo(a).

commence [kə'mɛns] vt, vi cominciare.

commend [kə'mɛnd] vt lodare; raccomandare.

commendable [kə'mɛndəbl] adj lodevole.

commendation [kɔmɛn'deɪʃən] n lode f; raccomandazione f; (*for bravery etc*) encomio.

commensurate [kə'mɛnʃərɪt] adj: ~ **with** proporzionato(a) a.

comment ['kɔmɛnt] n commento ♦ vi: **to** ~ **(on)** fare commenti (su); **to** ~ **that** osservare che; "**no** ~" "niente da dire".

commentary ['kɔməntərɪ] n commentario; (*SPORT*) radiocronaca; telecronaca.

commentator ['kɔmənteɪtə*] n commentatore/trice; (*SPORT*) radiocronista m/f; telecronista m/f.

commerce ['kɔmɜːs] n commercio.

commercial [kə'mɜːʃəl] adj commerciale ♦ n (*TV: also:* ~ **break**) pubblicità f inv.

commercial bank n banca commerciale.

commercial college n ≈ istituto commerciale.

commercialism [kə'mɜːʃəlɪzəm] n affarismo.

commercial television n televisione f commerciale.

commercial traveller n commesso viaggiatore.

commercial vehicle n veicolo commerciale.

commiserate [kə'mɪzəreɪt] vi: **to** ~ **with** condolersi con.

commission [kə'mɪʃən] n commissione f; (*for salesman*) commissione, provvigione f ♦ vt (*MIL*) nominare (al comando); (*work of art*) commissionare; **I get 10%** ~ ricevo il 10% sulle vendite; **out of** ~ (*NAUT*) in disarmo; (*machine*) fuori uso; **to** ~ **sb to do sth** incaricare qn di fare qc; **to** ~ **sth from sb** (*painting etc*) commissionare qc a qn; ~ **of inquiry** (*BRIT*) commissione f d'inchiesta.

commissionaire [kəmɪʃə'nɛə*] n (*BRIT: at shop, cinema etc*) portiere m in livrea.

commissioner [kə'mɪʃənə*] n commissionario; (*POLICE*) questore m.

commit [kə'mɪt] vt (*act*) commettere; (*to*

sb's care) affidare; **to** ~ **o.s. (to do)** impegnarsi (a fare); **to** ~ **suicide** suicidarsi; **to** ~ **sb for trial** rinviare qn a giudizio.

commitment [kə'mɪtmənt] n impegno.

committed [kə'mɪtɪd] adj (*writer*) impegnato(a); (*Christian*) convinto(a).

committee [kə'mɪtɪ] n comitato; **to be on a** ~ far parte di un comitato or di una commissione.

committee meeting n riunione f di comitato or di commissione.

commodity [kə'mɔdɪtɪ] n prodotto, articolo; (*food*) derrata.

commodity exchange n borsa f merci inv.

common ['kɔmən] adj comune; (*pej*) volgare; (*usual*) normale ♦ n terreno comune; **in** ~ in comune; **in** ~ **use** di uso comune; **it's** ~ **knowledge that** è di dominio pubblico che; **to the** ~ **good** nell'interesse generale, per il bene comune; *see also* **Commons**.

common cold n: **the** ~ il raffreddore.

common denominator n denominatore m comune.

commoner ['kɔmənə*] n cittadino/a (non nobile).

common ground n (*fig*) terreno comune.

common land n terreno di uso pubblico.

common law n diritto consuetudinario.

common-law ['kɔmənlɔː] adj: ~ **wife** convivente f more uxorio.

commonly ['kɔmənlɪ] adv comunemente, usualmente.

Common Market n Mercato Comune.

commonplace ['kɔmənpleɪs] adj banale, ordinario(a).

commonroom ['kɔmənrum] n sala di riunione; (*SCOL*) sala dei professori.

Commons ['kɔmənz] npl (*BRIT POL*): **the (House of)** ~ la Camera dei Comuni.

common sense n buon senso.

Commonwealth ['kɔmənwɛlθ] n: **the** ~ il Commonwealth.

Il **Commonwealth** è un'associazione di stati sovrani indipendenti e di alcuni territori annessi che facevano parte dell'antico Impero Britannico, e che nel 1931 assunsero il nome di Commonwealth of Nations, denominazione successivamente semplificata in Commonwealth.
Attualmente gli stati del Commonwealth riconoscono ancora il proprio capo di stato nel sovrano britannico e i loro rappresentanti si riuniscono per discutere questioni di comune interesse.

commotion [kə'məʊʃən] *n* confusione *f*, tumulto.

communal ['kɔmjuːnl] *adj* (*life*) comunale; (*for common use*) pubblico(a).

commune *n* ['kɔmjuːn] (*group*) comune *f* ♦ *vi* [kə'mjuːn]: **to ~ with** mettersi in comunione con.

communicate [kə'mjuːnɪkeɪt] *vt* comunicare, trasmettere ♦ *vi*: **to ~ (with)** comunicare (con).

communication [kəmjuːnɪ'keɪʃən] *n* comunicazione *f*.

communication cord *n* (*BRIT*) segnale *m* d'allarme.

communications network *n* rete *f* delle comunicazioni.

communications satellite *n* satellite *m* per telecomunicazioni.

communicative [kə'mjuːnɪkətɪv] *adj* (*gen*) loquace.

communion [kə'mjuːnɪən] *n* (*also:* **Holy C~**) comunione *f*.

communiqué [kə'mjuːnɪkeɪ] *n* comunicato.

communism ['kɔmjunɪzəm] *n* comunismo.

communist ['kɔmjunɪst] *adj*, *n* comunista (*m/f*).

community [kə'mjuːnɪtɪ] *n* comunità *f inv*.

community centre *n* circolo ricreativo.

community chest *n* (*US*) fondo di beneficenza.

community health centre *n* centro socio-sanitario.

community home *n* (*BRIT*) riformatorio.

community service *n* (*BRIT*) ≈ lavoro sostitutivo.

community spirit *n* spirito civico.

commutation ticket [kɔmju'teɪʃən-] *n* (*US*) biglietto di abbonamento.

commute [kə'mjuːt] *vi* fare il pendolare ♦ *vt* (*LAW*) commutare.

commuter [kə'mjuːtə*] *n* pendolare *m/f*.

compact *adj* [kəm'pækt] compatto(a) ♦ *n* ['kɔmpækt] (*also:* **powder ~**) portacipria *m inv*.

compact disc *n* compact disc *m inv*; **~ player** lettore *m* CD *inv*.

companion [kəm'pænjən] *n* compagno/a.

companionship [kəm'pænjənʃɪp] *n* compagnia.

companionway [kəm'pænjənweɪ] *n* (*NAUT*) scala.

company ['kʌmpənɪ] *n* (*also* COMM, MIL, THEAT*) compagnia; **he's good ~** è di buona compagnia; **we have ~** abbiamo ospiti; **to keep sb ~** tenere compagnia a qn; **to part ~ with** separarsi da; **Smith and C~** Smith e soci.

company car *n* macchina (di proprietà) della ditta.

company director *n* amministratore *m*, consigliere *m* di amministrazione.

company secretary *n* (*BRIT COMM*) segretario/a generale.

comparable ['kɔmpərəbl] *adj* comparabile.

comparative [kəm'pærətɪv] *adj* (*freedom, cost*) relativo(a); (*adjective, adverb etc*) comparativo(a); (*literature*) comparato(a).

comparatively [kəm'pærətɪvlɪ] *adv* relativamente.

compare [kəm'pɛə*] *vt*: **to ~ sth/sb with/to** confrontare qc/qn con/a ♦ *vi*: **to ~ (with)** reggere il confronto (con); **~d with** *or* **to** a paragone di, rispetto a; **how do the prices ~?** che differenza di prezzo c'è?

comparison [kəm'pærɪsn] *n* confronto; **in ~ (with)** a confronto (di).

compartment [kəm'pɑːtmənt] *n* compartimento; (*RAIL*) scompartimento.

compass ['kʌmpəs] *n* bussola; (**a pair of**) **~es** (*MATH*) compasso; **within the ~ of** entro i limiti di.

compassion [kəm'pæʃən] *n* compassione *f*.

compassionate [kəm'pæʃənɪt] *adj* compassionevole; **on ~ grounds** per motivi personali.

compassionate leave *n* congedo straordinario (*per gravi motivi di famiglia*).

compatibility [kəmpætɪ'bɪlɪtɪ] *n* compatibilità.

compatible [kəm'pætɪbl] *adj* compatibile.

compel [kəm'pɛl] *vt* costringere, obbligare.

compelling [kəm'pɛlɪŋ] *adj* (*fig: argument*) irresistibile.

compendium [kəm'pɛndɪəm] *n* compendio.

compensate ['kɔmpənseɪt] *vt* risarcire ♦ *vi*: **to ~ for** compensare.

compensation [kɔmpən'seɪʃən] *n* compensazione *f*; (*money*) risarcimento.

compère ['kɔmpɛə*] *n* presentatore/trice.

compete [kəm'piːt] *vi* (*take part*) concorrere; (*vie*): **to ~ (with)** fare concorrenza (a).

competence ['kɔmpɪtəns] *n* competenza.

competent ['kɔmpɪtənt] *adj* competente.

competing [kəm'piːtɪŋ] *adj* (*theories, ideas*) opposto(a); (*companies*) in concorrenza; **three ~ explanations (of)** tre spiegazioni contrastanti tra di loro (di).

competition [kɔmpɪ'tɪʃən] *n* gara, concorso; (*SPORT*) gara; (*ECON*) concorrenza; **in ~ with** in concorrenza con.

competitive [kəm'pɛtɪtɪv] *adj* (*sports*) agonistico(a); (*person*) che ha spirito di competizione; (*ECON*) concorrenziale.

competitive examination *n* concorso.

competitor [kəm'pɛtɪtə*] n concorrente m/f.
compile [kəm'paɪl] vt compilare.
complacency [kəm'pleɪsnsɪ] n compiacenza di sé.
complacent [kəm'pleɪsnt] adj compiaciuto(a) di sé.
complain [kəm'pleɪn] vi: **to ~ (about)** lagnarsi (di); (in shop etc) reclamare (per).
►**complain of** vt fus (MED) accusare.
complaint [kəm'pleɪnt] n lamento; reclamo; (MED) malattia.
complement n ['kɒmplɪmənt] complemento; (especially of ship's crew etc) effettivo ♦ vt ['kɒmplɪmɛnt] (enhance) accompagnarsi bene a.
complementary [kɒmplɪ'mɛntərɪ] adj complementare.
complete [kəm'pliːt] adj completo(a) ♦ vt completare; (a form) riempire; **it's a ~ disaster** è un vero disastro.
completely [kəm'pliːtlɪ] adv completamente.
completion [kəm'pliːʃən] n completamento; **to be nearing ~** essere in fase di completamento; **on ~ of contract** alla firma del contratto.
complex ['kɒmplɛks] adj complesso(a) ♦ n (PSYCH, buildings etc) complesso.
complexion [kəm'plɛkʃən] n (of face) carnagione f; (of event etc) aspetto.
complexity [kəm'plɛksɪtɪ] n complessità f inv.
compliance [kəm'plaɪəns] n acquiescenza; **in ~ with** (orders, wishes etc) in conformità con.
compliant [kəm'plaɪənt] adj acquiescente, arrendevole.
complicate ['kɒmplɪkeɪt] vt complicare.
complicated ['kɒmplɪkeɪtɪd] adj complicato(a).
complication [kɒmplɪ'keɪʃən] n complicazione f.
compliment n ['kɒmplɪmənt] complimento ♦ vt ['kɒmplɪmɛnt] fare un complimento a; **~s** npl complimenti mpl; rispetti mpl; **to pay sb a ~** fare un complimento a qn; **to ~ sb (on sth/on doing sth)** congratularsi or complimentarsi con qn (per qc/per aver fatto qc).
complimentary [kɒmplɪ'mɛntərɪ] adj complimentoso(a), elogiativo(a); (free) in omaggio.
complimentary ticket n biglietto d'omaggio.
compliments slip n cartoncino della società.
comply [kəm'plaɪ] vi: **to ~ with** assentire a;

conformarsi a.
component [kəm'pəʊnənt] adj, n componente (m).
compose [kəm'pəʊz] vt comporre; **to ~ o.s.** ricomporsi; **~d of** composto(a) di.
composed [kəm'pəʊzd] adj calmo(a).
composer [kəm'pəʊzə*] n (MUS) compositore/trice.
composite ['kɒmpəzɪt] adj composito(a); (MATH) composto(a).
composition [kɒmpə'zɪʃən] n composizione f.
compost ['kɒmpɒst] n composta, concime m.
composure [kəm'pəʊʒə*] n calma.
compound ['kɒmpaʊnd] n (CHEM, LING) composto; (enclosure) recinto ♦ adj composto(a) ♦ vt (fig: problem, difficulty) peggiorare.
compound fracture n frattura esposta.
compound interest n interesse m composto.
comprehend [kɒmprɪ'hɛnd] vt comprendere, capire.
comprehension [kɒmprɪ'hɛnʃən] n comprensione f.
comprehensive [kɒmprɪ'hɛnsɪv] adj comprensivo(a).
comprehensive insurance policy n polizza multi-rischio inv.
comprehensive (school) n (BRIT) scuola secondaria aperta a tutti.
compress vt [kəm'prɛs] comprimere ♦ n ['kɒmprɛs] (MED) compressa.
compression [kəm'prɛʃən] n compressione f.
comprise [kəm'praɪz] vt (also: **be ~d of**) comprendere.
compromise ['kɒmprəmaɪz] n compromesso ♦ vt compromettere ♦ vi venire a un compromesso ♦ cpd (decision, solution) di compromesso.
compulsion [kəm'pʌlʃən] n costrizione f; **under ~** sotto pressioni.
compulsive [kəm'pʌlsɪv] adj (PSYCH) incontrollabile; **he's a ~ smoker** non riesce a controllarsi nel fumare.
compulsory [kəm'pʌlsərɪ] adj obbligatorio(a).
compulsory purchase n espropriazione f.
compunction [kəm'pʌŋkʃən] n scrupolo; **to have no ~ about doing sth** non farsi scrupoli a fare qc.
computer [kəm'pjuːtə*] n computer m inv, elaboratore m elettronico.
computer game n computer game m inv.
computerization [kəmpjuːtəraɪ'zeɪʃən] n computerizzazione f.

computerize [kəm'pjuːtəraɪz] *vt* computerizzare.

computer language *n* linguaggio *m* macchina *inv.*

computer literate *adj*: **to be ~** essere in grado di usare il computer.

computer peripheral *n* unità periferica.

computer program *n* programma *m* di computer.

computer programmer *n* programmatore/trice.

computer programming *n* programmazione *f* di computer.

computer science *n* informatica.

computer scientist *n* informatico/a.

computing [kəm'pjuːtɪŋ] *n* informatica.

comrade ['kɔmrɪd] *n* compagno/a.

comradeship ['kɔmrɪdʃɪp] *n* cameratismo.

comsat ['kɔmsæt] *n abbr* = **communications satellite**.

con [kɔn] *vt* (*col*) truffare ♦ *n* truffa; **to ~ sb into doing sth** indurre qn a fare qc con raggiri.

concave ['kɔn'keɪv] *adj* concavo(a).

conceal [kən'siːl] *vt* nascondere.

concede [kən'siːd] *vt* concedere ♦ *vi* fare una concessione.

conceit [kən'siːt] *n* presunzione *f*, vanità.

conceited [kən'siːtɪd] *adj* presuntuoso(a), vanitoso(a).

conceivable [kən'siːvəbl] *adj* concepibile; **it is ~ that** ... può anche darsi che ....

conceivably [kən'siːvəblɪ] *adv*: **he may ~ be right** può anche darsi che abbia ragione.

conceive [kən'siːv] *vt* concepire ♦ *vi* concepire un bambino; **to ~ of sth/of doing sth** immaginare qc/di fare qc.

concentrate ['kɔnsəntreɪt] *vi* concentrarsi ♦ *vt* concentrare.

concentration [kɔnsən'treɪʃən] *n* concentrazione *f*.

concentration camp *n* campo di concentramento.

concentric [kɔn'sɛntrɪk] *adj* concentrico(a).

concept ['kɔnsɛpt] *n* concetto.

conception [kən'sɛpʃən] *n* concezione *f*; (*idea*) idea, concetto.

concern [kən'səːn] *n* affare *m*; (*COMM*) azienda, ditta; (*anxiety*) preoccupazione *f* ♦ *vt* riguardare; **to be ~ed (about)** preoccuparsi (di); **to be ~ed with** occuparsi di; **as far as I am ~ed** per quanto mi riguarda; **"to whom it may ~"** "a tutti gli interessati"; **the department ~ed** (*under discussion*) l'ufficio in questione; (*relevant*) l'ufficio competente.

concerning [kən'səːnɪŋ] *prep* riguardo a, circa.

concert ['kɔnsət] *n* concerto; **in ~** di concerto.

concerted [kən'səːtɪd] *adj* concertato(a).

concert hall *n* sala da concerti.

concertina [kɔnsə'tiːnə] *n* piccola fisarmonica ♦ *vi* ridursi come una fisarmonica.

concerto [kən'tʃəːtəu] *n* concerto.

concession [kən'sɛʃən] *n* concessione *f*.

concessionaire [kənsɛʃə'nɛə*] *n* concessionario.

concessionary [kən'sɛʃənərɪ] *adj* (*ticket, fare*) a prezzo ridotto.

conciliation [kənsɪlɪ'eɪʃən] *n* conciliazione *f*.

conciliatory [kən'sɪlɪətrɪ] *adj* conciliativo(a).

concise [kən'saɪs] *adj* conciso(a).

conclave ['kɔnkleɪv] *n* riunione *f* segreta; (*REL*) conclave *m*.

conclude [kən'kluːd] *vt* concludere ♦ *vi* (*speaker*) concludere; (*events*): **to ~ (with)** concludersi (con).

concluding [kən'kluːdɪŋ] *adj* (*remarks etc*) conclusivo(a), finale.

conclusion [kən'kluːʒən] *n* conclusione *f*; **to come to the ~ that** ... concludere che ..., arrivare alla conclusione che ....

conclusive [kən'kluːsɪv] *adj* conclusivo(a).

concoct [kən'kɔkt] *vt* inventare.

concoction [kən'kɔkʃən] *n* (*food, drink*) miscuglio.

concord ['kɔŋkɔːd] *n* (*harmony*) armonia, concordia; (*treaty*) accordo.

concourse ['kɔŋkɔːs] *n* (*hall*) atrio.

concrete ['kɔŋkriːt] *n* calcestruzzo ♦ *adj* concreto(a); (*CONSTR*) di calcestruzzo.

concrete mixer *n* betoniera.

concur [kən'kəː*] *vi* concordare.

concurrently [kən'kʌrntlɪ] *adv* simultaneamente.

concussion [kən'kʌʃən] *n* (*MED*) commozione *f* cerebrale.

condemn [kən'dɛm] *vt* condannare.

condemnation [kɔndɛm'neɪʃən] *n* condanna.

condensation [kɔndɛn'seɪʃən] *n* condensazione *f*.

condense [kən'dɛns] *vi* condensarsi ♦ *vt* condensare.

condensed milk *n* latte *m* condensato.

condescend [kɔndɪ'sɛnd] *vi* condiscendere; **to ~ to do sth** degnarsi di fare qc.

condescending [kɔndɪ'sɛndɪŋ] *adj* condiscendente.

condition [kən'dɪʃən] *n* condizione *f*; (*disease*) malattia ♦ *vt* condizionare, regolare; **in good/poor ~** in buone/cattive condizioni; **to have a heart ~**

soffrire di (mal di) cuore; **weather** ~**s** condizioni meteorologiche; **on** ~ **that** a condizione che + sub, a condizione di.
conditional [kən'dɪʃənl] adj condizionale; **to be** ~ **upon** dipendere da.
conditioner [kən'dɪʃənə*] n (for hair) balsamo.
condo ['kɔndəu] n abbr (US col) = **condominium.**
condolences [kən'dəulənsɪz] npl condoglianze fpl.
condom ['kɔndəm] n preservativo.
condominium [kɔndə'mɪnɪəm] n (US) condominio.
condone [kən'dəun] vt condonare.
conducive [kən'djuːsɪv] adj: ~ **to** favorevole a.
conduct n ['kɔndʌkt] condotta ♦ vt [kən'dʌkt] condurre; (manage) dirigere; amministrare; (MUS) dirigere; **to** ~ **o.s.** comportarsi.
conductor [kən'dʌktə*] n (of orchestra) direttore m d'orchestra; (on bus) bigliettaio; (US RAIL) controllore m; (ELEC) conduttore m.
conductress [kən'dʌktrɪs] n (on bus) bigliettaia.
conduit ['kɔndɪt] n condotto; tubo.
cone [kəun] n cono; (BOT) pigna.
confectioner [kən'fɛkʃənə*] n: ~'**s (shop)** ≈ pasticceria.
confectionery [kən'fɛkʃənərɪ] n dolciumi mpl.
confederate [kən'fɛdərɪt] adj confederato(a) ♦ n (pej) complice m/f; (US HISTORY) confederato.
confederation [kənfɛdə'reɪʃən] n confederazione f.
confer [kən'fəː*] vt: **to** ~ **sth on** conferire qc a ♦ vi conferire; **to** ~ **(with sb about sth)** consultarsi (con qn su qc).
conference ['kɔnfərns] n congresso; **to be in** ~ essere in riunione.
conference room n sala f conferenze inv.
confess [kən'fɛs] vt confessare, ammettere ♦ vi confessarsi.
confession [kən'fɛʃən] n confessione f.
confessional [kən'fɛʃənl] n confessionale m.
confessor [kən'fɛsə*] n confessore m.
confetti [kən'fɛtɪ] n coriandoli mpl.
confide [kən'faɪd] vi: **to** ~ **in** confidarsi con.
confidence ['kɔnfɪdns] n confidenza; (trust) fiducia; (also: **self-**~) sicurezza di sé; **to tell sb sth in strict** ~ dire qc a qn in via strettamente confidenziale; **to have (every)** ~ **that** ... essere assolutamente certo(a) che ...; **motion of no** ~ mozione f

di sfiducia.
confidence trick n truffa.
confident ['kɔnfɪdənt] adj sicuro(a); (also: **self-**~) sicuro(a) di sé.
confidential [kɔnfɪ'dɛnʃəl] adj riservato(a); (secretary) particolare.
confidentiality ['kɔnfɪdɛnʃɪ'ælɪtɪ] n riservatezza, carattere m confidenziale.
configuration [kən'fɪgju'reɪʃən] n (COMPUT) configurazione f.
confine [kən'faɪn] vt limitare; (shut up) rinchiudere; **to** ~ **o.s. to doing sth** limitarsi a fare qc; see also **confines.**
confined [kən'faɪnd] adj (space) ristretto(a).
confinement [kən'faɪnmənt] n prigionia; (MIL) consegna; (MED) parto.
confines ['kɔnfaɪnz] npl confini mpl.
confirm [kən'fəːm] vt confermare; (REL) cresimare.
confirmation [kɔnfə'meɪʃən] n conferma; cresima.
confirmed [kən'fəːmd] adj inveterato(a).
confiscate ['kɔnfɪskeɪt] vt confiscare.
confiscation [kɔnfɪs'keɪʃən] n confisca.
conflagration [kɔnflə'greɪʃən] n conflagrazione f.
conflict n ['kɔnflɪkt] conflitto ♦ vi [kən'flɪkt] essere in conflitto.
conflicting [kən'flɪktɪŋ] adj contrastante; (reports, evidence, opinions) contraddittorio(a).
conform [kən'fɔːm] vi: **to** ~ **(to)** conformarsi (a).
conformist [kən'fɔːmɪst] n conformista m/f.
confound [kən'faund] vt confondere; (amaze) sconcertare.
confounded [kən'faundɪd] adj maledetto(a).
confront [kən'frʌnt] vt confrontare; (enemy, danger) affrontare.
confrontation [kɔnfrən'teɪʃən] n scontro.
confrontational [kɔnfrən'teɪʃənəl] adj polemico(a), aggressivo(a).
confuse [kən'fjuːz] vt imbrogliare; (one thing with another) confondere.
confused [kən'fjuːzd] adj confuso(a); **to get** ~ confondersi.
confusing [kən'fjuːzɪŋ] adj che fa confondere.
confusion [kən'fjuːʒən] n confusione f.
congeal [kən'dʒiːl] vi (blood) congelarsi.
congenial [kən'dʒiːnɪəl] adj (person) simpatico(a); (place, work, company) piacevole.
congenital [kən'dʒɛnɪtl] adj congenito(a).
conger eel ['kɔŋgər-] n grongo.
congested [kən'dʒɛstɪd] adj congestionato(a); (telephone lines)

sovraccarico(a).
congestion [kən'dʒɛstʃən] *n* congestione *f.*
conglomerate [kən'glɔmərɪt] *n* (*COMM*) conglomerato.
conglomeration [kəngləmə'reɪʃən] *n* conglomerazione *f.*
Congo ['kɔŋgəu] *n* Congo.
congratulate [kən'grætjuleɪt] *vt*: **to ~ sb (on)** congratularsi con qn (per *or* di).
congratulations [kəngrætju'leɪʃənz] *npl*: **~ (on)** congratulazioni *fpl* (per) ♦ *excl* congratulazioni!, rallegramenti!
congregate ['kɔŋrɪgeɪt] *vi* congregarsi, riunirsi.
congregation [kɔŋgrɪ'geɪʃən] *n* congregazione *f.*
congress ['kɔŋgrɛs] *n* congresso; (*US POL*): **C~** il Congresso.

Il **Congress** *è l'assemblea statunitense che si riunisce a Washington D.C. nel* **Capitol** *per elaborare e discutere le leggi federali. È costituita dalla* **House of Representatives** *(435 membri, eletti nei vari stati in base al numero degli abitanti) e dal* **Senate** *(100 senatori, due per ogni stato). Sia i membri della House of Representatives che quelli del Senate sono eletti direttamente dal popolo.*

---

congressman ['kɔŋgrɛsmən] *n* (*US*) membro del Congresso.
congresswoman ['kɔŋgrɛswumən] *n* (*US*) (donna) membro del Congresso.
conical ['kɔnɪkl] *adj* conico(a).
conifer ['kɔnɪfə*] *n* conifero.
coniferous [kə'nɪfərəs] *adj* (*forest*) di conifere.
conjecture [kən'dʒɛktʃə*] *n* congettura ♦ *vt, vi* congetturare.
conjugal ['kɔndʒugl] *adj* coniugale.
conjugate ['kɔndʒugeɪt] *vt* coniugare.
conjugation [kɔndʒə'geɪʃən] *n* coniugazione *f.*
conjunction [kən'dʒʌŋkʃən] *n* congiunzione *f;* **in ~ with** in accordo con, insieme con.
conjunctivitis [kəndʒʌŋktɪ'vaɪtɪs] *n* congiuntivite *f.*
conjure ['kʌndʒə*] *vi* fare giochi di prestigio.
▶**conjure up** *vt* (*ghost, spirit*) evocare; (*memories*) rievocare.
conjurer ['kʌndʒərə*] *n* prestigiatore/trice, prestidigitatore/trice.
conjuring trick ['kʌndʒərɪŋ-] *n* gioco di prestigio.
conker ['kɔŋkə*] *n* (*BRIT col*) castagna (d'ippocastano).

conk out [kɔŋk-] *vi* (*col*) andare in panne.
conman ['kɔnmæn] *n* truffatore *m.*
Conn. *abbr* (*US*) = Connecticut.
connect [kə'nɛkt] *vt* connettere, collegare; (*ELEC*) collegare; (*fig*) associare ♦ *vi* (*train*): **to ~ with** essere in coincidenza con; **to be ~ed with** aver rapporti con; essere imparentato(a) con; **I am trying to ~ you** (*TEL*) sto cercando di darle la linea.
connection [kə'nɛkʃən] *n* relazione *f,* rapporto; (*ELEC*) connessione *f;* (*TEL*) collegamento; (*train etc*) coincidenza; **in ~ with** con riferimento a, a proposito di; **what is the ~ between them?** in che modo sono legati?; **business ~s** rapporti d'affari; **to miss/get one's ~** (*train etc*) perdere/prendere la coincidenza.
connexion [kə'nɛkʃən] *n* (*BRIT*) = **connection.**
conning tower ['kɔnɪŋ-] *n* torretta di comando.
connive [kə'naɪv] *vi*: **to ~ at** essere connivente in.
connoisseur [kɔnɪ'sə:*] *n* conoscitore/trice.
connotation [kɔnə'teɪʃən] *n* connotazione *f.*
connubial [kə'nju:bɪəl] *adj* coniugale.
conquer ['kɔŋkə*] *vt* conquistare; (*feelings*) vincere.
conqueror ['kɔŋkərə*] *n* conquistatore *m.*
conquest ['kɔŋkwɛst] *n* conquista.
cons [kɔnz] *npl see* **pro; convenience.**
conscience ['kɔnʃəns] *n* coscienza; **in all ~** onestamente, in coscienza.
conscientious [kɔnʃɪ'ɛnʃəs] *adj* coscienzioso(a).
conscientious objector *n* obiettore *m* di coscienza.
conscious ['kɔnʃəs] *adj* consapevole; (*MED*) conscio(a); (*deliberate: insult, error*) intenzionale, voluto(a); **to become ~ of sth/that** rendersi conto di qc/che.
consciousness ['kɔnʃəsnɪs] *n* consapevolezza; (*MED*) coscienza; **to lose/regain ~** perdere/riprendere coscienza.
conscript ['kɔnskrɪpt] *n* coscritto.
conscription [kən'skrɪpʃən] *n* coscrizione *f.*
consecrate ['kɔnsɪkreɪt] *vt* consacrare.
consecutive [kən'sɛkjutɪv] *adj* consecutivo(a); **on 3 ~ occasions** 3 volte di fila.
consensus [kən'sɛnsəs] *n* consenso; **the ~ of opinion** l'opinione *f* unanime *or* comune.
consent [kən'sɛnt] *n* consenso ♦ *vi*: **to ~ (to)** acconsentire (a); **age of ~** età legale (per avere rapporti sessuali); **by**

common ~ di comune accordo.
consenting adults [kən'sɛntɪŋ-] npl adulti mpl consenzienti.
consequence ['kɒnsɪkwəns] n conseguenza, risultato; importanza; **in** ~ di conseguenza.
consequently ['kɒnsɪkwəntlɪ] adv di conseguenza, dunque.
conservation [kɒnsə'veɪʃən] n conservazione f; (also: **nature** ~) tutela dell'ambiente; **energy** ~ risparmio energetico.
conservationist [kɒnsə'veɪʃənɪst] n fautore/trice della tutela dell'ambiente.
conservative [kən'sə:vətɪv] adj conservatore(trice); (cautious) cauto(a); **C~** adj, n (BRIT POL) conservatore(trice); **the C~ Party** il partito conservatore.
conservatory [kən'sə:vətrɪ] n (greenhouse) serra.
conserve [kən'sə:v] vt conservare ♦ n conserva.
consider [kən'sɪdə*] vt considerare; (take into account) tener conto di; **to** ~ **doing sth** considerare la possibilità di fare qc; **all things** ~**ed** tutto sommato or considerato; ~ **yourself lucky** puoi dirti fortunato.
considerable [kən'sɪdərəbl] adj considerevole, notevole.
considerably [kən'sɪdərəblɪ] adv notevolmente, decisamente.
considerate [kən'sɪdərɪt] adj premuroso(a).
consideration [kənsɪdə'reɪʃən] n considerazione f; (reward) rimunerazione f; **out of** ~ **for** per riguardo a; **under** ~ in esame; **my first** ~ **is my family** il mio primo pensiero è per la mia famiglia.
considered [kən'sɪdəd] adj: **it is my** ~ **opinion that ...** dopo lunga riflessione il mio parere è che ....
considering [kən'sɪdərɪŋ] prep in considerazione di; ~ **(that)** se si considera (che).
consign [kən'saɪn] vt consegnare; (send: goods) spedire.
consignee [kɒnsaɪ'ni:] n consegnatario/a, destinatario/a.
consignment [kən'saɪnmənt] n consegna; spedizione f.
consignment note n (COMM) nota di spedizione.
consignor [kən'saɪnə*] n mittente m/f.
consist [kən'sɪst] vi: **to** ~ **of** constare di, essere composto(a) di.
consistency [kən'sɪstənsɪ] n consistenza; (fig) coerenza.
consistent [kən'sɪstənt] adj coerente;

(constant) costante; ~ **with** compatibile con.
consolation [kɒnsə'leɪʃən] n consolazione f.
console vt [kən'səul] consolare ♦ n ['kɒnsəul] quadro di comando.
consolidate [kən'sɒlɪdeɪt] vt consolidare.
consols ['kɒnsɔlz] npl (STOCK EXCHANGE) titoli mpl del debito consolidato.
consommé [kən'sɔmeɪ] n consommé m inv, brodo ristretto.
consonant ['kɒnsənənt] n consonante f.
consort ['kɒnsɔ:t] n consorte m/f; **prince** ~ principe m consorte ♦ vi (often pej): **to** ~ **with sb** frequentare qn.
consortium [kən'sɔ:tɪəm] n consorzio.
conspicuous [kən'spɪkjuəs] adj cospicuo(a); **to make o.s.** ~ farsi notare.
conspiracy [kən'spɪrəsɪ] n congiura, cospirazione f.
conspiratorial [kənspɪrə'tɔ:rɪəl] adj cospiratorio(a).
conspire [kən'spaɪə*] vi congiurare, cospirare.
constable ['kʌnstəbl] n (BRIT: also: **police** ~) ≈ poliziotto, agente m di polizia.
constabulary [kən'stæbjulərɪ] n forze fpl dell'ordine.
constant ['kɒnstənt] adj costante; continuo(a).
constantly ['kɒnstəntlɪ] adv costantemente; continuamente.
constellation [kɒnstə'leɪʃən] n costellazione f.
consternation [kɒnstə'neɪʃən] n costernazione f.
constipated ['kɒnstɪpeɪtɪd] adj stitico(a).
constipation [kɒnstɪ'peɪʃən] n stitichezza.
constituency [kən'stɪtjuənsɪ] n collegio elettorale; (people) elettori mpl (del collegio).

> Con il termine **constituency** viene indicato sia un collegio elettorale che i suoi elettori. In Gran Bretagna ogni collegio elegge un rappresentante che in seguito incontra regolarmente i propri elettori in riunioni chiamate **surgery** per discutere questioni di interesse locale.

constituency party n sezione f locale (del partito).
constituent [kən'stɪtjuənt] n elettore/trice; (part) elemento componente.
constitute ['kɒnstɪtju:t] vt costituire.
constitution [kɒnstɪ'tju:ʃən] n costituzione f.
constitutional [kɒnstɪ'tju:ʃənl] adj costituzionale.

constitutional monarchy n monarchia costituzionale.

constrain [kən'streɪn] vt costringere.

constrained [kən'streɪnd] adj costretto(a).

constraint [kən'streɪnt] n (*restraint*) limitazione f, costrizione f; (*embarrassment*) imbarazzo, soggezione f.

constrict [kən'strɪkt] vt comprimere; opprimere.

construct [kən'strʌkt] vt costruire.

construction [kən'strʌkʃən] n costruzione f; (*fig: interpretation*) interpretazione f; **under** ~ in costruzione.

construction industry n edilizia, industria edile.

constructive [kən'strʌktɪv] adj costruttivo(a).

construe [kən'struː] vt interpretare.

consul ['kɔnsl] n console m.

consulate ['kɔnsjulɪt] n consolato.

consult [kən'sʌlt] vt: **to** ~ **sb (about sth)** consultare qn (su *or* riguardo a qc).

consultancy [kən'sʌltənsɪ] n consulenza.

consultancy fee n onorario di consulenza.

consultant [kən'sʌltənt] n (*MED*) consulente m medico; (*other specialist*) consulente ♦ cpd: ~ **engineer** n ingegnere m consulente; ~ **paediatrician** n specialista m/f in pediatria; **legal/ management** ~ consulente legale/ gestionale.

consultation [kɔnsəl'teɪʃən] n consultazione f; (*MED, LAW*) consulto; **in** ~ **with** consultandosi con.

consultative [kən'sʌltətɪv] adj di consulenza.

consulting room [kən'sʌltɪŋ-] n (*BRIT*) ambulatorio.

consume [kən'sjuːm] vt consumare.

consumer [kən'sjuːmə*] n consumatore/ trice; (*of electricity, gas etc*) utente m/f.

consumer credit n credito al consumatore.

consumer durables npl prodotti mpl di consumo durevole.

consumer goods npl beni mpl di consumo.

consumerism [kən'sjuːmərɪzəm] n (*consumer protection*) tutela del consumatore; (*ECON*) consumismo.

consumer society n società dei consumi.

consumer watchdog n comitato di difesa dei consumatori.

consummate ['kɔnsʌmeɪt] vt consumare.

consumption [kən'sʌmpʃən] n consumo; (*MED*) consunzione f; **not fit for human** ~ non commestibile.

cont. abbr (= *continued*) segue.

contact ['kɔntækt] n contatto; (*person*) conoscenza ♦ vt mettersi in contatto con; **to be in** ~ **with sb/sth** essere in contatto con qn/qc; **business** ~s contatti mpl d'affari.

contact lenses npl lenti fpl a contatto.

contagious [kən'teɪdʒəs] adj contagioso(a).

contain [kən'teɪn] vt contenere; **to** ~ **o.s.** contenersi.

container [kən'teɪnə*] n recipiente m; (*for shipping etc*) container m.

containerize [kən'teɪnəraɪz] vt mettere in container.

container ship n nave f container inv.

contaminate [kən'tæmɪneɪt] vt contaminare.

contamination [kəntæmɪ'neɪʃən] n contaminazione f.

cont'd abbr (= *continued*) segue.

contemplate ['kɔntəmpleɪt] vt contemplare; (*consider*) pensare a (*or* di).

contemplation [kɔntəm'pleɪʃən] n contemplazione f.

contemporary [kən'tempərərɪ] adj contemporaneo(a); (*design*) moderno(a) ♦ n contemporaneo/a; (*of the same age*) coetaneo/a.

contempt [kən'tempt] n disprezzo; ~ **of court** (*LAW*) oltraggio alla Corte.

contemptible [kən'temptəbl] adj sregevole, vergognoso(a).

contemptuous [kən'temptjuəs] adj sdegnoso(a).

contend [kən'tend] vt: **to** ~ **that** sostenere che ♦ vi: **to** ~ **with** lottare contro; **he has a lot to** ~ **with** ha un sacco di guai.

contender [kən'tendə*] n contendente m/f; concorrente m/f.

content [kən'tent] adj contento(a), soddisfatto(a) ♦ vt contentare, soddisfare ♦ n ['kɔntent] contenuto; ~s npl contenuto; (*of barrel etc: capacity*) capacità f inv; (**table of**) ~s indice m; **to be** ~ **with** essere contento di; **to** ~ **o.s. with sth/with doing sth** accontentarsi di qc/di fare qc.

contented [kən'tentɪd] adj contento(a), soddisfatto(a).

contentedly [kən'tentɪdlɪ] adv con soddisfazione.

contention [kən'tenʃən] n contesa; (*assertion*) tesi f inv; **bone of** ~ pomo della discordia.

contentious [kən'tenʃəs] adj polemico(a).

contentment [kən'tentmənt] n contentezza.

contest n ['kɔntest] lotta; (*competition*) gara, concorso ♦ vt [kən'test] contestare; (*LAW*) impugnare; (*compete for*) contendere.

contestant [kən'tɛstənt] *n* concorrente *m/f*; (*in fight*) avversario/a.

context ['kɔntɛkst] *n* contesto; **in/out of ~** nel/fuori dal contesto.

continent ['kɔntɪnənt] *n* continente *m*; **the C~** (*BRIT*) l'Europa continentale; **on the C~** in Europa.

continental [kɔntɪ'nɛntl] *adj* continentale ♦ *n* (*BRIT*) abitante *m/f* dell'Europa continentale.

continental breakfast *n* colazione *f* all'europea.

continental quilt *n* (*BRIT*) piumino.

contingency [kən'tɪndʒənsɪ] *n* eventualità *f* *inv*.

contingency plan *n* misura d'emergenza.

contingent [kən'tɪndʒənt] *n* contingenza ♦ *adj*: **to be ~ upon** dipendere da.

continual [kən'tɪnjuəl] *adj* continuo(a).

continually [kən'tɪnjuəlɪ] *adv* di continuo.

continuation [kəntɪnju'eɪʃən] *n* continuazione *f*; (*after interruption*) ripresa; (*of story*) seguito.

continue [kən'tɪnjuː] *vi* continuare ♦ *vt* continuare; (*start again*) riprendere; **to be ~d** (*story*) continua; **~d on page 10** segue *or* continua a pagina 10.

continuing education [kən'tɪnjuɪŋ-] *n* corsi *mpl* per adulti.

continuity [kɔntɪ'njuːɪtɪ] *n* continuità; (*CINE*) (ordine *m* della) sceneggiatura.

continuity girl *n* (*CINE*) segretaria di edizione.

continuous [kən'tɪnjuəs] *adj* continuo(a), ininterrotto(a); **~ performance** (*CINE*) spettacolo continuato; **~ stationery** (*COMPUT*) carta a moduli continui.

continuously [kən'tɪnjuəslɪ] *adv* (*repeatedly*) continuamente; (*uninterruptedly*) ininterrottamente.

contort [kən'tɔːt] *vt* contorcere.

contortion [kən'tɔːʃən] *n* contorcimento; (*of acrobat*) contorsione *f*.

contortionist [kən'tɔːʃənɪst] *n* contorsionista *m/f*.

contour ['kɔntuə*] *n* contorno, profilo; (*also*: **~ line**) curva di livello.

contraband ['kɔntrəbænd] *n* contrabbando ♦ *adj* di contrabbando.

contraception [kɔntrə'sɛpʃən] *n* contraccezione *f*.

contraceptive [kɔntrə'sɛptɪv] *adj* contraccettivo(a) ♦ *n* contraccettivo.

contract *n* ['kɔntrækt] contratto ♦ *cpd* ['kɔntrækt] (*price, date*) del contratto; (*work*) a contratto ♦ *vi* [kən'trækt] (*COMM*): **to ~ to do sth** fare un contratto per fare qc; (*become smaller*) contrarre; **to be**

under ~ to do sth aver stipulato un contratto per fare qc; **~ of employment** contratto di lavoro.

►**contract in** *vi* impegnarsi (con un contratto); (*BRIT ADMIN*) scegliere di pagare i contributi per una pensione.

►**contract out** *vi*: **to ~ out (of)** ritirarsi (da); (*BRIT ADMIN*) (scegliere di) non pagare i contributi per una pensione.

contraction [kən'trækʃən] *n* contrazione *f*.

contractor [kən'træktə*] *n* imprenditore *m*.

contractual [kən'træktjuəl] *adj* contrattuale.

contradict [kɔntrə'dɪkt] *vt* contraddire.

contradiction [kɔntrə'dɪkʃən] *n* contraddizione *f*; **to be in ~ with** discordare con.

contradictory [kɔntrə'dɪktərɪ] *adj* contraddittorio(a).

contralto [kən'træltəu] *n* contralto.

contraption [kən'træpʃən] *n* (*pej*) aggeggio.

contrary ['kɔntrərɪ] *adj* contrario(a); (*unfavourable*) avverso(a), contrario(a); [kən'trɛərɪ] (*perverse*) bisbetico(a) ♦ *n* contrario; **on the ~** al contrario; **unless you hear to the ~** a meno che non si disdica; **~ to what we thought** a differenza di *or* contrariamente a quanto pensavamo.

contrast *n* ['kɔntrɑːst] contrasto ♦ *vt* [kən'trɑːst] mettere in contrasto; **in ~ to** *or* **with** a differenza di, contrariamente a.

contrasting [kən'trɑːstɪŋ] *adj* contrastante, di contrasto.

contravene [kɔntrə'viːn] *vt* contravvenire.

contravention [kɔntrə'vɛnʃən] *n*: **~ (of)** contravvenzione *f* (a), infrazione *f* (di).

contribute [kən'trɪbjuːt] *vi* contribuire ♦ *vt*: **to ~ £10/an article to** dare 10 sterline/un articolo a; **to ~ to** contribuire a; (*newspaper*) scrivere per; (*discussion*) partecipare a.

contribution [kɔntrɪ'bjuːʃən] *n* contribuzione *f*.

contributor [kən'trɪbjutə*] *n* (*to newspaper*) collaboratore/trice.

contributory [kən'trɪbjutərɪ] *adj* (*cause*) che contribuisce; **it was a ~ factor in ...** quello ha contribuito a ....

contributory pension scheme *n* (*BRIT*) *sistema di pensionamento finanziato congiuntamente dai contributi del lavoratore e del datore di lavoro*.

contrite ['kɔntraɪt] *adj* contrito(a).

contrivance [kən'traɪvəns] *n* congegno; espediente *m*.

contrive [kən'traɪv] *vt* inventare;

escogitare ♦ *vi:* **to ~ to do** fare in modo di fare.

control [kən'trəul] *vt* dominare; (*firm, operation etc*) dirigere; (*check*) controllare; (*disease, fire*) arginare, limitare ♦ *n* controllo; **~s** *npl* comandi *mpl*; **to take ~ of** assumere il controllo di; **to be in ~ of** aver autorità su; essere responsabile di; controllare; **to ~ o.s.** controllarsi; **everything is under ~** tutto è sotto controllo; **the car went out of ~** la macchina non rispondeva ai comandi; **circumstances beyond our ~** circostanze *fpl* che non dipendono da noi.

control key *n* (*COMPUT*) tasto di controllo.

controller [kən'trəulə*] *n* controllore *m*.

controlling interest [kən'trəulɪŋ-] *n* (*COMM*) maggioranza delle azioni.

control panel *n* (*on aircraft, ship, TV etc*) quadro dei comandi.

control point *n* punto di controllo.

control room *n* (*NAUT, MIL*) sala di comando; (*RADIO, TV*) sala di regia.

control tower *n* (*AVIAT*) torre *f* di controllo.

control unit *n* (*COMPUT*) unità *f inv* di controllo.

controversial [kɔntrə'və:ʃl] *adj* controverso(a), polemico(a).

controversy ['kɔntrəvə:sɪ] *n* controversia, polemica.

conurbation [kɔnə:'beɪʃən] *n* conurbazione *f*.

convalesce [kɔnvə'lɛs] *vi* rimettersi in salute.

convalescence [kɔnvə'lɛsns] *n* convalescenza.

convalescent [kɔnvə'lɛsnt] *adj, n* convalescente (*m/f*).

convector [kən'vɛktə*] *n* convettore *m*.

convene [kən'vi:n] *vt* convocare; (*meeting*) organizzare ♦ *vi* convenire, adunarsi.

convenience [kən'vi:nɪəns] *n* comodità *f inv*; **at your ~** a suo comodo; **at your earliest ~** (*COMM*) appena possibile; **all modern ~s**, (*BRIT*) **all mod cons** tutte le comodità moderne.

convenience foods *npl* cibi *mpl* precotti.

convenient [kən'vi:nɪənt] *adj* conveniente, comodo(a); **if it is ~ to you** se per lei va bene, se non la incomoda.

conveniently [kən'vi:nɪəntlɪ] *adv* (*happen*) a proposito; (*situated*) in un posto comodo.

convent ['kɔnvənt] *n* convento.

convention [kən'vɛnʃən] *n* convenzione *f*; (*meeting*) convegno.

conventional [kən'vɛnʃənl] *adj* convenzionale.

convent school *n* scuola retta da suore.

converge [kən'və:dʒ] *vi* convergere.

conversant [kən'və:snt] *adj:* **to be ~ with** essere al corrente di; essere pratico(a) di.

conversation [kɔnvə'seɪʃən] *n* conversazione *f*.

conversational [kɔnvə'seɪʃənl] *adj* non formale; (*COMPUT*) conversazionale; **~ Italian** l'italiano parlato.

conversationalist [kɔnvə'seɪʃnəlɪst] *n* conversatore/trice.

converse *n* ['kɔnvə:s] contrario, opposto ♦ *vi* [kən'və:s]: **to ~ (with sb about sth)** conversare (con qn su qc).

conversely [kɔn'və:slɪ] *adv* al contrario, per contro.

conversion [kən'və:ʃən] *n* conversione *f*; (*BRIT: of house*) trasformazione *f*, rimodernamento.

conversion table *n* tavola di equivalenze.

convert *vt* [kən'və:t] (*REL, COMM*) convertire; (*alter*) trasformare ♦ *n* ['kɔnvə:t] convertito/a.

convertible [kən'və:təbl] *n* macchina decappottabile.

convex ['kɔnvɛks] *adj* convesso(a).

convey [kən'veɪ] *vt* trasportare; (*thanks*) comunicare; (*idea*) dare.

conveyance [kən'veɪəns] *n* (*of goods*) trasporto; (*vehicle*) mezzo di trasporto.

conveyancing [kən'veɪənsɪŋ] *n* (*LAW*) redazione *f* di transazioni di proprietà.

conveyor belt *n* nastro trasportatore.

convict *vt* [kən'vɪkt] dichiarare colpevole ♦ *n* ['kɔnvɪkt] carcerato/a.

conviction [kən'vɪkʃən] *n* condanna; (*belief*) convinzione *f*.

convince [kən'vɪns] *vt:* **to ~ sb (of sth/that)** convincere qn (di qc/che), persuadere qn (di qc/che).

convincing [kən'vɪnsɪŋ] *adj* convincente.

convincingly [kən'vɪnsɪŋlɪ] *adv* in modo convincente.

convivial [kən'vɪvɪəl] *adj* allegro(a).

convoluted ['kɔnvəlu:tɪd] *adj* (*shape*) attorcigliato(a), avvolto(a); (*argument*) involuto(a).

convoy ['kɔnvɔɪ] *n* convoglio.

convulse [kən'vʌls] *vt* sconvolgere; **to be ~d with laughter** contorcersi dalle risa.

convulsion [kən'vʌlʃən] *n* convulsione *f*.

coo [ku:] *vi* tubare.

cook [kuk] *vt* cucinare, cuocere; (*meal*) preparare ♦ *vi* cuocere; (*person*) cucinare ♦ *n* cuoco/a.

▶**cook up** *vt* (*col: excuse, story*) improvvisare, inventare.

cookbook ['kukbuk] *n* = **cookery book**.
cooker ['kukə*] *n* fornello, cucina.
cookery book *n* (*BRIT*) libro di cucina.
cookie ['kukɪ] *n* (*US*) biscotto.
cooking ['kukɪŋ] *n* cucina ♦ *cpd* (*apples, chocolate*) da cuocere; (*utensils, salt, foil*) da cucina.
cookout ['kukaut] *n* (*US*) pranzo (cucinato) all'aperto.
cool [kuːl] *adj* fresco(a); (*not afraid*) calmo(a); (*unfriendly*) freddo(a); (*impertinent*) sfacciato(a) ♦ *vt* raffreddare, rinfrescare ♦ *vi* raffreddarsi, rinfrescarsi; **it's** ~ (*weather*) fa fresco; **to keep sth** ~ *or* **in a** ~ **place** tenere qc in fresco.
►**cool down** *vi* raffreddarsi; (*fig: person, situation*) calmarsi.
coolant ['kuːlənt] *n* (liquido) refrigerante *m*.
cool box, (*US*) **cooler** ['kuːlə*] *n* borsa termica.
cooling ['kuːlɪŋ] *adj* (*breeze*) fresco(a).
cooling tower *n* torre *f* di raffreddamento.
coolly ['kuːlɪ] *adv* (*calmly*) con calma, tranquillamente; (*audaciously*) come se niente fosse; (*unenthusiastically*) freddamente.
coolness ['kuːlnɪs] *n* freschezza; sangue *m* freddo, calma.
coop [kuːp] *n* stia ♦ *vt*: **to** ~ **up** (*fig*) rinchiudere.
co-op ['kəuɔp] *n abbr* (= *cooperative* (*society*)) coop *f*.
cooperate [kəu'ɔpəreɪt] *vi* cooperare, collaborare.
cooperation [kəuɔpə'reɪʃən] *n* cooperazione *f*, collaborazione *f*.
cooperative [kəu'ɔpərətɪv] *adj* cooperativo(a) ♦ *n* cooperativa.
coopt [kəu'ɔpt] *vt*: **to** ~ **sb into sth** cooptare qn per qc.
coordinate *vt* [kəu'ɔːdɪneɪt] coordinare ♦ *n* [kəu'ɔːdɪnət] (*MATH*) coordinata; ~**s** *npl* (*clothes*) coordinati *mpl*.
coordination [kəuɔːdɪ'neɪʃən] *n* coordinazione *f*.
coot [kuːt] *n* folaga.
co-ownership [kəu'əunəʃɪp] *n* comproprietà.
cop [kɔp] *n* (*col*) sbirro.
cope [kəup] *vi* farcela; **to** ~ **with** (*problems*) far fronte a.
Copenhagen [kəupən'heɪgən] *n* Copenhagen *f*.
copier ['kɔpɪə*] *n* (*also*: **photo**~) (foto)copiatrice *f*.

co-pilot ['kəupaɪlət] *n* secondo pilota *m*.
copious ['kəupɪəs] *adj* copioso(a), abbondante.
copper ['kɔpə*] *n* rame *m*; (*col: policeman*) sbirro; ~**s** *npl* spiccioli *mpl*.
coppice ['kɔpɪs], **copse** [kɔps] *n* bosco ceduo.
copulate ['kɔpjuleɪt] *vi* accoppiarsi.
copy ['kɔpɪ] *n* copia; (*book etc*) esemplare *m*; (*material: for printing*) materiale *m*, testo ♦ *vt* (*gen, COMPUT*) copiare; (*imitate*) imitare; **rough/fair** ~ brutta/bella (copia); **to make good** ~ (*fig*) fare notizia.
►**copy out** *vt* ricopiare, trascrivere.
copycat ['kɔpɪkæt] *n* (*pej*) copione *m*.
copyright ['kɔpɪraɪt] *n* diritto d'autore; ~ **reserved** tutti i diritti riservati.
copy typist *n* dattilografo/a.
copywriter ['kɔpɪraɪtə*] *n* redattore *m* pubblicitario.
coral ['kɔrəl] *n* corallo.
coral reef *n* barriera corallina.
Coral Sea *n*: **the** ~ il mar dei Coralli.
cord [kɔːd] *n* corda; (*ELEC*) filo; (*fabric*) velluto a coste; ~**s** *npl* (*trousers*) calzoni *mpl* (di velluto) a coste.
cordial ['kɔːdɪəl] *adj*, *n* cordiale (*m*).
cordless ['kɔːdlɪs] *adj* senza cavo.
cordon ['kɔːdn] *n* cordone *m*.
►**cordon off** *vt* fare cordone intorno a.
corduroy ['kɔːdərɔɪ] *n* fustagno.
CORE [kɔː*] *n abbr* (*US*) = *Congress of Racial Equality*.
core [kɔː*] *n* (*of fruit*) torsolo; (*TECH*) centro; (*of earth, nuclear reactor*) nucleo; (*of problem etc*) cuore *m*, nocciolo ♦ *vt* estrarre il torsolo da; **rotten to the** ~ marcio fino al midollo.
Corfu [kɔː'fuː] *n* Corfù *f*.
coriander [kɔrɪ'ændə*] *n* coriandolo.
cork [kɔːk] *n* sughero; (*of bottle*) tappo.
corkage ['kɔːkɪdʒ] *n* somma da pagare se il cliente porta il proprio vino.
corked [kɔːkt], (*US*) **corky** ['kɔːkɪ] *adj* (*wine*) che sa di tappo.
corkscrew ['kɔːkskruː] *n* cavatappi *m inv*.
cormorant ['kɔːmərnt] *n* cormorano.
Corn *abbr* (*BRIT*) = **Cornwall**.
corn [kɔːn] *n* (*BRIT: wheat*) grano; (*US: maize*) granturco; (*on foot*) callo; ~ **on the cob** (*CULIN*) pannocchia cotta.
cornea ['kɔːnɪə] *n* cornea.
corned beef ['kɔːnd-] *n* carne *f* di manzo in scatola.
corner ['kɔːnə*] *n* angolo; (*AUT*) curva; (*FOOTBALL: also:* ~ **kick**) corner *m inv*, calcio d'angolo ♦ *vt* intrappolare; mettere con le spalle al muro; (*COMM: market*)

accaparrare ♦ vi prendere una curva; **to cut ~s** (fig) prendere una scorciatoia.

corner flag n (FOOTBALL) bandierina d'angolo.

corner kick n (FOOTBALL) calcio d'angolo.

cornerstone ['kɔːnəstəun] n pietra angolare.

cornet ['kɔːnɪt] n (MUS) cornetta; (BRIT: of ice-cream) cono.

cornflakes ['kɔːnfleɪks] npl fiocchi mpl di granturco.

cornflour ['kɔːnflauə*] n (BRIT) ≈ fecola di patate.

cornice ['kɔːnɪs] n cornicione m; cornice f.

Cornish ['kɔːnɪʃ] adj della Cornovaglia.

corn oil n olio di mais.

cornstarch ['kɔːnstɑːtʃ] n (US) = cornflour.

cornucopia [kɔːnjuːkəupɪə] n grande abbondanza.

Cornwall ['kɔːnwəl] n Cornovaglia.

corny ['kɔːnɪ] adj (col) trito(a).

corollary [kə'rɔlərɪ] n corollario.

coronary ['kɔrənərɪ] n: ~ **(thrombosis)** trombosi f coronaria.

coronation [kɔrə'neɪʃən] n incoronazione f.

coroner ['kɔrənə*] n magistrato incaricato di indagare la causa di morte in circostanze sospette.

coronet ['kɔrənɪt] n diadema m.

Corp. abbr = corporation.

corporal ['kɔːpərl] n caporalmaggiore m ♦ adj: ~ **punishment** pena corporale.

corporate ['kɔːpərɪt] adj comune; (COMM) costituito(a) (in corporazione).

corporate hospitality n omaggi mpl ai clienti (come biglietti per spettacoli, cene etc).

corporate identity, corporate image n (of organization) immagine f di marca.

corporation [kɔːpə'reɪʃən] n (of town) consiglio comunale; (COMM) ente m.

corporation tax n ≈ imposta societaria.

corps [kɔː*], pl **corps** [kɔːz] n corpo; **press ~** ufficio m stampa inv.

corpse [kɔːps] n cadavere m.

corpuscle ['kɔːpʌsl] n corpuscolo.

corral [kə'rɑːl] n recinto.

correct [kə'rɛkt] adj (accurate) corretto(a), esatto(a); (proper) corretto(a) ♦ vt correggere; **you are ~** ha ragione.

correction [kə'rɛkʃən] n correzione f.

correlate ['kɔrɪleɪt] vt mettere in correlazione ♦ vi: **to ~ with** essere in rapporto con.

correlation [kɔrɪ'leɪʃən] n correlazione f.

correspond [kɔrɪs'pɔnd] vi corrispondere.

correspondence [kɔrɪs'pɔndəns] n corrispondenza.

correspondence course n corso per corrispondenza.

correspondent [kɔrɪs'pɔndənt] n corrispondente m/f.

corridor ['kɔrɪdɔː*] n corridoio.

corroborate [kə'rɔbəreɪt] vt corroborare, confermare.

corrode [kə'rəud] vt corrodere ♦ vi corrodersi.

corrosion [kə'rəuʒən] n corrosione f.

corrosive [kə'rəuzɪv] adj corrosivo(a).

corrugated ['kɔrəgeɪtɪd] adj increspato(a); ondulato(a).

corrugated iron n lamiera di ferro ondulata.

corrupt [kə'rʌpt] adj corrotto(a) ♦ vt corrompere; ~ **practices** (dishonesty, bribery) pratiche fpl illecite.

corruption [kə'rʌpʃən] n corruzione f.

corset ['kɔːsɪt] n busto.

Corsica ['kɔːsɪkə] n Corsica.

Corsican ['kɔːsɪkən] adj, n corso(a).

cortège [kɔː'teɪʒ] n corteo.

cortisone ['kɔːtɪzəun] n cortisone m.

coruscating ['kɔrəskeɪtɪŋ] adj scintillante.

c.o.s. abbr (= cash on shipment) pagamento alla spedizione.

cosh [kɔʃ] n (BRIT) randello (corto).

cosignatory [kəu'sɪgnətərɪ] n cofirmatario/a.

cosiness ['kəuzɪnɪs] n intimità.

cos lettuce ['kɔs-] n lattuga romana.

cosmetic [kɔz'mɛtɪk] n cosmetico ♦ adj (preparation) cosmetico(a); (surgery) estetico(a); (fig: reforms) ornamentale.

cosmic ['kɔzmɪk] adj cosmico(a).

cosmonaut ['kɔzmənɔːt] n cosmonauta m/f.

cosmopolitan [kɔzmə'pɔlɪtn] adj cosmopolita.

cosmos ['kɔzmɔs] n cosmo.

cosset ['kɔsɪt] vt vezzeggiare.

cost [kɔst] n costo ♦ vb (pt, pp cost) vi costare ♦ vt stabilire il prezzo di; ~**s** npl (LAW) spese fpl; **it ~s £5/too much** costa 5 sterline/troppo; **it ~ him his life/job** gli costò la vita/il suo lavoro; **how much does it ~?** quanto costa?, quanto viene?; **what will it ~ to have it repaired?** quanto costerà farlo riparare?; ~ **of living** costo della vita; **at all ~s** a ogni costo.

cost accountant n analizzatore m dei costi.

co-star ['kəustɑː*] n attore/trice della stessa importanza del protagonista.

Costa Rica ['kɔstə'riːkə] n Costa Rica.

cost centre n centro di costo.

cost control n controllo dei costi.

cost-effective ['kɔstɪ'fɛktɪv] adj (gen)

conveniente, economico(a); (*COMM*) redditizio(a), conveniente.

cost-effectiveness [ˈkɔstɪˈfɛktɪvnɪs] *n* convenienza.

costing [ˈkɔstɪŋ] *n* (determinazione *f* dei) costi *mpl*.

costly [ˈkɔstlɪ] *adj* costoso(a), caro(a).

cost-of-living [ˈkɔstəvˈlɪvɪŋ] *adj*: ~ **allowance** indennità *f inv* di contingenza; ~ **index** indice *m* della scala mobile.

cost price *n* (*BRIT*) prezzo all'ingrosso.

costume [ˈkɔstjuːm] *n* costume *m*; (*lady's suit*) tailleur *m inv*; (*BRIT*: *also*: **swimming** ~) costume da bagno.

costume jewellery *n* bigiotteria.

cosy, (*US*) **cozy** [ˈkəuzɪ] *adj* intimo(a); (*room, atmosphere*) accogliente.

cot [kɔt] *n* (*BRIT*: *child's*) lettino; (*US*: *folding bed*) brandina.

cot death *n improvvisa e inspiegabile morte nel sonno di un neonato.*

Cotswolds [ˈkɔtswəuldz] *npl*: **the** ~ *zona collinare del Gloucestershire.*

cottage [ˈkɔtɪdʒ] *n* cottage *m inv*.

cottage cheese *n* fiocchi *mpl* di latte magro.

cottage industry *n industria artigianale basata sul lavoro a cottimo.*

cottage pie *n piatto a base di carne macinata in sugo e purè di patate.*

cotton [ˈkɔtn] *n* cotone *m*; ~ **dress** *etc* vestito *etc* di cotone.

►**cotton on** *vi* (*col*): **to** ~ **on (to sth)** afferrare (qc).

cotton wool *n* (*BRIT*) cotone *m* idrofilo.

couch [kautʃ] *n* sofà *m inv*; (*in doctor's surgery*) lettino ♦ *vt* esprimere.

couchette [kuːˈʃɛt] *n* cuccetta.

couch potato *n* (*col*) pigrone/a teledipendente.

cough [kɔf] *vi* tossire ♦ *n* tosse *f*.

cough drop *n* pasticca per la tosse.

cough mixture, cough syrup *n* sciroppo per la tosse.

could [kud] *pt of* **can**.

couldn't [ˈkudnt] = **could not**.

council [ˈkaunsl] *n* consiglio; **city** *or* **town** ~ consiglio comunale; **C~ of Europe** Consiglio d'Europa.

council estate *n* (*BRIT*) quartiere *m* di case popolari.

council house *n* (*BRIT*) casa popolare.

council housing *n* alloggi *mpl* popolari.

councillor [ˈkaunsələ*] *n* consigliere/a.

council tax *n* (*BRIT*) *tassa comunale sulla proprietà.*

counsel [ˈkaunsl] *n* avvocato; consultazione *f* ♦ *vt*: **to** ~ **sth/sb to do sth** consigliare

qc/a qn di fare qc; ~ **for the defence/the prosecution** avvocato difensore/di parte civile.

counsellor, (*US*) **counselor** [ˈkaunslə*] *n* consigliere/a; (*US*: *lawyer*) avvocato/essa.

count [kaunt] *vt, vi* contare ♦ *n* conto; (*nobleman*) conte *m*; **to** ~ **(up) to 10** contare fino a 10; **to** ~ **the cost of** calcolare il costo di; **not** ~**ing the children** senza contare i bambini; **10** ~**ing him** 10 compreso lui; ~ **yourself lucky** considerati fortunato; **it** ~**s for very little** non conta molto, non ha molta importanza; **to keep** ~ **of sth** tenere il conto di qc.

►**count on** *vt fus* contare su; **to** ~ **on doing sth** contare di fare qc.

►**count up** *vt* addizionare.

countdown [ˈkauntdaun] *n* conto alla rovescia.

countenance [ˈkauntɪnəns] *n* volto, aspetto ♦ *vt* approvare.

counter [ˈkauntə*] *n* banco; (*position: in post office, bank*) sportello; (*in game*) gettone *m*; (*TECH*) contatore *m* ♦ *vt* opporsi a; (*blow*) parare ♦ *adv*: ~ **to** contro; in opposizione a; **to buy under the** ~ (*fig*) comperare sottobanco; **to** ~ **sth with sth/by doing sth** rispondere a qc con qc/facendo qc.

counteract [kauntərˈækt] *vt* agire in opposizione a; (*poison etc*) annullare gli effetti di.

counterattack [ˈkauntərətæk] *n* contrattacco ♦ *vi* contrattaccare.

counterbalance [ˈkauntəbæləns] *vt* contrappesare.

counter-clockwise [ˈkauntəˈklɔkwaɪz] *adv* in senso antiorario.

counter-espionage [kauntərˈɛspɪɒnɑːʒ] *n* controspionaggio.

counterfeit [ˈkauntəfɪt] *n* contraffazione *f*, falso ♦ *vt* contraffare, falsificare ♦ *adj* falso(a).

counterfoil [ˈkauntəfɔɪl] *n* matrice *f*.

counterintelligence [ˈkauntərɪnˈtɛlɪdʒəns] *n* = **counter-espionage**.

countermand [ˈkauntəmɑːnd] *vt* annullare.

countermeasure [ˈkauntəmɛʒə*] *n* contromisura.

counteroffensive [ˈkauntərəˈfɛnsɪv] *n* controffensiva.

counterpane [ˈkauntəpeɪn] *n* copriletto *m inv*.

counterpart [ˈkauntəpɑːt] *n* (*of document etc*) copia; (*of person*) corrispondente *m/f*.

counterproductive [ˈkauntəprəˈdʌktɪv] *adj* controproducente.

counterproposal [ˈkauntəprəˈpəuzl] n controproposta.

countersign [ˈkauntəsain] vt controfirmare.

countersink [ˈkauntəsiŋk] vt (hole) svasare.

countess [ˈkauntis] n contessa.

countless [ˈkauntlis] adj innumerevole.

countrified [ˈkʌntrifaid] adj rustico(a), campagnolo(a).

country [ˈkʌntri] n paese m; (native land) patria; (as opposed to town) campagna; (region) regione f; **in the** ~ in campagna; **mountainous** ~ territorio montagnoso.

country and western (music) n musica country e western, country m.

country dancing n (BRIT) danza popolare.

country house n villa in campagna.

countryman [ˈkʌntrimən] n (national) compatriota m; (rural) contadino.

countryside [ˈkʌntrisaid] n campagna.

country-wide [ˈkʌntriˈwaid] adj diffuso(a) in tutto il paese ♦ adv in tutto il paese.

county [ˈkaunti] n contea.

county council n (BRIT) consiglio di contea.

county town n (BRIT) capoluogo.

coup, ~s [kuː, -z] n (also: ~ **d'état**) colpo di Stato; (triumph) bel colpo.

coupé [kuːˈpei] n coupé m inv.

couple [ˈkʌpl] n coppia ♦ vt (carriages) agganciare; (TECH) accoppiare; (ideas, names) associare; **a** ~ **of** un paio di.

couplet [ˈkʌplit] n distico.

coupling [ˈkʌpliŋ] n (RAIL) agganciamento.

coupon [ˈkuːpɔn] n (voucher) buono; (COMM) coupon m inv.

courage [ˈkʌridʒ] n coraggio.

courageous [kəˈreidʒəs] adj coraggioso(a).

courgette [kuəˈʒɛt] n (BRIT) zucchina.

courier [ˈkuriə*] n corriere m; (for tourists) guida.

course [kɔːs] n corso; (of ship) rotta; (for golf) campo; (part of meal) piatto; **first** ~ primo piatto; **of** ~ adv senz'altro, naturalmente; **(no) of** ~ **not!** certo che no!, no di certo!; **in the** ~ **of the next few days** nel corso dei prossimi giorni; **in due** ~ a tempo debito; ~ **(of action)** modo d'agire; **the best** ~ **would be to** ... la cosa migliore sarebbe ...; **we have no other** ~ **but to** ... non possiamo far altro che ...; ~ **of lectures** corso di lezioni; **a** ~ **of treatment** (MED) una cura.

court [kɔːt] n corte f; (TENNIS) campo ♦ vt (woman) fare la corte a; (fig: favour, popularity) cercare di conquistare; (: death, disaster) sfiorare, rasentare; **out of** ~ (LAW: settle) in via amichevole; **to take to** ~ citare in tribunale; **C~ of Appeal** corte d'appello.

courteous [ˈkəːtiəs] adj cortese.

courtesan [kɔːtiˈzæn] n cortigiana.

courtesy [ˈkəːtəsi] n cortesia; **by** ~ **of** per gentile concessione di.

courtesy light n (AUT) luce f interna.

court-house [ˈkɔːthaus] n (US) palazzo di giustizia.

courtier [ˈkɔːtiə*] n cortigiano/a.

courtmartial, pl courtsmartial [ˈkɔːtˈmɑːʃəl] n corte f marziale.

courtroom [ˈkɔːtrum] n tribunale m.

court shoe n scarpa f décolleté inv.

courtyard [ˈkɔːtjɑːd] n cortile m.

cousin [ˈkʌzn] n cugino/a.

cove [kəuv] n piccola baia.

covenant [ˈkʌvənənt] n accordo ♦ vt: **to** ~ **to do sth** impegnarsi (per iscritto) a fare qc.

Coventry [ˈkɔvəntri] n: **to send sb to** ~ (fig) dare l'ostracismo a qn.

cover [ˈkʌvə*] vt (gen) coprire; (distance) coprire, percorrere; (PRESS: report on) fare un servizio su ♦ n (of pan) coperchio; (over furniture) fodera; (of book) copertina; (shelter) riparo; (COMM, INSURANCE) copertura; **to take** ~ mettersi al coperto; **under** ~ al riparo; **under** ~ **of darkness** protetto dall'oscurità; **under separate** ~ (COMM) a parte, in plico separato; **£10 will** ~ **everything** 10 sterline saranno sufficienti.

▶**cover up** vt (child, object): **to** ~ **up (with)** coprire (di); (fig: hide: truth, facts) nascondere ♦ vi: **to** ~ **up for sb** (fig) coprire qn.

coverage [ˈkʌvəridʒ] n (PRESS, TV, RADIO): **to give full** ~ **to** fare un ampio servizio su.

coveralls [ˈkʌvərɔːlz] npl (US) tuta.

cover charge n coperto.

covering [ˈkʌvəriŋ] n copertura.

covering letter, (US) **cover letter** n lettera di accompagnamento.

cover note n (INSURANCE) polizza (di assicurazione) provvisoria.

cover price n prezzo di copertina.

covert [ˈkʌvət] adj nascosto(a); (glance) di sottecchi, furtivo(a).

cover-up [ˈkʌvərʌp] n occultamento (di informazioni).

covet [ˈkʌvit] vt bramare.

cow [kau] n vacca ♦ cpd femmina ♦ vt intimidire; ~ **elephant** n elefantessa.

cowardice [ˈkauədis] n vigliaccheria.

cowardly [ˈkauədli] adj vigliacco(a).

cowboy [ˈkaubɔi] n cow-boy m inv.

cower [ˈkauə*] vi acquattarsi.

cowshed ['kauʃed] *n* stalla.
cowslip ['kausltp] *n* (*BOT*) primula (odorata).
coxswain ['kɔksn] *n* (*abbr*: **cox**) timoniere *m*.
coy [kɔɪ] *adj* falsamente timido(a).
coyote [kɔɪ'autɪ] *n* coyote *m inv*.
cozy ['kəuzɪ] *adj* (*US*) = **cosy**.
CP *n abbr* (= *Communist Party*) P.C. *m*.
cp. *abbr* (= *compare*) cfr.
c/p *abbr* (*BRIT*) = **carriage paid**.
CPA *n abbr* (*US*) *see* **certified public accountant**.
CPI *n abbr* (*US*: = *Consumer Price Index*) *indice dei prezzi al consumo*.
Cpl. *abbr* = **corporal**.
CP/M *n abbr* (= *Control Program for Microcomputers*) CP/M *m*.
c.p.s. *abbr* (= *characters per second*) c.p.s.
CPSA *n abbr* (*BRIT*: = *Civil and Public Services Association*) *sindacato dei servizi pubblici*.
CPU *n abbr see* **central processing unit**.
cr. *abbr* = **credit; creditor**.
crab [kræb] *n* granchio.
crab apple *n* mela selvatica.
crack [kræk] *n* (*split, slit*) fessura, crepa; incrinatura; (*noise*) schiocco; (: *of gun*) scoppio; (*joke*) battuta; (*col: attempt*): **to have a ~ at sth** tentare qc; (*DRUGS*) crack *m inv* ♦ *vt* spaccare; incrinare; (*whip*) schioccare; (*nut*) schiacciare; (*case, mystery: solve*) risolvere; (*code*) decifrare ♦ *cpd* (*athlete*) di prim'ordine; **to ~ jokes** (*col*) dire battute, scherzare; **to get ~ing** (*col*) darsi una mossa.
▶**crack down on** *vt fus* prendere serie misure contro, porre freno a.
▶**crack up** *vi* crollare.
crackdown ['krækdaun] *n* repressione *f*.
cracked [krækt] *adj* (*col*) matto(a).
cracker ['krækə*] *n* cracker *m inv*; (*firework*) petardo; (*Christmas ~*) mortaretto natalizio (con sorpresa); **a ~ of a ...** (*BRIT col*) un(a) ... formidabile; **he's ~s** (*BRIT col*) è tocco.
crackle ['krækl] *vi* crepitare.
crackling ['kræklɪŋ] *n* crepitio; (*on radio, telephone*) disturbo; (*of pork*) cotenna croccante (del maiale).
crackpot ['krækpɔt] *n* (*col*) imbecille *m/f* con idee assurde, assurdo/a.
cradle ['kreɪdl] *n* culla ♦ *vt* (*child*) tenere fra le braccia; (*object*) reggere tra le braccia.
craft [krɑːft] *n* mestiere *m*; (*cunning*) astuzia; (*boat*) naviglio.
craftsman ['krɑːftsmən] *n* artigiano.
craftsmanship ['krɑːftsmənʃɪp] *n* abilità.

crafty ['krɑːftɪ] *adj* furbo(a), astuto(a).
crag [kræg] *n* roccia.
cram [kræm] *vt* (*fill*): **to ~ sth with** riempire qc di; (*put*): **to ~ sth into** stipare qc in.
cramming ['kræmɪŋ] *n* (*fig: pej*) sgobbare *m*.
cramp [kræmp] *n* crampo ♦ *vt* soffocare, impedire.
cramped [kræmpt] *adj* ristretto(a).
crampon ['kræmpən] *n* (*CLIMBING*) rampone *m*.
cranberry ['krænbərɪ] *n* mirtillo.
crane [kreɪn] *n* gru *f inv* ♦ *vt, vi*: **to ~ forward, to ~ one's neck** allungare il collo.
cranium, *pl* crania ['kreɪnɪəm, 'kreɪnɪə] *n* cranio.
crank [kræŋk] *n* manovella; (*person*) persona stramba.
crankshaft ['kræŋkʃɑːft] *n* albero a gomiti.
cranky ['kræŋkɪ] *adj* eccentrico(a); (*bad-tempered*): **to be ~** avere i nervi.
cranny ['krænɪ] *n see* **nook**.
crap [kræp] *n* (*col!*) fesserie *fpl*; **to have a ~** cacare (*!*).
crappy ['kræpɪ] *adj* (*col*) di merda (*!*).
crash [kræʃ] *n* fragore *m*; (*of car*) incidente *m*; (*of plane*) caduta; (*of business*) fallimento; (*STOCK EXCHANGE*) crollo ♦ *vt* fracassare ♦ *vi* (*plane*) fracassarsi; (*car*) avere un incidente; (*two cars*) scontrarsi; (*fig*) fallire, andare in rovina; **to ~ into** scontrarsi con; **he ~ed the car into a wall** andò a sbattere contro un muro con la macchina.
crash barrier *n* (*BRIT AUT*) guardrail *m inv*.
crash course *n* corso intensivo.
crash helmet *n* casco.
crash landing *n* atterraggio di fortuna.
crass [kræs] *adj* crasso(a).
crate [kreɪt] *n* gabbia.
crater ['kreɪtə*] *n* cratere *m*.
cravat(e) [krə'væt] *n* fazzoletto da collo.
crave [kreɪv] *vi*: **to ~ for** desiderare ardentemente.
craving ['kreɪvɪŋ] *n*: **~ (for)** (*for food, cigarettes etc*) (gran) voglia (di).
crawl [krɔːl] *vi* strisciare carponi; (*child*) andare a gattoni; (*vehicle*) avanzare lentamente ♦ *n* (*SWIMMING*) crawl *m*; **to ~ to sb** (*col: suck up*) arruffianarsi qn.
crawler lane ['krɔːlə*-] *n* (*BRIT AUT*) corsia riservata al traffico lento.
crayfish ['kreɪfɪʃ] *n* (*pl inv*) gambero (d'acqua dolce).
crayon ['kreɪən] *n* matita colorata.
craze [kreɪz] *n* mania.
crazed [kreɪzd] *adj* (*look, person*) folle, pazzo(a); (*pottery, glaze*) incrinato(a).

crazy ['kreɪzɪ] adj matto(a); **to go** ~ uscir di senno, impazzire; **to be** ~ **about sb** (col: keen) essere pazzo di qn; **to be** ~ **about sth** andare matto per qc.

crazy paving n (BRIT) lastricato a mosaico irregolare.

creak [kriːk] vi cigolare, scricchiolare.

cream [kriːm] n crema; (fresh) panna ♦ adj (colour) color crema inv; **whipped** ~ panna montata.

▶**cream off** vt (best talents, part of profits) portarsi via.

cream cake n torta alla panna.

cream cheese n formaggio fresco.

creamery ['kriːmərɪ] n (shop) latteria; (factory) caseificio.

creamy ['kriːmɪ] adj cremoso(a).

crease [kriːs] n grinza; (deliberate) piega ♦ vt sgualcire ♦ vi sgualcirsi.

crease-resistant ['kriːsrɪzɪstənt] adj ingualcibile.

create [kriː'eɪt] vt creare; (fuss, noise) fare.

creation [kriː'eɪʃən] n creazione f.

creative [kriː'eɪtɪv] adj creativo(a).

creativity [kriːeɪ'tɪvɪtɪ] n creatività.

creator [kriː'eɪtə*] n creatore/trice.

creature ['kriːtʃə*] n creatura.

crèche, creche [krɛʃ] n asilo infantile.

credence ['kriːdns] n credenza, fede f.

credentials [krɪ'dɛnʃlz] npl (papers) credenziali fpl; (letters of reference) referenze fpl.

credibility [krɛdɪ'bɪlɪtɪ] n credibilità.

credible ['krɛdɪbl] adj credibile; (witness, source) attendibile.

credit ['krɛdɪt] n credito; onore m; (SCOL: esp US) certificato del compimento di una parte del corso universitario ♦ vt (COMM) accreditare; (believe: also: **give** ~ **to**) credere, prestar fede a; **to** ~ **£5 to sb** accreditare 5 sterline a qn; **to** ~ **sb with sth** (fig) attribuire qc a qn; **on** ~ a credito; **to one's** ~ a proprio onore; **to take the** ~ **for** farsi il merito di; **to be in** ~ (person) essere creditore(trice); (bank account) essere coperto(a); **he's a** ~ **to his family** fa onore alla sua famiglia; see also **credits**.

creditable ['krɛdɪtəbl] adj che fa onore, degno(a) di lode.

credit account n conto di credito.

credit agency n (BRIT) agenzia di analisi di credito.

credit balance n saldo attivo.

credit bureau n (US) agenzia di analisi di credito.

credit card n carta di credito.

credit control n controllo dei crediti.

credit facilities npl agevolazioni fpl creditizie.

credit limit n limite m di credito.

credit note n (BRIT) nota di credito.

creditor ['krɛdɪtə*] n creditore/trice.

credits ['krɛdɪts] npl (CINE) titoli mpl.

credit transfer n bancogiro, postagiro.

creditworthy ['krɛdɪt'wɔːðɪ] adj autorizzabile al credito.

credulity [krɪ'djuːlɪtɪ] n credulità.

creed [kriːd] n credo; dottrina.

creek [kriːk] n insenatura; (US) piccolo fiume m.

creel [kriːl] n cestino per il pesce; (also: **lobster** ~) nassa.

creep [kriːp] vi (pt, pp **crept** [krɛpt]) avanzare furtivamente (or pian piano); (plant) arrampicarsi ♦ n (col): **he's a** ~ è un tipo viscido; **it gives me the** ~**s** (col) mi fa venire la pelle d'oca; **to** ~ **up on sb** avvicinarsi quatto quatto a qn; (fig: old age etc) cogliere qn alla sprovvista.

creeper ['kriːpə*] n pianta rampicante.

creepers ['kriːpəz] npl (US: rompers) tutina.

creepy ['kriːpɪ] adj (frightening) che fa accapponare la pelle.

creepy-crawly ['kriːpɪ'krɔːlɪ] n (col) bestiolina, insetto.

cremate [krɪ'meɪt] vt cremare.

cremation [krɪ'meɪʃən] n cremazione f.

crematorium, pl crematoria [krɛmə'tɔːrɪəm, -'tɔːrɪə] n forno crematorio.

creosote ['krɪəsəut] n creosoto.

crêpe [kreɪp] n crespo.

crêpe bandage n (BRIT) fascia elastica.

crêpe paper n carta crespa.

crêpe sole n suola di para.

crept [krɛpt] pt, pp of **creep**.

crescendo [krɪ'ʃɛndəu] n crescendo.

crescent ['krɛsnt] n (shape) mezzaluna; (street) strada semicircolare.

cress [krɛs] n crescione m.

crest [krɛst] n cresta; (of helmet) pennacchiera; (of coat of arms) cimiero.

crestfallen ['krɛstfɔːlən] adj mortificato(a).

Crete ['kriːt] n Creta.

crevasse [krɪ'væs] n crepaccio.

crevice ['krɛvɪs] n fessura, crepa.

crew [kruː] n equipaggio; (CINE) troupe f inv; (gang) banda, compagnia.

crew-cut ['kruːkʌt] n: **to have a** ~ avere i capelli a spazzola.

crew-neck ['kruːnɛk] n girocollo.

crib [krɪb] n culla; (REL) presepio ♦ vt (col) copiare.

cribbage ['krɪbɪdʒ] n tipo di gioco di carte.

crick [krɪk] n crampo; ~ **in the neck**

torcicollo.
cricket ['krɪkɪt] n (*insect*) grillo; (*game*) cricket m.
cricketer ['krɪkɪtə*] n giocatore m di cricket.
crime [kraɪm] n (*in general*) criminalità; (*instance*) crimine m, delitto.
crime wave n ondata di criminalità.
criminal ['krɪmɪnl] adj, n criminale (m/f); **C~ Investigation Department (CID)** ≈ polizia giudiziaria.
crimp [krɪmp] vt arricciare.
crimson ['krɪmzn] adj color cremisi inv.
cringe [krɪndʒ] vi acquattarsi; (*fig*) essere servile.
crinkle ['krɪŋkl] vt arricciare, increspare.
cripple ['krɪpl] n zoppo/a ♦ vt azzoppare; (*ship, plane*) avariare; (*production, exports*) rovinare; **~d with arthritis** sciancato(a) per l'artrite.
crippling ['krɪplɪŋ] adj (*taxes, debts*) esorbitante; (*disease*) molto debilitante.
crisis, pl **crises** ['kraɪsɪs, -siːz] n crisi f inv.
crisp [krɪsp] adj croccante; (*fig*) frizzante; vivace; deciso(a).
crisps [krɪsps] npl (*BRIT*) patatine fpl fritte.
criss-cross ['krɪskrɔs] adj incrociato(a) ♦ vt incrociarsi.
criterion, pl **criteria** [kraɪ'tɪərɪən, -'tɪərɪə] n criterio.
critic ['krɪtɪk] n critico/a.
critical ['krɪtɪkl] adj critico(a); **to be ~ of sb/sth** criticare qn/qc, essere critico verso qn/qc.
critically ['krɪtɪklɪ] adv criticamente; **~ ill** gravemente malato.
criticism ['krɪtɪsɪzəm] n critica.
criticize ['krɪtɪsaɪz] vt criticare.
critique [krɪ'tiːk] n critica, saggio critico.
croak [krəuk] vi gracchiare.
Croat ['krəuæt] adj, n = **Croatian.**
Croatia [krəu'eɪʃɪə] n Croazia.
Croatian [krəu'eɪʃɪən] adj croato(a) ♦ n croato/a; (*LING*) croato.
crochet ['krəuʃeɪ] n lavoro all'uncinetto.
crock [krɔk] n coccio; (*col: person: also:* **old ~**) rottame m; (*: car etc*) caffettiera, rottame m.
crockery ['krɔkərɪ] n vasellame m; (*plates, cups etc*) stoviglie fpl.
crocodile ['krɔkədaɪl] n coccodrillo.
crocus ['krəukəs] n croco.
croft [krɔft] n (*BRIT*) piccolo podere m.
crofter ['krɔftə*] n (*BRIT*) affittuario di un piccolo podere.
crone [krəun] n strega.
crony ['krəunɪ] n (*col*) amicone/a.
crook [kruk] n truffatore m; (*of shepherd*)

bastone m.
crooked ['krukɪd] adj curvo(a), storto(a); (*person, action*) disonesto(a).
crop [krɔp] n raccolto; (*produce*) coltivazione f; (*of bird*) gozzo, ingluvie f ♦ vt (*cut: hair*) tagliare, rapare; (*subj: animals: grass*) brucare.
▶**crop up** vi presentarsi.
cropper ['krɔpə*] n: **to come a ~** (*col*) fare fiasco.
crop spraying n spruzzatura di antiparassitari.
croquet ['krəukeɪ] n croquet m.
croquette [krə'kɛt] n crocchetta.
cross [krɔs] n croce f; (*BIOL*) incrocio ♦ vt (*street etc*) attraversare; (*arms, legs, BIOL*) incrociare; (*cheque*) sbarrare; (*thwart: person, plan*) contrastare, ostacolare ♦ vi: **the boat ~es from ... to ...** la barca fa la traversata da ... a ... ♦ adj di cattivo umore; **to ~ o.s.** fare il segno della croce, segnarsi; **we have a ~ed line** (*BRIT: on telephone*) c'è un'interferenza; **they've got their lines ~ed** (*fig*) si sono fraintesi; **to be/get ~ with sb (about sth)** essere arrabbiato(a)/arrabbiarsi con qn (per qc).
▶**cross out** vt cancellare.
▶**cross over** vi attraversare.
crossbar ['krɔsbɑː*] n traversa.
crossbow ['krɔsbəu] n balestra.
crossbreed ['krɔsbriːd] n incrocio.
cross-Channel ferry ['krɔs'tʃænl-] n traghetto che attraversa la Manica.
cross-check ['krɔstʃɛk] n controprova ♦ vi fare una controprova.
crosscountry (race) [krɔs'kʌntrɪ-] n cross-country m inv.
cross-dressing [krɔs'drɛsɪŋ] n travestitismo.
cross-examination ['krɔsɪgzæmɪ'neɪʃən] n (*LAW*) controinterrogatorio.
cross-examine ['krɔsɪg'zæmɪn] vt (*LAW*) sottoporre a controinterrogatorio.
cross-eyed ['krɔsaɪd] adj strabico(a).
crossfire ['krɔsfaɪə*] n fuoco incrociato.
crossing ['krɔsɪŋ] n incrocio; (*sea-passage*) traversata; (*also:* **pedestrian ~**) passaggio pedonale.
crossing point n valico di frontiera.
cross-purposes ['krɔs'pə:pəsɪz] npl: **to be at ~ with sb** (*misunderstand*) fraintendere qn; **to talk at ~** fraintendersi.
cross-question [krɔs'kwɛstʃən] vt (*LAW*) = **cross-examine**; (*fig*) sottoporre ad un interrogatorio.
cross-reference ['krɔs'rɛfərəns] n rinvio, rimando.

crossroads ['krɔsrəudz] *n* incrocio.
cross section *n* (*BIOL*) sezione *f* trasversale; (*in population*) settore *m* rappresentativo.
crosswalk ['krɔswɔːk] *n* (*US*) strisce *fpl* pedonali, passaggio pedonale.
crosswind ['krɔswɪnd] *n* vento di traverso.
crosswise ['krɔswaɪz] *adv* di traverso.
crossword ['krɔswəːd] *n* cruciverba *m inv*.
crotch [krɔtʃ] *n* (*ANAT*) inforcatura; (*of garment*) pattina.
crotchet ['krɔtʃɪt] *n* (*MUS*) semiminima.
crotchety ['krɔtʃɪtɪ] *adj* (*person*) burbero(a).
crouch [krautʃ] *vi* acquattarsi; rannicchiarsi.
croup [kruːp] *n* (*MED*) crup *m*.
crouton ['kruːtɔn] *n* crostino.
crow [krəu] *n* (*bird*) cornacchia; (*of cock*) canto del gallo ♦ *vi* (*cock*) cantare; (*fig*) vantarsi; cantar vittoria.
crowbar ['krəubɑː*] *n* piede *m* di porco.
crowd [kraud] *n* folla ♦ *vt* affollare, stipare ♦ *vi* affollarsi; ~**s of people** un sacco di gente.
crowded ['kraudɪd] *adj* affollato(a); ~ **with** stipato(a) di.
crowd scene *n* (*CINE, THEAT*) scena di massa.
crown [kraun] *n* corona; (*of head*) calotta cranica; (*of hat*) cocuzzolo; (*of hill*) cima ♦ *vt* incoronare; (*tooth*) incapsulare; **and to ~ it all** ... (*fig*) e per giunta ..., e come se non bastasse ....

Nel sistema legale inglese, la **crown court** *è un tribunale penale che si sposta da una città all'altra. È formata da una giuria e presieduta da un giudice. Vi si discutono i reati più gravi, mentre dei reati minori si occupano le* **magistrates' court**, *presiedute da un giudice di pace, ma senza giuria. È il giudice di pace che decide se passare o meno un caso alla crown court.*

---

crowning ['kraunɪŋ] *adj* (*achievement, glory*) supremo(a).
crown jewels *npl* gioielli *mpl* della Corona.
crown prince *n* principe *m* ereditario.
crow's-feet ['krəuzfiːt] *npl* zampe *fpl* di gallina.
crow's-nest ['krəuznɛst] *n* (*on sailing-ship*) coffa.
crucial ['kruːʃl] *adj* cruciale, decisivo(a); ~ **to** essenziale per.
crucifix ['kruːsɪfɪks] *n* crocifisso.
crucifixion [kruːsɪ'fɪkʃən] *n* crocifissione *f*.
crucify ['kruːsɪfaɪ] *vt* crocifiggere, mettere

in croce; (*fig*) distruggere, fare a pezzi.
crude [kruːd] *adj* (*materials*) greggio(a); non raffinato(a); (*fig: basic*) crudo(a), primitivo(a); (: *vulgar*) rozzo(a), grossolano(a).
crude (oil) *n* (petrolio) greggio.
cruel ['kruəl] *adj* crudele.
cruelty ['kruəltɪ] *n* crudeltà *f inv*.
cruet ['kruːɪt] *n* ampolla.
cruise [kruːz] *n* crociera ♦ *vi* andare a velocità di crociera; (*taxi*) circolare.
cruise missile *n* missile *m* cruise *inv*.
cruiser ['kruːzə*] *n* incrociatore *m*.
cruising speed ['kruːzɪŋ-] *n* velocità *f inv* di crociera.
crumb [krʌm] *n* briciola.
crumble ['krʌmbl] *vt* sbriciolare ♦ *vi* sbriciolarsi; (*plaster etc*) sgrettolarsi; (*land, earth*) franare; (*building, fig*) crollare.
crumbly ['krʌmblɪ] *adj* friabile.
crummy ['krʌmɪ] *adj* (*col: cheap*) di infima categoria; (: *depressed*) giù *inv*.
crumpet ['krʌmpɪt] *n* specie *di frittella*.
crumple ['krʌmpl] *vt* raggrinzare, spiegazzare.
crunch [krʌntʃ] *vt* sgranocchiare; (*underfoot*) scricchiolare ♦ *n* (*fig*) punto *or* momento cruciale.
crunchy ['krʌntʃɪ] *adj* croccante.
crusade [kruː'seɪd] *n* crociata ♦ *vi* (*fig*): **to ~ for/against** fare una crociata per/contro.
crusader [kruː'seɪdə*] *n* crociato; (*fig*): ~ **(for)** sostenitore/trice (di).
crush [krʌʃ] *n* folla; (*love*): **to have a ~ on sb** avere una cotta per qn; (*drink*): **lemon ~** spremuta di limone ♦ *vt* schiacciare; (*crumple*) sgualcire; (*grind, break up: garlic, ice*) tritare; (: *grapes*) pigiare.
crush barrier *n* (*BRIT*) transenna.
crushing ['krʌʃɪŋ] *adj* schiacciante.
crust [krʌst] *n* crosta.
crustacean [krʌs'teɪʃən] *n* crostaceo.
crusty ['krʌstɪ] *adj* (*bread*) croccante; (*person*) brontolone(a); (*remark*) brusco(a).
crutch [krʌtʃ] *n* (*MED*) gruccia; (*support*) sostegno; (*also*: **crotch**) pattina.
crux [krʌks] *n* nodo.
cry [kraɪ] *vi* piangere; (*shout: also*: ~ **out**) urlare ♦ *n* urlo, grido; (*of animal*) verso; **to ~ for help** gridare aiuto; **what are you ~ing about?** perché piangi?; **she had a good ~** si è fatta un bel pianto; **it's a far ~ from** ... (*fig*) è tutt'un'altra cosa da ....
►**cry off** *vi* ritirarsi.
crying ['kraɪɪŋ] *adj* (*fig*) palese; urgente.
crypt [krɪpt] *n* cripta.

cryptic ['krıptık] *adj* ermetico(a).
crystal ['krıstl] *n* cristallo.
crystal-clear ['krıstl'klıə*] *adj* cristallino(a); (*fig*) chiaro(a) (come il sole).
crystallize ['krıstəlaız] *vi* cristallizzarsi ♦ *vt* (*fig*) concretizzare, concretare; ~**d fruits** (*BRIT*) frutta candita.
CSA *n abbr* (*US*) = *Confederate States of America*; (*BRIT*: = *Child Support Agency*) *istituto a difesa dei figli di coppie separate, che si adopera affinché venga rispettato l'obbligo del mantenimento.*
CSC *n abbr* (= *Civil Service Commission*) *commissione per il reclutamento dei funzionari statali.*
CSE *n abbr* (*BRIT old*: = *Certificate of Secondary Education*) *diploma di istruzione superiore.*
CS gas *n* (*BRIT*) *tipo di gas lacrimogeno.*
CST *abbr* (*US*: = *central standard time*) *fuso orario.*
CT *abbr* (*US*) = *Connecticut*.
ct *abbr* = **carat**.
CTC *n abbr* (*BRIT*: = *city technology college*) *istituto tecnico superiore.*
cu. *abbr* = **cubic**.
cub [kʌb] *n* cucciolo; (*also*: ~ **scout**) lupetto.
Cuba ['kjuːbə] *n* Cuba.
Cuban ['kjuːbən] *adj*, *n* cubano(a).
cubbyhole ['kʌbıhəul] *n* angolino.
cube [kjuːb] *n* cubo ♦ *vt* (*MATH*) elevare al cubo.
cube root *n* radice *f* cubica.
cubic ['kjuːbık] *adj* cubico(a); ~ **metre** *etc* metro *etc* cubo; ~ **capacity** (*AUT*) cilindrata.
cubicle ['kjuːbıkl] *n* scompartimento separato; cabina.
cuckoo ['kuku:] *n* cucù *m inv*.
cuckoo clock *n* orologio a cucù.
cucumber ['kjuːkʌmbə*] *n* cetriolo.
cud [kʌd] *n*: **to chew the** ~ ruminare.
cuddle ['kʌdl] *vt* abbracciare, coccolare ♦ *vi* abbracciarsi.
cuddly ['kʌdlı] *adj* da coccolare.
cudgel ['kʌdʒl] *n* randello ♦ *vt*: **to** ~ **one's brains** scervellarsi, spremere le meningi.
cue [kjuː] *n* stecca; (*THEAT etc*) segnale *m*.
cuff [kʌf] *n* (*of shirt, coat etc*) polsino; (*US: on trousers*) = **turnup**; (*blow*) schiaffo ♦ *vt* dare uno schiaffo a; **off the** ~ *adv* improvvisando.
cufflink ['kʌflıŋk] *n* gemello.
cu. ft. *abbr* = *cubic feet*.
cu. in. *abbr* = *cubic inches*.
cuisine [kwı'ziːn] *n* cucina.

cul-de-sac ['kʌldəsæk] *n* vicolo cieco.
culinary ['kʌlınərı] *adj* culinario(a).
cull [kʌl] *vt* (*kill selectively: animals*) selezionare e abbattere.
culminate ['kʌlmıneıt] *vi*: **to** ~ **in** culminare con.
culmination [kʌlmı'neıʃən] *n* culmine *m*.
culottes [kjuː'lɔts] *npl* gonna *f* pantalone *inv*.
culpable ['kʌlpəbl] *adj* colpevole.
culprit ['kʌlprıt] *n* colpevole *m/f*.
cult [kʌlt] *n* culto.
cult figure *n* idolo.
cultivate ['kʌltıveıt] *vt* (*also fig*) coltivare.
cultivation [kʌltı'veıʃən] *n* coltivazione *f*.
cultural ['kʌltʃərəl] *adj* culturale.
culture ['kʌltʃə*] *n* (*also fig*) cultura.
cultured ['kʌltʃəd] *adj* colto(a).
cumbersome ['kʌmbəsəm] *adj* ingombrante.
cumin ['kʌmın] *n* (*spice*) cumino.
cumulative ['kjuːmjulətıv] *adj* cumulativo(a).
cunning ['kʌnıŋ] *n* astuzia, furberia ♦ *adj* astuto(a), furbo(a); (*clever: device, idea*) ingegnoso(a).
cunt [kʌnt] *n* (*col!*) *n* figa (*!*); (*insult*) stronzo/a (*!*).
cup [kʌp] *n* tazza; (*prize*) coppa; **a** ~ **of tea** una tazza di tè.
cupboard ['kʌbəd] *n* armadio.
cup final *n* (*BRIT FOOTBALL*) finale *f* di coppa.
Cupid ['kjuːpıd] *n* Cupido; (*figurine*): **c**~ cupido.
cupidity [kjuː'pıdıtı] *n* cupidigia.
cupola ['kjuːpələ] *n* cupola.
cuppa ['kʌpə] *n* (*BRIT col*) tazza di tè.
cup-tie ['kʌptaı] *n* (*BRIT FOOTBALL*) partita di coppa.
curable ['kjuərəbl] *adj* curabile.
curate ['kjuərıt] *n* cappellano.
curator [kjuə'reıtə*] *n* direttore *m* (*di museo etc*).
curb [kəːb] *vt* tenere a freno; (*expenditure*) limitare ♦ *n* freno; (*US*) = **kerb**.
curd cheese [kəːd-] *n* cagliata.
curdle ['kəːdl] *vi* cagliare.
curds [kəːdz] *npl* latte *m* cagliato.
cure [kjuə*] *vt* guarire; (*CULIN*) trattare; affumicare; essiccare ♦ *n* rimedio; **to be** ~**d of sth** essere guarito(a) da qc.
cure-all ['kjuərɔːl] *n* (*also fig*) panacea, toccasana *m inv*.
curfew ['kəːfjuː] *n* coprifuoco.
curio ['kjuərıəu] *n* curiosità *f inv*.
curiosity [kjuərı'ɔsıtı] *n* curiosità.
curious ['kjuərıəs] *adj* curioso(a); **I'm** ~

about him m'incuriosisce.
curiously ['kjuərɪəslɪ] *adv* con curiosità; (*strangely*) stranamente; ~ **enough, ...** per quanto possa sembrare strano, ...
curl [kəːl] *n* riccio; (*of smoke etc*) anello ♦ *vt* ondulare; (*tightly*) arricciare ♦ *vi* arricciarsi.
►**curl up** *vi* avvolgersi a spirale; rannicchiarsi.
curler ['kəːlə*] *n* bigodino; (*SPORT*) giocatore/trice di curling.
curlew ['kəːluː] *n* chiurlo.
curling ['kəːlɪŋ] *n* (*SPORT*) curling *m*.
curling tongs, (*US*) **curling irons** *npl* (*for hair*) arricciacapelli *m inv*.
curly ['kəːlɪ] *adj* ricciuto(a).
currant ['kʌrnt] *n* uva passa.
currency ['kʌrnsɪ] *n* moneta; **foreign** ~ divisa estera; **to gain** ~ (*fig*) acquistare larga diffusione.
current ['kʌrnt] *adj* corrente; (*tendency, price, event*) attuale ♦ *n* corrente *f*; **in** ~ **use** in uso corrente, d'uso comune; **the** ~ **issue of a magazine** l'ultimo numero di una rivista; **direct/alternating** ~ (*ELEC*) corrente continua/alternata.
current account *n* (*BRIT*) conto corrente.
current affairs *npl* attualità *fpl*.
current assets (*COMM*) attivo realizzabile e disponibile.
current liabilities *npl* (*COMM*) passività *fpl* correnti.
currently ['kʌrntlɪ] *adv* attualmente.
curriculum, *pl* ~**s** *or* **curricula** [kə'rɪkjuləm, -lə] *n* curriculum *m inv*.
curriculum vitae (CV) [-'viːtaɪ] *n* curriculum vitae *m inv*.
curry ['kʌrɪ] *n* curry *m inv* ♦ *vt:* **to** ~ **favour with** cercare di attirarsi i favori di; **chicken** ~ pollo al curry.
curry powder *n* curry *m*.
curse [kəːs] *vt* maledire ♦ *vi* bestemmiare ♦ *n* maledizione *f*; bestemmia.
cursor ['kəːsə*] *n* (*COMPUT*) cursore *m*.
cursory ['kəːsərɪ] *adj* superficiale.
curt [kəːt] *adj* secco(a).
curtail [kəː'teɪl] *vt* (*visit etc*) accorciare; (*expenses etc*) ridurre, decurtare.
curtain ['kəːtn] *n* tenda; (*THEAT*) sipario; **to draw the** ~**s** (*together*) chiudere *or* tirare le tende; (*apart*) aprire le tende.
curtain call *n* (*THEAT*) chinata alla ribalta.
curts(e)y ['kəːtsɪ] *n* inchino, riverenza ♦ *vi* fare un inchino *or* una riverenza.
curvature ['kəːvətʃə*] *n* curvatura.
curve [kəːv] *n* curva ♦ *vt* curvare ♦ *vi* curvarsi; (*road*) fare una curva.
curved [kəːvd] *adj* curvo(a).

cushion ['kuʃn] *n* cuscino ♦ *vt* (*shock*) fare da cuscinetto a.
cushy ['kuʃɪ] *adj* (*col*): **a** ~ **job** un lavoro di tutto riposo; **to have a** ~ **time** spassarsela.
custard ['kʌstəd] *n* (*for pouring*) crema.
custard powder *n* (*BRIT*) crema pasticcera in polvere.
custodial sentence [kʌs'təudɪəl-] *n* condanna a pena detentiva.
custodian [kʌs'təudɪən] *n* custode *m/f*; (*of museum etc*) soprintendente *m/f*.
custody ['kʌstədɪ] *n* (*of child*) custodia; (*for offenders*) arresto; **to take sb into** ~ mettere qn in detenzione preventiva; **in the** ~ **of** alla custodia di.
custom ['kʌstəm] *n* costume *m*, usanza; (*LAW*) consuetudine *f*; (*COMM*) clientela; *see also* **customs**.
customary ['kʌstəmərɪ] *adj* consueto(a); **it is** ~ **to do** è consuetudine fare.
custom-built ['kʌstəm'bɪlt] *adj see* **custom-made**.
customer ['kʌstəmə*] *n* cliente *m/f*; **he's an awkward** ~ (*col*) è un tipo incontentabile.
customer profile *n* profilo del cliente.
customized ['kʌstəmaɪzd] *adj* personalizzato(a); (*car*) fuoriserie *inv*.
custom-made ['kʌstəm'meɪd] *adj* (*clothes*) fatto(a) su misura; (*other goods: also:* **custom-built**) fatto(a) su ordinazione.
customs ['kʌstəmz] *npl* dogana; **to go through (the)** ~ passare la dogana.
Customs and Excise *n* (*BRIT*) Ufficio Dazi e Dogana.
customs officer *n* doganiere *m*.
cut [kʌt] *vb* (*pt, pp* **cut**) *vt* tagliare; (*shape, make*) intagliare; (*reduce*) ridurre; (*col: avoid: class, lecture, appointment*) saltare ♦ *vi* tagliare; (*intersect*) tagliarsi ♦ *n* taglio; (*in salary etc*) riduzione *f*; **cold** ~**s** *npl* (*US*) affettati *mpl*; **power** ~ mancanza di corrente elettrica; **to** ~ **one's finger** tagliarsi un dito; **to get one's hair** ~ farsi tagliare i capelli; **to** ~ **a tooth** mettere un dente; **to** ~ **sb/sth short** interrompere qn/qc; **to** ~ **sb dead** ignorare qn completamente.
►**cut back** *vt* (*plants*) tagliare; (*production, expenditure*) ridurre.
►**cut down** *vt* (*tree*) abbattere; (*consumption, expenses*) ridurre; **to** ~ **sb down to size** (*fig*) sgonfiare *or* ridimensionare qn.
►**cut down on** *vt fus* ridurre.
►**cut in** *vi* (*interrupt conversation*): **to** ~ **in (on)** intromettersi (in); (*AUT*) tagliare la

strada (a).
►**cut off** vt tagliare; (fig) isolare; **we've been ~ off** (TEL) è caduta la linea.
►**cut out** vt tagliare; (picture) ritagliare.
►**cut up** vt (gen) tagliare; (chop: food) sminuzzare.
cut-and-dried ['kʌtən'draɪd] adj (also: **cut-and-dry**) assodato(a).
cutaway ['kʌtəweɪ] adj, n: ~ **(drawing)** spaccato.
cutback ['kʌtbæk] n riduzione f.
cute [kjuːt] adj grazioso(a); (clever) astuto(a).
cut glass n cristallo.
cuticle ['kjuːtɪkl] n (on nail) pellicina, cuticola.
cutlery ['kʌtlərɪ] n posate fpl.
cutlet ['kʌtlɪt] n costoletta.
cutoff ['kʌtɔf] n (also: ~ **point**) limite m.
cutoff switch n interruttore m.
cutout ['kʌtaut] n (switch) interruttore m; (paper, cardboard figure) ritaglio.
cut-price ['kʌt'praɪs], (US) **cut-rate** ['kʌt'reɪt] adj a prezzo ridotto.
cutthroat ['kʌtθrəut] n assassino ♦ adj: ~ **competition** concorrenza spietata.
cutting ['kʌtɪŋ] adj tagliente; (fig) pungente ♦ n (BRIT: PRESS) ritaglio (di giornale); (: RAIL) trincea; (CINE) montaggio.
cutting edge n (of knife) taglio, filo; **on** or **at the ~ of sth** all'avanguardia di qc.
cuttlefish ['kʌtlfɪʃ] n seppia.
cut-up ['kʌtʌp] adj stravolto(a).
CV n abbr see **curriculum vitae.**
C & W n abbr = **country and western (music).**
CWO abbr = **cash with order.**
cwt. abbr = **hundredweight.**
cyanide ['saɪənaɪd] n cianuro.
cybernetics [saɪbə'nɛtɪks] n cibernetica.
cyclamen ['sɪkləmən] n ciclamino.
cycle ['saɪkl] n ciclo; (bicycle) bicicletta ♦ vi andare in bicicletta.
cycle race n gara or corsa ciclistica.
cycle rack n portabiciclette m inv.
cycling ['saɪklɪŋ] n ciclismo; **to go on a ~ holiday** (BRIT) fare una vacanza in bicicletta.
cyclist ['saɪklɪst] n ciclista m/f.
cyclone ['saɪkləun] n ciclone m.
cygnet ['sɪgnɪt] n cigno giovane.
cylinder ['sɪlɪndə*] n cilindro.
cylinder capacity n cilindrata.
cylinder head n testata.
cylinder head gasket n guarnizione f della testata del cilindro.
cymbals ['sɪmblz] npl cembali mpl.
cynic ['sɪnɪk] n cinico/a.

cynical ['sɪnɪkl] adj cinico(a).
cynicism ['sɪnɪsɪzəm] n cinismo.
CYO n abbr (US) = **Catholic Youth Organization.**
cypress ['saɪprɪs] n cipresso.
Cypriot ['sɪprɪət] adj, n cipriota (m/f).
Cyprus ['saɪprəs] n Cipro.
cyst [sɪst] n cisti f inv.
cystitis [sɪ'staɪtɪs] n cistite f.
CZ n abbr (US: = Canal Zone) zona del Canale di Panama.
czar [zɑː*] n zar m inv.
Czech [tʃɛk] adj ceco(a) ♦ n ceco/a; (LING) ceco; **the ~ Republic** la Repubblica Ceca.
Czechoslovak [tʃɛkə'sləuvæk] adj, n = **Czechoslovakian.**
Czechoslovakia [tʃɛkəslə'vækɪə] n Cecoslovacchia.
Czechoslovakian [tʃɛkəslə'vækɪən] adj, n cecoslovacco(a).

D d

D, d [diː] n (letter) D, d for m inv; (MUS): **D** re m; **D for David,** (US) **D for Dog** ≈ D come Domodossola.
D abbr (US POL) = **democrat(ic).**
d abbr (BRIT: old) = **penny.**
d. abbr = **died.**
DA n abbr (US) see **district attorney.**
dab [dæb] vt (eyes, wound) tamponare; (paint, cream) applicare (con leggeri colpetti); **a ~ of paint** un colpetto di vernice.
dabble ['dæbl] vi: **to ~ in** occuparsi (da dilettante) di.
Dacca ['dækə] n Dacca f.
dachshund ['dækshund] n bassotto.
dad, daddy [dæd, 'dædɪ] n babbo, papà m inv.
daddy-long-legs [dædɪ'lɔŋlɛgz] n tipula, zanzarone m.
daffodil ['dæfədɪl] n trombone m, giunchiglia.
daft [dɑːft] adj sciocco(a); **to be ~ about sb** perdere la testa per qn; **to be ~ about sth** andare pazzo per qc.
dagger ['dægə*] n pugnale m.
dahlia ['deɪljə] n dalia.
daily ['deɪlɪ] adj quotidiano(a), giornaliero(a) ♦ n quotidiano; (BRIT:

dainty - dart

96 ENGLISH-ITALIAN

servant) donna di servizio ♦ *adv* tutti i giorni; **twice** ~ due volte al giorno.

dainty ['deɪntɪ] *adj* delicato(a), grazioso(a).

dairy ['dɛərɪ] *n* (*shop*) latteria; (*on farm*) caseificio ♦ *cpd* caseario(a).

dairy cow *n* mucca da latte.

dairy farm *n* caseificio.

dairy produce *n* latticini *mpl*.

dais ['deɪɪs] *n* pedana, palco.

daisy ['deɪzɪ] *n* margherita.

daisy wheel *n* (*on printer*) margherita.

daisy-wheel printer ['deɪzɪwiːl-] *n* stampante *f* a margherita.

Dakar ['dækə*] *n* Dakar *f.*

dale [deɪl] *n* valle *f.*

dally ['dælɪ] *vi* trastullarsi.

dalmatian [dæl'meɪʃən] *n* (*dog*) dalmata *m.*

dam [dæm] *n* diga; (*reservoir*) bacino artificiale ♦ *vt* sbarrare; costruire dighe su.

damage ['dæmɪdʒ] *n* danno, danni *mpl*; (*fig*) danno ♦ *vt* danneggiare; (*fig*) recar danno a; ~ **to property** danni materiali.

damages ['dæmɪdʒɪz] *npl* (*LAW*) danni *mpl*; **to pay £5000 in** ~ pagare 5000 sterline di indennizzo.

damaging ['dæmɪdʒɪŋ] *adj*: ~ (**to**) nocivo(a) (a).

Damascus [də'mɑːskəs] *n* Damasco *f.*

dame [deɪm] *n* (*title*, *US col*) donna; (*THEAT*) vecchia signora (*ruolo comico di donna recitato da un uomo*).

damn [dæm] *vt* condannare; (*curse*) maledire ♦ *n* (*col*): **I don't give a** ~ non me ne importa un fico ♦ *adj* (*col*): **this** ~ ... questo maledetto ...; ~ (**it**)! accidenti!

damnable ['dæmnəbl] *adj* (*col: behaviour*) vergognoso(a); (: *weather*) schifoso(a).

damnation [dæm'neɪʃən] *n* (*REL*) dannazione *f* ♦ *excl* (*col*) dannazione!, diavolo!

damning ['dæmɪŋ] *adj* (*evidence*) schiacciante.

damp [dæmp] *adj* umido(a) ♦ *n* umidità, umido ♦ *vt* (*also*: ~**en**) (*cloth, rag*) inumidire, bagnare; (*enthusiasm etc*) spegnere.

dampcourse ['dæmpkɔːs] *n* strato *m* isolante antiumido *inv.*

damper ['dæmpə*] *n* (*MUS*) sordina; (*of fire*) valvola di tiraggio; **to put a** ~ **on sth** (*fig: atmosphere*) gelare; (: *enthusiasm*) far sbollire.

dampness ['dæmpnɪs] *n* umidità, umido.

damson ['dæmzən] *n* susina damaschina.

dance [dɑːns] *n* danza, ballo; (*ball*) ballo ♦ *vi* ballare; **to** ~ **about** saltellare.

dance hall *n* dancing *m inv*, sala da ballo.

dancer ['dɑːnsə*] *n* danzatore/trice; (*professional*) ballerino/a.

dancing ['dɑːnsɪŋ] *n* danza, ballo.

D and C *n abbr* (*MED*: = dilation and curettage) raschiamento.

dandelion ['dændɪlaɪən] *n* dente *m* di leone.

dandruff ['dændrəf] *n* forfora.

dandy ['dændɪ] *n* dandy *m inv*, elegantone *m* ♦ *adj* (*US col*) fantastico(a).

Dane [deɪn] *n* danese *m/f.*

danger ['deɪndʒə*] *n* pericolo; **there is a** ~ **of fire** c'è pericolo di incendio; **in** ~ in pericolo; **out of** ~ fuori pericolo; **he was in** ~ **of falling** rischiava di cadere.

danger list *n* (*MED*): **on the** ~ **list** in prognosi riservata.

dangerous ['deɪndʒrəs] *adj* pericoloso(a).

dangerously ['deɪndʒrəslɪ] *adv*: ~ **ill** in pericolo di vita.

danger zone *n* area di pericolo.

dangle ['dæŋgl] *vt* dondolare; (*fig*) far balenare ♦ *vi* pendolare.

Danish ['deɪnɪʃ] *adj* danese ♦ *n* (*LING*) danese *m.*

Danish pastry *n* dolce *m* di pasta sfoglia.

dank [dæŋk] *adj* freddo(a) e umido(a).

Danube ['dænjuːb] *n*: **the** ~ il Danubio.

dapper ['dæpə*] *adj* lindo(a).

Dardanelles [dɑːdə'nɛlz] *npl* Dardanelli *mpl.*

dare [dɛə*] *vt*: **to** ~ **sb to do** sfidare qn a fare ♦ *vi*: **to** ~ (**to**) **do sth** osare fare qc; **I** ~**n't tell him** (*BRIT*) non oso dirglielo; **I** ~ **say he'll turn up** immagino che spunterà.

daredevil ['dɛədɛvl] *n* scavezzacollo *m/f.*

Dar-es-Salaam ['dɑːrɛssə'lɑːm] *n* Dar-es-Salaam *f.*

daring ['dɛərɪŋ] *adj* audace, ardito(a).

dark [dɑːk] *adj* (*night, room*) buio(a), scuro(a); (*colour, complexion*) scuro(a); (*fig*) cupo(a), tetro(a), nero(a) ♦ *n*: **in the** ~ al buio; **it is/is getting** ~ è/si sta facendo buio; **in the** ~ **about** (*fig*) all'oscuro di; **after** ~ a notte fatta; ~ **chocolate** cioccolata amara.

darken ['dɑːkən] *vt* (*room*) oscurare; (*photo, painting*) far scuro(a) ♦ *vi* oscurarsi; imbrunirsi.

dark glasses *npl* occhiali *mpl* scuri.

dark horse *n* (*fig*) incognita.

darkly ['dɑːklɪ] *adv* (*gloomily*) cupamente, con aria cupa; (*in a sinister way*) minacciosamente.

darkness ['dɑːknɪs] *n* oscurità, buio.

darkroom ['dɑːkruːm] *n* camera oscura.

darling ['dɑːlɪŋ] *adj* caro(a) ♦ *n* tesoro.

darn [dɑːn] *vt* rammendare.

dart [dɑːt] *n* freccetta ♦ *vi*: **to** ~ **towards** (*also*: **make a** ~ **towards**) precipitarsi verso; **to ~ along** passare come un razzo; **to ~ away** guizzare via; *see also* **darts.**

dartboard ['dɑːtbɔːd] *n* bersaglio (per freccette).

darts [dɑːts] *n* tiro al bersaglio (con freccette).

dash [dæʃ] *n* (*sign*) lineetta; (*small quantity: of liquid*) goccio, goccino; (: *of soda*) spruzzo ♦ *vt* (*missile*) gettare; (*hopes*) infrangere ♦ *vi*: **to ~ towards** (*also*: **make a ~ towards**) precipitarsi verso.

►**dash away** *vi* scappare via.

dashboard ['dæʃbɔːd] *n* cruscotto.

dashing ['dæʃɪŋ] *adj* ardito(a).

dastardly ['dæstədlɪ] *adj* vile.

DAT *n abbr* (= *digital audio tape*) cassetta *f* digitale audio *inv*.

data ['deɪtə] *npl* dati *mpl*.

database ['deɪtəbeɪs] *n* database *m*, base *f* di dati.

data capture *n* registrazione *f* or rilevazione *f* di dati.

data processing *n* elaborazione *f* (elettronica) dei dati.

data transmission *n* trasmissione *f* di dati.

date [deɪt] *n* data; (*appointment*) appuntamento; (*fruit*) dattero ♦ *vt* datare; (*col: girl etc*) uscire con; **what's the ~ today?** quanti ne abbiamo oggi?; **~ of birth** data di nascita; **closing ~** scadenza, termine *m*; **to ~** *adv* fino a oggi; **out of ~** scaduto(a); (*old-fashioned*) passato(a) di moda; **up to ~** moderno(a); aggiornato(a); **to bring up to ~** (*correspondence, information*) aggiornare; (*method*) modernizzare; (*person*) aggiornare, mettere al corrente; **~d the 13th** datato il 13; **thank you for your letter ~d 5th July** or (*US*) **July 5th** la ringrazio per la sua lettera in data 5 luglio.

dated ['deɪtɪd] *adj* passato(a) di moda.

dateline ['deɪtlaɪn] *n* linea del cambiamento di data.

date rape *n stupro perpetrato da persona conosciuta*.

date stamp *n* timbro datario.

daub [dɔːb] *vt* imbrattare.

daughter ['dɔːtə*] *n* figlia.

daughter-in-law ['dɔːtərɪnlɔː] *n* nuora.

daunt [dɔːnt] *vt* intimidire.

daunting ['dɔːntɪŋ] *adj* non invidiabile.

dauntless ['dɔːntlɪs] *adj* intrepido(a).

dawdle ['dɔːdl] *vi* bighellonare; **to ~ over one's work** gingillarsi con il lavoro.

dawn [dɔːn] *n* alba ♦ *vi* (*day*) spuntare; (*fig*) venire in mente; **at ~** all'alba; **from ~ to dusk** dall'alba al tramonto; **it ~ed on him that ...** gli è venuto in mente che ....

dawn chorus *n* (*BRIT*) coro mattutino degli uccelli.

day [deɪ] *n* giorno; (*as duration*) giornata; (*period of time, age*) tempo, epoca; **the ~ before** il giorno avanti *or* prima; **the ~ after, the following ~** il giorno dopo, il giorno seguente; **the ~ before yesterday** l'altroieri; **the ~ after tomorrow** dopodomani; **(on) that ~** quel giorno; **(on) the ~ that ...** il giorno che *or* in cui ...; **to work an 8-hour ~** avere una giornata lavorativa di 8 ore; **by ~** di giorno; **~ by ~** giorno per giorno; **paid by the ~** pagato(a) a giornata; **these ~s, in the present ~** di questi tempi, oggigiorno.

daybook ['deɪbuk] *n* (*BRIT*) brogliaccio.

day boy *n* (*SCOL*) alunno esterno.

daybreak ['deɪbreɪk] *n* spuntar *m* del giorno.

day care centre *n* scuola materna.

daydream ['deɪdriːm] *n* sogno a occhi aperti ♦ *vi* sognare a occhi aperti.

day girl *n* (*SCOL*) alunna esterna.

daylight ['deɪlaɪt] *n* luce *f* del giorno.

daylight robbery *n*: **it's ~!** (*BRIT col*) è un vero furto!

Daylight Saving Time *n* (*US*) ora legale.

day release *n*: **to be on ~** *avere un giorno di congedo alla settimana per formazione professionale*.

day return (ticket) *n* (*BRIT*) biglietto giornaliero di andata e ritorno.

day shift *n* turno di giorno.

daytime ['deɪtaɪm] *n* giorno.

day-to-day ['deɪtə'deɪ] *adj* (*routine*) quotidiano(a); (*expenses*) giornaliero(a); **on a ~ basis** a giornata.

day trip *n* gita (di un giorno).

day tripper *n* gitante *m/f*.

daze [deɪz] *vt* (*subj: drug*) inebetire; (: *blow*) stordire ♦ *n*: **in a ~** inebetito(a); stordito(a).

dazzle ['dæzl] *vt* abbagliare.

dazzling ['dæzlɪŋ] *adj* (*light*) abbagliante; (*colour*) violento(a); (*smile*) smagliante.

dB *abbr* (= *decibel*) db.

DC *abbr* (*ELEC*: = *direct current*) c.c.; (*US*) = *District of Columbia*.

DCC ® *n abbr* = *digital compact cassette*.

DD *n abbr* (= *Doctor of Divinity*) titolo di studio.

dd. *abbr* (*COMM*) = *delivered*.

D/D *abbr* = **direct debit**.

D-day ['diːdeɪ] *n giorno dello sbarco alleato in Normandia*.

DDS *n abbr* (*US*: = *Doctor of Dental Science*; *Doctor of Dental Surgery*) *titoli di studio*.

DDT *n abbr* (= *dichlorodiphenyl trichloroethane*) D.D.T. *m*.
DE *abbr* (*US*) = *Delaware*.
DEA *n abbr* (*US:* = *Drug Enforcement Administration*) ≈ squadra narcotici.
deacon ['diːkən] *n* diacono.
dead [dɛd] *adj* morto(a); (*numb*) intirizzito(a) ♦ *adv* assolutamente, perfettamente; **the ~** *npl* i morti; **he was shot ~** fu colpito a morte; **~ on time** in perfetto orario; **~ tired** stanco(a) morto(a); **to stop ~** fermarsi in tronco; **the line has gone ~** (*TEL*) è caduta la linea.
dead beat *adj* (*col*) stanco(a) morto(a).
deaden ['dɛdn] *vt* (*blow, sound*) ammortire; (*make numb*) intirizzire.
dead end *n* vicolo cieco.
dead-end ['dɛdɛnd] *adj*: **a ~ job** un lavoro senza sbocchi.
dead heat *n* (*SPORT*): **to finish in a ~** finire alla pari.
dead-letter office [dɛd'lɛtə-] *n* ufficio della posta in giacenza.
deadline ['dɛdlaɪn] *n* scadenza; **to work to a ~** avere una scadenza.
deadlock ['dɛdlɔk] *n* punto morto.
dead loss *n* (*col*): **to be a ~** (*person, thing*) non valere niente.
deadly ['dɛdlɪ] *adj* mortale; (*weapon, poison*) micidiale ♦ *adv*: **~ dull** di una noia micidiale.
deadpan ['dɛdpæn] *adj* a faccia impassibile.
Dead Sea *n*: **the ~** il mar Morto.
deaf [dɛf] *adj* sordo(a); **to turn a ~ ear to sth** fare orecchi da mercante a qc.
deaf-aid ['dɛfeɪd] *n* apparecchio per la sordità.
deaf-and-dumb ['dɛfən'dʌm] *adj* (*person*) sordomuto(a); (*alphabet*) dei sordomuti.
deafen ['dɛfn] *vt* assordare.
deafening ['dɛfnɪŋ] *adj* fragoroso(a), assordante.
deaf-mute ['dɛfmjuːt] *n* sordomuto/a.
deafness ['dɛfnɪs] *n* sordità.
deal [diːl] *n* accordo; (*business ~*) affare *m* ♦ *vt* (*pt, pp* **dealt** [dɛlt]) (*blow, cards*) dare; **to strike a ~ with sb** fare un affare con qn; **it's a ~!** (*col*) affare fatto!; **he got a bad/fair ~ from them** l'hanno trattato male/bene; **a good ~ of, a great ~ of** molto(a).
▶**deal in** *vt fus* (*COMM*) occuparsi di.
▶**deal with** *vt fus* (*COMM*) fare affari con, trattare con; (*handle*) occuparsi di; (*be about: book etc*) trattare di.
dealer ['diːlə*] *n* commerciante *m/f*.
dealership ['diːləʃɪp] *n* rivenditore *m*.

dealings ['diːlɪŋz] *npl* rapporti *mpl*; (*in goods, shares*) transazioni *fpl*.
dealt [dɛlt] *pt, pp of* **deal**.
dean [diːn] *n* (*REL*) decano; (*SCOL*) preside *m* di facoltà (*or* di collegio).
dear [dɪə*] *adj* caro(a) ♦ *n*: **my ~** caro mio/cara mia; **~ me!** Dio mio!; **D~ Sir/Madam** (*in letter*) Egregio Signore/Egregia Signora; **D~ Mr/Mrs X** Gentile Signor/Signora X.
dearly ['dɪəlɪ] *adv* (*love*) moltissimo; (*pay*) a caro prezzo.
dear money *n* (*COMM*) denaro ad alto interesse.
dearth [dəːθ] *n* scarsità, carestia.
death [dɛθ] *n* morte *f*; (*ADMIN*) decesso.
deathbed ['dɛθbɛd] *n* letto di morte.
death certificate *n* atto di decesso.
death duty *n* (*BRIT*) imposta *or* tassa di successione.
deathly ['dɛθlɪ] *adj* di morte ♦ *adv* come un cadavere.
death penalty *n* pena di morte.
death rate *n* indice *m* di mortalità.
death row [-rəu] *n* (*US*): **to be on ~** essere nel braccio della morte.
death sentence *n* condanna a morte.
death squad *n* squadra della morte.
deathtrap ['dɛθtræp] *n* trappola mortale.
deb [dɛb] *n abbr* (*col*) = **debutante**.
debacle [deɪ'baːkl] *n* (*defeat*) disfatta; (*collapse*) sfacelo.
debar [dɪ'baː*] *vt*: **to ~ sb from a club** *etc* escludere qn da un club *etc*; **to ~ sb from doing** vietare a qn di fare.
debase [dɪ'beɪs] *vt* (*currency*) adulterare; (*person*) degradare.
debatable [dɪ'beɪtəbl] *adj* discutibile; **it is ~ whether ...** è in dubbio se ....
debate [dɪ'beɪt] *n* dibattito ♦ *vt* dibattere, discutere ♦ *vi* (*consider*): **to ~ whether** riflettere se.
debauchery [dɪ'bɔːtʃərɪ] *n* dissolutezza.
debenture [dɪ'bɛntʃə*] *n* (*COMM*) obbligazione *f*.
debilitate [dɪ'bɪlɪteɪt] *vt* debilitare.
debit ['dɛbɪt] *n* debito ♦ *vt*: **to ~ a sum to sb** *or* **to sb's account** addebitare una somma a qn.
debit balance *n* saldo debitore.
debit note *n* nota di addebito.
debonair [dɛbə'nɛə*] *adj* gioviale e disinvolto(a).
debrief [diː'briːf] *vt* chiamare a rapporto (a operazione ultimata).
debriefing [diː'briːfɪŋ] *n* rapporto.
debris ['dɛbriː] *n* detriti *mpl*.
debt [dɛt] *n* debito; **to be in ~** essere

indebitato(a); ~s of £5000 debiti per 5000 sterline; **bad** ~ debito insoluto.

debt collector *n* agente *m* di recupero crediti.

debtor ['dɛtə*] *n* debitore/trice.

debug [di:'bʌg] *vt* (*COMPUT*) localizzare e rimuovere errori in.

debunk [di:'bʌŋk] *vt* (*col: theory*) demistificare; (: *claim*) smentire; (: *person, institution*) screditare.

debut ['deɪbju:] *n* debutto.

debutante ['dɛbjutɑ:nt] *n* debuttante *f*.

Dec. *abbr* (= *December*) dic.

decade ['dɛkeɪd] *n* decennio.

decadence ['dɛkədəns] *n* decadenza.

decadent ['dɛkədənt] *adj* decadente.

de-caff ['di:kæf] *n* (*col*) decaffeinato.

decaffeinated [dɪ'kæfɪneɪtɪd] *adj* decaffeinato(a).

decamp [dɪ'kæmp] *vi* (*col*) filarsela, levare le tende.

decant [dɪ'kænt] *vt* (*wine*) travasare.

decanter [dɪ'kæntə*] *n* caraffa.

decarbonize [di:'kɑ:bənaɪz] *vt* (*AUT*) decarburare.

decathlon [dɪ'kæθlən] *n* decathlon *m*.

decay [dɪ'keɪ] *n* decadimento; imputridimento; (*fig*) rovina; (*also*: **tooth** ~) carie *f* ♦ *vi* (*rot*) imputridire; (*fig*) andare in rovina.

decease [dɪ'si:s] *n* decesso.

deceased [dɪ'si:st] *n*: **the** ~ il(la) defunto(a).

deceit [dɪ'si:t] *n* inganno.

deceitful [dɪ'si:tful] *adj* ingannevole, perfido(a).

deceive [dɪ'si:v] *vt* ingannare; **to** ~ **o.s.** illudersi, ingannarsi.

decelerate [di:'sɛləreɪt] *vt, vi* rallentare.

December [dɪ'sɛmbə*] *n* dicembre *m; for phrases see also* **July.**

decency ['di:sənsɪ] *n* decenza.

decent ['di:sənt] *adj* decente; **they were very** ~ **about it** si sono comportati da signori riguardo a ciò.

decently ['di:səntlɪ] *adv* (*respectably*) decentemente, convenientemente; (*kindly*) gentilmente.

decentralization [di:sɛntrəlaɪ'zeɪʃən] *n* decentramento.

decentralize [di:'sɛntrəlaɪz] *vt* decentrare.

deception [dɪ'sɛpʃən] *n* inganno.

deceptive [dɪ'sɛptɪv] *adj* ingannevole.

decibel ['dɛsɪbɛl] *n* decibel *m inv.*

decide [dɪ'saɪd] *vt* (*person*) far prendere una decisione a; (*question, argument*) risolvere, decidere ♦ *vi* decidere, decidersi; **to** ~ **to do/that** decidere di

fare/che; **to** ~ **on** decidere per; **to** ~ **against doing sth** decidere di non fare qc.

decided [dɪ'saɪdɪd] *adj* (*resolute*) deciso(a); (*clear, definite*) netto(a), chiaro(a).

decidedly [dɪ'saɪdɪdlɪ] *adv* indubbiamente; decisamente.

deciding [dɪ'saɪdɪŋ] *adj* decisivo(a).

deciduous [dɪ'sɪdjuəs] *adj* deciduo(a).

decimal ['dɛsɪməl] *adj, n* decimale (*m*); **to 3** ~ **places** al terzo decimale.

decimalize ['dɛsɪməlaɪz] *vt* (*BRIT*) convertire al sistema metrico decimale.

decimal point *n* ≈ virgola.

decimate ['dɛsɪmeɪt] *vt* decimare.

decipher [dɪ'saɪfə*] *vt* decifrare.

decision [dɪ'sɪʒən] *n* decisione *f*; **to make a** ~ prendere una decisione.

decisive [dɪ'saɪsɪv] *adj* (*victory, factor*) decisivo(a); (*influence*) determinante; (*manner, person*) risoluto(a), deciso(a); (*reply*) deciso(a), categorico(a).

deck [dɛk] *n* (*NAUT*) ponte *m*; (*of cards*) mazzo; (*of bus*): **top** ~ imperiale *m*; **to go up on** ~ salire in coperta; **below** ~ sotto coperta; **cassette** ~ piastra (di registrazione); **record** ~ piatto (giradischi).

deckchair ['dɛktʃeə*] *n* sedia a sdraio.

deck hand *n* marinaio.

declaration [dɛklə'reɪʃən] *n* dichiarazione *f*.

declare [dɪ'klɛə*] *vt* dichiarare.

declassify [di:'klæsɪfaɪ] *vt* rendere accessibile al pubblico.

decline [dɪ'klaɪn] *n* (*decay*) declino; (*lessening*) ribasso ♦ *vt* declinare; rifiutare ♦ *vi* declinare; diminuire; ~ **in living standards** abbassamento del tenore di vita; **to** ~ **to do sth** rifiutar(si) di fare qc.

declutch [di:'klʌtʃ] *vi* (*BRIT*) premere la frizione.

decode [di:'kəud] *vt* decifrare.

decoder [di:'kəudə*] *n* (*COMPUT, TV*) decodificatore *m*.

decompose [di:kəm'pəuz] *vi* decomporre.

decomposition [di:kɒmpə'zɪʃən] *n* decomposizione *f*.

decompression [di:kəm'prɛʃən] *n* decompressione *f*.

decompression chamber *n* camera di decompressione.

decongestant [di:kən'dʒɛstənt] *n* decongestionante *m*.

decontaminate [di:kən'tæmɪneɪt] *vt* decontaminare.

decontrol [di:kən'trəul] *vt* (*trade*) liberalizzare; (*prices*) togliere il controllo governativo a.

decor ['deɪkɔː*] *n* decorazione *f.*

decorate ['dɛkəreɪt] *vt* (*adorn, give a medal to*) decorare; (*paint and paper*) pitturare e tappezzare.

decoration [dɛkə'reɪʃən] *n* decorazione *f.*

decorative ['dɛkərətɪv] *adj* decorativo(a).

decorator ['dɛkəreɪtə*] *n* decoratore/trice.

decorum [dɪ'kɔːrəm] *n* decoro.

decoy ['diːkɔɪ] *n* zimbello; **they used him as a ~ for the enemy** l'hanno usato come esca per il nemico.

decrease *n* ['diːkriːs] diminuzione *f* ♦ *vt, vi* [diː'kriːs] diminuire; **to be on the ~** essere in diminuzione.

decreasing [diː'kriːsɪŋ] *adj* sempre meno *inv.*

decree [dɪ'kriː] *n* decreto ♦ *vt*: **to ~ (that)** decretare (che + *sub*); **~ absolute** sentenza di divorzio definitiva; **~ nisi** [-'naɪsaɪ] sentenza provvisoria di divorzio.

decrepit [dɪ'krɛpɪt] *adj* decrepito(a); (*building*) cadente.

decry [dɪ'kraɪ] *vt* condannare, deplorare.

dedicate ['dɛdɪkeɪt] *vt* consacrare; (*book etc*) dedicare.

dedicated ['dɛdɪkeɪtɪd] *adj* coscienzioso(a); (*COMPUT*) specializzato(a), dedicato(a).

dedication [dɛdɪ'keɪʃən] *n* (*devotion*) dedizione *f*; (*in book*) dedica.

deduce [dɪ'djuːs] *vt* dedurre.

deduct [dɪ'dʌkt] *vt*: **to ~ sth (from)** dedurre qc (da); (*from wage etc*) trattenere qc (da).

deduction [dɪ'dʌkʃən] *n* (*deducting*) deduzione *f*; (*from wage etc*) trattenuta; (*deducing*) deduzione *f*, conclusione *f.*

deed [diːd] *n* azione *f*, atto; (*LAW*) atto; **~ of covenant** atto di donazione.

deem [diːm] *vt* (*formal*) giudicare, ritenere; **to ~ it wise to do** ritenere prudente fare.

deep [diːp] *adj* profondo(a) ♦ *adv*: **~ in snow** affondato(a) nella neve; **spectators stood 20 ~** c'erano 20 file di spettatori; **knee-~ in water** in acqua fino alle ginocchia; **4 metres ~** profondo(a) 4 metri; **he took a ~ breath** fece un respiro profondo.

deepen ['diːpn] *vt* (*hole*) approfondire ♦ *vi* approfondirsi; (*darkness*) farsi più intenso(a).

deep-freeze [diːp'friːz] *n* congelatore *m* ♦ *vt* congelare.

deep-fry ['diːp'fraɪ] *vt* friggere in olio abbondante.

deeply ['diːplɪ] *adv* profondamente; **to regret sth ~** rammaricarsi sinceramente di qc.

deep-rooted ['diːp'ruːtɪd] *adj* (*prejudice*) profondamente radicato(a); (*affection*) profondo(a); (*habit*) inveterato(a).

deep-sea diver ['diːp'siː-] *n* palombaro.

deep-sea diving *n* immersione *f* in alto mare.

deep-sea fishing *n* pesca d'alto mare.

deep-seated ['diːp'siːtɪd] *adj* (*beliefs*) radicato(a).

deep-set ['diːpsɛt] *adj* (*eyes*) infossato(a).

deer [dɪə*] *n* (*pl inv*): **the ~** i cervidi (*ZOOL*); (**red**) **~** cervo; (**fallow**) **~** daino; (**roe**) **~** capriolo.

deerskin ['dɪəskɪn] *n* pelle *f* di daino.

deerstalker ['dɪəstɔːkə*] *n* berretto da cacciatore.

deface [dɪ'feɪs] *vt* imbrattare.

defamation [dɛfə'meɪʃən] *n* diffamazione *f.*

defamatory [dɪ'fæmətərɪ] *adj* diffamatorio(a).

default [dɪ'fɔːlt] *vi* (*LAW*) essere contumace; (*gen*) essere inadempiente ♦ *n* (*COMPUT*: *also*: **~ value**) default *m inv*; **by ~** (*LAW*) in contumacia; (*SPORT*) per abbandono; **to ~ on a debt** non onorare un debito.

defaulter [dɪ'fɔːltə*] *n* (*on debt*) inadempiente *m/f.*

default option *n* (*COMPUT*) opzione *f* di default.

defeat [dɪ'fiːt] *n* sconfitta ♦ *vt* (*team, opponents*) sconfiggere; (*fig: plans, efforts*) frustrare.

defeatism [dɪ'fiːtɪzəm] *n* disfattismo.

defeatist [dɪ'fiːtɪst] *adj, n* disfattista (*m/f*).

defecate ['dɛfəkeɪt] *vi* defecare.

defect *n* ['diːfɛkt] difetto ♦ *vi* [dɪ'fɛkt]: **to ~ to the enemy/the West** passare al nemico/all'Ovest; **physical ~** difetto fisico; **mental ~** anomalia mentale.

defective [dɪ'fɛktɪv] *adj* difettoso(a).

defector [dɪ'fɛktə*] *n* rifugiato(a) politico(a).

defence, (*US*) **defense** [dɪ'fɛns] *n* difesa; **in ~ of** in difesa di; **the Ministry of D~**, (*US*) **the Department of Defense** il Ministero della Difesa; **witness for the ~** teste *m/f* a difesa.

defenceless [dɪ'fɛnslɪs] *adj* senza difesa.

defend [dɪ'fɛnd] *vt* difendere; (*decision, action*) giustificare; (*opinion*) sostenere.

defendant [dɪ'fɛndənt] *n* imputato/a.

defender [dɪ'fɛndə*] *n* difensore/a.

defending champion *n* (*SPORT*) campione/essa in carica.

defending counsel *n* (*LAW*) avvocato difensore.

defense [dɪ'fɛns] *n* (*US*) = **defence**.

defensive [dɪ'fɛnsɪv] *adj* difensivo(a) ♦ *n* difensiva; **on the ~** sulla difensiva.

defer [dɪ'fə:*] vt (postpone) differire, rinviare ♦ vi (submit): **to ~ to sb/sth** rimettersi a qn/qc.

deference ['dɛfərəns] n deferenza; riguardo; **out of** or **in ~ to** per riguardo a.

defiance [dɪ'faɪəns] n sfida; **in ~ of** a dispetto di.

defiant [dɪ'faɪənt] adj (attitude) di sfida; (person) ribelle.

defiantly [dɪ'faɪəntlɪ] adv con aria di sfida.

deficiency [dɪ'fɪʃənsɪ] n deficienza; carenza; (COMM) ammanco.

deficiency disease n malattia da carenza.

deficient [dɪ'fɪʃənt] adj deficiente; insufficiente; **to be ~ in** mancare di.

deficit ['dɛfɪsɪt] n disavanzo.

defile vb [dɪ'faɪl] vt contaminare ♦ vi sfilare ♦ n ['di:faɪl] gola, stretta.

define [dɪ'faɪn] vt (gen, COMPUT) definire.

definite ['dɛfɪnɪt] adj (fixed) definito(a), preciso(a); (clear, obvious) ben definito(a), esatto(a); (LING) determinativo(a); **he was ~ about it** ne era sicuro.

definitely ['dɛfɪnɪtlɪ] adv indubbiamente.

definition [dɛfɪ'nɪʃən] n definizione f.

definitive [dɪ'fɪnɪtɪv] adj definitivo(a).

deflate [di:'fleɪt] vt sgonfiare; (ECON) deflazionare; (pompous person) fare abbassare la cresta a.

deflation [di:'fleɪʃən] n (ECON) deflazione f.

deflationary [di:'fleɪʃənrɪ] adj (ECON) deflazionistico(a).

deflect [dɪ'flɛkt] vt deflettere, deviare.

defog ['di:'fɔg] vt (US AUT) sbrinare.

defogger ['di:'fɔgə*] n (US AUT) sbrinatore m.

deform [dɪ'fɔ:m] vt deformare.

deformed [dɪ'fɔ:md] adj deforme.

deformity [dɪ'fɔ:mɪtɪ] n deformità f inv.

defraud [dɪ'frɔ:d] vt: **to ~ (of)** defraudare (di).

defray [dɪ'freɪ] vt: **to ~ sb's expenses** sostenere le spese di qn.

defrost [di:'frɔst] vt (fridge) disgelare; (frozen food) scongelare.

deft [dɛft] adj svelto(a), destro(a).

defunct [dɪ'fʌŋkt] adj defunto(a).

defuse [di:'fju:z] vt disinnescare; (fig) distendere.

defy [dɪ'faɪ] vt sfidare; (efforts etc) resistere a; (refuse to obey: person) rifiutare di obbedire a.

degenerate vi [dɪ'dʒɛnəreɪt] degenerare ♦ adj [dɪ'dʒɛnərɪt] degenere.

degradation [dɛgrə'deɪʃən] n degradazione f.

degrade [dɪ'greɪd] vt degradare.

degrading [dɪ'greɪdɪŋ] adj degradante.

degree [dɪ'gri:] n grado; (SCOL) laurea (universitaria); **10 ~s below freezing** 10 gradi sotto zero; **a (first) ~ in maths** una laurea in matematica; **a considerable ~ of risk** una grossa percentuale di rischio; **by ~s** (gradually) gradualmente, a poco a poco; **to some ~, to a certain ~** fino a un certo punto, in certa misura.

dehydrated [di:haɪ'dreɪtɪd] adj disidratato(a); (milk, eggs) in polvere.

dehydration [di:haɪ'dreɪʃən] n disidratazione f.

de-ice [di:'aɪs] vt (windscreen) disgelare.

de-icer ['di:aɪsə*] n sbrinatore m.

deign [deɪn] vi: **to ~ to do** degnarsi di fare.

deity ['di:ɪtɪ] n divinità f inv; dio/dea.

déjà vu [deɪʒɑː'vuː] n déjà vu m inv.

dejected [dɪ'dʒɛktɪd] adj abbattuto(a), avvilito(a).

dejection [dɪ'dʒɛkʃən] n abbattimento, avvilimento.

Del. abbr (US) = Delaware.

del. abbr = delete.

delay [dɪ'leɪ] vt (journey, operation) ritardare, rinviare; (travellers, trains) ritardare; (payment) differire ♦ n ritardo; **without ~** senza ritardo.

delayed-action [dɪ'leɪd'ækʃən] adj a azione ritardata.

delectable [dɪ'lɛktəbl] adj delizioso(a).

delegate n ['dɛlɪgɪt] delegato/a ♦ vt ['dɛlɪgeɪt] delegare; **to ~ sth to sb/sb to do sth** delegare qc a qn/qn a fare qc.

delegation [dɛlɪ'geɪʃən] n delegazione f; (of work etc) delega.

delete [dɪ'liːt] vt (gen, COMPUT) cancellare.

Delhi ['dɛlɪ] n Delhi f.

deli ['dɛlɪ] n = delicatessen.

deliberate adj [dɪ'lɪbərɪt] (intentional) intenzionale; (slow) misurato(a) ♦ vi [dɪ'lɪbəreɪt] deliberare, riflettere.

deliberately [dɪ'lɪbərɪtlɪ] adv (on purpose) deliberatamente.

deliberation [dɪlɪbə'reɪʃən] n (consideration) riflessione f; (discussion) discussione f, deliberazione f.

delicacy ['dɛlɪkəsɪ] n delicatezza.

delicate ['dɛlɪkɪt] adj delicato(a).

delicately ['dɛlɪkɪtlɪ] adv (gen) delicatamente; (act, express) con delicatezza.

delicatessen [dɛlɪkə'tɛsn] n ≈ salumeria.

delicious [dɪ'lɪʃəs] adj delizioso(a), squisito(a).

delight [dɪ'laɪt] n delizia, gran piacere m ♦ vt dilettare; **it is a ~ to the eyes** è un piacere guardarlo; **to take ~ in** divertirsi a; **to be the ~ of** essere la gioia di.

delighted [dɪ'laɪtɪd] *adj*: ~ **(at** *or* **with sth)** contentissimo(a) (di qc), felice (di qc); **to be ~ to do sth/that** essere felice di fare qc/che + *sub*; **I'd be ~** con grande piacere.

delightful [dɪ'laɪtfʊl] *adj (person, place, meal)* delizioso(a); *(smile, manner)* incantevole.

delimit [di:'lɪmɪt] *vt* delimitare.

delineate [dɪ'lɪnɪeɪt] *vt* delineare.

delinquency [dɪ'lɪŋkwənsɪ] *n* delinquenza.

delinquent [dɪ'lɪŋkwənt] *adj, n* delinquente *(m/f)*.

delirious [dɪ'lɪrɪəs] *adj (MED, fig)* delirante, in delirio; **to be ~** delirare; *(fig)* farneticare.

delirium [dɪ'lɪrɪəm] *n* delirio.

deliver [dɪ'lɪvə*] *vt (mail)* distribuire; *(goods)* consegnare; *(speech)* pronunciare; *(free)* liberare; *(MED)* far partorire; **to ~ a message** fare un'ambasciata; **to ~ the goods** *(fig)* partorire.

deliverance [dɪ'lɪvrəns] *n* liberazione *f*.

delivery [dɪ'lɪvərɪ] *n* distribuzione *f*; consegna; *(of speaker)* dizione *f*; *(MED)* parto; **to take ~ of** prendere in consegna.

delivery note *n* bolla di consegna.

delivery van, *(US)* **delivery truck** *n* furgoncino (per le consegne).

delta ['dɛltə] *n* delta *m*.

delude [dɪ'lu:d] *vt* deludere, illudere.

deluge ['dɛlju:dʒ] *n* diluvio ♦ *vt (fig)*: **to ~ (with)** subissare (di), inondare (di).

delusion [dɪ'lu:ʒən] *n* illusione *f*.

de luxe [də'lʌks] *adj* di lusso.

delve [dɛlv] *vi*: **to ~ into** frugare in; *(subject)* far ricerche in.

Dem. *abbr (US POL)* = **democrat(ic).**

demagogue ['dɛməgɔg] *n* demagogo.

demand [dɪ'mɑ:nd] *vt* richiedere ♦ *n* richiesta; *(ECON)* domanda; **to ~ sth (from** *or* **of sb)** pretendere qc (da qn), esigere qc (da qn); **in ~** ricercato(a), richiesto(a); **on ~** a richiesta.

demand draft *n (COMM)* tratta a vista.

demanding [dɪ'mɑ:ndɪŋ] *adj (boss)* esigente; *(work)* impegnativo(a).

demarcation [di:mɑ:'keɪʃən] *n* demarcazione *f*.

demarcation dispute *n (INDUSTRY)* controversia settoriale *(or* di categoria).

demean [dɪ'mi:n] *vt*: **to ~ o.s.** umiliarsi.

demeanour, *(US)* **demeanor** [dɪ'mi:nə*] *n* comportamento; contegno.

demented [dɪ'mɛntɪd] *adj* demente, impazzito(a).

demilitarized zone [di:'mɪlɪtəraɪzd-] *n* zona smilitarizzata.

demise [dɪ'maɪz] *n* decesso.

demist [di:'mɪst] *vt (BRIT AUT)* sbrinare.

demister [di:'mɪstə*] *n (BRIT AUT)* sbrinatore *m*.

demo ['dɛməʊ] *n abbr (col)* = **demonstration.**

demobilize [di:'məʊbɪlaɪz] *vt* smobilitare.

democracy [dɪ'mɔkrəsɪ] *n* democrazia.

democrat ['dɛməkræt] *n* democratico/a.

democratic [dɛmə'krætɪk] *adj* democratico(a); **the D~ Party** *(US)* il partito democratico.

demography [dɪ'mɔgrəfɪ] *n* demografia.

demolish [dɪ'mɔlɪʃ] *vt* demolire.

demolition [dɛmə'lɪʃən] *n* demolizione *f*.

demon ['di:mən] *n (also fig)* demonio ♦ *cpd*: **a ~ squash player** un mago dello squash; **a ~ driver** un guidatore folle.

demonstrate ['dɛmənstreɪt] *vt* dimostrare, provare ♦ *vi*: **to ~ (for/against)** dimostrare (per/contro), manifestare (per/contro).

demonstration [dɛmən'streɪʃən] *n* dimostrazione *f*, *(POL)* manifestazione *f*, dimostrazione; **to hold a ~** *(POL)* tenere una manifestazione, fare una dimostrazione.

demonstrative [dɪ'mɔnstrətɪv] *adj* dimostrativo(a).

demonstrator ['dɛmənstreɪtə*] *n (POL)* dimostrante *m/f*; *(COMM: sales person)* dimostratore/trice; (: *car, computer etc)* modello per dimostrazione.

demoralize [dɪ'mɔrəlaɪz] *vt* demoralizzare.

demote [dɪ'məʊt] *vt* far retrocedere.

demotion [dɪ'məʊʃən] *n* retrocessione *f*, degradazione *f*.

demur [dɪ'mə:*] *vi (formal)*: **to ~ (at)** sollevare obiezioni (a *or* su) ♦ *n*: **without ~** senza obiezioni.

demure [dɪ'mjʊə*] *adj* contegnoso(a).

demurrage [dɪ'mʌrɪdʒ] *n* diritti *mpl* di immagazzinaggio; spese *fpl* di controstallia.

den [dɛn] *n* tana, covo.

denationalization ['di:næʃnəlaɪ'zeɪʃən] *n* denazionalizzazione *f*.

denationalize [di:'næʃnəlaɪz] *vt* snazionalizzare.

denial [dɪ'naɪəl] *n* diniego; rifiuto.

denier ['dɛnɪə*] *n* denaro *(di filati, calze)*.

denigrate ['dɛnɪgreɪt] *vt* denigrare.

denim ['dɛnɪm] *n* tessuto di cotone ritorto; *see also* **denims.**

denim jacket *n* giubbotto di jeans.

denims ['dɛnɪmz] *npl* blue jeans *mpl*.

denizen ['dɛnɪzən] *n (inhabitant)* abitante *m/f*; *(foreigner)* straniero(a) naturalizzato(a).

Denmark ['dɛnmɑːk] *n* Danimarca.

denomination [dɪnɒmɪ'neɪʃən] *n* (*money*) valore *m*; (*REL*) confessione *f*.

denominator [dɪ'nɒmɪneɪtə*] *n* denominatore *m*.

denote [dɪ'nəʊt] *vt* denotare.

denounce [dɪ'naʊns] *vt* denunciare.

dense [dɛns] *adj* fitto(a); (*stupid*) ottuso(a), duro(a).

densely ['dɛnslɪ] *adv*: ~ **wooded** fittamente boscoso(a); ~ **populated** densamente popolato(a).

density ['dɛnsɪtɪ] *n* densità *f inv*; **single/double** ~ **disk** (*COMPUT*) disco a singola/doppia densità di registrazione.

dent [dɛnt] *n* ammaccatura ♦ *vt* (*also*: **make a** ~ **in**) ammaccare; (*fig*) intaccare.

dental ['dɛntl] *adj* dentale.

dental floss [-flɒs] *n* filo interdentale.

dental surgeon *n* medico/a dentista.

dentist ['dɛntɪst] *n* dentista *m/f*; ~'**s surgery** (*BRIT*) gabinetto dentistico.

dentistry ['dɛntɪstrɪ] *n* odontoiatria.

denture(s) ['dɛntʃə(z)] *n(pl)* dentiera.

denunciation [dɪnʌnsɪ'eɪʃən] *n* denuncia.

deny [dɪ'naɪ] *vt* negare; (*refuse*) rifiutare; **he denies having said it** nega di averlo detto.

deodorant [diː'əʊdərənt] *n* deodorante *m*.

depart [dɪ'pɑːt] *vi* partire; **to** ~ **from** (*leave*) allontanarsi da, partire da; (*fig*) deviare da.

departed [dɪ'pɑːtɪd] *adj* estinto(a) ♦ *n*: **the** ~ il caro estinto/la cara estinta.

department [dɪ'pɑːtmənt] *n* (*COMM*) reparto; (*SCOL*) sezione *f*, dipartimento; (*POL*) ministero; **that's not my** ~ (*also fig*) questo non è di mia competenza; **D~ of State** (*US*) Dipartimento di Stato.

departmental [diːpɑːt'mɛntl] *adj* (*dispute*) settoriale; (*meeting*) di sezione; ~ **manager** caporeparto *m/f*.

department store *n* grande magazzino.

departure [dɪ'pɑːtʃə*] *n* partenza *f*; (*fig*): ~ **from** deviazione *f* da; **a new** ~ una novità.

departure lounge *n* sala d'attesa.

depend [dɪ'pɛnd] *vi*: **to** ~ (**up**)**on** dipendere da; (*rely on*) contare su; (*be dependent on*) dipendere (economicamente) da, essere a carico di; **it** ~**s** dipende; ~**ing on the result** ... a seconda del risultato ....

dependable [dɪ'pɛndəbl] *adj* fidato(a); (*car etc*) affidabile.

dependant [dɪ'pɛndənt] *n* persona a carico.

dependence [dɪ'pɛndəns] *n* dipendenza.

dependent [dɪ'pɛndənt] *adj*: **to be** ~ (**on**) (*gen*) dipendere (da); (*child, relative*) essere a carico (di) ♦ *n* = **dependant**.

depict [dɪ'pɪkt] *vt* (*in picture*) dipingere; (*in words*) descrivere.

depilatory [dɪ'pɪlətərɪ] *n* (*also*: ~ **cream**) crema depilatoria.

depleted [dɪ'pliːtɪd] *adj* diminuito(a).

deplorable [dɪ'plɔːrəbl] *adj* deplorevole, lamentevole.

deplore [dɪ'plɔː*] *vt* deplorare.

deploy [dɪ'plɔɪ] *vt* dispiegare.

depopulate [diː'pɒpjuleɪt] *vt* spopolare.

depopulation ['diːpɒpju'leɪʃən] *n* spopolamento.

deport [dɪ'pɔːt] *vt* deportare; espellere.

deportation [diːpɔː'teɪʃən] *n* deportazione *f*.

deportation order *n* foglio di via obbligatorio.

deportee [diːpɔː'tiː] *n* deportato/a.

deportment [dɪ'pɔːtmənt] *n* portamento.

depose [dɪ'pəʊz] *vt* deporre.

deposit [dɪ'pɒzɪt] *n* (*COMM, GEO*) deposito; (*of ore, oil*) giacimento; (*CHEM*) sedimento; (*part payment*) acconto; (*for hired goods etc*) cauzione *f* ♦ *vt* depositare; dare in acconto; (*luggage etc*) mettere *or* lasciare in deposito; **to put down a** ~ **of £50** versare una caparra di 50 sterline.

deposit account *n* conto vincolato.

depositor [dɪ'pɒzɪtə*] *n* depositante *m/f*.

depository [dɪ'pɒzɪtərɪ] *n* (*person*) depositario/a; (*place*) deposito.

depot ['dɛpəʊ] *n* deposito.

depraved [dɪ'preɪvd] *adj* depravato(a).

depravity [dɪ'prævɪtɪ] *n* depravazione *f*.

deprecate ['dɛprɪkeɪt] *vt* deprecare.

deprecating ['dɛprɪkeɪtɪŋ] *adj* (*disapproving*) di biasimo; (*apologetic*): **a** ~ **smile** un sorriso di scusa.

depreciate [dɪ'priːʃɪeɪt] *vt* svalutare ♦ *vi* svalutarsi.

depreciation [dɪpriːʃɪ'eɪʃən] *n* svalutazione *f*.

depress [dɪ'prɛs] *vt* deprimere; (*press down*) premere.

depressant [dɪ'prɛsnt] *n* (*MED*) sedativo.

depressed [dɪ'prɛst] *adj* (*person*) depresso(a), abbattuto(a); (*area*) depresso(a); (*COMM: market, trade*) stagnante, in ribasso; **to get** ~ deprimersi.

depressing [dɪ'prɛsɪŋ] *adj* deprimente.

depression [dɪ'prɛʃən] *n* depressione *f*.

deprivation [dɛprɪ'veɪʃən] *n* privazione *f*; (*state*) indigenza; (*PSYCH*) carenza affettiva.

deprive [dɪ'praɪv] *vt*: **to** ~ **sb of** privare qn di.

deprived [dɪ'praɪvd] *adj* disgraziato(a).

dept. *abbr* = **department.**

depth [dɛpθ] *n* profondità *f inv*; **at a ~ of 3 metres** a una profondità di 3 metri, a 3 metri di profondità; **in the ~s of** nel profondo di; nel cuore di; **in the ~s of winter** in pieno inverno; **to study sth in ~** studiare qc in profondità; **to be out of one's ~** (*BRIT: swimmer*) essere dove non si tocca; (*fig*) non sentirsi all'altezza della situazione.

depth charge *n* carica di profondità.

deputation [dɛpju'teɪʃən] *n* deputazione *f*, delegazione *f*.

deputize ['dɛpjutaɪz] *vi*: **to ~ for** svolgere le funzioni di.

deputy ['dɛpjutɪ] *n* (*replacement*) supplente *m/f*; (*second in command*) vice *m/f* ♦ *cpd*: **~ chairman** vicepresidente *m*; **~ head** (*SCOL*) vicepreside *m/f*; **~ leader** (*BRIT POL*) sottosegretario.

derail [dɪ'reɪl] *vt* far deragliare; **to be ~ed** deragliare.

derailment [dɪ'reɪlmənt] *n* deragliamento.

deranged [dɪ'reɪndʒd] *adj*: **to be (mentally) ~** essere pazzo(a).

derby ['dəːbɪ] *n* (*US*) bombetta.

Derbys *abbr* (*BRIT*) = **Derbyshire.**

deregulate [diːˈrɛgjuleɪt] *vt* eliminare la regolamentazione di.

deregulation ['diːrɛgju'leɪʃən] *n* eliminazione *f* della regolamentazione.

derelict ['dɛrɪlɪkt] *adj* abbandonato(a).

deride [dɪ'raɪd] *vt* deridere.

derision [dɪ'rɪʒən] *n* derisione *f*.

derisive [dɪ'raɪsɪv] *adj* di derisione.

derisory [dɪ'raɪsərɪ] *adj* (*sum*) irrisorio(a).

derivation [dɛrɪ'veɪʃən] *n* derivazione *f*.

derivative [dɪ'rɪvətɪv] *n* derivato ♦ *adj* derivato(a).

derive [dɪ'raɪv] *vt*: **to ~ sth from** derivare qc da; trarre qc da ♦ *vi*: **to ~ from** derivare da.

dermatitis [dəːmə'taɪtɪs] *n* dermatite *f*.

dermatology [dəːmə'tɔlədʒɪ] *n* dermatologia.

derogatory [dɪ'rɔgətərɪ] *adj* denigratorio(a).

derrick ['dɛrɪk] *n* gru *f inv*; (*for oil*) derrick *m inv*.

derv [dəːv] *n* (*BRIT*) gasolio.

DES *n abbr* (*BRIT*: = *Department of Education and Science*) ≈ ministero della Pubblica Istruzione.

desalination [diːsælɪ'neɪʃən] *n* desalinizzazione *f*, dissalazione *f*.

descend [dɪ'sɛnd] *vt*, *vi* discendere, scendere; **to ~ from** discendere da; **in ~ing order of importance** in ordine decrescente d'importanza.

▶**descend on** *vt fus* (*subj: enemy, angry person*) assalire, piombare su; (: *misfortune*) arrivare addosso a; (: *fig*: *gloom, silence*) scendere su; **visitors ~ed (up)on us** ci sono arrivate visite tra capo e collo.

descendant [dɪ'sɛndənt] *n* discendente *m/f*.

descent [dɪ'sɛnt] *n* discesa; (*origin*) discendenza, famiglia.

describe [dɪs'kraɪb] *vt* descrivere.

description [dɪs'krɪpʃən] *n* descrizione *f*; (*sort*) genere *m*, specie *f*; **of every ~** di ogni genere e specie.

descriptive [dɪs'krɪptɪv] *adj* descrittivo(a).

desecrate ['dɛsɪkreɪt] *vt* profanare.

desert *n* ['dɛzət] deserto ♦ *vb* [dɪ'zəːt] *vt* lasciare, abbandonare ♦ *vi* (*MIL*) disertare; *see also* **deserts.**

deserter [dɪ'zəːtə*] *n* disertore *m*.

desertion [dɪ'zəːʃən] *n* diserzione *f*.

desert island *n* isola deserta.

deserts [dɪ'zəːts] *npl*: **to get one's just ~** avere ciò che si merita.

deserve [dɪ'zəːv] *vt* meritare.

deservedly [dɪ'zəːvɪdlɪ] *adv* meritatamente, giustamente.

deserving [dɪ'zəːvɪŋ] *adj* (*person*) meritevole, degno(a); (*cause*) meritorio(a).

desiccated ['dɛsɪkeɪtɪd] *adj* essiccato(a).

design [dɪ'zaɪn] *n* (*sketch*) disegno; (: *of dress, car*) modello; (*layout, shape*) linea; (*pattern*) fantasia; (*COMM*) disegno tecnico; (*intention*) intenzione *f* ♦ *vt* disegnare; progettare; **to have ~s on** aver mire su; **well-~ed** ben concepito(a); **industrial ~** disegno industriale.

designate *vt* ['dɛzɪgneɪt] designare ♦ *adj* ['dɛzɪgnɪt] designato(a).

designation [dɛzɪg'neɪʃən] *n* designazione *f*.

designer [dɪ'zaɪnə*] *n* (*TECH*) disegnatore/trice, progettista *m/f*; (*of furniture*) designer *m/f inv*; (*fashion ~*) disegnatore/trice di moda; (*of theatre sets*) scenografo/a.

desirability [dɪzaɪərə'bɪlɪtɪ] *n* desiderabilità; vantaggio.

desirable [dɪ'zaɪərəbl] *adj* desiderabile; **it is ~ that** è opportuno che + *sub*.

desire [dɪ'zaɪə*] *n* desiderio, voglia ♦ *vt* desiderare, volere; **to ~ sth/to do sth/that** desiderare qc/di fare qc/che + *sub*.

desirous [dɪ'zaɪərəs] *adj*: **~ of** desideroso(a) di.

desk [dɛsk] *n* (*in office*) scrivania; (*for pupil*) banco; (*BRIT*: *in shop, restaurant*) cassa; (*in* *hotel*) ricevimento; (*at airport*) accettazione *f*.

desk job *n* lavoro d'ufficio.

desktop computer ['dɛsktɔp-] *n* personal *m inv*, personal computer *m inv*.

desktop publishing *n* desktop publishing *m*.

desolate ['dɛsəlɪt] *adj* desolato(a).

desolation [dɛsə'leɪʃən] *n* desolazione *f*.

despair [dɪs'pɛə*] *n* disperazione *f* ♦ *vi*: **to ~ of** disperare di; **in ~** disperato(a).

despatch [dɪs'pætʃ] *n, vt* = **dispatch**.

desperate ['dɛspərɪt] *adj* disperato(a); (*measures*) estremo(a); (*fugitive*) capace di tutto; **we are getting ~** siamo sull'orlo della disperazione.

desperately ['dɛspərɪtlɪ] *adv* disperatamente; (*very*) terribilmente, estremamente; **~ ill** in pericolo di vita.

desperation [dɛspə'reɪʃən] *n* disperazione *f*; **in ~** per disperazione.

despicable [dɪs'pɪkəbl] *adj* disprezzabile.

despise [dɪs'paɪz] *vt* disprezzare, sdegnare.

despite [dɪs'paɪt] *prep* malgrado, a dispetto di, nonostante.

despondent [dɪs'pɔndənt] *adj* abbattuto(a), scoraggiato(a).

despot ['dɛspɔt] *n* despota *m*.

dessert [dɪ'zə:t] *n* dolce *m*; frutta.

dessertspoon [dɪ'zə:tspu:n] *n* cucchiaio da dolci.

destabilize [di:'steɪbɪlaɪz] *vt* privare di stabilità; (*fig*) destabilizzare.

destination [dɛstɪ'neɪʃən] *n* destinazione *f*.

destine ['dɛstɪn] *vt* destinare.

destined ['dɛstɪnd] *adj*: **to be ~ to do sth** essere destinato(a) a fare qc; **~ for London** diretto a Londra, con destinazione Londra.

destiny ['dɛstɪnɪ] *n* destino.

destitute ['dɛstɪtjuːt] *adj* indigente, bisognoso(a); **~ of** privo(a) di.

destroy [dɪs'trɔɪ] *vt* distruggere.

destroyer [dɪs'trɔɪə*] *n* (*NAUT*) cacciatorpediniere *m*.

destruction [dɪs'trʌkʃən] *n* distruzione *f*.

destructive [dɪs'trʌktɪv] *adj* distruttivo(a).

desultory ['dɛsəltərɪ] *adj* (*reading*) disordinato(a); (*conversation*) sconnesso(a); (*contact*) saltuario(a), irregolare.

detach [dɪ'tætʃ] *vt* staccare, distaccare.

detachable [dɪ'tætʃəbl] *adj* staccabile.

detached [dɪ'tætʃt] *adj* (*attitude*) distante.

detached house *n* villa.

detachment [dɪ'tætʃmənt] *n* (*MIL*) distaccamento; (*fig*) distacco.

detail ['diːteɪl] *n* particolare *m*, dettaglio;

(*MIL*) piccolo distaccamento ♦ *vt* dettagliare, particolareggiare; (*MIL*): **to ~ sb (for)** assegnare qn (a); **in ~** nei particolari; **to go into ~(s)** scendere nei particolari.

detailed ['diːteɪld] *adj* particolareggiato(a).

detain [dɪ'teɪn] *vt* trattenere; (*in captivity*) detenere.

detainee [diːteɪ'niː] *n* detenuto/a.

detect [dɪ'tɛkt] *vt* scoprire, scorgere; (*MED, POLICE, RADAR etc*) individuare.

detection [dɪ'tɛkʃən] *n* scoperta; individuazione *f*; **crime ~** indagini *fpl* criminali; **to escape ~** (*criminal*) eludere le ricerche; (*mistake*) passare inosservato(a).

detective [dɪ'tɛktɪv] *n* investigatore/trice; **private ~** investigatore *m* privato.

detective story *n* giallo.

detector [dɪ'tɛktə*] *n* rivelatore *m*.

détente [deɪ'tɑːnt] *n* distensione *f*.

detention [dɪ'tɛnʃən] *n* detenzione *f*; (*SCOL*) permanenza forzata per punizione.

deter [dɪ'tə:*] *vt* dissuadere.

detergent [dɪ'tə:dʒənt] *n* detersivo.

deteriorate [dɪ'tɪərɪəreɪt] *vi* deteriorarsi.

deterioration [dɪtɪərɪə'reɪʃən] *n* deterioramento.

determination [dɪtə:mɪ'neɪʃən] *n* determinazione *f*.

determine [dɪ'tə:mɪn] *vt* determinare; **to ~ to do sth** decidere di fare qc.

determined [dɪ'tə:mɪnd] *adj* (*person*) risoluto(a), deciso(a); **to be ~ to do sth** essere determinato *or* deciso a fare qc; **a ~ effort** uno sforzo di volontà.

deterrence [dɪ'tɛrəns] *n* deterrenza.

deterrent [dɪ'tɛrənt] *n* deterrente *m*; **to act as a ~** fungere da deterrente.

detest [dɪ'tɛst] *vt* detestare.

detestable [dɪ'tɛstəbl] *adj* detestabile, abominevole.

detonate ['dɛtəneɪt] *vi* detonare ♦ *vt* far detonare.

detonator ['dɛtəneɪtə*] *n* detonatore *m*.

detour ['diːtuə*] *n* deviazione *f*.

detract [dɪ'trækt] *vt*: **to ~ from** detrarre da.

detractor [dɪ'træktə*] *n* detrattore/trice.

detriment ['dɛtrɪmənt] *n*: **to the ~ of** a detrimento di; **without ~ to** senza danno a.

detrimental [dɛtrɪ'mentl] *adj*: **~ to** dannoso(a) a, nocivo(a) a.

deuce [djuːs] *n* (*TENNIS*) quaranta pari *m inv*.

devaluation [diːvæljuːˈeɪʃən] *n* svalutazione *f*.

devalue ['diː'væljuː] *vt* svalutare.

devastate ['dɛvəsteɪt] *vt* devastare; **he was ~d by the news** la notizia fu per lui un colpo terribile.

devastating ['dɛvəsteɪtɪŋ] *adj* devastatore(trice).

devastation [dɛvə'steɪʃən] *n* devastazione *f*.

develop [dɪ'vɛləp] *vt* sviluppare; (*habit*) prendere (gradualmente) ♦ *vi* svilupparsi; (*facts, symptoms: appear*) manifestarsi, rivelarsi; **to ~ a taste for sth** imparare a gustare qc; **to ~ into** diventare.

developer [dɪ'vɛləpə*] *n* (*PHOT*) sviluppatore *m*; **property ~** costruttore *m* (edile).

developing country [dɪ'vɛləpɪŋ-] *n* paese *m* in via di sviluppo.

development [dɪ'vɛləpmənt] *n* sviluppo.

development area *n* area di sviluppo industriale.

deviant ['di:vɪənt] *adj* deviante.

deviate ['di:vɪeɪt] *vi*: **to ~ (from)** deviare (da).

deviation [di:vɪ'eɪʃən] *n* deviazione *f*.

device [dɪ'vaɪs] *n* (*apparatus*) congegno; (*explosive ~*) ordigno esplosivo.

devil ['dɛvl] *n* diavolo; demonio.

devilish ['dɛvlɪʃ] *adj* diabolico(a).

devil-may-care ['dɛvlmeɪ'kɛə*] *adj* impudente.

devil's advocate *n*: **to play ~** fare l'avvocato del diavolo.

devious ['di:vɪəs] *adj* (*means*) indiretto(a), tortuoso(a); (*person*) subdolo(a).

devise [dɪ'vaɪz] *vt* escogitare, concepire.

devoid [dɪ'vɔɪd] *adj*: **~ of** privo(a) di.

devolution [di:və'lu:ʃən] *n* (*POL*) decentramento.

devolve [dɪ'vɔlv] *vi*: **to ~ (up)on** ricadere su.

devote [dɪ'vəut] *vt*: **to ~ sth to** dedicare qc a.

devoted [dɪ'vəutɪd] *adj* devoto(a); **to be ~ to** essere molto attaccato(a) a.

devotee [dɛvəu'ti:] *n* (*REL*) adepto/a; (*MUS, SPORT*) appassionato/a.

devotion [dɪ'vəuʃən] *n* devozione *f*, attaccamento; (*REL*) atto di devozione, preghiera.

devour [dɪ'vauə*] *vt* divorare.

devout [dɪ'vaut] *adj* pio(a), devoto(a).

dew [dju:] *n* rugiada.

dexterity [dɛks'tɛrɪtɪ] *n* destrezza.

dext(e)rous ['dɛkstrəs] *adj* (*skilful*) destro(a), abile; (*movement*) agile.

dg *abbr* (= *decigram*) dg.

DH *n abbr* = **Department of Health**; *see*

health.

DHSS *n abbr* (*BRIT: old*) = *Department of Health and Social Security.*

diabetes [daɪə'bi:ti:z] *n* diabete *m*.

diabetic [daɪə'bɛtɪk] *adj* diabetico(a); (*chocolate, jam*) per diabetici ♦ *n* diabetico/a.

diabolical [daɪə'bɔlɪkl] *adj* diabolico(a); (*col: dreadful*) infernale, atroce.

diaeresis [daɪ'ɛrɪsɪs] *n* dieresi *f inv*.

diagnose [daɪəg'nəuz] *vt* diagnosticare.

diagnosis, *pl* **diagnoses** [daɪəg'nəusɪs, -si:z] *n* diagnosi *f inv*.

diagonal [daɪ'ægənl] *adj, n* diagonale (*f*).

diagram ['daɪəgræm] *n* diagramma *m*.

dial ['daɪəl] *n* quadrante *m*; (*on telephone*) disco combinatore ♦ *vt* (*number*) fare; **to ~ a wrong number** sbagliare numero; **can I ~ London direct?** si può chiamare Londra in teleselezione?

dial. *abbr* = **dialect.**

dialect ['daɪəlɛkt] *n* dialetto.

dialling code ['daɪəlɪŋ-], (*US*) **dial code** *n* prefisso.

dialling tone ['daɪəlɪŋ-], (*US*) **dial tone** *n* segnale *m* di linea libera.

dialogue ['daɪəlɔg] *n* dialogo.

dialysis [daɪ'ælɪsɪs] *n* dialisi *f*.

diameter [daɪ'æmɪtə*] *n* diametro.

diametrically [daɪə'mɛtrɪklɪ] *adv*: **~ opposed (to)** diametralmente opposto(a) (a).

diamond ['daɪəmənd] *n* diamante *m*; (*shape*) rombo; **~s** *npl* (*CARDS*) quadri *mpl*.

diamond ring *n* anello di brillanti; (*with one diamond*) anello con brillante.

diaper ['daɪəpə*] *n* (*US*) pannolino.

diaphragm ['daɪəfræm] *n* diaframma *m*.

diarrhoea, (*US*) **diarrhea** [daɪə'ri:ə] *n* diarrea.

diary ['daɪərɪ] *n* (*daily account*) diario; (*book*) agenda; **to keep a ~** tenere un diario.

diatribe ['daɪətraɪb] *n* diatriba.

dice [daɪs] *n* (*pl inv*) dado ♦ *vt* (*CULIN*) tagliare a dadini.

dicey ['daɪsɪ] *adj* (*col*): **it's a bit ~** è un po' un rischio.

dichotomy [daɪ'kɔtəmɪ] *n* dicotomia.

dickhead ['dɪkhɛd] *n* (*BRIT col!*) testa *m* di cazzo(*!*).

Dictaphone ® ['dɪktəfəun] *n* dittafono.

dictate *vt* ['dɪk'teɪt] dettare ♦ *vi*: **to ~ to** (*person*) dare ordini a, dettar legge a ♦ *n* ['dɪkteɪt] dettame *m*; **I won't be ~d to** non ricevo ordini.

dictation [dɪk'teɪʃən] *n* dettato; (*to secretary etc*) dettatura; **at ~ speed** a velocità di dettatura.

dictator [dɪk'teɪtə*] n dittatore m.
dictatorship [dɪk'teɪtəʃɪp] n dittatura.
diction ['dɪkʃən] n dizione f.
dictionary ['dɪkʃənrɪ] n dizionario.
did [dɪd] pt of **do.**
didactic [daɪ'dæktɪk] adj didattico(a).
didn't = **did not.**
die [daɪ] n (pl: **dies**) conio; matrice f; stampo ♦ vi morire; **to be dying star** morendo; **to be dying for sth/to do sth** morire dalla voglia di qc/di fare qc; **to ~ (of or from)** morire (di).
▶**die away** vi spegnersi a poco a poco.
▶**die down** vi abbassarsi.
▶**die out** vi estinguersi.
diehard ['daɪhɑːd] n reazionario/a.
diesel ['diːzl] n diesel m.
diesel engine n motore m diesel inv.
diesel fuel, diesel oil n gasolio (per motori diesel).
diet ['daɪət] n alimentazione f; (restricted food) dieta ♦ vi (also: **be on a ~**) stare a dieta; **to live on a ~ of** nutrirsi di.
dietician [daɪə'tɪʃən] n dietologo/a.
differ ['dɪfə*] vi: **to ~ from sth** differire da qc; essere diverso(a) da qc; **to ~ from sb over sth** essere in disaccordo con qn su qc.
difference ['dɪfrəns] n differenza; (quarrel) screzio; **it makes no ~ to me** per me è lo stesso; **to settle one's ~s** risolvere la situazione.
different ['dɪfrənt] adj diverso(a).
differential [dɪfə'rɛnʃəl] n (AUT, wages) differenziale m.
differentiate [dɪfə'rɛnʃɪeɪt] vi differenziarsi; **to ~ between** discriminare fra, fare differenza fra.
differently ['dɪfrəntlɪ] adv diversamente.
difficult ['dɪfɪkəlt] adj difficile; **~ to understand** difficile da capire.
difficulty ['dɪfɪkəltɪ] n difficoltà f inv; **to have difficulties with** (police, landlord etc) avere noie con; **to be in ~** essere or trovarsi in difficoltà.
diffidence ['dɪfɪdəns] n mancanza di sicurezza.
diffident ['dɪfɪdənt] adj sfiduciato(a).
diffuse adj [dɪ'fjuːs] diffuso(a) ♦ vt [dɪ'fjuːz] diffondere, emanare.
dig [dɪg] vb (pt, pp **dug** [dʌg]) vt (hole) scavare; (garden) vangare ♦ vi scavare ♦ n (prod) gomitata; (fig) frecciata; (ARCHAEOLOGY) scavo, scavi mpl; **to ~ into** (snow, soil) scavare; **to ~ into one's pockets for sth** frugarsi le tasche cercando qc; **to ~ one's nails into** conficcare le unghie in; see also **digs.**

▶**dig in** vi (col: eat) attaccare a mangiare; (also: **~ o.s. in:** MIL) trincerarsi; (: fig) insediarsi, installarsi ♦ vt (compost) interrare; (knife, claw) affondare; **to ~ in one's heels** (fig) impuntarsi.
▶**dig out** vt (survivors, car from snow) tirar fuori (scavando), estrarre (scavando).
▶**dig up** vt scavare; (tree etc) sradicare.
digest [daɪ'dʒɛst] vt digerire.
digestible [dɪ'dʒɛstəbl] adj digeribile.
digestion [dɪ'dʒɛstʃən] n digestione f.
digestive [dɪ'dʒɛstɪv] adj digestivo(a); **~ system** apparato digerente.
digit ['dɪdʒɪt] n cifra; (finger) dito.
digital ['dɪdʒɪtəl] adj digitale.
digital compact cassette n piastra digitale per CD.
dignified ['dɪgnɪfaɪd] adj dignitoso(a).
dignitary ['dɪgnɪtərɪ] n dignitario.
dignity ['dɪgnɪtɪ] n dignità.
digress [daɪ'grɛs] vi: **to ~ from** divagare da.
digression [daɪ'grɛʃən] n digressione f.
digs [dɪgz] npl (BRIT col) camera ammobiliata.
dilapidated [dɪ'læpɪdeɪtɪd] adj cadente.
dilate [daɪ'leɪt] vt dilatare ♦ vi dilatarsi.
dilatory ['dɪlətərɪ] adj dilatorio(a).
dilemma [daɪ'lɛmə] n dilemma m; **to be in a ~** essere di fronte a un dilemma.
diligent ['dɪlɪdʒənt] adj diligente.
dill [dɪl] n aneto.
dilly-dally ['dɪlɪdælɪ] vi gingillarsi.
dilute [daɪ'luːt] vt diluire; (with water) annacquare ♦ adj diluito(a).
dim [dɪm] adj (light, eyesight) debole; (memory, outline) vago(a); (stupid) ottuso(a) ♦ vt (light: also: US AUT) abbassare; **to take a ~ view of sth** non vedere di buon occhio qc.
dime [daɪm] n (US) = **10 cents.**
dimension [dɪ'mɛnʃən] n dimensione f.
-dimensional [dɪ'mɛnʃənl] adj suffix: **two~** bi-dimensionale.
diminish [dɪ'mɪnɪʃ] vt, vi diminuire.
diminished [dɪ'mɪnɪʃt] adj: **~ responsibility** (LAW) incapacità d'intendere e di volere.
diminutive [dɪ'mɪnjutɪv] adj minuscolo(a) ♦ n (LING) diminutivo.
dimly ['dɪmlɪ] adv debolmente; indistintamente.
dimmer ['dɪmə*] n (also: **~ switch**) dimmer m inv, interruttore m a reostato; **~s** (US AUT) anabbaglianti mpl; (: parking lights) luci fpl di posizione.
dimple ['dɪmpl] n fossetta.
dim-witted ['dɪm'wɪtɪd] adj (col) sciocco(a), stupido(a).
din [dɪn] n chiasso, fracasso ♦ vt: **to ~ sth**

into sb (*col*) ficcare qc in testa a qn.
dine [daɪn] *vi* pranzare.
diner ['daɪnə*] *n* (*person: in restaurant*)
cliente *m*; (*RAIL*) carrozza *or* vagone *m*
ristorante; (*US: eating place*) tavola calda.
dinghy ['dɪŋgɪ] *n* battello pneumatico;
(*also:* **sailing ~**) dinghy *m inv*.
dingy ['dɪndʒɪ] *adj* grigio(a).
dining area ['daɪnɪŋ-] *n* zona pranzo *inv*.
dining car *n* vagone *m* ristorante.
dining room *n* sala da pranzo.
dinner ['dɪnə*] *n* pranzo; (*evening meal*)
cena; (*public*) banchetto; **~'s ready!** a
tavola!
dinner jacket *n* smoking *m inv*.
dinner party *n* cena.
dinner service *n* servizio da tavola.
dinner time *n* ora di pranzo (*or* cena).
dinosaur ['daɪnəsɔ:*] *n* dinosauro.
dint [dɪnt] *n*: **by ~ of (doing) sth** a forza di
(fare) qc.
diocese ['daɪəsɪs] *n* diocesi *f inv*.
dioxide [daɪ'ɔksaɪd] *n* biossido.
dip [dɪp] *n* (*slope*) discesa; (*in sea*) bagno
♦ *vt* immergere, bagnare; (*BRIT AUT: lights*)
abbassare ♦ *vi* (*road*) essere in pendenza;
(*bird, plane*) abbassarsi.
Dip. *abbr* (*BRIT*) = **diploma.**
diphtheria [dɪf'θɪərɪə] *n* difterite *f*.
diphthong ['dɪfθɔŋ] *n* dittongo.
diploma [dɪ'pləumə] *n* diploma *m*.
diplomacy [dɪ'pləuməsɪ] *n* diplomazia.
diplomat ['dɪpləmæt] *n* diplomatico.
diplomatic [dɪplə'mætɪk] *adj*
diplomatico(a); **to break off ~ relations**
rompere le relazioni diplomatiche.
diplomatic corps *n* corpo diplomatico.
diplomatic immunity *n* immunità *f inv*
diplomatica.
dipstick ['dɪpstɪk] *n* (*AUT*) indicatore *m* di
livello dell'olio.
dipswitch ['dɪpswɪtʃ] *n* (*BRIT AUT*) levetta
dei fari.
dire [daɪə*] *adj* terribile; estremo(a).
direct [daɪ'rɛkt] *adj* diretto(a); (*manner,
person*) franco(a), esplicito(a) ♦ *vt*
dirigere; **to ~ sb to do sth** dare direttive
a qn di fare qc; **can you ~ me to ...?** mi
può indicare la strada per ...?
direct cost *n* (*COMM*) costo diretto.
direct current *n* (*ELEC*) corrente *f*
continua.
direct debit *n* (*BANKING*) addebito
effettuato per ordine di un cliente di
banca.
direct dialling *n* (*TEL*) ≈ teleselezione *f*.
direct hit *n* (*MIL*) colpo diretto.
direction [dɪ'rɛkʃən] *n* direzione *f*; (*of play,*

film, programme) regia; **~s** *npl* (*advice*)
chiarimenti *mpl*; (*instructions: to a place*)
indicazioni *fpl*; **~s for use** istruzioni *fpl*; **to
ask for ~s** chiedere la strada; **sense of ~**
senso dell'orientamento; **in the ~ of** in
direzione di.
directive [dɪ'rɛktɪv] *n* direttiva, ordine *m*; **a
government ~** una disposizione
governativa.
direct labour *n* manodopera diretta.
directly [dɪ'rɛktlɪ] *adv* (*in straight line*)
direttamente; (*at once*) subito.
direct mail *n* pubblicità diretta.
direct mailshot *n* (*BRIT*) materiale *m*
pubblicitario ad approccio diretto.
directness [daɪ'rɛktnɪs] *n* (*of person, speech*)
franchezza.
director [dɪ'rɛktə*] *n* direttore/trice;
amministratore/trice; (*THEAT, CINE, TV*)
regista *m/f*; **D~ of Public Prosecutions
(DPP)** (*BRIT*) ≈ Procuratore *m* della
Repubblica.
directory [dɪ'rɛktərɪ] *n* elenco; (*street ~*)
stradario; (*trade ~*) repertorio del
commercio; (*COMPUT*) directory *m inv*.
directory enquiries, (*US*) **directory
assistance** *n* (*TEL*) servizio informazioni,
informazioni *fpl* elenco abbonati.
dirt [dɜ:t] *n* sporcizia; immondizia; **to treat
sb like ~** trattare qn come uno straccio.
dirt-cheap ['dɜ:t'tʃi:p] *adj* da due soldi.
dirt road *n* strada non asfaltata.
dirty ['dɜ:tɪ] *adj* sporco(a) ♦ *vt* sporcare; **~
story** storia oscena; **~ trick** brutto
scherzo.
disability [dɪsə'bɪlɪtɪ] *n* invalidità *f inv*;
(*LAW*) incapacità *f inv*.
disability allowance *n* pensione *f*
d'invalidità.
disable [dɪs'eɪbl] *vt* (*subj: illness, accident*)
rendere invalido(a); (*tank, gun*) mettere
fuori uso.
disabled [dɪs'eɪbld] *adj* invalido(a);
(*maimed*) mutilato(a); (*through illness, old
age*) inabile.
disadvantage [dɪsəd'vɑ:ntɪdʒ] *n*
svantaggio.
disadvantaged [dɪsəd'vɑ:ntɪdʒd] *adj*
(*person*) svantaggiato(a).
disadvantageous [dɪsædvɑ:n'teɪdʒəs] *adj*
svantaggioso(a).
disaffected [dɪsə'fɛktɪd] *adj*: **~ (to or
towards)** scontento(a) di, insoddisfatto(a)
di.
disaffection [dɪsə'fɛkʃən] *n* malcontento,
insoddisfazione *f*.
disagree [dɪsə'gri:] *vi* (*differ*) discordare;
(*be against, think otherwise*): **to ~ (with)**

essere in disaccordo (con), dissentire
(da); **I ~ with you** non sono d'accordo con
lei; **garlic ~s with me** l'aglio non mi va.
disagreeable [dɪsə'griːəbl] *adj* sgradevole;
(*person*) antipatico(a).
disagreement [dɪsə'griːmənt] *n*
disaccordo; (*quarrel*) dissapore *m*; **to have
a ~ with sb** litigare con qn.
disallow ['dɪsə'lau] *vt* respingere; (*BRIT
FOOTBALL: goal*) annullare.
disappear [dɪsə'pɪə*] *vi* scomparire.
disappearance [dɪsə'pɪərəns] *n* scomparsa.
disappoint [dɪsə'pɔɪnt] *vt* deludere.
disappointed [dɪsə'pɔɪntɪd] *adj* deluso(a).
disappointing [dɪsə'pɔɪntɪŋ] *adj* deludente.
disappointment [dɪsə'pɔɪntmənt] *n*
delusione *f*.
disapproval [dɪsə'pruːvəl] *n*
disapprovazione *f*.
disapprove [dɪsə'pruːv] *vi*: **to ~ of**
disapprovare.
disapproving [dɪsə'pruːvɪŋ] *adj* di
disapprovazione.
disarm [dɪs'ɑːm] *vt* disarmare.
disarmament [dɪs'ɑːməmənt] *n* disarmo.
disarming [dɪs'ɑːmɪŋ] *adj* (*smile*)
disarmante.
disarray [dɪsə'reɪ] *n*: **in ~** (*troops*) in rotta;
(*thoughts*) confuso(a); (*clothes*) in
disordine; **to throw into ~** buttare
all'aria.
disaster [dɪ'zɑːstə*] *n* disastro.
disaster area *n* zona disastrata.
disastrous [dɪ'zɑːstrəs] *adj* disastroso(a).
disband [dɪs'bænd] *vt* sbandare; (*MIL*)
congedare ♦ *vi* sciogliersi.
disbelief ['dɪsbə'liːf] *n* incredulità; **in ~**
incredulo(a).
disbelieve ['dɪsbə'liːv] *vt* (*person, story*) non
credere a, mettere in dubbio; **I don't ~
you** vorrei poterle credere.
disc [dɪsk] *n* disco.
disc. *abbr* (*COMM*) = **discount**.
discard [dɪs'kɑːd] *vt* (*old things*) scartare;
(*fig*) abbandonare.
disc brake *n* freno a disco.
discern [dɪ'səːn] *vt* discernere, distinguere.
discernible [dɪ'səːnəbl] *adj* percepibile.
discerning [dɪ'səːnɪŋ] *adj* perspicace.
discharge *vt* [dɪs'tʃɑːdʒ] (*duties*) compiere;
(*settle: debt*) pagare, estinguere; (*ELEC,
waste etc*) scaricare; (*MED*) emettere;
(*patient*) dimettere; (*employee*) licenziare;
(*soldier*) congedare; (*defendant*) liberare
♦ *n* ['dɪstʃɑːdʒ] (*ELEC*) scarica; (*MED, of gas,
chemicals*) emissione *f*; (*vaginal ~*) perdite
fpl (bianche); (*dismissal*) licenziamento;
congedo; liberazione *f*; **to ~ one's gun**

fare fuoco.
discharged bankrupt [dɪs'tʃɑːdʒd-] *n*
fallito cui il tribunale ha concesso la
riabilitazione.
disciple [dɪ'saɪpl] *n* discepolo.
disciplinary ['dɪsɪplɪnərɪ] *adj* disciplinare;
to take ~ action against sb prendere un
provvedimento disciplinare contro qn.
discipline ['dɪsɪplɪn] *n* disciplina ♦ *vt*
disciplinare; (*punish*) punire; **to ~ o.s. to
do sth** imporsi di fare qc.
disc jockey (DJ) *n* disc jockey *m inv*.
disclaim [dɪs'kleɪm] *vt* negare, smentire.
disclaimer [dɪs'kleɪmə*] *n* smentita; **to
issue a ~** pubblicare una smentita.
disclose [dɪs'kləuz] *vt* rivelare, svelare.
disclosure [dɪs'kləuʒə*] *n* rivelazione *f*.
disco ['dɪskəu] *n abbr* = **discothèque**.
discolour, (*US*) **discolor** [dɪs'kʌlə*] *vt*
scolorire; (*sth white*) ingiallire ♦ *vi*
sbiadire, scolorirsi; (*sth white*) ingiallire.
discolo(u)ration [dɪskʌlə'reɪʃən] *n*
scolorimento.
discolo(u)red [dɪs'kʌləd] *adj* scolorito(a);
ingiallito(a).
discomfort [dɪs'kʌmfət] *n* disagio; (*lack of
comfort*) scomodità *f inv*.
disconcert [dɪskən'səːt] *vt* sconcertare.
disconnect [dɪskə'nekt] *vt* sconnettere,
staccare; (*ELEC, RADIO*) staccare; (*gas,
water*) chiudere.
disconnected [dɪskə'nektɪd] *adj* (*speech,
thought*) sconnesso(a).
disconsolate [dɪs'kɔnsəlɪt] *adj*
sconsolato(a).
discontent [dɪskən'tent] *n* scontentezza.
discontented [dɪskən'tentɪd] *adj*
scontento(a).
discontinue [dɪskən'tɪnjuː] *vt* smettere,
cessare; "**~d**" (*COMM*) "sospeso".
discord ['dɪskɔːd] *n* disaccordo; (*MUS*)
dissonanza.
discordant [dɪs'kɔːdənt] *adj* discordante;
dissonante.
discothèque ['dɪskəutɛk] *n* discoteca.
discount *n* ['dɪskaunt] sconto ♦ *vt* [dɪs'kaunt]
scontare; (*report etc*) non badare a; **at a ~**
con uno sconto; **to give sb a ~ on sth** fare
uno sconto a qn su qc; **~ for cash** sconto
m cassa *inv*.
discount house *n* (*FINANCE*) casa di
sconto, discount house *f inv*; (*COMM: also*:
discount store) discount *m inv*.
discount rate *n* tasso di sconto.
discourage [dɪs'kʌrɪdʒ] *vt* scoraggiare;
(*dissuade, deter*) tentare di dissuadere.
discouragement [dɪs'kʌrɪdʒmənt] *n*
(*dissuasion*) disapprovazione *f*;

(_depression_) scoraggiamento; **to act as a ~ to** ostacolare.

discouraging [dɪsˈkʌrɪdʒɪŋ] _adj_ scoraggiante.

discourteous [dɪsˈkəːtɪəs] _adj_ scortese.

discover [dɪsˈkʌvə*] _vt_ scoprire.

discovery [dɪsˈkʌvərɪ] _n_ scoperta.

discredit [dɪsˈkrɛdɪt] _vt_ screditare; mettere in dubbio ♦ _n_ discredito.

discreet [dɪˈskriːt] _adj_ discreto(a).

discreetly [dɪˈskriːtlɪ] _adv_ con discrezione.

discrepancy [dɪˈskrɛpənsɪ] _n_ discrepanza.

discretion [dɪˈskrɛʃən] _n_ discrezione _f_; **use your own ~** giudichi lei.

discretionary [dɪsˈkrɛʃənərɪ] _adj_ (_powers_) discrezionale.

discriminate [dɪˈskrɪmɪneɪt] _vi_: **to ~ between** distinguere tra; **to ~ against** discriminare contro.

discriminating [dɪsˈkrɪmɪneɪtɪŋ] _adj_ (_ear, taste_) fine, giudizioso(a); (_person_) esigente; (_tax, duty_) discriminante.

discrimination [dɪskrɪmɪˈneɪʃən] _n_ discriminazione _f_; (_judgement_) discernimento; **racial/sexual ~** discriminazione razziale/sessuale.

discus [ˈdɪskəs] _n_ disco.

discuss [dɪˈskʌs] _vt_ discutere; (_debate_) dibattere.

discussion [dɪˈskʌʃən] _n_ discussione _f_; **under ~** in discussione.

disdain [dɪsˈdeɪn] _n_ disdegno.

disease [dɪˈziːz] _n_ malattia.

diseased [dɪˈziːzd] _adj_ malato(a).

disembark [dɪsɪmˈbɑːk] _vt, vi_ sbarcare.

disembarkation [dɪsɛmbɑːˈkeɪʃən] _n_ sbarco.

disembodied [dɪsɪmˈbɔdɪd] _adj_ disincarnato(a).

disembowel [dɪsɪmˈbauəl] _vt_ sbudellare, sventrare.

disenchanted [dɪsɪnˈtʃɑːntɪd] _adj_ disincantato(a); **~ (with)** deluso(a) (da).

disenfranchise [dɪsɪnˈfræntʃaɪz] _vt_ privare del diritto di voto; (_COMM_) revocare una condizione di privilegio commerciale a.

disengage [dɪsɪnˈgeɪdʒ] _vt_ disimpegnare; (_TECH_) distaccare; (_AUT_) disinnestare.

disentangle [dɪsɪnˈtæŋgl] _vt_ sbrogliare.

disfavour, (_US_**) disfavor** [dɪsˈfeɪvə*] _n_ sfavore _m_; disgrazia.

disfigure [dɪsˈfɪgə*] _vt_ sfigurare.

disgorge [dɪsˈgɔːdʒ] _vt_ (_subj: river_) riversare.

disgrace [dɪsˈgreɪs] _n_ vergogna; (_disfavour_) disgrazia ♦ _vt_ disonorare, far cadere in disgrazia.

disgraceful [dɪsˈgreɪsful] _adj_ scandaloso(a),

vergognoso(a).

disgruntled [dɪsˈgrʌntld] _adj_ scontento(a), di cattivo umore.

disguise [dɪsˈgaɪz] _n_ travestimento ♦ _vt_ travestire; (_voice_) contraffare; (_feelings etc_) mascherare; **to ~ o.s. as** travestirsi da; **in ~** travestito(a); **there's no disguising the fact that ...** non si può nascondere (il fatto) che ....

disgust [dɪsˈgʌst] _n_ disgusto, nausea ♦ _vt_ disgustare, far schifo a.

disgusting [dɪsˈgʌstɪŋ] _adj_ disgustoso(a).

dish [dɪʃ] _n_ piatto; **to do** _or_ **wash the ~es** fare i piatti.

▶**dish out** _vt_ (_food_) servire; (_advice_) elargire; (_money_) tirare fuori; (_exam papers_) distribuire.

▶**dish up** _vt_ (_food_) servire; (_facts, statistics_) presentare.

dishcloth [ˈdɪʃklɔθ] _n_ strofinaccio dei piatti.

dishearten [dɪsˈhɑːtn] _vt_ scoraggiare.

dishevelled, (_US_**) disheveled** [dɪˈʃɛvəld] _adj_ arruffato(a); scapigliato(a).

dishonest [dɪsˈɔnɪst] _adj_ disonesto(a).

dishonesty [dɪsˈɔnɪstɪ] _n_ disonestà.

dishonour, (_US_**) dishonor** [dɪsˈɔnə*] _n_ disonore _m_.

dishono(u)rable [dɪsˈɔnərəbl] _adj_ disonorevole.

dish soap _n_ (_US_) detersivo liquido (per stoviglie).

dishtowel [ˈdɪʃtauəl] _n_ strofinaccio dei piatti.

dishwasher [ˈdɪʃwɔʃə*] _n_ lavastoviglie _f inv_; (_person_) sguattero/a.

dishy [ˈdɪʃɪ] _adj_ (_BRIT col_) figo(a).

disillusion [dɪsɪˈluːʒən] _vt_ disilludere, disingannare ♦ _n_ disillusione _f_; **to become ~ed (with)** perdere le illusioni (su).

disillusionment [dɪsɪˈluːʒənmənt] _n_ disillusione _f_.

disincentive [dɪsɪnˈsɛntɪv] _n_: **to act as a ~ (to)** agire da freno (su); **to be a ~ to** scoraggiare.

disinclined [dɪsɪnˈklaɪnd] _adj_: **to be ~ to do sth** essere poco propenso(a) a fare qc.

disinfect [dɪsɪnˈfɛkt] _vt_ disinfettare.

disinfectant [dɪsɪnˈfɛktənt] _n_ disinfettante _m_.

disinflation [dɪsɪnˈfleɪʃən] _n_ disinflazione _f_.

disinformation [dɪsɪnfəˈmeɪʃən] _n_ disinformazione _f_.

disinherit [dɪsɪnˈhɛrɪt] _vt_ diseredare.

disintegrate [dɪsˈɪntɪgreɪt] _vi_ disintegrarsi.

disinterested [dɪsˈɪntrəstɪd] _adj_ disinteressato(a).

disjointed [dɪsˈdʒɔɪntɪd] _adj_ sconnesso(a).

disk [dɪsk] n (COMPUT) disco; **single-/ double-sided** ~ disco m monofaccia inv/a doppia faccia.

disk drive n disk drive m inv, unità f inv a dischi magnetici.

disk operating system (DOS) n sistema m operativo a disco.

diskette [dɪsˈkɛt] n (COMPUT) dischetto.

dislike [dɪsˈlaɪk] n antipatia, avversione f ♦ vt: **he ~s it** non gli piace; **I ~ the idea** l'idea non mi va; **to take a ~ to sb/sth** prendere in antipatia qn/qc.

dislocate [ˈdɪsləkeɪt] vt (MED) slogare; (fig) disorganizzare; **he ~d his shoulder** si è lussato una spalla.

dislodge [dɪsˈlɒdʒ] vt rimuovere, staccare; (enemy) sloggiare.

disloyal [dɪsˈlɔɪəl] adj sleale.

dismal [ˈdɪzml] adj triste, cupo(a).

dismantle [dɪsˈmæntl] vt smantellare, smontare; (fort, warship) disarmare.

dismast [dɪsˈmɑːst] vt disalberare.

dismay [dɪsˈmeɪ] n costernazione f ♦ vt sgomentare; **much to my** ~ con mio gran stupore.

dismiss [dɪsˈmɪs] vt congedare; (employee) licenziare; (idea) scacciare; (LAW) respingere ♦ vi (MIL) rompere i ranghi.

dismissal [dɪsˈmɪsəl] n congedo; licenziamento.

dismount [dɪsˈmaunt] vi scendere ♦ vt (rider) disarcionare.

disobedience [dɪsəˈbiːdɪəns] n disubbidienza.

disobedient [dɪsəˈbiːdɪənt] adj disubbidiente.

disobey [dɪsəˈbeɪ] vt disubbidire; (rule) trasgredire.

disorder [dɪsˈɔːdə*] n disordine m; (rioting) tumulto; (MED) disturbo; **civil** ~ disordini mpl interni.

disorderly [dɪsˈɔːdəlɪ] adj disordinato(a); tumultuoso(a).

disorderly conduct n (LAW) comportamento atto a turbare l'ordine pubblico.

disorganize [dɪsˈɔːgənaɪz] vt disorganizzare.

disorganized [dɪsˈɔːgənaɪzd] adj (person, life) disorganizzato(a); (system, meeting) male organizzato(a).

disorientated [dɪsˈɔːrɪənteɪtɪd] adj disorientato(a).

disown [dɪsˈəun] vt ripudiare.

disparaging [dɪsˈpærɪdʒɪŋ] adj spregiativo(a), sprezzante; **to be** ~ **about sb/sth** denigrare qn/qc.

disparate [ˈdɪspərɪt] adj disparato(a).

disparity [dɪsˈpærɪtɪ] n disparità f inv.

dispassionate [dɪsˈpæʃənət] adj calmo(a), freddo(a); imparziale.

dispatch [dɪsˈpætʃ] vt spedire, inviare; (deal with: business) sbrigare ♦ n spedizione f, invio; (MIL, PRESS) dispaccio.

dispatch department n reparto spedizioni.

dispatch rider n (MIL) corriere m, portaordini m inv.

dispel [dɪsˈpɛl] vt dissipare, scacciare.

dispensary [dɪsˈpɛnsərɪ] n farmacia; (in chemist's) dispensario.

dispense [dɪsˈpɛns] vt distribuire, amministrare; (medicine) preparare e dare; **to** ~ **sb from** dispensare qn da.

▶**dispense with** vt fus fare a meno di; (make unnecessary) rendere superfluo(a).

dispenser [dɪsˈpɛnsə*] n (container) distributore m.

dispensing chemist n (BRIT) farmacista m/f.

dispersal [dɪsˈpɔːsl] n dispersione f.

disperse [dɪsˈpɔːs] vt disperdere; (knowledge) disseminare ♦ vi disperdersi.

dispirited [dɪsˈpɪrɪtɪd] adj scoraggiato(a), abbattuto(a).

displace [dɪsˈpleɪs] vt spostare.

displaced person n (POL) profugo/a.

displacement [dɪsˈpleɪsmənt] n spostamento.

display [dɪsˈpleɪ] n mostra; esposizione f; (of feeling etc) manifestazione f; (military ~) parata (militare); (computer ~) display m inv; (pej) ostentazione f ♦ vt mostrare; (goods) esporre; (results) affiggere; (departure times) indicare; **on** ~ (gen) in mostra; (goods) in vetrina.

display advertising n pubblicità tabellare.

displease [dɪsˈpliːz] vt dispiacere a, scontentare; ~**d with** scontento(a) di.

displeasure [dɪsˈplɛʒə*] n dispiacere m.

disposable [dɪsˈpəuzəbl] adj (pack etc) a perdere; (income) disponibile; ~ **nappy** (BRIT) pannolino di carta.

disposal [dɪsˈpəuzl] n (of rubbish) evacuazione f; distruzione f; (of property etc: by selling) vendita; (: by giving away) cessione f; **at one's** ~ alla sua disposizione; **to put sth at sb's** ~ mettere qc a disposizione di qn.

dispose [dɪsˈpəuz] vt disporre.

▶**dispose of** vt fus (time, money) disporre di; (COMM: sell) vendere; (unwanted goods) sbarazzarsi di; (problem) eliminare.

disposed [dɪsˈpəuzd] adj: ~ **to do** disposto(a) a fare.

disposition [dɪspəˈzɪʃən] n disposizione f; (*temperament*) carattere m.
dispossess [ˈdɪspəˈzɛs] vt: **to ~ sb (of)** spossessare qn (di).
disproportion [dɪsprəˈpɔːʃən] n sproporzione f.
disproportionate [dɪsprəˈpɔːʃənət] adj sproporzionato(a).
disprove [dɪsˈpruːv] vt confutare.
dispute [dɪsˈpjuːt] n disputa; (*also:* **industrial ~**) controversia (sindacale) ♦ vt contestare; (*matter*) discutere; (*victory*) disputare; **to be in** or **under ~** (*matter*) essere in discussione; (*territory*) essere oggetto di contesa.
disqualification [dɪskwɔlɪfɪˈkeɪʃən] n squalifica; **~ (from driving)** (*BRIT*) ritiro della patente.
disqualify [dɪsˈkwɔlɪfaɪ] vt (*SPORT*) squalificare; **to ~ sb from sth/from doing** rendere qn incapace a qc/a fare; squalificare qn da qc/da fare; **to ~ sb from driving** (*BRIT*) ritirare la patente a qn.
disquiet [dɪsˈkwaɪət] n inquietudine f.
disquieting [dɪsˈkwaɪətɪŋ] adj inquietante, allarmante.
disregard [dɪsrɪˈgɑːd] vt non far caso a, non badare a ♦ n (*indifference*): **~ (for)** (*feelings*) insensibilità (a), indifferenza (verso); (*danger*) noncuranza (di); (*money*) disprezzo (di).
disrepair [dɪsrɪˈpɛə*] n cattivo stato; **to fall into ~** (*building*) andare in rovina; (*street*) deteriorarsi.
disreputable [dɪsˈrɛpjutəbl] adj (*person*) di cattiva fama; (*area*) malfamato(a), poco raccomandabile.
disrepute [ˈdɪsrɪˈpjuːt] n disonore m, vergogna; **to bring into ~** rovinare la reputazione di.
disrespectful [dɪsrɪˈspɛktful] adj che manca di rispetto.
disrupt [dɪsˈrʌpt] vt (*meeting, lesson*) disturbare, interrompere; (*public transport*) creare scompiglio in; (*plans*) scombussolare.
disruption [dɪsˈrʌpʃən] n disordine m; interruzione f.
disruptive [dɪsˈrʌptɪv] adj (*influence*) negativo(a), deleterio(a); (*strike action*) paralizzante.
dissatisfaction [dɪssætɪsˈfækʃən] n scontentezza, insoddisfazione f.
dissatisfied [dɪsˈsætɪsfaɪd] adj: **~ (with)** scontento(a) or insoddisfatto(a) (di).
dissect [dɪˈsɛkt] vt sezionare; (*fig*) sviscerare.

disseminate [dɪˈsɛmɪneɪt] vt disseminare.
dissent [dɪˈsɛnt] n dissenso.
dissenter [dɪˈsɛntə*] n (*REL, POL etc*) dissidente m/f.
dissertation [dɪsəˈteɪʃən] n (*SCOL*) tesi f inv, dissertazione f.
disservice [dɪsˈsəːvɪs] n: **to do sb a ~** fare un cattivo servizio a qn.
dissident [ˈdɪsɪdnt] adj dissidente; (*speech, voice*) di dissenso ♦ n dissidente m/f.
dissimilar [dɪˈsɪmɪlə*] adj: **~ (to)** dissimile or diverso(a) (da).
dissipate [ˈdɪsɪpeɪt] vt dissipare.
dissipated [ˈdɪsɪpeɪtɪd] adj dissipato(a).
dissociate [dɪˈsəuʃɪeɪt] vt dissociare; **to ~ o.s. from** dichiarare di non avere niente a che fare con.
dissolute [ˈdɪsəluːt] adj dissoluto(a), licenzioso(a).
dissolve [dɪˈzɔlv] vt dissolvere, sciogliere; (*COMM, POL, marriage*) sciogliere ♦ vi dissolversi, sciogliersi; (*fig*) svanire.
dissuade [dɪˈsweɪd] vt: **to ~ sb (from)** dissuadere qn (da).
distaff side [ˈdɪstɑːf-] n ramo femminile di una famiglia.
distance [ˈdɪstns] n distanza; **in the ~** in lontananza; **what's the ~ to London?** quanto dista Londra?; **it's within walking ~** ci si arriva a piedi; **at a ~ of 2 metres** a 2 metri di distanza.
distant [ˈdɪstnt] adj lontano(a), distante; (*manner*) riservato(a), freddo(a).
distaste [dɪsˈteɪst] n ripugnanza.
distasteful [dɪsˈteɪstful] adj ripugnante, sgradevole.
Dist. Atty. abbr (*US*) = **district attorney.**
distemper [dɪsˈtɛmpə*] n (*paint*) tempera; (*of dogs*) cimurro.
distend [dɪsˈtɛnd] vt dilatare ♦ vi dilatarsi.
distended [dɪsˈtɛndɪd] adj (*stomach*) dilatato(a).
distil, (*US*) **distill** [dɪsˈtɪl] vt distillare.
distillery [dɪsˈtɪlərɪ] n distilleria.
distinct [dɪsˈtɪŋkt] adj distinto(a); (*preference, progress*) definito(a); **as ~ from** a differenza di.
distinction [dɪsˈtɪŋkʃən] n distinzione f; (*in exam*) lode f; **to draw a ~ between** fare distinzione tra; **a writer of ~** uno scrittore di notevoli qualità.
distinctive [dɪsˈtɪŋktɪv] adj distintivo(a).
distinctly [dɪsˈtɪŋktlɪ] adv distintamente; (*remember*) chiaramente; (*unhappy, better*) decisamente.
distinguish [dɪsˈtɪŋgwɪʃ] vt distinguere; discernere ♦ vi: **to ~ (between)** distinguere (tra); **to ~ o.s.** distinguersi.

distinguished [dɪs'tɪŋgwɪʃt] *adj* (*eminent*) eminente; (*career*) brillante; (*refined*) distinto(a), signorile.
distinguishing [dɪs'tɪŋgwɪʃɪŋ] *adj* (*feature*) distinto(a), caratteristico(a).
distort [dɪs'tɔːt] *vt* (*also fig*) distorcere; (*account, news*) falsare; (*TECH*) deformare.
distortion [dɪs'tɔːʃən] *n* (*gen*) distorsione *f*; (*of truth etc*) alterazione *f*; (*of facts*) travisamento; (*TECH*) deformazione *f*.
distract [dɪs'trækt] *vt* distrarre.
distracted [dɪs'træktɪd] *adj* distratto(a).
distraction [dɪs'trækʃən] *n* distrazione *f*; **to drive sb to** ~ spingere qn alla pazzia.
distraught [dɪs'trɔːt] *adj* stravolto(a).
distress [dɪs'trɛs] *n* angoscia; (*pain*) dolore *m* ♦ *vt* affliggere; **in** ~ (*ship etc*) in pericolo, in difficoltà; **~ed area** (*BRIT*) zona sinistrata.
distressing [dɪs'trɛsɪŋ] *adj* doloroso(a), penoso(a).
distress signal *n* segnale *m* di pericolo.
distribute [dɪs'trɪbjuːt] *vt* distribuire.
distribution [dɪstrɪ'bjuːʃən] *n* distribuzione *f*.
distribution cost *n* costo di distribuzione.
distributor [dɪs'trɪbjutə*] *n* distributore *m*; (*COMM*) concessionario.
district ['dɪstrɪkt] *n* (*of country*) regione *f*; (*of town*) quartiere *m*; (*ADMIN*) distretto.
district attorney (DA) *n* (*US*) ≈ sostituto procuratore *m* della Repubblica.
district council *n* organo di amministrazione regionale.

In Inghilterra e in Galles, il **district council** è l'organo amministrativo indipendente dei **district** (*che sono 369, ripartiti in 53* **county**) e si occupa di questioni di interesse locale. È finanziato tramite una tassa locale e riceve un contributo da parte del governo che ne controlla le spese tramite un'apposita commissione. I district council vengono eletti ogni quattro anni.

district nurse *n* (*BRIT*) infermiera di quartiere.
distrust [dɪs'trʌst] *n* diffidenza, sfiducia ♦ *vt* non aver fiducia in.
distrustful [dɪs'trʌstful] *adj* diffidente.
disturb [dɪs'təːb] *vt* disturbare; (*inconvenience*) scomodare; **sorry to** ~ **you** scusi se la disturbo.
disturbance [dɪs'təːbəns] *n* disturbo; (*political etc*) tumulto; (*by drunks etc*) disordini *mpl*; ~ **of the peace** disturbo della quiete pubblica; **to cause a** ~

provocare disordini.
disturbed [dɪs'təːbd] *adj* turbato(a); **to be emotionally** ~ avere problemi emotivi; **to be mentally** ~ essere malato(a) di mente.
disturbing [dɪs'təːbɪŋ] *adj* sconvolgente.
disuse [dɪs'juːs] *n*: **to fall into** ~ cadere in disuso.
disused [dɪs'juːzd] *adj* abbandonato(a).
ditch [dɪtʃ] *n* fossa ♦ *vt* (*col*) piantare in asso.
dither ['dɪðə*] *vi* vacillare.
ditto ['dɪtəu] *adv* idem.
divan [dɪ'væn] *n* divano.
divan bed *n* divano letto *inv*.
dive [daɪv] *n* tuffo; (*of submarine*) immersione *f*; (*AVIAT*) picchiata; (*pej*) buco ♦ *vi* tuffarsi.
diver ['daɪvə*] *n* tuffatore/trice; (*deep-sea* ~) palombaro.
diverge [daɪ'vəːdʒ] *vi* divergere.
divergent [daɪ'vəːdʒənt] *adj* divergente.
diverse [daɪ'vəːs] *adj* vario(a).
diversification [daɪvəːsɪfɪ'keɪʃən] *n* diversificazione *f*.
diversify [daɪ'vəːsɪfaɪ] *vt* diversificare.
diversion [daɪ'vəːʃən] *n* (*BRIT AUT*) deviazione *f*; (*distraction*) divertimento.
diversionary tactics [daɪ'vəːʃənrɪ-] *npl* tattica *fsg* diversiva.
diversity [daɪ'vəːsɪtɪ] *n* diversità *f inv*, varietà *f inv*.
divert [daɪ'vəːt] *vt* (*traffic, river*) deviare; (*train, plane*) dirottare; (*amuse*) divertire.
divest [daɪ'vɛst] *vt*: **to** ~ **sb of** spogliare qn di.
divide [dɪ'vaɪd] *vt* dividere; (*separate*) separare ♦ *vi* dividersi; **to** ~ (**between** *or* **among**) dividere (tra), ripartire (tra); **40** ~**d by 5** 40 diviso 5.
▶**divide out** *vt*: **to** ~ **out** (**between** *or* **among**) (*sweets etc*) distribuire (tra); (*tasks*) distribuire *or* ripartire (tra).
divided [dɪ'vaɪdɪd] *adj* (*country*) diviso(a); (*opinions*) discordi.
divided highway *n* (*US*) strada a doppia carreggiata.
divided skirt *n* gonna *f* pantalone *inv*.
dividend ['dɪvɪdɛnd] *n* dividendo.
dividend cover *n* rapporto dividendo profitti.
dividers [dɪ'vaɪdəz] *npl* compasso a punte fisse.
divine [dɪ'vaɪn] *adj* divino(a) ♦ *vt* (*future*) divinare, predire; (*truth*) indovinare; (*water, metal*) individuare tramite radioestesia.
diving ['daɪvɪŋ] *n* tuffo.
diving board *n* trampolino.

diving suit _n_ scafandro.
divinity [dɪ'vɪnɪtɪ] _n_ divinità _f inv_; teologia.
division [dɪ'vɪʒən] _n_ divisione _f_;
separazione _f_; (_BRIT FOOTBALL_) serie _f inv_;
~ **of labour** divisione _f_ del lavoro.
divisive [dɪ'vaɪsɪv] _adj_ che è causa di
discordia.
divorce [dɪ'vɔːs] _n_ divorzio ♦ _vt_ divorziare
da.
divorced [dɪ'vɔːst] _adj_ divorziato(a).
divorcee [dɪvɔː'siː] _n_ divorziato/a.
divot ['dɪvət] _n_ (_GOLF_) zolla di terra
(_sollevata accidentalmente_).
divulge [daɪ'vʌldʒ] _vt_ divulgare, rivelare.
D.I.Y. _adj_, _n abbr_ (_BRIT_) _see_ **do-it-yourself.**
dizziness ['dɪzɪnɪs] _n_ vertigini _fpl._
dizzy ['dɪzɪ] _adj_ (_height_) vertiginoso(a); **to
make sb** ~ far girare la testa a qn; **to feel**
~ avere il capogiro; **I feel** ~ mi gira la
testa, ho il capogiro.
DJ _n abbr see_ **disc jockey.**
d.j. _n abbr_ = **dinner jacket.**
Djakarta [dʒə'kɑːtə] _n_ Giakarta.
DJIA _n abbr_ (_US STOCK EXCHANGE_: = _Dow-
Jones Industrial Average_) indice _m_ Dow-
Jones.
dl _abbr_ (= _decilitre_) dl.
DLit(t) _n abbr_ = _Doctor of Literature_; _Doctor of
Letters._
DLO _n abbr_ = **dead-letter office.**
dm _abbr_ (= _decimetre_) dm.
DMus _n abbr_ = _Doctor of Music._
DMZ _n abbr_ (= _demilitarized zone_) zona
smilitarizzata.
DNA _n abbr_ (= _deoxyribonucleic acid_) DNA _m._

=========================== _KEYWORD_

do [duː] (_pt_ **did**, _pp_ **done**) _n_ (_col:_ _party etc_)
festa; **it was rather a grand** ~ è stato un
ricevimento piuttosto importante
♦ _vb_ **1** (_in negative constructions_) _non
tradotto_; **I don't understand** non capisco
2 (_to form questions_) _non tradotto_; **didn't
you know?** non lo sapevi?; **why didn't you
come?** perché non sei venuto?
3 (_for emphasis, in polite expressions_): **she
does seem rather late** sembra essere
piuttosto in ritardo; **I DO wish I could ...**
magari potessi ...; **but I DO like it!** sì che
mi piace!; ~ **sit down** si accomodi la
prego, prego si sieda; ~ **take care!** mi
raccomando, stai attento!
4 (_used to avoid repeating vb_): **she swims
better than I** ~ lei nuota meglio di me; ~
you agree? — yes, I ~/**no, I don't** sei
d'accordo? — sì/no; **she lives in Glasgow
— so** ~ **I** lei vive a Glasgow — anch'io; **he
asked me to help him and I did** mi ha

chiesto di aiutarlo ed io l'ho fatto; **they
come here often —** ~ **they?** vengono qui
spesso — ah sì?, davvero?
5 (_in question tags_): **you like him, don't
you?** ti piace, vero?; **I don't know him,** ~
I? non lo conosco, vero?
♦ _vt_ (_gen, carry out, perform etc_) fare; **what
are you** ~**ing tonight?** che fai stasera?;
what can I ~ **for you?** (_in shop_) desidera?;
I'll ~ **all I can** farò tutto il possibile; **to** ~
the cooking cucinare; **to** ~ **the washing-
up** fare i piatti; **to** ~ **one's teeth** lavarsi i
denti; **to** ~ **one's hair/nails** farsi i
capelli/le unghie; **the car was** ~**ing 100** la
macchina faceva i 100 all'ora; **how** ~ **you
like your steak done?** come preferisce la
bistecca?; **well done** ben cotto(a)
♦ _vi_ **1** (_act, behave_) fare; ~ **as I** ~ faccia
come me, faccia come faccio io; **what did
he** ~ **with the cat?** che ne ha fatto del
gatto?
2 (_get on, fare_) andare; **he's** ~**ing well/
badly at school** va bene/male a scuola;
how ~ **you** ~? piacere!
3 (_suit_) andare bene; **this room will** ~
questa stanza va bene
4 (_be sufficient_) bastare; **will £10** ~?
basteranno 10 sterline?; **that'll** ~ basta
così; **that'll** ~**!** (_in annoyance_) ora basta!;
to make ~ (**with**) arrangiarsi (con)
▶**do away with** _vt fus_ (_kill_) far fuori;
(_abolish_) abolire
▶**do for** _vt fus_ (_BRIT col: clean for_) fare i
servizi per
▶**do out of** _vt fus:_ **to** ~ **sb out of sth**
fregare qc a qn
▶**do up** _vt_ (_laces_) allacciare; (_dress, buttons_)
abbottonare; (_renovate: room, house_)
rimettere a nuovo, rifare; **to** ~ **o.s. up**
farsi bello(a)
▶**do with** _vt fus_ (_need_) aver bisogno di; **I
could** ~ **with some help/a drink** un aiuto/
un bicchierino non guasterebbe; **it could**
~ **with a wash** una lavata non gli farebbe
male; (_be connected_): **what has it got to** ~
with you? e tu che c'entri?; **I won't have
anything to** ~ **with it** non voglio avere
niente a che farci; **it has to** ~ **with money**
si tratta di soldi
▶**do without** _vi_ fare senza ♦ _vt fus_ fare a
meno di.

──────────────────────────

do. _abbr_ = **ditto.**
DOA _abbr_ (= _dead on arrival_) morto(a)
durante il trasporto.
d.o.b. _abbr_ = **date of birth.**
doc [dɔk] _n_ (_col_) dottore/essa.
docile ['dəʊsaɪl] _adj_ docile.

dock [dɔk] n bacino; (wharf) molo; (LAW) banco degli imputati ♦ vi entrare in bacino ♦ vt (pay etc) decurtare.
dock dues npl diritti mpl di banchina.
docker ['dɔkə*] n scaricatore m.
docket ['dɔkɪt] n (on parcel etc) etichetta, cartellino.
dockyard ['dɔkjɑːd] n cantiere m navale.
doctor ['dɔktə*] n medico, dottore/essa; (PhD etc) dottore/essa ♦ vt (interfere with: food, drink) adulterare; (: text, document) alterare, manipolare; ~'s office (US) gabinetto medico, ambulatorio; **D~ of Philosophy (PhD)** dottorato di ricerca; (person) titolare m/f di un dottorato di ricerca.
doctorate ['dɔktərɪt] n dottorato.

Il **doctorate** è il riconoscimento accademico più prestigioso in tutti i campi del sapere e viene conferito in seguito alla presentazione di una tesi originale di fronte ad una commissione di esperti. Generalmente tale tesi è un compendio del lavoro svolto durante più anni di studi; vedi anche **Bachelor's degree, Master's degree**.

doctrine ['dɔktrɪn] n dottrina.
docudrama [dɔkjuː'drɑːmə] n (TV) ricostruzione f filmata.
document n ['dɔkjumənt] documento ♦ vt ['dɔkjumɛnt] documentare.
documentary [dɔkjuː'mɛntərɪ] adj documentario(a); (evidence) documentato(a) ♦ n documentario.
documentation [dɔkjumən'teɪʃən] n documentazione f.
DOD n abbr (US) = **Department of Defense**; see **defence**.
doddering ['dɔdərɪŋ] adj traballante.
doddery ['dɔdərɪ] adj malfermo(a).
doddle ['dɔdl] n: **it's a** ~ (col) è un gioco da ragazzi.
Dodecanese Islands [dəudɪkə'niːz-] npl Isole fpl del Dodecanneso.
dodge [dɔdʒ] n trucco; schivata ♦ vt schivare, eludere ♦ vi scansarsi; (SPORT) fare una schivata; **to** ~ **out of the way** scansarsi; **to** ~ **through the traffic** destreggiarsi nel traffico.
dodgems ['dɔdʒəmz] npl (BRIT) autoscontri mpl.
dodgy ['dɔdʒɪ] adj (col: uncertain) rischioso(a); (untrustworthy) sospetto(a).
DOE n abbr (BRIT) = **Department of the Environment**; ≈ Ministero dell'Ambiente; (US) = **Department of Energy**; see **energy**.
doe [dəu] n (deer) femmina di daino;

(rabbit) coniglia.
does [dʌz] see **do**.
doesn't ['dʌznt] = **does not**.
dog [dɔg] n cane m ♦ vt (follow closely) pedinare; (fig: memory etc) perseguitare; **to go to the** ~**s** (person) ridursi male, lasciarsi andare; (nation etc) andare in malora.
dog biscuits npl biscotti mpl per cani.
dog collar n collare m di cane; (fig) collarino.
dog-eared ['dɔgɪəd] adj (book) con orecchie.
dog food n cibo per cani.
dogged ['dɔgɪd] adj ostinato(a), tenace.
doggie, doggy ['dɔgɪ] n (col) cane m, cagnolino.
doggy bag n sacchetto per gli avanzi (da portare a casa).
dogma ['dɔgmə] n dogma m.
dogmatic [dɔg'mætɪk] adj dogmatico(a).
do-gooder [duː'gudə*] n (col pej): **to be a** ~ fare il filantropo.
dogsbody ['dɔgzbɔdɪ] n (BRIT) factotum m inv.
doily ['dɔɪlɪ] n centrino di carta sottopiatto.
doing ['duːɪŋ] n: **this is your** ~ è opera tua, sei stato tu.
doings ['duːɪŋz] npl attività fpl.
do-it-yourself (DIY) ['duːɪtjɔː'sɛlf] n il far da sé.
doldrums ['dɔldrəmz] npl (fig): **to be in the** ~ essere giù; (business) attraversare un momento difficile.
dole [dəul] n (BRIT) sussidio di disoccupazione; **to be on the** ~ vivere del sussidio.
▶**dole out** vt distribuire.
doleful ['dəulful] adj triste, doloroso(a).
doll [dɔl] n bambola.
▶**doll up** vt: **to** ~ **o.s. up** farsi bello(a).
dollar ['dɔlə*] n dollaro.
dollop ['dɔləp] n (of food) cucchiaiata.
dolly ['dɔlɪ] n bambola.
dolphin ['dɔlfɪn] n delfino.
domain [də'meɪn] n dominio; (fig) campo, sfera.
dome [dəum] n cupola.
domestic [də'mɛstɪk] adj (duty, happiness, animal) domestico(a); (policy, affairs, flights) nazionale; (news) dall'interno.
domesticated [də'mɛstɪkeɪtɪd] adj addomesticato(a); (person) casalingo(a).
domesticity [dəumɛs'tɪsɪtɪ] n vita di famiglia.
domestic servant n domestico/a.
domicile ['dɔmɪsaɪl] n domicilio.
dominant ['dɔmɪnənt] adj dominante.

dominate ['dɔmɪneɪt] *vt* dominare.
domination [dɔmɪ'neɪʃən] *n* dominazione *f.*
domineering [dɔmɪ'nɪərɪŋ] *adj* dispotico(a), autoritario(a).
Dominican Republic [də'mɪnɪkən-] *n* Repubblica Dominicana.
dominion [də'mɪnɪən] *n* dominio; sovranità; (*BRIT POL*) dominion *m inv.*
domino, ~es ['dɔmɪnəu] *n* domino; **~es** *n* (*game*) gioco del domino.
don [dɔn] *n* (*BRIT*) docente *m/f* universitario(a) ♦ *vt* indossare.
donate [də'neɪt] *vt* donare.
donation [də'neɪʃən] *n* donazione *f.*
done [dʌn] *pp of* **do.**
donkey ['dɔŋkɪ] *n* asino.
donkey-work ['dɔŋkɪwəːk] *n* (*BRIT col*) lavoro ingrato.
donor ['dəunə*] *n* donatore/trice.
donor card *n* tessera di donatore di organi.
don't [dəunt] *vb* = **do not.**
donut ['dəunʌt] *n* (*US*) = **doughnut.**
doodle ['duːdl] *n* scarabocchio ♦ *vi* scarabocchiare.
doom [duːm] *n* destino; rovina ♦ *vt*: **to be ~ed** (**to failure**) essere predestinato(a) (a fallire).
doomsday ['duːmzdeɪ] *n* il giorno del Giudizio.
door [dɔː*] *n* porta; (*of vehicle*) sportello, portiera; **from ~ to ~** di porta in porta.
doorbell ['dɔːbɛl] *n* campanello.
door handle *n* maniglia.
doorman ['dɔːmæn] *n* (*in hotel*) portiere *m* in livrea; (*in block of flats*) portinaio.
doormat ['dɔːmæt] *n* stuoia della porta.
doorstep ['dɔːstɛp] *n* gradino della porta.
door-to-door ['dɔːtə'dɔː*] *adj*: ~ **selling** vendita porta a porta.
doorway ['dɔːweɪ] *n* porta; **in the ~** nel vano della porta.
dope [dəup] *n* (*col: drugs*) roba; (: *information*) dati *mpl* ♦ *vt* (*horse etc*) drogare.
dopey ['dəupɪ] *adj* (*col*) inebetito(a).
dormant ['dɔːmənt] *adj* inattivo(a); (*fig*) latente.
dormer ['dɔːmə*] *n* (*also*: ~ **window**) abbaino.
dormice ['dɔːmaɪs] *npl of* **dormouse.**
dormitory ['dɔːmɪtrɪ] *n* dormitorio; (*US: hall of residence*) casa dello studente.
dormouse, *pl* **dormice** ['dɔːmaus, -maɪs] *n* ghiro.
Dors *abbr* (*BRIT*) = **Dorset.**
DOS [dɔs] *n abbr see* **disk operating system.**
dosage ['dəusɪdʒ] *n* (*on medicine bottle*) posologia.
dose [dəus] *n* dose *f*; (*BRIT*: *bout*) attacco ♦ *vt*: **to ~ sb with sth** somministrare qc a qn; **a ~ of flu** una bella influenza.
dosser ['dɔsə*] *n* (*BRIT col*) barbone/a.
doss house ['dɔs-] *n* (*BRIT*) asilo notturno.
dossier ['dɔsɪeɪ] *n* dossier *m inv.*
DOT *n abbr* (*US*) = **Department of Transportation;** *see* **transportation.**
dot [dɔt] *n* punto; macchiolina ♦ *vt*: **~ted with** punteggiato(a) di; **on the ~** in punto.
dot command *n* (*COMPUT*) dot command *m inv.*
dote [dəut]: **to ~ on** *vt fus* essere infatuato(a) di.
dot-matrix printer [dɔt'meɪtrɪks-] *n* stampante *f* a matrice a punti.
dotted line ['dɔtɪd-] *n* linea punteggiata; **to sign on the ~** firmare (nell'apposito spazio); (*fig*) accettare.
dotty ['dɔtɪ] *adj* (*col*) strambo(a).
double ['dʌbl] *adj* doppio(a) ♦ *adv* (*fold*) in due, doppio; (*twice*): **to cost ~** (**sth**) costare il doppio (di qc) ♦ *n* sosia *m inv*; (*CINE*) controfigura ♦ *vt* raddoppiare; (*fold*) piegare doppio *or* in due ♦ *vi* raddoppiarsi; **spelt with a ~ "l"** scritto con due elle *or* con doppia elle; ~ **five two six (5526)** (*BRIT TEL*) cinque cinque due sei; **on the ~,** (*BRIT*) **at the ~** a passo di corsa; **to ~ as** (*have two uses etc*) funzionare *or* servire anche da; *see also* **doubles.**
▶**double back** *vi* (*person*) tornare sui propri passi.
▶**double up** *vi* (*bend over*) piegarsi in due; (*share room*) dividere la stanza.
double bass *n* contrabbasso.
double bed *n* letto matrimoniale.
double-breasted ['dʌbl'brɛstɪd] *adj* a doppio petto.
double-check ['dʌbl'tʃɛk] *vt, vi* ricontrollare.
double-clutch ['dʌbl'klʌtʃ] *vi* (*US*) fare la doppietta.
double cream *n* (*BRIT*) doppia panna.
doublecross ['dʌbl'krɔs] *vt* fare il doppio gioco con.
doubledecker ['dʌbl'dɛkə*] *n* autobus *m inv* a due piani.
double declutch *vi* (*BRIT*) fare la doppietta.
double exposure *n* (*PHOT*) sovrimpressione *f.*
double glazing *n* (*BRIT*) doppi vetri *mpl.*
double-page ['dʌblpeɪdʒ] *adj*: ~ **spread** pubblicità a doppia pagina.
double parking *n* parcheggio in doppia

double room – doz.

fila.

double room *n* camera per due.

doubles ['dʌblz] *n* (TENNIS) doppio.

double time *n* tariffa doppia per lavoro straordinario.

double whammy [-'wæmɪ] *n* doppia mazzata (fig).

doubly ['dʌblɪ] *adv* doppiamente.

doubt [daut] *n* dubbio ♦ *vt* dubitare di; **to ~ that** dubitare che + *sub*; **without (a) ~** senza dubbio; **beyond ~** fuor di dubbio; **I ~ it very much** ho i miei dubbi, nutro seri dubbi in proposito.

doubtful ['dautful] *adj* dubbioso(a), incerto(a); (*person*) equivoco(a); **to be ~ about sth** avere dei dubbi su qc, non essere convinto di qc; **I'm a bit ~** non ne sono sicuro.

doubtless ['dautlɪs] *adv* indubbiamente.

dough [dəu] *n* pasta, impasto; (*col: money*) grana.

doughnut, (*US*) **donut** ['dəunʌt] *n* bombolone *m*.

dour [duə*] *adj* arcigno(a).

douse [daus] *vt* (*with water*) infradiciare; (*flames*) spegnere.

dove [dʌv] *n* colombo/a.

Dover ['dəuvə*] *n* Dover *f*.

dovetail ['dʌvteɪl] *n*: **~ joint** incastro a coda di rondine ♦ *vi* (*fig*) combaciare.

dowager ['dauədʒə*] *n* vedova titolata.

dowdy ['daudɪ] *adj* trasandato(a); malvestito(a).

Dow-Jones average ['dau'dʒəunz-] *n* (*US*) indice *m* Dow-Jones.

down [daun] *n* (*fluff*) piumino; (*hill*) collina, colle *m* ♦ *adv* giù, di sotto ♦ *prep* giù per ♦ *vt* (*col: drink*) scolarsi; **~ there** laggiù, là in fondo; **~ here** quaggiù; **I'll be ~ in a minute** scendo tra un minuto; **the price of meat is ~** il prezzo della carne è sceso; **I've got it ~ in my diary** ce l'ho sulla mia agenda; **to pay £2 ~** dare 2 sterline in acconto *or* di anticipo; **I've been ~ with flu** sono stato a letto con l'influenza; **England is two goals ~** l'Inghilterra sta perdendo per due goal; **to ~ tools** (*BRIT*) incrociare le braccia; **~ with X!** abbasso X!

down-and-out ['daunəndaut] *n* (*tramp*) barbone *m*.

down-at-heel ['daunət'hi:l] *adj* scalcagnato(a); (*fig*) trasandato(a).

downbeat ['daunbi:t] *n* (MUS) tempo in battere ♦ *adj* (*col*) volutamente distaccato(a).

downcast ['daunkɑ:st] *adj* abbattuto(a).

downer ['daunə*] *n* (*col: drug*) farmaco

depressivo; **to be on a ~** (*depressed*) essere giù.

downfall ['daunfɔ:l] *n* caduta; rovina.

downgrade ['daungreɪd] *vt* (*job, hotel*) declassare; (*employee*) degradare.

downhearted [daun'hɑ:tɪd] *adj* scoraggiato(a).

downhill ['daun'hɪl] *adv* verso il basso ♦ *n* (SKI: *also*: **~ race**) discesa libera; **to go ~** andare in discesa; (*business*) andare a rotoli.

Downing Street ['daunɪŋ-] *n*: **lo ~** residenza del primo ministro inglese.

Downing Street è la via di Westminster che porta da Whitehall al parco di St James dove, al numero 10, si trova la residenza del primo ministro inglese. Nella stessa via, al numero 11, si trova la residenza del **Chancellor of the Exchequer.** Spesso si usa Downing Street per indicare il governo britannico.

---

download ['daunləud] *vt* (COMPUT) trasferire (*per esempio da un grosso calcolatore ad un microcalcolatore*).

down-market ['daun'mɑ:kɪt] *adj* rivolto(a) ad una fascia di mercato inferiore.

down payment *n* acconto.

downplay ['daunpleɪ] *vt* (*US*) minimizzare.

downpour ['daunpɔ:*] *n* scroscio di pioggia.

downright ['daunraɪt] *adj* franco(a); (*refusal*) assoluto(a).

Downs [daunz] *npl* (*BRIT*): **the ~** colline ricche di gesso nel sud-est dell'Inghilterra.

downsize ['daunsaɪz] *vt* (*workforce*) ridurre.

Down's syndrome *n* sindrome *f* di Down.

downstairs ['daun'stɛəz] *adv* di sotto; al piano inferiore; **to come ~, go ~** scendere giù.

downstream ['daun'stri:m] *adv* a valle.

downtime ['dauntaɪm] *n* (COMM) tempi *mpl* morti.

down-to-earth ['dauntu'ə:θ] *adj* pratico(a).

downtown ['daun'taun] *adv* in città ♦ *adj* (*US*): **~ Chicago** il centro di Chicago.

downtrodden ['dauntrɔdn] *adj* oppresso(a).

down under *adv* agli antipodi.

downward ['daunwəd] *adj* in giù, in discesa; **a ~ trend** una diminuzione progressiva.

downward(s) ['daunwəd(z)] *adv* in giù, in discesa.

dowry ['dauri] *n* dote *f*.

doz. *abbr* = **dozen.**

doze [dəuz] *vi* sonnecchiare.
▶**doze off** *vi* appisolarsi.
dozen ['dʌzn] *n* dozzina; **a ~ books** una dozzina di libri; **80p a ~** 80 pence la dozzina; **~s of times** centinaia *or* migliaia di volte.
DPh, DPhil *n abbr* (= *Doctor of Philosophy*) ≈ dottorato di ricerca.
DPP *n abbr* (*BRIT*) *see* **Director of Public Prosecutions.**
DPT *n abbr* (*MED*: = *diphtheria, pertussis, tetanus*) vaccino.
DPW *n abbr* (*US*: = *Department of Public Works*) ≈ Ministero dei Lavori Pubblici.
Dr, Dr. *abbr* (= *doctor*) Dr, Dott./Dott.ssa.
dr *abbr* (*COMM*) = **debtor.**
Dr. *abbr* (*in street names*) = **drive.**
drab [dræb] *adj* tetro(a), grigio(a).
draft [drɑːft] *n* abbozzo; (*COMM*) tratta; (*US MIL*) contingente *m*; (: *call-up*) leva ♦ *vt* abbozzare; (*document, report*) stendere (in versione preliminare); *see also* **draught.**
drag [dræg] *vt* trascinare; (*river*) dragare ♦ *vi* trascinarsi ♦ *n* (*AVIAT, NAUT*) resistenza (aerodinamica); (*col: person*) noioso/a; (: *task*) noia; (*women's clothing*): **in ~** travestito (da donna).
▶**drag away** *vt*: **to ~ away (from)** tirare via (da).
▶**drag on** *vi* tirar avanti lentamente.
dragnet ['drægnɛt] *n* giacchio; (*fig*) rastrellamento.
dragon ['drægən] *n* drago.
dragonfly ['drægənflaɪ] *n* libellula.
dragoon [drə'guːn] *n* (*cavalryman*) dragone *m* ♦ *vt*: **to ~ sb into doing sth** (*BRIT*) costringere qn a fare qc.
drain [dreɪn] *n* canale *m* di scolo; (*for sewage*) fogna; (*on resources*) salasso ♦ *vt* (*land, marshes*) prosciugare; (*vegetables*) scolare; (*reservoir etc*) vuotare ♦ *vi* (*water*) defluire; **to feel ~ed** sentirsi svuotato(a), sentirsi sfinito(a).
drainage ['dreɪnɪdʒ] *n* prosciugamento; fognatura.
draining board ['dreɪnɪŋ-], **drainboard** (*US*) ['dreɪnbɔːd] *n* piano del lavello.
drainpipe ['dreɪnpaɪp] *n* tubo di scarico.
drake [dreɪk] *n* maschio dell'anatra.
dram [dræm] *n* bicchierino (di whisky *etc*).
drama ['drɑːmə] *n* (*art*) dramma *m*, teatro; (*play*) commedia; (*event*) dramma.
dramatic [drə'mætɪk] *adj* drammatico(a).
dramatically [drə'mætɪklɪ] *adv* in modo spettacolare.
dramatist ['dræmətɪst] *n* drammaturgo/a.
dramatize ['dræmətaɪz] *vt* (*events etc*) drammatizzare; (*adapt: novel: for TV*)

ridurre *or* adattare per la televisione; (: *for cinema*) ridurre *or* adattare per lo schermo.
drank [dræŋk] *pt of* **drink.**
drape [dreɪp] *vt* drappeggiare; *see also* **drapes.**
draper ['dreɪpə*] *n* (*BRIT*) negoziante *m/f* di stoffe.
drapes [dreɪps] *npl* (*US*) tende *fpl*.
drastic ['dræstɪk] *adj* drastico(a).
drastically ['dræstɪklɪ] *adv* drasticamente.
draught, (*US*) **draft** [drɑːft] *n* corrente *f* d'aria; (*NAUT*) pescaggio; **on ~** (*beer*) alla spina; *see also* **draughts.**
draught beer *n* birra alla spina.
draughtboard ['drɑːftbɔːd] *n* scacchiera.
draughts [drɑːfts] *n* (*BRIT*) (gioco della) dama.
draughtsman, (*US*) **draftsman** ['drɑːftsmən] *n* disegnatore *m*.
draughtsmanship, (*US*) **draftsmanship** ['drɑːftsmənʃɪp] *n* disegno tecnico; (*skill*) arte *f* del disegno.
draw [drɔː] *vb* (*pt* **drew,** *pp* **drawn** [druː, drɔːn]) *vt* tirare; (*attract*) attirare; (*picture*) disegnare; (*line, circle*) tracciare; (*money*) ritirare; (*formulate: conclusion*) trarre, ricavare; (: *comparison, distinction*): **to ~ (between)** fare (tra) ♦ *vi* (*SPORT*) pareggiare ♦ *n* (*SPORT*) pareggio; (*in lottery*) estrazione *f*; (*attraction*) attrazione *f*; **to ~ to a close** avvicinarsi alla conclusione; **to ~ near** *vi* avvicinarsi.
▶**draw back** *vi*: **to ~ back (from)** indietreggiare (di fronte a), tirarsi indietro (di fronte a).
▶**draw in** *vi* (*BRIT: car*) accostarsi; (: *train*) entrare in stazione.
▶**draw on** *vt* (*resources*) attingere a; (*imagination, person*) far ricorso a.
▶**draw out** *vi* (*lengthen*) allungarsi ♦ *vt* (*money*) ritirare.
▶**draw up** *vi* (*stop*) arrestarsi, fermarsi ♦ *vt* (*document*) compilare; (*plans*) formulare.
drawback ['drɔːbæk] *n* svantaggio, inconveniente *m*.
drawbridge ['drɔːbrɪdʒ] *n* ponte *m* levatoio.
drawee [drɔː'iː] *n* trattario.
drawer [drɔː*] *n* cassetto; ['drɔːə*] (*of cheque*) riscuotitore/trice.
drawing ['drɔːɪŋ] *n* disegno.
drawing board *n* tavola da disegno.
drawing pin *n* (*BRIT*) puntina da disegno.
drawing room *n* salotto.
drawl [drɔːl] *n* pronuncia strascicata.
drawn [drɔːn] *pp of* **draw** ♦ *adj* (*haggard: with tiredness*) tirato(a); (: *with pain*)

contratto(a) (dal dolore).
drawstring ['drɔːstrɪŋ] n laccio (per stringere maglie, sacche etc).
dread [drɛd] n terrore m ♦ vt tremare all'idea di.
dreadful ['drɛdful] adj terribile; **I feel** ~! (ill) mi sento uno straccio!; (ashamed) vorrei scomparire (dalla vergogna)!
dream [driːm] n sogno ♦ vt, vi (pt, pp **dreamed** or **dreamt** [drɛmt]) sognare; **to have a** ~ **about sb/sth** fare un sogno su qn/qc; **sweet** ~**s!** sogni d'oro!
▶**dream up** vt (reason, excuse) inventare; (plan, idea) escogitare.
dreamer ['driːmə*] n sognatore/trice.
dreamt [drɛmt] pt, pp of **dream**.
dreamy ['driːmɪ] adj (look, voice) sognante; (person) distratto(a), sognatore(trice).
dreary ['drɪərɪ] adj tetro(a); monotono(a).
dredge [drɛdʒ] vt dragare.
▶**dredge up** vt tirare alla superficie; (fig: unpleasant facts) rivangare.
dredger ['drɛdʒə*] n draga; (BRIT: also: **sugar** ~) spargizucchero m inv.
dregs [drɛgz] npl feccia.
drench [drɛntʃ] vt inzuppare; ~**ed to the skin** bagnato(a) fino all'osso, bagnato(a) fradicio(a).
dress [drɛs] n vestito; (clothing) abbigliamento ♦ vt vestire; (wound) fasciare; (food) condire; preparare; (shop window) allestire ♦ vi vestirsi; **to** ~ **o.s.**, **to get** ~**ed** vestirsi; **she** ~**es very well** veste molto bene.
▶**dress up** vi vestirsi a festa; (in fancy dress) vestirsi in costume.
dress circle n prima galleria.
dress designer n disegnatore/trice di moda.
dresser ['drɛsə*] n (THEAT) assistente m/f del camerino; (also: **window** ~) vetrinista m/f; (furniture) credenza.
dressing ['drɛsɪŋ] n (MED) benda; (CULIN) condimento.
dressing gown n (BRIT) vestaglia.
dressing room n (THEAT) camerino; (SPORT) spogliatoio.
dressing table n toilette f inv.
dressmaker ['drɛsmeɪkə*] n sarta.
dressmaking ['drɛsmeɪkɪŋ] n sartoria; confezioni fpl per donna.
dress rehearsal n prova generale.
dress shirt n camicia da sera.
dressy ['drɛsɪ] adj (col) elegante.
drew [druː] pt of **draw**.
dribble ['drɪbl] vi gocciolare; (baby) sbavare; (FOOTBALL) dribblare ♦ vt dribblare.

dried [draɪd] adj (fruit, beans) secco(a); (eggs, milk) in polvere.
drier ['draɪə*] n = **dryer**.
drift [drɪft] n (of current etc) direzione f; forza; (of sand, snow) cumulo; (general meaning) senso ♦ vi (boat) essere trasportato(a) dalla corrente; (sand, snow) ammucchiarsi; **to catch sb's** ~ capire dove qn vuole arrivare; **to let things** ~ lasciare che le cose vadano come vogliono; **to** ~ **apart** (friends) perdersi di vista; (lovers) allontanarsi l'uno dall'altro.
drifter ['drɪftə*] n persona che fa una vita da zingaro.
driftwood ['drɪftwud] n resti mpl della mareggiata.
drill [drɪl] n trapano; (MIL) esercitazione f ♦ vt trapanare; (soldiers) esercitare, addestrare; (pupils: in grammar) fare esercitare ♦ vi (for oil) fare trivellazioni.
drilling ['drɪlɪŋ] n (for oil) trivellazione f.
drilling rig n (on land) torre f di perforazione; (at sea) piattaforma (per trivellazioni subacquee).
drily ['draɪlɪ] adv = **dryly**.
drink [drɪŋk] n bevanda, bibita ♦ vt, vi (pt **drank**, pp **drunk** [dræŋk, drʌŋk]) bere; **to have a** ~ bere qualcosa; **a** ~ **of water** un bicchier d'acqua; **would you like something to** ~? vuole qualcosa da bere?; **we had** ~**s before lunch** abbiamo preso l'aperitivo.
▶**drink in** vt (subj: person: fresh air) aspirare; (: story) ascoltare avidamente; (: sight) ammirare, bersi con gli occhi.
drinkable ['drɪŋkəbl] adj (not poisonous) potabile; (palatable) bevibile.
drink-driving ['drɪŋk'draɪvɪŋ] n guida in stato di ebbrezza.
drinker ['drɪŋkə*] n bevitore/trice.
drinking ['drɪŋkɪŋ] n (drunkenness) il bere, alcoolismo.
drinking fountain n fontanella.
drinking water n acqua potabile.
drip [drɪp] n goccia; (~ping) sgocciolio; (MED) fleboclisi f inv; (col: spineless person) lavativo ♦ vi gocciolare; (washing) sgocciolare; (wall) trasudare.
drip-dry ['drɪp'draɪ] adj (shirt) che non si stira.
drip-feed ['drɪpfiːd] vt alimentare mediante fleboclisi.
dripping ['drɪpɪŋ] n (CULIN) grasso d'arrosto ♦ adj: ~ **wet** fradicio(a).
drive [draɪv] n passeggiata or giro in macchina; (also: ~**way**) viale m d'accesso; (energy) energia; (PSYCH) impulso;

bisogno; (*push*) sforzo eccezionale; campagna; (*SPORT*) drive *m inv*; (*TECH*) trasmissione *f*; (*COMPUT*: *also*: **disk** ~) disk drive *m inv*, unità *f inv* a dischi magnetici ♦ *vb* (*pt* **drove**, *pp* **driven** [drəuv, 'drɪvn]) *vt* (*vehicle*) guidare; (*nail*) piantare; (*push*) cacciare, spingere; (*TECH*: *motor*) azionare; far funzionare ♦ *vi* (*AUT*: *at controls*) guidare; (: *travel*) andare in macchina; **to go for a** ~ andare a fare un giro in macchina; **it's 3 hours'** ~ **from London** è a 3 ore di macchina da Londra; **left-/right-hand** ~ (*AUT*) guida a sinistra/ destra; **front-/rear-wheel** ~ (*AUT*) trazione *f* anteriore/posteriore; **to** ~ **sb to** (**do**) **sth** spingere qn a (fare) qc; **he** ~**s a taxi** fa il tassista; **to** ~ **at 50 km an hour** guidare *or* andare a 50 km all'ora.

▶**drive at** *vt fus* (*fig*: *intend*, *mean*) mirare a, voler dire.

▶**drive on** *vi* proseguire, andare (più) avanti ♦ *vt* (*incite*, *encourage*) sospingere, spingere.

drive-by ['draɪvbaɪ] *n* (*also*: ~ **shooting**) sparatoria dalla macchina; **he was killed in a** ~ **shooting** lo hanno ammazzato sparandogli da una macchina in corsa.

drive-in ['draɪvɪn] *adj*, *n* (*esp US*) drive-in (*m inv*).

drive-in window *n* (*US*) sportello di drive-in.

drivel ['drɪvl] *n* (*col*: *nonsense*) ciance *fpl*.

driven ['drɪvn] *pp of* **drive**.

driver ['draɪvə*] *n* conducente *m/f*; (*of taxi*) tassista *m*; (*of bus*) autista *m*.

driver's license *n* (*US*) patente *f* di guida.

driveway ['draɪvweɪ] *n* viale *m* d'accesso.

driving ['draɪvɪŋ] *adj*: ~ **rain** pioggia sferzante ♦ *n* guida.

driving force *n* forza trainante.

driving instructor *n* istruttore/trice di scuola guida.

driving lesson *n* lezione *f* di guida.

driving licence *n* (*BRIT*) patente *f* di guida.

driving school *n* scuola *f* guida *inv*.

driving test *n* esame *m* di guida.

drizzle ['drɪzl] *n* pioggerella ♦ *vi* piovigginare.

droll [drəul] *adj* buffo(a).

dromedary ['drɔmədərɪ] *n* dromedario.

drone [drəun] *n* ronzio; (*male bee*) fuco ♦ *vi* (*bee*, *aircraft*, *engine*) ronzare; (*also*: ~ **on**: *person*) continuare a parlare (in modo monotono); (: *voice*) continuare a ronzare.

drool [dru:l] *vi* sbavare; **to** ~ **over sb/sth** (*fig*) andare in estasi per qn/qc.

droop [dru:p] *vi* abbassarsi; languire.

drop [drɔp] *n* goccia; (*fall*: *in price*) calo,

ribasso; (: *in salary*) riduzione *f*, taglio; (*also*: **parachute** ~) lancio; (*steep incline*) salto ♦ *vt* lasciar cadere; (*voice, eyes, price*) abbassare; (*set down from car*) far scendere ♦ *vi* cascare; (*decrease*: *wind, temperature, price, voice*) calare; (*numbers, attendance*) diminuire; ~**s** *npl* (*MED*) gocce *fpl*; **cough** ~**s** pastiglie *fpl* per la tosse; **a** ~ **of 10%** un calo del 10%; **to** ~ **sb a line** mandare due righe a qn; **to** ~ **anchor** gettare l'ancora.

▶**drop in** *vi* (*col*: *visit*): **to** ~ **in** (**on**) fare un salto (da), passare (da).

▶**drop off** *vi* (*sleep*) addormentarsi ♦ *vt*: **to** ~ **sb off** far scendere qn.

▶**drop out** *vi* (*withdraw*) ritirarsi; (*student etc*) smettere di studiare.

droplet ['drɔplɪt] *n* gocciolina.

dropout ['drɔpaut] *n* (*from society/university*) chi ha abbandonato (la società/gli studi).

dropper ['drɔpə*] *n* (*MED etc*) contagocce *m inv*.

droppings ['drɔpɪŋz] *npl* sterco.

dross [drɔs] *n* scoria; scarto.

drought [draut] *n* siccità *f inv*.

drove [drəuv] *pt of* **drive** ♦ *n*: ~**s of people** una moltitudine di persone.

drown [draun] *vt* affogare; (*also*: ~ **out**: *sound*) coprire ♦ *vi* affogare.

drowse [drauz] *vi* sonnecchiare.

drowsy ['drauzɪ] *adj* sonnolento(a), assonnato(a).

drudge [drʌdʒ] *n* (*person*) uomo/donna di fatica; (*job*) faticaccia.

drudgery ['drʌdʒərɪ] *n* fatica improba; **housework is sheer** ~ le faccende domestiche sono alienanti.

drug [drʌg] *n* farmaco; (*narcotic*) droga ♦ *vt* drogare; **he's on** ~**s** si droga; (*MED*) segue una cura.

drug abuser [-ə'bjuːzə*] *n* chi fa uso di droghe.

drug addict *n* tossicomane *m/f*.

druggist ['drʌgɪst] *n* (*US*) farmacista *m/f*.

drug peddler *n* spacciatore/trice di droga.

drugstore ['drʌgstɔː*] *n* (*US*) *negozio di generi vari e di articoli di farmacia con un bar*.

drum [drʌm] *n* tamburo; (*for oil, petrol*) fusto ♦ *vt*: **to** ~ **one's fingers on the table** tamburellare con le dita sulla tavola; ~**s** *npl* (*MUS*) batteria.

▶**drum up** *vt* (*enthusiasm, support*) conquistarsi.

drummer ['drʌmə*] *n* batterista *m/f*.

drum roll *n* rullio di tamburi.

drumstick ['drʌmstɪk] *n* (*MUS*) bacchetta; (*chicken leg*) coscia di pollo.

drunk [drʌŋk] *pp of* **drink** ♦ *adj* ubriaco(a); ebbro(a) ♦ *n* ubriacone/a; **to get ~** ubriacarsi, prendere una sbornia.

drunkard ['drʌŋkəd] *n* ubriacone/a.

drunken ['drʌŋkən] *adj* ubriaco(a); da ubriaco; **~ driving** guida in stato di ebbrezza.

drunkenness ['drʌŋkənnɪs] *n* ubriachezza; ebbrezza.

dry [draɪ] *adj* secco(a); (*day, clothes, fig: humour*) asciutto(a); (*uninteresting: lecture, subject*) poco avvincente ♦ *vt* seccare; (*clothes, hair, hands*) asciugare ♦ *vi* asciugarsi; **on ~ land** sulla terraferma; **to ~ one's hands/hair/eyes** asciugarsi le mani/i capelli/gli occhi.

▶**dry up** *vi* seccarsi; (*source of supply*) esaurirsi; (*fig: imagination etc*) inaridirsi; (*fall silent: speaker*) azzittirsi.

dry-clean [draɪ'kliːn] *vt* pulire *or* lavare a secco.

dry-cleaner's [draɪ'kliːnəz] *n* lavasecco *m inv*.

dry-cleaning [draɪ'kliːnɪŋ] *n* pulitura a secco.

dry dock *n* (*NAUT*) bacino di carenaggio.

dryer ['draɪə*] *n* (*for hair*) föhn *m inv*, asciugacapelli *m inv*; (*for clothes*) asciugabiancheria *m inv*.

dry goods *npl* (*COMM*) tessuti *mpl* e mercerie *fpl*.

dry goods store *n* (*US*) negozio di stoffe.

dry ice *n* ghiaccio secco.

dryly ['draɪlɪ] *adv* con fare asciutto.

dryness ['draɪnɪs] *n* secchezza; (*of ground*) aridità.

dry rot *n* fungo del legno.

dry run *n* (*fig*) prova.

dry ski slope *n* pista artificiale.

DSc *n abbr* (= *Doctor of Science*) titolo di studio.

DSS *n abbr* (*BRIT*) = **Department of Social Security;** *see* **social security.**

DST *abbr* (*US*) = **Daylight Saving Time.**

DT *n abbr* (*COMPUT*) = **data transmission.**

DTI *n abbr* (*BRIT*) = **Department of Trade and Industry;** *see* **trade.**

DTP *n abbr* = **desktop publishing.**

DT's *n abbr* (*col*) = *delirium tremens.*

dual ['djuəl] *adj* doppio(a).

dual carriageway *n* (*BRIT*) strada a doppia carreggiata.

dual-control ['djuəlkən'trəul] *adj* con doppi comandi.

dual nationality *n* doppia nazionalità.

dual-purpose ['djuəl'pə:pəs] *adj* a doppio uso.

dubbed [dʌbd] *adj* (*CINE*) doppiato(a); (*nicknamed*) soprannominato(a).

dubious ['djuːbɪəs] *adj* dubbio(a); (*character, manner*) ambiguo(a), equivoco(a); **I'm very ~ about it** ho i miei dubbi in proposito.

Dublin ['dʌblɪn] *n* Dublino *f*.

Dubliner ['dʌblɪnə*] *n* dublinese *m/f*.

duchess ['dʌtʃɪs] *n* duchessa.

duck [dʌk] *n* anatra ♦ *vi* abbassare la testa ♦ *vt* spingere sotto (acqua).

duckling ['dʌklɪŋ] *n* anatroccolo.

duct [dʌkt] *n* condotto; (*ANAT*) canale *m*.

dud [dʌd] *n* (*shell*) proiettile *m* che fa cilecca; (*object, tool*): **it's a ~** è inutile, non funziona ♦ *adj* (*BRIT: cheque*) a vuoto; (*note, coin*) falso(a).

due [djuː] *adj* dovuto(a); (*expected*) atteso(a); (*fitting*) giusto(a) ♦ *n* dovuto ♦ *adv*: **~ north** diritto verso nord; **~s** *npl* (*for club, union*) quota; (*in harbour*) diritti *mpl* di porto; **in ~ course** a tempo debito; finalmente; **~ to** dovuto a; a causa di; **the rent's ~ on the 30th** l'affitto scade il 30; **the train is ~ at 8** il treno è atteso per le 8; **she is ~ back tomorrow** dovrebbe essere di ritorno domani; **I am ~ 6 days' leave** mi spettano 6 giorni di ferie.

due date *n* data di scadenza.

duel ['djuəl] *n* duello.

duet [djuː'ɛt] *n* duetto.

duff [dʌf] *adj* (*BRIT col*) barboso(a).

duffelbag, duffle bag ['dʌflbæg] *n* sacca da viaggio di tela.

duffelcoat, duffle coat ['dʌflkəut] *n* montgomery *m inv*.

duffer ['dʌfə*] *n* (*col*) schiappa.

dug [dʌg] *pt, pp of* **dig.**

dugout ['dʌgaut] *n* (*FOOTBALL*) panchina.

duke [djuːk] *n* duca *m*.

dull [dʌl] *adj* (*boring*) noioso(a); (*slow-witted*) ottuso(a); (*sound, pain*) sordo(a); (*weather, day*) fosco(a), scuro(a); (*blade*) smussato(a) ♦ *vt* (*pain, grief*) attutire; (*mind, senses*) intorpidire.

duly ['djuːlɪ] *adv* (*on time*) a tempo debito; (*as expected*) debitamente.

dumb [dʌm] *adj* muto(a); (*stupid*) stupido(a); **to be struck ~** (*fig*) ammutolire, restare senza parole.

dumbbell ['dʌmbɛl] *n* (*SPORT*) manubrio, peso.

dumbfounded [dʌm'faundɪd] *adj* stupito(a), stordito(a).

dummy ['dʌmɪ] *n* (*tailor's model*) manichino; (*SPORT*) finto; (*BRIT: for baby*) tettarella ♦ *adj* falso(a), finto(a).

dummy run *n* giro di prova.

dump [dʌmp] *n* mucchio di rifiuti; (*place*)

luogo di scarico; (*MIL*) deposito; (*COMPUT*) scaricamento, dump *m inv* ♦ *vt* (*put down*) scaricare; mettere giù; (*get rid of*) buttar via; (*COMM: goods*) svendere; (*COMPUT*) scaricare; **to be (down) in the ~s** (*col*) essere giù di corda.

dumping ['dʌmpɪŋ] *n* (*ECON*) dumping *m*; (*of rubbish*): **"no ~"** "vietato lo scarico".

dumpling ['dʌmplɪŋ] *n specie di gnocco.*

dumpy ['dʌmpɪ] *adj* tracagnotto(a).

dunce [dʌns] *n* asino.

dune [dju:n] *n* duna.

dung [dʌŋ] *n* concime *m*.

dungarees [dʌŋɡə'ri:z] *npl* tuta.

dungeon ['dʌndʒən] *n* prigione *f* sotterranea.

dunk [dʌŋk] *vt* inzuppare.

duo ['dju:əu] *n* (*gen, MUS*) duo *m inv*.

duodenal [dju:əu'di:nl] *adj* (*ulcer*) duodenale.

duodenum [dju:əu'di:nəm] *n* duodeno.

dupe [dju:p] *vt* gabbare, ingannare.

duplex ['dju:plɛks] *n* (*US: also: ~ apartment*) appartamento su due piani.

duplicate *n* ['dju:plɪkət] doppio; (*copy of letter etc*) duplicato ♦ *vt* ['dju:plɪkeɪt] raddoppiare; (*on machine*) ciclostilare ♦ *adj* (*copy*) conforme, esattamente uguale; **in ~** in duplice copia; **~ key** duplicato (della chiave).

duplicating machine ['dju:plɪkeɪtɪŋ-], **duplicator** ['dju:plɪkeɪtə*] *n* duplicatore *m*.

duplicity [dju:'plɪsɪtɪ] *n* doppiezza, duplicità.

Dur. *abbr* (*BRIT*) = *Durham.*

durability [djuərə'bɪlɪtɪ] *n* durevolezza; resistenza.

durable ['djuərəbl] *adj* durevole; (*clothes, metal*) resistente.

duration [djuə'reɪʃən] *n* durata.

duress [djuə'rɛs] *n*: **under ~** sotto costrizione.

Durex ® ['djuərɛks] *n* (*BRIT*) preservativo.

during ['djuərɪŋ] *prep* durante, nel corso di.

dusk [dʌsk] *n* crepuscolo.

dusky ['dʌskɪ] *adj* scuro(a).

dust [dʌst] *n* polvere *f* ♦ *vt* (*furniture*) spolverare; (*cake etc*): **to ~ with** cospargere con.

▶**dust off** *vt* rispolverare.

dustbin ['dʌstbɪn] *n* (*BRIT*) pattumiera.

duster ['dʌstə*] *n* straccio per la polvere.

dust jacket *n* sopraccoperta.

dustman ['dʌstmən] *n* (*BRIT*) netturbino.

dustpan ['dʌstpæn] *n* pattumiera.

dusty ['dʌstɪ] *adj* polveroso(a).

Dutch [dʌtʃ] *adj* olandese ♦ *n* (*LING*)

olandese *m* ♦ *adv*: **to go ~** *or* **d~** fare alla romana; **the ~** gli Olandesi.

Dutch auction *n* asta all'olandese.

Dutchman ['dʌtʃmən], **Dutchwoman** ['dʌtʃwumən] *n* olandese *m/f*.

dutiable ['dju:tɪəbl] *adj* soggetto(a) a dazio.

dutiful ['dju:tɪful] *adj* (*child*) rispettoso(a); (*husband*) premuroso(a); (*employee*) coscienzioso(a).

duty ['dju:tɪ] *n* dovere *m*; (*tax*) dazio, tassa; **duties** *npl* mansioni *fpl*; **on ~** di servizio; (*MED: in hospital*) di guardia; **off ~** libero(a), fuori servizio; **to make it one's ~ to do sth** assumersi l'obbligo di fare qc; **to pay ~ on sth** pagare il dazio su qc.

duty-free ['dju:tɪ'fri:] *adj* esente da dazio; **~ shop** duty free *m inv*.

duty officer *n* (*MIL etc*) ufficiale *m* di servizio.

duvet ['du:veɪ] *n* piumino, piumone *m*.

DV *abbr* (= *Deo volente*) D.V.

DVLA *n abbr* (= *Driver and Vehicle Licensing Authority*) ≈ I.M.C.T.C. *m* (= *Ispettorato Generale della Motorizzazione Civile e dei Trasporti in Concessione*).

DVLC *n abbr* (*BRIT*: = *Driver and Vehicle Licensing Office*) ≈ I.M.C.T.C. *m*.

DVM *n abbr* (*US*: = *Doctor of Veterinary Medicine*) titolo di studio.

dwarf [dwɔ:f] *n* nano/a ♦ *vt* far apparire piccolo.

dwell, *pt, pp* **dwelt** [dwɛl, dwɛlt] *vi* dimorare.

▶**dwell on** *vt fus* indugiare su.

dweller ['dwɛlə*] *n* abitante *m/f*; **city ~** cittadino/a.

dwelling ['dwɛlɪŋ] *n* dimora.

dwelt [dwɛlt] *pt, pp of* **dwell**.

dwindle ['dwɪndl] *vi* diminuire, decrescere.

dwindling ['dwɪndlɪŋ] *adj* (*strength, interest*) che si affievolisce; (*resources, supplies*) in diminuzione.

dye [daɪ] *n* colore *m*; (*chemical*) colorante *m*, tintura ♦ *vt* tingere; **hair ~** tinta per capelli.

dyestuffs ['daɪstʌfs] *npl* coloranti *mpl*.

dying ['daɪɪŋ] *adj* morente, moribondo(a).

dyke [daɪk] *n* diga; (*channel*) canale *m* di scolo; (*causeway*) sentiero rialzato.

dynamic [daɪ'næmɪk] *adj* dinamico(a).

dynamics [daɪ'næmɪks] *n or npl* dinamica.

dynamite ['daɪnəmaɪt] *n* dinamite *f* ♦ *vt* far saltare con la dinamite.

dynamo ['daɪnəməu] *n* dinamo *f inv*.

dynasty ['dɪnəstɪ] *n* dinastia.

dysentery ['dɪsntrɪ] *n* dissenteria.

dyslexia [dɪs'lɛksɪə] *n* dislessia.

dyslexic [dɪs'lɛksɪk] *adj, n* dislessico(a).

dyspepsia [dɪsˈpɛpsɪə] *n* dispepsia.
dystrophy [ˈdɪstrəfɪ] *n* distrofia; **muscular**
~ distrofia muscolare.

E e

E, e [iː] *n* (*letter*) E, e *f or m inv*; (*MUS*): **E** mi *m*;
E for Edward, (*US*) **E for Easy** ≈ E come
Empoli.
E *abbr* (= *east*) E ♦ *n abbr* (= *Ecstasy*) ecstasy
f inv.
E111 *n abbr* (*also*: **form** ~) E111 (*modulo CEE
per rimborso spese mediche*).
ea. *abbr* = **each.**
E.A. *n abbr* (*US*) = *educational age.*
each [iːtʃ] *adj* ogni, ciascuno(a) ♦ *pron*
ciascuno(a), ognuno(a); ~ **one** ognuno(a);
~ **other** si (*or* ci *etc*); **they hate** ~ **other** si
odiano (l'un l'altro); **you are jealous of** ~
other siete gelosi l'uno dell'altro; ~ **day**
ogni giorno; **they have 2 books** ~ hanno 2
libri ciascuno; **they cost £5** ~ costano 5
sterline l'uno; ~ **of us** ciascuno *or* ognuno
di noi.
eager [ˈiːgə*] *adj* impaziente;
desideroso(a); ardente; (*keen: pupil*)
appassionato(a), attento(a); **to be** ~ **to do**
sth non veder l'ora di fare qc; **to be** ~ **for** essere
desideroso di fare qc; **to be** ~ **for** essere
desideroso di, aver gran voglia di.
eagle [ˈiːgl] *n* aquila.
E and OE *abbr* (= *errors and omissions
excepted*) S.E.O.
ear [ɪə*] *n* orecchio; (*of corn*) pannocchia;
up to the ~**s in debt** nei debiti fino al
collo.
earache [ˈɪəreɪk] *n* mal *m* d'orecchi.
eardrum [ˈɪədrʌm] *n* timpano.
earful [ˈɪəful] *n*: **to give sb an** ~ fare una
ramanzina a qn.
earl [əːl] *n* conte *m.*
earlier [ˈəːlɪə*] *adj* (*date etc*) anteriore;
(*edition etc*) precedente, anteriore ♦ *adv*
prima; **I can't come any** ~ non posso
venire prima.
early [ˈəːlɪ] *adv* presto, di buon'ora; (*ahead
of time*) in anticipo ♦ *adj* precoce;
anticipato(a); che si fa vedere di
buon'ora; (*man*) primitivo(a); (*Christians,
settlers*) primo(a); ~ **in the morning/
afternoon** nelle prime ore del mattino/del

pomeriggio; **you're** ~! sei in anticipo!;
have an ~ **night/start** vada a letto/parta
presto; **in the** ~ *or* ~ **in the spring/19th
century** all'inizio della primavera/
dell'Ottocento; **she's in her** ~ **forties** ha
appena passato la quarantina; **at your
earliest convenience** (*COMM*) non appena
possibile.
early retirement *n* ritiro anticipato.
early warning system *n* sistema *m* del
preallarme.
earmark [ˈɪəmɑːk] *vt*: **to** ~ **sth for** destinare
qc a.
earn [əːn] *vt* guadagnare; (*rest, reward*)
meritare; (*COMM: yield*) maturare; **to** ~
one's living guadagnarsi da vivere; **this**
~**ed him much praise, he** ~**ed much
praise for this** si è attirato grandi lodi per
questo.
earned income *n* reddito da lavoro.
earnest [ˈəːnɪst] *adj* serio(a) ♦ *n* (*also*: ~
money) caparra; **in** ~ *adv* sul serio.
earnings [ˈəːnɪŋz] *npl* guadagni *mpl*; (*of
company etc*) proventi *mpl*; (*salary*)
stipendio.
ear, nose and throat specialist *n*
otorinolaringoiatra *m/f.*
earphones [ˈɪəfəunz] *npl* cuffia.
earplugs [ˈɪəplʌgz] *npl* tappi *mpl* per le
orecchie.
earring [ˈɪərɪŋ] *n* orecchino.
earshot [ˈɪəʃɔt] *n*: **out of/within** ~ fuori
portata/a portata d'orecchio.
earth [əːθ] *n* (*gen, also BRIT ELEC*) terra; (*of
fox etc*) tana ♦ *vt* (*BRIT ELEC*) mettere a
terra.
earthenware [ˈəːθənwɛə*] *n* terracotta;
stoviglie *fpl* di terracotta ♦ *adj* di
terracotta.
earthly [ˈəːθlɪ] *adj* terreno(a); ~ **paradise**
paradiso terrestre; **there is no** ~ **reason
to think** ... non vi è ragione di pensare ....
earthquake [ˈəːθkweɪk] *n* terremoto.
earth-shattering [ˈəːθʃætərɪŋ] *adj*
stupefacente.
earth tremor *n* scossa sismica.
earthworks [ˈəːθwəːks] *npl* lavori *mpl* di
sterro.
earthworm [ˈəːθwəːm] *n* lombrico.
earthy [ˈəːθɪ] *adj* (*fig*) grossolano(a).
earwax [ˈɪəwæks] *n* cerume *m.*
earwig [ˈɪəwɪg] *n* forbicina.
ease [iːz] *n* agio, comodo ♦ *vt* (*soothe*)
calmare; (*loosen*) allentare ♦ *vi* (*situation*)
allentarsi, distendersi; **life of** ~ vita
comoda; **with** ~ senza difficoltà; **at** ~ a
proprio agio; (*MIL*) a riposo; **to feel at** ~ /
ill at ~ sentirsi a proprio agio/a disagio;

to ~ sth out/in tirare fuori/infilare qc con delicatezza; facilitare l'uscita/l'entrata di qc.
▶**ease off, ease up** *vi* diminuire; (*slow down*) rallentarsi; (*fig*) rilassarsi.
easel ['i:zl] *n* cavalletto.
easily ['i:zɪlɪ] *adv* facilmente.
easiness ['i:zɪnɪs] *n* facilità, semplicità; (*of manners*) disinvoltura.
east [i:st] *n* est *m* ♦ *adj* dell'est ♦ *adv* a oriente; **the E~** l'Oriente *m*; (*POL*) i Paesi dell'Est.
Easter ['i:stə*] *n* Pasqua ♦ *adj* (*holidays*) pasquale, di Pasqua.
Easter egg *n* uovo di Pasqua.
Easter Island *n* isola di Pasqua.
easterly ['i:stəlɪ] *adj* dall'est, d'oriente.
Easter Monday *n* Pasquetta.
eastern ['i:stən] *adj* orientale, d'oriente; **E~ Europe** l'Europa orientale; **the E~ bloc** (*POL*) i Paesi dell'Est.
Easter Sunday *n* domenica di Pasqua.
East Germany *n* Germania dell'Est.
eastward(s) ['i:stwəd(z)] *adv* verso est, verso levante.
easy ['i:zɪ] *adj* facile; (*manner*) disinvolto(a); (*carefree: life*) agiato(a), tranquillo(a) ♦ *adv*: **to take it** *or* **things ~** prendersela con calma; **I'm ~** (*col*) non ho problemi; **easier said than done** tra il dire e il fare c'è di mezzo il mare; **payment on ~ terms** (*COMM*) facilitazioni *fpl* di pagamento.
easy chair *n* poltrona.
easy-going ['i:zɪ'gəʊɪŋ] *adj* accomodante.
eat, *pt* **ate**, *pp* **eaten** [i:t, eɪt, 'i:tn] *vt* mangiare.
▶**eat away** *vt* (*subj: sea*) erodere; (: *acid*) corrodere.
▶**eat away at, eat into** *vt fus* rodere.
▶**eat out** *vi* mangiare fuori.
▶**eat up** *vt* (*meal etc*) finire di mangiare; **it ~s up electricity** consuma un sacco di corrente.
eatable ['i:təbl] *adj* mangiabile; (*safe to eat*) commestibile.
eaten ['i:tn] *pp of* **eat**.
eau de Cologne ['əʊdəkə'ləʊn] *n* acqua di colonia.
eaves [i:vz] *npl* gronda.
eavesdrop ['i:vzdrɔp] *vi*: **to ~** (**on a conversation**) origliare (una conversazione).
ebb [ɛb] *n* riflusso ♦ *vi* rifluire; (*fig: also: ~ away*) declinare; **~ and flow** flusso e riflusso; **to be at a low ~** (*fig: person, spirits*) avere il morale a terra; (: *business*) andar male.

ebb tide *n* marea discendente.
ebony ['ɛbənɪ] *n* ebano.
ebullient [ɪ'bʌlɪənt] *adj* esuberante.
EC *n abbr* (= *European Community*) CE (= *Comunità Europea*).
eccentric [ɪk'sɛntrɪk] *adj*, *n* eccentrico(a).
ecclesiastic [ɪkliːzɪ'æstɪk] *n* ecclesiastico.
ecclesiastic(al) [ɪkliːzɪ'æstɪk(əl)] *adj* ecclesiastico(a).
ECG *n abbr see* **electrocardiogram**.
ECGD *n abbr* (= *Export Credits Guarantee Department*) *servizio di garanzia finanziaria per l'esportazione*.
echo, ~es ['ɛkəʊ] *n* eco *m or f* ♦ *vt* ripetere; fare eco a ♦ *vi* echeggiare; dare un eco.
éclair ['eɪklɛə*] *n* ≈ bignè *m inv*.
eclipse [ɪ'klɪps] *n* eclissi *f inv* ♦ *vt* eclissare.
ECM *n abbr* (*US*: = *European Common Market*) MEC *m*.
eco... ['i:kəʊ] *prefix* eco....
eco-friendly [i:kəʊ'frɛndlɪ] *adj* ecologico(a).
ecological [i:kə'lɔdʒɪkəl] *adj* ecologico(a).
ecologist [ɪ'kɔlədʒɪst] *n* ecologo/a.
ecology [ɪ'kɔlədʒɪ] *n* ecologia.
economic [i:kə'nɔmɪk] *adj* economico(a); (*profitable: price*) vantaggioso(a); (*business*) che rende.
economical [i:kə'nɔmɪkəl] *adj* economico(a); (*person*) economo(a).
economically [i:kə'nɔmɪklɪ] *adv* con economia; (*regarding economics*) dal punto di vista economico.
economics [i:kə'nɔmɪks] *n* economia ♦ *npl* aspetto *or* lato economico.
economist [ɪ'kɔnəmɪst] *n* economista *m/f*.
economize [ɪ'kɔnəmaɪz] *vi* risparmiare, fare economia.
economy [ɪ'kɔnəmɪ] *n* economia; **economies of scale** (*COMM*) economie *fpl* di scala.
economy class *n* (*AVIAT etc*) classe *f* turistica.
economy size *n* confezione *f* economica.
ecosystem ['i:kəʊsɪstəm] *n* ecosistema *m*.
eco-tourism [i:kəʊ'tʊərɪzəm] *n* ecoturismo.
ECSC *n abbr* (= *European Coal & Steel Community*) C.E.C.A. *f* (= *Comunità Europea del Carbone e dell'Acciaio*).
ecstasy ['ɛkstəsɪ] *n* estasi *f inv*; **to go into ecstasies over** andare in estasi davanti a; **E~** (*drug*) ecstasy *f inv*.
ecstatic [ɛks'tætɪk] *adj* estatico(a), in estasi.
ECT *n abbr see* **electroconvulsive therapy**.
ECU, ecu ['eɪkjuː] *n abbr* (= *European Currency Unit*) ECU *f inv*, ecu *f inv*.
Ecuador ['ɛkwədɔ:*] *n* Ecuador *m*.
ecumenical [i:kju'mɛnɪkl] *adj*

ecumenico(a).
eczema ['ɛksɪmə] *n* eczema *m*.
eddy ['ɛdɪ] *n* mulinello.
edge [ɛdʒ] *n* margine *m*; (*of table, plate, cup*) orlo; (*of knife etc*) taglio ♦ *vt* bordare ♦ *vi*: **to ~ away from** sgattaiolare da; **to ~ past** passar rasente; **to ~ forward** avanzare a poco a poco; **on ~** (*fig*) = **edgy; to have the ~ on** essere in vantaggio su.
edgeways ['ɛdʒweɪz] *adv* di fianco; **he couldn't get a word in ~** non riuscì a dire una parola.
edging ['ɛdʒɪŋ] *n* bordo.
edgy ['ɛdʒɪ] *adj* nervoso(a).
edible ['ɛdɪbl] *adj* commestibile; (*meal*) mangiabile.
edict ['iːdɪkt] *n* editto.
edifice ['ɛdɪfɪs] *n* edificio.
edifying ['ɛdɪfaɪŋ] *adj* edificante.
Edinburgh ['ɛdɪnbərə] *n* Edimburgo *f*.
edit ['ɛdɪt] *vt* curare; (*newspaper, magazine*) dirigere; (*COMPUT*) correggere e modificare, editare.
edition [ɪ'dɪʃən] *n* edizione *f*.
editor ['ɛdɪtə*] *n* (*in newspaper*) redattore/trice; redattore/trice capo; (*of sb's work*) curatore/trice; (*film ~*) responsabile *m/f* del montaggio.
editorial [ɛdɪ'tɔːrɪəl] *adj* redazionale, editoriale ♦ *n* editoriale *m*; **the ~ staff** la redazione.
EDP *n abbr see* **electronic data processing**.
EDT *abbr* (*US*: = *Eastern Daylight Time*) *ora legale di New York*.
educate ['ɛdjukeɪt] *vt* istruire; educare.
educated guess ['ɛdjukeɪtɪd-] *n* ipotesi *f* ben fondata.
education [ɛdju'keɪʃən] *n* (*teaching*) insegnamento; istruzione *f*; (*knowledge, culture*) cultura; (*SCOL: subject etc*) pedagogia; **primary** *or* (*US*) **elementary/secondary ~** scuola primaria/secondaria.
educational [ɛdju'keɪʃənl] *adj* pedagogico(a); scolastico(a); istruttivo(a); **~ technology** tecnologie *fpl* applicate alla didattica.
Edwardian [ɛd'wɔːdɪən] *adj* edoardiano(a).
EE *abbr* = **electrical engineer**.
EEC *n abbr* (= *European Economic Community*) C.E.E. *f* (= *Comunità Economica Europea*).
EEG *n abbr see* **electroencephalogram**.
eel [iːl] *n* anguilla.
EENT *n abbr* (*US MED*) = *eye, ear, nose and throat*.
EEOC *n abbr* (*US*) = **Equal Employment Opportunity Commission**.
eerie ['ɪərɪ] *adj* che fa accapponare la pelle.

EET *abbr* (= *Eastern European Time*) *fuso orario*.
effect [ɪ'fɛkt] *n* effetto ♦ *vt* effettuare; **to take ~** (*law*) entrare in vigore; (*drug*) fare effetto; **to have an ~ on sb/sth** avere *or* produrre un effetto su qn/qc; **to put into ~** (*plan*) attuare; **in ~** effettivamente; **his letter is to the ~ that** ... il contenuto della sua lettera è che ...; *see also* **effects**.
effective [ɪ'fɛktɪv] *adj* efficace; (*striking: display, outfit*) che fa colpo; **~ date** data d'entrata in vigore; **to become ~** (*law*) entrare in vigore.
effectively [ɪ'fɛktɪvlɪ] *adv* (*efficiently*) efficacemente; (*strikingly*) ad effetto; (*in reality*) di fatto; (*in effect*) in effetti.
effectiveness [ɪ'fɛktɪvnɪs] *n* efficacia.
effects [ɪ'fɛkts] *npl* (*THEAT*) effetti *mpl* scenici; (*property*) effetti *mpl*.
effeminate [ɪ'fɛmɪnɪt] *adj* effeminato(a).
effervescent [ɛfə'vɛsnt] *adj* effervescente.
efficacy ['ɛfɪkəsɪ] *n* efficacia.
efficiency [ɪ'fɪʃənsɪ] *n* efficienza; rendimento effettivo.
efficiency apartment *n* (*US*) miniappartamento.
efficient [ɪ'fɪʃənt] *adj* efficiente; (*remedy, product, system*) efficace; (*machine, car*) che ha un buon rendimento.
efficiently [ɪ'fɪʃəntlɪ] *adv* efficientemente; efficacemente.
effigy ['ɛfɪdʒɪ] *n* effigie *f*.
effluent ['ɛfluənt] *n* effluente *m*.
effort ['ɛfət] *n* sforzo; **to make an ~ to do sth** sforzarsi di fare qc.
effortless ['ɛfətlɪs] *adj* senza sforzo, facile.
effrontery [ɪ'frʌntərɪ] *n* sfrontatezza.
effusive [ɪ'fjuːsɪv] *adj* (*person*) espansivo(a); (*welcome, letter*) caloroso(a); (*thanks, apologies*) interminabile.
EFL *n abbr* (*SCOL*) = *English as a foreign language*.
EFTA ['ɛftə] *n abbr* (= *European Free Trade Association*) E.F.T.A. *f*.
e.g. *adv abbr* (= *exempli gratia: for example*) p.es.
egalitarian [ɪgælɪ'tɛərɪən] *adj* egualitario(a).
egg [ɛg] *n* uovo.
▶**egg on** *vt* incitare.
eggcup ['ɛgkʌp] *n* portauovo *m inv*.
eggplant ['ɛgplɑːnt] *n* (*esp US*) melanzana.
eggshell ['ɛgʃɛl] *n* guscio d'uovo ♦ *adj* (*colour*) guscio d'uovo *inv*.
egg-timer ['ɛgtaɪmə*] *n* clessidra (*per misurare il tempo di cottura delle uova*).
egg white *n* albume *m*, bianco d'uovo.

egg yolk *n* tuorlo, rosso (d'uovo).
ego ['i:gəu] *n* ego *m inv.*
egoism ['ɛgəuizəm] *n* egoismo.
egoist ['ɛgəuist] *n* egoista *m/f.*
egotism ['ɛgəutizəm] *n* egotismo.
egotist ['ɛgəutist] *n* egotista *m/f.*
ego trip *n*: **to be on an** ~ gasarsi.
Egypt ['i:dʒipt] *n* Egitto.
Egyptian [ɪ'dʒipʃən] *adj, n* egiziano(a).
eiderdown ['aidədaun] *n* piumino.
eight [eit] *num* otto.
eighteen ['ei'ti:n] *num* diciotto.
eighth [eitθ] *num* ottavo(a).
eighty [eiti] *num* ottanta.
Eire ['ɛərə] *n* Repubblica d'Irlanda.
EIS *n abbr* (= *Educational Institute of Scotland*) *principale sindacato degli insegnanti in Scozia.*
either ['aiðə*] *adj* l'uno(a) o l'altro(a); (*both, each*) ciascuno(a); **on** ~ **side** su ciascun lato ♦ *pron*: ~ **(of them)** (o) l'uno(a) o l'altro(a); **I don't like** ~ non mi piace né l'uno né l'altro ♦ *adv* neanche; **no, I don't** ~ no, neanch'io ♦ *conj*: ~ **good or bad** o buono o cattivo; **I haven't seen** ~ **one or the other** non ho visto né l'uno né l'altro.
ejaculation [idʒækju'leiʃən] *n* (*PHYSIOL*) eiaculazione *f.*
eject [ɪ'dʒɛkt] *vt* espellere; lanciare ♦ *vi* (*pilot*) catapultarsi.
ejector seat [ɪ'dʒɛktə-] *n* sedile *m* eiettabile.
eke [i:k]: **to** ~ **out** *vt* far durare; aumentare.
EKG *n abbr* (*US*) = **electrocardiogram.**
el [ɛl] *n abbr* (*US col*) *see* **elevated railroad.**
elaborate *adj* [ɪ'læbərit] elaborato(a), minuzioso(a) ♦ *vb* [ɪ'læbəreit] *vt* elaborare ♦ *vi* entrare in dettagli.
elapse [ɪ'læps] *vi* trascorrere, passare.
elastic [ɪ'læstik] *adj* elastico(a) ♦ *n* elastico.
elastic band *n* (*BRIT*) elastico.
elasticity [ɪlæs'tisiti] *n* elasticità.
elated [ɪ'leitid] *adj* pieno(a) di gioia.
elation [ɪ'leiʃən] *n* gioia.
elbow ['ɛlbəu] *n* gomito ♦ *vt*: **to** ~ **one's way through the crowd** farsi largo tra la folla a gomitate.
elbow grease *n*: **to use a bit of** ~ usare un po' di olio di gomiti.
elbowroom ['ɛlbəurum] *n* spazio.
elder ['ɛldə*] *adj* maggiore, più vecchio(a) ♦ *n* (*tree*) sambuco; **one's** ~**s** i più anziani.
elderly ['ɛldəli] *adj* anziano(a) ♦ *npl*: **the** ~ gli anziani.
elder statesman *n* anziano uomo politico in pensione, ma ancora influente; (*of company*) anziano/a consigliere/a.

eldest ['ɛldist] *adj, n*: **the** ~ **(child)** il(la) maggiore (dei bambini).
elect [ɪ'lɛkt] *vt* eleggere; (*choose*): **to** ~ **to do** decidere di fare ♦ *adj*: **the president** ~ il presidente designato.
election [ɪ'lɛkʃən] *n* elezione *f*; **to hold an** ~ indire un'elezione.
election campaign *n* campagna elettorale.
electioneering [ɪlɛkʃə'niəriŋ] *n* propaganda elettorale.
elector [ɪ'lɛktə*] *n* elettore/trice.
electoral [ɪ'lɛktərəl] *adj* elettorale.
electoral college *n* collegio elettorale.
electoral roll *n* (*BRIT*) registro elettorale.
electoral system *n* sistema *m* elettorale.
electorate [ɪ'lɛktərit] *n* elettorato.
electric [ɪ'lɛktrik] *adj* elettrico(a).
electrical [ɪ'lɛktrikəl] *adj* elettrico(a).
electrical engineer *n* ingegnere *m* elettrotecnico.
electrical failure *n* guasto all'impianto elettrico.
electric blanket *n* coperta elettrica.
electric chair *n* sedia elettrica.
electric cooker *n* cucina elettrica.
electric current *n* corrente *f* elettrica.
electric fire *n* (*BRIT*) stufa elettrica.
electrician [ɪlɛk'triʃən] *n* elettricista *m.*
electricity [ɪlɛk'trisiti] *n* elettricità; **to switch on/off the** ~ attaccare/staccare la corrente.
electricity board *n* (*BRIT*) ente *m* regionale per l'energia elettrica.
electric light *n* luce *f* elettrica.
electric shock *n* scossa (elettrica).
electrify [ɪ'lɛktrifai] *vt* (*RAIL*) elettrificare; (*audience*) elettrizzare.
electro... [ɪ'lɛktrəu] *prefix* elettro....
electrocardiogram (ECG) [ɪ'lɛktrə-'kɑ:diəgræm] *n* elettrocardiogramma *m.*
electro-convulsive therapy (ECT) [ɪ'lɛktrəkən'vʌlsiv-] *n* elettroshockterapia.
electrocute [ɪ'lɛktrəkju:t] *vt* fulminare.
electrode [ɪ'lɛktrəud] *n* elettrodo.
electroencephalogram (EEG) [ɪ'lɛktrəuen'sɛfələgræm] *n* (*MED*) elettroencefalogramma *m* (EEG).
electrolysis [ɪlɛk'trɔlisis] *n* elettrolisi *f.*
electromagnetic [ɪ'lɛktrəumæg'nɛtik] *n* elettromagnetico(a).
electron [ɪ'lɛktrɔn] *n* elettrone *m.*
electronic [ɪlɛk'trɔnik] *adj* elettronico(a); *see also* **electronics.**
electronic data processing (EDP) *n* elaborazione *f* elettronica di dati.
electronic mail *n* posta elettronica.
electronics [ɪlɛk'trɔniks] *n* elettronica.

electron microscope *n* microscopio elettronico.
electroplated [ɪ'lɛktrəu'pleɪtɪd] *adj* galvanizzato(a).
electrotherapy [ɪ'lɛktrəu'θerəpɪ] *n* elettroterapia.
elegance ['ɛlɪgəns] *n* eleganza.
elegant ['ɛlɪgənt] *adj* elegante.
element ['ɛlɪmənt] *n* elemento; (*of heater, kettle etc*) resistenza.
elementary [ɛlɪ'mɛntərɪ] *adj* elementare.

L'**elementary school**, negli Stati Uniti e in Canada, è un istituto scolastico dove i bambini ricevono un'istruzione per un periodo che va dai 6 agli 8 anni. Negli Stati Uniti si chiama anche **grade school** o **grammar school**.

elephant ['ɛlɪfənt] *n* elefante/essa.
elevate ['ɛlɪveɪt] *vt* elevare.
elevated railroad (el) *n* (*US*) (ferrovia) soprelevata.
elevation [ɛlɪ'veɪʃən] *n* elevazione *f*; (*height*) altitudine *f*.
elevator ['ɛlɪveɪtə*] *n* elevatore *m*; (*US: lift*) ascensore *m*.
eleven [ɪ'lɛvn] *num* undici.
elevenses [ɪ'lɛvnzɪz] *npl* (*BRIT*) caffè *m* a metà mattina.
eleventh [ɪ'lɛvnθ] *adj* undicesimo(a); **at the ~ hour** (*fig*) all'ultimo minuto.
elf, *pl* **elves** [ɛlf, ɛlvz] *n* elfo.
elicit [ɪ'lɪsɪt] *vt*: **to ~ (from)** trarre (da), cavare fuori (da); **to ~ sth (from sb)** strappare qc (a qn).
eligible ['ɛlɪdʒəbl] *adj* eleggibile; (*for membership*) che ha i requisiti; **to be ~ for a pension** essere pensionabile.
eliminate [ɪ'lɪmɪneɪt] *vt* eliminare.
elimination [ɪlɪmɪ'neɪʃən] *n* eliminazione *f*; **by process of ~** per eliminazione.
élite [eɪ'liːt] *n* élite *f inv*.
elitist [eɪ'liːtɪst] *adj* (*pej*) elitario(a).
elixir [ɪ'lɪksə*] *n* elisir *m inv*.
Elizabethan [ɪlɪzə'biːθən] *n* elisabettiano(a).
ellipse [ɪ'lɪps] *n* ellisse *f*.
elliptical [ɪ'lɪptɪkl] *adj* ellittico(a).
elm [ɛlm] *n* olmo.
elocution [ɛlə'kjuːʃən] *n* elocuzione *f*.
elongated ['iːlɔŋgeɪtɪd] *adj* allungato(a).
elope [ɪ'ləup] *vi* (*lovers*) scappare.
elopement [ɪ'ləupmənt] *n* fuga romantica.
eloquence ['ɛləkwəns] *n* eloquenza.
eloquent ['ɛləkwənt] *adj* eloquente.
else [ɛls] *adv* altro; **something ~** qualcos'altro; **somewhere ~** altrove;

everywhere ~ in qualsiasi altro luogo; **where ~?** in quale altro luogo?; **little ~** poco altro; **everyone ~** tutti gli altri; **nothing ~** nient'altro; **or ~** (*otherwise*) altrimenti; **is there anything ~ I can do?** posso fare qualcos'altro?
elsewhere [ɛls'wɛə*] *adv* altrove.
ELT *n abbr* (*SCOL*) = English Language Teaching.
elucidate [ɪ'luːsɪdeɪt] *vt* delucidare.
elude [ɪ'luːd] *vt* eludere.
elusive [ɪ'luːsɪv] *adj* elusivo(a); (*answer*) evasivo(a); **he is very ~** è proprio inafferrabile *or* irraggiungibile.
elves [ɛlvz] *npl of* **elf**.
emaciated [ɪ'meɪsɪeɪtɪd] *adj* emaciato(a).
E-mail, e-mail ['iːmeɪl] *n abbr* (= *electronic mail*) posta elettronica ♦ *vt*: **to ~ sb** comunicare con qn mediante posta elettronica.
emanate ['ɛməneɪt] *vi*: **to ~ from** emanare da.
emancipate [ɪ'mænsɪpeɪt] *vt* emancipare.
emancipation [ɪmænsɪ'peɪʃən] *n* emancipazione *f*.
emasculate [ɪ'mæskjuleɪt] *vt* (*fig*) rendere impotente.
embalm [ɪm'bɑːm] *vt* imbalsamare.
embankment [ɪm'bæŋkmənt] *n* (*of road, railway*) massicciata; (*riverside*) argine *m*; (*dyke*) diga.
embargo [ɪm'bɑːgəu] *n* (*pl ~es*: *COMM, NAUT*) embargo ♦ *vt* mettere l'embargo su; **to put an ~ on sth** mettere l'embargo su qc.
embark [ɪm'bɑːk] *vi*: **to ~ (on)** imbarcarsi (su) ♦ *vt* imbarcare; **to ~ on** (*fig*) imbarcarsi in; (*journey*) intraprendere.
embarkation [ɛmbɑː'keɪʃən] *n* imbarco.
embarkation card *n* carta d'imbarco.
embarrass [ɪm'bærəs] *vt* imbarazzare; **to be ~ed** essere imbarazzato(a).
embarrassing [ɪm'bærəsɪŋ] *adj* imbarazzante.
embarrassment [ɪm'bærəsmənt] *n* imbarazzo.
embassy ['ɛmbəsɪ] *n* ambasciata; **the Italian E~** l'ambasciata d'Italia.
embed [ɪm'bɛd] *vt* conficcare; incastrare.
embellish [ɪm'bɛlɪʃ] *vt* abbellire; **to ~ (with)** (*fig: story, truth*) infiorare (con).
embers ['ɛmbəz] *npl* braci *fpl*.
embezzle [ɪm'bɛzl] *vt* appropriarsi indebitamente di.
embezzlement [ɪm'bɛzlmənt] *n* appropriazione *f* indebita, malversazione *f*.

embezzler [ɪm'bɛzlə*] *n* malversatore/trice.
embitter [ɪm'bɪtə*] *vt* amareggiare; inasprire.
emblem ['ɛmbləm] *n* emblema *m*.
embodiment [ɪm'bɔdɪmənt] *n* personificazione *f*, incarnazione *f*.
embody [ɪm'bɔdɪ] *vt* (*features*) racchiudere, comprendere; (*ideas*) dar forma concreta a, esprimere.
embolden [ɪm'bəuldn] *vt* incitare.
embolism ['ɛmbəlɪzəm] *n* embolia.
embossed [ɪm'bɔst] *adj* in rilievo; goffrato(a); ~ **with** ... con in rilievo ....
embrace [ɪm'breɪs] *vt* abbracciare; (*include*) comprendere ♦ *vi* abbracciarsi ♦ *n* abbraccio.
embroider [ɪm'brɔɪdə*] *vt* ricamare; (*fig: story*) abbellire.
embroidery [ɪm'brɔɪdərɪ] *n* ricamo.
embroil [ɪm'brɔɪl] *vt*: **to become ~ed (in sth)** restare invischiato(a) (in qc).
embryo ['ɛmbrɪəu] *n* (*also fig*) embrione *m*.
emcee [ɛm'siː] *n abbr* = **master of ceremonies**.
emend [ɪ'mɛnd] *vt* (*text*) correggere, emendare.
emerald ['ɛmərəld] *n* smeraldo.
emerge [ɪ'məːdʒ] *vi* apparire, sorgere; **it ~s that** (*BRIT*) risulta che.
emergence [ɪ'məːdʒəns] *n* apparizione *f*; (*of nation*) nascita.
emergency [ɪ'məːdʒənsɪ] *n* emergenza; **in an ~** in caso di emergenza; **to declare a state of ~** dichiarare lo stato di emergenza.
emergency exit *n* uscita di sicurezza.
emergency landing *n* atterraggio forzato.
emergency lane *n* (*US AUT*) corsia d'emergenza.
emergency road service *n* (*US*) servizio riparazioni.
emergency service *n* servizio di pronto intervento.
emergency stop *n* (*BRIT AUT*) frenata improvvisa.
emergent [ɪ'məːdʒənt] *adj*: ~ **nation** paese *m* in via di sviluppo.
emery board ['ɛmərɪ-] *n* limetta di carta smerigliata.
emery paper *n* carta smerigliata.
emetic [ɪ'mɛtɪk] *n* emetico.
emigrant ['ɛmɪgrənt] *n* emigrante *m/f*.
emigrate ['ɛmɪgreɪt] *vi* emigrare.
emigration [ɛmɪ'greɪʃən] *n* emigrazione *f*.
émigré ['ɛmɪgreɪ] *n* emigrato/a.
eminence ['ɛmɪnəns] *n* eminenza.

eminent ['ɛmɪnənt] *adj* eminente.
eminently ['ɛmɪnəntlɪ] *adv* assolutamente, perfettamente.
emirate [ɛ'mɪərɪt] *n* emirato.
emission [ɪ'mɪʃən] *n* (*of gas, radiation*) emissione *f*.
emit [ɪ'mɪt] *vt* emettere.
emolument [ɪ'mɔljumənt] *n* (*often pl: formal*) emolumento.
emotion [ɪ'məuʃən] *n* emozione *f*; (*love, jealousy etc*) sentimento.
emotional [ɪ'məuʃənl] *adj* (*person*) emotivo(a); (*scene*) commovente; (*tone, speech*) carico(a) d'emozione.
emotionally [ɪ'məuʃnəlɪ] *adv* (*behave, be involved*) sentimentalmente; (*speak*) con emozione; ~ **disturbed** con turbe emotive.
emotive [ɪ'məutɪv] *adj* emotivo(a); ~ **power** capacità di commuovere.
empathy ['ɛmpəθɪ] *n* immedesimazione *f*; **to feel ~ with sb** immedesimarsi con i sentimenti di qn.
emperor ['ɛmpərə*] *n* imperatore *m*.
emphasis, *pl* **-ases** ['ɛmfəsɪs, -siːz] *n* enfasi *f inv*; importanza; **to lay** *or* **place ~ on sth** (*fig*) mettere in risalto *or* in evidenza qc; **the ~ is on sport** si dà molta importanza allo sport.
emphasize ['ɛmfəsaɪz] *vt* (*word, point*) sottolineare; (*feature*) mettere in evidenza.
emphatic [ɪm'fætɪk] *adj* (*strong*) vigoroso(a); (*unambiguous, clear*) netto(a); categorico(a).
emphatically [ɪm'fætɪkəlɪ] *adv* vigorosamente; nettamente.
emphysema [ɛmfɪ'siːmə] *n* (*MED*) enfisema *m*.
empire ['ɛmpaɪə*] *n* impero.
empirical [ɛm'pɪrɪkl] *adj* empirico(a).
employ [ɪm'plɔɪ] *vt* (*make use of: thing, method, person*) impiegare, servirsi di; (*give job to*) dare lavoro a, impiegare; **he's ~ed in a bank** lavora in banca.
employee [ɪmplɔɪ'iː] *n* impiegato/a.
employer [ɪm'plɔɪə*] *n* principale *m/f*, datore *m* di lavoro.
employment [ɪm'plɔɪmənt] *n* impiego; **to find ~** trovare impiego *or* lavoro; **without ~** disoccupato(a); **place of ~** posto di lavoro.
employment agency *n* agenzia di collocamento.
employment exchange *n* (*BRIT*) ufficio *m* collocamento *inv*.
empower [ɪm'pauə*] *vt*: **to ~ sb to do** concedere autorità a qn di fare.

empress ['ɛmprɪs] n imperatrice f.

emptiness ['ɛmptɪnɪs] n vuoto.

empty ['ɛmptɪ] adj vuoto(a); (street, area) deserto(a); (threat, promise) vano(a) ♦ n (bottle) vuoto ♦ vt vuotare ♦ vi vuotarsi; (liquid) scaricarsi; **on an ~ stomach** a stomaco vuoto; **to ~ into** (river) gettarsi in.

empty-handed [ɛmptɪ'hændɪd] adj a mani vuote.

empty-headed [ɛmptɪ'hɛdɪd] adj sciocco(a).

EMS n abbr (= European Monetary System) S.M.E. m.

EMT n abbr = emergency medical technician.

EMU n abbr (= European Monetary Union) Unità f monetaria europea.

emulate ['ɛmjuleɪt] vt emulare.

emulsion [ɪ'mʌlʃən] n emulsione f; (also: ~ paint) colore m a tempera.

enable [ɪ'neɪbl] vt: **to ~ sb to do** permettere a qn di fare.

enact [ɪn'ækt] vt (law) emanare; (play, scene) rappresentare.

enamel [ɪ'næməl] n smalto.

enamel paint n vernice f a smalto.

enamoured [ɪ'næməd] adj: **~ of** innamorato(a) di.

encampment [ɪn'kæmpmənt] n accampamento.

encased [ɪn'keɪst] adj: **~ in** racchiuso(a) in; rivestito(a) di.

enchant [ɪn'tʃɑːnt] vt incantare; (subj: magic spell) catturare.

enchanting [ɪn'tʃɑːntɪŋ] adj incantevole, affascinante.

encircle [ɪn'sɜːkl] vt accerchiare.

enc(l). abbr (on letters etc: = enclosed, enclosure) all., alleg.

enclose [ɪn'kləʊz] vt (land) circondare, recingere; (letter etc): **to ~ (with)** allegare (con); **please find ~d** trovi qui accluso.

enclosure [ɪn'kləʊʒə*] n recinto; (COMM) allegato.

encoder [ɪn'kəʊdə*] n (COMPUT) codificatore m.

encompass [ɪn'kʌmpəs] vt comprendere.

encore [ɔŋ'kɔː*] excl, n bis (m inv).

encounter [ɪn'kaʊntə*] n incontro ♦ vt incontrare.

encourage [ɪn'kʌrɪdʒ] vt incoraggiare; (industry, growth etc) favorire; **to ~ sb to do sth** incoraggiare qn a fare qc.

encouragement [ɪn'kʌrɪdʒmənt] n incoraggiamento.

encouraging [ɪn'kʌrɪdʒɪŋ] adj incoraggiante.

encroach [ɪn'krəʊtʃ] vi: **to ~ (up)on** (rights)

usurpare; (time) abusare di; (land) oltrepassare i limiti di.

encrusted [ɪn'krʌstɪd] adj: **~ with** incrostato(a) di.

encumbered [ɪn'kʌmbəd] adj: **to be ~ (with)** essere carico(a) di.

encyclop(a)edia [ɛnsaɪkləu'piːdɪə] n enciclopedia.

end [ɛnd] n fine f; (aim) fine m; (of table) bordo estremo; (of line, rope etc) estremità f inv; (of pointed object) punta; (of town) parte f ♦ vt finire; (also: **bring to an ~, put an ~ to**) mettere fine a ♦ vi finire; **from ~ to ~** da un'estremità all'altra; **to come to an ~** arrivare alla fine, finire; **to be at an ~** essere finito; **in the ~** alla fine; **at the ~ of the street** in fondo alla strada; **at the ~ of the day** (BRIT fig) in fin dei conti; **on ~** (object) ritto(a); **to stand on ~** (hair) rizzarsi; **for 5 hours on ~** per 5 ore di fila; **for hours on ~** per ore e ore; **to this ~, with this ~ in view** a questo fine; **to ~ (with)** concludere (con).

▶**end up** vi: **to ~ up in** finire in.

endanger [ɪn'deɪndʒə*] vt mettere in pericolo; **an ~ed species** una specie in via di estinzione.

endear [ɪn'dɪə*] vt: **to ~ o.s. to sb** accattivarsi le simpatie di qn.

endearing [ɪn'dɪərɪŋ] adj accattivante.

endearment [ɪn'dɪəmənt] n: **to whisper ~s** sussurrare tenerezze; **term of ~** vezzeggiativo, parola affettuosa.

endeavour, (US) **endeavor** [ɪn'dɛvə*] n sforzo, tentativo ♦ vi: **to ~ to do** cercare or sforzarsi di fare.

endemic [ɛn'dɛmɪk] adj endemico(a).

ending ['ɛndɪŋ] n fine f, conclusione f; (LING) desinenza.

endive ['ɛndaɪv] n (curly) indivia (riccia); (smooth, flat) indivia belga.

endless ['ɛndlɪs] adj senza fine; (patience, resources) infinito(a); (possibilities) illimitato(a).

endorse [ɪn'dɔːs] vt (cheque) girare; (approve) approvare, appoggiare.

endorsee [ɪndɔː'siː] n giratario/a.

endorsement [ɪn'dɔːsmənt] n (approval) approvazione f; (signature) firma; (BRIT: on driving licence) contravvenzione registrata sulla patente.

endorser [ɪn'dɔːsə*] n girante m/f.

endow [ɪn'dau] vt (prize) istituire; (hospital) fondare; (provide with money) devolvere denaro a; (equip): **to ~ with** fornire di, dotare di.

endowment [ɪn'daumənt] n istituzione f;

fondazione *f*; (*amount*) donazione *f*.
endowment mortgage *n mutuo che viene ripagato sotto forma di un'assicurazione a vita.*
endowment policy *n* polizza-vita mista.
end product *n* (*INDUSTRY*) prodotto finito; (*fig*) risultato.
end result *n* risultato finale.
endurable [ɪn'djuərəbl] *adj* sopportabile.
endurance [ɪn'djuərəns] *n* resistenza; pazienza.
endurance test *n* prova di resistenza.
endure [ɪn'djuə*] *vt* sopportare, resistere a ♦ *vi* durare.
enduring [ɪn'djuərɪŋ] *adj* duraturo(a).
end user *n* (*COMPUT*) consumatore(trice) effettivo(a).
enema ['enɪmə] *n* (*MED*) clistere *m*.
enemy ['enəmɪ] *adj*, *n* nemico(a); **to make an ~ of sb** inimicarsi qn.
energetic [enə'dʒetɪk] *adj* energico(a); attivo(a).
energy ['enədʒɪ] *n* energia; **Department of E~** Ministero dell'Energia.
energy crisis *n* crisi *f* energetica.
energy-saving ['enədʒɪ'seɪvɪŋ] *adj* (*policy*) del risparmio energetico; (*device*) che risparmia energia.
enervating ['enə:veɪtɪŋ] *adj* debilitante.
enforce [ɪn'fɔːs] *vt* (*LAW*) applicare, far osservare.
enforced [ɪn'fɔːst] *adj* forzato(a).
enfranchise [ɪn'fræntʃaɪz] *vt* (*give vote to*) concedere il diritto di voto a; (*set free*) affrancare.
engage [ɪn'geɪdʒ] *vt* (*hire*) assumere; (*lawyer*) incaricare; (*attention, interest*) assorbire; (*MIL*) attaccare; (*TECH*): **to ~ gear/the clutch** innestare la marcia/la frizione ♦ *vi* (*TECH*) ingranare; **to ~ in** impegnarsi in; **he is ~d in research/a survey** si occupa di ricerca/di un'inchiesta; **to ~ sb in conversation** attaccare conversazione con qn.
engaged [ɪn'geɪdʒd] *adj* (*BRIT: busy, in use*) occupato(a); (*betrothed*) fidanzato(a); **to get ~** fidanzarsi.
engaged tone *n* (*BRIT TEL*) segnale *m* di occupato.
engagement [ɪn'geɪdʒmənt] *n* impegno, obbligo; appuntamento; (*to marry*) fidanzamento; (*MIL*) combattimento; **I have a previous ~** ho già un impegno.
engagement ring *n* anello di fidanzamento.
engaging [ɪn'geɪdʒɪŋ] *adj* attraente.
engender [ɪn'dʒendə*] *vt* produrre, causare.

engine ['endʒɪn] *n* (*AUT*) motore *m*; (*RAIL*) locomotiva.
engine driver *n* (*BRIT: of train*) macchinista *m*.
engineer [endʒɪ'nɪə*] *n* ingegnere *m*; (*BRIT: for domestic appliances*) tecnico; (*US RAIL*) macchinista *m*; **civil/mechanical ~** ingegnere civile/meccanico.
engineering [endʒɪ'nɪərɪŋ] *n* ingegneria ♦ *cpd* (*works, factory, worker etc*) metalmeccanico(a).
engine failure *n* guasto al motore.
engine trouble *n* panne *f*.
England ['ɪŋglənd] *n* Inghilterra.
English ['ɪŋglɪʃ] *adj* inglese ♦ *n* (*LING*) inglese *m*; **the ~** *npl* gli Inglesi; **to be an ~ speaker** essere anglofono(a).
English Channel *n*: **the ~** il Canale della Manica.
Englishman ['ɪŋglɪʃmən], **Englishwoman** ['ɪŋglɪʃwumən] *n* inglese *m/f*.
English-speaking ['ɪŋglɪʃ'spiːkɪŋ] *adj* di lingua inglese.
engrave [ɪn'greɪv] *vt* incidere.
engraving [ɪn'greɪvɪŋ] *n* incisione *f*.
engrossed [ɪn'grəust] *adj*: **~ in** assorbito(a) da, preso(a) da.
engulf [ɪn'gʌlf] *vt* inghiottire.
enhance [ɪn'hɑːns] *vt* accrescere; (*position, reputation*) migliorare.
enigma [ɪ'nɪgmə] *n* enigma *m*.
enigmatic [enɪg'mætɪk] *adj* enigmatico(a).
enjoy [ɪn'dʒɔɪ] *vt* godere; (*have: success, fortune*) avere; (*have benefit of: health*) godere (di); **I ~ dancing** mi piace ballare; **to ~ o.s.** godersela, divertirsi.
enjoyable [ɪn'dʒɔɪəbl] *adj* piacevole.
enjoyment [ɪn'dʒɔɪmənt] *n* piacere *m*, godimento.
enlarge [ɪn'lɑːdʒ] *vt* ingrandire ♦ *vi*: **to ~ on** (*subject*) dilungarsi su.
enlarged [ɪn'lɑːdʒd] *adj* (*edition*) ampliato(a); (*MED: organ, gland*) ingrossato(a).
enlargement [ɪn'lɑːdʒmənt] *n* (*PHOT*) ingrandimento.
enlighten [ɪn'laɪtn] *vt* illuminare; dare chiarimenti a.
enlightened [ɪn'laɪtnd] *adj* illuminato(a).
enlightening [ɪn'laɪtnɪŋ] *adj* istruttivo(a).
enlightenment [ɪn'laɪtnmənt] *n* progresso culturale; chiarimenti *mpl*; (*HISTORY*): **the E~** l'Illuminismo.
enlist [ɪn'lɪst] *vt* arruolare; (*support*) procurare ♦ *vi* arruolarsi; **~ed man** (*US MIL*) soldato semplice.
enliven [ɪn'laɪvn] *vt* (*people*) rallegrare; (*events*) ravvivare.

enmity ['ɛnmɪtɪ] n inimicizia.
ennoble [ɪ'nəubl] vt nobilitare; (with title) conferire un titolo nobiliare a.
enormity [ɪ'nɔːmɪtɪ] n enormità f inv.
enormous [ɪ'nɔːməs] adj enorme.
enormously [ɪ'nɔːməslɪ] adv enormemente.
enough [ɪ'nʌf] adj, n: ~ **time/books** assai tempo/libri; **have you got ~?** ne ha abbastanza or a sufficienza? ♦ adv: **big ~** abbastanza grande; **he has not worked ~** non ha lavorato abbastanza; **~! basta!;** **it's hot ~ (as it is)!** fa abbastanza caldo così!; **will £5 be ~?** bastano 5 sterline?; **that's ~** basta; **I've had ~!** non ne posso più!; **he was kind ~ to lend me the money** è stato così gentile da prestarmi i soldi; **... which, funnily ~** ... che, strano a dirsi.
enquire [ɪn'kwaɪə*] vt, vi = **inquire.**
enrage [ɪn'reɪdʒ] vt fare arrabbiare.
enrich [ɪn'rɪtʃ] vt arricchire.
enrol, (US) enroll [ɪn'rəul] vt iscrivere; (at university) immatricolare ♦ vi iscriversi.
enrol(l)ment [ɪn'rəulmənt] n iscrizione f.
en route [ɔn'ruːt] adv: ~ **for/from/to** in viaggio per/da/a.
ensconced [ɪn'skɔnst] adj: ~ **in** ben sistemato(a) in.
ensemble [ɑ̃ːn'sɑ̃ːmbl] n (MUS) ensemble m inv.
enshrine [ɪn'ʃraɪn] vt conservare come una reliquia.
ensign n (NAUT) ['ɛnsən] bandiera; (MIL) ['ɛnsaɪn] portabandiera m inv.
enslave [ɪn'sleɪv] vt fare schiavo.
ensue [ɪn'sjuː] vi seguire, risultare.
ensure [ɪn'ʃuə*] vt assicurare; garantire; **to ~ that** assicurarsi che.
ENT n abbr (MED: = Ear, Nose & Throat) O.R.L.
entail [ɪn'teɪl] vt comportare.
entangle [ɪn'tæŋgl] vt (thread etc) impigliare; **to become ~d in sth** (fig) rimanere impegolato in qc.
enter ['ɛntə*] vt (gen) entrare in; (club) associarsi a; (profession) intraprendere; (army) arruolarsi in; (competition) partecipare a; (sb for a competition) iscrivere; (write down) registrare; (COMPUT: data) introdurre, inserire ♦ vi entrare.
▶**enter for** vt fus iscriversi a.
▶**enter into** vt fus (explanation) cominciare a dare; (debate) partecipare a; (agreement) concludere; (negotiations) prendere parte a.
▶**enter (up)on** vt fus cominciare.
enteritis [ɛntə'raɪtɪs] n enterite f.
enterprise ['ɛntəpraɪz] n (undertaking,

company) impresa; (spirit) iniziativa.
enterprising ['ɛntəpraɪzɪŋ] adj intraprendente.
entertain [ɛntə'teɪn] vt divertire; (invite) ricevere; (idea, plan) nutrire.
entertainer [ɛntə'teɪnə*] n comico/a.
entertaining [ɛntə'teɪnɪŋ] adj divertente ♦ n: **to do a lot of ~** avere molti ospiti.
entertainment [ɛntə'teɪnmənt] n (amusement) divertimento; (show) spettacolo.
entertainment allowance n spese fpl di rappresentanza.
enthral [ɪn'θrɔːl] vt affascinare, avvincere.
enthralled [ɪn'θrɔːld] adj affascinato(a).
enthralling [ɪn'θrɔːlɪŋ] adj avvincente.
enthuse [ɪn'θuːz] vi: **to ~ (about or over)** entusiasmarsi (per).
enthusiasm [ɪn'θuːzɪæzəm] n entusiasmo.
enthusiast [ɪn'θuːzɪæst] n entusiasta m/f; **a jazz etc ~** un appassionato di jazz etc.
enthusiastic [ɪnθuːzɪ'æstɪk] adj entusiasta, entusiastico(a); **to be ~ about sth/sb** essere appassionato di qc/entusiasta di qn.
entice [ɪn'taɪs] vt allettare, sedurre.
enticing [ɪn'taɪsɪŋ] adj allettante.
entire [ɪn'taɪə*] adj intero(a).
entirely [ɪn'taɪəlɪ] adv completamente, interamente.
entirety [ɪn'taɪərətɪ] n: **in its ~** nel suo complesso.
entitle [ɪn'taɪtl] vt (give right): **to ~ sb to sth/to do** dare diritto a qn a qc/a fare.
entitled [ɪn'taɪtld] adj (book) che si intitola; **to be ~ to sth/to do sth** avere diritto a qc/a fare qc.
entity ['ɛntɪtɪ] n entità f inv.
entrails ['ɛntreɪlz] npl interiora fpl.
entrance n ['ɛntrns] entrata, ingresso; (of person) entrata ♦ vt [ɪn'trɑːns] incantare, rapire; **to gain ~ to** (university etc) essere ammesso a.
entrance examination n (to school) esame m di ammissione.
entrance fee n tassa d'iscrizione; (to museum etc) prezzo d'ingresso.
entrance ramp n (US AUT) rampa di accesso.
entrancing [ɪn'trɑːnsɪŋ] adj incantevole.
entrant ['ɛntrnt] n partecipante m/f; concorrente m/f; (BRIT: in exam) candidato/a.
entreat [ɛn'triːt] vt supplicare.
entreaty [ɪn'triːtɪ] n supplica, preghiera.
entrée ['ɔntreɪ] n (CULIN) prima portata.
entrenched [ɛn'trɛntʃt] adj radicato(a).
entrepreneur ['ɔntrəprə'nəː*] n

imprenditore *m*.
entrepreneurial [ˈɔntrəprəˈnəːrɪəl] *adj*
imprenditoriale.
entrust [ɪnˈtrʌst] *vt*: **to ~ sth to** affidare qc
a.
entry [ˈɛntrɪ] *n* entrata; (*way in*) entrata,
ingresso; (*in dictionary*) voce *f*; (*in diary,
ship's log*) annotazione *f*; (*in account book,
ledger, list*) registrazione *f*; **"no ~"**
"vietato l'ingresso"; (*AUT*) "divieto di
accesso"; **single/double ~ book-keeping**
partita semplice/doppia.
entry form *n* modulo d'iscrizione.
entry phone *n* (*BRIT*) citofono.
entwine [ɪnˈtwaɪn] *vt* intrecciare.
E number *n sigla di additivo alimentare*.
enumerate [ɪˈnjuːməreɪt] *vt* enumerare.
enunciate [ɪˈnʌnsɪeɪt] *vt* enunciare;
pronunciare.
envelop [ɪnˈvɛləp] *vt* avvolgere,
avviluppare.
envelope [ˈɛnvələup] *n* busta.
enviable [ˈɛnvɪəbl] *adj* invidiabile.
envious [ˈɛnvɪəs] *adj* invidioso(a).
environment [ɪnˈvaɪərənmənt] *n* ambiente
m; **Department of the E~** (*BRIT*) ≈
Ministero dell'Ambiente.
environmental [ɪnvaɪərənˈmɛntl] *adj*
ecologico(a); ambientale; **~ studies** (*in
school etc*) ecologia.
environmentalist [ɪnˈvaɪərənˈmɛntəlɪst] *n*
studioso/a della protezione
dell'ambiente.
environmentally [ɪnvaɪərənˈmɛntəlɪ] *adv*: **~
sound/friendly** che rispetta l'ambiente.
**Environmental Protection Agency
(EPA)** *n* (*US*) ≈ Ministero dell'Ambiente.
envisage [ɪnˈvɪzɪdʒ] *vt* immaginare;
prevedere.
envision [ɪnˈvɪʒən] *vt* concepire,
prevedere.
envoy [ˈɛnvɔɪ] *n* inviato/a.
envy [ˈɛnvɪ] *n* invidia ♦ *vt* invidiare; **to ~ sb
sth** invidiare qn per qc.
enzyme [ˈɛnzaɪm] *n* enzima *m*.
EPA *n abbr* (*US*) *see* **Environmental
Protection Agency**.
ephemeral [ɪˈfɛmərəl] *adj* effimero(a).
epic [ˈɛpɪk] *n* poema *m* epico ♦ *adj* epico(a).
epicentre, (*US*) **epicenter** [ˈɛpɪsɛntə*] *n*
epicentro.
epidemic [ɛpɪˈdɛmɪk] *n* epidemia.
epilepsy [ˈɛpɪlɛpsɪ] *n* epilessia.
epileptic [ɛpɪˈlɛptɪk] *adj, n* epilettico(a).
epilogue [ˈɛpɪlɔg] *n* epilogo.
Epiphany [ɪˈpɪfənɪ] *n* Epifania.
episcopal [ɪˈpɪskəpəl] *adj* episcopale.
episode [ˈɛpɪsəud] *n* episodio.

epistle [ɪˈpɪsl] *n* epistola.
epitaph [ˈɛpɪtɑːf] *n* epitaffio.
epithet [ˈɛpɪθɛt] *n* epiteto.
epitome [ɪˈpɪtəmɪ] *n* epitome *f*;
quintessenza.
epitomize [ɪˈpɪtəmaɪz] *vt* (*fig*) incarnare.
epoch [ˈiːpɔk] *n* epoca.
epoch-making [ˈiːpɔkmeɪkɪŋ] *adj* che fa
epoca.
eponymous [ɪˈpɔnɪməs] *adj* dello stesso
nome.
equable [ˈɛkwəbl] *adj* uniforme; (*climate*)
costante; (*character*) equilibrato(a).
equal [ˈiːkwl] *adj, n* uguale (*m/f*) ♦ *vt*
uguagliare; **~ to** (*task*) all'altezza di.
equality [iːˈkwɔlɪtɪ] *n* uguaglianza.
equalize [ˈiːkwəlaɪz] *vt, vi* pareggiare.
equalizer [ˈiːkwəlaɪzə*] *n* punto del
pareggio.
equally [ˈiːkwəlɪ] *adv* ugualmente; **they are
~ clever** sono intelligenti allo stesso
modo.
Equal Opportunities Commission, (*US*)
**Equal Employment Opportunity
Commission** *n commissione contro
discriminazioni sessuali o razziali nel
mondo del lavoro*.
equal(s) sign *n* segno d'uguaglianza.
equanimity [ɛkwəˈnɪmɪtɪ] *n* serenità.
equate [ɪˈkweɪt] *vt*: **to ~ sth with**
considerare qc uguale a; (*compare*)
paragonare qc con; **to ~ A to B** mettere
in equazione A e B.
equation [ɪˈkweɪʃən] *n* (*MATH*) equazione *f*.
equator [ɪˈkweɪtə*] *n* equatore *m*.
Equatorial Guinea [ɛkwəˈtɔːrɪəl-] *n* Guinea
Equatoriale.
equestrian [ɪˈkwɛstrɪən] *adj* equestre ♦ *n*
cavaliere/amazzone.
equilibrium [iːkwɪˈlɪbrɪəm] *n* equilibrio.
equinox [ˈiːkwɪnɔks] *n* equinozio.
equip [ɪˈkwɪp] *vt* equipaggiare, attrezzare;
to ~ sb/sth with fornire qn/qc di; **~ped
with** (*machinery etc*) dotato(a) di; **he is
well ~ped for the job** ha i requisiti
necessari per quel lavoro.
equipment [ɪˈkwɪpmənt] *n* attrezzatura;
(*electrical etc*) apparecchiatura.
equitable [ˈɛkwɪtəbl] *adj* equo(a), giusto(a).
equities [ˈɛkwɪtɪz] *npl* (*BRIT COMM*) azioni *fpl*
ordinarie.
equity [ˈɛkwɪtɪ] *n* equità.
equity capital *n* capitale *m* azionario.
equivalent [ɪˈkwɪvələnt] *adj, n* equivalente
(*m*); **to be ~ to** equivalere a.
equivocal [ɪˈkwɪvəkl] *adj* equivoco(a); (*open
to suspicion*) dubbio(a).
equivocate [ɪˈkwɪvəkeɪt] *vi* esprimersi in

modo equivoco.

equivocation [ɪkwɪvəˈkeɪʃən] *n* parole *fpl* equivoche.

ER *abbr* (*BRIT*) = *Elizabeth Regina*.

ERA *n abbr* (*US POL*) = *Equal Rights Amendment*.

era [ˈɪərə] *n* era, età *f inv*.

eradicate [ɪˈrædɪkeɪt] *vt* sradicare.

erase [ɪˈreɪz] *vt* cancellare.

eraser [ɪˈreɪzə*] *n* gomma.

erect [ɪˈrɛkt] *adj* eretto(a) ♦ *vt* costruire; (*monument, tent*) alzare.

erection [ɪˈrɛkʃən] *n* (*also PHYSIOL*) erezione *f*; (*of building*) costruzione *f*; (*of machinery*) montaggio.

ergonomics [əːgəˈnɔmɪks] *n* ergonomia.

ERISA *n abbr* (*US*: = *Employee Retirement Income Security Act*) *legge relativa al pensionamento statale*.

Eritrea [ɛrɪˈtreɪə] *n* Eritrea.

ERM *n abbr* (= *Exchange Rate Mechanism*) meccanismo dei tassi di cambio.

ermine [ˈəːmɪn] *n* ermellino.

ERNIE [ˈəːnɪ] *n abbr* (*BRIT*: = *Electronic Random Number Indicator Equipment*) *sistema che seleziona i numeri vincenti di buoni del Tesoro*.

erode [ɪˈrəud] *vt* erodere; (*metal*) corrodere.

erogenous zone [ɪˈrɔdʒənəs-] *n* zona erogena.

erosion [ɪˈrəuʒən] *n* erosione *f*.

erotic [ɪˈrɔtɪk] *adj* erotico(a).

eroticism [ɪˈrɔtɪsɪzəm] *n* erotismo.

err [əː*] *vi* errare; (*REL*) peccare.

errand [ˈɛrənd] *n* commissione *f*; **to run ~s** fare commissioni; **~ of mercy** atto di carità.

errand boy *n* fattorino.

erratic [ɪˈrætɪk] *adj* imprevedibile; (*person, mood*) incostante.

erroneous [ɪˈrəunɪəs] *adj* erroneo(a).

error [ˈɛrə*] *n* errore *m*; **typing/spelling ~** errore di battitura/di ortografia; **in ~** per errore; **~s and omissions excepted** salvo errori ed omissioni.

error message *n* (*COMPUT*) messaggio di errore.

erstwhile [ˈəːstwaɪl] *adv* allora, un tempo ♦ *adj* di allora.

erudite [ˈɛrjudaɪt] *adj* erudito(a).

erupt [ɪˈrʌpt] *vi* erompere; (*volcano*) mettersi (*or* essere) in eruzione.

eruption [ɪˈrʌpʃən] *n* eruzione *f*; (*of anger, violence*) esplosione *f*.

ESA *n abbr* (= *European Space Agency*) ESA *f*.

escalate [ˈɛskəleɪt] *vi* intensificarsi; (*costs*) salire.

escalation [ɛskəˈleɪʃən] *n* escalation *f*; (*of prices*) aumento.

escalation clause *n* clausola di revisione.

escalator [ˈɛskəleɪtə*] *n* scala mobile.

escapade [ɛskəˈpeɪd] *n* scappatella; avventura.

escape [ɪˈskeɪp] *n* evasione *f*; fuga; (*of gas etc*) fuga, fuoriuscita ♦ *vi* fuggire; (*from jail*) evadere, scappare; (*fig*) sfuggire; (*leak*) uscire ♦ *vt* sfuggire a; **to ~ from sb** sfuggire a qn; **to ~ to** (*another place*) fuggire in; (*freedom, safety*) fuggire verso; **to ~ notice** passare inosservato(a).

escape artist *n* mago della fuga.

escape clause *n* clausola scappatoia.

escapee [ɪskeɪˈpiː] *n* evaso/a.

escape hatch *n* (*in submarine, space rocket*) portello di sicurezza.

escape key *n* (*COMPUT*) tasto di escape, tasto per cambio di codice.

escape route *n* percorso della fuga.

escapism [ɪsˈkeɪpɪzəm] *n* evasione *f* (dalla realtà).

escapist [ɪsˈkeɪpɪst] *adj* d'evasione ♦ *n* persona che cerca di evadere dalla realtà.

escapologist [ɛskəˈpɔlədʒɪst] *n* (*BRIT*) = **escape artist**.

escarpment [ɪsˈkɑːpmənt] *n* scarpata.

eschew [ɪsˈtʃuː] *vt* evitare.

escort *n* [ˈɛskɔːt] scorta; (*to dance etc*): **her ~** il suo cavaliere; **his ~** la sua dama ♦ *vt* [ɪsˈkɔːt] scortare; accompagnare.

escort agency *n* agenzia di hostess.

Eskimo [ˈɛskɪməu] *adj* eschimese ♦ *n* eschimese *m/f*; (*LING*) eschimese *m*.

ESL *n abbr* (*SCOL*) = *English as a Second Language*.

esophagus [iːˈsɔfəgəs] *n* (*US*) = **oesophagus**.

esoteric [ɛsəuˈtɛrɪk] *adj* esoterico(a).

ESP *n abbr see* **extrasensory perception**; (*SCOL*) = *English for Special Purposes*.

esp. *abbr* (= *especially*) spec.

especially [ɪˈspɛʃlɪ] *adv* specialmente; (*above all*) soprattutto; (*specifically*) espressamente; (*particularly*) particolarmente.

espionage [ˈɛspɪɑːnɑːʒ] *n* spionaggio.

esplanade [ɛspləˈneɪd] *n* lungomare *m*.

espouse [ɪˈspauz] *vt* abbracciare.

Esquire [ɪˈskwaɪə*] *n* (*BRIT*: *abbr* **Esq.**): **J. Brown, ~** Signor J. Brown.

essay [ˈɛseɪ] *n* (*SCOL*) composizione *f*; (*LITERATURE*) saggio.

essence [ˈɛsns] *n* essenza; **in ~** in sostanza;

speed is of the ~ la velocità è di estrema importanza.
essential [ɪ'sɛnʃəl] *adj* essenziale; (*basic*) fondamentale ♦ *n* elemento essenziale; **it is** ~ **that** è essenziale che + *sub*.
essentially [ɪ'sɛnʃəlɪ] *adv* essenzialmente.
EST *abbr* (*US*: = *Eastern Standard Time*) *fuso orario*.
est. *abbr* = *established*; *estimate(d)*.
establish [ɪ'stæblɪʃ] *vt* stabilire; (*business*) mettere su; (*one's power etc*) confermare; (*prove: fact, identity, sb's innocence*) dimostrare.
establishment [ɪs'tæblɪʃmənt] *n* stabilimento; (*business*) azienda; **the E~** la classe dirigente; l'establishment *m*; **a teaching** ~ un istituto d'istruzione.
estate [ɪ'steɪt] *n* proprietà *f inv*; (*LAW*) beni *mpl*, patrimonio; (*BRIT: also:* **housing** ~) complesso edilizio.
estate agency *n* (*BRIT*) agenzia immobiliare.
estate agent *n* (*BRIT*) agente *m* immobiliare.
estate car *n* (*BRIT*) giardiniera.
esteem [ɪ'stiːm] *n* stima ♦ *vt* considerare; stimare; **I hold him in high** ~ gode di tutta la mia stima.
esthetic [ɪs'θɛtɪk] *adj* (*US*) = **aesthetic**.
estimate *n* ['ɛstɪmət] stima; (*COMM*) preventivo ♦ *vt* ['ɛstɪmeɪt] *vt* stimare, valutare ♦ *vi* (*BRIT COMM*): **to** ~ **for** fare il preventivo per; **to give sb an** ~ **of** fare a qn una valutazione approssimativa (*or* un preventivo) di; **at a rough** ~ approssimativamente.
estimation [ɛstɪ'meɪʃən] *n* stima; opinione *f*; **in my** ~ a mio giudizio, a mio avviso.
Estonia [ɛ'stəʊnɪə] *n* Estonia.
Estonian [ɛ'stəʊnɪən] *adj* estone *inv* ♦ *n* estone *m/f*; (*LING*) estone *m*.
estranged [ɪ'streɪndʒd] *adj* separato(a).
estrangement [ɪs'treɪndʒmənt] *n* alienazione *f*.
estrogen ['iːstrəʊdʒən] *n* (*US*) = **oestrogen**.
estuary ['ɛstjʊərɪ] *n* estuario.
ET *abbr* (*US*: = *Eastern Time*) *fuso orario*; (*BRIT*: = *Employment Training*) *corso di formazione professionale per disoccupati*.
ETA *n abbr* (= *estimated time of arrival*) ora di arrivo prevista.
et al. *abbr* (= *et alii: and others*) ed altri.
etc. *abbr* (= *et cetera*) ecc., etc.
etch [ɛtʃ] *vt* incidere all'acquaforte.
etching ['ɛtʃɪŋ] *n* acquaforte *f*.
ETD *n abbr* (= *estimated time of departure*) ora di partenza prevista.

eternal [ɪ'təːnl] *adj* eterno(a).
eternity [ɪ'təːnɪtɪ] *n* eternità.
ether ['iːθə*] *n* etere *m*.
ethereal [ɪ'θɪərɪəl] *adj* etereo(a).
ethical ['ɛθɪkl] *adj* etico(a), morale.
ethics ['ɛθɪks] *n* etica ♦ *npl* morale *f*.
Ethiopia [iːθɪ'əʊpɪə] *n* Etiopia.
Ethiopian [iːθɪ'əʊpɪən] *adj, n* etiope (*m/f*).
ethnic ['ɛθnɪk] *adj* etnico(a).
ethnic cleansing [-'klɛnzɪŋ] *n* pulizia etnica.
ethnology [ɛθ'nɔlədʒɪ] *n* etnologia.
ethos ['iːθɔs] *n* (*of culture, group*) norma di vita.
etiquette ['ɛtɪkɛt] *n* etichetta.
ETV *n abbr* (*US*) = *Educational Television*.
etymology [ɛtɪ'mɔlədʒɪ] *n* etimologia.
EU *n abbr* (= *European Union*) UE *f*.
eucalyptus [juːkə'lɪptəs] *n* eucalipto.
eulogy ['juːlədʒɪ] *n* elogio.
euphemism ['juːfəmɪzəm] *n* eufemismo.
euphemistic [juːfə'mɪstɪk] *adj* eufemistico(a).
euphoria [juː'fɔːrɪə] *n* euforia.
Eurasia [juə'reɪʃə] *n* Eurasia.
Eurasian [juə'reɪʃən] *adj, n* eurasiano(a).
Euratom [juə'rætəm] *n abbr* (= *European Atomic Energy Community*) EURATOM *f*.
Euro- ['juərəʊ] *prefix* euro-.
Eurocheque ['juərəʊtʃɛk] *n* eurochèque *m inv*.
Eurocrat ['juərəʊkræt] *n* eurocrate *m/f*.
Eurodollar ['juərəʊdɔlə*] *n* eurodollaro.
Europe ['juərəp] *n* Europa.
European [juərə'piːən] *adj, n* europeo(a).
European Court of Justice *n* Corte *f* di Giustizia della Comunità Europea.
Euro-sceptic ['juərəʊskɛptɪk] *n* euroscettico/a.
euthanasia [juːθə'neɪzɪə] *n* eutanasia.
evacuate [ɪ'vækjueɪt] *vt* evacuare.
evacuation [ɪvækju'eɪʃən] *n* evacuazione *f*.
evacuee [ɪvækju'iː] *n* sfollato/a.
evade [ɪ'veɪd] *vt* eludere; (*duties etc*) sottrarsi a.
evaluate [ɪ'væljueɪt] *vt* valutare.
evangelist [ɪ'vændʒəlɪst] *n* evangelista *m*.
evangelize [ɪ'vændʒəlaɪz] *vt* evangelizzare.
evaporate [ɪ'væpəreɪt] *vi* evaporare ♦ *vt* far evaporare.
evaporated milk *n* latte *m* concentrato.
evaporation [ɪvæpə'reɪʃən] *n* evaporazione *f*.
evasion [ɪ'veɪʒən] *n* evasione *f*.
evasive [ɪ'veɪsɪv] *adj* evasivo(a).
eve [iːv] *n*: **on the** ~ **of** alla vigilia di.
even ['iːvn] *adj* regolare; (*number*) pari *inv* ♦ *adv* anche, perfino; ~ **if**, ~ **though** anche

se; ~ **more** ancora di più; **he loves her ~ more** la ama anche di più; ~ **faster** ancora più veloce; ~ **so** ciò nonostante; **not ~ ...** nemmeno ...; **to break ~** finire in pari *or* alla pari; **to get ~ with sb** dare la pari a qn.

▶**even out** *vi* pareggiare.

even-handed ['i:vn'hændɪd] *adj* imparziale, equo(a).

evening ['i:vnɪŋ] *n* sera; (*as duration, event*) serata; **in the ~** la sera; **this ~** stasera, questa sera; **tomorrow/yesterday ~** domani/ieri sera.

evening class *n* corso serale.

evening dress *n* (*woman's*) abito da sera; **in ~** (*man*) in abito scuro; (*woman*) in abito lungo.

evenly ['i:vənlɪ] *adv* (*distribute, space, spread*) uniformemente; (*divide*) in parti uguali.

evensong ['i:vnsɔŋ] *n* ≈ vespro.

event [ɪ'vɛnt] *n* avvenimento; (*SPORT*) gara; **in the ~ of** in caso di; **at all ~s** (*BRIT*), **in any ~** in ogni caso; **in the ~** in realtà, di fatto; **in the course of ~s** nel corso degli eventi.

eventful [ɪ'vɛntful] *adj* denso(a) di eventi.

eventing [ɪ'vɛntɪŋ] *n* (*HORSERIDING*) concorso ippico.

eventual [ɪ'vɛntʃuəl] *adj* finale.

eventuality [ɪvɛntʃu'ælɪtɪ] *n* possibilità *f inv*, eventualità *f inv*.

eventually [ɪ'vɛntʃuəlɪ] *adv* finalmente.

ever ['ɛvə*] *adv* mai; (*at all times*) sempre; **for ~** per sempre; **the best ~** il migliore che ci sia mai stato; **hardly ~** non ... quasi mai; **did you ~ meet him?** l'ha mai incontrato?; **have you ~ been there?** c'è mai stato?; ~ **so pretty** così bello(a); **thank you ~ so much** grazie mille; **yours ~** (*BRIT: in letters*) sempre tuo; ~ **since** *adv* da allora ♦ *conj* sin da quando.

Everest ['ɛvərɪst] *n* (*also*: **Mount ~**) Everest *m*.

evergreen ['ɛvəgri:n] *n* sempreverde *m*.

everlasting [ɛvə'lɑ:stɪŋ] *adj* eterno(a).

every ['ɛvrɪ] *adj* ogni; ~ **day** tutti i giorni, ogni giorno; ~ **other/third day** ogni due/ tre giorni; ~ **other car** una macchina su due; ~ **now and then** ogni tanto, di quando in quando; **I have ~ confidence in him** ho piena fiducia in lui.

everybody ['ɛvrɪbɔdɪ] *pron* ognuno, tutti *pl*; ~ **else** tutti gli altri; ~ **knows about it** lo sanno tutti.

everyday ['ɛvrɪdeɪ] *adj* quotidiano(a); di ogni giorno; (*use, occurrence, experience*) comune; (*expression*) di uso corrente.

everyone ['ɛvrɪwʌn] = **everybody**.

everything ['ɛvrɪθɪŋ] *pron* tutto, ogni cosa; ~ **is ready** è tutto pronto; **he did ~ possible** ha fatto tutto il possibile.

everywhere ['ɛvrɪwɛə*] *adv* in ogni luogo, dappertutto; (*wherever*) ovunque; ~ **you go you meet ...** ovunque si vada si trova ....

evict [ɪ'vɪkt] *vt* sfrattare.

eviction [ɪ'vɪkʃən] *n* sfratto.

eviction notice *n* avviso di sfratto.

evidence ['ɛvɪdəns] *n* (*proof*) prova; (*of witness*) testimonianza; (*sign*): **to show ~ of** dare segni di; **to give ~** deporre; **in ~** (*obvious*) in evidenza; in vista.

evident ['ɛvɪdənt] *adj* evidente.

evidently ['ɛvɪdəntlɪ] *adv* evidentemente.

evil ['i:vl] *adj* cattivo(a), maligno(a) ♦ *n* male *m*.

evince [ɪ'vɪns] *vt* manifestare.

evocative [ɪ'vɔkətɪv] *adj* evocativo(a).

evoke [ɪ'vəuk] *vt* evocare; (*admiration*) suscitare.

evolution [i:və'lu:ʃən] *n* evoluzione *f*.

evolve [ɪ'vɔlv] *vt* elaborare ♦ *vi* svilupparsi, evolversi.

ewe [ju:] *n* pecora.

ex- [ɛks] *prefix* ex; (*out of*): **the price ~ works** il prezzo franco fabbrica.

exacerbate [ɪk'sæsəbeɪt] *vt* (*pain*) aggravare; (*fig: relations, situation*) esacerbare, esasperare.

exact [ɪg'zækt] *adj* esatto(a) ♦ *vt*: **to ~ sth** (**from**) estorcere qc (da); esigere qc (da).

exacting [ɪg'zæktɪŋ] *adj* esigente; (*work*) faticoso(a).

exactitude [ɪg'zæktɪtju:d] *n* esattezza, precisione *f*.

exactly [ɪg'zæktlɪ] *adv* esattamente; ~! esatto!

exaggerate [ɪg'zædʒəreɪt] *vt, vi* esagerare.

exaggeration [ɪgzædʒə'reɪʃən] *n* esagerazione *f*.

exalt [ɪg'zɔːlt] *vt* esaltare; elevare.

exalted [ɪg'zɔːltɪd] *adj* (*rank, person*) elevato(a); (*elated*) esaltato(a).

exam [ɪg'zæm] *n abbr* (*SCOL*) = **examination**.

examination [ɪgzæmɪ'neɪʃən] *n* (*SCOL*) esame *m*; (*MED*) controllo; **to take** *or* (*BRIT*) **sit an ~** sostenere *or* dare un esame; **the matter is under ~** la questione è all'esame.

examine [ɪg'zæmɪn] *vt* esaminare; (*SCOL: orally, LAW: person*) interrogare; (*inspect: machine, premises*) ispezionare; (*luggage, passport*) controllare; (*MED*) visitare.

examiner [ɪg'zæmɪnə*] *n* esaminatore/ trice.

example [ɪgˈzɑːmpl] *n* esempio; **for** ~ ad *or* per esempio; **to set a good/bad** ~ dare il buon/cattivo esempio.

exasperate [ɪgˈzɑːspəreɪt] *vt* esasperare; ~**d by** (*or* at *or* with) esasperato da.

exasperating [ɪgˈzɑːspəreɪtɪŋ] *adj* esasperante.

exasperation [ɪgzɑːspəˈreɪʃən] *n* esasperazione *f*.

excavate [ˈɛkskəveɪt] *vt* scavare.

excavation [ɛkskəˈveɪʃən] *n* escavazione *f*.

excavator [ˈɛkskəveɪtə*] *n* scavatore *m*, scavatrice *f*.

exceed [ɪkˈsiːd] *vt* superare; (*one's powers, time limit*) oltrepassare.

exceedingly [ɪkˈsiːdɪŋlɪ] *adv* eccessivamente.

excel [ɪkˈsɛl] *vi* eccellere ♦ *vt* sorpassare; **to** ~ **o.s.** (*BRIT*) superare se stesso.

excellence [ˈɛksələns] *n* eccellenza.

Excellency [ˈɛksələnsɪ] *n*: **His** ~ Sua Eccellenza.

excellent [ˈɛksələnt] *adj* eccellente.

except [ɪkˈsɛpt] *prep* (*also*: ~ **for**, ~**ing**) salvo, all'infuori di, eccetto ♦ *vt* escludere; ~ **if/when** salvo se/quando; ~ **that** salvo che.

exception [ɪkˈsɛpʃən] *n* eccezione *f*; **to take** ~ **to** trovare a ridire su; **with the** ~ **of** ad eccezione di.

exceptional [ɪkˈsɛpʃənl] *adj* eccezionale.

excerpt [ˈɛksəːpt] *n* estratto.

excess [ɪkˈsɛs] *n* eccesso; **in** ~ **of** al di sopra di.

excess baggage *n* bagaglio in eccedenza.

excess fare *n* supplemento.

excessive [ɪkˈsɛsɪv] *adj* eccessivo(a).

excess supply *n* eccesso di offerta.

exchange [ɪksˈtʃeɪndʒ] *n* scambio; (*also*: **telephone** ~) centralino ♦ *vt*: **to** ~ (**for**) scambiare (con); **in** ~ **for** in cambio di; **foreign** ~ (*COMM*) cambio.

exchange control *n* controllo sui cambi.

exchange market *n* mercato dei cambi.

exchange rate *n* tasso di cambio.

Exchequer [ɪksˈtʃɛkə*] *n*: **the** ~ (*BRIT*) lo Scacchiere, ≈ il ministero delle Finanze.

excisable [ɪkˈsaɪzəbl] *adj* soggetto(a) a dazio.

excise *n* [ˈɛksaɪz] imposta, dazio ♦ *vt* [ɛkˈsaɪz] recidere.

excise duties *npl* dazi *mpl*.

excitable [ɪkˈsaɪtəbl] *adj* eccitabile.

excite [ɪkˈsaɪt] *vt* eccitare; **to get** ~**d** eccitarsi.

excitement [ɪkˈsaɪtmənt] *n* eccitazione *f*; agitazione *f*.

exciting [ɪkˈsaɪtɪŋ] *adj* avventuroso(a);

(*film, book*) appassionante.

excl. *abbr* (= *excluding, exclusive* (*of*)) escl.

exclaim [ɪkˈskleɪm] *vi* esclamare.

exclamation [ɛkskləˈmeɪʃən] *n* esclamazione *f*.

exclamation mark *n* punto esclamativo.

exclude [ɪkˈskluːd] *vt* escludere.

excluding [ɪkˈskluːdɪŋ] *prep*: ~ **VAT** IVA esclusa.

exclusion [ɪkˈskluːʒən] *n* esclusione *f*; **to the** ~ **of** escludendo.

exclusion clause *n* clausola di esclusione.

exclusion zone *n* area interdetta.

exclusive [ɪkˈskluːsɪv] *adj* esclusivo(a); (*club*) selettivo(a); (*district*) snob *inv* ♦ *adv* (*COMM*) non compreso; ~ **of VAT** IVA esclusa; ~ **of postage** spese postali escluse; ~ **of service** servizio escluso; **from 1st to 15th March** ~ dal 1° al 15 marzo esclusi; ~ **rights** *npl* (*COMM*) diritti *mpl* esclusivi.

exclusively [ɪkˈskluːsɪvlɪ] *adv* esclusivamente.

excommunicate [ɛkskəˈmjuːnɪkeɪt] *vt* scomunicare.

excrement [ˈɛkskrəmənt] *n* escremento.

excruciating [ɪkˈskruːʃɪeɪtɪŋ] *adj* straziante, atroce.

excursion [ɪkˈskəːʃən] *n* escursione *f*, gita.

excursion ticket *n* biglietto a tariffa escursionistica.

excusable [ɪkˈskjuːzəbl] *adj* scusabile.

excuse *n* [ɪkˈskjuːs] scusa ♦ *vt* [ɪkˈskjuːz] scusare; (*justify*) giustificare; **to make** ~**s for sb** trovare giustificazioni per qn; **to** ~ **sb from** (*activity*) dispensare qn da; ~ **me!** mi scusi!; **now if you will** ~ **me**, ... ora, mi scusi ma ...; **to** ~ **o.s. (for (doing) sth)** giustificarsi (per (aver fatto) qc).

ex-directory [ˈɛksdɪˈrɛktərɪ] *adj* (*BRIT*): ~ **(phone) number** numero non compreso nell'elenco telefonico.

execrable [ˈɛksɪkrəbl] *adj* (*gen*) pessimo(a); (*manners*) esecrabile.

execute [ˈɛksɪkjuːt] *vt* (*prisoner*) giustiziare; (*plan etc*) eseguire.

execution [ɛksɪˈkjuːʃən] *n* esecuzione *f*.

executioner [ɛksɪˈkjuːʃnə*] *n* boia *m inv*.

executive [ɪgˈzɛkjutɪv] *n* (*COMM*) dirigente *m*; (*POL*) esecutivo ♦ *adj* esecutivo(a); (*secretary*) di direzione; (*offices, suite*) della direzione; (*car, plane*) dirigenziale; (*position, job, duties*) direttivo(a).

executive director *n* amministratore/ trice.

executor [ɪgˈzɛkjutə*] *n* esecutore(trice) testamentario(a).

exemplary [ɪgˈzɛmplərɪ] *adj* esemplare.

exemplify [ɪg'zɛmplɪfaɪ] vt esemplificare.

exempt [ɪg'zɛmpt] adj: ~ **(from)** (person: from tax) esentato(a) (da); (: from military service etc) esonerato(a) (da); (goods) esente (da) ♦ vt: **to ~ sb from** esentare qn da.

exemption [ɪg'zɛmpʃən] n esenzione f.

exercise ['ɛksəsaɪz] n esercizio ♦ vt esercitare; (dog) portar fuori ♦ vi (also: take ~) fare del movimento or moto.

exercise bike n cyclette ® f inv.

exercise book n quaderno.

exert [ɪg'zəːt] vt esercitare; (strength, force) impiegare; **to ~ o.s.** sforzarsi.

exertion [ɪg'zəːʃən] n sforzo.

ex gratia ['ɛks'greɪʃə] adj: ~ **payment** gratifica.

exhale [ɛks'heɪl] vt, vi espirare.

exhaust [ɪg'zɔːst] n (also: ~ **fumes**) scappamento; (also: ~ **pipe**) tubo di scappamento ♦ vt esaurire; **to ~ o.s.** sfiancarsi.

exhausted [ɪg'zɔːstɪd] adj esaurito(a).

exhausting [ɪg'zɔːstɪŋ] adj estenuante.

exhaustion [ɪg'zɔːstʃən] n esaurimento; **nervous ~** sovraffaticamento mentale.

exhaustive [ɪg'zɔːstɪv] adj esauriente.

exhibit [ɪg'zɪbɪt] n (ART) oggetto esposto; (LAW) documento or oggetto esibito ♦ vt esporre; (courage, skill) dimostrare.

exhibition [ɛksɪ'bɪʃən] n mostra, esposizione f; (of rudeness etc) spettacolo; **to make an ~ of o.s.** dare spettacolo di sé.

exhibitionist [ɛksɪ'bɪʃənɪst] n esibizionista m/f.

exhibitor [ɪg'zɪbɪtə*] n espositore/trice.

exhilarating [ɪg'zɪləreɪtɪŋ] adj esilarante; stimolante.

exhilaration [ɪgzɪlə'reɪʃən] n esaltazione f, ebbrezza.

exhort [ɪg'zɔːt] vt esortare.

exile ['ɛksaɪl] n esilio; (person) esiliato/a ♦ vt esiliare; **in ~** in esilio.

exist [ɪg'zɪst] vi esistere.

existence [ɪg'zɪstəns] n esistenza; **to be in ~** esistere.

existentialism [ɛgzɪs'tɛnʃəlɪzəm] n esistenzialismo.

existing [ɪg'zɪstɪŋ] adj (laws, regime) attuale.

exit ['ɛksɪt] n uscita ♦ vi (COMPUT, THEAT) uscire.

exit poll n exit poll m inv, sondaggio all'uscita dei seggi.

exit ramp n (US AUT) rampa di uscita.

exit visa n visto d'uscita.

exodus ['ɛksədəs] n esodo.

ex officio ['ɛksə'fɪʃɪəu] adj, adv d'ufficio.

exonerate [ɪg'zɔnəreɪt] vt: **to ~ from** discolpare da.

exorbitant [ɪg'zɔːbɪtənt] adj (price) esorbitante; (demands) spropositato(a).

exorcize ['ɛksɔːsaɪz] vt esorcizzare.

exotic [ɪg'zɔtɪk] adj esotico(a).

expand [ɪk'spænd] vt (chest, economy etc) sviluppare; (market, operations) espandere; (influence) estendere; (horizons) allargare ♦ vi svilupparsi; (also gas) espandersi; (metal) dilatarsi; **to ~ on** (notes, story etc) ampliare.

expanse [ɪk'spæns] n distesa, estensione f.

expansion [ɪk'spænʃən] n (gen) espansione f; (of town, economy) sviluppo; (of metal) dilatazione f.

expansionism [ɪk'spænʃənɪzəm] n espansionismo.

expansionist [ɪk'spænʃənɪst] adj espansionistico(a).

expatriate n [ɛks'pætrɪət] espatriato/a ♦ vt [ɛks'pætrɪeɪt] espatriare.

expect [ɪk'spɛkt] vt (anticipate) prevedere, aspettarsi, prevedere or aspettarsi che + sub; (count on) contare su; (hope for) sperare; (require) richiedere, esigere; (suppose) supporre; (await, also baby) aspettare ♦ vi: **to be ~ing** essere in stato interessante; **to ~ sb to do** aspettarsi che qn faccia; **to ~ to do sth** pensare or contare di fare qc; **as ~ed** come previsto; **I ~ so** credo di sì.

expectancy [ɪk'spɛktənsɪ] n attesa; **life ~** probabilità fpl di vita.

expectant [ɪk'spɛktənt] adj pieno(a) di aspettative.

expectantly [ɪk'spɛktəntlɪ] adv (look, listen) con un'aria d'attesa.

expectant mother n gestante f.

expectation [ɛkspɛk'teɪʃən] n aspettativa; speranza; **in ~ of** in previsione di; **against** or **contrary to all ~(s)** contro ogni aspettativa; **to come** or **live up to sb's ~s** rispondere alle attese di qn.

expedience, expediency [ɪk'spiːdɪəns, ɪk'spiːdɪənsɪ] n convenienza; **for the sake of ~** per una questione di comodità.

expedient [ɪk'spiːdɪənt] adj conveniente; vantaggioso(a) ♦ n espediente m.

expedite ['ɛkspədaɪt] vt sbrigare; facilitare.

expedition [ɛkspə'dɪʃən] n spedizione f.

expeditionary force [ɛkspə'dɪʃənərɪ-] n corpo di spedizione.

expeditious [ɛkspə'dɪʃəs] adj sollecito(a), rapido(a).

expel [ɪk'spɛl] *vt* espellere.

expend [ɪk'spɛnd] *vt* spendere; (*use up*) consumare.

expendable [ɪk'spɛndəbl] *adj* sacrificabile.

expenditure [ɪk'spɛndɪtʃə*] *n* spesa; (*of time, effort*) dispendio.

expense [ɪk'spɛns] *n* spesa; (*high cost*) costo; ~**s** *npl* (*COMM*) spese *fpl*, indennità *fpl*; **to go to the** ~ **of** sobbarcarsi la spesa di; **at great** ~ con grande impiego di mezzi; **at the** ~ **of** a spese di.

expense account *n* conto *m* spese *inv*.

expensive [ɪk'spɛnsɪv] *adj* caro(a), costoso(a); **she has** ~ **tastes** le piacciono le cose costose.

experience [ɪk'spɪərɪəns] *n* esperienza ♦ *vt* (*pleasure*) provare; (*hardship*) soffrire; **to learn by** ~ imparare per esperienza.

experienced [ɪk'spɪərɪənst] *adj* che ha esperienza.

experiment *n* [ɪk'spɛrɪmənt] esperimento, esperienza ♦ *vi* [ɪk'spɛrɪmɛnt] fare esperimenti; **to perform** *or* **carry out an** ~ fare un esperimento; **as an** ~ a titolo di esperimento; **to** ~ **with a new vaccine** sperimentare un nuovo vaccino.

experimental [ɪksperɪ'mɛntl] *adj* sperimentale; **at the** ~ **stage** in via di sperimentazione.

expert ['ɛkspəːt] *adj, n* esperto(a); ~ **witness** (*LAW*) esperto/a; ~ **in** *or* **at doing sth** esperto nel fare qc; **an** ~ **on sth** un esperto di qc.

expertise [ɛkspəː'tiːz] *n* competenza.

expire [ɪk'spaɪə*] *vi* (*period of time, licence*) scadere.

expiry [ɪk'spaɪərɪ] *n* scadenza.

explain [ɪk'spleɪn] *vt* spiegare.

►**explain away** *vt* dar ragione di.

explanation [ɛksplə'neɪʃən] *n* spiegazione *f*; **to find an** ~ **for sth** trovare la spiegazione di qc.

explanatory [ɪk'splænətrɪ] *adj* esplicativo(a).

expletive [ɪk'spliːtɪv] *n* imprecazione *f*.

explicit [ɪk'splɪsɪt] *adj* esplicito(a); (*definite*) netto(a).

explode [ɪk'spləud] *vi* esplodere ♦ *vt* (*fig: theory*) demolire; **to** ~ **a myth** distruggere un mito.

exploit *n* ['ɛksplɔɪt] impresa ♦ *vt* [ɪk'splɔɪt] sfruttare.

exploitation [ɛksplɔɪ'teɪʃən] *n* sfruttamento.

exploration [ɛksplə'reɪʃən] *n* esplorazione *f*.

exploratory [ɪk'splɔrətrɪ] *adj* (*fig: talks*) esplorativo(a); ~ **operation** (*MED*) intervento d'esplorazione.

explore [ɪk'splɔː*] *vt* esplorare; (*possibilities*) esaminare.

explorer [ɪk'splɔːrə*] *n* esploratore/trice.

explosion [ɪk'spləuʒən] *n* esplosione *f*.

explosive [ɪk'spləusɪv] *adj* esplosivo(a) ♦ *n* esplosivo.

exponent [ɪk'spəunənt] *n* esponente *m/f*.

export *vt* [ɛk'spɔːt] esportare ♦ *n* ['ɛkspɔːt] esportazione *f*; articolo di esportazione ♦ *cpd* d'esportazione.

exportation [ɛkspɔː'teɪʃən] *n* esportazione *f*.

exporter [ɪk'spɔːtə*] *n* esportatore *m*.

export licence *n* licenza d'esportazione.

expose [ɪk'spəuz] *vt* esporre; (*unmask*) smascherare; **to** ~ **o.s.** (*LAW*) oltraggiare il pudore.

exposed [ɪk'spəuzd] *adj* (*land, house*) esposto(a); (*ELEC: wire*) scoperto(a); (*pipe, beam*) a vista.

exposition [ɛkspə'zɪʃən] *n* esposizione *f*.

exposure [ɪk'spəuʒə*] *n* esposizione *f*; (*PHOT*) posa; (*MED*) assideramento; **to die of** ~ morire assiderato(a).

exposure meter *n* esposimetro.

expound [ɪk'spaund] *vt* esporre; (*theory, text*) spiegare.

express [ɪk'sprɛs] *adj* (*definite*) chiaro(a), espresso(a); (*BRIT: letter etc*) espresso *inv* ♦ *n* (*train*) espresso ♦ *adv*: **to send sth** ~ spedire qc per espresso ♦ *vt* esprimere; **to** ~ **o.s.** esprimersi.

expression [ɪk'sprɛʃən] *n* espressione *f*.

expressionism [ɪk'sprɛʃənɪzəm] *n* espressionismo.

expressive [ɪk'sprɛsɪv] *adj* espressivo(a).

expressly [ɪk'sprɛslɪ] *adv* espressamente.

expressway [ɪk'sprɛsweɪ] *n* (*US*) autostrada che attraversa la città.

expropriate [ɛks'prəuprɪeɪt] *vt* espropriare.

expulsion [ɪk'spʌlʃən] *n* espulsione *f*.

exquisite [ɛk'skwɪzɪt] *adj* squisito(a).

ex-serviceman ['ɛks'səːvɪsmən] *n* ex combattente *m*.

ext. *abbr* (*TEL*: = *extension*) int. (= *interno*).

extemporize [ɪk'stɛmpəraɪz] *vi* improvvisare.

extend [ɪk'stɛnd] *vt* (*visit*) protrarre; (*road, deadline*) prolungare; (*building*) ampliare; (*offer*) offrire, porgere; (*COMM: credit*) accordare ♦ *vi* (*land*) estendersi.

extension [ɪk'stɛnʃən] *n* (*of road, term*) prolungamento; (*of contract, deadline*) proroga; (*building*) annesso; (*to wire, table*) prolunga; (*telephone*) interno; (: *in private house*) apparecchio supplementare; ~ **3718** (*TEL*) interno 3718.

extension cable *n* (*ELEC*) prolunga.

extensive [ɪk'stɛnsɪv] adj esteso(a),
ampio(a); (damage) su larga scala;
(alterations) notevole; (inquiries)
esauriente; (use) grande.

extensively [ɪk'stɛnsɪvlɪ] adv (altered,
damaged etc) radicalmente; **he's travelled
~** ha viaggiato molto.

extent [ɪk'stɛnt] n estensione f; (of
knowledge, activities, power) portata;
(degree: of damage, loss) proporzioni fpl; **to
some ~** fino a un certo punto; **to a
certain/large ~** in certa/larga misura; **to
what ~?** fino a che punto?; **to such an ~
that ...** a tal punto che ....

extenuating [ɪk'stɛnjueɪtɪŋ] adj: **~
circumstances** attenuanti fpl.

exterior [ɛk'stɪərɪə*] adj esteriore,
esterno(a) ♦ n esteriore m, esterno;
aspetto (esteriore).

exterminate [ɪk'stɜ:mɪneɪt] vt sterminare.

extermination [ɪkstɜ:mɪ'neɪʃən] n
sterminio.

external [ɛk'stɜ:nl] adj esterno(a), esteriore
♦ n: **the ~s** le apparenze; **for ~ use only**
(MED) solo per uso esterno; **~ affairs** (POL)
affari mpl esteri.

externally [ɛk'stɜːnəlɪ] adv esternamente.

extinct [ɪk'stɪŋkt] adj estinto(a).

extinction [ɪk'stɪŋkʃən] n estinzione f.

extinguish [ɪk'stɪŋgwɪʃ] vt estinguere.

extinguisher [ɪk'stɪŋgwɪʃə*] n estintore m.

extol, (US) **extoll** [ɪk'stəul] vt (merits,
virtues) magnificare; (person) celebrare.

extort [ɪk'stɔːt] vt: **to ~ sth (from)**
estorcere qc (da).

extortion [ɪk'stɔːʃən] n estorsione f.

extortionate [ɪk'stɔːʃənɪt] adj esorbitante.

extra ['ɛkstrə] adj extra inv, supplementare
♦ adv (in addition) di più ♦ n supplemento;
(THEAT) comparso; **wine will cost ~** il
vino è extra; **~ large sizes** taglie fpl forti.

extra... ['ɛkstrə] prefix extra....

extract vt [ɪk'strækt] estrarre; (money,
promise) strappare ♦ n ['ɛkstrækt]
estratto; (passage) brano.

extraction [ɪk'strækʃən] n estrazione f;
(descent) origine f.

extractor fan [ɪk'stræktə*-] n aspiratore m.

extracurricular [ɛkstrəkə'rɪkjulə*] adj
(SCOL) parascolastico(a).

extradite ['ɛkstrədaɪt] vt estradare.

extradition [ɛkstrə'dɪʃən] n estradizione f.

extramarital [ɛkstrə'mærɪtl] adj
extraconiugale.

extramural [ɛkstrə'mjuərl] adj fuori
dell'università.

extraneous [ɛk'streɪnɪəs] adj: **~ to**
estraneo(a) a.

extraordinary [ɪk'strɔːdnrɪ] adj
straordinario(a); **the ~ thing is that ...** la
cosa strana è che ....

extraordinary general meeting n
assemblea straordinaria.

extrapolation [ɪkstræpə'leɪʃən] n
estrapolazione f.

extrasensory perception (ESP)
[ɛkstrə'sɛnsərɪ-] n percezione f
extrasensoriale.

extra time n (FOOTBALL) tempo
supplementare.

extravagance [ɪk'strævəgəns] n (excessive
spending) sperpero; (thing bought)
stravaganza.

extravagant [ɪk'strævəgənt] adj
stravagante; (in spending: person)
prodigo(a); (: tastes) dispendioso(a).

extreme [ɪk'striːm] adj estremo(a) ♦ n
estremo; **~s of temperature** eccessivi
sbalzi mpl di temperatura; **the ~ left/right**
(POL) l'estrema sinistra/destra.

extremely [ɪk'striːmlɪ] adv estremamente.

extremist [ɪk'striːmɪst] adj, n estremista
(m/f).

extremity [ɪk'strɛmɪtɪ] n estremità f inv.

extricate ['ɛkstrɪkeɪt] vt: **to ~ sth (from)**
districare qc (da).

extrovert ['ɛkstrəvɜːt] n estroverso/a.

exuberance [ɪg'zuːbərəns] n esuberanza.

exuberant [ɪg'zjuːbərənt] adj esuberante.

exude [ɪg'zjuːd] vt trasudare; (fig)
emanare.

exult [ɪg'zʌlt] vi esultare, gioire.

exultant [ɪg'zʌltənt] adj (person, smile)
esultante; (shout, expression) di giubilo.

exultation [ɛgzʌl'teɪʃən] n giubilo; **in ~** per
la gioia.

eye [aɪ] n occhio; (of needle) cruna ♦ vt
osservare; **to keep an ~ on** tenere
d'occhio; **in the public ~** esposto(a) al
pubblico; **as far as the ~ can see** a
perdita d'occhio; **with an ~ to doing sth**
(BRIT) con l'idea di far qc; **to have an ~
for sth** avere occhio per qc; **there's more
to this than meets the ~** non è così
semplice come sembra.

eyeball ['aɪbɔːl] n globo dell'occhio.

eyebath ['aɪbɑːθ] n occhino.

eyebrow ['aɪbrau] n sopracciglio.

eyebrow pencil n matita per le
sopracciglia.

eye-catching ['aɪkætʃɪŋ] adj che colpisce
l'occhio.

eye cup n (US) = **eyebath**.

eyedrops ['aɪdrɒps] npl gocce fpl oculari,
collirio.

eyeful ['aɪful] n: **to get an ~ (of sth)** (col)

avere l'occasione di dare una bella
sbirciata (a qc).
eyeglass ['aɪglɑːs] *n* monocolo.
eyelash ['aɪlæʃ] *n* ciglio.
eyelet ['aɪlɪt] *n* occhiello.
eye-level ['aɪlɛvl] *adj* all'altezza degli
occhi.
eyelid ['aɪlɪd] *n* palpebra.
eyeliner ['aɪlaɪnə*] *n* eye-liner *m inv*.
eye-opener ['aɪəupnə*] *n* rivelazione *f*.
eyeshadow ['aɪʃædəu] *n* ombretto.
eyesight ['aɪsaɪt] *n* vista.
eyesore ['aɪsɔː*] *n* pugno nell'occhio.
eyestrain ['aɪstreɪn] *n*: **to get** ~ stancarsi
gli occhi.
eye-tooth, *pl* **-teeth** ['aɪtuːθ, -tiːθ] *n* canino
superiore; **to give one's eye-teeth for
sth/to do sth** (*fig*) dare non so che cosa
per qc/per fare qc.
eyewash ['aɪwɔʃ] *n* collirio; (*fig*)
sciocchezze *fpl*.
eye witness *n* testimone *m/f* oculare.
eyrie ['ɪərɪ] *n* nido (d'aquila).

Ff

F, f [ɛf] *n* (*letter*) F, f *f or m inv*; (*MUS*): F fa *m*;
F for Frederick, (*US*) **F for Fox** ≈ F come
Firenze.
F. *abbr* (= *Fahrenheit*) F.
FA *n abbr* (*BRIT*) = *Football Association.*
FAA *n abbr* (*US*) = *Federal Aviation
Administration.*
fable ['feɪbl] *n* favola.
fabric ['fæbrɪk] *n* stoffa, tessuto; (*ARCHIT*)
struttura.
fabricate ['fæbrɪkeɪt] *vt* fabbricare.
fabrication [fæbrɪ'keɪʃən] *n* fabbricazione *f*.
fabric ribbon *n* (*for typewriter*)
dattilonastro di tessuto.
fabulous ['fæbjuləs] *adj* favoloso(a); (*col:
super*) favoloso(a), fantastico(a).
façade [fə'sɑːd] *n* facciata; (*fig*) apparenza.
face [feɪs] *n* faccia, viso, volto; (*expression*)
faccia; (*grimace*) smorfia; (*of clock*)
quadrante *m*; (*of building*) facciata; (*side,
surface*) faccia; (*of mountain, cliff*) parete *f*
♦ *vt* fronteggiare; (*fig*) affrontare; ~
down (*person*) bocconi; (*object*) a faccia
in giù; **to lose/save** ~ perdere/salvare la
faccia; **to pull a** ~ fare una smorfia; **in**

the ~ **of** (*difficulties etc*) di fronte a; **on the**
~ **of it** a prima vista; **to** ~ **the fact that** ...
riconoscere *or* ammettere che ....
▶**face up to** *vt fus* affrontare, far fronte a.
face cloth *n* (*BRIT*) guanto di spugna.
face cream *n* crema per il viso.
faceless ['feɪslɪs] *adj* anonimo(a).
face lift *n* lifting *m inv*; (*of façade etc*)
ripulita.
face powder *n* cipria.
face-saving ['feɪsseɪvɪŋ] *adj* che salva la
faccia.
facet ['fæsɪt] *n* faccetta, sfaccettatura; (*fig*)
sfaccettatura.
facetious [fə'siːʃəs] *adj* faceto(a).
face-to-face ['feɪstə'feɪs] *adv* faccia a
faccia.
face value ['feɪs'væljuː] *n* (*of coin*) valore *m*
facciale *or* nominale; **to take sth at** ~ (*fig*)
giudicare qc dalle apparenze.
facia ['feɪʃɪə] *n* = **fascia.**
facial ['feɪʃəl] *adj* facciale ♦ *n* trattamento
del viso.
facile ['fæsaɪl] *adj* facile; superficiale.
facilitate [fə'sɪlɪteɪt] *vt* facilitare.
facility [fə'sɪlɪtɪ] *n* facilità; **facilities** *npl*
attrezzature *fpl*; **credit facilities**
facilitazioni *fpl* di credito.
facing ['feɪsɪŋ] *n* (*of wall etc*) rivestimento;
(*SEWING*) paramontura.
facsimile [fæk'sɪmɪlɪ] *n* facsimile *m inv*.
facsimile machine *n* telecopiatrice *f*.
fact [fækt] *n* fatto; **in** ~ infatti; **to know for**
a ~ **that** ... sapere per certo che ...; **the** ~
(**of the matter) is that** ... la verità è che ...;
the ~**s of life** (*sex*) i fatti riguardanti la
vita sessuale; (*fig*) le realtà della vita.
fact-finding ['fæktfaɪndɪŋ] *adj*: **a** ~ **tour/
mission** un viaggio/una missione
d'inchiesta.
faction ['fækʃən] *n* fazione *f*.
factional ['fækʃənl] *adj*: ~ **fighting** scontri
mpl tra fazioni.
factor ['fæktə*] *n* fattore *m*; (*COMM:
company*) organizzazione specializzata
nell'incasso di crediti per conto terzi; (:
agent) agente *m* depositario ♦ *vi* incassare
crediti per conto terzi; **human** ~
elemento umano; **safety** ~ coefficiente *m*
di sicurezza.
factory ['fæktərɪ] *n* fabbrica, stabilimento.
factory farming *n* (*BRIT*) allevamento su
scala industriale.
factory floor *n*: **the** ~ (*workers*) gli operai;
(*area*) il reparto produzione; **on the** ~ nel
reparto produzione.
factory ship *n* nave *f* fattoria *inv*.
factual ['fæktjuəl] *adj* che si attiene ai fatti.

faculty ['fækəltɪ] n facoltà f inv; (US: teaching staff) corpo insegnante.

fad [fæd] n mania; capriccio.

fade [feɪd] vi sbiadire, sbiadirsi; (light, sound, hope) attenuarsi, affievolirsi; (flower) appassire.

▶**fade in** vt (picture) aprire in dissolvenza; (sound) aumentare gradualmente d'intensità.

▶**fade out** vt (picture) chiudere in dissolvenza; (sound) diminuire gradualmente d'intensità.

faeces, (US) **feces** ['fiːsiːz] npl feci fpl.

fag [fæg] n (BRIT col: cigarette) cicca; (: chore) sfacchinata; (US col: homosexual) frocio.

fag end n (BRIT col) mozzicone m.

fagged out ['fægd-] adj (BRIT col) stanco(a) morto(a).

fail [feɪl] vt (exam) non superare; (candidate) bocciare; (subj: courage, memory) mancare a ♦ vi fallire; (student) essere respinto(a); (supplies) mancare; (eyesight, health, light: also: be ~ing) venire a mancare; (brakes) non funzionare; **to ~ to do sth** (neglect) mancare di fare qc; (be unable) non riuscire a fare qc; **without ~** senza fallo; certamente.

failing ['feɪlɪŋ] n difetto ♦ prep in mancanza di; ~ **that** se questo non è possibile.

failsafe ['feɪlseɪf] adj (device etc) di sicurezza.

failure ['feɪljə*] n fallimento; (person) fallito/a; (mechanical etc) guasto; (in exam) insuccesso, bocciatura; (of crops) perdita; **his ~ to come** il fatto che non sia venuto; **it was a complete ~** è stato un vero fiasco.

faint [feɪnt] adj debole; (recollection) vago(a); (mark) indistinto(a); (smell, breeze, trace) leggero(a) ♦ vi svenire; **to feel ~** sentirsi svenire.

faintest ['feɪntɪst] adj: **I haven't the ~ idea** non ho la più pallida idea.

faint-hearted [feɪnt'hɑːtɪd] adj pusillanime.

faintly ['feɪntlɪ] adv debolmente; vagamente.

faintness ['feɪntnɪs] n debolezza.

fair [feə*] adj (person, decision) giusto(a), equo(a); (hair etc) biondo(a); (skin, complexion) bianco(a); (weather) bello(a), clemente; (good enough) assai buono(a); (sizeable) bello(a) ♦ adv: **to play ~** giocare correttamente ♦ n fiera; (BRIT: funfair) luna park m inv; (also: **trade ~**) fiera campionaria; **it's not ~!** non è giusto!; **a ~ amount of** un bel po' di.

fair copy n bella copia.

fair game n: **to be ~** (person) essere bersaglio legittimo.

fairground ['feəgraund] n luna park m inv.

fair-haired [feə'heəd] adj (person) biondo(a).

fairly ['feəlɪ] adv equamente; (quite) abbastanza.

fairness ['feənɪs] n equità, giustizia; **in all ~** per essere giusti, a dire il vero.

fair play n correttezza.

fairy ['feərɪ] n fata.

fairy godmother n fata buona.

fairy lights npl (BRIT) lanternine fpl colorate.

fairy tale n fiaba.

faith [feɪθ] n fede f; (trust) fiducia; (sect) religione f, fede f; **to have ~ in sb/sth** avere fiducia in qn/qc.

faithful ['feɪθful] adj fedele.

faithfully ['feɪθfəlɪ] adv fedelmente; **yours ~** (BRIT: in letters) distinti saluti.

faith healer n guaritore/trice.

fake [feɪk] n imitazione f; (picture) falso; (person) impostore/a ♦ adj falso(a) ♦ vt (accounts) falsificare; (illness) fingere; (painting) contraffare; **his illness is a ~** fa finta di essere malato.

falcon ['fɔːlkən] n falco, falcone m.

Falkland Islands ['fɔːlklənd-] npl: **the ~** le isole Falkland.

fall [fɔːl] n caduta; (decrease) diminuzione f, calo; (in temperature) abbassamento; (in price) ribasso; (US: autumn) autunno ♦ vi (pt **fell**, pp **fallen** [fɛl, 'fɔːlən]) cadere; (temperature, price) abbassarsi; **a ~ of earth** uno smottamento; **a ~ of snow** (BRIT) una nevicata; **to ~ in love (with sb/sth)** innamorarsi (di qn/qc); **to ~ short of** (sb's expectations) non corrispondere a; **to ~ flat** vi (on one's face) cadere bocconi; (joke) fare cilecca; (plan) fallire; see also **falls**.

▶**fall apart** vi cadere a pezzi.

▶**fall back** vi indietreggiare; (MIL) ritirarsi.

▶**fall back on** vt fus ripiegare su; **to have sth to ~ back on** avere qc di riserva.

▶**fall behind** vi rimanere indietro; (fig: with payments) essere in arretrato.

▶**fall down** vi (person) cadere; (building, hopes) crollare.

▶**fall for** vt fus (person) prendere una cotta per; **to ~ for a trick** (or **a story** etc) cascarci.

▶**fall in** vi crollare; (MIL) mettersi in riga.

▶**fall in with** vt fus (sb's plans etc) trovarsi d'accordo con.

▶**fall off** vi cadere; (diminish) diminuire, abbassarsi.

►**fall out** *vi* (*friends etc*) litigare.
►**fall over** *vi* cadere.
►**fall through** *vi* (*plan, project*) fallire.
fallacy ['fæləsɪ] *n* errore *m*.
fallback ['fɔːlbæk] *adj*: ~ **position** posizione *f* di ripiego.
fallen ['fɔːlən] *pp of* **fall**.
fallible ['fælɪbl] *adj* fallibile.
falling ['fɔːlɪŋ] *adj*: ~ **market** (*COMM*) mercato in ribasso.
falling-off ['fɔːlɪŋ'ɔf] *n* calo.
fallopian tube [fə'ləupɪən-] *n* (*ANAT*) tuba di Falloppio.
fallout ['fɔːlaut] *n* fall-out *m*.
fallout shelter *n* rifugio antiatomico.
fallow ['fæləu] *adj* incolto(a); a maggese.
falls [fɔːlz] *npl* (*waterfall*) cascate *fpl*.
false [fɔːls] *adj* falso(a); **under** ~ **pretences** con l'inganno.
false alarm *n* falso allarme *m*.
falsehood ['fɔːlshud] *n* menzogna.
falsely ['fɔːlslɪ] *adv* (*accuse*) a torto.
false teeth *npl* (*BRIT*) denti *mpl* finti.
falsify ['fɔːlsɪfaɪ] *vt* falsificare; (*figures*) alterare.
falter ['fɔːltə*] *vi* esitare, vacillare.
fame [feɪm] *n* fama, celebrità.
familiar [fə'mɪlɪə*] *adj* familiare; (*common*) comune; (*close*) intimo(a); **to be** ~ **with** (*subject*) conoscere; **to make o.s.** ~ **with** familiarizzarsi con; **to be on** ~ **terms with** essere in confidenza con.
familiarity [fəmɪlɪ'ærɪtɪ] *n* familiarità; intimità.
familiarize [fə'mɪlɪəraɪz] *vt*: **to** ~ **sb with sth** far conoscere qc a qn.
family ['fæmɪlɪ] *n* famiglia.
family allowance *n* (*BRIT*) assegni *mpl* familiari.
family business *n* impresa familiare.
family credit *n* (*BRIT*) ≈ assegni *mpl* familiari.
family doctor *n* medico di famiglia.
family life *n* vita familiare.
family man *n* padre *m* di famiglia.
family planning clinic *n* consultorio familiare.
family tree *n* albero genealogico.
famine ['fæmɪn] *n* carestia.
famished ['fæmɪʃt] *adj* affamato(a); **I'm** ~! (*col*) ho una fame da lupo!
famous ['feɪməs] *adj* famoso(a).
famously ['feɪməslɪ] *adv* (*get on*) a meraviglia.
fan [fæn] *n* (*folding*) ventaglio; (*machine*) ventilatore *m*; (*person*) ammiratore/trice; (*SPORT*) tifoso/a ♦ *vt* far vento a; (*fire, quarrel*) alimentare.

►**fan out** *vi* spargersi (a ventaglio).
fanatic [fə'nætɪk] *n* fanatico/a.
fanatical [fə'nætɪkl] *adj* fanatico(a).
fan belt *n* cinghia del ventilatore.
fancied ['fænsɪd] *adj* immaginario(a).
fanciful ['fænsɪful] *adj* fantasioso(a); (*object*) di fantasia.
fan club *n* fan club *m inv*.
fancy ['fænsɪ] *n* immaginazione *f*, fantasia; (*whim*) capriccio ♦ *cpd* (di) fantasia *inv* ♦ *vt* (*feel like, want*) aver voglia di; (*imagine*) immaginare, credere; **to take a** ~ **to** incapricciarsi di; **it took** *or* **caught my** ~ mi è piaciuto; **when the** ~ **takes him** quando ne ha voglia; **to** ~ **that** immaginare che; **he fancies her** gli piace.
fancy dress *n* costume *m* (per maschera).
fancy-dress ball *n* ballo in maschera.
fancy goods *npl* articoli *mpl* di ogni genere.
fanfare ['fænfɛə*] *n* fanfara.
fanfold paper ['fænfəuld-] *n* carta a moduli continui.
fang [fæŋ] *n* zanna; (*of snake*) dente *m*.
fan heater *n* (*BRIT*) stufa ad aria calda.
fanlight ['fænlaɪt] *n* lunetta.
fanny ['fænɪ] *n* (*BRIT col!*) figa(!); (*US col*) culo(!).
fantasize ['fæntəsaɪz] *vi* fantasticare, sognare.
fantastic [fæn'tæstɪk] *adj* fantastico(a).
fantasy ['fæntəsɪ] *n* fantasia, immaginazione *f*; fantasticheria; chimera.
fanzine ['fænziːn] *n* rivista specialistica (*per appassionati*).
FAO *n abbr* (= *Food and Agriculture Organization*) FAO *f*.
FAQ *abbr* (= *free alongside quay*) franco lungo banchina.
far [fɑː*] *adj*: **the** ~ **side/end** l'altra parte/l'altro capo; **the** ~ **left/right** (*POL*) l'estrema sinistra/destra ♦ *adv* lontano; **is it** ~ **to London?** è lontana Londra?; **it's not** ~ **(from here)** non è lontano (da qui); ~ **away**, ~ **off** lontano, distante; ~ **better** assai migliore; ~ **from** lontano da; **by** ~ di gran lunga; **as** ~ **back as the 13th century** già nel duecento; **go as** ~ **as the farm** vada fino alla fattoria; **as** ~ **as I know** per quel che so; **as** ~ **as possible** nei limiti del possibile; **how** ~ **have you got with your work?** dov'è arrivato con il suo lavoro?
faraway ['fɑːrəweɪ] *adj* lontano(a); (*voice, look*) assente.
farce [fɑːs] *n* farsa.
farcical ['fɑːsɪkəl] *adj* farsesco(a).

fare [fɛə*] n (on trains, buses) tariffa; (in taxi) prezzo della corsa; (food) vitto, cibo ♦ vi passarsela.

Far East n: the ~ l'Estremo Oriente m.

farewell [fɛə'wɛl] excl, n addio ♦ cpd (party etc) d'addio.

far-fetched ['fɑː'fɛtʃt] adj (explanation) stiracchiato(a), forzato(a); (idea, scheme, story) inverosimile.

farm [fɑːm] n fattoria, podere m ♦ vt coltivare.

►**farm out** vt (work) dare in consegna.

farmer ['fɑːmə*] n coltivatore/trice; agricoltore/trice.

farmhand ['fɑːmhænd] n bracciante m agricolo.

farmhouse ['fɑːmhaus] n fattoria.

farming ['fɑːmɪŋ] n agricoltura; **intensive** ~ coltura intensiva; **sheep** ~ allevamento di pecore.

farm labourer n = **farmhand**.

farmland ['fɑːmlænd] n terreno da coltivare.

farm produce n prodotti mpl agricoli.

farm worker n = **farmhand**.

farmyard ['fɑːmjɑːd] n aia.

Faroe Islands ['fɛərəu-], **Faroes** ['fɛərəuz] npl: **the** ~ le isole Faeroer.

far-reaching ['fɑː'riːtʃɪŋ] adj di vasta portata.

far-sighted ['fɑː'saɪtɪd] adj presbite; (fig) lungimirante.

fart [fɑːt] (col!) n scoreggia(!) ♦ vi scoreggiare (!).

farther ['fɑːðə*] adv più lontano ♦ adj più lontano(a).

farthest ['fɑːðɪst] superlative of **far**.

FAS abbr (BRIT: = free alongside ship) franco banchina nave.

fascia ['feɪʃɪə] n (AUT) cruscotto.

fascinate ['fæsɪneɪt] vt affascinare.

fascinating ['fæsɪneɪtɪŋ] adj affascinante.

fascination [fæsɪ'neɪʃən] n fascino.

fascism ['fæʃɪzəm] n fascismo.

fascist ['fæʃɪst] adj, n fascista (m/f).

fashion ['fæʃən] n moda; (manner) maniera, modo ♦ vt foggiare, formare; **in** ~ alla moda; **out of** ~ passato(a) di moda; **after a** ~ (finish, manage etc) così così; **in the Greek** ~ alla greca.

fashionable ['fæʃənəbl] adj alla moda, di moda; (writer) di grido.

fashion designer n disegnatore/trice di moda.

fashion show n sfilata di moda.

fast [fɑːst] adj rapido(a), svelto(a), veloce; (clock): **to be** ~ andare avanti; (dye, colour) solido(a) ♦ adv rapidamente; (stuck,

held) saldamente ♦ n digiuno ♦ vi digiunare; ~ **asleep** profondamente addormentato; **as** ~ **as I can** più in fretta possibile; **my watch is 5 minutes** ~ il mio orologio va avanti di 5 minuti; **to make a boat** ~ (BRIT) ormeggiare una barca.

fasten ['fɑːsn] vt chiudere, fissare; (coat) abbottonare, allacciare ♦ vi chiudersi, fissarsi; abbottonarsi, allacciarsi.

►**fasten (up)on** vt fus (idea) cogliere al volo.

fastener ['fɑːsnə*], **fastening** ['fɑːsnɪŋ] n fermaglio, chiusura; (BRIT: zip ~) chiusura lampo.

fast food n fast food m inv.

fastidious [fæs'tɪdɪəs] adj esigente, difficile.

fast lane n (AUT) ≈ corsia di sorpasso.

fat [fæt] adj grasso(a) ♦ n grasso; **to live off the** ~ **of the land** vivere nel lusso, avere ogni ben di Dio.

fatal ['feɪtl] adj fatale; mortale; disastroso(a).

fatalism ['feɪtəlɪzəm] n fatalismo.

fatality [fə'tælɪtɪ] n (road death etc) morto/a, vittima.

fatally ['feɪtəlɪ] adv a morte.

fate [feɪt] n destino; (of person) sorte f; **to meet one's** ~ trovare la morte.

fated ['feɪtɪd] adj (governed by fate) destinato(a); (person, project etc) destinato(a) a finire male.

fateful ['feɪtful] adj fatidico(a).

fat-free ['fæt'friː] adj senza grassi.

father ['fɑːðə*] n padre m.

Father Christmas n Babbo Natale.

fatherhood ['fɑːðəhuːd] n paternità.

father-in-law ['fɑːðərɪnlɔː] n suocero.

fatherland ['fɑːðəlænd] n patria.

fatherly ['fɑːðəlɪ] adj paterno(a).

fathom ['fæðəm] n braccio (= 1828 mm) ♦ vt (mystery) penetrare, sondare.

fatigue [fə'tiːg] n stanchezza; (MIL) corvé f; **metal** ~ fatica del metallo.

fatness ['fætnɪs] n grassezza.

fatten ['fætn] vt, vi ingrassare; **chocolate is** ~**ing** la cioccolata fa ingrassare.

fatty ['fætɪ] adj (food) grasso(a) ♦ n (col) ciccione/a.

fatuous ['fætjuəs] adj fatuo(a).

faucet ['fɔːsɪt] n (US) rubinetto.

fault [fɔːlt] n colpa; (TENNIS) fallo; (defect) difetto; (GEO) faglia ♦ vt criticare; **it's my** ~ è colpa mia; **to find** ~ **with** trovare da ridire su; **at** ~ in fallo; **generous to a** ~ eccessivamente generoso.

faultless ['fɔːltlɪs] adj perfetto(a); senza difetto; impeccabile.

faulty ['fɔːltɪ] *adj* difettoso(a).

fauna ['fɔːnə] *n* fauna.

faux pas [fəu'pɑː] *n* gaffe *f inv*.

favour, (*US*) **favor** ['feɪvə*] *n* favore *m* ♦ *vt* (*proposition*) favorire, essere favorevole a; (*pupil etc*) favorire; (*team, horse*) dare per vincente; **to do sb a** ~ fare un favore *or* una cortesia a qn; **in** ~ **of** in favore di; **to be in** ~ **of sth/of doing sth** essere favorevole a qc/a fare qc; **to find** ~ **with sb** (*subj: person*) entrare nelle buone grazie di qn; (: *suggestion*) avere l'approvazione di qn.

favo(u)rable ['feɪvərəbl] *adj* favorevole.

favo(u)rably ['feɪvərəblɪ] *adv* favorevolmente.

favo(u)rite ['feɪvrɪt] *adj, n* favorito(a).

favo(u)ritism ['feɪvrɪtɪzəm] *n* favoritismo.

fawn [fɔːn] *n* daino ♦ *adj* (*also:* ~-**coloured**) marrone chiaro *inv* ♦ *vi:* **to** ~ (**up**)**on** adulare servilmente.

fax [fæks] *n* (*document, machine*) facsimile *m inv* ♦ *vt* teletrasmettere, spedire in facsimile.

FBI *n abbr* (*US:* = *Federal Bureau of Investigation*) FBI *f*.

FCC *n abbr* (*US*) = *Federal Communications Commission.*

FCO *n abbr* (*BRIT:* = *Foreign and Commonwealth Office*) ≈ Ufficio affari esteri.

FD *n abbr* (*US*) = **fire department.**

FDA *n abbr* (*US*) = *Food and Drug Administration.*

FE *n abbr* = **further education.**

fear [fɪə*] *n* paura, timore *m* ♦ *vt* aver paura di, temere ♦ *vi:* **to** ~ **for** temere per, essere in ansia per; ~ **of heights** vertigini *fpl;* **for** ~ **of** per paura di; **to** ~ **that** avere paura di (*or* che + *sub*), temere di (*or* che + *sub*).

fearful ['fɪəful] *adj* pauroso(a); (*sight, noise*) terribile, spaventoso(a); (*frightened*): **to be** ~ **of** temere.

fearfully ['fɪəfəlɪ] *adv* (*timidly*) timorosamente; (*col: very*) terribilmente, spaventosamente.

fearless ['fɪəlɪs] *adj* intrepido(a), senza paura.

fearsome ['fɪəsəm] *adj* (*opponent*) formidabile, terribile; (*sight*) terrificante.

feasibility [fiːzə'bɪlɪtɪ] *n* praticabilità.

feasibility study *n* studio delle possibilità di realizzazione.

feasible ['fiːzəbl] *adj* fattibile, realizzabile.

feast [fiːst] *n* festa, banchetto; (*REL: also:* ~ **day**) festa ♦ *vi* banchettare; **to** ~ **on** godersi, gustare.

feat [fiːt] *n* impresa, fatto insigne.

feather ['fɛðə*] *n* penna ♦ *cpd* (*mattress, bed, pillow*) di piume ♦ *vt:* **to** ~ **one's nest** (*fig*) arricchirsi.

feather-weight ['fɛðəweɪt] *n* peso *m* piuma *inv.*

feature ['fiːtʃə*] *n* caratteristica; (*article*) articolo ♦ *vt* (*subj: film*) avere come protagonista ♦ *vi* figurare; ~**s** *npl* (*of face*) fisionomia; **a** (**special**) ~ **on sth/sb** un servizio speciale su qc/qn; **it** ~**d prominently in** ... ha avuto un posto di prima importanza in ....

feature film *n* film *m inv* principale.

featureless ['fiːtʃəlɪs] *adj* anonimo(a), senza caratteri distinti.

Feb. [fɛb] *abbr* (= *February*) feb.

February ['fɛbruərɪ] *n* febbraio; *for phrases see also* **July.**

feces ['fiːsiːz] *npl* (*US*) = **faeces.**

feckless ['fɛklɪs] *adj* irresponsabile, incosciente.

Fed [fɛd] *abbr* (*US*) = **federal; federation.**

fed [fɛd] *pt, pp of* **feed; to be** ~ **up** essere stufo(a).

Fed. [fɛd] *n abbr* (*US col*) = **Federal Reserve Board.**

federal ['fɛdərəl] *adj* federale.

Federal Republic of Germany (FRG) *n* Repubblica Federale Tedesca (RFT).

Federal Reserve Board (Fed.) *n* (*US*) *organo di controllo del sistema bancario statunitense.*

Federal Trade Commission (FTC) *n* (*US*) *organismo di protezione contro le pratiche commerciali abusive.*

federation [fɛdə'reɪʃən] *n* federazione *f.*

fee [fiː] *n* pagamento; (*of doctor, lawyer*) onorario; (*for examination*) tassa d'esame; **school** ~**s** tasse *fpl* scolastiche; **entrance** ~, **membership** ~ quota d'iscrizione; **for a small** ~ per una somma modesta.

feeble ['fiːbl] *adj* debole.

feeble-minded [fiːbl'maɪndɪd] *adj* deficiente.

feed [fiːd] *n* (*of baby*) pappa ♦ *vt* (*pt, pp* **fed** [fɛd]) nutrire; (*horse etc*) dare da mangiare a; (*fire, machine*) alimentare ♦ *vi* (*baby, animal*) mangiare; **to** ~ **material into sth** introdurre materiale in qc; **to** ~ **data/information into sth** inserire dati/informazioni in qc.

▶**feed back** *vt* (*results*) riferire.

▶**feed on** *vt fus* nutrirsi di.

feedback ['fiːdbæk] *n* feed-back *m*; (*from person*) reazioni *fpl.*

feeder ['fiːdə*] *n* (*bib*) bavaglino.

feeding bottle ['fiːdɪŋ-] *n* (*BRIT*) biberon *m*

inv.

feel [fi:l] *n* sensazione *f*; (*sense of touch*) tatto; (*of substance*) consistenza ♦ *vt* (*pt, pp* **felt** [fɛlt]) toccare; palpare; tastare; (*cold, pain, anger*) sentire; (*grief*) provare; (*think, believe*): **to ~ (that)** pensare che; **I ~ that you ought to do it** penso che dovreste farlo; **to ~ hungry/cold** aver fame/freddo; **to ~ lonely/better** sentirsi solo/meglio; **I don't ~ well** non mi sento bene; **to ~ sorry for** dispiacersi per; **it ~s soft** è morbido al tatto; **it ~s colder out here** sembra più freddo qui fuori; **it ~s like velvet** sembra velluto (al tatto); **to ~ like** (*want*) aver voglia di; **to ~ about** *or* **around for** cercare a tastoni; **to ~ about** *or* **around in one's pocket for** frugarsi in tasca per cercare; **I'm still ~ing my way** (*fig*) sto ancora tastando il terreno; **to get the ~ of sth** (*fig*) abituarsi a qc.

feeler ['fi:lə*] *n* (*of insect*) antenna; **to put out ~s** (*fig*) fare un sondaggio.

feeling ['fi:lɪŋ] *n* sensazione *f*; sentimento; (*impression*) senso, impressione *f*; **to hurt sb's ~s** offendere qn; **what are your ~s about the matter?** che cosa ne pensa?; **my ~ is that** ... ho l'impressione che ...; **I got the ~ that** ... ho avuto l'impressione che ...; **~s ran high about it** la cosa aveva provocato grande eccitazione.

fee-paying school ['fi:peɪɪŋ-] *n* scuola privata.

feet [fi:t] *npl of* **foot**.

feign [feɪn] *vt* fingere, simulare.

felicitous [fɪ'lɪsɪtəs] *adj* felice.

fell [fɛl] *pt of* **fall** ♦ *vt* (*tree*) abbattere; (*person*) atterrare ♦ *adj*: **with one ~ blow** con un colpo terribile; **at one ~ swoop** in un colpo solo ♦ *n* (*BRIT: mountain*) monte *m*; (*: moorland*): **the ~s** la brughiera.

fellow ['fɛləu] *n* individuo, tipo; (*comrade*) compagno; (*of learned society*) membro; (*of university*) ≈ docente *m/f* ♦ *cpd*: **their ~ prisoners/students** i loro compagni di prigione/studio.

fellow citizen *n* concittadino/a.

fellow countryman *n* compatriota *m*.

fellow feeling *n* simpatia.

fellow men *npl* simili *mpl*.

fellowship ['fɛləuʃɪp] *n* associazione *f*; compagnia; (*SCOL*) specie di borsa di studio universitaria.

fellow traveller *n* compagno/a di viaggio; (*POL*) simpatizzante *m/f*.

fell-walking ['fɛlwɔ:kɪŋ] *n* (*BRIT*) passeggiate *fpl* in montagna.

felon ['fɛlən] *n* (*LAW*) criminale *m/f*.

felony ['fɛlənɪ] *n* (*LAW*) reato, crimine *m*.

felt [fɛlt] *pt, pp of* **feel** ♦ *n* feltro.

felt-tip pen ['fɛlttɪp-] *n* pennarello.

female ['fi:meɪl] *n* (*ZOOL*) femmina; (*pej: woman*) donna, femmina ♦ *adj* femminile; (*BIOL, ELEC*) femmina *inv*; **male and ~ students** studenti e studentesse.

female impersonator *n* (*THEAT*) attore comico che fa parti da donna.

feminine ['fɛmɪnɪn] *adj*, *n* femminile (*m*).

femininity [fɛmɪ'nɪnɪtɪ] *n* femminilità.

feminism ['fɛmɪnɪzəm] *n* femminismo.

feminist ['fɛmɪnɪst] *n* femminista *m/f*.

fen [fɛn] *n* (*BRIT*): **the F~s** la regione delle Fen.

fence [fɛns] *n* recinto; (*SPORT*) ostacolo; (*col: person*) ricettatore/trice ♦ *vt* (*also: ~ in*) recingere ♦ *vi* schermire; **to sit on the ~** (*fig*) rimanere neutrale.

fencing ['fɛnsɪŋ] *n* (*SPORT*) scherma.

fend [fɛnd] *vi*: **to ~ for o.s.** arrangiarsi.

▶**fend off** *vt* (*attack, attacker*) respingere, difendersi da; (*blow*) parare; (*awkward question*) eludere.

fender ['fɛndə*] *n* parafuoco; (*US*) parafango; paraurti *m inv*.

fennel ['fɛnl] *n* finocchio.

ferment *vi* [fə'mɛnt] fermentare ♦ *n* ['fə:mɛnt] agitazione *f*, eccitazione *f*.

fermentation [fə:mɛn'teɪʃən] *n* fermentazione *f*.

fern [fə:n] *n* felce *f*.

ferocious [fə'rəuʃəs] *adj* feroce.

ferocity [fə'rɔsɪtɪ] *n* ferocità.

ferret ['fɛrɪt] *n* furetto.

▶**ferret about, ferret around** *vi* frugare.

▶**ferret out** *vt* (*person*) scovare, scoprire; (*secret, truth*) scoprire.

ferry ['fɛrɪ] *n* (*small*) traghetto; (*large: also: ~boat*) nave *f* traghetto *inv* ♦ *vt* traghettare; **to ~ sth/sb across** *or* **over** traghettare qc/qn da una parte all'altra.

ferryman ['fɛrɪmən] *n* traghettatore *m*.

fertile ['fə:taɪl] *adj* fertile; (*BIOL*) fecondo(a); **~ period** periodo di fecondità.

fertility [fə'tɪlɪtɪ] *n* fertilità; fecondità.

fertility drug *n* farmaco fecondativo.

fertilize ['fə:tɪlaɪz] *vt* fertilizzare; fecondare.

fertilizer ['fə:tɪlaɪzə*] *n* fertilizzante *m*.

fervent ['fə:vənt] *adj* ardente, fervente.

fervour, (*US*) **fervor** ['fə:və*] *n* fervore *m*, ardore *m*.

fester ['fɛstə*] *vi* suppurare.

festival ['fɛstɪvəl] *n* (*REL*) festa; (*ART, MUS*) festival *m inv*.

festive ['fɛstɪv] *adj* di festa; **the ~ season** (*BRIT: Christmas*) il periodo delle feste.

festivities [fɛs'tɪvɪtɪz] npl festeggiamenti mpl.

festoon [fɛ'stuːn] vt: **to ~ with** ornare di; decorare con.

fetch [fɛtʃ] vt andare a prendere; (sell for) essere venduto(a) per; **how much did it ~?** a or per quanto lo ha venduto?

►**fetch up** vi (BRIT) andare a finire.

fetching ['fɛtʃɪŋ] adj attraente.

fête [feɪt] n festa.

fetid ['fɛtɪd] adj fetido(a).

fetish ['fɛtɪʃ] n feticcio.

fetter ['fɛtə*] vt (person) incatenare; (horse) legare; (fig) ostacolare.

fetters ['fɛtəz] npl catene fpl.

fettle ['fɛtl] n (BRIT): **in fine ~** in gran forma.

fetus ['fiːtəs] n (US) = **foetus**.

feud [fjuːd] n contesa, lotta ♦ vi essere in lotta; **a family ~** una lite in famiglia.

feudal ['fjuːdl] adj feudale.

feudalism ['fjuːdəlɪzəm] n feudalesimo.

fever ['fiːvə*] n febbre f; **he has a ~** ha la febbre.

feverish ['fiːvərɪʃ] adj (also fig) febbrile; (person) febbricitante.

few [fjuː] adj pochi(e) ♦ pron alcuni(e); **~ succeed** pochi ci riescono; **they were ~** erano pochi; **a ~ ...** qualche ...; **I know a ~** ne conosco alcuni; **a good ~, quite a ~** parecchi; **in the next ~ days** nei prossimi giorni; **in the past ~ days** negli ultimi giorni, in questi ultimi giorni; **every ~ days/months** ogni due o tre giorni/mesi; **a ~ more days** qualche altro giorno.

fewer ['fjuːə*] adj meno inv; meno numerosi(e) ♦ pron meno; **they are ~ now** adesso ce ne sono di meno.

fewest ['fjuːɪst] adj il minor numero di.

FFA n abbr = Future Farmers of America.

FH abbr (BRIT) = **fire hydrant**.

FHA n abbr (US) = Federal Housing Administration.

fiancé [fɪ'ɑːŋseɪ] n fidanzato.

fiancée [fɪ'ɑːŋseɪ] n fidanzata.

fiasco [fɪ'æskəu] n fiasco.

fib [fɪb] n piccola bugia.

fibre, (US) **fiber** ['faɪbə*] n fibra.

fibreboard, (US) **fiberboard** ['faɪbəbɔːd] n pannello di fibre.

fibre-glass, (US) **fiber-glass** ['faɪbəglɑːs] n fibra di vetro.

fibrositis [faɪbrə'saɪtɪs] n cellulite f.

FICA n abbr (US) = Federal Insurance Contributions Act.

fickle ['fɪkl] adj incostante, capriccioso(a).

fiction ['fɪkʃən] n narrativa; (sth made up) finzione f.

fictional ['fɪkʃənl] adj immaginario(a).

fictionalize ['fɪkʃənəlaɪz] vt romanzare.

fictitious [fɪk'tɪʃəs] adj fittizio(a).

fiddle ['fɪdl] n (MUS) violino; (cheating) imbroglio; truffa ♦ vt (BRIT: accounts) falsificare, falsare; **tax ~** frode f fiscale; **to work a ~** fare un imbroglio.

►**fiddle with** vt fus gingillarsi con.

fiddler ['fɪdlə*] n violinista m/f.

fiddly ['fɪdlɪ] adj (task) da certosino; (object) complesso(a).

fidelity [fɪ'dɛlɪtɪ] n fedeltà; (accuracy) esattezza.

fidget ['fɪdʒɪt] vi agitarsi.

fidgety ['fɪdʒɪtɪ] adj agitato(a).

fiduciary [fɪ'djuːʃɪərɪ] n fiduciario.

field [fiːld] n (gen, COMPUT) campo; **to lead the ~** (SPORT, COMM) essere in testa, essere al primo posto; **to have a ~ day** (fig) divertirsi, spassarsela.

field glasses npl binocolo (da campagna).

field hospital n ospedale m da campo.

field marshal (FM) n feldmaresciallo.

fieldwork ['fiːldwəːk] n ricerche fpl esterne; (ARCHEOLOGY, GEO) lavoro sul campo.

fiend [fiːnd] n demonio.

fiendish ['fiːndɪʃ] adj demoniaco(a).

fierce [fɪəs] adj (look, fighting) fiero(a); (wind) furioso(a); (attack) feroce; (enemy) acerrimo(a).

fiery ['faɪərɪ] adj ardente; infocato(a).

FIFA ['fiːfə] n abbr (= Fédération Internationale de Football Association) F.I.F.A. f.

fifteen [fɪf'tiːn] num quindici.

fifth [fɪfθ] num quinto(a).

fiftieth ['fɪftɪɪθ] num cinquantesimo(a).

fifty ['fɪftɪ] num cinquanta.

fifty-fifty ['fɪftɪ'fɪftɪ] adj, adv: **to go ~ with sb** fare a metà con qn; **we have a ~ chance of success** abbiamo una probabilità su due di successo.

fig [fɪg] n fico.

fight [faɪt] n zuffa, rissa; (MIL) battaglia, combattimento; (against cancer etc) lotta ♦ vb (pt, pp **fought** [fɔːt]) vt combattere; (cancer, alcoholism) lottare contro, combattere; (LAW: case) difendere ♦ vi battersi, combattere; (quarrel): **to ~ (with sb)** litigare (con qn); (fig): **to ~ (for/against)** lottare (per/contro).

►**fight back** vi difendersi; (SPORT, after illness) riprendersi ♦ vt (tears) ricacciare.

►**fight down** vt (anger, anxiety) vincere; (urge) reprimere.

►**fight off** vt (attack, attacker) respingere; (disease, sleep, urge) lottare contro.

►**fight out** vt: **to ~ it out** risolvere la

questione a pugni.

fighter ['faɪtə*] n combattente m; (plane) aeroplano da caccia.

fighter-bomber ['faɪtəbɔmə*] n cacciabombardiere m.

fighter pilot n pilota m di caccia.

fighting ['faɪtɪŋ] n combattimento; (in streets) scontri mpl.

figment ['fɪgmənt] n: **a ~ of the imagination** un parto della fantasia.

figurative ['fɪgjurətɪv] adj figurato(a).

figure ['fɪgə*] n (DRAWING, GEOM, person) figura; (number, cipher) cifra; (body, outline) forma ♦ vi (appear) figurare; (US: make sense) spiegarsi; essere logico(a) ♦ vt (US: think, calculate) pensare, immaginare; **public ~** personaggio pubblico; **~ of speech** figura retorica.

▶**figure on** vt fus (US) contare su.

▶**figure out** vt riuscire a capire; calcolare.

figurehead ['fɪgəhɛd] n (NAUT) polena; (pej) prestanome m/f inv.

figure skating n pattinaggio artistico.

Fiji (Islands) ['fi:dʒi:-] n(pl) le (isole) Figi.

filament ['fɪləmənt] n filamento.

filch [fɪltʃ] vt (col: steal) grattare.

file [faɪl] n (tool) lima; (for nails) limetta; (dossier) incartamento; (in cabinet) scheda; (folder) cartellina; (for loose leaf) raccoglitore m; (row) fila; (COMPUT) archivio, file m inv ♦ vt (nails, wood) limare; (papers) archiviare; (LAW: claim) presentare ♦ vi: **to ~ in/out** entrare/ uscire in fila; **to ~ past** marciare in fila davanti a; **to ~ a suit against sb** intentare causa contro qn.

file name n (COMPUT) nome m del file.

filibuster ['fɪlɪbʌstə*] (esp US POL) n (also: ~er) ostruzionista m/f ♦ vi fare ostruzionismo.

filing ['faɪlɪŋ] n archiviare m; see also **filings**.

filing cabinet n casellario.

filing clerk n archivista m/f.

filings ['faɪlɪŋz] npl limatura.

Filipino [fɪlɪ'pi:nəu] n filippino/a; (LING) tagal m.

fill [fɪl] vt riempire; (tooth) otturare; (job) coprire; (supply: order, requirements, need) soddisfare ♦ n: **to eat one's ~** mangiare a sazietà; **we've already ~ed that vacancy** abbiamo già assunto qualcuno per quel posto.

▶**fill in** vt (hole) riempire; (form) compilare; (details, report) completare ♦ vi: **to ~ in for sb** sostituire qn; **to ~ sb in on sth** (col) mettere qn al corrente di qc.

▶**fill out** vt (form, receipt) riempire.

▶**fill up** vt riempire ♦ vi (AUT) fare il pieno;

~ it up, please (AUT) mi faccia il pieno, per piacere.

fillet ['fɪlɪt] n filetto.

fillet steak n bistecca di filetto.

filling ['fɪlɪŋ] n (CULIN) impasto, ripieno; (for tooth) otturazione f.

filling station n stazione f di rifornimento.

fillip ['fɪlɪp] n incentivo, stimolo.

filly ['fɪlɪ] n puledra.

film [fɪlm] n (CINE) film m inv; (PHOT) pellicola; (thin layer) velo ♦ vt (scene) filmare.

film script n copione m.

film star n divo/a dello schermo.

filmstrip ['fɪlmstrɪp] n filmina.

film studio n studio cinematografico.

Filofax ® ['faɪləufæks] n agenda ad anelli.

filter ['fɪltə*] n filtro ♦ vt filtrare.

▶**filter in, filter through** vi (news) trapelare.

filter coffee n caffè m da passare al filtro.

filter lane n (BRIT AUT) corsia di svincolo.

filter tip n filtro.

filth [fɪlθ] n sporcizia; (fig) oscenità.

filthy ['fɪlθɪ] adj lordo(a), sozzo(a); (language) osceno(a).

fin [fɪn] n (of fish) pinna.

final ['faɪnl] adj finale, ultimo(a); definitivo(a) ♦ n (SPORT) finale f; ~s npl (SCOL) esami mpl finali; **~ demand** ingiunzione f di pagamento.

finale [fɪ'nɑ:lɪ] n finale m.

finalist ['faɪnəlɪst] n (SPORT) finalista m/f.

finality [faɪ'nælɪtɪ] n irrevocabilità; **with an air of ~** con risolutezza.

finalize ['faɪnəlaɪz] vt mettere a punto.

finally ['faɪnəlɪ] adv (lastly) alla fine; (eventually) finalmente; (once and for all) definitivamente.

finance [faɪ'næns] n finanza; (funds) fondi mpl, capitale m ♦ vt finanziare; ~s npl finanze fpl.

financial [faɪ'nænʃəl] adj finanziario(a); ~ **statement** estratto conto finanziario.

financially [faɪ'nænʃəlɪ] adv finanziariamente.

financial year n anno finanziario, esercizio finanziario.

financier [faɪ'nænsɪə*] n finanziatore m.

find [faɪnd] vt (pt, pp **found** [faund]) trovare; (lost object) ritrovare ♦ n trovata, scoperta; **to ~ (some) difficulty in doing sth** trovare delle difficoltà nel fare qc; **to ~ sb guilty** (LAW) giudicare qn colpevole.

▶**find out** vt informarsi di; (truth, secret) scoprire; (person) cogliere in fallo ♦ vi: **to ~ out about** informarsi su; (by chance) venire a sapere.

findings ['faɪndɪŋz] *npl* (*LAW*) sentenza, conclusioni *fpl*; (*of report*) conclusioni.

fine [faɪn] *adj* bello(a); ottimo(a); (*thin, subtle*) fine ♦ *adv* (*well*) molto bene; (*small*) finemente ♦ *n* (*LAW*) multa ♦ *vt* (*LAW*) multare; **he's** ~ sta bene; **the weather is** ~ il tempo è bello; **you're doing** ~ te la cavi benissimo; **to cut it** ~ (*of time, money*) farcela per un pelo.

fine arts *npl* belle arti *fpl*.

finely ['faɪnlɪ] *adv* (*splendidly*) in modo stupendo; (*chop*) finemente; (*adjust*) con precisione.

fine print *n*: **the** ~ i caratteri minuti.

finery ['faɪnərɪ] *n* abiti *mpl* eleganti.

finesse [fɪ'nɛs] *n* finezza.

fine-tooth comb ['faɪntuːθ-] *n*: **to go through sth with a** ~ (*fig*) passare qc al setaccio.

finger ['fɪŋgə*] *n* dito ♦ *vt* toccare, tastare.

fingernail ['fɪŋgəneɪl] *n* unghia.

fingerprint ['fɪŋgəprɪnt] *n* impronta digitale ♦ *vt* (*person*) prendere le impronte digitali di.

fingerstall ['fɪŋgəstɔːl] *n* ditale *m*.

fingertip ['fɪŋgətɪp] *n* punta del dito; **to have sth at one's** ~**s** (*fig*) avere qc sulla punta delle dita.

finicky ['fɪnɪkɪ] *adj* esigente, pignolo(a); minuzioso(a).

finish ['fɪnɪʃ] *n* fine *f*; (*SPORT: place*) traguardo; (*polish etc*) finitura ♦ *vt* finire; (*use up*) esaurire ♦ *vi* finire; (*session*) terminare; **to** ~ **doing sth** finire di fare qc; **to** ~ **first/second** (*SPORT*) arrivare primo/secondo; **she's** ~**ed with him** ha chiuso con lui.

▶**finish off** *vt* compiere; (*kill*) uccidere.

▶**finish up** *vi*, *vt* finire.

finished ['fɪnɪʃt] *adj* (*product*) finito(a); (*performance*) perfetto(a); (*col: tired*) sfinito(a).

finishing line ['fɪnɪʃɪŋ-] *n* linea d'arrivo.

finishing school *n* scuola privata di perfezionamento (*per signorine*).

finishing touches *npl* ultimi ritocchi *mpl*.

finite ['faɪnaɪt] *adj* limitato(a); (*verb*) finito(a).

Finland ['fɪnlənd] *n* Finlandia.

Finn [fɪn] *n* finlandese *m/f*.

Finnish ['fɪnɪʃ] *adj* finlandese ♦ *n* (*LING*) finlandese *m*.

fiord [fjɔːd] *n* fiordo.

fir [fəː*] *n* abete *m*.

fire [faɪə*] *n* fuoco; incendio ♦ *vt* (*discharge*): **to** ~ **a gun** scaricare un fucile; (*fig*) infiammare; (*dismiss*) licenziare ♦ *vi* sparare, far fuoco; **on** ~ in fiamme;

insured against ~ assicurato contro gli incendi; **electric/gas** ~ stufa elettrica/a gas; **to set** ~ **to sth, set sth on** ~ dar fuoco a qc, incendiare qc; **to be/come under** ~ (**from**) essere/finire sotto il fuoco *or* il tiro (di).

fire alarm *n* allarme *m* d'incendio.

firearm ['faɪərɑːm] *n* arma da fuoco.

fire brigade *n* (*BRIT*) (corpo dei) pompieri *mpl*.

fire chief *n* (*US*) = **fire master**.

fire department *n* (*US*) = **fire brigade**.

fire door *n* porta *f* rompifuoco *inv*.

fire drill *n* esercitazione *f* antincendio.

fire engine *n* autopompa.

fire escape *n* scala di sicurezza.

fire extinguisher *n* estintore *m*.

fireguard ['faɪəgɑːd] *n* (*BRIT*) parafuoco.

fire hazard *n*: **that's a** ~ comporta rischi in caso d'incendio.

fire hydrant *n* idrante *m*.

fire insurance *n* assicurazione *f* contro gli incendi.

fireman ['faɪəmən] *n* pompiere *m*.

fire master *n* (*BRIT*) comandante *m* dei vigili del fuoco.

fireplace ['faɪəpleɪs] *n* focolare *m*.

fireplug ['faɪəplʌg] *n* (*US*) = **fire hydrant**.

fire practice *n* = **fire drill**.

fireproof ['faɪəpruːf] *adj* resistente al fuoco.

fire regulations *npl* norme *fpl* antincendio.

fire screen *n* parafuoco.

fireside ['faɪəsaɪd] *n* angolo del focolare.

fire station *n* caserma dei pompieri.

firewood ['faɪəwud] *n* legna.

firework ['faɪəwəːk] *n* fuoco d'artificio.

firing ['faɪərɪŋ] *n* (*MIL*) spari *mpl*, tiro.

firing line *n* linea del fuoco; **to be in the** ~ (*fig*) essere sotto tiro.

firing squad *n* plotone *m* d'esecuzione.

firm [fəːm] *adj* fermo(a); (*offer, decision*) definitivo(a) ♦ *n* ditta, azienda; **to be a** ~ **believer in sth** credere fermamente in qc.

firmly ['fəːmlɪ] *adv* fermamente.

firmness ['fəːmnɪs] *n* fermezza.

first [fəːst] *adj* primo(a) ♦ *adv* (*before others*) il primo, la prima; (*before other things*) per primo; (*for the first time*) per la prima volta; (*when listing reasons etc*) per prima cosa ♦ *n* (*person: in race*) primo/a; (*BRIT SCOL*) laurea con lode; (*AUT*) prima; **at** ~ dapprima, all'inizio; ~ **of all** prima di tutto; **in the** ~ **instance** prima di tutto, in primo luogo; **I'll do it** ~ **thing tomorrow** lo farò per prima cosa domani; **from the (very)** ~ fin dall'inizio, fin dal primo momento; **the** ~ **of January** il primo (di) gennaio.

first aid n pronto soccorso.
first-aid kit ['fə:st'eɪd-] n cassetta pronto soccorso.
first-class ['fə:st'klɑːs] adj di prima classe.
first-class mail n ≈ espresso.
first-hand ['fə:st'hænd] adj di prima mano; diretto(a).
first lady n (US) moglie f del presidente.
firstly ['fə:stlɪ] adv in primo luogo.
first name n prenome m.
first night n (THEAT) prima.
first-rate ['fə:st'reɪt] adj di prima qualità, ottimo(a).
first-time buyer ['fə:sttaɪm-] n acquirente m/f di prima casa.
First World War n: the ~ la prima guerra mondiale.
fir tree n abete m.
FIS n abbr (BRIT: = Family Income Supplement) ≈ A.F. (= assegni familiari).
fiscal ['fɪskəl] adj fiscale; ~ **year** anno fiscale.
fish [fɪʃ] n (pl inv) pesce m ♦ vt, vi pescare; **to** ~ **a river** pescare in un fiume; **to go** ~**ing** andare a pesca.
▶**fish out** vt (from water) ripescare; (from box etc) tirare fuori.
fish-and-chip shop [fɪʃən'tʃɪp-] n ≈ friggitoria; see **chip shop**.
fishbone ['fɪʃbəun] n lisca, spina.
fisherman ['fɪʃəmən] n pescatore m.
fishery ['fɪʃərɪ] n zona da pesca.
fish factory n (BRIT) fabbrica per la lavorazione del pesce.
fish farm n vivaio.
fish fingers npl (BRIT) bastoncini mpl di pesce (surgelati).
fish hook n amo.
fishing boat ['fɪʃɪŋ-] n barca da pesca.
fishing industry n industria della pesca.
fishing line n lenza.
fishing net n rete f da pesca.
fishing rod n canna da pesca.
fishing tackle n attrezzatura da pesca.
fish market n mercato del pesce.
fishmonger ['fɪʃmʌŋɡə*] n pescivendolo; ~**'s (shop)** pescheria.
fish slice n (BRIT) posata per servire il pesce.
fish sticks npl (US) = **fish fingers**.
fishy ['fɪʃɪ] adj (fig) sospetto(a).
fission ['fɪʃən] n fissione f; **atomic/nuclear** ~ fissione atomica/nucleare.
fissure ['fɪʃə*] n fessura.
fist [fɪst] n pugno.
fistfight ['fɪstfaɪt] n scazzottata.
fit [fɪt] adj (MED, SPORT) in forma; (proper) adatto(a), appropriato(a); conveniente

♦ vt (subj: clothes) stare bene a; (match: facts etc) concordare con; (: description) corrispondere a; (adjust) aggiustare; (put in, attach) mettere; installare; (equip) fornire, equipaggiare ♦ vi (clothes) stare bene; (parts) andare bene, adattarsi; (in space, gap) entrare ♦ n (MED) attacco; ~ **to** in grado di; ~ **for** adatto(a) a; degno(a) di; **to keep** ~ tenersi in forma; ~ **for work** (after illness) in grado di riprendere il lavoro; **do as you think** or **see** ~ faccia come meglio crede; **this dress is a tight/good** ~ questo vestito è stretto/sta bene; ~ **of anger/enthusiasm** accesso d'ira/d'entusiasmo; **to have a** ~ (MED) avere un attacco di convulsioni; (col) andare su tutte le furie; **by** ~**s and starts** a sbalzi.
▶**fit in** vi accordarsi; adattarsi ♦ vt (object) far entrare; (fig: appointment, visitor) trovare il tempo per; **to** ~ **in with sb's plans** adattarsi ai progetti di qn.
▶**fit out** vt (BRIT: also: ~ **up**) equipaggiare.
fitful ['fɪtful] adj saltuario(a).
fitment ['fɪtmənt] n componibile m.
fitness ['fɪtnɪs] n (MED) forma fisica; (of remark) appropriatezza.
fitted ['fɪtɪd] adj: ~ **carpet** moquette f inv; ~ **cupboards** armadi mpl a muro; ~ **kitchen** (BRIT) cucina componibile.
fitter ['fɪtə*] n aggiustatore m or montatore m meccanico; (DRESSMAKING) sarto/a.
fitting ['fɪtɪŋ] adj appropriato(a) ♦ n (of dress) prova; (of piece of equipment) montaggio, aggiustaggio; see also **fittings**.
fitting room n (in shop) camerino.
fittings ['fɪtɪŋz] npl impianti mpl.
five [faɪv] num cinque.
five-day week ['faɪvdeɪ-] n settimana di 5 giorni (lavorativi).
fiver ['faɪvə*] n (col: BRIT) biglietto da cinque sterline; (: US) biglietto da cinque dollari.
fix [fɪks] vt fissare; (mend) riparare; (make ready: meal, drink) preparare ♦ n: **to be in a** ~ essere nei guai; **the fight was a** ~ (col) l'incontro è stato truccato.
▶**fix up** vt (arrange: date, meeting) fissare, stabilire; **to** ~ **sb up with sth** procurare qc a qn.
fixation [fɪk'seɪʃən] n (PSYCH, fig) fissazione f, ossessione f.
fixed [fɪkst] adj (prices etc) fisso(a); **there's a** ~ **charge** c'è una quota fissa; **how are you** ~ **for money?** (col) a soldi come stai?
fixed assets npl beni mpl patrimoniali.
fixture ['fɪkstʃə*] n impianto (fisso); (SPORT) incontro (del calendario sportivo).

fizz [fɪz] *vi* frizzare.

fizzle ['fɪzl] *vi* frizzare; (*also*: ~ **out**: *enthusiasm, interest*) smorzarsi, svanire; (: *plan*) fallire.

fizzy ['fɪzɪ] *adj* frizzante; gassato(a).

fjord [fjɔːd] *n* = **fiord**.

FL, Fla. *abbr* (US) = Florida.

flabbergasted ['flæbəgɑːstɪd] *adj* sbalordito(a).

flabby ['flæbɪ] *adj* flaccido(a).

flag [flæg] *n* bandiera; (*also*: ~**stone**) pietra da lastricare ♦ *vi* stancarsi; affievolirsi; ~ **of convenience** bandiera di convenienza.

▶**flag down** *vt* fare segno (di fermarsi) a.

flagon ['flægən] *n* bottiglione *m*.

flagpole ['flægpəul] *n* albero.

flagrant ['fleɪgrənt] *adj* flagrante.

flag stop *n* (US: *for bus*) fermata facoltativa, fermata a richiesta.

flair [flɛə*] *n* (*for business etc*) fiuto; (*for languages etc*) facilità.

flak [flæk] *n* (MIL) fuoco d'artiglieria; (*col*: *criticism*) critiche *fpl*.

flake [fleɪk] *n* (*of rust, paint*) scaglia; (*of snow, soap powder*) fiocco ♦ *vi* (*also*: ~ **off**) sfaldarsi.

flaky ['fleɪkɪ] *adj* (*paintwork*) scrostato(a); (*skin*) squamoso(a); ~ **pastry** (CULIN) pasta sfoglia.

flamboyant [flæm'bɔɪənt] *adj* sgargiante.

flame [fleɪm] *n* fiamma; **old** ~ (*col*) vecchia fiamma.

flamingo [flə'mɪŋgəu] *n* fenicottero, fiammingo.

flammable ['flæməbl] *adj* infiammabile.

flan [flæn] *n* (BRIT) flan *m inv*.

Flanders ['flɑːndəz] *n* Fiandre *fpl*.

flange [flændʒ] *n* flangia; (*on wheel*) suola.

flank [flæŋk] *n* fianco.

flannel ['flænl] *n* (BRIT: *also*: **face** ~) guanto di spugna; (*fabric*) flanella; ~**s** *npl* pantaloni *mpl* di flanella.

flannelette [flænə'lɛt] *n* flanella di cotone.

flap [flæp] *n* (*of pocket*) patta; (*of envelope*) lembo; (AVIAT) flap *m inv* ♦ *vt* (*wings*) battere ♦ *vi* (*sail, flag*) sbattere; (*col*: *also*: **be in a** ~) essere in agitazione.

flapjack ['flæpdʒæk] *n* (US: *pancake*) frittella; (BRIT: *biscuit*) biscotto di avena.

flare [flɛə*] *n* razzo; (*in skirt etc*) svasatura.

▶**flare up** *vi* andare in fiamme; (*fig*: *person*) infiammarsi di rabbia; (: *revolt*) scoppiare.

flared ['flɛəd] *adj* (*trousers*) svasato(a).

flash [flæʃ] *n* vampata; (*also*: **news** ~) notizia *f* lampo *inv*; (PHOT) flash *m inv*; (US: *torch*) torcia elettrica, lampadina tascabile ♦ *vt* accendere e spegnere;

(*send*: *message*) trasmettere; (*flaunt*) ostentare ♦ *vi* brillare; (*light on ambulance, eyes etc*) lampeggiare; **in a** ~ in un lampo; ~ **of inspiration** lampo di genio; **to** ~ **one's headlights** lampeggiare; **he** ~**ed by** *or* **past** ci passò davanti come un lampo.

flashback ['flæʃbæk] *n* flashback *m inv*.

flashbulb ['flæʃbʌlb] *n* cubo *m* flash *inv*.

flash card *n* (SCOL) scheda didattica.

flashcube ['flæʃkjuːb] *n* flash *m inv*.

flasher ['flæʃə*] *n* (AUT) lampeggiatore *m*.

flashlight ['flæʃlaɪt] *n* (*torch*) lampadina tascabile.

flashpoint ['flæʃpɔɪnt] *n* punto di infiammabilità; (*fig*) livello critico.

flashy ['flæʃɪ] *adj* (*pej*) vistoso(a).

flask [flɑːsk] *n* fiasco; (CHEM) beuta; (*also*: **vacuum** ~) thermos ® *m inv*.

flat [flæt] *adj* piatto(a); (*tyre*) sgonfio(a), a terra; (*battery*) scarico(a); (*denial*) netto(a); (MUS) bemolle *inv*; (: *voice*) stonato(a); (: *instrument*) scordato(a) ♦ *n* (BRIT: *rooms*) appartamento; (MUS) bemolle *m*; (AUT) pneumatico sgonfio ♦ *adv*: **(to work)** ~ **out** (lavorare) a più non posso; ~ **rate of pay** tariffa unica di pagamento.

flat-footed ['flæt'futɪd] *adj*: **to be** ~ avere i piedi piatti.

flatly ['flætlɪ] *adv* categoricamente, nettamente.

flatmate ['flætmeɪt] *n* (BRIT): **he's my** ~ divide l'appartamento con me.

flatness ['flætnɪs] *n* (*of land*) assenza di rilievi.

flat-screen ['flætskriːn] *adj* a schermo piatto.

flatten ['flætn] *vt* (*also*: ~ **out**) appiattire; (*house, city*) abbattere, radere al suolo.

flatter ['flætə*] *vt* lusingare; (*show to advantage*) donare a.

flatterer ['flætərə*] *n* adulatore/trice.

flattering ['flætərɪŋ] *adj* lusinghiero(a); (*clothes etc*) che dona, che abbellisce.

flattery ['flætərɪ] *n* adulazione *f*.

flatulence ['flætjuləns] *n* flatulenza.

flaunt [flɔːnt] *vt* fare mostra di.

flavour, (US) **flavor** ['fleɪvə*] *n* gusto, sapore *m* ♦ *vt* insaporire, aggiungere sapore a; **vanilla-~ed** al gusto di vaniglia.

flavo(u)ring ['fleɪvərɪŋ] *n* essenza (artificiale).

flaw [flɔː] *n* difetto.

flawless ['flɔːlɪs] *adj* senza difetti.

flax [flæks] *n* lino.

flaxen ['flæksən] *adj* biondo(a).

flea [fliː] *n* pulce *f*.

flea market *n* mercato delle pulci.

fleck [flɛk] n (of mud, paint, colour) macchiolina; (of dust) granello ♦ vt (with blood, mud etc) macchiettare; **brown ~ed with white** marrone screziato di bianco.

fled [flɛd] pt, pp of **flee**.

fledg(e)ling ['flɛdʒlɪŋ] n uccellino.

flee, pt, pp **fled** [fliː, flɛd] vt fuggire da ♦ vi fuggire, scappare.

fleece [fliːs] n vello ♦ vt (col) pelare.

fleecy ['fliːsɪ] adj (blanket) soffice; (cloud) come ovatta.

fleet [fliːt] n flotta; (of lorries etc) convoglio; (of cars) parco.

fleeting ['fliːtɪŋ] adj fugace, fuggitivo(a); (visit) volante.

Flemish ['flɛmɪʃ] adj fiammingo(a) ♦ n (LING) fiammingo; **the ~** npl i Fiamminghi.

flesh [flɛʃ] n carne f; (of fruit) polpa.

flesh wound n ferita superficiale.

flew [fluː] pt of **fly**.

flex [flɛks] n filo (flessibile) ♦ vt flettere; (muscles) contrarre.

flexibility [flɛksɪ'bɪlɪtɪ] n flessibilità.

flexible ['flɛksəbl] adj flessibile.

flexitime ['flɛksɪtaɪm] n orario flessibile.

flick [flɪk] n colpetto; see also **flicks**.

►**flick through** vt fus sfogliare.

flicker ['flɪkə*] vi tremolare ♦ n tremolio; **a ~ of light** un breve bagliore.

flick knife n (BRIT) coltello a serramanico.

flicks npl: **the ~** (col) il cine.

flier ['flaɪə*] n aviatore m.

flight [flaɪt] n volo; (escape) fuga; (also: ~ of steps) scalinata; **to take ~** darsi alla fuga; **to put to ~** mettere in fuga.

flight attendant n (US) steward m, hostess f inv.

flight crew n equipaggio.

flight deck n (AVIAT) cabina di controllo; (NAUT) ponte m di comando.

flight path n (of aircraft) rotta di volo; (of rocket, projectile) traiettoria.

flight recorder n registratore m di volo.

flimsy ['flɪmzɪ] adj (fabric) inconsistente; (excuse) meschino(a).

flinch [flɪntʃ] vi ritirarsi; **to ~ from** tirarsi indietro di fronte a.

fling, pt, pp **flung** [flɪŋ, flʌŋ] vt lanciare, gettare ♦ n (love affair) avventura.

flint [flɪnt] n selce f; (in lighter) pietrina.

flip [flɪp] n colpetto ♦ vt dare un colpetto a; (US: pancake) far saltare (in aria) ♦ vi: **to ~ for sth** (US) fare a testa e croce per qc.

►**flip through** vt fus (book, records) dare una scorsa a.

flippant ['flɪpənt] adj senza rispetto, irriverente.

flipper ['flɪpə*] n pinna.

flip side n (of record) retro.

flirt [fləːt] vi flirtare ♦ n civetta.

flirtation [fləː'teɪʃən] n flirt m inv.

flit [flɪt] vi svolazzare.

float [fləut] n galleggiante m; (in procession) carro; (sum of money) somma ♦ vi galleggiare; (bather) fare il morto; (COMM: currency) fluttuare ♦ vt far galleggiare; (loan, business) lanciare; **to ~ an idea** ventilare un'idea.

floating ['fləutɪŋ] adj a galla; **~ vote** voto oscillante; **~ voter** elettore m indeciso.

flock [flɔk] n gregge m; (of people) folla; (of birds) stormo.

floe [fləu] n (also: **ice ~**) banchisa.

flog [flɔg] vt flagellare.

flood [flʌd] n alluvione f; (of words, tears etc) diluvio ♦ vt inondare, allagare; (AUT: carburettor) ingolfare; **in ~** in pieno; **to ~ the market** (COMM) inondare il mercato.

flooding ['flʌdɪŋ] n inondazione f.

floodlight ['flʌdlaɪt] n riflettore m ♦ vt illuminare a giorno.

floodlit ['flʌdlɪt] pt, pp of **floodlight** ♦ adj illuminato(a) a giorno.

flood tide n alta marea, marea crescente.

floodwater ['flʌdwɔːtə*] n acque fpl (di inondazione).

floor [flɔː*] n pavimento; (storey) piano; (of sea, valley) fondo; (fig: at meeting): **the ~** il pubblico ♦ vt pavimentare; (knock down) atterrare; (baffle) confondere; (silence) far tacere; **on the ~** sul pavimento, per terra; **ground ~**, (US) **first ~** pianterreno; **first ~**, (US) **second ~** primo piano; **top ~** ultimo piano; **to have the ~** (speaker) prendere la parola.

floorboard ['flɔːbɔːd] n tavellone m di legno.

flooring ['flɔːrɪŋ] n (floor) pavimento; (material) materiale m per pavimentazioni.

floor lamp n (US) lampada a stelo.

floor show n spettacolo di varietà.

floorwalker ['flɔːwɔːkə*] n (esp US) ispettore m di reparto.

flop [flɔp] n fiasco ♦ vi (fail) far fiasco.

floppy ['flɔpɪ] adj floscio(a), molle ♦ n (COMPUT) = **floppy disk**; **~ hat** cappello floscio.

floppy disk n floppy disk m inv.

flora ['flɔːrə] n flora.

floral ['flɔːrl] adj floreale.

Florence ['flɔrəns] n Firenze f.

Florentine ['flɔrəntaɪn] adj fiorentino(a).

florid ['flɔrɪd] adj (complexion) florido(a); (style) fiorito(a).

florist ['flɔrɪst] n fioraio/a; **at the ~'s (shop)**

dal fioraio.

flotation [fləu'teɪʃən] n (COMM) lancio.

flounce [flauns] n balzo.

▶**flounce out** vi uscire stizzito(a).

flounder ['flaundə*] vi annaspare ♦ n (ZOOL) passera di mare.

flour ['flauə*] n farina.

flourish ['flʌrɪʃ] vi fiorire ♦ vt brandire ♦ n abbellimento; svolazzo; (of trumpets) fanfara.

flourishing ['flʌrɪʃɪŋ] adj prosperoso(a), fiorente.

flout [flaut] vt (order) contravvenire a; (convention) sfidare.

flow [fləu] n flusso; circolazione f; (of river, also ELEC) corrente f ♦ vi fluire; (traffic, blood in veins) circolare; (hair) scendere.

flow chart n schema m di flusso.

flow diagram n organigramma m.

flower ['flauə*] n fiore m ♦ vi fiorire; **in ~** in fiore.

flower bed n aiuola.

flowerpot ['flauəpɔt] n vaso da fiori.

flowery ['flauərɪ] adj fiorito(a).

flown [fləun] pp of **fly**.

flu [flu:] n influenza.

fluctuate ['flʌktjueɪt] vi fluttuare, oscillare.

fluctuation [flʌktju'eɪʃən] n fluttuazione f, oscillazione f.

flue [flu:] n canna fumaria.

fluency ['flu:ənsɪ] n facilità, scioltezza; **his ~ in English** la sua scioltezza nel parlare l'inglese.

fluent ['flu:ənt] adj (speech) facile, sciolto(a); **he's a ~ speaker/reader** si esprime/legge senza difficoltà; **he speaks ~ Italian, he's ~ in Italian** parla l'italiano correntemente.

fluently ['flu:əntlɪ] adv con facilità; correntemente.

fluff [flʌf] n lanugine f.

fluffy ['flʌfɪ] adj lanuginoso(a); (toy) di peluche.

fluid ['flu:ɪd] adj fluido(a) ♦ n fluido; (in diet) liquido.

fluid ounce n (BRIT) = 0.028 l; 0.05 pints.

fluke [flu:k] n (col) colpo di fortuna.

flummox ['flʌməks] vt rendere perplesso(a).

flung [flʌŋ] pt, pp of **fling**.

flunky ['flʌŋkɪ] n tirapiedi m/f inv.

fluorescent [fluə'rɛsnt] adj fluorescente.

fluoride ['fluəraɪd] n fluoruro.

fluorine ['fluəri:n] n fluoro.

flurry ['flʌrɪ] n (of snow) tempesta; **a ~ of activity/excitement** una febbre di attività/un'improvvisa agitazione.

flush [flʌʃ] n rossore m; (fig) ebbrezza ♦ vt

ripulire con un getto d'acqua; (also: ~ out: birds) far alzare in volo; (: animals, fig: criminal) stanare ♦ vi arrossire ♦ adj: ~ **with** a livello di, pari a; ~ **against** aderente a; **hot ~es** (MED) vampate fpl di calore; **to ~ the toilet** tirare l'acqua.

flushed [flʌʃt] adj tutto(a) rosso(a).

fluster ['flʌstə*] n agitazione f.

flustered ['flʌstəd] adj sconvolto(a).

flute [flu:t] n flauto.

flutter ['flʌtə*] n agitazione f; (of wings) frullio ♦ vi (bird) battere le ali.

flux [flʌks] n: **in a state of ~** in continuo mutamento.

fly [flaɪ] n (insect) mosca; (on trousers: also: **flies**) bracchetta ♦ vb (pt **flew**, pp **flown** [flu:, fləun]) vt pilotare; (passengers, cargo) trasportare (in aereo); (distances) percorrere ♦ vi volare; (passengers) andare in aereo; (escape) fuggire; (flag) sventolare; **to ~ open** spalancarsi all'improvviso; **to ~ off the handle** perdere le staffe, uscire dai gangheri.

▶**fly away** vi volar via.

▶**fly in** vi (plane) arrivare; (person) arrivare in aereo.

▶**fly off** vi volare via.

▶**fly out** vi (plane) partire; (person) partire in aereo.

fly-fishing ['flaɪfɪʃɪŋ] n pesca con la mosca.

flying ['flaɪɪŋ] n (activity) aviazione f; (action) volo ♦ adj: ~ **visit** visita volante; **with ~ colours** con risultati brillanti; **he doesn't like ~** non gli piace viaggiare in aereo.

flying buttress n arco rampante.

flying picket n picchetto (proveniente da fabbriche non direttamente coinvolte nello sciopero).

flying saucer n disco volante.

flying squad n (POLICE) (squadra) volante f.

flying start n: **to get off to a ~ start** partire come un razzo.

flyleaf ['flaɪli:f] n risguardo.

flyover ['flaɪəuvə*] n (BRIT: bridge) cavalcavia m inv.

flypast ['flaɪpɑ:st] n esibizione f della pattuglia aerea.

flysheet ['flaɪʃi:t] n (for tent) sopratetto.

flyweight ['flaɪweɪt] n (SPORT) peso m mosca inv.

flywheel ['flaɪwi:l] n volano.

FM abbr see **frequency modulation**; (BRIT MIL) see **Field Marshal**.

FMB n abbr (US) = Federal Maritime Board.

FMCS n abbr (US: = Federal Mediation and Conciliation Services) organismo di *conciliazione in caso di conflitti sul lavoro.*

FO *n abbr* (*BRIT*) *see* **Foreign Office.**

foal [fəul] *n* puledro.

foam [fəum] *n* schiuma ♦ *vi* schiumare.

foam rubber *n* gommapiuma ®.

FOB *abbr* (= *free on board*) franco a bordo.

fob [fɔb] *vt*: **to ~ sb off with** appioppare qn con; sbarazzarsi di qn con ♦ *n* (*also*: **watch ~**: *chain*) catena per orologio; (: *band of cloth*) nastro per orologio.

foc *abbr* (*BRIT*) = **free of charge.**

focal [ˈfəukəl] *adj* focale.

focal point *n* punto focale.

focus [ˈfəukəs] *n* (*pl* **~es**) fuoco; (*of interest*) centro ♦ *vt* (*field glasses etc*) mettere a fuoco; (*light rays*) far convergere ♦ *vi*: **to ~ on** (*with camera*) mettere a fuoco; (*person*) fissare lo sguardo su; **in ~** a fuoco; **out of ~** sfocato(a).

fodder [ˈfɔdə*] *n* foraggio.

FOE *n abbr* (= *Friends of the Earth*) Amici *mpl* della Terra; (*US*: = *Fraternal Order of Eagles*) organizzazione filantropica.

foe [fəu] *n* nemico.

foetus, (*US*) **fetus** [ˈfiːtəs] *n* feto.

fog [fɔg] *n* nebbia.

fogbound [ˈfɔgbaund] *adj* fermo(a) a causa della nebbia.

foggy [ˈfɔgɪ] *adj* nebbioso(a); **it's ~** c'è nebbia.

fog lamp, (*US*) **fog light** *n* (*AUT*) faro *m* antinebbia *inv*.

foible [ˈfɔɪbl] *n* debolezza, punto debole.

foil [fɔɪl] *vt* confondere, frustrare ♦ *n* lamina di metallo; (*also*: **kitchen ~**) foglio di alluminio; (*FENCING*) fioretto; **to act as a ~ to** (*fig*) far risaltare.

foist [fɔɪst] *vt*: **to ~ sth on sb** rifilare qc a qn.

fold [fəuld] *n* (*bend, crease*) piega; (*AGR*) ovile *m*; (*fig*) gregge *m* ♦ *vt* piegare; **to ~ one's arms** incrociare le braccia.

▶**fold up** *vi* (*map etc*) piegarsi; (*business*) crollare ♦ *vt* (*map etc*) piegare, ripiegare.

folder [ˈfəuldə*] *n* (*for papers*) cartella; cartellina; (*binder*) raccoglitore *m*.

folding [ˈfəuldɪŋ] *adj* (*chair, bed*) pieghevole.

foliage [ˈfəulɪɪdʒ] *n* fogliame *m*.

folk [fəuk] *npl* gente *f* ♦ *cpd* popolare; **~s** *npl* famiglia.

folklore [ˈfəuklɔː*] *n* folclore *m*.

folk music *n* musica folk *inv*.

folk singer *n* cantante *m/f* folk *inv*.

folksong [ˈfəuksɔŋ] *n* canto popolare.

follow [ˈfɔləu] *vt* seguire ♦ *vi* seguire; (*result*) conseguire, risultare; **to ~ sb's advice** seguire il consiglio di qn; **I don't**

quite ~ you non ti capisco *or* seguo affatto; **to ~ in sb's footsteps** seguire le orme di qn; **it ~s that** ... ne consegue che ...; **he ~ed suit** lui ha fatto lo stesso.

▶**follow on** *vi* (*continue*): **to ~ on from** seguire.

▶**follow out** *vt* (*implement: idea, plan*) eseguire, portare a termine.

▶**follow through** *vt* = **follow out.**

▶**follow up** *vt* (*victory*) sfruttare; (*letter, offer*) fare seguito a; (*case*) seguire.

follower [ˈfɔləuə*] *n* seguace *m/f*, discepolo/a.

following [ˈfɔləuɪŋ] *adj* seguente, successivo(a) ♦ *n* seguito, discepoli *mpl*.

follow-up [ˈfɔləuʌp] *n* seguito.

folly [ˈfɔlɪ] *n* pazzia, follia.

fond [fɔnd] *adj* (*memory, look*) tenero(a), affettuoso(a); **to be ~ of** volere bene a; **she's ~ of swimming** le piace nuotare.

fondle [ˈfɔndl] *vt* accarezzare.

fondly [ˈfɔndlɪ] *adv* (*lovingly*) affettuosamente; (*naïvely*): **he ~ believed that** ... ha avuto l'ingenuità di credere che ....

fondness [ˈfɔndnɪs] *n* affetto; **~ (for sth)** predilezione *f* (per qc).

font [fɔnt] *n* (*REL*) fonte *m* (battesimale); (*TYP*) stile *m* di carattere.

food [fuːd] *n* cibo.

food chain *n* catena alimentare.

food mixer *n* frullatore *m*.

food poisoning *n* intossicazione *f* alimentare.

food processor *n* tritatutto *m inv* elettrico.

food stamp *n* (*US*) buono alimentare dato agli indigenti.

foodstuffs [ˈfuːdstʌfs] *npl* generi *fpl* alimentari.

fool [fuːl] *n* sciocco/a; (*HISTORY: of king*) buffone *m*; (*CULIN*) frullato ♦ *vt* ingannare ♦ *vi* (*gen*: **~ around**) fare lo sciocco; **to make a ~ of sb** prendere in giro qn; **to make a ~ of o.s.** coprirsi di ridicolo; **you can't ~ me** non mi inganna.

▶**fool about, fool around** *vi* (*waste time*) perdere tempo.

foolhardy [ˈfuːlhɑːdɪ] *adj* avventato(a).

foolish [ˈfuːlɪʃ] *adj* scemo(a), stupido(a); imprudente.

foolishly [ˈfuːlɪʃlɪ] *adv* stupidamente.

foolishness [ˈfuːlɪʃnɪs] *n* stupidità.

foolproof [ˈfuːlpruːf] *adj* (*plan etc*) sicurissimo(a).

foolscap [ˈfuːlskæp] *n* carta protocollo.

foot [fut] *n* (*pl* **feet** [fiːt]) piede *m*; (*measure*) piede (= *304 mm; 12 inches*); (*of animal*) zampa; (*of page, stairs etc*) fondo ♦ *vt* (*bill*)

pagare; **on** ~ a piedi; **to put one's** ~
down (*AUT*) schiacciare l'acceleratore;
(*say no*) imporsi; **to find one's feet**
ambientarsi.

footage ['futɪdʒ] *n* (*CINE: length*) ≈
metraggio; (: *material*) sequenza.

foot and mouth (disease) *n* afta
epizootica.

football ['futbɔːl] *n* pallone *m*; (*sport*: *BRIT*)
calcio; (: *US*) football *m* americano.

footballer ['futbɔːlə*] *n* (*BRIT*) = **football
player**.

football ground *n* campo di calcio.

football match *n* (*BRIT*) partita di calcio.

football player *n* (*BRIT*) calciatore *m*; (*US*)
giocatore *m* di football americano.

footbrake ['futbreɪk] *n* freno a pedale.

footbridge ['futbrɪdʒ] *n* passerella.

foothills ['futhɪlz] *npl* contrafforti *fpl*.

foothold ['futhəuld] *n* punto d'appoggio.

footing ['futɪŋ] *n* (*fig*) posizione *f*; **to lose
one's** ~ mettere un piede in fallo; **on an
equal** ~ in condizioni di parità.

footlights ['futlaɪts] *npl* luci *fpl* della
ribalta.

footman ['futmən] *n* lacchè *m inv*.

footnote ['futnəut] *n* nota (a piè di pagina).

footpath ['futpɑːθ] *n* sentiero; (*in street*)
marciapiede *m*.

footprint ['futprɪnt] *n* orma, impronta.

footrest ['futrest] *n* poggiapiedi *m inv*.

footsie ['futsɪ] *n* (*col*): **to play** ~ **with sb**
fare piedino a qn.

Footsie (index) ['futsɪ-] *n* (*col*) = Financial
Times Stock Exchange 100 Index.

footsore ['futsɔː*] *adj*: **to be** ~ avere mal di
piedi.

footstep ['futstɛp] *n* passo.

footwear ['futwɛə*] *n* calzatura.

FOR *abbr* (= *free on rail*) franco vagone.

━━━━━━━━━━━━━━ *KEYWORD*

for [fɔː*] *prep* **1** (*indicating destination,
intention, purpose*) per; **the train** ~ **London**
il treno per Londra; **he went** ~ **the paper**
è andato a prendere il giornale; **it's time**
~ **lunch** è ora di pranzo; **what's it** ~? a
che serve?; **what** ~? (*why*) perché?

2 (*on behalf of, representing*) per; **to work**
~ **sb/sth** lavorare per qn/qc; **I'll ask him**
~ **you** glielo chiederò a nome tuo; **G** ~
George G come George

3 (*because of*) per, a causa di; ~ **this
reason** per questo motivo

4 (*with regard to*) per; **it's cold** ~ **July** è
freddo per luglio; ~ **everyone who voted
yes, 50 voted no** per ogni voto a favore
ce n'erano 50 contro

5 (*in exchange for*) per; **I sold it** ~ **£5** l'ho
venduto per 5 sterline

6 (*in favour of*) per, a favore di; **are you** ~
or against us? sei con noi o contro di
noi?; **I'm all** ~ **it** sono completamente a
favore

7 (*referring to distance, time*) per; **there are
roadworks** ~ **5 km** ci sono lavori in corso
per 5 km; **he was away** ~ **2 years** è stato
via per 2 anni; **she will be away** ~ **a
month** starà via un mese; **it hasn't rained**
~ **3 weeks** non piove da 3 settimane; **can
you do it** ~ **tomorrow?** può farlo per
domani?

8 (*with infinitive clauses*): **it is not** ~ **me to
decide** non sta a me decidere; **it would be
best** ~ **you to leave** sarebbe meglio che
lei se ne andasse; **there is still time** ~ **you
to do it** ha ancora tempo per farlo; ~ **this
to be possible** ... perché ciò sia possibile
...

9 (*in spite of*) nonostante; ~ **all his
complaints, he's very fond of her**
nonostante tutte le sue lamentele, le
vuole molto bene

♦ *conj* (*since, as*: *rather formal*) dal
momento che, poiché.

forage ['fɔrɪdʒ] *vi* foraggiare.

forage cap *n* bustina.

foray ['fɔreɪ] *n* incursione *f*.

forbad(e) [fə'bæd] *pt of* **forbid**.

forbearing [fɔː'bɛərɪŋ] *adj* paziente,
tollerante.

forbid, *pt* **forbad(e)**, *pp* **forbidden** [fə'bɪd,
-'bæd, -'bɪdn] *vt* vietare, interdire; **to** ~ **sb
to do sth** proibire a qn di fare qc.

forbidding [fə'bɪdɪŋ] *adj* arcigno(a),
d'aspetto minaccioso.

force [fɔːs] *n* forza ♦ *vt* forzare; (*obtain by
~: smile, confession*) strappare; **the F~s**
npl (*BRIT*) le forze armate; **in** ~ (*in large
numbers*) in gran numero; (*law*) in vigore;
to come into ~ entrare in vigore; **a** ~ **5
wind** un vento forza 5; **to join** ~**s** unire le
forze; **the sales** ~ (*COMM*) l'effettivo dei
rappresentanti; **to** ~ **sb to do sth**
costringere qn a fare qc.

▶**force back** *vt* (*crowd, enemy*) respingere;
(*tears*) ingoiare.

▶**force down** *vt* (*food*) sforzarsi di
mangiare.

forced [fɔːst] *adj* forzato(a).

force-feed ['fɔːsfiːd] *vt* sottoporre ad
alimentazione forzata.

forceful ['fɔːsful] *adj* forte, vigoroso(a).

forcemeat ['fɔːsmiːt] *n* (*BRIT CULIN*) ripieno.

forceps ['fɔːsɪps] *npl* forcipe *m*.

forcibly ['fɔːsəblɪ] *adv* con la forza;
  (*vigorously*) vigorosamente.
ford [fɔːd] *n* guado ♦ *vt* guadare.
fore [fɔː*] *n*: **to the** ~ **in** prima linea; **to**
  come to the ~ mettersi in evidenza.
forearm ['fɔːrɑːm] *n* avambraccio.
forebear ['fɔːbɛə*] *n* antenato.
foreboding [fɔː'bəʊdɪŋ] *n* presagio di male.
forecast ['fɔːkɑːst] *n* previsione *f;* (*weather*
  ~) previsioni *fpl* del tempo ♦ *vt* (*irreg: like*
  cast) prevedere.
foreclose [fɔː'kləʊz] *vt* (*LAW: also:* ~ **on**)
  sequestrare l'immobile ipotecato di.
foreclosure [fɔː'kləʊʒə*] *n* sequestro di
  immobile ipotecato.
forecourt ['fɔːkɔːt] *n* (*of garage*) corte *f*
  esterna.
forefathers ['fɔːfɑːðəz] *npl* antenati *mpl,* avi
  mpl.
forefinger ['fɔːfɪŋgə*] *n* (dito) indice *m.*
forefront ['fɔːfrʌnt] *n*: **in the** ~ **of**
  all'avanguardia di.
forego [fɔː'gəʊ] *vt* = **forgo.**
foregoing ['fɔːgəʊɪŋ] *adj* precedente.
foregone ['fɔːgɔn] *pp of* **forego** ♦ *adj*: **it's a** ~
  conclusion è una conclusione scontata.
foreground ['fɔːgraʊnd] *n* primo piano
  ♦ *cpd* (*COMPUT*) foreground *inv,* di primo
  piano.
forehand ['fɔːhænd] *n* (*TENNIS*) diritto.
forehead ['fɔrɪd] *n* fronte *f.*
foreign ['fɔrən] *adj* straniero(a); (*trade*)
  estero(a).
foreign body *n* corpo estraneo.
foreign currency *n* valuta estera.
foreigner ['fɔrənə*] *n* straniero/a.
foreign exchange *n* cambio di valuta;
  (*currency*) valuta estera.
foreign exchange market *n* mercato
  delle valute.
foreign exchange rate *n* cambio.
foreign investment *n* investimento
  all'estero.
foreign minister *n* ministro degli Affari
  esteri.
Foreign Office (FO) *n* (*BRIT*) Ministero
  degli Esteri.
foreign secretary *n* (*BRIT*) ministro degli
  Affari esteri.
foreleg ['fɔːlɛg] *n* zampa anteriore.
foreman ['fɔːmən] *n* caposquadra *m;* (*LAW:*
  of jury) portavoce *m* della giuria.
foremost ['fɔːməʊst] *adj* principale; più in
  vista ♦ *adv*: **first and** ~ innanzitutto.
forename ['fɔːneɪm] *n* nome *m* di
  battesimo.
forensic [fə'rɛnsɪk] *adj*: ~ **medicine**
  medicina legale; ~ **expert** esperto della

(polizia) scientifica.
foreplay ['fɔːpleɪ] *n* preliminari *mpl.*
forerunner ['fɔːrʌnə*] *n* precursore *m.*
foresee, *pt* **foresaw,** *pp* **foreseen** [fɔː'siː,
  -'sɔː, -'siːn] *vt* prevedere.
foreseeable [fɔː'siːəbl] *adj* prevedibile.
foreseen [fɔː'siːn] *pp of* **foresee.**
foreshadow [fɔː'ʃædəʊ] *vt* presagire, far
  prevedere.
foreshorten [fɔː'ʃɔːtn] *vt* (*figure, scene*)
  rappresentare in scorcio.
foresight ['fɔːsaɪt] *n* previdenza.
foreskin ['fɔːskɪn] *n* (*ANAT*) prepuzio.
forest ['fɔrɪst] *n* foresta.
forestall [fɔː'stɔːl] *vt* prevenire.
forestry ['fɔrɪstrɪ] *n* silvicoltura.
foretaste ['fɔːteɪst] *n* pregustazione *f.*
foretell, *pt,* *pp* **foretold** [fɔː'tɛl, -'təʊld] *vt*
  predire.
forethought ['fɔːθɔːt] *n* previdenza.
foretold [fɔː'təʊld] *pt, pp of* **foretell.**
forever [fə'rɛvə*] *adv* per sempre; (*fig*)
  sempre, di continuo.
forewarn [fɔː'wɔːn] *vt* avvisare in
  precedenza.
forewent [fɔː'wɛnt] *pt of* **forego.**
foreword ['fɔːwəːd] *n* prefazione *f.*
forfeit ['fɔːfɪt] *n* ammenda, pena ♦ *vt*
  perdere; (*one's happiness, health*) giocarsi.
forgave [fə'geɪv] *pt of* **forgive.**
forge [fɔːdʒ] *n* fucina ♦ *vt* falsificare;
  (*signature*) contraffare, falsificare;
  (*wrought iron*) fucinare, foggiare.
▶**forge ahead** *vi* tirare avanti.
forger ['fɔːdʒə*] *n* contraffattore *m.*
forgery ['fɔːdʒərɪ] *n* falso; (*activity*)
  contraffazione *f.*
forget, *pt* **forgot,** *pp* **forgotten** [fə'gɛt, -'gɔt,
  -'gɔtn] *vt, vi* dimenticare.
forgetful [fə'gɛtful] *adj* di corta memoria;
  ~ **of** dimentico(a) di.
forgetfulness [fə'gɛtfulnɪs] *n*
  smemoratezza; (*oblivion*) oblio.
forget-me-not [fə'gɛtmɪnɔt] *n*
  nontiscordardimé *m inv.*
forgive, *pt* **forgave,** *pp* **forgiven** [fə'gɪv,
  -'geɪv, -'gɪvn] *vt* perdonare; **to** ~ **sb for**
  sth/for doing sth perdonare qc a qn/a qn
  di aver fatto qc.
forgiveness [fə'gɪvnɪs] *n* perdono.
forgiving [fə'gɪvɪŋ] *adj* indulgente.
forgo, *pt* **forwent,** *pp* **forgone** [fɔː'gəʊ,
  -'wɛnt, -'gɔn] *vt* rinunciare a.
forgot [fə'gɔt] *pt of* **forget.**
forgotten [fə'gɔtn] *pp of* **forget.**
fork [fɔːk] *n* (*for eating*) forchetta; (*for*
  gardening) forca; (*of roads*) bivio; (*of*
  railways) inforcazione *f* ♦ *vi* (*road*)

biforcarsi.

▶**fork out** (*col: pay*) *vt* sborsare ♦ *vi* pagare.

forked [fɔːkt] *adj* (*lightning*) a zigzag.

fork-lift truck ['fɔːklɪft-] *n* carrello elevatore.

forlorn [fə'lɔːn] *adj* (*person*) sconsolato(a); (*deserted: cottage*) abbandonato(a); (*desperate: attempt*) disperato(a).

form [fɔːm] *n* forma; (*SCOL*) classe *f*; (*questionnaire*) modulo ♦ *vt* formare; (*circle, queue etc*) fare; **in the ~ of** a forma di, sotto forma di; **to be in good ~** (*SPORT, fig*) essere in forma; **in top ~** in gran forma; **to ~ part of sth** far parte di qc.

formal ['fɔːməl] *adj* (*offer, receipt*) vero(a) e proprio(a); (*person*) cerimonioso(a); (*occasion, dinner*) formale, ufficiale; (*ART, PHILOSOPHY*) formale; **~ dress** abito da cerimonia; (*evening dress*) abito da sera.

formality [fɔː'mælɪtɪ] *n* formalità *f inv*.

formalize ['fɔːməlaɪz] *vt* rendere ufficiale.

formally ['fɔːməlɪ] *adv* ufficialmente; formalmente; cerimoniosamente; **to be ~ invited** ricevere un invito ufficiale.

format ['fɔːmæt] *n* formato ♦ *vt* (*COMPUT*) formattare.

formation [fɔː'meɪʃən] *n* formazione *f*.

formative ['fɔːmətɪv] *adj*: **~ years** anni *mpl* formativi.

former ['fɔːmə*] *adj* vecchio(a) (*before n*), ex *inv* (*before n*); **the ~ president** l'ex presidente; **the ~ ... the latter** quello ... questo; **the ~ Yugoslavia/Soviet Union** l'ex Jugoslavia/Unione Sovietica.

formerly ['fɔːməlɪ] *adv* in passato.

form feed *n* (*on printer*) alimentazione *f* modulo.

formidable ['fɔːmɪdəbl] *adj* formidabile.

formula ['fɔːmjulə] *n* formula; **F~ One** (*AUT*) formula uno.

formulate ['fɔːmjuleɪt] *vt* formulare.

fornicate ['fɔːnɪkeɪt] *vi* fornicare.

forsake, *pt* forsook, *pp* forsaken [fə'seɪk, -'suk, -'seɪkən] *vt* abbandonare.

fort [fɔːt] *n* forte *m*; **to hold the ~** (*fig*) prendere le redini (della situazione).

forte ['fɔːtɪ] *n* forte *m*.

forth [fɔːθ] *adv* in avanti; **to go back and ~** andare avanti e indietro; **and so ~** e così via.

forthcoming [fɔːθ'kʌmɪŋ] *adj* prossimo(a); (*character*) aperto(a), comunicativo(a).

forthright ['fɔːθraɪt] *adj* franco(a), schietto(a).

forthwith [fɔːθ'wɪθ] *adv* immediatamente, subito.

fortieth ['fɔːtɪɪθ] *num* quarantesimo(a).

fortification [fɔːtɪfɪ'keɪʃən] *n* fortificazione *f*.

fortified wine *n* vino ad alta gradazione alcolica.

fortify ['fɔːtɪfaɪ] *vt* fortificare.

fortitude ['fɔːtɪtjuːd] *n* forza d'animo.

fortnight ['fɔːtnaɪt] *n* (*BRIT*) quindici giorni *mpl*, due settimane *fpl*; **it's a ~ since ...** sono due settimane da quando ....

fortnightly ['fɔːtnaɪtlɪ] *adj* bimensile ♦ *adv* ogni quindici giorni.

FORTRAN ['fɔːtræn] *n* FORTRAN *m*.

fortress ['fɔːtrɪs] *n* fortezza, rocca.

fortuitous [fɔː'tjuːɪtəs] *adj* fortuito(a).

fortunate ['fɔːtʃənɪt] *adj* fortunato(a); **he is ~ to have ...** ha la fortuna di avere ...; **it is ~ that** è una fortuna che + *sub*.

fortunately ['fɔːtʃənɪtlɪ] *adv* fortunatamente.

fortune ['fɔːtʃən] *n* fortuna; **to make a ~** farsi una fortuna.

fortuneteller ['fɔːtʃəntɛlə*] *n* indovino/a.

forty ['fɔːtɪ] *num* quaranta.

forum ['fɔːrəm] *n* foro; (*fig*) luogo di pubblica discussione.

forward ['fɔːwəd] *adj* (*movement, position*) in avanti; (*not shy*) sfacciato(a); (*COMM: delivery, sales, exchange*) a termine ♦ *n* (*SPORT*) avanti *m inv* ♦ *vt* (*letter*) inoltrare; (*parcel, goods*) spedire; (*fig*) promuovere, appoggiare; **to move ~** avanzare; **"please ~"** "si prega di inoltrare"; **~ planning** programmazione *f* in anticipo.

forward(s) ['fɔːwəd(z)] *adv* avanti.

forwent [fɔː'wɛnt] *pt of* forgo.

fossil ['fɔsl] *adj*, *n* fossile (*m*); **~ fuel** combustibile *m* fossile.

foster ['fɔstə*] *vt* incoraggiare, nutrire; (*child*) avere in affidamento.

foster brother *n* fratellastro.

foster child *n* bambino(a) preso(a) in affidamento.

foster mother *n* madre *f* affidataria.

fought [fɔːt] *pt*, *pp of* fight.

foul [faul] *adj* (*smell, food*) cattivo(a); (*weather*) brutto(a), orribile; (*language*) osceno(a); (*deed*) infame ♦ *n* (*FOOTBALL*) fallo ♦ *vt* sporcare; (*football player*) commettere un fallo su; (*entangle: anchor, propeller*) impigliarsi in.

foul play *n* (*SPORT*) gioco scorretto; **~ is not suspected** si è scartata l'ipotesi del delitto (*or* dell'attentato *etc*).

found [faund] *pt*, *pp of* find ♦ *vt* (*establish*) fondare.

foundation [faun'deɪʃən] *n* (*act*) fondazione *f*; (*base*) base *f*; (*also*: **~ cream**) fondo tinta; **~s** *npl* (*of building*) fondamenta *fpl*;

to lay the ~s gettare le fondamenta.
foundation stone *n* prima pietra.
founder ['faundə*] *n* fondatore/trice ♦ *vi* affondare.
founding ['faundıŋ] *adj*: ~ **fathers** (*US*) padri *mpl* fondatori; ~ **member** socio fondatore.
foundry ['faundrı] *n* fonderia.
fount [faunt] *n* fonte *f*; (*TYP*) stile *m* di carattere.
fountain ['fauntın] *n* fontana.
fountain pen *n* penna stilografica.
four [fɔ:*] *num* quattro; **on all ~s** a carponi.
four-letter word ['fɔ:lɛtə-] *n* parolaccia.
four-poster ['fɔ:'pəustə*] *n* (*also:* ~ **bed**) letto a quattro colonne.
foursome ['fɔ:səm] *n* partita a quattro; uscita in quattro.
fourteen ['fɔ:ti:n] *num* quattordici.
fourth [fɔ:θ] *num* quarto(a) ♦ *n* (*AUT: also:* ~ **gear**) quarta.
four-wheel drive ['fɔ:wi:l-] *n* (*AUT*): **with ~** con quattro ruote motrici.
fowl [faul] *n* pollame *m*; volatile *m*.
fox [fɔks] *n* volpe *f* ♦ *vt* confondere.
fox fur *n* volpe *f*, pelliccia di volpe.
foxglove ['fɔksglʌv] *n* (*BOT*) digitale *f*.
fox-hunting ['fɔkshʌntıŋ] *n* caccia alla volpe.
foyer ['fɔıeı] *n* atrio; (*THEAT*) ridotto.
FP *n abbr* (*BRIT*) = *former pupil*; (*US*) = **fireplug**.
FPA *n abbr* (*BRIT*: = *Family Planning Association*) ≈ A.I.E.D. *f* (= *Associazione Italiana Educazione Demografica*).
Fr. *abbr* (*REL*) = *father; friar*.
fr. *abbr* (= *franc*) fr.
fracas ['frækɑ:] *n* rissa, lite *f*.
fraction ['frækʃən] *n* frazione *f*.
fractionally ['frækʃnəlı] *adv* un tantino, minimamente.
fractious ['frækʃəs] *adj* irritabile.
fracture ['fræktʃə*] *n* frattura ♦ *vt* fratturare.
fragile ['frædʒaıl] *adj* fragile.
fragment ['frægmənt] *n* frammento.
fragmentary ['frægməntərı] *adj* frammentario(a).
fragrance ['freıgrəns] *n* fragranza, profumo.
fragrant ['freıgrənt] *adj* fragrante, profumato(a).
frail [freıl] *adj* debole, delicato(a).
frame [freım] *n* (*of building*) armatura; (*of human, animal*) ossatura, corpo; (*of picture*) cornice *f*; (*of door, window*) telaio; (*of spectacles: also:* ~**s**) montatura ♦ *vt* (*picture*) incorniciare; **to ~ sb** (*col*)

incastrare qn; ~ **of mind** stato d'animo.
framework ['freımwə:k] *n* struttura.
France [frɑ:ns] *n* Francia.
franchise ['fræntʃaız] *n* (*POL*) diritto di voto; (*COMM*) concessione *f*.
franchisee [fræntʃaı'zi:] *n* concessionaria.
franchiser ['fræntʃaızə*] *n* concedente *m*.
frank [fræŋk] *adj* franco(a), aperto(a) ♦ *vt* (*letter*) affrancare.
Frankfurt ['fræŋkfə:t] *n* Francoforte *f*.
frankfurter ['fræŋkfə:tə*] *n* würstel *m inv*.
franking machine ['fræŋkıŋ-] *n* macchina affrancatrice.
frankly ['fræŋklı] *adv* francamente, sinceramente.
frankness ['fræŋknıs] *n* franchezza.
frantic ['fræntık] *adj* (*activity, pace*) frenetico(a); (*desperate: need, desire*) pazzo(a), sfrenato(a); (: *search*) affannoso(a); (*person*) fuori di sé.
frantically ['fræntıklı] *adv* freneticamente; affannosamente.
fraternal [frə'tə:nl] *adj* fraterno(a).
fraternity [frə'tə:nıtı] *n* (*club*) associazione *f*; (*spirit*) fratellanza.
fraternize ['frætənaız] *vi* fraternizzare.
fraud [frɔ:d] *n* truffa; (*LAW*) frode *f*; (*person*) impostore/a.
fraudulent ['frɔ:djulənt] *adj* fraudolento(a).
fraught [frɔ:t] *adj* (*tense*) teso(a); ~ **with** pieno(a) di, intriso(a) da.
fray [freı] *n* baruffa ♦ *vt* logorare ♦ *vi* logorarsi; **to return to the** ~ tornare nella mischia; **tempers were getting ~ed** cominciavano ad innervosirsi; **her nerves were ~ed** aveva i nervi a pezzi.
FRB *n abbr* (*US*) = **Federal Reserve Board**.
FRCM *n abbr* (*BRIT*) = *Fellow of the Royal College of Music*.
FRCO *n abbr* (*BRIT*) = *Fellow of the Royal College of Organists*.
FRCP *n abbr* (*BRIT*) = *Fellow of the Royal College of Physicians*.
FRCS *n abbr* (*BRIT*) = *Fellow of the Royal College of Surgeons*.
freak [fri:k] *n* fenomeno, mostro; (*col: enthusiast*) fanatico/a ♦ *adj* (*storm, conditions*) anormale; (*victory*) inatteso(a).
▶**freak out** *vi* (*col*) andare fuori di testa.
freakish ['fri:kıʃ] *adj* (*result, appearance*) strano(a), bizzarro(a); (*weather*) anormale.
freckle ['frɛkl] *n* lentiggine *f*.
free [fri:] *adj* libero(a); (*gratis*) gratuito(a); (*liberal*) generoso(a) ♦ *vt* (*prisoner, jammed person*) liberare; (*jammed object*) districare; ~ **(of charge)** gratuitamente; **admission** ~ entrata libera; **to give sb a**

~ **hand** dare carta bianca a qn; ~ **and easy** rilassato.

freebie ['fri:bɪ] n (col): **it's a** ~ è in omaggio.

freedom ['fri:dəm] n libertà.

freedom fighter n combattente m/f per la libertà.

free enterprise n liberalismo economico.

Freefone ® ['fri:fəun] n (BRIT) ≈ numero verde.

free-for-all ['fri:fərɔ:l] n parapiglia m generale.

free gift n regalo, omaggio.

freehold ['fri:həuld] n proprietà assoluta.

free kick n (SPORT) calcio libero.

freelance ['fri:lɑ:ns] adj indipendente; ~ **work** collaborazione f esterna.

freeloader ['fri:ləudə*] n (pej) scroccone/a.

freely ['fri:lɪ] adv liberamente; (liberally) liberalmente.

free-market economy [fri:'mɑ:kɪt-] n economia di libero mercato.

freemason ['fri:meɪsn] n massone m.

freemasonry ['fri:meɪsnrɪ] n massoneria.

freepost ['fri:pəust] n affrancatura a carica del destinatario.

free-range ['fri:'reɪndʒ] adj (eggs) di gallina ruspante.

free sample n campione m gratuito.

free speech n libertà di parola.

freestyle ['fri:staɪl] n (in swimming) stile m libero.

free trade n libero scambio.

freeway ['fri:weɪ] n (US) superstrada.

freewheel [fri:'wi:l] vi andare a ruota libera.

freewheeling [fri:'wi:lɪŋ] adj a ruota libera.

free will n libero arbitrio; **of one's own** ~ di spontanea volontà.

freeze [fri:z] vb (pt **froze**, pp **frozen** [frəuz, 'frəuzn]) vi gelare ♦ vt gelare; (food) congelare; (prices, salaries) bloccare ♦ n gelo; blocco.

▶**freeze over** vi (lake, river) ghiacciarsi; (windows, windscreen) coprirsi di ghiaccio.

▶**freeze up** vi gelarsi.

freeze-dried ['fri:zdraɪd] adj liofilizzato(a).

freezer ['fri:zə*] n congelatore m.

freezing ['fri:zɪŋ] adj: **I'm** ~ mi sto congelando ♦ n (also: ~ **point**) punto di congelamento; **3 degrees below** ~ 3 gradi sotto zero.

freight [freɪt] n (goods) merce f, merci fpl; (money charged) spese fpl di trasporto; ~ **forward** spese a carico del destinatario; ~ **inward** spese di trasporto sulla merce in entrata.

freight car n (US) carro m merci inv.

freighter ['freɪtə*] n (NAUT) nave f da carico.

freight forwarder [-'fɔ:wədə*] n spedizioniere m.

freight train n (US) treno m merci inv.

French [frɛntʃ] adj francese ♦ n (LING) francese m; **the** ~ npl i Francesi.

French bean n fagiolino.

French Canadian adj, n franco-canadese (m/f).

French dressing n (CULIN) condimento per insalata.

French fried potatoes, (US) **French fries** npl patate fpl fritte.

French Guiana [-gaɪ'ænə] n Guiana francese.

French loaf n ≈ filoncino.

Frenchman ['frɛntʃmən] n francese m.

French Riviera n: **the** ~ la Costa Azzurra.

French stick n baguette f inv.

French window n portafinestra.

Frenchwoman ['frɛntʃwumən] n francese f.

frenetic [frə'nɛtɪk] adj frenetico(a).

frenzy ['frɛnzɪ] n frenesia.

frequency ['fri:kwənsɪ] n frequenza.

frequency modulation (FM) n modulazione f di frequenza (F.M.).

frequent adj ['fri:kwənt] frequente ♦ vt [frɪ'kwɛnt] frequentare.

frequently ['fri:kwəntlɪ] adv frequentemente, spesso.

fresco ['frɛskəu] n affresco.

fresh [frɛʃ] adj fresco(a); (new) nuovo(a); (cheeky) sfacciato(a); **to make a** ~ **start** cominciare da capo.

freshen ['frɛʃən] vi (wind, air) rinfrescare.

▶**freshen up** vi rinfrescarsi.

freshener ['frɛʃnə*] n: **skin** ~ tonico rinfrescante; **air** ~ deodorante m per ambienti.

fresher ['frɛʃə*] n (BRIT SCOL: col) = **freshman**.

freshly ['frɛʃlɪ] adv di recente, di fresco.

freshman ['frɛʃmən] n (SCOL) matricola.

freshness ['frɛʃnɪs] n freschezza.

freshwater ['frɛʃwɔ:tə*] adj (fish) d'acqua dolce.

fret [frɛt] vi agitarsi, affliggersi.

fretful ['frɛtful] adj (child) irritabile.

Freudian ['frɔɪdɪən] adj freudiano(a); ~ **slip** lapsus m inv freudiano.

FRG n abbr see **Federal Republic of Germany**.

Fri. abbr (= Friday) ven.

friar ['fraɪə*] n frate m.

friction ['frɪkʃən] n frizione f, attrito.

friction feed n (on printer) trascinamento ad attrito.

Friday ['fraɪdɪ] *n* venerdì *m inv; for phrases see also* **Tuesday**.

fridge [frɪdʒ] *n* (*BRIT*) frigo, frigorifero.

fridge-freezer ['frɪdʒ'friːzə*] *n* freezer *m inv*.

fried [fraɪd] *pt, pp of* **fry** ♦ *adj* fritto(a); **~ egg** uovo fritto.

friend [frɛnd] *n* amico/a; **to make ~s with** fare amicizia con.

friendliness ['frɛndlɪnɪs] *n* amichevolezza.

friendly ['frɛndlɪ] *adj* amichevole ♦ *n* (*also:* **~ match**) partita amichevole; **to be ~ with** essere amico di; **to be ~ to** essere cordiale con.

friendly fire *n* fuoco amico.

friendly society *n* società *f inv* di mutuo soccorso.

friendship ['frɛndʃɪp] *n* amicizia.

frieze [friːz] *n* fregio.

frigate ['frɪgɪt] *n* (*NAUT: modern*) fregata.

fright [fraɪt] *n* paura, spavento; **to take ~** spaventarsi; **she looks a ~!** guarda com'è conciata!

frighten ['fraɪtn] *vt* spaventare, far paura a.

►**frighten away, frighten off** *vt* (*birds, children etc*) scacciare (facendogli paura).

frightened ['fraɪtnd] *adj*: **to be ~ (of)** avere paura (di).

frightening ['fraɪtnɪŋ] *adj* spaventoso(a), pauroso(a).

frightful ['fraɪtful] *adj* orribile.

frightfully ['fraɪtfulɪ] *adv* terribilmente; **I'm ~ sorry** mi dispiace moltissimo.

frigid ['frɪdʒɪd] *adj* (*woman*) frigido(a).

frigidity [frɪ'dʒɪdɪtɪ] *n* frigidità.

frill [frɪl] *n* balza; **without ~s** (*fig*) senza fronzoli.

frilly ['frɪlɪ] *adj* (*clothes, lampshade*) pieno(a) di fronzoli.

fringe [frɪndʒ] *n* frangia; (*edge: of forest etc*) margine *m*; (*fig*): **on the ~** al margine.

fringe benefits *npl* vantaggi *mpl*.

fringe theatre *n* teatro d'avanguardia.

Frisbee ® ['frɪzbɪ] *n* frisbee ® *m inv*.

frisk [frɪsk] *vt* perquisire.

frisky ['frɪskɪ] *adj* vivace, vispo(a).

fritter ['frɪtə*] *n* frittella.

►**fritter away** *vt* sprecare.

frivolity [frɪ'vɔlɪtɪ] *n* frivolezza.

frivolous ['frɪvələs] *adj* frivolo(a).

frizzy ['frɪzɪ] *adj* crespo(a).

fro [frəʊ] *adv*: **to and ~** avanti e indietro.

frock [frɔk] *n* vestito.

frog [frɔg] *n* rana; **to have a ~ in one's throat** avere la voce rauca.

frogman ['frɔgmən] *n* uomo *m* rana *inv*.

frogmarch ['frɔgmɑːtʃ] *vt* (*BRIT*): **to ~ sb**

in/out portar qn dentro/fuori con la forza.

frolic ['frɔlɪk] *vi* sgambettare.

KEYWORD

from [frɔm] *prep* **1** (*indicating starting place, origin etc*) da; **where do you come ~?**, **where are you ~?** da dove viene?, di dov'è?; **where has he come ~?** da dove arriva?; **~ London to Glasgow** da Londra a Glasgow; **a letter ~ my sister** una lettera da mia sorella; **tell him ~ me that ...** gli dica da parte mia che ...

2 (*indicating time*) da; **~ one o'clock to** *or* **until** *or* **till two** dall'una alle due; **(as) ~ Friday** a partire da venerdì; **~ January (on)** da gennaio, a partire da gennaio

3 (*indicating distance*) da; **the hotel is 1 km ~ the beach** l'albergo è a 1 km dalla spiaggia

4 (*indicating price, number etc*) da; **~ a pound** da una sterlina in su; **prices range ~ £10 to £50** i prezzi vanno dalle 10 alle 50 sterline

5 (*indicating difference*) da; **he can't tell red ~ green** non sa distinguere il rosso dal verde

6 (*because of, on the basis of*): **~ what he says** da quanto dice lui; **weak ~ hunger** debole per la fame.

frond [frɔnd] *n* fronda.

front [frʌnt] *n* (*of house, dress*) davanti *m inv*; (*of train*) testa; (*of book*) copertina; (*promenade: also:* **sea ~**) lungomare *m*; (*MIL, POL, METEOR*) fronte *m*; (*fig: appearances*) fronte *f* ♦ *adj* primo(a); anteriore, davanti *inv* ♦ *vi*: **to ~ onto sth** dare su qc, guardare verso qc; **in ~ (of)** davanti (a).

frontage ['frʌntɪdʒ] *n* facciata.

frontal ['frʌntl] *adj* frontale.

front bench *n* posti in Parlamento occupati dai frontbencher.

Nel Parlamento britannico, si chiamano **front bench** gli scanni della **House of Commons** che si trovano alla sinistra e alla destra dello **Speaker** davanti ai **backbenches**. I *front bench* sono occupati dai **frontbencher**, parlamentari che ricoprono una carica di governo o che fanno parte dello **shadow cabinet** dell'opposizione.

frontbencher ['frʌnt'bentʃə*] *n* (*BRIT*) parlamentare con carica al governo o all'opposizione.

front desk *n* (*US: in hotel*) reception *f inv*; (:

at doctor's) accettazione *f.*

front door *n* porta d'entrata; (*of car*) sportello anteriore.

frontier ['frʌntɪə*] *n* frontiera.

frontispiece ['frʌntɪspiːs] *n* frontespizio.

front page *n* prima pagina.

front room *n* (*BRIT*) salotto.

front runner *n* (*fig*) favorito/a.

front-wheel drive ['frʌntwiːl-] *n* trasmissione *f* anteriore.

frost [frɔst] *n* gelo; (*also*: **hoar~**) brina.

frostbite ['frɔstbaɪt] *n* congelamento.

frosted ['frɔstɪd] *adj* (*glass*) smerigliato(a); (*US*: *cake*) glassato(a).

frosting ['frɔstɪŋ] *n* (*US*: *on cake*) glassa.

frosty ['frɔstɪ] *adj* (*window*) coperto(a) di ghiaccio; (*welcome*) gelido(a).

froth ['frɔθ] *n* spuma; schiuma.

frown [fraun] *n* cipiglio ♦ *vi* accigliarsi.

►frown on *vt fus* (*fig*) disapprovare.

froze [frəuz] *pt of* **freeze**.

frozen ['frəuzn] *pp of* **freeze** ♦ *adj* (*food*) congelato(a); (*COMM*: *assets*) bloccato(a).

FRS *n abbr* (*BRIT*) = Fellow of the Royal Society; (*US*: = Federal Reserve System) *sistema bancario degli Stati Uniti.*

frugal ['fruːgəl] *adj* frugale; (*person*) economo(a).

fruit [fruːt] *n* (*pl inv*) frutto; (*collectively*) frutta.

fruiterer ['fruːtərə*] *n* fruttivendolo; **at the ~'s (shop)** dal fruttivendolo.

fruit fly *n* mosca della frutta.

fruitful ['fruːtful] *adj* fruttuoso(a); (*plant*) fruttifero(a); (*soil*) fertile.

fruition [fruː'ɪʃən] *n*: **to come to ~** realizzarsi.

fruit juice *n* succo di frutta.

fruitless ['fruːtlɪs] *adj* (*fig*) vano(a), inutile.

fruit machine *n* (*BRIT*) macchina *f* mangiasoldi *inv*.

fruit salad *n* macedonia.

frump [frʌmp] *n*: **to feel a ~** sentirsi infagottato(a).

frustrate [frʌs'treɪt] *vt* frustrare.

frustrated [frʌs'treɪtɪd] *adj* frustrato(a).

frustrating [frʌs'treɪtɪŋ] *adj* (*job*) frustrante; (*day*) disastroso(a).

frustration [frʌs'treɪʃən] *n* frustrazione *f.*

fry, *pt, pp* **fried** [fraɪ, -d] *vt* friggere ♦ *npl*: **the small ~** i pesci piccoli.

frying pan ['fraɪɪŋ-] *n* padella.

FT *n abbr* (*BRIT*: = Financial Times) *giornale finanziario;* **the ~ index** l'indice FT.

ft. *abbr* = foot, feet.

FTC *n abbr* (*US*) *see* **Federal Trade Commission.**

FT-SE 100 Index *n abbr* = Financial Times

Stock Exchange 100 Index.

fuchsia ['fjuːʃə] *n* fucsia.

fuck [fʌk] *vt, vi* (*col!*) fottere (*!*); **~ off!** vaffanculo! (*!*).

fuddled ['fʌdld] *adj* (*muddled*) confuso(a); (*col: tipsy*) brillo(a).

fuddy-duddy ['fʌdɪdʌdɪ] *n* (*pej*) parruccone *m.*

fudge [fʌdʒ] *n* (*CULIN*) *specie di caramella a base di latte, burro e zucchero* ♦ *vt* (*issue, problem*) evitare.

fuel [fjuəl] *n* (*for heating*) combustibile *m*; (*for propelling*) carburante *m* ♦ *vt* (*furnace etc*) alimentare; (*aircraft, ship etc*) rifornire di carburante.

fuel oil *n* nafta.

fuel pump *n* (*AUT*) pompa del carburante.

fuel tank *n* deposito *m* nafta *inv*; (*on vehicle*) serbatoio (della benzina).

fug [fʌg] *n* (*BRIT*) aria viziata.

fugitive ['fjuːdʒɪtɪv] *n* fuggitivo/a, profugo/a; (*from prison*) evaso/a.

fulfil, (*US*) **fulfill** [ful'fɪl] *vt* (*function*) compiere; (*order*) eseguire; (*wish, desire*) soddisfare, appagare.

fulfilled [ful'fɪld] *adj* (*person*) realizzato(a), soddisfatto(a).

fulfil(l)ment [ful'fɪlmənt] *n* (*of wishes*) soddisfazione *f*, appagamento.

full [ful] *adj* pieno(a); (*details, skirt*) ampio(a); (*price*) intero(a) ♦ *adv*: **to know ~ well that** sapere benissimo che; **~ (up)** (*hotel etc*) al completo; **I'm ~ (up)** sono pieno; **a ~ two hours** due ore intere; **at ~ speed** a tutta velocità; **in ~** per intero; **to pay in ~** pagare tutto; **~ name** nome *m* e cognome *m*; **~ employment** piena occupazione; **~ fare** tariffa completa.

fullback ['fulbæk] *n* (*RUGBY, FOOTBALL*) terzino.

full-blooded ['ful'blʌdɪd] *adj* (*vigorous: attack*) energico(a); (*virile: male*) virile.

full-cream ['ful'kriːm] *adj*: **~ milk** (*BRIT*) latte *m* intero.

full-grown ['ful'grəun] *adj* maturo(a).

full-length ['ful'leŋθ] *adj* (*portrait*) in piedi; (*film*) a lungometraggio.

full moon *n* luna piena.

full-scale ['fulskeɪl] *adj* (*plan, model*) in grandezza naturale; (*search, retreat*) su vasta scala.

full-sized ['ful'saɪzd] *adj* (*portrait etc*) a grandezza naturale.

full stop *n* punto.

full-time ['ful'taɪm] *adj, adv* (*work*) a tempo pieno ♦ *n* (*SPORT*) fine *f* partita.

fully ['fulɪ] *adv* interamente, pienamente, completamente; (*at least*): **~ as big**

almeno così grosso.
fully-fledged ['fulɪ'flɛdʒd] *adj* (*bird*)
adulto(a); (*fig: teacher, member etc*) a tutti
gli effetti.
fulsome ['fulsəm] *adj* (*pej: praise*)
esagerato(a), eccessivo(a); (: *manner*)
insincero.
fumble ['fʌmbl] *vi* brancolare, andare a
tentoni ♦ *vt* (*ball*) lasciarsi sfuggire.
▶**fumble with** *vt fus* trafficare.
fume [fjuːm] *vi* essere furioso(a); ~**s** *npl*
esalazioni *fpl*, vapori *mpl*.
fumigate ['fjuːmɪɡeɪt] *vt* suffumicare.
fun [fʌn] *n* divertimento, spasso; **to have** ~
divertirsi; **for** ~ per scherzo; **it's not
much** ~ non è molto divertente; **to make**
~ **of** prendersi gioco di.
function ['fʌŋkʃən] *n* funzione *f*; cerimonia,
ricevimento ♦ *vi* funzionare; **to** ~ **as**
fungere da, funzionare da.
functional ['fʌŋkʃənl] *adj* funzionale.
function key *n* (*COMPUT*) tasto di funzioni.
fund [fʌnd] *n* fondo, cassa; (*source*) fondo;
(*store*) riserva; ~**s** *npl* (*money*) fondi *mpl*.
fundamental [fʌndə'mɛntl] *adj*
fondamentale; ~**s** *npl* basi *fpl*.
fundamentalism [fʌndə'mɛntəlɪzəm] *n*
fondamentalismo.
fundamentalist [fʌndə'mɛntəlɪst] *n*
fondamentalista *m/f*.
fundamentally [fʌndə'mɛntəlɪ] *adv*
essenzialmente, fondamentalmente.
funding ['fʌndɪŋ] *n* finanziamento.
fund-raising ['fʌndreɪzɪŋ] *n* raccolta di
fondi.
funeral ['fjuːnərəl] *n* funerale *m*.
funeral director *n* impresario di pompe
funebri.
funeral parlour *n* impresa di pompe
funebri.
funeral service *n* ufficio funebre.
funereal [fjuː'nɪərɪəl] *adj* funereo(a),
lugubre.
fun fair *n* luna park *m inv*.
fungus, *pl* **fungi** ['fʌŋɡəs, -ɡaɪ] *n* fungo;
(*mould*) muffa.
funicular [fjuː'nɪkjulə*] *adj* (*also:* ~ **railway**)
funicolare *f*.
funky ['fʌŋkɪ] *adj* (*music*) funky *inv*; (*col:
excellent*) figo(a).
funnel ['fʌnl] *n* imbuto; (*of ship*) ciminiera.
funnily ['fʌnɪlɪ] *adv* in modo divertente;
(*oddly*) stranamente.
funny ['fʌnɪ] *adj* divertente, buffo(a);
(*strange*) strano(a), bizzarro(a).
funny bone *n* osso cubitale.
fun run *n* marcia non competitiva.
fur [fəː*] *n* pelo; pelliccia; pelle *f*; (*BRIT: in*

kettle etc) deposito calcare.
fur coat *n* pelliccia.
furious ['fjuərɪəs] *adj* furioso(a); (*effort*)
accanito(a); (*argument*) violento(a).
furiously ['fjuərɪəslɪ] *adv* furiosamente;
accanitamente.
furl [fəːl] *vt* (*sail*) piegare.
furlong ['fəːlɔŋ] *n* = 201.17 m (*termine
ippico*).
furlough ['fəːləu] *n* (*US*) congedo,
permesso.
furnace ['fəːnɪs] *n* fornace *f*.
furnish ['fəːnɪʃ] *vt* ammobiliare; (*supply*)
fornire; ~**ed flat** *or* (*US*) **apartment**
appartamento ammobiliato.
furnishings ['fəːnɪʃɪŋz] *npl* mobili *mpl*,
mobilia.
furniture ['fəːnɪtʃə*] *n* mobili *mpl*; **piece of**
~ mobile *m*.
furore [fjuə'rɔːrɪ] *n* (*protests*) scalpore *m*;
(*enthusiasm*) entusiasmo.
furrier ['fʌrɪə*] *n* pellicciaio/a.
furrow ['fʌrəu] *n* solco ♦ *vt* (*forehead*)
segnare di rughe.
furry ['fəːrɪ] *adj* (*animal*) peloso(a); (*toy*) di
peluche.
further ['fəːðə*] *adj* supplementare,
altro(a); nuovo(a); più lontano(a) ♦ *adv*
più lontano; (*more*) di più; (*moreover*)
inoltre ♦ *vt* favorire, promuovere; **until** ~
notice fino a nuovo avviso; **how much** ~
is it? quanto manca *or* dista?; ~ **to your
letter of** ... (*COMM*) con riferimento alla
vostra lettera del ...; **to** ~ **one's interests**
fare i propri interessi.
further education *n* ≈ corsi *mpl* di
formazione.
furthermore [fəːðə'mɔː*] *adv* inoltre, per di
più.
furthermost ['fəːðəməust] *adj* più
lontano(a).
furthest ['fəːðɪst] *superlative of* **far**.
furtive ['fəːtɪv] *adj* furtivo(a).
fury ['fjuərɪ] *n* furore *m*.
fuse, (*US*) **fuze** [fjuːz] *n* fusibile *m*; (*for
bomb etc*) miccia, spoletta ♦ *vt* fondere;
(*ELEC*): **to** ~ **the lights** far saltare i
fusibili ♦ *vi* fondersi; **a** ~ **has blown** è
saltato un fusibile.
fuse box *n* cassetta dei fusibili.
fuselage ['fjuːzəlɑːʒ] *n* fusoliera.
fuse wire *n* filo (di fusibile).
fusillade [fjuːzɪ'leɪd] *n* scarica di fucileria;
(*fig*) fuoco di fila, serie *f inv* incalzante.
fusion ['fjuːʒən] *n* fusione *f*.
fuss [fʌs] *n* chiasso, trambusto, confusione
f; (*complaining*) storie *fpl* ♦ *vt* (*person*)
infastidire, scocciare ♦ *vi* agitarsi; **to**

make a ~ fare delle storie; **to make a ~ of sb** coprire qn di attenzioni.
▶**fuss over** _vt fus_ (_person_) circondare di premure.
fusspot ['fʌspɒt] _n_ (_col_): **he's such a ~** fa sempre tante storie.
fussy ['fʌsɪ] _adj_ (_person_) puntiglioso(a), esigente; che fa le storie; (_dress_) carico(a) di fronzoli; (_style_) elaborato(a); **I'm not ~** (_col_) per me è lo stesso.
fusty ['fʌstɪ] _adj_ (_pej: archaic_) stantio(a); (: _smell_) che sa di stantio.
futile ['fju:taɪl] _adj_ futile.
futility [fju:'tɪlɪtɪ] _n_ futilità.
futon ['fu:tɒn] _n_ futon _m inv_, letto giapponese.
future ['fju:tʃə*] _adj_ futuro(a) ♦ _n_ futuro, avvenire _m_; (_LING_) futuro; **in ~** in futuro; **in the near ~** in un prossimo futuro; **in the immediate ~** nell'immediato futuro.
futures ['fju:tʃəz] _npl_ (_COMM_) operazioni _fpl_ a termine.
futuristic [fju:tʃə'rɪstɪk] _adj_ futuristico(a).
fuze [fju:z] _n_, _vt_, _vi_ (_US_) = **fuse**.
fuzzy ['fʌzɪ] _adj_ (_PHOT_) indistinto(a), sfocato(a); (_hair_) crespo(a).
fwd. _abbr_ = **forward**.
fwy _abbr_ (_US_) = **freeway**.
FY _abbr_ = **fiscal year**.
FYI _abbr_ = **for your information**.

_G g_

G, g [dʒi:] _n_ (_letter_) G, g _f_ or _m inv_; (_MUS_): **G** sol _m_; **G for George** ≈ G come Genova.
G _n abbr_ (_BRIT SCOL: mark_: = _good_) ≈ buono; (_US CINE_: = _general audience_) per tutti.
g _abbr_ (= _gram; gravity_) g.
G7 _n abbr_ (_POL_: = _Group of Seven_) G7 _mpl_.
GA _abbr_ (_US POST_) = _Georgia_.
gab [gæb] _n_ (_col_): **to have the gift of the ~** avere parlantina.
gabble ['gæbl] _vi_ borbottare; farfugliare.
gaberdine [gæbə'di:n] _n_ gabardine _m inv_.
gable ['geɪbl] _n_ frontone _m_.
Gabon [gə'bɒn] _n_ Gabon _m_.
gad about [gæd-] _vi_ (_col_) svolazzare (qua e là).
gadget ['gædʒɪt] _n_ aggeggio.
Gaelic ['geɪlɪk] _adj_ gaelico(a) ♦ _n_ (_language_) gaelico.

gaffe [gæf] _n_ gaffe _f inv_.
gaffer ['gæfə*] _n_ (_BRIT col_) capo.
gag [gæg] _n_ bavaglio; (_joke_) facezia, scherzo ♦ _vt_ (_prisoner etc_) imbavagliare ♦ _vi_ (_choke_) soffocare.
gaga ['gɑ:gɑ:] _adj_: **to go ~** rimbambirsi.
gage [geɪdʒ] _n_, _vt_ (_US_) = **gauge**.
gaiety ['geɪɪtɪ] _n_ gaiezza.
gaily ['geɪlɪ] _adv_ allegramente.
gain [geɪn] _n_ guadagno, profitto ♦ _vt_ guadagnare ♦ _vi_ (_watch_) andare avanti; **to ~ in/by** aumentare di/con; **to ~ 3lbs (in weight)** aumentare di 3 libbre; **to ~ ground** guadagnare terreno.
▶**gain (up)on** _vt fus_ accorciare le distanze da, riprendere.
gainful ['geɪnful] _adj_ profittevole, lucrativo(a).
gainfully ['geɪnfəlɪ] _adv_: **to be ~ employed** avere un lavoro retribuito.
gainsay [geɪn'seɪ] _vt irreg_ (_like_ **say**) contraddire; negare.
gait [geɪt] _n_ andatura.
gal. _abbr_ = **gallon**.
gala ['gɑ:lə] _n_ gala; **swimming ~** manifestazione _f_ di nuoto.
Galapagos Islands [gə'læpəgəs-] _npl_: **the ~** le isole Galapagos.
galaxy ['gæləksɪ] _n_ galassia.
gale [geɪl] _n_ vento forte; burrasca; **~ force 10** vento forza 10.
gall [gɔ:l] _n_ (_ANAT_) bile _f_; (_fig: impudence_) fegato, faccia ♦ _vt_ urtare (i nervi a).
gall. _abbr_ = **gallon**.
gallant ['gælənt] _adj_ valoroso(a); (_towards ladies_) galante, cortese.
gallantry ['gæləntrɪ] _n_ valore _m_ militare; galanteria, cortesia.
gall bladder ['gɔ:l-] _n_ cistifellea.
galleon ['gælɪən] _n_ galeone _m_.
gallery ['gælərɪ] _n_ galleria; loggia; (_for spectators_) tribuna; (_in theatre_) loggione _m_, balconata; (_also: **art ~**: state-owned_) museo; (: _private_) galleria.
galley ['gælɪ] _n_ (_ship's kitchen_) cambusa; (_ship_) galea; (_also: **~ proof**_) bozza in colonna.
Gallic ['gælɪk] _adj_ gallico(a); (_French_) francese.
galling ['gɔ:lɪŋ] _adj_ irritante.
gallon ['gælən] _n_ gallone _m_ (_BRIT_ = 4.543 _l_; 8 pints; _US_ = 3.785 _l_).
gallop ['gæləp] _n_ galoppo ♦ _vi_ galoppare; **~ing inflation** inflazione _f_ galoppante.
gallows ['gæləuz] _n_ forca.
gallstone ['gɔ:lstəun] _n_ calcolo biliare.
Gallup Poll ['gæləp-] _n_ sondaggio a campione.

galore [gə'lɔː*] adv a iosa, a profusione.
galvanize ['gælvənaɪz] vt galvanizzare; **to ~ sb into action** (fig) galvanizzare qn, spronare qn all'azione.
Gambia ['gæmbɪə] n Gambia m.
gambit ['gæmbɪt] n (fig): **(opening) ~** prima mossa.
gamble ['gæmbl] n azzardo, rischio calcolato ♦ vt, vi giocare; **to ~ on** (fig) giocare su; **to ~ on the Stock Exchange** giocare in Borsa.
gambler ['gæmblə*] n giocatore/trice d'azzardo.
gambling ['gæmblɪŋ] n gioco d'azzardo.
gambol ['gæmbəl] vi saltellare.
game [geɪm] n gioco; (event) partita; (HUNTING) selvaggina ♦ adj coraggioso(a); (ready): **to be ~ (for sth/to do)** essere pronto(a) (a qc/a fare); **~s** npl (SCOL) attività fpl sportive; **big ~** selvaggina grossa.
game bird n uccello selvatico.
gamekeeper ['geɪmkiːpə*] n guardacaccia m inv.
gamely ['geɪmlɪ] adv coraggiosamente.
game reserve n riserva di caccia.
games console n console f inv dei videogame.
gameshow ['geɪmʃəu] n gioco a premi.
gamesmanship ['geɪmzmənʃɪp] n abilità.
gaming ['geɪmɪŋ] n gioco d'azzardo.
gammon ['gæmən] n (bacon) quarto di maiale; (ham) prosciutto affumicato.
gamut ['gæmət] n gamma.
gang [gæŋ] n banda, squadra ♦ vi: **to ~ up on sb** far combutta contro qn.
Ganges ['gændʒiːz] n: **the ~** il Gange.
gangland ['gæŋlænd] adj della malavita; **~ killer** sicario.
gangling ['gæŋglɪŋ] adj allampanato(a).
gangly ['gæŋglɪ] adj = gangling.
gangplank ['gæŋplæŋk] n passerella.
gangrene ['gæŋgriːn] n cancrena.
gangster ['gæŋstə*] n gangster m inv.
gangway ['gæŋweɪ] n passerella; (BRIT: of bus) passaggio.
gantry ['gæntrɪ] n (for crane, railway signal) cavalletto; (for rocket) torre f di lancio.
GAO n abbr (US: = General Accounting Office) ≈ Corte f dei Conti.
gaol [dʒeɪl] n, vt (BRIT) = jail.
gap [gæp] n buco; (in time) intervallo; (fig) lacuna; vuoto.
gape [geɪp] vi restare a bocca aperta.
gaping ['geɪpɪŋ] adj (hole) squarciato(a).
garage ['gærɑːʒ] n garage m inv.
garb [gɑːb] n abiti mpl, veste f.
garbage ['gɑːbɪdʒ] n immondizie fpl, rifiuti

mpl; (fig: film, book) porcheria, robaccia; (: nonsense) fesserie fpl.
garbage can n (US) bidone m della spazzatura.
garbage collector n (US) spazzino/a.
garbage disposal unit n tritarifiuti m inv.
garbage truck n (US) camion m inv della spazzatura.
garbled ['gɑːbld] adj deformato(a); ingarbugliato(a).
garden ['gɑːdn] n giardino ♦ vi lavorare nel giardino; **~s** npl (public) giardini pubblici; (private) parco.
garden centre n vivaio.
garden city n (BRIT) città f inv giardino inv.
gardener ['gɑːdnə*] n giardiniere/a.
gardening ['gɑːdnɪŋ] n giardinaggio.
gargle ['gɑːgl] vi fare gargarismi ♦ n gargarismo.
gargoyle ['gɑːgɔɪl] n gargouille f inv.
garish ['gɛərɪʃ] adj vistoso(a).
garland ['gɑːlənd] n ghirlanda; corona.
garlic ['gɑːlɪk] n aglio.
garment ['gɑːmənt] n indumento.
garner ['gɑːnə*] vt ammucchiare, raccogliere.
garnish ['gɑːnɪʃ] vt guarnire.
garret ['gærɪt] n soffitta.
garrison ['gærɪsn] n guarnigione f ♦ vt guarnire.
garrulous ['gærjuləs] adj ciarliero(a), loquace.
garter ['gɑːtə*] n giarrettiera; (US: suspender) gancio (di reggicalze).
garter belt n (US) reggicalze m inv.
gas [gæs] n gas m inv; (used as anaesthetic) etere m; (US: gasoline) benzina ♦ vt asfissiare con il gas; (MIL) gasare.
gas cooker n (BRIT) cucina a gas.
gas cylinder n bombola del gas.
gaseous ['gæsɪəs] adj gassoso(a).
gas fire n (BRIT) radiatore m a gas.
gas-fired ['gæsfaɪəd] adj (alimentato(a)) a gas.
gash [gæʃ] n sfregio ♦ vt sfregiare.
gasket ['gæskɪt] n (AUT) guarnizione f.
gas mask n maschera f antigas inv.
gas meter n contatore m del gas.
gasoline ['gæsəliːn] n (US) benzina.
gasp [gɑːsp] vi ansare, boccheggiare; (in surprise) restare senza fiato.
▶**gasp out** vt dire affannosamente.
gas ring n fornello a gas.
gas station n (US) distributore m di benzina.
gas stove n cucina a gas.
gassy ['gæsɪ] adj gassoso(a).
gas tank n (US AUT) serbatoio (di benzina).

gas tap n (on cooker) manopola del gas; (on pipe) rubinetto del gas.

gastric ['gæstrɪk] adj gastrico(a).

gastric ulcer n ulcera gastrica.

gastroenteritis ['gæstrəuɛntə'raɪtɪs] n gastroenterite f.

gastronomy [gæs'trɔnəmɪ] n gastronomia.

gasworks ['gæswəːks] n or npl impianto di produzione del gas.

gate [geɪt] n cancello; (of castle, town) porta; (at airport) uscita; (at level crossing) barriera.

gâteau, pl ~**x** ['gætəu, -z] n torta.

gatecrash ['geɪtkræʃ] vt partecipare senza invito a.

gatecrasher ['geɪtkræʃə*] n intruso(a), ospite m/f non invitato(a).

gatehouse ['geɪthaus] n casetta del custode (all'entrata di un parco).

gateway ['geɪtweɪ] n porta.

gather ['gæðə*] vt (flowers, fruit) cogliere; (pick up) raccogliere; (assemble) radunare; raccogliere; (understand) capire ♦ vi (assemble) radunarsi; (dust) accumularsi; (clouds) addensarsi; **to ~ speed** acquistare velocità; **to ~ (from/ that)** comprendere (da/che), dedurre (da/che); **as far as I can ~** da quel che ho potuto capire.

gathering ['gæðərɪŋ] n adunanza.

GATT [gæt] n abbr (= General Agreement on Tariffs and Trade) G.A.T.T. m.

gauche [gəuʃ] adj goffo(a), maldestro(a).

gaudy ['gɔːdɪ] adj vistoso(a).

gauge [geɪdʒ] n (standard measure) calibro; (RAIL) scartamento; (instrument) indicatore m ♦ vt misurare; (fig: sb's capabilities, character) valutare, stimare; **to ~ the right moment** calcolare il momento giusto; **petrol ~,** (US) **gas ~** indicatore m or spia della benzina.

gaunt [gɔːnt] adj scarno(a); (grim, desolate) desolato(a).

gauntlet ['gɔːntlɪt] n (fig): **to run the ~ through an angry crowd** passare sotto il fuoco di una folla ostile; **to throw down the ~** gettare il guanto.

gauze [gɔːz] n garza.

gave [geɪv] pt of **give**.

gawky ['gɔːkɪ] adj goffo(a), sgraziato(a).

gawp [gɔːp] vi: **to ~ at** guardare a bocca aperta.

gay [geɪ] adj (person) gaio(a), allegro(a); (colour) vivace, vivo(a); (col) omosessuale.

gaze [geɪz] n sguardo fisso ♦ vi: **to ~ at** guardare fisso.

gazelle [gə'zɛl] n gazzella.

gazette [gə'zɛt] n (newspaper) gazzetta; (official publication) gazzetta ufficiale.

gazetteer [gæzə'tɪə*] n (book) dizionario dei nomi geografici; (section of book) indice m dei nomi geografici.

gazump [gə'zʌmp] vt (BRIT): **to ~ sb** nella compravendita di immobili, venire meno all'impegno preso con un acquirente accettando un'offerta migliore fatta da altri.

GB abbr (= Great Britain) GB.

GBH n abbr (BRIT LAW: col) see **grievous bodily harm**.

GC n abbr (BRIT: = George Gross) decorazione al valore.

GCE n abbr (BRIT: = General Certificate of Education) ≈ diploma m di maturità.

GCHQ n abbr (BRIT: = Government Communications Headquarters) centro per l'intercettazione delle telecomunicazioni straniere.

GCSE n abbr (BRIT: = General Certificate of Secondary Education) diploma di istruzione secondaria conseguito a 16 anni in Inghilterra e Galles.

Gdns. abbr = gardens.

GDP n abbr = **gross domestic product**.

GDR n abbr see **German Democratic Republic**.

gear [gɪə*] n attrezzi mpl, equipaggiamento; (belongings) roba; (TECH) ingranaggio; (AUT) marcia ♦ vt (fig: adapt) adattare; **top** or (US) **high/low/ bottom ~** quarta (or quinta)/ seconda/ prima; **in ~** in marcia; **out of ~** in folle; **our service is ~ed to meet the needs of the disabled** la nostra organizzazione risponde espressamente alle esigenze degli handicappati.

▶**gear up** vi: **to ~ up (to do)** prepararsi (a fare).

gear box n scatola del cambio.

gear lever, (US) **gear shift** n leva del cambio.

GED n abbr (US SCOL) = general educational development.

geese [giːs] npl of **goose**.

geezer ['giːzə*] n (BRIT col) tizio.

Geiger counter ['gaɪgə-] n geiger m inv.

gel [dʒɛl] n gel m inv.

gelatin(e) ['dʒɛlətiːn] n gelatina.

gelignite ['dʒɛlɪgnaɪt] n nitroglicerina.

gem [dʒɛm] n gemma.

Gemini ['dʒɛmɪnaɪ] n Gemelli mpl; **to be ~** essere dei Gemelli.

gen [dʒɛn] n (BRIT col): **to give sb the ~ on sth** mettere qn al corrente di qc.

Gen. abbr (MIL: = General) Gen.

gen. *abbr* (= *general, generally*) gen.
gender ['dʒɛndə*] *n* genere *m*.
gene [dʒiːn] *n* (*BIOL*) gene *m*.
genealogy [dʒiːnɪ'ælədʒɪ] *n* genealogia.
general ['dʒɛnərl] *n* generale *m* ♦ *adj*
    generale; **in** ~ in genere; **the** ~ **public** il
    grande pubblico.
general anaesthetic *n* anestesia totale.
general delivery *n* (*US*) fermo posta *m*.
general election *n* elezioni *fpl* generali.
generalization ['dʒɛnrəlaɪ'zeɪʃən] *n*
    generalizzazione *f*.
generalize ['dʒɛnrəlaɪz] *vi* generalizzare.
generally ['dʒɛnrəlɪ] *adv* generalmente.
general manager *n* direttore *m* generale.
general practitioner (GP) *n* medico
    generico; **who's your GP?** qual'è il suo
    medico di fiducia.
general strike *n* sciopero generale.
generate ['dʒɛnəreɪt] *vt* generare.
generation [dʒɛnə'reɪʃən] *n* generazione *f*;
    (*of electricity etc*) produzione *f*.
generator ['dʒɛnəreɪtə*] *n* generatore *m*.
generic [dʒɪ'nɛrɪk] *adj* generico(a).
generosity [dʒɛnə'rɔsɪtɪ] *n* generosità.
generous ['dʒɛnərəs] *adj* generoso(a);
    (*copious*) abbondante.
genesis ['dʒɛnɪsɪs] *n* genesi *f*.
genetic [dʒɪ'nɛtɪk] *adj* genetico(a); ~
    engineering ingegneria genetica.
genetic fingerprinting [-fɪŋgəprɪntɪŋ] *n*
    rilevamento delle impronte genetiche.
genetics [dʒɪ'nɛtɪks] *n* genetica.
Geneva [dʒɪ'niːvə] *n* Ginevra; **Lake** ~ il
    lago di Ginevra.
genial ['dʒiːnɪəl] *adj* geniale, cordiale.
genitals ['dʒɛnɪtlz] *npl* genitali *mpl*.
genitive ['dʒɛnɪtɪv] *n* genitivo.
genius ['dʒiːnɪəs] *n* genio.
Genoa ['dʒɛnəuə] *n* Genova.
genocide ['dʒɛnəusaɪd] *n* genocidio.
Genoese [dʒɛnəu'iːz] *adj, n* (*pl inv*)
    genovese (*m/f*).
gent [dʒɛnt] *n abbr* (*BRIT col*)
    = **gentleman**.
genteel [dʒɛn'tiːl] *adj* raffinato(a),
    distinto(a).
gentle ['dʒɛntl] *adj* delicato(a); (*person*)
    dolce.
gentleman ['dʒɛntlmən] *n* signore *m*; (*well-
    bred man*) gentiluomo; ~'s **agreement**
    impegno sulla parola.
gentlemanly ['dʒɛntlmənlɪ] *adj* da
    gentiluomo.
gentleness ['dʒɛntlnɪs] *n* delicatezza;
    dolcezza.
gently ['dʒɛntlɪ] *adv* delicatamente.
gentry ['dʒɛntrɪ] *n* nobiltà minore.

gents [dʒɛnts] *n* W.C. *m* (per signori).
genuine ['dʒɛnjuɪn] *adj* autentico(a);
    sincero(a).
genuinely ['dʒɛnjuɪnlɪ] *adv* genuinamente.
geographer [dʒɪ'ɔgrəfə*] *n*
    geografo/a.
geographic(al) [dʒɪə'græfɪk(l)] *adj*
    geografico(a).
geography [dʒɪ'ɔgrəfɪ] *n* geografia.
geological [dʒɪə'lɔdʒɪkl] *adj* geologico(a).
geologist [dʒɪ'ɔlədʒɪst] *n* geologo/a.
geology [dʒɪ'ɔlədʒɪ] *n* geologia.
geometric(al) [dʒɪə'mɛtrɪk(l)] *adj*
    geometrico(a).
geometry [dʒɪ'ɔmətrɪ] *n* geometria.
Geordie ['dʒɔːdɪ] *n* (*col*) abitante *m/f*
    del Tyneside; originario/a del
    Tyneside.
Georgia ['dʒɔːdʒə] *n* Georgia.
Georgian ['dʒɔːdʒən] *adj* georgiano(a) ♦ *n*
    georgiano/a; (*LING*) georgiano.
geranium [dʒɪ'reɪnɪəm] *n* geranio.
geriatric [dʒɛrɪ'ætrɪk] *adj* geriatrico(a).
germ [dʒəːm] *n* (*MED*) microbo; (*BIOL, fig*)
    germe *m*.
German ['dʒəːmən] *adj* tedesco(a) ♦ *n*
    tedesco/a; (*LING*) tedesco.
German Democratic Republic (GDR) *n*
    Repubblica Democratica Tedesca
    (R.D.T.).
germane [dʒəː'meɪn] *adj* (*formal*): **to be** ~ **to**
    sth essere attinente a qc.
German measles *n* rosolia.
Germany ['dʒəːmənɪ] *n* Germania.
germination [dʒəːmɪ'neɪʃən] *n*
    germinazione *f*.
germ warfare *n* guerra batteriologica.
gerrymandering ['dʒɛrɪmændərɪŋ] *n*
    manipolazione *f* dei distretti
    elettorali.
gestation [dʒɛs'teɪʃən] *n* gestazione *f*.
gesticulate [dʒɛs'tɪkjuleɪt] *vi* gesticolare.
gesture ['dʒɛstjə*] *n* gesto; **as a** ~ **of**
    friendship in segno d'amicizia.

═══════════════════════════ *KEYWORD*

get [gɛt] (*pt, pp* **got**, (*US*) *pp* **gotten**) *vi* **1**
    (*become, be*) diventare, farsi; **to** ~ **drunk**
    ubriacarsi; **to** ~ **killed** venire *or* rimanere
    ucciso(a); **it's** ~**ting late** si sta facendo
    tardi; **to** ~ **old** invecchiare; **to** ~ **paid**
    venire pagato(a); **to** ~ **ready** prepararsi;
    to ~ **shaved** farsi la barba; **to** ~ **tired**
    stancarsi; **to** ~ **washed** lavarsi
    2 (*go*): **to** ~ **to/from** andare a/da; **to** ~
    home arrivare *or* tornare a casa; **how did**
    you ~ **here?** come sei venuto?; **he got**
    across the bridge ha attraversato il

ponte; **he got under the fence** è passato sotto il recinto
3 (*begin*) mettersi a, cominciare a; **to ~ to know sb** incominciare a conoscere qn; **let's ~ going** *or* **started** muoviamoci
4 (*modal aux vb*): **you've got to do it** devi farlo
♦ *vt* **1: to ~ sth done** (*do*) fare qc; (*have done*) far fare qc; **to ~ sth/sb ready** preparare qc/qn; **to ~ one's hair cut** tagliarsi *or* farsi tagliare i capelli; **to ~ sb to do sth** far fare qc a qn
2 (*obtain: money, permission, results*) ottenere; (*find: job, flat*) trovare; (*fetch: person, doctor*) chiamare; (: *object*) prendere; **to ~ sth for sb** prendere *or* procurare qc a qn; **~ me Mr Jones, please** (*TEL*) mi passi il signor Jones, per favore; **can I ~ you a drink?** le posso offrire da bere?
3 (*receive: present, letter, prize*) ricevere; (*acquire: reputation*) farsi; **how much did you ~ for the painting?** quanto le hanno dato per il quadro?
4 (*catch*) prendere; (*hit: target etc*) colpire; **to ~ sb by the arm/throat** afferrare qn per un braccio/alla gola; **~ him!** prendetelo!; **he really ~s me** (*fig*: *annoy*) mi dà proprio sui nervi
5 (*take, move*) portare; **to ~ sth to sb** far avere qc a qn; **do you think we'll ~ it through the door?** pensi che riusciremo a farlo passare per la porta?
6 (*catch, take: plane, bus etc*) prendere; **he got the last bus** ha preso l'ultimo autobus; **she got the morning flight to Milan** ha preso il volo per Milano del mattino
7 (*understand*) afferrare; (*hear*) sentire; **I've got it!** ci sono arrivato!, ci sono!; **I'm sorry, I didn't ~ your name** scusi, non ho capito (*or* sentito) come si chiama
8 (*have, possess*): **to have got** avere; **how many have you got?** quanti ne ha?
▶**get about** *vi* muoversi; (*news*) diffondersi
▶**get across** *vt*: **to ~ across (to)** (*message, meaning*) comunicare (a) ♦ *vi*: **to ~ across to** (*subj: speaker*) comunicare con
▶**get along** *vi* (*agree*) andare d'accordo; (*depart*) andarsene; (*manage*) = **get by**
▶**get at** *vt fus* (*attack*) prendersela con; (*reach*) raggiungere, arrivare a; **what are you ~ting at?** dove vuoi arrivare?
▶**get away** *vi* partire, andarsene; (*escape*) scappare
▶**get away with** *vt fus*: **he'll never ~ away with it!** non riuscirà a farla franca!

▶**get back** *vi* (*return*) ritornare, tornare ♦ *vt* riottenere, riavere; **to ~ back to** (*start again*) ritornare a; (*contact again*) rimettersi in contatto con
▶**get back at** *vt fus* (*col*): **to ~ back at sb (for sth)** rendere pan per focaccia a qn (per qc)
▶**get by** *vi* (*pass*) passare; (*manage*) farcela; **I can ~ by in Dutch** mi arrangio in olandese
▶**get down** *vi, vt fus* scendere ♦ *vt* far scendere; (*depress*) buttare giù
▶**get down to** *vt fus* (*work*) mettersi a (fare); **to ~ down to business** venire al dunque
▶**get in** *vi* entrare; (*train*) arrivare; (*arrive home*) ritornare, tornare ♦ *vt* (*bring in: harvest*) raccogliere; (: *coal, shopping, supplies*) fare provvista di; (*insert*) far entrare, infilare
▶**get into** *vt fus* entrare in; **to ~ into a rage** incavolarsi; **to ~ into bed** mettersi a letto
▶**get off** *vi* (*from train etc*) scendere; (*depart: person, car*) andare via; (*escape*) cavarsela ♦ *vt* (*remove: clothes, stain*) levare; (*send off*) spedire; (*have as leave: days, time*): **we got 2 days off** abbiamo avuto 2 giorni liberi ♦ *vt fus* (*train, bus*) scendere da; **to ~ off to a good start** (*fig*) cominciare bene
▶**get on** *vi*: **how did you ~ on?** com'è andata?; **he got on quite well** ha fatto bene, (gli) è andata bene; **to ~ on (with sb)** andare d'accordo (con qn); **how are you ~ting on?** come va la vita? ♦ *vt fus* montare in; (*horse*) montare su
▶**get on to** *vt fus* (*BRIT col: contact: on phone etc*) contattare, rintracciare; (: *deal with*) occuparsi di
▶**get out** *vi* uscire; (*of vehicle*) scendere ♦ *vt* tirar fuori, far uscire; **to ~ out (of)** (*money from bank etc*) ritirare (da)
▶**get out of** *vt fus* uscire da; (*duty etc*) evitare; **what will you ~ out of it?** cosa ci guadagni?
▶**get over** *vt fus* (*illness*) riaversi da; (*communicate: idea etc*) comunicare, passare; **let's ~ it over (with)** togliamoci il pensiero
▶**get round** *vt fus* aggirare; (*fig: person*) rigirare ♦ *vi*: **to ~ round to doing sth** trovare il tempo di fare qc
▶**get through** *vi* (*TEL*) avere la linea ♦ *vt fus* (*finish: work*) sbrigare; (: *book*) finire
▶**get through to** *vt fus* (*TEL*) parlare a
▶**get together** *vi* riunirsi ♦ *vt* raccogliere; (*people*) adunare
▶**get up** *vi* (*rise*) alzarsi ♦ *vt fus* salire su

per
►**get up to** *vt fus* (*reach*) raggiungere; (*prank etc*) fare.

getaway ['gɛtəweɪ] *n* fuga.
getaway car *n* macchina per la fuga.
get-together ['gɛttəgɛðə*] *n* (piccola) riunione *f*; (*party*) festicciola.
get-up ['gɛtʌp] *n* (*col: outfit*) tenuta.
get-well card [gɛt'wɛl-] *n* cartolina di auguri di pronta guarigione.
geyser ['giːzə*] *n* scaldabagno; (*GEO*) geyser *m inv*.
Ghana ['gɑːnə] *n* Ghana *m*.
Ghanaian [gɑːˈneɪən] *adj, n* ganaense (*m/f*).
ghastly ['gɑːstlɪ] *adj* orribile, orrendo(a).
gherkin ['gəːkɪn] *n* cetriolino.
ghetto ['gɛtəu] *n* ghetto.
ghetto blaster [-ˈblɑːstə*] *n* maxistereo portatile.
ghost [gəust] *n* fantasma *m*, spettro ♦ *vt* (*book*) fare lo scrittore ombra per.
ghostly ['gəustlɪ] *adj* spettrale.
ghostwriter ['gəustraɪtə*] *n* scrittore/trice ombra *inv*.
ghoul [guːl] *n* vampiro che si nutre di cadaveri.
ghoulish ['guːlɪʃ] *adj* (*tastes etc*) macabro(a).
GHQ *n abbr* (*MIL:* = *general headquarters*) ≈ comando di Stato maggiore.
GI *n abbr* (*US col:* = *government issue*) G.I. *m*, soldato americano.
giant ['dʒaɪənt] *n* gigante/essa ♦ *adj* gigante, enorme; ~ **(size) packet** confezione *f* gigante.
giant killer *n* (*SPORT*) *piccola squadra che riesce a batterne una importante.*
gibber ['dʒɪbə*] *vi* (*monkey*) squittire confusamente; (*idiot*) farfugliare.
gibberish ['dʒɪbərɪʃ] *n* parole *fpl* senza senso.
gibe [dʒaɪb] *n* frecciata ♦ *vi*: **to** ~ **at** lanciare frecciate a.
giblets ['dʒɪblɪts] *npl* frattaglie *fpl*.
Gibraltar [dʒɪˈbrɔːltə*] *n* Gibilterra.
giddiness ['gɪdɪnɪs] *n* vertigine *f*.
giddy ['gɪdɪ] *adj* (*dizzy*): **to be** ~ aver le vertigini; (*height*) vertiginoso(a); **I feel** ~ mi gira la testa.
gift [gɪft] *n* regalo; (*donation, ability*) dono; (*COMM: also:* **free** ~) omaggio; **to have a** ~ **for sth** (*talent*) avere il dono di qc.
gifted ['gɪftɪd] *adj* dotato(a).
gift token, gift voucher *n* buono (acquisto).
gig [gɪg] *n* (*col: of musician*) serata.
gigabyte [giːgəbaɪt] *n* gigabyte *m inv*.

gigantic [dʒaɪˈgæntɪk] *adj* gigantesco(a).
giggle ['gɪgl] *vi* ridere scioccamente ♦ *n* risolino (sciocco).
GIGO ['gaɪgəu] *abbr* (*COMPUT: col:* = *garbage in, garbage out*) qualità di input = qualità di output.
gild [gɪld] *vt* dorare.
gill [dʒɪl] *n* (*measure*) = 0.25 *pints* (*BRIT* = 0.148 *l; US* = 0.118 *l*).
gills [gɪlz] *npl* (*of fish*) branchie *fpl*.
gilt [gɪlt] *n* doratura ♦ *adj* dorato(a).
gilt-edged ['gɪltɛdʒd] *adj* (*stocks, securities*) della massima sicurezza.
gimlet ['gɪmlɪt] *n* succhiello.
gimmick ['gɪmɪk] *n* trucco; **sales** ~ trovata commerciale.
gin [dʒɪn] *n* (*liquor*) gin *m inv*.
ginger ['dʒɪndʒə*] *n* zenzero.
►**ginger up** *vt* scuotere; animare.
ginger ale, ginger beer *n* bibita gassosa allo zenzero.
gingerbread ['dʒɪndʒəbrɛd] *n* pan *m* di zenzero.
ginger group *n* (*BRIT*) gruppo di pressione.
ginger-haired ['dʒɪndʒə'hɛəd] *adj* rossiccio(a).
gingerly ['dʒɪndʒəlɪ] *adv* cautamente.
gingham ['gɪŋəm] *n* percalle *m* a righe (or quadretti).
ginseng ['dʒɪnsɛŋ] *n* ginseng *m*.
gipsy ['dʒɪpsɪ] *n* zingaro/a ♦ *adj* degli zingari.
giraffe [dʒɪˈrɑːf] *n* giraffa.
girder ['gəːdə*] *n* trave *f*.
girdle ['gəːdl] *n* (*corset*) guaina.
girl [gəːl] *n* ragazza; (*young unmarried woman*) signorina; (*daughter*) figlia, figliola; **a little** ~ una bambina.
girlfriend ['gəːlfrɛnd] *n* (*of girl*) amica; (*of boy*) ragazza.
girlish ['gəːlɪʃ] *adj* da ragazza.
Girl Scout *n* (*US*) Giovane Esploratrice *f*.
Giro ['dʒaɪrəu] *n*: **the National** ~ (*BRIT*) ≈ la or il Bancoposta.
giro ['dʒaɪrəu] *n* (*bank* ~) versamento bancario; (*post office* ~) postagiro.
girth [gəːθ] *n* circonferenza; (*of horse*) cinghia.
gist [dʒɪst] *n* succo.
give [gɪv] *n* (*of fabric*) elasticità ♦ *vb* (*pt* **gave**, *pp* **given** [geɪv, 'gɪvn]) *vt* dare ♦ *vi* cedere; **to** ~ **sb sth,** ~ **sth to sb** dare qc a qn; **to** ~ **a cry/sigh** emettere un grido/ sospiro; **how much did you** ~ **for it?** quanto (l')hai pagato?; **12 o'clock,** ~ **or take a few minutes** mezzogiorno, minuto più minuto meno; **to** ~ **way** *vi* cedere;

(*BRIT AUT*) dare la precedenza.
▶**give away** *vt* dare via; (*give free*) fare dono di; (*betray*) tradire; (*disclose*) rivelare; (*bride*) condurre all'altare.
▶**give back** *vt* rendere.
▶**give in** *vi* cedere ♦ *vt* consegnare.
▶**give off** *vt* emettere.
▶**give out** *vt* distribuire; annunciare ♦ *vi* (*be exhausted*: *supplies*) esaurirsi, venir meno; (*fail*: *engine*) fermarsi; (: *strength*) mancare.
▶**give up** *vi* rinunciare ♦ *vt* rinunciare a; **to ~ up smoking** smettere di fumare; **to ~ o.s. up** arrendersi.
give-and-take [gɪvən'teɪk] *n* (*col*) elasticità (da ambo le parti), concessioni *fpl* reciproche.
giveaway ['gɪvəweɪ] *n* (*col*): **her expression was a ~** le si leggeva tutto in volto; **the exam was a ~!** l'esame è stato uno scherzo! ♦ *cpd*: **~ prices** prezzi stracciati.
given ['gɪvn] *pp of* **give** ♦ *adj* (*fixed*: *time, amount*) dato(a), determinato(a) ♦ *conj*: **~ (that)** ... dato che ...; **~ the circumstances** ... date le circostanze ....
glacial ['gleɪsɪəl] *adj* glaciale.
glacier ['glæsɪə*] *n* ghiacciaio.
glad [glæd] *adj* lieto(a), contento(a); **to be ~ about sth/that** essere contento *or* lieto di qc/che + *sub*; **I was ~ of his help** gli sono stato grato del suo aiuto.
gladden ['glædn] *vt* rallegrare, allietare.
glade [gleɪd] *n* radura.
gladioli [glædɪ'əulaɪ] *npl* gladioli *mpl*.
gladly ['glædlɪ] *adv* volentieri.
glamorous ['glæmərəs] *adj* (*gen*) favoloso(a); (*person*) affascinante, seducente; (*occasion*) brillante, elegante.
glamour ['glæmə*] *n* fascino.
glance [glɑːns] *n* occhiata, sguardo ♦ *vi*: **to ~ at** dare un'occhiata a.
▶**glance off** *vt fus* (*bullet*) rimbalzare su.
glancing ['glɑːnsɪŋ] *adj* (*blow*) che colpisce di striscio.
gland [glænd] *n* ghiandola.
glandular ['glændjulə*] *adj*: **~ fever** (*BRIT*) mononucleosi *f*.
glare [glɛə*] *n* riverbero, luce *f* abbagliante; (*look*) sguardo furioso ♦ *vi* abbagliare; **to ~ at** guardare male.
glaring ['glɛərɪŋ] *adj* (*mistake*) madornale.
glasnost ['glæznɔst] *n* glasnost *f*.
glass [glɑːs] *n* (*substance*) vetro; (*tumbler*) bicchiere *m*; (*also*: **looking ~**) specchio; *see also* **glasses**.
glass-blowing ['glɑːsbləuɪŋ] *n* soffiatura del vetro.
glass ceiling *n* (*fig*) barriera invisibile.

glasses ['glɑːsɪz] *npl* (*spectacles*) occhiali *mpl*. .
glass fibre *n* fibra di vetro.
glasshouse ['glɑːshaus] *n* serra.
glassware ['glɑːswɛə*] *n* vetrame *m*.
glassy ['glɑːsɪ] *adj* (*eyes*) vitreo(a).
Glaswegian [glæs'wiːdʒən] *adj* di Glasgow ♦ *n* abitante *m/f* di Glasgow; originario/a di Glasgow.
glaze [gleɪz] *vt* (*door*) fornire di vetri; (*pottery*) smaltare; (*CULIN*) glassare ♦ *n* smalto; glassa.
glazed ['gleɪzd] *adj* (*eye*) vitreo(a); (*tiles, pottery*) smaltato(a).
glazier ['gleɪzɪə*] *n* vetraio.
gleam [gliːm] *n* barlume *m*; raggio ♦ *vi* luccicare; **a ~ of hope** un barlume di speranza.
gleaming ['gliːmɪŋ] *adj* lucente.
glean [gliːn] *vt* (*information*) racimolare.
glee [gliː] *n* allegrezza, gioia.
gleeful ['gliːful] *adj* allegro(a), gioioso(a).
glen [glɛn] *n* valletta.
glib [glɪb] *adj* dalla parola facile; facile.
glide [glaɪd] *vi* scivolare; (*AVIAT, birds*) planare ♦ *n* scivolata; planata.
glider ['glaɪdə*] *n* (*AVIAT*) aliante *m*.
gliding ['glaɪdɪŋ] *n* (*AVIAT*) volo a vela.
glimmer ['glɪmə*] *vi* luccicare ♦ *n* barlume *m*.
glimpse [glɪmps] *n* impressione *f* fugace ♦ *vt* vedere di sfuggita; **to catch a ~ of** vedere di sfuggita.
glint [glɪnt] *n* luccichio ♦ *vi* luccicare.
glisten ['glɪsn] *vi* luccicare.
glitter ['glɪtə*] *vi* scintillare ♦ *n* scintillio.
glitz [glɪts] *n* (*col*) vistosità, chiassosità.
gloat [gləut] *vi*: **to ~ (over)** gongolare di piacere (per).
global ['gləubl] *adj* globale; (*world-wide*) mondiale.
global warming *n* riscaldamento dell'atmosfera terrestre.
globe [gləub] *n* globo, sfera.
globetrotter ['gləubtrɔtə*] *n* giramondo *m/f inv*.
globule ['glɔbjuːl] *n* (*ANAT*) globulo; (*of water etc*) gocciolina.
gloom [gluːm] *n* oscurità, buio; (*sadness*) tristezza, malinconia.
gloomy ['gluːmɪ] *adj* fosco(a), triste; **to feel ~** sentirsi giù *or* depresso.
glorification [glɔːrɪfɪ'keɪʃən] *n* glorificazione *f*.
glorify ['glɔːrɪfaɪ] *vt* glorificare; celebrare, esaltare.
glorious ['glɔːrɪəs] *adj* glorioso(a); magnifico(a).

glory ['glɔ:rɪ] n gloria; splendore m ♦ vi: **to ~ in** gloriarsi di or in.

glory hole n (col) ripostiglio.

Glos abbr (BRIT) = Gloucestershire.

gloss [glɔs] n (shine) lucentezza; (also: ~ paint) vernice f a olio.

▶**gloss over** vt fus scivolare su.

glossary ['glɔsərɪ] n glossario.

glossy ['glɔsɪ] adj lucente ♦ n (also: ~ magazine) rivista di lusso.

glove [glʌv] n guanto.

glove compartment n (AUT) vano portaoggetti.

glow [gləu] vi ardere; (face) essere luminoso(a) ♦ n bagliore m; (of face) colorito acceso.

glower ['glauə*] vi: **to ~ (at sb)** guardare (qn) in cagnesco.

glowing ['gləuɪŋ] adj (fire) ardente; (complexion) luminoso(a); (fig: report, description etc) entusiasta.

glow-worm ['gləuwə:m] n lucciola.

glucose ['glu:kəus] n glucosio.

glue [glu:] n colla ♦ vt incollare.

glue-sniffing ['glu:snɪfɪŋ] n sniffare m (colla).

glum [glʌm] adj abbattuto(a).

glut [glʌt] n eccesso ♦ vt saziare; (market) saturare.

glutinous ['glu:tɪnəs] adj colloso(a), appiccicoso(a).

glutton ['glʌtn] n ghiottone/a; **a ~ for work** un(a) patito(a) del lavoro.

gluttonous ['glʌtənəs] adj ghiotto(a), goloso(a).

gluttony ['glʌtənɪ] n ghiottoneria; (sin) gola.

glycerin(e) ['glɪsəri:n] n glicerina.

gm abbr = gram.

GMAT n abbr (US: = Graduate Management Admissions Test) esame di ammissione all'ultimo biennio di scuola superiore.

GMB n abbr (BRIT) = General Municipal and Boilermakers (Union).

GMT abbr (= Greenwich Mean Time) T.M.G.

gnarled [nɑ:ld] adj nodoso(a).

gnash [næʃ] vt: **to ~ one's teeth** digrignare i denti.

gnat [næt] n moscerino.

gnaw [nɔ:] vt rodere.

gnome [nəum] n gnomo.

GNP n abbr = gross national product.

go [gəu] vb (pt **went**, pp **gone** [wɛnt, gɔn]) vi andare; (depart) partire, andarsene; (work) funzionare; (break etc) cedere; (be sold): **to ~ for £10** essere venduto per 10 sterline; (fit, suit): **to ~ with** andare bene con; (become): **to ~ pale** diventare pallido(a); **to ~ mouldy** ammuffire ♦ n (pl ~es): **to have a ~ (at)** provare; **to be on the ~** essere in moto; **whose ~ is it?** a chi tocca?; **to ~ by car/on foot** andare in macchina/a piedi; **he's ~ing to do** sta per fare; **to ~ for a walk** andare a fare una passeggiata; **to ~ dancing/shopping** andare a ballare/fare la spesa; **to ~ looking for sb/sth** andare in cerca di qn/qc; **to ~ to sleep** addormentarsi; **to ~ and see sb, to ~ to see sb** andare a trovare qn; **how is it ~ing?** come va (la vita)?; **how did it ~?** com'è andato?; **to ~ round the back/by the shop** passare da dietro/davanti al negozio; **my voice has gone** m'è andata via la voce; **the cake is all gone** il dolce è finito tutto; **I'll take whatever is ~ing** (BRIT) prendo quello che c'è; ... **to ~** (US: food) ... da portar via; **the money will ~ towards our holiday** questi soldi li mettiamo per la vacanza.

▶**go about** vi (also: ~ around) aggirarsi; (: rumour) correre, circolare ♦ vt fus: **how do I ~ about this?** qual'è la prassi per questo?; **to ~ about one's business** occuparsi delle proprie faccende.

▶**go after** vt fus (pursue) correr dietro a, rincorrere; (job, record etc) mirare a.

▶**go against** vt fus (be unfavourable to) essere contro; (be contrary to) andare contro.

▶**go ahead** vi andare avanti; **~ ahead!** faccia pure!

▶**go along** vi andare, avanzare ♦ vt fus percorrere; **to ~ along with** (accompany) andare con, accompagnare; (agree with: idea) sottoscrivere, appoggiare.

▶**go away** vi partire, andarsene.

▶**go back** vi tornare, ritornare; (go again) andare di nuovo.

▶**go back on** vt fus (promise) non mantenere.

▶**go by** vi (years, time) scorrere ♦ vt fus attenersi a, seguire (alla lettera); prestar fede a.

▶**go down** vi scendere; (ship) affondare; (sun) tramontare ♦ vt fus scendere; **that should ~ down well with him** dovrebbe incontrare la sua approvazione.

▶**go for** vt fus (fetch) andare a prendere; (like) andar matto(a) per; (attack) attaccare; saltare addosso a.

▶**go in** vi entrare.

▶**go in for** vt fus (competition) iscriversi a; (be interested in) interessarsi di.

▶**go into** vt fus entrare in; (investigate) indagare, esaminare; (embark on) lanciarsi in.

▶**go off** *vi* partire, andar via; (*food*) guastarsi; (*explode*) esplodere, scoppiare; (*lights etc*) spegnersi; (*event*) passare ♦ *vt fus*: **I've gone off chocolate** la cioccolata non mi piace più; **the gun went off** il fucile si scaricò; **the party went off well** la festa è andata *or* è riuscita bene; **to ~ off to sleep** addormentarsi.

▶**go on** *vi* continuare; (*happen*) succedere; (*lights*) accendersi ♦ *vt fus* (*be guided by: evidence etc*) basarsi su, fondarsi su; **to ~ on doing** continuare a fare; **what's ~ing on here?** che succede *or* che sta succedendo qui?

▶**go on at** *vt fus* (*nag*) assillare.

▶**go on with** *vt fus* continuare, proseguire.

▶**go out** *vi* uscire; (*fire, light*) spegnersi; (*ebb: tide*) calare; **to ~ out with sb** uscire con qn.

▶**go over** *vi* (*ship*) ribaltarsi ♦ *vt fus* (*check*) esaminare; **to ~ over sth in one's mind** pensare bene a qc.

▶**go round** *vi* (*circulate: news, rumour*) circolare; (*revolve*) girare; (*visit*): **to ~ round (to sb's)** passare (da qn); (*make a detour*): **to ~ round (by)** passare (per); (*suffice*) bastare (per tutti).

▶**go through** *vt fus* (*town etc*) attraversare; (*search through*) frugare in; (*examine: list, book*) leggere da capo a fondo; (*perform*) fare.

▶**go through with** *vt fus* (*plan, crime*) mettere in atto, eseguire; **I couldn't ~ through with it** non sono riuscito ad andare fino in fondo.

▶**go under** *vi* (*sink: ship*) affondare, colare a picco; (: *person*) andare sotto; (*fig: business, firm*) fallire.

▶**go up** *vi* salire ♦ *vt fus* salire su per; **to ~ up in flames** andare in fiamme.

▶**go without** *vt fus* fare a meno di.

goad [gəʊd] *vt* spronare.

go-ahead ['gəʊəhɛd] *adj* intraprendente ♦ *n*: **to give sb/sth the ~** dare l'okay a qn/qc.

goal [gəʊl] *n* (*SPORT*) gol *m*, rete *f*; (: *place*) porta; (*fig: aim*) fine *m*, scopo.

goal difference *n* differenza *f* reti *inv*.

goalie ['gəʊlɪ] *n* (*col*) portiere *m*.

goalkeeper ['gəʊlkiːpə*] *n* portiere *m*.

goalpost ['gəʊlpəʊst] *n* palo (della porta).

goat [gəʊt] *n* capra.

gobble ['gɔbl] *vt* (*also: ~ down, ~ up*) ingoiare.

go-between ['gəʊbɪtwiːn] *n* intermediario/a.

Gobi Desert ['gəʊbɪ-] *n*: **the ~** il Deserto dei Gobi.

goblet ['gɔblɪt] *n* calice *m*, coppa.

goblin ['gɔblɪn] *n* folletto.

go-cart ['gəʊkɑːt] *n* go-kart *m inv* ♦ *cpd*: **~ racing** *n* kartismo.

god [gɔd] *n* dio; **G~** Dio.

god-awful [gɔd'ɔːfəl] *adj* (*col*) di merda (*!*).

godchild ['gɔdtʃaɪld] *n* figlioccio/a.

goddamn(ed) ['gɔddæm(d)] (*esp US: col*) *excl*: **goddamn!** porca miseria! ♦ *adj* fottuto(a) (*!*), maledetto(a) ♦ *adv* maledettamente.

goddaughter ['gɔddɔːtə*] *n* figlioccia.

goddess ['gɔdɪs] *n* dea.

godfather ['gɔdfɑːðə*] *n* padrino.

god-fearing ['gɔdfɪərɪŋ] *adj* timorato(a) di Dio.

god-forsaken ['gɔdfəseɪkən] *adj* desolato(a), sperduto(a).

godmother ['gɔdmʌðə*] *n* madrina.

godparents ['gɔdpɛərənts] *npl*: **the ~** il padrino e la madrina.

godsend ['gɔdsɛnd] *n* dono del cielo.

godson ['gɔdsʌn] *n* figlioccio.

goes [gəʊz] *vb see* **go**.

gofer ['gəʊfə*] *n* (*col*) tuttofare *m/f*, tirapiedi *m/f inv*.

go-getter ['gəʊgɛtə*] *n* arrivista *m/f*.

goggle ['gɔgl] *vi*: **to ~ (at)** stare con gli occhi incollati *or* appiccicati (a *or* addosso a).

goggles ['gɔglz] *npl* occhiali *mpl* (di protezione).

going ['gəʊɪŋ] *n* (*conditions*) andare *m*, stato del terreno ♦ *adj*: **the ~ rate** la tariffa in vigore; **a ~ concern** un'azienda avviata; **it was slow ~** si andava a rilento.

going-over [gəʊɪŋ'əʊvə*] *n* (*col*) controllata; (*violent attack*) pestaggio.

goings-on ['gəʊɪŋz'ɔn] *npl* (*col*) fatti *mpl* strani, cose *fpl* strane.

go-kart ['gəʊkɑːt] *n* = **go-cart**.

gold [gəʊld] *n* oro ♦ *adj* d'oro; (*reserves*) aureo(a).

golden ['gəʊldən] *adj* (*made of gold*) d'oro; (*gold in colour*) dorato(a).

golden age *n* età d'oro.

golden handshake *n* (*BRIT*) gratifica di fine servizio.

golden rule *n* regola principale.

goldfish ['gəʊldfɪʃ] *n* pesce *m* dorato *or* rosso.

gold leaf *n* lamina d'oro.

gold medal *n* (*SPORT*) medaglia d'oro.

goldmine ['gəʊldmaɪn] *n* miniera d'oro.

gold-plated ['gəʊld'pleɪtɪd] *adj* placcato(a) oro *inv*.

goldsmith ['gəʊldsmɪθ] *n* orefice *m*, orafo.

gold standard *n* tallone *m* aureo.

golf [gɔlf] *n* golf *m*.
golf ball *n* pallina da golf.
golf club *n* circolo di golf; (*stick*) bastone *m* or mazza da golf.
golf course *n* campo di golf.
golfer ['gɔlfə*] *n* giocatore/trice di golf.
golfing ['gɔlfɪŋ] *n* il giocare a golf.
gondola ['gɔndələ] *n* gondola.
gondolier [gɔndə'lɪə*] *n* gondoliere *m*.
gone [gɔn] *pp of* **go**.
goner ['gɔnə*] *n* (*col*): **I thought you were a** ~ pensavo che ormai fossi spacciato.
gong [gɔŋ] *n* gong *m inv*.
good [gud] *adj* buono(a); (*kind*) buono(a), gentile; (*child*) bravo(a) ♦ *n* bene *m*; ~! bene!, ottimo!; **to be** ~ **at** essere bravo(a) in; **it's** ~ **for you** fa bene; **it's a** ~ **thing you were** meno male che c'era; **she is** ~ **with children/her hands** ci sa fare coi bambini/è abile nei lavori manuali; **to feel** ~ sentirsi bene; **it's** ~ **to see you** che piacere vederla; **he's up to no** ~ ne sta combinando qualcuna; **it's no** ~ **complaining** brontolare non serve a niente; **for the common** ~ nell'interesse generale, per il bene comune; **for** ~ (*for ever*) per sempre, definitivamente; **would you be** ~ **enough to ...?** avrebbe la gentilezza di ...?; **that's very** ~ **of you** è molto gentile da parte sua; **is this any** ~? (*will it do?*) va bene questo?; (*what's it like?*) com'è?; **a** ~ **deal (of)** molto(a), una buona quantità (di); **a** ~ **many** molti(e); ~ **morning!** buon giorno!; ~ **afternoon/ evening!** buona sera!; ~ **night!** buona notte!; *see also* **goods**.
goodbye [gud'baɪ] *excl* arrivederci!; **to say** ~ **to** (*person*) salutare.
good faith *n* buona fede.
good-for-nothing ['gudfənʌθɪŋ] *n* buono/a a nulla, vagabondo/a.
Good Friday *n* Venerdì Santo.
good-humoured [gud'hju:məd] *adj* (*person*) di buon umore; (*remark, joke*) bonario(a).
good-looking [gud'lukɪŋ] *adj* bello(a).
good-natured [gud'neɪtʃəd] *adj* (*person*) affabile; (*discussion*) amichevole, cordiale.
goodness ['gudnɪs] *n* (*of person*) bontà; **for** ~ **sake!** per amor di Dio!; ~ **gracious!** santo cielo!, mamma mia!
goods [gudz] *npl* (*COMM etc*) merci *fpl*, articoli *mpl*; ~ **and chattels** beni *mpl* e effetti *mpl*.
goods train *n* (*BRIT*) treno *m* merci *inv*.
goodwill [gud'wɪl] *n* amicizia, benevolenza; (*COMM*) avviamento.

goody-goody ['gudɪgudɪ] *n* (*pej*) santarellino/a.
gooey ['gu:ɪ] *adj* (*BRIT col*: sticky) appiccicoso(a); (*cake, dessert*) troppo zuccherato(a).
goose, *pl* **geese** [gu:s, gi:s] *n* oca.
gooseberry ['guzbərɪ] *n* uva spina; **to play** ~ (*BRIT*) tenere la candela.
gooseflesh ['gu:sfleʃ] *n*, **goosepimples** ['gu:spɪmplz] *npl* pelle *f* d'oca.
goose step *n* (*MIL*) passo dell'oca.
GOP *n abbr* (*US POL: col*: = Grand Old Party) partito repubblicano.
gopher ['gəufə*] *n* = **gofer**.
gore [gɔ:*] *vt* incornare ♦ *n* sangue *m* (coagulato).
gorge [gɔ:dʒ] *n* gola ♦ *vt*: **to** ~ **o.s. (on)** ingozzarsi (di).
gorgeous ['gɔ:dʒəs] *adj* magnifico(a).
gorilla [gə'rɪlə] *n* gorilla *m inv*.
gormless ['gɔ:mlɪs] *adj* (*BRIT col*) tonto(a); (: *stronger*) deficiente.
gorse [gɔ:s] *n* ginestrone *m*.
gory ['gɔ:rɪ] *adj* sanguinoso(a).
go-slow ['gəu'sləu] *n* (*BRIT*) rallentamento dei lavori (*per agitazione sindacale*).
gospel ['gɔspl] *n* vangelo.
gossamer ['gɔsəmə*] *n* (*cobweb*) fili *mpl* della Madonna *or* di ragnatela; (*light fabric*) stoffa sottilissima.
gossip ['gɔsɪp] *n* chiacchiere *fpl*; pettegolezzi *mpl*; (*person*) pettegolo/a ♦ *vi* chiacchierare; (*maliciously*) pettegolare; **a piece of** ~ un pettegolezzo.
gossip column *n* cronaca mondana.
got [gɔt] *pt, pp of* **get**.
Gothic ['gɔθɪk] *adj* gotico(a).
gotten ['gɔtn] (*US*) *pp of* **get**.
gouge [gaudʒ] *vt* (*also*: ~ **out**: *hole etc*) scavare; (: *initials*) scolpire; (: *sb's eyes*) cavare.
gourd [guəd] *n* zucca.
gourmet ['guəmeɪ] *n* buongustaio/a.
gout [gaut] *n* gotta.
govern ['gʌvən] *vt* governare; (*LING*) reggere.
governess ['gʌvənɪs] *n* governante *f*.
governing ['gʌvənɪŋ] *adj* (*POL*) al potere, al governo; ~ **body** consiglio di amministrazione.
government ['gʌvnmənt] *n* governo; (*BRIT: ministers*) ministero ♦ *cpd* statale; **local** ~ amministrazione *f* locale.
governmental [gʌvn'mɛntl] *adj* governativo(a).
government housing *n* (*US*) alloggi *mpl* popolari.
government stock *n* titoli *mpl* di stato.

governor ['gʌvənə*] n (*of state, bank*) governatore m; (*of school, hospital*) amministratore m; (*BRIT: of prison*) direttore/trice.

Govt *abbr* = **government**.

gown [gaun] n vestito lungo; (*of teacher, judge*) toga.

GP n *abbr* (*MED*) *see* **general practitioner**.

GPMU n *abbr* (*BRIT*) = **Graphical, Paper and Media Union**.

GPO n *abbr* (*BRIT: old*) = **General Post Office**; (*US*: = *Government Printing Office*) ≈ Poligrafici dello Stato.

gr. *abbr* (*COMM*) = **gross**.

grab [græb] vt afferrare, arraffare; (*property, power*) impadronirsi di ♦ vi: **to ~ at** tentare disperatamente di afferrare.

grace [greis] n grazia; (*graciousness*) garbo, cortesia ♦ vt onorare; **5 days' ~** dilazione f di 5 giorni; **to say ~** dire il benedicite; **with a good/bad ~** volentieri/ malvolentieri; **his sense of humour is his saving ~** il suo senso dell'umorismo è quello che lo salva.

graceful ['greisful] *adj* elegante, aggraziato(a).

gracious ['greiʃəs] *adj* grazioso(a); misericordioso(a) ♦ *excl*: (**good**) ~! madonna (mia)!

gradation [grə'deiʃən] n gradazione f.

grade [greid] n (*COMM*) qualità f *inv*; classe f; categoria; (*in hierarchy*) grado; (*US SCOL*) voto; classe; (*gradient*) pendenza, gradiente m ♦ vt classificare; ordinare; graduare; **to make the ~** (*fig*) farcela.

grade crossing n (*US*) passaggio a livello.

grade school n (*US*) scuola elementare *or* primaria.

gradient ['greidiənt] n pendenza, gradiente m.

gradual ['grædjuəl] *adj* graduale.

gradually ['grædjuəlɪ] *adv* man mano, a poco a poco.

graduate n ['grædjuit] laureato/a; (*US SCOL*) diplomato/a, licenziato/a ♦ vi ['grædjueit] laurearsi.

graduated pension ['grædjueitid-] n *pensione calcolata sugli ultimi stipendi*.

graduation [grædju'eiʃən] n cerimonia del conferimento della laurea; (*US SCOL*) consegna dei diplomi.

graffiti [grə'fi:ti] npl graffiti mpl.

graft [grɑ:ft] n (*AGR, MED*) innesto ♦ vt innestare; **hard ~** (*col*) duro lavoro.

grain [grein] n (*no pl: cereals*) cereali mpl; (*US: corn*) grano; (*of sand*) granello; (*of wood*) venatura; **it goes against the ~**

(*fig*) va contro la mia (*or* la sua *etc*) natura.

gram [græm] n grammo.

grammar ['græmə*] n grammatica.

grammar school n (*BRIT*) ≈ liceo; (*US*) ≈ scuola elementare.

grammatical [grə'mætikl] *adj* grammaticale.

gramme [græm] n = **gram**.

gramophone ['græməfəun] n (*BRIT*) grammofono.

granary ['grænərɪ] n granaio.

grand [grænd] *adj* grande, magnifico(a); grandioso(a) ♦ n (*col: thousand*) mille dollari mpl (*or* sterline fpl).

grandchild, pl **-children** ['græntʃaild, -tʃildrən] n nipote m.

granddad ['grændæd] n (*col*) nonno.

granddaughter ['grændɔːtə*] n nipote f.

grandeur ['grændjə*] n (*of style, house*) splendore m; (*of occasion, scenery etc*) grandiosità, maestà.

grandfather ['grændfɑːðə*] n nonno.

grandiose ['grændiəus] *adj* grandioso(a); (*pej*) pomposo(a).

grand jury n (*US*) giuria (*formata da 12 a 23 membri*).

grandma ['grænmɑː] n (*col*) nonna.

grandmother ['grænmʌðə*] n nonna.

grandpa ['grænpɑː] n (*col*) = **granddad**.

grandparent ['grænpɛərənt] n nonno/a.

grand piano n pianoforte m a coda.

Grand Prix ['grɑ̃:'pri:] n (*AUT*) Gran Premio, Grand Prix m *inv*.

grandson ['grænsʌn] n nipote m.

grandstand ['grændstænd] n (*SPORT*) tribuna.

grand total n somma complessiva.

granite ['grænit] n granito.

granny ['grænɪ] n (*col*) nonna.

grant [grɑ:nt] vt accordare; (*a request*) accogliere; (*admit*) ammettere, concedere ♦ n (*SCOL*) borsa; (*ADMIN*) sussidio, sovvenzione f; **to take sth for ~ed** dare qc per scontato.

granulated ['grænjuleitid] *adj*: ~ **sugar** zucchero cristallizzato.

granule ['grænju:l] n granello.

grape [greip] n chicco d'uva, acino; **a bunch of ~s** un grappolo d'uva.

grapefruit ['greipfru:t] n pompelmo.

grapevine ['greipvain] n vite f; **I heard it on the ~** (*fig*) me l'ha detto l'uccellino.

graph [grɑ:f] n grafico.

graphic ['græfik] *adj* grafico(a); (*vivid*) vivido(a); *see also* **graphics**.

graphic designer n grafico/a.

graphic equalizer n equalizzatore m

grafico.
graphics ['græfɪks] n (art, process) grafica; (pl: drawings) illustrazioni fpl.
graphite ['græfaɪt] n grafite f.
graph paper n carta millimetrata.
grapple ['græpl] vi: **to ~ with** essere alle prese con.
grappling iron ['græplɪŋ-] n (NAUT) grappino.
grasp [grɑːsp] vt afferrare ♦ n (grip) presa; (fig) potere m; comprensione f; **to have sth within one's ~** avere qc a portata di mano; **to have a good ~ of** (subject) avere una buona padronanza di.
▶**grasp at** vt fus (rope etc) afferrarsi a, aggrapparsi a; (fig: opportunity) non farsi sfuggire, approfittare di.
grasping ['grɑːspɪŋ] adj avido(a).
grass [grɑːs] n erba; (pasture) pascolo, prato; (BRIT col: informer) informatore/trice; (ex-terrorist) pentito/a.
grasshopper ['grɑːshɔpə*] n cavalletta.
grassland ['grɑːslænd] n prateria.
grass roots npl (fig) base f.
grass snake n natrice f.
grassy ['grɑːsɪ] adj erboso(a).
grate [greɪt] n graticola (del focolare) ♦ vi cigolare, stridere ♦ vt (CULIN) grattugiare.
grateful ['greɪtful] adj grato(a), riconoscente.
gratefully ['greɪtfulɪ] adv con gratitudine.
grater ['greɪtə*] n grattugia.
gratification [grætɪfɪ'keɪʃən] n soddisfazione f.
gratify ['grætɪfaɪ] vt appagare; (whim) soddisfare.
gratifying ['grætɪfaɪɪŋ] adj gradito(a); soddisfacente.
grating ['greɪtɪŋ] n (iron bars) grata ♦ adj (noise) stridente, stridulo(a).
gratitude ['grætɪtjuːd] n gratitudine f.
gratuitous [grə'tjuːɪtəs] adj gratuito(a).
gratuity [grə'tjuːɪtɪ] n mancia.
grave [greɪv] n tomba ♦ adj grave, serio(a).
gravedigger ['greɪvdɪgə*] n becchino.
gravel ['grævl] n ghiaia.
gravely ['greɪvlɪ] adv gravemente, solennemente; **~ ill** in pericolo di vita.
gravestone ['greɪvstəun] n pietra tombale.
graveyard ['greɪvjɑːd] n cimitero.
gravitate ['grævɪteɪt] vi gravitare.
gravity ['grævɪtɪ] n (all senses) gravità.
gravy ['greɪvɪ] n intingolo della carne; salsa.
gravy boat n salsiera.
gravy train n: **the ~** (col) l'albero della cuccagna.

gray [greɪ] adj (US) = **grey**.
graze [greɪz] vi pascolare, pascere ♦ vt (touch lightly) sfiorare; (scrape) escoriare ♦ n (MED) escoriazione f.
grazing ['greɪzɪŋ] n pascolo.
grease [griːs] n (fat) grasso; (lubricant) lubrificante m ♦ vt ingrassare; lubrificare; **to ~ the skids** (US: fig) spianare la strada.
grease gun n ingrassatore m.
greasepaint ['griːspeɪnt] n cerone m.
greaseproof paper ['griːspruːf-] n (BRIT) carta oleata.
greasy ['griːsɪ] adj grasso(a); untuoso(a); (BRIT: road, surface) scivoloso(a); (hands, clothes) unto(a).
great [greɪt] adj grande; (pain, heat) forte, intenso(a); (col) magnifico(a), meraviglioso(a); **they're ~ friends** sono grandi amici; **the ~ thing is that ...** il bello è che ...; **it was ~!** è stato fantastico!; **we had a ~ time** ci siamo divertiti un mondo.
Great Barrier Reef n: **the ~** la Grande Barriera Corallina.
Great Britain n Gran Bretagna.
great-grandchild, pl **-children** [greɪt'græntʃaɪld, -tʃɪldrən] n pronipote m/f.
great-grandfather [greɪt'grændfɑːðə*] n bisnonno.
great-grandmother [greɪt'grænmʌðə*] n bisnonna.
Great Lakes npl: **the ~** i Grandi Laghi.
greatly ['greɪtlɪ] adv molto.
greatness ['greɪtnɪs] n grandezza.
Grecian ['griːʃən] adj greco(a).
Greece [griːs] n Grecia.
greed [griːd] n (also: ~iness) avarizia; (for food) golosità, ghiottoneria.
greedily ['griːdɪlɪ] adv avidamente; golosamente.
greedy ['griːdɪ] adj avido(a); goloso(a), ghiotto(a).
Greek [griːk] adj greco(a) ♦ n greco/a; (LING) greco; **ancient/modern ~** greco antico/moderno.
green [griːn] adj (also POL) verde; (inexperienced) inesperto(a), ingenuo(a) ♦ n verde m; (stretch of grass) prato; (also: village ~) ≈ piazza del paese; **~s** npl (vegetables) verdura; (of golf course) green m inv; **to have ~ fingers** or (US) **a ~ thumb** (fig) avere il pollice verde; **the G~ Party** (BRIT POL) i Verdi.
green belt n (round town) cintura di verde.
green card n (AUT) carta verde.
greenery ['griːnərɪ] n verde m.
greenfly ['griːnflaɪ] n afide f.
greengage ['griːngeɪdʒ] n susina Regina

Claudia.

greengrocer ['gri:ngrəusə*] n (BRIT) fruttivendolo/a, erbivendolo/a.

greenhouse ['gri:nhaus] n serra.

greenhouse effect n: **the ~** l'effetto serra.

greenhouse gas n gas m inv responsabile dell'effetto serra.

greenish ['gri:nıʃ] adj verdastro(a).

Greenland ['gri:nlənd] n Groenlandia.

Greenlander ['gri:nləndə*] n groenlandese m/f.

green light n: **to give sb the ~** dare via libera a qn.

green pepper n peperone m verde.

greet [gri:t] vt salutare.

greeting ['gri:tıŋ] n saluto; **Christmas/ birthday ~s** auguri mpl di Natale/di compleanno; **Season's ~s** Buone Feste.

greeting(s) card n cartolina d'auguri.

gregarious [grə'gɛərıəs] adj gregario(a); socievole.

grenade [grə'neıd] n (also: **hand ~**) granata.

grew [gru:] pt of **grow**.

grey [greı] adj grigio(a); **to go ~** diventar grigio.

greyhound ['greıhaund] n levriere m.

grid [grıd] n grata; (ELEC) rete f; (US AUT) area d'incrocio.

griddle ['grıdl] n piastra.

gridiron ['grıdaıən] n graticola.

gridlock ['grıdlɔk] n (traffic jam) paralisi f inv del traffico.

grief [gri:f] n dolore m; **to come to ~** (plan) naufragare; (person) finire male.

grievance ['gri:vəns] n doglianza, lagnanza; (cause for complaint) motivo di risentimento.

grieve [gri:v] vi addolorarsi, soffrire ♦ vt addolorare; **to ~ for sb** compiangere qn; (dead person) piangere qn.

grievous bodily harm (GBH) ['gri:vəs-] n (LAW) aggressione f.

grill [grıl] n (on cooker) griglia ♦ vt (BRIT) cuocere ai ferri; (question) interrogare senza sosta; **~ed meat** carne f ai ferri or alla griglia.

grille [grıl] n grata; (AUT) griglia.

grill(room) ['grıl(rum)] n rosticceria.

grim [grım] adj sinistro(a); brutto(a).

grimace [grı'meıs] n smorfia ♦ vi fare smorfie.

grime [graım] n sudiciume m.

grimy ['graımı] adj sudicio(a).

grin [grın] n sorriso smagliante ♦ vi: **to ~ (at)** sorridere (a), fare un gran sorriso (a).

grind [graınd] vb (pt, pp **ground** [graund]) vt macinare; (US: meat) tritare, macinare; (make sharp) arrotare; (polish: gem, lens) molare ♦ vi (car gears) grattare ♦ n (work) sgobbata; **to ~ one's teeth** digrignare i denti; **to ~ to a halt** (vehicle) arrestarsi con uno stridio di freni; (fig: talks, scheme) insabbiarsi; (: work, production) cessare del tutto; **the daily ~** (col) il trantran quotidiano.

grinder ['graındə*] n (machine: for coffee) macinino.

grindstone ['graındstəun] n: **to keep one's nose to the ~** darci sotto.

grip [grıp] n presa; (holdall) borsa da viaggio ♦ vt afferrare; **to come to ~s with** affrontare; cercare di risolvere; **to ~ the road** (tyres) far presa sulla strada; (car) tenere bene la strada; **to lose one's ~** perdere or allentare la presa; (fig) perdere la grinta.

gripe [graıp] n (MED) colica; (col: complaint) lagna ♦ vi (col) brontolare.

gripping ['grıpıŋ] adj avvincente.

grisly ['grızlı] adj macabro(a), orrido(a).

grist [grıst] n (fig): **it's (all) ~ to the mill** tutto aiuta.

gristle ['grısl] n cartilagine f.

grit [grıt] n ghiaia; (courage) fegato ♦ vt (road) coprire di sabbia; **to ~ one's teeth** stringere i denti; **I've got a piece of ~ in my eye** ho un bruscolino nell'occhio.

grits [grıts] npl (US) macinato grosso (di avena etc).

grizzle ['grızl] vi (BRIT) piagnucolare.

grizzly ['grızlı] n (also: **~ bear**) orso grigio, grizzly m inv.

groan [grəun] n gemito ♦ vi gemere.

grocer ['grəusə*] n negoziante m di generi alimentari; **~'s (shop)** negozio di alimentari.

groceries ['grəusərız] npl provviste fpl.

grocery ['grəusərı] n (shop) (negozio di) alimentari.

grog [grɔg] n grog m inv.

groggy ['grɔgı] adj barcollante.

groin [grɔın] n inguine m.

groom [gru:m] n palafreniere m; (also: **bride~**) sposo ♦ vt (horse) strigliare; (fig): **to ~ sb for** avviare qn a.

groove [gru:v] n scanalatura, solco.

grope [grəup] vi andare a tentoni; **to ~ for sth** cercare qc a tastoni.

gross [grəus] adj grossolano(a); (COMM) lordo(a) ♦ n (pl inv) (twelve dozen) grossa ♦ vt (COMM) incassare, avere un incasso lordo di.

gross domestic product (GDP) n

prodotto interno lordo (P.I.L.).

grossly ['grəuslı] adv (greatly) molto.

gross national product (GNP) n prodotto nazionale lordo (P.N.L.).

grotesque [grəu'tɛsk] adj grottesco(a).

grotto ['grɔtəu] n grotta.

grotty ['grɔtı] adj (BRIT col) squallido(a).

grouch [grautʃ] (col) vi brontolare ♦ n (person) brontolone/a.

ground [graund] pt, pp of **grind** ♦ adj (coffee etc) macinato(a) ♦ n suolo, terra; (land) terreno; (SPORT) campo; (reason: gen pl) ragione f; (US: also: ~ **wire**) (presa a) terra ♦ vt (plane) tenere a terra; (US ELEC) mettere la presa a terra a ♦ vi (ship) arenarsi; ~**s** npl (of coffee etc) fondi mpl; (gardens etc) terreno, giardini mpl; **on/to the** ~ per/a terra; **below** ~ sottoterra; **common** ~ terreno comune; **to gain/lose** ~ guadagnare/perdere terreno; **he covered a lot of** ~ **in his lecture** ha toccato molti argomenti nel corso della conferenza.

ground cloth n (US) = **groundsheet**.

ground control n (AVIAT, SPACE) base f di controllo.

ground floor n pianterreno.

grounding ['graundıŋ] n (in education) basi fpl.

groundless ['graundlıs] adj infondato(a).

groundnut ['graundnʌt] n arachide f.

ground rent n (BRIT) canone m di affitto di un terreno.

ground rules npl regole fpl fondamentali.

groundsheet ['graundʃiːt] n (BRIT) telone m impermeabile.

groundsman ['graundzmən], (US) **groundskeeper** ['graundzkiːpə*] n (SPORT) custode m (di campo sportivo).

ground staff n personale m di terra.

groundswell ['graundswɛl] n maremoto; (fig) movimento.

ground-to-air ['graundtu'ɛə*] adj terra-aria inv.

ground-to-ground ['graundtə'graund] adj: ~ **missile** missile m terra-terra.

groundwork ['graundwəːk] n preparazione f.

group [gruːp] n gruppo; (MUS: pop ~) complesso, gruppo ♦ vt raggruppare ♦ vi raggrupparsi.

groupie ['gruːpı] n groupie m/f inv, fan m/f inv scatenato(a).

group therapy n terapia di gruppo.

grouse [graus] n (pl inv) (bird) tetraone m ♦ vi (complain) brontolare.

grove [grəuv] n boschetto.

grovel ['grɔvl] vi (fig): **to** ~ **(before)** strisciare (di fronte a).

grow, pt **grew,** pp **grown** [grəu, gruː, grəun] vi crescere; (increase) aumentare; (become): **to** ~ **rich/weak** arricchirsi/ indebolirsi ♦ vt coltivare, far crescere; **to** ~ **tired of waiting** stancarsi di aspettare.

▶**grow apart** vi (fig) estraniarsi.

▶**grow away from** vt fus (fig) allontanarsi da, staccarsi da.

▶**grow on** vt fus: **that painting is** ~**ing on me** quel quadro più lo guardo più mi piace.

▶**grow out of** vt fus (clothes) diventare troppo grande per indossare; (habit) perdere (col tempo); **he'll** ~ **out of it** gli passerà.

▶**grow up** vi farsi grande, crescere.

grower ['grəuə*] n coltivatore/trice.

growing ['grəuıŋ] adj (fear, amount) crescente; ~ **pains** (also fig) problemi mpl di crescita.

growl [graul] vi ringhiare.

grown [grəun] pp of **grow** ♦ adj adulto(a), maturo(a).

grown-up [grəun'ʌp] n adulto/a, grande m/f.

growth [grəuθ] n crescita, sviluppo; (what has grown) crescita; (MED) escrescenza, tumore m.

growth rate n tasso di crescita.

GRSM n abbr (BRIT) = Graduate of the Royal Schools of Music.

grub [grʌb] n larva; (col: food) roba (da mangiare).

grubby ['grʌbı] adj sporco(a).

grudge [grʌdʒ] n rancore m ♦ vt: **to** ~ **sb sth** dare qc a qn di malavoglia; invidiare qc a qn; **to bear sb a** ~ **(for)** serbar rancore a qn (per).

grudgingly ['grʌdʒıŋlı] adv di malavoglia, di malincuore.

gruelling, (US) **grueling** ['gruəlıŋ] adj estenuante.

gruesome ['gruːsəm] adj orribile.

gruff [grʌf] adj rozzo(a).

grumble ['grʌmbl] vi brontolare, lagnarsi.

grumpy ['grʌmpı] adj stizzito(a).

grunge [grʌndʒ] n (MUS) grunge m inv; (style) moda f grunge inv.

grunt [grʌnt] vi grugnire ♦ n grugnito.

G-string ['dʒiːstrıŋ] n (garment) tanga m inv.

GSUSA n abbr = Girl Scouts of the United States of America.

GT abbr (AUT: = gran turismo) GT.

GU abbr (US POST) = Guam.

guarantee [gærən'tiː] n garanzia ♦ vt garantire; **he can't** ~ **(that) he'll come** non può garantire che verrà.

guarantor [gærən'tɔː*] n garante m/f.

guard [gɑːd] n guardia; (*protection*) riparo, protezione f; (*BOXING*) difesa; (*one man*) guardia, sentinella; (*BRIT RAIL*) capotreno; (*safety device: on machine*) schermo protettivo; (*also*: **fire ~**) parafuoco ♦ vt fare la guardia a; **to ~ (against** or **from)** proteggere (da), salvaguardare (da); **to be on one's ~** (*fig*) stare in guardia.
▶**guard against** vi: **to ~ against doing sth** guardarsi dal fare qc.

guard dog n cane m da guardia.

guarded ['gɑːdɪd] adj (*fig*) cauto(a), guardingo(a).

guardian ['gɑːdɪən] n custode m; (*of minor*) tutore/trice.

guard's van n (*BRIT RAIL*) vagone m di servizio.

Guatemala [gwɑːtə'mɑːlə] n Guatemala m.

Guernsey ['gəːnzɪ] n Guernesey f.

guerrilla [gə'rɪlə] n guerrigliero.

guerrilla warfare n guerriglia.

guess [gɛs] vi indovinare ♦ vt indovinare; (*US*) credere, pensare ♦ n congettura; **to take** or **have a ~** cercare di indovinare; **my ~ is that** ... suppongo che ...; **to keep sb ~ing** tenere qn in sospeso or sulla corda; **I ~ you're right** mi sa che hai ragione.

guesstimate ['gɛstɪmɪt] n (*col*) stima approssimativa.

guesswork ['gɛswəːk] n: **I got the answer by ~** ho azzeccato la risposta.

guest [gɛst] n ospite m/f; (*in hotel*) cliente m/f; **be my ~** (*col*) fai come (se fossi) a casa tua.

guest-house ['gɛsthaus] n pensione f.

guest room n camera degli ospiti.

guff [gʌf] n (*col*) stupidaggini fpl, assurdità fpl.

guffaw [gʌ'fɔː] n risata sonora ♦ vi scoppiare di una risata sonora.

guidance ['gaɪdəns] n guida, direzione f; **marriage/vocational ~** consulenza matrimoniale/per l'avviamento professionale.

guide [gaɪd] n (*person, book etc*) guida; (*also*: **girl ~**) giovane esploratrice f ♦ vt guidare; **to be ~d by sb/sth** farsi or lasciarsi guidare da qn/qc.

guidebook ['gaɪdbuk] n guida.

guided missile n missile m telecomandato.

guide dog n (*BRIT*) cane m guida inv.

guidelines ['gaɪdlaɪnz] npl (*fig*) indicazioni fpl, linee fpl direttive.

guild [gɪld] n arte f, corporazione f; associazione f.

guildhall ['gɪldhɔːl] n (*BRIT*) palazzo municipale.

guile [gaɪl] n astuzia.

guileless ['gaɪllɪs] adj candido(a).

guillotine ['gɪlətiːn] n ghigliottina.

guilt [gɪlt] n colpevolezza.

guilty ['gɪltɪ] adj colpevole; **to feel ~ (about)** sentirsi in colpa (per); **to plead ~/not ~** dichiararsi colpevole/innocente.

Guinea ['gɪnɪ] n: **Republic of ~** Repubblica di Guinea.

guinea ['gɪnɪ] n (*BRIT*) ghinea (= *21 shillings: valuta ora fuori uso*).

guinea pig n cavia.

guise [gaɪz] n maschera.

guitar [gɪ'tɑː*] n chitarra.

guitarist [gɪ'tɑːrɪst] n chitarrista m/f.

gulch [gʌltʃ] n (*US*) burrone m.

gulf [gʌlf] n golfo; (*abyss*) abisso; **the (Persian) G~** il Golfo Persico.

Gulf States npl: **the ~** i paesi del Golfo Persico.

Gulf Stream n: **the ~** la corrente del Golfo.

gull [gʌl] n gabbiano.

gullet ['gʌlɪt] n gola.

gullibility [gʌlɪ'bɪlɪtɪ] n semplicioneria.

gullible ['gʌlɪbl] adj credulo(a).

gully ['gʌlɪ] n burrone m; gola; canale m.

gulp [gʌlp] vi deglutire; (*from emotion*) avere il nodo in gola ♦ vt (*also*: **~ down**) tracannare, inghiottire ♦ n (*of liquid*) sorso; (*of food*) boccone m; **in** or **at one ~** in un sorso, d'un fiato.

gum [gʌm] n (*ANAT*) gengiva; (*glue*) colla; (*sweet*) gelatina di frutta; (*also*: **chewing-~**) chewing-gum m ♦ vt incollare.
▶**gum up** vt: **to ~ up the works** (*col*) mettere il bastone tra le ruote.

gumboil ['gʌmbɔɪl] n ascesso (dentario).

gumboots ['gʌmbuːts] npl (*BRIT*) stivali mpl di gomma.

gumption ['gʌmpʃən] n buon senso, senso pratico.

gun [gʌn] n fucile m; (*small*) pistola, rivoltella; (*rifle*) carabina; (*shotgun*) fucile da caccia; (*cannon*) cannone m ♦ vt (*also*: **~ down**) abbattere a colpi di pistola or fucile; **to stick to one's ~s** (*fig*) tener duro.

gunboat ['gʌnbəut] n cannoniera.

gun dog n cane m da caccia.

gunfire ['gʌnfaɪə*] n spari mpl.

gung-ho ['gʌŋ'həu] adj (*col*) stupidamente entusiasta.

gunk [gʌŋk] n porcherie fpl.

gunman ['gʌnmən] n bandito armato.

gunner ['gʌnə*] n artigliere m.

gunpoint ['gʌnpɔɪnt] n: **at ~** sotto minaccia

di fucile.

gunpowder ['gʌnpaudə*] *n* polvere *f* da sparo.

gunrunner ['gʌnrʌnə*] *n* contrabbandiere d'armi.

gunrunning ['gʌnrʌnɪŋ] *n* contrabbando d'armi.

gunshot ['gʌnʃɔt] *n* sparo; **within** ~ a portata di fucile.

gunsmith ['gʌnsmɪθ] *n* armaiolo.

gurgle ['gəːgl] *n* gorgoglio ♦ *vi* gorgogliare.

guru ['guruː] *n* guru *m inv*.

gush [gʌʃ] *n* fiotto, getto ♦ *vi* sgorgare; (*fig*) abbandonarsi ad effusioni.

gushing ['gʌʃɪŋ] *adj* che fa smancerie, smorfioso(a).

gusset ['gʌsɪt] *n* gherone *m*; (*in tights, pants*) rinforzo.

gust [gʌst] *n* (*of wind*) raffica; (*of smoke*) buffata.

gusto ['gʌstəu] *n* entusiasmo.

gusty ['gʌstɪ] *adj* (*wind*) a raffiche; (*day*) tempestoso(a).

gut [gʌt] *n* intestino, budello; (*MUS etc*) minugia; ~**s** *npl* (*col: innards*) budella *fpl*; (: *of animals*) interiora *fpl*; (*courage*) fegato ♦ *vt* (*poultry, fish*) levare le interiora a, sventrare; (*building*) svuotare; (: *subj: fire*) divorare l'interno di; **to hate sb's** ~**s** odiare qn a morte.

gut reaction *n* reazione *f* istintiva.

gutsy ['gʌtsɪ] *adj* (*col: style*) che ha mordente; (*plucky*) coraggioso(a).

gutted ['gʌtɪd] *adv* (*col: upset*) scioccato(a).

gutter ['gʌtə*] *n* (*of roof*) grondaia; (*in street*) cunetta.

gutter press *n*: **the** ~ la stampa scandalistica.

guttural ['gʌtərl] *adj* gutturale.

guy [gaɪ] *n* (*also*: ~**rope**) cavo *or* corda di fissaggio; (*col: man*) tipo, elemento; (*figure*) effigie di Guy Fawkes.

Durante la notte del 5 novembre, la **Guy Fawkes' Night**, *che commemora il fallimento della Congiura delle Polveri contro Giacomo I nel 1605, vengono lanciati fuochi d'artificio e viene bruciata l'effigie di Guy Fawkes, uno dei cospiratori.*

Guyana [gaɪ'ænə] *n* Guyana *f*.

guzzle ['gʌzl] *vi* gozzovigliare ♦ *vt* trangugiare.

gym [dʒɪm] *n* (*also*: **gymnasium**) palestra; (*also*: **gymnastics**) ginnastica.

gymkhana [dʒɪm'kɑːnə] *n* gimkana.

gymnasium [dʒɪm'neɪzɪəm] *n* palestra.

gymnast ['dʒɪmnæst] *n* ginnasta *m/f*.

gymnastics [dʒɪm'næstɪks] *n*, *npl* ginnastica.

gym shoes *npl* scarpe *fpl* da ginnastica.

gym slip *n* (*BRIT*) grembiule *m* da scuola (*per ragazze*).

gynaecologist, (*US*) **gynecologist** [gaɪnɪ'kɔlədʒɪst] *n* ginecologo/a.

gynaecology, (*US*) **gynecology** [gaɪnə'kɔlədʒɪ] *n* ginecologia.

gypsy ['dʒɪpsɪ] *n* = **gipsy**.

gyrate [dʒaɪ'reɪt] *vi* girare.

gyroscope ['dʒaɪərəskəup] *n* giroscopio.

H h

H, h [eɪtʃ] *n* (*letter*) H, h *f or m inv*; **H for Harry**, (*US*) **H for How** ≈ H come Hotel.

habeas corpus ['heɪbɪəs'kɔːpəs] *n* (*LAW*) habeas corpus *m inv*.

haberdashery ['hæbədæʃərɪ] *n* merceria.

habit ['hæbɪt] *n* abitudine *f*; (*costume*) abito; (*REL*) tonaca; **to get out of/into the** ~ **of doing sth** perdere/prendere l'abitudine di fare qc.

habitable ['hæbɪtəbl] *adj* abitabile.

habitat ['hæbɪtæt] *n* habitat *m inv*.

habitation [hæbɪ'teɪʃən] *n* abitazione *f*.

habitual [hə'bɪtjuəl] *adj* abituale; (*drinker, liar*) inveterato(a).

habitually [hə'bɪtjuəlɪ] *adv* abitualmente, di solito.

hack [hæk] *vt* tagliare, fare a pezzi ♦ *n* (*cut*) taglio; (*blow*) colpo; (*old horse*) ronzino; (*pej: writer*) negro.

hacker ['hækə*] *n* (*COMPUT*) pirata *m* informatico.

hackles ['hæklz] *npl*: **to make sb's** ~ **rise** (*fig*) rendere qn furioso.

hackney cab ['hæknɪ-] *n* carrozza a nolo.

hackneyed ['hæknɪd] *adj* comune, trito(a).

hacksaw ['hæksɔː] *n* seghetto (per metallo).

had [hæd] *pt*, *pp of* **have**.

haddock ['hædək] *n* eglefino.

hadn't ['hædnt] = **had not**.

haematology, (*US*) **hematology** [hiːmə'tɔlədʒɪ] *n* ematologia.

haemoglobin, (*US*) **hemoglobin** [hiːməu'gləubɪn] *n* emoglobina.

haemophilia, (*US*) **hemophilia** [hiːməu'fɪlɪə] *n* emofilia.

haemorrhage, *(US)* **hemorrhage** ['hemərɪdʒ] *n* emorragia.
haemorrhoids, *(US)* **hemorrhoids** ['hemərɔɪdz] *npl* emorroidi *fpl.*
hag [hæg] *n (ugly)* befana; *(nasty)* megera; *(witch)* strega.
haggard ['hægəd] *adj* smunto(a).
haggis ['hægɪs] *n (Scottish)* insaccato a base di frattaglie di pecora e avena.
haggle ['hægl] *vi:* **to ~ (over)** contrattare (su); *(argue)* discutere (su).
haggling ['hæglɪŋ] *n* contrattazioni *fpl.*
Hague [heɪg] *n:* **The ~** L'Aia.
hail [heɪl] *n* grandine *f* ♦ *vt (call)* chiamare; *(greet)* salutare ♦ *vi* grandinare; **to ~ (as)** acclamare (come); **he ~s from Scotland** viene dalla Scozia.
hailstone ['heɪlstəun] *n* chicco di grandine.
hailstorm ['heɪlstɔːm] *n* grandinata.
hair [hɛə*] *n* capelli *mpl;* (*single hair: on head*) capello; (: *on body*) pelo; **to do one's ~** pettinarsi.
hairbrush ['hɛəbrʌʃ] *n* spazzola per capelli.
haircut ['hɛəkʌt] *n* taglio di capelli; **I need a ~** devo tagliarmi i capelli.
hairdo ['hɛəduː] *n* acconciatura, pettinatura.
hairdresser ['hɛədrɛsə*] *n* parrucchiere/a.
hair-dryer ['hɛədraɪə*] *n* asciugacapelli *m inv.*
-haired [hɛəd] *suffix:* **fair/long~** dai capelli biondi/lunghi.
hairgrip ['hɛəgrɪp] *n* forcina.
hairline ['hɛəlaɪn] *n* attaccatura dei capelli.
hairline fracture *n* incrinatura.
hairnet ['hɛənɛt] *n* retina (per capelli).
hair oil *n* brillantina.
hairpiece ['hɛəpiːs] *n* toupet *m inv.*
hairpin ['hɛəpɪn] *n* forcina.
hairpin bend, *(US)* **hairpin curve** *n* tornante *m.*
hair-raising ['hɛəreɪzɪŋ] *adj* orripilante.
hair remover *n* crema depilatoria.
hair spray *n* lacca per capelli.
hairstyle ['hɛəstaɪl] *n* pettinatura, acconciatura.
hairy ['hɛərɪ] *adj* irsuto(a); peloso(a); (*col: frightening*) spaventoso(a).
Haiti ['heɪtɪ] *n* Haiti *f.*
hake, *pl* **~** *or* **~s** [heɪk] *n* nasello.
halcyon ['hælsɪən] *adj* sereno(a).
hale [heɪl] *adj:* **~ and hearty** che scoppia di salute.
half [hɑːf] *n (pl* **halves** [hɑːvz]*)* mezzo, metà *f inv;* (*SPORT: of match*) tempo; (: *of ground*) metà campo ♦ *adj* mezzo(a) ♦ *adv* a mezzo, a metà; **~ an hour** mezz'ora; **~ a dozen** mezza dozzina; **~ a pound** mezza libbra;

two and a ~ due e mezzo; **a week and a ~** una settimana e mezza; **~ (of it)** la metà; **~ (of)** la metà di; **~ the amount of** la metà di; **to cut sth in ~** tagliare qc in due; **~ empty/closed** mezzo vuoto/chiuso, semivuoto/semichiuso; **~ past 3** le 3 e mezza; **to go halves (with sb)** fare a metà (con qn).
half-back ['hɑːfbæk] *n (SPORT)* mediano.
half-baked [hɑːf'beɪkt] *adj (fig col: idea, scheme)* mal combinato(a), che non sta in piedi.
half-breed ['hɑːfbriːd] *n =* **half-caste.**
half-brother ['hɑːfbrʌðə*] *n* fratellastro.
half-caste ['hɑːfkɑːst] *n* meticcio/a.
half-hearted [hɑːf'hɑːtɪd] *adj* tiepido(a).
half-hour [hɑːf'auə*] *n* mezz'ora.
half-mast ['hɑːf'mɑːst] *n:* **at ~** *(flag)* a mezz'asta.
halfpenny ['heɪpnɪ] *n* mezzo penny *m inv.*
half-price ['hɑːf'praɪs] *adj* a metà prezzo ♦ *adv (also:* **at ~**) a metà prezzo.
half term *n (BRIT SCOL)* vacanza a *or* di metà trimestre.
half-time [hɑːf'taɪm] *n (SPORT)* intervallo.
halfway [hɑːf'weɪ] *adv* a metà strada; **to meet sb ~** *(fig)* arrivare a un compromesso con qn.
halfway house *n (hostel)* ostello dove possono alloggiare temporaneamente ex detenuti; *(fig)* via di mezzo.
half-wit ['hɑːfwɪt] *n (col)* idiota *m/f.*
half-yearly [hɑːf'jɪəlɪ] *adv* semestralmente, ogni sei mesi ♦ *adj* semestrale.
halibut ['hælɪbət] *n (pl inv)* ippoglosso.
halitosis [hælɪ'təusɪs] *n* alitosi *f.*
hall [hɔːl] *n* sala, salone *m;* (*entrance way*) entrata; *(corridor)* corridoio; *(mansion)* grande villa, maniero; **~ of residence** *n (BRIT)* casa dello studente.
hallmark ['hɔːlmɑːk] *n* marchio di garanzia; *(fig)* caratteristica.
hallo [hə'ləu] *excl =* **hello.**
Hallowe'en ['hæləu'iːn] *n* vigilia d'Ognissanti.

Secondo la tradizione anglosassone, durante la notte di **Hallowe'en,** *il 31 di ottobre, è possibile vedere le streghe e i fantasmi. Negli Stati Uniti e in Scozia i bambini, travestiti da fantasmi e con in mano lanterne ricavate da zucche, vanno di porta in porta e raccolgono dolci e piccoli doni.*

hallucination [həluːsɪ'neɪʃən] *n* allucinazione *f.*
hallucinogenic [həluːsɪnəu'dʒɛnɪk] *adj* allucinogeno(a).

hallway ['hɔːlweɪ] n ingresso; corridoio.
halo ['heɪləu] n (of saint etc) aureola; (of sun) alone m.
halt [hɔːlt] n fermata ♦ vt fermare ♦ vi fermarsi; **to call a ~ (to sth)** (fig) mettere or porre fine (a qc).
halter ['hɔːltə*] n (for horse) cavezza.
halterneck ['hɔːltənɛk] adj allacciato(a) dietro il collo.
halve [hɑːv] vt (apple etc) dividere a metà; (expense) ridurre di metà.
halves [hɑːvz] npl of **half**.
ham [hæm] n prosciutto; (col: also: **radio ~**) radioamatore/trice; (also: **~ actor**) attore/trice senza talento.
Hamburg ['hæmbəːg] n Amburgo f.
hamburger ['hæmbəːgə*] n hamburger m inv.
ham-fisted ['hæm'fɪstɪd], (US) **ham-handed** ['hæm'hændɪd] adj maldestro(a).
hamlet ['hæmlɪt] n paesetto.
hammer ['hæmə*] n martello ♦ vt martellare; (fig) sconfiggere duramente ♦ vi (at door) picchiare; **to ~ a point home to sb** cacciare un'idea in testa a qn.
▶**hammer out** vt (metal) spianare (a martellate); (fig: solution, agreement) mettere a punto.
hammock ['hæmək] n amaca.
hamper ['hæmpə*] vt impedire ♦ n cesta.
hamster ['hæmstə*] n criceto.
hamstring ['hæmstrɪŋ] n (ANAT) tendine m del ginocchio.
hand [hænd] n mano f; (of clock) lancetta; (handwriting) scrittura; (at cards) mano; (: game) partita; (worker) operaio/a; (measurement: of horse) ≈ dieci centimetri ♦ vt dare, passare; **to give sb a ~** dare una mano a qn; **at ~** a portata di mano; **in ~** a disposizione; (work) in corso; **we have the matter in ~** ci stiamo occupando della cosa; **we have the situation in ~** abbiamo la situazione sotto controllo; **to be on ~** (person) essere disponibile; (emergency services) essere pronto(a) a intervenire; **to ~** (information etc) a portata di mano; **to force sb's ~** forzare la mano a qn; **to have a free ~** avere carta bianca; **to have in one's ~** (also fig) avere in mano or in pugno; **on the one ~ ..., on the other ~** da un lato ..., dall'altro.
▶**hand down** vt passare giù; (tradition, heirloom) tramandare; (US: sentence, verdict) emettere.
▶**hand in** vt consegnare.
▶**hand out** vt (leaflets) distribuire; (advice) elargire.

▶**hand over** vt passare; cedere.
▶**hand round** vt (BRIT: information, papers) far passare; (distribute: chocolates etc) far girare; (subj: hostess) offrire.
handbag ['hændbæg] n borsetta.
hand baggage n bagaglio a mano.
handball ['hændbɔːl] n pallamano f.
handbasin ['hændbeɪsn] n lavandino.
handbook ['hændbuk] n manuale m.
handbrake ['hændbreɪk] n freno a mano.
hand cream n crema per le mani.
handcuffs ['hændkʌfs] npl manette fpl.
handful ['hændful] n manciata, pugno.
hand-held ['hænd'hɛld] adj portatile.
handicap ['hændɪkæp] n handicap m inv ♦ vt handicappare; **to be mentally ~ped** essere un handicappato mentale; **to be physically ~ped** essere handicappato.
handicraft ['hændɪkrɑːft] n lavoro d'artigiano.
handiwork ['hændɪwəːk] n lavorazione f a mano; **this looks like his ~** (pej) qui c'è il suo zampino.
handkerchief ['hæŋkətʃɪf] n fazzoletto.
handle ['hændl] n (of door etc) maniglia; (of cup etc) ansa; (of knife etc) impugnatura; (of saucepan) manico; (for winding) manovella ♦ vt toccare, maneggiare; manovrare; (deal with) occuparsi di; (treat: people) trattare; **"~ with care"** "fragile".
handlebar(s) ['hændlbɑː(z)] n(pl) manubrio.
handling ['hændlɪŋ] n (AUT) maneggevolezza; (of issue) modo di affrontare.
handling charges npl commissione f per la prestazione; (for goods) spese fpl di trasporto; (BANKING) spese fpl bancarie.
hand-luggage ['hændlʌgɪdʒ] n bagagli mpl a mano.
handmade [hænd'meɪd] adj fatto(a) a mano; (biscuits etc) fatto(a) in casa.
handout ['hændaut] n (leaflet) volantino; (press ~) comunicato stampa.
hand-picked [hænd'pɪkt] adj (produce) scelto(a), selezionato(a); (staff etc) scelto(a).
handrail ['hændreɪl] n (on staircase etc) corrimano.
handset ['hændsɛt] n (TEL) ricevitore m.
handshake ['hændʃeɪk] n stretta di mano; (COMPUT) colloquio.
handsome ['hænsəm] adj bello(a); (reward) generoso(a); (profit, fortune) considerevole.
hands-on ['hændz'ɔn] adj: **~ experience** esperienza diretta or pratica.
handstand ['hændstænd] n: **to do a ~** fare

la verticale.

hand-to-mouth ['hændtə'mauθ] *adj* (*existence*) precario(a).

handwriting ['hændraɪtɪŋ] *n* scrittura.

handwritten ['hændrɪtn] *adj* scritto(a) a mano, manoscritto(a).

handy ['hændɪ] *adj* (*person*) bravo(a); (*close at hand*) a portata di mano; (*convenient*) comodo(a); (*useful: machine etc*) pratico(a), utile; **to come in** ~ servire.

handyman ['hændɪmæn] *n* tuttofare *m inv*; **tools for the** ~ arnesi per il fatelo-da-voi.

hang, *pt, pp* hung [hæŋ, hʌŋ] *vt* appendere; (*criminal: pt, pp* **hanged**) impiccare ♦ *vi* pendere; (*hair*) scendere; (*drapery*) cadere; **to get the** ~ **of (doing) sth** (*col*) cominiciare a capire (come si fa) qc.

►**hang about** *vi* bighellonare, ciondolare.

►**hang back** *vi* (*hesitate*): **to** ~ **back (from doing)** essere riluttante (a fare).

►**hang on** *vi* (*wait*) aspettare ♦ *vt fus* (*depend on: decision etc*) dipendere da; **to** ~ **on to** (*keep hold of*) aggrapparsi a, attaccarsi a; (*keep*) tenere.

►**hang out** *vt* (*washing*) stendere (fuori); (*col: live*) stare ♦ *vi* penzolare, pendere.

►**hang together** *vi* (*argument etc*) stare in piedi.

►**hang up** *vi* (*TEL*) riattaccare ♦ *vt* appendere; **to** ~ **up on sb** (*TEL*) metter giù il ricevitore a qn.

hangar ['hæŋə*] *n* hangar *m inv*.

hangdog ['hæŋdɔg] *adj* (*guilty: look, expression*) da cane bastonato.

hanger ['hæŋə*] *n* gruccia.

hanger-on [hæŋər'ɔn] *n* parassita *m*.

hang-glider ['hæŋglaɪdə*] *n* deltaplano.

hang-gliding ['hæŋglaɪdɪŋ] *n* volo col deltaplano.

hanging ['hæŋɪŋ] *n* (*execution*) impiccagione *f*.

hangman ['hæŋmən] *n* boia *m*, carnefice *m*.

hangover ['hæŋəuvə*] *n* (*after drinking*) postumi *mpl* di sbornia.

hang-up ['hæŋʌp] *n* complesso.

hank [hæŋk] *n* matassa.

hanker ['hæŋkə*] *vi*: **to** ~ **after** bramare.

hankering ['hæŋkərɪŋ] *n*: **to have a** ~ **for sth/to do sth** avere una gran voglia di qc/di fare qc.

hankie, hanky ['hæŋkɪ] *n abbr* = **handkerchief.**

Hants *abbr* (*BRIT*) = Hampshire.

haphazard [hæp'hæzəd] *adj* a casaccio, alla carlona.

hapless ['hæplɪs] *adj* disgraziato(a); (*unfortunate*) sventurato(a).

happen ['hæpən] *vi* accadere, succedere;

she ~**ed to be free** per caso era libera; **if anything** ~**ed to him** se dovesse succedergli qualcosa; **as it** ~**s** guarda caso; **what's** ~**ing?** cosa succede?, cosa sta succedendo?

►**happen (up)on** *vt fus* capitare su.

happening ['hæpnɪŋ] *n* avvenimento.

happily ['hæpɪlɪ] *adv* felicemente; fortunatamente.

happiness ['hæpɪnɪs] *n* felicità, contentezza.

happy ['hæpɪ] *adj* felice, contento(a); ~ **with** (*arrangements etc*) soddisfatto(a) di; **yes, I'd be** ~ **to** (certo,) con piacere, (ben) volentieri; ~ **birthday!** buon compleanno!; ~ **Christmas/New Year!** buon Natale/anno!

happy-go-lucky ['hæpɪgəu'lʌkɪ] *adj* spensierato(a).

happy hour *n orario in cui i pub hanno prezzi ridotti.*

harangue [hə'ræŋ] *vt* arringare.

harass ['hærəs] *vt* molestare.

harassed ['hærəst] *adj* assillato(a).

harassment ['hærəsmənt] *n* molestia.

harbour, (*US*) **harbor** ['ha:bə*] *n* porto ♦ *vt* dare rifugio a; (*retain: grudge etc*) covare, nutrire.

harbo(u)r dues *npl* diritti *mpl* portuali.

harbo(u)r master *n* capitano di porto.

hard [ha:d] *adj* duro(a) ♦ *adv* (*work*) sodo; (*think, try*) bene; **to look** ~ **at** guardare fissamente; esaminare attentamente; **to drink** ~ bere forte; ~ **luck!** peccato!; **no** ~ **feelings!** senza rancore!; **to be** ~ **of hearing** essere duro(a) d'orecchio; **to be** ~ **on sb** essere severo con qn; **to be** ~ **done by** essere trattato(a) ingiustamente; **I find it** ~ **to believe that** ... stento *or* faccio fatica a credere che ... + *sub*.

hard-and-fast ['ha:dən'fa:st] *adj* ferreo(a).

hardback ['ha:dbæk] *n* libro rilegato.

hardboard ['ha:dbɔ:d] *n* legno precompresso.

hard-boiled egg ['ha:d'bɔɪld-] *n* uovo sodo.

hard cash *n* denaro in contanti.

hard copy *n* (*COMPUT*) hard copy *f inv*, terminale *m* di stampa.

hard-core ['ha:d'kɔ:*] *adj* (*pornography*) hardcore *inv*; (*supporters*) irriducibile.

hard court *n* (*TENNIS*) campo in terra battuta.

hard disk *n* (*COMPUT*) hard disk *m inv*, disco rigido.

harden ['ha:dn] *vt* indurire; (*steel*) temprare; (*fig: determination*) rafforzare ♦ *vi* (*substance*) indurirsi.

hardened ['hɑːdnd] adj (criminal)
incallito(a); **to be ~ to sth** essere
(diventato) insensibile a qc.

hard graft n: **by sheer ~** lavorando da
matti.

hard-headed ['hɑːd'hɛdɪd] adj pratico(a).

hard-hearted ['hɑːd'hɑːtɪd] adj che non si
lascia commuovere, dal cuore duro.

hard-hitting ['hɑːd'hɪtɪŋ] adj molto duro(a);
a ~ documentary un documentario m
verità inv.

hard labour n lavori forzati mpl.

hardliner [hɑːd'laɪnə*] n fautore/trice della
linea dura.

hard-luck story [hɑːd'lʌk-] n storia
lacrimosa (con un fine ben preciso).

hardly ['hɑːdlɪ] adv (scarcely) appena, a
mala pena; **it's ~ the case** non è proprio il
caso; **~ anyone/anywhere** quasi
nessuno/da nessuna parte; **I can ~ believe
it** stento a crederci.

hardness ['hɑːdnɪs] n durezza.

hard-nosed ['hɑːd'nəʊzd] adj (people) con i
piedi per terra.

hard-pressed ['hɑːd'prɛst] adj in difficoltà.

hard sell n (COMM) intensa campagna
promozionale.

hardship ['hɑːdʃɪp] n avversità f inv;
privazioni fpl.

hard shoulder n (BRIT AUT) corsia
d'emergenza.

hard-up [hɑːd'ʌp] adj (col) al verde.

hardware ['hɑːdwɛə*] n ferramenta fpl;
(COMPUT) hardware m.

hardware shop n (negozio di) ferramenta
fpl.

hard-wearing [hɑːd'wɛərɪŋ] adj resistente,
robusto(a).

hard-won ['hɑːd'wʌn] adj sudato(a).

hard-working [hɑːd'wɔːkɪŋ] adj
lavoratore(trice).

hardy ['hɑːdɪ] adj robusto(a); (plant)
resistente al gelo.

hare [hɛə*] n lepre f.

hare-brained ['hɛəbreɪnd] adj folle;
scervellato(a).

harelip ['hɛəlɪp] n (MED) labbro leporino.

harem [hɑː'riːm] n harem m inv.

hark back [hɑːk-] vi: **to ~ back to** (former
days) rievocare; (earlier occasion)
ritornare a or su.

harm [hɑːm] n male m; (wrong) danno ♦ vt
(person) fare male a; (thing) danneggiare;
to mean no ~ non avere l'intenzione
d'offendere; **out of ~'s way** al sicuro;
there's no ~ in trying tentar non nuoce.

harmful ['hɑːmful] adj dannoso(a).

harmless ['hɑːmlɪs] adj innocuo(a);

inoffensivo(a).

harmonic [hɑː'mɒnɪk] adj armonico(a).

harmonica [hɑː'mɒnɪkə] n armonica.

harmonics [hɑː'mɒnɪks] npl armonia.

harmonious [hɑː'məʊnɪəs] adj
armonioso(a).

harmonium [hɑː'məʊnɪəm] n armonium m
inv.

harmonize ['hɑːmənaɪz] vt, vi armonizzare.

harmony ['hɑːmənɪ] n armonia.

harness ['hɑːnɪs] n bardatura, finimenti mpl
♦ vt (horse) bardare; (resources) sfruttare.

harp [hɑːp] n arpa ♦ vi: **to ~ on about**
insistere tediosamente su.

harpist ['hɑːpɪst] n arpista m/f.

harpoon [hɑː'puːn] n arpione m.

harpsichord ['hɑːpsɪkɔːd] n clavicembalo.

harrow ['hærəʊ] n (AGR) erpice m.

harrowing ['hærəʊɪŋ] adj straziante.

harry ['hærɪ] vt (MIL) saccheggiare; (person)
assillare.

harsh [hɑːʃ] adj (hard) duro(a); (severe)
severo(a); (unpleasant: sound) rauco(a);
(: colour) chiassoso(a); violento(a).

harshly ['hɑːʃlɪ] adv duramente;
severamente.

harshness ['hɑːʃnɪs] n durezza; severità.

harvest ['hɑːvɪst] n raccolto; (of grapes)
vendemmia ♦ vt fare il raccolto di,
raccogliere; vendemmiare ♦ vi fare il
raccolto; vendemmiare.

harvester ['hɑːvɪstə*] n (machine)
mietitrice f; (also: **combine ~**)
mietitrebbia; (person) mietitore/trice.

has [hæz] see **have**.

has-been ['hæzbiːn] n (col: person): **he's/
she's a ~** ha fatto il suo tempo.

hash [hæʃ] n (CULIN) specie di spezzatino
fatto con carne già cotta; (fig: mess)
pasticcio ♦ n abbr (col) = **hashish**.

hashish ['hæʃɪʃ] n hascisc m.

hasn't ['hæznt] = **has not**.

hassle ['hæsl] n (col) sacco di problemi.

haste [heɪst] n fretta.

hasten ['heɪsn] vt affrettare ♦ vi affrettarsi;
I ~ to add that ... mi preme di aggiungere
che ...

hastily ['heɪstɪlɪ] adv in fretta,
precipitosamente.

hasty ['heɪstɪ] adj affrettato(a),
precipitoso(a).

hat [hæt] n cappello.

hatbox ['hætbɒks] n cappelliera.

hatch [hætʃ] n (NAUT: also: **~way**)
boccaporto; (BRIT: also: **service ~**) portello
di servizio ♦ vi schiudersi ♦ vt covare; (fig:
scheme, plot) elaborare, mettere a punto.

hatchback ['hætʃbæk] n (AUT) tre (or

cinque) porte *f inv.*
hatchet ['hætʃɪt] *n* accetta.
hatchet job *n* (*col*) attacco spietato; **to do a ~ on sb** fare a pezzi qn.
hatchet man *n* (*col*) tirapiedi *m inv*, scagnozzo.
hate [heɪt] *vt* odiare, detestare ♦ *n* odio; **to ~ to do** *or* **doing** detestare fare; **I ~ to trouble you, but ...** mi dispiace disturbarla, ma ....
hateful ['heɪtful] *adj* odioso(a), detestabile.
hatred ['heɪtrɪd] *n* odio.
hat trick *n* (*BRIT SPORT, also fig*): **to get a ~** segnare tre punti consecutivi (*or* vincere per tre volte consecutive).
haughty ['hɔːtɪ] *adj* altero(a), arrogante.
haul [hɔːl] *vt* trascinare, tirare ♦ *n* (*of fish*) pescata; (*of stolen goods etc*) bottino.
haulage ['hɔːlɪdʒ] *n* trasporto; autotrasporto.
haulage contractor *n* (*BRIT: firm*) impresa di trasporti; (: *person*) autotrasportatore *m*.
haulier ['hɔːlɪə*], (*US*) **hauler** ['hɔːlə*] *n* autotrasportatore *m*.
haunch [hɔːntʃ] *n* anca; **a ~ of venison** una coscia di cervo.
haunt [hɔːnt] *vt* (*subj: fear*) pervadere; (: *person*) frequentare ♦ *n* rifugio; **a ghost ~s this house** questa casa è abitata da un fantasma.
haunted ['hɔːntɪd] *adj* (*castle etc*) abitato(a) dai fantasmi *or* dagli spiriti; (*look*) ossessionato(a), tormentato(a).
haunting ['hɔːntɪŋ] *adj* (*sight, music*) ossessionante, che perseguita.
Havana [hə'vænə] *n* l'Avana.

══════════════════ *KEYWORD*

have [hæv] (*pt, pp* **had**) *aux vb* **1** (*gen*) avere; essere; **to ~ arrived/gone** essere arrivato(a)/andato(a); **to ~ eaten/slept** avere mangiato/dormito; **he has been kind/promoted** è stato gentile/promosso; **having finished** *or* **when he had finished, he left** dopo aver finito, se n'è andato
2 (*in tag questions*): **you've done it, ~n't you?** l'hai fatto, (non è) vero?; **he hasn't done it, has he?** non l'ha fatto, vero?
3 (*in short answers and questions*): **you've made a mistake — no I ~n't/so I ~** ha fatto un errore — ma no, niente affatto/ sì, è vero; **we ~n't paid — yes we ~!** non abbiamo pagato — ma sì che abbiamo pagato!; **I've been there before, ~ you?** ci sono già stato, e lei?
♦ *modal aux vb* (*be obliged*): **to ~ (got) to do sth** dover fare qc; **I ~n't got** *or* **I don't ~**

to wear glasses non ho bisogno di portare gli occhiali; **I had better leave** è meglio che io vada
♦ *vt* **1** (*possess, obtain*) avere; **he has (got) blue eyes/dark hair** ha gli occhi azzurri/i capelli scuri; **~ you got** *or* **do you ~ a car/phone?** ha la macchina/il telefono?; **may I ~ your address?** potrebbe darmi il suo indirizzo?; **you can ~ it for £5** te lo do per 5 sterline
2 (*+noun: take, hold etc*): **to ~ a bath** fare un bagno; **to ~ breakfast** fare colazione; **to ~ a cigarette** fumare una sigaretta; **to ~ dinner** cenare; **to ~ a drink** bere qualcosa; **to ~ lunch** pranzare; **to ~ a party** dare *or* fare una festa; **to ~ an operation** avere *or* subire un'operazione; **to ~ a swim** fare una nuotata; **I'll ~ a coffee** prendo un caffè; **let me ~ a try** fammi *or* lasciami provare
3: **to ~ sth done** far fare qc; **to ~ one's hair cut** tagliarsi *or* farsi tagliare i capelli; **he had a suit made** si fece fare un abito; **to ~ sb do sth** far fare qc a qn; **he had me phone his boss** mi ha fatto telefonare al suo capo
4 (*experience, suffer*) avere; **to ~ a cold/ flu** avere il raffreddore/l'influenza; **she had her bag stolen** le hanno rubato la borsa
5 (*phrases*): **you've been had!** ci sei cascato!; **I won't ~ it!** (*accept*) non mi sta affatto bene!; *see also* **haves**
►**have in** *vt*: **to ~ it in for sb** (*col*) avercela con qn
►**have on** *vt* (*garment*) avere addosso; (*be busy with*) avere da fare; **I don't ~ any money on me** non ho soldi con me; **~ you anything on tomorrow?** (*BRIT*) ha qualcosa in programma per domani?; **to ~ sb on** (*BRIT col*) prendere in giro qn
►**have out** *vt*: **to ~ it out with sb** (*settle a problem etc*) mettere le cose in chiaro con qn.

haven ['heɪvn] *n* porto; (*fig*) rifugio.
haversack ['hævəsæk] *n* zaino.
haves [hævz] *npl* (*col*): **the ~ and the have- nots** gli abbienti e i non abbienti.
havoc ['hævək] *n* confusione *f*, subbuglio; **to play ~ with sth** scombussolare qc; **to wreak ~ on sth** mettere in subbuglio qc.
Hawaii [hə'waɪiː] *n* le Hawaii.
Hawaiian [hə'waɪjən] *adj* hawaiano(a) ♦ *n* hawaiano/a; (*LING*) lingua hawaiana.
hawk [hɔːk] *n* falco ♦ *vt* (*goods for sale*) vendere per strada.
hawker ['hɔːkə*] *n* venditore *m* ambulante.

hawkish ['hɔːkɪʃ] adj violento(a).
hawthorn ['hɔːθɔːn] n biancospino.
hay [heɪ] n fieno.
hay fever n febbre f da fieno.
haystack ['heɪstæk] n pagliaio.
haywire ['heɪwaɪə*] adj (col): **to go ~** perdere la testa; impazzire.
hazard ['hæzəd] n (chance) azzardo; (risk) pericolo, rischio ♦ vt (one's life) rischiare, mettere a repentaglio; (remark) azzardare; **to be a health/fire ~** essere pericoloso per la salute/in caso d'incendio; **to ~ a guess** tirare a indovinare.
hazardous ['hæzədəs] adj pericoloso(a), rischioso(a).
hazard pay n (US) indennità di rischio.
hazard warning lights npl (AUT) luci fpl di emergenza.
haze [heɪz] n foschia.
hazel ['heɪzl] n (tree) nocciolo ♦ adj (eyes) (color) nocciola inv.
hazelnut ['heɪzlnʌt] n nocciola.
hazy ['heɪzɪ] adj fosco(a); (idea) vago(a); (photograph) indistinto(a).
H-bomb ['eɪtʃbɒm] n bomba H.
h & c abbr (BRIT) = hot and cold (water).
HE abbr = high explosive; (REL, DIPLOMACY: = His (or Her) Excellency) S.E.
he [hiː] pron lui, egli; **it is ~ who** ... è lui che ...; **here ~ is** eccolo; **~-bear** etc orso etc maschio.
head [hɛd] n testa, capo; (leader) capo; (on tape recorder, computer etc) testina ♦ vt (list) essere in testa a; (group) essere a capo di; **~s (or tails)** testa (o croce), pari (o dispari); **~ first** a capofitto; **~ over heels in love** pazzamente innamorato(a); **£10 a** or **per ~** 10 sterline a testa; **to sit at the ~ of the table** sedersi a capotavola; **to have a ~ for business** essere tagliato per gli affari; **to have no ~ for heights** soffrire di vertigini; **to lose/keep one's ~** perdere/non perdere la testa; **to come to a ~** (fig: situation etc) precipitare; **to ~ the ball** (SPORT) dare di testa alla palla.
▶**head for** vt fus dirigersi verso.
▶**head off** vt (threat, danger) sventare.
headache ['hɛdeɪk] n mal m di testa; **to have a ~** aver mal di testa.
headband ['hɛdbænd] n fascia per i capelli.
headboard ['hɛdbɔːd] n testiera (del letto).
head cold n raffreddore m di testa.
headdress ['hɛddrɛs] n (of Indian etc) copricapo; (of bride) acconciatura.
headed notepaper ['hɛdɪd-] n carta intestata.
header ['hɛdə*] n (BRIT col: FOOTBALL) colpo

di testa; (: fall) caduta di testa.
head-first ['hɛd'fɜːst] adv a testa in giù; (fig) senza pensare.
headhunt ['hɛdhʌnt] vt: **to be ~ed** avere un'offerta di lavoro da un cacciatore di teste.
headhunter ['hɛdhʌntə*] n cacciatore m di teste.
heading ['hɛdɪŋ] n titolo; intestazione f.
headlamp ['hɛdlæmp] n (BRIT) = **headlight**.
headland ['hɛdlənd] n promontorio.
headlight ['hɛdlaɪt] n fanale m.
headline ['hɛdlaɪn] n titolo.
headlong ['hɛdlɒŋ] adv (fall) a capofitto; (rush) precipitosamente.
headmaster [hɛd'mɑːstə*] n preside m.
headmistress [hɛd'mɪstrɪs] n preside f.
head office n sede f (centrale).
head-on [hɛd'ɒn] adj (collision) frontale.
headphones ['hɛdfəʊnz] npl cuffia.
headquarters (HQ) [hɛd'kwɔːtəz] npl ufficio centrale; (MIL) quartiere m generale.
head-rest ['hɛdrɛst] n poggiacapo.
headroom ['hɛdrum] n (in car) altezza dell'abitacolo; (under bridge) altezza limite.
headscarf ['hɛdskɑːf] n foulard m inv.
headset ['hɛdsɛt] n = **headphones**.
headstone ['hɛdstəʊn] n (on grave) lapide f, pietra tombale.
headstrong ['hɛdstrɒŋ] adj testardo(a).
head waiter n capocameriere m.
headway ['hɛdweɪ] n: **to make ~** fare progressi or passi avanti.
headwind ['hɛdwɪnd] n controvento.
heady ['hɛdɪ] adj che dà alla testa; inebriante.
heal [hiːl] vt, vi guarire.
health [hɛlθ] n salute f; **Department of H~** ≈ Ministero della Sanità.
health care n assistenza sanitaria.
health centre n (BRIT) poliambulatorio.
health food(s) n(pl) alimenti mpl integrali.
health hazard n pericolo per la salute.
Health Service n: **the ~** (BRIT) ≈ il Servizio Sanitario Statale.
healthy ['hɛlθɪ] adj (person) in buona salute; (climate) salubre; (food) salutare; (attitude etc) sano(a); (economy) florido(a); (bank balance) solido(a).
heap [hiːp] n mucchio ♦ vt ammucchiare; **~s (of)** (col: lots) un sacco (di), un mucchio (di); **to ~ favours/praise/gifts** etc **on sb** ricolmare qn di favori/lodi/ regali etc.
hear, pt, pp **heard** [hɪə*, hɜːd] vt sentire; (news) ascoltare; (lecture) assistere a;

(*LAW: case*) esaminare ♦ *vi* sentire; **to ~ about** sentire parlare di; (*have news of*) avere notizie di; **did you ~ about the move?** ha sentito del trasloco?; **to ~ from sb** ricevere notizie da qn.

►**hear out** *vt* ascoltare senza interrompere.

hearing ['hɪərɪŋ] *n* (*sense*) udito; (*of witnesses*) audizione *f*; (*of a case*) udienza; **to give sb a ~** dare ascolto a qn.

hearing aid *n* apparecchio acustico.

hearsay ['hɪəseɪ] *n* dicerie *fpl*, chiacchiere *fpl*; **by ~** *adv* per sentito dire.

hearse [hɜːs] *n* carro funebre.

heart [hɑːt] *n* cuore *m*; **~s** *npl* (*CARDS*) cuori *mpl*; **at ~** in fondo; **by ~** (*learn, know*) a memoria; **to take ~** farsi coraggio *or* animo; **to lose ~** perdere coraggio, scoraggiarsi; **to have a weak ~** avere il cuore debole; **to set one's ~ on sth/on doing sth** tenere molto a qc/a fare qc; **the ~ of the matter** il nocciolo della questione.

heartache ['hɑːteɪk] *n* pene *fpl*, dolori *mpl*.

heart attack *n* attacco di cuore.

heartbeat ['hɑːtbiːt] *n* battito del cuore.

heartbreak ['hɑːtbreɪk] *n* immenso dolore *m*.

heartbreaking ['hɑːtbreɪkɪŋ] *adj* straziante.

heartbroken ['hɑːtbrəukən] *adj* affranto(a); **to be ~** avere il cuore spezzato.

heartburn ['hɑːtbɜːn] *n* bruciore *m* di stomaco.

-hearted ['hɑːtɪd] *suffix*: **a kind~ person** una persona molto gentile.

heartening ['hɑːtnɪŋ] *adj* incoraggiante.

heart failure *n* (*MED*) arresto cardiaco.

heartfelt ['hɑːtfelt] *adj* sincero(a).

hearth [hɑːθ] *n* focolare *m*.

heartily ['hɑːtɪlɪ] *adv* (*laugh*) di cuore; (*eat*) di buon appetito; (*agree*) in pieno, completamente; **to be ~ sick of** (*BRIT*) essere veramente stufo di, essere arcistufo di.

heartland ['hɑːtlænd] *n* zona centrale; **Italy's industrial ~** il cuore dell'industria italiana.

heartless ['hɑːtlɪs] *adj* senza cuore, insensibile; crudele.

heartstrings ['hɑːtstrɪŋz] *npl*: **to tug at sb's ~** toccare il cuore a qn, toccare qn nel profondo.

heart-throb ['hɑːtθrɔb] *n* rubacuori *m inv*.

heart-to-heart ['hɑːttə'hɑːt] *adj, adv* a cuore aperto.

heart transplant *n* trapianto del cuore.

heartwarming ['hɑːtwɔːmɪŋ] *adj* confortante, che scalda il cuore.

hearty ['hɑːtɪ] *adj* caloroso(a); robusto(a), sano(a); vigoroso(a).

heat [hiːt] *n* calore *m*; (*fig*) ardore *m*; fuoco; (*SPORT: also:* **qualifying ~**) prova eliminatoria; (*ZOOL*): **in** *or* (*BRIT*) **on ~** in calore ♦ *vt* scaldare.

►**heat up** *vi* (*liquids*) scaldarsi; (*room*) riscaldarsi ♦ *vt* riscaldare.

heated ['hiːtɪd] *adj* riscaldato(a); (*fig*) appassionato(a); acceso(a), eccitato(a).

heater ['hiːtə*] *n* stufa; radiatore *m*.

heath [hiːθ] *n* (*BRIT*) landa.

heathen ['hiːðn] *adj, n* pagano(a).

heather ['hɛðə*] *n* erica.

heating ['hiːtɪŋ] *n* riscaldamento.

heat-resistant ['hiːtrɪzɪstənt] *adj* termoresistente.

heat-seeking ['hiːtsiːkɪŋ] *adj* che cerca fonti di calore.

heatstroke ['hiːtstrəuk] *n* colpo di sole.

heatwave ['hiːtweɪv] *n* ondata di caldo.

heave [hiːv] *vt* sollevare (con forza) ♦ *vi* sollevarsi ♦ *n* (*push*) grande spinta; **to ~ a sigh** emettere *or* mandare un sospiro.

►**heave to** *vi* (*pt, pp* **hove**) *vi* (*NAUT*) mettersi in cappa.

heaven ['hɛvn] *n* paradiso, cielo; **~ forbid!** Dio ce ne guardi!; **for ~'s sake!** (*pleading*) per amor del cielo!, per carità!; (*protesting*) santo cielo!, in nome del cielo!; **thank ~!** grazie al cielo!

heavenly ['hɛvnlɪ] *adj* divino(a), celeste.

heavily ['hɛvɪlɪ] *adv* pesantemente; (*drink, smoke*) molto.

heavy ['hɛvɪ] *adj* pesante; (*sea*) grosso(a); (*rain*) forte; (*drinker, smoker*) gran (*before noun*); **it's ~ going** è una gran fatica; **~ industry** industria pesante.

heavy cream *n* (*US*) doppia panna.

heavy-duty ['hɛvɪ'djuːtɪ] *adj* molto resistente.

heavy goods vehicle (HGV) *n* (*BRIT*) veicolo per trasporti pesanti.

heavy-handed ['hɛvɪ'hændɪd] *adj* (*clumsy, tactless*) pesante.

heavy metal *n* (*MUS*) heavy metal *m*.

heavy-set ['hɛvɪ'sɛt] *adj* (*esp US*) tarchiato(a).

heavyweight ['hɛvɪweɪt] *n* (*SPORT*) peso massimo.

Hebrew ['hiːbruː] *adj* ebreo(a) ♦ *n* (*LING*) ebraico.

Hebrides ['hɛbrɪdiːz] *npl*: **the ~** le Ebridi.

heck [hɛk] (*col*) *excl*: **oh ~!** oh no! ♦ *n*: **a ~ of a lot of** un gran bel po' di.

heckle ['hɛkl] *vt* interpellare e dare noia a (*un oratore*).

heckler ['hɛklə*] *n* agitatore/trice.

hectare ['hɛktɑː*] n (BRIT) ettaro.
hectic ['hɛktɪk] adj movimentato(a); (busy) frenetico(a).
hector ['hɛktə*] vt usare le maniere forti con.
he'd [hiːd] = **he would; he had.**
hedge [hɛdʒ] n siepe f ♦ vi essere elusivo(a); **as a ~ against inflation** per cautelarsi contro l'inflazione; **to ~ one's bets** (fig) coprirsi dai rischi.
▸**hedge in** vt recintare con una siepe.
hedgehog ['hɛdʒhɔg] n riccio.
hedgerow ['hɛdʒrəu] n siepe f.
hedonism ['hiːdənɪzəm] n edonismo.
heed [hiːd] vt (also: **take ~ of**) badare a, far conto di ♦ n: **to pay (no) ~ to, to take (no) ~ of** (non) ascoltare, (non) tener conto di.
heedless ['hiːdlɪs] adj sbadato(a).
heel [hiːl] n (ANAT) calcagno; (of shoe) tacco ♦ vt (shoe) rifare i tacchi a; **to bring to ~** addomesticare; **to take to one's ~s** (col) darsela a gambe, alzare i tacchi.
hefty ['hɛftɪ] adj (person) solido(a); (parcel) pesante; (piece, price) grosso(a).
heifer ['hɛfə*] n giovenca.
height [haɪt] n altezza; (high ground) altura; (fig: of glory) apice m; (: of stupidity) colmo; **what ~ are you?** quanto sei alto?; **of average ~** di statura media; **to be afraid of ~s** soffrire di vertigini; **it's the ~ of fashion** è l'ultimo grido della moda.
heighten ['haɪtn] vt innalzare; (fig) accrescere.
heinous ['heɪnəs] adj nefando(a), atroce.
heir [ɛə*] n erede m.
heir apparent n erede m/f legittimo(a).
heiress ['ɛərɛs] n erede f.
heirloom ['ɛəluːm] n mobile m (or gioiello or quadro) di famiglia.
heist [haɪst] n (US col) rapina.
held [hɛld] pt, pp of **hold.**
helicopter ['hɛlɪkɔptə*] n elicottero.
heliport ['hɛlɪpɔːt] n eliporto.
helium ['hiːlɪəm] n elio.
hell [hɛl] n inferno; **a ~ of a ...** (col) un(a) maledetto(a) ...; **oh ~!** (col) porca miseria!, accidenti!
he'll [hiːl] = **he will, he shall.**
hell-bent [hɛl'bɛnt] adj (col): **to be ~ on doing sth** voler fare qc a tutti i costi.
hellish ['hɛlɪʃ] adj infernale.
hello [hə'ləu] excl buon giorno!; ciao! (to sb one addresses as "tu"); (surprise) ma guarda!
helm [hɛlm] n (NAUT) timone m.
helmet ['hɛlmɪt] n casco.
helmsman ['hɛlmzmən] n timoniere m.
help [hɛlp] n aiuto; (charwoman) donna di servizio; (assistant etc) impiegato/a ♦ vt aiutare; **~!** aiuto!; **with the ~ of** con l'aiuto di; **to be of ~ to sb** essere di aiuto or essere utile a qn; **to ~ sb (to) do sth** aiutare qn a far qc; **can I ~ you?** (in shop) desidera?; **~ yourself (to bread)** si serva (del pane); **I can't ~ saying** non posso evitare di dire; **he can't ~ it** non ci può far niente.
helper ['hɛlpə*] n aiutante m/f, assistente m/f.
helpful ['hɛlpful] adj di grande aiuto; (useful) utile.
helping ['hɛlpɪŋ] n porzione f.
helping hand n: **to give sb a ~** dare una mano a qn.
helpless ['hɛlplɪs] adj impotente; debole; (baby) indifeso(a).
helplessly ['hɛlplɪslɪ] adv (watch) senza poter fare nulla.
helpline ['hɛlplaɪn] n ≈ telefono amico; (COMM) servizio m informazioni inv (a pagamento).
Helsinki ['hɛlsɪŋkɪ] n Helsinki f.
helter-skelter ['hɛltə'skɛltə*] n (BRIT: in funfair) scivolo (a spirale).
hem [hɛm] n orlo ♦ vt fare l'orlo a.
▸**hem in** vt cingere; **to feel ~med in** (fig) sentirsi soffocare.
he-man ['hiːmæn] n (col) fusto.
hematology [hiːmə'tɔlədʒɪ] n (US) = **haematology.**
hemisphere ['hɛmɪsfɪə*] n emisfero.
hemlock ['hɛmlɔk] n cicuta.
hemoglobin [hiːməu'gləubɪn] n (US) = **haemoglobin.**
hemophilia [hiːməu'fɪlɪə] n (US) = **haemophilia.**
hemorrhage n (US) = **haemorrhage.**
hemorrhoids ['hɛmərɔɪdz] npl (US) = **haemorrhoids.**
hemp [hɛmp] n canapa.
hen [hɛn] n gallina; (female bird) femmina.
hence [hɛns] adv (therefore) dunque; **2 years ~** di qui a 2 anni.
henceforth [hɛns'fɔːθ] adv d'ora in poi.
henchman ['hɛntʃmən] n (pej) caudatario.
henna ['hɛnə] n henna.
hen night n (col) addio al nubilato.
hen party n (col) festa di sole donne.
henpecked ['hɛnpɛkt] adj dominato dalla moglie.
hepatitis [hɛpə'taɪtɪs] n epatite f.
her [həː*] pron (direct) la, l' + vowel; (indirect) le; (stressed, after prep) lei; see note at **she** ♦ adj il(la) suo(a), i(le) suoi(sue); **I see ~** la vedo; **give ~ a book** le dia un libro; **after ~** dopo (di)

lei.
herald ['hɛrəld] n araldo ♦ vt annunciare.
heraldic [hɛ'rældɪk] adj araldico(a).
heraldry ['hɛrəldrɪ] n araldica.
herb [həːb] n erba; ~s npl (CULIN) erbette fpl.
herbaceous [həː'beɪʃəs] adj erbaceo(a).
herbal ['həːbəl] adj di erbe; ~ **tea** tisana.
herbicide ['həːbɪsaɪd] n erbicida m.
herd [həːd] n mandria; (of wild animals, swine) branco ♦ vt (drive, gather: animals) guidare; (: people) radunare; ~**ed together** ammassati (come bestie).
here [hɪə*] adv qui, qua ♦ excl ehi!; ~! (at roll call) presente!; ~ **is**, ~ **are** ecco; ~'**s my sister** ecco mia sorella; ~ **she is** eccola; ~ **she comes** eccola che viene; **come** ~! vieni qui!; ~ **and there** qua e là.
hereabouts ['hɪərəbauts] adv da queste parti.
hereafter [hɪər'ɑːftə*] adv in futuro; dopo questo ♦ n: **the** ~ l'al di là m.
hereby [hɪə'baɪ] adv (in letter) con la presente.
hereditary [hɪ'rɛdɪtrɪ] adj ereditario(a).
heredity [hɪ'rɛdɪtɪ] n eredità.
heresy ['hɛrəsɪ] n eresia.
heretic ['hɛrətɪk] n eretico/a.
heretical [hɪ'rɛtɪkl] adj eretico(a).
herewith [hɪə'wɪð] adv qui accluso.
heritage ['hɛrɪtɪdʒ] n eredità; (of country, nation) retaggio; **our national** ~ il nostro patrimonio nazionale.
hermetically [həː'mɛtɪklɪ] adv ermeticamente; ~ **sealed** ermeticamente chiuso.
hermit ['həːmɪt] n eremita m.
hernia ['həːnɪə] n ernia.
hero, ~**es** ['hɪərəu] n eroe m.
heroic [hɪ'rəuɪk] adj eroico(a).
heroin ['hɛrəuɪn] n eroina (droga).
heroin addict n eroinomane m/f.
heroine ['hɛrəuɪn] n eroina (donna).
heroism ['hɛrəuɪzəm] n eroismo.
heron ['hɛrən] n airone m.
hero worship n divismo.
herring ['hɛrɪŋ] n aringa.
hers [həːz] pron il(la) suo(a), i(le) suoi(sue); **a friend of** ~ un suo amico; **this is** ~ questo è (il) suo.
herself [həː'sɛlf] pron (reflexive) si; (emphatic) lei stessa; (after prep) se stessa, sé.
Herts abbr (BRIT) = Hertfordshire.
he's [hiːz] = he is; he has.
hesitant ['hɛzɪtənt] adj esitante, indeciso(a); **to be** ~ **about doing sth** esitare a fare qc.

hesitate ['hɛzɪteɪt] vi: **to** ~ **(about/to do)** esitare (su/a fare); **don't** ~ **to ask (me)** non aver timore or paura di chiedermelo.
hesitation [hɛzɪ'teɪʃən] n esitazione f; **I have no** ~ **in saying (that)** ... non esito a dire che ....
hessian ['hɛsɪən] n tela di canapa.
heterogeneous [hɛtərəu'dʒiːnɪəs] adj eterogeneo(a).
heterosexual [hɛtərəu'sɛksjuəl] adj, n eterosessuale (m/f).
het up [hɛt'ʌp] adj agitato(a).
HEW n abbr (US: = Department of Health, Education and Welfare) ministero della sanità, della pubblica istruzione e della previdenza sociale.
hew [hjuː] vt tagliare (con l'accetta).
hex [hɛks] (US) n stregoneria ♦ vt stregare.
hexagon ['hɛksəgən] n esagono.
hexagonal [hɛk'sægənl] adj esagonale.
hey [heɪ] excl ehi!
heyday ['heɪdeɪ] n: **the** ~ **of** i bei giorni di, l'età d'oro di.
HF n abbr (= high frequency) AF.
HGV n abbr see heavy goods vehicle.
HI abbr (US) = Hawaii.
hi [haɪ] excl ciao!
hiatus [haɪ'eɪtəs] n vuoto; (LING) iato.
hibernate ['haɪbəneɪt] vi ibernare.
hibernation [haɪbə'neɪʃən] n letargo, ibernazione f.
hiccough, **hiccup** ['hɪkʌp] vi singhiozzare ♦ n singhiozzo; **to have (the)** ~**s** avere il singhiozzo.
hick [hɪk] n (US col) buzzurro/a.
hid [hɪd] pt of hide.
hidden ['hɪdn] pp of hide ♦ adj nascosto(a); **there are no** ~ **extras** è veramente tutto compreso nel prezzo; ~ **agenda** programma m occulto.
hide [haɪd] n (skin) pelle f ♦ vb (pt hid, pp hidden [hɪd, 'hɪdn]) vt: **to** ~ **sth (from sb)** nascondere qc (a qn) ♦ vi: **to** ~ **(from sb)** nascondersi (da qn).
hide-and-seek ['haɪdən'siːk] n rimpiattino.
hideaway ['haɪdəweɪ] n nascondiglio.
hideous ['hɪdɪəs] adj laido(a); orribile.
hide-out ['haɪdaut] n nascondiglio.
hiding ['haɪdɪŋ] n (beating) bastonata; **to be in** ~ (concealed) tenersi nascosto(a).
hiding place n nascondiglio.
hierarchy ['haɪərɑːkɪ] n gerarchia.
hieroglyphic [haɪərə'glɪfɪk] adj geroglifico(a); ~**s** npl geroglifici mpl.
hi-fi ['haɪ'faɪ] adj, n abbr (= high fidelity) hi-fi (m) inv.
higgledy-piggledy ['hɪgldɪ'pɪgldɪ] adv alla rinfusa.

high [haɪ] *adj* alto(a); (*speed, respect, number*) grande; (*wind*) forte; (*BRIT CULIN: meat, game*) frollato(a); (: *spoilt*) andato(a) a male; (*col: on drugs*) fatto(a); (: *on drink*) su di giri ♦ *adv* alto, in alto ♦ *n*: **exports have reached a new** ~ le esportazioni hanno toccato un nuovo record; **20m** ~ alto(a) 20m; **to pay a** ~ **price for sth** pagare (molto) caro qc.

highball ['haɪbɔːl] *n* (*US: drink*) whisky (*or* brandy) e soda con ghiaccio.

highboy ['haɪbɔɪ] *n* (*US*) cassettone *m*.

highbrow ['haɪbrau] *adj, n* intellettuale (*m/f*).

highchair ['haɪtʃɛə*] *n* seggiolone *m*.

high-class ['haɪ'klɑːs] *adj* (*neighbourhood*) elegante; (*hotel*) di prim'ordine; (*person*) di gran classe; (*food*) raffinato(a).

High Court *n* alta corte *f*.

> *Nel sistema legale inglese e gallese, la* **High Court** *e la* **Court of Appeal** *compongono la* **Supreme Court of Judicature**. *In Scozia, invece, la High Court è la corte che si occupa dei reati più gravi e corrisponde alla* **crown court** *inglese.*

higher ['haɪə*] *adj* (*form of life, study etc*) superiore ♦ *adv* più in alto, più in su.

higher education *n* istruzione *f* superiore, istruzione universitaria.

highfalutin [haɪfə'luːtɪn] *adj* (*col*) pretenzioso(a).

high finance *n* alta finanza.

high-flier, high-flyer [haɪ'flaɪə*] *n* (*giovane*) promessa *f* (*fig*).

high-flying [haɪ'flaɪɪŋ] *adj* (*fig*) promettente.

high-handed [haɪ'hændɪd] *adj* prepotente.

high-heeled [haɪ'hiːld] *adj* a tacchi alti.

highjack ['haɪdʒæk] *vt, n* = **hijack**.

high jump *n* (*SPORT*) salto in alto.

highlands ['haɪləndz] *npl* zona montuosa; **the H**~ le Highlands scozzesi.

high-level ['haɪlɛvl] *adj* (*talks etc, COMPUT*) ad alto livello.

highlight ['haɪlaɪt] *n* (*fig: of event*) momento culminante ♦ *vt* mettere in evidenza; ~**s** *npl* (*in hair*) colpi *mpl* di sole.

highlighter ['haɪlaɪtə*] *n* (*pen*) evidenziatore *m*.

highly ['haɪlɪ] *adv* molto; ~ **paid** pagato molto bene; **to speak** ~ **of** parlare molto bene di.

highly-strung ['haɪlɪ'strʌŋ] *adj* teso(a) di nervi, eccitabile.

High Mass *n* messa cantata *or* solenne.

highness ['haɪnɪs] *n* altezza; **Her H**~ Sua

Altezza.

high-pitched [haɪ'pɪtʃt] *adj* acuto(a).

high point *n*: **the** ~ il momento più importante.

high-powered ['haɪ'pauəd] *adj* (*engine*) molto potente, ad alta potenza; (*fig: person*) di prestigio.

high-pressure ['haɪprɛʃə*] *adj* ad alta pressione; (*fig*) aggressivo(a).

high-rise block ['haɪraɪz-] *n* palazzone *m*.

high school *n* (*BRIT*) scuola secondaria; (*US*) istituto d'istruzione secondaria.

> *Negli Stati Uniti la* **high school** *è un istituto di istruzione secondaria. Si suddivide in junior high school (dal settimo al nono anno di corso) e senior high school (dal decimo al dodicesimo), dove vengono impartiti sia insegnamenti accademici che di formazione professionale. In Gran Bretagna molte scuole secondarie si chiamano high school; vedi anche* **elementary school**.

high season *n* (*BRIT*) alta stagione.

high spirits *npl* buonumore *m*, euforia; **to be in** ~ essere euforico(a).

high street *n* (*BRIT*) strada principale.

highway ['haɪweɪ] *n* strada maestra; **the information** ~ l'autostrada telematica.

Highway Code *n* (*BRIT*) codice *m* della strada.

highwayman ['haɪweɪmən] *n* bandito.

hijack ['haɪdʒæk] *vt* dirottare ♦ *n* dirottamento; (*also*: ~**ing**) pirateria aerea.

hijacker ['haɪdʒækə*] *n* dirottatore/trice.

hike [haɪk] *vi* fare un'escursione a piedi ♦ *n* escursione *f* a piedi; (*col: in prices etc*) aumento ♦ *vt* (*col*) aumentare.

hiker ['haɪkə*] *n* escursionista *m/f*.

hiking ['haɪkɪŋ] *n* escursioni *fpl* a piedi.

hilarious [hɪ'lɛərɪəs] *adj* che fa schiantare dal ridere.

hilarity [hɪ'lærɪtɪ] *n* ilarità.

hill [hɪl] *n* collina, colle *m*; (*fairly high*) montagna; (*on road*) salita.

hillbilly ['hɪlbɪlɪ] *n* (*US*) montanaro/a dal sud degli Stati Uniti; (*pej*) zotico/a.

hillock ['hɪlək] *n* collinetta, poggio.

hillside ['hɪlsaɪd] *n* fianco della collina.

hill start *n* (*AUT*) partenza in salita.

hilly ['hɪlɪ] *adj* collinoso(a); montagnoso(a).

hilt [hɪlt] *n* (*of sword*) elsa; **to the** ~ (*fig: support*) fino in fondo.

him [hɪm] *pron* (*direct*) lo, l' + *vowel*; (*indirect*) gli; (*stressed, after prep*) lui; **I see** ~ lo vedo; **give** ~ **a book** gli dia un libro; **after** ~ dopo (di) lui.

Himalayas [hɪmə'leɪəz] *npl*: **the ~** l'Himalaia *m*.

himself [hɪm'sɛlf] *pron* (*reflexive*) si; (*emphatic*) lui stesso; (*after prep*) se stesso, sé.

hind [haɪnd] *adj* posteriore ♦ *n* cerva.

hinder ['hɪndə*] *vt* ostacolare; (*delay*) tardare; (*prevent*): **to ~ sb from doing** impedire a qn di fare.

hindquarters ['haɪndkwɔːtəz] *npl* (*ZOOL*) posteriore *m*.

hindrance ['hɪndrəns] *n* ostacolo, impedimento.

hindsight ['haɪndsaɪt] *n* senno di poi; **with the benefit of ~** con il senno di poi.

Hindu ['hɪnduː] *n* indù *m/f inv*.

hinge [hɪndʒ] *n* cardine *m* ♦ *vi* (*fig*): **to ~ on** dipendere da.

hint [hɪnt] *n* accenno, allusione *f*; (*advice*) consiglio ♦ *vt*: **to ~ that** lasciar capire che ♦ *vi*: **to ~ at** accennare a; **to drop a ~** lasciar capire; **give me a ~** (*clue*) dammi almeno un'idea, dammi un'indicazione.

hip [hɪp] *n* anca, fianco; (*BOT*) frutto della rosa canina.

hip flask *n* fiaschetta da liquore tascabile.

hip hop *n* hip-hop *m*.

hippie ['hɪpɪ] *n* hippy *m/f inv*.

hip pocket *n* tasca posteriore dei calzoni.

hippopotamus, *pl* **-es** *or* **hippopotami** [hɪpə'pɔtəməs, -'pɔtəmaɪ] *n* ippopotamo.

hippy ['hɪpɪ] *n* = **hippie**.

hire ['haɪə*] *vt* (*BRIT*: *car, equipment*) noleggiare; (*worker*) assumere, dare lavoro a ♦ *n* nolo, noleggio; **for ~** da nolo; (*taxi*) libero(a); **on ~** a nolo.

▶**hire out** *vt* noleggiare, dare a nolo *or* noleggio, affittare.

hire(d) car *n* (*BRIT*) macchina a nolo.

hire purchase (HP) *n* (*BRIT*) acquisto (*or* vendita) rateale; **to buy sth on ~** comprare qc a rate.

his [hɪz] *adj, pron* il(la) suo(sua), i(le) suoi(sue); **this is ~** questo è (il) suo.

hiss [hɪs] *vi* fischiare; (*cat, snake*) sibilare ♦ *n* fischio; sibilo.

histogram ['hɪstəgræm] *n* istogramma *m*.

historian [hɪ'stɔːrɪən] *n* storico/a.

historic(al) [hɪ'stɔrɪk(l)] *adj* storico(a).

history ['hɪstərɪ] *n* storia; **there's a long ~ of that illness in his family** ci sono molti precedenti (della malattia) nella sua famiglia.

histrionics [hɪstrɪ'ɔnɪks] *n* istrionismo.

hit [hɪt] *vt* (*pt, pp* **hit**) colpire, picchiare; (*knock against*) battere; (*reach: target*) raggiungere; (*collide with: car*) urtare contro; (*fig: affect*) colpire; (*find: problem*)

incontrare ♦ *n* colpo; (*success, song*) successo; **to ~ the headlines** far titolo; **to ~ the road** (*col*) mettersi in cammino; **to ~ it off with sb** andare molto d'accordo con qn.

▶**hit back** *vi*: **to ~ back at sb** restituire il colpo a qn.

▶**hit out at** *vt fus* sferrare dei colpi contro; (*fig*) attaccare.

▶**hit (up)on** *vt fus* (*answer*) imbroccare, azzeccare; (*solution*) trovare (per caso).

hit-and-run driver ['hɪtænd'rʌn-] *n* pirata *m* della strada.

hitch [hɪtʃ] *vt* (*fasten*) attaccare; (*also: ~ up*) tirare su ♦ *n* (*difficulty*) intoppo, difficoltà *f inv*; **technical ~** difficoltà tecnica; **to ~ a lift** fare l'autostop.

▶**hitch up** *vt* (*horse, cart*) attaccare.

hitch-hike ['hɪtʃhaɪk] *vi* fare l'autostop.

hitch-hiker ['hɪtʃhaɪkə*] *n* autostoppista *m/f*.

hi-tech ['haɪtɛk] *adj* high-tech *inv*, a tecnologia avanzata.

hitherto ['hɪðə'tuː] *adv* finora.

hit list *n* libro nero.

hitman ['hɪtmæn] *n* (*col*) sicario.

hit-or-miss ['hɪtə'mɪs] *adj* casuale; **it's ~ whether ...** è in dubbio se ...; **the service in this hotel is very ~** il servizio dell'albergo lascia a desiderare.

hit parade *n* hit-parade *f*.

HIV *n abbr* (= *human immunodeficiency virus*) virus *m inv* di immunodeficienza; **~-negative/-positive** sieronegativo(a)/ sieropositivo(a).

hive [haɪv] *n* alveare *m*; **the shop was a ~ of activity** (*fig*) c'era una grande attività nel negozio.

▶**hive off** *vt* (*col*) separare.

hl *abbr* (= *hectolitre*) hl.

HM *abbr* (= *His* (*or Her*) *Majesty*) S.M. (= *Sua Maestà*).

HMG *abbr* (*BRIT*) = *His* (*or Her*) *Majesty's Government*.

HMI *n abbr* (*BRIT SCOL*: = *His* (*or Her*) *Majesty's Inspector*) ≈ ispettore *m* scolastico.

HMO *n abbr* (*US*: = *health maintenance organization*) organo per la salvaguardia della salute pubblica.

HMS *abbr* (*BRIT*) = *His* (*or Her*) *Majesty's Ship*.

HMSO *n abbr* (*BRIT*: = *His* (*or Her*) *Majesty's Stationery Office*) ≈ Poligrafici *mpl* dello Stato.

HNC *n abbr* (*BRIT*: = *Higher National Certificate*) diploma di istituto tecnico o professionale.

HND *n abbr* (*BRIT*: = *Higher National Diploma*)

diploma in materie tecniche equivalente ad una laurea.

hoard [hɔːd] n (*of food*) provviste *fpl*; (*of money*) gruzzolo ♦ *vt* ammassare.

hoarding ['hɔːdɪŋ] n (*BRIT*) tabellone *m* per affissioni.

hoarfrost ['hɔːfrɔst] n brina.

hoarse [hɔːs] *adj* rauco(a).

hoax [həuks] n scherzo; falso allarme.

hob [hɔb] n piastra (con fornelli).

hobble ['hɔbl] *vi* zoppicare.

hobby ['hɔbɪ] n hobby *m inv*, passatempo.

hobby-horse ['hɔbɪhɔːs] n cavallo a dondolo; (*fig*) chiodo fisso.

hobnail(ed) boots ['hɔbneɪl(d)-] n scarponi *mpl* chiodati.

hobnob ['hɔbnɔb] *vi*: **to ~ (with)** mescolarsi (con).

hobo ['həubəu] n (*US*) vagabondo.

hock [hɔk] n (*BRIT: wine*) vino del Reno; (*of animal, CULIN*) garretto; (*col*): **to be in ~** avere debiti.

hockey ['hɔkɪ] n hockey *m*.

hocus-pocus ['həukəs'pəukəs] n (*trickery*) trucco; (*words: of magician*) abracadabra *m inv*; (: *jargon*) parolone *fpl*.

hod [hɔd] n (*TECH*) cassetta per portare i mattoni.

hodgepodge ['hɔdʒpɔdʒ] n = **hotchpotch.**

hoe [həu] n zappa ♦ *vt* (*ground*) zappare.

hog [hɔg] n maiale *m* ♦ *vt* (*fig*) arraffare; **to go the whole ~** farlo fino in fondo.

Hogmanay [hɔgmə'neɪ] n (*SCOTTISH*) ≈ San Silvestro.

hogwash ['hɔgwɔʃ] n (*col*) stupidaggini *fpl*.

hoist [hɔɪst] n paranco ♦ *vt* issare.

hoity-toity [hɔɪtɪ'tɔɪtɪ] *adj* (*col*) altezzoso(a).

hold [həuld] *vb* (*pt, pp* **held** [hɛld]) *vt* tenere; (*contain*) contenere; (*keep back*) trattenere; (*believe*) mantenere; considerare; (*possess*) avere, possedere; detenere ♦ *vi* (*withstand pressure*) tenere; (*be valid*) essere valido(a) ♦ n presa; (*fig*) potere *m*; (*NAUT*) stiva; **~ the line!** (*TEL*) resti in linea!; **to ~ office** (*POL*) essere in carica; **to ~ sb responsible for sth** considerare *or* ritenere qn responsabile di qc; **to ~ one's own** (*fig*) difendersi bene; **he ~s the view that ...** è del parere che ...; **to ~ firm** *or* **fast** resistere bene, tenere; **to catch** *or* **get (a) ~ of** afferrare; **to get ~ of** (*fig*) trovare; **to get ~ of o.s.** trattenersi.

►**hold back** *vt* trattenere; (*secret*) tenere celato(a); **to ~ sb back from doing sth** impedire a qn di fare qc.

►**hold down** *vt* (*person*) tenere a terra;

(*job*) tenere.

►**hold forth** *vi* fare *or* tenere una concione.

►**hold off** *vt* tener lontano ♦ *vi* (*rain*): **if the rain ~s off** se continua a non piovere.

►**hold on** *vi* tener fermo; (*wait*) aspettare; **~ on!** (*TEL*) resti in linea!

►**hold on to** *vt fus* tenersi stretto(a) a; (*keep*) conservare.

►**hold out** *vt* offrire ♦ *vi* (*resist*): **to ~ out (against)** resistere (a).

►**hold over** *vt* (*meeting etc*) rimandare, rinviare.

►**hold up** *vt* (*raise*) alzare; (*support*) sostenere; (*delay*) ritardare; (*traffic*) rallentare; (*rob: bank*) assaltare.

holdall ['həuldɔːl] n (*BRIT*) borsone *m*.

holder ['həuldə*] n (*of ticket, title*) possessore/posseditrice; (*of office etc*) incaricato/a; (*of passport, post*) titolare; (*of record*) detentore/trice.

holding ['həuldɪŋ] n (*share*) azioni *fpl*, titoli *mpl*; (*farm*) podere *m*, tenuta.

holding company n holding *f inv*.

holdup ['həuldʌp] n (*robbery*) rapina a mano armata; (*delay*) ritardo; (*BRIT: in traffic*) blocco.

hole [həul] n buco, buca ♦ *vt* bucare; **~ in the heart** (*MED*) morbo blu; **to pick ~s in** (*fig*) trovare da ridire su.

►**hole up** *vi* nascondersi, rifugiarsi.

holiday ['hɔlədɪ] n vacanza; (*from work*) ferie *fpl*; (*day off*) giorno di vacanza; (*public*) giorno festivo; **to be on ~** essere in vacanza; **tomorrow is a ~** domani è festa.

holiday camp n (*BRIT: for children*) colonia (di villeggiatura); (*also*: **holiday centre**) ≈ villaggio (di vacanze).

holiday-maker ['hɔlədɪmeɪkə*] n (*BRIT*) villeggiante *m/f*.

holiday pay n stipendio delle ferie.

holiday resort n luogo di villeggiatura.

holiday season n stagione *f* delle vacanze.

holiness ['həulɪnɪs] n santità.

holistic [həu'lɪstɪk] *adj* olistico(a).

Holland ['hɔlənd] n Olanda.

holler ['hɔlə*] *vi* gridare, urlare.

hollow ['hɔləu] *adj* cavo(a), vuoto(a); (*fig*) falso(a); vano(a) ♦ n cavità *f inv*; (*in land*) valletta, depressione *f*.

►**hollow out** *vt* scavare.

holly ['hɔlɪ] n agrifoglio.

hollyhock ['hɔlɪhɔk] n malvone *m*.

holocaust ['hɔləkɔːst] n olocausto.

hologram ['hɔləgræm] n ologramma *m*.

hols [hɔlz] *npl*: **the ~** le vacanze.

holster ['həulstə*] n fondina (di pistola).

holy ['həʊlɪ] *adj* santo(a); (*bread*) benedetto(a), consacrato(a); (*ground*) consacrato(a); **the H~ Father** il Santo Padre.

Holy Communion *n* la Santa Comunione.

Holy Ghost, Holy Spirit *n* Spirito Santo.

Holy Land *n*: **the ~** la Terra Santa.

holy orders *npl* ordini *mpl* (sacri).

homage ['hɔmɪdʒ] *n* omaggio; **to pay ~ to** rendere omaggio a.

home [həʊm] *n* casa; (*country*) patria; (*institution*) casa, ricovero ♦ *cpd* (*life*) familiare; (*cooking etc*) casalingo(a); (*ECON, POL*) nazionale, interno(a); (*SPORT: team*) di casa; (: *match, win*) in casa ♦ *adv* a casa; in patria; (*right in: nail etc*) fino in fondo; **at ~** a casa; **to go** (*or* **come**) **~** tornare a casa (*or* in patria); **it's near my ~** è vicino a casa mia; **make yourself at ~** si metta a suo agio.

▶**home in on** *vt fus* (*missiles*) dirigersi (automaticamente) verso.

home address *n* indirizzo di casa.

home-brew [həʊm'bruː] *n* birra *or* vino fatto(a) in casa.

homecoming ['həʊmkʌmɪŋ] *n* ritorno.

home computer *n* home computer *m inv*.

Home Counties *npl* contee *fpl* intorno a Londra.

home economics *n* economia domestica.

home ground *n* (*fig*): **to be on ~** essere sul proprio terreno.

home-grown [həʊm'grəʊn] *adj* nostrano(a), di produzione locale.

home help *n* (*BRIT*) collaboratore *familiare per persone bisognose stipendiato dal comune.*

homeland ['həʊmlænd] *n* patria.

homeless ['həʊmlɪs] *adj* senza tetto; spatriato(a); **the ~** *npl* i senzatetto.

home loan *n* prestito con garanzia immobiliare.

homely ['həʊmlɪ] *adj* semplice, alla buona; accogliente.

home-made [həʊm'meɪd] *adj* casalingo(a).

Home Office *n* (*BRIT*) ministero degli Interni.

homeopathy *etc* [həʊmɪ'ɔpəθɪ] (*US*) = **homoeopathy** *etc*.

home rule *n* autogoverno.

Home Secretary *n* (*BRIT*) ministro degli Interni.

homesick ['həʊmsɪk] *adj*: **to be ~** avere la nostalgia.

homestead ['həʊmstɛd] *n* fattoria e terreni.

home town *n* città *f inv* natale.

home truth *n*: **to tell sb a few ~s** dire a qn qualche amara verità.

homeward ['həʊmwəd] *adj* (*journey*) di ritorno.

homeward(s) ['həʊmwəd(z)] *adv* verso casa.

homework ['həʊmwəːk] *n* compiti *mpl* (per casa).

homicidal [hɔmɪ'saɪdl] *adj* omicida.

homicide ['hɔmɪsaɪd] *n* (*US*) omicidio.

homily ['hɔmɪlɪ] *n* omelia.

homing ['həʊmɪŋ] *adj* (*device, missile*) autocercante; **~ pigeon** piccione *m* viaggiatore.

homoeopath, (*US***) homeopath** ['həʊmɪəʊpæθ] *n* omeopatico.

homoeopathic, (*US***) homeopathic** ['həʊmɪəʊ'pæθɪk] *adj* omeopatico(a).

homoeopathy, (*US***) homeopathy** [həʊmɪ'ɔpəθɪ] *n* omeopatia.

homogeneous [hɔməʊ'dʒiːnɪəs] *adj* omogeneo(a).

homogenize [hə'mɔdʒənaɪz] *vt* omogenizzare.

homosexual [hɔməʊ'sɛksjʊəl] *adj, n* omosessuale (*m/f*).

Hon. *abbr* = **honourable; honorary**.

Honduras [hɔn'djʊərəs] *n* Honduras *m*.

hone [həʊn] *vt* (*sharpen*) affilare; (*fig*) affinare.

honest ['ɔnɪst] *adj* onesto(a); sincero(a); **to be quite ~ with you ...** se devo dirle la verità ....

honestly ['ɔnɪstlɪ] *adv* onestamente; sinceramente.

honesty ['ɔnɪstɪ] *n* onestà.

honey ['hʌnɪ] *n* miele *m*; (*US col*) tesoro, amore *m*.

honeycomb ['hʌnɪkəʊm] *n* favo ♦ *vt* (*fig*): **~ed with tunnels** *etc* pieno(a) di gallerie *etc*.

honeymoon ['hʌnɪmuːn] *n* luna di miele, viaggio di nozze.

honeysuckle ['hʌnɪsʌkl] *n* caprifoglio.

Hong Kong ['hɔŋ'kɔŋ] *n* Hong Kong *f*.

honk [hɔŋk] *n* (*AUT*) colpo di clacson ♦ *vi* suonare il clacson.

Honolulu [hɔnə'luːluː] *n* Honolulu *f*.

honorary ['ɔnərərɪ] *adj* onorario(a); (*duty, title*) onorifico(a).

honour, (*US***) honor** ['ɔnə*] *vt* onorare ♦ *n* onore *m*; **in ~ of** in onore di.

hono(u)rable ['ɔnərəbl] *adj* onorevole.

hono(u)r-bound ['ɔnə'baʊnd] *adj*: **to be ~ to do** dover fare per una questione di onore.

hono(u)rs degree *n* (*SCOL*) *laurea (con corso di studi di 4 o 5 anni).*

Il corso universitario di studi che porta al conferimento del **Bachelor's degree** *può avere una durata diversa a seconda del profitto dello studente. Dopo quattro o cinque anni di corso si ottiene l'***honours degree**, *il riconoscimento più alto, che, abbreviato in* **Hons.**, *viene posto dopo il titolo ottenuto (ad esempio BA Hons); vedi anche* **ordinary degree**.

honours list *n* (*BRIT*) elenco ufficiale dei destinati al conferimento di onorificenze.

La **honours list** *è un elenco di cittadini britannici e del Commonwealth che si sono distinti in campi come imprenditoria, forze armate, sport ecc, meritando il conferimento di un titolo o di una decorazione da parte del sovrano. Ogni anno vengono redatte dal primo ministro due* honours list, *una a Capodanno e una in occasione del compleanno del sovrano.*

Hons. [ɔnz] *abbr* (*SCOL*) = **hono(u)rs degree**.
hood [hud] *n* cappuccio; (*BRIT AUT*) capote *f*; (*US AUT*) cofano; (*col*) malvivente *m/f*.
hooded ['hudɪd] *adj* (*robber*) mascherato(a).
hoodlum ['huːdləm] *n* malvivente *m/f*.
hoodwink ['hudwɪŋk] *vt* infinocchiare.
hoof, *pl* ~**s** *or* **hooves** [huːf, huːvz] *n* zoccolo.
hook [huk] *n* gancio; (*for fishing*) amo ♦ *vt* uncinare; (*dress*) agganciare; **to be** ~**ed on** (*col*) essere fanatico di; ~**s and eyes** gancetti; **by** ~ **or by crook** in un modo o nell'altro.
▶**hook up** *vt* (*RADIO, TV etc*) allacciare, collegare.
hooligan ['huːlɪɡən] *n* giovinastro, teppista *m*.
hooliganism ['huːlɪɡənɪzəm] *n* teppismo.
hoop [huːp] *n* cerchio.
hoot [huːt] *vi* (*AUT*) suonare il clacson; (*owl*) gufare ♦ *n* colpo di clacson; **to** ~ **with laughter** farsi una gran risata.
hooter ['huːtə*] *n* (*AUT*) clacson *m inv*; (*NAUT, at factory*) sirena.
hoover ® ['huːvə*] *n* (*BRIT*) aspirapolvere *m inv* ♦ *vt* pulire con l'aspirapolvere.
hooves [huːvz] *npl of* **hoof**.
hop [hɔp] *vi* saltellare, saltare; (*on one foot*) saltare su una gamba ♦ *n* salto; *see also* **hops**.
hope [həup] *vt, vi* sperare ♦ *n* speranza; **I** ~ **so/not** spero di sì/no.
hopeful ['həupful] *adj* (*person*) pieno(a) di speranza; (*situation*) promettente; **I'm** ~ **that she'll manage to come** ho buone speranze che venga.
hopefully ['həupfulɪ] *adv* con speranza; ~ **he will recover** speriamo che si riprenda.
hopeless ['həuplɪs] *adj* senza speranza, disperato(a); (*useless*) inutile.
hopelessly ['həuplɪslɪ] *adv* (*live etc*) senza speranza; (*involved, complicated*) spaventosamente; (*late*) disperatamente, irrimediabilmente; **I'm** ~ **confused/lost** sono completamente confuso/perso.
hopper ['hɔpə*] *n* (*chute*) tramoggia.
hops [hɔps] *npl* luppoli *mpl*.
horde [hɔːd] *n* orda.
horizon [hə'raɪzn] *n* orizzonte *m*.
horizontal [hɔrɪ'zɔntl] *adj* orizzontale.
hormone ['hɔːməun] *n* ormone *m*.
hormone replacement therapy *n* terapia ormonale (*usata in menopausa*).
horn [hɔːn] *n* corno; (*AUT*) clacson *m inv*.
horned [hɔːnd] *adj* (*animal*) cornuto(a).
hornet ['hɔːnɪt] *n* calabrone *m*.
horny ['hɔːnɪ] *adj* corneo(a); (*hands*) calloso(a).
horoscope ['hɔrəskəup] *n* oroscopo.
horrendous [hə'rɛndəs] *n* orrendo(a).
horrible ['hɔrɪbl] *adj* orribile, tremendo(a).
horrid ['hɔrɪd] *adj* orrido(a); (*person*) antipatico(a).
horrific [hə'rɪfɪk] *adj* (*accident*) spaventoso(a); (*film*) orripilante.
horrify ['hɔrɪfaɪ] *vt* lasciare inorridito(a).
horrifying ['hɔrɪfaɪɪŋ] *adj* terrificante.
horror ['hɔrə*] *n* orrore *m*.
horror film *n* film *m inv* dell'orrore.
horror-struck ['hɔrəstrʌk], **horror-stricken** ['hɔrəstrɪkn] *adj* inorridito (a).
hors d'œuvre [ɔː'dəːvrə] *n* antipasto.
horse [hɔːs] *n* cavallo.
horseback ['hɔːsbæk]: **on** ~ *adj, adv* a cavallo.
horsebox ['hɔːsbɔks] *n* carro *or* furgone *m* per il trasporto dei cavalli.
horse chestnut *n* ippocastano.
horse-drawn ['hɔːsdrɔːn] *adj* tirato(a) da cavallo.
horsefly ['hɔːsflaɪ] *n* tafano, mosca cavallina.
horseman ['hɔːsmən] *n* cavaliere *m*.
horsemanship ['hɔːsmənʃɪp] *n* equitazione *f*.
horseplay ['hɔːspleɪ] *n* giochi *mpl* scatenati.
horsepower (hp) ['hɔːspauə*] *n* cavallo (vapore) (c/v).
horse-racing ['hɔːsreɪsɪŋ] *n* ippica.
horseradish ['hɔːsrædɪʃ] *n* rafano.
horseshoe ['hɔːsʃuː] *n* ferro di cavallo.

horse show n concorso ippico, gare fpl ippiche.

horse-trading ['hɔːstreɪdɪŋ] n mercanteggiamento.

horse trials npl = **horse show**.

horsewhip ['hɔːswɪp] vt frustare.

horsewoman ['hɔːswumən] n amazzone f.

horsey ['hɔːsɪ] adj (col: person) che adora i cavalli; (appearance) cavallino(a), da cavallo.

horticulture ['hɔːtɪkʌltʃə*] n orticoltura.

hose [həuz] n (also: ~pipe) tubo; (also: garden ~) tubo per annaffiare.

▶**hose down** vt lavare con un getto d'acqua.

hosepipe ['həuzpaɪp] n see **hose**.

hosiery ['həuzɪərɪ] n (in shop) (reparto di) calze fpl e calzini mpl.

hospice ['hɔspɪs] n ricovero, ospizio.

hospitable [hɔ'spɪtəbl] adj ospitale.

hospital ['hɔspɪtl] n ospedale m; **in** ~, (US) **in the** ~ all'ospedale.

hospitality [hɔspɪ'tælɪtɪ] n ospitalità.

hospitalize ['hɔspɪtəlaɪz] vt ricoverare (in or all'ospedale).

host [həust] n ospite m; (TV, RADIO) presentatore/trice; (REL) ostia; (large number): **a** ~ **of** una schiera di ♦ vt (TV programme, games) presentare.

hostage ['hɔstɪdʒ] n ostaggio/a.

host country n paese m ospite, paese che ospita.

hostel ['hɔstl] n ostello; (for students, nurses etc) pensionato; (for homeless people) ospizio, ricovero; (also: **youth** ~) ostello della gioventù.

hostelling ['hɔstəlɪŋ] n: **to go (youth)** ~ passare le vacanze negli ostelli della gioventù.

hostess ['həustɪs] n ospite f; (AVIAT) hostess f inv; (in nightclub) entraineuse f inv.

hostile ['hɔstaɪl] adj ostile.

hostility [hɔ'stɪlɪtɪ] n ostilità f inv.

hot [hɔt] adj caldo(a); (as opposed to only warm) molto caldo(a); (spicy) piccante; (fig) accanito(a); ardente; violento(a), focoso(a); **to be** ~ (person) aver caldo; (thing) essere caldo(a); (METEOR) far caldo.

▶**hot up** (BRIT col) vi (situation) farsi più teso(a); (party) scaldarsi ♦ vt (pace) affrettare; (engine) truccare.

hot-air balloon [hɔt'ɛə-] n mongolfiera.

hotbed ['hɔtbɛd] n (fig) focolaio.

hotchpotch ['hɔtʃpɔtʃ] n (BRIT) pot-pourri m.

hot dog n hot dog m inv.

hotel [həu'tɛl] n albergo.

hotelier [həu'tɛljeɪ] n albergatore/trice.

hotel industry n industria alberghiera.

hotel room n camera d'albergo.

hot flush n (BRIT) scalmana, caldana.

hotfoot ['hɔtfut] adv di gran carriera.

hothead ['hɔthɛd] n (fig) testa calda.

hotheaded [hɔt'hɛdɪd] adj focoso(a), eccitabile.

hothouse ['hɔthaus] n serra.

hot line n (POL) telefono rosso.

hotly ['hɔtlɪ] adv violentemente.

hotplate ['hɔtpleɪt] n fornello; piastra riscaldante.

hotpot ['hɔtpɔt] n (BRIT CULIN) stufato.

hot potato n (BRIT col) patata bollente; **to drop sb/sth like a** ~ mollare subito qn/qc.

hot seat n (fig) posto che scotta.

hot spot n (fig) zona calda.

hot spring n sorgente f termale.

hot-tempered [hɔt'tɛmpəd] adj irascibile.

hot-water bottle [hɔt'wɔːtə-] n borsa dell'acqua calda.

hot-wire ['hɔtwaɪə*] vt (col: car) avviare mettendo in contatto i fili dell'accensione.

hound [haund] vt perseguitare ♦ n segugio; **the** ~**s** la muta.

hour ['auə*] n ora; **at 30 miles an** ~ a 30 miglia all'ora; **lunch** ~ intervallo di pranzo; **to pay sb by the** ~ pagare qn a ore.

hourly ['auəlɪ] adj (ad) ogni ora; (rate) orario(a) ♦ adv ogni ora; ~ **paid** adj pagato(a) a ore.

house n [haus] (pl ~**s** ['hauzɪz]) (also: firm) casa; (POL) camera; (THEAT) sala; pubblico; spettacolo ♦ vt [hauz] (person) ospitare; **at** (or **to**) **my** ~ a casa mia; **the H**~ (**of Commons/Lords**) (BRIT) la Camera dei Comuni/Lords; **the H**~ (**of Representatives**) (US) ≈ la Camera dei Deputati; **on the** ~ (fig) offerto(a) dalla casa.

house arrest n arresti mpl domiciliari.

houseboat ['hausbəut] n house boat f inv.

housebound ['hausbaund] adj confinato(a) in casa.

housebreaking ['hausbreɪkɪŋ] n furto con scasso.

house-broken ['hausbrəukn] adj (US) = **house-trained**.

housecoat ['hauskəut] n vestaglia.

household ['haushəuld] n famiglia, casa.

householder ['haushəuldə*] n padrone/a di casa; (head of house) capofamiglia m/f.

household name n nome m che tutti conoscono.

househunting ['haushʌntɪŋ] n: **to go** ~

mettersi a cercar casa.
housekeeper ['hauskiːpə*] n governante f.
housekeeping ['hauskiːpɪŋ] n (work)
governo della casa; (also: ~ **money**) soldi
mpl per le spese di casa; (COMPUT) ausilio.
houseman ['hausmən] n (BRIT MED) ≈
interno.
house-owner ['hausəunə*] n possessore m/f
di casa.
house plant n pianta da appartamento.
house-proud ['hauspraud] adj che è
maniaco(a) della pulizia.
house-to-house ['haustə'haus] adj
(collection) di porta in porta; (search) casa
per casa.
house-train ['haustreɪn] vt (pet animal)
addestrare a non sporcare in casa.
house-trained ['haustreɪnd] adj (BRIT:
animal) che non sporca in casa.
house-warming party ['hauswɔːmɪŋ-] n
festa per inaugurare la casa nuova.
housewife ['hauswaɪf] n massaia,
casalinga.
housework ['hauswəːk] n faccende fpl
domestiche.
housing ['hauzɪŋ] n alloggio ♦ cpd (problem,
shortage) degli alloggi.
housing association n cooperativa
edilizia.
housing benefit n (BRIT) contributo
abitativo (ad affittuari e a coloro che
comprano una casa).
housing conditions npl condizioni fpl di
abitazione.
housing development, (BRIT) **housing
estate** n zona residenziale con case
popolari e/o private.
hovel ['hɔvl] n casupola.
hover ['hɔvə*] vi (bird) librarsi; (helicopter)
volare a punto fisso; **to ~ round sb**
aggirarsi intorno a qn.
hovercraft ['hɔvəkrɑːft] n hovercraft m inv.
hoverport ['hɔvəpɔːt] n porto per
hovercraft.
how [hau] adv come; ~ **are you?** come sta?;
~ **do you do?** piacere!, molto lieto!; ~ **far
is it to ...?** quanto è lontano ...?; ~ **long
have you been here?** da quanto tempo sta
qui?; ~ **lovely!** che bello!; ~ **many?**
quanti(e)?; ~ **much?** quanto(a)?; ~ **many
people/much milk?** quante persone/
quanto latte?; ~ **old are you?** quanti anni
ha?; ~'s **life?** (col) come va (la vita)?; ~
about a drink? che ne diresti di andare a
bere qualcosa?; ~ **is it that ...?** com'è che
... + sub?
however [hau'ɛvə*] adv in qualsiasi modo
or maniera che; (+ adjective) per quanto

+ sub; (in questions) come ♦ conj
comunque, però.
howitzer ['hauɪtsə*] n (MIL) obice m.
howl [haul] n ululato ♦ vi ululare.
howler ['haulə*] n marronata.
howling ['haulɪŋ] adj: **a ~ wind** or **gale** un
vento terribile.
HP n abbr (BRIT) see **hire purchase**.
hp abbr (AUT) see **horsepower**.
HQ n abbr (= headquarters) Q.G.
HR n abbr (US) = **House of Representatives**.
HRH abbr (= His (or Her) Royal Highness)
S.A.R.
hr(s) abbr (= hour(s)) h.
HRT n abbr = **hormone replacement
therapy**.
HS abbr (US) = **high school**.
HST abbr (= Hawaiian Standard Time) fuso
orario.
HT abbr (= high tension) A.T.
hub [hʌb] n (of wheel) mozzo; (fig) fulcro.
hubbub ['hʌbʌb] n baccano.
hubcap ['hʌbkæp] n (AUT) coprimozzo.
HUD n abbr (US) = Department of Housing
and Urban Development.
huddle ['hʌdl] vi: **to ~ together**
rannicchiarsi l'uno contro l'altro.
hue [hjuː] n tinta; ~ **and cry** n clamore m.
huff [hʌf] n: **in a ~** stizzito(a); **to take the ~**
mettere il broncio.
huffy ['hʌfɪ] adj (col) stizzito(a),
indispettito(a).
hug [hʌg] vt abbracciare; (shore, kerb)
stringere ♦ n abbraccio, stretta; **to give
sb a ~** abbracciare qn.
huge [hjuːdʒ] adj enorme, immenso(a).
hulk [hʌlk] n carcassa.
hulking ['hʌlkɪŋ] adj: ~ **(great)** grosso(a) e
goffo(a).
hull [hʌl] n (of ship) scafo.
hullabaloo [hʌləbə'luː] n (col: noise)
fracasso.
hullo [hə'ləu] excl = **hello**.
hum [hʌm] vt (tune) canticchiare ♦ vi
canticchiare; (insect, plane, tool) ronzare
♦ n (also ELEC) ronzio; (of traffic, machines)
rumore m; (of voices etc) mormorio,
brusio.
human ['hjuːmən] adj umano(a) ♦ n (also: ~
being) essere m umano.
humane [hjuː'meɪn] adj umanitario(a).
humanism ['hjuːmənɪzəm] n umanesimo.
humanitarian [hjuːmænɪ'tɛərɪən] adj
umanitario(a).
humanity [hjuː'mænɪtɪ] n umanità; **the
humanities** gli studi umanistici.
humanly ['hjuːmənlɪ] adv umanamente.
humanoid ['hjuːmənɔɪd] adj che sembra

umano(a) ♦ *n* umanoide *m/f.*

human rights *npl* diritti *mpl* dell'uomo.

humble ['hʌmbl] *adj* umile, modesto(a) ♦ *vt* umiliare.

humbly ['hʌmblɪ] *adv* umilmente, modestamente.

humbug ['hʌmbʌg] *n* inganno; sciocchezze *fpl*; (*BRIT: sweet*) caramella alla menta.

humdrum ['hʌmdrʌm] *adj* monotono(a), tedioso(a).

humid ['hjuːmɪd] *adj* umido(a).

humidifier [hjuːˈmɪdɪfaɪə*] *n* umidificatore *m.*

humidity [hjuːˈmɪdɪtɪ] *n* umidità.

humiliate [hjuːˈmɪlɪeɪt] *vt* umiliare.

humiliation [hjuːmɪlɪˈeɪʃən] *n* umiliazione *f.*

humility [hjuːˈmɪlɪtɪ] *n* umiltà.

humorist ['hjuːmərɪst] *n* umorista *m/f.*

humorous ['hjuːmərəs] *adj* umoristico(a); (*person*) buffo(a).

humour, (*US*) **humor** ['hjuːmə*] *n* umore *m* ♦ *vt* (*person*) compiacere; (*sb's whims*) assecondare; **sense of** ~ senso dell'umorismo; **to be in a good/bad** ~ essere di buon/cattivo umore.

humo(u)rless ['hjuːməlɪs] *adj* privo(a) di umorismo.

hump [hʌmp] *n* gobba.

humpback ['hʌmpbæk] *n* schiena d'asino; (*BRIT: also:* ~ **bridge**) ponte *m* a schiena d'asino.

humus ['hjuːməs] *n* humus *m.*

hunch [hʌntʃ] *n* gobba; (*premonition*) intuizione *f*; **I have a** ~ **that** ho la vaga impressione che.

hunchback ['hʌntʃbæk] *n* gobbo/a.

hunched [hʌntʃt] *adj* incurvato(a).

hundred ['hʌndrəd] *num* cento; **about a** ~ **people** un centinaio di persone; **~s of people** centinaia *fpl* di persone; **I'm a** ~ **per cent sure** sono sicuro al cento per cento.

hundredweight ['hʌndrɪdweɪt] *n* (*BRIT*) = *50.8 kg; 112 lb;* (*US*) = *45.3 kg; 100 lb.*

hung [hʌŋ] *pt, pp of* **hang.**

Hungarian [hʌŋˈgɛərɪən] *adj* ungherese ♦ *n* ungherese *m/f*; (*LING*) ungherese *m.*

Hungary ['hʌŋgərɪ] *n* Ungheria.

hunger ['hʌŋgə*] *n* fame *f* ♦ *vi*: **to** ~ **for** desiderare ardentemente.

hunger strike *n* sciopero della fame.

hungover [hʌŋˈəuvə*] *adj* (*col*): **to be** ~ avere i postumi della sbornia.

hungrily ['hʌŋgrəlɪ] *adv* voracemente; (*fig*) avidamente.

hungry ['hʌŋgrɪ] *adj* affamato(a); **to be** ~ aver fame; ~ **for** (*fig*) assetato di.

hung up *adj* (*col*) complessato(a).

hunk [hʌŋk] *n* bel pezzo.

hunt [hʌnt] *vt* (*seek*) cercare; (*SPORT*) cacciare ♦ *vi* andare a caccia ♦ *n* caccia.
►**hunt down** *vt* scovare.

hunter ['hʌntə*] *n* cacciatore *m*; (*BRIT: horse*) cavallo da caccia.

hunting ['hʌntɪŋ] *n* caccia.

hurdle ['hɜːdl] *n* (*SPORT, fig*) ostacolo.

hurl [hɜːl] *vt* lanciare con violenza.

hurling ['hɜːlɪŋ] *n* (*SPORT*) hurling *m.*

hurly-burly ['hɜːlɪ'bɜːlɪ] *n* chiasso, baccano.

hurrah, hurray [hu'rɑː, hu'reɪ] *excl* urra!, evviva!

hurricane ['hʌrɪkən] *n* uragano.

hurried ['hʌrɪd] *adj* affrettato(a); (*work*) fatto(a) in fretta.

hurriedly ['hʌrɪdlɪ] *adv* in fretta.

hurry ['hʌrɪ] *n* fretta ♦ *vi* affrettarsi ♦ *vt* (*person*) affrettare; (*work*) far in fretta; **to be in a** ~ aver fretta; **to do sth in a** ~ fare qc in fretta; **to** ~ **in/out** entrare/ uscire in fretta; **to** ~ **back/home** affrettarsi a tornare indietro/a casa.
►**hurry along** *vi* camminare in fretta.
►**hurry away, hurry off** *vi* andarsene in fretta.
►**hurry up** *vi* sbrigarsi.

hurt [hɜːt] *vb* (*pt, pp* **hurt**) *vt* (*cause pain to*) far male a; (*injure, fig*) ferire; (*business, interests etc*) colpire, danneggiare ♦ *vi* far male ♦ *adj* ferito(a); **I** ~ **my arm** mi sono fatto male al braccio; **where does it** ~? dove ti fa male?

hurtful ['hɜːtful] *adj* (*remark*) che ferisce.

hurtle ['hɜːtl] *vt* scagliare ♦ *vi*: **to** ~ **past/ down** passare/scendere a razzo.

husband ['hʌzbənd] *n* marito.

hush [hʌʃ] *n* silenzio, calma ♦ *vt* zittire; ~! zitto(a)!
►**hush up** *vt* (*fact*) cercare di far passare sotto silenzio.

hush-hush ['hʌʃ'hʌʃ] *adj* (*col*) segretissimo(a).

husk [hʌsk] *n* (*of wheat*) cartoccio; (*of rice, maize*) buccia.

husky ['hʌskɪ] *adj* roco(a) ♦ *n* cane *m* eschimese.

hustings ['hʌstɪŋz] *npl* (*BRIT POL*) comizi *mpl* elettorali.

hustle ['hʌsl] *vt* spingere, incalzare ♦ *n* pigia pigia *m inv*; ~ **and bustle** trambusto.

hut [hʌt] *n* rifugio; (*shed*) ripostiglio.

hutch [hʌtʃ] *n* gabbia.

hyacinth ['haɪəsɪnθ] *n* giacinto.

hybrid ['haɪbrɪd] *adj* ibrido(a) ♦ *n* ibrido.

hydrant ['haɪdrənt] *n* (*also:* **fire** ~) idrante *m.*

hydraulic [haɪ'drɒlɪk] *adj* idraulico(a).

hydraulics [haɪˈdrɔlɪks] *n* idraulica.
hydrochloric [haɪdrəˈklɔrɪk] *adj*: ~ **acid** acido cloridrico.
hydroelectric [haɪdrəʊˈlɛktrɪk] *adj* idroelettrico(a).
hydrofoil [ˈhaɪdrəfɔɪl] *n* aliscafo.
hydrogen [ˈhaɪdrədʒən] *n* idrogeno.
hydrogen bomb *n* bomba all'idrogeno.
hydrophobia [haɪdrəˈfəʊbɪə] *n* idrofobia.
hydroplane [ˈhaɪdrəʊpleɪn] *n* idrovolante *m*.
hyena [haɪˈiːnə] *n* iena.
hygiene [ˈhaɪdʒiːn] *n* igiene *f*.
hygienic [haɪˈdʒiːnɪk] *adj* igienico(a).
hymn [hɪm] *n* inno; cantica.
hype [haɪp] *n* (*col*) clamorosa pubblicità.
hyperactive [haɪpərˈæktɪv] *adj* iperattivo(a).
hypermarket [ˈhaɪpəmaːkɪt] *n* (*BRIT*) ipermercato.
hypertension [haɪpəˈtɛnʃən] *n* (*MED*) ipertensione *f*.
hyphen [ˈhaɪfn] *n* trattino.
hypnosis [hɪpˈnəʊsɪs] *n* ipnosi *f*.
hypnotic [hɪpˈnɔtɪk] *adj* ipnotico(a).
hypnotism [ˈhɪpnətɪzəm] *n* ipnotismo.
hypnotist [ˈhɪpnətɪst] *n* ipnotizzatore/trice.
hypnotize [ˈhɪpnətaɪz] *vt* ipnotizzare.
hypoallergenic [haɪpəʊæləˈdʒɛnɪk] *adj* ipoallergico(a).
hypochondriac [haɪpəˈkɔndrɪæk] *n* ipocondriaco/a.
hypocrisy [hɪˈpɔkrɪsɪ] *n* ipocrisia.
hypocrite [ˈhɪpəkrɪt] *n* ipocrita *m/f*.
hypocritical [hɪpəˈkrɪtɪkl] *adj* ipocrita.
hypodermic [haɪpəˈdəːmɪk] *adj* ipodermico(a) ♦ *n* (*syringe*) siringa ipodermica.
hypotenuse [haɪˈpɔtɪnjuːz] *n* ipotenusa.
hypothermia [haɪpəʊˈθəːmɪə] *n* ipotermia.
hypothesis, *pl* **hypotheses** [haɪˈpɔθɪsɪs, -siːz] *n* ipotesi *f inv*.
hypothetical [haɪpəʊˈθɛtɪkl] *adj* ipotetico(a).
hysterectomy [hɪstəˈrɛktəmɪ] *n* isterectomia.
hysteria [hɪˈstɪərɪə] *n* isteria.
hysterical [hɪˈstɛrɪkl] *adj* isterico(a); **to become** ~ avere una crisi isterica.
hysterics [hɪˈstɛrɪks] *npl* accesso di isteria; (*laughter*) attacco di riso; **to have** ~ avere una crisi isterica.

I i

I, i [aɪ] *n* (*letter*) I, i *f or m inv*; **I for Isaac,** (*US*) **I for Item** ≈ I come Imola.
I [aɪ] *pron* io ♦ *abbr* (= *island, isle*) Is.
IA *abbr* (*US*) = *Iowa*.
IAEA *n abbr* = **International Atomic Energy Agency.**
IBA *n abbr* (*BRIT:* = *Independent Broadcasting Authority*) *organo di controllo sulle reti televisive.*
Iberian [aɪˈbɪərɪən] *adj* iberico(a).
Iberian Peninsula *n:* **the** ~ la Penisola iberica.
IBEW *n abbr* (*US:* = *International Brotherhood of Electrical Workers*) *associazione internazionale degli elettrotecnici.*
ib(id). [ˈɪb(ɪd)] *abbr* (= *ibidem: from the same source*) ibid.
i/c *abbr* (*BRIT*) = **in charge.**
ICBM *n abbr* (= *intercontinental ballistic missile*) ICBM *m inv*.
ICC *n abbr* (= *International Chamber of Commerce*) C.C.I. *f*; (*US:* = *Interstate Commerce Commission*) *commissione per il commercio tra gli stati degli USA.*
ice [aɪs] *n* ghiaccio; (*on road*) gelo ♦ *vt* (*cake*) glassare; (*drink*) mettere in fresco ♦ *vi* (*also:* ~ **over**) ghiacciare; (*also:* ~ **up**) gelare; **to keep sth on** ~ (*fig: plan, project*) mettere da parte (per il momento), accantonare.
Ice Age *n* era glaciale.
ice axe *n* piccozza da ghiaccio.
iceberg [ˈaɪsbəːg] *n* iceberg *m inv*; **tip of the** ~ (*also fig*) punta dell'iceberg.
icebox [ˈaɪsbɔks] *n* (*US*) frigorifero; (*BRIT*) reparto ghiaccio; (*insulated box*) frigo portatile.
icebreaker [ˈaɪsbreɪkə*] *n* rompighiaccio *m inv*.
ice bucket *n* secchiello del ghiaccio.
ice-cap [ˈaɪskæp] *n* calotta polare.
ice-cold [aɪsˈkəʊld] *adj* gelato(a).
ice cream *n* gelato.
ice-cream soda *n* (gelato) affogato al seltz.
ice cube *n* cubetto di ghiaccio.
iced [aɪst] *adj* (*drink*) ghiacciato(a); (*coffee, tea*) freddo(a); (*cake*) glassato(a).

ice hockey *n* hockey *m* su ghiaccio.
Iceland ['aɪslənd] *n* Islanda.
Icelander ['aɪsləndə*] *n* islandese *m/f*.
Icelandic [aɪs'lændɪk] *adj* islandese ♦ *n* (*LING*) islandese *m*.
ice lolly *n* (*BRIT*) ghiacciolo.
ice pick *n* piccone *m* per ghiaccio.
ice rink *n* pista di pattinaggio.
ice-skate ['aɪsskeɪt] *n* pattino da ghiaccio ♦ *vi* pattinare sul ghiaccio.
ice-skating ['aɪsskeɪtɪŋ] *n* pattinaggio sul ghiaccio.
icicle ['aɪsɪkl] *n* ghiacciolo.
icing ['aɪsɪŋ] *n* (*AVIAT etc*) patina di ghiaccio; (*CULIN*) glassa.
icing sugar *n* zucchero a velo.
ICJ *n abbr see* **International Court of Justice.**
icon ['aɪkɔn] *n* icona; (*COMPUT*) immagine *f*.
ICR *n abbr* (*US*) = *Institute for Cancer Research.*
ICRC *n abbr* (= *International Committee of the Red Cross*) CICR *m*.
ICU *n abbr see* **intensive care unit.**
icy ['aɪsɪ] *adj* ghiacciato(a); (*weather, temperature*) gelido(a).
ID *abbr* (*US*) = *Idaho.*
I'd [aɪd] = **I would; I had.**
Ida. *abbr* (*US*) = *Idaho.*
ID card *n* = **identity card.**
IDD *n abbr* (*BRIT TEL*: = *International direct dialling*) teleselezione *f* internazionale.
idea [aɪ'dɪə] *n* idea; **good ~!** buon'idea!; **to have an ~ that** ... aver l'impressione che ...; **I haven't the least ~** non ne ho la minima idea.
ideal [aɪ'dɪəl] *adj, n* ideale (*m*).
idealist [aɪ'dɪəlɪst] *n* idealista *m/f*.
ideally [aɪ'dɪəlɪ] *adv* perfettamente, assolutamente; **~ the book should have** ... l'ideale sarebbe che il libro avesse ....
identical [aɪ'dɛntɪkl] *adj* identico(a).
identification [aɪdɛntɪfɪ'keɪʃən] *n* identificazione *f*; **means of ~** carta d'identità.
identify [aɪ'dɛntɪfaɪ] *vt* identificare ♦ *vi*: **to ~ with** identificarsi con.
Identikit ® [aɪ'dɛntɪkɪt] *n*: **~ (picture)** identikit *m inv*.
identity [aɪ'dɛntɪtɪ] *n* identità *f inv*.
identity card *n* carta d'identità.
identity parade *n* (*BRIT*) confronto all'americana.
ideological [aɪdɪə'lɔdʒɪkəl] *adj* ideologico(a).
ideology [aɪdɪ'ɔlədʒɪ] *n* ideologia.
idiocy ['ɪdɪəsɪ] *n* idiozia.
idiom ['ɪdɪəm] *n* idioma *m*; (*phrase*)

espressione *f* idiomatica.
idiomatic [ɪdɪə'mætɪk] *adj* idiomatico(a).
idiosyncrasy [ɪdɪəu'sɪŋkrəsɪ] *n* idiosincrasia.
idiot ['ɪdɪət] *n* idiota *m/f*.
idiotic [ɪdɪ'ɔtɪk] *adj* idiota.
idle ['aɪdl] *adj* inattivo(a); (*lazy*) pigro(a), ozioso(a); (*unemployed*) disoccupato(a); (*question, pleasures*) ozioso(a) ♦ *vi* (*engine*) girare al minimo; **to lie ~** stare fermo, non funzionare.
►**idle away** *vt* (*time*) sprecare, buttar via.
idleness ['aɪdlnɪs] *n* ozio; pigrizia.
idler ['aɪdlə*] *n* ozioso/a, fannullone/a.
idle time *n* tempi *mpl* morti.
idol ['aɪdl] *n* idolo.
idolize ['aɪdəlaɪz] *vt* idoleggiare.
idyllic [ɪ'dɪlɪk] *adj* idillico(a).
i.e. *abbr* (= *id est: that is*) cioè.
if [ɪf] *conj* se ♦ *n*: **there are a lot of ~s and buts** ci sono molti se e ma; **I'd be pleased ~ you could do it** sarei molto contento se potesse farlo; **~ necessary** (è) necessario; **~ only he were here** se solo fosse qui; **~ only to show him my gratitude** se non altro per esprimergli la mia gratitudine.
iffy ['ɪfɪ] *adj* (*col*) incerto(a).
igloo ['ɪglu:] *n* igloo *m inv*.
ignite [ɪg'naɪt] *vt* accendere ♦ *vi* accendersi.
ignition [ɪg'nɪʃən] *n* (*AUT*) accensione *f*; **to switch on/off the ~** accendere/spegnere il motore.
ignition key *n* (*AUT*) chiave *f* dell'accensione.
ignoble [ɪg'nəubl] *adj* ignobile.
ignominious [ɪgnə'mɪnɪəs] *adj* vergognoso(a), ignominioso(a).
ignoramus [ɪgnə'reɪməs] *n* ignorante *m/f*.
ignorance ['ɪgnərəns] *n* ignoranza; **to keep sb in ~ of sth** tenere qn all'oscuro di qc.
ignorant ['ɪgnərənt] *adj* ignorante; **to be ~ of** (*subject*) essere ignorante in; (*events*) essere ignaro(a) di.
ignore [ɪg'nɔ:*] *vt* non tener conto di; (*person, fact*) ignorare.
ikon ['aɪkɔn] *n* = **icon.**
IL *abbr* (*US*) = *Illinois.*
ILA *n abbr* (*US*: = *International Longshoremen's Association*) associazione internazionale degli scaricatori di porto.
ill [ɪl] *adj* (*sick*) malato(a); (*bad*) cattivo(a) ♦ *n* male *m*; **to take** *or* **be taken ~** ammalarsi; **to feel ~** star male; **to speak/think ~ of sb** parlar/pensar male di qn.
I'll [aɪl] = **I will, I shall.**

III. *abbr* (*US*) = *Illinois.*

ill-advised [ɪləd'vaɪzd] *adj* (*decision*) poco giudizioso(a); (*person*) mal consigliato(a).

ill-at-ease [ɪlət'iːz] *adj* a disagio.

ill-considered [ɪlkən'sɪdəd] *adj* (*plan*) avventato(a).

ill-disposed [ɪldɪs'pəuzd] *adj*: **to be ~ towards sb/sth** essere maldisposto(a) verso qn/qc *or* nei riguardi di qn/qc.

illegal [ɪ'liːgl] *adj* illegale.

illegally [ɪ'liːgəlɪ] *adv* illegalmente.

illegible [ɪ'lɛdʒɪbl] *adj* illeggibile.

illegitimate [ɪlɪ'dʒɪtɪmət] *adj* illegittimo(a).

ill-fated [ɪl'feɪtɪd] *adj* nefasto(a).

ill-favoured, (*US*) **ill-favored** [ɪl'feɪvəd] *adj* sgraziato(a), brutto(a).

ill feeling *n* rancore *m*.

ill-gotten [ˈɪlgɔtn] *adj*: **~ gains** maltolto.

ill health *n* problemi *mpl* di salute.

illicit [ɪ'lɪsɪt] *adj* illecito(a).

ill-informed [ɪlɪn'fɔːmd] *adj* (*judgement, speech*) pieno(a) di inesattezze; (*person*) male informato(a).

illiterate [ɪ'lɪtərət] *adj* analfabeta, illetterato(a); (*letter*) scorretto(a).

ill-mannered [ɪl'mænəd] *adj* maleducato(a), sgarbato(a).

illness [ˈɪlnɪs] *n* malattia.

illogical [ɪ'lɔdʒɪkl] *adj* illogico(a).

ill-suited [ɪl'suːtɪd] *adj* (*couple*) mal assortito(a); **he is ~ to the job** è inadatto a quel lavoro.

ill-timed [ɪl'taɪmd] *adj* intempestivo(a), inopportuno(a).

ill-treat [ɪl'triːt] *vt* maltrattare.

ill-treatment [ɪl'triːtmənt] *n* maltrattamenti *mpl*.

illuminate [ɪ'luːmɪneɪt] *vt* illuminare; **~d sign** insegna luminosa.

illuminating [ɪ'luːmɪneɪtɪŋ] *adj* chiarificatore(trice).

illumination [ɪluːmɪ'neɪʃən] *n* illuminazione *f*.

illusion [ɪ'luːʒən] *n* illusione *f*; **to be under the ~ that** avere l'impressione che.

illusive [ɪ'luːsɪv], **illusory** [ɪ'luːsərɪ] *adj* illusorio(a).

illustrate [ˈɪləstreɪt] *vt* illustrare.

illustration [ɪlə'streɪʃən] *n* illustrazione *f*.

illustrator [ˈɪləstreɪtə*] *n* illustratore/trice.

illustrious [ɪ'lʌstrɪəs] *adj* illustre.

ill will *n* cattiva volontà.

ILO *n abbr* (= *International Labour Organization*) OIL *f*.

ILWU *n abbr* (*US*: = *International Longshoremen's and Warehousemen's Union*) *sindacato internazionale degli scaricatori di porto e magazzinieri.*

I'm [aɪm] = **I am.**

image [ˈɪmɪdʒ] *n* immagine *f*; (*public face*) immagine (pubblica).

imagery [ˈɪmɪdʒərɪ] *n* immagini *fpl*.

imaginable [ɪ'mædʒɪnəbl] *adj* immaginabile, che si possa immaginare.

imaginary [ɪ'mædʒɪnərɪ] *adj* immaginario(a).

imagination [ɪmædʒɪ'neɪʃən] *n* immaginazione *f*, fantasia.

imaginative [ɪ'mædʒɪnətɪv] *adj* immaginoso(a).

imagine [ɪ'mædʒɪn] *vt* immaginare.

imbalance [ɪm'bæləns] *n* squilibrio.

imbecile [ˈɪmbəsiːl] *n* imbecille *m/f*.

imbue [ɪm'bjuː] *vt*: **to ~ sth with** impregnare qc di.

IMF *n abbr see* **International Monetary Fund.**

imitate [ˈɪmɪteɪt] *vt* imitare.

imitation [ɪmɪ'teɪʃən] *n* imitazione *f*.

imitator [ˈɪmɪteɪtə*] *n* imitatore/trice.

immaculate [ɪ'mækjulət] *adj* immacolato(a); (*dress, appearance*) impeccabile.

immaterial [ɪmə'tɪərɪəl] *adj* immateriale, indifferente; **it is ~ whether** poco importa se *or* che + *sub*.

immature [ɪmə'tjuə*] *adj* immaturo(a).

immaturity [ɪmə'tjuərɪtɪ] *n* immaturità, mancanza di maturità.

immeasurable [ɪ'mɛʒərəbl] *adj* incommensurabile.

immediacy [ɪ'miːdɪəsɪ] *n* immediatezza.

immediate [ɪ'miːdɪət] *adj* immediato(a).

immediately [ɪ'miːdɪətlɪ] *adv* (*at once*) subito, immediatamente; **~ next to** proprio accanto a.

immense [ɪ'mɛns] *adj* immenso(a); enorme.

immensity [ɪ'mɛnsɪtɪ] *n* (*of size, difference*) enormità; (*of problem etc*) vastità.

immerse [ɪ'məːs] *vt* immergere.

immersion heater [ɪ'məːʃən-] *n* (*BRIT*) scaldaacqua *m inv* a immersione.

immigrant [ˈɪmɪgrənt] *n* immigrante *m/f*; (*already established*) immigrato/a.

immigration [ɪmɪ'greɪʃən] *n* immigrazione *f*.

immigration authorities *npl* ufficio stranieri.

immigration laws *npl* leggi *fpl* relative all'immigrazione.

imminent [ˈɪmɪnənt] *adj* imminente.

immobile [ɪ'məubaɪl] *adj* immobile.

immobilize [ɪ'məubɪlaɪz] *vt* immobilizzare.

immoderate [ɪ'mɔdərɪt] *adj* (*person*) smodato(a), sregolato(a); (*opinion, reaction, demand*) eccessivo(a).

immodest [ɪ'mɔdɪst] *adj* (*indecent*)

indecente, impudico(a); (*boasting*)
presuntuoso(a).
immoral [ɪ'mɔrl] *adj* immorale.
immorality [ɪmɔ'rælɪtɪ] *n* immoralità.
immortal [ɪ'mɔːtl] *adj, n* immortale (*m/f*).
immortalize [ɪ'mɔːtəlaɪz] *vt* rendere
immortale.
immovable [ɪ'muːvəbl] *adj* (*object*) non
movibile; (*person*) irremovibile.
immune [ɪ'mjuːn] *adj*: ~ (**to**) immune (da).
immune system *n* sistema *m*
immunitario.
immunity [ɪ'mjuːnɪtɪ] *n* (*also fig: of
diplomat*) immunità; **diplomatic** ~
immunità diplomatica.
immunization [ɪmjunaɪ'zeɪʃən] *n*
immunizzazione *f*.
immunize ['ɪmjunaɪz] *vt* immunizzare.
imp [ɪmp] *n* folletto, diavoletto; (*child*)
diavoletto.
impact ['ɪmpækt] *n* impatto.
impair [ɪm'pɛə*] *vt* danneggiare.
impaired [ɪm'pɛəd] *adj* indebolito(a).
-impaired [ɪm'pɛəd] *suffix*: **visually**~
videoleso(a).
impale [ɪm'peɪl] *vt* impalare.
impart [ɪm'pɑːt] *vt* (*make known*)
comunicare; (*bestow*) impartire.
impartial [ɪm'pɑːʃl] *adj* imparziale.
impartiality [ɪmpɑːʃɪ'ælɪtɪ] *n* imparzialità.
impassable [ɪm'pɑːsəbl] *adj* insuperabile;
(*road*) impraticabile.
impasse [æm'pɑːs] *n* impasse *f inv*.
impassioned [ɪm'pæʃənd] *adj*
appassionato(a).
impassive [ɪm'pæsɪv] *adj* impassibile.
impatience [ɪm'peɪʃəns] *n* impazienza.
impatient [ɪm'peɪʃənt] *adj* impaziente; **to
get** *or* **grow** ~ perdere la pazienza.
impeach [ɪm'piːtʃ] *vt* accusare, attaccare;
(*public official*) mettere sotto accusa.
impeachment [ɪm'piːtʃmənt] *n* (*LAW*)
imputazione *f*.
impeccable [ɪm'pɛkəbl] *adj* impeccabile.
impecunious [ɪmpɪ'kjuːnɪəs] *adj* povero(a).
impede [ɪm'piːd] *vt* impedire.
impediment [ɪm'pɛdɪmənt] *n* impedimento;
(*also*: **speech** ~) difetto di pronuncia.
impel [ɪm'pɛl] *vt* (*force*): **to** ~ **sb** (**to do sth**)
costringere *or* obbligare qn (a fare qc).
impending [ɪm'pɛndɪŋ] *adj* imminente.
impenetrable [ɪm'pɛnɪtrəbl] *adj*
impenetrabile.
imperative [ɪm'pɛrətɪv] *adj* imperativo(a);
necessario(a), urgente; (*voice*)
imperioso(a) ♦ *n* (*LING*) imperativo.
imperceptible [ɪmpə'sɛptɪbl] *adj*
impercettibile.

imperfect [ɪm'pəːfɪkt] *adj* imperfetto(a);
(*goods etc*) difettoso(a) ♦ *n* (*LING: also*: ~
tense) imperfetto.
imperfection [ɪmpəː'fɛkʃən] *n*
imperfezione *f*; (*flaw*) difetto.
imperial [ɪm'pɪərɪəl] *adj* imperiale;
(*measure*) legale.
imperialism [ɪm'pɪərɪəlɪzəm] *n*
imperialismo.
imperil [ɪm'pɛrɪl] *vt* mettere in pericolo.
imperious [ɪm'pɪərɪəs] *adj* imperioso(a).
impersonal [ɪm'pəːsənl] *adj* impersonale.
impersonate [ɪm'pəːsəneɪt] *vt*
impersonare; (*THEAT*) imitare.
impersonation [ɪmpəːsə'neɪʃən] *n* (*LAW*)
usurpazione *f* d'identità; (*THEAT*)
imitazione *f*.
impersonator [ɪm'pəːsəneɪtə*] *n* (*gen,
THEAT*) imitatore/trice.
impertinence [ɪm'pəːtɪnəns] *n*
impertinenza.
impertinent [ɪm'pəːtɪnənt] *adj*
impertinente.
imperturbable [ɪmpə'təːbəbl] *adj*
imperturbabile.
impervious [ɪm'pəːvɪəs] *adj* impermeabile;
(*fig*): ~ **to** insensibile a; impassibile di
fronte a.
impetuous [ɪm'pɛtjuəs] *adj* impetuoso(a),
precipitoso(a).
impetus ['ɪmpətəs] *n* impeto.
impinge [ɪm'pɪndʒ]: **to** ~ **on** *vt fus* (*person*)
colpire; (*rights*) ledere.
impish ['ɪmpɪʃ] *adj* malizioso(a),
birichino(a).
implacable [ɪm'plækəbl] *adj* implacabile.
implant [ɪm'plɑːnt] *vt* (*MED*) innestare; (*fig:
idea, principle*) inculcare.
implausible [ɪm'plɔːzɪbl] *adj* non plausibile.
implement *n* ['ɪmplɪmənt] attrezzo; (*for
cooking*) utensile *m* ♦ *vt* ['ɪmplɪmɛnt]
effettuare.
implicate ['ɪmplɪkeɪt] *vt* implicare.
implication [ɪmplɪ'keɪʃən] *n* implicazione *f*;
by ~ implicitamente.
implicit [ɪm'plɪsɪt] *adj* implicito(a);
(*complete*) completo(a).
implicitly [ɪm'plɪsɪtlɪ] *adv* implicitamente.
implore [ɪm'plɔː*] *vt* implorare.
imply [ɪm'plaɪ] *vt* insinuare; suggerire.
impolite [ɪmpə'laɪt] *adj* scortese.
imponderable [ɪm'pɒndərəbl] *adj*
imponderabile.
import *vt* [ɪm'pɔːt] importare ♦ *n* ['ɪmpɔːt]
(*COMM*) importazione *f*; (*meaning*)
significato, senso ♦ *cpd* (*duty, licence etc*)
d'importazione.
importance [ɪm'pɔːtns] *n* importanza; **to be**

of great/little ~ importare molto/poco, essere molto/poco importante.

important [ɪm'pɔːtnt] adj importante; **it's not** ~ non ha importanza; **it is** ~ **that** è importante che + sub.

importantly [ɪm'pɔːtəntlɪ] adv (pej) con (un'aria d')importanza; **but, more** ~, ... ma, quel che più conta or importa, ...

importation [ɪmpɔː'teɪʃən] n importazione f.

imported [ɪm'pɔːtɪd] adj importato(a).

importer [ɪm'pɔːtə*] n importatore/trice.

impose [ɪm'pəuz] vt imporre ♦ vi: **to** ~ **on sb** sfruttare la bontà di qn.

imposing [ɪm'pəuzɪŋ] adj imponente.

imposition [ɪmpə'zɪʃən] n imposizione f; **to be an** ~ **on** (person) abusare della gentilezza di.

impossibility [ɪmpɔsə'bɪlɪtɪ] n impossibilità.

impossible [ɪm'pɔsɪbl] adj impossibile; **it is** ~ **for me to leave now** mi è impossibile venir via adesso.

impostor [ɪm'pɔstə*] n impostore/a.

impotence ['ɪmpətns] n impotenza.

impotent ['ɪmpətnt] adj impotente.

impound [ɪm'paund] vt confiscare.

impoverished [ɪm'pɔvərɪʃt] adj impoverito(a).

impracticable [ɪm'præktɪkəbl] adj impraticabile.

impractical [ɪm'præktɪkl] adj non pratico(a).

imprecise [ɪmprɪ'saɪs] adj impreciso(a).

impregnable [ɪm'pregnəbl] adj (fortress) inespugnabile; (fig) inoppugnabile; irrefutabile.

impregnate ['ɪmpregneɪt] vt impregnare; (fertilize) fecondare.

impresario [ɪmprɪ'sɑːrɪəu] n impresario/a.

impress [ɪm'pres] vt impressionare; (mark) imprimere, stampare; **to** ~ **sth on sb** far capire qc a qn.

impression [ɪm'preʃən] n impressione f; **to be under the** ~ **that** avere l'impressione che; **to make a good/bad** ~ **on sb** fare una buona/cattiva impressione a or su qn.

impressionable [ɪm'preʃnəbl] adj impressionabile.

impressionist [ɪm'preʃənɪst] n impressionista m/f.

impressive [ɪm'presɪv] adj impressionante.

imprint ['ɪmprɪnt] n (PUBLISHING) sigla editoriale.

imprinted [ɪm'prɪntɪd] adj: ~ **on** impresso(a) in.

imprison [ɪm'prɪzn] vt imprigionare.

imprisonment [ɪm'prɪznmənt] n imprigionamento.

improbable [ɪm'prɔbəbl] adj improbabile; (excuse) inverosimile.

impromptu [ɪm'prɔmptjuː] adj improvvisato(a) ♦ adv improvvisando, così su due piedi.

improper [ɪm'prɔpə*] adj scorretto(a); (unsuitable) inadatto(a), improprio(a); sconveniente, indecente.

impropriety [ɪmprə'praɪətɪ] n sconvenienza; (of expression) improprietà.

improve [ɪm'pruːv] vt migliorare ♦ vi migliorare; (pupil etc) fare progressi.

▶**improve (up)on** vt fus (offer) aumentare.

improvement [ɪm'pruːvmənt] n miglioramento; progresso; **to make** ~**s to** migliorare, apportare dei miglioramenti a.

improvisation [ɪmprəvaɪ'zeɪʃən] n improvvisazione f.

improvise ['ɪmprəvaɪz] vt, vi improvvisare.

imprudence [ɪm'pruːdns] n imprudenza.

imprudent [ɪm'pruːdnt] adj imprudente.

impudence ['ɪmpjudns] n impudenza.

impudent ['ɪmpjudnt] adj impudente, sfacciato(a).

impugn [ɪm'pjuːn] vt impugnare.

impulse ['ɪmpʌls] n impulso; **to act on** ~ agire d'impulso or impulsivamente.

impulse buy n acquisto fatto d'impulso.

impulsive [ɪm'pʌlsɪv] adj impulsivo(a).

impunity [ɪm'pjuːnɪtɪ] n: **with** ~ impunemente.

impure [ɪm'pjuə*] adj impuro(a).

impurity [ɪm'pjuərɪtɪ] n impurità f inv.

IN abbr (US) = Indiana.

════════════════ KEYWORD

in [ɪn] prep **1** (indicating place, position) in; ~ **the house/garden** in casa/giardino; ~ **the box** nella scatola; ~ **the fridge** nel frigorifero; **I have it** ~ **my hand** ce l'ho in mano; ~ **town/the country** in città/ campagna; ~ **school** a scuola; ~ **here/ there** qui/lì dentro

2 (with place names: of town, region, country): ~ **London** a Londra; ~ **England** in Inghilterra; ~ **the United States** negli Stati Uniti; ~ **Yorkshire** nello Yorkshire

3 (indicating time: during, in the space of) in; ~ **spring/summer** in primavera/ estate; ~ **1988** nel 1988; ~ **May** in or a maggio; **I'll see you** ~ **July** ci vediamo a luglio; ~ **the afternoon** nel pomeriggio; **at 4 o'clock** ~ **the afternoon** alle 4 del pomeriggio; **I did it** ~ **3 hours/days** l'ho fatto in 3 ore/giorni; **I'll see you ~ 2 weeks'** *or* **~ 2 weeks' time** ci vediamo tra 2 settimane; **once ~ a hundred years** una volta ogni cento anni

4 (*indicating manner etc*) a; **~ a loud/soft voice** a voce alta/bassa; **~ pencil** a matita; **~ English/French** in inglese/francese; **~ writing** per iscritto; **the boy ~ the blue shirt** il ragazzo con la camicia blu

5 (*indicating circumstances*): **~ the sun** al sole; **~ the shade** all'ombra; **~ the rain** sotto la pioggia; **a rise ~ prices** un aumento dei prezzi

6 (*indicating mood, state*): **~ tears** in lacrime; **~ anger** per la rabbia; **~ despair** disperato(a); **~ good condition** in buono stato, in buone condizioni; **to live ~ luxury** vivere nel lusso

7 (*with ratios, numbers*): **1 ~ 10** 1 su 10; **20 pence ~ the pound** 20 pence per sterlina; **they lined up ~ twos** si misero in fila per due; **~ hundreds** a centinaia

8 (*referring to people, works*) in; **the disease is common ~ children** la malattia è comune nei bambini; **~ (the works of) Dickens** in Dickens, nelle opere di Dickens

9 (*indicating profession etc*) in; **to be ~ teaching** fare l'insegnante, insegnare; **to be ~ publishing** lavorare nell'editoria

10 (*after superlative*) di; **the best ~ the class** il migliore della classe

11 (*with present participle*): **~ saying this** dicendo questo, nel dire questo

12: **~ that** *conj* poiché

♦ *adv*: **to be ~** (*person: at home, work*) esserci; (*train, ship, plane*) essere arrivato(a); (*in fashion*) essere di moda; **their party is ~** il loro partito è al potere; **to ask sb ~** invitare qn ad entrare; **to run/limp** *etc* **~** entrare di corsa/zoppicando *etc*

♦ *n*: **the ~s and outs of the problem** tutti gli aspetti del problema.

---

in., ins *abbr* = **inch(es)**.
inability [ɪnə'bɪlɪtɪ] *n* inabilità, incapacità; **~ to pay** impossibilità di pagare.
inaccessible [ɪnək'sɛsɪbl] *adj* inaccessibile.
inaccuracy [ɪn'ækjurəsɪ] *n* inaccuratezza; inesattezza; imprecisione *f*.
inaccurate [ɪn'ækjurət] *adj* inaccurato(a); (*figures*) inesatto(a); (*translation*) impreciso(a).
inaction [ɪn'ækʃən] *n* inazione *f*.
inactivity [ɪnæk'tɪvɪtɪ] *n* inattività.
inadequacy [ɪn'ædɪkwəsɪ] *n* insufficienza.
inadequate [ɪn'ædɪkwət] *adj* insufficiente.

inadmissible [ɪnəd'mɪsəbl] *adj* inammissibile.
inadvertent [ɪnəd'vəːtənt] *adj* involontario(a).
inadvertently [ɪnəd'vəːtntlɪ] *adv* senza volerlo.
inadvisable [ɪnəd'vaɪzəbl] *adj* sconsigliabile.
inane [ɪ'neɪn] *adj* vacuo(a), stupido(a).
inanimate [ɪn'ænɪmət] *adj* inanimato(a).
inapplicable [ɪn'æplɪkəbl] *adj* inapplicabile.
inappropriate [ɪnə'prəuprɪət] *adj* disadatto(a); (*word, expression*) improprio(a).
inapt [ɪn'æpt] *adj* maldestro(a); fuori luogo.
inaptitude [ɪn'æptɪtjuːd] *n* improprietà.
inarticulate [ɪnɑː'tɪkjulət] *adj* (*person*) che si esprime male; (*speech*) inarticolato(a).
inasmuch as [ɪnəz'mʌtʃæz] *adv* in quanto che; (*seeing that*) poiché.
inattention [ɪnə'tɛnʃən] *n* mancanza di attenzione.
inattentive [ɪnə'tɛntɪv] *adj* disattento(a); distratto(a); negligente.
inaudible [ɪn'ɔːdɪbl] *adj* che non si riesce a sentire.
inaugural [ɪ'nɔːgjurəl] *adj* inaugurale.
inaugurate [ɪ'nɔːgjureɪt] *vt* inaugurare; (*president, official*) insediare.
inauguration [ɪnɔːgju'reɪʃən] *n* inaugurazione *f*; insediamento in carica.
inauspicious [ɪnɔːs'pɪʃəs] *adj* poco propizio(a).
in-between [ɪnbɪ'twiːn] *adj* fra i (*or* le) due.
inborn [ɪn'bɔːn] *adj* (*feeling*) innato(a); (*defect*) congenito(a).
inbred [ɪn'brɛd] *adj* innato(a); (*family*) connaturato(a).
inbreeding [ɪn'briːdɪŋ] *n* incrocio ripetuto di animali consanguinei; unioni *fpl* fra consanguinei.
Inc. *abbr see* **incorporated**.
Inca ['ɪŋkə] *adj* (*also*: **~n**) inca *inv* ♦ *n* inca *m/f inv*.
incalculable [ɪn'kælkjuləbl] *adj* incalcolabile.
incapability [ɪnkeɪpə'bɪlɪtɪ] *n* incapacità.
incapable [ɪn'keɪpəbl] *adj*: **~ (of doing sth)** incapace (di fare qc).
incapacitate [ɪnkə'pæsɪteɪt] *vt*: **to ~ sb from doing** rendere qn incapace di fare.
incapacitated [ɪnkə'pæsɪteɪtɪd] *adj* (*LAW*) inabilitato(a).
incapacity [ɪnkə'pæsɪtɪ] *n* incapacità.
incarcerate [ɪn'kɑːsəreɪt] *vt* imprigionare.
incarnate *adj* [ɪn'kɑːnɪt] incarnato(a) ♦ *vt* ['ɪnkɑːneɪt] incarnare.
incarnation [ɪnkɑː'neɪʃən] *n* incarnazione *f*.

incendiary [ɪn'sɛndɪərɪ] *adj* incendiario(a) ♦ *n* (*bomb*) bomba incendiaria.

incense *n* ['ɪnsɛns] incenso ♦ *vt* [ɪn'sɛns] (*anger*) infuriare.

incense burner *n* incensiere *m*.

incentive [ɪn'sɛntɪv] *n* incentivo.

incentive scheme *n* piano di incentivazione.

inception [ɪn'sɛpʃən] *n* inizio, principio.

incessant [ɪn'sɛsnt] *adj* incessante.

incessantly [ɪn'sɛsntlɪ] *adv* di continuo, senza sosta.

incest ['ɪnsɛst] *n* incesto.

inch [ɪntʃ] *n* pollice *m* (= *25 mm*; *12 in a foot*); **within an ~ of** a un pelo da; **he wouldn't give an ~** (*fig*) non ha ceduto di un millimetro.

▶**inch forward** *vi* avanzare pian piano.

inch tape *n* (*BRIT*) metro a nastro (da sarto).

incidence ['ɪnsɪdns] *n* incidenza.

incident ['ɪnsɪdnt] *n* incidente *m*; (*in book*) episodio.

incidental [ɪnsɪ'dɛntl] *adj* accessorio(a), d'accompagnamento; (*unplanned*) incidentale; ~ **to** marginale a; ~ **expenses** *npl* spese *fpl* accessorie.

incidentally [ɪnsɪ'dɛntəlɪ] *adv* (*by the way*) a proposito.

incidental music *n* sottofondo (musicale), musica di sottofondo.

incident room *n* (*POLICE*) centrale *f* delle operazioni (*per indagini*).

incinerate [ɪn'sɪnəreɪt] *vt* incenerire.

incinerator [ɪn'sɪnəreɪtə*] *n* inceneritore *m*.

incipient [ɪn'sɪpɪənt] *adj* incipiente.

incision [ɪn'sɪʒən] *n* incisione *f*.

incisive [ɪn'saɪsɪv] *adj* incisivo(a); tagliante; acuto(a).

incisor [ɪn'saɪzə*] *n* incisivo.

incite [ɪn'saɪt] *vt* incitare.

incl. *abbr* = **including, inclusive (of)**.

inclement [ɪn'klɛmənt] *adj* inclemente.

inclination [ɪnklɪ'neɪʃən] *n* inclinazione *f*.

incline *n* ['ɪnklaɪn] pendenza, pendio ♦ *vb* [ɪn'klaɪn] *vt* inclinare ♦ *vi*: **to ~ to** tendere a; **to be ~d to do** tendere a fare; essere propenso(a) a fare; **to be well ~d towards sb** essere ben disposto(a) verso qn.

include [ɪn'kluːd] *vt* includere, comprendere; **the tip is/is not ~d** la mancia è compresa/esclusa.

including [ɪn'kluːdɪŋ] *prep* compreso(a), incluso(a); ~ **tip** mancia compresa, compresa la mancia.

inclusion [ɪn'kluːʒən] *n* inclusione *f*.

inclusive [ɪn'kluːsɪv] *adj* incluso(a), compreso(a); £50, ~ **of all surcharges** 50 sterline, incluse tutte le soprattasse.

inclusive terms *npl* (*BRIT*) prezzo tutto compreso.

incognito [ɪnkɔg'niːtəu] *adv* in incognito.

incoherent [ɪnkəu'hɪərənt] *adj* incoerente.

income ['ɪnkʌm] *n* reddito; **gross/net** ~ reddito lordo/netto; ~ **and expenditure account** conto entrate ed uscite.

income support *n* (*BRIT*) sussidio di indigenza *or* povertà.

income tax *n* imposta sul reddito.

income tax inspector *n* ispettore *m* delle imposte dirette.

income tax return *n* dichiarazione *f* annuale dei redditi.

incoming ['ɪnkʌmɪŋ] *adj* (*passengers*) in arrivo; (*government, tenant*) subentrante; ~ **tide** marea montante.

incommunicado [ɪnkəmjunɪ'kɑːdəu] *adj*: **to hold sb** ~ tenere qn in segregazione.

incomparable [ɪn'kɔmpərəbl] *adj* incomparabile.

incompatible [ɪnkəm'pætɪbl] *adj* incompatibile.

incompetence [ɪn'kɔmpɪtns] *n* incompetenza, incapacità.

incompetent [ɪn'kɔmpɪtnt] *adj* incompetente, incapace.

incomplete [ɪnkəm'pliːt] *adj* incompleto(a).

incomprehensible [ɪnkɔmprɪ'hɛnsɪbl] *adj* incomprensibile.

inconceivable [ɪnkən'siːvəbl] *adj* inimmaginabile.

inconclusive [ɪnkən'kluːsɪv] *adj* improduttivo(a); (*argument*) poco convincente.

incongruous [ɪn'kɔŋgruəs] *adj* poco appropriato(a); (*remark, act*) incongruo(a).

inconsequential [ɪnkɔnsɪ'kwɛnʃl] *adj* senza importanza.

inconsiderable [ɪnkən'sɪdərəbl] *adj*: **not** ~ non trascurabile.

inconsiderate [ɪnkən'sɪdərət] *adj* sconsiderato(a).

inconsistency [ɪnkən'sɪstənsɪ] *n* (*of actions etc*) incongruenza; (*of work*) irregolarità; (*of statement etc*) contraddizione *f*.

inconsistent [ɪnkən'sɪstnt] *adj* incoerente; poco logico(a); contraddittorio(a); ~ **with** in contraddizione con.

inconsolable [ɪnkən'səuləbl] *adj* inconsolabile.

inconspicuous [ɪnkən'spɪkjuəs] *adj* incospicuo(a); (*colour*) poco appariscente; (*dress*) dimesso(a); **to make o.s.** ~ cercare di passare inosservato(a).

inconstant [ɪn'kɒnstnt] *adj* incostante; mutevole.

incontinence [ɪn'kɒntɪnəns] *n* incontinenza.

incontinent [ɪn'kɒntɪnənt] *adj* incontinente.

incontrovertible [ɪnkɒntrə'və:təbl] *adj* incontrovertibile.

inconvenience [ɪnkən'vi:njəns] *n* inconveniente *m*; (*trouble*) disturbo ♦ *vt* disturbare; **to put sb to great ~** creare degli inconvenienti a qn; **don't ~ yourself** non si disturbi.

inconvenient [ɪnkən'vi:njənt] *adj* scomodo(a); **that time is very ~ for me** quell'ora mi è molto scomoda, non è un'ora adatta per me.

incorporate [ɪn'kɔ:pəreɪt] *vt* incorporare; (*contain*) contenere.

incorporated [ɪn'kɔ:pəreɪtɪd] *adj*: **~ company** (*US: abbr* **Inc.**) società *f inv* registrata.

incorrect [ɪnkə'rɛkt] *adj* scorretto(a); (*statement*) impreciso(a).

incorrigible [ɪn'kɔrɪdʒəbl] *adj* incorreggibile.

incorruptible [ɪnkə'rʌptɪbl] *adj* incorruttibile.

increase *n* ['ɪnkri:s] aumento ♦ *vi* [ɪn'kri:s] aumentare; **to be on the ~** essere in aumento; **an ~ of £5/10%** un aumento di 5 sterline/del 10%.

increasing [ɪn'kri:sɪŋ] *adj* (*number*) crescente.

increasingly [ɪn'kri:sɪŋli] *adv* sempre più.

incredible [ɪn'krɛdɪbl] *adj* incredibile.

incredulous [ɪn'krɛdjuləs] *adj* incredulo(a).

increment ['ɪnkrɪmənt] *n* aumento, incremento.

incriminate [ɪn'krɪmɪneɪt] *vt* compromettere.

incriminating [ɪn'krɪmɪneɪtɪŋ] *adj* incriminante.

incubate ['ɪnkjubeɪt] *vt* (*eggs*) covare ♦ *vi* (*egg*) essere in incubazione; (*disease*) avere un'incubazione.

incubation [ɪnkju'beɪʃən] *n* incubazione *f*.

incubation period *n* (periodo di) incubazione *f*.

incubator ['ɪnkjubeɪtə*] *n* incubatrice *f*.

inculcate ['ɪnkʌlkeɪt] *vt*: **to ~ sth in sb** inculcare qc a qn, istillare qc a qn.

incumbent [ɪn'kʌmbənt] *adj*: **it is ~ on him to do ...** è suo dovere fare ... ♦ *n* titolare *m/f*.

incur [ɪn'kə:*] *vt* (*expenses*) incorrere; (*debt*) contrarre; (*loss*) subire; (*anger, risk*) esporsi a.

incurable [ɪn'kjuərəbl] *adj* incurabile.

incursion [ɪn'kə:ʃən] *n* incursione *f*.

Ind. *abbr* (*US*) = *Indiana.*

indebted [ɪn'dɛtɪd] *adj*: **to be ~ to sb (for)** essere obbligato(a) verso qn (per).

indecency [ɪn'di:snsɪ] *n* indecenza.

indecent [ɪn'di:snt] *adj* indecente.

indecent assault *n* (*BRIT*) aggressione *f* a scopo di violenza sessuale.

indecent exposure *n* atti *mpl* osceni in luogo pubblico.

indecipherable [ɪndɪ'saɪfərəbl] *adj* indecifrabile.

indecision [ɪndɪ'sɪʒən] *n* indecisione *f*.

indecisive [ɪndɪ'saɪsɪv] *adj* indeciso(a); (*discussion*) non decisivo(a).

indeed [ɪn'di:d] *adv* infatti; veramente; **yes ~!** certamente!

indefatigable [ɪndɪ'fætɪgəbl] *adj* infaticabile, instancabile.

indefensible [ɪndɪ'fɛnsəbl] *adj* (*conduct*) ingiustificabile.

indefinable [ɪndɪ'faɪnəbl] *adj* indefinibile.

indefinite [ɪn'dɛfɪnɪt] *adj* indefinito(a); (*answer*) vago(a); (*period, number*) indeterminato(a).

indefinitely [ɪn'dɛfɪnɪtlɪ] *adv* (*wait*) indefinitamente.

indelible [ɪn'dɛlɪbl] *adj* indelebile.

indelicate [ɪn'dɛlɪkɪt] *adj* (*tactless*) indelicato(a), privo(a) di tatto; (*not polite*) sconveniente.

indemnify [ɪn'dɛmnɪfaɪ] *vt* indennizzare.

indemnity [ɪn'dɛmnɪtɪ] *n* (*insurance*) assicurazione *f*; (*compensation*) indennità, indennizzo.

indent [ɪn'dɛnt] *vt* (*TYP: text*) far rientrare dal margine.

indentation [ɪndɛn'teɪʃən] *n* dentellatura; (*TYP*) rientranza; (*dent*) tacca.

indented [ɪn'dɛntɪd] *adj* (*TYP*) rientrante.

indenture [ɪn'dɛntʃə*] *n* contratto *m* formazione *inv*.

independence [ɪndɪ'pɛndns] *n* indipendenza.

> *Negli Stati Uniti il 4 luglio si festeggia* l'**Independence Day**, *il giorno in cui è stata firmata, nel 1776, la Dichiarazione di Indipendenza con la quale tredici colonie britanniche dichiaravano la propria indipendenza dalla Gran Bretagna e la propria appartenenza agli Stati Uniti d'America.*

independent [ɪndɪ'pɛndnt] *adj* indipendente.

independently [ɪndɪ'pɛndntlɪ] *adv* indipendentemente; separatamente; **~ of** indipendentemente da.

in-depth ['ın'dɛpθ] *adj* approfondito(a).
indescribable [ındı'skraıbəbl] *adj* indescrivibile.
indestructible [ındı'strʌktəbl] *adj* indistruttibile.
indeterminate [ındı'tə:mınıt] *adj* indeterminato(a).
index ['ındɛks] *n* (*pl* ~**es**: *in book*) indice *m*; (: *in library etc*) catalogo; (*pl* **indices** ['ındısi:z]: *ratio, sign*) indice *m*.
index card *n* scheda.
index finger *n* (dito) indice *m*.
index-linked ['ındɛks'lıŋkt], (*US*) **indexed** ['ındɛkst] *adj* legato(a) al costo della vita.
India ['ındıə] *n* India.
Indian ['ındıən] *adj, n* indiano(a).
Indian ink *n* inchiostro di china.
Indian Ocean *n*: **the** ~ l'Oceano Indiano.
Indian Summer *n* (*fig*) estate *f* di San Martino.
India paper *n* carta d'India, carta bibbia.
India rubber *n* caucciù *m*.
indicate ['ındıkeıt] *vt* indicare ♦ *vi* (*BRIT AUT*): **to** ~ **left/right** mettere la freccia a sinistra/a destra.
indication [ındı'keıʃən] *n* indicazione *f*, segno.
indicative [ın'dıkətıv] *adj* indicativo(a) ♦ *n* (*LING*) indicativo; **to be** ~ **of sth** essere indicativo(a) *or* un indice di qc.
indicator ['ındıkeıtə*] *n* (*sign*) segno; (*AUT*) indicatore *m* di direzione, freccia.
indices ['ındısi:z] *npl of* **index**.
indict [ın'daıt] *vt* accusare.
indictable [ın'daıtəbl] *adj* passibile di pena; ~ **offence** atto che costituisce reato.
indictment [ın'daıtmənt] *n* accusa.
indifference [ın'dıfrəns] *n* indifferenza.
indifferent [ın'dıfrənt] *adj* indifferente; (*poor*) mediocre.
indigenous [ın'dıdʒınəs] *adj* indigeno(a).
indigestible [ındı'dʒɛstıbl] *adj* indigeribile.
indigestion [ındı'dʒɛstʃən] *n* indigestione *f*.
indignant [ın'dıgnənt] *adj*: ~ **(at sth/with sb)** indignato(a) (per qc/contro qn).
indignation [ındıg'neıʃən] *n* indignazione *f*.
indignity [ın'dıgnıtı] *n* umiliazione *f*.
indigo ['ındıgəu] *adj, n* indaco (*inv*).
indirect [ındı'rɛkt] *adj* indiretto(a).
indirectly [ındı'rɛktlı] *adv* indirettamente.
indiscreet [ındı'skri:t] *adj* indiscreto(a); (*rash*) imprudente.
indiscretion [ındı'skrɛʃən] *n* indiscrezione *f*; imprudenza.
indiscriminate [ındı'skrımınət] *adj* (*person*) che non sa discernere; (*admiration*) cieco(a); (*killings*) indiscriminato(a).
indispensable [ındı'spɛnsəbl] *adj* indispensabile.

indisposed [ındı'spəuzd] *adj* (*unwell*) indisposto(a).
indisposition [ındıspə'zıʃən] *n* (*illness*) indisposizione *f*.
indisputable [ındı'spju:təbl] *adj* incontestabile, indiscutibile.
indistinct [ındı'stıŋkt] *adj* indistinto(a); (*memory, noise*) vago(a).
indistinguishable [ındı'stıŋgwıʃəbl] *adj* indistinguibile.
individual [ındı'vıdjuəl] *n* individuo ♦ *adj* individuale; (*characteristic*) particolare, originale.
individualist [ındı'vıdjuəlıst] *n* individualista *m/f*.
individuality [ındıvıdju'ælıtı] *n* individualità.
individually [ındı'vıdjuəlı] *adv* singolarmente, uno(a) per uno(a).
indivisible [ındı'vızıbl] *adj* indivisibile.
Indochina ['ındəu'tʃaınə] *n* Indocina.
indoctrinate [ın'dɔktrıneıt] *vt* indottrinare.
indoctrination [ındɔktrı'neıʃən] *n* indottrinamento.
indolent ['ındələnt] *adj* indolente.
Indonesia [ındəu'ni:zıə] *n* Indonesia.
Indonesian [ındəu'ni:zıən] *adj, n* indonesiano(a); (*LING*) indonesiano.
indoor ['ındɔ:*] *adj* da interno; (*plant*) d'appartamento; (*swimming pool*) coperto(a); (*sport, games*) fatto(a) al coperto.
indoors [ın'dɔ:z] *adv* all'interno; (*at home*) in casa.
indubitable [ın'dju:bıtəbl] *adj* indubitabile.
induce [ın'dju:s] *vt* persuadere; (*bring about*) provocare; **to** ~ **sb to do sth** persuadere qn a fare qc.
inducement [ın'dju:smənt] *n* incitamento; (*incentive*) stimolo, incentivo.
induct [ın'dʌkt] *vt* insediare; (*fig*) iniziare.
induction [ın'dʌkʃən] *n* (*MED: of birth*) parto indotto.
induction course *n* (*BRIT*) corso di avviamento.
indulge [ın'dʌldʒ] *vt* (*whim*) compiacere, soddisfare; (*child*) viziare ♦ *vi*: **to** ~ **in sth** concedersi qc; abbandonarsi a qc.
indulgence [ın'dʌldʒəns] *n* lusso (che uno si permette); (*leniency*) indulgenza.
indulgent [ın'dʌldʒənt] *adj* indulgente.
industrial [ın'dʌstrıəl] *adj* industriale; (*injury*) sul lavoro; (*dispute*) di lavoro.
industrial action *n* azione *f* rivendicativa.
industrial estate *n* zona industriale.
industrialist [ın'dʌstrıəlıst] *n* industriale *m*.
industrialize [ın'dʌstrıəlaız] *vt*

industrializzare.
industrial park *n (US)* zona industriale.
industrial relations *npl* relazioni *fpl*
industriali.
industrial tribunal *n (BRIT)* ≈ Tribunale *m*
Amministrativo Regionale.
industrial unrest *n (BRIT)* agitazione *f*
(sindacale).
industrious [ɪn'dʌstrɪəs] *adj* industrioso(a),
assiduo(a).
industry ['ɪndəstrɪ] *n* industria; (*diligence*)
operosità.
inebriated [ɪ'niːbrɪeɪtɪd] *adj* ubriaco(a).
inedible [ɪn'ɛdɪbl] *adj* immangiabile; non
commestibile.
ineffective [ɪnɪ'fɛktɪv] *adj* inefficace.
ineffectual [ɪnɪ'fɛktʃuəl] *adj* inefficace;
incompetente.
inefficiency [ɪnɪ'fɪʃənsɪ] *n* inefficienza.
inefficient [ɪnɪ'fɪʃənt] *adj* inefficiente.
inelegant [ɪn'ɛlɪgənt] *adj* poco elegante.
ineligible [ɪn'ɛlɪdʒɪbl] *adj* (*candidate*)
ineleggibile; **to be** ~ **for sth** non avere il
diritto a qc.
inept [ɪ'nɛpt] *adj* inetto(a).
ineptitude [ɪ'nɛptɪtjuːd] *n* inettitudine *f*,
stupidità.
inequality [ɪnɪ'kwɔlɪtɪ] *n* ineguaglianza.
inequitable [ɪn'ɛkwɪtəbl] *adj* iniquo(a).
ineradicable [ɪnɪ'rædɪkəbl] *adj*
inestirpabile.
inert [ɪ'nəːt] *adj* inerte.
inertia [ɪ'nəːʃə] *n* inerzia.
inertia-reel seat belt [ɪ'nəːʃə'riːl-] *n*
cintura di sicurezza con arrotolatore.
inescapable [ɪnɪ'skeɪpəbl] *adj* inevitabile.
inessential [ɪnɪ'sɛnʃl] *adj* non essenziale.
inestimable [ɪn'ɛstɪməbl] *adj* inestimabile,
incalcolabile.
inevitable [ɪn'ɛvɪtəbl] *adj* inevitabile.
inevitably [ɪn'ɛvɪtəblɪ] *adv* inevitabilmente;
as ~ **happens** ... come immancabilmente
succede ....
inexact [ɪnɪg'zækt] *adj* inesatto(a).
inexcusable [ɪnɪks'kjuːzəbl] *adj*
imperdonabile.
inexhaustible [ɪnɪg'zɔːstɪbl] *adj*
inesauribile; (*person*) instancabile.
inexorable [ɪn'ɛksərəbl] *adj* inesorabile.
inexpensive [ɪnɪk'spɛnsɪv] *adj* poco
costoso(a).
inexperience [ɪnɪk'spɪərɪəns] *n*
inesperienza.
inexperienced [ɪnɪk'spɪərɪənst] *adj*
inesperto(a), senza esperienza; **to be** ~ **in
sth** essere poco pratico di qc.
inexplicable [ɪnɪk'splɪkəbl] *adj*
inesplicabile.

inexpressible [ɪnɪk'sprɛsəbl] *adj*
inesprimibile.
inextricable [ɪnɪk'strɪkəbl] *adj* inestricabile.
infallibility [ɪnfælə'bɪlɪtɪ] *n* infallibilità.
infallible [ɪn'fælɪbl] *adj* infallibile.
infamous ['ɪnfəməs] *adj* infame.
infamy ['ɪnfəmɪ] *n* infamia.
infancy ['ɪnfənsɪ] *n* infanzia.
infant ['ɪnfənt] *n* bambino/a.
infantile ['ɪnfəntaɪl] *adj* infantile.
infant mortality *n* mortalità infantile.
infantry ['ɪnfəntrɪ] *n* fanteria.
infantryman ['ɪnfəntrɪmən] *n* fante *m*.
infant school *n (BRIT)* scuola elementare
(*per bambini dall'età di 5 a 7 anni*).
infatuated [ɪn'fætjueɪtɪd] *adj*: ~ **with**
infatuato(a) di; **to become** ~ **(with sb)**
infatuarsi (di qn).
infatuation [ɪnfætjʊ'eɪʃən] *n* infatuazione *f*.
infect [ɪn'fɛkt] *vt* infettare; ~**ed with**
(*illness*) affetto(a) da; **to become** ~**ed**
(*wound*) infettarsi.
infection [ɪn'fɛkʃən] *n* infezione *f*.
infectious [ɪn'fɛkʃəs] *adj* (*disease*)
infettivo(a), contagioso(a); (*person,
laughter*) contagioso(a).
infer [ɪn'fəː*] *vt*: **to** ~ **(from)** dedurre (da),
concludere (da).
inference ['ɪnfərəns] *n* deduzione *f*,
conclusione *f*.
inferior [ɪn'fɪərɪə*] *adj* inferiore; (*goods*) di
qualità scadente ♦ *n* inferiore *m/f*; (*in rank*)
subalterno/a; **to feel** ~ sentirsi inferiore.
inferiority [ɪnfɪərɪ'ɔrɪtɪ] *n* inferiorità.
inferiority complex *n* complesso di
inferiorità.
infernal [ɪn'fəːnl] *adj* infernale.
inferno [ɪn'fəːnəʊ] *n* inferno.
infertile [ɪn'fəːtaɪl] *adj* sterile.
infertility [ɪnfəː'tɪlɪtɪ] *n* sterilità.
infested [ɪn'fɛstɪd] *adj*: ~ **(with)**
infestato(a) (di).
infidelity [ɪnfɪ'dɛlɪtɪ] *n* infedeltà.
in-fighting ['ɪnfaɪtɪŋ] *n* lotte *fpl* intestine.
infiltrate ['ɪnfɪltreɪt] *vt* (*troops etc*) far
penetrare; (*enemy line etc*) infiltrare ♦ *vi*
infiltrarsi.
infinite ['ɪnfɪnɪt] *adj* infinito(a); **an** ~
amount of time/money un'illimitata
quantità di tempo/denaro.
infinitely ['ɪnfɪnɪtlɪ] *adv* infinitamente.
infinitesimal [ɪnfɪnɪ'tɛsɪməl] *adj*
infinitesimale.
infinitive [ɪn'fɪnɪtɪv] *n* infinito.
infinity [ɪn'fɪnɪtɪ] *n* infinità; (*also MATH*)
infinito.
infirm [ɪn'fəːm] *adj* infermo(a).
infirmary [ɪn'fəːmərɪ] *n* ospedale *m*; (*in*

school, factory) infermeria.
infirmity [ɪnˈfəːmɪtɪ] n infermità f inv.
inflamed [ɪnˈfleɪmd] adj infiammato(a).
inflammable [ɪnˈflæməbl] adj infiammabile.
inflammation [ɪnfləˈmeɪʃən] n
infiammazione f.
inflammatory [ɪnˈflæmətərɪ] adj (speech)
incendiario(a).
inflatable [ɪnˈfleɪtəbl] adj gonfiabile.
inflate [ɪnˈfleɪt] vt (tyre, balloon) gonfiare;
(fig) esagerare; gonfiare; **to ~ the
currency** far ricorso all'inflazione.
inflated [ɪnˈfleɪtɪd] adj (style) gonfio(a);
(value) esagerato(a).
inflation [ɪnˈfleɪʃən] n (ECON) inflazione f.
inflationary [ɪnˈfleɪʃənərɪ] adj
inflazionistico(a).
inflexible [ɪnˈflɛksɪbl] adj inflessibile,
rigido(a).
inflict [ɪnˈflɪkt] vt: **to ~ on** infliggere a.
infliction [ɪnˈflɪkʃən] n inflizione f; afflizione
f.
in-flight [ˈɪnflaɪt] adj a bordo.
inflow [ˈɪnfləu] n afflusso.
influence [ˈɪnfluəns] n influenza ♦ vt
influenzare; **under the ~ of** sotto
l'influenza di; **under the ~ of drink** sotto
l'influenza or l'effetto dell'alcool.
influential [ɪnfluˈɛnʃl] adj influente.
influenza [ɪnfluˈɛnzə] n (MED) influenza.
influx [ˈɪnflʌks] n afflusso.
inform [ɪnˈfɔːm] vt: **to ~ sb (of)** informare
qn (di) ♦ vi: **to ~ on sb** denunciare qn; **to
~ sb about** mettere qn al corrente di.
informal [ɪnˈfɔːml] adj (person, manner) alla
buona, semplice; (visit, discussion)
informale; (announcement, invitation) non
ufficiale; **"dress ~"** "non è richiesto
l'abito scuro"; **~ language** linguaggio
colloquiale.
informality [ɪnfɔːˈmælɪtɪ] n semplicità,
informalità; carattere m non ufficiale.
informally [ɪnˈfɔːməlɪ] adv senza cerimonie;
(invite) in modo non ufficiale.
informant [ɪnˈfɔːmənt] n informatore/trice.
informatics [ɪnfəˈmætɪks] n informatica.
information [ɪnfəˈmeɪʃən] n informazioni
fpl; particolari mpl; **to get ~ on** informarsi
su; **a piece of ~** un'informazione; **for your
~** a titolo d'informazione, per sua
informazione.
information bureau n ufficio m
informazioni inv.
information processing n elaborazione f
delle informazioni.
information retrieval n ricupero delle
informazioni.
information technology (IT) n

informatica.
informative [ɪnˈfɔːmətɪv] adj istruttivo(a).
informed [ɪnˈfɔːmd] adj (observer) (ben)
informato(a); **an ~ guess** un'ipotesi
fondata.
informer [ɪnˈfɔːmə*] n informatore/trice.
infra dig [ˈɪnfrəˈdɪg] adj abbr (col: = infra
dignitatem: beneath one's dignity)
indecoroso(a).
infra-red [ɪnfrəˈrɛd] adj infrarosso(a).
infrastructure [ˈɪnfrəstrʌktʃə*] n
infrastruttura.
infrequent [ɪnˈfriːkwənt] adj infrequente,
raro(a).
infringe [ɪnˈfrɪndʒ] vt infrangere ♦ vi: **to ~
on** calpestare.
infringement [ɪnˈfrɪndʒmənt] n: **~ (of)**
infrazione f (di).
infuriate [ɪnˈfjuərɪeɪt] vt rendere
furioso(a).
infuriating [ɪnˈfjuərɪeɪtɪŋ] adj molto
irritante.
infuse [ɪnˈfjuːz] vt (with courage,
enthusiasm): **to ~ sb with sth** infondere
qc a qn, riempire qn di qc.
infusion [ɪnˈfjuːʒən] n (tea etc) infuso,
infusione f.
ingenious [ɪnˈdʒiːnjəs] adj ingegnoso(a).
ingenuity [ɪndʒɪˈnjuːɪtɪ] n ingegnosità.
ingenuous [ɪnˈdʒɛnjuəs] adj ingenuo(a).
ingot [ˈɪŋgət] n lingotto.
ingrained [ɪnˈgreɪnd] adj radicato(a).
ingratiate [ɪnˈgreɪʃɪeɪt] vt: **to ~ o.s. with sb**
ingraziarsi qn.
ingratiating [ɪnˈgreɪʃɪeɪtɪŋ] adj (smile,
speech) suadente, cattivante; (person)
compiacente.
ingratitude [ɪnˈgrætɪtjuːd] n ingratitudine f.
ingredient [ɪnˈgriːdɪənt] n ingrediente m;
elemento.
ingrowing [ˈɪngrəuɪŋ], **ingrown** [ˈɪngrəun]
adj: **~ (toe)nail** unghia incarnita.
inhabit [ɪnˈhæbɪt] vt abitare.
inhabitable [ɪnˈhæbɪtəbl] adj abitabile.
inhabitant [ɪnˈhæbɪtnt] n abitante m/f.
inhale [ɪnˈheɪl] vt inalare ♦ vi (in smoking)
aspirare.
inhaler [ɪnˈheɪlə*] n inalatore m.
inherent [ɪnˈhɪərənt] adj: **~ (in or to)**
inerente (a).
inherently [ɪnˈhɪərəntlɪ] adv (easy, difficult)
di per sé, di per se stesso(a); **~ lazy** pigro
di natura.
inherit [ɪnˈhɛrɪt] vt ereditare.
inheritance [ɪnˈhɛrɪtəns] n eredità.
inhibit [ɪnˈhɪbɪt] vt (PSYCH) inibire; **to ~ sb
from doing** impedire a qn di fare.
inhibited [ɪnˈhɪbɪtɪd] adj (person) inibito(a).

inhibiting [ɪn'hɪbɪtɪŋ] *adj* che inibisce.
inhibition [ɪnhɪ'bɪʃən] *n* inibizione *f.*
inhospitable [ɪnhɔs'pɪtəbl] *adj* inospitale.
in-house ['ɪn'haus] *adj* effettuato(a) da personale interno, interno(a) ♦ *adv* (*training*) all'interno dell'azienda.
inhuman [ɪn'hjuːmən] *adj* inumano(a), disumano(a).
inhumane [ɪnhjuː'meɪn] *adj* inumano(a), disumano(a).
inimitable [ɪ'nɪmɪtəbl] *adj* inimitabile.
iniquity [ɪ'nɪkwɪtɪ] *n* iniquità *f inv.*
initial [ɪ'nɪʃl] *adj* iniziale ♦ *n* iniziale *f* ♦ *vt* siglare; ~**s** *npl* iniziali *fpl*; (*as signature*) sigla.
initialize [ɪ'nɪʃəlaɪz] *vt* (*COMPUT*) inizializzare.
initially [ɪ'nɪʃəlɪ] *adv* inizialmente, all'inizio.
initiate [ɪ'nɪʃɪeɪt] *vt* (*start*) avviare; intraprendere; iniziare; (*person*) iniziare; **to ~ sb into sth** iniziare qn a qc; **to ~ proceedings against sb** (*LAW*) intentare causa *a or* contro qn.
initiation [ɪnɪʃɪ'eɪʃən] *n* iniziazione *f.*
initiative [ɪ'nɪʃətɪv] *n* iniziativa; **to take the ~** prendere l'iniziativa.
inject [ɪn'dʒɛkt] *vt* (*liquid*) iniettare; (*person*) fare una puntura a; (*fig: money*): **to ~ into** immettere in.
injection [ɪn'dʒɛkʃən] *n* iniezione *f*, puntura; **to have an ~** farsi fare un'iniezione *or* una puntura.
injudicious [ɪndʒu'dɪʃəs] *adj* poco saggio(a).
injunction [ɪn'dʒʌŋkʃən] *n* (*LAW*) ingiunzione *f*, intimazione *f.*
injure ['ɪndʒə*] *vt* ferire; (*wrong*) fare male *or* torto a; (*damage: reputation etc*) nuocere a; (*feelings*) offendere; **to ~ o.s.** farsi male.
injured ['ɪndʒəd] *adj* (*person, leg etc*) ferito(a); (*tone, feelings*) offeso(a); ~ **party** (*LAW*) parte *f* lesa.
injurious [ɪn'dʒuərɪəs] *adj*: ~ (**to**) nocivo(a) (a), pregiudizievole (per).
injury ['ɪndʒərɪ] *n* ferita; (*wrong*) torto; **to escape without ~** rimanere illeso.
injury time *n* (*SPORT*) tempo di recupero.
injustice [ɪn'dʒʌstɪs] *n* ingiustizia; **you do me an ~** mi fa un torto, è ingiusto verso di me.
ink [ɪŋk] *n* inchiostro.
ink-jet printer ['ɪŋkdʒɛt-] *n* stampante *f* a getto d'inchiostro.
inkling ['ɪŋklɪŋ] *n* sentore *m*, vaga idea.
inkpad ['ɪŋkpæd] *n* tampone *m*, cuscinetto per timbri.
inky ['ɪŋkɪ] *adj* macchiato(a) *or* sporco(a) d'inchiostro.

inlaid ['ɪnleɪd] *adj* incrostato(a); (*table etc*) intarsiato(a).
inland *adj* ['ɪnlənd] interno(a) ♦ *adv* [ɪn'lænd] all'interno; ~ **waterways** canali e fiumi *mpl* navigabili.
Inland Revenue *n* (*BRIT*) Fisco.
in-laws ['ɪnlɔːz] *npl* suoceri *mpl*; famiglia del marito (*or* della moglie).
inlet ['ɪnlɛt] *n* (*GEO*) insenatura, baia.
inlet pipe *n* (*TECH*) tubo d'immissione.
inmate ['ɪnmeɪt] *n* (*in prison*) carcerato/a; (*in asylum*) ricoverato/a.
inmost ['ɪnməust] *adj* più profondo(a), più intimo(a).
inn [ɪn] *n* locanda.
innards ['ɪnədz] *npl* (*col*) interiora *fpl*, budella *fpl.*
innate [ɪ'neɪt] *adj* innato(a).
inner ['ɪnə*] *adj* interno(a), interiore.
inner city *n* centro di una zona urbana.
innermost ['ɪnəməust] *adj* = **inmost**.
inner tube *n* camera d'aria.
innings ['ɪnɪŋz] *n* (*CRICKET*) turno di battuta; (*BRIT fig*): **he has had a good ~** ha avuto molto dalla vita.
innocence ['ɪnəsns] *n* innocenza.
innocent ['ɪnəsnt] *adj* innocente.
innocuous [ɪ'nɔkjuəs] *adj* innocuo(a).
innovation [ɪnəu'veɪʃən] *n* innovazione *f.*
innuendo, ~**es** [ɪnju'ɛndəu] *n* insinuazione *f.*
innumerable [ɪ'njuːmrəbl] *adj* innumerevole.
inoculate [ɪ'nɔkjuleɪt] *vt*: **to ~ sb with sth/ against sth** inoculare qc a qn/qn contro qc.
inoculation [ɪnɔkju'leɪʃən] *n* inoculazione *f.*
inoffensive [ɪnə'fɛnsɪv] *adj* inoffensivo(a), innocuo(a).
inopportune [ɪn'ɔpətjuːn] *adj* inopportuno(a).
inordinate [ɪ'nɔːdɪnɪt] *adj* eccessivo(a).
inordinately [ɪ'nɔːdɪnətlɪ] *adv* smoderatamente.
inorganic [ɪnɔː'gænɪk] *adj* inorganico(a).
in-patient ['ɪnpeɪʃənt] *n* ricoverato/a.
input ['ɪnput] *n* (*ELEC*) energia, potenza; (*of machine*) alimentazione *f*; (*of computer*) input *m* ♦ *vt* (*COMPUT*) inserire, introdurre.
inquest ['ɪnkwɛst] *n* inchiesta.
inquire [ɪn'kwaɪə*] *vi* informarsi ♦ *vt* domandare, informarsi *or* su; **to ~ about** informarsi di *or* su, chiedere informazioni su; **to ~ when/where/ whether** informarsi di quando/su dove/ se.
▶**inquire after** *vt fus* (*person*) chiedere di;

(*sb's health*) informarsi di.
▶**inquire into** *vt fus* indagare su, fare delle indagini *or* ricerche su.
inquiring [ɪnˈkwaɪərɪŋ] *adj* (*mind*) inquisitivo(a).
inquiry [ɪnˈkwaɪərɪ] *n* domanda; (*LAW*) indagine *f*, investigazione *f*; **to hold an ~ into sth** fare un'inchiesta su qc.
inquiry desk *n* (*BRIT*) banco delle informazioni.
inquiry office *n* (*BRIT*) ufficio *m* informazioni *inv.*
inquisition [ɪnkwɪˈzɪʃən] *n* inquisizione *f*, inchiesta; (*REL*): **the** ~ l'Inquisizione.
inquisitive [ɪnˈkwɪzɪtɪv] *adj* curioso(a).
inroads [ˈɪnrəudz] *npl*: **to make ~ into** (*savings, supplies*) intaccare (seriamente).
insane [ɪnˈseɪn] *adj* matto(a), pazzo(a); (*MED*) alienato(a).
insanitary [ɪnˈsænɪtərɪ] *adj* insalubre.
insanity [ɪnˈsænɪtɪ] *n* follia; (*MED*) alienazione *f* mentale.
insatiable [ɪnˈseɪʃəbl] *adj* insaziabile.
inscribe [ɪnˈskraɪb] *vt* iscrivere; (*book etc*): **to ~ (to sb)** dedicare (a qn).
inscription [ɪnˈskrɪpʃən] *n* iscrizione *f*; (*in book*) dedica.
inscrutable [ɪnˈskruːtəbl] *adj* imperscrutabile.
inseam [ˈɪnsiːm] *n* (*US*): **~ measurement** lunghezza interna.
insect [ˈɪnsɛkt] *n* insetto.
insect bite *n* puntura *or* morsicatura di insetto.
insecticide [ɪnˈsɛktɪsaɪd] *n* insetticida *m*.
insect repellent *n* insettifugo.
insecure [ɪnsɪˈkjuə*] *adj* malsicuro(a); (*person*) insicuro(a).
insecurity [ɪnsɪˈkjuərɪtɪ] *n* mancanza di sicurezza.
insensible [ɪnˈsɛnsɪbl] *adj* insensibile; (*unconscious*) privo(a) di sensi.
insensitive [ɪnˈsɛnsɪtɪv] *adj* insensibile.
insensitivity [ɪnsɛnsɪˈtɪvɪtɪ] *n* mancanza di sensibilità.
inseparable [ɪnˈsɛprəbl] *adj* inseparabile.
insert *vt* [ɪnˈsəːt] inserire, introdurre ♦ *n* [ˈɪnsəːt] inserto.
insertion [ɪnˈsəːʃən] *n* inserzione *f*.
in-service [ˈɪnˈsəːvɪs] *adj* (*course, training*) dopo l'assunzione.
inshore [ɪnˈʃɔː*] *adj* costiero(a) ♦ *adv* presso la riva; verso la riva.
inside [ˈɪnˈsaɪd] *n* interno, parte *f* interiore; (*of road*: *BRIT*) sinistra; (: *US, in Europe etc*) destra ♦ *adj* interno(a), interiore ♦ *adv* dentro, all'interno ♦ *prep* dentro, all'interno di; (*of time*): **~ 10 minutes**

entro 10 minuti; **~s** *npl* (*col*) ventre *m*; **~ out** *adv* alla rovescia; **to turn sth ~ out** rivoltare qc; **to know sth ~ out** conoscere qc a fondo; **~ information** informazioni *fpl* riservate; **~ story** storia segreta.
inside forward *n* (*SPORT*) mezzala, interno.
inside lane *n* (*AUT*) corsia di marcia.
inside leg measurement *n* (*BRIT*) lunghezza interna.
insider [ɪnˈsaɪdə*] *n* uno(a) che ha le mani in pasta.
insider dealing, insider trading *n* (*STOCK EXCHANGE*) insider trading *m inv.*
insidious [ɪnˈsɪdɪəs] *adj* insidioso(a).
insight [ˈɪnsaɪt] *n* acume *m*, perspicacia; (*glimpse, idea*) percezione *f*; **to gain** *or* **get an ~ into sth** potersi render conto di qc.
insignia [ɪnˈsɪgnɪə] *npl* insegne *fpl.*
insignificant [ɪnsɪgˈnɪfɪknt] *adj* insignificante.
insincere [ɪnsɪnˈsɪə*] *adj* insincero(a).
insincerity [ɪnsɪnˈsɛrɪtɪ] *n* falsità, insincerità.
insinuate [ɪnˈsɪnjueɪt] *vt* insinuare.
insinuation [ɪnsɪnjuˈeɪʃən] *n* insinuazione *f*.
insipid [ɪnˈsɪpɪd] *adj* insipido(a), insulso(a).
insist [ɪnˈsɪst] *vi* insistere; **to ~ on doing** insistere per fare; **to ~ that** insistere perché + *sub*; (*claim*) sostenere che.
insistence [ɪnˈsɪstəns] *n* insistenza.
insistent [ɪnˈsɪstənt] *adj* insistente.
insofar [ɪnsəuˈfɑː*] *conj*: **~ as** in quanto.
insole [ˈɪnsəul] *n* soletta; (*fixed part of shoe*) tramezza.
insolence [ˈɪnsələns] *n* insolenza.
insolent [ˈɪnsələnt] *adj* insolente.
insoluble [ɪnˈsɔljubl] *adj* insolubile.
insolvency [ɪnˈsɔlvənsɪ] *n* insolvenza.
insolvent [ɪnˈsɔlvənt] *adj* insolvente.
insomnia [ɪnˈsɔmnɪə] *n* insonnia.
insomniac [ɪnˈsɔmnɪæk] *n* chi soffre di insonnia.
inspect [ɪnˈspɛkt] *vt* ispezionare; (*BRIT*: *ticket*) controllare.
inspection [ɪnˈspɛkʃən] *n* ispezione *f*; controllo.
inspector [ɪnˈspɛktə*] *n* ispettore/trice; controllore *m*.
inspiration [ɪnspəˈreɪʃən] *n* ispirazione *f*.
inspire [ɪnˈspaɪə*] *vt* ispirare.
inspired [ɪnˈspaɪəd] *adj* (*writer, book etc*) ispirato(a); **in an ~ moment** in un momento d'ispirazione.
inspiring [ɪnˈspaɪərɪŋ] *adj* stimolante.
inst. [ɪnst] *abbr* (*BRIT COMM*: = *instant*) c.m. (=*corrente mese*).

instability [ɪnstə'bɪlɪtɪ] *n* instabilità.
install [ɪn'stɔːl] *vt* installare.
installation [ɪnstə'leɪʃən] *n* installazione *f*.
installment plan *n* (*US*) acquisto a rate.
instalment, (*US*) **installment**
[ɪn'stɔːlmənt] *n* rata; (*of TV serial etc*)
puntata; **to pay in ~s** pagare a rate.
instance ['ɪnstəns] *n* esempio, caso; **for ~**
per *or* ad esempio; **in that ~** in quel caso;
in the first ~ in primo luogo.
instant ['ɪnstənt] *n* istante *m*, attimo ♦ *adj*
immediato(a); urgente; (*coffee, food*) in
polvere; **the 10th ~** il 10 corrente (mese).
instantaneous [ɪnstən'teɪnɪəs] *adj*
istantaneo(a).
instantly ['ɪnstəntlɪ] *adv* immediatamente,
subito.
instant replay *n* (*US TV*) replay *m inv*.
instead [ɪn'stɛd] *adv* invece; **~ of** invece di;
~ of sb al posto di qn.
instep ['ɪnstɛp] *n* collo del piede; (*of shoe*)
collo della scarpa.
instigate ['ɪnstɪgeɪt] *vt* (*rebellion, strike,
crime*) istigare a; (*new ideas etc*)
promuovere.
instigation [ɪnstɪ'geɪʃən] *n* istigazione *f*; **at
sb's ~** per *or* in seguito al suggerimento
di qn.
instil [ɪn'stɪl] *vt*: **to ~ (into)** inculcare (in).
instinct ['ɪnstɪŋkt] *n* istinto.
instinctive [ɪn'stɪŋktɪv] *adj* istintivo(a).
instinctively [ɪn'stɪŋktɪvlɪ] *adv* per istinto.
institute ['ɪnstɪtjuːt] *n* istituto ♦ *vt* istituire,
stabilire; (*inquiry*) avviare; (*proceedings*)
iniziare.
institution [ɪnstɪ'tjuːʃən] *n* istituzione *f*;
istituto (d'istruzione); istituto
(psichiatrico).
institutional [ɪnstɪ'tjuːʃənl] *adj*
istituzionale; **~ care** assistenza presso un
istituto.
instruct [ɪn'strʌkt] *vt* istruire; **to ~ sb in
sth** insegnare qc a qn; **to ~ sb to do** dare
ordini a qn di fare.
instruction [ɪn'strʌkʃən] *n* istruzione *f*; **~s
(for use)** istruzioni per l'uso.
instruction book *n* libretto di istruzioni.
instructive [ɪn'strʌktɪv] *adj* istruttivo(a).
instructor [ɪn'strʌktə*] *n* istruttore/trice;
(*for skiing*) maestro/a.
instrument ['ɪnstrumənt] *n* strumento.
instrumental [ɪnstru'mɛntl] *adj* (*MUS*)
strumentale; **to be ~ in sth/in doing sth**
avere un ruolo importante in qc/nel fare
qc.
instrumentalist [ɪnstru'mɛntəlɪst] *n*
strumentista *m/f*.
instrument panel *n* quadro *m*

portastrumenti *inv*.
insubordinate [ɪnsə'bɔːdənɪt] *adj*
insubordinato(a).
insubordination [ɪnsəbɔːdə'neɪʃən] *n*
insubordinazione *f*.
insufferable [ɪn'sʌfrəbl] *adj* insopportabile.
insufficient [ɪnsə'fɪʃənt] *adj* insufficiente.
insufficiently [ɪnsə'fɪʃəntlɪ] *adv* in modo
insufficiente.
insular ['ɪnsjulə*] *adj* insulare; (*person*) di
mente ristretta.
insulate ['ɪnsjuleɪt] *vt* isolare.
insulating tape ['ɪnsjuleɪtɪŋ-] *n* nastro
isolante.
insulation [ɪnsju'leɪʃən] *n* isolamento.
insulin ['ɪnsjulɪn] *n* insulina.
insult *n* ['ɪnsʌlt] insulto, affronto ♦ *vt*
[ɪn'sʌlt] insultare.
insulting [ɪn'sʌltɪŋ] *adj* offensivo(a),
ingiurioso(a).
insuperable [ɪn'sjuːprəbl] *adj*
insormontabile, insuperabile.
insurance [ɪn'ʃuərəns] *n* assicurazione *f*;
fire/life ~ assicurazione contro gli
incendi/sulla vita; **to take out ~ (against)**
fare un'assicurazione (contro),
assicurarsi (contro).
insurance agent *n* agente *m*
d'assicurazioni.
insurance broker *n* broker *m inv*
d'assicurazioni.
insurance policy *n* polizza
d'assicurazione.
insurance premium *n* premio
assicurativo.
insure [ɪn'ʃuə*] *vt* assicurare; **to ~ sb** *or*
sb's life assicurare qn sulla vita; **to be ~d
for £5000** essere assicurato per 5000
sterline.
insured [ɪn'ʃuəd] *n*: **the ~** l'assicurato/a.
insurer [ɪn'ʃuərə*] *n* assicuratore/trice.
insurgent [ɪn'sɜːdʒənt] *adj* ribelle ♦ *n*
insorto/a, rivoltoso/a.
insurmountable [ɪnsə'mauntəbl] *adj*
insormontabile.
insurrection [ɪnsə'rɛkʃən] *n* insurrezione *f*.
intact [ɪn'tækt] *adj* intatto(a).
intake ['ɪnteɪk] *n* (*TECH*) immissione *f*; (*of
food*) consumo; (*of pupils etc*) afflusso.
intangible [ɪn'tændʒɪbl] *adj* intangibile.
integral ['ɪntɪgrəl] *adj* integrale; (*part*)
integrante.
integrate ['ɪntɪgreɪt] *vt* integrare.
integrated circuit *n* (*COMPUT*) circuito
integrato.
integration [ɪntɪ'greɪʃən] *n* integrazione *f*;
racial ~ integrazione razziale.
integrity [ɪn'tɛgrɪtɪ] *n* integrità.

intellect ['ɪntəlɛkt] n intelletto.
intellectual [ɪntə'lɛktjuəl] adj, n intellettuale (m/f).
intelligence [ɪn'tɛlɪdʒəns] n intelligenza; (MIL etc) informazioni fpl.
intelligence quotient (IQ) n quoziente m d'intelligenza (Q.I.).
Intelligence Service n servizio segreto.
intelligence test n test m inv d'intelligenza.
intelligent [ɪn'tɛlɪdʒənt] adj intelligente.
intelligible [ɪn'tɛlɪdʒɪbl] adj intelligibile.
intemperate [ɪn'tɛmpərət] adj immoderato(a); (drinking too much) intemperante nel bere.
intend [ɪn'tɛnd] vt (gift etc): **to ~ sth for** destinare qc a; **to ~ to do** aver l'intenzione di fare.
intended [ɪn'tɛndɪd] adj (insult) intenzionale; (effect) voluto(a); (journey, route) progettato(a).
intense [ɪn'tɛns] adj intenso(a); (person) di forti sentimenti.
intensely [ɪn'tɛnslɪ] adv intensamente; profondamente.
intensify [ɪn'tɛnsɪfaɪ] vt intensificare.
intensity [ɪn'tɛnsɪtɪ] n intensità.
intensive [ɪn'tɛnsɪv] adj intensivo(a).
intensive care n terapia intensiva; **~ unit (ICU)** n reparto terapia intensiva.
intent [ɪn'tɛnt] n intenzione f ♦ adj: **~ (on)** intento(a) (a), immerso(a) (in); **to all ~s and purposes** a tutti gli effetti; **to be ~ on doing sth** essere deciso a fare qc.
intention [ɪn'tɛnʃən] n intenzione f.
intentional [ɪn'tɛnʃənl] adj intenzionale, deliberato(a).
intentionally [ɪn'tɛnʃənəlɪ] adv apposta.
intently [ɪn'tɛntlɪ] adv attentamente.
inter [ɪn'təː*] vt sotterrare.
interact [ɪntər'ækt] vi agire reciprocamente, interagire.
interaction [ɪntər'ækʃən] n azione f reciproca, interazione f.
interactive [ɪntər'æktɪv] adj interattivo(a).
intercede [ɪntə'siːd] vi: **to ~ (with sb/on behalf of sb)** intercedere (presso qn/a favore di qn).
intercept [ɪntə'sɛpt] vt intercettare; (person) fermare.
interception [ɪntə'sɛpʃən] n intercettamento.
interchange n ['ɪntətʃeɪndʒ] (exchange) scambio; (on motorway) incrocio pluridirezionale ♦ vt [ɪntə'tʃeɪndʒ] scambiare; sostituire l'uno(a) per l'altro(a).
interchangeable [ɪntə'tʃeɪndʒəbl] adj

intercambiabile.
intercity [ɪntə'sɪtɪ] adj: **~ (train)** ≈ (treno) rapido.
intercom ['ɪntəkɔm] n interfono.
interconnect [ɪntəkə'nɛkt] vi (rooms) essere in comunicazione.
intercontinental ['ɪntəkɔntɪ'nɛntl] adj intercontinentale.
intercourse ['ɪntəkɔːs] n rapporti mpl; (sexual ~) rapporti sessuali.
interdependent [ɪntədɪ'pɛndənt] adj interdipendente.
interest ['ɪntrɪst] n interesse m; (COMM: stake, share) interessi mpl ♦ vt interessare; **compound/simple ~** interesse composto/semplice; **business ~s** attività fpl commerciali; **British ~s in the Middle East** gli interessi (commerciali) britannici nel Medio Oriente.
interested ['ɪntrɪstɪd] adj interessato(a); **to be ~ in** interessarsi di.
interest-free ['ɪntrɪst'friː] adj senza interesse.
interesting ['ɪntrɪstɪŋ] adj interessante.
interest rate n tasso di interesse.
interface ['ɪntəfeɪs] n (COMPUT) interfaccia.
interfere [ɪntə'fɪə*] vi: **to ~ in** (quarrel, other people's business) immischiarsi (in); **to ~ with** (object) toccare; (plans) ostacolare; (duty) interferire con.
interference [ɪntə'fɪərəns] n interferenza.
interfering [ɪntə'fɪərɪŋ] adj invadente.
interim ['ɪntərɪm] adj provvisorio(a) ♦ n: **in the ~** nel frattempo; **~ dividend** (COMM) acconto di dividendo.
interior [ɪn'tɪərɪə*] n interno; (of country) entroterra ♦ adj interiore, interno(a).
interior decorator, interior designer n decoratore/trice (d'interni).
interjection [ɪntə'dʒɛkʃən] n interiezione f.
interlock [ɪntə'lɔk] vi ingranarsi ♦ vt ingranare.
interloper ['ɪntələupə*] n intruso/a.
interlude ['ɪntəluːd] n intervallo; (THEAT) intermezzo.
intermarry [ɪntə'mærɪ] vi imparentarsi per mezzo di matrimonio; sposarsi tra parenti.
intermediary [ɪntə'miːdɪərɪ] n intermediario/a.
intermediate [ɪntə'miːdɪət] adj intermedio(a); (SCOL: course, level) medio(a).
interment [ɪn'təːmənt] n (formal) inumazione f.
interminable [ɪn'təːmɪnəbl] adj interminabile.
intermission [ɪntə'mɪʃən] n pausa; (THEAT,

CINE) intermissione *f*, intervallo.

intermittent [ɪntə'mɪtnt] *adj* intermittente.

intermittently [ɪntə'mɪtntlɪ] *adv* a intermittenza.

intern *vt* [ɪn'tə:n] internare ♦ *n* ['ɪntə:n] (*US*) medico interno.

internal [ɪn'tə:nl] *adj* interno(a); ~ **injuries** lesioni *fpl* interne.

internally [ɪn'tə:nəlɪ] *adv* all'interno; "**not to be taken ~**" "per uso esterno".

Internal Revenue (Service) (IRS) *n* (*US*) Fisco.

international [ɪntə'næʃənl] *adj* internazionale ♦ *n* (*BRIT SPORT*) partita internazionale.

International Atomic Energy Agency (IAEA) *n* Agenzia Internazionale per l'Energia Atomica (IAEA).

International Court of Justice (ICJ) *n* Corte *f* Internazionale di Giustizia.

international date line *n* linea del cambiamento di data.

internationally [ɪntə'næʃnəlɪ] *adv* a livello internazionale.

International Monetary Fund (IMF) *n* Fondo monetario internazionale (F.M.I.).

international relations *npl* rapporti *mpl* internazionali.

internecine [ɪntə'ni:saɪn] *adj* sanguinoso(a).

internee [ɪntə:'ni:] *n* internato/a.

internment [ɪn'tə:nmənt] *n* internamento.

interplay ['ɪntəpleɪ] *n* azione e reazione *f*.

Interpol ['ɪntəpɔl] *n* Interpol *f*.

interpret [ɪn'tə:prɪt] *vt* interpretare ♦ *vi* fare da interprete.

interpretation [ɪntə:prɪ'teɪʃən] *n* interpretazione *f*.

interpreter [ɪn'tə:prɪtə*] *n* interprete *m/f*.

interpreting [ɪn'tə:prɪtɪŋ] *n* (*profession*) interpretariato.

interrelated [ɪntərɪ'leɪtɪd] *adj* correlato(a).

interrogate [ɪn'tɛrəugeɪt] *vt* interrogare.

interrogation [ɪntɛrəu'geɪʃən] *n* interrogazione *f*; (*of suspect etc*) interrogatorio.

interrogative [ɪntə'rɔgətɪv] *adj* interrogativo(a) ♦ *n* (*LING*) interrogativo.

interrogator [ɪn'tɛrəgeɪtə*] *n* interrogante *m/f*.

interrupt [ɪntə'rʌpt] *vt* interrompere.

interruption [ɪntə'rʌpʃən] *n* interruzione *f*.

intersect [ɪntə'sɛkt] *vt* intersecare ♦ *vi* (*roads*) intersecarsi.

intersection [ɪntə'sɛkʃən] *n* intersezione *f*; (*of roads*) incrocio.

intersperse [ɪntə'spə:s] *vt*: **to ~ with** costellare di.

intertwine [ɪntə'twaɪn] *vt* intrecciare ♦ *vi* intrecciarsi.

interval ['ɪntəvl] *n* intervallo; (*BRIT SCOL*) ricreazione *f*, intervallo; **bright ~s** (*in weather*) schiarite *fpl*; **at ~s** a intervalli.

intervene [ɪntə'vi:n] *vi* (*time*) intercorrere; (*event, person*) intervenire.

intervention [ɪntə'vɛnʃən] *n* intervento.

interview ['ɪntəvju:] *n* (*RADIO, TV etc*) intervista; (*for job*) colloquio ♦ *vt* intervistare; avere un colloquio con.

interviewee [ɪntəvju'i:] *n* (*TV*) intervistato/a; (*for job*) chi si presenta ad un colloquio di lavoro.

interviewer ['ɪntəvju:ə*] *n* intervistatore/trice.

intestate [ɪn'tɛsteɪt] *adj* intestato(a).

intestinal [ɪn'tɛstɪnl] *adj* intestinale.

intestine [ɪn'tɛstɪn] *n* intestino; **large/small ~** intestino crasso/tenue.

intimacy ['ɪntɪməsɪ] *n* intimità.

intimate *adj* ['ɪntɪmət] intimo(a); (*knowledge*) profondo(a) ♦ *vt* ['ɪntɪmeɪt] lasciar capire.

intimately ['ɪntɪmɪtlɪ] *adv* intimamente.

intimation [ɪntɪ'meɪʃən] *n* annuncio.

intimidate [ɪn'tɪmɪdeɪt] *vt* intimidire, intimorire.

intimidation [ɪntɪmɪ'deɪʃən] *n* intimidazione *f*.

into ['ɪntu] *prep* dentro, in; **come ~ the house** vieni dentro la casa; **~ pieces** a pezzi; **~ Italian** in italiano; **to change pounds ~ dollars** cambiare delle sterline in dollari.

intolerable [ɪn'tɔlərəbl] *adj* intollerabile.

intolerance [ɪn'tɔlərns] *n* intolleranza.

intolerant [ɪn'tɔlərnt] *adj*: ~ **(of)** intollerante (di).

intonation [ɪntəu'neɪʃən] *n* intonazione *f*.

intoxicate [ɪn'tɔksɪkeɪt] *vt* inebriare.

intoxicated [ɪn'tɔksɪkeɪtɪd] *adj* inebriato(a).

intoxication [ɪntɔksɪ'keɪʃən] *n* ebbrezza.

intractable [ɪn'træktəbl] *adj* intrattabile; (*illness*) difficile da curare; (*problem*) insolubile.

intransigence [ɪn'trænsɪdʒəns] *n* intransigenza.

intransigent [ɪn'trænsɪdʒənt] *adj* intransigente.

intransitive [ɪn'trænsɪtɪv] *adj* intransitivo(a).

intra-uterine device (IUD) [ɪntrə'ju:təraɪn-] *n* dispositivo intrauterino (IUD).

intravenous [ɪntrə'vi:nəs] *adj* endovenoso(a).

in-tray ['ɪntreɪ] *n* raccoglitore *m* per le carte in arrivo.

intrepid [ɪn'trepɪd] *adj* intrepido(a).
intricacy ['ɪntrɪkəsɪ] *n* complessità *f inv.*
intricate ['ɪntrɪkət] *adj* intricato(a),
complicato(a).
intrigue [ɪn'triːg] *n* intrigo ♦ *vt* affascinare
♦ *vi* complottare, tramare.
intriguing [ɪn'triːgɪŋ] *adj* affascinante.
intrinsic [ɪn'trɪnsɪk] *adj* intrinseco(a).
introduce [ɪntrə'djuːs] *vt* introdurre; **to ~
sb (to sb)** presentare qn (a qn); **to ~ sb to**
(*pastime, technique*) iniziare qn a; **may I
~ ...?** permette che le presenti ...?
introduction [ɪntrə'dʌkʃən] *n* introduzione
f; (*of person*) presentazione *f*; **a letter of ~**
una lettera di presentazione.
introductory [ɪntrə'dʌktərɪ] *adj*
introduttivo(a); **an ~ offer** un'offerta di
lancio; **~ remarks** osservazioni *fpl*
preliminari.
introspection [ɪntrəu'spekʃən] *n*
introspezione *f.*
introspective [ɪntrəu'spektɪv] *adj*
introspettivo(a).
introvert ['ɪntrəuvɜːt] *adj*, *n* introverso(a).
intrude [ɪn'truːd] *vi* (*person*) intromettersi;
to ~ on (*person*) importunare; **~ on** *or*
into (*conversation*) intromettersi in; **am I
intruding?** disturbo?
intruder [ɪn'truːdə*] *n* intruso/a.
intrusion [ɪn'truːʒən] *n* intrusione *f.*
intrusive [ɪn'truːsɪv] *adj* importuno(a).
intuition [ɪntjuː'ɪʃən] *n* intuizione *f.*
intuitive [ɪn'tjuːɪtɪv] *adj* intuitivo(a);
dotato(a) di intuito.
inundate ['ɪnʌndeɪt] *vt*: **to ~ with** inondare
di.
inure [ɪn'juə*] *vt*: **to ~ (to)** assuefare (a).
invade [ɪn'veɪd] *vt* invadere.
invader [ɪn'veɪdə*] *n* invasore *m.*
invalid *n* ['ɪnvəlɪd] malato/a; (*with disability*)
invalido/a ♦ *adj* [ɪn'vælɪd] (*not valid*)
invalido(a), non valido(a).
invalidate [ɪn'vælɪdeɪt] *vt* invalidare.
invalid chair *n* (*BRIT*) sedia a rotelle.
invaluable [ɪn'væljuəbl] *adj* prezioso(a);
inestimabile.
invariable [ɪn'vɛərɪəbl] *adj* costante,
invariabile.
invariably [ɪn'vɛərɪəblɪ] *adv*
invariabilmente; **she is ~ late** è
immancabilmente in ritardo.
invasion [ɪn'veɪʒən] *n* invasione *f.*
invective [ɪn'vektɪv] *n* invettiva.
inveigle [ɪn'viːgl] *vt*: **to ~ sb into (doing)
sth** circuire qn per (fargli fare) qc.
invent [ɪn'vent] *vt* inventare.
invention [ɪn'venʃən] *n* invenzione *f.*
inventive [ɪn'ventɪv] *adj* inventivo(a).

inventiveness [ɪn'ventɪvnɪs] *n* inventiva.
inventor [ɪn'ventə*] *n* inventore *m.*
inventory ['ɪnvəntrɪ] *n* inventario.
inventory control *n* (*COMM*) controllo
delle giacenze.
inverse [ɪn'vɜːs] *adj* inverso(a) ♦ *n* inverso,
contrario; **in ~ proportion (to)** in modo
inversamente proporzionale (a).
inversely [ɪn'vɜːslɪ] *adv* inversamente.
invert [ɪn'vɜːt] *vt* invertire; (*object*)
rovesciare.
invertebrate [ɪn'vɜːtɪbrɪt] *n* invertebrato.
inverted commas [ɪn'vɜːtɪd-] *npl* (*BRIT*)
virgolette *fpl.*
invest [ɪn'vest] *vt* investire; (*fig: time, effort*)
impiegare; (*endow*): **to ~ sb with sth**
investire qn di qc ♦ *vi* fare investimenti;
to ~ in investire in, fare (degli)
investimenti in; (*acquire*) comprarsi.
investigate [ɪn'vestɪgeɪt] *vt* investigare,
indagare; (*crime*) fare indagini su.
investigation [ɪnvestɪ'geɪʃən] *n*
investigazione *f*; (*of crime*) indagine *f.*
investigative [ɪn'vestɪgətɪv] *adj*: **~
journalism** giornalismo investigativo.
investigator [ɪn'vestɪgeɪtə*] *n*
investigatore/trice; **a private ~** un
investigatore privato, un detective.
investiture [ɪn'vestɪtʃə*] *n* investitura.
investment [ɪn'vestmənt] *n* investimento.
investment income *n* reddito da
investimenti.
investment trust *n* fondo comune di
investimento.
investor [ɪn'vestə*] *n* investitore/trice;
(*shareholder*) azionista *m/f.*
inveterate [ɪn'vetərət] *adj* inveterato(a).
invidious [ɪn'vɪdɪəs] *adj* odioso(a); (*task*)
spiacevole.
invigilate [ɪn'vɪdʒɪleɪt] *vt, vi* (*BRIT SCOL*)
sorvegliare.
invigilator [ɪn'vɪdʒɪleɪtə*] *n* (*BRIT*) chi
sorveglia agli esami.
invigorating [ɪn'vɪgəreɪtɪŋ] *adj* stimolante;
vivificante.
invincible [ɪn'vɪnsɪbl] *adj* invincibile.
inviolate [ɪn'vaɪələt] *adj* inviolato(a).
invisible [ɪn'vɪzɪbl] *adj* invisibile.
invisible assets *npl* (*BRIT*) beni *mpl*
immateriali.
invisible ink *n* inchiostro simpatico.
invisible mending *n* rammendo
invisibile.
invitation [ɪnvɪ'teɪʃən] *n* invito; **by ~ only**
esclusivamente su *or* per invito; **at sb's
~** dietro invito di qn.
invite [ɪn'vaɪt] *vt* invitare; (*opinions etc*)
sollecitare; (*trouble*) provocare; **to ~ sb**

(to do) invitare qn (a fare); **to ~ sb to dinner** invitare qn a cena.
▶**invite out** *vt* invitare fuori.
▶**invite over** *vt* invitare (a casa).
inviting [ɪn'vaɪtɪŋ] *adj* invitante, attraente.
invoice ['ɪnvɔɪs] *n* fattura ♦ *vt* fatturare; **to ~ sb for goods** inviare a qn la fattura per le *or* delle merci.
invoke [ɪn'vəuk] *vt* invocare.
involuntary [ɪn'vɔləntrɪ] *adj* involontario(a).
involve [ɪn'vɔlv] *vt* (*entail*) richiedere, comportare; (*associate*): **to ~ sb (in)** implicare qn (in); coinvolgere qn (in); **to involve o.s. in sth** (*politics etc*) impegnarsi in qc.
involved [ɪn'vɔlvd] *adj* involuto(a), complesso(a); **to feel ~** sentirsi coinvolto(a); **to become ~ with sb** (*socially*) legarsi a qn; (*emotionally*) legarsi sentimentalmente a qn.
involvement [ɪn'vɔlvmənt] *n* implicazione *f*; coinvolgimento; impegno; partecipazione *f*.
invulnerable [ɪn'vʌlnərəbl] *adj* invulnerabile.
inward ['ɪnwəd] *adj* (*movement*) verso l'interno; (*thought, feeling*) interiore, intimo(a); *see also* **inward(s)**.
inwardly ['ɪnwədlɪ] *adv* (*feel, think etc*) nell'intimo, entro di sé.
inward(s) ['ɪnwəd(z)] *adv* verso l'interno.
I/O *abbr* (*COMPUT*: = *input/output*) I/O.
IOC *n abbr* (= *International Olympic Committee*) CIO *m* (= *Comitato Internazionale Olimpico*).
iodine ['aɪəudi:n] *n* iodio.
IOM *abbr* (*BRIT*) = *Isle of Man*.
ion ['aɪən] *n* ione *m*.
Ionian Sea [aɪ'əunɪən-] *n*: **the ~** il mare Ionio.
ioniser ['aɪənaɪzə*] *n* ionizzatore *m*.
iota [aɪ'əutə] *n* (*fig*) briciolo.
IOU *n abbr* (= *I owe you*) pagherò *m inv*.
IOW *abbr* (*BRIT*) = *Isle of Wight*.
IPA *n abbr* (= *International Phonetic Alphabet*) I.P.A. *m*.
IQ *n abbr* = **intelligence quotient**.
IRA *n abbr* (= *Irish Republican Army*) I.R.A. *f*; (*US*) = *individual retirement account*.
Iran [ɪ'rɑːn] *n* Iran *m*.
Iranian [ɪ'reɪnɪən] *adj* iraniano(a) ♦ *n* iraniano/a; (*LING*) iranico.
Iraq [ɪ'rɑːk] *n* Iraq *m*.
Iraqi [ɪ'rɑːkɪ] *adj* iracheno(a) ♦ *n* iracheno/a.
irascible [ɪ'ræsɪbl] *adj* irascibile.
irate [aɪ'reɪt] *adj* irato(a).

Ireland ['aɪələnd] *n* Irlanda; **Republic of ~** Repubblica d'Irlanda, Eire *f*.
iris, ~es ['aɪrɪs, -ɪz] *n* iride *f*; (*BOT*) giaggiolo, iride.
Irish ['aɪrɪʃ] *adj* irlandese ♦ *npl*: **the ~** gli Irlandesi.
Irishman ['aɪrɪʃmən] *n* irlandese *m*.
Irish Sea *n*: **the ~** il mar d'Irlanda.
Irishwoman ['aɪrɪʃwumən] *n* irlandese *f*.
irk [əːk] *vt* seccare.
irksome ['əːksəm] *adj* seccante.
IRN *n abbr* (= *Independent Radio News*) agenzia d'informazioni per la radio.
IRO *n abbr* (*US*: = *International Refugee Organization*) O.I.R. *f* (= *Organizzazione Internazionale per i Rifugiati*).
iron ['aɪən] *n* ferro; (*for clothes*) ferro da stiro ♦ *adj* di *or* in ferro ♦ *vt* (*clothes*) stirare; *see also* **irons**.
▶**iron out** *vt* (*crease*) appianare; (*fig*) spianare; far sparire.
Iron Curtain *n*: **the ~** la cortina di ferro.
iron foundry *n* fonderia.
ironic(al) [aɪ'rɔnɪk(l)] *adj* ironico(a).
ironically [aɪ'rɔnɪklɪ] *adv* ironicamente.
ironing ['aɪənɪŋ] *n* (*act*) stirare *m*; (*clothes*) roba da stirare.
ironing board *n* asse *f* da stiro.
iron lung *n* (*MED*) polmone *m* d'acciaio.
ironmonger ['aɪənmʌŋgə*] *n* (*BRIT*) negoziante *m* in ferramenta; **~'s (shop)** *n* negozio di ferramenta.
iron ore *n* minerale *m* di ferro.
irons ['aɪənz] *npl* (*chains*) catene *fpl*.
ironworks ['aɪənwəːks] *n* ferriera.
irony ['aɪrənɪ] *n* ironia.
irrational [ɪ'ræʃənl] *adj* irrazionale; irragionevole; illogico(a).
irreconcilable [ɪrɛkən'saɪləbl] *adj* irreconciliabile; (*opinion*): **~ with** inconciliabile con.
irredeemable [ɪrɪ'diːməbl] *adj* (*COMM*) irredimibile.
irrefutable [ɪrɪ'fjuːtəbl] *adj* irrefutabile.
irregular [ɪ'rɛgjulə*] *adj* irregolare.
irregularity [ɪrɛgju'lærɪtɪ] *n* irregolarità *f inv*.
irrelevance [ɪ'rɛləvəns] *n* inappropriatezza.
irrelevant [ɪ'rɛləvənt] *adj* non pertinente.
irreligious [ɪrɪ'lɪdʒəs] *adj* irreligioso(a).
irreparable [ɪ'rɛprəbl] *adj* irreparabile.
irreplaceable [ɪrɪ'pleɪsəbl] *adj* insostituibile.
irrepressible [ɪrɪ'prɛsəbl] *adj* irrefrenabile.
irreproachable [ɪrɪ'prəutʃəbl] *adj* irreprensibile.
irresistible [ɪrɪ'zɪstɪbl] *adj* irresistibile.
irresolute [ɪ'rɛzəluːt] *adj* irresoluto(a),

indeciso(a).
irrespective [ɪrɪ'spɛktɪv]: ~ **of** prep senza
riguardo a.
irresponsible [ɪrɪ'spɒnsɪbl] adj
irresponsabile.
irretrievable [ɪrɪ'triːvəbl] adj (object)
irrecuperabile; (loss, damage)
irreparabile.
irreverent [ɪ'rɛvərnt] adj irriverente.
irrevocable [ɪ'rɛvəkəbl] adj irrevocabile.
irrigate ['ɪrɪgeɪt] vt irrigare.
irrigation [ɪrɪ'geɪʃən] n irrigazione f.
irritable ['ɪrɪtəbl] adj irritabile.
irritant ['ɪrɪtənt] n sostanza irritante.
irritate ['ɪrɪteɪt] vt irritare.
irritation [ɪrɪ'teɪʃən] n irritazione f.
IRS n abbr (US) see **Internal Revenue
Service**.
is [ɪz] vb see **be**.
ISBN n abbr (= International Standard Book
Number) I.S.B.N. m.
Islam ['ɪzlɑːm] n Islam m.
island ['aɪlənd] n isola; (also: **traffic** ~)
salvagente m.
islander ['aɪləndə*] n isolano/a.
isle [aɪl] n isola.
isn't ['ɪznt] = **is not**.
isolate ['aɪsəleɪt] vt isolare.
isolated ['aɪsəleɪtɪd] adj isolato(a).
isolation [aɪsə'leɪʃən] n isolamento.
isolationism [aɪsə'leɪʃənɪzəm] n
isolazionismo.
isotope ['aɪsəutəup] n isotopo.
Israel ['ɪzreɪl] n Israele m.
Israeli [ɪz'reɪlɪ] adj, n israeliano(a).
issue ['ɪʃjuː] n questione f, problema m;
(outcome) esito, risultato; (of banknotes
etc) emissione f; (of newspaper etc)
numero; (offspring) discendenza ♦ vt
(rations, equipment) distribuire; (orders)
dare; (book) pubblicare; (banknotes,
cheques, stamps) emettere ♦ vi: **to** ~
(from) uscire (da), venir fuori (da); **at** ~
in gioco, in discussione; **to avoid the** ~
evitare la discussione; **to take** ~ **with sb
(over sth)** prendere posizione contro qn
(riguardo a qc); **to confuse** or **obscure the**
~ confondere le cose; **to make an** ~ **of
sth** fare un problema di qc; **to** ~ **sth to
sb**, ~ **sb with sth** consegnare qc a qn.
Istanbul [ɪstæn'buːl] n Istanbul f.
isthmus ['ɪsməs] n istmo.
IT n abbr see **information technology**.

—————————————————— KEYWORD

it [ɪt] pron **1** (specific: subject) esso(a) (mostly
omitted in Italian); (: direct object) lo(la), l';
(: indirect object) gli(le); **where's my book?**

— ~**'s on the table** dov'è il mio libro? — è
sulla tavola; **what is** ~**?** che cos'è?;
(what's the matter?) cosa c'è?; **where is** ~**?**
dov'è?; **I can't find** ~ non lo (or la) trovo;
give ~ **to me** dammelo (or dammela);
about/from/of ~ ne; **I spoke to him about**
~ gliene ho parlato; **what did you learn
from** ~**?** quale insegnamento ne hai
tratto?; **I'm proud of** ~ ne sono fiero; **in/
to/at** ~ ci; **put the book in** ~ mettici il
libro; **did you go to** ~**?** ci sei andato?; **I
wasn't at** ~ non c'ero; **above/over** ~
sopra; **below/under** ~ sotto; **in front of/
behind** ~ lì davanti/dietro
2 (impers): ~**'s raining** piove; ~**'s Friday
tomorrow** domani è venerdì; ~**'s 6
o'clock** sono le 6; ~**'s 2 hours on the train**
sono or ci vogliono 2 ore di treno; **who is**
~**?** — ~**'s me** chi è? — sono io.

ITA n abbr (BRIT: = initial teaching alphabet)
alfabeto fonetico semplificato per
insegnare a leggere.
Italian [ɪ'tæljən] adj italiano(a) ♦ n italiano/a;
(LING) italiano; **the** ~**s** gli Italiani.
italic [ɪ'tælɪk] adj corsivo(a); ~**s** npl corsivo.
Italy ['ɪtəlɪ] n Italia.
itch [ɪtʃ] n prurito ♦ vi (person) avere il
prurito; (part of body) prudere; **to be** ~**ing
to do** non veder l'ora di fare.
itchy ['ɪtʃɪ] adj che prude; **my back is** ~ ho
prurito alla schiena.
it'd ['ɪtd] = **it would**; **it had**.
item ['aɪtəm] n articolo; (on agenda) punto;
(in programme) numero; (also: **news** ~)
notizia; ~**s of clothing** capi mpl di
abbigliamento.
itemize ['aɪtəmaɪz] vt specificare,
dettagliare.
itemized bill ['aɪtəmaɪzd-] n conto
dettagliato.
itinerant [ɪ'tɪnərənt] adj ambulante.
itinerary [aɪ'tɪnərərɪ] n itinerario.
it'll ['ɪtl] = **it will**, **it shall**.
ITN n abbr (BRIT: = Independent Television
News) agenzia d'informazioni per la
televisione.
its [ɪts] adj, pron il(la) suo(a), i(le) suoi(sue).
it's [ɪts] = **it is**; **it has**.
itself [ɪt'sɛlf] pron (emphatic) esso(a)
stesso(a); (reflexive) si.
ITV n abbr (BRIT: = Independent Television)
rete televisiva indipendente.

La **ITV** è un'azienda televisiva privata che
comprende una serie di emittenti regionali,
la prima delle quali è stata aperta nel 1955.
Si autofinanzia tramite la pubblicità ed è

*sottoposta al controllo di un ente ufficiale,
la* **IBA**; *vedi anche* **BBC**.

IUD *n abbr* = **intra-uterine device.**
I've [aɪv] = **I have.**
ivory ['aɪvərɪ] *n* avorio.
Ivory Coast *n* Costa d'Avorio.
ivory tower *n* torre *f* d'avorio.
ivy ['aɪvɪ] *n* edera.

Ivy League *è il termine usato per indicare le
otto università più prestigiose degli Stati
Uniti nordorientali (Brown, Columbia,
Cornell, Dartmouth College, Harvard,
Princeton, University of Pennsylvania e
Yale).*

J j

J, j [dʒeɪ] *n* (*letter*) J, j *f or m inv;* **J for Jack,**
(*US*) **J for Jig** ≈ J come Jersey.
JA *n abbr see* **judge advocate.**
J/A *abbr see* **joint account.**
jab [dʒæb] *vt:* **to ~ sth into** affondare *or*
piantare qc dentro ♦ *vi:* **to ~ at** dare colpi
a ♦ *n* colpo; (*MED: col*) puntura.
jabber ['dʒæbə*] *vt, vi* borbottare.
jack [dʒæk] *n* (*AUT*) cricco; (*BOWLS*)
boccino, pallino; (*CARDS*) fante *m.*
▶**jack in** *vt* (*col*) mollare.
▶**jack up** *vt* sollevare sul cricco; (*raise:
prices etc*) alzare.
jackal ['dʒækl] *n* sciacallo.
jackass ['dʒækæs] *n* (*also fig*) asino, somaro.
jackdaw ['dʒækdɔː] *n* taccola.
jacket ['dʒækɪt] *n* giacca; (*of book*)
copertura; **potatoes in their ~s** (*BRIT*)
patate *fpl* con la buccia.
jacket potato *n patata cotta al forno con
la buccia.*
jack-in-the-box ['dʒækɪnðəbɒks] *n* scatola a
sorpresa (con pupazzo a molla).
jack-knife ['dʒæknaɪf] *vi:* **the lorry ~d**
l'autotreno si è piegato su se stesso.
jack-of-all-trades [dʒækəv'ɔːltreɪdz] *n* uno
che fa un po' di tutto.
jack plug *n* (*BRIT*) jack plug *f inv.*
jackpot ['dʒækpɒt] *n* primo premio (in
denaro).
Jacuzzi ® [dʒə'kuːzɪ] *n* vasca per

idromassaggio Jacuzzi ®.
jade [dʒeɪd] *n* (*stone*) giada.
jaded ['dʒeɪdɪd] *adj* sfinito(a), spossato(a).
jagged ['dʒægɪd] *adj* sboccencellato(a);
(*cliffs etc*) frastagliato(a).
jaguar ['dʒægjuə*] *n* giaguaro.
jail [dʒeɪl] *n* prigione *f* ♦ *vt* mandare in
prigione.
jailbird ['dʒeɪlbɜːd] *n* avanzo di galera.
jailbreak ['dʒeɪlbreɪk] *n* evasione *f.*
jailer ['dʒeɪlə*] *n* custode *m* del carcere.
jalopy [dʒə'lɒpɪ] *n* (*col*) macinino.
jam [dʒæm] *n* marmellata; (*of shoppers etc*)
ressa; (*also:* **traffic ~**) ingorgo ♦ *vt*
(*passage etc*) ingombrare, ostacolare;
(*mechanism, drawer etc*) bloccare; (*RADIO*)
disturbare con interferenze ♦ *vi*
(*mechanism, sliding part*) incepparsi,
bloccarsi; (*gun*) incepparsi; **to get sb out
of a ~** tirare qn fuori dai pasticci; **to ~**
sth into forzare qc dentro; infilare qc a
forza dentro; **the telephone lines are**
~med le linee sono sovraccariche.
Jamaica [dʒə'meɪkə] *n* Giamaica.
Jamaican [dʒə'meɪkən] *adj, n*
giamaicano(a).
jamb [dʒæm] *n* stipite *m.*
jam-packed [dʒæm'pækt] *adj:* **~ (with)**
pieno(a) zeppo(a) (di), strapieno(a)
(di).
jam session *n* improvvisazione *f*
jazzistica.
Jan. *abbr* (= *January*) gen., genn.
jangle ['dʒæŋgl] *vi* risuonare; (*bracelet*)
tintinnare.
janitor ['dʒænɪtə*] *n* (*caretaker*) portiere *m;*
(*SCOL*) bidello.
January ['dʒænjuərɪ] *n* gennaio; *for phrases
see also* **July.**
Japan [dʒə'pæn] *n* Giappone *m.*
Japanese [dʒæpə'niːz] *adj* giapponese ♦ *n* (*pl
inv*) giapponese *m/f;* (*LING*) giapponese *m.*
jar [dʒɑː*] *n* (*container*) barattolo, vasetto
♦ *vi* (*sound*) stridere; (*colours etc*)
stonare ♦ *vt* (*shake*) scuotere.
jargon ['dʒɑːgən] *n* gergo.
jarring ['dʒɑːrɪŋ] *adj* (*sound, colour*)
stonato(a).
Jas. *abbr* = *James.*
jasmin(e) ['dʒæzmɪn] *n* gelsomino.
jaundice ['dʒɔːndɪs] *n* itterizia.
jaundiced ['dʒɔːndɪst] *adj* (*fig*) invidioso(a)
e critico(a).
jaunt [dʒɔːnt] *n* gita.
jaunty ['dʒɔːntɪ] *adj* vivace; disinvolto(a),
spigliato(a).
Java ['dʒɑːvə] *n* Giava.
javelin ['dʒævlɪn] *n* giavellotto.

jaw [dʒɔː] n mascella; ~**s** (*TECH: of vice etc*) morsa.

jawbone ['dʒɔːbəun] n mandibola.

jay [dʒeɪ] n ghiandaia.

jaywalker ['dʒeɪwɔːkə*] n pedone(a) indisciplinato(a).

jazz [dʒæz] n jazz m.

▶**jazz up** vt rendere vivace.

jazz band n banda f jazz inv.

jazzy ['dʒæzɪ] adj vistoso(a), chiassoso(a).

JCB ® n scavatrice f.

JCS n abbr (*US*) = Joint Chiefs of Staff.

JD n abbr (*US*: = Doctor of Laws) titolo di studio; (: = Justice Department) ministero della Giustizia.

jealous ['dʒɛləs] adj geloso(a).

jealously ['dʒɛləslɪ] adv (enviously) con gelosia; (watchfully) gelosamente.

jealousy ['dʒɛləsɪ] n gelosia.

jeans [dʒiːnz] npl (blue-)jeans mpl.

Jeep ® [dʒiːp] n jeep m inv.

jeer [dʒɪə*] vi: **to ~ (at)** fischiare; beffeggiare; see also **jeers**.

jeering ['dʒɪərɪŋ] adj (crowd) che urla e fischia ♦ n fischi mpl; parole fpl di scherno.

jeers ['dʒɪəz] npl fischi mpl.

jelly ['dʒɛlɪ] n gelatina.

jellyfish ['dʒɛlɪfɪʃ] n medusa.

jeopardize ['dʒɛpədaɪz] vt mettere in pericolo.

jeopardy ['dʒɛpədɪ] n: **in ~** in pericolo.

jerk [dʒəːk] n sobbalzo, scossa; sussulto; (col) povero scemo ♦ vt dare una scossa a ♦ vi (vehicles) sobbalzare.

jerkin ['dʒəːkɪn] n giubbotto.

jerky ['dʒəːkɪ] adj a scatti; a sobbalzi.

jerry-built ['dʒɛrɪbɪlt] adj fatto(a) di cartapesta.

jerry can ['dʒɛrɪ-] n tanica.

Jersey ['dʒəːzɪ] n Jersey m.

jersey ['dʒəːzɪ] n maglia, jersey m.

Jerusalem [dʒə'ruːsələm] n Gerusalemme f.

jest [dʒɛst] n scherzo; **in ~** per scherzo.

jester ['dʒɛstə*] n (HISTORY) buffone m.

Jesus ['dʒiːzəs] n Gesù m; ~ **Christ** Gesù Cristo.

jet [dʒɛt] n (of gas, liquid) getto; (AUT) spruzzatore m; (AVIAT) aviogetto.

jet-black ['dʒɛt'blæk] adj nero(a) come l'ebano, corvino(a).

jet engine n motore m a reazione.

jet lag n (problemi mpl dovuti allo) sbalzo dei fusi orari.

jetsam ['dʒɛtsəm] n relitti mpl di mare.

jet-setter ['dʒɛtsɛtə*] n membro del jet set.

jettison ['dʒɛtɪsn] vt gettare in mare.

jetty ['dʒɛtɪ] n molo.

Jew [dʒuː] n ebreo.

jewel ['dʒuːəl] n gioiello.

jeweller, (US) **jeweler** ['dʒuːələ*] n orefice m, gioielliere/a; ~'**s** (**shop**) n oreficeria, gioielleria.

jewellery, (US) **jewelry** ['dʒuːəlrɪ] n gioielli mpl.

Jewess ['dʒuːɪs] n ebrea.

Jewish ['dʒuːɪʃ] adj ebreo(a), ebraico(a).

JFK n abbr (*US*) = John Fitzgerald Kennedy International Airport.

jib [dʒɪb] n (NAUT) fiocco; (of crane) braccio ♦ vi (horse) impennarsi; **to ~ at doing sth** essere restio a fare qc.

jibe [dʒaɪb] n beffa.

jiffy ['dʒɪfɪ] n (col): **in a ~** in un batter d'occhio.

jig [dʒɪg] n (dance, tune) giga.

jigsaw ['dʒɪgsɔː] n (tool) sega da traforo; (also: ~ **puzzle**) puzzle m inv.

jilt [dʒɪlt] vt piantare in asso.

jingle ['dʒɪŋgl] n (advert) sigla pubblicitaria ♦ vi tintinnare, scampanellare.

jingoism ['dʒɪŋgəʊɪzəm] n sciovinismo.

jinx [dʒɪŋks] n (col) iettatura; (person) iettatore/trice.

jitters ['dʒɪtəz] npl (col): **to get the ~** aver fifa.

jittery ['dʒɪtərɪ] adj (col) teso(a), agitato(a); **to be ~** aver fifa.

jiujitsu [dʒuː'dʒɪtsuː] n jujitsu m.

job [dʒɔb] n lavoro; (employment) impiego, posto; **a part-time/full-time ~** un lavoro a mezza giornata/a tempo pieno; **that's not my ~** non è compito mio; **he's only doing his ~** non fa che il suo dovere; **it's a good ~ that ...** meno male che ...; **just the ~!** proprio quello che ci vuole!

jobber ['dʒɔbə*] n (BRIT STOCK EXCHANGE) intermediario tra agenti di cambio.

jobbing ['dʒɔbɪŋ] adj (BRIT: workman) a ore, a giornata.

Jobcentre ['dʒɔbsɛntə*] n ufficio di collocamento.

job creation scheme n progetto per la creazione di nuovi posti di lavoro.

job description n caratteristiche fpl (di un lavoro).

jobless ['dʒɔblɪs] adj senza lavoro, disoccupato(a) ♦ npl: **the ~** i senza lavoro.

job lot n partita di articoli disparati.

job satisfaction n soddisfazione f nel lavoro.

job security n sicurezza del posto di lavoro.

job specification n caratteristiche fpl (di un lavoro).

Jock [dʒɔk] n (col) termine colloquiale per chiamare uno scozzese.

jockey ['dʒɔkɪ] *n* fantino, jockey *m inv* ♦ *vi*: **to ~ for position** manovrare per una posizione di vantaggio.

jockey box *n* (*US AUT*) vano portaoggetti.

jockstrap ['dʒɔkstræp] *n* conchiglia (*per atleti*).

jocular ['dʒɔkjulə*] *adj* gioviale; scherzoso(a).

jog [dʒɔg] *vt* urtare ♦ *vi* (*SPORT*) fare footing, fare jogging; **to ~ along** trottare; (*fig*) andare avanti pian piano; **to ~ sb's memory** stimolare la memoria di qn.

jogger ['dʒɔgə*] *n* persona che fa footing *or* jogging.

jogging ['dʒɔgɪŋ] *n* footing *m*, jogging *m*.

john [dʒɔn] *n* (*US col*): **the ~** il gabinetto.

join [dʒɔɪn] *vt* unire, congiungere; (*become member of*) iscriversi a; (*meet*) raggiungere; riunirsi a ♦ *vi* (*roads, rivers*) confluire ♦ *n* giuntura; **to ~ forces (with)** allearsi (con *or* a); (*fig*) mettersi insieme (a); **will you ~ us for dinner?** viene a cena con noi?; **I'll ~ you later** vi raggiungo più tardi.

▶**join in** *vt fus* unirsi a, prendere parte a, partecipare a ♦ *vi* partecipare.

▶**join up** *vi* arruolarsi.

joiner ['dʒɔɪnə*] *n* falegname *m*.

joinery ['dʒɔɪnərɪ] *n* falegnameria.

joint [dʒɔɪnt] *n* (*TECH*) giuntura; giunto; (*ANAT*) articolazione *f*, giuntura; (*BRIT CULIN*) arrosto; (*col: place*) locale *m* ♦ *adj* comune; (*responsibility*) collettivo(a); (*committee*) misto(a).

joint account (J/A) *n* (*at bank etc*) conto in comune.

jointly ['dʒɔɪntlɪ] *adv* in comune, insieme.

joint ownership *n* comproprietà.

joint-stock company ['dʒɔɪntstɔk-] *n* società *f inv* per azioni.

joist [dʒɔɪst] *n* trave *f*.

joke [dʒəuk] *n* scherzo; (*funny story*) barzelletta ♦ *vi* scherzare; **to play a ~ on** fare uno scherzo a.

joker ['dʒəukə*] *n* buffone/a, burlone/a; (*CARDS*) matta, jolly *m inv*.

joking ['dʒəukɪŋ] *n* scherzi *mpl*.

jollity ['dʒɔlɪtɪ] *n* allegria.

jolly ['dʒɔlɪ] *adj* allegro(a), gioioso(a) ♦ *adv* (*BRIT col*) veramente, proprio ♦ *vt* (*BRIT*): **to ~ sb along** cercare di tenere qn su (di morale); **~ good!** (*BRIT*) benissimo!

jolt [dʒəult] *n* scossa, sobbalzo ♦ *vt* urtare.

Jordan ['dʒɔːdən] *n* (*country*) Giordania; (*river*) Giordano.

Jordanian [dʒɔːˈdeɪnɪən] *adj, n* giordano(a).

joss stick ['dʒɔs-] *n* bastoncino d'incenso.

jostle ['dʒɔsl] *vt* spingere coi gomiti ♦ *vi* farsi spazio coi gomiti.

jot [dʒɔt] *n*: **not one ~** nemmeno un po'.

▶**jot down** *vt* annotare in fretta, buttare giù.

jotter ['dʒɔtə*] *n* (*BRIT*) quaderno; blocco.

journal ['dʒəːnl] *n* (*newspaper*) giornale *m*; (*periodical*) rivista; (*diary*) diario.

journalese [dʒəːnəˈliːz] *n* (*pej*) stile *m* giornalistico.

journalism ['dʒəːnəlɪzəm] *n* giornalismo.

journalist ['dʒəːnəlɪst] *n* giornalista *m/f*.

journey ['dʒəːnɪ] *n* viaggio; (*distance covered*) tragitto; **a 5-hour ~** un viaggio *or* un tragitto di 5 ore.

jovial ['dʒəuvɪəl] *adj* gioviale, allegro(a).

jowl [dʒaul] *n* mandibola; guancia.

joy [dʒɔɪ] *n* gioia.

joyful ['dʒɔɪful], **joyous** ['dʒɔɪəs] *adj* gioioso(a), allegro(a).

joyride ['dʒɔɪraɪd] *n*: **to go for a ~** rubare una macchina per farsi un giro.

joyrider ['dʒɔɪraɪdə*] *n* chi ruba una macchina per andare a farsi un giro.

joystick ['dʒɔɪstɪk] *n* (*AVIAT*) barra di comando; (*COMPUT*) joystick *m inv*.

JP *n abbr see* **Justice of the Peace.**

Jr. *abbr* = **junior.**

JTPA *n abbr* (*US*: = Job Training Partnership Act*) piano governativo di parziale sovvenzione per l'addestramento sul lavoro di apprendisti.

jubilant ['dʒuːbɪlnt] *adj* giubilante; trionfante.

jubilation [dʒuːbɪˈleɪʃən] *n* giubilo.

jubilee ['dʒuːbɪliː] *n* giubileo; **silver ~** venticinquesimo anniversario.

judge [dʒʌdʒ] *n* giudice *m/f* ♦ *vt* giudicare; (*consider*) ritenere; (*estimate: weight, size etc*) calcolare, valutare ♦ *vi*: **judging *or* to ~ by his expression** a giudicare dalla sua espressione; **as far as I can ~** a mio giudizio; **I ~d it necessary to inform him** ho ritenuto necessario informarlo.

judge advocate (JA) *n* (*MIL*) magistrato militare.

judg(e)ment ['dʒʌdʒmənt] *n* giudizio; (*punishment*) punizione *f*; **in my ~** a mio giudizio; **to pass ~ (on)** (*LAW*) pronunciare un giudizio (su); (*fig*) dare giudizi affrettati (su).

judicial [dʒuːˈdɪʃl] *adj* giudiziale, giudiziario(a).

judiciary [dʒuːˈdɪʃɪərɪ] *n* magistratura.

judicious [dʒuːˈdɪʃəs] *adj* giudizioso(a).

judo ['dʒuːdəu] *n* judo.

jug [dʒʌg] *n* brocca, bricco.

jugged hare [dʒʌgd-] *n* (*BRIT*) lepre *f* in salmì.

juggernaut ['dʒʌgənɔːt] n (BRIT: huge truck) bestione m.

juggle ['dʒʌgl] vi fare giochi di destrezza.

juggler ['dʒʌglə*] n giocoliere/a.

Jugoslav ['juːgəu'slɑːv] adj, n = **Yugoslav**.

jugular ['dʒʌgjulə*] adj: ~ **(vein)** vena giugulare.

juice [dʒuːs] n succo; (of meat) sugo; **we've run out of** ~ (col: petrol) siamo rimasti a secco.

juicy ['dʒuːsɪ] adj succoso(a).

jukebox ['dʒuːkbɔks] n juke-box m inv.

Jul. abbr (= July) lug., lu.

July [dʒuː'laɪ] n luglio; **the first of** ~ il primo luglio; **(on) the eleventh of** ~ l'undici luglio; **in the month of** ~ nel mese di luglio; **at the beginning/end of** ~ all'inizio/alla fine di luglio; **in the middle of** ~ a metà luglio; **during** ~ durante (il mese di) luglio; **in** ~ **of next year** a luglio dell'anno prossimo; **each** or **every** ~ ogni anno a luglio; ~ **was wet this year** ha piovuto molto a luglio quest'anno.

jumble ['dʒʌmbl] n miscuglio ♦ vt (also: ~ up, ~ together) mischiare, mettere alla rinfusa.

jumble sale n ≈ vendita di beneficenza.

La **jumble sale** è un mercatino dove vengono venduti vari oggetti, per lo più di seconda mano; viene organizzato in chiese, scuole o circoli ricreativi. I proventi delle vendite vengono devoluti in beneficenza o usati per una giusta causa.

---

jumbo ['dʒʌmbəu] adj: ~ **jet** jumbo-jet m inv; ~ **size** formato gigante.

jump [dʒʌmp] vi saltare, balzare; (start) sobbalzare; (increase) rincarare ♦ vt saltare ♦ n salto, balzo; sobbalzo; (SHOWJUMPING) salto; (fence) ostacolo; **to** ~ **the queue** (BRIT) passare davanti agli altri (in una coda).

▶**jump about** vi fare salti, saltellare.

▶**jump at** vt fus (fig) cogliere or afferrare al volo; **he** ~**ed at the offer** si affrettò ad accettare l'offerta.

▶**jump down** vi saltare giù.

▶**jump up** vi saltare in piedi.

jumped-up ['dʒʌmptʌp] adj (BRIT pej) presuntuoso(a).

jumper ['dʒʌmpə*] n (BRIT: pullover) maglia; (US: pinafore dress) scamiciato; (SPORT) saltatore/trice.

jump leads, (US) **jumper cables** npl cavi mpl per batteria.

jump-start ['dʒʌmpstɑːt] vt (car) far partire spingendo; (fig) dare una spinta a, rimettere in moto.

jump suit n tuta.

jumpy ['dʒʌmpɪ] adj nervoso(a), agitato(a).

Jun. abbr (= June) giu.

Jun., Junr abbr = junior.

junction ['dʒʌŋkʃən] n (BRIT: of roads) incrocio; (of rails) nodo ferroviario.

juncture ['dʒʌŋktʃə*] n: **at this** ~ in questa congiuntura.

June [dʒuːn] n giugno; for phrases see also **July**.

jungle ['dʒʌŋgl] n giungla.

junior ['dʒuːnɪə*] adj, n: **he's** ~ **to me (by 2 years), he's my** ~ **(by 2 years)** è più giovane di me (di 2 anni); **he's** ~ **to me** (seniority) è al di sotto di me, ho più anzianità di lui.

junior executive n giovane dirigente m.

junior high school n (US) scuola media (da 12 a 15 anni).

junior minister n (BRIT POL) ministro che non fa parte del Cabinet.

junior partner n socio meno anziano.

junior school n (BRIT) scuola elementare (da 8 a 11 anni).

junior sizes npl (COMM) taglie fpl per ragazzi.

juniper ['dʒuːnɪpə*] n: ~ **berry** bacca di ginepro.

junk [dʒʌŋk] n (rubbish) chincaglia; (ship) giunca ♦ vt disfarsi di.

junk bond n (COMM) titolo m spazzatura inv.

junk dealer n rigattiere m.

junket ['dʒʌŋkɪt] n (CULIN) giuncata; (BRIT col: also: ~ing): **to go on a** ~, **go** ~**ing** fare bisboccia.

junk food n porcherie fpl, cibo a scarso valore nutritivo.

junkie ['dʒʌŋkɪ] n (col) drogato/a.

junk mail n posta f spazzatura inv.

junk room n (US) ripostiglio.

junk shop n chincaglieria.

junta ['dʒʌntə] n giunta.

Jupiter ['dʒuːpɪtə*] n (planet) Giove m.

jurisdiction [dʒuərɪs'dɪkʃən] n giurisdizione f; **it falls** or **comes within/outside our** ~ è/non è di nostra competenza.

jurisprudence [dʒuərɪs'pruːdəns] n giurisprudenza.

juror ['dʒuərə*] n giurato/a.

jury ['dʒuərɪ] n giuria.

jury box n banco della giuria.

juryman ['dʒuərɪmən] n = **juror**.

just [dʒʌst] adj giusto(a) ♦ adv: **he's** ~ **done it/left** lo ha appena fatto/è appena partito; ~ **as I expected** proprio come me lo aspettavo; ~ **right** proprio giusto; ~ **2 o'clock** le 2 precise; **we were ~ going** stavamo uscendo; **I was ~ about to phone** stavo proprio per telefonare; ~ **as he was leaving** proprio mentre se ne stava andando; **it was ~ before/enough/ here** era poco prima/appena assai/ proprio qui; **it's ~ me** sono solo io; **it's ~ a mistake** non è che uno sbaglio; ~ **missed/caught** appena perso/preso; ~ **listen to this!** senta un po' questo!; ~ **ask someone the way** basta che tu chieda la strada a qualcuno; **it's ~ as good** è altrettanto buono; **it's ~ as well you didn't go** per fortuna non ci sei andato; **not ~ now** non proprio adesso; ~ **a minute!**, ~ **one moment!** un attimo!

justice ['dʒʌstɪs] n giustizia; **Lord Chief J~** (BRIT) presidente m della Corte d'Appello; **this photo doesn't do you ~** questa foto non ti fa giustizia.

Justice of the Peace (JP) n giudice m conciliatore.

justifiable [dʒʌstɪ'faɪəbl] adj giustificabile.

justifiably [dʒʌstɪ'faɪəblɪ] adv legittimamente, con ragione.

justification [dʒʌstɪfɪ'keɪʃən] n giustificazione f; (TYP) giustezza.

justify ['dʒʌstɪfaɪ] vt giustificare; (TYP etc) allineare, giustificare; **to be justified in doing sth** avere ragione di fare qc.

justly ['dʒʌstlɪ] adv giustamente.

justness ['dʒʌstnɪs] n giustezza.

jut [dʒʌt] vi (also: ~ **out**) sporgersi.

jute [dʒuːt] n iuta.

juvenile ['dʒuːvənaɪl] adj giovane, giovanile; (court) dei minorenni; (books) per ragazzi ♦ n giovane m/f, minorenne m/f.

juvenile delinquency n delinquenza minorile.

juvenile delinquent n delinquente m/f minorenne.

juxtapose ['dʒʌkstəpəuz] vt giustapporre.

juxtaposition [dʒʌkstəpə'zɪʃən] n giustapposizione f.

K k

K, k [keɪ] n (letter) K, k f or m inv; **K for King** ≈ K come Kursaal.

K n abbr (= one thousand) mille ♦ abbr (BRIT: = Knight) titolo; (= kilobyte) K.

kaftan ['kæftæn] n caffettano.

Kalahari Desert [kælə'hɑːrɪ-] n Deserto di Calahari.

kale [keɪl] n cavolo verde.

kaleidoscope [kə'laɪdəskəup] n caleidoscopio.

kamikaze [kæmɪ'kɑːzɪ] adj da kamikaze.

Kampala [kæm'pɑːlə] n Kampala f.

Kampuchea [kæmpu'tʃɪə] n Kampuchea f.

kangaroo [kæŋgə'ruː] n canguro.

Kans. abbr (US) = Kansas.

kaput [kə'put] adj (col) kaputt inv.

karaoke [kɑːrə'əukɪ] n karaoke m inv.

karate [kə'rɑːtɪ] n karate m.

Kashmir [kæʃ'mɪə*] n Kashmir m.

Kazakhstan [kæzæk'stɑːn] n Kazakistan m.

KC n abbr (BRIT LAW: = King's Counsel) avvocato della Corona; see also **QC**.

kd abbr (US: = knocked down) da montare.

kebab [kə'bæb] n spiedino.

keel [kiːl] n chiglia; **on an even ~** (fig) in uno stato normale.

▶**keel over** vi (NAUT) capovolgersi; (person) crollare.

keen [kiːn] adj (interest, desire) vivo(a); (eye, intelligence) acuto(a); (competition) serrato(a); (edge) affilato(a); (eager) entusiasta; **to be ~ to do** or **on doing sth** avere una gran voglia di fare qc; **to be ~ on sth** essere appassionato(a) di qc; **to be ~ on sb** avere un debole per qn; **I'm not ~ on going** non mi va di andare.

keenly ['kiːnlɪ] adv (enthusiastically) con entusiasmo; (acutely) vivamente; in modo penetrante.

keenness ['kiːnnɪs] n (eagerness) entusiasmo.

keep [kiːp] vb (pt, pp **kept** [kɛpt]) vt tenere; (hold back) trattenere; (feed: one's family etc) mantenere, sostentare; (a promise) mantenere; (chickens, bees, pigs etc) allevare ♦ vi (food) mantenersi; (remain: in a certain state or place) restare ♦ n (of *castle*) maschio; (*food etc*): **enough for his** ~ abbastanza per vitto e alloggio; **to** ~ **doing sth** continuare a fare qc; fare qc di continuo; **to** ~ **sb from doing/sth from happening** impedire a qn di fare/che qc succeda; **to** ~ **sb busy/a place tidy** tenere qn occupato(a)/un luogo in ordine; **to** ~ **sb waiting** far aspettare qn; **to** ~ **an appointment** andare ad un appuntamento; **to** ~ **a record** *or* **note of sth** prendere nota di qc; **to** ~ **sth to o.s.** tenere qc per sé; **to** ~ **sth (back) from sb** celare qc a qn; **to** ~ **time** (*clock*) andar bene; ~ **the change** tenga il resto; *see also* **keeps.**

▶**keep away** *vt*: **to** ~ **sth/sb away from sb** tenere qc/qn lontano da qn ♦ *vi*: **to** ~ **away (from)** stare lontano (da).

▶**keep back** *vt* (*crowds, tears, money*) trattenere ♦ *vi* tenersi indietro.

▶**keep down** *vt* (*control: prices, spending*) contenere, ridurre; (*retain: food*) trattenere, ritenere ♦ *vi* tenersi giù, stare giù.

▶**keep in** *vt* (*invalid, child*) tenere a casa; (*SCOL*) trattenere a scuola ♦ *vi* (*col*): **to** ~ **in with sb** tenersi buono qn.

▶**keep off** *vt* (*dog, person*) tenere lontano da ♦ *vi* stare alla larga; ~ **your hands off!** non toccare!, giù le mani!; **"**~ **off the grass"** "non calpestare l'erba".

▶**keep on** *vi* continuare; **to** ~ **on doing** continuare a fare.

▶**keep out** *vt* tener fuori ♦ *vi* restare fuori; **"**~ **out"** "vietato l'accesso".

▶**keep up** *vi* mantenersi ♦ *vt* continuare, mantenere; **to** ~ **up with** tener dietro a, andare di pari passo con; (*work etc*) farcela a seguire; **to** ~ **up with sb** (*in race etc*) mantenersi al passo con qn.

keeper ['kiːpə*] *n* custode *m/f*, guardiano/a.

keep-fit [kiːp'fɪt] *n* ginnastica.

keeping ['kiːpɪŋ] *n* (*care*) custodia; **in** ~ **with** in armonia con; in accordo con.

keeps [kiːps] *n*: **for** ~ (*col*) per sempre.

keepsake ['kiːpseɪk] *n* ricordo.

keg [kɛg] *n* barilotto.

Ken. *abbr* (*US*) = *Kentucky.*

kennel ['kɛnl] *n* canile *m*.

Kenya ['kɛnjə] *n* Kenia *m*.

Kenyan ['kɛnjən] *adj, n* Keniano(a), Keniota (*m/f*).

kept [kɛpt] *pt, pp of* **keep.**

kerb [kəːb] *n* (*BRIT*) orlo del marciapiede.

kerb crawler [-'krɔːlə*] *n chi va in macchina in cerca di una prostituta.*

kernel ['kəːnl] *n* nocciolo.

kerosene ['kɛrəsiːn] *n* cherosene *m*.

ketchup ['kɛtʃəp] *n* ketchup *m inv*.

kettle ['kɛtl] *n* bollitore *m*.

kettle drum *n* timpano.

key [kiː] *n* (*gen, MUS*) chiave *f*; (*of piano, typewriter*) tasto; (*on map*) leg(g)enda ♦ *cpd* (*vital: position, industry etc*) chiave *inv*.

▶**key in** *vt* (*text*) introdurre da tastiera.

keyboard ['kiːbɔːd] *n* tastiera ♦ *vt* (*text*) comporre su tastiera.

keyboarder ['kiːbɔːdə*] *n* dattilografo(a).

keyed up [kiːd'ʌp] *adj*: **to be** ~ essere agitato(a).

keyhole ['kiːhəul] *n* buco della serratura.

keyhole surgery *n* chirurgia mininvasiva.

keynote ['kiːnəut] *n* (*MUS*) tonica; (*fig*) nota dominante.

keypad ['kiːpæd] *n* tastierino numerico.

key ring *n* portachiavi *m inv*.

keystroke ['kiːstrəuk] *n* battuta (di un tasto).

kg *abbr* (= *kilogram*) Kg.

KGB *n abbr* KGB *m*.

khaki ['kɑːkɪ] *adj, n* cachi (*m*).

kibbutz [kɪ'buts] *n* kibbutz *m inv*.

kick [kɪk] *vt* calciare, dare calci a ♦ *vi* (*horse*) tirar calci ♦ *n* calcio; (*of rifle*) contraccolpo; (*thrill*): **he does it for** ~**s** lo fa giusto per il piacere di farlo.

▶**kick around** *vi* (*col*) essere in giro.

▶**kick off** *vi* (*SPORT*) dare il primo calcio.

kick-off ['kɪkɔf] *n* (*SPORT*) calcio d'inizio.

kick-start ['kɪkstɑːt] *n* (*also*: ~**er**) pedale *m* d'avviamento.

kid [kɪd] *n* ragazzino/a; (*animal, leather*) capretto ♦ *vi* (*col*) scherzare ♦ *vt* (*col*) prendere in giro.

kid gloves *npl*: **to treat sb with** ~ trattare qn coi guanti.

kidnap ['kɪdnæp] *vt* rapire, sequestrare.

kidnapper ['kɪdnæpə*] *n* rapitore/trice.

kidnapping ['kɪdnæpɪŋ] *n* sequestro (di persona).

kidney ['kɪdnɪ] *n* (*ANAT*) rene *m*; (*CULIN*) rognone *m*.

kidney bean *n* fagiolo borlotto.

kidney machine *n* rene *m* artificiale.

Kilimanjaro [kɪlɪmən'dʒɑːrəu] *n*: **Mount** ~ il monte Kilimangiaro.

kill [kɪl] *vt* uccidere, ammazzare; (*fig*) sopprimere; soppraffare; ammazzare ♦ *n* uccisione *f*; **to** ~ **time** ammazzare il tempo.

▶**kill off** *vt* sterminare; (*fig*) eliminare, soffocare.

killer ['kɪlə*] *n* uccisore *m*, killer *m inv*; assassino/a.

killer instinct *n*: **to have a/the** ~ essere

spietato(a).

killing ['kɪlɪŋ] n assassinio; (*massacre*) strage f; (*col*): **to make a ~** fare un bel colpo.

kill-joy ['kɪldʒɔɪ] n guastafeste m/f inv.

kiln [kɪln] n forno.

kilo ['kiːləʊ] n abbr (= *kilogram*) chilo.

kilobyte ['kɪləbaɪt] n kilobyte m inv.

kilogram(me) ['kɪləʊgræm] n chilogrammo.

kilometre, (*US*) **kilometer** ['kɪləmiːtə*] n chilometro.

kilowatt ['kɪləʊwɔt] n chilowatt m inv.

kilt [kɪlt] n gonnellino scozzese.

kilter ['kɪltə*] n: **out of ~** fuori fase.

kimono [kɪ'məʊnəʊ] n chimono.

kin [kɪn] n see **next of kin, kith.**

kind [kaɪnd] adj gentile, buono(a) ♦ n sorta, specie f; (*species*) genere m; **to be two of a ~** essere molto simili; **would you be ~ enough to ...?, would you be so ~ as to ...?** sarebbe così gentile da ...?; **it's very ~ of you (to do)** è molto gentile da parte sua (di fare); **in ~** (*COMM*) in natura; (*fig*): **to repay sb in ~** ripagare qn della stessa moneta.

kindergarten ['kɪndəgaːtn] n giardino d'infanzia.

kind-hearted [kaɪnd'haːtɪd] adj di buon cuore.

kindle ['kɪndl] vt accendere, infiammare.

kindling ['kɪndlɪŋ] n frasche fpl, ramoscelli mpl.

kindly ['kaɪndlɪ] adj pieno(a) di bontà, benevolo(a) ♦ adv con bontà, gentilmente; **will you ~ ...** vuole ... per favore; **he didn't take it ~** se l'è presa a male.

kindness ['kaɪndnɪs] n bontà, gentilezza.

kindred ['kɪndrɪd] adj imparentato(a); **~ spirit** spirito affine.

kinetic [kɪ'nɛtɪk] adj cinetico(a).

king [kɪŋ] n re m inv.

kingdom ['kɪŋdəm] n regno, reame m.

kingfisher ['kɪŋfɪʃə*] n martin m inv pescatore.

kingpin ['kɪŋpɪn] n (*TECH, fig*) perno.

king-size(d) ['kɪŋsaɪz(d)] adj super inv; gigante; (*cigarette*) extra lungo(a).

kink [kɪŋk] n (*of rope*) attorcigliamento; (*in hair*) ondina; (*fig*) aberrazione f.

kinky ['kɪŋkɪ] adj (*fig*) eccentrico(a); dai gusti particolari.

kinship ['kɪnʃɪp] n parentela.

kinsman ['kɪnzmən] n parente m.

kinswoman ['kɪnzwʊmən] n parente f.

kiosk ['kiːɔsk] n edicola, chiosco; (*BRIT: also*: **telephone ~**) cabina (telefonica); (: *also*: **newspaper ~**) edicola.

kipper ['kɪpə*] n aringa affumicata.

Kirghizia [kəːˈgɪzɪə] n Kirghizistan.

kiss [kɪs] n bacio ♦ vt baciare; **to ~** (**each other**) baciarsi; **to ~ sb goodbye** congedarsi da qn con un bacio; **~ of life** (*BRIT*) respirazione f bocca a bocca.

kissagram ['kɪsəgræm] n servizio di recapito a domicilio di messaggi e baci augurali.

kit [kɪt] n equipaggiamento, corredo; (*set of tools etc*) attrezzi mpl; (*for assembly*) scatola di montaggio; **tool ~** cassetta or borsa degli attrezzi.

▶**kit out** vt (*BRIT*) attrezzare, equipaggiare.

kitbag ['kɪtbæg] n zaino; sacco militare.

kitchen ['kɪtʃɪn] n cucina.

kitchen garden n orto.

kitchen sink n acquaio.

kitchen unit n (*BRIT*) elemento da cucina.

kitchenware ['kɪtʃɪnwɛə*] n stoviglie fpl; utensili mpl da cucina.

kite [kaɪt] n (*toy*) aquilone m; (*ZOOL*) nibbio.

kith [kɪθ] n: **~ and kin** amici e parenti mpl.

kitten ['kɪtn] n gattino/a, micino/a.

kitty ['kɪtɪ] n (*money*) fondo comune.

kiwi fruit ['kiːwiː-] n kiwi m inv.

KKK n abbr (*US*) = *Ku Klux Klan.*

Kleenex ® ['kliːnɛks] n fazzolettino di carta.

kleptomaniac [klɛptəʊ'meɪnɪæk] n cleptomane m/f.

km abbr (= *kilometre*) km.

km/h abbr (= *kilometres per hour*) km/h.

knack [næk] n: **to have a ~** (**for doing**) avere una pratica (per fare); **to have the ~ of** avere l'abilità di; **there's a ~ to doing this** c'è un trucco per fare questo.

knackered ['nækəd] adj (*col*) fuso(a).

knapsack ['næpsæk] n zaino, sacco da montagna.

knave [neɪv] n (*CARDS*) fante m.

knead [niːd] vt impastare.

knee [niː] n ginocchio.

kneecap ['niːkæp] n rotula ♦ vt gambizzare.

knee-deep ['niːdiːp] adj: **the water was ~** l'acqua ci arrivava alle ginocchia.

kneel [niːl] vi (pt, pp **knelt** [nɛlt]) inginocchiarsi.

kneepad ['niːpæd] n ginocchiera.

knell [nɛl] n rintocco.

knelt [nɛlt] pt, pp of **kneel.**

knew [njuː] pt of **know.**

knickers ['nɪkəz] npl (*BRIT*) mutandine fpl.

knick-knack ['nɪknæk] n ninnolo.

knife [naɪf] n (pl **knives**) coltello ♦ vt accoltellare, dare una coltellata a; **~, fork and spoon** coperto.

knife edge n: **to be on a ~** (*fig*) essere appeso(a) a un filo.

knight [naɪt] *n* cavaliere *m*; (*CHESS*) cavallo.

knighthood ['naɪthud] *n* cavalleria; (*title*): **to get a ~** essere fatto cavaliere.

knit [nɪt] *vt* fare a maglia; (*fig*): **to ~ together** unire ♦ *vi* lavorare a maglia; (*broken bones*) saldarsi.

knitted ['nɪtɪd] *adj* lavorato(a) a maglia.

knitting ['nɪtɪŋ] *n* lavoro a maglia.

knitting machine *n* macchina per maglieria.

knitting needle *n* ferro (da calza).

knitting pattern *n* modello (per maglia).

knitwear ['nɪtwɛə*] *n* maglieria.

knives [naɪvz] *npl of* **knife**.

knob [nɔb] *n* bottone *m*; manopola; (*BRIT*): **a ~ of butter** una noce di burro.

knobbly ['nɔblɪ], (*US*) **knobby** ['nɔbɪ] *adj* (*wood, surface*) nodoso(a); (*knee*) ossuto(a).

knock [nɔk] *vt* (*strike*) colpire; urtare; (*fig: col*) criticare ♦ *vi* (*engine*) battere; (*at door etc*): **to ~ at/on** bussare a ♦ *n* bussata; colpo, botta; **he ~ed at the door** ha bussato alla porta; **to ~ a nail into sth** conficcare un chiodo in qc.

►**knock down** *vt* abbattere; (*pedestrian*) investire; (*price*) abbassare.

►**knock off** *vi* (*col: finish*) smettere (di lavorare) ♦ *vt* (*strike off*) far cadere; (*col: steal*) sgraffignare, grattare; **to ~ off £10** fare uno sconto di 10 sterline.

►**knock out** *vt* stendere; (*BOXING*) mettere K.O., mettere fuori combattimento.

►**knock over** *vt* (*object*) far cadere; (*pedestrian*) investire.

knockdown ['nɔkdaun] *adj* (*price*) fortemente scontato(a).

knocker ['nɔkə*] *n* (*on door*) battente *m*.

knocking ['nɔkɪŋ] *n* colpi *mpl*.

knock-kneed [nɔk'niːd] *adj* che ha le gambe ad x.

knockout ['nɔkaut] *n* (*BOXING*) knock out *m inv*.

knockout competition *n* (*BRIT*) gara ad eliminazione.

knock-up ['nɔkʌp] *n* (*TENNIS etc*) palleggio; **to have a ~** palleggiare.

knot [nɔt] *n* nodo ♦ *vt* annodare; **to tie a ~** fare un nodo.

knotty ['nɔtɪ] *adj* (*fig*) spinoso(a).

know [nau] *vt* (*pt* **knew**, *pp* **known** [njuː, naun]) sapere; (*person, author, place*) conoscere ♦ *vi* sapere; **to ~ that** ... sapere che ...; **to ~ how to do** sapere fare; **to get to ~ sth** venire a sapere qc; **I ~ nothing about it** non ne so niente; **I don't ~ him** non lo conosco; **to ~ right from wrong**

distinguere il bene dal male; **as far as I ~** ... che io sappia ..., per quanto io ne sappia ...; **yes, I ~** sì, lo so; **I don't ~** non lo so.

know-all ['nauɔːl] *n* (*BRIT pej*) sapientone/a.

know-how ['nauhau] *n* tecnica; pratica.

knowing ['nauɪŋ] *adj* (*look etc*) d'intesa.

knowingly ['nauɪŋlɪ] *adv* consapevolmente; di complicità.

know-it-all ['nauɪtɔːl] *n* (*US*) = **know-all**.

knowledge ['nɔlɪdʒ] *n* consapevolezza; (*learning*) conoscenza, sapere *m*; **to have no ~ of** ignorare, non sapere; **not to my ~** che io sappia, no; **to have a working ~ of Italian** avere una conoscenza pratica dell'italiano; **without my ~** a mia insaputa; **it is common ~ that** ... è risaputo che ...; **it has come to my ~ that** ... sono venuto a sapere che ....

knowledgeable ['nɔlɪdʒəbl] *adj* ben informato(a).

known [naun] *pp of* **know** ♦ *adj* (*thief, facts*) noto(a); (*expert*) riconosciuto(a).

knuckle ['nʌkl] *n* nocca.

►**knuckle down** *vi* (*col*): **to ~ down to some hard work** mettersi sotto a lavorare.

►**knuckle under** *vi* (*col*) cedere.

knuckleduster ['nʌkldʌstə*] *n* tirapugni *m inv*.

KO *abbr* (= *knock out*) *n* K.O. *m* ♦ *vt* mettere K.O.

koala [kau'ɑːlə] *n* (*also*: **~ bear**) koala *m inv*.

kook [kuːk] *n* (*US col*) svitato/a.

Koran [kɔ'rɑːn] *n* Corano.

Korea [kə'riːə] *n* Corea; **North/South ~** Corea del Nord/Sud.

Korean [kə'riːən] *adj, n* coreano(a).

kosher ['kauʃə*] *adj* kasher *inv*.

kowtow ['kau'tau] *vi*: **to ~ to sb** mostrarsi ossequioso(a) verso qn.

Kremlin ['krɛmlɪn] *n*: **the ~** il Cremlino.

KS *abbr* (*US*) = *Kansas*.

Kt *abbr* (*BRIT*: = *Knight*) titolo.

Kuala Lumpur ['kwɑːlə'lumpuə*] *n* Kuala Lumpur *f*.

kudos ['kjuːdɔs] *n* gloria, fama.

Kurd [kəːd] *n* curdo/a.

Kuwait [ku'weɪt] *n* Kuwait *m*.

Kuwaiti [ku'weɪtɪ] *adj, n* kuwaitiano(a).

kw *abbr* (= *kilowatt*) kw.

KY, Ky. *abbr* (*US*) = *Kentucky*.

L l

L, I [εl] *n* (*letter*) L, l *f or m inv*; **L for Lucy**, (*US*)
L for Love ≈ L come Livorno.
L *abbr* (= *lake*) l; (= *large*) taglia grande;
(= *left*) sin.; (*BRIT AUT*) = **learner**.
I *abbr* (= *litre*) l.
LA *n abbr* (*US*) = *Los Angeles* ♦ *abbr* (*US*)
= *Louisiana*.
La. *abbr* (*US*) = *Louisiana*.
lab [læb] *n abbr* (= *laboratory*) laboratorio.
Lab. *abbr* (*Canada*) = *Labrador*.
label ['leɪbl] *n* etichetta, cartellino; (*brand*:
of record) casa ♦ *vt* etichettare;
classificare.
labor *etc* ['leɪbə*] (*US*) = **labour** *etc*.
laboratory [lə'bɔrətərɪ] *n* laboratorio.
Labor Day *n* (*US*) festa del lavoro.

> *Negli Stati Uniti e nel Canada il* **Labor Day**,
> *la festa del lavoro, cade il primo lunedì di*
> *settembre, contrariamente a quanto accade*
> *nella maggior parte dei paesi europei dove*
> *tale celebrazione ha luogo il primo maggio.*

laborious [lə'bɔːrɪəs] *adj* laborioso(a).
labor union *n* (*US*) sindacato.
Labour ['leɪbə*] *n* (*BRIT POL: also:* **the ~**
Party) il partito laburista, i laburisti.
labour, (*US*) **labor** ['leɪbə*] *n* (*task*) lavoro;
(*workmen*) manodopera; (*MED*) travaglio
del parto, doglie *fpl* ♦ *vi*: **to ~** (**at**) lavorare
duro (a); **to be in ~** (*MED*) avere le doglie.
labo(u)r camp *n* campo dei lavori forzati.
labo(u)r cost *n* costo del lavoro.
labo(u)r dispute *n* conflitto tra lavoratori
e datori di lavoro.
labo(u)red ['leɪbəd] *adj* (*breathing*)
affaticato(a), affannoso(a); (*style*)
elaborato(a), pesante.
labo(u)rer ['leɪbərə*] *n* manovale *m*; (*on*
farm) lavoratore *m* agricolo.
labo(u)r force *n* manodopera.
labo(u)r-intensive [leɪbərɪn'tɛnsɪv] *adj* che
assorbe molta manodopera.
labo(u)r market *n* mercato del lavoro.
labo(u)r pains *npl* doglie *fpl.*
labo(u)r relations *npl* relazioni *fpl*
industriali.
labo(u)r-saving ['leɪbəseɪvɪŋ] *adj* che fa

risparmiare fatica *or* lavoro.
labo(u)r unrest *n* agitazioni *fpl* degli
operai.
labyrinth ['læbɪrɪnθ] *n* labirinto.
lace [leɪs] *n* merletto, pizzo; (*of shoe etc*)
laccio ♦ *vt* (*shoe*) allacciare; (*drink*: *fortify*
with spirits) correggere.
lacemaking ['leɪsmeɪkɪŋ] *n* fabbricazione *f*
dei pizzi *or* dei merletti.
laceration [læsə'reɪʃən] *n* lacerazione *f*.
lace-up ['leɪsʌp] *adj* (*shoes etc*) con i lacci,
con le stringhe.
lack [læk] *n* mancanza, scarsità ♦ *vt*
mancare di; **through** *or* **for ~ of** per
mancanza di; **to be ~ing** mancare; **to be**
~ing in mancare di.
lackadaisical [lækə'deɪzɪkl] *adj*
disinteressato(a), noncurante.
lackey ['lækɪ] *n* (*also fig*) lacchè *m inv*.
lacklustre, (*US*) **lackluster** ['læklʌstə*] *adj*
(*surface*) opaco(a); (*style*) scialbo(a);
(*eyes*) spento(a).
laconic [lə'kɔnɪk] *adj* laconico(a).
lacquer ['lækə*] *n* lacca; **hair ~** lacca per
(i) capelli.
lacy ['leɪsɪ] *adj* (*like lace*) che sembra un
pizzo.
lad [læd] *n* ragazzo, giovanotto; (*BRIT: in*
stable etc) mozzo *or* garzone *m* di stalla.
ladder ['lædə*] *n* scala; (*BRIT: in tights*)
smagliatura ♦ *vt* smagliare ♦ *vi*
smagliarsi.
laden ['leɪdn] *adj*: **~ (with)** carico(a) *or*
caricato(a) (di); **fully ~** (*truck, ship*) a
pieno carico.
ladle ['leɪdl] *n* mestolo.
lady ['leɪdɪ] *n* signora; **L~ Smith** lady
Smith; **the ladies' (toilets)** i gabinetti per
signore; **a ~ doctor** una dottoressa.
ladybird ['leɪdɪbəːd], (*US*) **ladybug**
['leɪdɪbʌg] *n* coccinella.
lady-in-waiting ['leɪdɪɪn'weɪtɪŋ] *n* dama di
compagnia.
ladykiller ['leɪdɪkɪlə*] *n* dongiovanni *m inv*.
ladylike ['leɪdɪlaɪk] *adj* da signora,
distinto(a).
ladyship ['leɪdɪʃɪp] *n*: **your L~** signora
contessa *etc*.
lag [læg] *n* = **time ~** ♦ *vi* (*also:* **~ behind**)
trascinarsi ♦ *vt* (*pipes*) rivestire di
materiale isolante.
lager ['lɑːgə*] *n* lager *m inv*.
lager lout *n* (*BRIT col*) giovinastro ubriaco.
lagging ['lægɪŋ] *n* rivestimento di
materiale isolante.
lagoon [lə'guːn] *n* laguna.
Lagos ['leɪgɔs] *n* Lagos *f*.
laid [leɪd] *pt, pp of* **lay**.

laid-back [leɪd'bæk] *adj* (*col*) rilassato(a).

lain [leɪn] *pp of* **lie**.

lair [lɛə*] *n* covo, tana.

laissez-faire [lɛseɪ'fɛə*] *n* liberismo.

laity ['leɪətɪ] *n* laici *mpl*.

lake [leɪk] *n* lago.

Lake District *n*: **the ~** (*BRIT*) la regione dei laghi.

lamb [læm] *n* agnello.

lamb chop *n* cotoletta d'agnello.

lambskin ['læmskɪn] *n* (pelle *f* d')agnello.

lambswool ['læmzwul] *n* lamb's wool *m*.

lame [leɪm] *adj* zoppo(a); **~ duck** (*fig: person*) persona inetta; (: *firm*) azienda traballante.

lamely ['leɪmlɪ] *adv* (*fig*) in modo poco convincente.

lament [lə'mɛnt] *n* lamento ♦ *vt* lamentare, piangere.

lamentable ['læməntəbl] *adj* doloroso(a); deplorevole.

laminated ['læmɪneɪtɪd] *adj* laminato(a).

lamp [læmp] *n* lampada.

lamplight ['læmplaɪt] *n*: **by ~** a lume della lampada.

lampoon [læm'puːn] *n* satira.

lamppost ['læmppəust] *n* lampione *m*.

lampshade ['læmpʃeɪd] *n* paralume *m*.

lance [lɑːns] *n* lancia ♦ *vt* (*MED*) incidere.

lance corporal *n* (*BRIT*) caporale *m*.

lancet ['lɑːnsɪt] *n* (*MED*) bisturi *m inv*.

Lancs [læŋks] *abbr* (*BRIT*) = Lancashire.

land [lænd] *n* (*as opposed to sea*) terra (ferma); (*country*) paese *m*; (*soil*) terreno; (*estate*) terreni *mpl*, terre *fpl* ♦ *vi* (*from ship*) sbarcare; (*AVIAT*) atterrare; (*fig: fall*) cadere ♦ *vt* (*obtain*) acchiappare; (*passengers*) sbarcare; (*goods*) scaricare; **to go/travel by ~** andare/viaggiare per via di terra; **to own ~** possedere dei terreni, avere delle proprietà (terriere); **to ~ on one's feet** cadere in piedi; (*fig: to be lucky*) cascar bene.

▶**land up** *vi* andare a finire.

landed gentry ['lændɪd-] *n* proprietari *mpl* terrieri.

landfill site ['lændfɪl-] *n* discarica dove i rifiuti vengono sepolti.

landing ['lændɪŋ] *n* (*from ship*) sbarco; (*AVIAT*) atterraggio; (*of staircase*) pianerottolo.

landing card *n* carta di sbarco.

landing craft *n* mezzo da sbarco.

landing gear *n* (*AVIAT*) carrello d'atterraggio.

landing stage *n* pontile *m* da sbarco.

landing strip *n* pista d'atterraggio.

landlady ['lændleɪdɪ] *n* padrona or proprietaria di casa.

landlocked ['lændlɔkt] *adj* senza sbocco sul mare.

landlord ['lændlɔːd] *n* padrone *m or* proprietario di casa; (*of pub etc*) oste *m*.

landlubber ['lændlʌbə*] *n* marinaio d'acqua dolce.

landmark ['lændmɑːk] *n* punto di riferimento; (*fig*) pietra miliare.

landowner ['lændəunə*] *n* proprietario(a) terriero(a).

landscape ['lænskeɪp] *n* paesaggio.

landscape architect, landscape gardener *n* paesaggista *m/f*.

landscape painting *n* (*ART*) paesaggistica.

landslide ['lændslaɪd] *n* (*GEO*) frana; (*fig: POL*) valanga.

lane [leɪn] *n* (*in country*) viottolo; (*in town*) stradetta; (*AUT, in race*) corsia; **shipping ~** rotta (marittima).

language ['læŋgwɪdʒ] *n* lingua; (*way one speaks*) linguaggio; **bad ~** linguaggio volgare.

language laboratory *n* laboratorio linguistico.

languid ['læŋgwɪd] *adj* languente; languido(a).

languish ['læŋgwɪʃ] *vi* languire.

lank [læŋk] *adj* (*hair*) liscio(a) e opaco(a).

lanky ['læŋkɪ] *adj* allampanato(a).

lanolin(e) ['lænəlɪn] *n* lanolina.

lantern ['læntn] *n* lanterna.

Laos [lauz] *n* Laos *m*.

lap [læp] *n* (*of track*) giro; (*of body*): **in** or **on one's ~** in grembo ♦ *vt* (*also*: **~ up**) papparsi, leccare ♦ *vi* (*waves*) sciabordare.

▶**lap up** *vt* (*fig: compliments, attention*) bearsi di.

La Paz [læ'pæz] *n* La Paz *f*.

lapdog ['læpdɔg] *n* cane *m* da grembo.

lapel [lə'pɛl] *n* risvolto.

Lapland ['læplænd] *n* Lapponia.

Lapp [læp] *adj* lappone ♦ *n* lappone *m/f*; (*LING*) lappone *m*.

lapse [læps] *n* lapsus *m inv*; (*longer*) caduta; (*fault*) mancanza; (*in behaviour*) scorrettezza ♦ *vi* (*law, act*) cadere; (*ticket, passport*) scadere; **to ~ into bad habits** pigliare cattive abitudini; **~ of time** spazio di tempo; **a ~ of memory** un vuoto di memoria.

laptop ['læptɔp] *n* (*also*: **~ computer**) laptop *m inv*.

larceny ['lɑːsənɪ] *n* furto.

lard [lɑːd] *n* lardo.

larder ['lɑːdə*] *n* dispensa.

large [lɑːdʒ] *adj* grande; (*person, animal*) grosso(a) ♦ *adv*: **by and** ~ generalmente; **at** ~ (*free*) in libertà; (*generally*) in generale; nell'insieme; **to make** ~**r** ingrandire; **a** ~ **number of people** molta gente; **on a** ~ **scale** su vasta scala.

largely [ˈlɑːdʒlɪ] *adv* in gran parte.

large-scale [ˈlɑːdʒˈskeɪl] *adj* (*map, drawing etc*) in grande scala; (*reforms, business activities*) su vasta scala.

lark [lɑːk] *n* (*bird*) allodola; (*joke*) scherzo, gioco.

►**lark about** *vi* fare lo stupido.

larva [ˈlɑːvə], *pl* **larvae** [ˈlɑːvə, -iː] *n* larva.

laryngitis [lærɪnˈdʒaɪtɪs] *n* laringite *f*.

larynx [ˈlærɪŋks] *n* laringe *f*.

lasagne [ləˈzænjə] *n* lasagne *fpl*.

lascivious [ləˈsɪvɪəs] *adj* lascivo(a).

laser [ˈleɪzə*] *n* laser *m*.

laser beam *n* raggio *m* laser *inv*.

laser printer *n* stampante *f* laser *inv*.

lash [læʃ] *n* frustata; (*also*: **eye**~) ciglio ♦ *vt* frustare; (*tie*) legare.

►**lash down** *vt* assicurare (con corde) ♦ *vi* (*rain*) scrosciare.

►**lash out** *vi*: **to** ~ **out** (**at** *or* **against sb/sth**) attaccare violentemente (qn/qc); **to** ~ **out** (**on sth**) (*col: spend*) spendere un sacco di soldi (per qc).

lashing [ˈlæʃɪŋ] *n* (*beating*) frustata, sferzata; ~**s of** (*BRIT col*) un mucchio di, una montagna di.

lass [læs] *n* ragazza.

lasso [læˈsuː] *n* laccio ♦ *vt* acchiappare con il laccio.

last [lɑːst] *adj* ultimo(a); (*week, month, year*) scorso(a), passato(a) ♦ *adv* per ultimo ♦ *vi* durare; ~ **week** la settimana scorsa; ~ **night** ieri sera, la notte scorsa; **at** ~ finalmente, alla fine; ~ **but one** penultimo(a); **the** ~ **time** l'ultima volta; **it** ~**s (for) 2 hours** dura 2 ore.

last-ditch [ˈlɑːstˈdɪtʃ] *adj* ultimo(a) e disperato(a).

lasting [ˈlɑːstɪŋ] *adj* durevole.

lastly [ˈlɑːstlɪ] *adv* infine, per finire, per ultimo.

last-minute [ˈlɑːstmɪnɪt] *adj* fatto(a) (*or* preso(a) *etc*) all'ultimo momento.

latch [lætʃ] *n* serratura a scatto.

►**latch on to** *vt fus* (*cling to: person*) attaccarsi a, appiccicarsi a; (: *idea*) afferrare, capire.

latchkey [ˈlætʃkiː] *n* chiave *f* di casa.

late [leɪt] *adj* (*not on time*) in ritardo; (*far on in day etc*) tardi *inv*; tardo(a); (*recent*) recente, ultimo(a); (*former*) ex; (*dead*) defunto(a) ♦ *adv* tardi; (*behind time,*

schedule) in ritardo; **to be (10 minutes)** ~ essere in ritardo (di 10 minuti); **to work** ~ lavorare fino a tardi; ~ **in life** in età avanzata; **of** ~ di recente; **in the** ~ **afternoon** nel tardo pomeriggio; **in** ~ **May** verso la fine di maggio; **the** ~ **Mr X** il defunto Signor X.

latecomer [ˈleɪtkʌmə*] *n* ritardatario/a.

lately [ˈleɪtlɪ] *adv* recentemente.

lateness [ˈleɪtnɪs] *n* (*of person*) ritardo; (*of event*) tardezza, ora tarda.

latent [ˈleɪtnt] *adj* latente; ~ **defect** vizio occulto.

later [ˈleɪtə*] *adj* (*date etc*) posteriore; (*version etc*) successivo(a) ♦ *adv* più tardi; ~ **on today** oggi più tardi.

lateral [ˈlætərl] *adj* laterale.

latest [ˈleɪtɪst] *adj* ultimo(a), più recente; **at the** ~ al più tardi; **the** ~ **news** le ultime notizie.

latex [ˈleɪtɛks] *n* latice *m*.

lath, ~**s** [læθ, læðz] *n* assicella.

lathe [leɪð] *n* tornio.

lather [ˈlɑːðə*] *n* schiuma di sapone ♦ *vt* insaponare ♦ *vi* far schiuma.

Latin [ˈlætɪn] *n* latino ♦ *adj* latino(a).

Latin America *n* America Latina.

Latin American *adj* sudamericano(a).

latitude [ˈlætɪtjuːd] *n* latitudine *f*; (*fig: freedom*) libertà d'azione.

latrine [ləˈtriːn] *n* latrina.

latter [ˈlætə*] *adj* secondo(a); più recente ♦ *n*: **the** ~ quest'ultimo, il secondo.

latterly [ˈlætəlɪ] *adv* recentemente, negli ultimi tempi.

lattice [ˈlætɪs] *n* traliccio; graticolato.

lattice window *n* finestra con vetrata a losanghe.

Latvia [ˈlætvɪə] *n* Lettonia.

Latvian [ˈlætvɪən] *adj* lettone *inv* ♦ *n* lettone *m/f*; (*LING*) lettone *m*.

laudable [ˈlɔːdəbl] *adj* lodevole.

laudatory [ˈlɔːdətrɪ] *adj* elogiativo(a).

laugh [lɑːf] *n* risata ♦ *vi* ridere.

►**laugh at** *vt fus* (*misfortune etc*) ridere di; **I** ~**ed at his joke** la sua barzelletta mi fece ridere.

►**laugh off** *vt* prendere alla leggera.

laughable [ˈlɑːfəbl] *adj* ridicolo(a).

laughing [ˈlɑːfɪŋ] *adj* (*face*) ridente; **this is no** ~ **matter** non è una cosa da ridere.

laughing gas *n* gas *m* esilarante.

laughing stock *n*: **the** ~ **of** lo zimbello di.

laughter [ˈlɑːftə*] *n* riso; risate *fpl*.

launch [lɔːntʃ] *n* (*of rocket, product etc*) lancio; (*of new ship*) varo; (*boat*) scialuppa; (*also*: **motor** ~) lancia ♦ *vt* (*rocket, product*) lanciare; (*ship, plan*)

varare.
►**launch out** *vi:* **to ~ out (into)** lanciarsi (in).
launching ['lɔːntʃɪŋ] *n* lancio; varo.
launch(ing) pad *n* rampa di lancio.
launder ['lɔːndə*] *vt* lavare e stirare.
Launderette ® [lɔːn'drɛt], (*US*)
Laundromat ® ['lɔːndrəmæt] *n* lavanderia (automatica).
laundry ['lɔːndrɪ] *n* lavanderia; (*clothes*) biancheria; **to do the ~** fare il bucato.
laureate ['lɔːrɪət] *adj see* **poet laureate**.
laurel ['lɔrl] *n* lauro, alloro; **to rest on one's ~s** riposare *or* dormire sugli allori.
Lausanne [ləu'zæn] *n* Losanna.
lava ['lɑːvə] *n* lava.
lavatory ['lævətərɪ] *n* gabinetto.
lavatory paper *n* (*BRIT*) carta igienica.
lavender ['lævəndə*] *n* lavanda.
lavish ['lævɪʃ] *adj* abbondante; sontuoso(a); (*giving freely*): **~** with prodigo(a) di, largo(a) in ♦ *vt:* **to ~ sth on sb/sth** profondere qc a qn/qc.
lavishly ['lævɪʃlɪ] *adv* (*give, spend*) generosamente; (*furnished*) sontuosamente, lussuosamente.
law [lɔː] *n* legge *f;* **against the ~** contro la legge; **to study ~** studiare diritto; **to go to ~** (*BRIT*) ricorrere alle vie legali; **civil/ criminal ~** diritto civile/penale.
law-abiding ['lɔːəbaɪdɪŋ] *adj* ubbidiente alla legge.
law and order *n* l'ordine *m* pubblico.
lawbreaker ['lɔːbreɪkə*] *n* violatore/trice della legge.
law court *n* tribunale *m*, corte *f* di giustizia.
lawful ['lɔːful] *adj* legale.
lawfully ['lɔːfəlɪ] *adv* legalmente.
lawless ['lɔːlɪs] *adj* senza legge; illegale.
Law Lords *npl* ≈ Corte *f* Suprema.
lawmaker ['lɔːmeɪkə*] *n* legislatore *m*.
lawn [lɔːn] *n* tappeto erboso.
lawnmower ['lɔːnməuə*] *n* tosaerba *m or f inv.*
lawn tennis *n* tennis *m* su prato.
law school *n* facoltà *f inv* di legge.
law student *n* studente/essa di legge.
lawsuit ['lɔːsuːt] *n* processo, causa; **to bring a ~** intentare causa a.
lawyer ['lɔːjə*] *n* (*consultant, with company*) giurista *m/f*; (*for sales, wills etc*) ≈ notaio; (*partner, in court*) ≈ avvocato/essa.
lax [læks] *adj* (*conduct*) rilassato(a); (*person: careless*) negligente; (*: on discipline*) permissivo(a).
laxative ['læksətɪv] *n* lassativo.
laxity ['læksɪtɪ] *n* rilassatezza; negligenza.

lay [leɪ] *pt of* **lie** ♦ *adj* laico(a); secolare ♦ *vt* (*pt, pp* **laid** [leɪd]) posare, mettere; (*eggs*) fare; (*trap*) tendere; (*plans*) fare, elaborare; **to ~ the table** apparecchiare la tavola; **to ~ the facts/one's proposals before sb** presentare i fatti/delle proposte a qn; **to get laid** (*col!*) scopare (*!*); essere scopato(a) (*!*).
►**lay aside, lay by** *vt* mettere da parte.
►**lay down** *vt* mettere giù; **to ~ down the law** (*fig*) dettar legge.
►**lay in** *vt* fare una scorta di.
►**lay into** *vt fus* (*col: attack, scold*) aggredire.
►**lay off** *vt* (*workers*) licenziare.
►**lay on** *vt* (*water, gas*) installare, mettere; (*provide: meal etc*) fornire; (*paint*) applicare.
►**lay out** *vt* (*design*) progettare; (*display*) presentare; (*spend*) sborsare.
►**lay up** *vt* (*to store*) accumulare; (*ship*) mettere in disarmo; (*subj: illness*) costringere a letto.
layabout ['leɪəbaut] *n* sfaccendato/a, fannullone/a.
lay-by ['leɪbaɪ] *n* (*BRIT*) piazzola (di sosta).
lay days *npl* (*NAUT*) stallie *fpl*.
layer ['leɪə*] *n* strato.
layette [leɪ'ɛt] *n* corredino (per neonato).
layman ['leɪmən] *n* laico; profano.
lay-off ['leɪɔf] *n* sospensione *f*, licenziamento.
layout ['leɪaut] *n* lay-out *m inv*, disposizione *f*; (*PRESS*) impaginazione *f*.
laze [leɪz] *vi* oziare.
laziness ['leɪzɪnɪs] *n* pigrizia.
lazy ['leɪzɪ] *adj* pigro(a).
lb. *abbr* (= *libra: pound*) lb.
lbw *abbr* (*CRICKET:* = *leg before wicket*) *fallo dovuto al fatto che il giocatore ha la gamba davanti alla porta.*
LC *n abbr* (*US*) = *Library of Congress.*
lc *abbr* (*TYP*) = **lower case**.
L/C *abbr* = **letter of credit**.
LCD *n abbr see* **liquid crystal display**.
Ld *abbr* (*BRIT:* = *lord*) *titolo.*
LDS *n abbr* (= *Licentiate in Dental Surgery*) *specializzazione dopo la laurea;* (= *Latter-day Saints*) *Chiesa di Gesù Cristo dei Santi dell'Ultimo Giorno.*
LEA *n abbr* (*BRIT:* = *local education authority*) ≈ Provveditorato degli Studi.
lead [liːd] *n* (*front position*) posizione *f* di testa; (*distance, time ahead*) vantaggio; (*clue*) indizio; (*ELEC*) filo (elettrico); (*for dog*) guinzaglio; (*THEAT*) parte *f* principale; [lɛd] (*metal*) piombo; (*in pencil*) mina ♦ *vb* (*pt, pp* **led** [lɛd]) *vt* menare, guidare, condurre; (*induce*) indurre; (*be*

leader of) essere a capo di; (: *orchestra*: *BRIT*) essere il primo violino di; (: *US*) dirigere; (*SPORT*) essere in testa a ♦ *vi* condurre, essere in testa; **to be in the ~** (*SPORT*) essere in testa; **to take the ~** (*SPORT*) passare in testa; (*fig*) prendere l'iniziativa; **to ~ to** menare a; condurre a; portare a; **to ~ astray** sviare; **to ~ sb to believe that ...** far credere a qn che ...; **to ~ sb to do sth** portare qn a fare qc.

►**lead away** *vt* condurre via.

►**lead back** *vt* riportare, ricondurre.

►**lead off** *vt* portare ♦ *vi* partire da.

►**lead on** *vt* (*tease*) tenere sulla corda.

►**lead on to** *vt* (*induce*) portare a.

►**lead up to** *vt fus* portare a; (*fig*) preparare la strada per.

leaded ['lɛdɪd] *adj*: **~ windows** vetrate *fpl* (artistiche).

leaden ['lɛdn] *adj* di piombo.

leader ['liːdə*] *n* capo; leader *m inv*; (*in newspaper*) articolo di fondo; **they are ~s in their field** (*fig*) sono all'avanguardia nel loro campo; **the L~ of the House** (*BRIT*) il capo della maggioranza ministeriale.

leadership ['liːdəʃɪp] *n* direzione *f*; **under the ~ of ...** sotto la direzione *or* guida di ...; **qualities of ~** qualità *fpl* di un capo.

lead-free ['lɛdfriː] *adj* senza piombo.

leading ['liːdɪŋ] *adj* primo(a); principale; **a ~ question** una domanda tendenziosa; **~ role** ruolo principale.

leading lady *n* (*THEAT*) prima attrice.

leading light *n* (*person*) personaggio di primo piano.

leading man *n* (*THEAT*) primo attore.

lead pencil [lɛd-] *n* matita con la mina di grafite.

lead poisoning [lɛd-] *n* saturnismo.

lead time [liːd-] *n* (*COMM*) tempo di consegna.

lead weight [lɛd-] *n* piombino, piombo.

leaf [liːf] *n* (*pl* **leaves**) foglia; (*of table*) ribalta; **to turn over a new ~** (*fig*) cambiar vita; **to take a ~ out of sb's book** (*fig*) prendere esempio da qn.

►**leaf through** *vt* (*book*) sfogliare.

leaflet ['liːflɪt] *n* dépliant *m inv*; (*POL, REL*) volantino.

leafy ['liːfɪ] *adj* ricco(a) di foglie.

league [liːg] *n* lega; (*FOOTBALL*) campionato; **to be in ~ with** essere in lega con.

league table *n* classifica.

leak [liːk] *n* (*out*) fuga; (*in*) infiltrazione *f*; (*fig: of information*) fuga di notizie ♦ *vi* (*roof, bucket*) perdere; (*liquid*) uscire; (*shoes*) lasciar passare l'acqua ♦ *vt* (*liquid*) spandere; (*information*) divulgare.

►**leak out** *vi* uscire; (*information*) trapelare.

leakage ['liːkɪdʒ] *n* (*of water, gas etc*) perdita.

leaky ['liːkɪ] *adj* (*pipe, bucket, roof*) che perde; (*shoe*) che lascia passare l'acqua; (*boat*) che fa acqua.

lean [liːn] *adj* magro(a) ♦ *n* (*of meat*) carne *f* magra ♦ *vb* (*pt, pp* **leaned** *or* **leant** [lɛnt]) *vt*: **to ~ sth on** appoggiare qc su ♦ *vi* (*slope*) pendere; (*rest*): **to ~ against** appoggiarsi contro; essere appoggiato(a) a; **to ~ on** appoggiarsi a.

►**lean back** *vi* sporgersi indietro.

►**lean forward** *vi* sporgersi in avanti.

►**lean out** *vi*: **to ~ out (of)** sporgersi (da).

►**lean over** *vi* inclinarsi.

leaning ['liːnɪŋ] *n*: **~ (towards)** propensione *f* (per) ♦ *adj* inclinato(a), pendente; **the L~ Tower of Pisa** la torre (pendente) di Pisa.

leant [lɛnt] *pt, pp of* **lean**.

lean-to ['liːntuː] *n* (*roof*) tettoia; (*building*) *edificio con tetto appoggiato ad altro edificio*.

leap [liːp] *n* salto, balzo ♦ *vi* (*pt, pp* **leaped** *or* **leapt** [lɛpt]) saltare, balzare; **to ~ at an offer** afferrare al volo una proposta.

►**leap up** *vi* (*person*) alzarsi d'un balzo, balzare su.

leapfrog ['liːpfrɔg] *n* gioco della cavallina ♦ *vi*: **to ~ over sb/sth** saltare (alla cavallina) qn/qc.

leapt [lɛpt] *pt, pp of* **leap**.

leap year *n* anno bisestile.

learn, *pt, pp* **learned** *or* **learnt** [ləːn, -t] *vt, vi* imparare; **to ~ how to do sth** imparare a fare qc; **to ~ that ...** apprendere che ...; **to ~ about sth** (*SCOL*) studiare qc; (*hear*) apprendere qc; **we were sorry to ~ that it was closing down** la notizia della chiusura ci ha fatto dispiacere.

learned ['ləːnɪd] *adj* erudito(a), dotto(a).

learner ['ləːnə*] *n* principiante *m/f*; apprendista *m/f*; **he's a ~ (driver)** (*BRIT*) sta imparando a guidare.

learning ['ləːnɪŋ] *n* erudizione *f*, sapienza.

learnt [ləːnt] *pt, pp of* **learn**.

lease [liːs] *n* contratto d'affitto ♦ *vt* affittare; **on ~** in affitto.

►**lease back** *vt* effettuare un lease-back *inv*.

leaseback ['liːsbæk] *n* lease-back *m inv*.

leasehold ['liːshəuld] *n* (*contract*) contratto di affitto (*a lungo termine con responsabilità simili a quelle di un proprietario*) ♦ *adj* in affitto.

leash [liːʃ] *n* guinzaglio.

least [liːst] *adj*: **the ~ +** *noun* il(la) più piccolo(a), il(la) minimo(a); (*smallest* amount of) il(la) meno ♦ adv: the ~ + adjective: the ~ beautiful girl la ragazza meno bella; the ~ expensive il(la) meno caro(a); I have the ~ money ho meno denaro di tutti; at ~ almeno; not in the ~ affatto, per nulla.

leather ['lɛðə*] n (soft) pelle f; (hard) cuoio ♦ cpd di or in pelle; di cuoio; ~ goods pelletteria, pelletterie fpl.

leave [li:v] vb (pt, pp left [lɛft]) vt lasciare; (go away from) partire da ♦ vi partire, andarsene ♦ n (time off) congedo; (MIL, also: consent) licenza; to be left rimanere; there's some milk left over c'è rimasto del latte; to take one's ~ of congedarsi di; he's already left for the airport è già uscito per andare all'aeroporto; to ~ school finire la scuola; ~ it to me! ci penso io!, lascia fare a me!; on ~ in congedo; on ~ of absence in permesso; (public employee) in congedo; (MIL) in licenza.

▶**leave behind** vt (also fig) lasciare indietro; (forget) dimenticare.

▶**leave off** vt non mettere; (BRIT col: stop): to ~ off doing sth smetterla or piantarla di fare qc.

▶**leave on** vt lasciare su; (light, fire, cooker) lasciare acceso(a).

▶**leave out** vt omettere, tralasciare.

leaves [li:vz] npl of leaf.

leavetaking ['li:vteikiŋ] n commiato, addio.

Lebanese [lɛbə'ni:z] adj, n (pl inv) libanese (m/f).

Lebanon ['lɛbənən] n Libano.

lecherous ['lɛtʃərəs] adj lascivo(a), lubrico(a).

lectern ['lɛktə:n] n leggio.

lecture ['lɛktʃə*] n conferenza; (SCOL) lezione f ♦ vi fare conferenze; fare lezioni; (reprove) rimproverare, fare una ramanzina a; to ~ on fare una conferenza su; to give a ~ (on) (BRIT) fare una conferenza (su); fare lezione (su).

lecture hall n aula magna.

lecturer ['lɛktʃərə*] n (speaker) conferenziere/a; (BRIT: at university) professore/essa, docente m/f; assistant ~ (BRIT) ≈ professore(essa) associato(a); senior ~ (BRIT) ≈ professore(essa) ordinario(a).

lecture theatre n = lecture hall.

LED n abbr (ELEC: = light-emitting diode) diodo a emissione luminosa.

led [lɛd] pt, pp of lead.

ledge [lɛdʒ] n (of window) davanzale m; (on wall etc) sporgenza; (of mountain) cornice f, cengia.

ledger ['lɛdʒə*] n libro maestro, registro.

lee [li:] n lato sottovento; in the ~ of a ridosso di, al riparo di.

leech [li:tʃ] n sanguisuga.

leek [li:k] n porro.

leer [lɪə*] vi: to ~ at sb gettare uno sguardo voglioso (or maligno) su qn.

leeward ['li:wəd] adj sottovento inv ♦ n lato sottovento; to ~ sottovento.

leeway ['li:wei] n (fig): to have some ~ avere una certa libertà di agire.

left [lɛft] pt, pp of leave ♦ adj sinistra(a) ♦ adv a sinistra ♦ n sinistra; on the ~, to the ~ a sinistra; the L~ (POL) la sinistra.

left-hand drive ['lɛfthænd-] n (BRIT) guida a sinistra.

left-handed [lɛft'hændɪd] adj mancino(a); ~ scissors forbici fpl per mancini.

left-hand side ['lɛfthænd-] n lato or fianco sinistro.

leftie ['lɛftɪ] n: a ~ (col) uno/a di sinistra.

leftist ['lɛftɪst] adj (POL) di sinistra.

left-luggage (office) [lɛft'lʌgɪdʒ-] n deposito m bagagli inv.

left-overs ['lɛftəuvəz] npl avanzi mpl, resti mpl.

left wing n (MIL, SPORT) ala sinistra; (POL) sinistra ♦ adj: left-wing (POL) di sinistra.

left-winger [lɛft'wɪŋə*] n (POL) uno/a di sinistra; (SPORT) ala sinistra.

lefty ['lɛftɪ] n = leftie.

leg [lɛg] n gamba; (of animal) zampa; (of furniture) piede m; (CULIN: of chicken) coscia; (of journey) tappa; 1st/2nd ~ (SPORT) partita di andata/ritorno; ~ of lamb (CULIN) cosciotto d'agnello; to stretch one's ~s sgranchirsi le gambe.

legacy ['lɛgəsɪ] n eredità f inv; (fig) retaggio.

legal ['li:gl] adj legale; to take ~ action or proceedings against sb intentare un'azione legale contro qn, far causa a qn.

legal adviser n consulente m/f legale.

legality [lɪ'gælɪtɪ] n legalità.

legalize ['li:gəlaɪz] vt legalizzare.

legally ['li:gəlɪ] adv legalmente; ~ binding legalmente vincolante.

legal tender n moneta legale.

legation [lɪ'geɪʃən] n legazione f.

legend ['lɛdʒənd] n leggenda.

legendary ['lɛdʒəndərɪ] adj leggendario(a).

-legged ['lɛgɪd] suffix: two~ a due gambe (or zampe), bipede.

leggings ['lɛgɪŋz] npl ghette fpl.

leggy ['lɛgɪ] adj dalle gambe lunghe.

legibility [lɛdʒɪ'bɪlɪtɪ] n leggibilità.

legible ['lɛdʒəbl] adj leggibile.

legibly ['lɛdʒəblɪ] adv in modo leggibile.

legion ['liːdʒən] *n* legione *f*.
legionnaire [liːdʒə'nɛə*] *n* legionario; ~'s **disease** morbo del legionario.
legislate ['lɛdʒɪsleɪt] *vi* legiferare.
legislation [lɛdʒɪs'leɪʃən] *n* legislazione *f*; **a piece of** ~ una legge.
legislative ['lɛdʒɪslətɪv] *adj* legislativo(a).
legislator ['lɛdʒɪsleɪtə*] *n* legislatore/trice.
legislature ['lɛdʒɪslətʃə*] *n* corpo legislativo.
legitimacy [lɪ'dʒɪtɪməsɪ] *n* legittimità.
legitimate [lɪ'dʒɪtɪmət] *adj* legittimo(a).
legitimize [lɪ'dʒɪtɪmaɪz] *vt* (*gen*) legalizzare, rendere legale; (*child*) legittimare.
legless ['lɛglɪs] *adj* (*BRIT col*) sbronzo(a), fatto(a).
leg-room ['lɛgruːm] *n* spazio per le gambe.
Leics *abbr* (*BRIT*) = *Leicestershire*.
leisure ['lɛʒə*] *n* agio, tempo libero; ricreazioni *fpl*; **at** ~ all'agio; a proprio comodo.
leisure centre *n* centro di ricreazione.
leisurely ['lɛʒəlɪ] *adj* tranquillo(a); fatto(a) con comodo *or* senza fretta.
leisure suit *n* (*BRIT*) tuta (da ginnastica).
lemon ['lɛmən] *n* limone *m*.
lemonade [lɛmə'neɪd] *n* limonata.
lemon cheese, lemon curd *n* crema di limone (*che si spalma sul pane etc*).
lemon juice *n* succo di limone.
lemon squeezer *n* spremiagrumi *m inv*.
lemon tea *n* tè *m inv* al limone.
lend, *pt*, *pp* **lent** [lɛnd, lɛnt] *vt*: **to** ~ **sth (to sb)** prestare qc (a qn); **to** ~ **a hand** dare una mano.
lender ['lɛndə*] *n* prestatore/trice.
lending library ['lɛndɪŋ-] *n* biblioteca circolante.
length [lɛŋθ] *n* lunghezza; (*section: of road, pipe etc*) pezzo, tratto; ~ **of time** periodo (di tempo); **what** ~ **is it?** quant'è lungo?; **it is 2 metres in** ~ è lungo 2 metri; **to fall full** ~ cadere lungo disteso; **at** ~ (*at last*) finalmente, alla fine; (*lengthily*) a lungo; **to go to any** ~(**s**) **to do sth** fare qualsiasi cosa pur di *or* per fare qc.
lengthen ['lɛŋθən] *vt* allungare, prolungare ◆ *vi* allungarsi.
lengthways ['lɛŋθweɪz] *adv* per il lungo.
lengthy ['lɛŋθɪ] *adj* molto lungo(a).
leniency ['liːnɪənsɪ] *n* indulgenza, clemenza.
lenient ['liːnɪənt] *adj* indulgente, clemente.
leniently ['liːnɪəntlɪ] *adv* con indulgenza.
lens [lɛnz] *n* lente *f*; (*of camera*) obiettivo.
Lent [lɛnt] *n* Quaresima.
lent [lɛnt] *pt*, *pp of* **lend**.

lentil ['lɛntl] *n* lenticchia.
Leo ['liːəu] *n* Leone *m*; **to be** ~ essere del Leone.
leopard ['lɛpəd] *n* leopardo.
leotard ['liːətɑːd] *n* calzamaglia.
leper ['lɛpə*] *n* lebbroso/a.
leper colony *n* lebbrosario.
leprosy ['lɛprəsɪ] *n* lebbra.
lesbian ['lɛzbɪən] *n* lesbica ◆ *adj* lesbico(a).
lesion ['liːʒən] *n* (*MED*) lesione *f*.
Lesotho [lɪ'suːtu] *n* Lesotho *m*.
less [lɛs] *adj*, *pron*, *adv* meno; ~ **than you/ ever** meno di lei/che mai; ~ **than half** meno della metà; ~ **and** ~ sempre meno; **the** ~ **he works** ... meno lavora ...; ~ **than £1/a kilo/3 metres** meno di una sterlina/ un chilo/3 metri; ~ **5%** meno il 5%.
lessee [lɛ'siː] *n* affittuario/a, locatario/a.
lessen ['lɛsn] *vi* diminuire, attenuarsi ◆ *vt* diminuire, ridurre.
lesser ['lɛsə*] *adj* minore, più piccolo(a); **to a** ~ **extent** *or* **degree** in grado *or* misura minore.
lesson ['lɛsn] *n* lezione *f*; **a maths** ~ una lezione di matematica; **to give** ~**s in** dare *or* impartire lezioni di; **it taught him a** ~ (*fig*) gli è servito di lezione.
lessor ['lɛsɔː*, lɛ'sɔː*] *n* locatore/trice.
lest [lɛst] *conj* per paura di + *infinitive*, per paura che + *sub*.
let, *pt*, *pp* **let** [lɛt] *vt* lasciare; (*BRIT: lease*) dare in affitto; **to** ~ **sb do sth** lasciar fare qc a qn, lasciare che qn faccia qc; **to** ~ **sb know sth** far sapere qc a qn; **to** ~ **sb have sth** dare qc a qn; **he** ~ **me go** mi ha lasciato andare; ~ **the water boil and** ... fate bollire l'acqua e ...; ~'**s go** andiamo; ~ **him come** lo lasci venire; "**to** ~" "affittasi".
▶**let down** *vt* (*lower*) abbassare; (*dress*) allungare; (*hair*) sciogliere; (*disappoint*) deludere; (*BRIT: tyre*) sgonfiare.
▶**let go** *vi* mollare ◆ *vt* mollare; (*allow to go*) lasciare andare.
▶**let in** *vt* lasciare entrare; (*visitor etc*) far entrare; **what have you** ~ **yourself in for?** in che guai *or* pasticci sei andato a cacciarti?
▶**let off** *vt* (*allow to go*) lasciare andare; (*firework etc*) far partire; (*smell etc*) emettere; (*subj: taxi driver, bus driver*) far scendere; **to** ~ **off steam** (*fig col*) sfogarsi, scaricarsi.
▶**let on** *vi* (*col*): **to** ~ **on that** ... lasciar capire che ....
▶**let out** *vt* lasciare uscire; (*dress*) allargare; (*scream*) emettere; (*rent out*) affittare, dare in affitto.

▶**let up** *vi* diminuire.
let-down ['lɛtdaun] *n* (*disappointment*)
delusione *f*.
lethal ['li:θl] *adj* letale, mortale.
lethargic [lɛ'θɑːdʒɪk] *adj* letargico(a).
lethargy ['lɛθədʒɪ] *n* letargia.
letter ['lɛtə*] *n* lettera; **~s** *npl* (*LITERATURE*)
lettere; **small/capital** ~ lettera
minuscola/maiuscola; ~ **of credit** lettera
di credito; **documentary** ~ **of credit**
lettera di credito documentata.
letter bomb *n* lettera esplosiva.
letterbox ['lɛtəbɔks] *n* buca delle lettere.
letterhead ['lɛtəhɛd] *n* intestazione *f*.
lettering ['lɛtərɪŋ] *n* iscrizione *f*; caratteri
mpl.
letter-opener ['lɛtərəupnə*] *n* tagliacarte *m*
inv.
letterpress ['lɛtəprɛs] *n* (*method*)
rilievografia.
letter quality *n* (*of printer*) qualità di
stampa.
letters patent *npl* brevetto di invenzione.
lettuce ['lɛtɪs] *n* lattuga, insalata.
let-up ['lɛtʌp] *n* (*col*) interruzione *f*.
leukaemia, (*US*) **leukemia** [lu:'ki:mɪə] *n*
leucemia.
level ['lɛvl] *adj* piatto(a), piano(a);
orizzontale ♦ *n* livello; (*also:* **spirit** ~)
livella (a bolla d'aria) ♦ *vt* livellare,
spianare; (*gun*) puntare (verso);
(*accusation*): **to** ~ (**against**) lanciare (a *or*
contro) ♦ *vi* (*col*): **to** ~ **with sb** essere
franco(a) con qn; **to be** ~ **with** essere alla
pari di; **a** ~ **spoonful** (*CULIN*) un cucchiaio
raso; **to draw** ~ **with** (*team*) mettersi alla
pari di; (*runner, car*) affiancarsi a; **A ~s**
npl (*BRIT*) ≈ esami *mpl* di maturità; **O ~s**
npl (*BRIT:* formerly) diploma di istruzione
secondaria conseguito a 16 anni in
Inghilterra e Galles, ora sostituito dal
GCSE; **on the** ~ piatto(a); (*fig*) onesto(a).
▶**level off, level out** *vi* (*prices etc*)
stabilizzarsi; (*ground*) diventare
pianeggiante; (*aircraft*) volare in quota.
level crossing *n* (*BRIT*) passaggio a livello.
level-headed [lɛvl'hɛdɪd] *adj*
equilibrato(a).
levelling, (*US*) **leveling** ['lɛvlɪŋ] *adj*
(*process, effect*) di livellamento.
level playing field *n*: **to compete on a** ~
(*fig*) competere ad armi pari.
lever ['li:və*] *n* leva ♦ *vt*: **to** ~ **up/out**
sollevare/estrarre con una leva.
leverage ['li:vərɪdʒ] *n*: ~ (**on** *or* **with**)
ascendente *m* (su).
levity ['lɛvɪtɪ] *n* leggerezza, frivolità.
levy ['lɛvɪ] *n* tassa, imposta ♦ *vt* imporre.

lewd [lu:d] *adj* osceno(a), lascivo(a).
lexicographer [lɛksɪ'kɔgrəfə*] *n*
lessicografo/a.
lexicography [lɛksɪ'kɔgrəfɪ] *n* lessicografia.
LGV *n abbr* (= *Large Goods Vehicle*)
automezzo pesante.
LI *abbr* (*US*) = *Long Island*.
liabilities [laɪə'bɪlətɪz] *npl* debiti *mpl*; (*on
balance sheet*) passivo.
liability [laɪə'bɪlətɪ] *n* responsabilità *f inv*;
(*handicap*) peso.
liable ['laɪəbl] *adj* (*subject*): ~ **to** soggetto(a)
a; passibile di; (*responsible*): ~ (**for**)
responsabile (di); (*likely*): ~ **to do**
propenso(a) a fare; **to be** ~ **to a fine**
essere passibile di multa.
liaise [li:'eɪz] *vi*: **to** ~ (**with**) mantenere i
contatti (con).
liaison [li:'eɪzɔn] *n* relazione *f*; (*MIL*)
collegamento.
liar ['laɪə*] *n* bugiardo/a.
libel ['laɪbl] *n* libello, diffamazione *f* ♦ *vt*
diffamare.
libellous, (*US*) **libelous** ['laɪbləs] *adj*
diffamatorio(a).
liberal ['lɪbərl] *adj* liberale; (*generous*): **to be**
~ **with** distribuire liberalmente ♦ *n* (*POL*):
L~ liberale *m/f*.
Liberal Democrat *n* liberal-
democratico(a).
liberality [lɪbə'rælɪtɪ] *n* (*generosity*)
generosità, liberalità.
liberalize ['lɪbərəlaɪz] *vt* liberalizzare.
liberal-minded [lɪbərl'maɪndɪd] *adj*
tollerante.
liberate ['lɪbəreɪt] *vt* liberare.
liberation [lɪbə'reɪʃən] *n* liberazione *f*.
liberation theology *n* teologia della
liberazione.
Liberia [laɪ'bɪərɪə] *n* Liberia.
Liberian [laɪ'bɪərɪən] *adj, n* liberiano(a).
liberty ['lɪbətɪ] *n* libertà *f inv*; **at** ~ **to do**
libero(a) di fare; **to take the** ~ **of**
prendersi la libertà di, permettersi di.
libido [lɪ'bi:dəu] *n* libido *f*.
Libra ['li:brə] *n* Bilancia; **to be** ~ essere
della Bilancia.
librarian [laɪ'brɛərɪən] *n* bibliotecario/a.
library ['laɪbrərɪ] *n* biblioteca.
library book *n* libro della biblioteca.
libretto [lɪ'brɛtəu] *n* libretto.
Libya ['lɪbɪə] *n* Libia.
Libyan ['lɪbɪən] *adj, n* libico(a).
lice [laɪs] *npl of* **louse**.
licence, (*US*) **license** ['laɪsns] *n*
autorizzazione *f*, permesso; (*COMM*)
licenza; (*RADIO, TV*) canone *m*,
abbonamento; (*also:* **driving** ~, (*US*)

driver's ~) patente *f* di guida; (*excessive freedom*) licenza; **import** ~ licenza di importazione; **produced under** ~ prodotto su licenza.

licence number *n* (*BRIT AUT*) numero di targa.

license ['laɪsns] *n* (*US*) = **licence** ♦ *vt* dare una licenza a; (*car*) pagare la tassa di circolazione *or* il bollo di.

licensed ['laɪsnst] *adj* (*for alcohol*) che ha la licenza di vendere bibite alcoliche.

licensed trade *n* commercio di bevande alcoliche con licenza speciale.

licensee [laɪsən'siː] *n* (*BRIT: of pub*) detentore/trice di autorizzazione alla vendita di bevande alcoliche.

license plate *n* (*esp US AUT*) targa (automobilistica).

licentious [laɪ'sɛnʃəs] *adj* licenzioso(a).

lichen ['laɪkən] *n* lichene *m*.

lick [lɪk] *vt* leccare; (*col: defeat*) suonarle a, stracciare ♦ *n* leccata; **a** ~ **of paint** una passata di vernice.

licorice ['lɪkərɪs] *n* = **liquorice**.

lid [lɪd] *n* coperchio; **to take the** ~ **off sth** (*fig*) smascherare qc.

lido ['laɪdəu] *n* piscina all'aperto; (*part of the beach*) lido, stabilimento balneare.

lie [laɪ] *n* bugia, menzogna ♦ *vi* mentire, dire bugie; (*pt* **lay,** *pp* **lain** [leɪ, leɪn]) (*rest*) giacere, star disteso(a); (*in grave*) giacere, riposare; (*of object: be situated*) trovarsi, essere; **to tell** ~**s** raccontare *or* dire bugie; **to** ~ **low** (*fig*) latitare.

▶**lie about, lie around** *vi* (*things*) essere in giro; (*person*) bighellonare.

▶**lie back** *vi* stendersi.

▶**lie down** *vi* stendersi, sdraiarsi.

▶**lie up** *vi* (*hide*) nascondersi.

Liechtenstein ['lɪktənstaɪn] *n* Liechtenstein *m*.

lie detector *n* macchina della verità.

lie-down ['laɪdaun] *n* (*BRIT*): **to have a** ~ sdraiarsi, riposarsi.

lie-in ['laɪɪn] *n* (*BRIT*): **to have a** ~ rimanere a letto.

lieu [luː] *n*: **in** ~ **of** invece di, al posto di.

Lieut. *abbr* (= *lieutenant*) Ten.

lieutenant [lɛf'tɛnənt, (*US*) luː'tɛnənt] *n* tenente *m*.

lieutenant-colonel [lɛf'tɛnənt'kəːnl, (*US*) luː'tɛnənt'kəːnl] *n* tenente colonnello.

life [laɪf] *n* (*pl* **lives**) vita ♦ *cpd* di vita; della vita; a vita; **country/city** ~ vita di campagna/di città; **to be sent to prison for** ~ essere condannato all'ergastolo; **true to** ~ fedele alla realtà; **to paint from** ~ dipingere dal vero.

life annuity *n* rendita vitalizia.

life assurance *n* (*BRIT*) = **life insurance**.

lifebelt ['laɪfbɛlt] *n* (*BRIT*) salvagente *m*.

lifeblood ['laɪfblʌd] *n* (*fig*) linfa vitale.

lifeboat ['laɪfbəut] *n* scialuppa di salvataggio.

life expectancy *n* durata media della vita.

lifeguard ['laɪfgɑːd] *n* bagnino.

life imprisonment *n* ergastolo.

life insurance *n* assicurazione *f* sulla vita.

life jacket *n* giubbotto di salvataggio.

lifeless ['laɪflɪs] *adj* senza vita.

lifelike ['laɪflaɪk] *adj* che sembra vero(a); rassomigliante.

lifeline ['laɪflaɪn] *n* cavo di salvataggio.

lifelong ['laɪflɔŋ] *adj* per tutta la vita.

life preserver *n* (*US*) salvagente *m*; giubbotto di salvataggio; (*BRIT*) sfollagente *m inv*.

lifer ['laɪfə*] *n* (*col*) ergastolano/a.

life-raft ['laɪfrɑːft] *n* zattera di salvataggio.

life-saver ['laɪfseɪvə*] *n* bagnino.

life sentence *n* (condanna all')ergastolo.

life-sized ['laɪfsaɪzd] *adj* a grandezza naturale.

life span *n* (durata della) vita.

life style *n* stile *m* di vita.

life support system *n* (*MED*) respiratore *m* automatico.

lifetime ['laɪftaɪm] *n*: **in his** ~ durante la sua vita; **in a** ~ nell'arco della vita; in tutta la vita; **the chance of a** ~ un'occasione unica.

lift [lɪft] *vt* sollevare, levare; (*steal*) prendere, rubare ♦ *vi* (*fog*) alzarsi ♦ *n* (*BRIT: elevator*) ascensore *m*; **to give sb a** ~ (*BRIT*) dare un passaggio a qn.

▶**lift off** *vt* togliere ♦ *vi* (*rocket*) partire; (*helicopter*) decollare.

▶**lift out** *vt* tirar fuori; (*troops, evacuees etc*) far evacuare per mezzo di elicotteri (*or aerei*).

▶**lift up** *vt* sollevare, alzare.

lift-off ['lɪftɔf] *n* decollo.

ligament ['lɪgəmənt] *n* legamento.

light [laɪt] *n* luce, lume *m*; (*daylight*) luce, giorno; (*lamp*) lampada; (*AUT: rear* ~) luce di posizione; (*: headlamp*) fanale *m*; (*for cigarette etc*): **have you got a** ~**?** ha da accendere? ♦ *vt* (*pt, pp* **lighted** *or* **lit** [lɪt]) (*candle, cigarette, fire*) accendere; (*room*) illuminare ♦ *adj* (*room, colour*) chiaro(a); (*not heavy, also fig*) leggero(a) ♦ *adv* (*travel*) con poco bagaglio; ~**s** *npl* (*AUT: traffic* ~**s**) semaforo; **in the** ~ **of** alla luce di; **to turn the** ~ **on/off** accendere/ spegnere la luce; **to come to** ~ venire in luce; **to cast** *or* **shed** *or* **throw** ~ **on**

gettare luce su; **to make** ~ **of sth** (*fig*) prendere alla leggera qc, non dar peso a qc.
▶**light up** *vi* illuminarsi ♦ *vt* illuminare.
light bulb *n* lampadina.
lighten ['laɪtn] *vi* schiarirsi ♦ *vt* (*give light to*) illuminare; (*make lighter*) schiarire; (*make less heavy*) alleggerire.
lighter ['laɪtə*] *n* (*also:* **cigarette** ~) accendino; (*boat*) chiatta.
light-fingered [laɪt'fɪŋɡəd] *adj* lesto(a) di mano.
light-headed ['laɪt'hɛdɪd] *adj* stordito(a).
light-hearted ['laɪt'hɑːtɪd] *adj* gioioso(a), gaio(a).
lighthouse ['laɪthaus] *n* faro.
lighting ['laɪtɪŋ] *n* illuminazione *f*.
lighting-up time ['laɪtɪŋʌp-] *n* (*BRIT*) *orario per l'accensione delle luci*.
lightly ['laɪtlɪ] *adv* leggermente; **to get off** ~ cavarsela a buon mercato.
light meter *n* (*PHOT*) esposimetro.
lightness ['laɪtnɪs] *n* chiarezza; (*in weight*) leggerezza.
lightning ['laɪtnɪŋ] *n* lampo, fulmine *m*; **a flash of** ~ un lampo, un fulmine.
lightning conductor, (*US*) **lightning rod** *n* parafulmine *m*.
lightning strike *n* (*BRIT*) sciopero *m* lampo *inv*.
light pen *n* penna luminosa.
lightship ['laɪtʃɪp] *n* battello *m* faro *inv*.
lightweight ['laɪtweɪt] *adj* (*suit*) leggero(a); (*boxer*) peso leggero *inv*.
light year ['laɪtjɪə*] *n* anno *m* luce *inv*.
Ligurian [lɪ'ɡjuərɪən] *adj*, *n* ligure (*m/f*).
like [laɪk] *vt* (*person*) volere bene a; (*activity, object, food*): **I** ~ **swimming/that book/ chocolate** mi piace nuotare/quel libro/il cioccolato ♦ *prep* come ♦ *adj* simile, uguale ♦ *n*: **the** ~ uno(a) uguale; **I would** ~, **I'd** ~ mi piacerebbe, vorrei; **would you** ~ **a coffee?** gradirebbe un caffè?; **if you** ~ se vuoi; **to be/look** ~ **sb/sth** somigliare a qn/qc; **what's he** ~? che tipo è?, com'è?; **what's the weather** ~? che tempo fa?; **that's just** ~ **him** è proprio da lui; **something** ~ **that** qualcosa del genere; **I feel** ~ **a drink** avrei voglia di bere qualcosa; **there's nothing** ~ ... non c'è niente di meglio di *or* niente come ...; **his** ~**s and dislikes** i suoi gusti.
likeable ['laɪkəbl] *adj* simpatico(a).
likelihood ['laɪklɪhud] *n* probabilità; **in all** ~ con ogni probabilità, molto probabilmente.
likely ['laɪklɪ] *adj* probabile; plausibile; **he's** ~ **to leave** probabilmente partirà, è

probabile che parta; **not** ~! (*col*) neanche per sogno!
like-minded ['laɪk'maɪndɪd] *adj* che pensa allo stesso modo.
liken ['laɪkən] *vt*: **to** ~ **sth to** paragonare qc a.
likeness ['laɪknɪs] *n* (*similarity*) somiglianza.
likewise ['laɪkwaɪz] *adv* similmente, nello stesso modo.
liking ['laɪkɪŋ] *n*: ~ **(for)** simpatia (per); debole *m* (per); **to be to sb's** ~ essere di gusto *or* gradimento di qn; **to take a** ~ **to sb** prendere qn in simpatia.
lilac ['laɪlək] *n* lilla *m inv* ♦ *adj* lilla *inv*.
Lilo ® ['laɪləu] *n* materassino gonfiabile.
lilt [lɪlt] *n* cadenza.
lilting ['lɪltɪŋ] *adj* melodioso(a).
lily ['lɪlɪ] *n* giglio; ~ **of the valley** mughetto.
Lima ['liːmə] *n* Lima.
limb [lɪm] *n* membro; **to be out on a** ~ (*fig*) sentirsi spaesato *or* tagliato fuori.
limber ['lɪmbə*]: **to** ~ **up** *vi* riscaldarsi i muscoli.
limbo ['lɪmbəu] *n*: **to be in** ~ (*fig*) essere lasciato(a) nel dimenticatoio.
lime [laɪm] *n* (*tree*) tiglio; (*fruit*) limetta; (*GEO*) calce *f*.
lime juice *n* succo di limetta.
limelight ['laɪmlaɪt] *n*: **in the** ~ (*fig*) alla ribalta, in vista.
limerick ['lɪmərɪk] *n poesiola umoristica di cinque versi*.
limestone ['laɪmstəun] *n* pietra calcarea; (*GEO*) calcare *m*.
limit ['lɪmɪt] *n* limite *m* ♦ *vt* limitare; **weight/speed** ~ limite di peso/di velocità; **within** ~**s** entro certi limiti.
limitation [lɪmɪ'teɪʃən] *n* limitazione *f*, limite *m*.
limited ['lɪmɪtɪd] *adj* limitato(a), ristretto(a); ~ **edition** edizione *f* a bassa tiratura.
limited (liability) company (Ltd) *n* (*BRIT*) ≈ società *f inv* a responsabilità limitata (S.r.l.).
limitless ['lɪmɪtlɪs] *adj* illimitato(a).
limousine ['lɪməziːn] *n* limousine *f inv*.
limp [lɪmp] *n*: **to have a** ~ zoppicare ♦ *vi* zoppicare ♦ *adj* floscio(a), flaccido(a).
limpet ['lɪmpɪt] *n* patella.
limpid ['lɪmpɪd] *adj* (*poet*) limpido(a).
linchpin ['lɪntʃpɪn] *n* acciarino, bietta; (*fig*) perno.
Lincs *abbr* (*BRIT*) = Lincolnshire.
line [laɪn] *n* (*gen*, *COMM*) linea; (*rope*) corda; (*wire*) filo; (*of poem*) verso; (*row, series*) fila, riga; coda ♦ *vt* (*clothes*): **to** ~ **(with)** foderare (di); (*box*): **to** ~ **(with)** rivestire

or foderare (di); (*subj: trees, crowd*)
fiancheggiare; **to cut in** ~ (*US*) passare
avanti; **in his** ~ **of business** nel suo ramo
(di affari); **on the right** ~s sulla buona
strada; **a new** ~ **in cosmetics** una nuova
linea di cosmetici; **hold the** ~ **please** (*BRIT
TEL*) resti in linea per cortesia; **to be in** ~
for sth (*fig*) essere in lista per qc; **in** ~
with d'accordo con, in linea con; **to bring
sth into** ~ **with sth** mettere qc al passo
con qc; **to draw the** ~ **at (doing) sth** (*fig*)
rifiutarsi di fare qc; **to take the** ~ **that** ...
essere del parere che ....
►**line up** *vi* allinearsi, mettersi in fila ♦ *vt*
mettere in fila; **to have sth** ~d **up** avere
qc in programma; **to have sb** ~d **up**
avere qn in mente.
linear ['lɪnɪə*] *adj* lineare.
lined [laɪnd] *adj* (*paper*) a righe, rigato(a);
(*face*) rugoso(a); (*clothes*) foderato(a).
line feed *n* (*COMPUT*) avanzamento di una
interlinea.
linen ['lɪnɪn] *n* biancheria, panni *mpl*; (*cloth*)
tela di lino.
line printer *n* stampante *f* parallela.
liner ['laɪnə*] *n* nave *f* di linea; **dustbin** ~
sacchetto per la pattumiera.
linesman ['laɪnzmən] *n* guardalinee *m inv*,
segnalinee *m inv*.
line-up ['laɪnʌp] *n* allineamento, fila; (*also:*
police ~) confronto all'americana;
(*SPORT*) formazione *f* di gioco.
linger ['lɪŋgə*] *vi* attardarsi; indugiare;
(*smell, tradition*) persistere.
lingerie ['lænʒəriː] *n* biancheria intima
(femminile).
lingering ['lɪŋgərɪŋ] *adj* lungo(a);
persistente; (*death*) lento(a).
lingo, ~es ['lɪŋgəʊ] *n* (*pej*) gergo.
linguist ['lɪŋgwɪst] *n* linguista *m/f*; poliglotta
m/f.
linguistic [lɪŋ'gwɪstɪk] *adj* linguistico(a).
linguistics [lɪŋ'gwɪstɪks] *n* linguistica.
lining ['laɪnɪŋ] *n* fodera; (*TECH*)
rivestimento (interno); (*of brake*)
guarnizione *f*.
link [lɪŋk] *n* (*of a chain*) anello; (*connection*)
legame *m*, collegamento ♦ *vt* collegare,
unire, congiungere; **rail** ~ collegamento
ferroviario; *see also* **links**.
►**link up** *vt* collegare, unire ♦ *vi* riunirsi;
associarsi.
links [lɪŋks] *npl* pista *or* terreno da golf.
link-up ['lɪŋkʌp] *n* legame *m*; (*of roads*)
nodo; (*of spaceships*) aggancio; (*RADIO, TV*)
collegamento.
linoleum [lɪ'nəʊlɪəm] *n* linoleum *m inv*.
linseed oil ['lɪnsiːd-] *n* olio di semi di lino.

lint [lɪnt] *n* garza.
lintel ['lɪntl] *n* architrave *f*.
lion ['laɪən] *n* leone *m*.
lion cub *n* leoncino.
lioness ['laɪənɪs] *n* leonessa.
lip [lɪp] *n* labbro; (*of cup etc*) orlo; (*insolence*)
sfacciataggine *f*.
liposuction ['lɪpəʊsʌkʃən] *n* liposuzione *f*.
lipread ['lɪpriːd] *vi* leggere sulle labbra.
lip salve *n* burro di cacao.
lip service *n*: **to pay** ~ **to sth** essere
favorevole a qc solo a parole.
lipstick ['lɪpstɪk] *n* rossetto.
liquefy ['lɪkwɪfaɪ] *vt* liquefare ♦ *vi*
liquefarsi.
liqueur [lɪ'kjuə*] *n* liquore *m*.
liquid ['lɪkwɪd] *n* liquido ♦ *adj* liquido(a).
liquid assets *npl* attività *fpl* liquide, crediti
mpl liquidi.
liquidate ['lɪkwɪdeɪt] *vt* liquidare.
liquidation [lɪkwɪ'deɪʃən] *n* liquidazione *f*;
to go into ~ andare in liquidazione.
liquidator ['lɪkwɪdeɪtə*] *n* liquidatore *m*.
liquid crystal display (LCD) *n*
visualizzazione *f* a cristalli liquidi.
liquidity [lɪ'kwɪdɪtɪ] *n* (*COMM*) liquidità.
liquidize ['lɪkwɪdaɪz] *vt* (*BRIT CULIN*) passare
al frullatore.
liquidizer ['lɪkwɪdaɪzə*] *n* (*BRIT CULIN*)
frullatore *m* (a brocca).
liquor ['lɪkə*] *n* alcool *m*.
liquorice ['lɪkərɪs] *n* liquirizia.
Lisbon ['lɪzbən] *n* Lisbona.
lisp [lɪsp] *n* difetto nel pronunciare le
sibilanti.
lissom ['lɪsəm] *adj* leggiadro(a).
list [lɪst] *n* lista, elenco; (*of ship*)
sbandamento ♦ *vt* (*write down*) mettere in
lista; fare una lista di; (*enumerate*)
elencare; (*COMPUT*) stampare (un
prospetto di) ♦ *vi* (*ship*) sbandare;
shopping ~ lista *or* nota della spesa.
listed building ['lɪstəd-] *n* (*ARCHIT*) edificio
sotto la protezione delle Belle Arti.
listed company *n* società quotata in
Borsa.
listen ['lɪsn] *vi* ascoltare; **to** ~ **to** ascoltare.
listener ['lɪsnə*] *n* ascoltatore/trice.
listeria [lɪs'tɪərɪə] *n* listeria.
listing ['lɪstɪŋ] *n* (*COMPUT*) lista stampata.
listless ['lɪstlɪs] *adj* svogliato(a); apatico(a).
listlessly ['lɪstlɪslɪ] *adv* svogliatamente;
apaticamente.
list price *n* prezzo di listino.
lit [lɪt] *pt, pp* *of* **light**.
litany ['lɪtənɪ] *n* litania.
liter ['liːtə*] *n* (*US*) = **litre**.
literacy ['lɪtərəsɪ] *n* il sapere leggere e

scrivere.
literacy campaign n lotta contro l'analfabetismo.
literal ['lɪtərl] adj letterale.
literally ['lɪtərəlɪ] adv alla lettera, letteralmente.
literary ['lɪtərərɪ] adj letterario(a).
literate ['lɪtərɪt] adj che sa leggere e scrivere.
literature ['lɪtərɪtʃə*] n letteratura; (brochures etc) materiale m.
lithe [laɪð] adj agile, snello(a).
lithography [lɪ'θɔgrəfɪ] n litografia.
Lithuania [lɪθju'eɪnɪə] n Lituania.
Lithuanian [lɪθju'eɪnɪən] adj lituano(a) ♦ n lituano/a; (LING) lituano.
litigate ['lɪtɪgeɪt] vt muovere causa a ♦ vi litigare.
litigation [lɪtɪ'geɪʃən] n causa.
litmus ['lɪtməs] n: ~ **paper** cartina di tornasole.
litre, (US) **liter** ['li:tə*] n litro.
litter ['lɪtə*] n (rubbish) rifiuti mpl; (young animals) figliata ♦ vt sparpagliare; lasciare rifiuti in; ~**ed with** coperto(a) di.
litter bin n (BRIT) cestino per rifiuti.
litter lout, (US) **litterbug** ['lɪtəbʌg] n persona che butta per terra le cartacce o i rifiuti.
little ['lɪtl] adj (small) piccolo(a); (not much) poco(a) ♦ adv poco; **a** ~ un po' (di); **a** ~ **milk** un po' di latte; **with** ~ **difficulty** senza fatica or difficoltà; ~ **by** ~ a poco a poco; **as** ~ **as possible** il meno possibile; **for a** ~ **while** per un po'; **to make** ~ **of** dare poca importanza a; ~ **finger** mignolo.
little-known ['lɪtl'nəun] adj poco noto(a).
liturgy ['lɪtədʒɪ] n liturgia.
live vi [lɪv] vivere; (reside) vivere, abitare ♦ adj [laɪv] (animal) vivo(a); (issue) scottante, d'attualità; (wire) sotto tensione; (broadcast) diretto(a); (ammunition: not blank) carico(a); (unexploded) inesploso(a); **to** ~ **in London** abitare a Londra; **to** ~ **together** vivere insieme, convivere.
▶**live down** vt far dimenticare (alla gente).
▶**live in** vi essere interno(a); avere vitto e alloggio.
▶**live off** vi (land, fish etc) vivere di; (pej: parents etc) vivere alle spalle or a spese di.
▶**live on** vt fus (food) vivere di ♦ vi sopravvivere, continuare a vivere; **to** ~ **on £50 a week** vivere con 50 sterline la settimana.

▶**live out** vi (BRIT: students) essere esterno(a) ♦ vt: **to** ~ **out one's days** or **life** trascorrere gli ultimi anni.
▶**live up** vt: **to** ~ **it up** (col) fare la bella vita.
▶**live up to** vt fus tener fede a, non venir meno a.
live-in ['lɪvɪn] adj (col: partner) convivente; (servant) che vive in casa; **he has a** ~ **girlfriend** la sua ragazza vive con lui.
livelihood ['laɪvlɪhud] n mezzi mpl di sostentamento.
liveliness ['laɪvlɪnəs] n vivacità.
lively ['laɪvlɪ] adj vivace, vivo(a).
liven up ['laɪvn-] vt (room etc) ravvivare; (discussion, evening) animare.
liver ['lɪvə*] n fegato.
liverish ['lɪvərɪʃ] adj che soffre di mal di fegato; (fig) scontroso(a).
Liverpudlian [lɪvə'pʌdlɪən] adj di Liverpool ♦ n abitante m/f di Liverpool; originario/a di Liverpool.
livery ['lɪvərɪ] n livrea.
lives [laɪvz] npl of **life**.
livestock ['laɪvstɔk] n bestiame m.
live wire [laɪv-] n (col: fig): **to be a** ~ essere pieno(a) di vitalità.
livid ['lɪvɪd] adj livido(a); (furious) livido(a) di rabbia, furibondo(a).
living ['lɪvɪŋ] adj vivo(a), vivente ♦ n: **to earn** or **make a** ~ guadagnarsi la vita; **cost of** ~ costo della vita, carovita m; **within** ~ **memory** a memoria d'uomo.
living conditions npl condizioni fpl di vita.
living expenses npl spese fpl di mantenimento.
living room n soggiorno.
living standards npl tenore m di vita.
living wage n salario sufficiente per vivere.
lizard ['lɪzəd] n lucertola.
llama ['lɑːmə] n lama m inv.
LLB n abbr (= Bachelor of Laws) ≈ laurea in legge.
LLD n abbr (= Doctor of Laws) titolo di studio.
LMT abbr (US: = Local Mean Time) tempo medio locale.
load [ləud] n (weight) peso; (ELEC, TECH, thing carried) carico ♦ vt: **to** ~ **(with)** (lorry, ship) caricare (di); (gun, camera) caricare (con); **a** ~ **of,** ~**s of** (fig) un sacco di; **to** ~ **a program** (COMPUT) caricare un programma.
loaded ['ləudɪd] adj (dice) falsato(a); (question, word) capzioso(a); (col: rich) pieno(a) di soldi.
loading bay ['ləudɪŋ-] n piazzola di carico.

loaf [ləuf] n (pl **loaves**) pane m, pagnotta ♦ vi (also: ~ **about**, ~ **around**) bighellonare.
loam [ləum] n terra di marna.
loan [ləun] n prestito ♦ vt dare in prestito; **on** ~ in prestito.
loan account n conto dei prestiti.
loan capital n capitale m di prestito.
loan shark n (col: pej) strozzino(a).
loath [ləuθ] adj: **to be** ~ **to do** essere restio(a) a fare.
loathe [ləuð] vt detestare, aborrire.
loathing ['ləuðıŋ] n aborrimento, disgusto.
loathsome ['ləuðsəm] adj (gen) ripugnante; (person) detestabile, odioso(a).
loaves [ləuvz] npl of **loaf**.
lob [lɔb] vt (ball) lanciare.
lobby ['lɔbı] n atrio, vestibolo; (POL: pressure group) gruppo di pressione ♦ vt fare pressione su.
lobbyist ['lɔbııst] n appartenente m/f ad un gruppo di pressione.
lobe [ləub] n lobo.
lobster ['lɔbstə*] n aragosta.
lobster pot n nassa per aragoste.
local ['ləukl] adj locale ♦ n (BRIT: pub) ≈ bar m inv all'angolo; **the** ~**s** npl la gente della zona.
local anaesthetic n anestesia locale.
local authority n autorità locale.
local call n (TEL) telefonata urbana.
local government n amministrazione f locale.
locality [ləu'kælıtı] n località f inv; (position) posto, luogo.
localize ['ləukəlaız] vt localizzare.
locally ['ləukəlı] adv da queste parti; nel vicinato.
locate [ləu'keıt] vt (find) trovare; (situate) collocare.
location [ləu'keıʃən] n posizione f; **on** ~ (CINE) all'esterno.
loch [lɔx] n lago.
lock [lɔk] n (of door, box) serratura; (of canal) chiusa; (of hair) ciocca, riccio ♦ vt (with key) chiudere a chiave; (immobilize) bloccare ♦ vi (door etc) chiudersi; (wheels) bloccarsi, incepparsi; ~ **stock and barrel** (fig) in blocco; **on full** ~ (BRIT AUT) a tutto sterzo.
►**lock away** vt (valuables) tenere (rinchiuso(a)) al sicuro; (criminal) metter dentro.
►**lock out** vt chiudere fuori; **to** ~ **workers out** fare una serrata.
►**lock up** vi chiudere tutto (a chiave).
locker ['lɔkə*] n armadietto.
locket ['lɔkıt] n medaglione m.
lockjaw ['lɔkdʒɔː] n tetano.

lockout ['lɔkaut] n (INDUSTRY) serrata.
locksmith ['lɔksmıθ] n magnano.
lock-up ['lɔkʌp] n (prison) prigione f; (cell) guardina; (also: ~ **garage**) box m inv.
locomotive [ləukə'məutıv] n locomotiva.
locum ['ləukəm] n (MED) medico sostituto.
locust ['ləukəst] n locusta.
lodge [lɔdʒ] n casetta, portineria; (FREEMASONRY) loggia ♦ vi (person): **to** ~ **(with)** essere a pensione (presso or da) ♦ vt (appeal etc) presentare, fare; **to** ~ **a complaint** presentare un reclamo; **to** ~ **(itself) in/between** piantarsi dentro/fra.
lodger ['lɔdʒə*] n affittuario/a; (with room and meals) pensionante m/f.
lodging ['lɔdʒıŋ] n alloggio; see also **board**; **lodgings**.
lodging house n (BRIT) casa con camere in affitto.
lodgings ['lɔdʒıŋz] npl camera d'affitto; camera ammobiliata.
loft [lɔft] n soffitta; (AGR) granaio; (US) appartamento ricavato da solaio (or granaio etc).
lofty ['lɔftı] adj alto(a); (haughty) altezzoso(a); (sentiments, aims) nobile.
log [lɔg] n (of wood) ceppo; (book) = **logbook** ♦ n abbr = **logarithm** ♦ vt registrare.
►**log in, log on** vi (COMPUT) aprire una sessione (con codice di riconoscimento).
►**log off, log out** vi (COMPUT) terminare una sessione.
logarithm ['lɔgərıðm] n logaritmo.
logbook ['lɔgbuk] n (NAUT, AVIAT) diario di bordo; (AUT) libretto di circolazione; (of lorry driver) registro di viaggio; (of events, movement of goods etc) registro.
log cabin n capanna di tronchi.
log fire n fuoco di legna.
logger ['lɔgə*] n boscaiolo, tagliategna m inv.
loggerheads ['lɔgəhɛdz] npl: **at** ~ **(with)** ai ferri corti (con).
logic ['lɔdʒık] n logica.
logical ['lɔdʒıkəl] adj logico(a).
logically ['lɔdʒıkəlı] adv logicamente.
logistics [lɔ'dʒıstıks] n logistica.
logjam ['lɔgdʒæm] n: **to break the** ~ superare l'impasse.
logo ['ləugəu] n logo m inv.
loin [lɔın] n (CULIN) lombata; ~**s** npl reni fpl.
loin cloth n perizoma m.
loiter ['lɔıtə*] vi attardarsi; **to** ~ **(about)** indugiare, bighellonare.
loll [lɔl] vi (also: ~ **about**) essere stravaccato(a).
lollipop ['lɔlıpɔp] n lecca lecca m inv.

In Gran Bretagna il **lollipop man** e la **lollipop lady** sono persone incaricate di regolare il traffico in prossimità delle scuole e di aiutare i bambini ad attraversare la strada; usano una paletta la cui forma ricorda quella di un lecca lecca, in inglese, appunto, lollipop.

lollop ['lɔləp] vi (BRIT) camminare (or correre) goffamente.
lolly ['lɔlɪ] (col) n lecca lecca m inv; (also: ice ~) ghiacciolo; (money) grana.
Lombardy ['lɔmbədɪ] n Lombardia.
London ['lʌndən] n Londra.
Londoner ['lʌndənə*] n londinese m/f.
lone [ləun] adj solitario(a).
loneliness ['ləunlɪnɪs] n solitudine f, isolamento.
lonely ['ləunlɪ] adj solitario(a); (place) isolato(a); **to feel** ~ sentirsi solo(a).
lonely hearts adj: ~ **ads**, ~ **column** messaggi mpl personali; ~ **club** club m inv dei cuori solitari.
lone parent n (unmarried: mother) ragazza madre; (: father) ragazzo padre; (divorced) genitore m divorziato(a); (widowed) genitore rimasto vedovo.
loner ['ləunə*] n solitario/a.
lonesome ['ləunsəm] adj solo(a).
long [lɔŋ] adj lungo(a) ♦ adv a lungo, per molto tempo ♦ n: **the** ~ **and the short of it is that** ... (fig) a farla breve ... ♦ vi: **to** ~ **for sth/to do** desiderare qc/di fare; non veder l'ora di aver qc/di fare; **he had** ~ **understood that** ... aveva capito da molto tempo che ...; **how** ~ **is this river/course?** quanto è lungo questo fiume/corso?; **6 metres** ~ lungo 6 metri; **6 months** ~ che dura 6 mesi, di 6 mesi; **all night** ~ tutta la notte; **he no** ~**er comes** non viene più; ~ **before** molto tempo prima; **before** ~ (+ future) presto, fra poco; (+ past) poco tempo dopo; ~ **ago** molto tempo fa; **don't be** ~! faccia presto!; **I shan't be** ~ non ne avrò per molto; **at** ~ **last** finalmente; **in the** ~ **run** alla fin fine; **so or as** ~ **as** sempre che + sub.
long-distance [lɔŋ'dɪstəns] adj (race) di fondo; (call) interurbano(a).
long-haired ['lɔŋ'hɛəd] adj (person) dai capelli lunghi; (animal) dal pelo lungo.
longhand ['lɔŋhænd] n scrittura normale.
longing ['lɔŋɪŋ] n desiderio, voglia, brama ♦ adj di desiderio; pieno(a) di nostalgia.
longingly ['lɔŋɪŋlɪ] adv con desiderio (or nostalgia).
longitude ['lɔŋgɪtjuːd] n longitudine f.

long johns [-dʒɔnz] npl mutande fpl lunghe.
long jump n salto in lungo.
long-lost ['lɔŋlɔst] adj perduto(a) da tempo.
long-playing ['lɔŋpleɪɪŋ] adj: ~ **record (LP)** (disco) 33 giri m inv.
long-range [lɔŋ'reɪndʒ] adj a lunga portata; (weather forecast) a lungo termine.
longshoreman ['lɔŋʃɔːmən] n (US) scaricatore m (di porto), portuale m.
long-sighted [lɔŋ'saɪtɪd] adj (BRIT) presbite; (fig) lungimirante.
long-standing ['lɔŋstændɪŋ] adj di vecchia data.
long-suffering [lɔŋ'sʌfərɪŋ] adj estremamente paziente; infinitamente tollerante.
long-term ['lɔŋtəːm] adj a lungo termine.
long wave n (RADIO) onde fpl lunghe.
long-winded [lɔŋ'wɪndɪd] adj prolisso(a), interminabile.
loo [luː] n (BRIT col) W.C. m inv, cesso.
loofah ['luːfə] n luffa.
look [luk] vi guardare; (seem) sembrare, parere; (building etc): **to** ~ **south/on to the sea** dare a sud/sul mare ♦ n sguardo; (appearance) aspetto, aria; ~**s** npl aspetto; bellezza; **to** ~ **like** assomigliare a; **to** ~ **ahead** guardare avanti; **it** ~**s about 4 metres long** sarà lungo un 4 metri; **it** ~**s all right to me** a me pare che vada bene; **to have a** ~ **at sth** dare un'occhiata a qc; **to have a** ~ **for sth** cercare qc.
►**look after** vt fus occuparsi di, prendersi cura di; (keep an eye on) guardare, badare a.
►**look around** vi guardarsi intorno.
►**look at** vt fus guardare.
►**look back** vi: **to** ~ **back at sth/sb** voltarsi a guardare qc/qn; **to** ~ **back on** (event, period) ripensare a.
►**look down on** vt fus (fig) guardare dall'alto, disprezzare.
►**look for** vt fus cercare.
►**look forward to** vt fus non veder l'ora di; **I'm not** ~**ing forward to it** non ne ho nessuna voglia; ~**ing forward to hearing from you** (in letter) aspettando tue notizie.
►**look in** vi: **to** ~ **in on sb** (visit) fare un salto da qn.
►**look into** vt fus (matter, possibility) esaminare.
►**look on** vi fare da spettatore.
►**look out** vi (beware): **to** ~ **out (for)** stare in guardia (per).
►**look out for** vt fus cercare; (watch out for): **to** ~ **out for sb/sth** guardare se arriva qn/qc.
►**look over** vt (essay) dare un'occhiata a,

riguardare; (_town, building_) vedere; (_person_) esaminare.

►**look round** _vi_ (_turn_) girarsi, voltarsi; (_in shops_) dare un'occhiata; **to ~ round for sth** guardarsi intorno cercando qc.

►**look through** _vt fus_ (_papers, book_) scorrere; (_telescope_) guardare attraverso.

►**look to** _vt fus_ stare attento(a) a; (_rely on_) contare su.

►**look up** _vi_ alzare gli occhi; (_improve_) migliorare ♦ _vt_ (_word_) cercare; (_friend_) andare a trovare.

►**look up to** _vt fus_ avere rispetto per.

look-out ['lukaut] _n_ posto d'osservazione; guardia; **to be on the ~ (for)** stare in guardia (per).

look-up table ['lukʌp-] _n_ (_COMPUT_) tabella di consultazione.

LOOM _n abbr_ (_US_: = _Loyal Order of Moose_) organizzazione filantropica.

loom [luːm] _n_ telaio ♦ _vi_ sorgere; (_fig_) minacciare.

loony ['luːnɪ] _adj_, _n_ (_col_) pazzo(a).

loop [luːp] _n_ cappio; (_COMPUT_) anello.

loophole ['luːphəul] _n_ via d'uscita; scappatoia.

loose [luːs] _adj_ (_knot_) sciolto(a); (_screw_) allentato(a); (_stone_) cadente; (_clothes_) ampio(a), largo(a); (_animal_) in libertà, scappato(a); (_life, morals_) dissoluto(a); (_discipline_) allentato(a); (_thinking_) poco rigoroso(a), vago(a) ♦ _vt_ (_untie_) sciogliere; (_slacken_) allentare; (_free_) liberare; (_BRIT: arrow_) scoccare; **~ connection** (_ELEC_) filo che fa contatto; **to be at a ~ end** _or_ (_US_) **at ~ ends** (_fig_) non saper che fare; **to tie up ~ ends** (_fig_) avere ancora qualcosa da sistemare.

loose change _n_ spiccioli _mpl_, moneta.

loose-fitting ['luːsfɪtɪŋ] _adj_ ampio(a).

loose-leaf ['luːsliːf] _adj_: **~ binder** _or_ **folder** raccoglitore _m_.

loose-limbed [luːs'lɪmd] _adj_ snodato(a), agile.

loosely ['luːslɪ] _adv_ lentamente; approssimativamente.

loosely-knit ['luːslɪ'nɪt] _adj_ non rigidamente strutturato(a).

loosen ['luːsn] _vt_ sciogliere.

►**loosen up** _vi_ (_before game_) sciogliere i muscoli, scaldarsi; (_col: relax_) rilassarsi.

loot [luːt] _n_ bottino ♦ _vt_ saccheggiare.

looter ['luːtə*] _n_ saccheggiatore/trice.

looting ['luːtɪŋ] _n_ saccheggio.

lop [lɔp] _vt_ (_also_: **~ off**) tagliare via, recidere.

lop-sided ['lɔp'saɪdɪd] _adj_ non

equilibrato(a), asimmetrico(a).

lord [lɔːd] _n_ signore _m_; **L~ Smith** lord Smith; **the L~** (_REL_) il Signore; **the (House of) L~s** (_BRIT_) la Camera dei Lord.

lordly ['lɔːdlɪ] _adj_ nobile, maestoso(a); (_arrogant_) altero(a).

lordship ['lɔːdʃɪp] _n_ (_BRIT_): **your L~** Sua Eccellenza.

lore [lɔː*] _n_ tradizioni _fpl_.

lorry ['lɔrɪ] _n_ (_BRIT_) camion _m inv_.

lorry driver _n_ (_BRIT_) camionista _m_.

lose [luːz], _pt_, _pp_ **lost** [luːz, lɔst] _vt_ perdere; (_pursuers_) distanziare ♦ _vi_ perdere; **to ~ (time)** (_clock_) ritardare; **to ~ no time (in doing sth)** non perdere tempo (a fare qc); **to get lost** (_person_) perdersi, smarrirsi; (_object_) andare perso _or_ perduto.

loser ['luːzə*] _n_ perdente _m/f_; **to be a good/ bad ~** saper/non saper perdere.

loss [lɔs] _n_ perdita; **to cut one's ~es** rimetterci il meno possibile; **to make a ~** subire una perdita; **to sell sth at a ~** vendere qc in perdita; **to be at a ~** essere perplesso(a); **to be at a ~ to explain sth** non saper come fare a spiegare qc.

loss adjuster _n_ (_INSURANCE_) responsabile _m/f_ della valutazione dei danni.

loss leader _n_ (_COMM_) articolo a prezzo ridottissimo per attirare la clientela.

lost [lɔst] _pt_, _pp_ _of_ **lose** ♦ _adj_ perduto(a); **~ in thought** immerso _or_ perso nei propri pensieri; **~ and found property** _n_ (_US_) oggetti _mpl_ smarriti; **~ and found** _n_ (_US_) ufficio oggetti smarriti.

lost property _n_ (_BRIT_) oggetti _mpl_ smarriti; **~ office** _or_ **department** ufficio oggetti smarriti.

lot [lɔt] _n_ (_at auctions_) lotto; (_destiny_) destino, sorte _f_; **the ~** tutto(a) quanto(a); tutti(e) quanti(e); **a ~** molto; **a ~ of** una gran quantità di, un sacco di; **~s of** molto(a); **to draw ~s (for sth)** tirare a sorte (per qc).

lotion ['ləuʃən] _n_ lozione _f_.

lottery ['lɔtərɪ] _n_ lotteria.

loud [laud] _adj_ forte, alto(a); (_gaudy_) vistoso(a), sgargiante ♦ _adv_ (_speak etc_) forte; **out ~** ad alta voce.

loudhailer [laud'heɪlə*] _n_ (_BRIT_) portavoce _m inv_.

loudly ['laudlɪ] _adv_ fortemente, ad alta voce.

loudspeaker [laud'spiːkə*] _n_ altoparlante _m_.

lounge [laundʒ] _n_ salotto, soggiorno; (_of hotel_) salone _m_; (_of airport_) sala d'attesa ♦ _vi_ oziare; starsene colle mani in mano.

lounge bar _n_ bar _m inv_ con servizio a

tavolino.

lounge suit n (BRIT) completo da uomo.

louse [laus] n (pl **lice**) pidocchio.

▶**louse up** vt (col) rovinare.

lousy ['lauzı] adj (fig) orrendo(a), schifoso(a).

lout [laut] n zoticone m.

louvre, (US) **louver** ['lu:və*] adj (door, window) con apertura a gelosia.

lovable ['lʌvəbl] adj simpatico(a), carino(a); amabile.

love [lʌv] n amore m ♦ vt amare; voler bene a; **to ~ to do:** I ~ **to do** mi piace fare; **I'd ~ to come** mi piacerebbe molto venire; **to be in ~ with** essere innamorato(a) di; **to fall in ~ with** innamorarsi di; **to make ~** fare l'amore; **~ at first sight** amore a prima vista, colpo di fulmine; **to send one's ~ to sb** mandare i propri saluti a qn; **~ from Anne, ~, Anne** con affetto, Anne; **"15 ~"** (TENNIS) "15 a zero".

love affair n relazione f.

love child n figlio/a dell'amore.

loved ones [lʌvd-] npl: **my ~** i miei cari.

love-hate relationship ['lʌv'heıt-] n rapporto amore-odio inv.

love letter n lettera d'amore.

love life n vita sentimentale.

lovely ['lʌvlı] adj bello(a); (delicious: smell, meal) buono(a); **we had a ~ time** ci siamo divertiti molto.

lover ['lʌvə*] n amante m/f; (amateur): **a ~ of** un(un')amante di; un(un')appassionato(a) di.

lovesick ['lʌvsık] adj malato(a) d'amore.

lovesong ['lʌvsɔŋ] n canzone f d'amore.

loving ['lʌvıŋ] adj affettuoso(a), amoroso(a), tenero(a).

low [ləu] adj basso(a) ♦ adv in basso ♦ n (METEOR) depressione f ♦ vi (cow) muggire; **to feel ~** sentirsi giù; **he's very ~** (ill) è molto debole; **to reach a new** or **an all-time ~** toccare il livello più basso or il minimo; **to turn (down) ~** vt abbassare.

low-alcohol [ləu'ælkəhɔl] adj a basso contenuto alcolico.

lowbrow ['ləubrau] adj (person) senza pretese intellettuali.

low-calorie ['ləu'kælərı] adj a basso contenuto calorico.

low-cut ['ləukʌt] adj (dress) scollato(a).

low-down ['ləudaun] adj (mean) ignobile ♦ n (col): **he gave me the ~ on it** mi ha messo al corrente dei fatti.

lower ['ləuə*] adj, adv comparative of **low** ♦ vt (gen) calare; (reduce: price) abbassare, ridurre; (resistance) indebolire ♦ vi ['lauə*]

(person): **to ~ (at sb)** dare un'occhiataccia (a qn); (sky) minacciare.

lower case n minuscolo.

low-fat ['ləu'fæt] adj magro(a).

low-key ['ləu'ki:] adj moderato(a); (operation) condotto(a) con discrezione.

lowland ['ləulənd] n bassopiano, pianura.

low-level ['ləulɛvl] adj a basso livello; (flying) a bassa quota.

low-loader ['ləuləudə*] n camion m a pianale basso.

lowly ['ləulı] adj umile, modesto(a).

low-lying [ləu'laıŋ] adj a basso livello.

low-paid [ləu'peıd] adj mal pagato(a).

low-rise ['ləuraız] adj di altezza contenuta.

low-tech ['ləu'tɛk] adj a basso contenuto tecnologico.

loyal ['lɔıəl] adj fedele, leale.

loyalist ['lɔıəlıst] n lealista m/f.

loyalty ['lɔıəltı] n fedeltà, lealtà.

lozenge ['lɔzındʒ] n (MED) pastiglia; (GEOM) losanga.

LP n abbr (= long-playing record) LP m.

L-plate n = contrassegno P principiante.

Le **L-plate** sono delle tabelle bianche con
una L rossa che in Gran Bretagna i
guidatori principianti, **learners**, in possesso
di una **provisional licence**, che corrisponde
al nostro foglio rosa, devono applicare
davanti e dietro alla loro autovettura finché
non ottengono la patente.

LPN n abbr (US: = Licensed Practical Nurse) ≈ infermiera diplomata.

LRAM n abbr (BRIT: = Licentiate of the Royal Academy of Music) specializzazione dopo la laurea.

LSAT n abbr (US) = Law School Admission Test.

LSD n abbr (= lysergic acid diethylamide) L.S.D. m; (BRIT: = pounds, shillings and pence) sistema monetario in vigore in Gran Bretagna fino al 1971.

LSE n abbr = London School of Economics.

LT abbr (ELEC: = low tension) B.T.

Lt. abbr (= lieutenant) Ten.

Ltd abbr (COMM) = **limited.**

lubricant ['lu:brıkənt] n lubrificante m.

lubricate ['lu:brıkeıt] vt lubrificare.

lucid ['lu:sıd] adj lucido(a).

lucidity [lu:'sıdıtı] n lucidità.

luck [lʌk] n fortuna, sorte f; **bad ~** sfortuna, mala sorte; **good ~** (buona) fortuna; **to be in ~** essere fortunato(a); **to be out of ~** essere sfortunato(a).

luckily ['lʌkılı] adv fortunatamente, per fortuna.

luckless ['lʌklɪs] *adj* sventurato(a).
lucky ['lʌkɪ] *adj* fortunato(a); (*number etc*) che porta fortuna.
lucrative ['lu:krətɪv] *adj* lucrativo(a), lucroso(a), profittevole.
ludicrous ['lu:dɪkrəs] *adj* ridicolo(a), assurdo(a).
ludo ['lu:dəu] *n* ≈ gioco dell'oca.
lug [lʌg] *vt* trascinare.
luggage ['lʌgɪdʒ] *n* bagagli *mpl*.
luggage rack *n* portabagagli *m inv*.
luggage van, (*US*) **luggage car** *n* (*RAIL*) bagagliaio.
lugubrious [lu'gu:brɪəs] *adj* lugubre.
lukewarm ['lu:kwɔ:m] *adj* tiepido(a).
lull [lʌl] *n* intervallo di calma ♦ *vt* (*child*) cullare; (*person, fear*) acquietare, calmare.
lullaby ['lʌləbaɪ] *n* ninnananna.
lumbago [lʌm'beɪgəu] *n* lombaggine *f*.
lumber ['lʌmbə*] *n* roba vecchia ♦ *vt* (*BRIT col*): **to ~ sb with sth/sb** affibbiare *or* rifilare qc/qn a qn ♦ *vi* (*also:* **~ about**, **~ along**) muoversi pesantemente.
lumberjack ['lʌmbədʒæk] *n* boscaiolo.
lumber room *n* (*BRIT*) sgabuzzino.
lumber yard *n* segheria.
luminous ['lu:mɪnəs] *adj* luminoso(a).
lump [lʌmp] *n* pezzo; (*in sauce*) grumo; (*swelling*) gonfiore *m* ♦ *vt* (*also:* **~ together**) riunire, mettere insieme.
lump sum *n* somma globale.
lumpy ['lʌmpɪ] *adj* (*sauce*) grumoso(a).
lunacy ['lu:nəsɪ] *n* demenza, follia, pazzia.
lunar ['lu:nə*] *adj* lunare.
lunatic ['lu:nətɪk] *adj, n* pazzo(a), matto(a).
lunatic asylum *n* manicomio.
lunch [lʌntʃ] *n* pranzo, colazione *f*; **to invite sb to** *or* **for ~** invitare qn a pranzo *or* a colazione.
lunch break *n* intervallo del pranzo.
luncheon ['lʌntʃən] *n* pranzo.
luncheon meat *n* ≈ mortadella.
luncheon voucher *n* buono *m* pasto *inv*.
lunch hour *n* = **lunch break**.
lunchtime ['lʌntʃtaɪm] *n* ora di pranzo.
lung [lʌŋ] *n* polmone *m*.
lung cancer *n* cancro del polmone.
lunge [lʌndʒ] *vi* (*also:* **~ forward**) fare un balzo in avanti; **to ~ at sb** balzare su qn.
lupin ['lu:pɪn] *n* lupino.
lurch [lə:tʃ] *vi* vacillare, barcollare ♦ *n* scatto improvviso; **to leave sb in the ~** piantare in asso qn.
lure [luə*] *n* richiamo; lusinga ♦ *vt* attirare (con l'inganno).
lurid ['luərɪd] *adj* sgargiante; (*details etc*) impressionante.

lurk [lə:k] *vi* stare in agguato.
luscious ['lʌʃəs] *adj* succulento(a); delizioso(a).
lush [lʌʃ] *adj* lussureggiante.
lust [lʌst] *n* lussuria; cupidigia; desiderio; (*fig*): **~ for** sete *f* di.
▶**lust after** *vt fus* bramare, desiderare.
luster ['lʌstə*] *n* (*US*) = **lustre**.
lustful ['lʌstful] *adj* lascivo(a), voglioso(a).
lustre, (*US*) **luster** ['lʌstə*] *n* lustro, splendore *m*.
lusty ['lʌstɪ] *adj* vigoroso(a), robusto(a).
lute [lu:t] *n* liuto.
Luxembourg ['lʌksəmbɔ:g] *n* (*state*) Lussemburgo *m*; (*city*) Lussemburgo *f*.
luxuriant [lʌg'zjuərɪənt] *adj* lussureggiante.
luxurious [lʌg'zjuərɪəs] *adj* sontuoso(a), di lusso.
luxury ['lʌkʃərɪ] *n* lusso ♦ *cpd* di lusso.
LV *n abbr* (*BRIT*) = **luncheon voucher**.
LW *abbr* (*RADIO*: = *long wave*) O.L.
Lycra ® ['laɪkrə] *n* lycra ® *f inv*.
lying ['laɪɪŋ] *n* bugie *fpl*, menzogne *fpl* ♦ *adj* (*statement, story*) falso(a); (*person*) bugiardo(a).
lynch [lɪntʃ] *vt* linciare.
lynx [lɪŋks] *n* lince *f*.
Lyons ['laɪənz] *n* Lione *f*.
lyre ['laɪə*] *n* lira.
lyric ['lɪrɪk] *adj* lirico(a); **~s** *npl* (*of song*) parole *fpl*.
lyrical ['lɪrɪkl] *adj* lirico(a).
lyricism ['lɪrɪsɪzəm] *n* lirismo.

Mm

M, m [ɛm] *n* (*letter*) M, m *f or m inv*; **M for Mary**, (*US*) **M for Mike** ≈ M come Milano.
M *n abbr* (*BRIT*: = *motorway*): **the M8** ≈ l'A8 ♦ *abbr* (= *medium*) taglia media.
m *abbr* (= *metre*) m; = **mile**; **million**.
MA *n abbr* (*SCOL*) *see* **Master of Arts**; (*US*) = *military academy* ♦ (*US*) = *Massachusetts*.
mac [mæk] *n* (*BRIT*) impermeabile *m*.
macabre [mə'kɑ:brə] *adj* macabro(a).
macaroni [mækə'rəunɪ] *n* maccheroni *mpl*.
macaroon [mækə'ru:n] *n* amaretto (*biscotto*).
mace [meɪs] *n* mazza; (*spice*) macis *m or f*.
Macedonia [mæsɪ'dəunɪə] *n* Macedonia.
Macedonian [mæsɪ'dəunɪən] *adj* macedone

♦ n macedone *m/f*; (*LING*) macedone *m*.
machinations [mækɪ'neɪʃənz] *npl*
macchinazioni *fpl*, intrighi *mpl*.
machine [mə'ʃiːn] *n* macchina ♦ *vt* (*dress etc*) cucire a macchina; (*TECH*) lavorare (a macchina).
machine code *n* (*COMPUT*) codice *m* di macchina, codice assoluto.
machine gun *n* mitragliatrice *f*.
machine language *n* (*COMPUT*) linguaggio *m* macchina *inv*.
machine-readable [mə'ʃiːnriːdəbl] *adj* (*COMPUT*) leggibile dalla macchina.
machinery [mə'ʃiːnərɪ] *n* macchinario, macchine *fpl*; (*fig*) macchina.
machine shop *n* officina meccanica.
machine tool *n* macchina utensile.
machine washable *adj* lavabile in lavatrice.
machinist [mə'ʃiːnɪst] *n* macchinista *m/f*.
macho ['mætʃəu] *adj* macho *inv*.
mackerel ['mækrəl] *n* (*pl inv*) sgombro.
mackintosh ['mækɪntɔʃ] *n* impermeabile *m*.
macro... ['mækrəu] *prefix* macro....
macroeconomics ['mækrəuiːkə'nɔmɪks] *n* macroeconomia.
mad [mæd] *adj* matto(a), pazzo(a); (*foolish*) sciocco(a); (*angry*) furioso(a); **to go ~** impazzire, diventar matto; **~ (at or with sb)** furibondo(a) (con qn); **to be ~ (keen) about or on sth** (*col*) andar pazzo *or* matto per qc.
madam ['mædəm] *n* signora; **M~ Chairman** Signora Presidentessa.
madcap ['mædkæp] *adj* (*col*) senza senso, assurdo(a).
mad cow disease *n* encefalite *f* bovina spongiforme.
madden ['mædn] *vt* fare infuriare.
maddening ['mædnɪŋ] *adj* esasperante.
made [meɪd] *pt, pp of* **make**.
Madeira [mə'dɪərə] *n* (*GEO*) Madera; (*wine*) madera *m*.
made-to-measure ['meɪdtə'mɛʒə*] *adj* (*BRIT*) fatto(a) su misura.
madhouse ['mædhaus] *n* (*also fig*) manicomio.
madly ['mædlɪ] *adv* follemente; (*love*) alla follia.
madman ['mædmən] *n* pazzo, alienato.
madness ['mædnɪs] *n* pazzia.
Madrid [mə'drɪd] *n* Madrid *f*.
Mafia ['mæfɪə] *n* mafia *f*.
mag. [mæg] *n abbr* (*BRIT col*) = **magazine** (*PRESS*).
magazine [mægə'ziːn] *n* (*PRESS*) rivista; (*MIL: store*) magazzino, deposito; (*of firearm*) caricatore *m*.

maggot ['mægət] *n* baco, verme *m*.
magic ['mædʒɪk] *n* magia ♦ *adj* magico(a).
magical ['mædʒɪkəl] *adj* magico(a).
magician [mə'dʒɪʃən] *n* mago/a.
magistrate ['mædʒɪstreɪt] *n* magistrato; giudice *m/f*.
magistrates' court *n see* **crown court**.
magnanimous [mæg'nænɪməs] *adj* magnanimo(a).
magnate ['mægneɪt] *n* magnate *m*.
magnesium [mæg'niːzɪəm] *n* magnesio.
magnet ['mægnɪt] *n* magnete *m*, calamita.
magnetic [mæg'nɛtɪk] *adj* magnetico(a).
magnetic disk *n* (*COMPUT*) disco magnetico.
magnetic tape *n* nastro magnetico.
magnetism ['mægnɪtɪzəm] *n* magnetismo.
magnification [mægnɪfɪ'keɪʃən] *n* ingrandimento.
magnificence [mæg'nɪfɪsns] *n* magnificenza.
magnificent [mæg'nɪfɪsnt] *adj* magnifico(a).
magnify ['mægnɪfaɪ] *vt* ingrandire.
magnifying glass ['mægnɪfaɪɪŋ-] *n* lente *f* d'ingrandimento.
magnitude ['mægnɪtjuːd] *n* grandezza; importanza.
magnolia [mæg'nəulɪə] *n* magnolia.
magpie ['mægpaɪ] *n* gazza.
mahogany [mə'hɔgənɪ] *n* mogano ♦ *cpd* di *or* in mogano.
maid [meɪd] *n* domestica; (*in hotel*) cameriera; **old ~** (*pej*) vecchia zitella.
maiden ['meɪdn] *n* fanciulla ♦ *adj* (*aunt etc*) nubile; (*speech, voyage*) inaugurale.
maiden name *n* nome *m* nubile *or* da ragazza.
mail [meɪl] *n* posta ♦ *vt* spedire (per posta); **by ~** per posta.
mailbox ['meɪlbɔks] *n* (*US*) cassetta delle lettere; (*COMPUT*) mailbox *f inv*.
mailing list ['meɪlɪŋ-] *n* elenco d'indirizzi.
mailman ['meɪlmæn] *n* (*US*) portalettere *m inv*, postino.
mail-order ['meɪlɔːdə*] *n* vendita (*or* acquisto) per corrispondenza ♦ *cpd*: **~ firm** *or* **house** ditta di vendita per corrispondenza.
mailshot ['meɪlʃɔt] *n* mailing *m inv*.
mail train *n* treno postale.
mail truck *n* (*US AUT*) = **mail van**.
mail van *n* (*BRIT: AUT*) furgone *m* postale; (*:RAIL*) vagone *m* postale.
maim [meɪm] *vt* mutilare.
main [meɪn] *adj* principale ♦ *n* (*pipe*) conduttura principale; **the ~s** (*ELEC*) la linea principale; **~s operated** *adj* che funziona a elettricità; **in the ~** nel

complesso, nell'insieme.

main course n (*CULIN*) piatto principale, piatto forte.

mainframe ['meɪnfreɪm] n (*also:* ~ **computer**) mainframe m *inv*.

mainland ['meɪnlənd] n continente m.

mainline ['meɪnlaɪn] adj (*RAIL*) della linea principale ♦ vb (*drugs slang*) vt bucarsi di ♦ vi bucarsi.

main line n (*RAIL*) linea principale.

mainly ['meɪnlɪ] adv principalmente, soprattutto.

main road n strada principale.

mainstay ['meɪnsteɪ] n (*fig*) sostegno principale.

mainstream ['meɪnstriːm] n (*fig*) corrente f principale.

maintain [meɪn'teɪn] vt mantenere; (*affirm*) sostenere; **to** ~ **that** ... sostenere che ....

maintenance ['meɪntənəns] n manutenzione f; (*alimony*) alimenti mpl.

maintenance contract n contratto di manutenzione.

maintenance order n (*LAW*) obbligo degli alimenti.

maisonette [meɪzə'nɛt] n (*BRIT*) appartamento a due piani.

maize [meɪz] n granturco, mais m.

Maj. abbr (*MIL*) = **major**.

majestic [mə'dʒɛstɪk] adj maestoso(a).

majesty ['mædʒɪstɪ] n maestà f inv.

major ['meɪdʒə*] n (*MIL*) maggiore m ♦ adj (*greater, MUS*) maggiore; (*in importance*) principale, importante ♦ vi (*US SCOL*): **to** ~ **(in)** specializzarsi (in); **a** ~ **operation** (*MED*) una grossa operazione.

Majorca [mə'jɔːkə] n Maiorca.

major general n (*MIL*) generale m di divisione.

majority [mə'dʒɔrɪtɪ] n maggioranza ♦ cpd (*verdict*) maggioritario(a).

majority holding n (*COMM*): **to have a** ~ essere maggiore azionista.

make [meɪk] vt (*pt, pp* **made** [meɪd]) fare; (*manufacture*) fare, fabbricare; (*cause to be*): **to** ~ **sb sad** etc rendere qn triste etc; (*force*): **to** ~ **sb do sth** costringere qn a fare qc, far fare qc a qn; (*equal*): **2 and 2** ~ **4** 2 più 2 fa 4 ♦ n fabbricazione f; (*brand*) marca; **to** ~ **it** (*in time etc*) arrivare; (*succeed*) farcela; **what time do you** ~ **it?** che ora fai?; **to** ~ **good** vi (*succeed*) aver successo ♦ vt (*deficit*) colmare; (*losses*) compensare; **to** ~ **do with** arrangiarsi con.

▶**make for** vt fus (*place*) avviarsi verso.

▶**make off** vi svignarsela.

▶**make out** vt (*write out*) scrivere;

(*understand*) capire; (*see*) distinguere; (: *numbers*) decifrare; (*claim, imply*): **to** ~ **out (that)** voler far credere (che); **to** ~ **out a case for sth** presentare delle valide ragioni in favore di qc.

▶**make over** vt (*assign*): **to** ~ **over (to)** passare (a), trasferire (a).

▶**make up** vt (*invent*) inventare; (*parcel*) fare ♦ vi conciliarsi; (*with cosmetics*) truccarsi; **to be made up of** essere composto di *or* formato da.

▶**make up for** vt fus compensare; ricuperare.

make-believe ['meɪkbɪliːv] n: **a world of** ~ un mondo di favole; **it's just** ~ è tutta un'invenzione.

maker ['meɪkə*] n fabbricante m; creatore/trice, autore/trice.

makeshift ['meɪkʃɪft] adj improvvisato(a).

make-up ['meɪkʌp] n trucco.

make-up bag n borsa del trucco.

make-up remover n struccatore m.

making ['meɪkɪŋ] n (*fig*): **in the** ~ in formazione; **he has the** ~**s of an actor** ha la stoffa dell'attore.

maladjusted [mælə'dʒʌstɪd] adj disadattato(a).

maladroit [mælə'drɔɪt] adj maldestro(a).

malaise [mæ'leɪz] n malessere m.

malaria [mə'lɛərɪə] n malaria.

Malawi [mə'lɑːwɪ] n Malawi m.

Malay [mə'leɪ] adj malese ♦ n malese m/f; (*LING*) malese m.

Malaya [mə'leɪə] n Malesia.

Malayan [mə'leɪən] adj, n = **Malay**.

Malaysia [mə'leɪzɪə] n Malaysia.

Malaysian [mə'leɪzɪən] adj, n malaysiano(a).

Maldives ['mɔːldaɪvz] npl: **the** ~ le (isole) Maldive.

male [meɪl] n (*BIO, ELEC*) maschio ♦ adj (*gen, sex*) maschile; (*animal, child*) maschio(a); ~ **and female students** studenti e studentesse.

male chauvinist n maschilista m.

male nurse n infermiere m.

malevolence [mə'lɛvələns] n malevolenza.

malevolent [mə'lɛvələnt] adj malevolo(a).

malfunction [mæl'fʌŋkʃən] n funzione f difettosa.

malice ['mælɪs] n malevolenza.

malicious [mə'lɪʃəs] adj malevolo(a); (*LAW*) doloso(a).

malign [mə'laɪn] vt malignare su; calunniare.

malignant [mə'lɪɡnənt] adj (*MED*) maligno(a).

malingerer [mə'lɪŋɡərə*] n scansafatiche m/f inv.

mall [mɔːl] n (also: **shopping ~**) centro commerciale.

malleable ['mælɪəbl] adj malleabile.

mallet ['mælɪt] n maglio.

malnutrition [mælnjuː'trɪʃən] n denutrizione f.

malpractice [mæl'præktɪs] n prevaricazione f; negligenza.

malt [mɔːlt] n malto ♦ cpd (whisky) di malto.

Malta ['mɔːltə] n Malta.

Maltese [mɔːl'tiːz] adj, n (pl inv) maltese (m/f); (LING) maltese m.

maltreat [mæl'triːt] vt maltrattare.

mammal ['mæml] n mammifero.

mammoth ['mæməθ] n mammut m inv ♦ adj enorme, gigantesco(a).

man [mæn] n (pl **men**) uomo; (CHESS) pezzo; (DRAUGHTS) pedina ♦ vt fornire d'uomini; stare a; essere di servizio a.

Man. abbr (Canada) = Manitoba.

manacles ['mænəklz] npl manette fpl.

manage ['mænɪdʒ] vi farcela ♦ vt (be in charge of) occuparsi di; (shop, restaurant) gestire; **to ~ without sth/sb** fare a meno di qc/qn; **to ~ to do sth** riuscire a far qc.

manageable ['mænɪdʒəbl] adj maneggevole; (task etc) fattibile.

management ['mænɪdʒmənt] n amministrazione f, direzione f; gestione f; (persons: of business, firm) dirigenti mpl; (: of hotel, shop, theatre) direzione f; "**under new ~**" "sotto nuova gestione".

management accounting n contabilità di gestione.

management consultant n consulente m/f aziendale.

manager ['mænɪdʒə*] n direttore m; (of shop, restaurant) gerente m; (of artist) manager m inv; **sales ~** direttore m delle vendite.

manageress [mænɪdʒə'rɛs] n direttrice f; gerente f.

managerial [mænə'dʒɪərɪəl] adj dirigenziale.

managing director (MD) ['mænɪdʒɪŋ-] n amministratore m delegato.

Mancunian [mæŋ'kjuːnɪən] adj di Manchester ♦ n abitante m/f di Manchester; originario/a di Manchester.

mandarin ['mændərɪn] n (person, fruit) mandarino.

mandate ['mændeɪt] n mandato.

mandatory ['mændətərɪ] adj obbligatorio(a); ingiuntivo(a).

mandolin(e) ['mændəlɪn] n mandolino.

mane [meɪn] n criniera.

maneuver [mə'nuːvə*] etc (US) = **manoeuvre** etc.

manful ['mænful] adj coraggioso(a), valoroso(a).

manfully ['mænfəlɪ] adv valorosamente.

manganese [mæŋgə'niːz] n manganese m.

mangetout ['mɔnʒ'tuː] n pisello dolce, taccola.

mangle ['mæŋgl] vt straziare; mutilare ♦ n strizzatoio.

mango, ~es ['mæŋgəu] n mango.

mangrove ['mæŋgrəuv] n mangrovia.

mangy ['meɪndʒɪ] adj rognoso(a).

manhandle ['mænhændl] vt (treat roughly) malmenare; (move by hand: goods) spostare a mano.

manhole ['mænhəul] n botola stradale.

manhood ['mænhud] n età virile; virilità.

man-hour ['mænauə*] n ora di lavoro.

manhunt ['mænhʌnt] n caccia all'uomo.

mania ['meɪnɪə] n mania.

maniac ['meɪnɪæk] n maniaco/a.

manic ['mænɪk] adj maniacale.

manic-depressive ['mænɪkdɪ'prɛsɪv] adj maniaco-depressivo(a) ♦ n persona affetta da mania depressiva.

manicure ['mænɪkjuə*] n manicure f inv.

manicure set n trousse f inv della manicure.

manifest ['mænɪfɛst] vt manifestare ♦ adj manifesto(a), palese ♦ n (AVIAT, NAUT) manifesto.

manifestation [mænɪfɛs'teɪʃən] n manifestazione f.

manifesto [mænɪ'fɛstəu] n manifesto.

manifold ['mænɪfəuld] adj molteplice ♦ n (AUT etc): **exhaust ~** collettore m di scarico.

Manila [mə'nɪlə] n Manila.

manil(l)a [mə'nɪlə] adj (paper, envelope) manilla inv.

manipulate [mə'nɪpjuleɪt] vt (tool) maneggiare; (controls) azionare; (limb, facts) manipolare.

manipulation [mənɪpju'leɪʃən] n maneggiare m; capacità di azionare; manipolazione f.

mankind [mæn'kaɪnd] n umanità, genere m umano.

manliness ['mænlɪnɪs] n virilità.

manly ['mænlɪ] adj virile; coraggioso(a).

man-made ['mæn'meɪd] adj sintetico(a); artificiale.

manna ['mænə] n manna.

mannequin ['mænɪkɪn] n (dummy) manichino; (fashion model) indossatrice f.

manner ['mænə*] n maniera, modo; **~s** npl maniere fpl; (good) **~s** buona educazione f, buone maniere; **bad ~s** maleducazione f; **all ~ of** ogni sorta di.

mannerism ['mænərɪzəm] *n* vezzo, tic *m inv*.
mannerly ['mænəlɪ] *adj* educato(a), civile.
manoeuvrable, (*US*) **maneuverable**
[mə'nu:vrəbl] *adj* facile da manovrare;
(*car*) maneggevole.
manoeuvre, (*US*) **maneuver** [mə'nu:və*]
vt manovrare ♦ *vi* far manovre ♦ *n*
manovra; **to ~ sb into doing sth**
costringere abilmente qn a fare qc.
manor ['mænə*] *n* (*also*: **~ house**) maniero.
manpower ['mænpauə*] *n* manodopera.
Manpower Services Commission
(MSC) *n* (*BRIT*) *ente nazionale per
l'occupazione.*
manservant, *pl* **menservants**
['mænsə:vənt, 'men-] *n* domestico.
mansion ['mænʃən] *n* casa signorile.
manslaughter ['mænslɔ:tə*] *n* omicidio
preterintenzionale.
mantelpiece ['mæntlpi:s] *n* mensola del
caminetto.
mantle ['mæntl] *n* mantello.
man-to-man ['mæntə'mæn] *adj, adv* da
uomo a uomo.
Mantua ['mæntjuə] *n* Mantova.
manual ['mænjuəl] *adj, n* manuale (*m*).
manual worker *n* manovale *m*.
manufacture [mænju'fæktʃə*] *vt*
fabbricare ♦ *n* fabbricazione *f*,
manifattura.
manufactured goods *npl* manufatti *mpl*.
manufacturer [mænju'fæktʃərə*] *n*
fabbricante *m*.
manufacturing industries
[mænju'fæktʃərɪŋ-] *npl* industrie *fpl*
manifatturiere.
manure [mə'njuə*] *n* concime *m*.
manuscript ['mænjuskrɪpt] *n* manoscritto.
many ['menɪ] *adj* molti(e) ♦ *pron* molti(e),
un gran numero; **a great ~** moltissimi(e),
un gran numero (di); **~ a ...** molti(e) ...,
più di un(a) ...; **too ~ difficulties** troppe
difficoltà; **twice as ~** due volte tanto;
how ~? quanti(e)?
Maori ['mauri] *adj, n* maori (*m/f*) *inv*.
map [mæp] *n* carta (geografica) ♦ *vt* fare
una carta di.
►**map out** *vt* tracciare un piano di; (*fig:
career, holiday, essay*) pianificare.
maple ['meɪpl] *n* acero.
mar [mɑ:*] *vt* sciupare.
Mar. *abbr* (= *March*) mar.
marathon ['mærəθən] *n* maratona ♦ *adj:* **a ~
session** una seduta fiume.
marathon runner *n* maratoneta *m/f*.
marauder [mə'rɔ:də*] *n* saccheggiatore *m*;
predatore *m*.
marble ['mɑ:bl] *n* marmo; (*toy*) pallina,

bilia; **~s** *n* (*game*) palline, bilie.
March [mɑ:tʃ] *n* marzo; *for phrases see also*
July.
march [mɑ:tʃ] *vi* marciare; sfilare ♦ *n*
marcia; (*demonstration*) dimostrazione *f*;
to ~ into a room entrare a passo deciso
in una stanza.
marcher ['mɑ:tʃə*] *n* dimostrante *m/f*.
marching ['mɑ:tʃɪŋ] *n:* **to give sb his ~
orders** (*fig*) dare il benservito a qn.
march-past ['mɑ:tʃpɑ:st] *n* sfilata.
mare [mɛə*] *n* giumenta.
marg. [mɑ:dʒ] *n abbr* (*col*) = **margarine**.
margarine [mɑ:dʒə'ri:n] *n* margarina.
margin ['mɑ:dʒɪn] *n* margine *m*.
marginal ['mɑ:dʒɪnl] *adj* marginale; **~ seat**
(*POL*) *seggio elettorale ottenuto con una
stretta maggioranza.*
marginally ['mɑ:dʒɪnəlɪ] *adv* (*bigger, better*)
lievemente, di poco; (*different*) un po'.
marigold ['mærɪgəuld] *n* calendola.
marijuana [mærɪ'wɑ:nə] *n* marijuana.
marina [mə'ri:nə] *n* marina.
marinade *n* [mærɪ'neɪd] marinata ♦ *vt*
['mærɪneɪd] = **marinate**.
marinate ['mærɪneɪt] *vt* marinare.
marine [mə'ri:n] *adj* (*animal, plant*)
marino(a); (*forces, engineering*)
marittimo(a) ♦ *n* fante *m* di marina; (*US*)
marine *m inv*.
marine insurance *n* assicurazione *f*
marittima.
marital ['mærɪtl] *adj* maritale, coniugale; **~
status** stato coniugale.
maritime ['mærɪtaɪm] *adj* marittimo(a).
maritime law *n* diritto marittimo.
marjoram ['mɑ:dʒərəm] *n* maggiorana.
mark [mɑ:k] *n* segno; (*stain*) macchia; (*of
skid etc*) traccia; (*BRIT SCOL*) voto; (*SPORT*)
bersaglio; (*currency*) marco; (*BRIT TECH*):
M~ 2/3 1a/2a serie *f* ♦ *vt* segnare; (*stain*)
macchiare; (*BRIT SCOL*) dare un voto a;
correggere; (*SPORT: player*) marcare;
punctuation ~s segni di punteggiatura;
to be quick off the ~ (in doing) (*fig*) non
perdere tempo (per fare); **up to the ~** (*in
efficiency*) all'altezza; **to ~ time** segnare il
passo.
►**mark down** *vt* (*reduce: prices, goods*)
ribassare, ridurre.
►**mark off** *vt* (*tick off*) spuntare, cancellare.
►**mark out** *vt* delimitare.
►**mark up** *vt* (*price*) aumentare.
marked ['mɑ:kt] *adj* spiccato(a), chiaro(a).
markedly ['mɑ:kɪdlɪ] *adv* visibilmente,
notevolmente.
marker ['mɑ:kə*] *n* (*sign*) segno; (*bookmark*)
segnalibro.

market ['mɑːkɪt] n mercato ♦ vt (COMM) mettere in vendita; (promote) lanciare sul mercato; **to play the** ~ giocare or speculare in borsa; **to be on the** ~ essere (messo) in vendita or in commercio; **open** ~ mercato libero.

marketable ['mɑːkɪtəbl] adj commercializzabile.

market analysis n analisi f di mercato.

market day n giorno di mercato.

market demand n domanda del mercato.

market economy n economia di mercato.

market forces npl forze fpl di mercato.

market garden n (BRIT) orto industriale.

marketing ['mɑːkɪtɪŋ] n marketing m.

marketplace ['mɑːkɪtpleɪs] n (piazza del) mercato; (world of trade) piazza, mercato.

market price n prezzo di mercato.

market research n indagine f or ricerca di mercato.

market value n valore m di mercato.

marking ['mɑːkɪŋ] n (on animal) marcatura di colore; (on road) segnaletica orizzontale.

marksman ['mɑːksmən] n tiratore m scelto.

marksmanship ['mɑːksmənʃɪp] n abilità nel tiro.

mark-up ['mɑːkʌp] n (COMM: margin) margine m di vendita; (: increase) aumento.

marmalade ['mɑːməleɪd] n marmellata d'arance.

maroon [mə'ruːn] vt (fig): **to be ~ed (in** or **at)** essere abbandonato(a) (in) ♦ adj bordeaux inv.

marquee [mɑː'kiː] n padiglione m.

marquess, marquis ['mɑːkwɪs] n marchese m.

Marrakech, Marrakesh [mærə'kɛʃ] n Marrakesh f.

marriage ['mærɪdʒ] n matrimonio.

marriage bureau n agenzia matrimoniale.

marriage certificate n certificato di matrimonio.

marriage guidance, (US) marriage counseling n consulenza matrimoniale.

marriage of convenience n matrimonio di convenienza.

married ['mærɪd] adj sposato(a); (life, love) coniugale, matrimoniale.

marrow ['mærəu] n midollo; (vegetable) zucca.

marry ['mærɪ] vt sposare, sposarsi con; (subj: father, priest etc) dare in matrimonio ♦ vi (also: **get married**) sposarsi.

Mars [mɑːz] n (planet) Marte m.

Marseilles [mɑː'seɪlz] n Marsiglia.

marsh [mɑːʃ] n palude f.

marshal ['mɑːʃl] n maresciallo; (US: fire ~) capo; (: police ~) capitano; (for demonstration, meeting) membro del servizio d'ordine ♦ vt adunare.

marshalling yard ['mɑːʃlɪŋ-] n scalo smistamento.

marshmallow [mɑːʃ'mæləu] n (BOT) altea; (sweet) caramella soffice e gommosa.

marshy ['mɑːʃɪ] adj paludoso(a).

marsupial [mɑː'suːpɪəl] adj, n marsupiale (m).

martial ['mɑːʃl] adj marziale.

martial arts npl arti fpl marziali.

martial law n legge f marziale.

Martian ['mɑːʃən] n marziano/a.

martin ['mɑːtɪn] n (also: **house** ~) balestruccio.

martyr ['mɑːtə*] n martire m/f ♦ vt martirizzare.

martyrdom ['mɑːtədəm] n martirio.

marvel ['mɑːvl] n meraviglia ♦ vi: **to** ~ **(at)** meravigliarsi (di).

marvellous, (US) marvelous ['mɑːvələs] adj meraviglioso(a).

Marxism ['mɑːksɪzəm] n marxismo.

Marxist ['mɑːksɪst] adj, n marxista (m/f).

marzipan ['mɑːzɪpæn] n marzapane m.

mascara [mæs'kɑːrə] n mascara m inv.

mascot ['mæskət] n mascotte f inv.

masculine ['mæskjulɪn] adj maschile ♦ n genere m maschile.

masculinity [mæskju'lɪnɪtɪ] n mascolinità.

MASH [mæʃ] n abbr (US MIL: = mobile army surgical hospital) ospedale di campo di unità mobile dell'esercito.

mash [mæʃ] vt (CULIN) passare, schiacciare.

mashed [mæʃt] adj: ~ **potatoes** purè m di patate.

mask [mɑːsk] n (gen, ELEC) maschera ♦ vt mascherare.

masochism ['mæsəkɪzəm] n masochismo.

masochist ['mæsəkɪst] n masochista m/f.

mason ['meɪsn] n (also: **stone**~) scalpellino; (also: **free**~) massone m.

masonic [mə'sɔnɪk] adj massonico(a).

masonry ['meɪsnrɪ] n muratura.

masquerade [mæskə'reɪd] n ballo in maschera; (fig) mascherata ♦ vi: **to** ~ **as** farsi passare per.

mass [mæs] n moltitudine f, massa; (PHYSICS) massa; (REL) messa ♦ vi ammassarsi; **the ~es** le masse; **to go to** ~ andare a or alla messa.

Mass. abbr (US) = Massachusetts.

massacre ['mæsəkə*] n massacro ♦ vt massacrare.

massage ['mæsɑːʒ] n massaggio ♦ vt

massaggiare.
masseur [mæ'sə:*] *n* massaggiatore *m*.
masseuse [mæ'sə:z] *n* massaggiatrice *f*.
massive ['mæsɪv] *adj* enorme,
massiccio(a).
mass market *n* mercato di massa.
mass media *npl* mass media *mpl*.
mass meeting *n* (*of everyone concerned*)
riunione *f* generale; (*huge*) adunata
popolare.
mass-produce ['mæsprə'dju:s] *vt* produrre
in serie.
mass production *n* produzione *f* in serie.
mast [mɑ:st] *n* albero; (*RADIO, TV*) pilone *m*
(a traliccio).
mastectomy [mæs'tɛktəmɪ] *n*
mastectomia.
master ['mɑ:stə*] *n* padrone *m*; (*ART etc,
teacher: in primary school*) maestro; (: *in
secondary school*) professore *m*; (*title for
boys*): **M~ X** Signorino X ♦ *vt* domare;
(*learn*) imparare a fondo; (*understand*)
conoscere a fondo; ~ **of ceremonies (MC)**
n maestro di cerimonie.

Il **Master's degree** *è il riconoscimento che
viene conferito a chi segue un corso di
specializzazione dopo aver conseguito un
*Bachelor's degree. Vi sono diversi tipi di
Master's Degree; i più comuni sono il
Master of Arts (MA) e il Master of Science
(MSc) che si ottengono dopo aver seguito un
corso e aver presentato una tesi originale.
Per il Master of Letters (MLitt) e il Master
of Philosophy (MPhil) è invece sufficiente
presentare la tesi; vedi anche* **doctorate**.

---

master disk *n* (*COMPUT*) disco *m* master
inv, disco principale.
masterful ['mɑ:stəful] *adj* autoritario(a),
imperioso(a).
master key *n* chiave *f* maestra.
masterly ['mɑ:stəlɪ] *adj* magistrale.
mastermind ['mɑ:stəmaɪnd] *n* mente *f*
superiore ♦ *vt* essere il cervello di.
masterpiece ['mɑ:stəpi:s] *n* capolavoro.
master plan *n* piano generale.
master stroke *n* colpo maestro.
mastery ['mɑ:stərɪ] *n* dominio; padronanza.
mastiff ['mæstɪf] *n* mastino inglese.
masturbate ['mæstəbeɪt] *vi* masturbare.
masturbation [mæstə'beɪʃən] *n*
masturbazione *f*.
mat [mæt] *n* stuoia; (*also:* **door~**) stoino,
zerbino ♦ *adj* = **matt**.
match [mætʃ] *n* fiammifero; (*game*) partita,
incontro; (*fig*) uguale *m/f*; matrimonio;
partito ♦ *vt* intonare; (*go well with*) andare

benissimo con; (*equal*) uguagliare ♦ *vi*
intonarsi; **to be a good** ~ andare bene.
►**match up** *vt* intonare.
matchbox ['mætʃbɔks] *n* scatola per
fiammiferi.
matching ['mætʃɪŋ] *adj* ben assortito(a).
matchless ['mætʃlɪs] *adj* senza pari.
mate [meɪt] *n* compagno/a di lavoro; (*col:
friend*) amico/a; (*animal*) compagno/a; (*in
merchant navy*) secondo ♦ *vi* accoppiarsi
♦ *vt* accoppiare.
material [mə'tɪərɪəl] *n* (*substance*)
materiale *m*, materia; (*cloth*) stoffa ♦ *adj*
materiale; (*important*) essenziale; ~**s** *npl*
(*equipment etc*) materiali *mpl*; occorrente
m.
materialistic [mətɪərɪə'lɪstɪk] *adj*
materialistico(a).
materialize [mə'tɪərɪəlaɪz] *vi*
materializzarsi, realizzarsi.
materially [mə'tɪərɪəlɪ] *adv* dal punto di
vista materiale; sostanzialmente.
maternal [mə'tə:nl] *adj* materno(a).
maternity [mə'tə:nɪtɪ] *n* maternità ♦ *cpd* di
maternità; (*clothes*) pre-maman *inv*.
maternity benefit *n* sussidio di
maternità.
maternity hospital *n* ≈ clinica ostetrica.
matey ['meɪtɪ] *adj* (*BRIT col*) amicone(a).
math. [mæθ] *n abbr* (*US*) = **mathematics**.
mathematical [mæθə'mætɪkl] *adj*
matematico(a).
mathematician [mæθəmə'tɪʃən] *n*
matematico/a.
mathematics [mæθə'mætɪks] *n*
matematica.
maths [mæθs] *n abbr* (*BRIT*) = **mathematics**.
matinée ['mætɪneɪ] *n* matinée *f inv*.
mating ['meɪtɪŋ] *n* accoppiamento.
mating call *n* chiamata all'accoppiamento.
mating season *n* stagione *f* degli amori.
matriarchal [meɪtrɪ'ɑ:kl] *adj* matriarcale.
matrices ['meɪtrɪsi:z] *npl of* **matrix**.
matriculation [mətrɪkju'leɪʃən] *n*
immatricolazione *f*.
matrimonial [mætrɪ'məunɪəl] *adj*
matrimoniale, coniugale.
matrimony ['mætrɪmənɪ] *n* matrimonio.
matrix, pl matrices ['meɪtrɪks, 'meɪtrɪsi:z]
n matrice *f*.
matron ['meɪtrən] *n* (*in hospital*)
capoinfermiera; (*in school*) infermiera.
matronly ['meɪtrənlɪ] *adj* da matrona.
matt [mæt] *adj* opaco(a).
matted ['mætɪd] *adj* ingarbugliato(a).
matter ['mætə*] *n* questione *f*; (*PHYSICS*)
materia, sostanza; (*content*) contenuto;
(*MED: pus*) pus *m* ♦ *vi* importare; **it doesn't**

~ non importa; (*I don't mind*) non fa niente; **what's the** ~**?** che cosa c'è?; **no** ~ **what** qualsiasi cosa accada; **that's another** ~ quello è un altro affare; **as a** ~ **of course** come cosa naturale; **as a** ~ **of fact** in verità; **it's a** ~ **of habit** è una questione di abitudine; **printed** ~ stampe *fpl*; **reading** ~ (*BRIT*) qualcosa da leggere.

matter-of-fact [mætərəv'fækt] *adj* prosaico(a).

matting ['mætɪŋ] *n* stuoia.

mattress ['mætrɪs] *n* materasso.

mature [mə'tjuə*] *adj* maturo(a); (*cheese*) stagionato(a) ♦ *vi* maturare; stagionare; (*COMM*) scadere.

mature student *n* studente universitario che ha più di 25 anni.

maturity [mə'tjuərɪtɪ] *n* maturità.

maudlin ['mɔːdlɪn] *adj* lacrimoso(a).

maul [mɔːl] *vt* lacerare.

Mauritania [mɔrɪ'teɪnɪə] *n* Mauritania.

Mauritius [mə'rɪʃəs] *n* Maurizio.

mausoleum [mɔːsə'lɪəm] *n* mausoleo.

mauve [məuv] *adj* malva *inv*.

maverick ['mævərɪk] *n* (*fig*) chi sta fuori del branco.

mawkish ['mɔːkɪʃ] *adj* sdolcinato(a); insipido(a).

max. *abbr* = **maximum**.

maxim ['mæksɪm] *n* massima.

maxima ['mæksɪmə] *npl of* **maximum**.

maximize ['mæksɪmaɪz] *vt* (*profits etc*) massimizzare; (*chances*) aumentare al massimo.

maximum ['mæksɪməm] *adj* massimo(a) ♦ *n* (*pl* **maxima**) massimo.

May [meɪ] *n* maggio; *for phrases see also* **July**.

may [meɪ] *vi* (*conditional*: **might**) (*indicating possibility*): **he** ~ **come** può darsi che venga; (*be allowed to*): ~ **I smoke?** posso fumare?; ~ **I sit here?** le dispiace se mi siedo qua?; (*wishes*): ~ **God bless you!** Dio la benedica!; **he might be there** può darsi che ci sia; **he might come** potrebbe venire, può anche darsi che venga; **I might as well go** potrei anche andarmene; **you might like to try** forse le piacerebbe provare.

maybe ['meɪbiː] *adv* forse, può darsi; ~ **he'll** ... può darsi che lui ... +*sub*, forse lui ...; ~ **not** forse no, può darsi di no.

mayday ['meɪdeɪ] *n* S.O.S. *m*, mayday *m inv*.

May Day *n* il primo maggio.

mayhem ['meɪhɛm] *n* cagnara.

mayonnaise [meɪə'neɪz] *n* maionese *f*.

mayor [mɛə*] *n* sindaco.

mayoress ['mɛərɛs] *n* sindaco (*donna*); moglie *f* del sindaco.

maypole ['meɪpəul] *n* palo ornato di fiori attorno a cui si danza durante la festa di maggio.

maze [meɪz] *n* labirinto, dedalo.

MB *abbr* (*COMPUT*) = megabyte; (*Canada*) = Manitoba.

MBA *n abbr* (= *Master of Business Administration*) titolo di studio.

MBBS, MBChB *n abbr* (*BRIT*: = *Bachelor of Medicine and Surgery*) titolo di studio.

MBE *n abbr* (*BRIT*: = *Member of the Order of the British Empire*) titolo.

MC *n abbr see* **master of ceremonies**; (*US*: = *Member of Congress*) membro del Congresso.

MCAT *n abbr* (*US*: = *Medical College Admissions Test*) esame di ammissione a studi superiori di medicina.

MCP *n abbr* (*BRIT col*: = *male chauvinist pig*) sporco maschilista *m*.

MD *n abbr* (= *Doctor of Medicine*) titolo di studio; (*COMM*) *see* **managing director** ♦ *abbr* (*US*) = Maryland.

Md. *abbr* (*US*) = Maryland.

MDT *abbr* (*US*: = *Mountain Daylight Time*) ora legale delle Montagne Rocciose.

ME *abbr* (*US*) = Maine ♦ *n abbr* (*MED*: = *myalgic encephalomyelitis*) sindrome *f* da affaticamento cronico; (*US*) *see* **medical examiner**.

me [miː] *pron* mi, m' + *vowel*; (*stressed, after prep*) me; **it's** ~ sono io; **it's for** ~ è per me.

meadow ['mɛdəu] *n* prato.

meagre, (*US*) **meager** ['miːgə*] *adj* magro(a).

meal [miːl] *n* pasto; (*flour*) farina; **to go out for a** ~ mangiare fuori.

meals on wheels *n* (*BRIT*) distribuzione *f* di pasti caldi a domicilio (*per persone malate o anziane*).

mealtime ['miːltaɪm] *n* l'ora di mangiare.

mealy-mouthed ['miːlɪmauðd] *adj* che parla attraverso eufemismi.

mean [miːn] *adj* (*with money*) avaro(a), gretto(a); (*unkind*) meschino(a), maligno(a); (*US: vicious: animal*) cattivo(a); (: *person*) perfido(a); (*average*) medio(a) ♦ *vt* (*pt, pp* **meant** [mɛnt]) (*signify*) significare, voler dire; (*intend*): **to** ~ **to do** aver l'intenzione di fare ♦ *n* mezzo; (*MATH*) media; **to be meant for** essere destinato(a); **do you** ~ **it?** dice sul serio?; **what do you** ~**?** che cosa vuol dire?; *see also* **means**.

meander [mɪ'ændə*] *vi* far meandri; (*fig*) divagare.

meaning ['miːnɪŋ] *n* significato, senso.

meaningful ['mi:nɪŋful] *adj* significativo(a); (*relationship*) valido(a).
meaningless ['mi:nɪŋlɪs] *adj* senza senso.
meanness ['mi:nnɪs] *n* avarizia; meschinità.
means [mi:nz] *npl* mezzi *mpl*; **by ~ of** per mezzo di; (*person*) **a mezzo di; by all ~** ma certo, prego.
means test *n* (*ADMIN*) accertamento dei redditi (*per una persona che ha chiesto un aiuto finanziario*).
meant [mɛnt] *pt, pp of* **mean.**
meantime ['mi:ntaɪm], **meanwhile** ['mi:nwaɪl] *adv* (*also:* **in the ~**) nel frattempo.
measles ['mi:zlz] *n* morbillo.
measly ['mi:zlɪ] *adj* (*col*) miserabile.
measurable ['mɛʒərəbl] *adj* misurabile.
measure ['mɛʒə*] *vt, vi* misurare ♦ *n* misura; (*ruler*) metro; **a litre ~** una misura da un litro; **some ~ of success** un certo successo; **to take ~s to do sth** prendere provvedimenti per fare qc.
►**measure up** *vi:* **to ~ up (to)** dimostrarsi *or* essere all'altezza (di).
measured ['mɛʒəd] *adj* misurato(a).
measurement ['mɛʒəmənt] *n* (*act*) misurazione *f;* (*measure*) misura; **chest/ hip ~** giro petto/fianchi; **to take sb's ~s** prendere le misure di qn.
meat [mi:t] *n* carne *f;* **cold ~s** (*BRIT*) affettati *mpl;* **crab ~** polpa di granchio.
meatball ['mi:tbɔ:l] *n* polpetta di carne.
meat pie *n* torta salata in pasta frolla con ripieno di carne.
meaty ['mi:tɪ] *adj* che sa di carne; (*fig*) sostanzioso(a); (*of person*) corpulento(a); (*of part of body*) carnoso(a); **~ meal** pasto a base di carne.
Mecca ['mɛkə] *n* La Mecca; (*fig*): **a ~ (for)** la Mecca (di).
mechanic [mɪ'kænɪk] *n* meccanico; *see also* **mechanics.**
mechanical [mɪ'kænɪkəl] *adj* meccanico(a).
mechanical engineering *n* (*science*) ingegneria meccanica; (*industry*) costruzioni *fpl* meccaniche.
mechanics [mə'kænɪks] *n* meccanica ♦ *npl* meccanismo.
mechanism ['mɛkənɪzəm] *n* meccanismo.
mechanization [mɛkənaɪ'zeɪʃən] *n* meccanizzazione *f.*
MEd *n abbr* (= *Master of Education*) titolo di studio.
medal ['mɛdl] *n* medaglia.
medallion [mɪ'dælɪən] *n* medaglione *m.*
medallist, (*US*) **medalist** ['mɛdəlɪst] *n* (*SPORT*) vincitore/trice di medaglia.

meddle ['mɛdl] *vi:* **to ~ in** immischiarsi in, mettere le mani in; **to ~ with** toccare.
meddlesome ['mɛdlsəm], **meddling** ['mɛdlɪŋ] *adj* (*interfering*) che mette il naso dappertutto; (*touching things*) che tocca tutto.
media ['mi:dɪə] *npl* (*PRESS, RADIO, TV*) media *mpl;* (*means*) *pl of* **medium.**
media circus *n* carrozzone *m* dell'informazione.
mediaeval [mɛdɪ'i:vl] *adj* = **medieval.**
median ['mi:dɪən] *n* (*US: also:* **~ strip**) banchina *f* spartitraffico *inv.*
media research *n* sondaggio tra gli utenti dei mass media.
mediate ['mi:dɪeɪt] *vi* interporsi; fare da mediatore/trice.
mediation [mi:dɪ'eɪʃən] *n* mediazione *f.*
mediator ['mi:dɪeɪtə*] *n* mediatore/trice.
Medicaid ['mɛdɪkeɪd] *n* (*US*) assistenza medica ai poveri.
medical ['mɛdɪkl] *adj* medico(a); **~ (examination)** visita medica.
medical certificate *n* certificato medico.
medical examiner (ME) *n* (*US*) medico incaricato di indagare la causa di morte in circostanze sospette.
medical student *n* studente/essa di medicina.
Medicare ['mɛdɪkɛə*] *n* (*US*) assistenza medica agli anziani.
medicated ['mɛdɪkeɪtɪd] *adj* medicato(a).
medication [mɛdɪ'keɪʃən] *n* (*drugs etc*) medicinali *mpl,* farmaci *mpl.*
medicinal [mɛ'dɪsɪnl] *adj* medicinale.
medicine ['mɛdsɪn] *n* medicina.
medicine chest *n* armadietto farmaceutico.
medicine man *n* stregone *m.*
medieval [mɛdɪ'i:vl] *adj* medievale.
mediocre [mi:dɪ'əukə*] *adj* mediocre.
mediocrity [mi:dɪ'ɔkrɪtɪ] *n* mediocrità.
meditate ['mɛdɪteɪt] *vi:* **to ~ (on)** meditare (su).
meditation [mɛdɪ'teɪʃən] *n* meditazione *f.*
Mediterranean [mɛdɪtə'reɪnɪən] *adj* mediterraneo(a); **the ~ (Sea)** il (mare) Mediterraneo.
medium ['mi:dɪəm] *adj* medio(a) ♦ *n* (*pl* **media:** *means*) mezzo; (*pl* **mediums:** *person*) medium *m inv;* **the happy ~** una giusta via di mezzo; *see also* **media.**
medium-dry ['mi:dɪəm'draɪ] *adj* demisec *inv.*
medium-sized ['mi:dɪəmsaɪzd] *adj* (*tin etc*) di grandezza media; (*clothes*) di taglia media.
medium wave *n* (*RADIO*) onde *fpl* medie.

medley ['mɛdlɪ] *n* selezione *f.*

meek [miːk] *adj* dolce, umile.

meet, *pt, pp* **met** [miːt, mɛt] *vt* incontrare; (*for the first time*) fare la conoscenza di; (*fig*) affrontare; far fronte a; soddisfare; raggiungere ♦ *vi* incontrarsi; (*in session*) riunirsi; (*join: objects*) unirsi ♦ *n* (*BRIT HUNTING*) raduno (dei partecipanti alla caccia alla volpe); (*US SPORT*) raduno (sportivo); **I'll ~ you at the station** verrò a prenderla alla stazione; **pleased to ~ you!** lieto di conoscerla!, piacere!

▶**meet up** *vi*: **to ~ up with sb** incontrare qn.

▶**meet with** *vt fus* incontrare; **he met with an accident** ha avuto un incidente.

meeting ['miːtɪŋ] *n* incontro; (*session: of club etc*) riunione *f*; (*interview*) intervista; (*formal*) colloquio; (*SPORT: rally*) raduno; **she's at a ~** (*COMM*) è in riunione; **to call a ~** convocare una riunione.

meeting place *n* luogo d'incontro.

megabyte ['mɛgəbaɪt] *n* megabyte *m inv.*

megalomaniac [mɛgələu'meɪnɪæk] *n* megalomane *m/f.*

megaphone ['mɛgəfəun] *n* megafono.

megawatt ['mɛgəwɔt] *n* megawatt *m inv.*

melancholy ['mɛlənkəlɪ] *n* malinconia ♦ *adj* malinconico(a).

mellow ['mɛləu] *adj* (*wine, sound*) ricco(a); (*person, light*) dolce; (*colour*) caldo(a); (*fruit*) maturo(a) ♦ *vi* (*person*) addolcirsi.

melodious [mɪ'ləudɪəs] *adj* melodioso(a).

melodrama ['mɛləudrɑːmə] *n* melodramma *m.*

melodramatic [mɛlədrə'mætɪk] *adj* melodrammatico(a).

melody ['mɛlədɪ] *n* melodia.

melon ['mɛlən] *n* melone *m.*

melt [mɛlt] *vi* (*gen*) sciogliersi, struggersi; (*metals*) fondersi; (*fig*) intenerirsi ♦ *vt* sciogliere, struggere; fondere; (*person*) commuovere; **~ed butter** burro fuso.

▶**melt away** *vi* sciogliersi completamente.

▶**melt down** *vt* fondere.

meltdown ['mɛltdaun] *n* melt-down *m inv.*

melting point ['mɛltɪŋ-] *n* punto di fusione.

melting pot ['mɛltɪŋ-] *n* (*fig*) crogiolo; **to be in the ~** essere ancora in discussione.

member ['mɛmbə*] *n* membro; (*of club*) socio/a, iscritto/a; (*of political party*) iscritto/a; **~ country/state** *n* paese *m*/stato membro; **M~ of Parliament (MP)** *n* (*BRIT*) deputato; **M~ of the European Parliament (MEP)** *n* eurodeputato; **M~ of the House of Representatives (MHR)** *n* (*US*) membro della Camera dei Rappresentanti.

membership ['mɛmbəʃɪp] *n* iscrizione *f*; (numero d')iscritti *mpl*, membri *mpl.*

membership card *n* tessera (di iscrizione).

membrane ['mɛmbreɪn] *n* membrana.

memento [mə'mɛntəu] *n* ricordo, souvenir *m inv.*

memo ['mɛməu] *n* appunto; (*COMM etc*) comunicazione *f* di servizio.

memoir ['mɛmwɑː*] *n* memoria; **~s** *npl* memorie *fpl*, ricordi *mpl.*

memo pad *n* blocchetto per appunti.

memorable ['mɛmərəbl] *adj* memorabile.

memorandum, *pl* **memoranda** [mɛmə'rændəm, -də] *n* appunto; (*COMM etc*) comunicazione *f* di servizio; (*DIPLOMACY*) memorandum *m inv.*

memorial [mɪ'mɔːrɪəl] *n* monumento commemorativo ♦ *adj* commemorativo(a).

Negli Stati Uniti il **Memorial Day** *è una festa nazionale per la commemorazione di tutti i soldati americani caduti in guerra. Le celebrazioni sono tenute ogni anno l'ultimo lunedì di maggio.*

---

memorize ['mɛməraɪz] *vt* imparare a memoria.

memory ['mɛmərɪ] *n* (*gen, COMPUT*) memoria; (*recollection*) ricordo; **in ~ of** in memoria di; **to have a good/bad ~** aver buona/cattiva memoria; **loss of ~** amnesia.

men [mɛn] *npl of* **man.**

menace ['mɛnɪs] *n* minaccia; (*col: nuisance*) peste *f* ♦ *vt* minacciare; **a public ~** un pericolo pubblico.

menacing ['mɛnɪsɪŋ] *adj* minaccioso(a).

menagerie [mɪ'nædʒərɪ] *n* serraglio.

mend [mɛnd] *vt* aggiustare, riparare; (*darn*) rammendare ♦ *n* rammendo; **on the ~** in via di guarigione.

mending ['mɛndɪŋ] *n* rammendo; (*items to be mended*) roba da rammendare.

menial ['miːnɪəl] *adj* da servo, domestico(a); umile.

meningitis [mɛnɪn'dʒaɪtɪs] *n* meningite *f.*

menopause ['mɛnəupɔːz] *n* menopausa.

menservants ['mɛnsəːvənts] *npl of* **manservant.**

men's room *n*: **the ~** (*esp US*) la toilette degli uomini.

menstruate ['mɛnstrueɪt] *vi* mestruare.

menstruation [mɛnstru'eɪʃən] *n* mestruazione *f.*

menswear ['mɛnzwɛə*] *n* abbigliamento maschile.

mental ['mɛntl] *adj* mentale; **~ illness**

malattia mentale.
mental hospital *n* ospedale *m*
psichiatrico.
mentality [mɛn'tælɪtɪ] *n* mentalità *f inv.*
mentally ['mɛntlɪ] *adv*: **to be ~
handicapped** essere minorato psichico.
menthol ['mɛnθɔl] *n* mentolo.
mention ['mɛnʃən] *n* menzione *f* ♦ *vt*
menzionare, far menzione di; **don't ~ it!**
non c'è di che!, prego!; **I need hardly ~
that ...** inutile dire che ...; **not to ~**,
without ~ing per non parlare di, senza
contare.
mentor ['mɛntɔ:*] *n* mentore *m*.
menu ['mɛnju:] *n* (*set ~*, *COMPUT*) menù *m
inv*; (*printed*) carta.
menu-driven ['mɛnju:drɪvn] *adj* (*COMPUT*)
guidato(a) da menù.
MEP *n abbr see* **Member of the European
Parliament.**
mercantile ['mə:kəntaɪl] *adj* mercantile;
(*law*) commerciale.
mercenary ['mə:sɪnərɪ] *adj* venale ♦ *n*
mercenario.
merchandise ['mə:tʃəndaɪz] *n* merci *fpl* ♦ *vt*
commercializzare.
merchandiser ['mə:tʃəndaɪzə*] *n*
merchandiser *m inv.*
merchant ['mə:tʃənt] *n* (*trader*)
commerciante *m*; (*shopkeeper*) negoziante
m; **timber/wine ~** negoziante di legno/
vino.
merchant bank *n* (*BRIT*) banca d'affari.
merchantman ['mə:tʃəntmən] *n*
mercantile *m*.
merchant navy, (US) merchant marine
n marina mercantile.
merciful ['mə:sɪful] *adj* pietoso(a),
clemente.
mercifully ['mə:sɪflɪ] *adv* con clemenza;
(*fortunately*) per fortuna.
merciless ['mə:sɪlɪs] *adj* spietato(a).
mercurial [mə:'kjuərɪəl] *adj* (*unpredictable*)
volubile.
mercury ['mə:kjurɪ] *n* mercurio.
mercy ['mə:sɪ] *n* pietà; (*REL*) misericordia;
to have ~ on sb aver pietà di qn; **at the ~
of** alla mercè di.
mercy killing *n* eutanasia.
mere [mɪə*] *adj* semplice; **by a ~ chance**
per mero caso.
merely ['mɪəlɪ] *adv* semplicemente, non ...
che.
merge [mə:dʒ] *vt* unire; (*COMPUT: files, text*)
fondere ♦ *vi* fondersi, unirsi; (*COMM*)
fondersi.
merger ['mə:dʒə*] *n* (*COMM*) fusione *f.*
meridian [mə'rɪdɪən] *n* meridiano.

meringue [mə'ræŋ] *n* meringa.
merit ['mɛrɪt] *n* merito, valore *m* ♦ *vt*
meritare.
meritocracy [mɛrɪ'tɔkrəsɪ] *n* meritocrazia.
mermaid ['mə:meɪd] *n* sirena.
merriment ['mɛrɪmənt] *n* gaiezza, allegria.
merry ['mɛrɪ] *adj* gaio(a), allegro(a); **M~
Christmas!** Buon Natale!
merry-go-round ['mɛrɪgəuraund] *n*
carosello.
mesh [mɛʃ] *n* maglia; rete *f* ♦ *vi* (*gears*)
ingranarsi; **wire ~** rete metallica.
mesmerize ['mɛzməraɪz] *vt* ipnotizzare;
affascinare.
mess [mɛs] *n* confusione *f*, disordine *m*; (*fig*)
pasticcio; (*MIL*) mensa; **to be (in) a ~**
(*house, room*) essere in disordine (*or*
molto sporco); (*fig: marriage, life*) essere
un caos; **to be/get o.s. in a ~** (*fig*) essere/
cacciarsi in un pasticcio.
►**mess about, mess around** *vi* (*col*)
trastullarsi.
►**mess about** *or* **around with** *vt fus* (*col*)
gingillarsi con; (*plans*) fare un pasticcio
di.
►**mess up** *vt* sporcare; fare un pasticcio
di; rovinare.
message ['mɛsɪdʒ] *n* messaggio; **to get the
~** (*fig col*) capire l'antifona.
message switching *n* (*COMPUT*)
smistamento messaggi.
messenger ['mɛsɪndʒə*] *n* messaggero/a.
Messiah [mɪ'saɪə] *n* Messia *m.*
Messrs, Messrs. ['mɛsəz] *abbr* (*on letters*:
= *messieurs*) Spett.
messy ['mɛsɪ] *adj* sporco(a); disordinato(a);
(*confused: situation etc*) ingarbugliato(a).
Met [mɛt] *n abbr* (*US*) = *Metropolitan Opera.*
met [mɛt] *pt, pp of* **meet** ♦ *adj abbr*
(= *meteorological*): **the M~ Office** l'Ufficio
Meteorologico.
metabolism [mɛ'tæbəlɪzəm] *n*
metabolismo.
metal ['mɛtl] *n* metallo ♦ *vt* massicciare.
metallic
[mɛ'tælɪk] *adj* metallico(a).
metallurgy [mɛ'tælədʒɪ] *n* metallurgia.
metalwork ['mɛtlwə:k] *n* (*craft*) lavorazione
f del metallo.
metamorphosis, *pl* **-phoses**
[mɛtə'mɔ:fəsɪs, -i:z] *n* metamorfosi *f inv.*
metaphor ['mɛtəfə*] *n* metafora.
metaphysics [mɛtə'fɪzɪks] *n* metafisica.
mete [mi:t]: **to ~ out** *vt fus* infliggere.
meteor ['mi:tɪə*] *n* meteora.
meteoric [mi:tɪ'ɔrɪk] *adj* (*fig*) fulmineo(a).
meteorite ['mi:tɪəraɪt] *n* meteorite *m.*
meteorological [mi:tɪərə'lɔdʒɪkl] *adj*

meteorologico(a).
meteorology [miːtɪəˈrɔlədʒɪ] n
meteorologia.
meter ['miːtə*] n (instrument) contatore m;
(parking ~) parchimetro; (US) = **metre**.
methane ['miːθeɪn] n metano.
method ['mɛθəd] n metodo; ~ **of payment**
modo or modalità f inv di pagamento.
methodical [mɪˈθɔdɪkl] adj metodico(a).
Methodist ['mɛθədɪst] adj, n metodista
(m/f).
methylated spirits ['mɛθɪleɪtɪd-] n (BRIT:
also: **meths**) alcool m denaturato.
meticulous [mɛˈtɪkjuləs] adj meticoloso(a).
metre, (US) **meter** ['miːtə*] n metro.
metric ['mɛtrɪk] adj metrico(a); **to go ~**
adottare il sistema metrico decimale.
metrical ['mɛtrɪkl] adj metrico(a).
metrication [mɛtrɪˈkeɪʃən] n conversione f
al sistema metrico.
metric system n sistema m metrico
decimale.
metric ton n tonnellata.
metronome ['mɛtrənəum] n metronomo.
metropolis [mɪˈtrɔpəlɪs] n metropoli f inv.
metropolitan [mɛtrəˈpɔlɪtən] adj
metropolitano(a).
Metropolitan Police n (BRIT): **the ~** la
polizia di Londra.
mettle ['mɛtl] n coraggio.
mew [mjuː] vi (cat) miagolare.
mews [mjuːz] n (BRIT): ~ **flat**
appartamentino ricavato da una vecchia
scuderia.
Mexican ['mɛksɪkən] adj, n messicano(a).
Mexico ['mɛksɪkəu] n Messico.
Mexico City n Città del Messico.
mezzanine ['mɛtsəniːn] n mezzanino.
MFA n abbr (US: = Master of Fine Arts) titolo
di studio.
mfr abbr = **manufacture; manufacturer.**
mg abbr (= milligram) mg.
Mgr abbr (= Monseigneur, Monsignor)
mons.; (COMM) = **manager.**
MHR n abbr (US) see **Member of the House
of Representatives.**
MHz abbr (= megahertz) MHz.
MI abbr (US) = Michigan.
MI5 n abbr (BRIT: = Military Intelligence 5)
agenzia di controspionaggio.
MI6 n abbr (BRIT: = Military Intelligence 6)
agenzia di spionaggio.
MIA abbr = **missing in action.**
miaow [miːˈau] vi miagolare.
mice [maɪs] npl of **mouse.**
Mich. abbr (US) = Michigan.
microbe ['maɪkrəub] n microbio.
microbiology [maɪkrəubaɪˈɔlədʒɪ] n

microbiologia.
microchip ['maɪkrəutʃɪp] n microcircuito
integrato, chip m inv.
microcomputer [maɪkrəukəmˈpjuːtə*] n
microcomputer m inv.
microcosm ['maɪkrəukɔzəm] n
microcosmo.
microeconomics [maɪkrəuiːkəˈnɔmɪks] n
microeconomia.
microfiche ['maɪkrəufiːʃ] n microfiche f inv.
microfilm ['maɪkrəufɪlm] n microfilm m inv
♦ vt microfilmare.
microlight ['maɪkrəulaɪt] n aereo m biposto
inv.
micrometer [maɪˈkrɔmɪtə*] n micrometro,
palmer m inv.
microphone ['maɪkrəfəun] n microfono.
microprocessor [maɪkrəuˈprəusɛsə*] n
microprocessore m.
microscope ['maɪkrəskəup] n microscopio;
under the ~ al microscopio.
microscopic [maɪkrəˈskɔpɪk] adj
microscopico(a).
microwave ['maɪkrəuweɪv] n (also: ~ **oven**)
forno a microonde.
mid [mɪd] adj: ~ **May** metà maggio; ~
afternoon metà pomeriggio; **in** ~ **air** a
mezz'aria; **he's in his** ~ **thirties** avrà circa
trentacinque anni.
midday [mɪdˈdeɪ] n mezzogiorno.
middle ['mɪdl] n mezzo; centro; (waist) vita
♦ adj di mezzo; **I'm in the ~ of reading it**
sto proprio leggendolo ora; **in the ~ of
the night** nel mezzo della notte.
middle age n mezza età.
middle-aged [mɪdlˈeɪdʒd] adj di mezza età.
Middle Ages npl: **the ~** il Medioevo.
middle class adj (also: **middle-class**)
≈ borghese ♦ n: **the ~(es)** la borghesia.
Middle East n: **the ~** il Medio Oriente.
middleman ['mɪdlmæn] n intermediario;
agente m rivenditore.
middle management n quadri mpl
intermedi.
middle name n secondo nome m.
middle-of-the-road ['mɪdləvðəˈrəud] adj
moderato(a).
middleweight ['mɪdlweɪt] n (BOXING) peso
medio.
middling ['mɪdlɪŋ] adj medio(a).
midge [mɪdʒ] n moscerino.
midget ['mɪdʒɪt] n nano/a.
midi system ['mɪdɪ-] n (hi-fi) compatto.
Midlands ['mɪdləndz] npl contee del centro
dell'Inghilterra.
midnight ['mɪdnaɪt] n mezzanotte f; **at ~** a
mezzanotte.
midriff ['mɪdrɪf] n diaframma m.

midst [mɪdst] *n*: **in the** ~ **of** in mezzo a.

midsummer [mɪd'sʌmə*] *n* mezza *or* piena estate *f*.

midway [mɪd'weɪ] *adj, adv*: ~ **(between)** a mezza strada (fra).

midweek [mɪd'wi:k] *adv, adj* a metà settimana.

midwife, *pl* **midwives** ['mɪdwaɪf, -vz] *n* levatrice *f*.

midwifery ['mɪdwɪfərɪ] *n* ostetrica.

midwinter [mɪd'wɪntə*] *n* pieno inverno.

miffed [mɪft] *adj* (*col*) seccato(a), stizzito(a).

might [maɪt] *vb see* **may** ♦ *n* potere *m*, forza.

mighty ['maɪtɪ] *adj* forte, potente ♦ *adv* (*col*) molto.

migraine ['mi:greɪn] *n* emicrania.

migrant ['maɪgrənt] *n* (*bird, animal*) migratore *m*; (*person*) migrante *m/f*; nomade *m/f* ♦ *adj* migratore(trice); nomade; (*worker*) emigrato(a).

migrate [maɪ'greɪt] *vi* migrare.

migration [maɪ'greɪʃən] *n* migrazione *f*.

mike [maɪk] *n abbr* (= *microphone*) microfono.

Milan [mɪ'læn] *n* Milano *f*.

mild [maɪld] *adj* mite; (*person, voice*) dolce; (*flavour*) delicato(a); (*illness*) leggero(a) ♦ *n* birra leggera.

mildew ['mɪldju:] *n* muffa.

mildly ['maɪldlɪ] *adv* mitemente; dolcemente; delicatamente; leggeramente; **to put it** ~ a dire poco.

mildness ['maɪldnɪs] *n* mitezza; dolcezza; delicatezza; non gravità.

mile [maɪl] *n* miglio; **to do 20** ~**s per gallon** ≈ usare 14 litri per cento chilometri.

mileage ['maɪlɪdʒ] *n* distanza in miglia, ≈ chilometraggio.

mileage allowance *n* rimborso per miglio.

mileometer [maɪ'lɒmɪtə*] *n* (*BRIT*) = **milometer**.

milestone ['maɪlstəun] *n* pietra miliare.

milieu ['mi:ljə:] *n* ambiente *m*.

militant ['mɪlɪtnt] *adj, n* militante (*m/f*).

militarism ['mɪlɪtərɪzəm] *n* militarismo.

militaristic [mɪlɪtə'rɪstɪk] *adj* militaristico(a).

military ['mɪlɪtərɪ] *adj* militare ♦ *n*: **the** ~ i militari, l'esercito.

military service *n* servizio militare.

militate ['mɪlɪteɪt] *vi*: **to** ~ **against** essere d'ostacolo a.

militia [mɪ'lɪʃə] *n* milizia.

milk [mɪlk] *n* latte *m* ♦ *vt* (*cow*) mungere; (*fig*) sfruttare.

milk chocolate *n* cioccolato al latte.

milk float *n* (*BRIT*) furgone *m* del lattaio.

milking ['mɪlkɪŋ] *n* mungitura.

milkman ['mɪlkmən] *n* lattaio.

milk shake *n* frappé *m inv*.

milk tooth *n* dente *m* di latte.

milk truck *n* (*US*) = **milk float**.

milky ['mɪlkɪ] *adj* lattiginoso(a); (*colour*) latteo(a).

Milky Way *n* Via Lattea.

mill [mɪl] *n* mulino; (*small: for coffee, pepper etc*) macinino; (*factory*) fabbrica; (*spinning* ~) filatura ♦ *vt* macinare ♦ *vi* (*also*: ~ **about**) formicolare.

millennium, *pl* ~**s** *or* **millennia** [mɪ'lɛnɪəm, -'lɛnɪə] *n* millennio.

miller ['mɪlə*] *n* mugnaio.

millet ['mɪlɪt] *n* miglio.

milli... ['mɪlɪ] *prefix* milli....

milligram(me) ['mɪlɪgræm] *n* milligrammo.

millilitre, (*US*) **milliliter** ['mɪlɪli:tə*] *n* millilitro.

millimetre, (*US*) **millimeter** ['mɪlɪmi:tə*] *n* millimetro.

milliner ['mɪlɪnə*] *n* modista.

millinery ['mɪlɪnərɪ] *n* modisteria.

million ['mɪljən] *n* milione *m*.

millionaire [mɪljə'nɛə*] *n* milionario, ≈ miliardario.

millipede ['mɪlɪpi:d] *n* millepiedi *m inv*.

millstone ['mɪlstəun] *n* macina.

millwheel ['mɪlwi:l] *n* ruota di mulino.

milometer [maɪ'lɒmɪtə*] *n* ≈ contachilometri *m inv*.

mime [maɪm] *n* mimo ♦ *vt, vi* mimare.

mimic ['mɪmɪk] *n* imitatore/trice ♦ *vt* (*subj: comedian*) imitare; (: *animal, person*) scimmiottare.

mimicry ['mɪmɪkrɪ] *n* imitazioni *fpl*; (*ZOOL*) mimetismo.

Min. *abbr* (*BRIT POL*: = *ministry*) Min.

min. *abbr* (= *minute, minimum*) min.

minaret [mɪnə'rɛt] *n* minareto.

mince [mɪns] *vt* tritare, macinare ♦ *vi* (*in walking*) camminare a passettini ♦ *n* (*BRIT CULIN*) carne *f* tritata *or* macinata; **he does not** ~ **(his) words** parla chiaro e tondo.

mincemeat ['mɪnsmi:t] *n frutta secca tritata per uso in pasticceria.*

mince pie *n specie di torta con frutta secca.*

mincer ['mɪnsə*] *n* tritacarne *m inv*.

mincing ['mɪnsɪŋ] *adj* lezioso(a).

mind [maɪnd] *n* mente *f* ♦ *vt* (*attend to, look after*) badare a, occuparsi di; (*be careful*) fare attenzione a, stare attento(a) a; (*object to*): **I don't** ~ **the noise** il rumore non mi dà alcun fastidio; **do you** ~ **if ...?**

le dispiace se ...?; **I don't** ~ non
m'importa; ~ **you,** ... sì, però va detto che
...; **never** ~ non importa, non fa niente; **it
is on my** ~ mi preoccupa; **to change
one's** ~ cambiare idea; **to be in two** ~**s
about sth** essere incerto su qc; **to my** ~
secondo me, a mio parere; **to be out of
one's** ~ essere uscito(a) di mente; **to
keep sth in** ~ non dimenticare qc; **to bear
sth in** ~ tener presente qc; **to have sb/sth
in** ~ avere in mente qn/qc; **to have in** ~
to do aver l'intenzione di fare; **it went
right out of my** ~ mi è completamente
passato di mente, me ne sono
completamente dimenticato; **to bring** or
call sth to ~ riportare or richiamare qc
alla mente; **to make up one's** ~ decidersi;
"~ **the step**" "attenzione allo scalino".
mind-boggling ['maɪndbɔglɪŋ] adj (col)
sconcertante.
-minded ['maɪndɪd] adj: **fair**~ imparziale;
an industrially~ **nation** una nazione
orientata verso l'industria.
minder ['maɪndə*] n (child ~) bambinaia;
(bodyguard) guardia del corpo.
mindful ['maɪndful] adj: ~ **of** attento(a) a;
memore di.
mindless ['maɪndlɪs] adj idiota; (violence,
crime) insensato(a).
mine [maɪn] pron il(la) mio(a), pl i(le)
miei(mie); **this book is** ~ questo libro è
mio ♦ n miniera; (explosive) mina ♦ vt
(coal) estrarre; (ship, beach) minare.
mine detector n rivelatore m di mine.
minefield ['maɪnfiːld] n campo minato.
miner ['maɪnə*] n minatore m.
mineral ['mɪnərəl] adj minerale ♦ n
minerale m; ~**s** npl (BRIT: soft drinks)
bevande fpl gasate.
mineralogy [mɪnə'rælədʒɪ] n mineralogia.
mineral water n acqua minerale.
minesweeper ['maɪnswiːpə*] n dragamine
m inv.
mingle ['mɪŋgl] vt mescolare, mischiare
♦ vi: **to** ~ **with** mescolarsi a, mischiarsi
con.
mingy ['mɪndʒɪ] adj (col: amount) misero(a);
(: person) spilorcio(a).
miniature ['mɪnətʃə*] adj in miniatura ♦ n
miniatura.
minibus ['mɪnɪbʌs] n minibus m inv.
minicab ['mɪnɪkæb] n (BRIT) ≈ taxi m inv.
minicomputer ['mɪnɪkəm'pjuːtə*] n
minicomputer m inv.
minim ['mɪnɪm] n (MUS) minima.
minima ['mɪnɪmə] npl of **minimum.**
minimal ['mɪnɪml] adj minimo(a).
minimalist ['mɪnɪməlɪst] adj, n minimalista

(m/f).
minimize ['mɪnɪmaɪz] vt minimizzare.
minimum ['mɪnɪməm] n (pl **minima**)
minimo ♦ adj minimo(a); **to reduce to a** ~
ridurre al minimo; ~ **wage** salario
minimo garantito.
minimum lending rate (MLR) n (BRIT)
≈ tasso ufficiale di sconto (T.U.S.).
mining ['maɪnɪŋ] n industria mineraria
♦ adj minerario(a); di minatori.
minion ['mɪnjən] n (pej) caudatario;
favorito/a.
mini-series ['mɪnɪsɪəriːz] n miniserie f inv.
miniskirt ['mɪnɪskəːt] n minigonna.
minister ['mɪnɪstə*] n (BRIT POL) ministro;
(REL) pastore m ♦ vi: **to** ~ **to sb** assistere
qn; **to** ~ **to sb's needs** provvedere ai
bisogni di qn.
ministerial [mɪnɪs'tɪərɪəl] adj (BRIT POL)
ministeriale.
ministry ['mɪnɪstrɪ] n (BRIT POL) ministero;
(REL): **to go into the** ~ diventare pastore.
mink [mɪŋk] n visone m.
mink coat n pelliccia di visone.
Minn. abbr (US) = Minnesota.
minnow ['mɪnəu] n pesciolino d'acqua
dolce.
minor ['maɪnə*] adj minore, di poca
importanza; (MUS) minore ♦ n (LAW)
minorenne m/f.
Minorca [mɪ'nɔːkə] n Minorca.
minority [maɪ'nɔrɪtɪ] n minoranza; **to be in
a** ~ essere in minoranza.
minster ['mɪnstə*] n cattedrale f (annessa a
monastero).
minstrel ['mɪnstrəl] n giullare m,
menestrello.
mint [mɪnt] n (plant) menta; (sweet)
pasticca di menta ♦ vt (coins) battere; **the
(Royal) M**~, (US) **the (US) M**~ la Zecca; **in**
~ **condition** come nuovo(a) di zecca.
mint sauce n salsa di menta.
minuet [mɪnju'ɛt] n minuetto.
minus ['maɪnəs] n (also: ~ **sign**) segno
meno ♦ prep meno.
minuscule ['mɪnəskjuːl] adj minuscolo(a).
minute adj [maɪ'njuːt] minuscolo(a); (detail)
minuzioso(a) ♦ n ['mɪnɪt] minuto; (official
record) processo verbale, resoconto
sommario; ~**s** npl verbale m, verbali mpl;
it is 5 ~**s past 3** sono le 3 e 5 (minuti);
wait a ~! (aspetta) un momento!; **at the
last** ~ all'ultimo momento; **up to the** ~
ultimissimo; modernissimo; **in** ~ **detail**
minuziosamente.
minute book n libro dei verbali.
minute hand n lancetta dei minuti.
minutely [maɪ'njuːtlɪ] adv (by a small

amount) di poco; (*in detail)* minuziosamente.

minutiae [mɪ'njuːʃiː] *npl* minuzie *fpl.*

miracle ['mɪrəkl] *n* miracolo.

miraculous [mɪ'rækjuləs] *adj* miracoloso(a).

mirage ['mɪrɑːʒ] *n* miraggio.

mire ['maɪə*] *n* pantano, melma.

mirror ['mɪrə*] *n* specchio ♦ *vt* rispecchiare, riflettere.

mirror image *n* immagine *f* speculare.

mirth [məːθ] *n* gaiezza.

misadventure [mɪsəd'vɛntʃə*] *n* disavventura; **death by** ~ (*BRIT*) morte *f* accidentale.

misanthropist [mɪ'zænθrəpɪst] *n* misantropo/a.

misapply [mɪsə'plaɪ] *vt* impiegare male.

misapprehension ['mɪsæprɪ'hɛnʃən] *n* malinteso.

misappropriate [mɪsə'prəuprɪeɪt] *vt* appropriarsi indebitamente di.

misappropriation ['mɪsəprəuprɪ'eɪʃən] *n* appropriazione *f* indebita.

misbehave [mɪsbɪ'heɪv] *vi* comportarsi male.

misbehaviour, (*US*) **misbehavior** [mɪsbɪ'heɪvjə*] *n* comportamento scorretto.

misc. *abbr* = **miscellaneous.**

miscalculate [mɪs'kælkjuleɪt] *vt* calcolare male.

miscalculation ['mɪskælkju'leɪʃən] *n* errore *m* di calcolo.

miscarriage ['mɪskærɪdʒ] *n* (*MED*) aborto spontaneo; ~ **of justice** errore *m* giudiziario.

miscarry [mɪs'kærɪ] *vi* (*MED*) abortire; (*fail: plans)* andare a monte, fallire.

miscellaneous [mɪsɪ'leɪnɪəs] *adj* (*items)* vario(a); (*selection)* misto(a); ~ **expenses** spese varie.

miscellany [mɪ'sɛlənɪ] *n* raccolta.

mischance [mɪs'tʃɑːns] *n*: **by (some)** ~ per sfortuna.

mischief ['mɪstʃɪf] *n* (*naughtiness)* birichineria; (*harm)* male *m*, danno; (*maliciousness)* malizia.

mischievous ['mɪstʃɪvəs] *adj* (*naughty)* birichino(a); (*harmful)* dannoso(a).

misconception [mɪskən'sɛpʃən] *n* idea sbagliata.

misconduct [mɪs'kɔndʌkt] *n* cattiva condotta; **professional** ~ reato professionale.

misconstrue [mɪskən'struː] *vt* interpretare male.

miscount [mɪs'kaunt] *vt*, *vi* contare male.

misdeed [mɪs'diːd] *n* (*old)* misfatto.

misdemeanour, (*US*) **misdemeanor** [mɪsdɪ'miːnə*] *n* misfatto; infrazione *f.*

misdirect [mɪsdɪ'rɛkt] *vt* mal indirizzare.

miser ['maɪzə*] *n* avaro.

miserable ['mɪzərəbl] *adj* infelice; (*wretched)* miserabile; (*weather)* deprimente; **to feel** ~ sentirsi avvilito *or* giù di morale.

miserably ['mɪzərəblɪ] *adv* (*fail, live, pay)* miseramente; (*smile, answer)* tristemente.

miserly ['maɪzəlɪ] *adj* avaro(a).

misery ['mɪzərɪ] *n* (*unhappiness)* tristezza; (*pain)* sofferenza; (*wretchedness)* miseria.

misfire [mɪs'faɪə*] *vi* far cilecca; (*car engine)* perdere colpi.

misfit ['mɪsfɪt] *n* (*person)* spostato/a.

misfortune [mɪs'fɔːtʃən] *n* sfortuna.

misgiving(s) [mɪs'gɪvɪŋ(z)] *n(pl)* dubbi *mpl*, sospetti *mpl*; **to have ~s about sth** essere diffidente *or* avere dei dubbi per quanto riguarda qc.

misguided [mɪs'gaɪdɪd] *adj* sbagliato(a); poco giudizioso(a).

mishandle [mɪs'hændl] *vt* (*treat roughly)* maltrattare; (*mismanage)* trattare male.

mishap ['mɪshæp] *n* disgrazia.

mishear [mɪs'hɪə*] *vt*, *vi irreg* capire male.

mishmash ['mɪʃmæʃ] *n* (*col)* minestrone *m*, guazzabuglio.

misinform [mɪsɪn'fɔːm] *vt* informare male.

misinterpret [mɪsɪn'təːprɪt] *vt* interpretare male.

misinterpretation ['mɪsɪntəːprɪ'teɪʃən] *n* errata interpretazione *f.*

misjudge [mɪs'dʒʌdʒ] *vt* giudicare male.

mislay [mɪs'leɪ] *vt irreg* smarrire.

mislead [mɪs'liːd] *vt irreg* sviare.

misleading [mɪs'liːdɪŋ] *adj* ingannevole.

misled [mɪs'lɛd] *pt*, *pp of* **mislead.**

mismanage [mɪs'mænɪdʒ] *vt* gestire male; trattare male.

mismanagement [mɪs'mænɪdʒmənt] *n* cattiva amministrazione *f.*

misnomer [mɪs'nəumə*] *n* termine *m* sbagliato *or* improprio.

misogynist [mɪ'sɔdʒɪnɪst] *n* misogino.

misplace [mɪs'pleɪs] *vt* smarrire; collocare fuori posto; **to be ~d** (*trust etc)* essere malriposto(a).

misprint ['mɪsprɪnt] *n* errore *m* di stampa.

mispronounce [mɪsprə'nauns] *vt* pronunziare male.

misquote [mɪs'kwəut] *vt* citare erroneamente.

misread [mɪs'riːd] *vt irreg* leggere male.

misrepresent [mɪsrɛprɪ'zɛnt] *vt* travisare.

Miss [mɪs] n Signorina; **Dear ~ Smith** Cara Signorina; (more formal) Gentile Signorina.

miss [mɪs] vt (fail to get) perdere; (appointment, class) mancare a; (escape, avoid) evitare; (notice loss of: money etc) accorgersi di non avere più; (regret the absence of): **I ~ him/it** sento la sua mancanza, lui/esso mi manca ♦ vi mancare ♦ n (shot) colpo mancato; (fig): **that was a near ~** c'è mancato poco; **the bus just ~ed the wall** l'autobus per un pelo non è andato a finire contro il muro; **you're ~ing the point** non capisce.
▶**miss out** vt (BRIT) omettere.
▶**miss out on** vt fus (fun, party) perdersi; (chance, bargain) lasciarsi sfuggire.

Miss. abbr (US) = Mississippi.
missal ['mɪsl] n messale m.
misshapen [mɪs'ʃeɪpən] adj deforme.
missile ['mɪsaɪl] n (AVIAT) missile m; (object thrown) proiettile m.
missile base n base f missilistica.
missile launcher n lancia-missili m inv.
missing ['mɪsɪŋ] adj perso(a), smarrito(a); **to go ~** sparire; **~ person** scomparso/a, disperso/a; **~ in action** (MIL) disperso/a.
mission ['mɪʃən] n missione f; **on a ~ to sb** in missione da qn.
missionary ['mɪʃənrɪ] n missionario/a.
misspell [mɪs'spɛl] vt (irreg: like **spell**) sbagliare l'ortografia di.
misspent [mɪs'spɛnt] adj: **his ~ youth** la sua gioventù sciupata.
mist [mɪst] n nebbia, foschia ♦ vi (also: ~ over, ~ up) annebbiarsi; (BRIT: windows) appannarsi.
mistake [mɪs'teɪk] n sbaglio, errore m ♦ vt (irreg: like **take**) sbagliare di; fraintendere; **to ~ for** prendere per; **by ~** per sbaglio; **to make a ~** (in writing, calculating etc) fare uno sbaglio or un errore; **to make a ~ about sb/sth** sbagliarsi sul conto di qn/su qc.
mistaken [mɪs'teɪkən] pp of **mistake** ♦ adj (idea etc) sbagliato(a); **to be ~** sbagliarsi.
mistaken identity n errore m di persona.
mistakenly [mɪs'teɪkənlɪ] adv per errore.
mister ['mɪstə*] n (col) signore m; see **Mr.**
mistletoe ['mɪsltəu] n vischio.
mistook [mɪs'tuk] pt of **mistake.**
mistranslation [mɪstræns'leɪʃən] n traduzione f errata.
mistreat [mɪs'triːt] vt maltrattare.
mistress ['mɪstrɪs] n padrona; (lover) amante f; (BRIT SCOL) insegnante f.
mistrust [mɪs'trʌst] vt diffidare di ♦ n: ~ (of) diffidenza (nei confronti di).

mistrustful [mɪs'trʌstful] adj: ~ (of) diffidente (nei confronti di).
misty ['mɪstɪ] adj nebbioso(a), brumoso(a).
misty-eyed ['mɪstɪ'aɪd] adj trasognato(a).
misunderstand [mɪsʌndə'stænd] vt, vi irreg capire male, fraintendere.
misunderstanding [mɪsʌndə'stændɪŋ] n malinteso, equivoco.
misunderstood [mɪsʌndə'stud] pt, pp of **misunderstand.**
misuse n [mɪs'juːs] cattivo uso; (of power) abuso ♦ vt [mɪs'juːz] far cattivo uso di; abusare di.
MIT n abbr (US) = Massachusetts Institute of Technology.
mite [maɪt] n (small quantity) briciolo; (BRIT: small child): **poor ~!** povera creaturina!
miter ['maɪtə*] n (US) = **miter.**
mitigate ['mɪtɪgeɪt] vt mitigare; (suffering) alleviare; **mitigating circumstances** circostanze fpl attenuanti.
mitigation [mɪtɪ'geɪʃən] n mitigazione f; alleviamento.
mitre, (US) miter ['maɪtə*] n mitra; (CARPENTRY) giunto ad angolo retto.
mitt(en) ['mɪt(n)] n mezzo guanto; manopola.
mix [mɪks] vt mescolare ♦ vi mescolarsi ♦ n mescolanza; preparato; **to ~ sth with sth** mischiare qc a qc; **to ~ business with pleasure** unire l'utile al dilettevole; **cake ~** preparato per torta.
▶**mix in** vt (eggs etc) incorporare.
▶**mix up** vt mescolare; (confuse) confondere; **to be ~ed up in sth** essere coinvolto in qc.
mixed [mɪkst] adj misto(a).
mixed-ability ['mɪkstə'bɪlɪtɪ] adj (class etc) con alunni di capacità diverse.
mixed bag n miscuglio, accozzaglia; **it's a ~** c'è un po' di tutto.
mixed blessing n: **it's a ~** ha i suoi lati positivi e negativi.
mixed doubles npl (SPORT) doppio misto.
mixed economy n economia mista.
mixed grill n (BRIT) misto alla griglia.
mixed marriage n matrimonio misto.
mixed-up [mɪkst'ʌp] adj (confused) confuso(a).
mixer ['mɪksə*] n (for food: electric) frullatore m; (: hand) frullino; (person): **he is a good ~** è molto socievole.
mixer tap n miscelatore m.
mixture ['mɪkstʃə*] n mescolanza; (blend: of tobacco etc) miscela; (MED) sciroppo.
mix-up ['mɪksʌp] n confusione f.
MK abbr (BRIT TECH) = **mark.**
mk abbr = **mark** (currency).

mkt *abbr* = **market**.
MLitt *n abbr* (= *Master of Literature, Master of Letters*) *titolo di studio*.
MLR *n abbr* (*BRIT*) *see* **minimum lending rate**.
mm *abbr* (= *millimetre*) mm.
MN *abbr* (*BRIT*) = **Merchant Navy**; (*US*) = **Minnesota**.
MO *n abbr* = *medical officer,* (*US col*: = *modus operandi*) modo d'agire ♦ *abbr* (*US*) = Missouri.
m.o. *abbr* = **money order**.
moan [məun] *n* gemito ♦ *vi* gemere; (*col*: *complain*): **to ~ (about)** lamentarsi (di).
moaner ['məunə*] *n* (*col*) uno/a che si lamenta sempre.
moaning ['məunɪŋ] *n* gemiti *mpl*.
moat [məut] *n* fossato.
mob [mɔb] *n* folla; (*disorderly*) calca; (*pej*): **the ~** la plebaglia ♦ *vt* accalcarsi intorno a.
mobile ['məubaɪl] *adj* mobile ♦ *n* (*ART*) mobile *m inv*; **applicants must be ~** (*BRIT*) i candidati devono essere disposti a viaggiare.
mobile home *n* grande roulotte *f inv* (*utilizzata come domicilio*).
mobile phone *n* telefonino.
mobile shop *n* (*BRIT*) negozio ambulante.
mobility [məu'bɪlɪtɪ] *n* mobilità; (*of applicant*) disponibilità a viaggiare.
mobilize ['məubɪlaɪz] *vt* mobilitare ♦ *vi* mobilitarsi.
moccasin ['mɔkəsɪn] *n* mocassino.
mock [mɔk] *vt* deridere, burlarsi di ♦ *adj* falso(a).
mockery ['mɔkərɪ] *n* derisione *f*; **to make a ~ of** rendere ridicolo.
mocking ['mɔkɪŋ] *adj* derisorio(a).
mockingbird ['mɔkɪŋbə:d] *n* mimo (*uccello*).
mock-up ['mɔkʌp] *n* modello dimostrativo; abbozzo.
MOD *n abbr* (*BRIT*) = **Ministry of Defence**; *see* **defence**.
mod cons ['mɔd'kɔnz] *npl abbr* (*BRIT*) = **modern conveniences**.
mode [məud] *n* modo; (*of transport*) mezzo; (*COMPUT*) modalità *f inv*.
model ['mɔdl] *n* modello; (*person: for fashion*) indossatore/trice; (: *for artist*) modello/a ♦ *vt* modellare ♦ *vi* fare l'indossatore (*or* l'indossatrice) ♦ *adj* (*small-scale: railway etc*) in miniatura; (*child, factory*) modello *inv*; **to ~ clothes** presentare degli abiti; **to ~ sb/sth on** modellare qn/qc su.
modem ['məudɛm] *n* modem *m inv*.
moderate ['mɔdərɪt] *adj* moderato(a) ♦ *n*

(*POL*) moderato/a ♦ *vb* ['mɔdəreɪt] *vi* moderarsi, placarsi ♦ *vt* moderare.
moderately ['mɔdərɪtlɪ] *adv* (*act*) con moderazione; (*expensive, difficult*) non troppo; (*pleased, happy*) abbastanza, discretamente; **~ priced** a prezzo modico.
moderation [mɔdə'reɪʃən] *n* moderazione *f*, misura; **in ~** in quantità moderata, con moderazione.
moderator ['mɔdəreɪtə*] *n* moderatore/trice; (*REL*) *moderatore in importanti riunioni ecclesiastiche*.
modern ['mɔdən] *adj* moderno(a); **~ conveniences** comodità *fpl* moderne; **~ languages** lingue *fpl* moderne.
modernization [mɔdənaɪ'zeɪʃən] *n* rimodernamento, modernizzazione *f*.
modernize ['mɔdənaɪz] *vt* modernizzare.
modest ['mɔdɪst] *adj* modesto(a).
modesty ['mɔdɪstɪ] *n* modestia.
modicum ['mɔdɪkəm] *n*: **a ~ of** un minimo di.
modification [mɔdɪfɪ'keɪʃən] *n* modificazione *f*; **to make ~s** fare *or* apportare delle modifiche.
modify ['mɔdɪfaɪ] *vt* modificare.
modish ['məudɪʃ] *adj* (*liter*) à la page *inv*.
Mods [mɔdz] *n abbr* (*BRIT*: = (*Honour*) *Moderations*) esame all'università di Oxford.
modular ['mɔdjulə*] *adj* (*filing, unit*) modulare.
modulate ['mɔdjuleɪt] *vt* modulare.
modulation [mɔdju'leɪʃən] *n* modulazione *f*.
module ['mɔdju:l] *n* modulo.
Mogadishu [mɔgə'dɪʃu:] *n* Mogadiscio *f*.
mogul ['məugl] *n* (*fig*) magnate *m*, pezzo grosso; (*SKI*) cunetta.
MOH *n abbr* (*BRIT*: = *Medical Officer of Health*) ≈ ufficiale *m* sanitario.
mohair ['məuhɛə*] *n* mohair *m*.
Mohammed [məu'hæmɪd] *n* Maometto.
moist [mɔɪst] *adj* umido(a).
moisten ['mɔɪsn] *vt* inumidire.
moisture ['mɔɪstʃə*] *n* umidità; (*on glass*) goccioline *fpl* di vapore.
moisturize ['mɔɪstʃəraɪz] *vt* (*skin*) idratare.
moisturizer ['mɔɪstʃəraɪzə*] *n* idratante *f*.
molar ['məulə*] *n* molare *m*.
molasses [məu'læsɪz] *n* molassa.
mold [məuld] *etc* (*US*) = **mould** *etc*.
Moldavia [mɔl'deɪvɪə], **Moldova** [mɔl'dəuvə] *n* Moldavia.
Moldavian [mɔl'deɪvɪən], **Moldovan** [mɔl'dəuvən] *adj* moldavo(a).
mole [məul] *n* (*animal*) talpa; (*spot*) neo.
molecule ['mɔlɪkju:l] *n* molecola.
molehill ['məulhɪl] *n cumulo di terra sulla*

tana di una talpa.

molest [mǝu'lɛst] *vt* molestare.

mollusc, *(US)* **mollusk** ['mɔlǝsk] *n* mollusco.

mollycoddle ['mɔlɪkɔdl] *vt* coccolare, vezzeggiare.

Molotov cocktail ['mɔlǝtɔf-] *n* (bottiglia) Molotov *f inv.*

molt [mǝult] *vi (US)* = **moult.**

molten ['mǝultǝn] *adj* fuso(a).

mom [mɔm] *n (US)* = **mum.**

moment ['mǝumǝnt] *n* momento, istante *m*; importanza; **at the** ~ al momento, in questo momento; **for the** ~ per il momento, per ora; **in a** ~ tra un momento; **"one** ~ **please"** *(TEL)* "attenda, prego".

momentarily ['mǝumǝntǝrɪlɪ] *adv* per un momento; *(US: very soon)* da un momento all'altro.

momentary ['mǝumǝntǝrɪ] *adj* momentaneo(a), passeggero(a).

momentous [mǝu'mɛntǝs] *adj* di grande importanza.

momentum [mǝu'mɛntǝm] *n* velocità acquisita, slancio; *(PHYSICS)* momento; **to gather** ~ aumentare di velocità; *(fig)* prendere *or* guadagnare terreno.

mommy ['mɔmɪ] *n (US)* mamma.

Mon. *abbr (= Monday)* lun.

Monaco ['mɔnǝkǝu] *n* Monaco *f.*

monarch ['mɔnǝk] *n* monarca *m.*

monarchist ['mɔnǝkɪst] *n* monarchico/a.

monarchy ['mɔnǝkɪ] *n* monarchia.

monastery ['mɔnǝstǝrɪ] *n* monastero.

monastic [mǝ'næstɪk] *adj* monastico(a).

Monday ['mʌndɪ] *n* lunedì *m inv; for phrases see also* **Tuesday.**

Monegasque [mɔnǝ'gæsk] *adj, n* monegasco(a).

monetarist ['mʌnɪtǝrɪst] *n* monetarista *m/f.*

monetary ['mʌnɪtǝrɪ] *adj* monetario(a).

money ['mʌnɪ] *n* denaro, soldi *mpl*; **to make** ~ *(person)* fare (i) soldi; *(business)* rendere; **danger** ~ *(BRIT)* indennità di rischio; **I've got no** ~ **left** non ho più neanche una lira.

moneyed ['mʌnɪd] *adj* ricco(a).

moneylender ['mʌnɪlɛndǝ*] *n* prestatore *m* di denaro.

moneymaker ['mʌnɪmeɪkǝ*] *n (BRIT col: business)* affare *m* d'oro.

moneymaking ['mʌnɪmeɪkɪŋ] *adj* che rende (bene *or* molto), lucrativo(a).

money market *n* mercato monetario.

money order *n* vaglia *m inv.*

money-spinner ['mʌnɪspɪnǝ*] *n (col)* miniera d'oro *(fig).*

money supply *n* liquidità monetaria.

Mongol ['mɔŋgǝl] *n* mongolo/a; *(LING)* mongolo.

mongol ['mɔŋgǝl] *adj, n (MED)* mongoloide *(m/f).*

Mongolia [mɔŋ'gǝulɪǝ] *n* Mongolia.

Mongolian [mɔŋ'gǝulɪǝn] *adj* mongolico(a) ♦ *n* mongolo/a; *(LING)* mongolo.

mongoose ['mɔŋguːs] *n* mangusta.

mongrel ['mʌŋgrǝl] *n (dog)* cane *m* bastardo.

monitor ['mɔnɪtǝ*] *n (BRIT SCOL)* capoclasse *m/f*; *(US SCOL)* chi sorveglia agli esami; *(TV, COMPUT)* monitor *m inv* ♦ *vt* controllare; *(foreign station)* ascoltare le trasmissioni di.

monk [mʌŋk] *n* monaco.

monkey ['mʌŋkɪ] *n* scimmia.

monkey business *n (col)* scherzi *mpl.*

monkey nut *n (BRIT)* nocciolina americana.

monkey wrench *n* chiave *f* a rullino.

mono ['mɔnǝu] *adj* mono *inv*; *(broadcast)* in mono.

mono... ['mɔnǝu] *prefix* mono....

monochrome ['mɔnǝkrǝum] *adj* monocromo(a).

monocle ['mɔnǝkl] *n* monocolo.

monogamous [mǝ'nɔgǝmǝs] *adj* monogamo(a).

monogamy [mǝ'nɔgǝmɪ] *n* monogamia.

monogram ['mɔnǝgræm] *n* monogramma *m.*

monolith ['mɔnǝlɪθ] *n* monolito.

monologue ['mɔnǝlɔg] *n* monologo.

monoplane ['mɔnǝupleɪn] *n* monoplano.

monopolize [mǝ'nɔpǝlaɪz] *vt* monopolizzare.

monopoly [mǝ'nɔpǝlɪ] *n* monopolio; **Monopolies and Mergers Commission** *(BRIT)* commissione *f* antimonopoli.

monorail ['mɔnǝureɪl] *n* monorotaia.

monosodium glutamate (MSG) [mɔnǝ'sǝudɪǝm'gluːtǝmeɪt] *n* glutammato di sodio.

monosyllabic [mɔnǝsɪ'læbɪk] *adj* monosillabico(a); *(person)* che parla a monosillabi.

monosyllable ['mɔnǝsɪlǝbl] *n* monosillabo.

monotone ['mɔnǝtǝun] *n* pronunzia *(or* voce *f)* monotona; **to speak in a** ~ parlare con voce monotona.

monotonous [mǝ'nɔtǝnǝs] *adj* monotono(a).

monotony [mǝ'nɔtǝnɪ] *n* monotonia.

monoxide [mɔ'nɔksaɪd] *n*: **carbon** ~ ossido di carbonio.

monsoon [mɔn'suːn] *n* monsone *m.*

monster ['mɔnstə*] *n* mostro.
monstrosity [mɔn'strɔsɪtɪ] *n* mostruosità *f inv*.
monstrous ['mɔnstrəs] *adj* mostruoso(a).
Mont. *abbr* (*US*) = *Montana*.
montage [mɔn'tɑːʒ] *n* montaggio.
Mont Blanc [mɔ̃blɑ̃] *n* Monte *m* Bianco.
month [mʌnθ] *n* mese *m*; **300 dollars a ~** 300 dollari al mese; **every ~** (*happen*) tutti i mesi; (*pay*) mensilmente, ogni mese.
monthly ['mʌnθlɪ] *adj* mensile ♦ *adv* al mese; ogni mese ♦ *n* (*magazine*) rivista mensile; **twice ~** due volte al mese.
monument ['mɔnjumənt] *n* monumento.
monumental [mɔnju'mɛntl] *adj* monumentale; (*fig*) colossale.
monumental mason *n* lapidario.
moo [muː] *vi* muggire, mugghiare.
mood [muːd] *n* umore *m*; **to be in a good/ bad ~** essere di buon/cattivo umore; **to be in the ~ for** essere disposto(a) a, aver voglia di.
moody ['muːdɪ] *adj* (*variable*) capriccioso(a), lunatico(a); (*sullen*) imbronciato(a).
moon [muːn] *n* luna.
moonbeam ['muːnbiːm] *n* raggio di luna.
moon landing *n* allunaggio.
moonlight ['muːnlaɪt] *n* chiaro di luna ♦ *vi* fare del lavoro nero.
moonlighting ['muːnlaɪtɪŋ] *n* lavoro nero.
moonlit ['muːnlɪt] *adj* illuminato(a) dalla luna; **a ~ night** una notte rischiarata dalla luna.
moonshot ['muːnʃɔt] *n* lancio sulla luna.
moonstruck ['muːnstrʌk] *adj* lunatico(a).
moony ['muːnɪ] *adj* (*eyes*) sognante.
Moor [muə*] *n* moro/a.
moor [muə*] *n* brughiera ♦ *vt* (*ship*) ormeggiare ♦ *vi* ormeggiarsi.
moorings ['muərɪŋz] *npl* (*chains*) ormeggi *mpl*; (*place*) ormeggio.
Moorish ['muərɪʃ] *adj* moresco(a).
moorland ['muələnd] *n* brughiera.
moose [muːs] *n* (*pl inv*) alce *m*.
moot [muːt] *vt* sollevare ♦ *adj*: **~ point** punto discutibile.
mop [mɔp] *n* lavapavimenti *m inv*; (*also*: **~ of hair**) zazzera ♦ *vt* lavare con lo straccio; **to ~ one's brow** asciugarsi la fronte.
▶**mop up** *vt* asciugare con uno straccio.
mope [məup] *vi* fare il broncio.
▶**mope about, mope around** *vi* trascinarsi *or* aggirarsi con aria avvilita.
moped ['məupɛd] *n* (*BRIT*) ciclomotore *m*.

MOR *adj abbr* (*MUS*: = *middle-of-the-road*): **~ music** musica leggera.
moral ['mɔrəl] *adj* morale ♦ *n* morale *f*; **~s** *npl* moralità.
morale [mɔ'rɑːl] *n* morale *m*.
morality [mə'rælɪtɪ] *n* moralità.
moralize ['mɔrəlaɪz] *vi*: **to ~ (about)** fare il (*or* la) moralista (riguardo), moraleggiare (riguardo).
morally ['mɔrəlɪ] *adv* moralmente.
moral victory *n* vittoria morale.
morass [mə'ræs] *n* palude *f*, pantano.
moratorium [mɔrə'tɔːrɪəm] *n* moratoria.
morbid ['mɔːbɪd] *adj* morboso(a).

══════════════════════════ *KEYWORD*

more [mɔː*] *adj* **1** (*greater in number etc*) più; **~ people/letters than we expected** più persone/lettere di quante ne aspettavamo; **I have ~ wine/money than you** ho più vino/soldi di te; **I have ~ wine than beer** ho più vino che birra
2 (*additional*) altro(a), ancora; **do you want (some) ~ tea?** vuole dell'altro tè?, vuole ancora del tè?; **I have no** *or* **I don't have any ~ money** non ho più soldi
♦ *pron* **1** (*greater amount*) più; **~ than 10** più di 10; **it cost ~ than we expected** è costato più di quanto ci aspettassimo; **and what's ~ ...** e per di più ...
2 (*further or additional amount*) ancora; **is there any ~?** ce n'è ancora?; **there's no ~** non ce n'è più; **a little ~** ancora un po'; **many/much ~** molti(e)/molto(a) di più
♦ *adv*: **~ dangerous/easily (than)** più pericoloso/facilmente (di); **~ and ~** sempre di più; **~ and ~ difficult** sempre più difficile; **~ or less** più o meno; **~ than ever** più che mai; **once ~** ancora (una volta), un'altra volta; **no ~, not any ~** non ... più; **I have no ~ money, I haven't any ~ money** non ho più soldi.

moreover [mɔː'rəuvə*] *adv* inoltre, di più.
morgue [mɔːg] *n* obitorio.
MORI ['mɔːrɪ] *n abbr* (*BRIT*: = *Market & Opinion Research Institute*) istituto di sondaggio.
moribund ['mɔrɪbʌnd] *adj* moribondo(a).
morning ['mɔːnɪŋ] *n* mattina, mattino; (*duration*) mattinata; **in the ~** la mattina; **this ~** stamattina; **7 o'clock in the ~** le 7 di *or* della mattina.
morning-after pill ['mɔːnɪŋ'ɑːftə-] *n* pillola del giorno dopo.
morning sickness *n* nausee *fpl* mattutine.
Moroccan [mə'rɔkən] *adj*, *n* marocchino(a).
Morocco [mə'rɔkəu] *n* Marocco.

moron ['mɔːrɒn] n deficiente m/f.
moronic [mə'rɒnɪk] adj deficiente.
morose [mə'rəus] adj cupo(a), tetro(a).
morphine ['mɔːfiːn] n morfina.
morris dancing ['mɔrɪs-] n (BRIT) antica danza tradizionale inglese.
Morse [mɔːs] n (also: ~ **code**) alfabeto Morse.
morsel ['mɔːsl] n boccone m.
mortal ['mɔːtl] adj, n mortale (m).
mortality [mɔː'tælɪtɪ] n mortalità.
mortality rate n tasso di mortalità.
mortar ['mɔːtə*] n (CONSTR) malta; (dish) mortaio.
mortgage ['mɔːgɪdʒ] n ipoteca; (in house buying) mutuo ipotecario ♦ vt ipotecare; **to take out a** ~ contrarre un mutuo (or un'ipoteca).
mortgage company n (US) società f inv immobiliare.
mortgagee [mɔːgɪ'dʒiː] n creditore m ipotecario.
mortgagor ['mɔːgɪdʒə*] n debitore m ipotecario.
mortician [mɔː'tɪʃən] n (US) impresario di pompe funebri.
mortified ['mɔːtɪfaɪd] adj umiliato(a).
mortise lock ['mɔːtɪs-] n serratura incastrata.
mortuary ['mɔːtjuərɪ] n camera mortuaria; obitorio.
mosaic [məu'zeɪɪk] n mosaico.
Moscow ['mɒskəu] n Mosca.
Moslem ['mɒzləm] adj, n = **Muslim**.
mosque [mɒsk] n moschea.
mosquito, ~es [mɒs'kiːtəu] n zanzara.
mosquito net n zanzariera.
moss [mɒs] n muschio.
mossy ['mɒsɪ] adj muscoso(a).
most [məust] adj la maggior parte di; il più di ♦ pron la maggior parte ♦ adv più; (work, sleep etc) di più; (very) molto, estremamente; **the** ~ (also: + adjective) il(la) più; ~ **fish** la maggior parte dei pesci; ~ **of** la maggior parte di; ~ **of them** quasi tutti; **I saw** ~ ho visto più io; **at the (very)** ~ al massimo; **to make the** ~ **of** trarre il massimo vantaggio da.
mostly ['məustlɪ] adv per lo più.
MOT n abbr (BRIT: = Ministry of Transport): **the** ~ **(test)** revisione obbligatoria degli autoveicoli.
motel [məu'tɛl] n motel m inv.
moth [mɒθ] n farfalla notturna; tarma.
mothball ['mɒθbɔːl] n pallina di naftalina.
moth-eaten ['mɒθiːtn] adj tarmato(a).
mother ['mʌðə*] n madre f ♦ vt (care for) fare da madre a.

mother board n (COMPUT) scheda madre.
motherhood ['mʌðəhud] n maternità.
mother-in-law ['mʌðərɪnlɔː] n suocera.
mother-of-pearl [mʌðərəv'pɔːl] n madreperla.
mother's help n bambinaia.
mother-to-be [mʌðətə'biː] n futura mamma.
mother tongue n madrelingua.
mothproof ['mɒθpruːf] adj antitarmico(a).
motif [məu'tiːf] n motivo.
motion ['məuʃən] n movimento, moto; (gesture) gesto; (at meeting) mozione f; (BRIT: also: **bowel** ~) evacuazione f ♦ vt, vi: **to** ~ **(to) sb to do** fare cenno a qn di fare; **to be in** ~ (vehicle) essere in moto; **to set in** ~ avviare; **to go through the** ~**s of doing sth** (fig) fare qc pro forma.
motionless ['məuʃənlɪs] adj immobile.
motion picture n film m inv.
motivate ['məutɪveɪt] vt (act, decision) dare origine a, motivare; (person) spingere.
motivated ['məutɪveɪtɪd] adj motivato(a).
motivation [məutɪ'veɪʃən] n motivazione f.
motive ['məutɪv] n motivo ♦ adj motore(trice); **from the best** ~**s** con le migliori intenzioni.
motley ['mɒtlɪ] adj eterogeneo(a), molto vario(a).
motor ['məutə*] n motore m; (BRIT col: vehicle) macchina ♦ adj motore(trice).
motorbike ['məutəbaɪk] n moto f inv.
motorboat ['məutəbəut] n motoscafo.
motorcade ['məutəkeɪd] n corteo di macchine.
motorcar ['məutəkaː] n automobile f.
motorcoach ['məutəkəutʃ] n (BRIT) pullman m inv.
motorcycle ['məutəsaɪkl] n motocicletta.
motorcyclist ['məutəsaɪklɪst] n motociclista m/f.
motoring ['məutərɪŋ] n (BRIT) turismo automobilistico ♦ adj (accident) d'auto, automobilistico(a); (offence) di guida; ~ **holiday** vacanza in macchina.
motorist ['məutərɪst] n automobilista m/f.
motorize ['məutəraɪz] vt motorizzare.
motor oil n olio lubrificante.
motor racing n (BRIT) corse fpl automobilistiche.
motor scooter n motorscooter m inv.
motor vehicle n autoveicolo.
motorway ['məutəweɪ] n (BRIT) autostrada.
mottled ['mɒtld] adj chiazzato(a), marezzato(a).
motto, ~es ['mɒtəu] n motto.
mould, (US) mold [məuld] n forma, stampo; (mildew) muffa ♦ vt formare; (fig)

foggiare.

mo(u)lder ['məuldə*] *vi* (*decay*) ammuffire.

mo(u)lding ['məuldɪŋ] *n* (*ARCHIT*) modanatura.

mo(u)ldy ['məuldɪ] *adj* ammuffito(a).

moult, (*US*) **molt** [məult] *vi* far la muta.

mound [maund] *n* rialzo, collinetta.

mount [maunt] *n* monte *m*, montagna; (*horse*) cavalcatura; (*for jewel etc*) montatura ♦ *vt* montare; (*horse*) montare a; (*exhibition*) organizzare; (*attack*) sferrare, condurre; (*picture, stamp*) sistemare ♦ *vi* salire; (*get on a horse*) montare a cavallo; (*also*: ~ **up**) aumentare.

mountain ['mauntɪn] *n* montagna ♦ *cpd* di montagna; **to make a** ~ **out of a molehill** fare di una mosca un elefante.

mountain bike *n* mountain bike *f inv*.

mountaineer [mauntɪ'nɪə*] *n* alpinista *m/f*.

mountaineering [mauntɪ'nɪərɪŋ] *n* alpinismo; **to go** ~ fare dell'alpinismo.

mountainous ['mauntɪnəs] *adj* montagnoso(a).

mountain range *n* catena montuosa.

mountain rescue team *n* ≈ squadra di soccorso alpino.

mountainside ['mauntɪnsaɪd] *n* fianco della montagna.

mounted ['mauntɪd] *adj* a cavallo.

mourn [mɔːn] *vt* piangere, lamentare ♦ *vi*: **to** ~ (**for sb**) piangere (la morte di qn).

mourner ['mɔːnə*] *n* parente *m/f* (*or* amico/a) del defunto.

mourning ['mɔːnɪŋ] *n* lutto ♦ *cpd* (*dress*) da lutto; **in** ~ in lutto.

mouse, *pl* **mice** [maus, maɪs] *n* topo; (*COMPUT*) mouse *m inv*.

mousetrap ['maustræp] *n* trappola per i topi.

moussaka [mu'saːkə] *n* moussaka.

mousse [muːs] *n* mousse *f inv*.

moustache [məs'taːʃ] *n* baffi *mpl*.

mousy ['mausɪ] *adj* (*person*) timido(a); (*hair*) né chiaro(a) né scuro(a).

mouth, ~**s** [mauθ, -ðz] *n* bocca; (*of river*) bocca, foce *f*; (*opening*) orifizio.

mouthful ['mauθful] *n* boccata.

mouth organ *n* armonica.

mouthpiece ['mauθpiːs] *n* (*MUS*) bocchino; (*TEL*) microfono; (*of breathing apparatus*) boccaglio; (*person*) portavoce *m/f*.

mouth-to-mouth ['mauθtə'mauθ] *adj*: ~ **resuscitation** respirazione *f* bocca a bocca.

mouthwash ['mauθwɔʃ] *n* collutorio.

mouth-watering ['mauθwɔːtərɪŋ] *adj* che fa venire l'acquolina in bocca.

movable ['muːvəbl] *adj* mobile.

move [muːv] *n* (*movement*) movimento; (*in game*) mossa; (: *turn to play*) turno; (*change of house*) trasloco ♦ *vt* muovere, spostare; (*emotionally*) commuovere; (*POL: resolution etc*) proporre ♦ *vi* (*gen*) muoversi, spostarsi; (*traffic*) circolare; (*also*: ~ **house**) cambiar casa, traslocare; **to** ~ **towards** andare verso; **to** ~ **sb to do sth** indurre *or* spingere qn a fare qc; **to get a** ~ **on** affrettarsi, sbrigarsi; **to be** ~**d** (*emotionally*) essere commosso(a).

▶**move about, move around** *vi* (*fidget*) agitarsi; (*travel*) viaggiare.

▶**move along** *vi* muoversi avanti.

▶**move away** *vi* allontanarsi, andarsene.

▶**move back** *vi* indietreggiare; (*return*) ritornare.

▶**move forward** *vi* avanzare ♦ *vt* avanzare, spostare in avanti; (*people*) far avanzare.

▶**move in** *vi* (*to a house*) entrare (*in una nuova casa*).

▶**move off** *vi* partire.

▶**move on** *vi* riprendere la strada ♦ *vt* (*onlookers*) far circolare.

▶**move out** *vi* (*of house*) sgombrare.

▶**move over** *vi* spostarsi.

▶**move up** *vi* avanzare.

movement ['muːvmənt] *n* (*gen*) movimento; (*gesture*) gesto; (*of stars, water, physical*) moto; ~ (**of the bowels**) (*MED*) evacuazione *f*.

mover ['muːvə*] *n* proponente *m/f*.

movie ['muːvɪ] *n* film *m inv*; **the** ~**s** il cinema.

movie camera *n* cinepresa.

moviegoer ['muːvɪgəuə*] *n* (*US*) frequentatore/trice di cinema.

moving ['muːvɪŋ] *adj* mobile; (*causing emotion*) commovente; (*instigating*) animatore(trice).

mow, *pt* **mowed,** *pp* **mowed** *or* **mown** [məu, -n] *vt* falciare; (*grass*) tagliare.

▶**mow down** *vt* falciare.

mower ['məuə*] *n* (*also*: **lawn** ~) tagliaerba *m inv*.

mown [məun] *pp of* **mow**.

Mozambique [məuzəm'biːk] *n* Mozambico.

MP *n abbr* = *Military Police*; (*Canada*) = *Mounted Police*; (*BRIT*) *see* **Member of Parliament**.

mpg *n abbr* = *miles per gallon* (*30 mpg = 9.4 l. per 100 km*).

mph *n abbr* = *miles per hour* (*60 mph = 96 km/h*).

MPhil *n abbr* (*US*: = *Master of Philosophy*) titolo di studio.

MPS *n abbr* (*BRIT*) = *Member of the*

Pharmaceutical Society.
Mr, Mr. ['mɪstə*] *n*: ~ **X** Signor X, Sig. X.
MRC *n abbr* (*BRIT*: = *Medical Research
Council*) *ufficio governativo per la ricerca
medica in Gran Bretagna e nel
Commonwealth.*
MRCP *n abbr* (*BRIT*) = *Member of the Royal
College of Physicians.*
MRCS *n abbr* (*BRIT*) = *Member of the Royal
College of Surgeons.*
MRCVS *n abbr* (*BRIT*) = *Member of the Royal
College of Veterinary Surgeons.*
Mrs, Mrs. ['mɪsɪz] *n*: ~ **X** Signora X, Sig.ra
X.
MS *n abbr* (*US*: = *Master of Science*) *titolo di
studio*; (= *manuscript*) ms; (*MED*) =
multiple sclerosis ♦ *abbr* (*US*) = *Mississippi.*
Ms, Ms. [mɪz] *n* (= *Miss or Mrs*): ~ **X**
≈ Signora X, Sig.ra X.
MSA *n abbr* (*US*: = *Master of Science in
Agriculture*) *titolo di studio.*
MSc *n abbr see* **Master of Science.**
MSG *abbr see* **monosodium glutamate.**
MST *abbr* (*US*: = *Mountain Standard Time*)
ora invernale delle Montagne Rocciose.
MSW *n abbr* (*US*: = *Master of Social Work*)
titolo di studio.
MT *n abbr* = *machine translation* ♦ (*US*)
= *Montana.*
Mt *abbr* (*GEO*: = *mount*) M.
mth *abbr* (= *month*) m.
MTV *n abbr* = *music television.*

================= *KEYWORD*

much [mʌtʃ] *adj, pron* molto(a); **he's done so
~ work** ha lavorato così tanto; **I have as
~ money as you** ho tanti soldi quanti ne
hai tu; **how ~ is it?** quant'è?; **it's not ~**
non è tanto; **it costs too ~** costa troppo;
as ~ as you want quanto vuoi
♦ *adv* **1** (*greatly*) molto, tanto; **thank you
very ~** molte grazie; **I like it very/so ~** mi
piace moltissimo/così tanto; **~ to my
amazement** con mio enorme stupore;
he's very ~ the gentleman è il vero
gentiluomo; **I read as ~ as I can** leggo
quanto posso; **as ~ as you** tanto quanto te
2 (*by far*) molto; **it's ~ the biggest
company in Europe** è di gran lunga la più
grossa società in Europa
3 (*almost*) grossomodo, praticamente;
they're ~ the same sono praticamente
uguali.

muck [mʌk] *n* (*mud*) fango; (*dirt*) sporcizia.
▶**muck about, muck around** *vi* (*col*) fare
lo stupido; (: *waste time*) gingillarsi;
(*tinker*) armeggiare.

▶**muck in** *vi* (*BRIT col*) mettersi insieme.
▶**muck out** *vt* (*stable*) pulire.
▶**muck up** *vt* (*col*: *dirty*) sporcare; (: *spoil*)
rovinare.
muckraking ['mʌkreɪkɪŋ] *n* (*fig col*) caccia
agli scandali ♦ *adj* scandalistico(a).
mucky ['mʌkɪ] *adj* (*dirty*) sporco(a),
lordo(a).
mucus ['mjuːkəs] *n* muco.
mud [mʌd] *n* fango.
muddle ['mʌdl] *n* confusione *f*, disordine *m*;
pasticcio ♦ *vt* (*also*: ~ **up**) mettere
sottosopra; confondere; **to be in a ~**
(*person*) non riuscire a raccapezzarsi; **to
get in a ~** (*while explaining etc*)
imbrogliarsi.
▶**muddle along** *vi* andare avanti a
casaccio.
▶**muddle through** *vi* cavarsela alla meno
peggio.
muddle-headed [mʌdl'hedɪd] *adj* (*person*)
confusionario(a).
muddy ['mʌdɪ] *adj* fangoso(a).
mud flats *npl* distesa fangosa.
mudguard ['mʌdgɑːd] *n* parafango.
mudpack ['mʌdpæk] *n* maschera di fango.
mud-slinging ['mʌdslɪŋɪŋ] *n* (*fig*)
infangamento.
muesli ['mjuːzlɪ] *n* müsli *m inv*.
muff [mʌf] *n* manicotto ♦ *vt* (*shot, catch etc*)
mancare, sbagliare; **to ~ it** sbagliare
tutto.
muffin ['mʌfɪn] *n specie di pasticcino
soffice da tè.*
muffle ['mʌfl] *vt* (*sound*) smorzare, attutire;
(*against cold*) imbacuccare.
muffled ['mʌfld] *adj* smorzato(a),
attutito(a).
muffler ['mʌflə*] *n* (*scarf*) sciarpa
(pesante); (*US AUT*) marmitta; (*on
motorbike*) silenziatore *m*.
mufti ['mʌftɪ] *n*: **in ~** in borghese.
mug [mʌg] *n* (*cup*) tazzone *m*; (*for beer*)
boccale *m*; (*col*: *face*) muso; (: *fool*)
scemo/a ♦ *vt* (*assault*) assalire; **it's a ~'s
game** (*BRIT*) è proprio (una cosa) da fessi.
▶**mug up** *vt* (*BRIT col*: *also*: ~ **up on**)
studiare bene.
mugger ['mʌgə*] *n* aggressore *m*.
mugging ['mʌgɪŋ] *n* aggressione *f* (a scopo
di rapina).
muggins ['mʌgɪnz] *n* (*col*) semplicione/a,
sprovveduto/a.
muggy ['mʌgɪ] *adj* afoso(a).
mug shot *n* (*col*) foto *f inv* segnaletica.
mulatto, ~es [mjuː'lætəu] *n* mulatto/a.
mulberry ['mʌlbərɪ] *n* (*fruit*) mora (di
gelso); (*tree*) gelso, moro.

mule [mjuːl] *n* mulo.
mull [mʌl]: **to ~ over** *vt* rimuginare.
mulled [mʌld] *adj*: **~ wine** vino caldo.
multi... ['mʌltɪ] *prefix* multi....
multi-access [mʌltɪ'æksɛs] *adj* (*COMPUT*) ad accesso multiplo.
multicoloured, (*US*) **multicolored** ['mʌltɪkʌləd] *adj* multicolore, variopinto(a).
multifarious [mʌltɪ'fɛərɪəs] *adj* molteplice, svariato(a).
multilateral [mʌltɪ'lætərəl] *adj* (*POL*) multilaterale.
multi-level ['mʌltɪlɛvl] *adj* (*US*) = **multistorey**.
multimillionaire [mʌltɪmɪljə'nɛə*] *n* multimiliardario/a.
multinational [mʌltɪ'næʃənl] *adj, n* multinazionale (*f*).
multiple ['mʌltɪpl] *adj* multiplo(a); molteplice ♦ *n* multiplo; (*BRIT: also*: **~ store**) *grande magazzino che fa parte di una catena*.
multiple choice *n* esercizi *mpl* a scelta multipla.
multiple crash *n* serie *f inv* di incidenti a catena.
multiple sclerosis *n* sclerosi *f* a placche.
multiplex ['mʌltɪplɛks] *n* (*also*: **~ cinema**) cinema *m inv* multisale *inv*.
multiplication [mʌltɪplɪ'keɪʃən] *n* moltiplicazione *f*.
multiplication table *n* tavola pitagorica.
multiplicity [mʌltɪ'plɪsɪtɪ] *n* molteplicità.
multiply ['mʌltɪplaɪ] *vt* moltiplicare ♦ *vi* moltiplicarsi.
multiracial [mʌltɪ'reɪʃəl] *adj* multirazziale.
multistorey ['mʌltɪ'stɔːrɪ] *adj* (*BRIT: building, car park*) a più piani.
multitude ['mʌltɪtjuːd] *n* moltitudine *f*.
mum [mʌm] *n* (*BRIT*) mamma ♦ *adj*: **to keep ~** non aprire bocca; **~'s the word!** acqua in bocca!
mumble ['mʌmbl] *vt, vi* borbottare.
mumbo jumbo ['mʌmbəu-] *n* (*col*) parole *fpl* incomprensibili.
mummify ['mʌmɪfaɪ] *vt* mummificare.
mummy ['mʌmɪ] *n* (*BRIT: mother*) mamma; (*embalmed*) mummia.
mumps [mʌmps] *n* orecchioni *mpl*.
munch [mʌntʃ] *vt, vi* sgranocchiare.
mundane [mʌn'deɪn] *adj* terra a terra *inv*.
Munich ['mjuːnɪk] *n* Monaco *f* (di Baviera).
municipal [mjuː'nɪsɪpl] *adj* municipale.
municipality [mjuːnɪsɪ'pælɪtɪ] *n* municipio.
munitions [mjuː'nɪʃənz] *npl* munizioni *fpl*.
mural ['mjuərəl] *n* dipinto murale.
murder ['mɜːdə*] *n* assassinio, omicidio

♦ *vt* assassinare; **to commit ~** commettere un omicidio.
murderer ['mɜːdərə*] *n* omicida *m*, assassino.
murderess ['mɜːdərɪs] *n* omicida *f*, assassina.
murderous ['mɜːdərəs] *adj* micidiale.
murk [mɜːk] *n* oscurità, buio.
murky ['mɜːkɪ] *adj* tenebroso(a), buio(a).
murmur ['mɜːmə*] *n* mormorio ♦ *vt, vi* mormorare; **heart ~** (*MED*) soffio al cuore.
MusB(ac) *n abbr* (= *Bachelor of Music*) *titolo di studio*.
muscle ['mʌsl] *n* muscolo.
▶**muscle in** *vi* immischiarsi.
muscular ['mʌskjulə*] *adj* muscolare; (*person, arm*) muscoloso(a).
muscular dystrophy *n* distrofia muscolare.
MusD(oc) *n abbr* (= *Doctor of Music*) *titolo di studio*.
muse [mjuːz] *vi* meditare, sognare ♦ *n* musa.
museum [mjuː'zɪəm] *n* museo.
mush [mʌʃ] *n* pappa.
mushroom ['mʌʃrum] *n* fungo ♦ *vi* (*fig*) svilupparsi rapidamente.
mushy ['mʌʃɪ] *adj* (*of food*) spappolato(a); (*sentimental*) sdolcinato(a).
music ['mjuːzɪk] *n* musica.
musical ['mjuːzɪkəl] *adj* musicale ♦ *n* (*show*) commedia musicale.
music(al) box *n* carillon *m inv*.
musical chairs *n* gioco delle sedie (*in cui bisogna sedersi non appena cessa la musica*); (*fig*) scambio delle poltrone.
musical instrument *n* strumento musicale.
music centre *n* impianto *m* stereo *inv* monoblocco *inv*.
music hall *n* teatro di varietà.
musician [mjuː'zɪʃən] *n* musicista *m/f*.
music stand *n* leggio.
musk [mʌsk] *n* muschio.
musket ['mʌskɪt] *n* moschetto.
muskrat ['mʌskræt] *n* topo muschiato.
musk rose *n* (*BOT*) rosa muschiata.
Muslim ['mʌzlɪm] *adj, n* musulmano(a).
muslin ['mʌzlɪn] *n* mussola.
musquash ['mʌskwɔʃ] *n* (*fur*) rat musqué *m inv*.
mussel ['mʌsl] *n* cozza.
must [mʌst] *aux vb* (*obligation*): **I ~ do it** devo farlo; (*probability*): **he ~ be there by now** dovrebbe essere arrivato ormai; **I ~ have made a mistake** devo essermi sbagliato ♦ *n*: **this programme/trip is a ~**

è un programma/viaggio da non perdersi.

mustache ['mʌstæʃ] n (US) = **moustache**.

mustard ['mʌstəd] n senape f, mostarda.

mustard gas n iprite f.

muster ['mʌstə*] vt radunare; (also: ~ up: strength, courage) fare appello a.

mustiness ['mʌstɪnɪs] n odor di muffa or di stantio.

mustn't ['mʌsnt] = **must not**.

musty ['mʌstɪ] adj che sa di muffa or di rinchiuso.

mutant ['mjuːtənt] adj, n mutante (m).

mutate [mjuː'teɪt] vi subire una mutazione.

mutation [mjuː'teɪʃən] n mutazione f.

mute [mjuːt] adj, n muto(a).

muted ['mjuːtɪd] adj (noise) attutito(a), smorzato(a); (criticism) attenuato(a); (MUS) in sordina; (: trumpet) con sordina.

mutilate ['mjuːtɪleɪt] vt mutilare.

mutilation [mjuːtɪ'leɪʃən] n mutilazione f.

mutinous ['mjuːtɪnəs] adj (troops) ammutinato(a); (attitude) ribelle.

mutiny ['mjuːtɪnɪ] n ammutinamento ♦ vi ammutinarsi.

mutter ['mʌtə*] vt, vi borbottare, brontolare.

mutton ['mʌtn] n carne f di montone.

mutual ['mjuːtʃuəl] adj mutuo(a), reciproco(a).

mutually ['mjuːtʃuəlɪ] adv reciprocamente.

Muzak ® ['mjuːzæk] n (often pej) musica di sottofondo.

muzzle ['mʌzl] n muso; (protective device) museruola; (of gun) bocca ♦ vt mettere la museruola a.

MV abbr (= motor vessel) M/N, m/n.

MVP n abbr (US SPORT: = most valuable player) titolo ottenuto da sportivo.

MW abbr (RADIO: = medium wave) O.M.

my [maɪ] adj il(la) mio(a), pl i(le) miei(mie).

Myanmar ['maɪænmɑː*] n Myanma.

myopic [maɪ'ɔpɪk] adj miope.

myriad ['mɪrɪəd] n miriade f.

myself [maɪ'sɛlf] pron (reflexive) mi; (emphatic) io stesso(a); (after prep) me.

mysterious [mɪs'tɪərɪəs] adj misterioso(a).

mystery ['mɪstərɪ] n mistero.

mystery story n racconto del mistero.

mystic ['mɪstɪk] adj, n mistico(a).

mystical ['mɪstɪkəl] adj mistico(a).

mystify ['mɪstɪfaɪ] vt mistificare; (puzzle) confondere.

mystique [mɪs'tiːk] n fascino.

myth [mɪθ] n mito.

mythical ['mɪθɪkl] adj mitico(a).

mythological [mɪθə'lɔdʒɪkl] adj mitologico(a).

mythology [mɪ'θɔlədʒɪ] n mitologia.

N n

N, n [ɛn] n (letter) N, n f or m inv; **N for Nellie**, (US) **N for Nan** ≈ N come Napoli.

N abbr (= north) N.

NA n abbr (US: = Narcotics Anonymous) associazione in aiuto dei tossicodipendenti; (US) = National Academy.

n/a abbr (= not applicable) non pertinente; (COMM etc) = no account.

NAACP n abbr (US) = National Association for the Advancement of Colored People.

NAAFI ['næfɪ] n abbr (BRIT: = Navy, Army & Air Force Institute) organizzazione che gestisce negozi, mense ecc. per il personale militare.

nab [næb] vt (col) beccare, acchiappare.

NACU n abbr (US) = National Association of Colleges and Universities.

nadir ['neɪdɪə*] n (ASTRONOMY) nadir m; (fig) punto più basso.

nag [næg] n (pej: horse) ronzino; (person) brontolone/a ♦ vt tormentare ♦ vi brontolare in continuazione.

nagging ['nægɪŋ] adj (doubt, pain) persistente ♦ n brontolii mpl, osservazioni fpl continue.

nail [neɪl] n (human) unghia; (metal) chiodo ♦ vt inchiodare; **to ~ sb down to a date/ price** costringere qn a un appuntamento/ ad accettare un prezzo; **to pay cash on the ~** (BRIT) pagare a tamburo battente.

nailbrush ['neɪlbrʌʃ] n spazzolino da or per unghie.

nailfile ['neɪlfaɪl] n lima da or per unghie.

nail polish n smalto da or per unghie.

nail polish remover n acetone m, solvente m.

nail scissors npl forbici fpl da or per unghie.

nail varnish n (BRIT) = **nail polish**.

Nairobi [naɪ'rəubɪ] n Nairobi f.

naïve [naɪ'iːv] adj ingenuo(a).

naïveté [nɑːiːv'teɪ], **naivety** [naɪ'iːvtɪ] n ingenuità f inv.

naked ['neɪkɪd] adj nudo(a); **with the ~ eye** a occhio nudo.

nakedness ['neɪkɪdnɪs] n nudità.

NAM *n abbr* (*US*) = *National Association of Manufacturers*.

name [neɪm] *n* nome *m*; (*reputation*) nome, reputazione *f* ♦ *vt* (*baby etc*) chiamare; (*person, object*) identificare; (*price, date*) fissare; **by** ~ di nome; **she knows them all by** ~ li conosce tutti per nome; **in the** ~ **of** in nome di; **what's your** ~? come si chiama?; **my** ~ **is Peter** mi chiamo Peter; **to take sb's** ~ **and address** prendere nome e indirizzo di qn; **to make a** ~ **for o.s.** farsi un nome; **to get (o.s.) a bad** ~ farsi una cattiva fama *or* una brutta reputazione; **to call sb** ~**s** insultare qn.

name dropping *n menzionare qualcuno per fare bella figura.*

nameless ['neɪmlɪs] *adj* senza nome.

namely ['neɪmlɪ] *adv* cioè.

nameplate ['neɪmpleɪt] *n* (*on door etc*) targa.

namesake ['neɪmseɪk] *n* omonimo.

nan bread [nɑːn-] *n tipo di pane indiano poco lievitato di forma allungata.*

nanny ['nænɪ] *n* bambinaia.

nanny goat *n* capra.

nap [næp] *n* (*sleep*) pisolino; (*of cloth*) peluria ♦ *vi*: **to be caught** ~**ping** essere preso alla sprovvista; **to have a** ~ schiacciare un pisolino.

NAPA *n abbr* (*US*: = *National Association of Performing Artists*) associazione nazionale degli artisti di palcoscenico.

napalm ['neɪpɑːm] *n* napalm *m*.

nape [neɪp] *n*: ~ **of the neck** nuca.

napkin ['næpkɪn] *n* tovagliolo; (*BRIT: for baby*) pannolino.

Naples ['neɪplz] *n* Napoli *f*.

Napoleonic [nəpəʊlɪ'ɒnɪk] *adj* napoleonico(a).

nappy ['næpɪ] *n* (*BRIT*) pannolino.

nappy liner *n* (*BRIT*) fogliettino igienico.

narcissistic [nɑːsɪ'sɪstɪk] *adj* narcisistico(a).

narcissus, *pl* **narcissi** [nɑː'sɪsəs, -saɪ] *n* narciso.

narcotic [nɑː'kɒtɪk] *n* (*MED*) narcotico; ~**s** *npl* (*drugs*) narcotici, stupefacenti *mpl*.

nark [nɑːk] *vt* (*BRIT col*) scocciare.

narrate [nə'reɪt] *vt* raccontare, narrare.

narration [nə'reɪʃən] *n* narrazione *f*.

narrative ['nærətɪv] *n* narrativa ♦ *adj* narrativo(a).

narrator [nə'reɪtə*] *n* narratore/trice.

narrow ['nærəʊ] *adj* stretto(a); (*resources, means*) limitato(a), modesto(a); (*fig*): **to take a** ~ **view of** avere una visione limitata di ♦ *vi* restringersi; **to have a** ~ **escape** farcela per un pelo; **to** ~ **sth**

down to ridurre qc a.

narrow gauge *adj* (*RAIL*) a scartamento ridotto.

narrowly ['nærəʊlɪ] *adv*: **Maria** ~ **escaped drowning** per un pelo Maria non è affogata; **he** ~ **missed hitting the cyclist** per poco non ha investito il ciclista.

narrow-minded [nærəʊ'maɪndɪd] *adj* meschino(a).

NAS *n abbr* (*US*) = *National Academy of Sciences*.

NASA ['næsə] *n abbr* (*US*: = *National Aeronautics and Space Administration*) N.A.S.A. *f*.

nasal ['neɪzl] *adj* nasale.

Nassau ['næsɔː] *n* Nassau *f*.

nastily ['nɑːstɪlɪ] *adv* con cattiveria.

nastiness ['nɑːstɪnɪs] *n* (*of person, remark*) cattiveria; (: *spitefulness*) malignità.

nasturtium [nəs'tɜːʃəm] *n* cappuccina, nasturzio (indiano).

nasty ['nɑːstɪ] *adj* (*person, remark*) cattivo(a); (: *spiteful*) maligno(a); (*smell, wound, situation*) brutto(a); **to turn** ~ (*situation*) mettersi male; (*weather*) guastarsi; (*person*) incattivirsi; **it's a** ~ **business** è una brutta faccenda, è un brutto affare.

NAS/UWT *n abbr* (*BRIT*: = *National Association of Schoolmasters/Union of Women Teachers*) sindacato di insegnanti in Inghilterra e Galles.

nation ['neɪʃən] *n* nazione *f*.

national ['næʃənl] *adj* nazionale ♦ *n* cittadino/a.

national anthem *n* inno nazionale.

National Curriculum *n* (*BRIT*) ≈ programma *m* scolastico ministeriale (*in Inghilterra e Galles*).

national debt *n* debito pubblico.

national dress *n* costume *m* nazionale.

National Guard *n* (*US*) milizia nazionale (*volontaria, in ogni stato*).

National Health Service (NHS) *n* (*BRIT*) *servizio nazionale di assistenza sanitaria*, ≈ S.A.U.B. *f*.

National Insurance *n* (*BRIT*) ≈ Previdenza Sociale.

nationalism ['næʃnəlɪzəm] *n* nazionalismo.

nationalist ['næʃnəlɪst] *adj, n* nazionalista (*m/f*).

nationality [næʃə'nælɪtɪ] *n* nazionalità *f inv*.

nationalization [næʃnəlaɪ'zeɪʃən] *n* nazionalizzazione *f*.

nationalize ['næʃnəlaɪz] *vt* nazionalizzare.

nationally ['næʃnəlɪ] *adv* a livello nazionale.

national park *n* parco nazionale.

national press *n* stampa a diffusione

nazionale.
National Security Council n (US) consiglio nazionale di sicurezza.
national service n (MIL) servizio militare.
National Trust n sovrintendenza ai beni culturali e ambientali.

Fondato nel 1895, il **National Trust** *è un'organizzazione che si occupa della tutela e salvaguardia di edifici e monumenti di interesse storico e di territori di interesse ambientale.*

nation-wide ['neɪʃənwaɪd] adj diffuso(a) in tutto il paese ♦ adv in tutto il paese.
native ['neɪtɪv] n abitante m/f del paese; (in colonies) indigeno/a ♦ adj indigeno(a); (country) natio(a); (ability) innato(a); **a ~ of Russia** un nativo della Russia; **a ~ speaker of French** una persona di madrelingua francese; **~ language** madrelingua.
Native American n discendente di tribù dell'America settentrionale.
Nativity [nə'tɪvɪtɪ] n (REL): **the ~** la Natività.
nativity play n recita sulla Natività.
NATO ['neɪtəu] n abbr (= North Atlantic Treaty Organization) N.A.T.O. f.
natter ['nætə*] (BRIT col) vi chiacchierare ♦ n chiacchierata.
natural ['nætʃrəl] adj naturale; (ability) innato(a); (manner) semplice; **death from ~ causes** (LAW) morte f per cause naturali.
natural childbirth n parto indolore.
natural gas n gas m metano.
natural history n storia naturale.
naturalist ['nætʃrəlɪst] n naturalista m/f.
naturalization [nætʃrəlaɪ'zeɪʃən] n naturalizzazione f; acclimatazione f.
naturalize ['nætʃrəlaɪz] vt: **to be ~d** (person) naturalizzarsi; **to become ~d** (animal, plant) acclimatarsi.
naturally ['nætʃrəlɪ] adv naturalmente; (by nature: gifted) di natura.
naturalness ['nætʃrəlnɪs] n naturalezza.
natural resources npl risorse fpl naturali.
natural selection n selezione f naturale.
natural wastage n (INDUSTRY) diminuzione f di manodopera (per pensionamento, decesso etc).
nature ['neɪtʃə*] n natura; (character) natura, indole f; **by ~** di natura; **documents of a confidential ~** documenti mpl di natura privata.
-natured ['neɪtʃəd] suffix: **ill~** maldisposto(a).

nature reserve n (BRIT) parco naturale.
nature trail n percorso tracciato in parchi nazionali ecc con scopi educativi.
naturist ['neɪtʃərɪst] n naturista m/f, nudista m/f.
naught [nɔːt] n = **nought**.
naughtiness ['nɔːtɪnɪs] n cattiveria.
naughty ['nɔːtɪ] adj (child) birichino(a), cattivello(a); (story, film) spinto(a).
nausea ['nɔːsɪə] n (MED) nausea; (fig: disgust) schifo.
nauseate ['nɔːsɪeɪt] vt nauseare; far schifo a.
nauseating ['nɔːsɪeɪtɪŋ] adj nauseante; (fig) disgustoso(a).
nauseous ['nɔːsɪəs] adj nauseabondo(a); (feeling sick): **to be ~** avere la nausea.
nautical ['nɔːtɪkl] adj nautico(a).
nautical mile n miglio nautico or marino.
naval ['neɪvl] adj navale.
naval officer n ufficiale m di marina.
nave [neɪv] n navata centrale.
navel ['neɪvl] n ombelico.
navigable ['nævɪgəbl] adj navigabile.
navigate ['nævɪgeɪt] vt percorrere navigando ♦ vi navigare; (AUT) fare da navigatore.
navigation [nævɪ'geɪʃən] n navigazione f.
navigator ['nævɪgeɪtə*] n (NAUT, AVIAT) ufficiale m di rotta; (explorer) navigatore m; (AUT) copilota m/f.
navvy ['nævɪ] n manovale m.
navy ['neɪvɪ] n marina; **Department of the N~** (US) Ministero della Marina.
navy(-blue) ['neɪvɪ('bluː)] adj blu scuro inv.
Nazareth ['næzərɪθ] n Nazareth f.
Nazi ['nɑːtsɪ] adj, n nazista (m/f).
NB abbr (= nota bene) N.B.; (Canada) = New Brunswick.
NBA n abbr (US: = National Basketball Association) ≈ F.I.P. f (= Federazione Italiana Pallacanestro); = National Boxing Association.
NBC n abbr (US: = National Broadcasting Company) compagnia nazionale di radiodiffusione.
NBS n abbr (US: = National Bureau of Standards) ufficio per la normalizzazione.
NC abbr (COMM etc: = no charge) gratis; (US) = North Carolina.
NCC n abbr (= Nature Conservancy Council) organismo di protezione dei beni naturali; (US) = National Council of Churches.
NCCL n abbr (BRIT: = National Council for Civil Liberties) associazione per la difesa delle libertà civili.
NCO n abbr see **non-commissioned**.

ND, N. Dak. *abbr (US)* = *North Dakota*.
NE *abbr (US)* = *Nebraska; New England*.
NEA *n abbr (US)* = *National Education Association*.
neap [niːp] *n (also:* ~**tide**) marea di quadratura.
Neapolitan [nɪəˈpɔlɪtən] *adj, n* napoletano(a).
near [nɪə*] *adj* vicino(a); *(relation)* prossimo(a) ♦ *adv* vicino ♦ *prep (also:* ~ **to**) vicino a, presso; *(time)* verso ♦ *vt* avvicinarsi a; **to come** ~ avvicinarsi; ~ **here/there** qui/lì vicino; **£25,000 or** ~**est offer** *(BRIT)* 25.000 sterline trattabili; **in the** ~ **future** in un prossimo futuro; **the building is** ~**ing completion** il palazzo è quasi terminato *or* ultimato.
nearby [nɪəˈbaɪ] *adj* vicino(a) ♦ *adv* vicino.
Near East *n:* **the** ~ il Medio Oriente.
nearer [ˈnɪərə*] *adj* più vicino(a) ♦ *adv* più vicino.
nearly [ˈnɪəlɪ] *adv* quasi; **not** ~ non ... affatto; **I** ~ **lost it** per poco non lo perdevo; **she was** ~ **crying** era lì lì per piangere.
near miss *n:* **that was a** ~ c'è mancato poco.
nearness [ˈnɪənɪs] *n* vicinanza.
nearside [ˈnɪəsaɪd] *n (right-hand drive)* lato sinistro; *(left-hand drive)* lato destro ♦ *adj* sinistro(a); destro(a).
near-sighted [nɪəˈsaɪtɪd] *adj* miope.
neat [niːt] *adj (person, room)* ordinato(a); *(work)* pulito(a); *(solution, plan)* ben indovinato(a), azzeccato(a); *(spirits)* liscio(a).
neatly [ˈniːtlɪ] *adv* con ordine; *(skilfully)* abilmente.
neatness [ˈniːtnɪs] *n (tidiness)* ordine *m;* *(skilfulness)* abilità.
Nebr. *abbr (US)* = *Nebraska*.
nebulous [ˈnɛbjuləs] *adj* nebuloso(a); *(fig)* vago(a).
necessarily [ˈnɛsɪsrɪlɪ] *adv* necessariamente; **not** ~ non è detto, non necessariamente.
necessary [ˈnɛsɪsrɪ] *adj* necessario(a); **if** ~ se necessario.
necessitate [nɪˈsɛsɪteɪt] *vt* rendere necessario(a).
necessity [nɪˈsɛsɪtɪ] *n* necessità *f inv;* **in case of** ~ in caso di necessità.
neck [nɛk] *n* collo; *(of garment)* colletto ♦ *vi (col)* pomiciare, sbaciucchiarsi; ~ **and** ~ testa a testa; **to stick one's** ~ **out** *(col)* rischiare (forte).
necklace [ˈnɛklɪs] *n* collana.
neckline [ˈnɛklaɪn] *n* scollatura.

necktie [ˈnɛktaɪ] *n (esp US)* cravatta.
nectar [ˈnɛktə*] *n* nettare *m.*
nectarine [ˈnɛktərɪn] *n* nocepesca.
NEDC *n abbr (BRIT:* = *National Economic Development Council)* ≈ C.N.E.L. *m* (= *Consiglio Nazionale dell'Economia e del Lavoro*).
Neddy [ˈnɛdɪ] *n abbr (BRIT col)* = **NEDC**.
née [neɪ] *adj:* ~ **Scott** nata Scott.
need [niːd] *n* bisogno ♦ *vt* aver bisogno di; **I** ~ **to do it** lo devo fare, bisogna che io lo faccia; **you don't** ~ **to go** non deve andare, non c'è bisogno che lei vada; **a signature is** ~**ed** occorre *or* ci vuole una firma; **to be in** ~ **of, have** ~ **of** aver bisogno di; **£10 will meet my immediate** ~**s** 10 sterline mi basteranno per le necessità più urgenti; **in case of** ~ in caso di bisogno *or* necessità; **there's no** ~ **for** ... non c'è bisogno *or* non occorre che ...; **there's no** ~ **to do** ... non occorre fare ...; **the** ~**s of industry** le esigenze dell'industria.
needle [ˈniːdl] *n* ago; *(on record player)* puntina ♦ *vt* punzecchiare.
needlecord [ˈniːdlkɔːd] *n (BRIT)* velluto a coste sottili.
needless [ˈniːdlɪs] *adj* inutile; ~ **to say,** ... inutile dire che ....
needlessly [ˈniːdlɪslɪ] *adv* inutilmente.
needlework [ˈniːdlwəːk] *n* cucito.
needn't [ˈniːdnt] = **need not**.
needy [ˈniːdɪ] *adj* bisognoso(a).
negation [nɪˈgeɪʃən] *n* negazione *f.*
negative [ˈnɛgətɪv] *n (PHOT)* negativa, negativo; *(ELEC)* polo negativo; *(LING)* negazione *f* ♦ *adj* negativo(a); **to answer in the** ~ rispondere negativamente *or* di no.
negative equity *n situazione in cui l'ammontare del mutuo su un immobile supera il suo valore sul mercato.*
neglect [nɪˈglɛkt] *vt* trascurare ♦ *n (of person, duty)* negligenza; **state of** ~ stato di abbandono; **to** ~ **to do sth** trascurare *or* tralasciare di fare qc.
neglected [nɪˈglɛktɪd] *adj* trascurato(a).
neglectful [nɪˈglɛktful] *adj (gen)* negligente; **to be** ~ **of sb/sth** trascurare qn/qc.
negligee [ˈnɛglɪʒeɪ] *n* négligé *m inv.*
negligence [ˈnɛglɪdʒəns] *n* negligenza.
negligent [ˈnɛglɪdʒənt] *adj* negligente.
negligently [ˈnɛglɪdʒəntlɪ] *adv* con negligenza.
negligible [ˈnɛglɪdʒɪbl] *adj* insignificante, trascurabile.
negotiable [nɪˈgəuʃɪəbl] *adj* negoziabile; *(cheque)* trasferibile; *(road)* transitabile.
negotiate [nɪˈgəuʃɪeɪt] *vi* negoziare ♦ *vt*

(*COMM*) negoziare; (*obstacle*) superare; (*bend in road*) prendere; **to ~ with sb for sth** trattare con qn per ottenere qc.

negotiating table [nɪ'gəʊʃieɪtɪŋ-] *n* tavolo delle trattative.

negotiation [nɪgəʊʃɪ'eɪʃən] *n* trattativa; (*POL*) negoziato; **to enter into ~s with sb** entrare in trattative (*or* intavolare i negoziati) con qn.

negotiator [nɪ'gəʊʃieɪtə*] *n* negoziatore/trice.

Negress ['niːgrɪs] *n* negra.

Negro ['niːgrəʊ] *adj, n* (*pl* **~es**) negro(a).

neigh [neɪ] *vi* nitrire.

neighbour, (*US*) **neighbor** ['neɪbə*] *n* vicino/a.

neighbo(u)rhood ['neɪbəhud] *n* vicinato.

neighbourhood watch *n* (*BRIT: also:* **~ scheme**) *sistema di vigilanza reciproca in un quartiere.*

neighbo(u)ring ['neɪbərɪŋ] *adj* vicino(a).

neighbo(u)rly ['neɪbəlɪ] *adj:* **he is a ~ person** è un buon vicino.

neither ['naɪðə*] *adj, pron* né l'uno(a) né l'altro(a), nessuno(a) dei(delle) due ♦ *conj* neanche, nemmeno, neppure ♦ *adv:* **~ good nor bad** né buono né cattivo; **I didn't move and ~ did Claude** io non mi mossi e nemmeno Claude; ... **~ did I refuse ...,** ma non ho nemmeno rifiutato.

neo... ['niːəʊ] *prefix* neo....

neolithic [niːəʊ'lɪθɪk] *adj* neolitico(a).

neologism [nɪ'ɔlədʒɪzəm] *n* neologismo.

neon ['niːɔn] *n* neon *m*.

neon light *n* luce *f* al neon.

neon sign *n* insegna al neon.

Nepal [nɪ'pɔːl] *n* Nepal *m*.

nephew ['nɛvjuː] *n* nipote *m*.

nepotism ['nɛpətɪzəm] *n* nepotismo.

nerd [nɜːd] *n* (*col*) sfigato/a, povero(a) fesso/a.

nerve [nɜːv] *n* nervo; (*fig*) coraggio; (*impudence*) faccia tosta; **he gets on my ~s** mi dà ai nervi, mi fa venire i nervi; **a fit of ~s** una crisi di nervi; **to lose one's ~** (*self-confidence*) perdere fiducia in se stesso; **I lost my ~** (*courage*) mi è mancato il coraggio.

nerve centre *n* (*ANAT*) centro nervoso; (*fig*) cervello, centro vitale.

nerve gas *n* gas *m* nervino.

nerve-racking ['nɜːvrækɪŋ] *adj* che spezza i nervi.

nervous ['nɜːvəs] *adj* nervoso(a).

nervous breakdown *n* esaurimento nervoso.

nervously ['nɜːvəslɪ] *adv* nervosamente.

nervousness ['nɜːvəsnɪs] *n* nervosismo.

nervous wreck *n:* **to be a ~** (*col*) essere nevrastenico(a).

nervy ['nɜːvɪ] *adj* agitato(a), nervoso(a).

nest [nɛst] *n* nido; **~ of tables** tavolini *mpl* cicogna *inv.*

nest egg *n* (*fig*) gruzzolo.

nestle ['nɛsl] *vi* accoccolarsi.

nestling ['nɛslɪŋ] *n* uccellino di nido.

net [nɛt] *n* rete *f*; (*fabric*) tulle *m* ♦ *adj* netto(a) ♦ *vt* (*subj: person*) ricavare un utile netto di; (*deal, sale*) dare un utile netto di; **~ of tax** netto, al netto di tasse; **he earns £10,000 ~ per year** guadagna 10.000 sterline nette all'anno.

netball ['nɛtbɔːl] *n* specie di pallacanestro.

net curtains *npl* tende *fpl* di tulle.

Netherlands ['nɛðələndz] *npl:* **the ~** i Paesi Bassi.

net profit *n* utile *m* netto.

nett [nɛt] *adj* = **net.**

netting ['nɛtɪŋ] *n* (*for fence etc*) reticolato; (*fabric*) tulle *m.*

nettle ['nɛtl] *n* ortica.

network ['nɛtwɜːk] *n* rete *f.*

neuralgia [njʊə'rældʒə] *n* nevralgia.

neurological [njʊərə'lɔdʒɪkl] *adj* neurologico(a).

neurosis, *pl* **neuroses** [njʊə'rəʊsɪs, -siːz] *n* nevrosi *f inv.*

neurotic [njʊə'rɔtɪk] *adj, n* nevrotico(a).

neuter ['njuːtə*] *adj* neutro(a) ♦ *n* neutro ♦ *vt* (*cat etc*) castrare.

neutral ['njuːtrəl] *adj* neutro(a); (*person, nation*) neutrale ♦ *n* (*AUT*): **in ~** in folle.

neutrality [njuː'trælɪtɪ] *n* neutralità.

neutralize ['njuːtrəlaɪz] *vt* neutralizzare.

neutron bomb ['njuːtrɔn-] *n* bomba al neutrone.

Nev. *abbr* (*US*) = **Nevada.**

never ['nɛvə*] *adv* (non...) mai; **~ again** mai più; **I'll ~ go there again** non ci vado più; **~ in my life** mai in vita mia; *see also* **mind.**

never-ending [nɛvər'ɛndɪŋ] *adj* interminabile.

nevertheless [nɛvəðə'lɛs] *adv* tuttavia, ciò nonostante, ciò nondimeno.

new [njuː] *adj* nuovo(a); (*brand new*) nuovo(a) di zecca; **as good as ~** come nuovo.

New Age *adj, n* New Age (*f*) *inv.*

newborn ['njuːbɔːn] *adj* neonato(a).

newcomer ['njuːkʌmə*] *n* nuovo(a) venuto(a).

new-fangled ['njuːfæŋgld] *adj* (*pej*) stramoderno(a).

new-found ['njuːfaund] *adj* nuovo(a).

Newfoundland ['njuːfənlənd] *n* Terranova.

New Guinea *n* Nuova Guinea.

newly ['njuːlɪ] *adv* di recente.
newly-weds ['njuːlɪwɛdz] *npl* sposini *mpl*, sposi *mpl* novelli.
new moon *n* luna nuova.
newness ['njuːnɪs] *n* novità.
news [njuːz] *n* notizie *fpl*; (*RADIO*) giornale *m* radio; (*TV*) telegiornale *m*; **a piece of** ~ una notizia; **good/bad** ~ buone/cattive notizie; **financial** ~ (*PRESS*) pagina economica e finanziaria; (*RADIO, TV*) notiziario economico.
news agency *n* agenzia di stampa.
newsagent ['njuːzeɪdʒənt] *n* (*BRIT*) giornalaio.
news bulletin *n* (*RADIO, TV*) notiziario.
newscaster ['njuːzkɑːstə*] *n* (*RADIO, TV*) annunciatore/trice.
newsdealer ['njuːzdiːlə*] *n* (*US*) = **newsagent**.
newsflash ['njuːzflæʃ] *n* notizia *f* lampo *inv*.
newsletter ['njuːzlɛtə*] *n* bollettino (*di ditta, associazione*).
newspaper ['njuːzpeɪpə*] *n* giornale *m*; **daily** ~ quotidiano; **weekly** ~ settimanale *m*.
newsprint ['njuːzprɪnt] *n* carta da giornale.
newsreader ['njuːzriːdə*] *n* = **newscaster**.
newsreel ['njuːzriːl] *n* cinegiornale *m*.
newsroom ['njuːzrum] *n* (*PRESS*) redazione *f*; (*RADIO, TV*) studio.
news stand *n* edicola.
newsworthy ['njuːzwəːðɪ] *adj* degno(a) di menzione (*per radio, TV ecc*); **to be** ~ fare notizia.
newt [njuːt] *n* tritone *m*.
new town *n* (*BRIT*) nuovo centro urbano creato con fondi pubblici.
New Year *n* Anno Nuovo; **Happy** ~**!** Buon Anno!; **to wish sb a happy** ~ augurare Buon Anno a qn.
New Year's Day *n* il Capodanno.
New Year's Eve *n* la vigilia di Capodanno.
New York [-'jɔːk] *n* New York *f*, Nuova York *f*; (*also*: ~ **State**) stato di New York.
New Zealand [-'ziːlənd] *n* Nuova Zelanda ♦ *adj* neozelandese.
New Zealander [-'ziːləndə*] *n* neozelandese *m/f*.
next [nɛkst] *adj* prossimo(a) ♦ *adv* accanto; (*in time*) dopo; ~ **to** *prep* accanto a; ~ **to nothing** quasi niente; ~ **time** *adv* la prossima volta; ~ **week** la settimana prossima; **the** ~ **week** la settimana dopo *or* seguente; **the week after** ~ fra due settimane; **the** ~ **day** il giorno dopo, l'indomani; ~ **year** l'anno prossimo *or* venturo; "**turn to the** ~ **page**" "vedi pagina seguente"; **who's** ~**?** a chi tocca?;

when do we meet ~**?** quando ci rincontriamo?
next door *adv* accanto.
next of kin *n* parente *m/f* prossimo(a).
NF *n abbr* (*BRIT POL*: = *National Front*) partito di estrema destra ♦ *abbr* (*Canada*) = **Newfoundland**.
NFL *n abbr* (*US*) = *National Football League*.
Nfld. *abbr* (*Canada*) = **Newfoundland**.
NG *abbr* (*US*) = **National Guard**.
NGO *n abbr* (*US*) = *non-governmental organization*.
NH *abbr* (*US*) = *New Hampshire*.
NHL *n abbr* (*US*: = *National Hockey League*) ≈ F.I.H.P. *f* (= *Federazione Italiana Hockey e Pattinaggio*).
NHS *n abbr* (*BRIT*) *see* **National Health Service**.
NI *abbr* = **Northern Ireland**; (*BRIT*) = **National Insurance**.
Niagara Falls [naɪˈægərə-] *npl*: **the** ~ le cascate del Niagara.
nib [nɪb] *n* (*of pen*) pennino.
nibble ['nɪbl] *vt* mordicchiare.
Nicaragua [nɪkəˈrægjuə] *n* Nicaragua *m*.
Nicaraguan [nɪkəˈrægjuən] *adj, n* nicaraguense (*m/f*).
Nice [niːs] *n* Nizza.
nice [naɪs] *adj* (*holiday, trip*) piacevole; (*flat, picture*) bello(a); (*person*) simpatico(a), gentile; (*taste, smell, meal*) buono(a); (*distinction, point*) sottile.
nice-looking ['naɪslukɪŋ] *adj* bello(a).
nicely ['naɪslɪ] *adv* bene; **that will do** ~ andrà benissimo.
niceties ['naɪsɪtɪz] *npl* finezze *fpl*.
nick [nɪk] *n* tacca ♦ *vt* intaccare; tagliare; (*col: steal*) rubare; (: *BRIT: arrest*) beccare; **in the** ~ **of time** appena in tempo; **in good** ~ (*BRIT col*) decente, in buono stato; **to** ~ **o.s.** farsi un taglietto.
nickel ['nɪkl] *n* nichel *m*; (*US*) moneta da cinque centesimi di dollaro.
nickname ['nɪkneɪm] *n* soprannome *m* ♦ *vt* soprannominare.
Nicosia [nɪkəˈsiːə] *n* Nicosia.
nicotine ['nɪkətiːn] *n* nicotina.
nicotine patch *n* cerotto antifumo (*a base di nicotina*).
niece [niːs] *n* nipote *f*.
nifty ['nɪftɪ] *adj* (*col: car, jacket*) chic *inv*; (: *gadget, tool*) ingegnoso(a).
Niger ['naɪdʒə*] *n* Niger *m*.
Nigeria [naɪˈdʒɪərɪə] *n* Nigeria.
Nigerian [naɪˈdʒɪərɪən] *adj, n* nigeriano(a).
niggardly ['nɪgədlɪ] *adj* (*person*) tirchio(a), spilorcio(a); (*allowance, amount*) misero(a).

nigger ['nɪgə*] n (coll: highly offensive) negro/a.

niggle ['nɪgl] vt assillare ♦ vi fare il(la) pignolo(a).

niggling ['nɪglɪŋ] adj pignolo(a); (detail) insignificante; (doubt, pain) persistente.

night [naɪt] n notte f; (evening) sera; **at ~** la notte; la sera; **by ~** di notte; **in the ~, during the ~** durante la notte; **the ~ before last** l'altro ieri notte; l'altro ieri sera.

night-bird ['naɪtbɜːd] n uccello notturno; (fig) nottambulo/a.

nightcap ['naɪtkæp] n bicchierino prima di andare a letto.

night club n locale m notturno.

nightdress ['naɪtdrɛs] n camicia da notte.

nightfall ['naɪtfɔːl] n crepuscolo.

nightie ['naɪtɪ] n camicia da notte.

nightingale ['naɪtɪŋgeɪl] n usignolo.

night life n vita notturna.

nightly ['naɪtlɪ] adj di ogni notte or sera; (by night) notturno(a) ♦ adv ogni notte or sera.

nightmare ['naɪtmɛə*] n incubo.

night porter n portiere m di notte.

night safe n cassa continua.

night school n scuola serale.

nightshade ['naɪtʃeɪd] n: **deadly ~** (BOT) belladonna.

nightshift ['naɪtʃɪft] n turno di notte.

night-time ['naɪttaɪm] n notte f.

night watchman n guardiano notturno.

nihilism ['naɪɪlɪzəm] n nichilismo.

nil [nɪl] n nulla m; (SPORT) zero.

Nile [naɪl] n: **the ~** il Nilo.

nimble ['nɪmbl] adj agile.

nine [naɪn] num nove.

nineteen [naɪn'tiːn] num diciannove.

ninety ['naɪntɪ] num novanta.

ninth [naɪnθ] num nono(a).

nip [nɪp] vt pizzicare ♦ vi (BRIT col): **to ~ out/down/up** fare un salto fuori/giù/di sopra ♦ n (pinch) pizzico; (drink) goccio, bicchierino.

nipple ['nɪpl] n (ANAT) capezzolo.

nippy ['nɪpɪ] adj (weather) pungente; (BRIT: car, person) svelto(a).

nit [nɪt] n (of louse) lendine m; (col: idiot) cretino/a, scemo/a.

nit-pick ['nɪtpɪk] vi (col) cercare il pelo nell'uovo.

nitrogen ['naɪtrədʒən] n azoto.

nitroglycerin(e) [naɪtrəʊ'glɪsəriːn] n nitroglicerina.

nitty-gritty ['nɪtɪ'grɪtɪ] n (col): **to get down to the ~** venire al sodo.

nitwit ['nɪtwɪt] n (col) scemo/a.

NJ abbr (US) = New Jersey.

NLF n abbr (= National Liberation Front) ≈ F.L.N. m.

NLQ abbr (= near letter quality) qualità quasi di corrispondenza.

NLRB n abbr (US: = National Labor Relations Board) organismo per la tutela dei lavoratori.

NM, N. Mex. abbr (US) = New Mexico.

════════════════════════ KEYWORD

no [nəʊ] adv (opposite of "yes") no; **are you coming? — ~ (I'm not)** viene? — no (non vengo); **would you like some more? — ~ thank you** ne vuole ancora un po'? — no, grazie; **I have ~ more wine** non ho più vino

♦ adj (not any) nessuno(a); **I have ~ money/time/books** non ho soldi/tempo/libri; **~ student would have done it** nessuno studente lo avrebbe fatto; **there is ~ reason to believe ...** non c'è nessuna ragione per credere ...; **"~ parking"** "divieto di sosta"; **"~ smoking"** "vietato fumare"; **"~ entry"** "ingresso vietato"; **"~ dogs"** "vietato l'accesso ai cani"

♦ n (pl ~es) no m inv; **I won't take ~ for an answer** non accetterò un rifiuto.

no. abbr (= number) n.

nobble ['nɒbl] vt (BRIT col: bribe: person) comprare, corrompere; (: person to speak to, criminal) bloccare, beccare; (RACING: horse, dog) drogare.

Nobel prize [nəʊ'bɛl-] n premio Nobel.

nobility [nəʊ'bɪlɪtɪ] n nobiltà.

noble ['nəʊbl] adj, n nobile (m).

nobleman ['nəʊblmən] n nobile m, nobiluomo.

nobly ['nəʊblɪ] adv (selflessly) generosamente.

nobody ['nəʊbədɪ] pron nessuno.

no-claims bonus ['nəʊkleɪmz-] n bonus malus m inv.

nocturnal [nɒk'tɜːnl] adj notturno(a).

nod [nɒd] vi accennare col capo, fare un cenno; (sleep) sonnecchiare ♦ vt: **to ~ one's head** fare di sì col capo ♦ n cenno; **they ~ded their agreement** accennarono di sì (col capo).

▶**nod off** vi assopirsi.

no-fly zone [nəʊ'flaɪ-] n zona di interdizione aerea.

noise [nɔɪz] n rumore m; (din, racket) chiasso.

noiseless ['nɔɪzlɪs] adj silenzioso(a).

noisily ['nɔɪzɪlɪ] adv rumorosamente.

noisy ['nɔɪzɪ] adj (street, car) rumoroso(a); (person) chiassoso(a).

nomad ['nəumæd] *n* nomade *m/f*.
nomadic [nəu'mædɪk] *adj* nomade.
no man's land *n* terra di nessuno.
nominal ['nɔmɪnl] *adj* nominale.
nominate ['nɔmɪneɪt] *vt* (*propose*) proporre come candidato; (*elect*) nominare.
nomination [nɔmɪ'neɪʃən] *n* nomina; candidatura.
nominee [nɔmɪ'niː] *n* persona nominata; candidato/a.
non... [nɔn] *prefix* non....
non-alcoholic ['nɔnælkə'hɔlɪk] *adj* analcolico(a).
non-breakable [nɔn'breɪkəbl] *adj* infrangibile.
nonce word ['nɔns-] *n* parola coniata per l'occasione.
nonchalant ['nɔnʃələnt] *adj* incurante, indifferente.
non-commissioned [nɔnkə'mɪʃnd] *adj*: ~ **officer (NCO)** sottufficiale *m*.
non-committal [nɔnkə'mɪtl] *adj* evasivo(a).
nonconformist [nɔnkən'fɔːmɪst] *n* anticonformista *m/f*; (*BRIT REL*) dissidente *m/f* ♦ *adj* anticonformista.
non-contributory [nɔnkən'trɪbjutərɪ] *adj*: ~ **pension scheme** *or* (*US*) **plan** *sistema di pensionamento con i contributi interamente a carico del datore di lavoro.*
non-cooperation ['nɔnkəuɔpə'reɪʃən] *n* non cooperazione *f*, non collaborazione *f*.
nondescript ['nɔndɪskrɪpt] *adj* qualunque *inv*.
none [nʌn] *pron* (*not one thing*) niente; (*not one person*) nessuno(a); ~ **of you** nessuno(a) di voi; **I have** ~ non ne ho nemmeno uno; **I have** ~ **left** non ne ho più; ~ **at all** proprio niente; (*not one*) nemmeno uno; **he's** ~ **the worse for it** non ne ha risentito.
nonentity [nɔ'nɛntɪtɪ] *n* persona insignificante.
non-essential [nɔnɪ'sɛnʃl] *adj* non essenziale ♦ *n*: ~**s** superfluo, cose *fpl* superflue.
nonetheless ['nʌnðə'lɛs] *adv* nondimeno.
non-event [nɔnɪ'vɛnt] *n* delusione *f*.
non-executive [nɔnɪg'zɛkjutɪv] *adj*: ~ **director** direttore *m* senza potere esecutivo.
non-existent [nɔnɪg'zɪstənt] *adj* inesistente.
non-fiction [nɔn'fɪkʃən] *n* saggistica.
non-flammable [nɔn'flæməbl] *adj* ininfiammabile.
non-intervention ['nɔnɪntə'vɛnʃən] *n* non intervento.

no-no ['nəunəu] *n*: **it's a** ~! (*undesirable*) è inaccettabile!; (*forbidden*) non si può fare!
non obst. *abbr* (= *non obstante*: *notwithstanding*) nonostante.
no-nonsense [nəu'nɔnsəns] *adj* che va al sodo.
non-payment [nɔn'peɪmənt] *n* mancato pagamento.
nonplussed [nɔn'plʌst] *adj* sconcertato(a).
non-profit-making [nɔn'prɔfɪtmeɪkɪŋ] *adj* senza scopo di lucro.
nonsense ['nɔnsəns] *n* sciocchezze *fpl*; ~! che sciocchezze!, che assurdità!; **it is** ~ **to say that ...** è un'assurdità *or* non ha senso dire che ....
nonsensical [nɔn'sɛnsɪkl] *adj* assurdo(a), ridicolo(a).
non-shrink [nɔn'ʃrɪŋk] *adj* (*BRIT*) irrestringibile.
non-skid [nɔn'skɪd] *adj* antisdrucciolo(a).
non-smoker [nɔn'sməukə*] *n* non fumatore/trice.
non-starter [nɔn'staːtə*] *n*: **it's a** ~ è fallito in partenza.
non-stick [nɔn'stɪk] *adj* antiaderente, antiadesivo(a).
non-stop ['nɔn'stɔp] *adj* continuo(a); (*train, bus*) direttissimo(a) ♦ *adv* senza sosta.
non-taxable [nɔn'tæksəbl] *adj*: ~ **income** reddito non imponibile.
non-U [nɔn'juː] *adj abbr* (*BRIT col*) = *non-upper class*.
non-volatile [nɔn'vɔlətaɪl] *adj*: ~ **memory** (*COMPUT*) memoria permanente.
non-voting [nɔn'vəutɪŋ] *adj*: ~ **shares** azioni *fpl* senza diritto di voto.
non-white ['nɔn'waɪt] *adj* di colore ♦ *n* persona di colore.
noodles ['nuːdlz] *npl* taglierini *mpl*.
nook [nuk] *n*: ~**s and crannies** angoli *mpl*.
noon [nuːn] *n* mezzogiorno.
no one ['nəuwʌn] *pron* = **nobody**.
noose [nuːs] *n* nodo scorsoio, cappio; (*hangman's*) cappio.
nor [nɔː*] *conj* = **neither** ♦ *adv see* **neither**.
Norf *abbr* (*BRIT*) = Norfolk.
norm [nɔːm] *n* norma.
normal ['nɔːml] *adj* normale ♦ *n*: **to return to** ~ tornare alla normalità.
normality [nɔː'mælɪtɪ] *n* normalità.
normally ['nɔːməlɪ] *adv* normalmente.
Normandy ['nɔːməndɪ] *n* Normandia.
north [nɔːθ] *n* nord *m*, settentrione *m* ♦ *adj* nord *inv*, del nord, settentrionale ♦ *adv* verso nord.
North Africa *n* Africa del Nord.
North African *adj*, *n* nordafricano(a).

North America n America del Nord.
North American adj, n nordamericano(a).
Northants [nɔː'θænts] abbr (BRIT)
= Northamptonshire.
northbound ['nɔːθbaund] adj (traffic)
diretto(a) a nord; (carriageway) nord inv.
Northd abbr (BRIT) = Northumberland.
north-east [nɔːθ'iːst] n nord-est m.
northerly ['nɔːðəlɪ] adj (wind) del nord;
(direction) verso nord.
northern ['nɔːðən] adj del nord,
settentrionale.
Northern Ireland n Irlanda del Nord.
North Pole n: the ~ il Polo Nord.
North Sea n: the ~ il mare del Nord.
North Sea oil n petrolio del mare del
Nord.
northward(s) ['nɔːθwəd(z)] adv verso nord.
north-west [nɔːθ'wɛst] n nord-ovest m.
Norway ['nɔːweɪ] n Norvegia.
Norwegian [nɔː'wiːdʒən] adj norvegese ♦ n
norvegese m/f; (LING) norvegese m.
nos. abbr (= numbers) nn.
nose [nəuz] n naso; (of animal) muso ♦ vi
(also: ~ one's way) avanzare cautamente;
to pay through the ~ (for sth) (col) pagare
(qc) un occhio della testa.
▶**nose about, nose around** vi aggirarsi.
nosebleed ['nəuzbliːd] n emorragia nasale.
nose-dive ['nəuzdaɪv] n picchiata.
nose drops npl gocce fpl per il naso.
nosey ['nəuzɪ] adj curioso(a).
nostalgia [nɔs'tældʒɪə] n nostalgia.
nostalgic [nɔs'tældʒɪk] adj nostalgico(a).
nostril ['nɔstrɪl] n narice f; (of horse) frogia.
nosy ['nəuzɪ] adj = nosey.
not [nɔt] adv non; ~ **at all** niente affatto;
(after thanks) prego, s'immagini; **you must**
~ **or mustn't do this** non deve fare
questo; **he isn't** ... egli non è ...; **I hope** ~
spero di no.
notable ['nəutəbl] adj notevole.
notably ['nəutəblɪ] adv notevolmente; (in
particular) in particolare.
notary ['nəutərɪ] n (also: ~ **public**) notaio.
notation [nəu'teɪʃən] n notazione f.
notch [nɔtʃ] n tacca.
▶**notch up** vt (score, victory) marcare,
segnare.
note [nəut] n nota; (letter, banknote)
biglietto ♦ vt prendere nota di; **to take** ~
of prendere nota di; **to take** ~**s** prendere
appunti; **to compare** ~**s** (fig) scambiarsi
le impressioni; **of** ~ eminente,
importante; **just a quick** ~ **to let you**
know ... ti scrivo solo due righe per
informarti ....
notebook ['nəutbuk] n taccuino; (for

shorthand) bloc-notes m inv.
note-case ['nəutkeɪs] n (BRIT) portafoglio.
noted ['nəutɪd] adj celebre.
notepad ['nəutpæd] n bloc-notes m inv,
blocchetto.
notepaper ['nəutpeɪpə*] n carta da lettere.
noteworthy ['nəutwɔːðɪ] adj degno(a) di
nota, importante.
nothing ['nʌθɪŋ] n nulla m, niente m; **he**
does ~ non fa niente; ~ **new** niente di
nuovo; **for** ~ (free) per niente; ~ **at all**
proprio niente.
notice ['nəutɪs] n avviso; (of leaving)
preavviso; (BRIT: review: of play etc)
critica, recensione f ♦ vt notare,
accorgersi di; **to take** ~ **of** fare
attenzione a; **to bring sth to sb's** ~ far
notare qc a qn; **to give sb** ~ **of sth**
avvisare qn di qc; **to give** ~, **hand in**
one's ~ (subj: employee) licenziarsi;
without ~ senza preavviso; **at short** ~
con un breve preavviso; **until further** ~
fino a nuovo avviso; **advance** ~
preavviso; **to escape** or **avoid** ~ passare
inosservato; **it has come to my** ~ **that** ...
sono venuto a sapere che ...
noticeable ['nəutɪsəbl] adj evidente.
notice board n (BRIT) tabellone m per
affissi.
notification [nəutɪfɪ'keɪʃən] n annuncio;
notifica; denuncia.
notify ['nəutɪfaɪ] vt: **to** ~ **sth to sb** notificare
qc a qn; **to** ~ **sb of sth** avvisare qn di qc;
(police) denunciare qc a qn.
notion ['nəuʃən] n idea; (concept) nozione f.
notions ['nəuʃənz] npl (US: haberdashery)
merceria.
notoriety [nəutə'raɪətɪ] n notorietà.
notorious [nəu'tɔːrɪəs] adj famigerato(a).
notoriously [nəu'tɔːrɪəslɪ] adv
notoriamente.
Notts [nɔts] abbr (BRIT) = Nottinghamshire.
notwithstanding [nɔtwɪθ'stændɪŋ] adv
nondimeno ♦ prep nonostante, malgrado.
nougat ['nuːgɑː] n torrone m.
nought [nɔːt] n zero.
noun [naun] n nome m, sostantivo.
nourish ['nʌrɪʃ] vt nutrire.
nourishing ['nʌrɪʃɪŋ] adj nutriente.
nourishment ['nʌrɪʃmənt] n nutrimento.
Nov. abbr (= November) nov.
Nova Scotia ['nəuvə'skəuʃə] n Nuova
Scozia.
novel ['nɔvl] n romanzo ♦ adj nuovo(a).
novelist ['nɔvəlɪst] n romanziere/a.
novelty ['nɔvəltɪ] n novità f inv.
November [nəu'vɛmbə*] n novembre m; for
phrases see also **July**.

novice ['nɔvɪs] *n* principiante *m/f*; (*REL*) novizio/a.

NOW [nau] *n abbr* (*US*: = *National Organization for Women*) ≈ U.D.I. *f* (= *Unione Donne Italiane*).

now [nau] *adv* ora, adesso ♦ *conj*: ~ **(that)** adesso che, ora che; **right** ~ subito; **by** ~ ormai; **just** ~: **that's the fashion just** ~ è la moda del momento; **I saw her just** ~ l'ho vista proprio adesso; **I'll read it just** ~ lo leggo subito; ~ **and then**, ~ **and again** ogni tanto; **from** ~ **on** da ora in poi; **in 3 days from** ~ fra 3 giorni; **between** ~ **and Monday** da qui a lunedì, entro lunedì; **that's all for** ~ per ora basta.

nowadays ['nauədeɪz] *adv* oggidì.

nowhere ['nəuwɛə*] *adv* in nessun luogo, da nessuna parte; ~ **else** in nessun altro posto.

no-win situation [nəu'wɪn-] *n*: **to be in a** ~ aver perso in partenza.

noxious ['nɔkʃəs] *adj* nocivo(a).

nozzle ['nɔzl] *n* (*of hose etc*) boccaglio.

NP *n abbr* = **notary public**.

NS *abbr* (*Canada*) = **Nova Scotia**.

NSC *n abbr* (*US*) = **National Security Council**.

NSF *n abbr* (*US*) = *National Science Foundation*.

NSPCC *n abbr* (*BRIT*) = *National Society for the Prevention of Cruelty to Children*.

NSW *abbr* (*Australia*) = *New South Wales*.

NT *n abbr* (= *New Testament*) N.T. ♦ *abbr* (*Canada*) = *Northwest Territories*.

nth [ɛnθ] *adj*: **for the** ~ **time** (*col*) per l'ennesima volta.

nuance ['nju:ɑ̃:ns] *n* sfumatura.

nubile ['nju:baɪl] *adj* nubile; (*attractive*) giovane e desiderabile.

nuclear ['nju:klɪə*] *adj* nucleare; (*warfare*) atomico(a).

nuclear disarmament *n* disarmo nucleare.

nuclear family *n* famiglia nucleare.

nuclear-free zone ['nju:klɪə'fri:-] *n* zona denuclearizzata.

nucleus, pl nuclei ['nju:klɪəs, 'nju:klɪaɪ] *n* nucleo.

NUCPS *n abbr* (*BRIT*) = *National Union of Civil and Public Servants*.

nude [nju:d] *adj* nudo(a) ♦ *n* (*ART*) nudo; **in the** ~ tutto(a) nudo(a).

nudge [nʌdʒ] *vt* dare una gomitata a.

nudist ['nju:dɪst] *n* nudista *m/f*.

nudity ['nju:dɪtɪ] *n* nudità.

nugget ['nʌgɪt] *n* pepita.

nuisance ['nju:sns] *n*: **it's a** ~ è una seccatura; **he's a** ~ lui dà fastidio; **what a** ~! che seccatura!

NUJ *n abbr* (*BRIT*: = *National Union of Journalists*) sindacato nazionale dei giornalisti.

nuke [nju:k] *n* (*col*) bomba atomica.

null [nʌl] *adj*: ~ **and void** nullo(a).

nullify ['nʌlɪfaɪ] *vt* annullare.

NUM *n abbr* (*BRIT*: = *National Union of Mineworkers*) sindacato nazionale dei dipendenti delle miniere.

numb [nʌm] *adj* intorpidito(a) ♦ *vt* intorpidire; ~ **with** (*fear*) paralizzato(a) da; (*grief*) impietrito(a) da; ~ **with cold** intirizzito(a) (dal freddo).

number ['nʌmbə*] *n* numero ♦ *vt* numerare; (*include*) contare; **a** ~ **of** un certo numero di; **telephone** ~ numero di telefono; **wrong** ~ (*TEL*) numero sbagliato; **the staff** ~**s 20** gli impiegati sono in 20.

numbered account ['nʌmbəd-] *n* (*in bank*) conto numerato.

number plate *n* (*BRIT AUT*) targa.

Number Ten *n* (*BRIT*: = *10 Downing Street*) *residenza del Primo Ministro del Regno Unito*.

numbness ['nʌmnɪs] *n* intorpidimento; (*due to cold*) intirizzimento.

numbskull ['nʌmskʌl] *n* (*col*) imbecille *m/f*, idiota *m/f*.

numeral ['nju:mərəl] *n* numero, cifra.

numerate ['nju:mərɪt] *adj* (*BRIT*): **to be** ~ saper far di conto.

numerical [nju:'mɛrɪkl] *adj* numerico(a).

numerous ['nju:mərəs] *adj* numeroso(a).

nun [nʌn] *n* suora, monaca.

nunnery ['nʌnərɪ] *n* convento.

nuptial ['nʌpʃəl] *adj* nuziale.

nurse [nə:s] *n* infermiere/a; (*also*: ~**maid**) bambinaia ♦ *vt* (*patient, cold*) curare; (*baby*: *BRIT*) cullare; (: *US*) allattare, dare il latte a; (*hope*) nutrire.

nursery ['nə:sərɪ] *n* (*room*) camera dei bambini; (*institution*) asilo; (*for plants*) vivaio.

nursery rhyme *n* filastrocca.

nursery school *n* scuola materna.

nursery slope *n* (*BRIT SKI*) pista per principianti.

nursing ['nə:sɪŋ] *n* (*profession*) professione *f* di infermiere (*or* di infermiera) ♦ *adj* (*mother*) che allatta.

nursing home *n* casa di cura.

nurture ['nə:tʃə*] *vt* allevare; nutrire.

NUS *n abbr* (*BRIT*: = *National Union of Students*) sindacato nazionale degli studenti.

NUT *n abbr* (*BRIT*: = *National Union of Teachers*) sindacato nazionale degli

insegnanti.
nut [nʌt] n (*of metal*) dado; (*fruit*) noce f (*or* nocciola *or* mandorla *etc*) ♦ adj (*chocolate etc*) alla nocciola *etc*; **he's ~s** (*col*) è matto.
nutcase ['nʌtkeɪs] n (*col*) mattarello/a.
nutcrackers ['nʌtkrækəz] npl schiaccianoci m inv.
nutmeg ['nʌtmɛg] n noce f moscata.
nutrient ['njuːtrɪənt] adj nutriente ♦ n sostanza nutritiva.
nutrition [njuː'trɪʃən] n nutrizione f.
nutritionist [njuː'trɪʃənɪst] n nutrizionista m/f.
nutritious [njuː'trɪʃəs] adj nutriente.
nutshell ['nʌtʃɛl] n guscio di noce; **in a ~ in** poche parole.
nutty ['nʌtɪ] adj di noce (*or* nocciola *or* mandorla *etc*); (*BRIT col*) tocco(a), matto(a).
nuzzle ['nʌzl] vi: **to ~ up to** strofinare il muso contro.
NV abbr (*US*) = Nevada.
NWT abbr (*Canada*) = Northwest Territories.
NY abbr (*US*) = **New York**.
NYC abbr (*US*) = New York City.
nylon ['naɪlɔn] n nailon m; **~s** npl calze fpl di nailon.
nymph [nɪmf] n ninfa.
nymphomaniac [nɪmfəu'meɪnɪæk] adj, n ninfomane (f).
NYSE abbr (*US*) = New York Stock Exchange.

O o

O, o [əu] n (*letter*) O, o f or m inv; (*US SCOL: = outstanding*) ≈ ottimo; (*number: TEL etc*) zero; **O for Oliver,** (*US*) **O for Oboe** ≈ O come Otranto.
oaf [əuf] n zoticone m.
oak [əuk] n quercia ♦ cpd di quercia.
OAP n abbr (*BRIT*) see **old-age pensioner**.
oar [ɔː*] n remo; **to put** *or* **shove one's ~ in** (*fig col*) intromettersi.
oarsman ['ɔːzmən], **oarswoman** ['ɔːzwumən] n rematore/trice.
OAS n abbr (= Organization of American States) O.S.A. f (= Organizzazione degli Stati Americani).
oasis, pl **oases** [əu'eɪsɪs, əu'eɪsiːz] n oasi f inv.

oath [əuθ] n giuramento; (*swear word*) bestemmia; **to take the ~** giurare; **on ~** (*BRIT*) *or* **under ~** sotto giuramento.
oatmeal ['əutmiːl] n farina d'avena.
oats [əuts] npl avena.
OAU n abbr (= Organization of African Unity) O.A.U. f.
obdurate ['ɔbdjurɪt] adj testardo(a); incallito(a); ostinato(a), irremovibile.
OBE n abbr (*BRIT*: = Order of the British Empire*) titolo.
obedience [ə'biːdɪəns] n ubbidienza; **in ~ to** conformemente a.
obedient [ə'biːdɪənt] adj ubbidiente; **to be ~ to sb/sth** ubbidire a qn/qc.
obelisk ['ɔbɪlɪsk] n obelisco.
obese [əu'biːs] adj obeso(a).
obesity [əu'biːsɪtɪ] n obesità.
obey [ə'beɪ] vt ubbidire a; (*instructions, regulations*) osservare ♦ vi ubbidire.
obituary [ə'bɪtjuərɪ] n necrologia.
object n ['ɔbdʒɪkt] oggetto; (*purpose*) scopo, intento; (*LING*) complemento oggetto ♦ vi [əb'dʒɛkt]: **to ~ to** (*attitude*) disapprovare; (*proposal*) protestare contro, sollevare delle obiezioni contro; **I ~!** mi oppongo!; **he ~ed that ...** obiettò che ...; **do you ~ to my smoking?** la disturba se fumo?; **what's the ~ of doing that?** a che serve farlo?; **expense is no ~** non si bada a spese.
objection [əb'dʒɛkʃən] n obiezione f; (*drawback*) inconveniente m; **if you have no ~** se non ha obiezioni; **to make** *or* **raise an ~** sollevare un'obiezione.
objectionable [əb'dʒɛkʃənəbl] adj antipatico(a); (*smell*) sgradevole; (*language*) scostumato(a).
objective [əb'dʒɛktɪv] n obiettivo ♦ adj obiettivo(a).
objectivity [ɔbdʒɪk'tɪvɪtɪ] n obiettività.
object lesson n: **~ (in)** dimostrazione f (di).
objector [əb'dʒɛktə*] n oppositore/trice.
obligation [ɔblɪ'geɪʃən] n obbligo, dovere m; (*debt*) obbligo (di riconoscenza); **"without ~"** "senza impegno"; **to be under an ~ to sb/to do sth** essere in dovere verso qn/di fare qc.
obligatory [ə'blɪgətərɪ] adj obbligatorio(a).
oblige [ə'blaɪdʒ] vt (*force*): **to ~ sb to do** costringere qn a fare; (*do a favour*) fare una cortesia a; **to be ~d to sb for sth** essere grato a qn per qc; **anything to ~!** (*col*) questo e altro!
obliging [ə'blaɪdʒɪŋ] adj servizievole, compiacente.
oblique [ə'bliːk] adj obliquo(a); (*allusion*)

indiretto(a) ♦ *n* (*BRIT TYP*): ~ **(stroke)** barra.

obliterate [əˈblɪtəreɪt] *vt* cancellare.

oblivion [əˈblɪvɪən] *n* oblio.

oblivious [əˈblɪvɪəs] *adj*: ~ **of** incurante di; inconscio(a) di.

oblong [ˈɔblɔŋ] *adj* oblungo(a) ♦ *n* rettangolo.

obnoxious [əbˈnɔkʃəs] *adj* odioso(a); (*smell*) disgustoso(a), ripugnante.

o.b.o. *abbr* (*US*: = *or best offer*: *in classified ads*) o al miglior offerente.

oboe [ˈəubəu] *n* oboe *m*.

obscene [əbˈsiːn] *adj* osceno(a).

obscenity [əbˈsɛnɪtɪ] *n* oscenità *f inv*.

obscure [əbˈskjuə*] *adj* oscuro(a) ♦ *vt* oscurare; (*hide*: *sun*) nascondere.

obscurity [əbˈskjuərɪtɪ] *n* oscurità; (*obscure point*) punto oscuro; (*lack of fame*) anonimato.

obsequious [əbˈsiːkwɪəs] *adj* ossequioso(a).

observable [əbˈzəːvəbl] *adj* osservabile; (*appreciable*) notevole.

observance [əbˈzəːvns] *n* osservanza; **religious** ~**s** pratiche *fpl* religiose.

observant [əbˈzəːvnt] *adj* attento(a).

observation [ɔbzəˈveɪʃən] *n* osservazione *f*; (*by police etc*) sorveglianza.

observation post *n* (*MIL*) osservatorio.

observatory [əbˈzəːvətrɪ] *n* osservatorio.

observe [əbˈzəːv] *vt* osservare.

observer [əbˈzəːvə*] *n* osservatore/trice.

obsess [əbˈsɛs] *vt* ossessionare; **to be** ~**ed by** *or* **with sb/sth** essere ossessionato da qn/qc.

obsession [əbˈsɛʃən] *n* ossessione *f*.

obsessive [əbˈsɛsɪv] *adj* ossessivo(a).

obsolescence [ɔbsəˈlɛsns] *n* obsolescenza; **built-in** *or* **planned** ~ (*COMM*) obsolescenza programmata.

obsolescent [ɔbsəˈlɛsnt] *adj* obsolescente.

obsolete [ˈɔbsəliːt] *adj* obsoleto(a); (*word*) desueto(a).

obstacle [ˈɔbstəkl] *n* ostacolo.

obstacle race *n* corsa agli ostacoli.

obstetrician [ɔbstəˈtrɪʃən] *n* ostetrico/a.

obstetrics [ɔbˈstɛtrɪks] *n* ostetrica.

obstinacy [ˈɔbstɪnəsɪ] *n* ostinatezza.

obstinate [ˈɔbstɪnɪt] *adj* ostinato(a).

obstreperous [əbˈstrɛpərəs] *adj* turbolento(a).

obstruct [əbˈstrʌkt] *vt* (*block*) ostruire, ostacolare; (*halt*) fermare; (*hinder*) impedire.

obstruction [əbˈstrʌkʃən] *n* ostruzione *f*; ostacolo.

obstructive [əbˈstrʌktɪv] *adj* ostruttivo(a); che crea impedimenti.

obtain [əbˈteɪn] *vt* ottenere ♦ *vi* essere in uso; **to** ~ **sth (for o.s.)** procurarsi qc.

obtainable [əbˈteɪnəbl] *adj* ottenibile.

obtrusive [əbˈtruːsɪv] *adj* (*person*) importuno(a); (*smell*) invadente; (*building etc*) imponente e invadente.

obtuse [əbˈtjuːs] *adj* ottuso(a).

obverse [ˈɔbvəːs] *n* opposto, inverso.

obviate [ˈɔbvɪeɪt] *vt* ovviare a, evitare.

obvious [ˈɔbvɪəs] *adj* ovvio(a), evidente.

obviously [ˈɔbvɪəslɪ] *adv* ovviamente; ~! certo!; ~ **not!** certo che no!; **he was** ~ **not drunk** si vedeva che non era ubriaco; **he was not** ~ **drunk** non si vedeva che era ubriaco.

OCAS *n abbr* = *Organization of Central American States*.

occasion [əˈkeɪʒən] *n* occasione *f*; (*event*) avvenimento ♦ *vt* cagionare; **on that** ~ in quell'occasione, quella volta; **to rise to the** ~ mostrarsi all'altezza della situazione.

occasional [əˈkeɪʒənl] *adj* occasionale; **I smoke an** ~ **cigarette** ogni tanto fumo una sigaretta.

occasionally [əˈkeɪʒənəlɪ] *adv* ogni tanto; **very** ~ molto raramente.

occasional table *n* tavolino.

occult [ɔˈkʌlt] *adj* occulto(a) ♦ *n*: **the** ~ l'occulto.

occupancy [ˈɔkjupənsɪ] *n* occupazione *f*.

occupant [ˈɔkjupənt] *n* occupante *m/f*; (*of boat, car etc*) persona a bordo.

occupation [ɔkjuˈpeɪʃən] *n* occupazione *f*; (*job*) mestiere *m*, professione *f*; **unfit for** ~ (*house*) inabitabile.

occupational [ɔkjuˈpeɪʃənl] *adj* (*disease*) professionale; (*hazard*) del mestiere; ~ **accident** infortunio sul lavoro.

occupational guidance *n* (*BRIT*) orientamento professionale.

occupational pension scheme *n sistema pensionistico programmato dal datore di lavoro*.

occupational therapy *n* ergoterapia.

occupier [ˈɔkjupaɪə*] *n* occupante *m/f*.

occupy [ˈɔkjupaɪ] *vt* occupare; **to** ~ **o.s. by doing** occuparsi a fare; **to be occupied with sth/in doing sth** essere preso da qc/occupato a fare qc.

occur [əˈkəː*] *vi* accadere; (*difficulty, opportunity*) capitare; (*phenomenon, error*) trovarsi; **to** ~ **to sb** venire in mente a qn.

occurrence [əˈkʌrəns] *n* caso, fatto; presenza.

ocean [ˈəuʃən] *n* oceano; ~**s of** (*col*) un sacco di.

ocean bed *n* fondale *m* oceanico.

ocean-going ['əuʃəngəuɪŋ] *adj* d'alto mare.
Oceania [əuʃɪ'ɑːnɪə] *n* Oceania.
ocean liner *n* transatlantico.
ochre, (*US*) **ocher** ['əukə*] *adj* ocra *inv*.
o'clock [ə'klɔk] *adv*: **it is one** ~ è l'una; **it is 5** ~ sono le 5.
OCR *n abbr see* **optical character reader; optical character recognition.**
Oct. *abbr* (= *October*) ott.
octagonal [ɔk'tægənl] *adj* ottagonale.
octane ['ɔkteɪn] *n* ottano; **high-**~ **petrol** *or* (*US*) **gas** benzina ad alto numero di ottani.
octave ['ɔktɪv] *n* ottavo.
October [ɔk'təubə*] *n* ottobre *m*; *for phrases see also* **July.**
octogenarian [ɔktəudʒɪ'nɛərɪən] *n* ottuagenario/a.
octopus ['ɔktəpəs] *n* polpo, piovra.
odd [ɔd] *adj* (*strange*) strano(a), bizzarro(a); (*number*) dispari *inv*; (*left over*) in più; (*not of a set*) spaiato(a); **60-**~ 60 e oltre; **at** ~ **times** di tanto in tanto; **the** ~ **one out** l'eccezione *f*.
oddball ['ɔdbɔːl] *n* (*col*) eccentrico/a.
oddity ['ɔdɪtɪ] *n* bizzarria; (*person*) originale *m/f*.
odd-job man [ɔd'dʒɔb-] *n* tuttofare *m inv*.
odd jobs *npl* lavori *mpl* occasionali.
oddly ['ɔdlɪ] *adv* stranamente.
oddments ['ɔdmənts] *npl* (*BRIT COMM*) rimanenze *fpl*.
odds [ɔdz] *npl* (*in betting*) quota; **the** ~ **are against his coming** c'è poca probabilità che venga; **it makes no** ~ non importa; **at** ~ **in contesa; to succeed against all the** ~ riuscire contro ogni aspettativa; ~ **and ends** avanzi *mpl*.
odds-on [ɔdz'ɔn] *adj* (*col*) probabile; ~ **favourite** (*RACING*) favorito(a).
ode [əud] *n* ode *f*.
odious ['əudɪəs] *adj* odioso(a), ripugnante.
odometer [ɔ'dɔmɪtə*] *n* odometro.
odour, (*US*) **odor** ['əudə*] *n* odore *m*.
odo(u)rless ['əudəlɪs] *adj* inodoro(a).
OECD *n abbr* (= *Organization for Economic Cooperation and Development*) O.C.S.E. *f* (= *Organizzazione per la Cooperazione e lo Sviluppo Economico*).
oesophagus, (*US*) **esophagus** [iː'sɔfəgəs] *n* esofago.
oestrogen, (*US*) **estrogen** ['iːstrəudʒən] *n* estrogeno.

═══════════════════ *KEYWORD*

of [ɔv, əv] *prep* **1** (*gen*) di; **a boy** ~ **10** un ragazzo di 10 anni; **a friend** ~ **ours** un nostro amico; **that was kind** ~ **you** è stato molto gentile da parte sua
2 (*expressing quantity, amount, dates etc*) di; **a kilo** ~ **flour** un chilo di farina; **how much** ~ **this do you need?** quanto gliene serve?; **there were four** ~ **them** (*people*) erano in quattro; (*objects*) ce n'erano quattro; **three** ~ **us went** tre di noi sono andati; **the 5th** ~ **July** il 5 luglio; **a quarter** ~ **4** (*US*) le 4 meno un quarto
3 (*from, out of*) di, in; **made** ~ **wood** (*fatto*) di *or* in legno.

═══════════════════ *KEYWORD*

off [ɔf] *adv* **1** (*distance, time*): **it's a long way** ~ è lontano; **the game is 3 days** ~ la partita è tra 3 giorni
2 (*departure, removal*) via; **to go** ~ **to Paris** andarsene a Parigi; **I must be** ~ devo andare via; **to take** ~ **one's coat** togliersi il cappotto; **the button came** ~ il bottone è venuto via *or* si è staccato; **10%** ~ con lo sconto del 10%
3 (*not at work*): **to have a day** ~ avere un giorno libero; **to be** ~ **sick** essere assente per malattia
♦ *adj* (*engine*) spento(a); (*tap*) chiuso(a); (*cancelled*) sospeso(a); (*BRIT: food*) andato(a) a male; **to be well/badly** ~ essere/non essere benestante; **the lid was** ~ non c'era il coperchio; **I'm afraid the chicken is** ~ (*BRIT: not available*) purtroppo il pollo è finito; **on the** ~ **chance** nel caso; **to have an** ~ **day** non essere in forma; **that's a bit** ~, **isn't it?** (*fig col*) non è molto carino, vero?
♦ *prep* **1** (*motion, removal etc*) da; (*distant from*) a poca distanza da; **a street** ~ **the square** una strada che parte dalla piazza; **5km** ~ **the road** a 5km dalla strada; ~ **the coast** al largo della costa; **a house** ~ **the main road** una casa che non è sulla strada principale
2: **to be** ~ **meat** non mangiare più la carne.

offal ['ɔfl] *n* (*CULIN*) frattaglie *fpl*.
offbeat ['ɔfbiːt] *adj* eccentrico(a).
off-centre, (*US*) **off-center** [ɔf'sɛntə*] *adj* storto(a), fuori centro.
off-colour ['ɔf'kʌlə*] *adj* (*BRIT: ill*) malato(a), indisposto(a); **to feel** ~ sentirsi poco bene.
offence, (*US*) **offense** [ə'fɛns] *n* (*LAW*) contravvenzione *f*, (: *more serious*) reato; **to give** ~ **to** offendere; **to take** ~ **at** offendersi per; **to commit an** ~ commettere un reato.

offend [ə'fɛnd] *vt* (*person*) offendere ♦ *vi*: **to ~ against** (*law, rule*) trasgredire.
offender [ə'fɛndə*] *n* delinquente *m/f*; (*against regulations*) contravventore/trice.
offending [ə'fɛndɪŋ] *adj* (*often hum*): **the ~ word/object** la parola incriminata/ l'oggetto incriminato.
offense [ə'fɛns] *n* (*US*) = **offence**.
offensive [ə'fɛnsɪv] *adj* offensivo(a); (*smell etc*) sgradevole, ripugnante ♦ *n* (*MIL*) offensiva.
offer ['ɔfə*] *n* offerta, proposta ♦ *vt* offrire; **"on ~"** (*COMM*) "in offerta speciale"; **to make an ~ for sth** fare un'offerta per qc; **to ~ sth to sb, ~ sb sth** offrire qc a qn; **to ~ to do sth** offrirsi di fare qc.
offering ['ɔfərɪŋ] *n* offerta.
offhand [ɔf'hænd] *adj* disinvolto(a), noncurante ♦ *adv* all'impronto; **I can't tell you ~** non posso dirglielo su due piedi.
office ['ɔfɪs] *n* (*place*) ufficio; (*position*) carica; **doctor's ~** (*US*) ambulatorio; **to take ~** entrare in carica; **through his good ~s** con il suo prezioso aiuto; **O~ of Fair Trading** (*BRIT*) organismo di protezione contro le pratiche commerciali abusive.
office automation *n* automazione *f* d'ufficio, burotica.
office bearer *n* (*of club etc*) membro dell'amministrazione.
office block, (*US*) **office building** *n* complesso di uffici.
office boy *n* garzone *m*.
office hours *npl* orario d'ufficio; (*US MED*) orario di visite.
office manager *n* capoufficio *m/f*.
officer ['ɔfɪsə*] *n* (*MIL etc*) ufficiale *m*; (*of organization*) funzionario; (*also*: **police ~**) agente *m* di polizia.
office work *n* lavoro d'ufficio.
office worker *n* impiegato/a d'ufficio.
official [ə'fɪʃl] *adj* (*authorized*) ufficiale ♦ *n* ufficiale *m*; (*civil servant*) impiegato/a statale; funzionario.
officialdom [ə'fɪʃəldəm] *n* burocrazia.
officially [ə'fɪʃəlɪ] *adv* ufficialmente.
official receiver *n* curatore *m* fallimentare.
officiate [ə'fɪʃɪeɪt] *vi* (*REL*) ufficiare; **to ~ as Mayor** esplicare le funzioni di sindaco; **to ~ at a marriage** celebrare un matrimonio.
officious [ə'fɪʃəs] *adj* invadente.
offing ['ɔfɪŋ] *n*: **in the ~** (*fig*) in vista.
off-key [ɔf'kiː] *adj* stonato(a) ♦ *adv* fuori tono.
off-licence ['ɔflaɪsns] *n* (*BRIT*) spaccio di bevande alcoliche.

In Gran Bretagna e in Irlanda, gli **off-licence** *sono esercizi pubblici specializzati nella vendita strettamente regolamentata di bevande alcoliche, per la quale è necessario avere un'apposita licenza. In genere sono aperti fino a tarda sera.*

---

off-limits [ɔf'lɪmɪts] *adj* (*esp US*) in cui vige il divieto d'accesso.
off line *adj, adv* (*COMPUT*) off line *inv*, fuori linea; (: *switched off*) spento(a).
off-load ['ɔfləud] *vt* scaricare.
off-peak ['ɔf'piːk] *adj* (*ticket etc*) a tariffa ridotta; (*time*) non di punta.
off-putting ['ɔfputɪŋ] *adj* (*BRIT*) un po' scostante.
off-season ['ɔfsiːzn] *adj, adv* fuori stagione.
offset ['ɔfsɛt] *vt irreg* (*counteract*) controbilanciare, compensare ♦ *n* (*also*: **~ printing**) offset *m*.
offshoot ['ɔfʃuːt] *n* (*fig*) diramazione *f*.
offshore [ɔf'ʃɔː*] *adj* (*breeze*) di terra; (*island*) vicino alla costa; (*fishing*) costiero(a); **~ oilfield** giacimento petrolifero in mare aperto.
offside ['ɔf'saɪd] *adj* (*SPORT*) fuori gioco; (*AUT*: *with right-hand drive*) destro(a); (: *with left-hand drive*) sinistro(a) ♦ *n* destra; sinistra.
offspring ['ɔfsprɪŋ] *n* prole *f*, discendenza.
offstage [ɔf'steɪdʒ] *adv* dietro le quinte.
off-the-cuff [ɔfðə'kʌf] *adv* improvvisando.
off-the-job ['ɔfðə'dʒɔb] *adj*: **~ training** addestramento fuori sede.
off-the-peg ['ɔfðə'pɛg], (*US*) **off-the-rack** ['ɔfðə'ræk] *adv* prêt-à-porter.
off-the-record ['ɔfðə'rɛkɔːd] *adj* ufficioso(a) ♦ *adv* in via ufficiosa.
off-white ['ɔfwaɪt] *adj* bianco sporco *inv*.
Ofgas ['ɔfgæs] *n abbr* (*BRIT*: *Office of Gas Supply*) organo indipendente di controllo per la tutela dei consumatori.
Oftel ['ɔftɛl] *n abbr* (*BRIT*: *Office of Telecommunications*) organo indipendente di controllo per la tutela dei consumatori.
often ['ɔfn] *adv* spesso; **how ~ do you go?** quanto spesso ci va?; **as ~ as not** quasi sempre.
Ofwat ['ɔfwɔt] *n abbr* (*BRIT*: = *Office of Water Services*) in Inghilterra e Galles, organo indipendente di controllo per la tutela dei consumatori.
ogle ['əugl] *vt* occhieggiare.
ogre ['əugə*] *n* orco.

OH *abbr* (*US*) = Ohio.

oh [əu] *excl* oh!

OHMS *abbr* (*BRIT*) = On His (or Her) Majesty's Service.

oil [ɔɪl] *n* olio; (*petroleum*) petrolio; (*for central heating*) nafta ♦ *vt* (*machine*) lubrificare.

oilcan ['ɔɪlkæn] *n* oliatore *m* a mano; (*for storing*) latta da olio.

oil change *n* cambio dell'olio.

oilfield ['ɔɪfiːld] *n* giacimento petrolifero.

oil filter *n* (*AUT*) filtro dell'olio.

oil-fired ['ɔɪlfaɪəd] *adj* a nafta.

oil gauge *n* indicatore *m* del livello dell'olio.

oil industry *n* industria del petrolio.

oil level *n* livello dell'olio.

oil painting *n* quadro a olio.

oil refinery *n* raffineria di petrolio.

oil rig *n* derrick *m* inv; (*at sea*) piattaforma per trivellazioni subacquee.

oilskins ['ɔɪlskɪnz] *npl* indumenti *mpl* di tela cerata.

oil slick *n* chiazza d'olio.

oil tanker *n* petroliera.

oil well *n* pozzo petrolifero.

oily ['ɔɪlɪ] *adj* unto(a), oleoso(a); (*food*) untuoso(a).

ointment ['ɔɪntmənt] *n* unguento.

OK *abbr* (*US*) = Oklahoma.

O.K., okay [əu'keɪ] *excl* d'accordo! ♦ *vt* approvare ♦ *n*: **to give sth one's ~** approvare qc ♦ *adj*: **is it ~?, are you ~?** tutto bene?; **it's ~ with** *or* **by me** per me va bene; **are you ~ for money?** sei a posto coi soldi?

Okla. *abbr* (*US*) = Oklahoma.

old [əuld] *adj* vecchio(a); (*ancient*) antico(a), vecchio(a); (*person*) vecchio(a), anziano(a); **how ~ are you?** quanti anni ha?; **he's 10 years ~** ha 10 anni; **~er brother/sister** fratello/sorella maggiore; **any ~ thing will do** va bene qualsiasi cosa.

old age *n* vecchiaia.

old-age pensioner (OAP) ['əuldeɪdʒ-] *n* (*BRIT*) pensionato/a.

old-fashioned ['əuld'fæʃnd] *adj* antiquato(a), fuori moda; (*person*) all'antica.

old maid *n* zitella.

old people's home *n* ricovero per anziani.

old-style ['əuldstaɪl] *adj* (di) vecchio stampo *inv*.

old-time ['əuldtaɪm] *adj* di una volta.

old-timer [əuld'taɪmə*] *n* veterano/a.

old wives' tale *n* vecchia superstizione *f*.

O levels *npl* (*BRIT*: *formerly*) *diploma di istruzione secondaria conseguito a 16 anni in Inghilterra e Galles, ora sostituito dal GCSE.*

olive ['ɔlɪv] *n* (*fruit*) oliva; (*tree*) olivo ♦ *adj* (*also*: **~-green**) verde oliva *inv*.

olive oil *n* olio d'oliva.

Olympic [əu'lɪmpɪk] *adj* olimpico(a); **the ~ Games, the ~s** i giochi olimpici, le Olimpiadi.

OM *n abbr* (*BRIT*: = Order of Merit) titolo.

O & M *abbr* = organization and method.

Oman [əu'mɑːn] *n* Oman *m*.

OMB *n abbr* (*US*: = Office of Management and Budget) *servizio di consulenza al Presidente in materia di bilancio.*

omelet(te) ['ɔmlɪt] *n* omelette *f inv*; **ham/cheese ~** omelette al prosciutto/al formaggio.

omen ['əumən] *n* presagio, augurio.

ominous ['ɔmɪnəs] *adj* minaccioso(a); (*event*) di malaugurio.

omission [əu'mɪʃən] *n* omissione *f*.

omit [əu'mɪt] *vt* omettere; **to ~ to do sth** tralasciare *or* trascurare di fare qc.

omnivorous [ɔm'nɪvərəs] *adj* onnivoro(a).

ON *abbr* (*Canada*) = Ontario.

=========== *KEYWORD*

on [ɔn] *prep* **1** (*indicating position*) su; **~ the wall** sulla parete; **~ the left** a *or* sulla sinistra; **I haven't any money ~ me** non ho soldi con me

2 (*indicating means, method, condition etc*): **~ foot** a piedi; **~ the train/plane** in treno/ aereo; **~ the telephone** al telefono; **~ the radio/television** alla radio/televisione; **to be ~ drugs** drogarsi; **~ holiday** in vacanza; **he's ~ £16,000 a year** guadagna 16.000 sterline all'anno; **this round's ~ me** questo giro lo offro io

3 (*referring to time*): **~ Friday** venerdì; **~ Fridays** il *or* di venerdì; **~ June 20th** il 20 giugno; **~ Friday, June 20th** venerdì, 20 giugno; **a week ~ Friday** venerdì a otto; **his arrival** al suo arrivo; **~ seeing this** vedendo ciò

4 (*about, concerning*) su, di; **information ~ train services** informazioni sui collegamenti ferroviari; **a book ~ Goldoni/physics** un libro su Goldoni/di *or* sulla fisica

♦ *adv* **1** (*referring to dress, covering*): **to have one's coat ~** avere indosso il cappotto; **to put one's coat ~** mettersi il

cappotto; **what's she got** ~**?** cosa
indossa?; **she put her boots/gloves/hat** ~
si mise gli stivali/i guanti/il cappello;
screw the lid ~ **tightly** avvita bene il
coperchio
2 (*further, continuously*): **to walk** ~**, go** ~
etc continuare, proseguire; **to read** ~
continuare a leggere; ~ **and off** ogni
tanto; **from that day** ~ da quel giorno in
poi; **it was well** ~ **in the evening** era sera
inoltrata
♦ *adj* **1** (*in operation: machine, TV, light*)
acceso(a); (: *tap*) aperto(a); (: *brake*)
inserito(a); **is the meeting still** ~**?** (*in
progress*) la riunione è ancora in corso?;
(*not cancelled*) è confermato l'incontro?;
there's a good film ~ **at the cinema** danno
un buon film al cinema; **when is the film**
~**?** quando c'è questo film?; **my father's
always** ~ **at me to get a job** (*col*) mio
padre mi tormenta sempre perché trovi
un lavoro
2 (*col*): **that's not** ~**!** (*not acceptable*) non
si fa così!; (*not possible*) non se ne parla
neanche!

ONC *n abbr* (*BRIT.* = *Ordinary National
Certificate*) diploma in materie tecniche a
livello di maturità.
once [wʌns] *adv* una volta ♦ *conj* non
appena, quando; ~ **he had left/it was
done** dopo che se n'era andato/fu fatto; **at**
~ subito; (*simultaneously*) a un tempo; **all
at** ~ (tutto) a un tratto; ~ **a week** una
volta alla settimana; ~ **more** ancora una
volta; **I knew him** ~ un tempo *or* in
passato lo conoscevo; ~ **and for all** una
volta per sempre; ~ **upon a time there
was ...** c'era una volta ....
oncoming [ˈɔnkʌmɪŋ] *adj* (*traffic*) che viene
in senso opposto.
OND *n abbr* (*BRIT.* = *Ordinary National
Diploma*) diploma in materie tecniche
conseguito dopo un corso biennale.

========================= KEYWORD

one [wʌn] *num* uno(a); ~ **hundred and fifty**
centocinquanta; ~ **day** un giorno; **it's** ~
(o'clock) è l'una; **to be** ~ **up on sb** essere
avvantaggiato(a) rispetto a qn; **to be at** ~
(with sb) andare d'accordo (con qn)
♦ *adj* **1** (*sole*) unico(a); **the** ~ **book which**
l'unico libro che; **the** ~ **man who** l'unico
che
2 (*same*) stesso(a); **they came in the** ~
car sono venuti nella stessa macchina
♦ *pron* **1**: **this** ~ questo(a); **that** ~
quello(a); **which** ~ **do you want?** quale

vuole?; **I've already got** ~**/a red** ~ ne ho
già uno/uno rosso; ~ **by** ~ uno per uno
2: ~ **another** l'un l'altro; **to look at** ~
another guardarsi; **to help** ~ **another**
aiutarsi l'un l'altro *or* a vicenda
3 (*impersonal*) si; ~ **never knows** non si
sa mai; **to cut** ~**'s finger** tagliarsi un dito;
to express ~**'s opinion** esprimere la
propria opinione; ~ **needs to eat** bisogna
mangiare.

one-armed bandit [ˈwʌnɑːmd-] *n* slot-
machine *f inv*.
one-day excursion [ˈwʌndeɪ-] *n* (*US*)
biglietto giornaliero di andata e ritorno.
One-hundred share index [ˈwʌnhʌndrəd-]
n indice borsistico del Financial Times.
one-man [ˈwʌnˈmæn] *adj* (*business*)
diretto(a) *etc* da un solo uomo.
one-man band *n suonatore ambulante
con vari strumenti.*
one-off [wʌnˈɔf] (*BRIT col*) *n* fatto
eccezionale ♦ *adj* eccezionale.
one-parent family [ˈwʌnpɛərənt-] *n*
famiglia monogenitore.
one-piece [ˈwʌnpiːs] *adj* (*bathing suit*)
intero(a).
onerous [ˈɔnərəs] *adj* (*task, duty*)
gravoso(a); (*responsibility*) pesante.
oneself [wʌnˈsɛlf] *pron* si; (*after prep*) sé, se
stesso(a); **to do sth (by)** ~ fare qc da sé.
one-shot [wʌnˈʃɔt] *n* (*US*) = **one-off.**
one-sided [wʌnˈsaɪdɪd] *adj* (*decision, view*)
unilaterale; (*judgement, account*) parziale;
(*game, contest*) impari *inv*.
one-time [ˈwʌntaɪm] *adj* ex *inv*.
one-to-one [ˈwʌntəwʌn] *adj* (*relationship*)
univoco(a).
one-upmanship [wʌnˈʌpmənʃɪp] *n*: **the art
of** ~ l'arte *f* di primeggiare.
one-way [ˈwʌnweɪ] *adj* (*street, traffic*) a
senso unico.
ongoing [ˈɔngəʊɪŋ] *adj* in corso; in
attuazione.
onion [ˈʌnjən] *n* cipolla.
on line *adj* (*COMPUT*) on line *inv*, in linea;
(: *switched on*) acceso(a).
onlooker [ˈɔnlʊkə*] *n* spettatore/trice.
only [ˈəʊnlɪ] *adv* solo, soltanto ♦ *adj* solo(a),
unico(a) ♦ *conj* solo che, ma; **an** ~ **child** un
figlio unico; **not** ~ non solo; **I** ~ **took one**
ne ho preso soltanto uno, non ne ho preso
che uno; **I saw her** ~ **yesterday** l'ho vista
appena ieri; **I'd be** ~ **too pleased to help**
sarei proprio felice di essere d'aiuto; **I
would come,** ~ **I'm very busy** verrei
volentieri, solo che sono molto occupato.
ono *abbr* = **or nearest offer;** *see* **near.**

onset ['ɔnsɛt] n inizio; (of winter) arrivo.
onshore ['ɔnʃɔː*] adj (wind) di mare.
onslaught ['ɔnslɔːt] n attacco, assalto.
Ont. abbr (Canada) = Ontario.
on-the-job ['ɔnðə'dʒɔb] adj: ~ **training** addestramento in sede.
onto ['ɔntu] prep su, sopra.
onus ['əunəs] n onere m, peso; **the ~ is upon him to prove it** sta a lui dimostrarlo.
onward(s) ['ɔnwəd(z)] adv (move) in avanti; **from this time** ~ d'ora in poi.
onyx ['ɔnɪks] n onice f.
oops [ups] excl ops! (esprime rincrescimento per un piccolo contrattempo); ~-**a-daisy!** oplà!
ooze [uːz] vi stillare.
opacity [əu'pæsɪtɪ] n opacità.
opal ['əupl] n opale m or f.
opaque [əu'peɪk] adj opaco(a).
OPEC ['əupɛk] n abbr (= Organization of Petroleum-Exporting Countries) O.P.E.C. f.
open ['əupn] adj aperto(a); (road) libero(a); (meeting) pubblico(a); (admiration) evidente, franco(a); (question) insoluto(a); (enemy) dichiarato(a) ♦ vt aprire ♦ vi (eyes, door, debate) aprirsi; (flower) sbocciare; (shop, bank, museum) aprire; (book etc: commence) cominciare; **in the ~ (air)** all'aperto; **the ~ sea** il mare aperto, l'alto mare; ~ **ground** (among trees) radura; (waste ground) terreno non edificato; **to have an ~ mind (on sth)** non avere ancora deciso (su qc).
►**open on to** vt fus (subj: room, door) dare su.
►**open out** vt aprire ♦ vi aprirsi.
►**open up** vt aprire; (blocked road) sgombrare ♦ vi aprirsi.
open-air [əupn'ɛə*] adj all'aperto.
open-and-shut ['əupnən'ʃʌt] adj: ~ **case** caso indubbio.
open day n (BRIT) giornata di apertura al pubblico.
open-ended [əupn'ɛndɪd] adj (fig) aperto(a), senza limiti.
opener ['əupnə*] n (also: **can** ~, **tin** ~) apriscatole m inv.
open-heart [əupn'hɑːt] adj: ~ **surgery** chirurgia a cuore aperto.
opening ['əupnɪŋ] n apertura; (opportunity) occasione f, opportunità f inv; sbocco; (job) posto vacante.
opening night n (THEAT) prima.
open learning n sistema educativo secondo il quale lo studente ha maggior controllo e gestione delle modalità di apprendimento.
openly ['əupnlɪ] adv apertamente.

open-minded [əupn'maɪndɪd] adj che ha la mente aperta.
open-necked ['əupnnɛkt] adj col collo slacciato.
openness ['əupnnɪs] n (frankness) franchezza, sincerità.
open-plan ['əupn'plæn] adj senza pareti divisorie.
open prison n istituto di pena dove viene data maggiore libertà ai detenuti.
open sandwich n canapè m inv.
open shop n fabbrica o ditta dove sono accolti anche operai non iscritti ai sindacati.

La **Open University (OU)**, fondata in Gran Bretagna nel 1969, organizza corsi universitari per corrispondenza, basati anche su lezioni che vengono trasmesse dalla **BBC** per radio e per televisione e su corsi estivi.

---

opera ['ɔpərə] n opera.
opera glasses npl binocolo da teatro.
opera house n opera.
opera singer n cantante m/f d'opera or lirico(a).
operate ['ɔpəreɪt] vt (machine) azionare, far funzionare; (system) usare ♦ vi funzionare; (drug, person) agire; **to ~ on sb (for)** (MED) operare qn (di).
operatic [ɔpə'rætɪk] adj dell'opera, lirico(a).
operating ['ɔpəreɪtɪŋ] adj (COMM: costs etc) di gestione; (MED) operatorio(a).
operating room n (US) = **operating theatre**.
operating system n (COMPUT) sistema m operativo.
operating theatre n (MED) sala operatoria.
operation [ɔpə'reɪʃən] n operazione f; **to be in** ~ (machine) essere in azione or funzionamento; (system) essere in vigore; **to have an** ~ **(for)** (MED) essere operato(a) (di).
operational [ɔpə'reɪʃənl] adj operativo(a); (COMM) di gestione, d'esercizio; (ready for use or action) in attività, in funzione; **when the service is fully** ~ quando il servizio sarà completamente in funzione.
operative ['ɔpərətɪv] adj (measure) operativo(a) ♦ n (in factory) operaio/a; **the** ~ **word** la parola chiave.
operator ['ɔpəreɪtə*] n (of machine) operatore/trice; (TEL) centralinista m/f.
operetta [ɔpə'rɛtə] n operetta.
ophthalmologist [ɔfθæl'mɔlədʒɪst] n

oftalmologo/a.

opinion [ə'pɪnjən] n opinione f, parere m; **in my** ~ secondo me, a mio avviso; **to seek a second** ~ (MED etc) consultarsi con un altro medico etc.

opinionated [ə'pɪnjəneɪtɪd] adj dogmatico(a).

opinion poll n sondaggio di opinioni.

opium ['əupɪəm] n oppio.

opponent [ə'pəunənt] n avversario/a.

opportune ['ɔpətjuːn] adj opportuno(a).

opportunist [ɔpə'tjuːnɪst] n opportunista m/f.

opportunity [ɔpə'tjuːnɪtɪ] n opportunità f inv, occasione f; **to take the** ~ **to do** or **of doing** cogliere l'occasione per fare.

oppose [ə'pəuz] vt opporsi a; ~**d to** contrario(a) a; **as** ~**d to** in contrasto con.

opposing [ə'pəuzɪŋ] adj opposto(a); (team) avversario(a).

opposite ['ɔpəzɪt] adj opposto(a); (house etc) di fronte ♦ adv di fronte, dirimpetto ♦ prep di fronte a ♦ n opposto, contrario; (of word) contrario; "**see** ~ **page**" "vedere pagina a fronte".

opposite number n controparte f, corrispondente m/f.

opposite sex n: **the** ~ l'altro sesso.

opposition [ɔpə'zɪʃən] n opposizione f.

oppress [ə'prɛs] vt opprimere.

oppression [ə'prɛʃən] n oppressione f.

oppressive [ə'prɛsɪv] adj oppressivo(a).

opprobrium [ə'prəubrɪəm] n (formal) obbrobrio.

opt [ɔpt] vi: **to** ~ **for** optare per; **to** ~ **to do** scegliere di fare; **to** ~ **out of** (BRIT: of NHS) scegliere di non far più parte di; (of agreement, arrangement) scegliere di non partecipare a.

optical ['ɔptɪkl] adj ottico(a).

optical character reader/recognition (OCR) n lettore m ottico/lettura ottica di caratteri.

optical fibre n fibra ottica.

optician [ɔp'tɪʃən] n ottico.

optics ['ɔptɪks] n ottica.

optimism ['ɔptɪmɪzəm] n ottimismo.

optimist ['ɔptɪmɪst] n ottimista m/f.

optimistic [ɔptɪ'mɪstɪk] adj ottimistico(a).

optimum ['ɔptɪməm] adj ottimale.

option ['ɔpʃən] n scelta; (SCOL) materia facoltativa; (COMM) opzione f; **to keep one's** ~**s open** (fig) non impegnarsi; **I have no** ~ non ho scelta.

optional ['ɔpʃənl] adj facoltativo(a); (COMM) a scelta; ~ **extra** optional m inv.

opulence ['ɔpjuləns] n opulenza.

opulent ['ɔpjulənt] adj opulento(a).

OR abbr (US) = Oregon.

or [ɔː*] conj o, oppure; (with negative): **he hasn't seen** ~ **heard anything** non ha visto né sentito niente; ~ **else** se no, altrimenti; oppure.

oracle ['ɔrəkl] n oracolo.

oral ['ɔːrəl] adj orale ♦ n esame m orale.

orange ['ɔrɪndʒ] n (fruit) arancia ♦ adj arancione.

orangeade [ɔrɪndʒ'eɪd] n aranciata.

oration [ɔː'reɪʃən] n orazione f.

orator ['ɔrətə*] n oratore/trice.

oratorio [ɔrə'tɔːrɪəu] n oratorio.

orb [ɔːb] n orbe m.

orbit ['ɔːbɪt] n orbita ♦ vt orbitare intorno a; **to be in/go into** ~ **(round)** essere/entrare in orbita (attorno a).

orbital ['ɔːbɪtl] n (also: ~ **motorway**) raccordo anulare.

orchard ['ɔːtʃəd] n frutteto; **apple** ~ meleto.

orchestra ['ɔːkɪstrə] n orchestra; (US: seating) platea.

orchestral [ɔː'kɛstrəl] adj orchestrale; (concert) sinfonico(a).

orchestrate ['ɔːkɪstreɪt] vt (MUS, fig) orchestrare.

orchid ['ɔːkɪd] n orchidea.

ordain [ɔː'deɪn] vt (REL) ordinare; (decide) decretare.

ordeal [ɔː'diːl] n prova, travaglio.

order ['ɔːdə*] n ordine m; (COMM) ordinazione f ♦ vt ordinare; **to** ~ **sb to do** ordinare a qn di fare; **in** ~ in ordine; (of document) in regola; **in** ~ **of size** in ordine di grandezza; **in** ~ **to do** per fare; **in** ~ **that** affinché +sub; **a machine in working** ~ una macchina che funziona bene; **to be out of** ~ (machine, toilets) essere guasto(a); (telephone) essere fuori servizio; **to place an** ~ **for sth with sb** ordinare qc a qn; **to the** ~ **of** (BANKING) all'ordine di; **to be under** ~**s to do sth** avere l'ordine di fare qc; **a point of** ~ una questione di procedura; **to be on** ~ essere stato ordinato; **made to** ~ fatto su commissione; **the lower** ~**s** (pej) i ceti inferiori.

order book n copiacommissioni m inv.

order form n modulo d'ordinazione.

orderly ['ɔːdəlɪ] n (MIL) attendente m ♦ adj (room) in ordine; (mind) metodico(a); (person) ordinato(a), metodico(a).

order number n numero di ordinazione.

ordinal ['ɔːdɪnl] adj (number) ordinale.

ordinary ['ɔːdnrɪ] adj normale, comune; (pej) mediocre ♦ n: **out of the** ~ diverso dal solito, fuori dell'ordinario.

ordinary degree *n* laurea (*con corso di studi di 3 anni*).

Il corso universitario di studi che porta al conferimento del **Bachelor's degree** può avere una durata diversa, a seconda del profitto dello studente. Chi non è interessato a proseguire gli studi oltre tre anni di corso può optare per l'**ordinary degree**; *vedi anche* **honours degree**.

ordinary seaman (OS) *n* (*BRIT*) marinaio semplice.
ordinary shares *npl* azioni *fpl* ordinarie.
ordination [ɔːdɪˈneɪʃən] *n* ordinazione *f*.
ordnance [ˈɔːdnəns] *n* (*MIL: unit*) (reparto di) sussistenza.
Ordnance Survey map *n* (*BRIT*) ≈ carta topografica dell'IGM.
ore [ɔː*] *n* minerale *m* grezzo.
Ore(g). *abbr* (*US*) = Oregon.
organ [ˈɔːgən] *n* organo.
organic [ɔːˈgænɪk] *adj* organico(a).
organism [ˈɔːgənɪzəm] *n* organismo.
organist [ˈɔːgənɪst] *n* organista *m/f*.
organization [ɔːgənaɪˈzeɪʃən] *n* organizzazione *f*.
organization chart *n* organigramma *m*.
organize [ˈɔːgənaɪz] *vt* organizzare; **to get ~d** organizzarsi.
organized crime [ˈɔːgənaɪzd-] *n* criminalità organizzata.
organized labour [ˈɔːgənaɪzd-] *n* manodopera organizzata.
organizer [ˈɔːgənaɪzə*] *n* organizzatore/trice.
orgasm [ˈɔːgæzəm] *n* orgasmo.
orgy [ˈɔːdʒɪ] *n* orgia *f*.
Orient [ˈɔːrɪənt] *n*: **the ~** l'Oriente *m*.
oriental [ɔːrɪˈɛntl] *adj, n* orientale (*m/f*).
orientate [ˈɔːrɪənteɪt] *vt* orientare.
orifice [ˈɔrɪfɪs] *n* orifizio.
origin [ˈɔrɪdʒɪn] *n* origine *f*; **country of ~** paese *m* d'origine.
original [əˈrɪdʒɪnl] *adj* originale; (*earliest*) originario(a) ♦ *n* originale *m*.
originality [ərɪdʒɪˈnælɪtɪ] *n* originalità.
originally [əˈrɪdʒɪnəlɪ] *adv* (*at first*) all'inizio.
originate [əˈrɪdʒɪneɪt] *vi*: **to ~ from** venire da, essere originario(a) di; (*suggestion*) provenire da; **to ~ in** nascere in; (*custom*) avere origine in.
originator [əˈrɪdʒɪneɪtə*] *n* iniziatore/trice.
Orkneys [ˈɔːknɪz] *npl*: **the ~** (*also*: **the Orkney Islands**) le (isole) Orcadi.
ornament [ˈɔːnəmənt] *n* ornamento; (*trinket*) ninnolo.
ornamental [ɔːnəˈmɛntl] *adj* ornamentale.

ornamentation [ɔːnəmɛnˈteɪʃən] *n* decorazione *f*, ornamento.
ornate [ɔːˈneɪt] *adj* molto ornato(a).
ornithologist [ɔːnɪˈθɔlədʒɪst] *n* ornitologo/a.
ornithology [ɔːnɪˈθɔlədʒɪ] *n* ornitologia.
orphan [ˈɔːfn] *n* orfano/a ♦ *vt*: **to be ~ed** diventare orfano.
orphanage [ˈɔːfənɪdʒ] *n* orfanotrofio.
orthodox [ˈɔːθədɔks] *adj* ortodosso(a).
orthopaedic, (*US*) **orthopedic** [ɔːθəˈpiːdɪk] *adj* ortopedico(a).
OS *abbr* (*BRIT*: = *Ordnance Survey*) ≈ IGM *m* (= *Istituto Geografico Militare*); (: *NAUT*) *see* **ordinary seaman**; (: *DRESS*) = **outsize**.
O/S *abbr* = **out of stock**.
Oscar [ˈɔskə*] *n* Oscar *m inv*.
oscillate [ˈɔsɪleɪt] *vi* oscillare.
OSHA *n abbr* (*US*: = *Occupational Safety and Health Administration*) amministrazione per la sicurezza e la salute sul lavoro.
Oslo [ˈɔzləu] *n* Oslo *f*.
ostensible [ɔsˈtɛnsɪbl] *adj* preteso(a); apparente.
ostensibly [ɔsˈtɛnsɪblɪ] *adv* all'apparenza.
ostentation [ɔstɛnˈteɪʃən] *n* ostentazione *f*.
ostentatious [ɔstɛnˈteɪʃəs] *adj* pretenzioso(a); ostentato(a).
osteopath [ˈɔstɪəpæθ] *n* specialista *m/f* di osteopatia.
ostracize [ˈɔstrəsaɪz] *vt* dare l'ostracismo a.
ostrich [ˈɔstrɪtʃ] *n* struzzo.
OT *abbr* (= *Old Testament*) V.T.
OTB *n abbr* (*US*: = *off-track betting*) puntate effettuate fuori dagli ippodromi.
OTE *abbr* (= *on-target earnings*) stipendio compreso le commissioni.
other [ˈʌðə*] *adj* altro(a) ♦ *pron*: **the ~** l'altro(a); **the ~s** gli altri; **the ~ day** l'altro giorno; **some ~ people have still to arrive** (alcuni) altri devono ancora arrivare; **some actor or ~** un certo attore; **somebody or ~** qualcuno; **~ than** altro che; a parte; **the car was none ~ than Roberta's** la macchina era proprio di Roberta.
otherwise [ˈʌðəwaɪz] *adv, conj* altrimenti; **an ~ good piece of work** un lavoro comunque buono.
OTT *abbr* (*col*) = **over the top**; *see* **top**.
otter [ˈɔtə*] *n* lontra *f*.
OU *n abbr* (*BRIT*) *see* **Open University**.
ouch [autʃ] *excl* ohi!, ahi!
ought [ɔːt] *pt* **ought** *aux vb*: **I ~ to do it** dovrei farlo; **this ~ to have been corrected** questo avrebbe dovuto essere corretto; **he ~ to win** dovrebbe vincere; **you ~ to go and see it** dovreste andare a

vederlo, fareste bene ad andarlo a
vedere.
ounce [auns] *n* oncia (= *28.35 g; 16 in a
pound*).
our [auə*] *adj* il(la) nostro(a), *pl* i(le)
nostri(e).
ours [auəz] *pron* il(la) nostro(a), *pl* i(le)
nostri(e).
ourselves [auə'sɛlvz] *pron pl* (*reflexive*) ci;
(*after preposition*) noi; (*emphatic*) noi
stessi(e); **we did it (all) by ~** l'abbiamo
fatto (tutto) da soli.
oust [aust] *vt* cacciare, espellere.

=============================== *KEYWORD*

out [aut] *adv* (*gen*) fuori; **~ here/there** qui/
là fuori; **to speak ~ loud** parlare forte; **to
have a night ~** uscire una sera; **to be ~
and about** *or* (*US*) **around again** essere di
nuovo in piedi; **the boat was 10 km ~** la
barca era a 10 km dalla costa; **the
journey ~** l'andata; **3 days ~ from
Plymouth** a 3 giorni da Plymouth
♦ *adj*: **to be ~** (*gen*) essere fuori;
(*unconscious*) aver perso i sensi; (*style,
singer*) essere fuori moda; **before the
week was ~** prima che la settimana
fosse finita; **to be ~ to do sth** avere
intenzione di fare qc; **he's ~ for all he can
get** sta cercando di trarne il massimo
profitto; **to be ~ in one's calculations**
aver sbagliato i calcoli
♦ **out of** *prep* **1** (*outside, beyond*) fuori di;
to go ~ of the house uscire di casa; **to
look ~ of the window** guardare fuori
dalla finestra
2 (*because of*) per; **~ of pity** per pietà; **~
of boredom** per noia
3 (*origin*) da; **made ~ of wood** (fatto) di
or in legno; **to drink ~ of a cup** bere da
una tazza
4 (*from among*): **~ of 10** su 10
5 (*without*) senza; **~ of petrol** senza
benzina; **it's ~ of stock** (*COMM*) è
esaurito.

outage ['autɪdʒ] *n* (*esp US: power failure*)
interruzione *f or* mancanza di corrente
elettrica.
out-and-out ['autəndaut] *adj* vero(a) e
proprio(a).
outback ['autbæk] *n* zona isolata; (*in
Australia*) interno, entroterra.
outbid, *pt, pp* **outbid** [aut'bɪd] *vt* fare
un'offerta più alta di.
outboard ['autbɔːd] *n*: **~ (motor)** (motore
m) fuoribordo.
outbound ['autbaund] *adj*: **~ (for** *or* **from)** in

partenza (per *or* da).
outbreak ['autbreɪk] *n* scoppio; epidemia.
outbuilding ['autbɪldɪŋ] *n* dipendenza.
outburst ['autbəːst] *n* scoppio.
outcast ['autkɑːst] *n* esule *m/f*; (*socially*)
paria *m inv*.
outclass [aut'klɑːs] *vt* surclassare.
outcome ['autkʌm] *n* esito, risultato.
outcrop ['autkrɒp] *n* affioramento.
outcry ['autkraɪ] *n* protesta, clamore *m*.
outdated [aut'deɪtɪd] *adj* (*custom, clothes*)
fuori moda; (*idea*) sorpassato(a).
outdistance [aut'dɪstəns] *vt* distanziare.
outdo [aut'duː] *vt irreg* sorpassare.
outdoor [aut'dɔː*] *adj* all'aperto.
outdoors [aut'dɔːz] *adv* fuori; all'aria
aperta.
outer ['autə*] *adj* esteriore; **~ suburbs**
estrema periferia.
outer space *n* spazio cosmico.
outfit ['autfɪt] *n* equipaggiamento; (*clothes*)
abito; (*col: organization*) organizzazione *f*.
outfitter ['autfɪtə*] *n* (*BRIT*): **"(gent's) ~s"**
"confezioni da uomo".
outgoing ['autgəuɪŋ] *adj* (*president, tenant*)
uscente; (*means of transport*) in partenza;
(*character*) socievole.
outgoings ['autgəuɪŋz] *npl* (*BRIT: expenses*)
spese *fpl*.
outgrow [aut'grəu] *vt irreg* (*clothes*)
diventare troppo grande per.
outhouse ['authaus] *n* costruzione *f*
annessa.
outing ['autɪŋ] *n* gita; escursione *f*.
outlandish [aut'lændɪʃ] *adj* strano(a).
outlast [aut'lɑːst] *vt* sopravvivere a.
outlaw ['autlɔː] *n* fuorilegge *m/f* ♦ *vt*
(*person*) mettere fuori della legge;
(*practice*) proscrivere.
outlay ['autleɪ] *n* spesa.
outlet ['autlet] *n* (*for liquid etc*) sbocco,
scarico; (*for emotion*) sfogo; (*for goods*)
sbocco, mercato; (*also*: **retail ~**) punto di
vendita; (*US ELEC*) presa di corrente.
outline ['autlaɪn] *n* contorno, profilo;
(*summary*) abbozzo, grandi linee *fpl*.
outlive [aut'lɪv] *vt* sopravvivere a.
outlook ['autluk] *n* prospettiva, vista.
outlying ['autlaɪɪŋ] *adj* periferico(a).
outmanoeuvre, (*US*) **outmaneuver**
[autmə'nuːvə*] *vt* (*rival etc*) superare in
strategia.
outmoded [aut'məudɪd] *adj* passato(a) di
moda; antiquato(a).
outnumber [aut'nʌmbə*] *vt* superare in
numero.
out-of-court [autəv'kɔːt] *adj*
extragiudiziale ♦ *adv* (*settle*) senza

ricorrere al tribunale.

out-of-date [autəv'deɪt] *adj* (*passport, ticket*) scaduto(a); (*theory, idea*) sorpassato(a), superato(a); (*custom*) antiquato(a); (*clothes*) fuori moda.

out-of-the-way ['autəvðə'weɪ] *adj* (*remote*) fuori mano; (*unusual*) originale, insolito(a).

outpatient ['autpeɪʃənt] *n* paziente *m/f* esterno(a).

outpost ['autpəust] *n* avamposto.

outpouring ['autpɔːrɪŋ] *n* (*fig*) torrente *m*.

output ['autput] *n* produzione *f*; (COMPUT) output *m inv* ♦ *vt* emettere.

outrage ['autreɪdʒ] *n* oltraggio; scandalo ♦ *vt* oltraggiare.

outrageous [aut'reɪdʒəs] *adj* oltraggioso(a); scandaloso(a).

outrider ['autraɪdə*] *n* (*on motorcycle*) battistrada *m inv*.

outright *adv* [aut'raɪt] completamente; schiettamente; apertamente; sul colpo ♦ *adj* ['autraɪt] completo(a); schietto(a) e netto(a).

outrun [aut'rʌn] *vt irreg* superare (nella corsa).

outset ['autsɛt] *n* inizio.

outshine [aut'ʃaɪn] *vt irreg* (*fig*) eclissare.

outside [aut'saɪd] *n* esterno, esteriore *m* ♦ *adj* esterno(a), esteriore; (*remote, unlikely*): **an ~ chance** una vaga possibilità ♦ *adv* fuori, all'esterno ♦ *prep* fuori di, all'esterno di; **at the ~** (*fig*) al massimo; **~ left/right** *n* (FOOTBALL) ala sinistra/destra.

outside broadcast *n* (RADIO, TV) trasmissione *f* in esterno.

outside lane *n* (AUT) corsia di sorpasso.

outside line *n* (TEL) linea esterna.

outsider [aut'saɪdə*] *n* (*in race etc*) outsider *m inv*; (*stranger*) straniero/a.

outsize ['autsaɪz] *adj* enorme; (*clothes*) per taglie forti.

outskirts ['autskɜːts] *npl* sobborghi *mpl*.

outsmart [aut'smɑːt] *vt* superare in astuzia.

outspoken [aut'spəukən] *adj* molto franco(a).

outspread ['autsprɛd] *adj* (*wings*) aperto(a), spiegato(a).

outstanding [aut'stændɪŋ] *adj* eccezionale, di rilievo; (*unfinished*) non completo(a); non evaso(a); non regolato(a); **your account is still ~** deve ancora saldare il conto.

outstay [aut'steɪ] *vt*: **to ~ one's welcome** diventare un ospite sgradito.

outstretched [aut'strɛtʃt] *adj* (*hand*)

teso(a); (*body*) disteso(a).

outstrip [aut'strɪp] *vt* (*also fig*) superare.

out-tray ['auttreɪ] *n* raccoglitore *m* per le carte da spedire.

outvote [aut'vəut] *vt*: **to ~ sb (by)** avere la maggioranza rispetto a qn (per); **to ~ sth (by)** respingere qc (per).

outward ['autwəd] *adj* (*sign, appearances*) esteriore; (*journey*) d'andata.

outwardly ['autwədlɪ] *adv* esteriormente; in apparenza.

outweigh [aut'weɪ] *vt* avere maggior peso di.

outwit [aut'wɪt] *vt* superare in astuzia.

oval ['əuvl] *adj*, *n* ovale (*m*).

> L'**Oval Office** è una grande stanza di forma ovale nella **White House**, la Casa Bianca, dove ha sede l'ufficio del Presidente degli Stati Uniti. Spesso il termine è usato per indicare la stessa presidenza degli Stati Uniti.

ovarian [əu'vɛərɪən] *adj* ovarico(a).

ovary ['əuvərɪ] *n* ovaia.

ovation [əu'veɪʃən] *n* ovazione *f*.

oven ['ʌvn] *n* forno.

ovenproof ['ʌvnpruːf] *adj* da forno.

oven-ready ['ʌvnrɛdɪ] *adj* pronto(a) da infornare.

ovenware ['ʌvnwɛə*] *n* vasellame *m* da mettere in forno.

over ['əuvə*] *adv* al di sopra; (*excessively*) molto, troppo ♦ *adj* (*or adv*) (*finished*) finito(a), terminato(a); (*too much*) troppo; (*remaining*) che avanza ♦ *prep* su; sopra; (*above*) al di sopra di; (*on the other side of*) di là di; (*more than*) più di; (*during*) durante; **~ here** qui; **~ there** là; **all ~** (*everywhere*) dappertutto; (*finished*) tutto(a) finito(a); **~ and** ~ (*again*) più e più volte; **~ and above** oltre (a); **to ask sb ~** invitare qn (a passare); **now ~ to our Rome correspondent** diamo ora la linea al nostro corrispondente da Roma; **the world ~** in tutto il mondo; **she's not ~ intelligent** (BRIT) non è troppo intelligente; **they fell out ~ money** litigarono per una questione di denaro.

over... ['əuvə*] *prefix*: **~abundant** sovrabbondante.

overact [əuvər'ækt] *vi* (THEAT) esagerare *or* strafare la propria parte.

overall *adj*, *n* ['əuvərɔːl] *adj* totale ♦ *n* (BRIT) grembiule *m* ♦ *adv* [əuvər'ɔːl] nell'insieme, complessivamente; **~s** *npl* tuta (da lavoro).

overall majority *n* maggioranza assoluta.

overanxious [əuvər'æŋkʃəs] *adj* troppo ansioso(a).

overawe [əuvər'ɔː] *vt* intimidire.

overbalance [əuvə'bæləns] *vi* perdere l'equilibrio.

overbearing [əuvə'bɛərɪŋ] *adj* imperioso(a), prepotente.

overboard ['əuvəbɔːd] *adv* (*NAUT*) fuori bordo, in acqua; **to go ~ for sth** (*fig*) impazzire per qc.

overbook [əuvə'buk] *vt* sovrapprenotare.

overcapitalize [əuvə'kæpɪtəlaɪz] *vt* sovraccapitalizzare.

overcast ['əuvəkɑːst] *adj* coperto(a).

overcharge [əuvə'tʃɑːdʒ] *vt*: **to ~ sb for sth** far pagare troppo caro a qn per qc.

overcoat ['əuvəkəut] *n* soprabito, cappotto.

overcome [əuvə'kʌm] *vt irreg* superare; sopraffare; **~ with grief** sopraffatto(a) dal dolore.

overconfident [əuvə'kɔnfɪdənt] *adj* troppo sicuro(a) (di sé), presuntuoso(a).

overcrowded [əuvə'kraudɪd] *adj* sovraffollato(a).

overcrowding [əuvə'kraudɪŋ] *n* sovraffollamento; (*in bus*) calca.

overdo [əuvə'duː] *vt irreg* esagerare; (*overcook*) cuocere troppo; **to ~ it, to ~ things** (*work too hard*) lavorare troppo.

overdose ['əuvədəus] *n* dose *f* eccessiva.

overdraft ['əuvədrɑːft] *n* scoperto (di conto).

overdrawn [əuvə'drɔːn] *adj* (*account*) scoperto(a).

overdrive ['əuvədraɪv] *n* (*AUT*) overdrive *m inv*.

overdue [əuvə'djuː] *adj* in ritardo; (*recognition*) tardivo(a); (*bill*) insoluto(a); **that change was long ~** quel cambiamento ci voleva da tempo.

overemphasis [əuvər'ɛmfəsɪs] *n*: **~ on sth** importanza eccessiva data a qc.

overemphasize [əuvər'ɛmfəsaɪz] *vt* dare un'importanza eccessiva a.

overestimate [əuvər'ɛstɪmeɪt] *vt* sopravvalutare.

overexcited [əuvərɪk'saɪtɪd] *adj* sovraeccitato(a).

overexertion [əuvərɪg'zəːʃən] *n* logorio (fisico).

overexpose [əuvərɪk'spəuz] *vt* (*PHOT*) sovraesporre.

overflow *vi* [əuvə'fləu] traboccare ♦ *n* ['əuvəfləu] eccesso; (*also*: **~ pipe**) troppopieno.

overfly [əuvə'flaɪ] *vt irreg* sorvolare.

overgenerous [əuvə'dʒənərəs] *adj* troppo generoso(a).

overgrown [əuvə'grəun] *adj* (*garden*) ricoperto(a) di vegetazione; **he's just an ~ schoolboy** è proprio un bambinone.

overhang [əuvə'hæŋ] *irreg vt* sporgere da ♦ *vi* sporgere.

overhaul *vt* [əuvə'hɔːl] revisionare ♦ *n* ['əuvəhɔːl] revisione *f*.

overhead *adv* [əuvə'hɛd] di sopra ♦ *adj* ['əuvəhɛd] aereo(a); (*lighting*) verticale ♦ *n* (*US*) = **overheads**.

overheads ['əuvəhɛdz] *npl* (*BRIT*) spese *fpl* generali.

overhear [əuvə'hɪə*] *vt irreg* sentire (per caso).

overheat [əuvə'hiːt] *vi* surriscaldarsi.

overjoyed [əuvə'dʒɔɪd] *adj* pazzo(a) di gioia.

overkill ['əuvəkɪl] *n* (*fig*) strafare *m*.

overland ['əuvəlænd] *adj, adv* per via di terra.

overlap *vi* [əuvə'læp] sovrapporsi ♦ *n* ['əuvəlæp] sovrapposizione *f*.

overleaf [əuvə'liːf] *adv* a tergo.

overload [əuvə'ləud] *vt* sovraccaricare.

overlook [əuvə'luk] *vt* (*have view of*) dare su; (*miss*) trascurare; (*forgive*) passare sopra a.

overlord ['əuvəlɔːd] *n* capo supremo.

overmanning [əuvə'mænɪŋ] *n* eccedenza di manodopera.

overnight *adv* [əuvə'naɪt] (*happen*) durante la notte; (*fig*) tutto ad un tratto ♦ *adj* ['əuvənaɪt] di notte; fulmineo(a); **he stayed there ~** ci ha passato la notte; **if you travel ~ ...** se viaggia di notte ...; **he'll be away ~** passerà la notte fuori.

overpass ['əuvəpɑːs] *n* cavalcavia *m inv*.

overpay [əuvə'peɪ] *vt*: **to ~ sb by £50** pagare 50 sterline in più a qn.

overplay [əuvə'pleɪ] *vt* dare troppa importanza a; **to ~ one's hand** sopravvalutare la propria posizione.

overpower [əuvə'pauə*] *vt* sopraffare.

overpowering [əuvə'pauərɪŋ] *adj* irresistibile; (*heat, stench*) soffocante.

overproduction ['əuvəprə'dʌkʃən] *n* sovrapproduzione *f*.

overrate [əuvə'reɪt] *vt* sopravvalutare.

overreach [əuvə'riːtʃ] *vt*: **to ~ o.s.** volere strafare.

overreact [əuvəriː'ækt] *vi* reagire in modo esagerato.

override [əuvə'raɪd] *vt* (*irreg: like* **ride**) (*order, objection*) passar sopra a; (*decision*) annullare.

overriding [əuvə'raɪdɪŋ] *adj* preponderante.

overrule [əuvə'ruːl] *vt* (*decision*) annullare; (*claim*) respingere.

overrun [əuvə'rʌn] vt irreg (MIL: country etc) invadere; (time limit etc) superare, andare al di là di ♦ vi protrarsi; **the town is ~ with tourists** la città è invasa dai turisti.

overseas [əuvə'siːz] adv oltremare; (abroad) all'estero ♦ adj (trade) estero(a); (visitor) straniero(a).

oversee [əuvə'siː] vt irreg sorvegliare.

overseer ['əuvəsɪə*] n (in factory) caposquadra m.

overshadow [əuvə'ʃædəu] vt (fig) eclissare.

overshoot [əuvə'ʃuːt] vt irreg superare.

oversight ['əuvəsaɪt] n omissione f, svista; **due to an ~** per una svista.

oversimplify [əuvə'sɪmplɪfaɪ] vt rendere troppo semplice.

oversleep [əuvə'sliːp] vi irreg dormire troppo a lungo.

overspend [əuvə'spɛnd] vi irreg spendere troppo; **we have overspent by 5000 dollars** abbiamo speso 5000 dollari di troppo.

overspill ['əuvəspɪl] n eccedenza di popolazione.

overstaffed [əuvə'stɑːft] adj: **to be ~** avere troppo personale.

overstate [əuvə'steɪt] vt esagerare.

overstatement [əuvə'steɪtmənt] n esagerazione f.

overstay [əuvə'steɪ] vt: **to ~ one's welcome** trattenersi troppo a lungo (come ospite).

overstep [əuvə'stɛp] vt: **to ~ the mark** superare ogni limite.

overstock [əuvə'stɔk] vt sovrapprovvigionare, sovraimmagazzinare.

overstretched [əuvə'strɛtʃt] adj sovraccarico(a); (budget) arrivato(a) al limite.

overstrike n ['əuvəstraɪk] (on printer) sovrapposizione f (di caratteri) ♦ vt irreg [əuvə'straɪk] sovrapporre.

overt [əu'vəːt] adj palese.

overtake [əuvə'teɪk] vt irreg sorpassare.

overtaking [əuvə'teɪkɪŋ] n (AUT) sorpasso.

overtax [əuvə'tæks] vt (ECON) imporre tasse eccessive a, tassare eccessivamente; (fig: strength, patience) mettere alla prova, abusare di; **to ~ o.s.** chiedere troppo alle proprie forze.

overthrow [əuvə'θrəu] vt irreg (government) rovesciare.

overtime ['əuvətaɪm] n (lavoro) straordinario; **to do or work ~** fare lo straordinario.

overtime ban n rifiuto sindacale a fare gli straordinari.

overtone ['əuvətəun] n (also: ~s) sfumatura.

overture ['əuvətʃuə*] n (MUS) ouverture f inv; (fig) approccio.

overturn [əuvə'təːn] vt rovesciare ♦ vi rovesciarsi.

overview ['əuvəvjuː] n visione f d'insieme.

overweight [əuvə'weɪt] adj (person) troppo grasso(a); (luggage) troppo pesante.

overwhelm [əuvə'wɛlm] vt sopraffare; sommergere; schiacciare.

overwhelming [əuvə'wɛlmɪŋ] adj (victory, defeat) schiacciante; (desire) irresistibile; **one's ~ impression is of heat** l'impressione dominante è quella di caldo.

overwhelmingly [əuvə'wɛlmɪŋlɪ] adv in massa.

overwork [əuvə'wəːk] vt far lavorare troppo ♦ vi lavorare troppo, strapazzarsi.

overwrite [əuvə'raɪt] vt (COMPUT) ricoprire.

overwrought [əuvə'rɔːt] adj molto agitato(a).

ovulation [ɔvjuˈleɪʃən] n ovulazione f.

owe [əu] vt dovere; **to ~ sb sth, to ~ sth to sb** dovere qc a qn.

owing to ['əuɪŋtuː] prep a causa di.

owl [aul] n gufo.

own [əun] adj proprio(a) ♦ vt possedere ♦ vi (BRIT): **to ~ to sth** ammettere qc; **to ~ to having done sth** ammettere di aver fatto qc; **a room of my ~** la mia propria camera; **to get one's ~ back** vendicarsi; **on one's ~** tutto(a) solo(a); **can I have it for my (very) ~?** posso averlo tutto per me?; **to come into one's ~** mostrare le proprie qualità.

►**own up** vi confessare.

own brand n (COMM) etichetta propria.

owner ['əunə*] n proprietario/a.

owner-occupier ['əunər'ɔkjupaɪə*] n proprietario/a della casa in cui abita.

ownership ['əunəʃɪp] n possesso; **it's under new ~** ha un nuovo proprietario.

own goal n (also fig) autogol m inv.

ox, pl **oxen** [ɔks, 'ɔksn] n bue m.

Oxbridge ['ɔksbrɪdʒ] n le università di Oxford e/o Cambridge.

> La parola **Oxbridge** deriva dalla fusione dei nomi Ox(ford) e (Cam)bridge e fa riferimento a queste due antiche università e a coloro che le frequentano o le hanno frequentate.

Oxfam ['ɔksfæm] n abbr (BRIT: = Oxford Committee for Famine Relief) organizzazione per aiuti al terzo mondo.

oxide ['ɔksaɪd] *n* ossido.
Oxon. ['ɔksn] *abbr* (*BRIT*: = *Oxoniensis*) = *of Oxford.*
oxtail ['ɔksteɪl] *n*: ~ **soup** minestra di coda di bue.
oxyacetylene ['ɔksɪə'sɛtɪliːn] *adj* ossiacetilenico(a); ~ **burner,** ~ **lamp** cannello ossiacetilenico.
oxygen ['ɔksɪdʒən] *n* ossigeno.
oxygen mask *n* maschera ad ossigeno.
oxygen tent *n* tenda ad ossigeno.
oyster ['ɔɪstə*] *n* ostrica.
oz. *abbr* = **ounce.**
ozone ['əuzəun] *n* ozono.

P p

P, p [piː] *n* (*letter*) P, p *f or m inv*; **P for Peter** ≈ P come Padova.
P *abbr* = **president; prince.**
p *abbr* (= *page*) p; (*BRIT*) = **penny, pence.**
PA *n abbr see* **personal assistant; public address system** ♦ *abbr* (*US*) = **Pennsylvania.**
pa [pɑː] *n* (*col*) papà *m inv*, babbo.
p.a. *abbr* = **per annum.**
PAC *n abbr* (*US*) = **political action committee.**
pace [peɪs] *n* passo; (*speed*) passo; velocità ♦ *vi*: **to ~ up and down** camminare su e giù; **to keep ~ with** camminare di pari passo a; (*events*) tenersi al corrente di; **to put sb through his ~s** (*fig*) mettere qn alla prova; **to set the ~** (*running*) fare l'andatura; (*fig*) dare il la *or* il tono.
pacemaker ['peɪsmeɪkə*] *n* (*MED*) pacemaker *m inv*, stimolatore *m* cardiaco; (*SPORT*) chi fa l'andatura.
pacific [pə'sɪfɪk] *adj* pacifico(a) ♦ *n*: **the P~ (Ocean)** il Pacifico, l'Oceano Pacifico.
pacification [pæsɪfɪ'keɪʃən] *n* pacificazione *f.*
pacifier ['pæsɪfaɪə*] *n* (*US*: *dummy*) succhiotto, ciuccio (*col*).
pacifist ['pæsɪfɪst] *n* pacifista *m/f.*
pacify ['pæsɪfaɪ] *vt* pacificare; (*soothe*) calmare.
pack [pæk] *n* (*packet*) pacco; (*COMM*) confezione *f*; (*US: of cigarettes*) pacchetto; (*of goods*) balla; (*of hounds*) muta; (*of wolves*) branco; (*of thieves etc*) banda; (*of cards*) mazzo ♦ *vt* (*goods*) impaccare, imballare; (*in suitcase etc*) mettere; (*box*)

riempire; (*cram*) stipare, pigiare; (*press down*) tamponare; turare; (*COMPUT*) comprimere, impaccare ♦ *vi*: **to ~ (one's bags)** fare la valigia; **to send sb ~ing** (*col*) spedire via qn.
▶**pack in** (*BRIT col*) *vi* (*watch, car*) guastarsi ♦ *vt* mollare, piantare; ~ **it in!** piantala!
▶**pack off** *vt* (*person*) spedire.
▶**pack up** *vi* (*BRIT col*: *machine*) guastarsi; (: *person*) far fagotto ♦ *vt* (*belongings, clothes*) mettere in una valigia; (*goods, presents*) imballare.
package ['pækɪdʒ] *n* pacco; balla; (*also*: ~ **deal**) pacchetto; forfait *m inv* ♦ *vt* (*goods*) confezionare.
package holiday *n* (*BRIT*) vacanza organizzata.
package tour *n* viaggio organizzato.
packaging ['pækɪdʒɪŋ] *n* confezione *f*, imballo.
packed [pækt] *adj* (*crowded*) affollato(a); ~ **lunch** (*BRIT*) pranzo al sacco.
packer ['pækə*] *n* (*person*) imballatore/ trice.
packet ['pækɪt] *n* pacchetto.
packet switching [-swɪtʃɪŋ] *n* (*COMPUT*) commutazione *f* di pacchetto.
pack ice ['pækaɪs] *n* banchisa.
packing ['pækɪŋ] *n* imballaggio.
packing case *n* cassa da imballaggio.
pact [pækt] *n* patto, accordo; trattato.
pad [pæd] *n* blocco; (*for inking*) tampone *m*; (*col: flat*) appartamentino ♦ *vt* imbottire ♦ *vi*: **to ~ about/in** *etc* camminare/entrare *etc* a passi felpati.
padded cell ['pædɪd-] *n* cella imbottita.
padding ['pædɪŋ] *n* imbottitura; (*fig*) riempitivo.
paddle ['pædl] *n* (*oar*) pagaia ♦ *vi* sguazzare ♦ *vt* (*boat*) fare andare a colpi di pagaia.
paddle steamer *n* battello a ruote.
paddling pool ['pædlɪŋ-] *n* piscina per bambini.
paddock ['pædək] *n* recinto; paddock *m inv.*
paddy ['pædɪ] *n* (*also*: ~ **field**) risaia.
padlock ['pædlɔk] *n* lucchetto ♦ *vt* chiudere con il lucchetto.
padre ['pɑːdrɪ] *n* cappellano.
Padua ['pædjuə] *n* Padova.
paediatrician, (*US*) **pediatrician** [piːdɪə'trɪʃən] *n* pediatra *m/f.*
paediatrics, (*US*) **pediatrics** [piːdɪ'ætrɪks] *n* pediatria.
paedophile, (*US*) **pedophile** ['piːdəufaɪl] *adj*, *n* pedofilo(a).
pagan ['peɪgən] *adj*, *n* pagano(a).
page [peɪdʒ] *n* pagina; (*also*: ~ **boy**) fattorino; (: *at wedding*) paggio ♦ *vt* (*in*

hotel etc) (*far*) chiamare.
pageant ['pædʒənt] *n* spettacolo storico; grande cerimonia.
pageantry ['pædʒəntrɪ] *n* pompa.
page break *n* interruzione *f* di pagina.
pager ['peɪdʒə*] *n* cicalino, cercapersone *m*.
paginate ['pædʒɪneɪt] *vt* impaginare.
pagination [pædʒɪ'neɪʃən] *n* impaginazione *f*.
pagoda [pə'gəudə] *n* pagoda.
paid [peɪd] *pt, pp of* **pay** ♦ *adj* (*work, official*) rimunerato(a); **to put ~ to** (*BRIT*) mettere fine a.
paid-up ['peɪdʌp], (*US*) **paid in** ['peɪdɪn] *adj* (*member*) che ha pagato la sua quota; (*share*) interamente pagato(a); **~ capital** capitale *m* interamente versato.
pail [peɪl] *n* secchio.
pain [peɪn] *n* dolore *m*; **to be in ~** soffrire, aver male; **to have a ~ in** aver male *or* un dolore a; **to take ~s to do** mettercela tutta per fare; **on ~ of death** sotto pena di morte.
pained [peɪnd] *adj* addolorato(a), afflitto(a).
painful ['peɪnful] *adj* doloroso(a), che fa male; (*difficult*) difficile, penoso(a).
painfully ['peɪnfəlɪ] *adv* (*fig: very*) fin troppo.
painkiller ['peɪnkɪlə*] *n* antalgico, antidolorifico.
painstaking ['peɪnzteɪkɪŋ] *adj* sollecito(a).
paint [peɪnt] *n* (*for house etc*) tinta, vernice *f*; (*ART*) colore *m* ♦ *vt* (*ART, walls*) dipingere; (*door etc*) verniciare; **a tin of ~** un barattolo di tinta *or* vernice; **to ~ the door blue** verniciare la porta di azzurro; **to ~ in oils** dipingere a olio.
paintbox ['peɪntbɔks] *n* scatola di colori.
paintbrush ['peɪntbrʌʃ] *n* pennello.
painter ['peɪntə*] *n* (*artist*) pittore *m*; (*decorator*) imbianchino.
painting ['peɪntɪŋ] *n* (*activity: of artist*) pittura; (: *of decorator*) imbiancatura; verniciatura; (*picture*) dipinto, quadro.
paint-stripper ['peɪntstrɪpə*] *n* prodotto sverniciante.
paintwork ['peɪntwɜːk] *n* (*BRIT*) tinta; (: *of car*) vernice *f*.
pair [pɛə*] *n* (*of shoes, gloves etc*) paio; (*of people*) coppia; duo *m inv*; **a ~ of scissors/ trousers** un paio di forbici/pantaloni.
▶**pair off** *vi*: **to ~ off (with sb)** fare coppia (con qn).
pajamas [pə'dʒɑːməz] *npl* (*US*) pigiama *m*.
Pakistan [pɑːkɪ'stɑːn] *n* Pakistan *m*.
Pakistani [pɑːkɪ'stɑːnɪ] *adj, n* pakistano(a).
PAL [pæl] *n abbr* (*TV:* = *phase alternation line*) PAL *m*.

pal [pæl] *n* (*col*) amico/a, compagno/a.
palace ['pæləs] *n* palazzo.
palatable ['pælɪtəbl] *adj* gustoso(a).
palate ['pælɪt] *n* palato.
palatial [pə'leɪʃəl] *adj* sontuoso(a), sfarzoso(a).
palaver [pə'lɑːvə*] *n* chiacchiere *fpl*; storie *fpl*.
pale [peɪl] *adj* pallido(a) ♦ *vi* impallidire ♦ *n*: **to be beyond the ~** aver oltrepassato ogni limite; **to grow *or* turn ~** (*person*) diventare pallido(a), impallidire; **to ~ into insignificance (beside)** perdere d'importanza (nei confronti di); **~ blue** azzurro *or* blu pallido *inv*.
paleness ['peɪlnɪs] *n* pallore *m*.
Palestine ['pælɪstaɪn] *n* Palestina.
Palestinian [pælɪs'tɪnɪən] *adj, n* palestinese (*m/f*).
palette ['pælɪt] *n* tavolozza.
paling ['peɪlɪŋ] *n* (*stake*) palo; (*fence*) palizzata.
palisade [pælɪ'seɪd] *n* palizzata.
pall [pɔːl] *n* (*of smoke*) cappa ♦ *vi*: **to ~ (on)** diventare noioso(a) (a).
pallet ['pælɪt] *n* (*for goods*) paletta.
pallid ['pælɪd] *adj* pallido(a), smorto(a).
pallor ['pælə*] *n* pallore *m*.
pally ['pælɪ] *adj* (*col*) amichevole.
palm [pɑːm] *n* (*ANAT*) palma, palmo; (*also:* **~ tree**) palma ♦ *vt*: **to ~ sth off on sb** (*col*) rifilare qc a qn.
palmist ['pɑːmɪst] *n* chiromante *m/f*.
Palm Sunday *n* Domenica delle Palme.
palpable ['pælpəbl] *adj* palpabile.
palpitation [pælpɪ'teɪʃən] *n* palpitazione *f*; **to have ~s** avere le palpitazioni.
paltry ['pɔːltrɪ] *adj* derisorio(a); insignificante.
pamper ['pæmpə*] *vt* viziare, accarezzare.
pamphlet ['pæmflət] *n* dépliant *m inv*; (*political etc*) volantino, manifestino.
pan [pæn] *n* (*also:* **sauce~**) casseruola; (*also:* **frying ~**) padella ♦ *vi* (*CINE*) fare una panoramica; **to ~ for gold** (lavare le sabbie aurifere per) cercare l'oro.
panacea [pænə'sɪə] *n* panacea.
panache [pə'næʃ] *n* stile *m*.
Panama ['pænəmɑː] *n* Panama *m*.
Panama Canal *n* canale *m* di Panama.
Panamanian [pænə'meɪnɪən] *adj, n* panamense (*m/f*).
pancake ['pænkeɪk] *n* frittella.
Pancake Day *n* (*BRIT*) martedì *m* grasso.
pancake roll *n* crêpe ripiena di verdure alla cinese.
pancreas ['pæŋkrɪəs] *n* pancreas *m inv*.
panda ['pændə] *n* panda *m inv*.

panda car *n* (*BRIT*) auto *f* della polizia.
pandemonium [pændɪ'məʊnɪəm] *n* pandemonio.
pander ['pændə*] *vi*: **to** ~ **to** lusingare; concedere tutto a.
p & h *abbr* (*US*: = *postage and handling*) affrancatura e trasporto.
P & L *abbr* (= *profit and loss*) P.P.
p & p *abbr* (*BRIT*: = *postage and packing*) affrancatura ed imballaggio.
pane [peɪn] *n* vetro.
panel ['pænl] *n* (*of wood, cloth etc*) pannello; (*RADIO, TV*) giuria.
panel game *n* (*BRIT*) quiz *m inv* a squadre.
panelling, (*US*) **paneling** ['pænəlɪŋ] *n* rivestimento a pannelli.
panellist, (*US*) **panelist** ['pænəlɪst] *n* partecipante *m/f* (al quiz, alla tavola rotonda *etc*).
pang [pæŋ] *n*: **to feel** ~**s of remorse** essere torturato(a) dal rimorso; ~**s of hunger** spasimi *mpl* della fame; ~**s of conscience** morsi *mpl* di coscienza.
panhandler ['pænhændlə*] *n* (*US col*) accattone/a.
panic ['pænɪk] *n* panico ♦ *vi* perdere il sangue freddo.
panic buying [-baɪɪŋ] *n* accaparramento (*di generi alimentari etc*).
panicky ['pænɪkɪ] *adj* (*person*) pauroso(a).
panic-stricken ['pænɪkstrɪkən] *adj* (*person*) preso(a) dal panico, in preda al panico; (*look*) terrorizzato(a).
pannier ['pænɪə*] *n* (*on animal*) bisaccia; (*on bicycle*) borsa.
panorama [pænə'rɑːmə] *n* panorama *m*.
panoramic [pænə'ræmɪk] *adj* panoramico(a).
pansy ['pænzɪ] *n* (*BOT*) viola del pensiero, pensée *f inv*; (*col*) femminuccia.
pant [pænt] *vi* ansare.
pantechnicon [pæn'tɛknɪkən] *n* (*BRIT*) grosso furgone *m* per traslochi.
panther ['pænθə*] *n* pantera.
panties ['pæntɪz] *npl* slip *m*, mutandine *fpl*.
pantihose ['pæntɪhəʊz] *n* (*US*) collant *m inv*.
panto ['pæntəʊ] *n* (*BRIT col*) see **pantomime**.
pantomime ['pæntəmaɪm] *n* (*at Christmas*) spettacolo natalizio; (*tecnica*) pantomima.

In Gran Bretagna la **pantomime** (*abbreviata in* **panto**) *è una sorta di libera interpretazione delle favole più conosciute che vengono messe in scena nei teatri durante il periodo natalizio. Gli attori principali sono la dama,* **dame**, *che è un uomo vestito da donna, il protagonista,* **principal boy**, *che è una donna travestita da*

uomo, e il cattivo, **villain**. *È uno spettacolo per tutta la famiglia, che prevede la partecipazione del pubblico.*

pantry ['pæntrɪ] *n* dispensa.
pants [pænts] *npl* (*BRIT*) mutande *fpl*, slip *m*; (*US*: *trousers*) pantaloni *mpl*.
pantsuit ['pæntsuːt] *n* (*US*) completo *m or* tailleur *m inv* pantalone *inv*.
papacy ['peɪpəsɪ] *n* papato.
papal ['peɪpəl] *adj* papale, pontificio(a).
paparazzi [pæpə'rætsi:] *npl* paparazzi *mpl*.
paper ['peɪpə*] *n* carta; (*also*: **wall**~) carta da parati, tappezzeria; (*also*: **news**~) giornale *m*; (*study, article*) saggio; (*exam*) prova scritta ♦ *adj* di carta ♦ *vt* tappezzare; **a piece of** ~ (*odd bit*) un pezzo di carta; (*sheet*) un foglio (di carta); **to put sth down on** ~ mettere qc per iscritto; *see also* **papers**.
paper advance *n* (*on printer*) avanzamento della carta.
paperback ['peɪpəbæk] *n* tascabile *m*; edizione *f* economica ♦ *adj*: ~ **edition** edizione *f* tascabile.
paper bag *n* sacchetto di carta.
paperboy ['peɪpəbɔɪ] *n* (*selling*) strillone *m*; (*delivering*) ragazzo che recapita i giornali.
paper clip *n* graffetta, clip *f inv*.
paper handkerchief *n* fazzolettino di carta.
paper mill *n* cartiera.
paper money *n* cartamoneta, moneta cartacea.
paper profit *n* utile *m* teorico.
papers ['peɪpəz] *npl* (*also*: **identity** ~) carte *fpl*, documenti *mpl*.
paper shop *n* (*BRIT*) giornalaio (*negozio*).
paperweight ['peɪpəweɪt] *n* fermacarte *m inv*.
paperwork ['peɪpəwɜːk] *n* lavoro amministrativo.
papier-mâché ['pæpɪeɪ'mæʃeɪ] *n* cartapesta.
paprika ['pæprɪkə] *n* paprica.
Pap test, Pap smear ['pæp-] *n* (*MED*) pap-test *m inv*.
par [pɑː*] *n* parità, pari *f*; (*GOLF*) norma; **on a** ~ **with** alla pari con; **at/above/below** ~ (*COMM*) alla/sopra la/sotto la pari; **above/below** ~ (*gen, GOLF*) al di sopra/al di sotto della norma; **to feel below** *or* **under** *or* **not up to** ~ non sentirsi in forma.
parable ['pærəbl] *n* parabola (*REL*).
parabola [pə'ræbələ] *n* parabola (*MATH*).
parachute ['pærəʃuːt] *n* paracadute *m inv* ♦ *vi* scendere col paracadute.

parachute jump n lancio col paracadute.
parachutist ['pærəʃuːtɪst] n paracadutista
m/f.
parade [pə'reɪd] n parata; (*inspection*)
rivista, rassegna ♦ vt (*fig*) fare sfoggio di
♦ vi sfilare in parata; **a fashion** ~ (*BRIT*)
una sfilata di moda.
parade ground n piazza d'armi.
paradise ['pærədaɪs] n paradiso.
paradox ['pærədɔks] n paradosso.
paradoxical [pærə'dɔksɪkl] adj paradossale.
paradoxically [pærə'dɔksɪklɪ] adv
paradossalmente.
paraffin ['pærəfɪn] n (*BRIT*): ~ (**oil**)
paraffina; **liquid** ~ olio di paraffina.
paraffin heater n (*BRIT*) stufa al
cherosene.
paraffin lamp n (*BRIT*) lampada al
cherosene.
paragon ['pærəgən] n modello di
perfezione or di virtù.
paragraph ['pærəgrɑːf] n paragrafo; **to
begin a new** ~ andare a capo.
Paraguay ['pærəgwaɪ] n Paraguay m.
Paraguayan [pærə'gwaɪən] adj, n
paraguaiano(a).
parallel ['pærəlɛl] adj (*also COMPUT*)
parallelo(a); (*fig*) analogo(a) ♦ n (*line*)
parallela; (*fig, GEO*) parallelo; ~ (**with** or
to) parallelo(a) (a).
paralysis, pl paralyses [pə'rælɪsɪs, -siːz] n
paralisi f inv.
paralytic [pærə'lɪtɪk] adj paralitico(a); (*BRIT
col: drunk*) ubriaco(a) fradicio(a).
paralyze ['pærəlaɪz] vt paralizzare.
paramedic [pærə'mɛdɪk] n paramedico.
parameter [pə'ræmɪtə*] n parametro.
paramilitary [pærə'mɪlɪtərɪ] adj
paramilitare.
paramount ['pærəmaunt] adj: **of** ~
importance di capitale importanza.
paranoia [pærə'nɔɪə] n paranoia.
paranoid ['pærənɔɪd] adj paranoico(a).
paranormal [pærə'nɔːml] adj paranormale.
paraphernalia [pærəfə'neɪlɪə] n attrezzi mpl,
roba.
paraphrase ['pærəfreɪz] vt parafrasare.
paraplegic [pærə'pliːdʒɪk] n paraplegico(a).
parapsychology [pærəsaɪ'kɔlədʒɪ] n
parapsicologia.
parasite ['pærəsaɪt] n parassita m.
parasol ['pærəsɔl] n parasole m inv.
paratrooper ['pærətruːpə*] n paracadutista
m (*soldato*).
parcel ['pɑːsl] n pacco, pacchetto ♦ vt (*also:*
~ **up**) impaccare.
▶**parcel out** vt spartire.
parcel bomb n (*BRIT*) pacchetto esplosivo.

parcel post n servizio pacchi.
parch [pɑːtʃ] vt riardere.
parched ['pɑːtʃt] adj (*person*) assetato(a).
parchment ['pɑːtʃmənt] n pergamena.
pardon ['pɑːdn] n perdono; grazia ♦ vt
perdonare; (*LAW*) graziare; ~! scusi!; ~
me! mi scusi!; **I beg your** ~! scusi!; (**I beg
your**) ~?, (*US*) ~ **me?** prego?
pare [pɛə*] vt (*BRIT: nails*) tagliarsi; (*: fruit
etc*) sbucciare, pelare.
parent ['pɛərənt] n padre m (or madre f); ~**s**
npl genitori mpl.
parentage ['pɛərəntɪdʒ] n natali mpl; **of
unknown** ~ di genitori sconosciuti.
parental [pə'rɛntl] adj dei genitori.
parent company n società madre
f inv.
parenthesis, pl parentheses [pə'rɛnθɪsɪs,
-siːz] n parentesi f inv; **in parentheses** fra
parentesi.
parenthood ['pɛərənthud] n paternità or
maternità.
parenting ['pɛərəntɪŋ] n mestiere m di
genitore.
Paris ['pærɪs] n Parigi f.
parish ['pærɪʃ] n parrocchia; (*civil*)
≈ municipio ♦ adj parrocchiale.
parish council n (*BRIT*) ≈ consiglio
comunale.
parishioner [pə'rɪʃənə*] n parrocchiano/a.
Parisian [pə'rɪzɪən] adj, n parigino(a).
parity ['pærɪtɪ] n parità.
park [pɑːk] n parco; (*public*) giardino
pubblico ♦ vt, vi parcheggiare.
parka ['pɑːkə] n eskimo.
parking ['pɑːkɪŋ] n parcheggio; "**no** ~"
"sosta vietata".
parking lights npl luci fpl di posizione.
parking lot n (*US*) posteggio, parcheggio.
parking meter n parchimetro.
parking offence n (*BRIT*) infrazione f al
divieto di sosta.
parking place n posto di parcheggio.
parking ticket n multa per sosta vietata.
parking violation n (*US*) = **parking
offence.**
Parkinson's ['pɑːkɪnsənz] n (*also:* ~
disease) morbo di Parkinson.
parkway ['pɑːkweɪ] n (*US*) viale m.
parlance ['pɑːləns] n: **in common/modern**
~ nel gergo or linguaggio comune/
moderno.
parliament ['pɑːləmənt] n parlamento.

Nel Regno Unito il Parlamento, the
Parliament, *è formato da due camere: la*
House of Commons, *e la* **House of Lords.**
Nella House of Commons siedono 650

parlamentari, chiamati **MP**, *eletti per votazione diretta del popolo nelle rispettive circoscrizioni elettorali, le* **constituency**. *Le sessioni del Parlamento sono presiedute e moderate dal presidente della Camera, lo* **Speaker**. *Alla House of Lords, i cui poteri sono più limitati, si accede tramite nomina o carica ereditaria e non per elezione.*

parliamentary [pɑːlə'mɛntərɪ] *adj* parlamentare.

parlour, (*US*) **parlor** ['pɑːlə*] *n* salotto.

parlous ['pɑːləs] *adj* periglioso(a).

Parmesan [pɑːmɪ'zæn] *n* (*also*: ~ **cheese**) parmigiano.

parochial [pə'rəukɪəl] *adj* parrocchiale; (*pej*) provinciale.

parody ['pærədɪ] *n* parodia.

parole [pə'rəul] *n*: **on** ~ in libertà per buona condotta.

paroxysm ['pærəksɪzəm] *n* (*MED*) parossismo; (*of anger, laughter, coughing*) convulso; (*of grief*) attacco.

parquet ['pɑːkeɪ] *n*: ~ **floor(ing)** parquet *m*.

parrot ['pærət] *n* pappagallo.

parrot fashion *adv* in modo pappagallesco.

parry ['pærɪ] *vt* parare.

parsimonious [pɑːsɪ'məunɪəs] *adj* parsimonioso(a).

parsley ['pɑːslɪ] *n* prezzemolo.

parsnip ['pɑːsnɪp] *n* pastinaca.

parson ['pɑːsn] *n* prete *m*; (*Church of England*) parroco.

part [pɑːt] *n* parte *f*; (*of machine*) pezzo; (*THEAT etc*) parte, ruolo; (*MUS*) voce *f*; parte ♦ *adj* in parte ♦ *adv* = **partly** ♦ *vt* separare ♦ *vi* (*people*) separarsi; (*roads*) dividersi; **to take** ~ **in** prendere parte a; **to take sb's** ~ parteggiare per qn, prendere le parti di qn; **on his** ~ da parte sua; **for my** ~ per parte mia; **for the most** ~ in generale; nella maggior parte dei casi; **for the better** ~ **of the day** per la maggior parte della giornata; **to be** ~ **and parcel of** essere parte integrante di; **to take sth in good/bad** ~ prendere bene/male qc; ~ **of speech** (*LING*) parte del discorso.

▶**part with** *vt fus* separarsi da; rinunciare a.

partake [pɑː'teɪk] *vi irreg* (*formal*): **to** ~ **of sth** consumare qc, prendere qc.

part exchange *n* (*BRIT*): **in** ~ in pagamento parziale.

partial ['pɑːʃl] *adj* parziale; **to be** ~ **to** avere un debole per.

partially ['pɑːʃəlɪ] *adv* in parte, parzialmente.

participant [pɑː'tɪsɪpənt] *n*: ~ **(in)** partecipante *m/f* (a).

participate [pɑː'tɪsɪpeɪt] *vi*: **to** ~ **(in)** prendere parte (a), partecipare (a).

participation [pɑːtɪsɪ'peɪʃən] *n* partecipazione *f*.

participle ['pɑːtɪsɪpl] *n* participio.

particle ['pɑːtɪkl] *n* particella.

particular [pə'tɪkjulə*] *adj* particolare; speciale; (*fussy*) difficile; meticoloso(a); ~**s** *npl* particolari *mpl*, dettagli *mpl*; (*information*) informazioni *fpl*; **in** ~ in particolare, particolarmente; **to be very** ~ **about** essere molto pignolo(a) su; **I'm not** ~ per me va bene tutto.

particularly [pə'tɪkjuləlɪ] *adv* particolarmente; in particolare.

parting ['pɑːtɪŋ] *n* separazione *f*; (*BRIT: in hair*) scriminatura ♦ *adj* d'addio; ~ **shot** (*fig*) battuta finale.

partisan [pɑːtɪ'zæn] *n* partigiano/a ♦ *adj* partigiano(a); di parte.

partition [pɑː'tɪʃən] *n* (*POL*) partizione *f*; (*wall*) tramezzo.

partly ['pɑːtlɪ] *adv* parzialmente; in parte.

partner ['pɑːtnə*] *n* (*COMM*) socio/a; (*SPORT*) compagno/a; (*at dance*) cavaliere/dama.

partnership ['pɑːtnəʃɪp] *n* associazione *f*; (*COMM*) società *f inv*; **to go into** ~ **(with)**, **form a** ~ **(with)** mettersi in società (con), associarsi (a).

part payment *n* acconto.

partridge ['pɑːtrɪdʒ] *n* pernice *f*.

part-time ['pɑːt'taɪm] *adj*, *adv* a orario ridotto, part-time (*inv*).

part-timer ['pɑːt'taɪmə*] *n* (*also*: **part-time worker**) lavoratore/trice part-time.

party ['pɑːtɪ] *n* (*POL*) partito; (*team*) squadra; gruppo; (*LAW*) parte *f*; (*celebration*) ricevimento; serata; festa; **dinner** ~ cena; **to give** *or* **throw a** ~ dare una festa *or* un party; **to be a** ~ **to a crime** essere coinvolto in un reato.

party line *n* (*POL*) linea del partito; (*TEL*) duplex *m inv*.

party piece *n*: **to do one's** ~ (*BRIT col*) *esibirsi nel proprio pezzo forte a una festa, cena etc.*

party political broadcast *n* comunicato radiotelevisivo di propaganda.

pass [pɑːs] *vt* (*gen*) passare; (*place*) passare davanti a; (*exam*) passare, superare; (*candidate*) promuovere; (*overtake, surpass*) sorpassare, superare; (*approve*) approvare ♦ *vi* passare; (*SCOL*) essere promosso(a) ♦ *n* (*permit*) lasciapassare *m inv*; permesso; (*in mountains*) passo, gola;

(*SPORT*) passaggio; (*SCOL: also:* ~ **mark**): **to get a** ~ prendere la sufficienza; **to** ~ **for** passare per; **could you** ~ **the vegetables round?** potrebbe far passare i contorni?; **to make a** ~ **at sb** (*col*) fare delle proposte *or* delle avances a qn; **things have come to a pretty** ~ (*BRIT*) ecco a cosa siamo arrivati.
▶**pass away** *vi* morire.
▶**pass by** *vi* passare ♦ *vt* trascurare.
▶**pass down** *vt* (*customs, inheritance*) tramandare, trasmettere.
▶**pass on** *vi* (*die*) spegnersi, mancare ♦ *vt* (*hand on*): **to** ~ **on** (**to**) (*news, information, object*) passare (a); (*cold, illness*) attaccare (a); (*benefits*) trasmettere (a); (*price rises*) riversare (su).
▶**pass out** *vi* svenire; (*BRIT MIL*) uscire dall'accademia.
▶**pass over** *vi* (*die*) spirare ♦ *vt* lasciare da parte.
▶**pass up** *vt* (*opportunity*) lasciarsi sfuggire, perdere.
passable ['pɑːsəbl] *adj* (*road*) praticabile; (*work*) accettabile.
passage ['pæsɪdʒ] *n* (*gen*) passaggio; (*also:* ~**way**) corridoio; (*in book*) brano, passo; (*by boat*) traversata.
passenger ['pæsɪndʒə*] *n* passeggero/a.
passer-by [pɑːsə'baɪ] *n* passante *m/f*.
passing ['pɑːsɪŋ] *adj* (*fig*) fuggevole; **to mention sth in** ~ accennare a qc di sfuggita.
passing place *n* (*AUT*) piazzola (di sosta).
passion ['pæʃən] *n* passione *f*; amore *m*; **to have a** ~ **for sth** aver la passione di *or* per qc.
passionate ['pæʃənɪt] *adj* appassionato(a).
passion fruit *n* frutto della passione.
passion play *n* rappresentazione *f* della Passione di Cristo.
passive ['pæsɪv] *adj* (*also LING*) passivo(a).
passive smoking *n* fumo passivo.
passkey ['pɑːskiː] *n* passe-partout *m inv*.
Passover ['pɑːsəuvə*] *n* Pasqua ebraica.
passport ['pɑːspɔːt] *n* passaporto.
passport control *n* controllo *m* passaporti *inv*.
password ['pɑːswəːd] *n* parola d'ordine.
past [pɑːst] *prep* (*further than*) oltre, di là di; dopo; (*later than*) dopo ♦ *adv*: **to run** ~ passare di corsa; **to walk** ~ passare ♦ *adj* passato(a); (*president etc*) ex *inv* ♦ *n* passato; **quarter/half** ~ **four** le quattro e un quarto/e mezzo; **ten/twenty** ~ **four** le quattro e dieci/venti; **he's** ~ **forty** ha più di quarant'anni; **it's** ~ **midnight** è mezzanotte passata; **for the** ~ **few days**

da qualche giorno; in questi ultimi giorni; **for the** ~ **3 days** negli ultimi 3 giorni; **in the** ~ in *or* nel passato; (*LING*) al passato; **I'm** ~ **caring** non me ne importa più nulla; **to be** ~ **it** (*BRIT col: person*) essere finito(a).
pasta ['pæstə] *n* pasta.
paste [peɪst] *n* (*glue*) colla; (*CULIN*) pâté *m inv*; pasta ♦ *vt* collare; **tomato** ~ concentrato di pomodoro.
pastel ['pæstl] *adj* pastello *inv*.
pasteurized ['pæstəraɪzd] *adj* pastorizzato(a).
pastille ['pæstl] *n* pastiglia.
pastime ['pɑːstaɪm] *n* passatempo.
past master *n* (*BRIT*): **to be a** ~ **at** essere molto esperto(a) in.
pastor ['pɑːstə*] *n* pastore *m*.
pastoral ['pɑːstərl] *adj* pastorale.
pastry ['peɪstrɪ] *n* pasta.
pasture ['pɑːstʃə*] *n* pascolo.
pasty *n* ['pæstɪ] pasticcio di carne ♦ *adj* ['peɪstɪ] pastoso(a); (*complexion*) pallido(a).
pat [pæt] *vt* accarezzare, dare un colpetto (affettuoso) a ♦ *n*: **a** ~ **of butter** un panetto di burro; **to give sb/o.s. a** ~ **on the back** (*fig*) congratularsi *or* compiacersi con qn/se stesso; **he knows it (off)** ~, (*US*) **he has it down** ~ lo conosce *or* sa a menadito.
patch [pætʃ] *n* (*of material*) toppa; (*spot*) macchia; (*of land*) pezzo ♦ *vt* (*clothes*) rattoppare; **a bad** ~ (*BRIT*) un brutto periodo.
▶**patch up** *vt* rappezzare.
patchwork ['pætʃwəːk] *n* patchwork *m*.
patchy ['pætʃɪ] *adj* irregolare.
pate [peɪt] *n*: **a bald** ~ una testa pelata.
pâté ['pæteɪ] *n* pâté *m inv*.
patent ['peɪtnt] *n* brevetto ♦ *vt* brevettare ♦ *adj* patente, manifesto(a).
patent leather *n* cuoio verniciato.
patently ['peɪtntlɪ] *adv* palesemente.
patent medicine *n* specialità *f inv* medicinale.
patent office *n* ufficio brevetti.
paternal [pə'təːnl] *adj* paterno(a).
paternity [pə'təːnɪtɪ] *n* paternità.
paternity suit *n* (*LAW*) causa di riconoscimento della paternità.
path [pɑːθ] *n* sentiero, viottolo; viale *m*; (*fig*) via, strada; (*of planet, missile*) traiettoria.
pathetic [pə'θetɪk] *adj* (*pitiful*) patetico(a); (*very bad*) penoso(a).
pathological [pæθə'lɔdʒɪkl] *adj* patologico(a).

pathologist [pə'θɔlədʒɪst] *n* patologo/a.
pathology [pə'θɔlədʒɪ] *n* patologia.
pathos ['peɪθɔs] *n* pathos *m*.
pathway ['pɑːθweɪ] *n* sentiero, viottolo.
patience ['peɪʃns] *n* pazienza; (*BRIT CARDS*) solitario; **to lose one's** ~ spazientirsi.
patient ['peɪʃnt] *n* paziente *m/f*; malato/a ♦ *adj* paziente; **to be** ~ **with sb** essere paziente *or* aver pazienza con qn.
patiently ['peɪʃntlɪ] *adv* pazientemente.
patio ['pætɪəu] *n* terrazza.
patriot ['peɪtrɪət] *n* patriota *m/f*.
patriotic [pætrɪ'ɔtɪk] *adj* patriottico(a).
patriotism ['pætrɪətɪzəm] *n* patriottismo.
patrol [pə'trəul] *n* pattuglia ♦ *vt* pattugliare; **to be on** ~ fare la ronda; essere in ricognizione; essere in perlustrazione.
patrol boat *n* guardacoste *m inv.*
patrol car *n* autoradio *f inv* (della polizia).
patrolman [pə'trəulmən] *n* (*US*) poliziotto.
patron ['peɪtrən] *n* (*in shop*) cliente *m/f*; (*of charity*) benefattore/trice; ~ **of the arts** mecenate *m/f*.
patronage ['pætrənɪdʒ] *n* patronato.
patronize ['pætrənaɪz] *vt* essere cliente abituale di; (*fig*) trattare con condiscendenza.
patronizing ['pætrənaɪzɪŋ] *adj* condiscendente.
patron saint *n* patrono.
patter ['pætə*] *n* picchiettio; (*sales talk*) propaganda di vendita ♦ *vi* picchiettare.
pattern ['pætən] *n* modello; (*SEWING etc*) modello (di carta), cartamodello; (*design*) disegno, motivo; (*sample*) campione *m*; **behaviour** ~**s** tipi *mpl* di comportamento.
patterned ['pætənd] *adj* a disegni, a motivi; (*material*) fantasia *inv.*
paucity ['pɔːsɪtɪ] *n* scarsità.
paunch [pɔːntʃ] *n* pancione *m.*
pauper ['pɔːpə*] *n* indigente *m/f*; ~**'s grave** fossa comune.
pause [pɔːz] *n* pausa ♦ *vi* fare una pausa, arrestarsi; **to** ~ **for breath** fermarsi un attimo per riprender fiato.
pave [peɪv] *vt* pavimentare; **to** ~ **the way for** aprire la via a.
pavement ['peɪvmənt] *n* (*BRIT*) marciapiede *m*; (*US*) pavimentazione *f* stradale.
pavilion [pə'vɪlɪən] *n* padiglione *m*; tendone *m*; (*SPORT*) edificio annesso ad un campo sportivo.
paving ['peɪvɪŋ] *n* pavimentazione *f.*
paving stone *n* lastra di pietra.
paw [pɔː] *n* zampa ♦ *vt* dare una zampata a; (*subj: person: pej*) palpare.
pawn [pɔːn] *n* pegno; (*CHESS*) pedone *m*; (*fig*) pedina ♦ *vt* dare in pegno.

pawnbroker ['pɔːnbrəukə*] *n* prestatore *m* su pegno.
pawnshop ['pɔːnʃɔp] *n* monte *m* di pietà.
pay [peɪ] *n* (*gen*) paga ♦ *vb* (*pt, pp* **paid** [peɪd]) *vt* pagare; (*be profitable to: also fig*) convenire a ♦ *vi* pagare; (*be profitable*) rendere; **to** ~ **attention** (**to**) fare attenzione (a); **I paid £5 for that record** quel disco l'ho pagato 5 sterline; **how much did you** ~ **for it?** quanto l'ha pagato?; **to** ~ **one's way** pagare la propria parte; (*company*) coprire le spese; **to** ~ **dividends** (*fig*) dare buoni frutti.
▶**pay back** *vt* rimborsare.
▶**pay for** *vt fus* pagare.
▶**pay in** *vt* versare.
▶**pay off** *vt* (*debts*) saldare; (*creditor*) pagare; (*mortgage*) estinguere; (*workers*) licenziare ♦ *vi* (*scheme*) funzionare; (*patience*) dare dei frutti; **to** ~ **sth off in instalments** pagare qc a rate.
▶**pay out** *vt* (*money*) sborsare, tirar fuori; (*rope*) far allentare.
▶**pay up** *vt* saldare.
payable ['peɪəbl] *adj* pagabile; **to make a cheque** ~ **to sb** intestare un assegno a (nome di) qn.
pay award *n* aumento salariale.
pay day *n* giorno di paga.
PAYE *n abbr* (*BRIT*: = *pay as you earn*) *pagamento di imposte tramite ritenute alla fonte.*
payee [peɪ'iː] *n* beneficiario/a.
pay envelope *n* (*US*) busta *f* paga *inv.*
paying ['peɪɪŋ] *adj*: ~ **guest** ospite *m/f* pagante, pensionante *m/f.*
payload ['peɪləud] *n* carico utile.
payment ['peɪmənt] *n* pagamento; **advance** ~ (*part sum*) anticipo, acconto; (*total sum*) pagamento anticipato; **deferred** ~, ~ **by instalments** pagamento dilazionato *or* a rate; **in** ~ **for**, **in** ~ **of** in pagamento di; **on** ~ **of £5** dietro pagamento di 5 sterline.
pay packet *n* (*BRIT*) busta *f* paga *inv.*
payphone ['peɪfəun] *n* cabina telefonica.
payroll ['peɪrəul] *n* ruolo (organico); **to be on a firm's** ~ far parte del personale di una ditta.
pay slip *n* (*BRIT*) foglio *m* paga *inv.*
pay station *n* (*US*) cabina telefonica.
PBS *n abbr* (*US*: = *Public Broadcasting Service*) *servizio che collabora alla realizzazione di programmi per la rete televisiva nazionale.*
PBX *abbr* (= *private branch exchange*) *sistema telefonico con centralino.*
PC *n abbr see* **personal computer**; (*BRIT*) *see*

police constable ♦ abbr (BRIT) = Privy
Councillor **♦** adj abbr = politically correct.
pc abbr = per cent; (= postcard) C.P.
p/c abbr = petty cash.
PCB n abbr see printed circuit board.
pcm abbr = per calendar month.
PD n abbr (US) = police department.
pd abbr = paid.
PDQ abbr (col) = pretty damn quick.
PDSA n abbr (BRIT: = People's Dispensary for
Sick Animals) assistenza veterinaria
gratuita.
PDT abbr (US: = Pacific Daylight Time) ora
legale del Pacifico.
PE n abbr (= physical education) ed. fisica
♦ abbr (Canada) = Prince Edward Island.
pea [piː] n pisello.
peace [piːs] n pace f; (calm) calma,
tranquillità; **to be at ~ with sb/sth** essere
in pace con qn/qc; **to keep the ~** (subj:
policeman) mantenere l'ordine pubblico;
(: citizen) rispettare l'ordine pubblico.
peaceable ['piːsəbl] adj pacifico(a).
peaceful ['piːsful] adj pacifico(a), calmo(a).
peacekeeping ['piːskiːpɪŋ] n mantenimento
della pace; **~ force** forza di pace.
peace offering n (fig) dono in segno di
riconciliazione.
peach [piːtʃ] n pesca.
peacock ['piːkɔk] n pavone m.
peak [piːk] n (of mountain) cima, vetta;
(mountain itself) picco; (fig) massimo; (: of
career) acme f.
peak-hour ['piːkauə*] adj (traffic etc) delle
ore di punta.
peak hours npl ore fpl di punta.
peak period n periodo di punta.
peak rate n tariffa massima.
peaky ['piːkɪ] adj (BRIT col) sbattuto(a).
peal [piːl] n (of bells) scampanio, carillon m
inv; **~s of laughter** scoppi mpl di risa.
peanut ['piːnʌt] n arachide f, nocciolina
americana.
peanut butter n burro di arachidi.
pear [pɛə*] n pera.
pearl [pɜːl] n perla.
peasant ['pɛznt] n contadino/a.
peat [piːt] n torba.
pebble ['pɛbl] n ciottolo.
peck [pɛk] vt (also: ~ at) beccare; (: food)
mangiucchiare **♦** n colpo di becco; (kiss)
bacetto.
pecking order ['pɛkɪŋ-] n (fig) ordine m
gerarchico.
peckish ['pɛkɪʃ] adj (BRIT col): **I feel ~** ho un
languorino.
peculiar [pɪ'kjuːlɪə*] adj strano(a),
bizzarro(a); (particular: importance,

qualities) particolare; **~ to** tipico(a) di,
caratteristico(a) di.
peculiarity [pɪkjuːlɪ'ærɪtɪ] n peculiarità f inv;
(oddity) bizzarria.
pecuniary [pɪ'kjuːnɪərɪ] adj pecuniario(a).
pedal ['pɛdl] n pedale m **♦** vi pedalare.
pedal bin n (BRIT) pattumiera a pedale.
pedantic [pɪ'dæntɪk] adj pedantesco(a).
peddle ['pɛdl] vt (goods) andare in giro a
vendere; (drugs) spacciare; (gossip)
mettere in giro.
peddler ['pɛdlə*] n venditore m ambulante.
pedestal ['pɛdəstl] n piedestallo.
pedestrian [pɪ'dɛstrɪən] n pedone/a **♦** adj
pedonale; (fig) prosaico(a), pedestre.
pedestrian crossing n (BRIT) passaggio
pedonale.
pedestrian precinct n (BRIT) zona
pedonale.
pediatrics [piːdɪ'ætrɪks] n (US)
= paediatrics.
pedigree ['pɛdɪgriː] n stirpe f; (of animal)
pedigree m inv **♦** cpd (animal) di razza.
pedlar ['pɛdlə*] n = peddler.
pee [piː] vi (col) pisciare.
peek [piːk] vi guardare furtivamente.
peel [piːl] n buccia; (of orange, lemon)
scorza **♦** vt sbucciare **♦** vi (paint etc)
staccarsi.
▶**peel back** vt togliere, levare.
peeler [piːlə*] n: **potato ~** sbucciapatate m
inv.
peelings ['piːlɪŋz] npl bucce fpl.
peep [piːp] n (BRIT: look) sguardo furtivo,
sbirciata; (sound) pigolio **♦** vi (BRIT)
guardare furtivamente.
▶**peep out** vi (BRIT) mostrarsi
furtivamente.
peephole ['piːphəul] n spioncino.
peer [pɪə*] vi: **to ~ at** scrutare **♦** n (noble)
pari m inv; (equal) pari m/f inv, uguale m/f.
peerage ['pɪərɪdʒ] n dignità di pari; pari
mpl.
peerless ['pɪəlɪs] adj impareggiabile, senza
pari.
peeved [piːvd] adj stizzito(a).
peevish ['piːvɪʃ] adj stizzoso(a).
peg [pɛg] n (tent ~) picchetto; (for coat etc)
attaccapanni m inv; (BRIT: also: clothes ~)
molletta **♦** vt (clothes) appendere con le
mollette; (BRIT: groundsheet) fissare con i
picchetti; (fig: prices, wages) fissare,
stabilizzare; **off the ~** confezionato(a).
pejorative [pɪ'dʒɔrətɪv] adj peggiorativo(a).
Pekin [piː'kɪn], **Peking** [piː'kɪŋ] n Pechino f.
pekin(g)ese [piːkɪ'niːz] n pechinese m.
pelican ['pɛlɪkən] n pellicano.
pelican crossing n (BRIT AUT)

attraversamento pedonale con semaforo a controllo manuale.

pellet ['pɛlɪt] *n* pallottola, pallina.

pell-mell ['pɛl'mɛl] *adv* disordinatamente, alla rinfusa.

pelmet ['pɛlmɪt] *n* mantovana; cassonetto.

pelt [pɛlt] *vt*: **to ~ sb (with)** bombardare qn (con) ♦ *vi* (*rain*) piovere a dirotto ♦ *n* pelle *f*.

pelvis ['pɛlvɪs] *n* pelvi *f inv*, bacino.

pen [pɛn] *n* penna; (*for sheep*) recinto; (*US col: prison*) galera; **to put ~ to paper** prendere la penna in mano.

penal ['piːnl] *adj* penale.

penalize ['piːnəlaɪz] *vt* punire; (*SPORT*) penalizzare; (*fig*) svantaggiare.

penal servitude [-'səːvɪtjuːd] *n* lavori *mpl* forzati.

penalty ['pɛnltɪ] *n* penalità *f inv*; sanzione *f* penale; (*fine*) ammenda; (*SPORT*) penalizzazione *f*; (*FOOTBALL: also:* ~ **kick**) calcio di rigore.

penalty area *n* (*BRIT SPORT*) area di rigore.

penalty clause *n* penale *f*.

penalty kick *n* (*FOOTBALL*) calcio di rigore.

penalty shoot-out [-'ʃuːtaut] *n* (*FOOTBALL*) rigori *mpl*; **to beat a team in a ~** battere una squadra ai rigori.

penance ['pɛnəns] *n* penitenza.

pence [pɛns] *npl* (*BRIT*) of **penny**.

penchant ['pɑ̃ːʃɑ̃ːŋ] *n* debole *m*.

pencil ['pɛnsl] *n* matita ♦ *vt* (*also:* ~ **in**) scrivere a matita.

pencil case *n* astuccio per matite.

pencil sharpener *n* temperamatite *m inv*.

pendant ['pɛndnt] *n* pendaglio.

pending ['pɛndɪŋ] *prep* in attesa di ♦ *adj* in sospeso.

pendulum ['pɛndjuləm] *n* pendolo.

penetrate ['pɛnɪtreɪt] *vt* penetrare.

penetrating ['pɛnɪtreɪtɪŋ] *adj* penetrante.

penetration [pɛnɪ'treɪʃən] *n* penetrazione *f*.

penfriend ['pɛnfrɛnd] *n* (*BRIT*) corrispondente *m/f*.

penguin ['pɛŋgwɪn] *n* pinguino.

penicillin [pɛnɪ'sɪlɪn] *n* penicillina.

peninsula [pə'nɪnsjulə] *n* penisola.

penis ['piːnɪs] *n* pene *m*.

penitence ['pɛnɪtns] *n* penitenza.

penitent ['pɛnɪtnt] *adj* penitente.

penitentiary [pɛnɪ'tɛnʃərɪ] *n* (*US*) carcere *m*.

penknife ['pɛnnaɪf] *n* temperino.

Penn(a). *abbr* (*US*) = *Pennsylvania*.

pen name *n* pseudonimo.

pennant ['pɛnənt] *n* banderuola.

penniless ['pɛnɪlɪs] *adj* senza un soldo.

Pennines ['pɛnaɪnz] *npl*: **the ~** i Pennini.

penny, *pl* **pennies** *or* **pence** ['pɛnɪ, 'pɛnɪz, pɛns] *n* penny *m* (*pl* pence); (*US*) centesimo.

penpal ['pɛnpæl] *n* corrispondente *m/f*.

penpusher ['pɛnpuʃə*] *n* (*pej*) scribacchino/a.

pension ['pɛnʃən] *n* pensione *f*.

▶**pension off** *vt* mandare in pensione.

pensionable ['pɛnʃənəbl] *adj* (*person*) che ha diritto a una pensione, pensionabile; (*age*) pensionabile.

pensioner ['pɛnʃənə*] *n* (*BRIT*) pensionato/a.

pension fund *n* fondo pensioni.

pensive ['pɛnsɪv] *adj* pensoso(a).

pentagon ['pɛntəgən] *n* pentagono; **the P~** (*US POL*) il Pentagono.

---

*Il **Pentagon** è un edificio a pianta pentagonale che si trova ad Arlington, in Virginia, nel quale si trovano gli uffici del Ministero della Difesa degli Stati Uniti. Il termine Pentagon è usato anche per indicare la dirigenza militare del paese.*

Pentecost ['pɛntɪkɔst] *n* Pentecoste *f*.

penthouse ['pɛnthaus] *n* appartamento (di lusso) nell'attico.

pent-up ['pɛntʌp] *adj* (*feelings*) represso(a).

penultimate [pɪ'nʌltɪmət] *adj* penultimo(a).

penury ['pɛnjurɪ] *n* indigenza.

people ['piːpl] *npl* gente *f*; persone *fpl*; (*citizens*) popolo ♦ *n* (*nation, race*) popolo ♦ *vt* popolare; **old ~** i vecchi; **young ~** i giovani; **~ at large** il grande pubblico; **a man of the ~** un uomo del popolo; **4/ several ~ came** 4/parecchie persone sono venute; **the room was full of ~** la stanza era piena di gente; **~ say that ...** si dice *or* la gente dice che ....

PEP [pɛp] *n* = **personal equity plan**.

pep [pɛp] *n* (*col*) dinamismo.

▶**pep up** *vt* vivacizzare; (*food*) rendere più gustoso(a).

pepper ['pɛpə*] *n* pepe *m*; (*vegetable*) peperone *m* ♦ *vt* pepare.

peppermint ['pɛpəmɪnt] *n* (*plant*) menta peperita; (*sweet*) pasticca di menta.

pepperoni [pɛpə'rəunɪ] *n* salsiccia piccante.

pepperpot ['pɛpəpɔt] *n* pepaiola.

peptalk ['pɛptɔːk] *n* (*col*) discorso di incoraggiamento.

per [pəː*] *prep* per; a; **~ hour** all'ora; **~ kilo** *etc* il chilo *etc*; **~ day** al giorno; **~ week** alla settimana; **~ person** a testa, a *or* per persona; **as ~ your instructions** secondo le vostre istruzioni.

per annum *adv* all'anno.

per capita *adj, adv* pro capite.

perceive [pə'siːv] *vt* percepire; (*notice*) accorgersi di.

per cent *adv* per cento; **a 20 ~ discount** uno sconto del 20 per cento.

percentage [pə'sɛntɪdʒ] *n* percentuale *f*; **on a ~ basis** a percentuale.

percentage point *n* punto percentuale.

perceptible [pə'sɛptɪbl] *adj* percettibile.

perception [pə'sɛpʃən] *n* percezione *f*; sensibilità; perspicacia.

perceptive [pə'sɛptɪv] *adj* percettivo(a); perspicace.

perch [pəːtʃ] *n* (*fish*) pesce *m* persico; (*for bird*) sostegno, ramo ♦ *vi* appollaiarsi.

percolate ['pəːkəleɪt] *vt* filtrare.

percolator ['pəːkəleɪtə*] *n* caffettiera a pressione; caffettiera elettrica.

percussion [pə'kʌʃən] *n* percussione *f*; (*MUS*) strumenti *mpl* a percussione.

peremptory [pə'rɛmptərɪ] *adj* perentorio(a).

perennial [pə'rɛnɪəl] *adj* perenne ♦ *n* pianta perenne.

perfect *adj, n* ['pəːfɪkt] *adj* perfetto(a) ♦ *n* (*also:* ~ **tense**) perfetto, passato prossimo ♦ *vt* [pə'fɛkt] perfezionare; mettere a punto; **he's a ~ stranger to me** mi è completamente sconosciuto.

perfection [pə'fɛkʃən] *n* perfezione *f*.

perfectionist [pə'fɛkʃənɪst] *n* perfezionista *m/f*.

perfectly ['pəːfɪktlɪ] *adv* perfettamente; **I'm ~ happy with the situation** sono completamente soddisfatta della situazione; **you know ~ well** sa benissimo.

perforate ['pəːfəreɪt] *vt* perforare.

perforated ulcer ['pəːfəreɪtɪd-] *n* (*MED*) ulcera perforata.

perforation [pəːfə'reɪʃən] *n* perforazione *f*; (*line of holes*) dentellatura.

perform [pə'fɔːm] *vt* (*carry out*) eseguire, fare; (*symphony etc*) suonare; (*play, ballet*) dare; (*opera*) fare ♦ *vi* suonare; recitare.

performance [pə'fɔːməns] *n* esecuzione *f*; (*at theatre etc*) rappresentazione *f*, spettacolo; (*of an artist*) interpretazione *f*; (*of player etc*) performance *f*; (*of car, engine*) prestazione *f*; **the team put up a good ~** la squadra ha giocato una bella partita.

performer [pə'fɔːmə*] *n* artista *m/f*.

performing [pə'fɔːmɪŋ] *adj* (*animal*) ammaestrato(a).

performing arts *npl*: **the ~** le arti dello spettacolo.

perfume ['pəːfjuːm] *n* profumo ♦ *vt* profumare.

perfunctory [pə'fʌŋktərɪ] *adj* superficiale, per la forma.

perhaps [pə'hæps] *adv* forse; **~ he'll come** forse verrà, può darsi che venga; **~ so/ not** forse sì/no, può darsi di sì/di no.

peril ['pɛrɪl] *n* pericolo.

perilous ['pɛrɪləs] *adj* pericoloso(a).

perilously ['pɛrɪləslɪ] *adv*: **they came ~ close to being caught** sono stati a un pelo dall'esser presi.

perimeter [pə'rɪmɪtə*] *n* perimetro.

perimeter wall *n* muro di cinta.

period ['pɪərɪəd] *n* periodo; (*HISTORY*) epoca; (*SCOL*) lezione *f*; (*full stop*) punto; (*US FOOTBALL*) tempo; (*MED*) mestruazioni *fpl* ♦ *adj* (*costume, furniture*) d'epoca; **for a ~ of three weeks** per un periodo di *or* per la durata di tre settimane; **the holiday ~** (*BRIT*) il periodo delle vacanze.

periodic [pɪərɪ'ɔdɪk] *adj* periodico(a).

periodical [pɪərɪ'ɔdɪkl] *adj* periodico(a) ♦ *n* periodico.

periodically [pɪərɪ'ɔdɪklɪ] *adv* periodicamente.

period pains *npl* (*BRIT*) dolori *mpl* mestruali.

peripatetic [pɛrɪpə'tɛtɪk] *adj* (*salesman*) ambulante; (*BRIT: teacher*) peripatetico(a).

peripheral [pə'rɪfərəl] *adj* periferico(a) ♦ *n* (*COMPUT*) unità *f inv* periferica.

periphery [pə'rɪfərɪ] *n* periferia.

periscope ['pɛrɪskəup] *n* periscopio.

perish ['pɛrɪʃ] *vi* perire, morire; (*decay*) deteriorarsi.

perishable ['pɛrɪʃəbl] *adj* deperibile.

perishables ['pɛrɪʃəblz] *npl* merci *fpl* deperibili.

perishing ['pɛrɪʃɪŋ] *adj* (*BRIT col*): **it's ~ (cold)** fa un freddo da morire.

peritonitis [pɛrɪtə'naɪtɪs] *n* peritonite *f*.

perjure ['pəːdʒə*] *vt*: **to ~ o.s.** spergiurare.

perjury ['pəːdʒərɪ] *n* (*LAW: in court*) falso giuramento; (*breach of oath*) spergiuro.

perk [pəːk] *n* vantaggio.

▶**perk up** *vi* (*cheer up*) rianimarsi.

perky ['pəːkɪ] *adj* (*cheerful*) vivace, allegro(a).

perm [pəːm] *n* (*for hair*) permanente *f* ♦ *vt*: **to have one's hair ~ed** farsi fare la permanente.

permanence ['pəːmənəns] *n* permanenza.

permanent ['pəːmənənt] *adj* permanente; (*job, position*) fisso(a); (*dye, ink*) indelebile; **~ address** residenza fissa; **I'm not ~ here** non sono fisso qui.

permanently ['pəːmənəntlɪ] *adv*

definitivamente.
permeable ['pɔːmɪəbl] *adj* permeabile.
permeate ['pɔːmɪeɪt] *vi* penetrare ♦ *vt* permeare.
permissible [pɔ'mɪsɪbl] *adj* permissibile, ammissibile.
permission [pɔ'mɪʃən] *n* permesso; **to give sb ~ to do sth** dare a qn il permesso di fare qc.
permissive [pɔ'mɪsɪv] *adj* tollerante; **the ~ society** la società permissiva.
permit *n* ['pɔːmɪt] permesso; (*entrance pass*) lasciapassare *m* ♦ *vt*, *vi* [pɔ'mɪt] permettere; **fishing ~** licenza di pesca; **to ~ sb to do** permettere a qn di fare, dare il permesso a qn di fare; **weather ~ting** tempo permettendo.
permutation [pɔːmju'teɪʃən] *n* permutazione *f.*
pernicious [pɔː'nɪʃəs] *adj* pernicioso(a), nocivo(a).
pernickety [pɔ'nɪkɪtɪ] *adj* (*col: person*) pignolo(a); (: *task*) da certosino.
perpendicular [pɔːpən'dɪkjulə*] *adj*, *n* perpendicolare (*f*).
perpetrate ['pɔːpɪtreɪt] *vt* perpetrare, commettere.
perpetual [pɔ'pɛtjuəl] *adj* perpetuo(a).
perpetuate [pɔ'pɛtjueɪt] *vt* perpetuare.
perpetuity [pɔːpɪ'tjuːɪtɪ] *n*: **in ~** in perpetuo.
perplex [pɔ'plɛks] *vt* lasciare perplesso(a).
perplexing [pɔ'plɛksɪŋ] *adj* che lascia perplesso(a).
perquisites ['pɔːkwɪzɪts] *npl* (*also*: **perks**) benefici *mpl* collaterali.
persecute ['pɔːsɪkjuːt] *vt* perseguitare.
persecution [pɔːsɪ'kjuːʃən] *n* persecuzione *f.*
perseverance [pɔːsɪ'vɪərəns] *n* perseveranza.
persevere [pɔːsɪ'vɪə*] *vi* perseverare.
Persia ['pɔːʃə] *n* Persia.
Persian ['pɔːʃən] *adj* persiano(a) ♦ *n* (*LING*) persiano; **the (~) Gulf** il Golfo Persico.
Persian cat *n* gatto persiano.
persist [pɔ'sɪst] *vi*: **to ~ (in doing)** persistere (nel fare); ostinarsi (a fare).
persistence [pɔ'sɪstəns] *n* persistenza; ostinazione *f.*
persistent [pɔ'sɪstənt] *adj* persistente; ostinato(a); (*lateness, rain*) continuo(a); **~ offender** (*LAW*) delinquente *m/f* abituale.
persnickety [pɔ'snɪkɪtɪ] *adj* (*US col*) = **pernickety**.
person ['pɔːsn] *n* persona; **in ~** di *or* in persona, personalmente; **on** *or* **about**

one's ~ (*weapon*) su di sé; (*money*) con sé; **a ~ to ~ call** (*TEL*) una chiamata con preavviso.
personable ['pɔːsnəbl] *adj* di bell'aspetto.
personal ['pɔːsnl] *adj* personale; individuale; **~ belongings, ~ effects** oggetti *mpl* d'uso personale; **a ~ interview** un incontro privato.
personal allowance *n* (*TAX*) quota del reddito non imponibile.
personal assistant (PA) *n* segretaria personale.
personal call *n* (*TEL*) chiamata con preavviso.
personal column *n* messaggi *mpl* personali.
personal computer (PC) *n* personal computer *m inv.*
personal details *npl* dati *mpl* personali.
personal equity plan *n* (*FINANCE*) *fondo di investimento azionario con agevolazioni fiscali destinato al piccolo risparmiatore.*
personal identification number (PIN) *n* (*COMPUT, BANKING*) numero di codice segreto.
personality [pɔːsə'nælɪtɪ] *n* personalità *f inv.*
personally ['pɔːsnəlɪ] *adv* personalmente.
personal organizer *n* agenda; (*electronic*) agenda elettronica.
personal property *n* beni *mpl* personali.
personal stereo *n* walkman ® *m inv.*
personify [pɔː'sɔnɪfaɪ] *vt* personificare.
personnel [pɔːsə'nɛl] *n* personale *m.*
personnel department *n* ufficio del personale.
personnel manager *n* direttore/trice del personale.
perspective [pɔ'spɛktɪv] *n* prospettiva; **to get sth into ~** ridimensionare qc.
Perspex ® ['pɔːspɛks] *n* (*BRIT*) *tipo di resina termoplastica.*
perspicacity [pɔːspɪ'kæsɪtɪ] *n* perspicacia.
perspiration [pɔːspɪ'reɪʃən] *n* traspirazione *f*, sudore *m.*
perspire [pɔ'spaɪə*] *vi* traspirare.
persuade [pɔ'sweɪd] *vt*: **to ~ sb to do sth** persuadere qn a fare qc; **to ~ sb of sth/ that** persuadere qn di qc/che.
persuasion [pɔ'sweɪʒən] *n* persuasione *f*; (*creed*) convinzione *f*, credo.
persuasive [pɔ'sweɪsɪv] *adj* persuasivo(a).
pert [pɔːt] *adj* (*bold*) sfacciato(a), impertinente; (*hat*) spiritoso(a).
pertaining [pɔː'teɪnɪŋ]: **~ to** *prep* che riguarda.
pertinent ['pɔːtɪnənt] *adj* pertinente.
perturb [pɔ'tɔːb] *vt* turbare.

perturbing [pə'tə:bɪŋ] *adj* inquietante.
Peru [pə'ru:] *n* Perù *m*.
perusal [pə'ru:zl] *n* attenta lettura.
Peruvian [pə'ru:vjən] *adj, n* peruviano(a).
pervade [pə'veɪd] *vt* pervadere.
pervasive [pə:'veɪsɪv] *adj* (*smell*)
penetrante; (*influence*) dilagante; (*gloom*,
feelings) diffuso(a).
perverse [pə'və:s] *adj* perverso(a).
perversion [pə'və:ʃən] *n* pervertimento,
perversione *f*.
perversity [pə'və:sɪtɪ] *n* perversità.
pervert *n* ['pə:və:t] pervertito/a ♦ *vt*
[pə'və:t] pervertire.
pessimism ['pɛsɪmɪzəm] *n* pessimismo.
pessimist ['pɛsɪmɪst] *n* pessimista *m/f*.
pessimistic [pɛsɪ'mɪstɪk] *adj*
pessimistico(a).
pest [pɛst] *n* animale *m* (*or* insetto)
pestifero; (*fig*) peste *f*.
pest control *n* disinfestazione *f*.
pester ['pɛstə*] *vt* tormentare, molestare.
pesticide ['pɛstɪsaɪd] *n* pesticida *m*.
pestilence ['pɛstɪləns] *n* pestilenza.
pestle ['pɛsl] *n* pestello.
pet [pɛt] *n* animale *m* domestico; (*favourite*)
favorito/a ♦ *vt* accarezzare ♦ *vi* (*col*) fare
il petting; ~ **lion** *etc* leone *m etc*
ammaestrato.
petal ['pɛtl] *n* petalo.
peter ['pi:tə*]: **to ~ out** *vi* esaurirsi,
estinguersi.
petite [pə'ti:t] *adj* piccolo(a) e
aggraziato(a).
petition [pə'tɪʃən] *n* petizione *f* ♦ *vi*
richiedere; **to ~ for divorce** presentare
un'istanza di divorzio.
pet name *n* (*BRIT*) nomignolo.
petrified ['pɛtrɪfaɪd] *adj* (*fig*) morto(a) di
paura.
petrify ['pɛtrɪfaɪ] *vt* pietrificare; (*fig*)
terrorizzare.
petrochemical [pɛtrə'kɛmɪkl] *adj*
petrolchimico(a).
petrodollars ['pɛtrəudɔləz] *npl* petrodollari
mpl.
petrol ['pɛtrəl] *n* (*BRIT*) benzina.
petrol bomb *n* (*BRIT*) (bottiglia) molotov
f inv.
petrol can *n* (*BRIT*) tanica per benzina.
petrol engine *n* (*BRIT*) motore *m* a benzina.
petroleum [pə'trəuliəm] *n* petrolio.
petroleum jelly *n* vaselina.
petrol pump *n* (*BRIT*: *in car, at garage*)
pompa di benzina.
petrol station *n* (*BRIT*) stazione *f* di
rifornimento.
petrol tank *n* (*BRIT*) serbatoio della

benzina.
petticoat ['pɛtɪkəut] *n* sottana.
pettifogging ['pɛtɪfɔgɪŋ] *adj* cavilloso(a).
pettiness ['pɛtɪnɪs] *n* meschinità.
petty ['pɛtɪ] *adj* (*mean*) meschino(a);
(*unimportant*) insignificante.
petty cash *n* piccola cassa.
petty officer *n* sottufficiale *m* di marina.
petulant ['pɛtjulənt] *adj* irritabile.
pew [pju:] *n* panca (di chiesa).
pewter ['pju:tə*] *n* peltro.
Pfc *abbr* (*US MIL*) = *private first class*.
PG *n abbr* (*CINE*: = *parental guidance*)
consenso dei genitori richiesto.
PGA *n abbr* (= *Professional Golfers
Association*) *associazione dei giocatori di
golf professionisti*.
PH *n abbr* (*US MIL*: = *Purple Heart*)
*decorazione per ferite riportate in
guerra*.
PHA *n abbr* (*US*: = *Public Housing
Administration*) *amministrazione per
l'edilizia pubblica*.
phallic ['fælɪk] *adj* fallico(a).
phantom ['fæntəm] *n* fantasma *m*.
Pharaoh ['fɛərəu] *n* faraone *m*.
pharmaceutical [fɑːmə'sjuːtɪkl] *adj*
farmaceutico(a) ♦ *n*: ~**s** prodotti *mpl*
farmaceutici.
pharmacist ['fɑːməsɪst] *n* farmacista *m/f*.
pharmacy ['fɑːməsɪ] *n* farmacia.
phase [feɪz] *n* fase *f*, periodo ♦ *vt*: **to ~ sth
in/out** introdurre/eliminare qc
progressivamente.
PhD *n abbr* = *Doctor of Philosophy*.
pheasant ['fɛznt] *n* fagiano.
phenomenon, *pl* **phenomena**
[fə'nɔmɪnən, -nə] *n* fenomeno.
phew [fju:] *excl* uff!
phial ['faɪəl] *n* fiala.
philanderer [fɪ'lændərə*] *n* donnaiolo.
philanthropic [fɪlən'θrɔpɪk] *adj*
filantropico(a).
philanthropist [fɪ'lænθrəpɪst] *n* filantropo.
philatelist [fɪ'lætəlɪst] *n* filatelico/a.
philately [fɪ'lætəlɪ] *n* filatelia.
Philippines ['fɪlɪpiːnz] *npl* (*also*: **Philippine
Islands): the** ~ le Filippine.
philosopher [fɪ'lɔsəfə*] *n* filosofo/a.
philosophical [fɪlə'sɔfɪkl] *adj* filosofico(a).
philosophy [fɪ'lɔsəfɪ] *n* filosofia.
phlegm [flɛm] *n* flemma.
phlegmatic [flɛg'mætɪk] *adj* flemmatico(a).
phobia ['fəubjə] *n* fobia.
phone [fəun] *n* telefono ♦ *vt* telefonare a
♦ *vi* telefonare; **to be on the** ~ avere il
telefono; (*be calling*) essere al telefono.
▶**phone back** *vt, vi* richiamare.

phone book n guida del telefono, elenco telefonico.
phone box, phone booth n cabina telefonica.
phone call n telefonata.
phonecard ['fəʊnkɑːd] n scheda telefonica.
phone-in ['fəʊnɪn] n (*BRIT RADIO, TV*) *trasmissione radiofonica o televisiva con intervento telefonico degli ascoltatori.*
phone tapping [-tæpɪŋ] n intercettazioni *fpl* telefoniche.
phonetics [fə'nɛtɪks] n fonetica.
phoney ['fəʊnɪ] adj falso(a), fasullo(a) ♦ n (*person*) ciarlatano.
phonograph ['fəʊnəgrɑːf] n (*US*) giradischi m inv.
phony ['fəʊnɪ] adj, n = **phoney**.
phosphate ['fɔsfeɪt] n fosfato.
phosphorus ['fɔsfərəs] n fosforo.
photo ['fəʊtəʊ] n foto f inv.
photo... ['fəʊtəʊ] prefix foto....
photocall ['fəʊtəʊkɔːl] n *convocazione di fotoreporter a scopo pubblicitario.*
photocopier ['fəʊtəʊkɒpɪə*] n fotocopiatrice f.
photocopy ['fəʊtəʊkɒpɪ] n fotocopia ♦ vt fotocopiare.
photoelectric [fəʊtəʊɪ'lɛktrɪk] adj: ~ **cell** cellula fotoelettrica.
Photofit ® ['fəʊtəʊfɪt] n photofit m inv.
photogenic [fəʊtəʊ'dʒɛnɪk] adj fotogenico(a).
photograph ['fəʊtəgræf] n fotografia ♦ vt fotografare; **to take a** ~ **of sb** fare una fotografia a *or* fotografare qn.
photographer [fə'tɔgrəfə*] n fotografo.
photographic [fəʊtə'græfɪk] adj fotografico(a).
photography [fə'tɔgrəfɪ] n fotografia.
photo opportunity n *opportunità di scattare delle foto ad un personaggio importante.*
Photostat ® ['fəʊtəʊstæt] n fotocopia.
photosynthesis [fəʊtəʊ'sɪnθəsɪs] n fotosintesi f.
phrase [freɪz] n espressione f; (*LING*) locuzione f; (*MUS*) frase f ♦ vt esprimere; (*letter*) redigere.
phrasebook ['freɪzbuk] n vocabolarietto.
physical ['fɪzɪkl] adj fisico(a); ~ **examination** visita medica; ~ **education** educazione f fisica; ~ **exercises** ginnastica.
physically [fɪzɪklɪ] adv fisicamente.
physician [fɪ'zɪʃən] n medico.
physicist ['fɪzɪsɪst] n fisico.
physics ['fɪzɪks] n fisica.
physiological [fɪzɪə'lɔdʒɪkəl] adj fisiologico(a).

physiology [fɪzɪ'ɔlədʒɪ] n fisiologia.
physiotherapist [fɪzɪəʊ'θɛrəpɪst] n fisioterapista m/f.
physiotherapy [fɪzɪəʊ'θɛrəpɪ] n fisioterapia.
physique [fɪ'ziːk] n fisico.
pianist ['piːənɪst] n pianista m/f.
piano [pɪ'ænəʊ] n pianoforte m.
piano accordion n (*BRIT*) fisarmonica (a tastiera).
piccolo ['pɪkələʊ] n ottavino.
pick [pɪk] n (*tool: also:* ~-**axe**) piccone m ♦ vt scegliere; (*gather*) cogliere; (*scab, spot*) grattarsi ♦ vi: **to** ~ **and choose** scegliere con cura; **take your** ~ scelga; **the** ~ **of** il fior fiore di; **to** ~ **one's nose** mettersi le dita nel naso; **to** ~ **one's teeth** stuzzicarsi i denti; **to** ~ **sb's brains** farsi dare dei suggerimenti da qn; **to** ~ **pockets** borseggiare; **to** ~ **a fight/quarrel with sb** attaccar rissa/briga con qn; **to** ~ **one's way through** attraversare stando ben attento a dove mettere i piedi.
►**pick off** vt (*kill*) abbattere.
►**pick on** vt fus (*person*) avercela con.
►**pick out** vt scegliere; (*distinguish*) distinguere.
►**pick up** vi (*improve*) migliorarsi ♦ vt raccogliere; (*collect*) passare a prendere; (*AUT: give lift to*) far salire; (*learn*) imparare; (*RADIO, TV, TEL*) captare; **to** ~ **o.s. up** rialzarsi; **to** ~ **up where one left off** riprendere dal punto in cui ci si era fermati; **to** ~ **up speed** acquistare velocità.
pickaxe, (*US*) **pickax** ['pɪkæks] n piccone m.
picket ['pɪkɪt] n (*in strike*) scioperante m/f che fa parte di un picchetto; picchetto ♦ vt picchettare.
picket line n cordone m degli scioperanti.
pickings ['pɪkɪŋz] npl (*pilferings*): **there are good** ~ **to be had here** qui ci sono buone possibilità di intascare qualcosa sottobanco.
pickle ['pɪkl] n (*also:* ~**s**: *as condiment*) sottaceti mpl; (*fig*): **in a** ~ nei pasticci ♦ vt mettere sottaceto; mettere in salamoia.
pick-me-up ['pɪkmiːʌp] n tiramisù m inv.
pickpocket ['pɪkpɔkɪt] n borsaiolo.
pickup ['pɪkʌp] n (*BRIT: on record player*) pick-up m inv; (*small truck: also:* ~ **truck,** ~ **van**) camioncino.
picnic ['pɪknɪk] n picnic m inv ♦ vi fare un picnic.
picnicker ['pɪknɪkə*] n chi partecipa a un picnic.

pictorial [pɪk'tɔːrɪəl] *adj* illustrato(a).

picture ['pɪktʃə*] *n* quadro; (*painting*) pittura; (*photograph*) foto(grafia); (*drawing*) disegno; (*TV*) immagine *f*; (*film*) film *m inv* ♦ *vt* raffigurarsi; **the ~s** (*BRIT*) il cinema; **to take a ~ of sb/sth** fare una foto a qn/di qc; **we get a good ~ here** (*TV*) la ricezione qui è buona; **the overall ~** il quadro generale; **to put sb in the ~** mettere qn al corrente.

picture book *n* libro illustrato.

picturesque [pɪktʃə'rɛsk] *adj* pittoresco(a).

picture window *n* finestra panoramica.

piddling ['pɪdlɪŋ] *adj* (*col*) insignificante.

pidgin English ['pɪdʒɪn-] *n inglese semplificato misto ad elementi indigeni.*

pie [paɪ] *n* torta; (*of meat*) pasticcio.

piebald ['paɪbɔːld] *adj* pezzato(a).

piece [piːs] *n* pezzo; (*of land*) appezzamento; (*DRAUGHTS etc*) pedina; (*item*): **a ~ of furniture/advice** un mobile/ consiglio ♦ *vt*: **to ~ together** mettere insieme; **in ~s** (*broken*) in pezzi; (*not yet assembled*) smontato(a); **to take to ~s** smontare; **~ by ~** poco alla volta; **a 10p ~** (*BRIT*) una moneta da 10 pence; **a six-~ band** un complesso di sei strumentisti; **in one ~** (*object*) intatto; **to get back all in one ~** (*person*) tornare a casa incolume *or* sano e salvo; **to say one's ~** dire la propria.

piecemeal ['piːsmiːl] *adv* pezzo a pezzo, a spizzico.

piece rate *n* tariffa a cottimo.

piecework ['piːswəːk] *n* (lavoro a) cottimo.

pie chart *n* grafico a torta.

Piedmont ['piːdmɔnt] *n* Piemonte *m*.

pier [pɪə*] *n* molo; (*of bridge etc*) pila.

pierce [pɪəs] *vt* forare; (*with arrow etc*) trafiggere; **to have one's ears ~d** farsi fare i buchi per gli orecchini.

piercing ['pɪəsɪŋ] *adj* (*cry*) acuto(a).

piety ['paɪətɪ] *n* pietà, devozione *f*.

piffling ['pɪflɪŋ] *adj* insignificante.

pig [pɪg] *n* maiale *m*, porco.

pigeon ['pɪdʒən] *n* piccione *m*.

pigeonhole ['pɪdʒənhəul] *n* casella ♦ *vt* classificare.

pigeon-toed ['pɪdʒən'təud] *adj* che cammina con i piedi in dentro.

piggy bank ['pɪgɪ-] *n* salvadanaio.

pigheaded ['pɪg'hɛdɪd] *adj* caparbio(a), cocciuto(a).

piglet ['pɪglɪt] *n* porcellino.

pigment ['pɪgmənt] *n* pigmento.

pigmentation [pɪgmən'teɪʃən] *n* pigmentazione *f*.

pigmy ['pɪgmɪ] *n* = **pygmy**.

pigskin ['pɪgskɪn] *n* cinghiale *m*.

pigsty ['pɪgstaɪ] *n* porcile *m*.

pigtail ['pɪgteɪl] *n* treccina.

pike [paɪk] *n* (*spear*) picca; (*fish*) luccio.

pilchard ['pɪltʃəd] *n specie di sardina.*

pile [paɪl] *n* (*pillar, of books*) pila; (*heap*) mucchio; (*of carpet*) pelo ♦ *vb* (*also*: **~ up**) *vt* ammucchiare ♦ *vi* ammucchiarsi; **in a ~** ammucchiato; *see also* **piles**.

▶**pile on** *vt*: **to ~ it on** (*col*) esagerare, drammatizzare.

piles [paɪlz] *npl* (*MED*) emorroidi *fpl*.

pileup ['paɪlʌp] *n* (*AUT*) tamponamento a catena.

pilfer ['pɪlfə*] *vt* rubacchiare ♦ *vi* fare dei furtarelli.

pilfering ['pɪlfərɪŋ] *n* rubacchiare *m*.

pilgrim ['pɪlgrɪm] *n* pellegrino/a.

pilgrimage ['pɪlgrɪmɪdʒ] *n* pellegrinaggio.

pill [pɪl] *n* pillola; **to be on the ~** prendere la pillola.

pillage ['pɪlɪdʒ] *vt* saccheggiare.

pillar ['pɪlə*] *n* colonna.

pillar box *n* (*BRIT*) cassetta delle lettere (a colonnina).

pillion ['pɪljən] *n* (*of motor cycle*) sellino posteriore; **to ride ~** viaggiare dietro.

pillory ['pɪlərɪ] *n* berlina ♦ *vt* mettere alla berlina.

pillow ['pɪləu] *n* guanciale *m*.

pillowcase ['pɪləukeɪs], **pillowslip** ['pɪləuslɪp] *n* federa.

pilot ['paɪlət] *n* pilota *m/f* ♦ *cpd* (*scheme etc*) pilota *inv* ♦ *vt* pilotare.

pilot boat *n* pilotina.

pilot light *n* fiammella di sicurezza.

pimento [pɪ'mɛntəu] *n* peperoncino.

pimp [pɪmp] *n* mezzano.

pimple ['pɪmpl] *n* foruncolo.

pimply ['pɪmplɪ] *adj* foruncoloso(a).

PIN *n abbr see* **personal identification number**.

pin [pɪn] *n* spillo; (*TECH*) perno; (*BRIT*: *drawing ~*) puntina da disegno; (*BRIT ELEC*: *of plug*) spinotto ♦ *vt* attaccare con uno spillo; **~s and needles** formicolio; **to ~ sb against/to** inchiodare qn contro/a; **to ~ sth on sb** (*fig*) addossare la colpa di qc a qn.

▶**pin down** *vt* (*fig*): **to ~ sb down** obbligare qn a pronunziarsi; **there's something strange here but I can't quite ~ it down** c'è qualcosa di strano qua ma non riesco a capire cos'è.

pinafore ['pɪnəfɔː*] *n* grembiule *m* (senza maniche).

pinafore dress *n* scamiciato.

pinball ['pɪnbɔːl] *n* flipper *m inv*.

pincers ['pɪnsəz] *npl* pinzette *fpl*.

pinch [pɪntʃ] *n* pizzicotto, pizzico ♦ *vt* pizzicare; (*col: steal*) grattare ♦ *vi* (*shoe*) stringere; **at a** ~ in caso di bisogno; **to feel the** ~ (*fig*) trovarsi nelle ristrettezze.

pinched [pɪntʃt] *adj* (*drawn*) dai lineamenti tirati; (*short*): ~ **for money/space** a corto di soldi/di spazio; ~ **with cold** raggrinzito dal freddo.

pincushion ['pɪnkuʃən] *n* puntaspilli *m inv*.

pine [paɪn] *n* (*also*: ~ **tree**) pino ♦ *vi*: **to** ~ **for** struggersi dal desiderio di.
▶**pine away** *vi* languire.

pineapple ['paɪnæpl] *n* ananas *m inv*.

pine cone *n* pigna.

pine needles *npl* aghi *mpl* di pino.

ping [pɪŋ] *n* (*noise*) tintinnio.

Ping-Pong ® ['pɪŋpɔŋ] *n* ping-pong ® *m*.

pink [pɪŋk] *adj* rosa *inv* ♦ *n* (*colour*) rosa *m inv*; (*BOT*) garofano.

pinking shears ['pɪŋkɪŋ-] *n* forbici *fpl* a zigzag.

pin money *n* (*BRIT*) denaro per le piccole spese.

pinnacle ['pɪnəkl] *n* pinnacolo.

pinpoint ['pɪnpɔɪnt] *vt* indicare con precisione.

pinstripe ['pɪnstraɪp] *n* stoffa gessata; (*also*: ~ **suit**) gessato.

pint [paɪnt] *n* pinta (*BRIT* = *0.57 l*; *US* = *0.47 l*); (*BRIT col: of beer*) ≈ birra piccola.

pinup [pɪnʌp] *n* pin-up girl *f inv*.

pioneer [paɪə'nɪə*] *n* pioniere/a ♦ *vt* essere un pioniere in.

pious ['paɪəs] *adj* pio(a).

pip [pɪp] *n* (*seed*) seme *m*; (*time signal on radio*) segnale *m* orario.

pipe [paɪp] *n* tubo; (*for smoking*) pipa; (*MUS*) piffero ♦ *vt* portare per mezzo di tubazione; ~**s** *npl* (*also*: **bag**~**s**) cornamusa (*scozzese*).
▶**pipe down** *vi* (*col*) calmarsi.

pipe cleaner *n* scovolino.

piped music [paɪpt-] *n* musica di sottofondo.

pipe dream *n* vana speranza.

pipeline ['paɪplaɪn] *n* conduttura; (*for oil*) oleodotto; (*for natural gas*) metanodotto; **it is in the** ~ (*fig*) è in arrivo.

piper ['paɪpə*] *n* piffero; suonatore/trice di cornamusa.

pipe tobacco *n* tabacco da pipa.

piping ['paɪpɪŋ] *adv*: ~ **hot** bollente.

piquant ['piːkənt] *adj* (*sauce*) piccante; (*conversation*) stimolante.

pique [piːk] *n* picca.

piracy ['paɪərəsɪ] *n* pirateria.

pirate ['paɪərət] *n* pirata *m* ♦ *vt* (*record, video, book*) riprodurre abusivamente.

pirate radio *n* (*BRIT*) radio pirata *f inv*.

pirouette [pɪru'et] *n* piroetta ♦ *vi* piroettare.

Pisces ['paɪsiːz] *n* Pesci *mpl*; **to be** ~ essere dei Pesci.

piss [pɪs] *vi* (*col!*) pisciare; ~ **off!** vaffanculo! (*!*).

pissed [pɪst] *adj* (*BRIT col: drunk*) ubriaco(a) fradicio(a).

pistol ['pɪstl] *n* pistola.

piston ['pɪstən] *n* pistone *m*.

pit [pɪt] *n* buca, fossa; (*also*: **coal** ~) miniera; (*also*: **orchestra** ~) orchestra ♦ *vt*: **to** ~ **sb against sb** opporre qn a qn; ~**s** *npl* (*AUT*) box *m*; **to** ~ **o.s. against** opporsi a.

pitapat ['pɪtə'pæt] *adv* (*BRIT*): **to go** ~ (*heart*) palpitare, battere forte; (*rain*) picchiettare.

pitch [pɪtʃ] *n* (*throw*) lancia; (*MUS*) tono; (*of voice*) altezza; (*fig: degree*) grado, punto; (*also: sales* ~) discorso di vendita, imbonimento; (*BRIT SPORT*) campo; (*NAUT*) beccheggio; (*tar*) pece *f* ♦ *vt* (*throw*) lanciare ♦ *vi* (*fall*) cascare; (*NAUT*) beccheggiare; **to** ~ **a tent** piantare una tenda; **at this** ~ a questo ritmo.

pitch-black [pɪtʃ'blæk] *adj* nero(a) come la pece.

pitched battle [pɪtʃt-] *n* battaglia campale.

pitcher ['pɪtʃə*] *n* brocca.

pitchfork ['pɪtʃfɔːk] *n* forcone *m*.

piteous ['pɪtɪəs] *adj* pietoso(a).

pitfall ['pɪtfɔːl] *n* trappola.

pith [pɪθ] *n* (*of plant*) midollo; (*of orange*) parte *f* interna della scorza; (*fig*) essenza, succo; vigore *m*.

pithead ['pɪthɛd] *n* (*BRIT*) imbocco della miniera.

pithy ['pɪθɪ] *adj* conciso(a); vigoroso(a).

pitiable ['pɪtɪəbl] *adj* pietoso(a).

pitiful ['pɪtɪful] *adj* (*touching*) pietoso(a); (*contemptible*) miserabile.

pitifully ['pɪtɪfəlɪ] *adv* pietosamente; **it's** ~ **obvious** è penosamente chiaro.

pitiless ['pɪtɪlɪs] *adj* spietato(a).

pittance ['pɪtns] *n* miseria, magro salario.

pitted ['pɪtɪd] *adj*: ~ **with** (*potholes*) pieno(a) di; (*chickenpox*) butterato(a) da.

pity ['pɪtɪ] *n* pietà ♦ *vt* aver pietà di, compatire, commiserare; **to have** *or* **take** ~ **on sb** aver pietà di qn; **it is a** ~ **that you can't come** è un peccato che non possa venire; **what a** ~! che peccato!

pitying ['pɪtɪɪŋ] *adj* compassionevole.

pivot ['pɪvət] *n* perno ♦ *vi* impernarsi.

pixel ['pɪksl] *n* (*COMPUT*) pixel *m inv*.

pixie ['pıksı] *n* folletto.
pizza ['pi:tsə] *n* pizza.
placard ['plækɑːd] *n* affisso.
placate [plə'keɪt] *vt* placare, calmare.
placatory [plə'keɪtərı] *adj* conciliante.
place [pleɪs] *n* posto, luogo; (*proper position, rank, seat*) posto; (*house*) casa, alloggio; (*home*): **at/to his** ~ a casa sua; (*in street names*): **Laurel P~** via dei Lauri ♦ *vt* (*object*) posare, mettere; (*identify*) riconoscere; individuare; (*goods*) piazzare; **to take** ~ aver luogo; succedere; **out of** ~ (*not suitable*) inopportuno(a); **I feel rather out of** ~ **here** qui mi sento un po' fuori posto; **in the first** ~ in primo luogo; **to change** ~**s with sb** scambiare il posto con qn; **to put sb in his** ~ (*fig*) mettere a posto qn, mettere qn al suo posto; **from** ~ **to** ~ da un posto all'altro; **all over the** ~ dappertutto; **he's going** ~**s** (*fig col*) si sta facendo strada; **it is not my** ~ **to do it** non sta a me farlo; **how are you** ~**d next week?** com'è messo la settimana prossima?; **to** ~ **an order with sb (for)** (*COMM*) fare un'ordinazione a qn (di).
placebo [plə'si:bəu] *n* placebo *m inv.*
place mat *n* sottopiatto; (*in linen etc*) tovaglietta.
placement ['pleɪsmənt] *n* collocamento; (*job*) lavoro.
place name *n* toponimo.
placenta [plə'sɛntə] *n* placenta.
placid ['plæsıd] *adj* placido(a), calmo(a).
placidity [plə'sıdıtı] *n* placidità.
plagiarism ['pleɪdʒərızəm] *n* plagio.
plagiarist ['pleɪdʒərıst] *n* plagiario/a.
plagiarize ['pleɪdʒəraɪz] *vt* plagiare.
plague [pleɪg] *n* peste *f* ♦ *vt* tormentare; **to** ~ **sb with questions** assillare qn di domande.
plaice [pleɪs] *n* (*pl inv*) pianuzza.
plaid [plæd] *n* plaid *m inv.*
plain [pleɪn] *adj* (*clear*) chiaro(a), palese; (*simple*) semplice; (*frank*) franco(a), aperto(a); (*not handsome*) bruttino(a); (*without seasoning etc*) scondito(a); naturale; (*in one colour*) tinta unita *inv* ♦ *adv* francamente, chiaramente ♦ *n* pianura; **to make sth** ~ **to sb** far capire chiaramente qc a qn; **in** ~ **clothes** (*police*) in borghese.
plain chocolate *n* cioccolato fondente.
plainly ['pleɪnlı] *adv* chiaramente; (*frankly*) francamente.
plainness ['pleɪnnıs] *n* semplicità.
plain speaking *n*: **there has been some** ~ **between the two leaders** i due leader si

sono parlati chiaro.
plaintiff ['pleɪntıf] *n* attore/trice.
plaintive ['pleɪntıv] *adj* (*voice, song*) lamentoso(a); (*look*) struggente.
plait [plæt] *n* treccia ♦ *vt* intrecciare; **to** ~ **one's hair** farsi una treccia (*or* le trecce).
plan [plæn] *n* pianta; (*scheme*) progetto, piano ♦ *vt* (*think in advance*) progettare; (*prepare*) organizzare; (*intend*) avere in progetto ♦ *vi*: **to** ~ **(for)** far piani *or* progetti (per); **to** ~ **to do** progettare di fare, avere l'intenzione di fare; **how long do you** ~ **to stay?** quanto conta di restare?
plane [pleɪn] *n* (*AVIAT*) aereo; (*tree*) platano; (*tool*) pialla; (*ART, MATH etc*) piano ♦ *adj* piano(a), piatto(a) ♦ *vt* (*with tool*) piallare.
planet ['plænıt] *n* pianeta *m.*
planetarium [plænı'tɛərıəm] *n* planetario.
plank [plæŋk] *n* tavola, asse *f.*
plankton ['plæŋktən] *n* plancton *m.*
planned economy [plænd-] *n* economia pianificata.
planner ['plænə*] *n* pianificatore/trice; (*chart*) calendario; **town** *or* (*US*) **city** ~ urbanista *m/f.*
planning ['plænıŋ] *n* progettazione *f*; (*POL, ECON*) pianificazione *f*; **family** ~ pianificazione delle nascite.
planning permission *n* (*BRIT*) permesso di costruzione.
plant [plɑːnt] *n* pianta; (*machinery*) impianto; (*factory*) fabbrica ♦ *vt* piantare; (*bomb*) mettere.
plantation [plæn'teɪʃən] *n* piantagione *f.*
plant pot *n* (*BRIT*) vaso (di fiori).
plaque [plæk] *n* placca.
plasma ['plæzmə] *n* plasma *m.*
plaster ['plɑːstə*] *n* intonaco; (*also*: ~ **of Paris**) gesso; (*BRIT: also*: **sticking** ~) cerotto ♦ *vt* intonacare; ingessare; (*cover*): **to** ~ **with** coprire di; (*col: mud etc*) impiastricciare; **in** ~ (*BRIT: leg etc*) ingessato(a).
plasterboard ['plɑːstəbɔːd] *n* lastra di cartone ingessato.
plaster cast *n* (*MED*) ingessatura, gesso; (*model, statue*) modello in gesso.
plastered ['plɑːstəd] *adj* (*col*) ubriaco(a) fradicio(a).
plasterer ['plɑːstərə*] *n* intonacatore *m.*
plastic ['plæstık] *n* plastica ♦ *adj* (*made of plastic*) di *or* in plastica; (*flexible*) plastico(a), malleabile; (*art*) plastico(a).
plastic bag *n* sacchetto di plastica.
plastic bullet *n* pallottola di plastica.
plastic explosive *n* esplosivo al plastico.
plasticine ® ['plæstısi:n] *n* plastilina ®.

plastic surgery *n* chirurgia plastica.
plate [pleɪt] *n* (*dish*) piatto; (*sheet of metal*) lamiera; (*PHOT*) lastra; (*TYP*) cliché *m inv*; (*in book*) tavola; (*on door*) targa, targhetta; (*AUT: number* ~) targa; (*dishes*): **gold** ~ vasellame *m* d'oro; **silver** ~ argenteria.
plateau, ~s *or* **~x** ['plætəu, -z] *n* altipiano.
plateful ['pleɪtful] *n* piatto.
plate glass *n* vetro piano.
platen ['plætən] *n* (*on typewriter, printer*) rullo.
plate rack *n* scolapiatti *m inv*.
platform ['plætfɔːm] *n* (*stage, at meeting*) palco; (*BRIT: on bus*) piattaforma; (*RAIL*) marciapiede *m*; **the train leaves from** ~ **7** il treno parte dal binario 7.
platform ticket *n* (*BRIT*) biglietto d'ingresso ai binari.
platinum ['plætɪnəm] *n* platino.
platitude ['plætɪtjuːd] *n* luogo comune.
platoon [plə'tuːn] *n* plotone *m*.
platter ['plætə*] *n* piatto.
plaudits ['plɔːdɪts] *npl* plauso.
plausible ['plɔːzɪbl] *adj* plausibile, credibile; (*person*) convincente.
play [pleɪ] *n* gioco; (*THEAT*) commedia ♦ *vt* (*game*) giocare a; (*team, opponent*) giocare contro; (*instrument, piece of music*) suonare; (*play, part*) interpretare ♦ *vi* giocare; suonare; recitare; **to bring** *or* **call into** ~ (*plan*) mettere in azione; (*emotions*) esprimere; ~ **on words** gioco di parole; **to** ~ **a trick on sb** fare uno scherzo a qn; **they're** ~**ing at soldiers** stanno giocando ai soldati; **to** ~ **for time** (*fig*) cercare di guadagnar tempo; **to** ~ **into sb's hands** (*fig*) fare il gioco di qn.
▶**play about, play around** *vi* (*person*) divertirsi; **to** ~ **about** *or* **around with** (*fiddle with*) giocherellare con; (*idea*) accarezzare.
▶**play along** *vi*: **to** ~ **along with** (*fig: person*) stare al gioco di; (*: plan, idea*) fingere di assecondare ♦ *vt* (*fig*): **to** ~ **sb along** tenere qn in sospeso.
▶**play back** *vt* riascoltare, risentire.
▶**play down** *vt* minimizzare.
▶**play on** *vt fus* (*sb's feelings, credulity*) giocare su; **to** ~ **on sb's nerves** dare sui nervi a qn.
▶**play up** *vi* (*cause trouble*) fare i capricci.
playact ['pleɪækt] *vi* fare la commedia.
playboy ['pleɪbɔɪ] *n* playboy *m inv*.
played-out ['pleɪd'aut] *adj* spossato(a).
player ['pleɪə*] *n* giocatore/trice; (*THEAT*) attore/trice; (*MUS*) musicista *m/f*.
playful ['pleɪful] *adj* giocoso(a).

playgoer ['pleɪgəuə*] *n* assiduo(a) frequentatore(trice) di teatri.
playground ['pleɪgraund] *n* (*in school*) cortile *m* per la ricreazione; (*in park*) parco *m* giochi *inv*.
playgroup ['pleɪgruːp] *n* giardino d'infanzia.
playing card ['pleɪɪŋ-] *n* carta da gioco.
playing field ['pleɪɪŋ-] *n* campo sportivo.
playmaker ['pleɪmeɪkə*] *n* (*SPORT*) playmaker *m inv*.
playmate ['pleɪmeɪt] *n* compagno/a di gioco.
play-off ['pleɪɔf] *n* (*SPORT*) bella.
playpen ['pleɪpɛn] *n* box *m inv*.
playroom ['pleɪruːm] *n* stanza dei giochi.
plaything ['pleɪθɪŋ] *n* giocattolo.
playtime ['pleɪtaɪm] *n* (*SCOL*) ricreazione *f*.
playwright ['pleɪraɪt] *n* drammaturgo/a.
plc *abbr* (*BRIT*) *see* **public limited company**.
plea [pliː] *n* (*request*) preghiera, domanda; (*excuse*) scusa; (*LAW*) (argomento di) difesa.
plea bargaining *n* (*LAW*) patteggiamento.
plead [pliːd] *vt* patrocinare; (*give as excuse*) addurre a pretesto ♦ *vi* (*LAW*) perorare la causa; (*beg*): **to** ~ **with sb** implorare qn; **to** ~ **for sth** implorare qc; **to** ~ **guilty/not guilty** (*defendant*) dichiararsi colpevole/innocente.
pleasant ['plɛznt] *adj* piacevole, gradevole.
pleasantly ['plɛzntlɪ] *adv* piacevolmente.
pleasantry ['plɛzntrɪ] *n* (*joke*) scherzo; (*polite remark*): **to exchange pleasantries** scambiarsi i convenevoli.
please [pliːz] *vt* piacere a ♦ *vi* (*think fit*): **do as you** ~ faccia come le pare; ~! per piacere!; **my bill,** ~ il conto, per piacere; ~ **yourself!** come ti (*or* le) pare!; ~ **don't cry!** ti prego, non piangere!
pleased [pliːzd] *adj* (*happy*) felice, lieto(a); ~ (*with*) (*satisfied*) contento(a) (di); **we are** ~ **to inform you that** ... abbiamo il piacere di informarla che ...; ~ **to meet you!** piacere!
pleasing ['pliːzɪŋ] *adj* piacevole, che fa piacere.
pleasurable ['plɛʒərəbl] *adj* molto piacevole, molto gradevole.
pleasure ['plɛʒə*] *n* piacere *m*; **with** ~ con piacere, volentieri; **"it's a** ~**"** "prego"; **is this trip for business or** ~? è un viaggio d'affari o di piacere?
pleasure cruise *n* crociera.
pleat [pliːt] *n* piega.
plebiscite ['plɛbɪsɪt] *n* plebiscito.
plebs [plɛbz] *npl* (*pej*) plebe *f*.
plectrum ['plɛktrəm] *n* plettro.

pledge [plɛdʒ] n pegno; (promise) promessa ♦ vt impegnare; promettere; **to ~ support for sb** impegnarsi a sostenere qn; **to ~ sb to secrecy** far promettere a qn di mantenere il segreto.

plenary ['pliːnərɪ] adj plenario(a); **in ~ session** in seduta plenaria.

plentiful ['plɛntɪful] adj abbondante, copioso(a).

plenty ['plɛntɪ] n abbondanza; **~ of** tanto(a), molto(a); un'abbondanza di; **we've got ~ of time to get there** abbiamo un sacco di tempo per arrivarci.

pleurisy ['pluərɪsɪ] n pleurite f.

Plexiglas ® ['plɛksɪglɑːs] n (US) plexiglas ® m.

pliable ['plaɪəbl] adj flessibile; (person) malleabile.

pliers ['plaɪəz] npl pinza.

plight [plaɪt] n situazione f critica.

plimsolls ['plɪmsəlz] npl (BRIT) scarpe fpl da tennis.

plinth [plɪnθ] n plinto; piedistallo.

PLO n abbr (= Palestine Liberation Organization) O.L.P. f.

plod [plɔd] vi camminare a stento; (fig) sgobbare.

plodder ['plɔdə*] n sgobbone m.

plodding ['plɔdɪŋ] adj lento(a) e pesante.

plonk [plɔŋk] (col) n (BRIT: wine) vino da poco ♦ vt: **to ~ sth down** buttare giù qc bruscamente.

plot [plɔt] n congiura, cospirazione f; (of story, play) trama; (of land) lotto ♦ vt (mark out) fare la pianta di; rilevare; (: diagram etc) tracciare; (conspire) congiurare, cospirare ♦ vi congiurare; **a vegetable ~** (BRIT) un orticello.

plotter ['plɔtə*] n cospiratore/trice; (COMPUT) plotter m inv, tracciatore m di curve.

plough, (US) **plow** [plau] n aratro ♦ vt (earth) arare.

▶**plough back** vt (COMM) reinvestire.

▶**plough through** vt fus (snow etc) procedere a fatica in.

ploughing, (US) **plowing** ['plauɪŋ] n aratura.

ploughman, (US) **plowman** ['plaumən] n aratore m; **~'s lunch** (BRIT) semplice pasto a base di pane e formaggio.

ploy [plɔɪ] n stratagemma m.

pluck [plʌk] vt (fruit) cogliere; (musical instrument) pizzicare; (bird) spennare ♦ n coraggio, fegato; **to ~ one's eyebrows** depilarsi le sopracciglia; **to ~ up courage** farsi coraggio.

plucky ['plʌkɪ] adj coraggioso(a).

plug [plʌg] n tappo; (ELEC) spina; (AUT: also: **spark(ing) ~**) candela ♦ vt (hole) tappare; (col: advertise) spingere; **to give sb/sth a ~** fare pubblicità a qn/qc.

▶**plug in** (ELEC) vi inserire la spina ♦ vt attaccare a una presa.

plughole ['plʌghəul] n (BRIT) scarico.

plum [plʌm] n (fruit) susina ♦ cpd: **~ job** (col) impiego ottimo or favoloso.

plumage ['pluːmɪdʒ] n piume fpl, piumaggio.

plumb [plʌm] adj verticale ♦ n piombo ♦ adv (exactly) esattamente ♦ vt sondare.

▶**plumb in** vt (washing machine) collegare all'impianto idraulico.

plumber ['plʌmə*] n idraulico.

plumbing ['plʌmɪŋ] n (trade) lavoro di idraulico; (piping) tubature fpl.

plumbline ['plʌmlaɪn] n filo a piombo.

plume [pluːm] n piuma, penna; (decorative) pennacchio.

plummet ['plʌmɪt] vi cadere a piombo.

plump [plʌmp] adj grassoccio(a) ♦ vt: **to ~ sth (down) on** lasciar cadere qc di peso su.

▶**plump for** vt fus (col) decidersi per.

▶**plump up** vt sprimacciare.

plunder ['plʌndə*] n saccheggio ♦ vt saccheggiare.

plunge [plʌndʒ] n tuffo ♦ vt immergere ♦ vi (dive) tuffarsi; (fall) cadere, precipitare; **to take the ~** (fig) saltare il fosso; **to ~ a room into darkness** far piombare una stanza nel buio.

plunger ['plʌndʒə*] n (for blocked sink) sturalavandini m inv.

plunging ['plʌndʒɪŋ] adj (neckline) profondo(a).

pluperfect [pluːˈpəːfɪkt] n piuccheperfetto.

plural ['pluərl] adj, n plurale (m).

plus [plʌs] n (also: **~ sign**) segno più ♦ prep più ♦ adj (MATH, ELEC) positivo(a); **ten/twenty ~** più di dieci/venti; **it's a ~** (fig) è un vantaggio.

plus fours npl calzoni mpl alla zuava.

plush [plʌʃ] adj lussuoso(a) ♦ n felpa.

plutonium [pluːˈtəunɪəm] n plutonio.

ply [plaɪ] n (of wool) capo; (of wood) strato ♦ vt (tool) maneggiare; (a trade) esercitare ♦ vi (ship) fare il servizio; **three ~ (wool)** lana a tre capi; **to ~ sb with drink** dare da bere continuamente a qn.

plywood ['plaɪwud] n legno compensato.

PM n abbr (BRIT) see **prime minister**.

p.m. adv abbr (= post meridiem) del pomeriggio.

PMS n abbr (= premenstrual syndrome) sindrome f premestruale.

PMT *n abbr* (= *premenstrual tension*) sindrome *f* premestruale.

pneumatic [njuːˈmætɪk] *adj* pneumatico(a); ~ **drill** martello pneumatico.

pneumonia [njuːˈməʊnɪə] *n* polmonite *f*.

PO *n abbr* (= *Post Office*) ≈ P.T. (= *Poste e Telegrafi*) ♦ *abbr* (*NAUT*) = **petty officer.**

po *abbr* = **postal order.**

POA *n abbr* (*BRIT*: = *Prison Officers' Association*) sindacato delle guardie carcerarie.

poach [pəʊtʃ] *vt* (*cook*) affogare; (*steal*) cacciare (*or* pescare) di frodo ♦ *vi* fare il bracconiere.

poached [pəʊtʃt] *adj* (*egg*) affogato(a).

poacher [ˈpəʊtʃə*] *n* bracconiere *m*.

poaching [ˈpəʊtʃɪŋ] *n* caccia (*or* pesca) di frodo.

PO box *n abbr see* **post office box.**

pocket [ˈpɔkɪt] *n* tasca ♦ *vt* intascare; **to be out of** ~ rimetterci; **to be £5 in/out of** ~ (*BRIT*) trovarsi con 5 sterline in più/in meno; **air** ~ vuoto d'aria.

pocketbook [ˈpɔkɪtbuk] *n* (*wallet*) portafoglio; (*notebook*) taccuino; (*US*: *handbag*) busta.

pocket knife *n* temperino.

pocket money *n* paghetta, settimana.

pockmarked [ˈpɔkmɑːkt] *adj* (*face*) butterato(a).

pod [pɔd] *n* guscio ♦ *vt* sgusciare.

podgy [ˈpɔdʒɪ] *adj* grassoccio(a).

podiatrist [pɔˈdiːətrɪst] *n* (*US*) callista *m/f*, pedicure *m/f*.

podiatry [pɔˈdiːətrɪ] *n* (*US*) mestiere *m* di callista.

podium [ˈpəʊdɪəm] *n* podio.

POE *n abbr* = *port of embarkation*; *port of entry*.

poem [ˈpəʊɪm] *n* poesia.

poet [ˈpəʊɪt] *n* poeta/essa.

poetic [pəʊˈɛtɪk] *adj* poetico(a).

poet laureate *n* (*BRIT*) poeta *m* laureato.

> In Gran Bretagna un **poet laureate** è un poeta che riceve un vitalizio dalla casa reale britannica e che ha l'incarico di scrivere delle poesie commemorative in occasione delle festività ufficiali.

poetry [ˈpəʊɪtrɪ] *n* poesia.

poignant [ˈpɔɪnjənt] *adj* struggente.

point [pɔɪnt] *n* (*gen*) punto; (*tip*: *of needle etc*) punta; (*BRIT ELEC*: *also*: **power** ~) presa (di corrente); (*in time*) punto, momento; (*SCOL*) voto; (*main idea, important part*) nocciolo; (*also*: **decimal** ~): **2** ~ **3 (2.3)** 2 virgola 3 (2,3) ♦ *vt* (*show*)

indicare; (*gun etc*): **to** ~ **sth at** puntare qc contro ♦ *vi* mostrare a dito; ~**s** *npl* (*AUT*) puntine *fpl*; (*RAIL*) scambio; **to** ~ **to** indicare; (*fig*) dimostrare; **to make a** ~ fare un'osservazione; **to get the** ~ capire; **to come to the** ~ venire al fatto; **when it comes to the** ~ quando si arriva al dunque; **to be on the** ~ **of doing sth** essere sul punto di *or* stare (proprio) per fare qc; **to be beside the** ~ non entrarci; **to make a** ~ **of doing sth** non mancare di fare qc; **there's no** ~ **(in doing)** è inutile (fare); **in** ~ **of fact** a dire il vero; **that's the whole** ~! precisamente!, sta tutto lì!; **you've got a** ~ **there!** giusto!, hai ragione!; **the train stops at Carlisle and all** ~**s south** il treno ferma a Carlisle e in tutte le stazioni a sud di Carlisle; **good** ~**s** vantaggi *mpl*; (*of person*) qualità *fpl*; ~ **of departure** (*also fig*) punto di partenza; ~ **of order** mozione *f* d'ordine; ~ **of sale** (*COMM*) punto di vendita; ~ **of view** punto di vista.

▶**point out** *vt* far notare.

point-blank [ˈpɔɪntˈblæŋk] *adv* (*also*: **at** ~ **range**) a bruciapelo; (*fig*) categoricamente.

point duty *n* (*BRIT*): **to be on** ~ dirigere il traffico.

pointed [ˈpɔɪntɪd] *adj* (*shape*) aguzzo(a), appuntito(a); (*remark*) specifico(a).

pointedly [ˈpɔɪntɪdlɪ] *adv* in maniera inequivocabile.

pointer [ˈpɔɪntə*] *n* (*stick*) bacchetta; (*needle*) lancetta; (*clue*) indizio; (*advice*) consiglio; (*dog*) pointer *m*, cane *m* da punta.

pointless [ˈpɔɪntlɪs] *adj* inutile, vano(a).

poise [pɔɪz] *n* (*balance*) equilibrio; (*of head, body*) portamento; (*calmness*) calma ♦ *vt* tenere in equilibrio; **to be** ~**d for** (*fig*) essere pronto(a) a.

poison [ˈpɔɪzn] *n* veleno ♦ *vt* avvelenare.

poisoning [ˈpɔɪznɪŋ] *n* avvelenamento.

poisonous [ˈpɔɪznəs] *adj* velenoso(a); (*fumes*) venefico(a), tossico(a); (*ideas, literature*) pernicioso(a); (*rumours, individual*) perfido(a).

poke [pəʊk] *vt* (*fire*) attizzare; (*jab with finger, stick etc*) punzecchiare; (*put*): **to** ~ **sth in(to)** spingere qc dentro ♦ *n* (*jab*) colpetto; (*with elbow*) gomitata; **to** ~ **one's head out of the window** mettere la testa fuori dalla finestra; **to** ~ **fun at sb** prendere in giro qn.

▶**poke about** *vi* frugare.

poker [ˈpəʊkə*] *n* attizzatoio; (*CARDS*) poker *m*.

poker-faced [ˈpəʊkəˈfeɪst] *adj* dal viso

impassibile.
poky ['pəʊkɪ] *adj* piccolo(a) e stretto(a).
Poland ['pəʊlənd] *n* Polonia.
polar ['pəʊlə*] *adj* polare.
polar bear *n* orso bianco.
polarize ['pəʊləraɪz] *vt* polarizzare.
Pole [pəʊl] *n* polacco/a.
pole [pəʊl] *n* (*of wood*) palo; (*ELEC, GEO*) polo.
poleaxe, (*US*) **poleax** ['pəʊlæks] *vt* (*fig*) stendere.
pole bean *n* (*US*) fagiolino.
polecat ['pəʊlkæt] *n* puzzola; (*US*) moffetta.
Pol. Econ. ['pɒlɪkɒn] *n abbr* = *political economy*.
polemic [pɒ'lemɪk] *n* polemica.
pole star *n* stella polare.
pole vault *n* salto con l'asta.
police [pə'liːs] *n* polizia ♦ *vt* mantenere l'ordine in; (*streets, city, frontier*) presidiare; **a large number of** ~ **were hurt** molti poliziotti sono rimasti feriti.
police car *n* macchina della polizia.
police constable (PC) *n* (*BRIT*) agente *m* di polizia.
police department *n* (*US*) dipartimento di polizia.
police force *n* corpo di polizia, polizia.
policeman [pə'liːsmən] *n* poliziotto, agente *m* di polizia.
police officer *n* = **police constable**.
police record *n*: **to have a** ~ avere precedenti penali.
police state *n* stato di polizia.
police station *n* posto di polizia.
policewoman [pə'liːswʊmən] *n* donna *f* poliziotto *inv*.
policy ['pɒlɪsɪ] *n* politica; (*of newspaper, company*) linea di condotta, prassi *f inv*; (*also*: **insurance** ~) polizza (d'assicurazione); **to take out a** ~ (*INSURANCE*) stipulare una polizza di assicurazione.
policy holder *n* assicurato/a.
policy-making ['pɒlɪsɪmeɪkɪŋ] *n* messa a punto di programmi.
polio ['pəʊlɪəʊ] *n* polio *f*.
Polish ['pəʊlɪʃ] *adj* polacco(a) ♦ *n* (*LING*) polacco.
polish ['pɒlɪʃ] *n* (*for shoes*) lucido; (*for floor*) cera; (*for nails*) smalto; (*shine*) lucentezza, lustro; (*fig: refinement*) raffinatezza ♦ *vt* lucidare; (*fig: improve*) raffinare.
►**polish off** *vt* (*work*) sbrigare; (*food*) mangiarsi.
polished ['pɒlɪʃt] *adj* (*fig*) raffinato(a).
polite [pə'laɪt] *adj* cortese; **it's not** ~ **to do**

that non è educato *or* buona educazione fare questo.
politely [pə'laɪtlɪ] *adv* cortesemente.
politeness [pə'laɪtnɪs] *n* cortesia.
politic ['pɒlɪtɪk] *adj* diplomatico(a).
political [pə'lɪtɪkl] *adj* politico(a).
political asylum *n* asilo politico.
politically [pə'lɪtɪklɪ] *adv* politicamente.
politically correct *adj* politicamente corretto(a).
politician [pɒlɪ'tɪʃən] *n* politico.
politics ['pɒlɪtɪks] *n* politica ♦ *npl* idee *fpl* politiche.
polka ['pɒlkə] *n* polca.
polka dot *n* pois *m inv*.
poll [pəʊl] *n* scrutinio; (*votes cast*) voti *mpl*; (*also*: **opinion** ~) sondaggio (d'opinioni) ♦ *vt* ottenere; **to go to the** ~**s** (*voters*) andare alle urne; (*government*) indire le elezioni.
pollen ['pɒlən] *n* polline *m*.
pollen count *n* tasso di polline nell'aria.
pollination [pɒlɪ'neɪʃən] *n* impollinazione *f*.
polling ['pəʊlɪŋ] *n* (*BRIT POL*) votazione *f*, votazioni *fpl*; (*TEL*) interrogazione *f* ciclica.
polling booth *n* (*BRIT*) cabina elettorale.
polling day *n* (*BRIT*) giorno delle elezioni.
polling station *n* (*BRIT*) sezione *f* elettorale.
pollster ['pəʊlstə*] *n* chi esegue sondaggi d'opinione.
poll tax *n* (*BRIT*) imposta locale sulla persona fisica (non più in vigore).
pollutant [pə'luːtənt] *n* sostanza inquinante.
pollute [pə'luːt] *vt* inquinare.
pollution [pə'luːʃən] *n* inquinamento.
polo ['pəʊləʊ] *n* polo.
polo neck *n* collo alto; (*also*: ~ **sweater**) dolcevita ♦ *adj* a collo alto.
poly ['pɒlɪ] *n abbr* (*BRIT*) = **polytechnic**.
poly bag *n* (*BRIT col*) borsa di plastica.
polyester [pɒlɪ'estə*] *n* poliestere *m*.
polygamy [pə'lɪgəmɪ] *n* poligamia.
polygraph ['pɒlɪgrɑːf] *n* macchina della verità.
Polynesia [pɒlɪ'niːzɪə] *n* Polinesia.
Polynesian [pɒlɪ'niːzɪən] *adj, n* polinesiano(a).
polyp ['pɒlɪp] *n* (*MED*) polipo.
polystyrene [pɒlɪ'staɪriːn] *n* polistirolo.
polytechnic [pɒlɪ'teknɪk] *n* (*college*) istituto superiore ad indirizzo tecnologico.
polythene ['pɒlɪθiːn] *n* politene *m*.
polythene bag *n* borsa di plastica.
polyurethane ['pɒlɪ'jʊərɪθeɪn] *n* poliuretano.

pomegranate ['pɒmɪgrænɪt] n melagrana.
pommel ['pɒml] n pomo ♦ vt = **pummel**.
pomp [pɒmp] n pompa, fasto.
pompom ['pɒmpɒm] n pompon m inv.
pompous ['pɒmpəs] adj pomposo(a); (person) pieno(a) di boria.
pond [pɒnd] n stagno; (in park) laghetto.
ponder ['pɒndə*] vi riflettere, meditare ♦ vt ponderare, riflettere su.
ponderous ['pɒndərəs] adj ponderoso(a), pesante.
pong [pɒŋ] (BRIT col) n puzzo ♦ vi puzzare.
pontiff ['pɒntɪf] n pontefice m.
pontificate [pɒn'tɪfɪkeɪt] vi (fig): **to ~ (about)** pontificare (su).
pontoon [pɒn'tuːn] n pontone m; (BRIT CARDS) ventuno.
pony ['pəʊnɪ] n pony m inv.
ponytail ['pəʊnɪteɪl] n coda di cavallo.
pony trekking [-trekɪŋ] n (BRIT) escursione f a cavallo.
poodle ['puːdl] n barboncino, barbone m.
pooh-pooh [puː'puː] vt deridere.
pool [puːl] n (of rain) pozza; (pond) stagno; (artificial) vasca; (also: **swimming ~**) piscina; (sth shared) fondo comune; (COMM: consortium) pool m inv; (US: monopoly trust) trust m inv; (billiards) specie di biliardo a buca ♦ vt mettere in comune; **typing ~**, (US) **secretary ~** servizio comune di dattilografia; **to do the (football) ~s** ≈ fare la schedina, giocare al totocalcio.
poor [pʊə*] adj povero(a); (mediocre) mediocre, cattivo(a) ♦ npl: **the ~** i poveri.
poorly ['pʊəlɪ] adv poveramente; (badly) male ♦ adj indisposto(a), malato(a).
pop [pɒp] n (noise) schiocco; (MUS) musica pop; (US col: father) babbo; (col: drink) bevanda gasata ♦ vt (put) mettere (in fretta) ♦ vi scoppiare; (cork) schioccare; **she ~ped her head out** (of the window) sporse fuori la testa.
► **pop in** vi passare.
► **pop out** vi fare un salto fuori.
► **pop up** vi apparire, sorgere.
pop concert n concerto m pop inv.
popcorn ['pɒpkɔːn] n pop-corn m.
pope [pəʊp] n papa m.
poplar ['pɒplə*] n pioppo.
poplin ['pɒplɪn] n popeline f.
popper ['pɒpə*] n (BRIT) bottone m automatico, bottone a pressione.
poppy ['pɒpɪ] n papavero.
poppycock ['pɒpɪkɒk] n (col) scempiaggini fpl.
Popsicle ® ['pɒpsɪkl] n (US) ghiacciolo.
populace ['pɒpjʊləs] n popolo.

popular ['pɒpjʊlə*] adj popolare; (fashionable) in voga; **to be ~ (with)** (person) essere benvoluto(a) or ben visto(a) (da); (decision) essere gradito(a) (a); **a ~ song** una canzone di successo.
popularity [pɒpjʊ'lærɪtɪ] n popolarità.
popularize ['pɒpjʊləraɪz] vt divulgare; (science) volgarizzare.
populate ['pɒpjʊleɪt] vt popolare.
population [pɒpjʊ'leɪʃən] n popolazione f.
population explosion n forte espansione f demografica.
populous ['pɒpjʊləs] adj popolato(a).
porcelain ['pɔːslɪn] n porcellana.
porch [pɔːtʃ] n veranda.
porcupine ['pɔːkjʊpaɪn] n porcospino.
pore [pɔː*] n poro ♦ vi: **to ~ over** essere immerso(a) in.
pork [pɔːk] n carne f di maiale.
pork chop n braciola or costoletta di maiale.
porn [pɔːn] (col) n pornografia ♦ adj porno inv.
pornographic [pɔːnə'græfɪk] adj pornografico(a).
pornography [pɔː'nɒgrəfɪ] n pornografia.
porous ['pɔːrəs] adj poroso(a).
porpoise ['pɔːpəs] n focena.
porridge ['pɒrɪdʒ] n porridge m.
port1 [pɔːt] n porto; (opening in ship) portello; (NAUT: left side) babordo; (COMPUT) porta; **to ~** (NAUT) a babordo; **~ of call** (porto di) scalo.
port2 [pɔːt] n (wine) porto.
portable ['pɔːtəbl] adj portatile.
portal ['pɔːtl] n portale m.
portcullis [pɔːt'kʌlɪs] n saracinesca.
portent ['pɔːtent] n presagio.
porter ['pɔːtə*] n (for luggage) facchino, portabagagli m inv; (doorkeeper) portiere m, portinaio; (US RAIL) addetto ai vagoni letto.
portfolio [pɔːt'fəʊlɪəʊ] n (POL: office; ECON) portafoglio; (of artist) raccolta dei propri lavori.
porthole ['pɔːthəʊl] n oblò m inv.
portico ['pɔːtɪkəʊ] n portico.
portion ['pɔːʃən] n porzione f.
portly ['pɔːtlɪ] adj corpulento(a).
portrait ['pɔːtreɪt] n ritratto.
portray [pɔː'treɪ] vt fare il ritratto di; (character on stage) rappresentare; (in writing) ritrarre.
portrayal ['pɔːtreɪəl] n ritratto; rappresentazione f.
Portugal ['pɔːtjʊgl] n Portogallo.
Portuguese [pɔːtjʊ'giːz] adj portoghese ♦ n (pl inv) portoghese m/f; (LING) portoghese m.

Portuguese man-of-war [-mænəv'wɔ:*] *n* (*jellyfish*) medusa.

pose [pəuz] *n* posa ♦ *vi* posare; (*pretend*): to ~ as atteggiarsi a, posare a ♦ *vt* porre; **to strike a** ~ mettersi in posa.

poser ['pəuzə*] *n* domanda difficile; (*person*) = **poseur**.

poseur [pəu'zə:*] *n* (*pej*) persona affettata.

posh [pɔʃ] *adj* (*col*) elegante; (*family*) per bene ♦ *adv* (*col*): **to talk** ~ parlare in modo snob.

position [pə'zɪʃən] *n* posizione *f*; (*job*) posto ♦ *vt* mettere in posizione, collocare; **to be in a** ~ **to do sth** essere nella posizione di fare qc.

positive ['pɔzɪtɪv] *adj* positivo(a); (*certain*) sicuro(a), certo(a); (*definite*) preciso(a); definitivo(a).

posse ['pɔsɪ] *n* (*US*) drappello.

possess [pə'zɛs] *vt* possedere; **like one ~ed** come un ossesso; **whatever can have ~ed you?** cosa ti ha preso?

possession [pə'zɛʃən] *n* possesso; (*object*) bene *m*; **to take** ~ **of sth** impossessarsi *or* impadronirsi di qc.

possessive [pə'zɛsɪv] *adj* possessivo(a).

possessiveness [pə'zɛsɪvnɪs] *n* possessività.

possessor [pə'zɛsə*] *n* possessore/ posseditrice.

possibility [pɔsɪ'bɪlɪtɪ] *n* possibilità *f inv*; **he's a** ~ **for the part** è uno dei candidati per la parte.

possible ['pɔsɪbl] *adj* possibile; **it is** ~ **to do it** è possibile farlo; **if** ~ se possibile; **as big as** ~ il più grande possibile; **as far as** ~ nei limiti del possibile.

possibly ['pɔsɪblɪ] *adv* (*perhaps*) forse; **if you** ~ **can** se lo è possibile; **I cannot** ~ **come** proprio non posso venire.

post [pəust] *n* (*BRIT: mail, letters, delivery*) posta; (*: collection*) levata; (*job, situation*) posto; (*pole*) palo; (*trading* ~) stazione *f* commerciale ♦ *vt* (*BRIT: send by post*) impostare; (*MIL*) appostare; (*notice*) affiggere; (*BRIT: appoint*): **to** ~ **to** assegnare a; **by** ~ (*BRIT*) per posta; **by return of** ~ (*BRIT*) a giro di posta; **to keep sb ~ed** tenere qn al corrente.

post... [pəust] *prefix* post...; **~-1990** dopo il 1990.

postage ['pəustɪdʒ] *n* affrancatura.

postage stamp *n* francobollo.

postal ['pəustəl] *adj* postale.

postal order *n* vaglia *m inv* postale.

postbag ['pəustbæg] *n* (*BRIT*) sacco postale, sacco della posta.

postbox ['pəustbɔks] *n* cassetta delle lettere.

postcard ['pəustkɑːd] *n* cartolina.

postcode ['pəustkəud] *n* (*BRIT*) codice *m* (di avviamento) postale.

postdate ['pəust'deɪt] *vt* (*cheque*) postdatare.

poster ['pəustə*] *n* manifesto, affisso.

poste restante [pəust'rɛstɑ̃ːnt] *n* (*BRIT*) fermo posta *m*.

posterior [pɔs'tɪərɪə*] *n* (*col*) deretano, didietro.

posterity [pɔs'tɛrɪtɪ] *n* posterità.

poster paint *n* tempera.

post exchange (PX) *n* (*US MIL*) spaccio militare.

post-free [pəust'friː] *adj*, *adv* (*BRIT*) franco di porto.

postgraduate ['pəust'grædjuət] *n* laureato/a che continua gli studi.

posthumous ['pɔstjuməs] *adj* postumo(a).

posthumously ['pɔstjuməslɪ] *adv* dopo la mia (*or* sua *etc*) morte.

posting ['pəustɪŋ] *n* (*BRIT*) incarico.

postman ['pəustmən] *n* postino.

postmark ['pəustmɑːk] *n* bollo *or* timbro postale.

postmaster ['pəustmɑːstə*] *n* direttore *m* di un ufficio postale.

Postmaster General *n* ≈ ministro delle Poste.

postmistress ['pəustmɪstrɪs] *n* direttrice *f* di un ufficio postale.

post-mortem [pəust'mɔːtəm] *n* autopsia; (*fig*) analisi *f inv* a posteriori.

postnatal ['pəust'neɪtl] *adj* post-parto *inv*.

post office *n* (*building*) ufficio postale; (*organization*) poste *fpl*.

post office box (PO box) *n* casella postale (C.P.).

post-paid ['pəust'peɪd] *adj* già affrancato(a).

postpone [pəust'pəun] *vt* rinviare.

postponement [pəust'pəunmənt] *n* rinvio.

postscript ['pəustskrɪpt] *n* poscritto.

postulate ['pɔstjuleɪt] *vt* postulare.

posture ['pɔstʃə*] *n* portamento; (*pose*) posa, atteggiamento ♦ *vi* posare.

postwar ['pəust'wɔː*] *adj* del dopoguerra.

posy ['pəuzɪ] *n* mazzetto di fiori.

pot [pɔt] *n* (*for cooking*) pentola; casseruola; (*for plants, jam*) vaso; (*piece of pottery*) ceramica; (*col: marijuana*) erba ♦ *vt* (*plant*) piantare in vaso; **to go to** ~ (*col*) andare in malora; **~s of** (*BRIT col*) un sacco di.

potash ['pɔtæʃ] *n* potassa.

potassium [pə'tæsɪəm] *n* potassio.

potato, ~es [pə'teɪtəu] *n* patata.

potato crisps, (*US*) **potato chips** *npl*

patatine *fpl.*
potato flour *n* fecola di patate.
potato peeler *n* sbucciapatate *m inv.*
potbellied ['pɔtbɛlɪd] *adj (from overeating)* panciuto(a); *(from malnutrition)* dal ventre gonfio.
potency ['pəutnsɪ] *n* potenza; *(of drink)* forza.
potent ['pəutnt] *adj* potente, forte.
potentate ['pəutnteɪt] *n* potentato.
potential [pə'tɛnʃl] *adj* potenziale ♦ *n* possibilità *fpl*; **to have** ~ essere promettente.
potentially [pə'tɛnʃəlɪ] *adv* potenzialmente.
pothole ['pɔthəul] *n (in road)* buca; *(BRIT: underground)* marmitta.
potholer ['pɔthəulə*] *n (BRIT)* speleologo/a.
potholing ['pɔthəulɪŋ] *n (BRIT)*: **to go** ~ fare la speleologia.
potion ['pəuʃən] *n* pozione *f.*
potluck [pɔt'lʌk] *n*: **to take** ~ tentare la sorte.
potpourri [pəu'puriː] *n (dried petals etc)* miscuglio di petali essiccati profumati; *(fig)* pot-pourri *m inv.*
pot roast *n* brasato.
potshot ['pɔtʃɔt] *n*: **to take** ~s **at** tirare a casaccio contro.
potted ['pɔtɪd] *adj (food)* in conserva; *(plant)* in vaso; *(fig: shortened)* condensato(a).
potter ['pɔtə*] *n* vasaio ♦ *vi (BRIT)*: **to** ~ **around,** ~ **about** lavoracchiare; **to** ~ **round the house** sbrigare con calma le faccende di casa; ~'**s wheel** tornio (da vasaio).
pottery ['pɔtərɪ] *n* ceramiche *fpl*; **a piece of** ~ una ceramica.
potty ['pɔtɪ] *adj (BRIT col: mad)* tocco(a) ♦ *n (child's)* vasino.
potty-trained ['pɔtɪtreɪnd] *adj* che ha imparato a farla nel vasino.
pouch [pautʃ] *n* borsa; *(ZOOL)* marsupio.
pouf(fe) [puːf] *n (stool)* pouf *m inv.*
poultice ['pəultɪs] *n* impiastro, cataplasma *m.*
poultry ['pəultrɪ] *n* pollame *m.*
poultry farm *n* azienda avicola.
poultry farmer *n* pollicoltore/trice.
pounce [pauns] *vi*: **to** ~ **(on)** balzare addosso (a), piombare (su) ♦ *n* balzo.
pound [paund] *n (weight*: = *453g, 16 ounces)* libbra; *(money*: = *100 pence)* (lira) sterlina; *(for dogs)* canile *m* municipale ♦ *vt (beat)* battere; *(crush)* pestare, polverizzare ♦ *vi (beat)* battere, martellare; **half a** ~ mezza libbra; **a five-** ~ **note** una banconota da cinque sterline.

pounding ['paundɪŋ] *n*: **to take a** ~ *(fig)* prendere una batosta.
pound sterling *n* sterlina.
pour [pɔː*] *vt* versare ♦ *vi* riversarsi; *(rain)* piovere a dirotto.
►**pour away, pour off** *vt* vuotare.
►**pour in** *vi (people)* entrare in fiotto; **to come** ~**ing in** *(water)* entrare a fiotti; *(letters)* arrivare a valanghe; *(cars, people)* affluire in gran quantità.
►**pour out** *vi (people)* riversarsi fuori ♦ *vt* vuotare; versare.
pouring ['pɔːrɪŋ] *adj*: ~ **rain** pioggia torrenziale.
pout [paut] *vi* sporgere le labbra; fare il broncio.
poverty ['pɔvətɪ] *n* povertà, miseria.
poverty line *n* soglia di povertà.
poverty-stricken ['pɔvətɪstrɪkən] *adj* molto povero(a), misero(a).
poverty trap *n (BRIT)* circolo vizioso della povertà.
POW *n abbr* = **prisoner of war**.
powder ['paudə*] *n* polvere *f* ♦ *vt* spolverizzare; *(face)* incipriare; ~**ed milk** latte *m* in polvere; **to** ~ **one's nose** incipriarsi il naso; *(euphemism)* andare alla toilette.
powder compact *n* portacipria *m inv.*
powder keg *n (fig: area)* polveriera; *(: situation)* situazione *f* esplosiva.
powder puff *n* piumino della cipria.
powder room *n* toilette *f inv* (per signore).
powdery ['paudərɪ] *adj* polveroso(a).
power ['pauə*] *n (strength)* potenza, forza; *(ability, POL: of party, leader)* potere *m*; *(MATH)* potenza; *(ELEC)* corrente *f* ♦ *vt* fornire di energia; azionare; **to be in** ~ essere al potere; **to do all in one's** ~ **to help sb** fare tutto quello che si può per aiutare qn; **the world** ~**s** le grandi potenze; **mental** ~**s** capacità *fpl* mentali.
powerboat ['pauəbəut] *n (BRIT)* motobarca, imbarcazione *f* a motore.
power cut *n (BRIT)* interruzione *f or* mancanza di corrente.
powered ['pauəd] *adj*: ~ **by** azionato(a) da; **nuclear-**~ **submarine** sottomarino a propulsione atomica.
power failure *n* guasto alla linea elettrica.
powerful ['pauəful] *adj* potente, forte.
powerhouse ['pauəhaus] *n (fig: person)* persona molto dinamica; **a** ~ **of ideas** una miniera di idee.
powerless ['pauəlɪs] *adj* impotente, senza potere.
power line *n* linea elettrica.
power of attorney *n* procura.

power point n (BRIT) presa di corrente.
power station n centrale f elettrica.
power steering n (AUT: also: **power-assisted steering**) servosterzo.
powwow ['pauwau] n riunione f.
pp abbr (= pages) pp.; (= per procurationem: by proxy): ~ **J. Smith** per il Signor J. Smith.
PPE n abbr (BRIT SCOL: = philosophy, politics and economics) corso di laurea.
PPS n abbr (BRIT: = parliamentary private secretary) parlamentare che assiste un ministro; = post postscriptum.
PQ abbr (Canada) = Province of Quebec.
PR n abbr see proportional representation; **public relations ♦** abbr (US) = Puerto Rico.
Pr. abbr = prince.
practicability [præktɪkə'bɪlɪtɪ] n praticabilità.
practicable ['præktɪkəbl] adj (scheme) praticabile.
practical ['præktɪkl] adj pratico(a).
practicality [præktɪ'kælɪtɪ] n (of plan) fattibilità; (of person) senso pratico; **practicalities** dettagli mpl pratici.
practical joke n beffa.
practically ['præktɪklɪ] adv (almost) quasi, praticamente.
practice ['præktɪs] n pratica; (of profession) esercizio; (at football etc) allenamento; (business) gabinetto; clientela ♦ vt, vi (US) = **practise**; **in** ~ (in reality) in pratica; **out of** ~ fuori esercizio; **2 hours' piano** ~ 2 ore di esercizio al pianoforte; **it's common** ~ è d'uso; **to put sth into** ~ mettere qc in pratica; **target** ~ pratica di tiro.
practice match n partita di allenamento.
practise, (US) **practice** ['præktɪs] vt (work at: piano, one's backhand etc) esercitarsi a; (train for: skiing, running etc) allenarsi a; (a sport, religion) praticare; (method) usare; (profession) esercitare ♦ vi esercitarsi; (train) allenarsi; **to** ~ **for a match** allenarsi per una partita.
practised ['præktɪst] adj (BRIT: person) esperto(a); (: performance) da virtuoso(a); (: liar) matricolato(a); **with a** ~ **eye** con occhio esperto.
practising ['præktɪsɪŋ] adj (Christian etc) praticante; (lawyer) che esercita la professione; (homosexual) attivo(a).
practitioner [præk'tɪʃənə*] n professionista m/f; (MED) medico.
pragmatic [præg'mætɪk] adj prammatico(a).
Prague [prɑːg] n Praga.
prairie ['prɛərɪ] n prateria.

praise [preɪz] n elogio, lode f ♦ vt elogiare, lodare.
praiseworthy ['preɪzwəːðɪ] adj lodevole.
pram [præm] n (BRIT) carrozzina.
prance [prɑːns] vi (horse) impennarsi.
prank [præŋk] n burla.
prat [præt] n (BRIT col) cretino/a.
prattle ['prætl] vi cinguettare.
prawn [prɔːn] n gamberetto.
pray [preɪ] vi pregare.
prayer [prɛə*] n preghiera.
prayer book n libro di preghiere.
pre... [priː] prefix pre...; **~-1970** prima del 1970.
preach [priːtʃ] vt, vi predicare; **to** ~ **at sb** fare la predica a qn.
preacher ['priːtʃə*] n predicatore/trice; (US: minister) pastore m.
preamble [prɪ'æmbl] n preambolo.
prearranged [priːə'reɪndʒd] adj organizzato(a) in anticipo.
precarious [prɪ'kɛərɪəs] adj precario(a).
precaution [prɪ'kɔːʃən] n precauzione f.
precautionary [prɪ'kɔːʃənərɪ] adj (measure) precauzionale.
precede [prɪ'siːd] vt, vi precedere.
precedence ['prɛsɪdəns] n precedenza; **to take** ~ **over** avere la precedenza su.
precedent ['prɛsɪdənt] n precedente m; **to establish** or **set a** ~ creare un precedente.
preceding [prɪ'siːdɪŋ] adj precedente.
precept ['priːsɛpt] n precetto.
precinct ['priːsɪŋkt] n (round cathedral) recinto; (US: district) circoscrizione f; **~s** npl (neighbourhood) dintorni mpl, vicinanze fpl; **pedestrian** ~ zona pedonale; **shopping** ~ (BRIT) centro commerciale.
precious ['prɛʃəs] adj prezioso(a) ♦ adv (col): ~ **little/few** ben poco/pochi; **your** ~ **dog** (ironic) il suo amatissimo cane.
precipice ['prɛsɪpɪs] n precipizio.
precipitate adj [prɪ'sɪpɪtɪt] (hasty) precipitoso(a) ♦ vt [prɪ'sɪpɪteɪt] accelerare.
precipitation [prɪsɪpɪ'teɪʃən] n precipitazione f.
precipitous [prɪ'sɪpɪtəs] adj (steep) erto(a), ripido(a).
précis, pl **précis** ['preɪsiː, -z] n riassunto.
precise [prɪ'saɪs] adj preciso(a).
precisely [prɪ'saɪslɪ] adv precisamente; ~! appunto!
precision [prɪ'sɪʒən] n precisione f.
preclude [prɪ'kluːd] vt precludere, impedire; **to** ~ **sb from doing** impedire a qn di fare.
precocious [prɪ'kəʊʃəs] adj precoce.

preconceived [priːkənˈsiːvd] *adj* (*idea*) preconcetto(a).

preconception [priːkənˈsɛpʃən] *n* preconcetto.

precondition [priːkənˈdɪʃən] *n* condizione *f* necessaria.

precursor [priːˈkəːsə*] *n* precursore *m*.

predate [priːˈdeɪt] *vt* (*precede*) precedere.

predator [ˈprɛdətə*] *n* predatore *m*.

predatory [ˈprɛdətərɪ] *adj* predatore(trice).

predecessor [ˈpriːdɪsɛsə*] *n* predecessore/a.

predestination [priːdɛstɪˈneɪʃən] *n* predestinazione *f*.

predetermine [priːdɪˈtəːmɪn] *vt* predeterminare.

predicament [prɪˈdɪkəmənt] *n* situazione *f* difficile.

predicate [ˈprɛdɪkɪt] *n* (*LING*) predicativo.

predict [prɪˈdɪkt] *vt* predire.

predictable [prɪˈdɪktəbl] *adj* prevedibile.

predictably [prɪˈdɪktəblɪ] *adv* (*behave, react*) in modo prevedibile; ~ **she didn't arrive** come era da prevedere, non è arrivata.

prediction [prɪˈdɪkʃən] *n* predizione *f*.

predispose [priːdɪsˈpəuz] *vt* predisporre.

predominance [prɪˈdɔmɪnəns] *n* predominanza.

predominant [prɪˈdɔmɪnənt] *adj* predominante.

predominantly [prɪˈdɔmɪnəntlɪ] *adv* in maggior parte; soprattutto.

predominate [prɪˈdɔmɪneɪt] *vi* predominare.

pre-eminent [priːˈɛmɪnənt] *adj* preminente.

pre-empt [prɪˈɛmpt] *vt* acquistare per diritto di prelazione; (*fig*) anticipare.

pre-emptive [prɪˈɛmptɪv] *adj*: ~ **strike** azione *f* preventiva.

preen [priːn] *vt*: **to** ~ **itself** (*bird*) lisciarsi le penne; **to** ~ **o.s.** agghindarsi.

prefab [ˈpriːfæb] *n* casa prefabbricata.

prefabricated [priːˈfæbrɪkeɪtɪd] *adj* prefabbricato(a).

preface [ˈprɛfəs] *n* prefazione *f*.

prefect [ˈpriːfɛkt] *n* (*BRIT: in school*) studente/essa con funzioni disciplinari; (*in Italy*) prefetto.

prefer [prɪˈfəː*] *vt* preferire; (*LAW: charges, complaint*) sporgere; (*: action*) intentare; **to** ~ **coffee to tea** preferire il caffè al tè.

preferable [ˈprɛfrəbl] *adj* preferibile.

preferably [ˈprɛfrəblɪ] *adv* preferibilmente.

preference [ˈprɛfrəns] *n* preferenza; **in** ~ **to sth** piuttosto che qc.

preference shares *npl* (*BRIT*) azioni *fpl* privilegiate.

preferential [prɛfəˈrɛnʃəl] *adj* preferenziale; ~ **treatment** trattamento di favore.

preferred stock [prɪˈfəːd-] *npl* (*US*) = **preference shares**.

prefix [ˈpriːfɪks] *n* prefisso.

pregnancy [ˈprɛgnənsɪ] *n* gravidanza.

pregnancy test *n* test *m inv* di gravidanza.

pregnant [ˈprɛgnənt] *adj* incinta *adj f*; (*animal*) gravido(a); (*fig: remark, pause*) significativo(a); **3 months** ~ incinta di 3 mesi.

prehistoric [ˈpriːhɪsˈtɔrɪk] *adj* preistorico(a).

prehistory [priːˈhɪstərɪ] *n* preistoria.

prejudge [priːˈdʒʌdʒ] *vt* pregiudicare.

prejudice [ˈprɛdʒudɪs] *n* pregiudizio; (*harm*) torto, danno ♦ *vt* pregiudicare, ledere; (*bias*): **to** ~ **sb in favour of/against** disporre bene/male qn verso.

prejudiced [ˈprɛdʒudɪst] *adj* (*person*) pieno(a) di pregiudizi; (*view*) prevenuto(a); **to be** ~ **against sb/sth** essere prevenuto contro qn/qc.

prelate [ˈprɛlət] *n* prelato.

preliminaries [prɪˈlɪmɪnərɪz] *npl* preliminari *mpl*.

preliminary [prɪˈlɪmɪnərɪ] *adj* preliminare.

prelude [ˈprɛljuːd] *n* preludio.

premarital [ˈpriːˈmærɪtl] *adj* prematrimoniale.

premature [ˈprɛmətʃuə*] *adj* prematuro(a); (*arrival*) (molto) anticipato(a); **you are being a little** ~ è un po' troppo precipitoso.

premeditated [priːˈmɛdɪteɪtɪd] *adj* premeditato(a).

premeditation [priːmɛdɪˈteɪʃən] *n* premeditazione *f*.

premenstrual tension [priːˈmɛnstruəl-] *n* (*MED*) tensione *f* premestruale.

premier [ˈprɛmɪə*] *adj* primo(a) ♦ *n* (*POL*) primo ministro.

première [ˈprɛmɪɛə*] *n* prima.

premise [ˈprɛmɪs] *n* premessa.

premises [ˈprɛmɪsɪz] *npl* locale *m*; **on the** ~ sul posto; **business** ~ locali commerciali.

premium [ˈpriːmɪəm] *n* premio; **to be at a** ~ (*fig: housing etc*) essere ricercatissimo; **to sell at a** ~ (*shares*) vendere sopra la pari.

premium bond *n* (*BRIT*) obbligazione *f* a premio.

I **premium bonds** *sono delle obbligazioni emesse dal Tesoro britannico fin dal 1956. Non fruttano interessi, ma un premio periodico in denaro.*

---

premium deal *n* (*COMM*) offerta speciale.

premium gasoline *n* (*US*) super *f*.
premonition [prɛmə'nɪʃən] *n* premonizione *f*.
preoccupation [pri:ɔkju'peɪʃən] *n* preoccupazione *f*.
preoccupied [pri:'ɔkjupaɪd] *adj* preoccupato(a).
prep [prɛp] *n abbr* (*SCOL*: = *preparation*) studio ♦ *adj abbr*: ~ **school** = **preparatory school**.
prepackaged [pri:'pækɪdʒd] *adj* già impacchettato(a).
prepaid [pri:'peɪd] *adj* pagato(a) in anticipo; (*envelope*) affrancato(a).
preparation [prɛpə'reɪʃən] *n* preparazione *f*; ~**s** *npl* (*for trip, war*) preparativi *mpl*; **in ~ for sth** in vista di qc.
preparatory [prɪ'pærətərɪ] *adj* preparatorio(a); ~ **to sth/to doing sth** prima di qc/di fare qc.
preparatory school *n* (*BRIT*) scuola elementare privata; (*US*) scuola superiore privata.

In Gran Bretagna, la **prep(aratory) school** *è una scuola, generalmente privata, frequentata da bambini dai 7 ai 13 anni in vista dell'iscrizione alla* **public school**. *Negli Stati Uniti, invece, è una scuola superiore privata che prepara i ragazzi che si iscriveranno al* **college**.

---

prepare [prɪ'pɛə*] *vt* preparare ♦ *vi*: **to ~ for** prepararsi a.
prepared [prɪ'pɛəd] *adj*: ~ **for** preparato(a) a; ~ **to** pronto(a) a; **to be ~ to help sb** (*willing*) essere disposto *or* pronto ad aiutare qn.
preponderance [prɪ'pɔndərns] *n* preponderanza.
preposition [prɛpə'zɪʃən] *n* preposizione *f*.
prepossessing [pri:pə'zɛsɪŋ] *adj* simpatico(a), attraente.
preposterous [prɪ'pɔstərəs] *adj* assurdo(a).
prerecord ['pri:rɪ'kɔːd] *vt* registrare in anticipo; ~**ed broadcast** trasmissione *f* registrata; ~**ed cassette** (musi)cassetta.
prerequisite [pri:'rɛkwɪzɪt] *n* requisito indispensabile.
prerogative [prɪ'rɔgətɪv] *n* prerogativa.
presbyterian [prɛzbɪ'tɪərɪən] *adj, n* presbiteriano(a).
presbytery ['prɛzbɪtərɪ] *n* presbiterio.
preschool ['pri:'sku:l] *adj* (*age*) prescolastico(a); (*child*) in età prescolastica.
prescribe [prɪ'skraɪb] *vt* prescrivere; (*MED*) ordinare; ~**d books** (*BRIT SCOL*) testi *mpl*

in programma.
prescription [prɪ'skrɪpʃən] *n* prescrizione *f*; (*MED*) ricetta; **to make up** *or* (*US*) **fill a ~** preparare *or* fare una ricetta; "**only available on ~**" "ottenibile solo dietro presentazione di ricetta medica".
prescription charges *npl* (*BRIT*) ticket *m inv*.
prescriptive [prɪ'skrɪptɪv] *adj* normativo(a).
presence ['prɛzns] *n* presenza; ~ **of mind** presenza di spirito.
present ['prɛznt] *adj* presente; (*wife, residence, job*) attuale ♦ *n* regalo; (*also:* ~ **tense**) tempo presente ♦ *vt* [prɪ'zɛnt] presentare; (*give*): **to ~ sb with sth** offrire qc a qn; **to be ~ at** essere presente a; **those ~** i presenti; **at ~** al momento; **to make sb a ~ of sth** regalare qc a qn.
presentable [prɪ'zɛntəbl] *adj* presentabile.
presentation [prɛzn'teɪʃən] *n* presentazione *f*; (*gift*) regalo, dono; (*ceremony*) consegna ufficiale; **on ~ of the voucher** dietro presentazione del buono.
present-day ['prɛzntdeɪ] *adj* attuale, d'oggigiorno.
presenter [prɪ'zɛntə*] *n* (*BRIT RADIO, TV*) presentatore/trice.
presently ['prɛzntlɪ] *adv* (*soon*) fra poco, presto; (*at present*) al momento; (*US: now*) adesso, ora.
preservation [prɛzə'veɪʃən] *n* preservazione *f*, conservazione *f*.
preservative [prɪ'zə:vətɪv] *n* conservante *m*.
preserve [prɪ'zə:v] *vt* (*keep safe*) preservare, proteggere; (*maintain*) conservare; (*food*) mettere in conserva ♦ *n* (*for game, fish*) riserva; (*often pl: jam*) marmellata; (*: fruit*) frutta sciroppata.
preshrunk [pri:'ʃrʌŋk] *adj* irrestringibile.
preside [prɪ'zaɪd] *vi* presiedere.
presidency ['prɛzɪdənsɪ] *n* presidenza; (*US: of company*) direzione *f*.
president ['prɛzɪdənt] *n* presidente *m*; (*US: of company*) direttore/trice generale.
presidential [prɛzɪ'dɛnʃl] *adj* presidenziale.
press [prɛs] *n* (*tool, machine*) pressa; (*for wine*) torchio; (*newspapers*) stampa; (*crowd*) folla ♦ *vt* (*push*) premere, pigiare; (*doorbell*) suonare; (*squeeze*) spremere; (*: hand*) stringere; (*clothes: iron*) stirare; (*pursue*) incalzare; (*insist*): **to ~ sth on sb** far accettare qc da qn; (*urge, entreat*): **to ~ sb to do** *or* **into doing sth** fare pressione su qn affinché faccia qc ♦ *vi* premere; accalcare; **to go to ~**

(*newspaper*) andare in macchina; **to be in the** ~ (*in the newspapers*) essere sui giornali; **we are ~ed for time** ci manca il tempo; **to** ~ **for sth** insistere per avere qc; **to** ~ **sb for an answer** insistere perché qn risponda; **to** ~ **charges against sb** (*LAW*) sporgere una denuncia contro qn.

▶**press ahead** *vi*: **to** ~ **ahead (with)** andare avanti (con).

▶**press on** *vi* continuare.

press agency *n* agenzia di stampa.
press clipping *n* ritaglio di giornale.
press conference *n* conferenza stampa.
press cutting *n* = **press clipping**.
press-gang ['prɛsgæŋ] *vt*: **to** ~ **sb into doing sth** costringere qn a viva forza a fare qc.
pressing ['prɛsɪŋ] *adj* urgente ♦ *n* stiratura.
press officer *n* addetto/a stampa *inv*.
press release *n* comunicato stampa.
press stud *n* (*BRIT*) bottone *m* a pressione.
press-up ['prɛsʌp] *n* (*BRIT*) flessione *f* sulle braccia.
pressure ['prɛʃə*] *n* pressione *f* ♦ *vt* = **to put** ~ **on; high/low** ~ alta/bassa pressione; **to put** ~ **on sb** fare pressione su qn.
pressure cooker *n* pentola a pressione.
pressure gauge *n* manometro.
pressure group *n* gruppo di pressione.
pressurize ['prɛʃəraɪz] *vt* pressurizzare; (*fig*): **to** ~ **sb (into doing sth)** fare delle pressioni su qn (per costringerlo a fare qc).
pressurized ['prɛʃəraɪzd] *adj* pressurizzato(a).
Prestel ® ['prɛstɛl] *n* Videotel ® *m inv*.
prestige [prɛs'tiːʒ] *n* prestigio.
prestigious [prɛs'tɪdʒəs] *adj* prestigioso(a).
presumably [prɪ'zjuːməblɪ] *adv* presumibilmente; ~ **he did it** penso *or* presumo che l'abbia fatto.
presume [prɪ'zjuːm] *vt* supporre; **to** ~ **to do** (*dare*) permettersi di fare.
presumption [prɪ'zʌmpʃən] *n* presunzione *f*; (*boldness*) audacia.
presumptuous [prɪ'zʌmpʃəs] *adj* presuntuoso(a).
presuppose [priːsə'pəuz] *vt* presupporre.
pre-tax [priː'tæks] *adj* al lordo d'imposta.
pretence, (*US*) **pretense** [prɪ'tɛns] *n* (*claim*) pretesa; (*pretext*) pretesto, scusa; **to make a** ~ **of doing** far finta di fare; **on** *or* **under the** ~ **of doing sth** con il pretesto *or* la scusa di fare qc; **she is devoid of all** ~ non si nasconde dietro false apparenze.

pretend [prɪ'tɛnd] *vt* (*feign*) fingere ♦ *vi* far finta; (*claim*): **to** ~ **to sth** pretendere a qc; **to** ~ **to do** far finta di fare.
pretense [prɪ'tɛns] *n* (*US*) = **pretence**.
pretension [prɪ'tɛnʃən] *n* (*claim*) pretesa; **to have no ~s to being/to doing sth** non avere la pretesa di avere qc/di essere qc.
pretentious [prɪ'tɛnʃəs] *adj* pretenzioso(a).
preterite ['prɛtərɪt] *n* preterito.
pretext ['priːtɛkst] *n* pretesto; **on** *or* **under the** ~ **of doing sth** col pretesto di fare qc.
pretty ['prɪtɪ] *adj* grazioso(a), carino(a) ♦ *adv* abbastanza, assai.
prevail [prɪ'veɪl] *vi* (*win, be usual*) prevalere; (*persuade*): **to** ~ **(up)on sb to do** persuadere qn a fare.
prevailing [prɪ'veɪlɪŋ] *adj* dominante.
prevalent ['prɛvələnt] *adj* (*belief*) predominante; (*customs*) diffuso(a); (*fashion*) corrente; (*disease*) comune.
prevarication [prɪværɪ'keɪʃən] *n* tergiversazione *f*.
prevent [prɪ'vɛnt] *vt* prevenire; **to** ~ **sb from doing** impedire a qn di fare.
preventable [prɪ'vɛntəbl] *adj* evitabile.
preventative [prɪ'vɛntətɪv] *adj* preventivo(a).
prevention [prɪ'vɛnʃən] *n* prevenzione *f*.
preventive [prɪ'vɛntɪv] *adj* preventivo(a).
preview ['priːvjuː] *n* (*of film*) anteprima.
previous ['priːvɪəs] *adj* precedente; anteriore; **I have a** ~ **engagement** ho già (preso) un impegno; ~ **to doing** prima di fare.
previously ['priːvɪəslɪ] *adv* prima.
prewar ['priː'wɔː*] *adj* anteguerra *inv*.
prey [preɪ] *n* preda ♦ *vi*: **to** ~ **on** far preda di; **it was ~ing on his mind** gli rodeva la mente.
price [praɪs] *n* prezzo; (*BETTING: odds*) quotazione *f* ♦ *vt* (*goods*) fissare il prezzo di; valutare; **what is the** ~ **of ...?** quanto costa ...?; **to go up** *or* **rise in** ~ salire *or* aumentare di prezzo; **to put a** ~ **on sth** valutare *or* stimare qc; **he regained his freedom, but at a** ~ ha riconquistato la sua libertà, ma a caro prezzo; **what** ~ **his promises now?** (*BRIT*) a che valgono ora le sue promesse?; **to be ~d out of the market** (*article*) essere così caro da diventare invendibile; (*producer, nation*) non poter sostenere la concorrenza.
price control *n* controllo dei prezzi.
price-cutting ['praɪskʌtɪŋ] *n* riduzione *f* dei prezzi.
priceless ['praɪslɪs] *adj* di valore

inestimabile; (*col*: *amusing*) impagabile, spassosissimo(a).
price list *n* listino (dei) prezzi.
price range *n* gamma di prezzi; **it's within my** ~ rientra nelle mie possibilità.
price tag *n* cartellino del prezzo.
price war *n* guerra dei prezzi.
pricey ['praɪsɪ] *adj* (*col*) caruccio(a).
prick [prɪk] *n* puntura ♦ *vt* pungere; **to** ~ **up one's ears** drizzare gli orecchi.
prickle ['prɪkl] *n* (*of plant*) spina; (*sensation*) pizzicore *m*.
prickly ['prɪklɪ] *adj* spinoso(a); (*fig*: *person*) permaloso(a).
prickly heat *n* sudamina.
prickly pear *n* fico d'India.
pride [praɪd] *n* orgoglio; superbia ♦ *vt*: **to** ~ **o.s. on** essere orgoglioso(a) di; vantarsi di; **to take (a)** ~ **in** tenere molto a; essere orgoglioso di; **to take a** ~ **in doing** andare orgoglioso di fare; **to have** ~ **of place** (*BRIT*) essere al primo posto.
priest [priːst] *n* prete *m*, sacerdote *m*.
priestess ['priːstɪs] *n* sacerdotessa.
priesthood ['priːsthud] *n* sacerdozio.
prig [prɪg] *n*: **he's a** ~ è compiaciuto di se stesso.
prim [prɪm] *adj* pudico(a); contegnoso(a).
primacy ['praɪməsɪ] *n* primato.
prima facie ['praɪmə'feɪʃɪ] *adj*: **to have a** ~ **case** (*LAW*) presentare una causa in apparenza fondata.
primal ['praɪməl] *adj* primitivo(a), originario(a).
primarily ['praɪmərɪlɪ] *adv* principalmente, essenzialmente.
primary ['praɪmərɪ] *adj* primario(a); (*first in importance*) primo(a) ♦ *n* (*US*: *election*) primarie *fpl*.

> *Negli Stati Uniti, attraverso le* **primary** *viene fatta una prima scrematura dei candidati dei partiti alle elezioni presidenziali. La scelta definitiva del candidato da presentare alla presidenza si basa sui risultati delle primary e ha luogo durante le Convention dei partiti, che si tengono in luglio e in agosto.*

primary colour *n* colore *m* fondamentale.
primary school *n* (*BRIT*) scuola elementare.

> *In Gran Bretagna la* **primary school** *è la scuola elementare, frequentata dai bambini dai 5 agli 11 anni di età. È suddivisa in* **infant school** *(5-7 anni) e* **junior school** *(7-11 anni); vedi anche* **secondary school**.

primate *n* (*REL*: ['praɪmɪt], *ZOOL*: ['praɪmeɪt]) primate *m*.
prime [praɪm] *adj* primario(a), fondamentale; (*excellent*) di prima qualità ♦ *n*: **in the** ~ **of life** nel fiore della vita ♦ *vt* (*gun*) innescare; (*pump*) adescare; (*fig*) mettere al corrente.
prime minister (PM) *n* primo ministro.
primer ['praɪmə*] *n* (*book*) testo elementare; (*paint*) vernice *f* base *inv*.
prime time *n* (*RADIO, TV*) fascia di massimo ascolto.
primeval [praɪˈmiːvl] *adj* primitivo(a).
primitive ['prɪmɪtɪv] *adj* primitivo(a).
primrose ['prɪmrəuz] *n* primavera.
primus (stove) ® ['praɪməs-] *n* (*BRIT*) fornello a petrolio.
prince [prɪns] *n* principe *m*.
prince charming *n* principe *m* azzurro.
princess [prɪnˈsɛs] *n* principessa.
principal ['prɪnsɪpl] *adj* principale ♦ *n* (*of school, college etc*) preside *m/f*; (*money*) capitale *m*; (*in play*) protagonista *m/f*.
principality [prɪnsɪˈpælɪtɪ] *n* principato.
principally ['prɪnsɪplɪ] *adv* principalmente.
principle ['prɪnsɪpl] *n* principio; **in** ~ in linea di principio; **on** ~ per principio.
print [prɪnt] *n* (*mark*) impronta; (*letters*) caratteri *mpl*; (*fabric*) tessuto stampato; (*ART, PHOT*) stampa ♦ *vt* imprimere; (*publish*) stampare, pubblicare; (*write in capitals*) scrivere in stampatello; **out of** ~ esaurito(a).
▶**print out** *vt* (*COMPUT*) stampare.
printed circuit board (PCB) [prɪntɪd-] *n* circuito stampato.
printed matter [prɪntɪd-] *n* stampe *fpl*.
printer ['prɪntə*] *n* tipografo; (*machine*) stampante *m*.
printhead ['prɪnthɛd] *n* testa di stampa.
printing ['prɪntɪŋ] *n* stampa.
printing press *n* macchina tipografica.
print-out ['prɪntaut] *n* tabulato.
print wheel *n* margherita.
prior ['praɪə*] *adj* precedente ♦ *n* (*REL*) priore *m*; ~ **to doing** prima di fare; **without** ~ **notice** senza preavviso; **to have a** ~ **claim to sth** avere un diritto di precedenza su qc.
priority [praɪˈɔrɪtɪ] *n* priorità *f inv*, precedenza; **to have** *or* **take** ~ **over sth** avere la precedenza su qc.
priory ['praɪərɪ] *n* monastero.
prise [praɪz] *vt*: **to** ~ **open** forzare.
prism ['prɪzəm] *n* prisma *m*.
prison ['prɪzn] *n* prigione *f*.
prison camp *n* campo di prigionia.

prisoner ['prɪznə*] *n* prigioniero/a; **to take sb** ~ far prigioniero qn; **the** ~ **at the bar** l'accusato, l'imputato; ~ **of war** prigioniero/a di guerra.

prissy ['prɪsɪ] *adj* per benino.

pristine ['prɪstiːn] *adj* originario(a); intatto(a); puro(a).

privacy ['prɪvəsɪ] *n* solitudine *f*, intimità.

private ['praɪvɪt] *adj* privato(a); personale ♦ *n* soldato semplice; "~" (*on envelope*) "riservata"; **in** ~ in privato; **in (his)** ~ **life** nella vita privata; **he is a very** ~ **person** è una persona molto riservata; ~ **hearing** (*LAW*) udienza a porte chiuse; **to be in** ~ **practice** essere medico non convenzionato (con la mutua).

private enterprise *n* iniziativa privata.

private eye *n* investigatore *m* privato.

private limited company *n* (*BRIT*) società per azioni non quotata in Borsa.

privately ['praɪvɪtlɪ] *adv* in privato; (*within o.s.*) dentro di sé.

private parts *npl* (*ANAT*) parti *fpl* intime.

private property *n* proprietà privata.

private school *n* scuola privata.

privation [praɪ'veɪʃən] *n* (*state*) privazione *f*; (*hardship*) privazioni *fpl*, stenti *mpl*.

privatize ['praɪvɪtaɪz] *vt* privatizzare.

privet ['prɪvɪt] *n* ligustro.

privilege ['prɪvɪlɪdʒ] *n* privilegio.

privileged ['prɪvɪlɪdʒd] *adj* privilegiato(a); **to be** ~ **to do sth** avere il privilegio *or* l'onore di fare qc.

privy ['prɪvɪ] *adj*: **to be** ~ **to** essere al corrente di.

Privy Council *n* (*BRIT*) Consiglio della Corona.

Il **Privy Council**, *un gruppo di consiglieri del re, era il principale organo di governo durante il regno dei Tudor e degli Stuart. Col tempo ha perso la sua importanza e oggi è un organo senza potere effettivo formato da ministri e altre personalità politiche ed ecclesiastiche.*

Privy Councillor *n* (*BRIT*) Consigliere *m* della Corona.

prize [praɪz] *n* premio ♦ *adj* (*example, idiot*) perfetto(a); (*bull, novel*) premiato(a) ♦ *vt* apprezzare, pregiare.

prize-fighter ['praɪzfaɪtə*] *n* pugile *m* (*che si batte per conquistare un premio*).

prize giving *n* premiazione *f*.

prize money *n* soldi *mpl* del premio.

prizewinner ['praɪzwɪnə*] *n* premiato/a.

prizewinning ['praɪzwɪnɪŋ] *adj* vincente; (*novel, essay etc*) premiato(a).

PRO *n abbr* = **public relations officer**.

pro [prəu] *n* (*SPORT*) professionista *m/f*; **the** ~**s and cons** il pro e il contro.

pro- [prəu] *prefix* (*in favour of*) filo...; ~**Soviet** *adj* filosovietico(a).

pro-active [prəu'æktɪv] *adj*: **to be** ~ agire d'iniziativa.

probability [prɔbə'bɪlɪtɪ] *n* probabilità *f inv*; **in all** ~ con ogni probabilità.

probable ['prɔbəbl] *adj* probabile; **it is** ~ / **hardly** ~ **that** ... è probabile/poco probabile che ... + *sub*.

probably ['prɔbəblɪ] *adv* probabilmente.

probate ['prəubɪt] *n* (*LAW*) omologazione *f* (*di un testamento*).

probation [prə'beɪʃən] *n* (*in employment*) periodo di prova; (*LAW*) libertà vigilata; (*REL*) probandato; **on** ~ (*employee*) in prova; (*LAW*) in libertà vigilata.

probationary [prəu'beɪʃənərɪ] *adj*: ~ **period** periodo di prova.

probe [prəub] *n* (*MED, SPACE*) sonda; (*enquiry*) indagine *f*, investigazione *f* ♦ *vt* sondare, esplorare; indagare.

probity ['prəubɪtɪ] *n* probità.

problem ['prɔbləm] *n* problema *m*; **to have** ~**s with the car** avere dei problemi con la macchina; **what's the** ~? che cosa c'è?; **I had no** ~ **in finding her** non mi è stato difficile trovarla; **no** ~! ma certamente!, non c'è problema!

problematic [prɔblə'mætɪk] *adj* problematico(a).

problem-solving ['prɔbləmsɔlvɪŋ] *n* risoluzione *f* di problemi.

procedure [prə'siːdʒə*] *n* (*ADMIN, LAW*) procedura; (*method*) metodo, procedimento.

proceed [prə'siːd] *vi* (*go forward*) avanzare, andare avanti; (*go about it*) procedere; (*continue*): **to** ~ (**with**) continuare; **to** ~ **to** andare a; passare a; **to** ~ **to do** mettersi a fare; **to** ~ **against sb** (*LAW*) procedere contro qn; **I am not sure how to** ~ non so bene come fare.

proceedings [prə'siːdɪŋz] *npl* misure *fpl*; (*LAW*) procedimento; (*meeting*) riunione *f*; (*records*) rendiconti *mpl*; atti *mpl*.

proceeds ['prəusiːdz] *npl* profitto, incasso.

process ['prəusɛs] *n* processo; (*method*) metodo, sistema *m* ♦ *vt* trattare; (*information*) elaborare ♦ *vi* [prə'sɛs] (*BRIT formal: go in procession*) sfilare, procedere in corteo; **we are in the** ~ **of moving to** ... stiamo per trasferirci a ....

processed cheese, (*US*) **process cheese** *n* formaggio fuso.

processing ['prəusɛsɪŋ] *n* trattamento;

elaborazione *f*.
procession [prə'sɛʃən] *n* processione *f*,
corteo; **funeral** ~ corteo funebre.
pro-choice [prəu'tʃɔɪs] *adj* per la libertà di
scelta di gravidanza.
proclaim [prə'kleɪm] *vt* proclamare,
dichiarare.
proclamation [prɔklə'meɪʃən] *n*
proclamazione *f*.
proclivity [prə'klɪvɪtɪ] *n* tendenza,
propensione *f*.
procrastination [prəukræstɪ'neɪʃən] *n*
procrastinazione *f*.
procreation [prəukrɪ'eɪʃən] *n* procreazione
f.
Procurator Fiscal ['prɔkjureɪtə-] *n*
(*Scottish*) procuratore *m*.
procure [prə'kjuə*] *vt* (*for o.s.*) procurarsi;
(*for sb*) procurare.
procurement [prə'kjuəmənt] *n*
approvvigionamento.
prod [prɔd] *vt* dare un colpetto a ♦ *n* (*push,
jab*) colpetto.
prodigal ['prɔdɪgl] *adj* prodigo(a).
prodigious [prə'dɪdʒəs] *adj* prodigioso(a).
prodigy ['prɔdɪdʒɪ] *n* prodigio.
produce *n* ['prɔdjuːs] (*AGR*) prodotto,
prodotti *mpl* ♦ *vt* [prə'djuːs] produrre; (*to
show*) esibire, mostrare; (*proof of identity*)
produrre, fornire; (*cause*) cagionare,
causare; (*THEAT*) mettere in scena.
producer [prə'djuːsə*] *n* (*THEAT*) direttore/
trice; (*AGR, CINE*) produttore *m*.
product ['prɔdʌkt] *n* prodotto.
production [prə'dʌkʃən] *n* produzione *f*;
(*THEAT*) messa in scena; **to put into** ~
mettere in produzione.
production agreement *n* (*US*) accordo
sui tempi di produzione.
production line *n* catena di lavorazione.
production manager *n* production
manager *m inv*, direttore *m* della
produzione.
productive [prə'dʌktɪv] *adj* produttivo(a).
productivity [prɔdʌk'tɪvɪtɪ] *n* produttività.
productivity agreement *n* (*BRIT*) accordo
sui tempi di produzione.
productivity bonus *n* premio di
produzione.
Prof. *abbr* (= *professor*) Prof.
profane [prə'feɪn] *adj* profano(a); (*language*)
empio(a).
profess [prə'fɛs] *vt* professare; **I do not** ~
to be an expert non pretendo di essere un
esperto.
professed [prə'fɛst] *adj* (*self-declared*)
dichiarato(a).
profession [prə'fɛʃən] *n* professione *f*; **the**

~**s** le professioni liberali.
professional [prə'fɛʃnl] *n* (*SPORT*)
professionista *m/f* ♦ *adj* professionale;
(*work*) da professionista; **he's a** ~ **man** è
un professionista; **to take** ~ **advice**
consultare un esperto.
professionalism [prə'fɛʃnəlɪzəm] *n*
professionismo.
professionally [prə'fɛʃnəlɪ] *adv*
professionalmente, in modo
professionale; (*SPORT: play*) come
professionista; **I only know him** ~ con lui
ho solo rapporti di lavoro.
professor [prə'fɛsə*] *n* professore *m*
(*titolare di una cattedra*); (*US: teacher*)
professore/essa.
professorship [prə'fɛsəʃɪp] *n* cattedra.
proffer ['prɔfə*] *vt* (*remark*) profferire;
(*apologies*) porgere, presentare; (*one's
hand*) porgere.
proficiency [prə'fɪʃənsɪ] *n* competenza,
abilità.
proficient [prə'fɪʃənt] *adj* competente,
abile.
profile ['prəufaɪl] *n* profilo; **to keep a low** ~
(*fig*) cercare di passare inosservato *or* di
non farsi notare troppo; **to maintain a
high** ~ mettersi in mostra.
profit ['prɔfɪt] *n* profitto; beneficio ♦ *vi*: **to** ~
(**by** *or* **from**) approfittare (di); ~ **and loss
account** conto perdite e profitti; **to make
a** ~ realizzare un profitto; **to sell sth at a**
~ vendere qc con un utile.
profitability [prɔfɪtə'bɪlɪtɪ] *n* redditività.
profitable ['prɔfɪtəbl] *adj* redditizio(a); (*fig:
beneficial*) vantaggioso(a); (*: meeting, visit*)
fruttuoso(a).
profit centre *n* centro di profitto.
profiteering [prɔfɪ'tɪərɪŋ] *n* (*pej*) affarismo.
profit-making ['prɔfɪtmeɪkɪŋ] *adj* a scopo di
lucro.
profit margin *n* margine *m* di profitto.
profit-sharing ['prɔfɪtʃɛərɪŋ] *n*
compartecipazione *f* agli utili.
profits tax *n* (*BRIT*) imposta sugli utili.
profligate ['prɔflɪgɪt] *adj* (*dissolute:
behaviour*) dissipato(a); (*: person*)
debosciato(a); (*extravagant*): **he's very** ~
with his money è uno che sperpera i suoi
soldi.
pro forma ['prəu'fɔːmə] *adv*: ~ **invoice**
fattura proforma.
profound [prə'faund] *adj* profondo(a).
profuse [prə'fjuːs] *adj* infinito(a),
abbondante.
profusely [prə'fjuːslɪ] *adv* con grande
effusione.
profusion [prə'fjuːʒən] *n* profusione *f*,

abbondanza.

progeny ['prɒdʒɪnɪ] *n* progenie *f*; discendenti *mpl*.

programme, (*US*) **program** ['prəʊɡræm] *n* programma *m* ♦ *vt* programmare.

program(m)er ['prəʊɡræmə*] *n* programmatore/trice.

program(m)ing ['prəʊɡræmɪŋ] *n* programmazione *f*.

program(m)ing language *n* linguaggio di programmazione.

progress *n* ['prəʊɡrɛs] progresso ♦ *vi* [prə'ɡrɛs] (*go forward*) avanzare, procedere; (*in time*) procedere; (*also*: **make ~**) far progressi; **in ~** in corso.

progression [prə'ɡrɛʃən] *n* progressione *f*.

progressive [prə'ɡrɛsɪv] *adj* progressivo(a); (*person*) progressista.

progressively [prə'ɡrɛsɪvlɪ] *adv* progressivamente.

progress report *n* (*MED*) bollettino medico; (*ADMIN*) rendiconto dei lavori.

prohibit [prə'hɪbɪt] *vt* proibire, vietare; **to ~ sb from doing sth** vietare *or* proibire a qn di fare qc; **"smoking ~ed"** "vietato fumare".

prohibition [prəʊɪ'bɪʃən] *n* (*US*) proibizionismo.

prohibitive [prə'hɪbɪtɪv] *adj* (*price etc*) proibitivo(a).

project *n* ['prɒdʒɛkt] (*plan*) piano; (*venture*) progetto; (*SCOL*) studio, ricerca ♦ *vb* [prə'dʒɛkt] *vt* proiettare ♦ *vi* (*stick out*) sporgere.

projectile [prə'dʒɛktaɪl] *n* proiettile *m*.

projection [prə'dʒɛkʃən] *n* proiezione *f*; sporgenza.

projectionist [prə'dʒɛkʃənɪst] *n* (*CINE*) proiezionista *m/f*.

projection room *n* (*CINE*) cabina *or* sala di proiezione.

projector [prə'dʒɛktə*] *n* proiettore *m*.

proletarian [prəʊlɪ'tɛərɪən] *adj, n* proletario(a).

proletariat [prəʊlɪ'tɛərɪət] *n* proletariato.

pro-life [prəʊ'laɪf] *adj* per il diritto alla vita.

proliferate [prə'lɪfəreɪt] *vi* proliferare.

proliferation [prəlɪfə'reɪʃən] *n* proliferazione *f*.

prolific [prə'lɪfɪk] *adj* prolifico(a).

prologue, (*US*) **prolog** ['prəʊlɒɡ] *n* prologo.

prolong [prə'lɒŋ] *vt* prolungare.

prom [prɒm] *n abbr* = **promenade, promenade concert**; (*US: ball*) ballo studentesco.

In Gran Bretagna i **Prom** (= *promenade concert*) *sono concerti di musica classica, i più noti dei quali sono quelli eseguiti nella Royal Albert Hall a Londra. Prendono il nome dal fatto che in origine il pubblico li ascoltava stando in piedi o passeggiando. Negli Stati Uniti, invece, con prom si intende il ballo studentesco di un'università o di un college.*

---

promenade [prɒmə'nɑːd] *n* (*by sea*) lungomare *m*.

promenade concert *n* concerto (*con posti in piedi*).

promenade deck *n* (*NAUT*) ponte *m* di passeggiata.

prominence ['prɒmɪnəns] *n* prominenza; importanza.

prominent ['prɒmɪnənt] *adj* (*standing out*) prominente; (*important*) importante; **he is ~ in the field of ...** è un'autorità nel campo di ....

prominently ['prɒmɪnəntlɪ] *adv* (*display, set*) ben in vista; **he figured ~ in the case** ha avuto una parte di primo piano nella faccenda.

promiscuity [prɒmɪs'kjuːɪtɪ] *n* (*sexual*) rapporti *mpl* multipli.

promiscuous [prə'mɪskjuəs] *adj* (*sexually*) di facili costumi.

promise ['prɒmɪs] *n* promessa ♦ *vt, vi* promettere; **to make sb a ~** fare una promessa a qn; **a young man of ~** un giovane promettente; **to ~ (sb) to do sth** promettere (a qn) di fare qc.

promising ['prɒmɪsɪŋ] *adj* promettente.

promissory note ['prɒmɪsərɪ-] *n* pagherò *m inv*.

promontory ['prɒməntrɪ] *n* promontorio.

promote [prə'məʊt] *vt* promuovere; (*venture, event*) organizzare; (*product*) lanciare, reclamizzare; **the team was ~d to the second division** (*BRIT FOOTBALL*) la squadra è stata promossa in serie B.

promoter [prə'məʊtə*] *n* (*of sporting event*) organizzatore/trice; (*of cause etc*) sostenitore/trice.

promotion [prə'məʊʃən] *n* promozione *f*.

prompt [prɒmpt] *adj* rapido(a), svelto(a); puntuale; (*reply*) sollecito(a) ♦ *adv* (*punctually*) in punto ♦ *n* (*COMPUT*) guida ♦ *vt* incitare; provocare; (*THEAT*) suggerire a; **at 8 o'clock ~** alle 8 in punto; **to be ~ to do sth** essere sollecito nel fare qc; **to ~ sb to do** spingere qn a fare.

prompter ['prɒmptə*] *n* (*THEAT*) suggeritore *m*.

promptly ['promptlɪ] *adv* prontamente; puntualmente.

promptness ['promptnɪs] *n* prontezza; puntualità.

prone [prəun] *adj* (*lying*) prono(a); ~ **to** propenso(a) a, incline a; **to be** ~ **to illness** essere soggetto(a) a malattie; **she is** ~ **to burst into tears if** ... può facilmente scoppiare in lacrime se ....

prong [prɔŋ] *n* rebbio, punta.

pronoun ['prəunaun] *n* pronome *m*.

pronounce [prə'nauns] *vt* pronunziare ♦ *vi*: **to** ~ **(up)on** pronunziare su; **they** ~**d him unfit to drive** lo hanno dichiarato inabile alla guida.

pronounced [prə'naunst] *adj* (*marked*) spiccato(a).

pronouncement [prə'naunsmənt] *n* dichiarazione *f*.

pronunciation [prənʌnsɪ'eɪʃən] *n* pronunzia.

proof [pru:f] *n* prova; (*of book*) bozza; (*PHOT*) provino; (*of alcohol*): **70%** ~ ≈ 40° in volume ♦ *vt* (*tent, anorak*) impermeabilizzare ♦ *adj*: ~ **against** a prova di.

proofreader ['pru:fri:də*] *n* correttore/trice di bozze.

prop [prɔp] *n* sostegno, appoggio ♦ *vt* (*also*: ~ **up**) sostenere, appoggiare; (*lean*): **to** ~ **sth against** appoggiare qc contro *or* a.

Prop. *abbr* (*COMM*) = **proprietor**.

propaganda [prɔpə'gændə] *n* propaganda.

propagation [prɔpə'geɪʃən] *n* propagazione *f*.

propel [prə'pɛl] *vt* spingere (in avanti), muovere.

propeller [prə'pɛlə*] *n* elica.

propelling pencil [prə'pɛlɪŋ-] *n* (*BRIT*) matita a mina.

propensity [prə'pɛnsɪtɪ] *n* tendenza.

proper ['prɔpə*] *adj* (*suited, right*) adatto(a), appropriato(a); (*seemly*) decente; (*authentic*) vero(a); (*col*: *real*) *n* + vero(a) e proprio(a); **to go through the** ~ **channels** (*ADMIN*) seguire la regolare procedura.

properly ['prɔpəlɪ] *adv* decentemente; (*really, thoroughly*) veramente.

proper noun *n* nome *m* proprio.

property ['prɔpətɪ] *n* (*things owned*) beni *mpl*; (*land, building, CHEM etc*) proprietà *f inv*.

property developer *n* (*BRIT*) costruttore *m* edile.

property owner *n* proprietario/a.

property tax *n* imposta patrimoniale.

prophecy ['prɔfɪsɪ] *n* profezia.

prophesy ['prɔfɪsaɪ] *vt* predire, profetizzare.

prophet ['prɔfɪt] *n* profeta *m*.

prophetic [prə'fɛtɪk] *adj* profetico(a).

proportion [prə'pɔ:ʃən] *n* proporzione *f*; (*share*) parte *f* ♦ *vt* proporzionare, commisurare; **to be in/out of** ~ **to** *or* **with sth** essere in proporzione/sproporzionato rispetto a qc; **to see sth in** ~(*fig*) dare il giusto peso a qc.

proportional [prə'pɔ:ʃənl] *adj* proporzionale.

proportional representation (PR) *n* rappresentanza proporzionale.

proportionate [prə'pɔ:ʃənɪt] *adj* proporzionato(a).

proposal [prə'pəuzl] *n* proposta; (*plan*) progetto; (*of marriage*) proposta di matrimonio.

propose [prə'pəuz] *vt* proporre, suggerire ♦ *vi* fare una proposta di matrimonio; **to** ~ **to do** proporsi di fare, aver l'intenzione di fare.

proposer [prə'pəuzə*] *n* (*BRIT*: *of motion*) proponente *m/f*.

proposition [prɔpə'zɪʃən] *n* proposizione *f*; (*proposal*) proposta; **to make sb a** ~ proporre qualcosa a qn.

propound [prə'paund] *vt* proporre, presentare.

proprietary [prə'praɪətərɪ] *adj*: ~ **article** prodotto con marchio depositato; ~ **brand** marchio di fabbrica.

proprietor [prə'praɪətə*] *n* proprietario/a.

propriety [prə'praɪətɪ] *n* (*seemliness*) decoro, rispetto delle convenienze sociali.

propulsion [prə'pʌlʃən] *n* propulsione *f*.

pro rata [prəu'rɑːtə] *adv* in proporzione.

prosaic [prəu'zeɪɪk] *adj* prosaico(a).

Pros. Atty. *abbr* (*US*) = **prosecuting attorney**.

proscribe [prə'skraɪb] *vt* proscrivere.

prose [prəuz] *n* prosa; (*SCOL*: *translation*) traduzione *f* dalla madrelingua.

prosecute ['prɔsɪkjuːt] *vt* intentare azione contro.

prosecuting attorney ['prɔsɪkjuːtɪŋ-] *n* (*US*) ≈ procuratore *m*.

prosecution [prɔsɪ'kjuːʃən] *n* (*LAW*) azione *f* giudiziaria; (*accusing side*) accusa.

prosecutor ['prɔsɪkjuːtə*] *n* (*also*: **public** ~) ≈ procuratore *m* della Repubblica.

prospect *n* ['prɔspɛkt] prospettiva; (*hope*) speranza ♦ *vb* [prə'spɛkt] *vt* esplorare ♦ *vi*: **to** ~ **for gold** cercare l'oro; **there is every** ~ **of an early victory** tutto lascia prevedere una rapida vittoria; *see also* **prospects**.

prospecting [prə'spɛktɪŋ] *n* prospezione *f*.

prospective [prə'spɛktɪv] *adj* (*buyer*) probabile; (*legislation, son-in-law*) futuro(a).

prospector [prə'spɛktə*] *n* prospettore *m*; **gold** ~ cercatore *m* d'oro.

prospects ['prɔspɛkts] *npl* (*for work etc*) prospettive *fpl*.

prospectus [prə'spɛktəs] *n* prospetto, programma *m*.

prosper ['prɔspə*] *vi* prosperare.

prosperity [prɔ'spɛrɪtɪ] *n* prosperità.

prosperous ['prɔspərəs] *adj* prospero(a).

prostate ['prɔsteɪt] *n* (*also:* ~ **gland**) prostata, ghiandola prostatica.

prostitute ['prɔstɪtjuːt] *n* prostituta; **male** ~ uomo che si prostituisce.

prostitution [prɔstɪ'tjuːʃən] *n* prostituzione *f*.

prostrate *adj* ['prɔstreɪt] prostrato(a) ♦ *vt* [prɔ'streɪt]: **to** ~ **o.s.** (*before sb*) prostrarsi.

protagonist [prə'tægənɪst] *n* protagonista *m/f*.

protect [prə'tɛkt] *vt* proteggere, salvaguardare.

protection [prə'tɛkʃən] *n* protezione *f*; **to be under sb's** ~ essere sotto la protezione di qn.

protectionism [prə'tɛkʃənɪzəm] *n* protezionismo.

protection racket *n* racket *m inv*.

protective [prə'tɛktɪv] *adj* protettivo(a); ~ **custody** (*LAW*) protezione *f*.

protector [prə'tɛktə*] *n* protettore/trice.

protégé ['prəutɪʒeɪ] *n* protetto.

protégée ['prəutɪʒeɪ] *n* protetta.

protein ['prəutiːn] *n* proteina.

pro tem [prəu'tɛm] *adv abbr* (= *pro tempore:* *for the time being*) pro tempore.

protest *n* ['prəutɛst] protesta ♦ *vt, vi* [prə'tɛst] protestare; **to do sth under** ~ fare qc protestando; **to** ~ **against/about** protestare contro/per.

Protestant ['prɔtɪstənt] *adj, n* protestante (*m/f*).

protester, protestor [prə'tɛstə*] *n* (*in demonstration*) dimostrante *m/f*.

protest march *n* marcia di protesta.

protocol ['prəutəkɔl] *n* protocollo.

prototype ['prəutətaɪp] *n* prototipo.

protracted [prə'træktɪd] *adj* tirato(a) per le lunghe.

protractor [prə'træktə*] *n* (*GEOM*) goniometro.

protrude [prə'truːd] *vi* sporgere.

protuberance [prə'tjuːbərəns] *n* sporgenza.

proud [praud] *adj* fiero(a), orgoglioso(a); (*pej*) superbo(a); **to be** ~ **to do sth** essere onorato(a) di fare qc; **to do sb** ~ non far

mancare nulla a qn; **to do o.s.** ~ trattarsi bene.

proudly ['praudlɪ] *adv* con orgoglio, fieramente.

prove [pruːv] *vt* provare, dimostrare ♦ *vi*: **to** ~ **correct** *etc* risultare vero(a) *etc*; **to** ~ **o.s.** mostrare le proprie capacità; **to** ~ **o.s./itself (to be) useful** *etc* mostrarsi *or* rivelarsi utile *etc*; **he was** ~**d right in the end** alla fine i fatti gli hanno dato ragione.

Provence [prɔvãs] *n* Provenza.

proverb ['prɔvɜːb] *n* proverbio.

proverbial [prə'vɜːbɪəl] *adj* proverbiale.

provide [prə'vaɪd] *vt* fornire, provvedere; **to** ~ **sb with sth** fornire *or* provvedere qn di qc; **to be** ~**d with** essere dotato *or* munito di.

▶**provide for** *vt fus* provvedere a.

provided [prə'vaɪdɪd] *conj:* ~ **(that)** purché + *sub*, a condizione che + *sub*.

Providence ['prɔvɪdəns] *n* Provvidenza.

providing [prə'vaɪdɪŋ] *conj* purché + *sub*, a condizione che + *sub*.

province ['prɔvɪns] *n* provincia.

provincial [prə'vɪnʃəl] *adj* provinciale.

provision [prə'vɪʒən] *n* (*supply*) riserva; (*supplying*) provvista; rifornimento; (*stipulation*) condizione *f*; ~**s** *npl* (*food*) provviste *fpl*; **to make** ~ **for** (*one's family, future*) pensare a; **there's no** ~ **for this in the contract** il contratto non lo prevede.

provisional [prə'vɪʒənl] *adj* provvisorio(a) ♦ *n*: **P**~ (*Irish POL*) provisional *m inv*.

provisional licence *n* (*BRIT AUT*) ≈ foglio *m* rosa *inv*.

provisionally [prə'vɪʒnəlɪ] *adv* provvisoriamente; (*appoint*) a titolo provvisorio.

proviso [prə'vaɪzəu] *n* condizione *f*; **with the** ~ **that** a condizione che + *sub*, a patto che + *sub*.

Provo ['prɔvəu] *n abbr* (*col*) = **Provisional**.

provocation [prɔvə'keɪʃən] *n* provocazione *f*.

provocative [prə'vɔkətɪv] *adj* (*aggressive*) provocatorio(a); (*thought-provoking*) stimolante; (*seductive*) provocante.

provoke [prə'vəuk] *vt* provocare; incitare; **to** ~ **sb to sth/to do** *or* **into doing sth** spingere qn a qc/a fare qc.

provoking [prə'vəukɪŋ] *adj* irritante, esasperante.

provost ['prɔvəst] *n* (*BRIT: of university*) rettore *m*; (*Scottish*) sindaco.

prow [prau] *n* prua.

prowess ['prauɪs] *n* prodezza; **his** ~ **as a footballer** le sue capacità di calciatore.

prowl [praul] *vi* (*also*: ~ **about**, ~ **around**) aggirarsi furtivamente ♦ *n*: **on the** ~ in cerca di preda.

prowler ['praulə*] *n* tipo sospetto (*che s'aggira con l'intenzione di rubare, aggredire etc*).

proximity [prɔk'sɪmɪtɪ] *n* prossimità.

proxy ['prɔksɪ] *n* procura; **by** ~ per procura.

PRP *n abbr* (= *performance related pay*) retribuzione *f* commensurata al rendimento.

prude [pruːd] *n* puritano/a.

prudence ['pruːdns] *n* prudenza.

prudent ['pruːdnt] *adj* prudente.

prudish ['pruːdɪʃ] *adj* puritano(a).

prune [pruːn] *n* prugna secca ♦ *vt* potare.

pry [praɪ] *vi*: **to** ~ **into** ficcare il naso in.

PS *n abbr* (= *postscript*) P.S.

psalm [sɑːm] *n* salmo.

PSAT *n abbr* (*US*) = *Preliminary Scholastic Aptitude Test.*

PSBR *n abbr* (*BRIT*: = *public sector borrowing requirement*) fabbisogno di prestiti per il settore pubblico.

pseud ['sjuːd] *n* (*BRIT col*: *intellectually*) intellettualoide *m/f*; (: *socially*) snob *m/f inv.*

pseudo- ['sjuːdəu] *prefix* pseudo....

pseudonym ['sjuːdənɪm] *n* pseudonimo.

PST *abbr* (*US*: = *Pacific Standard Time*) *ora invernale del Pacifico.*

PSV *n abbr* (*BRIT*) *see* **public service vehicle**.

psyche ['saɪkɪ] *n* psiche *f*.

psychedelic [saɪkɪ'delɪk] *adj* psichedelico(a).

psychiatric [saɪkɪ'ætrɪk] *adj* psichiatrico(a).

psychiatrist [saɪ'kaɪətrɪst] *n* psichiatra *m/f*.

psychiatry [saɪ'kaɪətrɪ] *n* psichiatria.

psychic ['saɪkɪk] *adj* (*also*: ~**al**) psichico(a); (*person*) dotato(a) di qualità telepatiche.

psycho ['saɪkəu] *n* (*col*) folle *m/f*, psicopatico/a.

psychoanalyse [saɪkəu'ænəlaɪz] *vt* psicanalizzare.

psychoanalysis, *pl* **-ses** [saɪkəuə'nælɪsɪs, -siːz] *n* psicanalisi *f inv*.

psychoanalyst [saɪkəu'ænəlɪst] *n* psicanalista *m/f*.

psychological [saɪkə'lɔdʒɪkl] *adj* psicologico(a).

psychologist [saɪ'kɔlədʒɪst] *n* psicologo/a.

psychology [saɪ'kɔlədʒɪ] *n* psicologia.

psychopath ['saɪkəupæθ] *n* psicopatico/a.

psychosis, *pl* **psychoses** [saɪ'kəusɪs, -siːz] *n* psicosi *f inv*.

psychosomatic [saɪkəusə'mætɪk] *adj* psicosomatico(a).

psychotherapy [saɪkəu'θerəpɪ] *n* psicoterapia.

psychotic [saɪ'kɔtɪk] *adj*, *n* psicotico(a).

PT *n abbr* (*BRIT*: = *physical training*) ed. fisica.

pt *abbr* (= *pint*; *point*) pt.

Pt. *abbr* (*in place names*: = *Point*) Pt.

PTA *n abbr* (= *Parent-Teacher Association*) associazione genitori e insegnanti.

Pte. *abbr* (*BRIT MIL*) = **private**.

PTO *abbr* (= *please turn over*) v.r. (= *vedi retro*).

PTV *n abbr* (*US*) = *pay television*, *public television*.

pub [pʌb] *n abbr* (= *public house*) pub *m inv*.

In Gran Bretagna e in Irlanda i **pub** sono locali dove vengono servite bibite alcoliche ed analcoliche e dove è anche possibile mangiare. Sono punti di ritrovo dove spesso si può giocare a biliardo, a freccette o guardare la televisione. Le leggi che regolano la vendita degli alcolici sono molto severe in Gran Bretagna e quindi gli orari di apertura e di chiusura vengono osservati scrupolosamente.

pub crawl *n*: **to go on a** ~ (*BRIT col*) fare il giro dei pub.

puberty ['pjuːbətɪ] *n* pubertà.

pubic ['pjuːbɪk] *adj* pubico(a), del pube.

public ['pʌblɪk] *adj* pubblico(a) ♦ *n* pubblico; **in** ~ in pubblico; **the general** ~ il pubblico; **to make sth** ~ render noto *or* di pubblico dominio qc; **to be** ~ **knowledge** essere di dominio pubblico; **to go** ~ (*COMM*) emettere le azioni sul mercato.

public address system (PA) *n* impianto di amplificazione.

publican ['pʌblɪkən] *n* (*BRIT*) gestore *m* (*or* proprietario) di un pub.

publication [pʌblɪ'keɪʃən] *n* pubblicazione *f*.

public company *n* ≈ società *f inv* per azioni (*costituita tramite pubblica sottoscrizione*).

public convenience *n* (*BRIT*) gabinetti *mpl*.

public holiday *n* (*BRIT*) giorno festivo, festa nazionale.

public house *n* (*BRIT*) pub *m inv*.

publicity [pʌb'lɪsɪtɪ] *n* pubblicità.

publicize ['pʌblɪsaɪz] *vt* fare (della) pubblicità a, reclamizzare.

public limited company (plc) *n* ≈ società per azioni a responsabilità limitata (*quotata in Borsa*).

publicly ['pʌblɪklɪ] *adv* pubblicamente.

public opinion *n* opinione *f* pubblica.

public ownership *n* proprietà pubblica *or*

sociale; **to be taken into** ~ essere statalizzato(a).

public prosecutor *n* pubblico ministero; ~**'s office** ufficio del pubblico ministero.

public relations *n* pubbliche relazioni *fpl*.

public relations officer *n* addetto/a alle pubbliche relazioni.

public school *n* (*BRIT*) scuola privata; (*US*) scuola statale.

In Inghilterra le **public school** *sono scuole o collegi di istruzione secondaria, private, spesso di un certo prestigio. In Scozia e negli Stati Uniti, invece, le public school sono scuole pubbliche gratuite amministrate dallo stato.*

---

public sector *n* settore *m* pubblico.

public service vehicle (PSV) *n* (*BRIT*) mezzo pubblico.

public-spirited [pʌblɪk'spɪrɪtɪd] *adj* che ha senso civico.

public transport, (*US*) **public transportation** *n* mezzi *mpl* pubblici.

public utility *n* servizio pubblico.

public works *npl* lavori *mpl* pubblici.

publish ['pʌblɪʃ] *vt* pubblicare.

publisher ['pʌblɪʃə*] *n* editore *m*; (*firm*) casa editrice.

publishing ['pʌblɪʃɪŋ] *n* (*industry*) editoria; (*of a book*) pubblicazione *f*.

publishing company *n* casa *or* società editrice.

puce [pjuːs] *adj* color pulce *inv*.

puck [pʌk] *n* (*ICE HOCKEY*) disco.

pucker ['pʌkə*] *vt* corrugare.

pudding ['pudɪŋ] *n* budino; (*dessert*) dolce *m*; **black** ~, (*US*) **blood** ~ sanguinaccio; **rice** ~ budino di riso.

puddle ['pʌdl] *n* pozza, pozzanghera.

puerile ['pjuəraɪl] *adj* puerile.

Puerto Rico ['pwəːtəu'riːkəu] *n* Portorico.

puff [pʌf] *n* sbuffo; (*also:* **powder** ~) piumino ♦ *vt* (*also:* ~ **out:** *sails, cheeks*) gonfiare ♦ *vi* uscire a sbuffi; (*pant*) ansare; **to** ~ **out smoke** mandar fuori sbuffi di fumo; **to** ~ **one's pipe** tirare sboccate di fumo.

puffed [pʌft] *adj* (*col: out of breath*) senza fiato.

puffin ['pʌfɪn] *n* puffino.

puff pastry, (*US*) **puff paste** *n* pasta sfoglia.

puffy ['pʌfɪ] *adj* gonfio(a).

pugnacious [pʌg'neɪʃəs] *adj* combattivo(a).

pull [pul] *n* (*tug*) strattone *m*, tirata; (*of moon, magnet, the sea etc*) attrazione *f*; (*fig*) influenza ♦ *vt* tirare; (*muscle*) strappare, farsi uno strappo a ♦ *vi* tirare; **to give sth a** ~ tirare su qc; **to** ~ **a face** fare una smorfia; **to** ~ **to pieces** fare a pezzi; **to** ~ **one's punches** (*BOXING*) risparmiare l'avversario; **not to** ~ **one's punches** (*fig*) non avere peli sulla lingua; **to** ~ **one's weight** dare il proprio contributo; **to** ~ **o.s. together** ricomporsi, riprendersi; **to** ~ **sb's leg** prendere in giro qn; **to** ~ **strings (for sb)** muovere qualche pedina (per qn).

▶**pull about** *vt* (*BRIT: handle roughly: object*) strapazzare; (*: person*) malmenare.

▶**pull apart** *vt* (*break*) fare a pezzi.

▶**pull down** *vt* (*house*) demolire; (*tree*) abbattere.

▶**pull in** *vi* (*AUT: at the kerb*) accostarsi; (*RAIL*) entrare in stazione.

▶**pull off** *vt* (*deal etc*) portare a compimento.

▶**pull out** *vi* partire; (*withdraw*) ritirarsi; (*AUT: come out of line*) spostarsi sulla mezzeria ♦ *vt* staccare; far uscire; (*withdraw*) ritirare.

▶**pull over** *vi* (*AUT*) accostare.

▶**pull round** *vi* (*unconscious person*) rinvenire; (*sick person*) ristabilirsi.

▶**pull through** *vi* farcela.

▶**pull up** *vi* (*stop*) fermarsi ♦ *vt* (*uproot*) sradicare; (*stop*) fermare.

pulley ['pulɪ] *n* puleggia, carrucola.

pull-out ['pulaut] *n* inserto ♦ *cpd* staccabile.

pullover ['puləuvə*] *n* pullover *m inv*.

pulp [pʌlp] *n* (*of fruit*) polpa; (*for paper*) pasta per carta; (*magazines, books*) stampa di qualità e di tono scadenti; **to reduce sth to** ~ spappolare qc.

pulpit ['pulpɪt] *n* pulpito.

pulsate [pʌl'seɪt] *vi* battere, palpitare.

pulse [pʌls] *n* polso; **to feel** *or* **take sb's** ~ sentire *or* tastare il polso a qn.

pulses ['pʌlsɪz] *npl* (*CULIN*) legumi *mpl*.

pulverize ['pʌlvəraɪz] *vt* polverizzare.

puma ['pjuːmə] *n* puma *m inv*.

pumice (stone) ['pʌmɪs-] *n* (pietra) pomice *f*.

pummel ['pʌml] *vt* dare pugni a.

pump [pʌmp] *n* pompa; (*shoe*) scarpetta ♦ *vt* pompare; (*fig: col*) far parlare; **to** ~ **sb for information** cercare di strappare delle informazioni a qn.

▶**pump up** *vt* gonfiare.

pumpkin ['pʌmpkɪn] *n* zucca.

pun [pʌn] *n* gioco di parole.

punch [pʌntʃ] *n* (*blow*) pugno; (*fig: force*) forza; (*tool*) punzone *m*; (*drink*) ponce *m* ♦ *vt* (*hit*): **to** ~ **sb/sth** dare un pugno a qn/qc; **to** ~ **a hole (in)** fare un buco (in).

▶**punch in** *vi* (*US*) timbrare il cartellino (all'entrata).

▶**punch out** *vi* (*US*) timbrare il cartellino (all'uscita).

punch-drunk ['pʌntʃdrʌŋk] *adj* (*BRIT*) stordito(a).

punch(ed) card ['pʌntʃ(t)-] *n* scheda perforata.

punch line *n* (*of joke*) battuta finale.

punch-up ['pʌntʃʌp] *n* (*BRIT col*) rissa.

punctual ['pʌŋktjuəl] *adj* puntuale.

punctuality [pʌŋktju'ælɪtɪ] *n* puntualità.

punctually [pʌŋktjuəlɪ] *adv* puntualmente; **it will start** ~ **at 6** comincerà alle 6 precise *or* in punto.

punctuate ['pʌŋktjueɪt] *vt* punteggiare.

punctuation [pʌŋktju'eɪʃən] *n* interpunzione *f*, punteggiatura.

punctuation mark *n* segno d'interpunzione.

puncture ['pʌŋktʃə*] *n* (*BRIT*) foratura ♦ *vt* forare; **to have a** ~ (*AUT*) forare (una gomma).

pundit ['pʌndɪt] *n* sapientone/a.

pungent ['pʌndʒənt] *adj* piccante; (*fig*) mordace, caustico(a).

punish ['pʌnɪʃ] *vt* punire; **to** ~ **sb for sth/ for doing sth** punire qn per qc/per aver fatto qc.

punishable ['pʌnɪʃəbl] *adj* punibile.

punishing ['pʌnɪʃɪŋ] *adj* (*fig: exhausting*) sfiancante.

punishment ['pʌnɪʃmənt] *n* punizione *f*; (*fig col*): **to take a lot of** ~ (*boxer*) incassare parecchi colpi; (*car*) essere messo(a) a dura prova.

punk [pʌŋk] *n* (*person: also*: ~ **rocker**) punk *m/f inv*; (*music: also*: ~ **rock**) musica punk, punk rock *m*; (*US col: hoodlum*) teppista *m*.

punt [pʌnt] *n* (*boat*) barchino; (*FOOTBALL*) colpo a volo; (*Irish*) sterlina irlandese ♦ *vi* (*BRIT: bet*) scommettere.

punter ['pʌntə*] *n* (*BRIT: gambler*) scommettitore/trice.

puny ['pju:nɪ] *adj* gracile.

pup [pʌp] *n* cucciolo/a.

pupil ['pju:pl] *n* allievo/a; (*ANAT*) pupilla.

puppet ['pʌpɪt] *n* burattino.

puppet government *n* governo fantoccio.

puppy ['pʌpɪ] *n* cucciolo/a, cagnolino/a.

purchase ['pɜ:tʃɪs] *n* acquisto, compera; (*grip*) presa ♦ *vt* comprare; **to get a** ~ **on** (*grip*) trovare un appoggio su.

purchase order *n* ordine *m* d'acquisto, ordinazione *f*.

purchase price *n* prezzo d'acquisto.

purchaser ['pɜ:tʃɪsə*] *n* compratore/trice.

purchase tax *n* (*BRIT*) tassa d'acquisto.

purchasing power ['pɜ:tʃɪsɪŋ-] *n* potere *m* d'acquisto.

pure [pjuə*] *adj* puro(a); **a** ~ **wool jumper** un golf di pura lana; **it's laziness** ~ **and simple** è pura pigrizia.

purebred ['pjuəbrɛd] *adj* di razza pura.

purée ['pjuəreɪ] *n* purè *m inv*.

purely ['pjuəlɪ] *adv* puramente.

purge [pɜ:dʒ] *n* (*MED*) purga; (*POL*) epurazione *f* ♦ *vt* purgare; (*fig*) epurare.

purification [pjuərɪfɪ'keɪʃən] *n* purificazione *f*.

purify ['pjuərɪfaɪ] *vt* purificare.

purist ['pjuərɪst] *n* purista *m/f*.

puritan ['pjuərɪtən] *adj*, *n* puritano(a).

puritanical [pjuərɪ'tænɪkl] *adj* puritano(a).

purity ['pjuərɪtɪ] *n* purità.

purl [pɜ:l] *n* punto rovescio ♦ *vt* lavorare a rovescio.

purloin [pɜ:'lɔɪn] *vt* rubare.

purple ['pɜ:pl] *adj* di porpora; viola *inv*.

purport [pɜ:'pɔ:t] *vi*: **to** ~ **to be/do** pretendere di essere/fare.

purpose ['pɜ:pəs] *n* intenzione *f*, scopo; **on** ~ **apposta**, di proposito; **for illustrative** ~**s** a titolo illustrativo; **for teaching** ~**s** per l'insegnamento; **for the** ~**s of this meeting** agli effetti di questa riunione; **to no** ~ senza nessun risultato, inutilmente.

purpose-built ['pɜ:pəs'bɪlt] *adj* (*BRIT*) costruito(a) allo scopo.

purposeful ['pɜ:pəsful] *adj* deciso(a), risoluto(a).

purposely ['pɜ:pəslɪ] *adv* apposta.

purr [pɜ:*] *n* fusa *fpl* ♦ *vi* fare le fusa.

purse [pɜ:s] *n* borsellino; (*US: handbag*) borsetta, borsa ♦ *vt* contrarre.

purser ['pɜ:sə*] *n* (*NAUT*) commissario di bordo.

purse snatcher [-'snætʃə*] *n* (*US*) scippatore *m*.

pursue [pə'sju:] *vt* inseguire; essere alla ricerca di; (*inquiry, matter*) approfondire.

pursuer [pə'sju:ə*] *n* inseguitore/trice.

pursuit [pə'sju:t] *n* inseguimento; (*occupation*) occupazione *f*, attività *f inv*; **in (the)** ~ **of sth** alla ricerca di qc; **scientific** ~**s** ricerche *fpl* scientifiche.

purveyor [pə'veɪə*] *n* fornitore/trice.

pus [pʌs] *n* pus *m*.

push [puʃ] *n* spinta; (*effort*) grande sforzo; (*drive*) energia ♦ *vt* spingere; (*button*) premere; (*thrust*): **to** ~ **sth (into)** ficcare qc (in); (*fig*) fare pubblicità a ♦ *vi* spingere; premere; **to** ~ **a door open/ shut** aprire/chiudere una porta con una spinta *or* spingendola; **to be** ~**ed for time/money** essere a corto di tempo/

soldi; **she is ~ing 50** (*col*) va per i 50; **to ~
for** (*better pay, conditions etc*) fare
pressione per ottenere; "**~**" (*on door*)
"spingere"; (*on bell*) "suonare"; **at a ~**
(*BRIT col*) in caso di necessità.
▶**push aside** *vt* scostare.
▶**push in** *vi* introdursi a forza.
▶**push off** *vi* (*col*) filare.
▶**push on** *vi* (*continue*) continuare.
▶**push over** *vt* far cadere.
▶**push through** *vt* (*measure*) far
approvare.
▶**push up** *vt* (*total, prices*) far salire.
push-bike ['puʃbaɪk] *n* (*BRIT*) bicicletta.
push-button ['puʃbʌtn] *adj* a pulsante.
pushchair ['puʃtʃɛə*] *n* passeggino.
pusher ['puʃə*] *n* (*also:* **drug ~**)
spacciatore/trice (di droga).
pushover ['puʃəuvə*] *n* (*col*): **it's a ~** è un
lavoro da bambini.
push-up ['puʃʌp] *n* (*US*) flessione *f* sulle
braccia.
pushy ['puʃɪ] *adj* (*pej*) troppo
intraprendente.
puss, pussy(-cat) [pus, 'pusɪ(kæt)] *n* micio.
put, *pt, pp* **put** [put] *vt* mettere, porre; (*say*)
dire, esprimere; (*a question*) fare;
(*estimate*) stimare ♦ *adv*: **to stay ~** non
muoversi; **to ~ sb to bed** mettere qn a
letto; **to ~ sb in a good/bad mood**
mettere qn di buon/cattivo umore; **to ~
sb to a lot of trouble** scomodare qn; **to ~
a lot of time into sth** dedicare molto
tempo a qc; **to ~ money on a horse**
scommettere su un cavallo; **how shall I ~
it?** come dire?; **I ~ it to you that ...** (*BRIT*)
io sostengo che ....
▶**put about** *vi* (*NAUT*) virare di bordo ♦ *vt*
(*rumour*) diffondere.
▶**put across** *vt* (*ideas etc*) comunicare, far
capire.
▶**put aside** *vt* (*lay down: book etc*) mettere
da una parte, posare; (*save*) mettere da
parte; (*in shop*) tenere da parte.
▶**put away** *vt* (*clothes, toys etc*) mettere
via.
▶**put back** *vt* (*replace*) rimettere (a posto);
(*postpone*) rinviare; (*delay*) ritardare; (*set
back: watch, clock*) mettere indietro; **this
will ~ us back 10 years** questo ci farà
tornare indietro di 10 anni.
▶**put by** *vt* (*money*) mettere da parte.
▶**put down** *vt* (*parcel etc*) posare, mettere
giù; (*pay*) versare; (*in writing*) mettere
per iscritto; (*suppress: revolt etc*)
reprimere, sopprimere; (*attribute*)
attribuire.
▶**put forward** *vt* (*ideas*) avanzare,

proporre; (*date*) anticipare.
▶**put in** *vt* (*application, complaint*)
presentare.
▶**put in for** *vt fus* (*job*) far domanda per;
(*promotion*) far domanda di.
▶**put off** *vt* (*postpone*) rimandare, rinviare;
(*discourage*) dissuadere.
▶**put on** *vt* (*clothes, lipstick etc*) mettere;
(*light etc*) accendere; (*play etc*) mettere in
scena; (*concert, exhibition etc*) allestire,
organizzare; (*extra bus, train etc*) mettere
in servizio; (*food, meal*) servire; (*brake*)
mettere; (*assume: accent, manner*)
affettare; (*col: tease*) prendere in giro;
(*inform, indicate*): **to ~ sb on to sb/sth**
indicare qn/qc a qn; **to ~ on weight**
ingrassare; **to ~ on airs** darsi delle arie.
▶**put out** *vt* mettere fuori; (*one's hand*)
porgere; (*light etc*) spegnere; (*person:
inconvenience*) scomodare; (*dislocate:
shoulder, knee*) lussarsi; (*: back*) farsi uno
strappo a ♦ *vi* (*NAUT*): **to ~ out to sea**
prendere il largo; **to ~ out from
Plymouth** partire da Plymouth.
▶**put through** *vt* (*caller*) mettere in
comunicazione; (*call*) passare; **~ me
through to Miss Blair** mi passi la
signorina Blair.
▶**put together** *vt* mettere insieme,
riunire; (*assemble: furniture*) montare;
(*: meal*) improvvisare.
▶**put up** *vt* (*raise*) sollevare, alzare; (*pin up*)
affiggere; (*hang*) appendere; (*build*)
costruire, erigere; (*increase*) aumentare;
(*accommodate*) alloggiare; (*incite*): **to ~ sb
up to doing sth** istigare qn a fare qc; **to ~
sth up for sale** mettere in vendita qc.
▶**put upon** *vt fus*: **to be ~ upon** (*imposed
on*) farsi mettere sotto i piedi.
▶**put up with** *vt fus* sopportare.
putrid ['pju:trɪd] *adj* putrido(a).
putt [pʌt] *vt* (*ball*) colpire leggermente ♦ *n*
colpo leggero.
putter ['pʌtə*] *n* (*GOLF*) putter *m inv* ♦ *vi* (*US*)
= **potter**.
putting green ['pʌtɪŋ-] *n* green *m inv*;
campo da putting.
putty ['pʌtɪ] *n* stucco.
put-up ['putʌp] *adj*: **~ job** montatura.
puzzle ['pʌzl] *n* enigma *m*, mistero; (*jigsaw*)
puzzle *m* ♦ *vt* confondere, rendere
perplesso(a) ♦ *vi* scervellarsi; **to be ~d
about sth** domandarsi il perché di qc; **to
~ over** (*sb's actions*) cercare di capire;
(*mystery, problem*) cercare di risolvere.
puzzling ['pʌzlɪŋ] *adj* (*question*) poco
chiaro(a); (*attitude, set of instructions*)
incomprensibile.

PVC *n abbr* (= *polyvinyl chloride*) P.V.C. *m*.
Pvt. *abbr* (*US MIL*) = **private**.
PW *n abbr* (*US*) = **prisoner of war**.
pw *abbr* = *per week*.
PX *n abbr* (*US MIL*) *see* **post exchange**.
pygmy ['pɪgmɪ] *n* pigmeo/a.
pyjamas, (*US*) **pajamas** [pə'dʒɑːməz] *npl*
   pigiama *m*; **a pair of** ~ un pigiama.
pylon ['paɪlən] *n* pilone *m*.
pyramid ['pɪrəmɪd] *n* piramide *f*.
Pyrenean [pɪrə'niːən] *adj* pirenaico(a).
Pyrenees [pɪrə'niːz] *npl*: **the** ~ i Pirenei.
Pyrex ® ['paɪrɛks] *n* Pirex ® *m inv* ♦ *cpd*: ~
   dish pirofila.
python ['paɪθən] *n* pitone *m*.

Q q

Q, q [kjuː] *n* (*letter*) Q, q *f or m inv*; **Q for**
   Queen ≈ Q come Quarto.
Qatar [kæ'tɑː*] *n* Qatar *m*.
QC *n abbr* (*BRIT*: = *Queen's Counsel*)
   avvocato della Corona.
QED *abbr* (= *quod erat demonstrandum*) qed.
QM *n abbr see* **quartermaster**.
q.t. *n abbr* (*col*: = *quiet*): **on the** ~ di
   nascosto.
qty *abbr* = **quantity**.
quack [kwæk] *n* (*of duck*) qua qua *m inv*; (*pej*:
   doctor) ciarlatano/a.
quad [kwɔd] *n abbr* = **quadrangle**;
   quadruple; **quadruplet**.
quadrangle ['kwɔdræŋgl] *n* (*MATH*)
   quadrilatero; (*courtyard*: *abbr* **quad**)
   cortile *m*.
quadruped ['kwɔdrupɛd] *n* quadrupede *m*.
quadruple [kwɔ'drupl] *adj* quadruplo(a) ♦ *n*
   quadruplo ♦ *vt* quadruplicare ♦ *vi*
   quadruplicarsi.
quadruplet [kwɔ'druːplɪt] *n* uno/a di
   quattro gemelli.
quagmire ['kwægmaɪə*] *n* pantano.
quail [kweɪl] *n* (*ZOOL*) quaglia ♦ *vi*: **to** ~ **at**
   or **before** perdersi d'animo davanti a.
quaint [kweɪnt] *adj* bizzarro(a); (*old-*
   fashioned) antiquato(a) e pittoresco(a).
quake [kweɪk] *vi* tremare ♦ *n abbr*
   = **earthquake**.
Quaker ['kweɪkə*] *n* quacchero/a.
qualification [kwɔlɪfɪ'keɪʃən] *n* (*degree etc*)
   qualifica, titolo; (*ability*) competenza,

   qualificazione *f*; (*limitation*) riserva,
   restrizione *f*; **what are your** ~**s?** quali
   sono le sue qualifiche?
qualified ['kwɔlɪfaɪd] *adj* qualificato(a);
   (*able*) competente, qualificato(a); (*limited*)
   condizionato(a); ~ **for/to do**
   qualificato(a) per/per fare; **he's not** ~ **for**
   the job non ha i requisiti necessari per
   questo lavoro; **it was a** ~ **success** è stato
   un successo parziale.
qualify ['kwɔlɪfaɪ] *vt* abilitare; (*limit*:
   statement) modificare, precisare ♦ *vi*: **to** ~
   (**as**) qualificarsi (come); **to** ~ (**for**)
   acquistare i requisiti necessari (per);
   (*SPORT*) qualificarsi (per *or* a); **to** ~ **as an**
   engineer diventare un perito tecnico.
qualifying ['kwɔlɪfaɪɪŋ] *adj* (*exam*) di
   ammissione; (*round*) eliminatorio(a).
qualitative ['kwɔlɪtətɪv] *adj* qualitativo(a).
quality ['kwɔlɪtɪ] *n* qualità *f inv* ♦ *cpd* di
   qualità; **of good** ~ di buona qualità; **of**
   poor ~ scadente; ~ **of life** qualità della
   vita.
quality control *n* controllo di qualità.
quality papers *npl*, **quality press** *n* (*BRIT*):
   the ~ la stampa d'informazione.

Il termine **quality press** *si riferisce ai*
quotidiani o ai settimanali che offrono
un'informazione seria ed approfondita.
Questi giornali si differenziano da quelli
popolari, i **tabloid***, per formato e contenuti.*
Questa divisione tra tipi di giornali riflette il
tradizionale divario tra classi sociali nella
società britannica; vedi anche **tabloid press***.*

---

qualm [kwɑːm] *n* dubbio; scrupolo; **to have**
   ~**s about sth** avere degli scrupoli per
   qc.
quandary ['kwɔndrɪ] *n*: **in a** ~ in un
   dilemma.
quango ['kwæŋgəu] *n abbr* (*BRIT*: = *quasi-*
   autonomous non-governmental organization)
   commissione consultiva di nomina
   governativa.
quantifiable ['kwɔntɪfaɪəbl] *adj*
   quantificabile.
quantitative ['kwɔntɪtətɪv] *adj*
   quantitativo(a).
quantity ['kwɔntɪtɪ] *n* quantità *f inv*; **in** ~ in
   grande quantità.
quantity surveyor *n* (*BRIT*) geometra *m*
   (*specializzato nel calcolare la quantità e il*
   costo del materiale da costruzione).
quantum leap ['kwɔntəm-] *n* (*fig*) enorme
   cambiamento.
quarantine ['kwɔrntiːn] *n* quarantena.
quark [kwɑːk] *n* quark *m inv*.

quarrel ['kwɔrl] *n* lite *f*, disputa ♦ *vi* litigare; **to have a ~ with sb** litigare con qn; **I've no ~ with him** non ho niente contro di lui; **I can't ~ with that** non ho niente da ridire su questo.

quarrelsome ['kwɔrəlsəm] *adj* litigioso(a).

quarry ['kwɔrɪ] *n* (*for stone*) cava; (*animal*) preda ♦ *vt* (*marble etc*) estrarre.

quart [kwɔːt] *n* due pinte *fpl*, ≈ litro.

quarter ['kwɔːtə*] *n* quarto; (*of year*) trimestre *m*; (*district*) quartiere *m*; (*US, Canada: 25 cents*) quarto di dollaro, 25 centesimi ♦ *vt* dividere in quattro; (*MIL*) alloggiare; **~s** *npl* alloggio; (*MIL*) alloggi *mpl*, quadrato; **to pay by the ~** pagare trimestralmente; **a ~ of an hour** un quarto d'ora; **it's a ~ to 3**, (*US*) **it's a ~ of 3** sono le 3 meno un quarto, manca un quarto alle 3; **it's a ~ past 3**, (*US*) **it's a ~ after 3** sono le 3 e un quarto; **from all ~s** da tutte la parti *or* direzioni; **at close ~s** a distanza ravvicinata.

quarterback ['kwɔːtəbæk] *n* (*US FOOTBALL*) quarterback *m inv*.

quarter-deck ['kwɔːtədɛk] *n* (*NAUT*) cassero.

quarter final *n* quarto di finale.

quarterly ['kwɔːtəlɪ] *adj* trimestrale ♦ *adv* trimestralmente ♦ *n* periodico trimestrale.

quartermaster (QM) ['kwɔːtəmɑːstə*] *n* (*MIL*) furiere *m*.

quartet(te) [kwɔːˈtɛt] *n* quartetto.

quarto ['kwɔːtəu] *adj*, *n* in quarto (*m*) *inv*.

quartz [kwɔːts] *n* quarzo ♦ *cpd* di quarzo; (*watch, clock*) al quarzo.

quash [kwɔʃ] *vt* (*verdict*) annullare.

quasi- ['kweɪzaɪ] *prefix* quasi + *noun*; quasi, pressoché + *adjective*.

quaver ['kweɪvə*] *n* (*BRIT MUS*) croma ♦ *vi* tremolare.

quay [kiː] *n* (*also:* **~side**) banchina.

Que. *abbr* (*Canada*) = **Quebec**.

queasy ['kwiːzɪ] *adj* (*stomach*) delicato(a); **to feel ~** aver la nausea.

Quebec [kwɪˈbɛk] *n* Quebec *m*.

queen [kwiːn] *n* (*gen*) regina; (*CARDS etc*) regina, donna.

queen mother *n* regina madre.

Durante la sessione di apertura del Parlamento britannico il sovrano legge un discorso redatto dal primo ministro, il **Queen's speech** (se si tratta della regina), che contiene le linee generali del nuovo programma politico.

queer [kwɪə*] *adj* strano(a), curioso(a);

(*suspicious*) dubbio(a), sospetto(a); (*BRIT: sick*): **I feel ~** mi sento poco bene ♦ *n* (*col*) finocchio.

quell [kwɛl] *vt* domare.

quench [kwɛntʃ] *vt* (*flames*) spegnere; **to ~ one's thirst** dissetarsi.

querulous ['kwɛruləs] *adj* querulo(a).

query ['kwɪərɪ] *n* domanda, questione *f*; (*doubt*) dubbio ♦ *vt* mettere in questione; (*disagree with, dispute*) contestare.

quest [kwɛst] *n* cerca, ricerca.

question ['kwɛstʃən] *n* domanda, questione *f* ♦ *vt* (*person*) interrogare; (*plan, idea*) mettere in questione *or* in dubbio; **to ask sb a ~**, **put a ~ to sb** fare una domanda a qn; **to bring** *or* **call sth into ~** mettere in dubbio qc; **the ~ is ...** il problema è ...; **it's a ~ of doing** si tratta di fare; **there's some ~ of doing** c'è chi suggerisce di fare; **beyond ~** fuori di dubbio; **out of the ~** fuori discussione, impossibile.

questionable ['kwɛstʃənəbl] *adj* discutibile.

questioner ['kwɛstʃənə*] *n* interrogante *m/f*.

questioning ['kwɛstʃənɪŋ] *adj* interrogativo(a) ♦ *n* interrogatorio.

question mark *n* punto interrogativo.

questionnaire [kwɛstʃəˈnɛə*] *n* questionario.

queue [kjuː] *n* coda, fila ♦ *vi* fare la coda; **to jump the ~** passare davanti agli altri (in una coda).

quibble ['kwɪbl] *vi* cavillare.

quick [kwɪk] *adj* rapido(a), veloce; (*reply*) pronto(a); (*mind*) pronto(a), acuto(a) ♦ *adv* rapidamente, presto ♦ *n*: **cut to the ~** (*fig*) toccato(a) sul vivo; **be ~!** fa presto!; **to be ~ to act** agire prontamente; **she was ~ to see that ...** ha visto subito che ....

quicken ['kwɪkn] *vt* accelerare, affrettare; (*rouse*) animare, stimolare ♦ *vi* accelerare, affrettarsi.

quick fix *n* soluzione *f* tampone *inv*.

quicklime ['kwɪklaɪm] *n* calce *f* viva.

quickly ['kwɪklɪ] *adv* rapidamente, velocemente; **we must act ~** dobbiamo agire tempestivamente.

quickness ['kwɪknɪs] *n* rapidità; prontezza; acutezza.

quicksand ['kwɪksænd] *n* sabbie *fpl* mobili.

quickstep ['kwɪkstɛp] *n* tipo di ballo simile al fox-trot.

quick-tempered [kwɪkˈtɛmpəd] *adj* che si arrabbia facilmente.

quick-witted [kwɪkˈwɪtɪd] *adj* pronto(a) d'ingegno.

quid [kwɪd] *n* (*pl inv*: *BRIT col*) sterlina.

quid pro quo ['kwɪdprəu'kwəu] *n*

contraccambio.

quiet ['kwaɪət] *adj* tranquillo(a), quieto(a); (*reserved*) quieto(a), taciturno(a); (*ceremony*) semplice; (*not noisy: engine*) silenzioso(a); (*not busy: day*) calmo(a), tranquillo(a); (*colour*) discreto(a) ♦ *n* tranquillità, calma ♦ *vt, vi* (*US*) = **quieten**; **keep** ~! sta zitto!; **on the** ~ di nascosto; **I'll have a** ~ **word with him** gli dirò due parole in privato; **business is** ~ **at this time of year** questa è la stagione morta.

quieten ['kwaɪətn] (*BRIT: also:* ~ **down**) *vi* calmarsi, chetarsi ♦ *vt* calmare, chetare.

quietly ['kwaɪətlɪ] *adv* tranquillamente, calmamente; silenziosamente.

quietness ['kwaɪətnɪs] *n* tranquillità, calma; silenzio.

quill [kwɪl] *n* penna d'oca.

quilt [kwɪlt] *n* trapunta; **continental** ~ piumino.

quin [kwɪn] *n abbr* = **quintuplet**.

quince [kwɪns] *n* (mela) cotogna; (*tree*) cotogno.

quinine [kwɪ'niːn] *n* chinino.

quintet(te) [kwɪn'tɛt] *n* quintetto.

quintuplet [kwɪn'tjuːplɪt] *n* uno/a di cinque gemelli.

quip [kwɪp] *n* battuta di spirito.

quire ['kwaɪə*] *n* ventesima parte di una risma.

quirk [kwəːk] *n* ghiribizzo; **by some** ~ **of fate** per un capriccio della sorte.

quit, *pt, pp* **quit** *or* **quitted** [kwɪt] *vt* lasciare, partire da ♦ *vi* (*give up*) mollare; (*resign*) dimettersi; **to** ~ **doing** smettere di fare; ~ **stalling!** (*US col*) non tirarla per le lunghe!; **notice to** ~ (*BRIT*) preavviso (*dato all'inquilino*).

quite [kwaɪt] *adv* (*rather*) assai; (*entirely*) completamente, del tutto; **I** ~ **understand** capisco perfettamente; ~ **a few of them** non pochi di loro; ~ (**so**)! esatto!; ~ **new** proprio nuovo; **that's** ~ **right** non è proprio esatto; **she's** ~ **pretty** è piuttosto carina.

Quito ['kiːtəu] *n* Quito *m*.

quits [kwɪts] *adj*: ~ (**with**) pari (con); **let's call it** ~ adesso siamo pari.

quiver ['kwɪvə*] *vi* tremare, fremere ♦ *n* (*for arrows*) faretra.

quiz [kwɪz] *n* (*game*) quiz *m inv*; indovinello ♦ *vt* interrogare.

quizzical ['kwɪzɪkəl] *adj* enigmatico(a).

quoits [kwɔɪts] *npl* gioco degli anelli.

quorum ['kwɔːrəm] *n* quorum *m*.

quota ['kwəutə] *n* quota.

quotation [kwəu'teɪʃən] *n* citazione *f*; (*of shares etc*) quotazione *f*; (*estimate*)

preventivo.

quotation marks *npl* virgolette *fpl*.

quote [kwəut] *n* citazione *f* ♦ *vt* (*sentence*) citare; (*price*) dare, indicare, fissare; (*shares*) quotare ♦ *vi*: **to** ~ **from** citare; **to** ~ **for a job** dare un preventivo per un lavoro; ~**s** *npl* (*col*) = **quotation marks**; **in** ~**s** tra virgolette; ~ ... **unquote** (*in dictation*) aprire le virgolette ... chiudere le virgolette.

quotient ['kwəuʃənt] *n* quoziente *m*.

qv *abbr* (= *quod vide: which see*) v.

qwerty keyboard ['kwəːtɪ-] *n* tastiera qwerty *inv*.

R r

R, r [ɑː*] *n* (*letter*) R, r *f or m inv*; **R for Robert**, (*US*) **R for Roger** ≈ R come Roma.

R *abbr* (= *Réaumur (scale)*) R; (= *river*) F; (= *right*) D; (*US CINE:* = *restricted*) ≈ vietato; (*US POL*) = **republican**; (*BRIT*) = *Rex, Regina*.

RA *n abbr* (*BRIT*) = *Royal Academy, Royal Academician* ♦ *abbr* = **rear admiral**.

RAAF *n abbr* = *Royal Australian Air Force*.

Rabat [rə'bɑːt] *n* Rabat *f*.

rabbi ['ræbaɪ] *n* rabbino.

rabbit ['ræbɪt] *n* coniglio ♦ *vi*: **to** ~ (**on**) (*BRIT*) blaterare.

rabbit hole *n* tana di coniglio.

rabbit hutch *n* cogliera.

rabble ['ræbl] *n* (*pej*) canaglia, plebaglia.

rabid ['ræbɪd] *adj* rabbioso(a); (*fig*) fanatico(a).

rabies ['reɪbiːz] *n* rabbia.

RAC *n abbr* (*BRIT:* = *Royal Automobile Club*) ≈ A.C.I. *m* (= *Automobile Club d'Italia*).

raccoon [rə'kuːn] *n* procione *m*.

race [reɪs] *n* razza; (*competition, rush*) corsa ♦ *vt* (*person*) gareggiare (in corsa) con; (*horse*) far correre; (*engine*) imballare ♦ *vi* correre; **the human** ~ la razza umana; **he** ~**d across the road** ha attraversato la strada di corsa; **to** ~ **in/ out** *etc* precipitarsi dentro/fuori *etc*.

race car *n* (*US*) = **racing car**.

race car driver *n* (*US*) = **racing driver**.

racecourse ['reɪskɔːs] *n* campo di corse, ippodromo.

racehorse ['reɪshɔːs] *n* cavallo da corsa.
race relations *npl* rapporti razziali.
racetrack ['reɪstræk] *n* pista.
racial ['reɪʃl] *adj* razziale.
racial discrimination *n* discriminazione *f* razziale.
racialism ['reɪʃəlɪzəm] *n* razzismo.
racialist ['reɪʃəlɪst] *adj, n* razzista (*m/f*).
racing ['reɪsɪŋ] *n* corsa.
racing car *n* (*BRIT*) macchina da corsa.
racing driver *n* (*BRIT*) corridore *m* automobilista.
racism ['reɪsɪzəm] *n* razzismo.
racist ['reɪsɪst] *adj, n* (*pej*) razzista (*m/f*).
rack [ræk] *n* rastrelliera; (*also:* **luggage** ~) rete *f*, portabagagli *m inv*; (*also:* **roof** ~) portabagagli ♦ *vt* torturare, tormentare; **magazine** ~ portariviste *m inv*; **shoe** ~ scarpiera; **toast** ~ portatoast *m inv*; **to go to** ~ **and ruin** (*building*) andare in rovina; (*business*) andare in malora *or* a catafascio; **to** ~ **one's brains** scervellarsi.
▶**rack up** *vt* accumulare.
racket ['rækɪt] *n* (*for tennis*) racchetta; (*noise*) fracasso, baccano; (*swindle*) imbroglio, truffa; (*organized crime*) racket *m inv.*
racketeer [rækɪ'tɪə*] *n* (*US*) trafficante *m/f.*
racoon [rə'kuːn] *n* = **raccoon.**
racquet ['rækɪt] *n* racchetta.
racy ['reɪsɪ] *adj* brioso(a); piccante.
RADA ['rɑːdə] *n abbr* (*BRIT*) = *Royal Academy of Dramatic Art.*
radar ['reɪdɑː*] *n* radar *m* ♦ *cpd* radar *inv.*
radar trap *n* controllo della velocità con radar.
radial ['reɪdɪəl] *adj* (*also:* ~**-ply**) radiale.
radiance ['reɪdɪəns] *n* splendore *m*, radiosità.
radiant ['reɪdɪənt] *adj* raggiante; (*PHYSICS*) radiante.
radiate ['reɪdɪeɪt] *vt* (*heat*) irraggiare, irradiare ♦ *vi* (*lines*) irradiarsi.
radiation [reɪdɪ'eɪʃən] *n* irradiamento; (*radioactive*) radiazione *f.*
radiation sickness *n* malattia da radiazioni.
radiator ['reɪdɪeɪtə*] *n* radiatore *m.*
radiator cap *n* tappo del radiatore.
radiator grill *n* (*AUT*) mascherina, calandra.
radical ['rædɪkl] *adj* radicale.
radii ['reɪdɪaɪ] *npl of* **radius.**
radio ['reɪdɪəu] *n* radio *f inv* ♦ *vt* (*information*) trasmettere per radio; (*one's position*) comunicare via radio; (*person*) chiamare via radio ♦ *vi*: **to** ~ **to sb** comunicare via radio con qn; **on the** ~ alla radio.

radio... ['reɪdɪəu] *prefix* radio....
radioactive ['reɪdɪəu'æktɪv] *adj* radioattivo(a).
radioactivity ['reɪdɪəuæk'tɪvɪtɪ] *n* radioattività.
radio announcer *n* annunciatore/trice della radio.
radio-controlled ['reɪdɪəukən'trəuld] *adj* radiocomandato(a), radioguidato(a).
radiographer [reɪdɪ'ɔgrəfə*] *n* radiologo/a (*tecnico*).
radiography [reɪdɪ'ɔgrəfɪ] *n* radiografia.
radiologist [reɪdɪ'ɔlədʒɪst] *n* radiologo/a (*medico*).
radiology [reɪdɪ'ɔlədʒɪ] *n* radiologia.
radio station *n* stazione *f* radio *inv.*
radio taxi *n* radiotaxi *m inv.*
radiotelephone ['reɪdɪəu'tɛlɪfəun] *n* radiotelefono.
radiotherapist ['reɪdɪəu'θɛrəpɪst] *n* radioterapista *m/f.*
radiotherapy ['reɪdɪəu'θɛrəpɪ] *n* radioterapia.
radish ['rædɪʃ] *n* ravanello.
radium ['reɪdɪəm] *n* radio.
radius, *pl* **radii** ['reɪdɪəs, -ɪaɪ] *n* raggio; (*ANAT*) radio; **within a** ~ **of 50 miles** in un raggio di 50 miglia.
RAF *n abbr* (*BRIT*) *see* **Royal Air Force.**
raffia ['ræfɪə] *n* rafia.
raffish ['ræfɪʃ] *adj* dal look trasandato.
raffle ['ræfl] *n* lotteria ♦ *vt* (*object*) mettere in palio.
raft [rɑːft] *n* zattera.
rafter ['rɑːftə*] *n* trave *f.*
rag [ræg] *n* straccio, cencio; (*pej: newspaper*) giornalaccio; (*for charity*) iniziativa studentesca a scopo benefico ♦ *vt* (*BRIT*) prendere in giro; ~**s** *npl* stracci *mpl*, brandelli *mpl*; **in** ~**s** stracciato.

> *Durante il* **rag day/week**, *gli studenti universitari organizzano vari spettacoli e manifestazioni i cui proventi vengono devoluti in beneficenza.*

rag-and-bone man ['rægən'bəun-] *n* straccivendolo.
ragbag ['rægbæg] *n* (*fig*) guazzabuglio.
rag doll *n* bambola di pezza.
rage [reɪdʒ] *n* (*fury*) collera, furia ♦ *vi* (*person*) andare su tutte le furie; (*storm*) infuriare; **it's all the** ~ fa furore; **to fly into a** ~ andare *or* montare su tutte le furie.
ragged ['rægɪd] *adj* (*edge*) irregolare; (*cuff*) logoro(a); (*appearance*) pezzente.
raging ['reɪdʒɪŋ] *adj* (*all senses*) furioso(a);

in a ~ **temper** su tutte le furie.
rag trade n (col): **the ~** l'abbigliamento.
raid [reɪd] n (MIL) incursione f; (criminal) rapina; (by police) irruzione f ♦ vt fare un'incursione in; rapinare; fare irruzione in.
raider ['reɪdə*] n rapinatore/trice; (plane) aeroplano da incursione.
rail [reɪl] n (on stair) ringhiera; (on bridge, balcony) parapetto; (of ship) battagliola; (for train) rotaia; **~s** npl binario, rotaie fpl; **by ~** per ferrovia, in treno.
railcard ['reɪlkɑːd] n (BRIT) tessera di riduzione ferroviaria.
railing(s) ['reɪlɪŋ(z)] n(pl) ringhiere fpl.
railway ['reɪlweɪ], (US) **railroad** ['reɪlrəʊd] n ferrovia.
railway engine n (BRIT) locomotiva.
railway line n (BRIT) linea ferroviaria.
railwayman ['reɪlweɪmən] n (BRIT) ferroviere m.
railway station n (BRIT) stazione f ferroviaria.
rain [reɪn] n pioggia ♦ vi piovere; **in the ~** sotto la pioggia; **it's ~ing** piove; **it's ~ing cats and dogs** piove a catinelle.
rainbow ['reɪnbəʊ] n arcobaleno.
raincoat ['reɪnkəʊt] n impermeabile m.
raindrop ['reɪndrɒp] n goccia di pioggia.
rainfall ['reɪnfɔːl] n pioggia; (measurement) piovosità.
rainforest ['reɪnfɒrɪst] n foresta pluviale or equatoriale.
rainproof ['reɪnpruːf] adj impermeabile.
rainstorm ['reɪnstɔːm] n pioggia torrenziale.
rainwater ['reɪnwɔːtə*] n acqua piovana.
rainy ['reɪnɪ] adj piovoso(a).
raise [reɪz] n aumento ♦ vt (lift) alzare, sollevare; (build) erigere; (increase) aumentare; (a protest, doubt, question) sollevare; (cattle, family) allevare; (crop) coltivare; (army, funds) raccogliere; (loan) ottenere; (end: siege, embargo) togliere; **to ~ one's voice** alzare la voce; **to ~ sb's hopes** accendere le speranze di qn; **to ~ one's glass to sb/sth** brindare a qn/qc; **to ~ a laugh/a smile** far ridere/sorridere.
raisin ['reɪzn] n uva secca.
Raj [rɑːdʒ] n: **the ~** l'impero britannico (in India).
rajah ['rɑːdʒə] n ragià m inv.
rake [reɪk] n (tool) rastrello; (person) libertino ♦ vt (garden) rastrellare; (with machine gun) spazzare ♦ vi: **to ~ through** (fig: search) frugare tra.
rake-off ['reɪkɔf] n (col) parte f percentuale, fetta.

rakish ['reɪkɪʃ] adj dissoluto(a); disinvolto(a).
rally ['rælɪ] n (POL etc) riunione f; (AUT) rally m inv; (TENNIS) scambio ♦ vt riunire, radunare ♦ vi raccogliersi, radunarsi; (sick person, STOCK EXCHANGE) riprendersi.
▶**rally round** vt fus raggrupparsi intorno a; venire in aiuto di.
rallying point ['rælɪɪŋ-] n (POL, MIL) punto di riunione, punto di raduno.
RAM [ræm] n abbr (COMPUT: = random access memory) RAM f.
ram [ræm] n montone m, ariete m; (device) ariete ♦ vt conficcare; (crash into) cozzare, sbattere contro; percuotere; speronare.
ramble ['ræmbl] n escursione f ♦ vi (pej: also: ~ **on**) divagare.
rambler ['ræmblə*] n escursionista m/f; (BOT) rosa rampicante.
rambling ['ræmblɪŋ] adj (speech) sconnesso(a); (BOT) rampicante; (house) tutto(a) nicchie e corridoi.
rambunctious [ræm'bʌŋkʃəs] adj (US) = **rumbustious**.
RAMC n abbr (BRIT) = Royal Army Medical Corps.
ramification [ræmɪfɪ'keɪʃən] n ramificazione f.
ramp [ræmp] n rampa; (AUT) dosso artificiale.
rampage [ræm'peɪdʒ] n: **to go on the ~** scatenarsi in modo violento ♦ vi: **they went rampaging through the town** si sono scatenati in modo violento per la città.
rampant ['ræmpənt] adj (disease etc) che infierisce.
rampart ['ræmpɑːt] n bastione m.
ram raiding [-reɪdɪŋ] n il rapinare un negozio sfondandone la vetrina con un veicolo rubato.
ramshackle ['ræmʃækl] adj (house) cadente; (car etc) sgangherato(a).
RAN n abbr = Royal Australian Navy.
ran [ræn] pt of **run**.
ranch [rɑːntʃ] n ranch m inv.
rancher ['rɑːntʃə*] n (owner) proprietario di un ranch; (ranch hand) cowboy m inv.
rancid ['rænsɪd] adj rancido(a).
rancour, (US) **rancor** ['ræŋkə*] n rancore m.
R&B n abbr = rhythm and blues.
R&D n abbr see research and development.
random ['rændəm] adj fatto(a) or detto(a) per caso; (COMPUT, MATH) casuale ♦ n: **at ~** a casaccio.
random access n (COMPUT) accesso

casuale.

randy ['rændɪ] *adj* (*col*) arrapato(a); lascivo(a).

rang [ræŋ] *pt of* **ring**.

range [reɪndʒ] *n* (*of mountains*) catena; (*of missile, voice*) portata; (*of products*) gamma; (*MIL: also:* **shooting** ~) campo di tiro; (*also:* **kitchen** ~) fornello, cucina economica ♦ *vt* (*place*) disporre, allineare; (*roam*) vagare per ♦ *vi:* **to** ~ **over** coprire; **to** ~ **from ... to** andare da ... a; **price** ~ gamma di prezzi; **do you have anything else in this price** ~? ha nient'altro su *or* di questo prezzo?; **within (firing)** ~ **a** portata di tiro; ~**d left/right** (*text*) allineato(a) a destra/sinistra.

ranger ['reɪndʒə*] *n* guardia forestale.

Rangoon [ræŋ'ɡuːn] *n* Rangun *f*.

rank [ræŋk] *n* fila; (*MIL*) grado; (*BRIT: also:* **taxi** ~) posteggio di taxi ♦ *vi:* **to** ~ **among** essere nel numero di ♦ *adj* (*smell*) puzzolente; (*hypocrisy, injustice*) vero(a) e proprio(a); **the** ~**s** (*MIL*) la truppa; **the** ~ **and file** (*fig*) la gran massa; **to close** ~**s** (*MIL, fig*) serrare i ranghi; **I** ~ **him sixth** gli do il sesto posto, lo metto al sesto posto.

rankle ['ræŋkl] *vi:* **to** ~ **(with sb)** bruciare (a qn).

rank outsider *n* outsider *m/f inv*.

ransack ['rænsæk] *vt* rovistare; (*plunder*) saccheggiare.

ransom ['rænsəm] *n* riscatto; **to hold sb to** ~ (*fig*) esercitare pressione su qn.

rant [rænt] *vi* vociare.

ranting ['ræntɪŋ] *n* vociare *m*.

rap [ræp] *n* (*noise*) colpetti *mpl*; (*at a door*) bussata ♦ *vt* dare dei colpetti a; bussare a.

rape [reɪp] *n* violenza carnale, stupro ♦ *vt* violentare.

rape(seed) oil ['reɪp(siːd)-] *n* olio di ravizzone.

rapid ['ræpɪd] *adj* rapido(a).

rapidity [rə'pɪdɪtɪ] *n* rapidità.

rapidly ['ræpɪdlɪ] *adv* rapidamente.

rapids ['ræpɪdz] *npl* (*GEO*) rapida.

rapist ['reɪpɪst] *n* violentatore *m*.

rapport [ræ'pɔː*] *n* rapporto.

rapt [ræpt] *adj* (*attention*) rapito(a), profondo(a); **to be** ~ **in contemplation** essere in estatica contemplazione.

rapture ['ræptʃə*] *n* estasi *f inv*; **to go into** ~**s over** andare in solluchero per.

rapturous ['ræptʃərəs] *adj* estatico(a).

rare [rɛə*] *adj* raro(a); (*CULIN: steak*) al sangue; **it is** ~ **to find that ...** capita di rado *or* raramente che ... + *sub*.

rarebit ['rɛəbɪt] *n see* **Welsh rarebit**.

rarefied ['rɛərɪfaɪd] *adj* (*air, atmosphere*) rarefatto(a).

rarely ['rɛəlɪ] *adv* raramente.

raring ['rɛərɪŋ] *adj:* **to be** ~ **to go** (*col*) non veder l'ora di cominciare.

rarity ['rɛərɪtɪ] *n* rarità *f inv*.

rascal ['rɑːskl] *n* mascalzone *m*.

rash [ræʃ] *adj* imprudente, sconsiderato(a) ♦ *n* (*MED*) eruzione *f*; **to come out in a** ~ avere uno sfogo.

rasher ['ræʃə*] *n* fetta sottile (di lardo *or* prosciutto).

rasp [rɑːsp] *n* (*tool*) lima ♦ *vt* (*speak: also:* ~ **out**) gracchiare.

raspberry ['rɑːzbərɪ] *n* lampone *m*.

raspberry bush *n* lampone *m* (*pianta*).

rasping ['rɑːspɪŋ] *adj* stridulo(a).

Rastafarian [ræstə'fɛərɪən] *adj, n* rastafariano(a).

rat [ræt] *n* ratto.

ratable ['reɪtəbl] *adj* = **rateable**.

ratchet ['rætʃɪt] *n:* ~ **wheel** ruota dentata.

rate [reɪt] *n* (*proportion*) tasso, percentuale *f*; (*speed*) velocità *f inv*; (*price*) tariffa ♦ *vt* valutare; stimare; **to** ~ **sb/sth as** valutare qn/qc come; **to** ~ **sb/sth among** annoverare qn/qc tra; **to** ~ **sb/sth highly** stimare molto qn/qc; **at a** ~ **of 60 kph** alla velocità di 60 km all'ora; ~ **of exchange** tasso di cambio; ~ **of flow** flusso medio; ~ **of growth** tasso di crescita; ~ **of return** tasso di rendimento; **pulse** ~ frequenza delle pulsazioni; *see also* **rates**.

rateable value ['reɪtəbl-] *n* (*BRIT*) valore *m* imponibile (agli effetti delle imposte comunali).

ratepayer ['reɪtpeɪə*] *n* (*BRIT*) contribuente *m/f* (che paga le imposte comunali).

rates [reɪts] *npl* (*BRIT*) imposte *fpl* comunali.

rather ['rɑːðə*] *adv* piuttosto; (*somewhat*) abbastanza; (*to some extent*) un po'; **it's** ~ **expensive** è piuttosto caro; (*too much*) è un po' caro; **there's** ~ **a lot** ce n'è parecchio; **I would** *or* **I'd** ~ **go** preferirei andare; **I had** ~ **go** farei meglio ad andare; **I'd** ~ **not leave** preferirei non partire; **or** ~ (*more accurately*) anzi, per essere (più) precisi; **I** ~ **think he won't come** credo proprio che non verrà.

ratification [rætɪfɪ'keɪʃən] *n* ratificazione *f*.

ratify ['rætɪfaɪ] *vt* ratificare.

rating ['reɪtɪŋ] *n* classificazione *f*; punteggio di merito; (*NAUT: category*) classe *f*; (: *sailor: BRIT*) marinaio semplice.

ratings ['reɪtɪŋz] *npl* (*RADIO, TV*) indice *m* di ascolto.

ratio ['reɪʃɪəu] *n* proporzione *f*; **in the** ~ **of 2**

to 1 in rapporto di 2 a 1.
ration ['ræʃən] n razione f ♦ vt razionare.
rational ['ræʃənl] adj razionale, ragionevole; (solution, reasoning) logico(a).
rationale [ræʃə'nɑːl] n fondamento logico; giustificazione f.
rationalization [ræʃnəlaɪ'zeɪʃən] n razionalizzazione f.
rationalize ['ræʃnəlaɪz] vt razionalizzare.
rationally ['ræʃnəlɪ] adv razionalmente; logicamente.
rationing ['ræʃnɪŋ] n razionamento.
ratpack ['rætpæk] n (BRIT col) stampa scandalistica.
rat poison n veleno per topi.
rat race n carrierismo, corsa al successo.
rattan [ræ'tæn] n malacca.
rattle ['rætl] n tintinnio; (louder) rumore m di ferraglia; (object: of baby) sonaglino; (: of sports fan) raganella ♦ vi risuonare, tintinnare; fare un rumore di ferraglia ♦ vt agitare; far tintinnare; (col: disconcert) sconcertare.
rattlesnake ['rætlsneɪk] n serpente m a sonagli.
ratty ['rætɪ] adj (col) incavolato(a).
raucous ['rɔːkəs] adj sguaiato(a).
raucously ['rɔːkəslɪ] adv sguaiatamente.
raunchy ['rɔːntʃɪ] adj (col: person) allupato(a); (: voice, song) libidinoso(a).
ravage ['rævɪdʒ] vt devastare.
ravages ['rævɪdʒɪz] npl danni mpl.
rave [reɪv] vi (in anger) infuriarsi; (with enthusiasm) andare in estasi; (MED) delirare ♦ n: **a ~ (party)** un rave ♦ adj (scene, culture, music) del fenomeno rave ♦ cpd: **~ review** (col) critica entusiasta.
raven ['reɪvən] n corvo.
ravenous ['rævənəs] adj affamato(a).
ravine [rə'viːn] n burrone m.
raving ['reɪvɪŋ] adj: **~ lunatic** pazzo(a) furioso(a).
ravings ['reɪvɪŋz] npl vaneggiamenti mpl.
ravioli [rævɪ'əulɪ] n ravioli mpl.
ravish ['rævɪʃ] vt (delight) estasiare.
ravishing ['rævɪʃɪŋ] adj incantevole.
raw [rɔː] adj (uncooked) crudo(a); (not processed) greggio(a); (sore) vivo(a); (inexperienced) inesperto(a); **to get a ~ deal** (col: bad bargain) prendere un bidone; (: harsh treatment) venire trattato ingiustamente.
Rawalpindi [rɔːl'pɪndɪ] n Rawalpindi f.
raw material n materia prima.
ray [reɪ] n raggio.
rayon ['reɪɒn] n raion m.
raze [reɪz] vt radere, distruggere; (also: ~

to the ground) radere al suolo.
razor ['reɪzə*] n rasoio.
razor blade n lama di rasoio.
razzle(-dazzle) ['ræzl('dæzl)] n (BRIT col): **to be/go on the ~** darsi alla pazza gioia.
razzmatazz ['ræzmə'tæz] n (col) clamore m.
RC abbr = **Roman Catholic.**
RCAF n abbr = Royal Canadian Air Force.
RCMP n abbr = Royal Canadian Mounted Police.
RCN n abbr = Royal Canadian Navy.
RD abbr (US POST) = rural delivery.
Rd abbr = **road.**
RDC n abbr (BRIT) see **rural district council.**
RE n abbr (BRIT MIL: = Royal Engineers) ≈ G.M. (= Genio Militare); (BRIT) = **religious education.**
re [riː] prep con riferimento a.
reach [riːtʃ] n portata; (of river etc) tratto ♦ vt raggiungere; arrivare a ♦ vi stendersi; (stretch out hand: also: ~ **down,** ~ **over,** ~ **across** etc) allungare una mano; **out of/within ~** (object) fuori/a portata di mano; **within easy ~ (of)** (place) a breve distanza (di), vicino (a); **to ~ sb by phone** contattare qn per telefono; **can I ~ you at your hotel?** la posso contattare al suo albergo?
▶**reach out** vi: **to ~ out for** stendere la mano per prendere.
react [riː'ækt] vi reagire.
reaction [riː'ækʃən] n reazione f.
reactionary [riː'ækʃənrɪ] adj, n reazionario(a).
reactor [riː'æktə*] n reattore m.
read, pt, pp **read** [riːd, rɛd] vi leggere ♦ vt leggere; (understand) intendere, interpretare; (study) studiare; **do you ~ me?** (TEL) mi ricevete?; **to take sth as read** (fig) dare qc per scontato.
▶**read out** vt leggere ad alta voce.
▶**read over** vt rileggere attentamente.
▶**read through** vt (quickly) dare una scorsa a; (thoroughly) leggere da cima a fondo.
▶**read up** vt, **read up on** vt fus studiare bene.
readable ['riːdəbl] adj leggibile; che si legge volentieri.
reader ['riːdə*] n lettore/trice; (book) libro di lettura; (BRIT: at university) professore con funzioni preminenti di ricerca.
readership ['riːdəʃɪp] n (of paper etc) numero di lettori.
readily ['rɛdɪlɪ] adv volentieri; (easily) facilmente.
readiness ['rɛdɪnɪs] n prontezza; **in ~** (prepared) pronto(a).

reading ['ri:dɪŋ] *n* lettura; (*understanding*) interpretazione *f*; (*on instrument*) indicazione *f*.

reading lamp *n* lampada da studio.

reading room *n* sala di lettura.

readjust [ri:ə'dʒʌst] *vt* raggiustare ♦ *vi* (*person*): **to ~ (to)** riadattarsi (a).

ready ['rɛdɪ] *adj* pronto(a); (*willing*) pronto(a), disposto(a); (*quick*) rapido(a); (*available*) disponibile ♦ *n*: **at the ~** (*MIL*) pronto a sparare; (*fig*) tutto(a) pronto(a); **~ for use** pronto per l'uso; **to be ~ to do sth** essere pronto a fare qc; **to get ~** *vi* prepararsi ♦ *vt* preparare.

ready cash *n* denaro in contanti.

ready-cooked [rɛdɪ'kukt] *adj* già cotto(a).

ready-made [rɛdɪ'meɪd] *adj* prefabbricato(a); (*clothes*) confezionato(a).

ready reckoner [-'rɛkənə*] *n* (*BRIT*) prontuario di calcolo.

ready-to-wear [rɛdɪtə'wɛə*] *adj* prêt-à-porter *inv*.

reagent [ri:'eɪdʒənt] *n*: **chemical ~** reagente *m* chimico.

real [rɪəl] *adj* reale; vero(a) ♦ *adv* (*US col*: *very*) veramente, proprio; **in ~ terms** in realtà; **in ~ life** nella realtà.

real ale *n* birra ad effervescenza naturale.

real estate *n* beni *mpl* immobili.

realism ['rɪəlɪzəm] *n* (*also ART*) realismo.

realist ['rɪəlɪst] *n* realista *m/f*.

realistic [rɪə'lɪstɪk] *adj* realistico(a).

reality [ri:'ælɪtɪ] *n* realtà *f inv*; **in ~** in realtà, in effetti.

realization [rɪəlaɪ'zeɪʃən] *n* (*awareness*) presa di coscienza; (*of hopes, project etc*) realizzazione *f*.

realize ['rɪəlaɪz] *vt* (*understand*) rendersi conto di; (*a project, COMM: asset*) realizzare; **I ~ that** ... mi rendo conto *or* capisco che ....

really ['rɪəlɪ] *adv* veramente, davvero.

realm [rɛlm] *n* reame *m*, regno.

real time *n* (*COMPUT*) tempo reale.

Realtor ® ['rɪəltɔ:*] *n* (*US*) agente *m* immobiliare.

ream [ri:m] *n* risma; **~s** (*fig col*) pagine e pagine *fpl*.

reap [ri:p] *vt* mietere; (*fig*) raccogliere.

reaper ['ri:pə*] *n* (*machine*) mietitrice *f*.

reappear [ri:ə'pɪə*] *vi* ricomparire, riapparire.

reappearance [ri:ə'pɪərəns] *n* riapparizione *f*.

reapply [ri:ə'plaɪ] *vi*: **to ~ for** fare un'altra domanda per.

reappraisal [ri:ə'preɪzl] *n* riesame *m*.

rear [rɪə*] *adj* di dietro; (*AUT*: *wheel etc*) posteriore ♦ *n* didietro, parte *f* posteriore ♦ *vt* (*cattle, family*) allevare ♦ *vi* (*also*: **~ up**: *animal*) impennarsi.

rear admiral *n* contrammiraglio.

rear-engined ['rɪər'ɛndʒɪnd] *adj* (*AUT*) con motore posteriore.

rearguard ['rɪəɡɑ:d] *n* retroguardia.

rearm [ri:'ɑ:m] *vt, vi* riarmare.

rearmament [ri:'ɑ:məmənt] *n* riarmo.

rearrange [ri:ə'reɪndʒ] *vt* riordinare.

rear-view mirror ['rɪəvju:-] *n* (*AUT*) specchio retrovisivo.

reason ['ri:zn] *n* ragione *f*; (*cause, motive*) ragione, motivo ♦ *vi*: **to ~ with sb** far ragionare qn; **to have ~ to think** avere motivi per pensare; **it stands to ~ that** è ovvio che; **the ~ for/why** la ragione *or* il motivo di/per cui; **with good ~** a ragione; **all the more ~ why you should not sell it** ragione di più per non venderlo.

reasonable ['ri:znəbl] *adj* ragionevole; (*not bad*) accettabile.

reasonably ['ri:znəblɪ] *adv* ragionevolmente; **one can ~ assume that** ... uno può facilmente supporre che ....

reasoned ['ri:znd] *adj* (*argument*) ponderato(a).

reasoning ['ri:znɪŋ] *n* ragionamento.

reassemble [ri:ə'sɛmbl] *vt* riunire; (*machine*) rimontare.

reassert [ri:ə'sə:t] *vt* riaffermare.

reassurance [ri:ə'ʃuərəns] *n* rassicurazione *f*.

reassure [ri:ə'ʃuə*] *vt* rassicurare; **to ~ sb of** rassicurare qn di *or* su.

reassuring [ri:ə'ʃuərɪŋ] *adj* rassicurante.

reawakening [ri:ə'weɪknɪŋ] *n* risveglio.

rebate ['ri:beɪt] *n* rimborso.

rebel *n* ['rɛbl] ribelle *m/f* ♦ *vi* [rɪ'bɛl] ribellarsi.

rebellion [rɪ'bɛljən] *n* ribellione *f*.

rebellious [rɪ'bɛljəs] *adj* ribelle.

rebirth [ri:'bə:θ] *n* rinascita.

rebound *vi* [rɪ'baund] (*ball*) rimbalzare ♦ *n* ['ri:baund] rimbalzo.

rebuff [rɪ'bʌf] *n* secco rifiuto ♦ *vt* respingere.

rebuild [ri:'bɪld] *vt irreg* ricostruire.

rebuke [rɪ'bju:k] *n* rimprovero ♦ *vt* rimproverare.

rebut [rɪ'bʌt] *vt* rifiutare.

rebuttal [rɪ'bʌtl] *n* rifiuto.

recalcitrant [rɪ'kælsɪtrənt] *adj* recalcitrante.

recall [rɪ'kɔ:l] *vt* (*gen, COMPUT*) richiamare; (*remember*) ricordare, richiamare alla mente ♦ *n* richiamo; **beyond ~**

irrevocabile.

recant [rɪ'kænt] *vi* ritrattarsi; (*REL*) fare abiura.

recap ['riːkæp] *n* ricapitolazione *f* ♦ *vt* ricapitolare ♦ *vi* riassumere.

recapture [riː'kæptʃə*] *vt* riprendere; (*atmosphere*) ricreare.

recd. *abbr* = received.

recede [rɪ'siːd] *vi* allontanarsi; ritirarsi; calare.

receding [rɪ'siːdɪŋ] *adj* (*forehead, chin*) sfuggente; **he's got a ~ hairline** è stempiato.

receipt [rɪ'siːt] *n* (*document*) ricevuta; (*act of receiving*) ricevimento; **to acknowledge ~ of** accusare ricevuta di; **we are in ~ of** ... abbiamo ricevuto ....

receipts [rɪ'siːts] *npl* (*COMM*) introiti *mpl*.

receivable [rɪ'siːvəbl] *adj* (*COMM*) esigibile; (: *owed*) dovuto(a).

receive [rɪ'siːv] *vt* ricevere; (*guest*) ricevere, accogliere; "~d with thanks" (*COMM*) "per quietanza".

Si chiama **Received Pronunciation (RP)** *l'accento dell'inglese parlato in alcune parti del sud-est dell'Inghilterra. In esso si identifica l'inglese "standard" delle classi colte, privo di inflessioni regionali e adottato tradizionalmente dagli annunciatori della* **BBC**. *È anche l'accento standard dell'inglese insegnato come lingua straniera.*

---

receiver [rɪ'siːvə*] *n* (*TEL*) ricevitore *m*; (*RADIO*) apparecchio ricevente; (*of stolen goods*) ricettatore/trice; (*LAW*) curatore *m* fallimentare.

receivership [rɪ'siːvəʃɪp] *n* curatela; **to go into ~** andare in amministrazione controllata.

recent ['riːsnt] *adj* recente; **in ~ years** negli ultimi anni.

recently ['riːsntlɪ] *adv* recentemente; **as ~ as** ... soltanto ...; **until ~** fino a poco tempo fa.

receptacle [rɪ'sɛptɪkl] *n* recipiente *m*.

reception [rɪ'sɛpʃən] *n* (*gen*) ricevimento; (*welcome*) accoglienza; (*TV etc*) ricezione *f*.

reception centre *n* (*BRIT*) centro di raccolta.

reception desk *n* (*in hotel*) reception *f inv*; (*in hospital, at doctor's*) accettazione *f*; (*in large building, offices*) portineria.

receptionist [rɪ'sɛpʃənɪst] *n* receptionist *m/f inv*.

receptive [rɪ'sɛptɪv] *adj* ricettivo(a).

recess [rɪ'sɛs] *n* (*in room*) alcova; (*POL etc: holiday*) vacanze *fpl*; (*US LAW: short break*) sospensione *f*; (*US SCOL*) intervallo.

recession [rɪ'sɛʃən] *n* (*ECON*) recessione *f*.

recharge [riː'tʃɑːdʒ] *vt* (*battery*) ricaricare.

rechargeable ['riː'tʃɑːdʒəbl] *adj* ricaricabile.

recipe ['rɛsɪpɪ] *n* ricetta.

recipient [rɪ'sɪpɪənt] *n* beneficiario/a; (*of letter*) destinatario/a.

reciprocal [rɪ'sɪprəkl] *adj* reciproco(a).

reciprocate [rɪ'sɪprəkeɪt] *vt* ricambiare, contraccambiare.

recital [rɪ'saɪtl] *n* recital *m inv*; concerto (di solista).

recite [rɪ'saɪt] *vt* (*poem*) recitare.

reckless ['rɛkləs] *adj* (*driver etc*) spericolato(a); (*spender*) incosciente.

recklessly ['rɛkləslɪ] *adv* in modo spericolato; da incoscente.

reckon ['rɛkən] *vt* (*count*) calcolare; (*consider*) considerare, stimare; (*think*): **I ~ that** ... penso che ... ♦ *vi* contare, calcolare; **to ~ without sb/sth** non tener conto di qn/qc; **he is somebody to be ~ed with** è uno da non sottovalutare.

►**reckon on** *vt fus* contare su.

reckoning ['rɛknɪŋ] *n* conto; stima; **the day of ~** il giorno del giudizio.

reclaim [rɪ'kleɪm] *vt* (*land*) bonificare; (*demand back*) richiedere, reclamare.

reclamation [rɛklə'meɪʃən] *n* bonifica.

recline [rɪ'klaɪn] *vi* stare sdraiato(a).

reclining [rɪ'klaɪnɪŋ] *adj* (*seat*) ribaltabile.

recluse [rɪ'kluːs] *n* eremita *m*, recluso/a.

recognition [rɛkəg'nɪʃən] *n* riconoscimento; **to gain ~** essere riconosciuto(a); **in ~ of** in *or* come segno di riconoscimento per; **transformed beyond ~** irriconoscibile.

recognizable ['rɛkəgnaɪzəbl] *adj*: **~ (by)** riconoscibile (a *or* da).

recognize ['rɛkəgnaɪz] *vt*: **to ~ (by/as)** riconoscere (a *or* da/come).

recoil [rɪ'kɔɪl] *vi* (*gun*) rinculare; (*spring*) balzare indietro; (*person*): **to ~ (from)** indietreggiare (davanti a) ♦ *n* (*of gun*) rinculo.

recollect [rɛkə'lɛkt] *vt* ricordare.

recollection [rɛkə'lɛkʃən] *n* ricordo; **to the best of my ~** per quello che mi ricordo.

recommend [rɛkə'mɛnd] *vt* raccomandare; (*advise*) consigliare; **she has a lot to ~ her** ha molti elementi a suo favore.

recommendation [rɛkəmen'deɪʃən] *n* raccomandazione *f*; consiglio.

recommended retail price (RRP) [rɛkə'mɛndɪd-] *n* (*BRIT*) prezzo raccomandato al dettaglio.

recompense ['rɛkəmpɛns] *vt* ricompensare; (*compensate*) risarcire ♦ *n* ricompensa; risarcimento.

reconcilable ['rɛkənsaɪləbl] *adj* conciliabile.

reconcile ['rɛkənsaɪl] *vt* (*two people*) riconciliare; (*two facts*) conciliare, quadrare; **to ~ o.s. to** rassegnarsi a.

reconciliation [rɛkənsɪlɪ'eɪʃən] *n* riconciliazione *f*; conciliazione *f*.

recondite [rɪ'kɒndaɪt] *adj* recondito(a).

recondition [riːkən'dɪʃən] *vt* rimettere a nuovo; rifare.

reconnaissance [rɪ'kɒnɪsns] *n* (*MIL*) ricognizione *f*.

reconnoitre, (*US*) reconnoiter [rɛkə'nɔɪtə*] (*MIL*) *vt* fare una ricognizione di ♦ *vi* fare una ricognizione.

reconsider [riːkən'sɪdə*] *vt* riconsiderare.

reconstitute [riː'kɒnstɪtjuːt] *vt* ricostituire.

reconstruct [riːkən'strʌkt] *vt* ricostruire.

reconstruction [riːkən'strʌkʃən] *n* ricostruzione *f*.

reconvene [riːkən'viːn] *vt* riconvocare ♦ *vi* radunarsi.

record *n* ['rɛkɔːd] ricordo, documento; (*of meeting etc*) nota, verbale *m*; (*register*) registro; (*file*) pratica, dossier *m inv*; (*COMPUT*) record *m inv*, registrazione *f*; (*also:* **police ~**) fedina penale sporca; (*MUS: disc*) disco; (*SPORT*) record *m inv*, primato ♦ *vt* [rɪ'kɔːd] (*set down*) prendere nota di, registrare; (*relate*) raccontare; (*COMPUT, MUS: song etc*) registrare; **public ~s** archivi *mpl*; **Italy's excellent ~** i brillanti successi italiani; **in ~ time** a tempo di record; **to keep a ~ of** tener nota di; **to set the ~ straight** mettere le cose in chiaro; **off the ~** *adj* ufficioso(a) ♦ *adv* ufficiosamente; **he is on ~ as saying that …** ha dichiarato pubblicamente che ….

record card *n* (*in file*) scheda.

recorded delivery letter [rɪ'kɔːdɪd-] *n* (*BRIT POST*) lettera raccomandata.

recorder [rɪ'kɔːdə*] *n* (*LAW*) avvocato che funge da giudice; (*MUS*) flauto diritto.

record holder *n* (*SPORT*) primatista *m/f*.

recording [rɪ'kɔːdɪŋ] *n* (*MUS*) registrazione *f*.

recording studio *n* studio di registrazione.

record library *n* discoteca.

record player *n* giradischi *m inv*.

recount [rɪ'kaunt] *vt* raccontare, narrare.

re-count *n* ['riːkaunt] (*POL: of votes*) nuovo conteggio ♦ *vt* [riː'kaunt] ricontare.

recoup [rɪ'kuːp] *vt* ricuperare; **to ~ one's**

losses ricuperare le perdite, rifarsi.

recourse [rɪ'kɔːs] *n*: **to have ~ to** ricorrere a.

recover [rɪ'kʌvə*] *vt* ricuperare ♦ *vi* (*from illness*) rimettersi (in salute), ristabilirsi; (*country, person: from shock*) riprendersi.

re-cover [riː'kʌvə*] *vt* (*chair etc*) ricoprire.

recovery [rɪ'kʌvərɪ] *n* ricupero; ristabilimento; ripresa.

recreate [riːkrɪ'eɪt] *vt* ricreare.

recreation [rɛkrɪ'eɪʃən] *n* ricreazione *f*; svago.

recreational [rɛkrɪ'eɪʃənəl] *adj* ricreativo(a).

recreational drug *n* droga usata saltuariamente.

recreational vehicle (RV) *n* (*US*) camper *m inv*.

recrimination [rɪkrɪmɪ'neɪʃən] *n* recriminazione *f*.

recruit [rɪ'kruːt] *n* recluta ♦ *vt* reclutare.

recruiting office [rɪ'kruːtɪŋ-] *n* ufficio di reclutamento.

recruitment [rɪ'kruːtmənt] *n* reclutamento.

rectangle ['rɛktæŋgl] *n* rettangolo.

rectangular [rɛk'tæŋgjulə*] *adj* rettangolare.

rectify ['rɛktɪfaɪ] *vt* (*error*) rettificare; (*omission*) riparare.

rector ['rɛktə*] *n* (*REL*) parroco (*anglicano*); (*in Scottish universities*) *personalità eletta dagli studenti per rappresentarli.*

rectory ['rɛktərɪ] *n* presbiterio.

rectum ['rɛktəm] *n* (*ANAT*) retto.

recuperate [rɪ'kjuːpəreɪt] *vi* ristabilirsi.

recur [rɪ'kəː*] *vi* riaccadere; (*idea, opportunity*) riapparire; (*symptoms*) ripresentarsi.

recurrence [rɪ'kʌrəns] *n* ripresentarsi *m*; riapparizione *f*.

recurrent [rɪ'kʌrənt] *adj* ricorrente, periodico(a).

recurring [rɪ'kʌrɪŋ] *adj* (*MATH*) periodico(a).

recycle [riː'saɪkl] *vt* riciclare.

red [rɛd] *n* rosso; (*POL: pej*) rosso/a ♦ *adj* rosso(a); **in the ~** (*account*) scoperto; (*business*) in deficit.

red alert *n* allarme *m* rosso.

red-blooded ['rɛd'blʌdɪd] *adj* (*col*) gagliardo(a).

red-brick university ['rɛdbrɪk-] *n* *università di recente formazione.*

In Gran Bretagna, con **red-brick university** *(letteralmente, università di mattoni rossi) si indicano le università di recente formazione, cioè quelle istituite tra la fine dell'Ottocento e i primi del Novecento, per* *contraddistinguerle dalle università più antiche, i cui edifici sono di pietra; vedi anche* **Oxbridge.**

red carpet treatment *n* cerimonia col gran pavese.
Red Cross *n* Croce *f* Rossa.
redcurrant ['rɛdkʌrənt] *n* ribes *m inv*.
redden ['rɛdn] *vt* arrossare ♦ *vi* arrossire.
reddish ['rɛdɪʃ] *adj* rossiccio(a).
redecorate [riː'dɛkəreɪt] *vt* tinteggiare (e tappezzare) di nuovo.
redeem [rɪ'diːm] *vt* (*debt*) riscattare; (*sth in pawn*) ritirare; (*fig, also REL*) redimere.
redeemable [rɪ'diːməbl] *adj* con diritto di riscatto; redimibile.
redeeming [rɪ'diːmɪŋ] *adj* (*feature*) che salva.
redefine [riːdɪ'faɪn] *vt* ridefinire.
redemption [rɪ'dɛmpʃən] *n* (*REL*) redenzione *f*; **past** *or* **beyond** ~ irrecuperabile.
redeploy [riːdɪ'plɔɪ] *vt* (*MIL*) riorganizzare lo schieramento di; (*resources*) riorganizzare.
redeployment [riːdɪ'plɔɪmənt] *n* riorganizzazione *f*.
redevelop [riːdɪ'vɛləp] *vt* ristrutturare.
redevelopment [riːdɪ'vɛləpmənt] *n* ristrutturazione *f*.
red-handed [rɛd'hændɪd] *adj*: **to be caught** ~ essere preso(a) in flagrante *or* con le mani nel sacco.
redhead ['rɛdhɛd] *n* rosso/a.
red herring *n* (*fig*) falsa pista.
red-hot [rɛd'hɔt] *adj* arroventato(a).
redirect [riːdaɪ'rɛkt] *vt* (*mail*) far seguire.
redistribute [riːdɪ'strɪbjuːt] *vt* ridistribuire.
red-letter day ['rɛdlɛtə-] *n* giorno memorabile.
red light *n*: **to go through a** ~ (*AUT*) passare col rosso.
red-light district [rɛd'laɪt-] *n* quartiere *m* luce rossa *inv*.
red meat *n* carne *f* rossa.
redness ['rɛdnɪs] *n* rossore *m*; (*of hair*) rosso.
redo [riː'duː] *vt irreg* rifare.
redolent ['rɛdələnt] *adj*: ~ **of** che sa di; (*fig*) che ricorda.
redouble [riː'dʌbl] *vt*: **to** ~ **one's efforts** raddoppiare gli sforzi.
redraft [riː'drɑːft] *vt* fare una nuova stesura di.
redress [rɪ'drɛs] *n* riparazione *f* ♦ *vt* riparare; **to** ~ **the balance** ristabilire l'equilibrio.
Red Sea *n*: **the** ~ il mar Rosso.

redskin ['rɛdskɪn] *n* pellerossa *m/f*.
red tape *n* (*fig*) burocrazia.
reduce [rɪ'djuːs] *vt* ridurre; (*lower*) ridurre, abbassare; *"~ speed now"* (*AUT*) "rallentare"; **to** ~ **sth by/to** ridurre qc di/a; **to** ~ **sb to silence/despair/tears** ridurre qn al silenzio/alla disperazione/in lacrime.
reduced [rɪ'djuːst] *adj* (*decreased*) ridotto(a); **at a** ~ **price** a prezzo ribassato *or* ridotto; **"greatly** ~ **prices"** "grandi ribassi".
reduction [rɪ'dʌkʃən] *n* riduzione *f*; (*of price*) ribasso; (*discount*) sconto.
redundancy [rɪ'dʌndənsɪ] *n* licenziamento (per eccesso di personale); **compulsory** ~ licenziamento; **voluntary** ~ *forma di cassa integrazione volontaria.*
redundancy payment *n* (*BRIT*) indennità *f inv* di licenziamento.
redundant [rɪ'dʌndnt] *adj* (*BRIT: worker*) licenziato(a); (*detail, object*) superfluo(a); **to make** ~ (*BRIT*) licenziare (per eccesso di personale).
reed [riːd] *n* (*BOT*) canna; (*MUS: of clarinet etc*) ancia.
re-educate [riː'ɛdjukeɪt] *vt* rieducare.
reedy ['riːdɪ] *adj* (*voice, instrument*) acuto(a).
reef [riːf] *n* (*at sea*) scogliera; **coral** ~ barriera corallina.
reek [riːk] *vi*: **to** ~ (**of**) puzzare (di).
reel [riːl] *n* bobina, rocchetto; (*TECH*) aspo; (*FISHING*) mulinello; (*CINE*) rotolo ♦ *vt* (*TECH*) annaspare; (*also*: ~ **up**) avvolgere ♦ *vi* (*sway*) barcollare, vacillare; **my head is** ~**ing** mi gira la testa.
▶**reel off** *vt* snocciolare.
re-election [riːɪ'lɛkʃən] *n* rielezione *f*.
re-enter [riː'ɛntə*] *vt* rientrare in.
re-entry [riː'ɛntrɪ] *n* rientro.
re-export *vt* [riːɪk'spɔːt] riesportare ♦ *n* [riː'ɛkspɔːt] merce *f* riesportata, riesportazione *f*.
ref [rɛf] *n abbr* (*col*: = *referee*) arbitro.
ref. *abbr* (*COMM*: = *with reference to*) sogg.
refectory [rɪ'fɛktərɪ] *n* refettorio.
refer [rɪ'fəː*] *vt*: **to** ~ **sth to** (*dispute, decision*) deferire qc a; **to** ~ **sb to** (*inquirer: for information*) indirizzare qn a; (*reader: to text*) rimandare qn a; **he** ~**red me to the manager** mi ha detto di rivolgermi al direttore.
▶**refer to** *vt fus* (*allude to*) accennare a; (*apply to*) riferire a; (*consult*) rivolgersi a; ~**ring to your letter** (*COMM*) in riferimento alla Vostra lettera.
referee [rɛfə'riː] *n* arbitro; (*TENNIS*) giudice *m* di gara; (*BRIT: for job application*)

referenza ♦ *vt* arbitrare.
reference ['rɛfrəns] *n* riferimento;
(*mention*) menzione *f*, allusione *f*; (*for job application: letter*) referenza; lettera di raccomandazione; (: *person*) referenza; (*in book*) rimando; **with ~ to** riguardo a; (*COMM: in letter*) in *or* con riferimento a; **"please quote this ~"** (*COMM*) "si prega di far riferimento al numero di protocollo".
reference book *n* libro di consultazione.
reference library *n* biblioteca per la consultazione.
reference number *n* (*COMM*) numero di riferimento.
referendum, *pl* **referenda** [rɛfə'rɛndəm, -də] *n* referendum *m inv*.
referral [rɪ'fəːrəl] *n* deferimento; (*MED*) richiesta (di visita specialistica).
refill *vt* [riː'fɪl] riempire di nuovo; (*pen, lighter etc*) ricaricare ♦ *n* ['riːfɪl] (*for pen etc*) ricambio.
refine [rɪ'faɪn] *vt* raffinare.
refined [rɪ'faɪnd] *adj* raffinato(a).
refinement [rɪ'faɪnmənt] *n* (*of person*) raffinatezza.
refinery [rɪ'faɪnərɪ] *n* raffineria.
refit *n* ['riːfɪt] (*NAUT*) raddobbo ♦ *vt* [riː'fɪt] (*ship*) raddobbare.
reflate [riː'fleɪt] *vt* (*economy*) rilanciare.
reflation [riː'fleɪʃən] *n* rilancio.
reflationary [riː'fleɪʃənərɪ] *adj* nuovamente inflazionario(a).
reflect [rɪ'flɛkt] *vt* (*light, image*) riflettere; (*fig*) rispecchiare ♦ *vi* (*think*) riflettere, considerare.
►**reflect on** *vt fus* (*discredit*) rispecchiarsi su.
reflection [rɪ'flɛkʃən] *n* riflessione *f*; (*image*) riflesso; (*criticism*): ~ **on** giudizio su; attacco a; **on** ~ pensandoci sopra.
reflector [rɪ'flɛktə*] *n* (*also AUT*) catarifrangente *m*.
reflex ['riːflɛks] *adj* riflesso(a) ♦ *n* riflesso.
reflexive [rɪ'flɛksɪv] *adj* (*LING*) riflessivo(a).
reform [rɪ'fɔːm] *n* riforma ♦ *vt* riformare.
reformat [rɪ'fɔːmæt] *vt* (*COMPUT*) riformattare.
Reformation [rɛfə'meɪʃən] *n*: **the** ~ la Riforma.
reformatory [rɪ'fɔːmətərɪ] *n* (*US*) riformatorio.
reformed [rɪ'fɔːmd] *adj* cambiato(a) (per il meglio).
reformer [rɪ'fɔːmə*] *n* riformatore/trice.
refrain [rɪ'freɪn] *vi*: **to ~ from doing** trattenersi dal fare ♦ *n* ritornello.
refresh [rɪ'frɛʃ] *vt* rinfrescare; (*subj: food,*

sleep) ristorare.
refresher course [rɪ'frɛʃə-] *n* (*BRIT*) corso di aggiornamento.
refreshing [rɪ'frɛʃɪŋ] *adj* (*drink*) rinfrescante; (*sleep*) riposante, ristoratore(trice); (*change etc*) piacevole; (*idea, point of view*) originale.
refreshment [rɪ'frɛʃmənt] *n* (*eating, resting etc*) ristoro; ~**(s)** rinfreschi *mpl*.
refrigeration [rɪfrɪdʒə'reɪʃən] *n* refrigerazione *f*.
refrigerator [rɪ'frɪdʒəreɪtə*] *n* frigorifero.
refuel [riː'fjuəl] *vt* rifornire (di carburante) ♦ *vi* far rifornimento (di carburante).
refuge ['rɛfjuːdʒ] *n* rifugio; **to take ~ in** rifugiarsi in.
refugee [rɛfju'dʒiː] *n* rifugiato/a, profugo/a.
refugee camp *n* campo (di) profughi.
refund *n* ['riːfʌnd] rimborso ♦ *vt* [rɪ'fʌnd] rimborsare.
refurbish [riː'fəːbɪʃ] *vt* rimettere a nuovo.
refurnish [riː'fəːnɪʃ] *vt* ammobiliare di nuovo.
refusal [rɪ'fjuːzəl] *n* rifiuto; **to have first ~ on sth** avere il diritto d'opzione su qc.
refuse *n* ['rɛfjuːs] rifiuti *mpl* ♦ *vt, vi* [rɪ'fjuːz] rifiutare; **to ~ to do sth** rifiutare *or* rifiutarsi di fare qc.
refuse collection *n* raccolta di rifiuti.
refuse disposal *n* sistema *m* di scarico dei rifiuti.
refusenik [rɪ'fjuːznɪk] *n ebreo a cui il governo sovietico impediva di lasciare il paese.*
refute [rɪ'fjuːt] *vt* confutare.
regain [rɪ'geɪn] *vt* riguadagnare; riacquistare, ricuperare.
regal ['riːgl] *adj* regale.
regale [rɪ'geɪl] *vt*: **to ~ sb with sth** intrattenere qn con qc.
regalia [rɪ'geɪlɪə] *n* insegne *fpl* reali.
regard [rɪ'gɑːd] *n* riguardo, stima ♦ *vt* considerare, stimare; **to give one's ~s to** porgere i suoi saluti a; (*kind*) ~**s** cordiali saluti; **as ~s, with ~ to** riguardo a.
regarding [rɪ'gɑːdɪŋ] *prep* riguardo a, per quanto riguarda.
regardless [rɪ'gɑːdlɪs] *adv* lo stesso; ~ **of** a dispetto di, nonostante.
regatta [rɪ'gætə] *n* regata.
regency ['riːdʒənsɪ] *n* reggenza.
regenerate [rɪ'dʒɛnəreɪt] *vt* rigenerare; (*feelings, enthusiasm*) far rinascere ♦ *vi* rigenerarsi; rinascere.
regent ['riːdʒənt] *n* reggente *m*.
reggae ['rɛgeɪ] *n* reggae *m*.
régime [reɪ'ʒiːm] *n* regime *m*.
regiment *n* ['rɛdʒɪmənt] reggimento ♦ *vt*

['rɛdʒɪmɛnt] irreggimentare.
regimental [rɛdʒɪ'mɛntl] *adj* reggimentale.
regimentation [rɛdʒɪmɛn'teɪʃən] *n*
irreggimentazione *f*.
region ['riːdʒən] *n* regione *f*; **in the ~ of** (*fig*)
all'incirca di.
regional ['riːdʒənl] *adj* regionale.
regional development *n* sviluppo
regionale.
register ['rɛdʒɪstə*] *n* registro; (*also*:
electoral ~) lista elettorale ♦ *vt*
registrare; (*vehicle*) immatricolare;
(*luggage*) spedire assicurato(a); (*letter*)
assicurare; (*subj: instrument*) segnare ♦ *vi*
iscriversi; (*at hotel*) firmare il registro;
(*make impression*) entrare in testa; **to ~ a**
protest fare un esposto; **to ~ for a course**
iscriversi a un corso.
registered ['rɛdʒɪstəd] *adj* (*design*)
depositato(a); (*BRIT: letter*) assicurato(a);
(*student, voter*) iscritto(a).
registered company *n* società iscritta al
registro.
registered nurse *n* (*US*) infermiere(a)
diplomato(a).
registered office *n* sede *f* legale.
registered trademark *n* marchio
depositato.
registrar ['rɛdʒɪstrɑː*] *n* ufficiale *m* di stato
civile; segretario.
registration [rɛdʒɪs'treɪʃən] *n* (*act*)
registrazione *f*; iscrizione *f*; (*AUT: also*: ~
number) numero di targa.
registry ['rɛdʒɪstrɪ] *n* ufficio del registro.
registry office *n* (*BRIT*) anagrafe *f*; **to get**
married in a ~ ≈ sposarsi in municipio.
regret [rɪ'grɛt] *n* rimpianto, rincrescimento
♦ *vt* rimpiangere; **I ~ that I/he cannot**
help mi rincresce di non poter aiutare/
che lui non possa aiutare; **we ~ to inform**
you that ... siamo spiacenti di informarla
che ....
regretfully [rɪ'grɛtfəlɪ] *adv* con
rincrescimento.
regrettable [rɪ'grɛtəbl] *adj* deplorevole.
regrettably [rɪ'grɛtəblɪ] *adv* purtroppo,
sfortunatamente.
regroup [riː'gruːp] *vt* raggruppare ♦ *vi*
raggrupparsi.
regt *abbr* (= *regiment*) Reg.
regular ['rɛgjulə*] *adj* regolare; (*usual*)
abituale, normale; (*listener, reader*) fedele;
(*soldier*) dell'esercito regolare; (*COMM:*
size) normale ♦ *n* (*client etc*) cliente *m/f*
abituale.
regularity [rɛgju'lærɪtɪ] *n* regolarità *f inv*.
regularly ['rɛgjulәlɪ] *adv* regolarmente.
regulate ['rɛgjuleɪt] *vt* regolare.

regulation [rɛgju'leɪʃən] *n* (*rule*) regola,
regolamento; (*adjustment*) regolazione *f*
♦ *cpd* (*MIL*) di ordinanza.
rehabilitate [riːə'bɪlɪteɪt] *vt* (*criminal, drug*
addict, invalid) ricuperare, reinserire.
rehabilitation ['riːəbɪlɪ'teɪʃən] *n* (*see vb*)
ricupero, reinserimento.
rehash [riː'hæʃ] *vt* (*col*) rimaneggiare.
rehearsal [rɪ'həːsəl] *n* prova; **dress ~** prova
generale.
rehearse [rɪ'həːs] *vt* provare.
rehouse [riː'hauz] *vt* rialloggiare.
reign [reɪn] *n* regno ♦ *vi* regnare.
reigning ['reɪnɪŋ] *adj* (*monarch*) regnante;
(*champion*) attuale.
reimburse [riːɪm'bəːs] *vt* rimborsare.
rein [reɪn] *n* (*for horse*) briglia; **to give sb**
free ~ (*fig*) lasciare completa libertà a
qn.
reincarnation [riːɪnkɑː'neɪʃən] *n*
reincarnazione *f*.
reindeer ['reɪndɪə*] *n* (*pl inv*) renna.
reinforce [riːɪn'fɔːs] *vt* rinforzare.
reinforced concrete [riːɪn'fɔːst-] *n*
cemento armato.
reinforcement [riːɪn'fɔːsmənt] *n* (*action*)
rinforzamento; ~**s** *npl* (*MIL*) rinforzi *mpl*.
reinstate [riːɪn'steɪt] *vt* reintegrare.
reinstatement [riːɪn'steɪtmənt] *n*
reintegrazione *f*.
reissue [riː'ɪʃjuː] *vt* (*book*) ristampare,
ripubblicare; (*film*) distribuire di nuovo.
reiterate [riː'ɪtəreɪt] *vt* reiterare, ripetere.
reject *n* ['riːdʒɛkt] (*COMM*) scarto ♦ *vt*
[rɪ'dʒɛkt] rifiutare, respingere; (*COMM:*
goods) scartare.
rejection [rɪ'dʒɛkʃən] *n* rifiuto.
rejoice [rɪ'dʒɔɪs] *vi*: **to ~ (at or over)**
provare diletto (di).
rejoinder [rɪ'dʒɔɪndə*] *n* (*retort*) replica.
rejuvenate [rɪ'dʒuːvəneɪt] *vt* ringiovanire.
rekindle [riː'kɪndl] *vt* riaccendere.
relapse [rɪ'læps] *n* (*MED*) ricaduta.
relate [rɪ'leɪt] *vt* (*tell*) raccontare; (*connect*)
collegare ♦ *vi*: **to ~ to** (*refer to*) riferirsi a;
(*get on with*) stabilire un rapporto con.
related [rɪ'leɪtɪd] *adj* imparentato(a);
collegato(a), connesso(a); ~ **to**
imparentato(a) con; collegato(a) *or*
connesso(a) con.
relating [rɪ'leɪtɪŋ]: ~ **to** *prep* che riguarda,
rispetto a.
relation [rɪ'leɪʃən] *n* (*person*) parente *m/f*;
(*link*) rapporto, relazione *f*; **in ~ to** con
riferimento a; **diplomatic/international**
~**s** rapporti diplomatici/internazionali; **to**
bear a ~ to corrispondere a.
relationship [rɪ'leɪʃənʃɪp] *n* rapporto;

(*personal ties*) rapporti *mpl*, relazioni *fpl*; (*also*: **family** ~) legami *mpl* di parentela; (*affair*) relazione *f*; **they have a good** ~ vanno molto d'accordo.

relative ['rɛlətɪv] *n* parente *m/f* ♦ *adj* relativo(a); (*respective*) rispettivo(a).

relatively ['rɛlətɪvlɪ] *adv* relativamente; (*fairly, rather*) abbastanza.

relax [rɪ'læks] *vi* rilasciarsi; (*person: unwind*) rilassarsi ♦ *vt* rilasciare; (*mind, person*) rilassare; ~! (*calm down*) calma!

relaxation [riːlæk'seɪʃən] *n* rilasciamento; rilassamento; (*entertainment*) ricreazione *f*, svago.

relaxed [rɪ'lækst] *adj* rilasciato(a); rilassato(a).

relaxing [rɪ'læksɪŋ] *adj* rilassante.

relay ['riːleɪ] *n* (*SPORT*) corsa a staffetta ♦ *vt* (*message*) trasmettere.

release [rɪ'liːs] *n* (*from prison*) rilascio; (*from obligation*) liberazione *f*, (*of gas etc*) emissione *f*; (*of film etc*) distribuzione *f*; (*record*) disco; (*device*) disinnesto ♦ *vt* (*prisoner*) rilasciare; (*from obligation, wreckage etc*) liberare; (*book, film*) far uscire; (*news*) rendere pubblico(a); (*gas etc*) emettere; (*TECH: catch, spring etc*) disinnestare; (*let go*) rilasciare; lasciar andare; sciogliere; **to** ~ **one's grip** mollare la presa; **to** ~ **the clutch** (*AUT*) staccare la frizione.

relegate ['rɛləgeɪt] *vt* relegare; (*SPORT*): **to be** ~**d** essere retrocesso(a).

relent [rɪ'lɛnt] *vi* cedere.

relentless [rɪ'lɛntlɪs] *adj* implacabile.

relevance ['rɛləvəns] *n* pertinenza; ~ **of sth to sth** rapporto tra qc e qc.

relevant ['rɛləvənt] *adj* pertinente; (*chapter*) in questione; ~ **to** pertinente a.

reliability [rɪlaɪə'bɪlɪtɪ] *n* (*of person*) serietà; (*of machine*) affidabilità.

reliable [rɪ'laɪəbl] *adj* (*person, firm*) fidato(a), che dà affidamento; (*method*) sicuro(a); (*machine*) affidabile.

reliably [rɪ'laɪəblɪ] *adv*: **to be** ~ **informed** sapere da fonti sicure.

reliance [rɪ'laɪəns] *n*: ~ (**on**) dipendenza (da).

reliant [rɪ'laɪənt] *adj*: **to be** ~ **on sth/sb** dipendere da qc/qn.

relic ['rɛlɪk] *n* (*REL*) reliquia; (*of the past*) resto.

relief [rɪ'liːf] *n* (*from pain, anxiety*) sollievo; (*help, supplies*) soccorsi *mpl*; (*of guard*) cambio; (*ART, GEO*) rilievo; **by way of light** ~ come diversivo.

relief map *n* carta in rilievo.

relief road *n* (*BRIT*) circonvallazione *f*.

relieve [rɪ'liːv] *vt* (*pain, patient*) sollevare; (*bring help*) soccorrere; (*take over from: gen*) sostituire; (: *guard*) rilevare; **to** ~ **sb of sth** (*load*) alleggerire qn di qc; **to** ~ **sb of his command** (*MIL*) esonerare qn dal comando; **to** ~ **o.s.** (*euphemism*) fare i propri bisogni.

relieved [rɪ'liːvd] *adj* sollevato(a); **to be** ~ **that** ... essere sollevato(a) (dal fatto) che ...; **I'm** ~ **to hear it** mi hai tolto un peso con questa notizia.

religion [rɪ'lɪdʒən] *n* religione *f*.

religious [rɪ'lɪdʒəs] *adj* religioso(a).

religious education *n* religione *f*.

relinquish [rɪ'lɪŋkwɪʃ] *vt* abbandonare; (*plan, habit*) rinunziare a.

relish ['rɛlɪʃ] *n* (*CULIN*) condimento; (*enjoyment*) gran piacere *m* ♦ *vt* (*food etc*) godere; **to** ~ **doing** adorare fare.

relive [riː'lɪv] *vt* rivivere.

reload [riː'ləud] *vt* ricaricare.

relocate [riːləu'keɪt] *vt* (*business*) trasferire ♦ *vi*: **to** ~ **in** trasferire la propria sede a.

reluctance [rɪ'lʌktəns] *n* riluttanza.

reluctant [rɪ'lʌktənt] *adj* riluttante, mal disposto(a); **to be** ~ **to do sth** essere restio a fare qc.

reluctantly [rɪ'lʌktəntlɪ] *adv* di mala voglia, a malincuore.

rely [rɪ'laɪ]: **to** ~ **on** *vt fus* contare su; (*be dependent*) dipendere da.

remain [rɪ'meɪn] *vi* restare, rimanere; **to** ~ **silent** restare in silenzio; **I** ~, **yours faithfully** (*BRIT: in letters*) distinti saluti.

remainder [rɪ'meɪndə*] *n* resto; (*COMM*) rimanenza.

remaining [rɪ'meɪnɪŋ] *adj* che rimane.

remains [rɪ'meɪnz] *npl* resti *mpl*.

remand [rɪ'mɑːnd] *n*: **on** ~ in detenzione preventiva ♦ *vt*: **to** ~ **in custody** rinviare in carcere; trattenere a disposizione della legge.

remand home *n* (*BRIT*) riformatorio, casa di correzione.

remark [rɪ'mɑːk] *n* osservazione *f* ♦ *vt* osservare, dire; (*notice*) notare ♦ *vi*: **to** ~ **on sth** fare dei commenti su qc.

remarkable [rɪ'mɑːkəbl] *adj* notevole; eccezionale.

remarry [riː'mærɪ] *vi* risposarsi.

remedial [rɪ'miːdɪəl] *adj* (*tuition, classes*) di riparazione.

remedy ['rɛmədɪ] *n*: ~ (**for**) rimedio (per) ♦ *vt* rimediare a.

remember [rɪ'mɛmbə*] *vt* ricordare, ricordarsi di; **I** ~ **seeing it**, **I** ~ **having seen it** (mi) ricordo di averlo visto; **she** ~**ed to do it** si è ricordata di farlo; ~ **me**

to your wife and children! saluti sua moglie e i bambini da parte mia!
remembrance [rɪ'mɛmbrəns] n memoria; ricordo.

Nel Regno Unito, la domenica più vicina all'11 di novembre, data in cui fu firmato l'armistizio con la Germania nel 1918, ricorre il **Remembrance Sunday***, giorno in cui vengono commemorati i caduti in guerra. In questa occasione molti portano un papavero di carta appuntato al petto in segno di rispetto.*

---

remind [rɪ'maɪnd] vt: **to ~ sb of sth** ricordare qc a qn; **to ~ sb to do** ricordare a qn di fare; **that ~s me!** a proposito!
reminder [rɪ'maɪndə*] n richiamo; (*note etc*) promemoria m inv.
reminisce [rɛmɪ'nɪs] vi: **to ~ (about)** abbandonarsi ai ricordi (di).
reminiscences [rɛmɪ'nɪsnsɪz] npl reminiscenze fpl, memorie fpl.
reminiscent [rɛmɪ'nɪsnt] adj: ~ **of** che fa pensare a, che richiama.
remiss [rɪ'mɪs] adj negligente; **it was ~ of me** è stata una negligenza da parte mia.
remission [rɪ'mɪʃən] n remissione f; (*of fee*) esonero.
remit [rɪ'mɪt] vt rimettere.
remittance [rɪ'mɪtəns] n rimessa.
remnant ['rɛmnənt] n resto, avanzo; ~**s** npl (*COMM*) scampoli mpl; fine f serie.
remonstrate ['rɛmənstreɪt] vi protestare; **to ~ with sb about sth** fare le proprie rimostranze a qn circa qc.
remorse [rɪ'mɔːs] n rimorso.
remorseful [rɪ'mɔːsful] adj pieno(a) di rimorsi.
remorseless [rɪ'mɔːslɪs] adj (*fig*) spietato(a).
remote [rɪ'məut] adj remoto(a), lontano(a); (*person*) distaccato(a); **there is a ~ possibility that ...** c'è una vaga possibilità che ... + sub.
remote control n telecomando.
remote-controlled [rɪ'məutkən'trəuld] adj telecomandato(a).
remotely [rɪ'məutlɪ] adv remotamente; (*slightly*) vagamente.
remoteness [rɪ'məutnɪs] n lontananza.
remould ['riːməuld] n (*BRIT: tyre*) gomma rivestita.
removable [rɪ'muːvəbl] adj (*detachable*) staccabile.
removal [rɪ'muːvəl] n (*taking away*) rimozione f; soppressione f; (*from house*)

trasloco; (*from office: sacking*) destituzione f; (*MED*) ablazione f.
removal man n (*BRIT*) addetto ai traslochi.
removal van n (*BRIT*) furgone m per traslochi.
remove [rɪ'muːv] vt togliere, rimuovere; (*employee*) destituire; (*stain*) far sparire; (*doubt, abuse*) sopprimere, eliminare; **first cousin once ~d** cugino di secondo grado.
remover [rɪ'muːvə*] n (*for paint*) prodotto sverniciante; (*for varnish*) solvente m; **make-up ~** struccatore m.
remunerate [rɪ'mjuːnəreɪt] vt rimunerare.
remuneration [rɪmjuːnə'reɪʃən] n rimunerazione f.
Renaissance [rə'neɪsəns] n: **the ~** il Rinascimento.
rename [riː'neɪm] vt ribattezzare.
rend, pt, pp **rent** [rɛnd, rɛnt] vt lacerare.
render ['rɛndə*] vt rendere; (*CULIN: fat*) struggere.
rendering ['rɛndərɪŋ] n (*MUS etc*) interpretazione f.
rendez-vous ['rɔndɪvuː] n appuntamento; (*place*) luogo d'incontro; (*meeting*) incontro ♦ vi ritrovarsi; (*spaceship*) effettuare un rendez-vous.
rendition [rɛn'dɪʃən] n (*MUS*) interpretazione f.
renegade ['rɛnɪɡeɪd] n rinnegato/a.
renew [rɪ'njuː] vt rinnovare; (*negotiations*) riprendere.
renewable [rɪ'njuːəbl] adj riutilizzabile; ~ **energy**, ~**s** fonti mpl di energia rinnovabile.
renewal [rɪ'njuːəl] n rinnovamento; ripresa.
renounce [rɪ'nauns] vt rinunziare a; (*disown*) ripudiare.
renovate ['rɛnəveɪt] vt rinnovare; (*art work*) restaurare.
renovation [rɛnə'veɪʃən] n rinnovamento, restauro.
renown [rɪ'naun] n rinomanza.
renowned [rɪ'naund] adj rinomato(a).
rent [rɛnt] pt, pp of **rend** ♦ n affitto ♦ vt (*take for rent*) prendere in affitto; (*car, TV*) noleggiare, prendere a noleggio; (*also*: ~ **out**) dare in affitto; (*car, TV*) noleggiare, dare a noleggio.
rental ['rɛntl] n (*cost: on TV, telephone*) abbonamento; (: *on car*) nolo, noleggio.
rent boy n (*BRIT col*) giovane prostituto.
renunciation [rɪnʌnsɪ'eɪʃən] n rinnegamento; (*self-denial*) rinunzia.
reopen [riː'əupən] vt riaprire.
reopening [riː'əupnɪŋ] n riapertura.

reorder [riː'ɔːdə*] *vt* ordinare di nuovo; (*rearrange*) riorganizzare.
reorganize [riː'ɔːgənaɪz] *vt* riorganizzare.
Rep *abbr* (*US POL*) = **representative**; **republican**.
rep [rɛp] *n abbr* (*COMM*: = *representative*) rappresentante *m/f*; (*THEAT*: = *repertory*) teatro di repertorio.
repair [rɪ'pɛə*] *n* riparazione *f* ♦ *vt* riparare; **in good/bad** ~ in buona/cattiva condizione; **under** ~ in riparazione.
repair kit *n* corredo per riparazioni.
repair man *n* riparatore *m*.
repair shop *n* (*AUT etc*) officina.
repartee [rɛpɑː'tiː] *n* risposta pronta.
repast [rɪ'pɑːst] *n* (*formal*) pranzo.
repatriate [riː'pætrɪeɪt] *vt* rimpatriare.
repay [riː'peɪ] *vt irreg* (*money, creditor*) rimborsare, ripagare; (*sb's efforts*) ricompensare.
repayment [riː'peɪmənt] *n* rimborsamento; ricompensa.
repeal [rɪ'piːl] *n* (*of law*) abrogazione *f*, (*of sentence*) annullamento ♦ *vt* abrogare; annullare.
repeat [rɪ'piːt] *n* (*RADIO, TV*) replica ♦ *vt* ripetere; (*pattern*) riprodurre; (*promise, attack, also COMM*: *order*) rinnovare ♦ *vi* ripetere.
repeatedly [rɪ'piːtɪdlɪ] *adv* ripetutamente, spesso.
repeat order *n* (*COMM*): **to place a** ~ (**for**) rinnovare l'ordinazione (di).
repel [rɪ'pɛl] *vt* respingere.
repellent [rɪ'pɛlənt] *adj* repellente ♦ *n*: **insect** ~ prodotto *m* anti-insetti *inv*; **moth** ~ anti-tarmico.
repent [rɪ'pɛnt] *vi*: **to** ~ (**of**) pentirsi (di).
repentance [rɪ'pɛntəns] *n* pentimento.
repercussion [riːpə'kʌʃən] *n* (*consequence*) ripercussione *f*.
repertoire ['rɛpətwɑː*] *n* repertorio.
repertory ['rɛpətərɪ] *n* (*also*: ~ **theatre**) teatro di repertorio.
repertory company *n* compagnia di repertorio.
repetition [rɛpɪ'tɪʃən] *n* ripetizione *f*, (*COMM*: *of order etc*) rinnovo.
repetitious [rɛpɪ'tɪʃəs] *adj* (*speech*) pieno(a) di ripetizioni.
repetitive [rɪ'pɛtɪtɪv] *adj* (*movement*) che si ripete; (*work*) monotono(a); (*speech*) pieno(a) di ripetizioni.
replace [rɪ'pleɪs] *vt* (*put back*) rimettere a posto; (*take the place of*) sostituire; (*TEL*): "~ **the receiver**" "riattaccare".
replacement [rɪ'pleɪsmənt] *n* rimessa; sostituzione *f*; (*person*) sostituto/a.

replacement part *n* pezzo di ricambio.
replay ['riːpleɪ] *n* (*of match*) partita ripetuta; (*of tape, film*) replay *m inv*.
replenish [rɪ'plɛnɪʃ] *vt* (*glass*) riempire; (*stock etc*) rifornire.
replete [rɪ'pliːt] *adj*: ~ (**with**) ripieno(a) (di); (*well-fed*) sazio(a) (di).
replica ['rɛplɪkə] *n* replica, copia.
reply [rɪ'plaɪ] *n* risposta ♦ *vi* rispondere; **in** ~ **in** risposta; **there's no** ~ (*TEL*) non risponde (nessuno).
reply coupon *n* buono di risposta.
report [rɪ'pɔːt] *n* rapporto; (*PRESS etc*) cronaca; (*BRIT*: *also*: **school** ~) pagella ♦ *vt* riportare; (*PRESS etc*) fare una cronaca su; (*bring to notice*: *occurrence*) segnalare; (: *person*) denunciare ♦ *vi* (*make a report*) fare un rapporto (*or* una cronaca); (*present o.s.*): **to** ~ (**to sb**) presentarsi (a qn); **to** ~ (**on**) fare un rapporto (su); **it is** ~**ed that** si dice che; **it is** ~**ed from Berlin that** ... ci è stato riferito da Berlino che ....
report card *n* (*US, Scottish*) pagella.
reportedly [rɪ'pɔːtɪdlɪ] *adv*: **she is** ~ **living in Spain** si dice che vive in Spagna.
reported speech [rɪ'pɔːtɪd-] *n* (*LING*) discorso indiretto.
reporter [rɪ'pɔːtə*] *n* (*PRESS*) cronista *m/f*, reporter *m inv*; (*RADIO*) radiocronista *m/f*; (*TV*) telecronista *m/f*.
repose [rɪ'pəuz] *n*: **in** ~ in riposo.
repossess [riːpə'zɛs] *vt* rientrare in possesso di.
repossession order [riːpə'zɛʃən-] *n* ordine *m* di espropriazione.
reprehensible [rɛprɪ'hɛnsɪbl] *adj* riprensibile.
represent [rɛprɪ'zɛnt] *vt* rappresentare.
representation [rɛprɪzɛn'teɪʃən] *n* rappresentazione *f*; ~**s** *npl* (*protest*) protesta.
representative [rɛprɪ'zɛntətɪv] *n* rappresentativo/a; (*COMM*) rappresentante *m* (di commercio); (*US*: *POL*) deputato/a ♦ *adj*: ~ (**of**) rappresentativo/a (di).
repress [rɪ'prɛs] *vt* reprimere.
repression [rɪ'prɛʃən] *n* repressione *f*.
repressive [rɪ'prɛsɪv] *adj* repressivo(a).
reprieve [rɪ'priːv] *n* (*LAW*) sospensione *f* dell'esecuzione della condanna; (*fig*) dilazione *f* ♦ *vt* sospendere l'esecuzione della condanna a; accordare una dilazione a.
reprimand ['rɛprɪmɑːnd] *n* rimprovero ♦ *vt* rimproverare, redarguire.
reprint ['riːprɪnt] *n* ristampa ♦ *vt*

ristampare.

reprisal [rɪ'praɪzl] n rappresaglia; **to take**
~**s** fare delle rappresaglie.

reproach [rɪ'prəutʃ] n rimprovero ♦ vt: **to ~
sb with sth** rimproverare qn di qc;
beyond ~ irreprensibile.

reproachful [rɪ'prəutʃful] adj di
rimprovero.

reproduce [ri:prə'djuːs] vt riprodurre ♦ vi
riprodursi.

reproduction [ri:prə'dʌkʃən] n
riproduzione f.

reproductive [ri:prə'dʌktɪv] adj
riproduttore(trice); riproduttivo(a).

reproof [rɪ'pruːf] n riprovazione f.

reprove [rɪ'pruːv] vt (action) disapprovare;
(person): **to ~ (for)** biasimare (per).

reproving [rɪ'pruːvɪŋ] adj di
disapprovazione.

reptile ['reptaɪl] n rettile m.

Repub. abbr (US POL) = **republican.**

republic [rɪ'pʌblɪk] n repubblica.

republican [rɪ'pʌblɪkən] adj, n
repubblicano(a).

repudiate [rɪ'pjuːdɪeɪt] vt ripudiare.

repugnant [rɪ'pʌgnənt] adj ripugnante.

repulse [rɪ'pʌls] vt respingere.

repulsion [rɪ'pʌlʃən] n ripulsione f.

repulsive [rɪ'pʌlsɪv] adj ripugnante,
ripulsivo(a).

reputable ['repjutəbl] adj di buona
reputazione; (occupation) rispettabile.

reputation [repju'teɪʃən] n reputazione f;
he has a ~ for being awkward ha la fama
di essere un tipo difficile.

repute [rɪ'pjuːt] n reputazione f.

reputed [rɪ'pjuːtɪd] adj reputato(a); **to be ~
to be rich/intelligent** etc essere
ritenuto(a) ricco(a)/intelligente etc.

reputedly [rɪ'pjuːtɪdlɪ] adv secondo quanto
si dice.

request [rɪ'kwest] n domanda; (formal)
richiesta ♦ vt: **to ~ (of or from sb)**
chiedere (a qn); **at the ~ of** su richiesta
di; **"you are ~ed not to smoke"** "si prega
di non fumare".

request stop n (BRIT: for bus) fermata
facoltativa or a richiesta.

requiem ['rekwɪəm] n requiem m or f inv.

require [rɪ'kwaɪə*] vt (need: subj: person)
aver bisogno di; (: thing, situation)
richiedere; (want) volere; esigere; (order)
obbligare; **to ~ sb to do sth/sth of sb**
esigere che qn faccia qc/qc da qn; **what
qualifications are ~d?** che requisiti ci
vogliono?; ~**d by law** prescritto dalla
legge; **if** ~**d** in caso di bisogno.

required [rɪ'kwaɪəd] adj richiesto(a).

requirement [rɪ'kwaɪəmənt] n (need)
esigenza; (condition) requisito; **to meet
sb's** ~**s** soddisfare le esigenze di qn.

requisite ['rekwɪzɪt] n cosa necessaria ♦ adj
necessario(a); **toilet** ~**s** articoli mpl da
toletta.

requisition [rekwɪ'zɪʃən] n: ~ **(for)** richiesta
(di) ♦ vt (MIL) requisire.

reroute [riː'ruːt] vt (train etc) deviare.

resale ['riːseɪl] n rivendita.

resale price maintenance (RPM) n
prezzo minimo di vendita imposto.

rescind [rɪ'sɪnd] vt annullare; (law)
abrogare; (judgement) rescindere.

rescue ['reskjuː] n salvataggio; (help)
soccorso ♦ vt salvare; **to come/go to sb's
~** venire/andare in aiuto a or di qn.

rescue party n squadra di salvataggio.

rescuer ['reskjuə*] n salvatore/trice.

research [rɪ'səːtʃ] n ricerca, ricerche fpl
♦ vt fare ricerche su ♦ vi: **to ~ (into sth)**
fare ricerca (su qc); **a piece of** ~ un
lavoro di ricerca; ~ **and development
(R&D)** ricerca e sviluppo.

researcher [rɪ'səːtʃə*] n ricercatore/trice.

research work n ricerche fpl.

resell [riː'sel] vt irreg rivendere.

resemblance [rɪ'zembləns] n somiglianza;
to bear a strong ~ **to** somigliare
moltissimo a.

resemble [rɪ'zembl] vt assomigliare a.

resent [rɪ'zent] vt risentirsi di.

resentful [rɪ'zentful] adj pieno(a) di
risentimento.

resentment [rɪ'zentmənt] n risentimento.

reservation [rezə'veɪʃən] n (booking)
prenotazione f; (doubt) dubbio; (protected
area) riserva; (BRIT AUT: also: **central** ~)
spartitraffico m inv; **to make a** ~ **(in an
hotel/a restaurant/on a plane)** prenotare
(una camera/una tavola/un posto); **with**
~**s** (doubts) con le dovute riserve.

reservation desk n (US: in hotel) reception
f inv.

reserve [rɪ'zəːv] n riserva ♦ vt (seats etc)
prenotare; ~**s** npl (MIL) riserve fpl; **in** ~ in
serbo.

reserve currency n valuta di riserva.

reserved [rɪ'zəːvd] adj (shy) riservato(a);
(seat) prenotato(a).

reserve price n (BRIT) prezzo di riserva,
prezzo m base inv.

reserve team n (BRIT SPORT) seconda
squadra.

reservist [rɪ'zəːvɪst] n (MIL) riservista m.

reservoir ['rezəvwɑː*] n serbatoio; (artificial
lake) bacino idrico.

reset [riː'set] vt (COMPUT) azzerare.

reshape [riː'ʃeɪp] *vt* (*policy*) ristrutturare.
reshuffle [riː'ʃʌfl] *n*: **Cabinet** ~ (*POL*) rimpasto governativo.
reside [rɪ'zaɪd] *vi* risiedere.
residence ['rezɪdəns] *n* residenza; **to take up** ~ prendere residenza; **in** ~ (*queen etc*) in sede; (*doctor*) fisso.
residence permit *n* (*BRIT*) permesso di soggiorno.
resident ['rezɪdənt] *n* (*gen, COMPUT*) residente *m/f*; (*in hotel*) cliente *m/f* fisso(a) ♦ *adj* residente.
residential [rezɪ'denʃəl] *adj* di residenza; (*area*) residenziale.
residue ['rezɪdjuː] *n* resto; (*CHEM, PHYSICS*) residuo.
resign [rɪ'zaɪn] *vt* (*one's post*) dimettersi da ♦ *vi*: **to** ~ (**from**) dimettersi (da), dare le dimissioni (da); **to** ~ **o.s. to** rassegnarsi a.
resignation [rezɪg'neɪʃən] *n* dimissioni *fpl*; rassegnazione *f*; **to tender one's** ~ dare le dimissioni.
resilience [rɪ'zɪlɪəns] *n* (*of material*) elasticità, resilienza; (*of person*) capacità di recupero.
resilient [rɪ'zɪlɪənt] *adj* elastico(a); (*person*) che si riprende facilmente.
resin ['rezɪn] *n* resina.
resist [rɪ'zɪst] *vt* resistere a.
resistance [rɪ'zɪstəns] *n* resistenza.
resistant [rɪ'zɪstənt] *adj*: ~ (**to**) resistente (a).
resolute ['rezəluːt] *adj* risoluto(a).
resolution [rezə'luːʃən] *n* (*resolve*) fermo proposito, risoluzione *f*; (*determination*) risolutezza; (*on screen*) risoluzione *f*; **to make a** ~ fare un proposito.
resolve [rɪ'zɔlv] *n* risoluzione *f* ♦ *vi* (*decide*): **to** ~ **to do** decidere di fare ♦ *vt* (*problem*) risolvere.
resolved [rɪ'zɔlvd] *adj* risoluto(a).
resonance ['rezənəns] *n* risonanza.
resonant ['rezənənt] *adj* risonante.
resort [rɪ'zɔːt] *n* (*town*) stazione *f*; (*place*) località *f inv*; (*recourse*) ricorso ♦ *vi*: **to** ~ **to** far ricorso a; **seaside/winter sports** ~ stazione *f* balneare/di sport invernali; **as a last** ~ come ultima risorsa.
resound [rɪ'zaʊnd] *vi*: **to** ~ (**with**) risonare (di).
resounding [rɪ'zaʊndɪŋ] *adj* risonante.
resource [rɪ'sɔːs] *n* risorsa; ~**s** *npl* risorse *fpl*; **natural** ~**s** risorse naturali; **to leave sb to his** (*or* **her**) **own** ~**s** (*fig*) lasciare che qn si arrangi (per conto suo).
resourceful [rɪ'sɔːsful] *adj* pieno(a) di risorse, intraprendente.

resourcefulness [rɪ'sɔːsfəlnɪs] *n* intraprendenza.
respect [rɪs'pekt] *n* rispetto; (*point, detail*): **in some** ~**s** sotto certi aspetti ♦ *vt* rispettare; ~**s** *npl* ossequi *mpl*; **to have** *or* **show** ~ **for** aver rispetto per; **out of** ~ **for** per rispetto *or* riguardo a; **with** ~ **to** rispetto a, riguardo a; **in** ~ **of** quanto a; **in this** ~ per questo riguardo; **with (all) due** ~ **I** ... con rispetto parlando, io ....
respectability [rɪspektə'bɪlɪtɪ] *n* rispettabilità.
respectable [rɪs'pektəbl] *adj* rispettabile; (*quite big: amount etc*) considerevole; (*quite good: player, result etc*) niente male *inv*.
respectful [rɪs'pektful] *adj* rispettoso(a).
respective [rɪs'pektɪv] *adj* rispettivo(a).
respectively [rɪs'pektɪvlɪ] *adv* rispettivamente.
respiration [respɪ'reɪʃən] *n* respirazione *f*.
respirator ['respɪreɪtə*] *n* respiratore *m*.
respiratory ['respərətərɪ] *adj* respiratorio(a).
respite ['respaɪt] *n* respiro, tregua.
resplendent [rɪs'plendənt] *adj* risplendente.
respond [rɪs'pɔnd] *vi* rispondere.
respondent [rɪs'pɔndənt] *n* (*LAW*) convenuto/a.
response [rɪs'pɔns] *n* risposta; **in** ~ **to** in risposta a.
responsibility [rɪspɔnsɪ'bɪlɪtɪ] *n* responsabilità *f inv*; **to take** ~ **for sth/sb** assumersi *or* prendersi la responsabilità di qc/per qn.
responsible [rɪs'pɔnsɪbl] *adj* (*liable*): ~ (**for**) responsabile (di); (*trustworthy*) fidato(a); (*job*) di (grande) responsabilità; **to be** ~ **to sb (for sth)** dover rispondere a qn (di qc).
responsibly [rɪs'pɔnsəblɪ] *adv* responsabilmente.
responsive [rɪs'pɔnsɪv] *adj* che reagisce.
rest [rest] *n* riposo; (*stop*) sosta, pausa; (*MUS*) pausa; (*support*) appoggio, sostegno; (*remainder*) resto, avanzi *mpl* ♦ *vi* riposarsi; (*remain*) rimanere, restare; (*be supported*): **to** ~ **on** appoggiarsi su ♦ *vt* (*lean*): **to** ~ **sth on/against** appoggiare qc su/contro; **to set sb's mind at** ~ tranquillizzare qn; **the** ~ **of them** gli altri; **to** ~ **one's eyes** *or* **gaze on** posare lo sguardo su; ~ **assured that** ... stia tranquillo che ...; **it** ~**s with him to decide** sta a lui decidere.
restart [riː'stɑːt] *vt* (*engine*) rimettere in marcia; (*work*) ricominciare.
restaurant ['restərɔŋ] *n* ristorante *m*.

restaurant car – retrieval

restaurant car n (BRIT) vagone m ristorante.
rest cure n cura del riposo.
restful ['rɛstful] adj riposante.
rest home n casa di riposo.
restitution [rɛstɪ'tjuːʃən] n (act) restituzione f; (reparation) riparazione f.
restive ['rɛstɪv] adj agitato(a), impaziente; (horse) restio(a).
restless ['rɛstlɪs] adj agitato(a), irrequieto(a); **to get** ~ spazientirsi.
restlessly ['rɛstlɪslɪ] adv in preda all'agitazione.
restock [riː'stɔk] vt rifornire.
restoration [rɛstə'reɪʃən] n restauro; restituzione f.
restorative [rɪ'stɔrətɪv] adj corroborante, ristorativo(a) ♦ n ricostituente m.
restore [rɪ'stɔː*] vt (building) restaurare; (sth stolen) restituire; (peace, health) ristorare.
restorer [rɪs'tɔːrə*] n (ART etc) restauratore/trice.
restrain [rɪs'treɪn] vt (feeling) contenere, frenare; (person): **to** ~ **(from doing)** trattenere (dal fare).
restrained [rɪs'treɪnd] adj (style) contenuto(a), sobrio(a); (manner) riservato(a).
restraint [rɪs'treɪnt] n (restriction) limitazione f; (moderation) ritegno; **wage** ~ restrizioni fpl salariali.
restrict [rɪs'trɪkt] vt restringere, limitare.
restricted area [rɪs'trɪktɪd-] n (AUT) zona a velocità limitata.
restriction [rɪs'trɪkʃən] n restrizione f, limitazione f.
restrictive [rɪs'trɪktɪv] adj restrittivo(a).
restrictive practices npl (INDUSTRY) pratiche restrittive di produzione.
rest room n (US) toletta.
restructure [riː'strʌktʃə*] vt ristrutturare.
result [rɪ'zʌlt] n risultato ♦ vi: **to** ~ **in** avere per risultato; **as a** ~ **(of)** in or di conseguenza (a), in seguito a); **to** ~ **(from)** essere una conseguenza (di), essere causato(a) (da).
resultant [rɪ'zʌltənt] adj risultante, conseguente.
resume [rɪ'zjuːm] vt, vi (work, journey) riprendere; (sum up) riassumere.
résumé ['reɪzjuːmeɪ] n riassunto; (US: curriculum vitae) curriculum vitae m inv.
resumption [rɪ'zʌmpʃən] n ripresa.
resurgence [rɪ'sɜːdʒəns] n rinascita.
resurrection [rɛzə'rekʃən] n risurrezione f.
resuscitate [rɪ'sʌsɪteɪt] vt (MED) risuscitare.

resuscitation [rɪsʌsɪ'teɪʃən] n rianimazione f.
retail ['riːteɪl] n (vendita al) minuto ♦ cpd al minuto ♦ vt vendere al minuto ♦ vi: **to** ~ **at** essere in vendita al pubblico al prezzo di.
retailer ['riːteɪlə*] n commerciante m/f al minuto, dettagliante m/f.
retail outlet n punto di vendita al dettaglio.
retail price n prezzo al minuto.
retail price index n indice m dei prezzi al consumo.
retain [rɪ'teɪn] vt (keep) tenere, serbare.
retainer [rɪ'teɪnə*] n (servant) servitore m; (fee) onorario.
retaliate [rɪ'tælɪeɪt] vi: **to** ~ **(against)** vendicarsi (di); **to** ~ **on sb** fare una rappresaglia contro qn.
retaliation [rɪtælɪ'eɪʃən] n rappresaglie fpl; **in** ~ **for** per vendicarsi di.
retaliatory [rɪ'tælɪətərɪ] adj di rappresaglia, di ritorsione.
retarded [rɪ'tɑːdɪd] adj ritardato(a); (also: **mentally** ~) tardo(a) (di mente).
retch [rɛtʃ] vi aver conati di vomito.
retentive [rɪ'tentɪv] adj ritentivo(a).
rethink ['riː'θɪŋk] vt ripensare.
reticence ['rɛtɪsns] n reticenza.
reticent ['rɛtɪsnt] adj reticente.
retina ['rɛtɪnə] n retina.
retinue ['rɛtɪnjuː] n seguito, scorta.
retire [rɪ'taɪə*] vi (give up work) andare in pensione; (withdraw) ritirarsi, andarsene; (go to bed) andare a letto, ritirarsi.
retired [rɪ'taɪəd] adj (person) pensionato(a).
retirement [rɪ'taɪəmənt] n pensione f.
retirement age n età del pensionamento.
retiring [rɪ'taɪərɪŋ] adj (person) riservato(a); (departing: chairman) uscente.
retort [rɪ'tɔːt] n (reply) rimbecco; (container) storta ♦ vi rimbeccare.
retrace [riː'treɪs] vt ricostruire; **to** ~ **one's steps** tornare sui propri passi.
retract [rɪ'trækt] vt (statement) ritrattare; (claws, undercarriage, aerial) ritrarre, ritirare ♦ vi ritirarsi.
retractable [rɪ'træktəbl] adj retrattile.
retrain [riː'treɪn] vt (worker) riaddestrare.
retraining [rɪ'treɪnɪŋ] n riaddestramento.
retread vt [riː'trɛd] (AUT: tyre) rigenerare ♦ n ['riːtrɛd] gomma rigenerata.
retreat [rɪ'triːt] n ritirata; (place) rifugio ♦ vi battere in ritirata; (flood) ritirarsi; **to beat a hasty** ~ (fig) battersela.
retrial [riː'traɪəl] n nuovo processo.
retribution [rɛtrɪ'bjuːʃən] n castigo.
retrieval [rɪ'triːvəl] n ricupero.

retrieve [rɪ'triːv] _vt_ (_sth lost_) ricuperare, ritrovare; (_situation, honour_) salvare; (_COMPUT_) ricuperare.
retriever [rɪ'triːvə*] _n_ cane _m_ da riporto.
retroactive [rɛtrəu'æktɪv] _adj_ retroattivo(a).
retrograde ['rɛtrəugreɪd] _adj_ retrogrado(a).
retrospect ['rɛtrəspɛkt] _n_: **in** ~ guardando indietro.
retrospective [rɛtrə'spɛktɪv] _adj_ retrospettivo(a); (_law_) retroattivo(a) ♦ _n_ (_ART_) retrospettiva.
return [rɪ'təːn] _n_ (_going or coming back_) ritorno; (_of sth stolen etc_) restituzione _f_; (_COMM: from land, shares_) profitto, reddito; (_: of merchandise_) resa; (_report_) rapporto; (_reward_): **in** ~ **(for)** in cambio (di) ♦ _cpd_ (_journey, match_) di ritorno; (_BRIT: ticket_) di andata e ritorno ♦ _vi_ tornare, ritornare ♦ _vt_ rendere, restituire; (_bring back_) riportare; (_send back_) mandare indietro; (_put back_) rimettere; (_POL: candidate_) eleggere; ~**s** _npl_ (_COMM_) incassi _mpl_; profitti _mpl_; **by** ♦ **of post** a stretto giro di posta; **many happy** ~**s (of the day)!** auguri!, buon compleanno!
returnable [rɪ'təːnəbl] _adj_: ~ **bottle** vuoto a rendere.
returner [rɪ'təːnə*] _n_ donna che ritorna al lavoro dopo la maternità.
returning officer [rɪ'təːnɪŋ-] _n_ (_BRIT POL_) funzionario addetto all'organizzazione delle elezioni in un distretto.
return key _n_ (_COMPUT_) tasto di ritorno.
reunion [riː'juːnɪən] _n_ riunione _f_.
reunite [riːju:'naɪt] _vt_ riunire.
rev [rɛv] _n abbr_ (= _revolution: AUT_) giro ♦ _vb_ (_also_: ~ **up**) _vt_ imballare ♦ _vi_ imballarsi.
revaluation [riːvæljuˈeɪʃən] _n_ rivalutazione _f_.
revamp ['riː'væmp] _vt_ rinnovare; riorganizzare.
rev counter _n_ contagiri _m inv_.
Rev(d). _abbr_ = **reverend**.
reveal [rɪ'viːl] _vt_ (_make known_) rivelare, svelare; (_display_) rivelare, mostrare.
revealing [rɪ'viːlɪŋ] _adj_ rivelatore(trice); (_dress_) scollato(a).
reveille [rɪ'vælɪ] _n_ (_MIL_) sveglia.
revel ['rɛvl] _vi_: **to** ~ **in sth/in doing** dilettarsi di qc/a fare.
revelation [rɛvə'leɪʃən] _n_ rivelazione _f_.
reveller ['rɛvlə*] _n_ festaiolo/a.
revelry ['rɛvlrɪ] _n_ baldoria.
revenge [rɪ'vɛndʒ] _n_ vendetta; (_in game etc_) rivincita ♦ _vt_ vendicare; **to take** ~ vendicarsi; **to get one's** ~ **(for sth)** vendicarsi (di qc).

revengeful [rɪ'vɛndʒful] _adj_ vendicatore(trice); vendicativo(a).
revenue ['rɛvənjuː] _n_ reddito.
reverberate [rɪ'vəːbəreɪt] _vi_ (_sound_) rimbombare; (_light_) riverberarsi.
reverberation [rɪvəːbə'reɪʃən] _n_ (_of light, sound_) riverberazione _f_.
revere [rɪ'vɪə*] _vt_ venerare.
reverence ['rɛvərəns] _n_ venerazione _f_, riverenza.
Reverend ['rɛvərənd] _adj_ (_in titles_) reverendo(a).
reverent ['rɛvərənt] _adj_ riverente.
reverie ['rɛvərɪ] _n_ fantasticheria.
reversal [rɪ'vəːsl] _n_ capovolgimento.
reverse [rɪ'vəːs] _n_ contrario, opposto; (_back_) rovescio; (_AUT: also_: ~ **gear**) marcia indietro ♦ _adj_ (_order_) inverso(a); (_direction_) opposto(a) ♦ _vt_ (_turn_) invertire, rivoltare; (_change_) capovolgere, rovesciare; (_LAW: judgement_) cassare ♦ _vi_ (_BRIT AUT_) fare marcia indietro; **in** ~ **order** in ordine inverso; **to go into** ~ fare marcia indietro.
reversed charge call _n_ (_BRIT TEL_) telefonata con addebito al ricevente.
reverse video _n_ reverse video _m_.
reversible [rɪ'vəːsəbl] _adj_ (_garment_) double-face _inv_; (_procedure_) reversibile.
reversing lights [rɪ'vəːsɪŋ-] _npl_ (_BRIT AUT_) luci _fpl_ per la retromarcia.
reversion [rɪ'vəːʃən] _n_ ritorno.
revert [rɪ'vəːt] _vi_: **to** ~ **to** tornare a.
review [rɪ'vjuː] _n_ rivista; (_of book, film_) recensione _f_ ♦ _vt_ passare in rivista; fare la recensione di; **to come under** ~ essere preso in esame.
reviewer [rɪ'vjuːə*] _n_ recensore/a.
revile [rɪ'vaɪl] _vt_ insultare.
revise [rɪ'vaɪz] _vt_ (_manuscript_) rivedere, correggere; (_opinion_) emendare, modificare; (_study: subject, notes_) ripassare; ~**d edition** edizione riveduta.
revision [rɪ'vɪʒən] _n_ revisione _f_; ripasso; (_revised version_) versione _f_ riveduta e corretta.
revitalize [riː'vaɪtəlaɪz] _vt_ ravvivare.
revival [rɪ'vaɪvəl] _n_ ripresa; ristabilimento; (_of faith_) risveglio.
revive [rɪ'vaɪv] _vt_ (_person_) rianimare; (_custom_) far rivivere; (_hope, courage_) ravvivare; (_play, fashion_) riesumare ♦ _vi_ (_person_) rianimarsi; (_hope_) ravvivarsi; (_activity_) riprendersi.
revoke [rɪ'vəuk] _vt_ revocare; (_promise, decision_) rinvenire su.
revolt [rɪ'vəult] _n_ rivolta, ribellione _f_ ♦ _vi_ rivoltarsi, ribellarsi; **to** ~ **(against sb/**

sth) ribellarsi (a qn/qc).
revolting [rɪ'vəultɪŋ] adj ripugnante.
revolution [rɛvə'lu:ʃən] n rivoluzione f; (of wheel etc) rivoluzione, giro.
revolutionary [rɛvə'lu:ʃənrɪ] adj, n rivoluzionario(a).
revolutionize [rɛvə'lu:ʃənaɪz] vt rivoluzionare.
revolve [rɪ'vɔlv] vi girare.
revolver [rɪ'vɔlvə*] n rivoltella.
revolving [rɪ'vɔlvɪŋ] adj girevole.
revolving door n porta girevole.
revue [rɪ'vju:] n (THEAT) rivista.
revulsion [rɪ'vʌlʃən] n ripugnanza.
reward [rɪ'wɔ:d] n ricompensa, premio ♦ vt: **to ~ (for)** ricompensare (per).
rewarding [rɪ'wɔ:dɪŋ] adj (fig) soddisfacente; **financially ~** conveniente dal punto di vista economico.
rewind [ri:'waɪnd] vt irreg (watch) ricaricare; (ribbon etc) riavvolgere.
rewire [ri:'waɪə*] vt (house) rifare l'impianto elettrico di.
reword [ri:'wɔ:d] vt formulare or esprimere con altre parole.
rewrite [ri:'raɪt] vt irreg riscrivere.
Reykjavik ['reɪkjəvi:k] n Reykjavik f.
RFD abbr (US POST) = rural free delivery.
Rh abbr (= rhesus) Rh.
rhapsody ['ræpsədɪ] n (MUS) rapsodia; (fig) elogio stravagante.
rhesus negative ['ri:səs-] adj (MED) Rh-negativo(a).
rhesus positive adj (MED) Rh-positivo(a).
rhetoric ['rɛtərɪk] n retorica.
rhetorical [rɪ'tɔrɪkl] adj retorico(a).
rheumatic [ru:'mætɪk] adj reumatico(a).
rheumatism ['ru:mətɪzəm] n reumatismo.
rheumatoid arthritis ['ru:mətɔɪd-] n artrite f reumatoide.
Rhine [raɪn] n: **the ~** il Reno.
rhinestone ['raɪnstəun] n diamante m falso.
rhinoceros [raɪ'nɔsərəs] n rinoceronte m.
Rhodes [rəudz] n Rodi f.
Rhodesia [rəu'di:ʒə] n Rhodesia.
Rhodesian [rəu'di:ʒən] adj, n Rhodesiano(a).
rhododendron [rəudə'dɛndrn] n rododendro.
Rhone [rəun] n: **the ~** il Rodano.
rhubarb ['ru:bɑ:b] n rabarbaro.
rhyme [raɪm] n rima; (verse) poesia ♦ vi: **to ~ (with)** fare rima (con); **without ~ or reason** senza capo né coda.
rhythm ['rɪðm] n ritmo.
rhythmic(al) ['rɪðmɪk(əl)] adj ritmico(a).
rhythmically ['rɪðmɪkəlɪ] adv con ritmo.
rhythm method n metodo Ogino-Knauss.

RI abbr (US POST) = Rhode Island ♦ n abbr (BRIT) = religious instruction.
rib [rɪb] n (ANAT) costola ♦ vt (tease) punzecchiare.
ribald ['rɪbəld] adj licenzioso(a), volgare.
ribbed [rɪbd] adj (knitting) a coste.
ribbon ['rɪbən] n nastro; **in ~s** (torn) a brandelli.
rice [raɪs] n riso.
ricefield ['raɪsfi:ld] n risaia.
rice pudding n budino di riso.
rich [rɪtʃ] adj ricco(a); (clothes) sontuoso(a); **the ~** npl i ricchi; **~es** npl ricchezze fpl; **to be ~ in sth** essere ricco di qc.
richly ['rɪtʃlɪ] adv riccamente; (dressed) sontuosamente; (deserved) pienamente.
rickets ['rɪkɪts] n rachitismo.
rickety ['rɪkɪtɪ] adj zoppicante.
rickshaw ['rɪkʃɔ:] n risciò m inv.
ricochet ['rɪkəʃeɪ] n rimbalzo ♦ vi rimbalzare.
rid, pt, pp **rid** [rɪd] vt: **to ~ sb of** sbarazzare or liberare qn di; **to get ~ of** sbarazzarsi di.
riddance ['rɪdns] n: **good ~!** che liberazione!
ridden ['rɪdn] pp of ride.
riddle ['rɪdl] n (puzzle) indovinello ♦ vt: **to be ~d with** essere crivellato(a) di.
ride [raɪd] n (on horse) cavalcata; (outing) passeggiata; (distance covered) cavalcata; corsa ♦ vb (pt **rode**, pp **ridden** [rəud, 'rɪdn]) vi (as sport) cavalcare; (go somewhere: on horse, bicycle) andare (a cavallo or in bicicletta etc); (journey: on bicycle, motorcycle, bus) andare, viaggiare ♦ vt (a horse) montare, cavalcare; **to go for a ~** andare a fare una cavalcata; andare a fare un giro; **can you ~ a bike?** sai andare in bicicletta?; **we rode all day/all the way** abbiamo cavalcato tutto il giorno/per tutto il tragitto; **to ~ a horse/bicycle/camel** montare a cavallo/in bicicletta/in groppa a un cammello; **to ~ at anchor** (NAUT) essere alla fonda; **horse ~** cavalcata; **car ~** passeggiata in macchina; **to take sb for a ~** (fig) prendere in giro qn; fregare qn.
▶**ride out** vt: **to ~ out the storm** (fig) mantenersi a galla.
rider ['raɪdə*] n cavalcatore/trice; (jockey) fantino; (on bicycle) ciclista m/f; (on motorcycle) motociclista m/f; (in document) clausola addizionale, aggiunta.
ridge [rɪdʒ] n (of hill) cresta; (of roof) colmo; (of mountain) giogo; (on object) riga (in rilievo).
ridicule ['rɪdɪkju:l] n ridicolo ♦ vt mettere in

ridicolo; **to hold sb/sth up to** ~ mettere in ridicolo qn/qc.
ridiculous [rɪ'dɪkjʊləs] *adj* ridicolo(a).
riding ['raɪdɪŋ] *n* equitazione *f*.
riding school *n* scuola d'equitazione.
rife [raɪf] *adj* diffuso(a); **to be** ~ **with** abbondare di.
riffraff ['rɪfræf] *n* canaglia, gentaglia.
rifle ['raɪfl] *n* carabina ♦ *vt* vuotare.
►**rifle through** *vt fus* frugare.
rifle range *n* campo di tiro; (*at fair*) tiro a segno.
rift [rɪft] *n* fessura, crepatura; (*fig*: *disagreement*) incrinatura.
rig [rɪg] *n* (*also*: **oil** ~: *on land*) derrick *m inv* (*: at sea*) piattaforma di trivellazione ♦ *vt* (*election etc*) truccare.
►**rig out** *vt* (*BRIT*) attrezzare; (*pej*) abbigliare, agghindare.
►**rig up** *vt* allestire.
rigging ['rɪgɪŋ] *n* (*NAUT*) attrezzatura.
right [raɪt] *adj* giusto(a); (*suitable*) appropriato(a); (*not left*) destro(a) ♦ *n* (*title, claim*) diritto; (*not left*) destra ♦ *adv* (*answer*) correttamente; (*not on the left*) a destra ♦ *vt* raddrizzare; (*fig*) riparare ♦ *excl* bene!; **the** ~ **time** l'ora esatta; **to be** ~ (*person*) aver ragione; (*answer*) essere giusto(a) *or* corretto(a); **to get sth** ~ far giusto qc; **you did the** ~ **thing** ha fatto bene; **let's get it** ~ **this time!** cerchiamo di farlo bene stavolta!; **to put a mistake** ~ (*BRIT*) correggere un errore; ~ **now** proprio adesso; subito; ~ **away** subito; ~ **before/after** subito prima/dopo; **to go** ~ **to the end of sth** andare fino in fondo a qc; ~ **against the wall** proprio contro il muro; ~ **ahead** sempre diritto; proprio davanti; ~ **in the middle** proprio nel mezzo; **by** ~**s** di diritto; **on the** ~, **to the** ~ a destra; ~ **and wrong** il bene e il male; **to have a** ~ **to sth** aver diritto a qc; **film** ~**s** diritti di riproduzione cinematografica; ~ **of way** diritto di passaggio; (*AUT*) precedenza.
right angle *n* angolo retto.
righteous ['raɪtʃəs] *adj* retto(a), virtuoso(a); (*anger*) giusto(a), giustificato(a).
righteousness ['raɪtʃəsnɪs] *n* rettitudine *f*, virtù *f*.
rightful ['raɪtfʊl] *adj* (*heir*) legittimo(a).
rightfully ['raɪtfəlɪ] *adv* legittimamente.
right-handed [raɪt'hændɪd] *adj* (*person*) che adopera la mano destra.
right-hand man ['raɪthænd-] *n* braccio destro (*fig*).
right-hand side *n* lato destro.

rightly ['raɪtlɪ] *adv* bene, correttamente; (*with reason*) a ragione; **if I remember** ~ se mi ricordo bene.
right-minded [raɪt'maɪndɪd] *adj* sensato(a).
rights issue *n* (*STOCK EXCHANGE*) emissione *f* di azioni riservate agli azionisti.
right wing *n* (*MIL, SPORT*) ala destra; (*POL*) destra ♦ *adj*: **right-wing** (*POL*) di destra.
right-winger [raɪt'wɪŋə*] *n* (*POL*) uno/a di destra; (*SPORT*) ala destra.
rigid ['rɪdʒɪd] *adj* rigido(a); (*principle*) rigoroso(a).
rigidity [rɪ'dʒɪdɪtɪ] *n* rigidità.
rigidly ['rɪdʒɪdlɪ] *adv* rigidamente.
rigmarole ['rɪgmərəʊl] *n* tiritera; commedia.
rigor ['rɪgə*] *n* (*US*) = **rigour**.
rigor mortis ['rɪgə'mɔːtɪs] *n* rigidità cadaverica.
rigorous ['rɪgərəs] *adj* rigoroso(a).
rigorously ['rɪgərəslɪ] *adv* rigorosamente.
rigour, (*US*) **rigor** ['rɪgə*] *n* rigore *m*.
rig-out ['rɪgaʊt] *n* (*BRIT col*) tenuta.
rile [raɪl] *vt* irritare, seccare.
rim [rɪm] *n* orlo; (*of spectacles*) montatura; (*of wheel*) cerchione *m*.
rimless ['rɪmlɪs] *adj* (*spectacles*) senza montatura.
rimmed [rɪmd] *adj* bordato(a); cerchiato(a).
rind [raɪnd] *n* (*of bacon*) cotenna; (*of lemon etc*) scorza.
ring [rɪŋ] *n* anello; (*also*: **wedding** ~) fede *f*; (*of people, objects*) cerchio; (*of spies*) giro; (*of smoke etc*) spirale *f*; (*arena*) pista, arena; (*for boxing*) ring *m inv*; (*sound of bell*) scampanio; (*telephone call*) colpo di telefono ♦ *vb* (*pt* **rang**, *pp* **rung** [ræŋ, rʌŋ]) *vi* (*person, bell, telephone*) suonare; (*also*: ~ **out**: *voice, words*) risuonare; (*TEL*) telefonare ♦ *vt* (*BRIT TEL*: *also*: ~ **up**) telefonare a; **to give sb a** ~ (*TEL*) dare un colpo di telefono a qn; **that has the** ~ **of truth about it** questo ha l'aria d'essere vero; **to** ~ **the bell** suonare il campanello; **the name doesn't** ~ **a bell (with me)** questo nome non mi dice niente.
►**ring back** *vt, vi* (*BRIT TEL*) richiamare.
►**ring off** *vi* (*BRIT TEL*) mettere giù, riattaccare.
ring binder *n* classificatore *m* a anelli.
ring finger *n* anulare *m*.
ringing ['rɪŋɪŋ] *n* (*of bell*) scampanio; (*: louder*) scampanellata; (*of telephone*) squillo; (*in ears*) fischio, ronzio.
ringing tone *n* (*BRIT TEL*) segnale *m* di libero.
ringleader ['rɪŋliːdə*] *n* (*of gang*)

capobanda *m*.

ringlets ['rɪŋlɪts] *npl* boccoli *mpl*.

ring road *n* (*BRIT*) raccordo anulare.

rink [rɪŋk] *n* (*also*: **ice** ~) pista di pattinaggio; (*for roller-skating*) pista di pattinaggio (a rotelle).

rinse [rɪns] *n* risciacquatura; (*hair tint*) cachet *m inv* ♦ *vt* sciacquare.

Rio (de Janeiro) ['riːəu(dədʒə'nɪərəu)] *n* Rio de Janeiro *f*.

riot ['raɪət] *n* sommossa, tumulto ♦ *vi* tumultuare; **a** ~ **of colours** un'orgia di colori; **to run** ~ creare disordine.

rioter ['raɪətə*] *n* dimostrante *m/f* (*durante dei disordini*).

riot gear *n*: **in** ~ in assetto di guerra.

riotous ['raɪətəs] *adj* tumultuoso(a); che fa crepare dal ridere.

riotously ['raɪətəslɪ] *adv*: ~ **funny** che fa crepare dal ridere.

riot police *n* ≈ la Celere.

RIP *abbr* (= *rest in peace*) R.I.P.

rip [rɪp] *n* strappo ♦ *vt* strappare ♦ *vi* strapparsi.

▶**rip up** *vt* stracciare.

ripcord ['rɪpkɔːd] *n* cavo di spiegamento.

ripe [raɪp] *adj* (*fruit*) maturo(a); (*cheese*) stagionato(a).

ripen ['raɪpən] *vt* maturare ♦ *vi* maturarsi; stagionarsi.

ripeness ['raɪpnɪs] *n* maturità.

rip-off ['rɪpɔf] *n* (*col*): **it's a** ~! è un furto!

riposte [rɪ'pɔst] *n* risposta per le rime.

ripple ['rɪpl] *n* increspamento, ondulazione *f*; mormorio ♦ *vi* incresparsi ♦ *vt* increspare.

rise [raɪz] *n* (*slope*) salita, pendio; (*hill*) altura; (*increase: in wages*) aumento; (: *in prices, temperature*) rialzo, aumento; (*fig: to power etc*) ascesa ♦ *vi* (*pt* **rose**, *pp* **risen** [rəuz, 'rɪzn]) alzarsi, levarsi; (*prices*) aumentare; (*waters, river*) crescere; (*sun, wind*) levarsi; (*also*: ~ **up**: *rebel*) insorgere; ribellarsi; **to give** ~ **to** provocare, dare origine a; **to** ~ **to the occasion** dimostrarsi all'altezza della situazione.

rising ['raɪzɪŋ] *adj* (*increasing: number*) sempre crescente; (*prices*) in aumento; (*tide*) montante; (*sun, moon*) nascente, che sorge ♦ *n* (*uprising*) sommossa.

rising damp *n* infiltrazioni *fpl* d'umidità.

rising star *n* (*also fig*) astro nascente.

risk [rɪsk] *n* rischio ♦ *vt* rischiare; **to take** *or* **run the** ~ **of doing** correre il rischio di fare; **at** ~ in pericolo; **at one's own** ~ a proprio rischio e pericolo; **fire/health** ~ rischio d'incendio/per la salute; **I'll** ~ **it** ci

proverò lo stesso.

risk capital *n* capitale *m* di rischio.

risky ['rɪskɪ] *adj* rischioso(a).

risqué ['riːskeɪ] *adj* (*joke*) spinto(a).

rissole ['rɪsəul] *n* crocchetta.

rite [raɪt] *n* rito; **last** ~**s** l'estrema unzione.

ritual ['rɪtjuəl] *adj*, *n* rituale (*m*).

rival ['raɪvl] *n* rivale *m/f*; (*in business*) concorrente *m/f* ♦ *adj* rivale; che fa concorrenza ♦ *vt* essere in concorrenza con; **to** ~ **sb/sth in** competere con qn/qc in.

rivalry ['raɪvəlrɪ] *n* rivalità; concorrenza.

river ['rɪvə*] *n* fiume *m* ♦ *cpd* (*port, traffic*) fluviale; **up/down** ~ a monte/valle.

riverbank ['rɪvəbæŋk] *n* argine *m*.

riverbed ['rɪvəbɛd] *n* alveo (fluviale).

riverside ['rɪvəsaɪd] *n* sponda del fiume.

rivet ['rɪvɪt] *n* ribattino, rivetto ♦ *vt* ribadire; (*fig*) concentrare, fissare.

riveting ['rɪvɪtɪŋ] *adj* (*fig*) avvincente.

Riviera [rɪvɪ'ɛərə] *n*: **the (French)** ~ la Costa Azzurra; **the Italian** ~ la Riviera.

Riyadh [rɪ'jɑːd] *n* Riad *f*.

RMT *n abbr* (= *Rail, Maritime and Transport*) *sindacato dei Ferrovieri, Marittimi e Trasportatori*.

RN *n abbr* (*BRIT*) = **Royal Navy**; (*US*) = **registered nurse**.

RNA *n abbr* (= *ribonucleic acid*) R.N.A. *m*.

RNLI *n abbr* (*BRIT*: = *Royal National Lifeboat Institution*) *associazione volontaria che organizza e dispone di scialuppe di salvataggio*.

RNZAF *n abbr* = *Royal New Zealand Air Force*.

RNZN *n abbr* = *Royal New Zealand Navy*.

road [rəud] *n* strada; (*small*) cammino; (*in town*) via; **main** ~ strada principale; **major/minor** ~ strada con/senza diritto di precedenza; **it takes 4 hours by** ~ sono 4 ore di macchina (*or* in camion *etc*); **on the** ~ **to success** sulla via del successo; **"~ up"** (*BRIT*) "attenzione: lavori in corso".

roadblock ['rəudblɔk] *n* blocco stradale.

road haulage *n* autotrasporti *mpl*.

roadhog ['rəudhɔg] *n* pirata *m* della strada.

road map *n* carta stradale.

road safety *n* sicurezza sulle strade.

roadside ['rəudsaɪd] *n* margine *m* della strada; **by the** ~ a lato della strada.

roadsign ['rəudsaɪn] *n* cartello stradale.

roadsweeper ['rəudswiːpə*] *n* (*BRIT*: *person*) spazzino.

road user *n* utente *m/f* della strada.

roadway ['rəudweɪ] *n* carreggiata.

roadworks ['rəudwɜːks] *npl* lavori *mpl* stradali.

roadworthy [ˈrəʊdwəːðɪ] *adj* in buono stato di marcia.

roam [rəʊm] *vi* errare, vagabondare ♦ *vt* vagare per.

roar [rɔː*] *n* ruggito; (*of crowd*) tumulto; (*of thunder, storm*) muggito ♦ *vi* ruggire; tumultuare; muggire; **to ~ with laughter** scoppiare dalle risa.

roaring [ˈrɔːrɪŋ] *adj*: **a ~ fire** un bel fuoco; **to do a ~ trade** fare affari d'oro; **a ~ success** un successo strepitoso.

roast [rəʊst] *n* arrosto ♦ *vt* (*meat*) arrostire.

roast beef *n* arrosto di manzo.

roasting [ˈrəʊstɪŋ] *n* (*col*): **to give sb a ~** dare una lavata di capo a qn.

rob [rɔb] *vt* (*person*) rubare; (*bank*) svaligiare; **to ~ sb of sth** derubare qn di qc; (*fig: deprive*) privare qn di qc.

robber [ˈrɔbə*] *n* ladro; (*armed*) rapinatore *m*.

robbery [ˈrɔbərɪ] *n* furto; rapina.

robe [rəʊb] *n* (*for ceremony etc*) abito; (*also*: **bath~**) accappatoio ♦ *vt* vestire.

robin [ˈrɔbɪn] *n* pettirosso.

robot [ˈrəʊbɔt] *n* robot *m inv*.

robotics [ˈrəʊbɔtɪks] *n* robotica.

robust [rəʊˈbʌst] *adj* robusto(a); (*material*) solido(a).

rock [rɔk] *n* (*substance*) roccia; (*boulder*) masso; roccia; (*in sea*) scoglio; (*BRIT: sweet*) zucchero candito ♦ *vt* (*swing gently: cradle*) dondolare; (: *child*) cullare; (*shake*) scrollare, far tremare ♦ *vi* dondolarsi; oscillare; **on the ~s** (*drink*) col ghiaccio; (*ship*) sugli scogli; (*marriage etc*) in crisi; **to ~ the boat** (*fig*) piantare grane.

rock and roll *n* rock and roll *m*.

rock-bottom [ˈrɔkˈbɔtəm] *n* (*fig*) stremo; **to reach** *or* **touch ~** (*price*) raggiungere il livello più basso; (*person*) toccare il fondo.

rock climber *n* rocciatore/trice, scalatore/trice.

rock climbing *n* roccia.

rockery [ˈrɔkərɪ] *n* giardino roccioso.

rocket [ˈrɔkɪt] *n* razzo; (*MIL*) razzo, missile *m* ♦ *vi* (*prices*) salire alle stelle.

rocket launcher [-lɔːntʃə*] *n* lanciarazzi *m inv*.

rock face *n* parete *f* della roccia.

rock fall *n* caduta di massi.

rocking chair [ˈrɔkɪŋ-] *n* sedia a dondolo.

rocking horse *n* cavallo a dondolo.

rocky [ˈrɔkɪ] *adj* (*hill*) roccioso(a); (*path*) sassoso(a); (*unsteady: table*) traballante.

Rocky Mountains *npl*: **the ~** le Montagne Rocciose.

rod [rɔd] *n* (*metallic, TECH*) asta; (*wooden*) bacchetta; (*also*: **fishing ~**) canna da

pesca.

rode [rəʊd] *pt of* **ride**.

rodent [ˈrəʊdnt] *n* roditore *m*.

rodeo [ˈrəʊdɪəʊ] *n* rodeo.

roe [rəʊ] *n* (*species: also*: **~ deer**) capriolo; (*of fish: also*: **~**) uova *fpl* di pesce; **soft ~** latte *m* di pesce.

roe deer *n* (*species*) capriolo; (*female deer*: *pl inv*) capriolo femmina.

rogue [rəʊg] *n* mascalzone *m*.

roguish [ˈrəʊgɪʃ] *adj* birbantesco(a).

role [rəʊl] *n* ruolo.

role model *n* modello (di comportamento).

role-play [ˈrəʊlpleɪ], **role-playing** [ˈrəʊlpleɪɪŋ] *n* il recitare un ruolo, role-playing *m inv*.

roll [rəʊl] *n* rotolo; (*of banknotes*) mazzo; (*also*: **bread ~**) panino; (*register*) lista; (*sound: of drums etc*) rullo; (*movement: of ship*) rullio ♦ *vt* rotolare; (*also*: **~ up**: *string*) aggomitolare; (*also*: **~ out**: *pastry*) stendere ♦ *vi* rotolare; (*wheel*) girare; **cheese ~** panino al formaggio.

▶**roll about, roll around** *vi* rotolare qua e là; (*person*) rotolarsi.

▶**roll by** *vi* (*time*) passare.

▶**roll in** *vi* (*mail, cash*) arrivare a bizzeffe.

▶**roll over** *vi* rivoltarsi.

▶**roll up** *vi* (*col: arrive*) arrivare ♦ *vt* (*carpet, cloth, map*) arrotolare; (*sleeves*) rimboccare; **to ~ o.s. up into a ball** raggomitolarsi.

roll call *n* appello.

rolled gold [rəʊld-] *adj* d'oro laminato.

roller [ˈrəʊlə*] *n* rullo; (*wheel*) rotella.

roller blind *n* (*BRIT*) avvolgibile *m*.

roller coaster *n* montagne *fpl* russe.

roller skates *npl* pattini *mpl* a rotelle.

rollicking [ˈrɔlɪkɪŋ] *adj* allegro(a) e chiassoso(a); **to have a ~ time** divertirsi pazzamente.

rolling [ˈrəʊlɪŋ] *adj* (*landscape*) ondulato(a).

rolling mill *n* fabbrica di laminati.

rolling pin *n* matterello.

rolling stock *n* (*RAIL*) materiale *m* rotabile.

roll-on-roll-off [ˈrəʊlɔnˈrəʊlɔf] *adj* (*BRIT: ferry*) roll-on roll-off *inv*.

roly-poly [ˈrəʊlɪˈpəʊlɪ] *n* (*BRIT CULIN*) rotolo di pasta con ripieno di marmellata.

ROM [rɔm] *n abbr* (*COMPUT*: = *read-only memory*) ROM *f*.

Roman [ˈrəʊmən] *adj, n* romano(a).

Roman Catholic *adj, n* cattolico(a).

romance [rəˈmæns] *n* storia (*or* avventura *or* film *m inv*) romantico(a); (*charm*) poesia; (*love affair*) idillio.

Romanesque [rəumə'nɛsk] *adj* romanico(a).

Romania [rəu'meɪnɪə] *n* Romania.

Romanian [rəu'meɪnɪən] *adj* romeno(a) ♦ *n* romeno/a; (*LING*) romeno.

Roman numeral *n* numero romano.

romantic [rə'mæntɪk] *adj* romantico(a); sentimentale.

romanticism [rə'mæntɪsɪzəm] *n* romanticismo.

Romany ['rɔmənɪ] *adj* zingaresco(a) ♦ *n* (*person*) zingaro/a; (*LING*) lingua degli zingari.

Rome [rəum] *n* Roma.

romp [rɔmp] *n* gioco chiassoso ♦ *vi* (*also*: ~ **about**) giocare chiassosamente; **to** ~ **home** (*horse*) vincere senza difficoltà, stravincere.

rompers ['rɔmpəz] *npl* pagliaccetto.

rondo ['rɔndəu] *n* (*MUS*) rondò *m inv*.

roof [ruːf] *n* tetto; (*of tunnel, cave*) volta ♦ *vt* coprire (con un tetto); ~ **of the mouth** palato.

roof garden *n* giardino pensile.

roofing ['ruːfɪŋ] *n* materiale *m* per copertura.

roof rack *n* (*AUT*) portabagagli *m inv*.

rook [ruk] *n* (*bird*) corvo nero; (*CHESS*) torre *f* ♦ *vt* (*cheat*) truffare, spennare.

rookie ['rukɪ] *n* (*col: esp MIL*) pivellino/a.

room [ruːm] *n* (*in house*) stanza, camera; (*in school etc*) sala; (*space*) posto, spazio; ~**s** *npl* (*lodging*) alloggio; "~**s to let**", (*US*) "~**s for rent**" "si affittano camere"; **is there** ~ **for this?** c'è spazio per questo?, ci sta anche questo?; **to make** ~ **for sb** far posto a qn; **there is** ~ **for improvement** si potrebbe migliorare.

rooming house ['ruːmɪŋ-] *n* (*US*) casa in cui si affittano camere o appartamentini ammobiliati.

roommate ['ruːmmeɪt] *n* compagno/a di stanza.

room service *n* servizio da camera.

room temperature *n* temperatura ambiente.

roomy ['ruːmɪ] *adj* spazioso(a); (*garment*) ampio(a).

roost [ruːst] *n* appollaiato ♦ *vi* appollaiarsi.

rooster ['ruːstə*] *n* gallo.

root [ruːt] *n* radice *f* ♦ *vt* (*plant, belief*) far radicare; **to take** ~ (*plant*) attecchire, prendere; (*idea*) far presa; **the** ~ **of the problem is that** ... il problema deriva dal fatto che ....

▶**root about** *vi* (*fig*) frugare.

▶**root for** *vt fus* (*col*) fare il tifo per.

▶**root out** *vt* estirpare.

root beer *n* (*US*) bibita dolce a base di estratti di erbe e radici.

rope [rəup] *n* corda, fune *f*; (*NAUT*) cavo ♦ *vt* (*box*) legare; (*climbers*) legare in cordata; **to** ~ **sb in** (*fig*) coinvolgere qn; **to know the** ~**s** (*fig*) conoscere i trucchi del mestiere.

rope ladder *n* scala di corda.

ropey ['rəupɪ] *adj* (*col*) scadente, da quattro soldi; **to feel** ~ (*ill*) sentirsi male.

rosary ['rəuzərɪ] *n* rosario; roseto.

rose [rəuz] *pt of* **rise** ♦ *n* rosa; (*also*: ~ **bush** rosaio; (*on watering can*) rosetta ♦ *adj* rosa *inv*.

rosé ['rəuzeɪ] *n* vino rosato.

rosebed ['rəuzbɛd] *n* roseto.

rosebud ['rəuzbʌd] *n* bocciolo di rosa.

rosebush ['rəuzbuʃ] *n* rosaio.

rosemary ['rəuzmərɪ] *n* rosmarino.

rosette [rəu'zɛt] *n* coccarda.

ROSPA ['rɔspə] *n abbr* (*BRIT*: = Royal Society for the Prevention of Accidents*) ≈ E.N.P.I. *m* (= Ente Nazionale Prevenzione Infortuni*).

roster ['rɔstə*] *n*: **duty** ~ ruolino di servizio.

rostrum ['rɔstrəm] *n* tribuna.

rosy ['rəuzɪ] *adj* roseo(a).

rot [rɔt] *n* (*decay*) putrefazione *f*; (*col: nonsense*) stupidaggini *fpl* ♦ *vt, vi* imputridire, marcire; **dry/wet** ~ *funghi parassiti del legno*; **to stop the** ~ (*BRIT fig*) salvare la situazione.

rota ['rəutə] *n* tabella dei turni; **on a** ~ **basis** a turno.

rotary ['rəutərɪ] *adj* rotante.

rotate [rəu'teɪt] *vt* (*revolve*) far girare; (*change round: crops*) avvicendare; (*: jobs*) fare a turno ♦ *vi* (*revolve*) girare.

rotating [rəu'teɪtɪŋ] *adj* (*movement*) rotante.

rotation [rəu'teɪʃən] *n* rotazione *f*; **in** ~ a turno, in rotazione.

rote [rəut] *n*: **to learn sth by** ~ imparare qc a memoria.

rotor ['rəutə*] *n* rotore *m*.

rotten ['rɔtn] *adj* (*decayed*) putrido(a), marcio(a); (*: teeth*) cariato(a); (*dishonest*) corrotto(a); (*col: bad*) brutto(a); (*: action*) vigliacco(a); **to feel** ~ (*ill*) sentirsi proprio male.

rotting ['rɔtɪŋ] *adj* in putrefazione.

rotund [rəu'tʌnd] *adj* grassoccio(a); tondo(a).

rouble, (*US*) **ruble** ['ruːbl] *n* rublo.

rouge [ruːʒ] *n* belletto.

rough [rʌf] *adj* aspro(a); (*person, manner: coarse*) rozzo(a), aspro(a); (*: violent*) brutale; (*district*) malfamato(a); (*weather*) cattivo(a); (*plan*) abbozzato(a); (*guess*) approssimativo(a) ♦ *n* (*GOLF*) macchia; ~ **estimate** approssimazione *f*; **to** ~ **it** far vita dura; **to play** ~ far il gioco pesante; **to sleep** ~ (*BRIT*) dormire all'addiaccio; **to feel** ~ (*BRIT*) sentirsi male; **to have a** ~ **time (of it)** passare un periodaccio; **the sea is** ~ **today** c'è mare grosso oggi.

▶**rough out** *vt* (*draft*) abbozzare.

roughage ['rʌfɪdʒ] *n* alimenti *mpl* ricchi di cellulosa.

rough-and-ready ['rʌfən'rɛdɪ] *adj* rudimentale.

rough-and-tumble ['rʌfən'tʌmbl] *n* zuffa.

roughcast ['rʌfkɑːst] *n* intonaco grezzo.

rough copy, rough draft *n* brutta copia.

roughen ['rʌfn] *vt* (*a surface*) rendere ruvido(a).

rough justice *n* giustizia sommaria.

roughly ['rʌflɪ] *adv* (*handle*) rudemente, brutalmente; (*make*) grossolanamente; (*approximately*) approssimativamente; ~ **speaking** grosso modo, ad occhio e croce.

roughness ['rʌfnɪs] *n* asprezza; rozzezza; brutalità.

roughshod ['rʌfʃɔd] *adv*: **to ride** ~ **over** (*person*) mettere sotto i piedi; (*objection*) passare sopra a.

rough work *n* (*at school etc*) brutta copia.

roulette [ruːˈlɛt] *n* roulette *f*.

Roumania *etc* [ruːˈmeɪnɪə] = **Romania** *etc*.

round [raund] *adj* rotondo(a) ♦ *n* tondo, cerchio; (*BRIT*: *of toast*) fetta; (*duty*: *of policeman, milkman etc*) giro; (: *of doctor*) visite *fpl*; (*game*: *of cards, in competition*) partita; (*BOXING*) round *m inv*; (*of talks*) serie *f inv* ♦ *vt* (*corner*) girare; (*bend*) prendere; (*cape*) doppiare ♦ *prep* intorno a ♦ *adv*: **right** ~, **all** ~ tutt'attorno; **the long way** ~ il giro più lungo; **all the year** ~ tutto l'anno; **in** ~ **figures** in cifra tonda; **it's just** ~ **the corner** (*also fig*) è dietro l'angolo; **to ask sb** ~ invitare qn (a casa propria); **I'll be** ~ **at 6 o'clock** ci sarò alle 6; **to go** ~ fare il giro; **to go** ~ **to sb's (house)** andare da qn; **to go** ~ **an obstacle** aggirare un ostacolo; **go** ~ **the back** passi da dietro; **to go** ~ **a house** visitare una casa; **enough to go** ~ abbastanza per tutti; **she arrived** ~ **(about) noon** è arrivata intorno a mezzogiorno; ~ **the clock** 24 ore su 24; **to go the** ~**s** (*illness*) diffondersi; (*story*) circolare, passare di bocca in bocca; **the daily** ~ (*fig*) la routine quotidiana; ~ **of ammunition** cartuccia; ~ **of applause** applausi *mpl*; ~ **of drinks** giro di bibite; ~ **of sandwiches** (*BRIT*) sandwich *m inv*.

▶**round off** *vt* (*speech etc*) finire.

▶**round up** *vt* radunare; (*criminals*) fare una retata di; (*prices*) arrotondare.

roundabout ['raundəbaut] *n* (*BRIT AUT*) rotatoria; (*at fair*) giostra ♦ *adj* (*route, means*) indiretto(a).

rounded ['raundɪd] *adj* arrotondato(a); (*style*) armonioso(a).

rounders ['raundəz] *npl* (*game*) gioco simile al baseball.

roundly ['raundlɪ] *adv* (*fig*) chiaro e tondo.

round robin *n* (*SPORT*: *also*: ~ **tournament**) ≈ torneo all'italiana.

round-shouldered [raundˈʃəuldəd] *adj* dalle spalle tonde.

round trip *n* (viaggio di) andata e ritorno.

roundup ['raundʌp] *n* raduno; (*of criminals*) retata; **a** ~ **of the latest news** un sommario *or* riepilogo delle ultime notizie.

rouse [rauz] *vt* (*wake up*) svegliare; (*stir up*) destare; provocare; risvegliare.

rousing ['rauzɪŋ] *adj* (*speech, applause*) entusiastico(a).

rout [raut] *n* (*MIL*) rotta ♦ *vt* mettere in rotta.

route [ruːt] *n* itinerario; (*of bus*) percorso; (*of trade, shipping*) rotta; "**all** ~**s**" (*AUT*) "tutte le direzioni"; **the best** ~ **to London** la strada migliore per andare a Londra; **en** ~ **for** in viaggio verso; **en** ~ **from ... to** viaggiando da ... a..

route map *n* (*BRIT*: *for journey*) cartina di itinerario; (*for trains etc*) pianta dei collegamenti.

routine [ruːˈtiːn] *adj* (*work*) corrente, abituale; (*procedure*) solito(a) ♦ *n* (*pej*) routine *f*, tran tran *m*; (*THEAT*) numero; (*COMPUT*) sottoprogramma *m*; **daily** ~ orario quotidiano; ~ **procedure** prassi *f*.

roving ['rəuvɪŋ] *adj* (*life*) itinerante.

roving reporter *n* reporter *m inv* volante.

row[1] [rəu] *n* (*line*) riga, fila; (*KNITTING*) ferro; (*behind one another: of cars, people*) fila ♦ *vi* (*in boat*) remare; (*as sport*) vogare ♦ *vt* (*boat*) manovrare a remi; **in a** ~ (*fig*) di fila.

row[2] [rau] *n* (*noise*) baccano, chiasso; (*dispute*) lite *f* ♦ *vi* litigare; **to make a** ~ far baccano; **to have a** ~ litigare.

rowboat ['rəubəut] *n* (*US*) barca a remi.

rowdiness ['raudɪnɪs] *n* baccano; (*fighting*) zuffa.

rowdy ['raudɪ] *adj* chiassoso(a); turbolento(a) ♦ *n* teppista *m/f*.

rowdyism ['raudɪɪzəm] *n* teppismo.

rowing ['rəuɪŋ] *n* canottaggio.

rowing boat n (BRIT) barca a remi.
rowlock ['rɒlək] n scalmo.
royal ['rɔɪəl] adj reale.

L'Accademia Reale d'Arte britannica, **Royal Academy (of the Arts)**, è un'istituzione fondata nel 1768 al fine di incoraggiare la pittura, la scultura e l'architettura. Ogni anno organizza una mostra estiva d'arte contemporanea.

Royal Air Force (RAF) n (BRIT) aeronautica militare britannica.
royal blue adj blu reale inv.
royalist ['rɔɪəlɪst] adj, n realista (m/f).
Royal Navy (RN) n (BRIT) marina militare britannica.
royalty ['rɔɪəltɪ] n (royal persons) (membri mpl della) famiglia reale; (payment: to author) diritti mpl d'autore; (: to inventor) diritti di brevetto.
RP n abbr (BRIT: = received pronunciation) pronuncia standard.
RPM abbr = **resale price maintenance**.
rpm abbr (= revolutions per minute) giri/min.
RR abbr (US = railroad) Ferr.
R&R n abbr (US MIL: = rest and recreation) permesso per militari.
RRP n abbr (BRIT) see **recommended retail price**.
RSA n abbr (BRIT) = Royal Society of Arts; Royal Scottish Academy.
RSI n abbr (MED: = repetitive strain injury) lesione al braccio tipica di violinisti e terminalisti.
RSPB n abbr (BRIT: = Royal Society for the Protection of Birds) ≈ L.I.P.U. f (= Lega Italiana Protezione Uccelli).
RSPCA n abbr (BRIT: = Royal Society for the Prevention of Cruelty to Animals) ≈ E.N.P.A. m (= Ente Nazionale per la Protezione degli Animali).
RSVP abbr (= répondez s'il vous plaît) R.S.V.P.
RTA n abbr (= road traffic accident) incidente m stradale.
Rt Hon. abbr (BRIT: = Right Honourable) ≈ On. (= Onorevole).
Rt Rev. abbr (= Right Reverend) Rev.
rub [rʌb] n (with cloth) fregata, strofinata; (on person) frizione f, massaggio ♦ vt fregare, strofinare; frizionare; **to ~ sb up** or (US) **~ sb the wrong way** lisciare qn contro pelo.
▶**rub down** vt (body) strofinare, frizionare; (horse) strigliare.
▶**rub in** vt (ointment) far penetrare (massaggiando or frizionando).

▶**rub off** vi andare via; **to ~ off on** lasciare una traccia su.
▶**rub out** vt cancellare ♦ vi cancellarsi.
rubber ['rʌbə*] n gomma.
rubber band n elastico.
rubber bullet n pallottola di gomma.
rubber plant n ficus m inv.
rubber ring n (for swimming) ciambella.
rubber stamp n timbro di gomma.
rubber-stamp [rʌbə'stæmp] vt (fig) approvare senza discussione.
rubbery ['rʌbərɪ] adj gommoso(a).
rubbish ['rʌbɪʃ] n (from household) immondizie fpl, rifiuti mpl; (fig: pej) cose fpl senza valore; robaccia; (nonsense) sciocchezze fpl ♦ vt (col) sputtanare; **what you've just said is ~** quello che ha appena detto è una sciocchezza.
rubbish bin n (BRIT) pattumiera.
rubbish dump n luogo di scarico.
rubbishy ['rʌbɪʃɪ] adj (BRIT col) scadente, che non vale niente.
rubble ['rʌbl] n macerie fpl; (smaller) pietrisco.
ruble ['ruːbl] n (US) = **rouble**.
ruby ['ruːbɪ] n rubino.
RUC n abbr (BRIT: = Royal Ulster Constabulary) forza di polizia dell'Irlanda del Nord.
rucksack ['rʌksæk] n zaino.
ructions ['rʌkʃənz] npl putiferio, finimondo.
rudder ['rʌdə*] n timone m.
ruddy ['rʌdɪ] adj (face) fresco(a); (col: damned) maledetto(a).
rude [ruːd] adj (impolite: person) scortese, rozzo(a); (: word, manners) grossolano(a), rozzo(a); (shocking) indecente; **to be ~ to sb** essere maleducato con qn.
rudely ['ruːdlɪ] adv scortesemente; grossolanamente.
rudeness ['ruːdnɪs] n scortesia; grossolanità.
rudiment ['ruːdɪmənt] n rudimento.
rudimentary [ruːdɪ'mɛntərɪ] adj rudimentale.
rue [ruː] vt pentirsi amaramente di.
rueful ['ruːful] adj mesto(a), triste.
ruff [rʌf] n gorgiera.
ruffian ['rʌfɪən] n briccone m, furfante m.
ruffle ['rʌfl] vt (hair) scompigliare; (clothes, water) increspare; (fig: person) turbare.
rug [rʌg] n tappeto; (BRIT: for knees) coperta.
rugby ['rʌgbɪ] n (also: ~ **football**) rugby m.
rugged ['rʌgɪd] adj (landscape) aspro(a); (features, determination) duro(a); (character) brusco(a).
rugger ['rʌgə*] n (col) rugby m.

ruin ['ru:ɪn] *n* rovina ♦ *vt* rovinare; (*spoil: clothes*) sciupare; ~s *npl* rovine *fpl*, ruderi *mpl*; **in ~s** in rovina.
ruination [ru:ɪ'neɪʃən] *n* rovina.
ruinous ['ru:ɪnəs] *adj* rovinoso(a); (*expenditure*) inverosimile.
rule [ru:l] *n* (*gen*) regola; (*regulation*) regolamento, regola; (*government*) governo; (*dominion etc*): **under British ~** sotto la sovranità britannica ♦ *vt* (*country*) governare; (*person*) dominare; (*decide*) decidere ♦ *vi* regnare; decidere; (*LAW*) dichiarare; **to ~ against/in favour of/on** (*LAW*) pronunciarsi a sfavore di/in favore di/su; **it's against the ~s** è contro le regole *or* il regolamento; **by ~ of thumb** a lume di naso; **as a ~** normalmente, di regola.
▶**rule out** *vt* escludere; **murder cannot be ~d out** non si esclude che si tratti di omicidio.
ruled [ru:ld] *adj* (*paper*) vergato(a).
ruler ['ru:lə*] *n* (*sovereign*) sovrano/a; (*leader*) capo (dello Stato); (*for measuring*) regolo, riga.
ruling ['ru:lɪŋ] *adj* (*party*) al potere; (*class*) dirigente ♦ *n* (*LAW*) decisione *f*.
rum [rʌm] *n* rum *m* ♦ *adj* (*BRIT col*) strano(a).
Rumania *etc* [ru:'meɪnɪə] = **Romania** *etc*.
rumble ['rʌmbl] *n* rimbombo; brontolio ♦ *vi* rimbombare; (*stomach, pipe*) brontolare.
rumbustious [rʌm'bʌstʃəs] *adj* (*person*): **to be ~** essere un terremoto.
rummage ['rʌmɪdʒ] *vi* frugare.
rumour, (*US*) **rumor** ['ru:mə*] *n* voce *f* ♦ *vt*: **it is ~ed that** corre voce che.
rump [rʌmp] *n* (*of animal*) groppa.
rumple ['rʌmpl] *vt* (*hair*) arruffare, scompigliare; (*clothes*) spiegazzare, sgualcire.
rump steak *n* bistecca di girello.
rumpus ['rʌmpəs] *n* (*col*) baccano; (*: quarrel*) rissa; **to kick up a ~** fare un putiferio.
run [rʌn] *n* corsa; (*outing*) gita (in macchina); (*distance travelled*) percorso, tragitto; (*series*) serie *f inv*; (*THEAT*) periodo di rappresentazione; (*SKI*) pista ♦ *vb* (*pt* **ran,** *pp* **run** [ræn, rʌn]) *vt* (*operate: business*) gestire, dirigere; (*: competition, course*) organizzare; (*: hotel*) gestire; (*: house*) governare; (*COMPUT: program*) eseguire; (*water, bath*) far scorrere; (*force through: rope, pipe*): **to ~ sth through** far passare qc attraverso; (*to pass: hand, finger*): **to ~ sth over** passare qc su ♦ *vi* correre; (*pass: road etc*) passare; (*work: machine, factory*) funzionare, andare; (*bus,*

train: operate) far servizio; (*: travel*) circolare; (*continue: play, contract*) durare; (*slide: drawer, flow: river, bath*) scorrere; (*colours, washing*) stemperarsi; (*in election*) presentarsi come candidato; **to go for a ~** andare a correre; (*in car*) fare un giro (in macchina); **to break into a ~** mettersi a correre; **a ~ of luck** un periodo di fortuna; **to have the ~ of sb's house** essere libero di andare e venire in casa di qn; **there was a ~ on ...** c'era una corsa a ...; **in the long ~** alla lunga; in fin dei conti; **in the short ~** sulle prime; **on the ~** in fuga; **to make a ~ for it** scappare, tagliare la corda; **I'll ~ you to the station** la porto alla stazione; **to ~ a risk** correre un rischio; **to ~ errands** andare a fare commissioni; **the train ~s between Gatwick and Victoria** il treno collega Gatwick alla stazione Victoria; **the bus ~s every 20 minutes** c'è un autobus ogni 20 minuti; **it's very cheap to ~** comporta poche spese; **to ~ on petrol** *or* (*US*) **gas/on diesel/off batteries** andare a benzina/a diesel/a batterie; **to ~ for the bus** fare una corsa per prendere l'autobus; **to ~ for president** presentarsi come candidato per la presidenza; **their losses ran into millions** le loro perdite hanno raggiunto i milioni; **to be ~ off one's feet** (*BRIT*) doversi fare in quattro.
▶**run about** *vi* (*children*) correre qua e là.
▶**run across** *vt fus* (*find*) trovare per caso.
▶**run away** *vi* fuggire.
▶**run down** *vi* (*clock*) scaricarsi ♦ *vt* (*AUT*) investire; (*criticize*) criticare; (*BRIT: reduce: production*) ridurre gradualmente; (*: factory, shop*) rallentare l'attività di; **to be ~ down** (*battery*) essere scarico(a); (*person*) essere giù (di corda).
▶**run in** *vt* (*BRIT: car*) rodare, fare il rodaggio di.
▶**run into** *vt fus* (*meet: person*) incontrare per caso; (*: trouble*) incontrare, trovare; (*collide with*) andare a sbattere contro; **to ~ into debt** trovarsi nei debiti.
▶**run off** *vi* fuggire ♦ *vt* (*water*) far defluire; (*copies*) fare.
▶**run out** *vi* (*person*) uscire di corsa; (*liquid*) colare; (*lease*) scadere; (*money*) esaurirsi.
▶**run out of** *vt fus* rimanere a corto di; **I've ~ out of petrol** *or* (*US*) **gas** sono rimasto senza benzina.
▶**run over** *vt* (*AUT*) investire, mettere sotto ♦ *vt fus* (*revise*) rivedere.
▶**run through** *vt fus* (*instructions*) dare una scorsa a.

▶**run up** *vt* (*debt*) lasciar accumulare; **to ~ up against** (*difficulties*) incontrare.

runaround ['rʌnəraund] *n* (*col*): **to give sb the ~** far girare a vuoto qn.

runaway ['rʌnəweɪ] *adj* (*person*) fuggiasco/a; (*horse*) in libertà; (*truck*) fuori controllo; (*inflation*) galoppante.

rundown ['rʌndaun] *n* (*BRIT: of industry etc*) riduzione *f* graduale dell'attività di.

rung [rʌŋ] *pp of* **ring** ◆ *n* (*of ladder*) piolo.

run-in ['rʌnɪn] *n* (*col*) scontro.

runner ['rʌnə*] *n* (*in race*) corridore *m*; (*on sledge*) pattino; (*for drawer etc, carpet*) guida.

runner bean *n* (*BRIT*) fagiolino.

runner-up [rʌnər'ʌp] *n* secondo(a) arrivato(a).

running ['rʌnɪŋ] *n* corsa; direzione *f*; organizzazione *f*; funzionamento ◆ *adj* (*water*) corrente; (*commentary*) simultaneo(a); **6 days ~** 6 giorni di seguito; **to be in/out of the ~ for sth** essere/non essere più in lizza per qc.

running costs *npl* (*of business*) costi *mpl* d'esercizio; (*of car*) spese *fpl* di mantenimento.

running head *n* (*TYP, WORD PROCESSING*) testata, titolo corrente.

running mate *n* (*US POL*) candidato alla vicepresidenza.

runny ['rʌnɪ] *adj* che cola.

run-off ['rʌnɔf] *n* (*in contest, election*) confronto definitivo; (*extra race*) spareggio.

run-of-the-mill ['rʌnəvðə'mɪl] *adj* solito(a), banale.

runt [rʌnt] *n* (*also pej*) omuncolo; (*ZOOL*) animale *m* più piccolo del normale.

run-through ['rʌnθruː] *n* prova.

run-up ['rʌnʌp] *n* (*BRIT*): **~ to sth** periodo che precede qc.

runway ['rʌnweɪ] *n* (*AVIAT*) pista (di decollo).

rupture ['rʌptʃə*] *n* (*MED*) ernia ◆ *vt*: **to ~ o.s.** farsi venire un'ernia.

rural ['ruərl] *adj* rurale.

rural district council (RDC) *n* (*BRIT*) consiglio (amministrativo) di distretto rurale.

ruse [ruːz] *n* trucco.

rush [rʌʃ] *n* corsa precipitosa; (*of crowd*) afflusso; (*hurry*) furia, fretta; (*current*) flusso; (*BOT*) giunco ◆ *vt* mandare *or* spedire velocemente; (*attack: town etc*) prendere d'assalto ◆ *vi* precipitarsi; **is there any ~ for this?** è urgente?; **we've had a ~ of orders** abbiamo avuto una valanga di ordinazioni; **I'm in a ~ (to do)**

ho fretta *or* premura (di fare); **gold ~** corsa all'oro; **to ~ sth off** spedire con urgenza qc; **don't ~ me!** non farmi fretta!

▶**rush through** *vt* (*meal*) mangiare in fretta; (*book*) dare una scorsa frettolosa a; (*town*) attraversare in fretta; (*COMM: order*) eseguire d'urgenza ◆ *vt fus* (*work*) sbrigare frettolosamente.

rush hour *n* ora di punta.

rush job *n* (*urgent*) lavoro urgente.

rush matting *n* stuoia.

rusk [rʌsk] *n* fetta biscottata.

Russia ['rʌʃə] *n* Russia.

Russian ['rʌʃən] *adj* russo(a) ◆ *n* russo/a; (*LING*) russo.

rust [rʌst] *n* ruggine *f* ◆ *vi* arrugginirsi.

rustic ['rʌstɪk] *adj* rustico(a) ◆ *n* (*pej*) cafone/a.

rustle ['rʌsl] *vi* frusciare ◆ *vt* (*paper*) far frusciare; (*US: cattle*) rubare.

rustproof ['rʌstpruːf] *adj* inossidabile.

rustproofing ['rʌstpruːfɪŋ] *n* trattamento antiruggine.

rusty ['rʌstɪ] *adj* arrugginito(a).

rut [rʌt] *n* solco; (*ZOOL*) fregola; **to be in a ~** (*fig*) essersi fossilizzato(a).

rutabaga [ruːtə'beɪgə] *n* (*US*) rapa svedese.

ruthless ['ruːθlɪs] *adj* spietato(a).

ruthlessness ['ruːθlɪsnɪs] *n* spietatezza.

RV *abbr* (= *revised version*) *versione riveduta della Bibbia* ◆ *n abbr* (*US*) *see* **recreational vehicle.**

rye [raɪ] *n* segale *f*.

S s

S, s [ɛs] *n* (*letter*) S, s *f or m inv*; (*US SCOL: = satisfactory*) ≈ sufficiente; **S for Sugar** ≈ S come Savona.

S *abbr* (= *saint*) S.; (= *south*) S; (*on clothes*) = *small*.

SA *abbr* = **South Africa; South America.**

Sabbath ['sæbəθ] *n* (*Jewish*) sabato; (*Christian*) domenica.

sabbatical [sə'bætɪkl] *adj*: **~ year** anno sabbatico.

sabotage ['sæbətɑːʒ] *n* sabotaggio ◆ *vt* sabotare.

saccharin(e) ['sækərɪn] *n* saccarina.

sachet ['sæʃeɪ] *n* bustina.

sack [sæk] n (*bag*) sacco ♦ vt (*dismiss*) licenziare, mandare a spasso; (*plunder*) saccheggiare; **to get the** ~ essere mandato a spasso; **to give sb the** ~ licenziare qn, mandare qn a spasso.

sackful ['sækful] n: **a** ~ **of** un sacco di.

sacking ['sækɪŋ] n tela di sacco; (*dismissal*) licenziamento.

sacrament ['sækrəmənt] n sacramento.

sacred ['seɪkrɪd] adj sacro(a).

sacred cow n (*fig: person*) intoccabile m/f; (: *institution*) caposaldo; (: *idea, belief*) dogma m.

sacrifice ['sækrɪfaɪs] n sacrificio ♦ vt sacrificare; **to make** ~**s (for sb)** fare (dei) sacrifici (per qn).

sacrilege ['sækrɪlɪdʒ] n sacrilegio.

sacrosanct ['sækrəusæŋkt] adj sacrosanto(a).

sad [sæd] adj triste; (*deplorable*) deplorevole.

sadden ['sædn] vt rattristare.

saddle ['sædl] n sella ♦ vt (*horse*) sellare; **to be** ~**d with sth** (*col*) avere qc sulle spalle.

saddlebag ['sædlbæg] n bisaccia; (*on bicycle*) borsa.

sadism ['seɪdɪzəm] n sadismo.

sadist ['seɪdɪst] n sadico/a.

sadistic [sə'dɪstɪk] adj sadico(a).

sadly ['sædlɪ] adv tristemente; (*regrettably*) sfortunatamente; ~ **lacking in** penosamente privo di.

sadness ['sædnɪs] n tristezza.

sadomasochism [seɪdəu'mæsəkɪzəm] n sadomasochismo.

sae abbr (*BRIT*) = **stamped addressed envelope;** see **stamp.**

safari [sə'fɑːrɪ] n safari m inv.

safari park n zoosafari m inv.

safe [seɪf] adj sicuro(a); (*out of danger*) salvo(a), al sicuro; (*cautious*) prudente ♦ n cassaforte f; ~ **from** al sicuro da; ~ **and sound** sano(a) e salvo(a); ~ **journey!** buon viaggio!; **(just) to be on the** ~ **side** per non correre rischi; **to play** ~ giocare sul sicuro; **it is** ~ **to say that** ... si può affermare con sicurezza che ....

safe bet n: **it's a** ~ è una cosa sicura.

safe-breaker ['seɪfbreɪkə*] n (*BRIT*) scassinatore m.

safe-conduct [seɪf'kɔndʌkt] n salvacondotto.

safe-cracker ['seɪfkrækə*] n = **safe-breaker.**

safe-deposit ['seɪfdɪpɔzɪt] n (*vault*) caveau m inv; (*box*) cassetta di sicurezza.

safeguard ['seɪfgɑːd] n salvaguardia ♦ vt salvaguardare.

safe haven n zona sicura or protetta.

safekeeping ['seɪf'kiːpɪŋ] n custodia.

safely ['seɪflɪ] adv sicuramente; sano(a) e salvo(a); prudentemente; **I can** ~ **say** ... posso tranquillamente asserire ....

safe passage n passaggio sicuro.

safe sex n sesso sicuro.

safety ['seɪftɪ] n sicurezza; ~ **first!** la prudenza innanzitutto!

safety belt n cintura di sicurezza.

safety catch n sicura.

safety net n rete f di protezione.

safety pin n spilla di sicurezza.

safety valve n valvola di sicurezza.

saffron ['sæfrən] n zafferano.

sag [sæg] vi incurvarsi; afflosciarsi.

saga ['sɑːgə] n saga; (*fig*) odissea.

sage [seɪdʒ] n (*herb*) salvia; (*man*) saggio.

Sagittarius [sædʒɪ'tɛərɪəs] n Sagittario; **to be** ~ essere del Sagittario.

sago ['seɪgəu] n sagù m.

Sahara [sə'hɑːrə] n: **the** ~ **Desert** il Deserto del Sahara.

Sahel [sæ'hɛl] n Sahel m.

said [sɛd] pt, pp of **say.**

Saigon [saɪ'gɔn] n Saigon f.

sail [seɪl] n (*on boat*) vela; (*trip*): **to go for a** ~ fare un giro in barca a vela ♦ vt (*boat*) condurre, governare ♦ vi (*travel: ship*) navigare; (: *passenger*) viaggiare per mare; (*set off*) salpare; (*SPORT*) fare della vela; **they** ~**ed into Genoa** entrarono nel porto di Genova.

▶**sail through** vt fus (*fig*) superare senza difficoltà ♦ vi farcela senza difficoltà.

sailboat ['seɪlbəut] n (*US*) barca a vela.

sailing ['seɪlɪŋ] n (*sport*) vela; **to go** ~ fare della vela.

sailing boat n barca a vela.

sailing ship n veliero.

sailor ['seɪlə*] n marinaio.

saint [seɪnt] n santo/a.

saintly ['seɪntlɪ] adj da santo(a); santo(a).

sake [seɪk] n: **for the** ~ **of** per, per amore di; **for pity's** ~ per pietà; **for the** ~ **of argument** tanto per fare un esempio; **art for art's** ~ l'arte per l'arte.

salad ['sæləd] n insalata; **tomato** ~ insalata di pomodori.

salad bowl n insalatiera.

salad cream n (*BRIT*) (tipo di) maionese f.

salad dressing n condimento per insalata.

salad oil n olio da tavola.

salami [sə'lɑːmɪ] n salame m.

salaried ['sælərɪd] adj stipendiato(a).

salary ['sælərɪ] n stipendio.

salary scale n scala dei salari.

sale [seɪl] n vendita; (*at reduced prices*) svendita, liquidazione f; **"for** ~**"** "in vendita"; **on** ~ in vendita; **on** ~ **or return** da vendere o rimandare; **a closing-down** or (US) **liquidation** ~ una liquidazione; ~ **and lease back** n lease back m inv.

saleroom ['seɪlrum] n sala delle aste.

sales assistant n (BRIT) commesso/a.

sales clerk n (US) commesso/a.

sales conference n riunione f marketing e vendite.

sales drive n campagna di vendita, sforzo promozionale.

sales force n personale m addetto alle vendite.

salesman ['seɪlzmən] n commesso; (representative) rappresentante m.

sales manager n direttore m commerciale.

salesmanship ['seɪlzmənʃɪp] n arte f del vendere.

sales tax n (US) imposta sulle vendite.

saleswoman ['seɪlzwumən] n commessa.

salient ['seɪlɪənt] adj saliente.

saline ['seɪlaɪn] adj salino(a).

saliva [sə'laɪvə] n saliva.

sallow ['sæləu] adj giallastro(a).

sally forth, sally out ['sælɪ–] vi uscire di gran carriera.

salmon ['sæmən] n (pl inv) salmone m.

salmon trout n trota (di mare).

saloon [sə'luːn] n (US) saloon m inv, bar m inv; (BRIT AUT) berlina; (ship's lounge) salone m.

SALT [sɔːlt] n abbr (= Strategic Arms Limitation Talks/Treaty) S.A.L.T. m.

salt [sɔːlt] n sale m ♦ vt salare ♦ cpd di sale; (CULIN) salato(a); **an old** ~ un lupo di mare.

▶**salt away** vt ammucchiare, mettere via.

salt cellar n saliera.

salt-free ['sɔːlt'friː] adj senza sale.

saltwater ['sɔːltwɔːtə*] adj (fish etc) di mare.

salty ['sɔːltɪ] adj salato(a).

salubrious [sə'luːbrɪəs] adj salubre; (fig: district etc) raccomandabile.

salutary ['sæljutərɪ] adj salutare.

salute [sə'luːt] n saluto ♦ vt salutare.

salvage ['sælvɪdʒ] n (saving) salvataggio; (things saved) beni mpl salvati or recuperati ♦ vt salvare, mettere in salvo.

salvage vessel n scialuppa di salvataggio.

salvation [sæl'veɪʃən] n salvezza.

Salvation Army n Esercito della Salvezza.

salver ['sælvə*] n vassoio.

salvo, ~es ['sælvəu] n salva.

Samaritan [sə'mærɪtən] n: **the ~s** (organization) ≈ telefono amico.

same [seɪm] adj stesso(a), medesimo(a) ♦ pron: **the** ~ lo(la) stesso(a), gli(le) stessi(e); **the** ~ **book as** lo stesso libro di (or che); **on the** ~ **day** lo stesso giorno; **at the** ~ **time** allo stesso tempo; **all** or **just the** ~ tuttavia; **to do the** ~ fare la stessa cosa; **to do the** ~ **as sb** fare come qn; **the** ~ **again** (in bar etc) un altro; **they're one and the** ~ (person/thing) sono la stessa persona/cosa; **and the** ~ **to you!** altrettanto a lei!; ~ **here!** anch'io!

sample ['sɑːmpl] n campione m ♦ vt (food) assaggiare; (wine) degustare; **to take a** ~ prelevare un campione; **free** ~ campione omaggio.

sanatorium, pl **sanatoria** [sænə'tɔːrɪəm, -rɪə] n sanatorio.

sanctify ['sæŋktɪfaɪ] vt santificare.

sanctimonious [sæŋktɪ'məunɪəs] adj bigotto(a), bacchettone(a).

sanction ['sæŋkʃən] n sanzione f ♦ vt sancire, sanzionare; **to impose economic** ~**s on** or **against** adottare sanzioni economiche contro.

sanctity ['sæŋktɪtɪ] n santità.

sanctuary ['sæŋktjuərɪ] n (holy place) santuario; (refuge) rifugio; (for wildlife) riserva.

sand [sænd] n sabbia ♦ vt cospargere di sabbia; (also: ~ **down**: wood etc) cartavetrare; see also **sands**.

sandal ['sændl] n sandalo.

sandbag ['sændbæg] n sacco di sabbia.

sandblast ['sændblɑːst] vt sabbiare.

sandbox ['sændbɔks] n (US: for children) buca di sabbia.

sandcastle ['sændkɑːsl] n castello di sabbia.

sand dune n duna di sabbia.

sander ['sændə*] n levigatrice f.

sandpaper ['sændpeɪpə*] n carta vetrata.

sandpit ['sændpɪt] n (BRIT: for children) buca di sabbia.

sands [sændz] npl spiaggia.

sandstone ['sændstəun] n arenaria.

sandstorm ['sændstɔːm] n tempesta di sabbia.

sandwich ['sændwɪtʃ] n tramezzino, panino, sandwich m inv ♦ vt (also: ~ **in**) infilare; **cheese/ham** ~ sandwich al formaggio/prosciutto; **to be** ~**ed between** essere incastrato(a) fra.

sandwich board n cartello pubblicitario (portato da un uomo sandwich).

sandwich course n (BRIT) corso di formazione professionale.

sandwich man n uomo m sandwich inv.

sandy ['sændɪ] adj sabbioso(a); (colour)

color sabbia *inv*, biondo(a) rossiccio(a).
sane [seɪn] *adj* (*person*) sano(a) di mente;
(*outlook*) sensato(a).
sang [sæŋ] *pt of* **sing**.
sanguine ['sæŋgwɪn] *adj* ottimista.
sanitarium, *pl* **sanitaria** [sænɪ'tɛərɪəm,
-rɪə] *n* (*US*) = **sanatorium**.
sanitary ['sænɪtərɪ] *adj* (*system,
arrangements*) sanitario(a); (*clean*)
igienico(a).
sanitary towel, (*US*) **sanitary napkin** *n*
assorbente *m* (igienico).
sanitation [sænɪ'teɪʃən] *n* (*in house*) impianti
mpl sanitari; (*in town*) fognature *fpl*.
sanitation department *n* (*US*) nettezza
urbana.
sanity ['sænɪtɪ] *n* sanità mentale; (*common
sense*) buon senso.
sank [sæŋk] *pt of* **sink**.
San Marino [sænmə'riːnəu] *n* San Marino *f*.
Santa Claus [sæntə'klɔːz] *n* Babbo Natale.
Santiago [sæntɪ'ɑːgəu] *n* (*also:* ~ **de Chile**)
Santiago (del Cile) *f*.
sap [sæp] *n* (*of plants*) linfa ♦ *vt* (*strength*)
fiaccare.
sapling ['sæplɪŋ] *n* alberello.
sapphire ['sæfaɪə*] *n* zaffiro.
sarcasm ['sɑːkæzm] *n* sarcasmo.
sarcastic [sɑː'kæstɪk] *adj* sarcastico(a); **to
be** ~ fare del sarcasmo.
sarcophagus, *pl* **sarcophagi** [sɑː'kɔfəgəs,
-gaɪ] *n* sarcofago.
sardine [sɑː'diːn] *n* sardina.
Sardinia [sɑː'dɪnɪə] *n* Sardegna.
Sardinian [sɑː'dɪnɪən] *adj, n* sardo(a).
sardonic [sɑː'dɔnɪk] *adj* sardonico(a).
sari ['sɑːrɪ] *n* sari *m inv*.
sartorial [sɑː'tɔːrɪəl] *adj* di sartoria.
SAS *n abbr* (*BRIT MIL*: = *Special Air Service*)
*reparto dell'esercito britannico
specializzato in operazioni clandestine*.
SASE *n abbr* (*US*: = *self-addressed stamped
envelope*) *busta affrancata e con
indirizzo*.
sash [sæʃ] *n* fascia.
sash window *n* finestra a ghigliottina.
Sask. *abbr* (*Canada*) = *Saskatchewan*.
SAT *n abbr* (*US*) = *Scholastic Aptitude Test*.
sat [sæt] *pt, pp of* **sit**.
Sat. *abbr* (= *Saturday*) sab.
Satan ['seɪtən] *n* Satana *m*.
satanic [sə'tænɪk] *adj* satanico(a).
satchel ['sætʃl] *n* cartella.
sated ['seɪtɪd] *adj* soddisfatto(a); sazio(a).
satellite ['sætəlaɪt] *adj, n* satellite (*m*).
satellite television *n* televisione *f* via
satellite.
satiate ['seɪʃɪeɪt] *vt* saziare.

satin ['sætɪn] *n* satin *m* ♦ *adj* di *or* in satin;
with a ~ **finish** satinato(a).
satire ['sætaɪə*] *n* satira.
satirical [sə'tɪrɪkl] *adj* satirico(a).
satirist ['sætərɪst] *n* (*writer etc*)
scrittore(trice) *etc* satirico(a);
(*cartoonist*) caricaturista *m/f*.
satirize ['sætɪraɪz] *vt* satireggiare.
satisfaction [sætɪs'fækʃən] *n* soddisfazione
f; **has it been done to your** ~? ne è
rimasto soddisfatto?
satisfactory [sætɪs'fæktərɪ] *adj*
soddisfacente.
satisfied ['sætɪsfaɪd] *adj* (*customer*)
soddisfatto(a); **to be** ~ (**with sth**) essere
soddisfatto(a) (di qc).
satisfy ['sætɪsfaɪ] *vt* soddisfare; (*convince*)
convincere; **to** ~ **the requirements**
rispondere ai requisiti; **to** ~ **sb** (**that**)
convincere qn (che), persuadere qn
(che); **to** ~ **o.s. of sth** accertarsi di qc.
satisfying ['sætɪsfaɪɪŋ] *adj* soddisfacente.
satsuma [sæt'suːmə] *n* agrume di
provenienza giapponese.
saturate ['sætʃəreɪt] *vt*: **to** ~ (**with**)
saturare (di).
saturated fat ['sætʃəreɪtɪd-] *n* grassi *mpl*
saturi.
saturation [sætʃə'reɪʃən] *n* saturazione *f*.
Saturday ['sætədɪ] *n* sabato; *for phrases see
also* **Tuesday**.
sauce [sɔːs] *n* salsa; (*containing meat, fish*)
sugo.
saucepan ['sɔːspən] *n* casseruola.
saucer ['sɔːsə*] *n* piattino.
saucy ['sɔːsɪ] *adj* impertinente.
Saudi Arabia ['saudɪ-] *n* Arabia Saudita.
Saudi (Arabian) *adj, n* saudita (*m/f*).
sauna ['sɔːnə] *n* sauna.
saunter ['sɔːntə*] *vi* andare a zonzo,
bighellonare.
sausage ['sɔsɪdʒ] *n* salsiccia; (*salami etc*)
salame *m*.
sausage roll *n* rotolo di pasta sfoglia
ripieno di salsiccia.
sauté ['səuteɪ] *adj* (*CULIN*: *potatoes*)
saltato(a); (: *onions*) soffritto(a) ♦ *vt* far
saltare; far soffriggere.
savage ['sævɪdʒ] *adj* (*cruel, fierce*)
selvaggio(a), feroce; (*primitive*)
primitivo(a) ♦ *n* selvaggio/a ♦ *vt*
attaccare selvaggiamente.
savagery ['sævɪdʒrɪ] *n* crudeltà, ferocia.
save [seɪv] *vt* (*person, belongings, COMPUT*)
salvare; (*money*) risparmiare, mettere da
parte; (*time*) risparmiare; (*food*)
conservare; (*avoid: trouble*) evitare ♦ *vi*
(*also:* ~ **up**) economizzare ♦ *n* (*SPORT*)

parata ♦ *prep* salvo, a eccezione di; **it will ~ me an hour** mi farà risparmiare un'ora; **to ~ face** salvare la faccia; **God ~ the Queen!** Dio salvi la Regina!

saving ['seɪvɪŋ] *n* risparmio ♦ *adj*: **the ~ grace** of l'unica cosa buona di; **~s** *npl* risparmi *mpl*; **to make ~s** fare economia.

savings account *n* libretto di risparmio.

savings bank *n* cassa di risparmio.

saviour, (US) savior ['seɪvjə*] *n* salvatore *m*.

savour, (US) savor ['seɪvə*] *n* sapore *m*, gusto ♦ *vt* gustare.

savoury, (US) savory ['seɪvərɪ] *adj* saporito(a); (*dish: not sweet*) salato(a).

savvy ['sævɪ] *n* (*col*) arguzia.

saw [sɔ:] *pt of* **see** ♦ *n* (*tool*) sega ♦ *vt* (*pt* **sawed**, *pp* **sawed** *or* **sawn** [sɔ:n]) segare; **to ~ sth up** fare a pezzi qc con la sega.

sawdust ['sɔ:dʌst] *n* segatura.

sawmill ['sɔ:mɪl] *n* segheria.

sawn [sɔ:n] *pp of* **saw**.

sawn-off ['sɔ:nɔf], (US) **sawed-off** ['sɔ:dɔf] *adj*: **~ shotgun** fucile *m* a canne mozze.

saxophone ['sæksəfəun] *n* sassofono.

say [seɪ] *n*: **to have one's ~** fare sentire il proprio parere; **to have a** *or* **some ~** avere voce in capitolo ♦ *vt* (*pt, pp* **said** [sɛd]) dire; **could you ~ that again?** potrebbe ripeterlo?; **to ~ yes/no** dire di sì/di no; **she said (that) I was to give you this** ha detto di darle questo; **my watch ~s 3 o'clock** il mio orologio fa le 3; **shall we ~ Tuesday?** facciamo martedì?; **that doesn't ~ much for him** non torna a suo credito; **when all is said and done** a conti fatti; **there is something** *or* **a lot to be said for it** ha i suoi lati positivi; **that is to ~** cioè, vale a dire; **to ~ nothing of** per non parlare di; **~ that** ... mettiamo *or* diciamo che ...; **that goes without ~ing** va da sé.

saying ['seɪɪŋ] *n* proverbio, detto.

SBA *n abbr* (*US:* = Small Business Administration*) organismo ausiliario per piccole imprese.

SC *n abbr* (*US*) = **supreme court** ♦ *abbr* (*US*) = South Carolina.

s/c *abbr* (= *self-contained*) indipendente.

scab [skæb] *n* crosta; (*pej*) crumiro/a.

scabby ['skæbɪ] *adj* crostoso(a).

scaffold ['skæfəuld] *n* impalcatura; (*gallows*) patibolo.

scaffolding ['skæfəldɪŋ] *n* impalcatura.

scald [skɔ:ld] *n* scottatura ♦ *vt* scottare.

scalding ['skɔ:ldɪŋ] *adj* (*also:* **~ hot**) bollente.

scale [skeɪl] *n* scala; (*of fish*) squama ♦ *vt*

(*mountain*) scalare; **pay ~** scala dei salari; **~ of charges** tariffa; **on a large ~** su vasta scala; **to draw sth to ~** disegnare qc in scala; **small-~ model** modello in scala ridotta; *see also* **scales**.

▸**scale down** *vt* ridurre (proporzionalmente).

scaled-down [skeɪld'daun] *adj* su scala ridotta.

scale drawing *n* disegno in scala.

scale model *n* modello in scala.

scales [skeɪlz] *npl* bilancia.

scallion ['skæljən] *n* cipolla; (*US: shallot*) scalogna; (: *leek*) porro.

scallop ['skɔləp] *n* pettine *m*.

scalp [skælp] *n* cuoio capelluto ♦ *vt* scotennare.

scalpel ['skælpl] *n* bisturi *m inv*.

scalper ['skælpə*] *n* (*US col: of tickets*) bagarino.

scam [skæm] *n* (*col*) truffa.

scamp [skæmp] *n* (*col: child*) peste *f*.

scamper ['skæmpə*] *vi*: **to ~ away**, **~ off** darsela a gambe.

scampi ['skæmpɪ] *npl* scampi *mpl*.

scan [skæn] *vt* scrutare; (*glance at quickly*) scorrere, dare un'occhiata a; (*poetry*) scandire; (*TV*) analizzare; (*RADAR*) esplorare ♦ *n* (*MED*) ecografia.

scandal ['skændl] *n* scandalo; (*gossip*) pettegolezzi *mpl*.

scandalize ['skændəlaɪz] *vt* scandalizzare.

scandalous ['skændələs] *adj* scandaloso(a).

Scandinavia [skændɪ'neɪvɪə] *n* Scandinavia.

Scandinavian [skændɪ'neɪvɪən] *adj, n* scandinavo(a).

scanner ['skænə*] *n* (*RADAR, MED*) scanner *m inv*.

scant [skænt] *adj* scarso(a).

scantily ['skæntɪlɪ] *adv*: **~ clad** *or* **dressed** succintamente vestito(a).

scanty ['skæntɪ] *adj* insufficiente; (*swimsuit*) ridotto(a).

scapegoat ['skeɪpgəut] *n* capro espiatorio.

scar [skɑ:*] *n* cicatrice *f* ♦ *vt* sfregiare.

scarce [skɛəs] *adj* scarso(a); (*copy, edition*) raro(a).

scarcely ['skɛəslɪ] *adv* appena; **~ anybody** quasi nessuno; **I can ~ believe it** faccio fatica a crederci.

scarcity ['skɛəsɪtɪ] *n* scarsità, mancanza.

scarcity value *n* valore *m* di rarità.

scare [skɛə*] *n* spavento, paura ♦ *vt* spaventare, atterrire; **to ~ sb stiff** spaventare a morte qn; **bomb ~** evacuazione *f* per sospetta presenza di un ordigno esplosivo.

▸**scare away, scare off** *vt* mettere in

fuga.

scarecrow ['skɛəkrəu] n spaventapasseri m inv.

scared [skɛəd] adj: **to be ~** aver paura.

scaremonger ['skɛəmʌŋgə*] n allarmista m/f.

scarf, pl **scarves** [skɑːf, skɑːvz] n (long) sciarpa; (square) fazzoletto da testa, foulard m inv.

scarlet ['skɑːlɪt] adj scarlatto(a).

scarlet fever n scarlattina.

scarper ['skɑːpə*] vi (BRIT col) darsela a gambe.

scarves [skɑːvz] npl of **scarf**.

scary ['skɛərɪ] adj (col) che fa paura.

scathing ['skeɪðɪŋ] adj aspro(a); **to be ~ about sth** essere molto critico rispetto a qc.

scatter ['skætə*] vt spargere; (crowd) disperdere ♦ vi disperdersi.

scatterbrained ['skætəbreɪnd] adj scervellato(a), sbadato(a).

scattered ['skætəd] adj sparso(a), sparpagliato(a).

scatty ['skætɪ] adj (col) scervellato(a), sbadato(a).

scavenge ['skævɪndʒ] vi (person): **to ~ (for)** frugare tra i rifiuti (alla ricerca di); (hyenas etc) nutrirsi di carogne.

scavenger ['skævəndʒə*] n spazzino.

SCE n abbr = Scottish Certificate of Education.

scenario [sɪˈnɑːrɪəu] n (THEAT, CINE) copione m; (fig) situazione f.

scene [siːn] n (THEAT, fig etc) scena; (of crime, accident) scena, luogo; (sight, view) vista, veduta; **behind the ~s** (also fig) dietro le quinte; **to appear** or **come on the ~** (also fig) entrare in scena; **the political ~ in Italy** il quadro politico in Italia; **to make a ~** (col: fuss) fare una scenata.

scenery ['siːnərɪ] n (THEAT) scenario; (landscape) panorama m.

scenic ['siːnɪk] adj scenico(a); panoramico(a).

scent [sɛnt] n odore m, profumo; (sense of smell) olfatto, odorato; (fig: track) pista; **to put** or **throw sb off the ~** (fig) far perdere le tracce a qn, sviare qn.

sceptic, (US) skeptic ['skɛptɪk] n scettico/a.

sceptical, (US) skeptical ['skɛptɪkl] adj scettico(a).

scepticism, (US) skepticism ['skɛptɪsɪzm] n scetticismo.

sceptre, (US) scepter ['sɛptə*] n scettro.

schedule ['ʃɛdjuːl, (US) 'skɛdjuːl] n programma m, piano; (of trains) orario; (of prices etc) lista, tabella ♦ vt fissare; **as ~d** come stabilito; **on ~** in orario; **to be ahead of/behind ~** essere in anticipo/ ritardo sul previsto; **we are working to a very tight ~** il nostro programma di lavoro è molto intenso; **everything went according to ~** tutto è andato secondo i piani or secondo il previsto.

scheduled ['ʃɛdjuːld, (US) 'skɛdjuːld] adj (date, time) fissato(a); (visit, event) programmato(a); (train, bus, stop) previsto(a) (sull'orario); **~ flight** volo di linea.

schematic [skɪˈmætɪk] adj schematico(a).

scheme [skiːm] n piano, progetto; (method) sistema m; (dishonest plan, plot) intrigo, trama; (arrangement) disposizione f, sistemazione f ♦ vt progettare; (plot) ordire ♦ vi fare progetti; (intrigue) complottare; **colour ~** combinazione f di colori.

scheming ['skiːmɪŋ] adj intrigante ♦ n intrighi mpl, macchinazioni fpl.

schism ['skɪzəm] n scisma m.

schizophrenia [skɪtsəˈfriːnɪə] n schizofrenia.

schizophrenic [skɪtsəˈfrɛnɪk] adj, n schizofrenico(a).

scholar ['skɔlə*] n erudito/a.

scholarly ['skɔləlɪ] adj dotto(a), erudito(a).

scholarship ['skɔləʃɪp] n erudizione f; (grant) borsa di studio.

school [skuːl] n scuola; (in university) scuola, facoltà f inv ♦ cpd scolare, scolastico(a) ♦ vt (animal) addestrare.

school age n età scolare.

schoolbook ['skuːlbuk] n libro scolastico.

schoolboy ['skuːlbɔɪ] n scolaro.

schoolchild, pl **-children** ['skuːltʃaɪld, -'tʃɪldrən] n scolaro/a.

schooldays ['skuːldeɪz] npl giorni mpl di scuola.

schoolgirl ['skuːlgɜːl] n scolara.

schooling ['skuːlɪŋ] n istruzione f.

school-leaver ['skuːlliːvə*] n (BRIT) ≈ neodiplomato(a).

schoolmaster ['skuːlmɑːstə*] n (primary) maestro; (secondary) insegnante m.

schoolmistress ['skuːlmɪstrɪs] n (primary) maestra; (secondary) insegnante f.

school report n (BRIT) pagella.

schoolroom ['skuːlruːm] n classe f, aula.

schoolteacher ['skuːltiːtʃə*] n insegnante m/f, docente m/f; (primary) maestro/a.

schoolyard ['skuːljɑːd] n (US) cortile m della scuola.

schooner ['skuːnə*] n (ship) goletta, schooner m inv; (glass) bicchiere m alto da sherry.

sciatica [saɪ'ætɪkə] n sciatica.

science ['saɪəns] n scienza; **the ~s** le scienze; (SCOL) le materie scientifiche.

science fiction n fantascienza.

scientific [saɪən'tɪfɪk] adj scientifico(a).

scientist ['saɪəntɪst] n scienziato/a.

sci-fi ['saɪfaɪ] n abbr (col) = **science fiction**.

Scilly Isles ['sɪlɪ'aɪlz] npl, **Scillies** ['sɪlɪz] npl: **the ~** le isole Scilly.

scintillating ['sɪntɪleɪtɪŋ] adj scintillante; (wit, conversation, company) brillante.

scissors ['sɪzəz] npl forbici fpl; **a pair of ~** un paio di forbici.

sclerosis [sklɪ'rəʊsɪs] n sclerosi f.

scoff [skɒf] vt (BRIT col: eat) tranguiare, ingozzare ♦ vi: **to ~ (at)** (mock) farsi beffe (di).

scold [skəʊld] vt rimproverare.

scolding ['skəʊldɪŋ] n lavata di capo, sgridata.

scone [skɒn] n focaccina da tè.

scoop [skuːp] n mestolo; (for ice cream) cucchiaio dosatore; (PRESS) colpo giornalistico, notizia (in) esclusiva.

▶**scoop out** vt scavare.

▶**scoop up** vt tirare su, sollevare.

scooter ['skuːtə*] n (motor cycle) motoretta, scooter m inv; (toy) monopattino.

scope [skəʊp] n (capacity: of plan, undertaking) portata; (: of person) capacità fpl; (opportunity) possibilità fpl; **to be within the ~ of** rientrare nei limiti di; **it's well within his ~ to ...** è perfettamente in grado di ...; **there is plenty of ~ for improvement** (BRIT) ci sono notevoli possibilità di miglioramento.

scorch [skɔːtʃ] vt (clothes) strinare, bruciacchiare; (earth, grass) seccare, bruciare.

scorched earth policy [skɔːtʃt-] n tattica della terra bruciata.

scorcher ['skɔːtʃə*] n (col: hot day) giornata torrida.

scorching ['skɔːtʃɪŋ] adj cocente, scottante.

score [skɔː*] n punti mpl, punteggio; (MUS) partitura, spartito; (twenty): **a ~** venti ♦ vt (goal, point) segnare, fare; (success) ottenere; (cut: leather, wood, card) incidere ♦ vi segnare; (FOOTBALL) fare un goal; (keep score) segnare i punti; **on that ~** a questo riguardo; **to have an old ~ to settle with sb** (fig) avere un vecchio conto da saldare con qn; **~s of people** (fig) un sacco di gente; **to ~ 6 out of 10** prendere 6 su 10.

▶**score out** vt cancellare con un segno.

scoreboard ['skɔːbɔːd] n tabellone m segnapunti.

scorecard ['skɔːkɑːd] n cartoncino segnapunti.

scoreline ['skɔːlaɪn] n (SPORT) risultato.

scorer ['skɔːrə*] n marcatore/trice; (keeping score) segnapunti m inv.

scorn [skɔːn] n disprezzo ♦ vt disprezzare.

scornful ['skɔːnful] adj sprezzante.

Scorpio ['skɔːpɪəʊ] n Scorpione m; **to be ~** essere dello Scorpione.

scorpion ['skɔːpɪən] n scorpione m.

Scot [skɒt] n scozzese m/f.

Scotch [skɒtʃ] n whisky m scozzese, scotch m.

scotch [skɒtʃ] vt (rumour etc) soffocare.

Scotch tape ® n scotch ® m.

scot-free ['skɒt'friː] adj impunito(a); **to get off ~** (unpunished) farla franca; (unhurt) uscire illeso(a).

Scotland ['skɒtlənd] n Scozia.

Scots [skɒts] adj scozzese.

Scotsman ['skɒtsmən] n scozzese m.

Scotswoman ['skɒtswumən] n scozzese f.

Scottish ['skɒtɪʃ] adj scozzese; **the ~ National Party** partito nazionalista scozzese.

scoundrel ['skaundrl] n farabutto/a; (child) furfantello/a.

scour ['skauə*] vt (clean) pulire strofinando; raschiare via; ripulire; (search) battere, perlustrare.

scourer ['skauərə*] n (pad) paglietta; (powder) (detersivo) abrasivo.

scourge [skɜːdʒ] n flagello.

scout [skaut] n (MIL) esploratore m; (also: boy ~) giovane esploratore, scout m inv.

▶**scout around** vi cercare in giro.

scowl [skaul] vi accigliarsi, aggrottare le sopracciglia; **to ~ at** guardare torvo.

scrabble ['skræbl] vi (claw): **to ~ (at)** graffiare, grattare; **to ~ about or around for sth** cercare affannosamente qc ♦ n: **S~** ® Scarabeo ®.

scraggy ['skrægɪ] adj scarno(a), molto magro(a).

scram [skræm] vi (col) filare via.

scramble ['skræmbl] n arrampicata ♦ vi inerpicarsi; **to ~ out** etc uscire etc in fretta; **to ~ for** azzuffarsi per; **to go scrambling** (SPORT) fare il motocross.

scrambled eggs npl uova fpl strapazzate.

scrap [skræp] n pezzo, pezzetto; (fight) zuffa; (also: ~ **iron**) rottami mpl di ferro, ferraglia ♦ vt demolire; (fig) scartare; **~s** npl (waste) scarti mpl; **to sell sth for ~** vendere qc come ferro vecchio.

scrapbook ['skræpbuk] n album m inv di ritagli.

scrap dealer n commerciante m di

ferraglia.

scrape [skreɪp] *vt, vi* raschiare, grattare ♦ *n*: **to get into a** ~ cacciarsi in un guaio.

▶**scrape through** *vi* (*succeed*) farcela per un pelo, cavarsela ♦ *vt fus* (*exam*) passare per miracolo, passare per il rotto della cuffia.

scraper ['skreɪpə*] *n* raschietto.

scrap heap *n* mucchio di rottami; **to throw sth on the** ~ (*fig*) mettere qc nel dimenticatoio.

scrap merchant *n* (*BRIT*) commerciante *m* di ferraglia.

scrap metal *n* ferraglia.

scrap paper *n* cartaccia.

scrappy ['skræpɪ] *adj* frammentario(a), sconnesso(a).

scrap yard *n* deposito di rottami; (*for cars*) cimitero delle macchine.

scratch [skrætʃ] *n* graffio ♦ *cpd*: ~ **team** squadra raccogliticcia ♦ *vt* graffiare, rigare; (*COMPUT*) cancellare ♦ *vi* grattare, graffiare; **to start from** ~ cominciare *or* partire da zero; **to be up to** ~ essere all'altezza.

scratch pad *n* (*US*) notes *m inv*, blocchetto.

scrawl [skrɔːl] *n* scarabocchio ♦ *vi* scarabocchiare.

scrawny ['skrɔːnɪ] *adj* scarno(a), pelle e ossa *inv*.

scream [skriːm] *n* grido, urlo ♦ *vi* urlare, gridare; **to** ~ **at sb (to do sth)** gridare a qn (di fare qc); **it was a** ~ (*fig col*) era da crepar dal ridere; **he's a** ~ (*fig col*) è una sagoma, è uno spasso.

scree [skriː] *n* ghiaione *m*.

screech [skriːtʃ] *n* strido; (*of tyres, brakes*) stridore *m* ♦ *vi* stridere.

screen [skriːn] *n* schermo; (*fig*) muro, cortina, velo ♦ *vt* schermare, fare schermo a; (*from the wind etc*) riparare; (*film*) proiettare; (*book*) adattare per lo schermo; (*candidates etc*) passare al vaglio; (*for illness*) sottoporre a controlli medici.

screen editing [-ɛdɪtɪŋ] *n* (*COMPUT*) correzione *f* e modifica su schermo.

screening ['skriːnɪŋ] *n* (*MED*) dépistage *m inv*; (*of film*) proiezione *f*; (*for security*) controlli *mpl* (di sicurezza).

screen memory *n* (*COMPUT*) memoria di schermo.

screenplay ['skriːnpleɪ] *n* sceneggiatura.

screen test *n* provino (cinematografico).

screw [skruː] *n* vite *f*; (*propeller*) elica ♦ *vt* avvitare; **to** ~ **sth to the wall** fissare qc al muro con viti.

▶**screw up** *vt* (*paper, material*) spiegazzare;

(*col: ruin*) mandare a monte; **to** ~ **up one's face** fare una smorfia.

screwdriver ['skruːdraɪvə*] *n* cacciavite *m*.

screwed-up ['skruːdʌp] *adj* (*col*): **she's totally** ~ è nel pallone.

screwy ['skruːɪ] *adj* (*col*) svitato(a).

scribble ['skrɪbl] *n* scarabocchio ♦ *vt* scribacchiare ♦ *vi* scarabocchiare; **to** ~ **sth down** scribacchiare qc.

scribe [skraɪb] *n* scriba *m*.

script [skrɪpt] *n* (*CINE etc*) copione *m*; (*in exam*) elaborato *or* compito d'esame; (*writing*) scrittura.

scripted ['skrɪptɪd] *adj* (*RADIO, TV*) preparato(a).

Scripture ['skrɪptʃə*] *n* Sacre Scritture *fpl*.

scriptwriter ['skrɪptraɪtə*] *n* soggettista *m/f*.

scroll [skrəul] *n* rotolo di carta ♦ *vt* (*COMPUT*) scorrere.

scrotum ['skrəutəm] *n* scroto.

scrounge [skraundʒ] *vt* (*col*): **to** ~ **sth (off or from sb)** scroccare qc (a qn) ♦ *vi*: **to** ~ **on sb** vivere alle spalle di qn.

scrounger ['skraundʒə*] *n* scroccone/a.

scrub [skrʌb] *n* (*clean*) strofinata; (*land*) boscaglia ♦ *vt* pulire strofinando; (*reject*) annullare.

scrubbing brush ['skrʌbɪŋ-] *n* spazzolone *m*.

scruff [skrʌf] *n*: **by the** ~ **of the neck** per la collottola.

scruffy ['skrʌfɪ] *adj* sciatto(a).

scrum(mage) ['skrʌm(ɪdʒ)] *n* mischia.

scruple ['skruːpl] *n* scrupolo; **to have no** ~**s about doing sth** non avere scrupoli a fare qc.

scrupulous ['skruːpjuləs] *adj* scrupoloso(a).

scrupulously ['skruːpjuləslɪ] *adv* scrupolosamente; **he tries to be** ~ **fair/ honest** cerca di essere più imparziale/ onesto che può.

scrutinize ['skruːtɪnaɪz] *vt* scrutare, esaminare attentamente.

scrutiny ['skruːtɪnɪ] *n* esame *m* accurato; **under the** ~ **of sb** sotto la sorveglianza di qn.

scuba ['skuːbə] *n* autorespiratore *m*.

scuba diving *n* immersioni *fpl* subacquee.

scuff [skʌf] *vt* (*shoes*) consumare strascicando.

scuffle ['skʌfl] *n* baruffa, tafferuglio.

scullery ['skʌlərɪ] *n* retrocucina *m or f*.

sculptor ['skʌlptə*] *n* scultore *m*.

sculpture ['skʌlptʃə*] *n* scultura.

scum [skʌm] *n* schiuma; (*pej: people*) feccia.

scupper ['skʌpə*] *vt* (*BRIT*) autoaffondare; (*fig*) far naufragare.

scurrilous ['skʌrɪləs] *adj* scurrile, volgare.
scurry ['skʌrɪ] *vi* sgambare, affrettarsi.
scurvy ['skə:vɪ] *n* scorbuto.
scuttle ['skʌtl] *n* (*NAUT*) portellino; (*also:* **coal ~**) secchio del carbone ♦ *vt* (*ship*) autoaffondare ♦ *vi* (*scamper*): **to ~ away, ~ off** darsela a gambe, scappare.
scythe [saɪð] *n* falce *f*.
SD, S. Dak. *abbr* (*US*) = *South Dakota*.
SDI *n abbr* (= *Strategic Defense Initiative*) S.D.I. *f*.
SDLP *n abbr* (*BRIT POL*) = *Social Democratic and Labour Party*.
SDP *n abbr* (*BRIT POL*) = *Social Democratic Party*.
sea [si:] *n* mare *m* ♦ *cpd* marino(a), del mare; (*ship, port*) marittimo(a), di mare; **on the ~** (*boat*) in mare; (*town*) di mare; **to go by ~** andare per mare; **by** *or* **beside the ~** (*holiday*) al mare; (*village*) sul mare; **to look out to ~** guardare il mare; **(out) at ~** al largo; **heavy** *or* **rough ~(s)** mare grosso *or* agitato; **a ~ of faces** (*fig*) una marea di gente; **to be all at ~** (*fig*) non sapere che pesci pigliare.
sea bed *n* fondo marino.
sea bird *n* uccello di mare.
seaboard ['si:bɔ:d] *n* costa.
sea breeze *n* brezza di mare.
seafarer ['si:fɛərə*] *n* navigante *m*.
seafaring ['si:fɛərɪŋ] *adj* (*community*) marinaro(a); (*life*) da marinaio.
seafood ['si:fu:d] *n* frutti *mpl* di mare.
sea front *n* lungomare *m*.
seagoing ['si:gəuɪŋ] *adj* (*ship*) d'alto mare.
seagull ['si:gʌl] *n* gabbiano.
seal [si:l] *n* (*animal*) foca; (*stamp*) sigillo; (*impression*) impronta del sigillo ♦ *vt* sigillare; (*decide: sb's fate*) segnare; (: *bargain*) concludere; **~ of approval** beneplacito.
►**seal off** *vt* (*close*) sigillare; (*forbid entry to*) bloccare l'accesso a.
sea level *n* livello del mare.
sealing wax ['si:lɪŋ-] *n* ceralacca.
sea lion *n* leone *m* marino.
sealskin ['si:lskɪn] *n* pelle *f* di foca.
seam [si:m] *n* cucitura; (*of coal*) filone *m*; **the hall was bursting at the ~s** l'aula era piena zeppa.
seaman ['si:mən] *n* marinaio.
seamanship ['si:mənʃɪp] *n* tecnica di navigazione.
seamless ['si:mlɪs] *adj* senza cucitura.
seamy ['si:mɪ] *adj* malfamato(a); squallido(a).
seance ['seɪɔns] *n* seduta spiritica.

seaplane ['si:pleɪn] *n* idrovolante *m*.
seaport ['si:pɔ:t] *n* porto di mare.
search [sə:tʃ] *n* (*for person, thing*) ricerca; (*of drawer, pockets*) esame *m* accurato; (*LAW: at sb's home*) perquisizione *f* ♦ *vt* perlustrare, frugare; (*scan, examine*) esaminare minuziosamente; (*COMPUT*) ricercare ♦ *vi*: **to ~ for** ricercare; **in ~ of** alla ricerca di; "**~ and replace**" (*COMPUT*) "ricercare e sostituire".
►**search through** *vt fus* frugare.
searcher ['sə:tʃə*] *n* chi cerca.
searching ['sə:tʃɪŋ] *adj* minuzioso(a); penetrante; (*question*) pressante.
searchlight ['sə:tʃlaɪt] *n* proiettore *m*.
search party *n* squadra di soccorso.
search warrant *n* mandato di perquisizione.
searing ['sɪərɪŋ] *adj* (*heat*) rovente; (*pain*) acuto(a).
seashore ['si:ʃɔ:*] *n* spiaggia; **on the ~** sulla riva del mare.
seasick ['si:sɪk] *adj* che soffre il mal di mare; **to be ~** avere il mal di mare.
seaside ['si:saɪd] *n* spiaggia; **to go to the ~** andare al mare.
seaside resort *n* stazione *f* balneare.
season ['si:zn] *n* stagione *f* ♦ *vt* condire, insaporire; **to be in/out of ~** essere di/fuori stagione; **the busy ~** (*for shops*) il periodo di punta; (*for hotels etc*) l'alta stagione; **the open ~** (*HUNTING*) la stagione della caccia.
seasonal ['si:zənl] *adj* stagionale.
seasoned ['si:znd] *adj* (*wood*) stagionato(a); (*fig: worker, actor, troops*) con esperienza; **a ~ campaigner** un veterano.
seasoning ['si:znɪŋ] *n* condimento.
season ticket *n* abbonamento.
seat [si:t] *n* sedile *m*; (*in bus, train: place*) posto; (*PARLIAMENT*) seggio; (*centre: of government etc, of infection*) sede *f*; (*buttocks*) didietro; (*of trousers*) fondo ♦ *vt* far sedere; (*have room for*) avere *or* essere fornito(a) di posti a sedere per; **are there any ~s left?** ci sono posti?; **to take one's ~** prendere posto; **to be ~ed** essere seduto(a); **please be ~ed** accomodatevi per favore.
seat belt *n* cintura di sicurezza.
seating arrangements ['si:tɪŋ-] *npl* sistemazione *f or* disposizione *f* dei posti.
seating capacity *n* posti *mpl* a sedere.
SEATO ['si:təu] *n abbr* (= *Southeast Asia Treaty Organization*) SEATO *f*.
sea water *n* acqua di mare.
seaweed ['si:wi:d] *n* alghe *fpl*.
seaworthy ['si:wə:ðɪ] *adj* atto(a) alla

navigazione.

SEC *n abbr* (*US*: = *Securities and Exchange Commission*) *commissione di controllo sulle operazioni in Borsa.*

sec. *abbr* = **second.**

secateurs [sɛkəˈtəːz] *npl* forbici *fpl* per potare.

secede [sɪˈsiːd] *vi:* **to** ~ **(from)** ritirarsi (da).

secluded [sɪˈkluːdɪd] *adj* isolato(a), appartato(a).

seclusion [sɪˈkluːʒən] *n* isolamento.

second [ˈsɛkənd] *num* secondo(a) ♦ *adv* (*in race etc*) al secondo posto; (*RAIL*) in seconda ♦ *n* (*unit of time*) secondo; (*in series, position*) secondo/a; (*BRIT SCOL*) *laurea con punteggio discreto*; (*AUT*: *also*: ~ **gear**) seconda; (*COMM*: *imperfect*) scarto ♦ *vt* (*motion*) appoggiare; [sɪˈkɒnd] (*employee*) distaccare; **Charles the S**~ Carlo Secondo; **just a** ~**!** un attimo!; ~ **floor** (*BRIT*) secondo piano; (*US*) primo piano; **to ask for a** ~ **opinion** (*MED*) chiedere un altro *or* ulteriore parere; **to have** ~ **thoughts (about doing sth)** avere dei ripensamenti (quanto a fare qc); **on** ~ **thoughts** *or* (*US*) **thought** a ripensarci, ripensandoci bene.

secondary [ˈsɛkəndərɪ] *adj* secondario(a).

secondary school *n* scuola secondaria.

In Gran Bretagna la **secondary school** *è la scuola frequentata dai ragazzi dagli 11 ai 18 anni. Alcuni ragazzi la lasciano a 16 anni, età fino alla quale è obbligatorio andare a scuola; vedi anche* **primary school.**

---

second-best [sɛkəndˈbɛst] *n* ripiego; **as a** ~ in mancanza di meglio.

second-class [sɛkəndˈklaːs] *adj* di seconda classe ♦ *adv:* **to travel** ~ viaggiare in seconda (classe); **to send sth** ~ spedire qc per posta ordinaria; ~ **citizen** cittadino di second'ordine.

second cousin *n* cugino di secondo grado.

seconder [ˈsɛkəndə*] *n* sostenitore/trice.

second-guess [ˈsɛkəndˈgɛs] *vt* (*predict*) anticipare; (*after the event*) giudicare col senno di poi.

second hand *n* (*on clock*) lancetta dei secondi.

second-hand [sɛkəndˈhænd] *adj* di seconda mano, usato(a) ♦ *adv* (*buy*) di seconda mano; **to hear sth** ~ venire a sapere qc da terze persone.

second-in-command [ˈsɛkəndɪnkəˈmaːnd] *n* (*MIL*) comandante *m* in seconda; (*ADMIN*) aggiunto.

secondly [ˈsɛkəndlɪ] *adv* in secondo luogo.

secondment [sɪˈkɒndmənt] *n* (*BRIT*) distaccamento.

second-rate [sɛkəndˈreɪt] *adj* scadente.

Second World War *n:* **the** ~ la seconda guerra mondiale.

secrecy [ˈsiːkrəsɪ] *n* segretezza.

secret [ˈsiːkrɪt] *adj* segreto(a) ♦ *n* segreto; **in** ~ in segreto, segretamente; **to keep sth** ~ **(from sb)** tenere qc segreto (a qn), tenere qc nascosto (a qn); **keep it** ~ **che** rimanga un segreto; **to make no** ~ **of sth** non far mistero di qc.

secret agent *n* agente *m* segreto.

secretarial [sɛkrɪˈtɛərɪəl] *adj* (*work*) da segretario/a; (*college, course*) di segretariato.

secretariat [sɛkrɪˈtɛərɪət] *n* segretariato.

secretary [ˈsɛkrətrɪ] *n* segretario/a; **S**~ **of State** (*US POL*) ≈ Ministro degli Esteri; **S**~ **of State (for)** (*BRIT POL*) ministro (di).

secretary-general [ˈsɛkrətrɪˈdʒɛnərl] *n* segretario generale.

secrete [sɪˈkriːt] *vt* (*MED, ANAT, BIOL*) secernere; (*hide*) nascondere.

secretion [sɪˈkriːʃən] *n* secrezione *f*.

secretive [ˈsiːkrətɪv] *adj* riservato(a).

secretly [ˈsiːkrɪtlɪ] *adv* in segreto, segretamente.

secret police *n* polizia segreta.

secret service *n* servizi *mpl* segreti.

sect [sɛkt] *n* setta.

sectarian [sɛkˈtɛərɪən] *adj* settario(a).

section [ˈsɛkʃən] *n* sezione *f*; (*of document*) articolo ♦ *vt* sezionare, dividere in sezioni; **the business** ~ (*PRESS*) la pagina economica.

sector [ˈsɛktə*] *n* settore *m*.

secular [ˈsɛkjulə*] *adj* secolare.

secure [sɪˈkjuə*] *adj* (*free from anxiety*) sicuro(a); (*firmly fixed*) assicurato(a), ben fermato(a); (*in safe place*) al sicuro ♦ *vt* (*fix*) fissare, assicurare; (*get*) ottenere, assicurarsi; (*COMM*: *loan*) garantire; **to make sth** ~ fissare bene qc; **to** ~ **sth for sb** procurare qc per *or* a qn.

secured creditor [sɪˈkjuəd-] *n* creditore *m* privilegiato.

security [sɪˈkjuərɪtɪ] *n* sicurezza; (*for loan*) garanzia; **securities** *npl* (*STOCK EXCHANGE*) titoli *mpl*; **to increase/tighten** ~ aumentare/intensificare la sorveglianza; ~ **of tenure** garanzia del posto di lavoro, garanzia di titolo *or* di godimento.

Security Council *n:* **the** ~ il Consiglio di Sicurezza.

security forces *npl* forze *fpl* dell'ordine.

security guard *n* guardia giurata.

security risk *n* rischio per la sicurezza.

secy. *abbr* = **secretary.**
sedan [sə'dæn] *n* (*US AUT*) berlina.
sedate [sɪ'deɪt] *adj* posato(a); calmo(a) ♦ *vt* calmare.
sedation [sɪ'deɪʃən] *n* (*MED*): **to be under ~** essere sotto l'azione di sedativi.
sedative ['sɛdɪtɪv] *n* sedativo, calmante *m*.
sedentary ['sɛdntrɪ] *adj* sedentario(a).
sediment ['sɛdɪmənt] *n* sedimento.
sedition [sɪ'dɪʃən] *n* sedizione *f*.
seduce [sɪ'djuːs] *vt* sedurre.
seduction [sɪ'dʌkʃən] *n* seduzione *f*.
seductive [sɪ'dʌktɪv] *adj* seducente.
see [siː] *vb* (*pt* **saw**, *pp* **seen** [sɔː, siːn]) *vt* vedere; (*accompany*): **to ~ sb to the door** accompagnare qn alla porta ♦ *vi* vedere; (*understand*) capire ♦ *n* sede *f* vescovile; **to ~ that** (*ensure*) badare che + *sub*, fare in modo che + *sub*; **to go and ~ sb** andare a trovare qn; **~ you soon/later/ tomorrow!** a presto/più tardi/domani!; **as far as I can ~** da quanto posso vedere; **there was nobody to be ~**n non c'era anima viva; **let me ~** (*show me*) fammi vedere; (*let me think*) vediamo (un po'); **~ for yourself** vai a vedere con i tuoi occhi; **I don't know what she ~s in him** non so che cosa ci trovi in lui.
▶**see about** *vt fus* (*deal with*) occuparsi di.
▶**see off** *vt* salutare alla partenza.
▶**see through** *vt* portare a termine ♦ *vt fus* non lasciarsi ingannare da.
▶**see to** *vt fus* occuparsi di.
seed [siːd] *n* seme *m*; (*fig*) germe *m*; (*TENNIS*) testa di serie; **to go to ~** fare seme; (*fig*) scadere.
seedless ['siːdlɪs] *adj* senza semi.
seedling ['siːdlɪŋ] *n* piantina di semenzaio.
seedy ['siːdɪ] *adj* (*shabby: person*) sciatto(a); (: *place*) cadente.
seeing ['siːɪŋ] *conj:* **~ (that)** visto che.
seek [siːk], *pt*, *pp* **sought** *vt* cercare; **to ~ advice/help from sb** chiedere consiglio/ aiuto a qn.
▶**seek out** *vt* (*person*) andare a cercare.
seem [siːm] *vi* sembrare, parere; **there ~s to be ...** sembra che ci sia ...; **it ~s (that) ...** sembra *or* pare che ... + *sub*; **what ~s to be the trouble?** cosa c'è che non va?
seemingly ['siːmɪŋlɪ] *adv* apparentemente.
seen [siːn] *pp* of **see.**
seep [siːp] *vi* filtrare, trapelare.
seer [sɪə*] *n* profeta/essa, veggente *m/f*.
seersucker ['sɪəsʌkə*] *n* cotone *m* indiano.
seesaw ['siːsɔː] *n* altalena a bilico.
seethe [siːð] *vi* ribollire; **to ~ with anger** fremere di rabbia.
see-through ['siːθruː] *adj* trasparente.

segment ['sɛgmənt] *n* segmento.
segregate ['sɛgrɪgeɪt] *vt* segregare, isolare.
segregation [sɛgrɪ'geɪʃən] *n* segregazione *f*.
Seine [seɪn] *n* Senna.
seismic ['saɪzmɪk] *adj* sismico(a).
seize [siːz] *vt* (*grasp*) afferrare; (*take possession of*) impadronirsi di; (*LAW*) sequestrare.
▶**seize up** *vi* (*TECH*) grippare.
▶**seize (up)on** *vt fus* ricorrere a.
seizure ['siːʒə*] *n* (*MED*) attacco; (*LAW*) confisca, sequestro.
seldom ['sɛldəm] *adv* raramente.
select [sɪ'lɛkt] *adj* scelto(a); (*hotel, restaurant*) chic *inv*; (*club*) esclusivo(a) ♦ *vt* scegliere, selezionare; **a ~ few** pochi eletti *mpl*.
selection [sɪ'lɛkʃən] *n* selezione *f*, scelta.
selection committee *n* comitato di selezione.
selective [sɪ'lɛktɪv] *adj* selettivo(a).
selector [sɪ'lɛktə*] *n* (*person*) selezionatore/trice; (*TECH*) selettore *m*.
self [sɛlf] *n* (*pl* **selves** [sɛlvz]): **the ~** l'io *m* ♦ *prefix* auto....
self-addressed ['sɛlfə'drɛst] *adj:* **~ envelope** busta col proprio nome e indirizzo.
self-adhesive [sɛlfəd'hiːzɪv] *adj* autoadesivo(a).
self-assertive [sɛlfə'səːtɪv] *adj* autoritario(a).
self-assurance [sɛlfə'ʃuərəns] *n* sicurezza di sé.
self-assured [sɛlfə'ʃuəd] *adj* sicuro(a) di sé.
self-catering [sɛlf'keɪtərɪŋ] *adj* (*BRIT*) in cui ci si cucina da sé; **~ apartment** appartamento (per le vacanze).
self-centred, (*US*) **self-centered** [sɛlf'sɛntəd] *adj* egocentrico(a).
self-cleaning [sɛlf'kliːnɪŋ] *adj* autopulente.
self-confessed [sɛlfkən'fɛst] *adj* (*alcoholic etc*) dichiarato(a).
self-confidence [sɛlf'kɔnfɪdəns] *n* sicurezza di sé.
self-conscious [sɛlf'kɔnʃəs] *adj* timido(a).
self-contained [sɛlfkən'teɪnd] *adj* (*BRIT: flat*) indipendente.
self-control [sɛlfkən'trəul] *n* autocontrollo.
self-defeating [sɛlfdɪ'fiːtɪŋ] *adj* futile.
self-defence, (*US*) **self-defense** [sɛlfdɪ'fɛns] *n* autodifesa; (*LAW*) legittima difesa.
self-discipline [sɛlf'dɪsɪplɪn] *n* autodisciplina.
self-employed [sɛlfɪm'plɔɪd] *adj* che lavora

in proprio.

self-esteem [sɛlfɪ'stiːm] *n* amor proprio *m*.

self-evident [sɛlf'ɛvɪdənt] *adj* evidente.

self-explanatory [sɛlfɪk'splænətərɪ] *adj* ovvio(a).

self-governing [sɛlf'gʌvənɪŋ] *adj* autonomo(a).

self-help ['sɛlf'hɛlp] *n* iniziativa individuale.

self-importance [sɛlfɪm'pɔːtns] *n* sufficienza.

self-indulgent [sɛlfɪn'dʌldʒənt] *adj* indulgente verso se stesso(a).

self-inflicted [sɛlfɪn'flɪktɪd] *adj* autoinflitto(a).

self-interest [sɛlf'ɪntrɪst] *n* interesse *m* personale.

selfish ['sɛlfɪʃ] *adj* egoista.

selfishly ['sɛlfɪʃlɪ] *adv* egoisticamente.

selfishness ['sɛlfɪʃnɪs] *n* egoismo.

selfless ['sɛlflɪs] *adj* altruista.

selflessly ['sɛlflɪslɪ] *adv* altruisticamente.

selflessness ['sɛlflɪsnɪs] *n* altruismo.

self-made man ['sɛlfmeɪd-] *n* self-made man *m inv*, uomo che si è fatto da sé.

self-pity [sɛlf'pɪtɪ] *n* autocommiserazione *f*.

self-portrait [sɛlf'pɔːtrɪt] *n* autoritratto.

self-possessed [sɛlfpə'zɛst] *adj* controllato(a).

self-preservation ['sɛlfprɛzə'veɪʃən] *n* istinto di conservazione.

self-raising [sɛlf'reɪzɪŋ], (*US*) **self-rising** [sɛlf'raɪzɪŋ] *adj*: ~ **flour** miscela di farina e lievito.

self-reliant [sɛlfrɪ'laɪənt] *adj* indipendente.

self-respect [sɛlfrɪs'pɛkt] *n* rispetto di sé, amor proprio.

self-respecting [sɛlfrɪs'pɛktɪŋ] *adj* che ha rispetto di sé.

self-righteous [sɛlf'raɪtʃəs] *adj* soddisfatto(a) di sé.

self-rising [sɛlf'raɪzɪŋ] *adj* (*US*) = **self-raising**.

self-sacrifice [sɛlf'sækrɪfaɪs] *n* abnegazione *f*.

self-same ['sɛlfseɪm] *adj* stesso(a).

self-satisfied [sɛlf'sætɪsfaɪd] *adj* compiaciuto(a) di sé.

self-sealing [sɛlf'siːlɪŋ] *adj* autosigillante.

self-service [sɛlf'səːvɪs] *n* autoservizio, self-service *m*.

self-styled [sɛlf'staɪld] *adj* sedicente.

self-sufficient [sɛlfsə'fɪʃənt] *adj* autosufficiente.

self-supporting [sɛlfsə'pɔːtɪŋ] *adj* economicamente indipendente.

self-taught [sɛlf'tɔːt] *adj* autodidatta.

self-test ['sɛlftɛst] *n* (*COMPUT*) autoverifica.

sell, *pt*, *pp* **sold** [sɛl, səuld] *vt* vendere ♦ *vi* vendersi; **to** ~ **at** *or* **for 1000 lire** essere in vendita a 1000 lire; **to** ~ **sb an idea** (*fig*) far accettare un'idea a qn.

▶**sell off** *vt* svendere, liquidare.

▶**sell out** *vt* vendere (tutto) (a qn/qc) ♦ *vt* esaurire; **the tickets are all sold out** i biglietti sono esauriti.

▶**sell up** *vi* vendere (tutto).

sell-by date ['sɛlbaɪ-] *n* scadenza.

seller ['sɛlə*] *n* venditore/trice; ~**'s market** mercato favorevole ai venditori.

selling price ['sɛlɪŋ-] *n* prezzo di vendita.

Sellotape ® ['sɛləuteɪp] *n* (*BRIT*) nastro adesivo, scotch ® *m*.

sellout ['sɛlaut] *n* (*betrayal*) tradimento; (*of tickets*): **it was a** ~ registrò un tutto esaurito.

selves [sɛlvz] *npl of* **self**.

semantic [sɪ'mæntɪk] *adj* semantico(a).

semantics [sɪ'mæntɪks] *n* semantica.

semaphore ['sɛməfɔː*] *n* segnali *mpl* con bandiere; (*RAIL*) semaforo.

semblance ['sɛmbləns] *n* parvenza, apparenza.

semen ['siːmən] *n* sperma *m*.

semester [sɪ'mɛstə*] *n* (*US*) semestre *m*.

semi... ['sɛmɪ] *prefix* semi... ♦ *n*: **semi** = **semidetached (house)**.

semi-breve ['sɛmɪbriːv] *n* (*BRIT*) semibreve *f*.

semicircle ['sɛmɪsəːkl] *n* semicerchio.

semicircular ['sɛmɪ'səːkjulə*] *adj* semicircolare.

semicolon [sɛmɪ'kəulən] *n* punto e virgola.

semiconductor [sɛmɪkən'dʌktə*] *n* semiconduttore *m*.

semiconscious [sɛmɪ'kɔnʃəs] *adj* parzialmente cosciente.

semidetached (house) [sɛmɪdɪ'tætʃt-] *n* (*BRIT*) casa gemella.

semifinal [sɛmɪ'faɪnl] *n* semifinale *f*.

seminar ['sɛmɪnɑː*] *n* seminario.

seminary ['sɛmɪnərɪ] *n* (*REL: for priests*) seminario.

semiprecious [sɛmɪ'prɛʃəs] *adj* semiprezioso(a).

semiquaver ['sɛmɪkweɪvə*] *n* (*BRIT*) semicroma.

semiskilled ['sɛmɪ'skɪld] *adj*: ~ **worker** operaio(a) non specializzato(a).

semi-skimmed ['sɛmɪ'skɪmd] *adj* parzialmente scremato(a).

semitone ['sɛmɪtəun] *n* (*MUS*) semitono.

semolina [sɛmə'liːnə] *n* semolino.

SEN *n abbr* (*BRIT*: = *State Enrolled Nurse*) *infermiera diplomata (dopo corso* *biennale*).

Sen., sen. *abbr* = **senator; senior.**

senate ['sɛnɪt] *n* senato.

senator ['sɛnɪtə*] *n* senatore/trice.

send [sɛnd], *pt, pp* **sent** *vt* mandare; **to ~ by post** *or* (*US*) **mail** spedire per posta; **to ~ sb for sth** mandare qn a prendere qc; **to ~ word that ...** mandare a dire che ...; **she ~s (you) her love** ti saluta affettuosamente; **to ~ sb to Coventry** (*BRIT*) dare l'ostracismo a qn; **to ~ sb to sleep/into fits of laughter** far addormentare/scoppiare dal ridere qn; **to ~ sth flying** far volare via qc.

▶**send away** *vt* (*letter, goods*) spedire; (*person*) mandare via.

▶**send away for** *vt fus* richiedere per posta, farsi spedire.

▶**send back** *vt* rimandare.

▶**send for** *vt fus* mandare a chiamare, far venire; (*by post*) ordinare per posta.

▶**send in** *vt* (*report, application, resignation*) presentare.

▶**send off** *vt* (*goods*) spedire; (*BRIT SPORT*: *player*) espellere.

▶**send on** *vt* (*BRIT*: *letter*) inoltrare; (*luggage etc*: *in advance*) spedire in anticipo.

▶**send out** *vt* (*invitation*) diramare; (*emit*: *light, heat*) mandare, emanare; (: *signals*) emettere.

▶**send round** *vt* (*letter, document etc*) far circolare.

▶**send up** *vt* (*person, price*) far salire; (*BRIT*: *parody*) mettere in ridicolo.

sender ['sɛndə*] *n* mittente *m/f.*

send-off ['sɛndɔf] *n*: **to give sb a good ~** festeggiare la partenza di qn.

Senegal [sɛnɪ'ɡɔːl] *n* Senegal *m.*

Senegalese [sɛnɪɡə'liːz] *adj, n* senegalese (*m/f*).

senile ['siːnaɪl] *adj* senile.

senility [sɪ'nɪlɪtɪ] *n* senilità *f.*

senior ['siːnɪə*] *adj* (*older*) più vecchio(a); (*of higher rank*) di grado più elevato ♦ *n* persona più anziana; (*in service*) persona con maggiore anzianità; **P. Jones ~ P.** Jones senior, P. Jones padre.

senior citizen *n* anziano/a.

senior high school *n* (*US*) ≈ liceo.

seniority [siːnɪ'ɔrɪtɪ] *n* anzianità; (*in rank*) superiorità.

sensation [sɛn'seɪʃən] *n* sensazione *f*; **to create a ~** fare scalpore.

sensational [sɛn'seɪʃənl] *adj* sensazionale; (*marvellous*) eccezionale.

sense [sɛns] *n* senso; (*feeling*) sensazione *f*, senso; (*meaning*) senso, significato; (*wisdom*) buonsenso ♦ *vt* sentire,

percepire; ~**s** *npl* (*sanity*) ragione *f*; **it makes ~** ha senso; **there is no ~ in (doing) that** non ha senso (farlo); ~ **of humour** (senso dell')umorismo; **to come to one's ~s** (*regain consciousness*) riprendere i sensi; (*become reasonable*) tornare in sé; **to take leave of one's ~s** perdere il lume *or* l'uso della ragione.

senseless ['sɛnslɪs] *adj* sciocco(a); (*unconscious*) privo(a) di sensi.

sensibilities [sɛnsɪ'bɪlɪtɪz] *npl* sensibilità *fsg.*

sensible ['sɛnsɪbl] *adj* sensato(a), ragionevole.

sensitive ['sɛnsɪtɪv] *adj*: ~ (**to**) sensibile (a); **he is very ~ about it** è un tasto che è meglio non toccare con lui.

sensitivity [sɛnsɪ'tɪvɪtɪ] *n* sensibilità.

sensual ['sɛnsjuəl] *adj* sensuale.

sensuous ['sɛnsjuəs] *adj* sensuale.

sent [sɛnt] *pt, pp of* **send.**

sentence ['sɛntns] *n* (*LING*) frase *f*; (*LAW*: *judgement*) sentenza; (: *punishment*) condanna ♦ *vt*: **to ~ sb to death/to 5 years** condannare qn a morte/a 5 anni; **to pass ~ on sb** condannare qn.

sentiment ['sɛntɪmənt] *n* sentimento; (*opinion*) opinione *f.*

sentimental [sɛntɪ'mɛntl] *adj* sentimentale.

sentimentality [sɛntɪmɛn'tælɪtɪ] *n* sentimentalità, sentimentalismo.

sentry ['sɛntrɪ] *n* sentinella.

sentry duty *n*: **to be on ~** essere di sentinella.

Seoul [səul] *n* Seul *f.*

separable ['sɛprəbl] *adj* separabile.

separate *adj* ['sɛprɪt] separato(a) ♦ *vb* ['sɛpəreɪt] *vt* separare ♦ *vi* separarsi; ~ **from** separato da; **under ~ cover** (*COMM*) in plico a parte; **to ~ into** dividere in; *see also* **separates.**

separately ['sɛprɪtlɪ] *adv* separatamente.

separates ['sɛprɪts] *npl* (*clothes*) coordinati *mpl.*

separation [sɛpə'reɪʃən] *n* separazione *f.*

Sept. *abbr* (= *September*) sett., set.

September [sɛp'tɛmbə*] *n* settembre *m*; *for phrases see also* **July.**

septic ['sɛptɪk] *adj* settico(a); (*wound*) infettato(a); **to go ~** infettarsi.

septicaemia, (*US*) **septicemia** [sɛptɪ'siːmɪə] *n* setticemia.

septic tank *n* fossa settica.

sequel ['siːkwl] *n* conseguenza; (*of story*) seguito.

sequence ['siːkwəns] *n* (*series*) serie *f inv*; (*order*) ordine *m*; **in ~** in ordine, di seguito; ~ **of tenses** concordanza dei tempi.

sequential [sɪ'kwɛnʃəl] *adj*: ~ **access** (*COMPUT*) accesso sequenziale.

sequin ['siːkwɪn] *n* lustrino, paillette *f inv*.

Serb [səːb] *adj, n* = **Serbian**.

Serbia ['səːbɪə] *n* Serbia.

Serbian ['səːbɪən] *adj* serbo(a) ♦ *n* serbo/a; (*LING*) serbo.

Serbo-Croat ['səːbəu'krəuæt] *n* (*LING*) serbocroato.

serenade [sɛrə'neɪd] *n* serenata ♦ *vt* fare la serenata a.

serene [sɪ'riːn] *adj* sereno(a), calmo(a).

serenity [sɪ'rɛnɪtɪ] *n* serenità, tranquillità.

sergeant ['sɑːdʒənt] *n* sergente *m*; (*POLICE*) brigadiere *m*.

sergeant major *n* maresciallo.

serial ['sɪərɪəl] *n* (*PRESS*) romanzo a puntate; (*RADIO, TV*) trasmissione *f* a puntate ♦ *cpd* (*number*) di serie; (*COMPUT*) seriale.

serialize ['sɪərɪəlaɪz] *vt* pubblicare a puntate; trasmettere a puntate.

serial killer *n* serial killer *m inv*.

serial number *n* numero di serie.

series ['sɪəriːz] *n* (*pl inv*) serie *f inv*; (*PUBLISHING*) collana.

serious ['sɪərɪəs] *adj* serio(a), grave; **are you ~ (about it)?** parla sul serio?

seriously ['sɪərɪəslɪ] *adv* seriamente; **he's ~ rich** (*col: extremely*) ha un casino di soldi; **to take sth/sb ~** prendere qc/qn sul serio.

seriousness ['sɪərɪəsnɪs] *n* serietà, gravità.

sermon ['səːmən] *n* sermone *m*.

serrated [sɪ'reɪtɪd] *adj* seghettato(a).

serum ['sɪərəm] *n* siero.

servant ['səːvənt] *n* domestico/a.

serve [səːv] *vt* (*employer etc*) servire, essere a servizio di; (*purpose*) servire a; (*customer, food, meal*) servire; (*apprenticeship*) fare; (*prison term*) scontare ♦ *vi* (*also TENNIS*) servire; (*soldier etc*) prestare servizio; (*be useful*): **to ~ as/for/to do** servire da/per/per fare ♦ *n* (*TENNIS*) servizio; **are you being ~d?** la stanno servendo?; **to ~ on a committee/jury** far parte di un comitato/una giuria; **it ~s him right** ben gli sta, se l'è meritata; **it ~s my purpose** fa al caso mio, serve al mio scopo.

▶**serve out, serve up** *vt* (*food*) servire.

service ['səːvɪs] *n* servizio; (*AUT: maintenance*) revisione *f*; (*REL*) funzione *f* ♦ *vt* (*car, washing machine*) revisionare; **the S~s** *npl* le forze armate; **to be of ~ to sb, to do sb a ~** essere d'aiuto a qn; **to put one's car in for (a) ~** portare la

macchina in officina per una revisione; **dinner ~** servizio da tavola.

serviceable ['səːvɪsəbl] *adj* pratico(a), utile; (*usable, working*) usabile.

service area *n* (*on motorway*) area di servizio.

service charge *n* (*BRIT*) servizio.

service industries *npl* settore *m* terziario.

serviceman ['səːvɪsmən] *n* militare *m*.

service station *n* stazione *f* di servizio.

serviette [səːvɪ'ɛt] *n* (*BRIT*) tovagliolo.

servile ['səːvaɪl] *adj* servile.

session ['sɛʃən] *n* (*sitting*) seduta, sessione *f*; (*SCOL*) anno scolastico (*or* accademico); **to be in ~** essere in seduta.

session musician *n* musicista *m/f* di studio.

set [sɛt] *n* serie *f inv*; (*RADIO, TV*) apparecchio; (*TENNIS*) set *m inv*; (*group of people*) mondo, ambiente *m*; (*CINE*) scenario; (*THEAT: stage*) scene *fpl*; (*: scenery*) scenario; (*MATH*) insieme *m*; (*HAIRDRESSING*) messa in piega ♦ *adj* (*fixed*) stabilito(a), determinato(a); (*ready*) pronto(a) ♦ *vb* (*pt, pp* **set**) (*place*) posare, mettere; (*fix*) fissare; (*assign: task, homework*) dare, assegnare; (*adjust*) regolare; (*decide: rules etc*) stabilire, fissare; (*TYP*) comporre ♦ *vi* (*sun*) tramontare; (*jam, jelly*) rapprendersi; (*concrete*) fare presa; **to be ~ on doing** essere deciso a fare; **to be all ~ to do sth** essere pronto fare qc; **to be (dead) ~ against** essere completamente contrario a; **~ in one's ways** abitudinario; **a novel ~ in Rome** un romanzo ambientato a Roma; **to ~ to music** mettere in musica; **to ~ on fire** dare fuoco a; **to ~ free** liberare; **to ~ sth going** mettere in moto qc; **to ~ sail** prendere il mare; **a ~ phrase** una frase fatta; **a ~ of false teeth** una dentiera; **a ~ of dining-room furniture** una camera da pranzo.

▶**set about** *vt fus* (*task*) intraprendere, mettersi a; **to ~ about doing sth** mettersi a fare qc.

▶**set aside** *vt* mettere da parte.

▶**set back** *vt* (*progress*) ritardare; **to ~ back (by)** (*in time*) mettere indietro (di); **a house ~ back from the road** una casa a una certa distanza dalla strada.

▶**set in** *vi* (*infection*) svilupparsi; (*complications*) intervenire; **the rain has ~ in for the day** ormai pioverà tutto il giorno.

▶**set off** *vi* partire ♦ *vt* (*bomb*) far scoppiare; (*cause to start*) mettere in moto; (*show up well*) dare risalto a.

▶**set out** vi partire; (aim): **to ~ out to do** proporsi di fare ♦ vt (arrange) disporre; (state) esporre, presentare.

▶**set up** vt (organization) fondare, costituire; (record) stabilire; (monument) innalzare.

setback ['sɛtbæk] n (hitch) contrattempo, inconveniente m; (in health) ricaduta.

set menu n menù m inv fisso.

set square n squadra.

settee [sɛ'tiː] n divano, sofà m inv.

setting ['sɛtɪŋ] n ambiente m; (scenery) sfondo; (of jewel) montatura.

setting lotion n fissatore m.

settle ['sɛtl] vt (argument, matter) appianare; (problem) risolvere; (pay: bill, account) regolare, saldare; (MED: calm) calmare; (colonize: land) colonizzare ♦ vi (bird, dust etc) posarsi; (sediment) depositarsi; (also: ~ down) sistemarsi, stabilirsi; (become calmer) calmarsi; **to ~ to sth** applicarsi a qc; **to ~ for sth** accontentarsi di qc; **to ~ on sth** decidersi per qc; **that's ~d then** allora è deciso; **to ~ one's stomach** calmare il mal di stomaco.

▶**settle in** vi sistemarsi.

▶**settle up** vi: **to ~ up with sb** regolare i conti con qn.

settlement ['sɛtlmənt] n (payment) pagamento, saldo; (agreement) accordo; (colony) colonia; (village etc) villaggio, comunità f inv; **in ~ of our account** (COMM) a saldo del nostro conto.

settler ['sɛtlə*] n colonizzatore/trice.

setup ['sɛtʌp] n (arrangement) sistemazione f; (situation) situazione f.

seven ['sɛvn] num sette.

seventeen [sɛvn'tiːn] num diciassette.

seventh ['sɛvnθ] num settimo(a).

seventy ['sɛvntɪ] num settanta.

sever ['sɛvə*] vt recidere, tagliare; (relations) troncare.

several ['sɛvərl] adj, pron alcuni(e), diversi(e); **~ of us** alcuni di noi; **~ times** diverse volte.

severance ['sɛvərəns] n (of relations) rottura.

severance pay n indennità di licenziamento.

severe [sɪ'vɪə*] adj severo(a); (serious) serio(a), grave; (hard) duro(a); (plain) semplice, sobrio(a).

severely [sɪ'vɪəlɪ] adv (gen) severamente; (wounded, ill) gravemente.

severity [sɪ'vɛrɪtɪ] n severità; gravità; (of weather) rigore m.

sew, pt **sewed**, pp **sewn** [səu, səud, səun] vt,

vi cucire.

▶**sew up** vt ricucire; **it is all sewn up** (fig) è tutto apposto.

sewage ['suːɪdʒ] n acque fpl di scolo.

sewage works n stabilimento per la depurazione dei liquami.

sewer ['suːə*] n fogna.

sewing ['səuɪŋ] n cucito.

sewing machine n macchina da cucire.

sewn [səun] pp of **sew**.

sex [sɛks] n sesso; **to have ~ with** avere rapporti sessuali con.

sex act n atto sessuale.

sex appeal n sex appeal m inv.

sex education n educazione f sessuale.

sexism ['sɛksɪzəm] n sessismo.

sexist ['sɛksɪst] adj sessista.

sex life n vita sessuale.

sex object n oggetto sessuale; **to be treated like a ~** (woman) essere trattata da donna oggetto.

sextet [sɛks'tɛt] n sestetto.

sexual ['sɛksjuəl] adj sessuale; **~ assault** violenza carnale; **~ harassment** molestie fpl sessuali; **~ intercourse** rapporti mpl sessuali.

sexy ['sɛksɪ] adj provocante, sexy inv.

Seychelles [seɪ'ʃɛlz] npl: **the ~** le Seicelle.

SF n abbr = **science fiction**.

SG n abbr (US) = **Surgeon General**.

Sgt. abbr (= sergeant) serg.

shabbiness ['ʃæbɪnɪs] n trasandatezza; squallore m; meschinità.

shabby ['ʃæbɪ] adj trasandato(a); (building) squallido(a), malandato(a); (behaviour) meschino(a).

shack [ʃæk] n baracca, capanna.

shackles ['ʃæklz] npl ferri mpl, catene fpl.

shade [ʃeɪd] n ombra; (for lamp) paralume m; (of colour) tonalità f inv; (US: window ~) veneziana; (small quantity): **a ~ of** un po' or un'ombra di ♦ vt ombreggiare, fare ombra a; **~s** npl (US: sunglasses) occhiali mpl da sole; **in the ~** all'ombra; **a ~ smaller** un tantino più piccolo.

shadow ['ʃædəu] n ombra ♦ vt (follow) pedinare; **without** or **beyond a ~ of doubt** senz'ombra di dubbio.

shadow cabinet n (BRIT POL) governo m ombra inv.

shadowy ['ʃædəuɪ] adj ombreggiato(a), ombroso(a); (dim) vago(a), indistinto(a).

shady ['ʃeɪdɪ] adj ombroso(a); (fig: dishonest) losco(a), equivoco(a).

shaft [ʃɑːft] n (of arrow, spear) asta; (AUT, TECH) albero; (of mine) pozzo; (of lift) tromba; (of light) raggio; **ventilator ~** condotto di ventilazione.

shaggy ['ʃægɪ] *adj* ispido(a).

shake [ʃeɪk] *vb* (*pt* **shook**, *pp* **shaken** [ʃuk, 'ʃeɪkn]) *vt* scuotere; (*bottle, cocktail*) agitare ♦ *vi* tremare ♦ *n* scossa; **to ~ one's head** scuotere la testa; **to ~ hands with** sb stringere *or* dare la mano a qn.

▶**shake off** *vt* scrollare (via); (*fig*) sbarazzarsi di.

▶**shake up** *vt* scuotere.

shake-up ['ʃeɪkʌp] *n* riorganizzazione *f* drastica.

shakily ['ʃeɪkɪlɪ] *adv* (*reply*) con voce tremante; (*walk*) con passo malfermo; (*write*) con mano tremante.

shaky ['ʃeɪkɪ] *adj* (*hand, voice*) tremante; (*memory*) labile; (*knowledge*) incerto(a); (*building*) traballante.

shale [ʃeɪl] *n* roccia scistosa.

shall [ʃæl] *aux vb*: **I ~ go** andrò.

shallot [ʃə'lɔt] *n* (*BRIT*) scalogna.

shallow ['ʃæləʊ] *adj* poco profondo(a); (*fig*) superficiale.

sham [ʃæm] *n* finzione *f*, messinscena; (*jewellery, furniture*) imitazione *f* ♦ *adj* finto(a) ♦ *vt* fingere, simulare.

shambles ['ʃæmblz] *n* confusione *f*, baraonda, scompiglio; **the economy is (in) a complete ~** l'economia è nel caos più totale.

shambolic [ʃæm'bɔlɪk] *adj* (*col*) incasinato(a).

shame [ʃeɪm] *n* vergogna ♦ *vt* far vergognare; **it is a ~ (that/to do)** è un peccato (che + *sub*/fare); **what a ~!** che peccato!; **to put sb/sth to ~** (*fig*) far sfigurare qn/qc.

shamefaced ['ʃeɪmfeɪst] *adj* vergognoso(a).

shameful ['ʃeɪmful] *adj* vergognoso(a).

shameless ['ʃeɪmlɪs] *adj* sfrontato(a); (*immodest*) spudorato(a).

shampoo [ʃæm'pu:] *n* shampoo *m inv* ♦ *vt* fare lo shampoo a; **~ and set** shampoo e messa in piega.

shamrock ['ʃæmrɔk] *n* trifoglio (*simbolo nazionale dell'Irlanda*).

shandy ['ʃændɪ] *n* birra con gassosa.

shan't [ʃɑ:nt] = **shall not**.

shanty town ['ʃæntɪ-] *n* bidonville *f inv.*

SHAPE [ʃeɪp] *n abbr* (= *Supreme Headquarters Allied Powers, Europe*) supremo quartier generale delle Potenze Alleate in Europa.

shape [ʃeɪp] *n* forma ♦ *vt* (*clay, stone*) dar forma a; (*fig: ideas, character*) formare; (: *course of events*) determinare; (*statement*) formulare; (*sb's ideas*) condizionare ♦ *vi* (*also: ~ up*: *events*) andare, mettersi; (: *person*)

cavarsela; **to take ~** prendere forma; **in the ~ of a heart** a forma di cuore; **to get o.s. into ~** rimettersi in forma; **I can't bear gardening in any ~ or form** detesto il giardinaggio d'ogni genere e specie.

-shaped [ʃeɪpt] *suffix*: **heart-~** a forma di cuore.

shapeless ['ʃeɪplɪs] *adj* senza forma, informe.

shapely ['ʃeɪplɪ] *adj* ben proporzionato(a).

share [ʃɛə*] *n* (*thing received, contribution*) parte *f*; (*COMM*) azione *f* ♦ *vt* dividere; (*have in common*) condividere, avere in comune; **to ~ out (among or between)** dividere (tra); **to ~ in** partecipare a.

share capital *n* capitale *m* azionario.

share certificate *n* certificato azionario.

shareholder ['ʃɛəhəuldə*] *n* azionista *m/f.*

share index *n* listino di Borsa.

shark [ʃɑ:k] *n* squalo, pescecane *m.*

sharp [ʃɑ:p] *adj* (*razor, knife*) affilato(a); (*point*) acuto(a), acuminato(a); (*nose, chin*) aguzzo(a); (*outline*) netto(a); (*curve, bend*) stretto(a), accentuato(a); (*cold, pain*) pungente; (*voice*) stridulo(a); (*person: quick-witted*) sveglio(a); (: *unscrupulous*) disonesto(a); (*MUS*): **C ~ do diesis** ♦ *n* (*MUS*) diesis *m inv* ♦ *adv*: **at 2 o'clock ~** alle due in punto; **turn ~ left** giri tutto a sinistra; **to be ~ with sb** rimproverare qn; **look ~!** sbrigati!

sharpen ['ʃɑ:pən] *vt* affilare; (*pencil*) fare la punta a; (*fig*) aguzzare.

sharpener ['ʃɑ:pnə*] *n* (*also*: **pencil ~**) temperamatite *m inv*; (*also*: **knife ~**) affilacoltelli *m inv.*

sharp-eyed [ʃɑ:p'aɪd] *adj* dalla vista acuta.

sharpish ['ʃɑ:pɪʃ] *adv* (*BRIT col*: *quickly*) subito.

sharply ['ʃɑ:plɪ] *adv* (*abruptly*) bruscamente; (*clearly*) nettamente; (*harshly*) duramente, aspramente.

sharp-tempered [ʃɑ:p'tempəd] *adj* irascibile.

shatter ['ʃætə*] *vt* mandare in frantumi, frantumare; (*fig: upset*) distruggere; (: *ruin*) rovinare ♦ *vi* frantumarsi, andare in pezzi.

shattered ['ʃætəd] *adj* (*grief-stricken*) sconvolto(a); (*exhausted*) a pezzi, distrutto(a).

shatterproof ['ʃætəpru:f] *adj* infrangibile.

shave [ʃeɪv] *vt* radere, rasare ♦ *vi* radersi, farsi la barba ♦ *n*: **to have a ~** farsi la barba.

shaven ['ʃeɪvn] *adj* (*head*) rasato(a), tonsurato(a).

shaver ['ʃeɪvə*] *n* (*also*: **electric ~**) rasoio

elettrico.

shaving ['ʃeɪvɪŋ] n (action) rasatura; ~s npl (of wood etc) trucioli mpl.

shaving brush n pennello da barba.

shaving cream n crema da barba.

shaving soap n sapone m da barba.

shawl [ʃɔːl] n scialle m.

she [ʃiː] pron ella, lei; **there** ~ **is** eccola; ~-**bear** orsa; ~-**elephant** elefantessa; NB: for ships, countries follow the gender of your translation.

sheaf, pl **sheaves** [ʃiːf, ʃiːvz] n covone m.

shear [ʃɪə*] vt (pt ~**ed,** pp ~**ed** or **shorn** [ʃɔːn]) (sheep) tosare.

▶**shear off** vi (break off) spezzarsi.

shears ['ʃɪəz] npl (for hedge) cesoie fpl.

sheath [ʃiːθ] n fodero, guaina; (contraceptive) preservativo.

sheathe [ʃiːð] vt rivestire; (sword) rinfoderare.

sheath knife n coltello (con fodero).

sheaves [ʃiːvz] npl of **sheaf.**

shed [ʃɛd] n capannone m ♦ vt (pt, pp **shed**) (leaves, fur etc) perdere; (tears) versare; **to** ~ **light on** (problem, mystery) far luce su.

she'd [ʃiːd] = she had; she would.

sheen [ʃiːn] n lucentezza.

sheep [ʃiːp] n (pl inv) pecora.

sheepdog ['ʃiːpdɔg] n cane m da pastore.

sheep farmer n allevatore m di pecore.

sheepish ['ʃiːpɪʃ] adj vergognoso(a), timido(a).

sheepskin ['ʃiːpskɪn] n pelle f di pecora.

sheepskin jacket n (giacca di) montone m.

sheer [ʃɪə*] adj (utter) vero(a) (e proprio(a)); (steep) a picco, perpendicolare; (transparent) trasparente ♦ adv a picco; **by** ~ **chance** per puro caso.

sheet [ʃiːt] n (on bed) lenzuolo; (of paper) foglio; (of glass) lastra; (of metal) foglio, lamina.

sheet feed n (on printer) alimentazione f di fogli.

sheet lightning n lampo diffuso.

sheet metal n lamiera.

sheet music n fogli mpl di musica.

sheik(h) [ʃeɪk] n sceicco.

shelf, pl **shelves** [ʃɛlf, ʃɛlvz] n scaffale m, mensola.

shelf life n (COMM) durata di conservazione.

shell [ʃɛl] n (on beach) conchiglia; (of egg, nut etc) guscio; (explosive) granata; (of building) scheletro, struttura ♦ vt (peas) sgranare; (MIL) bombardare, cannoneggiare.

▶**shell out** vi (col): **to** ~ **out (for)** sganciare

soldi (per).

she'll [ʃiːl] = she will; she shall.

shellfish ['ʃɛlfɪʃ] n (pl inv) (crab etc) crostaceo; (scallop etc) mollusco; (pl: as food) crostacei; molluschi.

shellsuit ['ʃɛlsuːt] n tuta di acetato.

shelter ['ʃɛltə*] n riparo, rifugio ♦ vt riparare, proteggere; (give lodging to) dare rifugio or asilo a ♦ vi ripararsi, mettersi al riparo; **to take** ~ **(from)** mettersi al riparo (da).

sheltered ['ʃɛltəd] adj (life) ritirato(a); (spot) riparato(a), protetto(a).

shelve [ʃɛlv] vt (fig) accantonare, rimandare.

shelves [ʃɛlvz] npl of **shelf.**

shelving ['ʃɛlvɪŋ] n scaffalature fpl.

shepherd ['ʃɛpəd] n pastore m ♦ vt (guide) guidare.

shepherdess ['ʃɛpədɪs] n pastora.

shepherd's pie n timballo di carne macinata e purè di patate.

sherbet ['ʃəːbət] n (BRIT: powder) polvere effervescente al gusto di frutta; (US: water ice) sorbetto.

sheriff ['ʃɛrɪf] n sceriffo.

sherry ['ʃɛrɪ] n sherry m inv.

she's [ʃiːz] = she is; she has.

Shetland ['ʃɛtlənd] n (also: **the** ~**s, the** ~ **Isles**) le (isole) Shetland.

Shetland pony n pony m inv delle Shetland.

shield [ʃiːld] n scudo ♦ vt: **to** ~ **(from)** riparare (da), proteggere (da or contro).

shift [ʃɪft] n (change) cambiamento; (of workers) turno ♦ vt spostare, muovere; (remove) rimuovere ♦ vi spostarsi, muoversi; **in demand** (COMM) variazione f della domanda; **the wind has** ~**ed to the south** il vento si è girato e soffia da sud.

shift key n (on typewriter) tasto delle maiuscole.

shiftless ['ʃɪftlɪs] adj fannullone(a).

shift work n lavoro a squadre; **to do** ~ fare i turni.

shifty ['ʃɪftɪ] adj ambiguo(a); (eyes) sfuggente.

Shiite ['ʃiːaɪt] adj, n sciita (m/f).

shilling ['ʃɪlɪŋ] n (BRIT) scellino (= 12 old pence; 20 in a pound).

shilly-shally ['ʃɪlɪʃælɪ] vi tentennare, esitare.

shimmer ['ʃɪmə*] vi brillare, luccicare.

shimmering ['ʃɪmərɪŋ] adj (gen) luccicante, scintillante; (haze) tremolante; (satin etc) cangiante.

shin [ʃɪn] n tibia ♦ vi: **to** ~ **up/down a tree**

arrampicarsi in cima a/scivolare giù da un albero.

shindig ['ʃɪndɪg] *n* (*col*) festa chiassosa.

shine [ʃaɪn] *n* splendore *m*, lucentezza ♦ *vb* (*pt, pp* **shone** [ʃɔn]) *vi* (ri)splendere, brillare ♦ *vt* far brillare, far risplendere; (*torch*): **to ~ sth on** puntare qc verso.

shingle ['ʃɪŋgl] *n* (*on beach*) ciottoli *mpl*; (*on roof*) assicella di copertura.

shingles ['ʃɪŋglz] *n* (*MED*) herpes zoster *m*.

shining ['ʃaɪnɪŋ] *adj* (*surface, hair*) lucente; (*light*) brillante.

shiny ['ʃaɪnɪ] *adj* lucente, lucido(a).

ship [ʃɪp] *n* nave *f* ♦ *vt* trasportare (via mare); (*send*) spedire (via mare); (*load*) imbarcare, caricare; **on board ~ a bordo**.

shipbuilder ['ʃɪpbɪldə*] *n* costruttore *m* navale.

shipbuilding ['ʃɪpbɪldɪŋ] *n* costruzione *f* navale.

ship chandler [-'tʃɑːndlə*] *n* fornitore *m* marittimo.

shipment ['ʃɪpmənt] *n* carico.

shipowner ['ʃɪpəʊnə*] *n* armatore *m*.

shipper ['ʃɪpə*] *n* spedizioniere *m* (marittimo).

shipping ['ʃɪpɪŋ] *n* (*ships*) naviglio; (*traffic*) navigazione *f*.

shipping agent *n* agente *m* marittimo.

shipping company *n* compagnia di navigazione.

shipping lane *n* rotta (di navigazione).

shipping line *n* = **shipping company**.

shipshape ['ʃɪpʃeɪp] *adj* in perfetto ordine.

shipwreck ['ʃɪprɛk] *n* relitto; (*event*) naufragio ♦ *vt*: **to be ~ed** naufragare, fare naufragio.

shipyard ['ʃɪpjɑːd] *n* cantiere *m* navale.

shire ['ʃaɪə*] *n* (*BRIT*) contea.

shirk [ʃəːk] *vt* sottrarsi a, evitare.

shirt [ʃəːt] *n* (*man's*) camicia; **in ~ sleeves** in maniche di camicia.

shirty ['ʃəːtɪ] *adj* (*BRIT col*) incavolato(a).

shit [ʃɪt] *excl* (*col!*) merda(*!*).

shiver ['ʃɪvə*] *n* brivido ♦ *vi* rabbrividire, tremare.

shoal [ʃəʊl] *n* (*of fish*) banco.

shock [ʃɔk] *n* (*impact*) urto, colpo; (*ELEC*) scossa; (*emotional*) colpo, shock *m inv*; (*MED*) shock ♦ *vt* colpire, scioccare; scandalizzare; **to give sb a ~** far venire un colpo a qn; **to be suffering from ~** essere in stato di shock; **it came as a ~ to hear that ...** è stata una grossa sorpresa sentire che ....

shock absorber *n* ammortizzatore *m*.

shocker ['ʃɔkə*] *n*: **it was a real ~** (*col*) è stata una vera bomba.

shocking ['ʃɔkɪŋ] *adj* scioccante, traumatizzante; (*scandalous*) scandaloso(a); (*very bad: weather, handwriting*) orribile; (: *results*) disastroso(a).

shockproof ['ʃɔkpruːf] *adj* antiurto *inv*.

shock therapy, shock treatment *n* (*MED*) shockterapia.

shock wave *n* onda d'urto; (*fig: usually pl*) impatto *msg*.

shod [ʃɔd] *pt, pp of* **shoe**.

shoddy ['ʃɔdɪ] *adj* scadente.

shoe [ʃuː] *n* scarpa; (*also:* **horse~**) ferro di cavallo; (*brake ~*) ganascia (del freno) ♦ *vt* (*pt, pp* **shod** [ʃɔd]) (*horse*) ferrare.

shoebrush ['ʃuːbrʌʃ] *n* spazzola per le scarpe.

shoehorn ['ʃuːhɔːn] *n* calzante *m*.

shoelace ['ʃuːleɪs] *n* stringa.

shoemaker ['ʃuːmeɪkə*] *n* calzolaio.

shoe polish *n* lucido per scarpe.

shoeshop ['ʃuːʃɔp] *n* calzoleria.

shoestring ['ʃuːstrɪŋ] *n* stringa (delle scarpe); **on a ~** (*fig: do sth*) con quattro soldi.

shoetree ['ʃuːtriː] *n* forma per scarpe.

shone [ʃɔn] *pt, pp of* **shine**.

shoo [ʃuː] *excl* sciò!, via! ♦ *vt* (*also:* **~ away, ~ off**) cacciare (via).

shook [ʃuk] *pt of* **shake**.

shoot [ʃuːt] *n* (*on branch, seedling*) germoglio; (*shooting party*) partita di caccia; (*competition*) gara di tiro ♦ *vb* (*pt, pp* **shot** [ʃɔt]) *vt* (*game: BRIT*) cacciare, andare a caccia di; (*person*) sparare a; (*execute*) fucilare; (*film*) girare ♦ *vi* (*with gun*): **to ~** (**at**) sparare (a), fare fuoco (su); (*with bow*): **to ~** (**at**) tirare (su); (*FOOTBALL*) sparare, tirare (forte); **to ~ past sb** passare vicino a qn come un fulmine; **to ~ in/out** entrare/uscire come una freccia.

▶**shoot down** *vt* (*plane*) abbattere.

▶**shoot up** *vi* (*fig*) salire alle stelle.

shooting ['ʃuːtɪŋ] *n* (*shots*) sparatoria; (*murder*) uccisione *f* (a colpi d'arma da fuoco); (*HUNTING*) caccia; (*CINE*) riprese *fpl*.

shooting range *n* poligono (di tiro), tirassegno.

shooting star *n* stella cadente.

shop [ʃɔp] *n* negozio; (*workshop*) officina ♦ *vi* (*also:* **go ~ping**) fare spese; **repair ~** officina di riparazione; **to talk ~** (*fig*) parlare di lavoro.

▶**shop around** *vi* fare il giro dei negozi.

shopaholic ['ʃɔpə'hɔlɪk] *n* (*col*) maniaco/a dello shopping.

shop assistant n (BRIT) commesso/a.
shop floor n (BRIT: fig) operai mpl, maestranze fpl.
shopkeeper ['ʃɔpkiːpə*] n negoziante m/f, bottegaio/a.
shoplift ['ʃɔplɪft] vi taccheggiare.
shoplifter ['ʃɔplɪftə*] n taccheggiatore/trice.
shoplifting ['ʃɔplɪftɪŋ] n taccheggio.
shopper ['ʃɔpə*] n compratore/trice.
shopping ['ʃɔpɪŋ] n (goods) spesa, acquisti mpl.
shopping bag n borsa per la spesa.
shopping centre n centro commerciale.
shop-soiled ['ʃɔpsɔɪld] adj sciupato(a) a forza di stare in vetrina.
shop steward n (BRIT INDUSTRY) rappresentante m sindacale.
shop window n vetrina.
shore [ʃɔː*] n (of sea) riva, spiaggia; (of lake) riva ♦ vt: **to ~ (up)** puntellare; **on ~** a terra.
shore leave n (NAUT) franchigia.
shorn [ʃɔːn] pp of **shear**.
short [ʃɔːt] adj (not long) corto(a); (soon finished) breve; (person) basso(a); (curt) brusco(a), secco(a); (insufficient) insufficiente ♦ n (also: ~ **film**) cortometraggio; **it is ~ for** è l'abbreviazione or il diminutivo di; **a ~ time ago** poco tempo fa; **in the ~ term** nell'immediato futuro; **to be ~ of sth** essere a corto di or mancare di qc; **to run ~ of sth** rimanere senza qc; **to be in ~ supply** scarseggiare; **I'm 3 ~** me ne mancano 3; **in ~** in breve; **~ of doing** a meno che non si faccia; **everything ~ of** tutto fuorché; **to cut ~** (speech, visit) accorciare, abbreviare; (person) interrompere; **to fall ~ of** venire meno a; non soddisfare; **to stop ~** fermarsi di colpo; **to stop ~ of** non arrivare fino a; see also **shorts**.
shortage ['ʃɔːtɪdʒ] n scarsezza, carenza.
shortbread ['ʃɔːtbrɛd] n biscotto di pasta frolla.
short-change [ʃɔːt'tʃeɪndʒ] vt: **to ~ sb** imbrogliare qn sul resto.
short-circuit [ʃɔːt'səːkɪt] n cortocircuito ♦ vt cortocircuitare ♦ vi fare cortocircuito.
shortcoming ['ʃɔːtkʌmɪŋ] n difetto.
short(crust) pastry ['ʃɔːt(krʌst)-] n (BRIT) pasta frolla.
shortcut ['ʃɔːtkʌt] n scorciatoia.
shorten ['ʃɔːtn] vt accorciare, ridurre.
shortening ['ʃɔːtnɪŋ] n grasso per pasticceria.
shortfall ['ʃɔːtfɔːl] n deficienza.

shorthand ['ʃɔːthænd] n (BRIT) stenografia; **to take sth down in ~** stenografare qc.
shorthand notebook n (BRIT) bloc-notes m inv per stenografia.
shorthand typist n (BRIT) stenodattilografo/a.
short list n (BRIT: for job) rosa dei candidati.
short-lived ['ʃɔːt'lɪvd] adj effimero(a), di breve durata.
shortly ['ʃɔːtlɪ] adv fra poco.
shortness ['ʃɔːtnɪs] n brevità; insufficienza.
shorts [ʃɔːts] npl (also: **a pair of ~**) i calzoncini.
short-sighted [ʃɔːt'saɪtɪd] adj (BRIT) miope; (fig) poco avveduto(a).
short-staffed [ʃɔːt'stɑːft] adj a corto di personale.
short story n racconto, novella.
short-tempered [ʃɔːt'tɛmpəd] adj irascibile.
short-term ['ʃɔːttəːm] adj (effect) di or a breve durata.
short time n (INDUSTRY): **to work ~, be on ~** essere or lavorare a orario ridotto.
short wave n (RADIO) onde fpl corte.
shot [ʃɔt] pt, pp of **shoot** ♦ n sparo, colpo; (shotgun pellets) pallottole fpl; (person) tiratore m; (try) prova; (injection) iniezione f; (PHOT) foto f inv; **like a ~** come un razzo; (very readily) immediatamente; **to fire a ~ at sb/sth** sparare un colpo a qn/qc; **to have a ~ at sth/doing sth** provarci con qc/a fare qc; **a big ~** (col) un pezzo grosso, un papavero; **to get ~ of sb/sth** (col) sbarazzarsi di qn/qc.
shotgun ['ʃɔtgʌn] n fucile m da caccia.
should [ʃud] aux vb: **I ~ go now** dovrei andare ora; **he ~ be there now** dovrebbe essere arrivato ora; **I ~ go if I were you** se fossi in lei andrei; **I ~ like to** mi piacerebbe; **~ he phone** ... se telefonasse ....
shoulder ['ʃəuldə*] n spalla; (BRIT: of road): **hard ~** corsia d'emergenza ♦ vt (fig) addossarsi, prendere sulle proprie spalle; **to look over one's ~** guardarsi alle spalle; **to rub ~s with sb** (fig) essere a contatto con qn; **to give sb the cold ~** (fig) trattare qn con freddezza.
shoulder bag n borsa a tracolla.
shoulder blade n scapola.
shoulder strap n bretella, spallina.
shouldn't ['ʃudnt] = **should not**.
shout [ʃaut] n urlo, grido ♦ vt gridare ♦ vi urlare, gridare; **to give sb a ~** chiamare qn gridando.
▶**shout down** vt zittire gridando.

shouting ['ʃautɪŋ] *n* urli *mpl*.
shouting match *n* (*col*) vivace scambio di opinioni.
shove [ʃʌv] *vt* spingere; (*col*: *put*): **to ~ sth in** ficcare qc in ♦ *n* spintone *m*; **he ~d me out of the way** mi ha spinto da parte.
▶**shove off** *vi* (*NAUT*) scostarsi.
shovel ['ʃʌvl] *n* pala ♦ *vt* spalare.
show [ʃəu] *n* (*of emotion*) dimostrazione *f*, manifestazione *f*; (*semblance*) apparenza; (*exhibition*) mostra, esposizione *f*; (*THEAT*, *CINE*) spettacolo; (*COMM*, *TECH*) salone *m*, fiera ♦ *vb* (*pt* ~**ed**, *pp* **shown** [ʃəun]) *vt* far vedere, mostrare; (*courage etc*) dimostrare, dar prova di; (*exhibit*) esporre ♦ *vi* vedersi, essere visibile; **to ~ sb to his seat/to the door** accompagnare qn al suo posto/alla porta; **to ~ a profit/ loss** (*COMM*) registrare un utile/una perdita; **it just goes to ~ that** ... il che sta a dimostrare che ...; **to ask for a ~ of hands** chiedere che si voti per alzata di mano; **to be on ~** essere esposto; **it's just for ~** è solo per far scena; **who's running the ~ here?** (*col*) chi è il padrone qui?
▶**show in** *vt* far entrare.
▶**show off** *vi* (*pej*) esibirsi, mettersi in mostra ♦ *vt* (*display*) mettere in risalto; (*pej*) mettere in mostra.
▶**show out** *vt* accompagnare alla porta.
▶**show up** *vi* (*stand out*) essere ben visibile; (*col*: *turn up*) farsi vedere ♦ *vt* mettere in risalto; (*unmask*) smascherare.
showbiz ['ʃəubɪz] *n* (*col*) = **show business**.
show business *n* industria dello spettacolo.
showcase ['ʃəukeɪs] *n* vetrina, bacheca.
showdown ['ʃəudaun] *n* prova di forza.
shower ['ʃauə*] *n* (*also*: ~ **bath**) doccia; (*rain*) acquazzone *m*; (*of stones etc*) pioggia; (*US*: *party*) festa (*di fidanzamento etc*) *in cui si fanno regali alla persona festeggiata* ♦ *vi* fare la doccia ♦ *vt*: **to ~ sb with** (*gifts, abuse etc*) coprire qn di; (*missiles*) lanciare contro qn una pioggia di; **to have** *or* **take a ~** fare la doccia.
shower cap *n* cuffia da doccia.
showerproof ['ʃauəpruːf] *adj* impermeabile.
showery ['ʃauərɪ] *adj* (*weather*) con piogge intermittenti.
showground ['ʃəugraund] *n* terreno d'esposizione.
showing ['ʃəuɪŋ] *n* (*of film*) proiezione *f*.
show jumping *n* concorso ippico (di salto ad ostacoli).

showman ['ʃəumən] *n* (*at fair, circus*) impresario; (*fig*) attore *m*.
showmanship ['ʃəumənʃɪp] *n* abilità d'impresario.
shown [ʃəun] *pp of* **show**.
show-off ['ʃəuɔf] *n* (*col*: *person*) esibizionista *m/f*.
showpiece ['ʃəupiːs] *n* (*of exhibition*) pezzo forte; **that hospital is a ~** è un ospedale modello.
showroom ['ʃəurum] *n* sala d'esposizione.
show trial *n* processo a scopo dimostrativo (*spesso ideologico*).
showy ['ʃəuɪ] *adj* vistoso(a), appariscente.
shrank [ʃræŋk] *pt of* **shrink**.
shrapnel ['ʃræpnl] *n* shrapnel *m*.
shred [ʃrɛd] *n* (*gen pl*) brandello; (*fig*: *of truth, evidence*) briciolo ♦ *vt* fare a brandelli; (*CULIN*) sminuzzare, tagliuzzare; (*documents*) distruggere, sminuzzare.
shredder ['ʃrɛdə*] *n* (*for documents, papers*) distruttore *m* di documenti, sminuzzatrice *f*.
shrew [ʃruː] *n* (*ZOOL*) toporagno; (*fig*: *pej*: *woman*) strega.
shrewd [ʃruːd] *adj* astuto(a), scaltro(a).
shrewdness ['ʃruːdnɪs] *n* astuzia.
shriek [ʃriːk] *n* strillo ♦ *vt*, *vi* strillare.
shrift [ʃrɪft] *n*: **to give sb short ~** sbrigare qn.
shrill [ʃrɪl] *adj* acuto(a), stridulo(a), stridente.
shrimp [ʃrɪmp] *n* gamberetto.
shrine [ʃraɪn] *n* reliquario; (*place*) santuario.
shrink [ʃrɪŋk] *vb* (*pt* **shrank**, *pp* **shrunk** [ʃræŋk, ʃrʌŋk]) *vi* restringersi; (*fig*) ridursi ♦ *vt* (*wool*) far restringere ♦ *n* (*col*: *pej*) psicanalista *m/f*; **to ~ from doing sth** rifuggire dal fare qc.
shrinkage ['ʃrɪŋkɪdʒ] *n* restringimento.
shrink-wrap ['ʃrɪŋkræp] *vt* confezionare con plastica sottile.
shrivel ['ʃrɪvl] (*also*: ~ **up**) *vt* raggrinzare, avvizzire ♦ *vi* raggrinzirsi, avvizzire.
shroud [ʃraud] *n* sudario ♦ *vt*: ~**ed in mystery** avvolto(a) nel mistero.
Shrove Tuesday ['ʃrəuv-] *n* martedì *m* grasso.
shrub [ʃrʌb] *n* arbusto.
shrubbery ['ʃrʌbərɪ] *n* arbusti *mpl*.
shrug [ʃrʌg] *n* scrollata di spalle ♦ *vt*, *vi*: **to ~ (one's shoulders)** alzare le spalle, fare spallucce.
▶**shrug off** *vt* passare sopra a; (*cold, illness*) sbarazzarsi di.
shrunk [ʃrʌŋk] *pp of* **shrink**.

shrunken ['ʃrʌŋkən] *adj* rattrappito(a).
shudder ['ʃʌdə*] *n* brivido ♦ *vi*
rabbrividire.
shuffle ['ʃʌfl] *vt* (*cards*) mescolare; **to ~
(one's feet)** strascicare i piedi.
shun [ʃʌn] *vt* sfuggire, evitare.
shunt [ʃʌnt] *vt* (*RAIL: direct*) smistare; (:
divert) deviare ♦ *vi*: **to ~ (to and fro)** fare
la spola.
shunting yard *n* fascio di smistamento.
shush [ʃuʃ] *excl* zitto(a)!
shut, *pt, pp* **shut** [ʃʌt] *vt* chiudere ♦ *vi*
chiudersi, chiudere.
▶**shut down** *vt, vi* chiudere
definitivamente.
▶**shut off** *vt* (*stop: power*) staccare; (:
water) chiudere; (: *engine*) spegnere;
(*isolate*) isolare.
▶**shut out** *vt* (*person, noise, cold*) non far
entrare; (*block: view*) impedire, bloccare;
(: *memory*) scacciare.
▶**shut up** *vi* (*col: keep quiet*) stare zitto(a) ♦ *vt*
(*close*) chiudere; (*silence*) far tacere.
shutdown ['ʃʌtdaun] *n* chiusura.
shutter ['ʃʌtə*] *n* imposta; (*PHOT*)
otturatore *m*.
shuttle ['ʃʌtl] *n* spola, navetta; (*also: ~
service*) servizio *m* navetta *inv* ♦ *vi* (*subj:
vehicle, person*) fare la spola ♦ *vt* (*to and
fro: passengers*) portare (avanti e
indietro).
shuttlecock ['ʃʌtlkɔk] *n* volano.
shuttle diplomacy *n* frequenti
mediazioni *fpl* diplomatiche.
shy [ʃaɪ] *adj* timido(a) ♦ *vi*: **to ~ away from
doing sth** (*fig*) rifuggire dal fare qc; **to
fight ~ of** tenersi alla larga da; **to be ~ of
doing sth** essere restio a fare qc.
shyness ['ʃaɪnɪs] *n* timidezza.
Siam [saɪ'æm] *n* Siam *m*.
Siamese [saɪə'miːz] *adj*: **~ cat** gatto
siamese; **~ twins** fratelli *mpl* (*or* sorelle
fpl) siamesi.
Siberia [saɪ'bɪərɪə] *n* Siberia.
sibling ['sɪblɪŋ] *n* (*formal*) fratello/sorella.
Sicilian [sɪ'sɪlɪən] *adj, n* siciliano(a).
Sicily ['sɪsɪlɪ] *n* Sicilia.
sick [sɪk] *adj* (*ill*) malato(a); (*vomiting*): **to be
~** vomitare; (*humour*) macabro(a); **to feel
~** avere la nausea; **to be ~ of** (*fig*) averne
abbastanza di; **a ~ person** un malato; **to
be (off) ~** essere assente perché malato;
to fall *or* **take ~** ammalarsi.
sickbag ['sɪkbæg] *n* sacchetto (*da usarsi in
caso di malessere*).
sick bay *n* infermeria.
sick building syndrome *n* *malattia
causata da mancanza di ventilazione e
luce naturale.*

sicken ['sɪkn] *vt* nauseare ♦ *vi*: **to be ~ing
for sth** (*cold, flu etc*) covare qc.
sickening ['sɪknɪŋ] *adj* (*fig*) disgustoso(a),
rivoltante.
sickle ['sɪkl] *n* falcetto.
sick leave *n* congedo per malattia.
sickle-cell anaemia ['sɪklsɛl-] *n* anemia
drepanocitica.
sickly ['sɪklɪ] *adj* malaticcio(a); (*causing
nausea*) nauseante.
sickness ['sɪknɪs] *n* malattia; (*vomiting*)
vomito.
sickness benefit *n* indennità di malattia.
sick pay *n* sussidio per malattia.
sickroom ['sɪkruːm] *n* stanza di malato.
side [saɪd] *n* (*gen*) lato; (*of person, animal*)
fianco; (*of lake*) riva; (*face, surface: gen*)
faccia; (: *of paper*) facciata; (*fig: aspect*)
aspetto, lato; (*team: SPORT*) squadra; (:
POL etc) parte *f* ♦ *cpd* (*door, entrance*)
laterale ♦ *vi*: **to ~ with sb** parteggiare per
qn, prendere le parti di qn; **by the ~ of** a
fianco di; (*road*) sul ciglio di; **~ by ~**
fianco a fianco; **to take ~s (with)**
schierarsi (con); **the right/wrong ~** il
dritto/rovescio; **from ~ to ~** da una parte
all'altra; **~ of beef** quarto di bue.
sideboard ['saɪdbɔːd] *n* credenza.
sideboards ['saɪdbɔːdz] (*BRIT*), **sideburns**
['saɪdbəːnz] *npl* (*whiskers*) basette *fpl*.
sidecar ['saɪdkɑː*] *n* sidecar *m inv*.
side dish *n* contorno.
side drum *n* (*MUS*) piccolo tamburo.
side effect *n* (*MED*) effetto collaterale.
sidekick ['saɪdkɪk] *n* (*col*) compagno/a.
sidelight ['saɪdlaɪt] *n* (*AUT*) luce *f* di
posizione.
sideline ['saɪdlaɪn] *n* (*SPORT*) linea laterale;
(*fig*) attività secondaria.
sidelong ['saɪdlɔŋ] *adj* obliquo(a); **to give a
~ glance at sth** guardare qc con la coda
dell'occhio.
side plate *n* piattino.
side road *n* strada secondaria.
sidesaddle ['saɪdsædl] *adv* all'amazzone.
side show *n* attrazione *f*.
sidestep ['saɪdstɛp] *vt* (*question*) eludere;
(*problem*) scavalcare ♦ *vi* (*BOXING etc*)
spostarsi di lato.
side street *n* traversa.
sidetrack ['saɪdtræk] *vt* (*fig*) distrarre.
sidewalk ['saɪdwɔːk] *n* (*US*) marciapiede *m*.
sideways ['saɪdweɪz] *adv* (*move*) di lato, di
fianco; (*look*) con la coda dell'occhio.
siding ['saɪdɪŋ] *n* (*RAIL*) binario di raccordo.
sidle ['saɪdl] *vi*: **to ~ up (to)** avvicinarsi
furtivamente (a).

SIDS *n* (= *sudden infant death syndrome*) *see* **cot death**.

siege [siːdʒ] *n* assedio; **to lay ~ to** porre l'assedio a.

siege economy *n* economia da stato d'assedio.

Sierra Leone [sɪˈɛrəliˈəun] *n* Sierra Leone *f*.

sieve [sɪv] *n* setaccio ♦ *vt* setacciare.

sift [sɪft] *vt* passare al crivello; (*fig*) vagliare ♦ *vi*: **to ~ through** esaminare minuziosamente.

sigh [saɪ] *n* sospiro ♦ *vi* sospirare.

sight [saɪt] *n* (*faculty*) vista; (*spectacle*) spettacolo; (*on gun*) mira ♦ *vt* avvistare; **in ~** in vista; **out of ~** non visibile; **at first ~** a prima vista; **to catch ~ of sth/sb** scorgere qc/qn; **to lose ~ of sb/sth** perdere di vista qn/qc; **to set one's ~s on sth/on doing sth** mirare a qc/a fare qc; **at ~** a vista; **I know her by ~** la conosco di vista.

sighted [ˈsaɪtɪd] *adj* che ha il dono della vista; **partially ~** parzialmente cieco.

sightseeing [ˈsaɪtsiːɪŋ] *n* turismo; **to go ~** visitare una località.

sightseer [ˈsaɪtsiːə*] *n* turista *m/f*.

sign [saɪn] *n* segno; (*with hand etc*) segno, gesto; (*notice*) insegna, cartello; (*road ~*) segnale *m* ♦ *vt* firmare; **as a ~ of** in segno di; **it's a good/bad ~** è buon/brutto segno; **to show ~s/no ~ of doing sth** accennare/non accennare a fare qc; **plus/minus ~** segno del più/meno; **to ~ one's name** firmare, apporre la propria firma.

▶**sign away** *vt* (*rights etc*) cedere (con una firma).

▶**sign in** *vi* firmare il registro (all'arrivo).

▶**sign off** *vi* (*RADIO, TV*) chiudere le trasmissioni.

▶**sign on** *vi* (*MIL etc: enlist*) arruolarsi; (*as unemployed*) iscriversi sulla lista (dell'ufficio di collocamento); (*begin work*) prendere servizio; (*enrol*): **to ~ on for a course** iscriversi a un corso.

▶**sign out** *vi* firmare il registro (alla partenza).

▶**sign over** *vt*: **to ~ sth over to sb** cedere qc con scrittura legale a qn.

▶**sign up** (*MIL*) *vt* arruolare ♦ *vi* arruolarsi.

signal [ˈsɪgnl] *n* segnale *m* ♦ *vt* segno a; (*message*) comunicare per mezzo di segnali ♦ *vi*: **to ~ to sb (to do sth)** far segno a qn (di fare qc); **to ~ a left/right turn** (*AUT*) segnalare un cambiamento di direzione a sinistra/ destra.

signal box *n* (*RAIL*) cabina di manovra.

signalman [ˈsɪgnlmən] *n* (*RAIL*) deviatore *m*.

signatory [ˈsɪgnətərɪ] *n* firmatario/a.

signature [ˈsɪgnətʃə*] *n* firma.

signature tune *n* sigla musicale.

signet ring [ˈsɪgnət-] *n* anello con sigillo.

significance [sɪgˈnɪfɪkəns] *n* (*of remark*) significato; (*of event*) importanza; **that is of no ~** ciò non ha importanza.

significant [sɪgˈnɪfɪkənt] *adj* (*improvement, amount*) notevole; (*discovery, event*) importante; (*evidence, smile*) significativo(a); **it is ~ that ...** è significativo che ....

significantly [sɪgˈnɪfɪkəntlɪ] *adv* (*smile*) in modo eloquente; (*improve, increase*) considerevolmente, decisamente.

signify [ˈsɪgnɪfaɪ] *vt* significare.

sign language *n* linguaggio dei muti.

signpost [ˈsaɪnpəust] *n* cartello indicatore.

silage [ˈsaɪlɪdʒ] *n* insilato.

silence [ˈsaɪlns] *n* silenzio ♦ *vt* far tacere, ridurre al silenzio.

silencer [ˈsaɪlənsə*] *n* (*on gun, BRIT AUT*) silenziatore *m*.

silent [ˈsaɪlnt] *adj* silenzioso(a); (*film*) muto(a); **to keep** *or* **remain ~** tacere, stare zitto(a).

silently [ˈsaɪlntlɪ] *adv* silenziosamente, in silenzio.

silent partner *n* (*COMM*) socio accomandante.

silhouette [sɪluːˈɛt] *n* silhouette *f inv* ♦ *vt*: **to be ~d against** stagliarsi contro.

silicon [ˈsɪlɪkən] *n* silicio.

silicon chip *n* chip *m inv* al silicone.

silicone [ˈsɪlɪkəun] *n* silicone *m*.

silk [sɪlk] *n* seta ♦ *cpd* di seta.

silky [ˈsɪlkɪ] *adj* di seta, come la seta.

sill [sɪl] *n* (*window~*) davanzale *m*; (*AUT*) predellino.

silly [ˈsɪlɪ] *adj* stupido(a), sciocco(a); **to do something ~** fare una sciocchezza.

silo [ˈsaɪləu] *n* silo.

silt [sɪlt] *n* limo.

silver [ˈsɪlvə*] *n* argento; (*money*) *monete da 5, 10, 20* o *50 pence*; (*also*: **~ware**) argenteria ♦ *cpd* d'argento.

silver foil, (*BRIT*) **silver paper** *n* carta argentata, (carta) stagnola.

silver-plated [sɪlvəˈpleɪtɪd] *adj* argentato(a).

silversmith [ˈsɪlvəsmɪθ] *n* argentiere *m*.

silverware [ˈsɪlvəwɛə*] *n* argenteria, argento.

silvery [ˈsɪlvərɪ] *adj* (*colour*) argenteo(a); (*sound*) argentino(a).

similar [ˈsɪmɪlə*] *adj*: **~ (to)** simile (a).

similarity [sɪmɪˈlærɪtɪ] *n* somiglianza,

rassomiglianza.

similarly ['sɪmɪləlɪ] *adv* (*in a similar way*) allo stesso modo; (*as is similar*) così pure.

simile ['sɪmɪlɪ] *n* similitudine *f*.

simmer ['sɪmə*] *vi* cuocere a fuoco lento.

►**simmer down** *vi* (*fig col*) calmarsi.

simper ['sɪmpə*] *vi* fare lo(la) smorfioso(a).

simpering ['sɪmpərɪŋ] *adj* lezioso(a), smorfioso(a).

simple ['sɪmpl] *adj* semplice; **the ~ truth** la pura verità.

simple interest *n* (*MATH, COMM*) interesse *m* semplice.

simple-minded [sɪmpl'maɪndɪd] *adj* sempliciotto(a).

simpleton ['sɪmpltən] *n* semplicione/a, sempliciotto/a.

simplicity [sɪm'plɪsɪtɪ] *n* semplicità.

simplification [sɪmplɪfɪ'keɪʃən] *n* semplificazione *f*.

simplify ['sɪmplɪfaɪ] *vt* semplificare.

simply ['sɪmplɪ] *adv* semplicemente.

simulate ['sɪmjuleɪt] *vt* fingere, simulare.

simulation [sɪmju'leɪʃən] *n* simulazione *f*.

simultaneous [sɪməl'teɪnɪəs] *adj* simultaneo(a).

simultaneously [sɪməl'teɪnɪəslɪ] *adv* simultaneamente, contemporaneamente.

sin [sɪn] *n* peccato ♦ *vi* peccare.

Sinai ['saɪnaɪ] *n* Sinai *m*.

since [sɪns] *adv* da allora ♦ *prep* da ♦ *conj* (*time*) da quando; (*because*) poiché, dato che; **~ then** da allora; **~ Monday** da lunedì; **(ever) ~ I arrived** (fin) da quando sono arrivato.

sincere [sɪn'sɪə*] *adj* sincero(a).

sincerely [sɪn'sɪəlɪ] *adv* sinceramente; **Yours ~** (*at end of letter*) distinti saluti.

sincerity [sɪn'sɛrɪtɪ] *n* sincerità.

sine [saɪn] *n* (*MATH*) seno.

sinew ['sɪnjuː] *n* tendine *m*; **~s** *npl* (*muscles*) muscoli *mpl*.

sinful ['sɪnful] *adj* peccaminoso(a).

sing, *pt* **sang**, *pp* **sung** [sɪŋ, sæŋ, sʌŋ] *vt, vi* cantare.

Singapore [sɪŋgə'pɔː*] *n* Singapore *f*.

singe [sɪndʒ] *vt* bruciacchiare.

singer ['sɪŋə*] *n* cantante *m/f*.

Singhalese [sɪŋə'liːz] *adj* = **Sinhalese**.

singing ['sɪŋɪŋ] *n* (*of person, bird*) canto; (*of kettle, bullet, in ears*) fischio.

single ['sɪŋgl] *adj* solo(a), unico(a); (*unmarried: man*) celibe; (: *woman*) nubile; (*not double*) semplice ♦ *n* (*BRIT: also:* **~ ticket**) biglietto di (sola) andata; (*record*) 45 giri *m inv*; **not a ~ one was left** non ne è rimasto nemmeno uno; **every ~ day** tutti i santi giorni; *see also* **singles**.

►**single out** *vt* scegliere; (*distinguish*) distinguere.

single bed *n* letto a una piazza.

single-breasted ['sɪŋglbrɛstɪd] *adj* a un petto.

Single European Market *n*: **the ~** il Mercato Unico.

single file *n*: **in ~** in fila indiana.

single-handed [sɪŋgl'hændɪd] *adv* senza aiuto, da solo(a).

single-minded [sɪŋgl'maɪndɪd] *adj* tenace, risoluto(a).

single parent *n* ragazzo padre/ragazza madre; genitore *m* separato.

single room *n* camera singola.

singles ['sɪŋglz] *npl* (*TENNIS*) singolo; (*US*: *single people*) single *m/f pl*.

singles bar *n* (*esp US*) bar *m inv* per single.

single-sex school ['sɪŋgl'sɛks-] *n* (*for boys*) scuola maschile; (*for girls*) scuola femminile.

singlet ['sɪŋglɪt] *n* canottiera.

singly ['sɪŋglɪ] *adv* separatamente.

singsong ['sɪŋsɔŋ] *adj* (*tone*) cantilenante ♦ *n* (*songs*): **to have a ~** farsi una cantata.

singular ['sɪŋgjulə*] *adj* (*LING*) singolare; (*unusual*) strano(a), singolare ♦ *n* (*LING*) singolare *m*; **in the feminine ~** al femminile singolare.

singularly ['sɪŋgjuləlɪ] *adv* stranamente.

Sinhalese [sɪnhə'liːz] *adj* singalese.

sinister ['sɪnɪstə*] *adj* sinistro(a).

sink [sɪŋk] *n* lavandino, acquaio ♦ *vb* (*pt* **sank**, *pp* **sunk** [sæŋk, sʌŋk]) *vt* (*ship*) (fare) affondare, colare a picco; (*foundations*) scavare; (*piles etc*): **to ~ sth into** conficcare qc in ♦ *vi* affondare, andare a fondo; (*ground etc*) cedere, avvallarsi; **he sank into a chair/the mud** sprofondò in una poltrona/nel fango.

►**sink in** *vi* penetrare; **it took a long time to ~ in** ci ho (*or* ha *etc*) messo molto a capirlo.

sinking ['sɪŋkɪŋ] *adj*: **that ~ feeling** una stretta allo stomaco.

sinking fund *n* (*COMM*) fondo d'ammortamento.

sink unit *n* blocco lavello.

sinner ['sɪnə*] *n* peccatore/trice.

Sinn Féin [ʃɪn'feɪn] *n* movimento separatista irlandese.

sinuous ['sɪnjuəs] *adj* sinuoso(a).

sinus ['saɪnəs] *n* (*ANAT*) seno.

sip [sɪp] *n* sorso ♦ *vt* sorseggiare.

siphon ['saɪfən] *n* sifone *m* ♦ *vt* (*funds*) trasferire.

►**siphon off** *vt* travasare (con un sifone).

sir [sə*] *n* signore *m*; **S~ John Smith** Sir

John Smith; **yes** ~ sì, signore; **Dear S~** (*in letter*) Egregio signor (*followed by name*); **Dear S~s** Spettabile ditta.

siren ['saɪərn] *n* sirena.

sirloin ['sɜːlɔɪn] *n* controfiletto.

sirloin steak *n* bistecca di controfiletto.

sirocco [sɪ'rɔkəu] *n* scirocco.

sisal ['saɪsəl] *n* sisal *f inv*.

sissy ['sɪsɪ] *n* (*col*) femminuccia.

sister ['sɪstə*] *n* sorella; (*nun*) suora; (*nurse*) infermiera *f* caposala *inv* ♦ *cpd*: ~ **organization** organizzazione *f* affine; ~ **ship** nave *f* gemella.

sister-in-law ['sɪstərɪnlɔː] *n* cognata.

sit, *pt, pp* **sat** [sɪt, sæt] *vi* sedere, sedersi; (*dress etc*) cadere; (*assembly*) essere in seduta ♦ *vt* (*exam*) sostenere, dare; **to** ~ **on a committee** far parte di una commissione.

▶**sit about, sit around** *vi* star seduto(a) (senza far nulla).

▶**sit back** *vi* (*in seat*) appoggiarsi allo schienale.

▶**sit down** *vi* sedersi; **to be** ~**ting down** essere seduto(a).

▶**sit in** *vi*: **to** ~ **in on a discussion** assistere ad una discussione.

▶**sit up** *vi* tirarsi su a sedere; (*not go to bed*) stare alzato(a) fino a tardi.

sitcom ['sɪtkɔm] *n abbr* (*TV*: = *situation comedy*) sceneggiato a episodi (*comico*).

sit-down ['sɪtdaun] *adj*: ~ **strike** sciopero bianco (con occupazione della fabbrica); **a** ~ **meal** un pranzo.

site [saɪt] *n* posto; (*also*: **building** ~) cantiere *m* ♦ *vt* situare.

sit-in ['sɪtɪn] *n* (*demonstration*) sit-in *m inv*.

siting ['saɪtɪŋ] *n* ubicazione *f*.

sitter ['sɪtə*] *n* (*for painter*) modello/a; (*also*: **baby** ~) babysitter *m/f inv*.

sitting ['sɪtɪŋ] *n* (*of assembly etc*) seduta; (*in canteen*) turno.

sitting member *n* (*POL*) deputato/a in carica.

sitting room *n* soggiorno.

sitting tenant *n* (*BRIT*) attuale affittuario.

situate ['sɪtjueɪt] *vt* collocare.

situated ['sɪtjueɪtɪd] *adj* situato(a).

situation [sɪtju'eɪʃən] *n* situazione *f*; "~**s vacant/wanted**" (*BRIT*) "offerte/domande di impiego".

situation comedy *n* (*THEAT*) commedia di situazione.

six [sɪks] *num* sei.

six-pack ['sɪkspæk] *n* (*esp US*) confezione *f* da sei.

sixteen [sɪks'tiːn] *num* sedici.

sixth [sɪksθ] *num* sesto(a) ♦ *n*: **the upper/**

lower ~ (*BRIT SCOL*) l'ultimo/il penultimo anno di scuola superiore.

sixty ['sɪkstɪ] *num* sessanta.

size [saɪz] *n* dimensioni *fpl*; (*of clothing*) taglia, misura; (*of shoes*) numero; (*glue*) colla; **I take** ~ **14 in a dress** ≈ porto la 44 di vestiti; **I'd like the small/large** ~ (*of soap powder etc*) vorrei la confezione piccola/grande.

▶**size up** *vt* giudicare, farsi un'idea di.

sizeable ['saɪzəbl] *adj* considerevole.

sizzle ['sɪzl] *vi* sfrigolare.

SK *abbr* (*Canada*) = *Saskatchewan*.

skate [skeɪt] *n* pattino; (*fish*: *pl inv*) razza ♦ *vi* pattinare.

▶**skate over, skate around** *vi* (*problem, issue*) prendere alla leggera, prendere sottogamba.

skateboard ['skeɪtbɔːd] *n* skateboard *m inv*.

skater ['skeɪtə*] *n* pattinatore/trice.

skating ['skeɪtɪŋ] *n* pattinaggio.

skating rink *n* pista di pattinaggio.

skeleton ['skɛlɪtn] *n* scheletro.

skeleton key *n* passe-partout *m inv*.

skeleton staff *n* personale *m* ridotto.

skeptic *etc* ['skɛptɪk] (*US*) = **sceptic** *etc*.

sketch [skɛtʃ] *n* (*drawing*) schizzo, abbozzo; (*THEAT etc*) scenetta comica, sketch *m inv* ♦ *vt* abbozzare, schizzare.

sketch book *n* album *m inv* per schizzi.

sketch pad *n* blocco per schizzi.

sketchy ['skɛtʃɪ] *adj* incompleto(a), lacunoso(a).

skew [skjuː] *n* (*BRIT*): **on the** ~ di traverso.

skewer ['skjuːə*] *n* spiedo.

ski [skiː] *n* sci *m inv* ♦ *vi* sciare.

ski boot *n* scarpone *m* da sci.

skid [skɪd] *n* slittamento; (*sideways slip*) sbandamento ♦ *vi* slittare; sbandare; **to go into a** ~ slittare; sbandare.

skid mark *n* segno della frenata.

skier ['skiːə*] *n* sciatore/trice.

skiing ['skiːɪŋ] *n* sci *m*.

ski instructor *n* maestro/a di sci.

ski jump *n* (*ramp*) trampolino; (*event*) salto con gli sci.

skilful, (*US*) **skillful** ['skɪlful] *adj* abile.

ski lift *n* sciovia.

skill [skɪl] *n* abilità *f inv*, capacità *f inv*; (*technique*) tecnica.

skilled [skɪld] *adj* esperto(a); (*worker*) qualificato(a), specializzato(a).

skillet ['skɪlɪt] *n* padella.

skillful *etc* ['skɪlful] (*US*) = **skilful** *etc*.

skil(l)fully ['skɪlfəlɪ] *adv* abilmente.

skim [skɪm] *vt* (*milk*) scremare; (*soup*) schiumare; (*glide over*) sfiorare ♦ *vi*: **to** ~ **through** (*fig*) scorrere, dare una scorsa a.

skimmed milk n latte m scremato.
skimp [skɪmp] vi: **to ~ on**, vt (work) fare alla carlona; (cloth etc) lesinare.
skimpy ['skɪmpɪ] adj misero(a); striminzito(a); frugale.
skin [skɪn] n pelle f; (of fruit, vegetable) buccia; (on pudding, paint) crosta ♦ vt (fruit etc) sbucciare; (animal) scuoiare, spellare; **wet** or **soaked to the ~** bagnato fino al midollo.
skin cancer n cancro alla pelle.
skin-deep [skɪn'diːp] adj superficiale.
skin diver n subacqueo.
skin diving n nuoto subacqueo.
skinflint ['skɪnflɪnt] n taccagno/a, tirchio/a.
skin graft n innesto epidermico.
skinhead ['skɪnhɛd] n skinhead m/f inv.
skinny ['skɪnɪ] adj molto magro(a), pelle e ossa inv.
skin test n prova di reazione cutanea.
skintight ['skɪntaɪt] adj aderente.
skip [skɪp] n saltello, balzo; (container) benna ♦ vi saltare; (with rope) saltare la corda ♦ vt (pass over) saltare; **to ~ school** (US) marinare la scuola.
ski pants npl pantaloni mpl da sci.
ski pole n racchetta (da sci).
skipper ['skɪpə*] n (NAUT, SPORT) capitano.
skipping rope ['skɪpɪŋ-] n (BRIT) corda per saltare.
ski resort n località f inv sciistica.
skirmish ['skɜːmɪʃ] n scaramuccia.
skirt [skɜːt] n gonna, sottana ♦ vt fiancheggiare, costeggiare.
skirting board ['skɜːtɪŋ-] n (BRIT) zoccolo.
ski run n pista (da sci).
ski suit n tuta da sci.
skit [skɪt] n parodia; scenetta satirica.
ski tow n = **ski lift**.
skittle ['skɪtl] n birillo; **~s** n (game) (gioco dei) birilli mpl.
skive [skaɪv] vi (BRIT col) fare il lavativo.
skulk [skʌlk] vi muoversi furtivamente.
skull [skʌl] n cranio, teschio.
skullcap ['skʌlkæp] n (worn by Jews) zucchetto; (worn by Pope) papalina.
skunk [skʌŋk] n moffetta.
sky [skaɪ] n cielo; **to praise sb to the skies** portare alle stelle qn.
sky-blue [skaɪ'bluː] adj azzurro(a), celeste.
sky-diving ['skaɪdaɪvɪŋ] n caduta libera, paracadutismo acrobatico.
sky-high [skaɪ'haɪ] adv (throw) molto in alto ♦ adj (col) esorbitante; **prices have gone ~** (col) i prezzi sono saliti alle stelle.
skylark ['skaɪlɑːk] n allodola.
skylight ['skaɪlaɪt] n lucernario.
skyline ['skaɪlaɪn] n (horizon) orizzonte m;

(of city) profilo.
skyscraper ['skaɪskreɪpə*] n grattacielo.
slab [slæb] n lastra; (of wood) tavola; (of meat, cheese) pezzo.
slack [slæk] adj (loose) allentato(a); (slow) lento(a); (careless) negligente; (COMM: market) stagnante; (: demand) scarso(a); (period) morto(a) ♦ n (in rope etc) parte f non tesa; **business is ~** l'attività commerciale è scarsa; see also **slacks**.
slacken ['slækn] (also: **~ off**) vi rallentare, diminuire ♦ vt allentare; (pressure) diminuire.
slacks [slæks] npl pantaloni mpl.
slag [slæg] n scorie fpl.
slag heap n ammasso di scorie.
slain [sleɪn] pp of **slay**.
slake [sleɪk] vt (one's thirst) spegnere.
slalom ['slɑːləm] n slalom m.
slam [slæm] vt (door) sbattere; (throw) scaraventare; (criticize) stroncare ♦ vi sbattere.
slammer ['slæmə*] n: **the ~** (col) la gattabuia.
slander ['slɑːndə*] n calunnia; (LAW) diffamazione f ♦ vt calunniare; diffamare.
slanderous ['slɑːndrəs] adj calunnioso(a); diffamatorio(a).
slang [slæŋ] n gergo, slang m.
slanging match ['slæŋɪŋ-] n (BRIT col) rissa verbale.
slant [slɑːnt] n pendenza, inclinazione f; (fig) angolazione f, punto di vista.
slanted ['slɑːntɪd] adj tendenzioso(a).
slanting ['slɑːntɪŋ] adj in pendenza, inclinato(a).
slap [slæp] n manata, pacca; (on face) schiaffo ♦ vt dare una manata a; schiaffeggiare ♦ adv (directly) in pieno; **fell ~ in the middle** cadde proprio nel mezzo.
slapdash ['slæpdæʃ] adj abborracciato(a).
slaphead ['slæphɛd] n (BRIT col) imbecille m/f.
slapstick ['slæpstɪk] n (comedy) farsa grossolana.
slap-up ['slæpʌp] adj (BRIT): **a ~ meal** un pranzo (or una cena) coi fiocchi.
slash [slæʃ] vt squarciare; (face) sfregiare; (fig: prices) ridurre drasticamente, tagliare.
slat [slæt] n (of wood) stecca.
slate [sleɪt] n ardesia ♦ vt (fig: criticize) stroncare, distruggere.
slaughter ['slɔːtə*] n (of animals) macellazione f; (of people) strage f, massacro ♦ vt macellare; trucidare, massacrare.

slaughterhouse ['slɔːtəhaus] *n* macello, mattatoio.

Slav [slɑːv] *adj, n* slavo(a).

slave [sleɪv] *n* schiavo/a ♦ *vi* (*also:* ~ **away**) lavorare come uno schiavo; **to** ~ (**away**) **at sth/at doing sth** ammazzarsi di fatica *or* sgobbare per qc/per fare qc.

slave driver *n* (*col, pej*) schiavista *m/f*.

slave labour *n* lavoro degli schiavi; (*fig*): **we're just** ~ **here** siamo solamente sfruttati qui dentro.

slaver ['slævə*] *vi* (*dribble*) sbavare.

slavery ['sleɪvərɪ] *n* schiavitù *f*.

Slavic ['slævɪk] *adj* slavo(a).

slavish ['sleɪvɪʃ] *adj* servile; pedissequo(a).

slavishly ['sleɪvɪʃlɪ] *adv* (*copy*) pedissequamente.

Slavonic [slə'vɔnɪk] *adj* slavo(a).

slay, *pt* **slew**, *pp* **slain** [sleɪ, sluː, sleɪn] *vt* (*formal*) uccidere.

SLD *n abbr* (*BRIT*) = Social and Liberal Democrats.

sleazy ['sliːzɪ] *adj* trasandato(a).

sledge [sledʒ] *n* slitta.

sledgehammer ['sledʒhæmə*] *n* martello da fabbro.

sleek [sliːk] *adj* (*hair, fur*) lucido(a), lucente; (*car, boat*) slanciato(a), affusolato(a).

sleep [sliːp] *n* sonno ♦ *vi* (*pt, pp* **slept** [slept]) dormire ♦ *vt*: **we can** ~ **4** abbiamo 4 posti letto, possiamo alloggiare 4 persone; **to have a good night's** ~ farsi una bella dormita; **to go to** ~ addormentarsi; **to** ~ **lightly** avere il sonno leggero; **to put to** ~ (*patient*) far addormentare; (*animal: euphemistic: kill*) abbattere; **to** ~ **with sb** (*euphemistic: have sex*) andare a letto con qn.

►**sleep in** *vi* (*lie late*) alzarsi tardi; (*oversleep*) dormire fino a tardi.

sleeper ['sliːpə*] *n* (*person*) dormiente *m/f*; (*BRIT RAIL: on track*) traversina; (: *train*) treno di vagoni letto.

sleepily ['sliːpɪlɪ] *adv* con aria assonnata.

sleeping ['sliːpɪŋ] *adj* addormentato(a).

sleeping bag *n* sacco a pelo.

sleeping car *n* vagone *m* letto *inv*, carrozza *f* letto *inv*.

sleeping partner *n* (*BRIT COMM*) = **silent partner**.

sleeping pill *n* sonnifero.

sleeping sickness *n* malattia del sonno.

sleepless ['sliːplɪs] *adj* (*person*) insonne; **a** ~ **night** una notte in bianco.

sleeplessness ['sliːplɪsnɪs] *n* insonnia.

sleepwalk ['sliːpwɔːk] *vi* camminare nel sonno; (*as a habit*) essere sonnambulo(a).

sleepwalker ['sliːpwɔːkə*] *n* sonnambulo/a.

sleepy ['sliːpɪ] *adj* assonnato(a), sonnolento(a); (*fig*) addormentato(a); **to be** *or* **feel** ~ avere sonno.

sleet [sliːt] *n* nevischio.

sleeve [sliːv] *n* manica; (*of record*) copertina.

sleeveless ['sliːvlɪs] *adj* (*garment*) senza maniche.

sleigh [sleɪ] *n* slitta.

sleight [slaɪt] *n*: ~ **of hand** gioco di destrezza.

slender ['slendə*] *adj* snello(a), sottile; (*not enough*) scarso(a), esiguo(a).

slept [slept] *pt, pp of* **sleep**.

sleuth [sluːθ] *n* (*col*) segugio.

slew [sluː] *vi* (*also:* ~ **round**) girare ♦ *pt of* **slay**.

slice [slaɪs] *n* fetta ♦ *vt* affettare, tagliare a fette; ~**d bread** pane *m* a cassetta.

slick [slɪk] *adj* (*clever*) brillante; (*insincere*) untuoso(a), falso(a) ♦ *n* (*also:* **oil** ~) chiazza di petrolio.

slid [slɪd] *pt, pp of* **slide**.

slide [slaɪd] *n* (*in playground*) scivolo; (*PHOT*) diapositiva; (*microscope* ~) vetrino; (*BRIT: also:* **hair** ~) fermaglio (per capelli); (*in prices*) caduta ♦ *vb* (*pt, pp* **slid** [slɪd]) *vt* far scivolare ♦ *vi* scivolare; **to let things** ~ (*fig*) lasciare andare tutto, trascurare tutto.

slide projector *n* proiettore *m* per diapositive.

slide rule *n* regolo calcolatore.

sliding ['slaɪdɪŋ] *adj* (*door*) scorrevole; ~ **roof** (*AUT*) capotte *f inv*.

sliding scale *n* scala mobile.

slight [slaɪt] *adj* (*slim*) snello(a), sottile; (*frail*) delicato(a), fragile; (*trivial*) insignificante; (*small*) piccolo(a) ♦ *n* offesa, affronto ♦ *vt* (*offend*) offendere, fare un affronto a; **the** ~**est** il minimo (*or* la minima); **not in the** ~**est** affatto, neppure per sogno.

slightly ['slaɪtlɪ] *adv* lievemente, un po'; ~ **built** esile.

slim [slɪm] *adj* magro(a), snello(a) ♦ *vi* dimagrire, fare (*or* seguire) una dieta dimagrante.

slime [slaɪm] *n* limo, melma; viscidume *m*.

slimming ['slɪmɪŋ] *adj* (*diet, pills*) dimagrante.

slimy ['slaɪmɪ] *adj* (*also fig: person*) viscido(a); (*covered with mud*) melmoso(a).

sling [slɪŋ] *n* (*MED*) benda al collo ♦ *vt* (*pt, pp* **slung** [slʌŋ]) lanciare, tirare; **to have one's arm in a** ~ avere un braccio al collo.

slink, *pt, pp* **slunk** [slɪŋk, slʌŋk] *vi*: **to ~ away,
~ off** svignarsela.
slinky ['slɪŋkɪ] *adj* (*clothing*) aderente,
attillato(a).
slip [slɪp] *n* scivolata, scivolone *m*; (*mistake*)
errore *m*, sbaglio; (*underskirt*) sottoveste *f*;
(*paper*) bigliettino, talloncino ♦ *vt* (*slide*)
far scivolare ♦ *vi* (*slide*) scivolare; (*move
smoothly*): **to ~ into/out of** scivolare in/
via da; (*decline*) declinare; **to give sb the
~** sfuggire qn; **a ~ of paper** un foglietto;
a ~ of the tongue un lapsus linguae; **to ~
sth on/off** infilarsi/togliersi qc; **to let a
chance ~ by** lasciarsi scappare
un'occasione; **it ~ped from her hand** le
sfuggì di mano.
▶**slip away** *vi* svignarsela.
▶**slip in** *vt* introdurre casualmente.
▶**slip out** *vi* uscire furtivamente.
slip-on ['slɪpɔn] *adj* (*gen*) comodo(a) da
mettere; (*shoes*) senza allacciatura.
slipped disc ['slɪpt-] *n* spostamento delle
vertebre.
slipper ['slɪpə*] *n* pantofola.
slippery ['slɪpərɪ] *adj* scivoloso(a); **it's ~** si
scivola.
slip road *n* (*BRIT*: *to motorway*) rampa di
accesso.
slipshod ['slɪpʃɔd] *adj* sciatto(a),
trasandato(a).
slip-up ['slɪpʌp] *n* granchio *m* (*fig*).
slipway ['slɪpweɪ] *n* scalo di costruzione.
slit [slɪt] *n* fessura, fenditura; (*cut*) taglio;
(*tear*) strappo ♦ *vt* (*pt, pp* **slit**) tagliare; **to ~
sb's throat** tagliare la gola a qn.
slither ['slɪðə*] *vi* scivolare, sdrucciolare.
sliver ['slɪvə*] *n* (*of glass, wood*) scheggia;
(*of cheese, sausage*) fettina.
slob [slɔb] *n* (*col*) sciattone/a.
slog [slɔg] (*BRIT*) *n* faticata ♦ *vi* lavorare con
accanimento, sgobbare.
slogan ['sləugən] *n* motto, slogan *m inv.*
slop [slɔp] *vi* (*also*: **~ over**) traboccare;
versarsi ♦ *vt* spandere; versare ♦ *npl*: **~s**
acqua sporca; sbobba.
slope [sləup] *n* pendio; (*side of mountain*)
versante *m*; (*of roof*) pendenza; (*of floor*)
inclinazione *f* ♦ *vi*: **to ~ down** declinare;
to ~ up essere in salita.
sloping ['sləupɪŋ] *adj* inclinato(a).
sloppy ['slɔpɪ] *adj* (*work*) tirato a via;
(*appearance*) sciatto(a); (*film etc*)
sdolcinato(a).
slosh [slɔʃ] *vi* (*col*): **to ~ about** *or* **around**
(*person*) sguazzare; (*liquid*) guazzare.
sloshed [slɔʃt] *adj* (*col*: *drunk*) sbronzo(a).
slot [slɔt] *n* fessura ♦ (*fig*: *in timetable, RADIO,
TV*) spazio ♦ *vt*: **to ~ into** introdurre in

una fessura.
sloth [sləuθ] *n* (*vice*) pigrizia, accidia;
(*ZOOL*) bradipo.
slot machine *n* (*BRIT*: *vending machine*)
distributore *m* automatico; (*for
amusement*) slot-machine *f inv.*
slot meter *n* contatore *m* a gettoni.
slouch [slautʃ] *vi* (*when walking*)
camminare dinoccolato(a); **she was ~ed
in a chair** era sprofondata in una
poltrona.
▶**slouch about, slouch around** *vi* (*laze*)
oziare.
Slovak ['sləuvæk] *adj* slovacco(a) ♦ *n*
slovacco/a; (*LING*) slovacco; **the ~
Republic** la Repubblica Slovacca.
Slovakia [sləu'vækɪə] *n* Slovacchia.
Slovakian [sləu'vækɪən] *adj, n* = **Slovak**.
Slovene ['sləuviːn] *adj* sloveno(a) ♦ *n*
sloveno/a; (*LING*) sloveno.
Slovenia [sləu'viːnɪə] *n* Slovenia.
Slovenian [sləu'viːnɪən] *adj, n* = **Slovene**.
slovenly ['slʌvənlɪ] *adj* sciatto(a),
trasandato(a).
slow [sləu] *adj* lento(a); (*watch*): **to be ~**
essere indietro ♦ *adv* lentamente ♦ *vt, vi*
(*also*: **~ down, ~ up**) rallentare; **"~"**
(*road sign*) "rallentare"; **at a ~ speed** a
bassa velocità; **to be ~ to act/decide**
essere lento ad agire/a decidere; **my
watch is 20 minutes ~** il mio orologio è
indietro di 20 minuti; **business is ~**
(*COMM*) gli affari procedono a rilento; **to
go ~** (*driver*) andare piano; (*in industrial
dispute*) fare uno sciopero bianco.
slow-acting ['sləu'æktɪŋ] *adj* che agisce
lentamente, ad azione lenta.
slowly ['sləulɪ] *adv* lentamente; **to drive ~**
andare piano.
slow motion *n*: **in ~** al rallentatore.
slowness ['sləunɪs] *n* lentezza.
sludge [slʌdʒ] *n* fanghiglia.
slug [slʌg] *n* lumaca; (*bullet*) pallottola.
sluggish ['slʌgɪʃ] *adj* lento(a); (*business,
market, sales*) stagnante, fiacco(a).
sluice [sluːs] *n* chiusa ♦ *vt*: **to ~ down** *or* **out**
lavare (con abbondante acqua).
slum [slʌm] *n* catapecchia.
slumber ['slʌmbə*] *n* sonno.
slump [slʌmp] *n* crollo, caduta; (*economic*)
depressione *f*, crisi *f inv* ♦ *vi* crollare; **he
was ~ed over the wheel** era curvo sul
volante.
slung [slʌŋ] *pt, pp of* **sling**.
slunk [slʌŋk] *pt, pp of* **slink**.
slur [sləː*] *n* pronuncia indistinta; (*stigma*)
diffamazione *f*, calunnia; (*MUS*) legatura;
(*smear*): **~ (on)** macchia (su) ♦ *vt*

pronunciare in modo indistinto; **to cast a**
~ **on sb** calunniare qn.
slurp [slə:p] *vt, vi* bere rumorosamente ♦ *n*
rumore fatto bevendo.
slurred [slə:d] *adj (pronunciation)*
inarticolato(a), disarticolato(a).
slush [slʌʃ] *n* neve *f* mista a fango.
slush fund *n* fondi *mpl* neri.
slushy ['slʌʃɪ] *adj (snow)* che si scioglie;
(*BRIT: fig*) sdolcinato(a).
slut [slʌt] *n* donna trasandata, sciattona.
sly [slaɪ] *adj* furbo(a), scaltro(a); **on the** ~
di soppiatto.
SM *n abbr* (= *sadomasochism*)
sadomasochismo.
smack [smæk] *n (slap)* pacca; (*on face*)
schiaffo ♦ *vt* schiaffeggiare; (*child*)
picchiare ♦ *vi*: **to** ~ **of** puzzare di; **to** ~
one's lips fare uno schiocco con le
labbra.
smacker ['smækə*] *n (col: kiss)* bacio;
(: *BRIT: pound note*) sterlina; (: *US: dollar
bill*) dollaro.
small [smɔ:l] *adj* piccolo(a); (*in height*)
basso(a); (*letter*) minuscolo(a) ♦ *n*: **the** ~
of the back le reni; **to get** *or* **grow** ~**er**
(*stain, town*) rimpicciolire; (*debt,
organization, numbers*) ridursi; **to make**
~**er** (*amount, income*) ridurre; (*garden,
object, garment*) rimpicciolire; **in the** ~
hours alle ore piccole; **a** ~ **shopkeeper** un
piccolo negoziante.
small ads *npl* (*BRIT*) piccoli annunci *mpl.*
small arms *npl* armi *fpl* portatili *or*
leggere.
small business *n* piccola impresa.
small change *n* moneta, spiccioli *mpl.*
smallholder ['smɔ:lhəuldə*] *n* (*BRIT*) piccolo
proprietario.
smallholding ['smɔ:lhəuldɪŋ] *n* (*BRIT*)
piccola tenuta.
smallish ['smɔ:lɪʃ] *adj* piccolino(a).
small-minded [smɔ:l'maɪndɪd] *adj*
meschino(a).
smallpox ['smɔ:lpɔks] *n* vaiolo.
small print *n* caratteri *mpl* piccoli; (*on
document*) parte scritta in piccolo.
small-scale ['smɔ:lskeɪl] *adj (map, model)* in
scala ridotta; (*business, farming*)
modesto(a).
small talk *n* chiacchiere *fpl.*
small-time ['smɔ:ltaɪm] *adj (col)* da poco; **a**
~ **thief** un ladro di polli.
small-town ['smɔ:ltaun] *adj (pej)*
provinciale, di paese.
smarmy ['smɑ:mɪ] *adj* (*BRIT pej*) untuoso(a),
strisciante.
smart [smɑ:t] *adj* elegante; (*also fig: clever*)

intelligente; (*quick*) sveglio(a) ♦ *vi*
bruciare; **the** ~ **set** il bel mondo; **to look**
~ essere elegante; **my eyes are** ~**ing** mi
bruciano gli occhi.
smartcard ['smɑ:tkɑ:d] *n* smartcard *f inv*,
carta intelligente.
smarten up ['smɑ:tn-] *vi* farsi bello(a) ♦ *vt*
(*people*) fare bello(a); (*things*) abbellire.
smash [smæʃ] *n (also:* ~**-up**) scontro,
collisione *f*; (*sound*) fracasso ♦ *vt*
frantumare, fracassare; (*opponent*)
annientare, schiacciare; (*hopes*)
distruggere; (*SPORT: record*) battere ♦ *vi*
frantumarsi, andare in pezzi.
▶**smash up** *vt (car)* sfasciare; (*room*)
distruggere.
smash-hit [smæʃ'hɪt] *n* successone *m.*
smashing ['smæʃɪŋ] *adj (col)* favoloso(a),
formidabile.
smattering ['smætərɪŋ] *n*: **a** ~ **of**
un'infarinatura di.
smear [smɪə*] *n* macchia; (*MED*) striscio;
(*insult*) calunnia ♦ *vt* ungere; (*fig*)
denigrare, diffamare; **his hands were**
~**ed with oil/ink** aveva le mani sporche
di olio/inchiostro.
smear campaign *n* campagna
diffamatoria.
smear test *n* (*BRIT MED*) Pap-test *m inv.*
smell [smɛl] *n* odore *m*; (*sense*) olfatto,
odorato ♦ *vb* (*pt, pp* **smelt** *or* **smelled**
[smɛlt, smɛld]) *vt* sentire (l')odore di ♦ *vi*
(*food etc*): **to** ~ (**of**) avere odore (di); (*pej*)
puzzare, avere un cattivo odore; **it** ~**s
good** ha un buon odore.
smelly ['smɛlɪ] *adj* puzzolente.
smelt [smɛlt] *pt, pp of* **smell** ♦ *vt (ore)*
fondere.
smile [smaɪl] *n* sorriso ♦ *vi* sorridere.
smiling ['smaɪlɪŋ] *adj* sorridente.
smirk [smə:k] *n* sorriso furbo; sorriso
compiaciuto.
smith [smɪθ] *n* fabbro.
smithy ['smɪðɪ] *n* fucina.
smitten ['smɪtn] *adj*: ~ **with** colpito(a) da.
smock [smɔk] *n* grembiule *m*, camice *m.*
smog [smɔg] *n* smog *m.*
smoke [sməuk] *n* fumo ♦ *vt, vi* fumare; **to
have a** ~ fumarsi una sigaretta; **do you**
~? fumi?; **to go up in** ~ (*house etc*)
bruciare, andare distrutto dalle fiamme;
(*fig*) andare in fumo.
smoked [sməukt] *adj (bacon, glass)*
affumicato(a).
smokeless fuel ['sməuklɪs-] *n* carburante
m che non dà fumo.
smokeless zone *n* (*BRIT*) zona dove sono
vietati gli scarichi di fumo.

smoker ['sməukə*] n (person) fumatore/trice; (RAIL) carrozza per fumatori.

smoke screen n cortina fumogena or di fumo; (fig) copertura.

smoke shop n (US) tabaccheria.

smoking ['sməukɪŋ] n fumo; "no ~" (sign) "vietato fumare"; **he's given up ~** ha smesso di fumare.

smoking compartment, (US) smoking car n carrozza (per) fumatori.

smoky ['sməukɪ] adj fumoso(a); (surface) affumicato(a).

smolder ['sməuldə*] vi (US) = smoulder.

smoochy ['smu:tʃɪ] adj (col) romantico(a).

smooth [smu:ð] adj liscio(a); (sauce) omogeneo(a); (flavour, whisky) amabile; (cigarette) leggero(a); (movement) regolare; (person) mellifluo(a); (landing, take-off, flight) senza scosse ♦ vt lisciare, spianare; (also: ~ out: difficulties) appianare.

▶**smooth over** vt: **to ~ things over** (fig) sistemare le cose.

smoothly ['smu:ðlɪ] adv (easily) liscio; **everything went ~** tutto andò liscio.

smother ['smʌðə*] vt soffocare.

smoulder, (US) smolder ['sməuldə*] vi covare sotto la cenere.

smudge [smʌdʒ] n macchia; sbavatura ♦ vt imbrattare, sporcare.

smug [smʌg] adj soddisfatto(a), compiaciuto(a).

smuggle ['smʌgl] vt contrabbandare; **to ~ in/out** (goods etc) far entrare/uscire di contrabbando.

smuggler ['smʌglə*] n contrabbandiere/a.

smuggling ['smʌglɪŋ] n contrabbando.

smut [smʌt] n (grain of soot) granello di fuliggine; (mark) segno nero; (in conversation etc) sconcezze fpl.

smutty ['smʌtɪ] adj (fig) osceno(a), indecente.

snack [snæk] n spuntino; **to have a ~** fare uno spuntino.

snack bar n tavola calda, snack bar m inv.

snag [snæg] n intoppo, ostacolo imprevisto.

snail [sneɪl] n chiocciola.

snake [sneɪk] n serpente m.

snap [snæp] n (sound) schianto, colpo secco; (photograph) istantanea; (game) rubamazzo ♦ adj improvviso(a) ♦ vt (far) schioccare; (break) spezzare di netto; (photograph) scattare un'istantanea di ♦ vi spezzarsi con un rumore secco; (fig: person) crollare; **to ~ at sb** rivolgersi a qn con tono brusco; (subj: dog) cercare di mordere qn; **to ~ open/shut** aprirsi/chiudersi di scatto; **to ~ one's fingers at**

(fig) infischiarsi di; **a cold ~** (of weather) un'improvvisa ondata di freddo.

▶**snap off** vt (break) schiantare.

▶**snap up** vt afferrare.

snap fastener n bottone m automatico.

snappy ['snæpɪ] adj rapido(a); **make it ~!** (col: hurry up) sbrigati!, svelto!

snapshot ['snæpʃɔt] n istantanea.

snare [snɛə*] n trappola.

snarl [snɑːl] vi ringhiare ♦ vt: **to get ~ed up** (wool, plans) ingarbugliarsi; (traffic) intasarsi.

snatch [snætʃ] n (fig) furto; (BRIT: small amount): **~es of** frammenti mpl di ♦ vt strappare (con violenza); (steal) rubare ♦ vi: **don't ~!** non strappare le cose di mano!; **to ~ a sandwich** mangiarsi in fretta un panino; **to ~ some sleep** riuscire a dormire un po'.

▶**snatch up** vt raccogliere in fretta.

snazzy ['snæzɪ] adj (col: clothes) sciccoso(a).

sneak [sni:k] vi: **to ~ in/out** entrare/uscire di nascosto ♦ vt: **to ~ a look at sth** guardare di sottecchi qc.

sneakers ['sni:kəz] npl scarpe fpl da ginnastica.

sneaking ['sni:kɪŋ] adj: **to have a ~ feeling/suspicion that ...** avere la vaga impressione/il vago sospetto che ....

sneaky ['sni:kɪ] adj falso(a), disonesto(a).

sneer [snɪə*] n ghigno, sogghigno ♦ vi ghignare, sogghignare; **to ~ at sb/sth** farsi beffe di qn/qc.

sneeze [sni:z] n starnuto ♦ vi starnutire.

snide [snaɪd] adj maligno(a).

sniff [snɪf] n fiutata, annusata ♦ vi fiutare, annusare; tirare su col naso; (in contempt) arricciare il naso ♦ vt fiutare, annusare; (glue, drug) sniffare.

▶**sniff at** vt fus: **it's not to be ~ed at** non è da disprezzare.

sniffer dog ['snɪfə-] n cane m poliziotto (per stupefacenti o esplosivi).

snigger ['snɪgə*] n riso represso ♦ vi ridacchiare, ridere sotto i baffi.

snip [snɪp] n pezzetto; (bargain) (buon) affare m, occasione f ♦ vt tagliare.

sniper ['snaɪpə*] n franco tiratore m, cecchino.

snippet ['snɪpɪt] n frammento.

snivelling ['snɪvlɪŋ] adj piagnucoloso(a).

snob [snɔb] n snob m/f inv.

snobbery ['snɔbərɪ] n snobismo.

snobbish ['snɔbɪʃ] adj snob inv.

snog [snɔg] vi (col) pomiciare.

snooker ['snu:kə*] n tipo di gioco del biliardo.

snoop [snu:p] vi: **to ~ on sb** spiare qn; **to ~**

about curiosare.

snooper ['snu:pə*] *n* ficcanaso *m/f*.

snooty ['snu:tɪ] *adj* borioso(a), snob *inv*.

snooze [snu:z] *n* sonnellino, pisolino ♦ *vi* fare un sonnellino.

snore [snɔ:*] *vi* russare.

snoring ['snɔ:rɪŋ] *n* russare *m*.

snorkel ['snɔ:kl] *n* (*of swimmer*) respiratore *m* a tubo.

snort [snɔ:t] *n* sbuffo ♦ *vi* sbuffare ♦ *vt* (*drugs slang*) sniffare.

snotty ['snɔtɪ] *adj* moccioso(a).

snout [snaut] *n* muso.

snow [snəu] *n* neve *f* ♦ *vi* nevicare ♦ *vt*: **to be ~ed under with work** essere sommerso di lavoro.

snowball ['snəubɔ:l] *n* palla di neve.

snowbound ['snəubaund] *adj* bloccato(a) dalla neve.

snow-capped ['snəukæpt] *adj* (*mountain*) con la cima coperta di neve; (*peak*) coperto(a) di neve.

snowdrift ['snəudrɪft] *n* cumulo di neve (*ammucchiato dal vento*).

snowdrop ['snəudrɔp] *n* bucaneve *m inv*.

snowfall ['snəufɔ:l] *n* nevicata.

snowflake ['snəufleɪk] *n* fiocco di neve.

snowman ['snəumæn] *n* pupazzo di neve.

snowplough, (*US*) **snowplow** ['snəuplau] *n* spazzaneve *m inv*.

snowshoe ['snəuʃu:] *n* racchetta da neve.

snowstorm ['snəustɔ:m] *n* tormenta.

snowy ['snəuɪ] *adj* nevoso(a).

SNP *n abbr* (*BRIT POL*) = *Scottish National Party*.

snub [snʌb] *vt* snobbare ♦ *n* offesa, affronto.

snub-nosed [snʌb'nəuzd] *adj* dal naso camuso.

snuff [snʌf] *n* tabacco da fiuto ♦ *vt* (*also*: ~ **out**: *candle*) spegnere.

snuff movie *n* (*col*) film porno dove una persona viene uccisa realmente.

snug [snʌg] *adj* comodo(a); (*room, house*) accogliente, comodo(a); **it's a ~ fit** è attillato.

snuggle ['snʌgl] *vi*: **to ~ down in bed** accovacciarsi a letto; **to ~ up to sb** stringersi a qn.

snugly ['snʌglɪ] *adv* comodamente; **it fits ~** (*object in pocket etc*) entra giusto giusto; (*garment*) sta ben attillato.

SO *abbr* (*BANKING*) = **standing order**.

━━━━━━━━━━━━ *KEYWORD*

so [səu] *adv* **1** (*thus, likewise*) così; **if ~** se è così, quand'è così; **I didn't do it — you did ~!** non l'ho fatto io — sì che l'hai fatto!;

~ **do I**, ~ **am I** anch'io; **it's 5 o'clock — ~ it is!** sono le 5 — davvero!; **I hope ~** lo spero; **I think ~** penso di sì; **quite ~!** esattamente!; **even ~** comunque; ~ **far** finora, fin qui; (*in past*) fino ad allora

2 (*in comparisons etc: to such a degree*) così; ~ **big (that)** così grande (che); **she's not ~ clever as her brother** lei non è (così) intelligente come suo fratello

3: ~ **much** *adj* tanto(a) ♦ *adv* tanto; **I've got ~ much work/money** ho tanto lavoro/ tanti soldi; **I love you ~ much** ti amo tanto; ~ **many** tanti(e)

4 (*phrases*): **10 or ~** circa 10; ~ **long!** (*col: goodbye*) ciao!, ci vediamo!; ~ **to speak** per così dire; ~ **what?** (*col*) e allora?, e con questo?

♦ *conj* **1** (*expressing purpose*): ~ **as to do** in modo *or* così da fare; **we hurried ~ as not to be late** ci affrettammo per non fare tardi; ~ **(that)** affinché + *sub*, perché + *sub*

2 (*expressing result*): **he didn't arrive ~ I left** non è venuto così me ne sono andata; ~ **you see, I could have gone** vedi, sarei potuto andare; ~ **that's the reason!** allora è questo il motivo!, ecco perché!

soak [səuk] *vt* inzuppare; (*clothes*) mettere a mollo ♦ *vi* inzupparsi; (*clothes*) essere a mollo; **to be ~ed through** essere fradicio.

▶**soak in** *vi* penetrare.

▶**soak up** *vt* assorbire.

soaking ['səukɪŋ] *adj* (*also*: ~ **wet**) fradicio(a).

so-and-so ['səuənsəu] *n* (*somebody*) un tale; **Mr/Mrs ~** signor/signora tal dei tali.

soap [səup] *n* sapone *m*.

soapbox ['səupbɔks] *n* palco improvvisato (*per orazioni pubbliche*).

soapflakes ['səupfleɪks] *npl* sapone *m* in scaglie.

soap opera *n* soap opera *f inv*.

soap powder *n* detersivo.

soapsuds ['səupsʌdz] *npl* saponata.

soapy ['səupɪ] *adj* insaponato(a).

soar [sɔ:*] *vi* volare in alto; (*price, morale, spirits*) salire alle stelle.

sob [sɔb] *n* singhiozzo ♦ *vi* singhiozzare.

s.o.b. *n abbr* (*US col!*: = *son of a bitch*) figlio di puttana (*!*).

sober ['səubə*] *adj* non ubriaco(a); (*sedate*) serio(a); (*moderate*) moderato(a); (*colour, style*) sobrio(a).

▶**sober up** *vt* far passare la sbornia a ♦ *vi* farsi passare la sbornia.

sobriety [səu'braɪətɪ] *n* (*not being drunk*) sobrietà; (*seriousness, sedateness*) sobrietà, pacatezza.

sob story n (col, pej) storia lacrimosa.
Soc. abbr (= society) Soc.
so-called ['səu'kɔːld] adj cosiddetto(a).
soccer ['sɔkə*] n calcio.
soccer pitch n campo di calcio.
soccer player n calciatore m.
sociable ['səuʃəbl] adj socievole.
social ['səuʃl] adj sociale ♦ n festa, serata.
social climber n arrampicatore/trice sociale, arrivista m/f.
social club n club m inv sociale.
Social Democrat n socialdemocratico/a.
social insurance n (US) assicurazione f sociale.
socialism ['səuʃəlɪzəm] n socialismo.
socialist ['səuʃəlɪst] adj, n socialista (m/f).
socialite ['səuʃəlaɪt] n persona in vista nel bel mondo.
socialize ['səuʃəlaɪz] vi frequentare la gente; farsi degli amici; **to ~ with** socializzare con.
social life n vita sociale.
socially ['səuʃəlɪ] adv socialmente, in società.
social science n scienze fpl sociali.
social security n previdenza sociale; **Department of S~ S~ (DSS)** (BRIT) ≈ Istituto di Previdenza Sociale.
social services npl servizi mpl sociali.
social welfare n assistenza sociale.
social work n servizio sociale.
social worker n assistente m/f sociale.
society [sə'saɪətɪ] n società f inv; (club) società, associazione f; (also: **high ~**) alta società ♦ cpd (party, column) mondano(a).
socioeconomic ['səusɪəui:kə'nɔmɪk] adj socio-economico(a).
sociological [səusɪə'lɔdʒɪkl] adj sociologico(a).
sociologist [səusɪ'ɔlədʒɪst] n sociologo/a.
sociology [səusɪ'ɔlədʒɪ] n sociologia.
sock [sɔk] n calzino ♦ vt (hit) dare un pugno a; **to pull one's ~s up** (fig) darsi una regolata.
socket ['sɔkɪt] n cavità f inv; (of eye) orbita; (ELEC: also: **wall ~**) presa di corrente; (: for light bulb) portalampada m inv.
sod [sɔd] n (of earth) zolla erbosa; (BRIT col!) bastardo/a (!).
►**sod off** vi: ~ **off!** (BRIT col!) levati dalle palle! (!).
soda ['səudə] n (CHEM) soda; (also: ~ **water**) acqua di seltz; (US: also: ~ **pop**) gassosa.
sodden ['sɔdn] adj fradicio(a).
sodium ['səudɪəm] n sodio.
sodium chloride n cloruro di sodio.
sofa ['səufə] n sofà m inv.
Sofia ['səufɪə] n Sofia.

soft [sɔft] adj (not rough) morbido(a); (not hard) soffice; (not loud) sommesso(a); (kind) gentile; (: look, smile) dolce; (not strict) indulgente; (weak) debole; (stupid) stupido(a).
soft-boiled ['sɔftbɔɪld] adj (egg) alla coque.
soft drink n analcolico.
soft drugs npl droghe fpl leggere.
soften ['sɔfn] vt ammorbidire; addolcire; attenuare ♦ vi ammorbidirsi; addolcirsi; attenuarsi.
softener ['sɔfnə*] n ammorbidente m.
soft fruit n (BRIT) ≈ frutti di bosco.
soft furnishings npl tessuti mpl d'arredo.
soft-hearted [sɔft'hɑːtɪd] adj sensibile.
softly ['sɔftlɪ] adv dolcemente; morbidamente.
softness ['sɔftnɪs] n dolcezza; morbidezza.
soft option n soluzione f (più) facile.
soft sell n persuasione f all'acquisto.
soft target n obiettivo civile (e quindi facile da colpire).
soft touch n (col): **to be a ~** lasciarsi spillare facilmente denaro.
soft toy n giocattolo di peluche.
software ['sɔftwɛə*] n software m.
software package n pacchetto di software.
soft water n acqua non calcarea.
soggy ['sɔgɪ] adj inzuppato(a).
soil [sɔɪl] n (earth) terreno, suolo ♦ vt sporcare; (fig) macchiare.
soiled [sɔɪld] adj sporco(a), sudicio(a).
sojourn ['sɔdʒəːn] n (formal) soggiorno.
solace ['sɔlɪs] n consolazione f.
solar ['səulə*] adj solare.
solarium, pl **solaria** [sə'lɛərɪəm, -rɪə] n solarium m inv.
solar plexus [-'plɛksəs] n (ANAT) plesso solare.
solar power n energia solare.
sold [səuld] pt, pp of **sell**.
solder ['səuldə*] vt saldare ♦ n saldatura.
soldier ['səuldʒə*] n soldato, militare m ♦ vi: **to ~ on** perseverare; **toy ~** soldatino.
sold out adj (COMM) esaurito(a).
sole [səul] n (of foot) pianta (del piede); (of shoe) suola; (fish: pl inv) sogliola ♦ adj solo(a), unico(a); (exclusive) esclusivo(a).
solely ['səullɪ] adv solamente, unicamente; **I will hold you ~ responsible** la considererò il solo responsabile.
solemn ['sɔləm] adj solenne; grave; serio(a).
sole trader n (COMM) commerciante m in proprio.
solicit [sə'lɪsɪt] vt (request) richiedere, sollecitare ♦ vi (prostitute) adescare i

passanti.

solicitor [sə'lısıtə*] *n* (*BRIT: for wills etc*) ≈ notaio; (*in court*) ≈ avvocato.

---

*Il **solicitor** appartiene a una delle due branche della professione legale britannica (vedi anche **barrister**). È compito dei solicitor agire come consulenti in materia legale, redarre documenti legali, preparare i casi per i barrister. Contrariamente a questi ultimi, i solicitor non sono qualificati a rappresentare una parte nelle corti investite della potestà di decidere sui reati più gravi.*

---

solid ['sɔlıd] *adj* (*not hollow*) pieno(a); (*strong, sound, reliable, not liquid*) solido(a); (*meal*) sostanzioso(a); (*line*) ininterrotto(a); (*vote*) unanime ♦ *n* solido; **to be on ~ ground** essere su terraferma; (*fig*) muoversi su terreno sicuro; **we waited 2 ~ hours** abbiamo aspettato due ore buone.

solidarity [sɔlı'dærıtı] *n* solidarietà.

solid fuel *n* combustibile *m* solido.

solidify [sə'lıdıfaı] *vi* solidificarsi ♦ *vt* solidificare.

solidity [sə'lıdıtı] *n* solidità.

solid-state ['sɔlıdsteıt] *adj* (*ELEC*) a transistor.

soliloquy [sə'lıləkwı] *n* soliloquio.

solitaire [sɔlı'tɛə*] *n* (*game, gem*) solitario.

solitary ['sɔlıtərı] *adj* solitario(a).

solitary confinement *n* (*LAW*): **to be in ~** essere in cella d'isolamento.

solitude ['sɔlıtju:d] *n* solitudine *f*.

solo ['səuləu] *n* (*MUS*) assolo.

soloist ['səuləuıst] *n* solista *m/f*.

Solomon Islands ['sɔləmən-] *n*: **the ~** le isole Salomone.

solstice ['sɔlstıs] *n* solstizio.

soluble ['sɔljubl] *adj* solubile.

solution [sə'lu:ʃən] *n* soluzione *f*.

solve [sɔlv] *vt* risolvere.

solvency ['sɔlvənsı] *n* (*COMM*) solvenza, solvibilità.

solvent ['sɔlvənt] *adj* (*COMM*) solvibile ♦ *n* (*CHEM*) solvente *m*.

solvent abuse *n* abuso di colle e solventi.

Som. *abbr* (*BRIT*) = Somerset.

Somali [sə'mɑ:lı] *adj* somalo(a).

Somalia [səu'mɑ:lıə] *n* Somalia.

Somaliland [səu'mɑ:lılænd] *n* paesi *mpl* del corno d'Africa.

sombre, (*US*) **somber** ['sɔmbə*] *adj* scuro(a); (*mood, person*) triste.

════════════════════ *KEYWORD*

some [sʌm] *adj* **1** (*a certain amount or number of*): ~ **tea/water/cream** del tè/dell'acqua/della panna; **there's ~ milk in the fridge** c'è (del) latte nel frigo; ~ **children/apples** dei bambini/delle mele; **after ~ time** dopo un po'; **at ~ length** a lungo

2 (*certain: in contrasts*) certo(a); ~ **people say that ...** alcuni dicono che ..., certa gente dice che ...

3 (*unspecified*) un(a) certo(a), qualche; ~ **woman was asking for you** una tale chiedeva di lei; ~ **day** un giorno; ~ **day next week** un giorno della prossima settimana; **in ~ form or other** in una forma o nell'altra

♦ *pron* **1** (*a certain number*) alcuni(e), certi(e); **I've got ~** (*books etc*) ne ho alcuni; ~ (**of them**) **have been sold** alcuni sono stati venduti

2 (*a certain amount*) un po'; **I've got ~** (*money, milk*) ne ho un po'; **I've read ~ of the book** ho letto parte del libro; ~ (**of it**) **was left** ne è rimasto un po'; **could I have ~ of that cheese?** potrei avere un po' di quel formaggio?

♦ *adv*: ~ **10 people** circa 10 persone.

somebody ['sʌmbədı] *pron* qualcuno; ~ **or other** qualcuno.

someday ['sʌmdeı] *adv* uno di questi giorni, un giorno o l'altro.

somehow ['sʌmhau] *adv* in un modo o nell'altro, in qualche modo; (*for some reason*) per qualche ragione.

someone ['sʌmwʌn] *pron* = **somebody**.

someplace ['sʌmpleıs] *adv* (*US*) = **somewhere**.

somersault ['sʌməsɔ:lt] *n* capriola; (*in air*) salto mortale ♦ *vi* fare una capriola (*or* un salto mortale); (*car*) cappottare.

something ['sʌmθıŋ] *pron* qualcosa; ~ **interesting** qualcosa di interessante; ~ **to do** qualcosa da fare; **he's ~ like me** mi assomiglia un po'; **it's ~ of a problem** è un bel problema.

sometime ['sʌmtaım] *adv* (*in future*) una volta o l'altra; (*in past*): ~ **last month** durante il mese scorso; **I'll finish it** ~ lo finirò prima o poi.

sometimes ['sʌmtaımz] *adv* qualche volta.

somewhat ['sʌmwɔt] *adv* piuttosto.

somewhere ['sʌmwɛə*] *adv* in *or* da qualche parte; ~ **else** da qualche altra parte.

son [sʌn] *n* figlio.

sonar ['səunɑː*] n sonar m.
sonata [sə'nɑːtə] n sonata.
song [sɔŋ] n canzone f.
songbook ['sɔŋbuk] n canzoniere m.
songwriter ['sɔŋraɪtə*] n compositore/trice di canzoni.
sonic ['sɔnɪk] adj (boom) sonico(a).
son-in-law ['sʌnɪnlɔː] n genero.
sonnet ['sɔnɪt] n sonetto.
sonny ['sʌnɪ] n (col) ragazzo mio.
soon [suːn] adv presto, fra poco; (early) presto; ~ **afterwards** poco dopo; **very/ quite** ~ molto/abbastanza presto; **as** ~ **as possible** prima possibile; **I'll do it as** ~ **as I can** lo farò appena posso; **how** ~ **can you be ready?** fra quanto tempo sarà pronto?; **see you** ~! a presto!
sooner ['suːnə*] adv (time) prima; (preference): **I would** ~ **do** preferirei fare; ~ **or later** prima o poi; **no** ~ **said than done** detto fatto; **the** ~ **the better** prima è meglio è; **no** ~ **had we left than ...** eravamo appena partiti, quando ....
soot [sut] n fuliggine f.
soothe [suːð] vt calmare.
soothing ['suːðɪŋ] adj (ointment etc) calmante; (tone, words etc) rassicurante.
SOP n abbr = standard operating procedure.
sop [sɔp] n: **that's only a** ~ è soltanto un contentino.
sophisticated [sə'fɪstɪkeɪtɪd] adj sofisticato(a); raffinato(a); (film, mind) sottile.
sophistication [səfɪstɪ'keɪʃən] n raffinatezza; (of machine) complessità; (of argument etc) sottigliezza.
sophomore ['sɔfəmɔː*] n (US) studente/ essa del secondo anno.
soporific [sɔpə'rɪfɪk] adj soporifero(a).
sopping ['sɔpɪŋ] adj (also: ~ **wet**) bagnato(a) fradicio(a).
soppy ['sɔpɪ] adj (pej) sentimentale.
soprano [sə'prɑːnəu] n (voice) soprano m; (singer) soprano m/f.
sorbet ['sɔːbeɪ] n sorbetto.
sorcerer ['sɔːsərə*] n stregone m, mago.
sordid ['sɔːdɪd] adj sordido(a).
sore [sɔː*] adj (painful) dolorante; (col: offended) offeso(a) ♦ n piaga; **my eyes are** ~, **I have** ~ **eyes** mi fanno male gli occhi; ~ **throat** mal m di gola; **it's a** ~ **point** (fig) è un punto delicato.
sorely ['sɔːlɪ] adv (tempted) fortemente.
sorrel ['sɔrəl] n acetosa.
sorrow ['sɔrəu] n dolore m.
sorrowful ['sɔrəuful] adj triste.
sorry ['sɔrɪ] adj spiacente; (condition, excuse) misero(a), pietoso(a); (sight,

failure) triste; ~! scusa! (or scusi! or scusate!); **to feel** ~ **for sb** rincrescersi per qn; **I'm** ~ **to hear that** ... mi dispiace (sentire) che ...; **to be** ~ **about sth** essere dispiaciuto or spiacente di qc.
sort [sɔːt] n specie f, genere m; (make: of coffee, car etc) tipo ♦ vt (also: ~ **out**: papers) classificare; ordinare; (: letters etc) smistare; (: problems) risolvere; (COMPUT) ordinare; **what** ~ **of car?** che tipo di macchina?; **I shall do nothing of the** ~! nemmeno per sogno!; **it's** ~ **of awkward** (col) è piuttosto difficile.
sortie ['sɔːtɪ] n sortita.
sorting office ['sɔːtɪŋ-] n ufficio m smistamento inv.
SOS n abbr (= save our souls) S.O.S. m inv.
so-so ['səusəu] adv così così.
soufflé ['suːfleɪ] n soufflé m inv.
sought [sɔːt] pt, pp of **seek.**
sought-after ['sɔːtɑːftə*] adj richiesto(a).
soul [səul] n anima; **the poor** ~ **had nowhere to sleep** il poveraccio non aveva dove dormire; **I didn't see a** ~ non ho visto anima viva.
soul-destroying ['səuldɪ'strɔɪɪŋ] adj demoralizzante.
soulful ['səulful] adj pieno(a) di sentimento.
soulless ['səullɪs] adj senz'anima, inumano(a).
soul mate n anima gemella.
soul-searching ['səulsɑːtʃɪŋ] n: **after much** ~ dopo un profondo esame di coscienza.
sound [saund] adj (healthy) sano(a); (safe, not damaged) solido(a), in buono stato; (reliable, not superficial) solido(a); (sensible) giudizioso(a), di buon senso; (valid: argument, policy, claim) valido(a) ♦ adv: ~ **asleep** profondamente addormentato ♦ n (noise) suono; rumore m; (GEO) stretto ♦ vt (alarm) suonare; (also: ~ **out**: opinions) sondare ♦ vi suonare; (fig: seem) sembrare; **to be of** ~ **mind** essere sano di mente; **I don't like the** ~ **of it** (fig: of film etc) non mi dice niente; (: of news) è preoccupante; **it** ~s **as if** ... ho l'impressione che ...; **it** ~s **like French** somiglia al francese; **that** ~s **like them arriving** mi sembra di sentirli arrivare.
▶**sound off** vi (col): **to** ~ **off (about)** (give one's opinions) fare dei grandi discorsi (su).
sound barrier n muro del suono.
soundbite ['saundbaɪt] n frase f incisiva.
sound effects npl effetti mpl sonori.
sound engineer n tecnico del suono.
sounding ['saundɪŋ] n (NAUT etc) scandagliamento.

sounding board n (_MUS_) cassa di risonanza; (_fig_): **to use sb as a ~ for one's ideas** provare le proprie idee su qn.

soundly ['saundlɪ] adv (_sleep_) profondamente; (_beat_) duramente.

soundproof ['saundpruːf] vt insonorizzare, isolare acusticamente ♦ adj insonorizzato(a), isolato(a) acusticamente.

sound system n impianto m audio _inv_.

soundtrack ['saundtræk] n (_of film_) colonna sonora.

soup [suːp] n minestra; (_clear_) brodo; (_thick_) zuppa; **in the ~** (_fig_) nei guai.

soup course n minestra.

soup kitchen n mensa per i poveri.

soup plate n piatto fondo.

soupspoon ['suːpspuːn] n cucchiaio da minestra.

sour ['sauə*] adj aspro(a); (_fruit_) acerbo(a); (_milk_) acido(a), fermentato(a); (_fig_) acido(a); **to go or turn ~** (_milk, wine_) inacidirsi; (_fig: relationship, plans_) guastarsi; **it's ~ grapes** (_fig_) è soltanto invidia.

source [sɔːs] n fonte f, sorgente f; (_fig_) fonte; **I have it from a reliable ~ that ...** ho saputo da fonte sicura che ....

south [sauθ] n sud m, meridione m, mezzogiorno ♦ adj del sud, sud _inv_, meridionale ♦ adv verso sud; **(to the) ~ of** a sud di; **the S~ of France** il sud della Francia; **to travel ~** viaggiare verso sud.

South Africa n Sudafrica m.

South African adj, n sudafricano(a).

South America n Sudamerica m, America del sud.

South American adj, n sudamericano(a).

southbound ['sauθbaund] adj (_gen_) diretto(a) a sud; (_carriageway_) sud _inv_.

south-east [sauθ'iːst] n sud-est m.

South-East Asia n Asia m sudorientale.

southerly ['sʌðəlɪ] adj del sud.

southern ['sʌðən] adj del sud, meridionale; (_wall_) esposto(a) a sud; **the ~ hemisphere** l'emisfero australe.

South Pole n Polo Sud.

South Sea Islands npl: **the ~** le isole dei Mari del Sud.

South Seas npl: **the ~** i Mari del Sud.

South Vietnam n Vietnam m del Sud.

southward(s) ['sauθwəd(z)] adv verso sud.

south-west [sauθ'wɛst] n sud-ovest m.

souvenir [suːvə'nɪə*] n ricordo, souvenir m _inv_.

sovereign ['sɔvrɪn] adj, n sovrano(a).

sovereignty ['sɔvrəntɪ] n sovranità.

soviet ['səuvɪət] adj sovietico(a).

Soviet Union n: **the ~** l'Unione f Sovietica.

sow n [sau] scrofa ♦ vt [səu] (_pt ~ed, pp_ **sown** [səun]) seminare.

soya ['sɔɪə], (_US_) **soy** [sɔɪ] n: **~ bean** seme m di soia; **~ sauce** salsa di soia.

sozzled ['sɔzld] adj (_BRIT col_) sbronzo(a).

spa [spɑː] n (_resort_) stazione f termale; (_US: also_: **health ~**) centro di cure estetiche.

space [speɪs] n spazio; (_room_) posto; spazio; (_length of time_) intervallo ♦ cpd spaziale ♦ vt (_also_: **~ out**) distanziare; **in a confined ~** in un luogo chiuso; **to clear a ~ for sth** fare posto per qc; **in a short ~ of time** in breve tempo; **(with)in the ~ of an hour/ three generations** nell'arco di un'ora/di tre generazioni.

space bar n (_on typewriter_) barra spaziatrice.

spacecraft ['speɪskrɑːft] n (_pl inv_) veicolo spaziale.

spaceman ['speɪsmæn] n astronauta m, cosmonauta m.

spaceship ['speɪsʃɪp] n astronave f, navicella spaziale.

space shuttle n shuttle m _inv_.

spacesuit ['speɪssuːt] n tuta spaziale.

spacewoman ['speɪswumən] n astronauta f, cosmonauta f.

spacing ['speɪsɪŋ] n spaziatura; **single/ double ~** (_TYP etc_) spaziatura singola/ doppia.

spacious ['speɪʃəs] adj spazioso(a), ampio(a).

spade [speɪd] n (_tool_) vanga; pala; (_child's_) paletta; **~s** npl (_CARDS_) picche fpl.

spadework ['speɪdwəːk] n (_fig_) duro lavoro preparatorio.

spaghetti [spə'gɛtɪ] n spaghetti mpl.

Spain [speɪn] n Spagna.

span [spæn] n (_of bird, plane_) apertura alare; (_of arch_) campata; (_in time_) periodo; durata ♦ vt attraversare; (_fig_) abbracciare.

Spaniard ['spænjəd] n spagnolo/a.

spaniel ['spænjəl] n spaniel m _inv_.

Spanish ['spænɪʃ] adj spagnolo(a) ♦ n (_LING_) spagnolo; **the ~** npl gli Spagnoli; **~ omelette** frittata di cipolle, pomodori e peperoni.

spank [spæŋk] vt sculacciare.

spanner ['spænə*] n (_BRIT_) chiave f inglese.

spar [spɑː*] n asta, palo ♦ vi (_BOXING_) allenarsi.

spare [spɛə*] adj di riserva, di scorta; (_surplus_) in più, d'avanzo ♦ n (_part_) pezzo di ricambio ♦ vt (_do without_) fare a meno di; (_afford to give_) concedere; (_refrain from hurting, using_) risparmiare; **to ~** (_surplus_) d'avanzo; **there are 2 going** ~ (BRIT) ce ne sono 2 in più; **to** ~ **no expense** non badare a spese; **can you** ~ **the time?** ha tempo?; **I've a few minutes to** ~ ho un attimino di tempo; **there is no time to** ~ non c'è tempo da perdere; **can you** ~ **(me) £10?** puoi prestarmi 10 sterline?

spare part n pezzo di ricambio.

spare room n stanza degli ospiti.

spare time n tempo libero.

spare tyre n (AUT) gomma di scorta.

spare wheel n (AUT) ruota di scorta.

sparing ['spɛərɪŋ] adj (amount) scarso(a); (use) parsimonioso(a); **to be** ~ **with** essere avaro(a) di.

sparingly ['spɛərɪŋlɪ] adv moderatamente.

spark [spɑːk] n scintilla.

spark(ing) plug ['spɑːk(ɪŋ)-] n candela.

sparkle ['spɑːkl] n scintillio, sfavillio ♦ vi scintillare, sfavillare; (bubble) spumeggiare, frizzare.

sparkler ['spɑːklə*] n fuoco d'artificio.

sparkling ['spɑːklɪŋ] adj scintillante, sfavillante; (wine) spumante.

sparring partner ['spɑːrɪŋ-] n sparring partner m inv; (fig) interlocutore abituale in discussioni, dibattiti, tavole rotonde ecc.

sparrow ['spærəu] n passero.

sparse [spɑːs] adj sparso(a), rado(a).

spartan ['spɑːtən] adj (fig) spartano(a).

spasm ['spæzəm] n (MED) spasmo; (fig) accesso, attacco.

spasmodic [spæz'mɔdɪk] adj spasmodico(a); (fig) intermittente.

spastic ['spæstɪk] n spastico/a.

spat [spæt] pt, pp of **spit** ♦ n (US) battibecco.

spate [speɪt] n (fig): ~ **of** diluvio or fiume m di; **in** ~ (river) in piena.

spatial ['speɪʃəl] adj spaziale.

spatter ['spætə*] vt, vi schizzare.

spatula ['spætjulə] n spatola.

spawn [spɔːn] vt deporre; (pej) produrre ♦ vi deporre le uova ♦ n uova fpl.

SPCA n abbr (US: = Society for the Prevention of Cruelty to Animals) ≈ E.N.P.A. m (= Ente Nazionale per la Protezione degli Animali).

SPCC n abbr (US) = Society for the Prevention of Cruelty to Children.

speak, pt **spoke,** pp **spoken** [spiːk, spəuk, 'spəukn] vt (language) parlare; (truth) dire ♦ vi parlare; **to** ~ **to sb/of** or **about sth** parlare a qn/di qc; ~ **up!** parli più forte!; **to** ~ **at a conference/in a debate** partecipare ad una conferenza/ad un dibattito; ~**ing!** (on telephone) sono io!; **to** ~ **one's mind** dire quello che si pensa; **he has no money to** ~ **of** non si può proprio

dire che sia ricco.

▶**speak for** vt fus: **to** ~ **for sb** parlare a nome di qn; **that picture is already spoken for** (in shop) quel quadro è già stato venduto.

speaker ['spiːkə*] n (in public) oratore/trice; (also: **loud**~) altoparlante m; (POL): **the S**~ il presidente della Camera dei Comuni (BRIT) or dei Rappresentanti (US); **are you a Welsh** ~? parla gallese?

speaking ['spiːkɪŋ] adj parlante; **Italian-**~ **people** persone che parlano italiano; **to be on** ~ **terms** parlarsi.

spear [spɪə*] n lancia.

spearhead ['spɪəhɛd] n punta di lancia; (MIL) reparto d'assalto ♦ vt (attack etc) condurre.

spearmint ['spɪəmɪnt] n (BOT etc) menta verde.

spec [spɛk] n (BRIT col): **on** ~ sperando bene; **to buy sth on** ~ comprare qc sperando di fare un affare.

special ['spɛʃl] adj speciale ♦ n (train) treno supplementare; **nothing** ~ niente di speciale; **take** ~ **care** siate particolarmente prudenti.

special agent n agente m segreto.

special correspondent n inviato speciale.

special delivery n (POST): **by** ~ per espresso.

special effects npl (CINE) effetti mpl speciali.

specialist ['spɛʃəlɪst] n specialista m/f; **a heart** ~ (MED) un cardiologo.

speciality [spɛʃɪ'ælɪtɪ], (esp US) **specialty** n specialità f inv.

specialize ['spɛʃəlaɪz] vi: **to** ~ **(in)** specializzarsi (in).

specially ['spɛʃəlɪ] adv specialmente, particolarmente.

special offer n (COMM) offerta speciale.

specialty ['spɛʃəltɪ] n (esp US) = **speciality.**

species ['spiːʃiːz] n (pl inv) specie f inv.

specific [spə'sɪfɪk] adj specifico(a); preciso(a); **to be** ~ **to** avere un legame specifico con.

specifically [spə'sɪfɪklɪ] adv (explicitly: state, warn) chiaramente, esplicitamente; (especially: design, intend) appositamente.

specification [spɛsɪfɪ'keɪʃən] n specificazione f; (esp sth): ~**s** npl (of car, machine) dati mpl caratteristici; (for building) dettagli mpl.

specify ['spɛsɪfaɪ] vt specificare, precisare; **unless otherwise specified** salvo indicazioni contrarie.

specimen ['spɛsɪmən] n esemplare m, modello; (MED) campione m.

specimen copy n campione m.
specimen signature n firma depositata.
speck [spɛk] n puntino, macchiolina; (particle) granello.
speckled ['spɛkld] adj macchiettato(a).
specs [spɛks] npl (col) occhiali mpl.
spectacle ['spɛktəkl] n spettacolo; see also **spectacles**.
spectacle case n (BRIT) fodero per gli occhiali.
spectacles ['spɛktəklz] npl (BRIT) occhiali mpl.
spectacular [spɛk'tækjulə*] adj spettacolare ♦ n (CINE etc) film m inv etc spettacolare.
spectator [spɛk'teɪtə*] n spettatore/trice.
spectator sport n sport m inv come spettacolo.
spectra ['spɛktrə] npl of **spectrum**.
spectre, (US) specter ['spɛktə*] n spettro.
spectrum, pl spectra ['spɛktrəm, -rə] n spettro; (fig) gamma.
speculate ['spɛkjuleɪt] vi speculare; (try to guess): **to ~ about** fare ipotesi su.
speculation [spɛkju'leɪʃən] n speculazione f; congetture fpl.
speculative ['spɛkjulətɪv] adj speculativo(a).
speculator ['spɛkjuleɪtə*] n speculatore/trice.
sped [spɛd] pt, pp of **speed**.
speech [spiːtʃ] n (faculty) parola; (talk) discorso; (manner of speaking) parlata; (language) linguaggio; (enunciation) elocuzione f.
speech day n (BRIT SCOL) giorno della premiazione.
speech impediment n difetto di pronuncia.
speechless ['spiːtʃlɪs] adj ammutolito(a), muto(a).
speech therapy n cura dei disturbi del linguaggio.
speed [spiːd] n velocità f inv; (promptness) prontezza; (AUT: gear) marcia ♦ vi (pt, pp **sped** [spɛd]): **to ~ along** procedere velocemente; **the years sped by** gli anni sono volati; (AUT: exceed ~ limit) andare a velocità eccessiva; **at ~** (BRIT) velocemente; **at full or top ~** a tutta velocità; **at a ~ of 70 km/h** a una velocità di 70 km l'ora; **shorthand/typing ~s** numero di parole al minuto in stenografia/dattilografia; **a five-~ gearbox** un cambio a cinque marce.
▶**speed up**, pt, pp **~ed up** vi, vt accelerare.
speedboat ['spiːdbəut] n motoscafo; fuoribordo m inv.

speedily ['spiːdɪlɪ] adv velocemente; prontamente.
speeding ['spiːdɪŋ] n (AUT) eccesso di velocità.
speed limit n limite m di velocità.
speedometer [spɪ'dɔmɪtə*] n tachimetro.
speed trap n (AUT) tratto di strada sul quale la polizia controlla la velocità dei veicoli.
speedway ['spiːdweɪ] n (SPORT) pista per motociclismo.
speedy ['spiːdɪ] adj veloce, rapido(a); (reply) pronto(a).
speleologist [spɛlɪ'ɔlədʒɪst] n speleologo/a.
spell [spɛl] n (also: **magic ~**) incantesimo; (period of time) (breve) periodo ♦ vt (pt, pp **spelt** or **~ed** [spɛlt, spɛld]) (in writing) scrivere (lettera per lettera); (aloud) dire lettera per lettera; (fig) significare; **to cast a ~ on sb** fare un incantesimo a qn; **he can't ~** fa errori di ortografia; **how do you ~ your name?** come si scrive il suo nome?; **can you ~ it for me?** me lo può dettare lettera per lettera?
spellbound ['spɛlbaund] adj incantato(a), affascinato(a).
spelling ['spɛlɪŋ] n ortografia.
spelt [spɛlt] pt, pp of **spell**.
spend, pt, pp **spent** [spɛnd, spɛnt] vt (money) spendere; (time, life) passare; **to ~ time/money/effort on sth** dedicare tempo/soldi/energie a qc.
spending ['spɛndɪŋ] n: **government ~** spesa pubblica.
spending money n denaro per le piccole spese.
spending power n potere m d'acquisto.
spendthrift ['spɛndθrɪft] n spendaccione/a.
spent [spɛnt] pt, pp of **spend** ♦ adj (patience) esaurito(a); (cartridge, bullets, match) usato(a).
sperm [spəːm] n sperma m.
sperm bank n banca dello sperma.
sperm whale n capodoglio.
spew [spjuː] vt vomitare.
sphere [sfɪə*] n sfera.
spherical ['sfɛrɪkl] adj sferico(a).
sphinx [sfɪŋks] n sfinge f.
spice [spaɪs] n spezia ♦ vt aromatizzare.
spick-and-span ['spɪkən'spæn] adj impeccabile.
spicy ['spaɪsɪ] adj piccante.
spider ['spaɪdə*] n ragno; **~'s web** ragnatela.
spiel [spiːl] n (col) tiritera.
spike [spaɪk] n punta; **~s** npl (SPORT) scarpe fpl chiodate.
spike heel n (US) tacco a spillo.

spiky ['spaɪkɪ] adj (bush, branch) spinoso(a); (animal) ricoperto(a) di aculei.

spill, pt, pp **spilt** or ~**ed** [spɪl, -t, -d] vt versare, rovesciare ♦ vi versarsi, rovesciarsi; **to ~ the beans** (col) vuotare il sacco.

►**spill out** vi riversarsi fuori.

►**spill over** vi: **to ~ over (into)** (liquid) versarsi (in); (crowd) riversarsi (in).

spillage ['spɪlɪdʒ] n (event) fuoriuscita; (substance) sostanza fuoriuscita.

spin [spɪn] n (revolution of wheel) rotazione f; (AVIAT) avvitamento; (trip in car) giretto ♦ vb (pt, pp **spun** [spʌn]) vt (wool etc) filare; (wheel) far girare; (BRIT: clothes) mettere nella centrifuga ♦ vi girare; **to ~ a yarn** raccontare una storia; **to ~ a coin** (BRIT) lanciare in aria una moneta.

►**spin out** vt far durare.

spina bifida ['spaɪnə'bɪfɪdə] n spina bifida.

spinach ['spɪnɪtʃ] n spinacio; (as food) spinaci mpl.

spinal ['spaɪnl] adj spinale.

spinal column n colonna vertebrale, spina dorsale.

spinal cord n midollo spinale.

spindly ['spɪndlɪ] adj lungo(a) e sottile, filiforme.

spin doctor n (col) pierre addetto alla difesa di provvedimenti impopolari con interviste, interventi in TV ecc.

spin-dry ['spɪn'draɪ] vt asciugare con la centrifuga.

spin-dryer [spɪn'draɪə*] n (BRIT) centrifuga.

spine [spaɪn] n spina dorsale; (thorn) spina.

spine-chilling ['spaɪntʃɪlɪŋ] adj agghiacciante.

spineless ['spaɪnlɪs] adj invertebrato(a), senza spina dorsale; (fig) smidollato(a).

spinner ['spɪnə*] n (of thread) tessitore/ trice.

spinning ['spɪnɪŋ] n filatura.

spinning top n trottola.

spinning wheel n filatoio.

spin-off ['spɪnɔf] n applicazione f secondaria.

spinster ['spɪnstə*] n nubile f; zitella.

spiral ['spaɪərl] n spirale f ♦ adj a spirale ♦ vi (prices) salire vertiginosamente; **the inflationary ~** la spirale dell'inflazione.

spiral staircase n scala a chiocciola.

spire ['spaɪə*] n guglia.

spirit ['spɪrɪt] n (soul) spirito, anima; (ghost) spirito, fantasma m; (mood) stato d'animo, umore m; (courage) coraggio; ~**s** npl (drink) alcolici mpl; **in good ~s** di buon umore; **in low ~s** triste, abbattuto(a); **community ~**, **public ~** senso civico.

spirit duplicator n duplicatore m a spirito.

spirited ['spɪrɪtɪd] adj vivace, vigoroso(a); (horse) focoso(a).

spirit level n livella a bolla (d'aria).

spiritual ['spɪrɪtjuəl] adj spirituale ♦ n (also: **Negro ~**) spiritual m inv.

spiritualism ['spɪrɪtjuəlɪzəm] n spiritismo.

spit [spɪt] n (for roasting) spiedo; (spittle) sputo; (saliva) saliva ♦ vi (pt, pp **spat** [spæt]) sputare; (fire, fat) scoppiettare.

spite [spaɪt] n dispetto ♦ vt contrariare, far dispetto a; **in ~ of** nonostante, malgrado.

spiteful ['spaɪtful] adj dispettoso(a); (tongue, remark) maligno(a), velenoso(a).

spitroast ['spɪt'rəust] vt cuocere allo spiedo.

spitting ['spɪtɪŋ] n: "~ **prohibited**" "vietato sputare" ♦ adj: **to be the ~ image of sb** essere il ritratto vivente or sputato di qn.

spittle ['spɪtl] n saliva; sputo.

spiv [spɪv] n (BRIT col) imbroglione m.

splash [splæʃ] n spruzzo; (sound) tonfo; (of colour) schizzo ♦ vt spruzzare ♦ vi (also: ~ **about**) sguazzare; **to ~ paint on the floor** schizzare il pavimento di vernice.

splashdown ['splæʃdaun] n ammaraggio.

splay [spleɪ] adj: ~ **footed** che ha i piedi piatti.

spleen [spliːn] n (ANAT) milza.

splendid ['splendɪd] adj splendido(a), magnifico(a).

splendour, (US) **splendor** ['splendə*] n splendore m.

splice [splaɪs] vt (rope) impiombare; (wood) calettare.

splint [splɪnt] n (MED) stecca.

splinter ['splɪntə*] n scheggia ♦ vi scheggiarsi.

splinter group n gruppo dissidente.

split [splɪt] n spaccatura; (fig: division, quarrel) scissione f ♦ vb (pt, pp **split**) vt spaccare; (party) dividere; (work, profits) spartire, ripartire ♦ vi (divide) dividersi; **to do the ~s** fare la spaccata; **to ~ the difference** dividersi la differenza.

►**split up** vi (couple) separarsi, rompere; (meeting) sciogliersi.

split-level ['splɪtlevl] adj (house) a piani sfalsati.

split peas npl piselli mpl secchi spaccati.

split personality n doppia personalità.

split second n frazione f di secondo.

splitting ['splɪtɪŋ] adj: **a ~ headache** un mal di testa da impazzire.

splutter ['splʌtə*] vi farfugliare; sputacchiare.

spoil, pt, pp **spoilt** or ~**ed** [spɔɪl, -t, -d] vt (damage) rovinare, guastare; (mar) sciupare; (*child*) viziare; (*ballot paper*) rendere nullo(a), invalidare; **to be ~ing for a fight** morire dalla voglia di litigare.

spoils [spɔɪlz] *npl* bottino.

spoilsport ['spɔɪlspɔːt] *n* guastafeste *m/f inv*.

spoilt [spɔɪlt] *pt, pp of* **spoil** ♦ *adj* (*child*) viziato(a); (*ballot paper*) nullo(a).

spoke [spəuk] *pt of* **speak** ♦ *n* raggio.

spoken ['spəukn] *pp of* **speak**.

spokesman ['spəuksmən], **spokeswoman** [-wumən] *n* portavoce *m/f inv*.

spokesperson ['spəukspəːsn] *n* portavoce *m/f*.

sponge [spʌndʒ] *n* spugna; (*CULIN: also:* ~ **cake**) pan *m* di Spagna ♦ *vt* spugnare, pulire con una spugna ♦ *vi*: **to ~ on** *or* (*US*) **off of** scroccare a.

sponge bag *n* (*BRIT*) nécessaire *m inv*.

sponge cake *n* pan *m* di Spagna.

sponger ['spʌndʒə*] *n* (*pej*) parassita *m/f*, scroccone/a.

spongy ['spʌndʒɪ] *adj* spugnoso(a).

sponsor ['spɔnsə*] *n* (*RADIO, TV, SPORT etc*) sponsor *m inv*; (*of enterprise, bill, for fund-raising*) promotore/trice ♦ *vt* sponsorizzare; patrocinare; (*POL: bill*) presentare; **I ~ed him at 3p a mile** (*in fund-raising race*) ho offerto in beneficenza 3 penny per ogni miglio che fa.

sponsorship ['spɔnsəʃɪp] *n* sponsorizzazione *f*; patrocinio.

spontaneity [spɔntə'neɪɪtɪ] *n* spontaneità.

spontaneous [spɔn'teɪnɪəs] *adj* spontaneo(a).

spoof [spuːf] *n* presa in giro, parodia.

spooky ['spuːkɪ] *adj* che fa accapponare la pelle.

spool [spuːl] *n* bobina.

spoon [spuːn] *n* cucchiaio.

spoon-feed ['spuːnfiːd] *vt* nutrire con il cucchiaio; (*fig*) imboccare.

spoonful ['spuːnful] *n* cucchiaiata.

sporadic [spə'rædɪk] *adj* sporadico(a).

sport [spɔːt] *n* sport *m inv*; (*person*) persona di spirito; (*amusement*) divertimento ♦ *vt* sfoggiare; **indoor/outdoor ~s** sport *mpl* al chiuso/all'aria aperta; **to say sth in ~** dire qc per scherzo.

sporting ['spɔːtɪŋ] *adj* sportivo(a); **to give sb a ~ chance** dare a qn una possibilità (di vincere).

sport jacket *n* (*US*) = **sports jacket**.

sports car *n* automobile *f* sportiva.

sports ground *n* campo sportivo.

sports jacket *n* giacca sportiva.

sportsman ['spɔːtsmən] *n* sportivo.

sportsmanship ['spɔːtsmənʃɪp] *n* spirito

sportivo.

sports page *n* pagina sportiva.

sportswear ['spɔːtsweə*] *n* abiti *mpl* sportivi.

sportswoman ['spɔːtswumən] *n* sportiva.

sporty ['spɔːtɪ] *adj* sportivo(a).

spot [spɔt] *n* punto; (*mark*) macchia; (*dot: on pattern*) pallino; (*pimple*) foruncolo; (*place*) posto; (*also:* ~ **advertisement**) spot *m inv*; (*small amount*): **a ~ of** un po' di ♦ *vt* (*notice*) individuare, distinguere; **on the ~** sul posto; **to do sth on the ~** fare qc immediatamente *or* lì per lì; **to put sb on the ~** mettere qn in difficoltà; **to come out in ~s** coprirsi di foruncoli.

spot check *n* controllo senza preavviso.

spotless ['spɔtlɪs] *adj* immacolato(a).

spotlight ['spɔtlaɪt] *n* proiettore *m*; (*AUT*) faro ausiliario.

spot-on [spɔt'ɔn] *adj* (*BRIT*) esatto(a).

spot price *n* (*COMM*) prezzo del pronto.

spotted ['spɔtɪd] *adj* macchiato(a); a puntini, a pallini; ~ **with** punteggiato(a) di.

spotty ['spɔtɪ] *adj* (*face*) foruncoloso(a).

spouse [spauz] *n* sposo/a.

spout [spaut] *n* (*of jug*) beccuccio; (*of liquid*) zampillo, getto ♦ *vi* zampillare.

sprain [spreɪn] *n* storta, distorsione *f* ♦ *vt*: **to ~ one's ankle** storcersi una caviglia.

sprang [spræŋ] *pt of* **spring**.

sprawl [sprɔːl] *vi* sdraiarsi (in modo scomposto) ♦ *n*: **urban ~** sviluppo urbanistico incontrollato; **to send sb ~ing** mandare qn a gambe all'aria.

spray [spreɪ] *n* spruzzo; (*container*) nebulizzatore *m*, spray *m inv*; (*of flowers*) mazzetto ♦ *cpd* (*deodorant*) spray *inv* ♦ *vt* spruzzare; (*crops*) irrorare.

spread [sprɛd] *n* diffusione *f*; (*distribution*) distribuzione *f*; (*PRESS, TYP: two pages*) doppia pagina; (*: across columns*) articolo a più colonne; (*CULIN*) pasta (da spalmare) ♦ *vb* (*pt, pp* **spread**) *vt* (*cloth*) stendere, distendere; (*butter etc*) spalmare; (*disease, knowledge*) propagare, diffondere ♦ *vi* stendersi, distendersi; spalmarsi; propagarsi, diffondersi; **middle-age ~** pancetta; **repayments will be ~ over 18 months** i versamenti saranno scaglionati lungo un periodo di 18 mesi.

spread-eagled ['sprɛdiːgld] *adj*: **to be** *or* **lie ~** essere disteso(a) a gambe e braccia aperte.

spreadsheet ['sprɛdʃiːt] *n* (*COMPUT*) foglio elettronico.

spree [spriː] *n*: **to go on a ~** fare baldoria.

sprig [sprɪg] n ramoscello.
sprightly ['spraɪtlɪ] adj vivace.
spring [sprɪŋ] n (leap) salto, balzo; (bounciness) elasticità; (coiled metal) molla; (season) primavera; (of water) sorgente f ♦ vi (pt **sprang**, pp **sprung** [spræŋ, sprʌŋ]) saltare, balzare ♦ vt: **to ~ a leak** (pipe etc) cominciare a perdere; **to walk with a ~ in one's step** camminare con passo elastico; **in ~**, **in the ~** in primavera; **to ~ from** provenire da; **to ~ into action** entrare (rapidamente) in azione; **he sprang the news on me** mi ha sorpreso con quella notizia.
▶**spring up** vi (problem) presentarsi.
springboard ['sprɪŋbɔːd] n trampolino.
spring-clean [sprɪŋ'kliːn] n (also: ~**ing**) grandi pulizie fpl di primavera.
spring onion n (BRIT) cipollina.
spring roll n involtino fritto di verdure o carne tipico della cucina cinese.
springtime ['sprɪŋtaɪm] n primavera.
springy ['sprɪŋɪ] adj elastico(a).
sprinkle ['sprɪŋkl] vt spruzzare; spargere; **to ~ water** etc **on**, ~ **with water** etc spruzzare dell'acqua etc su; **to ~ sugar** etc **on**, ~ **with sugar** etc spolverizzare di zucchero etc; ~**d with** (fig) cosparso(a) di.
sprinkler ['sprɪŋklə*] n (for lawn etc) irrigatore m; (for fire-fighting) sprinkler m inv.
sprinkling ['sprɪŋklɪŋ] n (of water) qualche goccia; (of salt, sugar) pizzico.
sprint [sprɪnt] n scatto ♦ vi scattare; **the 200-metres** ~ i 200 metri piani.
sprinter ['sprɪntə*] n velocista m/f.
sprite [spraɪt] n elfo, folletto.
spritzer ['sprɪtsə*] n spritz m inv.
sprocket ['sprɔkɪt] n (on printer etc) dente m, rocchetto.
sprout [spraut] vi germogliare.
sprouts [sprauts] npl (also: **Brussels** ~) cavolini mpl di Bruxelles.
spruce [spruːs] n abete m rosso ♦ adj lindo(a); azzimato(a).
▶**spruce up** vt (tidy) mettere in ordine; (smarten up: room etc) abbellire; **to ~ o.s. up** farsi bello(a).
sprung [sprʌŋ] pp of **spring**.
spry [spraɪ] adj arzillo(a), sveglio(a).
SPUC n abbr (= Society for the Protection of Unborn Children) associazione anti-abortista.
spun [spʌn] pt, pp of **spin**.
spur [spəː*] n sperone m; (fig) sprone m, incentivo ♦ vt (also: ~ **on**) spronare; **on the ~ of the moment** lì per lì.

spurious ['spjuərɪəs] adj falso(a).
spurn [spəːn] vt rifiutare con disprezzo, sdegnare.
spurt [spəːt] n getto; (of energy) esplosione f ♦ vi sgorgare; zampillare; **to put in** or **on a ~** (runner) fare uno scatto; (fig: in work etc) affrettarsi, sbrigarsi.
sputter ['spʌtə*] vi = **splutter**.
spy [spaɪ] n spia ♦ cpd (film, story) di spionaggio ♦ vi: **to ~ on** spiare ♦ vt (see) scorgere.
spying ['spaɪɪŋ] n spionaggio.
Sq. abbr (in address) = **square**.
sq. abbr (MATH etc) = **square**.
squabble ['skwɔbl] n battibecco ♦ vi bisticciarsi.
squad [skwɔd] n (MIL) plotone m; (POLICE) squadra; **flying** ~ (POLICE) volante f.
squad car n (BRIT POLICE) automobile f della polizia.
squaddie ['skwɔdɪ] n (MIL col) burba.
squadron ['skwɔdrn] n (MIL) squadrone m; (AVIAT, NAUT) squadriglia.
squalid ['skwɔlɪd] adj sordido(a).
squall [skwɔːl] n burrasca.
squalor ['skwɔlə*] n squallore m.
squander ['skwɔndə*] vt dissipare.
square [skwɛə*] n quadrato; (in town) piazza; (US: block of houses) blocco, isolato; (instrument) squadra ♦ adj quadrato(a); (honest) onesto(a); (col: ideas, person) di vecchio stampo ♦ vt (arrange) regolare; (MATH) elevare al quadrato ♦ vi (agree) accordarsi; **a ~ meal** un pasto abbondante; **2 metres** ~ di 2 metri per 2; **1 ~ metre** 1 metro quadrato; **we're back to ~ one** (fig) siamo al punto di partenza; **all ~** pari; **to get one's accounts** ~ mettere in ordine i propri conti; **I'll ~ it with him** (col) sistemo io le cose con lui; **can you ~ it with your conscience?** (reconcile) puoi conciliarlo con la tua coscienza?
▶**square up** vi (BRIT: settle) saldare, pagare; **to ~ up with sb** regolare i conti con qn.
square bracket n (TYP) parentesi f inv quadra.
squarely ['skwɛəlɪ] adv (directly) direttamente; (honestly, fairly) onestamente.
square root n radice f quadrata.
squash [skwɔʃ] n (BRIT: drink): **lemon/ orange** ~ sciroppo di limone/arancia; (vegetable) zucca; (SPORT) squash m ♦ vt schiacciare.
squat [skwɔt] adj tarchiato(a), tozzo(a) ♦ vi accovacciarsi; (on property) occupare

abusivamente.

squatter ['skwɔtə*] *n* occupante *m/f* abusivo(a).

squawk [skwɔ:k] *vi* emettere strida rauche.

squeak [skwi:k] *vi* squittire ♦ *n* (*of hinge, wheel etc*) cigolio; (*of shoes*) scricchiolio; (*of mouse etc*) squittio.

squeaky ['skwi:kɪ] *adj* (*col*) cigolante; **to be ~ clean** (*fig*) avere un'immagine pulita.

squeal [skwi:l] *vi* strillare.

squeamish ['skwi:mɪʃ] *adj* schizzinoso(a); disgustato(a).

squeeze [skwi:z] *n* pressione *f*; (*also ECON*) stretta; (*credit ~*) stretta creditizia ♦ *vt* premere; (*hand, arm*) stringere ♦ *vi*: **to ~ in** infilarsi; **to ~ past/under sth** passare vicino/sotto a qc con difficoltà; **a ~ of lemon** una spruzzata di limone.

▶**squeeze out** *vt* spremere.

squelch [skweltʃ] *vi* fare ciac; sguazzare.

squib [skwɪb] *n* petardo.

squid [skwɪd] *n* calamaro.

squint [skwɪnt] *vi* essere strabico(a); (*in the sunlight*) strizzare gli occhi ♦ *n*: **he has a ~** è strabico; **to ~ at sth** guardare qc di traverso; (*quickly*) dare un'occhiata a qc.

squire ['skwaɪə*] *n* (*BRIT*) proprietario terriero.

squirm [skwə:m] *vi* contorcersi.

squirrel ['skwɪrəl] *n* scoiattolo.

squirt [skwə:t] *n* schizzo ♦ *vi* schizzare; zampillare.

Sr *abbr* = **senior; sister** (*REL*).

SRC *n abbr* (*BRIT*: = *Students' Representative Council*) *comitato di rappresentanza studenti*.

Sri Lanka [srɪ'læŋkə] *n* Sri Lanka *m*.

SRN *n abbr* (*BRIT*: = *State Registered Nurse*) infermiera diplomata (*dopo corso triennale*).

SRO *abbr* (*US*: = *standing room only*) solo posti in piedi.

SS *abbr* = **steamship**.

SSA *n abbr* (*US*: = *Social Security Administration*) ≈ Previdenza Sociale.

SST *n abbr* (*US*: = *supersonic transport*).

ST *abbr* (*US*: = *Standard Time*) *ora ufficiale*.

St *abbr* = **saint; street**.

stab [stæb] *n* (*with knife etc*) pugnalata; (*col: try*): **to have a ~ at (doing) sth** provare a fare qc ♦ *vt* pugnalare; **to ~ sb to death** uccidere qn a coltellate.

stabbing ['stæbɪŋ] *n*: **there's been a ~** qualcuno è stato pugnalato ♦ *adj* (*pain, ache*) lancinante.

stability [stə'bɪlɪtɪ] *n* stabilità.

stabilization [steɪbəlaɪ'zeɪʃən] *n* stabilizzazione *f*.

stabilize ['steɪbəlaɪz] *vt* stabilizzare ♦ *vi* stabilizzarsi.

stabilizer ['steɪbəlaɪzə*] *n* (*AVIAT, NAUT*) stabilizzatore *m*.

stable ['steɪbl] *n* (*for horses*) scuderia; (*for cattle*) stalla ♦ *adj* stabile; **riding ~s** maneggio.

staccato [stə'kɑ:təu] *adv* in modo staccato ♦ *adj* (*MUS*) staccato(a); (*sound*) scandito(a).

stack [stæk] *n* catasta, pila; (*col*) mucchio, sacco ♦ *vt* accatastare, ammucchiare; **there's ~s of time to finish it** (*BRIT col*) abbiamo un sacco di tempo per finirlo.

stadium ['steɪdɪəm] *n* stadio.

staff [stɑ:f] *n* (*work force: gen*) personale *m*; (: *BRIT: SCOL*) personale insegnante; (: *servants*) personale di servizio; (*MIL*) stato maggiore; (*stick*) bastone *m* ♦ *vt* fornire di personale.

staffroom ['stɑ:fru:m] *n* sala dei professori.

Staffs *abbr* (*BRIT*) = **Staffordshire**.

stag [stæg] *n* cervo; (*BRIT STOCK EXCHANGE*) rialzista *m/f* su nuove emissioni.

stage [steɪdʒ] *n* (*platform*) palco; (*in theatre*) palcoscenico; (*profession*): **the ~** il teatro, la scena; (*point*) fase *f*, stadio ♦ *vt* (*play*) allestire, mettere in scena; (*demonstration*) organizzare; (*fig: perform: recovery etc*) effettuare; **in ~s** per gradi; **a tappe; in the early/final ~s** negli stadi iniziali/finali; **to go through a difficult ~** attraversare un periodo difficile.

stagecoach ['steɪdʒkəutʃ] *n* diligenza.

stage door *n* ingresso degli artisti.

stage fright *n* paura del pubblico.

stagehand ['steɪdʒhænd] *n* macchinista *m*.

stage-manage ['steɪdʒmænɪdʒ] *vt* allestire le scene per; montare.

stage manager *n* direttore *m* di scena.

stagger ['stægə*] *vi* barcollare ♦ *vt* (*person*) sbalordire; (*hours, holidays*) scaglionare.

staggering ['stægərɪŋ] *adj* (*amazing*) incredibile, sbalorditivo(a).

staging post ['steɪdʒɪŋ-] *n* passaggio obbligato.

stagnant ['stægnənt] *adj* stagnante.

stagnate [stæg'neɪt] *vi* (*also fig*) stagnare.

stagnation [stæg'neɪʃən] *n* stagnazione *f*, ristagno.

stag night, stag party *n* festa di addio al celibato.

staid [steɪd] *adj* posato(a), serio(a).

stain [steɪn] *n* macchia; (*colouring*) colorante *m* ♦ *vt* macchiare; (*wood*) tingere.

stained glass window ['steɪnd-] *n*
vetrata.
stainless ['steɪnlɪs] *adj (steel)* inossidabile.
stain remover *n* smacchiatore *m*.
stair [stɛə*] *n (step)* gradino; **~s** *npl (flight of
~s)* scale *fpl*, scala.
staircase ['stɛəkeɪs], **stairway** ['stɛəweɪ] *n*
scale *fpl*, scala.
stairwell ['stɛəwɛl] *n* tromba delle scale.
stake [steɪk] *n* palo, piolo; *(BETTING)*
puntata, scommessa ♦ *vt (bet)*
scommettere; *(risk)* rischiare; *(also: ~
out: area)* delimitare con paletti; **to be at
~** essere in gioco; **to have a ~ in sth**
avere un interesse in qc; **to ~ a claim (to
sth)** rivendicare (qc).
stakeout ['steɪkaut] *n* sorveglianza.
stalactite ['stæləktaɪt] *n* stalattite *f*.
stalagmite ['stæləgmaɪt] *n* stalagmite *f*.
stale [steɪl] *adj (bread)* raffermo(a),
stantio(a); *(beer)* svaporato(a); *(smell)* di
chiuso.
stalemate ['steɪlmeɪt] *n* stallo; *(fig)* punto
morto.
stalk [stɔ:k] *n* gambo, stelo ♦ *vt* inseguire
♦ *vi* camminare impettito(a).
stall [stɔ:l] *n (BRIT: in street, market etc)*
bancarella; *(in stable)* box *m inv* di stalla
♦ *vt (AUT)* far spegnere ♦ *vi (AUT)*
spegnersi, fermarsi; *(fig)* temporeggiare;
~s *npl (BRIT: in cinema, theatre)* platea;
newspaper/flower ~ chiosco del
giornalaio/del fioraio.
stallholder ['stɔ:lhəuldə*] *n (BRIT)*
bancarellista *m/f*.
stallion ['stæljən] *n* stallone *m*.
stalwart ['stɔ:lwət] *n* membro fidato.
stamen ['steɪmɛn] *n* stame *m*.
stamina ['stæmɪnə] *n* vigore *m*, resistenza.
stammer ['stæmə*] *n* balbuzie *f* ♦ *vi*
balbettare.
stamp [stæmp] *n (postage ~)* francobollo;
(implement) timbro; *(mark, also fig)*
marchio, impronta; *(on document)* bollo;
timbro ♦ *vi (also: ~ one's foot)* battere il
piede ♦ *vt* battere; *(letter)* affrancare;
(mark with a ~) timbrare; **~ed addressed
envelope (sae)** busta affrancata per la
risposta.
▶**stamp out** *vt (fire)* estinguere; *(crime)*
eliminare; *(opposition)* soffocare.
stamp album *n* album *m inv* per
francobolli.
stamp collecting *n* filatelia.
stamp duty *n (BRIT)* bollo.
stampede [stæm'pi:d] *n* fuggi fuggi *m inv*;
(of cattle) fuga precipitosa.
stamp machine *n* distributore *m*

automatico di francobolli.
stance [stæns] *n* posizione *f*.
stand [stænd] *n (position)* posizione *f*; *(MIL)*
resistenza; *(structure)* supporto, sostegno;
(at exhibition) stand *m inv*; *(at market)*
bancarella; *(booth)* chiosco; *(SPORT)*
tribuna; *(also: music ~)* leggio *m* ♦ *vb (pt,
pp stood* [stud]*) vi* stare in piedi; *(rise)*
alzarsi in piedi; *(be placed)* trovarsi ♦ *vt
(place)* mettere, porre; *(tolerate, withstand)*
resistere, sopportare; **to make a ~**
prendere posizione; **to take a ~ on an
issue** prendere posizione su un
problema; **to ~ for parliament** *(BRIT)*
presentarsi come candidato (per il
parlamento); **to ~ guard** *or* **watch** *(MIL)*
essere di guardia; **it ~s to reason** è
logico; **as things ~** stando così le cose; **to
~ sb a drink/meal** offrire da bere/un
pranzo a qn; **I can't ~ him** non lo
sopporto.
▶**stand aside** *vi* farsi da parte, scostarsi.
▶**stand by** *vi (be ready)* tenersi pronto(a)
♦ *vt fus (opinion)* sostenere.
▶**stand down** *vi (withdraw)* ritirarsi; *(LAW)*
lasciare il banco dei testimoni.
▶**stand for** *vt fus (signify)* rappresentare,
significare; *(tolerate)* sopportare,
tollerare.
▶**stand in for** *vt fus* sostituire.
▶**stand out** *vi (be prominent)* spiccare.
▶**stand up** *vi (rise)* alzarsi in piedi.
▶**stand up for** *vt fus* difendere.
▶**stand up to** *vt fus* tener testa a, resistere
a.
stand-alone ['stændələun] *adj (COMPUT)*
stand-alone *inv*.
standard ['stændəd] *n* modello, standard *m
inv*; *(level)* livello; *(flag)* stendardo ♦ *adj
(size etc)* normale, standard *inv*; *(practice)*
normale; *(model)* di serie; **~s** *npl (morals)*
principi *mpl*, valori *mpl*; **to be** *or* **come up
to ~** rispondere ai requisiti; **below** *or* **not
up to ~** *(work)* mediocre; **to apply a
double ~** usare metri diversi (nel
giudicare *or* fare *etc*); **~ of living** livello
di vita.
standardization [stændədaɪ'zeɪʃən] *n*
standardizzazione *f*.
standardize ['stændədaɪz] *vt* normalizzare,
standardizzare.
standard lamp *n (BRIT)* lampada a stelo.
standard time *n* ora ufficiale.
stand-by ['stændbaɪ] *n* riserva, sostituto; **to
be on ~** *(gen)* tenersi pronto(a); *(doctor)*
essere di guardia; **a ~ ticket** un biglietto
standby; **to fly ~** essere in lista d'attesa
per un volo.

stand-by generator *n* generatore *m* d'emergenza.

stand-by passenger *n* (*AVIAT*) passeggero/a in lista d'attesa.

stand-by ticket *n* (*AVIAT*) biglietto senza garanzia.

stand-in ['stændɪn] *n* sostituto/a; (*CINE*) controfigura.

standing ['stændɪŋ] *adj* diritto(a), in piedi; (*permanent: committee*) permanente; (: *rule*) fisso(a); (: *army*) regolare; (*grievance*) continuo(a); (*duration*): **of 6 months'** ~ che dura da 6 mesi ♦ *n* rango, condizione *f*, posizione *f*; **it's a** ~ **joke** è diventato proverbiale; **he was given a** ~ **ovation** tutti si alzarono per applaudirlo; **a man of some** ~ un uomo di una certa importanza.

standing committee *n* commissione *f* permanente.

standing order *n* (*BRIT: at bank*) ordine *m* di pagamento (permanente); ~**s** *npl* (*MIL*) regolamento.

standing room *n* posto all'impiedi.

stand-off ['stændɔf] *n* (*esp US: stalemate*) situazione *f* di stallo.

standoffish [stænd'ɔfɪʃ] *adj* scostante, freddo(a).

standpat ['stændpæt] *adj* (*US*) irremovibile.

standpipe ['stændpaɪp] *n* fontanella.

standpoint ['stændpɔɪnt] *n* punto di vista.

standstill ['stændstɪl] *n*: **at a** ~ fermo(a); (*fig*) a un punto morto; **to come to a** ~ fermarsi; giungere a un punto morto.

stank [stæŋk] *pt of* **stink**.

stanza ['stænzə] *n* stanza (*poesia*).

staple ['steɪpl] *n* (*for papers*) graffetta; (*chief product*) prodotto principale ♦ *adj* (*food etc*) di base; (*crop, industry*) principale ♦ *vt* cucire.

stapler ['steɪplə*] *n* cucitrice *f*.

star [stɑ:*] *n* stella; (*celebrity*) divo/a; (*principal actor*) vedette *f inv* ♦ *vi*: **to** ~ **(in)** essere il (*or* la) protagonista (di) ♦ *vt* (*CINE*) essere interpretato(a) da; **four-**~ **hotel** ≈ albergo di prima categoria; **2-**~ **petrol** (*BRIT*) ≈ benzina normale; **4-**~ **petrol** (*BRIT*) ≈ super *f*.

star attraction *n* numero principale.

starboard ['stɑːbəd] *n* dritta; **to** ~ a dritta.

starch [stɑːtʃ] *n* amido.

starched ['stɑːtʃt] *adj* (*collar*) inamidato(a).

starchy ['stɑːtʃɪ] *adj* (*food*) ricco(a) di amido.

stardom ['stɑːdəm] *n* celebrità.

stare [stɛə*] *n* sguardo fisso ♦ *vi*: **to** ~ **at** fissare.

starfish ['stɑːfɪʃ] *n* stella di mare.

stark [stɑːk] *adj* (*bleak*) desolato(a); (*simplicity, colour*) austero(a); (*reality, poverty, truth*) crudo(a) ♦ *adv*: ~ **naked** completamente nudo(a).

starkers ['stɑːkəz] *adj*: **to be** ~ (*BRIT col*) essere nudo(a) come un verme.

starlet ['stɑːlɪt] *n* (*CINE*) stellina.

starlight ['stɑːlaɪt] *n*: **by** ~ alla luce delle stelle.

starling ['stɑːlɪŋ] *n* storno.

starlit ['stɑːlɪt] *adj* stellato(a).

starry ['stɑːrɪ] *adj* stellato(a).

starry-eyed [stɑːrɪ'aɪd] *adj* (*idealistic, gullible*) ingenuo(a); (*from wonder*) meravigliato(a).

Stars and Stripes *npl*: **the** ~ la bandiera a stelle e strisce.

star sign *n* segno zodiacale.

star-studded ['stɑːstʌdɪd] *adj*: **a** ~ **cast** un cast di attori famosi.

start [stɑːt] *n* inizio; (*of race*) partenza; (*sudden movement*) sobbalzo; (*advantage*) vantaggio ♦ *vt* cominciare, iniziare; (*found: business, newspaper*) fondare, creare ♦ *vi* cominciare; (*on journey*) partire, mettersi in viaggio; (*jump*) sobbalzare; **to** ~ **doing sth** (in)cominciare a fare qc; **at the** ~ all'inizio; **for a** ~ tanto per cominciare; **to make an early** ~ partire di buon'ora; **to** ~ **(off) with ...** (*firstly*) per prima cosa ...; (*at the beginning*) all'inizio; **to** ~ **a fire** provocare un incendio.

▶**start off** *vi* cominciare; (*leave*) partire.

▶**start over** *vi* (*US*) ricominciare.

▶**start up** *vi* cominciare; (*car*) avviarsi ♦ *vt* iniziare; (*car*) avviare.

starter ['stɑːtə*] *n* (*AUT*) motorino d'avviamento; (*SPORT: official*) starter *m inv*; (: *runner, horse*) partente *m/f*; (*BRIT CULIN*) primo piatto.

starting handle ['stɑːtɪŋ-] *n* (*BRIT*) manovella d'avviamento.

starting point *n* punto di partenza.

starting price *n* prezzo *m* base *inv*.

startle ['stɑːtl] *vt* far trasalire.

startling ['stɑːtlɪŋ] *adj* sorprendente, sbalorditivo(a).

star turn *n* (*BRIT*) attrazione *f* principale.

starvation [stɑː'veɪʃən] *n* fame *f*, inedia; **to die of** ~ morire d'inedia.

starve [stɑːv] *vi* morire di fame; soffrire la fame ♦ *vt* far morire di fame, affamare; **I'm starving** muoio di fame.

stash [stæʃ] *vt*: **to** ~ **sth away** (*col*) nascondere qc.

state [steɪt] *n* stato; (*pomp*): **in** ~ in pompa ♦ *vt* dichiarare, affermare; annunciare;

to be in a ~ essere agitato(a); **the** ~ **of the art** il livello di tecnologia (or cultura etc); ~ **of emergency** stato di emergenza; ~ **of mind** stato d'animo.

state control n controllo statale.

stated ['steɪtɪd] adj fissato(a), stabilito(a).

State Department n (US) Dipartimento di Stato, ≈ Ministero degli Esteri.

state education n (BRIT) istruzione f pubblica or statale.

stateless ['steɪtlɪs] adj apolide.

stately ['steɪtlɪ] adj maestoso(a), imponente.

statement ['steɪtmənt] n dichiarazione f; (LAW) deposizione f; (FINANCE) rendiconto; **official** ~ comunicato ufficiale; ~ **of account, bank** ~ estratto conto.

state-owned ['steɪt'əund] adj statalizzato(a).

States [steɪts] npl: **the** ~ (USA) gli Stati Uniti.

state school n scuola statale.

statesman ['steɪtsmən] n statista m.

statesmanship ['steɪtsmənʃɪp] n abilità politica.

static ['stætɪk] n (RADIO) scariche fpl ♦ adj statico(a); ~ **electricity** elettricità statica.

station ['steɪʃən] n stazione f; (rank) rango, condizione f ♦ vt collocare, disporre; **action** ~**s** posti mpl di combattimento; **to be** ~**ed in** (MIL) essere di stanza in.

stationary ['steɪʃənərɪ] adj fermo(a), immobile.

stationer ['steɪʃənə*] n cartolaio/a; ~**'s shop** cartoleria.

stationery ['steɪʃənərɪ] n articoli mpl di cancelleria; (writing paper) carta da lettere.

station master n (RAIL) capostazione m.

station wagon n (US) giardinetta.

statistic [stə'tɪstɪk] n statistica; see also **statistics**.

statistical [stə'tɪstɪkəl] adj statistico(a).

statistics [stə'tɪstɪks] n (science) statistica.

statue ['stætjuː] n statua.

statuesque [stætju'ɛsk] adj statuario(a).

statuette [stætju'ɛt] n statuetta.

stature ['stætʃə*] n statura.

status ['steɪtəs] n posizione f, condizione f sociale; (prestige) prestigio; (legal, marital) stato.

status quo [-'kwəu] n: **the** ~ lo statu quo.

status symbol n simbolo di prestigio.

statute ['stætjuːt] n legge f; ~**s** npl (of club etc) statuto.

statute book n codice m.

statutory ['stætjutərɪ] adj stabilito(a) dalla legge, statutario(a); ~ **meeting** (COMM) assemblea ordinaria.

staunch [stɔːntʃ] adj fidato(a), leale ♦ vt (flow) arrestare; (blood) arrestare il flusso di.

stave [steɪv] n (MUS) rigo ♦ vt: **to** ~ **off** (attack) respingere; (threat) evitare.

stay [steɪ] n (period of time) soggiorno, permanenza ♦ vi rimanere; (reside) alloggiare, stare; (spend some time) trattenersi, soggiornare; ~ **of execution** (LAW) sospensione f dell'esecuzione; **to** ~ **put** non muoversi; **to** ~ **with friends** stare presso amici; **to** ~ **the night** passare la notte.

►**stay behind** vi restare indietro.

►**stay in** vi (at home) stare in casa.

►**stay on** vi restare, rimanere.

►**stay out** vi (of house) rimanere fuori (di casa); (strikers) continuare lo sciopero.

►**stay up** vi (at night) rimanere alzato(a).

staying power ['steɪɪŋ-] n capacità di resistenza.

STD n abbr (BRIT: = subscriber trunk dialling) teleselezione f; (= sexually transmitted disease) malattia venerea.

stead [stɛd] n (BRIT): **in sb's** ~ al posto di qn; **to stand sb in good** ~ essere utile a qn.

steadfast ['stɛdfɑːst] adj fermo(a), risoluto(a).

steadily ['stɛdɪlɪ] adv continuamente; (walk) con passo sicuro.

steady ['stɛdɪ] adj stabile, solido(a), fermo(a); (regular) costante; (boyfriend etc) fisso(a); (person) calmo(a), tranquillo(a) ♦ vt stabilizzare; calmare; **to** ~ **o.s.** ritrovare l'equilibrio.

steak [steɪk] n (meat) bistecca; (fish) trancia.

steakhouse ['steɪkhaus] n ristorante specializzato in bistecche.

steal, pt **stole**, pp **stolen** [stiːl, stəul, 'stəuln] vt rubare ♦ vi (thieve) rubare.

►**steal away, steal off** vi svignarsela, andarsene alla chetichella.

stealth [stɛlθ] n: **by** ~ furtivamente.

stealthy ['stɛlθɪ] adj furtivo(a).

steam [stiːm] n vapore m ♦ vt trattare con vapore; (CULIN) cuocere a vapore ♦ vi fumare; (ship): **to** ~ **along** filare; **to let off** ~ (fig) sfogarsi; **under one's own** ~ (fig) da solo, con i propri mezzi; **to run out of** ~ (fig: person) non farcela più.

►**steam up** vi (window) appannarsi; **to get** ~**ed up about sth** (fig) andare in bestia per qc.

steam engine n macchina a vapore; (*RAIL*) locomotiva a vapore.

steamer ['stiːmə*] n piroscafo, vapore m; (*CULIN*) pentola a vapore.

steam iron n ferro a vapore.

steamroller ['stiːmrəulə*] n rullo compressore.

steamship ['stiːmʃɪp] n piroscafo, vapore m.

steamy ['stiːmɪ] adj pieno(a) di vapore; (*window*) appannato(a).

steed [stiːd] n (*literary*) corsiero, destriero.

steel [stiːl] n acciaio ♦ cpd di acciaio.

steel band n banda di strumenti a percussione (*tipica dei Caribi*).

steel industry n industria dell'acciaio.

steel mill n acciaieria.

steelworks ['stiːlwəːks] n acciaieria.

steely ['stiːlɪ] adj (*determination*) inflessibile; (*gaze*) duro(a); (*eyes*) freddo(a) come l'acciaio.

steep [stiːp] adj ripido(a), scosceso(a); (*price*) eccessivo(a) ♦ vt inzuppare; (*washing*) mettere a mollo.

steeple ['stiːpl] n campanile m.

steeplechase ['stiːpltʃeɪs] n corsa a ostacoli, steeplechase m inv.

steeplejack ['stiːpldʒæk] n chi ripara campanili e ciminiere.

steer [stɪə*] n manzo ♦ vt (*ship*) governare; (*car*) guidare ♦ vi (*NAUT: person*) governare; (: *ship*) rispondere al timone; (*car*) guidarsi; **to ~ clear of sb/sth** (*fig*) tenersi alla larga da qn/qc.

steering ['stɪərɪŋ] n (*AUT*) sterzo.

steering column n piantone m dello sterzo.

steering committee n comitato direttivo.

steering wheel n volante m.

stem [stɛm] n (*of flower, plant*) stelo; (*of tree*) fusto; (*of glass*) gambo; (*of fruit, leaf*) picciolo ♦ vt contenere, arginare.

▶**stem from** vt fus provenire da, derivare da.

stench [stɛntʃ] n puzzo, fetore m.

stencil ['stɛnsl] n (*of metal, cardboard*) stampino, mascherina; (*in typing*) matrice f.

stenographer [stɛ'nɔgrəfə*] n (*US*) stenografo/a.

stenography [stɛ'nɔgrəfɪ] n (*US*) stenografia.

step [stɛp] n passo; (*stair*) gradino, scalino; (*action*) mossa, azione f ♦ vi: **to ~ forward** fare un passo avanti; **~s** npl (*BRIT*) = **stepladder**; **~ by ~** un passo dietro l'altro; (*fig*) poco a poco; **to be in/out of ~ with** (*also fig*) stare/non stare al passo con.

▶**step down** vi (*fig*) ritirarsi.

▶**step in** vi fare il proprio ingresso.

▶**step off** vt fus scendere da.

▶**step over** vt fus scavalcare.

▶**step up** vt aumentare; intensificare.

step aerobics n step m inv.

stepbrother ['stɛpbrʌðə*] n fratellastro.

stepchild ['stɛptʃaɪld] n figliastro/a.

stepdaughter ['stɛpdɔːtə*] n figliastra.

stepfather ['stɛpfɑːðə*] n patrigno.

stepladder ['stɛplædə*] n scala a libretto.

stepmother ['stɛpmʌðə*] n matrigna.

stepping stone ['stɛpɪŋ-] n pietra di un guado; (*fig*) trampolino.

step Reebok ® [-'riːbɔk] n step m inv.

stepsister ['stɛpsɪstə*] n sorellastra.

stepson ['stɛpsʌn] n figliastro.

stereo ['stɛrɪəu] n (*system*) sistema m stereofonico; (*record player*) stereo m inv ♦ adj (*also*: ~**phonic**) stereofonico(a); **in ~** in stereofonia.

stereotype ['stɪərɪətaɪp] n stereotipo.

sterile ['stɛraɪl] adj sterile.

sterility [stɛ'rɪlɪtɪ] n sterilità.

sterilization [stɛrɪlaɪ'zeɪʃən] n sterilizzazione f.

sterilize ['stɛrɪlaɪz] vt sterilizzare.

sterling ['stəːlɪŋ] adj (*gold, silver*) di buona lega; (*fig*) autentico(a), genuino(a) ♦ n (*ECON*) (*lira*) sterlina; **a pound ~** una lira sterlina.

sterling area n area della sterlina.

stern [stəːn] adj severo(a) ♦ n (*NAUT*) poppa.

sternum ['stəːnəm] n sterno.

steroid ['stɛrɔɪd] n steroide m.

stethoscope ['stɛθəskəup] n stetoscopio.

stevedore ['stiːvɪdɔː*] n scaricatore m di porto.

stew [stjuː] n stufato ♦ vt, vi cuocere in umido; ~**ed tea** tè lasciato troppo in infusione; ~**ed fruit** frutta cotta.

steward ['stjuːəd] n (*AVIAT, NAUT, RAIL*) steward m inv; (*in club etc*) dispensiere m; (*shop* ~) rappresentante m/f sindacale.

stewardess ['stjuːədɛs] n assistente f di volo, hostess f inv.

stewardship ['stjuːədʃɪp] n amministrazione f.

stewing steak ['stjuːɪŋ-], (*US*) **stew meat** n carne f (di manzo) per stufato.

St. Ex. abbr = **stock exchange**.

stg abbr = **sterling**.

stick [stɪk] n bastone m; (*of rhubarb, celery*) gambo ♦ vb (pt, pp **stuck** [stʌk]) vt (*glue*) attaccare; (*thrust*): **to ~ sth into** conficcare or piantare or infiggere qc in; (*col: put*) ficcare; (: *tolerate*) sopportare

♦ *vi* conficcarsi; tenere; (*remain*) restare, rimanere; (*get jammed: door, lift*) bloccarsi; **to ~ to** (*one's word, promise*) mantenere; (*principles*) tener fede a; **to get hold of the wrong end of the ~** (*fig*) capire male; **it stuck in my mind** mi è rimasto in mente.

▶**stick around** *vi* (*col*) restare, fermarsi.

▶**stick out, stick up** *vi* sporgere, spuntare ♦ *vt*: **to ~ it out** (*col*) tener duro.

▶**stick up for** *vt fus* difendere.

sticker ['stɪkə*] *n* cartellino adesivo.

sticking plaster ['stɪkɪŋ-] *n* cerotto adesivo.

sticking point *n* (*fig*) punto di stallo, impasse *f inv.*

stickleback ['stɪklbæk] *n* spinarello.

stickler ['stɪklə*] *n*: **to be a ~ for** essere pignolo(a) su, tenere molto a.

stick-on ['stɪkɔn] *adj* (*label*) adesivo(a).

stick shift *n* (*US AUT*) cambio manuale.

stick-up ['stɪkʌp] *n* (*col*) rapina a mano armata.

sticky ['stɪkɪ] *adj* attaccaticcio(a), vischioso(a); (*label*) adesivo(a).

stiff [stɪf] *adj* rigido(a), duro(a); (*muscle*) legato(a), indolenzito(a); (*difficult*) difficile, arduo(a); (*cold: manner etc*) freddo(a), formale; (*strong*) forte; (*high: price*) molto alto(a); **to be** *or* **feel ~** (*person*) essere *or* sentirsi indolenzito; **to have a ~ neck/back** avere il torcicollo/ mal di schiena; **to keep a ~ upper lip** (*BRIT fig*) conservare il sangue freddo.

stiffen ['stɪfn] *vt* irrigidire; rinforzare ♦ *vi* irrigidirsi; indurirsi.

stiffness ['stɪfnɪs] *n* rigidità; indolenzimento; difficoltà; freddezza.

stifle ['staɪfl] *vt* soffocare.

stifling ['staɪflɪŋ] *adj* (*heat*) soffocante.

stigma, *pl* (*BOT, MED*) **~ta**, (*fig*) **~s** ['stɪgmə, stɪg'mɑːtə] *n* stigma *m*.

stigmata [stɪg'mɑːtə] *npl* (*REL*) stigmate *fpl.*

stile [staɪl] *n* cavalcasiepe *m*; cavalcasteccato.

stiletto [stɪ'lɛtəu] *n* (*also*: **~ heel**) tacco a spillo.

still [stɪl] *adj* fermo(a); (*quiet*) silenzioso(a); (*orange juice etc*) non gassato(a) ♦ *adv* (*up to this time, even*) ancora; (*nonetheless*) tuttavia, ciò nonostante ♦ *n* (*CINE*) fotogramma *m*; **keep ~!** stai fermo!; **he ~ hasn't arrived** non è ancora arrivato.

stillborn ['stɪlbɔːn] *adj* nato(a) morto(a).

still life *n* natura morta.

stilt [stɪlt] *n* trampolo *m*; (*pile*) palo.

stilted ['stɪltɪd] *adj* freddo(a), formale; artificiale.

stimulant ['stɪmjulənt] *n* stimolante *m.*

stimulate ['stɪmjuleɪt] *vt* stimolare.

stimulating ['stɪmjuleɪtɪŋ] *adj* stimolante.

stimulation [stɪmju'leɪʃən] *n* stimolazione *f.*

stimulus, *pl* **stimuli** ['stɪmjuləs, 'stɪmjulaɪ] *n* stimolo.

sting [stɪŋ] *n* puntura; (*organ*) pungiglione *m*; (*col*) trucco ♦ *vt* (*pt, pp* **stung** [stʌŋ]) pungere ♦ *vi* bruciare; **my eyes are ~ing** mi bruciano gli occhi.

stingy ['stɪndʒɪ] *adj* spilorcio(a), tirchio(a).

stink [stɪŋk] *n* fetore *m*, puzzo ♦ *vi* (*pt* **stank**, *pp* **stunk** [stæŋk, stʌŋk]) puzzare.

stinker ['stɪŋkə*] *n* (*col*) porcheria; (*person*) fetente *m/f.*

stinking ['stɪŋkɪŋ] *adj* (*col*): **a ~** ... uno schifo di ..., un(a) maledetto(a) ...; **~ rich** ricco(a) da far paura.

stint [stɪnt] *n* lavoro, compito ♦ *vi*: **to ~ on** lesinare su.

stipend ['staɪpɛnd] *n* stipendio, congrua.

stipendiary [staɪ'pɛndɪərɪ] *adj*: **~ magistrate** magistrato stipendiato.

stipulate ['stɪpjuleɪt] *vt* stipulare.

stipulation [stɪpju'leɪʃən] *n* stipulazione *f.*

stir [stə:*] *n* agitazione *f*, clamore *m* ♦ *vt* rimescolare; (*move*) smuovere, agitare ♦ *vi* muoversi; **to give sth a ~** mescolare qc; **to cause a ~** fare scalpore.

▶**stir up** *vt* provocare, suscitare.

stir-fry ['stə:'fraɪ] *vt* saltare in padella ♦ *n* pietanza al salto.

stirring ['stə:rɪŋ] *adj* eccitante; commovente.

stirrup ['stɪrəp] *n* staffa.

stitch [stɪtʃ] *n* (*SEWING*) punto; (*KNITTING*) maglia; (*MED*) punto (di sutura); (*pain*) fitta ♦ *vt* cucire, attaccare; suturare.

stoat [stəut] *n* ermellino.

stock [stɔk] *n* riserva, provvista; (*COMM*) giacenza, stock *m inv*; (*AGR*) bestiame *m*; (*CULIN*) brodo; (*FINANCE*) titoli *mpl*, azioni *fpl*; (*RAIL*: *also*: **rolling ~**) materiale *m* rotabile; (*descent, origin*) stirpe *f* ♦ *adj* (*fig: reply etc*) consueto(a); solito(a), classico(a); (*greeting*) usuale; (*COMM: goods, size*) standard *inv* ♦ *vt* (*have in stock*) avere, vendere; **well-~ed** ben fornito(a); **to have sth in ~** avere qc in magazzino; **out of ~** esaurito(a); **to take ~** (*fig*) fare il punto; **~s and shares** valori *mpl* di borsa; **government ~** titoli di Stato.

▶**stock up** *vi*: **to ~ up (with)** fare provvista (di).

stockade [stɔ'keɪd] *n* palizzata.

stockbroker ['stɔkbrəukə*] *n* agente *m* di cambio.

stock control *n* gestione *f* magazzino.

stock cube *n* (*BRIT CULIN*) dado.
stock exchange *n* Borsa (valori).
stockholder ['stɔkhəuldə*] *n* (*FINANCE*) azionista *m/f*.
Stockholm ['stɔkhəum] *n* Stoccolma.
stocking ['stɔkɪŋ] *n* calza.
stock-in-trade ['stɔkɪn'treɪd] *n* (*fig*): **it's his** ~ è la sua specialità.
stockist ['stɔkɪst] *n* (*BRIT*) fornitore *m*.
stock market *n* (*BRIT*) Borsa, mercato finanziario.
stock phrase *n* cliché *m inv*.
stockpile ['stɔkpaɪl] *n* riserva ♦ *vt* accumulare riserve di.
stockroom ['stɔkrum] *n* magazzino.
stocktaking ['stɔkteɪkɪŋ] *n* (*BRIT COMM*) inventario.
stocky ['stɔkɪ] *adj* tarchiato(a), tozzo(a).
stodgy ['stɔdʒɪ] *adj* pesante, indigesto(a).
stoic ['stəuɪk] *n* stoico/a.
stoical ['stəuɪkəl] *adj* stoico(a).
stoke [stəuk] *vt* alimentare.
stoker ['stəukə*] *n* fochista *m*.
stole [stəul] *pt of* **steal** ♦ *n* stola.
stolen ['stəuln] *pp of* **steal**.
stolid ['stɔlɪd] *adj* impassibile.
stomach ['stʌmək] *n* stomaco; (*abdomen*) ventre *m* ♦ *vt* sopportare, digerire.
stomach ache *n* mal *m* di stomaco.
stomach pump *n* pompa gastrica.
stomach ulcer *n* ulcera allo stomaco.
stomp [stɔmp] *vi*: **to** ~ **in/out** *etc* entrare/uscire *etc* con passo pesante.
stone [stəun] *n* pietra; (*pebble*) sasso, ciottolo; (*in fruit*) nocciolo; (*MED*) calcolo; (*BRIT: weight*) = 6.348 kg.; 14 libbre ♦ *cpd* di pietra ♦ *vt* lapidare; **within a ~'s throw of the station** a due passi dalla stazione.
Stone Age *n*: **the** ~ l'età della pietra.
stone-cold [stəun'kəuld] *adj* gelido(a).
stoned [stəund] *adj* (*col: drunk*) sbronzo(a); (*on drugs*) fuori *inv*.
stone-deaf [stəun'dɛf] *adj* sordo(a) come una campana.
stonemason ['stəunmeɪsn] *n* scalpellino.
stonewall [stəun'wɔːl] *vi* fare ostruzionismo ♦ *vt* ostacolare.
stonework ['stəunwɜːk] *n* muratura.
stony ['stəunɪ] *adj* pietroso(a), sassoso(a).
stood [stud] *pt, pp of* **stand**.
stooge [stuːdʒ] *n* (*col*) tirapiedi *m/f inv*.
stool [stuːl] *n* sgabello.
stoop [stuːp] *vi* (*also*: **have a** ~) avere una curvatura; (*bend*) chinarsi, curvarsi; **to** ~ **to sth/doing sth** abbassarsi a qc/a fare qc.
stop [stɔp] *n* arresto; (*stopping place*) fermata; (*in punctuation*) punto ♦ *vt*

arrestare, fermare; (*break off*) interrompere; (*also*: **put a** ~ **to**) porre fine a; (*prevent*) impedire ♦ *vi* fermarsi; (*rain, noise etc*) cessare, finire; **to** ~ **doing sth** cessare *or* finire di fare qc; **to** ~ **sb (from) doing sth** impedire a qn di fare qc; **to** ~ **dead** fermarsi di colpo; ~ **it!** smettila!, basta!
►**stop by** *vi* passare, fare un salto.
►**stop off** *vi* sostare brevemente.
►**stop up** *vt* (*hole*) chiudere, turare.
stopcock ['stɔpkɔk] *n* rubinetto di arresto.
stopgap ['stɔpgæp] *n* (*person*) tappabuchi *m/f inv*; (*measure*) ripiego ♦ *cpd* (*measures, solution*) di fortuna.
stoplights ['stɔplaɪts] *npl* (*AUT*) stop *mpl*.
stopover ['stɔpəuvə*] *n* breve sosta; (*AVIAT*) scalo.
stoppage ['stɔpɪdʒ] *n* arresto, fermata; (*of pay*) trattenuta; (*strike*) interruzione *f* del lavoro.
stopper ['stɔpə*] *n* tappo.
stop press *n* ultimissime *fpl*.
stopwatch ['stɔpwɔtʃ] *n* cronometro.
storage ['stɔːrɪdʒ] *n* immagazzinamento; (*COMPUT*) memoria.
storage heater *n* (*BRIT*) radiatore *m* elettrico che accumula calore.
store [stɔː*] *n* provvista, riserva; (*depot*) deposito; (*BRIT: department* ~) grande magazzino; (*US: shop*) negozio ♦ *vt* mettere da parte; conservare; (*grain, goods*) immagazzinare; (*COMPUT*) registrare; **to set great/little** ~ **by sth** dare molta/poca importanza a qc; **who knows what is in** ~ **for us?** chissà cosa ci riserva il futuro?
►**store up** *vt* mettere in serbo, conservare.
storehouse ['stɔːhaus] *n* magazzino, deposito.
storekeeper ['stɔːkiːpə*] *n* (*US*) negoziante *m/f*.
storeroom ['stɔːrum] *n* dispensa.
storey, (*US*) **story** ['stɔːrɪ] *n* piano.
stork [stɔːk] *n* cicogna.
storm [stɔːm] *n* tempesta; (*also*: **thunder**~) temporale *m* ♦ *vi* (*fig*) infuriarsi ♦ *vt* prendere d'assalto.
storm cloud *n* nube *f* temporalesca.
storm door *n* controporta.
stormy ['stɔːmɪ] *adj* tempestoso(a), burrascoso(a).
story ['stɔːrɪ] *n* storia; racconto; (*PRESS*) articolo; (*US*) = **storey**.
storybook ['stɔːrɪbuk] *n* libro di racconti.
storyteller ['stɔːrɪtɛlə*] *n* narratore/trice.
stout [staut] *adj* solido(a), robusto(a);

(*brave*) coraggioso(a); (*fat*) corpulento(a), grasso(a) ♦ *n* birra scura.

stove [stəuv] *n* (*for cooking*) fornello; (: *small*) fornelletto; (*for heating*) stufa; **gas/electric** ~ cucina a gas/elettrica.

stow [stəu] *vt* mettere via.

stowaway ['stəuəweɪ] *n* passeggero(a) clandestino(a).

straddle ['strædl] *vt* stare a cavalcioni di.

strafe [strɑːf] *vt* mitragliare.

straggle ['strægl] *vi* crescere (*or* estendersi) disordinatamente; trascinarsi; rimanere indietro; ~**d along the coast** disseminati(e) lungo la costa.

straggler ['stræglə*] *n* sbandato/a.

straggling ['stræglɪŋ], **straggly** ['stræglɪ] *adj* (*hair*) in disordine.

straight [streɪt] *adj* (*continuous, direct*) dritto(a); (*frank*) onesto(a), franco(a); (*plain, uncomplicated*) semplice; (*THEAT: part, play*) serio(a); (*col: heterosexual*) eterosessuale ♦ *adv* diritto; (*drink*) liscio ♦ *n*: **the** ~ **la linea retta;** (*RAIL*) il rettilineo; (*SPORT*) la drittura d'arrivo; **to put** *or* **get** ~ mettere in ordine, mettere ordine in; **to be (all)** ~ (*tidy*) essere a posto, essere sistemato; (*clarified*) essere chiaro; **ten** ~ **wins** dieci vittorie di fila; ~ **away,** ~ **off** (*at once*) immediatamente; ~ **off,** ~ **out** senza esitare; **I went** ~ **home** sono andato direttamente a casa.

straighten ['streɪtn] *vt* (*also*: ~ **out**) raddrizzare; **to** ~ **things out** mettere le cose a posto.

straight-faced [streɪt'feɪst] *adj* impassibile, imperturbabile ♦ *adv* con il viso serio.

straightforward [streɪt'fɔːwəd] *adj* semplice; (*frank*) onesto(a), franco(a).

strain [streɪn] *n* (*TECH*) sollecitazione *f*; (*physical*) sforzo; (*mental*) tensione *f*; (*MED*) strappo; (*streak, trace*) tendenza; elemento; (*breed*) razza; (*of virus*) tipo ♦ *vt* tendere; (*muscle*) slogare; (*ankle*) storcere; (*friendship, marriage*) mettere a dura prova; (*filter*) colare, filtrare ♦ *vi* sforzarsi; ~**s** *npl* (*MUS*) note *fpl*; **she's under a lot of** ~ è molto tesa, è sotto pressione.

strained [streɪnd] *adj* (*laugh etc*) forzato(a); (*relations*) teso(a).

strainer ['streɪnə*] *n* passino, colino.

strait [streɪt] *n* (*GEO*) stretto; **to be in dire** ~**s** (*fig*) essere nei guai.

straitjacket ['streɪtdʒækɪt] *n* camicia di forza.

strait-laced [streɪt'leɪst] *adj* puritano(a).

strand [strænd] *n* (*of thread*) filo.

strange [streɪndʒ] *adj* (*not known*) sconosciuto(a); (*odd*) strano(a), bizzarro(a).

strangely ['streɪndʒlɪ] *adv* stranamente.

stranger ['streɪndʒə*] *n* (*unknown*) sconosciuto/a; (*from another place*) estraneo/a; **I'm a** ~ **here** non sono del posto.

strangle ['stræŋgl] *vt* strangolare.

stranglehold ['stræŋglhəuld] *n* (*fig*) stretta (mortale).

strangulation [stræŋgju'leɪʃən] *n* strangolamento.

strap [stræp] *n* cinghia; (*of slip, dress*) spallina, bretella ♦ *vt* legare con una cinghia; (*child etc*) punire (con una cinghia).

straphanging ['stræphæŋɪŋ] *n* viaggiare *m* in piedi (*su mezzi pubblici reggendosi a un sostegno*).

strapless ['stræplɪs] *adj* (*bra, dress*) senza spalline.

strapped [stræpt] *adj*: ~ **for cash** a corto di soldi; **financially** ~ finanziariamente a terra.

strapping ['stræpɪŋ] *adj* ben piantato(a).

Strasbourg ['stræzbəːg] *n* Strasburgo *f*.

strata ['strɑːtə] *npl of* **stratum**.

stratagem ['strætɪdʒəm] *n* stratagemma *m*.

strategic [strə'tiːdʒɪk] *adj* strategico(a).

strategist ['strætɪdʒɪst] *n* stratega *m*.

strategy ['strætɪdʒɪ] *n* strategia.

stratosphere ['strætəsfɪə*] *n* stratosfera.

stratum, *pl* **strata** ['strɑːtəm, 'strɑːtə] *n* strato.

straw [strɔː] *n* paglia; (*drinking* ~) cannuccia; **that's the last** ~! è la goccia che fa traboccare il vaso!

strawberry ['strɔːbərɪ] *n* fragola.

stray [streɪ] *adj* (*animal*) randagio(a) ♦ *vi* perdersi; allontanarsi, staccarsi (dal gruppo); ~ **bullet** proiettile *m* vagante.

streak [striːk] *n* striscia; (*fig: of madness etc*): **a** ~ **of** una vena di ♦ *vt* striare, screziare ♦ *vi*: **to** ~ **past** passare come un fulmine; **to have** ~**s in one's hair** avere le mèche nei capelli; **a winning/losing** ~ un periodo fortunato/sfortunato.

streaker ['striːkə*] *n* streaker *m/f inv*.

streaky ['striːkɪ] *adj* screziato(a), striato(a).

streaky bacon *n* (*BRIT*) ≈ pancetta.

stream [striːm] *n* ruscello; corrente *f*; (*of people*) fiume *m* ♦ *vt* (*SCOL*) dividere in livelli di rendimento ♦ *vi* scorrere; **to** ~ **in/out** entrare/uscire a fiotti; **against the** ~ controcorrente; **on** ~ (*new power plant etc*) in funzione, in produzione.

streamer ['striːmə*] *n* (*of paper*) stella filante.

stream feed *n* (*on photocopier etc*) alimentazione *f* continua.

streamline ['stri:mlaɪn] *vt* dare una linea aerodinamica a; (*fig*) razionalizzare.

streamlined ['stri:mlaɪnd] *adj* aerodinamico(a), affusolato(a); (*fig*) razionalizzato(a).

street [stri:t] *n* strada, via; **the back ~s** le strade secondarie; **to be on the ~s** (*homeless*) essere senza tetto; (*as prostitute*) battere il marciapiede.

streetcar ['stri:tkɑ:*] *n* (*US*) tram *m inv*.

street cred [-krɛd] *n* (*col*) credibilità presso i giovani.

street lamp *n* lampione *m*.

street lighting *n* illuminazione *f* stradale.

street map, street plan *n* pianta (di una città).

street market *n* mercato all'aperto.

streetwise ['stri:twaɪz] *adj* (*col*) esperto(a) dei bassifondi.

strength [strɛŋθ] *n* forza; (*of girder, knot etc*) resistenza, solidità; (*of chemical solution*) concentrazione *f*; (*of wine*) gradazione *f* alcolica; **on the ~ of** sulla base di, in virtù di; **below/at full ~** con gli effettivi ridotti/al completo.

strengthen ['strɛŋθən] *vt* rinforzare; (*muscles*) irrobustire; (*economy, currency*) consolidare.

strenuous ['strɛnjuəs] *adj* vigoroso(a), energico(a); (*tiring*) duro(a), pesante.

stress [strɛs] *n* (*force, pressure*) pressione *f*; (*mental strain*) tensione *f*; (*accent*) accento; (*emphasis*) enfasi *f* ♦ *vt* insistere su, sottolineare; **to be under ~** essere sotto tensione; **to lay great ~ on sth** dare grande importanza a qc.

stressful ['strɛsful] *adj* (*job*) difficile, stressante.

stretch [strɛtʃ] *n* (*of sand etc*) distesa; (*of time*) periodo ♦ *vi* stirarsi; (*extend*): **to ~ to** *or* **as far as** estendersi fino a; (*be enough*: *money, food*): **to ~ (to)** bastare (per) ♦ *vt* tendere, allungare; (*spread*) distendere; (*fig*) spingere (al massimo); **at a ~** ininterrottamente; **to ~ a muscle** tendere un muscolo; **to ~ one's legs** sgranchirsi le gambe.

▶**stretch out** *vi* allungarsi, estendersi ♦ *vt* (*arm etc*) allungare, tendere; (*to spread*) distendere; **to ~ out for sth** allungare la mano per prendere qc.

stretcher ['strɛtʃə*] *n* barella, lettiga.

stretcher-bearer ['strɛtʃəbɛərə*] *n* barelliere *m*.

stretch marks *npl* smagliature *fpl*.

strewn [stru:n] *adj*: **~ with** cosparso(a) di.

stricken ['strɪkən] *adj* provato(a); affranto(a); **~ with** colpito(a) da.

strict [strɪkt] *adj* (*severe*) rigido(a), severo(a); (: *order, rule*) rigoroso(a); (: *supervision*) stretto(a); (*precise*) preciso(a), stretto(a); **in ~ confidence** in assoluta confidenza.

strictly ['strɪktlɪ] *adv* severamente; rigorosamente; strettamente; **~ confidential** strettamente confidenziale; **~ speaking** a rigor di termini; **~ between ourselves ...** detto fra noi ....

stride [straɪd] *n* passo lungo ♦ *vi* (*pt* **strode**, *pp* **stridden** [strəud, 'strɪdn]) camminare a grandi passi; **to take in one's ~** (*fig*: *changes etc*) prendere con tranquillità.

strident ['straɪdnt] *adj* stridente.

strife [straɪf] *n* conflitto; litigi *mpl*.

strike [straɪk] *n* sciopero; (*of oil etc*) scoperta; (*attack*) attacco ♦ *vb* (*pt, pp* **struck** [strʌk]) *vt* colpire; (*oil etc*) scoprire, trovare; (*produce, make: coin, medal*) coniare; (: *agreement, deal*) concludere ♦ *vi* far sciopero, scioperare; (*attack*) attaccare; (*clock*) suonare; **to go on** *or* **come out on ~** mettersi in sciopero; **to ~ a match** accendere un fiammifero; **to ~ a balance** (*fig*) trovare il giusto mezzo.

▶**strike back** *vi* (*MIL*) fare rappresaglie; (*fig*) reagire.

▶**strike down** *vt* (*fig*) atterrare.

▶**strike off** *vt* (*from list*) cancellare; (: *doctor etc*) radiare.

▶**strike out** *vt* depennare.

▶**strike up** *vt* (*MUS*) attaccare; **to ~ up a friendship with** fare amicizia con.

strikebreaker ['straɪkbreɪkə*] *n* crumiro/a.

striker ['straɪkə*] *n* scioperante *m/f*; (*SPORT*) attaccante *m*.

striking ['straɪkɪŋ] *adj* impressionante.

Strimmer ® ['strɪmə*] *n* tagliabordi *m inv*.

string [strɪŋ] *n* spago; (*row*) fila; sequenza; catena; (*COMPUT*) stringa, sequenza; (*MUS*) corda ♦ *vt* (*pt, pp* **strung** [strʌŋ]): **~ out** disporre di fianco; **to ~ together** mettere insieme; **the ~s** *npl* (*MUS*) gli archi; **~ of pearls** filo di perle; **with no ~s attached** (*fig*) senza vincoli, senza obblighi; **to get a job by pulling ~s** ottenere un lavoro a forza di raccomandazioni.

string bean *n* fagiolino.

string(ed) instrument *n* (*MUS*) strumento a corda.

stringent ['strɪndʒənt] *adj* rigoroso(a); (*reasons, arguments*) stringente, impellente.

string quartet *n* quartetto d'archi.

strip – stuff

strip [strɪp] n striscia; (SPORT): **wearing the Celtic** ~ con la divisa del Celtic ♦ vt spogliare; (also: ~ **down**: machine) smontare ♦ vi spogliarsi.
strip cartoon n fumetto.
stripe [straɪp] n striscia, riga.
striped ['straɪpt] adj a strisce or righe.
strip light n (BRIT) tubo al neon.
stripper ['strɪpə*] n spogliarellista.
strip-search ['strɪpsə:tʃ] vt: **to** ~ **sb** perquisire qn facendolo(a) spogliare ♦ n perquisizione f (facendo spogliare il perquisito).
striptease ['strɪpti:z] n spogliarello.
strive, pt **strove**, pp **striven** [straɪv, strəuv, 'strɪvn] vi: **to** ~ **to do** sforzarsi di fare.
strobe [strəub] n (also: ~ **light**) luce f stroboscopica.
strode [strəud] pt of **stride**.
stroke [strəuk] n colpo; (of piston) corsa; (MED) colpo apoplettico; (SWIMMING: style) nuoto; (caress) carezza ♦ vt accarezzare; **at a** ~ in un attimo; **on the** ~ **of 5** alle 5 in punto, allo scoccare delle 5; **a** ~ **of luck** un colpo di fortuna; **two-**~ **engine** motore a due tempi.
stroll [strəul] n giretto, passeggiata ♦ vi andare a spasso; **to go for a** ~, **have** or **take a** ~ andare a fare un giretto or due passi.
stroller ['strəulə*] n (US) passeggino.
strong [strɒŋ] adj (gen) forte; (sturdy: table, fabric etc) solido(a); (concentrated, intense: bleach, acid) concentrato(a); (protest, letter, measures) energico(a) ♦ adv: **to be going** ~ (company) andare a gonfie vele; (person) essere attivo(a); **they are 50** ~ sono in 50; ~ **language** (swearing) linguaggio volgare.
strong-arm ['strɒŋɑ:m] adj (tactics, methods) energico(a).
strongbox ['strɒŋbɒks] n cassaforte f.
stronghold ['strɒŋhəuld] n fortezza, roccaforte f.
strongly ['strɒŋlɪ] adv fortemente, con forza; solidamente; energicamente; **to feel** ~ **about sth** avere molto a cuore qc.
strongman ['strɒŋmæn] n personaggio di spicco.
strongroom ['strɒŋrum] n camera di sicurezza.
stroppy ['strɒpɪ] adj (BRIT col) scontroso(a), indisponente.
strove [strəuv] pt of **strive**.
struck [strʌk] pt, pp of **strike**.
structural ['strʌktʃərəl] adj strutturale; (CONSTR) di costruzione; di struttura.
structurally ['strʌktʃrəlɪ] adv dal punto di

vista della struttura.
structure ['strʌktʃə*] n struttura; (building) costruzione f, fabbricato.
struggle ['strʌgl] n lotta ♦ vi lottare; **to have a** ~ **to do sth** avere dei problemi per fare qc.
strum [strʌm] vt (guitar) strimpellare.
strung [strʌŋ] pt, pp of **string**.
strut [strʌt] n sostegno, supporto ♦ vi pavoneggiarsi.
strychnine ['strɪkni:n] n stricnina.
stub [stʌb] n mozzicone m; (of ticket etc) matrice f, talloncino ♦ vt: **to** ~ **one's toe (on sth)** urtare or sbattere il dito del piede (contro qc).
▶**stub out** vt: **to** ~ **out a cigarette** spegnere una sigaretta.
stubble ['stʌbl] n stoppia; (on chin) barba ispida.
stubborn ['stʌbən] adj testardo(a), ostinato(a).
stubby ['stʌbɪ] adj tozzo(a).
stucco ['stʌkəu] n stucco.
stuck [stʌk] pt, pp of **stick** ♦ adj (jammed) bloccato(a); **to get** ~ bloccarsi.
stuck-up [stʌk'ʌp] adj presuntuoso(a).
stud [stʌd] n bottoncino; borchia; (of horses) scuderia, allevamento di cavalli; (also: ~ **horse**) stallone m ♦ vt (fig): ~**ded with** tempestato(a) di.
student ['stju:dənt] n studente/essa ♦ cpd studentesco(a); universitario(a); degli studenti; **a law/medical** ~ uno studente di legge/di medicina.
student driver n (US) conducente m/f principiante.
students' union n (BRIT: association) circolo universitario; (: building) sede f del circolo universitario.
studied ['stʌdɪd] adj studiato(a), calcolato(a).
studio ['stju:dɪəu] n studio.
studio flat, (US) **studio apartment** n appartamento monolocale.
studious ['stju:dɪəs] adj studioso(a); (studied) studiato(a), voluto(a).
studiously ['stju:dɪəslɪ] adv (carefully) deliberatamente, di proposito.
study ['stʌdɪ] n studio ♦ vt studiare; esaminare ♦ vi studiare; **to make a** ~ **of sth** fare uno studio su qc; **to** ~ **for an exam** prepararsi a un esame.
stuff [stʌf] n (substance) roba; (belongings) cose fpl, roba ♦ vt imbottire; (animal: for exhibition) impagliare; (CULIN) farcire; **my nose is** ~**ed up** ho il naso chiuso; **get** ~**ed!** (col!) va' a farti fottere! (!); ~**ed toy** giocattolo di peluche.

stuffing ['stʌfɪŋ] n imbottitura; (*CULIN*) ripieno.

stuffy ['stʌfɪ] adj (*room*) mal ventilato(a), senz'aria; (*ideas*) antiquato(a).

stumble ['stʌmbl] vi inciampare; **to ~ across** (*fig*) imbattersi in.

stumbling block ['stʌmblɪŋ-] n ostacolo, scoglio.

stump [stʌmp] n ceppo; (*of limb*) moncone m ♦ vt: **to be ~ed for an answer** essere incapace di rispondere.

stun [stʌn] vt stordire; (*amaze*) sbalordire.

stung [stʌŋ] pt, pp of **sting**.

stunk [stʌŋk] pp of **stink**.

stunning ['stʌnɪŋ] adj (*piece of news etc*) sbalorditivo(a); (*girl, dress*) favoloso(a), stupendo(a).

stunt [stʌnt] n bravata; trucco pubblicitario; (*AVIAT*) acrobazia ♦ vt arrestare.

stunted ['stʌntɪd] adj stentato(a), rachitico(a).

stuntman ['stʌntmæn] n cascatore m.

stupefaction [stjuːpɪ'fækʃən] n stupefazione f, stupore m.

stupefy ['stjuːpɪfaɪ] vt stordire; intontire; (*fig*) stupire.

stupendous [stjuː'pɛndəs] adj stupendo(a), meraviglioso(a).

stupid ['stjuːpɪd] adj stupido(a).

stupidity [stjuː'pɪdɪtɪ] n stupidità.

stupidly ['stjuːpɪdlɪ] adv stupidamente.

stupor ['stjuːpə*] n torpore m.

sturdy ['stəːdɪ] adj robusto(a), vigoroso(a); solido(a).

sturgeon ['stəːdʒən] n storione m.

stutter ['stʌtə*] n balbuzie f ♦ vi balbettare.

Stuttgart ['ʃtutgart] n Stoccarda.

sty [staɪ] n (*of pigs*) porcile m.

stye [staɪ] n (*MED*) orzaiolo.

style [staɪl] n stile m; (*distinction*) eleganza, classe f; (*hair ~*) pettinatura; (*of dress etc*) modello, linea; **in the latest ~** all'ultima moda.

styli ['staɪlaɪ] npl of **stylus**.

stylish ['staɪlɪʃ] adj elegante.

stylist ['staɪlɪst] n: **hair ~** parrucchiere/a.

stylized ['staɪlaɪzd] adj stilizzato(a).

stylus, pl **styli** or **styluses** ['staɪləs, -laɪ] n (*of record player*) puntina.

Styrofoam ® ['staɪrəfəum] n (*US*) = **polystyrene** ♦ adj (*cup*) di polistirene.

suave [swɑːv] adj untuoso(a).

sub [sʌb] n abbr = **submarine; subscription**.

sub... [sʌb] prefix sub..., sotto....

subcommittee ['sʌbkəmɪtɪ] n sottocomitato.

subconscious [sʌb'kɔnʃəs] adj, n subcosciente (m).

subcontinent [sʌb'kɔntɪnənt] n: **the (Indian) ~** il subcontinente (indiano).

subcontract n [sʌb'kɔntrækt] subappalto ♦ vt [sʌbkən'trækt] subappaltare.

subcontractor ['sʌbkən'træktə*] n subappaltatore/trice.

subdivide [sʌbdɪ'vaɪd] vt suddividere.

subdivision ['sʌbdɪvɪʒən] n suddivisione f.

subdue [səb'djuː] vt sottomettere, soggiogare.

subdued [səb'djuːd] adj pacato(a); (*light*) attenuato(a); (*person*) poco esuberante.

sub-editor ['sʌb'ɛdɪtə*] n (*BRIT*) redattore(trice) aggiunto(a).

subject ['sʌbdʒɪkt] n soggetto; (*citizen etc*) cittadino/a; (*SCOL*) materia ♦ adj (*liable*): **~ to** soggetto(a) a ♦ vt [səb'dʒɛkt]: **to ~ to** sottomettere a; esporre a; **~ to confirmation in writing** a condizione di ricevere conferma scritta; **to change the ~** cambiare discorso.

subjection [səb'dʒɛkʃən] n sottomissione f, soggezione f.

subjective [səb'dʒɛktɪv] adj soggettivo(a).

subject matter n argomento; contenuto.

sub judice [sʌb'dʒuːdɪsɪ] adj (*LAW*) sub iudice.

subjugate ['sʌbdʒugeɪt] vt sottomettere, soggiogare.

subjunctive [səb'dʒʌŋktɪv] adj congiuntivo(a) ♦ n congiuntivo.

sublet [sʌb'lɛt] vt, vi irreg subaffittare.

sublime [sə'blaɪm] adj sublime.

subliminal [sʌb'lɪmɪnl] adj subliminale.

submachine gun ['sʌbmə'ʃiːn-] n mitra m inv.

submarine [sʌbmə'riːn] n sommergibile m.

submerge [səb'məːdʒ] vt sommergere; immergere ♦ vi immergersi.

submersion [səb'məːʃən] n sommersione f; immersione f.

submission [səb'mɪʃən] n sottomissione f; (*to committee etc*) richiesta, domanda.

submissive [səb'mɪsɪv] adj remissivo(a).

submit [səb'mɪt] vt sottomettere; (*proposal, claim*) presentare ♦ vi sottomettersi.

subnormal [sʌb'nɔːməl] adj subnormale.

subordinate [sə'bɔːdɪnət] adj, n subordinato(a).

subpoena [səb'piːnə] n (*LAW*) citazione f, mandato di comparizione ♦ vt (*LAW*) citare in giudizio.

subroutine ['sʌbruːtiːn] n (*COMPUT*) sottoprogramma m.

subscribe [səb'skraɪb] vi contribuire; **to ~ to** (*opinion*) approvare, condividere; (*fund*) sottoscrivere; (*newspaper*) abbonarsi a; essere abbonato(a) a.

subscriber [səb'skraıbə*] n (to periodical, telephone) abbonato/a.

subscript ['sʌbskrıpt] n deponente m.

subscription [səb'skrıpʃən] n sottoscrizione f; abbonamento; **to take out a ~ to** abbonarsi a.

subsequent ['sʌbsıkwənt] adj (later) successivo(a); (further) ulteriore; **~ to** in seguito a.

subsequently ['sʌbsıkwəntlı] adv in seguito, successivamente.

subservient [səb'sə:vıənt] adj: **~ (to)** remissivo(a) (a), sottomesso(a) (a).

subside [səb'saıd] vi cedere, abbassarsi; (flood) decrescere; (wind) calmarsi.

subsidence [səb'saıdns] n cedimento, abbassamento.

subsidiarity [səbsıdı'ærıtı] n (POL) principio del decentramento del potere.

subsidiary [səb'sıdıərı] adj sussidiario(a); accessorio(a); (BRIT SCOL: subject) complementare ♦ n filiale f.

subsidize ['sʌbsıdaız] vt sovvenzionare.

subsidy ['sʌbsıdı] n sovvenzione f.

subsist [səb'sıst] vi: **to ~ on sth** vivere di qc.

subsistence [səb'sıstəns] n esistenza; mezzi mpl di sostentamento.

subsistence allowance n indennità f inv di trasferta.

subsistence level n livello minimo di vita.

substance ['sʌbstəns] n sostanza; (fig) essenza; **to lack ~** (argument) essere debole.

substance abuse n abuso di sostanze tossiche.

substandard [sʌb'stændəd] adj (goods, housing) di qualità scadente.

substantial [səb'stænʃl] adj solido(a); (amount, progress etc) notevole; (meal) sostanzioso(a).

substantially [səb'stænʃəlı] adv sostanzialmente; **~ bigger** molto più grande.

substantiate [səb'stænʃıeıt] vt comprovare.

substitute ['sʌbstıtju:t] n (person) sostituto/a; (thing) succedaneo, surrogato ♦ vt: **to ~ sth/sb for** sostituire qc/qn a.

substitute teacher n (US) supplente m/f.

substitution [sʌbstı'tju:ʃən] n sostituzione f.

subterfuge ['sʌbtəfju:dʒ] n sotterfugio.

subterranean [sʌbtə'reınıən] adj sotterraneo(a).

subtitle ['sʌbtaıtl] n (CINE) sottotitolo.

subtle ['sʌtl] adj sottile; (flavour, perfume) delicato(a).

subtlety ['sʌtltı] n sottigliezza.

subtly ['sʌtlı] adv sottilmente; delicatamente.

subtotal [sʌb'təutl] n somma parziale.

subtract [səb'trækt] vt sottrarre.

subtraction [səb'trækʃən] n sottrazione f.

suburb ['sʌbə:b] n sobborgo; **the ~s** la periferia.

suburban [sə'bə:bən] adj suburbano(a).

suburbia [sə'bə:bıə] n periferia, sobborghi mpl.

subversion [səb'və:ʃən] n sovversione f.

subversive [səb'və:sıv] adj sovversivo(a).

subway ['sʌbweı] n (US: underground) metropolitana; (BRIT: underpass) sottopassaggio.

subzero [sʌb'zıərəu] adj: **~ temperatures** temperature fpl sotto zero.

succeed [sək'si:d] vi riuscire, avere successo ♦ vt succedere a; **to ~ in doing** riuscire a fare.

succeeding [sək'si:dıŋ] adj (following) successivo(a); **~ generations** generazioni fpl future.

success [sək'sɛs] n successo.

successful [sək'sɛsful] adj (venture) coronato(a) da successo, riuscito(a); **to be ~ (in doing)** riuscire (a fare).

successfully [sək'sɛsfəlı] adv con successo.

succession [sək'sɛʃən] n successione f; **in ~** di seguito.

successive [sək'sɛsıv] adj successivo(a); consecutivo(a); **on 3 ~ days** per 3 giorni consecutivi or di seguito.

successor [sək'sɛsə*] n successore m.

succinct [sək'sıŋkt] adj succinto(a), breve.

succulent ['sʌkjulənt] adj succulento(a) ♦ n (BOT): **~s** piante fpl grasse.

succumb [sə'kʌm] vi soccombere.

such [sʌtʃ] adj tale; (of that kind): **~ a book** un tale libro, un libro del genere; **~ books** tali libri, libri del genere; (so much): **~ courage** tanto coraggio ♦ adv: **~ a long trip** un viaggio così lungo; **~ good books** libri così buoni; **~ a lot of** talmente or così tanto(a); **making ~ a noise that** facendo un rumore tale che; **~ a long time ago** tanto tempo fa; **~ as** (like) come; **a noise ~ as to** un rumore tale da; **~ books as I have** quei pochi libri che ho; **as ~ come or** in quanto tale; **I said no ~ thing** non ho detto niente del genere.

such-and-such ['sʌtʃənsʌtʃ] adj tale (after noun).

suchlike ['sʌtʃlaık] pron (col): **and ~** e così via.

suck [sʌk] vt succhiare; (subj: baby)

poppare; (: *pump, machine*) aspirare.
sucker ['sʌkə*] *n* (*ZOOL, TECH*) ventosa;
(*BOT*) pollone *m*; (*col*) gonzo/a, babbeo/a.
suckle ['sʌkl] *vt* allattare.
sucrose ['su:krəuz] *n* saccarosio.
suction ['sʌkʃən] *n* succhiamento; (*TECH*)
aspirazione *f*.
suction pump *n* pompa aspirante.
Sudan [su:'dɑ:n] *n* Sudan *m*.
Sudanese [su:də'ni:z] *adj, n* sudanese (*m/f*).
sudden ['sʌdn] *adj* improvviso(a); **all of a ~**
improvvisamente, all'improvviso.
sudden-death [sʌdn'dɛθ] *n* (*also*: ~ **playoff**)
(*SPORT*) spareggio, bella.
suddenly ['sʌdnlɪ] *adv* bruscamente,
improvvisamente, di colpo.
suds [sʌdz] *npl* schiuma (di sapone).
sue [su:] *vt* citare in giudizio ♦ *vi*: **to ~ (for)**
intentare causa (per); **to ~ for divorce**
intentare causa di divorzio; **to ~ sb for**
damages citare qn per danni.
suede [sweɪd] *n* pelle *f* scamosciata ♦ *cpd*
scamosciato(a).
suet ['suɪt] *n* grasso di rognone.
Suez ['su:ɪz] *n*: **the ~ Canal** il Canale di
Suez.
Suff. *abbr* (*BRIT*) = *Suffolk*.
suffer ['sʌfə*] *vt* soffrire, patire; (*bear*)
sopportare, tollerare; (*undergo: loss,*
setback) subire ♦ *vi* soffrire; **to ~ from**
soffrire di; **to ~ from the effects of**
alcohol/a fall risentire degli effetti
dell'alcool/di una caduta.
sufferance ['sʌfərəns] *n*: **he was only there**
on ~ era più che altro sopportato lì.
sufferer ['sʌfərə*] *n* (*MED*): ~ **(from)**
malato/a (di).
suffering ['sʌfərɪŋ] *n* sofferenza; (*hardship,*
deprivation) privazione *f*.
suffice [sə'faɪs] *vi* essere sufficiente,
bastare.
sufficient [sə'fɪʃənt] *adj* sufficiente; ~
money abbastanza soldi.
sufficiently [sə'fɪʃəntlɪ] *adv*
sufficientemente, abbastanza.
suffix ['sʌfɪks] *n* suffisso.
suffocate ['sʌfəkeɪt] *vi* (*have difficulty*
breathing) soffocare; (*die through lack of*
air) asfissiare.
suffocation [sʌfə'keɪʃən] *n* soffocamento;
(*MED*) asfissia.
suffrage ['sʌfrɪdʒ] *n* suffragio.
suffuse [sə'fju:z] *vt*: **to ~ (with)** (*colour*)
tingere (di); (*light*) soffondere (di); **her**
face was ~d with joy la gioia si dipingeva
sul suo volto.
sugar ['ʃugə*] *n* zucchero ♦ *vt* zuccherare.
sugar beet *n* barbabietola da zucchero.

sugar bowl *n* zuccheriera.
sugar cane *n* canna da zucchero.
sugar-coated ['ʃugəkəutɪd] *adj* ricoperto(a)
di zucchero.
sugar lump *n* zolletta di zucchero.
sugar refinery *n* raffineria di zucchero.
sugary ['ʃugərɪ] *adj* zuccherino(a), dolce;
(*fig*) sdolcinato(a).
suggest [sə'dʒɛst] *vt* proporre, suggerire;
(*indicate*) indicare; **what do you ~ I do?**
cosa mi suggerisce di fare?
suggestion [sə'dʒɛstʃən] *n* suggerimento,
proposta.
suggestive [sə'dʒɛstɪv] *adj* suggestivo(a);
(*indecent*) spinto(a), indecente.
suicidal [suɪ'saɪdl] *adj* suicida *inv*; (*fig*)
fatale, disastroso(a).
suicide ['suɪsaɪd] *n* (*person*) suicida *m/f*; (*act*)
suicidio; **to commit ~** suicidarsi.
suicide attempt, suicide bid *n* tentato
suicidio.
suit [su:t] *n* (*man's*) completo; (*woman's*)
completo, tailleur *m inv*; (*law~*) causa;
(*CARDS*) seme *m*, colore *m* ♦ *vt* andar bene
a *or* per; essere adatto(a) a *or* per;
(*adapt*): **to ~ sth to** adattare qc a; **to be**
~ed to sth (*suitable for*) essere adatto a
qc; **well ~ed** (*couple*) fatti l'uno per
l'altro; **to bring a ~ against sb** intentare
causa a qn; **to follow ~** (*fig*) fare
altrettanto.
suitable ['su:təbl] *adj* adatto(a);
appropriato(a); **would tomorrow be ~?**
andrebbe bene domani?; **we found**
somebody ~ abbiamo trovato la persona
adatta.
suitably ['su:təblɪ] *adv* (*dress*) in modo
adatto; (*thank*) adeguatamente.
suitcase ['su:tkeɪs] *n* valigia.
suite [swi:t] *n* (*of rooms*) appartamento;
(*MUS*) suite *f inv*; (*furniture*): **bedroom/**
dining room ~ arredo *or* mobilia per la
camera da letto/sala da pranzo; **a three-**
piece ~ un salotto comprendente un
divano e due poltrone.
suitor ['su:tə*] *n* corteggiatore *m*,
spasimante *m*.
sulfate ['sʌlfeɪt] *n* (*US*) = **sulphate**.
sulfur *etc* ['sʌlfə*] (*US*) = **sulphur** *etc*.
sulk [sʌlk] *vi* fare il broncio.
sulky ['sʌlkɪ] *adj* imbronciato(a).
sullen ['sʌlən] *adj* scontroso(a); cupo(a).
sulphate, (*US***) sulfate** ['sʌlfeɪt] *n* solfato;
copper ~ solfato di rame.
sulphur, (*US***) sulfur** ['sʌlfə*] *n* zolfo.
sulphur dioxide *n* biossido di zolfo.
sulphuric, (*US***) sulfuric** [sʌl'fjuərɪk] *adj*: ~
acid acido solforico.

sultan ['sʌltən] n sultano.
sultana [sʌl'tɑːnə] n (fruit) uva (secca) sultanina.
sultry ['sʌltrɪ] adj afoso(a).
sum [sʌm] n somma; (SCOL etc) addizione f.
▶**sum up** vt riassumere; (evaluate rapidly) valutare, giudicare ♦ vi riassumere.
Sumatra [su'mɑːtrə] n Sumatra.
summarize ['sʌməraɪz] vt riassumere, riepilogare.
summary ['sʌmərɪ] n riassunto ♦ adj (justice) sommario(a).
summer ['sʌmə*] n estate f ♦ cpd d'estate, estivo(a); **in (the)** ~ d'estate.
summer camp n (US) colonia (estiva).
summerhouse ['sʌməhaus] n (in garden) padiglione m.
summertime ['sʌmətaɪm] n (season) estate f.
summer time n (by clock) ora legale (estiva).
summery ['sʌmərɪ] adj estivo(a).
summing-up [sʌmɪŋ'ʌp] n (LAW) ricapitolazione f del processo.
summit ['sʌmɪt] n cima, sommità; (POL) vertice m.
summit conference n conferenza al vertice.
summon ['sʌmən] vt chiamare, convocare; **to** ~ **a witness** citare un testimone.
▶**summon up** vt raccogliere, fare appello a.
summons n ordine m di comparizione ♦ vt citare; **to serve a** ~ **on sb** notificare una citazione a qn.
sumo ['suːməu] n (also: ~ **wrestling**) sumo.
sump [sʌmp] n (AUT) coppa dell'olio.
sumptuous ['sʌmptjuəs] adj sontuoso(a).
Sun. abbr (= Sunday) dom.
sun [sʌn] n sole m; **in the** ~ al sole; **to catch the** ~ prendere sole; **they have everything under the** ~ hanno tutto ciò che possono desiderare.
sunbathe ['sʌnbeɪð] vi prendere un bagno di sole.
sunbeam ['sʌnbiːm] n raggio di sole.
sunbed ['sʌnbed] n lettino solare.
sunburn ['sʌnbɜːn] n (tan) abbronzatura; (painful) scottatura.
sunburnt ['sʌnbɜːnt], **sunburned** ['sʌnbɜːnd] adj abbronzato(a); (painfully) scottato(a) dal sole.
sun cream n crema solare.
sundae ['sʌndeɪ] n coppa di gelato guarnita.
Sunday ['sʌndɪ] n domenica; for phrases see also **Tuesday**.
Sunday paper n giornale m della domenica.

I **Sunday papers** sono i giornali che escono di domenica. Sono generalmente corredati da supplementi e riviste di argomento culturale, sportivo e di attualità ed hanno un'alta tiratura.

Sunday school n ≈ scuola di catechismo.
sundial ['sʌndaɪəl] n meridiana.
sundown ['sʌndaun] n tramonto.
sundries ['sʌndrɪz] npl articoli diversi, cose diverse.
sundry ['sʌndrɪ] adj vari(e), diversi(e); **all and** ~ tutti quanti.
sunflower ['sʌnflauə*] n girasole m.
sung [sʌŋ] pp of **sing**.
sunglasses ['sʌnglɑːsɪz] npl occhiali mpl da sole.
sunk [sʌŋk] pp of **sink**.
sunken ['sʌŋkən] adj sommerso(a); (eyes, cheeks) infossato(a); (bath) incassato(a).
sunlamp ['sʌnlæmp] n lampada a raggi ultravioletti.
sunlight ['sʌnlaɪt] n (luce f del) sole m.
sunlit ['sʌnlɪt] adj assolato(a), soleggiato(a).
sunny ['sʌnɪ] adj assolato(a), soleggiato(a); (fig) allegro(a), felice; **it is** ~ c'è il sole.
sunrise ['sʌnraɪz] n levata del sole, alba.
sunroof ['sʌnruːf] n (on building) tetto a terrazzo; (AUT) tetto apribile.
sunscreen ['sʌnskriːn] n crema solare protettiva.
sunset ['sʌnset] n tramonto.
sunshade ['sʌnʃeɪd] n parasole m.
sunshine ['sʌnʃaɪn] n (luce f del) sole m.
sunspot ['sʌnspɒt] n macchia solare.
sunstroke ['sʌnstrəuk] n insolazione f, colpo di sole.
suntan ['sʌntæn] n abbronzatura.
suntanned ['sʌntænd] adj abbronzato(a).
suntan oil n olio solare.
suntrap ['sʌntræp] n luogo molto assolato, angolo pieno di sole.
super ['suːpə*] adj (col) fantastico(a).
superannuation [suːpərænjuˈeɪʃən] n contributi mpl pensionistici; pensione f.
superb [suːˈpɜːb] adj magnifico(a).
Super Bowl n (US SPORT) Super Bowl m inv.
supercilious [suːpəˈsɪlɪəs] adj sprezzante, sdegnoso(a).
superconductor [suːpəkənˈdʌktə*] n superconduttore m.
superficial [suːpəˈfɪʃəl] adj superficiale.
superficially [suːpəˈfɪʃəlɪ] adv superficialmente.

superfluous [su'pə:fluəs] *adj* superfluo(a).
superglue ['su:pəglu:] *n* colla a presa rapida.
superhighway ['su:pəhaıweı] *n* (*US*) autostrada; **the information** ~ l'autostrada telematica.
superhuman [su:pə'hju:mən] *adj* sovrumano(a).
superimpose ['su:pərım'pəuz] *vt* sovrapporre.
superintend [su:pərın'tɛnd] *vt* dirigere, sovraintendere.
superintendent [su:pərın'tɛndənt] *n* direttore/trice; (*POLICE*) ≈ commissario (capo).
superior [su'pıərıə*] *adj* superiore; (*COMM:* goods, quality) di prim'ordine, superiore; (*smug: person*) che fa il superiore ♦ *n* superiore *m/f*; **Mother S**~ (*REL*) Madre *f* Superiora, Superiora.
superiority [supıərı'ɔrıtı] *n* superiorità.
superlative [su'pə:lətıv] *adj* superlativo(a), supremo(a) ♦ *n* (*LING*) superlativo.
superman ['su:pəmæn] *n* superuomo.
supermarket ['su:pəmɑ:kıt] *n* supermercato.
supermodel ['su:pəmɔdl] *n* top model *m/f* inv.
supernatural [su:pə'nætʃərəl] *adj* soprannaturale.
supernova [su:pə'nəuvə] *n* supernova.
superpower ['su:pəpauə*] *n* (*POL*) superpotenza.
superscript ['su:pəskrıpt] *n* esponente *m*.
supersede [su:pə'si:d] *vt* sostituire, soppiantare.
supersonic ['su:pə'sɔnık] *adj* supersonico(a).
superstar ['su:pəstɑ:*] *adj, n* superstar (*f*) inv.
superstition [su:pə'stıʃən] *n* superstizione *f.*
superstitious [su:pə'stıʃəs] *adj* superstizioso(a).
superstore ['su:pəstɔ:*] *n* (*BRIT*) grande supermercato.
supertanker ['su:pətæŋkə*] *n* superpetroliera.
supertax ['su:pətæks] *n* soprattassa.
supervise ['su:pəvaız] *vt* (*person etc*) sorvegliare; (*organization*) soprintendere a.
supervision [su:pə'vıʒən] *n* sorveglianza, supervisione *f*; **under medical** ~ sotto controllo medico.
supervisor ['su:pəvaızə*] *n* sorvegliante *m/f*, soprintendente *m/f*; (*in shop*) capocommesso/a; (*at university*) relatore/

trice.
supervisory ['su:pəvaızərı] *adj* di sorveglianza.
supine ['su:paın] *adj* supino(a).
supper ['sʌpə*] *n* cena; **to have** ~ cenare.
supplant [sə'plɑ:nt] *vt* soppiantare.
supple ['sʌpl] *adj* flessibile; agile.
supplement *n* ['sʌplımənt] supplemento ♦ *vt* [sʌplı'mɛnt] completare, integrare.
supplementary [sʌplı'mɛntərı] *adj* supplementare.
supplementary benefit *n* (*BRIT*) *forma di indennità assistenziale.*
supplier [sə'plaıə*] *n* fornitore *m.*
supply [sə'plaı] *vt* (*goods*): **to** ~ **sth (to sb)** fornire qc (a qn); (*people, organization*): **to** ~ **sb (with sth)** fornire a qn (qc); (*system, machine*): **to** ~ **sth (with sth)** alimentare qc (con qc); (*a need*) soddisfare ♦ *n* riserva, provvista; (*supplying*) approvvigionamento; (*TECH*) alimentazione *f*; **supplies** *npl* (*food*) viveri *mpl*; (*MIL*) sussistenza; **office supplies** forniture *fpl* per ufficio; **to be in short** ~ scarseggiare, essere scarso(a); **the electricity/water/gas** ~ l'erogazione *f* di corrente/d'acqua/di gas; ~ **and demand** la domanda e l'offerta; **the car comes supplied with a radio** l'auto viene fornita completa di radio.
supply teacher *n* (*BRIT*) supplente *m/f.*
support [sə'pɔ:t] *n* (*moral, financial etc*) sostegno, appoggio; (*TECH*) supporto ♦ *vt* sostenere; (*financially*) mantenere; (*uphold*) sostenere, difendere; (*SPORT: team*) fare il tifo per; **they stopped work in** ~ (**of**) hanno smesso di lavorare per solidarietà (con); **to** ~ **o.s.** (*financially*) mantenersi.
supporter [sə'pɔ:tə*] *n* (*POL etc*) sostenitore/trice, fautore/trice; (*SPORT*) tifoso/a.
supporting [sə'pɔ:tıŋ] *adj* (*wall*) di sostegno.
supporting actor *n* attore *m* non protagonista.
supporting actress *n* attrice *f* non protagonista.
supporting role *n* ruolo non protagonista.
supportive [sə'pɔ:tıv] *adj* d'appoggio; **I have a** ~ **wife/family** mia moglie/la mia famiglia mi appoggia.
suppose [sə'pəuz] *vt, vi* supporre; immaginare; **to be** ~**d to do** essere tenuto(a) a fare; **always supposing (that) he comes** ammesso e non concesso che venga; **I don't** ~ **she'll come** non credo che venga; **he's** ~**d to be an expert**

dicono che sia un esperto, passa per un esperto.

supposedly [sə'pəuzɪdlɪ] *adv* presumibilmente; (*seemingly*) apparentemente.

supposing [sə'pəuzɪŋ] *conj* se, ammesso che + *sub*.

supposition [sʌpə'zɪʃən] *n* supposizione *f*, ipotesi *f inv*.

suppository [sə'pɒzɪtərɪ] *n* supposta, suppositorio.

suppress [sə'prɛs] *vt* reprimere; sopprimere; tenere segreto(a).

suppression [sə'prɛʃən] *n* repressione *f*; soppressione *f*.

suppressor [sə'prɛsə*] *n* (*ELEC etc*) soppressore *m*.

supremacy [su'prɛməsɪ] *n* supremazia.

supreme [su'priːm] *adj* supremo(a).

Supreme Court *n* (*US*) Corte *f* suprema; ~ **of Judicature** *corte di giudizio suprema dell'Inghilterra e del Galles.*

supremo [su'priːməu] *n* autorità *f inv* massima.

Supt. *abbr* (*POLICE*) = **superintendent.**

surcharge ['səːtʃɑːdʒ] *n* supplemento; (*extra tax*) soprattassa.

sure [ʃuə*] *adj* sicuro(a); (*definite, convinced*) sicuro(a), certo(a) ♦ *adv* (*col: US*): **that ~ is pretty, that's ~ pretty è** veramente *or* davvero carino; ~**!** (*of course*) senz'altro!, certo!; ~ **enough** infatti; **to make ~ of** assicurarsi di; **to be ~ of sth** essere sicuro di qc; **to be ~ of o.s.** essere sicuro di sé; **I'm not ~ how/ why/when** non so bene come/perché/ quando + *sub*.

sure-fire ['ʃuəfaɪə*] *adj* (*col*) infallibile.

sure-footed [ʃuə'futɪd] *adj* dal passo sicuro.

surely ['ʃuəlɪ] *adv* sicuramente; certamente; ~ **you don't mean that!** non parlerà sul serio!

surety ['ʃuərətɪ] *n* garanzia; **to go** *or* **stand ~ for sb** farsi garante per qn.

surf [səːf] *n* (*waves*) cavalloni *mpl*; (*foam*) spuma.

surface ['səːfɪs] *n* superficie *f* ♦ *vt* (*road*) asfaltare ♦ *vi* risalire alla superficie; (*fig: person*) venire a galla, farsi vivo(a); **on the ~ it seems that ...** (*fig*) superficialmente sembra che ....

surface area *n* superficie *f*.

surface mail *n* posta ordinaria.

surface-to-surface ['səːfɪstə'səːfɪs] *adj* (*MIL*) terra-terra *inv*.

surfboard ['səːfbɔːd] *n* tavola per surfing.

surfeit ['səːfɪt] *n*: **a ~ of** un eccesso di;

un'indigestione di.

surfer ['səːfə*] *n* chi pratica il surfing.

surfing ['səːfɪŋ] *n* surfing *m*.

surge [səːdʒ] *n* (*strong movement*) ondata; (*of feeling*) impeto; (*ELEC*) sovracorrente *f* ♦ *vi* (*waves*) gonfiarsi; (*ELEC: power*) aumentare improvvisamente; **to ~ forward** buttarsi avanti.

surgeon ['səːdʒən] *n* chirurgo.

Surgeon General *n* (*US*) ≈ Ministro della Sanità.

surgery ['səːdʒərɪ] *n* chirurgia; (*BRIT MED: room*) studio *or* gabinetto medico, ambulatorio; (*: session*) visita ambulatoriale; (*BRIT: of MP etc*) incontri *mpl* con gli elettori; **to undergo ~** subire un intervento chirurgico.

surgery hours *npl* (*BRIT*) orario delle visite *or* di consultazione.

surgical ['səːdʒɪkl] *adj* chirurgico(a).

surgical spirit *n* (*BRIT*) alcool denaturato.

surly ['səːlɪ] *adj* scontroso(a), burbero(a).

surmise [səː'maɪz] *vt* supporre, congetturare.

surmount [səː'maunt] *vt* sormontare.

surname ['səːneɪm] *n* cognome *m*.

surpass [səː'pɑːs] *vt* superare.

surplus ['səːpləs] *n* eccedenza; (*ECON*) surplus *m inv* ♦ *adj* eccedente, d'avanzo; **it is ~ to our requirements** eccede i nostri bisogni; ~ **stock** merce *f* in sovrappiù.

surprise [sə'praɪz] *n* sorpresa; (*astonishment*) stupore *m* ♦ *vt* sorprendere; stupire; **to take by ~** (*person*) cogliere di sorpresa; (*MIL: town, fort*) attaccare di sorpresa.

surprising [sə'praɪzɪŋ] *adj* sorprendente, stupefacente.

surprisingly [se'praɪzɪŋlɪ] *adv* sorprendentemente; (**somewhat**) ~**, he agreed** cosa (alquanto) sorprendente, ha accettato.

surrealism [sə'rɪəlɪzəm] *n* surrealismo.

surrealist [sə'rɪəlɪst] *adj*, *n* surrealista (*m/f*).

surrender [sə'rɛndə*] *n* resa, capitolazione *f* ♦ *vi* arrendersi ♦ *vt* (*claim, right*) rinunciare a.

surrender value *n* (*COMM*) valore *m* di riscatto.

surreptitious [sʌrəp'tɪʃəs] *adj* furtivo(a).

surrogate ['sʌrəgɪt] *n* (*BRIT: substitute*) surrogato ♦ *adj* surrogato(a).

surrogate mother *n* madre *f* sostitutiva.

surround [sə'raund] *vt* circondare; (*MIL etc*) accerchiare.

surrounding [sə'raundɪŋ] *adj* circostante.

surroundings [sə'raundɪŋz] *npl* dintorni *mpl*; (*fig*) ambiente *m*.

surtax ['sə:tæks] *n* soprattassa.

surveillance [sə:'veɪləns] *n* sorveglianza, controllo.

survey *n* ['sə:veɪ] (*comprehensive view: of situation, development*) quadro generale; (*study*) indagine *f*, studio; (*in housebuying etc*) perizia; (*of land*) rilevamento, rilievo topografico ♦ *vt* [sə:'veɪ] osservare; esaminare; (*SURVEYING: building*) fare una perizia di; (: *land*) fare il rilevamento di.

surveying [sə'veɪɪŋ] *n* (*of land*) agrimensura.

surveyor [sə'veɪə*] *n* perito; (*of land*) agrimensore *m*.

survival [sə'vaɪvl] *n* sopravvivenza; (*relic*) reliquia, vestigio.

survival course *n* corso di sopravvivenza.

survival kit *n* equipaggiamento di prima necessità.

survive [sə'vaɪv] *vi* sopravvivere ♦ *vt* sopravvivere a.

survivor [sə'vaɪvə*] *n* superstite *m/f*, sopravvissuto/a.

susceptible [sə'sɛptəbl] *adj*: ~ (**to**) sensibile (a); (*disease*) predisposto(a) (a).

suspect *adj, n* ['sʌspɛkt] *adj* sospetto(a) ♦ *n* persona sospetta ♦ *vt* [səs'pɛkt] sospettare; (*think likely*) supporre; (*doubt*) dubitare di.

suspected [səs'pɛktɪd] *adj* presunto(a); **to have a ~ facture** avere una sospetta frattura.

suspend [səs'pɛnd] *vt* sospendere.

suspended animation *n*: **in a state of ~** in stato comatoso.

suspended sentence *n* condanna con la condizionale.

suspender belt [səs'pɛndə*-] *n* (*BRIT*) reggicalze *m inv*.

suspenders [sə'spɛndəz] *npl* (*BRIT*) giarrettiere *fpl*; (*US*) bretelle *fpl*.

suspense [səs'pɛns] *n* apprensione *f*; (*in film etc*) suspense *m*.

suspension [səs'pɛnʃən] *n* (*gen, AUT*) sospensione *f*; (*of driving licence*) ritiro temporaneo.

suspension bridge *n* ponte *m* sospeso.

suspicion [səs'pɪʃən] *n* sospetto; **to be under ~** essere sospettato; **arrested on ~ of murder** arrestato come presunto omicida.

suspicious [səs'pɪʃəs] *adj* (*suspecting*) sospettoso(a); (*causing suspicion*) sospetto(a); **to be ~ of** *or* **about sb/sth** nutrire sospetti nei riguardi di qn/qc.

suss out *vt* (*BRIT col*): **I've ~ed it/him out** ho capito come stanno le cose/che tipo è.

sustain [səs'teɪn] *vt* sostenere; sopportare; (*suffer*) subire.

sustainable [səs'teɪnəbl] *adj* sostenibile.

sustained [sə'steɪnd] *adj* (*effort*) prolungato(a).

sustenance ['sʌstɪnəns] *n* nutrimento; mezzi *mpl* di sostentamento.

suture ['su:tʃə*] *n* sutura.

SW *abbr* (*RADIO*: = *short wave*) O.C.

swab [swɔb] *n* (*MED*) tampone *m* ♦ *vt* (*NAUT: also*: ~ **down**) radazzare.

swagger ['swægə*] *vi* pavoneggiarsi.

swallow ['swɔləu] *n* (*bird*) rondine *f*; (*of food*) boccone *m*; (*of drink*) sorso ♦ *vt* inghiottire; (*fig: story*) bere.

►**swallow up** *vt* inghiottire.

swam [swæm] *pt of* **swim**.

swamp [swɔmp] *n* palude *f* ♦ *vt* sommergere.

swampy ['swɔmpɪ] *adj* palludoso(a), pantanoso(a).

swan [swɔn] *n* cigno.

swank [swæŋk] *vi* (*col: talk boastfully*) fare lo spaccone; (: *show off*) mettersi in mostra.

swan song *n* (*fig*) canto del cigno.

swap [swɔp] *n* scambio ♦ *vt*: **to ~ (for)** scambiare (con).

SWAPO ['swɑːpəu] *n abbr* = *South-West Africa People's Organization*.

swarm [swɔːm] *n* sciame *m* ♦ *vi* formicolare; (*bees*) sciamare.

swarthy ['swɔːðɪ] *adj* di carnagione scura.

swashbuckling ['swɔʃbʌklɪŋ] *adj* (*role, hero*) spericolato(a).

swastika ['swɔstɪkə] *n* croce *f* uncinata, svastica.

SWAT [swɔt] *n abbr* (*US*: = *Special Weapons and Tactics*) reparto speciale di polizia; **a ~ team** uno squadrone del reparto speciale (di polizia).

swat [swɔt] *vt* schiacciare ♦ *n* (*BRIT: also*: **fly ~**) ammazzamosche *m inv*.

swathe [sweɪð] *n* fascio ♦ *vt*: **to ~ in** (*bandages, blankets*) avvolgere in.

swatter ['swɔtə*] *n* (*also*: **fly ~**) ammazzamosche *m inv*.

sway [sweɪ] *vi* (*building*) oscillare; (*tree*) ondeggiare; (*person*) barcollare ♦ *vt* (*influence*) influenzare ♦ *n* (*rule, power*): ~ (**over**) influenza (su); **to hold ~ over sb** dominare qn.

Swaziland ['swɑːzɪlænd] *n* Swaziland *m*.

swear, *pt* **swore**, *pp* **sworn** [swɛə*, swɔː*, swɔːn] *vi* (*witness etc*) giurare; (*curse*) bestemmiare, imprecare ♦ *vt*: **to ~ an oath** prestare giuramento; **to ~ to sth** giurare qc.

►**swear in** *vt* prestare giuramento a.

swearword ['swɛəwɔːd] n parolaccia.
sweat [swɛt] n sudore m, traspirazione f
♦ vi sudare; **in a ~** in un bagno di sudore.
sweatband ['swɛtbænd] n (SPORT) fascia
elastica (per assorbire il sudore).
sweater ['swɛtə*] n maglione m.
sweatshirt ['swɛtʃəːt] n maglione m in
cotone felpato.
sweatshop ['swɛtʃɔp] n azienda o fabbrica
dove i dipendenti sono sfruttati.
sweaty ['swɛtɪ] adj sudato(a); bagnato(a) di
sudore.
Swede [swiːd] n svedese m/f.
swede [swiːd] n (BRIT) rapa svedese.
Sweden ['swiːdn] n Svezia.
Swedish ['swiːdɪʃ] adj svedese ♦ n (LING)
svedese m.
sweep [swiːp] n spazzata; (curve) curva;
(expanse) distesa; (range) portata; (also:
chimney ~) spazzacamino ♦ vb (pt, pp
swept [swɛpt]) vt spazzare, scopare; (subj:
fashion, craze) invadere ♦ vi camminare
maestosamente; precipitarsi, lanciarsi;
(e)stendersi.
▶**sweep away** vt spazzare via; trascinare
via.
▶**sweep past** vi sfrecciare accanto;
passare accanto maestosamente.
▶**sweep up** vt, vi spazzare.
sweeper ['swiːpə*] n (person) spazzino/a;
(machine) spazzatrice f; (FOOTBALL)
libero.
sweeping ['swiːpɪŋ] adj (gesture) ampio(a);
(changes, reforms) ampio(a), radicale; **a ~
statement** un'affermazione generica.
sweepstake ['swiːpsteɪk] n lotteria (spesso
abbinata alle corse dei cavalli).
sweet [swiːt] n (BRIT) dolce m; (candy)
caramella ♦ adj dolce; (fresh) fresco(a);
(kind) gentile; (cute) carino(a) ♦ adv: **to
smell/taste ~** avere un odore/sapore
dolce; **~ and sour** adj agrodolce.
sweetbread ['swiːtbrɛd] n animella.
sweetcorn ['swiːtkɔːn] n granturco dolce.
sweeten ['swiːtn] vt addolcire; zuccherare.
sweetener ['swiːtnə*] n (CULIN)
dolcificante m.
sweetheart ['swiːthaːt] n innamorato/a.
sweetly ['swiːtlɪ] adv dolcemente.
sweetness ['swiːtnɪs] n sapore m dolce;
dolcezza.
sweet pea n pisello odoroso.
sweet potato n patata americana, patata
dolce.
sweetshop ['swiːtʃɔp] n (BRIT) ≈
pasticceria.
sweet tooth n: **to have a ~** avere un
debole per i dolci.

swell [swɛl] n (of sea) mare m lungo ♦ adj
(col: excellent) favoloso(a) ♦ vb (pt ~**ed**, pp
swollen, ~**ed** ['swəulən]) vt gonfiare,
ingrossare; (numbers, sales etc)
aumentare ♦ vi gonfiarsi, ingrossarsi;
(sound) crescere; (MED) gonfiarsi.
swelling ['swɛlɪŋ] n (MED) tumefazione f,
gonfiore m.
sweltering ['swɛltərɪŋ] adj soffocante.
swept [swɛpt] pt, pp of **sweep**.
swerve [swəːv] vi deviare; (driver) sterzare;
(boxer) scartare.
swift [swɪft] n (bird) rondone m ♦ adj
rapido(a), veloce.
swiftly ['swɪftlɪ] adv rapidamente,
velocemente.
swiftness ['swɪftnɪs] n rapidità, velocità.
swig [swɪg] n (col: drink) sorsata.
swill [swɪl] n broda ♦ vt (also: ~ **out**, ~
down) risciacquare.
swim [swɪm] n: **to go for a ~** andare a fare
una nuotata ♦ vb (pt **swam**, pp **swum**
[swæm, swʌm]) vi nuotare; (SPORT) fare
del nuoto; (head, room) girare ♦ vt (river,
channel) attraversare or percorrere a
nuoto; **to go ~ming** andare a nuotare; **to
~ a length** fare una vasca (a nuoto).
swimmer ['swɪmə*] n nuotatore/trice.
swimming ['swɪmɪŋ] n nuoto.
swimming baths npl (BRIT) piscina.
swimming cap n cuffia.
swimming costume n (BRIT) costume m
da bagno.
swimmingly ['swɪmɪŋlɪ] adv: **to go ~**
(wonderfully) andare a gonfie vele.
swimming pool n piscina.
swimming trunks npl costume m da
bagno (per uomo).
swimsuit ['swɪmsuːt] n costume m da
bagno.
swindle ['swɪndl] n truffa ♦ vt truffare.
swindler ['swɪndlə*] n truffatore/trice.
swine [swaɪn] n (pl inv) maiale m, porco;
(col!) porco (!).
swing [swɪŋ] n altalena; (movement)
oscillazione f; (MUS) ritmo; (also: ~
music) swing m ♦ vb (pt, pp **swung** [swʌŋ])
vt dondolare, far oscillare; (also: ~ **round**)
far girare ♦ vi oscillare, dondolare; (also:
~ **round**: object) roteare; (: person)
girarsi, voltarsi; **to be in full ~** (activity)
essere in piena attività; (party etc) essere
nel pieno; **a ~ to the left** (POL) una svolta
a sinistra; **to get into the ~ of things**
entrare nel pieno delle cose; **the road ~s
south** la strada prende la direzione sud.
swing bridge n ponte m girevole.
swing door n (BRIT) porta battente.

swingeing ['swɪndʒɪŋ] adj (BRIT: defeat) violento(a); (: price increase) enorme.
swinging ['swɪŋɪŋ] adj (step) cadenzato(a), ritmico(a); (rhythm, music) trascinante; ~ **door** (US) porta battente.
swipe [swaɪp] n forte colpo; schiaffo ♦ vt (hit) colpire con forza; dare uno schiaffo a; (col: steal) sgraffignare; (credit card etc) far passare (nell'apposita macchinetta).
swirl [swəːl] n turbine m, mulinello ♦ vi turbinare, far mulinello.
swish [swɪʃ] adj (col: smart) all'ultimo grido, alla moda ♦ n (sound: of whip) sibilo; (: of skirts, grass) fruscio ♦ vi sibilare.
Swiss [swɪs] adj, n (pl inv) svizzero(a).
Swiss French adj svizzero(a) francese.
Swiss German adj svizzero(a) tedesco(a).
switch [swɪtʃ] n (for light, radio etc) interruttore m; (change) cambiamento ♦ vt (also: ~ round, ~ over) cambiare; scambiare.
▶**switch off** vt spegnere.
▶**switch on** vt accendere; (engine, machine) mettere in moto, avviare; (AUT: ignition) inserire; (BRIT: water supply) aprire.
switchback ['swɪtʃbæk] n (BRIT) montagne fpl russe.
switchblade ['swɪtʃbleɪd] n (also: ~ knife) coltello a scatto.
switchboard ['swɪtʃbɔːd] n centralino.
switchboard operator n centralinista m/f.
Switzerland ['swɪtsələnd] n Svizzera.
swivel ['swɪvl] vi (also: ~ round) girare.
swollen ['swəulən] pp of **swell** ♦ adj (ankle etc) gonfio(a).
swoon [swuːn] vi svenire.
swoop [swuːp] n (by police etc) incursione f; (of bird etc) picchiata ♦ vi (also: ~ down) scendere in picchiata; (police): to ~ (on) fare un'incursione (in).
swop [swɔp] n, vt = **swap**.
sword [sɔːd] n spada.
swordfish ['sɔːdfɪʃ] n pesce m spada inv.
swore [swɔː*] pt of **swear**.
sworn [swɔːn] pp of **swear**.
swot [swɔt] vt sgobbare su ♦ vi sgobbare.
swum [swʌm] pp of **swim**.
swung [swʌŋ] pt, pp of **swing**.
sycamore ['sɪkəmɔː*] n sicomoro.
sycophant ['sɪkəfənt] n leccapiedi m/f.
sycophantic [sɪkə'fæntɪk] adj ossequioso(a), adulatore(trice).
Sydney ['sɪdnɪ] n Sydney f.
syllable ['sɪləbl] n sillaba.
syllabus ['sɪləbəs] n programma m; **on the** ~ in programma d'esame.

symbol ['sɪmbl] n simbolo.
symbolic(al) [sɪm'bɔlɪk(l)] adj simbolico(a); **to be** ~ **of sth** simboleggiare qc.
symbolism ['sɪmbəlɪzəm] n simbolismo.
symbolize ['sɪmbəlaɪz] vt simbolizzare.
symmetrical [sɪ'mɛtrɪkl] adj simmetrico(a).
symmetry ['sɪmɪtrɪ] n simmetria.
sympathetic [sɪmpə'θɛtɪk] adj (showing pity) compassionevole; (kind) comprensivo(a); ~ **towards** ben disposto(a) verso; **to be** ~ **to a cause** (well-disposed) simpatizzare per una causa.
sympathetically [sɪmpə'θɛtɪklɪ] adv in modo compassionevole; con comprensione.
sympathize ['sɪmpəθaɪz] vi: **to** ~ **with sb** compatire qn; partecipare al dolore di qn; (understand) capire qn.
sympathizer ['sɪmpəθaɪzə*] n (POL) simpatizzante m/f.
sympathy ['sɪmpəθɪ] n compassione f; **in** ~ **with** d'accordo con; (strike) per solidarietà con; **with our deepest** ~ con le nostre più sincere condoglianze.
symphonic [sɪm'fɔnɪk] adj sinfonico(a).
symphony ['sɪmfənɪ] n sinfonia.
symphony orchestra n orchestra sinfonica.
symposium [sɪm'pəuzɪəm] n simposio.
symptom ['sɪmptəm] n sintomo; indizio.
symptomatic [sɪmptə'mætɪk] adj: ~ **(of)** sintomatico(a) (di).
synagogue ['sɪnəgɔg] n sinagoga.
sync [sɪŋk] n (col): **in/out of** ~ in/fuori sincronia; (fig: people) **they are in** ~ sono in sintonia.
synchromesh [sɪŋkrəu'mɛʃ] n cambio sincronizzato.
synchronize ['sɪŋkrənaɪz] vt sincronizzare ♦ vi: **to** ~ **with** essere contemporaneo(a) a.
synchronized swimming n nuoto sincronizzato.
syncopated ['sɪŋkəpeɪtɪd] adj sincopato(a).
syndicate ['sɪndɪkɪt] n sindacato; (PRESS) agenzia di stampa.
syndrome ['sɪndrəum] n sindrome f.
synonym ['sɪnənɪm] n sinonimo.
synonymous [sɪ'nɔnɪməs] adj: ~ **(with)** sinonimo(a) (di).
synopsis, pl **synopses** [sɪ'nɔpsɪs, -siːz] n sommario, sinossi f inv.
syntax ['sɪntæks] n sintassi f inv.
synthesis, pl **syntheses** ['sɪnθəsɪs, -siːz] n sintesi f inv.
synthesizer ['sɪnθəsaɪzə*] n (MUS) sintetizzatore m.

synthetic [sɪn'θetɪk] *adj* sintetico(a) ♦ *n* prodotto sintetico; (*TEXTILES*) fibra sintetica.
syphilis ['sɪfɪlɪs] *n* sifilide *f*.
syphon ['saɪfən] *n*, *vb* = **siphon**.
Syria ['sɪrɪə] *n* Siria.
Syrian ['sɪrɪən] *adj*, *n* siriano(a).
syringe [sɪ'rɪndʒ] *n* siringa.
syrup ['sɪrəp] *n* sciroppo; (*also*: **golden ~**) melassa raffinata.
syrupy ['sɪrəpɪ] *adj* sciropposo(a).
system ['sɪstəm] *n* sistema *m*; (*network*) rete *f*; (*ANAT*) apparato; **it was a shock to his ~** è stato uno shock per il suo organismo.
systematic [sɪstə'mætɪk] *adj* sistematico(a).
system disk *n* (*COMPUT*) disco del sistema.
systems analyst *n* analista *m/f* di sistemi.

T t

T, t [tiː] *n* (*letter*) T, t *m* or *f* inv; **T for Tommy** ≈ T come Taranto.
TA *n* abbr (*BRIT*) = **Territorial Army**.
ta [taː] *excl* (*BRIT col*) grazie!
tab [tæb] *n* abbr = **tabulator** ♦ *n* (*loop on coat etc*) laccetto; (*label*) etichetta; **to keep ~s on** (*fig*) tenere d'occhio.
tabby ['tæbɪ] *n* (*also*: **~ cat**) (gatto) soriano, gatto tigrato.
tabernacle ['tæbənækl] *n* tabernacolo.
table ['teɪbl] *n* tavolo, tavola; (*chart*) tabella ♦ *vt* (*motion etc*) presentare; **to lay** *or* **set the ~** apparecchiare *or* preparare la tavola; **to clear the ~** sparecchiare; **league ~** (*FOOTBALL*, *RUGBY*) classifica; **~ of contents** indice *m*.
tablecloth ['teɪblklɔθ] *n* tovaglia.
table d'hôte [taːbl'dəut] *adj* (*meal*) a prezzo fisso.
table lamp *n* lampada da tavolo.
tablemat ['teɪblmæt] *n* sottopiatto.
table salt *n* sale *m* fino *or* da tavola.
tablespoon ['teɪblspuːn] *n* cucchiaio da tavola; (*also*: **~ful**: *as measurement*) cucchiaiata.
tablet ['tæblɪt] *n* (*MED*) compressa; (: *for sucking*) pastiglia; (*for writing*) blocco; (*of stone*) targa; **~ of soap** (*BRIT*) saponetta.
table tennis *n* tennis *m* da tavolo, ping-

pong ® *m*.
table wine *n* vino da tavola.
tabloid ['tæblɔɪd] *n* (*newspaper*) tabloid *m* inv (*giornale illustrato di formato ridotto*); **the ~s** i giornali popolari.

Il termine **tabloid press** *si riferisce ai quotidiani o ai settimanali popolari che, rispetto ai* **quality papers** *hanno un formato ridotto e presentano le notizie in modo più sensazionalistico e meno approfondito; vedi anche* **quality press**.

---

taboo [tə'buː] *adj*, *n* tabù (*m inv*).
tabulate ['tæbjuleɪt] *vt* (*data, figures*) tabulare, disporre in tabelle.
tabulator ['tæbjuleɪtə*] *n* tabulatore *m*.
tachograph ['tækəgraːf] *n* tachigrafo.
tachometer [tæ'kɔmɪtə*] *n* tachimetro.
tacit ['tæsɪt] *adj* tacito(a).
taciturn ['tæsɪtəːn] *adj* taciturno(a).
tack [tæk] *n* (*nail*) bulletta; (*stitch*) punto d'imbastitura; (*NAUT*) bordo, bordata ♦ *vt* imbullettare; imbastire ♦ *vi* bordeggiare; **to change ~** virare di bordo; **on the wrong ~** (*fig*) sulla strada sbagliata; **to ~ sth on to (the end of) sth** (*of letter, book*) aggiungere qc alla fine di qc.
tackle ['tækl] *n* (*equipment*) attrezzatura, equipaggiamento; (*for lifting*) paranco; (*RUGBY*) placcaggio; (*FOOTBALL*) contrasto ♦ *vt* (*difficulty*) affrontare; (*RUGBY*) placcare; (*FOOTBALL*) contrastare.
tacky ['tækɪ] *adj* colloso(a), appiccicaticcio(a); ancora bagnato(a); (*col: shabby*) scadente.
tact [tækt] *n* tatto.
tactful ['tæktful] *adj* delicato(a), discreto(a); **to be ~** avere tatto.
tactfully ['tæktfəlɪ] *adv* con tatto.
tactical ['tæktɪkl] *adj* tattico(a).
tactical voting *n* voto tattico.
tactician [tæk'tɪʃən] *n* tattico/a.
tactics ['tæktɪks] *n*, *npl* tattica.
tactless ['tæktlɪs] *adj* che manca di tatto.
tactlessly ['tæktlɪslɪ] *adv* senza tatto.
tadpole ['tædpəul] *n* girino.
taffy ['tæfɪ] *n* (*US*) caramella *f* mou inv.
tag [tæg] *n* etichetta; **price/name ~** etichetta del prezzo/con il nome.
▶**tag along** *vi* seguire.
Tahiti [tə'hiːti] *n* Tahiti *f*.
tail [teɪl] *n* coda; (*of shirt*) falda ♦ *vt* (*follow*) seguire, pedinare; **to turn ~** voltare la schiena; *see also* **head**.
▶**tail away, tail off** *vi* (*in size, quality etc*) diminuire gradatamente.
tailback ['teɪlbæk] *n* (*BRIT*) ingorgo.

tail coat *n* marsina.
tail end *n* (*of train, procession etc*) coda; (*of meeting etc*) fine *f*.
tailgate ['teɪlgeɪt] *n* (*AUT*) portellone *m* posteriore.
tail light *n* (*AUT*) fanalino di coda.
tailor ['teɪlə*] *n* sarto ♦ *vt*: **to ~ sth (to)** adattare qc (alle esigenze di); **~'s (shop)** sartoria (da uomo).
tailoring ['teɪlərɪŋ] *n* (*cut*) taglio.
tailor-made ['teɪlə'meɪd] *adj* (*also fig*) fatto(a) su misura.
tailwind ['teɪlwɪnd] *n* vento di coda.
taint [teɪnt] *vt* (*meat, food*) far avariare; (*fig: reputation*) infangare.
tainted ['teɪntɪd] *adj* (*food*) guasto(a); (*water, air*) infetto(a); (*fig*) corrotto(a).
Taiwan [taɪ'wɑːn] *n* Taiwan *m*.
Tajikistan [tɑːdʒɪkɪ'stɑːn] *n* Tagikistan *m*.
take [teɪk] *vb* (*pt* **took**, *pp* **taken** [tuk, 'teɪkn]) *vt* prendere; (*gain: prize*) ottenere, vincere; (*require: effort, courage*) occorrere, volerci; (*tolerate*) accettare, sopportare; (*hold: passengers etc*) contenere; (*accompany*) accompagnare; (*bring, carry*) portare; (*conduct: meeting*) condurre; (*exam*) sostenere, presentarsi a ♦ *vi* (*dye, fire etc*) prendere; (*injection*) fare effetto; (*plant*) attecchire ♦ *n* (*CINE*) ripresa; **I ~ it that** suppongo che; **to ~ for a walk** (*child, dog*) portare a fare una passeggiata; **to ~ sb's hand** prendere qn per mano; **to ~ it upon o.s. to do sth** prendersi la responsabilità di fare qc; **to be ~n ill** avere un malore; **to be ~n with sb/sth** (*attracted*) essere tutto preso da qn/qc; **it won't ~ long** non ci vorrà molto tempo; **it ~s a lot of time/courage** occorre *or* ci vuole molto tempo/ coraggio; **it will ~ at least 5 litres** contiene almeno 5 litri; **~ the first on the left** prenda la prima a sinistra; **to ~ Russian at university** fare russo all'università; **I took him for a doctor** l'ho preso per un dottore.
▶**take after** *vt fus* assomigliare a.
▶**take apart** *vt* smontare.
▶**take away** *vt* portare via; togliere; **to ~ away (from)** sottrarre (da).
▶**take back** *vt* (*return*) restituire; riportare; (*one's words*) ritirare.
▶**take down** *vt* (*building*) demolire; (*dismantle: scaffolding*) smontare; (*letter etc*) scrivere.
▶**take in** *vt* (*lodger*) prendere, ospitare; (*orphan*) accogliere; (*stray dog*) raccogliere; (*SEWING*) stringere; (*deceive*) imbrogliare, abbindolare; (*understand*)

capire; (*include*) comprendere, includere.
▶**take off** *vi* (*AVIAT*) decollare ♦ *vt* (*remove*) togliere; (*imitate*) imitare.
▶**take on** *vt* (*work*) accettare, intraprendere; (*employee*) assumere; (*opponent*) sfidare, affrontare.
▶**take out** *vt* portare fuori; (*remove*) togliere; (*licence*) prendere, ottenere; **to ~ sth out of** tirare qc fuori da; estrarre qc da; **don't ~ it out on me!** non prendertela con me!
▶**take over** *vt* (*business*) rilevare ♦ *vi*: **to ~ over from sb** prendere le consegne *or* il controllo da qn.
▶**take to** *vt fus* (*person*) prendere in simpatia; (*activity*) prendere gusto a; (*form habit of*): **to ~ to doing sth** prendere *or* cominciare a fare qc.
▶**take up** *vt* (*one's story*) riprendere; (*dress*) accorciare; (*absorb: liquids*) assorbire; (*accept: offer, challenge*) accettare; (*occupy: time, space*) occupare; (*engage in: hobby etc*) mettersi a; **to ~ up with sb** fare amicizia con qn.
takeaway ['teɪkəweɪ] *adj* (*BRIT: food*) da portar via.
take-home pay ['teɪkhəum-] *n* stipendio netto.
taken ['teɪkn] *pp of* **take**.
takeoff ['teɪkɔf] *n* (*AVIAT*) decollo.
takeout ['teɪkaut] *adj* (*US*) = **takeaway**.
takeover ['teɪkəuvə*] *n* (*COMM*) assorbimento.
takeover bid *n* offerta di assorbimento.
takings ['teɪkɪŋz] *npl* (*COMM*) incasso.
talc [tælk] *n* (*also*: **~um powder**) talco.
tale [teɪl] *n* racconto, storia; (*pej*) fandonia; **to tell ~s** fare la spia.
talent ['tælənt] *n* talento.
talented ['tæləntɪd] *adj* di talento.
talent scout *n* talent scout *m/f inv*.
talisman ['tælɪzmən] *n* talismano.
talk [tɔːk] *n* discorso; (*gossip*) chiacchiere *fpl*; (*conversation*) conversazione *f*; (*interview*) discussione *f* ♦ *vi* parlare; (*chatter*) chiacchierare; **to give a ~** tenere una conferenza; **to ~ about** parlare di; (*converse*) discorrere *or* conversare su; **to ~ sb out of/into doing** dissuadere qn da/convincere qn a fare; **to ~ shop** parlare del lavoro *or* degli affari; **~ing of films, have you seen ...?** a proposito di film, ha visto ...?
▶**talk over** *vt* discutere.
talkative ['tɔːkətɪv] *adj* loquace, ciarliero(a).
talking point ['tɔːkɪŋ-] *n* argomento di conversazione.

talking-to ['tɔːkɪŋtuː] *n*: **to give sb a good ~** fare una bella paternale a qn.
talk show *n* (*TV*, *RADIO*) intervista (informale), talk show *m inv*.
tall [tɔːl] *adj* alto(a); **to be 6 feet ~** ≈ essere alto 1 metro e 80; **how ~ are you?** quanto è alto?
tallboy ['tɔːlbɔɪ] *n* (*BRIT*) cassettone *m* alto.
tallness ['tɔːlnɪs] *n* altezza.
tall story *n* panzana, frottola.
tally ['tælɪ] *n* conto, conteggio ♦ *vi*: **to ~ (with)** corrispondere (a); **to keep a ~ of sth** tener il conto di qc.
talon ['tælən] *n* artiglio.
tambourine [tæmbə'riːn] *n* tamburello.
tame [teɪm] *adj* addomesticato(a); (*fig: story, style*) insipido(a), scialbo(a).
Tamil ['tæmɪl] *adj* tamil *inv* ♦ *n* tamil *m/f inv*; (*LING*) tamil *m*.
tamper ['tæmpə*] *vi*: **to ~ with** manomettere.
tampon ['tæmpɔn] *n* tampone *m*.
tan [tæn] *n* (*also: suntan~*) abbronzatura ♦ *vt* abbronzare ♦ *vi* abbronzarsi ♦ *adj* (*colour*) marrone rossiccio *inv*; **to get a ~** abbronzarsi.
tandem ['tændəm] *n* tandem *m inv*.
tandoori [tæn'duərɪ] *adj nella cucina indiana, detto di carni o verdure cucinate allo spiedo in particolari forni.*
tang [tæŋ] *n* odore *m* penetrante; sapore *m* piccante.
tangent ['tændʒənt] *n* (*MATH*) tangente *f*; **to go off at a ~** (*fig*) partire per la tangente.
tangerine [tændʒə'riːn] *n* mandarino.
tangible ['tændʒəbl] *adj* tangibile; **~ assets** patrimonio reale.
Tangier [tæn'dʒɪə*] *n* Tangeri *f*.
tangle ['tæŋgl] *n* groviglio ♦ *vt* aggrovigliare; **to get in(to) a ~** finire in un groviglio.
tango ['tæŋgəu] *n* tango.
tank [tæŋk] *n* serbatoio; (*for processing*) vasca; (*for fish*) acquario; (*MIL*) carro armato.
tankard ['tæŋkəd] *n* boccale *m*.
tanker ['tæŋkə*] *n* (*ship*) nave *f* cisterna *inv*; (*for oil*) petroliera; (*truck*) autobotte *f*, autocisterna.
tanned [tænd] *adj* abbronzato(a).
tannin ['tænɪn] *n* tannino.
tanning ['tænɪŋ] *n* (*of leather*) conciatura.
tannoy ® ['tænɔɪ] *n* (*BRIT*) altoparlante *m*; **over the ~** per altoparlante.
tantalizing ['tæntəlaɪzɪŋ] *adj* allettante.
tantamount ['tæntəmaunt] *adj*: **~ to** equivalente a.
tantrum ['tæntrəm] *n* accesso di collera; **to**

throw a ~ fare le bizze.
Tanzania [tænzə'nɪə] *n* Tanzania.
Tanzanian [tænzə'nɪən] *adj*, *n* tanzaniano(a).
tap [tæp] *n* (*on sink etc*) rubinetto; (*gentle blow*) colpetto ♦ *vt* dare un colpetto a; (*resources*) sfruttare, utilizzare; (*telephone conversation*) intercettare; (*telephone*) mettere sotto controllo; **on ~** (*beer*) alla spina; (*fig: resources*) a disposizione.
tap-dancing ['tæpdɑːnsɪŋ] *n* tip tap *m*.
tape [teɪp] *n* nastro; (*also: magnetic ~*) nastro (magnetico) ♦ *vt* (*record*) registrare (su nastro); **on ~** (*song etc*) su nastro.
tape deck *n* piastra di registrazione.
tape measure *n* metro a nastro.
taper ['teɪpə*] *n* candelina ♦ *vi* assottigliarsi.
tape-record ['teɪprɪkɔːd] *vt* registrare (su nastro).
tape recorder *n* registratore *m* (a nastro).
tape recording *n* registrazione *f*.
tapered ['teɪpəd], **tapering** ['teɪpərɪŋ] *adj* affusolato(a).
tapestry ['tæpɪstrɪ] *n* arazzo; tappezzeria.
tape-worm ['teɪpwɔːm] *n* tenia, verme *m* solitario.
tapioca [tæpɪ'əukə] *n* tapioca.
tappet ['tæpɪt] *n* punteria.
tar [tɑː*] *n* catrame *m*; **low-/middle-~ cigarettes** sigarette a basso/medio contenuto di nicotina.
tarantula [tə'ræntjulə] *n* tarantola.
tardy ['tɑːdɪ] *adj* tardo(a); tardivo(a).
target ['tɑːgɪt] *n* bersaglio; (*fig: objective*) obiettivo; **to be on ~** (*project*) essere nei tempi (di lavorazione).
target practice *n* tiro al bersaglio.
tariff ['tærɪf] *n* tariffa.
tarmac ['tɑːmæk] *n* (*BRIT*: *on road*) macadam *m* al catrame; (*AVIAT*) pista di decollo ♦ *vt* (*BRIT*) macadamizzare.
tarnish ['tɑːnɪʃ] *vt* offuscare, annerire; (*fig*) macchiare.
tarot ['tærəu] *n* tarocco.
tarpaulin [tɑː'pɔːlɪn] *n* tela incatramata.
tarragon ['tærəgən] *n* dragoncello.
tart [tɑːt] *n* (*CULIN*) crostata; (*BRIT col*: *pej*: *woman*) sgualdrina ♦ *adj* (*flavour*) aspro(a), agro(a).
▶**tart up** *vt* (*col*): **to ~ o.s. up** farsi bello(a); (*pej*) agghindarsi.
tartan ['tɑːtn] *n* tartan *m inv*.
tartar ['tɑːtə*] *n* (*on teeth*) tartaro.
tartar sauce *n* salsa tartara.
task [tɑːsk] *n* compito; **to take to ~**

rimproverare.

task force *n* (*MIL, POLICE*) unità operativa.

taskmaster ['tɑːskmɑːstə*] *n*: **he's a hard ~** è un vero tiranno.

Tasmania [tæz'meɪnɪə] *n* Tasmania.

tassel ['tæsl] *n* fiocco.

taste [teɪst] *n* gusto; (*flavour*) sapore *m*, gusto; (*fig: glimpse, idea*) idea ♦ *vt* gustare; (*sample*) assaggiare ♦ *vi*: **to ~ of** (*fish etc*) sapere di, avere sapore di; **what does it ~ like?** che sapore *or* gusto ha?; **it ~s like fish** sa di pesce; **you can ~ the garlic (in it)** (ci) si sente il sapore dell'aglio; **can I have a ~ of this wine?** posso assaggiare un po' di questo vino?; **to have a ~ of sth** assaggiare qc; **to have a ~ for sth** avere un'inclinazione per qc; **to be in bad** *or* **poor ~** essere di cattivo gusto.

taste bud *n* papilla gustativa.

tasteful ['teɪstful] *adj* di buon gusto.

tastefully ['teɪstfəlɪ] *adv* con gusto.

tasteless ['teɪstlɪs] *adj* (*food*) insipido(a); (*remark*) di cattivo gusto.

tasty ['teɪstɪ] *adj* saporito(a), gustoso(a).

tattered ['tætəd] *adj see* **tatters**.

tatters ['tætəz] *npl*: **in ~** (*also*: **tattered**) a brandelli, sbrindellato(a).

tattoo [tə'tuː] *n* tatuaggio; (*spectacle*) parata militare ♦ *vt* tatuare.

tatty ['tætɪ] *adj* (*BRIT col*) malandato(a).

taught [tɔːt] *pt, pp of* **teach**.

taunt [tɔːnt] *n* scherno ♦ *vt* schernire.

Taurus ['tɔːrəs] *n* Toro; **to be ~** essere del Toro.

taut [tɔːt] *adj* teso(a).

tavern ['tævən] *n* taverna.

tawdry ['tɔːdrɪ] *adj* pacchiano(a).

tawny ['tɔːnɪ] *adj* fulvo(a).

tax [tæks] *n* imposta, tassa; (*on income*) imposte *fpl*, tasse *fpl* ♦ *vt* tassare; (*fig: strain: patience etc*) mettere alla prova; **free of ~** esentasse *inv*, esente da imposte; **before/after ~** al lordo/netto delle tasse.

taxable ['tæksəbl] *adj* imponibile.

tax allowance *n* detrazione *f* d'imposta.

taxation [tæk'seɪʃən] *n* tassazione *f*; tasse *fpl*, imposte *fpl*; **system of ~** sistema *m* fiscale.

tax avoidance *n l'evitare legalmente il pagamento di imposte.*

tax collector *n* esattore *m* delle imposte.

tax disc *n* (*BRIT AUT*) ≈ bollo.

tax evasion *n* evasione *f* fiscale.

tax exemption *n* esenzione *f* fiscale.

tax exile *n chi ripara all'estero per evadere le imposte.*

tax-free [tæks'friː] *adj* esente da imposte.

tax haven *n* paradiso fiscale.

taxi ['tæksɪ] *n* taxi *m inv* ♦ *vi* (*AVIAT*) rullare.

taxidermist ['tæksɪdəːmɪst] *n* tassidermista *m/f.*

taxi driver *n* tassista *m/f.*

tax inspector *n* (*BRIT*) ispettore *m* delle tasse.

taxi rank, (*US*) **taxi stand** *n* posteggio dei taxi.

tax payer *n* contribuente *m/f.*

tax rebate *n* rimborso fiscale.

tax relief *n* sgravio fiscale.

tax return *n* dichiarazione *f* dei redditi.

tax shelter *n* paradiso fiscale.

tax year *n* anno fiscale.

TB *n abbr* (= *tuberculosis*) TBC *f.*

TD *n abbr* (*US*) = **Treasury Department**; (: *FOOTBALL*) = **touchdown**.

tea [tiː] *n* tè *m inv*; (*BRIT: snack: for children*) merenda; **high ~** (*BRIT*) cena leggera (*presa nel tardo pomeriggio*).

tea bag *n* bustina di tè.

tea break *n* (*BRIT*) intervallo per il tè.

teacake ['tiːkeɪk] *n* (*BRIT*) panino dolce all'uva.

teach, *pt, pp* **taught** [tiːtʃ, tɔːt] *vt*: **to ~ sb sth, ~ sth to sb** insegnare qc a qn ♦ *vi* insegnare; **it taught him a lesson** (*fig*) gli è servito da lezione.

teacher ['tiːtʃə*] *n* (*gen*) insegnante *m/f*; (*in secondary school*) professore/essa; (*in primary school*) maestro/a; **French ~** insegnante di francese.

teacher training college *n* (*for primary schools*) ≈ istituto magistrale; (*for secondary schools*) scuola universitaria *per l'abilitazione all'insegnamento nelle medie superiori.*

teaching ['tiːtʃɪŋ] *n* insegnamento.

teaching aids *npl* materiali *mpl* per l'insegnamento.

teaching hospital *n* (*BRIT*) clinica universitaria.

teaching staff *n* (*BRIT*) insegnanti *mpl*, personale *m* insegnante.

tea cosy *n* copriteiera *m inv.*

teacup ['tiːkʌp] *n* tazza da tè.

teak [tiːk] *n* teak *m.*

tea leaves *npl* foglie *fpl* di tè.

team [tiːm] *n* squadra; (*of animals*) tiro.

►**team up** *vi*: **to ~ up (with)** mettersi insieme (a).

team games *npl* giochi *mpl* di squadra.

teamwork ['tiːmwəːk] *n* lavoro di squadra.

tea party *n* tè *m inv* (*ricevimento*).

teapot ['tiːpɔt] *n* teiera.

tear *n* [tɛə*] strappo; [tɪə*] lacrima ♦ *vb*

[tɛə*] (pt **tore**, pp **torn** [tɔː*, tɔːn]) vt
strappare ♦ vi strapparsi; **in ~s** in
lacrime; **to burst into ~s** scoppiare in
lacrime; **to ~ to pieces** or **to bits** or **to
shreds** (also fig) fare a pezzi or a
brandelli.
►**tear along** vi (rush) correre
all'impazzata.
►**tear apart** vt (also fig) distruggere.
►**tear away** vt: **to ~ o.s. away (from sth)**
(fig) staccarsi (da qc).
►**tear out** vt (sheet of paper, cheque)
staccare.
►**tear up** vt (sheet of paper etc) strappare.
tearaway ['tɛərəweɪ] n (col) monello/a.
teardrop ['tɪədrɒp] n lacrima.
tearful ['tɪəful] adj piangente, lacrimoso(a).
tear gas n gas m lacrimogeno.
tearoom ['tiːruːm] n sala da tè.
tease [tiːz] vt canzonare; (unkindly)
tormentare.
tea set n servizio da tè.
teashop ['tiːʃɒp] n (BRIT) sala da tè.
Teasmaid ® ['tiːzmeɪd] n macchinetta per
fare il tè.
teaspoon ['tiːspuːn] n cucchiaino da tè;
(also: ~**ful**: as measurement) cucchiaino.
tea strainer n colino da tè.
teat [tiːt] n capezzolo; (of bottle) tettarella.
teatime ['tiːtaɪm] n ora del tè.
tea towel n (BRIT) strofinaccio (per i
piatti).
tea urn n bollitore m per il tè.
tech [tɛk] n abbr (col) = **technical college**;
technology.
technical ['tɛknɪkl] adj tecnico(a).
technical college n ≈ istituto tecnico.
technicality [tɛknɪ'kælɪtɪ] n tecnicità;
(detail) dettaglio tecnico; **on a legal ~**
grazie a un cavillo legale.
technically ['tɛknɪklɪ] adv dal punto di vista
tecnico.
technician [tɛk'nɪʃən] n tecnico/a.
technique [tɛk'niːk] n tecnica.
techno ['tɛknəu] n (MUS) techno f inv.
technocrat ['tɛknəkræt] n tecnocrate m/f.
technological [tɛknə'lɒdʒɪkl] adj
tecnologico(a).
technologist [tɛk'nɒlədʒɪst] n tecnologo/a.
technology [tɛk'nɒlədʒɪ] n tecnologia.
teddy (bear) ['tɛdɪ-] n orsacchiotto.
tedious ['tiːdɪəs] adj noioso(a), tedioso(a).
tedium ['tiːdɪəm] n noia, tedio.
tee [tiː] n (GOLF) tee m inv.
teem [tiːm] vi abbondare, brulicare; **to ~
with** brulicare di; **it is ~ing (with rain)**
piove a dirotto.
teenage ['tiːneɪdʒ] adj (fashions etc) per

giovani, per adolescenti.
teenager ['tiːneɪdʒə*] n adolescente m/f.
teens [tiːnz] npl: **to be in one's ~** essere
adolescente.
tee-shirt ['tiːʃəːt] n = **T-shirt**.
teeter ['tiːtə*] vi barcollare, vacillare.
teeth [tiːθ] npl of **tooth**.
teethe [tiːð] vi mettere i denti.
teething ring ['tiːðɪŋ-] n dentaruolo.
teething troubles npl (fig) difficoltà fpl
iniziali.
teetotal ['tiː'təutl] adj astemio(a).
teetotaller, (US) **teetotaler** ['tiː'təutlə*] n
astemio/a.
TEFL ['tɛfl] n abbr = Teaching of English as a
Foreign Language.
Teflon ® ['tɛflɒn] n teflon ® m.
Tehran [tɛə'rɑːn] n Tehran f.
tel. abbr (= telephone) tel.
Tel Aviv ['tɛlə'viːv] n Tel Aviv f.
telecast ['tɛlɪkɑːst] vt, vi teletrasmettere.
telecommunications ['tɛlɪkəmjuːnɪ
'keɪʃənz] n telecomunicazioni fpl.
telegram ['tɛlɪgræm] n telegramma m.
telegraph ['tɛlɪgrɑːf] n telegrafo.
telegraphic [tɛlɪ'græfɪk] adj telegrafico(a).
telegraph pole n palo del telegrafo.
telegraph wire n filo del telegrafo.
telepathic [tɛlɪ'pæθɪk] adj telepatico(a).
telepathy [tə'lɛpəθɪ] n telepatia.
telephone ['tɛlɪfəun] n telefono ♦ vt
(person) telefonare a; (message)
telefonare; **to have a ~**, (BRIT) **to be on
the ~** (subscriber) avere il telefono; **to be
on the ~** (be speaking) essere al telefono.
telephone booth, (BRIT) **telephone box**
n cabina telefonica.
telephone call n telefonata.
telephone directory n elenco telefonico.
telephone exchange n centralino
telefonico.
telephone number n numero di telefono.
telephone operator n centralinista m/f.
telephone tapping n intercettazione f
telefonica.
telephonist [tə'lɛfənɪst] n (BRIT) telefonista
m/f.
telephoto lens ['tɛlɪfəutəu-] n
teleobiettivo.
teleprinter ['tɛlɪprɪntə*] n telescrivente f.
Teleprompter ® ['tɛlɪprɒmptə*] n (US)
gobbo.
telesales ['tɛlɪseɪlz] n vendita per telefono.
telescope ['tɛlɪskəup] n telescopio ♦ vi
chiudersi a telescopio; (fig: vehicles)
accartocciarsi.
telescopic [tɛlɪs'kɒpɪk] adj telescopico(a);
(umbrella) pieghevole.

Teletext ® ['tɛlɪtɛkst] *n (system)* teletext *m inv; (in Italy)* televideo.

telethon ['tɛlɪθɒn] *n* maratona televisiva.

televise ['tɛlɪvaɪz] *vt* teletrasmettere.

television ['tɛlɪvɪʒən] *n* televisione *f*; **on ~** alla televisione.

television licence *n (BRIT)* abbonamento alla televisione.

television programme *n* programma *m* televisivo.

television set *n* televisore *m*.

telex ['tɛlɛks] *n* telex *m inv* ♦ *vt* trasmettere per telex ♦ *vi* mandare un telex; **to ~ sb (about sth)** informare qn via telex (di qc).

tell, *pt, pp* **told** [tɛl, təʊld] *vt* dire; *(relate: story)* raccontare; *(distinguish):* **to ~ sth from** distinguere qc da ♦ *vi (have effect)* farsi sentire, avere effetto; **to ~ sb to do** dire a qn di fare; **to ~ sb about sth** dire a qn di qc; raccontare qc a qn; **to ~ the time** leggere l'ora; **can you ~ me the time?** può dirmi l'ora?; **(I) ~ you what ...** so io che cosa fare ...; **I couldn't ~ them apart** non riuscivo a distinguerli.

►**tell off** *vt* rimproverare, sgridare.

►**tell on** *vt fus (inform against)* denunciare.

teller ['tɛlə*] *n (in bank)* cassiere/a.

telling ['tɛlɪŋ] *adj (remark, detail)* rivelatore(trice).

telltale ['tɛlteɪl] *adj (sign)* rivelatore(trice) ♦ *n* malalingua, pettegolo/a.

telly ['tɛlɪ] *n abbr (BRIT col: = television)* tivù *f inv.*

temerity [tə'mɛrɪtɪ] *n* temerarietà.

temp [tɛmp] *abbr (BRIT col: = temporary)* *n* impiegato(a) straordinario(a) ♦ *vi* lavorare come impiegato(a) straordinario(a).

temper ['tɛmpə*] *n (nature)* carattere *m*; *(mood)* umore *m*; *(fit of anger)* collera ♦ *vt (moderate)* temperare, moderare; **to be in a ~** essere in collera; **to keep one's ~** restare calmo; **to lose one's ~** andare in collera.

temperament ['tɛmprəmənt] *n* temperamento.

temperamental [tɛmprə'mɛntl] *adj* capriccioso(a).

temperance ['tɛmpərns] *n* moderazione *f*; *(in drinking)* temperanza nel bere.

temperate ['tɛmprət] *adj* moderato(a); *(climate)* temperato(a).

temperature ['tɛmprətʃə*] *n* temperatura; **to have** *or* **run a ~** avere la febbre.

tempered ['tɛmpəd] *adj (steel)* temprato(a).

tempest ['tɛmpɪst] *n* tempesta.

tempestuous [tɛm'pɛstjuəs] *adj*

(relationship, meeting) burrascoso(a).

tempi ['tɛmpiː] *npl of* **tempo**.

template, *(US)* **templet** ['tɛmplɪt] *n* sagoma.

temple ['tɛmpl] *n (building)* tempio; *(ANAT)* tempia.

templet ['tɛmplɪt] *n (US)* = **template**.

tempo, **~s** *or* **tempi** ['tɛmpəʊ, 'tɛmpiː] *n* tempo; *(fig: of life etc)* ritmo.

temporal ['tɛmpərl] *adj* temporale.

temporarily ['tɛmpərərɪlɪ] *adv* temporaneamente.

temporary ['tɛmpərərɪ] *adj* temporaneo(a); *(job, worker)* avventizio(a), temporaneo(a); **~ secretary** segretaria temporanea; **~ teacher** supplente *m/f.*

temporize ['tɛmpəraɪz] *vi* temporeggiare.

tempt [tɛmpt] *vt* tentare; **to ~ sb into doing** indurre qn a fare; **to be ~ed to do sth** essere tentato di fare qc.

temptation [tɛmp'teɪʃən] *n* tentazione *f.*

tempting ['tɛmptɪŋ] *adj* allettante, seducente.

ten [tɛn] *num* dieci ♦ *n* dieci; **~s of thousands** decine di migliaia.

tenable ['tɛnəbl] *adj* sostenibile.

tenacious [tə'neɪʃəs] *adj* tenace.

tenacity [tə'næsɪtɪ] *n* tenacia.

tenancy ['tɛnənsɪ] *n* affitto; condizione *f* di inquilino.

tenant ['tɛnənt] *n* inquilino/a.

tend [tɛnd] *vt* badare a, occuparsi di; *(sick etc)* prendersi cura di ♦ *vi:* **to ~ to do** tendere a fare; *(colour):* **to ~ to** tendere a.

tendency ['tɛndənsɪ] *n* tendenza.

tender ['tɛndə*] *adj* tenero(a); *(sore)* sensibile; *(fig: subject)* delicato(a) ♦ *n (COMM: offer)* offerta; *(money):* **legal ~** valuta (a corso legale) ♦ *vt* offrire; **to put in a ~ (for)** fare un'offerta (per); **to put work out to ~ (BRIT)** dare lavoro in appalto; **to ~ one's resignation** presentare le proprie dimissioni.

tenderize ['tɛndəraɪz] *vt (CULIN)* far intenerire.

tenderly ['tɛndəlɪ] *adv* teneramente.

tenderness ['tɛndənɪs] *n* tenerezza; sensibilità.

tendon ['tɛndən] *n* tendine *m*.

tenement ['tɛnəmənt] *n* casamento.

Tenerife [tɛnə'riːf] *n* Tenerife *f.*

tenet ['tɛnət] *n* principio.

Tenn. *abbr (US)* = *Tennessee.*

tenner ['tɛnə*] *n (BRIT col)* (banconota da) dieci sterline *fpl.*

tennis ['tɛnɪs] *n* tennis *m.*

tennis ball *n* palla da tennis.

tennis court n campo da tennis.
tennis elbow n (MED) gomito del tennista.
tennis match n partita di tennis.
tennis player n tennista m/f.
tennis racket n racchetta da tennis.
tennis shoes npl scarpe fpl da tennis.
tenor ['tɛnə*] n (MUS, of speech etc) tenore m.
tenpin bowling ['tɛnpɪn-] n (BRIT) bowling m.
tense [tɛns] adj teso(a) ♦ n (LING) tempo ♦ vt (tighten: muscles) tendere.
tenseness ['tɛnsnɪs] n tensione f.
tension ['tɛnʃən] n tensione f.
tent [tɛnt] n tenda.
tentacle ['tɛntəkl] n tentacolo.
tentative ['tɛntətɪv] adj esitante, incerto(a); (conclusion) provvisorio(a).
tenterhooks ['tɛntəhuks] npl: on ~ sulle spine.
tenth [tɛnθ] num decimo(a).
tent peg n picchetto da tenda.
tent pole n palo da tenda, montante m.
tenuous ['tɛnjuəs] adj tenue.
tenure ['tɛnjuə*] n (of property) possesso; (of job) incarico; (guaranteed employment): **to have** ~ essere di ruolo.
tepid ['tɛpɪd] adj tiepido(a).
term [təːm] n (limit) termine m; (word) vocabolo, termine; (SCOL) trimestre m; (LAW) sessione f ♦ vt chiamare, definire; ~**s** npl (conditions) condizioni fpl; (COMM) prezzi mpl, tariffe fpl; ~ **of imprisonment** periodo di prigionia; **during his** ~ **of office** durante il suo incarico; **in the short/long** ~ a breve/lunga scadenza; **"easy** ~**s"** (COMM) "facilitazioni di pagamento"; **to be on good** ~**s with** essere in buoni rapporti con; **to come to** ~**s with** (person) arrivare a un accordo con; (problem) affrontare.
terminal ['təːmɪnl] adj finale, terminale; (disease) nella fase terminale ♦ n (ELEC, COMPUT) terminale m; (AVIAT, for oil, ore etc) terminal m inv; (BRIT: also: **coach** ~) capolinea m.
terminate ['təːmɪneɪt] vt mettere fine a ♦ vi: **to** ~ **in** finire in or con.
termination [təːmɪ'neɪʃən] n fine f; (of contract) rescissione f; ~ **of pregnancy** (MED) interruzione f della gravidanza.
termini ['təːmɪnaɪ] npl of **terminus**.
terminology [təːmɪ'nɔlədʒɪ] n terminologia.
terminus, pl termini ['təːmɪnəs, 'təːmɪnaɪ] n (for buses) capolinea m; (for trains) stazione f terminale.
termite ['təːmaɪt] n termite f.

term paper n (US UNIVERSITY) saggio scritto da consegnare a fine trimestre.
Ter(r). abbr = **terrace**.
terrace ['tɛrəs] n terrazza; (BRIT: row of houses) fila di case a schiera; **the** ~**s** npl (BRIT SPORT) le gradinate.
terraced ['tɛrɪst] adj (garden) a terrazze; (in a row: house, cottage etc) a schiera.
terrain [tɛ'reɪn] n terreno.
terrible ['tɛrɪbl] adj terribile; (weather) bruttissimo(a); (performance, report) pessimo(a).
terribly ['tɛrəblɪ] adv terribilmente; (very badly) malissimo.
terrier ['tɛrɪə*] n terrier m inv.
terrific [tə'rɪfɪk] adj incredibile, fantastico(a); (wonderful) formidabile, eccezionale.
terrify ['tɛrɪfaɪ] vt terrorizzare; **to be terrified** essere atterrito(a).
territorial [tɛrɪ'tɔːrɪəl] adj territoriale.
territorial waters npl acque fpl territoriali.
territory ['tɛrɪtərɪ] n territorio.
terror ['tɛrə*] n terrore m.
terrorism ['tɛrərɪzəm] n terrorismo.
terrorist ['tɛrərɪst] n terrorista m/f.
terrorize ['tɛrəraɪz] vt terrorizzare.
terse [təːs] adj (style) conciso(a); (reply) laconico(a).
tertiary ['təːʃərɪ] adj (gen) terziario(a); ~ **education** (BRIT) educazione f superiore post-scolastica.
Terylene ® ['tɛrəliːn] n (BRIT) terital ® m, terilene ® m.
TESL ['tɛsl] n abbr = Teaching of English as a Second Language.
TESSA ['tɛsə] n abbr (BRIT: = Tax Exempt Special Savings Account) deposito a risparmio esente da tasse.
test [tɛst] n (trial, check) prova; (: of goods in factory) controllo, collaudo; (MED) esame m; (CHEM) analisi f inv; (exam: of intelligence etc) test m inv; (: in school) compito in classe; (also: **driving** ~) esame m di guida ♦ vt provare; controllare, collaudare; esaminare; analizzare; sottoporre ad esame; **to put sth to the** ~ mettere qc alla prova; **to** ~ **sth for sth** analizzare qc alla ricerca di qc; **to** ~ **sb in history** esaminare qn in storia.
testament ['tɛstəmənt] n testamento; **the Old/New T**~ il Vecchio/Nuovo testamento.
test ban n (also: **nuclear** ~) divieto di esperimenti nucleari.
test case n (LAW, fig) caso che farà testo.
testes ['tɛstiːz] npl testicoli mpl.
test flight n volo di prova.

testicle ['tɛstɪkl] *n* testicolo.

testify ['tɛstɪfaɪ] *vi* (*LAW*) testimoniare, deporre; **to ~ to sth** (*LAW*) testimoniare qc; (*gen*) comprovare *or* dimostrare qc; (*be sign of*) essere una prova di qc.

testimonial [tɛstɪ'məʊnɪəl] *n* (*BRIT: reference*) benservito; (*gift*) testimonianza di stima.

testimony ['tɛstɪmənɪ] *n* (*LAW*) testimonianza, deposizione *f*.

testing ['tɛstɪŋ] *adj* (*difficult: time*) duro(a).

test match *n* (*CRICKET, RUGBY*) partita internazionale.

testosterone [tɛs'tɔstərəʊn] *n* testosterone *m*.

test paper *n* (*SCOL*) interrogazione *f* scritta.

test pilot *n* pilota *m* collaudatore.

test tube *n* provetta.

test-tube baby ['tɛsttjuːb-] *n* bambino(a) concepito(a) in provetta.

testy ['tɛstɪ] *adj* irritabile.

tetanus ['tɛtənəs] *n* tetano.

tetchy ['tɛtʃɪ] *adj* irritabile, irascibile.

tether ['tɛðə*] *vt* legare ♦ *n*: **at the end of one's ~** al limite (della pazienza).

Tex. *abbr* (*US*) = *Texas*.

text [tɛkst] *n* testo.

textbook ['tɛkstbʊk] *n* libro di testo.

textile ['tɛkstaɪl] *n* tessile *m*; **~s** *npl* tessuti *mpl*.

textual ['tɛkstjʊəl] *adj* testuale, del testo.

texture ['tɛkstʃə*] *n* tessitura; (*of skin, paper etc*) struttura.

TGIF *abbr* (*col*) = *thank God it's Friday*.

TGWU *n abbr* (*BRIT*: = *Transport and General Workers' Union*) sindacato degli operai dei trasporti e non specializzati.

Thai [taɪ] *adj* tailandese ♦ *n* tailandese *m/f*; (*LING*) tailandese *m*.

Thailand ['taɪlænd] *n* Tailandia.

thalidomide ® [θə'lɪdəmaɪd] *n* talidomide ® *m*.

Thames [tɛmz] *n*: **the ~** il Tamigi.

than [ðæn, ðən] *conj* che; (*with numerals, pronouns, proper names*): **more ~ 10/me/Maria** più di 10/me/Maria; **you know her better ~ I do** la conosce meglio di me *or* di quanto non la conosca io; **she has more apples ~ pears** ha più mele che pere; **it is better to phone ~ to write** è meglio telefonare che scrivere; **no sooner did he leave ~ the phone rang** non appena uscì il telefono suonò.

thank [θæŋk] *vt* ringraziare; **~ you (very much)** grazie (tante); **~ heavens/God!** grazie al cielo/a Dio!; *see also* **thanks**.

thankful ['θæŋkful] *adj*: **~ (for)** riconoscente

(per); **~ for/that** (*relieved*) sollevato(a) da/dal fatto che.

thankfully ['θæŋkfəlɪ] *adv* con riconoscenza; con sollievo; **~ there were few victims** grazie al cielo ci sono state poche vittime.

thankless ['θæŋklɪs] *adj* ingrato(a).

thanks [θæŋks] *npl* ringraziamenti *mpl*, grazie *fpl* ♦ *excl* grazie!; **~ to** *prep* grazie a.

Thanksgiving (Day) ['θæŋksgɪvɪŋ-] *n* giorno del ringraziamento.

> Negli Stati Uniti il quarto giovedì di novembre ricorre il **Thanksgiving (Day)**, festa nazionale in ricordo della celebrazione con cui i Padri Pellegrini, i puritani inglesi che fondarono la colonia di Plymouth nel Massachusetts, ringraziarono Dio del buon raccolto del 1621.

═══════════════════════════════════ *KEYWORD*

that [ðæt] (*pl* **those**) *adj* (*demonstrative*) quel(quell', quello) *m*; quella(quell') *f*; **~ man/woman/book** quell'uomo/quella donna/quel libro; (*not "this"*) quell'uomo/quella donna/quel libro là; **~ one** quello là

♦ *pron* **1** (*demonstrative*) ciò; (*not "this one"*) quello(a); **who's ~?** chi è quello là?; **what's ~?** cos'è quello?; **is ~ you?** sei tu?; **I prefer this to ~** preferisco questo a quello; **~'s what he said** questo è ciò che ha detto; **after ~** dopo; **what happened after ~?** che è successo dopo?; **~ is (to say)** cioè; **at** *or* **with ~ she ...** con ciò lei ...; **do it like ~** fallo così

2 (*relative: direct*) che; (: *indirect*) cui; **the book (~) I read** il libro che ho letto; **the box (~) I put it in** la scatola in cui l'ho messo; **the people (~) I spoke to** le persone con cui *or* con le quali ho parlato; **not ~ I know of** non che io sappia

3 (*relative: of time*) in cui; **the day (~) he came** il giorno in cui è venuto

♦ *conj* che; **he thought ~ I was ill** pensava che io fossi malato

♦ *adv* (*demonstrative*) così; **I can't work ~ much** non posso lavorare (così) tanto; **~ high** così alto; **the wall's about ~ high and ~ thick** il muro è alto circa così e spesso circa così.

thatched [θætʃt] *adj* (*roof*) di paglia; **~ cottage** cottage *m inv* col tetto di paglia.

Thatcherism ['θætʃərɪzəm] *n* thatcherismo.

thaw [θɔː] *n* disgelo ♦ *vi* (*ice*) sciogliersi;

(*food*) scongelarsi ♦ *vt* (*food*) (fare) scongelare; **it's ~ing** (*weather*) sta sgelando.

================================ *KEYWORD*

the [ðiː, ðə] *def art* **1** (*gen*) il(lo, l') *m*; la(l') *f*; i(gli) *mpl*; le *fpl*; ~ **boy/girl/ink** il ragazzo/la ragazza/l'inchiostro; ~ **books/pencils** i libri/le matite; ~ **history of** ~ **world** la storia del mondo; **give it to** ~ **postman** dallo al postino; **I haven't** ~ **time/money** non ho tempo/soldi; ~ **rich and** ~ **poor** i ricchi e i poveri; **1700 lire to** ~ **dollar** 1700 lire per un dollaro; **paid by** ~ **hour** pagato a ore
2 (*in titles*): **Elizabeth** ~ **First** Elisabetta prima; **Peter** ~ **Great** Pietro il Grande
3 (*in comparisons*): ~ **more he works,** ~ **more he earns** più lavora più guadagna; ~ **sooner** ~ **better** prima è meglio è.

theatre, (*US*) **theater** ['θɪətə*] *n* teatro.
theatre-goer ['θɪətəɡəʊə*] *n* frequentatore/trice di teatri.
theatrical [θɪ'ætrɪkl] *adj* teatrale.
theft [θɛft] *n* furto.
their [ðɛə*] *adj* il(la) loro, *pl* i(le) loro.
theirs [ðɛəz] *pron* il(la) loro, *pl* i(le) loro; **it is** ~ è loro; **a friend of** ~ un loro amico.
them [ðɛm, ðəm] *pron* (*direct*) li(le); (*indirect*) gli, loro (*after vb*); (*stressed, after prep*: *people*) loro; (: *people, things*) essi(e); **I see** ~ li vedo; **give** ~ **the book** dà loro *or* dagli il libro; **give me a few of** ~ dammene un po' *or* qualcuno.
theme [θiːm] *n* tema *m*.
theme park *n* parco dei divertimenti a soggetto.
theme song, theme tune *n* tema musicale.
themselves [ðəm'sɛlvz] *pl pron* (*reflexive*) si; (*emphatic*) loro stessi(e); (*after prep*) se stessi(e); **between** ~ tra (di) loro.
then [ðɛn] *adv* (*at that time*) allora; (*next*) poi, dopo; (*and also*) e poi ♦ *conj* (*therefore*) perciò, dunque, quindi ♦ *adj*: **the** ~ **president** il presidente di allora; **from** ~ **on** da allora in poi; **until** ~ fino ad allora; **and** ~ **what?** e poi?, e allora?; **what do you want me to do** ~? allora cosa vuole che faccia?
theologian [θɪə'ləʊdʒən] *n* teologo/a.
theological [θɪə'lɒdʒɪkl] *adj* teologico(a).
theology [θɪ'ɒlədʒɪ] *n* teologia.
theorem ['θɪərəm] *n* teorema *m*.
theoretical [θɪə'rɛtɪkl] *adj* teorico(a).
theorize ['θɪəraɪz] *vi* teorizzare.
theory ['θɪərɪ] *n* teoria; **in** ~ in teoria.

therapeutic(al) [θɛrə'pjuːtɪk(l)] *adj* terapeutico(a).
therapist ['θɛrəpɪst] *n* terapista *m/f*.
therapy ['θɛrəpɪ] *n* terapia.

================================ *KEYWORD*

there [ðɛə*] *adv* **1**: ~ **is,** ~ **are** c'è, ci sono; ~ **are 3 of them** (*people*) sono in 3; (*things*) ce ne sono 3; ~ **is no-one here** non c'è nessuno qui; ~ **has been an accident** c'è stato un incidente
2 (*referring to place*) là, lì; **it's** ~ è là *or* lì; **up/in/down** ~ lassù/là dentro/laggiù; **back** ~ là dietro; **on** ~ lassù; **over** ~ là; **through** ~ di là; **he went** ~ **on Friday** ci è andato venerdì; **it takes two hours to go** ~ **and back** ci vogliono due ore per andare e tornare; **I want that book** ~ voglio quel libro là *or* lì; ~ **he is!** eccolo!
3: ~, ~ (*esp to child*) su, su.

thereabouts ['ðɛərəbauts] *adv* (*place*) nei pressi, da quelle parti; (*amount*) giù di lì, all'incirca.
thereafter [ðɛər'ɑːftə*] *adv* da allora in poi.
thereby [ðɛə'baɪ] *adv* con ciò.
therefore ['ðɛəfɔː*] *adv* perciò, quindi.
there's [ðɛəz] = **there is; there has**.
thereupon [ðɛərə'pɒn] *adv* (*at that point*) a quel punto; (*formal: on that subject*) in merito.
thermal ['θəːml] *adj* (*currents, spring*) termale; (*underwear, printer*) termico(a); (*paper*) termosensibile.
thermodynamics [θəːməʊdaɪ'næmɪks] *n* termodinamica.
thermometer [θə'mɒmɪtə*] *n* termometro.
thermonuclear ['θəːməʊ'njuːklɪə*] *adj* termonucleare.
Thermos ® ['θəːməs] *n* (*also:* ~ **flask**) thermos ® *m inv*.
thermostat ['θəːməstæt] *n* termostato.
thesaurus [θɪ'sɔːrəs] *n* dizionario dei sinonimi.
these [ðiːz] *pl pron, adj* questi(e).
thesis, pl theses ['θiːsɪs, 'θiːsiːz] *n* tesi *f inv*.
they [ðeɪ] *pl pron* essi(esse); (*people only*) loro; ~ **say that ...** (*it is said that*) si dice che ....
they'd [ðeɪd] = **they would; they had**.
they'll [ðeɪl] = **they will; they shall**.
they're [ðɛə*] = **they are**.
they've [ðeɪv] = **they have**.
thick [θɪk] *adj* spesso(a); (*crowd*) compatto(a); (*stupid*) ottuso(a), lento(a) ♦ *n*: **in the** ~ **of** nel folto di; **it's 20 cm** ~ ha uno spessore di 20 cm.
thicken ['θɪkən] *vi* ispessire ♦ *vt* (*sauce etc*)

ispessire, rendere più denso(a).
thicket ['θɪkɪt] n boscaglia.
thickly ['θɪklɪ] adv (spread) a strati spessi; (cut) a fette grosse; (populated) densamente.
thickness ['θɪknɪs] n spessore m.
thickset [θɪk'sɛt] adj tarchiato(a), tozzo(a).
thickskinned [θɪk'skɪnd] adj (fig) insensibile.
thief, pl **thieves** [θi:f, θi:vz] n ladro/a.
thieving ['θi:vɪŋ] n furti mpl.
thigh [θaɪ] n coscia.
thighbone ['θaɪbəun] n femore m.
thimble ['θɪmbl] n ditale m.
thin [θɪn] adj sottile; (person) magro(a); (soup) poco denso(a); (hair, crowd) rado(a); (fog) leggero(a) ♦ vt (hair) sfoltire ♦ vi (fog) diradarsi; (also: ~ out: crowd) disperdersi; **to ~ (down)** (sauce, paint) diluire; **his hair is ~ning** sta perdendo i capelli.
thing [θɪŋ] n cosa; (object) oggetto; (contraption) aggeggio; **~s** npl (belongings) cose fpl; **for one ~** tanto per cominciare; **the best ~ would be to** la cosa migliore sarebbe di; **the ~ is ...** il fatto è che ...; **the main ~ is to ...** la cosa più importante è di ...; **first ~ (in the morning)** come or per prima cosa (di mattina); **last ~ (at night)** come or per ultima cosa (di sera); **poor ~** poveretto/a; **she's got a ~ about mice** è terrorizzata dai topi; **how are ~s?** come va?
think, pt, pp **thought** [θɪŋk, θɔ:t] vi pensare, riflettere ♦ vt pensare, credere; (imagine) immaginare; **to ~ of** pensare a; **what did you ~ of them?** cosa ne ha pensato?; **to ~ about sth/sb** pensare a qc/qn; **I'll ~ about it** ci penserò; **to ~ of doing** pensare di fare; **I ~ so** penso or credo di sì; **to ~ well of** avere una buona opinione di; **to ~ aloud** pensare ad alta voce; **~ again!** rifletti!, pensaci su!
▶**think out** vt (plan) elaborare; (solution) trovare.
▶**think over** vt riflettere su; **I'd like to ~ things over** vorrei pensarci su.
▶**think through** vt riflettere a fondo su.
▶**think up** vt ideare.
thinking ['θɪŋkɪŋ] n: **to my (way of) ~** a mio parere.
think tank n gruppo di esperti.
thinly ['θɪnlɪ] adv (cut) a fette sottili; (spread) in uno strato sottile.
thinness ['θɪnnɪs] n sottigliezza; magrezza.
third [θɜ:d] n terzo(a) ♦ n terzo/a; (fraction) terzo, terza parte f; (BRIT SCOL: degree) laurea col minimo dei voti.

third-degree burns ['θɜ:ddɪ'gri:-] npl ustioni fpl di terzo grado.
thirdly ['θɜ:dlɪ] adv in terzo luogo.
third party insurance n (BRIT) assicurazione f contro terzi.
third-rate [θɜ:d'reɪt] adj di qualità scadente.
Third World n: **the ~** il Terzo Mondo.
thirst [θɜ:st] n sete f.
thirsty ['θɜ:stɪ] adj (person) assetato(a), che ha sete; **to be ~** aver sete.
thirteen [θɜ:'ti:n] num tredici.
thirtieth ['θɜ:tɪɪθ] num trentesimo(a).
thirty ['θɜ:tɪ] num trenta.

====================== *KEYWORD*

this [ðɪs] (pl **these**) adj (demonstrative) questo(a); **~ man/woman/book** quest'uomo/questa donna/questo libro; (not "that") quest'uomo/questa donna/ questo libro qui; **~ one** questo(a) qui; **~ time** questa volta; **~ time last year** l'anno scorso in questo periodo; **~ way** (in this direction) da questa parte; (in this fashion) così
♦ pron (demonstrative) questo(a); (not "that one") questo(a) qui; **who/what is ~?** chi è/che cos'è questo?; **I prefer ~ to that** preferisco questo a quello; **~ is where I live** io abito qui; **~ is what he said** questo è ciò che ha detto; **they were talking of ~ and that** stavano parlando del più e del meno; **~ is Mr Brown** (in introductions, photo) questo è il signor Brown; (on telephone) sono il signor Brown
♦ adv (demonstrative): **~ high/long etc** alto/lungo etc così; **it's about ~ high** è alto circa così; **I didn't know things were ~ bad** non sapevo andasse così male.

thistle ['θɪsl] n cardo.
thong [θɔŋ] n cinghia.
thorn [θɔ:n] n spina.
thorny ['θɔ:nɪ] adj spinoso(a).
thorough ['θʌrə] adj (person) preciso(a), accurato(a); (search) minuzioso(a); (knowledge, research) approfondito(a), profondo(a); (cleaning) a fondo.
thoroughbred ['θʌrəbrɛd] n (horse) purosangue m/f inv.
thoroughfare ['θʌrəfɛə*] n strada transitabile; **"no ~"** (BRIT) "divieto di transito".
thoroughgoing ['θʌrəgəuɪŋ] adj (analysis) approfondito(a); (reform) totale.
thoroughly ['θʌrəlɪ] adv accuratamente; minuziosamente; in profondità; a fondo; **he ~ agreed** fu completamente

d'accordo.

thoroughness ['θʌrənɪs] n precisione f.

those [ðəuz] pl pron quelli(e) ♦ pl adj quei(quegli) mpl; quelle fpl.

though [ðəu] conj benché, sebbene ♦ adv comunque, tuttavia; **even** ~ anche se; **it's not so easy,** ~ tuttavia non è così facile.

thought [θɔːt] pt, pp of **think** ♦ n pensiero; (opinion) opinione f; (intention) intenzione f; **after much** ~ dopo molti ripensamenti; **I've just had a** ~ mi è appena venuta un'idea; **to give sth some** ~ prendere qc in considerazione, riflettere su qc.

thoughtful ['θɔːtful] adj pensieroso(a), pensoso(a); ponderato(a); (considerate) premuroso(a).

thoughtfully ['θɔːtfəlɪ] adv (pensively) con aria pensierosa.

thoughtless ['θɔːtlɪs] adj sconsiderato(a); (behaviour) scortese.

thoughtlessly ['θɔːtlɪslɪ] adv sconsideratamente; scortesemente.

thought-provoking ['θɔːtprəvəukɪŋ] adj stimolante.

thousand ['θauzənd] num mille; **one** ~ mille; ~**s of** migliaia di.

thousandth ['θauzəntθ] num millesimo(a).

thrash [θræʃ] vt picchiare; bastonare; (defeat) battere.

▶**thrash about** vi dibattersi.

▶**thrash out** vt dibattere, sviscerare.

thrashing ['θræʃɪŋ] n: **to give sb a** ~ = **to thrash sb**.

thread [θrɛd] n filo; (of screw) filetto ♦ vt (needle) infilare; **to** ~ **one's way between** infilarsi tra.

threadbare ['θrɛdbɛə*] adj consumato(a), logoro(a).

threat [θrɛt] n minaccia; **to be under** ~ **of** (closure, extinction) rischiare di; (exposure) essere minacciato(a) di.

threaten ['θrɛtn] vi (storm) minacciare ♦ vt: **to** ~ **sb with sth/to do** minacciare qn con qc/di fare.

threatening ['θrɛtnɪŋ] adj minaccioso(a).

three [θriː] num tre.

three-dimensional [θriːdaɪ'mɛnʃənl] adj tridimensionale.

three-piece ['θriː'piːs]: ~ **suit** n completo (con gilè); ~ **suite** n salotto comprendente un divano e due poltrone.

three-ply [θriː'plaɪ] adj (wood) a tre strati; (wool) a tre fili.

three-quarters [θriː'kwɔːtəz] npl tre quarti mpl; ~ **full** pieno per tre quarti.

three-wheeler [θriː'wiːlə*] n (car) veicolo a tre ruote.

thresh [θrɛʃ] vt (AGR) trebbiare.

threshing machine ['θrɛʃɪŋ-] n trebbiatrice f.

threshold ['θrɛʃhəuld] n soglia; **to be on the** ~ **of** (fig) essere sulla soglia di.

threshold agreement n (ECON) ≈ scala mobile.

threw [θruː] pt of **throw**.

thrift [θrɪft] n parsimonia.

thrifty ['θrɪftɪ] adj economico(a), parsimonioso(a).

thrill [θrɪl] n brivido ♦ vi eccitarsi, tremare ♦ vt (audience) elettrizzare; **I was** ~**ed to get your letter** la tua lettera mi ha fatto veramente piacere.

thriller ['θrɪlə*] n film m inv (or dramma m or libro) del brivido.

thrilling ['θrɪlɪŋ] adj (book, play etc) pieno(a) di suspense; (news, discovery) entusiasmante.

thrive, pt **thrived, throve,** pp **thrived, thriven** [θraɪv, θrəuv, 'θrɪvn] vi crescere or svilupparsi bene; (business) prosperare; **he** ~**s on it** gli fa bene, ne gode.

thriving ['θraɪvɪŋ] adj (industry etc) fiorente.

throat [θrəut] n gola; **to have a sore** ~ avere (un or il) mal di gola.

throb [θrɔb] n (of heart) battito; (of engine) vibrazione f; (of pain) fitta ♦ vi (heart) palpitare; (engine) vibrare; (with pain) pulsare; **my head is** ~**bing** mi martellano le tempie.

throes [θrəuz] npl: **in the** ~ **of** alle prese con; in preda a; **in the** ~ **of death** in agonia.

thrombosis [θrɔm'bəusɪs] n trombosi f.

throne [θrəun] n trono.

throng [θrɔŋ] n moltitudine f ♦ vt affollare.

throttle ['θrɔtl] n (AUT) valvola a farfalla; (on motorcycle) (manopola del) gas ♦ vt strangolare.

through [θruː] prep attraverso; (time) per, durante; (by means of) per mezzo di; (owing to) a causa di ♦ adj (ticket, train, passage) diretto(a) ♦ adv attraverso; **(from) Monday** ~ **Friday** (US) da lunedì a venerdì; **I am halfway** ~ **the book** sono a metà libro; **to let sb** ~ lasciar passare qn; **to put sb** ~ **to sb** (TEL) passare qn a qn; **to be** ~ (TEL) ottenere la comunicazione; (have finished) avere finito; **"no** ~ **traffic"** (US) "divieto d'accesso"; **"no** ~ **road"** (BRIT) "strada senza sbocco".

throughout [θruː'aut] prep (place) dappertutto in; (time) per or durante tutto(a) ♦ adv dappertutto; sempre.

throughput ['θruːput] n (of goods, materials) materiale m in lavorazione; (COMPUT) volume m di dati immessi.

throve [θrəuv] *pt of* **thrive**.
throw [θrəu] *n* tiro, getto; (*SPORT*) lancio
♦ *vt* (*pt* **threw**, *pp* **thrown** [θruː, θrəun])
tirare, gettare; (*SPORT*) lanciare; (*rider*)
disarcionare; (*fig*) confondere; (*pottery*)
formare al tornio; **to ~ a party** dare una
festa; **to ~ open** (*doors, windows*)
spalancare; (*house, gardens etc*) aprire al
pubblico; (*competition, race*) aprire a tutti.
▶**throw about, throw around** *vt* (*litter
etc*) spargere.
▶**throw away** *vt* gettare *or* buttare via.
▶**throw off** *vt* sbarazzarsi di.
▶**throw out** *vt* buttare fuori; (*reject*)
respingere.
▶**throw together** *vt* (*clothes, meal etc*)
mettere insieme; (*essay*) buttar giù.
▶**throw up** *vi* vomitare.
throwaway ['θrəuəweɪ] *adj* da buttare.
throwback ['θrəubæk] *n*: **it's a ~ to** (*fig*) ciò
risale a.
throw-in ['θrəuɪn] *n* (*SPORT*) rimessa in
gioco.
thrown [θrəun] *pp of* **throw**.
thru [θruː] *prep, adj, adv* (*US*) = **through**.
thrush [θrʌʃ] *n* (*ZOOL*) tordo; (*MED: esp in
children*) mughetto; (: *BRIT: in women*)
candida.
thrust [θrʌst] *n* (*TECH*) spinta ♦ *vt* (*pt, pp*
thrust) spingere con forza; (*push in*)
conficcare.
thrusting ['θrʌstɪŋ] *adj* (*troppo*)
intraprendente.
thud [θʌd] *n* tonfo.
thug [θʌg] *n* delinquente *m*.
thumb [θʌm] *n* (*ANAT*) pollice *m* ♦ *vt* (*book*)
sfogliare; **to ~ a lift** fare l'autostop; **to
give sb/sth the ~s up/down** approvare/
disapprovare qn/qc.
thumb index *n* indice *m* a rubrica.
thumbnail ['θʌmneɪl] *n* unghia del pollice.
thumbnail sketch *n* descrizione *f* breve.
thumbtack ['θʌmtæk] *n* (*US*) puntina da
disegno.
thump [θʌmp] *n* colpo forte; (*sound*) tonfo
♦ *vt* battere su ♦ *vi* picchiare, battere.
thunder ['θʌndə*] *n* tuono ♦ *vi* tuonare;
(*train etc*): **to ~ past** passare con un
rombo.
thunderbolt ['θʌndəbəult] *n* fulmine *m*.
thunderclap ['θʌndəklæp] *n* rombo di
tuono.
thunderous ['θʌndərəs] *adj* fragoroso(a).
thunderstorm ['θʌndəstɔːm] *n* temporale
m.
thunderstruck ['θʌndəstrʌk] *adj* (*fig*)
sbigottito(a).
thundery ['θʌndərɪ] *adj* temporalesco(a).

Thur(s). *abbr* (= *Thursday*) gio.
Thursday ['θəːzdɪ] *n* giovedì *m inv; for
phrases see also* **Tuesday**.
thus [ðʌs] *adv* così.
thwart [θwɔːt] *vt* contrastare.
thyme [taɪm] *n* timo.
thyroid ['θaɪrɔɪd] *n* tiroide *f*.
tiara [tɪ'ɑːrə] *n* (*woman's*) diadema *m*.
Tiber ['taɪbə*] *n*: **the ~** il Tevere.
Tibet [tɪ'bet] *n* Tibet *m*.
Tibetan [tɪ'betən] *adj* tibetano(a) ♦ *n*
(*person*) tibetano/a; (*LING*) tibetano.
tibia ['tɪbɪə] *n* tibia.
tic [tɪk] *n* tic *m inv*.
tick [tɪk] *n* (*sound: of clock*) tic tac *m inv*;
(*mark*) segno; spunta; (*ZOOL*) zecca; (*BRIT
col*): **in a ~** in un attimo; (*BRIT col: credit*):
to buy sth on ~ comprare qc a credito
♦ *vi* fare tic tac ♦ *vt* spuntare; **to put a ~
against sth** fare un segno di fianco a qc.
▶**tick off** *vt* spuntare; (*person*) sgridare.
▶**tick over** *vi* (*BRIT: engine*) andare al
minimo.
ticker tape ['tɪkə-] *n* nastro di
telescrivente; (*US: in celebrations*) stelle
fpl filanti.
ticket ['tɪkɪt] *n* biglietto; (*in shop: on goods*)
etichetta; (: *from cash register*) scontrino;
(*for library*) scheda; (*US POL*) lista dei
candidati; **to get a (parking) ~** (*AUT*)
prendere una multa (per sosta vietata).
ticket agency *n* (*THEAT*) agenzia di vendita
di biglietti.
ticket collector *n* bigliettaio.
ticket holder *n* persona munita di
biglietto.
ticket inspector *n* controllore *m*.
ticket office *n* biglietteria.
tickle ['tɪkl] *n* solletico ♦ *vt* fare il solletico
a, solleticare; (*fig*) stuzzicare; piacere a;
far ridere.
ticklish ['tɪklɪʃ] *adj* che soffre il solletico;
(*which tickles: blanket, cough*) che provoca
prurito.
tidal ['taɪdl] *adj* di marea.
tidal wave *n* onda anomala.
tidbit ['tɪdbɪt] *n* (*US*) = **titbit**.
tiddlywinks ['tɪdlɪwɪŋks] *n* gioco della
pulce.
tide [taɪd] *n* marea; (*fig: of events*) corso
♦ *vt*: **will £20 ~ you over till Monday?** ti
basteranno 20 sterline fino a lunedì?;
high/low ~ alta/bassa marea; **the ~ of
public opinion** l'orientamento
dell'opinione pubblica.
tidily ['taɪdɪlɪ] *adv* in modo ordinato; **to
arrange ~** sistemare; **to dress ~** vestirsi
per benino.

tidiness ['taɪdɪnɪs] n ordine m.

tidy ['taɪdɪ] adj (room) ordinato(a), lindo(a); (dress, work) curato(a), in ordine; (person) ordinato(a); (mind) organizzato(a) ♦ vt (also: ~ **up**) riordinare, mettere in ordine; **to ~ o.s. up** rassettarsi.

tie [taɪ] n (string etc) legaccio; (BRIT: also: **neck~**) cravatta; (fig: link) legame m; (SPORT: draw) pareggio (: match) incontro; (US RAIL) traversina ♦ vt (parcel) legare; (ribbon) annodare ♦ vi (SPORT) pareggiare; "**black/white ~**" "smoking/abito di rigore"; **family ~s** legami familiari; **to ~ sth in a bow** annodare qc; **to ~ a knot in sth** fare un nodo a qc.

▶**tie down** vt fissare con una corda; (fig): **to ~ sb down to** costringere qn ad accettare.

▶**tie in** vi: **to ~ in (with)** (correspond) corrispondere (a).

▶**tie on** vt (BRIT: label etc) attaccare.

▶**tie up** vt (parcel, dog) legare; (boat) ormeggiare; (arrangements) concludere; **to be ~d up** (busy) essere occupato or preso.

tie-break(er) ['taɪbreɪk(ə*)] n (TENNIS) tie-break m inv; (in quiz) spareggio.

tie-on ['taɪɔn] adj (BRIT: label) volante.

tie-pin ['taɪpɪn] n (BRIT) fermacravatta m inv.

tier [tɪə*] n fila; (of cake) piano, strato.

Tierra del Fuego [tɪ'ɛrədɛl'fweɪgəu] n Terra del Fuoco.

tie tack n (US) fermacravatta m inv.

tiff [tɪf] n battibecco.

tiger ['taɪgə*] n tigre f.

tight [taɪt] adj (rope) teso(a), tirato(a); (clothes) stretto(a); (budget, programme, bend) stretto(a); (control) severo(a), fermo(a); (col: drunk) sbronzo(a) ♦ adv (squeeze) fortemente; (shut) ermeticamente; **to be packed ~** (suitcase) essere pieno zeppo; (people) essere pigiati; **everybody hold ~!** tenetevi stretti!; see also **tights**.

tighten ['taɪtn] vt (rope) tendere; (screw) stringere; (control) rinforzare ♦ vi tendersi; stringersi.

tight-fisted [taɪt'fɪstɪd] adj avaro(a).

tight-lipped ['taɪt'lɪpt] adj: **to be ~** essere reticente; (angry) tenere le labbra serrate.

tightly ['taɪtlɪ] adv (grasp) bene, saldamente.

tightrope ['taɪtrəup] n corda (da acrobata).

tightrope walker n funambolo/a.

tights [taɪts] npl (BRIT) collant m inv.

tigress ['taɪgrɪs] n tigre f (femmina).

tilde ['tɪldə] n tilde f.

tile [taɪl] n (on roof) tegola; (on floor) mattonella; (on wall) piastrella ♦ vt (floor, bathroom etc) piastrellare.

tiled [taɪld] adj rivestito(a) di tegole; a mattonelle; a piastrelle.

till [tɪl] n registratore m di cassa ♦ vt (land) coltivare ♦ prep, conj = **until**.

tiller ['tɪlə*] n (NAUT) barra del timone.

tilt [tɪlt] vt inclinare, far pendere ♦ vi inclinarsi, pendere ♦ n (slope) pendio; **to wear one's hat at a ~** portare il cappello sulle ventitrè; **(at) full ~** a tutta velocità.

timber ['tɪmbə*] n (material) legname m; (trees) alberi mpl da legname.

time [taɪm] n tempo; (epoch: often pl) epoca, tempo; (by clock) ora; (moment) momento; (occasion, also MATH) volta; (MUS) tempo ♦ vt (race) cronometrare; (programme) calcolare la durata di; (remark etc): **to ~ sth well/badly** scegliere il momento più/meno opportuno per qc; **a long ~** molto tempo; **for the ~ being** per il momento; **from ~ to ~** ogni tanto; **~ after ~, ~ and again** mille volte; **in ~** (soon enough) in tempo; (after some time) col tempo; (MUS) a tempo; **at ~s** a volte; **to take one's ~** prenderla con calma; **in a week's ~** fra una settimana; **in no ~** in un attimo; **on ~** puntualmente; **to be 30 minutes behind/ahead of ~** avere 30 minuti di ritardo/anticipo; **by the ~ he arrived** quando è arrivato; **5 ~s 5** 5 volte 5, 5 per 5; **what ~ is it?** che ora è?, che ore sono?; **what ~ do you make it?** che ora fa?; **to have a good ~** divertirsi; **they had a hard ~ of it** è stato duro per loro; **~'s up!** è (l')ora!; **to be behind the ~s** vivere nel passato; **I've no ~ for it** (fig) non ho tempo da perdere con cose del genere; **he'll do it in his own (good) ~** (without being hurried) lo farà quando avrà (un minuto di) tempo; **he'll do it in** or (US) **on his own ~** (out of working hours) lo farà nel suo tempo libero; **the bomb was ~d to explode 5 minutes later** la bomba era stata regolata in modo da esplodere 5 minuti più tardi.

time-and-motion study ['taɪmənd 'məuʃən-] n analisi f inv dei tempi e dei movimenti.

time bomb n bomba a orologeria.

time card n cartellino (da timbrare).

time clock n orologio m marcatempo inv.

time-consuming ['taɪmkənsjuːmɪŋ] adj che richiede molto tempo.

time difference n differenza di fuso orario.

time frame n tempi mpl.

time-honoured, (*US*) **time-honored** ['taɪmɔnəd] *adj* consacrato(a) dal tempo.

timekeeper ['taɪmkiːpə*] *n* (*SPORT*) cronometrista *m/f*.

time lag *n* intervallo, ritardo; (*in travel*) differenza di fuso orario.

timeless ['taɪmlɪs] *adj* eterno(a).

time limit *n* limite *m* di tempo.

timely ['taɪmlɪ] *adj* opportuno(a).

time off *n* tempo libero.

timer ['taɪmə*] *n* (*in kitchen*) contaminuti *m inv*; (*TECH*) timer *m inv*, temporizzatore *m*.

time-saving ['taɪmseɪvɪŋ] *adj* che fa risparmiare tempo.

time scale *n* tempi *mpl* d'esecuzione.

time-sharing ['taɪmʃɛərɪŋ] *n* (*COMPUT*) divisione *f* di tempo.

time sheet *n* = **time card**.

time signal *n* segnale *m* orario.

time switch *n* interruttore *m* a tempo.

timetable ['taɪmteɪbl] *n* orario; (*programme of events etc*) programma *m*.

time zone *n* fuso orario.

timid ['tɪmɪd] *adj* timido(a); (*easily scared*) pauroso(a).

timidity [tɪ'mɪdɪtɪ] *n* timidezza.

timing ['taɪmɪŋ] *n* sincronizzazione *f*; (*fig*) scelta del momento opportuno, tempismo; (*SPORT*) cronometraggio.

timing device *n* (*on bomb*) timer *m inv*.

timpani ['tɪmpənɪ] *npl* timpani *mpl*.

tin [tɪn] *n* stagno; (*also*: ~ **plate**) latta; (*BRIT: can*) barattolo (di latta), lattina, scatola; (*for baking*) teglia; **a** ~ **of paint** un barattolo di tinta *or* vernice.

tin foil *n* stagnola.

tinge [tɪndʒ] *n* sfumatura ♦ *vt*: ~**d with** tinto(a) di.

tingle ['tɪŋgl] *vi* (*cheeks, skin: from cold*) pungere, pizzicare; (*: from bad circulation*) formicolare.

tinker ['tɪŋkə*] *n* stagnino ambulante; (*gipsy*) zingaro/a.

▶**tinker with** *vt fus* armeggiare intorno a; cercare di riparare.

tinkle ['tɪŋkl] *vi* tintinnare ♦ *n* (*col*): **to give sb a** ~ dare un colpo di telefono a qn.

tin mine *n* miniera di stagno.

tinned [tɪnd] *adj* (*BRIT: food*) in scatola.

tinnitus [tɪ'naɪtəs] *n* (*MED*) ronzio auricolare.

tinny ['tɪnɪ] *adj* metallico(a).

tin-opener ['tɪnəupnə*] *n* (*BRIT*) apriscatole *m inv*.

tinsel ['tɪnsl] *n* decorazioni *fpl* natalizie (*argentate*).

tint [tɪnt] *n* tinta; (*for hair*) shampoo *m inv*

colorante ♦ *vt* (*hair*) fare uno shampoo colorante a.

tinted ['tɪntɪd] *adj* (*hair*) tinto(a); (*spectacles, glass*) colorato(a).

tiny ['taɪnɪ] *adj* minuscolo(a).

tip [tɪp] *n* (*end*) punta; (*protective: on umbrella etc*) puntale *m*; (*gratuity*) mancia; (*for coal*) discarica; (*for rubbish*) immondezzaio; (*advice*) suggerimento ♦ *vt* (*waiter*) dare la mancia a; (*tilt*) inclinare; (*overturn: also*: ~ **over**) capovolgere; (*empty: also*: ~ **out**) scaricare; (*predict: winner*) pronosticare; (*: horse*) dare vincente; **he** ~**ped out the contents of the box** ha rovesciato il contenuto della scatola.

▶**tip off** *vt* fare una soffiata a.

tip-off ['tɪpɔf] *n* (*hint*) soffiata.

tipped ['tɪpt] *adj* (*BRIT: cigarette*) col filtro; **steel-**~ con la punta d'acciaio.

Tipp-Ex ® ['tɪpɛks] *n* (*BRIT*) liquido correttore.

tipple ['tɪpl] (*BRIT*) *vi* sbevazzare ♦ *n*: **to have a** ~ prendere un bicchierino.

tipster ['tɪpstə*] *n* (*RACING*) chi vende informazioni sulle corse e altre manifestazioni oggetto di scommesse.

tipsy ['tɪpsɪ] *adj* brillo(a).

tiptoe ['tɪptəu] *n*: **on** ~ in punta di piedi.

tiptop ['tɪptɔp] *adj*: **in** ~ **condition** in ottime condizioni.

tirade [taɪ'reɪd] *n* filippica.

tire ['taɪə*] *vt* stancare ♦ *vi* stancarsi ♦ *n* (*US*) = **tyre**.

▶**tire out** *vt* sfinire, spossare.

tired ['taɪəd] *adj* stanco(a); **to be/feel/look** ~ essere/sentirsi/sembrare stanco; **to be** ~ **of** essere stanco *or* stufo di.

tiredness ['taɪədnɪs] *n* stanchezza.

tireless ['taɪəlɪs] *adj* instancabile.

tiresome ['taɪəsəm] *adj* noioso(a).

tiring ['taɪərɪŋ] *adj* faticoso(a).

tissue ['tɪʃuː] *n* tessuto; (*paper handkerchief*) fazzolettino di carta.

tissue paper *n* carta velina.

tit [tɪt] *n* (*bird*) cinciallegra; (*col: breast*) tetta; **to give** ~ **for tat** rendere pan per focaccia.

titanium [tɪ'teɪnɪəm] *n* titanio.

titbit ['tɪtbɪt], (*US*) **tidbit** ['tɪdbɪt] *n* (*food*) leccornia; (*news*) notizia ghiotta.

titillate ['tɪtɪleɪt] *vt* titillare.

titivate ['tɪtɪveɪt] *vt* agghindare.

title ['taɪtl] *n* titolo; (*LAW: right*): ~ **(to)** diritto (a).

title deed *n* (*LAW*) titolo di proprietà.

title page *n* frontespizio.

title role *n* ruolo *or* parte *f* principale.

titter ['tɪtə*] *vi* ridere scioccamente.

tittle-tattle ['tɪtltætl] *n* chiacchiere *fpl*, pettegolezzi *mpl*.

titular ['tɪtjulə*] *adj* (*in name only*) nominale.

tizzy ['tɪzɪ] *n* (*col*): **to be in a** ~ essere in agitazione.

T-junction ['tiː'dʒʌŋkʃən] *n* incrocio a T.

TM *n abbr* (= *transcendental meditation*) M.T. *f*; (*COMM*) = **trademark**.

TN *abbr* (*US*) = *Tennessee*.

TNT *n abbr* (= *trinitrotoluene*) T.N.T. *m*.

================= *KEYWORD*

to [tuː, tə] *prep* **1** (*direction*) a; **to go** ~ **France/London/school** andare in Francia/a Londra/a scuola; **to go** ~ **town** andare in città; **to go** ~ **Paul's/the doctor's** andare da Paul/dal dottore; **the road** ~ **Edinburgh** la strada per Edimburgo; ~ **the left/right** a sinistra/destra

2 (*as far as*) (fino) a; **from here** ~ **London** da qui a Londra; **to count** ~ **10** contare fino a 10; **from 40** ~ **50 people** da 40 a 50 persone

3 (*with expressions of time*): **a quarter** ~ **5** le 5 meno un quarto; **it's twenty** ~ **3** sono le 3 meno venti

4 (*for, of*): **the key** ~ **the front door** la chiave della porta d'ingresso; **a letter** ~ **his wife** una lettera per la moglie

5 (*expressing indirect object*) a; **to give sth** ~ **sb** dare qc a qn; **give it** ~ **me** dammelo; **to talk** ~ **sb** parlare a qn; **it belongs** ~ **him** gli appartiene, è suo; **to be a danger** ~ **sb/sth** rappresentare un pericolo per qn/qc

6 (*in relation to*) a; **3 goals** ~ **2** 3 goal a 2; **30 miles** ~ **the gallon** ≈ 11 chilometri con un litro; **4 apples** ~ **the kilo** 4 mele in un chilo

7 (*purpose, result*): **to come** ~ **sb's aid** venire in aiuto a qn; **to sentence sb** ~ **death** condannare a morte qn; ~ **my surprise** con mia sorpresa

♦ *with vb* **1** (*simple infinitive*): ~ **go/eat** *etc* andare/mangiare *etc*

2 (*following another vb*): **to want/try/start** ~ **do** volere/cercare di/cominciare a fare

3 (*with vb omitted*): **I don't want** ~ non voglio (farlo); **you ought** ~ devi (farlo)

4 (*purpose, result*) per; **I did it** ~ **help you** l'ho fatto per aiutarti

5 (*equivalent to relative clause*): **I have**

things ~ **do** ho da fare; **the main thing is** ~ **try** la cosa più importante è provare

6 (*after adjective etc*): **ready** ~ **go** pronto(a) a partire; **too old/young** ~ ... troppo vecchio(a)/giovane per ...

♦ *adv*: **to push the door** ~ accostare la porta; **to go** ~ **and fro** andare e tornare.

toad [təud] *n* rospo.

toadstool ['təudstuːl] *n* fungo (velenoso).

toady ['təudɪ] *vi* adulare.

toast [təust] *n* (*CULIN*) toast *m*, pane *m* abbrustolito; (*drink, speech*) brindisi *m inv* ♦ *vt* (*CULIN*) abbrustolire; (*drink to*) brindare a; **a piece** *or* **slice of** ~ una fetta di pane abbrustolito.

toaster ['təustə*] *n* tostapane *m inv*.

toastmaster ['təustmɑːstə*] *n* direttore *m* dei brindisi.

toast rack *n* portatoast *m inv*.

tobacco [tə'bækəu] *n* tabacco; **pipe** ~ tabacco da pipa.

tobacconist [tə'bækənɪst] *n* tabaccaio/a; ~**'s (shop)** tabaccheria.

Tobago [tə'beɪgəu] *n see* **Trinidad and Tobago**.

toboggan [tə'bɔgən] *n* toboga *m inv*; (*child's*) slitta.

today [tə'deɪ] *adv, n* (*also fig*) oggi (*m inv*); **what day is it** ~? che giorno è oggi?; **what date is it** ~? quanti ne abbiamo oggi?; ~ **is the 4th of March** (oggi) è il 4 di marzo; ~**'s paper** il giornale di oggi; **a fortnight** ~ quindici giorni a oggi.

toddler ['tɔdlə*] *n* bambino/a che impara a camminare.

toddy ['tɔdɪ] *n* grog *m inv*.

to-do [tə'duː] *n* (*fuss*) storie *fpl*.

toe [təu] *n* dito del piede; (*of shoe*) punta ♦ *vt*: **to** ~ **the line** (*fig*) stare in riga, conformarsi; **big** ~ alluce *m*; **little** ~ mignolino.

TOEFL ['təufl] *n abbr* = *Test(ing) of English as a Foreign Language*.

toehold ['təuhəuld] *n* punto d'appoggio.

toenail ['təuneɪl] *n* unghia del piede.

toffee ['tɔfɪ] *n* caramella.

toffee apple *n* (*BRIT*) mela caramellata.

tofu ['təufuː] *n* tofu *m* (*latte di soia non fermentato*).

toga ['təugə] *n* toga.

together [tə'gɛðə*] *adv* insieme; (*at same time*) allo stesso tempo; ~ **with** insieme a.

togetherness [tə'gɛðənɪs] *n* solidarietà; intimità.

toggle switch ['tɔgl-] *n* (*COMPUT*) tasto bistabile.

Togo ['təugəu] *n* Togo.

togs [tɔgz] *npl* (*col: clothes*) vestiti *mpl*.

toil [tɔil] *n* travaglio, fatica ♦ *vi* affannarsi; sgobbare.

toilet ['tɔilət] *n* (*BRIT: lavatory*) gabinetto ♦ *cpd* (*soap etc*) da toletta; **to go to the** ~ andare al gabinetto *or* al bagno.

toilet bag *n* (*BRIT*) nécessaire *m inv* da toilette.

toilet bowl *n* vaso *or* tazza del gabinetto.

toilet paper *n* carta igienica.

toiletries ['tɔilitriz] *npl* articoli *mpl* da toletta.

toilet roll *n* rotolo di carta igienica.

toilet water *n* acqua di colonia.

to-ing and fro-ing ['tuːiŋən'frəuiŋ] *n* (*BRIT*) andirivieni *m inv*.

token ['təukən] *n* (*sign*) segno; (*voucher*) buono ♦ *cpd* (*fee, strike*) simbolico(a); **book/record** ~ (*BRIT*) buono-libro/-disco; **by the same** ~ (*fig*) per lo stesso motivo.

tokenism ['təukənizəm] *n* (*POL*) concessione *f* pro forma *inv*.

Tokyo ['təukjəu] *n* Tokyo *f*.

told [təuld] *pt, pp of* **tell**.

tolerable ['tɔlərəbl] *adj* (*bearable*) tollerabile; (*fairly good*) passabile.

tolerably ['tɔlərəbli] *adv* (*good, comfortable*) abbastanza.

tolerance ['tɔlərns] *n* (*also TECH*) tolleranza.

tolerant ['tɔlərnt] *adj*: ~ (**of**) tollerante (nei confronti di).

tolerate ['tɔləreit] *vt* sopportare; (*MED, TECH*) tollerare.

toleration [tɔlə'reiʃən] *n* tolleranza.

toll [təul] *n* (*tax, charge*) pedaggio ♦ *vi* (*bell*) suonare; **the accident** ~ **on the roads** il numero delle vittime della strada.

tollbridge ['təulbridʒ] *n* ponte *m* a pedaggio.

toll call *n* (*US TEL*) (telefonata) interurbana.

toll-free ['təul'friː] (*US*) *adj* senza addebito, gratuito(a) ♦ *adv* gratuitamente; ~ **number** ≈ numero verde.

tomato, ~**es** [tə'mɑːtəu] *n* pomodoro.

tomb [tuːm] *n* tomba.

tombola [tɔm'bəulə] *n* tombola.

tomboy ['tɔmbɔi] *n* maschiaccio.

tombstone ['tuːmstəun] *n* pietra tombale.

tomcat ['tɔmkæt] *n* gatto.

tomorrow [tə'mɔrəu] *adv, n* (*also fig*) domani (*m inv*); **the day after** ~ dopodomani; **a week** ~ domani a otto; ~ **morning** domani mattina.

ton [tʌn] *n* tonnellata (*BRIT*: = 1016 kg; 20 cwt; *US* = 907 kg; *metric* = 1000 kg); (*NAUT: also*: **register** ~) tonnellata di stazza (= 2.83 cu.m; 100 cu.ft); ~**s of** (*col*) un

mucchio *or* sacco di.

tonal ['təunl] *adj* tonale.

tone [təun] *n* tono; (*of musical instrument*) timbro ♦ *vi* intonarsi.

▶**tone down** *vt* (*colour, criticism, sound*) attenuare.

▶**tone up** *vt* (*muscles*) tonificare.

tone-deaf [təun'dɛf] *adj* che non ha orecchio (musicale).

toner ['təunə*] *n* (*for photocopier*) colorante *m* organico, toner *m*.

Tonga ['tɔŋgə] *n* isole *fpl* Tonga.

tongs [tɔŋz] *npl* tenaglie *fpl*; (*for coal*) molle *fpl*; (*for hair*) arricciacapelli *m inv*.

tongue [tʌŋ] *n* lingua; ~ **in cheek** (*fig*) ironicamente.

tongue-tied ['tʌŋtaid] *adj* (*fig*) muto(a).

tongue-twister ['tʌŋtwistə*] *n* scioglilingua *m inv*.

tonic ['tɔnik] *n* (*MED*) ricostituente *m*; (*skin* ~) tonico; (*MUS*) nota tonica; (*also*: ~ **water**) acqua tonica.

tonight [tə'nait] *adv* stanotte; (*this evening*) stasera ♦ *n* questa notte; questa sera; **I'll see you** ~ ci vediamo stasera.

tonnage ['tʌnidʒ] *n* (*NAUT*) tonnellaggio, stazza.

tonne [tʌn] *n* (*BRIT: metric ton*) tonnellata.

tonsil ['tɔnsl] *n* tonsilla; **to have one's** ~**s out** farsi operare di tonsille.

tonsillitis [tɔnsi'laitis] *n* tonsillite *f*; **to have** ~ avere la tonsillite.

too [tuː] *adv* (*excessively*) troppo; (*also*) anche; **it's** ~ **sweet** è troppo dolce; **I went** ~ ci sono andato anch'io; ~ **much** *adv* troppo ♦ *adj* troppo(a); ~ **many** *adj* troppi(e); ~ **bad!** tanto peggio!; peggio così!

took [tuk] *pt of* **take**.

tool [tuːl] *n* utensile *m*, attrezzo; (*fig: person*) strumento ♦ *vt* lavorare con un attrezzo.

tool box *n* cassetta *f* portautensili *inv*.

tool kit *n* cassetta di attrezzi.

toot [tuːt] *vi* suonare; (*with car horn*) suonare il clacson.

tooth, *pl* **teeth** [tuːθ, tiːθ] *n* (*ANAT, TECH*) dente *m*; **to clean one's teeth** lavarsi i denti; **to have a** ~ **out** *or* (*US*) **pulled** farsi togliere un dente; **by the skin of one's teeth** per il rotto della cuffia.

toothache ['tuːθeik] *n* mal *m* di denti; **to have** ~ avere il mal di denti.

toothpaste ['tuːθpeist] *n* dentifricio.

toothpick ['tuːθpik] *n* stuzzicadenti *m inv*.

tooth powder *n* dentifricio in polvere.

top [tɔp] *n* (*of mountain, page, ladder*) cima; (*of box, cupboard, table*) sopra *m inv*, parte *f*

superiore; (*lid: of box, jar*) coperchio; (: *of bottle*) tappo; (*toy*) trottola; (*DRESS: blouse etc*) camicia (*or* maglietta *etc*); (*of pyjamas*) giacca ♦ *adj* più alto(a); (*in rank*) primo(a); (*best*) migliore ♦ *vt* (*exceed*) superare; (*be first in*) essere in testa a; **on ~ of** sopra, in cima a; (*in addition to*) oltre a; **from ~ to toe** (*BRIT*) dalla testa ai piedi; **at the ~ of the stairs/page/street** in cima alle scale/alla pagina/alla strada; **the ~ of the milk** (*BRIT*) la panna; **at ~ speed** a tutta velocità; **at the ~ of one's voice** (*fig*) a squarciagola; **over the ~** (*col: behaviour etc*) eccessivo(a); **to go over the ~** esagerare.
▶**top up,** (*US*) **top off** *vt* riempire.
topaz ['təupæz] *n* topazio.
top-class ['tɔp'klɑːs] *adj* di prim'ordine.
topcoat ['tɔpkəut] *n* soprabito.
topflight ['tɔpflaɪt] *adj* di primaria importanza.
top floor *n* ultimo piano.
top hat *n* cilindro.
top-heavy [tɔp'hɛvɪ] *adj* (*object*) con la parte superiore troppo pesante.
topic ['tɔpɪk] *n* argomento.
topical ['tɔpɪkəl] *adj* d'attualità.
topless ['tɔplɪs] *adj* (*bather etc*) col seno scoperto; **~ swimsuit** topless *m inv*.
top-level ['tɔplɛvl] *adj* (*talks*) ad alto livello.
topmost ['tɔpməust] *adj* il(la) più alto(a).
top-notch ['tɔp'nɔtʃ] *adj* (*col: player, performer*) di razza; (: *school, car*) eccellente.
topography [tə'pɔgrəfɪ] *n* topografia.
topping ['tɔpɪŋ] *n* (*CULIN*) guarnizione *f*.
topple ['tɔpl] *vt* rovesciare, far cadere ♦ *vi* cadere; traballare.
top-ranking ['tɔp'ræŋkɪŋ] *adj* di massimo grado.
top-secret ['tɔp'siːkrɪt] *adj* segretissimo(a).
top-security ['tɔpsɪ'kjuərɪtɪ] *adj* (*BRIT*) di massima sicurezza.
topsy-turvy ['tɔpsɪ'təːvɪ] *adj, adv* sottosopra (*inv*).
top-up ['tɔpʌp] *n*: **would you like a ~?** vuole che le riempia il bicchiere (*or* la tazza *etc*)?
top-up loan *n* (*BRIT*) prestito integrativo.
torch [tɔːtʃ] *n* torcia; (*BRIT: electric*) lampadina tascabile.
tore [tɔː*] *pt of* **tear**.
torment *n* ['tɔːmɛnt] tormento ♦ *vt* [tɔː'mɛnt] tormentare; (*fig: annoy*) infastidire.
torn [tɔːn] *pp of* **tear** ♦ *adj*: **~ between** (*fig*) combattuto(a) tra.
tornado, **~es** [tɔː'neɪdəu] *n* tornado.

torpedo, **~es** [tɔː'piːdəu] *n* siluro.
torpedo boat *n* motosilurante *f*.
torpor ['tɔːpə*] *n* torpore *m*.
torrent ['tɔrnt] *n* torrente *m*.
torrential [tɔ'rɛnʃl] *adj* torrenziale.
torrid ['tɔrɪd] *adj* torrido(a); (*fig*) denso(a) di passione.
torso ['tɔːsəu] *n* torso.
tortoise ['tɔːtəs] *n* tartaruga.
tortoiseshell ['tɔːtəʃɛl] *adj* di tartaruga.
tortuous ['tɔːtjuəs] *adj* tortuoso(a).
torture ['tɔːtʃə*] *n* tortura ♦ *vt* torturare.
torturer ['tɔːtʃərə*] *n* torturatore/trice.
Tory ['tɔːrɪ] *adj* tory *inv*, conservatore(trice) ♦ *n* tory *m/f inv*, conservatore/trice.
toss [tɔs] *vt* gettare, lanciare; (*BRIT: pancake*) far saltare; (*head*) scuotere ♦ *n* (*movement: of head etc*) movimento brusco; (*of coin*) lancio; **to win/lose the ~** vincere/perdere a testa o croce; (*SPORT*) vincere/perdere il sorteggio; **to ~ a coin** fare a testa o croce; **to ~ up for sth** fare a testa o croce per qc; **to ~ and turn** (*in bed*) girarsi e rigirarsi.
tot [tɔt] *n* (*BRIT: drink*) bicchierino; (*child*) bimbo/a.
▶**tot up** *vt* (*BRIT: figures*) sommare.
total ['təutl] *adj* totale ♦ *n* totale *m* ♦ *vt* (*add up*) sommare; (*amount to*) ammontare a; **in ~** in tutto.
totalitarian [təutælɪ'tɛərɪən] *adj* totalitario(a).
totality [təu'tælɪtɪ] *n* totalità.
totally ['təutəlɪ] *adv* completamente.
tote bag ['təut-] *n* sporta.
totem pole ['təutəm-] *n* totem *m inv*.
totter ['tɔtə*] *vi* barcollare; (*object, government*) vacillare.
touch [tʌtʃ] *n* tocco; (*sense*) tatto; (*contact*) contatto; (*FOOTBALL*) fuori gioco *m* ♦ *vt* toccare; **a ~ of** (*fig*) un tocco di; un pizzico di; **to get in ~ with** mettersi in contatto con; **to lose ~** (*friends*) perdersi di vista; **I'll be in ~** mi farò sentire; **to be out of ~ with events** essere tagliato fuori; **the personal ~** una nota personale; **to put the finishing ~es to sth** dare gli ultimi ritocchi a qc.
▶**touch on** *vt fus* (*topic*) sfiorare, accennare a.
▶**touch up** *vt* (*improve*) ritoccare.
touch-and-go ['tʌtʃən'gəu] *adj* incerto(a); **it was ~ with the sick man** il malato era tra la vita e la morte.
touchdown ['tʌtʃdaun] *n* atterraggio; (*on sea*) ammaraggio; (*US FOOTBALL*) meta.
touched [tʌtʃt] *adj* commosso(a); (*col*)

tocco(a), toccato(a).

touching ['tʌtʃɪŋ] adj commovente.

touchline ['tʌtʃlaɪn] n (SPORT) linea laterale.

touch-sensitive ['tʌtʃ'sɛnsɪtɪv] adj sensibile al tatto.

touch-type ['tʌtʃtaɪp] vi dattilografare (senza guardare i tasti).

touchy ['tʌtʃɪ] adj (person) suscettibile.

tough [tʌf] adj duro(a); (resistant) resistente; (meat) duro(a), tiglioso(a); (journey) faticoso(a), duro(a); (person: rough) violento(a), brutale ♦ n (gangster etc) delinquente m/f; ~ **luck!** che sfortuna!

toughen ['tʌfn] vt indurire, rendere più resistente.

toughness ['tʌfnɪs] n durezza; resistenza.

toupee ['tu:peɪ] n parrucchino.

tour [tuə*] n viaggio; (also: **package** ~) viaggio organizzato or tutto compreso; (of town, museum) visita; (by artist) tournée f inv ♦ vt visitare; **to go on a** ~ **of** (region, country) fare il giro di; (museum, castle) visitare; **to go on** ~ andare in tournée.

touring ['tuərɪŋ] n turismo.

tourism ['tuərɪzəm] n turismo.

tourist ['tuərɪst] n turista m/f ♦ adv (travel) in classe turistica ♦ cpd turistico(a); **the** ~ **trade** il turismo.

tourist class n (AVIAT) classe f turistica.

tourist office n pro loco f inv.

tournament ['tuənəmənt] n torneo.

tourniquet ['tuənɪkeɪ] n (MED) laccio emostatico, pinza emostatica.

tour operator n (BRIT) operatore m turistico.

tousled ['tauzld] adj (hair) arruffato(a).

tout [taut] vi: **to** ~ **for** procacciare, raccogliere; cercare clienti per ♦ n (BRIT: also: **ticket** ~) bagarino; **to** ~ **sth (around)** (BRIT) cercare di (ri)vendere qc.

tow [təu] vt rimorchiare ♦ n rimorchio; "**on** ~", (US) "**in** ~" (AUT) "veicolo rimorchiato"; **to give sb a** ~ rimorchiare qn.

toward(s) [tə'wɔːd(z)] prep verso; (of attitude) nei confronti di; (of purpose) per; ~ **noon/the end of the year** verso mezzogiorno/la fine dell'anno; **to feel friendly** ~ **sb** provare un sentimento d'amicizia per qn.

towel ['tauəl] n asciugamano; (also: **tea** ~) strofinaccio; **to throw in the** ~ (fig) gettare la spugna.

towelling ['tauəlɪŋ] n (fabric) spugna.

towel rail, (US) **towel rack** n portasciugamano.

tower ['tauə*] n torre f ♦ vi (building, mountain) innalzarsi; **to** ~ **above** or **over sb/sth** sovrastare qn/qc.

tower block n (BRIT) palazzone m.

towering ['tauərɪŋ] adj altissimo(a), imponente.

towline ['təulaɪn] n (cavo da) rimorchio.

town [taun] n città f inv; **to go to** ~ andare in città; (fig) mettercela tutta; **in (the)** ~ in città; **to be out of** ~ essere fuori città.

town centre n centro (città).

town clerk n segretario comunale.

town council n consiglio comunale.

town crier [-'kraɪə*] n (BRIT) banditore/trice.

town hall n ≈ municipio.

townie ['taunɪ] n (BRIT col) uno/a di città.

town plan n pianta della città.

town planner n urbanista m/f.

town planning n urbanistica.

township ['taunʃɪp] n township f inv.

townspeople ['taunzpi:pl] npl cittadinanza, cittadini mpl.

towpath ['təupɑːθ] n alzaia.

towrope ['təurəup] n (cavo da) rimorchio.

tow truck n (US) carro m attrezzi inv.

toxic ['tɒksɪk] adj tossico(a).

toxin ['tɒksɪn] n tossina.

toy [tɔɪ] n giocattolo.

▶**toy with** vt fus giocare con; (idea) accarezzare, trastullarsi con.

toyshop ['tɔɪʃɒp] n negozio di giocattoli.

trace [treɪs] n traccia ♦ vt (draw) tracciare; (follow) seguire; (locate) rintracciare; **without** ~ (disappear) senza lasciare traccia; **there was no** ~ **of it** non ne restava traccia.

trace element n oligoelemento.

trachea [trə'kɪə] n (ANAT) trachea.

tracing paper ['treɪsɪŋ-] n carta da ricalco.

track [træk] n (mark: of person, animal) traccia; (on tape, SPORT; path: gen) pista; (: of bullet etc) traiettoria; (: of suspect, animal) pista, tracce fpl; (RAIL) binario, rotaie fpl; (COMPUT) traccia, pista ♦ vt seguire le tracce di; **to keep** ~ **of** seguire; **to be on the right** ~ (fig) essere sulla buona strada.

▶**track down** vt (prey) scovare; snidare; (sth lost) rintracciare.

tracker dog ['trækə-] n (BRIT) cane m poliziotto inv.

track events npl (SPORT) prove fpl su pista.

tracking station ['trækɪŋ-] n (SPACE) osservatorio spaziale.

track meet n (US) meeting m inv di atletica.

track record n: **to have a good** ~ (fig) avere un buon curriculum.

tracksuit ['træksu:t] *n* tuta sportiva.
tract [trækt] *n* (*GEO*) tratto, estensione *f*; (*pamphlet*) opuscolo, libretto; **respiratory** ~ (*ANAT*) apparato respiratorio.
traction ['trækʃən] *n* trazione *f*.
tractor ['træktə*] *n* trattore *m*.
trade [treɪd] *n* commercio; (*skill, job*) mestiere *m*; (*industry*) industria, settore *m* ♦ *vi* commerciare; **to** ~ **with/in** commerciare con/in; **foreign** ~ commercio estero; **Department of T~ and Industry (DTI)** (*BRIT*) ≈ Ministero del Commercio.
▶**trade in** *vt* (*old car etc*) dare come pagamento parziale.
trade barrier *n* barriera commerciale.
trade deficit *n* bilancio commerciale in deficit.
Trade Descriptions Act *n* (*BRIT*) legge *f* a tutela del consumatore.
trade discount *n* sconto sul listino.
trade fair *n* fiera campionaria.
trade-in ['treɪdɪn] *n*: **to take as a** ~ accettare in permuta.
trade-in price *n* prezzo di permuta.
trademark ['treɪdmɑːk] *n* marchio di fabbrica.
trade mission *n* missione *f* commerciale.
trade name *n* marca, nome *m* depositato.
trade-off ['treɪdɔf] *n* compromesso, accomodamento.
trader ['treɪdə*] *n* commerciante *m/f*.
trade secret *n* segreto di fabbricazione.
tradesman ['treɪdzmən] *n* fornitore *m*; (*shopkeeper*) negoziante *m*.
trade union *n* sindacato.
trade unionist [-'juːnjənɪst] *n* sindacalista *m/f*.
trade wind *n* aliseo.
trading ['treɪdɪŋ] *n* commercio.
trading estate *n* (*BRIT*) zona industriale.
trading stamp *n* bollo premio.
tradition [trə'dɪʃən] *n* tradizione *f*; ~**s** *npl* tradizioni, usanze *fpl*.
traditional [trə'dɪʃənl] *adj* tradizionale.
traffic ['træfɪk] *n* traffico ♦ *vi*: **to** ~ **in** (*pej*: *liquor, drugs*) trafficare in.
traffic calming [-'kɑːmɪŋ] *n uso di accorgimenti per rallentare il traffico in zone abitate*.
traffic circle *n* (*US*) isola rotatoria.
traffic island *n* salvagente *m*, isola *f* spartitraffico *inv*.
traffic jam *n* ingorgo (del traffico).
trafficker ['træfɪkə*] *n* trafficante *m/f*.
traffic lights *npl* semaforo.
traffic offence *n* (*BRIT*) infrazione *f* al codice stradale.

traffic sign *n* cartello stradale.
traffic violation *n* (*US*) = **traffic offence**.
traffic warden *n* addetto/a al controllo del traffico e del parcheggio.
tragedy ['trædʒədɪ] *n* tragedia.
tragic ['trædʒɪk] *adj* tragico(a).
trail [treɪl] *n* (*tracks*) tracce *fpl*, pista; (*path*) sentiero; (*of smoke etc*) scia ♦ *vt* trascinare, strascicare; (*follow*) seguire ♦ *vi* essere al traino; (*dress etc*) strusciare; (*plant*) arrampicarsi; strisciare; **to be on sb's** ~ essere sulle orme di qn.
▶**trail away, trail off** *vi* (*sound*) affievolirsi; (*interest, voice*) spegnersi a poco a poco.
▶**trail behind** *vi* essere al traino.
trailer ['treɪlə*] *n* (*AUT*) rimorchio; (*US*) roulotte *f inv*; (*CINE*) prossimamente *m inv*.
trailer truck *n* (*US*) autoarticolato.
train [treɪn] *n* treno; (*of dress*) coda, strascico; (*BRIT*: *series*): ~ **of events** serie *f* di avvenimenti a catena ♦ *vt* (*apprentice, doctor etc*) formare; (*sportsman*) allenare; (*dog*) addestrare; (*memory*) esercitare; (*point*: *gun etc*): **to** ~ **sth on** puntare qc contro ♦ *vi* formarsi; allenarsi; (*learn a skill*) fare pratica, fare tirocinio; **to go by** ~ andare in *or* col treno; **one's** ~ **of thought** il filo dei propri pensieri; **to** ~ **sb to do sth** preparare qn a fare qc.
train attendant *n* (*US*) addetto/a ai vagoni letto.
trained [treɪnd] *adj* qualificato(a); allenato(a); addestrato(a).
trainee [treɪ'niː] *n* allievo/a; (*in trade*) apprendista *m/f*; **he's a** ~ **teacher** sta facendo tirocinio come insegnante.
trainer ['treɪnə*] *n* (*SPORT*) allenatore/trice; (*of dogs etc*) addestratore/trice; ~**s** *npl* (*shoes*) scarpe *fpl* da ginnastica.
training ['treɪnɪŋ] *n* formazione *f*; allenamento; addestramento; **in** ~ (*SPORT*) in allenamento; (*fit*) in forma.
training college *n* istituto professionale.
training course *n* corso di formazione professionale.
traipse [treɪps] *vi*: **to** ~ **in/out** *etc* entrare/ uscire *etc* trascinandosi.
trait [treɪt] *n* tratto.
traitor ['treɪtə*] *n* traditore/trice.
trajectory [trə'dʒɛktərɪ] *n* traiettoria.
tram [træm] *n* (*BRIT*: *also*: ~**car**) tram *m inv*.
tramline ['træmlaɪn] *n* linea tranviaria.
tramp [træmp] *n* (*person*) vagabondo/a; (*col*: *pej*: *woman*) sgualdrina ♦ *vi* camminare con passo pesante ♦ *vt* (*walk through*: *town, streets*) percorrere a piedi.
trample ['træmpl] *vt*: **to** ~ (**underfoot**)

calpestare.

trampoline ['træmpəliːn] *n* trampolino.

trance [trɑːns] *n* trance *f inv*; (*MED*) catalessi *f inv*; **to go into a** ~ cadere in trance.

tranquil ['træŋkwɪl] *adj* tranquillo(a).

tranquillity, (*US*) **tranquility** [træŋ'kwɪlɪtɪ] *n* tranquillità.

tranquillizer, (*US*) **tranquilizer** ['træŋkwɪlaɪzə*] *n* (*MED*) tranquillante *m*.

transact [træn'zækt] *vt* (*business*) trattare.

transaction [træn'zækʃən] *n* transazione *f*; ~**s** *npl* (*minutes*) atti *mpl*; **cash** ~ operazione *f* in contanti.

transatlantic ['trænzət'læntɪk] *adj* transatlantico(a).

transcend [træn'sɛnd] *vt* trascendere; (*excel over*) superare.

transcendental [trænsɛn'dɛntl] *adj*: ~ **meditation** meditazione *f* trascendentale.

transcribe [træn'skraɪb] *vt* trascrivere.

transcript ['trænskrɪpt] *n* trascrizione *f*.

transcription [træn'skrɪpʃən] *n* trascrizione *f*.

transept ['trænsɛpt] *n* transetto.

transfer *n* ['trænsfə*] (*gen, also SPORT*) trasferimento; (*POL: of power*) passaggio; (*picture, design*) decalcomania; (: *stick-on*) autoadesivo ♦ *vt* [træns'fəː*] trasferire; passare; decalcare; **by bank** ~ tramite trasferimento bancario; **to** ~ **the charges** (*BRIT TEL*) telefonare con addebito al ricevente.

transferable [træns'fəːrəbl] *adj* trasferibile; **not** ~ non cedibile, personale.

transfix [træns'fɪks] *vt* trafiggere; (*fig*): ~**ed with fear** paralizzato dalla paura.

transform [træns'fɔːm] *vt* trasformare.

transformation [trænsfə'meɪʃən] *n* trasformazione *f*.

transformer [træns'fɔːmə*] *n* (*ELEC*) trasformatore *m*.

transfusion [træns'fjuːʒən] *n* trasfusione *f*.

transgress [træns'grɛs] *vt* (*go beyond*) infrangere; (*violate*) trasgredire, infrangere.

tranship [træn'ʃɪp] *vt* trasbordare.

transient ['trænzɪənt] *adj* transitorio(a), fugace.

transistor [træn'zɪstə*] *n* (*ELEC*) transistor *m inv*; (*also*: ~ **radio**) radio *f inv* a transistor.

transit ['trænzɪt] *n*: **in** ~ in transito.

transit camp *n* campo (di raccolta) profughi.

transition [træn'zɪʃən] *n* passaggio, transizione *f*.

transitional [træn'zɪʃənl] *adj* di transizione.

transitive ['trænzɪtɪv] *adj* (*LING*)

transitivo(a).

transit lounge *n* (*AVIAT*) sala di transito.

transitory ['trænzɪtərɪ] *adj* transitorio(a).

translate [trænz'leɪt] *vt* tradurre; **to** ~ **(from/into)** tradurre (da/in).

translation [trænz'leɪʃən] *n* traduzione *f*; (*SCOL: as opposed to prose*) versione *f*.

translator [trænz'leɪtə*] *n* traduttore/trice.

translucent [trænz'luːsnt] *adj* traslucido(a).

transmission [trænz'mɪʃən] *n* trasmissione *f*.

transmit [trænz'mɪt] *vt* trasmettere.

transmitter [trænz'mɪtə*] *n* trasmettitore *m*.

transparency [træns'pɛərnsɪ] *n* (*PHOT*) diapositiva.

transparent [træns'pærnt] *adj* trasparente.

transpire [træns'paɪə*] *vi* (*happen*) succedere; **it finally** ~**d that** ... alla fine si è venuto a sapere che ....

transplant *vt* [træns'plɑːnt] trapiantare ♦ *n* ['trænsplɑːnt] trapianto; **to have a heart** ~ subire un trapianto cardiaco.

transport *n* ['trænspɔːt] trasporto ♦ *vt* [træns'pɔːt] trasportare; **public** ~ mezzi *mpl* pubblici; **Department of T**~(*BRIT*) Ministero dei Trasporti.

transportation ['trænspɔː'teɪʃən] *n* (mezzo di) trasporto; (*of prisoners*) deportazione *f*; **Department of T**~ (*US*) Ministero dei Trasporti.

transport café *n* (*BRIT*) trattoria per camionisti.

transpose [træns'pəuz] *vt* trasporre.

transsexual [trænz'sɛksjuəl] *adj, n* transessuale (*m/f*).

transverse ['trænzvəːs] *adj* trasversale.

transvestite [trænz'vɛstaɪt] *n* travestito/a.

trap [træp] *n* (*snare, trick*) trappola; (*carriage*) calesse *m* ♦ *vt* prendere in trappola, intrappolare; (*immobilize*) bloccare; (*jam*) chiudere, schiacciare; **to set** *or* **lay a** ~ **(for sb)** tendere una trappola (a qn); **to** ~ **one's finger in the door** chiudersi il dito nella porta; **shut your** ~**!** (*col*) chiudi quella boccaccia!

trap door *n* botola.

trapeze [trə'piːz] *n* trapezio.

trapper ['træpə*] *n* cacciatore *m* di animali da pelliccia.

trappings ['træpɪŋz] *npl* ornamenti *mpl*; indoratura, sfarzo.

trash [træʃ] *n* (*pej: goods*) ciarpame *m*; (: *nonsense*) sciocchezze *fpl*; (*US: rubbish*) rifiuti *mpl*, spazzatura.

trash can *n* (*US*) secchio della spazzatura.

trashy ['træʃɪ] *adj* (*col*) scadente.

trauma ['trɔːmə] *n* trauma *m*.

traumatic [trɔː'mætɪk] *adj* (*PSYCH*, *fig*) traumatico(a), traumatizzante.

travel ['trævl] *n* viaggio; viaggi *mpl* ♦ *vi* viaggiare; (*move*) andare, spostarsi ♦ *vt* (*distance*) percorrere; **this wine doesn't ~ well** questo vino non resiste agli spostamenti.

travel agency *n* agenzia (di) viaggi.

travel agent *n* agente *m* di viaggio.

travel brochure *n* dépliant *m* di viaggi.

traveller, (*US*) **traveler** ['trævlə*] *n* viaggiatore/trice; (*COMM*) commesso viaggiatore.

traveller's cheque, (*US*) **traveler's check** *n* assegno turistico.

travelling, (*US*) **traveling** ['trævlɪŋ] *n* viaggi *mpl* ♦ *adj* (*circus*, *exhibition*) itinerante ♦ *cpd* (*bag*, *clock*) da viaggio; (*expenses*) di viaggio.

travel(l)ing salesman *n* commesso viaggiatore.

travelogue ['trævəlɔg] *n* (*book*, *film*) diario *or* documentario di viaggio; (*talk*) conferenza sui viaggi.

travel sickness *n* mal *m* d'auto (*or* di mare *or* d'aria).

traverse ['trævəs] *vt* traversare, attraversare.

travesty ['trævəstɪ] *n* parodia.

trawler ['trɔːlə*] *n* peschereccio (a strascico).

tray [treɪ] *n* (*for carrying*) vassoio; (*on desk*) vaschetta.

treacherous ['trɛtʃərəs] *adj* traditore(trice); **road conditions today are** ~ oggi il fondo stradale è pericoloso.

treachery ['trɛtʃərɪ] *n* tradimento.

treacle ['triːkl] *n* melassa.

tread [trɛd] *n* passo; (*sound*) rumore *m* di passi; (*of tyre*) battistrada *m inv* ♦ *vi* (*pt* **trod**, *pp* **trodden** [trɔd, 'trɔdn]) camminare.
▶**tread on** *vt fus* calpestare.

treadle ['trɛdl] *n* pedale *m*.

treas. *abbr* = **treasurer**.

treason ['triːzn] *n* tradimento.

treasure ['trɛʒə*] *n* tesoro ♦ *vt* (*value*) tenere in gran conto, apprezzare molto; (*store*) custodire gelosamente.

treasure hunt *n* caccia al tesoro.

treasurer ['trɛʒərə*] *n* tesoriere/a.

treasury ['trɛʒərɪ] *n* tesoreria; (*POL*): **the T~**, (*US*) **the T~ Department** ≈ il Ministero del Tesoro.

treasury bill *n* buono del tesoro.

treat [triːt] *n* regalo ♦ *vt* trattare; (*MED*) curare; (*consider*) considerare; **it was a ~** mi (*or* ci *etc*) ha fatto veramente piacere; **to ~ sb to sth** offrire qc a qn; **to ~ sth as**

a joke considerare qc uno scherzo.

treatise ['triːtɪz] *n* trattato.

treatment ['triːtmənt] *n* trattamento; **to have ~ for sth** (*MED*) farsi curare qc.

treaty ['triːtɪ] *n* patto, trattato.

treble [trɛbl] *adj* triplo(a), triplice ♦ *n* (*MUS*) soprano *m/f* ♦ *vt* triplicare ♦ *vi* triplicarsi.

treble clef *n* chiave *f* di violino.

tree [triː] *n* albero.

tree-lined ['triːlaɪnd] *adj* fiancheggiato(a) da alberi.

treetop ['triːtɔp] *n* cima di un albero.

tree trunk *n* tronco d'albero.

trek [trɛk] *n* (*hike*) spedizione *f*; (*tiring walk*) camminata sfiancante ♦ *vi* (*as holiday*) fare dell'escursionismo.

trellis ['trɛlɪs] *n* graticcio, pergola.

tremble ['trɛmbl] *vi* tremare; (*machine*) vibrare.

trembling ['trɛmblɪŋ] *n* tremito ♦ *adj* tremante.

tremendous [trɪ'mɛndəs] *adj* (*enormous*) enorme; (*excellent*) meraviglioso(a), formidabile.

tremendously [trɪ'mɛndəslɪ] *adv* incredibilmente; **he enjoyed it** ~ gli è piaciuto da morire.

tremor [trɛmə*] *n* tremore *m*, tremito; (*also*: **earth** ~) scossa sismica.

trench [trɛntʃ] *n* trincea.

trench coat *n* trench *m inv*.

trench warfare *n* guerra di trincea.

trend [trɛnd] *n* (*tendency*) tendenza; (*of events*) corso; (*fashion*) moda; ~ **towards/ away from** tendenza a/ad allontanarsi da; **to set the** ~ essere all'avanguardia; **to set a** ~ lanciare una moda.

trendy ['trɛndɪ] *adj* (*idea*) di moda; (*clothes*) all'ultima moda.

trepidation [trɛpɪ'deɪʃən] *n* trepidazione *f*, agitazione *f*.

trespass ['trɛspəs] *vi*: **to ~ on** entrare abusivamente in; (*fig*) abusare di; **"no ~ing"** "proprietà privata", "vietato l'accesso".

trespasser ['trɛspəsə*] *n* trasgressore *m*; **"~s will be prosecuted"** "i trasgressori saranno puniti secondo i termini di legge".

trestle ['trɛsl] *n* cavalletto.

trestle table *n* tavola su cavalletti.

trial ['traɪəl] *n* (*LAW*) processo; (*test: of machine etc*) collaudo; (*hardship*) prova, difficoltà *f inv*; (*worry*) cruccio; ~**s** *npl* (*ATHLETICS*) prove *fpl* di qualificazione; **horse** ~**s** concorso ippico; **to be on** ~ essere sotto processo; ~ **by jury** processo penale con giuria; **to be sent for** ~ essere

rinviato a giudizio; **to bring sb to ~ (for a crime)** portare qn in giudizio (per un reato); **by ~ and error** a tentoni.
trial balance n (*COMM*) bilancio di verifica.
trial basis n: **on a ~** in prova.
trial run n periodo di prova.
triangle ['traɪæŋgl] n (*MATH, MUS*) triangolo.
triangular [traɪ'æŋgjulə*] adj triangolare.
triathlon [traɪ'æθlən] n triathlon m inv.
tribal ['traɪbəl] adj tribale.
tribe [traɪb] n tribù f inv.
tribesman ['traɪbzmən] n membro della tribù.
tribulation [trɪbju'leɪʃən] n tribolazione f.
tribunal [traɪ'bju:nl] n tribunale m.
tributary ['trɪbju:tərɪ] n (*river*) tributario, affluente m.
tribute ['trɪbju:t] n tributo, omaggio; **to pay ~ to** rendere omaggio a.
trice [traɪs] n: **in a ~** in un attimo.
trick [trɪk] n trucco; (*clever act*) stratagemma m; (*joke*) tiro; (*CARDS*) presa ♦ vt imbrogliare, ingannare; **to play a ~ on sb** giocare un tiro a qn; **it's a ~ of the light** è un effetto ottico; **that should do the ~** (*col*) vedrai che funziona; **to ~ sb into doing sth** convincere qn a fare qc con l'inganno; **to ~ sb out of sth** fregare qc a qn.
trickery ['trɪkərɪ] n inganno.
trickle ['trɪkl] n (*of water etc*) rivolo; gocciolio ♦ vi gocciolare; **to ~ in/out** (*people*) entrare/uscire alla spicciolata.
trick question n domanda f trabocchetto inv.
trickster ['trɪkstə*] n imbroglione/a.
tricky ['trɪkɪ] adj difficile, delicato(a).
tricycle ['traɪsɪkl] n triciclo.
trifle ['traɪfl] n sciocchezza; (*BRIT CULIN*) ≈ zuppa inglese ♦ adv: **a ~ long** un po' lungo ♦ vi: **to ~ with** prendere alla leggera.
trifling ['traɪflɪŋ] adj insignificante.
trigger ['trɪgə*] n (*of gun*) grilletto.
▶**trigger off** vt dare l'avvio a.
trigonometry [trɪgə'nɔmətrɪ] n trigonometria.
trilby ['trɪlbɪ] n (*BRIT: also:* **~ hat**) cappello floscio di feltro.
trill [trɪl] n (*of bird, MUS*) trillo.
trilogy ['trɪlədʒɪ] n trilogia.
trim [trɪm] adj ordinato(a); (*house, garden*) ben tenuto(a); (*figure*) snello(a) ♦ n (*haircut etc*) spuntata, regolata; (*embellishment*) finiture fpl; (*on car*) guarnizioni fpl ♦ vt spuntare; (*decorate*): **to ~ (with)** decorare (con); (*NAUT: a sail*) orientare; **to keep in (good) ~**

mantenersi in forma.
trimmings ['trɪmɪŋz] npl decorazioni fpl; (*extras: gen CULIN*) guarnizione f.
Trinidad and Tobago ['trɪnɪdæd-] n Trinidad e Tobago m.
Trinity ['trɪnɪtɪ] n: **the ~** la Trinità.
trinket ['trɪŋkɪt] n gingillo; (*piece of jewellery*) ciondolo.
trio ['tri:əu] n trio.
trip [trɪp] n viaggio; (*excursion*) gita, escursione f; (*stumble*) passo falso ♦ vi inciampare; (*go lightly*) camminare con passo leggero; **on a ~** in viaggio.
▶**trip up** vi inciampare ♦ vt fare lo sgambetto a.
tripartite [traɪ'pɑ:taɪt] adj (*agreement*) tripartito(a); (*talks*) a tre.
tripe [traɪp] n (*CULIN*) trippa; (*pej: rubbish*) sciocchezze fpl, fesserie fpl.
triple ['trɪpl] adj triplo(a) ♦ adv: **~ the distance/the speed** tre volte più lontano/più veloce.
triple jump n triplo salto.
triplets ['trɪplɪts] npl bambini(e) trigemini(e).
triplicate ['trɪplɪkət] n: **in ~** in triplice copia.
tripod ['traɪpɔd] n treppiede m.
Tripoli ['trɪpəlɪ] n Tripoli f.
tripper ['trɪpə*] n (*BRIT*) gitante m/f.
tripwire ['trɪpwaɪə*] n filo in tensione che fa scattare una trappola, allarme etc.
trite [traɪt] adj banale, trito(a).
triumph ['traɪʌmf] n trionfo ♦ vi: **to ~ (over)** trionfare (su).
triumphal [traɪ'ʌmfl] adj trionfale.
triumphant [traɪ'ʌmfənt] adj trionfante.
trivia ['trɪvɪə] npl banalità fpl.
trivial ['trɪvɪəl] adj (*matter*) futile; (*excuse, comment*) banale; (*amount*) irrisorio(a); (*mistake*) di poco conto.
triviality [trɪvɪ'ælɪtɪ] n frivolezza; (*trivial detail*) futilità.
trivialize ['trɪvɪəlaɪz] vt sminuire.
trod [trɔd] pt of **tread**.
trodden ['trɔdn] pp of **tread**.
trolley ['trɔlɪ] n carrello; (*in hospital*) lettiga.
trolley bus n filobus m inv.
trollop ['trɔləp] n prostituta.
trombone [trɔm'bəun] n trombone m.
troop [tru:p] n gruppo; (*MIL*) squadrone m; **~s** npl (*MIL*) truppe fpl; **~ing the colour** (*BRIT: ceremony*) sfilata della bandiera.
▶**troop in** vi entrare a frotte.
▶**troop out** vi uscire a frotte.
troop carrier n (*plane*) aereo per il trasporto (di) truppe; (*NAUT: also:*

troopship) nave *f* per il trasporto (di) truppe.

trooper ['truːpə*] *n* (*MIL*) soldato di cavalleria; (*US: policeman*) poliziotto (della polizia di stato).

troopship ['truːpʃɪp] *n* nave *f* per il trasporto (di) truppe.

trophy ['trəufɪ] *n* trofeo.

tropic ['trɔpɪk] *n* tropico; **in the ~s** ai tropici; **T~ of Cancer/Capricorn** tropico del Cancro/Capricorno.

tropical ['trɔpɪkəl] *adj* tropicale.

trot [trɔt] *n* trotto ♦ *vi* trottare; **on the ~** (*BRIT fig*) di fila, uno(a) dopo l'altro(a).

▶**trot out** *vt* (*excuse, reason*) tirar fuori; (*names, facts*) recitare di fila.

trouble ['trʌbl] *n* (*problems*) difficoltà *fpl*, problemi *mpl*; (*worry*) preoccupazione *f*; (*bother, effort*) sforzo; (*with sth mechanical*) noie *fpl*; (*POL*) conflitti *mpl*, disordine *m*; (*MED*): **stomach** *etc* ~ disturbi *mpl* gastrici *etc* ♦ *vt* disturbare; (*worry*) preoccupare ♦ *vi*: **to ~ to do** disturbarsi a fare; **~s** *npl* (*POL etc*) disordini *mpl*; **to be in ~** avere dei problemi; (*for doing wrong*) essere nei guai; (*for doing*) darsi la pena di fare; **it's no ~!** di niente!; **what's the ~?** cosa c'è che non va?; **the ~ is ...** c'è che ..., il guaio è che ...; **to have ~ doing sth** avere della difficoltà a fare qc; **please don't ~ yourself** non si disturbi.

troubled ['trʌbld] *adj* (*person*) preoccupato(a), inquieto(a); (*epoch, life*) agitato(a), difficile.

trouble-free ['trʌblfriː] *adj* senza problemi.

troublemaker ['trʌblmeɪkə*] *n* elemento disturbatore, agitatore/trice.

troubleshooter ['trʌblʃuːtə*] *n* (*in conflict*) conciliatore *m*.

troublesome ['trʌblsəm] *adj* fastidioso(a), seccante.

trouble spot *n* zona calda.

troubling ['trʌblɪŋ] *adj* (*thought*) preoccupante; **these are ~ times** questi sono tempi difficili.

trough [trɔf] *n* (*also: drinking ~*) abbeveratoio; (*also: feeding ~*) trogolo, mangiatoia; (*channel*) canale *m*; ~ **of low pressure** (*METEOROLOGY*) depressione *f*.

trounce [trauns] *vt* (*defeat*) sgominare.

troupe [truːp] *n* troupe *f inv*.

trouser press *n* stirapantaloni *m inv*.

trousers ['trauzəz] *npl* pantaloni *mpl*, calzoni *mpl*; **short ~** (*BRIT*) calzoncini *mpl*.

trouser suit *n* (*BRIT*) completo *m or* tailleur *m inv* pantalone *inv*.

trousseau, *pl* **~x** *or* **~s** ['truːsəu, -z] *n* corredo da sposa.

trout [traut] *n* (*pl inv*) trota.

trowel ['trauəl] *n* cazzuola.

truant ['truənt] *n*: **to play ~** (*BRIT*) marinare la scuola.

truce [truːs] *n* tregua.

truck [trʌk] *n* autocarro, camion *m inv*; (*RAIL*) carro merci aperto; (*for luggage*) carrello *m* portabagagli *inv*.

truck driver, (*US*) **trucker** ['trʌkə*] *n* camionista *m/f*.

truck farm *n* (*US*) orto industriale.

trucking ['trʌkɪŋ] *n* (*esp US*) autotrasporto.

trucking company *n* (*esp US*) impresa di trasporti.

truculent ['trʌkjulənt] *adj* aggressivo(a), brutale.

trudge [trʌdʒ] *vi* trascinarsi pesantemente.

true [truː] *adj* vero(a); (*accurate*) accurato(a), esatto(a); (*genuine*) reale; (*faithful*) fedele; (*wall, beam*) a piombo; (*wheel*) centrato(a); **to come ~** avverarsi; **~ to life** verosimile.

truffle ['trʌfl] *n* tartufo.

truly ['truːlɪ] *adv* veramente; (*truthfully*) sinceramente; (*faithfully*) fedelmente; **yours ~** (*in letter-writing*) distinti saluti.

trump [trʌmp] *n* (*CARDS*) atout *m inv*; **to turn up ~s** (*fig*) fare miracoli.

trump card *n* atout *m inv*; (*fig*) asso nella manica.

trumped-up [trʌmpt'ʌp] *adj* inventato(a).

trumpet ['trʌmpɪt] *n* tromba.

truncated [trʌŋ'keɪtɪd] *adj* tronco(a).

truncheon ['trʌntʃən] *n* sfollagente *m inv*.

trundle ['trʌndl] *vt, vi*: **to ~ along** rotolare rumorosamente.

trunk [trʌŋk] *n* (*of tree, person*) tronco; (*of elephant*) proboscide *f*; (*case*) baule *m*; (*US AUT*) bagagliaio.

trunk call *n* (*BRIT TEL*) (telefonata) interurbana.

trunk road *n* (*BRIT*) strada principale.

trunks [trʌŋks] *npl* (*also: swimming ~*) calzoncini *mpl* da bagno.

truss [trʌs] *n* (*MED*) cinto erniario ♦ *vt*: **to ~ (up)** (*CULIN*) legare.

trust [trʌst] *n* fiducia; (*LAW*) amministrazione *f* fiduciaria; (*COMM*) trust *m inv* ♦ *vt* (*have confidence in*) fidarsi di; (*rely on*) contare su; (*entrust*): **to ~ sth to sb** affidare qc a qn; (*hope*): **to ~ (that)** sperare (che); **you'll have to take it on ~** deve credermi sulla parola; **in ~** (*LAW*) in amministrazione fiduciaria.

trust company *n* trust *m inv*.

trusted ['trʌstɪd] *adj* fidato(a).

trustee [trʌs'tiː] *n* (*LAW*) amministratore(trice) fiduciario(a); (*of*

school etc) amministratore/trice.
trustful ['trʌstful] *adj* fiducioso(a).
trust fund *n* fondo fiduciario.
trusting ['trʌstɪŋ] *adj* = **trustful**.
trustworthy ['trʌstwəːðɪ] *adj* fidato(a), degno(a) di fiducia.
trusty ['trʌstɪ] *adj* fidato(a).
truth, ~s [truːθ, truːðz] *n* verità *f inv*.
truthful ['truːθful] *adj (person)* sincero(a); *(description)* veritiero(a), esatto(a).
truthfully ['truːθfəlɪ] *adv* sinceramente.
truthfulness ['truːθfəlnɪs] *n* veracità.
try [traɪ] *n* prova, tentativo; *(RUGBY)* meta ♦ *vt (LAW)* giudicare; *(test: sth new)* provare; *(strain: patience, person)* mettere alla prova ♦ *vi* provare; **to ~ to do** provare a fare; *(seek)* cercare di fare; **to give sth a ~** provare qc; **to ~ one's (very) best** *or* **one's (very) hardest** mettercela tutta.
►**try on** *vt (clothes)* provare, mettere alla prova; **to ~ it on** *(fig)* cercare di farla.
►**try out** *vt* provare, mettere alla prova.
trying ['traɪɪŋ] *adj (day, experience)* logorante, pesante; *(child)* difficile, insopportabile.
tsar [zɑː*] *n* zar *m inv*.
T-shirt ['tiːʃəːt] *n* maglietta.
T-square ['tiːskwɛə*] *n* riga a T.
TT *adj abbr (BRIT col)* = **teetotal** ♦ *abbr (US)* = Trust Territory.
tub [tʌb] *n* tinozza; mastello; *(bath)* bagno.
tuba ['tjuːbə] *n* tuba.
tubby ['tʌbɪ] *adj* grassoccio(a).
tube [tjuːb] *n* tubo; *(BRIT: underground)* metropolitana; *(for tyre)* camera d'aria; *(col: television)*: **the ~** la tele.
tubeless ['tjuːblɪs] *adj (tyre)* senza camera d'aria.
tuber ['tjuːbə*] *n (BOT)* tubero.
tuberculosis (TB) [tjubəːkjuˈləusɪs] *n* tubercolosi *f*.
tube station *n (BRIT)* stazione *f* del metrò.
tubing ['tjuːbɪŋ] *n* tubazione *f*; **a piece of ~** un tubo.
tubular ['tjuːbjulə*] *adj* tubolare.
TUC *n abbr (BRIT:* = *Trades Union Congress)* confederazione *f* dei sindacati britannici.
tuck [tʌk] *n (SEWING)* piega ♦ *vt (put)* mettere.
►**tuck away** *vt* riporre.
►**tuck in** *vt* mettere dentro; *(child)* rimboccare ♦ *vi (eat)* mangiare di buon appetito; abbuffarsi.
►**tuck up** *vt (child)* rimboccare.
tuck shop *n* negozio di pasticceria *(in una scuola)*.
Tue(s). *abbr (= Tuesday)* mar.
Tuesday ['tjuːzdɪ] *n* martedì *m inv*; **(the**

date) today is ~ 23rd March oggi è martedì 23 marzo; **on ~** martedì; **on ~s** di martedì; **every ~** tutti i martedì; **every other ~** ogni due martedì; **last/next ~** martedì scorso/prossimo; **~ next** martedì prossimo; **the following ~** *(in past)* il martedì successivo; *(in future)* il martedì dopo; **a week/fortnight on ~, ~ week/ fortnight** martedì fra una settimana/ quindici giorni; **the ~ before last** martedì di due settimane fa; **the ~ after next** non questo martedì ma il prossimo; **~ morning/lunchtime/afternoon/evening** martedì mattina/all'ora di pranzo/ pomeriggio/sera; **~ night** martedì sera; *(overnight)* martedì notte; **~'s newspaper** il giornale di martedì.
tuft [tʌft] *n* ciuffo.
tug [tʌg] *n (ship)* rimorchiatore *m* ♦ *vt* tirare con forza.
tug-of-love [tʌgəvˈlʌv] *n* contesa per la custodia dei figli; **~ children** bambini *mpl* coinvolti nella contesa per la custodia.
tug-of-war [tʌgəvˈwɔː*] *n* tiro alla fune.
tuition [tjuːˈɪʃən] *n (BRIT: lessons)* lezioni *fpl*; *(US: fees)* tasse *fpl* scolastiche *(or* universitarie).
tulip ['tjuːlɪp] *n* tulipano.
tumble ['tʌmbl] *n (fall)* capitombolo ♦ *vi* capitombolare, ruzzolare; *(somersault)* fare capriole ♦ *vt* far cadere; **to ~ to sth** *(col)* realizzare qc.
tumbledown ['tʌmbldaun] *n* cadente, diroccato(a).
tumble dryer *n (BRIT)* asciugatrice *f*.
tumbler ['tʌmblə*] *n* bicchiere *m* (senza stelo).
tummy ['tʌmɪ] *n (col)* pancia.
tumour, (US) tumor ['tjuːmə*] *n* tumore *m*.
tumult ['tjuːmʌlt] *n* tumulto.
tumultuous [tjuːˈmʌltjuəs] *adj* tumultuoso(a).
tuna ['tjuːnə] *n (pl inv) (also: ~ fish)* tonno.
tune [tjuːn] *n (melody)* melodia, aria ♦ *vt* *(MUS)* accordare; *(RADIO, TV, AUT)* regolare, mettere a punto; **to be in/out of ~** *(instrument)* essere accordato(a)/ scordato(a); *(singer)* essere intonato(a)/ stonato(a); **to the ~ of** *(fig: amount)* per la modesta somma di; **in ~ with** *(fig)* in accordo con.
►**tune in** *vi (RADIO, TV)*: **to ~ in (to)** sintonizzarsi (su).
►**tune up** *vi (musician)* accordare lo strumento.
tuneful ['tjuːnful] *adj* melodioso(a).
tuner ['tjuːnə*] *n (radio set)* sintonizzatore *m*; **piano ~** accordatore/trice di

pianoforte.

tuner amplifier n amplificatore m di sintonia.

tungsten ['tʌŋstn] n tungsteno.

tunic ['tjuːnɪk] n tunica.

tuning ['tjuːnɪŋ] n messa a punto.

tuning fork n diapason m inv.

Tunis ['tjuːnɪs] n Tunisi f.

Tunisia [tjuːˈnɪzɪə] n Tunisia.

Tunisian [tjuːˈnɪzɪən] adj, n tunisino(a).

tunnel ['tʌnl] n galleria ♦ vi scavare una galleria.

tunnel vision n (MED) riduzione f del campo visivo; (fig) visuale f ristretta.

tunny ['tʌnɪ] n tonno.

turban ['təːbən] n turbante m.

turbid ['təːbɪd] adj torbido(a).

turbine ['təːbaɪn] n turbina.

turbo ['təːbəʊ] n turbo m inv.

turbojet ['təːbəʊˈdʒɛt] n turboreattore m.

turboprop ['təːbəʊˈprɔp] n turboelica m inv.

turbot ['təːbət] n (pl inv) rombo gigante.

turbulence ['təːbjʊləns] n turbolenza.

turbulent ['təːbjʊlənt] adj turbolento(a); (sea) agitato(a).

tureen [təˈriːn] n zuppiera.

turf [təːf] n terreno erboso; (clod) zolla ♦ vt coprire di zolle erbose; **the T~** l'ippodromo.

►**turf out** vt (col) buttar fuori.

turf accountant n (BRIT) allibratore m.

turgid ['təːdʒɪd] adj (speech) ampolloso(a), pomposo(a).

Turin [tjʊəˈrɪn] n Torino f.

Turk [təːk] n turco/a.

Turkey ['təːkɪ] n Turchia.

turkey ['təːkɪ] n tacchino.

Turkish ['təːkɪʃ] adj turco(a) ♦ n (LING) turco.

Turkish bath n bagno turco.

Turkish delight n gelatine ricoperte di zucchero a velo.

turmeric ['təːmərɪk] n curcuma.

turmoil ['təːmɔɪl] n confusione f, tumulto.

turn [təːn] n giro m; (in road) curva; (tendency: of mind, events) tendenza; (performance) numero; (MED) crisi f inv, attacco ♦ vt girare, voltare; (milk) far andare a male; (shape: wood, metal) tornire; (change): **to ~ sth into** trasformare qc in ♦ vi girare; (person: look back) girarsi, voltarsi; (reverse direction) girarsi indietro; (change) cambiare; (become) diventare; **to ~ into** trasformarsi in; **a good ~** un buon servizio; **a bad ~** un brutto tiro; **it gave me quite a ~** mi ha fatto prendere un bello spavento; **"no left ~"** (AUT) "divieto di svolta a sinistra"; **it's your ~**

tocca a lei; **in ~** a sua volta; a turno; **to take ~s (at sth)** fare (qc) a turno; **at the ~ of the year/century** alla fine dell'anno/del secolo; **to take a ~ for the worse** (situation, events) volgere al peggio; (patient, health) peggiorare; **to ~ left/right** girare a sinistra/destra.

►**turn about** vi girarsi indietro.

►**turn away** vi girarsi (dall'altra parte) ♦ vt (reject: person) mandar via; (: business) rifiutare.

►**turn back** vi ritornare, tornare indietro.

►**turn down** vt (refuse) rifiutare; (reduce) abbassare; (fold) ripiegare.

►**turn in** vi (col: go to bed) andare a letto ♦ vt (fold) voltare in dentro.

►**turn off** vi (from road) girare, voltare ♦ vt (light, radio, engine etc) spegnere.

►**turn on** vt (light, radio etc) accendere; (engine) avviare.

►**turn out** vt (light, gas) chiudere, spegnere; (produce: goods) produrre; (: novel, good pupils) creare ♦ vi (appear, attend: troops, doctor etc) presentarsi; **to ~ out to be ...** rivelarsi ..., risultare ....

►**turn over** vi (person) girarsi; (car etc) capovolgersi ♦ vt girare.

►**turn round** vi girare; (person) girarsi.

►**turn up** vi (person) arrivare, presentarsi; (lost object) saltar fuori ♦ vt (collar, sound, gas etc) alzare.

turnabout ['təːnəbaʊt], **turnaround** ['təːnəraʊnd] n (fig) dietrofront m inv.

turncoat ['təːnkəʊt] n voltagabbana m/f inv.

turned-up ['təːndʌp] adj (nose) all'insù.

turning ['təːnɪŋ] n (in road) curva; (side road) strada laterale; **the first ~ on the right** la prima a destra.

turning circle n (BRIT) diametro di sterzata.

turning point n (fig) svolta decisiva.

turning radius n (US) = turning circle.

turnip ['təːnɪp] n rapa.

turnout ['təːnaʊt] n presenza, affluenza.

turnover ['təːnəʊvə*] n (COMM: amount of money) giro di affari; (: of goods) smercio; (CULIN): **apple** etc ~ sfogliatella alle mele etc; **there is a rapid ~ in staff** c'è un ricambio molto rapido di personale.

turnpike ['təːnpaɪk] n (US) autostrada a pedaggio.

turnstile ['təːnstaɪl] n tornella.

turntable ['təːnteɪbl] n (on record player) piatto.

turn-up ['təːnʌp] n (BRIT: on trousers) risvolto.

turpentine ['təːpəntaɪn] n (also: **turps**)

acqua ragia.

turquoise [təːkwɔɪz] n (*stone*) turchese m ◆ adj color turchese; di turchese.

turret ['tʌrɪt] n torretta.

turtle ['təːtl] n testuggine f.

turtleneck (sweater) ['təːtlnɛk-] n maglione m con il collo alto.

Tuscan ['tʌskən] adj, n toscano(a).

Tuscany ['tʌskənɪ] n Toscana.

tusk [tʌsk] n zanna.

tussle ['tʌsl] n baruffa, mischia.

tutor ['tjuːtə*] n (*in college*) docente m/f (*responsabile di un gruppo di studenti*); (*private teacher*) precettore m.

tutorial [tjuːˈtɔːrɪəl] n (SCOL) lezione f con discussione (*a un gruppo limitato*).

tuxedo [tʌkˈsiːdəu] n (US) smoking m inv.

TV [tiːˈviː] n abbr (= *television*) tivù f inv.

TV dinner n pasto surgelato pronto in due minuti.

twaddle ['twɔdl] n scemenze fpl.

twang [twæŋ] n (*of instrument*) suono vibrante; (*of voice*) accento nasale ◆ vi vibrare ◆ vt (*guitar*) pizzicare le corde di.

tweak [twiːk] vt (*nose*) pizzicare; (*ear, hair*) tirare.

tweed [twiːd] n tweed m inv.

tweezers ['twiːzəz] npl pinzette fpl.

twelfth [twɛlfθ] num dodicesimo(a).

Twelfth Night n la notte dell'Epifania.

twelve [twɛlv] num dodici; **at** ~ alle dodici, a mezzogiorno; (*midnight*) a mezzanotte.

twentieth ['twɛntɪɪθ] num ventesimo(a).

twenty ['twɛntɪ] num venti.

twerp [twəːp] n (*col*) idiota m/f.

twice [twaɪs] adv due volte; ~ **as much** due volte tanto; ~ **a week** due volte alla settimana; **she is** ~ **your age** ha il doppio dei suoi anni.

twiddle ['twɪdl] vt, vi: **to** ~ **(with) sth** giocherellare con qc; **to** ~ **one's thumbs** (*fig*) girarsi i pollici.

twig [twɪg] n ramoscello ◆ vt, vi (*col*) capire.

twilight ['twaɪlaɪt] n (*evening*) crepuscolo; (*morning*) alba; **in the** ~ nella penombra.

twill [twɪl] n spigato m.

twin [twɪn] adj, n gemello(a).

twin(-bedded) room ['twɪn('bɛdɪd)-] n stanza con letti gemelli.

twin beds npl letti mpl gemelli.

twin-carburettor ['twɪnkɑːbjuˈrɛtə*] adj a doppio carburatore.

twine [twaɪn] n spago, cordicella ◆ vi (*plant*) attorcigliarsi; (*road*) serpeggiare.

twin-engined ['twɪnˈɛndʒɪnd] adj a due motori; ~ **aircraft** bimotore m.

twinge [twɪndʒ] n (*of pain*) fitta; **a** ~ **of conscience/regret** un rimorso/rimpianto.

twinkle ['twɪŋkl] n scintillio ◆ vi scintillare; (*eyes*) brillare.

twin town n città f inv gemella.

twirl [twəːl] n piroetta ◆ vt far roteare ◆ vi roteare.

twist [twɪst] n torsione f; (*in wire, flex*) storta; (*in story*) colpo di scena; (*bend*) svolta, piega ◆ vt attorcigliare; (*weave*) intrecciare; (*roll around*) arrotolare; (*fig*) deformare ◆ vi attorcigliarsi; arrotolarsi; (*road*) serpeggiare; **to** ~ **one's ankle/wrist** (MED) slogarsi la caviglia/il polso.

twisted ['twɪstɪd] adj (*wire, rope*) attorcigliato(a); (*ankle, wrist*) slogato(a); (*fig: logic, mind*) contorto(a).

twit [twɪt] n (*col*) minchione/a.

twitch [twɪtʃ] n tiratina; (*nervous*) tic m inv ◆ vi contrarsi; avere un tic.

two [tuː] num due; ~ **by** ~, **in** ~**s** a due a due; **to put** ~ **and** ~ **together** (*fig*) trarre le conclusioni.

two-bit [tuːˈbɪt] adj (*esp US: col, pej*) da quattro soldi.

two-door [tuːˈdɔː*] adj (AUT) a due porte.

two-faced ['tuːˈfeɪst] adj (*pej: person*) falso(a).

twofold ['tuːfəuld] adv: **to increase** ~ aumentare del doppio ◆ adj (*increase*) doppio(a); (*reply*) in due punti.

two-piece ['tuːˈpiːs] n (*also:* ~ **suit**) due pezzi m inv; (*also:* ~ **swimsuit**) (costume m da bagno a) due pezzi m inv.

two-seater ['tuːˈsiːtə*] n (*plane*) biposto; (*car*) macchina a due posti.

twosome ['tuːsəm] n (*people*) coppia.

two-stroke ['tuːstrəuk] n (*engine*) due tempi m inv ◆ adj a due tempi.

two-tone ['tuːtəun] adj (*colour*) bicolore.

two-way ['tuːweɪ] adj (*traffic*) a due sensi; ~ **radio** radio f inv ricetrasmittente.

TX abbr (US) = *Texas*.

tycoon [taɪˈkuːn] n: **(business)** ~ magnate m.

type [taɪp] n (*category*) genere m; (*model*) modello; (*example*) tipo; (TYP) tipo, carattere m ◆ vt (*letter etc*) battere (a macchina), dattilografare; **what** ~ **do you want?** che tipo vuole?; **in bold/italic** ~ in grassetto/corsivo.

type-cast ['taɪpkɑːst] adj (*actor*) a ruolo fisso.

typeface ['taɪpfeɪs] n carattere m tipografico.

typescript ['taɪpskrɪpt] n dattiloscritto.

typeset ['taɪpsɛt] vt comporre.

typesetter ['taɪpsɛtə*] n compositore m.

typewriter – unacceptable

typewriter ['taɪpraɪtə*] n macchina da scrivere.
typewritten ['taɪprɪtn] adj dattiloscritto(a), battuto(a) a macchina.
typhoid ['taɪfɔɪd] n tifoidea.
typhoon [taɪ'fuːn] n tifone m.
typhus ['taɪfəs] n tifo.
typical ['tɪpɪkl] adj tipico(a).
typify ['tɪpɪfaɪ] vt essere tipico(a) di.
typing ['taɪpɪŋ] n dattilografia.
typing error n errore m di battitura.
typing pool n ufficio m dattilografia inv.
typist ['taɪpɪst] n dattilografo/a.
typo ['taɪpəu] n abbr (col: = typographical error) refuso.
typography [taɪ'pɒgrəfɪ] n tipografia.
tyranny ['tɪrənɪ] n tirannia.
tyrant ['taɪərnt] n tiranno.
tyre, (US) **tire** ['taɪə*] n pneumatico, gomma.
tyre pressure n pressione f (delle gomme).
Tyrol [tɪ'rəul] n Tirolo.
Tyrolean [tɪrə'liːən], **Tyrolese** [tɪrə'liːz] adj, n tirolese (m/f).
Tyrrhenian Sea [tɪ'riːnɪən-] n: **the** ~ il mar Tirreno.

U u

U, u [juː] n (letter) U, u m or f inv; **U for Uncle** ≈ U come Udine.
U n abbr (BRIT CINE: = universal) per tutti.
UAW n abbr (US: = United Automobile Workers) sindacato degli operai automobilistici.
UB40 n abbr (BRIT: = unemployment benefit form 40) modulo per la richiesta del sussidio di disoccupazione.
U-bend ['juːbend] n (in pipe) sifone m.
ubiquitous [juː'bɪkwɪtəs] adj onnipresente.
UCAS ['juːkæs] n abbr (BRIT) = Universities and Colleges Admissions Service.
UDA n abbr (BRIT: = Ulster Defence Association) organizzazione paramilitare protestante.
UDC n abbr (BRIT) = Urban District Council.
udder ['ʌdə*] n mammella.
UDI abbr (BRIT POL) = unilateral declaration of independence.
UDR n abbr (BRIT: = Ulster Defence Regiment) reggimento dell'esercito britannico in Irlanda del Nord.

UEFA [juː'eɪfə] n abbr (= Union of European Football Associations) U.E.F.A. f.
UFO ['juːfəu] n abbr (= unidentified flying object) UFO m inv.
Uganda [juː'gændə] n Uganda.
Ugandan [juː'gændən] adj, n ugandese (m/f).
UGC n abbr (BRIT: = University Grants Committee) organo che autorizza sovvenzioni alle università.
ugh [əːh] excl puah!
ugliness ['ʌglɪnɪs] n bruttezza.
ugly ['ʌglɪ] adj brutto(a).
UHF abbr = ultra-high frequency.
UHT adj abbr (= ultra-heat treated): ~ **milk** n latte m UHT.
UK n abbr see **United Kingdom**.
Ukraine [juː'kreɪn] n Ucraina.
Ukrainian [juː'kreɪnɪən] adj ucraino(a) ♦ n (person) ucraino/a; (LING) ucraino.
ulcer ['ʌlsə*] n ulcera; **mouth** ~ afta.
Ulster ['ʌlstə*] n Ulster m.
ulterior [ʌl'tɪərɪə*] adj ulteriore; ~ **motive** secondo fine m.
ultimata [ʌltɪ'meɪtə] npl of **ultimatum**.
ultimate ['ʌltɪmɪt] adj ultimo(a), finale; (authority) massimo(a), supremo(a) ♦ n: **the** ~ **in luxury** il non plus ultra del lusso.
ultimately ['ʌltɪmɪtlɪ] adv alla fine; in definitiva, in fin dei conti.
ultimatum, pl ~**s** or **ultimata** [ʌltɪ'meɪtəm, -tə] n ultimatum m inv.
ultrasonic [ʌltrə'sɒnɪk] adj ultrasonico(a).
ultrasound [ʌltrə'saund] n (MED) ecografia.
ultraviolet ['ʌltrə'vaɪəlɪt] adj ultravioletto(a).
umbilical [ʌm'bɪlɪkl] adj: ~ **cord** cordone m ombelicale.
umbrage ['ʌmbrɪdʒ] n: **to take** ~ offendersi, impermalirsi.
umbrella [ʌm'brelə] n ombrello; **under the** ~ **of** (fig) sotto l'egida di.
umlaut ['umlaut] n Umlaut m inv.
umpire ['ʌmpaɪə*] n arbitro.
umpteen [ʌmp'tiːn] adj non so quanti(e); **for the** ~**th time** per l'ennesima volta.
UMW n abbr (= United Mineworkers of America) unione dei minatori d'America.
UN n abbr see **United Nations**.
unabashed [ʌnə'bæʃt] adj imperturbato(a).
unabated [ʌnə'beɪtɪd] adj non diminuito(a).
unable [ʌn'eɪbl] adj: **to be** ~ **to** non potere, essere nell'impossibilità di; (not to know how to) essere incapace di, non sapere.
unabridged [ʌnə'brɪdʒd] adj integrale.
unacceptable [ʌnək'septəbl] adj (proposal, behaviour) inaccettabile; (price)

impossibile.

unaccompanied [ʌnə'kʌmpənɪd] *adj (child, lady)* non accompagnato(a); *(singing, song)* senza accompagnamento.

unaccountably [ʌnə'kauntəblɪ] *adv* inesplicabilmente.

unaccounted [ʌnə'kauntɪd] *adj*: **two passengers are ~ for** due passeggeri mancano all'appello.

unaccustomed [ʌnə'kʌstəmd] *adj* insolito(a); **to be ~ to sth** non essere abituato(a) a qc.

unacquainted [ʌnə'kweɪntɪd] *adj*: **to be ~ with** *(facts)* ignorare, non essere al corrente di.

unadulterated [ʌnə'dʌltəreɪtɪd] *adj (gen)* puro(a); *(wine)* non sofisticato(a).

unaffected [ʌnə'fɛktɪd] *adj (person, behaviour)* naturale, spontaneo(a); *(emotionally)*: **to be ~ by** non essere toccato(a) da.

unafraid [ʌnə'freɪd] *adj*: **to be ~** non aver paura.

unaided [ʌn'eɪdɪd] *adv* senza aiuto.

unanimity [juːnə'nɪmɪtɪ] *n* unanimità.

unanimous [juː'nænɪməs] *adj* unanime.

unanimously [juː'nænɪməslɪ] *adv* all'unanimità.

unanswered [ʌn'ɑːnsəd] *adj (question, letter)* senza risposta; *(criticism)* non confutato(a).

unappetizing [ʌn'æpɪtaɪzɪŋ] *adj* poco appetitoso(a).

unappreciative [ʌnə'priːʃɪətɪv] *adj* che non apprezza.

unarmed [ʌn'ɑːmd] *adj (person)* disarmato(a); *(combat)* senz'armi.

unashamed [ʌnə'ʃeɪmd] *adj* sfacciato(a); senza vergogna.

unassisted [ʌnə'sɪstɪd] *adj, adv* senza nessun aiuto.

unassuming [ʌnə'sjuːmɪŋ] *adj* modesto(a), senza pretese.

unattached [ʌnə'tætʃt] *adj* senza legami, libero(a).

unattended [ʌnə'tɛndɪd] *adj (car, child, luggage)* incustodito(a).

unattractive [ʌnə'træktɪv] *adj* privo(a) di attrattiva, poco attraente.

unauthorized [ʌn'ɔːθəraɪzd] *adj* non autorizzato(a).

unavailable [ʌnə'veɪləbl] *adj (article, room, book)* non disponibile; *(person)* impegnato(a).

unavoidable [ʌnə'vɔɪdəbl] *adj* inevitabile.

unavoidably [ʌnə'vɔɪdəblɪ] *adv (detained)* per cause di forza maggiore.

unaware [ʌnə'wɛə*] *adj*: **to be ~ of** non

sapere, ignorare.

unawares [ʌnə'wɛəz] *adv* di sorpresa, alla sprovvista.

unbalanced [ʌn'bælənst] *adj* squilibrato(a).

unbearable [ʌn'bɛərəbl] *adj* insopportabile.

unbeatable [ʌn'biːtəbl] *adj* imbattibile.

unbeaten [ʌn'biːtn] *adj (team, army)* imbattuto(a); *(record)* insuperato(a).

unbecoming [ʌnbɪ'kʌmɪŋ] *adj (unseemly: language, behaviour)* sconveniente; *(unflattering: garment)* che non dona.

unbeknown(st) [ʌnbɪ'nəun(st)] *adv*: **~ to** all'insaputa di.

unbelief [ʌnbɪ'liːf] *n* incredulità.

unbelievable [ʌnbɪ'liːvəbl] *adj* incredibile.

unbelievingly [ʌnbɪ'liːvɪŋlɪ] *adv* con aria incredula.

unbend [ʌn'bɛnd] *vb (irreg) vi* distendersi ♦ *vt (wire)* raddrizzare.

unbending [ʌn'bɛndɪŋ] *adj (fig)* inflessibile, rigido(a).

unbias(s)ed [ʌn'baɪəst] *adj* obiettivo(a), imparziale.

unblemished [ʌn'blɛmɪʃt] *adj* senza macchia.

unblock [ʌn'blɒk] *vt (pipe, road)* sbloccare.

unborn [ʌn'bɔːn] *adj* non ancora nato(a).

unbounded [ʌn'baundɪd] *adj* sconfinato(a), senza limite.

unbreakable [ʌn'breɪkəbl] *adj* infrangibile.

unbridled [ʌn'braɪdld] *adj* sbrigliato(a).

unbroken [ʌn'brəukən] *adj (intact)* intero(a); *(continuous)* continuo(a); *(record)* insuperato(a).

unbuckle [ʌn'bʌkl] *vt* slacciare.

unburden [ʌn'bɔːdn] *vt*: **to ~ o.s.** sfogarsi.

unbutton [ʌn'bʌtn] *vt* sbottonare.

uncalled-for [ʌn'kɔːldfɔː*] *adj (remark)* fuori luogo *inv*; *(action)* ingiustificato(a).

uncanny [ʌn'kænɪ] *adj* misterioso(a), strano(a).

unceasing [ʌn'siːsɪŋ] *adj* incessante.

unceremonious [ʌnsɛrɪ'məunɪəs] *adj (abrupt, rude)* senza tante cerimonie.

uncertain [ʌn'sɜːtn] *adj* incerto(a); **it's ~ whether ...** non è sicuro se ...; **in no ~ terms** chiaro e tondo, senza mezzi termini.

uncertainty [ʌn'sɜːtntɪ] *n* incertezza.

unchallenged [ʌn'tʃælɪndʒd] *adj* incontestato(a); **to go ~** non venire contestato, non trovare opposizione.

unchanged [ʌn'tʃeɪndʒd] *adj* immutato(a).

uncharitable [ʌn'tʃærɪtəbl] *adj* duro(a), severo(a).

uncharted [ʌn'tʃɑːtɪd] *adj* inesplorato(a).

unchecked [ʌn'tʃɛkt] *adj* incontrollato(a).

uncivilized [ʌn'sɪvɪlaɪzd] *adj (gen)*

selvaggio(a); (*fig*) incivile, barbaro(a).

uncle ['ʌŋkl] *n* zio.

unclear [ʌn'klɪə*] *adj* non chiaro(a); **I'm still ~ about what I'm supposed to do** non ho ancora ben capito cosa dovrei fare.

uncoil [ʌn'kɔɪl] *vt* srotolare ♦ *vi* srotolarsi, svolgersi.

uncomfortable [ʌn'kʌmfətəbl] *adj* scomodo(a); (*uneasy*) a disagio, agitato(a); (*situation*) sgradevole.

uncomfortably [ʌn'kʌmfətəblɪ] *adv* scomodamente; (*uneasily: say*) con voce inquieta; (: *think*) con inquietudine.

uncommitted [ʌnkə'mɪtɪd] *adj* (*attitude, country*) neutrale.

uncommon [ʌn'kɔmən] *adj* raro(a), insolito(a), non comune.

uncommunicative [ʌnkə'mju:nɪkətɪv] *adj* poco comunicativo(a), chiuso(a).

uncomplicated [ʌn'kɔmplɪkeɪtɪd] *adj* semplice, poco complicato(a).

uncompromising [ʌn'kɔmprəmaɪzɪŋ] *adj* intransigente, inflessibile.

unconcerned [ʌnkən'sə:nd] *adj* (*unworried*) tranquillo(a); **to be ~ about** non darsi pensiero di, non preoccuparsi di *or* per.

unconditional [ʌn'kən'dɪʃənl] *adj* incondizionato(a), senza condizioni.

uncongenial [ʌnkən'dʒi:nɪəl] *adj* (*work, surroundings*) poco piacevole.

unconnected [ʌnkə'nɛktɪd] *adj* (*unrelated*) senza connessione, senza rapporto; **to be ~ with** essere estraneo(a) a.

unconscious [ʌn'kɔnʃəs] *adj* privo(a) di sensi, svenuto(a); (*unaware*) inconsapevole, inconscio(a) ♦ *n*: **the ~** l'inconscio; **to knock sb ~** far perdere i sensi a qn con un pugno.

unconsciously [ʌn'kɔnʃəslɪ] *adv* inconsciamente.

unconstitutional [ʌnkɔnstɪ'tju:ʃənl] *adj* incostituzionale.

uncontested [ʌnkən'tɛstɪd] *adj* (*champion*) incontestato(a); (*POL: seat*) non disputato(a).

uncontrollable [ʌnkən'trəuləbl] *adj* incontrollabile, indisciplinato(a).

uncontrolled [ʌnkən'trəuld] *adj* (*child, dog, emotion*) sfrenato(a); (*inflation, price rises*) che sfugge al controllo.

unconventional [ʌnkən'vɛnʃənl] *adj* poco convenzionale.

unconvinced [ʌnkən'vɪnst] *adj*: **to be** *or* **remain ~** non essere convinto(a).

unconvincing [ʌnkən'vɪnsɪŋ] *adj* non convincente, poco persuasivo(a).

uncork [ʌn'kɔ:k] *vt* stappare.

uncorroborated [ʌnkə'rɔbəreɪtɪd] *adj* non

convalidato(a).

uncouth [ʌn'ku:θ] *adj* maleducato(a), grossolano(a).

uncover [ʌn'kʌvə*] *vt* scoprire.

unctuous ['ʌŋktjuəs] *adj* untuoso(a).

undamaged [ʌn'dæmɪdʒd] *adj* (*goods*) in buono stato; (*fig: reputation*) intatto(a).

undaunted [ʌn'dɔ:ntɪd] *adj* intrepido(a).

undecided [ʌndɪ'saɪdɪd] *adj* indeciso(a).

undelivered [ʌndɪ'lɪvəd] *adj* non recapitato(a); **if ~ return to sender** in caso di mancato recapito rispedire al mittente.

undeniable [ʌndɪ'naɪəbl] *adj* innegabile, indiscutibile.

under ['ʌndə*] *prep* sotto; (*less than*) meno di; al disotto di; (*according to*) secondo, in conformità a ♦ *adv* (al) disotto; **from ~ sth** da sotto *a or* dal disotto di qc; **~ there** là sotto; **in ~ 2 hours** in meno di 2 ore; **~ anaesthetic** sotto anestesia; **~ discussion** in discussione; **~ repair** in riparazione; **~ the circumstances** date le circostanze.

under... ['ʌndə*] *prefix* sotto..., sub....

under-age [ʌndər'eɪdʒ] *adj* minorenne.

underarm ['ʌndərɑ:m] *n* ascella ♦ *adj* ascellare ♦ *adv* da sotto in su.

undercapitalized [ʌndə'kæpɪtəlaɪzd] *adj* carente di capitali.

undercarriage ['ʌndəkærɪdʒ] *n* (*BRIT AVIAT*) carrello d'atterraggio.

undercharge [ʌndə'tʃɑːdʒ] *vt* far pagare di meno a.

underclass ['ʌndəklɑːs] *n* sottoproletariato.

underclothes ['ʌndəkləuðz] *npl* biancheria (intima).

undercover ['ʌndəkʌvə*] *adj* segreto(a), clandestino(a).

undercurrent ['ʌndəkʌrənt] *n* corrente *f* sottomarina.

undercut [ʌndə'kʌt] *vt irreg* vendere a prezzo minore di.

underdeveloped ['ʌndədɪ'vɛləpt] *adj* sottosviluppato(a).

underdog ['ʌndədɔg] *n* oppresso/a.

underdone [ʌndə'dʌn] *adj* (*CULIN*) poco cotto(a).

under-employment [ʌndərɪm'plɔɪmənt] *n* sottoccupazione *f*.

underestimate [ʌndər'ɛstɪmeɪt] *vt* sottovalutare.

underexposed [ʌndərɪks'pəuzd] *adj* (*PHOT*) sottoesposto(a).

underfed [ʌndə'fɛd] *adj* denutrito(a).

underfoot [ʌndə'fut] *adv* sotto i piedi.

under-funded ['ʌndə'fʌndɪd] *adj* insufficientemente sovvenzionato(a).

undergo [ʌndə'gəu] *vt irreg* subire;

(*treatment*) sottoporsi a; **the car is ~ing repairs** la macchina è in riparazione.

undergraduate [ʌndə'grædjuɪt] *n* studente(essa) universitario(a) ♦ *cpd:* ~ **courses** corsi *mpl* di laurea.

underground ['ʌndəgraund] *n* metropolitana; (*POL*) movimento clandestino ♦ *adj* sotterraneo(a); (*fig*) clandestino(a); (*ART, CINE*) underground *inv* ♦ *adv* sottoterra; clandestinamente.

undergrowth ['ʌndəgrəuθ] *n* sottobosco.

underhand(ed) [ʌndə'hænd(ɪd)] *adj* (*fig*) furtivo(a), subdolo(a).

underinsured [ʌndərɪn'ʃuəd] *adj* non sufficientemente assicurato(a).

underlie [ʌndə'laɪ] *vt irreg* essere alla base di; **the underlying cause** il motivo di fondo.

underline [ʌndə'laɪn] *vt* sottolineare.

underling ['ʌndəlɪŋ] *n* (*pej*) subalterno/a, tirapiedi *m/f inv*.

undermanning [ʌndə'mænɪŋ] *n* carenza di personale.

undermentioned [ʌndə'mɛnʃənd] *adj* (riportato(a)) qui sotto *or* qui di seguito.

undermine [ʌndə'maɪn] *vt* minare.

underneath [ʌndə'ni:θ] *adv* sotto, disotto ♦ *prep* sotto, al di sotto di.

undernourished [ʌndə'nʌrɪʃt] *adj* denutrito(a).

underpaid [ʌndə'peɪd] *adj* mal pagato(a).

underpants ['ʌndəpænts] *npl* (*BRIT*) mutande *fpl*, slip *m inv*.

underpass ['ʌndəpɑːs] *n* (*BRIT*) sottopassaggio.

underpin [ʌndə'pɪn] *vt* puntellare; (*argument, case*) corroborare.

underplay [ʌndə'pleɪ] *vt* minimizzare.

underpopulated [ʌndə'pɔpjuleɪtɪd] *adj* scarsamente popolato(a), sottopopolato(a).

underprice [ʌndə'praɪs] *vt* vendere a un prezzo inferiore al dovuto.

underprivileged [ʌndə'prɪvɪlɪdʒd] *adj* svantaggiato(a).

underrate [ʌndə'reɪt] *vt* sottovalutare.

underscore [ʌndə'skɔː*] *vt* sottolineare.

underseal ['ʌndəsiːl] *vt* rendere stagno il fondo di.

undersecretary [ʌndə'sɛkrətrɪ] *n* sottosegretario.

undersell ['ʌndə'sɛl] *vt irreg* (*competitors*) vendere a prezzi più bassi di.

undershirt ['ʌndəʃəːt] *n* (*US*) maglietta.

undershorts ['ʌndəʃɔːts] *npl* (*US*) mutande *fpl*, slip *m inv*.

underside ['ʌndəsaɪd] *n* disotto.

undersigned ['ʌndəsaɪnd] *adj, n* sottoscritto(a).

underskirt ['ʌndəskəːt] *n* sottoveste *f*.

understaffed [ʌndə'stɑːft] *adj* a corto di personale.

understand [ʌndə'stænd] *vb* (*irreg: like* **stand**) *vt, vi* capire, comprendere; **I ~ that** ... sento che ...; credo di capire che ...; **to make o.s. understood** farsi capire.

understandable [ʌndə'stændəbl] *adj* comprensibile.

understanding [ʌndə'stændɪŋ] *adj* comprensivo(a) ♦ *n* comprensione *f*; (*agreement*) accordo; **on the ~ that** ... a patto che *or* a condizione che ...; **to come to an ~ with sb** giungere ad un accordo con qn.

understate [ʌndə'steɪt] *vt* minimizzare, sminuire.

understatement [ʌndə'steɪtmənt] *n*: **that's an ~!** a dire poco!

understood [ʌndə'stud] *pt, pp of* **understand** ♦ *adj* inteso(a); (*implied*) sottinteso(a).

understudy ['ʌndəstʌdɪ] *n* sostituto/a, attore/trice supplente.

undertake [ʌndə'teɪk] *vt irreg* intraprendere; **to ~ to do sth** impegnarsi a fare qc.

undertaker ['ʌndəteɪkə*] *n* impresario di pompe funebri.

undertaking [ʌndə'teɪkɪŋ] *n* impresa; (*promise*) promessa.

undertone ['ʌndətəun] *n* (*low voice*) tono sommesso; (*of criticism etc*) vena, sottofondo; **in an ~** sottovoce.

undervalue [ʌndə'væljuː] *vt* svalutare, sottovalutare.

underwater [ʌndə'wɔːtə*] *adv* sott'acqua ♦ *adj* subacqueo(a).

underwear ['ʌndəwɛə*] *n* biancheria (intima).

underweight [ʌndə'weɪt] *adj* al di sotto del giusto peso; (*person*) sottopeso *inv*.

underworld ['ʌndəwəːld] *n* (*of crime*) malavita.

underwrite ['ʌndəraɪt] *vt* (*FINANCE*) sottoscrivere; (*INSURANCE*) assicurare.

underwriter ['ʌndəraɪtə*] *n* sottoscrittore/trice; assicuratore/trice.

undeserving [ʌndɪ'zəːvɪŋ] *adj*: **to be ~ of** non meritare, non essere degno di.

undesirable [ʌndɪ'zaɪərəbl] *adj* indesiderabile, sgradito(a).

undeveloped [ʌndɪ'vɛləpt] *adj* (*land, resources*) non sfruttato(a).

undies ['ʌndɪz] *npl* (*col*) robina, biancheria intima da donna.

undiluted [ʌndaɪ'luːtɪd] *adj* non diluito(a).

undiplomatic [ʌndɪplə'mætɪk] *adj* poco

diplomatico(a).

undischarged [ˈʌndɪsˈtʃɑːdʒd] *adj*: ~ **bankrupt** fallito non riabilitato.

undisciplined [ʌnˈdɪsɪplɪnd] *adj* indisciplinato(a).

undisguised [ʌndɪsˈgaɪzd] *adj* (*dislike, amusement etc*) palese.

undisputed [ʌndɪsˈpjuːtɪd] *adj* indiscusso(a).

undistinguished [ʌndɪsˈtɪŋgwɪʃt] *adj* mediocre, qualunque.

undisturbed [ʌndɪsˈtəːbd] *adj* tranquillo(a); **to leave sth ~** lasciare qc così com'è.

undivided [ʌndɪˈvaɪdɪd] *adj*: **I want your ~ attention** esigo tutta la sua attenzione.

undo [ʌnˈduː] *vt irreg* disfare.

undoing [ʌnˈduːɪŋ] *n* rovina, perdita.

undone [ʌnˈdʌn] *pp of* **undo**; **to come ~** slacciarsi.

undoubted [ʌnˈdautɪd] *adj* sicuro(a), certo(a).

undoubtedly [ʌnˈdautɪdlɪ] *adv* senza alcun dubbio.

undress [ʌnˈdrɛs] *vi* spogliarsi.

undrinkable [ʌnˈdrɪŋkəbl] *adj* (*unpalatable*) imbevibile; (*poisonous*) non potabile.

undue [ʌnˈdjuː] *adj* eccessivo(a).

undulating [ˈʌndjuleɪtɪŋ] *adj* ondeggiante; ondulato(a).

unduly [ʌnˈdjuːlɪ] *adv* eccessivamente.

undying [ʌnˈdaɪɪŋ] *adj* imperituro(a).

unearned [ʌnˈəːnd] *adj* (*praise, respect*) immeritato(a); ~ **income** rendita.

unearth [ʌnˈəːθ] *vt* dissotterrare; (*fig*) scoprire.

unearthly [ʌnˈəːθlɪ] *adj* soprannaturale; (*hour*) impossibile.

uneasy [ʌnˈiːzɪ] *adj* a disagio; (*worried*) preoccupato(a); **to feel ~ about doing sth** non sentirsela di fare qc.

uneconomic(al) [ˈʌniːkəˈnɔmɪk(l)] *adj* non economico(a), antieconomico(a).

uneducated [ʌnˈɛdjukeɪtɪd] *adj* senza istruzione, incolto(a).

unemployed [ʌnɪmˈplɔɪd] *adj* disoccupato(a) ♦ *npl*: **the ~** i disoccupati.

unemployment [ʌnɪmˈplɔɪmənt] *n* disoccupazione *f*.

unemployment benefit, (*US*) **unemployment compensation** *n* sussidio di disoccupazione.

unending [ʌnˈɛndɪŋ] *adj* senza fine.

unenviable [ʌnˈɛnvɪəbl] *adj* poco invidiabile.

unequal [ʌnˈiːkwəl] *adj* (*length, objects*) disuguale; (*amounts*) diverso(a); (*division of labour*) ineguale.

unequalled, (*US*) **unequaled** [ʌnˈiːkwəld]

adj senza pari, insuperato(a).

unequivocal [ʌnɪˈkwɪvəkəl] *adj* (*answer*) inequivocabile; (*person*) esplicito(a), chiaro(a).

unerring [ʌnˈəːrɪŋ] *adj* infallibile.

UNESCO [juːˈnɛskəu] *n abbr* (= *United Nations Educational, Scientific and Cultural Organization*) U.N.E.S.C.O. *f*.

unethical [ʌnˈɛθɪkəl] *adj* (*methods*) poco ortodosso(a), non moralmente accettabile; (*doctor's behaviour*) contrario(a) all'etica professionale.

uneven [ʌnˈiːvn] *adj* ineguale; (*ground*) disuguale, accidentato(a); (*heartbeat*) irregolare.

uneventful [ʌnɪˈvɛntful] *adj* senza sorprese, tranquillo(a).

unexceptional [ʌnɪkˈsɛpʃənl] *adj* che non ha niente d'eccezionale.

unexciting [ʌnɪkˈsaɪtɪŋ] *adj* (*news*) poco emozionante; (*film, evening*) poco interessante.

unexpected [ʌnɪkˈspɛktɪd] *adj* inatteso(a), imprevisto(a).

unexpectedly [ʌnɪkˈspɛktɪdlɪ] *adv* inaspettatamente.

unexplained [ʌnɪkˈspleɪnd] *adj* inspiegato(a).

unexploded [ʌnɪkˈspləudɪd] *adj* inesploso(a).

unfailing [ʌnˈfeɪlɪŋ] *adj* (*supply, energy*) inesauribile; (*remedy*) infallibile.

unfair [ʌnˈfɛə*] *adj*: ~ **(to)** ingiusto(a) (nei confronti di); **it's ~ that ...** non è giusto che ... + *sub*.

unfair dismissal *n* licenziamento ingiustificato.

unfairly [ʌnˈfɛəlɪ] *adv* ingiustamente.

unfaithful [ʌnˈfeɪθful] *adj* infedele.

unfamiliar [ʌnfəˈmɪlɪə*] *adj* sconosciuto(a), strano(a); **to be ~ with sth** non essere pratico di qc, non avere familiarità con qc.

unfashionable [ʌnˈfæʃnəbl] *adj* (*clothes*) fuori moda *inv*; (*district*) non alla moda.

unfasten [ʌnˈfɑːsn] *vt* slacciare; sciogliere.

unfathomable [ʌnˈfæðəməbl] *adj* insondabile.

unfavourable, (*US*) **unfavorable** [ʌnˈfeɪvərəbl] *adj* sfavorevole.

unfavo(u)rably [ʌnˈfeɪvərəblɪ] *adv*: **to look ~ upon** vedere di malocchio.

unfeeling [ʌnˈfiːlɪŋ] *adj* insensibile, duro(a).

unfinished [ʌnˈfɪnɪʃt] *adj* incompiuto(a).

unfit [ʌnˈfɪt] *adj* inadatto(a); (*ill*) non in forma; (*incompetent*): ~ **(for)** incompetente (in); (: *work, MIL*) inabile

(a); ~ **for habitation** inabitabile.
unflagging [ʌn'flægɪŋ] *adj* instancabile.
unflappable [ʌn'flæpəbl] *adj* calmo(a),
composto(a).
unflattering [ʌn'flætərɪŋ] *adj* (*dress,
hairstyle*) che non dona.
unflinching [ʌn'flɪntʃɪŋ] *adj* che non
indietreggia, risoluto(a).
unfold [ʌn'fauld] *vt* spiegare; (*fig*) rivelare
♦ *vi* (*view*) distendersi; (*story*) svelarsi.
unforeseeable ['ʌnfɔː'siːəbl] *adj*
imprevedibile.
unforeseen [ʌnfɔː'siːn] *adj* imprevisto(a).
unforgettable [ʌnfə'gɛtəbl] *adj*
indimenticabile.
unforgivable [ʌnfə'gɪvəbl] *adj*
imperdonabile.
unformatted [ʌn'fɔːmætɪd] *adj* (*disk, text*)
non formattato(a).
unfortunate [ʌn'fɔːtʃnɪt] *adj* sfortunato(a);
(*event, remark*) infelice.
unfortunately [ʌn'fɔːtʃnɪtlɪ] *adv*
sfortunatamente, purtroppo.
unfounded [ʌn'faundɪd] *adj* infondato(a).
unfriendly [ʌn'frɛndlɪ] *adj* poco
amichevole, freddo(a).
unfulfilled [ʌnful'fɪld] *adj* (*ambition*) non
realizzato(a); (*prophecy*) che non si è
avverato(a); (*desire*) insoddisfatto(a);
(*promise*) non mantenuto(a); (*terms of
contract*) non rispettato(a); (*person*)
frustrato(a).
unfurl [ʌn'fɔːl] *vt* spiegare.
unfurnished [ʌn'fɔːnɪʃt] *adj* non
ammobiliato(a).
ungainly [ʌn'geɪnlɪ] *adj* goffo(a),
impacciato(a).
ungodly [ʌn'gɔdlɪ] *adj* empio(a); **at an** ~
hour a un'ora impossibile.
ungrateful [ʌn'greɪtful] *adj* ingrato(a).
unguarded [ʌn'gɑːdɪd] *adj*: **in an** ~ **moment**
in un momento di distrazione.
unhappily [ʌn'hæpɪlɪ] *adv* (*unfortunately*)
purtroppo, sfortunatamente.
unhappiness [ʌn'hæpɪnɪs] *n* infelicità.
unhappy [ʌn'hæpɪ] *adj* infelice; ~ **with**
(*arrangements etc*) insoddisfatto(a) di.
unharmed [ʌn'hɑːmd] *adj* incolume,
sano(a) e salvo(a).
UNHCR *n abbr* (= *United Nations High
Commission for Refugees*) Alto
Commissariato delle Nazioni Unite per
Rifugiati.
unhealthy [ʌn'hɛlθɪ] *adj* (*gen*) malsano(a);
(*person*) malaticcio(a).
unheard-of [ʌn'hɔːdɔv] *adj* inaudito(a),
senza precedenti.
unhelpful [ʌn'hɛlpful] *adj* poco disponibile.

unhesitating [ʌn'hɛzɪteɪtɪŋ] *adj* (*loyalty*)
che non vacilla; (*reply, offer*) pronto(a),
immediato(a).
unholy [ʌn'hauli] *adj*: **an** ~ **alliance**
un'alleanza nefasta; **he returned at an** ~
hour è tornato ad un'ora indecente.
unhook [ʌn'huk] *vt* sganciare; sfibbiare.
unhurt [ʌn'hɔːt] *adj* incolume, sano(a) e
salvo(a).
unhygienic [ʌnhaɪ'dʒiːnɪk] *adj* non
igienico(a).
UNICEF ['juːnɪsɛf] *n abbr* (= *United Nations
International Children's Emergency Fund*)
U.N.I.C.E.F. *m*.
unicorn ['juːnɪkɔːn] *n* unicorno.
unidentified [ʌnaɪ'dɛntɪfaɪd] *adj* non
identificato(a).
uniform ['juːnɪfɔːm] *n* uniforme *f*, divisa
♦ *adj* uniforme.
uniformity [juːnɪ'fɔːmɪtɪ] *n* uniformità.
unify ['juːnɪfaɪ] *vt* unificare.
unilateral [juːnɪ'lætərəl] *adj* unilaterale.
unimaginable [ʌnɪ'mædʒɪnəbl] *adj*
inimmaginabile, inconcepibile.
unimaginative [ʌnɪ'mædʒɪnətɪv] *adj*
privo(a) di fantasia, a corto di idee.
unimpaired [ʌnɪm'pɛəd] *adj* intatto(a), non
danneggiato(a).
unimportant [ʌnɪm'pɔːtənt] *adj* senza
importanza, di scarsa importanza.
unimpressed [ʌnɪm'prɛst] *adj* niente
affatto impressionato(a).
uninhabited [ʌnɪn'hæbɪtɪd] *adj*
disabitato(a).
uninhibited [ʌnɪn'hɪbɪtɪd] *adj* senza
inibizioni; senza ritegno.
uninjured [ʌn'ɪndʒəd] *adj* incolume.
uninspiring [ʌnɪn'spaɪərɪŋ] *adj* banale.
unintelligent [ʌnɪn'tɛlɪdʒənt] *adj* poco
intelligente.
unintentional [ʌnɪn'tɛnʃənəl] *adj*
involontario(a).
unintentionally [ʌnɪn'tɛnʃnəlɪ] *adv* senza
volerlo, involontariamente.
uninvited [ʌnɪn'vaɪtɪd] *adj* non invitato(a).
uninviting [ʌnɪn'vaɪtɪŋ] *adj* (*place, food*) non
invitante, poco invitante; (*offer*) poco
allettante.
union ['juːnjən] *n* unione *f*; (*also*: **trade** ~)
sindacato ♦ *cpd* sindacale; **the U**~ (*US*) gli
stati dell'Unione.
unionize ['juːnjənaɪz] *vt* sindacalizzare,
organizzare in sindacato.
Union Jack *n bandiera nazionale
britannica*.
**Union of Soviet Socialist Republics
(USSR)** *n* Unione *f* delle Repubbliche
Socialiste Sovietiche (U.R.S.S.).

union shop n stabilimento in cui tutti gli operai sono tenuti ad aderire ad un sindacato.

unique [juːˈniːk] adj unico(a).

unisex [ˈjuːnɪsɛks] adj unisex inv.

Unison [ˈjuːnɪsn] n (trade union) sindacato generale dei funzionari.

unison [ˈjuːnɪsn] n: **in ~** all'unisono.

unit [ˈjuːnɪt] n unità f inv; (section: of furniture etc) elemento; (team, squad) reparto, squadra; **production ~** reparto m produzione inv; **sink ~** blocco m lavello inv.

unit cost n costo unitario.

unite [juːˈnaɪt] vt unire ♦ vi unirsi.

united [juːˈnaɪtɪd] adj unito(a); (efforts) congiunto(a).

United Arab Emirates npl Emirati mpl Arabi Uniti.

United Kingdom (UK) n Regno Unito.

United Nations (Organization) (UN, UNO) n (Organizzazione f delle) Nazioni Unite (O.N.U.).

United States (of America) (US, USA) n Stati mpl Uniti (d'America) (USA).

unit price n prezzo unitario.

unit trust n (BRIT COMM) fondo d'investimento.

unity [ˈjuːnɪtɪ] n unità.

Univ. abbr = **university**.

universal [juːnɪˈvɜːsl] adj universale.

universe [ˈjuːnɪvɜːs] n universo.

university [juːnɪˈvɜːsɪtɪ] n università f inv ♦ cpd (student, professor, education) universitario(a); (year) accademico(a).

university degree n laurea.

unjust [ʌnˈdʒʌst] adj ingiusto(a).

unjustifiable [ʌndʒʌstɪˈfaɪəbl] adj ingiustificabile.

unjustified [ʌnˈdʒʌstɪfaɪd] adj ingiustificato(a); (TYP) non allineato(a).

unkempt [ʌnˈkɛmpt] adj trasandato(a); spettinato(a).

unkind [ʌnˈkaɪnd] adj poco gentile, villano(a).

unkindly [ʌnˈkaɪndlɪ] adv (speak) in modo sgarbato; (treat) male.

unknown [ʌnˈnəʊn] adj sconosciuto(a); **~ to me** ... a mia insaputa ...; **~ quantity** (MATH, fig) incognita.

unladen [ʌnˈleɪdn] adj (ship, weight) a vuoto.

unlawful [ʌnˈlɔːful] adj illecito(a), illegale.

unleaded [ˈʌnˈlɛdɪd] adj senza piombo; **~ petrol** benzina verde or senza piombo.

unleash [ʌnˈliːʃ] vt sguinzagliare; (fig) scatenare.

unleavened [ʌnˈlɛvnd] adj non lievitato(a), azzimo(a).

unless [ʌnˈlɛs] conj a meno che (non) + sub; **~ otherwise stated** salvo indicazione contraria; **~ I am mistaken** se non mi sbaglio.

unlicensed [ʌnˈlaɪsənst] adj (BRIT) senza licenza per la vendita di alcolici.

unlike [ʌnˈlaɪk] adj diverso(a) ♦ prep a differenza di, contrariamente a.

unlikelihood [ʌnˈlaɪklɪhud] adj improbabilità.

unlikely [ʌnˈlaɪklɪ] adj improbabile; (explanation) inverosimile.

unlimited [ʌnˈlɪmɪtɪd] adj illimitato(a).

unlisted [ʌnˈlɪstɪd] adj (US TEL): **to be ~** non essere sull'elenco; (STOCK EXCHANGE) non quotato(a).

unlit [ʌnˈlɪt] adj (room) senza luce; (road) non illuminato(a).

unload [ʌnˈləud] vt scaricare.

unlock [ʌnˈlɔk] vt aprire.

unlucky [ʌnˈlʌkɪ] adj sfortunato(a); (object, number) che porta sfortuna, di malaugurio; **to be ~** (person) essere sfortunato, non avere fortuna.

unmanageable [ʌnˈmænɪdʒəbl] adj (tool, vehicle) poco maneggevole; (situation) impossibile.

unmanned [ʌnˈmænd] adj (spacecraft) senza equipaggio.

unmannerly [ʌnˈmænəlɪ] adj maleducato(a).

unmarked [ʌnˈmɑːkt] adj (unstained) pulito(a), senza macchie; **~ police car** civetta della polizia.

unmarried [ʌnˈmærɪd] adj non sposato(a); (man only) scapolo, celibe; (woman only) nubile.

unmarried mother n ragazza f madre inv.

unmask [ʌnˈmɑːsk] vt smascherare.

unmatched [ʌnˈmætʃt] adj senza uguali.

unmentionable [ʌnˈmɛnʃnəbl] adj (vice, topic) innominabile; (word) irripetibile.

unmerciful [ʌnˈmɔːsɪful] adj spietato(a).

unmistakable [ʌnmɪsˈteɪkəbl] adj indubbio(a); facilmente riconoscibile.

unmitigated [ʌnˈmɪtɪgeɪtɪd] adj (disaster etc) totale, assoluto(a).

unnamed [ʌnˈneɪmd] adj (nameless) senza nome; (anonymous) anonimo(a).

unnatural [ʌnˈnætʃrəl] adj innaturale; contro natura.

unnecessary [ʌnˈnɛsəsərɪ] adj inutile, superfluo(a).

unnerve [ʌnˈnɜːv] vt (subj: accident) sgomentare; (: hostile attitude) bloccare; (: long wait, interview) snervare.

unnoticed [ʌnˈnəʊtɪst] adj: **to go** or **pass ~** passare inosservato(a).

UNO ['juːnəu] *n abbr see* **United Nations Organization.**

unobservant [ʌnəb'zəːvənt] *adj*: **to be ~** non avere spirito di osservazione.

unobtainable [ʌnəb'teɪnəbl] *adj* (*TEL*) non ottenibile.

unobtrusive [ʌnəb'truːsɪv] *adj* discreto(a).

unoccupied [ʌn'ɔkjupaɪd] *adj* (*house*) vuoto(a); (*seat, MIL: zone*) libero(a), non occupato(a).

unofficial [ʌnə'fɪʃl] *adj* non ufficiale; (*strike*) non dichiarato(a) dal sindacato.

unopened [ʌn'əupənd] *adj* (*letter*) non aperto(a); (*present*) ancora incartato(a).

unopposed [ʌnə'pəuzd] *adj* senza incontrare opposizione.

unorthodox [ʌn'ɔːθədɔks] *adj* non ortodosso(a).

unpack [ʌn'pæk] *vi* disfare la valigia (*or* le valigie).

unpaid [ʌn'peɪd] *adj* (*holiday*) non pagato(a); (*work*) non retribuito(a); (*bill, debt*) da pagare.

unpalatable [ʌn'pælətəbl] *adj* (*food*) immangiabile; (*drink*) imbevibile; (*truth*) sgradevole.

unparalleled [ʌn'pærəlɛld] *adj* incomparabile, impareggiabile.

unpatriotic ['ʌnpætrɪ'ɔtɪk] *adj* (*person*) poco patriottico(a); (*speech, attitude*) antipatriottico(a).

unplanned [ʌn'plænd] *adj* (*visit*) imprevisto(a); (*baby*) non previsto(a).

unpleasant [ʌn'plɛznt] *adj* spiacevole; (*person, remark*) antipatico(a); (*day, experience*) brutto(a).

unplug [ʌn'plʌg] *vt* staccare.

unpolluted [ʌnpə'luːtɪd] *adj* non inquinato(a).

unpopular [ʌn'pɔpjulə*] *adj* impopolare; **to make o.s. ~ (with)** rendersi antipatico (a); (*subj: politician etc*) alienarsi le simpatie (di).

unprecedented [ʌn'prɛsɪdəntɪd] *adj* senza precedenti.

unpredictable [ʌnprɪ'dɪktəbl] *adj* imprevedibile.

unprejudiced [ʌn'prɛdʒudɪst] *adj* (*not biased*) obiettivo(a), imparziale; (*having no prejudices*) senza pregiudizi.

unprepared [ʌnprɪ'pɛəd] *adj* (*person*) impreparato(a); (*speech*) improvvisato(a).

unprepossessing [ʌnpriːpə'zɛsɪŋ] *adj* insulso(a).

unpretentious [ʌnprɪ'tɛnʃəs] *adj* senza pretese.

unprincipled [ʌn'prɪnsɪpld] *adj* senza scrupoli.

unproductive [ʌnprə'dʌktɪv] *adj* improduttivo(a); (*discussion*) sterile.

unprofessional ['ʌnprə'fɛʃənl] *adj*: **~ conduct** scorrettezza professionale.

unprofitable [ʌn'prɔfɪtəbl] *adj* (*financially*) non redditizio(a); (*job, deal*) poco lucrativo(a).

UNPROFOR ['ʌnprəfɔː*] *n abbr* (= *United Nations Protection Force*) reparto di protezione dell'ONU.

unprotected ['ʌnprə'tɛktɪd] *adj* (*sex*) non protetto(a).

unprovoked [ʌnprə'vəukt] *adj* non provocato(a).

unpunished [ʌn'pʌnɪʃt] *adj*: **to go ~** restare impunito(a).

unqualified [ʌn'kwɔlɪfaɪd] *adj* (*worker*) non qualificato(a); (*in professions*) non abilitato(a); (*success*) assoluto(a), senza riserve.

unquestionably [ʌn'kwɛstʃənəblɪ] *adv* indiscutibilmente.

unquestioning [ʌn'kwɛstʃənɪŋ] *adj* (*obedience, acceptance*) cieco(a).

unravel [ʌn'rævl] *vt* dipanare, districare.

unreal [ʌn'rɪəl] *adj* irreale.

unrealistic [ʌnrɪə'lɪstɪk] *adj* (*idea*) illusorio(a); (*estimate*) non realistico(a).

unreasonable [ʌn'riːznəbl] *adj* irragionevole; **to make ~ demands on sb** voler troppo da qn.

unrecognizable [ʌn'rɛkəgnaɪzəbl] *adj* irriconoscibile.

unrecognized [ʌn'rɛkəgnaɪzd] *adj* (*talent, genius*) misconosciuto(a); (*POL: regime*) non ufficialmente riconosciuto(a).

unrecorded [ʌnrɪ'kɔːdɪd] *adj* non documentato(a), non registrato(a).

unrefined [ʌnrɪ'faɪnd] *adj* (*sugar, petroleum*) greggio(a); (*person*) rozzo(a).

unrehearsed [ʌnrɪ'həːst] *adj* (*THEAT etc*) improvvisato(a); (*spontaneous*) imprevisto(a).

unrelated [ʌnrɪ'leɪtɪd] *adj*: **~ (to)** senza rapporto (con); (*by family*) non imparentato(a) (con).

unrelenting [ʌnrɪ'lɛntɪŋ] *adj* implacabile; accanito(a).

unreliable [ʌnrɪ'laɪəbl] *adj* (*person, machine*) che non dà affidamento; (*news, source of information*) inattendibile.

unrelieved [ʌnrɪ'liːvd] *adj* (*monotony*) uniforme.

unremitting [ʌnrɪ'mɪtɪŋ] *adj* incessante, infaticabile.

unrepeatable [ʌnrɪ'piːtəbl] *adj* (*offer*) unico(a).

unrepentant [ʌnrɪ'pɛntənt] *adj* impenitente.

unrepresentative [ʌnrɛprɪ'zɛntətɪv] *adj* atipico(a), poco rappresentativo(a).

unreserved [ʌnrɪ'zɜːvd] *adj* (*seat*) non prenotato(a), non riservato(a); (*approval, admiration*) senza riserve.

unresponsive [ʌnrɪs'pɒnsɪv] *adj* che non reagisce.

unrest [ʌn'rɛst] *n* agitazione *f.*

unrestricted [ʌnrɪ'strɪktɪd] *adj* (*power, time*) illimitato(a); (*access*) libero(a).

unrewarded [ʌnrɪ'wɔːdɪd] *adj* non ricompensato(a).

unripe [ʌn'raɪp] *adj* acerbo(a).

unrivalled, (*US*) **unrivaled** [ʌn'raɪvəld] *adj* senza pari.

unroll [ʌn'rəʊl] *vt* srotolare.

unruffled [ʌn'rʌfld] *adj* (*person*) calmo(a) e tranquillo(a), imperturbato(a); (*hair*) a posto.

unruly [ʌn'ruːlɪ] *adj* indisciplinato(a).

unsafe [ʌn'seɪf] *adj* pericoloso(a), rischioso(a); ~ **to drink** non potabile; ~ **to eat** non commestibile.

unsaid [ʌn'sɛd] *adj*: **to leave sth** ~ passare qc sotto silenzio.

unsaleable, (*US*) **unsalable** [ʌn'seɪləbl] *adj* invendibile.

unsatisfactory ['ʌnsætɪs'fæktərɪ] *adj* che lascia a desiderare, insufficiente.

unsavoury, (*US*) **unsavory** [ʌn'seɪvərɪ] *adj* (*fig: person*) losco(a); (: *reputation, subject*) disgustoso(a), ripugnante.

unscathed [ʌn'skeɪðd] *adj* incolume.

unscientific ['ʌnsaɪən'tɪfɪk] *adj* poco scientifico(a).

unscrew [ʌn'skruː] *vt* svitare.

unscrupulous [ʌn'skruːpjuləs] *adj* senza scrupoli.

unseat [ʌn'siːt] *vt* (*rider*) disarcionare; (*fig: an official*) spodestare.

unsecured [ʌnsɪ'kjuəd] *adj*: ~ **creditor** creditore *m* chirografario.

unseeded [ʌn'siːdɪd] *adj* (*SPORT*) che non è una testa di serie.

unseemly [ʌn'siːmlɪ] *adj* sconveniente.

unseen [ʌn'siːn] *adj* (*person*) inosservato(a); (*danger*) nascosto(a).

unselfish [ʌn'sɛlfɪʃ] *adj* (*person*) altruista; (*act*) disinteressato(a).

unsettled [ʌn'sɛtld] *adj* (*person, future*) incerto(a); (*question*) non risolto(a); (*weather, market*) instabile; **to feel** ~ sentirsi disorientato(a).

unsettling [ʌn'sɛtlɪŋ] *adj* inquietante.

unshak(e)able [ʌn'ʃeɪkəbl] *adj* irremovibile.

unshaven [ʌn'ʃeɪvn] *adj* non rasato(a).

unsightly [ʌn'saɪtlɪ] *adj* brutto(a), sgradevole a vedersi.

unskilled [ʌn'skɪld] *adj*: ~ **worker** manovale *m.*

unsociable [ʌn'səʊʃəbl] *adj* (*person*) poco socievole; (*behaviour*) antipatico(a).

unsocial [ʌn'səʊʃəl] *adj*: ~ **hours** orario sconveniente.

unsold [ʌn'səʊld] *adj* invenduto(a).

unsolicited [ʌnsə'lɪsɪtɪd] *adj* non richiesto(a).

unsophisticated [ʌnsə'fɪstɪkeɪtɪd] *adj* semplice, naturale.

unsound [ʌn'saʊnd] *adj* (*health*) debole, cagionevole; (*in construction: floor, foundations*) debole, malsicuro(a); (*policy, advice*) poco sensato(a); (*judgment, investment*) poco sicuro(a).

unspeakable [ʌn'spiːkəbl] *adj* (*bad*) abominevole.

unspoken [ʌn'spəʊkən] *adj* (*words*) non detto(a); (*agreement, approval*) tacito(a).

unsteady [ʌn'stɛdɪ] *adj* instabile, malsicuro(a).

unstinting [ʌn'stɪntɪŋ] *adj* (*support*) incondizionato(a); (*generosity*) illimitato(a); (*praise*) senza riserve.

unstuck [ʌn'stʌk] *adj*: **to come** ~ scollarsi; (*fig*) fare fiasco.

unsubstantiated [ʌnsəb'stænʃɪeɪtɪd] *adj* (*rumour, accusation*) infondato(a).

unsuccessful [ʌnsək'sɛsful] *adj* (*writer, proposal*) che non ha successo; (*marriage, attempt*) mal riuscito(a), fallito(a); **to be** ~ (*in attempting sth*) non riuscire; non avere successo; (*application*) non essere considerato(a).

unsuccessfully [ʌnsək'sɛsfəlɪ] *adv* senza successo.

unsuitable [ʌn'suːtəbl] *adj* inadatto(a); (*moment*) inopportuno(a).

unsuited [ʌn'suːtɪd] *adj*: **to be** ~ **for** *or* **to** non essere fatto(a) per.

unsung ['ʌn'sʌŋ] *adj*: **an** ~ **hero** un eroe misconosciuto.

unsupported [ʌnsə'pɔːtɪd] *adj* (*claim*) senza fondamento; (*theory*) non dimostrato(a).

unsure [ʌn'ʃuə*] *adj*: ~ (**of** *or* **about**) incerto(a) (su); **to be** ~ **of o.s.** essere insicuro(a).

unsuspecting [ʌnsə'spɛktɪŋ] *adj* che non sospetta niente.

unsweetened [ʌn'swiːtnd] *adj* senza zucchero.

unswerving [ʌn'swɜːvɪŋ] *adj* fermo(a).

unsympathetic ['ʌnsɪmpə'θɛtɪk] *adj* (*attitude*) poco incoraggiante; (*person*) antipatico(a); ~ **(to)** non solidale (verso).

untangle [ʌn'tæŋgl] *vt* sbrogliare.

untapped [ʌn'tæpt] *adj (resources)* non sfruttato(a).

untaxed [ʌn'tækst] *adj (goods)* esente da imposte; *(income)* non imponibile.

unthinkable [ʌn'θɪŋkəbl] *adj* impensabile, inconcepibile.

unthinkingly ['ʌn'θɪŋkɪŋlɪ] *adv* senza pensare.

untidy [ʌn'taɪdɪ] *adj (room)* in disordine; *(appearance, work)* trascurato(a); *(person, writing)* disordinato(a).

untie [ʌn'taɪ] *vt (knot, parcel)* disfare; *(prisoner, dog)* slegare.

until [ʌn'tɪl] *prep* fino a; *(after negative)* prima di ♦ *conj* finché, fino a quando; *(in past, after negative)* prima che + *sub*, prima di + *infinitive*; ~ **now** finora; ~ **then** fino ad allora; **from morning** ~ **night** dalla mattina alla sera.

untimely [ʌn'taɪmlɪ] *adj* intempestivo(a), inopportuno(a); *(death)* prematuro(a).

untold [ʌn'təuld] *adj* incalcolabile; indescrivibile.

untouched [ʌn'tʌtʃt] *adj (not used etc)* non toccato(a), intatto(a); *(safe: person)* incolume; *(unaffected)*: ~ **by** insensibile a.

untoward [ʌntə'wɔːd] *adj* sfortunato(a), sconveniente.

untrained ['ʌn'treɪnd] *adj (worker)* privo(a) di formazione professionale; *(troops)* privo(a) di addestramento; **to the** ~ **eye** ad un occhio inesperto.

untrammelled [ʌn'træmld] *adj* illimitato(a).

untranslatable [ʌntrænz'leɪtəbl] *adj* intraducibile.

untrue [ʌn'truː] *adj (statement)* falso(a), non vero(a).

untrustworthy [ʌn'trʌstwəːðɪ] *adj* di cui non ci si può fidare.

unusable [ʌn'juːzəbl] *adj* inservibile, inutilizzabile.

unused [ʌn'juːzd] *adj (new)* nuovo(a); *(not made use of)* non usato(a), non utilizzato(a); **to be** ~ **to sth/to doing sth** non essere abituato(a) a qc/a fare qc.

unusual [ʌn'juːʒuəl] *adj* insolito(a), eccezionale, raro(a).

unusually [ʌn'juːʒuəlɪ] *adv* insolitamente.

unveil [ʌn'veɪl] *vt* scoprire, svelare.

unwanted [ʌn'wɔntɪd] *adj* non desiderato(a).

unwarranted [ʌn'wɔrəntɪd] *adj* ingiustificato(a).

unwary [ʌn'wɛərɪ] *adj* incauto(a).

unwavering [ʌn'weɪvərɪŋ] *adj* fermo(a), incrollabile.

unwelcome [ʌn'wɛlkəm] *adj (gen)* non gradito(a); **to feel** ~ sentire che la propria presenza non è gradita.

unwell [ʌn'wɛl] *adj* indisposto(a); **to feel** ~ non sentirsi bene.

unwieldy [ʌn'wiːldɪ] *adj* poco maneggevole.

unwilling [ʌn'wɪlɪŋ] *adj*: **to be** ~ **to do** non voler fare.

unwillingly [ʌn'wɪlɪŋlɪ] *adv* malvolentieri.

unwind [ʌn'waɪnd] *vb (irreg)* *vt* svolgere, srotolare ♦ *vi (relax)* rilassarsi.

unwise [ʌn'waɪz] *adj (decision, act)* avventato(a).

unwitting [ʌn'wɪtɪŋ] *adj* involontario(a).

unworkable [ʌn'wəːkəbl] *adj (plan etc)* inattuabile.

unworthy [ʌn'wəːðɪ] *adj* indegno(a); **to be** ~ **of sth/to do sth** non essere degno di qc/di fare qc.

unwrap [ʌn'ræp] *vt* disfare; *(present)* aprire.

unwritten [ʌn'rɪtn] *adj (agreement)* tacito(a).

unzip [ʌn'zɪp] *vt* aprire (la chiusura lampo di).

=================================== *KEYWORD*

up [ʌp] *prep* su; **he went** ~ **the stairs/the hill** è salito su per le scale/sulla collina; **the cat was** ~ **a tree** il gatto era su un albero; **they live further** ~ **the street** vivono un po' più su nella stessa strada

♦ *adv* **1** *(upwards, higher)* su, in alto; ~ **in the sky/the mountains** su nel cielo/in montagna; ~ **there** lassù; ~ **above** su in alto; ~ **with Leeds United!** viva il Leeds United!

2: **to be** ~ *(out of bed)* essere alzato(a); *(prices, level)* essere salito(a); *(building)* essere terminato(a); *(tent)* essere piantato(a); *(curtains, shutters, wallpaper)* essere su; **"this side** ~**"** "alto"; **to be** ~ **(by)** *(in price, value)* essere salito(a) *or* aumentato(a) (di); **when the year was** ~ *(finished)* finito l'anno; **time's** ~ il tempo è scaduto; **he's well** ~ **in** *or* **on politics** *(BRIT)* è molto informato di *or* sulla politica

3: ~ **to** *(as far as)* fino a; ~ **to now** finora

4: **to be** ~ **to** *(depending on)*: **it's** ~ **to you** sta a lei, dipende da lei; *(equal to)*: **he's not** ~ **to it** *(job, task etc)* non ne è all'altezza; *(col: be doing)*: **what is he** ~ **to?** cosa sta combinando?; **what's** ~**?** *(col: wrong)* che c'è?; **what's** ~ **with him?** che ha?, che gli prende?

♦ *n*: ~**s and downs** alti e bassi *mpl*

◆ *vi (col)*: **she ~ped and left** improvvisamente se ne andò.

up-and-coming ['ʌpənd'kʌmɪŋ] *adj* pieno(a) di promesse, promettente.

upbeat ['ʌpbiːt] *n (MUS)* tempo in levare; *(in economy, prosperity)* incremento ◆ *adj (col)* ottimistico(a).

upbraid [ʌp'breɪd] *vt* rimproverare.

upbringing['ʌpbrɪŋɪŋ] *n* educazione *f*.

upcoming ['ʌpkʌmɪŋ] *adj* imminente, prossimo(a).

update [ʌp'deɪt] *vt* aggiornare.

upend [ʌp'ɛnd] *vt* rovesciare.

upfront [ʌp'frʌnt] *adj (col)* franco(a), aperto(a) ◆ *adv (pay)* subito.

upgrade [ʌp'greɪd] *vt* promuovere; *(job)* rivalutare; *(COMPUT)* far passare a potenza superiore.

upheaval [ʌp'hiːvl] *n* sconvolgimento; tumulto.

uphill [ʌp'hɪl] *adj* in salita; *(fig: task)* difficile ◆ *adv*: **to go ~** andare in salita, salire.

uphold [ʌp'həuld] *vt irreg* approvare; sostenere.

upholstery [ʌp'həulstərɪ] *n* tappezzeria.

upkeep ['ʌpkiːp] *n* manutenzione *f*.

up-market [ʌp'mɑːkɪt] *adj (product)* che si rivolge ad una fascia di mercato superiore.

upon [ə'pɔn] *prep* su.

upper ['ʌpə*] *adj* superiore ◆ *n (of shoe)* tomaia; **the ~ class** ≈ l'alta borghesia.

upper case *n* maiuscolo.

upper-class [ʌpə'klɑːs] *adj* dell'alta borghesia; *(district)* signorile; *(accent)* aristocratico(a); *(attitude)* snob *inv*.

uppercut ['ʌpəkʌt] *n* uppercut *m inv*, montante *m*.

upper hand *n*: **to have the ~** avere il coltello dalla parte del manico.

Upper House *n*: **the ~** *(in Britain)* la Camera Alta, la Camera dei Lords; *(in US etc)* il Senato.

uppermost ['ʌpəməust] *adj* il(la) più alto(a); predominante; **it was ~ in my mind** è stata la mia prima preoccupazione.

Upper Volta [-'vɔltə] *n* Alto Volta *m*.

upright ['ʌpraɪt] *adj* diritto(a); verticale; *(fig)* diritto(a), onesto(a) ◆ *n* montante *m*.

uprising ['ʌpraɪzɪŋ] *n* insurrezione *f*, rivolta.

uproar ['ʌprɔː*] *n* tumulto, clamore *m*.

uproarious [ʌp'rɔːrɪəs] *adj* clamoroso(a); *(hilarious)* esilarante; **~ laughter** risata sonora.

uproot [ʌp'ruːt] *vt* sradicare.

upset *n* ['ʌpsɛt] turbamento ◆ *vt* [ʌp'sɛt] *(irreg: like* **set***) (glass etc)* rovesciare; *(plan, stomach)* scombussolare; *(person: offend)* contrariare; *(: grieve)* addolorare; sconvolgere ◆ *adj* [ʌp'sɛt] contrariato(a); addolorato(a); *(stomach)* scombussolato(a), disturbato(a); **to have a stomach ~** *(BRIT)* avere lo stomaco in disordine *or* scombussolato; **to get ~** contrariarsi; addolorarsi.

upset price *n (US, Scottish)* prezzo di riserva.

upsetting [ʌp'sɛtɪŋ] *adj (saddening)* sconvolgente; *(offending)* offensivo(a); *(annoying)* fastidioso(a).

upshot ['ʌpʃɔt] *n* risultato; **the ~ of it all was that ...** la conclusione è stata che ....

upside down ['ʌpsaɪd-] *adv* sottosopra; **to turn ~** capovolgere; *(fig)* mettere sottosopra.

upstage ['ʌp'steɪdʒ] *vt*: **to ~ sb** rubare la scena a qn.

upstairs [ʌp'stɛəz] *adv, adj* di sopra, al piano superiore ◆ *n* piano di sopra.

upstart ['ʌpstɑːt] *n* parvenu *m inv*.

upstream [ʌp'striːm] *adv* a monte.

upsurge ['ʌpsəːdʒ] *n (of enthusiasm etc)* ondata.

uptake ['ʌpteɪk] *n*: **he is quick/slow on the ~** è pronto/lento di comprendonio.

uptight [ʌp'taɪt] *adj (col)* teso(a).

up-to-date ['ʌptə'deɪt] *adj* moderno(a); aggiornato(a).

upturn ['ʌptəːn] *n (in luck)* svolta favorevole; *(in value of currency)* rialzo.

upturned ['ʌptəːnd] *adj (nose)* all'insù.

upward ['ʌpwəd] *adj* ascendente; verso l'alto.

upwardly-mobile ['ʌpwədlɪ'məubaɪl] *n*: **to be ~** salire nella scala sociale.

upward(s) ['ʌpwəd(z)] *adv* in su, verso l'alto.

URA *n abbr (US: = Urban Renewal Administration) amministrazione per il rinnovamento urbano.

Ural Mountains ['juərəl-] *npl*: **the ~** *(also:* **the Urals***)* gli Urali, i Monti Urali.

uranium [juə'reɪnɪəm] *n* uranio.

Uranus [juə'reɪnəs] *n (planet)* Urano.

urban ['əːbən] *adj* urbano(a).

urbane [əː'beɪn] *adj* civile, urbano(a), educato(a).

urbanization [əːbənaɪ'zeɪʃən] *n* urbanizzazione *f*.

urchin ['əːtʃɪn] *n* monello; **sea ~** riccio di mare.

Urdu ['uəduː] *n* urdu *m inv*.

urge [əːdʒ] *n* impulso, stimolo ◆ *vt (caution*

etc) raccomandare vivamente; **to ~ sb to do** esortare qn a fare, spingere qn a fare; raccomandare a qn di fare.

▶**urge on** *vt* spronare.

urgency ['ɔːdʒənsɪ] *n* urgenza; (*of tone*) insistenza.

urgent ['ɔːdʒənt] *adj* urgente; (*earnest, persistent: plea*) pressante; (: *tone*) insistente, incalzante.

urgently ['ɔːdʒəntlɪ] *adv* d'urgenza, urgentemente; con insistenza.

urinal ['juərɪnl] *n* (*BRIT: building*) vespasiano; (: *vessel*) orinale *m*, pappagallo.

urinate ['juərɪneɪt] *vi* orinare.

urine ['juərɪn] *n* orina.

urn [əːn] *n* urna; (*also:* **tea ~**) bollitore *m* per il tè.

Uruguay ['juərəgwaɪ] *n* Uruguay *m*.

Uruguayan [juərə'gwaɪən] *adj, n* uruguaiano(a).

US *n abbr see* **United States**.

us [ʌs] *pron* ci; (*stressed, after prep*) noi.

USA *n abbr* (*GEO*) *see* **United States (of America)**; (*MIL*) = *United States Army*.

usable ['juːzəbl] *adj* utilizzabile, usabile.

USAF *n abbr* = *United States Air Force*.

usage ['juːzɪdʒ] *n* uso.

USCG *n abbr* = *United States Coast Guard*.

USDA *n abbr* = *United States Department of Agriculture*.

USDAW ['ʌzdɔː] *n abbr* (*BRIT*: = *Union of Shop, Distributive and Allied Workers*) sindacato dei dipendenti di negozi, reti di distribuzione e simili.

USDI *n abbr* = *United States Department of the Interior*.

use *n* [juːs] uso; impiego, utilizzazione *f* ♦ *vt* [juːz] usare, utilizzare, servirsi di; **she ~d to do it** lo faceva (una volta), era solita farlo; **in ~** in uso; **out of ~** fuori uso; **to be of ~** essere utile, servire; **to make ~ of sth** far uso di qc, utilizzare qc; **ready for ~** pronto per l'uso; **it's no ~** non serve, è inutile; **to have the ~ of** poter usare; **what's this ~d for?** a che serve?; **to be ~d to** avere l'abitudine di; **to get ~d to** abituarsi a, fare l'abitudine a.

▶**use up** *vt* finire; (*supplies*) dare fondo a; (*left-overs*) utilizzare.

used [juːzd] *adj* (*car*) d'occasione.

useful ['juːsful] *adj* utile; **to come in ~** fare comodo, tornare utile.

usefulness ['juːsfəlnɪs] *n* utilità.

useless ['juːslɪs] *adj* inutile; (*unusable: object*) inservibile.

user ['juːzə*] *n* utente *m/f*; (*of petrol, gas etc*) consumatore/trice.

user-friendly ['juːzə'frɛndlɪ] *adj* orientato(a) all'utente.

USES *n abbr* = *United States Employment Service*.

usher ['ʌʃə*] *n* usciere *m*; (*in cinema*) maschera ♦ *vt*: **to ~ sb in** far entrare qn.

usherette [ʌʃə'rɛt] *n* (*in cinema*) maschera.

USIA *n abbr* = *United States Information Agency*.

USM *n abbr* = *United States Mint*; *United States Mail*.

USN *n abbr* = *United States Navy*.

USPHS *n abbr* = *United States Public Health Service*.

USPO *n abbr* = *United States Post Office*.

USS *abbr* = *United States Ship* (*or Steamer*).

USSR *n abbr see* **Union of Soviet Socialist Republics**.

usu. *abbr* = *usually*.

usual ['juːʒuəl] *adj* solito(a); **as ~** come al solito, come d'abitudine.

usually ['juːʒuəlɪ] *adv* di solito.

usurer ['juːʒərə*] *adj* usuraio/a.

usurp [juː'zəːp] *vt* usurpare.

UT *abbr* (*US*) = *Utah*.

utensil [juː'tɛnsl] *n* utensile *m*.

uterus ['juːtərəs] *n* utero.

utilitarian [juːtɪlɪ'tɛərɪən] *adj* utilitario(a).

utility [juː'tɪlɪtɪ] *n* utilità; (*also:* **public ~**) servizio pubblico.

utility room *n* locale adibito alla stiratura dei panni *etc*.

utilization [juːtɪlaɪ'zeɪʃən] *n* utilizzazione *f*.

utilize ['juːtɪlaɪz] *vt* utilizzare; sfruttare.

utmost ['ʌtməust] *adj* estremo(a) ♦ *n*: **to do one's ~** fare il possibile *or* di tutto; **of the ~ importance** della massima importanza; **it is of the ~ importance that ...** è estremamente importante che ... + *sub*.

utter ['ʌtə*] *adj* assoluto(a), totale ♦ *vt* pronunciare, proferire; emettere.

utterance ['ʌtərəns] *n* espressione *f*; parole *fpl*.

utterly ['ʌtəlɪ] *adv* completamente, del tutto.

U-turn ['juːtəːn] *n* inversione *f* a U; (*fig*) voltafaccia *m inv*.

Uzbekistan [ʌzbɛkɪ'staːn] *n* Uzbekistan.

V v

V, v [viː] n (letter) V, v m or f inv; **V for Victor**
≈ V come Venezia.
v abbr (= verse; = vide: see) v.; (= volt) V.;
(= versus) contro.
VA, Va. abbr (US) = Virginia.
vac [væk] n abbr (BRIT col) = **vacation.**
vacancy ['veɪkənsɪ] n (job) posto libero;
(room) stanza libera; **"no vacancies"**
"completo"; **have you any vacancies?**
(office) avete bisogno di personale?;
(hotel) avete una stanza?
vacant ['veɪkənt] adj (job, seat etc) libero(a);
(expression) assente.
vacant lot n terreno non occupato; (for
sale) terreno in vendita.
vacate [və'keɪt] vt lasciare libero(a).
vacation [və'keɪʃən] n (esp US) vacanze fpl;
to take a ~ prendere una vacanza,
prendere le ferie; **on** ~ in vacanza, in
ferie.
vacation course n corso estivo.
vaccinate ['væksɪneɪt] vt vaccinare.
vaccination [væksɪ'neɪʃən] n vaccinazione
f.
vaccine ['væksiːn] n vaccino.
vacuum ['vækjum] n vuoto.
vacuum bottle n (US) = **vacuum flask.**
vacuum cleaner n aspirapolvere m inv.
vacuum flask n (BRIT) thermos ® m inv.
vacuum-packed ['vækjum'pækt] adj
confezionato(a) sottovuoto.
vagabond ['vægəbɔnd] n vagabondo/a.
vagary ['veɪgərɪ] n capriccio.
vagina [və'dʒaɪnə] n vagina.
vagrancy ['veɪgrənsɪ] n vagabondaggio.
vagrant ['veɪgrənt] n vagabondo/a.
vague [veɪg] adj vago(a); (blurred: photo,
memory) sfocato(a); **I haven't the ~st idea**
non ho la minima or più pallida idea.
vaguely ['veɪglɪ] adv vagamente.
vain [veɪn] adj (useless) inutile, vano(a);
(conceited) vanitoso(a); **in** ~ inutilmente,
invano.
valance ['væləns] n volant m inv, balza.
valedictory [vælɪ'dɪktərɪ] adj di commiato.
valentine ['væləntaɪn] n (also: ~ **card**)
cartolina or biglietto di San Valentino.
valet ['vælɪt] n cameriere m personale.

valet parking n parcheggio effettuato da
un dipendente (dell'albergo etc).
valet service n (for clothes) servizio di
lavanderia; (for car) servizio completo di
lavaggio.
valiant ['vælɪənt] adj valoroso(a),
coraggioso(a).
valid ['vælɪd] adj valido(a), valevole;
(excuse) valido(a).
validate ['vælɪdeɪt] vt (contract, document)
convalidare; (argument, claim)
comprovare.
validity [və'lɪdɪtɪ] n validità.
valise [və'liːz] n borsa da viaggio.
valley ['vælɪ] n valle f.
valour, (US) **valor** ['vælə*] n valore m.
valuable ['væljuəbl] adj (jewel) di (grande)
valore; (time) prezioso(a); ~**s** npl oggetti
mpl di valore.
valuation [vælju'eɪʃən] n valutazione f,
stima.
value ['væljuː] n valore m ♦ vt (fix price)
valutare, dare un prezzo a; (cherish)
apprezzare, tenere a; **to be of great** ~ **to
sb** avere molta importanza per qn; **to
lose (in)** ~ (currency) svalutarsi; (property)
perdere (di) valore; **to gain (in)** ~
(currency) guadagnare; (property)
aumentare di valore; **you get good** ~ **(for
money) in that shop** si compra bene in
quel negozio.
value added tax (VAT) n (BRIT) imposta
sul valore aggiunto (I.V.A.).
valued ['væluːd] adj (appreciated)
stimato(a), apprezzato(a).
valuer ['væljuə*] n stimatore/trice.
valve [vælv] n valvola.
vampire ['væmpaɪə*] n vampiro.
van [væn] n (AUT) furgone m; (BRIT RAIL)
vagone m.
V and A n abbr (BRIT) = Victoria and Albert
Museum.
vandal ['vændl] n vandalo/a.
vandalism ['vændəlɪzəm] n vandalismo.
vandalize ['vændəlaɪz] vt vandalizzare.
vanguard ['vængɑːd] n avanguardia.
vanilla [və'nɪlə] n vaniglia ♦ cpd (ice cream)
alla vaniglia.
vanish ['vænɪʃ] vi svanire, scomparire.
vanity ['vænɪtɪ] n vanità.
vanity case n valigetta per cosmetici.
vantage ['vɑːntɪdʒ] n: ~ **point** posizione f or
punto di osservazione; (fig) posizione
vantaggiosa.
vaporize ['veɪpəraɪz] vt vaporizzare ♦ vi
vaporizzarsi.
vapour, (US) **vapor** ['veɪpə*] n vapore m.
variable ['vɛərɪəbl] adj variabile; (mood)

mutevole ♦ *n* fattore *m* variabile, variabile *f*.

variance ['vɛərɪəns] *n*: **to be at ~ (with)** essere in disaccordo (con); (*facts*) essere in contraddizione (con).

variant ['vɛərɪənt] *n* variante *f*.

variation [vɛərɪ'eɪʃən] *n* variazione *f*; (*in opinion*) cambiamento.

varicose ['værɪkəus] *adj*: **~ veins** varici *fpl*.

varied ['vɛərɪd] *adj* vario(a), diverso(a).

variety [və'raɪətɪ] *n* varietà *f inv*; (*quantity*): **a wide ~ of ...** una vasta gamma di ...; **for a ~ of reasons** per una serie di motivi.

variety show *n* spettacolo di varietà.

various ['vɛərɪəs] *adj* vario(a), diverso(a); (*several*) parecchi(e), molti(e); **at ~ times** in momenti diversi; (*several*) diverse volte.

varnish ['vɑːnɪʃ] *n* vernice *f*; (*for nails*) smalto ♦ *vt* verniciare; **to ~ one's nails** mettersi lo smalto sulle unghie.

vary ['vɛərɪ] *vt*, *vi* variare, mutare; **to ~ (with *or* according to)** variare (con *or* a seconda di).

varying ['vɛərɪɪŋ] *adj* variabile.

vase [vɑːz] *n* vaso.

vasectomy [væ'sɛktəmɪ] *n* vasectomia.

Vaseline ® ['væsɪliːn] *n* vaselina.

vast [vɑːst] *adj* vasto(a); (*amount, success*) enorme.

vastly ['vɑːstlɪ] *adv* enormemente.

vastness ['vɑːstnɪs] *n* vastità.

VAT [væt] *n abbr* (*BRIT*) *see* **value added tax**.

vat [væt] *n* tino.

Vatican ['vætɪkən] *n*: **the ~** il Vaticano.

vatman ['vætmæn] *n* (*BRIT col*): **the ~** ≈ l'ispettore *m* dell'IVA; (*Inland Revenue*) (il) fisco.

vault [vɔːlt] *n* (*of roof*) volta; (*tomb*) tomba; (*in bank*) camera blindata; (*jump*) salto ♦ *vt* (*also*: **~ over**) saltare (d'un balzo).

vaunted ['vɔːntɪd] *adj*: **much-~** tanto celebrato(a).

VC *n abbr* (*BRIT*: = *Victoria Cross*) medaglia al coraggio; = **vice-chairman**.

VCR *n abbr see* **video cassette recorder**.

VD *n abbr see* **venereal disease**.

VDU *n abbr see* **visual display unit**.

veal [viːl] *n* vitello.

veer [vɪə*] *vi* girare; virare.

veg. [vɛdʒ] *n abbr* (*BRIT col*: = *vegetable(s)*) ≈ contorno.

vegan ['viːgən] *n* (*BRIT*) vegetaliano/a.

vegeburger, veggieburger ['vɛdʒɪbɜːgə*] *n* hamburger *m inv* vegetariano.

vegetable ['vɛdʒɪtəbl] *n* verdura, ortaggio ♦ *adj* vegetale.

vegetable garden *n* orto.

vegetarian [vɛdʒɪ'tɛərɪən] *adj*, *n* vegetariano(a).

vegetate ['vɛdʒɪteɪt] *vi* vegetare.

vegetation [vɛdʒɪ'teɪʃən] *n* vegetazione *f*.

vegetative ['vɛdʒɪtətɪv] *adj* (*also BOT*) vegetativo(a).

vehemence ['viːɪməns] *n* veemenza, violenza.

vehement ['viːɪmənt] *adj* veemente, violento(a); profondo(a).

vehicle ['viːɪkl] *n* veicolo; (*fig*) mezzo.

vehicular [vɪ'hɪkjulə*] *adj*: **"no ~ traffic"** "chiuso al traffico di veicoli".

veil [veɪl] *n* velo ♦ *vt* velare; **under a ~ of secrecy** (*fig*) protetto da una cortina di segretezza.

veiled [veɪld] *adj* (*also fig*) velato(a).

vein [veɪn] *n* vena; (*on leaf*) nervatura; (*fig*: *mood*) vena, umore *m*.

Velcro ® ['vɛlkrəu] *n* velcro ® *m inv*.

vellum ['vɛləm] *n* (*writing paper*) carta patinata.

velocity [vɪ'lɒsɪtɪ] *n* velocità *f inv*.

velour [və'luə*] *n* velours *m inv*.

velvet ['vɛlvɪt] *n* velluto.

vending machine ['vɛndɪŋ-] *n* distributore *m* automatico.

vendor ['vɛndə*] *n* venditore/trice; **street ~** venditore ambulante.

veneer [və'nɪə*] *n* impiallacciatura; (*fig*) vernice *f*.

venerable ['vɛnərəbl] *adj* venerabile.

venereal disease (VD) [vɪ'nɪərɪəl-] *n* malattia venerea.

Venetian [vɪ'niːʃən] *adj*, *n* veneziano(a).

Venetian blind *n* (tenda alla) veneziana.

Venezuela [vɛnɪ'zweɪlə] *n* Venezuela *m*.

Venezuelan [vɛnɪ'zweɪlən] *adj*, *n* venezuelano(a).

vengeance ['vɛndʒəns] *n* vendetta; **with a ~** (*fig*) davvero; furiosamente.

vengeful ['vɛndʒful] *adj* vendicativo(a).

Venice ['vɛnɪs] *n* Venezia.

venison ['vɛnɪsn] *n* carne *f* di cervo.

venom ['vɛnəm] *n* veleno.

venomous ['vɛnəməs] *adj* velenoso(a).

vent [vɛnt] *n* foro, apertura; (*in dress, jacket*) spacco ♦ *vt* (*fig*: *one's feelings*) sfogare, dare sfogo a.

ventilate ['vɛntɪleɪt] *vt* (*room*) dare aria a, arieggiare.

ventilation [vɛntɪ'leɪʃən] *n* ventilazione *f*.

ventilation shaft *n* condotto di aerazione.

ventilator ['vɛntɪleɪtə*] *n* ventilatore *m*.

ventriloquist [vɛn'trɪləkwɪst] *n* ventriloquo/a.

venture ['vɛntʃə*] *n* impresa (rischiosa) ♦ *vt* rischiare, azzardare ♦ *vi* arrischiarsi, azzardarsi; **a business ~** un'iniziativa commerciale; **to ~ to do sth** azzardarsi a fare qc.

venture capital *n* capitale *m* di rischio.

venue ['vɛnjuː] *n* luogo di incontro; (*SPORT*) luogo (designato) per l'incontro.

Venus ['viːnəs] *n* (*planet*) Venere *m*.

veracity [vəˈræsɪtɪ] *n* veridicità.

veranda(h) [vəˈrændə] *n* veranda.

verb [vəːb] *n* verbo.

verbal ['vəːbəl] *adj* verbale; (*translation*) letterale.

verbally ['vəːbəlɪ] *adv* a voce.

verbatim [vəːˈbeɪtɪm] *adv, adj* parola per parola.

verbose [vəːˈbəus] *adj* verboso(a).

verdict ['vəːdɪkt] *n* verdetto; (*opinion*) giudizio, parere *m*; **~ of guilty/not guilty** verdetto di colpevolezza/non colpevolezza.

verge [vəːdʒ] *n* bordo, orlo; **"soft ~s"** (*BRIT*) "banchina cedevole"; **on the ~ of doing** sul punto di fare.

▶**verge on** *vt fus* rasentare.

verger ['vəːdʒə*] *n* (*REL*) sagrestano.

verification [vɛrɪfɪˈkeɪʃən] *n* verifica.

verify ['vɛrɪfaɪ] *vt* verificare; (*prove the truth of*) confermare.

veritable ['vɛrɪtəbl] *adj* vero(a).

vermin ['vəːmɪn] *npl* animali *mpl* nocivi; (*insects*) insetti *mpl* parassiti.

vermouth ['vəːməθ] *n* vermut *m inv*.

vernacular [vəˈnækjulə*] *n* vernacolo.

versatile ['vəːsətaɪl] *adj* (*person*) versatile; (*machine, tool etc*) (che si presta a) molti usi.

verse [vəːs] *n* (*of poem*) verso; (*stanza*) stanza, strofa; (*in bible*) versetto; (*no pl: poetry*) versi *mpl*; **in ~** in versi.

versed [vəːst] *adj*: **(well-)~ in** versato(a) in.

version ['vəːʃən] *n* versione *f*.

versus ['vəːsəs] *prep* contro.

vertebra, *pl* **~e** ['vəːtɪbrə, -briː] *n* vertebra.

vertebrate ['vəːtɪbrɪt] *n* vertebrato.

vertebrae ['vəːtɪbriː] *npl of* **vertebra**.

vertical ['vəːtɪkl] *adj, n* verticale (*m*).

vertically ['vəːtɪklɪ] *adv* verticalmente.

vertigo ['vəːtɪgəu] *n* vertigine *f*; **to suffer from ~** soffrire di vertigini.

verve [vəːv] *n* brio; entusiasmo.

very ['vɛrɪ] *adv* molto ♦ *adj*: **the ~ book which** proprio il libro che; **~ much** moltissimo; **~ well** molto bene; **~ little** molto poco; **at the ~ end** proprio alla fine; **the ~ last** proprio l'ultimo; **at the ~ least** almeno; **the ~ thought (of it) alarms me** il solo pensiero mi spaventa, sono spaventato solo al pensiero.

vespers ['vɛspəz] *npl* vespro.

vessel ['vɛsl] *n* (*ANAT*) vaso; (*NAUT*) nave *f*; (*container*) recipiente *m*.

vest [vɛst] *n* (*BRIT*) maglia; (: *sleeveless*) canottiera; (*US: waistcoat*) gilè *m inv* ♦ *vt*: **to ~ sb with sth, to ~ sth in sb** conferire qc a qn.

vested interest *n*: **to have a ~ in doing** avere tutto l'interesse a fare; **~s** *npl* (*COMM*) diritti *mpl* acquisiti.

vestibule ['vɛstɪbjuːl] *n* vestibolo.

vestige ['vɛstɪdʒ] *n* vestigio.

vestment ['vɛstmənt] *n* (*REL*) paramento liturgico.

vestry ['vɛstrɪ] *n* sagrestia.

Vesuvius [vɪˈsuːvɪəs] *n* Vesuvio.

vet [vɛt] *n abbr* (= *veterinary surgeon*) veterinario ♦ *vt* esaminare minuziosamente; (*text*) rivedere; **to ~ sb for a job** raccogliere delle informazioni dettagliate su qn prima di offrirgli un posto.

veteran ['vɛtərn] *n* veterano; (*also*: **war ~**) reduce *m* ♦ *adj*: **she's a ~ campaigner for** ... lotta da sempre per ....

veteran car *n* auto *f inv* d'epoca (*anteriore al 1919*).

veterinarian [vɛtrɪˈnɛərɪən] *n* (*US*) = **veterinary surgeon**.

veterinary ['vɛtrɪnərɪ] *adj* veterinario(a).

veterinary surgeon *n* (*BRIT*) veterinario.

veto ['viːtəu] *n* (*pl* **~es**) veto ♦ *vt* opporre il veto a; **to put a ~ on** opporre il veto a.

vetting ['vɛtɪŋ] *n*: **positive ~** *indagine per accertare l'idoneità di un aspirante ad una carica ufficiale*.

vex [vɛks] *vt* irritare, contrariare.

vexed [vɛkst] *adj* (*question*) controverso(a), dibattuto(a).

VFD *n abbr* (*US*) = *voluntary fire department*.

VG *abbr* (*BRIT. SCOL etc*: = *very good*) ottimo.

VHF *abbr* (= *very high frequency*) VHF.

VI *abbr* (*US*) = *Virgin Islands*.

via ['vaɪə] *prep* (*by way of*) via; (*by means of*) tramite.

viability [vaɪəˈbɪlɪtɪ] *n* attuabilità.

viable ['vaɪəbl] *adj* attuabile; vitale.

viaduct ['vaɪədʌkt] *n* viadotto.

vial ['vaɪəl] *n* fiala.

vibes [vaɪbz] *npl* (*col*): **I got good/bad ~** ho trovato simpatica/antipatica l'atmosfera.

vibrant ['vaɪbrənt] *adj* (*sound*) vibrante; (*colour*) vivace, vivo(a).

vibraphone ['vaɪbrəfəun] *n* vibrafono.

vibrate [vaɪˈbreɪt] *vi*: **to ~ (with)** vibrare (di); (*resound*) risonare (di).

vibration [vaɪˈbreɪʃən] *n* vibrazione *f*.

vibrator [vaɪˈbreɪtə*] *n* vibratore *m*.

vicar ['vɪkə*] n pastore m.

vicarage ['vɪkərɪdʒ] n presbiterio.

vicarious [vɪ'kɛərɪəs] adj sofferto(a) al posto di un altro; **to get ~ pleasure out of sth** trarre piacere indirettamente da qc.

vice [vaɪs] n (evil) vizio; (TECH) morsa.

vice- [vaɪs] prefix vice ....

vice-chairman [vaɪs'tʃɛəmən] n vicepresidente m.

vice-chancellor [vaɪs'tʃɑːnsələ*] n (BRIT SCOL) rettore m (per elezione).

vice-president [vaɪs'prɛzɪdənt] n vicepresidente m.

viceroy ['vaɪsrɔɪ] n viceré m inv.

vice squad n (squadra del) buon costume f.

vice versa ['vaɪsɪ'vəːsə] adv viceversa.

vicinity [vɪ'sɪnɪtɪ] n vicinanze fpl.

vicious ['vɪʃəs] adj (remark) maligno(a), cattivo(a); (blow) violento(a); **a ~ circle** un circolo vizioso.

viciousness ['vɪʃəsnɪs] n malignità, cattiveria; ferocia.

vicissitudes [vɪ'sɪsɪtjuːdz] npl vicissitudini fpl.

victim ['vɪktɪm] n vittima; **to be the ~ of** essere vittima di.

victimization [vɪktɪmaɪ'zeɪʃən] n persecuzione f; rappresaglie fpl.

victimize ['vɪktɪmaɪz] vt perseguitare; compiere delle rappresaglie contro.

victor ['vɪktə*] n vincitore m.

Victorian [vɪk'tɔːrɪən] adj vittoriano(a).

victorious [vɪk'tɔːrɪəs] adj vittorioso(a).

victory ['vɪktərɪ] n vittoria; **to win a ~ over sb** riportare una vittoria su qn.

video ['vɪdɪəu] cpd video... ♦ n (~ film) video m inv; (also: ~ **cassette**) videocassetta; (also: ~ **cassette recorder**) videoregistratore m.

video camera n videocamera.

video cassette n videocassetta.

video (cassette) recorder n videoregistratore m.

videodisc ['vɪdɪəudɪsk] n disco ottico.

video game n videogioco.

video nasty n video estremamente violento o porno.

videophone ['vɪdɪəufəun] n videotelefono.

video recording n registrazione f su video.

video tape n videotape m inv.

vie [vaɪ] vi: **to ~ with** competere con, rivaleggiare con.

Vienna [vɪ'ɛnə] n Vienna.

Vietnam, Viet Nam [vjɛt'næm] n Vietnam m.

Vietnamese [vjɛtnə'miːz] adj vietnamita

♦ n vietnamita m/f; (LING) vietnamita m.

view [vjuː] n vista, veduta; (opinion) opinione f ♦ vt (situation) considerare; (house) visitare; **on ~** (in museum etc) esposto(a); **to be in** or **within ~ (of sth)** essere in vista (di qc); **in full ~ of sb** sotto gli occhi di qn; **an overall ~ of the situation** una visione globale della situazione; **in my ~** a mio avviso, secondo me; **in ~ of the fact that** considerato che; **to take** or **hold the ~ that ...** essere dell'opinione che ...; **with a ~ to doing sth** con l'intenzione di fare qc.

viewdata ['vjuːdeɪtə] n (BRIT) sistema di televideo.

viewer ['vjuːə*] n (viewfinder) mirino; (small projector) visore m; (TV) telespettatore/trice.

viewfinder ['vjuːfaɪndə*] n mirino.

viewpoint ['vjuːpɔɪnt] n punto di vista.

vigil ['vɪdʒɪl] n veglia; **to keep ~** vegliare.

vigilance ['vɪdʒɪləns] n vigilanza.

vigilant ['vɪdʒɪlənt] adj vigile.

vigilante [vɪdʒɪ'læntɪ] n cittadino che si fa giustizia da solo.

vigorous ['vɪgərəs] adj vigoroso(a).

vigour, (US) **vigor** [vɪgə*] n vigore m.

vile [vaɪl] adj (action) vile; (smell) disgustoso(a), nauseante; (temper) pessimo(a).

vilify ['vɪlɪfaɪ] vt diffamare.

villa ['vɪlə] n villa.

village ['vɪlɪdʒ] n villaggio.

villager ['vɪlɪdʒə*] n abitante m/f di villaggio.

villain ['vɪlən] n (scoundrel) canaglia; (criminal) criminale m; (in novel etc) cattivo.

VIN n abbr (US) = vehicle identification number.

vinaigrette [vɪneɪ'grɛt] n vinaigrette f inv.

vindicate ['vɪndɪkeɪt] vt comprovare; giustificare.

vindication [vɪndɪ'keɪʃən] n: **in ~ of** per giustificare; a discolpa di.

vindictive [vɪn'dɪktɪv] adj vendicativo(a).

vine [vaɪn] n vite f; (climbing plant) rampicante m.

vinegar ['vɪnɪgə*] n aceto.

vine grower n viticoltore m.

vine-growing ['vaɪngrəuɪŋ] adj viticolo(a) ♦ n viticoltura.

vineyard ['vɪnjɑːd] n vigna, vigneto.

vintage ['vɪntɪdʒ] n (year) annata, produzione f; **the 1970 ~** il vino del 1970.

vintage car n auto f inv d'epoca.

vintage wine n vino d'annata.

vinyl ['vaɪnl] n vinile m.

viola [vɪˈəʊlə] n viola.
violate [ˈvaɪəleɪt] vt violare.
violation [vaɪəˈleɪʃən] n violazione f; **in ~ of sth** violando qc.
violence [ˈvaɪələns] n violenza; (*POL etc*) incidenti *mpl* violenti.
violent [vaɪələnt] adj violento(a); **a ~ dislike of sb/sth** una violenta avversione per qn/qc.
violently [ˈvaɪələntlɪ] adv violentemente; (*ill, angry*) terribilmente.
violet [ˈvaɪələt] adj (*colour*) viola inv, violetto(a) ♦ n (*plant*) violetta.
violin [vaɪəˈlɪn] n violino.
violinist [vaɪəˈlɪnɪst] n violinista *m/f*.
VIP n abbr (= *very important person*) V.I.P. *m/f* inv.
viper [ˈvaɪpə*] n vipera.
viral [ˈvaɪərəl] adj virale.
virgin [ˈvɜːdʒɪn] n vergine f ♦ adj vergine inv; **she is a ~** lei è vergine; **the Blessed V~** la Beatissima Vergine.
virginity [vɜːˈdʒɪnɪtɪ] n verginità.
Virgo [ˈvɜːɡəʊ] n (*sign*) Vergine f; **to be ~** essere della Vergine.
virile [ˈvɪraɪl] adj virile.
virility [vɪˈrɪlɪtɪ] n virilità.
virtual [ˈvɜːtjʊəl] adj effettivo(a), vero(a); (*COMPUT, PHYSICS*) virtuale; (*in effect*): **it's a ~ impossibility** è praticamente impossibile; **the ~ leader** il capo all'atto pratico.
virtually [ˈvɜːtjʊəlɪ] adv (*almost*) praticamente; **it is ~ impossible** è praticamente impossibile.
virtual reality n realtà f inv virtuale.
virtue [ˈvɜːtjuː] n virtù f inv; (*advantage*) pregio, vantaggio; **by ~ of** grazie a.
virtuosity [vɜːtjʊˈɔsɪtɪ] n virtuosismo.
virtuoso [vɜːtjʊˈəʊzəʊ] n virtuoso.
virtuous [ˈvɜːtjʊəs] adj virtuoso(a).
virulent [ˈvɪrʊlənt] adj virulento(a).
virus [ˈvaɪərəs] n virus *m* inv.
visa [ˈviːzə] n visto.
vis-à-vis [viːzəˈviː] prep rispetto a, nei riguardi di.
viscount [ˈvaɪkaʊnt] n visconte *m*.
viscous [ˈvɪskəs] adj viscoso(a).
vise [vaɪs] n (*US TECH*) = **vice**.
visibility [vɪzɪˈbɪlɪtɪ] n visibilità.
visible [ˈvɪzəbl] adj visibile; **~ exports/imports** esportazioni *fpl*/importazioni *fpl* visibili.
visibly [ˈvɪzəblɪ] adv visibilmente.
vision [ˈvɪʒən] n (*sight*) vista; (*foresight, in dream*) visione f.
visionary [ˈvɪʒənərɪ] n visionario/a.
visit [ˈvɪzɪt] n visita; (*stay*) soggiorno ♦ vt

(*person*) andare a trovare; (*place*) visitare; **to pay a ~ to** (*person*) fare una visita a; (*place*) andare a visitare; **on a private/official ~** in visita privata/ufficiale.
visiting [ˈvɪzɪtɪŋ] adj (*speaker, professor, team*) ospite.
visiting card n biglietto da visita.
visiting hours *npl* orario delle visite.
visitor [ˈvɪzɪtə*] n visitatore/trice; (*guest*) ospite *m/f*.
visitors' book n libro d'oro; (*in hotel*) registro.
visor [ˈvaɪzə*] n visiera.
VISTA [ˈvɪstə] n abbr (= *Volunteers in Service to America*) volontariato in zone depresse degli Stati Uniti.
vista [ˈvɪstə] n vista, prospettiva.
visual [ˈvɪzjʊəl] adj visivo(a); visuale; ottico(a).
visual aid n sussidio visivo.
visual arts *npl* arti *fpl* figurative.
visual display unit (VDU) n unità f inv di visualizzazione.
visualize [ˈvɪzjʊəlaɪz] vt immaginare, figurarsi; (*foresee*) prevedere.
visually [ˈvɪzjʊəlɪ] adv: **~ appealing** piacevole a vedersi; **~ handicapped** con una menomazione della vista.
vital [ˈvaɪtl] adj vitale; **of ~ importance (to sb/sth)** di vitale importanza (per qn/qc).
vitality [vaɪˈtælɪtɪ] n vitalità.
vitally [ˈvaɪtəlɪ] adv estremamente.
vital statistics *npl* (*of population*) statistica demografica; (*col: woman's*) misure *fpl*.
vitamin [ˈvɪtəmɪn] n vitamina.
vitiate [ˈvɪʃɪeɪt] vt viziare.
vitreous [ˈvɪtrɪəs] adj (*rock*) vetroso(a); (*china, enamel*) vetrificato(a).
vitriolic [vɪtrɪˈɔlɪk] adj (*fig*) caustico(a).
viva [ˈvaɪvə] n (*also: ~ voce*) (*esame m*) orale.
vivacious [vɪˈveɪʃəs] adj vivace.
vivacity [vɪˈvæsɪtɪ] n vivacità.
vivid [ˈvɪvɪd] adj vivido(a).
vividly [ˈvɪvɪdlɪ] adv (*describe*) vividamente; (*remember*) con precisione.
vivisection [vɪvɪˈsɛkʃən] n vivisezione f.
vixen [ˈvɪksn] n volpe f femmina; (*pej: woman*) bisbetica.
viz abbr (= *vide licet: namely*) cioè.
VLF abbr (= *very low frequency*) bassissima frequenza.
V-neck [ˈviːnɛk] n maglione *m* con lo scollo a V.
VOA n abbr (= *Voice of America*) voce f dell'America (*alla radio*).
vocabulary [vəʊˈkæbjʊlərɪ] n vocabolario.

vocal ['vəukl] *adj* (*MUS*) vocale; (*communication*) verbale; (*noisy*) rumoroso(a).
vocal cords *npl* corde *fpl* vocali.
vocalist ['vəukəlıst] *n* cantante *m/f* (*in un gruppo*).
vocation [vəu'keıʃən] *n* vocazione *f*.
vocational [vəu'keıʃənl] *adj* professionale; ~ **guidance** orientamento professionale; ~ **training** formazione *f* professionale.
vociferous [və'sıfərəs] *adj* rumoroso(a).
vodka ['vɔdkə] *n* vodka *f inv*.
vogue [vəug] *n* moda; (*popularity*) popolarità, voga; **to be in** ~, **be the** ~ essere di moda.
voice [vɔıs] *n* voce *f* ♦ *vt* (*opinion*) esprimere; **in a loud/soft** ~ a voce alta/bassa; **to give** ~ **to** esprimere.
voice-over ['vɔısəuvə*] *n* voce *f* fuori campo *inv*.
void [vɔıd] *n* vuoto ♦ *adj*: ~ **of** privo(a) di.
voile [vɔıl] *n* voile *m*.
vol. *abbr* (= *volume*) vol.
volatile ['vɔlətaıl] *adj* volatile; (*fig*) volubile.
volcanic [vɔl'kænık] *adj* vulcanico(a).
volcano, ~**es** [vɔl'keınəu] *n* vulcano.
volition [və'lıʃən] *n*: **of one's own** ~ di propria volontà.
volley ['vɔlı] *n* (*of gunfire*) salva; (*of stones etc*) raffica, gragnola; (*TENNIS etc*) volata.
volleyball ['vɔlıbɔ:l] *n* pallavolo *f*.
volt [vəult] *n* volt *m inv*.
voltage ['vəultıdʒ] *n* tensione *f*, voltaggio; **high/low** ~ alta/bassa tensione.
voluble ['vɔljubl] *adj* loquace, ciarliero(a).
volume ['vɔlju:m] *n* volume *m*; (*of tank*) capacità *f inv*; ~ **one/two** (*of book*) volume primo/secondo; **his expression spoke** ~**s** la sua espressione lasciava capire tutto.
volume control *n* (*RADIO, TV*) regolatore *m or* manopola del volume.
volume discount *n* (*COMM*) vantaggio sul volume di vendita.
voluminous [və'lu:mınəs] *adj* voluminoso(a); (*notes etc*) abbondante.
voluntarily ['vɔləntrılı] *adv* volontariamente; gratuitamente.
voluntary ['vɔləntərı] *adj* volontario(a); (*unpaid*) gratuito(a), non retribuito(a).
voluntary liquidation *n* (*COMM*) liquidazione *f* volontaria.
volunteer [vɔlən'tıə*] *n* volontario/a ♦ *vi* (*MIL*) arruolarsi volontario; **to** ~ **to do** offrire (volontariamente) di fare.
voluptuous [və'lʌptjuəs] *adj* voluttuoso(a).
vomit ['vɔmıt] *n* vomito ♦ *vt, vi* vomitare.
voracious [və'reıʃəs] *adj* (*appetite*) smisurato(a); (*reader*) avido(a).

vote [vəut] *n* voto, suffragio; (*cast*) voto; (*franchise*) diritto di voto ♦ *vi* votare ♦ *vt* (*gen*) votare; (*sum of money etc*) votare a favore di; **to** ~ **to do sth** votare a favore di fare qc; **he was** ~**d secretary** è stato eletto segretario; **to put sth to the** ~, **to take a** ~ **on sth** mettere qc ai voti; ~ **for/against** voto a favore/contrario; **to pass a** ~ **of confidence/no confidence** dare il voto di fiducia/sfiducia; ~ **of thanks** discorso di ringraziamento.
voter ['vəutə*] *n* elettore/trice.
voting ['vəutıŋ] *n* scrutinio.
voting paper *n* (*BRIT*) scheda elettorale.
voting right *n* diritto di voto.
vouch [vautʃ]: **to** ~ **for** *vt fus* farsi garante di.
voucher ['vautʃə*] *n* (*for meal, petrol*) buono; (*receipt*) ricevuta; **travel** ~ voucher *m inv*, tagliando.
vow [vau] *n* voto, promessa solenne ♦ *vi* giurare; **to take** *or* **make a** ~ **to do sth** fare voto di fare qc.
vowel ['vauəl] *n* vocale *f*.
voyage ['vɔııdʒ] *n* viaggio per mare, traversata.
voyeur [vwɑ:'jə:*] *n* guardone/a.
VP *n abbr* (= *vice-president*) V.P.
vs *abbr* (= *versus*) contro.
VSO *n abbr* (*BRIT*: = *Voluntary Service Overseas*) servizio volontario in paesi sottosviluppati.
VT, Vt. *abbr* (*US*) = *Vermont*.
vulgar ['vʌlgə*] *adj* volgare.
vulgarity [vʌl'gærıtı] *n* volgarità.
vulnerability [vʌlnərə'bılıtı] *n* vulnerabilità.
vulnerable ['vʌlnərəbl] *adj* vulnerabile.
vulture ['vʌltʃə*] *n* avvoltoio.

W w

W, w ['dʌblju:] *n* (*letter*) W, w *m or f inv*; **W for William** ≈ W come Washington.
W *abbr* (= *west*) O; (*ELEC*: = *watt*) w.
WA *abbr* (*US*) = *Washington*.
wad [wɔd] *n* (*of cotton wool, paper*) tampone *m*; (*of banknotes etc*) fascio.
wadding ['wɔdıŋ] *n* imbottitura.
waddle ['wɔdl] *vi* camminare come una papera.

wade [weɪd] *vi*: **to ~ through** camminare a stento in ♦ *vt* guadare.

wafer ['weɪfə*] *n* (*CULIN*) cialda; (*REL*) ostia; (*COMPUT*) wafer *m inv*.

wafer-thin ['weɪfə'θɪn] *adj* molto sottile.

waffle ['wɔfl] *n* (*CULIN*) cialda; (*col*) ciance *fpl*; riempitivo ♦ *vi* cianciare; parlare a vuoto.

waffle iron *n* stampo per cialde.

waft [wɔft] *vt* portare ♦ *vi* diffondersi.

wag [wæg] *vt* agitare, muovere ♦ *vi* agitarsi; **the dog ~ged its tail** il cane scodinzolò.

wage [weɪdʒ] *n* (*also*: ~s) salario, paga ♦ *vt*: **to ~ war** fare la guerra; **a day's ~s** un giorno di paga.

wage claim *n* rivendicazione *f* salariale.

wage differential *n* differenza di salario.

wage earner *n* salariato/a.

wage freeze *n* blocco dei salari.

wage packet *n* (*BRIT*) busta *f* paga *inv*.

wager ['weɪdʒə*] *n* scommessa.

waggle ['wægl] *vt* dimenare, agitare ♦ *vi* dimenarsi, agitarsi.

wag(g)on ['wægən] *n* (*horse-drawn*) carro; (*truck*) furgone *m*; (*BRIT RAIL*) vagone *m* (merci).

wail [weɪl] *n* gemito; (*of siren*) urlo ♦ *vi* gemere; urlare.

waist [weɪst] *n* vita, cintola.

waistcoat ['weɪskəut] *n* panciotto, gilè *m inv*.

waistline ['weɪstlaɪn] *n* (giro di) vita.

wait [weɪt] *n* attesa ♦ *vi* aspettare, attendere; **to ~ for** aspettare; **to keep sb ~ing** far aspettare qn; **~ a moment!** (aspetti) un momento!; **"repairs while you ~"** "riparazioni lampo"; **I can't ~ to ...** (*fig*) non vedo l'ora di ...; **to lie in ~ for** stare in agguato a.

▶**wait behind** *vi* rimanere (ad aspettare).

▶**wait on** *vt fus* servire.

▶**wait up** *vi* restare alzato(a) (ad aspettare); **don't ~ up for me** non rimanere alzato per me.

waiter ['weɪtə*] *n* cameriere *m*.

waiting ['weɪtɪŋ] *n*: **"no ~"** (*BRIT AUT*) "divieto di sosta".

waiting list *n* lista d'attesa.

waiting room *n* sala d'aspetto *or* d'attesa.

waitress ['weɪtrɪs] *n* cameriera.

waive [weɪv] *vt* rinunciare a, abbandonare.

waiver ['weɪvə*] *n* rinuncia.

wake [weɪk] *vb* (*pt* **woke**, ~**d**, *pp* **woken**, ~**d** [wəuk, 'wəukn]) *vt* (*also*: ~ **up**) svegliare ♦ *vi* (*also*: ~ **up**) svegliarsi ♦ *n* (*for dead person*) veglia funebre; (*NAUT*) scia; **to ~ up to sth** (*fig*) rendersi conto di qc; **in the**

~ of sulla scia di; **to follow in sb's ~** (*fig*) seguire le tracce di qn.

waken ['weɪkn] *vt, vi* = **wake**.

Wales [weɪlz] *n* Galles *m*.

walk [wɔːk] *n* passeggiata; (*short*) giretto; (*gait*) passo, andatura; (*path*) sentiero; (*in park etc*) sentiero, vialetto ♦ *vi* camminare; (*for pleasure, exercise*) passeggiare ♦ *vt* (*distance*) fare *or* percorrere a piedi; (*dog*) accompagnare, portare a passeggiare; **10 minutes' ~ from** 10 minuti di cammino *or* a piedi da; **to go for a ~** andare a fare quattro passi; andare a fare una passeggiata; **from all ~s of life** di tutte le condizioni sociali; **to ~ in one's sleep** essere sonnambulo(a); **I'll ~ you home** ti accompagno a casa.

▶**walk out** *vi* (*go out*) uscire; (*as protest*) uscire (in segno di protesta); (*strike*) scendere in sciopero; **to ~ out on sb** piantare in asso qn.

walkabout ['wɔːkəbaut] *n*: **to go (on a) ~** avere incontri informali col pubblico (*durante una visita ufficiale*).

walker ['wɔːkə*] *n* (*person*) camminatore/trice.

walkie-talkie ['wɔːkɪ'tɔːkɪ] *n* walkie-talkie *m inv*.

walking ['wɔːkɪŋ] *n* camminare *m*; **it's within ~ distance** ci si arriva a piedi.

walking holiday *n* vacanza fatta di lunghe camminate.

walking shoes *npl* scarpe *fpl* da passeggio.

walking stick *n* bastone *m* da passeggio.

Walkman ® ['wɔːkmən] *n* walkman ® *m inv*.

walk-on ['wɔːkɔn] *adj* (*THEAT: part*) da comparsa.

walkout ['wɔːkaut] *n* (*of workers*) sciopero senza preavviso *or* a sorpresa.

walkover ['wɔːkəuvə*] *n* (*col*) vittoria facile, gioco da ragazzi.

walkway ['wɔːkweɪ] *n* passaggio pedonale.

wall [wɔːl] *n* muro; (*internal, of tunnel, cave*) parete *f*; **to go to the ~** (*fig: firm etc*) fallire.

▶**wall in** *vt* (*garden etc*) circondare con un muro.

wall cupboard *n* pensile *m*.

walled [wɔːld] *adj* (*city*) fortificato(a).

wallet ['wɔlɪt] *n* portafoglio.

wallflower ['wɔːlflauə*] *n* violacciocca; **to be a ~** (*fig*) fare da tappezzeria.

wall hanging *n* tappezzeria.

wallop ['wɔləp] *vt* (*col*) pestare.

wallow ['wɔləu] *vi* sguazzare, rotolarsi; **to ~ in one's grief** crogiolarsi nel proprio dolore.

wallpaper ['wɔːlpeɪpə*] *n* carta da parati.

wall-to-wall ['wɔːltə'wɔːl] *adj:* ~ **carpeting** moquette *f*.

walnut ['wɔːlnʌt] *n* noce *f*; (*tree*) noce *m*.

walrus, *pl* ~ *or* ~**es** ['wɔːlrəs] *n* tricheco.

waltz [wɔːlts] *n* valzer *m inv* ♦ *vi* ballare il valzer.

wan [wɔn] *adj* pallido(a), smorto(a); triste.

wand [wɔnd] *n* (*also:* **magic** ~) bacchetta (magica).

wander ['wɔndə*] *vi* (*person*) girare senza meta, girovagare; (*thoughts*) vagare; (*river*) serpeggiare.

wanderer ['wɔndərə*] *n* vagabondo/a.

wandering ['wɔndrɪŋ] *adj* (*tribe*) nomade; (*minstrel, actor*) girovago(a); (*path, river*) tortuoso(a); (*glance, mind*) distratto(a).

wane [weɪn] *vi* (*moon*) calare; (*reputation*) declinare.

wangle ['wæŋgl] (*BRIT col*) *vt* procurare (con l'astuzia) ♦ *n* astuzia.

wanker ['wæŋkə*] *n* (*col!*) segaiolo (*!*); (*as insult*) coglione (*!*) *m*.

want [wɔnt] *vt* volere; (*need*) aver bisogno di; (*lack*) mancare di ♦ *n* (*poverty*) miseria, povertà; ~**s** *npl* (*needs*) bisogni *mpl*; **for** ~ **of** per mancanza di; **to** ~ **to do** volere fare; **to** ~ **sb to do** volere che qn faccia; **you're** ~**ed on the phone** la vogliono al telefono; *"cook* ~*ed" "cercasi cuoco"*.

want ads *npl* (*US*) piccoli annunci *mpl*.

wanting ['wɔntɪŋ] *adj:* **to be** ~ (**in**) mancare (di); **to be found** ~ non risultare all'altezza.

wanton ['wɔntn] *adj* sfrenato(a); senza motivo.

war [wɔː*] *n* guerra; **to go to** ~ entrare in guerra.

warble ['wɔːbl] *n* (*of bird*) trillo ♦ *vi* trillare.

war cry *n* grido di guerra.

ward [wɔːd] *n* (*in hospital: room*) corsia; (*: section*) reparto; (*POL*) circoscrizione *f*; (*LAW: child*) pupillo/a.

►**ward off** *vt* parare, schivare.

warden ['wɔːdn] *n* (*of institution*) direttore/trice; (*of park, game reserve*) guardiano/a; (*BRIT: also:* **traffic** ~) addetto/a al controllo del traffico e del parcheggio.

warder ['wɔːdə*] *n* (*BRIT*) guardia carceraria.

wardrobe ['wɔːdrəub] *n* (*cupboard*) guardaroba *m inv*, armadio; (*clothes*) guardaroba; (*THEAT*) costumi *mpl*.

warehouse ['wɛəhaus] *n* magazzino.

wares [wɛəz] *npl* merci *fpl*.

warfare ['wɔːfɛə*] *n* guerra.

war game *n* war game *m inv*.

warhead ['wɔːhɛd] *n* (*MIL*) testata, ogiva.

warily ['wɛərɪlɪ] *adv* cautamente, con prudenza.

warlike ['wɔːlaɪk] *adj* guerriero(a).

warm [wɔːm] *adj* caldo(a); (*welcome, applause*) caloroso(a); (*person, greeting*) cordiale; (*heart*) d'oro; (*supporter*) convinto(a); **it's** ~ fa caldo; **I'm** ~ ho caldo; **to keep sth** ~ tenere qc al caldo; **with my** ~**est thanks** con i miei più sentiti ringraziamenti.

►**warm up** *vi* scaldarsi, riscaldarsi; (*athlete, discussion*) riscaldarsi ♦ *vt* scaldare, riscaldare; (*engine*) far scaldare.

warm-blooded ['wɔːm'blʌdɪd] *adj* a sangue caldo.

war memorial *n* monumento ai caduti.

warm-hearted [wɔːm'hɑːtɪd] *adj* affettuoso(a).

warmly ['wɔːmlɪ] *adv* caldamente; calorosamente; vivamente.

warmonger ['wɔːmʌŋgə*] *n* guerrafondaio.

warmongering ['wɔːmʌŋgrɪŋ] *n* bellicismo.

warmth [wɔːmθ] *n* calore *m*.

warm-up ['wɔːmʌp] *n* (*SPORT*) riscaldamento.

warn [wɔːn] *vt* avvertire, avvisare; **to** ~ **sb not to do sth** *or* **against doing sth** avvertire qn di non fare qc.

warning ['wɔːnɪŋ] *n* avvertimento; (*notice*) avviso; **without (any)** ~ senza preavviso; **gale** ~ avviso di burrasca.

warning light *n* spia luminosa.

warning triangle *n* (*AUT*) triangolo.

warp [wɔːp] *n* (*TEXTILES*) ordito ♦ *vi* deformarsi ♦ *vt* deformare; (*fig*) corrompere.

warpath ['wɔːpɑːθ] *n:* **to be on the** ~ (*fig*) essere sul sentiero di guerra.

warped [wɔːpt] *adj* (*wood*) curvo(a); (*fig: character, sense of humour etc*) contorto(a).

warrant ['wɔrnt] *n* (*LAW: to arrest*) mandato di cattura; (*: to search*) mandato di perquisizione ♦ *vt* (*justify, merit*) giustificare.

warrant officer (WO) *n* sottufficiale *m*.

warranty ['wɔrəntɪ] *n* garanzia; **under** ~ (*COMM*) in garanzia.

warren ['wɔrən] *n* (*of rabbits*) tana.

warring ['wɔːrɪŋ] *adj* (*interests etc*) opposto(a), in lotta; (*nations*) in guerra.

warrior ['wɔrɪə*] *n* guerriero/a.

Warsaw ['wɔːsɔː] *n* Varsavia.

warship ['wɔːʃɪp] *n* nave *f* da guerra.

wart [wɔːt] *n* verruca.

wartime ['wɔːtaɪm] *n:* **in** ~ in tempo di guerra.

wary ['wɛərɪ] *adj* prudente; **to be** ~ **about**

or **of doing sth** andare cauto nel fare qc.
was [wɔz] *pt of* be.
wash [wɔʃ] *vt* lavare; (*sweep, carry: sea etc*) portare, trascinare ♦ *vi* lavarsi ♦ *n*: **to give sth a** ~ lavare qc, dare una lavata a qc; **to have a** ~ lavarsi; **he was** ~**ed overboard** fu trascinato in mare (dalle onde).
▶**wash away** *vt* (*stain*) togliere lavando; (*subj: river etc*) trascinare via.
▶**wash down** *vt* lavare.
▶**wash off** *vi* andare via con il lavaggio.
▶**wash up** *vi* lavare i piatti; (*US: have a wash*) lavarsi.
Wash. *abbr* (*US*) = Washington.
washable ['wɔʃəbl] *adj* lavabile.
washbasin ['wɔʃbeɪsn] *n* lavabo.
washcloth ['wɔʃklɔθ] *n* (*US*) pezzuola (per lavarsi).
washer ['wɔʃə*] *n* (*TECH*) rondella.
washing ['wɔʃɪŋ] *n* (*BRIT: linen etc*) bucato; **dirty** ~ biancheria da lavare.
washing line *n* (*BRIT*) corda del bucato.
washing machine *n* lavatrice *f*.
washing powder *n* (*BRIT*) detersivo (in polvere).
Washington ['wɔʃɪŋtən] *n* Washington *f*.
washing-up [wɔʃɪŋ'ʌp] *n* (*dishes*) piatti *mpl* sporchi; **to do the** ~ lavare i piatti, rigovernare.
washing-up liquid *n* (*BRIT*) detersivo liquido (per stoviglie).
wash-out ['wɔʃaut] *n* (*col*) disastro.
washroom ['wɔʃrum] *n* gabinetto.
wasn't ['wɔznt] = **was not**.
Wasp, WASP [wɔsp] *n abbr* (*US*: = White Anglo-Saxon Protestant*) W.A.S.P. *m* (*protestante bianco anglosassone*).
wasp [wɔsp] *n* vespa.
waspish ['wɔspɪʃ] *adj* litigioso(a).
wastage ['weɪstɪdʒ] *n* spreco; (*in manufacturing*) scarti *mpl*.
waste [weɪst] *n* spreco; (*of time*) perdita; (*rubbish*) rifiuti *mpl* ♦ *adj* (*material*) di scarto; (*food*) avanzato(a); (*energy, heat*) sprecato(a); (*land, ground: in city*) abbandonato(a); (: *in country*) incolto(a) ♦ *vt* sprecare; (*time, opportunity*) perdere; ~**s** *npl* distesa desolata; **it's a** ~ **of money** sono soldi sprecati; **to go to** ~ andare sprecato; **to lay** ~ devastare.
▶**waste away** *vi* deperire.
wastebasket ['weɪstbɑːskɪt] *n* = **wastepaper basket**.
waste disposal (unit) *n* (*BRIT*) eliminatore *m* di rifiuti.
wasteful ['weɪstful] *adj* sprecone(a); (*process*) dispendioso(a).

waste ground *n* (*BRIT*) terreno incolto *or* abbandonato.
wasteland ['weɪstlænd] *n* terra desolata.
wastepaper basket ['weɪstpeɪpə-] *n* cestino per la carta straccia.
waste pipe *n* tubo di scarico.
waste products *npl* (*INDUSTRY*) materiali *mpl* di scarto.
waster ['weɪstə*] *n* (*col*) buono/a a nulla.
watch [wɔtʃ] *n* (*wrist*~) orologio; (*act of watching*) sorveglianza; (*guard: MIL, NAUT*) guardia; (*NAUT: spell of duty*) quarto ♦ *vt* (*look at*) osservare; (: *match, programme*) guardare; (*spy on, guard*) sorvegliare, tenere d'occhio; (*be careful of*) fare attenzione a ♦ *vi* osservare, guardare; (*keep guard*) fare *or* montare la guardia; **to keep a close** ~ **on sb/sth** tener bene d'occhio qn/qc; ~ **how you drive/what you're doing** attento a come guidi/quel che fai.
▶**watch out** *vi* fare attenzione.
watchband ['wɔtʃbænd] *n* (*US*) cinturino da orologio.
watchdog ['wɔtʃdɔg] *n* cane *m* da guardia; (*fig*) sorvegliante *m/f*.
watchful ['wɔtʃful] *adj* attento(a), vigile.
watchmaker ['wɔtʃmeɪkə*] *n* orologiaio/a.
watchman ['wɔtʃmən] *n* guardiano; (*also*: **night** ~) guardiano notturno.
watch stem *n* (*US*) corona di carica.
watch strap *n* cinturino da orologio.
watchword ['wɔtʃwɔːd] *n* parola d'ordine.
water [wɔːtə*] *n* acqua ♦ *vt* (*plant*) annaffiare ♦ *vi* (*eyes*) piangere; **in British** ~**s** nelle acque territoriali britanniche; **I'd like a drink of** ~ vorrei un bicchier d'acqua; **to pass** ~ orinare; **to make sb's mouth** ~ far venire l'acquolina in bocca a qn.
▶**water down** *vt* (*milk*) diluire; (*fig: story*) edulcorare.
water closet *n* (*BRIT*) W.C. *m inv*, gabinetto.
watercolour, (*US***) watercolor** ['wɔːtəkʌlə*] *n* (*picture*) acquerello; ~**s** *npl* colori *mpl* per acquerelli.
water-cooled ['wɔːtəkuːld] *adj* raffreddato(a) ad acqua.
watercress ['wɔːtəkrɛs] *n* crescione *m*.
waterfall ['wɔːtəfɔːl] *n* cascata.
waterfront ['wɔːtəfrʌnt] *n* (*seafront*) lungomare *m*; (*at docks*) banchina.
water heater *n* scaldabagno.
water hole *n* pozza d'acqua.
water ice *n* (*BRIT*) sorbetto.
watering can ['wɔːtərɪŋ-] *n* annaffiatoio.
water level *n* livello dell'acqua; (*of flood*) livello delle acque.

water lily *n* ninfea.

waterline ['wɔːtəlaɪn] *n* (*NAUT*) linea di galleggiamento.

waterlogged ['wɔːtəlɔgd] *adj* saturo(a) d'acqua; imbevuto(a) d'acqua; (*football pitch etc*) allagato(a).

watermark ['wɔːtəmɑːk] *n* (*on paper*) filigrana.

watermelon ['wɔːtəmɛlən] *n* anguria, cocomero.

water polo *n* pallanuoto *f*.

waterproof ['wɔːtəpruːf] *adj* impermeabile.

water-repellent ['wɔːtərɪ'pɛlənt] *adj* idrorepellente.

watershed ['wɔːtəʃɛd] *n* (*GEO, fig*) spartiacque *m*.

water-skiing ['wɔːtəskiːɪŋ] *n* sci *m* acquatico.

water softener *n* addolcitore *m*; (*substance*) anti-calcare *m*.

water tank *n* serbatoio d'acqua.

watertight ['wɔːtətaɪt] *adj* stagno(a).

water vapour *n* vapore *m* acqueo.

waterway ['wɔːtəweɪ] *n* corso d'acqua navigabile.

waterworks ['wɔːtəwəːks] *npl* impianto idrico.

watery ['wɔːtərɪ] *adj* (*colour*) slavato(a); (*coffee*) acquoso(a).

watt [wɔt] *n* watt *m inv*.

wattage ['wɔtɪdʒ] *n* wattaggio.

wattle ['wɔtl] *n* graticcio.

wave [weɪv] *n* onda; (*of hand*) gesto, segno; (*in hair*) ondulazione *f*; (*fig: of enthusiasm, strikes etc*) ondata ♦ *vi* fare un cenno con la mano; (*flag*) sventolare ♦ *vt* (*handkerchief*) sventolare; (*stick*) brandire; (*hair*) ondulare; **short/medium/long** ~ (*RADIO*) onde corte/medie/lunghe; **the new** ~ (*CINE, MUS*) la new wave; **to** ~ **sb goodbye, to** ~ **goodbye to sb** fare un cenno d'addio a qn; **he** ~**d us over to his table** ci invitò con un cenno al suo tavolo.

▶**wave aside, wave away** *vt* (*person*): **to** ~ **sb aside** fare cenno a qn di spostarsi; (*fig: suggestion, objection*) respingere, rifiutare; (: *doubts*) scacciare.

waveband ['weɪvbænd] *n* gamma di lunghezze d'onda.

wavelength ['weɪvlɛŋθ] *n* lunghezza d'onda.

waver ['weɪvə*] *vi* vacillare; (*voice*) tremolare.

wavy ['weɪvɪ] *adj* ondulato(a); ondeggiante.

wax [wæks] *n* cera ♦ *vt* dare la cera a; (*car*) lucidare ♦ *vi* (*moon*) crescere.

waxworks ['wækswəːks] *npl* cere *fpl*; museo delle cere.

way [weɪ] *n* via, strada; (*path, access*) passaggio; (*distance*) distanza; (*direction*) parte *f*, direzione *f*; (*manner*) modo, stile *m*; (*habit*) abitudine *f*; (*condition*) condizione *f*; **which** ~? — **this** ~ da che parte *or* in quale direzione? — da questa parte *or* per di qua; **to crawl one's** ~ **to ...** raggiungere ... strisciando; **he lied his** ~ **out of it** se l'è cavata mentendo; **to lose one's** ~ perdere la strada; **on the** ~ (*en route*) per strada; (*expected*) in arrivo; **you pass it on your** ~ **home** ci passi davanti andando a casa; **to be on one's** ~ essere in cammino *or* sulla strada; **to be in the** ~ bloccare il passaggio; (*fig*) essere tra i piedi *or* d'impiccio; **to keep out of sb's** ~ evitare qn; **it's a long** ~ **away** è molto lontano da qui; **the village is rather out of the** ~ il villaggio è abbastanza fuori mano; **to go out of one's** ~ **to do** (*fig*) mettercela tutta *or* fare di tutto per fare; **to be under** ~ (*work, project*) essere in corso; **to make** ~ **(for sb/sth)** far strada (a qn/qc); (*fig*) lasciare il posto *or* far largo (a qn/qc); **to get one's own** ~ fare come si vuole; **put it the right** ~ **up** (*BRIT*) mettilo in piedi dalla parte giusta; **to be the wrong** ~ **round** essere al contrario; **he's in a bad** ~ è ridotto male; **in a** ~ in un certo senso; **in some** ~**s** sotto certi aspetti; **in the** ~ **of** come; **by** ~ **of** (*through*) attraverso; (*as a sort of*) come; "~ **in**" "entrata", "ingresso"; "~ **out**" "uscita"; **the** ~ **back** la via del ritorno; **this** ~ **and that** di qua e di là; **"give** ~"" (*BRIT AUT*) "dare la precedenza"; **no** ~! (*col*) assolutamente no!

waybill ['weɪbɪl] *n* (*COMM*) bolla di accompagnamento.

waylay [weɪ'leɪ] *vt irreg* tendere un agguato a; attendere al passaggio; (*fig*): **I got waylaid** ho avuto un contrattempo.

wayside ['weɪsaɪd] *n* bordo della strada; **to fall by the** ~ (*fig*) perdersi lungo la strada.

way station *n* (*US RAIL*) stazione *f* secondaria; (*fig*) tappa.

wayward ['weɪwəd] *adj* capriccioso(a); testardo(a).

WC *n abbr* (*BRIT*: = *water closet*) W.C. *m inv*, gabinetto.

WCC *n abbr* (= *World Council of Churches*) Consiglio Ecumenico delle Chiese.

we [wiː] *pl pron* noi; **here** ~ **are** eccoci.

weak [wiːk] *adj* debole; (*health*) precario(a); (*beam etc*) fragile; (*tea, coffee*) leggero(a); **to grow** ~(**er**) indebolirsi.

weaken ['wiːkən] *vi* indebolirsi ♦ *vt* indebolire.

weak-kneed ['wiːk'niːd] *adj* (*fig*) debole, codardo(a).

weakling ['wiːklɪŋ] *n* smidollato/a; debole *m/f*.

weakly ['wiːklɪ] *adj* deboluccio(a), gracile ♦ *adv* debolmente.

weakness ['wiːknɪs] *n* debolezza; (*fault*) punto debole, difetto.

wealth [wɛlθ] *n* (*money, resources*) ricchezza, richezze *fpl*; (*of details*) abbondanza, profusione *f*.

wealth tax *n* imposta sul patrimonio.

wealthy ['wɛlθɪ] *adj* ricco(a).

wean [wiːn] *vt* svezzare.

weapon ['wɛpən] *n* arma.

wear [wɛə*] *n* (*use*) uso; (*deterioration through use*) logorio, usura; (*clothing*): **sports/baby** ~ abbigliamento sportivo/ per neonati ♦ *vb* (*pt* **wore**, *pp* **worn** [wɔː*, wɔːn]) *vt* (*clothes*) portare; mettersi; (*look, smile, beard etc*) avere; (*damage: through use*) consumare ♦ *vi* (*last*) durare; (*rub etc through*) consumarsi; ~ **and tear** usura, consumo; **town/evening** ~ abiti *mpl* or tenuta da città/sera; **to** ~ **a hole in sth** bucare qc a furia di usarlo.

▶**wear away** *vt* consumare; erodere ♦ *vi* consumarsi; essere eroso(a).

▶**wear down** *vt* consumare; (*strength*) esaurire.

▶**wear off** *vi* sparire lentamente.

▶**wear on** *vi* passare.

▶**wear out** *vt* consumare; (*person, strength*) esaurire.

wearable ['wɛərəbl] *adj* indossabile.

wearily ['wɪərɪlɪ] *adv* stancamente.

weariness ['wɪərɪnɪs] *n* stanchezza.

wearisome ['wɪərɪsəm] *adj* (*tiring*) estenuante; (*boring*) noioso(a).

weary ['wɪərɪ] *adj* stanco(a); (*tiring*) faticoso(a) ♦ *vt* stancare ♦ *vi*: **to** ~ **of** stancarsi di.

weasel ['wiːzl] *n* (*ZOOL*) donnola.

weather ['wɛðə*] *n* tempo ♦ *vt* (*wood*) stagionare; (*storm, crisis*) superare; **what's the** ~ **like?** che tempo fa?; **under the** ~ (*fig: ill*) poco bene.

weather-beaten ['wɛðəbiːtn] *adj* (*person*) segnato(a) dalle intemperie; (*building*) logorato(a) dalle intemperie.

weather forecast *n* previsioni *fpl* del tempo, bollettino meteorologico.

weatherman ['wɛðəmæn] *n* meteorologo.

weatherproof ['wɛðəpruːf] *adj* (*garment*) impermeabile.

weather report *n* bollettino meteorologico.

weather vane *n* = **weather cock.**

weave, *pt* **wove,** *pp* **woven** [wiːv, wəuv, 'wəuvn] *vt* (*cloth*) tessere; (*basket*) intrecciare ♦ *vi* (*fig: pt, pp* ~**d**: *move in and out*) zigzagare.

weaver ['wiːvə*] *n* tessitore/trice.

weaving ['wiːvɪŋ] *n* tessitura.

web [wɛb] *n* (*of spider*) ragnatela; (*on foot*) palma; (*fabric, also fig*) tessuto.

webbed [wɛbd] *adj* (*foot*) palmato(a).

webbing ['wɛbɪŋ] *n* (*on chair*) cinghie *fpl*.

wed [wɛd] *vt* (*pt, pp* **wedded**) sposare ♦ *n*: **the newly-**~**s** gli sposi novelli.

Wed. *abbr* (= *Wednesday*) mer.

we'd [wiːd] = **we had; we would.**

wedded ['wɛdɪd] *pt, pp of* **wed.**

wedding ['wɛdɪŋ] *n* matrimonio; **silver/ golden** ~ nozze *fpl* d'argento/d'oro.

wedding anniversary *n* anniversario di matrimonio.

wedding day *n* giorno delle nozze *or* del matrimonio.

wedding dress *n* abito nuziale.

wedding present *n* regalo di nozze.

wedding ring *n* fede *f*.

wedge [wɛdʒ] *n* (*of wood etc*) cuneo; (*under door etc*) zeppa; (*of cake*) spicchio, fetta ♦ *vt* mettere una zeppa sotto (*or* in); **to** ~ **a door open** tenere aperta una porta con un fermo.

wedge-heeled shoes ['wɛdʒhiːld-] *npl* scarpe *fpl* con tacco a zeppa.

wedlock ['wɛdlɔk] *n* vincolo matrimoniale.

Wednesday ['wɛdnzdɪ] *n* mercoledì *m inv*; *for phrases see also* **Tuesday.**

wee [wiː] *adj* (*Scottish*) piccolo(a).

weed [wiːd] *n* erbaccia ♦ *vt* diserbare.

▶**weed out** *vt* fare lo spoglio di.

weed-killer ['wiːdkɪlə*] *n* diserbante *m*.

weedy ['wiːdɪ] *adj* (*man*) allampanato.

week [wiːk] *n* settimana; **once/twice a** ~ una volta/due volte alla settimana; **in 2** ~**s' time** fra 2 settimane, fra 15 giorni; **Tuesday** ~, **a** ~ **on Tuesday** martedì a otto.

weekday ['wiːkdeɪ] *n* giorno feriale; (*COMM*) giornata lavorativa; **on** ~**s** durante la settimana.

weekend [wiːk'ɛnd] *n* fine settimana *m or f inv*, weekend *m inv*.

weekend case *n* borsa da viaggio.

weekly ['wiːklɪ] *adv* ogni settimana, settimanalmente ♦ *adj, n* settimanale (*m*).

weep, *pt, pp* **wept** [wiːp, wɛpt] *vi* (*person*) piangere; (*MED: wound etc*) essudare.

weeping willow ['wiːpɪŋ-] *n* salice *m* piangente.

weepy ['wi:pɪ] *n* (*col*) film *m inv or* storia strappalacrime.

weft [wɛft] *n* (*TEXTILES*) trama.

weigh [weɪ] *vt, vi* pesare; **to ~ anchor** salpare *or* levare l'ancora; **to ~ the pros and cons** valutare i pro e i contro.

▶**weigh down** *vt* (*branch*) piegare; (*fig:* *with worry*) opprimere, caricare.

▶**weigh out** *vt* (*goods*) pesare.

▶**weigh up** *vt* valutare.

weighbridge ['weɪbrɪdʒ] *n* bascula.

weighing machine ['weɪɪŋ-] *n* pesa.

weight [weɪt] *n* peso; **sold by ~** venduto(a) a peso; **~s and measures** pesi e misure; **to put on/lose ~** ingrassare/dimagrire.

weighting ['weɪtɪŋ] *n:* **~ allowance** indennità *f inv* speciale (*per carovita etc*).

weightlessness ['weɪtlɪsnɪs] *n* mancanza di peso.

weightlifter ['weɪtlɪftə*] *n* pesista *m*.

weight training *n:* **to do ~** allenarsi con i pesi.

weighty ['weɪtɪ] *adj* pesante; (*fig*) importante, grave.

weir [wɪə*] *n* diga.

weird [wɪəd] *adj* strano(a), bizzarro(a); (*eerie*) soprannaturale.

weirdo ['wɪədəu] *n* (*col*) tipo/a allucinante.

welcome ['wɛlkəm] *adj* benvenuto(a) ♦ *n* accoglienza, benvenuto ♦ *vt* accogliere cordialmente; (*also:* **bid ~**) dare il benvenuto a; (*be glad of*) rallegrarsi di; **to be ~** essere il(la) benvenuto(a); **to make sb ~** accogliere bene qn; **you're ~** (*after thanks*) prego; **you're ~ to try** provi pure.

welcoming ['wɛlkəmɪŋ] *adj* accogliente.

weld [wɛld] *n* saldatura ♦ *vt* saldare.

welder ['wɛldə*] *n* (*person*) saldatore *m*.

welding ['wɛldɪŋ] *n* saldatura (autogena).

welfare ['wɛlfɛə*] *n* benessere *m*.

welfare state *n* stato assistenziale.

welfare work *n* assistenza sociale.

well [wɛl] *n* pozzo ♦ *adv* bene ♦ *adj:* **to be ~** (*person*) stare bene ♦ *excl* allora!; ma!; ebbene!; **~ done!** bravo(a)!; **get ~ soon!** guarisci presto!; **to do ~ in sth** riuscire in qc; **to be doing ~** stare bene; **to think ~ of sb** avere una buona opinione di qn; **I don't feel ~** non mi sento bene; **as ~** (*in addition*) anche; **X as ~ as Y** sia X che Y; **he did as ~ as he could** ha fatto come meglio poteva; **you might as ~ tell me** potresti anche dirmelo; **it would be as ~ to ask** sarebbe bene chiedere; **~, as I was saying** ... dunque, come stavo dicendo ....

▶**well up** *vi* (*tears, emotions*) sgorgare.

we'll [wi:l] = **we will; we shall**.

well-behaved ['wɛlbɪ'heɪvd] *adj* ubbidiente.

well-being ['wɛl'bi:ɪŋ] *n* benessere *m*.

well-bred ['wɛl'brɛd] *adj* educato(a), beneducato(a).

well-built ['wɛl'bɪlt] *adj* (*person*) ben fatto(a).

well-chosen ['wɛl'tʃəuzn] *adj* (*remarks, words*) ben scelto(a), appropriato(a).

well-developed ['wɛldɪ'vɛləpt] *adj* sviluppato(a).

well-disposed ['wɛldɪs'pəuzd] *adj:* **~ to(wards)** bendisposto(a) verso.

well-dressed ['wɛl'drɛst] *adj* ben vestito(a), vestito(a) bene.

well-earned ['wɛl'ə:nd] *adj* (*rest*) meritato(a).

well-groomed ['wɛl'gru:md] *adj* curato(a), azzimato(a).

well-heeled ['wɛl'hi:ld] *adj* (*col: wealthy*) agiato(a), facoltoso(a).

well-informed ['wɛlin'fɔ:md] *adj* ben informato(a).

Wellington ['wɛlɪŋtən] *n* Wellington *f*.

wellingtons ['wɛlɪŋtənz] *npl* (*also:* **wellington boots**) stivali *mpl* di gomma.

well-kept ['wɛl'kɛpt] *adj* (*house, grounds, secret*) ben tenuto(a); (*hair, hands*) curato(a).

well-known ['wɛl'nəun] *adj* noto(a), famoso(a).

well-mannered ['wɛl'mænəd] *adj* ben educato(a).

well-meaning ['wɛl'mi:nɪŋ] *adj* ben intenzionato(a).

well-nigh ['wɛl'naɪ] *adv:* **~ impossible** quasi impossibile.

well-off ['wɛl'ɔf] *adj* benestante, danaroso(a).

well-read ['wɛl'rɛd] *adj* colto(a).

well-spoken ['wɛl'spəukn] *adj* che parla bene.

well-stocked ['wɛl'stɔkt] *adj* (*shop, larder*) ben fornito(a).

well-timed ['wɛl'taɪmd] *adj* opportuno(a).

well-to-do ['wɛltə'du:] *adj* abbiente, benestante.

well-wisher ['wɛlwɪʃə*] *n* ammiratore/ trice; **letters from ~s** lettere *fpl* di incoraggiamento.

well-woman clinic ['wɛlwumən-] *n* ≈ consultorio (familiare).

Welsh [wɛlʃ] *adj* gallese ♦ *n* (*LING*) gallese *m*; **the ~** *npl* i gallesi.

Welshman, Welshwoman ['wɛlʃmən, -wumən] *n* gallese *m/f*.

Welsh rarebit *n* crostino al formaggio.

welter ['wɛltə*] *n* massa, mucchio.

went [wɛnt] *pt of* **go**.

wept [wɛpt] *pt, pp of* **weep**.

were [wə:*] *pt of* **be.**

we're [wɪə*] = **we are.**

weren't [wə:nt] = **were not.**

werewolf, *pl* **-wolves** ['wɪəwulf, -wulvz] *n* licantropo, lupo mannaro (*col*).

west [wɛst] *n* ovest *m*, occidente *m*, ponente *m* ♦ *adj* (a) ovest *inv*, occidentale ♦ *adv* verso ovest; **the W~** l'Occidente.

westbound ['wɛstbaund] *adj* (*traffic*) diretto(a) a ovest; (*carriageway*) ovest *inv*.

West Country *n*: **the ~** il sud-ovest dell'Inghilterra.

westerly ['wɛstəlɪ] *adj* (*wind*) occidentale, da ovest.

western ['wɛstən] *adj* occidentale, dell'ovest ♦ *n* (*CINE*) western *m inv*.

westerner ['wɛstənə*] *n* occidentale *m/f*.

westernized ['wɛstənaɪzd] *adj* occidentalizzato(a).

West German *adj*, *n* tedesco(a) occidentale.

West Germany *n* Germania Occidentale.

West Indian *adj* delle Indie Occidentali ♦ *n* abitante *m/f* (*or* originario/a) delle Indie Occidentali.

West Indies [-'ɪndɪz] *npl*: **the ~** le Indie Occidentali.

Westminster ['wɛstmɪnstə*] *n* il parlamento (britannico).

westward(s) ['wɛstwəd(z)] *adv* verso ovest.

wet [wɛt] *adj* umido(a), bagnato(a); (*soaked*) fradicio(a); (*rainy*) piovoso(a) ♦ *vt*: **to ~ one's pants** *or* **o.s.** farsi la pipì addosso; **to get ~** bagnarsi; "**~ paint**" "vernice fresca".

wet blanket *n* (*fig*) guastafeste *m/f inv*.

wetness ['wɛtnɪs] *n* umidità.

wet suit *n* tuta da sub.

we've [wi:v] = **we have.**

whack [wæk] *vt* picchiare, battere.

whacked [wækt] *adj* (*col*: *tired*) sfinito(a), a pezzi.

whale [weɪl] *n* (*ZOOL*) balena.

whaler ['weɪlə*] *n* (*ship*) baleniera.

whaling ['weɪlɪŋ] *n* caccia alla balena.

wharf, *pl* **wharves** [wɔ:f, wɔ:vz] *n* banchina.

=========== **KEYWORD**

what [wɔt] *adj* **1** (*in direct/indirect questions*) che; quale; **~ size is it?** che taglia è?; **~ colour is it?** di che colore è?; **~ books do you want?** quali *or* che libri vuole?; **for ~ reason?** per quale motivo?
2 (*in exclamations*) che; **~ a mess!** che disordine!
♦ *pron* **1** (*interrogative*) che cosa, cosa, che;

~'s in there? cosa c'è lì dentro?; **~ is his address?** qual è il suo indirizzo?; **~ will it cost?** quanto costerà?; **~ are you doing?** che *or* (che) cosa fai?; **~ are you talking about?** di che cosa parli?; **~'s happening?** che *or* (che) cosa succede?; **~ is it called?** come si chiama?; **~ about me?** e io?; **~ about doing ...?** e se facessimo ...?
2 (*relative*) ciò che, quello che; **I saw ~ you did** ho visto quello che hai fatto; **I saw ~ was on the table** ho visto cosa c'era sul tavolo; **~ I want is a cup of tea** ciò che voglio adesso è una tazza di tè
3 (*indirect use*) (che) cosa; **he asked me ~ she had said** mi ha chiesto che cosa avesse detto; **tell me ~ you're thinking about** dimmi a cosa stai pensando; **I don't know ~ to do** non so cosa fare
♦ *excl* (*disbelieving*) cosa!, come!

whatever [wɔt'ɛvə*] *adj*: **~ book** qualunque *or* qualsiasi libro + *sub*
♦ *pron*: **do ~ is necessary/you want** faccia qualunque *or* qualsiasi cosa sia necessaria/lei voglia; **~ happens** qualunque cosa accada; **no reason ~** *or* **whatsoever** nessuna ragione affatto *or* al mondo; **~ it costs** costi quello che costi.

whatsoever [wɔtsəu'ɛvə*] *adj*, *pron* = **whatever.**

wheat [wi:t] *n* grano, frumento.

wheatgerm ['wi:tdʒə:m] *n* germe *m* di grano.

wheatmeal ['wi:tmi:l] *n* farina integrale di frumento.

wheedle ['wi:dl] *vt*: **to ~ sb into doing sth** convincere qn a fare qc (con lusinghe); **to ~ sth out of sb** ottenere qc da qn (con lusinghe).

wheel [wi:l] *n* ruota; (*AUT*: *also*: **steering ~**) volante *m*; (*NAUT*) (ruota del) timone *m* ♦ *vt* spingere ♦ *vi* (*also*: **~ round**) girare.

wheelbarrow ['wi:lbærəu] *n* carriola.

wheelbase ['wi:lbeɪs] *n* interasse *m*.

wheelchair ['wi:ltʃeə*] *n* sedia a rotelle.

wheel clamp *n* (*AUT*) morsetto *m* bloccaruota *inv*.

wheeler-dealer ['wi:lə'di:lə*] *n* trafficone *m*, maneggione *m*.

wheelie-bin ['wi:lɪbɪn] *n* (*BRIT*) bidone *m* (della spazzatura) a rotelle.

wheeling ['wi:lɪŋ] *n*: **~ and dealing** maneggi *mpl*.

wheeze [wi:z] *n* respiro affannoso ♦ *vi* ansimare.

wheezy ['wi:zɪ] *adj* (*person*) che respira con affanno; (*breath*) sibilante.

======================= *KEYWORD*

when [wɛn] *adv* quando; ~ **did it happen?** quando è successo?
♦ *conj* **1** (*at, during, after the time that*) quando; **she was reading** ~ **I came in** quando sono entrato lei leggeva; **that was** ~ **I needed you** era allora che avevo bisogno di te
2 (*on, at which*): **on the day** ~ **I met him** il giorno in cui l'ho incontrato; **one day** ~ **it was raining** un giorno che pioveva
3 (*whereas*) quando, mentre; **you said I was wrong** ~ **in fact I was right** mi hai detto che avevo torto, quando in realtà avevo ragione.

whenever [wɛn'ɛvə*] *adv* quando mai ♦ *conj* quando; (*every time that*) ogni volta che; **I go** ~ **I can** ci vado ogni volta che posso.
where [wɛə*] *adv, conj* dove; **this is** ~ è qui che; ~ **are you from?** di dov'è?; ~ **possible** quando è possibile, se possibile.
whereabouts ['wɛərəbauts] *adv* dove ♦ *n*: **sb's** ~ luogo dove qn si trova.
whereas [wɛər'æz] *conj* mentre.
whereby [wɛə'baɪ] *adv* (*formal*) per cui.
whereupon [wɛərə'pɔn] *adv* al che.
wherever [wɛər'ɛvə*] *adv* dove mai ♦ *conj* dovunque + *sub*; **sit** ~ **you like** si sieda dove vuole.
wherewithal ['wɛəwɪðɔːl] *n*: **the** ~ **(to do sth)** i mezzi (per fare qc).
whet [wɛt] *vt* (*tool*) affilare; (*appetite etc*) stimolare.
whether ['wɛðə*] *conj* se; **I don't know** ~ **to accept or not** non so se accettare o no; **it's doubtful** ~ è poco probabile che; ~ **you go or not** che lei vada o no.
whey [weɪ] *n* siero.

======================= *KEYWORD*

which [wɪtʃ] *adj* **1** (*interrogative: direct, indirect*) quale; ~ **picture do you want?** quale quadro vuole?; ~ **one?** quale?; ~ **one of you did it?** chi di voi lo ha fatto?; **tell me** ~ **one you want** mi dica quale vuole
2: **in** ~ **case** nel qual caso; **by** ~ **time** e a quel punto
♦ *pron* **1** (*interrogative*) quale; ~ **(of these) are yours?** quali di questi sono suoi?; ~ **of you are coming?** chi di voi viene?
2 (*relative*) che; (*: indirect*) cui, il (la) quale; **the apple** ~ **you ate**/~ **is on the table** la mela che hai mangiato/che è sul tavolo; **the chair on** ~ **you are sitting** la sedia sulla quale *or* su cui sei seduto; **the**

book of ~ **we were speaking** il libro del quale stavamo parlando; **he said he knew,** ~ **is true** ha detto che lo sapeva, il che è vero; **I don't mind** ~ non mi importa quale; **after** ~ dopo di che.

whichever [wɪtʃ'ɛvə*] *adj*: **take** ~ **book you prefer** prenda qualsiasi libro che preferisce; ~ **book you take** qualsiasi libro prenda; ~ **way you** ... in qualunque modo lei ... + *sub*.
whiff [wɪf] *n* odore *m*; **to catch a** ~ **of sth** sentire l'odore di qc.
while [waɪl] *n* momento ♦ *conj* mentre; (*as long as*) finché; (*although*) sebbene + *sub*; **for a** ~ per un po'; **in a** ~ tra poco; **all the** ~ tutto il tempo; **we'll make it worth your** ~ faremo in modo che le valga la pena.
▶**while away** *vt* (*time*) far passare.
whilst [waɪlst] *conj* = **while**.
whim [wɪm] *n* capriccio.
whimper ['wɪmpə*] *n* piagnucolio ♦ *vi* piagnucolare.
whimsical ['wɪmzɪkl] *adj* (*person*) capriccioso(a); (*look*) strano(a).
whine [waɪn] *n* gemito ♦ *vi* gemere; uggiolare; piagnucolare.
whip [wɪp] *n* frusta; (*for riding*) frustino; (*POL: person*) capogruppo ♦ *vt* frustare; (*CULIN: cream etc*) sbattere; (*snatch*) sollevare (*or* estrarre) bruscamente.
▶**whip up** *vt* (*cream*) montare, sbattere; (*col: meal*) improvvisare; (*: stir up: support, feeling*) suscitare, stimolare.

Nel Parlamento britannico i **whip** *sono parlamentari incaricati di mantenere la disciplina tra i deputati del loro partito durante le votazioni e di verificare la loro presenza in aula.*

whiplash ['wɪplæʃ] *n* (*MED: also:* ~ **injury**) colpo di frusta.
whipped cream ['wɪpt-] *n* panna montata.
whipping boy ['wɪpɪŋ-] *n* (*fig*) capro espiatorio.
whip-round ['wɪpraund] *n* (*BRIT*) colletta.
whirl [wəːl] *n* turbine *m* ♦ *vt* (*far*) girare rapidamente; (*far*) turbinare ♦ *vi* turbinare; (*dancers*) volteggiare; (*leaves, dust*) sollevarsi in un vortice.
whirlpool ['wəːlpuːl] *n* mulinello.
whirlwind ['wəːlwɪnd] *n* turbine *m*.
whirr [wəː*] *vi* ronzare.
whisk [wɪsk] *n* (*CULIN*) frusta; frullino ♦ *vt* sbattere, frullare; **to** ~ **sb away** *or* **off** portar via qn a tutta velocità.
whiskers ['wɪskəz] *npl* (*of animal*) baffi *mpl*;

(*of man*) favoriti *mpl*.
whisky, (*Irish, US*) **whiskey** ['wiski] *n*
whisky *m inv*.
whisper ['wispə*] *n* bisbiglio, sussurro;
(*rumour*) voce *f* ♦ *vt, vi* bisbigliare,
sussurrare; **to ~ sth to sb** bisbigliare qc
a qn.
whispering ['wispəriŋ] *n* bisbiglio.
whist [wist] *n* (*BRIT*) whist *m*.
whistle ['wisl] *n* (*sound*) fischio; (*object*)
fischietto ♦ *vi, vt* fischiare; **to ~ a tune**
fischiettare un motivetto.
whistle-stop ['wislstɔp] *adj:* **~ tour** (*POL,
fig*) rapido giro.
Whit [wit] *n* Pentecoste *f*.
white [wait] *adj* bianco(a); (*with fear*)
pallido(a) ♦ *n* bianco; (*person*) bianco/a;
to turn *or* **go ~** (*person*) sbiancare; (*hair*)
diventare bianco; **the ~s** (*washing*)
i capi bianchi; **tennis ~s** completo
da tennis.
whitebait ['waitbeit] *n* bianchetti
mpl.
white-collar worker ['waitkɔlə-] *n*
impiegato/a.
white elephant *n* (*fig*) oggetto (*or*
progetto) costoso ma inutile.
white goods *npl* (*appliances*)
elettrodomestici *mpl*; (*linens*) biancheria
per la casa.
white-hot [wait'hɔt] *adj* (*metal*)
incandescente.
White House *n:* **the ~** la Casa Bianca.

La **White House** *è la residenza ufficiale del
presidente degli Stati Uniti e ha sede a
Washington DC. Spesso il termine viene
usato per indicare l'esecutivo del governo
statunitense.*

---

white lie *n* bugia pietosa.
whiteness ['waitnis] *n* bianchezza.
white noise *n* rumore *m* bianco.
white paper *n* (*POL*) libro bianco.
whitewash ['waitwɔʃ] *n* (*paint*) bianco di
calce ♦ *vt* imbiancare; (*fig*)
coprire.
whiting ['waitiŋ] *n* (*pl inv*) merlango.
Whit Monday *n* lunedì *m inv* di
Pentecoste.
Whitsun ['witsn] *n* Pentecoste *f*.
whittle ['witl] *vt:* **to ~ away, ~ down**
ridurre, tagliare.
whizz [wiz] *vi* passare sfrecciando.
whizz kid *n* (*col*) prodigio.
WHO *n abbr* (= *World Health Organization*)
O.M.S. *f* (= *Organizzazione mondiale della
sanità*).

═══════════════ KEYWORD

who [hu:] *pron* **1** (*interrogative*) chi; **~ is it?,
~'s there?** chi è?
2 (*relative*) che; **the man ~ spoke to me**
l'uomo che ha parlato con me; **those ~
can swim** quelli che sanno nuotare.

---

whodunit [hu:'dʌnit] *n* (*col*) giallo.
whoever [hu:'ɛvə*] *pron:* **~ finds it**
chiunque lo trovi; **ask ~ you like** lo
chieda a chiunque vuole; **~ told you that?**
chi mai gliel'ha detto?
whole [həul] *adj* (*complete*) tutto(a),
completo(a); (*not broken*) intero(a),
intatto(a) ♦ *n* (*total*) totale *m*; (*sth not
broken*) tutto; **the ~ lot (of it)** tutto; **the ~
lot (of them)** tutti; **the ~ of the time** tutto
il tempo; **the ~ of the town** la città
intera; **on the ~, as a ~** nel complesso,
nell'insieme; **~ villages were destroyed**
interi paesi furono distrutti.
wholehearted [həul'hɑ:tid] *adj*
sincero(a).
wholemeal ['həulmi:l] *adj* (*BRIT: flour, bread*)
integrale.
whole note *n* (*US*) semibreve *f*.
wholesale ['həulseil] *n* commercio *or*
vendita all'ingrosso ♦ *adj* all'ingrosso;
(*destruction*) totale.
wholesaler ['həulseilə*] *n* grossista
m/f.
wholesome ['həulsəm] *adj* sano(a);
(*climate*) salubre.
wholewheat ['həulwi:t] *adj* = **wholemeal.**
wholly ['həuli] *adv* completamente, del
tutto.

═══════════════ KEYWORD

whom [hu:m] *pron* **1** (*interrogative*) chi; **~
did you see?** chi hai visto?; **to ~ did you
give it?** a chi lo hai dato?
2 (*relative*) che, *prep* + il (la) quale; **the
man ~ I saw** l'uomo che ho visto; **the
man to ~ I spoke** l'uomo al *or* con il quale
ho parlato; **those to ~ I spoke** le persone
alle *or* con le quali ho parlato.

---

whooping cough ['hu:piŋ-] *n* pertosse
f.
whoops [wu:ps] *excl:* **~-a-daisy!** ops!
whoosh [wuʃ] *n:* **it came out with a ~**
(*sauce etc*) è uscito di getto; (*air*) è uscito
con un sibilo.
whopper ['wɔpə*] *n* (*col: lie*) balla; (: *large
thing*) cosa enorme.
whopping ['wɔpiŋ] *adj* (*col: big*) enorme.
whore [hɔ:*] *n* (*pej*) puttana.

════════════════════ *KEYWORD*

whose [huːz] *adj* **1** (*possessive: interrogative*)
di chi; ~ **book is this?**, ~ **is this book?** di
chi è questo libro?; ~ **daughter are you?**
di chi sei figlia?; ~ **pencil have you
taken?** di chi è la matita che hai preso?
2 (*possessive: relative*): **the man ~ son
you rescued** l'uomo il cui figlio hai
salvato *or* a cui hai salvato il figlio; **the
girl ~ sister you were speaking to** la
ragazza alla cui sorella stavi parlando
♦ *pron* di chi; ~ **is this?** di chi è questo?; **I
know ~ it is** so di chi è.

Who's Who ['huːz'huː] *n elenco di
personalità.*

why [waɪ] *adv, conj* perché ♦ *excl* (*surprise*)
ma guarda un po'!; (*remonstrating*) ma
(via)!; (*explaining*) ebbene!; ~ **not?**
perché no?; ~ **not do it now?** perché non
farlo adesso?; **the reason ~** il motivo per
cui.

whyever [waɪ'ɛvə*] *adv* perché mai.

WI *n abbr* (*BRIT*: = *Women's Institute*) circolo
femminile ♦ *abbr* (*GEO*) = **West Indies**;
(*US*) = **Wisconsin**.

wick [wɪk] *n* lucignolo, stoppino.

wicked ['wɪkɪd] *adj* cattivo(a), malvagio(a);
(*mischievous*) malizioso(a); (*terrible: prices,
weather*) terribile.

wicker ['wɪkə*] *n* vimine *m*; (*also*: ~**work**)
articoli *mpl* di vimini.

wicket ['wɪkɪt] *n* (*CRICKET*) porta; area tra
le due porte.

wicket keeper *n* (*CRICKET*) ≈ portiere *m*.

wide [waɪd] *adj* largo(a); (*region, knowledge*)
vasto(a); (*choice*) ampio(a) ♦ *adv*: **to open
~** spalancare; **to shoot ~** tirare a vuoto
or fuori bersaglio; **it is 3 metres ~** è largo
3 metri.

wide-angle lens ['waɪdæŋgl-] *n*
grandangolare *m*.

wide-awake [waɪdə'weɪk] *adj*
completamente sveglio(a).

wide-eyed [waɪd'aɪd] *adj* con gli occhi
spalancati.

widely ['waɪdlɪ] *adv* (*different*) molto,
completamente; (*believed*) generalmente;
~ **spaced** molto distanziati(e); **to be ~
read** (*author*) essere molto letto; (*reader*)
essere molto colto.

widen ['waɪdn] *vt* allargare, ampliare.

wideness ['waɪdnɪs] *n* larghezza; vastità;
ampiezza.

wide open *adj* spalancato(a).

wide-ranging [waɪd'reɪndʒɪŋ] *adj* (*survey,
report*) vasto(a); (*interests*) svariato(a).

widespread ['waɪdsprɛd] *adj* (*belief etc*)
molto *or* assai diffuso(a).

widow ['wɪdəu] *n* vedova.

widowed ['wɪdəud] *adj* (che è rimasto(a))
vedovo(a).

widower ['wɪdəuə*] *n* vedovo.

width [wɪdθ] *n* larghezza; **it's 7 metres in ~**
è largo 7 metri.

widthways ['wɪdθweɪz] *adv*
trasversalmente.

wield [wiːld] *vt* (*sword*) maneggiare;
(*power*) esercitare.

wife, *pl* **wives** [waɪf, waɪvz] *n* moglie *f*.

wig [wɪg] *n* parrucca.

wigging ['wɪgɪŋ] *n* (*BRIT col*) lavata di capo.

wiggle ['wɪgl] *vt* dimenare, agitare ♦ *vi*
(*loose screw etc*) traballare; (*worm*)
torcersi.

wiggly ['wɪglɪ] *adj* (*line*) ondulato(a),
sinuoso(a).

wild [waɪld] *adj* (*animal, plant*) selvatico(a);
(*countryside, appearance*) selvaggio(a);
(*sea*) tempestoso(a); (*idea, life*) folle; (*col:
angry*) arrabbiato(a), furibondo(a);
(*enthusiastic*): **to be ~ about** andar
pazzo(a) per ♦ *n*: **the ~** la natura; ~**s** *npl*
regione *f* selvaggia.

wild card *n* (*COMPUT*) wild card *m inv*.

wildcat ['waɪldkæt] *n* gatto(a) selvatico(a).

wildcat strike *n* ≈ sciopero selvaggio.

wilderness ['wɪldənɪs] *n* deserto.

wildfire ['waɪldfaɪə*] *n*: **to spread like ~**
propagarsi rapidamente.

wild-goose chase [waɪld'guːs-] *n* (*fig*) pista
falsa.

wildlife ['waɪldlaɪf] *n* natura.

wildly ['waɪldlɪ] *adv* (*applaud*)
freneticamente; (*hit, guess*) a casaccio;
(*happy*) follemente.

wiles [waɪlz] *npl* astuzie *fpl*.

wilful, (*US*) **willful** ['wɪlful] *adj* (*person*)
testardo(a); ostinato(a); (*action*)
intenzionale; (*crime*) premeditato(a).

════════════════════ *KEYWORD*

will [wɪl] *aux vb* **1** (*forming future tense*): **I ~
finish it tomorrow** lo finirò domani; **I ~
have finished it by tomorrow** lo finirò
entro domani; ~ **you do it? – yes I ~/no I
won't** lo farai? – sì (lo farò)/no (non lo
farò); **the car won't start** la macchina non
parte
2 (*in conjectures, predictions*): **he ~** *or* **he'll
be there by now** dovrebbe essere
arrivato a quest'ora; **that ~ be the
postman** sarà il postino
3 (*in commands, requests, offers*): ~ **you be
quiet!** vuoi stare zitto?; ~ **you sit down?**

(*politely*) prego, si accomodi; (*angrily*) vuoi metterti seduto?; ~ **you come?** vieni anche tu?; ~ **you help me?** mi aiuti?, mi puoi aiutare?; **you won't lose it,** ~ **you?** non lo perderai, vero?; ~ **you have a cup of tea?** vorrebbe una tazza di tè?; **I won't put up with it!** non lo accetterò!

♦ *vt* (*pt, pp* ~**ed**): **to** ~ **sb to do** pregare tra sé perché qn faccia; **he** ~**ed himself to go on** continuò grazie a un grande sforzo di volontà

♦ *n* **1** (*desire*) volontà; **against sb's** ~ contro la volontà *or* il volere di qn; **to do sth of one's own free** ~ fare qc di propria volontà

2 (*LAW*) testamento; **to make a/one's** ~ fare testamento.

willful ['wɪlful] *adj* (*US*) = **wilful**.

willing ['wɪlɪŋ] *adj* volonteroso(a) ♦ *n*: **to show** ~ dare prova di buona volontà; ~ **to do** disposto(a) a fare.

willingly ['wɪlɪŋlɪ] *adv* volentieri.

willingness ['wɪlɪŋnɪs] *n* buona volontà.

will-o'-the-wisp [wɪləðə'wɪsp] *n* (*also fig*) fuoco fatuo.

willow ['wɪləu] *n* salice *m*.

will power *n* forza di volontà.

willy-nilly ['wɪlɪ'nɪlɪ] *adv* volente o nolente.

wilt [wɪlt] *vi* appassire.

Wilts [wɪlts] *abbr* (*BRIT*) = **Wiltshire**.

wily ['waɪlɪ] *adj* furbo(a).

wimp [wɪmp] *n* (*col*) mezza calzetta.

win [wɪn] *n* (*in sports etc*) vittoria ♦ *vb* (*pt, pp* **won** [wʌn]) *vt* (*battle, prize*) vincere; (*money*) guadagnare; (*popularity*) conquistare; (*contract*) aggiudicarsi ♦ *vi* vincere.

▶**win over,** (*BRIT*) **win round** *vt* convincere.

wince [wɪns] *n* trasalimento, sussulto ♦ *vi* trasalire.

winch [wɪntʃ] *n* verricello, argano.

Winchester disk ['wɪntʃɪstə-] *n* (*COMPUT*) disco Winchester.

wind *n* [wɪnd] vento; (*MED*) flatulenza, ventosità ♦ *vb* [waɪnd] (*pt, pp* **wound** [waund]) *vt* attorcigliare; (*wrap*) avvolgere; (*clock, toy*) caricare; (*take breath away*: [wɪnd]) far restare senza fiato ♦ *vi* (*road, river*) serpeggiare; **the** ~**(s)** (*MUS*) i fiati; **into** *or* **against the** ~ controvento; **to get** ~ **of sth** venire a sapere qc; **to break** ~ scoreggiare (*col*).

▶**wind down** *vt* (*car window*) abbassare; (*fig: production, business*) diminuire.

▶**wind up** *vt* (*clock*) caricare; (*debate*) concludere.

windbreak ['wɪndbreɪk] *n* frangivento.

windcheater ['wɪndtʃiːtə*], (*US*) **windbreaker** ['wɪndbreɪkə*] *n* giacca a vento.

winder ['waɪndə*] *n* (*BRIT: on watch*) corona di carica.

windfall ['wɪndfɔːl] *n* colpo di fortuna.

winding ['waɪndɪŋ] *adj* (*road*) serpeggiante; (*staircase*) a chiocciola.

wind instrument *n* (*MUS*) strumento a fiato.

windmill ['wɪndmɪl] *n* mulino a vento.

window ['wɪndəu] *n* (*gen, COMPUT*) finestra; (*in car, train*) finestrino; (*in shop etc*) vetrina; (*also*: ~ **pane**) vetro.

window box *n* cassetta da fiori.

window cleaner *n* (*person*) pulitore *m* di finestre.

window dressing *n* allestimento della vetrina.

window envelope *n* busta a finestra.

window frame *n* telaio di finestra.

window ledge *n* davanzale *m*.

window pane *n* vetro.

window-shopping ['wɪndəuʃɔpɪŋ] *n*: **to go** ~ andare a vedere le vetrine.

windowsill ['wɪndəusɪl] *n* davanzale *m*.

windpipe ['wɪndpaɪp] *n* trachea.

wind power *n* energia eolica.

windscreen ['wɪndskriːn], (*US*) **windshield** ['wɪndʃiːld] *n* parabrezza *m inv*.

windscreen washer *n* lavacristallo.

windscreen wiper *n* tergicristallo.

windshield ['wɪndʃiːld] *n* (*US*) = **windscreen**.

windsurfing ['wɪndsəːfɪŋ] *n* windsurf *m inv*.

windswept ['wɪndswɛpt] *adj* spazzato(a) dal vento.

wind tunnel *n* galleria aerodinamica *or* del vento.

windy ['wɪndɪ] *adj* ventoso(a); **it's** ~ c'è vento.

wine [waɪn] *n* vino ♦ *vt*: **to** ~ **and dine sb** offrire un ottimo pranzo a qn.

wine bar *n* enoteca.

wine cellar *n* cantina.

wine glass *n* bicchiere *m* da vino.

wine list *n* lista dei vini.

wine merchant *n* commerciante *m* di vino.

wine tasting *n* degustazione *f* dei vini.

wine waiter *n* sommelier *m inv*.

wing [wɪŋ] *n* ala; ~**s** *npl* (*THEAT*) quinte *fpl*.

winger ['wɪŋə*] *n* (*SPORT*) ala.

wing mirror *n* (*BRIT*) specchietto retrovisore esterno.

wing nut *n* galletto.

wingspan ['wɪŋspæn], **wingspread** ['wɪŋsprɛd] *n* apertura alare, apertura d'ali.

wink [wɪŋk] *n* occhiolino, strizzatina d'occhi ♦ *vi* ammiccare, fare l'occhiolino.

winkle ['wɪŋkl] *n* litorina.

winner ['wɪnə*] *n* vincitore/trice.

winning ['wɪnɪŋ] *adj* (*team*) vincente; (*goal*) decisivo(a); (*charming*) affascinante; *see also* **winnings**.

winning post *n* traguardo.

winnings ['wɪnɪŋz] *npl* vincite *fpl*.

winsome ['wɪnsəm] *adj* accattivante.

winter ['wɪntə*] *n* inverno; **in ~** d'inverno, in inverno.

winter sports *npl* sport *mpl* invernali.

wintry ['wɪntrɪ] *adj* invernale.

wipe [waɪp] *n* pulita, passata ♦ *vt* pulire (strofinando); (*dishes*) asciugare; **to give sth a ~** dare una pulita *or* una passata a qc; **to ~ one's nose** soffiarsi il naso.

►**wipe off** *vt* cancellare; (*stains*) togliere strofinando.

►**wipe out** *vt* (*debt*) pagare, liquidare; (*memory*) cancellare; (*destroy*) annientare.

►**wipe up** *vt* asciugare.

wire ['waɪə*] *n* filo; (*ELEC*) filo elettrico; (*TEL*) telegramma *m* ♦ *vt* (*ELEC: house*) fare l'impianto elettrico di; (: *circuit*) installare; (*also:* **~ up**) collegare, allacciare.

wire brush *n* spazzola metallica.

wire cutters [-kʌtəz] *npl* tronchese *m or f*.

wireless ['waɪəlɪs] *n* (*BRIT*) telegrafia senza fili; (*set*) (apparecchio *m*) radio *f inv*.

wire netting *n* rete *f* metallica.

wire service *n* (*US*) = **news agency**.

wire-tapping ['waɪə'tæpɪŋ] *n* intercettazione *f* telefonica.

wiring ['waɪərɪŋ] *n* (*ELEC*) impianto elettrico.

wiry ['waɪərɪ] *adj* magro(a) e nerboruto(a).

Wis(c). *abbr* (*US*) = Wisconsin.

wisdom ['wɪzdəm] *n* saggezza; (*of action*) prudenza.

wisdom tooth *n* dente *m* del giudizio.

wise [waɪz] *adj* saggio(a); (*advice, remark*) prudente; **I'm none the ~r** ne so come prima.

►**wise up** *vi* (*col*): **to ~ up to** divenire più consapevole di.

... wise [waɪz] *suffix*: **time~** per quanto riguarda il tempo, in termini di tempo.

wisecrack ['waɪzkræk] *n* battuta spiritosa.

wish [wɪʃ] *n* (*desire*) desiderio; (*specific desire*) richiesta ♦ *vt* desiderare, volere; **best ~es** (*on birthday etc*) i migliori

auguri; **with best ~es** (*in letter*) cordiali saluti, con i migliori saluti; **give her my best ~es** le faccia i migliori auguri da parte mia; **to ~ sb goodbye** dire arrivederci a qn; **he ~ed me well** mi augurò di riuscire; **to ~ to do/sb to do** desiderare *or* volere fare/che qn faccia; **to ~ for** desiderare; **to ~ sth on sb** rifilare qc a qn.

wishbone ['wɪʃbəun] *n* forcella.

wishful ['wɪʃful] *adj*: **it's ~ thinking** è prendere i desideri per realtà.

wishy-washy ['wɪʃɪ'wɔʃɪ] *adj* insulso(a).

wisp [wɪsp] *n* ciuffo, ciocca; (*of smoke, straw*) filo.

wistful ['wɪstful] *adj* malinconico(a); (*nostalgic*) nostalgico(a).

wit [wɪt] *n* (*gen pl*) intelligenza; presenza di spirito; (*wittiness*) spirito, arguzia; (*person*) bello spirito; **to be at one's ~s' end** (*fig*) non sapere più cosa fare; **to have** *or* **keep one's ~s about one** avere presenza di spirito; **to ~** *adv* cioè.

witch [wɪtʃ] *n* strega.

witchcraft ['wɪtʃkrɑːft] *n* stregoneria.

witch doctor *n* stregone *m*.

witch-hunt ['wɪtʃhʌnt] *n* (*fig*) caccia alle streghe.

═══════════════════════════ *KEYWORD*

with [wɪð, wɪθ] *prep* **1** (*in the company of*) con; **I was ~ him** ero con lui; **we stayed ~ friends** siamo stati da amici; **I'll be ~ you in a minute** vengo subito

2 (*descriptive*) con; **a room ~ a view** una camera con vista (sul mare *or* sulle montagne *etc*); **the man ~ the grey hat/ blue eyes** l'uomo con il cappello grigio/ gli occhi blu

3 (*indicating manner, means, cause*): **~ tears in her eyes** con le lacrime agli occhi; **red ~ anger** rosso(a) dalla rabbia; **to shake ~ fear** tremare di paura; **covered ~ snow** coperto(a) di neve

4: I'm ~ you (*I understand*) la seguo; **I'm not really ~ it today** (*col*) oggi sono un po' fuori.

withdraw [wɪθ'drɔː] *vb* (*irreg*) *vt* ritirare; (*money from bank*) ritirare, prelevare ♦ *vi* ritirarsi; **to ~ into o.s.** chiudersi in se stesso.

withdrawal [wɪθ'drɔːəl] *n* ritiro; prelievo; (*of army*) ritirata; (*MED*) stato di privazione.

withdrawal symptoms *npl* crisi *f* di astinenza.

withdrawn [wɪθ'drɔːn] *pp of* **withdraw** ♦ *adj*

wither – word

distaccato(a).

wither ['wɪðə*] vi appassire.

withered ['wɪðəd] adj appassito(a); (limb) atrofizzato(a).

withhold [wɪθ'həuld] vt irreg (money) trattenere; (permission): **to ~ (from)** rifiutare (a); (information): **to ~ (from)** nascondere (a).

within [wɪð'ɪn] prep all'interno di; (in time, distances) entro ♦ adv all'interno, dentro; **~ sight of** in vista di; **~ a mile of** entro un miglio da; **~ the week** prima della fine della settimana; **~ an hour from now** da qui a un'ora; **to be ~ the law** restare nei limiti della legge.

without [wɪð'aut] prep senza; **to go** or **do ~ sth** fare a meno di qc; **~ anybody knowing** senza che nessuno lo sappia.

withstand [wɪθ'stænd] vt irreg resistere a.

witness ['wɪtnɪs] n (person) testimone m/f ♦ vt (event) essere testimone di; (document) attestare l'autenticità di ♦ vi: **to ~ to sth/having seen sth** testimoniare qc/di aver visto qc; **to bear ~ to sth** testimoniare qc; **~ for the prosecution/ defence** testimone a carico/discarico.

witness box, (US) **witness stand** n banco dei testimoni.

witticism ['wɪtɪsɪzəm] n spiritosaggine f.

witty ['wɪtɪ] adj spiritoso(a).

wives [waɪvz] npl of **wife**.

wizard ['wɪzəd] n mago.

wizened ['wɪznd] adj raggrinzito(a).

wk abbr = **week**.

Wm. abbr = **William**.

WO n abbr see **warrant officer**.

wobble ['wɔbl] vi tremare; (chair) traballare.

wobbly ['wɔblɪ] adj (hand, voice) tremante; (table, chair) traballante; (object about to fall) che oscilla pericolosamente.

woe [wəu] n dolore m; disgrazia.

woeful ['wəuful] adj (sad) triste; (deplorable) deplorevole.

wok [wɔk] n wok m inv (padella concava usata nella cucina cinese).

woke [wəuk] pt of **wake**.

woken ['wəukn] pp of **wake**.

wolf, pl **wolves** [wulf, wulvz] n lupo.

woman, pl **women** ['wumən, 'wɪmɪn] n donna ♦ cpd: **~ doctor** n dottoressa; **~ friend** n amica; **~ teacher** n insegnante f; **women's page** n (PRESS) rubrica femminile.

womanize ['wumənaɪz] vi essere un donnaiolo.

womanly ['wumənlɪ] adj femminile.

womb [wu:m] n (ANAT) utero.

women ['wɪmɪn] npl of **woman**.

Women's (Liberation) Movement n (also: **Women's Lib**) Movimento per la Liberazione della Donna.

won [wʌn] pt, pp of **win**.

wonder ['wʌndə*] n meraviglia ♦ vi: **to ~ whether** domandarsi se; **to ~ at** essere sorpreso(a) di; meravigliarsi di; **to ~ about** domandarsi di; pensare a; **it's no ~ that** c'è poco or non c'è da meravigliarsi che + sub.

wonderful ['wʌndəful] adj meraviglioso(a).

wonderfully ['wʌndəfəlɪ] adv (+ adjective) meravigliosamente; (+ verb) a meraviglia.

wonky ['wɔŋkɪ] adj (BRIT col) traballante.

wont [wəunt] n: **as is his/her ~** com'è solito/a fare.

won't [wəunt] = **will not**.

woo [wu:] vt (woman) fare la corte a.

wood [wud] n legno; (timber) legname m; (forest) bosco ♦ cpd di bosco, silvestre.

wood carving n scultura in legno, intaglio.

wooded ['wudɪd] adj boschivo(a); boscoso(a).

wooden ['wudn] adj di legno; (fig) rigido(a); inespressivo(a).

woodland ['wudlənd] n zona boscosa.

woodpecker ['wudpɛkə*] n picchio.

wood pigeon n colombaccio, palomba.

woodwind ['wudwɪnd] npl (MUS): **the ~** i legni.

woodwork ['wudwə:k] n parti fpl in legno; (craft, subject) falegnameria.

woodworm ['wudwə:m] n tarlo del legno.

woof [wuf] n (of dog) bau bau m ♦ vi abbaiare; **~, ~!** bau bau!

wool [wul] n lana; **to pull the ~ over sb's eyes** (fig) fargliela a qn.

woollen, (US) **woolen** ['wulən] adj di lana ♦ n: **~s** indumenti mpl di lana.

woolly, (US) **wooly** ['wulɪ] adj lanoso(a); (fig: ideas) confuso(a).

woozy ['wu:zɪ] adj (col) stordito(a).

word [wə:d] n parola; (news) notizie fpl ♦ vt esprimere, formulare; **~ for ~** parola per parola, testualmente; **what's the ~ for "pen" in Italian?** come si dice "pen" in italiano?; **to put sth into ~s** esprimere qc a parole; **in other ~s** in altre parole; **to have a ~ with sb** scambiare due parole con qn; **to have ~s with sb** (quarrel with) avere un diverbio con qn; **to break/keep one's ~** non mantenere/mantenere la propria parola; **I'll take your ~ for it** la crederò sulla parola; **to send ~ of** avvisare di; **to leave ~ (with** or **for sb) that ...** lasciare detto (a qn) che ....

wording ['wɔːdɪŋ] *n* formulazione *f*.
word of mouth *n* passaparola *m*; **I learned it by** *or* **through** ~ lo so per sentito dire.
word-perfect ['wɔːd'pəfɪkt] *adj* (*speech etc*) imparato(a) a memoria.
word processing *n* word processing *m*, elaborazione *f* testi.
word processor *n* word processor *m inv*.
wordwrap ['wɔːdræp] *n* (*COMPUT*) ritorno carrello automatico.
wordy ['wɔːdɪ] *adj* verboso(a), prolisso(a).
wore [wɔː*] *pt of* **wear**.
work [wɔːk] *n* lavoro; (*ART, LITERATURE*) opera ♦ *vi* lavorare; (*mechanism, plan etc*) funzionare; (*medicine*) essere efficace ♦ *vt* (*clay, wood etc*) lavorare; (*mine etc*) sfruttare; (*machine*) far funzionare; **to be at** ~ **(on sth)** lavorare (a qc); **to set to** ~, **to start** ~ mettersi all'opera; **to go to** ~ andare al lavoro; **to be out of** ~ essere disoccupato(a); **to** ~ **one's way through a book** riuscire a leggersi tutto un libro; **to** ~ **one's way through college** lavorare per pagarsi gli studi; **to** ~ **hard** lavorare sodo; **to** ~ **loose** allentarsi; *see also* **works**.
▶**work on** *vt fus* lavorare su; (*principle*) basarsi su; **he's** ~**ing on the car** sta facendo dei lavori alla macchina.
▶**work out** *vi* (*plans etc*) riuscire, andare bene; (*SPORT*) allenarsi ♦ *vt* (*problem*) risolvere; (*plan*) elaborare; **it** ~**s out at £100** fa 100 sterline.
workable ['wɔːkəbl] *adj* (*solution*) realizzabile.
workaholic [wɔːkə'hɔlɪk] *n* stacanovista *m/f*.
workbench ['wɔːkbɛntʃ] *n* banco (da lavoro).
worked up *adj*: **to get** ~ andare su tutte le furie; eccitarsi.
worker ['wɔːkə*] *n* lavoratore/trice; (*esp AGR, INDUSTRY*) operaio/a; **office** ~ impiegato/a.
work force *n* forza lavoro.
work-in ['wɔːkɪn] *n* (*BRIT*) sciopero alla rovescia.
working ['wɔːkɪŋ] *adj* (*day*) feriale; (*tools, conditions*) di lavoro; (*clothes*) da lavoro; (*wife*) che lavora; (*partner*) attivo(a); **in** ~ **order** funzionante; ~ **knowledge** conoscenza pratica.
working capital *n* (*COMM*) capitale *m* d'esercizio.
working class *n* classe *f* operaia *or* lavoratrice ♦ *adj*: **working-class** operaio(a).
working man *n* lavoratore *m*.
working party *n* (*BRIT*) commissione *f*.

working week *n* settimana lavorativa.
work-in-progress ['wɔːkɪn'prəugrɛs] *n* (*products*) lavoro in corso; (*value*) valore *m* del manufatto in lavorazione.
workload ['wɔːkləud] *n* carico di lavoro.
workman ['wɔːkmən] *n* operaio.
workmanship ['wɔːkmənʃɪp] *n* (*of worker*) abilità; (*of thing*) fattura.
workmate ['wɔːkmeɪt] *n* collega *m/f*.
workout ['wɔːkaut] *n* (*SPORT*) allenamento.
work permit *n* permesso di lavoro.
works [wɔːks] *n* (*BRIT: factory*) fabbrica ♦ *npl* (*of clock, machine*) meccanismo; **road** ~ **opere stradali**.
works council *n* consiglio aziendale.
work sheet *n* (*COMPUT*) foglio col programma di lavoro.
workshop ['wɔːkʃɔp] *n* officina.
work station *n* stazione *f* di lavoro.
work study *n* studio di organizzazione del lavoro.
worktop ['wɔːktɔp] *n* piano di lavoro.
work-to-rule ['wɔːktə'ruːl] *n* (*BRIT*) sciopero bianco.
world [wɔːld] *n* mondo ♦ *cpd* (*tour*) del mondo; (*record, power, war*) mondiale; **all over the** ~ in tutto il mondo; **to think the** ~ **of sb** pensare un gran bene di qn; **out of this** ~ (*fig*) formidabile; **what in the** ~ **is he doing?** che cavolo sta facendo?; **to do sb a** ~ **of good** fare un gran bene a qn; **W**~ **War One/Two** la prima/seconda guerra mondiale.
world champion *n* campione/essa mondiale.
World Cup *n* (*FOOTBALL*) Coppa del Mondo.
world-famous [wɔːld'feɪməs] *adj* di fama mondiale.
worldly ['wɔːldlɪ] *adj* di questo mondo.
world music *n* musica etnica.
World Series *n*: **the** ~ (*US BASEBALL*) la finalissima di baseball.
world-wide ['wɔːld'waɪd] *adj* universale.
worm [wɔːm] *n* verme *m*.
worn [wɔːn] *pp of* **wear** ♦ *adj* usato(a).
worn-out ['wɔːnaut] *adj* (*object*) consumato(a), logoro(a); (*person*) sfinito(a).
worried ['wʌrɪd] *adj* preoccupato(a); **to be** ~ **about sth** essere preoccupato per qc.
worrier ['wʌrɪə*] *n* ansioso/a.
worrisome ['wʌrɪsəm] *adj* preoccupante.
worry ['wʌrɪ] *n* preoccupazione *f* ♦ *vt* preoccupare ♦ *vi* preoccuparsi; **to** ~ **about** *or* **over sth/sb** preoccuparsi di qc/ per qn.
worrying ['wʌrɪɪŋ] *adj* preoccupante.

worse [wəːs] *adj* peggiore ♦ *adv, n* peggio; **a change for the** ~ un peggioramento; **to get** ~, **to grow** ~ peggiorare; **he is none the** ~ **for it** non ha avuto brutte conseguenze; **so much the** ~ **for you!** tanto peggio per te!

worsen ['wəːsn] *vt, vi* peggiorare.

worse off *adj* in condizioni (economiche) peggiori; (*fig*): **you'll be** ~ **this way** così sarà peggio per lei; **he is now** ~ **than before** ora è in condizioni peggiori di prima.

worship ['wəːʃɪp] *n* culto ♦ *vt* (*God*) adorare, venerare; (*person*) adorare; **Your W**~ (*to mayor*) signor sindaco; (*to judge*) signor giudice.

worshipper ['wəːʃɪpə*] *n* adoratore/trice; (*in church*) fedele *m/f*, devoto/a.

worst [wəːst] *adj* il(la) peggiore ♦ *adv, n* peggio; **at** ~ al peggio, per male che vada; **to come off** ~ avere la peggio; **if the** ~ **comes to the** ~ nel peggior dei casi.

worst-case ['wəːst'keɪs] *adj*: **the** ~ **scenario** la peggiore delle ipotesi.

worsted ['wustɪd] *n*: **(wool)** ~ lana pettinata.

worth [wəːθ] *n* valore *m* ♦ *adj*: **to be** ~ valere; **how much is it** ~? quanto vale?; **it's** ~ **it** ne vale la pena; **it's not** ~ **the trouble** non ne vale la pena; **50 pence** ~ **of apples** 50 pence di mele.

worthless ['wəːθlɪs] *adj* di nessun valore.

worthwhile ['wəːθ'waɪl] *adj* (*activity*) utile; (*cause*) lodevole; **a** ~ **book** un libro che vale la pena leggere.

worthy ['wəːðɪ] *adj* (*person*) degno(a); (*motive*) lodevole; ~ **of** degno di.

=========================== *KEYWORD*

would [wud] *aux vb* **1** (*conditional tense*): **if you asked him he** ~ **do it** se glielo chiedesse lo farebbe; **if you had asked him he** ~ **have done it** se glielo avesse chiesto lo avrebbe fatto

2 (*in offers, invitations, requests*): ~ **you like a biscuit?** vorrebbe *or* vuole un biscotto?; ~ **you ask him to come in?** lo faccia entrare, per cortesia; ~ **you open the window please?** apra la finestra, per favore

3 (*in indirect speech*): **I said I** ~ **do it** ho detto che l'avrei fatto

4 (*emphatic*): **it WOULD have to snow today!** doveva proprio nevicare oggi!

5 (*insistence*): **she** ~**n't do it** non ha voluto farlo

6 (*conjecture*): **it** ~ **have been midnight**

sarà stata mezzanotte; **it** ~ **seem so** sembrerebbe proprio di sì

7 (*indicating habit*): **he** ~ **go there on Mondays** andava lì ogni lunedì.

_____

would-be ['wudbiː] *adj* (*pej*) sedicente.

wound *vb* [waund] *pt, pp of* **wind** ♦ *n, vt* [wuːnd] *n* ferita ♦ *vt* ferire; ~**ed in the leg** ferito(a) alla gamba.

wove [wəuv] *pt of* **weave.**

WP *abbr* (*BRIT col*: = *weather permitting*) tempo permettendo ♦ *n abbr* = **word processing; word processor.**

WPC *n abbr* (*BRIT*: = *woman police constable*) donna poliziotto.

wpm *abbr* (= *words per minute*) p.p.m.

WRAC *n abbr* (*BRIT*: = *Women's Royal Army Corps*) ausiliarie dell'esercito.

WRAF *n abbr* (*BRIT*: = *Women's Royal Air Force*) ausiliarie dell'aeronautica militare.

wrangle ['ræŋgl] *n* litigio ♦ *vi* litigare.

wrap [ræp] *n* (*stole*) scialle *m*; (*cape*) mantellina ♦ *vt* (*also*: ~ **up**) avvolgere; (*parcel*) incartare; **under** ~**s** segreto.

wrapper ['ræpə*] *n* (*of book*) copertina; (*on chocolate*) carta.

wrapping paper ['ræpɪŋ-] *n* carta da pacchi; (*for gift*) carta da regali.

wrath [rɔθ] *n* collera, ira.

wreak [riːk] *vt* (*destruction*) portare, causare; **to** ~ **vengeance on** vendicarsi su; **to** ~ **havoc on** portare scompiglio in.

wreath, ~s [riːθ, riːðz] *n* corona.

wreck [rɛk] *n* (*sea disaster*) naufragio; (*ship*) relitto; (*pej: person*) rottame *m* ♦ *vt* demolire; (*ship*) far naufragare; (*fig*) rovinare.

wreckage ['rɛkɪdʒ] *n* rottami *mpl*; (*of building*) macerie *fpl*; (*of ship*) relitti *mpl*.

wrecker ['rɛkə*] *n* (*US: breakdown van*) carro *m* attrezzi *inv*.

WREN [rɛn] *n abbr* (*BRIT*) *membro del WRNS.*

wren [rɛn] *n* (*ZOOL*) scricciolo.

wrench [rɛntʃ] *n* (*TECH*) chiave *f*; (*tug*) torsione *f* brusca; (*fig*) strazio ♦ *vt* strappare; storcere; **to** ~ **sth from** strappare qc a *or* da.

wrest [rɛst] *vt*: **to** ~ **sth from sb** strappare qc a qn.

wrestle ['rɛsl] *vi*: **to** ~ **(with sb)** lottare (con qn); **to** ~ **with** (*fig*) combattere *or* lottare contro.

wrestler ['rɛslə*] *n* lottatore/trice.

wrestling ['rɛslɪŋ] *n* lotta; (*also*: **all-in** ~: *BRIT*) catch *m*, lotta libera.

wrestling match *n* incontro di lotta (*or*

lotta libera).

wretch [rɛtʃ] *n* disgraziato/a, sciagurato/a; **little ~!** (*often humorous*) birbante!

wretched ['rɛtʃɪd] *adj* disgraziato(a); (*col: weather, holiday*) orrendo(a), orribile; (: *child, dog*) pestifero(a).

wriggle ['rɪgl] *n* contorsione *f* ♦ *vi* dimenarsi; (*snake, worm*) serpeggiare, muoversi serpeggiando.

wring *pt, pp* **wrung** [rɪŋ, rʌŋ] *vt* torcere; (*wet clothes*) strizzare; (*fig*): **to ~ sth out of** strappare qc a.

wringer ['rɪŋə*] *n* strizzatoio (manuale).

wringing ['rɪŋɪŋ] *adj* (*also:* **~ wet**) bagnato(a) fradicio(a).

wrinkle ['rɪŋkl] *n* (*on skin*) ruga; (*on paper etc*) grinza ♦ *vt* corrugare; raggrinzire ♦ *vi* corrugarsi; raggrinzirsi.

wrinkled ['rɪŋkld], **wrinkly** ['rɪŋklɪ] *adj* (*fabric, paper*) stropicciato(a); (*surface*) corrugato(a), increspato(a); (*skin*) rugoso(a).

wrist [rɪst] *n* polso.

wristband ['rɪstbænd] *n* (*of shirt*) polsino; (*of watch*) cinturino.

wrist watch *n* orologio da polso.

writ [rɪt] *n* ordine *m*; mandato; **to issue a ~ against sb, serve a ~ on sb** notificare un mandato di comparizione a qn.

write, *pt* **wrote,** *pp* **written** [raɪt, rəut, 'rɪtn] *vt, vi* scrivere; **to ~ sb a letter** scrivere una lettera a qn.

▶**write away** *vi:* **to ~ away for** (*information*) richiedere per posta; (*goods*) ordinare per posta.

▶**write down** *vt* annotare; (*put in writing*) mettere per iscritto.

▶**write off** *vt* (*debt*) cancellare; (*depreciate*) deprezzare; (*smash up: car*) distruggere.

▶**write out** *vt* scrivere; (*copy*) ricopiare.

▶**write up** *vt* redigere.

write-off ['raɪtɔf] *n* perdita completa; **the car is a ~** la macchina va bene per il demolitore.

write-protect ['raɪtprə'tɛkt] *vt* (*COMPUT*) proteggere contro scrittura.

writer ['raɪtə*] *n* autore/trice, scrittore/trice.

write-up ['raɪtʌp] *n* (*review*) recensione *f*.

writhe [raɪð] *vi* contorcersi.

writing ['raɪtɪŋ] *n* scrittura; (*of author*) scritto, opera; **in ~** per iscritto; **in my own ~** scritto di mio pugno.

writing case *n* nécessaire *m inv* per la corrispondenza.

writing desk *n* scrivania, scrittoio.

writing paper *n* carta da scrivere.

written ['rɪtn] *pp of* **write**.

WRNS *n abbr* (*BRIT:* = *Women's Royal Naval Service*) ausiliarie della marina militare.

wrong [rɔŋ] *adj* sbagliato(a); (*not suitable*) inadatto(a); (*wicked*) cattivo(a); (*unfair*) ingiusto(a) ♦ *adv* in modo sbagliato, erroneamente ♦ *n* (*evil*) male *m*; (*injustice*) torto ♦ *vt* fare torto a; **to be ~** (*answer*) essere sbagliato; (*in doing, saying*) avere torto; **you are ~ to do it** ha torto a farlo; **you are ~ about that, you've got it ~** si sbaglia; **to be in the ~** avere torto; **what's ~?** cosa c'è che non va?; **there's nothing ~** va tutto bene; **what's ~ with the car?** cos'ha la macchina che non va?; **to go ~** (*person*) sbagliarsi; (*plan*) fallire, non riuscire; (*machine*) guastarsi; **it's ~ to steal, stealing is ~** è male rubare.

wrongdoer ['rɔŋduːə*] *n* malfattore/trice.

wrong-foot [rɔŋ'fut] *vt* (*SPORT; also fig*) prendere in contropiede.

wrongful ['rɔŋful] *adj* illegittimo(a); ingiusto(a); **~ dismissal** licenziamento ingiustificato.

wrongly ['rɔŋlɪ] *adv* (*accuse, dismiss*) a torto; (*answer, do, count*) erroneamente; (*treat*) ingiustamente.

wrong number *n:* **you have the ~** (*TEL*) ha sbagliato numero.

wrong side *n* (*of cloth*) rovescio.

wrote [rəut] *pt of* **write**.

wrought [rɔːt] *adj:* **~ iron** ferro battuto.

wrung [rʌŋ] *pt, pp of* **wring**.

WRVS *n abbr* (*BRIT*) = *Women's Royal Voluntary Service*.

wry [raɪ] *adj* storto(a).

wt. *abbr* = **weight**.

WV, W. Va. *abbr* (*US*) = *West Virginia*.

WY, Wyo. *abbr* (*US*) = *Wyoming*.

WYSIWYG ['wɪzɪwɪg] *abbr* (*COMPUT*) = *what you see is what you get*.

Xx

X, x [ɛks] *n* (*letter*) X, x *f* or *m inv*; (*BRIT CINE: old*) ≈ film vietato ai minori di 18 anni; **X for Xmas** ≈ X come Xeres.

Xerox ® ['zɪərɔks] *n* (*also:* **~ machine**) fotocopiatrice *f*; (*photocopy*) fotocopia ♦ *vt* fotocopiare.

XL *abbr* = *extra large*.

Xmas ['ɛksməs] *n abbr* = **Christmas**.

X-rated ['ɛks'reɪtɪd] *adj* (*US*: *film*) ≈ vietato ai minori di 18 anni.
X-ray ['ɛks'reɪ] *n* raggio X; (*photograph*) radiografia ♦ *vt* radiografare; **to have an** ~ farsi fare una radiografia.
xylophone ['zaɪləfəun] *n* xilofono.

Y y

Y, y [waɪ] *n* (*letter*) Y, y *f or m inv*; **Y for Yellow**, (*US*) **Y for Yoke** ≈ Y come Yacht.
yacht [jɔt] *n* panfilo, yacht *m inv*.
yachting ['jɔtɪŋ] *n* yachting *m*, sport *m* della vela.
yachtsman ['jɔtsmən] *n* yachtsman *m inv*.
yam [jæm] *n* igname *m*; (*sweet potato*) patata dolce.
Yank [jæŋk], **Yankee** ['jæŋkɪ] *n* (*pej*) yankee *m/f inv*, nordamericano/a.
yank [jæŋk] *n* strattone *m* ♦ *vt* tirare, dare uno strattone a.
yap [jæp] *vi* (*dog*) guaire.
yard [jɑːd] *n* (*of house etc*) cortile *m*; (*US*: *garden*) giardino; (*measure*) iarda (= *914 mm; 3 feet*); **builder's** ~ deposito di materiale da costruzione.
yardstick ['jɑːdstɪk] *n* (*fig*) misura, criterio.
yarn [jɑːn] *n* filato; (*tale*) lunga storia.
yawn [jɔːn] *n* sbadiglio ♦ *vi* sbadigliare.
yawning ['jɔːnɪŋ] *adj* (*gap*) spalancato(a).
yd. *abbr* = **yard**.
yeah [jɛə] *adv* (*col*) sì.
year [jɪə*] *n* (*gen, SCOL*) anno; (*referring to harvest, wine etc*) annata; **every** ~ ogni anno, tutti gli anni; **this** ~ quest'anno; ~ **in,** ~ **out** anno dopo anno; **she's three** ~**s old** ha tre anni; **a** *or* **per** ~ all'anno.
yearbook ['jɪəbuk] *n* annuario.
yearly ['jɪəlɪ] *adj* annuale ♦ *adv* annualmente; **twice-**~ semestrale.
yearn [jɜːn] *vi*: **to** ~ **for sth/to do** desiderare ardentemente qc/di fare.
yearning ['jɜːnɪŋ] *n* desiderio intenso.
yeast [jiːst] *n* lievito.
yell [jɛl] *n* urlo ♦ *vi* urlare.
yellow ['jɛləu] *adj* giallo(a).
yellow fever *n* febbre *f* gialla.
yellowish ['jɛləuɪʃ] *adj* giallastro(a), giallognolo(a).
Yellow Pages ® *npl* pagine *fpl* gialle.
Yellow Sea *n*: **the** ~ il mar Giallo.

yelp [jɛlp] *n* guaito, uggiolio ♦ *vi* guaire, uggiolare.
Yemen ['jɛmən] *n* Yemen *m*.
yen [jɛn] *n* (*currency*) yen *m inv*; (*craving*): ~ **for/to do** gran voglia di/di fare.
yeoman ['jəumən] *n*: **Y** ~ **of the Guard** guardiano della Torre di Londra.
yes [jɛs] *adv, n* sì (*m inv*); **to say** ~ (**to**) dire di sì (a), acconsentire (a).
yesterday ['jɛstədɪ] *adv, n* ieri (*m inv*); ~ **morning/evening** ieri mattina/sera; **the day before** ~ l'altro ieri; **all day** ~ ieri tutto il giorno.
yet [jɛt] *adv* ancora; già ♦ *conj* ma, tuttavia; **it is not finished** ~ non è ancora finito; **the best** ~ il migliore finora; **as** ~ finora; ~ **again** di nuovo; **must you go just** ~? deve andarsene di già?; **a few days** ~ ancora qualche giorno.
yew [juː] *n* tasso (*albero*).
Y-fronts ® ['waɪfrʌnts] *npl* (*BRIT*) slip *m inv* da uomo.
YHA *n abbr* (*BRIT*: = *Youth Hostels Association*) Y.H.A. *f*.
Yiddish ['jɪdɪʃ] *n* yiddish *m*.
yield [jiːld] *n* resa; (*of crops etc*) raccolto ♦ *vt* produrre, rendere; (*surrender*) cedere ♦ *vi* cedere; (*US AUT*) dare la precedenza; **a** ~ **of 5%** un profitto *or* un interesse del 5%.
YMCA *n abbr* (= *Young Men's Christian Association*) Y.M.C.A. *m*.
yob(bo) ['jɔb(əu)] *n* (*BRIT col*) bullo.
yodel ['jəudl] *vi* cantare lo jodel *or* alla tirolese.
yoga ['jəugə] *n* yoga *m*.
yog(h)ourt, yog(h)urt ['jəugət] *n* iogurt *m inv*.
yoke [jəuk] *n* giogo ♦ *vt* (*also*: ~ **together**: *oxen*) aggiogare.
yolk [jəuk] *n* tuorlo, rosso d'uovo.
yonder ['jɔndə*] *adv* là.
yonks [jɔŋks] *npl*: **for** ~ (*col*) da una vita.
Yorks [jɔːks] *abbr* (*BRIT*) = **Yorkshire**.

━━━━━━━━━━━━━━━━━━━━━ *KEYWORD*

you [juː] *pron* **1** (*subject*) tu; (*: polite form*) lei; (*: pl*) voi; (*: very formal*) loro; ~ **Italians enjoy your food** a voi italiani piace mangiare bene; ~ **and I will go** andiamo io e te (*or* lei ed io); **if I was** *or* **were** ~ se fossi in te (*or* lei *etc*)
2 (*object: direct*) ti; la; vi; loro (*after vb*); (*: indirect*) ti; le; vi; loro (*after vb*); **I know** ~ ti (*or* la *or* vi) conosco; **I'll see** ~ **tomorrow** ci vediamo domani; **I gave it to** ~ te l'ho dato; gliel'ho dato; ve l'ho dato; l'ho dato loro

3 (*stressed, after prep, in comparisons*) te; lei; voi; loro; **I told YOU to do it** ho detto a TE (*or* a LEI *etc*) di farlo; **she's younger than** ~ è più giovane di te (*or* lei *etc*) **4** (*impers: one*) si; **fresh air does** ~ **good** l'aria fresca fa bene; ~ **never know** non si sa mai.

you'd [ju:d] = **you had; you would**.
you'll [ju:l] = **you will; you shall**.
young [jʌŋ] *adj* giovane ♦ *npl* (*of animal*) piccoli *mpl*; (*people*): **the** ~ i giovani, la gioventù; **a** ~ **man** un giovanotto; **a** ~ **lady** una signorina; **a** ~ **woman** una giovane donna; **the** ~**er generation** la nuova generazione; **my** ~**er brother** il mio fratello minore.
youngish [ˈjʌŋɪʃ] *adj* abbastanza giovane.
youngster [ˈjʌŋstə*] *n* giovanotto/a; (*child*) bambino/a.
your [jɔ:*] *adj* il(la) tuo(a), *pl* i(le) tuoi(tue); (*polite form*) il(la) suo(a), *pl* i(le) suoi(sue); (*pl*) il(la) vostro(a), *pl* i(le) vostri(e); (: *very formal*) il(la) loro, *pl* i(le) loro.
you're [juə*] = **you are**.
yours [jɔ:z] *pron* il(la) tuo(a), *pl* i(le) tuoi(tue); (*polite form*) il(la) suo(a), *pl* i(le) suoi(sue); (*pl*) il(la) vostro(a), *pl* i(le) vostri(e); (: *very formal*) il(la) loro, *pl* i(le) loro; ~ **sincerely/faithfully** (*in letter*) cordiali/distinti saluti; **a friend of** ~ un tuo (*or* suo *etc*) amico; **is it** ~**?** è tuo (*or* suo *etc*)?
yourself [jɔ:ˈsɛlf] *pron* (*reflexive*) ti; (: *polite form*) si; (*after prep*) te; se; (*emphatic*) tu stesso(a); lei stesso(a); **you** ~ **told me** me l'hai detto proprio tu, tu stesso me l'hai detto.
yourselves [jɔ:ˈsɛlvz] *pl pron* (*reflexive*) vi; (: *polite form*) si; (*after prep*) voi; loro; (*emphatic*) voi stessi(e); loro stessi(e).
youth [ju:θ] *n* gioventù *f*; (*young man: pl* ~**s** [ju:ðz]) giovane *m*, ragazzo *m*; **in my** ~ da giovane, quando ero giovane.
youth club *n* centro giovanile.
youthful [ˈju:θful] *adj* giovane; da giovane; giovanile.
youthfulness [ˈju:θfəlnɪs] *n* giovinezza.
youth hostel *n* ostello della gioventù.
youth movement *n* movimento giovanile.
you've [ju:v] = **you have**.
yowl [jaul] *n* (*of dog, person*) urlo; (*of cat*) miagolio ♦ *vi* urlare; miagolare.
yr *abbr* = **year**.
YT *abbr* (*Canada*) = *Yukon Territory*.
Yugoslav [ˈju:gəuslɑ:v] *adj*, *n* jugoslavo(a).
Yugoslavia [ju:gəuˈslɑ:vɪə] *n* Jugoslavia.
Yugoslavian [ju:gəuˈslɑ:vɪən] *adj*, *n*

jugoslavo(a).
Yule log [ju:l-] *n ceppo nel caminetto a Natale*.
yuppie [ˈjʌpɪ] *adj*, *n* (*col*) yuppie (*m/f*) *inv*.
YWCA *n abbr* (= *Young Women's Christian Association*) Y.W.C.A. *m*.

Z z

Z, z [zɛd, (*US*) zi:] *n* (*letter*) Z, z *f or m inv*; **Z for Zebra** ≈ Z come Zara.
Zaire [zɑ:ˈɪə*] *n* Zaire *m*.
Zambia [ˈzæmbɪə] *n* Zambia *m*.
Zambian [ˈzæmbɪən] *adj*, *n* zambiano(a).
zany [ˈzeɪnɪ] *adj* un po' pazzo(a).
zap [zæp] *vt* (*COMPUT*) cancellare.
zeal [zi:l] *n* zelo; entusiasmo.
zealot [ˈzɛlət] *n* zelota *m/f*.
zealous [ˈzɛləs] *adj* zelante; premuroso(a).
zebra [ˈzi:brə] *n* zebra.
zebra crossing *n* (*BRIT*) (passaggio pedonale a) strisce *fpl*, zebre *fpl*.
zenith [ˈzɛnɪθ] *n* zenit *m inv*; (*fig*) culmine *m*.
zero [ˈzɪərəu] *n* zero; **5° below** ~ 5° sotto zero.
zero hour *n* l'ora zero.
zero option *n* (*POL*) opzione *f* zero.
zero-rated [ˈzɪərəuˈreɪtɪd] *adj* (*BRIT*) ad aliquota zero.
zest [zɛst] *n* gusto; (*CULIN*) buccia.
zigzag [ˈzɪgzæg] *n* zigzag *m inv* ♦ *vi* zigzagare.
Zimbabwe [zɪmˈbɑ:bwɪ] *n* Zimbabwe *m*.
Zimbabwean [zɪmˈbɑ:bwɪən] *adj* dello Zimbabwe.
Zimmer ® [ˈzɪmə*] *n* (*also:* ~ **frame**) deambulatore *m*.
zinc [zɪŋk] *n* zinco.
Zionism [ˈzaɪənɪzəm] *n* sionismo.
Zionist [ˈzaɪənɪst] *adj* sionistico(a) ♦ *n* sionista *m/f*.
zip [zɪp] *n* (*also:* ~ **fastener**, (*US*) ~**per**) chiusura *f or* cerniera *f* lampo *inv*; (*energy*) energia, forza ♦ *vt* (*also:* ~ **up**) chiudere con una cerniera lampo.
zip code *n* (*US*) codice *m* di avviamento postale.
zither [ˈzɪðə*] *n* cetra.
zodiac [ˈzəudɪæk] *n* zodiaco.
zombie [ˈzɔmbɪ] *n* (*fig*): **like a** ~ come un morto che cammina.

zone [zəun] *n* zona.
zoo [zu:] *n* zoo *m inv*.
zoological [zuə'lɔdʒɪkl] *adj* zoologico(a).
zoologist [zu:'ɔlədʒɪst] *n* zoologo/a.
zoology [zu:'ɔlədʒɪ] *n* zoologia.
zoom [zu:m] *vi*: **to ~ past** sfrecciare; **to ~ in**
(**on sb/sth**) (*PHOT, CINE*) zumare (su qn/qc).
zoom lens *n* zoom *m inv*, obiettivo a
focale variabile.
zucchini [zu:'ki:nɪ] *n* (*pl inv*) (*US*) zucchina.
Zulu ['zu:lu:] *adj*, *n* zulù (*m/f*) *inv*.
Zürich ['zjuərɪk] *n* Zurigo *f*.